8/9u

THE COLUMBIA GRANGER'S® DICTIONARY OF POETRY QUOTATIONS

Other Columbia University Press Reference Works

The Columbia Granger's® Index to Poetry, Ninth Edition
Edith P. Hazen and Deborah J. Fryer, eds. (1990)

The Columbia Granger's® Guide to Poetry Anthologies
William Katz and Linda Sternberg Katz, eds. (1990)

The Concise Columbia Book of Poetry
William Harmon, ed. (1990)

The Columbia Granger's® World of Poetry CD ROM (1991)

The Concise Columbia Dictionary of Quotations
Robert Andrews, ed. (1989)

The Concise Columbia Encyclopedia, Second Edition (1989)

The Columbia Literary History of the United States
Emory Elliott, ed. (1988)

The Columbia History of the American Novel
Emory Elliott, ed. (1991)

THE COLUMBIA GRANGER'S®
DICTIONARY OF
POETRY
QUOTATIONS

EDITED BY
EDITH P. HAZEN

COLUMBIA UNIVERSITY PRESS · NEW YORK

COLUMBIA UNIVERSITY PRESS

NEW YORK   OXFORD

COPYRIGHT © 1992 COLUMBIA UNIVERSITY PRESS

LIBRARY OF CONGRESS CATALOGING-IN-PUBLICATION DATA

The Columbia Granger's dictionary of poetry quotations / edited by
Edith P. Hazen.
   p. cm.
   Includes indexes.
   ISBN 0-231-07546-4 : $99.00
   1. Quotations, English.   I. Hazen, Edith P. II. Title:
Dictionary of poetry quotations.
PN6082.C57 1992
808.881—dc20   91-42240
                                          CIP

Casebound editions of Columbia University Press books are Smyth-
sewn and printed on permanent and durable acid-free paper.

PRINTED IN THE UNITED STATES OF AMERICA

c 10 9 8 7 6 5 4 3 2 1

The quotations contained in this dictionary were selected on the basis of valuable advice provided by the following Columbia University professors of English:

- Annette Wheeler Cafarelli
- Carl Hovde
- David Kastan
- John Middendorf

- James Shapiro
- George Stade
- Edward Tayler
- Carl Woodring, Emeritus

CONTENTS

PREFACE

Carl Woodring

Dictionaries of familiar quotations are used most often as an anodyne to relieve the pain of not remembering where those familiar or half-familiar words came from. Professors in the humanities, when asked "Who wrote these lines I've written down here?" answer, "It will take me a couple of hours to remember," and then rush to the dictionaries of quotations. A fortunate few have been wise or lucky enough to discover that dictionaries of quotations can also stimulate as "a good read."

The present volume is a collection of striking, memorable passages from favored poems. If "favorite poems" are those, whatever their quality, enjoyed by the majority of readers, "favored" poems are selected by editors and readers after emerging at birth from superior poets or, occasionally, from an average poet at a superior moment.

The poet, among other virtues, is a phrase-maker, as a major poet of our century has said (if there were a dictionary of prose quotations as good as the present collection of poetry quotations, I could say when and where he said it). Familiarity with apt phrases sometimes results from their repetition in melodic refrains; more often, phrases are recollected and learned because they wrap in golden language a striking thought. An assembly of highlights from favored poems has a special advantage over other collections because it gathers the best thoughts in the best language. Coleridge wrote in *Biographia Literaria* that "a poem of any length neither can be, or ought to be, all poetry." The finest passages of poetry in the best poems meet Coleridge's requirement of fusing matter with manner; only in such passages, he insists, is the whole soul of the poet made present. *The Columbia Granger's® Dictionary of Poetry Quotations* is a collection of just such passages.

Speakers and truant readers can seek and find in this volume ways to awaken cheer and even exultation. There are also cries herein from a pit below the heart, and lessons that contradict each other could be culled, as from popular proverbs or fortune cookies, but it would take special effort to draw from this volume much encouragement of cynicism, unless in the contrast between select language and common practice.

Here one can encounter with Hopkins "things counter, original, spare, strange," can meditate in the "delicious solitude" of Marvell's "Garden," and can travel with Keats in "realms of gold."

INTRODUCTION

"Not marble, nor the gilded monuments
Of princes, shall outlive this powerful rhyme"
—William Shakespeare, *Sonnet LV*

The Columbia Granger's® Dictionary of Poetry Quotations is a treasury of the most memorable lines written by the greatest poets in our language. The quotations are arranged alphabetically by poet, so the book can be read for enjoyment as an anthology of the most notable offerings by individual poets, from Shakespeare to Eliot, from Chaucer to Auden. It will also be consulted as a fine new reference work.

The book will be used to verify the precise wording of a quotation half remembered; it will be used to find the author and/or title of a poem some of whose lines have stayed in the memory; and it will be used to find a suitable quotation on a particular subject or occasion.

It will also be used, like *The Columbia Granger's® Index to Poetry*, to find poems in current anthologies. Each quotation here carries the anthology codes familiar to users of *Granger's®*, and the list of anthologies at the beginning of the book, arranged by code, is the same as in the Ninth Edition of *The Columbia Granger's® Index to Poetry* (edited by Edith P. Hazen and Deborah J. Fryer, 1990). Now searchers can locate a poem not only by its first line or title, using *Granger's®*, but by the keywords in some famous lines within it, using this book. In this sense, *The Columbia Granger's® Index to Poetry Quotations* is a logical extension of *Granger's®*.

The quotations were selected by eight distinguished Columbia University specialists from the 4,000 poems that have been most anthologized, as shown by *The Columbia Granger's® Index to Poetry*. Our eight consultants added quotations from the long works of such poets as Chaucer, Shakespeare, Pope, Byron, and Whitman, who would otherwise have been under-represented, because anthologists do not always select the same passages from long works.

This book is a full presentation of the essence, the distillation, of great poetry in English in all its variety. It is offered as a useful reference and research tool, but also as a pleasure in itself, as page after page of great writing.

LIST OF ANTHOLOGIES

Listed below are the anthologies, with their abbreviated codes, from which the quotations in this book are selected. These codes are listed at the end of the quotations from each poem.

AA American Anthology, An, 1787–1900. *Edmund Clarence Stedman, ed.* (1900) Houghton Mifflin Company

AAA Age Ago, An; a Selection of Nineteenth-Century Russian Poetry. *Alan Myers, comp. and tr.* (1988) Farrar, Straus and Giroux

AAS Anchor Anthology of Sixteenth-Century Verse, The. *Richard S. Sylvester, ed.* (1974) Doubleday Anchor Books

ACKP Anthology of Contemporary Korean Poetry. *Koh Chang-soo, comp.* (1987) Seoul International Publishing House

ACP Anthology of Catholic Poets, An. *Shane Leslie, ed.* (Rev. ed., 1952) The Macmillan Company (later published by The Newman Press)

AH American Hymns Old and New, Vols. I–II. Vol. I, with music; Vol. II, notes on the hymns and biographies of the authors and composers. *Albert Christ-Janer, Charles W. Hughes, and Carleton Sprague Smith, eds.* (1980) Columbia University Press

AiP America in Poetry. *Charles Sullivan, ed.* (1988) Harry N. Abrams

AIW Ain't I a Woman! a Book of Women's Poetry from around the World. *Illona Linthwaite, ed.* (1988) Peter Bedrick Books

AmFN America Forever New; a Book of Poems. *Sara Brewton and John E. Brewton, comps.* (1968) Thomas Y. Crowell Company

AmFP American Folk Poetry; an Anthology. *Duncan Emrich, ed.* (1974) Little, Brown & Company

AmMo Amazing Monsters; Verses to Thrill and Chill. *Robert Fisher, ed.* (1982) Faber and Faber

AmNP American Negro Poetry. *Arna Bontemps, ed* (Rev. ed., 1974) Hill and Wang

AmPA American Poetry Anthology, The. *Daniel Halpern, ed.* (1975) Avon Books

AmPP American Poetry and Prose. *Norman Foerster, Norman S. Grabo, Russel B. Nye, E. Fred Carlisle, and Robert Falk, eds.* (5th ed., 1970) Houghton Mifflin Company

AnAmPo Anthology of American Poetry. *George Gesner, ed.* (1983) Avenel Books

AnAn Antaeus Anthology, The. *Daniel Halpern, ed.* (1986) Bantam Books

AnIL Anthology of Irish Literature, An. *David H Greene, ed.* (1954) The Modern Library

AnOE Anthology of Old English Poetry, An. *Charles W. Kennedy, tr.* (1960) Oxford University Press

BoWoP	Book of Women Poets from Antiquity to Now, A. *Aliki Barnstone and Willis Barnstone, eds.* (1980) Schocken Books
BPo	Black Poets, The. *Dudley Randall, ed.* (1971) Bantam Books
BrPo	British Poetry 1880–1920; Edwardian Voices. *Paul L. Wiley and Harold Orel, eds.* (1969) Appleton-Century-Crofts
BrRo	Bread and Roses; an Anthology of Nineteenth- and Twentieth-Century Poetry by Women Writers. *Diana Scott, comp.* (1982) Virago Press
BrSi	Breaking Silence; an Anthology of Contemporary Asian American Poets. *Joseph Bruchac, ed.* (1983) The Greenfield Review Press
BwV	Burning with a Vision; Poetry of Science and the Fantastic. *Robert Frazier, ed.* (1984) Owlswick Press
BXAP	Brand-X Anthology of Poetry, The: Burnt Norton Edition. *William Zaranka, ed.* (1981) Apple-Wood Books
CaP	Canadian Poetry in English (Canadian Literature Series). *Bliss Carman, Lorne Pierce, and V. B. Rhodenizer, eds.* (Rev. and enl. ed., 1954) The Ryerson Press
CaPo	Cavalier Poets; Selected Poems. *Thomas Clayton, ed.* (1978) Oxford University Press
CAPP	Contemporary American Poetry. *A. Poulin, Jr., ed.* (4th ed., 1985) Houghton Mifflin Company
CBAP	Collins Book of Australian Poetry, The. *Rodney Hall, comp.* (1981, 1984) Fontana/Collins
CBWP 1–4	Collected Black Women's Poetry, Vols. I–IV. *Joan R. Sherman, ed.* (1988) Oxford University Press
CCP	Contemporary Chicana Poetry; a Critical Approach to an Emerging Literature. *Marta Ester Sánchez, ed.* (1985) University of California Press
CDC	Caroling Dusk; an Anthology of Verse by Negro Poets. *Countee Cullen, ed.* (1927) Harper & Brothers
CDW	Carriers of the Dream Wheel; Contemporary Native American Poetry. *Duane Niatum, ed.* (1975) Harper & Row
CenHV	Century of Humorous Verse, A, 1850–1950 (Everyman's Library). *Roger Lancelyn Green, ed.* (1959) E. P. Dutton & Company
CH	Come Hither. *Walter de la Mare, comp.* (3d ed., 1957) Alfred A. Knopf
ChER	Choice of English Romantic Poetry, A. *Stephen Spender, ed.* (1947) The Dial Press
ChTr	Cherry-Tree, The. *Geoffrey Grigson, comp.* (1959) Phoenix House
CIP	Contemporary Irish Poetry; an Anthology. *Anthony Bradley, ed.* (New and rev. ed., 1988) University of California Press
CMoP	Chief Modern Poets of Britain and America. *Gerald DeWitt Sanders, John Herbert Nelson, and M. L. Rosenthal, eds.* (5th ed., 1970) Macmillan Publishing Company
CN	Chaos of the Night; Women's Poetry and Verse of the Second World War. *Catherine W. Reilly, ed.* (1984) Virago Press

FL	First Lines; Poems Written in Youth, from Herbert to Heaney. *Jon Stallworthy, ed.* (1987) Carcanet
FM	Fellow Mortals; an Anthology of Animal Verse. *Roy Fuller, comp.* (1981) Macdonald and Evans Ltd.
FOC	Face of Creation, The; Contemporary Hungarian Poetry. *Jascha Kessler, tr.* (1988) Coffee House Press
FPL	Favorite Poems in Large Print. *Virginia S. Reiser, ed.* (1981) G. K. Hall & Company
FYAP	Fifty Years of American Poetry; Anniversary Volume for the Academy of American Poets. Introduction by Robert Penn Warren. (1984) Harry N. Abrams
GBL	Gambit Book of Love Poems, The. *Geoffrey Grigson, ed.* (1975) Gambit (originally published in Great Britain by Faber and Faber as The Faber Book of Love Poems)
GBP	Gambit Book of Popular Verse, The. *Geoffrey Grigson, ed.* (1971) Gambit (also published in Great Britain as The Faber Book of Popular Verse)
GeTw	Generation of 2000, The; Contemporary American Poets. *William Heyen, ed.* (1984) Ontario Review Press
GLP	Gay & Lesbian Poetry in Our Time; an Anthology. *Carl Morse and Joan Larkin, eds.* (1988) St. Martin's Press
GN	Golden Numbers. *Kate Douglas Wiggin and Nora Archibald Smith, eds.* (1902) Doubleday, Doran & Company
GOA	Gift Outright, The; America to Her Poets. *Helen Plotz, ed.* (1977) Greenwillow Books
GoJo	Golden Journey, The; Poems for Young People. *Louise Bogan and William Jay Smith, comps.* (1965) Reilly & Lee Company
GOS	Gathering of Spirit, A; Writing and Art by North American Indian Women. *Beth Brant, ed.* (1984) Sinister Wisdom Books
GoT	Golden Tradition, The; an Anthology of Urdu Poetry. *Ahmed Ali, ed. and tr.* (1973) Columbia University Press
GoTS	Golden Treasury of Scottish Poetry, The. *Hugh MacDiarmid, ed.* (1941) The Macmillan Company
GoYe	Golden Year, The; the Poetry Society of America Anthology, 1910–1960. *Melville Cane, John Farrar, and Louise Townsend Nicholl, eds.* (1960) The Fine Editions Press
GOYP	Going Over to Your Place; Poems for Each Other. *Paul B. Janeczko, comp.* (1987) Bradbury Press
GrPl	Green Place, A; Modern Poems. *William Jay Smith, comp.* (1982) Delacorte Press/Seymour Lawrence
GTBS	Golden Treasury of the Best Songs and Lyrical Poems in the English Language. *Francis Palgrave, comp.* (1929) Oxford University Press
GTBS-P	Golden Treasury of the Best Songs & Lyrical Poems in the English Language. *Francis Turner Palgrave, comp. With a fifth book selected by John Press.* (5th ed., 1964) Oxford University Press

HAP   Harper Anthology of Poetry, The. *John Frederick Nims, ed.* (1981) Harper & Row

HATNAP   Harper's Anthology of 20th Century Native American Poetry. *Duane Niatum, ed.* (1988) Harper & Row

HCAP   Harvard Book of Contemporary American Poetry, The. *Helen Vendler, ed.* (1985) The Belknap Press of Harvard University Press

HeIP   Heath Introduction to Poetry, The. *Joseph de Roche, ed.* (3d ed., 1988) D. C. Heath and Company

HoPM   How Does a Poem Mean? *John Ciardi and Miller Williams, eds.* (2d ed., 1975) Houghton Mifflin Company

IAT   In the American Tree. *Ron Silliman, ed.* (1986) The National Poetry Foundation

IDB   I Am the Darker Brother; an Anthology of Modern Poems by Negro Americans. *Arnold Adoff, ed.* (1968) The Macmillan Company

IFON   Isle Full of Noises, The; Modern Chinese Poetry from Taiwan. *Dominic Cheung, ed. and tr.* (1987) Columbia University Press

IHMS   I Hear My Sisters Saying; Poems by Twentieth-Century Women. *Carol Konek and Dorothy Walters, eds.* (1976) Thomas Y. Crowell Company

ILY   I Like You, If You Like Me; Poems of Friendship (Margaret K. McElderry Books). *Myra Cohn Livingston, ed.* (1987) Macmillan Publishing Company

ImOP   Imagination's Other Place; Poems of Science and Mathematics. *Helen Plotz, comp.* (1955) Thomas Y. Crowell Company

InPK   Introduction to Poetry, An. *X. J. Kennedy, ed.* (6th ed., 1986) Little, Brown & Company

InPS   Introduction to Poetry, An. *Louis Simpson, ed.* (3d ed., 1986) St. Martin's Press

InvP   Invitation to Poetry; a Round of Poems from John Skelton to Dylan Thomas. *Lloyd Frankenberg, ed.* (1956) Doubleday & Company

InW   Inventing a Word; an Anthology of Twentieth-Century Puerto Rican Poetry. *Julio Marzán, ed.* (1980) Columbia University Press (in association with The Center for Inter-American Relations)

IP   Israeli Poetry; a Contemporary Anthology. *Warren Bargad and Stanley F. Chyet, comps. and trs.* (1986) Indiana University Press

IPY   Irish Poetry after Yeats; Seven Poets. *Maurice Harmon, ed.* (1979) Little, Brown & Company

JB   Jump Bad; a New Chicago Anthology. *Gwendolyn Brooks, ed.* (1971) Broadside Press

JCP   Jacobean and Caroline Poetry; an Anthology. *T. G. S. Cain, ed.* (1981) Methuen

JLIC 1–2   Japanese Literature in Chinese, Vols. I–II. Vol. I: Poetry and Prose in Chinese by Japanese Writers of the Early Period; Vol.

NBP   New Black Poetry, The. *Clarence Major, ed.* (1969) International Publishers Company

NeAC   New American and Canadian Poetry. *John Gill, ed.* (1971) Beacon Press

NeAP   New American Poetry, The, 1945–1960. *Donald M. Allen, ed.* (1960) Grove Press

NeIP   New Irish Poets. *Devin A. Garrity, ed.* (1948) The Devin-Adair Company

NePoEA   New Poets of England and America. *Donald Hall, Robert Pack, and Louis Simpson, eds.* (1957) Meridian Books

NePoEA–2   New Poets of England and America; Second Selection. *Donald Hall and Robert Pack, eds.* (1962) Meridian Books

NIP   Norton Introduction to Poetry, The. *J. Paul Hunter, ed.* (3d ed., 1986) W. W. Norton & Company

NItP   New Italian Poetry, The, 1945 to the Present; a Bilingual Anthology. *Lawrence R. Smith, ed. and tr.* (1981) University of California Press

NMM   No More Masks! an Anthology of Poems by Women. *Florence Howe and Ellen Bass, eds.* (1973) Doubleday Anchor Books

NNaP   New Naked Poetry, The; Recent American Poetry in Open Forms. *Stephen Berg and Robert Mezey, eds.* (1976) The Bobbs-Merrill Company

NoAM   Norton Anthology of Modern Poetry, The. *Richard Ellmann and Robert O'Clair, eds.* (2d ed., 1988) W. W. Norton & Company

NOBA   New Oxford Book of American Verse, The. *Richard Ellmann, ed.* (1976) Oxford University Press

NOBC   New Oxford Book of Canadian Verse in English, The. *Margaret Atwood, comp.* (1982) Oxford University Press

NOBE   New Oxford Book of English Verse, The, 1250–1950. *Helen Gardner, ed.* (1972) Oxford University Press

NOBL   New Oxford Book of English Light Verse, The. *Kingsley Amis, ed.* (1978) Oxford University Press

NOBVV   New Oxford Book of Victorian Verse, The. *Christopher Ricks, ed.* (1987) Oxford University Press

NOCV   New Oxford Book of Christian Verse, The. *Donald Davie, ed.* (1981) Oxford University Press

NOEC   New Oxford Book of Eighteenth Century Verse, The. *Roger Lonsdale, ed.* (1984) Oxford University Press

NOIV   New Oxford Book of Irish Verse, The. *Thomas Kinsella, ed. and tr.* (1986) Oxford University Press

NoP   Norton Anthology of Poetry, The. *Alexander W. Allison and others, eds.* (3d ed., 1983) W. W. Norton & Company

NOVW   New and Old Voices of Wah'kon-tah; Contemporary Native American Poetry. *Robert K. Dodge and Joseph B. McCullough, eds.* (1985) International Publishers Company

NPGG   19 New American Poets of the Golden Gate. *Philip Dow, ed.* (1984) Harcourt Brace Jovanovich

OBTV   Oxford Book of Travel Verse, The. *Kevin Crossley-Holland, ed.* (1986) Oxford University Press

OBVE   Oxford Book of Verse in English Translation, The. *Charles Tomlinson, ed.* (1980) Oxford University Press

OBWP   Oxford Book of War Poetry, The. *Jon Stallworthy, ed.* (1984) Oxford University Press

OBWVE Oxford Book of Welsh Verse in English, The. *Gwyn Jones, comp.* (1977) Oxford University Press

OFD   O Frabjous Day! Poetry for Holidays and Special Occasions. *Myra Cohn Livingston, ed.* (1977) Atheneum

OHFP   One Hundred and One Famous Poems. *Roy J. Cook, comp.* (Rev. ed., 1958) Reilly & Lee Company; reprinted 1981 by Contemporary Books

OHIP   Our Holidays in Poetry. *Mildred P. Harrington and Josephine H. Thomas, comps.* (1929) The H. W. Wilson Company

OnMSP 100 More Story Poems. *Elinor Parker, comp.* (1960) Thomas Y. Crowell Company

OnUR   Once upon a Rhyme; 101 Poems for Young Children. *Sara Corrin and Stephen Corrin, eds.* (1982) Faber and Faber

OPOP   100 Poems by 100 Poets; an Anthology. *Harold Pinter, Geoffrey Godbert, and Anthony Astbury, comps.* (1986) Grove Press

OPP   101 Patriotic Poems. (1986) Contemporary Books

OV   Other Voice, The; Twentieth-Century Women's Poetry in Translation. *Joanna Bankier and others, eds.* (1976) W. W. Norton & Company

OxBA   Oxford Book of American Verse, The. *F. O. Matthiessen, ed.* (1950) Oxford University Press

OxBB   Oxford Book of Ballads, The. *James Kinsley, ed.* (1969) Oxford University Press

OxBC   Oxford Book of Contemporary Verse, The; 1945–1980. *D. J. Enright, comp.* (1980) Oxford University Press

OxBChV Oxford Book of Children's Verse, The. *Iona Opie and Peter Opie, eds.* (1973) Oxford University Press

OxBLMV Oxford Book of Late Medieval Verse and Prose, The. *Douglas Gray, ed.* (1985) Clarendon Press

OxBoLi Oxford Book of Light Verse, The. *W. H. Auden, ed.* (1938) Oxford University Press

OxBS   Oxford Book of Scottish Verse, The. *John MacQueen and Tom Scott, comps.* (1966) Oxford University Press

OxBSP Oxford Book of Short Poems, The. *P. J. Kavanagh and James Michie, eds.* Oxford University Press

OxBSS Oxford Book of Sea Songs, The. *Roy Palmer, ed.* (1986) Oxford University Press

OxBTC Oxford Book of Twentieth-Century English Verse, The. *Philip Larkin, ed.* (1973) Oxford University Press

OxNR   Oxford Nursery Rhyme Book, The. *Iona Opie and Peter Opie, comps.* (1955) Oxford University Press

WiR   Wind and the Rain, The; an Anthology of Poems for Young People. *John Hollander and Harold Bloom, eds.* (1961) Doubleday & Company

WMBCH   When My Brothers Come Home; Poems from Central and Southern Africa. *Frank Mkalawile Chipasula, ed.* (1985) Wesleyan University Press

WPE   Women Poets in English, The; an Anthology. *Ann Stanford, ed.* (1972) McGraw-Hill Book Company

WPOW   Women Poets of the World. *Joanna Bankier and Deirdre Lashgari, eds.* (1983) Macmillan Publishing Company

WS   Watchers and Seekers; Creative Writing by Black Women. *Rhonda Cobham and Merle Collins, eds.* (1988) Peter Bedrick Books

WSC   Why Am I Grown So Cold? Poems of the Unknowable. *Myra Cohn Livingston, ed.* (1982) Atheneum

WT   Women Troubadours, The. *Meg Bogin, ed.* (1980) W. W. Norton & Company

WTO   World Treasury of Oral Poetry, A. *Ruth Finnegan, ed.* (1978) Indiana University Press

ZPCJ   Zen Poems of China & Japan; the Crane's Bill. *Lucien Stryk, Takashi Ikemoto, and Taigan Takayama, trs.* (1973) Grove Press

THE COLUMBIA
GRANGER'S®
DICTIONARY OF
POETRY
QUOTATIONS

POETRY QUOTATIONS

Poetry Quotations are arranged alphabetically by poet, with those from poems without known authors listed first. Under each poet, the poems from which the quotations derive are listed alphabetically. Also under each poet, all quotations are listed numerically. The codes at the end of all the quotations from a given poem indicate the anthologies in which the texts of the poem appear. These anthologies are listed on page xiii. Some quotations from long poems, for instance by Shakespeare and Samuel Johnson, have been included here even though the quotations themselves were not included in the anthologies listed. Line numbers are given except for quotations from most long poems or where there are differing versions of a poem.

UNKNOWN

Adam Lay Ibounden

1 Adam lay y-bounden,
  Bounden in a bond; (l. 1–2)

2 And al was for an appel, (l. 5)

ACP; CH; ChTr; CTC; HAP; InPS; MeEL; NAEL-1; NOBE; NOCV; NoP; OAEL-1; OxBLMV; OxBoLi; PoE; PoEL-1; TOF; WeW

The Agincourt Carol

3 Our king went forth to Normandy,
  With grace and might of chivalry,
  The God for him wrought marvellously,
  Wherefore England may call and cry
  Deo gratias, Deo gratias Anglia
  Redde pro victoria. (l. 1–6)

EBEV; MeEL; OAEL-1; OBET

Alison

4 From alle wymmen mi love is lent
  And lyht on Alysoun. (l. 11–12)

MeEL; NAEL-1; NoP; OAEL-1; OBEV

Alison Gross

5 And she straiked me three times o'er her knee;
  She changed me again to my ain proper shape,
  And I nae mair maun toddle about the tree.

CH; ESPB; FaBoCh; OxBB; WSC

All Seasons in One

6 April is in my mistress' face,
  And July in her eyes hath place,
  Within her bosom is September,
  But in her heart a cold December.

GBL; HeIP; OBSC; TrGrPo

Animal Fair

7 The elephant sneezed
  And fell on his knees,
  And that was the end of the monk,
  the monk, the monk.

AS; BLPA; FaBoBe; FPL; MoShBr; NTCP; RHPC

As I Sat on a Sunny Bank

8 I saw three ships come sailing by,
  Come sailing by, come sailing by,
  I saw three ships come sailing by,
  On Christmas Day in the morning.

9 O he did whistle and she did sing,
  And all the bells on earth did ring
  For joy our Saviour Christ was born
  On Christmas Day in the morning.

ChTr; GBP; OxBoLi; OxNR

As I Walked by Myself

10 'Look to thyself,
   Take care of thyself,
   For nobody cares for thee.' (l. 4–6)

ChTr; FaBoEE; NA; OxBSP; OxNR

As I Walked Out in the Streets of Laredo

11 'Oh beat the drum slowly and play the fife lowly,
Play the Dead March as you carry me along;
Take me to the green valley, there lay the sod o'er me,
For I'm a young cowboy and I know I've done wrong.
(l. 5—8)

AmFP; AS; ChTr; FaFP; GBP; RB

As I was going by Charing Cross

12 As I was going by Charing Cross,
I saw a black man upon a black horse;
They told me it was King Charles the First — (l. 1—3)

CH; FaBoCh; GBP; OxNR

As Joseph Was a-Walking

13 "He neither shall be christened
In white wine or red,
But with fair spring water,
With which we were christenèd." (l. 17—20)

BoTP; GN; OHIP; PChr

Babylon; or, The Bonnie Banks o' Fordie

14 Its whether will ye be a rank robber's wife,
Or will ye die by my wee pen knife?

Its I'll not be a rank robber's wife,
But I'll rather die by your wee pen knife.

He 's killed this may and he 's laid her by,
For to bear the red rose company. (l. 9—14)

AmFP; ESPB; OxBB; SeCePo

The Bailiff's Daughter of Islington

15 There was a youthe, and a well-loved youthe,
And he was a squires son:
He loved the bayliffes daughter deare,
That lived in Islington. (l. 1—4)

16 O staye, O staye, thou goodlye youthe,
She standeth by thy side;
She is here alive, she is not dead,
And readye to be thy bride. (l. 45—48)

17 O farewell griefe, and welcome joye,
Ten thousand times therefore; (l. 49—50)

ESPB; FaBoBa; GN; OBET; OxBB; OxBoLi

Battle of Brunanburh

18 Athelstan King,
Lord among Earls,
Bracelet-bestower and
Baron of Barons, (l. 1—4)

19 Slew with the sword-edge (l. 9)

20 Brake the shield-wall,
Hewed the lindenwood,
Hacked the battleshield, (l. 11—13)

21 Then with their nailed prows
Parted the Norsemen, (l. 93—94)

22 Shamed in their souls. (l. 99)

AnOE; OBVE; OBWP; TrGrPo; WaaP

The Bells of London

23 Gay go up and gay go down,
To ring the bells of London town.
Halfpence and farthings,
Say the bells of St. Martin's.
Oranges and lemons,
Say the bells of St. Clement's. (l. 1—6)

24 Pancakes and fritters,
Say the bells of St. Peter's.
Two sticks and an apple,
Say the bells of Whitechapel.

Kettles and pans,
Say the bells of St. Ann's. (l. 7—12)

25 You owe me ten shillings,
Say the bells of St. Helen's.
When will you pay me?
Say the bells of Old Bailey.
When I grow rich,
Say the bells of Shoreditch.
Pray when will that be?
Say the bells of Stepney.
I am sure I don't know,
Says the great bell of Bow. (l. 13—22)

BoTP; ChTr; LiTB; OxBoLi; OxNR; PoRA

The Big Rock Candy Mountains

26 I'm headed for a land that's far away
Beside the crystal fountains.
So come with me, we'll go and see
The Big Rock Candy Mountains. (l. 5—8)

AmFP; ChTr; GBP; OBAL; TTTS

Billy Boy

27 "Oh, where have you been, Billy boy, Billy boy?
Oh, where have you been, charming Billy?"
"I've been to seek a wife,
She's the joy of my life,
She's a young thing, and cannot leave her mother."
(l. 1–5)

28 "How old is she, Billy boy, Billy boy?
How old is she, charming Billy?"
Past six, past seven,
Past twenty and eleven,
She's a young thing, and cannot leave her mother."
(l. 21–25)

AmFP; BLPA; HoPM; OBET; OxNR

Binnorie; or, The Two Sisters

29 There were twa sisters sat in a bour;
Binnorie, O Binnorie!
There cam a knight to be their wooer,
By the bonnie milldams o' Binnorie. (l. 1–4)

30 The youngest stood upon a stane,
The eldest cam and push'd her in. (l. 15–16)

31 Sometimes she sank, sometimes she swam,
Until she cam to the miller's dam. (l. 21–22)

32 He's made a harp of her breast-bane,
Whose sound wad melt a heart of stane.

He's ta'en three locks o' her yellow hair,
And wi' them strung his harp sae rare. (l. 41–44)

33 "And yonder stands my brother Hugh,
But by him my William, sweet and true." (l. 51–52)

34 "Woe to my sister, false Helen!" (l. 55)

CH; EnSB; OBEV; PoE; TrGrPo

The Bitter Withy

35 our Saviour asked his dear mother
If he could play at ball. (l. 3–4)

36 'Oh the withy, the withy, the bitter withy
That has caused me to smart,
The withy shall be the very first tree
Fort to perish all at the heart.' (l. 31–34)

OBET

Bonnie George Campbell

37 Bonnie George Campbell rode out on a day.
He saddled, he bridled, and gallant rode he,
And hame cam his guid horse, but never cam he.
(l. 2–4)

AmFP; CH; ELP; EnRP; ESPB; FaBoBa; GBP; GoTS;
NoP; OxBB; OxBoLi

Bonny Barbara Allan

38 It was in and about the Martinmas time,
When the green leaves were afalling,
That Sir John Graeme, in the West Country,
Fell in love with Barbara Allan. (l. 1–4)

39 "O mother, mother, make my bed!
O make it saft and narrow!
Since my love died for me today,
I'll die for him tomorrow." (l. 33–36)

AWP; BoLoP; CH; ESPB; HeIP; InPK; LiTB; NAEL-1;
NoP; OxBB; TrGrPo

The Bonny Earl of Murray

40 Ye Highlands and ye Lawlands.
Oh! where hae ye been?
They hae slain the Earl of Murray,
And hae laid him on the green. (l. 1–4)

ESPB; FaBoBa; OBEV; OxBB; OxBS; PrIm

Brian O'Linn

41 Brian O'Linn was a gentleman born,
He lived at a time when no clothes they were worn.
(l. 1–2)

FaBoBa; FaBoNo; GBP; NBLV; RB

Bring Us In Good Ale

42 Bring us in no browne bred, for that is made of brane,
Nor bring us in no white bred, for therein is no gane,
But bring us in good ale!

Bring us in no befe, for there is many bones,
But bring us in good ale, for that goth downe at ones,
And bring us in good ale! (l. 3–8)

CH; EBEV; FaBoCo; MeEL; OAEL-1; SeCePo

Broom, Green Broom

43 There was an old man lived out in the wood,
His trade was a-cutting of Broom, green Broom;
He had but one son without thrift, without good,
Who lay in his bed till 'twas noon, bright noon.
(l. 1–4)

44 At market and fair, all folks do declare,
There is none like the Boy that sold Broom, green
Broom. (l. 23–24)

CH; LiTB; OxBoLi; PoRA

The Brown Girl

45 "I am as brown as brown can be,
And my eyes as black as sloe;
I am as brisk as brisk can be,
And wild as forest doe. (l. 1—4)

46 "Me did he send a love-letter,
He sent it from the town,
Saying no more he loved me,
For that I was so brown. (l. 9—12)

47 "My faith and troth I give back to thee,
So may thy soul have rest." (l. 51—52)

48 I'll dance above your green, green grave
Where you do lie beneath." (l. 59—60)

ELP; ESPB; OBET; OxBB

Brown Robyn's Confession

49 Till by and came Our Blessed Lady,
Her dear young son her wi.

"Will ye gang to your men again?
Or will ye gang wi me?
Will ye gang to the high heavens,
Wi my dear son and me?" (l. 23—28)

ACP; CH; ESPB; GBP

Bury Me Not on the Lone Prairie

50 "Oh bury me not on the lone prairie,
Where the wild cayotes will howl o'er me,
In a narrow grave just six by three, (l. 9—12)

AS; FaBoBe; FaBV; FaFP

Carol of the Numbers

51 Green grow the rushes-O
What is your one-O? (l. 2—3)

52 Ten for the Ten Commandments

Eleven for the 'leven that went to heaven

Twelve for the twelve Apostles (l. 30—32)

AmFP; GBP; OBET; OxBoLi

Casey Jones

53 Come all you rounders if you want to hear
A story 'bout a brave engineer;
Casey Jones, that was the rounder's name
On a heavy eight-wheeler he rode to fame. (l. 1—4)

54 Poor Casey Jones he was all right,
He stuck by his duty both day an' night,

55 Casey Jones, mounted to the cabin,
Casey Jones, throttle in his hand,
Casey Jones mounted to the cabin,
Took his farewell journey to the Promised Land.
(l. 49—52)

AmFP; AS; BeLS; FaBV; OxBoLi; RR; TrGrPo

The Cauld Lad of Hilton or, The Wandering Spectre

56 The acorn's not yet
Fallen from the tree
That's to grow the wood,
That's to make the cradle,
That's to rock the bairn,
That's to grow a man,
That's to lay me. (l. 2—8)

CH; ChTr; FaBoCh; GBP; OxBoLi

The Cherry-Tree Carol

57 Then bowed down the highest tree
unto his mother's hand;
Then she cried, "See, Joseph,
I have cherries at command." (l. 26—28)

AmFP; ChTr; EBEV; ELP; EnSB; ESPB; FaBoBa; GBP;
HeIP; OAEL-1; OBCP; OBET; OFD; OnMSP; OxBB;
OxBoLi; TrGrPo

Chevy Chase

58 God prosper long our noble king,
Our liffes and saftyes all!
A woefull hunting once there did
In Chevy Chase befall. (l. 1—4)

59 The hounds ran swiftly through the woods
The nimble deere to take,
That with their cryes the hills and dales
An eccho shrill did make. (l. 37—40)

60 Erle Douglas on his milk-white steede,
Most like a baron bold,
Rode foremost of his company,
Whose armor shone like gold. (l. 65—68)

61 At last these two stout erles did meet,
Like captaines of great might; (l. 121—122)

62 'Erle Dowglas, for thy life,
Wold I had lost my hand; (l. 151—152)

63 God save our king, and blesse this land
With plentye, ioy, and peace,
And grant hencforth that foule debate
Twixt noble men may ceaze! (l. 253–256)

FaBoBa; GN; OBET

Child Waters

64 Shee said, Lullabye, my owne deere child!
Lullabye, deere child, deere!
I wold thy father were a king,
Thy mother layd on a beere!

'Peace now,' he said, 'good Faire Ellen,
And be of good cheere, I thee pray,
And the bridall and the churching both,
They shall bee upon one day.' (l. 157–164)

ESPB; FaBoBa; OBET; OxBB

Clerk Colvill

65 Then louder cry'd the Clerk Colvill,
O sairer, sairer akes my head;
And sairer, sairer ever will,
The maiden crys, 'till you be dead. (l. 33–36)

EnSB; ESPB; FaBoBa; GBP; OxBB

Clerk Saunders

66 Your faith an' trouth yese never get
Nor our trew Love shall never twain
Till ye come within my bower
And kiss me both cheek and chin.

My mouth it is full cold, Margret,
It has the smell now of the ground;
An' if I kiss thy com'ly mouth
Thy life days will not be long. (l. 109–116)

ESPB; FaBoBa; OBEV; OxBS

Cocaine Lil

67 Did you ever hear about Cocaine Lil?
She lived in Cocaine town on Cocaine hill,
She had a cocaine dog and a cocaine cat,
They fought all night with a cocaine rat, (l. 1–4)

68 On her headstone you'll find this refrain:
'She died as she lived, sniffing cocaine.' (l. 27–28)

AS; GBP; MAT; OxBoLi; RB

Corpus Christi Carol

69 By that bedes side ther kneleth a may,
And she wepeth both nyght and day.

And by that beddes side ther stondith a ston,
'Corpus Christi' wretyn theron. (l. 11–14)

ACP; CH; ChTr; EBEV; FaBoBa; GBP; HAP; LiTB;
MeEL; NAEL-1; NOBE; NoP; NU; OAEL-1; OBD;
OBEV; SCV; TrGrPo; WeW

Coventry Carol

70 Herod, the king,
In his raging,
Charged he hath, this day,
His men of might
In his owne sight
All yonge children to slay. (l. 10–15)

ELP; MeEL; OFD; PChr; TTTS

The Cruel Mother

71 She's taen out her little pen-knife,
Fine flowers in the valley,
And twinned the sweet babe o' its life,
And the green leaves they grow rarely. (l. 9–12)

AmFP; ESPB; FaBoBa; InPK; OBET; OxBB

The Cuckoo

72 The cuckoo is a merry bird,
He sings as he flies,
He brings us glad tidings
And tells us no lies. (l. 1–4)

73 The cuckoo is a lazy bird,
She never builds a nest,
She makes herself busy
By singing to the rest. (l. 9–12)

AmFP; ChTr; OBET; OxNR; PBBP

Dear, If You Change

74 Dear, if you change, I'll never choose again;
Sweet, if you shrink, I'll never think of love;
Fair, if you fail, I'll judge all beauty vain;
Wise, if too weak, moe wits I'll never prove. (l. 1–4)

EIL; EnLoPo; InvP; OBSC; PoEL-2

The Death of Queen Jane

75 Queen Jane was in labor
Six weeks and some more;
The women grew wearied,
And the midwife gave o'er. (l. 1–4)

76 Just pierce my right side open
And save my baby." (l. 7–8)

AmFP; ESPB; OBET

Dives and Lazarus

77 'Thou art none of mine, brother Lazarus,
That lies begging at my gate.
No meat, no drink, will I give thee,
For Jesus Christ his sake.' (l. 13–16)

78 There is a place prepared in hell,
For to sit upon a serpent's knee.' (l. 39–40)

ELP; ESPB; FaBoBa; OBET; OxBB

The Dowie Houms o' Yarrow

79 "O haud your tongue, my father dear,
An' dinna grieve your Sarah;
A better lord was never born
Than him I lost on Yarrow. (l. 53–56)

ESPB; GoTS; OBEV; OBS; OxBS

Down in the Valley

80 Down in the valley,
Valley so low,
Hang your head over,
Hear the train blow. (l. 1–4)

81 Write me a letter,
Write it out plain,
And send it me care of
The Barbourville Jail. (l. 33–36)

AS; FaFP; GBP; WTO

The Dying Airman

82 'Take the cylinders out of my kidneys,
The connecting-rod out of my brain,
Take the cam-shaft from out of my backbone,
And Assemble the engine again.' (l. 5–8)

AS; FaBoNo; FaFP; OxBoLi; RB

Eadwacer

83 Wulf, my Wulf! Waiting for you
has made me ill, your seldom coming,
this sorrowing mood — not lack of meat.

Do you hear, Eadwacer? Our poor whelp
a wolf bears off to the wood. (l. 13–17)

BoWoP; CIP; PBWP; TrGrPo; WPE

Earl Brand

84 To a maiden true he'll give his hand,
Hey lillie, ho lillie lallie,
To the king's daughter o' fair England,
To a prize that was won by a slain brother's brand,
I' the brave nights so early. (l. 67–71)

OxBB

Edward

85 "Why does your brand so drop with blood,
Edward, Edward? (l. 1–2)

86 "O I have killed my hawk so good,
Mother, mother; (l. 5–6)

87 "And what will you leave to your own mother dear,
Edward, Edward?
And what will ye leave to your own mother dear,
My dear son, now tell me, O?"
"The curse of hell from me shall ye bear,
Mother, mother; (l. 49–54)

AmFP; CH; EBEV; ELP; EnRP; ESPB; FaBoBa; FaPoR;
GoTS; HAP; HoPM; InPK; InPS; LiTB; Mes; NAEL-1;
NOBE; NoP; OBEV; OxBB; OxBS; PoEL-1; PoRA; PrIm;
SoSe; TrGrPo; TW; WeW

Epitaph on John Knott

88 Here lies John Knott:
His father was Knott before him,
He lived Knott, died Knott, (l. 1–3)

ChTr; FaBoEE; OBS; SeCV-1

Erith, on the Thames

89 There are men in the village of Erith
Whom nobody seeth or heareth,
And there looms, on the marge
Of the river, a barge
That nobody roweth or steereth. (l. 1–5)

ChTr; FaBoPP; GBP; WSC

Everyman

90 O Death! thou comest when I had thee least in mind!
(l. 119)

91 Everyman, I will go with thee, and be thy guide
In thy most need to go by thy side. (l. 522–523)

92 All earthly things is but vanity:
Beauty, Strength, and Discretion do man forsake,
Foolish friends and kinsmen, that fair spake —
All fleeth save Good Deeds, and that am I.
　　　　　　　　　　　　　　(l. 870–873)

NAWM-1; OAEL-1; OxBLMV; PoEL-1

Fair Annie

93 The reivers they stole Fair Annie,
As she walked by the sea;
But a noble knight was her ransom soon,
Wi' gowd and white monie. (l. 1–4)

CH; ESPB; FaBoBa; OxBB

Fara Diddle Dyno

94 Ha ha! ha ha! This world doth pass
Most merrily I'll be sworn,
For many an honest Indian ass
Goes for a unicorn. (l. 1–4)

95 Call Tullia's ape a marmasyte
And Leda's goose a swan. (l. 7–8)

ElL; FaBoCh; FaBoCo; FaBoNo; OxBoLi

Fine Knacks for Ladies

96 Fine knacks for ladies, cheap, choice, brave and new,
Good pennyworths, — but money cannot move:
I keep a fair but for the Fair to view, —
A beggar may be liberal of love.
Though all my wares be trash, the heart is true,

CH; EBEV; ElL; HAP; LiTB; NoP; OAEL-1; OBSC; QFR

Five Little Chickens

97 Said the first little chicken,
With a queer little squirm,
"I wish I could find
A fat little worm" (l. 1–4)

98 "If you want any breakfast,
Just come here and scratch." (l. 23–24)

FaPON; MoShBr; PDV; RAR

The Foggy, Foggy Dew

99 When I was a bachelor, I lived by myself
And I worked at the weaver's trade;
The only, only, thing that I ever did wrong

Was to woo a fair young maid.
I wooed her in the winter time,
And in the summer too;
And the only, only thing that I ever did wrong
Was to keep her from the foggy, foggy dew. (l. 1–8)

AS; CoMu; ELP; GBP; LiTB; OBET; OxBoLi

Fowls in the Frith

100 Fowls in the frith,
Fishes in the flood,
And I must wax wod:
Much sorrow I walk with
For best of bone and blood.

HAP; MeEL; NAEL-1; OxBSP

Frankie and Johnny

101 Frankie and Johnny were lovers, O lordy how they
　　could love
Swore to be true to each other, true as the stars above;
He was her man but he done her wrong. (l. 1–3)

102 Frankie threw back her kimono, she took out her forty-
　　four
Root-a-toot-toot, three times she shot, right through
　　that hardwood door. (l. 25–27)

103 The very last words he ever said were, "High-low Jack
　　and the game." (l. 44)

104 "It's as plain as plain can be;
This woman shot her lover, it's murder in the second
　　degree, (l. 73–74)

105 Frankie mounted to the scaffold as calm as a girl can
　　be, (l. 85)

AmFP; AS; BeLS; FaFP; FF; NIP; NOBA; OxBoLi; RB;
TrGrPo; UnPo

The Friendly Beasts

106 Jesus our brother, strong and good,
Was humbly born in a stable rude,
And the friendly beasts around Him stood,
Jesus our brother, strong and good.

"I", said the donkey, shaggy and brown (l. 1–5)

107 "I," said the cow, all white and red, (l. 9)

108 "I," said the sheep, with curly horn, (l. 13)

109 "I," said the dove, from the rafters high, (l. 17)

FaPON ILY; OnMSP; PChr

The Frog

110 What a wonderful bird the frog are —
When he stand he sit almost;
When he hop, he fly almost.
He ain't got no sense hardly;
He ain't got no tail hardly either.
When he sit, he sit on what he ain't got almost.
(l. 1–6)

MoShBr; NBLV; NTCP; RB

The Gaberlunzie Man

111 'O fy gar ride, and fy gar rin,
And haste ye find these traitors again;
For she's be burnt and he's be slain,
The wearifu' gaberlunzie man.' (l. 49–52)

112 'Wi' cauk and keel I'll win your bread,
And spindles and whorles for them wha need
Whilk is a gentle trade indeed,
To carry the gaberlunzie on. (l. 73–76)

113 A cripple or blind they will ca' me,
While we shall be merry and sing.' (l. 79–80)

EnSB; GoTS; OxBB; OxBS

Get Up and Bar the Door

114 They made a paction tween them twa,
They made it firm and sure,
That the first word whaeer shoud speak,
Shoud rise and bar the door. (l. 13–16)

ESPB; FaBoBa; GoTS; HeIP; NoP; OnMSP; OxBS; PDV;
TrGrPo

Go Down, Moses

115 Go down, Moses
'Way down in Egypt land,
Tell ole Pharaoh,
To let my people go. (l. 1–4)

AH; AnAmPo; BPo; EaLo; NOBA

God Bless the Master of This House

116 God bless the master of this house,
Likewise the mistress too: (l. 1–2)

117 Love and joy come to you,
And to your wassail too, (l. 5–6)

BoTP; MoShBr; OHIP

The Golden Vanity

118 And they wrapped him up in an old cow's hide,
And they sunk him in the Lowland sea,
And they sunk him in the Lowlands low. (l. 43–45)

CH; ELP; FaBoCh; OBET; WiR

The Grass on the Mountain

119 long long
The snow has possessed the mountains. (l. 1–2)

120 Loud are the thunder drums
In the tents of the mountains. (l. 6–7)

121 We are wearied of our huts
And the smoky smell of our garments.
We are sick with desire of the sun
And the grass on the mountains. (l. 11–14)

AmFN; AWP; FaPON; GOA

The Great Silkie of Sule Skerry

122 "I am a man upo the lan,
An' I am a silkie in the sea,
And when I'm far and far frae lan,
My dwelling is in Sule Skerrie." (l. 9–12)

ChTr; ESPB; FaBoBa; FaBoCh; GBP; MAT; MOS; OxBB

Green Grass

123 She shall get a duke, my dear,
As duck do get a drake;
And she shall have a young prince,
For her own fair sake. (l. 9–12)

BoTP; CH; GBP; OxBoLi; OxNR

Greensleeves

124 Alas, my Love! ye do me wrong
To cast me off discourteously:
And I have loved you so long,
Delighting in your company. (l. 5–8)

ElL; FaBoCh; GBL; OBSC; PoEL-2; TTTS

Gypsies in the Wood

125 My mother said that I never should
Play with the gypsies in the wood, (l. 1–2)

BoTP; OxBoLi; OxBSP; OxNR

The Gypsy Laddie

126 'Will ye go with me, my hinny and my heart?
Will you go with me, my dearie?
And I will swear by the hilt of my spear,
That your lord shall no more come near thee.'
(l. 13–16)

ChTr; EnSB; ESPB; FaBoBa

Helen of Kirconnell

127 I wish I were where Helen lies,
Night and day on me she cries;
And I am weary of the skies,
For her sake that died for me. (l. 37–40)

AWP; CH; ELP; FaFP; GoTS; GTBS; GTBS-P; LiTB;
OBEV

Hey Nonny No!

128 Men are fools that wish to die!
Is 't not fine to dance and sing
When the bells of death do ring? (l. 2–4)

CH; ChTr; EBEV; ElL; FaBoCh; OBEV; TrGrPo

The Holly and the Ivy

129 The holly and the ivy
Are plants that are well known
Of all the trees that grow in the woods
The holly bears the crown. (l. 1–4)

130 shows its berries red
In token of the drops of blood
Which on Calvary were shed. (l. 10–12)

131 in the holly prickles
You can plainly see
The crown of thorns our Saviour wore (l. 13–15)

CH; ChTr; ELP; GBP; OBET; OFD; PChr

Hugh of Lincoln

132 He kicked the ball with his right foot,
And catched it with his knee,
And through and through the Jew's window
He gared the bonny ball flee. (l. 5–8)

133 'Throw down the ball, ye Jew's daughter,
Throw down the ball to me!'
'Never a bit,' says the Jew's daughter,
'Till up to me come ye.' (l. 13–16)

134 Now Lady Maisry is gone home,
Made him a winding sheet,
And at the back of merry Lincoln
The dead corpse did her meet.

And all the bells of merry Lincoln,
Without men's hands were rung, (l. 61–66)

ACP; EnSB; ESPB; OxBB

I Asked My Mother

135 I asked my mother for fifty cents
To see the elephant jump the fence.
He jumped so high he reached the sky,
And didn't get back till the Fourth of July. (l. 1–4)

FaFP; MoShBr; OxBoLi; RHPC

I Eat My Peas with Honey

136 I eat my peas with honey, (l. 1)

137 It makes the peas taste funny,
But it keeps them on the knife (l. 3–4)

CenHV; FaBoUs; FaPON; NTCP; OnUR; RHPC

I Heard a Noise and Wishèd for a Sight

138 But what it was, alas, I cannot tell,
Because of it I had no perfect view;
But as it was, by guess, I wish it well
And will until I see the same anew.
Shadow, or she, or both, or choose you whither:
Blest be the thing that brought the shadow hither.
(l. 13–18)

EBEV; ElL; HAP; InvP; OAEL-1

I Know Where I'm Going

139 I know who I love,
But the dear knows who I'll marry. (l. 3–4)

140 I say he's bonny,
He's the flower of them all,
My handsome, winsome Johnny. (l. 14–16)

ELP; GEP; MoShBr; OBET; WTO

I Saw My Lady Weep

141 I saw my lady weep,
And Sorrow proud to be advanced so
In those fair eyes where all perfections keep.
Her face was full of woe;

But such a woe, believe me, as wins more hearts
Than Mirth can do with her enticing parts. (l. 1–6)

EBEV; ElL; ELP; EnLoPo; LiTB; NOBE; OBEV; OBSC;
TrGrPo

I See the Moon

142 I see the moon,
And the moon sees me;
God bless the moon,
And God bless me.

GBP; NTCP; OxNR; PYC; RAR

I Sing of a Maiden

143 Mother and maiden
Was never none but she;
Well may such a lady
Goddes mother be. (l. 17–20)

InPK; NAEL-1; PoE; TOF

If All the World Were Paper

144 If all things were eternall,
And nothing their end bringing;
If this should be, then how should we
Here make an end of singing? (l. 21–24)

FaBoCo; FaBoNo; GBP; NTCP; OxNR; PYC; TTTS

If You Have a Friend

145 If your work is made more easy
By a friendly, helping hand,
Say so. (l. 31–33)

BLPA; FaFP; PWR; WBLP

In the Night

146 her nose was long and cold,
And her shoes were full of feet. (l. 3–4)

FaBoNo; NA; NBLV

Jerusalem, My Happy Home

147 O happy harbour of the saints,
O sweet and pleasant soil,
In thee no sorrow may be found
No grief, no care, no toil. (l. 5–8)

PoE

Jesse James

148 But the dirty little coward that shot Mister Howard,
He laid poor Jesse in his grave. (Chorus)

149 They robbed the Danville train.
And the people they did say, for many miles away,
'Twas the outlaws Frank and Jesse James. (l. 6–8)

AS; BeLS; FaBoBe; UnPo; WiR

Jimmy's Enlisted; or, The Recruited Collier

150 Oh, what's the matter wi' you, my lass,
An' where's your dashin Jimmy?
The sowdger boys have picked him up
And sent him far, far frae me. (l. 1–4)

151 And he'd better gone to the gallows. (l. 8)

CoMu; EBEV; OBET

John Henry

152 When John Henry was a little fellow,
You could hold him in the palm of your hand,
He said to his pa, "When I grow up
I'm gonna be a steel-driving man.
Gonna be a steel-driving man." (l. 1–5)

AmFN; AmFP; AS; BeLS; BPo; FaBoBa; FaBoBe; FaFP;
NOBA; OxBoLi; TrGrPo

Johnie Armstrong

153 There dwelt a man in faire Westmerland,
Jonnë Armstrong men did him call,
He had nither lands nor rents coming in,
Yet he kept eight score men in his hall. (l. 1–4)

154 But Jonnë had a bright sword by his side,
And it was made of the mettle so free,
That had not the king stept his foot aside,
He had smitten his head from his faire bodde.
(l. 45–48)

155 rather then men shall say we were hange'd,
Let them report how we were slaine.' (l. 51–52)

ESPB; FaBoBa; HoPM; NoP; TrGrPo

Johnny, I Hardly Knew Ye

156 With drums and guns, and guns and drums
The enemy nearly slew ye,
My darling dear, you look so queer,
Och, Johnny, I hardly knew ye! (Chorus.)

BIrV; ELP; FaBoBa; GBP; OxBoLi; WaaP

Jolly Jankin

157 As I went on Yule day
In our procession,
Knew I jolly Jankin
By his merry tone —
Kyrie eleison.

GBP; MeEL; NOBE; NoP; OxBLMV; OxBoLi; PoE

Joshua Fit De Battle of Jericho

158 Joshua fit de battle ob Jerico, Jerico, Jerico,
Joshua fit de battle ob Jerico,
An' de walls come tumblin' down. (l. 1–3)

BPo; NOBA; TAP; TrGrPo

King John and the Abbot of Canterbury

159 a notable prince that was called King John;
And he ruled England with main and with might,
For he did great wrong, and maintained little right.
(l. 2–4)

160 Thou must tell me to one penny what I am worth.
(l. 28)

161 How soon I may ride the whole world about;
And at the third question thou must not shrink,
But tell me here truly what I do think." (l. 30–32)

162 For and if thou canst answer my questions three,
Thy life and thy living both saved shall be. (l. 75–76)

163 And then your grace need not make any doubt
But in twenty-four hours you'll ride it about."
(l. 91–92)

164 But I'm his poor shepherd, as plain you may see,
That am come to beg pardon for him and for me."
(l. 99–100)

165 Thou hast brought him a pardon from good King
John." (l. 108)

BoTP; EnSB; GN; TrGrPo

The Lady Prayeth the Return of Her Lover Abiding on the Seas

166 open thou thy manly mouth, and say that thou wilt
come;
Whereby my heart may think, although I see not thee,
That thou wilt come, thy word so sware, if thou a
livesman be. (l. 4–6)

167 if thou slip thy troth and do not come at all.
As minutes in the clock do strike so call for death I
shall:
To please both thy false heart, and rid myself from
woe,
That rather had to die in troth than live forsaken so.
(l. 19–22)

ElL; GBL; OBEV; OBSC

The Laily Worm and the Machrel of the Sea

168 For she has made me the laily worm
That lies at the fit o' the tree,
An' my sister Masery she's made
The machrel of the sea. (l. 5–8)

ChTr; ESPB; InvP; OxBB; PoEL-1

A Lament for the Priory of Walsingham

169 thou Prince of Walsingham,
Graunt me to frame
Bitter plaints to rue thy wrong,
Bitter woe for thy name. (l. 5–8)

170 Blessing turned to blasphemies,
Holy deeds to despites.

Sin is where our Lady sat,
Heaven turned is to hell,
Sathan sits where our Lord did sway,
Walsingham, Oh farewell! (l. 39–44)

ACP; ChTr; FaBoPP; GBP; PoEL-2

The Lament of the Border Widow

171 Nae living man I'll love again,
Since that my lovely knight is slain.
Wi ae lock of his yellow hair
I'll chain my heart for evermair. (l. 25–28)

CH; GBP; Mes; OxBB

The Lincolnshire Poacher

172 When I was bound apprentice, in famous Lincolnshire,
Full well I served my master for more than seven year,
Till I took up poaching, as you shall quickly hear:
Oh, 'tis my delight on a shining night, in the season of
the year. (l. 1–4)

CH; GBP; OnMSP; OxBoLi; SD; WiR

Little Musgrave and Lady Barnard

173 Quoth she. "I have loved thee, Little Musgrave,
Full long and many a day;"
"So have I loved you, faire lady,
Yet never a word durst I say."

"I have a bower at Bucklesfordbery,
Full daintyly it is deight;
If thou wilt wend thither, thou Little Musgrave,
Thou's lig in mine armes all night." (l. 17–24)

174 "Arise, arise, thou Littell Musgrave,
And put they clothes on;
It shall nere be said in my country
I have killed a naked man. (l. 81–84)

ErPo; ESPB; FaBoBa; InvP; OBET; OxBB

London Bridge

175 London Bridge is broken down,
Dance o'er my lady lee,
London Bridge is broken down,
With a gay lady.

How shall we build it up again?
Dance o'er my lady lee, (l. 1–6)

CH; ChTr; EyDe; GBP; OxBoLi; OxNR

Long, Long Ago

176 Winds through the olive trees
Softly did blow,
Round little Bethlehem
Long, long ago. (l. 1–4)

BoTP; FaPON; OHIP; PChr; PDV

Lord Lovel

177 Lord Lovel he stood at his castle gate
A-combing his milk-white steed,
When along came Lady Nancy Bell
A-wishing her lover good speed, speed, speed, (l. 1–4)

178 And out of her bosom there grew a red rose
And out of Lord Lovel's a briar, briar, briar,
And out of Lord Lovel's a briar. (l. 38–40)

AmFP; AS; BLPA; ESPB; FaPON

Lord Thomas and Fair Annet

179 Lord Thomas was buried in the church,
Fair Ellinor in the choir;
And out from her bosom there grew a red rose
And out of Lord Thomas a briar. (l. 77–80)

180 there it entwined like a true love's knot
For all true loves to admire. (l. 83–84)

ESPB

Love Not Me for Comely Grace

181 Love not me for comely grace,
For my pleasing eye or face,
Nor for any outward part:
No, nor for a constant heart! (l. 1–4)

182 love me still, but know not why! (l. 8)

BLPL; CH; ElL; ELP; FaFP; GTBS; GTBS-P; LiTB;
OBEV; OxBSP; PoLF

Love Will Find Out the Way

183 if once the message greet him
That his True Love doth stay,
If Death should come and meet him,
Love will find out the way! (l. 53–56)

FaBoCh; FaFP; GBL; GN; GTBS; GTBS-P; OBEV; WiR

Love Winged My Hopes and Taught Me How to Fly

184 Love wing'd my Hopes and taught me how to fly (l. 1)

185 true pleasure
Lives in measure,
Which if men forsake,
Blinded they into folly run and grief for pleasure take.
(l. 3–6)

ElL; OBEV; OBSC; TrGrPo

Lyke-Wake Dirge, The

186 This ae nighte, this ae nighte,
— Every nighte and alle,
Fire and fleet and candle-lighte,
And Christe receive thy saule. (l. 33–36)

ACP; CH; ChTr; EaLo; EnSB; FaBoCh; FaBoRV; GBP;
HAP; HoPM; NOBE; NoP; OBEV; PoEL-1; WeW

Mary Hamilton

187 Word's gane to the kitchen,
And word's gane to the ha',
That Marie Hamilton gangs wi' bairn
To the hichest Stewart of a'. (l. 1–4)

188 "Last night there was four Maries,
The night there'll be but three;
There was Marie Seton, and Marie Beton,
And Marie Carmichael, and me." (l. 69–72)

AmFP; ESPB; FaBoBa; NoP

A Maxim Revised

189   In controlling men:
      If at first you don't succeed,
      Why, cry, cry, again. (l. 3–4)

BLPA; FPL; NBLV; WBLP

Merry It Is

190   I, being done so great a wrong,
      Sorrow and mourn and fast. (l. 6–7)

HAP; MeEL

My Love in Her Attire

191   No beauty she doth miss,
      When all her robes are on;
      But Beauty's self she is,
      When all her robes are gone. (l. 5–8)

BLPL; BoLoP; ElL; FF; GTBS; GTBS-P; HeIP; LiTB;
NAEL-1; NIP; NOBE; OBEV; OBSC; OxBSP

The Night before Larry Was Stretched

192   For when the gallows is high
      Your journey is shorter to heaven. (l. 57–58)

BIrV; FaBoBa; GBP; NOBL; NOIV; OxBoLi

Now I Lay Me Down to Take My Sleep

193   Now I lay me down to sleep,
      I pray the Lord my soul to keep;
      If I should die before I wake,
      I pray the Lord my soul to take. (l. 1–4)

BLRP; FaFP; GBP; OxNR

Odd but True

194   Oh that my lungs could bleat like butter'd pease;
      But bleating of my lungs hath caught the itch,
      And are as mangy as the Irish Seas,
      That doth ingender windmills on a bitch. (l. 1–4)

FaBoCo; FaBoNo; NA; NOBL

The Old Orange Flute

195   In the County Tyrone, in the town of Dungannon, (l. 1)

196   there's nothing compared with the ould Orange flute.
                                                   (l. 8)

197   blow as he would, though it made a great noise,
      The flute would play only 'The Protestant Boys'.
                                                   (l. 23–24)

198   So the old flute was doomed and its fate was pathetic,
      'Twas fastened and burned at the stake as heretic,
      While the flames roared around it they heard a strange
         noise —
      'Twas the old flute still whistling 'The Protestant Boys'.
                                                   (l. 37–40)

FaBoBa; GBP; OxBoLi; WTO

On a Clergyman's Horse Biting Him

199   The steed bit his master;
      How came this to pass?
      He heard the good pastor
      Cry, 'All flesh is grass.' (l. 1–4)

FaBoCo; FaBoEE; NBLV; OxBoLi

On Prince Frederick

200   But since 'tis only Fred,
      Who was alive and is dead,
      There's no more to be said. (l. 11–13)

FaBoCo; FaBoEE; NOBL; OxBoLi

The Outlaw of Loch Lene

201   Oh, many a day have I made good ale in the glen,
      That came not of stream, or malt, like the brewing of
         men;
      My bed was the ground, my roof the greenwood above,
      And the wealth that I sought, one far kind glance from
         my love. (l. 1–4)

BIrV; CH; GBL; OBEV

Pangur Bán

202   I and Pangur Bán, my cat,
      'Tis a like task we are at;
      Hunting mice is his delight,
      Hunting words I sit all night. (l. 1–4)

203   So in peace our tasks we ply,
      Pangur Ban, my cat, and I;
      In our arts we find our bliss,
      I have mine and he has his. (l. 25–28)

AnIL; CRH; FaBoCh; RB

Phillida Flouts Me

204 Come to me, pretty peat, let me embrace thee!
Though thou be fair and feat, do not disgrace me;
For I will constant prove (make no denial!)
And be thy dearest love — proof maketh trial.
If ought do breed thy pain,
I can procure thy gain;
Yet, bootless, I complain —
Phyllida flouts me. (l. 65–72)

CoMu; ElL; InvP; OBEV; OBSC; TrGrPo

Quia Amore Langueo

205 In the vale of restless mind
I sought in mountain and in mead,
Trusting a true love for to find. (l. 1–3)

206 A voice I heard — and near I yede —
In great dolour complaining tho:
'See, dear soul, my sides bleed,
Quia amore langueo. (l. 5–8)

NOBE; NOCV; OBEV; PoEL-1

The Rantin Laddie

207 Oft have I played at cards and dice,
Because they were so enticing;
But this is a sad and sorrowful day
To see my apron rising. (l. 1–4)

208 now I must sit at my father's fireboard,
And rock my bastard baby. (l. 11–12)

209 Ye lassies all, where'er ye be,
And ye lie with an east-shore laddie,
Ye'll happy be and ye'll happy be,
For they are frank and free. (l. 49–52)

AmFP; ESPB; HAP; OxBA; TAP

Robin Hood and Allen-a-Dale

210 And then having ended this merry wedding,
The bride looked as fresh as a queen;
And so they returned to the merry greenwood,
Amongst the leaves so green. (l. 105–108)

ESPB; FaBoBe; GBP; MoShBr

Robin Hood's Death

211 'Lay me a green sod under my head,
And another at my feet;
And lay my bent bow at my side,
Which was my music sweet;

And make my grave of gravel and green,
Which is most right and meet. (l. 65–70)

ESPB; FaBoBa; OBET; TrGrPo

St. Stephen and King Herod

212 Seynt Stevene was a clerk in Kyng Herowdes halle.
And servyd him of bred and cloth, as every kyng
   befalle. (l. 1–2)

213 I forsak the, Kyng Herowdes, and thi werkes alle;
Ther is a chyld in Bedlem born is beter than we alle.'
                                              (l. 6–8)

CH; ESPB; NoP; OxBB; OxBoLi; TrGrPo

The Second Shepherd's Play

214 Hail, comly and clene,
Hail, yong child!
Hail, maker, as I meene,
Of a maden so milde!

ChTr; NAEL-1; NAs; OAEL-1; OBEV; OxBoLi; PoEL-1

The Seven Virgins

215 I met with virgins seven,
And one of them was Mary mild,
Our Lord's mother from heaven. (l. 2–4)

216 Oh the rose, the rose, the gentle rose,
And the fennel that grows so green!
God give us grace in every place
To pray for our king and queen. (l. 41–44)

CH; ChTr; GBP; OBET; OBEV

The Shan Van Vocht

217 Don't you hear his cannons roar?
We'll be Orangemen no more
Says the Shan Van Vocht. (l. 10–12)

AnIL; FaBoPV; GBP; OxBoLi

She Was Poor but She Was Honest

218 She was poor, but she was honest,
Victim of the squire's whim:
First he loved her, then he left her,
And she lost her honest name. (l. 1–4)

219 'It's the same the whole world over;
   It's the poor that gets the blame,
   It's the rich that gets the pleasure.
   Isn't it a blooming shame?' (l. 37—40)

ErPo; FaBoCo; FiBHP; GBP; NBLV; NOBL; RB

Since First I Saw Your Face

220 I that loved and you that liked, shall we begin to
      wrangle?
   No, no, no, my heart is fast, and cannot disentangle.
                                          (l. 3—4)

ELP; LiTB; OBEV; OBSC; OxBSP

Sir Andrew Barton

221 Our noble King, King Henery the eighth,
   Ouer the riuer of Thames past hee.

222 Saint Andrews crosse, that is his guide;

223 Strike on your drummes, spread out your ancyents!
   Sound out your trumpetts, sound out amaine!

224 Itt is verry true, as the Welchman sayd,
   Couetousness getts no gaine.

225 I am hurt but I am not slaine;
   Ile lay mee downe and bleed a-while
   And then Ile rise and ffight againe.

226 Fight on for Scotland and Saint Andrew
   Till you heare my whistle blowe.

EnSB

Sir Patrick Spens

227 Late late yestreen I saw the new moone,
   Wi the auld moone in hir arme,
   And I feir, I feir, my deir master,
   That we will cum to harme.' (l. 25—28)

228 Haf owre, haf owre to Aberdour,
   It's fiftie fadom deip,
   And thair lies guid Sir Patrick Spence,
   Wi the Scots lords at his feit. (l. 41—44)

AmFP; AWP; CH; EBEV; ELP; EnRP; EnSB; ESPB;
FaBoBa; FaBoCh; FaPoR; FF; GN; GoJo; HAP; HoPM;
InPK; InPS; InvP; LiTB; MOS; NAEL-1; NIP; NIP;
NOBE; NoP; OAEL-1; OBEV; OxBB; OxBS; PoEL-1;
PoE; PPP; PrIm; RB; TrGrPo; UnPo; WeW

Sister, Awake!

229 Therefore awake! make haste, I say,
   And let us, without staying,
   All in our gowns of green so gay
   Into the Park a-maying! (l. 9—12)

BoTP; CH; EIL; NOBE; OBEV

Sonnet Found in a Deserted Madhouse

230 Oh that my soul a marrow-bone might seize!
   For the old egg of my desire is broken, (l. 1—2)

FaBoCc; FaBoNo; InvP; NA

Squire and Milkmaid; or, Blackberry Fold

231 It's of a rich squire in Bristol doth dwell,
   There are ladies of honour that love him well,
   But all was in vain, in vain was said,
   For he was in love with a charming milkmaid. (l. 1—4)

232 And they both went a walking to Blackberry Fold.
                                          (l. 20)

233 It's better to be honest if ever so poor,
   For he's made her his lady instead of his whore.
                                          (l. 39—40)

CoMu; OBET; OBET; OxBB

Summer Is Icumen In

234 Sumer is icumen in,
   Lhude sing cuccu; (l. 1—2)

AWP; ChT; EBEV; FF; HAP; HeIP; InPK; InPS; InvP;
MeEL; NBLV; NIP; NOBE; NoP; OAEL-1; OBEV; PBBP;
TEP; TrGrPo

A Swarm of bees in May

235 A swarm of bees in May
   Is worth a load of hay;
   A swarm of bees in June
   Is worth a silver spoon;
   A swarm of bees in July
   Is not worth a fly. (l. 1—6)

FaBoBe; OxNR

Sweet Betsey from Pike

236 Did you ever hear tell of Sweet Betsy from Pike.
   Who crossed the wide mountains with her lover Ike,
                                          (l. 1—2)

AmFP; AS; FaBoBa; OBAL; OxBoLi

Sweet, Let Me Go!

237 Sweet, let me go! Sweet, let me go!
     What do you mean to vex me so?
     Cease, cease, cease your pleading force! (l. 1–3)

ElL; InvP; OxBSP; TrGrPo

Tam Lin

238 O I forbid you, maidens a'
     That wear gowd on your hair,
     To come, or gae by Carterhaugh,
     For young Tom-lin is there. (l. 1–4)

239 Out then spak her father dear,
     And he spak meek and mild,
     And ever alas, sweet Janet, he says,
     I think thou gaes wi' child.

     If that I gae wi' child, father,
     Mysel maun bear the blame;
     There's ne'er a laird about your ha',
     Shall get the bairn's name. (l. 53–60)

ESPB; FaBoBa; NOBE; OBEV; OBNV; OxBB; OxBS;
WSC

There Was a Young Lady of Lynn

240 That when she essayed
     To drink lemonade,
     She slipped through the straw and fell in. (l. 3–5)

There was an old man of Peru

241 There was an old man from Peru
     Who dreamed he was eating his shoe;
     He woke in a fright
     In the middle of the night
     And found it was perfectly true. (l. 1–5)

CenHV; FaFP; NTCP; OnUR; PDV; SoSe

This Is the Key

242 This is the Key of the Kingdom:
     In that Kingdom is a city; (l. 1–2)

243 A fiery red dragon
     They spied on the grass;
     The lady wept sorely, (l. 34–36)

244 The knight slew the dragon,
     The lady was gay,
     They rode on together,
     Away, away. (l. 38–41)

BoTP; CH; FaBoCh; FaFP; MoShBr; OxBoLi; OxNR; Prf

Thomas the Rhymer

245 True Thomas lay on Huntlie bank;
     A ferlie he spied wi' his e'e;
     And there he saw a lady bright,
     Come riding down by the Eildon Tree. (l. 1–4)

246 That weird shall never daunten me."
     Syne he has kissed her rosy lips,
     All underneath the Eildon Tree. (l. 22–24)

247 And ye maun serve me seven years,
     Through weal or woe as may chance to be." (l. 27–28)

248 "Now haud thy peace!" the lady said,
     "For as I say, so must it be." (l. 75–76)

249 till seven years were gane and past,
     True Thomas on earth was never seen. (l. 79–80)

CH; ChTr; ELP; EnSB; ESPB; FaBoBa; FaBoCh; GoTS;
HAP; InPK; InPS; LiTB; NOBE; OAEL-1; OBEV;
OnMSP; OxBB; OxBS; PoE; Prf; RB; TrGrPo

The Thousand and One Nights

250 For him nor deep nor hill there is,
     But all's one level plain he hunts for flowers.

AWP

251 An early dew woos the half-opened flowers

252 Your mouth, dear child, is envied of the bees.

AWP

253 I passed a tomb among green shades
     Where seven anemones with down-dropped heads
     Wept tears of dew upon the stone beneath.

254 I pray that Allah may be moved
     To drop sleep on her eyes because she loved.

255 I please
     To plant some more dew-wet anemones
     That they may weep.

AWP

256 No hand has been allowed to touch
     The rose I hide,
     Though eyes have looked upon it and desired it.

ErPo

257 Love was before the light began,
     When light if over, love shall be

AWP

Three Young Rats

258 Three young rats with black felt hats,
Three young ducks with white straw flats, (l. 1–2)

259 But suddenly it chanced to rain,
And so they all went home again. (l. 7–8)

ChTr; FaBoNo; GBP; InvP; OxBoLi; OxNR

'Tis the Gift to Be Simple

260 'Tis the gift to be simple 'tis the gift to be free
'Tis the gift to come down where you ought to be
And when we find ourselves in the place just right
'Twill be in the valley of love and delight.

AH

To Be or Not to Be

261 I sometimes think I'd rather crow
And be a rooster than to roost
And be a crow. (l. 1–3)

FaBoCo; FaFP; MoShBr; RHPC

To Market, to Market, to Buy a Fat Pig

262 To market, to market, to buy a fat pig;
Home again, home again, jiggety jig.
To market, to market, to buy a fine hog;
Home again, home again, joggety jog. (l. 1–4)

BoTP; FaBoBe; FaFP; OxNR

Tom o' Bedlam's Song

263 Come dame or maid, be not afraid,
Poor Tom will injure nothing. (l. 11–12)

264 The palsy plagues my pulses (l. 37)

265 By a knight of ghosts and shadows
I summon'd am to a tourney
Ten leagues beyond the wide world's end:
Methinks it is no journey. (l. 57–60)

CH; ChTr; EBEV; EnSB; FaBoCh; HAP; InvP; LiTB;
Mes; NOBE; OAEL-1; OxBoLi; PoEL-2; PoRA; RB;
TrGrPo; WeW; WiR

Try Smiling

266 When the weather suits you not,
Try smiling;
When your coffee isn't hot,
Try smiling; (l. 1–4)

267 And it seems to help your case,
Brightens up a gloomy place;
Then, it sort of rests your face —
Just smiling. (l. 13–16)

BLPA; FaFP; PWR; WBLP

The Twa Brothers

268 There were twa brethren in the north, (l. 1)

269 They warsled up, they warsled down,
Till Sir John fell to the ground,
And there was a knife in Sir Willie's pouch,
Gied him a deadlie wound. (l. 5–8)

270 "Oh tell her I lie in Kirk-land fair,
And home shall never come." (l. 39–40)

CH; EBEV; ESPB; OxBB

The Twa Corbies

271 I heard twa corbies making a mane;
The tane unto the t'other say,
"Where sall we gang and dine today?" (l. 2–4)

AWP; CH; ELP; EnSB; ESPB; FaBoBa; FaBoCh; GoTS;
GTBS; GTBS-P; HAP; InPK; NoP; OBEV; OxBS; PBBP;
PPP; RB; SeCePo; UnPo

The Twa Magicians

272 I'd rather I were dead and gone,
And my body laid in grave,
Ere a rusty stock o coal-black smith
My maidenhead should have (l. 17–20)

ChTr; ESPB; GBP; OAEL-1; OxBB; OxBoLi

The Twa Sisters

273 The miller quickly drew the dam,
An' there he found a drown'd woman.

You cou'dna see her yellow hair
For gold and pearle that were so rare. (l. 32–35)

ESPB; FaBoBa; NoP; OxBS

The Twelve Days of Christmas

274 The first day of Christmas,
My true love sent to me
A partridge in a pear tree. (l. 1–3)

275 The second day of Christmas,
My true love sent to me
Two turtle doves, (l. 4–6)

276 The third day of Christmas,
My true love sent to me
Three French hens, (l. 8–10)

277 The fourth day of Christmas,
My true love sent to me
Four colly birds, (l. 13–15)

278 The fifth day of Christmas,
My true love sent to me
Five gold rings, (l. 19–21)

279 The sixth day of Christmas,
My true love sent to me
Six geese a-laying, (l. 26–28)

280 The seventh day of Christmas,
My true love sent to me
Seven swans a-swimming. (l. 34–36)

281 The eighth day of Christmas,
My true love sent to me
Eight maids a-milking, (l. 43–45)

282 The ninth day of Christmas,
My true love sent to me
Nine drummers drumming, (l. 53–55)

283 The tenth day of Christmas,
My true love sent to me
Ten pipers piping, (l. 64–66)

284 The eleventh day of Christmas,
My true love sent to me
Eleven ladies dancing, (l. 76–78)

285 The twelfth day of Christmas,
My true love sent to me
Twelve lords a-leaping. (l. 89–91)

AmFP; FaFP; OxBoLi; OxNR; PChr

The Two Sisters

286 Jelly flower jan;
The rose marie;
The jury hangs o'er
The rose marie.

AmFP; MAT; PrIm; TrGrPo

Ubi Sunt Qui ante Nos Fuerunt?

287 Where beth they biforen us weren, (l. 1)

288 Eten and drounken and maden hem glad; (l. 7)

289 Al that joye is went away,
That wele is comen to weylaway,
To manie harde stoundes.

Hoere paradis hy nomen here,
And now they lien in helle ifere: (l. 16–20)

EBEV; HAP; MeEL; MeEL; NoP; PrIm; WeW

The Unfaithful Shepherdess

290 While that the sun with his beams hot
Scorched the fruits in vale and mountain,
Philon the shepherd, late forgot,
Sitting beside a crystal fountain, (l. 1–4)

291 Adieu Love, adieu Love, untrue Love, (l. 7)

ElL; GTBS; GTBS-P; NOBE; OBEV; OBSC

The Unquiet Grave

292 "The wind doth blow today, my love,"
And a few small drops of rain;
I never had but one true love,
In cold grave she was lain. (l. 1–4)

293 "The stalk is withered dry, my love,
So will our hearts decay;
So make yourself content, my love,
Till God calls you away." (l. 25–28)

CH; ELP; ESPB; GBP; HAP; HeIP; NoP; OAEL-1; OBD;
OxBB; PoEL-1; RB; WeW

Upon Sir Francis Drake's Return from His Voyage about the World, and the Queen's Meeting Him

294 Sir Francis, Sir Francis, Sir Francis is come; (l. 1)

295 Then came the Lord Chamberlain with his white staff,
And all the people began to laugh;
And then the Queen began to speak,
'You're welcome home, Sir Francis Drake.' (l. 5–8)

CoMu; ElL; FaBoCh; OxBSS

Van Dieman's Land

296 The first day that we landed upon that fatal shore
The planters they came round us full twenty score or
more,
They rank'd us up like horses, and sold us out of hand

Then yok'd us unto ploughs, my boys, to plow Van
Dieman's Land. (l. 9–12)

CoMu; FaBoBa; OBET; OBTV

The Vicar of Bray

297 And this is law, I will maintain,
Until my dying day, Sir,
That whatsoever king shall reign,
I'll be the Vicar of Bray, Sir. (l. 9–12)

FaBoPV; GBP; InvP; NOBE; NOBL; OBSV; OxBoLi

Waly, Waly

298 And oh! if my young babe were born,
And set upon the nurse's knee,
And I my self were dead and gone
For a maid again I'll never be. (l. 37–40)

ELP; EnLoPo; EnSB; ESPB; FaBoBa; GBP; GoTS;
GTBS; GTBS-P; HAP; OBEV; OBS; OxBB; OxBS; PrIm

The Wearing of the Green

299 O Paddy dear, an' did ye hear the news that's goin'
round?
The shamrock is by law forbid to grow on Irish ground!
No more Saint Patrick's Day we'll keep, his colour can't
be seen,
For there's a cruel law agin the wearin' o' the Green!

AnIL; AWP; FaFP; FaPoR; GBP; OxBoLi; WTO

The Wee Wee Man

300 Four and twenty at her back
And they were a' clad out in green;
Tho the King of Scotland had been there
The warst o' them might hae been his Queen.

On we lap and awa we rade
Till we cam to yon bonny ha'
Whare the roof was o' the beaten gold
And the floor was o' the cristal a'. (l. 21–28)

CH; EBEV; ELP; ESPB; FaBoCh; GBP; OAEL-1; OxBB

Weep You No More, Sad Fountains

301 Sleep is a reconciling,
A rest that peace begets. (l. 10–11)

CH; ChTr; EBEV; ElL; ELP; EnLoPo; GBL; HAP; NcP;
OBSC; PoE; PoEL-2; SoSe; TrGrPo

Western Wind

302 Westron wind, when will thou blow?
The small rain down can rain.
Christ, that my love were in my arms,
And I in my bed again. (l. 1–4)

BoLoP CTC; EBEV; EnLoPo; FaBoCh; FF; GBL; GBP;
HAP; HeIP InPK; InvP; LLLT; MAT; MeEL; NAEL-1;
NIP; NOBE; NoP; OAEL-1; OBEV; OBSC; OBTV;
OxBLMV; OxBSP; PoE; PoEL-1; PPP; PrIm; TEP; UnPo;
WeW

What's in the Cupboard?

303 What's in the cupboard?
Says Mr. Hubbard.
A knuckle of veal,
Says Mr. Beal. (l. 1–4)

CH; ChTr; GBP; OxNR

Whistle, Daughter, Whistle

304 Mother I longs to get married
I longs to be a bride
I longs to lay by that young man
And close to by his side (l. 1–4)

305 Daughter daughter whistle
And you shall have a sheep (l. 17–18)

AIW; AmFP; ErPo; ErPo; OBET; OxNR

The Wife of Usher's Well

306 There lived a wife at Usher's Well,
And a wealthy wife was she;
She had three stout and stalwart sons,
And sent them o'er the sea. (l. 1–4)

307 'The cock doth craw, the day doth daw,
The channerin worm doth chide;
Gin we be mist out o our place,
A sair pain we maun bide.' (l. 41–44)

AmFP; AWP; CH; ChTr; EBEV; EnRP; EnSB; ESPB;
FaBoBa; GoTS; LiTB; NAEL-1; NOBE; NoP; OAEL-1;
OBEV; OnMSP; OxBB; OxBS; PoEL-1; PrIm; RB;
TrGrPo

The Wife's Lament

308 My lord endures
much care of mind.He remembers too often
a happier dwelling.Woe be to them
that for a loved onemust wait in longing. (l. 50–53)

AnOE; BoWoF; PBWP; WPE

The Wind

309 The King o' Scots, and a' his power
Canna turn Arthur O'Bower. (l. 3—4)

ChTr; FaBoCh; GBP; OxNR

Words from an Old Spanish Carol

310 Shall I tell you who will come
to Bethlehem on Christmas Morn,
Who will kneel them gently down
before the Lord, new-born? (l. 1—4)

FaPON; OBCP; PChr; PDV

The Wraggle Taggle Gipsies

311 There were three gipsies a-come to my door,
And down-stairs ran this a-lady, O! (l. 1—2)

312 "What care I for a goose-feather bed,
With the sheet turned down so bravely, O?
For to-night I shall sleep in a cold open field,
Along with the wraggle taggle gipsies, O!" (l. 33—36)

BoTP; CH; FaPON; FaPON; MAT; WiR

Yet if His Majesty, Our Sovereign Lord

313 'tis a duteous thing
To show all honor to an earthly king; (l. 21—22)

314 But at the coming of the King of Heaven
All's set at six and seven:
We wallow in our sin;
Christ cannot finde a chamber in the inn. (l. 25—28)

315 We entertain him always like a stranger,
And, as at first, still lodge him in the manger.
(l. 29—30)

CH; EaLo; FaBoCh; NOBE; NoP; OBEV; OBS; PoRA;
TrCP; TrGrPo

Young Beichan

316 Lord Bateman was a noble lord,
A noble lord of high degree, (l. 1—2)

317 He sailed east, he sailed west,
He sailed into proud Turkey, (l. 5—6)

318 'What news, what news, my proud young porter,
What news, what news has thou brought to me?'
(l. 57—58)

319 'She has got rings on every finger,
Round one of them she have got three.
She have gold enough around her middle
To buy Northumberland that belongs to thee.
(l. 61—64)

320 Lord Bateman prepared for another marriage,
So both their hearts so full of glee.
'I will range no more to foreign countries
Now since Sophia have a-crossed the sea.' (l. 81—84)

AmFP; EnSB; ESPB; FaBoBa; OBET

PETER ABRAHAMS (b. 1919)

Tell Freedom

1 There are three kinds of people:
White people, Colored people
and Black people.

2 Joseph and his mother come from the
black kings who were before the white man.

PBA

LÉONIE ADAMS (1899—1988)

Country Summer

1 O lovely time of beggars' luck — (l. 15)

2 All stars stand close in summer air
And tremble, and look mild as amber;
When wicks are lighted in the chamber
You might say stars were settling there. (l. 27—30)

GoJo; LiTM; MoAB; MoAmPo; TrGrPo

SARAH FLOWER ADAMS (1805—48)

Nearer, My God, to Thee

1 Though like the wanderer,
The sun gone down,
Darkness be over me,
My rest a stone;
Yet in my dreams I'd be
Nearer, my God, to Thee, (l. 8—13)

BLRP; FaBoBe; FaFP; PoLF; WBLP; WGRP

JOSEPH ADDISON (1672–1719)

A Letter from Italy

1 Immortal glories in my mind revive,
And in my soul a thousand passions strive,
When Rome's exalted beauties I descry
Magnificent in piles of ruin lie.

2 We envy not the warmer clime, that lies
In ten degrees of more indulgent skies,
Nor at the coarseness of our heaven repine,
Though o'er our heads the frozen Pleiads shine:
'Tis Liberty that crowns Britannia's Isle,
And makes her barren rocks and her bleak mountains
smile.

NOEC; OBTV

The Spacious Firmament on High

3 The Spacious Firmament on high,
With all the blue Ethereal Sky,
And spangled Heav'ns, a Shining Frame,
Their great Original proclaim:
Th' unwearied Sun, from day to day,
Does his Creator's Pow'r display,
And publishes to every Land
The Work of an Almighty Hand. (l. 1–8)

4 In Reason's Ear they all rejoice,
And utter forth a glorious Voice,
For ever singing, as they shine,
The Hand that made us is Divine. (l. 21–24)

BLPA; EaLo; ELP; FaBoBe; FaPoR; FPL; GN; HeIP;
NOCV; NOEC; PoEL-3; TOF

"Æ" (pseudonym of GEORGE WILLIAM RUSSELL) (1867–1935)

Germinal

1 Let thy young wanderer dream on:
Call him not home.
A door opens, a breath a voice
From the ancient room,
Speaks to him now. Be it dark or bright
He is knit with his doom. (l. 37–42)

BIrV; MoBrPo; OBEV; OBMV

The Great Breath

2 I saw how all the trembling ages past,
Molded to her by deep and deeper breath,
Neared to the hour when Beauty breathes her last
And knows herself in death. (l. 9–12)

MoBrPo; OBEV; OBMV; WGRP

Immortality

3 We must pass like smoke or live within the spirit's fire;
For we can no more than smoke unto the flame return
If our thought has changed to dream, our will unto
desire,
As smoke we vanish though the fire may burn. (l. 1–4)

AWP; OBMV; TIRV; WGRP

CONRAD AIKEN (1889–1973)

Discordants

1 Music I heard with you was more than music,
And bread I broke with you was more than bread;

AWP; BLPL; CMoP; FaFP; LiTA; LiTM; MoAB;
MoAmPo; NOBA; OxBA; PoRA

Preludes for Memnon; or, Preludes to Attitude

2 Rimbaud and Verlaine, precious pair of poets,
Genius in both (but what is genius?) playing
Chess on a marble table at an inn

3 'Rimbaud, there is one thing to do:
We must take rhetoric, and wring its neck! . . .'

4 Time in the heart and sequence in the brain —

Such as destroyed Rimbaud and fooled Verlaine.
And let us then take godhead by the neck —

And strangle it, and with it, rhetoric.

FaBoMo; LiTA; LiTM; NoAM; TwCP

Priapus and the Pool

5 This is the shape of the tree,
And the flower and the leaf, and the three pale
beautiful pilgrims:
This is what you are to me.

CMoP; GoJo; MoAB; MoAmPo; NOBA; OxBA; TrGrPo

Senlin; a Biography

6 It is morning, Senlin says, and in the morning
When the light drips through the shutters like the dew,
I arise, I face the sunrise,
And do the things my fathers learned to do.

7 in the morning
Should I not pause in the light to remember God?
Upright and firm I stand on a star unstable,
He is immense and lonely as a cloud.

8 I ascend from darkness
And depart on the winds of space for I know not where;
My watch is wound, a key is in my pocket,
And the sky is darkened as I descend the stair.

CMoP; LiTA; LiTM; MoAB; MoAmPo; NoAM; OxBA;
TrGrPo

Tetélestai

9 How shall we praise the magnificence of the dead,
The great man humbled, the haughty brought to dust?
(l. 1–2)

10 Should I not hear, as I lie down in dust,
The horns of glory blowing above my burial?
(l. 23–24)

11 I, the restless one; the circler of circles;
Herdsman and roper of stars, who could not capture
The secret of self; (l. 47–49)

12 ... Look! this flesh how it crumbles to dust and is
blown!
These bones, how they grind in the granite of frost and
are nothing!
This skull, how it yawns for a flicker of time in the
darkness,
Yet laughs not and sees not! (l. 68–71)

LiTA; LiTM; MoAB; MoAmPo; PrIm

MARK AKENSIDE (1721–70)

Inscription for a Grotto

1 He with cowslips pale,
Primrose, and purple lychnis, decked the green
Before my threshold, and my shelving walls
With honeysuckle covered. (l. 5–8)

2 here my clustering fruits I tend;
Or from the humid flowers, at break of day,
Fresh garlands weave, and chase from all my bounds
Each thing impure or noxious. (l. 10–14)

NOEC; PoEL-3; SeCePo; SeCePo

NANINA ALBA (1917–1968)

For Malcolm X

1 Words pouring out to resurrect the dead
Who walk among us, as Baldwin has said. (l. 5–6)

PoBA

NICCOLÒ DEGLI ALBIZZI (*fl.* 13th century)

Prolonged Sonnet: When the Troops Were Returning from Milan

1 Their empty victual-wagons up the street
Over the bridge dreadfully sound and sway;
Their eyes, as hanged men's, turning the wrong way;
And nothing on their backs, or heads, or feet.
One sees the ribs and all the skeletons
Of their gaunt horses; and a sorry sight
Are the torn saddles, crammed with straw and stones.
(l. 5–11)

2 silent as a man being shaved. (l. 16)

AWP; OBVE; PFI; WaaP

HENRY ALDRICH (1647–1710)

If all be true that I do think

1 If all be true that I do think,
There are five reasons we should drink:
Good wine, a friend, or being dry,
Or lest we should be by and by,
Or any other reason why. (l. 1–5)

FaBoCo; FaBoEE; FF; InvP; OBS; OxBSP

THOMAS BAILEY ALDRICH (1836–1907)

Memory

1 My mind lets go a thousand things,
Like dates of wars and deaths of kings, (l. 1–2)

2 The wind came briskly up this way,
Crisping the brook beside the road;
Then, pausing here, set down its load
Of pine-scents, and shook listlessly
Two petals from that wild-rose tree. (l. 6–10)

AA; AnAmPo; BoNaP; PoLF

CECIL FRANCES ALEXANDER (1818–1895)

All Things Bright and Beautiful

1 All things bright and beautiful,
All creatures great and small,
All things wise and wonderful,
The Lord God made them all. (l. 1–4)

2 He gave us eyes to see them,
And lips that we might tell,
How great is God Almighty,
Who has made all things well. (l. 17–20)

FaPON; FaPoR; OHIP; OxBChV; RHPC; TIRV

The Burial of Moses

3 That was the grandest funeral
That ever passed on earth;
Yet no man heard the trampling, (l. 9–11)

4 Noiselessly as the daylight
Comes when the night is done, (l. 13–14)

5 Noiselessly as the spring-time
Her crown of verdure weaves, (l. 17–18)

6 This was the bravest warrior
That ever buckled sword;
This the most gifted poet
That ever breathed a word; (l. 49–52)

7 God hath his mysteries of grace,
Ways that we cannot tell,
He hides them deep, like the secret sleep
Of him he loved so well. (l. 77–80)

BeLS; BLPA; BLRP; GN; WBLP

There Is a Green Hill Far Away

8 There is a green hill far away,
Without a city wall,
Where the dear Lord was crucified,
Who died to save us all. (l. 1–4)

9 There was no other good enough
To pay the price of sin;
He only could unlock the gate
Of heaven and let us in. (l. 17–20)

BLRP; OxBChV; TIRV; WGRP

SAMUEL ALLEN ("PAUL VESEY") (b. 1917)

To Satch

1 one fine mornin
I'm gonna reach up and grab me a handfulla stars
Swing out my long lean leg

And whip three hot strikes burnin down the heavens
And look over at God and say
How about that! (l. 3–8)

AmNP; IDB; PoBA; PoNe; SD; SoSe; TTY

WILLIAM ALLINGHAM (1824–1889)

The Fairies

1 Up the airy mountain,
Down the rushy glen,
We daren't go a-hunting
For fear of little men; (l. 1–4)

AnIL; CH; ChTr; FaBoCh; FaBoPP; FaBV; FaFP; FaPON;
Mes; NOBE; NOBVV; OBEV; OnMSP; OxBChV; PDV;
RHPC; WSC

Robin Redbreast

2 Bright yellow, red, and orange,
The leaves come down in hosts;
The trees are Indian princes,
But soon they'll turn to ghosts; (l. 13–16)

3 The fireside for the cricket,
The wheatstack for the mouse,
When trembling night-winds whistle
And moan all round the house; (l. 25–28)

4 Alas! in winter, dead and dark,
Where can poor Robin go? (l. 31–32)

FaBoBe MoShBr; OxBChV; PBBP

Wishing

5 Before a day was over,
Home comes the rover,
For mother's kiss — sweeter this
Than any other thing! (l. 21–24)

BoTP; FaPON; OHIP; OxBChV

KINGSLEY AMIS (b. 1922)

An Ever-Fixed Mark

1 Sex stops when you pull up your pants,
Love never lets you go. (l. 29–30)

ErPo; MoP; NoAM; PeHV

ARCHIE RANDOLPH AMMONS (b. 1926)

The City Limits

1 When you consider the radiance, that it does not
      withhold
   itself but pours its abundance without selection into
      every
   nook and cranny (l. 1–3)

2 air or vacuum, snow or shale, squid or wolf, rose or
      lichen,
   each is accepted into as much light as it will take,
                                            (l. 13–14)

CAPP; HCAP; MoP; NAAL-2; NoAM; NOBA; NoP

Corsons Inlet

3 the walk liberating, I was released from forms,
   from the perpendiculars,
   straight lines, blocks, boxes, binds
   of thought
   into the hues, shadings, rises, flowing bends and blends
   of sight: (l. 13–18)

4 but Overall is beyond me: is the sum of these events
   I cannot draw, the ledger I cannot keep, the accounting
   beyond the account: (l. 30–32)

5 I have reached no conclusions, have erected no
      boundaries,
   shutting out and shutting in, separating inside
   from outside: I have
   drawn no lines: (l. 41–44)

6 risk is full: every living thing in
   siege: the demand is life, to keep life: the small
   white blacklegged egret, how beautiful, quietly stalks
      and spears
   the shallows, darts to shore
   to stab — (l. 70–74)

7 the possibility of rule as the sum of rulelessness:
                                            (l. 92)

8 no arranged terror: no forcing of image, plan,
   or thought:
   no propaganda, no humbling of reality to precept:

   terror pervades but is not arranged, all possibilities
   of escape open: no route shut, (l. 114–118)

9 to fasten into order enlarging grasps of disorder,
      widening
   scope, but enjoying the freedom that
   Scope eludes my grasp, that there is no finality of
      vision,
   that I have perceived nothing completely,
   that tomorrow a new walk is a new walk.
                                            (l. 124–128)

CoAP; MoP; NAAL-2; NoAM; NOBA; NoP; PoE; PPP

Cut the Grass

10 The wonderful workings of the world: wonderful,
   wonderful: I'm surprised half the time: (l. 1–2)

11 the ocean, multiple to a blinding
   oneness (l. 14–15)

12 only total expression

   expresses hiding: I'll have to say everything
   to take on the roundness and withdrawal of the deep
      dark:
   less than total is a bucketful of radiant toys.
                                            (l. 15–18)

CAPP; HAP; PPP; TAP; WeW

Easter Morning

13 I have a life that did not become,
   that turned aside and stopped,
   astonished: (l. 1–3)

14 just about everybody older
   (and some younger) collected in one place
   waiting, particularly, but not for
   me, (l. 27–30)

15 the child in me that could not become
   was not ready for others to go, (l. 36–37)

16 a dance sacred as the sap in
   the trees, (l. 99–100)

HCAP; NAAL-2; NoAM; NoP

Gravelly Run

17 for it is not so much to know the self
   as to know it as it is known
   by galaxy and cedar cone,
   as if birth had never found it

   and death could never end it: (l. 7–11)

18 stranger,
   hoist your burdens, get on down the road (l. 29–30)

CoAP; NAAL-2; NoAM; PoA; Prf

Laser

19 the focused beam
   folds all energy in:
   the image glares filling all space:
   the head falls and
   hangs and cannot wake itself. (l. 24–28)

CAPP; NAAL-2; NoAM; NOBA

So I Said I Am Ezra

20 a word too much repeated
falls out of being (l. 21–22)

NAAL-2; NoAM; NOBA; NoP

MATTHEW ARNOLD (1822–1888)

Dover Beach

1 The sea is calm to-night.
The tide is full, the moon lies fair
Upon the straits; — (l. 1–3)

2 Sophocles long ago
Heard it on the Aegaean, and it brought
Into his mind the turbid ebb and flow
Of human misery; we
Find also in the sound a thought,
Hearing it by this distant northern sea. (l. 15–20)

3 Ah, love, let us be true
To one another! for the world, which seems
To lie before us like a land of dreams,
So various, so beautiful, so new,
Hath really neither joy, nor love, nor light,
Nor certitude, nor peace, nor help for pain; (l. 29–34)

4 And we are here as on a darkling plain
Swept with confused alarms of struggle and flight,
Where ignorant armies clash by night. (l. 35–37)

AWP; BLPA; EaLo; EBVV; FaBoBe; FaBoPP; FaBoRV;
FaBV; FaFP; FF; FiP; FPL; GTBS-P; HAP; HeIP; HoPM;
InPK; InPS; InvP; LiTB; MAT; MOS; NAEL-2; NIP;
NOBE; NOBVV; NoP; NU; OAEL-2; OBNC; OPOP; PoE;
PoEL-5; PoRA; PPP; Prf; PrIm; SCV; SeCePo; TOF

A Dream

5 One moment, on the rapid's top, our boat
Hung poised — and then the darting river of Life
(Such now, methought, it was), the river of Life,
Loud thundering, bore us by; swift, swift it foamed.
Black under cliffs it raced, round headlands shone.
(l. 30–34)

6 us burning plains,
Bristled with cities, us the sea received. (l. 36–37)

GBL; GTBS-P; OBTV; SeCePo

Empedocles on Etna

7 In the moonlight the shepherds,
Soft lull'd by the rills,
Lie wrapt in their blankets
Asleep on the hills. (l. 17–20)

8 The day in his hotness,
The strife with the palm;
The night in her silence,
The stars in their calm ... (l. 61–64)

ChTr; FaBoRV; FiP; NOBE; OAEL-2; OBEV; WiR

The Forsaken Merman

9 Come, dear children, let us away;
Down and away below!
Now my brothers call from the bay,
Now the great winds shoreward blow,
Now the salt tides seaward flow;
Now the wild white horses play,
Champ and chafe and toss in the spray. (l. 1–7)

10 Come away, away children;
Come children, come down!
The hoarse wind blows coldly;
Lights shine in the town. (l. 18–21)

BeLS; EBEV; FaBoCh; FaPoR; FiP; GN; MOS; NAEL-2;
OBNV

Growing Old

11 What is it to grow old?
Is it to lose the glory of the form,
The luster of the eye?
Is it for beauty to forego her wreath?
—Yes, but not this alone. (l. 1–5)

12 'Tis not to see the world
As from a height, with rapt prophetic eyes,
And heart profoundly stirred;
And weep, and feel the fullness of the past,
The years that are not more. (l. 16–20)

FaFP; FiP; NAEL-2; NOBVV; OAEL-2; PoEL-5

The Last Word

13 They out-talked thee, hissed thee, tore thee?
Better men fared thus before thee; (l. 9–10)

14 Charge once more, then, and be dumb!
Let the victors, when they come,
When the forts of folly fall,
Find thy body by the wall! (l. 13–16)

FiP; NOBE; OAEL-2; OBNC; PoEL-5; TrGrPo

Palladium

15 We shall renew the battle in the plain
Tomorrow — red with blood will Xanthus be;
Hector and Ajax will be there again,
Helen will come upon the wall to see. (l. 13–16)

16 Then we shall rust in shade, or shine in strife,
And fluctuate 'twixt blind hopes and blind despairs,
And fancy that we put forth all our life,
And never know how with the soul it fares. (l. 17–20)

17 Still doth the soul, from its lone fastness high,
Upon our life a ruling effluence send.
And when it fails, fight as we will, we die;
And while it lasts, we cannot wholly end. (l. 21–24)

GTBS-P; OAEL-2; OBNC; PPP

Philomela

18 Still, after many years, in distant lands,
Still nourishing in thy bewildered brain
That wild, unquenched, deep-sunken, old-world pain —
Say, will it never heal? (l. 6–9)

19 Eternal passion!
Eternal pain! (l. 31–32)

OAEL-2; OBEV; PBBP; PPP; UnPo

Requiescat

20 Strew on her roses, roses,
And never a spray of yew!
In quiet she reposes;
Ah, would that I did too! (l. 1–4)

21 Her cabined, ample spirit,
It fluttered and failed for breath.
Tonight it doth inherit
The vasty hall of death. (l. 13–16)

AWP; ELP; FiP; HeIP; InvP; LiTB; NOBE; OBD; OBEV;
PoRA; TrGrPo

The Scholar-Gipsy

22 — No, no thou hast not felt the lapse of hours!
For what wears out the life of mortal men?
'Tis that from change to change their being rolls;
'Tis that repeated shocks, again, again,
Exhaust the energy of strongest souls
And numb the elastic powers. (l. 140–146)

23 The generations of thy peers are fled.
And we ourselves shall go;
But thou possessest an immortal lot,
And we imagine thee exempt from age (l. 155–158)

24 O life unlike to ours!
Who fluctuate idly without term or scope,
Of whom each strives, nor knows for what he strives,
And each half lives a hundred different lives;
Who wait like thee, but not, like thee, in hope.
(l. 166–170)

25 Thou waitest for the spark from heaven! (l. 171)

26 each year we see
Breeds new beginnings, disappointments new;
(l. 176–177)

27 O born in days when wits were fresh and clear,
And life ran gaily as the sparkling Thames;
Before this strange disease of modern life,
With its sick hurry, its divided aims,
Its head o'ertaxed, its palsied hearts, was rife —
(l. 201–205)

28 Still nursing the unconquerable hope,
Still clutching the inviolable shade, (l. 211–212)

ChTr; EBEV; EBVV; FaBoPP; FiP; HAP; HeIP; NAEL-2;
NOBE; NOBVV; NoP; OAEL-2; OBEV; OBNC; PoE;
PoEL-5; TEP

Shakespeare

29 All pains the immortal spirit must endure,
All weakness that impairs, all griefs that bow,
Find their sole voice in that victorious brow.
(l. 12–14)

FiP; HeIP; InvP; NoP; OBEV; Son; TrGrPo

Stanzas from the Grande Chartreuse

30 For rigorous teachers seized my youth,
And purged its faith, and trimm'd its fire,
Show'd me the high, white star of Truth,
There bade me gaze, and there aspire.
Even now their whispers pierce the gloom:
What dost thou in this living tomb? (l. 67–72)

31 So much unlearnt, so much resign'd —
I come not here to be your foe!
I seek these anchorites, not in ruth,
To curse and to deny your truth; (l. 75–78)

32 Wandering between two worlds, one dead,
The other powerless to be born,
With nowhere yet to rest my head,
Like these, on earth I wait forlorn.
Their faith, my tears, the world deride —
I come to shed them at their side. (l. 85–90)

33 But — if you cannot give us ease —
Last of the race of them who grieve
Here leave us to die out with these
Last of the people who believe!
Silent, while years engrave the brow;
Silent — the best are silent now. (l. 109–114)

34 Our fathers water'd with their tears
This sea of time whereon we sail,
Their voices were in all men's ears

Who pass'd within their puissant hail.
Still the same ocean round us raves,
But we stand mute, and watch the waves.
(l. 121–126)

35 What helps it now, that Byron bore,
With haughty scorn which mock'd the smart,
Through Europe to the Aetolian shore
The pageant of his bleeding heart?
That thousands counted every groan,
And Europe made his woe her own? (l. 133–138)

36 Years hence, perhaps, may dawn an age,
More fortunate, alas! than we,
Which without hardness will be sage,
And gay without frivolity.
Sons of the world, oh, speed those years;
But, while we wait, allow our tears! (l. 157–162)

37 Allow them! We admire with awe
The exulting thunder of your race;
You give the universe your law,
You triumph over time and space!
Your pride of life, your tireless powers,
We laud them, but they are not ours. (l. 163–168)

38 But, where the road runs near the stream,
Oft through the trees they catch a glance
Of passing troops in the sun's beam —
Pennon, and plume, and flashing lance!
Forth to the world those soldiers fare,
To life, to cities, and to war! (l. 175–180)

39 The banners flashing through the trees
Make their blood dance and chain their eyes;
That bugle-music on the breeze
Arrests them with a charm'd surprise.
Banner by turns and bugle woo:
Ye shy recluses, follow too! (l. 187–192)

40 "Fenced early in this cloistral round
Of reverie, of shade, of prayer,
How should we grow in other ground?
How can we flower in foreign air?
— Pass, banners, pass, and bugles, cease;
And leave our desert to its peace!" (l. 205–210)

EBVV; NAEL-2; OAEL-2; PoE; PoEL-5; TEP

Switzerland

41 Yes! in sea of life enisled,
With echoing straits between us thrown,
Dotting the shoreless watery wild,
We mortal millions live alone. (l. 1–4)

42 Who ordered, that their longing's fire
Should be, as soon as kindled, cooled?
Who renders vain their deep desire? —
A God, a God their severance ruled!

And bade betwixt their shores to be
The unplumbed, salt, estranging sea. (l. 19–24)

BoLoP; EBEV; EBVV; ELP; FiP; GTBS-P; MOS; NOBE;
NoP; OAEL-2; OBEV; OBNC; PoEL-5; PPP; PrIm; TEP

Thyrsis

43 Once pass'd I blindfold here, at any hour,
Now seldom come I, since I came with him.
That single elm-tree bright
Against the west — I miss it! is it gone? (l. 24–27)

44 Too rare, too rare, grow now my visits here,
But once I knew each field, each flower, each stick;
(l. 31–32)

45 I fell her finger light
Laid pausefully upon life's headlong train; —
The foot less prompt to meet the morning dew,
The heart less bounding at emotion new,
And hope, once crush'd, less quick to spring again.
(l. 137–141)

46 Unbreachable the fort
Of the long-batter'd world uplifts its wall;
And strange and vain the earthly turmoil grows,
And near and real the charm of thy repose,
And night as welcome as a friend would fall.
(l. 146–150)

FaBoPP; FiP; Mes; NAEL-2; NOBE; NoP; OBEV; OBNC

JOHN ASHBERY (b. 1927)

The Instruction Manual

1 As I sit looking out of a window of the building
I wish I did not have to write the instructional manual
   on the uses of a new metal.
I look down into the street and see people, each
   walking with an inner peace,
And envy them — they are so far away from me!
Not one of them has to worry about getting out this
   manual on schedule (l. 1–5)

2 There is the rich quarter, with its houses of pink and
   white, and its crumbling, leafy terraces.
There is the poorer quarter, its homes a deep blue.
There is the market, where men are selling hats and
   swatting flies (l. 60–62)

3 I turn my gaze
Back to the instruction manual which has made me
   dream of Guadalajara. (l. 73–74)

HAP; InPS; MoP; NeAP; NoAM; NOBA; PoM; SOTW;
WeW

The Painter

4 How could he explain to them his prayer
That nature, not art, might unsurp the canvas?
(l. 13—14)

5 Imagine a painter crucified by his subject! (l. 25)

HCAP; NOBA; NoP; PoE; SOTW

MARGARET ATWOOD (b. 1939)

You Fit into Me

1 you fit into me
like a hook into an eye (l. 1—2)

InPK; NoAM; NoP; TW

WYSTAN HUGH AUDEN (1907—1973)

As I Walked Out One Evening

1 "I'll love you dear, I'll love you
Till China and Africa meet,
And the river jumps over the mountain
And the salmon sing in the street. (l. 9—12)

2 all the clocks in the city
Began to whirr and chime:
"O let not Time deceive you,
You cannot conquer Time. (l. 21—24)

3 "The glacier knocks in the cupboard,
The desert sighs in the bed,
And the crack in the tea-cup opens
A lane to the land of the dead. (l. 41—44)

FF; HeIP; InPK; LiTM; MoAB; MoBrPo; NoAM; NOBE;
NoP; OAEL-2; PrIm; RB; TwCP; UnPo

Epitaph on a Tyrant

4 He knew human folly like the back of his hand, (l. 3)

5 When he laughed, respectable senators burst with
laughter,
And when he cried the little children died in the
streets. (l. 5—6)

HeIP; NoAM; OxBSP; RB

The Fall of Rome

6 All the literati keep
An imaginary friend. (l. 11—12)

7 Caesar's double-bed is warm
As an unimportant clerk
Writes i do not like my work
On a pink official form. (l. 17—20)

8 vast
Herds of reindeer move across
Miles and miles of golden moss,
Silently and very fast. (l. 25—28)

InPS; MAT; OAEL-2; OxBTC; UnPo

Fish in the unruffled lakes

9 Swans in the winter air
A white perfection have, (l. 3—4)

10 We till shadowed days are done,
We must weep and sing
Duty's conscious wrong,
The Devil in the clock, (l. 10—13)

11 Sighs for folly said and done
Twist our narrow days; (l. 19—20)

BoLoP; CMoP; MoAB; MoBrPo; MoP

For the Time Being; A Christmas Oratorio

12 These are enough
Left overs to do, warmed-up, for the rest of the week —
Not that we have much appetite, having drunk such a
lot,
Stayed up so late, attempted — quite unsuccessfully —
To love all our relatives, and in general
Grossly overestimated our powers.

13 Once again we have sent Him away,
Begging though to remain His disobedient servant,

14 the moderate Aristotelian city
Of darning and the Eight-Fifteen, where Euclid's
geometry
And Newton's mechanics would account for our
experience,
And the kitchen table exists because I scrub it.

15 Remembering the stable where for once in our lives
Everything became a You and nothing was an It.

16 'Lead us not into temptation and evil for our sake.'
They will come all right, don't worry; probably in a
form

That we do not expect, and certainly with a force
More dreadful than we can imagine.

17 There are bills to be paid,machines to keep in repair,
Irregular verbs to learn, the Time Being to redeem
From insignificance.

18 and the Soul endure
A silence that is neither for nor against her faith
That God's Will will be done, that, in spite of her
 prayers,
God will cheat no one, not even the world of its
 triumph.

LiTA; MoAB; MoBrPo; OAEL-2; OBCP; OxBA

Hearing of Harvests Rotting in the Valleys

19 We honor founders of these starving cities,
Whose honor is the image of our sorrow. (l. 5–6)

20 Dreaming of evening walks through learned cities,
(l. 9)

21 They built by rivers and at night the water
Running past windows comforted their sorrow;
(l. 13–14)

22 There was still gold and silver in the mountains,
And hunger was a more immediate sorrow; (l. 21–22)

23 It is the sorrow; shall it melt? Ah, water
Would gush, flush, green these mountains and these
 valleys
And we rebuild our cities, not dream of islands.
(l. 37–39)

LiTB; MoAB; MoBrPo; OAEL-2; UnPo

In Memory of Sigmund Freud

24 every day they die
Among us, those who were doing us some good,
And knew it was never enough but
Hoped to improve a little by living. (l. 5–8)

25 An important Jew who died in exile. (l. 24)

26 All that he did was to remember
Like the old and be honest like children. (l. 31–32)

27 Like a poetry lesson til sooner
Or later it faltered at the line where (l. 35–36)

28 Long ago the accusations had begun,
And suddenly knew by whom it had been judged
(l. 37–38)

29 technique of unsettlement (l. 46)

30 what evil is: not as we thought
Deeds that must be punished, but our lack of faith,
Our dishonest mood of denial,
The concupiscence of the oppressor. (l. 57–60)

31 If often he was wrong and at times absurd,
To us he is no more a person
Now but a whole climate of opinion. (l. 66–68)

32 the child unlucky in his little State,
Some hearth where freedom is excluded,
A hive whose honey is fear and worry,

Feels calmer now and somehow assured of escape;
(l. 78–81)

33 to be free
Is often to be lonely; (l. 89–90)

34 One rational voice is dumb: over a grave
The household of Impulse mourns one dearly loved.
Sad is Eros, builder of cities,
And weeping anarchic Aphrodite. (l. 109–112)

HAP; LiTB; NcAM; OAEL-2; OxBA

In Memory of W. B. Yeats

35 He disappeared in the dead of winter. (l. 1)

36 The mercury sank in the mouth of the dying day.
What instruments we have agree
The day of his death was a dark cold day. (l. 4–6)

37 An afternoon of nurses and rumours;
The provinces of his body revolted,
The squares of his mind were empty,
Silence invaded the suburbs, (l. 13–16)

38 The words of a dead man
Are modified in the guts of the living. (l. 22–23)

39 each in the cell of himself is almost convinced of his
 freedom, (l. 27)

40 Mad Ireland hurt you into poetry. (l. 34)

41 For poetry makes nothing happen: (l. 36)

42 it survives,
A way of happening, a mouth. (l. 40–41)

43 Earth, receive an honoured guest:
William Yeats is laid to rest.
Let the Irish vessel lie
Emptied of its poetry. (l. 42–45)

44 Intellectual disgrace
Stares from every human face,
And the seas of pity lie
Locked and frozen in each eye. (l. 50–53)

45 With the farming of a verse
Make a vineyard of the curse, (l. 58–59)

46 In the deserts of the heart
Let the healing fountain start,
In the prison of his days
Teach the free man how to praise. (l. 62–65)

CMoP; FaFP; HAP; HeIP; HoPM; LiTB; LiTM; MoAB;
MoBrPo; NoAM; NOBE; OAEL-2; OxBTC; PPP; PrIm;
TrGrPo; UnPo; WeW

In Praise of Limestone

47 If it form the one landscape that we the inconstant ones
Are consistently homesick for, this is chiefly
Because it dissolves in water. (l. 1–3)

48 unable
To conceive a god whose temper-tantrums are moral
And not to be pacified by a clever line
Or a good lay: (l. 26–29)

49 to become a pimp
Or deal in fake jewelry or ruin a fine tenor voice
For effects that bring down the house could happen to
all
But the best and the worst of us ... (l. 40–43)

50 There is no love;
There are only the various envies, all of them sad."
(l. 59–60)

51 music
Which can be made anywhere, is invisible,
And does not smell. (l. 82–84)

52 Dear, I know nothing of
Either, but when I try to imagine a faultless love
Or the life to come, what I hear is the murmur
Of underground streams, what I see is a limestone
landscape. (l. 91–94)

CMoP; FaBoPV; FYAP; HAP; MoAB; MoP; NAEL-2;
NoAM; NoP; OAEL-2; PPP

In Time of War

53 Only the sculptors and the poets were half sad,
And the pert retinue from the magician's house
Grumbled and went elsewhere. The vanquished powers
were glad

To be invisible and free: (l. 9–12)

Son

Lay your sleeping head, my love

54 Time and fevers burn away
Individual beauty from
Thoughtful children, and the grave
Proves the child ephemeral: (l. 3–6)

55 in my arms till break of day
Let the living creature lie,
Mortal, guilty, but to me
The entirely beautiful.

Soul and body have no bounds: (l. 7–11)

56 their ordinary swoon, (l. 14)

57 The hermit's carnal ecstasy. (l. 20)

BoLoP; CMoP; EnLoPo; GLP; HAP; LLLT; MoP;
NAEL-2; NoAM; NOBE; OAEL-2; OxBTC; PoE; PPP;
UnPo; WeW

Mundus et Infans

58 Kicking his mother until she let go of his soul
Has given his a healthy appetite: clearly, her role
In the New Order must be
To supply and deliver his raw materials free; (l. 1–4)

59 With one fist clenched behind his head, heel drawn up
to thigh
The cocky little ogre dozes off, ready,
Though, to take on the rest
Of the world at the drop of a hat or the mildest
Nudge of the impossible, (l. 9–13)

60 to his eyes, Funnyface Or Elephant as yet
Mean nothing. His distinction between Me and Us
Is a matter of taste; his seasons are Dry and Wet;
He thinks as his mouth does. (l. 20–24)

61 let us rejoice
That he lets us hope, for
He may never become a fashionable or
Important personage:
However bad he may be, he has not yet gone mad;
(l. 42–46)

LiTB; LiTM; MoAB; MoBrPo; NAs; NoAM

Musée des Beaux Arts

62 About suffering they were never wrong,
The Old Masters: how well they understood
Its human position; how it takes place
While someone else is eating or opening a window or
just walking dully along; (l. 1–4)

63 even the dreadful martyrdom must run its course
Anyhow in a corner, some untidy spot
Where the dogs go on with their doggy life and the
torturer's horse
Scratches its innocent behind on a tree. (l. 10–13)

64 the expensive delicate ship that must have seen
Something amazing, a boy falling out of the sky,
Had somewhere to get to and sailed calmly on.
(l. 19–21)

CMoP; FaFP; FF; GTBS-P; HAP; HeIP; InPK; InPS;
LiTB; LiTM; MoAB; MoP; NAEL-2; NIP; NoAM; NOBE;
NoP; PoE; PoRA; PPP; PrIm; SCV; SeCePo; SoSe; TEP;
TrCP; TrGrPo; TwCP; WeW

O What Is That Sound

65 O where are you going? stay with me here.
Were the vows you swore me deceiving, deceiving?
No, I promised to love you, my dear,
But I must be leaving. (l. 29–32)

66 Their feet are heavy on the floor
And their eyes are burning. (l. 35–36)

CMoP; FaBoPV; LiTB; MoAB; MoBrPo; PoE; SoSe; WaP

The Orators

67 Behind you swiftly the figure comes softly,
The spot on your skin is a shocking disease.'

CMoP; FaBoCh; LiTB; LiTM; NoAM; NOBE; OAEL-2;
SoSe

Petition

68 the distortions of ingrown virginity. (l. 6)

69 Harrow the house of the dead; look shining at
New styles of architecture, a change of heart.
(l. 13–14)

CMoP; LiTB; NAEL-2; Son

September 1, 1939

70 I sit in one of the dives
On Fifty-second Street
Uncertain and afraid
As the clever hopes expire
Of a low dishonest decade: (l. 1–5)

71 I and the public know
What all schoolchildren learn,
Those to whom evil is done
Do evil in return. (l. 19–22)

72 Exiled Thucydides knew
All that a speech can say
About Democracy, (l. 23–25)

73 The habit-forming pain,
Mismanagement and grief:
We must suffer them all again. (l. 31–33)

74 blind skyscrapers use
Their full height to proclaim
The strength of Collective Man, (l. 35–37)

75 Faces along the bar
Cling to their average day:
The lights must never go out,
The music must always play, (l. 45–48)

76 Lost in a haunted wood,
Children afraid of the night
Who have never been happy or good. (l. 53–55)

77 the error bred in the bone
Of each woman and each man
Craves what it cannot have,
Not universal love
But to be loved alone. (l. 62–66)

78 May I, composed like them
Of Eros and of dust,
Beleaguered by the same
Negation and despair,
Show an affirming flame. (l. 84–88)

CMoP; LiTA; MoAB; MoBrPo; OxBA; PoE; PrIm; WaP

The Shield of Achilles

79 A million eyes, a million boots in line,
Without expression, waiting for a sigh. (l. 14–15)

80 Out of the air a voice without a face
Proved by statistics that some cause was just
(l. 16–17)

81 A crowd of ordinary decent folk
Watched from without and neither moved nor spoke
As three pale figures were led forth and bound
To three posts driven upright in the ground.
(l. 34–37)

82 That girls are raped, that two boys knife a third,
Were axioms to him, who'd never heard
Of any world where promises were kept,
Or one could weep because another wept. (l. 56–59)

83 the strong
Iron-hearted man-slaying Achilles
Who would not live long. (l. 65–67)

EBEV; FaBoMo; FaBoPV; GTBS-P; HAP; NAEL-2;
NoAM; NOBE; NOCV; NoP; PoA; PoE; WeW

Spain, 1937

84 Yesterday the theological feuds in the taverns
And the miraculous cure at the fountain;
Yesterday the Sabbath of Witches. But today the
struggle. (l. 14–16)

85 O descend as a dove or
A furious papa or a mild engineer: but descend.'
(l. 43–44)

86 Very well, I accept, for
I am your choice, your decision: yes, I am Spain.'
(l. 55–56)

87 that arid square, that fragment nipped off from hot
Africa, soldered so crudely to inventive Europe,
(l. 65–66)

88 the research on fatigue
And the movements of packers; the gradual exploring of
all the
Octaves of radiation;
Tomorrow the enlarging of consciousness by diet and
breathing. (l. 69–72)

89 the poets exploding like bombs, (l. 77)

90 the expending of powers
On the flat ephemeral pamphlet and the boring
meeting. (l. 83–84)

91 We are left alone with our day, and the time is short
and
History to the defeated
May say Alas but cannot help or pardon. (l. 90–92)

FaBoPV; LiTB; NAEL-2; OBWP; WaP

This Lunar Beauty

92 For time is inches
And the heart's changes,
Where ghost has haunted
Lost and wanted. (l. 12–15)

MoAB; MoBrPo; OBMV; OxBTC; RB; SOTW

The Unknown Citizen

93 all the reports on his conduct agree
That, in the modern sense of an old-fashioned word, he
was a saint,
For in everything he did he served the Greater
Community. (l. 3–5)

94 he held the proper opinions for the time of year;
When there was peace, he was for peace; when there
was war, he went.
He was married and added five children to the
population,
Which our Eugenist says was the right number for a
parent of his generation,
And our teachers report that he never interfered with
their education.
Was he free? Was he happy? The question is absurd.
(l. 23–28)

FF; HeIP; InPK; LiTA; LiTM; MoAB; NBLV; NIP;
NOBL; NYBP; OBSV; PoRA; SoSe; UnPo

The Wanderer

95 Doom is dark and deeper than any sea-dingle. (l. 1)

96 head falls forward, fatigued at evening,
And dreams of home, (l. 14–15)

97 gradual ruin spreading like a stain; (l. 26)

CMoP; LiTB; MoP; NoAM; RB; SOTW; WeW

Who's Who

98 A shilling life will give you all the facts:
How Father beat him, how he ran away,
What were the struggles of his youth, what acts
Made him the greatest figure of his day: (l. 1–4)

99 Love made him weep his pints like you and me. (l. 8)

100 he sighed for one
Who, say astonished critics, lived at home;
Did little jobs about the house with skill
And nothing else; (l. 9–14)

101 answered some
Of his long marvelous letters but kept none.

MoAB; MoBrPo; MoP; NoAM; Son

MARY AUSTIN   (1868–1934)
Grizzly Bear

1 if you ever, ever, dare
To stop a grizzly bear,
You will never meet another grizzly bear. (l. 5–7)

FaPON; GoJo; OnUR; PDV

SIR ROBERT AYTON   (1570–1638)
To His Forsaken Mistress

1 The morning rose, that untouched stands
Armed with her briars, how sweet she smells!
But plucked and strained through ruder hands,
Her sweets no longer with her dwells,
But scent and beauty both are gone,
And leaves fall from her, one by one. (l. 13–18)

2 And I shall sigh, when some will smile,
To see thy love to every one
Hath brought thee to be loved by none. (l. 22–24)

ElL; ErPo; GBL; OBEV; OBS; SeCePo

WILLIAM EDMONSTOUNE AYTOUN
(1813–1865)

The Massacre of the Macpherson

1 For he did resolve
To extirpate the vipers,
With four-and-twenty men
And five-and-thirty pipers. (l. 5–8)

BXAP; CenHV; ChTr; FaBoCo

FRANCIS BACON   (1561–1626)

The Life of Man

1 The world 's a bubble, and the life of man
Less then a span:
In his conception wretched, from the womb
So to the tomb;
Curst from his cradle, and brought up to years
With cares and fears. (l. 1–6)

2 What life is best?
Courts are but only superficial schools
To dandle fools:
The rural parts are turned into a den
Of savage men:
And where 's a city from all vice so free,
But may be termed the worst of all the three?
                    (l. 10–16)

ElL; GTBS; GTBS-P; OBSC

WILLIAM BALDWIN   (*fl.* 1547–1549)

Christ, My Beloved

1 My Love in me and I in him,
Conjoined by love, will till abide
Among the faithful lilies
Till day do break, and truth do dim
All shadows dark and cause them slide,
According as his will is. (l. 7–12)

ElL; ELP; NOCV; OBSC; OxBSP

JOHN KENDRICK BANGS   (1862–1922)

The Little Elf

1 I met a little Elf-man, once,
Down where the lilies blow.
I asked him why he was so small
And why he didn't grow. (l. 1–4)

2 "I'm quite as big for me, " said he,
"As you are big for you." (l. 7–8)

AA; FaBoBe; NTCP; OBCA; OnUR; PDV; RAR

GEORGE LINNAEUS BANKS
(1821–1881)

What I Live For

1 I live for those who love me,
Whose hearts are kind and true;
For the Heaven that smiles above me,
And awaits my spirit too;
For all human ties that bind me,
For the task by God assigned me,
For the bright hopes yet to find me,
And the good that I can do. (l. 1–8)

2 I live to hold communion
With all that is divine,
To feel there is a union
'Twixt Nature's heart and mine; (l. 17–20)

3 I live for those who love me,
For those who know me true, (l. 33–34)

4 For the wrong that needs resistance,
For the future in the distance,
And the good that I can do. (l. 38–40)

BLPA; FaBoBe; PWR; WBLP

IMAMU AMIRI BARAKA (LEROI JONES)
(b. 1934)

An Agony. As Now

1 I am inside someone
who hates me. (l. 1–2)

2 It burns the thing
inside it. And that thing
screams. (l. 43–45)

AmPP; BPo; LiTM; NAAL-2; PoE; PPP

Babylon Revisited

3 the great witch of euro-american legend
who sucked the life
from some unknown nigger (l. 13–15)

BPo; MoP; NoAM; TW

In Memory of Radio

4 Who has ever stopped to think of the divinity of
   Lamont Cranston? (l. 1)

5 Love is an evil word.
   Turn it backwards/ see, what I mean? (l. 14–15)

6 Saturday mornings we listened to Red Lantern& his
   undersea folk.
   At 11, Let's Pretend/& we did/& I, the poet, still do,
   Thank God! (l. 19–20)

   NAAL-2; NeAP; NoP; PoM

The Invention of Comics

7 I am a soul in the world: in
   the world of my soul the whirled
   light from the day
   the sacked land
   of my father. (l. 1–5)

8 Kind
   death. O
   my dark and sultry
   love. (l. 31–34)

   AmNP; CRP; LiTM; PoBA

Legacy

9 the cluttered eyes
   of early mysterious night. (l. 4–5)

10 Riding out
   from this town, to another, where
   it is also black. (l. 12–14)

   MoP; NoAM; NOBA; PoBA

A Poem for Black Hearts

11 Malcolm's words
   fire darts, the victor's tireless
   thrusts, words hung above the world
   change as it may, he said it, and
   for this he was killed, (l. 5–9)

12 his address
   to the grey monsters of the world, (l. 13–14)

13 For all of him dead and
   gone and vanished from us, and all of him which
   clings to our speech black god of our time. (l. 17–19)

   IDB; PoBA; PoM; SOTW

Political Poem

14 Luxury, then is a way of
   being ignorant, comfortably
   An approach to the open market
   of least information. (l. 1–4)

   CoAP; MoP; NAAL-2; NoAM

Preface to a Twenty Volume Suicide Note

15 Lately, I've become accustomed to the way
   The ground opens up and envelopes me
   Each time I go out to walk the dog. (l. 3–5)

16 Nobody sings anymore. (l. 13)

   AmNP; PoBA; PoM; PoNe; PPP; TTY

W. W.

17 Back home the black women are all beautiful (l. 1)

   HeIP; NBP; NOBA; PoBA

ANNA LAETITIA BARBAULD
(1743–1825)

Life

1 Life! I know not what thou art,
   But know that thou and I must part;
   And when, or how, or where we met
   I own to me's a secret yet. (l. 1–4)

   BLPA; FaFP; GTBS; GTBS-P; OBEV; PWR

JOHN BARBOUR (1316?–1395)

The Bruce

1 Ah! Freedom is a noble thing!
   Freedom makes man to have liking:
   Freedom all solace to man gives:
   He lives at ease that freely lives!

2 That is coupled to foul thraldom.
   But if he had assayed it,
   Then all perquer he should it wit;
   And should think freedom more to prize
   Than all the gold in world that is.

   FaBoCh; GoTS; OBEV; OxBS; TrGrPo

GEORGE BARKER (b. 1913)

O Golden Fleece

1 The love that kisses with a homicide
In robes of red generation resurrects. (l. 14–15)

2 The imperial multiplicatornothing can nonplus:
My mother Nature is the origin of it all. (l. 19–20)

ErPo; LiTM; MoAB; MoBrPo

Sonnet to My Mother

3 Most near, most dear, most loved and most far,
Under the window where I often found her
Sitting as huge as Asia, seismic with laughter, (l. 1–3)

4 She is a procession no one can follow after
But be like a little dog following a brass band. (l. 7–8)

FaBoMo; FaFP; FF; LiTB; LiTM; MoAB; OxBTC;
SeCePo; Son; TwCP; WaP

JOEL BARLOW (1754–1812)

Advice to a Raven in Russia, December, 1812

1 No Raven's wing can stretch the flight so far
As the torn bandrols of Napoleon's war.
Choose then your climate, fix your best abode,
He'll make you deserts and he'll bring you blood.
How could you fear a dearth? have not mankind,
Tho slain by millions, millions left behind?
Has not conscription still the power to weild
Her annual faulchion o'er the human field?
A faithful harvester! (l. 29–37)

AmPP; NAAL-1; NOBA; OBWP; OxBA

WILLIAM BARNES (1801–1886)

Leaves

1 Leaves of the summer, lovely summer's pride,
Sweet is the shade below your silent tree, (l. 1–2)

BoNaP; ChTr; FaBoRV; OBNC

The Wife a-Lost

2 Since I do miss your vaice an' feace
In prayer at eventide,
I'll pray wi' woone said vaice vor greace
To goo where you do bide; (l. 25–28)

BoLoP; EBVV; ELP; EnLoPo; HAP; OBEV

The Wind at the Door

3 But no. Too soon I voun' my charm abroke.
Noo comely soul in white like her —
Noo soul a-steppen light like her —
An' nwone o' comely height like her —
Went by, but all my grief agean awoke. (l. 21–25)

ELP; GBL; GTBS-P; PoEL-4

A Winter Night

4 It was a chilly winter's night;
And frost was glitt'ring on the ground,
And evening stars were twinkling bright;

5 And I alone of all mankind
Were left in loneliness behind. (l. 13–14)

ChTr; FaBoRV; NOBE; OBNC

RICHARD BARNFIELD (1574–1629)

The Affectionate Shepherd

1 In the merry month of May,
Sitting in a pleasant shade,
Which a grove of myrtles made,
Beasts did leap, and birds did sing,
Trees did grow, and plants did spring:
Every thing did banish moan,
Save the Nightingale alone.

AWP; CH; ElL; GBL; GTBS; GTBS-P; NOBE; OBEV;
OBSC; PBBP

To His Friend Master R.L., in Praise of Music and Poetry

2 If music and sweet poetry agree,
As they must needs (the sister and the brother),
Then must the love be great 'twixt thee and me,
Because thou lov'st the one, and I the other. (l. 1–4)

AAS; ElL; Son; UnS

KATHARINE LEE BATES (1859–1929)

America the Beautiful

1 O beautiful for spacious skies,
For amber waves of grain,
For purple mountain majesties
Above the fruited plain! (l. 1–4)

2 O beautiful for heroes proved
In liberating strife,
Who more than self their country loved,
And mercy more than life! (l. 17–20)

3 Thine alabaster cities gleam
Undimmed by human tears! (l. 27–28)

BLPA; EaLo; FaBoBe; FaBV; FaFP; FaPON; GOA; OPP;
TAP; WBLP; WGRP

FRANCIS BEAUMONT (1584–1616)

The Masque of the Inner Temple and Gray's Inne

1 Shake off your heavy trance,
and leap into a dance,
Such as no mortals use to tread,
fit only for Apollo
To play to, for the Moon to lead,
And all the Stars to follow.

ChTr; ElL; FaBoCh; OBS; TrGrPo

FRANCIS BEAUMONT (1584–1616) AND WILLIAM BASSE (fl. c. 1602)

Lines on the Tombs in Westminster (attributed to Beaumont and to Basse)

1 Mortality, behold, and fear,
What a change of flesh is here!
Think how many royal bones
Sleep within this heap of stones,
Hence removed from beds of ease,
Dainty fare, and what might please, (l. 1–6)

2 Know from this the world's a snare,
How that greatness is but care,
How all pleasures are but pain,
And how short they do remain: (l. 15–18)

3 Where from their pulpits sealed with dust
They preach: 'In greatness is no trust'. (l. 21–22)

4 Here the bones of birth have cried,
'Though Gods they were, as men they died'. (l. 27–28)

5 this scythe that mows down kings
Exempts no meaner mortal things. (l. 35–36)

6 Bid her paint till day of doom,
To this favour she must come.
Bid the merchant gather wealth,
The usurer exact by stealth,

The proud man beat it from his thought,
Yet to this shape all must be brought. (l. 43–48)

ACP; CH; ElL; FaBoCh; FaPoR; GTBS; GTBS-P; HAP;
NOBE; OBEV; OBS; TrGrPo

FRANCIS BEAUMONT (1584–1616) AND JOHN FLETCHER (1579–1625)

The Captain

1 Away delights, go seek some other dwelling,
For I must die:

2 For ever will I sleep, while poor maids cry,
Alas, for pity stay,
And let us die
With thee, men cannot mock us in the clay.

ElL; GBL; NOBE; OBEV

The Maid's Tragedy

3 Lay a garland on my hearse,
Of the dismal yew;
Maidens, willow branches bear;
Say I died true.

AWP; CH; ElL; GBL; HAP; NOBE; OBEV; OBS; TrGrPo

4 Hold back thy hours,dark Night, till we have done;
The Day will come too soon.
Young maids will curse thee, if thou steal'st away
And leav'st their losses open to the day.
Stay, stay, and hide
The blushes of the bride.

ElL; ErPo; OxBSP; TrGrPo

THOMAS LOVELL BEDDOES
(1803–1849)

Death's Jest Book

1 We have bathed, where none have seen us,
In the lake and in the fountain,
Underneath the charmed statue
Of the timid, bending Venus,

ChER; GBL; NOBVV; OBNC; PoEL-4

2 The swallow leaves her nest,
The soul my weary breast;

ELP; NOBE; OBNC; PoEL-4; WiR

3 But wilt thou cure thine heart
Of love and all its smart,
Then die, dear, die;

EnRP; LiTB; NOBE; OBEV; OBNC; PoEL-4

4 Old Adam, the carrion crow,

5 Is that the wind dying? O no;
It's only two devils, that blow
Through a murderer's bones, to and fro,
In the ghosts' moonshine.

ChER; EBEV; ELP; EnRP; LiTB; OAEL-2; PBBP;
PoEL-4; TrGrPo; WiR

6 Squats on a toad-stool under a tree
A bodiless childfull of life in the gloom,
Crying with frog voice, "What shall I be?
Poor unborn ghost, for my mother killed me
Scarcely alive in her wicked womb.

7 I'll be a new bird with the head of an ass,
Two pigs' feet, two men's feet, and two of a hen

InvP; NOBVV; OBD; OBNC; PrIm

8 We are afraid
They would envy our delight,
In our graves by glow-worm night.

ELP; NOBE; NOBVV; OBNC; WiR

Dream-Pedlary

9 If there were dreams to sell,
Merry and sad to tell,
And the crier rung the bell,
What would you buy?

BoTP; CH; EnRP; FaBoBe; HAP; LiTB; NOBE; OBEV;
OBNC; PoEL-4; TrGrPo; WiR

The Last Man

10 Hard by the lilied Nile I saw
A duskish river dragon stretched along.
The brown habergeon of his limbs enamelled
With sanguine alamandines and rainy pearl:
And on his back there lay a young one sleeping,
No bigger than a mouse; (l. 1–6)

FM; NOBVV; OBTV; RB

The Phantom-Wooer

11 Young soul put off your flesh, and come
With me into the quiet tomb,
Our bed is lovely, dark, and sweet;

The earth will swing us, as she goes,
Beneath our coverlid of snows, (l. 11–15)

EnRP; NAEL-2; TrGrPo; WiR

Torrismond

12 Tell me how many beads there are
In a silver chain
Of evening rain,
Unravelled from the tumbling main,
And threading the eye of a yellow star: —
So many times do I love again. (l. 9–14)

ELP; EnRP; LiTB; NAEL-2; PoEL-4; TrGrPo

MAX BEERBOHM (1872–1956)

A Luncheon

1 Lift latch, step in, be welcome, Sir,
Albiet to see you I'm unglad (l. 1–2)

FaBoCo; NOBL; OBSV; OxBTC

APHRA BEHN (1640–1689)

Abdelazer

1 Love in fantastic triumph sat,
Whilst bleeding hearts around him flowed,

2 But 'twas from mine, he took desire,
Enough to undo the amorous world.

NOBE; OBEV; OBS; TrGrPo; WPE

HILAIRE BELLOC (1870–1953)

Epitaph on the Politician Himself

1 The Politician's corpse was laid away.
While all of his acquaintance sneered and slanged,
I wept: for I had longed to see him hanged. (l. 2–4)

FaBoEE; MoBrPo; NBLV; OBSV; TW

The False Heart

2 "How goes it?" Heart replied,
"Right as a Ribstone Pippin!" (l. 1–2)

FaBoCh; FaBoEE; MoBrPo; OxBSP

Fatigue

3 I'm tired of Love: (l. 1)

4 Money gives me pleasure all the time. (l. 2)

FaBoCo; NBLV; NOBL; OxBTC

The Frog

5 Be kind and tender to the Frog,
And do not call him names,
As 'Slimy skin', or 'Polly-wog', (l. 1–3)

6 No animal will more repay
A treatment kind and fair;
At least so lonely people say
Who keep a frog (and, by the way,
They are extremely rare). (l. 9–13)

FaBoBe; FaBV; FaPON; FiBHP; GoJo; MoShBr; NA;
NTCP; OxBChV; RHPC

Ha'nacker Mill

7 Wind and Thistle for pipe and dancers
And never a ploughman under the Sun.
Never a ploughman. Never a one. (l. 13–15)

FaPoR; MoBrPo; OxBTC; RB

Henry King, Who Chewed Bits of String, and Was Early Cut Off in Dreadful Agonies

8 The Chief Defect of Henry King
Was chewing little bits of String.
At last he swallowed some which tied
Itself in ugly Knots inside. (l. 1–4)

CenHV; FaBoNo; FaBoUs; NBLV

The Hippopotamus

9 I shoot the Hippopotamus
With bullets made of platinum, (l. 1–2)

CenHV; FaBoNo; FiBHP; InPK

Jim, Who Ran Away from His Nurse, and Was Eaten by a Lion

10 He slipped his hand and ran away!
He hadn't gone a yard when — Bang!
With open jaws, a lion sprang,
And hungrily began to eat
The boy: beginning at his feet. (l. 18–22)

11 always keep a-hold of Nurse
For fear of finding something worse. (l. 53–54)

CenHV; ChTr; NoAM; OxBChV

Lines to a Don

12 Don here-and-there, Don epileptic;
Don puffed and empty, Don dyspeptic;
Don middle-class, Don sycophantic,
Don dull, Don brutish, Don pedantic; (l. 13–16)

13 Don different from those regal Dons!
With hearts of gold and lungs of bronze,
Who shout and bang and roar and brawl
The Absolute across the hall, (l. 21–24)

14 There is a Canon which confines
A Rhymed Octosyllabic Curse
If written in Iambic Verse
To fifty lines.

FaBoCo; MoBrPo; OBSV; TW

Lord Finchley

15 It is the business of the wealthy man
To give employment to the artisan. (l. 3–4)

FaBoCo; FaBoEE; FiBHP; NBLV; NoAM; NOBL;
OxBoLi

Matilda

16 For every time She shouted 'Fire!'
They only answered 'Little Liar'! (l. 47–50)

CenHV; FaBoCh; NOBE; OnMSP; OxBChV

On a General Election

17 The accursed power which stands on Privilege
(And goes with Women, and Champagne and Bridge)
(l. 1–2)

FaBoCo; FaBoEE; NOBE; NOBL; OBSV; OxBoLi;
OxBTC

On His Books

18 When I am dead, I hope it may be said:
'His sins were scarlet, but his books were read.'
(l. 1–2)

ACP; FaBoCo; FaBoEE; MoBrPo; NBLV; OxBoLi; WeW

Tarantella

19 Do you remember an Inn, Miranda,
Do you remember an Inn?
And the cheers and the jeers of the young muleteers
Who hadn't got a penny, (l. 10–13)

CH; FaBoCh; MoBrPo; MoShBr; OBMV; RB; RR

The Yak

20 As a friend to the children commend me the Yak.
You will find it exactly the thing:
It will carry and fetch, you can ride on its back,
Or lead it about with a string. (l. 1–4)

FaBV; FaPON; MoBrPo; NA; NBLV; NoAM; NOBL;
OxBChV

STEPHEN VINCENT BENÉT
(1898–1943)

American Names

1 I have fallen in love with American names, (l. 1)

2 Seine and Piave are silver spoons,
But the spoonbowl-metal is thin and worn, (l. 6–7)

3 I am tired of loving a foreign muse. (l. 20)

4 Bury my heart at Wounded Knee. (l. 35)

AmFN; GOA; OBAL; OPP; OxBA

ARNOLD BENNETT (1867–1931)

There was a young man of Montrose

1 There was a young man of Montrose
Who had pockets in none of his clothes. (l. 1–2)

2 'Darling, I pay through the nose.' (l. 5)

CenHV; FaBoNo; FaFP; OxBoLi

GWENDOLYN B. BENNETT (1902–1981)
Hatred

1 Hating you shall be a game
Played with cool hands
And slim fingers. (l. 9–11)

2 Memory will lay its hands
Upon your breast
And you will understand
My hatred. (l. 18–21)

AmNP; BANP; BlSi; CDC; PoBA

He came in silvern armor, trimmed with black

3 All eager-lipped I kissed the mouth of Death. (l. 14)

AmNP; CDC; PoBA; PoNe

Heritage

4 I want to hear the chanting
Around a heathen fire
Of a strange black race. (l. 10–12)

5 I want to feel the surging
Of my sad people's soul
Hidden by a minstrel-smile. (l. 16–18)

AmNP; EANP; BlSi; PoBA

To a Dark Girl

6 Something of old forgotten queens
Lurks in the lithe abandon of your walk, (l. 5–6)

7 Oh, little brown girl, born for sorrow's mate,
Keep all you have of queenliness,
Forgetting that you once were slave,
And let your full lips laugh at Fate! (l. 9–12)

BANP; BlSi; CDC; PoBA

HENRY HOLCOMB BENNETT
(1863–1924)

The Flag Goes By

1 Hats off!
The flag is passing by! (l. 5–6)

2 Days of plenty and years of peace;
March of a strong land's swift increase;
Equal justice, right and law,
Stately honor and reverend awe; (l. 16–19)

FaBoBe; FaFP; FaPON; GN; OHFP; OPP; PWR; WBLP

EDMUND CLERIHEW BENTLEY
(1875–1956)

George the Third

1 George the Third
Ought never to have occurred. (l. 1–2)

FaBoCo; FiBHP; NOBL; OxBoLi

GEORGE BERKELEY (1685–1753)

On the Prospect of Planting Arts and Learning in America

1 Westward the course of empire takes its way;
The four first acts already past,
A fifth shall close the drama with the day;
Time's noblest offspring is the last. (l. 21–24)

AiP; FaFP; NOEC; OBTV; SeCePo; TrGrPo

WENDELL BERRY (b. 1934)

The Peace of Wild Things

1 I come into the peace of wild things
who do not tax their lives with forethought
of grief. (l. 6–8)

GeTw; HeIP; MT; NIP; NU; PCP; VGW

JOHN BERRYMAN (1914–1972)

The Ball Poem

1 What is the boy now, who has lost his ball,
What, what is he to do? (l. 1–2)

2 He is learning, well behind his desperate eyes,
The epistemology of loss, (l. 15–16)

3 I am everywhere,
I suffer and move, my mind and my heart move
With all that move me, (l. 22–24)

ASP; CoAP; FF; MoAmPo; NoAM; NOBA; NoP

DREAM SONGS (the following 5 poems)

Filling Her Compact

4 Filling her compact & delicious body
with chicken paprika, she glanced at me
twice. (l. 1–3)

5 only the fact of her husband & four other people
kept me from springing on her (l. 5–7)

6 Where did it all go wrong? There ought to be a law
against Henry. (l. 18–19)

BoLoP; CAPP; HAP; HCAP; NoP; OBAL; OPOP; WeW

Henry's Confession

7 Nothing very bad happen to me lately.
How you explain that? — I explain that, Mr Bones,
terms o' your bafflin odd sobriety.
Sober as man can get, no girls, no telephones,
what could happen bad to Mr Bones? (l. 1–5)

LCAP; MoP; NAAL-2; NoAM; PoE; TwCP

Huffy Henry Hid the Day

8 What he has now to say is a long
wonder the world can bear & be. (l. 13–14)

9 Hard on the land wears the strong sea
and empty grows every bed. (l. 17–18)

CAPP; HCAP; NAAL-2; NoP; PoE

Life, friends, is boring

10 Life, friends, is boring. We must not say so. (l. 1)

11 literature bores me, especially great literature, (l. 10)

12 And the tranquil hills, & gin, look like a drag (l. 14)

CAPP; HAP; HCAP; HeIP; LiTM; MoP; NAAL-2; NaP; NoAM; NOBA; PrIm; TAP; TwCP

There Sat Down Once

13 But never did Henry, as he thought he did,
end anyone and hacks her body up
and hide the pieces, where they may be found.
He knows: he went over everyone, & nobody's missing.
(l. 13–16)

CAPP; HAP; HCAP; NoP; PoE

Henry's Understanding

14 I'd take off all my clothes
& cross the damp cold lawn & down the bluff
into the terrible water & walk forever
under it out toward the island. (l. 15–18)

CAPP; MoP; NoAM; NOBA

A Professor's Song

15 "A poet is a man speaking to men":
But I am then a poet, am I not? — (l. 10–11)

HeIP; MoP; NAAL-2; NoAM; NOBA; OxBC

BERTRANS DE BORN (*fl.* 12th century)

Well Pleaseth Me the Sweet Time of Easter

1 it pleaseth me when I see through the meadows
The tents and pavilions set up, and great joy have I
When I see o'er the campana knights armed and horses
arrayed.

And it pleaseth me when the scouts set in flight the folk
with their goods;
And it pleaseth me when I see coming together after
them an host of armed men. (l. 5–9)

AWP; CTC; InvP; WaaP

SIR JOHN BETJEMAN (1906–1984)

The Arrest of Oscar Wilde at the Cadogan Hotel

1 Approval of what is approved of
Is as false as a well-kept vow. (l. 15–16)

2 He rose, and he put down The Yellow Book.
He staggered — and, terrible-eyed,
He brushed past the palms on the staircase
And was helped to a hansom outside. (l. 33–36)

CMoP; EBEV; InvP; MoBrPo; MoP; NoAM; NoP; OxBTC

The Cottage Hospital

3 Down came the hairy talons
and horrible poison blade
And none of the garden noticed
that fizzing, hopeless fight. (l. 21–24)

GTBS-P; MoBrPo; NoAM; NOBE; OBD; UnPo

In Westminster Abbey

4 Think of what our Nation stands for,
Books from Boots and country lanes,
Free speech, free passes, class distinction,
Democracy and proper drains. (l. 19–22)

5 Lord, reserve for me a crown,
And do not let my shares go down. (l. 29–30)

6 What a treat to hear Thy Word
Where the bones of leading statesmen,
Have so often been interred. (l. 38–40)

CMoP; FaBcCo; InPK; NBLV; NIP; NoAM; NOBL;
OAEL-2 OBSV; TOF

"New King Arrives in His Capital by Air..." — Daily Newspaper

7 The big blue eyes are shut which saw wrong clothing
And favourite fields and coverts from a horse; (l. 5–6)

8 Old men who never cheated, never doubted,
Communicated monthly, sit and stare
At the new suburb stretched beyond the run-way
Where a young man lands hatless from the air.
(l. 9–12)

NOBE; OxBoLi

A Subaltern's Love-Song

9 Miss J, Hunter Dunn, Miss J: Hunter Dunn,
Furnish'd and burnish'd by Aldershot sun,
What strenous singles we played after tea,
We in the tournament — you against me! (l. 1–4)

10 Oh! full Surrey twilight! importunate band!
Oh! strongly adorable tennis-girl's hand! (l. 35–36)

11 and the words never said,
And the ominous, ominous dancing ahead.
We sat in the car park till twenty to one
And now I'm engaged to Miss Joan Hunter Dunn.
(l. 41–44)

BoLoP; HAP; NoAM; NOBL; OxBTC; TwCP

BIBLE, *OLD TESTAMENT*

Ecclesiastes

1 To every thing there is a season, and a time to every
purpose under the heaven:
A time to be born, and a time to die; a time to plant,
and a time to pluck up that which is planted;
(III, 1–2)

2 A time to weep, and a time to laugh; a time to mourn,
and a time to dance; (III, 4)

3 A time to love, and a time to hate; a time of war, and a
time of peace. (III, 8)

DL; FF; NAWM-1; OBVE; TrGrPo

4 the race is not to the swift, nor the battle to the strong, neither yet bread to the wise, nor yet riches to men of understanding, nor yet favour to men of skill; but time and chance happeneth to them all. (IX, 11)

5 man also knoweth not his time: as the fishes that are taken in an evil net, and as the birds that are caught in the snare; so are the sons of men snared in an evil time, (IX, 12)

Prf

6 Or ever the silver cord be loosed, or the golden bowl be broken, or the pitcher be broken at the fountain, or the wheel broken at the cistern.
Then shall the dust return to the earth as it was: and the spirit shall return unto God who gave it.
Vanity of vanities, saith the preacher, all is vanity.
(XII, 6–7)

7 of making many books there is no end; and much study is a weariness of the flesh.
Let us hear the conclusion of the whole matter: Fear God, and keep his commandments: for this is the whole duty of man. (XII, 13)

AWP; ChTr; OBVE; TrGrPo; TrJP

First Samuel

8 The Lord killeth, and maketh alive; he bringeth down to the grave, and bringeth up.
The Lord maketh poor, and maketh rich: he bringeth low, and lifteth up.
He raiseth up the poor out of the dust, and lifteth up the beggar from the dunghill, to set them among princes, and to make them inherit the throne of glory: for the pillars of the earth are the Lord's and he hath set the world upon them.
He will keep the feet of his saints, and the wicked shall be silent in darkness; for by strength shall no man prevail.
The adversaries of the Lord shall be broken to pieces; out of heaven shall he thunder upon them: the Lord shall judge the ends of the earth; and he shall give strength unto his king, and exalt the horn of his anointed. (II, 6–10)

AWP; TrCP

Job

9 Let the day perish wherein I was born, and the night in which it was said, There is a man child conceived.
(III, 3)

10 Because it shut not up the doors of my mother's womb, nor hid sorrow from mine eyes.
Why died I not from the womb? (III, 10–11)

11 There the wicked cease from troubling; and there the weary be at rest.
There the prisoners rest together; they hear not the voice of the oppressor. (III, 17–18)

12 Wherefore is light given to him that is in misery, and life unto the bitter in soul;
Which long for death, (III, 20–21)

AWP; NAs; NAWM-1; OBVE; TrGrPo; TrJP

13 Where wast thou when I laid the foundations of the earth? (XXXVIII, 4)

14 When the morning stars sang together, and all the sons of God shouted for joy? (XXXVIII, 7)

15 Where is the way where light dwelleth? and as for darkness, where is the place thereof, (XXXVIII, 19)

16 Gavest thou the goodly wings unto the peacocks? or wings and feathers unto the ostrich?
Which leaveth her eggs in the earth, and warmeth them in dust, (XXXIX, 13–14)

17 What time she lifteth up herself on high, she scorneth the horse and his rider.
Hast thou given the horse strength? hast thou clothed his neck with thunder? (XXXIX, 17–19)

AWP; NAWM-1

Judges

18 Speak, ye that ride on white asses, ye that sit in judgment, and walk by the way.
They that are delivered from the noise of archers in the places of drawing water, there shall they rehearse the righteous acts of the Lord, (V, 10–11)

19 He asked water, and she gave him milk; she brought forth butter in a lordly dish.
She put her hand to the nail, and her right hand to the workmen's hammer; and with the hammer she smote Sis'e-ra, she smote off his head, when she had pierced and stricken through his temples. (V, 25–26)

20 So let all thine enemies perish, O Lord: (V, 31)

AWP; BoWoP; PBWP; TrJP

PSALMS (the following 18 psalms)

Psalm I

21 Blessed is the man that walketh not in the counsel of the ungodly, nor standeth in the way of sinners, nor sitteth in the seat of the scornful.
But his delight is in the law of the Lord; and in his law doth he meditate day and night.

And he shall be like a tree planted by the rivers of
water, that bringeth forth his fruit in his season; his
leaf also shall not wither; and whatsoever he doeth
shall prosper. (I, 1–3)

22 the way of the ungodly shall perish. (I, 6)

AWP; SCAP; TrJP; WGRP

Psalm VIII

23 Out of the mouth of babes and sucklings hast thou
ordained strength because of thine enemies, that thou
mightest still the enemy and the avenger. (VIII, 2)

24 When I consider thy heavens, the work of thy fingers,
the moon and the stars, which thou hast ordained;
What is man, that thou art mindful of him?
(VIII, 3–4)

25 For thou hast made him a little lower than the angels,
and hast crowned him with glory and honor.
Thou madest him to have dominion over the works of
thy hands; (VIII, 5–6)

AWP; NAWM-1; OBVE; TrGrPo; TrJP

Psalm XIX

26 The heavens declare the glory of God; and the
firmament sheweth his handiwork. (XIX, 1)

27 In them hath he set a tabernacle for the sun.
Which is as a bridegroom coming out of his chamber.
(XIX, 4–5)

28 The law of the Lord is perfect, converting the soul: the
testimony of the Lord is sure, making wise the
simple. (XIX, 7)

29 Keep back thy servant also from presumptuous sins;
(XIX, 13)

30 Let the words of my mouth, and the meditation of my
heart, be acceptable in thy sight, O Lord, my
strength, and my redeemer. (XIX, 14)

AWP; FaPON; NAWM-1; OBVE; WBLP

Psalm XXIII

31 The Lord is my shepherd; I shall not want.
He maketh me to lie down in green pastures: he
leadeth me beside the still waters.
He restoreth my soul: he leadeth me in the paths of
righteousness for his name's sake.
Yea, though I walk through the valley of the shadow of
death, I will fear no evil: for thou art with me; thy
rod and thy staff they comfort me.

Thou preparest a table before me in the presence of
mine enemies: thou anointest my head with oil;my
cup runneth over.
Surely goodness and mercy shall follow me all the days
of my life: and I will dwell in the house of the Lord
for ever. (XXIII, 1–6)

AH; AWP; ELPL; FaBoBe; FaPON; FPL; JCP; NAWM-1;
NIP; OBCA; OBVE; OHIP; PoLF; TrGrPo; TrJP; WBLP;
WGRP

Psalm XXIV

32 The earth is the Lord's, and the fullness thereof; the
world, and they that dwell therein. (XXIV, 1)

33 He that hath clean hands, and a pure heart; who hath
not lifted up his soul unto vanity, nor sworn
deceitfully.
He shall receive the blessing from the Lord, and
righteousness from the God of his salvation.
(XXIV, 4–5)

34 Lift up your heads, O ye gates; and be ye lift up, ye
everlasting doors; and the King of glory shall come
in. (XXIV, 7)

AWP; EaLo; FaPON; TrGrPo; TrJP

Psalm XLII

35 As the hart panteth after the water brooks, so panteth
my soul after thee, O God. (XLII, 1)

36 Why art thou cast down, O my soul? and why art thou
disquieted within me? hope thou in God: for I shall
yet praise him, who is the health of my countenance,
and my God. (XLII, 11)

AWP; TrGrPo; TrJP; WGRP

Psalm LV

37 Give ear to my prayer, O God; and hide not thyself
from my supplication.
Attend unto me, and hear me: I mourn in my
complaint, and make a noise; (LV, 1–2)

38 And I said, Oh that I had wings like a dove! for then
would I fly away, and be at rest. (LV, 6)

39 For it was not an enemy that reproached me; then I
could have borne it: neither was it he that hated me
that did magnify himself against me; then I would
have hid myself from him:
But it was thou, a man mine equal, my guide, and mine
acquaintance.
We took sweet counsel together, and walked unto the
house of God in company. (LV, 12–14)

40 The words of his mouth were smoother than butter, but
   war was in his heart: his words were softer than oil,
   yet were they drawn swords.
   Cast thy burden upon the Lord, and he shall sustain
   thee: he shall never suffer the righteous to be moved.
   (LV, 21–22)

AWP; OBVE; WPE

Psalm LVIII (*Paraphrased by* The Countess of
Pembroke)

41 And call ye this to utter what is just,
   You that of justice hold the sov'reign throne?
   And call ye this to yield, O sons of dust,
   To wronged brethren ev'ry man his own? (l. 1–4)

42 Lord, crack their teeth! Lord, crush these lions' jaws!
   So let them sink as water in the sand;
   When deadly bow their aiming fury draws,
   Shiver the shaft ere past the shooter's hand.
   So make them melt as the dishoused snail (l. 17–21)

BoWoP; NAEL-1; NOCV; WPE

Psalm LXXXIV

43 Behold, O God our shield, and look upon the face of
   thine anointed.
   For a day in thy courts is better than a thousand. I had
   rather be a doorkeeper in the house of my God, than
   to dwell in the tents of wickedness.
   For the Lord God is a sun and shield: the Lord will
   give grace and glory: (LXXXIV, 9–11)

44 blessed is the man that trusteth in thee.
   (LXXXIV, 12)

FaPON; TrJP; TrPWD

Psalm XCVIII

45 O sing unto the Lord a new song, (XCVIII, 1)

46 Sing unto the Lordwith the harp, with the harp, and
   the voice of a psalm.
   With trumpets and sound of cornet make a joyful noise
   before the Lord, (XCVIII, 5–6)

47 Let the floods clap their hands; let the hills be joyful
   together.
   Before the Lord; for he cometh to judge the earth; with
   righteousness shall he judge the world, and the
   people with equity. (XCVIII, 8–9)

BLRP; EaLo; TrGrPo; TrJP

Psalm C

48 Make a joyful noise unto the Lord, all ye lands.
   Serve the Lord with gladness: come before his presence
   with singing. (C, 1–2)

49 we are his people, and the sheep of his pasture. (C, 3)

50 Enter into his gates with thanksgiving, and into his
   courts with praise: be thankful unto him, and bless
   his name.
   For the Lord is good; his mercy is everlasting; and his
   truth endureth to all generations. (C, 4–5)

BLRP; FaPON; FaPoR; NOCV; OFD; OHIP; WGRP

Psalm CIV

51 O Lord, how manifold are thy works! in wisdom hast
   thou made them all: the earth is full of thy riches.
   (CIV, 24)

52 there is that leviathan, whom thou hast made to play
   therein. (CIV, 26)

53 Thou hidest thy face,they are troubled:thou takest away
   their breath, they die, and return to their dust.
   (CIV, 29)

NAWM-1; OHIP; TrJP; WGRP

Psalm CVII (Bay Psalm Book)

54 O Give yee thanks unto the Lord,
   Because that good is hee:
   Because his loving kindenes lasts
   To perpetuitee. (l. 1–4)

55 O that men would Jehovah prayse
   For his great goodness then: (l. 69–70)

56 They that goe downe to 'th sea in ships:
   Their busines there to doo
   In waters great. The Lords work see,
   I'th deep his wonders too. (l. 77–80)

57 Then did they to Jehovah cry
   When they were in distress:
   And therupon he bringeth them
   Out of their anguishes. (l. 89–92)

SCAP

Psalm CXXI

58 I will lift up mine eyes unto the hills, from whence
   cometh my help. (CXXI, 1)

59 The Lord is thy keeper; the Lord is thy shade upon thy
right hand.
The sun shall not smite thee by day, nor the moon by
night.
The Lord shall preserve thee from all evil; he shall
preserve thy soul.
The Lord shall preserve thy going out and thy coming
in from this time forth, and even for evermore.
(CXXI, 5–8)

AWP; FaPON; OBCA; TrGrPo; WGRP

Psalm CXXX

60 Out of the depths have I cried unto thee, O Lord.
(CXXX, 1)

61 Let Israel hope in the Lord, for with the Lord there is
mercy,
And with him is plenteous redemption. And he shall
redeem Israel from all his iniquities. (CXXX, 7–8)

BLRP; OBVE; TrGrPo; TrJP; WGRP

Psalm CXXXVII

62 By the rivers of Babylon, there we sat down, yea, we
wept, then we remembered Zion. (CXXXVII, 1)

63 How shall we sing the Lord's song in a strange land?
If I forget thee, O Jerusalem, let my right hand forget
her cunning. (CXXXVII, 4–5)

AWP; NAWM-1; OAEL-1; OBS; OBVE; TrJP

Psalm CXXXIX (*Paraphrased by* The Countess of Pembroke)

64 If forth I march, thou goest before;
If back I turn, thou comest behind; (l. 15–16)

65 Well I thy wisdom may adore,
But never reach with earthy mind. (l. 20–21)

NOCV; OBSC; OBVE; WPE

Psalm CXLVII (*Paraphrased by* The Countess of Pembroke)

66 And tell so readily, he knoweth well
How ev'ry star by proper name to call? (l. 13–14)

67 O make harmonious mix of voice and string
To him by whom the skies with clouds are lin'd;
By whom the rain, from clouds to drop assign'd,
Supples the clods of summer-scorched fields,
(l. 21–24)

OBVE; TrGrPo; TrJP

Second Samuel

68 The beauty of Israel is slain upon thy high places how
are the mighty fallen!
Tell it not in Gath, publish it not in the streets of
Askelon; (I, 19–20)

69 Saul and Jonathan were lovely and pleasant in their
lives, and in their death they were not divided: they
were swifter than eagles, they were stronger than
lions.
Ye daughters of Israel, weep over Saul, who clothed
you in scarlet, with other delights, who put on
ornaments of gold upon your apparel.
How are the mighty fallen in the midst of the battle! O
Jonathan, thou wast slam in thine high places.
(I, 23–25)

AWP; ChTr; FF; OBVE; OBWP; TrGrPo; TrJP; WaaP

The Song of Solomon

70 I am the rose of Sharon, and the lily of the valleys.
(II, 1)

71 My beloved is like a roe or a young hart: (II, 9)

72 My beloved spake, and said unto me, Rise up, my love,
my fair one, and come away.
For lo, the winter is past, the rain is over and gone;
The flowers appear on the earth; the time of the singing
of birds is come, and the voice of the turtle is heard
in our land; (II, 10–12)

73 Take us the foxes, the little foxes, that spoil the vines:
for our vines have tender grapes. (II, 15)

AWP; BoLoP; ChTr; FF; GBL; LLLT; OBVE; TrGrPo

LAURENCE BINYON (1869–1943)

For the Fallen

1 With proud thanksgiving, a mother for her children,
England mourns for her dead across the sea, (l. 1–2)

2 Death august and royal
Sings sorrow up into immortal spheres. (l. 5–6)

3 They shall grow not old, as we that are left grow old:
Age shall not weary them, nor the years condemn.
(l. 13–14)

NOBE; OBEV; OBWP; OxBTC

The Little Dancers

4 the little street
Into its gloom retires, secluded and shy.

5 Two children, all alone and no one by,
Holding their tattered frocks, thro'an airy maze
Of motion lightly threaded with nimble feet
Dance sedately; face to face they gaze,
Their eyes shining, grave with a perfect pleasure.
(l. 8–12)

BoTP; CH; MoBrPo; OxBTC

EARLE BIRNEY (b. 1904)

The Bear on the Delhi Road

1 Unreal, tall as a myth, (l. 1)

2 an ambling bear
four-footed in berries. (l. 24–25)

3 It is not easy to free
myth from reality
or rear this fellow up
to lutch, lurch with them
in the tranced dancing of men. (l. 31–35)

HeIP; MoCV; NoAM; NOBC; NoP; NYBP; PrIm

Bushed

4 a fuzzed moth in a flannel of storm (l. 9)

5 ospreys
would fall like valkyries (l. 15–16)

6 owls in the beardusky woods (l. 22)

MoCV; NoAM; NOBC; NoP; OBCV

ELIZABETH BISHOP (1911–1979)

The Armadillo

1 light
that comes and goes, like hearts. (l. 7–8)

2 O falling fire and piercing cry
and panic, and a weak mailed fist
clenched ignorant against the sky! (l. 37–40)

CAPP; HCAP; MoP; NAAL-2; NoAM; NOBA; NoP;
NYBP; SM; TAP; VGW

At the Fishhouses

3 creamy iridescent coats of mail,
with small iridescent flies crawling on them.
(l. 24–25)

4 Cold dark deep and absolutely clear,
element bearable to no mortal, (l. 47–48)

5 I have seen it over and over, the same sea, the same,
slightly, indifferently swinging above the stones,
icily free above the stones,
above the stones and then the world. (l. 67–70)

6 It is what we imagine knowledge to be:
dark, salt, clear, moving, utterly free,
drawn from the cold hard mouth
of the world, derived from the rocky breasts
forever, flowing and drawn, and since
our knowledge is historical, flowing, and flown.
(l. 78–83)

CoAP; FaBoWP; HAP; HCAP; LCAP; LiTM; NAAL-2;
NoP; NYBP; PoRA

The Bight

7 One can smell it turning to gas; if one were Baudelaire
one could probably hear it turning to marimba music.
(l. 7–8)

8 The frowsy sponge boats keep coming in
with the obliging air of retrievers, (l. 20–21)

9 The bight is littered with old correspondences. (l. 32)

10 All the untidy activity continues,
awful but cheerful. (l. 35–36)

FaBoWP; HCAP; NAAL-2; NYBP; RB

Filling Station

11 Oh, but it is dirty!
— this little filling station,
oil-soaked, oil-permeated
to a disturbing, over-all
black translucency.
Be careful with that match! (l. 1–6)

12 a set of crushed and grease-
impregnated wickerwork;
on the wicker sofa
a dirty dog, quite comfy. (l. 17–20)

13 Somebody
arranges the rows of cans
so that they softly say:

esso — so — so — so
to high-strung automobiles.
Somebody loves us all. (l. 36—41)

FaBoMo; HAP; HCAP; InPK; NoP; NYBP; WeW

First Death in Nova Scotia

14 His breast was deep and white,
cold and caressable;
his eyes were red glass,
much to be desired. (l. 17—20)

15 Arthur was very small.
He was all white, like a doll
that hadn't been painted yet. (l. 31—33)

CoAP; FaBoWP; LCAP; NOBA; NYBP

The Fish

16 his gills were breathing in
the terrible oxygen (l. 22—23)

17 They shifted a little, but not
to return my stare. (l. 41—42)

18 I saw
that from his lower lip
if you could call it a lip —
grim, wet, and weaponlike,
hung five old pieces of fish-line, (l. 47—52)

19 everything
was rainbow, rainbow, rainbow!
And I let the fish go. (l. 74—76)

ASP; CAPP; FaBoWP; GoJo; HAP; HeIP; HoPM; InPK;
LiTM; MoAB; MoAmPo; MoP; MOS; NAAL-2; NoAM;
NOBA; NoP; NU; OPOP; PoE; RB; TrGrPo; WeW

The Imaginary Iceberg

20 Icebergs behoove the soul
(both being self-made from elements least visible
to see them so; fleshed, fair, erected indivisible.
(l. 31—33)

FaBoWP; LiTM; MoAB; MoAmPo

In the Waiting Room

21 The waiting room
was full of grown-up people,
arctics and overcoats,
lamps and magazines. (l. 7—10)

22 blacks, naked women with necks
wound round and round with wire
like the necks of light blubs,
Their breasts were horrifying. (l. 28—31)

23 How had I come to be here,
like them, and overhear
a cry of pain that could have
got loud and worse but hadn't? (l. 86—89)

FaEoWP; HeIP; InPS; LCAP; NAAL-2; NoAM; NOBA;
PoE; Pre

Large Bad Picture

24 Remembering the Strait of Belle Isle or
some northerly harbor of Labrador,
before he became a schoolteacher
a great-uncle painted a big picture. (l. 1—4)

25 On the middle of that quiet floor
sits a fleet of small black ships,
square-rigged, sails furled, motionless,
their spars like burned matchsticks. (l. 13—16)

26 In the pink light
the small red sun goes rolling, rolling,
round and round and round at the same height
in perpetual sunset, (l. 25—28)

27 Apparently they have reached their destination.
It would be hard to say what brought them there,
commerce or contemplation. (l. 30—32)

EyDe; NoP; NYBP; OxBC

Little Exercise at 4 a.m.

28 Think of the storm roaming the sky uneasily
like a dog looking for a place to sleep in,
listen to it growling. (l. 1—3)

CoAP; MoAB; MoAmPo; NYBP; UnPo

The Man-Moth

29 The whole shadow of Man is only as big as his hat.
(l. 2)

CAPP; LiTA; LiTM; MAT; MoAB; MoAmPo; MoP;
NoAM; NOBA; PPP

The Monument

30 The strong sunlight, the wind from the sea,
all the conditions of its existence,
may have faked off the paint, if ever it was painted,
and made it homelier than it was. (l. 50—53)

HCAP; LiTA; NoAM; NOBA

One Art

31 The art of losing isn't hard to master;
so many things seem filled with the intent
to be lost that their loss is no disaster.

Lose something every day. (l. 1–4)

CAPP; DiPo; HAP; NAAL-2; NoAM; PoE; SM; SoSe

Over Two Thousand Illustrations and a Complete Concordance

32 Thus should have been our travels:
serious, engravable. (l. 1–2)

33 Always the silence, the gesture, the specks of birds
suspended on invisible threads above the Site,
(l. 17–18)

34 Open the book. (The gilt rubs off the edges
of the pages and pollinates the fingertips.) (l. 66–67)

35 — the dark ajar, the rocks breaking with light,
and undisturbed, unbreathing flame,
colorless, sparkless, freely fed on straw,
and, lulled within, a family with pets,
— and looked and looked our infant sight away.
(l. 70–74)

HCAP; LCAP; NAAL-2; NoAM

The Prodigal

36 Light-lashed, self-righteous, above moving snouts,
the pigs' eyes followed him, a cheerful stare,
even to the sow that always ate her young —

37 The pigs stuck out their little feet and snored. (l. 21)

38 his shuddering insights, beyond his control,
touching him. But it took him a long time
finally to make his mind up to go home. (l. 26–28)

CoAP; InvP; LCAP; LiTM; MoAB; NYBP; PPP; TwCP

Sandpiper

39 The roaring alongside he takes for granted,
and that every so often the world is bound to shake.
He runs, he runs to the south, finical, awkward,
in a state of controlled panic, a student of Blake.
(l. 1–4)

40 The beach hisses like fat. (l. 5)

41 His beak is focussed; he is preoccupied,

looking for something, something, something.
Poor bird, he is obsessed! (l. 16–18)

42 The millions of grains are black, white, tan, and gray,
and mixed with quartz grains, rose and amethyst.
(l. 19–20)

AiP; HeIP; NYBP; RB; TOF

Seascape

43 this cartoon by Raphael for a tapestry for a Pope:
(l. 12)

44 Heaven is not like flying or swimming,
but has something to do with blackness and a strong
glare (l. 20–21)

FaBoWP; MoAB; MOS; OxBC; PPP

September rain falls on the house

45 I know what I know, says the almanac. (l. 26)

46 With crayons the child draws a rigid house
and a winding pathway. Then the child
puts in a man with buttons like tears (l. 27–29)

47 Time to plant tears, says the almanac.
The grandmother sings to the marvellous stove
and the child draws another inscrutable house.
(l. 37–39)

InPK; LCAP; NoP; PoE; SM; WeW

WILLIAM BLAKE (1757–1827)

Auguries of Innocence

1 To see a World in a Grain of Sand
And a Heaven in a Wild Flower,
Hold Infinity in the palm of your hand
And Eternity in an hour. (l. 1–4)

2 A Robin Redbreast in a Cage
Puts all Heaven in a Rage. (l. 5–6)

3 A dog starv'd at his Master's Gate
Predicts the ruin of the State. (l. 9–10)

4 Each outcry of the hunted Hare
A fibre from the Brain does tear. (l. 13–14)

5 A truth that's told with bad intent
Beats all the Lies you can invent. (l. 53–54)

6 The Beggar's Rags, fluttering in Air,
Does to Rags the Heavens tear. (l. 75–76)

7 He who shall teach the Child to Doubt
The rotting Grave shall ne'er get out. (l. 87–88)

8 The Child's Toys and the Old Man's Reasons
Are the Fruits of the Two seasons. (l. 91–92)

9 The Questioner, who sits so sly,
Shall never know how to Reply. (l. 93–94)

10 The Emmet's Inch and Eagle's Mile
Make Lame Philosophy to smile. (l. 105–106)

11 We are led to Believe a Lie
When we see not Thro' the Eye (l. 125–126)

BLPL; EBEV; EnRP; FaBoCh; FaBV; FaFP; FaPoR; FM;
ImOP; InPK; LiTB; OAEL-1; OBNC; OxBoLi; PoEL-4;
RHPC; TrGrPo; WGRP

The Book of Thel

12 Does the Eagle know what is in the pit
Or wilt thou go ask the Mole?
Can wisdom be put in a silver rod,
Or love in a golden bowl?

13 "O life of this our Spring! why fades the lotus of the
water?
Why fade these children of the Spring,born but to smile
and fall?

14 Ah! gentle may I lay me down, and gentle rest my
head,
And gentle sleep the sleep of death, and gentle hear the
voice
Of Him that walketh in the garden in the evening
time!"

15 Every thing that lives
Lives not alone nor for itself.

16 She saw the couches of the dead, and where the fibrous
root
Of every heart on earth infixes deep its restless twists:

17 "Why cannot the ear be closed to its own destruction?
Or the glistening eye to the poison of a smile?

18 Why a tender curb upon the youthful burning boy?
Why a little curtain of flesh on the bed of our desire?"

ChER; ChTr; EnRP; NAEL-2; NoP; OAEL-2; OBNC;
PoE; PoEL-4; TEP

The Crystal Cabinet

19 The Maiden caught me in the Wild,
Where I was dancing merrily;
She put me into her Cabinet
And Lock'd me up with a golden Key. (l. 1–4)

CH; FaBoCh; OAEL-2; OBNC; PoEL-4

The Gates of Paradise

20 Truly, My Satan, thou art but a Dunce,
And dost not know the Garment from the Man.
Every Harlot was a Virgin once,
Nor can'st thou ever change Kate into Nan.

HAP; NcP; OAEL-2; OBNC; OxBSP; PoE; TrGrPo; WeW

GNOMIC VERSES (the following 2 poems)
Abstinence sows sand all over

21 Abstinence sows sand all over
The ruddy limbs and flaming hair,
But Desire Gratified
Plants fruits of life and beauty there.

EBEV; FaBoEE; FF; GBL; TrGrPo

The Angel that presided o'er my birth

22 The Angel that presided o'er my birth
Said, "Little creature, formed of Joy and Mirth,
Go love without the help of any thing on earth. (l. 1-3)

InPK; NAs; OxBSP; RB; TrGrPo

How sweet I roam'd from field to field

23 How sweet I roam'd from field to field
And tasted all the summer's pride,
Till I the Prince of Love beheld
Who in the sunny beams did glide! (l. 1–4)

24 With sweet May dews my wings were wet,
And Phoebus fir'd my vocal rage;
He caught me in his silken net,
And shut me in his golden cage.

He loves to sit and hear me sing,
Then, laughing, sports and plays with me;
Then stretches out my golden wing,
And mocks my loss of liberty. (l. 9–16)

ChER; ChTr; CH; EnLoPo; EnRP; FL; LiTB; NAEL-2;
NOBE; NOEC; NoP; OAEL-2; OBNC; PoEL-4; SeCePo;
TrGrPo

I Askèd a Thief

25 I askèd a thief to steal me a peach
He turned up his eyes
I ask'd a lithe lady to lie her down
Holy & meek she cries —

As soon as I went
An angel came.
He wink'd at the thief
And smild at the dame —

And without one word said
Had a peach from the tree
And still as a maid
Enjoy'd the lady. (l. 1–12)

LiTB; NAEL-2; NoP; OBNC; PoE

JERUSALEM (the following poem)

Fields from Islington to Marybone

26 The Divine Vision still was seen,
Still was the human form divine
Weeping in weak & mortal clay;
O Jesus, still the form was thine!

27 A man's worst enemies are those
Of his own house & family;
And he who makes his law a curse,
By his own law shall surely die.

ChTr; FaBoPV; OBNC; OBNV

King Edward the Third

28 Prepare your hearts for Death's cold hand! prepare
Your souls for flight, your bodies for the earth;
Prepare your arms for glorious victory;
Prepare your eyes to meet a holy God!
Prepare, prepare!

CH; OHIP; WaaP

The Mental Traveller

29 I traveld thro' a Land of Men
A Land of Men & Women too,
And heard & saw such dreadful things
As cold Earth wanderers never knew. (l. 1–4)

30 we Reap in joy the fruit
Which we in bitter tears did sow. (l. 7–8)

31 And if the Babe is born a Boy
He's given to a Woman Old,
Who nails him down upon a rock
Catches his shrieks in cups of gold. (l. 9–12)

32 And she grows young as he grows old. (l. 20)

33 For the Eye altering alters all;
The Senses roll themselves in fear
And the flat Earth becomes a Ball. (l. 62–64)

EnRP; NAEL-2; OAEL-2; OPOP; PoE; PoEL-4

Milton

34 And was Jerusalem builded here,
Among these dark Satanic Mills?

35 Bring me my Bow of burning gold:
Bring me my Arrows of desire:
Bring me my Spear: O clouds unfold!
Bring me my Chariot of fire!

I will not cease from Mental Fight,
Nor shall my Sword sleep in my hand,
Till we have built Jerusalem
In England's green & pleasant Land.

AWP; BoTP; EaLo; EnRP; FaBoCh; FaBoPV; FaBV;
FaPoR; HAP; HeIP; InPS; LiTB; MAT; NAEL-2;
NAWM-2; NOBE; NOCV; NoP; OAEL-2; OBEV; OBNC;
PoE; PoEL-4; PoRA; PrIm; RB; TrGrPo; WaaP; WGRP

36 The lark sitting upon his earthy bed, just as the morn
Appears, listens silent, then springing from the waving
   Corn-field, loud
He leads the Choir of Day —

37 His little throat labours with inspiration, every feather
On throat and breast and wings vibrates with the
   effluence Divine.

EnRP; NOBE; OBNC; PBBP; WiR

Mock On, Mock On, Voltaire, Rousseau

38 Mock on, mock on, Voltaire, Rousseau!
Mock on, mock on — 'Tis all in vain! (l. 1–2)

39 The atoms of Democritus
And Newton's particles of light
Are sands upon the Red Sea shore,
Where Israel's tents do shine so bright. (l. 9–12)

EnRP; HAP; LiTB; NAEL-2; NAWM-2; NoP; OAEL-2;
OBNC; OxBSP; PoE; PoEL-4; PPP; PrIm; UnPo

My silks and fine array

40 My silks and fine array,
My smiles and languish'd air,
By Love are driv'n away;
And mournful lean Despair

Brings me yew to deck my grave:
Such end true lovers have. (l. 1–6)

41 Bring me an axe and spade,
Bring me a winding-sheet;
When I my grave have made
Let winds and tempests beat:
Then down I'll lie as cold as clay.
True love doth pass away! (l. 13–18)

ChTr; ELP; EnRP; GBL; OBNC; TEP; TrGrPo; UnPo

Never Seek to Tell Thy Love

42 Never seek to tell thy love
Love that never told can be; (l. 1–2)

43 I told my love, I told my love,
I told her all my heart,
Trembling, cold, in ghastly fears —
Ah, she doth depart. (l. 5–8)

ChER; ELP; EnLoPo; EnRP; FaBV; InPS; NAEL-2;
NOBE; OAEL-2; OBNC; PoEL-4

POETICAL SKETCHES (the following poem)

Mad Song

44 Come higher, Sleep,
And my griefs enfold: (l. 3–4)

45 Like a fiend in a cloud
With howling woe,
After night I do crowd,
And with night will go; (l. 17–20)

46 For light doth seize my brain
With frantic pain. (l. 23–24)

EnRP; NAEL-2; NOEC; OAEL-2; PoE; PoE; PoEL-4;
PrIm; TEP; TrGrPo

SEVERAL QUESTIONS ANSWERED (the following poem)

Eternity

47 He who binds to himself a joy
Does the winged life destroy;
But he who kisses the joy as it flies
Lives in eternity's sun rise.

AWP; EBEV; FaBoEE; NOBE; NoP; OBNC; OxBSP; RB;
TrGrPo

The Question Answer'd

48 What is it men in women do require?
The lineaments of gratified desire.
What is it women do in men require?
The lineaments of gratified desire.

ErPo; FaBoEE; GBL; NoP; OAEL-2

Sir Joshua Reynolds

49 When Sir Joshua Reynolds died
All Nature was degraded; (l. 1–2)

FaBoCo; FaBoEE; FiBHP; OxBoLi; TW

Sleep, sleep, beauty bright

50 Sweet babe, in thy face
Soft desires I can trace,
Secret joys and secret smiles,
Little pretty infant wiles. (l. 5–8)

51 O the cunning wiles that creep
In thy little heart asleep!
When thy little heart doth wake,
Then the dreadful night shall break. (l. 13–16)

EnRP; FPL; OBEV; PoLF

Soft Snow

52 I walked abroad in a snowy day;
I asked the soft snow with me to play;
She played and she melted in all her prime,
And the winter called it a dreadful crime. (l. 1–4)

FF; SoSe; TEP; TEP

SONGS OF EXPERIENCE (the following 17 poems)

Ah Sun-flower!

53 Ah Sun-flower! weary of time,

54 Where the Youth pined away with desire,
And the pale Virgin shrouded in snow,
Arise from their graves and aspire,
Where my Sun-flower wishes to go.

AWP; ChTr; EBEV; ELP; EnRP; FaBoRV; HAP;
NAEL-2; NIP; NOEC; NoP; OAEL-2; OBNC; PoE; PoEL-
4; PPP; PrIm; RB; TEP; TOF; TrGrPo; UnPo; WeW

The Chimney Sweeper

55 A little black thing among the snow
Crying "'weep, 'weep," in notes of woe!
"Where are thy father & mother? say?"
"They are both gone up to the church to pray.

56 "And because I am happy, & dance & sing,
They think they have done me no injury,
And are gone to praise God & his Priest & King,
Who make up a heaven of our misery."

NAEL-2; NAWM-2; NOEC; OAEL-2; PPP; RB; SaC; TEP

The Clod and the Pebble

57   "Love seeketh not Itself to please,
Nor for itself hath any care,
But for another gives its ease,
And builds a Heaven in Hell's despair."

58   "Love seeketh only Self to please,
To bind another to Its delight,
Joys in another's loss of ease,
And builds a Hell in Heaven's despite."

EnLoPo; EnRP; FaBV; InPS; NAEL-2; NOBE; NoP;
OBNC; OxBSP; PoE; PrIm; RB; SCV; TEP; TrGrPo

A Divine Image

59   Cruelty nas a Human Heart,
And Jealousy a Human Face;

ChTr; NAEL-2; NoP; OBNC; RB; TEP

Earth's Answer

60   Can delight
Chained in night
The virgins of youth and morning bear?

61   Does the sower
Sow by night,
Or the ploughman in darkness plough?

62   'Break this heavy chain
That does freeze my bones around.
Selfish, vain,
Eternal bane!
That free love with bondage bound.'

EnRP; InPS; NAEL-2; NAWM-2; NOEC; OAEL-2; PoE

The Fly

63   If thought is life
And strength & breath,
And the want
Of thought is death;

Then am I
A happy fly,
If I live,
Or if I die.

FM; NAEL-2; NBLV; TrGrPo

The Garden of Love

64   I went to the Garden of Love,
And saw what I never had seen:
A Chapel was built in the midst,
Where I used to play on the green.

And the gates of this Chapel were shut,
And 'Thou shalt not' writ over the door;

65   And I saw it was filled with graves,
And tomb-stones where flowers should be;
And Priests in black gowns were walking their rounds,
And binding with briars my joys and desires.

AWP; EnLoPo; EnRP; FaBV; GBL; HAP; LiTB; MAT;
NAEL-2; NoP; PoE; RB; SoSe; TEP; TOF

Hear the voice of the Bard

66   Hear the voice of the Bard!
Who Present, Past and Future, sees;

67   'O Earth, O Earth, return!
'Arise from out the dewy grass;
'Night is worn,
'And the morn
'Rises from the slumberous mass.

ChTr; EBEV; ELP; EnRP; HAP; In^t-S; NAEL-2;
NAWM-2; NOBE; NOEC; NoP; NU; OAEL-2; OBEV;
PoE; PoEL-4; RB; TEP; WGRP

Holy Thursday

68   Is this a holy thing to see
In a rich and fruitful land,
Babes reduced to misery,
Fed with cold and usurous hand?

69   For where'er the sun does shine,
And where'er the rain does fall,
Babe can never hunger there,
Nor poverty the mind appall.

EnRP; FF; InPS; NAEL-2; NOEC; NoP; OAEL-2; TEP

The Human Abstract

70   Pity would be no more,
If we did not make somebody poor;
And mercy no more could be,
If all were as happy as we;

71   The gods of the earth and sea
Sought through nature to find this tree.
But their search was all in vain:
There grows one in the human brain.

EnRP; NAEL-2; NOEC; OAEL-2; PoE; PoEL-4; PPP

Infant Sorrow

72   My mother groaned, my father wept.
Into the dangerous world I leapt:
Helpless, naked, piping loud,
Like a fiend hid in a cloud.

73 Struggling in my father's hands,
Striving against my swaddling bands,
Bound and weary, I thought best
To sulk upon my mother's breast.

InPS; NAEL-2; NAs; OBNC; OxBSP; PoEL-4; RB

London

74 In every cry of every Man,
In every Infants cry of fear,
In every voice: in every ban,
The mind-forg'd manacles I hear

75 How the Chimney-sweepers cry
Every blackning Church appalls,
And the hapless Soldiers sigh
Runs in blood down Palace walls

76 But most thro' midnight streets I hear
How the youthful Harlots curse
Blasts the new-born Infants tear
And blights with plagues the Marriage hearse

AWP; ChER; ChTr; EnRP; FaBoPP; FaBoPV; FF; HAP;
HeIP; InPK; InPS; LiTB; MAT; Mes; NAEL-2; NAWM-2;
NIP; NOBE; NOEC; NoP; OAEL-2; OBNC; PoE; PoEL-4;
PrIm; RB; SCV; SeCePo; TEP; UnPo; WeW

Nurse's Song

77 When the voices of children are heard on the green
And laughing is heard on the hill,
My heart is at rest within my breast
And everything else is still.

EnRP; FF

A Poison Tree

78 I was angry with my friend:
I told my wrath, my wrath did end.
I was angry with my foe:
I told it not, my wrath did grow.

79 In the morning glad I see
My foe outstretch'd beneath the tree.

AWP; EnRP; FaFP; HAP; HoPM; LiTB; NAEL-2; NoP;
PoEL-4; PPP; RB; SCV; SoSe; TrGrPo; TW; WeW

The Sick Rose

80 O Rose, thou art sick.
The invisible worm
That flies in the night.
In the howling storm,

Has found out thy bed
Of crimson joy:
And his dark secret love
Does thy life destroy.

AWP; BoLoP; ChER; ChTr; ELP; EnLoPo; HAP; HeIP;
InPK; InPS; NAEL-2; NAWM-2; NIP; NOBE; NOEC;
NoP; OAEL-2; OBNC; OxBSP; PoE; PoEL-4; PPP; PrIm;
RB; SoSe; TrGrPo; WeW

The Tiger

81 Tiger, Tiger, burning bright
In the forests of the night,
What immortal hand or eye
Could frame thy fearful symmetry?

82 What the hammer?What the chain?
In what furnace was thy brain?
What the anvil?What dread grasp
Dare its deadly terrors clasp?

83 Did he smile his work to see?
Did he who made the Lamb make thee?

84 Tiger, Tiger, burning bright
In the forests of the night,
What immortal hand or eye
Dare frame thy fearful symmetry?

AWP; BoTP; CH; ChTr; EaLo; EnRP; FaBoBe; FaBoCh;
FaBoPV; FaBV; FaFP; FaPON; FaPoR; FF; FM; FPL;
GN; HAP; HeIP; HoPM; InPK; InPS; LiTB; Mes;
NAWM-2; NIP; NOBE; NOEC; NoP; OAEL-2; OBEV;
OBNC; FoE; PoEL-4; PoLF; PoRA; PPP; PrIm; RB; SCV;
SeCePo; SoSe; TEP; TTTS; UnPo; WGRP

To Tirzah

85 Whate'er is Born of Mortal Birth
Must be consumed with the Earth

EnRP; NAEL-2; NOBE; OAEL-2

SONGS OF INNOCENCE (the following 12 poems)

The Chimney Sweeper

86 When my mother died I was very young,
And my father sold me while yet my tongue,
Could scarcely cry weep weep weep weep.
So your chimneys I sweep & in soot I sleep.

87 And the Angel told Tom if he'd be a good boy,
He'd have God for his father & never want joy.

And so Tom awoke and we rose in the dark
And got with our bags & our brushes to work.
Tho' the morning was cold, Tom was happy & warm,
So if all do their duty, they need not fear harm.

CH; EnRP; FaBoPV; FF; HeIP; InPK; NAEL-2;
NAWM-2 NOEC; OAEL-2; OxBChV; PoE; PPP; SaC;
SoSe; TEP

The Divine Image

88 For Mercy has a human heart,
Pity, a human face;
And Love, the human form divine,
And Peace, the human dress.

89 And all must love the human form,
In heathen, Turk, or Jew.
Where Mercy, Love, and Pity dwell
There God is dwelling too.

BoTP; EnRP; NAEL-2; NOBE; NOEC; NoP; OAEL-2;
OBNC; PoE; PoEL-4; PPP; TEP; WGRP

The Echoing Green

90 "Such, such were the joys
When we all, girls and boys,
In our youth time were seen
On the Echoing Green."

BoTP; CH; NAEL-2; PoE; UnPo; WiR

Holy Thursday

91 The hum of multitudes was there, but multitudes of
lambs,
Thousands of little boys and girls raising their innocent
hands.

92 Beneath them sit the aged men, wise guardians of the
poor;
Then cherish pity, lest you drive an angel from your
door.

CH; EnRP; InPS; NAEL-2; NAWM-2; NOBE; NOEC;
NoP; OAEL-2; OFD; PoE; SCV; TEP; TrCP

Infant Joy

93 I have no name.
I am but two days old.
What shall I call thee?
I happy am,
Joy is my name.
Sweet joy befall thee!

FaPON; GoJo; NAEL-2; NAs; OxBSP; PoLF; TEP

The Lamb

94 Little Lamb, who made thee?
Dost thou know who made thee?

95 He is called by thy name,
For he calls himself a Lamb,
He is meek, and he is mild;

He became a little child.
I a child, and thou a lamb,
We are called by his name.

BLPL; BoTP; CH; EaLo; EnRP; FaBoBe; FaBoCh;
FaPON; GoJo; HeIP; InPS; LiTB; NAEL-2; NAWM-2;
NIP; NOEC; NoP; OAEL-2; OxBChV; PoE; SoSe; TEP;
TrCP; TrGrPo; UnPo; WGRP

Laughing Song

96 When the painted birds laugh in the shade,
When our table with cherries and nuts is spread:
Come live, and be merry, and join with me
To sing the sweet chorus of 'Ha, ha, he!'

BoTP; CH; EnRP; GoJo; NAEL-2; NBLV; OxBChV

The Little Black Boy

97 My mother bore me in the southern wild,
And I am black, but O! my soul is white;

98 "And we are put on earth a little space,
That we may learn to bear the beams of love,

99 When I from black and he from white cloud free,
And round the tent of Godlike lambs we joy,

I'll shade him from the heat till he can bear
To lean in joy upon our father's knee;
And then I'll stand and stroke his silver hair,
And be like him, and he will then love me.

AWP; CH; EnRP; HeIP; NAEL-2; NAWM-2; NOEC; NoP;
OAEL-2; OBEV; OBNC; OxBChV; PoE; PoEL-4; PoNe;
TrGrPo

Night

100 The sun descending in the west,
The evening star does shine;
The birds are silent in their nest,
And I must seek for mine.

101 Farewell green fields and happy groves,
Where flocks have took delight.

BLPL; BoNaP; BoTP; CH; EnRP; FaBoBe; FaPON;
OBEV; OxBChV; PoLF; WiR

On Another's Sorrow

102 Can I see a falling tear,
And not feel my sorrow's share?

103 Think not thou canst sigh a sigh
And thy maker is not by;
Think not thou canst weep a tear
And thy maker is not near.

AWP; EnRP; FaBV; PoEL-4

Piping Down the Valleys Wild

104 On a cloud I saw a child,
And he laughing said to me,

"Pipe a song about a Lamb";
So I piped with merry chear.
"Piper pipe that song again" —
So I piped, he wept to hear.

"Drop thy pipe thy happy pipe
Sing thy songs of happy chear";
So I sung the same again
While he wept with joy to hear.

AWP; EnRP; FaBoBe; FaBoCh; FaBV; GoJo; HeIP; InPS;
InvP; LiTB; NAEL-2; NAWM-2; NIP; NOBE; NOEC;
NoP; OAEL-2; OBEV; OBNC; OnUR; OxBChV; PDV;
PoE; PoEL-4; RHPC; SoSe; TEP; TrGrPo

Spring

105 Sound the Flute!
Now it's mute.
Birds delight
Day and Night;

106 Little Boy
Full of joy;
Little Girl,
Sweet and small;

107 Little Lamb,
Here I am;
Come and lick
My white neck;

BoTP; FaBoCh; FaPON; MoShBr; TTTS

To Spring

108 O thou, with dewy locks, who lookest down
Through the clear windows of the morning; turn
Thine angel eyes upon our western isle,
Which in full choir hails thy approach, O Spring!
                                                (l. 1–4)

BLPL; BoNaP; BoTP; EnRP; NAEL-2; NOEC; OAEL-2;
OBEV; PoEL-4; PoLF; PPP; WiR

To the Evening Star

109 Thou Fair-haired Angel of the Evening,
Now, whilst the sun rests on the mountains, light
Thy bright torch of love; thy radiant crown
Put on, and smile upon our evening bed! (l. 1–4)

110 Let thy West Wind sleep on
The lake; speak silence with thy glimmering eyes,
And wash the dusk with silver. (l. 8–10)

BoNaP; CH; ChER; ChTr; EnRP; FaBoRV; FaBV; FPL;
NAEL-2; NOEC; NoP; OAEL-2; PoLF; TEP; TrGrPo;
WiR

To the Muses

111 How have you left the ancient love
That bards of old enjoyed in you!
The languid strings do scarcely move!
The sound is forced, the notes are few! (l. 13–16)

ChER; ChTr; EnRP; HAP; HeIP; LiTB; NAEL-2; NOBE;
NOEC; NoP; OAEL-2; OBEV; TrGrPo

To William Hayley

112 Your friendship oft has made my heart to ache:
Do be my enemy for friendship's sake. (l. 1–2)

FaBoCo FaBoEE; FF; TrGrPo

When a Man Has Married a Wife

113 When a man has married a wife, he finds out whether
Her knees and elbows are only glued together. (l. 1–2)

ErPo; FaBoEE; FF; OAEL-2; OxBoLi

EDMUND BLUNDEN (1896–1974)

Forefathers

1 On the green they watched their sons
Playing till too dark to see,
As their fathers watched them once,
As my father once watched me; (l. 19–22)

2 Like the bee that now is blown,
Honey-heavy on my hand,
From his toppling tansy-throne
In the green tempestuous land — (l. 31–34)

3 I'm in clover now, nor know
Who made honey long ago. (l. 35–36)

NOBE; OBEV OBMV OxBTC

The Midnight Skaters

4 But not the tallest there, 'tis said,
Could fathom to this pond's black bed. (l. 5–6)

FaBoTw; GoJo; GTBS-P; MoBrPo; NOBE; OBD

Report on Experience

5 I have seen a green country, useful to the race,
   Knocked silly with guns and mines, its villages
     vanished, (l. 5–6)

FaBoTw; GTBS-P; NOBE; OBMV; OBWP

ROBERT BLY (b. 1926)

Driving to Town Late to Mail a Letter

1 There is a privacy I love in this snowy night.
   Driving around, I will waste more time. (l. 4–5)

BoNaP; CAPP; HeIP; InPK; NaP; VGW

My Father's Wedding

2 Some men live with an invisible limp,
   stagger, or drag
   a leg. Their sons are often angry. (l. 7–9)

3 If a man, cautious,
   hides his limp,
   Somebody has to limp it! Things
   do it; the surroundings limp.
   House walls get scars,
   the car breaks down; matter, in drudgery, takes it up.
               (l. 25–30)

4 sympathy

   he longed for, didn't need, and wouldn't accept.
              (l. 48–49)

CAPP; DiL; InPS; NoAM

Waking from Sleep

5 Now we sing, and do tiny dances on the kitchen floor.
   Our whole body is like a harbor at dawn;
   We know that our master has left us for the day.
             (l. 10–12)

CAPP; EAS; NOBA; NoP

LOUISE BOGAN (1897–1970)

Cassandra

1 Song, like a wing, tears through my breast, my side,
   And madness chooses out my voice again,
   Again. (l. 4–6)

HAP; MoAmPo; PBWP; VGW

The Dream

2 O God, in the dream the terrible horse began
   To paw at the air, and make for me with his blows.
             (l. 1–2)

3 The terrible beast, that no one may understand,
   Came to my side, and put down his head in love.
             (l. 15–16)

InPK; LiTA; LiTM; MAT; MoAB; MoAmPo; NoAM

Evening in the Sanitarium

4 The women rest their tired half-healed hearts; they are
   almost well. (l. 6)

5 O fortunate bride, who never again will become elated
   after childbirth!
   O lucky older wife, who has been cured of feeling
     unwanted! (l. 11–12)

6 You will be again as normal and selfish and heartless
   as anybody else. (l. 15)

7 The cats will be glad; the fathers feel justified; the
   mothers relieved.
   The sons and husbands will no longer need to pay the
     bills.
   Childhoods will be put away, the obscene nightmare
     abated. (l. 21–23)

FaBoWP; FYAP; IHMS; TwCP

Medusa

8 the bare eyes were before me
   And the hissing hair,
   Held up at a window, seen through a door.
   The stiff bald eyes, the serpents on the forehead
   Formed in the air. (l. 5–9)

AWP; BoWoP; HoPM; MoAB; MoAmPo; NoAM; NoP;
WPE

Simple Autumnal

9 The measured blood beats out the year's delay. (l. 1)

MoAB; MoAmPo; QFR; Son

Song for the Last Act

10 yet another summer loath to go
   Although the scythes hang in the apple trees. (l. 7–8)

11 Now that I have your face by heart, I look. (l. 9)

12 the anchor weeps
Its red rust downward, (l. 24–25)

13 Now that I have your heart by heart, I see. (l. 27)

NoP; NYBP; UnPo; WPE

Women

14 Women have no wilderness in them,
They are provident instead,
Content in the tight hot cell of their hearts
To eat dusty bread. (l. 1–4)

15 Their love is an eager meaninglessness
Too tense, or too lax. (l. 15–16)

16 They hear in every whisper that speaks to them
A shout and a cry.
As like as not, when they take life over their door-sills
They should let it go by. (l. 17–20)

LiTA; MoAB; MoAmPo; NoAM; TwCP; VGW; WPE

GEORGE BOLEYN (d. 1536) *AND* ANNE BOLEYN (1507–1536)

O Death, Rock Me Asleep (*attributed to* George Boleyn *and to* Anne Boleyn)

1 O Death, rock me asleep,
Bring me to quiet rest,
Let pass my weary guiltless ghost
Out of my careful breast. (l. 1–4)

2 Toll on, thou passing bell;
Ring out my doleful knell; (l. 23–24)

ChTr; ElL; FaBoRV; FF; OBSC; TrGrPo; WPE

EDMUND BOLTON (1575?–1633?)

A Palinode

1 So melts, so vanisheth, so fades, so withers
The rose, the shine, the bubble, and the snow
Of praise, pomp, glory, joy (which short life gathers),
Fair praise, vain pomp, sweet glory, brittle joy.
(l. 5–8)

ElL; InvP; OBSC; PoEL-2; PrIm

THOMAS BONHAM (d. 1629?)

In Praise of Ale (*attributed to* Bonham)

1 Whenas the Chill Sirocco blowes,
And Winter tells a heavy tale;
When Pyes and Dawes and Rookes and Crows,
Sit cursing of the frosts and snowes;
Then give me Ale. (l. 1–5)

FaBoCh; OBEV; OBS

ARNA BONTEMPS (1902–1973)

A Black Man Talks of Reaping

1 Yet what I sowed and what the orchard yields
My brother's sons are gathering stalk and root,
Small wonder then my children glean in fields
They have not sown, and feed on bitter fruit. (l. 9–12)

AmNP; BANP; BPo; CDC; FB; IDB; PoBA; PoNe

Close Your Eyes!

2 Go through the gates with closed eyes.
Stand erect and let your black face front the west.
(l. 1–2)

AmNP; CDC; FB; PoBA; PoNe

The Day-Breakers

3 Yet would we die as some have done:
Beating a way for the rising sun. (l. 5–6)

AmNP; CDC; IDB; PoBA; PoNe

God Give to Men

4 Give blue-eyed men their swivel chairs
To whirl in tall buildings.
Allow them many ships at sea,
And on land, soldiers
And policemen. (l. 6–10)

5 God suffer little men
The taste of soul's desire. (l. 16–17)

BANP; BPo; CDC; PoNe

Nocturne at Bethesda

6 why
Do our black faces search the empty sky?

Is there something we have forgotten? some precious
    thing
We have lost, wandering in strange lands? (l. 12–16)

7 There will be better days when I am gone
And healing pools where I cannot be healed.
Fragrant stars will gleam forever and ever
Above the place where I lie desolate. (l. 30–33)

8 There is something I have forgotten, some precious
    thing.
I shall be seeking ornaments of ivory,
I shall be dying for a jungle fruit.

You do not hear, Bethesda.
O still green water in a stagnant pool! (l. 45–50)

AmNP; BANP; CDC; PoNe

Southern Mansion

9 There is a sound of music echoing
Through the open door
And in the field there is
Another sound tinkling in the cotton:
Chains of bondmen dragging on the ground. (l. 6–10)

AiP; AmFN; AmNP; BANP; CNA; FB; FF; IDB; LiTM;
PoBA; PoNe; TTY; WSC

JOHN COLLINS BOSSIDY (1860–1928)

Boston

1 I come from the city of Boston,
The home of the bean and the cod, (l. 1–2)

FaBoCo; FaBoEE; NBLV; OBAL; OxBoLi

FRANCIS WILLIAM BOURDILLON
(1852–1921)

The Night Has a Thousand Eyes

1 The night has a thousand eyes,
And the day but one;
Yet the light of the bright world dies
With the dying sun. (l. 1–4)

2 the light of a whole life dies
When love is gone. (l. 7–8)

BLPA; BLPL; BoLoP; FaBoBe; FaFP; OBEV; OHFP;
OxBSP; WBLP

CHARLES SYNGE CHRISTOPHER
BOWEN, BARON BOWEN (1835–1896)

The Rain It Raineth

1 The rain it raineth on the just
And also on the unjust fella;
But chiefly on the just, because
The unjust steals the just's umbrella. (l. 1–4)

CenHV; FiBHP; NBLV; NTCP

EDGAR BOWERS (b. 1924)

The Stoic: for Laura von Courten

1 Sometimes outside beneath a bombers' moon
You stood alone to watch the searchlights trace

Their careful webs against the boding sky, (l. 3–5)

2 Eternal Venice sinking by degrees
Into the very water that she lights; (l. 19–20)

CoAP; MT; NePoEA; QFR

MARK ALEXANDER BOYD (1563–1601)

Fra Bank to Bank, Fra Wood to Wood I Rin

1 Unhappy is the man for evermair
That tills the sand and sawis in the air;
But twice unhappier is he, I lairn,
That feidis in his hairt a mad desire
And follows on a woman thro the fire,
Led by a blind and teachit by a bairn. (l. 9–14)

EBEV; GoTS; HAP; InPK; NoP; OBEV; Prf; QFR; Son

ANNE BRADSTREET (c. 1612–1672)

As Weary Pilgrim, Now at Rest

1 A pilgrim I on earth perplext,
with sinns, with cares and sorrows vext,
By age and paines brought to decay,
and my Clay house mouldring away,
Oh how I long to be at rest
and soare on high among the blest! (l. 19–24)

AnAmPo; LiTA; NAAL-1; PoEL-3; SCAP

Before the Birth of One of Her Children

2 That when that knot's untied that made us one,
I may seem thine, who in effect am none.
And if I see not half my dayes that's due,
What nature would, God grant to yours and you;
(l. 11–14)

3 These o protect from step Dames injury.
And if chance to thine eyes shall bring this verse,
With some sad sighs honour my absent Herse;
And kiss this paper for thy loves dear sake,
Who with salt tears this last Farewel did take.
(l. 24–28)

BoWoP; MAT; NAAL-1; NAs; NOBA; WPE; WPOW

Contemplations

4 When I behold the heavens as in their prime,
And then the earth (though old) still clad in green,
The stones and trees, insensible of time,
Nor age nor wrinkle on their front are seen;
(l. 120–124)

5 But man grows old, lies down, remains where once he's
laid. (l. 126)

6 Nor youth, nor strength, nor wisdom spring again.
Nor habitations long their names retain,
But in oblivion to the final day remain. (l. 131–133)

7 O Time the fatal wrack of mortal things,
That draws oblivion's curtains over kings;
(l. 225–226)

8 But he whose name is graved in the white stone
Shall last and shine when all of these are gone.
(l. 231–232)

AmPP; PoEL-3; SCAP; WPE

The Flesh and the Spirit

9 Sisters we are, yea, twins we be,
Yet deadly feud 'twixt thee and me;
For from one father are we not,
Thou by old Adam wast begot,
But my arise is from above, (l. 43–47)

AmPP; AnAmPo; LiTA; NAAL-1; NOBA; OxBA; SCAP;
TAP

In Memory of My Dear Grandchild Elizabeth Bradstreet Who Deceased August, 1665, Being a Year and a Half Old

10 And time brings down what is both strong and tall.
But plants new set to be eradicate,
And buds new blown, to have so short a date,
Is by his hand alone that guides nature and fate.
(l. 11–14)

NAAL-1; NOCV; SCAP; WPE

A Letter to Her Husband, Absent upon Public Employment

11 The welcome house of him my dearest guest.
Where ever, ever stay, and go not thence,
Till natures sad decree shall call thee hence;
Flesh of thy flesh, bone of thy bone,
I here, thou there, yet both but one. (l. 22–26)

HAP; HeIP; NAAL-1; NoP; SCAP

Some Verses upon the Burning of Our House, July 10, 1666

12 Thou hast an house on high erect,
Framed by that mighty Architect,
With glory richly furnished,
Stands permanent though this be fled. (l. 43–46)

AiP; AnAmPo; BoWoP; NAAL-1; NOBA; NoP; OxBA;
SCAP; TAP; WPE

To My Dear and Loving Husband

13 If ever two were one, then surely we.
If ever man were lov'd by wife, then thee; (l. 1–2)

14 Thy love is such I can no way repay,
The heavens reward thee manifold I pray.
Then while we live, in love lets so persever,
That when we live no more, we may live ever.
(l. 9–12)

AmPP; AnAmPo; BLPL; BoWoP; FF; HAP; HeIP; NAAL-
1; NIP; NOBA; NOCV; OPOP; OxBA; OxBSP; PoE;
PoEL-3; PoLF; PrIm; SCAP; TAP; WeW; WPE

To sing of wars, of captains, and of kings

15 A Bartas can do what a Bartas will
But simple I according to my skill. (l. 11–12)

16 I am obnoxious to each carping tongue
Who says my hand a needle better fits, (l. 25–26)

17 For such despite they cast on female wits:
If what I do prove well, it won't advance,
They'll say it's stol'n, or else it was by chance.
(l. 28–30)

BoWoP; NAAL-1; NOBA; OxBA; PoE; SCAP; TAP; WPE

NICHOLAS BRETON (1542–1626)

Come, little babe, come, silly soul

1 Come little babe, come silly soul,
Thy fathers shame, thy mother's grief, (l. 1–2)

2 dost thou smile? O, thy sweet face!
Would God Himself He might thee see! —
No doubt thou wouldst soon purchase grace,
I know right well, for thee and me: (l. 19–22)

3 Come, little boy, and rock asleep;
Sing lullaby and be thou still;
I, that can do naught else but weep,
Will sit by thee and wail my fill:
God bless my babe, and lullaby
From this thy father's quality. (l. 43–48)

ElL; NOBE; OBEV; OBSC

The Passionate Shepherd

4 Who can live in heart so glad
As the merry country lad?

5 While he hears in every spring
How the birds do chirp and sing:
Or before the hounds in cry
See the hare go stealing by:
Or along the shallow brook,
Angling with a baited hook,
See the fishes leap and play
In a blessed sunny day:

CH; ElL; ELP; OBSC

A Report Song

6 Shall we go dance the hay, the hay?
Never pipe could ever play
Better shepherd's roundelay. (l. 1–3)

7 Shall we go learn to kiss, to kiss?
Never heart could ever miss
Comfort, where true meaning is. (l. 10–12)

GBL; NOBE; OBSC; SeCePo; TrGrPo

NICHOLAS BRETON *AND OTHERS*

The Honourable Entertainment Given to the Queen's Majesty in Progress at Elvetham, 1591

1 In the merry month of May,

2 Much ado there was, God wot,
He would love and she would not.
She said, never man was true;
He said, none was false to you.

ElL; NOBE; OBEV; OBSC; SeCePo; TrGrPo; TTTS

"MADELINE BRIDGES" (*pseudonym of* MARY AINGE DE VERE) (*fl.* c. 1840)

Life's Mirror

1 There are loyal hearts, there are spirits brave,
There are souls that are pure and true;
Then give to the world the best you have,
And the best will come back to you. (l. 1–4)

2 Have faith, and a score of hearts will show
Their faith in your word and deed. (l. 7–8)

3 Give truth, and your gift will be paid in kind,
And honor will honor meet; (l. 9–10)

4 Give sorrow and pity to those who mourn; (l. 13)

5 For life is the mirror of king and slave — (l. 17)

BLPA; FaBoBe; PWR; WBLP

ROBERT BRIDGES (1844–1930)

Awake, My Heart, to Be Loved

1 Awake, my heart, to be loved, awake, awake!
The darkness silvers away, the morn doth break,
It leaps in the sky: (l. 1–3)

2 Awake! the land is scattered with light, and see,
Uncanopied sleep is flying from field and tree:
(l. 13–14)

GTBS-P; MoAB; MoBrPo; NOBE; OBEV

Eros

3 Why hast thou nothing in thy face?
Thou idol of the human race,
Thou tyrant of the human heart,
The flower of lovely youth that art; (l. 1–4)

4 Surely thy body is thy mind,
For in thy face is nought to find,
Only thy soft unchristened smile,
That shadows neither love nor guile, (l. 13–16)

CMoP; LiTB; NOBE; PoEL-5; QFR

I Love All Beauteous Things

5 I love all beauteous things,
I seek and adore them; (l. 1–2)

6 to-morrow it seem
Like the empty words of a dream
Remembered on waking. (l. 8–10)

BoTP; BrPo; CMoP; EBEV; TrCP

I Will Not Let Thee Go

7 I will not let thee go.
I hold thee by too many bands:
Thou sayest farewell, and lo!
I have thee by the hands,
And will not let thee go. (l. 31–35)

BeLS; BLPL; CMoP; EnLoPo; FaBoBe; OBNC

London Snow

8 When men were all asleep the snow came flying,
In large white flakes falling on the city brown,
Stealthily and perpetually settling and loosely lying,
Hushing the latest traffic of the drowsy town. (l. 1–4)

9 They gathered up the crystal manna to freeze
Their tongues with tasting, their hands with
snowballing;
Or rioted in a drift, plunging up to the knees.
(l. 20–22)

BoNaP; BrPo; CH; ChTr; CMoP; EBEV; EBVV; FaBoPP;
GTBS-P; LiTB; LiTM; MoAB; MoBrPo; MoP; NoAM;
NOBE; NOBVV; OAEL-2; OBNC; OxBTC; PoEL-5;
SeCePo; TrGrPo; WiR

Low Barometer

10 On such a night, when Air has loosed
Its guardian grasp on blood and brain,
Old terrors then of god or ghost
Creep from their caves to life again; (l. 5–8)

11 And Reason kens he herits in
A haunted house. Tenants unknown
Assert their squalid lease of sin
With earlier title than his own. (l. 9–12)

CMoP; LiTB; MoP; NoAM; NOCV; OBNC; QFR

My Delight and Thy Delight

12 My delight and thy delight
Walking, like two angels white, (l. 1–2)

13 My desire and thy desire
Twining to a tongue of fire, (l. 4–5)

CMoP; NOBE; OBEV; PoEL-5

Nightingales

14 As night is withdrawn
From these sweet-springing meads and bursting boughs
of May,
Dream, while the innumerable choir of day
Welcome the dawn. (l. 15–18)

BrPo; CMoP; LiTB; LiTM; MoAB; MoBrPo; NOBE;
OAEL-2; OBEV; OBMV; OBNC; PBBP; TrGrPo; UnPo

Noel Christmas Eve 1913

15 The constellated sounds
ran sprinkling on earth's floor
As the dark vault above
with stars was spangled o'er. (l. 9–12)

16 Angels' song, comforting
as the comfort of Christ
When he spake tenderly
to his sorrowful flock: (l. 35–38)

LiTB; NOCV; OBCP; PoEL-5

On a Dead Child

17 Perfect little body, without fault or stain on thee,
With promise of strength and manhood full and fair!
(l. 1–2)

BrPo; CMoP; EBEV; LiTB; LiTM; NoAM; NOBE;
NOBVV; OBMV; OBNC

The storm is over, the land hushes to rest

18 The storm is over, the land hushes to rest:
The tyrannous wind, its strength fordone,
Is fallen back in the west (l. 1–3)

19 the broad cloud-driving moon in the clear sky
Lifts o'er the firs her shining shield,
And in her tranquil light
Sleep falls on forest and field.
See! sleep hath fallen: the trees are asleep:
The night is come. The land is wrapt in sleep.
(l. 38–43)

BrPo; GTBS-P; LiTB; LiTM; OBMV

MARY DOW BRINE (1816–1913)

Somebody's Mother

1 The woman was old and ragged and gray
And bent with the chill of the Winter's day. (l. 1–2)

2 At last came one of the merry troop,
The gayest laddie of all the group;

He paused beside her and whispered low,
"I'll help you cross, if you wish to go." (l. 19–22)

3 "She's somebody's mother, boys, you know,
For all she's aged and poor and slow,

"And I hope some fellow will lend a hand
To help my mother, you understand,

"If ever she's poor and old and gray,
When her own dear boy is far away." (l. 29–34)

BeLS; BLPA; FaFP; WBLP

ANTHONY BRODE (b. 1923)

Breakfast with Gerard Manley Hopkins

1 Sprung rhythm sprang, and I found (the mind fact-
mining at last)
An influence Father-Hopkins-fathered on the copy-
writing racket. (l. 3–4)

2 Parenthesis-proud, bracket-bold, happiest with hyphens,
The writers stagger intoxicated by terms, adjective-
unsteadied— (l. 5–6)

3 All things, crisp, crunchy, malted, tangy, sugared and
shredded. (l. 8)

BXAP; FaBoPa; FiBHP; NOBL; Par

EMILY BRONTË ("ELLIS BELL")
(1818–1848)

Fall, Leaves, Fall

1 I shall smile when wreaths of snow
Blossom where the rose should grow;
I shall sing when night's decay
Ushers in a drearier day. (l. 5–8)

CH; ELP; FaBoCh; FaBoRV; FaBV; OxBSP; PoEL-5;
TrGrPo

Night Is Darkening round Me

2 The night is darkening round me,
The wild winds coldly blow;
But a tyrant spell has bound me
And I cannot, cannot go. (l. 1–4)

NOBE; NOBVV; OBNC; PoEL-5

The Night Wind

3 I sat in silent musing —
The soft wind waved my hair;
It told me heaven was glorious
And sleeping earth was fair. (l. 5–8)

4 And when thy heart is laid to rest
Beneath the church-yard stone
I shall have time enough to mourn
And thou to be alone." (l. 33–36)

ChER; ChTr; EBVV; NAEL-2; TEP

Often rebuked, yet always back returning
(*attributed to* Brontë)

5 I'll walk, but not in old heroic traces,
And not in paths of high morality,
And not among the half-distinguished faces,
The clouded forms of long-past history. (l. 9–12)

6 I'll walk where my own nature would be leading:
It vexes me to choose another guide:
Where the grey flocks in ferny glens are feeding;
Where the wild wind blows on the mountain-side.
(l. 13–16)

ChER; LiTB; NOBVV; OAEL-2; OBEV; OBNC; PBWP

The Old Stoic

7 And if I pray, the only prayer
That moves my lips for me
Is — 'Leave the heart that now I bear,
And give me liberty.' (l. 5–8)

8 Yes, as my swift days near their goal,
'Tis all that I implore —
Through life and death, a chainless soul,
With courage to endure! (l. 9–12)

FaPoR; FPL; NOBE; OBEV; OBNC; PoLF; TrGrPo

The Prisoner

9 Still let my tyrants know, I am not doomed to wear
Year after year in gloom, and desolate despair;
A messenger of Hopecomes every night to me,
And offers for short life, eternal liberty. (l. 1–4)

10 "But, first a hush of peace — a soundless calm descends;
The struggle of distress, and fierce impatience ends;
Mute music soothes my breast — unuttered harmony,
That I could never dream, till Earth was lost to me.
(l. 13–16)

ChER; NOBE; NoP; OBEV; OBNC

Remembrance

11 Sweet Love of youth, forgive, if I forget thee,
   While the world's tide is bearing me along;
   Sterner desires and darker hopes beset me,
   Hopes which obscure, but cannot do thee wrong.
   (l. 13–16)

12 No other sun has lightened up my heaven,
   No other star has ever shone for me;
   All my life's bliss from thy dear life was given,
   All my life's bliss is in the grave with thee. (l. 17–20)

13 And, even yet, I dare not let it languish,
   Dare not indulge in memory's rapturous pain;
   Once drinking deep of that divinest anguish,
   How could I seek the empty world again? (l. 29–32)

   BLPL; BoLoP; BoWoP; BrRo; CH; EBEV; EBVV;
   EnLoPo; FaFP; HAP; LiTB; NAEL-2; NOBE; NOBVV;
   NoP; OBNC; OPOP; PBWP; PoE; PoEL-5; TEP; TrGrPo;
   WeW; WPE

The Visionary

14 Silent is the house: all are laid asleep:
   One alone looks out o'er the snow-wreaths deep,
   Watching every cloud, dreading every breeze
   That whirls the 'wildering drift, and bends the groaning
   trees. (l. 1–5)

   BLPL; BrRo; CH; ELP; LiTB; NOBE; NOBVV; OBNC;
   PBWP; SCV

RUPERT BROOKE (1887–1915)

Clouds

1 Down the blue night the unending columns press
  In noiseless tumult, break and wave and flow, (l. 1–2)

  BrPo; OBEV; OBMV; OxBTC

The Great Lover

2 The pain, the calm, and the astonishment,
  Desire illimitable, and still content,
  And all dear names men use, to cheat despair, (l. 3–5)

3 White plates and cups, clean-gleaming,
  Ringed with blue lines; and feathery, faery dust;
  (l. 27–28)

4 Then, the cool kindliness of sheets, that soon
  Smooth away trouble; and the rough male kiss
  Of blankets; grainy wood; live hair that is

Shining and free; blue-massing clouds; the keen
Unpassioned beauty of a great machine; (l. 35–39)

5 The comfortable smell of friendly fingers,
  Hair's fragrance, and the musty reek that lingers
  About dead leaves and last year's ferns. . . . (l. 42–44)

6 Sleep; and high places; footprints in the dew; (l. 55)

7 But the best I've known
  Stays here, and changes, breaks, grows old, is blown
  About the winds of the world, and fades from brains
  Of living men, and dies. (l. 68–71)

8 Nothing remains.
  O dear my loves, O faithless, once again
  This one last gift I give: that after men
  Shall know, and later lovers, far-removed
  Praise you, "All these were lovely"; say, "He loved."
  (l. 72–76)

  BrPo; FaFP; FPL; HoPM; LiTB; LiTM; MoBrPo; PoRA;
  TrGrPo; WaP

Heaven

9 Fish (fly-replete, in depth of June,
  Dawdling away their wat'ry noon) (l. 1–2)

10 Mud unto mud! — Death eddies near —
   Not here the appointed End, not here!
   But somewhere, beyond Space and Time,
   Is wetter water, slimier slime! (l. 15–18)

   BrPo; EBEV; HoPM; LiTB; LiTM; MoBrPo; NOBE;
   PoRA; WGRP

1914

11 He leaves a white
   Unbroken glory, a gathered radiance,
   A width, a shining peace, under the night.

   BrPo; CH; LiTB; MMA; PoA

12 But only agony, and that has ending;
   And the worst friend and enemy is but Death.

   MMA; OBWP; PoA; WGRP

13 If I should die, think only this of me:
   That there's some corner of a foreign field
   That is for ever England.

14 dreams happy as her day;
   And laughter, learnt of friends; and gentleness,
   In hearts at peace, under an English heaven.

   BrPo; FaBV; FaFP; FaPoR; FF; FPL; HeIP; LiTB; LiTM;
   MoBrPo; NAEL-2; NIP; NOBE; NoP; OBEV; OBWP;
   OxBTC; PoA; PoLF; PoRA; Son; TEP; TrGrPo; WaP

The Old Vicarage, Grantchester

15 Just now the lilac is in bloom,
All before my little room;

16 Here tulips bloom as they are told;
Unkempt about those hedges blows
An English unofficial rose;

17 εἴθε γενοίμηο . . . would I were
In Grantchester, in Grantchester! —

18 For Cambridge people rarely smile,
Being urban, squat, and packed with guile;

19 The women there do all they ought;
The men observe the Rules of Thought;
They love the Good; they worship Truth;
They laugh uproariously in youth;
(And when they get to feeling old,
They up and shoot themselves, I'm told). . .

20 Say, is there Beauty yet to find?
And Certainty? And Quiet kind?
Deep meadows yet, for to forget
The lies, and truths, and pain? . . . oh!
Stands the Church clock at ten to three?
And is there honey still for tea?

BrPo; FaBoPP; FaBV; MoBrPo; OBTV; OxBTC; PoRA

GWENDOLYN BROOKS (b. 1917)

The Bean Eaters

1 As they lean over the beans in their rented back room
that
is full of beads and receipts and dolls and cloths,
tobacco crumbs, vases and fringes. (l. 11–13)

AIW; BlSi; GrPl; HAP; HeIP; MAT; NoP; PoBA; PoE;
PrIm; TAP; TTY; WeW

Boy Breaking Glass

2 "I shall create! If not a note, a hole.
If not an overture, a desecration." (l. 7–8)

3 Each to his grief, each to
his loneliness and fidgety revenge. (l. 13–14)

4 The music is in minors. (l. 17)

5 Who has not Congress, lobster, love, luau,
the Regency Room, the Statue of Liberty,
runs. (l. 22–24)

AiP; MoP; NAAL-2; NoAM; NoP

The Lovers of the Poor

6 The pink paint on the innocence of fear;
Walk in a gingerly manner up the hall. (l. 5–6)

7 The worthy poor. The very very worthy
And beautiful poor. Perhaps just not too swarthy?
Perhaps just not too dirty nor too dim
Nor — passionate. (l. 22–25)

8 The stench; the urine, cabbage, and dead beans,
Dead porridges of assorted dusty grains,
The old smoke, heavy diapers, and, they're told,
Something called chitterlings. (l. 32–35)

9 They own Spode, Lowestoft, candelabra,
Mantels, and hostess gowns, and sunburst clocks,
Turtle soup, Chippendale, red stain "hangings,"
Aubussons and Hattie Carnegie. (l. 67–70)

10 Oh Squalor! This sick four-story hulk, this fibre
With fissures everywhere! (l. 75–76)

CAPP; MoP; NAAL-2; NoAM; NOBA

Malcolm X

11 And in a soft and fundamental hour
a sorcery devout and vertical
beguiled the world. (l. 8–10)

CNA; OFD; PoBA; TTY

Sadie and Maud

12 Maud went to college.
Sadie stayed at home.
Sadie scraped life
With a fine-tooth comb. (l. 1–4)

13 Sadie was one of the livingest chits
In all the land. (l. 7–8)

InPK; MoP; NoAM; NOBA; TAP

The Sermon on the Warpland

14 Prepare to meet
(sisters, brothers) the brash and terrible weather;
the pains;
the bruising; the collapse of bestials, idols. (l. 8–11)

15 Build with lithe love. With love like lion-eyes.
With love like morningrise.
With love like black, our black —
luminously indiscreet;
complete; continuous." (l. 17–21)

BPo; LiTM; NOBA; PoBA

A Street in Bronzeville

16 But could a dream send up through onion fumes
Its white and violet, fight with fried potatoes
And yesterday's garbage ripening in the hall,
Flutter, or sing an aria down these rooms

Even if we were willing to let it in,

BlSi; BPo; CAPP; FaBoWP; FF; NAAL-2; NMM; NoP;
PoE; PoNe; UnPo

17 Abortions will not let you forget.
You remember the children you got that you did not
get,

18 I have eased
My dim dears at the breasts they could never suck.

BlSi; BPo; CAPP; FaBoWP; NMM

19 I've stayed in the front yard all my life.
I want a peek at the back
Where it's rough and untended and hungry weed grows.
A girl gets sick of a rose.

BlSi; BPo; CAPP; FaBoWP; IDB; NAAL-2; NMM; NoAM;
NOBA; PoBA

We Real Cool

20 We

Sing sin. We
Thin gin. We

Jazz June. We
Die soon. (l. 4−8)

CAPP; FF; HAP; HeIP; HoPM; IDB; InPK; NoP; PoA;
PoBA; PoE; PrIm; SM; SoSe; TAP; TTY; WeW

The Womanhood

21 Even now she does the snake-hips with a hiss,
Slops the bad wine across her shantung, talks
Of pregnancy,guitars and bridgework,walks
In parks or alleys, comes haply on the verge
Of happiness, haply hysterics. Is.

BPo; HAP; WeW; WPE

PHILLIPS BROOKS (1835−1893)

Christmas Everywhere

1 Everywhere, everywhere, Christmas tonight ! (l. 1)

2 For the Christ-child who comes is the Master of all;
No palace too great, no cottage too small. (l. 11−12)

BLRP; FaFP; OHFP; OHIP; PWR; WBLP

O Little Town of Bethlehem

3 O little town of Bethlehem,
How still we see thee lie!
Above thy deep and dreamless sleep
The silent stars go by;
Yet in thy dark streets shineth
The Everlasting Light;
The hopes and fears of all the years
Are met in thee tonight. (l. 1−8)

4 For Christ is born of Mary; (l. 9)

5 And praises sing to God the King,
And peace to men on earth. (l. 15−16)

6 No ear may hear His coming,
But in this world of sin,
Where meek souls will receive him still,
The dear Christ enters in. (l. 21−24)

7 O holy Child of Bethlehem!
Descend to us, we pray; (l. 25−26)

8 O come to us, abide with us,
Our Lord, Immanuel. (l. 31−32)

AA; AH; AnAmPo; BLRP; FaFP; FaPON; GN; OHIP;
WBLP; WGRP

SHIRLEY BROOKS (1816−1874)

More Luck to Honest Poverty

1 More luck to honest poverty,
It claims respect, and a' that;
But honest wealth's a better thing.
We dare be rich for a' that. (l. 1−4)

BXAP; FaBoCo; NOBL; Par

ANNA GORDON BROWN (1747−1810)

The Gay Goshawk (*attributed to* Brown)

1 Lay down, lay down the bigly bier,
Lat me the dead look on;
Wi' cherry cheeks and ruby lips
She lay an' smil'd on him.

O ae sheave o' your bread, true-love,
An' ae glass o' your wine,
For I hae fasted for your sake
These fully day[is] nine. (l. 101–108)

ESPB; GN; OxBB; WPE

BEATRICE CURTIS BROWN (1901–1974)

Jonathan Bing

1 Poor old Jonathan Bing
Went home and addressed a short note to the King:
If you please will excuse me
I won't come to tea;
For home's the best place for
All people like me! (l. 15–20)

FaPON; OnMSP; PDV; RHPC

STERLING ALLEN BROWN (b. 1901)

Old Lem

1 Whippersnapper clerks
Call us out of our name
We got to say mister
To spindling boys (l. 11–14)

BPo; FB; IDB; PoBA; PoNe; TTY

Southern Road

2 My ole man died — hunh —
Cussin' me;
Ole lady rocks, bebby,
Huh misery. (l. 21–24)

3 White man tells me — hunh —
Damn yo' soul;
White man tells me — hunh —
Damn yo' soul;
Got no need, bebby,
To be tole. (l. 31–36)

BANP; BPo; FB; PoBA

Strong Men

4 They dragged you from homeland,
They chained you in coffles,
They huddled you spoon-fashion in filthy hatches,
They sold you to give a few gentlemen ease. (l. 1–4)

5 You sang:
Me an' muh baby gonna shine, shine
Me an' muh baby gonna shine.
The strong men keep a-comin' on
The strong men git stronger ... (l. 36–40)

BANP; BPo; CNA; FB; PoBA; TTY

THOMAS EDWARD BROWN (1830–1897)

My Garden

1 A garden is a lovesome thing, God wot! (l. 1)

BLPL; FaBV; InPK; OBEV; PoLF; WBLP; WGRP

WILLIAM BROWNE (1591–1643)

Epitaph in Obitum M.S., X° Maij, 1614

1 May! Be thou never graced with birds that sing,
Nor Flora's pride!
In thee all flowers and roses spring,
Mine only died. (l. 1–4)

ElL; FaBoEE; JCP; NOBE; OBEV; OBS

The Inner Temple Masque

2 be a while our guests:
For stars, gaze on our eyes.
The compass love shall hourly sing,
And as he goes about the ring,
We will not miss
To tell each point he nameth with a kiss. (l. 13–18)

ChTr; ElL; GBL; NOBE; OBEV; OBS

On the Countess Dowager of Pembroke
(*attributed to* Browne)

3 Underneath this sable hearse
Lies the subject of all verse:
Sidney's sister, Pembroke's mother;
Death ere thou has slain another,
Fair, and learned, and good as she,
Time shall throw a dart at thee. (l. 1–6)

AWP; FaBoEE; HAP; InvP; JCP; NIP; NOBE; NoP;
OAEL-1; OBEV; OBS; PoEL-2; PoRA; WeW

ELIZABETH BARRETT BROWNING
(1806–1861)

Grief

1 I tell you, hopeless grief is passionless;
That only men incredulous of despair,

Half-taught in anguish, through the midnight air
Beat upward to God's throne in loud access
Of shrieking and reproach. Full desertness,
In souls as countries, lieth silent-bare
Under the blanching, vertical eye-glare
Of the absolute Heavens. (l. 1–8)

FPL; HeIP; InPK; NOBVV; OBEV; OBNC; PoLF;
TrGrPo; WPE

A Musical Instrument

2 What was he doing, the great god Pan,
Down in the reeds by the river?
Spreading ruin and scattering ban,
Splashing and paddling with hoofs of a goat,
And breaking the golden lilies afloat
With the dragon-fly on the river. (l. 1–6)

EBVV; FaBoBe; FaPON; NAEL-2; NoP; OAEL-2; OBEV;
OnMSP; PoE; WiR; WPE

SONNETS FROM THE PORTUGUESE (the following 5 poems)

First time he kissed me

3 First time he kissed me, he but only kiss'd
The fingers of this hand wherewith I write; (l. 1–2)

BLPA; BLPL; CTC; FaBoBe

How do I love thee?

4 How do I love thee? Let me count the ways. (l. 1)

5 I love thee to the level of everyday's
Most quiet need, by sun and candle-light.
I love thee freely, as men strive for Right;
I love thee purely, as they turn from Praise.
I love thee with the passion put to use
In my old griefs, and with my childhood's faith.
(l. 5–10)

6 I love thee with a love I seemed to lose
With my lost saints, — I love thee with the breath,
Smiles, tears, of all my life! — and, if God choose,
I shall but love thee better after death. (l. 11–14)

BoLoP; CTC; EBVV; FaBoBe; FaBV; FaFP; FF; FPL;
HeIP; HoPM; InPK; LiTB; NAEL-2; NIP; NoP; PoE;
PoLF; PoRA; Son; TEP; TrGrPo; UnPo; WPE

I thought once how Theocritus had sung

7 I saw, in gradual vision through my tears,
The sweet, sad years, the melancholy years, . . .
(l. 6–7)

8 'Guess now who holds thee?' — 'Death,' I said. But,
there,
The silver answer rang, . . . 'Not Death, but Love.'
(l. 13–14)

EBVV; GBL; NOBE; NoP; OBEV; OBNC; WPE

If thou must love me

9 If thou must love me, let it be for nought
Except for love's sake only. Do not say
"I love her for her smile — her look — her way
Of speaking gently, — for a trick of thought
That falls in well with mine, and certes brought
A sense of pleasant ease on such a day" — (l. 1–6)

CTC; FaFP; HeIP; InPS; LiTB; OBEV; OBNC; TrGrPo

When we two souls

10 When our two souls stand up erect and strong,
Face to face, silent, drawing nigh and nigher,
Until the lengthening wings break into fire (l. 1–3)

BoWoP; NAEL-2; NOBE; OBEV; TrGrPo; WPE

ELIZABETH BARRETT BROWNING *AND* LOUISE IMOGEN GUINEY

Out in the Fields with God (attributed to Browning *and* to Guiney)

1 The foolish fears of what might happen.
I cast them all away
Among the clover-scented grass,
Among the new-mown hay,
Among the husking of the corn,
Where drowsy poppies nod
Where ill thoughts die and good are born —
Out in the fields with God.

BLPA; BLRP; WBLP; WGRP

ROBERT BROWNING (1812–1889)

Abt Vogler

1 Ye know why the forms are fair, ye hear how the tale is
told:
It is all triumphant art, but art in obedience to laws,
(l. 46–48)

2 On the earth the broken arcs; in the heaven a perfect
round. (l. 72)

3 The high that proved too high, the heroic for earth too
    hard,
  The passion that left the ground to lose itself in the sky,
  Are music sent up to God by the lover and the bard;
  Enough that he heard it once; we shall hear it by and
    by. (l. 77–80)

4 Sorrow is hard to bear, and doubt is slow to clear,
  Each sufferer says his say, his scheme of the weal and
    woe:
  But God has a few of us whom he whispers in the ear;
  The rest may reason and welcome; 'tis we musicians
    know. (l. 85–88)

5 Give me the keys. I feel for the common chord again,
  Sliding by semi-tones till I sink to a minor, — yes,
  And I blunt it into a ninth, and I stand on alien
    ground,
  Surveying a while the heights I rolled from into the
    deep;
  Which, hark, I have dared and done, for my resting-
    place is found,
  The C Major of this life: so, now I will try to sleep.
    (l. 91–96)

NAEL-2; OAEL-2; TOF; WGRP

Andrea del Sarto

6 Let us try.
  To-morrow, how you shall be glad for this! (l. 19–20)

7 the whole seems to fall into a shape
  As if I saw alike my work and self
  And all that I was born to be and do,
  A twilight-piece. Love, we are in God's hand.
    (l. 46–49)

8 I do what many dream of, all their lives, (l. 69)

9 less is more, Lucrezia: (l. 78)

10 You called me, and I came home to your heart.
    (l. 171)

CTC; NAEL-2; NOBVV; NoP; OAEL-2; PoE; PoEL-5

Asolando

11 Oh to love so, be so loved,yet so mistaken!

12 One who never turned his back but marched breast
    forward,
  Never doubted clouds would break,
  Never dreamed, though right were worsted, wrong
    would triumph,
  Held we fall to rise, are baffled to fight better,
  Sleep to wake

FaBV; FiP; NAEL-1; NOBE; OBNC; OHFP; TEP; TrGrPo

The Bishop Orders His Tomb at Saint Praxed's Church

13 Vanity, saith the preacher, vanity! (l. 1)

14 And as she died so must we die ourselves,
  And thence ye may perceive the world's a dream.
  Life, how and what is it? 8–10

AWP; EBVV; FiP; HAP; HeIP; NAEL-2; NAWM-2;
NOBVV; NoP; OAEL-2; OBAL; PoE; PPP; PrIm; TEP

Caliban upon Setebos; or, Natural Theology in the Island

15 Letting the rank tongue blossom into speech. (l. 23)

16 He made all these and more,
  Made all we see; and us, in spite: how else?
  He could not, Himself, make a second self
  To be His mate: as well have made Himself:
  He would not make what He mislikes or slights,
  An eyesore to Him, or not worth His pains;
  But did, in envy, listlessness, or sport,
  Make what Himself would fain, in a manner, be —
  Weaker in most points, stronger in a few,
  Worthy, and yet mere playthings all the while,
  Things He admires and mocks too, — (l. 56–66)

17 Well then, 'supposeth He is good i' the main,
  Placable if His mind and ways were guessed,
  But rougher than His handiwork, be sure!
    (l. 110–112)

18 What knows, — the something over Setebos
  That made Him, or He, may be, found and fought,
  Worsted, drove off and did to nothing, perchance.
  There may be something quiet o'er His head,
  Out of His reach, that feels nor joy nor grief,
  Since both derive from weakness in some way.
    (l. 130–135)

19 Those at His mercy, — why, they please Him most
    (l. 222)

AWP; EBEV; NAEL-2; NOBVV; NoP; OAEL-2; WGRP

Childe Roland to the Dark Tower Came

20 My first thought was, he lied in every word,
  That hoary cripple, with malicious eye (l. 1–2)

21 I think I never saw
  Such starved ignoble nature; (l. 55–56)

22 'Tis the Last Judgment's fire must cure this place,
    (l. 65)

NAEL-2; NOBVV; NoP; OAEL-2; OBNV; PoE; PPP

Confessions

23 What is he buzzing in my ears?
'Now that I come to die,
Do I view the world as a vale of tears?'
Ah, reverend sir, not I! (l. 1–4)

24 How sad and bad and mad it was —
But then, how it was sweet! (l. 35–36)

ELP; GTBS-P; NOBE; NOBVV

Fra Lippo Lippi

25 He's Judas to a tittle, that man is! (l. 25)

26 Take away love, and our earth is a tomb!
Flower o' the quince,
I let Lisa go, and what good in life since? (l. 55–57)

27 Flower o' the clove,
All the Latin I construe is "amo," I love! (l. 111–112)

28 Your business is not to catch men with show,
With homage to the perishable clay,
But lift them over it, ignore it all,
Make them forget there's such a thing as flesh.
Your business is to paint the souls of men —
(l. 180–184)

29 The world and life's too big to pass for a dream,
(l. 252)

30 We're made so that we love
First when we see them painted, things we have passed
Perhaps a hundred times nor cared to see;
And so they are better, painted — better to us,
Which is the same thing. Art was given for that;
God uses us to help each other so, (l. 301–306)

CTC; EBVV; NoP; OAEL-2; TEP

Hervé Riel

31 Praise is deeper than the lips: (l. 107)

BeLS; FaBoBe; GN; MOS; OnMSP

Home Thoughts from Abroad

32 Oh, to be in England
Now that April's there, (l. 1–2)

AWP; BoNaP; BoTP; EBVV; FaBoBe; FaBV; FaFP;
FaPON; FaPoR; FiP; FPL; GN; HeIP; LiTB; NAEL-2;
NOBE; NOBVV; NoP; OBEV; OBNC; OBTV; PoLF;
PoRA; PrIm; TEP; TrGrPo

How It Strikes a Contemporary

33 His very serviceable suit of black
Was courtly once and conscientious still, (l. 5–6)

34 — you stared at him,
And found, less to your pleasure than surprise,
He seemed to know you and expect as much.
(l. 33–35)

CTC; FaBoPV; GTBS-P; OAEL-2

How They Brought the Good News from Ghent to Aix

35 I sprang to the stirrup, and Joris and he;
I galloped, Dirck galloped, we galloped all three;
"Good speed!" cried the watch as the gate-bolts undrew,
"Speed!" echoed the wall to us galloping through.
Behind shut the postern, the lights sank to rest,
And into the midnight we galloped abreast. (l. 1–6)

36 I poured down his throat our last measure of wine,
Which (the burgesses voted by common consent)
Was no more than his due who brought good news
from Ghent. (l. 58–60)

BeLS; BLPL; FaBoBe; FaFP; FaPoR; GN; HoPM; NAEL-
2

In a Gondola

37 The moth's kiss first!
Kiss me as if you made believe
You were not sure, this eve,
How my face, your flower, had pursed
Its petals up; so, here and there
You brush it, till I grow aware
Who wants me, and wide ope I burst. (l. 1–7)

BoLoP GBL; OBEV; TrGrPo

Incident of the French Camp

38 'You're wounded!' 'Nay,' his soldier's pride
Touched to the quick, he said:
'I'm killed, Sire!' And his Chief beside,
Smiling the boy fell dead. (l. 37–40)

BeLS; FaPoR; GN; OBWP; TrGrPo

The Last Ride Together

39 Who knows but the world may end tonight? (l. 22)

40 Fail I alone, in words and deeds?
Why, all men strive and who succeeds?
We rode; it seemed my spirit flew, (l. 45–46)

41 you tell
What we felt only; (l. 68–69)

42 I sink back shuddering from the quest.
Earth being so good, would Heaven seem best?
Now, Heaven and she are beyond this ride. (l. 97–99)

43 we two
With life forever old yet new,
Changed not in kind but in degree,
The instant made eternity — (l. 105–108)

BoLoP; FiP; LiTB; NAEL-2; OBEV; PoEL-5; UnPo

The Lost Leader

44 Just for a handful of silver he left us,
Just for a riband to stick in his coat — (l. 1–2)

45 We that had loved him so, followed him, honored him,
Lived in his mild and magnificent eye,
Learned his great language, caught his clear accents,
Made him our pattern to live and to die! (l. 9–12)

FaBoPV; NAEL-2; PWR; TrGrPo

The Lost Mistress

46 All's over, then: does truth sound bitter
As one at first believes? (l. 1–2)

BoLoP; FiP; NOBE; OBEV; OBNC

Love among the Ruins

47 Where the quiet-coloured end of evening smiles (l. 1)

43 Where a multitude of men breathed joy and woe
Long ago;
Lust of glory pricked their hearts up, dread of shame
Struck them tame; (l. 31–34)

49 Oh, heart! oh, blood that freezes, blood that burns!
Earth's returns
For whole centuries of folly, noise and sin!
Shut them in,
With their triumphs and their glories and the rest!
Love is best. (l. 79–84)

FaBV; HAP; NAEL-2; NOBE; OAEL-2; OBEV; PoEL-5; PrIm

Love in a Life

50 Yet the day wears,
And door succeeds door;
I try the fresh fortune —
Range the wide house from the wing to the centre,

Still the same chance! she goes out as I enter.
Spend my whole day in the quest, — who cares?
(l. 9–14)

InvP; NOBE; NOBVV; OBNC

Meeting at Night

51 Then the two hearts beating each to each! (l. 12)

AWP; BoLoP; ELP; FaBV; FF; FiP; GBL; HeIP; InPS;
InvP; MOS; NOBE; NOBVV; OBEV; OBNC; OPOP;
OxBSP; PoRA; SCV; SeCePo; SoSe; TrGrPo; UnPo;
WeW

Memorabilia

52 Ah, did you once see Shelley plain,
And did he stop and speak to you,
And did you speak to him again?
How strange it seems and new! (l. 1–4)

53 For there I picked up on the heather
And there I put inside my breast
A moulted feather, an eagle-feather!
Well, I forget the rest. (l. 13–16)

FiP; NAEL-2; NOBVV; NoP; OAEL-2; OBNC; PoE; RB;
SeCePo

My Last Duchess

54 That's my last Duchess painted on the wall,
Looking as if she were alive. I call (l. 1–2)

55 She had
A heart — how shall I say? — too soon made glad,
Too easily impressed; she liked whate'er
She looked on, and her looks went everywhere.
(l. 21–24)

56 She thanked men, — good! but thanked
Somehow — I know not how — as if she ranked
My gift of a nine-hundred-years-old name
With anybody's gift. (l. 31–34)

57 — E'en then would be some stooping; and I choose
Never to stoop. Oh sir, she smiled, no doubt,
Whene'er I passed her; but who passed without
Much the same smile? This grew; I gave commands;
Then all smiles stopped together. There she stands
As if alive. (l. 42–47)

AWP; BeLS; EBVV; FaBoPV; FaFP; FF; FiP; FPL;
GTBS-P; HAP; HeIP; HoPM; InPK; InPS; LiTB; MAT;
NAEL-2; NIP; NOBE; NOBVV; NoP; OAEL-2; OBNC;
PoE; PoEL-5; PoLF; PPP; PrIm; SCV; SoSe; TEP;
TrGrPo; WeW

Parting at Morning

58 Round the cape of a sudden came the sea,
And the sun looked over the mountain's rim:
And straight was a path of gold for him,
And the need of a world of men for me. (l. 1–4)

AWP; FaBV; FF; FiP; HeIP; InPS; MOS; NAEL-2;
NOBE; OBEV; OBNC; OxBSP; SoSe; UnPo; WiR

The Pied Piper of Hamelin

59 Hamelin Town's in Brunswick,
By famous Hanover city; (l. 1–2)

60 Rats!
They fought the dogs, and kill'd the cats,
And bit the babies in the cradles,
And ate the cheeses out of the vats,
And lick'd the soup from the cook's own ladles,
Split open the kegs of salted sprats,
Made nests inside men's Sunday hats,
And even spoil'd the women's chats,
By drowning their speaking
With shrieking and squeaking
In fifty different sharps and flats. (l. 10–20)

61 "Please your honors," said he, "I'm able,
By means of a secret charm, to draw
All creatures living beneath the sun,
That creep, or swim, or fly, or run,
After me so as you never saw!
And I chiefly use my charm
On creatures that do people harm,
The mole, and toad, and newt, and viper;
And people call me the Pied Piper." (l. 71–79)

62 Out came the children running.
All the little boys and girls,
With rosy cheeks and flaxen curls,
And sparkling eyes and teeth like pearls,
Tripping and skipping, ran merrily after
The wonderful music with shouting and laughter.
                    (l. 202–207)

63 The music stopp'd, and I stood still,
And found myself outside the Hill,
Left alone against my will,
To go now limping as before,
And never hear of that country more!" (l. 251–255)

64 Alas, alas for Hamelin!
There came into many a burgher's pate
A text which says that Heaven's Gate
Opes to the rich at as easy rate
As the needle's eye takes a camel in! (l. 256–260)

65 So, Willy, let you and me be wipers
Of scores out with all men—especially pipers;
And, whether they pipe us free, from rats or from mice,
If we've promised them aught, let us keep our promise.
                    (l. 300–303)

BeLS; BLPL; FaBoBe; FaBoCh; FaFP; GN; OBNV;
OxBChV

Pippa Passes

66 The year's at the spring,
And day's at the morn;
Morning's at seven;
The hillside's dew-pearled;
The lark's on the wing;
The snail's on the thorn:
God's in His Heaven—
All's right with the world!

BLPA; BLPL; BoTP; FaBoBe; FaBV; FaFP; FaPON;
GoJo; LiTB; NTCP; OBEV; OHIP; PDV; SoSe; TEP;
TrCP; TrGrPo; UnPo; WGRP

Porphyria's Lover

67 And all night long we have not stirred,
And yet God has not said a word! (l. 59–60)

AWP; BeLS; HAP; NAEL-2; OBEV; TEP; TrGrPo

Prospice

68 Fear death?—to feel the fog in my throat,
The mist in my face,
When the snows begin, and the blasts denote
I am nearing the place,
The power of the night, the press of the storm,
The post of the foe;
Where he stands, the Arch Fear in a visible form,
Yet the strong man must go: (l. 1–8)

69 No! let me taste the whole of it, fare like my peers
The heroes of old,
Bear the brunt, in a minute pay glad life's arrears
Of pain, darkness and cold. (l. 17–20)

70 O thou soul of my soul! I shall clasp thee again,
And with God be the rest! (l. 27–28)

BLPL; DL; FaBV; FiP; LiTB; NAEL-2; OBD; PoLF;
PoRA; TrCP; TrGrPo; WGRP

Rabbi Ben Ezra

71 Grow old along with me!
The best is yet to be,
The last of life, for which the first was made: (l. 1–3)

72 Poor vaunt of life indeed,
Were man but formed to feed
On joy, to solely seek and find and feast: (l. 19–21)

73 Then, welcome each rebuff
That turns earth's smoothness rough,
Each sting that bids nor sit nor stand but go!
                    (l. 31–33)

74 Shall life succeed in that it seems to fail:
What I aspired to be,
And was not, comforts me: (l. 39–41)

75 Therefore I summon age
To grant youth's heritage,
Life's struggle having so far reached its term:
(l. 73–75)

76 Look not thou down but up! (l. 175)

BLPL; FaBV; FaFP; FiP; NAEL-2; OBNC; TEP; WGRP

Soliloquy of the Spanish Cloister

77 What's the Latin name for 'parsley'?
What's the Greek name for Swine's Snout? (l. 15–16)

78 There's a great text in Galatians,
Once you trip on it, entails
Twenty-nine distinct damnations,
One sure, if another fails: (l. 48–51)

FaBoCo; InPK; LiTB; NAEL-2; NIP; NOBL; NOBVV;
NoP; OAEL-2; TEP; TOF; TrGrPo; TW

A Toccata of Galuppi's

79 What of soul was left, I wonder, when the kissing had
to stop?

Dust and ashes?' So you creak it, and I want the heart
to scold.
Dear dead women, with such hair, too — what's become
of all the gold
Used to hang and brush their bosoms? — I feel chilly
and grown old. (l. 42–45)

EBVV; GTBS-P; HAP; LiTB; Mes; NAEL-2; NOBE;
NOBVV; NoP; OAEL-2; TEP

Two in the Campagna

80 Silence and passion, joy and peace,
An everlasting wash of air —
Rome's ghost since her
decease. (l. 23–25)

81 Let us be unashamed of soul,
As earth lies bare to heaven above!
How is it under our control
To love or not to love? (l. 32–35)

82 Only I discern —
Infinite passion, and the pain
Of finite hearts that yearn. (l. 58–60)

EBEV; EBVV; ELP; GTBS-P; NAEL-2; NOBE; NOBVV;
NoP; OAEL-2; OBNC; PoE; PoEL-5; SeCePo; TOF;
TrGrPo

Up at a Villa — Down in the City

83 Had I but plenty of money, money enough and to spare,
The house for me, no doubt, were a house in the city-
square;
Ah, such a life, such a life, as one leads at the window
there! (l. 1–3)

84 Oh, a day in the city-square, there is no such pleasure
in life! (l. 65)

FaBoPP; GTBS-P; InPS; NOBE; OBTV; PoRA; PPP

A Woman's Last Word

85 Let's contend no more, Love,
Strive nor weep:
All be as before, Love,
— Only sleep! (l. 1–4)

BLPA; BLPL; FaBoBe; FaFP; NAEL-2; TrGrPo

WILLIAM CULLEN BRYANT
(1794–1878)

The Battle-Field

1 Once this soft turf, this rivulet's sands,
Were trampled by a hurrying crowd, (l. 1–2)

2 Ah! never shall the land forget
How gushed the life-blood of her brave —
Gushed, warm with hope and courage yet,
Upon the soil they fought to save. (l. 5–8)

3 Truth, crushed to earth, shall rise again;
Th' eternal years of God are hers;
But Error, wounded, writhes in pain,
And dies among his worshippers. (l. 33–36)

4 Another hand thy sword shall wield,
Another hand the standard wave,
Till from the trumpet's mouth is pealed
The blast of triumph o'er thy grave. (l. 41–44)

AA; AnAmPo; FPL; PoLF

The Death of Lincoln

5 In sorrow by thy bier we stand,
Amid the awe that hushes all,
And speak the anguish of a land
That shook with horror at thy fall. (l. 5–8)

6 Pure was thy life; its bloody close
Hath placed thee with the sons of light,
Among the noble host of those
Who perished in the cause of Right. (l. 13–16)

NAAL-1; OHIP; PAH; TAP

The Death of the Flowers

7 The melancholy days are come, the saddest of the
year —
Of wailing winds and naked woods and meadows
brown and sear. (l. 1–2)

8 Where are the flowers, the fair young flowers, that
lately sprang and stood
In brighter light and softer airs, a beauteous
sisterhood?
Alas! they all are in their graves; (l. 7–9)

9 And then I think of one who in her youthful beauty
died,
The fair meek blossom that grew up and faded by my
side, (l. 25–26)

10 And we wept that one so lovely should have a life so
brief;

11 So gentle and so beautiful, should perish with the
flowers. (l. 28–30)

AA; AnAmPo; BLPL; BoNaP; GN; OBCA; PoLF; WBLP

Oh Mother of a Mighty Race

12 Oh mother of a mighty race,
Yet lovely in thy youthful grace!
The elder dames, thy haughty peers,
Admire and hate thy blooming years.

13 There's freedom at thy gates and rest
For Earth's downtrodden and oppressed, (l. 31–32)

14 on thy brow
Shall sit a nobler grace than now.
Deep in the brightness of the skies
The thronging years in glory rise.
And, as they fleet,
Drop strength and riches at thy feet. (l. 37–42)

AA; FaBoBe; OPP; PAH

The Prairies

15 These are the Gardens of the Desert, these
The unshorn fields, boundless and beautiful,
And fresh as the young earth, ere man had sinned —
(l. 1–3)

16 Man hath no part in all this glorious work:
The hand that built the firmament hath heaved
And smoothed these verdant swells, and sown their
slopes
With herbage, (l. 24–27)

17 Thus change the forms of being. Thus arise
Races of living things, glorious in strength,
And perish, as the quickening breath of God
Fills them, or is withdrawn. (l. 86–89)

18 All at once
A fresher wind sweeps by, and breaks my dream,
And I am in the wilderness alone. (l. 122–124)

AmPP; NAAL-1; NOBA; OPP; OxBA; PoEL-4; TAP

Robert of Lincoln

19 Merrily swinging on brier and weed,
Near to the nest of his little dame,
Over the mountainside or mead,
Robert of Lincoln is telling his name:
Bob-o'-link, bob-o'-link, (l. 1–5)

20 Summer wanes; the children are grown;
Fun and frolic no more he knows; (l. 62–63)

21 When you can pipe that merry old strain,
Robert of Lincoln, come back again. (l. 68–69)

FaBoBe; FaPCN; OBCA; WBLP

Thanatopsis

22 To him who, in the love of Nature, holds
Communion with her visible forms, she speaks
A various language: for his gayer hours

23 Go forth under the open sky, and list
To Nature's teachings.

24 So live that when thy summons comes to join
The innumerable caravan that moves
To that mysterious realm, where each shall take
His chamber in the silent halls of death,
Thou go not, like the quarry-slave at night,
Scourged to his dungeon, but, sustained and soothed
By an unfaltering trust, approach thy grave
Like one who wraps the drapery of his couch
About him and lies down to pleasant dreams.

AA; AmPP; AnAmPo; AWP; BLPL; BoNaP; DL; FaBoBe;
FaFP; LiTA NAAL-1; NOBA; OBEV; OHFP; OxBA;
PWR; TAP; TrGrPo; WBLP; WGRP

To a Waterfowl

25 While glow the heavens with the last steps of day,
Far, through their rosy depths, dost thou pursue
Thy solitary way! (l. 2–4)

26 There is a power whose care
Teaches thy way along that pathless coast, —
(l. 13–14)

27 He who, from zone to zone,
Guides through the boundless sky thy certain flight,
In the long way that I must tread alone,
Will lead my steps aright. (l. 29–32)

AA; AmPP; AnAmPo; AWP; BLPL; CH; FaBoBe; FaFP;
GN; HoPM; LiTA; NAAL-1; NOBA; NoP; OHFP; OxBA;
PoEL-4; PoLF; PrIm; PWR; SoSe; TAP; TrGrPo; WBLP;
WGRP

To Cole, the Painter, Departing for Europe

28 Thine eyes shall see the light of distant skies:
Yet, Cole! thy heart shall bear to Europe's strand
A living image of our own bright land,
Such as upon thy glorious canvas lies; (l. 1–4)

29 Fair scenes shall greet thee where thou goest — fair,
But different — (l. 9–10)

30 Gaze on them, till the tears shall dim thy sight,
But keep that earlier, wilder image bright. (l. 13–14)

AiP; AmPP; NAAL-1; TAP

To the Fringed Gentian

31 Thou blossom bright with autumn dew,
And colored with the heaven's own blue, (l. 1–2)

32 Thou waitest late and com'st alone,
When woods are bare and birds are flown, (l. 9–10)

33 I shall see
The hour of death draw near to me,
Hope, blossoming within my heart, (l. 17–19)

AA; AnAmPo; AWP; FaBoBe; FPL; GN; NoP; PoLF; TAP

The Yellow Violet

34 When beechen buds begin to swell,
And woods the blue-bird's warble know,
The yellow violet's modest bell
Peeps from the last year's leaves below. (l. 1–4)

35 Thy early smile has stayed my walk;
But midst the gorgeous blooms of May,
I passed thee on thy humble stalk. (l. 22–24)

36 So they, who climb to wealth, forget
The friends in darker fortunes tried.
I copied them — but I regret
That I should ape the ways of pride. (l. 25–28)

BLPL; NAAL-1; PoLF; TAP

ARTHUR BULLER (1874–1944)

There was a young lady named Bright (attributed to Buller)

1 There was a young lady named Bright,
Who traveled much faster than light. (l. 1–2)

2 And returned on the previous night. (l. 5)

CenHV; FaBoCo; FaFP; FaPON; ImOP; NOBL; OxBoLi

JOHN BUNYAN (1628–1688)

The Pilgrim's Progress

1 Who would true Valour see,
Let him come hither; (l. 1–2)

2 There's no Discouragement,
Shall make him once relent,
His first avow'd intent,
To be a Pilgrim. (l. 5–8)

3 Hobgoblin nor foul Fiend
Can daunt his spirit;
He knows he at the end
Shall Life inherit. (l. 17–20)

4 He'll fear not what men say,
He'll labour night and day
To be a Pilgrim. (l. 22–24)

BoTP; CoMu; EBEV; ELP; FaPoR; GN; NOCV; OBS;
WiR

5 He that is down needs fear no fall, (l. 1)

6 Fullness to such a burden is
That go on pilgrimage;
Here little, and hereafter bliss,
Is best from age to age. (l. 9–12)

BLRP; BoTP; EaLo; EBEV; GN; NOBE; OBEV; OBS;
OxBSP; WGRP

GELETT BURGESS (1866–1951)

Ah, Yes, I Wrote the "Purple Cow"

1 I'm Sorry, now, I Wrote it,
But I can Tell you Anyhow,
I'll Kill you if you Quote it. (l. 2–4)

CenHV; FaBoCo; FaBoNo; FiBHP; NBLV; OBAL

The Purple Cow

2 I never saw a Purple Cow,
I never hope to see one; (l. 1–2)

3 I'd rather see than be one. (l. 4)

CenHV; FaBoCo; FaBoNo; FaFP; FaPON; FiBHP; FPL;
GrPl; NA; NBLV; NTCP; OBAL; OBCA; PDV; PoLF;
RHPC

ROBERT BURNS (1759–1796)

Address to the Deil

1 O thou, whatever title suit thee!
Auld Hornie, Satan, Nick, or Clootie, (l. 1–2)

2 Hear me, auld Hangie, for a wee,
An' let poor, damned bodies bee;
I'm sure sma' pleasure it can gie,
Ev'n to a deil,
To skelp an' scaud poor dogs like me,
An' hear us squeel! (l. 7–12)

3 Then you, ye auld, snick-drawing dog!
Ye cam to Paradise incog,
An' played on a man a cursed brogue,
(Black be your fa'!)
An' gied the infant warld a shog,
'Maist ruined a'. (l. 91–96)

EnRP; GoTS; NOEC; OAEL-1; OxBS; PoEL-4

Address to the Unco Guid, or the Rigidly Righteous

4 O ye wha are sae guid yoursel,
Sae pious and sae holy,
Ye've nought to do but mark and tell
Your neebour's fauts and folly! (l. 1–4)

5 Think, when your castigated pulse
Gies now and then a wallop,
What ragings must his veins convulse,
That still eternal gallop: (l. 25–28)

6 See Social-life and Glee sit down,
All joyous and unthinking,
Till, quite transmugrified, they're grown
Debauchery and Drinking: (l. 33–36)

7 Then gently scan your brother Man,
Still gentler sister Woman;
Though they may gang a kennin wrang,
To step aside is human: (l. 49–52)

8 Who made the heart, 'tis He alone
Decidedly can try us, (l. 57–58)

9 What's done we partly may compute,
But know not what's resisted. (l. 63–64)

EnRP; NOBE; NOCV; NoP; OxBS; TrGrPo

Ae Fond Kiss

10 Ae fond kiss, and then we sever!
Ae fareweel, alas, for ever! (l. 1–2)

11 But to see her, was to love her;
Love but her, and love for ever. (l. 11–12)

12 Had we never lov'd sae kindly,
Had we never lov'd sae blindly,
Never met — or never parted,
We had ne'er been broken hearted. (l. 13–16)

BoLoP; ELP; EnRP; FaFP; NAEL-2; NOEC; OAEL-1;
OBEV; PoEL-4; PPP

Auld Lang Syne

13 Should auld acquaintance be forgot,
And never brought to mind?
Should auld acquaintance be forgot,
And auld lang syne? (l. 1–4)

14 For auld lang syne, by dear,
For auld lang syne,
We'll tak a cup o' kindness yet
For auld lang syne! (l. 5–8)

AWP; BLPL; EnRP; FaFP; GoTS; LiTB; NAEL-2; NOBE;
OBEV; OxBS; PoLF; TEP

The Banks of Doon

15 Ye banks and braes o' bonnie Doon,
How can ye bloom sae fresh and fair?
How can ye chant, ye little birds,
And I sae weary fu' o' care?
Thou'lt break my heart, thou warbling bird,
That wantons thro' the flowering thorn:
Thou minds me o' departed joys,
Departed never to return. (l. 1–8)

AWP; BoLoP; CH; ELP; EnRP; GTBS; GTBS-P; NAEL-2;
NOBE; NOEC; NoP; OBEV; PoEL-4; PrIm; TrGrPo;
UnPo; WBLP

Bonnie Lesley

16 To see her is to love her,
And love but her for ever;
For Nature made her what she is,
And never made anither! (l. 5–8)

CTC; GTBS; GTBS-P; NOBE; OBEV; OxBS

A Child's Grace

17 Some hae meat and canna eat,
And some wad eat that want it;
But we hae meat and we can eat,
And sae the Lord be thankit. (l. 1—4)

FaBoCh; FaPON; MoShBr

The Cotter's Saturday Night

18 Wi' joy unfeigned brothers and sisters meet,
An' each for other's weelfare kindly spiers:
The social hours, swift-winged, unnoticed fleet;
Each tells the uncos that he sees or hears;
The parents, partial, eye their hopeful years;
Anticipation forward points the view: (l. 37—42)

19 If Heaven a draught of heavenly pleasure spare,
One cordial in this melancholy vale,
'T is when a youthful, loving, modest pair
In other's arms breathe out the tender tale, (l. 77—80)

20 From scenes like these old Scotia's grandeur springs,
That makes her loved at home, revered abroad;
Princes and lords are but the breath of kings,
"An honest man's the noblest work of God!"
(l. 163—166)

21 O Scotia! my dear, my native soil!
For whom my warmest wish to Heaven is sent,
(l. 172—173)

BeLS; EnRP; FaBoBe; PoLF; WGRP

Flow Gently, Sweet Afton

22 Flow gently, sweet Afton! among thy green braes,
Flow gently, I'll sing thee a song in thy praise;
My Mary's asleep by thy murmuring stream,
Flow gently, sweet Afton, disturb not her dream.
(l. 1—4)

AWP; BLPL; BoNaP; EnRP; FaBoBe; FaBoPP; FaFP;
HeIP; LiTB; NAEL-2; TrGrPo

For A' That and A' That

23 Is there for honest poverty
That hings his head, and a' that? (l. 1—2)

24 The rank is but the guinea stamp —
The man's the gowd for a' that! (l. 7—8)

25 Gie fools their silks, and knaves their wine —
A man's a man for a' that! (l. 11—12)

26 The honest man, though e'er sae poor,
Is king o' men, for a' that! (l. 15—16)

27 Then let us pray that come it may, —
As come it will for a' that, —
That sense and worth, o'er a' the earth,
May bear the gree, an' a' that.
For a' that, and a' that,
It's comin' yet, for a' that —
That man to man, the warld o'er,
Shall brithers be for a' that. (l. 33—40)

EnRP; FaBoBe; FaBoPV; FaFP; FaPoR; LiTB; NAEL-2;
NOEC; OAEL-1; OHFP; OPOP; OxBS; TEP; TrGrPo;
WBLP

Green Grow the Rashes, O

28 Green grow the rashes, O;
Green grow the rashes, O;
The sweetest hours that e'er I spend,
Are spent amang the lasses, O. (l. 1—4)

29 There's nought but care on ev'ry han',
In ev'ry hour that passes, O:
What signifies the life o' man,
An' 'twere na for the lasses, O. (l. 5—8)

30 Auld Nature swears, the lovely Dears
Her noblest work she classes, O:
Her prentice han' she try'd on man,
An' then she made the lasses, O. (l. 21—24)

AWP; CoMu; CTC; EnRP; ErPo; FaFP; GBP; LiTB;
NAEL-2; NoP; OAEL-1; PPP; SeCePo

Highland Mary

31 O pale, pale now, those rosy lips,
I aft hae kissed sae fondly;
And closed for ay, the sparkling glance
That dwalt on me sae kindly;
And moldering now in silent dust
That heart that lo'ed me dearly! (l. 25—30)

AWP; EnRP; GTBS; GTBS-P; OBEV; TrGrPo; WBLP

Holy Willie's Prayer

32 O thou that in the heavens does dwell!
Wha, as it pleases best thysel',
Sends ane to heaven and ten to hell,
A' for thy glory!
And no for ony gude or ill
They've done before thee. — (l. 1—6)

33 But Lord, remember me and mine
Wi' mercies temporal and divine!
That I for grace and gear may shine,

Excelled by nane!
And a' the glory shall be thine!
Amen! Amen! (l. 97–102)

EBEV; EnRP; GoTS; InPS; NOEC; NoP; OAEL-1;
OBSV; OxBoLi; OxBS; PoEL-4; PoE; PPP; TW

It Was A' for Our Rightfu' King

34 The soger frae the wars returns,
The sailor frae the main,
But I hae parted frae my Love,
Never to meet again, my dear,
Never to meet again. (l. 16–20)

CH; EnRP; GoTS; OBEV; PoEL-4

John Anderson, My Jo

35 John Anderson my jo, John,
We clamb the 'hill the gither;
And mony a canty day, John,
We've had wi' ane anither:
Now we maun totter down, John,
And hand in hand we'll go;
And sleep the gither at the foot,
John Anderson my Jo. (l. 9–16)

AWP; BoLoP; EnRP; FaBV; FF; GTBS; GTBS-P; HeIP;
InPK; LiTB; NOBE; NOEC; NoP; OBEV; PoE; PrIm;
TrGrPo; WBLP

Lament for Culloden

36 Now wae to thee, thou cruel lord,
A bluidy man I trow thou be;
For mony a heart thou hast made sair
That ne'er did wrong to thine or thee. (l. 13–16)

GoTS; GTBS; GTBS-P; OBEV

Mary Morison

37 O Mary, at thy window be,
It is the wish'd, the trysted hour! (l. 1–2)

38 O Mary, canst thou wreck his peace,
Wha for thy sake wad gladly die?
Or canst thou break that heart of his,
Whase only faut is loving thee? (l. 17–20)

AWP; EnRP; GTBS; GTBS-P; OBEV; OxBS; TrGrPo

O, Wert Thou in the Cauld Blast

39 O wert thou in the cauld blast,
On yonder lea, on yonder lea,
My plaidie to the angry airt,
I'd shelter thee, I'd shelter thee. (l. 1–4)

40 Or were I in the wildest waste,
Sae black and bare, sae black and bare,
The desert were a Paradise,
If thou wert there, if thou wert there. (l. 9–12)

EBEV; ELP; EnRP; HAP; HeIP; NOBE; NoP; OxBS;
TrGrPo

Of A' the Airts

41 Of a' the airts the wind can blaw,
I dearly like the west,
For there the bonnie lassie lives,
The lassie I lo'e best; (l. 1–4)

42 I see her in the dewy flowers,
I see her sweet and fair:
I hear her in the tunefu' birds,
I hear her charm the air: (l. 9–12)

AWP; EnRP; GN; GoTS; GTBS; GTBS-P; NoP; OBEV;
OxBS; TrGrPo

A Poet's Welcome to His Love-begotten Daughter

43 Wee image of my bonnie Betty,
I fatherly will kiss and daut thee,
As dear an' near my heart I set thee
Wi' as guid will,
As a' the priests had seen me get thee
That's out o' hell. (l. 7–12)

44 Gude grant that thou may aye inherit
Thy mither's person, grace, an' merit,
An' thy poor worthless daddy's spirit,
Without his failins
'Twill please me mair to see and hear o't,
Than stockit mailins. (l. 43–48)

LiTB; NAs; NOEC; OxBoLi; PoEL-4

A Red, Red Rose

45 O My Luve's like a red, red rose,
That's newly sprung in June;
O My Luve's like the melodie
That's sweetly played in tune. (l. 1–4)

AWP; BoLoP; ChTr; FaBV; FaFP; FF; FPL; GBL; HAP;
HeIP; InvP; NAEL-2; NIP; NOBE; NOEC; NoP; OAEL-1;
OBEV; OxBS; PoEL-4; PoLF; PrIm; SoSe; TEP; TrGrPo

The Rigs o' Barley

46 The time flew by, wi' tentless heed;
Till, 'tween the late and early,
Wi' sma' persuasion she agreed
To see me thro' the barley. (l. 5–8)

BoLoP; ErPo; LiTB; OxBS

Scots Wha Hae

47 Scots, wha hae wi' Wallace bled,
Scots, wham Bruce has aften led,
Welcome to your gory bed,
Or to victory. (l. 1–4)

48 Lay the proud usurpers low!
Tyrants fall in every foe!
Liberty's in every blow!
Let us do, or die! (l. 21–24)

EnRP; FaBoCh; FaPoR; NAEL-2; OAEL-1; OxBS; TEP

The Silver Tassie

49 The trumpets sound, the banners fly,
The glittering spears are ranked ready;
The shouts o' war are heard afar,
The battle closes thick and bloody;
But it's no the roar o' sea or shore
Wad mak me langer wish to tarry;
Nor shout o' war that's heard afar,
Its leaving thee, my bonnie Mary. (l. 9–16)

GTBS; GTBS-P; NOBE; OBEV

Tam o' Shanter

50 our sulky, sullen dame,
Gathering her brows like gathering storm,
Nursing her wrath to keep it warm. (l. 10–12)

51 Ah, gentle dames! it gars me greet,
To think how mony counsels sweet,
How mony lengthen'd, sage advices,
The husband frae the wife despises! (l. 33–36)

52 Ae market night,
Tam had got planted unco right,
Fast by an ingle, bleezing finely,
Wi' reaming swats that drank divinely; (l. 37–40)

53 The minutes wing'd their way wi' pleasure:
Kings may be blest, but Tam was glorious,
O'er a' the ills o' life victorious! (l. 56–58)

54 But pleasures are like poppies spread,
You seize the flow'r, its bloom is shed;
Or like the snow falls in the river,
A moment white — then melts for ever; (l. 59–62)

55 Inspiring bold John Barleycorn!
What dangers thou canst make us scorn!
Wi' tippeny, we fear nae evil;
Wi' usquabae, we'll face the devil! (l. 105–108)

56 Ae spring brought off her master hale,
But left behind her ain grey tail: (l. 215–216)

BeLS; EnRP; GoTS; NAEL-2; NoP; OAEL-1; OBNV;
OxBS; SeCePo; TrGrPo

To a Louse

57 Ye ugly, creepin, blastit wonner,
Detested, shunn'd by saunt an' sinner,
How dare ye set your fit upon her,
Sae fine a lady! (l. 7–10)

58 O wad some Pow'r the giftie gie us
To see oursels as others see us!
It wad frae monie a blunder free us
And foolish notion:
What airs in dress an' gait wad lea'e us,
And ev'n Devotion!

BLPA; EnRP; FaFP; InvP; LiTB; NAEL-2; NOEC; OxBS;
PrIm

To a Mountain Daisy

59 Wee, modest, crimson-tipped flow'r,
Thou's met me in an evil hour;
For I maun crush amang the stoure
Thy slender stem:
To spare thee now is past my pow'r,
Thou bonnie gem. (l. 1–6)

60 Such is the fate of simple Bard,
On life's rough ocean luckless starr'd: (l. 37–38)

61 Ev'n thou who mourn'st the Daisy's fate,
That fate is thine — no distant date;
Stern Ruin's ploughshare drives , elate,
Full on thy bloom,
Till crush'd beneath the furrow's weight,
Shall be thy doom. (l. 49–54)

BoNaP; EnRP; GN; PoLF; WBLP

To a Mouse on Turning Her Up in Her Nest with the Plough

62 Wee, sleeket, cowran, tim'rous beastie,
O, what a panic's in thy breastie!
Thou need na start awa sae hasty,
Wi' bickering brattle!
I wad be laith to rin an' chase thee,
Wi' murd'ring pattle! (l. 1–6)

63 The best laid schemes o' Mice an' Men,
Gang aft agley,
An' lea'e us nought but grief an' pain,
For promis'd joy! (l. 39–42)

EnRP; FaFP; FF; FM; GoTS; GTBS; GTBS-P; HAP;
HeIP; InPS; NAEL-2; NOEC; NoP; OAEL-1; OxBS; PoE;
PoLF; PPP; PrIm; TEP; TrGrPo

Whistle, and I'll Come to You, My Lad

64 O whistle, and I'll come to you, my lad;
O whistle, and I'll come to you, my lad:
Tho' father and mither and a' should gae mad,
O whistle, and I'll come to you, my lad. (l. 1–4)

OxBoLi

SAMUEL BUTLER (1612–1680)

Hudibras

1 When civil fury first grew high,
And men fell out, they knew not why;
When hard words, jealousies, and fears,
Set folks together by the ears,
And made them fight, like mad or drunk,
For Dame Religion, as for punk;

2 For rhetoric, he could not ope
His mouth, but out there flew a trope;
And when he happen'd to break off
I' th' middle of his speech, or cough,
H' had hard words ready to show why,
And tell what rules he did it by;

3 For all a rhetorician's rules
Teach nothing but to name his tools.

4 'Twas English cut on Greek and Latin,
Like fustian heretofore on satin;

5 For he could coin, or counterfeit
New words, with little or no wit;
Words so debas'd and hard, no stone
Was hard enough to touch them on;
And when with hasty noise he spoke 'em;
The ignorant for current took 'em;

6 And when we can with Meeter safe,
We'll call him so, if not plain Ralph,
For Rhime the Rudder is of Verses,
With which like Ships they steer their courses.

7 This Light inspires, and plays upon
The nose of Saint like Bag-pipe drone,
And speaks through hollow empty Soul,
As through a Trunk, or whisp'ring hole,
Such language as no mortal Ear
But spiritual Eve-droppers can hear.

8 He could foretell whats'ever was
By consequence to come to pass.
As Death of Great Men, Alterations,
Diseases, Battels, Inundations.
All this without th' Eclipse of Sun,
Or dreadful Comet, he hath done
By inward Light, a way as good,

EBEV; NAEL-1; OAEL-1; SeCV-2

GEORGE GORDON NOEL BYRON, 6TH BARON BYRON (1788–1824)

Childe Harold's Pilgrimage

1 There is a pleasure in the pathless woods,
There is a rapture on the lonely shore,

There is society where none intrudes
By the deep sea, and music in its roar:
I love not man the less, but nature more,

2 Roll on, thou deep and dark blue Ocean, — roll!
Ten thousand fleets sweep over thee in vain;
Man marks the earth with ruin, — his control
Stops with the shore;

3 Time writes no wrinkles on thine azure brow;
Such as creation's dawn beheld, thou rollest now.

4 Dark-heaving; boundless, endless, and sublime,
The image of Eternity, — the throne
Of the Invisible!

OBNC; PoEL-4

5 There was a sound of revelry by night,
And Belgium's capital had gathered then
Her beauty and her chivalry, and bright
The lamps shone o'er fair women and brave men;
A thousand hearts beat happily; and when
Music arose with its voluptuous swell,
Soft eyes looked love to eyes which spake again,
And all went merry as a marriage-bell;
But hush! hark! a deep sound strikes like a rising knell!
(l. 1–9)

6 Did ye not hear it? — No; 'twas but the wind,
Or the car rattling o'er the stony street;
On with the dance! let joy be unconfined;
No sleep till morn, when Youth and Pleasure meet
To chase the glowing Hours with flying feet.
(l. 10–14)

7 He rushed into the field, and, foremost fighting, fell.
(l. 27)

8 The earth is covered thick with other clay,
Which her own clay shall cover, heaped and pent,
Rider and horse, — friend, foe, — in one red burial blent!
(l. 70–72)

9 They mourn, but smile at length; and, smiling, mourn;
The tree will wither long before it fall; (l. 100–101)

BeLS; EBEV; FaBoBe; FaBoCh; FaBV; FaFP; FiP; GN;
NOBE; OBNC; OBWP; TrGrPo; WaaP; WBLP

Darkness

10 I had a dream, which was not all a dream. (l. 1)

11 All earth was but one thought — and that was death,
Immediate and inglorious; and the pang
Of famine fed upon all entrails — men

Died, and their bones were tombless as their flesh;
The meagre by the meagre were devour'd, (l. 42–46)

EnRP; LiTB; NAEL-2; OAEL-2; OPOP; PoE; PoEL-4;
TEP

The Destruction of Sennacherib

12 The Assyrian came down like the wolf on the fold,
And his cohorts were gleaming in purple and gold:
(l. 1–2)

13 And the might of the Gentile, unsmote by the sword,
Hath melted like snow in the glance of the Lord!
(l. 23–24)

BeLS; BLPL; EnRP; FaBoBe; FaBoCh; FaFP; FaPON;
FaPoR; FF; GN; HAP; HeIP; InPS; NoP; OBWP;
OnMSP; PoLF; RB; TrCP; WBLP; WeW; WGRP

Don Juan

14 And Coleridge, too, has lately taken wing,
But like a hawk encumber'd with his hood, —
Explaining Metaphysics to the nation —
I wish he would explain his Explanation.

15 complaint of present days
Is not the certain path to future praise.

16 Would he adore a sultan? he obey
The intellectual eunuch Castlereagh?

17 The vulgarest tool that Tyranny could want,
With just enough of talent, and no more,
To lengthen fetters by another fixed,
And offer poison long already mixed.

CTC; EnRP; FiP; OAEL-2; OBSV; TrGrPo

18 The same things change their names at such a rate;
For instance — passion in a lover's glorious,
But in a husband is pronounced uxorious.

19 Milton's the prince of poets — so we say;
A little heavy, but no less divine:
An independent being in his day —

OAEL-2

20 I don't choose to say much upon this head,
I'm a plain man, and in a single station,
But — Oh! ye lords of ladies intellectual,
Inform us truly, have they not hen-peck'd you all?

21 And if his passions now and then outran
Discretion, and were not so peaceable
As Numa's (who was also named Pompilius),
He had been ill brought up, and was born bilious.

22 she
Was married, charming, chaste, and twenty-three.

23 Even innocence itself has many a wile,
And will not dare to trust itself with truth,
And love is taught hypocrisy from youth.

24 A quiet conscience makes one so serene!
Christians have burnt each other, quite persuaded
That all the Apostles would have done as they did.

25 They are a sort of post-house,where the Fates
Change horses, making history change its tune,
Then spur away o'er empires and o'er states,
Leaving at last not much besides chronology,
Excepting the post-obits of theology.

26 But who, alas! can love, and then be wise?
Not that remorse did not oppose temptation;
A little still she strove, and much repented,
And whispering 'I will ne'er consent' — consented.

27 Sweet to the miser are his glittering heaps,
Sweet to the father is his first-born's birth,
Sweet is revenge — especially to women,

28 dear the schoolboy spot
We ne'er forget, though there we are forgot.

29 If ever I should condescend to prose,
I'll write poetical commandments, which
Shall supersede beyond all doubt all those
That went before; in these I shall enrich
My text with many things that no one knows,
And carry precept to the highest pitch:
I'll call the work 'Longinus o'er a Bottle,
Or, Every Poet his own Aristotle.'

30 Thou shalt not set up Wordsworth, Coleridge, Southey;
Because the first is crazed beyond all hope,
The second drunk, the third so quaint and mouthy:

31 Ambition was my idol, which was broken
Before the shrines of Sorrow, and of Pleasure;

EnRP; NAEL-2; NoP; OAEL-2; PoE

32 I wonder if his appetite was good?
Or, if it were, if also his digestion?
Methinks at meals some odd thoughts might intrude,
And conscience ask a curious sort of question,
About the right divine how far we should
Sell flesh and blood.

OAEL-2

33 I say — the future is a serious matter —
And so — for God's sake — hock and soda-water!

CTC; FiP; NAEL-2; NOBL; NoP; OAEL-2; OxBSP; PrIm

34 The conqueror at least; who, ere Time renders
His last award, will have the long grass grow
Above his burnt-out brain and sapless cinders.
If I might augur, I should rate but low
Their chances: they are too numerous, like the thirty
Mock tyrants, when Rome's annals wax'd but dirty.

35 Now, were I once at home, and in good satire,
I'd try conclusions with those Janizaries,
And show them what an intellectual war is.

36 'Where is the world?' cries Young, at eighty. 'Where
The world in which a man was born?'

37 Statesmen, chiefs, orators, queens, patriots, kings,
And dandies, all are gone on the wind's wings.

38 But carpe diem, Juan, carpe, carpe!
To-morrow sees another race as gay
And transient, and devour'd by the same harpy.

39 Be hypocritical, be cautious, be
Not what you seem, but always what you see.

OxBoLi

40 The isles of Greece! the isles of Greece
Where burning Sappho loved and sung,

41 The mountains look on Marathon —
And Marathon looks on the sea;
And musing there an hour alone,
I dreamed that Greece might still be free;
For standing on the Persians' grave,
I could not deem myself a slave.

42 Fill high the bowl with Samian wine!
Our virgins dance beneath the shade —
I see their glorious black eyes shine;
But gazing on each glowing maid,
My own the burning tear-drop laves,
To think such breasts must suckle slaves.

AWP; ChTr; FaPoR; FiP; LiTB; NOBE; OBEV; OBTV

43 When over Catholics the ocean rolls,
They must wait several weeks before a mass
Takes off one peck of purgatorial coals,
Because, till people know what's come to pass,
They won't lay out their money on the dead —
It costs three francs for every mass that's said.

44 And had it been the dove from Noah's ark,
Returning there from her successful search,
Which in their way that moment chanced to fall,
They would have eat her, olive-branch and all.

45 A better swimmer you could scarce see ever,
He could, perhaps, have pass'd the Hellespont,
As once (a feat on which ourselves we prided)
Leander, Mr. Ekenhead, and I did.

46 They turn'd to rest; and, each clasp'd by an arm,
Yielded to the deep twilight's purple charm.

MOS

47 Of coursers also spake they: Henry rid
Well, like most Englishmen, and loved the races;
And Juan, like a true-born Andalusian,
Could back a horse, as despots ride a Russian.

48 Man's pity for himself, or for his son,
Always premising that said son at college
Has not contracted much more debt than knowledge.

49 Attorneys-general, awful to the sight,
As hinting more (unless our judgments warp us)
Of the "Star Chamber"than of "Habeas Corpus."

50 There now are no Squire Westerns as of old;
And our Sophias are not so emphatic,
But fair as then, or fairer to behold.
We have no accomplish'd blackguards, like Tom Jones,
But gentlemen in stays, as stiff as stones.

PoEL-4

51 Ye could not know where lies a thing so fair,
No stone is there to show, no tongue to say,
What was; no dirge, except the hollow sea's,
Mourns o'er the beauty of the Cyclades.

EBEV

52 —The man who has stood on the Acropolis,
And look'd down over Attica; or he
Who has sailed where picturesque Constantinople is,
Or seen Timbuctoo, or hath taken tea
In small-eyed China'scrockery-ware metropolis,
Or sat amidst the bricks of Nineveh,
May not think much of London's first appearance —
But ask him what he thinks of it a year hence!

53 Here laws are all inviolate — none lay
Traps for the traveller — every highway's clear —
Here" — he was interrupted by a knife,
With — "Damn your eyes your money or your life!" —

InPS; OESV

Fare Thee Well

54 Fare thee well! and if for ever,
Still for ever, fare thee well: (l. 1–2)

BLPA; ErRP; FaFP; FPL; OBNC; PoEL-4

Maid of Athens

55 Maid of Athens, ere we part,
Give, oh, give me back my heart!
Or, since that has left my breast,
Keep it now, and take the rest! (l. 1–4)

EBEV; ErRP; FaBV; FaFP; PrIm

Oh! snatch'd away in beauty's bloom!

56 Oh! snatch'd away in beauty's bloom,
On thee shall press no ponderous tomb;
But on thy turf shall roses rear
Their leaves, the earliest of the year; (l. 1–4)

EnRP; FiP; GTBS; GTBS-P

On This Day I Complete My Thirty-sixth Year

57 My days are in the yellow leaf;
The flowers and fruits of Love are gone;
The worm, the canker, and the grief
Are mine alone! (l. 5–8)

EnRP; FiP; NAs; NoP; OAEL-2; OBWP; PoE

The Prisoner of Chillon

58 Eternal Spirit of the chainless Mind!
Brightest in dungeons, Liberty! thou art, (l. 1–2)

BeLS; EnRP; FiP; GTBS; GTBS-P; LiTB; PoLF; TrGrPo

Prometheus

59 Thy Godlike crime was to be kind,
To render with thy precepts less
The sum of human wretchedness,
And strengthen Man with his own mind; (l. 35–38)

60 Man is in part divine,
A troubled stream from a pure source;
And Man in portions can foresee
His own funereal destiny; (l. 47–50)

EnRP; HeIP; InPS; NOBE; NoP; OAEL-2

She Walks in Beauty

61 She walks in Beauty, like the night
Of cloudless climes and starry skies;
And all that's best of dark and bright
Meet in her aspect and her eyes:
Thus mellowed to that tender light
Which Heaven to gaudy day denies. (l. 1–6)

AWP; BLPA; BoLoP; ChER; ELP; EnRP; FaBoBe; FaFP;
FF; FiP; FPL; GTBS; GTBS-P; HeIP; InPS; LiTB; NAEL-
2; NIP; NOBE; NoP; OBEV; OBNC; PoE; PoEL-4; PrIm;
TrGrPo

So we'll go no more a-roving

62 So, we'll go no more a-roving
So late into the night, (l. 1–2)

63 For the sword outwears its sheath,
And the soul outwears the breast, (l. 5–6)

AWP; BLPL; BoLoP; CH; ELP; EnRP; FaBV; FaFP;
FaPoR; FF; FiP; HAP; HeIP; LiTB; NAEL-2; NOBE;
NoP; OAEL-2; OBEV; OxBS; OxBSP; PoE; PoEL-4;
PoLF; PoRA; PrIm; TrGrPo; TTTS; WeW

Stanzas for Music

64 There be none of beauty's daughters
With a magic like thee;
And like music on the waters
Is thy sweet voice to me:

AWP; ChER; ELP; EnRP; FiP; GTBS; GTBS-P; LiTB;
NAEL-2; NoP; OAEL-2; PoRA; TrGrPo

65 There's not a joy the world can give like that it takes
away,

EnRP; GTBS; GTBS-P; HAP

Stanzas Written on the Road between Florence and Pisa

66 Oh, talk not to me of a name great in story—
The days of our youth are the days of our glory;
(l. 1–2)

EnRP; GTBS; GTBS-P; NAEL-2

The Vision of Judgment

67 Saint Peter sat by the celestial gate:
His keys were rusty, and the lock was dull, (l. 1–2)

68 The angels all were singing out of tune,
And hoarse with having little else to do,
Excepting to wind up the sun and moon,
Or curb a runaway young star or two, (l. 9–12)

69 It seemed the mockery of hell to fold
The rottenness of eighty years in gold. (l. 79–80)

70 Except that household virtue, most uncommon,
Of constancy to a bad, ugly woman. (l. 95–96)

71 I know one may be damned
For hoping no one else may e'er be so; (l. 106–107)

EnRP; OAEL-2; OBSV; OxBoLi; TEP

When a man hath no freedom to fight for at home

72 When a man hath no freedom to fight for at home,
Let him combat for that of his neighbors;
Let him think of the glories of Greece and of Rome,
And get knocked on the head for his labors. (l. 1–4)

EnRP; FaBoEE; NAEL-2; NBLV; NoP; PoLF; TrGrPo

When we two parted

73 When we two parted
In silence and tears, (l. 1–2)

74 If I should meet thee
After long years,
How should I greet thee?
With silence and tears. (l. 29–32)

BoLoP; ChER; EnRP; FiP; FPL; GTBS; GTBS-P; HoPM;
NAEL-2; NOBE; NoP; OBEV; OBNC; PoLF; TrGrPo

Written after Swimming from Sestos to Abydos

75 Leander, who was nightly wont
(What maid will not the tale remember?)
To cross thy stream, broad Hellespont! (l. 2–4)

76 Sad mortals! thus the gods still plague you!
He lost his labor, I my jest;
For he was drowned, and I've the ague. (l. 18–20)

MOS; NAEL-2; NBLV; NoP; OBTV

"J. C." (fl. c. 1595)

Alcilia

1 These cheeks were wont more fresh and fair to be;
But now, what once made me so much admired
Is least regarded, and of none desired.' (l. 4–6)

ElL

CHARLES STUART CALVERLEY
(1831–1884)

The auld wife sat at her ivied door

1 The farmer's daughter hath soft brown hair;
(Butter and eggs and a pound of cheese)
And I met with a ballad, I can't say where,
Which wholly consisted of lines like these. (l. 21–24)

2 Her sheep follow'd her, as their tails did them.
(Butter and eggs and a pound of cheese)
And this song is consider'd a perfect gem,
And as to the meaning, it's what you please.
(l. 37–40)

BXAP; CenHV; FaBoCo; FiBHP; NA; NBLV; Par; WiR

Lines on Hearing the Organ

3 Grinder, who serenely grindest
At my door the Hundredth Psalm, (l. 1–2)

4 Tell me, Grinder, if thou grindest
Always, always out of tune. (l. 19–20)

5 'Tis not that thy mien is stately,
'Tis not that thy tones are soft; (l. 93–94)

6 But I've heard mankind abuse thee;
And perhaps it's rather strange,
But I thought that I would choose thee
For encomium, as a change. (l. 97–100)

CenHV; FaBoCo; FiBHP; NOBL

NORMAN CAMERON (b. 1905)

The Compassionate Fool

1 And even as he stabbed me through and through
I pitied him for his small strategy. (l. 11–12)

GTBS-P; OxBSP; OxBTC; RB

Forgive Me, Sire

2 I, who should command a regiment,
Do amble amiably here, O God,
One of the neat ones in your awkward squad. (l. 2–4)

FaBoEE; GTBS-P; OxBS; OxBSP

Green, Green Is El Aghir

3 Green, green is El Aghir . It has a railway station,
And the wealth of its soil has borne many another fruit:
A mairie, a school and an elegant Salle de Fetes.
Such blessings, as I remarked, in effect, to the waiter,
Are added unto them that have plenty of water.
(l. 24–28)

FaBoTw; MoBS; OEWP; OxBTC

ROY CAMPBELL (1902–1957)

Autumn

1 I love to see, when leaves depart,
The clear anatomy arrive, (l. 1–2)

2 the clanging chains
  of geese are harnessed to the moon: (l. 6–7)

GTBS-P; MoBrPo; OBMV; OxBTC

Horses on the Camargue

3 the white-crested fillies of the surge
  And the white horses of the windy plain. (l. 35–36)

4 out of hardship bred,
  Spirits of power and beauty and delight
  Have ever on such frugal pastures fed
  And loved to course with tempests through the night.
                                         (l. 45–48)

GTBS-P; OBTV; PeSA; SeCePo

On Some South African Novelists

5 They use the snaffle and the curb all right;
  But where's the bloody horse? (l. 3–4)

FaBoCo; FaBoEE; GTBS-P; InPK; MoBrPo; NOBL;
OxBTC

The Serf

6 The timeless, surly patience of the serf
  That moves the nearest to the naked earth
  And ploughs down palaces, and thrones, and towers.
                                         (l. 12–14)

GTBS-P; LiTB; MoBrPo; OBMV

The Sisters

7 Bored with the foolish things that girls must dream
  Because their beds are empty of delight, (l. 3–4)

8 The frost stings sweetly with a burning kiss
  As intimate as love, as cold as death: (l. 13–14)

BoLoP; ErPo; FaBoTw; OBMV

THOMAS CAMPBELL (1774–1844)
Battle of the Baltic

1 There was silence deep as death;
  And the boldest held his breath
  For a time. (l. 16–18)

2 'Ye are brothers! ye are men!
  And we conquer but to save: —
  So peace instead of death let us bring: (l. 39–41)

EnRP; FaPoR; GN; GTBS; GTBS-P; OBEV

Hohenlinden

3 On Linden, when the sun was low,
  All bloodless lay the untrodden snow,
  And dark as winter was the flow
  Of Iser, rolling rapidly. (l. 1–4)

4 Few, few shall part, where many meet!
  The snow shall be their winding sheet,
  And every turf, beneath their feet,
  Shall be a soldier's sepulchre. (l. 29–32)

BeLS; CH; ChTr; EnRP; FaBoCh; FaBoRV; FaPoR; GN;
GTBS; GTBS-P; NOBE; OBNC; OBWP; OnMSP; WaaP;
WBLP

Lord Ullin's Daughter

5 I'll meet the raging of the skies,
  But not an angry father.' (l. 35–36)

6 The waters wild went o'er his child,
  And he was left lamenting. (l. 55–56)

BeLS; BoTP; EnRP; FaPON; FaPoR; GN; GTBS; GTBS-
P; WBLP

The River of Life

7 It may be strange — yet who would change
  Time's course to slower speeding,
  When one by one our friends have gone
  And left our bosoms bleeding? (l. 17–20)

FaFP; GTBS; GTBS-P; LiTB; OBNC

The Soldier's Dream

8 And the sentinel stars set their watch in the sky; (l. 2)

9 'Stay — stay with us! — rest — thou art weary and
    worn!' —
  And fain was their war-broken soldier to stay; —
  But sorrow return'd with the dawning of morn,
  And the voice in my dreaming ear melted away.
                                         (l. 21–24)

BeLS; EnRP; FaPoR; GTBS; GTBS-P

Ye Mariners of England

10 Ye Mariners of England
That guard our native seas!
Whose flag has braved a thousand years
The battle and the breeze! (l. 1–4)

11 Britannia needs no bulwarks,
No towers along the steep;
Her march is o'er the mountain-waves,
Her home is on the deep. (l. 21–24)

BLPA; EnRP; FaPoR; GN; GTBS; GTBS-P; NOBE;
OBEV; OBWP

THOMAS CAMPION (1567–1620)

Follow Thy Fair Sun

1 Followe thy faire sunne, unhappy shadowe,
Though thou be blacke as night,
And she made all of light,
Yet follow thy faire sun, unhappie shadowe. (l. 1–4)

AAS; CH; ElL; ELP; EnLoPo; LiTB; NOBE; NoP;
OBEV; OBSC; PoEL-2; Prf; UnPo

Follow Your Saint

2 Follow your saint, follow with accents sweet;
Haste you, sad notes, fall at her flying feet.
There, wrapped in cloud of sorrow, pity move,
And tell the ravisher of my soul I perish for her love.
(l. 1–4)

AAS; EBEV; ElL; EnLoPo; HAP; NOBE; OAEL-1;
OBEV; OBSC; PoE; SeCePo; TrGrPo

Hark, All You Ladies

3 Hark, all you ladies that do sleep!
The fairy queen
Bids you awake, and pity them that weep.
You may do in the dark
What the day doth forbid.
Fear not the dogs that bark;
Night will have all hid. (l. 1–7)

4 The fairy queen
Bids you increase that loving humour more.
They that have not yet fed
On delight amorous,
She vows that they shall lead
Apes in Avernus. (l. 30–35)

AAS; EBEV; ElL; OBSC; PoEL-2

A Hymn in Praise of Neptune

5 And every sea-god pays a gem,
Yearly out of his watery cell,
To deck great Neptune's diadem. (l. 8–10)

BoNaP; MOS; NOBE; OBEV; OBSC; WiR

I Care Not for These Ladies

6 I care not for these ladies,
That must be wooed and prayed;
Give me kind Amaryllis,
The wanton country maid.
Nature art disdaineth;
Her beauty is her own. (l. 1–6)

7 "Forsooth, let go!"
But when we come where comfort is,
She never will say no. (l. 8–10)

AAS; ErPo; HAP; NAEL-1; NIP; NoP; OBSC; PoE

Jack and Joan they think no ill

8 Jack and Joan they think no ill,
But loving live, and merry still;
Do their week-days' work, and pray
Devoutly on the holy day,
Skip and trip it on the green,
And help to choose the Summer Queen; (l. 1–6)

9 Now you courtly dames and knights,
That study only strange delights,
Though you scorn the home-spun gray
And revel in your rich array;
Though your tongues dissemble deep
And can your heads from danger keep:
Yet for all your pomp and train,
Securer lives the silly swain. (l. 25–32)

AAS; FaBoCh; FaPoR; OBSC

Kind Are Her Answers

10 Kind are her answers,
But her performance keeps no day;
Breaks time, as dancers,
From their own music when they stray. (l. 1–4)

11 Lost is our freedom
When we submit to women so:
Why do we need 'em
When, in their best, they work our woe? (l. 10–13)

12 Never were days yet called two
But one night went betwixt. (l. 17–18)

BoLoP; ELP; OBSC; PoEL-2; TrGrPo

The Man of Life Upright

13 The man whose silent days
In harmless joys are spent,
Whom hopes cannot delude,
Nor sorrow discontent:

That man needs neither towers
Nor armour for defence,
Nor secret vaults to fly
From thunder's violence. (l. 5–12)

AAS; ElL; OBSC; PoRA

My Life's Delight

14 Love loves no delay; (l. 3)

15 Thou all sweetness dost enclose
Like a little world of bliss.
Beauty guards thy looks: the rose
In them pure and eternal is. (l. 7–10)

ElL; InvP; OBSC; TrGrPo

My Sweetest Lesbia

16 If all would lead their lives in love like me,
Then bloody swords and armor should not be;
No drum nor trumpet peaceful sleeps should move,
Unless alarm came from the camp of love. (l. 7–10)

AAS; AWP; EBEV; ElL; FF; GBL; HAP; HeIP; InPS;
NAEL-1; NIP; NoP; OAEL-1; OBSC; OBVE; PoE; PoRA;
PrIm; TEP; TrGrPo; WeW

Never Weather-beaten Sail

17 Never weather-beaten sail more willing bent to shore,
Never tired pilgrim's limbs affected slumber more,
Than my weary spright now longs to fly out of my
troubled breast.
O! come quickly, sweetest Lord, and take my soul to
rest. (l. 1–4)

ChTr; ElL; NOBE; OAEL-1; OBEV; OBSC; OxBSP;
PoEL-2

Now Winter Nights Enlarge

18 The summer hath his joys
And winter his delights;
Though love and all his pleasures are but toys,
They shorten tedious nights. (l. 21–24)

AAS; EBEV; ElL; ELP; HeIP; NoP; OBSC; QFR;
SeCePo; TEP

Rose-cheeked Laura, Come

19 Only beauty purely loving
Knows no discord,

But still moves delight,
Like clear springs renewed by flowing,
Ever perfect, ever in them-
Selves eternal. (l. 11–16)

AAS; ElL; EnLoPo; InPK; InPS; InvP; NAEL-1; NOBE;
NoP; OAEL-1; OBEV; OBSC; PoE; PoEL-2; SeCePo;
TrGrPo; UnS

Shall I Come, Sweet Love, to Thee?

20 Shall I come, sweet Love, to thee,
When the ev'ning beams are set? (l. 1–2)

21 But to let such dangers pass,
Which a lover's thoughts disdain,
'Tis enough in such a place
To attend love's joys in vain. (l. 13–16)

AAS; EBEV; ElL; GBL; HAP; NOBE; OBSC; OxBoLi;
PoEL-2

Sleep, Angry Beauty

22 Plead, Sleep, my cause, and make her soft like thee,
That she in peace may wake and pity me. (l. 11–12)

ElL; ErPo; FF; OxBSP; TrGrPo

There Is a Garden in Her Face

23 There is a garden in her face,
Where roses and white lilies grow;
A heavenly paradise is that place,
Wherein all pleasant fruits do flow. (l. 1–4)

24 Yet them nor peer nor prince can buy,
Till 'Cherry-ripe' themselves do cry. (l. 11–12)

AAS; ElL; ELP; GoJo; HeIP; InPK; NAEL-1; NIP; NoP;
OAEL-1; OBSC; OPOP; PoE; PoEL-2; PrIm; TrGrPo

Thou Art Not Fair

25 Thou art not fair, for all thy red and white,
For all those rosy ornaments in thee.
Thou art not sweet, though made of mere delight
(l. 1–3)

26 Thou shalt prove
That beauty is no beauty without love. (l. 5–6)

AAS; ElL; EnLoPo; InvP; OBSC

To Music Bent Is My Retired Mind

27 From heav'nly thoughts all true delight doth spring.
(l. 4)

AAS; NOCV; TrPWD; UnS

What Faire Pompe

28 now I discerne they goe on a Pilgrimage
Towards Loves holy land, faire Paphos or Cyprus.
Such devotion is meete for a blithesome age;
With sweet youth, it agrees well to be amorous.
Let olde angrie fathers lurke in an Hermitage:
Come, weele associate this jolly Pilgrimage! (l. 25–30)

GBL; OBSC; PoEL-2; Prf

What If a Day

29 Fortune, honour, beauty, youth,
Are but blossoms dying;
Wanton pleasures, doting love,
Are but shadows flying. (l. 5–8)

30 All our joys
Are but toys, (l. 9–10)

31 Secret fates
Guide our states
Both in mirth and mourning. (l. 26–28)

AAS; EBEV; ElL; PrIm

When Thou Must Home to Shades of Underground

32 Then tell, O! tell, how thou didst murder me. (l. 12)

AWP; ChTr; ElL; EnLoPo; NoP; OBSC; OxBSP; PoEL-2;
PoRA

GEORGE CANNING (1770–1827)

A Political Despatch

1 In matters of commerce the fault of the Dutch
Is offering too little and asking too much. (l. 1–2)

FaBoCo; OBTV; OxBoLi

THOMAS CAREW (1589–1639)

Ask Me No More Where Jove Bestows

1 Ask me no more where Jove bestows,
When June is past, the fading rose;
For in your beauty's orient deep
These flowers, as in their causes, sleep.

Ask me no more whither do stray
The golden atoms of the day;
For in pure love heaven did prepare
Those powders to enrich your hair. (l. 1–8)

AWP; CaPo; CH; ELP; EnLoPo; FaFP; GBL; HAP; HeIP;
HoPM; InPS; LiTB; MeLP; MePo; NAEL-1; NOBE; NoP;
OBEV; OBS; PoE; PoEL-3; PoRA; PPP; SeCePo; SeCP;
SeCV-1; TEP; TrGrPo

Boldness in Love

2 But when with moving accents thou
Shalt constant faith and service vow,
Thy Celia shall receive those charms
With open ears, and with unfolded arms. (l. 13–16)

CaPo; ErPo; MePo; SeCV-1

An Elegy upon the Death of the Dean of St. Paul's, Dr. John Donne

3 Since to the awe of thy imperious wit
Our troublesome language bends, made only fit
With her tough thick-ribbed hoops to gird about
Thy giant fancy, which had proved too stout
For their soft melting phrases. (l. 48–52)

4 Here lies a King that ruled as he thought fit
The universal monarchy of wit;
Here lies two flamens, and both those the best,
Apollo's first, at last the true God's priest. (l. 93–96)

CaPo; JCP; MeLP; MePo; NoP; OAEL-1; OBS; SeCP;
SeCV-1

Epitaph on the Lady Mary Villiers

5 The Lady Mary Villiers lies
Under this stone; with weeping eyes
The parents that first gave her birth,
And their sad friends, laid her in earth. (l. 1–4)

6 For thou perhaps at thy return
May'st find thy Darling in an urn. (l. 11–12)

CaPo; FaBoEE; NOBE; OBEV; SeCV-1

Ingrateful Beauty Threatened

7 Know Celia, (since thou art so proud),
'Twas I that gave thee thy renowne:
Thou hadst, in the forgotten crowd
Of common beauties, liv'd unknowne,
Had not my verse exhal'd thy name,
And with it, ympt the wings of fame. (l. 1–6)

CaPo; InvP; MeLP; OBEV; OBS; SeCP; SeCV-1

Maria Wentworth

8 And here the precious dust is layd;
Whose purely temper'd Clay was made
So fine, that it the guest betray'd.

Else the soule grew so fast within,
It broke the outward shell of sinne,
And so was hatch'd a Cherubin. (l. 1–6)

CaPo; JCP; MeLP; MePo; OBD; OBS; SeCV-1

Persuasions to Enjoy

9 If the quick spirits in your eye
Now languish and anon must die; (l. 1–2)

10 Then, Celia, let us reap our joys
Ere Time such goodly fruit destroys. (l. 5–6)

11 Thus either Time his sickle brings
In vain, or else in vain his wings. (l. 13–14)

CaPo; MePo; NAEL-1; NOBE; OBEV; SeCP; SeCV-1

A Rapture

12 There shall the Queens of Love and Innocence,
Beauty, and Nature banish all offense
From our close ivy twines, there I'll behold
Thy bared snow and thy unbraided gold.
There my enfranchised hand on every side
Shall o'er thy naked polished ivory slide. (l. 25–30)

13 All things are lawful there that may delight
Nature or unrestrained appetite.
Like and enjoy, to will and act is one;
We only sin when love's rites are not done.
                              (l. 111–114)

CaPo; ErPo; JCP; NAEL-1; OAEL-1; SeCP

The Spring

14 Welcome the comming of the long'd-for May.
Now all things smile; onely my Love doth lowre;
Nor hath the scalding noon-day sunne the power
To melt that marble yce, which still doth hold
Her heart congeal'd, and makes her pittie cold.
                              (l. 12–16)

15 Time with the season: only shee doth carry
June in her eyes, in her heart January. (l. 23–24)

CaPo; GN; NoP; PoE; PoEL-3; SeCV-1; TEP; TrGrPo;
WiR

To a Lady That Desired I Would Love Her

16 Then give me leave to love, & love me too
Not with designe
To raise, as Loves curst Rebels doe,
When puling Poets whine,
Fame to their beauty, from their blubbr'd eyn.
                              (l. 11–15)

CaPo; MeLP; MePo; OBS; SeCV-1

To My Inconstant Mistress

17 When thou, poor Excommunicate
From all the joys of love, shalt see
The full reward and glorious fate
Which my strong faith shall purchase me,
Then curse thine own inconstancy! (l. 1–5)

CaPo; EnLoPo; GBL; JCP; MeLP; MePo; NOBE; NoP;
OBEV; OBS; SeCePo; SeCP; SeCV-1; TrGrPo

To My Worthy Friend Master George Sands, on His Translation of the Psalms

18 I press not to the quire, nor dare I greet
The holy place with my unhallowed feet;
My unwashed Muse pollutes not things divine,
Nor mingles her profaner notes with thine;
Here humbly at the porch she listening stays,
And with glad ears sucks in thy sacred lays. (l. 1–6)

CaPo; JCP; MeLP; MePo; OBS; SeCV-1

To Saxham

19 Yet, Saxham, thou within thy gate
Art of thyself so delicate,
So full of native sweets that bless
Thy roof with inward happiness,
As neither from nor to thy store
Winter takes aught, or spring adds more. (l. 5–10)

20 Those cheerful beams send forth their light (l. 35)

21 The weary pilgrim to thy roof;
Where if, refresh'd, he will away,
He's fairly welcome; or if stay,
Far more; which he shall hearty find
Both from the master and the hind. (l. 38–42)

CaPo; JCP; NoP; OBS

HENRY CAREY (1693?–1743)

Namby-Pamby; or, A Panegyric on the New Versification

1 Naughty Paughty Jack-a-Dandy,
Stole a Piece of Sugar Candy
From the Grocer's Shoppy-Shop,
And away did hoppy-hop. (l. 1–4)

2 All ye poets of the age,
  All ye witlings of the stage,
  Learn your jingles to reform,
  Crop your numbers to conform.
  Let your little verses flow
  Gently, sweetly, row by row;
  Let the verse the subject fit,
  Little subject, little wit.
  Namby-Pamby is your guide,
  Albion's joy, Hibernia's pride. (l. 5–14)

3 Now he sings of Jacky Horner,
  Sitting in the chimney corner,
  Eating of a Christmas pie,
  Putting in his thumb, O fie!
  Putting in, O fie! his thumb,
  Pulling out, O strange, a plum. (l. 63–68)

FaBoNo; FaBoPa; NOEC; OBSV; Par

Sally in Our Alley

4 Of all the girls that are so smart
  There's none like pretty Sally;
  She is the darling of my heart,
  And she lives in our alley. (l. 1–4)

5 But when my seven long years are out,
  O, then I'll marry Sally;
  O, then we'll wed, and then we'll bed —
  But not in our alley! (l. 53–56)

AnAmPo; AWP; BLPL; BoLoP; CoMu; FaBoBe; FaFP;
GTBS; GTBS-P; NOBE; NOEC; OBEV

BLISS CARMAN (1861–1929)

Lord of My Heart's Elation

1 Lord of my heart's elation,
  Spirit of things unseen,
  Be thou my aspiration
  Consuming and serene! (l. 1–4)

2 Be thou my exaltation
  Or fortitude of mien,
  Lord of the world's elation,
  Thou breath of things unseen! (l. 21–24)

AH; NOBC; OBCV; TrPWD

JULIA A. FLETCHER CARNEY
(1823–1908)

Little Things (attributed to Carney)

1 Little drops of water,
  Little grains of sand,
  Make the mighty ocean
  And the beauteous land. (l. 1–4)

2 Little deeds of kindness,
  Little words of love,
  Make our earth an Eden,
  Like the heaven above. (l. 13–16)

BLPA; BLPL; FaBoBe; FaFP; FaPON; OxBChV

"LEWIS CARROLL" (pseudonym of CHARLES LUTWIDGE DODGSON)
(1832–1898)

Alice's Adventures in Wonderland

1 'Tis the voice of the Lobster; I heard him declare,
  'You have baked me too brown, I must sugar my hair.'

FaBoCo; FaBoNo; NOBL; OxBChV; Par

2 Speak roughly to your little boy,
  And beat him when he sneezes:
  He only does it to annoy,
  Because he knows it teases.

FaBoCh; FaBoCo; FaBoNo; NBLV; Par; RHPC

3 They told me you had been to her,
  And mentioned me to him:
  She gave me a good character,
  But said I could not swim.

4 Don't let him know she liked them best,
  For this must ever be
  A secret kept from all the rest,
  Between yourself and me.

FaBoCo; FaBoNo; FaFP; GTBS-P; NOBVV; OxBoLi

5 "You are old, Father William," the young man said,
  "And your hair has become very white;
  And yet you incessantly stand on your head —
  Do you think, at your age, it is right?"

6 "In my youth," said his father, "I took to the law,
  And argued each case with my wife;
  And the muscular strength, which it gave to my jaw,
  Has lasted the rest of my life."

7 "I have answered three questions, and that is enough,"
  Said his father; "don't give yourself airs!
  Do you think I can listen all day to such stuff?
  Be off, or I'll kick you downstairs!"

BXAP; FaBoCo; FaBoNo; FaBoPa; FaPON; FiBHP; FPL;
GoJo; HoPM; LiTB; NOBL; NOBVV; OxBChV; Par;
PDV; PoLF; PoRA; RHPC; TrGrPo; UnPo

8 How doth the little crocodile
  Improve his shining tail,

9 How cheerfully he seems to grin,
How neatly spreads his claws,

FaBoCh; FaBoCo; FaBoEE; FaBoNo; FaFP; FaPON;
HoPM; MoShBr; NBLV; NOBL; NOBVV; Par; RB;
RHPC; TrGrPo; TTTS

10 "Will you walk a little faster?" said a whiting to a snail,
"There's a porpoise close behind us, and he's treading
on my tail.

BoTP; ChTr; FaBoNo; FaPON; MoShBr; NoAM;
OxBChV; Par; RR

The Hunting of the Snark

11 "Just the place for a Snark!" the Bellman cried,
As he landed his crew with care;
Supporting each man on the top of the tide
By a finger entwined in his hair. (l. 1–4)

12 The crew was complete: it included a Boots —
A maker of Bonnets and Hoods —
A Barrister, brought to arrange their disputes —
And a Broker, to value their goods. (l. 9–12)

13 A Billiard-marker, whose skill was immense, (l. 13)

14 But a Banker, engaged at enormous expense, (l. 15)

15 There was also a Beaver, that paced on the deck,
(l. 17)

16 He had forty-two boxes, all carefully packed,
With his name painted clearly on each:
But, since he omitted to mention the fact,
They were all left behind on the beach. (l. 25–28)

17 This was charming, no doubt: but they shortly found
out
That the Captain they trusted so well
Had only one notion for crossing the ocean,
And that was to tingle his bell. (l. 105–108)

18 'Friends, Romans, and countrymen, lend me your ears!'
(They were all of them fond of quotations:
So they drank to his health, and they gave him three
cheers,
While he served out additional rations). (l. 133–136)

19 They roused him with muffins — they roused him with
ice —
They roused him with mustard and cress —
They roused him with jam and judicious advice —
They set him conundrums to guess. (l. 173–176)

20 And my heart is like nothing so much as a bowl
Brimming over with quivering curds! (l. 215–216)

21 'You may charge me with murder — or want of sense —
(We are all of us weak at times):
But the slightest approach to a false pretence
Was never among my crimes! (l. 241–244)

22 'I said it in Hebrew — I said it in Dutch —
I said it in German and Greek;
But I wholly forgot (and it vexes me much)
That English is what you speak! (l. 245–248)

23 In his genial way he proceeded to say
(Forgetting all laws of propriety,
And that giving instruction, without introduction,
Would have caused quite a thrill in Society),
(l. 377–380)

24 They sought it with thimbles, they sought it with care;
They pursued it with forks and hope;
They threatened its life with a railway-share;
They charmed it with smiles and soap. (l. 417–420)

25 He dreamed that he stood in a shadowy Court,
Where the Snark, with a glass in its eye,
Dressed in gown, bands, and wig, was defending a pig
On the charge of deserting its sty. (l. 425–428)

26 The indictment had never been clearly expressed,
And it seemed that the Snark had begun,
And had spoken three hours, before any one guessed
What the pig was supposed to have done. (l. 433–436)

27 So the Snark found the verdict, although as it owned,
It was spent with the toils of the day:
When it said the word 'GUILTY!' the Jury all groaned,
And some of them fainted away. (l. 465–468)

28 To the horror of all who were present that day,
He uprose in full evening dress,
And with senseless grimaces endeavoured to say
What his tongue could no longer express. (l. 517–520)

FaBoNo; FiBHP; NA; OBNC; OBNV; OnMSP; PoEL-5

Sylvie and Bruno

29 He thought he saw an Elephant,
That practiced on a fife:
He looked again, and found it was
A letter from his wife.
"At length I realize," he said,
"The bitterness of Life!"

30 He thought he saw an Argument
That proved he was the Pope:
He looked again, and found it was
A Bar of Mottled Soap.

BLPL; FaBoCo; FaBoNo; FiBHP; NA; OnUR; OxBChV;
WiR

Through the Looking-Glass

31 In winter, when the fields are white,
 I sing this song for your delight —

32 In spring, when woods are getting green,
 I'll try and tell you what I mean:

33 In summer, when the days are long,
 Perhaps you'll understand the song:

34 In autumn, when the leaves are brown,
 Take pen and ink, and write it down.

 ChTr; EBEV; FaBoCo; FaBoNo; FiBHP; GTBS-P; Mes;
 NOBVV; OnMSP; OxBChV; OxBoLi

35 'Twas brillig, and the slithy toves
 Did gyre and gimble in the wabe;
 All mimsy were the borogoves,
 And the mome raths outgrabe.

 "Beware the Jabberwock, my son!
 The jaws that bite, the claws that catch!

36 O frabjous day! Callooh! Callay!"
 He chortled in his joy.

 AmMo; EBEV; EBVV; FaBoBe; FaBoCo; FaBoNo; FaBV;
 FaFP; FaPON; FF; FiBHP; FPL; GoJo; HeIP; HoPM;
 InPK; InPS; LiTB; NA; NAEL-2; NBLV; NIP; NoAM;
 NOBE; NOBL; NOBVV; NoP; NTCP; OAEL-2; OPOP;
 OxBChV; PoRA; PPP; RB; RHPC; TEP; TTTS

37 The sun was shining on the sea,
 Shining with all his might:
 He did his very best to make
 The billows smooth and bright —
 And this was odd, because it was
 The middle of the night. (l. 1–6)

38 The Walrus and the Carpenter
 Were walking close at hand:
 They wept like anything to see
 Such quantities of sand: (l. 19–22)

39 "The time has come," the Walrus said,
 "To talk of many things:
 Of shoes — and ships — and sealing wax —
 Of cabbages — and kings —
 And why the sea is boiling hot —
 And whether pigs have wings." (l. 61–66)

40 "A loaf of bread," the Walrus said,
 "Is what we chiefly need: (l. 73–74)

 BeLS; BLPA; FaBoBe; FaBoCo; FaBoNo; FaBV; FaFP;
 FaPON; FiBHP; FPL; GN; LiTB; NAEL-2; NA; NoAM;
 NOBL; NOBVV; OxBChV; PoRA; TEP

41 So, having no reply to give
 To what the old man said,
 I cried, 'Come, tell me how you live!'
 And thumped him on the head.

42 But I was thinking of a way
 To feed oneself on batter,
 And so go on from day to day
 Getting a little fatter.

 BXAP; FaBoCh; FaBoCo; FaBoNo; FaBoPa; FiBHP;
 HAP; InPS; InvF; NA; NAEL-2; NoAM; NOBE; NOBL;
 NoP; OAEL-2; OxBChV; Par; PoRA

WILLIAM HERBERT CARRUTH
(1859–1929)

Each in His Own Tongue

1 A jellyfish and a saurian,
 And caves where the cave men dwell;
 Then a sense of law and beauty,
 And a face turned from the clod —
 Some call it Evolution,
 And others call it God. (l. 3–8)

2 Socrates drinking the hemlock,
 And Jesus on the rood,
 And millions who, humble and nameless,
 The straight, hard pathway plod —
 Some call it Consecration,
 And others call it God. (l. 27–32)

 BLPA; OHFP; WBLP; WGRP

CHARLES EDWARD CARRYL
(1841–1920)

The Admiral's Caravan

1 there's never a question
 About my digestion —
 Anything does for me. (l. 5–7)

2 a camel comes handy
 Wherever it's sandy —
 Anywhere does for me. (l. 19–21)

3 But a camel's all lumpy
 And bumpy and humpy —
 Any shape does for me. (l. 33–35)

 FaPON; OBCA; OxBChV; RHPC

Davy and the Goblin

4 The night was thick and hazy
When the "Piccadilly Daisy"
Carried down the crew and captain in the sea;
And I think the water downed 'em;
For they never, never found 'em,
And I know they didn't come ashore with me.

5 I live on toasted lizards,
Prickly pears, and parrot gizzards,
And I'm really very fond of beetle-pie.

6 We take along a carrot
As refreshment for the parrot,
And a little can of jungleberry tea.

7 we carry home as prizes
Funny bugs, of handy sizes,
Just to give the day a scientific tone.

AA; BeLS; FiBHP; PoRA

8 Oh, a capital ship for an ocean trip,
Was the Walloping Window Blind;
No gale that blew dismayed her crew
Or troubled the captain's mind.

9 The boatswain's mate was very sedate,
Yet fond of amusement, too;
And he played hopscotch with the starboard watch,
While the captain tickled the crew.

10 The captain sat in a commodore's hat
And dined in a royal way
On toasted pigs and pickles and figs
And gummery bread each day.

11 we cast the vessel ashore
On the Gulliby Isles where the Pooh-pooh smiles,
And the Rumbletum bunders roar.

FaPON; MoShBr; NA; NBLV; OBAL; OBCA

WILLIAM CARTWRIGHT (1611–1643)

No Platonic Love

1 I was that silly thing that once was wrought
To practise this thin love;
I climbed from sex to soul, from soul to thought;
But thinking there to move,
Headlong I rolled from thought to soul, and then
From soul I lighted at the sex again. (l. 7–12)

ErPo; GBL; InvP; JCP; LiTB; OAEL-1; PoEL-2

To Chloe, Who Wished Herself Young Enough for Me

2 There are two births: the one when light
First strikes the new awakened sense;
The other when two souls unite,
And we must count our life from thence,
When you loved me and I loved you,
Then both of us were born anew. (l. 7–12)

JCP; LiTB; MePo; OBS

ADELBERT VON CHAMISSO (1781–1838)

A Tragic Story

1 There lived a sage in days of yore,
And he a handsome pigtail wore;
But wondered much, and sorrowed more,
Because it hung behind him. (l. 1–4)

BoTP; FaPON; MoShBr; OnMSP

ARTHUR CHAPMAN (1873–1935)

Out Where the West Begins

1 Out where the hand-clasp's a little stronger,
Out where the smile dwells a little longer,
That's where the West begins; (l. 1–3)

2 Where there's more of singing and less of sighing,
Where there's more of giving and less of buying,
And a man makes friends without half trying
That's where the West begins. (l. 18–21)

AiP; BLPA; FaBoBe; FaFP

GEORGE CHAPMAN (1559?–1634)

A Coronet for His Mistress Philosophy

1 The majesty and riches of the mind,
But dwell in darkness; for your God is blind.

ElL; OBSC; SeCePo; Son

CHARLEMAGNE (742?–814) *AND* HRABANUS MAURUS (1631–1700)

Veni Creator Spiritus (*attributed to* Charlemagne *and to* Hrabanus Maurus)

1 Make us eternal truths receive,
And practice all that we believe:
Give us thyself, that we may see

The Father and the Son, by thee. (l. 30–33)

AWP; FaPoR; SeCV-2; WGRP

THOMAS CHATTERTON (1752–1770)

Aella; a Tragycal Enterlude

1 Mie love ys dedde,
Gon to hys death-bedde,
Al under the wyllowe tree.

Waterre wytches, crownede wythe reytes,
Bere mee to yer leathalle tyde.
I die; I comme; mie true love waytes.
Thos the damselle spake, and dyed. (l. 54–60)

CH; EnLoPo; EnRP; HAP; LiTB; Mes; NOBE; NOEC;
OBEV; TrGrPo; WiR

An Excelente Balade of Charitie

2 Liste! now the thunder's rattling clymmynge sound
Cheves slowlie on, and then embollen clangs,
Shakes the hie spyre, and losst, dispended, drown'd.
Still on the gallard eare of terroure hanges;
The windes are up; the lofty elmen swanges;
Again the levynne and the thunder poures,
And the full cloudes are braste attenes in stonen
    showers. (l. 36–42)

EBEV; EnRP; LiTB; NOEC; SeCePo

GEOFFREY CHAUCER (1340?–1400)

Balade de Bon Conseill

1 Flee from the press and dwell with soothfastness;
Suffice unto thy good though it be small,
For hoard hath hate and climbing ticklishness,
Press hath envy and weal blent overall;

2 Hold the high way and let they ghost thee lead
And Truthe shall deliver, it is no dread.

ACP; AWP; MeEL; NAEL-1; NoP; OAEL-1; TrGrPo

THE CANTERBURY TALES *(the following 7 poems)*

General Prologue

3 Whan that Aprill with his shoures soote
The droghte of March hath perced to the roote,
And bathed every veyne in swich licour
Of which vertu engendred is the flour;

Whan Zephirus eek with his sweete breeth
Inspired hath in every holt and heeth (l. 1–6)

4 the yonge sonne
Hath in the Ram his halfe cours yronne,
And smale foweles maken melodye,
That slepen al the nyght with open eye —
So priketh hem nature in hir corages —
Thanne longen folk to goon on pilgrimages, (l. 7–12)

5 And specially from every shires ende
Of Engelond to Caunterbury they wende
The hooly blisful martir for to seke
That hem hath holpen whan that they were seeke.
                                                    (l. 15–18)

6 in that seson on a day
In Southwerk at the Tabard as I lay
Redy to wenden on my pilgrymage
To Caunterbury with ful devout corage,
At nyght was come into that hostelrye
Wel nyne and twenty in a compaignye (l. 19–24)

7 A knyght ther was, and that a worthy man,
That fro the tyme that he first bigan
To riden out, he loved chivalrie,
Trouthe and honour, fredom and curteisie.
Ful worthy was he in his lordes werre,
And therto hadde he riden, no man ferre,
As wel in cristendom as in hethenesse,
And evere honoured for his worthynesse. (l. 43–50)

8 With hym ther was his sone, a yong squier,
A lovyere and a lusty bacheler,
With lokkes crulle as they were leyd in presse.
Of twenty yeer of age he was, I gesse.
Of his stature he was of evene lengthe,
And wonderly delyvere, and of greet strengthe.
                                                    (l. 79–84)

9 And born hym weel, as of so litel space,
In hope to stonden in his lady grace.
Embrouded was he, as it were a meede
Al ful of fresshe floures, whyte and reede.
Syngynge he was or floytynge al the day.
He was as fressh as in the monthe of May. (l. 87–92)

10 Short was his gowne, with sleves longe and wyde.
Wel koude he sitte on hors and faire ryde. (l. 93–94)

11 Curteis he was, lowely, and servysable,
And carf biforn his fader at the table. (l. 99–100)

12 A yeman hadde he and servantz namo
At that tyme, for hym liste ride so,
And he was clad in cote and hood of grene.
                                                    (l. 101–103)

13 There was also a Nonne, a prioresse,
That of hir smylyng was ful symple and coy;
Hire gretteste ooth was but by Seint Loy.
And she was cleped madame Eglentyne. (l. 118–121)

14 Ful weel she soong the service dyvyne,
Entuned in hir nose ful semely,
And Frenssh she spak ful faire and fetisly,
After the scole of Stratford atte Bowe,
For Frenssh of Parys was to hire unknowe.
(l. 122–126)

15 She leet no morsel from hir lippes falle,
Ne wette hir fyngres in hir sauce depe.
Wel koude she carie a morsel and wel kepe
That no drope ne fille upon hire brest.
In curteisie was set ful muchel hir lest. (l. 128–132)

16 She was so charitable and so pitous
She wolde wepe, if that she saugh a mous
Kaught in a trappe, if it were deed or bledde.
(l. 143–145)

17 Of smale houndes hadde she that she fedde
With rosted flessh, or milk and wastel-breed.
But soore wepte she if oon of hem were deed,
Or if men smoot it with a yerde smerte —
And al was conscience and tendre herte. (l. 146–150)

18 A monk ther was, a fair for the maistrie,
An outridere, that lovede venerie,
A manly man, to been an abbot able. (l. 165–167)

19 whan he rood, men myghte his brydel heere
Gynglen in a whistlynge wynd als cleere
And eek as loude as dooth the chapel belle.
(l. 169–171)

20 A frere ther was, a wantowne and a merye,
A lymytour, a ful solempne man.
In alle the ordres foure is noon that kan
So muchel of daliaunce and fair langage.
He hadde maad ful many a mariage
Of yonge wommen at his owene cost.
Unto his ordre he was a noble post. (l. 208–214)

21 A marchant was therwith a forked berd,
In mottelee, and hye on horse he sat,
Upon his heed a Flaundryssh bevere hat,
His bootes clasped faire and fetisly.
His resons he spak ful solempnely, (l. 272–276)

22 A clerk ther was of Oxenford also
That unto logyk hadde longe ygo.
As leene was his hors as is a rake,
And he nas nat right fat, I undertake,
But looked holwe, and therto sobrely. (l. 287–291)

23 For hym was levere have at his beddes heed

24 A sergeant of the lawe, war and wys,
That often hadde been at the Parvys,
Ther was also, ful riche of excellence. (l. 311–313)

25 A frankeleyn was in his compaignye. (l. 333)

26 An haberdasshere and a carpenter,
A webbe, a dyere, and a tapycer,
And they were clothed alle in o lyveree
Of a solempne and a greet fraternitee. (l. 363–366)

27 A cook they hadde with hem for the nones
To boille the chiknes with the marybones.
(l. 381–382)

28 A shipman was ther, wonynge fer by weste.
For aught I woot, he was of Dertemouthe.
(l. 390–391)

29 With us ther was a doctour of phisik;
In al this world ne was ther noon hym lik,
To speke of phisik and of a surgerye,
For he was grounded in astronomye. (l. 413–416)

30 He kepte that he wan in pestilence,
For gold in phisik is a cordial;
Therefore he lovede gold in special. (l. 444–446)

31 A good wif was ther ofbiside bathe,
But she was somde, deef, and that was scathe.
Of clooth makyng the hadde swich an haunt,
She passed hem of Ypres and of Gaunt. (l. 447–450)

32 Boold was hir face, and fair, and reed of hewe.
She was a worthy womman al hir lyve.
Housbondes at chirche dore she hadde fyve,
Withouten oother compaignye in youthe —
But therof nedeth nat to speke as nowthe.
(l. 460–464)

33 A good man was ther of religioun,
And was a poure persoun of a toun,
But riche he was of hooly thoght and werk.
He was also a lerned man, a clerk,
That Cristes gospel trewely wolde preche.
His parisshens devoutly wolde he teche. (l. 479–484)

34 This noble ensample to his sheep he yaf,
That first he wroghte, and afterward he taughte.
Out of the gospel he tho wordes caughte,
And this figure he added eek therto,
That if gold ruste, what shal iren do? (l. 498–502)

35 A bettre preest I trowe that nowher noon ys.
He waited after no pompe and reverence
Ne maked hym a spiced conscience,
But Cristes loore and his apostles twelve
He taughte, but first he folwed it hymselve.
(l. 526–530)

36 With hym ther was a plowman, was his brother,
That hadde ylad of dong ful many a fother.
(l. 531–532)

37 The millere was a stout carl for the nones; (l. 547)

38 His berd as any sowe or fox was reed,
And therto brood, as though it were a spade.
Upon the cop right of his nose he hade
A werte, and theron stood a toft of herys
Reed as the brustles of a sowes erys.
His nosethirles blake were and wyde. (l. 554–559)

39 A gentil maunciple was ther of a temple,
Of which achatours myghte take exemple
For to be wise in byynge of vitaille. (l. 569–571)

40 The reve was a sclendre colerik man.
His berd was shave as ny as ever he kan. (l. 589–590)

41 A somonour was ther with us in that place
That hadde a fyr-reed cherubynnes face,
For sawcefleem he was, with eyen narwe.
As hoot he was and lecherous as a sparwe,
                    (l. 625–628)

42 With hym ther rood a gentil pardoner
Of Rouncivale, his freend and his compeer,
That streight was comen fro the court of Rome.
                    (l. 671–673)

43 This Pardoner hadde heer as yelow as wex,
But smothe it heeng as dooth a strike of flex.
                    (l. 677–678)

44 ech of yow, to shorte with oure weye,
In this viage shal telle tales tweye
To Caunterbury-ward, I mene it so,
And homward he shal tellen othere two,
Of aventures that whilom han bifalle. (l. 793–797)

NoP; OAEL-1; PPP

The Knight's Tale

45 But in the dome of mighty Mars the red,

46 Heaven froze above, severe; the clouds congeal,
And through the crystal vault appeared the standing
hail.

47 There saw I how the secret felon wrought,
And treason labouring in the traitor's thought,
And midwife Time the ripened plot to murder brought.

48 There was the murdered corpse, in covert laid,
And violent death in thousand shapes displayed;
The city to the soldier's rage resigned;
Successless wars, and poverty behind;
Ships burnt in fight, or forced on rocky shores,
And the rash hunter strangled by the boars;
The newborn babe by nurses overlaid;
And the cook caught within the raging fire he made.

The Miller's Tale

49 This carpenter hadde wedded newe a wif
Which that he loved more than his lif.

50 Jalous he was, and heeld hire narwe in cage,
For she was wilde and yong, and he was old,

51 Men sholde wedden after hir estat,
For youthe and elde is often at debat.

52 She was so propre and sweete and likerous,
I dar wel sayn, if she hadde been a mous,
And he a cat, he wolde hire hente anoon.

53 on a Saterday
This carpenter was goon til Oseney,
And hende Nicholas and Alisoun
Accorded been to this conclusioun,
That Nicholas shal shapen hem a wile
This sely jalous housbonde to bigile,

54 I have yfounde in myn astrologye,
As I have looked in the moone bright,
That now a Monday next, at quarter night,
Shal falle a rain, and that so wilde and wood,
That half so greet was nevere Noees flood.

55 "Hastou nat herd," quod Nicholas, "also
The sorwe of Noee with his felaweshipe?"

56 Lo, which a greet thing is affeccioun!
Men may dien of imaginacioun,
So deepe may impression be take.

57 Whan that the firste cok hath crowe, anoon
Up rist this joly lovere Absolon,
And him arrayeth gay at point devis.
But first he cheweth grain and licoris,
To smellen sweete, er he hadde kembd his heer.

58 I have swich love-longinge,
That lik a turtle trewe is my moorninge:
I may nat ete namore than a maide."

59 Derk was the night as pich or as the cole,
And at the windowe out she putte hir hole,
And Absolon, him fil no bet ne wers,
But with his mouth he kiste hir naked ers,

60 Abak he sterte, and thoughte it was amis,
For wel he wiste a womman hath no beerd.

61 "Teehee," quod she, and clapte the windowe to.
And Absolon gooth forth a sory pas.
"A beerd, a beerd!" quod hende Nicholas,
"By Goddes corpus, this gooth faire and weel."

62 This Nicholas was risen for to pisse,
And thoughte he wolde amenden al the jape:
He sholde kisse his ers er that he scape.
And up the windowe dide he hastily,
And out his ers he putteth prively,
Over the buttok to the haunche-boon.

63　This Nicholas anoon leet flee a fart
　　As greet as it hadde been a thonder-dent

64　And he was redy with his iren hoot,
　　And Nicholas amidde the ers he smoot:

　　NAEL-1; NAWM-1; OAEL-1; OxBoLi; TEP

The Nun's Priest's Tale

65　A poore widow, some deal stape in age,
　　Was whilom dwelling in a narrow cottage,
　　Beside a grove, standing in a dale.

66　she had a cock, hight Chanticleer.
　　In all the land, of crowing n'as his peer;
　　His voice was merrier than the merry organ
　　On masse-days that in the churche gone.
　　Well sikerer was his crowing in his lodge
　　Than is a clock or an abbey horologe.

67　We all desiren, if it mighte be,
　　To han husbandes hardy, wise, and free,
　　And secret, and no niggard, ne no fool,
　　Ne him that is aghast of every tool,
　　Ne none avaunter, by that God above!

68　Certes this dream, which ye han met tonight,
　　Cometh of the great superfluity
　　Of your redde colera,

69　Right as the humour of melancholy
　　Causeth full many a man in sleep to cry
　　For fear of blacke bears, or bulles black,
　　Or elles blacke devils will them take.

70　'O blissful God, that art so just and true,
　　Lo, how that thou bewrayest murder alway!
　　Murder will out, that see we day by day.
　　Murder is so wlatsom and abominable

71　Murder will out, this my conclusion.

72　Macrobius, that writ the avision
　　In Afrique of the worthy Scipio,
　　Affirmeth dreams, and sayeth that they been
　　Warning of thinges that men after seen.

73　Read eek of Joseph, and there shall ye see
　　Where dreames ben sometime — I say not all —
　　Warning of thinges that shall after fall.

74　Whoso will seeken acts of sundry realms
　　May read of dreames many a wonder thing.

75　when I see the beauty of your face,
　　Ye been so scarlet red about your eyen,
　　It maketh all my dreade for to dyen;

76　"Woman is mannes joy and all his bliss."
　　For when I feel a-night your softe side,
　　Albeit that I may not on you ride,
　　For that our perch is made so narrowe, alas!
　　I am so full of joy and of solace
　　That I defye bothe sweven and dream.'

77　Madame Pertelote, my worldes bliss,
　　Harkneth these blissful birdes how they sing,
　　And see the freshe flowers how they spring;
　　Full is mine heart of revel and solace!'
　　But suddenly him fell a sorrowful case,
　　For ever the latter end of joy is woe.

78　My tale is of a cock, as ye may hear,
　　That took his counsel of his wife, with sorrow,
　　To walken in the yard upon that morrow
　　That he had met the dream that I you told.
　　Womenes counsels been full ofte cold;

79　Alas! ye lordes, many a false flatterer
　　Is in your courts, and many a losenger,
　　That pleasen you well more, by my faith,
　　Than he that soothfastness unto you saith.
　　Readeth Ecclesiasticus of flattery;
　　Beeth ware, ye lordes of her treachery.

80　They yelleden as fiendes doon in hell;
　　The duckes cryden as men would them quell;
　　The geese for feare flewen over the trees;
　　Out of the hive came the swarm of bees.

81　So hideous was the noise, ah! benedicite!
　　Certes, he Jacke Straw and his meinie
　　Ne made never shoutes half so shrill
　　When that they woulden any Fleming kill,
　　As thilke day was made upon the fox.

82　But yet that holden this tale a folly,
　　As of a fox, or of a cock and hen,
　　Taketh the morality, good men.
　　For Saint Paul saith that all that written is,
　　To our doctrine it is y-writ, ywis;
　　Taketh the fruit, and let the chaff be still.

　　FiP; NAEL-1; NAWM-1; NoP; OAEL-1; OBNV; OBVE;
　　PoEL-1; TrGrPo

The Pardoner's Prologue and Tale

83　I preche of nothing but for coveityse.
　　Therfor my theme is yet, and ever was —
　　Radix malorum est cupiditas.

84　But, though myself be gilty in that sinne,
　　Yet can I maken other folk to twinne
　　From avaryce, and sore to repente.

　　NAEL-1; NAWM-1; NoP; OAEL-1; PoE

85 And thou shalt kisse the relikes everychon,
    Ye, for a grote!Unbokele anon thy purs.'

FiP; HAP; NAEL-1; NAWM-1; NoP; OAEL-1; PoE; PoEL-1; SCV

The Wife of Bath's Prologue

86 Experience, though noon auctoritee
    Were in this world, is right ynough for me
    To speke of wo that is in mariage:

87 Housbondes at chirche dore I have had five
    (If I so ofte mighte han wedded be),
    And alle were worthy men in hir degree.

88 Men may divine and glosen up and down,
    But wel I woot, expres, withouten lie,
    God bad us for to wexe and multiplye:
    That gentil text can I wel understonde.

89 th'Apostle saith that I am free
    To wedde, a Goddes half, where it liketh me.
    He saide that to be wedded is no sinne:
    Bet is to be wedded than to brinne.

90 Where can ye saye in any manere age
    That hye God defended mariage
    By expres word? I praye you, telleth me.
    Or where comanded he virginitee?

91 Men may conseile a womman to be oon,
    But conseiling nis no comandement.
    He putte it in oure owene juggement.
    For hadde God comanded maidenhede,
    Thanne hadde he dampned wedding with the deede;

92 And certes, if there were no seed ysowe,
    Virginitee, thanne wherof sholde it growe?

93 Virginitee is greet perfeccioun,
    And continence eek with devocioun,

94 nat every wight he sholde go selle
    Al that he hadde and yive it to the poore,
    And in swich wise folwe him and his fore:
    He spak to hem that wolde live parfitly —
    And lordinges, by youre leve, that am nat I.

95 I wol bistowe the flour of al myn age
    In th'actes and in fruit of mariage.

96 So that the clerkes be nat with me wrothe,
    I saye this, that they been maad for bothe —
    That is to sayn, for office and for ese
    Of engendrure, ther we nat God displese.

97 Ye wise wives, that conne understonde,
    Thus sholde ye speke and bere him wrong on honde —
    For half so boldely can ther no man
    Swere and lie as a woman can.

98 Thou saist that dropping houses and eek smoke
    And chiding wives maken men to flee
    Out of hir owene hous: a, benedicite,
    What aileth swich an old man for to chide?

99 I wolde no lenger in the bed abide
    If that I felte his arm over my side,
    Til he hadde maad his raunson unto me;
    Thanne wolde I suffre him do his nicetee.
    And therfore every man this tale I telle:
    Winne whoso may, for al is for to selle;
    With empty hand men may no hawkes lure.

100 And I was yong and ful of ragerye,
    Stibourne and strong and joly as a pie:
    How coude I daunce to an harpe smale,
    And singe, ywis, as any nightingale,
    Whan I hadde dronke a draughte of sweete win.

101 But age, allas that al wol envenime,
    Hath me biraft my beautee and my pith —
    Lat go, farewel the devel go therwith!
    The flour is goon, ther is namore to telle:

102 Forbede us thing, and that desiren we;
    Preesse on us faste, and thanne wol we flee.
    With daunger oute we al oure chaffare:
    Greet prees at market maketh dere ware,
    And too greet chepe is holden at litel pris.

103 Gat-toothed was I, and that bicam me weel;
    I hadde the prente of Sainte Venus seel.
    As help me God, I was a lusty oon,

104 mine housbondes tolde me,
    I hadde the beste quoniam mighte be.

105 Venus me yaf my lust, my likerousnesse,
    And Mars yaf me my sturdy hardinesse.

106 Of Eva first, that for hir wikkednesse
    Was al mankinde brought to wrecchednesse,
    For which that Jesu Crist himself was slain
    That boughte us with his herte blood again —
    Lo, heer expres of wommen may ye finde
    That womman was the los of al mankinde.

107 He yaf me al the bridel in myn hand,
    To han the governance of hous and land,
    And of his tonge and his hand also;

108 "Myn owene trewe wif,
    Do as thee lust the terme of al thy lif;
    Keep thyn honour, and keep eek myn estat,"
    After that day we hadde nevere debat.

NAEL-1; OAEL-1; OxBoLi; PoEL-1

The Wife of Bath's Tale

109 Somme seyde, wommen loven best richesse,
    Somme seyde honour,somme seyde, jolynesse;
    Somme, riche array, somme seyden, lust abedde,
    And ofte tyme to be widwe and wedde.

110   I wol nat lye;
A man shal winne us best with flaterye;
And with attendance, and with bisinesse,
Been we ylymed, bothe more and lesse.

111   'Wommen desyren to have sovereyntee
As wel over hir housbond as hir love,
And for to been in maistrie him above;
This is your moste desyr, thogh ye me kille,
Doth as yow list, I am heer at your wille.'

112   men may wel often finde
A lordes sone do shame and vileinye;
And he that wol han prys of his gentrye
For he was boren of a gentil hous,

113   For vileyns sinful dedes make a cherl.

114   Povert is hateful good, and, as I gesse,
A ful greet bringer out of bisiness;

115   Povert ful ofte, whan a man is lowe,
Maketh his God and eek himself to knowe.
Povert a spectacle is, as thinketh me,
Thurgh which he may his verray frendes see.

116   Jesu Crist us sende
Housbondes meke, yonge, and fresshe abedde,
And grace t'overbyde hem that we wedde.
And eek I preye Jesu shorte hir lyves
That wol nat be governed by hir wyves;
And olde and angry nigardes of dispence,
God sende hem sone verray pestilence.

NAEL-1; OAEL-1

The Complaint of Chaucer to His Empty Purse

117   Ye purs, that been to me my lives light
And saviour, as in this world down here,
Out of this tonne helpe me thurgh your might,
(l. 15–17)

118   For I am shave as neigh as any frere.
But yit I praye unto youre curteisye:
Beeth hevy again, or elles moot I die. (l. 19–21)

MeEL; NAEL-1; NoP; OAEL-1; TrGrPo

Merciles Beaute

119   Your yen two wol slee me sodenly,
I may the beaute of hem not sustene,
So woundeth hit through-out my herte kene. (l. 1–3)

120   So hath your beaute fro your herte chaced (l. 14)

ACP; BoLoP; CTC; EBEV; EnLoPo; HAP; MeEL; NAEL-1; NoP; TrGrPo

The Parlement of Foules

121   Now welcom, somer, with thy sonne softe,
That hast this wintres wedres overshake,
And driven away the longe nyghtes blake.

CTC; EnLoPo; HAP; MeEL; OAEL-1; OxBSP; SeCePo; TrGrPo

To Rosamond

122   Madame, ye been alle beautee shrine
As fer as cercled is the mapemounde:
For as the crystal glorious ye shine,
And like ruby been youre cheekes rounde.

123   whan that I see you daunce
It is an oinement unto my wounde,
Though ye to me ne do no daliaunce.

MeEL; NoP; OAEL-1; PoE

GILBERT KEITH CHESTERTON
(1874–1936)

Antichrist, or the Reunion of Christendom; an Ode

1   For your God of dream or devil
You will answer, not to me.
Talk about the pews and steeples
And the Cash that goes therewith!
But the souls of Christian peoples . . .
Chuck it, Smith! (l. 43–48)

FaBoCo; NOBE; NOBL; OBSV; SeCePo

The Christ-child lay on Mary's lap

2   The Christ-child lay on Mary's lap,
His hair was like a light.
(O weary, weary were the world,
But here is all aright. (l. 1–4)

BoTP; FaFP; OBCP; OHIP

The Donkey

3   With monstrous head and sickening cry
And ears like errant wings,
The devil's walking parody
On all four-footed things. (l. 5–8)

4   Fools! For I also had my hour;
One far fierce hour and sweet:
There was a shout about my ears,
And palms before my feet. (l. 13–16)

ACP; FaBV; FaPoR; FPL; InPK; MoBrPo; OBEV; PoLF; RB; WGRP

Elegy in a Country Churchyard

5 And they that rule in England
In stately conclave met,
Alas, alas, for England
They have no graves as yet. (l. 9–12)

FaPoR; MMA; MoBrPo; OBWP; OxBSP; TrGrPo

The Flying Inn

6 And Noah he often said to his wife when he sat down
    to dine,
"I don't care where the water goes if it doesn't get into
    the wine."

7 The seven heavens came roaring down for the throats of
    hell to drink,
And Noah he cocked his eye and said, "It looks like
    rain, I think,
The water has drowned the Matterhorn as deep as a
    Mendip mine,
But I don't care where the water goes if it doesn't get
    into the wine."

ACP; CenHV; FaBoCo; FiBHP; MoBrPo

Lepanto

8 And the Pope has cast his arms abroad for agony and
    loss,
And called the kings of Christendom for swords about
    the Cross, (l. 9–11)

9 Love-light of Spain — hurrah!
Death-light of Africa!
Don John of Austria
Is riding to the sea. (l. 35–38)

10 the green hells of the sea
Where fallen skies and evil hues and eyeless creatures
    be;
On them the sea-valves cluster and the grey sea-forests
    curl,
Splashed with a splended sickness, the sickness of the
    pearl; (l. 54–57)

11 The North is full of tangled things and texts and aching
    eyes
And dead is all the innocence of anger and surprise,
And Christian killeth Christian in a narrow dusty room,
And Christian dreadeth Christ that hath a newer face of
    doom,
And Christian hateth Mary that God kissed in Galilee,
                                                (l. 86–90)

FaBV; FaPoR; MoBrPo; MOS; OBMV; OBNV; RB

A Prayer in Darkness

12 This much, O heaven — if I should brood or rave,
Pity me not; but let the world be fed,
Yea, in my madness if I strike me dead, (l. 1–3)

13 He that hung upon the Torturing Tree
Heard all the crickets singing, and was glad.
                                                (l. 15–16)

FPL; MoBrPo; PoLF; TrGrPo

The Rolling English Road

14 Before the Roman came to Rye or out to Severn strode,
The rolling English drunkard made the rolling English
    road. (l. 1–2)

FaBoCh; NOBE; NOBL; OBEV; OBMV; OxBTC

Variations on an Air: After W. B. Yeats

15 Of an old King in a story
From the grey sea-folk I have heard,
Whose heart was no more broken
Than the wings of a bird. (l. 1–4)

BXAP; FaBoPa; NOBL; Par

Variations on an Air Composed on Having to Appear in a Pageant as Old King Cole

16 I perceive that you drink.
(I am drinking with you. I am as drunk as you are.)
                                                (l. 8–9)

17 I see you are inhaling tobacco, puffing, smoking,
    spitting
(I do not object to your spitting), (l. 10–11)

18 I see in you also there are movements, tremors, tears,
    desire for the melodious,
I salute your three violinists, endlessly making
    vibrations,
Rigid, relentless, capable of going on for ever;
                                                (l. 14–17)

BXAP; FaBoPa; NOBL; Par

COLLEY CIBBER (1671–1757)

The Blind Boy

1 Then let not what I cannot have
My cheer of mind destroy.
Whilst thus I sing, I am a king,
Although a poor blind boy! (l. 17–20)

GTBS; GTBS-P; NOEC; OxBChV

JOHN CLARE (1793–1864)

Autumn

1 Burning hot is the ground, liquid gold is the air;
Whoever looks round sees Eternity there. (l. 11–12)

BoNaP; HAP; NU; PoEL-4; WeW

Badger

2 He turns agen and drives the noisy crowd
And beats the dogs in noises loud.
He drives away and beats them every one,
And then they loose them all and set them on.
He falls as dead and kicked by boys and men,
Then starts and grins and drives the crowd agen;
Till kicked and torn and beaten out he lies
And leaves his hold and cackles, groans, and dies.
(l. 33–40)

EnRP; HAP; LiTB; NoP; NU; OAEL-2; PoEL-4; PrIm;
WeW; WiR

Clock-a-Clay

3 In the cowslips peeps I lie,
Hidden from the buzzing fly,
While green grass beneath me lies,
Pearled wi' dew like fishes' eyes,
Here I lye, a clock-a-clay,
Waiting for the time o' day. (l. 1–6)

EBEV; EBVV; FaPON; LiTB; NAEL-2; OAEL-2; OBNC;
PoEL-4; TrGrPo

First Love

4 Are flowers the winter's choice?
Is love's bed always snow? (l. 17–18)

5 I never saw so sweet a face
As that I stood before:
My heart has left its dwelling-place
And can return no more. (l. 21–24)

BoLoP; ChTr; ELP; EnLoPo; GBL; HAP; NOBVV; NoP

Hesperus

6 Hesperus thy twinkling ray
Beams in the blue of heaven
And tells the traveller on his way
That earth shall be forgiven (l. 13–16)

ChTr; EBVV; FaBoRV; GTBS-P; NOBVV; OAEL-2

I Am

7 I am — yet what I am none cares or knows,
My friends forsake me like a memory lost;
I am the self-consumer of my woes,
They rise and vanish in oblivions host,
Like shadows in love's frenzied stifled throes (l. 1–5)

EBEV; EBVV; EnRP; GTBS-P; HAP; InvP; LiTB;
NAEL-2; NOBE; NOBVV; NoP; OAEL-2; OBEV; OBNC;
PoEL-4; Prf; PrIm; TOF; TrGrPo

An Invite to Eternity

8 The land of shadows wilt thou trace
And look nor know each other's face
The present mixed with reasons gone
And past and present all as one
Say maiden can thy life be led
To join the living with the dead
Then trace thy footsteps on with me
We're wed to one eternity (l. 25–32)

NAEL-2; NOBVV; OAEL-2; OBNC

Language has not the power to speak what love indites

9 Language has not the power to speak what love indites:
The Soul lies buried in the ink that writes. (l. 1–2)

FaBoEE; OAEL-2; OBNC; OxBSP; PoEL-4

Little Trotty Wagtail

10 Little Trotty Wagtail, he waddled in the mud,
And left his little footmarks, trample where he would.
He waddled in the water-pudge, and waggle went his
    tail,
And chirrup up his wings to dry upon the garden rail.
(l. 5–8)

BoTP; FaPON; OnUR; RB; UnPo

Mouse's Nest

11 When out an old mouse bolted in the wheats
With all her young ones hanging at her teats; (l. 5–6)

ChTr; InPK; LiTB; NAEL-2; RB

Secret Love

12 I hid my love when young till I
Couldn't bear the buzzing of a fly;
I hid my life to my despite
Till I could not bear to look at light:

I dare not gaze upon her face
But left her memory in each place;
Where'er I saw a wild flower lie
I kissed and bade my love good-bye. (l. 1–8)

FaBV; NOBVV; OAEL-2; OBNC; PoE; PoEL-4; RB;
TrGrPo

To Mary: It Is the Evening Hour

13 Spirit of her I love,
Whispering to me,
Stories of sweet visions, as I rove,
Here stop, and crop with me
Sweet flowers that in the still hour grew, (l. 7–11)

BoLoP; ChTr; EnLoPo; GBL; Mes

A Vision

14 I lost the love of heaven above,
I spurned the lust of earth below,
I felt the sweets of fancied love,
And hell itself my only foe. (l. 1–4)

15 I loved, but woman fell away;
I hid me from her faded fame.
I snatched the sun's eternal ray
And wrote till earth was but a name. (l. 9–12)

ChTr; EBVV; ELP; FaBoRV; GTBS-P; NAEL-2; NOBVV;
OAEL-2; OBNC; OPOP; PoE; PPP

AUSTIN CLARKE (1896–1974)

Night and Morning

1 Thought can but share
Belief — and the tormented soul,
Changing confession to despair,
Must wear a borrowed robe. (l. 6–9)

2 How many councils and decrees
Have perished in the simple prayer
That gave obedience to the knee; (l. 19–21)

AnIL; CIP; IPY; MoAB; NeIP

Penal Law

3 Burn Ovid with the rest. Lovers will find
A hedge-school for themselves and learn by heart
All that the clergy banish from the mind, (l. 1–3)

BoLoP; GTBS-P; IPY; NOIV

JOSEPH I. C. CLARKE (1846–1925)

The Fighting Race

1 Shea — they call him Scholar Jack —
Went down the list of the dead.
Officers, seamen, gunners, marines,
The crews of the gig and yawl,
The bearded man and the lad in his teens,
Carpenters, coal-passers — all. (l. 3–8)

2 "Wherever there's Kellys there's trouble," said Burke,
"Wherever fighting's the game,
Or a spice of danger in grown man's work,"
Said Kelly, "you'll find my name. (l. 15–18)

3 My grandfather fell on Vinegar Hill,
And fighting was not his trade;
But his rusty pike's in the cabin still,
With Hessian blood on the blade." (l. 33–36)

4 "Oh, the fighting races don't die out,
If they seldom die in bed,
For love is first in their hearts, no doubt," (l. 57–59)

AA; AnAmPo; BLPA; BLPL; PAH

CAROLE GREGORY CLEMMONS
(b. 1945)

Ghetto Lovesong — Migration

1 when her husband came,
complaining about the tobacco spit on him,
they decided to run North
for a free evening. (l. 4–7)

NBP; NMM; PoBA

JOHN CLEVELAND (1613–1658)

Epitaph on the Earl of Strafford

1 The People's violent Love and Hate;
One in extreames lov'd and abhor'd.
Riddles lie here, or in a word,
Here lies Blood; and let it lie
Speechlesse still and never crie. (l. 10–14)

FaBoEE; FaBoPV; JCP; MePo; NOBE; OBS; SeCePo;
TrGrPo

On the Memory of Mr. Edward King, Drowned in the Irish Seas

2 I am no Poet here; my pen 's the spout,
Where the rain water of my eyes run out,
In pity of that name, whose fate wee see

Thus copied out in griefs Hydrography:
The Muses are not Mer-maids, though upon
His death the Ocean might turn Helicon (l. 5–10)

HAP; OAEL-1; OBS; SeCP

LUCILLE CLIFTON (b. 1936)

Good Times

1 My Mama has made bread
and Grampaw has come
and everybody is drunk
and dancing in the kitchen (l. 9–12)

AmNP; AmPA; BPo; CNA; FF; GrPl; InPS; PoBA; TAP;
TwCP

ARTHUR HUGH CLOUGH (1819–1861)

Dipsychus

1 As I sat at the cafe, I said to myself,
They may talk as they please about what they call pelf,
They may sneer as they like about eating and drinking,
But help it I cannot, I cannot help thinking
How pleasant it is to have money, heigh ho!
How pleasant it is to have money. (l. 1–6)

ELP; FaBoCo; FaBoPV; FiBHP; GTBS; NOBE; NOBVV;
OAEL-2; OxBoLi; SeCePo

2 "There is no God," the wicked saith,
"And truly it's a blessing,
For what he might have done with us
It's better only guessing." (l. 1–4)

3 But country folks who live beneath
The shadow and the steeple;
The parson and the parson's wife,
And mostly married people; (l. 21–24)

4 And almost every one when age,
Disease, or sorrows strike him,
Inclines to think there is a God,
Or something very like Him. (l. 29–32)

BLPL; NAEL-2; NOBE; NOBVV

The Latest Decalogue

5 Thou shalt have one God only; who
Would be at the expense of two?
No graven images may be
Worshipped, except the currency: (l. 1–4)

6 Thou shalt not kill; but need'st not strive
Officiously to keep alive:
Do not adultery commit;
Advantage rarely comes of it: (l. 11–14)

7 Thou shalt not covet, but tradition
Approves all forms of competition. (l. 19–20)

ChTr; EBEV; EBVV; FaBoCo; FaBoEE; FF; GTBS-P;
HAP; HoPM; NAEL-2; NIP; NOBE; NOBVV; OAEL-2;
OBNC; OBSV; OPOP; PPP; WeW; WGRP

Say Not the Struggle Nought Availeth

8 Say not the struggle nought availeth,
The labour and the wounds are vain,
The enemy faints not, nor faileth,
And as things have been they remain. (l. 1–4)

9 And not by eastern windows only,
When daylight comes, comes in the light;
In front the sun climbs slow, how slowly!
But westward, look, the land is bright! (l. 13–16)

AWP; EaLo; EBVV; FaBoRV; FaBV; FaFP; FaPoR;
GTBS-P; LiTB; MoShBr; NAEL-2; NOBE; NOBVV;
OAEL-2; OBEV; OBNC; SoSe; TEP; TrGrPo; WaaP;
WGRP

ELIZABETH JANE COATSWORTH
(b. 1893)

The Mouse

1 "Little I ask
And that little is not granted."
There are few crumbs
In this world any more. (l. 5–8)

BoTP; FaPON; MoShBr; OBCA

On a Night of Snow

2 Mistress, there are portents abroad of magic and might,
And things that are yet to be done. Open the door!
(l. 13–14)

CRH; MoAmPo; MoShBr; OBCA

HARTLEY COLERIDGE (1796–1849)

He Lived amidst th' Untrodden Ways

1 A bard whom there were none to praise,
And very few to read. (l. 3–4)

FaBoCo; FaBoPa; FiBHP; NOBL; Par

Long Time a Child

2 For I have lost the race I never ran,
A rathe December blights my lagging May; (l. 11–12)

EnRP; OBNC; PoEL-4; Son

MARY ELIZABETH COLERIDGE
(1861–1907)

Unwelcome

1 We were young, we were merry, we were very very
wise,
And the door stood open at our feast,
When there passed us a woman with the West in her
eyes,
And a man with his back to the East. (l. 1–4)

CH; OBEV; OBNC; WPE

SAMUEL TAYLOR COLERIDGE
(1772–1834)

Answer to a Child's Question

1 But the lark is so brimful of gladness and love,
The green fields below him, the blue sky above,
That he sings, and he sings; and for ever sings he —
'I love my Love, and my Love loves me!' (l. 7–10)

BoTP; EnRP; FaBoBe; OxBChV

Christabel

2 And the Spring comes slowly up this way. (l. 22)

3 Carved with figures strange and sweet,
All made out of the carver's brain, (l. 179–180)

4 Behold! her bosom and half her side
A sight to dream of, not to tell! (l. 252–253)

CH; EnRP; FiP; NAEL-2; OAEL-2; SeCePo

Cologne

5 I counted two and seventy stenches,
All well defined and several stinks!
Ye Nymphs that reign o'er sewers and sinks,
The river Rhine, it is well known,
Doth wash your city of Cologne;

But tell me, Nymphs! what power divine
Shall henceforth wash the river Rhine? (l. 4–10)

FaBoEE; NBLV; OBTV; TW

Dejection; an Ode

6 Well! If the Bard was weather-wise, who made
The grand old ballad of Sir Patrick Spence, (l. 1–2)

7 A grief without a pant, void, dark, and drear, (l. 21)

8 I see them all so excellently fair,
I see, not feel, how beautiful they are! (l. 37–38)

9 O Lady! we receive but what we give,
And in our life alone does Nature live: (l. 47–48)

10 But oh! each visitation
Suspends what nature gave me any my birth,
My shaping spirit of Imagination. (l. 84–86)

EnRP; FiP; HeLP; LiTB; NAEL-2; NAWM-2; NOBE;
NoP; OAEL-2; OBNC; PoE; PoEL-4; PPP; SeCePo; TOF

The Eolian Harp

11 O! the one Life within us and abroad, (l. 27)

12 And what if all of animated nature
Be but organic Harps diversely framed,
That tremble into thought, as o'er them sweeps
Plastic and vast, one intellectual breeze,
At once the Soul of each, and God of all? (l. 45–49)

EnRP; NAEL-2; NoP; OAEL-2

Frost at Midnight

13 The Frost performs its secret ministry,
Unhelped by any wind. The owlet's cry
Came loud — and hark, again! loud as before. (l. 1–3)

14 Only that film, which fluttered on the grate,
Still flutters there, the sole unquiet thing. (l. 15–16)

15 The lovely shapes and sounds intelligible
Of that eternal language, which thy God
Utters, who from eternity doth teach
Himself in all, and all things in himself. (l. 60–63)

16 Therefore all seasons shall be sweet to thee,
Whether the summer clothe the general earth
With greenness, or the redbreast sit and sing
Betwixt the tufts of snow on the bare branch
Of mossy apple-tree,

17   the eave-drops fall
Heard only in the trances of the blast,
Or if the secret ministry of frost
Shall hang them up in silent icicles,
Quietly shining to the quiet Moon.

EBEV; EnRP; FiP; HAP; NAEL-2; NAs; NOBE; NoP;
OAEL-2; OBNC; PoE; PoEL-4; PPP; PrIm; TOF

The Knight's Tomb

18   The Knight's bones are dust,
And his good sword rust: —
His soul is with the saints, I trust. (l. 9–11)

EnRP; FaBoCh; GN; RB

Kubla Khan; or, A Vision in a Dream

19   In Xanadu did Kubla Khan
A stately pleasure-dome decree:
Where Alph, the sacred river, ran
Through caverns measureless to man
Down to a sunless sea. (l. 1–5)

20   But oh! that deep romantic chasm which slanted
Down the green hill athwart a cedarn cover!
A savage place! as holy and enchanted
As e'er beneath a waning moon was haunted
By woman wailing for her demon-lover! (l. 12–16)

21   Five miles meandering with a mazy motion (l. 25)

22   Weave a circle round him thrice,
And close your eyes with holy dread,
For he on honey-dew hath fed,
And drunk the milk of Paradise. (l. 51–54)

AWP; CH; ChER; ChTr; ELP; EnRP; EyDe; FaBoBe;
FaBoCh; FaBV; FaFP; FF; FiP; FPL; GN; GoJo; HAP;
HeIP; HoPM; InPK; InPS; InvP; LiTB; MAT; NAEL-2;
NAWM-2; NIP; NOBE; NoP; OAEL-2; OBEV; OBNC;
OPOP; PoE; PoEL-4; PoRA; PrIm; SCV; SoSe; TEP; TOF

Love

23   All thoughts, all passions, all delights,
Whatever stirs this mortal frame,
Are all but ministers of Love,
And feed his sacred flame. (l. 1–4)

BeLS; ChER; EnRP; GTBS; GTBS-P; OBEV

Metrical Feet: Lesson for a Boy

24   Iambics march from short to long; —
With a leap and a bound the swift Anapaests throng;
(l. 5–6)

FaBoUs; NIP; OxBChV; SoSe

On Donne's Poetry

25   Wit's forge and fire-blast, meaning's press and screw.
(l. 4)

InvP; NAEL-2; NoP; OAEL-2; SeCePo

On My Joyful Departure from the City of Cologne

26   Mr. Mum's Rudesheimer
And the church of St. Geryon
Are the two things alone
That deserve to be known
In the body-and-soul-stinking town of Cologne. (l. 3–7)

FaBoCo; InvP; NBLV; OBTV; TW

The Pains of Sleep

27   I could not know
Whether I suffered, or I did:
For all seemed guilt, remorse or woe,
My own or others still the same
Life-stifling fear, soul-stifling shame. (l. 28–32)

28   To be beloved is all I need,
And whom I love, I love indeed. (l. 51–52)

EnRP; NAEL-2; OBNC; OxBChV; SeCePo; TEP; TrPWD

The Rime of the Ancient Mariner

29   He holds him with his glittering eye —
The Wedding Guest stood still,
And listens like a three years' child:
The Mariner hath his will. (l. 13–16)

30   Nor dim nor red, like God's own head,
The glorious Sun uprist: (l. 97–98)

31   We were the first that ever burst
Into that silent sea. (l. 105–106)

32   As idle as a painted ship
Upon a painted ocean. (l. 117–118)

33   Water, water, everywhere,
Nor any drop to drink. (l. 121–122)

34   Yea, slimy things did crawl with legs
Upon the slimy sea. (l. 125–126)

35   The souls did from their bodies fly —
They fled to bliss or woe!
And every soul, it passed me by,
Like the whizz of my cross-bow! (l. 220–223)

36 A spring of love gushed from my heart,
And I blessed them unaware: (l. 285–286)

37 Oh sleep! it is a gentle thing
Beloved from pole to pole! (l. 293–294)

38 He prayeth best, who loveth best
All things both great and small;
For the dear God who loveth us,
He made and loveth all. (l. 615–618)

39 A sadder and a wiser man,
He rose the morrow morn. (l. 625–626)

BeLS; CH; ChER; EBEV; EnRP; FaBoBe; FaBoCh;
FaBV; FaFP; FiP; HAP; HeIP; HoPM; InPS; LiTB; MOS;
NOBE; NoP; OAEL-2; OBEV; OBNC; OBNV; PoE;
PoEL-4; PrIm; TEP; TOF; TrGrPo

Stop, Christian passer-by! — Stop, child of God

40 Beneath this sod
A poet lies, or that which once seem'd he. (l. 2–3)

CH; EnRP; FiP; NAEL-2; NOCV; NoP; OAEL-2

This Lime-Tree Bower My Prison

41 Henceforth I shall know
That Nature ne'er deserts the wise and pure;
(l. 59–60)

42 my gentle-hearted Charles, to whom
No sound is dissonant which tells of Life. (l. 75–76)

EnRP; FaBoPP; HeIP; NAEL-2; NIP; PoE; PoEL-4; TOF

Time, Real and Imaginary

43 On the wide level of a mountain's head,
(I knew not where, but 'twas some faery place),
Their pinions, ostrich-like, for sails outspread,
Two lovely children run an endless race, (l. 1–4)

44 This far outstripped the other;
Yet ever runs she with reverted face,
And looks and listens for the boy behind:
For he, alas! is blind!
O'er rough and smooth with even step he passed,
And knows not whether he be first or last. (l. 6–11)

EnRP; NOBE; OBEV; OxBSP

Work without Hope

45 And I, the while, the sole unbusy thing,
Nor honey make, nor pair, nor build, nor sing. (l. 5–6)

46 Work without Hope draws nectar in a sieve,
And Hope without an object cannot live. (l. 13–14)

BoNaP; BoTP; EnRP; FiP; NAEL-2; NOBE; NoP; OBEV;
SaC; Son; TEP

Youth and Age

47 Life went a-maying
With Nature, Hope, and Poesy,
When I was young! (l. 3–5)

48 Nought cared this body for wind or weather
When Youth and I lived in't together. (l. 16–17)

BLPL; EnRP; FiP; GTBS; GTBS-P; OBEV; OBNC; PoLF

SARA COLERIDGE (1802–1852)

Trees

1 The Poplar grows up straight and tall,
The Pear-tree spreads along the wall, (l. 3–4)

BoTP; OHIP; OxBChV; RHPC

WILLIAM COLLINS (1721–1759)

A Fidele

1 To fair Fidele's grassy tomb
Soft maids and village hinds shall bring
Each opening sweet of earliest bloom,
And rifle all the breathing spring. (l. 1–4)

2 Each lonely scene shall thee restore;
For thee the tear be duly shed;
Beloved till life can charm no more,
And mourn'd till Pity's self be dead. (l. 21–24)

ELP; EnRP; Mes; NOBE; NOEC; OBEV; SeCePo

How Sleep the Brave

3 How sleep the brave who sink to rest
By all their country's wishes blest! (l. 1–2)

AWP; ELP; EnRP; GN; GTBS; GTBS-P; HAP; HeIP;
NAEL-1; NOEE; NOEC; NoP; OBEV; OxBSP; PoE;
PoEL-3; TrGrPo

Ode Occasioned by the Death of Mr. Thomson

4 In yonder Grave a Druid lies
Where slowly winds the Stealing Wave!
The Year's best Sweets shall duteous rise
To deck its Poet's sylvan Grave! (l. 1–4 –1748)

NAEL-1; NOEC; PoE; SeCePo

Ode on the Poetical Character

5 Happier, hopeless fair, if never
Her baffled hand with vain endeavour
Had touched that fatal zone to her denied! (l. 14–16)

6 Long by the loved Enthusiast wooed,
Himself in some diviner mood, (l. 29–30)

7 And thou, thou rich-haired youth of morn,
And all thy subject life was born! (l. 39–40)

8 And Truth, in sunny vest arrayed,
By whose the tarsel's eyes were made; (l. 45–46)

9 All the shad'wy tribes of Mind,
In braided dance their murmurs joined, (l. 47–48)

EnRP; NAEL-1; NOEC; OAEL-1; PoE; PoEL-3; TEP

Ode to Evening

10 Now Air is hush'd, save where the weak-ey'd Bat,
With short shrill Shriek flits by on leathern Wing,
Or where the Beetle winds
His small but sullen Horn, (l. 9–12)

AWP; EBEV; EnRP; FaBoBe; GTBS; GTBS-P; HAP;
LiTB; NAEL-1; NOBE; NOEC; NoP; OAEL-1; OBEV;
PoE; PoEL-3; PPP; SeCePo; TrGrPo

Ode to Simplicity

11 But com'st a decent maid,
In Attic robe array'd,
O chaste, unboastful nymph, to thee I call! (l. 10–12)

12 Though taste, though genius bless
To some divine excess,
Faint's the cold work till thou inspire the whole;
What each, what all supply,
May court, may charm our eye,
Thou, only thou, canst raise the meeting soul!
(l. 43–48)

EnRP; NOBE; OBEV; TEP

GEORGE COLMAN, THE YOUNGER
(1762–1836)

Unfortunate Miss Bailey

1 One night betimes he went to rest, for he had caught a
fever.
Says he, 'I am a handsome man, but I'm a gay
deceiver.' (l. 6–7)

2 'Dear Captain Smith,' the ghost replied, 'you've used
me ungenteelly.
The crowner's quest goes hard with me because I've
acted fraily,
And Parson Biggs won't bury me, though I am dead
Miss Bailey.' (l. 12–14)

FaBoBa; FiBHP; GBP; OxBoLi

PADRAIC COLUM   (1881–1972)

A Drover

1 To Meath of the pastures,
From wet hills by the sea,
Through Leitrim and Longford,
Go my cattle and me. (l. 1–4)

2 O farmer, strong farmer!
You can spend at the fair,
But your face you must turn
To your crops and your care; (l. 13–16)

AnIL; AWP; MoBrPo; OBMV; RB

An Old Woman of the Roads

3 Oh, to have a little house!
To own the hearth and stool and all!
The heaped-up sods upon the fire,
The pile of turf against the wall! (l. 1–4)

BoTP; CH; FaBoBe; FaPON; FYAP; MoBrPo; NOIV;
OBEV; PoRA; TIRV

WILLIAM CONGREVE   (1670–1729)

False Though She Be

1 False though she be to me and Love,
I'll ne'er pursue Revenge;
For still the Charmer I approve,
Tho' I deplore her change. (l. 1–4)

BoLoP; EnLoPo; NOBE; OBEV; OxBSP

Pious Selinda

2 Pious Selinda goes to prayers,
  If I but ask the favour;
  And yet the tender fool's in tears,
  When she believes I'll leave her.

  Would I were free from this restraint,
  Or else had hopes to win her;
  Would she would make of me a saint,
  Or I of her a sinner. (l. 1–8)

BoLoP; ELP; ErPo; FaBoCo; NBLV; NOBE; NOEC;
OxBSP

HENRY CONSTABLE (1562–1613)

On the Death of Sir Philip Sidney

1 I did not know that thou wert dead before;
  I did not feel the grief I did sustain;
  The greater stroke astonisheth the more;
  Astonishment takes from us sense of pain.
  I stood amazed when other's tears begun,
  And now begin to weep when they have done.
  (l. 9–14)

ElL; OBEV; OBSC; SeCePo

HENRY CONSTABLE *AND* HENRY CHETTLE (c. 1560–c. 1607)

Diaphenia (*attributed to* Constable *and to* Chettle)

1 Diaphenia, like the daffadowndilly,
  White as the sun, fair as the lily,
  Heigh ho, how I do love thee! (l. 1–3)

2 I do love thee as each flower
  Loves the sun's life-giving power,
  For, dead, thy breath to life might move me.
  (l. 10–12)

CH; ElL; ELP; GTBS; GTBS-P; NOBE; OBSC; PoEL-2

ELIZA COOK (1818–1889)

The Old Arm-Chair

1 I love it, I love it; and who shall dare
  To chide me for loving that old arm-chair? (l. 1–2)

AnAmPo; BrRo; InPK; WBLP

GEORGE COOPER (1838–1927)

Only One Mother

1 Hundreds of dewdrops to greet the dawn,
  Hundreds of bees in the purple clover,
  Hundreds of butterflies on the lawn,
  But only one mother the wide world over. (l. 5–8)

AA; BoTP; FaPON; OHIP

RICHARD CORBET (1582–1635)

To His Son, Vincent Corbet

1 I wish thee peace in all thy ways,
  Nor lazy nor contentious days;
  And when thy soul and body part,
  As innocent as now thou art. (l. 17–20)

FaBoCh; OES; OxBChV; TrGrPo

FRANCES (DARWIN) CORNFORD (1886–1960)

All Souls' Night

1 He put his hand upon my shoulder,
  He did not think me strange or older, (l. 4–5)

EnLoPo; OBD; OxBSP; OxBTC

To a Fat Lady Seen from the Train

2 O fat white woman whom nobody loves,
  Why do you walk through the fields in gloves,
  When the grass is soft as the breast of doves
  And shivering-sweet to the touch? (l. 3–6)

BLPA; FaBoWP; GoJo; MoBrPo; OBMV; WeW

The Watch

3 I thought it said in every tick:
  I am so sick, so sick, so sick:
  O death, come quick, come quick, come quick,
  Come quick, come quick, come quick, come quick.... (l. 7–10)

HeIP; InPK; MoBrPo; OxBTC; RR

GREGORY CORSO (b. 1930)

Marriage

1 Should I get married? Should I be good?
  Astound the girl next door with my velvet suit and
    faustus hood? (l. 1–2)

2 O how terrible it must be for a young man —
  seated before a family and the family thinking
  We never saw him before! He wants our Mary Lou!
  After tea and homemade cookies they ask What do you
    do for a living (l. 16–19)

3 O God, and the wedding! All her family and her friends
  and only a handful of mine all scroungy and bearded
  just wait to get at the drinks and food — (l. 24–26)

4 The indifferent clerk he knowing what was going to
    happen
  The lobby zombies they knowing what
  The whistling elevator man he knowing
  The winking bellboy knowing
  Everybody knowing! I'd be almost inclined not to do
    anything! (l. 37–41)

5 she in the kitchen
  aproned young and lovely wanting my baby
  and so happy about me she burns the roast beef
  and comes crying to me and I get up from my big papa
    chair
  saying Christmas teeth! Radiant brains! Apple deaf!
                                              (l. 52–56)

6 when Mrs Kindhead comes to collect for the
    Community Chest
  grab her and tell her There are unfavorable omens in
    the sky!
  And when the mayor comes to get my vote tell him
  When are you going to stop people killing whales!
                                              (l. 62–65)

7 a fat Reichian wife screeching over potatoes Get a job!
  And five nose running brats in love with Batman
                                              (l. 83–84)

8 it's just that I see love as odd as wearing shoes —
  I never wanted to marry a girl who was like my mother
  And Ingrid Bergman was always impossible
                                              (l. 100–103)

9 what if I'm 60 years old and not married,
  all alone in a furnished room with pee stains on my
    underwear
  and everybody else is married! (l. 106–108)

CoAP; LiTM; MoP; NeAP; NoP; OBAL; PPP; PrIm; TAP

JOSEPH SEAMON COTTER, JR.
(1895–1919)

And What Shall You Say?

1 Brother, come!
  And let us go unto our God.

And when we stand before Him
I shall say —
"Lord, I do not hate,
I am hated. (l. 1–6)

BANP; CDC; PoBA; PoNe

CHARLES COTTON (1630–1687)

Evening

1 And now on benches all are sat
  In the cool air to sit and chat,
  Till Phoebus, dipping in the West,
  Shall lead the world the way to rest. (l. 33–36)

ChTr; PoEL-3; TrGrPo; WiR

NOËL COWARD (1899–1973)

Mad Dogs and Englishmen

1 Mad dogs and Englishmen
  Go out in the midday sun. (l. 9–10)

2 It's such a surprise for the Eastern eyes to see,
  That though the English are effete
  They're quite impervious to heat. (l. 25–27)

3 In Rangoon the heat of noon
  Is just what the natives shun.
  They put their Scotch or rye down
  And lie down. (l. 37–40)

CenHV; FiBHP; NBLV; NOBL; OBTV

ABRAHAM COWLEY (1618–1667)

Drinking

1 The thirsty earth soaks up the rain,
  And drinks and gapes for drink again; (l. 1–2)

2 Nothing in Nature's sober found,
  But an eternal health goes round.
  Fill up the bowl, then, fill it high,
  Fill all the glasses there — for why
  Should every creature drink but I?
  Why, man of morals, tell me why? (l. 15–20)

BLPL; FF; HeIP; MePo; NOBE; OBEV; OBVE; SeCePo;
SeCP; SeCV-1; TrGrPo; WiR

The Grasshopper

3 Happy Insect, happy Thou,
  Dost neither Age, nor Winter know.

  But when thou'st drunk, and danc'd, and sung
  Thy fill, the flowry Leaves among,
  (Voluptuous, and Wise withal,
  Epicurean Animal!)
  Satiated with thy Summer Feast,
  Thou retir'st to endless Rest. (l. 27–34)

  AWP; FM; OAEL-1; OBVE; SeCV-1; WiR

Hymn: To Light

4 Even Lust the Master of a hardned Face,
  Blushes if thou beest in the place,
  To darkness' Curtains he retires,
  In Sympathizing Night he rowls his smoaky Fires.

  When, Goddess, thou liftst up thy wakened Head,
  Out of the Mornings purple bed,
  Thy Quire of Birds about thee play,
  And all the joyful world salutes the rising day.
                                        (l. 57–64)

  MeLP; MePo; OBS; SeCV-1

The Mistress

5 Fair Hope! our earlier Heaven! by thee
  Young Time is taster to Eternity.
  The generous wine with age grows strong, not sour,
  Nor need we kill thy fruit to smell thy flower.
  Thy golden head never hangs down
  Till in the lap of Love's full noon
  It falls and dies: Oh no, it melts away
  As doth the dawn into the day,
  As lumps of sugar lose themselves, and twine
  Their subtle essence with the soul of wine. (l. 41–50)

  LiTB; MeLP; MePo; NOBE; OBS; SeCV-1

6 Oh take my Heart, and by that means you'll prove
  Within too stor'd enough of Love:
  Give me but Yours, I'll by that change so thrive,
  That Love in all my parts shall live.
  So powerful is this change, it render can,
  My outside Woman, and your inside Man.

  MeLP; MePo; OBS; SeCP; SeCV-1

7 How could it be so fair, and you away?
  How could the Trees be beauteous, Flowers so gay?
  Could they remember but last year,
  How you did Them, They you delight,
  The sprouting leaves which saw you here,
  And call'd their Fellows to the sight,

Would, looking round for the same sight in vain,
Creep back into their silent Barks again.

HAP; JCP; MeLP; OBS

8 Ah, yet, ere I descend to the grave,
  May I a small house and large garden have;
  And a few friends, and many books, both true,
  Both wise, and both delightful too!
  And since love ne'er will from me flee,
  A mistress moderately fair,
  And good as guardian angels are,
  Only beloved and loving me.

  LiTB; NOBE; NoP; OBEV; OBS; SeCV-1; TrGrPo

Ode: Of Wit

9 'Tis not such lines as almost crack the stage
  When Bajazet begins to rage;
  Nor a tall met'phor in the bombast way,
  Nor the dry chips of short-lunged Seneca.
  Nor upon all things to obtrude
  And force some odd similitude.
  What is it then, which like the power divine
  We only can by negatives define? (l. 49–56)

10 In a true piece of Wit all things must be,
   Yet all things there agree,
   As in the ark, joined without force or strife,
   All creatures dwelt: all creatures that had life;
   Or as the primitive forms of all
   (If we compare great things with small)
   Which without discord or confusion lie
   In that strange mirror of the Deity. (l. 57–64)

   MeLP; MePo; NAEL-1; OAEL-1; OBS; SeCP; SeCV-1

On the Death of Mr. Crashaw

11 Ah wretched We, Poets of Earth! but Thou
   Wert Living the same Poet which thou'rt Now,
   Whilst Angelssing to thee their ayres divine,
   And joy in an applause so great as thine.
   Equal society with them to hold,
   Thou need'st not make new Songs, but say the Old.
                                        (l. 9–14)

12 Thy spotless Muse, like Mary, did contain
   The boundless Godhead; she did well disdain
   That her eternal Verse employ'd should be
   On a less subject than Eternitie; (l. 29–32)

13 Pardon, my Mother Church, if I consent
   That Angels led him when from thee he went,
   For even in Error sure no Danger is
   When joyn'd with so much Piety as His. (l. 47–50)

   MeLP; MePo; OBS; SeCP; SeCV-1

On the Death of Mr. William Hervey

14 Thy soul and body, when death's agony
Besieged around thy noble heart,
Did not with more reluctance part
Than I, my dearest Friend, do part from thee.
(l. 13–16)

15 We spent them not in toys, in lusts, or wine,
But search of deep Philosophy,
Wit, Eloquence, and Poetry,
Arts which I loved, for they, my Friend, were thine.

EBEV; FaBoRV; NOBE; OBEV; OBS; SeCP; SeCV-1

The Swallow

16 Foolish prater, What dost thou
So early at my window do?
Cruel bird, thou'st ta'en away
A dream out of my arms to-day;
A dream that ne'er must equall'd be
By all that waking eyes may see.
Thou this damage to repair
Nothing half so sweet and fair,
Nothing half so good, canst bring,
Tho' men say thou bring'st the Spring. (l. 1–10)

EBEV; FM; OBEV; PBBP

WILLIAM COWPER (1731–1800)

The Castaway

1 Obscurest night involv'd the sky,
Th' Atlantic billows roar'd,
When such a destin'd wretch as I,
Wash'd headlong from on board,
Of friends, of hope, of all bereft,
His floating home for ever left. (l. 1–6)

2 But misery still delights to trace
Its 'semblance in another's case.

No voice divine the storm allay'd,
No light propitious shone;
When, snatch'd from all effectual aid,
We perish'd, each alone:
But I beneath a rougher sea,
And whelm'd in deeper gulphs than he. (l. 59–66)

ELP; EnRP; FiP; HeIP; MOS; NAEL-1; NOBE; NOEC;
NoP; OAEL-1; PoE; PoEL-3; PPP

Epitaph on a Hare

3 I kept him for his humour's sake,
For he would oft beguile
My heart of thoughts that made it ache,
And force me to a smile. (l. 33–36)

FiP; FM; HAP; HeIP; NOEC; NoP; PoEL-3

God moves in a mysterious way

4 God moves in a mysterious way,
His wonders to perform;
He plants his footsteps in the sea,
And rides upon the storm. (l. 1–4)

5 His purposes will ripen fast,
Unfolding ev'ry hour;
The bud may have a bitter taste,
But sweet will be the flow'r. (l. 17–20)

EaLo; EBEV; ELP; EnRP; FaBoCh; FaFP; FiP; FPL;
HeIP; LiTB; NOBE; NOCV; NOEC; NoP; PoEL-3; PWR;
SeCePo; TOF; TrGrPo; WGRP

John Gilpin

6 John Gilpin was a citizen
Of credit and renown,
A train-band captain eke was he
Of famous London town. (l. 1–4)

7 Now let us sing, Long live the king,
And Gilpin long live he;
And when he next doth ride abroad,
May I be there to see! (l. 249–252)

BeLS; FaBoBe; FiP; GN; InvP; OBNV

On the Loss of the Royal George

8 Toll for the brave —
The brave! that are no more:
All sunk beneath the wave,
Fast by their native shore. (l. 1–4)

EBEV; FaPoR; FiP; GN; GTBS; GTBS-P; NOBE; TrGrPo

On the Receipt of My Mother's Picture out of Norfolk

9 O that those lips had language! Life has passed
With me but roughly since I heard thee last. (l. 1–2)

10 My Mother! when I learnt that thou wast dead,
Say, wast thou conscious of the tears I shed?
Hovered thy spirit o'er thy sorrowing son,
Wretch even then, life's journey just begun? (l. 7–10)

11 I heard the bell tolled on thy burial day,
I saw the hearse that bore thee slow away,
And, turning from my nursery window, drew
A long, long sigh, and wept a last adieu! (l. 14–17)

12 By contemplation's help,not sought in vain,
I seem t' have liv'd my childhood o'er again;
To have renew'd the joys that once were mine,
(l. 114–116)

EnRP; FiP; NOEC

The Poplar Field

13 The poplars are felled, farewell to the shade
And the whispering sound of the cool colonnade,
(l. 1–2)

CH; ChTr; ELP; FaBoPP; FaBoRV; FiP; GTBS; GTBS-P;
HAP; NOBE; NOEC; PoEL-3; TrGrPo; WiR

The Task

14 Hatred and vengeance, my eternal portion,
Scarce can endure delay of execution: —
Wait, with impatient readiness, to seize my
Soul in a moment.

15 Man disavows, the Deity disowns me.
Hell might afford my miseries a shelter;
Therefore hell keeps her everhungry mouths all
Bolted against me.

16 Him, the vindictive rod of angry justice
Sent, quick and howling, to the centre headlong;
I, fed with judgements,in a fleshy tomb, am
Buried above ground.

EBEV; FaBoRV; FiP; HAP; NOEC; NoP; OAEL-1; OPOP;
PPP; Prf; TW

17 How oft upon yon eminence our pace
Has slackened to a pause, and we have borne
The ruffling wind, scarce conscious that it blew,
While admiration, feeding at the eye,
And still unsated, dwelt upon the scene.
(I, l. 154–158)

18 Scenes must be beautiful, which, daily viewed,
Please daily, and whose novelty survives
Long knowledge and the scrutiny of years —
(I, l. 177–179)

19 Nor rural sights alone, but rural sounds,
Exhilarate the spirit, and restore
The tone of languid Nature. (I, l. 181–183)

20 Nature inanimate employs sweet sounds,
But animated nature sweeter still,
To soothe and satisfy the human ear. (I, l. 197–199)

NAEL-1

To Mary

21 The twentieth year is well-nigh past;
Since first our sky was overcast,
Ah would that this might be the last!
My Mary!
Thy spirits have a fainter flow,
I see thee daily weaker grow —
'Twas my distress that brought thee low,

My Mary!
Thy needles, once a shining store,
For my sake restless heretofore,
Now rust disus'd, and shine no more,
My Mary! (l. 1–12)

EnLoPo; EnRP; FiP; GTBS; GTBS-P; NOEC; OBEV

To Mary Unwin

22 There is a Book
By seraphs writ with beams of heavenly light,
On which the eyes of God not rarely look,

A chronicle of actions just and bright —
There all thy deeds, my faithful Mary, shine;
And since thou own'st that praise, I spare thee mine.
(l. 9–14)

GTBS; GTBS-P OBEV; TrGrPo

Verses Supposed to Be Written by Alexander Selkirk during His Solitary Abode on the Island of Juan Fernandez

23 I am monarch of all I survey;
My right there is none to dispute;
From the center all round to the sea
I am lord of the fowl and the brute.
O Solitude! where are the charms
That sages have seen in thy face?
Better dwell in the midst of alarms,
Than reign in this horrible place. (l. 1–8)

24 When I think of my own native land,
In a moment I seem to be there;
But alas! recollection at hand
Soon hurries me back to despair. (l. 45–48)

FiP; FPL; GTBS; GTBS-P; LiTB; NOEC; PoEL-3; PoLF

Walking with God

25 Oh! for a closer walk with God,
A calm and heav'nly frame;
A light to shine upon the road
That leads me to the Lamb! (l. 1–4)

EnRP; FiP; NOCV; NOEC; PoEL-3; TEP; TOF

GEORGE CRABBE (1754–1832)

The Borough: Peter Grimes

1 Here dull and hopeless he'd lie down and trace
How sidelong crabs had scrawled their crooked race;

EnRP; NoP; OBNV; PoEL-4; TEP

A Marriage Ring

2 Worn with life's care, love yet was love. (l. 4)

BoLoP; EnLoPo; NOBE; OBEV; OBNC; UnAS

The Parish Register

3 What I behold are feverish fits of strife,
'Twixt fears of dying and desire of life:

OAEL-1

The Village

4 Because the Muses never knew their pains.
They boast their peasants' pipes, but peasants now
Resign their pipes and plod behind the plough;

5 I sought the simple life that Nature yields;

6 Ye gentle souls, who dream of rural ease,
Whom the smooth stream and smoother sonnet please;
Go! if the peaceful cot your praises share,
Go, look within, and ask if peace be there:
If peace be his — that drooping weary sire,
Of theirs, that offspring round their feeble fire,
Or hers, that matron pale, whose trembling hand
Turns on the wretched hearth th' expiring brand.

7 And the cold charities of man to man:

8 A potent quack, long versed in human ills,
Who first insults the victim whom he kills;
Whose murd'rous hand a drowsy bench protect,
And whose most tender mercy is neglect.

EnRP; NAEL-1; NOEC; OAEL-1; PoE; PoEL-4

DINAH MARIA MULOCK CRAIK
(1826–1887)

God Rest You Merry, Gentlemen

1 God rest you merry, gentlemen,
Let nothing you dismay,
For Jesus Christ, our Saviour,
Was born upon this day,
To save us all from Satan's power
When we were gone astray.
O tidings of comfort and joy!
For Jesus Christ, our Saviour,
Was born on Christmas Day. (l. 1–9)

FaFP; GN; LiTB

HART CRANE (1899–1932)
At Melville's Tomb

1 Often beneath the wave, wide from this ledge
The dice of drowned men's bones he saw bequeath
An embassy. (l. 1–3)

2 This fabulous shadow only the sea keeps. (l. 16)

HAP; MoAmPo; MoP; MOS; NAAL-2; NoAM; NoP; PoA;
TAP; UnPo; VGW

Black Tambourine

3 The interests of a black man in a cellar
Mark tardy judgment on the world's closed door.
(l. 1–2)

InPK; InPS; NoAM; OxBA; OxBSP; PPP; TAP

The Bridge

4 from above, thin squeaks of radio static,
The captured fume of space foams in our ears —

5 But the star-glistered salver of infinity,
The circle, blind crucible of endless space,
Is sluiced by motion, — subjugated never.

6 each prison crypt,
of canyoned traffic . . . Confronting the Exchange,
Surviving in a world of stocks, —

7 Stars prick the eyes with sharp ammoniac proverbs,

8 Stars scribble on our eyes the frosty sagas,
The gleaming cantos of unvanquished space . . .

9 O sinewy silver biplane, nudging the wind's withers!
There, from Kill Devils Hill at Kitty Hawk
Two brothers in their twinship left the dune;
Warping the gale, the Wright wind wrestlers veered
Capeward, then blading the wind's flank, banked and
spun.

10 Wheeled swiftly, wings emerge from larval-silver
hangars.
Taut motors surge, space-gnawing, into flight;

11 O thou Dirigible, enormous Lounger
Of pendulous auroral beaches, —

12 The stars have grooved our eyes with old persuasions
Of love and hatred, birth, — surcease of nations . . .

13 Thou, pallid there as chalk,
Hast kept of wounds, O Mourner, all that sum
That then from Appomattox stretched to Somme!

14 Familiar, thou, as mendicants in public places;

15 To course that span of consciousness thou'st named
The Open Road — thy vision is reclaimed!
What heritage thou'st signalled to our hands!

InPS; LiTA; MoAB; MoAmPo; NAAL-2

16 So the 20th Century — so
whizzed the Limited — roared by and left
three men, still hungry on the tracks, ploddingly
watching the tail lights wizen and converge, slipping gimleted and neatly out of sight.

17 The last bear, shot drinking in the Dakotas
Loped under wires that span the mountain stream.

18 Keen instruments, strung to a vast precision
Bind town to town and dream to ticking dream.

19 Under a world of whistles, wires and steam
Caboose-like they go ruminating through
Ohio, Indiana — blind baggage —
To Cheyenne tagging . . . Maybe Kalamazoo. See
    Vagagonds

20 Behind
My father's cannery works I used to see
Rail-squatters ranged in nomad raillery,

21 John, Jake or Charley, hopping the slow freight
— Memphis to Tallahassee — riding the rods,
Blind fists of nothing, humpty-dumpty clods.

22 Papooses crying on the wind's long mane
Screamed red skin dynasties that fled the brain,

23 The River, spreading, flows — and spends your dream.
What are you, lost within this tideless spell?
You are your father's father, and the stream —
A liquid theme that floating niggers swell.

LiTA; NAAL-2

24 legs waken salads in the brain

25 Always and last, before the final ring
When all the fireworks blare, begins
A tom-tom scrimmage with a somewhere violin,
Some cheapest echo of them all — begins.

26 Yet, to the empty trapeze of your flesh,
O Magdalene, each comes back to die alone.
Then you, the burlesque of our lust — and faith,
Lug us back lifeward — bone by infant bone.

LiTA; NAAL-2

27 The seagull's wings shall dip and pivot him,
Shedding white rings of tumult, building high
Over the chained bay waters Liberty —

Then, with inviolate curve, forsake our eyes

28 And Thee, across the harbor, silver-paced
As though the sun took step of thee, yet left
Some motion ever unspent in thy stride, —
Implicitly thy freedom staying thee!

29 O Sleepless as the river under thee,
Vaulting the sea, the prairies dreaming sod,
Unto us lowliest sometime sweep, descend
As of the curveship lend a myth to God.

AiP; AmFP; AmPP; BLPL; CMoP; EyDe; HAP; HeIP;
InPS; LiTA; LiTM; MoAB; MoAmPo; NAAL-2; NoAM;
NOBA; NoP; OxBA; PoE; PrIm; TAP; WeW

30 subways, rivered under streets
and rivers . . . in the car
the overtone of motion
underground, the monotone
of motion is the sound
of other faces, also underground —

31 The phonographs of hades in the brain
Are tunnels that re-wind themselves, and love
A burnt match skating in a urinal —

32 The intent escalator lifts a serenade
Stilly
Of shoes, umbrellas, each eye attending its shoe, then
Bolting outright somewhere above where streets
Burst suddenly in rain. . . .

33 The train rounds, bending to a scream,
Taking the final level for the dive
Under the river —

34 And this thy harbor, O my City, I have driven under,
Tossed from the coil of ticking towers. . . . Tomorrow,
And to be . . . . Here by the River that is East —

CMoP; LiTA; MAT; MoAB; MoAmPo; NAAL-2; OxBA

The Broken Tower

35 The bells, I say, the bells break down their tower;
And swing I know not where. (l. 9–10)

36 And so it was I entered the broken world
To trace the visionary company of love, (l. 17–18)

AmPP; CMoP; LiTM; MoAB; MoAmPo; NoAM; NOBA;
NoP; OxBA; TrGrPo

Chaplinesque

37 We will sidestep, and to the final smirk
Dally the doom of that inevitable thumb
That slowly chafes its puckered index toward us,
                                    (l. 9–11)

CMoP; LiTM; MoP; NAAL-2; NoAM; NOBA; OxBA;
VGW

The Hurricane

38　Lo, Lord, Thou ridest!
　　Lord, Lord, Thy swifting heart

　　Naught stayeth, naught now bideth
　　But's smithereened apart! (l. 1–4)

　　CMoP; MoAB; MoAmPo; OxBA; TrCP

My Grandmother's Love Letters

39　There are no stars to-night
　　But those of memory.
　　Yet how much room for memory there is
　　In the loose girdle of soft rain. (l. 1–4)

40　they are brown and soft,
　　And liable to melt as snow. (l. 10–11)

　　BLPL; CMoP; FaBoBe; HeIP; InPK; MoAB; NoAM;
　　NOBA; NoP

Praise for an Urn

41　His thoughts, delivered to me
　　From the white coverlet and pillow,
　　I see now, were inheritances —
　　Delicate riders of the storm. (l. 5–8)

42　Scatter these well-meant idioms
　　Into the smoky spring that fills
　　The suburbs, where they will be lost.
　　They are no trophies of the sun. (l. 21–24)

　　AWP; CMoP; HAP; LiTM; MoAB; MoAmPo; NoAM;
　　NOBA; OxBA; PPP; WeW

Repose of Rivers

43　I could never remember
　　That seething, steady leveling of the marshes
　　Till age had brought me to the sea. (l. 3–5)

44　There, beyond the dykes

　　I heard wind flaking sapphire, like this summer,
　　And willows could not hold more steady sound.
　　　　　　　　　　　　　　　　　(l. 21–23)

　　AWP; CMoP; LiTM; MoAB; MoAmPo; NOBA; OxBA;
　　PoE

Royal Palm

45　It grazes the horizons, launched above

　　Mortality — ascending emerald-bright,
　　A fountain at salute, a crown in view — (l. 12–14)

　　CMoP; MoAB; MoAmPo; MoP; NoAM; NoP; TrGrPo

To Emily Dickinson

46　You who desired so much — in vain to ask —
　　Yet fed your hunger like an endless task,
　　Dared dignify the labor, bless the quest —
　　Achieved that stillness ultimately best, (l. 1–4)

　　CMoP; NIP; NoAM; NOBA; NoP; Son; TAP

Voyages

47　O brilliant kids, frisk with your dog,
　　Fondle your shells and sticks, bleached
　　By time and the elements; but there is a line
　　You must not cross

48　The bottom of the sea is cruel.

49　And yet this great wink of eternity,

50　Bind us in time, O seasons clear, and awe.
　　O minstrel galleons of Carib fire,
　　Bequeath us to no earthly shore until
　　Is answered in the vortex of our grave
　　The seal's wide spindrift gaze toward paradise.

　　AmPP; CMoP; MoP; MOS; NAAL-2; NoAM; NOBA; NoP;
　　OxBA; PoE; TAP; VGW

51　Creation's blithe and petaled word
　　To the lounged goddess when she rose
　　Conceding dialogue with eyes
　　That smile unsearchable repose —

52　The imaged word, it is that holds
　　Hushed willows anchored in its glow.
　　It is the unbetrayable reply
　　Whose accent no farewell can know.

　　CMoP; HAP; MoAB; MoAmPo; NoAM; NOBA; NoP; TAP;
　　UnPo

The Wine Menagerie

53　when wine redeems the sight,
　　Narrowing the mustard scansions of the eyes, (l. 1–2)

54　Petrushka's valentine pivots on its pin." (l. 49)

　　NoAM; NOBA; OxBA; VGW

STEPHEN CRANE　(1871–1900)

The Black Riders

1　I saw a man pursuing the horizon; (l. 1)

2 "It is futile," I said,
"You can never — "

AmPP; FF; HoPM; LiTA; LiTM; MAT; MoAmPo; NOBA

3 I saw a creature, naked, bestial,
Who, squatting upon the ground,
Held his heart in his hands,
And ate of it.

4 "But I like it
Because it is bitter,
And because it is my heart."

FaBoEE; HoPM; LiTM; MoAmPo; NOBA; OxBSP; TAP;
TW

5 A youth in apparel that glittered
Went to walk in a grim forest.
There he met an assassin

6 "I am enchanted, believe me,
To die, thus,
In this mediæval fashion,
According to the best legends;

7 Then took he the wound, smiling,
And died, content.

AA; LiTA; MoAmPo; NAAL-2

War Is Kind

8 Do not weep, maiden, for war is kind

9 Swift blazing flag of the regiment,
Eagle with crest of red and gold,
These men were born to drill and die.
Point for them the virtue of slaughter,
Make plain to them the excellence of killing
And a field where a thousand corpses lie.

AmPP; FPL; LiTA; LiTM; NAAL-2; NOBA; OBWP; PoLF;
TAP; WaaP

RICHARD CRASHAW (1613?–1649)

An Epitaph upon Husband and Wife Who Died
and Were Buried Together

1 To these, whom Death again did wed,
This grave's the second Marriage-bed. (l. 1–2)

2 (Pillow hard, and sheets not warm)
Love made the bed; they'll take no harm. (l. 13–14)

EBEV; ELP; FaBoEE; NOBE; OBEV; OBS; SeCePo;
SeCP; TrGrPo

The Flaming Heart

3 O thou undaunted daughter of desires!
By all thy dower of lights and fires;
By all the eagle in thee, all the dove;
By all thy lives and deaths of love;
By thy large draughts of intellectual day,
And by thy thirsts of love more large then they;
By all thy brim-fill'd Bowls of fierce desire,
By thy last Morning's draught of liquid fire;
By the full kingdom of that final kiss
That seiz'd thy parting Soul, and seal'd thee his;
(l. 93–102)

LiTB; NAEL-1; OAEL-1; PoEL-2; SeCePo; SeCV-1; TEP

In the Holy Nativity of Our Lord God

4 We saw Thee in Thy balmy nest,
Young Dawn of our Eternal Day!
We saw Thine eyes break from the East
And chase the trembling shades away.
We saw Thee and we blest the sight,
We saw Thee by Thine own sweet light. (l. 31–36)

5 Welcome, all wonders in one night!
Eternity shut in a span,
Summer in winter, day in night,
Heaven in earth, and God in man.
Great Little One! Whose all-embracing birth
Lifts earth to heaven, stoops heaven to earth.
(l. 79–84)

HAP; MeLP; MePo; OBS; PoEL-2; SeCV-1; WGRP

Music's Duel

6 Runs to and fro, complaining his sweet cares
Because those pretious mysteries that dwell
In musick's ravish't soule hee dare not tell,
But whisper to the world: thus doe they vary
Each string his Note, as if they meant to carry
Their Masters blest soule (snatcht out at his Eares
By a strong Extasy) through all the sphæres
Of Musicks heaven; and seat it there on high
In th' Empyrum of pure Harmony. (l. 142–150)

OAEL-1; OBS; SeCP; SeCV-1

Saint Mary Magdalene

7 Every Morne from hence,
A brisk Cherub something sips,
Whose sacred influence
Adds sweetnes to his sweetest lips,
Then to his Musick, and his song
Tastes of his breakfast all day long. (l. 25–30)

8 And now where e're he strayes
Among the Galilaean mountains,
Or more unwelcome wayes,
Hee's follow'd by two faithfull fountaines,
Two walking Baths, two weeping motions;
Portable and compendious Oceans. (l. 109–114)

FaBoCo; MeLP; MePo; OAEL-1; OBEV; Par; SeCP; SeCV-1

To the Infant Martyrs

9 Go, smiling souls, your new-built cages break,
In heaven you'll learn to sing, ere here to speak,
Nor let the milky fonts that bathe your thirst
Be your delay;
The place that calls you hence is, at the worst,
Milk all the way. (l. 1–6)

NAEL-1; NoP; OxBSP; SeCV-1

To the Noblest and Best of Ladies, the Countess of Denbigh

10 What heaven-entreated heart is this
Stands trembling at the gate of bliss;
Holds fast the door, yet dares not venture
Fairly to open it and enter?
Whose definition is a doubt
'Twixt life and death, 'twixt in and out? (l. 1–6)

JCP; MeLP; MePo; SeCP

Upon the Body of Our Blessed Lord, Naked and Bloody

11 They have left thee naked, Lord, O that they had!
This garment too I wish they had deny'd.
Thee with thy self they have too richly clad;
Opening the purple wardrobe in thy side.
O never could there be garment too good
For thee to wear, but this of thine own Blood. (l. 1–6)

ACP; HoPM; InvP; OAEL-1; OBS; OxBSP; SeCP; SeCV-1; TrCP

Wishes to His Supposed Mistress

12 Who ere shee bee,
That not impossible shee
That shall command my heart and mee; (l. 1–3)

13 In her whole frame,
Have Nature all the Name,
Art and ornament the shame.

Her flattery,
Picture and Poesy,
Her counsell her owne vertue bee. (l. 97–102)

BoLoP; EBEV; GTBS; GTBS-P; MeLP; MePo; OBEV; PoEL-2; SeCP; SeCV-1

ROBERT CREELEY (b. 1926)

Ballad of the Despairing Husband

1 My wife and I lived all alone,
contention was our only bone.
I fought with her, she fought with me,
and things went on right merrily. (l. 1–4)

2 Oh come home soon, I write to her.
Go screw yourself, is her answer.
Now what is that, for Christian word?
I hope she feeds on dried goose turd. (l. 9–12)

3 And I will wear what dresses I choose!
And I will dance, and what's to lose!
I'm free of you, you little prick,
and I'm the one can make it stick. (l. 29–32)

4 Oh lovely lady, morning or evening or afternoon.
Oh lovely lady, eating with or without a spoon.
Oh most lovely lady, whether dressed or undressed or
     partly.
Oh most lovely lady, getting up or going to bed or
     sitting only. (l. 40–43)

NeAP; NoP; OBAL; SM

The Door

5 It is hard going to the door
cut so small in the wall where
the vision which echoes loneliness
brings a scent of wild flowers in the wood. (l. 1–4)

6 Mighty magic is a mother,
in her there is another issue
of fixture, repeated form, the race renewal,
the charge of the command. (l. 25–28)

7 The Lady has always moved to the next town
and you stumble on after Her. (l. 55–56)

8 I will go to the garden.
I will be a romantic. I will sell
myself in hell,
in heaven also I will be. (l. 77–80)

NaP; NeAP; NoAM; PoM; VGW

I Know a Man

9 shall we &
why not, buy a goddamn big car,

drive, he sd, for
christ's sake, look
out where yr going. (l. 8–12)

CAPP; InPS; MAT; NOBA; OxBSP; PoM; PPP

If You

10 Dead. Died. Will die. Want.
Morning, midnight. I asked you

if you were going to get a pet
what kind of animal would you get. (l. 13–16)

MoP; NeAP; NoAM; NOBA; SM

The Rain

11 Love, if you love me,
lie next to me.
Be for me, like rain,
the getting out

of the tiredness, the fatuousness, the semi-
lust of intentional indifference. (l. 17–22)

CAPP; CoAP; PoE; VGW

The Way

12 My love's manners in bed
are not to be discussed by me, (l. 1–2)

13 Oh well, I will say here,
knowing each man,
let you find a good wife too,
and love her as hard as you can. (l. 8–11)

BoLoP; LiTM; NeAP; PPP

The Whip

14 my love was a feather, a flat

sleeping thing. (l. 2–3)

EOEF; MoP; NaP; NeAP; PoE; PoM

A Wicker Basket

15 Comes the time when it's later
and onto your table the headwaiter
puts the bill, (l. 1–3)

16 There are very huge stars, man, in the sky, (l. 21)

CAPP; HAP; MoP; NoAM; NoP; SM

The Window

17 Position is where you
put it, where it is. (l. 1–2)

CAPP; NoAM; NOBA; TAP; VGW

COUNTEE CULLEN   (1903–1946)

For a Lady I Know

1 poor black cherubs rise at seven
To do celestial chores. (l. 3–4)

AmNP; CDC; HeIP; IDB; InPK; MoAmPo; NIP; OBAL;
PoBA; PoNe; TAP

From the Dark Tower

2 We shall not always plant while others reap (l. 1)

3 The night whose sable breast relieves the stark,
White stars, is no less lovely being dark, (l. 9–10)

4 So in the dark we hide the heart that bleeds,
And wait, and tend our agonizing seeds. (l. 13–14)

BANP; BPo; CDC; IDB; LiTM; NAAL-2; PoBA; PoNe;
Son

Heritage

5 What is Africa to me:
Copper sun or scarlet sea,
Jungle star or jungle track,
Strong bronzed men, or regal black
Women from whose loins I sprang
When the birds of Eden sang? (l. 1–6)

6 Africa? A book one thumbs
Listlessly, till slumber comes. (l. 31–32)

7 What is last year's snow to me,
Last year's anything? The tree
Budding yearly must forget
How its past arose or set — (l. 52–55)

8 Quaint, outlandish heathen gods
Black men fashion out of rods, (l. 85–86)

9 Father, Son, and Holy Ghost,
So I make an idle boast;
Jesus of the twice-turned cheek
Lamb of God, although I speak
With my mouth thus, in my heart
Do I play a double part. (l. 93–98)

10 Lord, I fashion dark gods, too,
Daring even to give You
Dark despairing features (l. 107–108)

11 All day long and all night through,
One thing only must I do:
Quench my pride and cool my blood,
Lest I perish in the flood. (l. 116–119)

12 Not yet has my heart or head
In the least way realized
They and I are civilized. (l. 125–127)

AmNP; BANP; BPo; FaBV; HeIP; MoAmPo; NAAL-2;
NoAM; NoP; PoBA; TTY

Incident

13 Now I was eight and very small,
And he was no whit bigger,
And so I smiled, but he poked out
His tongue, and called me, "Nigger." (l. 5–8)

BPo; CDC; FF; IDB; NAAL-2; NoAM; NTCP; OBCA;
PoBA; PoNe; SoSe; VGW

Saturday's Child

14 I cut my teeth as the black raccoon —
For implements of battle. (l. 3–4)

15 Dame Poverty gave me my name,
And Pain godfathered me. (l. 11–12)

16 Death cut the strings that gave me life,
And handed me to Sorrow,
The only kind of middle wife
My folks could beg or borrow. (l. 17–20)

LiTM; NAs; OFD; PoBA; SaC

Simon the Cyrenian Speaks

17 At first I said, "I will not bear
His cross upon my back;
He only seeks to place it there
Because my skin is black." (l. 5–8)

AmNP; BPo; HAP; MoAmPo; TrCP; TTY

Yet Do I Marvel

18 I doubt not God is good, well-meaning, kind, (l. 1)

19 Inscrutable His ways are, and immune
To catechism by a mind too strewn
With petty cares to slightly understand
What awful brain compels His awful hand.
Yet do I marvel at this curious thing:
To make a poet black, and bid him sing! (l. 9–14)

AmNP; BANP; BPo; CDC; FF; IDB; NAAL-2; NoAM;
PoBA; PoNe; Son; TAP; TTY

EDWARD ESTLIN CUMMINGS
(1894–1962)

all ignorance toboggans into know

1 all ignorance toboggans into know
and trudges up to ignorance again:
but winter's not forever, even snow
melts; and if spring should spoil the game, what then?

all history's a winter sport or three: (l. 1–5)

2 — tomorrow is our permanent address (l. 12)

NAAL-2; NOBA; OxBA; WaP

All in green went my love riding

3 All in green went my love riding (l. 1)

CMoP; FaBV; GoJo; HeIP; LiTA; LiTM; MoP; NoAM;
NoP; OxBA; PoRA; SD

anyone lived in a pretty how town

4 anyone lived in a pretty how town
(with up so floating many bells down)
spring summer autumn winter
he sang his didn't he danced his did. (l. 1–4)

5 someones married their everyones
laughed their cryings and did their dance
(sleep wake hope and then) they
said their nevers they slept their dream (l. 17–20)

6 one day anyone died i guess
(and noone stooped to kiss his face)
busy folk buried them side by side
little by little and was by was (l. 25–28)

CMoP; FPL; HAP; InPK; LiTA; LiTM; MoAB; MoAmPo;
NAAL-2; NIP; NOBA; NoP; PoA; PrIm; RB; TAP; TwCP;
VGW; WeW

As Freedom Is a Breakfastfood

7 hopes dance best on bald men's hair (l. 9)

8 worms are the words but joy's the voice (l. 22)

9 deeds cannot dream what dreams can do
— time is a tree (this life one leaf)
but love is the sky and i am for you
just so long and long enough (l. 25–28)

CMoP; LiTA; LiTM; MAT; NOBA; OxBA; TAP; VGW

Buffalo Bill's

10 Buffalo Bill's
defunct (l. 1–2)

11 how do you like your blueeyed boy
Mister Death (l. 10–11)

AmFN; AmPP; CMoP; HeIP; InPK; LiTA; NAAL-2; NIP;
NOBA; OBD; OxBSP; PoE; RB; TAP; VGW

Chansons Innocentes

12 in Just-
spring when the world is mud-
luscious the little
lame balloonman

whistles far and wee

AmPP; FaBV; FaPON; HeIP; InPK; MoAB; MoAmPo;
MoShBr; NAAL-2; NIP; NoP; PrIm; SoSe; WeW

13 look the spangles
that sleep all the year in a dark box
dreaming of being taken out and allowed to shine,
the balls the chains red and gold the fluffy threads,

put up your little arms
and i'll give them all to you to hold

NTCP; OBCP; PChr; PDV

i sing of olaf glad and big

14 i sing of Olaf glad and big
whose warmest heart recoiled at war:
a conscientious object-or (l. 1–3)

15 Olaf (being to all intents
a corpse and wanting any rag
Upon what god unto him gave)
responds, without getting annoyed
"I will not kiss your f.ing flag" (l. 15–19)

16 (a yearning nation's blueeyed pride) (l. 23)

17 our president. being of which
assertions duly notified
threw the yellowsonofabitch
into a dungeon, where he died (l. 34–37)

18 and Olaf, too

preponderatingly because
unless statistics lie he was
more brave than me: more blond than you. (l. 39–42)

HeIP; LiTA; LiTM; MoP; NAAL-2; NoAM; NOBA; NoP;
OBSV; O3WP; VGW; WaP

i thank you god for most this amazing

19 i thank You God for most this amazing
day: for the leaping greenly spirits of trees
and a blue true dream of sky; and for everything
which is natural which is infinite which is yes
(l. 1–4)

EaLo; MoA3; TAP; TrCP

If I Have Made, My Lady, Intricate

20 lady through whose profound and fragile lips
the sweet small clumsy feet of April came

into the ragged meadow of my soul. (l. 13–15)

CMoP; FaBV; NOBA; PoRA

Maggie and Milly and Molly and May

21 For whatever we lose (like a you or a me)
it's always ourselves we find in the sea (l. 11–12)

NoAM; NOBA; RB; RHPC

A Man Who Had Fallen among Thieves

22 fate per a somewhat more than less
emancipated evening
had in return for consciousness
endowed him with a changeless grin (l. 5–8)

HAP; LiTM; MoP; NoAM; NOBA; OxBA; TAP

may I feel said he

23 may i feel said he
(i'll squeal said she
just once said he)
it's fun said she (l. 1–4)

24 (cccome? said he
   ummm said she)
   you're divine! said he
   (you are Mine said she) (l. 29–32)

   BoLoP; ErPo; FF; HeIP; LiTA; NBLV; NOBE

my father moved through dooms of love

25 my father moved through dooms of love
   through sames of am through haves of give,
   singing each morning out of each night
   my father moved through depths of height (l. 1–4)

   CMoP; DiL; FYAP; HAP; LiTA; MoAB; MoP; NAAL-2;
   NoAM; NOBA; NoP; OxBA; TAP; UnPo

My Sweet Old Etcetera

26 my
   mother hoped that

   i would die etcetera
   bravely of course my father used
   to become hoarse talking about how it was
   a privilege and if only he
   could (l. 12–17)

27 (dreaming,
   et
   cetera, of
   Your smile
   eyes knees and of your Etcetera) (l. 21–25)

   AmPP; AnAmPo; CMoP; FF; HeIP; InPS; OBAL; OBWP;
   OxBA; PPP; SOTW; WaaP; WaP

next to of course god america i

28 next to of course god america i
   love you land of the pilgrims' and so forth (l. 1–2)

29 these heroic happy dead
   who rushed like lions to the roaring slaughter
   they did not stop to think they died instead
   then shall the voice of liberty be mute?

   He spoke. And drank rapidly a glass of water
                                    (l. 10–14)

   AmFN; AmPP; FaBoPV; InPK; LiTM; NAAL-2; NBLV;
   NoP; OBWP; OFD; OPOP; OxBA; TAP; VGW; WaaP

Nobody Loses All the Time

30 my Uncle Sol's farm
   failed because the chickens
   ate the vegetables so

my Uncle Sol had a
chicken farm till the
skunks ate the chickens when (l. 14–19)

31 (and down went
   my Uncle
   Sol

   and started a worm farm) (l. 35–38)

   CMoP; DL; FaBoCo; FF; LiTM; NAAL-2; NBLV; NOBA;
   RB; TwCP

o sweet spontaneous

32 O sweet spontaneous
   earth (l. 1–2)

33 the
   doting

   fingers of
   prurient philosophers (l. 3–6)

34 the naughty thumb
   of science (l. 10–11)

   MoP; NAAL-2; NoAM; NoP; PrIm

pity this busy monster, manunkind

35 pity this busy monster, manunkind,

   not. Progress is a comfortable disease: (l. 1–2)

36 A world of made
   is not a world of born- (l. 8–9)

   AmPP; LiTA; LiTM; NAAL-2; NOBA; OxBA; PPP; TAP

plato told him

37 plato told

   him: he couldn't
   believe it (l. 1–3)

38 it took
   a nipponized bit of
   the old sixth
   avenue
   el; in the top of his head: to tell

   him (l. 20–25)

   AmFN; AmPP; CTC; MoP; NoAM; NOBA; OxBA; PoE;
   WaP

Poem, or Beauty Hurts Mr. Vinal

39 of you i
   sing: land of Abraham Lincoln and Lydia E. Pinkham,
   land above all of Just Add Hot Water And Serve —
   from every B. V. D.

   let freedom ring (l. 10–14)

40 perpetually crouched, quivering, upon the
   sternly allotted sandpile
   — how silently
   emit a tiny violet flavoured nuisance: Odor?

   o no.
   comes out like a ribbon lies flat on the brush
                                    (l. 50–55)

   InPS; MoAB; MoAmPo; NAAL-2; OBAL; OxBA

a politician

41 a politician is an arse (l. 1)

   FaBoEE; InPK; NBLV; OBAL; TW

R-P-O-P-H-E-S-S-A-G-R

42 to
   rea(be)rran(com)gi(e)ngly
   , grasshopper; (l. 14–16)

   AmPP; NoP; PoE; PPP

she being brand-new

43 she being brand

   -new; and you
   know consequently a
   little stiff i was
   careful of her (l. 1–5)

   ErPo; MoP; NOBA; OxBA

since feeling is first

44 since feeling is first
   who pays any attention
   to the syntax of things
   will never wholly kiss you; (l. 1–4)

45 to be a fool
   while Spring is in the world
   my blood approves, (l. 5–7)

46 for life's not a paragraph (l. 15)

47 And death i think is no parenthesis (l. 16)

   MoAB; MoAmPo; NoP; PrIm

Somewhere I have never travelled, gladly beyond

48 in your most frail gesture are things which enclose me,
   or which i cannot touch because they are too near
                                    (l. 3–4)

49 you open always petal by petal myself as Spring opens
   (touching skilfully, mysteriously) her first rose
                                    (l. 7–8)

   BoLoP; InPS; LiTA; LiTM; MoAB; MoAmPo; NAAL-2;
   NoP; SOTW; TrGrPo; TwCP; UnAS; VGW

Sonnets — Actualities

50 i like my body when it is with your
   body. (l. 1–2)

51 And eyes big love-crumbs,

   and possibly i like the thrill

   of under me you so quite new (l. 12–14)

   BoLoP; ErFo; LLLT; Son; VGW

Sonnets — Realities

52 the Cambridge ladies who live in furnished souls
   are unbeautiful and have comfortable minds (l. 1–2)

53 they believe in Christ and Longfellow, both dead, (l. 5)

   AmPP; HeIP; MoP; NAAL-2; NoAM; NOBA; NoP; OBAL;
   OxBA; TAP

Spring is like a perhaps hand

54 Spring is like a perhaps hand (l. 1)

55 moving a perhaps
   fraction of flower here placing
   an inch of air there) and

   without breaking anything. (l. 16–19)

   AmPP; NoP; SOTW; TAP; VGW

what if a much of a which of a wind

56 what if a much of a which of a wind
   gives the truth to summer's lie;
   bloodies with dizzying leaves the sun
   and yanks immortal stars awry? (l. 1–4)

57 — all nothing's only our hugest home;
the most who die, the more we live (l. 23–24)

BLPL; FaFP; LiTA; LiTM; MoAmPo; NAAL-2; NOBA;
NoP; OxBA; PoA; PoRA; PPP; SoSe; WaP

WARING CUNEY (1906–1976)

No Images

1 She does not know
Her beauty,
She thinks her brown body
Has no glory. (l. 1–4)

AmNP; BANP; CDC; MAT; NIP; TTY

ALLAN CUNNINGHAM (1784–1842)

A Wet Sheet and a Flowing Sea

1 A wet sheet and a flowing sea,
A wind that follows fast
And fills the white and rustling sail
And bends the gallant mast; (l. 1–4)

2 While the hollow oak our palace is,
Our heritage the sea. (l. 23–24)

BoTP; EnRP; FaBoBe; FaPoR; GN; GoTS; GTBS; GTBS-
P

JAMES VINCENT CUNNINGHAM
(1911–1985)

And what is love? Misunderstanding, pain

1 Like an old brandy after a long rain,
Distinguished, and familiar, and aloof. (l. 3–4)

CRP; HAP; HoPM; PoA

Epitaph for Someone or Other

2 Naked I came, naked I leave the scene, (l. 1)

OBAL; SM; VGW

I had gone broke, and got set to come back

3 a long shot at long odds, a black mare
By Hatred out of Envy by Despair. (l. 3–4)

OxBSP; QFR

Montana Pastoral

4 no images of pastoral will,
But fear, thirst, hunger, and and huddled chill.
(l. 9–10)

MAT; MoAmPo; PrIm; VGW

DAVID DAICHES (b. 1912)

To Kate, Skating Better than Her Date

1 Wait, Kate! You skate at such a rate
You leave behind your skating mate.
Your splendid speed won't you abate?
He's lagging far behind you, Kate. (l. 1–4)

2 He's anxious to expatiate
On how he wants you for his mate.
And don't you want to hear him, Kate? (l. 26–28)

ASP; FiBHP; NYBP; SD

GEORGE DANIEL (1616–1657)

The Robin

1 There, full in notes, to ravish all
My Earth, I wonder what to call
My dullness; when
I heare thee, prettie Creature, bring
Thy better odes of Praise, and Sing,
To puzzle men:
Poore pious Elfe!
I am instructed by thy harmonie,
To sing the Time's uncertaintie,
Safe in my Selfe. (l. 21–30)

FaBoRV; FM; OBS; PBBP

SAMUEL DANIEL (1562–1619)

Hymen's Triumph

1 Love is a torment of the mind,
A tempest everlasting;
And Jove hath made it of a kind
Not well, nor full, nor fasting.

ElL; ELP; NOBE; OBEV; OBSC; PoEL-2

Tethy's Festival

2 Are they shadows that we see?
And can shadows pleasures give?
Pleasures only shadows be,
Cast by bodies we conceive;

3 Pleasures are not, if they last;
In their passing is their best:
Glory is more bright and gay
In a flash, and so away.

4 When your eyes have done their part
Thought must length'n it in the heart.

CH; ElL; InvP; NOBE; NoP; OBSC; PoEL-2

To Delia

5 Beauty, sweet Love, is like the morning dew,
Whose short refresh upon the tender green
Cheers for a time, but till the sun doth shew,
And straight 'tis gone as it had never been.

6 Short is the glory of the blushing rose,
The hue which thou so carefully dost nourish,
Yet which at length thou must be forced to lose.

7 But ah, no more! this must not be foretold,
For women grieve to think they must be old.

ElL; NOBE; OBEV; OBSC

8 Care-charmer Sleep, son of the sable Night,
Brother to Death, in silent darkness born,
Relieve my languish, and restore the light,
With dark forgetting of my cares return.

AAS; ElL; GTBS; GTBS-P; InPS; LiTB; NAEL-1; NIP;
NOBE; NoP; OAEL-1; OBSC; PoEL-2; Son; TrGrPo

9 Fair is my Love, and cruel as she's fair
Her brow shades frowns, although her eyes are sunny;
Her smiles are lightning, though her pride despair;
And her disdains are gall, her favours honey.
A modest maid, decked with a blush of honour,
Whose feet do tread green paths of youth and love,

AAS; ElL; HoPM; LiTB; NOBE; NoP; OBEV; OBSC;
TEP; TrGrPo

10 If this be love, to clothe me with dark thoughts,
Haunting untrodden paths to wail apart;
My pleasures horror, music tragic notes,
Tears in mine eyes and sorrow at my heart.
If this be love, to live a living death,
Then do I love and draw this weary breath.

AAS; GBL; OBSC; TrGrPo

11 Let others sing of knights and paladins
In aged accents and untimely words,
Paint shadows, in imaginary lines,

12 These are the arks, the trophies, I erect,
That fortify thy name against old age;
And these thy sacred virtues must protect
Against the dark and Time's consuming rage.

13 Suffice they show I lived, and loved thee dear.

AAS; ElL; NOBE; NoP; OBEV; OBSC

14 No April can revive thy withered flowers,
Whose blooming grace adorns thy glory now;
Swift speeding Time, feathered with flying hours,
Dissolves the beauty of the fairest brow.
Oh let not then such riches waste in vain,
But love whilst that thou mayst be loved again.

ElL; HeIP; NoP; OBSC; SeCePo

15 When men shall find thy flow'r, thy glory, pass,
And thou with careful brow, sitting alone,
Received hast this message from thy glass,
That tells the truth and says that All is gone;

16 My faith shall wax, when thou art in thy waning.
The world shall find this miracle in me,
That fire can burn when all the matter's spent:
Then what my faith hath been thyself shalt see,
And that thou wast unkind thou may'st repent. —
Thou may'st repent that thou hast scorn'd my tears,
When Winter snows upon thy sable hairs.

ElL; NAEL-1; NOBE; NoP; OBEV; OBSC; Son; TrGrPo

17 When winter snows upon thy sable hairs,
And frost of age hath nipped thy beauties near;
When dark shall seem thy day that never clears,
And all lies withered that was held so dear,
Then take this picture which I here present thee,
Limned with a pencil not all unworthy;

CTC; OBSC; Son; TEP

Ulysses and the Siren

18 Fair nymph, if fame or honour were
To be attained with ease,
Then would I come and rest me there, (l. 9—11)

19 To spend the time luxuriously
Becomes not men of worth. (l. 15—16)

20 This honour is a thing conceived
And rests on others' fame; (l. 19—20)

21 The best thing of our life, our rest,
And give us up to toil. (l. 23—24)

22 To purge the mischiefs that increase
And all good order mar,
For oft we see a wicked peace
To be well changed for war. (l. 61–64)

ElL; HAP; NAEL-1; NOBE; NoP; OBEV; OBSC; PoEL-2;
PoE; TEP

DANTE ALIGHIERI (1265–1321)

Of the Lady Pietra degli Scrovigni

1 Utterly frozen is this youthful lady,
Even as the snow that lies within the shade;
For she is no more moved than is the stone
By the sweet season which makes warm the hills
(l. 7–10)

AWP; OAEL-2; OBVE; PFI

HUGH ANTOINE D'ARCY (1843–1925)

The Face upon the Floor

1 'Twas a balmy summer evening, and a goodly crowd
was there.
Which well-nigh filled Joe's barroom on the corner of
the square, (l. 1–2)

2 "Come, boys, I know there's kindly hearts among so
good a crowd —
To be in such good company would make a deacon
proud. (l. 11–12)

3 And then I met a woman — now comes the funny part —
With eyes that petrified my brain, and sunk into my
heart. (l. 39–40)

4 the vagabond began
To sketch a face that well might buy the soul of any
man.
Then, as he placed another lock upon the shapely head,
With a fearful shriek, he leaped and fell across the
picture — dead. (l. 65–68)

BeLS; BLPA; FaBoBe; FaFP; FPL

GEORGE DARLEY (1795–1846)

It Is Not Beauty I Demand

1 There's many a white hand holds an urn
With lovers' hearts to dust consumed. (l. 23–24)

GTBS; GTBS-P; NAEL-2; OAEL-2; OBNC

The Mermaiden's Vesper Hymn

2 In his green den the murmuring seal
Close by his sleek companion lies;
While singly we to bedward steal,
And close in fruitless sleep our eyes. (l. 9–12)

BIrV; FaBoRV; GBL; NAEL-2; OBNC; PoEL-4; WSC

Nepenthe

3 Her gorgeous death-bed! her rich pyre
Burnt up with aromatic fire!

BIrV; ChER; ChTr; FaBoCh; FaBoRV; NOBE; OAEL-2;
OBEV; OBNC; PBBP; WiR

SIR WILLIAM DAVENANT (1606–1668)

The Christian's Reply to the Philosopher

1 O harmless Death! whom still the valiant brave,
The wise expect, the sorrowful invite,
And all the good embrace, who know the grave
A short dark passage to eternal light. (l. 9–12)

MeLP; OBS

Endimion Porter and Olivia

2 Before we shall again behold
In his diurnal race the world's great eye,
We may as silent be and cold
As are the shades where buried lovers lie. (l. 1–4)

MeLP; MePo; NOBE; OBS

For the Lady Olivia Porter; a Present upon a New Year's Day

3 Go! climb that rock, and when thou there hast found
A star, contracted in a diamond, (l. 5–6)

4 Go! dive into the Southern Sea, and when
Th'ast found, to trouble the nice sight of men,
A swelling pearl, and such whose single worth
Boasts all the wonders which the seas bring forth,
Give it Endymion's love, whose ev'ry tear
Would more enrich the skilful jeweller. (l. 9–14)

JCP; MeLP; MePo; OBS

The Law against Lovers

5 In every grave make room, make room!
The world's at an end, and we come, we come.

ELP; FaBoCh; HAP; SeCePo

Lover and Philosopher

6 Your Beauty, ripe, and calm, and fresh,
As Eastern Summers are,
Must now, forsaking Time and Flesh,
Add light to some small Star. (l. 1–4)

ACP; MePo; NOBE; OBEV; Prf

JOHN DAVIDSON (1857–1909)

A Ballad of Hell

1 How long she stayed I cannot tell;
But when she felt this perfidy,
She marched across the floor of hell;
And all the damned stood up to see. (l. 77–80)

2 Seraphs and saints with one great voice
Welcomed that soul that knew not fear.
Amazed to find it could rejoice,
Hell raised a hoarse, half-human cheer. (l. 93–96)

EBVV; HoPM; MoBrPo; OHIP

In Romney Marsh

3 Masts in the offing wagged their tops;
The swinging waves pealed on the shore;
The saffron beach, all diamond drops
And beads of surge, prolonged the roar. (l. 13–16)

4 Night sank: like flakes of silver fire
The stars in one great shower came down; (l. 21–22)

EBVV; FaBoPP; GoTS; OxBTC

A Runnable Stag

5 A stag of warrant, a stag, a stag,
A runnable stag, a kingly crop,
Brow, bay and tray and three on top,
A stag, a runnable stag (l. 6–9)
and Hunters

BrPo; FaPoR; FM; GoTS; HAP; OBEV; OxBTC; PrIm;
SD; WiR

Thirty Bob a Week

6 For like a mole I journey in the dark,
A-travelling along the underground (l. 13–14)

7 But the difficultest go to understand,
And the difficultest job a man can do.
Is to come it brave and meek with thirty bob a week,
And feel that that's the proper thing for you.
(l. 87–90)

EBEV; EBVV; FaBoPV; FaBoTw; FaFP; LiTB; NOBE;
NOBVV OAEL-2; OBNC; OxBS; OxBTC

SIR JOHN DAVIES (1569–1626)

Nosce Teipsum

1 And as the sun above the light doth bring,
Though we behold it in the air below,
So from th' eternal Light the soul doth spring,
Though in the body she her powers do show.

CTC; LiTB; NOBE; OBSC; PoEL-2; SiPS

JOHN DAVIES, OF HEREFORD
(c. 1565–1618)

The Scourge of Folly

1 If there were, oh! an Hellespont of cream
Between us, milk-white mistress, I would swim
To you, to show to both my love's extreme,
Leander-like, — yea! dive from brim to brim.

ChTr; ElL; FaBoCh; FaBoNo; Son

WILLIAM HENRY DAVIES (1871–1940)

The Inquest

1 And I could see that child's one eye
Which seemed to laugh, and say with glee:
'What caused my death you'll never know —
Perhaps my mother murdered me.' (l. 25–28)

GTBS-P; NOBE; OxBTC; RB

Leisure

2 What is this life if, full of care,
We have no time to stand and stare. (l. 1–2)

AWP; BoNaP; BoTP; CH; FaBoBe; FaFP; FaPON; LiTB;
LiTM; MoBrPo; MoShBr; NOBE; OBEV; OBMV; PoRA;
SeCePo; TrGrPo

The Villain

3 I turned my head and saw the wind,
  Not far from where I stood,
  Dragging the corn by her golden hair,
  Into a dark and lonely wood. (l. 7–10)

MoBrPo; OxBSP; OxBTC; SoSe

FRANK MARSHALL DAVIS (b. 1905)

Flowers of Darkness

1 Slowly the night blooms, unfurling
  Flowers of darkness, covering
  The trellised sky, becoming
  A bouquet of blackness (l. 1–4)

2 The young woman-smell
  Of your poppy body
  Rises to my brain as opium (l. 18–20)

AmNP; IDB; NoP; PoBA; PoNe

Four Glimpses of Night

3 Night comes to the room of the world (l. 3)

4 Night is a curious child, wandering
  Between earth and sky, creeping
  In windows and doors, daubing
  The entire neighborhood
  With purple paint. (l. 1–5)

5 Night's brittle song, silver-thin
  Shatters into a billion fragments
  Of quiet shadows
  At the blaring jazz
  Of a morning sun. (l. 1–3)

AmNP; NoP; PoBA; PoNe

Robert Whitmore

6 Robert Whitmore
  died of apoplexy
  when a stranger from Georgia
  mistook him
  for a former Macon waiter. (l. 7–11)

BPo; NoP; PoBA; PoNe

CECIL DAY LEWIS (1904–1972)

Come live with me

1 Come, live with me and be my love,
  And we will all the pleasures prove
  Of peace and plenty, bed and board,
  That chance employment may afford. (l. 1–4)

2 Hunger shall make thy modest zone
  And cheat fond death of all but bone — (l. 13–14)

BoLoP; HAP; NIP; NoAM; NoP; OBMV

The Conflict

3 I sang as one
  Who on a tilting deck sings
  To keep men's courage up, though the wake hangs
  That shall cut off their sun. (l. 1–4)

4 Singing I was at peace,
  Above the clouds, outside the ring:
  For sorrow finds a swift release in song ·
  And pride its poise. (l. 13–16)

5 Move then with new desires,
  For where we used to build and love
  Is no man's land, and only ghosts can live
  Between two fires. (l. 29–32)

LiTB; LiTM; MoAB; MoBrPo; NoP

Do Not Expect Again a Phoenix Hour

6 Draw up the dew. Swell with pacific violence.
  Take shape in silence. Grow as the clouds grew.
  Beautiful brood the cornlands, and you are heavy;
  Leafy the boughs — they also hide big fruit. (l. 1–4)

CMoP; FaBoMo; LiTB; LiTM; MoAB; MoBrPo; NoAM;
OxBTC; PoRA

The Magnetic Mountain

7 Nearing again the legendary isle
  Where sirens sang and mariners were skinned,
  We wonder now what was there to beguile
  That such stout fellows left their bones behind.
                              (l. 1–4)

8 Lips that sealed up the sense from gnawing time
  Now beg the favor with a graveyard grin. (l. 7–8)

FaBoTw; LiTB; MoAB; MoBrPo

9 Father who endest all,
  Pity our broken sleep;
  For we lie down with tears
  And waken but to weep. (l. 21–24)

MoAB; MoBrPo; OBMV; PoA

Sheepdog Trials in Hyde Park

10 The shepherd is the brain behind the dog's brain,
   But his control of dog, like dog's of sheep
   Is never absolute — that's the beauty of it. (l. 30–32)

11 The guided missiles,
    The black-and-white angels follow each quirk and jink
       of
    The evasive sheep, play grandmother's-steps behind
       them,
    Freeze to the ground, or leap to head off a straggler
                                              (l. 33—36)

12 To lift, to fetch, to drive, to shed, to pen,
    Are acts I recognize, with all they mean
    Of shepherding the unruly, for a kind of
    Controlled woolgathering is my work too. (l. 45—48)

MoP; NoAM; NoP; OxBTC

Where Are the War Poets?

13 It is the logic of our times,
    No subject for immortal verse —
    That we who lived by honest dreams
    Defend the bad against the worse. (l. 5—8)

FaBoMo; OBWP; OxBSP; OxBTC

WALTER DE LA MARE ("WALTER RAMAL") (1873—1956)

All but Blind

1 All but blind
   In his chambered hole
   Gropes for worms
   The four-clawed Mole. (l. 1—4)

2 So, blind to Someone
   I must be. (l. 15—16)

FaPON; MoAB; MoBrPo; PDV; WeW

All That's Past

3 Oh, no man knows
   Through what wild centuries
   Roves back the rose. (l. 7—8)

4 We wake and whisper awhile,
   But, the day gone by,
   Silence and sleep like fields
   Of amaranth lie. (l. 21—24)

GoJo; MoAB; NOBE; OAEL-2; OBMV; OxBTC; TrGrPo

Bunches of Grapes

5 "Bunches of grapes," says Timothy;
   "Pomegranates pink," says Elaine;
   "A junket of cream and a cranberry tart." (l. 1—3)

6 "A bumpity ride in a wagon of hay
   For me," says Jane. (l. 11—12)

GoJo; G-Pl; MoShBr; OxBChV

The Ghost

7 'Who knocks?' 'I, who was beautiful,
   Beyond all dreams to restore,
   I from the roots of the dark thorn am hither,
   And knock on the door.' (l. 1—4)

8 A face peered. All the grey night
   In chaos of vacancy shone;
   Naught but vast sorrow was there —
   The sweet cheat gone. (l. 18—20)

BrPo; CMoP; ELP; EnLoPo; LiTM; MoAB; MoBrPo;
NOBE; OAEL-2; OxBTC

Here lies a most beautiful lady

9 But beauty vanishes; beauty passes;
   However rare — rare it be;
   And when I crumble, who will remember
   This lady of the West Country? (l. 5—8)

LiTB; LiTM; MoAB; MoBrPo; OBEV; RB

Jim Jay

10 Do diddle di do.
    Poor Jim Jay
    Got stuck fast
    In Yesterday. (l. 1—4)

BrPo; CenHV; SD; SO

The Listeners

11 "Is there anybody there?" said the Traveller,
    Knocking on the moonlit door; (l. 1—2)

12 "Tell them I came, and no one answered,
    That I kept my word," he said. (l. 27—28)

13 Ay, they heard his foot upon the stirrup,
    And the sound of iron on stone,
    And how the silence surged softly backward,
    When the plunging hoofs were gone. (l. 33—36)

AWP; BLFL; BrPo; CMoP; FaFP; FaPON; HAP; HeIP;
HoPM; InPK; IrvP; LiTB; LiTM; MoAB; MoBrPo; MoP;
NoAM; NOBE; NoP; OBEV; OBMV; OnMSP; PoRA;
SoSe; TrGrPo; WeW; WSC

Miss T.

14 It's a very odd thing —
As odd as can be —
That whatever Miss T. eats
Turns into Miss T.; (l. 1—4)

CenHV; FaBoBe; GoJo; GrPl; MoShBr; NTCP; OnUR;
PDV

Napoleon

15 'What is the world, O soldiers?
It is I,
I, this incessant snow,
This northern sky; (l. 1—4)

FaBoCh; FaBoTw; NOBE; RB

Nod

16 Softly along the road of evening,
In a twilight dim with rose,
Wrinkled with age, and drenched with dew
Old Nod, the shepherd, goes. (l. 1—4)

17 His are the quiet steeps of dreamland,
The waters of no-more-pain;
His ram's bell rings 'neath an arch of stars,
"Rest, rest, and rest again." (l. 17—20)

BoTP; MoAB; MoBrPo; OxBTC

The Old Summerhouse

18 for beauty with sorrow
Is a burden hard to be borne;
The evening light on the foam, and the swans, there;
That music, remote, forlorn. (l. 10—13)

CMoP; FaBoPP; FaBoRV; GTBS-P

Sam

9 Wonderful lovely there she sat,
Singing the night away,
All in the solitudinous sea
Of that there lonely bay. (l. 29—31)

FaBV; MoAB; MoBrPo; OnMSP

The Scribe

20 What lovely things
Thy hand hath made: (l. 1—2)

CMoP; FaBoCh; OBMV; TrCP; TrPWD

Silver

21 Slowly, silently, now the moon
Walks the night in her silver shoon; (l. 1—2)

22 A harvest mouse goes scampering by,
With silver claws and silver eye;
And moveless fish in the water gleam,
By silver reeds in a silver stream. (l. 11—14)

BoNaP; BoTP; FaPON; MoAB; MoBrPo; PoRA; PYC;
RHPC; TTTS

Some one came knocking

23 Some one came knocking
At my wee, small door;
Some one came knocking,
I'm sure — sure — sure; (l. 1—4)

FaPON; MoBrPo; PDV; RHPC

The Song of the Mad Prince

24 Who said, 'All Time's delight
Hath she for narrow bed;
Life's troubled bubble broken'? —
That's what I said. (l. 13—16)

EBEV; FaBoCh; GoJo; MoP; NoAM; NOBE; OxBChV

Summer Evening

25 Old Rover in his moss-greened house
Mumbles a bone, and barks at a mouse. (l. 3—4)

26 Dobbin at manger pulls his hay:
Gone is another summer's day. (l. 7—8)

FM; MoAB; MoBrPo; MoShBr

Tired Tim

27 Poor tired Tim! It's sad for him
He lags the long bright morning through,
Ever so tired of nothing to do; (l. 1—3)

BoTP; FaPON; MoShBr; NTCP; RHPC

JOHN BYRNE LEICESTER WARREN, 3RD BARON DE TABLEY (1835—1895)

The Churchyard on the Sands

1 My love lies in the gates of foam,
The last dear wreck of shore;
The naked sea-marsh binds her home,
The sand her chamber door. (l. 1—4)

2 Sleep, and forget all things but one,
Heard in each wave of sea, —
How lonely all the years will run
Until I rest by thee. (l. 97–100)

CH; FaBoPP; GBL; OBNC

EDWARD DE VERE, 17TH EARL OF OXFORD (1550–1604)

A Choice

1 Were I a king, I could command content;
Were I obscure, hidden should be my cares; (l. 1–2)

2 A doubtful choice, of these three which to crave,
A kingdom, or a cottage, or a grave. (l. 5–6)

EIL; FaBoEE; OBSC; OxBSP

PETER DE VRIES (b. 1910)

Bacchanal

1 And she, by passion once demented
— That woman out of Botticelli —
She brews and bottles, unfermented,
The stupid and abiding jelly. (l. 9–12)

BXAP; NBLV; NIP; NOBL; OBAL

THOMAS DEKKER (1572?–1632?)

The Shoemaker's Holiday

1 Troll the bowl, the jolly nut-brown bowl,
And here, kind mate, to thee!
Let's sing a dirge for Saint Hugh's soul,
And down it merrily.

EIL; OBSC; SeCePo; TrGrPo

2 Now the nightingale, the pretty nightingale,
The sweetest singer in all the forest's choir,
Entreats thee, sweet Peggy, to hear thy true Love's tale:
Lo! yonder she sitteth, her breast against a briar.

EIL; OBSC; PBBP; TrGrPo

THOMAS DEKKER AND OTHERS

The Pleasant Comedy of Patient Grissell

1 Golden slumbers kiss your eyes,
Smiles awake you when you rise.
Sleep, pretty wantons, do not cry,

And I will sing a lullaby:
Rock them, rock them, lullaby.

EIL; ELP; OBSC; OxBChV; TrGrPo

2 Work apace, apace, apace, apace;
Honest labour bears a lovely face;

CH; EIL; GTBS; GTBS-P; HAP; InPS; OBEV; OBSC;
RB; TrGrPo; UnPo

DENIS DEVLIN (1908–1959)

Ank'hor Vat

1 Buddha has covered the walls of the great temple
With the vegetative speed of his imagery (l. 4–5)

2 There is no mystery in the luminous lines
Of that high, animal face
The smile, sad, humouring and equal
Blesses without obliging
Loves without condescension; (l. 12–15)

BIrV; CIP; IPY; NOIV

CHARLES DICKENS (1812–1890)

The Fine Old English Gentleman; New Version

1 I'll sing you a new ballad, and I'll warrant it first-rate,
Of the days of that old gentleman who had that old
estate;
When they spent the public money at a bountiful old
rate
On ev'ry mistress, pimp, and scamp, at ev'ry noble
gate,
In the fine old English Tory times; (l. 1–5)

2 In those rare days, the press was seldom known to
snarl or bark,
But sweetly sang of men in pow'r, like any tuneful lark;
Grave judges, too, to all their evil deeds were in the
dark;
And not a man in twenty score knew how to make his
mark.
Oh the fine old English Tory times; (l. 25–30)

CoMu; FaEoBa; NOBVV; OBSV

JAMES DICKEY (b. 1923)

Buckdancer's Choice

1 The air split into nine levels,
Some gift of tongues of the whistler (l. 2–3)

2 For years, they have all been dying
  Out, the classic buck-and-wing men (l. 8–9)

3 Proclaiming what choices there are
  For the last dancers of their kind,

  For ill women and for all slaves
  Of death, (l. 26–29)

4 Not dancing but nearly risen
  Through barnlike, theatrelike houses
  On the winds of the buck and wing. (l. 31–33)

  HeIP; NoAM; NOBA; NoP; NYBP; PoNe

Cherrylog Road

5 Off Highway 106
  At Cherrylog Road I entered
  The '34 Ford without wheels,
  Smothered in kudzu,
  With a seat pulled out to run
  Corn whiskey down from the hills, (l. 1–6)

6 the parking lot of the dead. (l. 25)

7 Drunk on the wind in my mouth,
  Wringing the handlebar for speed,
  Wild to be wreckage forever. (l. 106–108)

  CoAP; HAP; HCAP; InPS; MT; NAAL-2; NIP; NYBP;
  PrIm; TwCP; WeW

Falling

8 with the plane nowhere and her body taking by the
    throat
  The undying cry of the void falling living beginning to
    be something
  That no one has ever been and lived through screaming
    without enough air (l. 9–11)

9 neat lipsticked stockinged girdled by regulation (l. 12)

10 sailing
   In sunlight smiling under their goggles swapping
     batons back and forth
   And He who jumped without a chute and was handed
     one by a diving
   Buddy. (l. 59–62)

11 She is watching her country lose its evoked master
     shape watching it lose
   And gain get back its houses and peoples watching it
     bring up
   Its local lights single homes lamps on barn roofs
                                          (l. 66–68)

12 all the fine
   Points of diving feet together toes pointed hands shaped
     right
   To insert her into water like a needle (l. 71–73)

13 who knows when what correct young woman must take
     up her body
   And fly (l. 85–86)

14 under chenille bed spreads
   The farm girls are feeling the goddess in them struggle
     and rise brooding (l. 93–94)

15 Boys finding for the first time their loins filled with
     heart's blood
   Widowed farmers whose hands float under light covers
     to find themselves
   Arisen at sunrise (l. 135–137)

16 a little sight left in the corner
   Of one eye fading seeing something wave lies believing
   That she could have made it (l. 159–161)

   LCAP; MT; NoAM; NYBP

The Heaven of Animals

17 Here they are. The soft eyes open.
   If they have lived in a wood
   It is a wood.
   If they have lived on plains
   It is grass rolling
   Under their feet forever. (l. 1–6)

18 These hunt, as they have done
   But with claws and teeth grown perfect,

   More deadly than they can believe. (l. 20–22)

19 those that are hunted
   Know this as their life,
   Their reward: to walk

   Under such trees in full knowledge
   Of what is in glory above them,
   And to feel no fear, (l. 29–34)

   CAPP; CoAP; HeIP; LiTM; MT; NAAL-2; NoAM; NOBA;
   PoE; TAP

The Hospital Window ·

20 I have just come down from my father.
   Higher and higher he lies
   Above me in a blue light
   Shed by a tinted window. (l. 1–4)

21 Ceremoniously, gravely, and weakly,
   Dozens of pale hands are waving (l. 19–20)

22 I am not afraid for my father —
Look! He is grinning; he is not

Afraid for my life, either, (l. 35–37)

CAPP; DiL; HCAP; MT; NoAM

The Performance

23 Dust fanned in scraped puffs from the earth
Between his arms, and blood turned his face inside out,
To demonstrate its suppleness
Of veins, as he perfected his role. (l. 13–16)

24 The back somersault, the kip-up —
And at last, the stand on his hands,
Perfect, with his feet together,
His head down, evenly breathing. (l. 32–35)

25 the thin, long human frame
Upside down in its own strange joy, (l. 39–40)

CAPP; CoAP; LiTM; MoP; NePoEA-2; NOBA; PoE

The Sheep Child

26 Farm boys wild to couple
With anything with soft-wooded trees
With mounds of earthmounds
Of pine straw will keep themselves off
Animals by legends of their own: (l. 1–5)

27 It was something like love
From another world that seized her
From behind, and she gave, not lifting her head
Out of dew, without ever looking, her best
Self to that great need. (l. 31–35)

28 I saw for a blazing moment
The great grassy world from both sides,
Man and beast in the round of their need, (l. 41–43)

CAPP; HCAP; MoP; MT; NoAM; NOBA; Prf; TAP

EMILY DICKINSON (1830–1886)

After great pain, a formal feeling comes

1 After great pain, a formal feeling comes — (l. 1)

2 This is the Hour of Lead —
Remembered, if outlived,
As Freezing persons, recollect the Snow —

First — Chill — then Stupor — then the letting go —
(l. 10–13)

AmPP; BoWoP; HAP; InPS; LiTA; MoAB; MoAmPo;
NAAL-1; NAWM-2; NoAM; NOBA; NoP; PoE; PrIm;
TAP; UnPo

Ample make this bed

3 Ample make this bed.
Make this bed with awe;
In it wait till judgment break
Excellent and fair. (l. 1–4)

MoAB; MoAmPo; NAAL-1; OxBA; PoEL-5

Apparently with no surprise

4 Apparently with no surprise
To any happy flower,
The frost beheads it at its play (l. 1–3)

5 The sun proceeds unmoved
To measure off another day
For an approving God. (l. 6–8)

AmPP; NAAL-1; NoP; PPP; SoSe; TrGrPo

As imperceptibly as Grief

6 As imperceptibly as Grief
The Summer lapsed away — (l. 1–2)

7 A courteous, yet harrowing Grace,
As Guest, that would be gone — (l. 11–12)

8 Our Summer made her light escape
Into the Beautiful. (l. 15–16)

CMoP; LiTA; NAAL-1; NOBA; NoP; PBWP; PoE;
PoEL-5; QFR

Because I could not stop for Death

9 Because I could not stop for Death —
He kindly stopped for me — (l. 1–2)

10 We paused before a House that seemed
A Swelling of the Ground — (l. 17–18)

11 Since then — 'tis Centuries — and yet
Feels shorter than the Day
I first surmised the Horses Heads
Were toward Eternity — (l. 21–24)

AmPP; AnAmPo; AWP; BoWoP; CMoP; DL; FF; FPL;
HAP; HeIP; InPK; LiTA; LiTM; Mes; MoAB; MoAmPo;
MoP; NAAL-1; NAWM-2; NIP; NoAM; NoP; OBD; OxBA;
PBWP; PoE; PoEL-5; SCV; SoSe; SOTW; TAP; UnPo;
WeW; WGRF; WPE

A Bird came down the Walk

12 A Bird came down the Walk —
He did not know I saw —
He bit an Angleworm in halves (l. 1–3)

13 And he unrolled his feathers
And rowed him softer home —

Than Oars divide the Ocean,
Too silver for a seam —
Or Butterflies, off Banks of Noon
Leap, plashless as they swim. (l. 15–20)

AmPP; BLPL; CMoP; FaPON; FF; FM; GoJo; InvP;
LiTA; LiTM; Mes; MoAmPo; NAAL-1; NoAM; NOBA;
NoP; NTCP; OBAL; OBCA; OxBA; PDV; PoLF; PoRA

The Brain is wider than the Sky

14 The Brain — is wider than the Sky — (l. 1)

15 The Brain is just the weight of God —
For — Heft them — Pound for Pound —
And they will differ — if they do —
As Syllable from Sound — (l. 9–12)

MoAB; MoAmPo; MoP; NAAL-1; NAWM-2; OxBA

The Bustle in a House

16 The Bustle in a House
The Morning after Death (l. 1–2)

17 The Sweeping up the Heart
And putting Love away
We shall not want to use again
Until Eternity. (l. 5–8)

FaBV; FPL; HAP; HeIP; NAAL-1; NoP; OBD; OxBA;
PoEL-5; PoLF; WGRP

A Clock stopped

18 A Clock stopped —
Not the Mantel's —
Geneva's farthest skill
Can't put the puppet bowing —
That just now dangled still — (l. 1–5)

19 Decades of Arrogance between
The Dial life —
And Him — (l. 16–18)

AmPP; NAAL-1; NoP; PoEL-5

Elysium is as far as to

20 Elysium is as far as to
The very nearest room,
If in that room a friend await
Felicity of doom. (l. 1–4)

AWP; GrPl; MoAB; MoAmPo; OxBA; WPE

"Faith" is a fine invention

21 "Faith" is a fine invention (l. 1)

22 But Microscopes are prudent
In an Emergency. (l. 3–4)

AmPP; FaBV; NAAL-1; NOBA; OxBA; TAP

Farther in summer than the birds

23 Farther in summer than the birds,
Pathetic from the grass,
A minor nation celebrates
Its unobtrusive mass. (l. 1–4)

24 Remit as yet no grace,
No furrow on the glow,
Yet a druidic difference
Enhances nature now. (l. 13–16)

AmPP; LiTA; NOBA; NoP; PoE; PoEL-5; QFR

The first Day's Night had come

25 The first Day's Night had come —
And grateful that a thing
So terrible — had been endured —
I told my Soul to sing — (l. 1–4)

26 And then — a Day as huge
As Yesterdays in pairs,
Unrolled its horror in my face —
Until it blocked my eyes — (l. 9–12)

LiTA; LiTM; OxBA; PoE; WPOW

The Heart asks Pleasure — first

27 The Heart asks Pleasure — first —
And then — Excuse from Pain — (l. 1–2)

28 The privilege to die — (l. 8)

AmPP; CMoP; MoAB; MoAmPo; NAAL-1; NOBA; NoP;
OxBA; PPP; PrIm; TrGrPo; WPE

"Hope" is the thing with feathers

29 "Hope" is the thing with feathers —
That perches in the soul — (l. 1–2)

30 Yet, never, in Extremity,
It asked a crumb — of Me. (l. 11–12)

AmPP; BLPL; MoAB; MoAmPo; MoShBr; NOBA; OxBA;
TAP

How many times these low feet staggered

31 How many times these low feet staggered —
Only the soldered mouth can tell — (l. 1–2)

32 Fearless — the cobweb swings from the ceiling —
Indolent Housewife — in Daisies — lain! (l. 11–12)

AmPP; HAP; NAAL-1; PoEL-5; WeW

I cannot live with you

33 I cannot live with you. (l. 1)

34 I could not die with you, (l. 13)

35 Nor could I rise with you,
Because your face
Would put out Jesus', (l. 21–23)

36 You there, I here,
With just the door ajar
That oceans are,
And prayer,
And that pale sustenance,
Despair! (l. 46–51)

AmPP; MAT; MoAB; MoAmPo; NAAL-1; NOBA; NoP;
OxBA; PoEL-5

I died for Beauty — but was scarce

37 I died for Beauty — but was scarce
Adjusted in the Tomb
When One who died for Truth, was lain
In an adjoining Room — (l. 1–4)

38 We talked between the Rooms —
Until the Moss had reached our lips —
And covered up — our names — (l. 10–12)

AnAmPo; AWP; BLPL; BoWoP; FaFP; LiTA; LiTM;
MoAB; MoAmPo; NAAL-2; NAWM-2; NOBA; NoP

I dreaded that first robin, so

39 I dreaded that first robin so,
But he is mastered now, (l. 1–2)

40 I dared not meet the daffodils, (l. 9)

41 I could not bear the bees should come, (l. 17)

42 They're here, though; not a creature failed,
No blossom stayed away
In gentle deference to me,
The Queen of Calvary.

Each one salutes me as he goes, (l. 21–25)

AmPP; HAP; MoAmPo; NAAL-1

I dwell in Possibility

43 I dwell in Possibility —
A fairer House than Prose — (l. 1–2)

44 For Occupation — This —
The spreading wide my narrow Hands
To gather Paradise — (l. 10–12)

NAWM-2; NIP; NoAM; NOBA; OxBA

I felt a Funeral, in my Brain

45 I felt a Funeral, in my Brain, (l. 1)

46 A Service like a Drum —
Kept beating — beating — till I thought
My Mind was going numb — (l. 6–8)

47 And then a Plank in Reason, broke,
And I dropped down, and down —
And hit a World, at every plunge,
And Finished knowing — then — (l. 17–20)

AmPP; AnAmPo; BoWoP; CMoP; LiTA; NAAL-1; NOBA;
NoP; OxBA; PBWP; PoE; PoEL-5; PoRA; SCV; TAP

I heard a Fly buzz — when I died

48 I heard a Fly buzz — when I died — (l. 1)

49 — and then it was
There interposed a Fly —

With Blue — uncertain stumbling Buzz —
Between the light — and me —
And then the Windows failed — and then
I could not see to see — (l. 12–16)

AmPP; AnAmPo; BoWoP; CMoP; DL; FF; HAP; HoPM;
InPK; LiTA; LiTM; MoAB; MoAmPo; MoP; NAAL-1;
NAWM-2; NoAM; NOBA; NoP; OBD; OxBA; PoE; PoRA;
PPP; SCV; SOTW; TAP; TOF; WeW

I know some lonely houses off the road

50 I know some lonely houses off the road
A robber'd like the look of, —
Wooden barred,
And windows hanging low, (l. 1–4)

51 There's plunder — where?
Tankard, or spoon,
Earring, or stone,
A watch, some ancient brooch
To match the grandmamma,
Staid sleeping there. (l. 25–30)

52 While the old couple, just astir,
Fancy the sunrise left the door ajar! (l. 39–40)

MoAB; MoAmPo; OxBA; PoRA; SO; WSC

I like a look of Agony

53 I like a look of Agony,
Because I know it's true — (l. 1–2)

54 The Eyes glaze once — and that is Death —
Impossible to feign (l. 5–6)

InPS; NAAL-1; NoP; OxBSP; PoE; TAP

I like to see it lap the Miles

55 I like to see it lap the Miles —
And lick the Valleys up — (l. 1–2)

56 And neigh like Boanerges —
Then — punctual as a Star
Stop — docile and omnipotent
At its own stable door — (l. 14–17)

AnAmPo; BoWoP; FaBV; FaPON; InPK; LiTA; LiTM;
MoAB; MoAmPo; MoShBr; NAAL-1; NAWM-2; NoAM;
NOBA; OBAL; OBCA; OxBA; PDV; PrIm; SoSe

I never lost as much but twice

57 I never lost as much but twice,
And that was in the sod. (l. 1–2)

58 Burglar! Banker — Father!
I am poor once more!

BLPL; MoAB; MoAmPo; NAAL-1; NoAM; NOBA; NoP;
TAP

I never saw a Moor

59 I never saw a Moor — (l. 1)

60 Yet know I how the heather looks (l. 3)

61 I never spoke with God
Nor visited in Heaven —
Yet certain am I of the spot
As if the Checks were given — (l. 5–8)

AA; FaFP; FaPON; FPL; GN; HeIP; LiTA; LiTM; MoAB;
MoAmPo; PoLF; TAP; TrGrPo; WGRP

I started Early — Took my Dog

62 I started Early — Took my Dog —
And visited the Sea — (l. 1–2)

63 But no Man moved Me — till the Tide
Went past my simple Shoe — (l. 9–10)

64 And He — He followed — close behind — (l. 17)

65 Until We met the Solid Town —
No One He seemed to know —
And bowing — with a Mighty look —
At me — The Sea withdrew — (l. 21–24)

AmPP; HAP; InPK; LiTA; LiTM; MOS; NAAL-1; PoEL-5;
WeW

I stepped from Plank to Plank

66 I stepped from Plank to Plank
A slow and cautious way (l. 1–2)

67 This gave me that precarious Gait
Some call Experience. (l. 7–8)

CMoP; NOBA; NOCV; OxBSP

I taste a liquor never brewed

68 I taste a liquor never brewed —
From Tankards scooped in Pearl! — (l. 1–2)

69 Inebriate of Air — am I —
And Debauchee of Dew — (l. 5–6)

70 And Saints — to windows run —
To see the little Tippler
Leaning against the — Sun — (l. 14–16)

AmPP; CMoP; FaBV; FF; HeIP; LiTA; LiTM; MoAmPo;
NAAL-1; NoAM; NOBA; NoP; OxBA; PoEL-5; SoSe;
TAP; WPE

I Years had been from Home

71 I Years had been from Home
And now before the Door
I dared not enter, (l. 1–3)

72 I fitted to the Latch
My Hand, with trembling care (l. 17–18)

73 Then moved my Fingers off
As cautiously as Glass
And held my ears, and like a Thief
Fled gasping from the House — (l. 21–24)

BLPL; NOBA; OxBA; PoRA

If I can stop one heart from breaking

74 If I can stop one heart from breaking
I shall not live in vain: (l. 1–2)

AH; FPL; OHFP; PoLF; PWR

If you were coming in the Fall

75 If you were coming in the Fall,
I'd brush the Summer by (l. 1–2)

76 If I could see you in a year,
I'd wind the months in balls – (l. 5–6)

77 If only Centuries, delayed,
I'd count them on my Hand, (l. 9–10)

78 If certain, when this life was out –
That your's and mine, should be –
I'd toss it yonder, like a Rind,
And take Eternity – (l. 13–16)

AmPP; NOBA; OxBA; PoRA

I'll tell you how the Sun rose

79 I'll tell you how the Sun rose –
A Ribbon at a time – (l. 1–2)

80 But how he set – I know not – (l. 9)

81 A Dominie in Gray –
Put gently up the evening Bars –
And led the flock away – (l. 14–16)

AmPP; FaBV; MoShBr; PDV; PoEL-5; TAP

I'm nobody! who are you?

82 I'm nobody, who are you? (l. 1)

83 How dreary to be somebody
How public – like a frog –
To tell your name the livelong June
To an admiring bog. (l. 5–8)

AmPP; AnAmPo; BoWoP; NBLV; NOBA; OBCA; OxBSP;
PDV; RHPC; SO; TAP; WPE

In winter in my room

84 In winter, in my room,
I came upon a worm, (l. 1–2)

85 Not quite with him at home –
Secured him by a string
To something neighboring, (l. 6–8)

86 A trifle afterward (l. 10)

87 A snake, with mottles rare,
Surveyed my chamber floor,
In feature as the worm before,
But ringed with power. (l. 14–17)

88 That time I flew, (l. 32)

89 Till, in a distant town,
Towns on from mine –
I sat me down;
This was a dream. (l. 36–39)

AmPP; EsPo; LiTA; MoP; NAAL-1; NoAM; NOBA; OxBA

It dropped so low – in my regard

90 It dropped so low in my regard
I heard it hit the ground,
And go to pieces on the stones
At bottom of my mind; (l. 1–4)

CMoP; HAP; InPK; OxBA; OxBSP

It sounded as if the streets were running

91 It sounded as if the streets were running,
And then the streets stood still. (l. 1–2)

92 Nature was in her beryl apron,
Mixing fresher air. (l. 7–8)

AnAmPo; NAAL-1; OxBSP; PBWP

I've seen a Dying Eye

93 I've seen a Dying Eye (l. 1)

94 And then – be soldered down
Without disclosing what it be
'Twere blessed to have seen – (l. 6–8)

AmPP; BoWoP; FPL; NOBA; PoEL-5; PoLF

Just lost, when I was saved!

95 Just lost, when I was saved! (l. 1)

96 Just girt me for the onset with Eternity,
When breath blew back,
And on the other side
I heard recede the disappointed tide! (l. 3–6)

97 Next time, to tarry,
While the Ages steal —
Slow tramp the Centuries,
And the Cycles wheel! (l. 16–19)

AA; AmPP; MoAmPo; NOBA; NOCV; Prf

The last Night that She lived

98 The last Night that She lived
It was a Common Night
Except the Dying — this to Us
Made Nature different (l. 1–4)

99 Too jostled were Our Souls to speak
At length the notice came. (l. 19–20)

100 struggled scarce —
Consented, and was dead —

And We — We placed the Hair —
And drew the Head erect —
And then an awful leisure was
Belief to regulate — (l. 23–28)

BoWoP; CMoP; LiTA; NAAL-1; OxBA; PoEL-5; QFR;
SOTW

A light exists in spring

101 A light exists in spring
Not present on the year
At any other period. (l. 1–3)

102 It passes, and we stay:

A quality of loss
Affecting our content,
As trade had suddenly encroached
Upon a sacrament. (l. 16–20)

BoWoP; LiTA; NOBA; OxBA

The morns are meeker than they were

103 The morns are meeker than they were,
The nuts are getting brown;
The berry's cheek is plumper,
The rose is out of town. (l. 1–4)

104 Lest I should be old-fashioned,
I'll put a trinket on. (l. 7–8)

AA; BoNaP; FaPON; OBCA

Much madness is divinest sense

105 Much madness is divinest sense
To a discerning eye;
Much sense the starkest madness. (l. 1–3)

106 Assent, and you are sane;
Demur, — you're straightway dangerous,
And handled with a chain. (l. 6–8)

AmPP; BoWoP; CMoP; HeIP; LiTA; LiTM; MAT; NAAL-
1; NAWM-2; NoAM; NOBA; NoP; OxBA; WPE

My life closed twice before its close

107 My life closed twice before its close — (l. 1)

108 Parting is all we know of heaven,
And all we need of hell. (l. 7–8)

AmPP; BoLoP; BoWoP; GBL; HeIP; MoAB; MoAmPo;
MoP; NAAL-1; NIP; NoAM; NOBA; OxBA; OxBSP; PPP;
SCV; SoSe; TrGrPo

My Life had stood — a Loaded Gun

109 My Life had stood — a Loaded Gun —
In Corners — till a Day
The Owner passed — identified —
And carried Me away — (l. 1–4)

110 Though I than He — may longer live
He longer must — than I —
For I have but the power to kill,
Without — the power to die — (l. 21–24)

AmPP; HAP; InPK; NAAL-1; NAWM-2; NIP; NoP; WeW;
WPOW

A narrow Fellow in the Grass

111 A narrow Fellow in the Grass
Occasionally rides — (l. 1–2)

112 But never met this Fellow
Attended, or alone
Without a tighter breathing
And Zero at the Bone — (l. 21–24)

AmPP; BoWoP; CMoP; FaFP; FM; FPL; GoJo; HAP;
HoPM; LiTA; LiTM; MoAB; NAAL-1; NIP; NoAM;
NOBA; NoP; OBCA; OxBA; PoE; PoEL-5; PoLF; PPP;
RB; SoSe; TAP; WeW

Of all the souls that stand create

113 Of all the souls that stand create —
I have elected — One — (l. 1–2)

114 Behold the Atom — I preferred —
To all the lists of Clay! (l. 11–12)

AA; AmPP; NAAL-1; TrGrPo

Our journey had advanced

115 Our journey had advanced; (l. 1)

116 Retreat was out of hope, —
Behind, a sealed route,
Eternity's white flag before,
And God at every gate. (l. 9—12)

LiTA; LiTM; MoAB; NOCV; PoEL-5; QFR

Pain has an element of blank

117 Pain has an element of blank — (l. 1)

118 It has no future but itself —
Its infinite contain
Its past — enlightened to perceive
New periods of pain. (l. 5—8)

LiTA; LiTM; MoAB; MoAmPo; NAAL-1; PPP

The pedigree of Honey

119 The pedigree of Honey
Does not concern the Bee, (l. 1—2)

120 The right of way to Tripoli
A more essential thing. (l. 7—8)

BLPL; FaBV; MoP; NOBA

Remorse is Memory awake

121 Remorse — is Memory — awake —
Her Parties all astir — (l. 1—2)

122 Remorse is cureless — the Disease
Not even God — can heal —
For 'tis His institution — and
The Adequate of Hell — (l. 9—12)

NAAL-1; NOBA; NOCV; NoP

A Route of Evanescence

123 A Route of Evanescence
With a revolving Wheel — (l. 1—2)

124 The mail from Tunis, probably,
An easy Morning's Ride — (l. 7—8)

NAAL-1; NoP; PoEL-5; SoSe

Safe in their Alabaster Chambers

125 Safe in their Alabaster Chambers —
Untouched by Morning
And untouched by Noon —
Sleep the meek members of the Resurrection —
(l. 1—4)

126 Grand go the Years — in the Crescent — above them —
(l. 17)

127 Soundless as dots — on a Disc of Snow — (l. 21)

AmPP; NAAL-1; NAWM-2; NOBA; NoP; OxBA; WPE

The sky is low, the clouds are mean

128 The sky is low, the clouds are mean,

129 Nature, like us, is sometimes caught
Without her diadem.

AA; BoNaP; FaBV; MoAmPo; OxBA; PoEL-5

Some keep the Sabbath going to church

130 Some keep the Sabbath going to church;
I keep it staying at home, (l. 1—2)

131 God preaches — a noted clergyman, —
And the sermon is never long;
So instead of getting to heaven at last,
I'm going all along! (l. 9—12)

MoAB; MoAmPo; SoSe; WGRP

The Soul selects her own Society

132 The Soul selects her own Society —
Then — shuts the Door — (l. 1—2)

133 I've known her — from an ample nation —
Choose One —
Then — close the Valves of her attention —
Like Stone —

AmPP; AWP; BLFL; BoWoP; CMoP; InPK; InPS; MoAB;
MoAmPo; NAAL-1; NAWM-2; NoAM; NOBA; NoP;
OxBA; PoE PoEL-5; TAP; TrGrPo; UnPo; WPE

Success is counted sweetest

134 Success is counted sweetest
By those who ne'er succeed. (l. 1—2)

135 On whose forbidden ear
The distant strains of triumph
Burst agonized and clear! (l. 9–12)

AnAmPo; AWP; CMoP; FPL; GoJo; InPS; LiTA; LiTM;
MoAB; MoAmPo; NAAL-1; NOBA; OxBA; PoRA; TAP;
WaaP; WPE

Tell all the truth but tell it slant

136 Tell all the truth but tell it slant,
Success in circuit lies, (l. 1–2)

137 The truth must dazzle gradually
Or every man be blind. (l. 7–8)

AmPP; HeIP; LiTA; NAAL-1; NAWM-2; NoAM; NOBA;
NoP; PPP; TAP; UnPo; WeW

There came a Wind like a Bugle

138 There came a Wind like a Bugle — (l. 1)

139 How much can come
And much can go,
And yet abide the World! (l. 15–17)

CMoP; MoAB; NAAL-1; NAWM-2; NOBA; OPOP; OxBA;
RB

There is no Frigate like a Book

140 There is no Frigate like a Book (l. 1)

141 How frugal is the Chariot
That bears the Human soul. (l. 7–8)

FaPON; FPL; GoJo; MoAmPo; NIP; OBCA; PoLF; SoSe;
TAP; TrGrPo

There's a certain Slant of light

142 There's a certain Slant of light,
Winter Afternoons — (l. 1–2)

143 None may teach it — Any —
'Tis the Seal Despair — (l. 9–10)

144 When it comes, the Landscape listens —
Shadows — hold their breath —
When it goes, 'tis like the Distance
On the look of Death — (l. 13–16)

AmPP; BLPL; BoWoP; CMoP; HAP; HeIP; LiTA; LiTM;
MoAB; MoAmPo; MoP; NAAL-1; NAWM-2; NoAM;
NOBA; NoP; OxBA; PoE; PoEL-5; PPP; QFR; RB; TOF;
WPE

This is my letter to the world

145 This is my letter to the world,
That never wrote to me —
The simple news that Nature told, (l. 1–3)

146 For love of her, sweet countrymen,
Judge tenderly of me! (l. 7–8)

AmPP; MoP; NAAL-1; NoAM; NOBA; OxBA; SCV; TAP;
WPE

This quiet Dust was Gentlemen and Ladies

147 This quiet Dust was Gentlemen and Ladies,
And Lads and Girls; (l. 1–2)

CMoP; DL; MoAB; MoAmPo; OxBA

To make a prairie it takes a clover and one bee

148 To make a prairie it takes a clover and one bee, —
(l. 1)

149 The revery alone will do
If bees are few. (l. 4–5)

BoWoP; HeIP; Mes; NBLV; OBCA; OxBA

'Twas like a Maelstrom, with a notch

150 'Twas like a Maelstrom, with a notch,
That nearer, every Day,
Kept narrowing its boiling Wheel (l. 1–3)

151 And you dropt, lost,
When something broke —
And let you from a Dream — (l. 7–9)

152 When God — remembered — and the Fiend
Let go, then, Overcome — (l. 16–17)

153 Which Anguish was the utterest — then —
To perish, or to live? (l. 24–25)

CMoP; LiTA; LiTM; PoE

'Twas warm — at first — like Us

154 Twas warm — at first — like Us —
Until there crept upon
A Chill — like frost upon a Glass — (l. 1–3)

CMoP; LiTA; NAWM-2; QFR; SoSe

What soft, cherubic creatures

155 What soft, cherubic creatures
These gentlewomen are! (l. 1–2)

156 Redemption, brittle lady,
Be so ashamed of thee. (l. 11–12)

AmPP; HAP; MoAB; MoAmPo; SoSe; WPE

Wild Nights! — Wild Nights!

157 Wild Nights — Wild Nights!
Were I with thee
Wild Nights should be
Our luxury! (l. 1–4)

158 Rowing in Eden — Ah, the Sea!
Might I but moor — Tonight —
In Thee! (l. 10–12)

AmPP; NAAL-1; NIP; NcAM; NOBA; NoP; OxBA;
PBWP; TAP; UnAS; WPE

The Wind begun to rock the Grass

159 The Wind begun to rock the Grass
With threatening Tunes and low — (l. 1–2)

160 The Dust did scoop itself like Hands
And threw away the Road. (l. 7–8)

161 The Lightning showed a Yellow Beak
And then a livid Claw. (l. 11–12)

BoNaP; HAP; NAAL-1; WeW

The Wind — tapped like a tired Man

162 The Wind — tapped like a tired Man —
And like a Host — 'Come in'
I boldly answered — entered then
My Residence within

A Rapid — footless Guest — (l. 1–5)

163 Again, He tapped — 'twas flurriedly —
And I became alone — (l. 19–20)

Mes; MoAB; MoAmPo; TOF

RICHARD WATSON DIXON   (1833–1900)

The feathers of the willow

1 The feathers of the willow
Are half of them grown yellow
Above the swelling stream;

And ragged are the bushes,
And rusty now the rushes,
And wild the clouded gleam. (l. 1–6)

BoNaP; CH; FaBoCh; GTBS-P; NOBE; OBEV; OBNC

GEORGE WASHINGTON DOANE
(1799–1859)

Evening Contemplation

1 Softly now the light of day
Fades upon my sight away;
Free from care, from labor free,
Lord, I would commune with Thee. (l. 1–4)

2 Thou who, sinless, yet hast known
All of man's infirmity!
Then, from Thine eternal throne,
Jesus, look with pitying eye. (l. 13–16)

AA; AH; BLPA; BLPL; FaBoBe

MARY MAPES DODGE   (1831–1905)

The Two Mysteries

1 We know not what it is, dear, this sleep so deep and
   still;
The folded hands, the awful calm, the cheek so pale
   and chill;
The lids that will not lift again, though we may call
   and call;
The strange white solitude of peace that settles over all.
   (l. 1–4)

2 The child who enters life comes not with knowledge or
   intent,
So those who enter death must go as little children
   sent.
Nothing is known. But I believe that God is overhead;
And as life is to the living, so death is to the dead.
   (l. 17–20)

AA; PWR; TrCP; WGRP

OWEN DODSON   (b. 1914)

Yardbird's Skull

1 The bird is lost,
Dead, with all the music:
While sunsets heard the brain's music
Faded to last horizon notes. (l. 1–4)

2 O I shall hear skull skull,
Hear your lame music,
Believe music rejects undertaking,
Limps back. (l. 25–28)

AmNP; CNA; IDB; PoBA; VGW

JOHN DONNE (1572–1631)

Air and Angels

1 Love must not be, but take a body too,
And therefore what thou wert, and who,
I bid Love aske, and now
That it assume thy body, I allow,
And fixe it selfe in thy lip, eye, and brow. (l. 10–14)

JCP; MeLP; MePo; NAEL-1; OAEL-1; OBS; Prf; SeCP;
SeCV-1

The Anniversary

2 All other things to their destruction draw,
Only our love hath no decay;
This no tomorrow hath, nor yesterday, (l. 6–8)

3 Two graves must hide thine and my corse;
If one might, death were no divorce. (l. 11–12)

BoLoP; HAP; HoPM; JCP; LiTB; MeLP; MePo; NOBE;
NoP; OAEL-1; OBS; SeCP; SeCV-1; WeW

The Apparition

4 When by thy scorn, O murderess, I am dead,
And that thou think'st thee free
From all solicitation from me,
Then shall my ghost come to thy bed, (l. 1–4)

EnLoPo; GBL; HeIP; MePo; NAEL-1; NAWM-1; NOBE;
NOBL; OAEL-1; OBD; OBEV; OBS; PoE; SCV; SeCP;
SeCV-1

At the round earth's imagined corners (Holy Sonnets)

5 At the round earth's imagined corners, blow
Your trumpets, angels, and arise, arise
From death, you numberless infinities
Of souls, and to your scattered bodies go,

BLPL; ChTr; EaLo; EBEV; FaBoRV; HAP; HeIP; InPS;
JCP; LiTB; MeLP; MePo; NAEL-1; NAWM-1; NOBE;
NoP; OAEL-1; OBD; OBS; PoE; PoEL-2; PPP; QFR;
SeCP; SeCV-1; Son; TEP; TOF

The Bait

6 Come live with me, and be my love,
And we will some new pleasures prove
Of golden sands, and crystal brooks,
With silken lines, and silver hooks.

7 For thee, thou need'st no such deceit,
For, thou thyself art thine own bait;
That fish, that is not catch'd thereby,
Alas, is wiser far than I. (l. 25–28)

ErPo; HoPM; InPK; InPS; NAEL-1; NIP; OAEL-1; PoRA;
RB; SD; TEP

Batter my heart three-personed God (Holy Sonnets)

8 Batter my heart, three-personed God;

9 Divorce me, untie, or break that knot again,
Take me to you, imprison me, for I
Except you enthral me, never shall be free,
Nor ever chaste, except you ravish me.

BLPL; EaLo; EBEV; FaFP; FF; HAP; HeIP; HoPM;
InPK; InPS; JCP; LiTB; MeLP; MePo; NAEL-1; NIP;
NOBE; NoP; OAEL-1; OBS; PoE; PoEL-2; PPP; PrIm;
SeCePo; SeCP; SeCV-1; Son; SoSe; TEP; TOF; TrCP;
TrGrPo; TrPWD

The Blossom

10 Various content
To your eyes, ears, and tongue, and every part.
If then your body go, what need you a heart?
(l. 22–24)

11 Well, then, stay here; but know,
When thou hast stayed and done thy most,
A naked thinking heart that makes no show
Is to a woman but a kind of ghost.
How shall she know my heart; or, having none,
Know thee for one?
Practice may make her know some other part,
But take my word, she doth not know a heart.
(l. 25–32)

AWP; LiTB; MeLP; NAEL-1; OBS; SeCP; UnPo

Break of Day (attributed to John Donne)

12 Stay, O sweet, and do not rise;
The light that shines comes from thine eyes;
The day breaks not, it is my heart,
Because that you and I must part. (l. 1–4)

ElL; TrGrPo; BoLoP; NOBE; OBEV

A Burnt Ship

13 So all were lost, which in the ship were found,
They in the sea being burnt, they in the burnt ship
   drown'd. (l. 5–6)

EBEV; InPK; OBWP; WaaP

The Canonization

14 Call us what you will, we are made such by love;
Call her one, me another fly,
We're tapers too, and at our own cost die,
And we in us find the eagle and the dove
The phoenix riddle hath more wit
By us; we two being one are it.
So to one neutral thing both sexes fit,
We die and rise the same, and prove
Mysterious by this love. (l. 19–27)

BLPL; ElL; EnLoPo; HAP; JCP; LiTB; MePo; NAEL-1;
NAWM-1; NIP; NOBE; NoP; OAEL-1; OBS; PoE; PoEL-
2; PPP; SeCePo; SeCP; SeCV-1; TEP; TrGrPo; UnPo

Come, madam, come, all rest my powers defy (Elegies)

15 License my roving hands, and let them go
Before, behind, between, above, below.
O my America! my new-found-land,
My kingdom, safeliest when with one man manned,
My mine of precious stones, my empery,
How blest am I in this discovering thee!
To enter in these bonds is to be free;
Then where my hand is set, my seal shall be.

16 Then, since that I may know,
As liberally as to a midwife, show
Thyself: cast all, yea, this white linen hence,
Here is no penance, much less innocence.
To teach thee, I am naked first; why than,
What needst thou have more covering than a man.

BoLoP; EBEV; ErPo; JCP; LiTB; MePo; NAEL-1; NoP;
OAEL-1; PoE; PPP; SeCP; TEP

Death, be not proud (Holy Sonnets)

17 Death, be not proud, though some have called thee
Mighty and dreadful, for thou art not so;

18 One short sleep past, we wake eternally,
And Death shall be no more: Death, thou shalt die.

ChTr; DL; ElL; FaBoRV; FaBV; FaFP; FF; FPL; HAP;
HeIP; InPK; InPS; InvP; JCP; LiTB; MeLP; MePo;
NAEL-1; NAWM-1; NIP; NOBE; NoP; OAEL-1; OBD;
OBEV; OBS; PoE; PoEL-2; PoRA; PPP; PrIm; SCV;
SeCP; SeCV-1; TEP; TrCP; TrGrPo; WeW

The Dream

19 My dream thou brok'st not, but continued'st it.
Thou art so true that thoughts of thee suffice
To make dreams truths and fables histories;
Enter these arms, for since thou thought'st it best
Not to dream all my dream, let's act the rest.
                                    (l. 6–10)

ElL; InvP; LiTB; MeLP; MePo; OAEL-1; OBEV; OBS;
SeCP; TOF

The Ecstasy

20 And whilst our souls negotiate there,
We like sepulchral statues lay;
All day, the same our postures were,
And we said nothing, all the day. (l. 17–20)

21 But oh alas, so long, so far
Our bodies why do we forbear?
They are ours, though they are not we; we are
The intelligences, they the sphere. (l. 49–52)

22 Love's mysteries in souls do grow,
But yet the body is his book.
And if some lover, such as we,
Have heard this dialogue of one,
Let him still mark us, he shall see
Small change, when we're to bodies gone." (l. 71–76)

BoLoP; EnLoPo; FPL; HAP; InPS; JCP; LiTB; MeLP;
MePo; NAEL-1; NOBE; NoP; OAEL-1; OBEV; OBS;
PoEL-2; PoE; PrIm; SeCePo; SeCP; SeCV-1; TEP; TOF;
TrGrPo

The Expiration

23 Go; and if that word have not quite killed thee,
Ease me with death by bidding me got too.
Oh, if it have, let my word work on me,
And a just office on a murderer do.
Except it be too late to kill me so,
Being double dead: going, and bidding go. (l. 7–12)

ElL; MeLP; MePo; OxBSP; SeCP

The Flea

24 A sinne, nor shame, nor losse of maidenhead, (l. 6)

25 This flea is you and I, and this
Our mariage bed, and mariage temple is;
Though parents grudge, and you, w'are met,
And cloystered in these living walls of Jet. (l. 12–15)

BLPL; BoLoP; EBEV; FF; FM; HoPM; InPK; InPS; JCP;
LiTB; MAT; MePo; NAEL-1; NBLV; NIP; OAEL-1; PoE;
SCV; SeCP; SeCV-1; SoSe; TEP; TrGrPo

The Funeral

26 Whate'er she meant by it, bury it with me,
For since I am
Love's martyr, it might breed idolatry,
If into others' hands these Reliques came;
As 'twas humility
To afford to it all that a Soul can do,
So, 'tis some bravery,
That since you would save none of me, I bury some of
    you. (l. 18–25)

AWP; BoLoP; EBEV; EnLoPo; HeIP; MeLP; NAEL-1;
NAWM-1; NoP; OAEL-1; OBEV; OBS; PoEL-2; PoRA;
SeCP; SeCV-1

Go and catch a falling star

27 Though she were true, when you met her,
And last, till you write your letter,
Yet she
Will be
False, ere I come, to two, or three. (l. 23–27)

AWP; EBEV; ElL; ELP; FaBV; FaFP; FPL; HAP; HeIP;
HoPM; InPK; InPS; JCP; LiTB; MeLP; MePo; NAEL-1;
NAWM-1; NBLV; NIP; NOBE; NoP; OBEV; PoE; PoEL-
2; SeCP; SeCV-1; SoSe; TrGrPo

Good Friday 1613, Riding Westward

28 Who sees God's face, that is self life, must die;
What a death were it then to see God die!
It made his own lieutenant, Nature, shrink;
It made his footstool crack, and the sun wink.
                                    (l. 17–20)

InPS; JCP; MeLP; MePo; NAEL-1; NOCV; NoP; OAEL-1;
OBS; PoEL-2; PoE; PPP; SeCP; SeCV-1; TEP

The Good-Morrow

29 And now good morrow to our waking souls,
Which watch not one another out of fear;
For love all love of other sights controls,
And makes one little room an everywhere.
Let sea-discoverers to new worlds have gone,
Let maps to other, worlds on worlds have shown,
Let us possess one world; each hath one, and is one.
                                    (l. 8–14)

AWP; BoLoP; EBEV; ElL; EnLoPo; FaBoBe; FaBV;
FaBV; FF; FPL; HoPM; InPS; InvP; JCP; LiTB; MeLP;
MePo; NAEL-1; NAWM-1; NIP; NoP; OAEL-1; OBS;
PoEL-2; PoE; PoRA; PPP; SCV; SeCP; SeCV-1; SoSe;
TEP; TrGrPo

A Hymn to God the Father

30 Sweare by thy selfe, that at my death thy Sonne
Shall shine as he shines now, and heretofore;

And having done that, thou hast done,
I feare no more. (l. 15–18)

AWP; EaLo; EBEV; HAP; InPK; JCP; LiTB; MeLP;
MePo; NAEL-1; NOBE; OAEL-1; OBS; PoEL-2; PoRA;
SCV; SeCP; SeCV-1; TOF; TrGrPo; TrPWD; WGRP

A Hymne to Christ, at the Author's Last Going into Germany

31 Not thou nor thy religion dost controule,
The amorousnesse of an harmonious Soule,
But thou would'st have that love thy selfe: As thou
Art jealous, Lord, so I am jealous now,
Thou lov'st not, till from loving more, thou free
My soule: Who ever gives, takes libertie:
O, if thou car'st not whom I love
Alas, thou lov'st not mee. (l. 17–24)

EBEV; LiTB; MeLP; MePo; NAEL-1; OBS; SeCV-1

Hymne to God My God, In My Sicknesse

32 We thinke that Paradise and Calvarie,
Christs Crosse, and Adams tree, stood in one place;
Looke, Lord, and finde both Adams met in me;
As the first Adams sweat surrounds my face,
May the last Adams blood my soule embrace.
                                    (l. 21–25)

ChTr; EBEV; HeIP; InPS; MeLP; MePo; NAEL-1; NIP;
NoP; OAEL-1; OBD; OBS; PoEL-2; PoE; PPP; SeCP;
SeCV-1; TOF; TrPWD

I am a little world (Holy Sonnets)

33 I am a little world made cunningly
Of elements, and an angelic sprite;
But black sin hath betrayed to endless night
My world's both parts, and Oh! both parts must die.

NAEL-1; NIP; NoP; OBS; PoE; SeCP; Son; TEP

If poisonous minerals (Holy Sonnets)

34 O God, oh! of thine only worthy blood,
And my tears, make a heavenly Lethean flood,
And drown in it my sins' black memory.
That thou remember them, some claim as debt;
I think it mercy, if thou wilt forget. (l. 10–14)

EBEV; JCP; LiTB; MePo; NAEL-1; NoP; OAEL-1; OBS;
PoEL-2; PPP; SeCP; Son; UnPo

The Indifferent

35 I can love both fair and brown;
Her whom abundance melts, and her whom want
    betrays;

Her who loves loneness best, and her who masks and
   plays;
Her whom the country formed, and whom the town;
Her who believes, and her who tries;
Her who still weeps with spongy eyes;
And her who is dry cork, and never cries.
I can love her, and her, and you and you,
I can love any, so she be not true. (l. 1–9)

BoLoP; NAEL-1; NAWM-1; SeCV-1; TEP

A Lecture upon the Shadow

36 Love is a growing, or full constant light;
And his first minute, after noone, is night. (l. 25–26)

AWP; NAEL-1; OBS; SeCP; TEP; UnPo

Lovers' Infiniteness

37 Loves riddles are, that though thy heart depart,
It stayes at home, and thou with losing savest it:
But wee will have a way more liberall,
Then changing hearts, to joyne them, so wee shall
Be one, and one anothers All. (l. 29–33)

ElL; LiTB; MeLP; OAEL-1; OBS; PoEL-2; SeCP; SeCV-1

Love's Alchemy

38 That loving wretch that swears
'Tis not the bodies marry, but the minds,
Which he in her angelic finds,
Would swear as justly that he hears,
In that day's rude hoarse minstrelsy, the spheres.
Hope not for mind in women; at their best
Sweetness and wit, they're but Mummy, possessed.
          (l. 18–24)

MePo; NAEL-1; NoP; OAEL-1; PoE; SeCP

Love's Deity

39 I long to talk with some old lover's ghost
Who died before the god of love was born.
I cannot think that he who then loved most,
Sunk so low as to love one which did scorn. (l. 1–4)

40 Rebel and atheist too, why murmur I,
As though I felt the worst that love could do?
Love may make me leave loving, or might try
A deeper plague, to make her love me too;
Which, since she loves before, I'm loth to see.
Falsehood is worse than hate; and that must be,
If she whom I love, should love me. (l. 22–28)

AWP; ElL; GBL; LiTB; MePo; SeCePo; SeCP; SeCV-1

Love's Growth

41 And yet no greater, but more eminent,
Love by the spring is grown;
As, in the firmament,
Stars by the sun are not enlarged, but shown,
Gentle love deeds, as blossoms on a bough,
From love's awakened root do bud out now. (l. 15–20)

JCP; MePo; NoP; SeCV-1

No spring, nor summer beauty hath such grace (Elegies)

42 No spring, nor summer beauty hath such grace,
As I have seen in one autumnal face.
Young beauties force our love, and that's a rape,

InPS; JCP; PoEL-2; SeCV-1; TEP

A Nocturnal upon Saint Lucy's Day, Being the Shortest Day

43 Study me then, you who shall lovers be
At the next world, that is, at the next spring:
For I am every dead thing,
In whom love wrought new alchemy.
For his art did express
A quintessence even from nothingness,
From dull privations, and lean emptiness:
He ruined me, and I am re-begot
Of absence, darkness, death: things which are not.
          (l. 10–18)

EBEV; GBL; JCP; LiTB; MeLP; MePo; NAEL-1; NOBE;
NoP; OAEL-1; OBS; PoEL-2; PoE; PPP; SeCP; SeCV-1;
TEP

O my black soul! (Holy Sonnets)

44 O my black soul! Now thou art summoned
By sickness, death's herald, and champion;
Thou art like a pilgrim, which abroad hath done
Treason, (l. 1–3)

EBEV; JCP; OAEL-1; OBS; Son; TEP; TOF

Oh, to vex me (Holy Sonnets)

45 Oh, to vex me, contraries meet in one:
Inconstancy unnaturally hath begot
A constant habit; that when I would not
I change in vows, and in devotion.
As humorous is my contrition
As my profane Love, and as soon forgot:
As ridlingly distempered, cold and hot, (l. 1–7)

OAEL-1; PoEL-2; SeCePo; Son

On His Mistress (Elegies)

46 By our first strange and fatal interview,

47 I conjure thee, and all the oaths which I
And thou have sworn to seal joint constancy,
Here I unswear, and overswear them thus,
Thou shalt not love by ways so dangerous.
Temper, O fair Love, love's impetuous rage,
Be my true Mistress still, not my feign'd Page;
I'll go, and, by thy kind leave, leave behind
Thee, only worthy to nurse in my mind
Thirst to come back;

BoLoP; EBEV; GBL; LiTB; MeLP; MePo; NAEL-1;
NOBE; PoEL-2; SeCP; SeCV-1

The Prohibition

48 Yet, love and hate mee too,
So, these extreames shall neithers office doe;
Love mee, that I may die the gentler way;
Hate mee, because thy love is too great for mee;
(l. 17–20)

ElL; GBL; MeLP; OBS

The Relic

49 A bracelet of bright hair about the bone,
Will he not let us alone,
And think that there a loving couple lies
Who thought that this device might be some way
To make their souls, at the last busy day,
Meet at this grave, and make a little stay? (l. 5–11)

ElL; GBL; HAP; HeIP; LiTB; MeLP; MePo; NOBE; NoP;
OAEL-1; OBS; PoEL-2; PPP; SeCP; SeCV-1

Satires

50 So doth, so is Religion; and this blind-
ness too much light breeds; but unmoved thou
Of force must one, and forc'd but one allow;
And the right; ask thy father which is she,
let him ask his; though truth and falsehood be
Near twins, yet truth a little elder is;

51 On a huge hill,
Cragged, and steep, Truth stands, and he that will
Reach her, about must, and about must go;
And what the hill's suddenness resists, win so;
Yet strive so, that before age, death's twilight,
Thy Soul rest, for none can work in that night.
To will, implies delay, therefore now do:
Hard deeds, the body's pains; hard knowledge too
The mind's endeavours reach, and mysteries
Are like the Sun, dazzling, yet plain to all eyes.

EBEV; JCP; MeLP; MePo; NAEL-1; NoP; OAEL-1; OBS;
PoE; PoEL-2; SeCP; SeCV-1

Show me, dear Christ, Thy spouse (Holy Sonnets)

52 Betray, kind husband, Thy spouse to our sights,
And let mine amorous soul court Thy mild Dove,
Who is most true and pleasing to Thee then
When she is embraced and open to most men.
(l. 11–14)

MeLP; NAEL-1; NoP; OBS; PoE; Son

Since she whom I loved (Holy Sonnets)

53 Since she whom I loved hath paid her last debt
To Nature, and to hers, and my good is dead,
And her soul early into heaven ravished,
Wholly on heavenly things my mind is set. (l. 1–4)

JCP; MePo; NAEL-1; Son

Spit in my face, you Jews (Holy Sonnets)

54 God clothed himself in vile man's flesh, that so
He might be weak enough to suffer woe. (l. 13–14)

JCP; OBS; Son; TOF

The Sun Rising

55 Busy old fool, unruly sun,
Why dost thou thus
Through windows, and through curtains call on us?
(l. 1–3)

56 Thine age asks ease, and since thy duties be
To warm the world, that's done in warming us.
Shine here to us, and thou art everywhere;
This bed thy center is, these walls, thy sphere.
(l. 27–30)

BoLoP; FF; GBL; HAP; HeIP; InPS; InvP; JCP; LiTB;
MeLP; MePo; NAEL-1; NIP; NOBE; NoP; OAEL-1; PoE;
PoEL-2; PPP; SCV; SeCePo; SeCP; SeCV-1; SoSe; TEP;
TrGrPo; WeW

Sweetest love, I do not go

57 Sweetest love, I do not go
For weariness of thee,
Nor in hope the world can show
A fitter love for me;
But since that I
Must die at last, 'tis best
To use myself in jest
Thus by feigned deaths to die. (l. 1–8)

AWP; BoLoP; ElL; ELP; HeIP; InPS; InvP; JCP; MeLP;
MePo; NOBE; NoP; OAEL-1; OBS; PoEL-2; SeCP; SeCV-
1; TEP; TrGrPo

This is my playes last scene (Holy Sonnets)

58 This is my playes last scene, here heavens appoint
My pilgrimages last mile; and my race
Idly, yet quickly runne, hath this last pace,
My spans last inch, my minutes last point,
And gluttonous death, will instantly unjoynt
My body, and soule, and I shall sleepe a space.
(l. 1–6)

EBEV; JCP; MeLP; MePo; OBS; SeCP; Son; TEP

Thou hast made me (Holy Sonnets)

59 Thou hast made me, and shall thy work decay?
Repair me now, for now mine end doth haste;
I run to death, and death meets me as fast,
And all my pleasures are like yesterday. (l. 1–4)

60 But our old subtle foe so tempteth me
That not one hour I can myself sustain.
Thy grace may wing me to prevent his art,
And thou like adamant draw mine iron heart.
(l. 11–14)

EBEV; MeLP; NAEL-1; NOBE; NOCV; NoP; OBS;
PoEL-2; SeCP; Son; TEP

Twickenham Garden

61 Nor can you more judge womans thoughts by tears,
Than by her shadow, what she weares.
O perverse sexe, where none is true but shee,
Who's therefore true, because her truth kills mee.
(l. 24–27)

EBEV; EnLoPo; FaBoPP; MeLP; MePo; OBS; OPOP;
PoEL-2; PoE; SeCP; TEP

A Valediction: Forbidding Mourning

62 As virtuous men pass mildly away,
And whisper to their souls to go,
Whilst some of their sad friends do say,
The breath goes now, and some say, no; (l. 1–4)

63 Dull sublunary lovers' love,
Whose soul is sense, cannot admit
Absence, because it doth remove
Those things which elemented it.

But we by a love so much refined
That our selves know not what it is,
Interassured of the mind,
Careless eyes, lips, and hands to miss.

Our two souls therefore, which are one,
Though I must go, endure not yet
A breach, but an expansion,
Like gold to airy thinness beat. (l. 13–24)

64 If they be two, they are two so
As stiff twin compasses are two;
Thy soul, the fixed foot, makes no show
To move, but doth if th' other do. (l. 25–28)

BLPL; FF; HAP; HeIP; HoPM; InPS; JCP; LiTB; MeLP;
MePo; NAEL-1; NIP; NOBE; NoP; OAEL-1; OBS;
PoEL-2; PoE; PPP; PrIm; SeCP; SeCV-1; SoSe; TEP;
UnPo; WeW

A Valediction: Of Weeping

65 On a round ball
A workman that hath copies by, can lay
An Europe, Afric, and an Asia,
And quickly make that, which was nothing, all;
So doth each tear,
Which thee doth wear,
A globe, yea world, by that impression grow,
Till thy tears mixed with mine do overflow
This world, by waters sent from thee, my heaven
dissolved so. (l. 10–18)

HAP; HeIP; InPS; MeLP; MePo; NAEL-1; NoP; OAEL-1;
OBS; PoE; SeCP; WeW

What if this present (Holy Sonnets)

66 What if this present were the world's last night?
Mark in my heart, O Soul, where thou dost dwell,
The picture of Christ crucified, and tell
Whether that countenance can thee affright, (l. 1–4)

67 No, no; but as in my idolatry
I said to all my profane mistresses,
Beauty, of pity, foulness only is
A sign of rigour: so I say to thee,
To wicked spirits are horrid shapes assign'd,
This beauteous form assures a piteous mind. (l. 9–14)

EBEV; HeIP; InPS; JCP; LiTB; MeLP; NAEL-1; NOCV;
OBS; PoE; Son; TEP

Why are we by all creatures waited on (Holy Sonnets)

68 But wonder at a greater wonder, for to us
Created nature doth these things subdue,
But their Creator, whom sin nor nature tied,
For us, his Creatures and his foes, hath died.
(l. 11–14)

JCP; NOCV; OBS; PoE; PoEL-2; TrCP

HILDA DOOLITTLE ("H. D.")
(1886–1961)

Evening

1 The light passes
from ridge to ridge,
from flower to flower – (l. 1–3)

2 shadow seeks shadow,
  then both leaf
  and leaf-shadow are lost. (l. 17–19)

  CMoP; FaBoMo; VGW; WPE

The Garden

3 O wind, rend open the heat,
  cut apart the heat,
  rend it to tatters.

  Fruit cannot drop
  through this thick air —

  CMoP; HeIP; InPK; LiTA; MoAmPo; NoAM; OxBA;
  PrIm; TAP; UnPo

Helen

4 Greece sees, unmoved,
  God's daughter, born of love,
  the beauty of cool feet
  and slenderest knees, (l. 12–15)

  AnAmPo; BoWoP; FaBoWP; LiTM; MoAmPo; NAAL-2;
  NoAM; NOBA; NoP; TAP; TW

Lethe

5 Nor skin nor hide nor fleece
  shall cover you,
  nor curtain of crimson nor fine
  shelter of cedar-wood be over you,
  nor the fir-tree
  nor the pine. (l. 1–6)

  AnAmPo; CMoP; FaBoWP; LiTM; MoAmPo; PoRA;
  TrGrPo; VGW

The Mysteries Remain

6 The mysteries remain,
  I keep the same
  cycle of seed-time
  and of sun and rain; (l. 1–4)

  NOBA; TAP; VGW; WPOW

Orchard

7 you have flayed us
  with your blossoms,
  spare us the beauty
  of fruit-trees. (l. 9–12)

  CMoP; LiTA; LiTM; MoAmPo; OxBA

Oread

8 Whirl up, sea— (l. 1)

  AWP; CMoP; GoJo; HeIP; InPS; MoAmPo; MoP;
  NAAL-2; NoAM; NOBA; OxBA; TAP

Pear Tree

9 O, white pear,
  your flower-tufts
  thick on the branch
  bring summer and ripe fruits
  in their purple hearts. (l. 12–16)

  BoWoP; CMoP; MoAmPo; NOBA; PoE; UnPo

Sea Rose

10 Rose, harsh rose,
   marred and with stint of petals,
   meager flower, thin,
   sparse of leaf, (l. 1–4)

   FaBoMo; HeIP; NoAM; NoP

KEITH DOUGLAS (1920–1944)

Aristocrats

1 How can I live among this gentle
  absolescent breed of heroes, and not weep?
  Unicorns, almost,
  for they are falling into two legends
  in which their stupidity and chivalry
  are celebrated. Each, fool and herb, will be an
     immortal. (l. 9–14)

  FaBoMo; NAEL-2; NePoEA; NoAM; OBWP

Vergissmeinnicht

2 For here the lover and killer are mingled
  who had one body and one heart.
  And death who had the soldier singled
  has done the lover mortal hurt. (l. 21–24)

  FaBoMo; GTBS-P; InPS; NAEL-2; NePoEA; NoAM;
  OBD; OBWP; OxBTC; RB; SoSe

WILLIAM DOUGLAS (1672?–1748)

Annie Laurie

1 Annie Laurie
  Gie'd me her promise true;
  Gie'd me her promise true,

Which ne'er forgot will be;
And for bonnie Annie Laurie
I'd lay me doune and dee. (l. 3–8)

FaBoBe; FaBV; FaFP; GN; WBLP

JOHN DOWLAND (1562–1626)

Come Away, Come, Sweet Love (*attributed to* Dowland)

1 Come away, come sweet Love,
The golden morning breakes:
All the earth, all the ayre,
Of love and pleasure speakes. (l. 1–4)

ElL; ELP; GBL; NAEL-1; OBSC; PoEL-2

ERNEST CHRISTOPHER DOWSON (1867–1900)

Extreme Unction

1 From troublous sights and sounds set free;
In such a twilight hour of breath,
Shall one retrace his life or see,
Through shadows, the true face of death? (l. 9–12)

2 Yet, when the walls of flesh grow weak,
In such an hour it may well be,
Through mist and darkness, light will break,
And each anointed sense will see. (l. 17–20)

ACP; MoBrPo; OAEL-2; OBMV

Non Sum Qualis Eram Bonae sub Regno Cynarae

3 I have been faithful to thee, Cynara! in my fashion.
(l. 6)

AWP; BeLS; BLPA; BoLoP; BrPo; EBVV; EnLoPo;
FaBoBe; FaFP; FPL; GBL; GTBS-P; HAP; HeIP; LiTB;
MoBrPo; NAEL-2; NOBE; NoP; OAEL-2; OBEV; OBMV;
OBNC; PoRA; PrIm; TEP; TrGrPo; UnPo

To One in Bedlam

4 Better than mortal flowers,
Thy moon-kissed roses seem: better than love or sleep,
The star-crowned solitude of thine oblivious hours!
(l. 12–14)

ACP; BrPo; MoBrPo; OBMV; Son

Vitae Summa Brevis Spem Nos Vetat Incohare Longam

5 They are not long, the weeping and the laughter,
Love and desire and hate:
I think they have no portion in us after
We pass the gate. (l. 1–4)

6 They are not long, the days of wine and roses:
Out of a misty dream
Our path emerges for a while, then closes
Within a dream. (l. 5–8)

AWP; BrPo; ChTr; EBVV; FaBoRV; HAP; MoBrPo;
NAEL-2; NOBE; NOBVV; NoP; OBEV; OxBSP; PCP;
PoRA; TrGrPo; WGRP

JOSEPH RODMAN DRAKE (1795–1820)

The American Flag

1 When Freedom, from her mountain height,
Unfurled her standard to the air,
She tore the azure robe of night,
And set the stars of glory there; (l. 1–4)

2 And when the cannon-mouthings loud
Heave in wild wreaths the battle-shroud, (l. 36–37)

3 Then shall thy meteor glances glow,
And cowering foes shall shrink beneath
Each gallant arm that strikes below
That lovely messenger of death. (l. 40–43)

4 Forever float that standard sheet!
Where breathes the foe but falls before us,
With Freedom's soil beneath our feet,
And Freedom's banner streaming o'er us! (l. 58–61)

AA; AnAmPo; FaBoBe; FaFP; GN; OPP; PAH; WBLP

MICHAEL DRAYTON (1563–1631)

Agincourt

1 Fair stood the wind for France,
When we our sails advance,
Nor now to prove our chance
Longer will tarry; (l. 1–4)

2 Upon Saint Crispin's day
Fought was this noble fray,
Which fame did not delay
To England to carry.
On when shall Englishmen

With such acts fill a pen,
Or England breed again
Such a King Harry? (l. 113–120)

BeLS; ElL; FaBoBe; FaBoCh; OBEV

Idea

3 Dear, why should you command me to my rest,
When now the night doth summon all to sleep?
Methinks this time becometh lovers best;
Night was ordained together friends to keep.
How happy are all other living things,
Which though the day disjoin by several flight,
The quiet evening yet together brings,
And each returns unto his love at night.

AAS; ElL; LiTB; NOBE; OBSC; PoEL-2; Son

4 An evil spirit, your beauty, haunts me still,
Wherewith, alas! I have been long possessed,

5 Before my face it lays down my despairs,
And hastes me on unto a sudden death,

6 Thus am I still provoked to every evil
By this good wicked spirit, sweet angel devil.

AAS; ElL; GBL; NOBE; OBSC

7 How many paltry, foolish, painted things
That now in coaches trouble every street
Shall be forgotten, whom no poet sings,
Ere they be well wrapped in their winding-sheet!

8 Virgins and matrons, reading these my rimes,
Shall be so much delighted with thy story
That they shall grieve they lived not in these times
To have seen thee, their sex's only glory.
So shalt thou fly above the vulgar throng
Still to survive in my immortal song.

AAS; ElL; EnLoPo; GBL; HAP; HeIP; NAEL-1; NIP;
NoP; OAEL-1; OBSC; PrIm; TEP

9 No far-fetched sigh shall ever wound my breast,
Love from mine eye a tear shall never wring,
Nor in Ah me's my whining sonnets dressed,
A libertine, fantastically I sing.
My verse is the true image of my mind,
Ever in motion, still desiring change;

10 If he from heaven that filched that living fire
Condemned by Jove to endless torment be,
I greatly marvel how you still go free
That far beyond Prometheus did aspire

11 But you broke into heaven's immortal store,
Where virtue, honor, wit, and beauty lay;
Which taking thence you have escaped away,
Yet stand as free as ere you did before;

12 My name shall mount upon Eternitie.

13 Now if thou wouldst, when all have given him over,
From death to life thou mightst him yet recover.

14 Or if no thing but death will serve thy turn,
Still thirsting for subversion of my state,
Do what thou canst, raze, massacre, and burn,
Let the world see the utmost of thy hate;

AAS; NAEL-1; NoP; Son

15 Since there's no help, come let us kiss and part;
Nay, I have done, you get no more of me,
And I am glad, yea, glad with all my heart
That thus so cleanly I myself can free;
Shake hands for ever, cancel all our vows,
And when we meet at any time again,
Be it not seen in either of our brows
That we one jot of former love retain.

AAS; AWP; BLPL; BoLoP; ElL; EnLoPo; GBL; GTBS;
GTBS-P; HAP; HeIP; InPS; JCP; LiTB; NAEL-1; NOBE;
NoP; OAEL-1; OBEV; OBSC; PoEL-2; PrIm; SCV;
SeCePo; Son; SoSe; TEP; TrGrPo

16 To nothing fitter can I thee compare
Than to the son of some rich pennyfather,
Who, having now brought on his end with care,
Leaves to his son all he had heaped together;

ElL; OBSC; Son; TrGrPo

To the Virginian Voyage

17 Virginia,
Earth's only paradise. (l. 23–24)

18 And the ambitious vine
Crowns with his purple mass
The cedar reaching high
To kiss the sky,
The cypress, pine,
And useful sassafras. (l. 31–36)

AiP; HAP; NAEL-1; NOBE; OBEV; OBS; PAH; PoEL-2;
SeCePo; TEP

JOHN DRINKWATER (1882–1937)

Moonlit Apples

1 At the top of the house the apples are laid in rows,
(l. 1)

BoNaP; BoTP; OBMV; OxBTC; PoRA

LOUISE DRISCOLL (b. 1875)

Hold Fast Your Dreams

1 Hold fast your dreams!
  Within your heart
  Keep one still, secret spot
  Where dreams may go, (l. 1–4)

BLPA; FaBoBe; FaPON; FPL

WILLIAM DRUMMOND, OF HAWTHORNDEN (1585–1649)

Like the Idalian Queen

1 The Graces naked danced about the place,
  The winds and trees amazed
  With silence on her gazed,
  The flowers did smile, like those upon her face;
  And as their aspen stalks those fingers band,
  That she might read my case,
  A hyacinth I wished me in her hand. (l. 8–14)

ElL; ELP; GBL; GoTS; InvP; NOBE; OAEL-1; OBEV;
OBS; PoEL-2; SeCePo

Madrigal

2 My thoughts hold mortal strife;
  I do detest my life, (l. 1–2)

3 —But he, grim grinning King,
  Who caitiffs scorns, and doth the blest surprise,
  Late having deck'd with beauty's rose his tomb,
  Disdains to crop a weed, and will not come. (l. 6–9)

ElL; GTBS; GTBS-P; NOBE; OBEV; OBS; OxBSP

My lute, be as thou wast when thou didst grow

4 My lute, be as thou wert when thou didst grow
  With thy green mother in some shady grove,
  When immelodious winds but made thee move,
  And birds their ramage did on thee bestow. (l. 1–4)

ElL; GTBS-P; GTBS; OBS; Son

Saint John Baptist

5 The last and greatest Herald of Heaven's King,
  Girt with rough skins, hies to the deserts wild,
  Among that savage brood the woods forth bring,
  Which he than man more harmless found and mild.
                                            (l. 1–4)

6 Parched body, hollow eyes, some uncouth thing
  Made him appear, long since from earth exiled.
                                            (l. 7–8)

7 Repent, repent, and from old errors turn!'
  Who listened to his voice, obeyed his cry?
  Only the echoes, which he made relent,
  Rung from their marble caves 'Repent! Repent!'
                                            (l. 11–14)

EaLo; GoTS; GTBS; GTBS-P; NOBE; OBEV; OBS;
TrCP; TrGrPo

JOHN DRYDEN (1631–1700)

Absalom and Achitophel, Pt. I

1 But, when to Sin our byast Nature leans,
  The careful Devil is still at hand with means;
  And providently Pimps for ill desires:
  The Good Old Cause, reviv'd, a Plot requires,
  Plots, true or false, are necessary things,
  To raise up Common-wealths and ruine Kings.
                                            (l. 79–84)

2 Great Wits are sure to Madness near alli'd
  And thin Partitions do their Bounds divide;
  Else, why should he, with Wealth and Honour blest,
  Refuse his Age the needful hours of Rest? (l. 163–166)

3 Nor let his Love enchant your generous Mind;
  'Tis Natures trick to propagate her Kind.
  Our fond Begetters, who would never die,
  Love but themselves in their Posterity. (l. 423–426)

4 Oh that my Pow'r to Saving were confin'd:
  Why am I forc'd, like Heav'n, against my mind,
  To make Examples of another Kind?
  Must I at length the Sword of Justice draw?
  Oh curst Effects of necessary Law!
  How ill my Fear they by my Mercy scan,
  Beware the Fury of a Patient Man. (l. 999–1005)

FaBoPV; HAP; NoP; NoP; OAEL-1; PoE; SeCV-2

Alexander's Feast; or, The Power of Music

5 Softly sweet in Lydian measures
  Soon he soothed his soul to pleasures.
  'War', he sung, 'is toil and trouble;
  Honour but an empty bubble.
  Never ending, still beginning,
  Fighting still, and still destroying;
  If the world be worth thy winning,
  Think, O think it worth enjoying.
  Lovely Thais sits beside thee,
  Take the good the Gods provide thee.' (l. 97–106)

ACP; FaPoR; FiP; GN; GTBS-P; GTBS; LiTB; NAEL-1;
NOBE; OAEL-1; OBS; SeCV-2; TrGrPo; WiR

Amphitryon

6 The Legend of Love no Couple can find
So easie to part, or so equally join'd.

AWP; OxBSP; PoEL-3; SeCV-2

Annus Mirabilis

7 Already, labouring with a mighty fate,
She shakes the rubbish from her mounting brow
And seems to have renewed her charter's date
Which Heaven will to the death of time allow.

FaBoCh; NOBE; OBS; SeCePo

Aureng-Zebe

8 But he has now another taste of Wit;
And, to confess a truth (though out of time,)
Grows weary of his long-loved mistress Rhyme.
Passion's too fierce to be in fetters bound,
And Nature flies him like enchanted ground:

FiP; OBS; OxBoLi; SeCV-2

Cleomenes

9 Time and death shall depart and say in flying
Love has found out a way to live, by dying.

LiTB; OBEV; QFR; SeCV-2

Lines Printed under the Engraved Portrait of Milton

10 Three poets, in three distant ages born,
Greece, Italy, and England did adorn.
The first in loftiness of thought surpassed,
The next in majesty, in both the last:
The force of Nature could no farther go;
To make a third she joined the former two. (l. 1–6)

ACP; HeIP; InPK; OAEL-1; SeCV-2; TrGrPo

MacFlecknoe; or, A Satire upon the True-Blue Protestant Poet T. S.

11 The rest to some faint meaning make pretense,
But Shnever deviates into sense.

12 Here stopped the good old sire, and wept for joy
In silent raptures of the hopeful boy.
All arguments, but most his plays, persuade
That for anointed dullness he was made.

13 High on a throne of his own labors reared.
At his right hand our young Ascanius sate,
Rome's other hope and pillar of the state.
His brows thick fogs, instead of glories, grace,
And lambent dullness played around his face.

14 The sire then shook the honors of his head,
And from his brows damps of oblivion shed
Full on the filial dullness:

FiP; HAP; NAEL-1; NOBE; NoP; OAEL-1; OBS; OBSV;
OxBoLi; PoE; PPP; QFR; SCV; SeCV-2; TEP; TrGrPo

Marriage à la Mode

15 Thus intranc'd they did lie,
Till Alexis did try
To recover new breath, that again he might die:
Then often they died; but the more they did so,
The nymph died more quick, and the shepherd more
  slow.

BoLoP; ErPo; FF; PrIm

16 We lov'd, and we lov'd, as long as we could,
Till our love was lov'd out in us both;
But our marriage is dead, when the pleasure is fled:
'Twas pleasure first made it an oath.

AWP; HeIP; NAEL-1; NIP; SeCV-2

Religio Laici

17 For granting we have sinned, and that the offence
Of man is made against Omnipotence,
Some price that bears proportion must be paid,
And infinite with infinite be weighed. (l. 111–114)

18 Then for the Style; Majestick and Divine,
It speaks no less than God in every Line:
Commanding words; whose Force is still the same
As the first Fiat that produc'd our Frame.
(l. 152–155)

19 That, if the Gentiles, (whom no Law inspir'd,)
By Nature did what was by Law requir'd;
They, who the written Rule and never known,
Were to themselves both Rule and Law alone:
To Natures plain Indictment they shall plead;
And, by their Conscience, be condemn'd or freed.
(l. 200–205)

20 More Safe, and much more modest 'tis, to say
God wou'd not leave Mankind without a way:
And that the Scriptures, though not every where
Free from Corruption, or intire, or clear,
Are uncorrupt, sufficient, clear, intire,
In all things which our needfull Faith require.
If others in the same Glass better see
'Tis for Themselves they look, but not for me:

For MY Salvation must its Doom receive
Not from what OTHERS, but what I believe.
(l. 295–304)

21 This good had full as bad a Consequence:
The Book thus put in every vulgar hand,
Which each presum'd he best cou'd understand,
The Common Rule was made the common Prey;
And at the mercy of the Rabble lay.
The tender Page with horney Fists was gual'd;
And he was gifted most that loudest baul'd:
The Spirit gave the Doctoral Degree:
And every member of a Company
Was of his Trade, and of the Bible free.
(l. 399–408)

22 Thus have I made my own opinions clear;
Yet neither praise expect, nor censure fear:
And this unpolished, rugged verse I chose,
As fittest for discourse and nearest prose; (l. 451–454)

FiP; OAEL-1; OBS; SeCV-2

The Secular Masque

23 Inspire the Vocal Brass, Inspire;
The World is past its Infant Age:
Arms and Honour,
Arms and Honour,
Set the Martial Mind on Fire,
And kindle Manly Rage.

24 Calms appear, when Storms are past;
Love will have his Hour at last:
Nature is my kindly Care;
Mars destroys, and I repair;
Take me, take me, while you may,
Venus comes not ev'ry Day.

NAEL-1; PoE; PoEL-3; PrIm; SeCV-2

Song for Saint Cecilia's Day 1687

25 From Harmony, from heavenly Harmony
This universal Frame began:
From Harmony to Harmony
Through all the Compass of the Notes it ran,
The Diapason closing full in Man. (l. 11–15)

26 The soft complaining FLUTE
In dying Notes discovers
The Woes of hopeless Lovers,
Whose Dirge is whisper'd by the warbling LUTE.
(l. 33–36)

27 So, when the last and dreadful Hour
This crumbling Pageant shall devour,
The TRUMPET shall be heard on high,

The dead shall live, the living die,
And MUSICK shall untune the Sky. (l. 59–63)

AWP; FaBoTw; GTBS; GTBS-P; HAP; InPS; LiTB;
OAEL-1; OBEV; OPOP; PoEL-3; PPP; SeCV-2; TEP;
TrGrPo; UnS

The Spanish Friar

28 Your love by ours we measure
Till we have lost our treasure,
But dying is a pleasure,
When living is a pain.

ACP; BoLoP; ELP; EnLoPo; FiP; HAP; LiTB; NOBE;
OBS; SeCV-2

To My Dear Friend Mr. Congreve

29 But what we gain'd in Skill we lost in Strength.
Our Builders were with Want of Genius curst;
The second Temple was not like the first;
Till you, the best Vitruvius, come at length,
Our Beauties equal, but excel our Strength. (l. 12–16)

30 Yet this I Prophesie; Thou shalt be seen,
(Tho' with some short Parenthesis between:)
High on the Throne of Wit; and, seated there,
Nor mine (that's little) but thy Lawrel wear,
(l. 51–54)

EBEV; FiP; OAEL-1; OBS; PoEL-3; SeCV-2

**To the Pious Memory of the Accomplished
Young Lady, Mrs. Anne Killigrew**

31 Hear, then, a mortal Muse thy praise rehearse,
In no ignoble verse;
But such as thy own voice did practise here,
When thy first-fruits of Poesy were given,
To make thyself a welcome inmate there;
While yet a young probationer,
And candidate of Heaven. (l. 16–22)

NAEL-1; OAEL-1 OBEV; PoEL-3; SeCV-2

JOHN DRYDEN (1631–1700) *AND*
NAHUM TATE (1652–1715)

Absalom and Achitophel, Pt. II

1 Railing in other men may be a crime,
But ought to pass for mere instinct in him:
Instinct he follows and no farther knows,
For to write verse with him is to transprose;

2 But though Heaven made him poor, with reverence
    speaking,
He never was a poet of God's making;
The midwife laid her hand on his thick skull,
With this prophetic blessing — Be thou dull;

AWP; FiP; TW

ALAN DUGAN (b. 1923)

Love Song: I and Thou

1 Nothing is plumb, level or square:
the studs are bowed, the joists
are shaky by nature, (l. 1–3)

2 bent nails
dance all over the surfacing
like maggots (l. 5–7)

3 I can nail my left palm
to the left-hand cross-piece but
I can't do everything myself.
I need a hand to nail the right,
a help, a love, a you, a wife. (l. 27–31)

CAPP; FF; HoPM; InPK; MoP; NoAM; SoSe

PAUL LAURENCE DUNBAR (1872–1906)

Dawn

1 An angel, robed in spotless white,
Bent down and kissed the sleeping Night.
Night woke to blush; the sprite was gone.
Men saw the blush and called it Dawn. (l. 1–4)

AmNP; AnAmPo; PoLF; PoNe

A Death Song

2 Lay me down beneaf de willers in de grass,
Whah de branch'll go a-singin' as it pass. (l. 1–2)

3 Fu' I t'ink de las' long res'
Gwine to soothe my sperrit bes'
If I's layin' 'mong de t'ings I's allus knowed.
        (l. 13–15)

BANP; CDC; PoLF; PoNe

The Debt

4 This is the debt I pay
Just for one riotous day, (l. 1–2)

5 Slight was the thing I bought,
Small was the debt I thought,
Poor was the loan at best —
God! but the interest! (l. 9–12)

AmNP; BANP; CDC; SoSe

Ships That Pass in the Night

6 Out in the sky the great dark clouds are massing;
I look far out into the pregnant night, (l. 1–2)

7 And catch the gleaming of a random light,
That tells me that the ship I seek is passing, passing.
        (l. 4–5)

8 Is there no hope for me? Is there no way
That I may sight and check that speeding bark
Which out of sight and sound is passing, passing?
        (l. 13–15)

AnAmPo; BANP; CDC; MOS

Sympathy

9 I know what the caged bird feels, alas! (l. l)

10 It is not a carol of joy or glee,
But a prayer that he sends from his heart's deep core,
But a plea, that upward to Heaven he flings —
I know why the caged bird sings! (l. 18–21)

AmNP; CDC; IDB; PoBA; PoNe

We Wear the Mask

11 We wear the mask that grins and lies, (l. 1)

12 With torn and bleeding hearts we smile,
And mouth with myriad subtleties. (l. 4–5)

13 We sing, but oh the clay is vile
Beneath our feet, and long the mile;
But let the world dream otherwise,
We wear the mask! (l. 12–15)

AmNP; CDC; FF; IDB; NIP; NoP; PoBA; TTY; UnPo

WILLIAM DUNBAR (c. 1465–c. 1530)

Done Is a Battle

1 Done is battell on the dragon blak,
Our campioun Chryst confountet hes his force; (l. 1–2)

2 He for our saik that sufferit to be slane,
And lyk a lamb in sacrifice wes dicht,
Is lyk a lyone rissin up agane,
And as gyane raxit him on hicht;
Sprungin is Aurora radius and bricht,
On loft is gone the glorius Appollo,
The blisfull day depairtit fro the nycht:
Surrexit Dominus de sepulchro. (l. 17–24)

NOCV; NoP; OxBLMV; OxBS; PoEL-1

Lament for the Makaris

3 Our pleasance here is all vain glory,
This false world is but transitory;
The flesh is bruckle, the Fiend is slee: —
Timor Mortis conturbat me. (l. 5–8)

ACP; ChTr; EBEV; FaBoRV; GoTS; HAP; MeEL; NOBE;
NoP; OAEL-1; OBEV; OxBS; PoEL-1

To the City of London

4 London, thou art of townes A per se.
Soveraign of cities, semeliest in sight,
Of high renoun, riches, and royaltie;
Of lordis, barons, and many goodly knyght;
Of most delectable lusty ladies bright;
Of famous prelatis in habitis clericall;
Of merchauntis full of substaunce and myght:
London, thou art the flour of Cities all (l. 1–8)

5 Strong be thy wallis that about the standis;
Wise be the people that within the dwellis;
Fresh is thy ryver with his lusty strandis;
Blith be thy chirches, wele sownyng be thy bellis;
Riche be thy merchauntis in substance that excellis
Fair be thy wives, right lovesom, white and small;
Clere be thy virgyns, lusty under kellis:
London, thou art the flour of Cities all. (l. 41–48)

ChTr; EBEV; FaBoPP; OBEV

ROBERT DUNCAN (b. 1919)

Often I Am Permitted to Return to a Meadow

1 Often I am permitted to return to a meadow
as if it were a given property of the mind
that certain bounds hold against chaos,

that is a place of first permission,
everlasting omen of what is. (l. 19–23)

CAPP; CMoP; HeIP; NOBA; NU

This Place Rumor'd to Have Been Sodom

2 This was once
a city among men, a gathering together of spirit.
It was measured by the Lord and found wanting.
(l. 5–7)

3 The devout have laid out gardens in the desert. (l. 17)

4 The world like Great Sodom lies under Love
and knows not the hand of the Lord that moves.
(l. 29–30)

NeAP; NOBA; PoM; PPP

RAY DUREM (1915–1963)

Award

1 You've watched me all your life,
I've clothed your wife,
put your two sons through college.
What good has it done?
Sun keeps rising every morning. (l. 7–11)

2 See, I'm so light, it don't seem right
to go to the colored rest room;
my daughter's brown, and folks frown on that in Texas,
I just don't know how to go to the bathroom in the free
world! (l. 27–30)

BPo; IDB; FoBA; SoSe; TTY

SIR EDWARD DYER (c. 1540–1607)

My Mind to Me a Kingdom Is (attributed to Dyer)

1 My mind to me a kingdom is;
Such present joys therein I find
That it excels all other bliss
That earth affords or grows by kind.
Though much I want which most would have,
Yet still my mind forbids to crave. (l. 1–6)

2 Some have too much, yet still do crave;
I little have, and seek no more.
They are but poor, though much they have,
And I am rich with little store.
They poor, I rich; they beg, I give;
They lack, I leave; they pine, I live. (l. 25–30)

BLPL; ElL; FaBoBe; LiTB; NAEL-1; NIP; NOBE; OBSC;
PoEL-1; TrGrPo; WGRP

JOHN DYER (1699–1758)

Grongar Hill

1 Below me trees unnumbered rise,
Beautiful in various dyes:
The gloomy pine, the poplar blue,
The yellow beech, the sable yew,
The slender fir that taper grows,
The sturdy oak with broad-spread boughs.

2 Ever charming, ever new,
When will the landscape tire the view!
The fountain's fall, the river's flow,
The woody valleys, warm and low;
The windy summit, wild and high,
Roughly rushing on the sky!
The pleasant seat, the ruined tow'r,
The naked rock, the shady bow'r;
The town and village, dome and farm,
Each give each a double charm,
As pearls upon an Ethiop's arm.

ChTr; EnRP; FaBoPP; NOEC; NoP; PoEL-3

RICHARD EBERHART (b. 1904)

For a Lamb

1 I saw on the slant hill a putrid lamb,
Propped with daisies. (l. 1–2)

CMoP; LiTM; OxBSP; RB

The Fury of Aerial Bombardment

2 You would think the fury of aerial bombardment
Would rouse God to relent; (l. 1–2)

3 Was man made stupid to see his own stupidity?
Is God by definition indifferent, beyond us all?
Is the eternal truth man's fighting soul
Wherein the Beast ravens in its own avidity? (l. 9–12)

4 Names on a list, whose faces I do not recall
But they are gone to early death, who late in school
Distinguished the belt feed lever from the belt holding
pawl. (l. 14–16)

CMoP; FaBoMo; FF; FYAP; HeIP; HoPM; InPK; LiTA;
LiTM; MoP; NIP; NoAM; NoP; OBWP; PrIm; RB; TAP;
TwCP; UnPo; VGW; WaP

The Horse Chestnut Tree

5 we, outlaws on God's property,
Fling out imagination beyond the skies,
Wishing a tangible good from the unknown.

And likewise death will drive us from the scene
With the great flowering world unbroken yet,
Which we held in idea, a little handful. (l. 19–24)

CMoP; LiTM; MoAB; MoAmPo

If I Could Only Live at the Pitch That Is near Madness

6 If I could only live at the pitch that is near madness
When everything is as it was in my childhood
Violent, vivid, and of infinite possibility:
That the sun and the moon broke over my head.
(l. 1–4)

7 And the truth wailing there like a red babe. (l. 16)

FF; LiTM; MAT; MoAB

On a Squirrel Crossing the Road in Autumn, in New England

8 He obeys the orders of nature
Without knowing them
It is what he does not know
That makes him beautiful.
Such a knot of little purposeful nature! (l. 8–12)

9 It is what man does not know of God
Composes the visible poem of the world. (l. 15–16)

HeIP; LiTM; Psk

"GEORGE ELIOT" (pseudonym of MARY ANN EVANS LEWES CROSS) (1727–1805)

The Choir Invisible

1 O may I join the choir invisible
Of those immortal dead who live again
In minds made better by their presence: (l. 1–3)

EBVV; OBD; OBNC; OHFP; WBLP; WGRP

THOMAS STEARNS ELIOT (1888–1965)

Ash Wednesday

1 Because I do not hope to turn again
Because I do not hope
Because I do not hope to turn (l. 1–3)

2 (Why should the aged eagle stretch its wings?) (l. 6)

3 Because I do not hope to know again
  The infirm glory of the positive hour (l. 9–10)

4 Consequently I rejoice, having to construct something
  Upon which to rejoice (l. 24–25)

5 And pray to God to have mercy upon us
  And I pray that I may forget
  These matters that with myself I too much discuss
  Too much explain (l. 26–29)

6 Lady, three white leopards sat under a juniper-tree
  In the cool of the day, having fed to satiety
  On my legs my heart my liver and that which had been
    contained
  In the hollow round of my skull. And God said
  Shall these bones live? shall these
  Bones live? (l. 42–47)

7 Let the whiteness of bones atone to forgetfulness.
  There is no life in them. As I am forgotten
  And would be forgotten, so I would forget
  Thus devoted, concentrated in purpose. (l. 59–62)

8 And the bones sang chirping
  With the burden of the grasshopper, (l. 64–65)

9 Lady of silences
  Calm and distressed
  Torn and most whole (l. 66–68)

10 Terminate torment
   Of love unsatisfied
   The greater torment
   Of love satisfied (l. 76–79)

11 Blown hair is sweet, brown hair over the mouth blown,
   Lilac and brown hair; (l. 112–113)

12 Redeem
   The time. Redeem.
   The unread vision in the higher dream
   While jewelled unicorns draw by the gilded hearse.
                                    (l. 137–140)

13 Against the Word the unstilled world still whirled
   About the center of the silent Word. (l. 156–157)

14 No place of grace for those who avoid the face
   No time to rejoice for those who walk among noise and
     deny the voice (l. 166–168)

LiTA; MoAB; MoAmPo; OxBA; VGW

Burnt Norton (Four Quartets)

15 Time present and time past
   Are both perhaps present in time future,
   And time future contained in time past.

If all time is eternally present
All time is unredeemable.

16 Footfalls echo in the memory
   Down the passage which we did not take
   Towards the door we never opened
   Into the rose-garden.

17 the roses
   Had the look of flowers that are looked at.

18 Go, said the bird, for the leaves were full of children,
   Hidden excitedly, containing laughter.

19 human kind
   Cannot bear very much reality.
   Time past and time future
   What might have been and what has been
   Point to one end, which is always present.

20 Except for the point, the still point,
   There would be no dance, and there is only the dance.

21 Desiccation of the world of sense,
   Evacuation of the world of fancy,
   Inoperancy of the world of spirit;
   This is the one way, and the other
   Is the same, not in movement
   But abstention from movement;

22 Words move, music moves
   Only in time; but that which is only living
   Can only die. Words, after speech, reach
   Into the silence.

23 Only by the form, the pattern,
   Can words or music reach
   The stillness, as a Chinese jar still
   Moves perpetually in its stillness.

24 Words strain,
   Crack and sometimes break, under the burden,
   Under the tension, slip, slide, perish,
   Decay with imprecision, will not stay in place,
   Will not stay still.

25 The Word in the desert
   Is most attacked by voices of temptation,
   The crying shadow in the funeral dance,
   The loud lament of the disconsolate chimera.

CMoP; LiTM; MoAB; MoAmPo; NAAL-2; PoE

The Dry Salvages (Four Quartets)

26 I do not know much about gods; but I think that the
     river
   Is a strong brown god —

27 Useful, untrustworthy, as a conveyor of commerce;
Then only a problem confronting the builder of bridges.

28 Unhonoured, unpropitiated
By worshippers of the machine, but waiting, watching
and waiting.

29 It tosses up our losses, the torn seine,
The shattered lobster pot, the broken oar
And the gear of foreign dead men. The sea has many
voices,
Many gods and many voices.

AiP; LiTB; NoP; OxBA; SeCePo

Gerontion

30 Here I am, an old man in a dry month,
Being read to by a boy, waiting for rain. (l. 1–2)

31 In the juvescence of the year
Came Christ the tiger (l. 19–20)

32 After such knowledge, what forgiveness? Think now
History has many cunning passages, contrived corridors
And issues, (l. 33–35)

33 Neither fear nor courage saves us. Unnatural vices
Are fathered by our heroism. Virtues
Are forced upon us by our impudent crimes.
(l. 44–46)

34 The tiger springs in the new year. Us he devours.
(l. 48)

35 Tenants of the house,
Thoughts of a dry brain in a dry season. (l. 74–75)

AmPP; CMoP; EBEV; GTBS-P; HAP; InPS; LiTA; LiTM;
MoP; NAAL-2; NoAM; NOBA; OAEL-2; OxBA; PPP;
SeCePo; TAP

The Hippopotamus

36 The broad-backed hippopotamus
Rests on his belly in the mud;
Although he seems so firm to us
He is merely flesh and blood. (l. 1–4)

37 While the True Church can never fail
For it is based upon a rock. (l. 7–8)

38 The hippopotamus's day
Is passed in sleep; at night he hunts;
God works in a mysterious way —
The Church can sleep and feed at once. (l. 21–24)

39 He shall be washed as white as snow,
By all the martyr'd virgins kist,
While the True Church remains below
Wrapt in the old miasmal mist. (l. 33–36)

AWP; HoPM; LiTB; NAEL-2; OBMV; VGW

The Hollow Men

40 We are the hollow men
We are the stuffed men (l. 1–2)

41 Our dried voices, when
We whisper together
Are quiet and meaningless
As wind in dry grass
Or rats' feet over broken glass (l. 5–9)

42 Those who have crossed
With direct eyes, to death's other Kingdom
Remember us — if at all — not as lost
Violent souls, but only
As the hollow men
The stuffed men. (l. 13–18)

43 Eyes I dare not meet in dreams
In death's dream kingdom
These do not appear: (l. 19–21)

44 This is the dead land
This is cactus land
Here the stone images
Are raised, here they receive
The supplication of a dead man's hand
Under the twinkle of a fading star. (l. 39–44)

45 Lips that would kiss
Form prayers to broken stone. (l. 50–51)

46 The eyes are not here
There are no eyes here
In this valley of dying stars
In this hollow valley (l. 52–55)

47 Sightless, unless
The eyes reappear
As the perpetual star
Multifoliate rose
Of death's twilight kingdom (l. 61–65)

48 This is the way the world ends
This is the way the world ends
This is the way the world ends
Not with a bang but a whimper. (l. 95–98)

InPS; LiTA; LiTM; MoAB; MoAmPo; NAAL-2; OAEL-2;
OBMV

Journey of the Magi

49 A cold coming we had of it,
Just the worst time of the year
For a journey, and such a long journey: (l. 1–3)

50 Then at dawn we came down to a temperate valley,
    Wet, below the snow line, smelling of vegetation,
    (l. 21–22)

51 were we led all that way for
    Birth or Death? (l. 35–36)

52 We returned to our places, these Kingdoms,
    But no longer at ease here, in the old dispensation,
    With an alien people clutching their gods.
    I should be glad of another death. (l. 40–43)

    EaLo; FaBoCh; FaBoMo; FaFP; HAP; HeIP; InPK; LiTA;
    LiTM; MoAB; MoAmPo; NAEL-2; NIP; NOCV; NoP;
    OBCP; OBMV; OxBTC; PChr; PoE; SoSe; TAP; TrGrPo;
    TwCP

La Figlia Che Piange

53 Weave, weave the sunlight in your hair — (l. 3)

54 Sometimes these cogitations still amaze
    The troubled midnight and the noon's repose.
    (l. 24–25)

    FaBoTw; GBL; HeIP; LiTA; MAT; OPOP; OxBTC; PoA;
    UnPo; VGW

LANDSCAPES (the following 3 poems)

Cape Ann

55 O quick quick quick, quick hear the song sparrow,
    Swamp sparrow, fox sparrow, vesper sparrow
    At dawn and dusk.

56 All are delectable. Sweet sweet sweet
    But resign this land at the end, resign it
    To its true owner, the tough one, the sea gull.
    The palaver is finished.

    GoJo; NAEL-2; NoAM; RB

New Hampshire

57 Children's voices in the orchard
    Between the blossom- and the fruit-time:

58 Cling, swing,
    Spring, sing,
    Swing up into the apple tree.

    FaBoCh; GTBS-P; NoAM; RB; WeW

Rannoch by Glencoe

59 Here the crow starves, here the patient stag
    Breeds for the rifle.

    FaBoPP; NAEL-2; PoSH; RB

Little Gidding (Four Quartets)

60 Midwinter spring is its own season
    Sempiternal though sodden towards sundown,
    Suspended in time,between pole and tropic.

61 Between melting and freezing
    The soul's sap quivers.

62 Now the hedgerow
    Is blanched for an hour with transitory blossom
    Of snow, a bloom more sudden
    Than that of summer,

63 And prayer is more
    Than an order of words, the conscious occupation
    Of the praying mind, or the sound of the voice praying.

64 the communication
    Of the dead is tongued with fire beyond the language of
       the living.

65 in the brown baked features
    The eyes of a familiar compound ghost
    Both intimate and unidentifiable.

66 Last season's fruit is eaten
    And the fullfed beast shall kick the empty pail.
    For last year's words belong to last year's language
    And next year's words await another voice.

67 our concern was speech, and speech impelled us
    To purify the dialect of the tribe
    And urge the mind to aftersight and foresight,

68 First, the cold friction of expiring sense
    Without enchantment, offering no promise
    But bitter tastelessness of shadow fruit
    As body and soul begin to fall asunder.
    Second, the conscious impotence of rage
    At human folly,

69 Whatever we inherit from the fortunate
    We have taken from the defeated
    What they had to leave us — a symbol:
    A symbol perfected in death.

70 Love is the unfamiliar Name
    Behind the hands that wove
    The intolerable shirt of flame
    Which human power cannot remove.

71 What we call the beginning is often the end
    And to make an end is to make a beginning.
    The end is where we start from.

72 We die with the dying:
    See, they depart, and we go with them.
    We are born with the dead:
    See, they return, and bring us with them.

73 We shall not cease from exploration
And the end of all our exploring
Will be to arrive where we started
And know the place for the first time.

74 And all shall be well and
All manner of thing shall be well
When the tongues of flame are in-folded
Into the crowned knot of fire
And the fire and the rose are one.

FaBoMo; FaBoPV; FaBoTw; GTBS-P; MoP; NAEL-2;
NAWM-2; NoAM; NOBA; NOBE; OAEL-2; OxBTC;
PrIm; TAP

The Love Song of J. Alfred Prufrock

75 Let us go then, you and I,
When the evening is spread out against the sky
Like a patient etherized upon a table; (l. 1–3)

76 restless nights in one-night cheap hotels
And sawdust restaurants with oyster-shells:
Streets that follow like a tedious argument
Of insidious intent (l. 6–9)

77 Oh, do not ask, "What is it?"
Let us go and make our visit.

In the room the women come and go
Talking of Michelangelo. (l. 11–14)

78 The yellow fog that rubs its back upon the window-
panes,
The yellow smoke that rubs its muzzle on the window-
panes (l. 15–16)

And seeing that it was a soft October night,
Curled once about the house, and fell asleep.
(l. 21–22)

79 Time for you and time for me,
And time yet for a hundred indecisions,
And for a hundred visions and revisions,
Before the taking of a toast and tea. (l. 31–34)

80 Time to turn back and descend the stair,
With a bald spot in the middle of my hair —
(They will say: "How his hair is growing thin!")
(l. 39–41)

81 Do I dare
Disturb the universe? (l. 45–46)

82 I have measured out my life with coffee spoons; (l. 51)

83 The eyes that fix you in a formulated phrase, (l. 56)

84 Then how should I begin
To spit out all the butt-ends of my days and ways?
And how should I presume? (l. 59–61)

85 Arms that are braceleted and white and bare
(But in the lamplight, downed with light brown hair!)
Is it perfume from a dress
That makes me so digress? (l. 63–66)

86 I should have been a pair of ragged claws
Scuttling across the floors of silent seas. (l. 73–74)

87 Though I have seen my head (grown slightly bald)
brought in upon a platter,
I am no prophet — and here's no great matter;
I have seen the moment of my greatness flicker,
And I have seen the eternal Footman hold my coat, and
snicker,
And in short, I was afraid. (l. 82–86)

88 If one, settling a pillow by her head,
Should say: "That is not what I meant at all.
That is not it, at all." (l. 96–98)

89 No! I am not Prince Hamlet, nor was meant to be;
Am an attendant lord, one that will do
To swell a progress, start a scene or two, (l. 111–113)

90 I grow old . . . I grow old . . .
I shall wear the bottoms of my trousers rolled.

Shall I part my hair behind? Do I dare to eat a peach?
I shall wear white flannel trousers, and walk upon the
beach.
I have heard the mermaids singing, each to each.

I do not think that they will sing to me. (l. 120–125)

91 We have lingered in the chambers of the sea
By sea-girls wreathed with seaweed red and brown
Till human voices wake us, and we drown.
(l. 129–131)

AmPP; AWP; CMoP; EBEV; FF; HAP; HeIP; HoPM;
InPK; InPS; LiTB; LiTM; MoAB; MoAmPo; MoP;
NAAL-2; NAEL-2; NAWM-2; NIP; NoAM; NOBA; NOBE;
NoP; OAEL-2; OxBTC; PoA; PoE; PoRA; PPP; PrIm;
SoSe; SOTW; TAP; TrGrPo; TwCP; WeW

Macavity: The Mystery Cat

92 Macavity's a Mystery Cat; he's called the Hidden Paw —
For he's the master criminal who can defy the Law.
(l. 1–2)

93 Macavity, Macavity, there's no one like Macavity,
He's broken every human law, he breaks the law of
gravity. (l. 5–6)

94 He sways his head from side to side, with movements
like a snake;
And when you think he's half asleep, he's always wide
awake. (l. 15–16)

95 And they say that all the Cats whose wicked deeds are
widely known
(I might mention Mungojerrie, I might mention
Griddlebone)

Are nothing more than agents for the Cat who all the time
Just controls their operations: the Napoleon of Crime!
(l. 39—42)

CenHV; CRH; FaBoCo; InPS; NBLV; NOBL; OBCA; OnUR; OxBChV; PoRA; RB

Marina

96 This form, this face, this life
Living to live in a world of time beyond me; let me
Resign my life for this life, my speech for that unspoken,
The awakened, lips parted, the hope, the new ships.
(l. 29—32)

CMoP; FaBoMo; GTBS-P; HeIP; LiTA; MOS; NAEL-2; NOBE; NOCV; PoE; TOF

Preludes (I–IV)

97 The winter evening settles down
With smell of steaks in passageways.
Six o'clock.
The burnt-out ends of smoky days. (l. 1—4)

98 One thinks of all the hands
That are raising dingy shades
In a thousand furnished rooms. (l. 21—23)

99 The thousand sordid images
Of which your soul was constituted; (l. 27—28)

100 Sitting along the bed's edge, where
You curled the papers from your hair,
Or clasped the yellow soles of feet
In the palms of both soiled hands. (l. 35—38)

101 The notion of some infinitely gentle
Infinitely suffering thing. (l. 50—51)

102 The worlds revolve like ancient women
Gathering fuel in vacant lots. (l. 53—54)

HeIP; LiTA; MoShBr; NoP; OBMV; PPP; SeCePo; SOTW; TwCP; UnPo; VGW; WeW

Rhapsody on a Windy Night

103 through the spaces of the dark
Midnight shakes the memory
As a madman shakes a dead geranium. (l. 10—12)

104 She winks a feeble eye,
She smiles into corners.
She smooths the hair of the grass.
The moon has lost her memory. (l. 52—55)

105 Smells of chestnuts in the streets,
And female smells in shuttered rooms,
And cigarettes in corridors
And cocktail smells in bars. (l. 65—68)

CMoP; HeIP; InPS; PoE

The Rum Tum Tugger

106 Yes the Rum Tum Tugger is a Curious Cat—
And there isn't any call for me to shout it:
For he will do
As he do do
And there's no doing anything about it! (l. 7—11)

107 When you let him in, then he wants to be out;
He's always on the wrong side of every door,
And as soon as he's at home, then he'd like to get about. (l. 13—15)

FaBoNo; FaBV; FaPON; PDV

A Song for Simeon

108 Lord, the Roman hyacinths are blooming in bowls and
The winter sun creeps by the snow hills;
The stubborn season has made stand. (l. 1—3)

109 Who shall remember my house, where shall live my children's children
When the time of sorrow is come? (l. 13—14)

110 I am tired with my own life and the lives of those after me,
I am dying in my own death and the deaths of those after me. (l. 34—35)

EaLo; LiTB; NAs; NOCV

Sweeney among the Nightingales

111 Apeneck Sweeney spreads his knees
Letting his arms hang down to laugh,
The zebra stripes along his jaw
Swelling to maculate giraffe. (l. 1—4)
The person in the Spanish cape
Tries to sit on Sweeney's knees

Slips and pulls the table cloth
Overturns a coffee-cup,
Reorganized upon the floor
She yawns and draws a stocking up; (l. 11—16)

112 The nightingales are singing near
The Convent of the Sacred Heart,

And sang within the bloody wood
When Agamemnon cried aloud,
And let their liquid siftings fall
To stain the stiff dishonored shroud. (l. 35—40)

AmPP; AnAmPo; CMoP; FaBoMo; HAP; HeIP; InvP; LiTA; LiTM; MoP; NAAL-2; NAEL-2; NoAM; NOBA; NOBE; NcP; OBMV; OxBA; PPP; WeW

The Waste Land

113　April is the cruellest month, breeding
　　Lilacs out of the dead land, mixing
　　Memory and desire, stirring
　　Dull roots with spring rain.
　　Winter kept us warm, covering
　　Earth in forgetful snow, (l. 1–6)

114　In the mountains, there you feel free. (l. 17)

115　There is shadow under this red rock,
　　(Come in under the shadow of this red rock),
　　And I will show you something different from either
　　Your shadow at morning striding behind you
　　Or your shadow at evening rising to meet you;
　　I will show you fear in a handful of dust. (l. 25–30)

116　Madame Sosostris, famous clairvoyante,
　　Had a bad cold, nevertheless
　　Is known to be the wisest woman in Europe,
　　With a wicked pack of cards. (l. 43–46)

117　I do not find
　　The Hanged Man. Fear death by water.
　　I see crowds of people, walking round in a ring.
　　Thank you. (l. 54–57)

118　Unreal city,
　　Under the brown fog of a winter dawn,
　　A crowd flowed over London Bridge, so many,
　　I had not thought death had undone so many.
　　　　　　　　　　　　　(l. 60–64)

119　With a dead sound on the final stroke of nine. (l. 68)

120　"That corpse you planted last year in your garden,
　　"Has it begun to sprout? Will it bloom this year?
　　"Or has the sudden frost disturbed its bed?
　　"O keep the Dog far hence, that's friend to men,
　　"Or with his nails he'll dig it up again! (l. 71–75)

121　In vials of ivory and coloured glass
　　Unstoppered, lurked her strange synthetic perfumes,
　　Unguent, powdered, or liquid — troubled, confused
　　And drowned the sense in odours; stirred by the air
　　　　　　　　　　　　　(l. 86–89)

122　The change of Philomel, by the barbarous king
　　So rudely forced: yet there the nightingale
　　Filled all the desert with inviolable voice
　　And still she cried, and still the world pursues,
　　"Jug Jug" to dirty ears. (l. 99–103)

123　Under the firelight, under the brush, her hair
　　Spread out in fiery points
　　Glowed into words, then would be savagely still.
　　　　　　　　　　　　　(l. 108–110)

124　I think we are in rats' alley
　　Where the dead men lost their bones. (l. 115–116)

125　OOOO that Shakespeherian Rag —
　　It's so elegant
　　So intelligent (l. 128–130)

126　And we shall play a game of chess,
　　Pressing lidless eyes and waiting for a knock upon the
　　　door. (l. 137–138)

127　It's them pills I took, to bring it off, she said.
　　(She's had five already, and nearly died of young
　　　George.)
　　The chemist said it would be all right, but I've never
　　　been the same.
　　You are a proper fool, I said. (l. 159–162)

128　Hurry up please its time
　　Goonight Bill. Goonight Lou. Goonight May. Goonight.
　　Ta ta. Goonight. Goonight.
　　Good night, ladies, good night, sweet ladies, good night,
　　　good night. (l. 169–172)

129　Sweet Thames, run softly, till I end my song.
　　The river bears no empty bottles, sandwich papers,
　　Silk handkerchiefs, cardboard boxes, cigarette ends
　　Or other testimony of summer nights. The nymphs are
　　　departed. (l. 176–179)

130　A rat crept softly through the vegetation
　　Dragging its slimy belly on the bank
　　While I was fishing in the dull canal (l. 187–189)

131　But at my back from time to time I hear
　　The sound of horns and motors, which shall bring
　　Sweeney to Mrs. Porter in the spring. (l. 196–198)

132　Twit twit twit
　　Jug jug jug jug jug jug
　　So rudely forc'd.
　　Tereu (l. 203–206)

133　At the violet hour, when the eyes and back
　　Turn upward from the desk when the human engine
　　　waits
　　Like a taxi throbbing waiting, (l. 215–217)

134　At the violet hour, the evening hour that strives
　　Homeward, and brings the sailor home from sea,
　　The typist home at teatime, clears her breakfast, lights
　　Her stove, and lays out food in tins. (l. 220–223)

135　I Tiresias, old man with wrinkled dugs
　　Perceived the scene, and foretold the rest —
　　I too awaited the expected guest.
　　He, the young man carbuncular, arrives, (l. 228–231)

136　The time is now propitious, as he guesses,
　　The meal is ended, she is bored and tired,
　　Endeavours to engage her in caresses
　　Which still are unreproved, if undesired.
　　Flushed and decided, he assaults at once;
　　Exploring hands encounter no defence; (l. 235–240)

137 She turns and looks a moment in the glass,
Hardly aware of her departed lover;
Her brain allows one half-formed thought to pass:
"Well now that's done: and I'm glad it's over."
(l. 249–252)

138 The river sweats
Oil and tar
The barges drift
With the turning tide (l. 266–269)

139 Highbury bore me. Richmond and Kew
Undid me. By Richmond I raised my knees
Supine on the floor of a narrow canoe."

"My feet are at Moorgate, and my heart
Under my feet. (l. 293–297)

140 To Carthage then I came (l. 307)

141 O Lord Thou pluckest

burning (l. 310–311)

142 Phlebas the Phoenician, a fortnight dead,
Forgot the cry of gulls, and the deep sea swell
And the profit and loss. (l. 312–314)

143 He who was living is now dead
We who were living are now dying
With a little patience (l. 328–330)

144 Here is no water but only rock (l. 331)

145 There is not even silence in the mountains
But dry sterile thunder without rain
There is not even solitude in the mountains
(l. 341–343)

146 A spring,
A pool among the rock
If there were the sound of water only (l. 351–353)

147 But sound of water over a rock
Where the hermit-thrush sings in the pine trees
Drip drop drip drop drop drop drop
But there is no water (l. 356–359)

148 Cracks and reforms and bursts in the violet air
Falling towers
Jerusalem Athens Alexandria
Vienna London (l. 373–376)

149 A woman drew her long black hair out tight
And fiddled whisper music on those strings
(l. 378–379)

150 And upside down in air were towers
Tolling reminiscent bells, that kept the hours
And voices singing out of empty cisterns and exhausted
wells (l. 383–385)

151 There is the empty chapel, only the wind's home.
It has no windows, and the door swings,
Dry bones can harm no one. (l. 389–391)

152 Then spoke the thunder
Da
Datta: what have we given? (l. 400–402)

153 The awful daring of a moment's surrender
Which an age of prudence can never retract
(l. 404–405)

154 Only at nightfall, aethereal rumours
Revive for a moment a broken Coriolanus
(l. 416–417)

155 I sat upon the shore
Fishing, with the arid plain behind me
Shall I at least set my lands in order? (l. 424–426)

156 These fragments I have shored against my ruins
(l. 431)

AmPP; CMoP; FaBoMo; HAP; LiTA; LiTM; MoAB;
MoAmPo; MoP; NAAL-2; NAEL-2; NAWM-2; NoAM;
NOBA; NOBE; NoP; OAEL-2; OxBA; OxBTC; PoE; TAP;
UnPo

Whispers of Immortality

157 Webster was much possessed by death
And saw the skull beneath the skin;
And breastless creatures under ground
Leaned backward with a lipless grin.

Daffodil bulbs instead of balls
Stared from the sockets of the eyes! (l. 1–6)

158 Donne, I suppose, was such another
Who found no substitute for sense, (l. 9–10)

159 Grishkin is nice: her Russian eye
Is underlined for emphasis;
Uncorseted, her friendly lust
Gives promise of pneumatic bliss. (l. 17–20)

160 The sleek Brazilian jaguar
Does not in its arboreal gloom
Distil so rank a feline smell
As Grishkin in a drawing-room. (l. 25–28)

CMoP; CTC; LiTA; NoAM; NOBA; NoP; OBMV

ELIZABETH I, QUEEN OF ENGLAND
(1533–1603)

The Doubt of Future Foes

1 The daughter of debate, that eke discord doth sow,
Shall reap no gain where former rule hath taught still
peace to grow.

No foreign banished wight shall anchor in this port;
Our realm it brooks no stranger's force, let them
    elsewhere resort. (l. 11–14)

CTC; NAEL-1; OBSC; PBWP; WPE

When I Was Fair and Young

2 When I was fair and young, and favor graced me,
Of many was I sought, their mistress for to be;
But I did scorn them all, and answered them therefore,
"Go, go, go seek some otherwhere!
Importune me no more!" (l. 1–5)

CTC; NIP; NoP; OBSC; PoRA

JEAN ELLIOT (1727–1805)

The Flowers of the Forest

1 I've heard the lilting at our yowe-milking, (l. 1)

2 Dule and wae for the order sent our lads to the Border;
The English, for ance, by guile won the day:
The Flowers of the Forest, that foucht aye the foremost,
The prime o' our land, are cauld in the clay.
                                    (l. 17–20)

CH; FaBoCh; FaBoRV; GoTS; GTBS-P; GTBS; OBEV;
OxBS; WPE

RALPH WALDO EMERSON (1803–1882)

Bacchus

1 Bring me wine, but wine which never grew
In the belly of the grape, (l. 1–2)

2 Let its grapes the morn salute
From a nocturnal root, (l. 6–7)

3 And turns the woe of Night,
By its own craft, to a more rich delight. (l. 10–11)

4 The rich results of the divine consents (l. 51)

5 The nectar and ambrosia, are withheld;
And in the midst of spoils and slaves, we thieves
And pirates of the universe, shut out
Daily to a more thin and outward rind,
Turn pale and starve. Therefore, to our sick eyes,
The stunted trees look sick, the summer short,

Clouds shade the sun, which will not tan our hay,
And nothing thrives to reach its natural term;
                                    (l. 53–60)

AmPP; AWP; LiTA; NOBA; OBEV; OxBA; PoEL-4

Brahma

6 If the red slayer think he slays,
Or if the slain think he is slain,
They know not well the subtle ways
I keep, and pass, and turn again. (l. 1–4)

7 They reckon ill who leave me out;
When me they fly, I am the wings;
I am the doubter and the doubt,
And I the hymn the Brahmin sings.

The strong gods pine for my abode,
And pine in vain the sacred Seven;
But thou, meek lover of the good!
Find me, and turn thy back on heaven. (l. 9–16)

AA; AmPP; AWP; EaLo; HAP; LiTA; NOBA; NoP;
OBEV; OxBA; PoE; PoRA; TAP; TrGrPo; UnPo; WGRP

Compensation

8 The wings of Time are black and white,
Pied with morning and with night. (l. 1–2)

9 The lonely Earth amid the balls
That hurry through the eternal halls,
A makeweight flying to the void,
Supplemental asteroid,
Or compensatory spark,
Shoots across the neutral Dark. (l. 9–14)

10 Hast not thy share? On winged feet,
Lo! it rushes thee to meet;
And all that Nature made thy own,
Floating in air or pent in stone,
Will rive the hills and swim the sea,
And, like thy shadow, follow thee. (l. 23–28)

AmPP; FPL; LiTA; NOBA; TAP

Concord Hymn

11 By the rude bridge that arched the flood,
Their flag to April's breeze unfurled,
Here once the embattled farmers stood
And fired the shot heard round the world. (l. 1–4)

12 Spirit, that made those heroes dare
To die, and leave their children free,
Bid Time and Nature gently spare
The shaft we raise to them and thee. (l. 13–16)

AA; AiP; AmFN; AmPP; AnAmPo; AWP; BLPA; BLPL;
FaBoBe; FaFP; FaPON; FaPoR; GN; GOA; HAP; HeIP;
LiTA; NAAL-1; NOBA; NoP; OBWP; OHFP; OPP; OxBA;
PAH; TAP; TrGrPo; WaaP

Days

13 Daughters of Time, the hypocritic Days,
Muffled and dumb like barefoot dervishes, (l. 1–2)

14 To each they offer gifts after his will, (l. 5)

15 I, in my pleached garden, watched the pomp, (l. 7)

16 Took a few herbs and apples, and the Day
Turned and departed silent. I, too late,
Under her solemn fillet saw the scorn. (l. 9–11)

AA; AmPP; AnAmPo; HAP; HeIP; LiTA; NAAL-1; NOBA;
NoP; OxBA; OxBSP; PoEL-4; PoE; TAP; TrGrPo

Each and All

17 Little thinks, in the field, yon red-cloaked clown, (l. 1)

18 The sexton, tolling his bell at noon,
Deems not that great Napoleon
Stops his horse, and lists with delight,
Whilst his files sweep round yon Alpine height;
Nor knowest thou what argument
Thy life to thy neighbor's creed has lent.
All are needed by each one;
Nothing is fair or good alone. (l. 5–12)

19 Beauty through my senses stole;
I yielded myself to the perfect whole. (l. 50–51)

AA; AmPP; AnAmPo; AWP; BLPL; NAAL-1; NOBA;
OHFP; OxBA; TAP; WGRP

Experience

20 The lords of life, the lords of life,—
I saw them pass
In their own guise,
Like and unlike,
Portly and grim,—
Use and surprise,
Surface and dream,
Succession swift, and spectral wrong,
Temperament without a tongue,
And the inventor of the game
Omnipresent without name;— (l. 1–11)

21 Dearest Nature, strong and kind,
Whispered, "Darling, never mind!
Tomorrow they will wear another face,
The founder thou; these are thy race!" (l. 18–21)

FPL; LiTA; PoEL-4; TAP

Forbearance

22 Hast thou named all the birds without a gun?
Loved the wood rose, and left it on its stalk?
At rich men's tables eaten bread and pulse?
Unarmed, faced danger with a heart of trust? (l. 1–4)

23 Nobility more nobly to repay?
O, be my friend, and teach me to be thine! (l. 7–8)

AA; AnAmPo; GN; LiTA; TAP; TrGrPo; WGRP

Give All to Love

24 Cling with life to the maid;
But when the surprise,
First vague shadow of surmise
Flits across her bosom young,
Of a joy apart from thee,
Free be she, fancy-free;
Nor thou detain her vesture's hem,
Nor the palest rose she flung
From her summer diadem. (l. 34–42)

25 Though her parting dims the day,
Stealing grace from all alive;
Heartily know,
When half-gods go,
The gods arrive. (l. 45–49)

AmPP; AnAmPo; AWP; FaFP; FPL; LiTA; NOBA; OBEV;
OxBA; PoEL-4; PoLF; TAP; TrGrPo

Good-bye

26 Good-bye, proud world! I'm Going home;
Thou art not my friend, and I'm not thine.
Long through thy weary crowds I roam;
A river-ark on the ocean brine, (l. 1–4)

27 Good-bye to flattery's fawning face,
To grandeur, with his wise grimace,
To upstart wealth's averted eye, (l. 7–9)

28 I am going to my own hearthstone,
Bosom'd in yon green hills alone—
A secret nook in a pleasant land, (l. 15–17)

29 I laugh at the lore and pride of man
At the sophist schools, and the learned clan;
For what are they all, in their high conceit,
When man in the bush with God may meet? (l. 27–30)

AnAmPo; FaFP; LiTA; PWR; TAP; WGRP

The Humble-Bee

30 Burly, dozing humble-bee,
Where thou art is clime for me. (l. 1–2)

31 Wiser far than human seer,
Yellow-breeched philosopher!
Seeing only what is fair,
Sipping only what is sweet,

Thou dost mock at fate and care,
Leave the chaff, and take the wheat, (l. 52–57)

32 Woe and want thou canst outsleep;
Want and woe, which torture us,
Thy sleep makes ridiculous. (l. 61–63)

AA; AnAmPo; FaPON; FM; GN; NOBA; OxBA

Merlin

33 Great is the art,
Great be the manners, of the bard.
He shall not his brain encumber
With the coil of rhythm and number;
But, leaving rule and pale forethought,
He shall aye climb
For his rhyme.
"Pass in, pass in," the angels say, (l. 27–34)

34 But mount to paradise
By the stairway of surprise." (l. 37–38)

AA; AmPP; NAAL-2; NOBA; OxBA

The Mountain and the Squirrel

35 The mountain and the squirrel
Had a quarrel,
And the former called the latter " Little Prig";
                                    (l. 1–3)

36 Talents differ; all is well and wisely put;
If I cannot carry forests on my back,
Neither can you crack a nut. (l. 17–19)

AmPP; AnAmPo; BeLS; BLPL; BoTP; FaBoBe; FaBV;
FaFP; FaPON; GoJo; LiTA; NBLV; OBAL; OBCA;
OnMSP

The Past

37 None can re-enter there —
No thief so politic,
No Satan with a royal trick
Steal in by window, chink, or hole,
To bind or unbind, add what lacked,
Insert a leaf, or forge a name,
New-face or finish what is packed,
Alter or mend eternal fact. (l. 14–21)

FaBoCh; FPL; LiTA; PoEL-4; TAP

The Problem

38 I like a church; I like a cowl;
I love a prophet of the soul;
And on my heart monastic aisles

Fall like sweet strains, or pensive smiles;
Yet not for all his faith can see
Would I that cowled churchman be. (l. 1–6)

39 These temples grew as grows the grass;
Art might obey, but not surpass. (l. 45–46)

40 I know what say the fathers wise, —
The Book itself before me lies,
Old Chrysostom, best Augustine. (l. 63–65)

41 Taylor, the Shakespeare of divines.
His words are music in my ear, (l. 68–69)

AA; AmPP; AnAmPo; AWP; LiTA; NAAL-1; NOBA; NoP;
OxBA; TAP; WGRP

The Rhodora

42 Rhodora! if the sages ask thee why
This charm is wasted on the earth and sky,
Tell them, dear, that if eyes were made for seeing,
Then Beauty is its own excuse for being:
Why thou wert there, O rival of the rose!
I never thought to ask, I never knew:
But, in my simple ignorance, suppose
The self-same Power that brought me there brought
    you. (l. 9–16)

AA; AmPP; AnAmPo; AWP; BoNaP; FaBV; FaFP; GN;
HeIP; LiTA; NAAL-1; NOBA; NoP; OHFP; OxBA; PoE;
PWR; TAP; TrGrPo

The Snow-Storm

43 Announced by all the trumpets of the sky,
Arrives the snow, and, driving o'er the fields,
Seems nowhere to alight: the whited air
Hides hills and woods, the river, and the heaven,
                                    (l. 1–4)

44 Come see the north wind's masonry.
Out of an unseen quarry evermore
Furnished with tile, the fierce artificer
Curves his white bastions with projected roof
                                    (l. 10–13)

45 And when his hours are numbered, and the world
Is all his own, retiring, as he were not,
Leaves, when the sun appears, astonished Art
To mimic in slow structures, stone by stone,
Built in an age, the mad wind's night-work,
The frolic architecture of the snow. (l. 23–28)

AA; AmPP; AnAmPo; BLPL; BoNaP; FaBoBe; GN; LiTA;
NAAL-1; NOBA; NoP; OHFP; OxBA; PoEL-4; PoE;
PoLF; Prf; TAP; TrGrPo; UnPo; WiR

Terminus

46 It is time to be old,
To take in sail: — (l. 1–2)

47 As the bird trims her to the gale,
I trim myself to the storm of time,
I man the rudder, reef the sail,
Obey the voice at eve obeyed at prime:
"Lowly faithful, banish fear,
Right onward drive unharmed;
The port, well worth the cruise, is near,
And every wave is charmed." (l. 33–40)

AA; AmPP; AWP; FPL; NOBA; OxBA; PoEL-4; PoLF;
TAP

Two Rivers

48 Thy summer voice, Musketaquit,
Repeats the music of the rain;
But sweeter rivers pulsing flit
Through thee, as thou through Concord Plain. (l. 1–4)

49 So forth and brighter fares my stream, —
Who drink it shall not thirst again;
No darkness stains its equal gleam,
And ages drop in it like rain. (l. 17–20)

AmPP; NOBA; OxBA; PoE; TrGrPo

Uriel

50 'Line in nature is not found;
Unit and universe are round;
In vain produced, all rays return;
Evil will bless, and ice will burn.'
As Uriel spoke with piercing eye,
A shudder ran around the sky; (l. 21–26)

51 And, shrilling from the solar course,
Or from fruit of chemic force,
Procession of a soul in matter,
Or the speeding change of water,
Or out of the good of evil born,
Came Uriel's voice of cherub scorn,
And a blush tinged the upper sky,
And the gods shook, they knew not why. (l. 49–56)

LiTA; NAAL-1; NOBA; OxBA

DANIEL DECATUR EMMETT
(1815–1904)

Dixie

1 I wish I was in de land ob cotton,
Old times dar am not forgotten,
Look away! Look away! Look away! Dixie Land.

In Dixie Land whar I was born in
Early on one frosty mornin', (l. 1–5)

2 To lib and die in Dixie!
Away, away, away down South in Dixie! (l. 9–10)

AnAmPo; FaFP; FaPON; TrGrPo

WILLIAM EMPSON (1906–1984)
Homage to the British Museum

1 Attending there let us absorb the cultures of nations
And dissolve into our judgement all their codes.
Then, being clogged, with a natural hesitation
(People are continually asking one the way out),
Let us stand here and admit that we have no road.
(l. 8–12)

CMoP; FaBoMo; LiTM; MoAB; MoBrPo; PoE

Hours before dawn we were woken by the quake

2 Hours before dawn we were woken by the quake.
My house was on a cliff. The thing could take
Bookloads off shelves, break bottles in a row.
Then the long pause and then the bigger shake.
It seemed the best thing to be up and go. (l. 1–5)

FaBoMo; FaBoTw; LiTB; OxBTC

Ignorance of Death

3 Buddhists and Christians contrive to agree about death

Making death their ideal basis for different ideals.
The Communists however disapprove of death
Except when practical. (l. 3–6)

4 Liberal hopefulness
Regards death as a mere border to an improving
picture. (l. 11–12)

CMoP; LiTM; NoAM; OBD

It is the pain, it is the pain, endures

5 It is the pain, it is the pain, endures. (l. 1)

6 Poise of my hands reminded me of yours. (l. 3)

7 My heart pumps yet the poison draught of you. (l. 14)

CMoP; EnLoPc; MoP; NoAM; OAEL-2; PoE

Just a Smack at Auden

8 Shall I make it clear, boys, for all to apprehend,
Those that will not hear, boys, waiting for the end,
Knowing it is near, boys, trying to pretend,
Sitting in cold fear, boys, waiting for the end?
(l. 14—17)

FaBoCo; LiTM; MoBrPo; UnPo

Legal Fiction

9 Law makes long spokes of the short stakes of men.
(l. 1)

10 Your rights reach down where all owners meet, in
Hell's
Pointed exclusive conclave, at earth's centre
(Your spun farm's root still on that axis dwells);
And up, through galaxies, a growing sector. (l. 9—12)

CMoP; FaBoMo; LiTB; LiTM; MoP; NoAM; NoP

Let It Go

11 It is this deep blankness is the real thing strange.
The more things happen to you the more you can't
Tell or remember even what they were. (l. 1—3)

FaBoMo; OPOP; OxBSP; OxBTC

Missing Dates

12 Slowly the poison the whole blood stream fills.
It is not the effort nor the failure tires.
The waste remains, the waste remains and kills.
(l. 1—3)

CMoP; HAP; LiTB; LiTM; MoAB; MoBrPo; MoP; NoAM;
NOBE; NoP; OAEL-2; PoE; UnPo

This Last Pain

13 This last pain for the damned the Fathers found:
"They knew the bliss with which they were not
crowned." (l. 1—2)

14 Man, as the prying housemaid of the soul, (l. 5)

15 All those large dreams by which men long live well
Are magic-lanterned on the smoke of hell; (l. 21—22)

16 Feign then what's by a decent tact believed
And act that state is only so conceived,
And build an edifice of form
For house where phantoms may keep warm.
(l. 29—32)

17 What could not possible be there,
And learn a style from a despair. (l. 35—36)

CMoP; EBEV; FaBoMo; GTBS-P; LiTM; MoAB; MoBrPo;
NoAM; OAEL-2; SeCePo

To an Old Lady

18 her in her cooling planet
Revere; do not presume to think her wasted. (l. 1—2)

19 Gods cool in turn, by the sun long outlasted. (l. 4)

FaBoTw; GTBS-P; MoAB; NoAM; NOBE

ANTHONY EUWER (1877—1955)

The Limeratomy

1 my face I don't mind it,
Because I'm behind it —
'Tis the folks in the front that I jar.

FaFP; InvP; OBAL; PoLF

MARI E. EVANS

The Rebel

1 When I
die
I'm sure
I will have a
Big Funeral (l. 1—5)

2 if I
am really
Dead (l. 9—11)

AmNP; CRP; IDB; IHMS; PoBA

CATHERINE MARIA FANSHAWE
(1765—1834)

Fragment in Imitation of Wordsworth

1 It were a blessed sight to see
That child become a willow tree,
His brother trees among.
He'd be four times as tall as me,
And live three times as long. (l. 46—50)

BXAP; FaBoNo; FaBoPa; NA; Par

SIR RICHARD FANSHAWE (1608–1666)

Il Pastor Fido

1 If thee thy brittle beauty so deceives,
  Know then the thing that swells thee is thy bane:
  For the same beauty doth, in bloody leaves,
  The sentence of thy early death contain. (l. 5–8)

AWP; OBEV; OBS; PoEL-2; SeCePo

ELEANOR FARJEON (1881–1965)

A Dragonfly

1 When the heat of the summer
  Made drowsy the land,
  A dragon-fly came
  And sat on my hand; (l. 1–4)

FaPON; OnUR; PDV; RHPC

The Night Will Never Stay

2 Though you bind it with the blowing wind
  And buckle it with the moon,
  The night will slip away
  Like sorrow or a tune. (l. 5–8)

BoTP; CH; NTCP; OxBChV

KENNETH FEARING (1902–1961)

1-2-3 was the number he played but today the number came 3-2-1

1 Denouement to denouement, he took a personal pride
    in the
  certain, certain way he lived his own, private life,
  but nevertheless, they shut off his gas; nevertheless,
  the bank foreclosed; nevertheless, the landlord called;
  nevertheless, the radio broke,

  And twelve o'clock arrived just once too often,
                          (l. 10–15)

2 And wow he died as wow he lived,
  going whop to the office and blooie home to sleep and
  biff got married and bam had children and oof got
    fired,
  zowie did he live and zowie did he die, (l. 20–23)

FF; HeIP; HoPM; NIP; PoRA; RB; TrJP

LAWRENCE FERLINGHETTI (b. 1919)

A Coney Island of the Mind

1 Constantly risking absurdity
  and death
  whenever he performs
  above the heads
  of his audience
  the poet like an acrobat

2 Beauty stands and waits
  with gravity
  to start her death-defying leap

CAPP; LiTM; NeAP; PoM; TAP

3 In Goya's greatest scenes we seem to see
  the people of the world
  exactly at the moment when
  they first attained the title of
  'suffering humanity'

4 freeways fifty lanes wide
  on a concrete continent
  spaced with bland billboards
  illustrating imbecile illusions of happiness

FF; HeIP; LiTM; NeAP; NoAM; PoM; TAP

5 The pennycandystore beyond the El
  is where I first
  fell in love
  with unreality

CAPP; HeIP; PoM; TAP

EUGENE FIELD (1850–1895)

The Duel

1 The gingham dog and the calico cat
  Side by side on the table sat; (l. 1–2)

2 They found no trace of dog or cat;
  And some folks think unto this day
  That burglars stole that pair away!
  But the truth about the cat and pup
  Is this: they ate each other up!
  Now what do you really think of that!
  The old Dutch clock it told me so,
  And that is how I came to know.) (l. 29–36)

BeLS; CenHV; FaBoBe; FaFP; FaPON; FPL; MoShBr;
OBAL; OBCA; OHFP; OnMSP; PoLF; PoRA; RHPC

Jest 'fore Christmas

3 Father calls me William, sister calls me Will,
  Mother calls me Willie, but the fellers call me Bill!

4 Love to chawnk green apples an' go swimmin' in the
lake. —
Hate to take the castor-ile they give for belly-ache!
'Most all the time, the whole year round, there ain't no
flies on me,
But jest 'fore Christmas I'm as good as I kin be!
(l. 5—8)

5 Say "Yessum" to the ladies, an' "Yessur" to the men,
And when they's company, don't pass yer plate for pie
again;
But, thinkin' of the things yer'd like to see upon that
tree,
Jes 'fore Christmas be as good as yer kin be!
(l. 37—40)

FaBV; FaFP; FaPON; FPL; OHFP; PoLF

Little Boy Blue

6 The little toy dog is covered with dust,
But sturdy and stanch he stands;
And the little toy soldier is red with rust,
And the musket moulds in his hands.
Time was when the little toy dog was new,
And the soldier was passing fair;
And that was the time when our Little Boy Blue
Kissed them and put them there. (l. 1—8)

7 And they wonder, as waiting the long years through
In the dust of that little chair,
What has become of our Little Boy Blue,
Since he kissed them and put them there. (l. 21—24)

AA; AnAmPo; BeLS; FaFP; FaPON; FPL; OBAL; OBCA;
OHFP; PoLF; SoSe

Wynken, Blynken, and Nod

8 Wynken, Blynken, and Nod one night
Sailed off in a wooden shoe —
Sailed on a river of crystal light,
Into a sea of dew. (l. 1—4)

9 Wynken and Blynken are two little eyes,
And Nod is a little head,
And the wooden shoe that sailed the skies
Is a wee one's trundle-bed. (l. 37—40)

AA; AnAmPo; BeLS; BLPA; BoTP; FaBoBe; FaFP;
FaPON; FPL; NBLV; NTCP; OBAL; OBCA; OxBChV;
PoRA; PYC

RACHEL LYMAN FIELD (1894—1942)

Some People

1 Isn't it strange some people make
You feel so tired inside,
Your thoughts begin to shrivel up
Like leaves all brown and dried! (l. 1—4)

FaPON; NTCP; PDV; RHPC

Something Told the Wild Geese

2 Something told the wild geese
It was time to go.
Though the fields lay golden
Something whispered — "Snow." (l. 1—4)

NTCP; OBCA; OnUR; PDV; RHPC

FRANCIS MILES FINCH (1827—1907)

The Blue and the Gray

1 By the flow of the inland river,
Whence the fleets of iron have fled,
Where the blades of the grave-grass quiver,
Asleep are the ranks of the dead: — (l. 1—4)

2 No more shall the war cry sever,
Or the winding rivers be red:
They banish our anger forever
When they laurel the graves of our dead!
Under the sod and the dew,
Waiting the Judgment Day: —
Love and tears for the Blue;
Tears and love for the Gray. (l. 24—31)

AA; AnAmPo; BLPA; BLPL; FaBoBe; OPP; PAH; WBLP

ROBERT FITZGERALD (1910—1985)

Cobb Would Have Caught It

1 In sunburnt parks where Sundays lie,
Or the wide wastes beyond the cities,
Teams in grey deploy through sunlight.

Talk it up, boys, a little practice. (l. 1—4)

2 Innings and afternoons. Fly lost in sunset.
Throwing arm gone bad. There's your old ball game.
Cool reek of the field. Reek of companions. (l. 23—25)

GrPl; HAP; InvP; SD; TwCP; WeW

THOMAS FLATMAN (1637—1688)

On Marriage

1 How happy a thing were a wedding,
And a bedding,
If a man might purchase a wife
For a twelvemonth and a day; (l. 1—4)

2 Till she grows as grey as a cat, (l. 7)

EnLoPo; FaBoUs; FiBHP; NOBL

JAMES ELROY FLECKER (1884–1919)

The Golden Journey to Samarkand

1 We who with songs beguile your pilgrimage
And swear that Beauty lives though lilies die,
We Poets of the proud old lineage
Who sing to find your hearts, we know not why,

2 They know time comes, not only you and I,
But the whose world shall whiten, here or there;

3 When the great markets by the sea shut fast
All that calm Sunday that goes on and on:
When even lovers find their peace at last,
And Earth is but a star, that once had shone.

BrPo; FaBoRV; FaPoR; GoJo; OBMV; OxBTC

The Old Ships

4 I have seen old ships sail like swans asleep (l. 1)

5 It was so old a ship — who knows, who knows?
— And yet so beautiful, I watched in vain
To see the mast burst open with a rose,
And the whole deck put on its leaves again. (l. 28–31)

BrPo; CH; FaBoRV; MoBrPo; MOS; OBMV; PoRA

Stillness

6 When the words rustle no more,
And the last work's done,
When the bolt lies deep in the door, (l. 1–3)

7 And Space with gaunt grey eyes and her brother Time
Wheeling and whispering come, (l. 8–9)

BrPo; CH; GoJo; MoBrPo

To a Poet a Thousand Years Hence

8 But have you wine and music still,
And statues and a bright-eyed love,
And foolish thoughts of good and ill,
And prayers to them who sit above? (l. 9–12)

9 O friend unseen, unborn, unknown,
Student of our sweet English tongue,
Read out my words at night, alone:
I was a poet, I was young. (l. 17–20)

ChTr; FaBoRV; MoBrPo; PoRA

MARJORY FLEMING (1803–1811)

A Sonnet on a Monkey

1 I could not get a rhyme for roman
And was obliged to call him woman. (l. 14–15)

FaBoCo; FaFP; FiBHP; NBLV

GILES FLETCHER, THE ELDER
(c. 1549–1611)

Licia

1 In time the strong and stately turrets fall,
In time the rose and silver lilies die,
In time the monarchs captive are, and thrall,
In time the sea and rivers are made dry;
The hardest flint in time doth melt asunder;
Still living fame in time doth fade away;
The mountains proud we see in time come under;
And earth, for age, we see in time decay.
The sun in time forgets for to retire
From out the east where he was wont to rise;
The basest thoughts we see in time aspire,
And greedy minds in time do wealth despise.
Thus all, sweet Fair, in time must have an end,
Except thy beauty, virtues, and thy friend.

AAS; EBEV; NIP; OBSC

GILES FLETCHER, THE YOUNGER
(1585–1623)

Christ's Victory and Triumph

1 And yet it is a kind of inward feast,
A harmony that sounds within the breast,
An odour, light, embrace, in which the soul doth rest,
(IV: l. 22–24)

2 The saints with their beau-peers whole worlds outwear,
And things unseen do see, and things unheard do hear.
(IV: l. 31–32)

JOHN FLETCHER (1579–1625)

The Faithful Shepherdess

1 Now, good night! may Sweetest Slumbers
And soft Silence fall in numbers
On your Eye-lids: So, farewell;
Thus I end my Evening knell. (II, i)

CH; ElL; GN; OBS

2 Do not fear to put thy feet
Naked in the river sweet;
Think not leech, or newt, or toad
Will bite thy foot when thou hast trod;
Nor let the water, rising high,
As thou wadest, make thee cry,
And sob; but ever live with me,
And not a wave shall trouble thee. (III, i)

ElL; FaPON; MoShBr; OBS

The Nice Valor

3 Then stretch our bones in a still gloomy valley;
Nothing's so dainty sweet as lovely melancholy.
(III, iii)

GTBS; GTBS-P; OBEV; OBS; PoEL-2; TrGrPo

The Tragedy of Valentinian

4 Care-charming Sleep, thou easer of all woes,
Brother to Death, sweetly thyself dispose (V, ii)

ELP; FaBoRV; OBS; OxBoLi; OxBSP; PoEL-2; PoRA;
SeCePo; TrGrPo

5 Hear, ye ladies that despise,
What the mighty Love has done;
Fear examples, and be wise: (II, v)

ElL; ELP; NOBE; OBEV; PoEL-2; TrGrPo

6 All Love's Emblems and all cry,
Ladies, if not pluckt we dye, (II, v)

BoLoP; ElL; ELP; ErPo; FF; NIP; NOBE

JOHN FLETCHER (1579–1625) *AND*
WILLIAM SHAKESPEARE (1564–1616)

King Henry VIII

1 Orpheus with his Lute made Trees,
And the Mountaine tops that freeze,
Bow themselves when he did sing.
To his Musicke, Plants and Flowers
Ever spring; as Sunne and Showres,
There had been a lasting Spring.
Every thing that heard him play,
Even the Billowes of the Sea,
Hung their heads, and then lay by.
In sweet Musicke is such Art,

Killing care, and griefe of heart,
Fall asleepe, or hearing dye. (III, i)

ChTr; ElL; FaBoCh; GN; NOBE; OBEV; OBS; PoEL-2;
TrGrPo; UnS

2 No man's pie, is freed
From his ambitious finger. (I, i)

3 I have ventured,
Like little wanton boys that swim on bladders,
This many summers in a sea of glory.
But far beyond my depth. My high-blown pride
At length broke under me and now has left me,
Weary and old with service, to the mercy
Of a rude stream that must forever hide me. (III, ii)

4 I have touched the highest point of all my greatness,
And from that full meridian of my glory
I haste now to my setting. I shall fall
Like a bright exhalation in the evening,
And no man see me more. (III, ii)

5 Had I but served my God with half the zeal
I served my king, he would not in mine age
Have left me naked to mine enemies. (III, ii)

The Two Noble Kinsmen

6 Come, all sad and solemn shows,
That are quick-eyed Pleasure's foes!
We convent nought else but woes,
We convent nought else but woes. (I, v)

ChTr; ElL; OBEV; OBS

JOHN FLETCHER (1579–1625) *AND*
OTHERS

The Queen of Corinth

1 Joys as winged dreams fly fast,
Why should sadness longer last?
Grief is but a wound to woe;
Gentlest fair, mourn, mourn no moe. (III, ii)

CH; ElL; OBEV; TrGrPo

ELIZA LEE FOLLEN (CABOT)
(1787–1860) *AND* ELIZA COOK
(1818–1889)

The Three Little Kittens (attributed to Follen and to Cook)

1 Three little kittens
They lost their mittens,
And they began to cry,

Oh, mother dear,
We sadly fear
Our mittens we have lost.
What! lost your mittens,
You naughty kittens!
Then you shall have no pie. (l. 1–9)

BoTP; FaPON; OBCA; OxNR

SAMUEL FOOTE (1720–1777)

The Great Panjandrum Himself

1 And there were present
the Picninnies,
and the Jobillies,
and the Garyulies,
and the great Panjandrum himself,
with the little round button at top;
and they all fell to playing the game
of catch-as-catch-can,
till the gunpowder ran out at the heels of their boots.
(l. 10–18)

FaBoCh; FaBoCo; MoShBr; Par; PoLF

JOHN FORD (1586–1640?)

The Broken Heart

1 Love is dead; let lovers' eyes,
Locked in endless dreams,
The extremes of all extremes,
Ope no more, for now Love dies. (IV, iii)

ELP; GBL; NOBE; OBS; OxBSP; PoEL-2; SeCePo

THOMAS FORD (1580–1648)

There Is a Lady Sweet and Kind (attributed to Ford)

1 There is a lady sweet and kind,
Was never face so pleased my mind;
I did but see her passing by,
And yet I love her till I die. (l. 1–4)

CH; EBEV; ElL; ELP; FaFP; GBL; HeIP; LiTB; NOBE;
NoP; OBEV; OBS; TrGrPo

SAM WALTER FOSS (1858–1911)

The House by the Side of the Road

1 There are hermit souls that live withdrawn
In the place of their self-content;
There are souls like stars, that dwell apart,

In a fellowless firmament;
There are pioneer souls that blaze their paths
Where highways never ran — (l. 1–6)

2 Let me live in a house by the side of the road
And be a friend to man. (l. 15–16)

3 Let me live in my house by the side of the road —
It's here the race of men go by.
They are good, they are bad, they are weak, they are strong,
Wise, foolish — so am I; (l. 33–36)

AnAmPo BLPA; BLPL; FaBoBe; FaFP; OHFP; WBLP;
WGRP

STEPHEN COLLINS FOSTER (1826–1884)

My Old Kentucky Home

1 The sun shines bright in the old Kentucky home;
'Tis summer, the darkeys are gay;
The corn-top's ripe, and the meadow's in the bloom,
(l. 1–3)

2 The head must bow, and the back will have to bend,
Wherever the darkey may go;
A few more days, and the trouble all will end,
In the field where the sugar-canes grow.
A few more days for to tote the weary load, —
No matter 't will never be light;
A few more days till we totter on the road: —
Then my old Kentucky home, good-night! (l. 21–28)

AA; AnAmPo; FaBoBe; FaBV; FaFP; PoLF; TrGrPo

The Old Folks at Home

3 'Way down upon de Swanee ribber,
Far, far away,
Dere's where my heart is turning ebber,
Dere's where de old folks stay. (l. 1–4)

4 Sadly I roam,
Still longing for de old plantation,
And for de old folks at home. (l. 6–8)

AA; AnAmPc; FaBoBe; FaFP; WBLP

ROBERT FRANCIS (b. 1901)

Pitcher

1 His art is eccentricity, his aim
How not to hit the mark he seems to aim at, (l. 1–2)

OxBSP; SD; SoSe; WeW

BENJAMIN FRANKLIN (1706–1790)

Jack and Roger (attributed to Franklin)

1 Jack, eating rotten cheese, did say,
  'Like Samson I my thousands slay.' (l. 1–2)

2 And with the self-same weapon, too! (l. 4)

ChTr; FaBoEE; NOBL

CAROL FREEMAN (b. 1941)

Christmas Morning I

1 grandmama
  sewing a new
  button on my last year
  ragdoll. (l. 6–9)

PChr; PoBA; PoNe; TTY

WILLIAM PERCY FRENCH (1854–1920)

"Are Ye Right There, Michael?" (A Lay of the Wild West Clare)

1 'Are ye right there, Michael? are ye right?
  Do you think that we'll be there before the night?
  Ye've been so long in startin',
  That ye couldn't say for sartin' —
  Still ye might now, Michael, so ye might!' (l. 11–15)

2 Have ye got the parcel there for Mrs White?
  Ye haven't! Oh, begorra!
  Say it's comin' down tomorra —
  And it might now, Michael, so it might!' (l. 27–30)

3 ''Tis all dependin' whether
  The ould engin' howlds together — '
  'And it might now, Michael, so it might!' (l. 58–60)

WTO

PHILIP FRENEAU (1752–1832)

The Indian Burying Ground

1 In spite of all the learned have said,
  I still my old opinion keep;
  The posture, that we give the dead,
  Points out the soul's eternal sleep.

Not so the ancients of these lands—
The Indian, when from life released,
Again is seated with his friends,
And shares again the joyous feast. (l. 1–8)

2 And long shall timorous fancy see
  The painted chief, and pointed spear,
  And Reason's self shall bow the knee
  To shadows and delusions here. (l. 37–40)

AA; Ampp; AnAmPo; HAP; LiTA; NAAL-1; NOBA; NoP;
OBD; OxBA; PoEL-4; PoLF; TAP

To the Memory of the Brave Americans

3 At Eutaw Springs the valiant died;
  Their limbs with dust are covered o'er —
  Weep on, ye springs, your tearful tide;
  How many heroes are no more! (l. 1–4)

4 Now rest in peace, our patriot band;
  Though far from nature's limits thrown,
  We trust they find a happier land,
  A brighter sunshine of their own. (l. 29–32)

AA; AiP; AmPP; AnAmPo; BeLS; PAH; PoLF

The Wild Honeysuckle

5 Fair flower, that dost so comely grow,
  Hid in this silent, dull retreat, (l. 1–2)

6 The flowers that did in Eden bloom;
  Unpitying frosts, and Autumn's power
  Shall leave no vestige of this flower. (l. 16–18)

7 At first thy little being came:
  If nothing once, you nothing lose,
  For when you die you are the same;
  The space between, is but an hour,
  The frail duration of a flower. (l. 20–24)

AA; AmPP; AnAmPo; BLPL; LiTA; NAAL-1; NOBA;
OxBA; PoEL-4; PoLF; TAP; TrGrPo

ROBERT FROST (1874–1963)

Acquainted with the Night

1 I have been one acquainted with the night.
  I have walked out in rain — and back in rain.
  I have outwalked the furthest city light. (l. 1–3)

2 One luminary clock against the sky
  Proclaimed the time was neither wrong nor right.
  I have been one acquainted with the night. (l. 12–14)

ChTr; CMoP; FPL; HAP; LiTM; MoAmPo; MoP; NoAM;
NOBA; PDV; PoE; PoLF; PPP; Son; SoSe; TAP; TwCP;
VGW; WeW

After Apple-picking

3 My long two-pointed ladder's sticking through a tree
   Toward heaven still,
   And there's a barrel that I didn't fill
   Beside it, and there may be two or three
   Apples I didn't pick upon some bough.
   But I am done with apple-picking now. (l. 1–6)

4 Magnified apples appear and disappear,
   Stem end and blossom end,
   And every fleck of russet showing clear. (l. 18–20)

5 For I have had too much
   Of apple-picking: I am overtired
   Of the great harvest I myself desired.

6 Were he not gone,
   The woodchuck could say whether it's like his
   Long sleep, as I describe its coming on,
   Or just some human sleep.

   AmPP; AnAmPo; CMoP; FPL; InPS; LiTA; MoAB;
   MoAmPo; MoP; NAAL-2; NoAM; NOBA; NU; OxBA;
   PoE; PPP; PrIm; TAP; UnPo

Bereft

7 Where had I heard this wind before
   Change like this to a deeper roar? (l. 1–2)

8 Leaves got up in a coil and hissed,
   Blindly struck at my knee and missed. (l. 9–10)

9 Word I was in my life alone,
   Word I had no one left but God. (l. 15–16)

   LiTM; MoAB; MoAmPo; OxBA; SoSe

Birches

10 When I see birches bend to left and right
   Across the lines of straighter darker trees,
   I like to think some boy's been swinging them. (l. 1–3)

11 they seem not to break; though once they are bowed
   So low for long, they never right themselves:
                                    (l. 15–16)

12 But I was going to say when Truth broke in
   With all her matter-of-fact about the ice-storm
                                    (l. 21–22)

13 I'd like to get away from earth awhile
   And then come back to it and begin over.
   May no fate willfully misunderstand me
   And half grant what I wish and snatch me away
   Not to return. Earth's the right place for love:
   I don't know where it's likely to go better. (l. 48–53)

14 That would be good both going and coming back.
   One could do worse than be a swinger of birches.
                                    (l. 58–59)

   AmPP; CMoP; FaBV; FPL; HeIP; LiTA; LiTM; MoAB;
   MoAmPo; MoP; NAAL-2; NIP; NoAM; NoP; OxBA;
   PoLF; PoRA; RB; TAP; TrGrPo

Come In

15 As I came to the edge of the woods,
   Thrush music — hark!
   Now if it was dusk outside,
   Inside it was dark. (l. 1–4)

16 Almost like a call to come in
   To the dark and lament.

   But no, I was out for stars:
   I would not come in.
   I meant not even if asked,
   And I hadn't been. (l. 15–20)

   AmPP; BoNaP; FaBV; LiTA; LiTM; MoAB; MoAmPo;
   NOBA; NoP; TrGrPo

The Cow in Apple Time

17 Something inspires the only cow of late
   To make no more of a wall than an open gate,
   And think no more of wall-builders than fools. (l. 1–3)

18 Having tasted fruit,
   She scorns a pasture withering to the root. (l. 5–6)

   MoAB; MoAmPo; OxBSP; PoLF

The Death of the Hired Man

19 Mary sat musing on the lamp-flame at the table
   Waiting for Warren. (l. 1–2)

20 "When was I ever anything but kind to him?
   But I'll not have the fellow back," he said.
   "I told him so last haying, didn't I?
   'If he left then,' I said, 'that ended it.'
   What good is he? Who else will harbor him
   At his age for the little he can do? (l. 11–16)

21 Surely you wouldn't grudge the poor old man
   Some humble way to save his self-respect.
   He added, if you really care to know,
   He meant to clear the upper pasture, too. (l. 51–54)

22 I sympathize, I know just how it feels
   To think of the right thing to say too late. (l. 78–79)

23 He said he couldn't make the boy believe
He could find water with a hazel prong —
Which showed how much good school had ever done
　　him. (l. 84–86)

24 He bundles every forkful in its place,
And tags and numbers it for future reference,
So he can find and easily dislodge it
In the unloading. Silas does that well.
He takes it out in bunches like birds' nests. (l. 91–95)

25 And nothing to look backward to with pride,
And nothing to look forward to with hope, 102–103

26 Part of a moon was falling down the west,
Dragging the whole sky with it to the hills.
Its light poured softly in her lap. She saw
And spread her apron to it. (l. 105–108)

27 "Home is the place where, when you have to go there,
They have to take you in."

"I should have called it
Something you somehow haven't to deserve."
　　　　　　　　　　　　　　(l. 121–124)

28 He never did a thing so very bad.
He don't know why he isn't quite as good
As anyone. Worthless though he is,
He won't be made ashamed to please his brother."
　　　　　　　　　　　　(l. 148–151)

29 Warren returned — too soon, it seemed to her,
Slipped to her side, caught up her hand and waited.

"Warren?" she questioned.

"Dead," was all he answered. (l. 171–174)

AmPP; CMoP; HeIP; HoPM; MoAB; MoAmPo; NAAL-2;
NoP; OxBA; SoSe; TrGrPo

Departmental

30 An ant on the tablecloth
Ran into a dormant moth
Of many times his size.
He showed not the least surprise.
His business wasn't with such.
He gave it scarcely a touch, (l. 1–6)

31 Ants are a curious race; (l. 13)

32 Then word goes forth in Formic:
"Death's come to Jerry McCormic,
Our selfless forager Jerry. (l. 22–24)

33 Go bring him home to his people.
Lay him in state on a sepal.
Wrap him for shroud in a petal.

Embalm him with ichor of nettle.
This is the word of your Queen." (l. 28–32)

34 It couldn't be called ungentle.
But how thoroughly departmental. (l. 42–43)

GoYe; HeIP; HoPM; MoAB; MoAmPo; NAAL-2; NOBA;
NOBL; OBAL; SoSe

Desert Places

35 And lonely as it is, that loneliness
Will be more lonely ere it will be less — (l. 9–10)

36 They cannot scare me with their empty spaces
Between stars — on stars where no human race is.
I have it in me so much nearer home
To scare myself with my own desert places. (l. 13–16)

AmPP; CMoP; InPK; MoAB; MoAmPo; MoP; NAAL-2;
NoAM; NOBA; OxBA; PoE; PPP; RB; TAP; UnPo

Design

37 I found a dimpled spider, fat and white,
On a white heal-all, holding up a moth
Like a white piece of rigid satin cloth —
Assorted characters of death and blight (l. 1–4)

38 What but design of darkness to appall? —
If design govern in a thing so small. (l. 13–14)

BLPL; CMoP; HeIP; InPK; InPS; MoP; NAAL-2; NIP;
NoAM; NOBA; NoP; PPP; PrIm; Son; SoSe; TAP

Directive

39 Back out of all this now too much for us,
Back in a time made simple by the loss
Of detail, burned, dissolved, and broken off
Like graveyard marble sculpture in the weather,
　　　　　　　　　　　　　　(l. 1–4)

40 The chisel work of an enormous Glacier
That braced his feet against the Arctic Pole.
　　　　　　　　　　　　(l. 16–17)

41 First there's the children's house of make believe,
Some shattered dishes underneath a pine,
The playthings in the playhouse of the children.
Weep for what little things could make them glad.
　　　　　　　　　　　　(l. 41–44)

42 Then for the house that is no more a house,
But only a belilaced cellar hole, (l. 45–46)

43 A brook that was the water of the house,
Cold as a spring as yet so near its source,
Too lofty and original to rage. (l. 50–52)

44 Here are your waters and your watering place.
Drink and be whole again beyond confusion.
(l. 61–62)

AmPP; BLPL; CMoP; HAP; InPS; LiTA; LiTM; MAT;
MoAB; MoAmPo; NAAL-2; NoAM; NOBA; NoP; PoE;
PPP; PrIm

The Draft Horse

45 And a man came out of the trees
And took our horse by the head
And reaching back to his ribs
Deliberately stabbed him dead. (l. 5–8)

CMoP; HeIP; HoPM; PoE

Dust of Snow

46 The way a crow
Shook down on me
The dust of snow
From a hemlock tree. (l. 1–4)

CMoP; MoShBr; OxBA; OxBSF; PDV; PrIm; RHPC;
SoSe; TAP; UnPo; WeW

Fire and Ice

47 Some say the world will end in fire,
Some say in ice. (l. 1–2)

48 I think I know enough of hate
To say that for destruction ice
Is also great
And would suffice. (l. 6–9)

AmPP; CMoP; FaBoEE; FaFP; FF; FPL; HeIP; HoPM;
InPK; LiTA; LiTM; MoAB; MoAmPo; MoP; NAAL-2;
NIP; NoAM; NOBA; OxBA; PPP; PrIm; SoSe; TAP;
TrGrPo; TW

The Gift Outright

49 The land was our before we were the land's.
She was our land more than a hundred years
Before we were her people. (l. 1–3)

50 Such as we were we gave ourselves outright
(The deed of gift was many deeds of war)
To the land vaguely realizing westward,
But still unstoried, artless, unenhanced,
Such as she was, such as she would become.
(l. 12–16)

AiP; AmFN; AmPP; CMoP; GOA; LiTM; MoAB;
MoAmPo; MoP; NAAL-2; NoAM; NOBA; NoP; OPP;
OxBA; PPP; WaP

The Hardship of Accounting

51 Nobody was ever meant
To remember or invent
What he did with every cent. (l. 3–5)

FaBoCh FaBoCo; FaFP; OBAL

The Hill Wife

52 One ought not to have to care
So much as you and I
Care when the birds come round the house
To seem to say good-by; (l. 1–4)

CMoP; HAP; InPS; LiTM; NoP

The Last Word of a Bluebird

53 But he sent her Good-by,
And said to be good,
And wear her red hood,
And look for skunk tracks
In the snow with an ax —
And do everything! (l. 15–20)

FaPON; GoJo; GrPl; SO

The Lovely Shall Be Choosers

54 She would refuse love safe with wealth and honor!
The lovely shall be choosers, shall they?
Then let them choose!' (l. 6–8)

MoAB; MoAmPo; NOBA; OxBA; PoE

Mending Wall

55 Something there is that doesn't love a wall, (l. 1)

56 I let my neighbor know beyond the hill;
And on a day we meet to walk the line
And set the wall between us once again.
We keep the wall between us as we go. (l. 12–15)

57 He only says, 'Good fences make good neighbors.'
(l. 27)

58 Before I built a wall I'd ask to know
What I was walling in or walling out,
And to whom I was like to give offense.
Something there is that doesn't love a wall,
That wants it down.' (l. 32–36)

AmFN; AmPP; AnAmPo; CMoP; FaBoPV; FaBV; FaFP;
FPL; HAF; HeIP; HoPM; InPS; LiTA; LiTM; MoAB;
MoAmPo; MoP; NAAL-2; NoAM; NOBA; NoP; OHFP;
OxBA; PoE; PrIm; SCV; SoSe; TAP; VGW; WeW

The Most of It

59 He thought he kept the universe alone; (l. 1)

60 He would cry out on life, that what it wants
Is not its own love back in copy speech,
But counter-love, original response. (l. 6–8)

61 As a great buck it powerfully appeared,
Pushing the crumpled water up ahead,
And landed pouring like a waterfall,
And stumbled through the rocks with horny tread,
And forced the underbrush — and that was all.
(l. 16–20)

HAP; NAAL-2; NoP; NU; TOF; WeW

Mowing

62 There was never a sound beside the wood but one,
And that was my long scythe whispering to the ground.
(l. 1–2)

63 The fact is the sweetest dream that labor knows.
My long scythe whispered and left the hay to make.
(l. 13–14)

AnAmPo; BLPL; CMoP; HoPM; LiTA; NAAL-2; NOBA;
OxBA; PPP; VGW

The Need of Being Versed in Country Things

64 The house had gone to bring again
To the midnight sky a sunset glow.
Now the chimney was all of the house that stood,
Like a pistil after the petals go. (l. 1–4)

65 The birds that came to it through the air
At broken windows flew out and in,
Their murmur more like the sigh we sigh
From too much dwelling on what has been. (l. 13–16)

66 One had to be versed in country things
Not to believe the phoebes wept. (l. 23–24)

NoAM; NOBA; OxBA; UnPo

Neither Out Far nor In Deep

67 The land may vary more;
But wherever the truth may be —
The water comes ashore,
And the people look at the sea. (l. 9–12)

68 They cannot look out far.
They cannot look in deep.
But when was that ever a
To any watch they keep? (l. 13–16)

AmPP; ChTr; HAP; LiTA; MoAB; MoP; MOS; NAAL-2;
NoAM; NOBA; NoP; TAP; WeW

Never Again Would Birds' Song Be the Same

69 He would declare and could himself believe
That the birds there in all the garden round
From having heard the daylong voice of Eve
Had added to their own an oversound,
Her tone of meaning but without the words. (l. 1–5)

FYAP; HAP; InPK; NIP; NoAM; NoP; Son; VGW

Nothing Gold Can Stay

70 Nature's first green is gold, (l. 1)

71 Then leaf subsides to leaf.
So Eden sank to grief,
So dawn goes down to day.
Nothing gold can stay. (l. 5–8)

AmPP; GrPl; MoAB; MoAmPo; NAAL-2; NOBA; PPP;
SoSe; TAP; VGW

An Old Man's Winter Night

72 All out of doors looked darkly in at him
Through the thin frost, almost in separate stars,
That gathers on the pane in empty rooms. (l. 1–3)

73 What kept him from remembering what it was
That brought him to that creaking room was age.
(l. 6–7)

74 A light he was to no one but himself. (l. 15)

75 One aged man — one man — can't keep a house,
A farm, a countryside, or if he can,
It's thus he does it of a winter night. (l. 26–28)

AWP; HAP; MoAB; MoAmPo; NAAL-2; NoAM; OxBA;
VGW

Once by the Pacific

76 The shattered water made a misty din.
Great waves looked over others coming in,
And thought of doing something to the shore
That water never did to land before. (l. 1–4)

77 You could not tell, and yet it looked as if
The shore was lucky in being backed by cliff,
The cliff in being backed by continent;
It looked as if a night of dark intent
Was coming, and not only a night, an age. (l. 7–11)

CMoP; HAP; HeIP; LiTA; LiTM; MoAB; MoAmPo; MOS;
NAAL-2; NOBA; PrIm; Son; VGW; WeW

The Onset

78 At last the gathered snow lets down as white
As may be in dark woods, and with a song
It shall not make again all winter long
Of hissing on the yet uncovered ground, (l. 2–5)

79 As one who overtaken by the end
Gives up his errand, and lets death descend
Upon him where he is, with nothing done
To evil, no important triumph won,
More than if life had never been begun. (l. 7–11)

80 I know that winter death has never tried
The earth but it has failed: (l. 13–14)

81 Nothing will be left white but here a birch,
And there a clump of houses with a church. (l. 22–23)

CMoP; MoAB; MoAmPo; OxBA; PPP

Out, Out

82 The buzz saw snarled and rattled in the yard
And made dust and dropped stove-length sticks of
wood,
Sweet-scented stuff when the breeze drew across it.
(l. 1–3)

83 "Don't let him cut my hand off—
The doctor, when he comes. Don't let him, sister!"
So. But the hand was gone already. (l. 25–27)

84 They listened at his heart.
Little—less—nothing!—and that ended it.
No more to build on there. And they, since they
Were not the one dead, turned to their affairs.
(l. 31–34)

DL; FF; HAP; HeIP; NAAL-2; OxBA; RB; SoSe; UnPo;
VGW; WeW

The Oven Bird

85 And comes that other fall we name the fall. (l. 9)

86 The bird would cease and be as other birds
But that he knows in singing not to sing.
The question that he frames in all but words
Is what to make of a diminished thing. (l. 11–14)

AmPP; AWP; HeIP; MoP; NAAL-2; NoAM; NOBA; NoP;
OxBA; PoE; PPP; Son; TAP

The Pasture

87 I'm going out to fetch the little calf
That's standing by the mother. It's so young,
It totters when she licks it with her tongue.
I sha'n't be gone long.—You come too. (l. 5–8)

BLPL; CMoP; FaPON; GoJo; MoAB; MoAmPo; MoShBr;
NAAL-2; NOBA; OxBA; PDV; PoE; TTTS

Provide, Provide

88 The witch that came (the withered hag)
To wash the steps with pail and rag,
Was once the beauty Abishag, (l. 1–3)

89 Die early and avoid the fate.
Of if predestined to die late,
Make up your mind to die in state. (l. 7–9)

90 Better to go down dignified
With boughten friendship at your side
Than none at all. Provide, provide! (l. 19–21)

AmPP; CMoP; HAP; MoAB; MoP; NAAL-2; NIP; NoAM;
NOBA; NoP; OPOP; PoE; PPP; TAP; TwCP; UnPo; WeW

Range-finding

91 On the bare upland pasture there had spread
O'ernight 'twixt mullein stalks a wheel of thread
And straining cables wet with silver dew. (l. 9–11)

MoP; NIP; NoAM; NoP; OBWP; RB

Reluctance

92 The leaves are all dead on the ground,
Save those that the oak is keeping (l. 7–8)

93 Ah, when to the heart of man
Was it ever less than a treason
To go with the drift of things
To yield with a grace to reason,
And bow and accept the end
Of a love or a season? (l. 19–24)

CMoP; MoAB; MoAmPo; NOBA; OxBA

The Road Not Taken

94 Two roads diverged in a yellow wood,
And sorry I could not travel both
And be one traveler, long I stood
And looked down one as far as I could (l. 1–4)

95 Two roads diverged in a wood, and I—
I took the one less traveled by,
And that has made all the difference. (l. 18–20)

AiP; AmPP; ChTr; CMoP; FaBoCh; FaFP; FPL; HAP;
HeIP; LiTA; LiTM; MoAB; MoAmPo; MoP; NAAL-2;
NIP; NoAM; NoP; OxBA; PoLF; RFM; SoSe; TAP; TwCP

The Rose Family

96 The rose is a rose.
And was always a rose.
But the theory now goes
That the apple's a rose, (l. 1–4)

97 You, of course, are a rose —
But were always a rose. (l. 9–10)

NIP; OBAL; OBCA; SoSe

The Runaway

98 A little Morgan had one forefoot on the wall,
The other curled at his breast. He dipped his head
And snorted at us. And then he had to bolt.
We heard the miniature thunder where he fled,
(l. 3–6)

99 And now he comes again with clatter of stone,
And mounts the wall again with whited eyes
And all his tail that isn't hair up straight. (l. 15–17)

100 'Whoever it is that leaves him out so late,
When other creatures have gone to stall and bine,
Ought to be told to come and take him in.' (l. 19–21)

AWP; CH; FaBoCh; FaPON; GoJo; MoAB; MoAmPo;
PDV; TwCP; VGW

The Silken Tent

101 She is as in a field a silken tent
At midday when a sunny summer breeze
Has dried the dew and all its ropes relent, (l. 1–3)

102 loosely bound
By countless silken ties of love and thought
To everything on earth the compass round, (l. 9–11)

AmPP; BLPL; InPK; NOBA; Son; SoSe; TAP; TwCP

A Soldier

103 He is that fallen lance that lies as hurled,
That lies unlifted now, come dew, come rust,
But still lies pointed as it plowed the dust. (l. 1–3)

104 Our missiles always make too short an arc:
They fall, they rip the grass, they intersect
The curve of earth, and striking, break their own;
(l. 8–10)

105 But this we know, the obstacle that checked
And tripped the body, shot the spirit on
Further than target ever showed or shone. (l. 12–14)

OFD; OPP; WaaP; WaP

Spring Pools

106 The trees that have it in their pent-up buds
To darken nature and be summer woods — (l. 7–8)

AmPP; MoAB; NAAL-2; NoAM; NOBA; NoP; OxBA

Stopping by Woods on a Snowy Evening

107 Whose woods these are I think I know.
His house is in the village though;
He will not see me stopping here
To watch his woods fill up with snow. (l. 1–4)

108 The woods are lovely, dark and deep,
But I have promises to keep,
And miles to go before I sleep,
And miles to go before I sleep. (l. 13–16)

AmPP; BoNaP; CMoP; FaBoCh; FaBV; FaFP; FaPON;
FF; FPL; GoJo; GrPl; HAP; HeIP; HoPM; InPK; InPS;
LiTA; LiTM; MoAB; MoAmPo; MoP; MoShBr; NAAL-2;
NIP; NoAM; NOBA; NoP; NTCP; OBCA; OxBA; PDV;
PoE; PoRA; PrIm; PYC; RB; RHPC; SCV; SoSe; TAP;
TOF; TTTS

The Subverted Flower

109 She drew back; he was calm
'It is this that had the power,'
And he lashed his open palm
With the tender-headed flower. (l. 1–4)

110 She had to lean away.
She dared not stir a foot,
Lest movement should provoke
The demon of pursuit
That slumbers in a brute. (l. 30–34)

111 A girl could only see
That a flower had marred a man,
But what she could not see
Was that the flower might be
Other than base and fetid: (l. 48–52)

CMoP; HAP; MoP; NoAM; NOBA; OxBA; PoE; WeW

To Earthward

112 Love at the lips was touch
As sweet as I could bear;
And once that seemed too much;
I lived on air (l. 1–4)

113 Now no joy but lacks salt
That is not dashed with pain
And weariness and fault; (l. 17–19)

114 The hurt is not enough:
I long for weight and strength
To feel the earth as rough
To all my length. (l. 29–32)

BLPL; LiTA; MoAB; MoAmPo; MoP; NoAM; NOBA;
NoP; OxBA; TAP

Tree at My Window

115 Tree at my window, window tree,
My sash is lowered when night comes on;
But let there never be curtain drawn
Between you and me. (l. 1–4)

116 Your head so much concerned with outer,
Mine with inner, weather. (l. 15–16)

BLPL; BoNaP; FaBoBe; MoAB; MoAmPo; NoAM; OxBA;
TAP; TrGrPo

The Tuft of Flowers

117 I went to turn the grass once after one
Who mowed it in the dew before the sun. (l. 1–2)

118 But he had gone his way, the grass all mown,
And I must be, as he had been, — alone,

'As all must be,' I said within my heart,
'Whether they work together or apart.' (l. 7–10)

119 A leaping tongue of bloom the scythe had spared
Beside a reedy brook the scythe had bared.

The mower in the dew had loved them thus,
By leaving them to flourish, not for us,

Nor yet to draw one thought of ours to him,
But from sheer morning gladness at the brim.
(l. 23–28)

120 'Men work together,' I told him from the heart,
'Whether they work together or apart.' (l. 39–40)

AWP; GoYe; LiTA; MoAB; MoAmPo; NAAL-2; OxBA

Two Tramps in Mud Time

121 Out of the mud two strangers came (l. 1)

122 Good blocks of oak it was I split,
As large around as the chopping block;
And every piece I squarely hit
Fell splinterless as a cloven rock. (l. 9–12)

123 The water for which we may have to look
In summertime with a witching wand,
In every wheelrut's now a brook,
In every print of a hoof a pond. (l. 33–36)

124 Men of the woods and lumberjacks,
They judged me by their appropriate tool.
Except as a fellow handled an ax,
They had no way of knowing a fool. (l. 53–56)

125 My right might be love but theirs was need.
And where the two exist in twain
Theirs was the better right — agreed. (l. 62–64)

126 Only where love and need are one,
And the work is play for mortal stakes,
Is the deed every really done
For Heaven and the future's sakes. (l. 69–72)

BLPL; CMoP; LiTA; LiTM; MoAB; MoAmPo; MoP;
NAAL-2; NoAM; PrIm; TrGrPo

Two Witches

127 Summoning spirits isn't 'Button, button,
Who's got the button,' I would have them know.

128 He said the dead had souls, but when I asked him
How could that be — I thought the dead were souls,
He broke my trance. Don't that make you suspicious
That there's something the dead are keeping back?

129 But the bones didn't try
The door; they halted helpless on the landing,
Waiting for things to happen in their favor.

130 I had a vision of them put together
Not like a man, but like a chandelier.

131 And set off briskly for so slow a thing,
Still going every which way in the joints, though,
So that it looked like lightning or a scribble.

132 When they sometimes
Come down the stairs at night and stand perplexed
Behind the door and headboard of the bed,
Brushing their chalky skull with chalky fingers,
With sounds like the dry rattling of a shutter,

133 She hadn't found the finger-bone she wanted
Among the buttons poured out in her lap.

CMoP; InPS; LiTM; MoAB; MoP; NoAM; NOBA; PoE

West-running Brook

134 It must be the brook
Can trust itself to go by contraries
The way I can with you — and you with me —
Because we re — we're — I don't know
What we are. (l. 8–11)

135 (The black stream, catching on a sunken rock,
Flung backward on itself in one white wave,
And the white water rode the black forever. (l. 24–26)

136 "Speaking of contraries, see how the brook
In that white wave runs counter to itself.
It is from that in water we were from
Long, long before we were from any creature.
(l. 43–46)

137 Some say existence like a Pirouot
   And Pirouette, forever in one place,
   Stands still and dances, but it runs away;
   It seriously, sadly, runs away
   To fill the abyss's void with emptiness. (l. 50–54)

138 Our life runs down in sending up the clock.
   The brook runs down in sending up our life.
   The sun runs down in sending up the brook.
   And there is something sending up the sun. (l. 69–72)

   BLPL; MoAB; MoAmPo; NOBA; NoP

The Wood-Pile

139 He thought that I was after him for a feather —
   The white one in his tail; like one who takes
   Everything said as personal to himself. (l. 14–16)

140 it was older sure than this year's cutting,
   Or even last year's or the year's before.
   The wood was gray and the bark warping off it
   And the pile somewhat sunken. Clematis
   Had wound strings round and round it like a bundle.
                              (l. 27–31)

141 To warm the frozen swamp as best it could
   With the slow smokeless burning of decay. (l. 39–40)

   AnAmPo; InPK; LiTA; NAAL-2; NoAM; NoP; VGW

ROY FULLER (b. 1912)

Autobiography of a Lungworm

1 Strangely, it is the pig himself becomes
  The god inside the car: (l. 25–26)

2 What does this mean? The individual,
  Nature, mutation, strife?
  I fell, though I am simple, still the whole
  Is complex; and that life,
  A huge, doomed throbbing — has a wiry soul
  That must escape the knife. (l. 37–42)

  MoP; NoAM; NoP; OxBC

January 1940

3 Water inflated the belly
  Of Hart Crane, and of Shelly.
  Coleridge was a dope.
  Southwell died on a rope. (l. 9–12)

4 I envy not only their talents
  And fertile lack of balance
  But the appearance of choice
  In their sad and fatal voice. (l. 21–24)

  HoPM; LiTM; SeCePo; WaP

ROSE FYLEMAN (1877–1957)

Mice

1 I think mice
  Are rather nice.

  Their tails are long,
  Their faces small,
  They haven't any
  Chins at all. (l. 1–6)

  BoTP; FaPON; NTCP; PDV; RAR; RHPC

JOHN GALT (1779–1839) *AND* "CHRISTOPHER NORTH"

Canadian Boat Song (attributed to Galt and "North")

1 The hearts that would have given their blood like
     water,
  Beat heavily beyond the Atlantic roar.
  Fair these broad meads — these hoary woods are grand:
  But we are exiles from our fathers' land. (l. 21–29)

  BLPA; CaP; FaBoCh; FaPoR; OBEV; OBNC

JEAN GARRIGUE (1914–1972)

The Stranger

1 Fear, then, so wounded me
  As fell upon my ear
  The voice a blind man dreams
  And broke on me the smile
  I dreamed as deaf men hear, (l. 19–23)

2 I suffered her to disappear
  Who hunger in the prison of my fear. (l. 30–31)

  LiTA; LiTM; NOBA; TwCP

GEORGE GASCOIGNE (1539–1577)

The Lullaby of a Lover

1 Sing lullaby, as women do,
  Wherewith they bring their babies to rest;
  And lullaby can I sing too,
  As womanly as can the best. (l. 1–4)

2 Full many wanton babes have I,
Which must be stilled with lullaby. (l. 7–8)

AAS; EBEV; ElL; HAP; InvP; NAEL-1; NoP; OBEV;
PoEL-1; QFR; TrGrPo

JOHN GAY (1685–1732)

Acis and Galatea

1 O ruddier than the cherry,
O sweeter than the berry,
O Nymph more bright
Than moonshine night,
Like kidlings blithe and merry.
Ripe as the melting cluster,
No lily has such lustre,
Yet hard to tame,
As raging flame,
And fierce as storms that bluster. (l. 1–10)

ELP; NAEL-1; NOBE; NOEC

The Beggar's Opera

2 Before the Barn-Door crowing,
The Cock by Hens attended,
His Eyes around him throwing,
Stands for a while suspended:
Then One he singles from the Crew,
And cheers the happy Hen;
With how do you do, and how do you do,
And how do you do again. (II,i)

ErPo; OAEL-1; OxBSP; PBBP; PoEL-3

3 If the heart of a man is deprest with cares,
The mist is dispell'dwhen a woman appears;
Like the notes of a fiddle, she sweetly, sweetly
Raises the spirits, and charms our ears. (II, ii)

ELP; EnLoPo; HeIP; NAEL-1; OAEL-1; TEP

4 Were I laid on Greenland'sCoast,
And in my Arms embrac'd my Lass;
Warm amidst eternal Frost,
Too soon the Half Year's Night would pass. (I,i)

5 And I would love you all the Day,
Every Night would kiss and play,
If with me you'd fondly stray
Over the Hills and far away.

EnLoPo; NAEL-1; NOBE; NOEC; OAEL-1; OxBoLi;
PoEL-3; PrIm

My Own Epitaph

6 Life is a jest: and all things show it.
I thought so once; but now I know it. (l. 1–2)

FaBoEE; FF; NIP; NOEC; OBD; SeCePo

Sweet William's Farewell to Black-eyed Susan

7 "O Susan, Susan, lovely dear,
My vows shall ever true remain;
Let me kiss off that falling tear,
We only part to meet again.
Change, as ye list, ye winds; my heart shall be
The faithful compass that still points to thee.

'Believe not what the landmen say,
Who tempt with doubts thy constant mind:
They'll tell thee, sailors, when away,
In ev'ry port a mistress find.
Yes, yes, believe them when they tell thee so,
For thou art present wheresoe'er I go. (l. 19–30)

AmFP; BeLS; BoLoP; GTBS; GTBS-P; MOS; NOEC

ORLANDO GIBBONS (1583–1625)

The Silver Swan (attributed to Gibbons)

1 O death, come close mine eyes;
More geese than swans now live, more fools than wise.
(l. 5–6)

ChTr; ElL; ELF; FaBoCh; HAP; HeIP; InPK; NAEL-1;
NoP; OBD; OxBSP; PBBP; PoEL-2; RB

SIR WILLIAM SCHWENCK GILBERT
(1836–1911)

The Bishop of Rum-ti-Foo

1 Among them was a Bishop, who
Had lately been appointed to
The balmy isle of Rum-ti-Foo,
And Peter was his name. (l. 5–8)

2 They played the eloquent tum-tum,
And lived on scalps served up in rum —
The only sauce they knew. (l. 10–12)

3 'Come, walk like this,' the dancer said,
'Stick you your toes — stick in your head,
Stalk on with quick, galvanic tread —

Your fingers thus extend;
The attitude's considered quaint,' (l. 57–61)

CenHV

Captain Reece

4 A feather bed had every man,
Warm slippers and hot-water can,
Brown windsor from the captain's store,
A valet, too, to every four. (l. 13–16)

5 The sisters, cousins, aunts, and niece,
And widowed ma of Captain Reece,
Attended there as they were bid;
It was their duty, and they did. (l. 89–90)

CenHV; FiBHP; GN

The Disagreeable Man

6 If you give me your attention, I will tell you what I am:
I'm a genuine philanthropist — all other kinds are sham.
Each little fault of temper and each social defect
In my erring fellow creatures, I endeavor to correct.

7 I do all the good I can —
Yet everybody says I'm such a disagreeable man!
And I can't think why!

8 I know everybody's income and what everybody earns,
And I carefully compare it with the income-tax returns;

9 I've an irritating chuckle, I've a celebrated sneer,
I've an entertaining snigger, I've a fascinating leer;
To everybody's prejudice I know a thing or two;
I can tell a woman's age in half a minute — and I do —

FiBHP

Etiquette

10 And down in fathoms many went the captain and the
crew;
Down went the owners — greedy men whom hope of
gain allured:
Oh, dry the starting tear, for they were heavily insured.
(l. 2–4)

11 They soon became like brothers from community of
wrongs;
They wrote each other little odes and sang each other
songs;
They told each other anecdotes disparaging their wives;
On several occasions, too, they saved each other's lives.
(l. 49–52)

CenHV; FaBoCh; FaBoCo; FiBHP

Ferdinando and Elvira; or, The Gentle Pieman

12 find out who it is that writes those lovely cracker
mottoes!'

'Tell me, Henry Wadsworth, Alfred, Poet Close, or
Mister Tupper,
Do you write the bonbon mottoes my Elvira pulls at
supper?' (l. 28–30)

13 'Then I polish all the silver, which a supper-table
lacquers;
Then I write the pretty mottoes which you find inside
the crackers' — (l. 53–54)

FaBoCo; FaBoNo; FiBHP

The Gondoliers

14 In enterprise of martial kind,
When there was any fighting,
He led his regiment from behind
(He found it less exciting).

15 No soldier in that gallant band
Hid half as well as he did.

16 That very knowing,
Overflowing,
Easygoing
Paladin,
The Duke of Plaza-Toro!

FaPON; FiBHP

17 a highly respectable gondolier,
Who promised the Royal babe to rear
And teach him the trade of a timoneer
With his own beloved brattling.

18 A taste for drink,combined with gout,
Had doubled him up forever.

19 Now owing, I'm much disposed to fear,
To his terrible taste for tippling,
That highly respectable gondolier
Could never declare with a mind sincere
Which of the two was his offspring dear
And which the Royal stripling.

OnMSP

H. M. S. Pinafore

20 he might have been a Roosian,
A French, or Turk, or Proosian,
Or perhaps Itali-an!

But in spite of all temptations,
To belong to other nations,
He remains an Englishman!

NOBL

Iolanthe

21 He exercises of his brains,
That is, assuming that he's got any.

22 I often think it's comical
How Nature always does contrive
That every boy and every gal,
That's born into the world alive,
Is either a little Liberal,
Or else a little Conservative!

23 If they've a brain and cerebellum, too,
They've got to leave that brain outside,
And vote just as their leaders tell 'em to.

FiBHP

24 When Wellington thrashed Bonaparte,
As every child can tell,
The House of Peers,throughout the war,
Did nothing in particular,
And did it very well:

NAEL-2; TrGrPo

25 When you're lying awake with a dismal headache, and
repose is taboo'd by anxiety,
I conceive you may use any language you choose to
indulge in without impropriety;

FaBoNo; NOBL; NoP; OxBoLi; PoRA

The Mikado

26 As some day it may happen that a victim must be
found,
I've got a little list — I've got a little list
Of society offenders who might well be underground,
And who never would be missed — who never would be
missed!

27 And that singular anomaly, the lady novelist —
I don't think she'd be missed — I'm sure she'd not be
missed!

LiTB

28 My object all sublime
I shall achieve in time —
To let the punishment fit the crime —
The punishment fit the crime;

LiTB

29 On a tree by a river a little tom-tit
Sang "Willow, titwillow, titwillow!"
And I said to him, "Dicky-bird, why do you sit
Singing, 'Willow, titwillow, titwillow'?
Is it a weakness of intellect, birdie?" I cried,
"Or a rather tough worm in your little inside?"

FaFP; LiTB; NoP

Patience

30 If you're anxious for to shine in the high esthetic line as
a man of culture rare,
You must get up all the germs of the transcendental
terms, and plant them everywhere.
You must lie upon the daisies and discourse in novel
phrases of your complicated state of mind,
The meaning doesn't matter if it's only idle chatterof a
transcendental kind.

31 Of course you will pooh-pooh whatever's fresh and new,
and declare it's crude and mean;

32 Then a sentimental passion of a vegetable fashion must
excite your languid spleen,
An attachment a la Plato for a bashful young potato, or
a not-too-French French bean!

EBVV; FiBHP; LiTB; OAEL-2

33 "If I can wheedle
A knife or a needle,
Why not a Silver Churn?"

34 While this magnetic,
Peripatetic
Lover he lived to learn,
By no endeavor
Can a magnet ever
Attract a Silver Churn!

FaPON; OnMSP

The Pirates of Penzance

35 I am the very patternof a modern Major-Gineral,
I've information vegetable, animal, and mineral;
I know the kings of England, and I quote the fights
historical,
From Marathon to Waterloo,in order categorical;

NBLV; NOBL; NoP

36 That most ingenious paradox!
We've quips and quibbles heard in flocks,
But none to beat that paradox!

NAs

37 When a felon's not engagedin his employment
Or maturing his felonious little plans,
His capacity for innocent enjoyment
Is just as great as any honest man's.

38 When the enterprising burglar isn't burgling,
When the cut-throat isn't occupied in crime,
He loves to hear the little brook a-gurgling,
And listen to the merry village chime.

NOBL; SaC; TrGrPo

Princess Ida

39 It's very hot,
And weighs a lot,
As many a guardsman knows,
So off that helmet goes.

40 A man is but an ass
Who fights in a cuirass,

41 They turn one's legs
To cribbage pegs —

FiBHP

Ruddigore

42 And I'll wager in their joy they kissed each other's
cheek
(Which is what them furriners do),
And they blessed their lucky stars
We were hardy British tars
Who had pity on a poor Parley-voo,

NOBL

The Story of Prince Agib

43 Strike the concertina's melancholy string!
Blow the spirit-stirring harp like any thing!
Let the piano's martial blast
Rouse the Echoes of the Past, (l. 1–4)

44 He would diligently play
On the Zoetrope all day,
And blow the gay Pantechnicon all night. (l. 13–15)

45 On my face extended flat
I was walloped with a cat
For listening at the key-hole of the door. (l. 68–70)

46 I shall carry to the Catacombs of Age,
Photographically lined
On the tablet of my mind, (l. 82–84)

FaBoCo; NA

To the Terrestrial Globe

47 Roll on, thou ball, roll on!
Through pathless realms of Space (l. 1–2)

48 What though I cannot meet my bills?
What though I suffer toothache's ills?
What though I swallow countless pills? (l. 4–6)

49 It's true I've got no shirts to wear;
It's true my butcher's bill is due;
It's true my prospects all look blue —
But don't let that unsettle you: (l. 12–15)

FaBoNo; NBLV; TrGrPo

Utopia Unlimited

50 Society has quite forsaken all her wicked courses,
Which empties our police courts, and abolishes
divorces.

51 (They haven't any slummeries in England.)

52 poverty is obsolete and hunger is abolished —

53 Utopia's quite another land;
In her enterprising movements,
She is England — with improvements,

54 Who knows but we may count among our intellectual
chickens
Like them an Earl of Thackeray and p'raps a Duke of
Dickens —

OBSV

The Yarn of the Nancy Bell

55 'Oh, I am a cook and a captain bold,
And the mate of the Nancybrig,
And a bos'un tight, and a midshipmite,
And the crew of the captain's gig!'''

BeLS; BLPA; CenHV; FaBoBe; FaBoCh; FaBoCo; FaBV;
FaFP; HoPM; MoShBr; MOS; NOBL; OnMSP; TrGrPo

Yeoman of the Guard

56 Oh! a private buffoon is a light-hearted loon,
If you listen to popular rumour;
From morning to night he's so joyous and bright,
And he bubbles with wit and good humour!

57 There are one or two rules,
Half-a-dozen, maybe,
That all family fools,

Of whatever degree,
Must observe if they love their profession.

58 If your master is surly, from getting up early
(And tempers are short in the morning),
An inopportune joke is enough to provoke
Him to give you, at once, a month's warning.

59 If the jests that you crackhave an orthodox smack,
You may get a bland smile from these sages;
But should it, by chance, be imported from France,
Half-a-crown is stopped out of your wages!

60 Bless your heart, they don't mind — they're exceedingly
kind —
They don't blame you — as long as you're funny!

NBLV

61 A man who would woo a fair maid,
Should 'prentice himself to the trade;
And study all day,
In methodical way,
How to flatter, cajole, and persuade

62 every Jack
He must study the knack
If he wants to make sure of his Jill!

FaBoUs

GARY GILDNER (b. 1938)

First Practice

1 if we are to win
that title I want to see how.
But I don't want to see
any marks when you're dressed,
he said. He said, Now. (l. 23–27)

AmPA; Psk; TSL; TW

JOSEPH HENRY GILMORE (1834–1918)

He Leadeth Me

1 He leadeth me O blessed thought,
O words with heavenly comfort fraught,
Whate'er I do, where'er I be,
Still 'tis God's hand that leadeth me.

AH; BLRP; WBLP; WGRP

ALLEN GINSBERG (b. 1926)

America

1 America, I've given you all and now I'm nothing. (l. 1)

2 America when will you be angelic?
When will you take off your clothes?
When will you look at yourself through the grave?
When will you be worothy of your million Trotskyites?
(l. 8–11)

3 Are you being sinister or is this some form of practical
joke?
I'm trying to come to the point.
I refuse to give up my obsession.
America stop pushing I know what I'm doing.
America the plum blossoms are falling. (l. 21–25)

4 Asia is rising against me.
I haven't got a chinaman's chance. (l. 48–49)

5 America how can I write a holy litany in your silly
mood? (l. 55)

6 I'd better get right down to the job.
It's true I don't want to join the Army or turn lathes in
precision parts factories, I'm nearsighted and
psychopathic anyway.
America I'm putting my queer shoulder to the wheel.
(l. 72–74)

CAPP; CoAP; HCAP; InPS; NaP; NoAM; PoE; PoM; PPP

Howl

7 I saw the best minds of my generation destroyed by
madness, starving hysterical naked,

8 angelheaded hipsters burning for the ancient heavenly
connection to the starry dynamo in the machinery of
night,

9 who chained themselves to subways for the endless ride
from Battery to holy Bronxon benzedrine until the
noise of wheels and children brought them down
shuddering mouth-wracked and battered bleak of
brain and drained of brilliance in the drear light of
Zoo,

10 vanished into nowhere Zen New Jersey leaving a trail
of ambiguous picture postcards of Atlantic City Hall,

11 who let themselves be fucked in the ass by saintly
motorcyclists, and screamed with joy,
who blew and were blown by those human seraphim,
the sailors, caresses of Atlantic and Caribbean love,

12 who lost their loveboys to the three old shrews of fate
the one eyed shrew of the heterosexual dollar the one
eyed shrew that winksout of the womb and the one
eyed shrew that does nothing but sit on her ass and
snip the intellectual golden threads of the craftsman's
loom,

13 who scribbled all nightrocking and rolling over lofty

incantations which in the yellow morning were stanzas of gibberish,

14 who cooked rotten animalslung heart feet tailborscht & tortillas dreaming of the pure vegetable kingdom,

15 concrete void of insulinmetrasol electricity hydrotherapypsychotherapy occupational therapypingpong & amnesia,

16 Moloch! Solitude! Filth! Ugliness! Ashcans and unobtainable dollars! Children screaming under the stairways! Boys sobbing in armies! Old men weeping in the parks!

17 Moloch whose love is endless oil and stone! Moloch whose soul is electricity and banks! Moloch whose poverty is the specter of genius! Moloch whose fate is a cloud of sexless hydrogen! Moloch whose name is the Mind!

18 Dreams! adorations! illuminations! religions! the whole boatload of sensitive bullshit!

19 Real holy laughter in the river! They saw it all! the wild eyes! the holy yells! They bade farewell! They jumped off the roof! to solitude! waving! carrying flowers! Down to the river! into the street!

AmPP; CAPP; GLP; InPS; MoP; NaP; NeAP; NIP; NoAM; NoP; PoM; SOTW; TAP

Kaddish

20 Strange now to think of you, gone without corsets and eyes while I walk on the sunny pavement of Greenwich Village. (l. 1)

21 Toward education marriage nervous breakdown, operation, teaching school, and learning to be mad, in a dream — what is this life? (l. 17)

22 Ai! ai! we do worse! We are in a fix! And you're out, Death let you out, Death had the Mercy, you're done with your century, done with God, done with the path thru it — (l. 25)

23 To go where? In that Dark — that — in that God? a radiance? A Lord in the Void? Like an eye in the black cloud in a dream? Adonoi at last, with you?
(l. 37)

24 All the accumulations of life, that wear us out — clocks, bodies, consciousness, shoe, breasts — begotten sons — your Communism — 'Paranoia' into hospitals. (l. 44)

25 This is the end, the redemption from Wilderness, way for the Wonderer, House sought for All, black handkerchief washed clean by weeping — page beyond Psalm — Last change of mine and Naomi — to Gods perfect Darkness — Death, stay thy phantoms! (l. 55)

26 'Don't be afraid of me because I'm just coming back home from the mental hospital — I'm your mother — '
(l. 79)

27 'Yesterday I saw God. What did he look like? Well, in the afternoon I climbed up a ladder — he as a cheap cabin in the country, like Monroe, NY the chicken farms in the wood. He was a lonely old man with a white beard. (l. 98)

28 'I told him, Look at all those fightings and killings down there, What's the matter? Why don't you put a stop to it?
'I try, he said — That's all he could do, he looked tired. He's a bachelor so long, and he likes lentil soup.'
(l. 100–101)

29 what can he do to escape that fatal Mama — (l. 128)

30 One hand stiff — heaviness of forties & menopause reduced by one heart stroke, lame now — wrinkles — a scar on her head, the lobotomy — ruin, the hand dipping downwards to death — (l. 151)

31 holy mother, now you smile on your love, your world is born anew, children run naked in the field spotted with dandelions, (l. 154)

32 'The key is in the window, the key is in the sunlight at the window — I have the key — Get married Allen don't take drugs — the key is in the bars, in the sunlight in the window.
Love,
your mother' (l. 163–165)

HCAP; NAAL-2; NeAP; NOBA; PoM; VWA

Sunflower Sutra

33 I walked on the banks of the tincan banana dock and sat down under the huge shade of a Southern Pacific locomotive to look at the sunset over the box house hills and cry. (l. 1)

34 corolla of bleary spikes pushed down and broken like a battered crown, seeds fallen out of its face, soon-to-be- toothless mouth of sunny air, sunrays obliterated on its hairy head like a dried wire spiderweb, (l. 8)

35 A perfect beauty of a sunflower! a perfect excellent lovely sunflower existence! a sweet natural eye to the new hip moon, woke up alive and excited grasping in the sunset shadow sunrise golden monthly breeze!
(l. 15)

AmPP; CoAP; HCAP; InPS; MAT; NAAL-2; NeAP; NOBA

A Supermarket in California

36 What thoughts I have of you tonight, Walt Whitman,
(l. 1)

37 What peaches and what penumbras! Whole families
shopping at night! Aisles full of husbands! Wives in
the avocados, babies in the tomatoes! — and you,
Garcia Lorca, what were you doing down by the
watermelons? (l. 3)

38 I saw you, Walt Whitman, childless, lonely old grubber,
poking among the meats in the refrigerator and
eyeing the grocery boys. (l. 4)

AmPP; CoAP; HAP; HCAP; HeIP; InPK; InPS; LiTM;
NAAL-2; NaP; NeAP; NoAM; NOBA; PoM; PrIm; SOTW;
TAP; TwCP; UnPo

To Aunt Rose

39 last time I saw you was the hospital
pale skull protruding under ashen skin
blue veined unconscious girl
in an oxygen tent
the war in Spain has ended long ago
Aunt Rose (l. 49–54)

LiTM; NAAL-2; NoP; PoE; VGW

Wales Visitation

40 of the satanic thistle that raises its horned symmetry
flowering above sister grass-daisies' pink tiny
bloomlets angelic as lightbulbs — (l. 14–16)

41 All the Valley quivered one extended motion, wind
undulating on mossy hills (l. 24–25)

42 No imperfection in budded mountain,
Valleys breathe, heaven and earth move together,
daisies push inches of yellow air, vegetables tremble,
green atoms shimmer in grassy mandalas,
sheep speckle the mountainside, revolving their jaws
    with empty eyes,
horses dance in the warm rain, (l. 48–53)

43 Fall on the ground, O great Wetness, O Mother, No
harm on thy body! (l. 60)

44 Groan thru breast and neck, a great Oh! to earth heart
(l. 76)

45 The great secret is no secret
Senses fit the winds,
Visible is visible,
rain-mist curtains wave through the bearded vale,
grey atoms wet the wind's Kaballah (l. 78–82)

46 What did I notice? Particulars! The
vision of the great One is myriad — (l. 93–94)

CAPP; NNaP; NOBA; NYBP; Prf

NIKKI GIOVANNI (b. 1943)
Knoxville, Tennessee

1 I always like summer
best (l. 1–2)

2 go barefoot
and be warm
all the time
not only when you go to bed
and sleep (l. 20–24)

AmNP; B Si; BPo; CNA; PoBA; SO

Nikki-Rosa

3 Childhood remembrances are always a drag
if you're Black (l. 1–2)

4 and I really hope no white person ever has cause to
    write about me
because they never understand Black love is Black
    wealth and they'll
probably talk about my hard childhood and never
    understand that
all the while I was quite happy. (l. 24–27)

AIW; AmNP; BlSi; HeIP; IHMS; MoP; NBP; PoBA; TAP

WASHINGTON GLADDEN (1836–1918)
O Master, Let Me Walk with Thee

1 O Master, let me walk with thee
In lowly paths of service free;
Tell me thy secret; help me bear
The strain of toil, the fret of care; (l. 1–4)

2 Teach me thy patience; still with thee
In closer, dearer company,
In work that keeps faith sweet and strong,
In trust that triumphs over wrong, (l. 17–20)

AH; BLRP; PWR; WGRP

LOUISE GLÜCK (b. 1943)
The Racer's Widow

1 soon the birds and ancients
Will be starting to arrive, bereaving points
South. (l. 3–5)

2 even he did not get to keep that lovely body. (l. 12)

AmPA; ASP; GeTw; NYBP; SM

SIDNEY GODOLPHIN (1610–1693)

Lord, when the wise men came from far

1 Lord, when the wise men came from far,
Led to thy cradle by a star,
Then did the shepherds too rejoice,
Instructed by thy angel's voice.
Blest were the wise men in their skill,
And shepherds in their harmless will. (l. 1–6)

BLPL; HAP; JCP; MeLP; MePo; NOBE; NOCV; OBS

JOHANN WOLFGANG VON GOETHE (1799–1832)

The Erl-King

1 "O father! O father! now, now, keep your hold,
The Erl-King has seized me — his grasp is so cold!

Sore trembled the father; he spurr'd thro' the wild,
Clasping close to his bosom his shuddering child;
He reaches his dwelling in doubt and in dread,
But, clasp'd to his bosom, the infant was dead.
(l. 27–32)

AWP; NU; OBVE; WSC

OLIVER ST. JOHN GOGARTY (1878–1957)

What should we know

1 What should we know,
For better or worse,
Of the Long Ago,
Were it not for Verse: (l. 1–4)

2 Where the Muse herself
All Time fulfils,
Who cuts with his scythe
All things but hers;
All but the blithe
Hexameters. (l. 15–20)

AnIL; FaBoCh; OBMV; PoRA

OLIVER GOLDSMITH (1730?–1774)

The Deserted Village

1 Sweet Auburn, loveliest village of the plain,
Where health and plenty cheered the labouring swain,
Where smiling spring its earliest visit paid,
And parting summer's lingering blooms delayed,
Dear lovely bowers of innocence and ease,
Seats of my youth, when every sport could please,
How often have I loitered o'er the green,
Where humble happiness endeared each scene. (l. 1–8)

BeLS; EnRP; FaFP; LaA; LiTB; NOBE; NOEC; NoP;
OAEL-1; PoEL-3; SeCePo; TEP; TrGrPo

2 Sweet smiling village, loveliest of the lawn,
Thy sports are fled and all thy charms withdrawn;
Amidst thy bowers the tyrant's hand is seen,
And desolation saddens all thy green;
One only master grasps the whole domain,
And half a tillage stints thy smiling plain; (l. 35–40)

3 Ill fares the land, to hastening ills a prey,
Where wealth accumulates, and men decay:
Princes and lords may flourish, or may fade;
A breath can make them, as a breath has made;
But a bold peasantry, their country's pride,
When once destroyed, can never be supplied.
(l. 51–56)

BeLS; EnRP; FaFP; LaA; NOEC; NoP; OAEL-1; OBSV;
PoEL-3; TEP

Retaliation

4 To coxcombs averse, yet most civilly steering,
When they judged without skill he was still hard of
hearing:
When they talked of their Raphaels, Corregios and stuff,
He shifted his trumpet, and only took snuff.

FaBoEE; LaA; NOEC; OBD; OxBoLi; SeCePo

She Stoops to Conquer

5 Let school-masters puzzle their brain.
With grammar, and nonsense, and learning;
Good liquor, I stoutly maintain,
Gives genus a better discerning. (l. 1–4)

6 When Methodist preachers come down
A-preaching that drinking is sinful,
I'll wager the rascals a crown
They always preach best with a skinful. (l. 10–14)

BIrV; ELP; NOIV; PoRA

The Vicar of Wakefield

7 This dog and man at first were friends;
But when a pique began,
The dog, to gain some private ends,
Went mad and bit the man.

8 But soon a wonder came to light,
That showed the rogues they lied:
The man recover'd of the bite,
The dog it was that died. (Fr. ch. 17)

BeLS; BLPA; FaBoBe; FaBoCh; FaBoCo; FaFP; FPL;
GN; NA; NBLV; NOBE; NOEC; NOIV; OBNV; TEP

9 When lovely woman stoops to folly,
And finds too late that men betray,
What charm can soothe her melancholy,
What art can wash her guilt away?

The only art her guilt to cover,
To hide her shame from every eye,
To give repentance to her lover,
And wring his bosom — is to die. (Fr. Ch. 24)

AWP; BoLoP; ELP; FPL; GTBS; GTBS-P; HAP; HeIP;
LiTB; NOBE; NOEC; NoP; OBEV; PrIm; SeCePo;
TrGrPo; UnPo

BARNABE GOOGE   (1540–1594)

Of Money

1 Give money me, take friendship whoso list,
For friends are gone come once adversity.
When money yet remaineth safe in chest,
That quickly can thee bring from misery.
Fair face show friends when riches do abound; (l. 1–5)

ElL; FF; NBLV; NoP

Out of Sight, Out of Mind

2 The oftener seen, the more I lust, (l. 1)

3 Thy absence therefore like I best. (l. 6)

ElL; InPS; InvP; OPOP

HARRY GRAHAM ("COL. D. STREAMER")   (1874–1936)

Mr. Jones

1 "Your servant's cut in half; he's dead!" (l. 2)

2 Send me the half that's got my keys." (l. 4)

CenHV; FaBoCo; FaFP; FiBHP

Some Ruthless Rhymes

3 Billy, in one of his nice new sashes,
Fell in the fire and was burnt to ashes; (l. 1–4)

4 I haven't the heart to poke poor Billy. (l. 7–8)

CenHV; FaBoCo; FaFP; NA; NBLV; RHPC

ROBERT GRAHAM (ROBERT CUNNINGHAME-GRAHAM)   (1735–1797)

If Doughty Deeds ("If daughty deeds my lady pleases.")

1 For you alone I ride the ring,
For you I wear the blue;
For you alone I strive to sing,
O tell me how to woo! (l. 25–29)

GoTS; GTBS; GTBS-P; OBEV

KENNETH GRAHAME   (1859–1932)

The Wind in the Willows

1 All along the backwater,
Through the rushes tall,
Ducks are a-dabbling,
Up tails all! (l. 1–4)

BoTP; FaFON; GoJo; MoShBr; NTCP; OxBChV; PDV;
RHPC

2 The world has held great Heroes,
As history books have showed;
But never a name to go down to fame
Compared with that of Toad! (l. 1–4)

FaPON; FiBHP; GoJo; NOBL

ROBERT GRAVES   (1895–1985)

The Blue-Fly

1 Magnified one thousand times, the insect
Looks farcically human; laugh if you will!
Bald head, stage-fairy wings, blear eyes,

A caved-in chest, hairy black mandibles,
Long spindly thighs. (l. 6—10)

2 Nature, doubtless, has some compelling cause
To glut the carriers of her epidemics —
Nor did the peach complain. (l. 18—20)

CMoP; NAEL-2; NoAM; NYBP

The Cool Web

3 There's a cool web of language winds us in,
Retreat from too much joy or too much fear:
We grow sea-green at last and coldly die
In brininess and volubility. (l. 9—12)

AWP; GTBS-P; MoP; NAEL-2; NIP; NoAM; NoP;
OxBTC; PoA; PrIm; SCV

Counting the Beats

4 Counting the beats,
Counting the slow heart beats,
The bleeding to death of time in slow heart beats,
Wakeful they lie. (l. 5—8)

ELP; GBL; GTBS-P; HAP; OxBTC; WeW

The Devil's Advice to Story-tellers

5 Assemble, first, all casual bits and scraps
That may shake down into a world perhaps;
People this world, by chance created so,
With random persons whom you do not know —
(l. 11—14)

6 Sigh then, or frown, but leave (as in despair)
Motive and end and moral in the air;
Nice contradiction between fact and fact
Will make the whole read human and exact.
(l. 19—22)

LiTM; MoP; NAEL-2; NoAM

Down, Wanton, Down!

7 Down, wanton, down! Have you no shame
That at the whisper of Love's name,
Or Beauty's, presto! up you raise
Your angry head and stand at gaze? (l. 1—4)

BoLoP; CMoP; ErPo; FaBoTw; HeIP; InPK; LiTM; MoP;
NAEL-2; NoAM; NoP; OAEL-2; PoE; TEP

Flying Crooked

8 The butterfly, a cabbage-white,
(His honest idiocy of flight)
Will never now, it is too late,
Master the art of flying straight, (l. 1—4)

FaBoMo; LiTM; OxBSP; PCP; RB; TwCP

A Frosty Night

9 Your eyes were frosted starlight,
Your heart fire and snow.
Who was it said, "I love you"?
alice: Mother, let me go! (l. 25—28)

CH; MoAB; MoBrPo; MoBS; OxBTC

Full Moon

10 Like man and wife who nightly keep
Inconsequent debate in sleep
As they dream side by side. (l. 12—14)

11 And love went by upon the wind
As though it had not been. (l. 34—35)

NOBE

Henry and Mary

12 "Then let us play at queen and king
As down the garden walks we go." (l. 13—14)

BrPo; GoJo; ILY; MoShBr; SO

In the Wilderness

13 Christ of His gentleness
Thirsting and hungering,
Walked in the wilderness;
Soft words of grace He spoke
Unto lost desert-folk
That listened wondering. (l. ´1—6)

14 The guileless old scapegoat;
For forty nights and days
Followed in Jesus' ways,
Sure guard behind Him kept,
Tears like a lover wept. (l. 26—30)

CH; MoAB; MoBrPo; SeCePo

Lost Love

15 This man is quickened so with grief.
He wanders god-like or like thief
Inside and out, below, above,
Without relief seeking lost love. (l. 21—24)

AWP; CH; FaBoCh; Mes; MoAB; MoBrPo; NoP

A Love Story

16 Her image was my ensign: snows melted,
Hedges sprouted, the moon tenderly shone,
The owls trilled with tongues of nightingale.
(l. 13—15)

17 her image
    Warped in the weather, turned beldamish.
    Then back came winter on me at a bound,
    The pallid sky heaved with a moon-quake. (l. 17–20)

CMoP; FaBoTw; LiTB; NAEL-2

Ogres and Pygmies

18 Those famous men of old, the Ogres —
    They had long beards and stinking arm-pits,
    They were wide-mouthed, long-yarded and great-bellied
    Yet not of taller stature, Sirs, than you. (l. 1–4)

19 the sweet-cupid-lipped and tassel-yarded
    Delicate-stomached dwellers
    In Pygmy Alley, (l. 25–27)

CMoP; FaBoMo; LiTB; LiTM; MoP; NoAM; SeCePo

The Persian Version

20 Truth-loving Persians do not dwell upon
    The trivial skirmish fought near Marathon. (l. 1–2)

CMoP; FaBoCo; LiTB; LiTM; MoP; NoAM; NOBL;
OBWP; WeW

Recalling War

21 Entrance and exit wounds are silvered clean,
    The track aches only when the rain reminds.
    The one-legged man forgets his leg of wood.
    The one-armed man his jointed wooden arm.
    The blinded man sees with his ears and hands
    As much or more than once with both his eyes.
                                        (l. 1–6)

22 What, then, was war? No mere discord of flags
    But an infection of the common sky
    That sagged ominously upon the earth (l. 11–13)

23 War was return of earth to ugly earth,
    War was foundering of sublimities,
    Extinction of each happy art and faith
    By which the world had still kept head in air.
                                        (l. 31–34)

CMoP; LiTM; MMA; NoAM; OAEL-2; OBWP; WaP

She Tells Her Love while Half Asleep

24 She tells her love while half asleep
    In the dark hours,
    With half-words whispered low: (l. 1–3)

BoLoP; EBEV; FaBoTw; GBL; NOBE; OxBTC

Sick Love

25 Take your delight in momentariness,
    Walk between dark and dark — a shining space
    With the grave's narrowness, though not its peace.
                                        (l. 10–12)

BoLoP; CMoP; EBEV; FaBoMo; GTBS-P; HAP; NOBE;
OAEL-2

A Slice of Wedding Cake

26 Why have such scores of lovely, gifted girls
    Married impossible men?
    Simple self-sacrifice may be ruled out,
    And missionary endeavour, nine times out of ten.
                                        (l. 1–4)

27 Has God's supply of tolerable husbands
    Fallen, in fact, so low?
    Or do I always over-value woman
    At the expense of man?
    Do I?
    It might be so. (l. 13–18)

BoLoP; NAEL-2 NOBE; OxBTC

Spoils

28 When all is over and you march for home,
    The spoils of war are easily disposed of: (l. 1–2)

29 never dare entrust them to a safe
    For fear they burn a hole through two-foot steel.
                                        (l. 13–14)

HAP; NYBP; Son; WeW

Star-Talk

30 "Are you cold too, poor Pleiads,
    This frosty night?"
    "Yes, and so are the Hyads:
    See us cuddle and hug," says the Pleiads,
    "All six in a ring: it keeps us warm:
    We huddle together like birds in a storm: (l. 9–14)

BoNaP; GoJo; MoBrPo; OxBTC

The Thieves

31 After, when they disentwine
    You from me and yours from mine,
    Neither can be certain who
    Was that I whose mine was you.
    To the act again they go
    More completely not to know. (l. 7–12)

32 Lovers, the conclusion is
Doubled sighs and jealousies
In a single heart that grieves
For lost honour among thieves. (l. 15–18)

BoLoP; CMoP; GTBS-P; LiTM; OAEL-2

To Juan at the Winter Solstice

33 There is one story and one story only
That will prove worth your telling,
Whether as learned bard or gifted child; (l. 1–3)

34 each new victim treads unfalteringly
The never altered circuit of his fate,
Bringing twelve peers as witness
Both to his starry rise and starry fall. (l. 15–18)

35 Dwell on her graciousness, dwell on her smiling,
Do not forget what flowers
The great boar trampled down in ivy time.
Her brow was creamy as the crested wave,
Her sea-blue eyes were wild
But nothing promised that is not performed.
(l. 37–42)

CMoP; EBEV; FaBoMo; LiTB; LiTM; MoBrPo; MoP;
NAEL-2; NoAM; OAEL-2; PoE; TwCP

The Traveler's Curse after Misdirection

36 May they stumble, stage by stage
On an endless pilgrimage,
Dawn and dusk, mile after mile,
At each and every step, a stile; (l. 1–4)

BrPo; CMoP; FiBHP; HoPM; LiTM; MoAB; MoBrPo;
NBLV; TW

Ulysses

37 One, two and many: flesh had made him blind,
Flesh had one pleasure only in the act,
Flesh set one purpose only in the mind –
Triumph of flesh and afterwards to find
Still those same terrors wherewith flesh was racked.
(l. 16–20)

38 he was nothing to be won or lost.
All lands to him were Ithaca: love-tossed
He loathed to fraud, yet would not bed alone.
(l. 23–25)

CMoP; FaBoTw; MoP; NoAM; PrIm

Warning to Children

39 Children, if you dare to think
Of the greatness, rareness, muchness,
Fewness of this precious only
Endless world in which you say
You live, (l. 1–5)

FaBoCh; FaFP; NoP; OAEL-2; SO

Welsh Incident

40 The populations of Pwllheli, Criccieth,
Portmadoc, Borth, Tremadoc, Penrhyndeudraeth,
Were all assembled. Criccieth's mayor addressed them
First in good Welsh and then in fluent English,
(l. 31–34)

CMoP; NOBE; OxBTC; WSC

The White Goddess

41 All saints revile her, and all sober men
Ruled by the God Apollo's golden mean – (l. 1–2)

42 Whom we desired above all things to know,
Sister of the mirage and echo. (l. 5–6)

43 We forget cruelty and past betrayal,
Heedless of where the next bright bolt may fall.
(l. 21–22)

MoBrPo; NAEL-2; OAEL-2; OPOP

THOMAS GRAY (1716–1771)

The Bard, a Pindaric Ode

1 'Ruin seize thee, ruthless king!
Confusion on thy banners wait, (l. 1–2)

2 Nor even thy virtues, tyrant, shall avail
To save thy secret soul from nightly fears,
From Cambria's curse, from Cambria's tears!' (l. 6–8)

3 On a rock, whose haughty brow,
Frowns o'er old Conway's foaming flood,
Robed in the sable garb of woe,
With haggard eyes the Poet stood; (l. 1–4)

4 Modred, whose magic song
Made huge Plinlimmon bow his cloud-topped head.
(l. 5–6)

5 "'Weave the warp and weave the woof,
The winding-sheet of Edward's race. (l. 1–2)

6 Fierce war and faithful love,
And truth severe, by fairy fiction dressed. (l. 2–3)

EnRP; GTBS; GTBS-P; NOBE; NOEC; OAEL-1

Elegy Written in a Country Churchyard

7 The curfew tolls the knell of parting day,
The lowing herd wind slowly o'er the lea,
The plowman homeward plods his weary way,
And leaves the world to darkness and to me. (l. 1–4)

8 Let not Ambition mock their useful toil,
Their homely joys, and destiny obscure;
Nor Grandeur hear with a disdainful smile,
The short and simple annals of the poor. (l. 29–32)

9 The paths of glory lead but to the grave. (l. 36)

10 Full many a gem of purest ray serene,
The dark unfathom'd caves of ocean bear:
Full many a flower is born to blush unseen,
And waste its sweetness on the desert air. (l. 53–56)

11 Far from the madding crowd's ignoble strife,
Their sober wishes never learn'd to stray; (l. 73–74)

12 Here rests his head upon the lap of Earth
A Youth to Fortune and to Fame unknown,
Fair Science frown'd not on his humble birth,
And Melancholy mark'd him for her own. (l. 117–120)

AWP; DL; EBEV; EnRP; FaBcBe; FaBoPP; FaBoPV;
FaBoRV; FaFP; FaPoR; FPL; GN; GTBS; GTBS-P; HAP;
HeIP; InPK; InPS; LaA; LiTB; NOBE; NOEC; NoP;
OAEL-1; OBEV; OHFP; PoEL-3; PoLF; PPP; PrIm; SCV;
TEP; TrGrPo; UnPo; WBLP; WeW

Ode on a Distant Prospect of Eton College

13 Ah happy hills! ah pleasing shade!
Ah fields beloved in vain!
Where once my careless childhood stray'd, (l. 11–13)

14 My weary soul they seem to soothe,
And, redolent of joy and youth,
To breathe a second spring. (l. 17–19)

15 Still as they run they look behind,
They hear a voice in every wind,
And snatch a fearful joy. (l. 37–39)

16 Alas! regardless of their doom
The litte victims play; (l. 50–51)

17 No more; — where ignorance is bliss
'Tis folly to be wise. (l. 98–99)

BLPL; GTBS; GTBS-P; HeIP; LiTB; NAEL-1; NOBE;
NOEC; NoP; OAEL-1; PoE; PoEL-3; PrIm

Ode on the Death of a Favourite Cat, Drowned in a Tub of Gold Fishes

18 Twas on a lofty vase's side,
Where China's gayest art had dyed
The azure flowers that blow;
Demurest of the tabby kind,
The pensive Selima reclined,
Gazed on the lake below. (l. 1–6)

19 The hapless Nymph with wonder saw:
A whisker first and then a claw,
With many an ardent wish,
She stretch'd in vain to reach the prize.
What female heart can gold despise?
What Cat's averse to fish? (l. 19–24)

20 Not all that tempts your wand'ring eyes
And heedless hearts, is lawful prize;
Nor all that glisters, gold. (l. 40–42)

BeLS; EBEV; FaBoBe; FaBoCo; FM; FPL; GN; GTBS;
GTBS-P; HoPM; InPS; InvP; LiTB; NAEL-1; NBLV;
NOBE; NOBL; NOEC; NoP; OAEL-1; OBEV; PoE;
PoEL-3; PoLF; PoRA; PPP; TEP; WiR

On Lord Holland's Seat near Margate, Kent

21 Old and abandoned by each venal friend,
Here H[olland] took the pious resolution
To smuggle some few years and strive to mend
A broken character and constitution. (l. 1–4)

22 And mimic desolation covers all. (l. 16)

NOEC; OAEL-1; OPOP; SeCePo; TW

The Progress of Poesy

23 From Helicon's harmonious springs
A thousand rills their mazy progress take: (l. 3–4)

24 Now the rich stream of Music winds along
Deep, majestic, smooth, and strong, (l. 7–8)

25 O Sovereign of the willing soul,
Parent of sweet and solemn-breathing airs,
Enchanting shell! (l. 13–15)

26 Man's feeble race what ills await!
Labour, and Penury, the racks of Pain,
Disease, and Sorrow's weeping train,
And Death, sad refuge from the storms of Fate!
(l. 42–44)

27 Her track, where'er the Goddess roves,
Glory pursue, and generous Shame,
Th' unconquerable Mind, and Freedom's holy flame.
(l. 62–64)

28 Far from the sun and summer-gale
In thy green lap was Nature's Darling laid,
What time, where lucid Avon stray'd,
To him the mighty mother did unveil
Her awful face: (l. 82–86)

29 Nor second He, that rode sublime
Upon the seraph-wings of Ecstasy
The secrets of the Abyss to spy: (l. 94–96)

30 He saw: but blasted with excess of light,
Closed his eyes in endless night. (l. 100–101)

31 Yet shall he mount, and keep his distant way
Beyond the limits of a vulgar fate:
Beneath the Good how far — but far above the Great.
(l. 120–122)

AWP; EnRP; GTBS; GTBS-P; NOEC; OBEV

Sonnet on the Death of Mr. Richard West

32 In vain to me the smiling Mornings shine,
And redd'ning Phoebus lifts his golden Fire:
The Birds in vain their amorous Descant join;
Or cheerful Fields resume their green Attire: (l. 1–4)

33 To warm their little Loves the Birds complain: (l. 12)

EnRP; NOBE; NOEC; NoP; OBD; PeHV; PoE; PoEL-3;
SeCePo; Son; TrGrPo

ROBERT GREENE (1558?–1592)

Farewell to Folly

1 Sweet are the thoughts that savour of content,
The quiet mind is richer than a crown;
Sweet are the nights in careless slumber spent,
The poor estate scorns Fortune's angry frown.
Such sweet content, such minds, such sleep, such bliss,
Beggars enjoy, when princes oft do miss.

CTC; ElL; OBSC; PoEL-2; TrGrPo; UnPo

Menaphon

2 Weep not, my wanton, smile upon my knee;
When thou art old there's grief enough for thee.

ElL; ELP; NOBE; OBEV; OBSC; PoEL-2; SeCePo;
TrGrPo

Pandosto

3 Ah were she pitiful as she is fair,
Or but as mild as she is seeming so,
Then were my hopes greater than my despair,
Then all the world were heaven, nothing woe.

4 Sovran of beauty! like the spray she grows,
Compassed she is with thorns and cankered bower.
Yet were she willing to be plucked and worn,
She would be gathered, though she grew on thorn.

OBEV; OBSC; PoEL-2; TrGrPo

JULIAN GRENFELL (1888–1915)

Into Battle

1 And he is dead who will not fight;
And who dies fighting has increase. (l. 7–8)

2 The horses show him nobler powers;
O patient eyes, courageous hearts! (l. 33–34)

3 Through joy and blindness he shall know,
Not caring much to know, that still
Nor lead nor steel shall reach him, (l. 39–41)

4 The thundering line of battle stands,
And in the air Death moans and sings:
But Day shall clasp him with strong hands,
And Night shall fold him in soft wings. (l. 43–46)

FaPoR; MMA; OBEV; OBMV; OBWP; OxBTC; WaaP

FULKE GREVILLE, 1ST BARON BROOKE (1554–1628)

Caelica

1 Sweet Cupid's shafts, like destiny,
Doth causeless good or ill decree.
Desert is born out of his bow,
Reward upon his wing doth go.
What fools are they that have not known
That Love likes no laws but his own!

2 The worth that worthiness should move
Is love, that is the bow of Love.
And love as well the foster can
As can the mighty nobleman.
Sweet saint, 'tis true you worthy be,
Yet without love nought worth to me.

ElL; ELP; NoP; OBSC

3 I bow'd not to thy image for succession,
Nor bound thy bow to shoot reformed kindness,
Thy plays of hope and fear were my confession,
The spectacles to my life was thy blindness;
But Cupid now farewell, I will go play me,
With thoughts that please me less and less betray me.

FaBoRV; GBL; OBSC; QFR; Son

4 In night when colours all to black are cast,
Distinction lost, or gone down with the light;
The eye — a watch to inward senses placed,
Not seeing, yet still having power of sight —
Gives vain alarums to the inward sense

5 And images of self-confusednesses
  Which hurt imaginations only see —
  And from this nothing seen, tells news of devils,
  Which but expressions be of inward evils.

  AAS; OAEL-1; QFR; Son

6 Man, dreame no more of curious mysteries,
  As what was here before the world was made,
  The first Mans life, the state of Paradise,
  Where heaven is, or hell's eternall shade,
  For Gods works are like him, all infinite;
  And curious search, but craftie sinnes delight.

  JCP; MePo; OBS; QFR

7 Three things there be in man's opinion dear,
  Fame, many friends, and fortune's dignities:
  False visions all, which in our sense appear,
  To sanctify desire's idolatry.

  LiTB; NOCV; OBS; PoEL-1

8 when this life is from the body fled,
  To see it selfe in that eternall Glasse,
  Where time doth end, and thoughts accuse the dead,
  Where all to come, is one with all that was;
  Then living men aske how he left his breath,
  That while he lived never thought of death.

  LiTB; MePo; OBS; PoEL-1

Mustapha

9 O wearisome condition of humanity!
  Born under one law, to another bound;
  Vainly begot, and yet forbidden vanity,
  Created sick, commanded to be sound.
  What meaneth nature by these diverse laws?
  Passion and reason self-division cause.

10 We that are bound by vows and by promotion,
  With pomp of holy sacrifice and rites,
  To teach belief in good and still devotion,
  To preach of heaven's wonders and delights —
  Yet, when each of us in his own heart looks,
  He finds the God there far unlike his books.

  HAP; InvP; JCP; LiTB; MePo; NAEL-1; NOBE; OAEL-1;
  OBS; PoEL-1; PPP; SeCePo

FULKE GREVILLE (1554–1628) *AND*
SIR EDWARD DYER (c. 1540–1607)

Epitaph on Sir Philip Sidney (attributed to
Greville)

1 Silence augmenteth grief, writing increaseth rage,
                                              (l. 1)

2 Hard-hearted minds relent and rigor's tears abound,
  And envy strangely rues his end, in whom no fault was
    found.
  Knowledge her light hath lost, valor hath slain her
    knight,
  Sidney is dead, dead is my friend, dead is the world's
    delight. (l. 5–8)

  LiTB; OBSC; Prf

BARTHOLOMEW GRIFFIN (d. 1602)

Fidessa, More Chaste than Kind

1 See where my Love sits in the beds of spices,
  Beset all round with camphor, myrrh, and roses,
  And interlaced with curious devices
  Which her apart from all the world incloses!
  There doth she tune her lute for her delight,
  And with sweet music makes the ground to move,
  Whilst I, poor I, do sit in heavy plight,
  Wailing alone my unrespected love;

  EIL; ErPo; GBL; PoEL-2; TrGrPo

EDGAR ALBERT GUEST (1881–1959)

Home

1 It takes a heap o' livin' in a house t' make it home,
  A heap o' sun an' shadder, an' ye sometimes have t'
    roam
  Afore ye really 'preciate the things ye lef' behind,
  An' hunger fer 'em somehow, with 'em allus on yer
    mind. (l. 1–4)

2 It ain't home t' ye, though it be the palace of a king,
  Until somehow yer soul is sort o' wrapped round
    everything. (l. 7–8)

3 Ye've got t' weep t' make it home, ye've got t' sit an'
  sigh (l. 17)

  BLPA; BLPL; FaBoBe; OBAL; OHFP; PWR

It Couldn't Be Done

4 Somebody said that it couldn't be done,
  But he with a chuckle replied
  That "maybe it couldn't," but he would be one
  Who wouldn't say so till he'd tried. (l. 1–4)

5 Just start to sing as you tackle the thing
  That "cannot be done," and you'll do it. (l. 23–24)

  BLPA; FaBoBe; FaFP; FPL; WBLP

ARTHUR GUITERMAN (1891–1943)

Habits of the Hippopotamus

1 The hippopotamus is strong
And huge of head and broad of bustle;
The limbs on which he rolls along
Are big with hippopotomuscle. (l. 1–4)

FaBV; FiBHP; OBCA; OnUR; RHPC

On the Vanity of Earthly Greatness

2 The grizzly bear whose potent hug
Was feared by all, is now a rug.

Great Caesar's bust is on the shelf,
And I don't feel so well myself. (l. 5–8)

BXAP; HeIP; HoPM; OBCA; TrJP

THOM GUNN (b. 1929)

The Byrnies

1 Thus for each blunt-faced ignorant one
The great grey rigid uniform combined
Safety with virtue of the sun.
Thus concepts linked like chainmail in the mind.
(l. 25–28)

MoP; NePoEA-2; NoAM; OxBTC

Considering the Snail

2 He
moves in a wood of desire,

pale antlers barely stirring
as he hunts. I cannot tell
what power is at work, drenched there
with purpose, knowing nothing. (l. 5–10)

3 the slow passion
to that deliberate progress. (l. 17–18)

GrPl; LiTM; NAEL-2; NePoEA-2; TwCP

In Santa Maria del Popolo

4 O wily painter, limiting the scene
From a cacophony of dusty forms
To the one convulsion, (l. 13–15)

5 The painter saw what was, an alternate
Candor and secrecy inside the skin. (l. 19–20)

CMoP; FaBoMo; GTBS-P; NePoEA-2; OxBC; PoE; QFR

Moly

6 These seem like bristles, and the hide is tough.
No claw or web here: each foot ends in hoof. (l. 9–10)

7 Direct me gods, whose changes are all holy,
To where it flickers deep in grass, the moly:
(l. 21–22)

8 From this fat dungeon I could rise to skin
And human title, putting pig within. (l. 25–26)

HAP; MoP; NoAM; PrIm

My Sad Captains

9 One by one they appear in
the darkness: a few friends, and
a few with historical
names. How late they start to shine!
but before they fade they stand
perfectly embodied, (l. 1–6)

CMoP; FaBoMo; LiTM; NAEL-2; NePoEA-2; NoAM

On the Move

10 the dull thunder of approximate words. (l. 8)

11 Small, black, as flies hanging in heat, the Boys,
Until the distance throws them forth, their hum
Bulges to thunder held by calf and thigh. (l. 10–12)

12 Much that is natural, to the will must yield.
Men manufacture both machine and soul,
And use what they imperfectly control
To dare a future from the taken routes. (l. 21–24)

13 One joins the movement in a valueless world,
Choosing it, till both hurler and the hurled,
One moves as well, always toward, toward. (l. 30–32)

14 At worst, one is in motion; and at best,
Reaching no absolute, in which to rest,
One is always nearer by not keeping still. (l. 38–40)

CMoP; HAP; LiTM; NePoEA-2; NoP; OAEL-2; OxBTC;
PoE; PPP; TwCP

DOROTHY FRANCES GURNEY
(1858–1932)

The Lord God Planted a Garden

1 The kiss of the sun for pardon,
The song of the birds for mirth, —
One is nearer God's heart in a garden

Than anywhere else on earth. (l. 13–16)

BLPA; FaBoBe; FPL; WGRP

while the long moon drifts
toward Asia (l. 13–18)

BoNaP; CoAP; HeIP; LCAP; NU

MRS. FLEETWOOD HABERGHAM

The Seeds of Love (*attributed to* Habergham)

1 I sowed the seeds of love,
It was all in the spring,
In April, May, and June, likewise,
When small birds they do sing. (l. 1–4)

2 My garden is run wild!
Where shall I plant anew —
For my bed, that once was covered with thyme,
Is all overrun with rue? (l. 37–40)

ELP; FaBoCh; GBP; OBET; OxBoLi; WiR

WILLIAM HABINGTON (1605–1654)

Castara

1 They hear but when the mermaid sings,
And only see the falling star,
Who ever dare
Affirm no woman chaste and fair. (II, l. 3–6)

JCP; MePo; OBS; SeCP

2 My soule her wings doth spread
And heaven-ward flies,
Th' Almighty's Mysteries to read
In the large volumes of the skies. (III, l. 5–8)

ACP; JCP; MeLP; MePo; NOBE; OBEV; OBS

3 Then that which living gave you roome,
Your glorious sepulcher shall be.
There wants no marble for a tombe,
Whose brest hath marble beene to me. (I, l. 13–16)

EnLoPo; MeLP; OBEV; SeCP

JOHN HAINES (b. 1924)

If the Owl Calls Again

1 And then we'll sit
in the shadowy spruce and
pick the bones
of careless mice,

SARAH JOSEPHA BUELL HALE
(1788–1879)

Mary's Lamb

1 Mary had a little lamb,
Its fleece was white as snow,
And every where that Mary went
The lamb was sure to go;
He followed her to school one day —
That was against the rule,
It made the children laugh and play,
To see a lamb at school. (l. 1–8)

2 "And you each gentle animal
In confidence may bind,
And make them follow at your call,
If you are always kind." (l. 21–24)

FaBoBe; FaFP; FaPON; OBCA; OxBChV; OxNR

DONALD HALL (b. 1928)

My Son, My Executioner

1 Sweet death, small son, our instrument
Of immortality,
Your cries and hungers document
Our bodily decay. (l. 5–8)

CAPP; DiL; NePoEA; SM

Names of Horses

2 Generation on generation, your neck rubbed the
windowsill
of the stall, smoothing the wood as the sea smooths
glass. (l. 15–16)

3 For a hundred and fifty years, in the pasture of dead
horses,
roots of pine trees pushed through the pale curves of
your ribs,
yellow blossoms flourished above you in autumn, and
in winter
frost heaved your bones in the ground — old toilers, soil
makers:

O Roger, Mackerel, Riley, Ned, Nellie, Chester, Lady
Ghost. (l. 25–29)

CAPP; HAP; InPK; LCAP; LLLT

Ox Cart Man

4 He packs wool sheared in April, honey
in combs, linen, leather
tanned from deerhide,
and vinegar in a barrel
hooped by hand at the forge's fire. (l. 6–10)

CAPP; FYAP; InPS; LCAP

The Sleeping Giant

5 I was afraid the waking arm would break
From the loose earth and rub against his eyes
A fist of trees, and the whole country tremble
In the exultant labor of his rise; (l. 5–8)

GrPl; NePoEA; NYBP; Psk; TwCP

Valentine

6 Chipmunks jump, and
Greensnakes slither.
Rather burst than
Not be with her. (l. 1–4)

GrPl; LLLT; NTCP; PCP

THOMAS HARDY   (1840–1928)

After a Journey

1 you are leading me on
To the spots we knew when we haunted here together,
(l. 17–18)

2 a voice still so hollow
That it seems to call out to me from forty years ago,
When you were all aglow,
And not the thin ghost that I now frailly follow!
(l. 21–24)

3 bring me here again!
I am just the same as when
Our days were a joy, and our paths through flowers.
(l. 30–32)

CMoP; EBEV; ELP; EnLoPo; FaBoPP; GBL; GTBS-P;
OBNC; OxBTC; PoE; PoEL-5

Afterwards

4 will the neighbors say,
"He was a man who used to notice such things"?
(l. 3–4)

5 Will this thought rise on those who will meet my face
no more,
"He was one who had an eye for such mysteries"?
(l. 15–16)

BoNaP; CH; ChTr; CMoP; EBEV; FaBoRV; GTBS-P;
InPS; LiTB; LiTM; MoAB; MoBrPo; NOBE; NoP;
OAEL-2; OBNC; PoEL-5; QFR; TOF; TrGrPo

Ah, Are You Digging on My Grave?

6 "Ah, are you digging on my grave
My beloved one? — planting rue?" (l. 1–2)

7 That one true heart was left behind!
What feeling do we ever find
To equal among human kind
A dog's fidelity!" (l. 27–30)

8 I am sorry, but I quite forgot
It was your resting-place." (l. 35–36)

BrPo; DL; MoAB; MoBrPo; NAEL-2; OBD; TEP

And There Was a Great Calm

9 There had been years of Passion — scorching, cold,
And much Despair, and Anger heaving high, (l. 1–2)

10 So, when old hopes that earth was bettering slowly
Were dead and damned, there sounded 'War is done!'
One morrow. Said the bereft, and meek, and lowly,
'Will men some day be given to grace? yea, wholly,
And in good sooth, as our dreams used to run?'
(l. 21–25)

11 Calm fell. From Heaven distilled a clemency;
There was peace on earth, and silence in the sky;
Some could, some could not, shake off misery:
The Sinister Spirit sneered: 'It had to be!'
And again the Spirit of Pity whispered, 'Why?'
(l. 41–45)

ChTr; CMoP; FaBoRV; LiTM; OAEL-2

At Castle Boterel

12 I look back at it amid the rain
For the very last time; for my sand is sinking,
And I shall traverse old love's domain
Never again. (l. 32–35)

EBEV; GTBS-P; NOBE; OBNC; PoE; SCV

Channel Firing

13 That night your great guns, unawares,
Shook all our coffins as we lay,
And broke the chancel window-squares,
We thought it was the Judgment-day (l. 1–4)

14 It's gunnery practice out at sea
Just as before you went below;
The world is as it used to be (l. 10–12)

15 Again the guns disturbed the hour,
Roaring their readiness to avenge,
As far inland a Stourton Tower,
And Camelot, and starlit Stonehenge. (l. 33–36)

BrPo; CMoP; EBEV; HAP; HeIP; LiTB; MoP; NAEL-2;
NIP; NoAM; NoP; OAEL-2; OxBTC; PoE; PoEL-5; PoRA;
PrIm; RB; SoSe; UnPo; WaaP

The Convergence of the Twain (Lines on the Loss of the Titanic)

16 Till the Spinner of the Years
Said "Now!" And each one hears,
And consummation comes, and jars two hemispheres.
(l. 31–33)

BrPo; FaBoTw; HeIP; InPK; InPS; LiTB; LiTM; MoAB;
MoBrPo; MoP; MOS; NAEL-2; NIP; NoAM; NoP; OAEL-
2; OxBTC; PrIm; TEP

The Darkling Thrush

17 I leant upon a coppice gate
When Frost was spectre-gray (l. 1–2)

18 An aged thrush, frail, gaunt, and small,
In blast-beruffled plume,
Had chosen thus to fling his soul
Upon the growing gloom. (l. 21–24)

BrPo; CMoP; EBVV; FaFP; FPL; HAP; InPS; LiTB;
LiTM; MoAB; MoBrPo; MoP; NAEL-2; NIP; NoAM;
NOBE; NOBVV; NoP; OAEL-2; OBEV; OBNC; PBBP;
PoE; PPP; RB; SoSe; TEP; TOF; TrGrPo; UnPo; WaP

Drummer Hodge

19 They throw in Drummer Hodge, to rest
Uncoffined — just as found:
His landmark is a kopje-crest
That breaks the veldt around; (l. 1–4)

20 His homely Northern breast and brain
Grow to some Southern tree,
And strange-eyed constellations reign
His stars eternally. (l. 15–18)

AWP; BrPo; EBEV; GTBS-P; HAP; InPS; MoP; NAEL-2;
NoAM; NOBVV; NoP; OBWP; WeW

The Dynasts

21 The victors and the vanquished then the storm it tossed
and tore,
As hard they strove, those worn-out men, upon that
surly shore;
Dead Nelson and his half-dead crew, his foes from near
and far,
Were rolled together on the deep that night at
Trafalgar!

CH; ChTr; FaBoCh; MoBrPo; MOS; OBMV

Friends Beyond

22 at mothy curfew-tide,
And at midnight when the noon-heat breathes it back
from walls and leads,
They've a way of whispering to me — fellow-wight who
yet abide — (l. 8–10)

EBVV; FaBoRV; GTBS-P; NOBVV; OBEV

The Going

23 Why did you give no hint that night
That quickly after the morrow's dawn,
And calmly, as if indifferent quite,
You would close your term here, up and be gone
(l. 1–4)

EBEV; ELP; LiTB; NOBE; UnPo

Hap

24 If but some vengeful god would call to me
From up the sky, and laugh: "Thou suffering thing,
Know that thy sorrow is my ecstasy,
That thy love's loss is my hate's profiting!" (l. 1–4)

AWP; CMoP; EaLo; EBVV; MoBrPo; NAEL-2; NIP;
NoAM; NoP; OAEL-2; PPP; Son; TEP

He Never Expected Much

25 Since as a child I used to lie
Upon the leaze and watch the sky,
Never, I own, expected I
That life would all be fair. (l. 5–8)

NAEL-2; NAs; NoAM; OxBTC; SCV

Heredity

26 The years-heired feature that can
In curve and voice and eye
Despise the human span

Of durance — that is I;
The eternal thing in man,
That heeds no call to die. (l. 7–12)

CTC; EBEV; ImOP; RB

I Look into My Glass

27 Time, to make me grieve,
Part steals, lets part abide;
And shakes this fragile frame at eve
With throbbings of noontide. (l. 9–12)

BrPo; EBEV; FaBoTw; HAP; NAEL-2; NOBE; NOBVV;
NoP; OxBSP; PrIm; SCV; WeW

The Impercipient

28 Yet I would bear my shortcomings
With meet tranquility,
But for the charge that blessed things
I'd liefer not have be.
O, doth a bird deprived of wings
Go earth-bound wilfully! (l. 25–30)

EBVV; NAEL-2; PrIm; TrGrPo; WGRP

In Time of "The Breaking of Nations"

29 Only a man harrowing clods
In a slow silent walk
With an old horse that stumbles and nods
Half asleep as they stalk. (l. 1–4)

30 Yonder a maid and her wight
Come whispering by:
War's annals will cloud into night
Ere their story die. (l. 9–12)

BoLoP; CMoP; EBEV; HAP; LiTB; LiTM; MMA; MoAB;
MoBrPo; MoP; NAEL-2; NoAM; NOBE; NoP; OAEL-2;
OBEV; OBWP; PPP; QFR; RB; WeW

The Man He Killed

31 'Yes; quaint and curious war is!
You shoot a fellow down
You'd treat if met where any bar is,
Or help to half-a-crown.' (l. 17–20)

BrPo; CMoP; DL; FaFP; FF; HAP; HeIP; LiTB; LiTM;
MoAB; MoBrPo; NIP; OBWP; RB; WaaP; WeW

The Oxen

32 Christmas Eve, and twelve of the clock.
"Now they are all on their knees," (l. 1–2)

33 "Come; see the oxen kneel,

"In the lonely barton by yonder coomb
Our childhood used to know,"
I should go with him in the gloom,
Hoping it might be so. (l. 12–16)

BoTP; CMoP; EBEV; HAP; InPK; LiTM; MoAB;
MoBrPo; MoP; NoAM; NOBE; OAEL-2; OBCP; OxBTC;
PChr; PPP; RB; SoSe; TOF; WeW

The Roman Road

34 The Roman Road runs straight and bare
As the pale parting-line in hair
Across the heath. (l. 1–3)

35 Uprises there
A mother's form upon my ken,
Guiding my infant steps, as when
We walked that ancient, thoroughfare,
The Roman Road. (l. 11–15)

BrPo; FaBoPP; GoJo; MoBrPo; NOBE

The Ruined Maid

36 whence such fair garments, such prosperi-ty?' —
'O didn't you know I'd been ruined?' said she. (l. 3–4)

37 — 'I wish I had feathers, a fine sweeping gown,
And a delicate face, and could strut about Town!' —
'My dear — a raw country girl, such as you be,
Cannot quite expect that. You ain't ruined,' said she.
(l. 21–24)

BoLoP; BrPo; CMoP; ErPo; FiBHP; HeIP; LiTB; NAEL-
2; NBLV; NOBL; NoP; OxBTC; SCV; TEP; WeW

Satires of Circumstance

38 preacher glides to the vestry-door,
And shuts it, and thinks he is seen no more.

39 re-enact at the vestry-glass
Each pulpit gesture in deft dumb-show
That had moved the congregation so.

BrPo; InPK; MoAB; MoBrPo; SCV

The Self-Unseeing

40 Here is the ancient floor,
Footworn and hollowed and thin
Here was the former door
Where the dead feet walked in. (l. 1–4)

EBEV; HAP; MoBrPo; NOBE; NOBVV; OBNC; PrIm;
RB; WeW

Shut Out That Moon

41 Shut out that stealing moon,
    She wears too much the guise she wore
    Before our lutes were strewn
    With years-deep dust, and names we read
    On a white stone were hewn. (l. 2–6)

BrPo; CMoP; NoAM; NOBE

Snow in the Suburbs

42 Some flakes have lost their way, and grope back
        upward, when
    Meeting those meandering down they turn and descend
        again. (l. 5–6)

43 A sparrow enters the tree,
    Whereon immediately
    A snow lump thrice his own slight size
    Descends on him and showers his head and eyes,
    And overturns him, (l. 9–13)

BoNaP; CMoP; GoJo; MoAB; MoBrPo; OAEL-2; OBMV;
OxBTC; PPP

The Subalterns

44 "Come hither, Son," I heard Death say;
    "I did not will a grave
    Should end thy pilgrimage today,
    But I, too, am a slave!" (l. 13–16)

CMoP; MoAB; MoBrPo; MoP; NoAM; NOBVV; OAEL-2;
PPP; TEP

Thoughts of Phena

45 It may be the more
    That no line of her writing have I,
    Nor a thread of her hair,
    No mark of her late time as dame in her dwelling,
        whereby
    I may picture her there. (l. 20–24)

EBVV; NOBVV; NoP; OxBTC

A Thunderstorm in Town

46 I should have kissed her if the rain
    Had lasted a minute more. (l. 9–10)

BoLoP; EnLoPo; GBL; OxBSP

To an Unborn Pauper Child

47 And such are we —
    Unreasoning, sanguine, visionary —
    That I can hope

Health, love, friends, scope
In full for thee; can dream thou'lt find
Joys seldom yet attained by humankind! (l. 31–36)

FaBoRV; GTBS-P; LiTB; NAs

Under the Waterfall

48 There lies intact that chalice of ours,
    And its presence adds to the rhyme of love
    Persistently sung by the fall above.
    No lip has touched it since his and mine
    In turns therefrom sipped lover's wine." (l. 48–52)

BoLoP; CTC; LiTB; NAEL-2

Weather

49 This is the weather the cuckoo likes,
    And so do I;
    When showers betumble the chestnut spikes,
    And nestlings fly: (l. 1–4)

50 This is the weather the shepherd shuns,
    And so do I;
    When beeches drip in browns and duns,
    And thresh, and ply; (l. 10–13)

BoTP; CH; FaBoCh; FaBV; MoAB; MoBrPo; OBMV; RB;
SeCePo

Wessex Heights

51 In the lowlands I have no comrade, not even the lone
        man's friend — (l. 5)

52 In the towns I am tracked by phantoms having weird
        detective ways — (l. 9)

53 And ghosts then keep their distance; and I know some
        liberty. (l. 32)

CMoP; EBVV; FaBoPP; OAEL-2; OBNC; PoEL-5

MAURICE EVAN HARE (1886–1967)

There once was a man who said, "Damn!"

1 I am
    An engine that moves
    In predestinate grooves,
    I'm not even a 'bus I'm a tram." (l. 2–5)

CenHV; FaBoCo; NOBL; OxBoLi

SIR JOHN HARINGTON   (1561–1612)

Fair, Rich, and Young

1 Fair, rich, and young: how rare is her perfection,
Were it not mingled with one foul infection!
I mean, so proud a heart, so curst a tongue,
As makes her seem nor fair, nor rich, nor young.
                                    (l. 1–4)

ElL; FaBoEE; NIP; SeCePo

Of Treason

2 Treason doth never prosper; what's the reason?
For if it prosper, none dare call it treason. (l. 1–2)

FaBoCo; FaBoEE; FF; FiBHP; InPK; InvP; OxBoLi

JOY HARJO   (b. 1951)

The Woman Hanging from the Thirteenth Floor Window

1 She is the woman hanging from the 13th floor
window. (l. 1–2)

2 Sometimes they are little cats mewing and scratching
at the door, sometimes they are her grandmother's
voice,
and sometimes they are gigantic men of light
whispering
to her to get up, to get up, to get up. (l. 35–38)

3 She thinks of the 4 a.m. lonelinesses that have folded
her up like death, discordant, without logical and
beautiful conclusion. Her teeth break off at the edges.
She would speak. (l. 56–59)

ER; GLP; HATNAP; NOVW

MICHAEL S. HARPER   (b. 1938)

Grandfather

1 as his weight wilts
and he is on a porch
that won't hold my arms,
or the legs of the race run
forwards, or the film
played backwards on his grandson's eyes. (l. 42–47)

CAPP; GeTw; LCAP; TAP

Nightmare Begins Responsibility

2 I place these numbed wrists to the pane
watching white uniforms whisk over
him in the tube-kept
prison
fear what they will do in experiment (l. 1–5)

3 and of my distrusting self
white-doctor-who-breathed-for-him-all-night
say it for two sons gone,
say nightmare, say it loud
panebreaking heartmadness:
nightmare begins responsibility. (l. 24–29)

CAPP; DiL; GeTw; HCAP; LCAP; TAP

We Assume: On the Death of Our Son, Reuben Masai Harper

4 A woman who'd lost her first son
consoled us with an angel gone ahead
to pray for our family —
gone into that sky
seeking oxygen,
gone into autopsy, (l. 21–26)

5 We assume
you did not know we loved you. (l. 29–30)

AmPA; DiL; GeTw; LCAP

BRET HARTE (FRANCIS BRET HARTE) (1836–1902)

Plain Language from Truthful James

1 Which I wish to remark —
And my language is plain —
That for ways that are dark
And for tricks that are vain,
The heathen Chinee is peculiar:
Which the same I would rise to explain. (l. 1–6)

2 In his sleeves, which were long,
He had twenty-four packs, —
Which was coming it strong,
Yet I state but the facts;
And we found on his nails, which were taper,
What is frequent in tapers, — that's wax. (l. 49–54)

AnAmPo; BeLS; BLPA; CenHV; CTC; FaBoBe; FaBoCo;
NOBL; OBAL

The Society upon the Stanislaus

3 I reside at Table Mountain, and my name is Truthful
James;
I am not up to small deceit, or any sinful games;

And I'll tell in simple language what I know about the
  row
That broke up our society upon the Stanislow.

But first I would remark, that it is not a proper plan
For any scientific man to whale his fellow-man,
                                        (l. 1–6)

4 Now, I hold it is not decent for a scientific gent
To say another is an ass — at least, to all intent;
Nor should the individual who happens to be meant
Reply by heaving rocks at him to any great extent.
                                        (l. 21–24)

AA; AnAmPo; BeLS; FaBoCo; OBAL

ROBERT HASS (b. 1941)

Meditation at Lagunitas

1 All the new thinking is about loss.
In this it resembles all the old thinking. (l. 1–2)

2 a word is elegy to what it signifies. (l. 11)

3 Longing, we say, because desire is full
of endless distances. (l. 24–25)

4 There are moments when the body is as numinous
as words, days that are the good flesh continuing
Such tenderness, those afternoons and evenings,
saying blackberry, blackberry, blackberry. (l. 28–31)

AnAn; MAYP; NoP; NPGG

STEPHEN HAWES (1474–1528)

The Pastime of Pleasure

1 O mortal folk, you may behold and see
How I lie here, sometime a mighty knight;
The end of joy and all prosperity
Is death at last, thorough his course and might;
                                        (l. 1–4)

2 in your mind inwardly despise
The brittle world so full of doubleness,
With the vile flesh, and right soon arise
Out of your sleep of mortal heaviness;
Subdue the devil with grace and mekeness, (l. 15–19)

ACP; ChTr; EBEV; FaBoEE; FaBoRV; OBEV; OBSC;
TrGrPo

JOHN MILTON HAY (1838–1905)

Good Luck and Bad

1 Good luck is the gayest of all gay girls;
Long in one place, she will not stay: (l. 1–2)

2 But Madame Bad Luck soberly comes
And stays — no fancy has she for flitting; (l. 5–6)

AnAmPo; FaBoEE; NBLV; OBAL

Jim Bludso of the Prairie Belle

3 Whar have you been for the last three year
That you haven't heard folks tell
How Jimmy Bludso passed in his checks
The night of the Prairie Belle? (l. 5–8)

4 He weren't no saint — but at Jedgment
I'd run my chance with Jim,
'Longside of some pious gentlemen
That wouldn't shook hands with him.
He seen his duty, a dead-sure thing, —
And went for it, thar an' then:
And Christ ain't a-goin' to be too hard
On a man that died for me. (l. 49–56)

AA; AnAmPo; BeLS; FaBoBe; FaFP

Little Breeches

5 I don't pan out on the prophets
An' free-will, an' that sort of thing —
But I b'lieve in God an' the angels,
Ever sence one night last spring. (l. 5–8)

6 We found it at last, an' a little shed
Where they shut up the lamb at night.
We looked in an' seen them huddled thar,
So warm an' sleepy an' white;
An' THAR sot Little Breeches an' chirped,
As peart as ever you see,
"I wants a chaw of terbacky,
An' that's what's the matter of me." (l. 41–48)

AA; AnAmPo; BeLS; FaBoBe

ROBERT EARL HAYDEN (1913–1980)

A Ballad of Remembrance

1 Quadroon mermaids, Afro angels, black saints
balanced upon the switchblades of that air
and sang. (l. 1–3)

2 As well have a talon as a finger, a muzzle as a mouth,
as well have a hollow as a heart. (l. 25–26)

3 Then you arrived, meditative, ironic,
   richly human; and your presence was shore where I
      rested
   released from the hoodoo of that dance, where I spoke
   with my true voice again. (l. 34–37)

4 Mark Van Doren,
   a poem of remembrance, a gift, a souvenir for you.
                                          (l. 43–44)

AmNP; BPo; IDB; PoBA; PoNe

Frederick Douglass

5 this freedom, this liberty, this beautiful
   and terrible thing, needful to man as air,
   usable as earth; (l. 1–3)

6 this man, this Douglass, this former slave, this Negro
   beaten to his knees, exiled, visioning a world
   where none is lonely, none hunted, alien,
   this man, superb in love and logic, this man
   shall be remembered. (l. 7–11)

AmNP; CAPP; CNA; GOA; HCAP; IDB; NIP; PoBA;
PoNe; Son; TTY

Homage to the Empress of the Blues

7 She came out on the stage in yards of pearls, emerging
      like
   a favorite scenic view, flashed her golden smile and
   sang. (l. 5–6)

CNA; HCAP; LCAP; PoBA; PoNe

Middle Passage

8 "10 April 1800 —
   Blacks rebellious. Crew uneasy. Our linguist says
   their moaning is a prayer for death,
   ours and their own. (l. 8–11)

9 Standing to America, bringing home
   black gold, black ivory, black seed. (l. 15–16)

10 Shuttles in the rocking loom of history,
   the dark ships move, the dark ships move,
   their bright ironical names
   like jests of kindness on a murderer's mouth;
                                          (l. 94–97)

11 Voyage through death
   to life upon these shores. (l. 176–177)

AmNP; BPo; IDB; InPS; NoAM; PoBA

Mourning Poem for the Queen of Sunday

12 Lord's lost Him His mockingbird,
   His fancy warbler;
   Satan sweet-talked her,
   four bullets hushed her.
   Who would have thought
   she'd end that way? (l. 1–6)

13 Oh who and oh who will sing Jesus down
   to help with struggling and doing without and being
      colored
   all through blue Monday?
   Till way next Sunday? (l. 10–13)

HCAP; NoAM; NoP; PoBA

Night, Death, Mississippi

14 Time was. Time was.
   White robes like moonlight

   In the sweetgum dark.
   Unbucked that one then
   and him squealing bloody Jesus
   as we cut it off. (l. 11–16)

CAPP; FF; LCAP; VGW

The Night-blooming Cereus

15 the bud packed
   tight with its miracle swayed
   stiffly on breaths
   of air, moved

   as though impelled
   by stirrings within itself. (l. 9–14)

16 tribal sentience
   in the cactus, focused
   energy of will. (l. 38–40)

17 Luna presence,
   foredoomed, already dying,
   it charged the room
   with plangency

   older than human
   cries, (l. 57–62)

CAPP; FB; NoP; NU

O Daedalus, Fly Away Home

18 Night is juba, night is conjo.
   Pretty Malinda, dance with me. (l. 4–5)

HAP; IDB; PoBA; PoNe; WeW

Runagate Runagate

19 Runs falls rises stumbles on from darkness into
    darkness
    and the darkness thicketed with shapes of terror
    and the hunters pursuing and the hounds pursuing
    and the night cold and the night long and the river
    to cross and the jack-muh-lanterns beckoning beckoning
    and blackness ahead (l. 1–6)

20 If you see my Pompey, 30 yrs of age,
    new breeches, plain stockings, negro shoes;
    if you see my Anna, likely young mulatto
    branded E on the right cheek, R on the left,
    catch them if you can and notify subscriber.
                                    (l. 21–25)

21 Harriet Tubman,

    woman of earth, whipscarred,
    a summoning, a shinning (l. 38–40)

22 Midnight Special on a sabre track movering movering,
    first stop Mercy and the last Hallelujah. (l. 69–70)

    BPo; CNA; IDB; InPS; LCAP; PoBA; PoNe

Those Winter Sundays

23 What did I know, what did I know
    of love's austere and lonely offices? (l. 13–14)

    CAPP; CNA; DiL; FF; GrPl; HAP; HCAP; IDB; InPK;
    LCAP; MoP; NIP; NoAM; NoP; PoBA; PPP; SoSe; UnPo;
    WeW

The Whipping

24 My head gripped in bony vise
    of knees, the writhing struggle
    to wrench free, the blows, the fear
    worse than blows that hateful

    Words could bring, the face that I
    no longer knew or loved.... (l. 13–18)

    GrPl; IDB; PoBA; PoE; TW

SEAMUS HEANEY (b. 1939)

Bogland

1 We have no prairies
   To slice a big sun at evening —
   Everywhere the eye concedes to
   Encroaching horizon,

Is wooed into the cyclops' eye
Of a tarn. (l. 1–6)

2 An astounding crate full of air. (l. 12)

3 The bogholes might be Atlantic seepage.
   The wet centre is bottomless. (l. 27–28)

   FaBCIP; HeIP; IPY; NoAM; NOIV; NoP

Casualty

4 At closing time would go
   In waders and peaked cap
   Into the showery dark,
   A dole-kept breadwinner
   But a natural for work. (l. 11–15)

5 It was a day of cold
   Raw silence, wind-blown
   Surplice and soutane:
   Rained-on, flower-laden
   Coffin after coffin
   Seemed to float from the door (l. 47–52)

6 the habitual
   Slow consolation
   Of a dawdling engine, (l. 92–94)

7 smile
   As you find a rhythm
   Working you, slow mile by mile,
   Into your proper haunt
   Somewhere, well out, beyond ... (l. 105–109)

8 Dawn-sniffing revenant,
   Plodder through midnight rain,
   Question me again. (l. 110–112)

   FaBoPV; IPY; NAEL-2; PoE

Death of a Naturalist

9 and wait and watch until
   The fattening dots burst into nimble-
   Swimming tadpoles. (l. 13–15)

10 Right down the dam gross-bellied frogs were cocked
    On sods; their loose necks pulsed like sails. Some
        hopped:
    The slap and plop were obscene threats. Some sat
    Poised like mud grenades, their blunt heads farting.
                                    (l. 27–30)

    HAP; NoAM; OxBC; WeW

Digging

11 By God, the old man could handle a spade.
    Just like his old man. (l. 15–16)

12 The cold smell of potato mould, the squelch and slap
Of soggy peat, the curt cuts of an edge
Through living roots awaken in my head.
But I've no spade to follow men like them. (l. 25–28)

13 The squat pen rests.
I'll dig with it. (l. 30–31)

BIrV; CIP; InPS; IPY; NAEL-2; TwCP

Docker

14 God is a foreman with certain definite views
Who orders life in shifts of work and leisure.
(l. 10–11)

15 He sits, strong and blunt as a Celtic cross,
Clearly used to silence and an armchair:
Tonight the wife and children will be quiet
At slammed door and smoker's cough in the hall.
(l. 13–16)

HeIP; MoP; NOIV; TW

Punishment

16 Little adulteress,
before they punished you

you were flaxen-haired,
undernourished, and your
tar-black face was beautiful. (l. 23–27)

17 who would connive
in civilized outrage
yet understand the exact
and tribal, intimate revenge. (l. 41–44)

FaBoPV; InPS; NAEL-2; NoAM; NoP

Requiem for the Croppies

18 Until, on Vinegar Hill, the fatal conclave.
Terraced thousands died, shaking scythes at cannon.
The hillside blushed, soaked in our broken wave.
They buried us without shroud or coffin
And in August the barley grew up out of the grave.
(l. 10–14)

BIrV; CIP; FaBCIP; FaBoMo; OBWP

The Skunk

19 Up, black, striped and damasked like the chasuble
At a funeral mass, the skunk's tail
Paraded the skunk. (l. 1–3)

20 After eleven years I was composing
Love-letters again, broaching the word 'wife'
Like a stored cask, (l. 9–11)

FaBCIP; NAEL-2; OxBC; PoE

The Strand at Lough Beg

21 What blazed ahead of you? A faked road block?
The red lamp swung, the sudden brakes and stalling
Engine, voices, heads hooded and the cold-nosed gun?
(l. 9–11)

AnAn; CIP; NoAM; NoP; OBWP

The Tollund Man

22 Some day I will go to Aarhus
To see his peat-brown head,
The mild pods of his eye-lids,
His pointed skin cap. (l. 1–4)

BIrV; CIP; EBEV; FaBCIP; FaBoMo; IPY; NoP; TEP

ANTHONY HECHT (b. 1923)
Birdwatchers of America

1 It's all very well to dream of a dove that saves,
Picasso's or the Pope's
The one that annually coos in Our Lady's ear
Half the world's hopes, (l. 1–4)

2 The air was clear. He seemed in ultimate peace

Except that he had no eyes. Rigid and bright
Upon the forehead, furred
With a light frost, crouched an outrageous bird.
(l. 21–24)

HoPM; NoAM; NOBA; PPP

The Dover Bitch

3 So there stood Matthew Arnold and this girl
With the cliffs of England crumbling away behind
them,
And he said to her, "Try to be true to me,
And I'll do the same for you, for things are bad
All over, etc., etc." (l. 1–5)

4 But all the time he was talking she had in mind
The notion of what his whiskers would feel like
On the back of her neck. (l. 9–11)

BXAP; MAT; NBLV; NePoEA-2; NIP; NOBA; NOBL;
OBAL; PPP; UnPo; VGW

The End of the Weekend

5 an endless wind
Whips at the headstones of the dead and wails
In the trees for all who have and have not sinned.
(l. 8—10)

6 The eventual shapes of all our formless prayers,
This dark, this cabin of loose imaginings,
Wind, lake, lip, everything awaits
The slow unloosening of her underthings. (l. 13—16)

7 A great black presence beats its wings in wrath.
Above the boneyard burn its golden eyes.
Some small grey fur is pulsing in its grip. (l. 24—26)

FaBoMo; HAP; LiTM; NePoEA-2; SM; WeW

The Feast of Stephen

8 The coltish horseplay of the locker room,
Moist with steam of the tiled shower stalls, (l. 1—2)

9 If the heart has its reasons, perhaps the body
Has its own lumbering sort of carnal spirit,
Felt in the tingling bruises of collision,
And known to captains as esprit de corps. (l. 15—18)

10 Mens sana in men's sauna, in the flush
Of health and toilets, private and corporal glee,
(l. 21—22)

11 Think of those barren places where men gather
To act in the terrible name of rectitude,
Of acned shame, punk's pride, muscle or turf
The bully's thin superiority. (l. 29—32)

HAP; KS; NoAM; NoP

It Out-Herods Herod. Pray You, Avoid It

12 And in their fairy tales
The warty giant and witch
Get sealed in doorless jails
And the match-girl strikes it rich. (l. 5—8)

13 And that their sleep be sound
I say this childermas
Who could not, at one time,
Have saved them from the gas. (l. 33—36)

CoAP; NIP; NoAM; NOBA; OxBC

"More Light! More Light!"

14 Composed in the Tower before his execution
These moving verses, and being brought at that time
Painfully to the stake, submitted, declaring thus:

"I implore my God to witness that I have made no
crime." (l. 1—4)

15 No prayers or incense rose up in those hours
Which grew to be years, and every day came mute
Ghosts from the ovens, sitting through crisp air,
And settled upon his eyes in a black soot. (l. 29—32)

CoAP; HAP; NePoEA-2; NoAM; NOBA; NoP; OBWP; RB;
SM; SoSe; TwCP; UnPo; VGW; VWA

Samuel Sewall

16 Samuel Sewall, in a world of wigs,
Flouted opinion in his personal hair;
For foppery he gave not any figs,
But in his right and honor took the air. (l. 1—4)

LiTM; NBLV; NePoEA; PoRA; TwCP

FELICIA DOROTHEA HEMANS
(1783—1835)

Casabianca

1 The boy stood on the burning deck,
Whence all but he had fled;
The flame that lit the battle's wreck,
Shone round him o'er the dead.

Yet beautiful and bright he stood,
As born to rule the storm;
A creature of heroic blood,
A proud though childlike form. (l. 1—8)

2 There came a burst of thunder sound;
The boy—Oh! where was he?
—Ask of the winds, that far around
With fragments strewed the sea;— (l. 32—35)

BeLS; BLPA; FaBoBe; FaBoPa; FaFP; FaPON; FPL;
WBLP

The Landing of the Pilgrim Fathers

3 The breaking waves dashed high
On a stern and rock-bound coast, (l. 1—2)

4 And the heavy night hung dark
The hills and waters o'er,
When a band of exiles moored their bark
On the wild New England shore. (l. 5—8)

5 What sought they thus afar?
Bright jewels of the mine?
The wealthy of seas, the spoils of war?—
They sought a faith's pure shrine!

Ay, call it holy ground,
The soil where first they trod;
They have left unstained what there they found, —
Freedom to worship God. (l. 33–40)

BeLS; BLPA; BoTP; FaBoBe; FaBV; FaFP; FaPON; GN;
OHIP; OPP; PAH; WBLP; WPE

WILLIAM ERNEST HENLEY
(1849–1903)

England, My England

1 What have I done for you,
England, my England?
What is there I would not do,
England, my own? (l. 1–4)

BLPL; MoBrPo; OBEV; PoLF

Falmouth

2 O, there's a wind a-blowing, a-blowing from the west,
And that of all the winds is the one I like the best,
For it blows at our backs, and it shakes our pennon
   free,
And it soon will blow us home to the old countrie.
                                    (l. 19–22)

3 For it's home, dearie, home — it's home I want to be.
Our topsails are hoisted, and we'll away to sea.
O, the oak and the ash and the bonnie birken tree
They're all growing green in the old countrie.
                                    (l. 23–26)

GN; MoBrPo; MOS; PoLF

Madam Life's a Piece in Bloom

4 Madam Life's a piece in bloom
Death goes dogging everywhere:
She's the tenant of the room,
He's the ruffian on the stair. (l. 1–4)

EBVV; MoBrPo; NAEL-2; NOBVV; OBD; OPOP; TrGrPo

Villon's Straight Tip to All Cross Coves

5 It's up the spout and Charley Wag
With wipes and tickers and what not
Until the squeezer nips your scrag,
Booze and the blowens cop the lot. (l. 25–28)

AWP; CenHV; FaBoCo; InvP; NA; SeCePo

HENRY VIII, KING OF ENGLAND
(1491–1547)

Pastime

1 Pastime with good company
I love and shall, until I die.
Grudge who list, but none deny!
So God be pleased, thus live will I. (l. 1–4)

2 My heart is set.
All goodly sport
For my comfort
Who shall me let? (l. 7–10)

CTC; EBEV; OBSC; TrGrPo

GEORGE HERBERT (1593–1633)

Aaron

1 Holinesse on the head,
Light and perfections on the breast,
Harmonious bells below, raising the dead
To leade them unto life and rest.
Thus are true Aarons drest. (l. 1–5)

2 Christ is my onely head,
My alone onely heart and breast,
My onely musick, striking me ev'n dead; (l. 16–18)

MeLP; MePo; OAEL-1; OBS

Affliction

3 At first thou gav'st me milk and sweetnesses;
I had my wish and way:
My dayes were straw'd with flow'rs and happinesse;
There was no month but May.
But with my yeares sorrow did twist and grow,
And made a partie unawares for wo. (l. 19–24)

4 Thus thinne and lean without a fence or friend,
I was blown through with ev'ry storm and winde.
                                    (l. 35–36)

5 Now I am here, what thou wilt do with me
None of my books will show:
I reade, and sigh, and wish I were a tree; (l. 55–57)

6 Ah my deare God! though I am clean forgot, Let me not
   love thee, if I love thee not. (l. 65–66)

JCP; LiTB; MeLP; MePo; NAEL-1; NOBE; NoP; OBS;
SeCP

The Altar

7 A broken altar, Lord, thy servant rears,
   Made of a heart, and cemented with tears:
   Whose parts are as thy hand did frame;
   No workman's tool hath touched the same. (l. 1–4)

8 That, if I chance to hold my peace,
   These stones to praise thee may not cease.
   Oh let thy blessed sacrifice be mine,
   And sanctify this altar to be thine. (l. 13–16)

   HoPM; InPS; JCP; NAEL-1; OAEL-1; SeCP; SeCV-1;
   TrCP; TrGrPo

Artillerie

9 I, who had heard of music in the spheres,
   But not of speech in stars, began to muse:
   But turning to my God, whose ministers
   The stars and all things are; If I refuse,
   Dread Lord, said I, so oft my good;
   Then I refuse not ev'n with blood
   To wash away my stubborn thought:
   For I will do or suffer what I ought. (l. 9–16)

   InPS; NoP; PoEL-2; SeCV-1

Bitter-sweet

10 Ah my dear angry Lord,
    Since thou dost love, yet strike;
    Cast down, yet help afford;
    Sure I will do the like. (l. 1–4)

    NOBE; NoP; OxBSP; TrPWD

Church Monuments

11 thou mayst know,
    That flesh is but the glass, which holds the dust
    That measures all our time; (l. 19–21)

    HAP; JCP; NAEL-1; NOCV; NoP; OAEL-1; PoE; QFR

The Church-Floor

12 Mark you the floore? that square & speckled stone,
    Which looks so firm and strong,
    Is Patience: (l. 1–3)

13 th' other black and grave, wherewith each one
    Is checker'd all along,
    Humilitie: (l. 4–6)

14 gentle rising, which on either hand
    Leads to the Quire above,
    Is Confidence: (l. 7–9)

15 But the sweet cement, which in one sure band
    Ties the whole frame, is Love
    And Charitie. (l. 10–12)

16 Sometimes Death, puffing at the doore,
    Blows all the dust about the floore:
    But while he thinks to spoil the room, he sweeps.
    Blest be the Architect, whose art
    Could build so strong in a weak heart. (l. 16–20)

    EBEV; MeLP; OAEL-1; OBS; SeCePo

The Collar

17 I struck the board, and cried, 'No more,
    I will abroad!
    What? shall I ever sigh and pine?
    My lines and life are free, free as the road,
    Loose as the wind, as large as store.
    Shall I be still in suit? (l. 1–6)

18 But as I raved and grew more fierce and wild
    At every word,
    Me thoughts, I heard one calling, 'Child!'
    And I replied, 'My Lord.' (l. 33–36)

    AWP; BLPL; EaLo; EBEV; HAP; HeIP; InPS; JCP; LiTB;
    MeLP; MePc; NAEL-2; NOBE; NOCV; NoP; OAEL-1;
    OBS; OBWVE; PoE; PoEL-2; PoRA; PPP; SCV; SeCePo;
    SeCP; SeCV-1; TEP; TOF; TrGrPo; WeW

Death

19 Death, thou wast once an uncouth hideous thing,
    Nothing but bones,
    The sad effect of sadder grones;
    Thy mouth was open, but thou couldst not sing.
                                            (l. 1–4)

20 But since our Saviours death did put some bloud
    Into thy face;
    Thou art grown fair and full of grace,
    Much in request, much sought for as a good.
                                            (l. 13–16)

    JCP; MeFo; NAEL-1; NoP; OBS; SeCP; SeCV-1

Denial

21 my soul lay out of sight,
    Untuned, unstrung; (l. 21–22)

22 O cheer and tune my heartless breast,
    Defer no time;
    That so thy favours granting my request,
    They and my mind may chime,
    And mend my rhyme. (l. 26–30)

    JCP; MePo; NAEL-1; NOBE; NoP; OAEL-1; PoEL-2;
    TOF

Discipline

23 Who can 'scape his bow?
That which wrought on thee, (l. 25–26)

24 Throw away thy rod:
Though man frailties hath,
Thou art God:
Throw away thy wrath. (l. 29–32)

FPL; LiTB; MeLP; MePo; NAEL-1; NOBE; NOCV; NoP;
OBEV; OBS; PoLF; SeCePo; TrGrPo

Easter

25 I got me flowers to straw thy way;
I got me boughs off many a tree;
But thou wast up by break of day,
And brought'st thy sweets along with thee. (l. 1–4)

BoTP; CH; FaBoCh; NAEL-1; NOBE; OBEV; OBS;
OHIP; TrGrPo

Easter Wings

26 Lord, who createdst man in wealth and store,
Though foolishly he lost the same,
Decaying more and more, (l. 1–3)

27 My tender age in sorrow did begin:
And still with sicknesses and shame
Thou did'st so punish sin,
That I became
Most thin.
With Thee
Let me combine
And feel this day Thy victory; (l. 11–18)

HAP; HeIP; InPK; InPS; LiTB; MeLP; MePo; NAEL-1;
NIP; NoP; OAEL-1; OBS; PoE; PoEL-2; PPP; SeCP;
TEP; TOF; TrCP; WeW

The Elixir

28 A man that looks on glass
On it may stay his eye;
Or, if he pleaseth, through it pass
And then the heaven espy. (l. 5–8)

BoTP; FaBoCh; GN; NoP; OHIP; SeCV-1; TrGrPo;
WGRP

Employment

29 Man is no starre, but a quick coal
Of mortall fire:
Who blows it not, nor doth controll
A faint desire,
Lets his own ashes choke his soul. (l. 6–10)

30 Life is a businesse, not good cheer;
Ever in warres.
The sunne still shineth there or here,
Whereas the starres
Watch an advantage to appeare. (l. 16–20)

JCP; OBS; SeCP; TEP

The Flower

31 These are thy wonders, Lord of power,
Killing and quickning, bringing down to hell
And up to heaven in an houre;
Making a chiming of a passing-bell. (l. 15–18)

32 Thy word is all, if we could spell. (l. 21)

33 These are thy wonders, Lord of love,
To make us see we are but flowers that glide.
Which when we once can finde and prove,
Thou hast a garden for us where to bide. (l. 43–46)

AWP; ELP; FaBoRV; JCP; MePo; NAEL-1; NOBE;
NOCV; NoP; OBS; PoEL-2; SeCP; SeCV-1

The Forerunners

34 The harbingers are come. See, see their mark:
White is their color, and behold my head.
But must they have my brain? Must they dispark
Those sparkling notions, which therein were bred?
Must dullness turn me to a clod?
Yet have they left me, Thou art still my God. (l. 1–6)

35 Lovely enchanting language, sugar-cane,
Honey of roses, wither wilt thou fly? (l. 19–20)

36 True beauty dwells on high: ours is a flame
But borrowed thence to light us thither.
Beauty and beauteous words should go together.
(l. 28–30)

37 Go, birds of spring: let winter have his fee;
Let a bleak paleness chalk the door,
So all within be livelier than before. (l. 34–36)

JCP; MePo; NAEL-1; NoP; TOF

Heaven

38 Thou Echo, thou art mortal, all men know. (l. 3)

39 Light, joy, and leisure; but shall they persever?
Echo Ever. (l. 19–20)

SeCP; TrCP; TrGrPo; TTTS

Jordan

40 When first my lines of heavenly joys made mention,
    Such was their luster, they did so excel,
    That I sought out quaint words and trim invention;
    My thoughts began to burnish, sprout, and swell,
    Curling with metaphors a plain intention,
    Decking the sense as if it were to sell.

41 I often blotted what I had begun:
    This was not quick enough, and that was dead.

42 As flames do work and wind when they ascend,
    So did I weave myself into the sense.

43 'How wide is all this long pretense!
    There is in love a sweetness ready penned,
    Copy out only that, and save expense."

    MePo; NAEL-1; OAEL-1; OBS; OBWVE; PPP; SeCP

44 Who says that fictions only and false hair
    Become a verse? Is there in truth no beauty?

45 Must all be veiled, while he that reads, divines,
    Catching the sense at two removes?

46 I envy no man's nightingale or spring;
    Nor let them punish me with loss of rhyme,
    Who plainly say, My God, My King.

    HAP; InPS; JCP; LiTB; MeLP; MePo; NAEL-1; NOCV;
    NoP; OAEL-1; OBS; PoE; PoEL-2; PPP; SeCP; TEP;
    TrCP

Life

47 Farewell deare flowers, sweetly your time ye spent,
    Fit, while ye liv'd, for smell or ornament,
    And after death for cures.
    I follow straight without complaints or grief,
    Since if my sent be good, I care not, if
    It be as short as yours. (l. 13–18)

    FaBoRV; JCP; LiTB; MeLP; MePo; NoP; OBS; SeCP;
    SeCV-1

Love

48 Love bade me welcome: yet my soul drew back,
    Guilty of dust and sin.
    But quick-eyed Love, observing me grow slack
    From my first entrance in,
    Drew nearer to me, sweetly questioning,
    If I lacked any thing. (l. 1–6)

49 'You must sit down,' says Love,' and taste my meat:
    So I did sit and eat. (l. 17–18)

    AWP; CH; ChTr; EBEV; FaBV; HeIP; InPK; JCP; LiTB;
    MAT; MeLP; MePo; NAEL-1; NOBE; NOCV; NoP;
    OAEL-1; OBEV; OBS; OBWVE; PoEL-2; PoLF; PPP; Prf;
    SCV; SeCePo; SeCP; SeCV-1; TEP; TOF; TrCP; TrGrPo;
    WeW

Man

50 Man is ev'ry thing,
    And more: (l. 7–8)

51 Reason and speech we onely bring. (l. 10)

52 Man is all symmetrie,
    Full of proportions, one limbe to another, (l. 13–14)

53 Each part may call the furthest, brother:
    For head with foot hath private amitie,
    And both with moons and tides. (l. 16–18)

    MePo; NAEL-1; NoP; PoEL-2; SeCP; SeCV-1; TrGrPo;
    TrPWD

Peace

54 At length I met a reverend good old man, (l. 19)

55 "There was a Prince of old
    At Salem dwelt, who lived with good increase
    Of flock and fold.

    He sweetly lived; yet sweetness did not save
    His life from foes. (l. 22–26)

56 virtue lies therein,
    A secret virtue bringing peace and mirth
    By flight of sin. (l. 34–36)

57 Take of this grain, which in my garden grows, (l. 37)

58 that repose
    And peace, which everywhere
    With so much earnestness you do pursue,
    Is only there. (l. 39–42)

    AWP; ChTr; ELP; NOCV; TEP

The Pearl

59 I know the wayes of learning; both the head
    And pipes that feed the presse, and make it runne;
    (l. 1–2)

60 Both th' old discoveries, and the new-found seas,
    The stock and surplus, cause and historie:
    All these stand open, or I have the keyes:
    Yet I love thee. (l. 7–10)

    EBEV; HAP; JCP; MePo; NOCV; OAEL-1; PoEL-2; SeCP;
    SeCV-1

The Pulley

61 When God at first made man,
    Having a glass of blessings standing by,
    "Let us," said He, "pour on him all we can:

Let the world's riches, which dispersed lie,
Contract into a span." (l. 1–5)

62 When almost all was out, God made a stay,
Perceiving that alone of all His treasure
Rest in the bottom lay. (l. 8–10)

63 "Yet let him keep the rest,
But keep them with repining restlessness:
Let him be rich and weary, that at least,
If goodness lead him not, yet weariness
May toss him to My breast." (l. 16–20)

AWP; EaLo; GTBS; GTBS-P; HAP; HeIP; InPK; InPS;
LiTB; MePo; Mes; NAEL-1; NOBE; NOCV; NoP; OAEL-
1; OBEV; OBS; PPP; PrIm; SeCP; SeCV-1; TEP; TrGrPo

The Quip

64 Yet when the houre of thy designe
To answer these fine things shall come,
Speak not at large, say, I am thine;
And then they have their answer home. (l. 21–24)

JCP; LiTB; OBS; SeCP; SeCV-1

The Temper

65 Whether I flie with angels, fall with dust,
Thy hands made both, and I am there:
Thy power and love, my love and trust
Make one place ev'rywhere. (l. 25–28)

MePo; NOCV; NoP; OBS; PoEL-2

The Temple

66 Prayer the Churches banquet, Angels age,
Gods breath in man returning to his birth,
The soul in paraphrase, heart in pilgrimage,
The Christian plummet sounding heav'n and earth;
(l. 1–4)

67 The six-daies world-transposing in an houre,
A kinde of tune, which all things heare and fear;
(l. 7–8)

68 Church-bels beyond the starres heard, the souls bloud,
The land of spices; something understood. (l. 13–14)

BLPL; EBEV; ELP; InPS; JCP; MePo; NAEL-1; NOBE;
NoP; OAEL-1; OBS; OBWVE; PoE; PoEL-2; SeCV-1;
Son; TOF

69 Having been tenant long to a rich Lord,
Not thriving, I resolved to be bold,
And make a suit unto him, to afford
A new small-rented lease, and cancel th' old. (l. 1–4)

70 They told me there, that he was lately gone
About some land, which he had dearly bought
Long since on earth, to take possession. (l. 6–8)

71 At length I heard a ragged noise and mirth
Of thieves and murderers: there I him espied
Who straight, Your suit is granted,said, and died.
(l. 12–14)

EaLo; FF; HAP; InPK; InPS; JCP; LiTB; MeLP; MePo;
NAEL-1; NOBE; NOCV; NoP; OBS; PoE; SCV; SeCP;
SeCV-1; Son; SoSe; TEP; TrCP; WeW

Virtue

72 all must die.

Only a sweet and virtuous soul,
Like seasoned timber, never gives;
But though the whole world turn to coal,
Then chiefly lives. (l. 12–16)

AWP; CH; ELP; FaBoRV; HAP; HeIP; InPS; InvP; JCP;
MeLP; MePo; NAEL-1; NOBE; NOCV; NoP; OAEL-1;
OBD; OBEV; OBS; PoE; PoRA; PPP; SeCP; SeCV-1;
SoSe; TEP; TrGrPo; WGRP

The Windows

73 Lord, how can man preach thy eternall word?
He is a brittle crazie glasse:
Yet in thy temple thou dost him afford
This glorious and transcendent place,
To be a window, through thy grace. (l. 1–5)

MeLP; NAEL-1; NOCV; NoP; OBS; PoE; SeCP; SeCV-1;
TrCP

A Wreath

74 A wreathed garland of deserved praise,
Of praise deserved, unto Thee I give,
I give to Thee, who knowest all my ways,
My crooked winding ways, wherein I live, (l. 1–4)

75 life is straight,
Straight as a line, and ever tends to Thee, (l. 5–6)

76 Give me simplicity, that I may live,
So live and like, that I may know Thy ways,
Know them and practise them: then shall I give
For this poor wreath, give Thee a crown of praise.
(l. 9–12)

JCP; OAEL-1; OxBSP; SeCP

EDWARD HERBERT, 1ST BARON HERBERT OF CHERBURY (1583–1648)

Elegy over a Tomb

1 Where all the beauties that those ashes owed

Are now bestowed? (l. 11–12)

2 Tell us, alas, that cannot tell our grief,
Or hope relief. (l. 35–36)

ElL; MeLP; MePo; NOBE; OBEV; OBS; OBWVE;
PoEL-2; QFR

An Ode, upon a Question Moved, Whether Love Should Continue Forever?

3 Having interr'd her Infant-birth,
The watry ground that late did mourn,
Was strew'd with flow'rs for the return
Of the wish'd Bridegroom of the earth. (l. 1–4)

4 Only if loves fire with the breath
Of life be kindled, I doubt,
With our last air 'twill be breath'd out,
And quenched with the cold of death. (l. 49–52)

JCP; MeLP; MePo; NOBE; OBS; SeCP

To His Watch, When He Could Not Sleep

5 making what's new
Ill and good, old, for as we die in you,
You die in Time, Time in Eternity. (l. 10–12)

JCP; MePo; NOBE; PoEL-2

OLIVER HERFORD (1863–1935)

The Chimpanzee

1 Children, behold the Chimpanzee:
He sits on the ancestral tree
From which we sprang in ages gone. (l. 1–3)

CenHV; FaBV; FiBHP; NA

The Elf and the Dormouse

2 Sudden the wee Elf
Smiled a wee smile,

Tugged till the toadstool
Toppled in two.
Holding it over him
Gaily he flew. (l. 15–20)

AA; FaBoBe; FaPON; OnMSP; RHPC

I Heard a Bird Sing

3 "We are nearer to Spring
Than we were in September,"
I heard a bird sing
In the dark of December. (l. 5–8)

NTCP; PDV; PoLF; RHPC

ROBERT HERRICK (1591–1674)

The Argument of His Book

1 I sing of brooks, of blossoms, birds and bowers,
Of April, May, of June and July-flowers;
I sing of May-poles, hock-carts, wassails, wakes,
Of bridegrooms, brides and of their bridal cakes;
I write of youth, of love, and have access
By these to sing of cleanly wantonness; (l. 1–6)

AWP; CaPo; EBEV; HAP; HeIP; InvP; JCP; NAEL-1;
NoP; OAEL-1; OBS; PoE; PoEL-3; PoRA; SeCePo; SeCP;
SeCV-1; TEP; TrGrPo; TTTS

The Bad Season Makes the Poet Sad

2 But if that Golden Age would come again,
And Charles here rule as he before did reign; (l. 7–8)

3 I should delight to have my curls half drowned
In Tyrian dews, and head with roses crowned,
And once more yet (ere I am laid out dead)
Knock at a star with my exalted head. (l. 11–14)

CaPo; LiTB; NAEL-1; PrIm

Ceremonies for Christmas

4 My merrie, merrie boyes,
The Christmas Log to the firing; (l. 2–3)

GN; OBCP; OHIP; TEP

Cherry-ripe

5 'Cherry-ripe, ripe, ripe', I cry,
'Full and fair ones; come and buy': (l. 1–2)

CaPo; CH; ELP; OBEV; SeCV-1; TEP

Corinna's Going a-Maying

6 Rise and put on your foliage, and be seen
To come forth, like the springtime, fresh and green,
(l. 15–16)

7 Many a kiss, both odd and even;
Many a glance, too, has been sent
From out the eye, love's firmament;
Many a jest told of the keys betraying
This night, and locks picked; yet we're not a-Maying!
(l. 62–67)

BoNaP; CaPo; GN; HAP; InPS; JCP; NAEL-1; NIP;
NOBE; NoP; OAEL-1; OBEV; OBS; PoE; PoEL-3; PPP;
PrIm; SeCP; SeCV-1; TEP; TrGrPo

Delight in Disorder

8 A sweet disorder in the dress
Kindles in clothes a wantonness:
A lawn about the shoulders thrown
Into a fine distraction:
An erring lace, which here and there
Enthralls the crimson stomacher:
A cuff neglectful, and thereby
Ribbands to flow confusedly:
A winning wave (deserving note)
In the tempestuous petticoat:
A careless shoestring, in whose tie
I see a wild civility:
Do more bewitch me than when art
Is too precise in every part. (l. 1–14)

AWP; BLPL; CaPo; EBEV; EnLoPo; ErPo; FaBV; FF;
GTBS; GTBS-P; HAP; HeIP; InPK; InPS; JCP; LiTB;
NAEL-1; NIP; NOBE; NoP; OAEL-1; OBEV; OBS; PoE;
PoRA; PPP; PrIm; SeCePo; SeCP; SeCV-1; TEP; TrGrPo;
WeW

Dreams

9 Here we are all, by day; by night we are hurled
By dreams, each one into a several world. (l. 1–2)

CaPo; HAP; NAEL-1; OxBSP

An Epitaph upon a Virgin

10 Or a sigh of such as bring
Cowslips for her covering. (l. 5–6)

CaPo; FaBoEE; OxBoLi; PoEL-3; SeCV-1

Grace for a Child

11 Here a little child I stand,
Heaving up my either hand; (l. 1–2)

12 For a Benizon to fall
On our meat, and on us all. (l. 5–6)

AWP; BoTP; ChTr; EaLo; FaBoCh; FaPON; GoJo; HeIP;
InPS; InvP; MoShBr; NAEL-1; OBEV; OBS; OxBChV;
PoE; SeCV-1; TrGrPo

Here a pretty baby lies

13 Here a pretty Baby lies
Sung asleep with Lullabies:
Pray be silent, and not stirre
Th' easie earth that covers her. (l. 1–4)

OBEV; OBS; SeCV-1; TrGrPo

His Farewell to Sack

14 or the warm soft side
Of the resigning yet resisting bride.
The kiss of virgins first-fruits of the bed;
Soft speech, smooth touch, the lips, the maidenhead;
These and a thousand sweets could never be
So near or dear as thou wast once to me. (l. 5–10)

15 O thou, the drink of gods and angels! Wine (l. 11)

16 'Tis not Apollo can, or those thrice three
Castalian sisters sing, if wanting thee.
Horace, Anacreon both had lost their fame.
Had'st thou not filled them with thy fire and flame.
(l. 29–32)

17 Let my muse
Fail of thy former helps, and only use
Her inadulterate strength. What's done by me
Hereafter shall smell of the lamp, not thee. (l. 51–54)

CaPo; NAEL-1; SeCP; SeCV-1

His Grange, or Private Wealth

18 A Cat
I keep, that playes about my House,
Grown fat,
With eating many a miching Mouse.
To these
A Trasy I do keep, whereby
I please
The more my rurall privacie:
Which are
But toyes, to give my heart some ease:
Where care
None is, slight things do lightly please. (l. 21–32)

CaPo; FM; GoJo; SeCV-1

His Litany to the Holy Spirit

19 In the hour of my distress,
When temptations me oppress,
And when I my sins confess,
Sweet Spirit comfort me! (l. 1–4)

20 When the tempter me pursueth
   With the sins of all my youth,
   And half damns me with untruth,
   Sweet Spirit, comfort me!' (l. 37–40)

BLPL; ELP; JCP; OBEV; OBS; PoLF; QFR; SeCePo;
SeCV-1; TEP

His Poetry His Pillar

21 Onely a little more
   I have to write,
   Then I'll give o'er,
   And bid the world Good-night. (l. 1–4)

22 O time that cut'st down all!
   And scarce leav'st here
   Memoriall
   Of any men that were. (l. 9–12)

CaPo; JCP; OBS; QFR; SeCP

His Prayer to Ben Jonson

23 When I a verse shall make,
   Know I have prayed thee,
   For old religion's sake,
   Saint Ben, to aid me. (l. 1–4)

CaPo; JCP; NAEL-1; NoP; OBS; OxBoLi; OxBSP;
SeCV-1; TrGrPo

His Return to London

24 O native country, repossessed by thee!
   For, rather than I'll to the West return,
   I'll beg of thee first here to have mine urn.
   Weak I am grown, and must in short time fall;
   Give thou my sacred relics burial. (l. 16–20)

CaPo; FaBoPP; FF; NAEL-1

The Hock-Cart, or Harvest Home

25 Feed him ye must, whose food fills you.
   And that this pleasure is like raine,
   Not sent ye for to drowne your paine,
   But for to make it spring againe. (l. 52–55)

CaPo; EBEV; FaBoPV; JCP; NAEL-1; OBS; SeCP;
SeCV-1

The Lilly in a Christal

26 You have beheld a smiling Rose
   When Virgins hands have drawn
   O'r it a Cobweb-Lawne:

And here, you see, this Lilly shows,
   Tomb'd in a Christal stone,
   More faire in this transparent case,
   Than when it grew alone;
   And had but single grace. (l. 1–8)

27 Thus let this Christal'd Lilliebe
   A Rule, how far to teach,
   Your nakednesse must reach:
   And that, no further, than we see
   Those glaring colours laid
   By Arts wise hand, but to this end
   They sho'd obey a shade;
   Lest they too far extend. (l. 41–48)

NAEL-1; NAEL-1; NoP; PoEL-3; SeCePo; SeCP

Love Me Little, Love Me Long

28 Love me little, love me long,
   Is the burden of my song: (l. 1–2)

BLPA; CaPo ElL; FaBoBe; FaFP; NoP

Lovers How They Come and Part

29 And air-like leave no pression to be seen
   Where'er they met, or parting place has been. (l. 7–8)

GBL; OxBoLi; OxBSP; PoEL-3

The Mad Maid's Song

30 Ah woe is me, woe, woe is me,
   Alack and welladay!
   For pity, sir, find out that bee
   Which bore my love away. (l. 9–12)

AWP; CaPo; CH; EnLoPo; OAEL-1; OBEV; SeCV-1;
TrGrPo; WiR

A Meditation for His Mistress

31 You are the Queen all flowers among,
   But die you must (faire Maid) ere long,
   As He, the maker of this Song. (l. 19–21)

CaPo; JCP; NOBE; OBEV; OBS; SeCP

The Night-Piece, to Julia

32 Her eyes the glow-worm lend thee,
   The shooting stars attend thee; (l. 1–2)

33 And when I shall meet,
Thy silv'ry feet
My soul I'll pour into thee. (l. 18–20)

BoTP; CaPo; CH; ELP; InvP; JCP; LiTB; NAEL-1; NoP;
OAEL-1; OBEV; OBS; PoE; PoEL-3; PoRA; SeCP;
SeCV-1; TEP

A Nuptial Song, or Epithalamie, on Sir Clipseby Crew and His Lady

34 See where she comes, and smell how all the street,
Breathes vineyards and pomegranates: oh, how sweet!
As a fired altar is each stone,
Perspiring pounded cinnamon.
The phoenix-nest,
Built up of odours, burneth in her breast.
Who therein would not consume
His soul to ash-heaps in that rich perfume, (l. 21–28)

35 And to your more bewitching, see the proud,
Plump bed bear up, and swelling like a cloud,
Tempting the two too modest; can
Ye see it brustle like a swan,
And you be cold
To meet it when it woos and seems to fold
The arms to hug you? Throw, throw
Yourselves into the mighty overflow
Of that white pride, and drown
The night with you in floods of down. (l. 111–120)

CaPo; JCP; PoEL-3; SeCP; SeCV-1

An Ode for Ben Jonson

36 Where we such clusters had,
As made us nobly wild, not mad;
And yet each verse of thine
Outdid the meat, outdid the frolic wine. (l. 7–10)

AWP; CaPo; InvP; NoP; OBS; SeCP; SeCV-1; TrGrPo

The Pillar of Fame

37 Fame's pillar here, at last, we set,
Out-during marble, brass, or jet, (l. 1–2)

CaPo; JCP; NIP; SeCP

A Ternarie of Littles, upon a Pipkin of Jellie Sent to a Lady

38 A little meat best fits a little belly,
As sweetly Lady, give me leave to tell ye,
This little Pipkin fits this little Jelly. (l. 16–18)

BoTP; FaBoCh; FaBoUs; GoJo; PoEL-3

A Thanksgiving to God for His House

39 Lord, Thou hast given me a cell
Wherein to dwell;
And little house, whose humble roof
Is weather-proof; (l. 1–4)

BLPL; ChTr; FaBoBe; HAP; OBS; OFD; OHIP; PoRA;
SeCP; SeCV-1; TrCP; TrPWD; WGRP

To Anthea, Who May Command Him Anything

40 Thou art my life, my love, my heart,
The very eyes of me:
And hast command of every part
To live and die for thee. (l. 17–20)

CaPo; GTBS; GTBS-P; JCP; NOBE; OAEL-1; OBEV;
OBS; SeCP; SeCV-1; TrGrPo

To Blossoms

41 And after they have shown their pride
Like you a while, they glide
Into the grave. (l. 16–18)

BoNaP; CaPo; GTBS; GTBS-P; JCP; NAEL-1; OBEV;
OBS; SeCP; SeCV-1

To Daffodils

42 Fair daffodils, we weep to see
You haste away so soon: (l. 1–2)

43 We die,
As your hours do, and dry
Away,
Like to the summer's rain;
Or as the pearls of morning's dew (l. 15–19)

AWP; BoNaP; CaPo; ELP; FaBoCh; GN; GoJo; GTBS;
GTBS-P; InPS; JCP; LiTB; NOBE; NoP; OBEV; OBS;
PoEL-3; PoRA; PPP; QFR; SeCP; SeCV-1; TrGrPo;
TTTS; UnPo

To Daisies, Not to Shut So Soon

44 Shut not so soon; the dull-eyed night
Has not yet begun
To make a seizure on the light,
Or to seal up the sun. (l. 1–4)

CaPo; CH; ELP; GBL; OBEV; OBS; OxBSP; SeCV-1;
TrGrPo

To Dianeme

45 When as that Rubie, which you weare,
Sunk from the tip of your soft eare,
Will last to be a precious Stone,
When all your world of Beautie 's gone. (l. 7–10)

CaPo; GTBS; GTBS-P; JCP; NOBE; OBEV; OBS;
SeCV-1; TrGrPo

To Electra

46 I dare not ask a kiss,
I dare not beg a smile,
Lest having that, or this,
I might grow proud the while.

No, no, the utmost share
Of my desire shall be
Only to kiss that air
That lately kissed thee. (l. 1–8)

BLPL; CaPo; HoPM; OBEV; OBS; SeCV-1

To His Saviour, a Child; a Present, by a Child

47 Go, pretty child, and bear this flower
Unto thy little Saviour;
And tell Him, by that bud now blown,
He is the Rose of Sharon known. (l. 1–4)

OHIP; OxBChV; SeCP; TrCP

To Live Merrily, and to Trust to Good Verses

48 Now is the time for mirth,
Nor cheek or tongue be dumb;
For with the flowery earth
The golden pomp is come. (l. 1–4)

49 And when all bodies meet
In Lethe to be drowned,
Then only numbers sweet
With endless life are crowned. (l. 49–52)

AWP; CaPo; InvP; OBS; SeCP; SeCV-1

To Meadows

50 Ye have been fresh and green,
Ye have been fill'd with flowers:
And ye the Walks have been
Where Maids have spent their houres. (l. 1–4)

AWP; CaPo; CH; JCP; NOBE; OBEV; OBS; PoEL-3;
QFR; SeCP; SeCV-1

To Music, to Becalm His Fever

51 That having ease me given,
With full delight,
I leave this light;

And take my flight
For Heaven. (l. 29–33)

CaPo; GoJo; OBEV; OBS; QFR; SeCV-1; UnS

To Perilla

52 Then, lastly, let some weekly strewings be
Devoted to the memory of me:
Then shall my ghost not walk about, but keep
Still in the cool and silent shades of sleep. (l. 15–18)

CaPo; OBS; SeCP; SeCV-1

To Robin Redbreast

53 Laid out for death, let thy last kindness be
With leaves and moss-work for to cover me:
And while the wood-nymphs my cold corpse inter,
Sing thou my dirge, sweet-warbling chorister!
For epitaph, in foliage, next write this:
Here, here the tomb of Robin Herrick is. (l. 1–6)

OBS; PBBP; PoE; TrGrPo

To the Reverend Shade of His Religious Father

54 Thou gav'st me life, but mortal; for that one
Favour I'll make full satisfaction:
For my life mortal, rise from out thy hearse,
And take a life immortal from my verse. (l. 13–16)

CaPo; JCP; OBS; SeCV-1

To the Virgins, to Make Much of Time

55 Gather ye rosebuds while ye may:
Old Time is still a-flying;
And this same flower that smiles today,
Tomorrow will be dying. (l. 1–4)

AWP; BLPA; BoLoP; CaPo; ChTr; ELP; EnLoPo; ErPo;
FaBV; FaFP; FF; FPL; GBL; GTBS; GTBS-P; HAP;
HeIP; InPK; InPS; JCP; LiTB; NAEL-1; NBLV; NIP;
NOBE; NoP; OAEL-1; OBEV; OBS; PoE; PoEL-3; PrIm;
QFR; SCV; SeCP; SeCV-1; SoSe; TEP; TrGrPo

To Violets

56 Y'are the maiden posies,
And so graced
To be placed
'Fore damask roses.

Yet though thus respected
By-and-by

Ye do lie,
Poor girls, neglected. (l. 9–16)

CaPo; JCP; OBEV; OBS; SeCP; TrGrPo

Upon a Child That Died

57 Here she lies, a pretty bud,
Lately made of flesh and blood: (l. 1–2)

58 Give her strewings, but not stir
The earth that lightly covers her. (l. 5–6)

CaPo; CH; InPK; NoP; OBD; OBEV; SeCV-1

Upon a Maid

59 Here she lies (in bed of spice)
Fair as Eve in Paradise:
For her beauty it was such
Poets could not praise too much.
Virgins come, and in a ring
Her supremest requiem sing;
When depart, but see ye tread
Lightly, lightly o'er the dead. (l. 1–8)

CaPo; ChTr; FaBoCh; FaBoEE; OxBoLi

Upon Ben Jonson

60 Here lies Jonson with the rest
Of the poets; but the best.
Reader, would'st thou more have known?
Ask his story, not this stone.
That will speak what this can't tell
Of his glory. So farewell. (l. 1–6)

CaPo; FaBoEE; NoP; OBS; SeCV-1

Upon Julia's Clothes

61 Whenas in silks my Julia goes,
Then, then, methinks, how sweeetly flows
That liquefaction of her clothes. (l. 1–3)

62 Next, when I cast mine eyes and see
That brave vibration each way free,
O how that glittering taketh me! (l. 4–6)

AWP; BLPA; CaPo; ChTr; EBEV; EnLoPo; FaBV; FaFP;
FF; FPL; GBL; GTBS; GTBS-P; HAP; HeIP; HoPM;
InPS; JCP; LiTB; NAEL-1; NBLV; NIP; NOBE; NoP;
OAEL-1; OBEV; OBS; OPOP; OxBSP; PoE; PoEL-3;
PPP; SeCP; SeCV-1; TEP; TrGrPo; TTTS; WeW

Upon Julia's Voice

63 So smooth, so sweet, so silvery, is thy voice
As, could they hear, the damned would make no noise,
But listen to thee (walking in thy chamber)
Melting melodious words to lutes of amber. (l. 1–4)

InPK; JCP; NOBE; SeCePo; SeCP; SoSe

Upon Prue, His Maid

64 In this little urn is laid
Prudence Baldwin (once my maid)
From whose happy spark here let
Spring the purple violet. (l. 1–5)

CaPo; JCP; NAEL-1; NoP; SeCV-1

Upon the Loss of His Mistresses

65 I have lost, and lately, these
Many dainty mistresses: (l. 1–2)

66 Only Herrick's left alone,
For to number sorrow by
Their departures hence and die. (l. 12–14)

CaPo; NAEL-1; PoE; SeCV-1

The Vine

67 I dreamed this mortal part of mine
Was metamorphosed to a vine, (l. 1–2)

68 Methought her long, small legs and thighs
I with my tendrils did surprise;
Her belly, buttocks, and her waist
By my soft nervelets were embraced; (l. 5–8)

69 And found (ah me!) this flesh of mine
More like a stock than like a vine. (l. 22–23)

CaPo; ErPo; NAEL-2; NoP

The Vision

70 And, chiding me, said, 'Hence, remove,
Herrick, thou art too coarse to love.' (l. 21–22)

CaPo; ErPo; JCP; SeCP

When He Would Have His Verses Read

71 In sober mornings do not thou rehearse
The holy incantation of a verse; (l. 1–2)

72 When the rose reigns, and locks with ointments shine,
Let rigid Cato read these lines of mine. (l. 9–10)

CaPo; NOBE; OBS; SeCV-1

The White Island; or, The Place of the Blest

73 In that whiter Island, where
Things are evermore sincere;
Candor here, and lustre there
Delighting: (l. 9–12)

ChTr; JCP; NoP; OAEL-1; OBS; TOF; WiR

THOMAS HEYWOOD   (1575?–1650)
The Rape of Lucrece

1 Pack, clouds, away, and welcome, day!
With night we banish sorrow. (l. 1–2)

2 Wake from thy nest, robin redbreast!
Sing, birds, in every furrow,
And from each bill let music shrill
Give my fair Love good morrow! (l. 11–14)

BoTP; CH; ElL; GBL; GTBS; GTBS-P; OBEV; PBBP;
SoSe

GEOFFREY HILL   (b. 1932)
An Apology for the Revival of Christian Architecture in England

1 Autumn resumes the land,ruffles the woods
with smoky wings, entangles them.

2 Platonic England, house of solitudes,
rests in its laurels and its injured stone,

NAEL-2; NoAM; NoP; PoE

Genesis

3 'Beware
The soft-voiced owl, the ferret's smile,
The hawk's deliberate stoop in air,
Cold eyes, and bodies hooped in steel,
Forever bent upon the kill.' (l. 16–20)

4 By blood we live, the hot, the cold,
To ravage and redeem the world:
There is no bloodless myth will hold. (l. 40–42)

HAP; NePoEA; OAEL-2; OxBC; TOF

In Memory of Jane Fraser

5 When snow like sheep lay in the fold (l. 1)

MoP; NAEL-2; NePoEA; NoAM; OxBTC

The Princess of Mercia

6 In the schoolyard,in the cloakrooms, the children
boasted their scars of dried snot;wrists and knees
garnished with impetigo.

HAP; NAEL-2; NoAM; NoP; PoE

September Song

7 As estimated. you died. Things marched,
sufficient, to that end.
Just so much Zyklon and leather, patented
terror, so many routine cries. (l. 4–7)

NAEL-2; NoAM; NoP; OBWP

JOE HILL   (1879–1914)
The Preacher and the Slave (attributed to Hill)

1 You will eat, bye and bye,
In that glorious land in the sky;
Work and pray, live on hay,
You'll get pie in the sky when you die. (Chorus)

2 Long-haired preachers come out every night,
Try to tell you what's wrong and what's right; (l. 1–2)

3 Holy Rollers and Jumpers come out,
And they roller, they jump and they shout, (l. 9–10)

4 You will eat, bye and bye,
When you've learned how to cook and to fry;
Chop some wood, 'twill do you good,
And you'll eat in the sweet bye and bye. (l. 21–24)

AS; GBP; GBP; WTO

ARTHUR CLEMENT HILTON   (1851–1877)
Octopus

1 Strange beauty, eight-limbed and eight-handed
Whence camest to dazzle our eyes? (l. 1–2)

2 Is thy home European or Asian,
O mystical monster marine? (l. 5–6)

3 Art thou innocent, art thou immoral, (l. 15–16)

4 Clinging close with the crush of the Python,
When she maketh her murderous meal! (l. 27–28)

BXAP; CenHV; FaBoCo; FaBoPa; Par

EDWARD HIRSCH (b. 1950)

Fast Break

1 A hook shot kisses the rim and
hangs there, helplessly, but doesn't drop

and for once our gangly starting center
boxes out his man and times his jump

perfectly, gathering the orange leather
from the air like a cherished possession (l. 1–6)

ASP; DiPo; EOEF; TSL

RALPH HODGSON (c. 1871–1962)

The Bells of Heaven

1 For tamed and shabby tigers
And dancing dogs and bears,
And wretched, blind pit ponies
And little hunted hares. (l. 7–10)

BoTP; BrPo; EaLo; GoJo; LiTM; MoAB; MoBrPo;
NOBE; OBEV; OxBSP

The Bull

2 See an old unhappy bull,
Sick in soul and body both,
Slouching in the undergrowth
Of the forest beautiful, (l. 1–4)

3 With his mother gaunt and lean
In the valley warm and green,
Full of baby wonderment,
Blinking out of silly eyes
At a hundred mysteries; (l. 68–72)

4 Pity him, this dupe of dream,
Leader of the herd again
Only in his daft old brain,
Once again the bull supreme
And bull enough to bear the part
Only in his tameless heart. (l. 164–168)

5 Turns to meet the loathly birds
Flocking round him from the skies,
Waiting for the flesh that dies. (l. 178–180)

BrPo; LiTM; MoAB; MoBrPo; OBMV; OxBTC

Eve

6 "Eva!" Each syllable
Light as a flower fell;
"Eva!" he whispered the
Wondering maid; (l. 17–20)

7 Picture that orchard sprite,
Eve, with her body white,
Supple and smooth to her
Slim finger tips, (l. 25–28)

BrPo; CH; LiTB; LiTM; MoAB; MoBrPo; OnMSP; TrCP;
TrGrPo; UnPo

The Hammers

8 Other hammers, muffled hammers,
Silent hammers of decay. (l. 11–12)

GoJo; MoBrPo; NOBE; OxBTC

The Mystery

9 I did not pray Him to lay bare
The mystery to me,
Enough the rose was Heaven to smell,
And His own face to see. (l. 5–8)

CH; MoAB; MoBrPo; WGRP

Stupidity Street

10 And in the shops nothing
For people to eat;
Nothing for sale in
Stupidity Street. (l. 9–12)

BrPo; CH; LiTM; MoAB; MoBrPo; OBD; OxBTC; PDV

Time, You Old Gypsy Man

11 Time, you old gipsy man,
Will you not stay,
Put up your caravan
Just for one day? (l. 1–4)

BoTP; BrPo; CH; FaPON; LiTM; MoAB; MoBrPo;
MoShBr; TrGrPo

HEINRICH HOFFMANN (1809–1894)

The Story of Augustus, Who Would Not Have Any Soup

1 He scream'd out — 'Take the soup away!
O take the nasty soup away!
I won't have any soup to-day.' (l. 8–10)

FaBoUs; GoJo; MoShBr; NBLV: OxBChV; RHPC

JAMES HOGG ("THE ETTRICK SHEPHERD") (1770–1835)

A Boy's Song

1 Where the blackbird sings the latest,
Where the hawthorn blooms the sweetest,
Where the nestlings chirp and flee,
That's the way for Billy and me. (l. 5–8)

BoTP; CH; FaPON; FaPoR; ILY; MoShBr; OBEV;
OnUR; OxBChV; WiR

JOHN HOLLANDER (b. 1929)

The Great Bear

1 the trouble lies in pointing
At any stars. For one's own finger aims
Always elsewhere: the man beside one seems
Never to get the point. "No! The bright star
Just above my fingertip." (l. 24–28)

2 To understand
The signs that stars compose, we need depend
Only on stars that are entirely there
And the apparent space between them. There

Never need be lines between them, puzzling
Our sense of what is what. (l. 53–58)

3 The world is everything that happens to
Be true. The stars at night seem to suggest
The shapes of what might be. If it were best,
Even, to have it there (such a great bear!
All hung with stars!), there still would be no bear.
(l. 80–84)

LiTM; NePoEA-2; NoAM: NYBP; TwCP

The Lady's-Maid 's Song

4 When Adam found his rib was gone
He cursed and sighed and cried and swore
And looked with cold resentment on
The creature God has used it for. (l. 1–4)

5 Though shoulder, bosom, lip, and knee
Are praised in every kind of art,
Here is love's true anatomy:
His rib is gone; he'll have her heart. (l. 17–20)

ErPo; LiTM; NePoEA; TwCP; TW

LUCY ARIEL WILLIAMS HOLLOWAY (b. 1905)

Northboun'

1 Since Norf is up,
An' Souf is down,
An' Hebben is up,
I'm upward boun'. (l. 25–28)

BANP; BlSi; CDC; PoNe

OLIVER WENDELL HOLMES (1809–1894)

THE AUTOCRAT OF THE BREAKFAST TABLE
(the following 3 poems)

Intramural Aestivation

1 Me wretched! Let me curr to quercine shades!
Effund your albid hausts, lactiferous maids!
O, might I vole to some umbrageous clump, —
Depart, — be off, — excede, — evade, — erump!

ChTr; FaBoNo; NA; NOBL; OBAL

The Chambered Nautilus

2 Year after year beheld the silent toil
That spread his lustrous coil;
Still as the spiral grew,
He left the past year's dwelling for the new,
Stole with soft step its shining archway through,
Built up its idle door,
Stretched in his last-found home, and knew the old no
more. (l. 15–21)

3 Build thee more stately mansions, O my soul,
As the swift seasons roll!
Leave thy low-vaulted past!
Let each new temple, nobler than the last,
Shut thee from heaven with a dome more vast,
Till thou at length art free,
Leaving thine outgrown shell by life's unresting sea!
(l. 29–35)

AA; AmPP; FaBoBe; FaFP; FPL; GN; HoPM; LiTA;
MOS; NOBA; NoP; OHFP; PoEL-5; PoLF; PrIm; WGRP

The Deacon's Masterpiece

4 Have you heard of the wonderful one-hoss shay,
That was built in such a logical way
It ran a hundred years to a day, (l. 1–3)

5 Seventeen hundred and fifty-five.
Georgius Secundus was then alive, —
Snuffy old drone from the German hive. (l. 9–11)

6 He sent for lancewood to make the thills;
The crossbars were ash, from the straightest trees;
The panels of white-wood, that cuts like cheese,
But lasts like iron for things like these;
The hubs of logs from the "Settler's ellum," —
Last of its timber, — they couldn't sell 'em, (l. 41–46)

7 Little of all we value here
Wakes on the morn of its hundredth year
Without both feeling and looking queer.
In fact, there's nothing that keeps its youth,
So far as I know, but a tree and truth. (l. 73–77)

8 The parson was workinghis Sunday's text, —
Had got to fifthly, and stopped perplexed
At what the — Moses — was coming next. (l. 101–103)

9 — First a shiver, and then a thrill,
Then something decidedly like a spill, —
And the parson was sitting up on a rock,
At half-past nine by the meet'n'-house clock, —
Just the hour of the Earthquake shock!
— What do you think the parson found,
When he got up and stared around?
The poor old chaise in a heap or mound,
As if it had been to the mill and ground! (l. 106–114)

AmPP; BeLS; FaBoBe; FaFP; FPL; LiTA; MoShBr;
NOBA; OBAL; OBCA; OHFP; OxBA; PoLF; PoRA; TAP;
WBLP

The Ballad of the Oysterman

10 It was a tall young oysterman lived by the river-side,
His shop was just upon the bank, his boat was on the
tide;
The daughter of a fisherman, that was so straight and
slim,
Lived over on the other bank, right opposite to him.
(l. 1–4)

11 Alas for those two loving ones! she waked not from her
swound,
And he was taken with the cramp, and in the waves
was drowned,
But Fate has metamorphosed them, in pity of their
woe,
And now they keep an oyster-shop for mermaids down
below. (l. 25–28)

AnAmPo; FaFP; MoShBr; MOS

The Height of the Ridiculous

12 He took the paper, and I watched,
And saw him peep within;
At the first line he read, his face
Was all upon the grin. (l. 17–20)

13 The fourth; he broke into a roar;
The fifth; his waistband split;
The sixth; he burst five buttons off,
And tumbled in a fit. (l. 25–28)

14 Ten days and nights, with sleepless eye,
I watched that wretched man,
And since, I never dare to write
As funny as I can. (l. 29–32)

AA; FaFP; FiBHP; FPL; MoShBr; OBAL; OBCA

The Last Leaf

15 They say that in his prime,
Ere the pruning-knife of Time
Cut him down,
Not a better man was found
By the Crier on his round
Through the town. (l. 7–12)

16 And if I should live to be
The last leaf upon the tree
In the spring,
Let them smile, as I do now,
At the old forsaken bough
Where I cling. (l. 43–48)

AA; AmPP; AnAmPo; FaBoBe; FaPON; NAAL-1; PoLF;
PWR; WBLP

Old Ironsides

17 Ay, tear her tattered ensign down!
Long has it waved on high,
And many an eye has danced to see
That banner in the sky; (l. 1–4)

18 O, better that her shattered hulk
Should sink beneath the wave;
Her thunders shook the mighty deep,
And there should be her grave;
Nail to the mast her holy flag,
Set every threadbare sail,
And give her to the god of storms,
The lightning and the gale! (l. 17–24)

AA; AiP; AnAmPo; BLPA; FaBoBe; FaFP; FaPON; FPL;
GN; GOA; MOS; NAAL-1; OPP; PAH; PWR; TAP

THOMAS HOOD (1799–1845)

Autumn

1 I saw old Autumn in the misty morn
Stand shadowless like Silence, listening

To silence, (l. 1–3)

BLPL; LiTB; OAEL-2; OBEV; OBNC; PoEL-4; UnPo

The Bridge of Sighs

2 One more Unfortunate,
Weary of breath,
Rashly importunate,
Gone to her death!

Take her up tenderly,
Lift her with care;
Fashioned so slenderly,
Young, and so fair! (l. 1–8)

BeLS; EBEV; EnRP; FaPoR; FPL; GTBS; GTBS-P;
OBEV; WBLP

The Death-Bed

3 We thought her dying when she slept,
And sleeping when she died. (l. 11–12)

EnRP; GTBS; GTBS-P; NOBE; OBD; OBEV; OBNC

Faithless Nelly Gray

4 Ben Battle was a soldier bold,
And used to war's alarms;
But a cannon-ball took off his legs,
So he laid down his arms. (l. 1–4)

BXAP; EnRP; FaBoCo; NA; NOBL

I Remember, I Remember

5 I remember, I remember
The fir trees dark and high;
I used to think their slender tops
Were close against the sky;
It was a childish ignorance,
But now 'tis little joy
To know I'm further off from Heaven
Than when I was a boy. (l. 25–32)

BLPA; CH; ELP; EnRP; FaBoBe; FaBV; FaFP; FaPON;
FaPoR; FPL; GTBS; GTBS-P; LiTB; NOBE; PoEL-4

No!

6 No shade, no shine, no butterflies, no bees,
No fruits, no flowers, no leaves, no birds — November!
(l. 22–23)

ChTr; FiBHP; GN

The Poet's Fate

7 The Critic spits on what is done, —
Gives it a wipe, — and all is gone. (l. 3–4)

FaBoEE; FiBHP; TW

Ruth

8 She stood breast high amid the corn,
Clasp'd by the golden light of morn, (l. 1–2)

9 Thus she stood amid the stooks,
Praising God with sweetest looks: — (l. 15–16)

BoLoP; EnLoPo; EnRP; GN; NOBE; OBEV; OBNC

Silence

10 There is a silence where hath been no sound,
There is a silence where no sound may be,
In the cold grave — under the deep, deep sea,
Or in wide desert where no life is found, (l. 1–4)

CH; EBEV; EnRP; NOBE; OBEV; OBNC; PoEL-4; Son

The Song of the Shirt

11 With fingers weary and worn,
With eyelids heavy and red,
A woman sat, in unwomanly rags
Plying her needle and thread —
Stitch! stitch! stitch!
In poverty, hunger, and dirt, (l. 1–6)

12 It is not linen you're wearing out
But human creatures' lives!
Stitch — stitch — stitch,
In poverty, hunger, and dirt,
Sewing at once, with a double thread,
A Shroud as well as a Shirt. (l. 27–32)

13 Oh, God, that bread should be so dear,
And flesh and blood so cheap! (l. 39–40)

EBVV; EnRP; FaPoR; SaC; TEP; WBLP

To Minerva

14 My brain is dull, my sight is foul,
I cannot write a verse, or read —
Then, Pallas, take away thine Owl,
And let us have a lark instead. (l. 5–8)

ChTr; FaBoCo; FaBoNo; FiBHP; NBLV; NOBL; OxBoLi

ALEC DERWENT HOPE (b. 1907)

Imperial Adam

1 Adam had learned the jolly deed of kind:
He took her in his arms and there and then
Like the clean beasts, embracing from behind,
Began in joy to found the breed of men. (l. 25–28)

2 quaking muscles in the act of birth,
Between her legs a pigmy face appear,
And the first murderer lay upon the earth. (l. 42–44)

CBAP; ErPo; HAP; NIP; NoAM; NoP

"LAURENCE HOPE" (pseudonym of ADELA FLORENCE CORY NICOLSON) (1865–1904)

Kashmiri Song

1 Pale hands I love beside the Shalimar,
Where are you now? Who lies beneath your spell?
(l. 1–2)

2 Or, pale dispensers of my Joys and Pains,
Holding the doors of Heaven and of Hell, (l. 5–6)

3 Pale hands, pink-tipped, like Lotus buds that float
On those cool waters where we used to dwell,
I would have rather felt you round my throat
Crushing out life than waving me farewell! (l. 9–12)

BLPA; BLPL; FaBoBe; FaFP

GERARD MANLEY HOPKINS (1844–1889)

As Kingfishers Catch Fire

1 As kingfishers catch fire, dragonflies draw flame; (l. 1)

CMoP; EaLo; EBEV; EBVV; FaBoMo; LiTM; MoAB;
MoBrPo; NAEL-2; NOBVV; NOCV; NoP; PoE; PrIm; RB

Binsey Poplars, Felled 1879

2 My aspens dear, whose airy cages quelled,
Quelled or quenched in leaves the leaping sun,
All felled, felled, are all felled; (l. 1–3)

3 When we hew or delve:
After-comers cannot guess the beauty been. (l. 18–19)

BoNaP; BrPo; EBVV; ELP; FaBoPP; InPS; Mes;
NAEL-2; NoAM; NoP; RB

Carrion Comfort

4 Not, I'll not, carrion comfort, Despair, not feast on thee:
(l. 1)

CMoP; HeIP; LiTB; NAEL-2; NoAM; NoP; OAEL-2;
OBNC; PoE; PoEL-5; PPP; Son; TEP; TOF

The Cuckoo

5 Repeat that, repeat,
Cuckoo, bird, (l. 1–2)

FM; MoAB; MoBrPo; OxBSP; PBBP; RB; TTTS

Felix Randal

6 poor Felix Randal;

How far from then forethought of, all thy more
boisterous years,
When thou at the random grim forge, powerful amidst
peers,
Didst fettle for the great gray drayhorse his bright and
battering sandal! (l. 11–14)

BrPo; EBEV; EBVV; FaBoMo; GTBS-P; HAP; InPS;
LiTB; LiTM; MoAB; MoBrPo; MoP; NAEL-2; NoAM;
NOBE; NoP; OBD; OBEV; OBNC; PoE; PoRA; PrIm;
Son; SOTW; WeW

God's Grandeur

7 The world is charged with the grandeur of God. (l. 1)

8 morning, at the brown brink eastward, springs —
Because the Holy Ghost over the bent
World broods with warm breast and with ah! bright
wings. (l. 12–14)

AWP; BLPL; BrPo; CMoP; EBVV; FaFP; FF; HAP; InPK;
InvP; LiTB; LiTM; MoAB; MoBrPo; MoP; NAEL-2; NIP;
NoAM; NOBE; NOBVV; NoP; OAEL-2; OBNC; PoE;
PPP; PrIm; Son; SoSe; SOTW; TEP; TrCP; TrGrPo;
UnPo; WeW

Heaven-Haven

9 I have desired to go
Where springs not fail,
To fields where flies no sharp and sided hail
And a few lilies blow. (l. 1–4)

10 And I have asked to be
Where no storms come,
Where the green swell is in the havens dumb,
And out of the swing of the sea. (l. 5–8)

ACP; BrPo; HeIP; MoAB; MoBrPo; MoP; MOS; NoAM;
NOBE; NOCV; OBEV; OBNC; OxBSP; RB; SoSe;
SOTW; TOF; TrGrPo

Inversnaid

11 What would the world be, once bereft
Of wet and of wildness? Let them be left,
O let them be left, wildness and wet;
Long live the weeds and the wilderness yet. (l. 13–16)

ACP; BLPL; BrPo; CMoP; FaBoPP; GTBS-P; LiTB;
LiTM; MoAB; MoBrPo; NoAM; OAEL-2; PoRA; PoSH;
RB; RR; UnPo

The Leaden Echo and the Golden Echo

12 Give beauty back, beauty, beauty, beauty, back to God,
beauty's self and beauty's giver. (l. 34–35)

BrPo; CMoP; FaFP; GTBS-P; LiTB; LiTM; MoAB;
MoBrPo; NOBVV; OBMV; OBNC; SOTW

Moonrise

13 I awoke in the Midsummer not-to-call night, in the
white and the walk of the morning: (l. 1)

FaBoPP; MoAB; MoBrPo; NOBVV; RB; SeCePo

My own heart let me more have pity on

14 My own heart let me more have pity on; let
Me live to my sad self hereafter kind,
Charitable; not live this tormented mind
With this tormented mind tormenting
yet. (l. 1–4)

BrPo; FaBoMo; InPS; LiTM; MoAB; MoBrPo; NOBVV;
NoP; TOF

No Worst, There Is None

15 all
Life death does end and each day dies with sleep.
(l. 13–14)

BrPo; CMoP; EBVV; FaBoMo; GTBS-P; HeIP; InPS;
LiTB; LiTM; MoAB; MoBrPo; MoP; NAEL-2; NoAM;
NOBE; NOBVV; NoP; OAEL-2; OBNC; OPOP; PoE;
PoEL-5; PPP; SeCePo

Patience, hard thing! the hard thing but to pray

16 Natural heart's ivy, Patience masks
Our ruins of wrecked past purpose. (l. 6–7)

NOBVV; OBNC; Prf; Son

Peace

17 That piecemeal peace is poor peace. What pure peace
allows
Alarms of wars, the daunting wars, the death of it?
(l. 5–6)

ELP; GTBS-P; OxBSP; TrCP

Pied Beauty

18 Glory be to God for dappled things — (l. 1)

19 All things counter, original, spare, strange;
Whatever is fickle, freckled (who knows how?)
With swift, slow; sweet, sour; adazzle, dim;
He fathers-forth whose beauty is past change:
Praise him. (l. 7–11)

AWP; BrPo; CMoP; EaLo; EBVV; FaBoMo; FaFP; GoJo;
GTBS-P; HAP; HeIP; HoPM; InPK; InPS; InvP; LiTB;
LiTM; MoAB; MoBrPo; MoP; NAEL-2; NoAM; NOBE;
NOBVV; NoP; OAEL-2; OBEV; OBMV; OBNC; OxBSP;
PoE; PoRA; PPP; PrIm; RB; SCV; SoSe; SOTW; TEP;
TrGrPo; TTTS; WeW

Spring

20 Nothing is so beautiful as Spring —
When weeds, in wheels, shoot long and lovely and lush;
(l. 1–2)

BoNaP; BrPo; EBVV; FaBV; HAP; InvP; LiTM; MoAB;
MoBrPo; NAEL-2; NoAM; NOBE; NOBVV; OAEL-2;
OBMV; OBNC; RB; SoSe; TrCP

Spring and Fall

21 Margaret, are you grieving
Over Goldengrove unleaving? (l. 1–2)

22 It is the blight man was born for, (l. 14)

BrPo; ChTr; CMoP; EBEV; ELP; FaBoUs; FF; GoJo;
GTBS-P; HAP; HeIP; HoPM; InPK; InPS; LiTB; LiTM;
MAT; MoAB; NAEL-2; NIP; NoAM; NOBE; NoP; OBD;
PoE; PoEL-5; PPP; RB; SCV; SOTW; TEP; TOF; WeW

The Starlight Night

23 Look at the stars! look, look up the skies!
O look at all the fire-folk sitting in the air! (l. 1–2)

24 This piece-bright paling shuts the spouse
Christ home, Christ and his mother and all his hallows.
(l. 13–14)

ACP; BrPo; GTBS-P; InPS; LiTM; MoAB; MoBrPo;
NAEL-2; PoE; PPP; SeCePo; WSC

Thou Art Indeed Just, Lord, If I Contend

25 Thou art indeed just, Lord, if I contend
With thee; but, sir, so what I plead is just.
Why do sinners' ways prosper? and why must
Disappointment all I endeavour end? (l. 1–4)

AWP; BrPo; CMoP; EaLo; EBEV; EBVV; GTBS-P; HAP;
HoPM; InPK; LiTM; MoAB; MoBrPo; NAEL-2; NoAM;
NOBE; NOBVV; NoP; OAEL-2; TOF; TrPWD; UnPo

To R. B.

26 Sweet fire the sire of muse, my soul needs this;
I want the one rapture of an inspiration.
O then if in my lagging lines you miss (l. 9–11)

CMoP; GTBS-P; InvP; OAEL-2

The Windhover

27 I caught this morning morning's minion, kingdom of daylight's dauphin, dapple-dawn-drawn Falcon,
in his riding
Of the rolling level underneath him steady air, and
striding
High there, how he rung upon the rein of a wimpling
wing
In his ecstasy! (l. 1–5)

ACP; BrPo; CMoP; EaLo; EBVV; GTBS-P; HAP; InPK;
InPS; InvP; LiTB; LiTM; MoAB; MoBrPo; MoP; NAEL-
2; NoAM; NOBE; NOBVV; NoP; OAEL-2; OBNC; PBBP;
PoE; PoEL-5; PoRA; PPP; PrIm; RB; SCV; TEP; TOF;
UnPo; WeW

JOSEPH HOPKINSON (1770–1842)

Hail, Columbia

1 Hail, Columbia! happy land!
Hail, ye heroes! heaven-born band!
Who fought and bled in Freedom's cause,
Who fought and bled in Freedom's cause,
And when the storm of war was gone,
Enjoyed the peace your valor won.
Let independence be our boast,
Ever mindful what it cost; (l. 1–8)

2 Firm, united, let us be,
Rallying round our Liberty;
As a band of brothers joined,
Peace and safety we shall find. (l. 11–14)

AA; AnAmPo; FaBoBe; FaFP; OPP; PAH

HORACE (QUINTUS HORATIUS FLACCUS) (65–8 B.C.)

Odes

1 Ribald romeosless and less berattle
your shut window with impulsive pebbles.

2 For insolent old lechers
you will weep soon on the lonely curbing (I, 25)

BoLoP; MAT; OBVE

3 What slender Youth bedew'd with liquid odours
Courts thee on Roses in some pleasant Cave,

4 Me in my vow'd
Picture the sacred wall declares t'have hung
My dank and dropping weeds
To the stern God of Sea. (I, 5)

AWP; EBEV; EnLoPo; OAEL-1; OBVE; PoEL-3; WiR

5 Receive, dear friend, the truths I teach,
So shalt thou live beyond the reach
Of adverse Fortune's pow'r;
Not always tempt the distant deep,
Nor always timorously creep
Along the treach'rous shore.

6 He, that holds fast the golden mean,
And lives contentedly between
The little and the great,
Feels not the wants that pinch the poor,
Nor plagues that haunt the rich man's door,
Imbitt'ring all his state. (II, 10)

AWP; OBVE

7 Pompeius, best of all my comrades, you and I
Often faced death when we were rebels.

8 Finally, your lengthy service ended,
Lay your weariness beneath my laurel tree.

9 Pour ointment from the shells, and comb
It in your hair. I will drink like any toper. (II, 7)

OBWP; WaaP

10 Come, give thy soul a loose, and taste the pleasures of
the poor.
Sometimes 'tis grateful for the rich to try
A short vicissitude, and fit of poverty:
A savory dish, a homely treat,
Where all is plain, where all is neat,
Without the stately spacious room,
The Persian carpet, or the Tyrian loom,
Clear up the cloudy foreheads of the great. (III, 29)

AWP; FaPoR; OBVE; SeCV-1; SeCV-2

11 Boy, I hate their empty shows,
Persian garlands I detest,
Bring me not the late-blown rose
Lingering after all the rest:
Plainer myrtle pleases me
Thus outstretched beneath my vine,
Myrtle more becoming thee,
Waiting with thy master's wine. (I, 38)

AWP; InPK; NBLV; NBLV; OBVE

FRANK HORNE (b. 1899)

Kid Stuff

1 The wise guys
tell me
that Christmas
is Kid Stuff ... (l. 1–4)

AmNP; PChr; PoBA; PoNe

On Seeing Two Brown Boys in a Catholic Church

2 They will nail you up twixt thieves
And gamble for your little garments.

And in this you will exceed God
For on this earth
You shall know Hell — (l. 23–27)

BANP; CDC; PoBA; PoNe; TTY

JOHN HOSKYNS (1566–1638)

Absence (attributed to Hoskyns)

1 Absence, hear my protestation
Against thy strength
Distance and length,
Do what thou canst for alteration:
For hearts of truest metal
Absence doth join, and Time doth settle. (l. 1–6)

MeLP; OPOP

ALFRED EDWARD HOUSMAN (1859–1936)

Because I Liked You Better

1 Halt by the headstone naming
The heart no longer stirred,
And say the lad that loved you
Was one that kept his word. (l. 13–16)

GBL; NOBVV; OxBTC; PeHV

Could Man Be Drunk for Ever

2 Could man be drunk for ever
With liquor, love, or fights,
Lief should I rouse at morning
And lief lie down of nights. (l. 1–4)

LiTM; NAEL-2; OBMV; PPP

Crossing Alone the Nighted Ferry

3 The brisk fond lackey to fetch and carry,
The true, sick-hearted slave,
Expect him not in the just city
And free land of the grave. (l. 5–8)

FaBoRV; GTBS-P; NOBE; NoP; OxBSP

Easter Hymn

4 If in that Syrian garden, ages slain,
You sleep, and know not you are dead in vain,
Nor even in dreams behold how dark and bright
Ascends in smoke and fire by day and night
The hate you died to quench and could but fan,
Sleep well and see no morning, son of man. (l. 1–6)

EaLo; EBEV; MoAB; OFD

Eight O'Clock

5 He stood, and heard the steeple
Sprinkle the quarters on the morning town.
One, two, three, four, to market-place and people
It tossed them down. (l. 1–4)

BrPo; CMoP; InFK; MoAB; MoBrPo; MoP; NoAM; NoP;
OxBSP; PoE; SoSe; TrGrPo

Fragment of a Greek Tragedy

6 O suitably-attired-in-leather-boots
Head of a traveler, wherefore seeking whom
Whence by what way how purposed art thou come
To this well-nigh-ingaled vicinity? (l. 1–4)

7 What? for I know not yet what you will say.
alc: Nor will you ever, if you interrupt.
Proceed, and I will hold my speechless tongue.
(l. 18–20)

8 Go chase into the house a lucky foot.
And, O my son, be, on the one hand, good,
And do not, on the other hand, be bad;
For that is very much the safest plan. (l. 24–27)

9 Why should I mention Io? Why indeed?
I have no notion why.

10 O, I am smitten with a hatchet's jaw;
    And that in deed and not in word alone.
    chorus: I thought I heard a sound within the house
    Unlike the voice of one that jumps for joy.
    He splits my skull, not in a friendly way,
    Once more: he purposes to kill me dead

11 O! O! another stroke! that makes the third.
    He stabs me to the heart against my wish.
    If that be so, thy state of health is poor;
    But thine arithmetic is quite correct.

    CenHV; FaBoNo; NOBL; Par

Her Strong Enchantments Failing

12 O Queen of air and darkness,
    I think 'tis truth you say,
    And I shall die to-morrow;
    But you will die to-day. (l. 9–12)

    FaBoTw; MAT; NOBE; NOBVV; OAEL-2; OPOP

Here dead lie we because we did not choose

13 Life, to be sure, is nothing much to lose;
    But young men think it is, and we were young.
                                    (l. 3–4)

    FaBoEE; FPL; NOBVV; NoP; OAEL-2; PoLF

In valleys green and still

14 The soldier's is the trade:
    In any wind or weather
    He steals the heart of maid
    And man together.

    The lover and his lass
    Beneath the hawthorn lying, (l. 9–14)

    BrPo; FaBoTw; OAEL-2; SCV

Infant Innocence

15 The infant child is not aware
    It has been eaten by the bear. (l. 3–4)

    CenHV; ChTr; FaBoCh; FaBoCo; FaBoNo; FaFP; LiTB;
    NOBL; OxBoLi

The Laws of God, the Laws of Man

16 The laws of God, the laws of man,
    He may keep that will and can;
    Not I: let God and man decree
    Laws for themselves and not for me; (l. 1–4)

17 Please yourselves, say I, and they
    Need only look the other way. (l. 9–10)

18 I, a stranger and afraid
    In a world I never made. (l. 17–18)

    MoAB; MoBrPo; NOBVV; OBSV; OxBoLi; PeHV; PPP

The Night Is Freezing Fast

19 The night is freezing fast,
    To-morrow comes December. (l. 1–2)

20 made of earth and sea
    His overcoat for ever,
    And wears the turning globe. (l. 10–12)

    CMoP; LiTM; OxBSP; PrIm

Oh Who Is That Young Sinner with the Handcuffs on His Wrists?

21 Oh who is that young sinner with the handcuffs on his
        wrists?
    And what has he been after that they groan and shake
        their fists?
    And wherefore is he wearing such a conscience-stricken
        air?
    Oh they're taking him to prison for the colour of his
        hair. (l. 1–4)

    FaBoTw; NOBVV; PeHV; SoSe

A SHROPSHIRE LAD (the following 21 poems)
Along the field as we came by

22 "Oh who are these that kiss and pass?
    A country lover and his lass;
    Two lovers looking to be wed;
    And time shall put them both to bed,
    But she shall lie with earth above,
    And he beside another love." (XXVI)

    HAP; MoAB; MoBrPo; WeW

Be still, my soul

23 Be still, my soul, be still; the arms you bear are brittle,

24 Ay, look: high heaven and earth ail from the prime
        foundation;
    All thoughts to rive the heart are here, and all are vain:
    Horror and scorn and hate and fear and indignation —
    Oh, why did I awake? When shall I sleep again?
                                    (XLVIII)

    MoAB; MoBrPo; NOBVV; OAEL-2; OBNC; TrGrPo

In Summertime on Breda

25 Here of a Sunday morning
My love and I would lie,
And see the colored counties,
And hear the larks so high
About us in the sky.

26 My love rose up so early
And stole out unbeknown
And went to church alone.

27 The bells they sound on Bredon,
And still the steeples hum.
"Come all to church, good people, — "
Oh, noisy bells, be dumb:
I hear you, I will come. (XXI)

BrPo; EBVV; FaBoPP; MoAB; MoBrPo; NAEL-2; SoSe

Farewell to barn and stack and tree

28 "Farewell to barn and stack and tree,
Farewell to Severn shore.
Terence, look your last at me,
For I come home no more.

29 "My mother thinks us long away;
'Tis time the field were mown.
She had two sons at rising day,
To-night she'll be alone.

30 "Long for me the rick will wait,
And long will wait the fold,
And long will stand the empty plate,
And dinner will be cold." (VIII)

CMoP; MoAB; MoBrPo; SoSe; UnPo

From Clee to heaven the beacon burns

31 The saviors come not home tonight:
Themselves they could not save.

32 Oh, God will save her, fear you not:
Be you the men you've been,
Get you the sons your fathers got,
And God will save the Queen. (I)

FaPoR; NIP; NOBVV; PrIm; UnPo

I hoed and trenched and weeded

33 So up and down I sow them
For lads like me to find,
When I shall lie below them,
A dead man out of mind. (LXIII)

LiTM; MoBrPo; TrGrPo; UnPo; WeW

Into my heart an air that kills

34 Into my heart an air that kills
From yon far country blows:

35 That is the land of lost content
I see it shining plain,
The happy highways where I went
And cannot come again. (XL)

ChTr; CMoP; EBEV; LiTB; LiTM; Mes; MoAB; MoBrPo;
NoAM; NOBE; NOBVV; OAEL-2; OxBTC; SeCePo

Is my team ploughing

36 Is my team ploughing,
That I was used to drive
And hear the harness jingle
When I was man alive?

37 Yes, lad, I lie easy,
I lie as lads would choose;
I cheer a dead man's sweetheart,
Never ask me whose. (XXVII)

CMoP; EBVV; LiTM; MoAB; MoBrPo; NoAM; NoP;
OBD; OBEV; TrGrPo

Loveliest of trees

38 Loveliest of trees, the cherry now
Is hung with bloom along the bough,

39 Now, of my threescore years and ten,
Twenty will not come again,
And take from seventy springs a score,
It only leaves me fifty more.

40 And since to look at things in bloom
Fifty springs are little room, (II)

AWP; BLPL; BoNaP; ChTr; CMoP; ELP; FaBoBe; FaBV;
FaFP; FF; HAP; HeIP; InPK; LiTB; LiTM; MoAB;
MoBrPo; MoP; NAs; NoAM; NoP; OAEL-2; OHIP;
OxBTC; PoE; PoLF; PrIm; RB; SoSe; TEP; TrGrPo

Oh, when I was in love with you

41 Oh, when I was in love with you,
Then I was clean and brave,
And miles around the wonder grew
How well did I behave. (XVIII)

BoLoP; FaBV; LiTB; MoBrPo; TTTS

On the idle hill of summer

42 On the idle hill of summer,
Sleepy with the flow of streams,

43 East and west on fields forgotten
   Bleach the bones of comrades slain,
   Lovely lads and dead and rotten;
   None that go return again. (XXXV)

   MoBrPo; NOBE; OAEL-2; OBNC; OBWP; SoSe

On Wenlock Edge

44 On Wenlock Edge the wood's in trouble;
   His forest fleece the Wrekin heaves;
   The gale, it plies the saplings double,
   And thick on Severn snow the leaves.

45 The gale, it plies the saplings double,
   It blows so hard, 'twill soon be gone:
   To-day the Roman and his trouble
   Are ashes under Uricon. (XXXI)

   BrPo; GTBS-P; LiTB; Mes; MoAB; MoBrPo; NAEL-2;
   NOBE; NoP; OBNC; OxBTC; PoEL-5; PoRA; PrIm; RB

Others, I am not the first

46 More than I, if truth were told,
   Have stood and sweated hot and cold,
   And through their veins in ice and fire
   Fear contended with desire. (XXX)

   CMoP; LiTB; MoBrPo; NOBVV; OxBTC; PoE; PPP

Reveille

47 Up, lad: thews that lie and cumber
   Sunlit pallets never thrive;
   Morns abed and daylight slumber
   Were not meant for man alive.

48 Up, lad: when the journey's over
   There'll be time enough to sleep. (IV)

   CMoP; FaFP; FPL; LiTB; LiTM; MoAB; MoBrPo; NoP;
   PoLF; SoSe

Terence, this is stupid stuff

49 "Terence, this is stupid stuff:
   You eat your victuals fast enough;
   There can't be much amiss, 'tis clear,
   To see the rate you drink your beer.

50 Pretty friendship 'tis to rhyme
   Your friends to death before their time
   Moping melancholy mad:
   Come, pipe a tune to dance to, lad."

51 And malt does more than Milton can
   To justify God's ways to man.

52 Therefore, since the world has still
   Much good, but much less good than ill,

53 They put arsenic in his meat
   And stared aghast to watch him eat;
   They poured strychnine in his cup
   And shook to see him drink it up:

54 — I tell the tale that I heard told.
   Mithridates, he died old. (LXII)

   CMoP; HeIP; InPK; LiTB; LiTM; MoAB; MoBrPo; MoP;
   NAEL-2; NIP; NoAM; NoP; PrIm; TrGrPo

To an Athlete Dying Young

55 The time you won your town the race
   We chaired you through the market-place;
   Man and boy stood cheering by,
   And home we brought you shoulder-high.

56 Smart lad, to slip betimes away
   From fields where glory does not stay,
   And early though the laurel grows
   It withers quicker than the rose.

57 Runners whom renown outran
   And the name died before the man.

58 And round that early-laurelled head
   Will flock to gaze the strengthless dead,
   And find unwithered on its curls
   The garland briefer than a girl's. (XIX)

   BLPL; BrPo; CMoP; DL; HAP; HeIP; InPK; LiTB; LiTM;
   MoAB; MoBrPo; MoP; NAEL-2; NIP; NoAM; NoP; PoE;
   PoEL-5; PoRA; PrIm; SoSe; TEP; TrGrPo; UnPo; WeW

When I was one-and-twenty

59 When I was one-and-twenty
   I heard a wise man say,
   "Give crowns and pounds and guineas
   But not your heart away;

60 And I am two-and-twenty,
   And oh, 'tis true, 'tis true. (XIII)

   CMoP; ELP; FaBV; FaFP; FPL; HeIP; InPK; LiTB;
   LiTM; MoAB; MoBrPo; NAEL-2; NoAM; PoE; PoLF;
   SoSe; TrGrPo

When I watch the living meet

61 Lovers lying two and two
   Ask not whom they sleep beside,
   And the bridegroom all night through
   Never turns him to the bride. (XII)

   CMoP; MoBrPo; NOBVV; NoP; TrGrPo

With rue my heart is laden

62 With rue my heart is laden
For golden friends I had,
For many a rose-lipt maiden
And many a lightfoot lad. (LIV)

AWP; BLPL; CMoP; FaFP; HAP; HeIP; HoPM; InPK;
LiTB; LiTM; MoAB; MoBrPo; NAEL-2; NoAM; NoP;
PoE; PrIm; SoSe; TrGrPo; UnPo

From far, from eve and morning

63 From far, from eve and morning
And yon twelve-winded sky,
The stuff of life to knit me
Blew hither: here am I. (XXXII)

CMoP; HAP; HeIP; MoBrPo; NoP; PoEL-5; PrIm

White in the moon the long road lies

64 White in the moon the long road lies,
The moon stands blank above;
White in the moon the long road lies
That leads me from my love. (XXXVI)

AWP; CMoP; ELP; LiTB

Tell Me Not Here

65 For nature, heartless, witless nature,
Will neither care nor know
What stranger's feet may find the meadow
And trespass there and go,
Nor ask amid the dews of morning
If they are mine or no. (l. 25–30)

ELP; GTBS-P; LiTM; NoAM; NOBE; OAEL-2; OBNC;
OxBTC; SCV

JULIA WARD HOWE (1819–1910)

The Battle Hymn of the Republic

1 Mine eyes have seen the glory of the coming of the
Lord;
He is trampling out the vintage where the grapes of
wrath are stored;
He hath loosed the fateful lightning of His terrible swift
sword; (l. 1–3)

2 Glory! Glory! Hallelujah!
Glory! Glory! Hallelujah!
Glory! Glory! Hallelujah!
His truth is marching on. (l. 6–9)

3 In the beauty of the lilies Christ was born across the
sea,
With a glory in His bosom that transfigures you and
me;
As He died to make men holy, let us die to make men
free; (l. 26–28)

AA; AH; AnAmPo; BLPA; CH; EaLo; FaBoBe; FaFP;
FaPON; FaPoR; GN; NOBA; NOCV; OBWP; OHIP; OPP;
PAH; PWR; SCV; TAP; WBLP; WGRP; WPE

MARY HOWITT (1799–1888)

The Spider and the Fly

1 "Will you walk into my parlor? " said the spider to the
fly;
"'Tis the prettiest little parlor that ever you did spy.
The way into my parlor is up a winding stair,
And I have many pretty things to show when you are
there." (l. 1–4)

2 And now, dear little children, who may this story read,
To idle, silly, flattering words, I pray you ne'er give
heed;
Unto an evil counselor close heart, and ear, and eye,
And take a lesson from this tale of the Spider and the
Fly. (l 41–44)

BeLS; FaFP; FaPON; OHFP; OnUR; OxBChV; Par;
PWR; WBLP

LANGSTON HUGHES (1902–1967)

April Rain Song

1 The rain makes still pools on the sidewalk.
The rain makes running pools in the gutter.
The rain plays a little sleep-song on our roof at night —
(l. 4–6)

FaPON; NTCP; OBCA; PDV; RHPC

Brass Spittoons

2 Clean the spittoons.
The steam in hotel kitchens,
And the smoke in hotel lobbies,
And the slime in hotel spittoons:
Part of my life. (l. 6–10)

3 Babies and gin and church
And women and Sunday
All mixed with dimes and
Dollars and clean spittoons
And house rent to pay. (l. 26–30)

AmNP; BANP; MoAmPo; NoAM

Dream Variation

4 Night coming tenderly
Black like me. (l. 16–17)

AmNP; CDC; HAP; IDB; NAAL-2; NOBA; PoBA; PoNe;
WeW

Harlem Sweeties

5 Brown sugar lassie,
Caramel treat,
Honey-gold baby
Sweet enough to eat.
Peach-skinned girlie, (l. 5–9)

LiTM; NoP; PoNe; TTY

I, Too

6 I, too, sing America.

I am the darker brother.
They send me to eat in the kitchen
When company comes, (l. 1–4)

7 They'll see how beautiful I am
And be ashamed —

I, too, am America. (l. 16–18)

AmNP; CDC; FF; HCAP; HeIP; IDB; OPP; PoBA; PoLF;
PoNe

Juke Box Love Song

8 I could take the Harlem night
and wrap around you,
Take the neon lights and make a crown,
Take the Lenox Avenue buses,
Taxis, subways,
And for your love song tone their rumble down.
(l. 1–6)

GrPl; IDB; PoBA; TTTS

Lenox Avenue Mural

9 What happens to a dream deferred?

Does it dry up
like a raisin in the sun? (l. 1–3)

10 Maybe it just sags
like a heavy load.

Or does it explode? (l. 9–11)

AiP; AmNP; AmPP; FF; GLP; HCAP; HeIP; HoPM; InPK;
InPS; LiTM; NIP; NoP; PoBA; PoNe; PPP; SoSe

Morning After

11 I was so sick last night I
Didn't hardly know my mind.
So sick last night I
Didn't know my mind.
I drunk some bad licker that
Almost made me blind. (l. 1–6)

MoP; NAAL-2; NBLV; NoAM

The Negro Speaks of Rivers

12 I've known rivers:
Ancient, dusky rivers.

My soul has grown deep like the rivers. (l. 11–13)

AiP; AmFN; AmNP; BANP; BPo; CDC; HAP; HCAP;
HeIP; IDB; NAAL-2; NIP; NoAM; NOBA; NoP; OBCA;
PoBA; PoNe; TAP; TTY; WeW

Song for a Dark Girl

13 Way Down South in Dixie
(Break the heart of me)
They hung my black young lover
To a cross roads tree. (l. 1–4)

14 Love is a naked shadow
On a gnarled and naked tree. (l. 11–12)

AmPP; CDC; IDB; NAAL-2; PoBA

Theme for English B

15 here
to this college on the hill above Harlem
I am the only colored student in my class. (l. 8–10)

16 So will my page be colored that I write?
Being me, it will not be white.
But it will be
a part of you, instructor.
You are white —
yet a part of me, as I am a part of you. (l. 27–32)

17 As I learn from you,
I guess you learn from me —
although you're older — and white —
and somewhat more free.

This is my page for English B. (l. 37–41)

HCAP; MoP; NIP; NoAM; NOBA; NoP

The Weary Blues

18 Droning a drowsy syncopated tune,
Rocking back and forth to a mellow croon,
I heard a Negro play.

Down on Lenox Avenue the other night
By the pale dull pallor of an old gas light (l. 1–5)

19 The singer stopped playing and went to bed
While the Weary Blues echoed through his head.
He slept like a rock or a man that's dead.

FaBV; MoP; NoAM; NOBA; NoP; PoNe

TED HUGHES (b. 1930)

Hawk Roosting

1 I sit in the top of the wood, my eyes closed.
Inaction, no falsifying dream
Between my hooked head and hooked feet:
Or in sleep rehearse perfect kills and eat. (l. 1–4)

2 Now I hold Creation in my foot

Or fly up, and revolve it all slowly —
I kill where I please because it is all mine.
There is no sophistry in my body:
My manners are tearing off heads —

The allotment of death. (l. 12–17)

CMoP; GTBS-P; HAP; HeIP; LiTM; NePoEA-2; OxBTC;
PPP; TwCP; UnPo

November

3 The mouth of the drowned dog. After long rain the land
Was sodden as the bed of an ancient lake,
Treed with iron and birdless. (l. 1–3)

CMoP; GTBS-P; NePoEA-2; NoP

An Otter

4 Underwater eyes, an eel's
Oil of water body, neither fish nor beast is the otter:
(l. 1–2)

5 So the self under the eye lies,
Attendant and withdrawn. (l. 27–28)

6 The heart beats thick,
Big trout muscle out of the dead cold; (l. 33–34)

7 he will lick
The fishbone bare. And can take stolen hold

On a bitch otter in a field full
Of nervous horses, but linger nowhere.
Yanked above hounds, reverts to nothing at all,
To this long pelt over the back of a chair. (l. 35–40)

CMoP; MoP; NePoEA-2; NoAM

Pibroch

8 The sea cries with its meaningless voice,
Treating alike its dead and its living, (l. 1–2)

9 Minute after minute, aeon after aeon,
Nothing lets up or develops.
And this is neither a bad variant nor a tryout.
This is where the staring angels go through.
This is where all the stars bow down. (l. 21–25)

FaBoMo; NePoEA-2; OAEL-2

Pike

10 Pike, three inches long, perfect
Pike in all parts, green tigering the gold.
Killers from the egg: the malevolent aged grin.
They dance on the surface among the flies. (l. 1–4)

11 The jaws' hooked clamp and fangs
Not to be changed at this date;
A life subdued to its instrument; (l. 13–15)

12 Stilled legendary depth:
It was as deep as England: it held
Pike too immense to stir, so immense and old
That past nightfall I dared not cast (l. 33–36)

CMoP; FaBoMo; HAP; HeIP; InPS; LiTM; MAT;
NAEL-2; NePoEA-2; OxBTC; PoE; SoSe; WeW

The Thought-Fox

13 A fox's nose touches twig, leaf;
Two eyes serve a movement, that now
And again now, and now, and now

Sets neat prints into the snow (l. 10–13)

14 Coming about its own business

Till, with a sudden sharp hot stink of fox
It enters the dark hole of the head.
The window is starless still; the clock ticks,
The page is printed. (l. 20–24)

FaBoMo; HeIP; InPS; MoP; NePoEA-2; NoAM; NoP;
NYBP; SCV

RICHARD HUGO (1923–1982)

Degrees of Gray in Philipsburg

1 You might come here Sunday on a whim.
Say your life broke down. The last good kiss
you had was years ago. (l. 1–3)

2 Isn't this your life? That ancient kiss
  still burning out your eyes? Isn't this defeat
  so accurate, the church bell simply seems
  a pure announcement: ring and no one comes?
                                      (l. 23–26)

CAPP; CoAP; NAAL-2; NoAM; NoP

The Lady in Kicking Horse Reservoir

3 Off south, the bison multiply so fast
  a slaughter's mandatory every spring
  and every spring the creeks get fat
  and Kicking Horse fills up. (l. 43–46)

CoAP; LCAP; NAAL-2; NoAM; NoP

The Way a Ghost Dissolves

4 She planted corn and left the rest
  to elements, convinced that God
  with giant faucets regulates the rain
  and saves the crops from frost or foreign wind.
                                      (l. 4–7)

5 Rub a half potato on your wart
  and wrap it in a damp cloth. Close
  your eyes and whirl three times and throw.
  Then bury rag and spud exactly where they fall.
                                      (l. 9–13)

6 Or driven wild
  by snakes that kept the carrots clean,
  she butchered snakes and carrots with a hoe.
                                      (l. 17–19)

7 work until my heart is short,
  then go out slowly with a feeble grin,
  my fingers flexing but my eyes gone gray
  from cramps and the lack of oxygen. (l. 25–28)

NAAL-2; NoAM; NoP; SM

THOMAS ERNEST HULME (1883–1917)
The Embankment

1 Once, in finesse of fiddles found I ecstasy, (l. 1)

2 Oh, God, make small
  The old star-eaten blanket of the sky,
  That I may fold it round me and in comfort lie.
                                      (l. 5–7)

EBEV; FaBoMo; GTBS-P; OxBSP; OxBTC; SeCePo

TOBIAS HUME (d. 1645)

Fain Would I Change That Note (*attributed to* Hume)

1 'Love is the perfect sum
  Of all delight,' (l. 6–7)

EBEV; ElL; ELP; GBL; NOBE; OBS; PoEL-2; TrGrPo

LEIGH HUNT (1784–1859)
Abou Ben Adhem

1 Abou Ben Adhem (may his tribe increase!) (l. 1)

2 Write me as one that loves his fellow-men. (l. 14)

3 And showed the names whom love of God had blessed,
  And, lo! Ben Adhem's name led all the rest! (l. 17–18)

BeLS; BLPA; EnRP; FaBoBe; FaBoRV; FaBV; FaFP;
FaPON; FaPoR; FPL; GN; NOBE; OBEV; OHFP; PWR;
WBLP; WGRP

The Glove and the Lions

4 "No love," quothe he, "but vanity, sets love a task like
  that." (l. 24)

BeLS; FaPON; GN; WBLP

Jenny Kiss'd Me

5 Say I'm weary, say I'm sad,
  Say that health and wealth have missed me,
  Say I'm growing old, but add,
  Jenny kissed me. (l. 5–8)

BLPA; EnRP; FaBoBe; FaBV; FaFP; FF; FPL; HoPM;
InPK; NBLV; NOBE; NOBVV; NTCP; OBEV; PoRA;
TEP

The Nile

6 It flows through old hushed Egypt and its sands,
  Like some grave mighty thought threading a dream,
                                      (l. 1–2)

7 The laughing queen that caught the world's great
  hands. (l. 8)

EBEV; EnRP; NOBE; OBNC

To the Grasshopper and the Cricket

8 Green little vaulter in the sunny grass, (l. 1)

EnRP; GN; OBNC; Son

DAVID IGNATOW (b. 1914)

The Dream

1 Someone approaches to say his life is ruined
   and to fall down at your feet
   and pound his head upon the sidewalk. (l. 1–3)

CoAP; MAT; NNaP; VWA

JEAN INGELOW (1820–1897)

High Tide on the Coast of Lincolnshire, 1571

1 Alle fresh the level pasture lay,
   And not a shadowe mote by seene,
   Save where full fyve good miles away
   The steeple towered from out the greene, (l. 50–53)

BeLS; EBVV; FaBoPP; GN; Mes; OnMSP

VALENTIN IREMONGER (b. 1918)

This Houre Her Vigill

1 Elizabeth, frigidly stretched,
   On a spring day surprised us
   With her starched dignity and the quietness
   Of her hands clasping a black cross. (l. 1–4)

CIP; NeIP; NOIV; OxBTC

CHRISTOPHER ISHERWOOD
(1904–1986)

The Common Cormorant

1 The common cormorant or shag
   Lays eggs inside a paper bag. (l. 1–2)

ChTr; FaBoCh; FaBoCo; FaBoNo; FiBHP; NBLV; PYC;
RHPC

HELEN HUNT JACKSON ("H. H."; "SAXE HOLM") (1830–1885)

October's Bright Blue Weather

1 O suns and skies and clouds of June,
   And flowers of June together,
   Ye cannot rival for one hour
   October's bright blue weather. (l. 1–4)

2 O suns and skies and flowers of June,
   Count all your boasts together,
   Love loveth best of all the year
   October's bright blue weather. (l. 29–32)

BLPA; BLPL; FaBoBe; GN

September

3 The goldenrod is yellow,
   The corn is turning brown,
   The trees in apple orchards
   With fruit are bending down. (l. 1–4)

4 By all these lovely tokens
   September days are here,
   With summer's best of weather
   And autumn's best of cheer. (l. 17–20)

FaPON; FPL; GoJo; OBCA; PoLF

RANDALL JARRELL (1914–1965)

Bats

1 A bat is born
   Naked and blind and pale.
   His mother makes a pocket of her tail
   And catches him. He clings to her long fur
   By his thumbs and toes and teeth. (l. 1–5)

2 Bunched upside down, they sleep in air.
   Their sharp ears, their sharp teeth, their quick sharp
      faces
   Are dull and slow and mild.
   All the bright day, as the mother sleeps,
   She folds her wings about her sleeping child.
                                             (l. 30–34)

GrPl; NTCP; NU; OBCA; RFM

A Camp in the Prussian Forest

3 One year
   They sent a million here:

Here men were drunk like water, burnt like wood.
The fat of good
And evil, the breast's star of hope
Were rendered into soap. (l. 15–20)

4 A filmy trash
Litters the black woods with the death
Of men; and one last breath

Curls from the monstrous chimney. . . . (l. 30–33)

CMoP; MoAmPo; OBWP; OxBC

The Death of the Ball Turret Gunner

5 I woke to black flak and the nightmare fighters.
When I died they washed me out of the turret with a
hose. (l. 4–5)

CAPP; CMoP; FF; HAP; HeIP; HoPM; InPK; LCAP;
LiTM; MoAmPo; MT; NAAL-2; NAs; NIP; NoAM; NOBA;
NoP; OBD; OBWP; OxBA; PoE; PPP; PrIm; RB; SoSe;
TAP; UnPo; VGW; WaaP; WaP

A Girl in a Library

6 An object among dreams, you sit here with your shoes
off
And curl your legs up under you; (l. 1–2)

7 These calves, grown muscular with certainties;
This nose, three medium-sized pink strawberries
(l. 9–10)

8 bars of that strange speech
In which each sound sets out to seek each other,
Murders its own father, marries its own mother,
And ends as one grand transcendental vowel.
(l. 13–16)

9 The soul has no assignments, neither cooks
Nor referees: it wastes its time.
It wastes its time. (l. 33–35)

10 The blind date that has stood you up: your life. (l. 87)

11 The firelight of a long, blind, dreaming story
Lingers upon your lips; and I have seen
Firm, fixed forever in your closing eyes,
The Corn King beckoning to his Spring Queen.
(l. 104–107)

NAAL-2; NoAM; NOBA; NoP

In Montecito

12 They have thrown away her electric toothbrush,
someone else slips
The key into the lock of her safety-deposit box

At the Crocker-Anglo Bank; her seat at the cricket
matches
Is warmed by buttocks less delectable than hers.
(l. 12–15)

CoAP; MAT; NoP; NYBP; VGW

Losses

13 It was not dying: everybody died. (l. 1)

14 We died like aunts of pets or foreigners. (l. 10)

15 In bombers named for girls, we burned
The cities we had learned about in school —
Till our lives wore out; our bodies lay among
The people we had killed and never seen. (l. 22–25)

16 They said, "Here are the maps"; we burned the cities.
It was not dying — no, not ever dying;
But the night I died I dreamed that I was dead,
And the cities said to me: "Why are you dying?
We are satisfied, if you are; but why did I die?"
(l. 28–32)

HCAP; LCAP; LiTM; OxBA; PoA; TAP; UnPo; WaP

Next Day

17 Now that I'm old, my wish
Is womanish:
That the boy putting groceries in my car

See me. (l. 16–19)

18 My friend's cold made-up face, granite among its
flowers,
Her undressed, operated-on, dressed body
Were my face and body. (l. 51–53)

19 But really no one is exceptional,
No one has anything, I'm anybody,
I stand beside my grave
Confused with my life, that is commonplace and
solitary. (l. 57–60)

HAP; HCAP; MoP; NAAL-2; NoAM; NoP; NYBP; WeW

90 North

20 — Here, the flag snaps in the glare and silence
Of the unbroken ice. I stand here,
The dogs bark, my beard is black, and I stare
At the North Pole. . .
And now what? Why, go back.

Turn as I please, my step is to the south. (l. 9–14)

21 I wrung from the darkness — that the darkness flung
  me —
  Is worthless as ignorance: nothing comes from nothing,
  The darkness from the darkness. Pain comes from the
  darkness
  And we call it wisdom. It is pain. (l. 30–33)

CAPP; CoAP; FYAP; MoAB; MT; NAAL-2; NoAM; NOBA;
TAP

The Orient Express

22 It is like any other work of art.
  It is and never can be changed.
  Behind everything there is always
  The unknown unwanted life. (l. 32–35)

CMoP; CoAP; NOBA; PoE

Second Air Force

23 The head withdraws into its hatch (a boy's),
  The engines rise to their blind laboring roar,
  And the green, made beasts run home to air.
  Now in each aspect death is pure. (l. 17–20)

CMoP; LiTM; NAAL-2; WaP

A Sick Child

24 If I can think of it, it isn't what I want.
  I want . . . I want a ship from some near star
  To land in the yard, (l. 13–15)

25 And yet somewhere there must be
  Something that's different from everything.
  All that I've never thought of — think of me!
                        (l. 18–20)

InPK; InvP; OxBC; SO; VGW

Well Water

26 the rusty
  Pump pumps over your sweating face the clear
  Water, cold, so cold! you cup your hands
  And gulp from them the dailiness of life. (l. 10–13)

InPK; NAAL-2; NOBA; NoP; OxBSP; VGW

The Woman at the Washington Zoo

27 The world goes by my cage and never sees me. (l. 20)

28 The wild beasts, sparrows pecking the llamas' grain,
  Pigeons settling on the bears' bread, buzzards
  Tearing the meat the flies have clouded. . . .
                        (l. 22–24)

CAPP; CoAP; HAP; HCAP; LiTM; OxBC; TAP; TwCP;
UnPo

ROBINSON JEFFERS (1887–1962)
Apology for Bad Dreams

1 This coast crying out for tragedy like all beautiful
  places, (l. 21)

2 what are we,
  The beast that walks upright, with speaking lips
  And little hair, to think we should always be fed,
  Sheltered, intact, and self-controlled? (l. 33–36)

3 the ghosts of the tribe
  Crouch in the nights beside the ghost of a fire, they try
  to remember the sunlight,
  Light has died out of their skies. (l. 43–45)

4 Unmeasured power, incredible passion, enormous craft:
  no thought apparent but burns darkly
  Smothered with its own smoke in the human brain-
  vault: no thought outside; a certain measure in
  phenomena:
  The fountains of the boiling stars, the flowers on the
  foreland, the ever-returning roses of dawn.
                        (l. 66–68)

AmPP; LiTA; MoAB; MoAmPo; NOBA; OxBA

Ave Caesar

5 We are easy to manage, a gregarious people,
  Full of sentiment, clever at mechanics, and we love our
  luxuries. (l. 7–8)

FaBoPV; MoP; NoAM; NOBA; OxBA; OxBSP

Boats in a Fog

6 Sports and gallantries, the stage, the arts, the antics of
  dancers,
  The exuberant voices of music,
  Have charm for children but lack nobility; it is bitter
  earnestness
  That makes beauty; the mind
  Knows, grown adult. (l. 1–5)

7 all the arts lose virtue
  Against the essential reality

Of creatures going about their business among the
equally
Earnest elements of nature. (l. 20–23)

MOS; NAAL-2; NoP; OxBA

Cassandra

8 The mad girl with the staring eyes and long white
fingers
Hooked in the stones of the wall, (l. 1–2)

9 Truly men hate the truth; they'd liefer
Meet a tiger on the road.
Therefore the poets honey their truth with lying; but
religion-
Vendors and political men
Pour from the barrel, new lies on the old, (l. 7–9)

HeIP; LiTA; LiTM; WaP

Eagle Valor, Chicken Mind

10 Unhappy country what wings you have (l. 1)

11 Unhappy, eagle wings and bleak, chicken brain. (l. 5)

LiTA; OxBA; OxBSP; WaP

The Eye

12 headland beyond stormy headland plunging like
dolphins through the gray sea-smoke
Into pale sea, look west at the hill of water: it is half
the planet: this dome, this half-globe, this bulging
Eyeball of water, (l. 10–12)

LiTA; LiTM; NoAM; NOBA; OxBA; WaP

Hurt Hawks

13 The broken pillar of the wing jags from the clotted
shoulder,
The wing trails like a banner in defeat, (l. 1–2)

14 He is strong and pain is worse to the strong, incapacity
is worse. (l. 9)

15 I'd sooner, except the penalties, kill a man than a
hawk; (l. 18)

16 I gave him the lead gift in the twilight. What fell was
relaxed,
Owl-downy, soft feminine feathers; but what

Soared: the fierce rush: the night-herons by the flooded
river cried fear at its rising
Before it was quite unsheathed from reality. (l. 24–27)

AmPP; CMoP; FYAP; LiTA; LiTM; MoAB; MoAmPo;
MoP; NAAL-2; NoAM; NOBA; NoP; OxBA; PrIm; RB;
TAP; UnPo

Love the Wild Swan

17 "I hate my verses, every line, every word.
Oh pale and brittle pencils ever to try
One grass-blade's curve, or the throat of one bird
That clings to twig, (l. 1–4)

18 This wild swan of a world is no hunter's game. (l. 9)

19 Love your eyes that can see, your mind that can
Hear the music, the thunder of the wings. Love the
wild swan. (l. 13–14)

MoAB; MoAmPo; NoAM; Son; TW

May – June, 1940

20 Forseen for so many years: these evils, this monstrous
violence, these massive agonies: no easier to bear.
(l. 1)

21 It would be better for men
To be few and live far apart, where none could infect
another; then slowly the sanity of field and mountain
And the cold ocean and glittering stars might enter
their minds. (l. 5–7)

22 the dive-bomber's screaming orgasm
As beautiful as other passions; (l. 12–13)

23 And why do you cry, my dear, why do you cry?
It is all in the whirling circles of time.
If millions are born millions must die, (l. 16–18)

24 If civilization goes down, that
Would be an event to contemplate.
It will not be in our time, alas, my dear,
It will not be in our time. (l. 22–25)

LiTA; LiTM; MoAB; MoAmPo; WaP

New Mexican Mountain

25 They dance with reluctance, they are growing civilized;
the old men persuade them. (l. 4)

26 Only the drum is confident, it thinks the world has not
changed; (l. 5)

27 civilization is a transient sickness. (l. 12)

GOA; InPS; MoP; NoAM

Night

28 the splendor without rays, the shining shadow,
Peace-bringer, the matrix of all shining and quieter of
shining. (l. 10–11)

29 O passionately at peace when will that tide draw
shoreward, (l. 47)

30 And life, the flicker of men and moths and the wolf on
the hill,
Though furious for continuance, passionately feeding,
passionately
Remaking itself upon its mates, remembers deep
inward
The calm mother, the quietness of the womb and the
egg, (l. 51–54)

31 Life is grown sweeter and lonelier,
And death is no evil. (l. 64–65)

AWP; LiTA; MoAmPo; NOBA; OxBA

Prescription of Painful Ends

32 The future is ever a misted landscape, no man
foreknows it, but at cyclical turns
There is a change felt in the rhythm of events:
(l. 3–4)

33 come peace or war, the progress of America and Europe
Becomes a long process of deterioration — (l. 7–8)

34 Lucretius
Sings his great theory of natural origins and of wise
conduct; Plato smiling carves dreams, bright cells
Of incorruptible wax to hive the Greek honey.
(l. 11–13)

LiTA; MoAB; MoAmPo; OxBA

Promise of Peace

35 The heads of strong old age are beautiful
Beyond all grace of youth. (l. 1–2)

36 How shall the dead taste the deep treasure they have?
(l. 14)

LiTA; LiTM; MoAB; MoAmPo

Shine, Perishing Republic

37 While this America settles in the mould of its vulgarity,
heavily thickening to empire,
And protest, only a bubble in the molten mass, pops
and sighs out, and the mass hardens, (l. 1–2)

38 A mortal splendor: meteors are not needed less than
mountains: shine, perishing republic. (l. 6)

39 And boys, be in nothing so moderate as in love of man,
a clever servant, insufferable master.
There is the trap that catches noblest spirits, that
caught — they say — God, when he walked on earth.
(l. 17–20)

CMoP; FF; LiTA; LiTM; MAT; McAB; MoP; NAAL-2;
NoAM; NOBA; NoP; OxBA; PrIm; TAP; UnPo; VGW

Shine, Republic

40 The love of freedom has been the quality of Western
man. (l. 2)

41 And you, America, that passion made you. You were
not born to prosperity, you were born to love
freedom.
You did not say "en masse," you said "independence."
But we cannot have all the luxuries and freedom also.
(l. 7–8)

42 Be great, carve deep your heel-marks.
The states of the next age will no doubt remember you,
and edge their love of freedom with contempt of
luxury. (l. 11–12)

AmFN; FaBoPV; GOA; OPP

To the Stone-Cutters

43 man will be blotted out, the blithe earth die, the brave
sun
Die blind and blacken to the heart:
Yet stones have stood for a thousand years, and pained
thoughts found
The honey of peace in old poems. (l. 7–10)

AmPP; MoAB; MoAmPo; NAAL-2; NOBA; NoP; OxBA;
PoRA; PrIm; TrGrPo

Vulture

44 I tell you solemnly
That I was sorry to have disappointed him. To be eaten
by that beak and become part of him, to share those
wings and those eyes —
What a sublime end of one's body, what an enskyment;
what a life after death. (l. 9–11)

NAAL-2; NoAM; NOBA; NoP

FRANCIS JEFFREY, LORD JEFFREY
(1773–1850)

On Peter Robinson

1 Here lies the preacher, judge, and poet, Peter
Who broke the laws of God, and man and metre.
(l. 1–2)

FaBoCo; FaBoEE; NBLV; OxBoLi

ELIZABETH JENNINGS (b. 1926)

One Flesh

1 Chastity faces them, a destination
For which their whole lives were a preparation.
(l. 11–12)

2 Do they know they're old,
These two who are my father and my mother
Whose fire from which I came, has now grown cold?
(l. 16–18)

AIW; FaBoWP; OxBTC; PBWP

FENTON JOHNSON (1886–1958)

Tired

1 Throw the children into the river; civilization has given
us too many.
It is better to die than to grow up and find that you are
colored.
Pluck the stars out of the heavens. The stars mark our
destiny. The stars marked my destiny.
I am tired of civilization. (l. 6–8)

BANP; IDB; PoBA; PoLF; PoNe; TTY

GEORGIA DOUGLAS JOHNSON
(1886–1966)

The Heart of a Woman

1 The heart of a woman falls back with the night,
And enters some alien cage in its plight,
And tries to forget it has dreamed of the stars,
While it breaks, breaks, breaks on the sheltering bars.
(l. 5–8)

BANP; BlSi; CDC; PoLF; PoNe

I Want to Die While You Love Me

2 I want to die while you love me,
And never, never see
The glory of this perfect day
Grow dim, or cease to be! (l. 13–16)

AmNP; BANP; BlSi; CDC

My Little Dreams

3 I'm folding up my little dreams
Within my heart tonight,
And praying I may soon forget
The torture of their sight. (l. 1–4)

BANP; BlSi; CDC; PoNe

HELENE JOHNSON (b. 1907)

Little brown boy

1 Gee, boy, when you sing, I can close my ears
And hear tom-toms just as plain.
Listen to me, will you, what do I know
About tom-toms? But I like the word, sort of,
Don't you? It belongs to us. (l. 19–23)

AmNP; BANP; CDC; PoBA

Magalu

2 Would you sell the colors of your sunset and the
fragrance
Of your flowers, and the passionate wonder of your
forest
For a creed that will not let you dance? (l. 22–24)

BlSi; CDC; PoBA; PoNe

The Road

3 Ah, little road, brown as my race is brown,
Your trodden beauty like our trodden pride,
Dust of the dust, they must not bruise you down.
Rise to one brimming golden, spilling cry! (l. 5–8)

AmNP; BANP; BlSi; CDC; PoNe

Sonnet to a Negro in Harlem

4 You are disdainful and magnificent —
Your perfect body and your pompous gait,
Your dark eyes flashing solemnly with hate, (l. 1–3)

AmNP; BANP; CDC; NIP

JAMES WELDON JOHNSON (1871–1938)

The Creation

1 And God stepped out on space,
And He looked around and said,
"I'm lonely —
I'll make me a world." (l. 1–4)

2 So God stepped over to the edge of the world
And He spat out the seven seas;
He batted His eyes, and the lightnings flashed;
He clapped His hands, and the thunders rolled;
And the waters above the earth came down,
The cooling waters came down. (l. 36–41)

3 This Great God,
Like a mammy bending over her baby,
Kneeled down in the dust
Toiling over a lump of clay
Till He shaped it in His own image; (l. 84–88)

BANP; CDC; FaBV; MoAmPo; PoBA; PoRA; TrCP

The Glory of the Day Was in Her Face

4 The glory of the day was in her face,
The beauty of the night was in her eyes. (l. 1–2)

BANP; CDC; IDB; PoBA

O Black and Unknown Bards

5 O black and unknown bards of long ago,
How came your lips to touch the sacred fire? (l. 1–2)

6 Whose starward eye
Saw chariot "swing low"? And who was he
That breathed that comforting, melodic sigh,
"Nobody knows de trouble I see"? (l. 13–16)

7 You sang far better than you knew; the songs
That for your listeners' hungry hearts sufficed
Still live, — but more than this to you belongs:
You sang a race from wood and stone to Christ.
(l. 45–48)

AmNP; BANP; BPo; HeIP; PoBA; PoNe; TTY; UnPo

LIONEL PIGOT JOHNSON (1867–1902)

By the Statue of King Charles at Charing Cross

1 Sombre and rich, the skies;
Great glooms, and starry plains.
Gently the night wind sighs;
Else a vast silence reigns. (l. 1–4)

2 The saddest of all kings
Crowned, and again discrowned. (l. 7–8)

3 Alone he rides, alone,
The fair and fatal king:
Dark night is all his own,
That strange and solemn thing. (l. 17–20)

4 Vanquished in life, his death
By beauty made amends:
The passing of his breath
Won his defeated ends. (l. 29–32)

5 Yet, when the city sleeps;
When all the cries are still:
The stars and heavenly deeps
Work out a perfect will. (l. 49–52)

BrPo; FaBoRV; MoBrPo; NOBE; OBEV; OBMV; OBNC;
PoEL-5

The Dark Angel

6 Dark Angel with thine aching lust
To rid the world of penitence:
Malicious Angel, who still dost
My soul such subtile violence!

Because of thee, no thought, no thing,
Abides for me undesecrate:
Dark Angel, ever on the wing,
Who never reachest me too late! (l. 1–8)

7 Because of thee, the land of dreams
Becomes a gathering place of fears:
Until tormented slumber seems
One vehemence of useless tears. (l. 17–20)

ACP; GTBS-P; LiTB; MoBrPo; NOBE; NOBVV; OAEL-2;
OBMV

SAMUEL JOHNSON (1709–1784)

London

1 Slow rises worth, by poverty depressed: (l. 177)

On the Death of Mr. Robert Levet, a Practiser in Physic

2 Condemned to Hope's delusive mine,
As on we toil from day to day,
By sudden blasts or slow decline
Our social comforts drop away. (l. 1–4)

3 His virtues walked their narrow round,
Nor made a pause, nor left a void;
And sure the Eternal Master found
The single talent well employed. (l. 25–28)

4 Then with no fiery throbbing pain,
No cold gradations of decay,
Death broke at once the vital chain,
And freed his soul the nearest way. (l. 33–36)

EBEV; HeIP; InPS; NAEL-1; NOBE; NOEC; NoP;
OAEL-1; OBEV; PoE; PoEL-3; PPP; SCV; TEP

Prologue Spoken by Mr. Garrick

5 When Learning's Triumph o'er her barb'rous Foes
First rear'd the Stage, immortal Shakespear rose;
Each Change of many-colour'd Life he drew,
Exhausted Worlds, and then imagin'd new: (l. 1–4)

6 Their Cause was gen'ral, their Supports were strong,
Their Slaves were willing, and their Reign was long;
(l. 25–26)

7 From Bard, to Bard, the frigid Caution crept,
Till Declamation roar'd, while Passion slept.
(l. 31–32)

8 Hard is his lot, that here by Fortune plac'd,
Must watch the wild Vicissitudes of Taste; (l. 47–48)

9 The Stage but echoes back the publick Voice.
The Drama's Laws the Drama's Patrons give,
For we that live to please, must please to live.
(l. 52–54)

EBEV; NAEL-1; NOEC; NoP

A Short Song of Congratulation

10 Long-expected one and twenty
Ling'ring year at last is flown,
Pomp and pleasure, pride and plenty,
Great Sir John, are all your own. (l. 1–4)

11 Loosened from the minor's tether;
Free to mortgage or to sell,
Wild as wind, and light as feather
Bid the slaves of thrift farewell. (l. 5–8)

12 If the guardian or the mother
Tell the woes of willful waste,
Scorn their counsel and their pother,
You can hang or drown at last. (l. 25–28)

EBEV; ELP; HAP; InPK; InPS; InvP; NOBE; NOEC;
NoP; OBSV; PoE; PoEL-3; TEP; UnPo

The Vanity of Human Wishes: The Tenth Satire of Juvenal Imitated

13 But grant, the virtues of a temp'rate prime
Bless with an age exempt from scorn or crime;
An age that melts with unperceived decay,
And glides in modest Innocence away; (l. 291–294)

14 Year chases year, decay pursues decay,
Still drops some joy from with'ring life away;
New forms arise, and diff'rent views engage,
(l. 305–307)

EBEV; HeIP; LaA; NOEC; NoP; OAEL-1; PoEL-3; PrIm;
SeCePo; TEP

15 Let observation with extensive view;
Survey mankind, from China to Peru; (l. 1–2)

16 Fate wings with every wish th' afflictive dart,
Each gift of nature, and each grace of art, (l. 15–16)

17 When first the college rolls receive his name,
The young enthusiast quilts his ease for fame;
Through all his veins the fever of renown
Burns from the strong contagion of the gown;
(l. 135–138)

18 There mark what ills the scholar's life assail,
Toil, envy, want, the patron, and the jail.
(l. 159–160)

19 He left the name, at which the worldgrew pale,
To point a moral, or adorn a tale. (l. 221–222)

20 That life protracted is protracted woe. (l. 258)

21 Superfluous lags the veteran on the stage,
Till pitying Nature signs the last release,
And bids afflicted worth retire to peace. (l. 308–310)

22 Still raise for good the supplicating voice,
But leave to heaven the measure and the choice,
(l. 351–352)

23 Pour forth thy fervors for a healthful mind,
Obedient passions, and a will resigned; (l. 359–360)

SAMUEL JOHNSON (1822–1882)

Life of Ages, Richly Poured

1 Life of Ages, richly poured,
Love of God unspent and free,
Flowing in the Prophet's word
And the People's liberty!

Never was to chosen race
That unstinted tide confined;
Thine is every time and place,
Fountain sweet of heart and mind! (l. 1–8)

AA; AH; TrPWD; WGRP

BEN JONSON (1572–1637)

A Celebration of Charis in Ten Lyrick Peeces

1 Let it not your wonder move,
Less your laughter, that I love.
Though I now write fifty years,
I have had, and have, my peers;
Poets, though divine, are men:

Some have loved as old again.
And it is not always face,
Clothes, or fortune gives the grace,
Or the feature, or the youth;
But the language, and the truth,
With the ardour and the passion,
Gives the lover weight and fashion. (l. 1–12)

JCP; PoEL-2; QFR; SeCP; SeCV-1

2 Have you seen but a bright lily grow
Before rude hands have touch'd it?
Have you mark'd but the fall of the snow
Before the soil hath smutch'd it?
Have you felt the wool of the beaver,
Or swan's down ever?
Or have smelt of the bud of the brier,
Or the nard in the fire?
Or have tasted the bag of the bee?
O so white, O so soft, O so sweet is she! (l. 21–30)

CTC; EBEV; ElL; ELP; InvP; JCP; LiTB; NOBE; NoP;
OBEV; OPOP; PoEL-2; PrIm; SeCP; SeCV-1

Cynthia's Revels

3 Queen and huntress, chaste and fair,
Now the sun is laid to sleep,
Seated in thy silver chair,
State in wonted manner keep:
Hesperus entreats thy light,
Goddess excellently bright.

AWP; CH; ChTr; ElL; GN; GTBS; GTBS-P; HAP; HeIP;
InPS; JCP; NAEL-1; NOBE; NoP; OAEL-1; OBEV; OBS;
PoE; PoEL-2; PoRA; PrIm; QFR; SeCePo; SeCP; SeCV-1;
TrGrPo; WiR

4 Slow, slow, fresh fount, keep time with my salt tears;
Yet slower yet, oh faintly gentle springs:
List to the heavy part the music bears,
"Woe weeps out her division when she sings."
Droop herbs and flowers;
Fall grief in showers;
"Our beauties are not ours":
Oh, I could still,
Like melting snow upon some craggy hill,
Drop, drop, drop, drop,
Since nature's pride is, now, a withered daffodil.

CH; ChTr; ElL; ELP; InPS; JCP; NoP; OAEL-1; OBS;
OxBSP; PoEL-2; PrIm; SeCP; SeCV-1; TrGrPo

Epicoene; or, The Silent Woman

5 Give me a look, give me a face,
That makes simplicity a grace;
Robes loosely flowing, hair as free:
Such sweet neglect more taketh me

Than all the adulteries of art;
They strike mine eyes, but not my heart. (l. 7–12)

AWP; ElL; FF; GBL; HAP; HeIP; HoPM; InPS; JCP;
NOBE; NoP; OAEL-1; OBEV; OBS; PoE; PPP; PrIm;
SeCePo; SeCP; SeCV-1; TEP; TrGrPo; WeW

Epitaph on Elizabeth, L. H.

6 Wouldst thou hear what man can say
In a little? Reader, stay.
Underneath this stone doth lie
As much beauty as could die; (l. 1–4)

ElL; ELP; FaBoEE; HAP; HeIP; NAEL-1; NIP; NoP;
OBEV; OBS; PoE; SeCP; SeCV-1

Epitaph on S. P., a Child of Queen Elizabeth's Chapel

7 Weep with me, all you that read
This little story;
And know, for whom a tear you shed
Death's self is sorry. (l. 1–4)

8 And have sought, to give new birth,
In baths to steep him;
But, being so much too good for earth,
Heaven vows to keep him. (l. 21–24)

ElL; HeIP; HoPM; JCP; MePo; Mes; NAEL-1; NOBE;
NoP; OAEL-1; OBD; OBEV; OBS; PoEL-2; PPP; SeCP;
SeCV-1; TrGrPo; UnPo

A Fit of Rime against Rime

9 Rhyme, the rack of finest wits,
That expresseth but by fits
True conceit,
Spoiling senses of their treasure,
Cozening judgment with a measure,
But false weight;
Wresting words from their true calling;
Propping verse for fear of falling
To the ground;
Jointing syllables, drowning letters,
Fastening vowels, as with fetters
They were bound! (l. 1–12)

InvP; MAT; OAEL-1; PoEL-2; SeCP; SeCV-1; TEP

The Gypsies Metamorphosed

10 The faery beam upon you,
The stars to glisten on you,
A moon of light
In the noon of night
Till the firedrake hath o'er gone you. (l. 1–5)

11 The wheel of fortune guide you,
The boy with the bow beside you
Run aye in the way
Till the bird of day
And the luckier lot betide you. (l. 6–7)

EBEV; FaBoCh; OxBSP; SeCV-1; TEP

The Hourglass

12 Do but consider this small dust, here running in the
glass,
By atoms moved.
Could you believe that this the body was
Of one that loved?
And in his mistress' flame playing like a fly,
Turned to cinders by her eye?
Yes, and in death as life unblest,
To have't expressed,
Even ashes of lovers find no rest. (l. 1–9)

EnLoPo; NIP; OAEL-1; SeCP

A Hymn to God the Father

13 Heare mee, O God!
A broken heart,
Is my best part:
Use still thy rod,
That I may prove
Therein, thy Love.

If thou hadst not
Beene stern to mee.
But left me free.
I had forgot
My selfe and thee. (l. 1–11)

MePo; NoP; OBS; SeCP; SeCV-1; TrCP; TrPWD

Inviting a Friend to Supper

14 Tonight, grave sir, both my poore house, and I
Doe equally desire your companie:
Not that we thinke us worthy such a ghest,
But that your worth will dignifie our feast, (l. 1–4)

15 How so ere, my man
Shall reade a piece of virgil, tacitus,
livie, or some better booke to us,
Of which wee'll speake our minds, amidst our meate:
And Ile professe no verses to repeate: (l. 19–23)

AWP; JCP; LiTB; NOBE; NoP; OAEL-1; OBS; OxBoLi;
PoEL-2; PPP; SeCP; SeCV-1

The Masque of Queens

16 The owl is abroad, the bat and the toad,
And so is the cat-a-mountain;
The ant and the mole sit both in a hole,
And frog peeps out o' the fountain. (l. 1–4)

17 With pictures full, of wax and of wool,
Their livers I stick with needles quick;
There lacks but the blood to make up the flood.
(l. 10–12)

ElL; WSC

My Picture Left in Scotland

18 I now thinke, Love is rather deafe, than blind,
For else it could not be,
That she,
Whom I adore so much, should so slight me,
And cast my love behind:
I'm sure my language to her, was as sweet,
And every close did meet
In sentence, of as subtile feet,
As hath the youngest Hee, (l. 1–9)

MePo; NAEL-1; PoEL-2; QFR; SeCP; SeCV-1

Oberon, the Fairy Prince

19 Buz, quoth the blue fly,
Hum, quoth the bee,
Buz and hum they cry,
And so do we:
In his ear, in his nose, thus, do you see?
He ate the dormouse, else it was he. (l. 1–6)

ElL; FaBoNo; FM; NA; OxNR; TEP

Ode to Himself

20 Come leave the loathed stage,
And the more loathsome age,
Where pride and impudence in faction knit
Usurp the chair of wit:
Indicting and arraigning every day,
Something they call a play.
Let their fastidious, vain
Commission of the brain,
Run on and rage, sweat, censure, and condemn:
They were not made for thee, less thou for them.
(l. 1–10)

NAEL-1; OAEL-1; OBS; SeCP

An Ode: To Himselfe

21 And since our Daintie age,
Cannot indure reproofe,
Make not thy selfe a Page,
To that strumpet the Stage,
But sing high and aloofe,
Safe from the wolves black jaw, and the dull Asses
hoofe. (l. 31–36)

HAP; JCP; LiTB; NOBE; NoP; OBS; PoEL-2; PrIm;
QFR; SeCePo; SeCP; SeCV-1

On My First Daughter

22 Here lies each her parents' ruth,
  Mary, the daughter of their youth:
  Yet, all heaven's gifts, being heaven's due,
  It makes the father, less, to rue.
  At six months' end, she parted hence
  With safety of her innocence;
  Whose soul heaven's Queen, (whose name she bears)
  In comfort of her mother's tears,
  Hath placed amongst her virgin-train:
  Where, while that severed doth remain,
  This grave partakes the fleshly birth.
  Which cover lightly, gentle earth. (l. 1–12)

EBEV; FaBoEE; HoPM; InPS; JCP; NAEL-1; NOBE;
NoP; OBS; PoE; SeCP; SeCV-1; TEP

On My First Son

23 Farewell, thou child of my right hand, and joy;
  My sin was too much hope of thee, loved boy.
  Seven years thou wert lent to me, and I thee pay,
  Exacted by thy fate, on the just day.
  Oh, could I lose all father now! For why
  Will man lament the state he should envy?
  To have so soon 'scaped world's and flesh's rage,
  And, if no other misery, yet age?
  Rest in soft peace, and. asked, say here doth lie
  Ben Jonson his best piece of poetry;
  For whose sake, henceforth, all his vows be such,
  As what he loves may never like too much. (l. 1–12)

AWP; EBEV; ElL; FaBoEE; FF; HAP; HeIP; HoPM;
InPK; InPS; JCP; LiTB; NAEL-1; NIP; NOBE; NoP;
OAEL-1; OBD; OBS; OxBSP; PoE; PoEL-2; QFR; RB;
SeCP; SeCV-1; TEP; WeW

On Something, That Walks Somewhere

24 At court I met it, in clothes brave enough
  To be a courtier, and looks grave enough
  To seem a statesman. (l. 1–3)

25 "A lord, it cried, buried in flesh and blood,
  And such from whom let no man hope least good,
  For I will do none; and as little ill,
  For I will dare none." Good Lord, walk dead still.
                                      (l. 5–8)

NAEL-1; OxBSP; PoE; SeCP; SeCV-1

Pleasure Reconciled to Virtue

26 Room, room, make room for the bouncing belly,
  First father of sauce, and deviser of jelly, (l. 1–2)

27 Hail, hail, plump paunch, O the founder of taste
  For fresh meats, or powdered, or pickle, or paste;
  Devourer of broiled, baked, roasted or sod,

And emptier of cups, be they even or odd;
  All which have now made thee so wide i' the waist
  As scarce with no pudding thou art to be laced;
  But eating and drinking until thou dost nod,
  Thou break'st all thy girdles, and break'st forth a god.
                                      (l. 17–24)

EIL; NAEL-1; OAEL-1; SeCePo

The Sad Shepherd

28 Though I am young and cannot tell
  Either what death or love is well,
  Yet I have heard they both bear darts,
  And both do aim at human hearts:
  And then again, I have been told,
  Love wounds with heat, as death with cold; (l. 1–6)

ELP; NOBE; NoP; PoEL-2; SeCP; TEP

That Women Are but Men's Shadows

29 Follow a shaddow, it still flies you;
  Seeme to flye it, it will pursue:
  So court a mistris, shee denyes you;
  Let her alone, shee will court you.
  Say, are not women truely, then,
  Stil'd but the shaddowes of us men?
  At morne, and even, shades are longest;
  At noone, they are or short, or none:
  So men at weakest, they are strongest,
  But grant us perfect, they're not knowne.
  Say, are not women truely, then,
  Stil'd but the shaddowes of us men? (l. 1–12)

EIL; NOBE; OBEV; OBS; OxBSP; SeCP; WBLP

Though beauty be the mark of praise

30 Though beautie be the marke of praise,
  And yours of whom I sing be such
  As not the world can praise too much,
  Yet is't your vertue now I raise. (l. 1–4)

NoP; OBEV; QFR; SeCV-1

To Celia

31 Drink to me only with thine eyes
  And I will pledge with mine;
  Or leave a kiss but in the cup,
  And I'll not look for wine.
  The thirst that from the soul doth rise
  Doth ask a drink divine;
  But might I of Jove's nectar sup,
  I would not change for thine. (l. 1–8)

AWP; BoLoP; ElL; ELP; EnLoPo; FaBoBe; FaBV; FaFP;
FPL; GBL; GTBS; GTBS-P; HeIP; InPK; LiTB; NAEL-1;
NOBE; NoP; OAEL-1; OBEV; OBS; OBVE; PoE;
PoEL-2; PoLF; PrIm; SeCP; SeCV-1; TEP; TrGrPo

To Fine Lady Would-Be

32 Fine Madam Would-Be, wherefore should you fear,
That love to make so well, a child to bear?
The world reputes you barren; but I know
Your 'pothecary, and his drug says no.
Is it the pain affrights? That's soon forgot,
Or your complexion's loss? You have a pot
That can restore that. Will it hurt your feature?
To make amends, you're thought a wholesome creature.
What should the cause be? Oh, you live at court,
And there's both loss of time and loss of sport
In a great belly. Write, then, on thy womb,
Of the not born, yet buried, here's the tomb. (l. 1–12)

FaBoEE; JCP; NoP; OxBSP

To Heaven

33 I know my state, both full of shame and scorn,
Conceived in sin, and unto labor born,
Standing with fear, and must with horror fall,
And destined unto judgment, after all. (l. 17–20)

HAP; JCP; LiTB; NAEL-1; NOCV; OBS; QFR; SeCP;
TrPWD; UnPo

To John Donne

34 My title's sealed. Those that for claps do write,
Let pui'nies, porters', players' praise delight,
And, till they burst, their backs like asses load:
A man should seek great glory, and not broad.
(l. 9–12)

JCP; NoP; SeCP; SeCV-1

To Penshurst

35 Thou art not, Penshurst, built to envious show,
Of touch or marble; nor canst boast a row
Of polished pillars, or a roof of gold;
Thou hast no lantern whereof tales are told,
Or stair, or courts; but stand'st an ancient pile,
(l. 1–5)

36 Some bring a capon, some a rural cake,
Some nuts, some apples; some that think they make
The better cheeses bring 'em, or else send
By their ripe daughters, whom they would commend
This way to husbands, and whose baskets bear
An emblem of themselves in plum or pear. (l. 51–56)

37 Now, Penshurst, they that will proportion thee
With other edifices, when they see
Those proud, ambitious heaps, and nothing else,
May say, their lords have built, but thy lord dwells.
(l. 99–102)

FaBoPP; FaBoPV; JCP; NAEL-1; NIP; NoP; OAEL-1;
OBS; PoE; PoEL-2; PPP; SeCP; SeCV-1; TEP

To the Immortal Memory and Friendship of That Noble Pair, Sir Lucius Cary and Sir Henry Morison

38 Wise child, didst hastily return
And mad'st thy mother's womb thine urn.
How summed a circle didst thou leave mankind
Of deepest lore, could we the center find! (l. 7–10)

39 He stood, a soldier, to the last right end,
A perfect patriot and a noble friend,
But most a virtuous son.
All offices were done
By him, so ample, full, and round
In weight in measure, number, sound,
As, though his age imperfect might appear,
His life was of humanity the sphere. (l. 45–52)

40 Not lived; for life doth her great actions spell,
By what was done and wrought
In season, and so brought
To light: her measures are, how well
Each syllab'e answered, and was formed how fair;
These make the lines of life, and that's her air.
(l. 59–64)

41 It is not growing like a tree
In bulk, doth make man better be,
Or standing long an oak, three hundred year,
To fall a log at last, dry, bald, and sere:
A lily of a day
Is fairer far in May
Although it fall and die that night;
It was the plant and flower of light.
In small proportions we just beauties see,
And in short measures life may perfect be. (l. 65–74)

42 This made you first to know the Why
You liked, then after to apply
That liking; and approach so one the tother,
Till either grew a portion of the other;
Each styled by his end,
The copy of his friend. (l. 107–112)

NAEL-1; NOBE; NoP; OAEL-1; OBS; PoEL-2; SeCP;
SeCV-1

To the Memory of My Beloved Master William Shakespeare

43 Thou art a monument without a tomb,
And art alive still while thy book doth live
And we have wits to read and praise to give.
(l. 17–19)

44 He was not of an age, but for all time! (l. 38)

45 Yet must I not give Nature all; thy art,
My gentle Shakespeare, must enjoy a part.
For though the poet's matter Nature be,
His art doth give the fashion; and, that he

Who casts to write a living line, must sweat
(Such as thine are) and strike the second heat
Upon the Muses' anvil; turn the same
(And himself with it) that he thinks to frame,
Or, for the laurel, he may gain a scorn;
For a good poet's made, as well as born. (l. 50–59)

46 Sweet Swan of Avon! what a sight it were
To see thee in our waters yet appear, (l. 66–67)

HeIP; JCP; LiTB; NoP; OAEL-1; OBS; PoEL-2; SeCP;
SeCV-1; TrGrPo

To William Camden

47 Camden, most reverend head, to whom I owe
All that I am in arts, all that I know.
(How nothing's that!) to whom my countrey owes
The great renowne and name wherewith she goes.
Than thee the age sees not that thing more grave,
More high, more holy, that shee more would crave.
What name, what skill, what faith hast thou in things!
What sight in searching the most antique springs!
What weight, and what authority in thy speech!
Man scarce can make that doubt, but thou canst teach.
Pardon free truth, and let thy modesty,
Which conquers all, be once overcome by thee.
Many of thine this better could, than I,
But for their powers, accept my piety. (l. 1–14)

AWP; JCP; NAEL-1; OBS; SeCV-1

Volpone

48 Come, my Celia, let us prove
While we may the sports of love;
Time will not be ours forever,
He at length our good will sever. (l. 1–4)

49 'Tis no sin love's fruit to steal;
But the sweet theft to reveal,
To be taken, to be seen,
These have crimes accounted been. (l. 15–18)

ElL; ErPo; FaBV; FF; HeIP; JCP; NoP; OAEL-1; OBS;
OBVE; SeCP; SeCV-1; TEP; TrGrPo

THOMAS JORDAN (1612?–1685)

The Careless Gallant

1 In frolics dispose your pounds, shillings, and pence,
For we shall be nothing a hundred years hence.

We'll sport and be free with Frank, Betty, and Dolly,
Have lobsters and oysters to cure melancholy;
Fish dinners will make a man spring like a flea,
Dame Venus, love's lady, was born of the sea;

With her and with Bacchus we'll tickle the sense,
For we shall be past it a hundred years hence.
(l. 5–12)

CoMu HAP; NOBE; OBEV; OxBoLi

JENNY JOSEPH

Warning

1 When I am an old woman I shall wear purple
With a red hat which doesn't go, and doesn't suit me,
And I shall spend my pension on brandy and summer
    gloves
And satin sandals, and say we've no money for butter.
(l. 1–4)

AIW; FaBoWP; GOYP; OxBTC

JAMES JOYCE (1882–1941)

Ecce Puer

1 Of the dark past
A child is born
With joy and grief
My heart is torn

2 A child is sleeping:
An old man gone.
O father forsaken,
Forgive your son!

BIrV; EBEV; MoP; NAs; NoAM; OPOP; TrCP

On the Beach at Fontana

3 Wind whines and whines the shingle,
The crazy pierstakes groan; (l. 1–2)

4 Around us fear, descending
Darkness of fear above
And in my heart how deep unending
Ache of love (l. 9–12)

MoBrPo; OBMV; PoA; RB; SoSe

DONALD JUSTICE (b. 1925)

Anonymous Drawing

1 The artist will have had his revenge for being made to
    wait,
A revenge not only necessary but right and clever —
Simply to leave him out of the scene forever.
(l. 20–22)

CoAP; EyDe; HeIP; NePoEA-2

Counting the Mad

2   This one was put in a jacket,
    This one was sent home,
    This one was given bread and meat
    But would eat none,
    And this one cried No No No No
    All day long. (l. 1–6)

CAPP; FF; NePoEA; NIP; UnPo

In Bertram's Garden

3   Jane looks down at her organdy skirt
    As if it somehow were the thing disgraced,
    For being there, on the floor, in the dirt, (l. 1–3)

4   Soon the purple dark must bruise
    Lily and bleeding-heart and rose,
    And the little Cupid lose
    Eyes and ears and chin and nose, (l. 13–16)

BoLoP; ErPo; MT; NePoEA; VGW

Men at Forty

5   Men at forty
    Learn to close softly
    The doors to rooms they will not be
    Coming back to. (l. 1–4)

6   the face of that father,
    Still warm with the mystery of lather.
    They are more fathers than sons themselves now.
    Something is filling them, something

    That is like the twilight sound
    Of the crickets, immense, (l. 13–18)

CAPP; DiL; LCAP; MT; NoAM; PPP; Prf

Sestina: Here in Katmandu

7   We have climbed the mountain,
    There's nothing more to do.
    It is terrible to come down
    To the valley
    Where, amidst many flowers,
    One thinks of snow, (l. 1–6)

CoAP; HeIP; RFM; SM

PATRICK KAVANAGH   (1905–1969)

Canal Bank Walk

1   Leafy-with-love banks and the green waters of the canal
    Pouring redemption for me, (l. 1–2)

2   O unworn world enrapture me, enrapture me in a web
    Of fabulous grass and eternal voices by a beech,
                                               (l. 9–10)

3   For this soul needs to be honoured (l. 13)

    CIP; CMoP; FaBoTw; IPY; MoBrPo; NoAM

Epic

4   I have lived in important places, times
    When great events were decided, (l. 1–2)

5   Homer's ghost came whispering to my mind.
    He said: I made the Iliad from such
    A local row. Gods make their own importance.
                                               (l. 12–14)

    BIrV; CIP; FaBCIP; IPY; NOIV

Father Mat

6   The knife of penance fell so like a blade
    Of grass that no one was afraid. (l. 10–11)

7   ancient Ireland sweeping
    In again with all its unbaptized beauty:
    The calm evening,
    The whitethorn blossoms,
    The smell from ditches that were not Christian.
                                               (l. 13–17)

8   His curate passed on a bicycle —
    He had the haughty intellectual look
    Of the man who never reads in brook or book;
                                               (l. 30–32)

9   The Holy Ghost descends
    At random like the muse
    On wise man and fool,
    And why should poet in the twilight choose?
                                               (l. 45–48)

10 On the stem
    Of memory imaginations blossom. (l. 79–80)

11 A secret lover is saying
    Three Hail Marys that she who knows
    The ways of women will bring
    Cathleen O'Hara (he names her) home to him.
                                               (l. 85–88)

12 "Ah lad, upon the road of life
    'Tis best to dance with Chance's wife
    And let the rains that come in time
    Erase the footprints of the crime." (l. 113–116)

13 I broke away
And rule all dominions that are rare;
I took with me all the answers to every prayer
That young men and girls pray for: love, happiness,
   riches — " (l. 124–127)

14 "God the Gay is not the Wise." (l. 132)

15 "Take your choice, take your choice,"
Called the breeze through the bridge's eye.
"The domestic Virgin and Her Child
Or Venus with her ecstasy." (l. 133–136)

AnIL; CMoP

If Ever You Go to Dublin Town

16 If ever you go to Dublin town
In a hundred years or so
Inquire for me in Baggot Street
And what I was like to know. (l. 1–4)

17 He had the knack of making men feel
As small as they really were
Which meant as great as God had made them
But as males they disliked his air. (l. 33–36)

18 He knew that posterity has no use
For anything but the soul,
The lines that speak the passionate heart,
The spirit that lives alone. (l. 57–60)

AnIL; CMoP; InPS; IPY

In Memory of My Mother

19 I do not think of you lying in the wet clay
Of a Monaghan graveyard; (l. 1–2)

20 O you are not lying in the wet clay,
For it is a harvest evening now and we
Are piling up the ricks against the moonlight
And you smile up at us — eternally. (l. 17–20)

BIrV; CIP; FaBCIP; MoP; NoAM

Inniskeen Road: July Evening

21 And there's the half-talk code of mysteries
And the wink-and-elbow language of delight. (l. 3–4)

22 A road, a mile of kingdom, I am king
Of banks and stones and every blooming thing.
                                        (l. 13–14)

CIP; FaBCIP; IPY; MoP; NoAM; NoP

Lines Written on a Seat on the Grand Canal, Dublin

23 O commemorate me where there is water,
Canal water preferably, so stilly
Greeny at the heart of summer. (l. 1–3)

24 O commemorate me with no hero-courageous
Tomb — just a canal-bank seat for the passer-by.
                                        (l. 13–14)

BIrV; CMcP; InPS; IPY; NOIV

Shancoduff

25 My black hills have never seen the sun rising,
Eternally they look north towards Armagh. (l. 1–2)

26 "Who owns them hungry hills
That the water-hen and snipe must have forsaken?
A poet? Then by heavens he must be poor."
I hear and is my heart not badly shaken? (l. 13–16)

BIrV; CIP; FaBCIP; FaBoTw; IPY; NoP

Spraying the Potatoes

27 And poet lost to potato-fields,
Remembering the lime and copper smell
Of the spraying barrels he is not lost
Or till blossomed stalks cannot weave a spell.
                                        (l. 29–32)

BIrV; FaBCIP; IPY; NoP

Tinker's Wife

28 Her face had streaks of care
Like wires across it, (l. 6–7)

CIP; InPS; MoP; NoAM

JOHN KEATS (1795–1821)

After Dark Vapours

1 After dark vapours have oppress'd our plains
For a long dreary season, comes a day
Born of the gentle South, and clears away
From the sick heavens all unseemly stains (l. 1–4)

EnRP; FaBoRV; OBNC; TEP

Bards of passion and of mirth

2 Bards of Passion and of Mirth
Ye have left your souls on earth!
Have ye souls in heaven too,

ChER; EnRP; GTBS; GTBS-P; OBEV

Bright Star, Would I Were Steadfast as Thou Art!

3 The moving waters at their priestlike task
Of pure ablution round earth's human shores, (l. 5–6)

BLPL; EnLoPo; GBL; GTBS; GTBS-P; HAP; InPK; InPS;
LiTB; NAEL-2; NAWM-2; NIP; OAEL-2; PoE; PPP;
PrIm; SCV; Son; TrGrPo

Endymion

4 A thing of beauty is a joy for ever:
Its loveliness increases; it will never
Pass into nothingness; (l. 1–3)

BLPL; CTC; EnRP; FaBV; FaFP; FiP; LiTB; NIP; OBNC;
PrIm

The Eve of St. Agnes

5 Music's golden tongue
Flattered to tears this aged man and poor; (l. 20–21)

6 The silver, snarling trumpets 'gan to chide: (l. 31)

7 The music, yearning like a God in pain,
She scarcely heard: (l. 56–57)

8 Sudden a thought came like a full-blown rose, (l. 136)

9 A poor, weak, palsy-stricken, churchyard thing, (l. 155)

10 Full on this casement shone the wintry moon,
And threw warm gules on Madeline's fair breast,
(l. 17–18)

11 As though a rose should shut, and be a bud again.
(l. 243)

12 Noiseless as fear in a wide wilderness, (l. 250)

13 spiced dainties, every one,
From silken Samarcand to cedared Lebanon.
(l. 269–270)

14 in chords that tenderest be,
He played an ancient ditty, long since mute,
In Provence called, "La belle dame sans merci":

15 Into her dream he melted, as the rose
Blendeth its odor with the violet —
Solution sweet: (l. 320–322)

BeLS; ChER; EnRP; FiP; HAP; HoPM; NAEL-2; NIP;
NoP; OAEL-2; OBNC; OBNV; PoE; PoEL-4; PoLF; TEP;
TrGrPo; WeW

Fancy

16 Ever let the Fancy roam!
Pleasure never is at home: (l. 1–2)

17 Everything is spoilt by use:
Where's the cheek that doth not fade,
Too much gazed at? Where's the maid
Whose lip mature is ever new?
Where's the eye, however, blue,
Doth not weary? Where's the face
One would meet in every place? (l. 68–74)

EnRP; GTBS; GTBS-P; OBEV

Fragment of an Ode to Maia, Written on May Day, 1818

18 Rich in the simple worship of a day. (l. 14)

EnRP; OAEL-2; OBEV; PoEL-4

The Human Seasons

19 Four seasons fill the measure of the year;
There are four seasons in the mind of man: (l. 1–2)

EnRP; FaFP; GTBS; GTBS-P; WiR

Hyperion

20 His old right hand lay nerveless, listless, dead,
Unsceptred; and his realmless eyes were closed;
(l. 18–19)

21 How beautiful, if sorrow had not made
Sorrow more beautiful than Beauty's self. (l. 35–36)

22 Those green-rob'd senators of mighty woods,
Tall oaks, branch-charmed by the earnest stars,
Dream, and so dream all night without a stir,
(l. 73–75)

23 I am gone
Away from my own bosom: (l. 112–113)

24 He enter'd, but he enter'd full of wrath; (l. 213)

25 For as in theatres of crowded men
Hubbub increases more they call out "Hush!"
(l. 253–254)

26 symbols divine,
"Manifestations of that beauteous life
"Diffus'd unseen throughout eternal space:
(l. 316–318)

ChER; EnRP; FiP; OAEL-2; OBNC; PoEL-4; TrGrPo

I Had a Dove and the Sweet Dove Died

27 I had a dove and the sweet dove died;
And I have thought it died of grieving:
O what could it grieve for? Its feet were tied,
With a silken thread of my own hand's weaving;
(l. 1–4)

CH; FaPON; FM; PBBP

In a Drear-nighted December

28 In a drear-nighted December,
Too happy, happy tree,
Thy branches ne'er remember
Their green felicity: (l. 1–4)

29 To know the change and feel it, (l. 21)

CH; ChER; ELP; EnRP; NOBE; OBEV; OBNC; TEP

Keen, Fitful Gusts

30 For I am brimfull of the friendliness
That in a little cottage I have found; (l. 9–10)

EnRP; PoEL-4; Son; TEP

La Belle Dame sans Merci

31 The sedge has wither'd from the lake,
And no birds sing. (l. 3–4)

32 I saw pale kings, and princes too,
Pale warriors, death pale were they all;
They cried — "La belle dame sans merci
Hath thee in thrall!" (l. 37–40)

AWP; BeLS; BLPA; CH; ChTr; ELP; EnRP; FaBoBe;
FaBoCh; FaFP; FiP; FPL; GoJo; GTBS; GTBS-P; HAP;
HeIP; InPS; InvP; LiTB; NAEL-2; NAWM-2; NOBE;
NoP; OAEL-2; OBEV; OBNC; PoE; PoEL-4; PoRA; Prf;
PrIm; RB; SCV; SoSe; TEP; TrGrPo; UnPo; VVA; WeW

Lines on the Mermaid Tavern

33 Souls of Poets dead and gone,
What Elysium have ye known
Happy field or mossy cavern,
Choicer than the Mermaid Tavern? (l. 1–4)

BLPL; FaBoBe; GTBS; GTBS-P

Meg Merrilies

34 Old Meg she was a Gipsy
And liv'd upon the Moors: (l. 1–2)

35 Her wine was dew o' the wild white rose
Her book a churchyard tomb. (l. 7–8)

BoTP; ELP; FaBoCh; FaPON; FiP; OxBChV; TEP

Ode on a Grecian Urn

36 Thou still unravished bride of quietness,
Thou foster-child of silence and slow time, (l. 1–2)

37 What men or gods are these? What maidens loth?
What mad pursuit? What struggle to escape?
What pipes and timbrels? What wild ecstasy?
(l. 8–10)

38 Heard melodies are sweet, but those unheard
Are sweeter; therefore, ye soft pipes, play on;
Not to the sensual ear, but, more endeared,
Pipe to the spirit ditties of no tone: (l. 9–12)

39 More happy love! more happy, happy love!
For ever warm and still to be enjoyed,
For ever panting, and for ever young;
All breathing human passion far above,
That leaves a heart high-sorrowful and cloyed,
A burning forehead, and a parching tongue. (l. 25–30)

40 When old age shall this generation waste,
Thou shalt remain, in midst of other woe
Than ours, a friend to man, to whom thou say'st,
Beauty is truth, truth beauty, — that is all
Ye know on earth, and all ye need to know. (l. 46–50)

AWP; ChER; EBEV; EnRP; FaBoBe; FaFP; FF; FiP;
FPL; HAP; HeIP; HoPM; InPS; LiTB; NAEL-2;
NAWM-2; NIP; NOBE; NoP; OAEL-2; OBEV; OBNC;
OHFP; PoE; PoEL-4; PPP; PrIm; SoSe; TEP; TOF;
TrGrPo; UnPo

Ode on Indolence

41 Ripe was the drowsy hour;
The blissful cloud of summer-indolence
Benumb'd my eyes; (l. 16–17)

EnRP; LiTB; NAEL-2; OBNC

Ode on Melancholy

42 No, no, go not to Lethe, neither twist
Wolf's-bane, tight-rooted, for its poisonous wine;
(l. 1–2)

43 Ay, in the very temple of Delight
Veil'd Melancholy has her sovran shrine, (l. 25–26)

EnRP; FiP; HAP; HeIP; InPK; InPS; LiTB; MAT;
NAEL-2; NAWM-2; NOBE; NoP; OAEL-2; OBEV;
OBNC; PoE; PoEL-4; PoRA; PPP; PrIm; TEP; TrGrPo

Ode to a Nightingale

44 My heart aches, and a drowsy numbness pains
My sense, as though of hemlock I had drunk,
Or emptied some dull opiate to the drains
One minute past, and Lethe-wards had sunk: (l. 1–4)

45 O for a beaker full of the warm South,
Full of the true, the blushful Hippocrene,
With beaded bubbles winking at the brim,
And purple-stained mouth; (l. 15–18)

46 That I might drink, and leave the world unseen,
And with thee fade away into the forest dim:
(l. 19–20)

47 Here, where men sit and hear each other groan;
Where palsy shakes a few, sad, last gray hairs,
Where youth grows pale, and specter-thin, and dies;
Where but to think is to be full of sorrow
And leaden-eyed despairs,
Where Beauty cannot keep her lustrous-eyes,
Or new Love pine at them beyond tomorrow.
(l. 24–30)

48 Not charioted by Bacchus and his pards,
But on the viewless wings of Poesy,
Though the dull brain perplexes and retards:
Already with thee! tender is the night,
And haply the Queen-Moon is on her throne,
(l. 32–36)

49 Darkling I listen; and for many a time
I have been half in love with easeful Death, (l. 51–52)

50 The voice I hear this passing night was heard
In ancient days by emperor and clown:
Perhaps the self-same song that found a path
Through the sad heart of Ruth, when sick for home,
She stood in tears amid the alien corn;
The same that oft-times hath
Charmed magic casements, opening on the foam
Of perilous seas, in faery lands forlorn. (l. 63–70)

51 Was it a vision, or a waking dream?
Fled is that music: — Do I wake or sleep? (l. 79–80)

AWP; BLPL; ChER; ChTr; EBEV; EnRP; FaBoBe; FaFP;
FiP; GTBS; GTBS-P; HAP; HeIP; InPS; LiTB; NAEL-2;
NAWM-2; NOBE; NoP; OAEL-2; OBEV; OBNC; OPOP;
PBBP; PoE; PoEL-4; PoRA; PPP; PrIm; SoSe; TEP; TOF;
TrGrPo; UnPo; WeW

Ode to Psyche

52 O latest-born and loveliest vision far
Of all Olympus' faded hierarchy! (l. 24–25)

53 Yes, I will be thy priest, and build a fane
In some untrodden region of my mind, (l. 50–51)

54 A bright torch, and a casement ope at night,
To let the warm Love in! (l. 66–67)

ChER; EnRP; InPS; LiTB; NAEL-2; NOBE; NoP;
OAEL-2; OBEV; OBNC; PoE; PoEL-4; PPP; TOF

On First Looking into Chapman's Homer

55 Much have I traveled in the realms of gold, (l. 1)

56 Then felt I like some watcher of the skies
When a new planet swims into his ken;
Or like stout Cortez when with eagle eyes
He stared at the Pacific — and all his men
Looked at each other with a wild surmise —
Silent, upon a peak in Darien. (l. 9–14)

BLPA; CH; ChER; ChTr; EnRP; FaBoBe; FaBoCh;
FaBV; FaFP; FF; FiP; FPL; GN; GTBS; GTBS-P; HAP;
HeIP; HoPM; InPK; LiTB; NAEL-2; NAWM-2; NIP;
NOBE; NoP; OAEL-2; OBAL; OBEV; OBNC; PoE;
PoEL-4; PPP; PrIm; Son; SoSe; TEP; TrGrPo

On Sitting Down to Read "King Lear" Once Again

57 When through the old oak forest I am gone,
Let me not wander in a barren dream,
But when I am consumed in the fire,
Give me new Phoenix wings to fly at my desire.
(l. 11–14)

EBEV; EnRP; NAEL-2; NoP

On the Grasshopper and Cricket

58 The poetry of earth is never dead: (l. 1)

BoTP; EnRP; FaBoBe; GN; LiTB; NIP; OAEL-2; Son;
TrGrPo; TTTS; WiR

On the Sea

59 It keeps eternal whisperings around
Desolate shores, (l. 1–2)

EnRP; FF; LiTB; MOS; NoP; OAEL-2; SeCePo; TEP;
TrGrPo

There Was a Naughty Boy

60 He ran away to Scotland
The people for to see —
There he found
That the ground
Was as hard
That a yard
Was as long, (l. 94—100)

BoTP; EBEV; FaBoCh; FaBoCo; InvP; LiTB; MoShBr;
OnUR; OxBChV; PoEL-4

This Living Hand, Now Warm and Capable

61 That thou wouldst wish thine own heart dry of blood
So in my veins red life might stream again, (l. 5—6)

BoLoP; HAP; InPK; InPS; NOBE; NoP; OAEL-2; OxBSP

To Autumn

62 Season of mists and mellow fruitfulness,
Close bosom-friend of the maturing sun;
Conspiring with him how to load and bless
With fruit the vines that round the thatch-eves run;
(l. 1—4)

63 Where are the songs of spring? Ay, where are they?
Think not of them, thou hast thy music too, —
(l. 23—24)

AWP; BoNaP; BoTP; CH; ChER; EBEV; EnRP; FaBoRV;
FaBV; FF; FiP; FPL; GTBS; GTBS-P; HAP; HeIP; InPK;
InPS; InvP; LiTB; Mes; NAEL-2; NAWM-2; NIP; NOBE;
NoP; NU; OAEL-2; OBEV; OBNC; PoE; PoEL-4; PoLF;
PPP; Prf; PrIm; RB; SCV; SoSe; TEP; TrGrPo; UnPo;
WeW

To Fanny

64 O! let me have thee whole, — all — all — be mine!
That shape, the fairness, that sweet minor zest
Of love, your kiss, — those hands, those eyes divine,
That warm, white, lucent, million-pleasured breast, —
(l. 5—8)

BoLoP; EBEV; EnRP; PPP; Son; TrGrPo

To Homer

65 Aye, on the shores of darkness there is light,
And precipices show untrodden green; (l. 9—10)

ChER; EBEV; NAEL-2; NoP; Son

To One Who Has Been Long in City Pent

66 To one who has been long in city pent,
'Tis very sweet to look into the fair
And open face of heaven, — (l. 1—3)

BLPA; EnRP; FaBoBe; FPL; LiTB; TrGrPo

To Sleep

67 O soft embalmer of the still midnight, (l. 1)

ChTr; EnRP; FaBoRV; NAEL-2; NIP; OBEV; PoEL-4;
PrIm; Son; TEP

When I Have Fears

68 When I have fears that I may cease to be
Before my pen has gleaned my teeming brain, (l. 1—2)

69 then on the shore
Of the wide world I stand alone, and think
Till love and fame to nothingness do sink. (l. 12—14)

AWP; BLPL; EBEV; EnRP; FiP; HAP; HeIP; HoPM;
InPS; LiTB; NAEL-2; NIP; NoP; OAEL-2; OBEV; OBNC;
PoE; PoRA; PrIm; Son; TEP; TrGrPo; UnPo

X. J. KENNEDY (b. 1929)

In a Prominent Bar in Secaucus One Day

1 'In a car like the Roxy I'd roll to the track,
A steel-guitar trio, a bar in the back,
And the wheels made no noise, they turned over so fast,
Still it took you ten minutes to see me go past.
(l. 21—24)

2 'Let you hold in mind, girls, that your beauty must
pass
Like a lovely white clover that rusts with its grass.
Keep your bottoms off barstools and marry you young
Or be left — an old barrel with many a bung.
(l. 29—32)

AiP; FYAP; HoPM; NBLV; NIP; OBAL; PPP

DAVID KEPPEL (1849?—1939)

Trouble

1 Better never trouble Trouble
Until Trouble troubles you;
For you only make your trouble
Double-trouble when you do; (l. 1—4)

FaFP; FPL; PoLF; WBLP

FRANCIS SCOTT KEY (1779–1843)

The Star-spangled Banner

1 O! say can you see by the dawn's early light,
What so proudly we hail'd at the twilight's last
  gleaming,
Whose broad stripes and bright stars, through the
  perilous fight,
O'er the ramparts we watched were so gallantly
  streaming?
And the rocket's red glare, the bombs bursting in air,
Gave proof through the night that our flag was still
  there;
O! say does that star-spangled banner yet wave,
O'er the land of the free, and the home of the brave?
                                            (l. 1–8)

AA; AiP; AnAmPo; BLPA; FaBoBe; FaFP; FaPON; OPP;
PAH; TAP; WBLP

JOYCE KILMER (1886–1918)

Trees

1 I think that I shall never see
A poem lovely as a tree. (l. 1–2)

2 Poems are made by fools like me,
But only God can make a tree. (l. 11–12)

BLPA; FaBoBe; FaFP; FaPON; FPL; OHFP; WBLP;
WGRP

BEN KING (BENJAMIN FRANKLIN KING) (1857–1899)

The Pessimist

1 Nothing to do but work,
Nothing to eat but food, (l. 1–2)

2 Nowhere to fall but off,
Nowhere to stand but on. (l. 7–8)

3 Nothing to weep but tears,
Nothing to bury but dead. (l. 11–12)

AnAmPo; BLPA; CTC; FaBoCo; FaBoNo; FaFP; NA;
NBLV; OBAL

HENRY KING, BISHOP OF CHICHESTER (1592–1669)

A Contemplation upon Flowers

1 Oh teach me to see death, and not to fear,
But rather to take truce;
How often have I seen you at a bier,
And there look fresh and spruce.
You fragrant flowers then teach me that my breath
Like yours may sweeten and perfume my death.
                                            (l. 13–18)

BoNaP; ELP; MeLP; MePo; NoP; OBEV; OBS; SeCP;
TrGrPo

The Exequy

2 But what I practise with mine eyes.
By which wet glasses I find out
How lazily time creeps about
To one that mourns: this, only this
My exercise and bus'ness is:
So I compute the weary hours
With sighs dissolved into showers. (l. 14–20)

3 That fit of fire
Once off, our bodies shall aspire
To our souls' bliss: then we shall rise,
And view ourselves with clearer eyes
In that calm region, where no night
Can hide us from each other's sight. (l. 55–60)

4 But hark! My pulse, like a soft drum
Beats my approach, tells thee I come;
And slow howe'er my marches be,
I shall at last sit down by thee.

BoLoP; GBL; HAP; InvP; JCP; MeLP; MePo; NOBE;
NoP; OBEV; OBS; PoEL-2; PrIm; QFR; SeCePo; SeCP;
TEP

Sic Vita (attributed to King)

5 Even such is man, whose borrowed light
Is straight called in, and paid to night.

The wind blows out, the bubble dies;
The spring entombed in autumn lies;
The dew dries up, the star is shot;
The flight is past: and man forgot. (l. 7–12)

ELP; FF; MePo; NOBE; OBS; OxBSP; SeCePo; SeCP;
TrGrPo

The Surrender

6 We must in tears
Unwind a love knit up in many years.
In this last kiss I here surrender thee
Back to thyself, so thou again art free;
Thou in another, sad as that, resend
The truest heart that lover e'er did lend. (l. 29–34)

BoLoP; EBEV; JCP; MePo; TrGrPo

Tell me no more how fair she is

7 Tell me no more how fair she is,
I have no minde to hear
The story of that distant bliss
I never shall come near:
By sad experience I have found
That her perfection is my wound. (l. 1–6)

EnLoPo; MeLP; MePo; OBS; SeCP; TrGrPo

CHARLES KINGSLEY (1819–1875)

The Last Buccaneer

1 Oh England is a pleasant place for them that's rich and
high,
But England is a cruel place for such poor folks as I;
(l. 1–2)

2 And now I'm old and going — I'm sure I can't tell
where;
One comfort is, this world's so hard, I can't be worse
off there: (l. 29–30)

BeLS; EBVV; FaBoBe; MoShBr

The Three Fishers

3 For men must work, and women must weep,
And there's little to earn, and many to keep,
Though the harbour bar be moaning. (l. 5–7)

4 And the sooner it's over, the sooner to sleep;
And good-bye to the bar and its moaning. (l. 20–21)

BeLS; EBVV; FaPoR; OnMSP; PoLF; PWR; WBLP

The Water Babies

5 When all the world is young, lad,
And all the trees are green;
And every goose a swan, lad,
And every lass a queen;

6 Young bloodmust have its course, lad,
And every dog his day.

7 When all the world is old, lad,
And all the trees are brown;

8 The spent and maimed among:
God grant you find one face there,
You loved when all was young.

BLPL; BoTP; EBEV; FaBoBe; FaFP; FaPoR; OxBChV;
PoLF

HUGH KINGSMILL (1889–1949)

What, still alive at twenty–two

1 What, still alive at twenty-two,
A clean upstanding chap like you? (l. 1–2)

2 Like enough, you won't be glad,
When they come to hang you, lad:
But bacon's not the only thing
That's cured by hanging from a string. (l. 5–8)

BXAP; FaBoCo; FaBoPa; InPK; NBLV; NOBL

GALWAY KINNELL (b. 1927)

After Making Love We Hear Footsteps

1 after making love, quiet, touching along the length of
our bodies,
familiar touch of the long-married, (l. 10–11)

2 this one whom habit of memory propels to the ground
of his making,
sleeper only the mortal sounds can sing awake,
this blessing love gives again into our arms.
(l. 21–23)

DiL; InPS; NIP; NoAM

The Bear

3 I take a wolf's rib and whittle
it sharp at both ends
and coil it up
and freeze it in blubber and place it out
on the fairway of the bears. (l. 9–13)

4 the rest of my days I spend
wandering: wondering
what, anyway,
was that sticky infusion, that rank flavor of blood, that
poetry, by which I lived? (l. 90–94)

CAPP; CoAP; InPS; NNaP; RFM; TAP; VGW

The Correspondence School Instructor Says
Goodbye to His Poetry Students

5 you in San Quentin,
who wrote, "Being German my hero is Hitler,"
instead of "Sincerely yours," at the end of long,
neat-scripted letters demolishing
the pre-Raphaelites: (l. 9–13)

6 And now,
  in this poem, or chopped prose, not any better,
  I realize, than those troubled lines
  I kept sending back to you, (l. 22–25)

7 Goodbye,
  you who are, for me, the postmarks again
  of shattered towns — Xenia, Burnt Cabins, Hornell —
  their loneliness
  given away in poems, only their solitude kept.
                                    (l. 32–36)

  NoAM; NOBA; NoP; TAP

First Song

8 A boy's hunched body loved out of a stalk
  The first song of his happiness, and the song woke
  His heart to the darkness and into the sadness of joy.
                                    (l. 16–18)

  CAPP; GoJo; GOYP; GrPl; LiTM; NoP; TwCP

Flower Herding on Mount Monadnock

9 There is something joyous in the elegies
  Of birds. They seem
  Caught up in a formal delight,
  Though the mourning dove whistles of despair.
                                    (l. 25–28)

10 The appeal to heaven breaks off.
   The petals begin to fall, in self-forgiveness.
   It is a flower. On this mountainside it is dying.
                                    (l. 75–78)

   LCAP; NaP; NoAM; NOBA

The Fundamental Project of Technology

11 a ring of skull-
   bone fused to the inside of a helmet; a pair of
     eyeglasses
   taken off the eyes of an eyewitness, without glass,
   which vanished, when a white flash sparkled. (l. 4–7)

12 To de-animalize human mentality, to purge it of
     obsolete
   evolutionary characteristics, in particular of death,
   which foreknowledge terrorizes the contents of skulls
     with,
   is the fundamental project of technology; (l. 29–32)

13 twice already on earth sparkled a flash, a white flash.
                                    (l. 42)

   BLA; CAPP; SM; SV

Saint Francis and the Sow

14 The bud
   stands for all things,
   even for those things that don't flower, (l. 1–3)

15 the sheer blue milken dreaminess spurting and
     shuddering
   from the fourteen teats into the fourteen mouths
     sucking and blowing beneath them:
   the long, perfect loveliness of sow. (l. 21–23)

   CAPP; FYAP; InPK; NIP; RB

To Christ Our Lord

16 The Christmas grace chilled
   The cooked bird, being long-winded and the room cold.
                                    (l. 7–8)

17 The stars glittered on the snow and nothing answered.
   Then the Swan spread her wings, cross of the cold
     north,
   The pattern and mirror of the acts of earth. (l. 28–30)

   NIP; PrIm; RFM; SM; TwCP

Vapor Trail Reflected in the Frog Pond

18 The young, heads
   trailed by the beginnings of necks,
   shiver,
   in the guarantee they shall be bodies. (l. 3–6)

19 crack of deputies' rifles practicing their aim on stray
     dogs
   at night,
   sput of cattleprod,
   TV groaning at the smells of the human body,
   curses of the soldier as he poisons, burns, grinds, and
     stabs
   the rice of the world, (l. 14–18)

   CAPP; NoP; OBWP; VGW

THOMAS KINSELLA (b. 1929)

Ancestor

1 Ancestor . . . among sweet- and fruit-boxes.
  Her black heart . . .
  Was that a sigh?
  — brushing by me in the shadows,
  with her heaped aprons, through the red hangings
  to the scullery, and down to the back room. (l. 16–21)

  BIrV; FaBCIP; NOIV; PoE

Baggot Street Deserta

2 The window is wide
On a crawling arch of stars, and the night
Reacts faintly to the mathematic
Passion of a cello suite
Plotting the quiet of my attic. (l. 4–8)

3 Versing, like an exile, makes
A virtuoso of the heart,
Interpreting the old mistakes
And discords in a work of Art (l. 24–28)

4 The goddess who had light for thighs
Grows feet of dung and takes to bed,
Affronting horror-stricken eyes,
The marsh bird that children dread. (l. 50–53)

CIP; CMoP; FaBCIP; IPY; NoAM

Mirror in February

5 I towel my shaven jaw and stop, and stare,
Riveted by a dark exhausted eye,
A dry downturning mouth. (l. 5–7)

6 In slow distaste
I fold my towel with what grace I can,
Not young, and not renewable, but man. (l. 19–21)

CIP; FaBCIP; GTBS-P; NoAM

RUDYARD KIPLING (1865–1936)

The Ballad of East and West

1 Oh, East is East, and West is West, and never the twain
shall meet, (l. 1)

2 The Colonel's son has taken a horse, and a raw rough
dun was he,
With the mouth of a bell and the heart of Hell and the
head of a gallows-tree. (l. 21–22)

3 But there is neither East nor West, Border, nor Breed,
nor Birth,
When two strong men stand face to face, though they
come from the ends of the earth! (l. 95–96)

BeLS; BLPL; BrPo; FaBoBe; FaBV; FaPoR; OBNV

Boots

4 I — 'ave — marched — six — weeks in 'Ell an' certify
It — is — not — fire — devils, dark or anything,

But boots — boots — boots — boots — movin' up an' down
again,
An' there's no discharge in the war! (l. 29–32)

BLPA; FaPoR; FPL; MoBrPo

Danny Deever

5 For they're hangin' Danny Deever, you can hear the
Dead March play,
The Regiment's in 'ollow square — they're hangin' him
today;
They've taken of his buttons off an' cut his stripes
away,
An' they're hangin' Danny deever in the mornin'.
(l. 5–8)

BrPo; EBVV; FaBoBa; FaPoR; FPL; GTBS-P; InPS;
LiTB; MoBrPo; NAEL-2; NoAM; NOBE; NOBVV;
OxBoLi; OxBTC; PoLF; SCV; SeCePo; TEP; TrGrPo;
UnPo; WaaP

The Gods of the Copybook Headings

6 As I pass through my incarnations in every age and
race,
I make my proper prostrations to the Gods of the
Market-Place.
Peering through reverent fingers I watch them flourish
and fall,
And the Gods of the Copybook Headings, I notice,
outlast them all. (l. 1–4)

FaPoR; NoAM; OBSV; OHFP; OPOP; OxBTC; TW

If

7 If you can keep your head when all about you
Are losing theirs and blaming it on you; (l. 1–2)

8 If you can fill the unforgiving minute
With sixty seconds' worth of distance run,
Yours is the Earth and everything that's in it,
And — which is more — you'll be a Man, my son!
(l. 29–32)

BLPA; FaBoBe; FaFP; FaPoR; FPL; OHFP; OxBChV;
OxBTC; PWR; WBLP

Mandalay

9 By the old Moulmein Pagoda, lookin' eastward to the
sea,
There's a Burma girl a-settin', and I know she thinks o'
me;
For the wind is in the palm-trees, and the temple-bells
they say:

"Come you back, you British soldier; come you back to Mandalay!" (l. 1–4)

10 An' I seed her first a-smokin' of a whackin' white cheroot,
An' a-wastin' Christian kisses on an 'eathen idol's foot: (l. 13–14)

11 An' I'm learnin' 'ere in London what the ten-year soldier tells:
"If you've 'eard the East a-callin', you won't never 'eed naught else." (l. 29–30)

12 I've a neater, sweeter maiden in a cleaner, greener land! (l. 41)

13 Ship me somewheres east of Suez, where the best is like the worst,
Where there aren't no Ten Commandments an' a man can raise a thirst; (l. 43–44)

BrPo; FaBV; FPL; LiTB; MoBrPo; NOBE; OBTV; TrGrPo

Puck of Pook's Hill

14 Cities and Thrones and Powers
Stand in Time's eye,
Almost as long as flowers,
Which daily die: (l. 1–4)

GoJo; NOBE; OBNC; OxBTC; PoEL-5

15 What is a woman that you forsake her,
And the hearth-fire and the home-acre,
To go with the old grey Widow-maker? (l. 1–3)

16 She has no strong white arms to fold you,
But the ten-times-fingering weed to hold you —
Out on the rocks where the tide has rolled you. (l. 7–9)

HAP; OBNC; PoRA; SeCePo

Recessional

17 Lord God of Hosts, be with us yet,
Lest we forget — lest we forget! (l. 5–6)

18 The tumult and the shouting dies;
The Captains and the Kings depart:
Still stands Thine ancient sacrifice,
An humble and a contrite heart. (l. 7–10)

AWP; BLPA; BLPL; BLRP; BrPo; FaBoPV; FaBV; FaFP; GN; LiTB; MoBrPo; NoAM; NOBE; NOBVV; NoP; OBEV; OBNC; OHFP; PWR; TrGrPo; UnPo; WBLP; WGRP

Sestina of the Tramp-Royal

19 For 'im that doth not work must surely die;
But that's no reason man should labour all
'Is life on one same shift — life's none so long. (l. 22–24)

20 It's like a book, I think, this bloomin' world,
Which you can read and care for just so long, (l. 31–32)

21 Gawd bless this world! Whatever she 'ath done —
Excep' when awful long — I've found it good.
So write, before I die, "E liked it all!' (l. 37–39)

BrPo; FPL; LiTB; MoBrPo; PrIm

Song of the Galley-slaves

22 We pulled for you when the wind was against us and the sails were low.
Will you never let us go? (l. 1–2)

ChTr; GTBS-P; HAP; PoEL-5

A St. Helena Lullaby

23 'How far is St. Helena from an Emperor of France?'
I cannot see — I cannot tell — the Crowns they dazzle so.
The Kings sit down to dinner, and the Queens stand up to dance.
(After open weather you may look for snow!) (l. 13–16)

EBEV; FaBoCh; OBMV; PoEL-5

The Story of the Gadsbys

24 What is the moral? Who rides may read. (l. 1)

25 Down to Gehenna or up to the Throne,
He travels the fastest who travels alone. (l. 6)

26 One may fall but he falls by himself —
Falls by himself with himself to blame, (l. 13–14)

BLPA; FaPoR; FPL; MoBrPo; TrGrPo

The Vampire

27 A fool there was and he made his prayer
(Even as you and I!)
To a rag and a bone and a hank of hair,
(We called her the woman who did not care),
But the fool he called her his lady fair —
(Even as you and I!) (l. 1–6)

BLPA; BLPL; NOBVV; VVA

The Way through the Woods

28 The old lost road through the woods. . . .
    But there is no road through the woods. (l. 24–25)

CH; FaBoCh; FaPON; NOBE; OBEV; OBNC; OxBChV;
OxBTC; RFM

When Earth's last picture is painted, and the tubes are twisted and dried

29 And no one shall work for money, and no one shall
        work for fame,
    But each for the joy of the working, and each, in his
        separate star,
    Shall draw the Thing as he sees It for the God of
        Things as They are! (l. 10–12)

FaFP; LiTB; OHFP; PWR; WGRP

The Widow at Windsor

30 'Ave you 'eard o' the Widow at Windsor
    With a hairy gold crown on 'er 'ead?
    She 'as ships on the foam — she 'as millions at 'ome,
    An' she pays us poor beggars in red. (l. 1–4)

31 Walk wide o' the Widow at Windsor,
    For 'alf o' Creation she owns:
    We 'ave bought 'er the same with the sword an' the
        flame,
    An' we've salted it down with our bones. (l. 16–19)

BrPo; NAEL-2; NoAM; NoP

JAMES KIRKUP (b. 1923)

A Correct Compassion

1 Cleanly, sir, you went to the core of the matter.
   Using the purest kind of wit, a balance of belief and
       art,
   You with a curious nervous elegance laid bare
   The root of life, and put your finger on its beating
       heart. (l. 1–4)

2 She who does not know she is a patient lies
   Within a tent of green, and sleeps without a sound
                                        (l. 13–14)

3 We find we breathe again, and hear the surgeon hum.
   Outside, in the street, a car starts up. The heart
       regularly
   Thunders. — (l. 66–68)

4 with proper grace
   Informing a correct compassion, that performs its love,
       and makes it live. (l. 71–72)

FaBoTw; ImOP; OxBTC; SeCePo

CAROLYN KIZER (b. 1925)

The Intruder

1 My mother — preferring the strange to the tame:
   Dove-note, bone marrow, deer dung,
   Frog's belly distended with funny young, (l. 1–3)

2 The soft mouse body, the hard feral glint
   In the caught eyes. (l. 14–15)

3 Whose denizens can turn upon the world
   With spitting tongue, an odor, talon, claw,
   To sting or soil benevolence, alien
   As our clumsy traps, our random scatter of shot.
   She swept to the kitchen. Turning on the tap,
   She washed and washed the pity from her hands.
                                        (l. 25–30)

BoWoP; ER; InPK; NePoEA-2

ABRAHAM MOSES KLEIN (1909–1972)

Heirloom

1 And my tears, too, have stained this heirloomed ground,
   When reading in these treatises some weird
   Miracle, I turned a leaf and found
   A white hair fallen from my father's beard. (l. 17–20)

NIP; NCBC; OBCV; TrJP

Indian Reservation: Caughnawaga

2 Where are the braves, the faces like autumn fruit,
   who stared at the child from the coloured frontispiece?
                                        (l. 1–2)

3 for the tourist's
   brown pennies scattered at the old church door,
   the ragged papooses jump, and bite the dust.
                                        (l. 19–21)

4 This is a grassy ghetto, and no home. (l. 29)

LiTM; NOBC; NoP; OBCV

ETHERIDGE KNIGHT (1933–1991)

Eastern guard tower

1 convicts rest
Like lizards on rocks. (l. 2–3)

BPo; MoP; NeAC; SM; TAP

For Black Poets Who Think of Suicide

2 Black Poets should live — not leap
From steel bridges, like the white boys do. (l. 1–2)

3 Let all Black Poets die as trumpets,
And be buried in the dust of marching feet. (l. 13–14)

CNA; HeIP; InPK; PoBA

Hard Rock Returns to Prison from the Hospital for the Criminal Insane

4 Hard Rock was "known not to take no shit
From nobody," and he had the scars to prove it:
(l. 1–2)

5 The WORD was that Hard Rock wasn't a mean nigger
Anymore, that the doctors had bored a hole in his head,
Cut out part of his brain, and shot electricity
Through the rest. (l. 7–10)

InPS; MoP; NIP; NNaP; TAP; UnPo

He Sees through Stone

6 He sees through stone
he has the secret
eyes this old black one (l. 1–3)

MT; NBP; NNaP; PoBA

The Idea of Ancestry

7 Each Fall the graves of my grandfathers call me, the
brown
hills and red gullies of mississippi send out their
electric
messages, galvanizing my genes. (l. 22–24)

8 This yr there is a gray stone wall damming my stream,
and when
the falling leaves stir my genes, I pace my cell or flop
on my bunk
and stare at 47 black faces across the space. I am all of
them,

they are all of me, I am me, they are thee, and I have
no sons
to float in the space between. (l. 35–39)

BPo; CNA; NIP; NNaP; PoBA; SV

WILLIAM KNOX (1789–1825)

Oh! Why Should the Spirit of Mortal Be Proud?

1 Oh! why should the spirit of mortal be proud?
Like a swift-fleeting meteor, a fast-flying cloud,
A flash of the lightning, a break of the wave,
Man passeth from life to his rest in the grave. (l. 1–4)

2 The hand of the king that the scepter hath borne;
The brow of the priest that the miter hath worn;
The eye of the sage, and the heart of the brave,
Are hidden and lost in the depth of the grave.
(l. 17–20)

3 From the gilded saloon to the bier and the shroud —
Oh! why should the spirit of mortal be proud?
(l. 55–56)

BLPA; FaFP; WBLP; WGRP

KENNETH KOCH (b. 1925)

Mending Sump

1 "Something there is that doesn't hump a sump,"
He said; and through his head she saw a cloud
That seemed to twinkle. (l. 5–7)

2 He's come to die
Or else to laugh, for hay is dried-up grass
When you're alone." (l. 9–11)

BXAP; HeIP; InPK; MoP; NeAP; NoAM

Permanently

3 One day the Nouns were clustered in the street.
An Adjective walked by, with her dark beauty.
The Nouns were struck, moved, changed.
The next day a Verb drove up, and created the
Sentence. (l. 1–4)

4 As the adjective is lost in the sentence,
So I am lost in your eyes, ears, nose, and throat —
You have enchanted me with a single kiss
Which can never be undone
Until the destruction of language. (l. 11–15)

CoAP; NoP; PoA; PoM; PPP

Variations on a Theme by William Carlos Williams

5 I chopped down the house that you had been saving to
    live in next summer.
  I am sorry, but it was morning, and I had nothing to
    do and its wooden beams were so inviting. (l. 1–2)

BXAP; CAPP; FF; NBLV; NIP; NoAM; NoP; PoM

You Were Wearing

6 You were wearing your Edgar Allen Poe printed cotton
    blouse.
  In each divided-up square of the blouse was a picture
    of Edgar Allan Poe. (l. 1–2)

7 In the yard across the street we saw a snowman
    holding a garbage can lid. smashed into a likeness of
    the mad English king, George the Third. (l. 13)

AiP; CoAP; EAS; MoP; NIP; NNaP; NoP

MAXINE W. KUMIN (b. 1925)

400-Meter Freestyle

1 T
   h
   e
  astonishing whites of the soles of his feet rise
                                                  a
                                                  n
                                                  d
  salute us on the turns. (l. 9–10)

ASP; SD; SoSe; TSL

STANLEY JASSPON KUNITZ (b. 1905)

End of Summer

1 Already the iron door of the north
  Clangs open: birds, leaves, snows
  Order their populations forth,
  And a cruel wind blows. (l. 13–16)

CAPP; MoAmPo; Psk; VGW

Father and Son

2 Him, steeped in the odor of ponds, whose indomitable
    love
  Kept me in chains. (l. 8–9)

3 The papers are delivered every day;
  I am alone and never shed a tear." (l. 21–22)

4 Instruct
  Your son, whirling between two wars,
  In the Gemara of your gentleness, (l. 26–28)

CAPP; DiL; MoP; TwCP

SIR FRANCIS KYNASTON (1587–1642)

To Cynthia, on Concealment of Her Beauty

1 Do not conceale no beauty grace,
  That's either in thy minde or face,
  Least vertue overcome by vice,
  Make men beleeve no Paradice. (l. 25–28)

MeLP; MePo; NOBE; OBS

JEAN DE LA FONTAINE (1621–1695)

The Wolf and the Stork

1 Such gluttony second to none
  Almost ended fatally
  When a bone choked a wolf as he gulped what he ate;

2 "Compensate?" he inquired with bared teeth,
  "A humorist, I infer!
  You should be glad that you draw breath.
  Thrust your beak down my throat and you somehow
    escaped death?
  Be off. You are unappreciative;

FM; OBVE

CHARLES LAMB (1775–1834)

Hester

1 gone before
  To that unknown and silent shore, (l. 25–26)

EnRP; GTBS; GTBS-P; OBEV

The Old Familiar Faces

2 I have had playmates, I have had companions,
  In my days of childhood, in my joyful school-days,
  All, all are gone, the old familiar faces. (l. 1–3)

AWP; BLPA; EnRP; FaBoBe; FaBoRV; FaFP; FaPoR;
FPL; GTBS; GTBS-P; NOBE; OBEV; RB

On an Infant Dying as Soon as Born

3 A flow'ret crushed in the bud,
A nameless piece of Babyhood,
Was in her cradle-coffin lying;
Extinct, with scarce the sense of dying: (l. 3–6)

4 Why should kings and nobles have
Pictured trophies to their grave,
And we, churls, to thee deny
Thy pretty toys with thee to lie —
A more harmless vanity? (l. 60–64)

GTBS; GTBS-P; OBEV

WALTER SAVAGE LANDOR (1775–1864)

Death Stands above Me

1 Death stands above me, whispering low
I know not what into my ear; (l. 1–2)

EnRP; LiTB; NOBE; NoP; OAEL-2; OBNC; OxBSP;
PoEL-4; SoSe; TrGrPo

The Georges

2 George the First was always reckoned
Vile, but viler George the Second;
And what mortal ever heard
Any good of George the Third?
When from earth the Fourth descended
(God be praised!) the Georges ended. (l. 1–6)

ChTr; FaBoCo; FaBoCo; FaBoEE; FiBHP; NIP; OBSV

The Hellenics

3 For, surely, surely, where
Your voice and graces are,
Nothing of death can any feel or know.

ELP; NOBE; OBNC; PoEL-4

Ianthe

4 From you, Ianthe, little troubles pass
Like little ripples down a sunny river;

GBL; NOBE; OBEV; OBNC; TrGrPo

5 Verse calls them forth; 'tis verse that gives
Immortal youth to mortal maids. (l. 3–4)

AWP; CTC; ELP; EnLoPo; EnRP; GBL; HAP; HeIP;
LiTB; NAEL-2; NOBE; NoP; OBEV; OBNC; PoEL-4;
PoRA; TrGrPo; WeW

6 I have since written what no tide
Shall ever wash away,what men
Unborn shall read o'er ocean wide
And find Ianthe's name agen.

HAP; OBNC; TrGrPo; TrGrPo

Ireland Never Was Contented

7 And about her courts were seen
Liveried angels robed in green,
Wearing, by St Patrick's bounty,
Emeralds big as half the county. (l. 7–10)

FaBoCo; FaBoEE; GTBS-P; OxBoLi; OxBSP

The Last Fruit Off an Old Tree

8 I strove with none, for none was worth my strife:
Nature I loved, and next to Nature, Art:

AWP; BLPL; ChTr; EBEV; EnRP; FaBoEE; FaPoR;
GTBS-P; HeIP; LiTB; NOBE; NOBVV; NoP; OAEL-2;
OBEV; OBNC; SeCePo; TrGrPo

Lately Our Poets

9 Lately our poets loiter'd in green lanes,
Content to catch the ballads of the plains; (l. 1–2)

10 My slumber broken and my doublet torn,
I find the laurel also bears a thorn. (l. 9–10)

FaBoEE; GTBS-P; LiTB; OAEL-2; PoEL-4

Mother, I Cannot Mind

11 Mother, I cannot mind my wheel;
My fingers ache, my lips are dry: (l. 1–2)

12 No longer could I doubt him true
All other men may use deceit;
He always said my eyes were blue,
And often swore my lips were sweet. (l. 5–8)

Pericles and Aspasia

13 Stand close around,ye Stygian set,
With Dirce in one boat convey'd,
Or Charon, seeing, may forget
That he is old, and she a shade.

AWP; ChTr; CTC; EBEV; EnRP; FaBoEE; GBL; HAP;
LiTB; NOBE; NoP; OAEL-2; OBEV; OBNC; OxBSP;
PoEL-4; PoRA; TrGrPo; WeW

Plays

14 But when we play the fool, how wide
The theatre expands! beside,
How long the audience sits before us!
How many prompters! what a chorus! (l. 5–8)

EnRP; NBLV; NoP; OxBoLi; OxBSP

Rose Aylmer

15 Rose Aylmer, whom these wakeful eyes
May weep, but never see,
A night of memories and of sighs
I consecrate to thee. (l. 5–8)

AWP; BoLoP; CH; ELP; EnLoPo; EnRP; FaFP; GBL;
HAP; HeIP; HoPM; LiTB; NAEL-2; NOBE; NoP;
OAEL-2; OBEV; OBNC; PoEL-4; TEP; TrGrPo; UnPo;
WeW

Twenty Years Hence

16 Twenty years hence my eyes may grow
If not quite dim, yet rather so,
Still yours from others they shall know (l. 1–3)

GBL; NAEL-2; NOBVV; TrGrPo

ANDREW LANG (1844–1912)

Brahma

1 If the wild bowler thinks he bowls,
Or if the batsman thinks he's bowled,
They know not, poor misguided souls,
They, too, shall perish unconsoled. (l. 1–4)

2 bowler and the ball,
The umpire, the pavilion cat,
The roller, pitch, and stumps, and all. (l. 6–8)

BXAP; CenHV; FaBoCo; NOBL

The Odyssey

3 So gladly, from the songs of modern speech
Men turn, and see the stars, and feel the free
Shrill wind beyond the close of heavy flowers,
And through the music of the languid hours,
They hear like ocean on a western beach
The surge and thunder of the Odyssey. (l. 9–14)

OBEV; OBNC; PoLF; PoRA

WILLIAM LANGLAND (1330–1400)

The Vision of Piers Plowman

1 on a May morwening upon Malverne hilles
Me befel a ferly, of fairye me thoughte;
I was wery ofwandred and wente me to reste
Under a brod bankby a bournes side;
And as I lay and lenede and lookede on the watres,
I slomerede into a sleeping, it swyede so merye.

2 I saw a towr on a toft tryely y-maked;
A deep dale benethe, a dungeoun thereinne
With deepe dikes and derke and dredful of sight.

3 A fair feeld ful of folk fand I there-betwene,
Of alle maner of men, the mene and the riche,
Worching and wandringe as the world asketh.
Some putte hem to plow, playede ful selde,
In setting and sowing swunke ful harde,
Wonne that these wastours with glotonye destroyeth.

4 And some chosen to chaffare, they chevede the betere,
As it seemeth to oure sight that suche men thriven.
And some merthes to make, as minstrales cunne,
And gete gold with here glee giltles, I trowe.

FaBoPP; OAEL-1; PoE; PoEL-1

SIDNEY LANIER (1842–1881)

A Ballad of Trees and the Master

1 Into the woods my Master went,
Clean forspent, forspent.
Into the woods my Master came,
Forspent with love and shame,
But the olives they were not blind to Him; (l. 1–5)

2 Out of the woods my Master came,
Content with death and shame.
When Death and Shame would woo Him last,
From under the trees they drew Him last:
'Twas on a tree they slew Him — last
When out of the woods He came. (l. 11–16)

AA; AnAmPo; FPL; LiTA; NOBA; OxBA; PoEL-5; PoLF;
WGRP

The Marshes of Glynn

3 Beautiful glooms, soft dusks in the noon-day fire, —
Wildwood privacies, closets of lone desire,
Chamber from chamber parted with wavering arras of
    leaves, —
Cells for the passionate pleasure of prayer to the soul
    that grieves,

Pure with a sense of the passing of saints through the
  wood,
Cool for the dutiful weighing of ill with good; —

4 And my spirit is grown to a lordly great compass
  within,
That the length and the breadth and the sweep of the
  marshes of Glynn
Will work me no fear like the fear they have wrought
  me of yore
When length was failure, and when breadth was but
  bitterness sore,
And when terror and shrinking and dreary unnamable
  pain
Drew over me out of the merciless miles of the plain, —
Oh, now, unafraid, I am fain to face
The vast sweet visage of space.

AA; AmPP; AnAmPo; LiTA; NOBA; OxBA; PrIm; WGRP

Song of the Chattahoochee

5 But oh, not the hills of Habersham,
And oh, not the valleys of Hall
Avail: I am fain for to water the plain.
Downward, the voices of Duty call —
Downward, to toil and be mixed with the main,
The dry fields burn, and the mills are to turn,
And a myriad flowers mortally yearn,
And the lordly main from beyond the plain
Calls o'er the hills of Habersham,
Calls through the valleys of Hall. (l. 41–50)

AA; AmFN; AnAmPo; BoNaP; FaBoBe; FaBV; LiTA;
OHFP

GEORGE THOMAS LANIGAN
(1845–1886)

What, what, what/ What's the news from Swat?

1 With the noise of the mourning of the Swattish nation!
Fallen is at length
Its tower of strength;
Its sun is dimmed ere it had nooned;
Dead lies the great Ahkoond,
The great Ahkoond of Swat
Is not! (l. 46–52)

AA; AnAmPo; CaP; CenHV; FiBHP; NA; NBLV

PHILIP LARKIN   (1922–1985)

Annus Mirabilis

1 Sexual intercourse began
In nineteen sixty-three
(Which was rather late for me) —

Between the end of the Chatterley ban
And the Beatles' first LP. (l. 1–5)

NBLV; NIP; NOBL; OBAL

At Grass

2 Do memories plague their ears like flies?
They shake their heads. (l. 19–20)

3 Almanacked, their names live; they
Have slipped their names, and stand at ease,
Or gallop for what must be joy, (l. 24–26)

HAP; NePoEA; OxBTC; RB; SD; WeW

Church Going

4 wondering, too,
When churches fall completely out of use
What we shall turn them into, if we shall keep
A few cathedrals chronically on show, (l. 21–24)

5 But superstition, like belief, must die,
And what remains when disbelief has gone?
Grass, weedy pavement, brambles, buttress, sky,
                    (l. 34–36)

6 A serious house on serious earth it is,
In whose blent air all our compulsions meet,
Are recognised, and robed as destinies,
And that much never can be obsolete, (l. 55–58)

CMoP; GTBS-P; HeIP; LiTM; MoBrPo; MoP; NAEL-2;
NePoEA; NIP; NoAM; NoP; OAEL-2; PPP; PrIm; SCV;
TwCP; UnPo

Cut Grass

7 Cut grass lies frail:
Brief is the breath
Mown stalks exhale, (l. 1–3)

NoAM; OxBC; PrIm; RB

Days

8 What are days for?
Days are where we live.
They come, they wake us
Time and time over. (l. 1–4)

EBEV; FaBoMo; Mes; OxBC; OxBSP; RB; TOF

Deceptions

9 All the unhurried day
Your mind lay open like a drawer of knives. (l. 8–9)

10 What can be said,
Except that suffering is exact, but where
Desire takes charge, readings will grow erratic?
(l. 11–13)

CMoP; ErPo; GTBS-P; NePoEA

The Explosion

11 for a second
Wives saw men of the explosion

Larger than in life they managed —
Gold as on a coin, or walking
Somehow from the sun towards them, (l. 20–24)

EBEV; FaBoMo; HAP; NAEL-2; NoAM; OxBC; RB; SCV;
WeW

Lines on a Young Lady's Photograph Album

12 All your ages
Matt and glossy on the thick black pages! (l. 2–3)

13 But o, photography! as no art is,
Faithful and disappointing! (l. 16–17)

14 Those flowers, that gate,
These misty parks and motors, lacerate
Simply by being over; you
Contract my heart by looking out of date. (l. 27–30)

15 calm and dry,
It holds you like a heaven, and you lie
Unvariably lovely there,
Smaller and clearer as the years go by. (l. 42–45)

EnLoPo; HAP; OAEL-2; WeW

Mr. Bleaney

16 the dread

That how we live measures our own nature,
And at his age having no more to show
Than one hired box should make him pretty sure
He warranted no better, (l. 24–28)

HoPM; InPS; NePoEA-2; OxBC; PoE

Myxomatosis

17 I'm glad I can't explain
Just in what jaws you were to suppurate:
You may have thought things would come right again
If you could only keep quite still and wait. (l. 6–9)

CMoP; MoP; NoAM; NoP

MCMXIV

18 the men
Leaving the gardens tidy,
The thousands of marriages
Lasting a little while longer:
Never such innocence again. (l. 28–32)

EBEV; NAEL-2; NoAM; OBWP

A Study of Reading Habits

19 Don't read much now: the dude
Who lets the girl down before
The hero arrives, the chap
Who's yellow and keeps the store,
Seem far too familiar. Get stewed:
Books are a load of crap. (l. 13–18)

InPK; NOBL; PoPo; PPP; SoSe; TW

Toads

20 Why should I let the toad work
Squat on my life?
Can't I use my wit as a pitchfork
And drive the brute off? (l. 1–4)

CMoP; NePoEA; NoAM; NOBL; OxBTC; PoE; SoSe

The Whitsun Weddings

21 children frowned
At something dull; fathers had never known

Success so huge and wholly farcical;
The women shared
The secret like a happy funeral; (l. 49–53)

22 none
Thought of the others they would never meet
Or how their lives would all contain this hour.
I thought of London spread out in the sun,
Its postal districts packed like squares of wheat:
(l. 66–70)

FaBoMo; HeIP; MoP; NePoEA-2; NoAM; NoP; OxBTC

DAVID HERBERT LAWRENCE
(1885–1930)

Bat

1 A circle swoop, and a quick parabola under the bridge
arches
Where light pushes through;
A sudden turning upon itself of a thing in the air.
A dip to the water. (l. 12–15)

2 At a wavering instant the swallows gave way to bats
By the Ponte Vecchio . . .
Changing guard. (l. 29–31)

3 Creatures that hang themselves up like an old rag, to
     sleep;
And disgustingly upside down.
Hanging upside down like rows of disgusting old rags
And grinning in their sleep.
Bats! (l. 40–44)

BrPo; GTBS-P; HAP; OAEL-2; OBTV

Bavarian Gentians

4 Reach me a gentian, give me a torch!
let me guide myself with the blue, forked torch of this
     flower (l. 11–12)

5 Persephone herself is but a voice
or a darkness invisible enfolded in the deeper dark
of the arms Plutonic, and pierced with the passion of
     dense gloom,
among the splendor of torches of darkness, shedding
     darkness on the
lost bride and her groom. (l. 16–20)

CMoP; FaBoCh; FaBoMo; GoJo; GTBS-P; HAP; InPK;
InPS; LiTB; MoP; NAEL-2; NoAM; NOBE; NoP;
OAEL-2; PoE; SOTW; TTTS

The Elephant Is Slow to Mate

6 The elephant, the huge old beast,
is slow to mate; (l. 1–2)

7 So slowly the hot elephant hearts
grow full of desire,
and the great beasts mate in secret at last,
hiding their fire. (l. 13–16)

8 their massive blood
moves as the moon-tides, near, more near,
till they touch in flood. (l. 22–24)

LiTB; LiTM; PPP; TEP

Giorno dei Morti

9 Along the avenue of cypresses,
All in their scarlet cloaks and surplices
Of linen, go the chanting choristers,
The priests in gold and black, the villagers. . . .
                (l. 1–4)

BrPo; FaBoRV; NOBE; SeCePo

Gloire de Dijon

10 When she rises in the morning
I linger to watch her; (l. 1–2)

11 her swung breasts
Sway like full-blown yellow
Gloire de Dijon roses. (l. 8–10)

12 She drips herself with water, and her shoulders
Glisten as silver, they crumple up
Like wet and falling roses, (l. 9–11)

BrPo; CMoP; ELP; EnLoPo; ErPo; GBL; NoAM

How Beastly the Bourgeois Is

13 How beastly the bourgeois is
especially the male of the species — (l. 1–2)

14 Isn't it god's own image? tramping his thirty miles a
     day
after partridges, or a little rubber ball?
wouldn't you like to be like that, well off, and quite the
     thing? (l. 7–9)

15 And even so, he's stale, he's been there too long.
Touch him, and you'll find he's all gone inside
just like an old mushroom, all wormy inside, and
     hollow
under a smooth skin and an upright appearance.
                (l. 23–26)

ChTr; LiTM; NAEL-2; OBSV; TW

Humming-Bird

16 I believe there were no flowers then,
In the world where the humming-bird flashed ahead of
     creation.
I believe he pierced the slow vegetable veins with his
     long beak. (l. 9–11)

CMoP; InPS; LiTB; LiTM; NoAM; RB; SeCePo

Hymn to Priapus

17 My love lies underground
With her face upturned to mine,
And her mouth unclosed in a last long kiss
That ended her life and mine. (l. 1–4)

18 Grief, grief, I suppose and sufficient
Grief makes us free
To be faithless and faithful together
As we have to be. (l. 57–60)

CMoP; MoAB; OBMV; PoE

Kangaroo

19 But the yellow antipodal Kangaroo, when she sits up,
    Who can useat her, like a liquid drop that is heavy, and
        just touches earth. (l. 11–12)

20 Her little loose hands, and dropping Victorian
        shoulders.
    And then her great weight below the waist, her vast
        pale belly
    With a thin young yellow little paw hanging out, and
        straggle of a long thin ear, like ribbon,
    Like a funny trimming to the middle of her belly, thin
        little dangle of an immature paw, and one thin ear.
                                        (l. 23–26)

21 Wistfully watching, with wonderful liquid eyes.
    And all her weight, all her blood, dripping sack-wise
        down towards the earth's center,
    And the live little-one taking in its paw at the door of
        her belly. (l. 47–49)

EBEV; InPS; OBTV; OxBTC

Little Fish

22 The tiny fish enjoy themselves
    in the sea. (l. 1–2)

OxBTC; RB; SOTW; TTTS

Love on the Farm

23 I see a redness suddenly come
    Into the evening's anxious breast —
    'Tis the wound of love goes home! (l. 6–8)

24 The rabbit presses back her ears,
    Turns back her liquid, anguished eyes
    And crouches low; then with wild spring
    Spurts from the terror of his oncoming; (l. 36–39)

25 ah! the uplifted sword
    Of his hand again my bosom! and oh, the broad
    Blade of his glance that asks me to applaud
    His coming! (l. 54–57)

26 God, I am caught in a snare!
    I know not what fine wire is round my throat;
    I only know I let him finger there
    My pulse of life, and let him nose like a stoat
    Who sniffs with joy before he drinks the blood.
                                        (l. 59–63)

27 his lips meet mine, and a flood
    Of sweet fire sweeps across me, so I drown
    Against him, die and find death good. (l. 66–68)

CMoP; ErPo; FaBV; FF; MoAB; MoBrPo; NAEL-2;
NoAM; TrGrPo

Mountain Lion

28 They hesitate
    We hesitate.
    They have a gun.
    We have no gun. (l. 6–9)

29 So, she will never leap up that way again, with the
        yellow flash of a mountain lion's long shoot! (l. 37)

30 And I think in this empty world there was room for me
        and a mountain lion.
    And I think in the world beyond, how easily we might
        spare a million or two of humans
    And never miss them. (l. 44–46)

Mes; OBTV; OxBTC; RB; RFM

Piano

31 Softly, in the dusk, a woman is singing to me;
    Taking me back down the vista of years, till I see
    A child sitting under the piano, in the boom of the
        tingling strings
    And pressing the small, poised feet of a mother who
        smiles as she sings. (l. 1–4)

32 So now it is vain for the singer to burst into clamor
    With the great black piano appassionato. The glamour
    Of childish days is upon me, my manhood is cast
    Down in the flood of remembrance, I weep like a child
        for the past. (l. 9–12)

BLPL; CMoP; GrPl; GTBS-P; HAP; HeIP; InPK; InvP;
LiTB; MoAB; MoBrPo; MoP; NAEL-2; NIP; NoAM;
NOBE; NoP; OAEL-2; OxBSP; PoE; PPP; RB; UnPo;
WeW

River Roses

33 By the Isar, in the twilight
    We were wandering and singing, (l. 1–2)

34 We whispered: 'No one knows us.
    Let it be as the snake disposes
    Here in this simmering marsh.' (l. 13–15)

BrPo; CMoP; GBL; OAEL-2

The Ship of Death

35 Now it is autumn and the falling fruit
    and the long journey towards oblivion. (l. 1–2)

36 Have you built your ship of death, O have you?
    O build your ship of death, for you will need it.
                                        (l. 8–9)

37 And can a man his own quietus make
with a bare bodkin? (l. 17–18)

38 We are dying, we are dying, we are all of us dying
and nothing will stay the death-flood rising within us
and soon it will rise on the world, on the outside world.
(l. 43–45)

39 Now launch the small ship, now as the body dies
and life departs, launch out, the fragile soul
in the fragile ship of courage, the ark of faith
with its store of food and little cooking pans
and change of clothes, (l. 56–60)

40 And everything is gone, the body is gone
completely under, gone, entirely gone. (l. 75–76)

41 And yet out of eternity, a thread
separates itself on the blackness,
a horizontal thread
that fumes a little with pallor upon the dark.
(l. 82–85)

42 The flood subsides, and the body, like a worn sea-shell
emerges strange and lovely. (l. 96–97)

CMoP; FaBoRV; FaBoTw; GTBS-P; LiTB; MoAB;
MoBrPo; MoP; MOS; NAEL-2; NoAM; NoP; OAEL-2;
PrIm

Snake

43 But must I confess how I liked him,
How glad I was he had come like a guest in quiet, to
drink at my water-trough
And depart peaceful, pacified, and thankless,
Into the burning bowels of this earth? (l. 27–30)

44 that part of him that was left behind convulsed in
undignified haste,
Writhed like lightning, and was gone
Into the black hole, the earth-lipped fissure in the wall-
front, (l. 59–61)

45 Like a king in exile, uncrowned in the underworld,
Now due to be crowned again. (l. 69–70)

46 And so, I missed my chance with one of the lords
Of life.
And I have something to expiate;
A pettiness. (l. 71–74)

BrPo; CMoP; FaBoMo; HeIP; HoPM; LiTB; LiTM;
MoAB; NoAM; NOBE; NoP; NU; OAEL-2; PoRA; PPP;
PrIm; SOTW

Song of a Man Who Has Come Through

47 Not I, not I, but the wind that blows through me!
A fine wind is blowing the new direction of Time.
(l. 1–2)

48 Oh, for the wonder that bubbles into my soul,
I would be a good fountain, a good well-head,
Would blur no whisper, spoil no expression. (l. 11–13)

49 It is somebody wants to do us harm.

No, no, it is the three strange angels.
Admit them, admit them. (l. 16–18)

CMoP; FaBoMo; GTBS-P; InPS; LiTM; OxBTC; PoE

Sorrow

50 Why does the thin grey strand
Floating up from the forgotten
Cigarette between my fingers,
Why does it trouble me? (l. 1–4)

CMoP; GTBS-P; OBD; OBMV

Spring Morning

51 Among the pink and blue
Of the sky and the almond flowers
A sparrow flutters.
— We have come through. (l. 5–8)

52 With nothing to fight any more —
In each other, at least.
See, how gorgeous the world is
Outside the door! (l. 25–28)

BrPo; CMoP; MoAB; MoBrPo

Tortoise-Shell

53 The Cross, the Cross
Goes deeper in than we know,
Deeper into life;
Right into the marrow
And through the bone. (l. 1–5)

54 Fives, and tens,
Threes and fours and twelves,
All the volte face of decimals,
The whirligig of dozens and the pinnacle of seven.
(l. 26–29)

55 The Lord wrote it all down on the little slate
Of the baby tortoise.
Outward and visible indication of the plan within,
The complex, manifold involvedness of an individual
creature (l. 45–48)

CMoP; FM; NAEL-2; OAEL-2

Trees in the Garden

56 they stand so still
in the thunder air, all strangers to one another
as the green grass glows upwards, strangers in the
garden. (l. 14–16)

CMoP; MoAB; MoBrPo; NoP

Whales Weep Not!

57 They say the sea is cold, but the sea contains
the hottest blood of all, and the wildest, the most
    urgent.

All the whales in the wider deeps, hot are they, as they
    urge
on and on, and dive beneath the icebergs.
The right whales, the sperm-whales, the hammer-heads,
    the killers
there they blow, there they blow, hot wild white breath
    out of the sea! (l. 1–6)

58 and Venus among the fishes skips and is a she-dolphin
she is the gay, delighted porpoise sporting with love
    and the sea
she is the female tunny-fish, round and happy among
    the males
and dense with happy blood, dark rainbow bliss in the
    sea. (l. 33–36)

CMoP; MOS; NoAM; NU

A Youth Mowing

59 There are four men mowing down by the Isar;
I can hear the swish of the scythe-strokes, four
Sharp breaths taken; (l. 1–3)

60 Lad, thou hast gotten a child in me,
Laddie, a man thou'lt ha'e to be,
Yea, though I'm sorry for thee. (l. 14–16)

InPK; MoAB; MoBrPo; NoAM; TrGrPo

IRVING LAYTON (b. 1912)

The Birth of Tragedy

1 And me happiest when I compose poems:
Love, power, the huzza of battle
are something, are much:
yet a poem includes them like a pool
water and reflection. (l. 1–4)

2 how seasonably
leaf and blossom uncurl
and living things arrange their death,
while someone from afar off
blows birthday candles for the world. (l. 28–32)

MoCV; NoAM; NoP; OBCV

EMMA LAZARUS (1849–1887)

The New Colossus

1 Not like the brazen giant of Greek fame,
With conquering limbs astride from land to land,
Here at our sea-washed, sunset gates shall stand

A mighty woman with a torch, whose flame
Is the imprisoned lightning, and her name
Mother of Exiles. From her beacon-hand
Glows world-wide welcome; her mild eyes command
The air-bridged harbor that twin cities frame. (l. 1–8)

2 With silent lips. "Give me your tired, your poor,
Your huddled masses yearning to breathe free,
The wretched refuse of your teeming shore.
Send these, the homeless, tempest-tost to me.
I lift my lamp beside the golden door!" (l. 10–14)

AiP; AmFN; FaBV; FaFP; FaPON; FPL; OPP; PoLF;
PrIm; Son; WPE

EDWARD LEAR (1812–1888)

The Ahkond of Swat

1 Who, or why, or which, or what,
Is the Ahkond of Swat? (l. 1–2)

CenHV; FaBoCh; FaBoCo; FaBoNo; FiBHP; NA

Calico Pie

2 Calico Pie,
The little Birds fly
Down to the calico tree,
Their wings were blue,
And they sang "Tilly-loo!"
Till away they flew —
And they never came back to me! (l. 1–6)

FaBoCh; FaPON; PYC; TrGrPo

Cold Are the Crabs

3 When wily walruses in congress meet —
Such such is life — (l. 13–14)

CenHV; FaBoNo; GoJo; NAEL-2

The Courtship of the Yonghy-Bonghy-Bo

4 On the Coast of Coromandel
Where the early pumpkins blow,
In the middle of the woods
Lived the Yonghy-Bonghy-Bo.
Two old chairs, and half a candle, —
One old jug without a handle, —
These were all his worldly goods:
In the middle of the woods, (l. 1–8)

5 I would be your wife most gladly!'
(Here she twirled her fingers madly)
'But in England I've a mate!

Yes! you've asked me far too late,
For in England I've a mate, (l. 46—50)

EnLoPo; FaBoNo; NA; NA; OAEL-2; OnMSP; WiR

The Dong with a Luminous Nose

6 When awful darkness and silence reign
Over the great Gromboolian plain,
Through the long, long wintry nights; — (l. 1—3)

AmMo; CenHV; ChTr; EBVV; FaBoCo; FaBoNo; FaBV;
NOBVV; PoEL-5; WiR

How Pleasant to Know Mr. Lear

7 'How pleasant to know Mr. Lear!'
Who has written such volumes of stuff!
Some think him ill-tempered and queer,
But a few think him pleasant enough. (l. 1—4)

ChTr; EBEV; FaBoCh; FaBoCo; FiBHP; HAP; NBLV;
NOBE; NOBL; NOBVV; NoP; WeW

The Jumblies

8 They went to sea in a Sieve, they did,
In a Sieve they went to sea:
In spite of all their friends could say,
On a winter's morn, on a stormy day, (l. 1—4)

9 Far and few, far and few,
Are the lands where the Jumblies live;
Their heads are green, and their hands are blue,
And they went to sea in a Sieve. (l. 11—14)

BLPL; ChTr; EBEV; FaBoBe; FaBoNo; FaFP; GoJo;
LiTB; MOS; NA; NAEL-2; OnMSP; OxBChV; OxBoLi;
PoRA; TEP; WiR

The Owl and the Pussy-cat

10 The Owl and the Pussy-cat went to sea
In a beautiful pea-green boat,
They took some honey, and plenty of money,
Wrapped up in a five-pound note. (l. 1—4)

11 They sailed away, for a year and a day,
To the land where the Bong-Tree grows, (l. 16—17)

12 And hand in hand, on the edge of the sand,
They danced by the light of the moon, (l. 29—30)

BeLS; BoTP; FaBoBe; FaBoCh; FaBoNo; FaFP; FaPON;
FPL; GoJo; GTBS-P; MoShBr; NA; NBLV; NOBE; NoP;
NTCP; OxBChV; OxBoLi; PDV; PoLF; PoRA; PYC;
RHPC; TrGrPo; TTTS

The Quangle Wangle's Hat

13 On the top of the Crumpetty Tree
The Quangle Wangle sat,
But his face you could not see,
On account of his Beaver Hat. (l. 1—4)

AmMo; EBEV; ILY; OnUR

There was an old man in a tree

14 There was an Old Man in a tree,
Who was horribly bored by a bee; (l. 1—2)

FaBoNo; InvP; MoShBr; NoP; OxBChV; TEP

There was an old man of Thermopylae

15 There was an old man of Thermopylae,
Who never did anything properly; (l. 1—2)

EBEV; FaBoNo; NA; NOBL

There was an old man who said, "Hush!"

16 There was an Old Man who said, 'Hush!
I perceive a young bird in this bush!' (l. 1—2)

FaBoCo; GoJo; NA; NOBL; OxBChV; OxBoLi; TEP

There was an old man who supposed

17 There was an Old Man who supposed,
That the street door was partially closed; (l. 1—2)

NA; NAEL-2; NOBVV; NoP

There was an old man with a beard

18 There was an old man with a beard,
who said, "It is just as I feared! —
Two owls and a hen, four larks and a wren,
Have all built their nests in my beard!" (l. 1—3)

ChTr; FaBoCo; FaBoNo; FaPON; NOBL; NTCP;
OxBChV; PDV; PYC; TEP

There was an old party of Lyme (attributed to Lear)

19 There was an old party of Lyme
Who married three wives at one time. (l. 1—2)

20 And bigamy, sir, is a crime.' (l. 5)

FaBoCo; FF; NA; OxBoLi

DON L. LEE (HAKI R. MADHUBUTI) (b. 1942)

Assassination

1 they came running.
with
guns
drawn
they came running
toward the King — (l. 10–15)

AmNP; FF; NeAC; OFD; PoBA

But He Was Cool; or, He Even Stopped for Green Lights

2 super-cool
ultrablack (l. 1–2)

3 cool-cool ultracool was bop-cool/ice box cool so cool
cold cool (l. 18)

4 to be black
is
to be
very-hot. (l. 29–32)

AmNP; BPo; MoP; PoBA

WINIFRED M. LETTS (1887–1972)

The Spires of Oxford

1 I saw the spires of Oxford
As I was passing by,
The grey spires of Oxford
Against a pearl-grey sky;
My heart was with the Oxford men
Who went abroad to die. (l. 1–6)

FaFP; OHFP; PoLF; PoRA; WGRP

DENISE LEVERTOV (b. 1923)

The Ache of Marriage

1 The ache of marriage;

thigh and tongue, beloved,
are heavy with it, (l. 1–3)

2 looking for joy, some joy
not to be known outside it

two by two in the ark of
the ache of it. (l. 10–13)

FF; InPK; NoAM; NOBA; PoM; TAP

Bedtime

3 We are a meadow where the bees hum:
mind and body are almost one (l. 1–2)

4 though the fall cold

surrounds our warm bed, and though
by day we are singular and often lonely. (l. 8–10)

IHMS; NaP; SM; TwCP

The Goddess

5 She in whose lip service
I passed my time,
whose name I knew, but not her face,
came upon me where I lay in Lie Castle! (l. 1–4)

6 without whom nothing
flowers, fruits, sleeps in season,
without whom nothing
speaks in its own tongue, but returns
lie for lie! (l. 27–31)

LiTM; NeAP; NOBA; PoM

Hypocrite Women

7 Hypocrite women, how seldom we speak
of our own doubts, while dubiously
we mother man in his doubt! (l. 1–3)

8 And our dreams,

with what frivolity we have pared them
like toenails, clipped them like ends of
split hair. (l. 18–21)

CAPP; MAT; NMM; PoM

Illustrious Ancestors

9 poems direct as what the birds said,
hard as a floor, sound as a bench,
mysterious as the silence when the tailor
would pause with his needle in the air. (l. 15–18)

AmPP; MoP; NAAL-2; NOBA; VGW

The Jacob's Ladder

10 The stairway is not
a thing of gleaming strands
a radiant evanescence
for angels' feet that only glance in their tread, and need
    not
touch the stone. (l. 1–5)

11 and a man climbing
must scrape his knees, and bring
the grip of his hands into play. The cut stone
consoles his groping feet. Wings brush past him.
The poem ascends. (l. 16–20)

AmPP; CAPP; PoM; PPP

Losing Track

12 in the pleasure of that communion

I lose track,
the moon I watch goes down, the

tide swings you away before
I know I'm
alone again long since, (l. 10–15)

HeIP; MoP; NaP; NOBA; PoE; PoM

Matins

13 The authentic! Shadows of it
sweep past in dreams, (l. 1–2)

14 The authentic! I said
rising from the toilet seat. (l. 12–13)

15 the real, the new-laid
egg whose speckled shell
the poet fondles and must break
if he will be nourished. (l. 29–32)

16 Marvelous Truth, confront us
at every turn,
in every guise, (l. 81–83)

17 Thrust close your smile
that we know you, terrible joy. (l. 92–93)

AmPP; FaBoWP; IHMS; MoP; NoAM; NOBA

O Taste and See

18 The world is
not with us enough.
O taste and see (l. 1–3)

NoP; PBWP; PPP; TAP

Pleasures

19 I like to find
what's not found
at once, but lies

within something of another nature,
in repose, distinct. (l. 1–5)

CAPP; NeAP; NoAM; NOBA; PoE

Scenes from the Life of the Peppertrees

20 After a while
it walks over and taps
on the upstairs window with a bunch
of red berries. Will he wake? (l. 42–45)

LiTM; NeAP; NoP; PoM

Song for Ishtar

21 The moon is a sow
and grunts in my throat
Her great shining shines through me (l. 1–3)

MoP; NaP; NMM; NoAM; PoM

To the Snake

22 Green Snake, when I hung you round my neck
and stroked your cold, pulsing throat (l. 1–2)

AmPP; LiTM; NePoEA-2; NMM; PoA

What Were They Like?

23 1) Did the people of Vietnam
use lanterns of stone? (l. 1–2)

24 2) Perhaps they gathered once to delight in blossom,
but after the children were killed
there were no more buds. (l. 13–15)

HeIP; NIP; OBWP; VGW; WPE

PHILIP LEVINE (b. 1928)

Animals Are Passing from Our Lives

1 It's wonderful how I jog
on four-honed-down ivory toes
my massive buttocks slipping
like oiled parts with each light step. (l. 1–4)

2 I can smell
   the blade that opens the hole
   and the pudgy white fingers

   that shake out the intestines
   like a hankie. (l. 6–10)

   CAPP; CoAP; NOBA; SM; TAP; TW

To a Child Trapped in a Barber Shop

3 You've gotten in through the transom
   and you can't get out
   till Monday morning or, worse,
   till the cops come. (l. 1–4)

4 We've all been here before,
   we took our turn
   under the electric storm
   of the vibrator

   and stiffened our wills to meet
   the close clippers (l. 17–22)

   CAPP; InPK; MoP; NoAM; NOBA; TAP; VGW

ALUN LEWIS (1915–1944)

All Day It Has Rained

1 And we talked of girls, and dropping bombs on Rome,
   And thought of the quiet dead and the loud celebrities
   Exhorting us to slaughter, (l. 17–19)

2 but now it is the rain
   Possesses us entirely, the twilight and the rain.
                                    (l. 23–24)

3 To the Shoulder o' Mutton where Edward Thomas
      brooded long
   On death and beauty – till a bullet stopped his song.
                                    (l. 30–31)

   GTBS-P; NAEL-2; NOBE; OBWP; OBWVE; OxBTC

The First Month of His Absence

4 The first month of his absence
   I was numb and sick
   And where he'd left his promise
   Life did not turn or kick.
   The seed, the seed of love was sick. (l. 1–5)

5 And he was lost among the waves,
   His ship rolled helpless in the sea,
   The fourth month of his voyage
   He shouted grievously
   "Beloved, do not think of me." (l. 16–20)

6 All this slowness, all this hardness,
   The nearness that is waiting in my bed,
   The gradual self-effacement of the dead. (l. 33–35)

   LiTM; NAEL-2; OBWP; WaaP

Goodbye

7 So we must say Goodbye, my darling,
   And go, as lovers go, for ever;
   Tonight remains, to pack and fix on labels
   And make an end of lying down together. (l. 1–4)

8 Your kisses close my eyes and yet you stare
   As though God struck a child with nameless fears;
                                    (l. 17–18)

   BoLoP; NAEL-2; OBWP; OxBTC

LI PO (701–762)

Lament of the Frontier Guard

1 By the North Gate, the wind blows full of sand,
   Lonely from the beginning of time until now!
   Trees fall, the grass goes yellow with autumn. (l. 1–3)

2 Ah, how shall you know the dreary sorrow at the North
      Gate,
   With Li Po's name forgotten,
   And we guardsmen fed to the tigers. (l. 21–23)

   OBVE; OBWP; VGW; WaaP

The River Merchant's Wife; a Letter

3 While my hair was still cut straight across my forehead
   I played about the front gate, pulling flowers.
   You came by on bamboo stilts, playing horse,
   You walked about my seat, playing with blue plums
                                    (l. 1–4)

4 At fourteen I married My Lord you. (l. 7)

5 I desired my dust to be mingled with yours
   Forever and forever and forever.
   Why should I climb the look out? (l. 12–14)

6 The paired butterflies are already yellow with August
   Over the grass in the West garden;
   They hurt me. I grow older. (l. 23–25)

7 Please let me know beforehand,
   And I will come out to meet you
   As far as Cho-fu-Sa. (l. 27–29)

   AmPP; AWP; BoLoP; FYAP; HAP; HeIP; InPK; InPS;
   LiTA; MoAB; MoAmPo; MoP; NAAL-2; NIP; NoAM;
   NOBA; NOBE; NoP; OBMV; OBVE; OxBA; PPP; PrIm;
   RB; SOTW; TAP; TTTS; TwCP; UnPo; WeW

ABRAHAM LINCOLN (1809–1865)

Memory

1 O memory! thou midway world
  'Twixt earth and paradise,
  Where things decayed and loved ones lost
  In dreamy shadows rise, (l. 5–8)

2 I range the fields with pensive tread,
  And pace the hollow rooms,
  And feel (companion of the dead)
  I'm living in the tombs. (l. 37–40)

BLPA; FaBoBe; FPL; WBLP

LADY ANNE LINDSAY (1750–1825)

Auld Robin Gray

1 When the sheep are in the fauld, and the kye at hame,
  And a' the warld to rest are gane,
  The waes o' my heart fa' in showers frae my e'e,
  While my gudeman lies sound by me.

  Young Jamie lo'ed me weel, and sought me for his
    bride;

2 But I'll do my best a gude wife ay to be,
  For auld Robin Gray he is kind unto me.

AIW; BeLS; CH; GoTS; GTBS; GTBS-P; NOEC; OBEV;
WPE

VACHEL LINDSAY (1879–1931)

Abraham Lincoln Walks at Midnight

1 here at midnight, in our little town
  A mourning figure walks, and will not rest,
  Near the old court-house pacing up and down, (l. 2–4)

2 A bronzed, lank man! His suit of ancient black,
  A famous high top-hat and plain worn shawl
  Make him the quaint great figure that men love,
  The prairie-lawyer, master of us all.

3 It breaks his heart that kings must murder still,
  That all his hours of travail here for men
  Seem yet in vain. And who will bring white peace
  That he may sleep upon his hill again? (l. 29–32)

AmFN; AmPP; CMoP; FaBV; FaFP; FaPON; GOA; LiTA;
MoAmPo; NOBA; OFD; OHFP; OHIP; OxBA; PAH; TAP;
VGW

Bryan, Bryan, Bryan, Bryan

4 I brag and chant of Bryan, Bryan, Bryan,
  Candidate for president who sketched a silver Zion,
  The one American Poet who could sing outdoors,
                                                    (l. 4–6)

5 Where is McKinley, Mark Hanna's McKinley,
  His slave, his echo, his suit of clothes?
  Gone to join the shadows, with the pomps of that time,
                                                    (l. 223–225)

6 Where is Hanna, bulldog Hanna,
  Low-browed Hanna, who said: "Stand pat"?
  Gone to his place with old Pierpont Morgan.
                                                    (l. 230–232)

7 Where is Roosevelt, the young dude cowboy,
  Who hated Bryan, then aped his way?
  Gone to join the shadows with mighty Cromwell
  And tall King Saul, till the Judgment day.
                                                    (l. 234–237)

CMoP; LiTA; OxBA; OxBoLi

The Congo

8 Fat black bucks in a wine-barrel room,
  Barrel-house kings, with feet unstable,
  Sagged and reeled and pounded on the table,
  Pounded on the table,
  Beat an empty barrel with the handle of a broom,
  Hard as they were able, (l. 1–6)

9 Boomlay, boomlay, boomlay, Boom,"
  A roaring, epic, ragtime tune
  From the mouth of the Congo
  To the Mountains of the Moon. (l. 26–29)

10 Boom, steal the pygmies,
  Boom, kill the Arabs,
  Boom, kill the white men, (l. 33–35)

11 "Be careful what you do,
  Or Mumbo-Jumbo, god of the Congo,
  And all of the other
  Gods of the Congo,
  Mumbo-Jumbo will hoo-doo you, (l. 45–49)

12 Coal-black maidens with pearls in their hair,
  Knee skirts trimmed with the jassamine sweet,
  And bells on their ankles and little black feet.
                                                    (l. 84–86)

CMoP; FaFP; LiTA; MoAB; MoAmPo; NOBA; OxBA;
PoNe; PoRA; TAP

The Eagle That Is Forgotten

13 Sleep softly . . . eagle forgotten . . . under the stone.
                                                    (l. 1)

14 Sleep on, O brave-hearted, O wise man, that kindled
    the flame —
  To live in mankind is far more than to live in a name,
                                                    (l. 19–20)

AWP; CMoP; LiTA; MoAB; McAmPo; NOBA; OxBA

Factory Windows Are Always Broken

15 Factory windows are always broken.
   Somebody's always throwing bricks,
   Somebody's always heaving cinders,
   Playing ugly Yahoo tricks. (l. 1–4)

FaFP; LiTA; OBCA; OxBSP

The Flower-fed Buffaloes

16 The flower-fed buffaloes of the spring
   In the days of long ago,
   Ranged where the locomotives sing
   And the prairie flowers lie low: — (l. 1–4)

AmFN; ChTr; CMoP; FaPON; GoJo; MoAmPo; NOBA;
OBCA; PoE; RB; RFM; VGW

The Leaden-eyed

17 Not that they die, but that they die like sheep.

CMoP; FaBoEE; LiTA; OxBSP; PoE; RB

The Little Turtle

18 He snapped at a mosquito.
   He snapped at a flea.
   He snapped at a minnow.
   And he snapped at me.

FaPON; GoJo; NTCP; OBAL; OBCA; PDV; RAR

The Moon's the North Wind's Cooky

19 The Moon's the North Wind's cooky, (l. 1)

20 The South Wind is a baker. (l. 5)

FaFP; FaPON; OBCA; PDV; RAR; RHPC

The Mysterious Cat

21 Did you ever hear of a thing like that?
   Oh, what a proud mysterious cat. (l. 19–20)

ChTr; FaPON; GoJo; OBCA

LENORE M. LINK

Holding Hands

1 Elephants walking
  Along the trails

  Are holding hands
  By holding tails. (l. 1–4)

FaPON; MoShBr; NTCP; RAR; RHPC

THOMAS LODGE   (1558?–1625)

Phyllis

1 I would in rich and golden coloured raine,
  With tempting showers in pleasant sort discend,

2 Into faire Phillis lappe (my lovely friend)
  When sleepe hir sence with slomber doth restraine.
  I would be chaunged to a milk-white Bull,
  When midst the gladsome fieldes she should appeare,

3 I were content to wearie out my paine,
  To bee Narsissus so she were a spring
  To drowne in hir those woes my heart do wring:
  And more I wish transformed to remaine:
  That whilest I thus in pleasures lappe did lye,
  I might refresh desire, which else would die.

AAS

4 My Phillis hath prime-feathered flowers
  That smile when she treads on them;
  And Phillis hath a gallant flock
  That leaps since she doth own them.
  But Phillis hath so hard a heart —

5 As yields no mercy to desert,
  Nor grace to those that crave it.
  Sweet sun, when thou lookest on,
  Pray her regard my moan;
  Sweet birds, when you sing to her,
  To yield some pity, woo her;

ACP; ElL; OBEV; OBSC

Rosalynde; or, Euphues' Golden Legacy

6 Nature herself her shape admires;
  The gods are wounded in her sight;
  And Love forsakes his heavenly fires
  And at her eyes his brand doth light:
  Heigh ho, would she were mine!

7 Since for a fair there's fairer none,
Nor for her virtues so divine:
Heigh ho, fair Rosaline!
Heigh ho, my heart! would God that she were mine!

ElL; GTBS; GTBS-P; LiTB; OBEV; OBSC; TrGrPo

HENRY WADSWORTH LONGFELLOW
(1809–1882)

The Arrow and the Song

1 I shot an arrow into the air,
It fell to earth, I knew not where; (l. 1–2)

2 I breathed a song into the air,
It fell to earth, I knew not where; (l. 5–6)

3 Long, long, afterward, in an oak
I found the arrow, still unbroke;
And the song, from beginning to end,
I found again in the heart of a friend. (l. 9–12)

AA; AnAmPo; FaFP; PWR

The Builders

4 All are architects of Fate,
Working in these walls of Time;
Some with massive deeds and great,
Some with ornaments of rhyme. (l. 1–4)

5 For the structure that we raise,
Time is with materials filled;
Our to-days and yesterdays
Are the blocks with which we build. (l. 9–12)

AnAmPo; FaFP; OHFP; PWR

The Building of the Ship

6 Thou, too, sail on, O Ship of State!
Sail on, O Union, strong and great!
Humanity with all its fears,
With all the hopes of future years,
Is hanging breathless on thy fate!

7 In spite of rock and tempest's roar,
In spite of false lights on the shore,
Sail on, nor fear to breast the sea!
Our hearts, our hopes, are all with thee,
Our hearts, our hopes, our prayers, our tears,
Our faith triumphant o'er our fears,
Are all with thee, — are all with thee!

AA; FaBoBe; FaFP; FaPON; MOS; OHIP; OPP; PAH;
PWR; WGRP

Chaucer

8 He is the poet of the dawn, who wrote
The Canterbury Tales and his old age
Made beautiful with song; and as I read
I hear the crowing cock, I hear the note
Of lark and linnet, and from every page
Rise odors of ploughed field or flowery mead.
(l. 9–14)

AA; AWP; HeIP; InvP; NOBA; NoP; OBEV; OxBA; PoE;
PoRA; PrIm; Son; TAP; TrGrPo

The Children's Hour

9 Between the dark and the daylight,
When the night is beginning to lower,
Comes a pause in the day's occupations,
That is known as the Children's Hour. (l. 1–4)

10 I have you fast in my fortress,
And will not let you depart,
But put you down into the dungeon
In the round-tower of my heart.

And there will I keep you forever,
Yes, forever and a day,
Till the walls shall crumble to ruin,
And moulder in dust away! (l. 33–40)

AA; AnAmPo; FaBoBe; FaBV; FaFP; FaPON; FPL;
OBAL; OBCA; OHFP; PoEL-5; PoLF; WBLP

Christmas Bells

11 I heard the bells, on Christmas Day,
Their old, familiar carols play,
And wild and sweet
The words repeat
Of peace on earth, good will to men. (l. 1–5)

12 Then pealed the bells more loud and deep:
"God is not dead; nor doth He sleep;
The wrong shall fail,
The right prevail,
With peace on earth, good will to men." (l. 16–20)

AH; AnAmPo; BLRP; FaFP; FaPON; OBCP; PChr; WBLP

The Cross of Snow

13 In the long, sleepless watches of the night,
A gentle face — the face of one long dead —
Looks at me from the wall, (l. 1–3)

14 There is a mountain in the distant West
That, sun-defying, in its deep ravines
Displays a cross of snow upon its side.
Such is the cross I wear upon my breast

These eighteen years, through all the changing scenes
And seasons, changeless since the day she died.
(l. 9–14)

HeIP; NOBA; OxBA; TAP

The Day Is Done

15   Come, read to me some poem,
Some simple and heartfelt lay,
That shall soothe this restless feeling,
And banish the thoughts of day.

Not from the grand old masters,
Not from the bards sublime,
Whose distant footsteps echo
Through the corridors of Time. (l. 13–20)

16   And the night shall be filled with music,
And the cares, that infest the day,
Shall fold their tents, like the Arabs,
And as silently steal away. (l. 41–44)

AnAmPo; BLPA; FaBoBe; FaFP; FPL; NOBA; OHFP;
OxBA; PoRA; PWR; TrGrPo

Daybreak

17   A wind came up out of the sea,
And said, "O mists, make room for me." (l. 1–2)

18   It whispered to the fields of corn,
"Bow down, and hail the coming morn."

It shouted through the belfry tower,
"Awake, O bell! proclaim the hour."

It crossed the churchyard with a sigh,
And said, "Not yet! in quiet lie." (l. 13–18)

BoTP; FPL; PoLF; PWR

Divina Commedia (translated by Longfellow)

19   O star of morning and of liberty!

20   Repeat thy song, till the familiar lines
Are footpaths for the thought of Italy!
Thy flame is blown abroad from all the heights,
Through all the nations, and a sound is heard,
As of a mighty wind, and men devout,
Strangers of Rome, and the new proselytes,
In their own language hear thy wondrous word,
And many are amazed and many doubt.

AmPP; HAP; OBEV; OxBA; Son; TAP

Excelsior

21   The shades of night were falling fast,
As through an Alpine village passed
A youth, who bore, 'mid snow and ice,

A banner with the strange device,
Excelsior! (l. 1–5)

22   "Beware the pine-tree's withered branch!
Beware the awful avalanche!"
This was the peasant's last Good-night,
A voice replied, far up the height,
Excelsior! (l. 26–30)

23   There in the twilight cold and gray,
Lifeless, but beautiful, he lay,
And from the sky, serene and far,
A voice fell, like a falling star,
Excelsior! (l. 41–45)

FaPON; FaPoR; NAAL-1; OBCA; OnMSP; PrIm; WBLP

Hymn to the Night

24   I heard the trailing garments of the Night
Sweep through her marble halls!
I saw her sable skirts all fringed with light
From the celestial walls! (l. 1–4)

25   O holy Night! from thee I learn to bear
What man has borne before!
Thou layest thy finger on the lips of Care,
And they complain no more. (l. 17–20)

AA; BLPL; NOBA; OxBA; PWR; TAP; TrGrPo

The Jewish Cemetery at Newport

26   Pride and humiliation hand in hand
Walked with them through the world where'er they
went;
Trampled and beaten were they as the sand,
And yet unshaken as the continent. (l. 45–48)

27   And all the great traditions of the Past
They saw reflected in the coming time.

And thus forever with reverted look
The mystic volume of the world they read,
Spelling it backward, like a Hebrew book,
Till life became a Legend of the Dead. (l. 51–56)

AmPP; HAP; HeIP; HoPM; NOBA; NoP; OxBA; TAP

Mezzo Cammin

28   Half of my life is gone, and I have let
The years slip from me and have not fulfilled
The aspiration of my youth, to build
Some tower of song with lofty parapet. (l. 1–4)

29   half-way up the hill, I see the Past
Lying beneath me with its sounds and sights, —
A city in the twilight dim and vast,

With smoking roofs, soft bells, and gleaming lights, —
And hear above me on the autumnal blast
The cataract of Death far thundering from the heights.
(l. 9–14)

FPL; NAAL-1; NoP; PoE; TAP

Milton

30 So in majestic cadence rise and fall
The mighty undulations of thy song,
O sightless bard, England's Monides!
And ever and anon, high over all
Uplifted, a ninth wave superb and strong,
Floods all the soul with its melodious seas. (l. 9–14)

AA; AmPP; AWP; NoP; TAP; TrGrPo

My Lost Youth

31 Often I think of the beautiful town
That is seated by the sea; (l. 1–2)

32 And my youth comes back to me.
And a verse of a Lapland song
Is haunting my memory still:
"A boy's will is the wind's will,
And the thoughts of youth are long, long thoughts."
(l. 5–9)

AA; AmPP; AnAmPo; AWP; FaBoBe; FaBV; FaFP;
FaPON; FaPoR; FPL; GoJo; LiTA; NAAL-1; NOBA;
OBEV; OxBA; PoEL-5; PoLF; PoRA; TAP

Nature

33 As a fond mother, when the day is o'er,
Leads by the hand her little child to bed,
Half willing, half reluctant to be led, (l. 1–3)

34 So Nature deals with us, and takes away
Our playthings one by one, and by the hand
Leads us to rest so gently, that we go
Scarce knowing if we wish to go or stay,
Being too full of sleep to understand
How far the unknown transcends the what we
know. (l. 9–14)

AA; BoNaP; FaBoBe; FPL; PoLF; TAP; TrGrPo

Paul Revere's Ride (Tales of a Wayside Inn)

35 Listen, my children, and you shall hear
Of the midnight ride of Paul Revere,
On the eighteenth of April, in Seventy-five;
Hardly a man is now alive
Who remembers that famous day and year. (l. 1–5)

36 Hang a lantern aloftin the belfry arch
Of the North Church toweras a signal light, —
One, if by land, and two, if by sea;
And I on the opposite shore will be,
Ready to ride and spread the alarm
Through every Middlesex village and farm, (l. 8–13)

37 And so through the nightwent his cry of alarm
To every Middlesex village and farm, —
A cry of defiance, and not of fear,
A voice in the darkness, a knock at the door,
And a word that shall echo for evermore! (l. 120–124)

AiP; AnAmPo; BeLS; BLPA; FaBoBe; FaBoTw; FaBV;
FaFP; FaPON; FaPoR; FPL; OBAL; OBCA; OBNV;
OHFP; OPP; PAH; PWR; TrGrPo; WBLP

A Psalm of Life

38 Tell me not, in mournful numbers,
Life is but an empty dream! —
For the soul is dead that slumbers,
And things are not what they seem.

Life is real! Life is earnest!
And the grave is not its goal;
Dust thou art, to dust returnest,
Was not spoken of the soul. (l. 1–8)

39 Lives of great men all remind us
We can make our lives sublime,
And, departing, leave behind us
Footprints on the sands of time; (l. 25–28)

40 Let us, then, be up and doing,
With a heart for any fate;
Still achieving, still pursuing,
Learn to labor and to wait. (l. 33–36)

AA; AH; AnAmPo; FaBoBe; FPL; NAAL-1; OBCA; OHFP;
PoLF; PrIm; PWR; TAP; WBLP

Snow-Flakes

41 Out of the bosom of the Air,
Out of the cloud-folds of her garments shaken,
Over the woodlands brown and bare,
Over the harvest-fields forsaken,
Silent, and soft, and slow
Descends the snow. (l. 1–6)

42 This is the poem of the air,
Slowly in silent syllables recorded;
This is the secret of despair,
Long in its cloudy bosom hoarded,
Now whispered and revealed
To wood and field. (l. 13–18)

BoTP; ChTr; FaBoRV; FPL; NOBA; NoP; PoEL-5; TAP;
UnPo; WiR

The Song of Hiawatha

43 By the shores of Gitche Gumee,
By the shining Big-Sea-Water,
Stood the wigwam of Nokomis,
Daughter of the Moon, Nokomis.

44 There the wrinkled old Nokomis
Nursed the little Hiawatha,
Rocked him in his linden cradle,
Bedded softin moss and rushes,

45 Then the little Hiawatha
Learned of every bird its language,
Learned their names and all their secrets,

BoTP; FaBV; FaPON; OHFP; WBLP

The Tide Rises, the Tide Falls

46 The tide rises, the tide falls,
The twilight darkens, the curlew calls;
Along the sea-sands damp and brown
The traveler hastens toward the town,
And the tide rises, the tide falls. (l. 1–5)

47 The morning breaks; the steeds in their stalls
Stamp and neigh, as the hostler calls;
The day returns, but nevermore
Returns the traveler to the shore,
And the tide rises, the tide falls. (l. 11–15)

AA; AmPP; BLPL; ChTr; FaFP; MOS; NOBA; OxBA;
PoE; PoRA; TAP; WiR

The Village Blacksmith

48 Under a spreading chestnut-tree
The village smithy stands;
The smith, a mighty man is he,
With large and sinewy hands;
And the muscles of his brawny arms
Are strong as iron bands. (l. 1–6)

49 Toiling, — rejoicing, — sorrowing,
Onward through life he goes;
Each morning sees some task begin,
Each evening sees its close;
Something attempted, something done,
Has earned a night's repose. (l. 37–42)

50 Thanks, thanks to thee, my worthy friend,
For the lesson thou hast taught!
Thus at the flaming forge of life
Our fortunes must be wrought;
Thus on its sounding anvil shaped
Each burning deed and thought! (l. 43–48)

AA; AiP; AnAmPo; BLPL; FaBoBe; FaFP; FaPON;
FaPoR; OBAL; OBCA; PWR; WBLP

The Wreck of the Hesperus

51 It was the schooner Hesperus,
That sailed the wintry sea;
And the skipper had taken his little daughter,
To bear him company. (l. 1–4)

52 At daybreak, on the bleak sea-beach,
A fisherman stood aghast,
To see the form of a maiden fair,
Lashed close to a drifting mast. (l. 77–80)

53 Such as the wreck of the Hesperus,
In the midnight and the snow!
Christ save us all from a death like this,
On the reef of Norman's Woe! (l. 85–88)

AnAmPo; BeLS; BLPA; FaBoBe; FaFP; FPL; GN; MOS;
OBCA; OBNV; PAH; WBLP

AUDRE LORDE (b. 1934)

Coal

1 Some words live in my throat
breeding like adders. Others know sun
seeking like gypsies over my tongue
to explode through my lips (l. 16–19)

2 Some words
bedevil me. (l. 21–22)

3 I am Black because I come from the earth's inside
now take my word for jewel in the open light.
(l. 25–26)

BlSi; CNA; NoAM; NoP; PoBA

Hanging Fire

4 I am fourteen
and my skin has betrayed me
the boy I cannot live without
still sucks his thumb
in secret (l. 1–5)

5 I have nothing to wear tomorrow
will I live long enough
to grow up
and momma's in the bedroom
with the door closed. (l. 31–35)

ER; NIP; NoAM; NoP

RICHARD LOVELACE (1618–1658)

The Grasshopper

1 Poor verdant fool, and now green ice! thy joys,
Large and as lasting as thy perch of grass,
Bid us lay in 'gainst winter rain, and poise

Their floods with an o'erflowing glass. (l. 17–20)

CaPo; EBEV; FaBoPV; JCP; MeLP; MePo; NAEL-1;
NOBE; NoP; OAEL-1; OBEV; OBS; PPP; SeCePo;
SeCV-1

La Bella Bona Roba

2 Then Love, I beg, when next thou takest thy bow,
Thy angry shafts, and dost heart-chasing go,
Pass rascal deer, strike me the largest doe. (l. 13–15)

CaPo; EBEV; OAEL-1; PoEL-3; SeCP

Love Made in the First Age: To Chloris

3 Love, then unstinted, Love did sip,
And cherries plucked fresh from the lip;
On cheeks and roses free he fed;
Lasses like autumn plums did drop,
And lads indifferently did crop
A flower and a maidenhead. (l. 13–18)

CaPo; JCP; NAEL-1; OAEL-1; SeCP

The Scrutiny

4 Then, if when I have lov'd my round,
Thou prov'st the pleasant she,
With spoils of meaner beauties crown'd
I laden will return to thee,
Ev'n sated with variety. (l. 16–20)

BoLoP; CaPo; ELP; EnLoPo; GBL; MeLP; MePo; NoP;
OBS; SeCP; TrGrPo

To Althea, from Prison

5 Stone walls do not a prison make,
Nor iron bars a cage;
Minds innocent and quiet take
That for an hermitage;
If I have freedom in my love
And in my soul am free,
Angels alone, that soar above,
Enjoy such liberty. (l. 25–32)

AWP; BLPA; CaPo; FaBoBe; FPL; GBL; GTBS; GTBS-P;
HAP; HeIP; InPS; JCP; LiTB; MeLP; MePo; NAEL-1;
NOBE; NoP; OBEV; OBS; PoE; PoRA; SeCP; SeCV-1;
SoSe; TEP; TrGrPo

To Amarantha, That She Would Dishevel Her Hair

6 Here we'll strip and cool our fire
In cream below, in milk-baths higher;
And when all wells are drawn dry,
I'll drink a tear out of thine eye. (l. 21–24)

CaPo; HoPM; MePo; NIP; NoP; OBEV; PoE; SeCP;
SeCV-1; TrGrPo

To Lucasta, Going beyond the Seas

7 Though seas and land be 'twixt us both,
Our faith and troth,
Like separated souls,
All time and space controls:
Above the highest sphere we meet
Unseen, unknown, and greet as angels greet.
(l. 13–18)

CaPo; GTBS; GTBS-P; LiTB; MeLP; MOS; OBEV; OBS;
SeCP; SeCV-1

To Lucasta, Going to the Wars

8 Tell me not, sweet, I am unkind,
That from the nunnery
Of thy chaste breast and quiet mind
To war and arms I fly. (l. 1–4)

9 Yet this inconstancy is such
As you too shall adore;
I could not love thee, dear, so much,
Loved I not honor more. (l. 9–12)

AWP; CaPo; ELP; EnLoPo; FaBV; FaFP; FF; FPL; GBL;
GTBS; GTBS-P; HAP; HeIP; HoPM; InPK; InPS; JCP;
LiTB; MeLP; MePo; NAEL-1; NIP; NOBE; NoP;
OAEL-1; OBEV; OBS; OBWP; OxBSP; PoE; PoEL-3;
PoRA; SCV; SeCePo; SeCP; SeCV-1; TrGrPo; WeW

AMY LOWELL   (1874–1925)

Lilacs

1 Lilacs,
False blue,
White,
Purple,
Colour of lilac. (l. 1–5)

2 The dead fed you
Amid the slant stones of graveyards.
Pale ghosts who planted you
Came in the night-time
And let their thin hair blow through your clustered
stems. (l. 41–45)

3 Because it is my country
And I speak to it of itself
And sing of it with my own voice
Since certainly it is mine. (l. 106–109)

BLPL; MoAmPo; OxBA; PoRA

Patterns

4 I walk down the garden-paths,
And all the daffodils
Are blowing, and the bright blue squills. (l. 1–3)

5 In my stiff, brocaded gown.
With my powdered hair and jeweled fan,
I too am a rare
Pattern. (l. 5–8)

6 Not a softness anywhere about me,
Only whalebone and brocade. (l. 17–18)

7 And I weep;
For the lime-tree is in blossom
And one small flower has dropped upon my bosom.
(l. 25–27)

8 Underneath my stiffened gown
Is the softness of a woman bathing in a marble basin,
(l. 32–33)

9 I am very like to swoon
With the weight of this brocade,
For the sun sifts through the shade. (l. 56–58)

10 I shall go
Up and down
In my gown.
Gorgeously arrayed,
Boned and stayed. (l. 97–101)

11 For the man who should loose me is dead,
Fighting with the Duke in Flanders,
In a pattern called a war.
Christ! What are patterns for? (l. 104–107)

AWP; BoWoP; DL; FaFP; FPL; LiTA; MoAmPo; OnMSP;
OxBA; TrGrPo

JAMES RUSSELL LOWELL (1819–1891)

A Fable for Critics

1 "There is Hawthorne, with genius so shrinking and rare
That you hardly at first see the strength that is there;
A frame so robust, with a nature so sweet,
So earnest, so graceful, so lithe and so fleet,
Is worth a descent from Olympus to meet;

2 His strength is so tender, his wildness so meek,

3 When Nature was shaping him, clay was not granted
For making so full-sized a man as she wanted,
So, to fill out her model, a little she spared
From some finer-grained stuff for a woman prepared,
And she could not have hit a more excellent plan
For making him fully and perfectly man.

AmPP; NOBA; OxBA; TAP

4 "There is Lowell, who's striving Parnassus to climb
With a whole bale of isms tied together with rhyme,
He might get on alone, spite of brambles and boulders,

But he can't with that bundle he has on his shoulders,
The top of the hill he will ne'er come nigh reaching
Till he learns the distinction 'twixt singing and
preaching;

AA; AmPP; NOBA; OxBA; TAP

5 "There comes Poe, with his raven, like Barnaby Rudge,
Three fifths of him genius and two fifths sheer fudge,
Who talks like a book of iambs and pentameters,
In a way to make people of common sense damn
metres,
Who has written some things quite the best of their
kind,
But the heart somehow seems all squeezed out by the
mind,

6 You may say that he's smooth and all that till you're
hoarse,
But remember that elegance also is force;
After polishing granite as much as you will,
The heart keeps its tough old persistency still;

7 Had Theocritus written in English, not Greek,
I believe that his exquisite sense would scarce change a
line
In that rare, tender, virgin-like pastoral Evangeline.
That 's not ancient nor modern, its place is apart
Where time has no sway, in the realm of pure Art,
'T is a shrine of retreat from Earth's hubbub and strife
As quiet and chaste as the author's own life.

AmPP; NOBA; OxBA; TAP

8 "There comes Emerson first, whose rich words, every
one,
Are like gold nails in temples to hang trophies on,
Whose prose is grand verse, while his verse, the Lord
knows,
Is some of it pr — No, 't is not even prose;
I'm speaking of metres;

9 He seems, to my thinking (although I'm afraid
The comparison must, long ere this, have been made),
A Plotinus-Montaigne, where the Egyptian's gold mist
And the Gascon's shrewd wit cheek-by-jowl coexist;
All admire, and yet scarcely six converts he's got
To I don't (nor they either) exactly know what;
For though he builds glorious temples, 't is odd
He leaves never a doorway to get in a god.

10 In whose mind all creation is duly respected
As parts of himself — just a little projected;

AmPP; NAAL-1; NOBA; OxBA; TAP

The First Snowfall

11 The snow had begun in the gloaming,
And busily all the night
Had been heaping field and highway
With a silence deep and white. (l. 1–4)

12 I thought of a mound in sweet Auburn
Where a little headstone stood;
How the flakes were folding it gently,
As did robins the babes in the wood.

Up spoke our own little Mabel,
Saying, "Father, who makes it snow?"
And I told of the good All-father
Who cares for us here below. (l. 17–24)

13 Then, with eyes that saw not, I kissed her;
And she, kissing back, could not know
That my kiss was given to her sister,
Folded close under deepening snow. (l. 37–40)

AnAmPo; BLPA; BLPL; FaBoBe; FaPON; TAP; WBLP

Ode Recited at the Harvard Commemoration

14 'Be proud! for she is saved, and all have helped to save
    her!
She that lifts up the manhood of the poor,
She of the open soul and open door,
With room about her hearth for all mankind!
The fire is dreadful in her eyes no more;
From her bold front the helm she doth unbind,
Sends all her handmaid armies back to spin,
And bids her navies, that so lately hurled
Their crashing battle, hold their thunders in,
Swimming like birds of calm along the unharmful
    shore.
No challenge sends she to the elder world,
That looked askance and hated; a light scorn
Plays o'er her mouth, as round her mighty knees
She calls her children back, and waits the morn
Of nobler day, enthroned between her subject seas.'

AA; NOBA; OBWP; PAH

To the Dandelion

15 Dear common flower, that grow'st beside the way,
Fringing the dusty road with harmless gold,
First pledge of blithesome May,
Which children pluck, and, full of pride, uphold,
Hight-hearted buccaneers, o'erjoyed that they
An Eldorado in the grass have found,
Which not the rich earth's ample round
May match in wealth — thou art more dear to me
Than all the prouder summer-blooms may be. (l. 1–9)

16 How like a prodigal doth nature seem,
When thou, for all thy gold, so common art!
Thou teachest me to deem
More sacredly of every human heart,
Since each reflects in joy its scanty gleam
Of Heaven, and could some wondrous secret show,
Did we but pay the love we owe,
And with a child's undoubting wisdom look
On all these living pages of God's book. (l. 73–81)

AnAmPo; FaPON; GN; NAAL-1

The Vision of Sir Launfal

17 And what is so rare as a day in June?
Then, if ever, come perfect days;
Then Heaven tries earth if it be in tune,
And over it softly her warm ear lays:
Whether we look, or whether we listen,
We hear life murmur, or see it glisten;

18 Joy comes, grief goes, we know not how;
Everything is happy now,
Everything is upward striving;

19 Who knows whither the clouds have fled?
In the unscarred heaven they leave no wake,
And the eyes forget the tears they have shed,
The heart forgets its sorrow and ache;
The soul partakes the season's youth,
And the sulphurous rifts of passion and woe
Lie deep 'neath a silence pure and smooth,
Like burnt-out craters healed with snow.

BLPL; FaBoBe; FaBV; FaFP; FaPON; OnMSP

Yussouf

20 A stranger came one night to Yussouf's tent,
Saying, "Behold one outcast and in dread,
Against whose life the bow of power is bent,
Who flies, and hath not where to lay his head;
I come to thee for shelter and for food,
To Yussouf, called through all our tribes 'The Good.'"

"This tent is mine," said Yussouf, "but no more
Than it is God's; come in, and be at peace; (l. 1–8)

21 As one lamp lights another, nor grows less,
So nobleness enkindleth nobleness. (l. 17–18)

22 First-born, for whom by day and night I yearn,
Balanced and just are all of God's decrees;
Thou art avenged, my first-born, sleep in peace!"
                                    (l. 28–30)

BeLS; BLPA; BLPL; BoTP; FaBoBe

ROBERT LOWELL (1917–1977)

After the Surprising Conversions

1 At it in its familiar twang: "My friend,
Cut your own throat. Cut your own throat. Now! Now!"
September twenty-second, Sir, the bough
Cracks with the unpicked apples, and at dawn
The small-mouth bass breaks water, gorged with
    spawn. (l. 42–46)

AmPP; HAP; NAAL-2; NePoEA; NoAM; NoP; PPP

As a Plane Tree by the Water

2 this planned
Babel of Boston where our money talks (l. 2–3)

3 And all the streets
To our Atlantic wall are singing: "Sing,
Sing for the resurrection of the King,"
Flies, flies are on the plane tree, on the streets.
(l. 27–30)

CMoP; CoAP; LiTM; MoAB; MoAmPo; NePoEA; NOBA;
OxBA; TrGrPo

Children of Light

4 Our fathers wrung their bread from stocks and stones
And fenced their gardens with the Redman's bones;
(l. 1–2)

5 the pivoting searchlights probe to shock
The riotous glass houses built on rock,
And candles gutter by an empty altar,
And light is where the landless blood of Cain
Is burning, burning the unburied grain. (l. 6–10)

CMoP; MoAB; NAAL-2; OxBA

Colloquy in Black Rock

6 O mud
For watermelons gutted to the crust,
Mud for the mole-tide harbor, mud for mouse,
Mud for the armored Diesel fishing tubs that thud
A year and a day to wind and tide; the dust
Is on this skipping heart that shakes my house,
(l. 11–16)

7 the mud
Flies from his hunching wings and beak — my heart,
The blue kingfisher dives on you in fire. (l. 24–26)

CAPP; MoAB; MoAmPo; NAAL-2

The Dead in Europe

8 After the planes unloaded, we fell down
Buried together, unmarried men and women; (l. 1–2)

9 Our Mother, shall we rise on Mary's day
In Maryland, wherever corpses married
Under the rubble, bundled together? (l. 8–10)

10 Mary, hear,
O Mary, marry earth, sea, air and fire;
Our sacred earth in our day is our curse. (l. 19–21)

LiTM; NePoEA; OxBA; OxBC

The Drunken Fisherman

11 Wallowing in this bloody sty,
I cast for fish that pleased my eye (l. 1–2)

12 Once fishing was a rabbit's foot —
O wind blow cold, O wind blow hot, (l. 17–18)

13 Here tantrums thrash to a whale's rage.
This is the pot-hole of old age. (l. 31–32)

14 I will catch Christ with a greased worm,
And when the Prince of Darkness stalks
My bloodstream to its Stygian term ...
On water the Man-Fisher walks. (l. 37–40)

AmPP; CMoP; LiTA; LiTM; NOBA; OxBA; VGW

Ezra Pound

15 Eliot dead, you saying,
"And who is left to understand my jokes?
My old Brother in the arts ... and besides, he was a
smash of poet." (l. 7–9)

16 And I, "Who else has been in Purgatory?"
And he, "To begin with a swelled head and end with
swelled feet." (l. 13–14)

MoP; NAAL-2 NoAM; NOBA

For the Union Dead

17 Colonel Shaw
and his bell-cheeked Negro infantry
on St. Gaudens shaking Civil War relief,
propped by a plank splint against the garage's
earthquake. (l. 21–24)

18 Their monument sticks like a fishbone
in the city's throat.
Its Colonel is as lean
as a compass-needle. (l. 29–32)

19 wasp-waisted, they doze over muskets
and muse through their sideburns ...

Shaw's father wanted no monument
except the ditch,
where his son's body was thrown
and lost with his "niggers." (l. 47–52)

20 Space is nearer.
When I crouch to my television set,
the drained faces of Negro school-children rise like
balloons. (l. 56–58)

21 The Aquarium is gone. Everywhere,
giant finned cars nose forward like fish;
a savage servility
slides by on grease. (l. 63–66)

AmPP; CoAP; FaBoPV; FYAP; HAP; HCAP; HeIP; InPS;
LCAP; LiTM; MoP; NAAL-2; NaP; NoAM; NOBA; NoP;
OBWP; PoE; SCV; TwCP; UnPo; WeW

The Holy Innocents

22 King Herod shrieking vengeance at the curled
   Up knees of Jesus choking in the air,

   A king of speechless clods and infants. Still
   The world out-Herods Herod; (l. 9–12)

23 and the oxen near
   The worn foundations of their resting-place,
   The holy manger where their bed is corn
   And holly torn for Christmas. If they die,
   As Jesus, in the harness, who will mourn?
   Lamb of the shepherds, Child, how still you lie.
                                    (l. 15–20)

   InvP; MoAB; MoAmPo; NePoEA; OBCP; OxBC

In the Cage

24 It is night,
   And it is vanity, and age
   Blackens the heart of Adam. Fear,
   The yellow chirper, beaks its cage. (l. 11–14)

   FF; NOBA; SM; Son

July in Washington

25 The elect, the elected . . . they come here bright as
      dimes,
   and die dishevelled and soft. (l. 11–12)

26 but we wish the river had another shore,
   some further range of delectable mountains, (l. 15–16)

   LCAP; NAAL-2; NaP; Prf

Man and Wife

27 Tamed by Miltown, we lie on Mother's bed; (l. 1)

28 All night I've held your hand,
   as if you had
   a fourth time faced the kingdom of the mad —
   its hackneyed speech, its homicidal eye —
   and dragged me home alive. . . . (l. 8–12)

29 your old fashioned tirade —
   loving, rapid, merciless —
   breaks like the Atlantic Ocean on my head. (l. 26–28)

   AmPP; BoLoP; CAPP; NAAL-2

Memories of West Street and Lepke

30 I have a nine months' daughter,
   young enough to be my granddaughter.

Like the sun she rises in her flame-flamingo infants'
   wear. (l. 9–11)

31 so vegetarian,
   he wore rope shoes and preferred fallen fruit.
                                    (l. 29–30)

32 Flabby, bald, lobotomized,
   he drifted in a sheepish calm,
   where no agonizing reappraisal
   jarred his concentration of the electric chair —
   hanging like an oasis in his air
   of lost connections. . . . (l. 48–53)

   AmPP; CAPP; CMoP; InPS; NAAL-2; NaP; NoAM;
   NOBA; PoE

Mr. Edwards and the Spider

33 I saw the spiders marching through the air, (l. 1)

34 A very little thing, a little worm,
   Or hourglass-blazoned spider, it is said,
   Can kill a tiger. (l. 19–21)

35 It's well
   If God who holds you to the pit of hell,
   Much as one holds a spider, will destroy,

   Baffle and dissipate your soul. (l. 24–27)

36 the blaze
   Is infinite, eternal: this is death,
   To die and know it. This is the Black Widow, death.
                                    (l. 43–45)

   CAPP; CMoP; CoAP; FaBoMo; HeIP; InPS; LiTM; MoAB;
   NAAL-2; NePoEA; NOBA; NoP; SM; SoSe; TwCP

The Quaker Graveyard in Nantucket

37 Light
   Flashed from his matted head and marble feet,
   He grappled at the net
   With the coiled, hurdling muscles of his thighs:
   The corpse was bloodless, a botch of reds and whites,
                                    (l. 4–8)

38 this old Quaker graveyard where the bones
   Cry out in the long night for the hurt beast
   Bobbing by Ahab's whaleboats in the East. (l. 42–44)

   CMoP; HAP; LiTM; MoAB; MoP; MOS; NAAL-2; NoAM;
   NOBA; NoP; OxBA; TAP; UnPo

Skunk Hour

39 I watched for love-cars. Lights turned down,
   they lay together, hull to hull,
   where the graveyard shelves on the town. . . .
   My mind's not right. (l. 27–30)

40 I myself am hell;
    nobody's here — (l. 35–36)

41 I stand on top
    of our back steps and breathe the rich air —
    a mother skunk with her column of kittens swills the
        garbage pail.
    She jabs her wedge-head in a cup
    of sour cream, drops her ostrich tail,
    and will not scare. (l. 43–48)

    AmPP; CAPP; CMoP; CoAP; FaBoMo; HAP; HCAP; HeIP;
    InPK; InPS; LCAP; MoAmPo; MoP; NAAL-2; NIP;
    NoAM; NOBA; NoP; OPOP; OxBC; PoE; PPP; PrIm;
    SCV; TAP; WeW

Those blessed structures, plot and rhyme

42 Those blessed structures, plot and rhyme —
    why are they no help to me now
    I want to make
    something imagined, not recalled? (l. 1–4)

43 But sometimes everything I write
    with the threadbare art of my eye
    seems a snapshot, (l. 8–10)

44 We are poor passing facts,
    warned by that to give
    each figure in the photograph
    his living name. (l. 20–23)

    CAPP; HCAP; NAAL-2; NoAM; NoP

"To Speak of Woe That Is in Marriage"

45 Life begins to happen.
    My hoppped up husband drops his home disputes,
    and hits the streets to cruise for prostitutes, (l. 2–4)

46 Gored by the climacteric of his want,
    he stalls above me like an elephant. (l. 13–14)

    CAPP; MoP; NAAL-2; NoAM

Waking Early Sunday Morning

47 O to break loose, like the chinook
    salmon jumping and falling back,
    nosing up to the impossible
    stone and bone-crushing waterfall — (l. 1–4)

48 Better dressed and stacking birch,
    or lost with the Faithful at Church —
    anywhere, but somewhere else! (l. 43–45)

49 O Bible chopped and crucified
    in hymns we hear but do not read, (l. 49–50)

50 Only man thinning out his kind
    sounds through the Sabbath noon, the blind
    swipe of the pruner and his knife
    busy about the tree of life . . . (l. 101–104)

51 Pity the planet, all joy gone
    from this sweet volcanic cone; (l. 105–106)

52 in small war on the heels of small
    war — until the end of time
    to police the earth, a ghost
    orbiting forever lost
    in our monotonous sublime. (l. 108–112)

    FaBoMo; HCAP; NOBA; OxBC

Waking in the Blue

53 Absence! My heart grows tense
    as though a harpoon were sparring for the kill.
                                        (l. 8–9)

54 In between the limits of day,
    hours and hours go by under the crew haircuts
    and slightly too little nonsensical bachelor twinkle
    of the Roman Catholic attendants. (l. 34–37)

55 see the shaky future grow familiar
    in the pinched, indigenous faces
    of these thoroughbred mental cases,
    twice my age and half my weight.
    We are all old-timers,
    each of us holds a locked razor. (l. 45–50)

    CoAP; HCAP; MoAmPo; UnPo

Water

56 It was a Maine lobster town —
    each morning boatloads of hands
    pushed off for granite
    quarries on the islands. (l. 1–4)

57 Remember? We sat on a slab of rock.
    From this distance in time,
    it seems the color
    of iris, rotting and turning purpler,

    but it was only
    the usual gray rock (l. 13–18)

58 We wished our two souls
    might return like gulls
    to the rock. In the end,
    the water was too cold for us. (l. 29–32)

    CMoP; HeIP; LCAP; NOBA; NoP; PoE; SM

Where the Rainbow Ends

59 the scythers, Time and Death,
Helmed locusts, move upon the tree of breath; (l. 8–9)

60 In Boston serpents whistle at the cold. (l. 21)

61 What can the dove of Jesus give
You now but wisdom, exile? Stand and live,
The dove has brought an olive branch to eat.
　　　　　　　　　　　　　　　　(l. 28–30)

HCAP; MoAB; MoAmPo; NePoEA; TrGrPo

LUCRETIUS (TITUS LUCRETIUS CARUS) (94–55 B.C.)

De Rerum Natura (On the Nature of Things)

1 What has this bugbear Death to frighten man,
If souls can die, as well as bodies can?

2 When heaven and earth were in confusion hurl'd
For the debated empire of the world,
Which awed with dreadful expectation lay,
Soon to be slaves, uncertain who should sway:

3 So, when our mortal frame shall be disjoin'd,
The lifeless lump uncoupled from the mind,
From sense of grief and pain we shall be free;
We shall not feel, because we shall not be.

AWP; DL; FaBoRV; OAEL-1; OBVE

4 Thy seas in delicate haze
Go off; those mooned sands forsake their place;
And where they are, shall other seas in turn
Mow with their scythes of whiteness other bays.

5 — Nature whose heedless might,
Casts, like some shipwrecked sailor, the poor babe,
Naked and bleating on the shores of light?

6 Oh Science, lift aloud thy voice that stills
The pulse of fear,

AWP; ImOP

MARTIN LUTHER (1483–1546)

Away in a Manger (attributed to Luther)

1 Away in a manger, no crib for a bed,
The little Lord Jesus laid down His sweet head.
The stars in the bright sky looked down where He lay —
The little Lord Jesus asleep in the hay. (l. 1–4)

AH; BoTP; FaPON; OHIP

A Mighty Fortress Is Our God

2 A mighty fortress is our God
A bulwark never failing;
Our helper he amid the flood
Of mortal ills prevailing. (l. 1–4)

3 Were not the right man on our side,
The man of God's own choosing.
Dost ask who that may be?
Christ Jesus, it is he,
Lord Sabaoth is his name,
From age to age the same,
And he must win the battle. (l. 12–18)

AA; AWP; CTC; EaLo; PWR; WGRP

JOHN LYLY (1553–1606)

Alexander and Campaspe

1 Cupid and my Campaspe played
At cards for kisses,

2 With these, the crystal of his brow,
And then the dimple of his chin:
All these did my Campaspe win
At last, he set her both his eyes;
She won, and Cupid blind did rise. (Fr. III,v)

ElL; GBL; GTBS; GTBS-P; HeIP; HoPM; NOBE; NoP;
OBEV; OBSC; PoRA; TrGrPo

3 What bird so sings, yet so does wail?
O, 'tis the ravished nightingale!
"Jug, jug, jug, jug, tereu," she cries,
And still her woes at midnight rise.
Brave prick-song! who is't now we hear?
None but the lark so shrill and clear;

4 Hark, hark, with what a pretty throat
Poor robin-redbreast tunes his note;
Hark, how the jolly cuckoos sing
Cuckoo — to welcome in the spring!
Cuckoo — to welcome in the spring!

CH; ElL; NOBE; OBEV; OBSC; PBBP; TrGrPo

Midas

5 Pan's Syrinx was a girl indeed,
Though now she's turned into a reed;
From that dear reed Pan's pipe does come,
A pipe that strikes Apollo dumb;
Nor flute, nor lute, nor gittern can
So chant it, as the pipe of Pan;

6 When Pan sounds up his minstrelsy;
His minstrelsy! O base! This quill,
Which at my mouth with wind I fill,
Puts me in mind, though her I miss,
That still my Syrinx' lips I kiss.

ElL; ELP; OBSC; SeCePo

HENRY FRANCIS LYTE (1793–1847)

Abide with Me

1 Abide with me: fast falls the eventide;
The darkness deepens; Lord with me abide: (l. 1–2)

2 I fear no foe with Thee at hand to bless;
Ills have no weights, and tears no bitterness;
(l. 25–26)

BLRP; EBVV; FaBoBe; FaFP; FaPoR; NOCV; PWR;
TIRV; WBLP; WGRP

THOMAS BABINGTON MACAULAY, 1ST BARON MACAULAY (1800–1859)

The Armada

1 Such night in England ne'er had been, nor e'er again
shall be. (l. 34)

BeLS; FaBoCh; FaPoR; GN; WBLP

Horatius at the Bridge (Lays of Ancient Rome)

2 "To every man upon this earth
Death cometh soon or late.
And how can man die better
Than facing fearful odds
For the ashes of his fathers
And the temples of his gods,

3 Was none who would be foremost
To lead such dire attack;
But those behind cried "Forward!"
And those before cried "Back!"

BeLS; FaBoCh; FaFP; FaPoR; OBNV; OBWP; OHFP;
PoLF

A Jacobite's Epitaph

4 Forget all feuds, and shed one English tear
O'er English dust. A broken heart lies here. (l. 17–18)

EBEV; FaPoR; NOBE; NOBVV; OBEV; OBNC

"HUGH MACDIARMID" (pseudonym of CHRISTOPHER MURRAY GRIEVE) (1892–1978)

Another Epitaph on an Army of Mercenaries

1 It is a God-damned lie to say that these
Saved, or knew, anything worth any man's pride.
(l. 1–2)

2 In spite of all their kind some elements of worth
With difficulty persist here and there on earth.
(l. 5–6)

InPK; MoP; NAEL-2; NIP; NoAM; OBWP; RB

Cattle Show

3 I shall go among red faces and virile voices,
See stylish sheep, with fine heads and well-wooled,
And great bulls mellow to the touch, (l. 1–3)

FaBoMo; GoTS; HAP; MoBrPo; OBMV; OxBTC

The Innumerable Christ

4 An' when the earth's as cauld's the mune
An' a' its folk are lang syne deid,
On coontless stars the Babe maun cry
An' the Crucified maun bleed. (l. 13–16)

EaLo; EBEV; NoP; OxBS

Parley of Beasts

5 Auld Noah was at hame wi' them a',
The lion and the lamb,
Pair by pair they entered the Ark
And he took them as they cam'. (l. 1–4)

MoBrPo; MoP; NoAM; NoP; OBMV

The Skeleton of the Future

6 The eternal lightning of Lenin's bones. (l. 4)

GoTS; MoBrPo; OBMV; OBTV

GEORGE MACDONALD (1824–1905)

At the Back of the North Wind

1 Where did you come from, Baby dear?
Out of the everywhere into the here.

Where did you get your eyes so blue?
Out of the sky as I came through. (l. 1–4)

BLPA; FaFP; FaPON; OxBChV

PATRICK MACDONOGH (1902–1961)

She Walked Unaware

1 O, she walked unaware of her own increasing beauty
That was holding men's thoughts from market or
plough, (l. 1–2)

2 God pity me now and all desolate sinners
Demented with beauty! (l. 21–22)

3 To-night she will spread her brown hair on his pillow,
But I shall be hearing the harsh cries of wild fowl.
(l. 25–26)

BoLoP; ErPo; FaBoTw; NeIP

ARCHIBALD MACLEISH (1892–1982)

Ars Poetica

1 A poem should be palpable and mute
As a globed fruit,
Dumb
As old medallions to the thumb, (l. 1–4)

2 A poem should be equal to:
Not true.

For all the history of grief
An empty doorway and a maple leaf. (l. 17–20)

3 A poem should not mean
But be. (l. 23–24)

AmPP; AWP; CMoP; FPL; HAP; HeIP; HoPM; InPK;
LiTA; LiTM; MoAB; MoAmPo; NAAL-2; NIP; NOBA;
NoP; OxBA; PoA; PoRA; SoSe; TAP; WeW

The End of the World

4 There with vast wings across the canceled skies,
There in the sudden blackness the black pall
Of nothing, nothing, nothing — nothing at all.
(l. 12–14)

BLPL; CMoP; HoPM; InPK; LiTM; MAT; MoAB;
MoAmPo; NoAM; NOBA; OBAL; OxBA; Son; TAP;
TrGrPo; VGW

Epistle to Be Left in the Earth

5 As for the nights I warn you the nights are dangerous
The wind changes at night and the dreams come

It is very cold
there are strange stars near Arcturus

Voices are crying an unknown name in the sky
(l. 28–31)

CMoP; ImOP; MoAB; MoAmPo; NOBA; TrGrPo

Immortal Autumn

6 It is the human season on this sterile air
Do words outcarry breath the sound goes on and on.
I hear a dead man's cry from autumn long since gone.

I cry to you beyond upon his bitter air. (l. 17–20)

CMoP; LiTA; MoAB; MoAmPo; NAAL-2; TrGrPo

L'An Trentiesme de Mon Eage

7 By words, by voices, a lost way —
And here above the chimney stack
The unknown constellations sway —
And by what way shall I go back? (l. 17–20)

LiTM; MoAmPo; MoP; NOBA

Memorial Rain

8 Ambassador Puser the ambassador
Reminds himself in French, felicitous tongue,
What these (young men no longer) lie here for
In rows that once, and somewhere else, were young . . .
(l. 1–4)

9 The roots of the grass strain,
Tighten, the earth is rigid, waits — he is waiting —

And suddenly, and all at once, the rain! (l. 37–39)

AmPP; CMoP; LiTA; MoAB; MoAmPo; OBWP

"Not Marble nor the Gilded Monuments"

10 (What is a dead girl but a shadowy ghost
Or a dead man's voice but a distant and vain
affirmation
Like dream words most) (l. 26–28)

11 I will not speak of the famous beauty of dead women:
I will say the shape of a leaf lay once on your hair.
Till the world ends and the eyes are out and the
mouths broken,
Look! It is there! (l. 34–38)

BoLoP; CMoP; HoPM; MoAB; PoRA; TwCP

The Too-late Born

12 And crossed the dark defile at last, and found
At Roncevaux upon the darkening plain
The dead against the dead and on the silent ground
The silent slain — (l. 9–12)

CMoP; GoJo; LiTM; MoAB; McAmPo; OxBA; WaP

You, Andrew Marvell

13 Nor now the long light on the sea —
And here face downward in the sun
To feel how swift how secretly
The shadow of the night comes on ... (l. 33–36)

AWP; CMoP; FaBV; FYAP; HAP; HeIP; HoPM; LiTA;
LiTM; MoAB; MoAmPo; MoP; NAAL-2; NoAM; NOBA;
NoP; OxBA; PoRA; PPP; PrIm; SoSe; TrGrPo; TwCP;
WeW

LOUIS MACNEICE (1907–1963)

Among These Turf-Stacks

1 a fortress against ideas and against the
Shuddering insidious shock of the theory-vendors
The little sardine men crammed in a monster toy
Who tilt their aggregate beast against our crumbling
Troy. (l. 9–12)

2 blind wantons like the gulls who scream
And rip the edge off any ideal or dream. (l. 17–18)

LiTB; LiTM; OBMV; SeCePo; WaP

Autumn Journal

3 And I envy the intransigence of my own
Countrymen who shoot to kill and never
See the victim's face become their own
Or find his motive sabotage their motives.

4 Up the Rebels,To Hell with the Pope,
And God Save — as you prefer — the King or Ireland.
The land of scholars and saints:
Scholars and saints my eye, the land of ambush,
Purblind manifestoes, never-ending complaints,

5 Why do we like being Irish? Partly because
It gives us a hold on the sentimental English
As members of a world that never was,
Baptized with fairy water;

6 A city built upon mud;
A culture built upon profit;
Free speech nipped in the bud,

The minority always guilty.
Why should I want to go back
To you, Ireland, my Ireland?

7 she gives her children neither sense nor money
Who slouch arouond the world with a gesture and a
brogue
And a faggot of useless memories.

AnIL; BIrV; CIP; FaBCIP

Bagpipe Music

8 It's no go the merry-go-round, it's no go the rickshaw
All we want is a limousine and a ticket for the
peepshow. (l. 1–2)

9 It's no go the picture palace, it's no go the stadium,
It's no go the country cot with a pot of pink geraniums.
It's no go the Government grants, it's no go the
elections,
Sit on your arse for fifty years and hang your hat on a
pension. (l. 39–43)

CMoP; GTBS-P; LiTB; LiTM; MoP; NAEL-2; NBLV;
NoAM; NOBE; NOBL; NoP; OAEL-2; OBSV; OxBTC;
RB; SeCePo

The British Museum Reading Room

10 Some on commission, some for the love of learning,
Some because they have nothing better to do
Or because they hope these walls of books will deaden
The drumming of the demon in their ears. (l. 4–7)

11 There seeps from heavily jowled or hawk-like foreign
faces
The guttural sorrow of the refugees. (l. 20–21)

LiTM; MoAB; MoBrPo; NOBE; SeCePo; WaP

Brother Fire

12 Thus were we weaned to knowledge of the Will
That wills the natural world but wills us dead.
(l. 11–12)

13 O delicate walker, babbler, dialectician Fire,
O enemy and image of ourselves, (l. 13–14)

MoAB; MoP; NoAM; NOBE; WaaP

Carrickfergus

14 I was the rector's son, born to the anglican order,
Banned for ever from the candles of the Irish poor;
The Chichesters knelt in marble at the end of a transept
With ruffs about their necks, their portion sure.
(l. 17–20)

AnIL; FaBCIP; FaBoPP; NAEL-2; NoAM; NOIV

Prayer before Birth

15 I am not yet born; O hear me.
   Let not the bloodsucking bat or the rat or the stoat or
       the
   club-footed ghoul come near me. (l. 1–3)

16 I am not yet born; O fill me
   With strength against those who would freeze my
   humanity, would dragoon me into a lethal automaton
   would make me a cog in a machine, a thing with
   one face, a thing, (l. 28–32)

17 Let them not make me a stone and let them not spill
       me.
   Otherwise kill me. (l. 38–39)

   FaBCIP; GTBS-P; LiTB; NAs; TIRV; TwCP

Snow

18 World is crazier and more of it than we think,
   Incorrigibly plural. (l. 5–6)

   CIP; CMoP; FaBCIP; FaBoMo; FPL; LiTM; MoP; NoAM;
   NOBE; OPOP; OxBSP; OxBTC

Soap Suds

19 This brand of soap has the same smell as once in the
       big
   House he visited when he was eight: (l. 1–2)

20 But the ball is lost and the mallet slipped long since
       from the hands
   Under the running tap that are not the hands of a
       child. (l. 15–16)

   FaBCIP; FaBoMo; NAEL-2; NOIV; NoP; SCV

Sunday Morning

21 Down the road someone is practicing scales,
   The notes like little fishes vanish with a wink of tails,
                                                    (l. 1–2)

22 But listen, up the road, something gulps, the church
       spire
   Opens its eight bells out, skulls' mouths which will not
       tire
   To tell how there is no music or movement which
       secures
   Escape from the weekday time. Which deadens and
       endures. (l. 11–15)

   FaBCIP; FaBoMo; HeIP; LiTB; MoAB; MoBrPo; NAEL-2;
   NIP; Son

The Sunlight on the Garden

23 The sunlight on the garden
   Hardens and grows cold,
   We cannot cage the minute
   Within its nets of gold, (l. 1–4)

24 The earth compels, (l. 17)

   CMoP; EBEV; GTBS-P; HAP; InPS; LiTB; NAEL-2;
   NOBE; NOIV; NoP; OxBTC; PrIm; TwCP

Thalassa

25 You know the worst: your wills are fickle,
   Your values blurred, your hearts impure
   And your past life a ruined church —
   But let your poison be your cure. (l. 9–12)

26 By a high star our course is set,
   Our end is Life. Put out to sea. (l. 17–18)

   BIrV; FaBoMo; FaBoRV; NOBE

OWEN ROE MACWARD   (d. 1849) *AND* HUGH O'DONNELL

Dark Rosaleen (*attributed to* MacWard *and to* O'Donnell)

1 All day long in unrest,
  To and fro do I move,
  The very soul within my breast
  Is wasted for you, love! (l. 25–28)

  ACP; AnIL; AWP; BIrV; CH; EnRP; NOIV; OBEV

DEREK MAHON   (b. 1941)

A Disused Shed in Co. Wexford

1 And in a disused shed in Co. Wexford,

  Deep in the grounds of a burnt-out hotel,
  Among the bathtubs and the washbasins
  A thousand mushrooms crowd to a keyhole. (l. 10–13)

2 They have been waiting for us in a foetor
  Of vegetable sweat since civil war days,
  Since the gravel-crunching, interminable departure
  Of the expropriated mycologist. (l. 21–24)

3 Grown beyond nature now, soft food for worms,
  They lift frail heads in gravity and good faith.
                                                    (l. 49–50)

  AnAn; CIP; FaBCIP; FaBoPV; NOIV; OxBC

The Snow Party

4 Snow is falling on Nagoya
And farther south
On the tiles of Kyoto. (l. 10–12 oto, Japan)

5 Elsewhere they are burning
Witches and heretics
In the boiling squares, (l. 16–18)

CIP; FaBCIP; FaBoPV; OxBC

FRANCIS SYLVESTER MAHONY ("FATHER PROUT") (1805–1866)

The Bells of Shandon

1 With deep affection and recollection
I often think of the Shandon bells, (l. 1–2)

2 On this I ponder where'er I wander,
And thus grow fonder, sweet Cork, of thee;
With thy bells of Shandon, (l. 5–7)

ACP; CH; ChTr; OBEV

JAMES CLARENCE MANGAN (1803–1849)

Gone in the Wind

1 Solomon! where is thy throne? It is gone in the wind.
Babylon! where is thy might? It is gone in the wind.
Happy in death are they only whose hearts have
consigned
All Earth's affections and longings and cares to the
wind. (l. 25–28)

ACP; SeCePo; TIRV

The Nameless One

2 Roll forth, my song, like the rushing river,
That sweeps along to the mighty sea; (l. 1–2)

3 He, too, had tears for all souls in trouble,
Here and in hell. (l. 55–56)

ACP; BIrV; EnRP; NOIV; OBEV

JOHN STREETER MANIFOLD (b. 1915)

Fife Tune

1 She ran down the stair
A twelve-year-old darling
And laughing and calling
She tossed her bright hair; (l. 9–12)

CBAP; FaFP; GoJo; InPS; LiTB; LiTM; Mes; NBLV;
WaaP; WaP

The Sirens

2 Odysseus saw the sirens; they were charming,
Blonde, with snub breasts and little neat posteriors,
(l. 9–10)

LiTB; LiTM; MoBrPo; Son; WaP

EDWIN MARKHAM (1852–1940)

A Creed

1 There is a destiny that makes us brothers;
None goes his way alone:
All that we send into the lives of others
Comes back into our own. (l. 1–4)

BLPA; BLPL; FaBoBe; FaFP

Lincoln, the Man of the People

2 Sprung from the West,
He drank the valorous youth of a new world.
The strength of virgin forests braced his mind,
The hush of spacious prairies stilled his soul.
His words were oaks in acorns; and his thoughts
Were roots that firmly gript the granite truth.
(l. 30–35)

3 The grip that swung the ax in Illinois
Was on the pen that set a people free. (l. 44–45)

4 he went down
As when a lordly cedar, green with boughs,
Goes down with a great shout upon the hills,
And leaves a lonesome place against the sky.
(l. 53–56)

GN; MoAmPo; OHFP; OHIP; PAH; TrGrPo

The Man with the Hoe

5 Bowed by the weight of centuries he leans
Upon his hoe and gazes on the ground,
The emptiness of ages in his face,
And on his back the burden of the world. (l. 1–4)

6 Who loosened and let down this brutal jaw? (l. 8)

7 Slave of the wheel of labor, what to him
Are Plato and the swing of Pleiades? (l. 23–24)

8 How will it be with kingdoms and with kings —
With those who shaped him to the thing he is —
When this dumb Terror shall rise to judge the world,
After the silence of the centuries? (l. 46–49)

AA; AnAmPo; BLPA; BLPL; EaLo; FaFP; LiTA;
MoAmPo; OHFP; PrIm; SaC; TrGrPo; WBLP; WGRP

CHRISTOPHER MARLOWE (1564–1593)

Doctor Faustus

1 Ah, Faustus,
Now hast thou but one bare hour to live,
And then thou must be damned perpetually!
Stand still, you ever-moving spheres of heaven,
That time may cease and midnight never come!
Fair Nature's eye, rise, rise again and make
Perpetual day; or let this hour be but
A year, a month, a week, a natural day,
That Faustus may repent and save his soul! (V, ii)

2 See, see where Christ's blood streams in the firmament!
One drop would save my soul — half a drop! ah, my
  Christ! —
Ah, rend not my heart for naming of my Christ! —
Yet will I call on him! — O, spare me, Lucifer! —
Where is it now? 'T is gone; and see where God
Stretcheth out his arm, and bends his ireful brows! —
Mountains and hills, come, come and fall on me,
And hide me from the heavy wrath of God!

ChTr; HeIP; NAEL-1; OAEL-1; PoEL-2; TrGrPo

3 Was this the face that launched a thousand ships,
And burnt the topless towers of Ilium?
Sweet Helen, make me immortal with a kiss. —
Her lips suck forth my soul; see where it flies! —
Come, Helen, come, give me my soul again.
Here will I dwell, for heaven be in these lips,
And all is dross that is not Helena. (V, i)

BLPL; EBEV; FaBV; FaFP; FF; GBL; HeIP; LiTB;
NAEL-1; NIP; OAEL-1; TrGrPo

Hero and Leander

4 On Hellespont guiltie of True-loves blood,
In view and opposit two citties stood,
Seaborders, disjoin'd by Neptunes might:
The one Abydos, the other Sestos hight.

5 At Sestos, Hero dwelt; Hero the faire,
Whom young Apollo, courted for her haire,
And offred as a dower his burning throne,
Where she should sit for men to gaze upon.

6 Amorous Leander, beautifull and yoong,
(Whose tragedie divine Musæus soong)
Dwelt at Abidus,

7 The men of wealthie Sestos, everie yeare,
(For his sake whom their goddesse held so deare,
Rose-cheekt Adonis) kept a solemne feast,
Thither resorted many a wandring guest,
To meet their loves;

8 It lies not in our power to love, or hate,
For will in us is over-rul'd by fate.

9 And one especiallie doe we affect,
Of two gold Ingots like in each respect,
The reason no man knowes, let it suffise,
What we behold is censur'd by our eies.
Where both deliberat, the love is slight,
Who ever lov'd, that lov'd not at first sight?

10 One is no number, mayds are nothing then,
Without the sweet societie of men.
Wilt thou live single still? one shalt thou bee,
Though never-singling Hymen couple thee.

11 This idoll which you terme Virginitie,
Is neither essence subject to the eie,
No, nor to any one exterior sence,
Nor hath it any place of residence,
Nor is't of earth or mold celestiall,
Or capable of any forme at all.

12 All women are ambitious naturallie,

13 He askt, she gave, and nothing was denied,
Both to each other quickly were affied.
Looke how their hands, so were their hearts united,
And what he did, she willingly requited.
(Sweet are the kisses, the imbracements sweet,
When like desires and affections meet),

14 Like to the tree of Tantalus she fled,
And seeming lavish, sav'de her maydenhead.
Ne're king more sought to keepe his diademe;
Than Hero this inestimable gemme.

15 Jewels being lost are found againe, this never,
T'is lost but once, and once lost, lost for ever.

16 O none but gods have power their love to hide,
Affection by the count'nance is descride.
The light of hidden fire it selfe discovers,
And love that is conceal'd, betraies poore lovers.

17 Love is not ful of pittie (as men say)
But deaffe and cruell, where he meanes to pray.

AAS; NoP; OAEL-1; OBSC; PoE; PoEL-2; SeCePo; TEP

The Passionate Shepherd to His Love

18 Come live with me and be my Love,
And we will all the pleasures prove
That hills and valleys, dales and fields,
Or woods or steepy mountain yields.

And we will sit upon the rocks,
And see the shepherds feed their flocks
By shallow rivers, to whose falls
Melodious birds sing madrigals. (l. 1–8)

19 And I will make thee beds of roses (l. 9)

20 if these pleasures may thee move,
Come live with me and be my Love. (l. 19–20)

21 The shepherd swains shall dance and sing
For thy delight each May morning:
If these delights thy mind may move,
Then live with me and be my Love. (l. 21–24)

AAS; AWP; BoLoP; CTC; ElL; ELP; FaBoBe; FaFP; FF;
FPL; GN; GTBS; GTBS-P; HAP; HeIP; HoPM; InPK;
InPS; LiTB; NAEL-1; NBLV; NIP; NOBE; NoP; OAEL-1;
OBEV; OBSC; PoE; PoLF; PoRA; PPP; RB; SCV;
SeCePo; SiPS; TrGrPo; TTTS; WeW

MARTIAL (MARCUS VALERIUS MARTIALIS) (c. 40–c. 104)

The Happy Life

1 Martial, the things for to attain
The happy life be these, I find:
The riches left, not got with pain;
The fruitful ground, the quiet mind;
The equal friend; no grudge nor strife;
No charge of rule nor governance; (l. 1–6)

2 The night discharged of all care
Where wine may bear no sovereignty;
The chaste wife wise, without debate;
Such sleeps as may beguile the night;
Contented with thine own estate;
Neither wish death, nor fear his might. (l. 10–16)

ElL; FaBoEE; NAEL-1; NOBE; NoP; OBEV; OBSC;
OBVE; SiPS; TrGrPo

SARAH CATHERINE MARTIN (1768–1826)

Old Mother Hubbard

1 Old Mother Hubbard
Went to the cupboard
To get her poor dog a bone:

But when she got there
The cupboard was bare,
And so the poor dog had none. (l. 1–6)

FaBoBe; OnMSP; OxBChV; OxNR

ANDREW MARVELL (1621–1678)

Bermudas

1 He hangs in shades the orange bright,
Like golden lamps in a green night,
And does in the pomegranates close
Jewels more rich than Ormus shows;
He makes the figs our mouths to meet,
And throws the melons at our feet;
But apples plants of such a price
No tree could ever bear them twice. (l. 17–24)

2 Oh! let our voice His praise exalt,
Till it arrive at Heaven's vault,
Which, thence (perhaps) rebounding, may
Echo beyond the Mexique bay." (l. 33–36)

AWP; CH; ChTr; FaBoCh; GN; GTBS; GTBS-P; JCP;
MePo; MOS; NAEL-1; NOBE; NOCV; NoP; OBEV; OBS;
OBTV; PAH; PoE; RB; SeCP; SeCV-1

The Character of Holland

3 'Tis probable Religion after this
Came next in order; which they could not miss.
How could the Dutch but be converted, when
The Apostles were so many fishermen?
Besides the waters of themselves did rise,
And, as their land, so them did re-baptize. (l. 55–60)

ChTr; NOBL; OBSV

The Coronet

4 Alas I find the Serpent old
That, twining in his speckled breast,
About the flow'rs disguis'd does fold,
With wreaths of Fame and Interest. (l. 13–16)

5 Or shatter too with him my curious frame:
And let these wither, so that he may die,
Though set with Skill and chosen out with Care.
That they, while Thou on both their Spoils dost tread,
May crown thy Feet, that could not crown thy Head.
(l. 22–26)

MeLP; MePo; NAEL-1; NOCV; NoP; OBS; PoE; SeCV-1;
TOF

The Definition of Love

6 It was begotten by despair
Upon impossibility. (l. 3–4)

7 Therefore the love which us doth bind,
But fate so enviously debars,
Is the conjunction of the mind,
And opposition of the stars. (l. 29–32)

BLPL; BoLoP; EBEV; GBL; HoPM; InPS; JCP; LiTB;
MeLP; MePo; NAEL-1; NOBE; NoP; OAEL-1; OBEV;
OBS; PoEL-2; SeCePo; SeCP; SeCV-1; TEP; TrGrPo;
UnPo

A Dialogue between the Resolved Soul and Created Pleasure

8 And shew that Nature wants an Art
To conquer one resolved Heart. (l. 9–10)

9 Welcome the Creations Guest,
Lord of Earth, and Heavens Heir.
Lay aside that Warlike Crest,
And of Nature's banquet share:
Where the Souls of fruits and flow'rs
Stand prepar'd to heighten yours. (l. 11–16)

10 Had I but any time to lose,
On this I would it all dispose.
Cease Tempter. None can chain a mind
Whom this sweet Chordage cannot bind.

MeLP; MePo; OAEL-1; OBS; SeCP; SeCV-1

A Dialogue between the Soul and Body

11 O who shall from this dungeon raise
A soul enslaved so many ways?
With bolts of bones, that fettered stands
In feet; and manacled in hands:
Here blinded with an eye; and there
Deaf with the drumming of an ear;
A soul hung up, as 'twere, in chains
Of nerves, and arteries, and veins; (l. 1–8)

12 But physic yet could never reach
The maladies thou me dost teach:
Whom first the cramp of hope does tear;
And then the palsy shakes of fear;
The pestilence of love does heat;
Or hatred's hidden ulcer eat;
Joy's cheerful madness does perplex,
Or sorrow's other madness vex;
Which knowledge forces me to know,
And memory will not forgo.
What but a soul could have the wit
To build me up for sin so fit?

So architects do square and hew
Green trees that in the forest grew. (l. 31–44)

HAP; InPS; JCP; MeLP; MePo; NAEL-1; NoP; OAEL-1;
OBS; PoEL-2; PPP; SeCP; SeCV-1; TEP; WeW

The Fair Singer

13 To make a final conquest of all me,
Love did compose so sweet an enemy,
In whom both beauties to my death agree,
Joining themselves in fatal harmony;
That while she with her eyes my heart does bind,
She with her voice might captivate my mind. (l. 1–6)

EnLoPo; MeLP; MePo; NOBE; NoP; PoEL-2

The Gallery

14 Here thou art painted in the dress
Of an inhuman murderess;
Examining upon our hearts
Thy fertile shop of cruel arts:
Engines more keen than ever yet
Adorned tyrant's cabinet,
Of which the most tormenting are
Black eyes, red lips, and curled hair. (l. 9–16)

15 Like an enchantress here thou show'st,
Vexing thy restless lover's ghost;
And, by a light obscure, dost rave
Over his entrails, in the cave;
Divining thence, with horrid care,
How long thou shalt continue fair;
And (when informed) them throw'st away,
To be the greedy vulture's prey. (l. 25–32)

MeLP; NoP; OBS; PoE

The Garden

16 Society is all but rude,
To this delicious solitude.

No white nor red was ever seen
So amorous as this lovely green.
Fond lovers, cruel as their flame,
Cut in these trees their mistress' name:
Little, alas, they know or heed
How far these beauties hers exceed!
Fair trees, wheresoe'er your barks I wound,
No name shall but your own be found. (l. 15–23)

17 What wondrous life in this I lead!
Ripe apples drop about my head;
The luscious clusters of the vine
Upon my mouth do crush their wine;
The nectarine and curious peach
Into my hands themselves do reach;

Stumbling on melons, as I pass,
Ensnared with flowers, I fall on grass. (l. 33–40)

18 Meanwhile the mind from pleasure less
Withdraws into its happiness;
The mind, that ocean where each kind
Does straight its own resemblance find;
Yet it creates, transcending these,
Far other worlds and other seas,
Annihilating all that's made
To a green thought in a green shade, (l. 41–48)

19 Here at the fountain's sliding foot,
Or at some fruit-tree's mossy root,
Casting the body's vest aside,
My soul into the boughs does glide:
There, like a bird, it sits and sings,
Then whets and combs its silver wings,
And, till prepared for longer flights,
Waves in its plumes the various light. (l. 49–56)

AWP; BLPL; GTBS; GTBS-P; HAP; InPS; InvP; JCP;
LiTB; MeLP; MePo; NAEL-1; NIP; NOBE; NoP; OAEL-
1; OBEV; OBS; PoE; PoEL-2; PoLF; PoRA; PPP; QFR;
SeCePo; SeCP; SeCV-1; TEP; TOF; TrGrPo

An Horatian Ode upon Cromwell's Return from Ireland

20 The forward Youth that would appear
Must now forsake his Muses dear,
Nor in the Shadows sing
His Numbers languishing. (l. 1–4)

21 Though Justice against Fate complain,
And plead the antient Rights in vain:
But those do hold or break
As Men are strong or weak. (l. 37–40)

22 Henothing common did, or mean,
Upon the memorable Scene:
But with his keener Eye
The Axes edge did try: (l. 57–60)

23 March indefatigably on,
And for the last effect
Still keep thy Sword erect:
Besides the force it has to fright
The Spirits of the shady Night;
The same Arts that did gain
A Pow'r must it maintain. (l. 115–122)

EBEV; GTBS; GTBS-P; HAP; InPS; JCP; MePo; NOBE;
NoP; OAEL-1; OBEV; OBS; OBWP; PoEL-2; SeCP;
SeCV-1

The Mower against Gardens

24 Luxurious Man, to bring his Vice in use,
Did after him the World seduce:
And from the fields the Flow'rs and Plants allure,
(l. 1–3)

25 And yet these Rarities might be allow'd,
To Man, that sov'raign thing and proud;
Had he not dealt between the Bark and Tree,
Forbidden mixtures there to see.
No Plant now knew the Stock from which it came;
He grafts upon the Wild the Tame: (l. 19–24)

EBEV; FaBoPV; LiTB; NAEL-1; NoP; OAEL-1; PoE;
PoEL-2; PoE; PPP; SeCV-1

The Mower to the Glow-Worms

26 Your courteous lights in vain you waste,
Since Juliana here is come,
For she my mind hath so displaced
That I shall never find my home. (l. 13–16)

AWP; ELP; EnLoPo; InvP; MePo; NAEL-1; NOBE; NoP;
OAEL-1; OBS; OxBoLi; PoEL-2; PPP; SeCP; TrGrPo

The Mower's Song

27 My mind was once the true survey
Of all these meadows fresh and gay,
And in the greenness of the grass
Did see its hopes as in a glass;
When Juliana came, and she,
What I do to the grass, does to my thoughts and me.
(l. 1–6)

NAEL-1; PoEL-2; PPP; SeCP; SeCV-1

The Nymph Complaining for the Death of Her Fawn

28 With sweetest milk, and sugar, first
I it as mine own fingers nurst.
And as it grew, so every day
It wax'd more white and sweet than they.
It had so sweet a Breath! (l. 55–59)

29 But all its chief delight was still
On Roses thus its self to fill:
And its pure virgin Limbs to fold
In whitest sheets of Lillies cold.
Had it liv'd long it would have been
Lillies without, Roses within. (l. 87–92)

30 For I so truly thee bemoane,
That I shall weep though I be Stone:
Until my Tears, still drooping, wear
My breast, themselves engraving there.
There at me feet shalt thou be laid,
Of purest Alabaster made:
For I would have thine Image be
White as I can, though not as Thee. (l. 115–122)

CH; FM; HeIP; MePo; NAEL-1; OAEL-1; OBS; PoEL-2;
SeCP; SeCV-1

On a Drop of Dew

31 So the soul, that drop, that ray
Of the clear fountain of eternal day,
Could it within the human flower be seen,
Remembering still its former height,
Shuns the sweet leaves and blossoms green;
And, recollecting its own light,
Does, in its pure and circling thoughts, express
The greater heaven in an heaven less. (l. 19–26)

HAP; JCP; LiTB; MeLP; MePo; NIP; OBS; SeCP;
SeCV-1; TEP

The Picture of Little T. C. in a Prospect of Flowers

32 But O, young beauty of the woods,
Whom Nature courts with fruits and flowers,
Gather the flowers, but spare the buds;
Lest Flora, angry at thy crime
To kill her infants in their prime,
Do quickly make the example yours;
And ere we see,
Nip in the blossom all our hopes and thee. (l. 33–40)

JCP; LiTB; MeLP; MePo; NAEL-1; NOBE; NoP;
OAEL-1; OBEV; OBS; PoE; PPP; PrIm; SeCP; SeCV-1

To His Coy Mistress

33 Had we but world enough, and time,
This coyness, Lady, were no crime. (l. 1–2)

34 But at my back I always hear
Time's winged chariot hurrying near;
And yonder all before us lie
Deserts of vast eternity.
Thy beauty shall no more be found,
Nor, in thy marble vault, shall sound
My echoing song: then worms shall try
That long preserved virginity:
And your quaint honor turn to dust,
And into ashes all my lust:
The grave's a fine and private place,
But none, I think, do there embrace. (l. 21–32)

35 Let us roll all our strength, and all
Our sweetness, up into one ball:
And tear our pleasures with rough strife
Thorough the iron gates of life.
Thus, though we cannot make our sun
Stand still, yet we will make him run. (l. 41–46)

AWP; BoLoP; EBEV; ELP; EnLoPo; ErPo; FaBV; FaFP;
FF; FPL; GBL; HAP; HeIP; HoPM; InPK; InPS; InvP;
JCP; LiTB; MAT; MeLP; MePo; NAEL-1; NIP; NOBE;
NoP; OAEL-1; OBD; OBEV; OBS; OPOP; PoE; PoEL-2;
PoLF; PoRA; PPP; PrIm; SCV; SeCePo; SeCP

JOHN MASEFIELD (1878–1967)

Cargoes

1 Quinquireme of Nineveh from distant Ophir
Rowing home to haven in sunny Palestine, (l. 1–2)

2 Dirty British coaster with a salt-caked smoke stack
(l. 11)

BLPL; CMoP; FaBV; FaPON; FaPoR; InPK; LiTM;
MoAB; MoBrPo; MOS; NOBE; OBEV; OBMV; PoRA;
TEP

On Growing Old

3 Be with me, Beauty, for the fire is dying;
My dog and I are old, too old for roving. (l. 1–2)

4 Summer of man its sunlight and its flower,
Spring-time of man all April in a face. (l. 17–18)

5 Let me have wisdom, Beauty, wisdom and passion,
Bread to the soul, rain when the summers parch.
Give me but these, and though the darkness close
Even the night will blossom as the rose. (l. 25–28)

CMoP; FaFP; FPL; LiTB; LiTM; MoAB; MoBrPo; PoLF;
PoRA

The Passing Strange

6 Out of the earth to rest or range
Perpetual in perpetual change,
The unknown passing through the strange. (l. 1–3)

7 Since moons decay and suns decline,
How else should end this life of mine? (l. 46–47)

8 They change, and we, who pass like foam,
Like dust blown through the streets of Rome,
Change ever, too; we have no home, (l. 61–63)

9 But gathering as we stray, a sense
Of Life, so lovely and intense,
It lingers when we wander hence,

That those who follow feel behind
Their backs, when all before is blind,
Our joy, a rampart to the mind. (l. 67–72)

LiTB; MoAB; MoBrPo; OBEV

Sea Change

10 'When freezing aloft in a snorter, I tell you I wish —
(Though maybe it ain't like a Christian) — I wish I could
be

A haughty old copper-bound albatross dipping for fish
And coming the proud over all o' the birds o' the sea.'
                                    (l. 13–16)

FaBoTw; MOS; OBMV; RB

Sea Fever

11 I must down to the seas again, to the lonely sea and
     the sky,
   And all I ask is a tall ship and a star to steer her by,
                                    (l. 1–2)

12 I must down to the seas again, for the call of the
     running tide
   Is a wild call and a clear call that may not be denied;
                                    (l. 5–6)

FaBoBe; FaBV; FaPON; FaPoR; FPL; MoAB; MoBrPo;
MOS; OBTV; OHFP; OxBTC; PDV; PoLF; TrGrPo

The West Wind

13 It's a warm wind, the west wind, full of birds' cries;
   I never hear the west wind but tears are in my eyes.
                                    (l. 1–2)

14 It's a fine land, the west land, for hearts as tired as
     mine,
   Apple orchards blossom there, and the air's like wine.
                                    (l. 5–6)

FaFP; FPL; LiTB; LiTM; MoAB; MoBrPo

EDGAR LEE MASTERS (1869–1950)

Anne Rutledge (Spoon River Anthology)

1 Out of me unworthy and unknown
  The vibrations of deathless music;

2 I am Anne Rutledge who sleep beneath these weeds,
  Beloved in life of Abraham Lincoln,
  Wedded to him, not through union,
  But through separation

AmFN; CMoP; FaFP; HAP; LiTA; LiTM; MoAmPo; MoP;
NoAM; NOBA; OFD; OHFP; OxBA; TrGrPo

Carl Hamblin (Spoon River Anthology)

3 The eye-balls were seared with a milky mucus;
  The madness of a dying soul
  Was written on her face —
  But the multitude saw why she wore the bandage."

CMoP; LiTA; LiTM; OBSV

Editor Whedon (Spoon River Anthology)

4 To be able to see every side of every question;
  To be on every side, to be everything, to be nothing
    long;
  To pervert truth, to ride it for a purpose,

  To use great feelings and passions of the human family
  For base designs, for cunning ends;

5 To be an editor, as I was.
  Then to lie here close by the river over the place
  Where the sewage flows from the village,
  And the empty cans and garbage are dumped,
  And abortions are hidden.

CMoP; FaBoEE; NOBA; OBSV; OxBA

The Hill (Spoon River Anthology)

6 Where are Elmer, Herman, Bert, Tom and Charley,
  The weak of will, the strong of arm, the clown, the
    boozer, the fighter?
  All, all, are sleeping on the hill.

7 Lo! he babbles of the fish-frys of long ago,
  Of the horse-races of long ago at Clary's Grove,
  Of what Abe Lincoln said
  One time at Springfield.

CMoP; FYAP; LiTA; LiTM; NoAM; NOBA; OxBA; TAP

Lucinda Matlock (Spoon River Anthology)

8 by Spoon Rivergathering many a shell,
  And many a flower and medicinal weed —
  Shouting to the wooded hills, singing to the green
    valleys.
  At ninety-six I had lived enough, that is all,
  And passed to a sweet repose.

9 Degenerate sons and daughters,
  Life is too strong for you —
  It takes life to love Life.

CMoP; FaBV; FF; HAP; LiTA; LiTM; MoAmPo; MoP;
NoAM; NOBA; OxBA

Petit the Poet (Spoon River Anthology)

10 Ballades by the score with the same old thought:
   The snows and the roses of yesterday are vanished;
   And what is love but a rose that fades?

11 Woodlands, meadows,streams and rivers —
   Blind to all of it all my life long.
   Triolets, villanelles,rondels, rondeaus,
   Seeds in a dry pod, tick, tick, tick,

CMoP; MoAmPo; NoAM; NOBA; OxBA; TAP

JAMES CLERK MAXWELL (1831–1879)

Rigid Body Sings

1 Gin a body meet a body
Flyin' through the air,
Gin a body hit a body,
Will it fly? and where? (l. 1–4)

BXAP; FaBoCo; FaBoPa; Par

JOHN MCCRAE (1872–1918)

In Flanders Fields

1 In Flanders fields the poppies blow
Between the crosses, row on row, (l. 1–2)

2 We are the Dead. Short days ago
We lived, felt dawn, saw sunset glow,
Loved and were loved, and now we lie
In Flanders fields. (l. 6–9)

3 If ye break faith with us who die
We shall not sleep, though poppies grow
In Flanders fields. (l. 13–15)

BLPA; CaP; FaBV; FaFP; FaPoR; FPL; NOBC; OBCV;
OBWP; OHFP; OPP; WBLP

JOHN LUCKEY MCCREERY (1835–1906)

There Is No Death

1 There is no death! The stars go down
To rise upon some other shore,
And bright in heaven's jewelled crown
They shine forevermore. (l. 1–4)

2 There is no death! The leaves may fall,
And flowers may fade and pass away —
They only wait, through wintry hours,
The warm, sweet breath of May. (l. 13–16)

3 They are not dead! They have but passed
Beyond the mists that blind us here
Into the new and larger life
Of that serener sphere. (l. 41–44)

4 For all the boundless universe
Is Life — there are no dead! (l. 63–64)

BLPA; FaBoBe; PWR; WBLP

CLAUDE MCKAY (1889–1948)

After the Winter

1 The shivering birds beneath the eaves
Have sheltered for the night. (l. 3–4)

BANP; IDB; PoBA; PoNe

America

2 Although she feeds me bread of bitterness,
And sinks into my throat her tiger's tooth,
Stealing my breath of life, I will confess
I love this cultured hell that tests my youth! (l. 1–4)

CDC; MoP; NIP; NoAM; OPP; PoBA; PoNe; TAP; TTY

Flame-Heart

3 I have forgotten much, but still remember
The poinsettia's red, blood-red in warm December.
(l. 9–10)

4 Oh some I know! I have embalmed the days,
Even the sacred moments when we played,
All innocent of passion, uncorrupt,
At noon and evening in the flame-heart's shade.
(l. 26–29)

AmNP; BANP; CDC; PoNe

The Harlem Dancer

5 The wine-flushed, bold-eyed boys, and even the girls,
Devoured her with their eager, passionate gaze;
But looking at her falsely-smiling face,
I knew her self was not in that strange place.
(l. 11–14)

BANP; BPo; FF; NoAM; Son; TAP

If We Must Die

6 If we must die, O let us nobly die,
So that our precious blood may not be shed
In vain; then even the monsters we defy
Shall be constrained to honor us though dead!

7 Like men we'll face the murderous, cowardly pack,
Pressed to the wall, dying, but fighting back!

AmPP; BANP; BPo; FaBV; IDB; MoP; NoAM; PBCV;
PoBA; PoNe; PPP; Son; TTY; UnPo

The Tropics in New York

8 And, hungry for the old, familiar ways,
  I turned aside and bowed my head and wept.
                                    (l. 11–12)

AmNP; NoAM; PoBA; PoNe; TTY

The White City

9 Deep in the secret chambers of my heart
  I muse my life-long hate, and without flinch
  I bear it nobly as I live my part. (l. 2–4)

BPo; NoAM; TAP; TW

The White House

10 The pavement slabs burn loose beneath my feet,
  A chafing savage, down the decent street;
  And passion rends my vitals as I pass,
  Where boldly shines your shuttered door of glass.
                                    (l. 5–8)

11 Oh, I must keep my heart inviolate
  Against the potent poison of your hate. (l. 13–14)

AmNP; AmPP; NIP; PoBA; PoNe

JOÃO CABRAL DE MELO NETO
(b. 1920)

The End of the World

1 his fear of the word "veil";
  and in the shape of a ship,
  still another who slept.

ATCBP

HERMAN MELVILLE (1819–1891)

The Berg

1 I saw a ship of martial build
  (Her standards set, her brave apparel on)
  Directed as by madness mere
  Against a stolid iceberg steer,
  Nor budge it, though the infatuate ship went down.
                                    (l. 1–5)

2 Adrift dissolving, bound for death;
  Though lumpish thou, a lumbering one —
  A lumbering lubbard loitering slow,

Impingers rue thee and go down,
Sounding thy precipice below,
Nor stir the slimy slug that sprawls
Along thy dead indifference of walls.

AmPP; LiTA; NOBA; NoP; PoEL-5; TAP

Billy Budd, Foretopman

3 through the port comes the moon-shine astray!
  It tips the guard's cutlass and silvers this nook;
  But 'twill die in the dawning of Billy's last day.
  A jewel-block they'll make of me to-morrow,
  Pendant pearl from the yard-arm-end
  Like the ear-drop I gave to Bristol Molly —
  O, 'tis me, not the sentence they'll suspend.

4 Fathoms down, fathoms down, how I'll dream fast
  asleep.

5 I am sleepy, and the oozy weeds about me twist.

HAP; NAAL-1; NAWM-2; NOBA; OxBoLi; PoEL-5

Commemorative of a Naval Victory

6 In social halls a favored guest
  In years that follow victory won,
  How sweet to feel your festal fame
  In woman's glance instinctive thrown:
  Repose is yours — your deed is known, (l. 10–14)

7 But seldom the laurel wreath is seen
  Unmixed with pensive pansies dark;
  There's a light and a shadow on every man
  Who at last attains his lifted mark —
  Nursing through night the ethereal spark.
  Elate he never can be;
  He feels that spirits which glad had hailed his worth,
  Sleep in oblivion. — The shark
  Glides white through the phosphorus sea. (l. 19–27)

AiP; HAP; MOS; UnPo

Fragments of a Lost Gnostic Poem of the Twelfth Century

8 Found a family, build a state,
  The pledged event is still the same:
  Matter in end will never abate
  His ancient brutal claim. (l. 1–4)

9 Indolence is heaven's ally here,
  And energy the child of hell:
  The Good Man pouring from his pitcher clear
  But brims the poisoned well. (l. 5–8)

NOBA; NoP; OxBSP; PoEL-5

The House-Top

10 No sleep. The sultriness pervades the air
And binds the brain — a dense oppression, such
As tawny tigers feel in matted shades,
Vexing their blood and making apt for ravage. (l. 1–4)

11 man rebounds whole æons back in nature. (l. 16)

12 Wise Draco comes, deep in the midnight roll
Of black artillery; he comes, though late;
In code corroborating Calvin's creed
And cynic tyrannies of honest kings;
He comes, nor parlies; and the Town, redeemed,
Gives thanks devout; nor, being thankful, heeds
The grimy slur on the Republic's faith implied,
Which holds that Man is naturally good,
And — more — is Nature's Roman, never to be scourged.
(l. 19–27)

LiTA; NAAL-1; NOBA; Prf

The Maldive Shark

13 About the Shark, phlegmatical one,
Pale sot of the Maldive sea,
The sleek little pilot-fish, azure and slim, (l. 1–3)

14 They are friends; and friendly they guide him to prey
Yet never partake of the treat —
Eyes and brains to the dotard lethargic and dull,
Pale ravener of horrible meat. (l. 13–16)

AmPP; AnAmPo; MOS; NAAL-1; NOBA; NoP; OxBA;
PoE; PoEL-5; RB; TAP; TW

Malvern Hill

15 Ye elms that wave on Malvern Hill
In prime of morn and May,
Recall ye how McClellan's men
Here stood at bay? (l. 1–4)

16 The battle-smoked flag, with stars eclipsed,
We followed (it never fell!) —
In silence husbanded our strength —
Received their yell;
Till on this slope we patient turned
With cannon ordered well;
Reverse we proved was not defeat;
But ah, the sod what thousands meet! —
Does Malvern Wood
Bethink itself, and muse and brood? (l. 21–30)

AmPP; FPL; PAH; TAP

The March into Virginia

17 Did all the lets and bars appear
To every just or larger end,
Whence should come the trust and cheer?

Youth must its ignorant impulse lend —
Age finds place in the rear.
All wars are boyish, and are fought by boys,
The champions and enthusiasts of the state: (l. 1–7)

18 But some who this blithe mood present,
As on in lightsome files they fare,
Shall die experienced ere three days be spent —
Perish, enlightened by the vollied glare;
Or shame survive, and, like to adamant,
Thy after shock, Manassas, share. (l. 31–36)

BLPL; HAP; LiTA; NAAL-1; NoP; PoE; TAP; TrGrPo;
WaaP

The Portent

19 Hidden in the cap
Is the anguish none can draw;
So your future veils its face,
Shenandoah!
But the streaming beard is shown
(Weird John Brown),
The meteor of the war.

AmPP; AnAmPo; InPK; NAAL-1; NOBA; NoP; OBWP;
OxBA; PoE; PoEL-5; PrIm; TAP; WiR

Shiloh; a Requiem

20 Foemen at morn, but friends at eve —
Fame or country least their care:
(What like a bullet can undeceive!)
But now they lie low,
While over them the swallows skim,
And all is hushed at Shiloh.

AmFN; AnAmPo; FF; LiTA; NOBA; NoP; OBWP; OxBA;
SCV; WiR

To Ned

21 Where is the world we roved, Ned Bunn?
Hollows thereof lay rich in shade
By voyagers old inviolate thrown
Ere Paul Pry cruised with Pelf and Trade.
To us old lads some thoughts come home
Who roamed a world young lads no more shall roam.
(l. 1–6)

22 But we, in anchor-watches calm,
The Indian Psyche's languor won,
And, musing, breathed primeval balm
From Edens ere yet over-run;
Marvelling mild if mortal twice,
Here and hereafter, touch a Paradise. (l. 25–30)

MOS; NAAL-1; NOBA; PoEL-5

The Tuft of Kelp

23 All dripping in tangles green,
Cast up by a lonely sea, (l. 1–2)

ChTr; FaBoEE; FaBoRV; MOS

GEORGE MEREDITH (1828–1909)

Dirge in Woods

1 Not a breath of wild air;
Still as the mosses that glow
On the flooring and over the lines (l. 3–5)

2 The pine-tree drops its dead;
They are quiet, as under the sea. (l. 7–8)

3 As the clouds the clouds chase;
And we go,
And we drop like the fruits of the tree,
Even we,
Even so. (l. 11–15)

FF; NAEL-2; OBEV; OBNC; OPOP; WiR

Love in the Valley

4 She whom I love is hard to catch and conquer,
Hard, but O the glory of the winning were she won!
(l. 15–16)

5 Darker grows the valley, more and more forgetting:
So were it with me if forgetting could be willed.
Tell the grassy hollow that holds the bubbling well-
spring
Tell it to forget the source that keeps it filled.
(l. 37–40)

6 Love that so desires would fain keep her changeless;
Fain would fling the net, and fain have her free.
(l. 47–48)

7 Could I find a place to be alone with heaven,
I would speak my heart out heaven is my need.
(l. 81–82)

AWP; EBVV; ErPo; LiTB; NOBE; OAEL-2; OBEV;
TrGrPo

Lucifer in Starlight

8 On a starred night Prince Lucifer uprose,
Tired of his dark dominion, swung the fiend
Above the rolling ball in cloud part screened, (l. 1–3)

AWP; CH; EBVV; FF; HAP; InPK; LiTB; Mes; NAEL-2;
NOBE; NOBVV; NoP; OAEL-2; OBEV; OBNC; PoE;
PoEL-5; Son; TrGrPo; UnPo; WeW

Modern Love

9 She keeps
The Topic over intellectual deeps
In buoyancy afloat. They see no ghost.
With sparkling surface-eyes we ply the ball:
It is in truth a most contagious game:
Hiding the Skeleton, shall be its name.

HeIP; NOBVV; NoP; PoE; Son

10 By this he knew she wept with waking eyes:

EnLoPo; HeIP; HoPM; NAEL-2; NOBVV; NoP; OAEL-2;
PoE; PoEL-5; Son

11 Mark where the pressing wind shoots javelin-like
Its skeleton shadow on the broad-backed wave!
Here is a fitting spot to dig Love's grave;

12 In tragic life, God wot,
No villain need be! Passions spin the plot:
We are betrayed by what is false within.

EnLoPo; GBL; NOBE; OBEV; OBNC; PoEL-5; TEP

13 Thus piteously Love closed what he begat:
The union of this ever-diverse pair!
These two were rapid falcons in a snare,
Condemned to do the flitting of the bat.

EBEV; EnLoPo; GTBS-P; HAP; NOBE; NOBVV; NoP;
OAEL-2; OBNC; PoE; PoEL-5; SeCePo; Son; TrGrPo

14 Love that had robbed us of immortal things,
This little moment mercifully gave,
Where I have seen across the twilight wave
The swan sail with her young beneath her wings.

ELP; EnLoPo; GTBS-P; Mes; NOBE; NOBVV; OAEL-2;
OBNC

15 What are we first? First, animals; and next
Intelligences at a leap; on whom
Pale lies the distant shadow of the tomb,

16 Swift doth young Love flee,
And we stand wakened, shivering from our dream.

GBL; HAP; NoP; PoEL-5

"OWEN MEREDITH" (*pseudonym of* EDWARD ROBERT BULWER-LYTTON, 1ST EARL OF LYTTON) (1831–1891)

Aux Italiens

1 And the one bird singing alone to his nest,
And the one star over the tower.

I thought of our little quarrels and strife,
And the letter that brought me back my ring;
And it all seem'd then, in the waste of life, (l. 51–55)

2 For I thought of her grave below the hill,
Which the sentinel cypress tree stands over,
And I thought, "Were she only living still,
How I could forgive her, and love her!" (l. 59–60)

3 The world is filled with folly and sin,
And Love must cling where it can, I say:
For Beauty is easy enough to win;
But one isn't loved every day. (l. 101–104)

4 There's a moment when all would go smooth and even,
If only the dead could find out when
To come back, and be forgiven. (l. 106–108)

BeLS; BLPA; BLPL; FaBoBe

WILLIAM MEREDITH (b. 1919)

The Open Sea

1 Oh, there are people, all right, settled in the sea;
It is as populous as Maine today,
But no one who will give you the time of day. (l. 4–6)

CoAP; GrPl; MOS; NePoEA; TAP; UnPo

JAMES MERRILL (b. 1926)

The Broken Home

1 In a room on the floor below,
Sunless, cooler — a brimming
Saucer of wax, marbly and dim —
I have lit what's left of my life. (l. 5–8)

2 What had the man done? Oh, made history.
Her business (he had implied) was giving birth,
Tending the house, mending the socks. (l. 37–39)

3 Always the same old story —
Father Time and Mother Earth,
A marriage on the rocks. (l. 40–42)

4 Tonight they have stepped out onto the gravel.
The party is over. It's the fall
Of 1931. They love each other still. (l. 57–59)

5 I see those two hearts, I'm afraid,
Still. Cool here in the graveyard of good and evil,
They are even so to be honored and obeyed. (l. 68–70)

6 Nor do I try to keep a garden, only
An avocado in a glass of water — (l. 79–80)

HAP; HCAP; MoP; NAAL-2; NoAM; NOBA; NYBP; PPP; WeW

Days of 1964

7 I had gone so long without loving
I hardly knew what I was thinking.

Where I hid my face, your touch, quick, merciful
Blindfolded me. A god breathed from my lips.
If that was illusion, I wanted it to last long;
                                    (l. 59–63)

8 But you were everywhere beside me, masked,
As who was not, in laughter, pain, and love. (l. 73–74)

CoAP; HCAP; NAAL-2; PoE

Laboratory Poem

9 He thought of certain human hearts, their climb
Through violence into exquisite disciplines
Of which, as it now appeared, they all expired.
                                    (l. 14–16)

CAPP; InPK; MAT; NePoEA-2; TwCP

The Mad Scene

10 the sheets and towels of a life we were going to share,
The milk-stiff bibs, the shroud, each rag to be ever
Trampled or soiled, bled on or groped for blindly,
Came swooning out of an enormous willow hamper
Onto moon-marbly boards. (l. 2–6)

11 The opera house sparkled with tiers
And tiers of eyes, like mine enlarged by belladonna,
                                    (l. 9–10)

CoAP; NOBA; PoA; PoE; TAP

WILLIAM STANLEY MERWIN (b. 1927)

The Asians Dying

1 The ghosts of the villages trail in the sky
Making a new twilight (l. 8–9)

2 Rain falls into the open eyes of the dead
Again again with its pointless sound
When the moon finds them they are the color of
  everything (l. 10–12)

CoAP; HCAP; NaP; NOBA; NYBP

The Drunk in the Furnace

3 Where he gets his spirits
It's a mystery. But the stuff keeps him musical:
(l. 15–16)

4 all afternoon
Their witless offspring flock like piped rats to its siren
Crescendo, and agape on the crumbling ridge
Stand in a row and learn. (l. 25–28)

CAPP; LiTM; MAT; MoP; NAAL-2; NePoEA-2; NoAM;
NoP; PoE; SM; TwCP

For the Anniversary of My Death

5 Every year without knowing it I have passed the day
When the last fires will wave to me (l. 1–2)

6 Then I will no longer
Find myself in life as in a strange garment (l. 6–7)

CoAP; HCAP; InPK; NAAL-2; NaP; NOBA

Leviathan

7 This is the black sea-brute bulling through wave-wrack,
(l. 1)

8 who should moor at his edge
And fare on afoot would find gates of no gardens,
But the hill of dark underfoot diving,
Closing overhead, the cold deep, and drowning.
He is called Leviathan, and named for rolling,
(l. 18–22)

9 The sea curling,
Star-climbed, wind-combed, cumbered with itself still
As at first it was, is the hand no yet contented
Of the Creator. And he waits for the world to begin.
(l. 36–39)

MoP; NePoEA; NoAM; NOBA

Separation

10 Your absence has gone through me
Like thread through a needle. (l. 1–2)

HAP; ILY; NoP; PCP

CHARLOTTE MEW (1870–1928)

Beside the Bed

1 Because all night you have not turned to us or spoken
It is time for you to wake; (l. 12–13)

2 This is only a most piteous pretense of sleep! (l. 17)

MoAB; MoBrPo; OxBSP; TrGrPo; WPE

The Farmer's Bride

3 She does the work about the house
As well as most, but like a mouse:
Happy enough to chat and play
With birds and rabbits and such as they,
So long as men-folk keep away. (l. 20–24)

4 Oh! my God! the down,
The soft young down of her, the brown,
The brown of her—her eyes, her hair, her hair . . .
(l. 44–46)

BoLoP; ErPo; FaBoWP; MoAB; MoBrPo; OxBTC;
TrGrPo; WPE

Old Shepherd's Prayer

5 And if I may not walk in th' old ways and look on
th' old faces
I wud sooner sleep. (l. 17–19)

EaLo; MoAB; MoBrPo; OBD; OxBTC; WPE

Sea Love

6 An' him no more to me nor me to him
Than the wind goin' over my hand. (l. 7–8)

MoAB; MoBrPo; OxBTC; TrGrPo

ALICE MEYNELL (MRS. WILFRID MEYNELL) (1847–1922)

Chimes

1 From the shaken tower
A flock of bells take flight,
And go with the hour. (l. 2–4)

BoTP; CH; MoBrPo; WPE

"I Am the Way"

2 Thou art the Way.
Hadst Thou been nothing but the goal,
I cannot say
If Thou hadst ever met my soul. (l. 1–4)

ACP; NOBVV; OBMV; OxBSP

The Shepherdess

3 She walks — the lady of my delight —
   A shepherdess of sheep.
   Her flocks are thoughts. She keeps them white;
   She guards them from the steep. (l. 1–4)

4 She is so circumspect and right;
   She has her soul to keep. (l. 15–16)

   ACP; AWP; MoBrPo; NOBVV; OBEV

MICHELANGELO BUONARROTI
(1474–1564)

For Inspiration

1 The prayers I make will then be sweet indeed,
   If thou the spirit give by which I pray;
   My unassisted heart is barren clay,
   Which of its native self can nothing feed; (l. 1–4)

2 Do thou, then breathe those thoughts into my mind
   By which such virtue may in me be bred
   That in thy holy footsteps I may tread:
   The fetters of my tongue do thou unbind,
   That I may have the power to sing of thee
   And sound thy praises everlastingly (l. 9–14)

   AWP; PFI; TrPWD; WGRP

Yes! hope may with my strong desire keep pace

3 His hope is treacherous only whose love dies
   With beauty, which is varying every hour;
   But, in chaste hearts uninfluenced by the power
   Of outward change, there blooms a deathless flower,
   That breathes on earth the air of paradise. (l. 10–14)

   AWP; CTC; OBVE; PFI

WILLIAM JULIUS MICKLE (1735–1788)

The Sailor's Wife (attributed to Mickle)

1 And are ye sure the news is true?
   And are ye sure he's weel? (l. 1–2)

   BeLS; GN; GTBS; GTBS-P; NOEC

JOSEPHINE MILES (1911–1985)

Belief

1 Therefore it was surprising that, as we kept the
      newspapers from Mother,
   She died feeling responsible for a disaster unverified,

Murmuring, in her sleep as it seemed, the ancient
   slogan
Noblesse oblige. (l. 13–16)

   FaBoWP; MoP; NoAM; TAP

Reason

2 Said, All you needed to do was just explain;
   Reason Reason is my middle name. (l. 14–15)

   InPK; NoAM; NoP; TAP

EDNA ST. VINCENT MILLAY ("NANCY BOYD") (1892–1950)

Afternoon on a Hill

1 I will be the gladdest thing
   Under the sun!
   I will touch a hundred flowers
   And not pick one. (l. 1–4)

   AnAmPo; BoTP; FaPON; GrPl; NTCP; OBCA; OxBA;
   PDV; TTTS

And You as Well Must Die, Beloved Dust

2 this wonder fled,
   Altered, estranged, disintegrated, lost.
   Nor shall my love avail you in your hour. (l. 7–9)

3 It mattering not how beautiful you were,
   Or how beloved above all else that dies. (l. 13–14)

   FPL; PoLF; PoRA; TAP

The Cameo

4 Clear and diminished like a scene cut in cameo
   The lighthouse, and the boat on the beach, and the two
      shapes
   Of the woman and the man; (l. 8–11)

5 O troubled forms, O early love unfortunate and hard,
   Time has estranged you into a jewel cold and pure;
                                          (l. 16–17)

   FYAP; LiTA; MoAmPo; UnPo; WPE

Dirge without Music

6 Down, down, down into the darkness of the grave
   Gently they go, the beautiful, the tender, the kind;
   Quietly they go, the intelligent, the witty, the brave.
   I know. But I do not approve. And I am not resigned.
                                          (l. 13–16)

   CMoP; DL; LiTA; TrGrPo

Euclid Alone Has Looked on Beauty Bare

7 Euclid alone has looked on Beauty bare, (l. 1)

8 let geese
Gabble and hiss, but heroes seek release
From dusty bondage into luminous air. (l. 6–8)

9 Fortunate they
Who, though once only and then but far away,
Have heard her massive sandal set on stone.
(l. 12–14)

CMoP; ImOP; MoAB; MoAmPo; NAAL-2; NoP; Son; TAP

Figs from Thistles

10 My candle burns at both ends;
It will not last the night; (l. 1–2)

FaBV; NoP; PoA

God's World

11 Lord, I do fear
Thou'st made the world too beautiful this year;
My soul is all but out of me, — let fall
No burning leaf; prithee, let no bird call. (l. 13–17)

BLPL; CMoP; FaBoBe; FaBV; MoAmPo; TrCP

Hearing your words, and not a word among them

12 Hearing your words, and not a word among them
Tuned to my liking, on a salty day
When inland woods were pushed by winds, that flung them
Hissing to leeward like a ton of spray, (l. 1–4)

13 The wind of their endurance, driving south,
Flattened your words against your speaking mouth.
(l. 13–14)

CMoP; MoP; NoAM; VGW

I, Being Born a Woman and Distressed

14 I, being born a woman and distressed
By all the needs and notions of my kind,
Am urged by your propinquity to find
Your person fair, and feel a certain zest
To bear your body's weight upon my breast: (l. 1–5)

15 I find this frenzy insufficient reason
For conversation when we meet again. (l. 13–14)

BoLoP; ErPo; NIP; NoP; OPOP

Love is not all; it is not meat nor drink.

16 Love is not all: it is not meat nor drink
Nor slumber nor a roof against the rain; (l. 1–2)

17 I might be driven to sell your love for peace,
Or trade the memory of this night for food.
It well may be. I do not think I would. (l. 12–14)

CMoP; FPL; HAP; HeIP; InPS; NoAM; OxBA; PrIm; TAP

Memorial to D. C.

18 On and on eternally
Shall your altered fluid run,
Bud and bloom and go to seed;
But your singing days are done;

19 All your lovely words are spoken.
Once the ivory box is broken,
Beats the golden bird no more.

CMoP; MoAB; MoAmPo; OxBA; PoRA

Oh, Sleep Forever in the Latmian Cave

20 And deep into her crystal body poured
The hot and sorrowful sweetness of the dust:
Whereof she wanders mad, being all unfit
For mortal love, that might not die of it. (l. 12–15)

CMoP; LiTM; MoAmPo; NoAM; NoP

On Hearing a Symphony of Beethoven

21 Sweet sounds, oh, beautiful music, do not cease!
Reject me not into the world again.
With you alone is excellence and peace,
Mankind made plausible, his purpose plain. (l. 1–4)

22 Music my rampart, and my only one. (l. 14)

LiTA; LiTM; MoAB; MoAmPo; TrGrPo

Passer Mortuus Est

23 After all my erstwhile dear,
My no longer cherished,
Need we say it was not love,
Just because it perished? (l. 9–12)

CMoP; FaBoWP; MoAmPo; OBD; OxBA

Pity me not

24 Pity me that the heart is slow to learn
What the swift mind beholds at every turn. (l. 13–14)

CMoP; FaBoWP; MoAB; MoAmPo; OxBA; TrGrPo

Portrait by a Neighbor

25 Before she has her floor swept
Or her dishes done.
Any day you'll find her
A-sunning in the sun! (l. 1–4)

FaPON; MoShBr; OBCA; PDV

Recuerdo

26 We were very tired, we were very merry —
We had gone back and forth all night on the ferry.
(l. 1–2)

AmFN; FaFP; FPL; LiTA; LiTM; NAAL-2; NoAM; OxBA;
PoA; TAP

Renascence

27 All I could see from where I stood
Was three long mountains and a wood; (l. 1–2)

28 I screamed, and — lo! — Infinity
Came down and settled over me; (l. 39–40)

29 The gossiping of friendly spheres,
The creaking of the tented sky,
The ticking of Eternity. (l. 58–60)

30 The world stands out on either side
No wider than the heart is wide;
Above the world is stretched the sky, —
No higher than the soul is high. (l. 275–280)

31 And he whose soul is flat — the sky
Will cave in on him by and by. (l. 291–292)

FaFP; MoAB; MoAmPo; OHFP; PDV

The Return

32 Earth does not understand her child,
Who from the loud gregarious town
Returns, depleted and defiled,
To the still woods, to fling him down. (l. 1–4)

33 But she is early up and out,
To trim the year or strip its bones; (l. 9–10)

LiTA; MoAB; MoAmPo; MoP; NoAM; OxBA

Sonnet to Gath

34 Country of hunchbacks! — where the strong, straight
spine
Jeered at by crooked children, makes his way
Through by-streets at the kindest hour of day, (l. 1–3)

35 Dust in an urn long since, dispersed and dead
Is great Apollo; and the happier he; (l. 9–10)

BoWoP; CMoP; MoAB; MoAmPo

Spring

36 To what purpose, April, do you return again?
Beauty is not enough. (l. 1–2)

37 Life in itself
Is nothing,
An empty cup, a flight of uncarpeted stairs.
It is not enought that yearly, down this hill,
April
Comes like an idiot, babbling and strewing flowers.
(l. 13–18)

BoWoP; MoAB; MoAmPo; NoP

Travel

38 My heart is warm with the friends I make,
And better friends I'll not be knowing,
Yet there isn't a train I wouldn't take,
No matter where it's going. (l. 9–12)

FaPON; MoShBr; OBCA; PDV; RHPC

What Lips My Lips Have Kissed

39 What lips my lips have kissed, and where, and why,
I have forgotten, and what arms have lain
Under my head till morning; out the rain
Is full of ghosts tonight, (l. 1–4)

40 I cannot say what loves have come and gone;
I only know that summer sang in me
A little while, that in me sings no more. (l. 13–15)

BoLoP; HeIP; HoPM; LiTA; LLLT; MoAB; MoAmPo;
NAAL-2; NIP; PrIm; Son

Wild Swans

41 Tiresome heart, forever living and dying,
House without air, I leave you and lock your door.
Wild swans, come over the town, come over
The town again, trailing your legs and crying! (l. 5–8)

CMoP; MoAmPo; PBWP; UnPo

VASSAR MILLER   (b. 1924)

Bout with Burning

1 I have tossed hours upon the tides of fever,
Upon the billows of my bood have ridden,
Where fish of fancy teem as neither river
Nor ocean spawns from India to Sweden. (l. 1–4)

LiTM; MoAmPo; MT; NePoEA

WILLIAM MILLER (1810–1872)

Wee Willie Winkie rins through the town

1 Wee Willie Winkie rins through the town,
  Up stairs and doon stairs in his nicht-gown,
  Tirling at the window, crying at the lock,
  'Are the weans in their bed, for it's now ten o'clock?'
  (l. 1–4)

FaFP; NOBVV; OxBChV; OxNR

ALAN ALEXANDER MILNE (1882–1956)

The More It Snows

1 The more it
  GOES-tiddely-pom
  The more it
  GOES-tiddely-pom
  On
  Snowing. (l. 3–8)

NTCP; PYC; RAR; RHPC

Puppy and I

2 "Where are you going this nice fine day?"
  (I said to the Puppy as he went by).
  "Up in the hills to roll and play."
  "I'll come with you, Puppy," said I. (l. 32–35)

BoTP; FaPON; OnUR; PDV; PYC

The Three Foxes

3 Once upon a time there were three little foxes
  Who didn't wear stockings, and they didn't wear
    sockses,
  But they all had handkerchiefs to blow their noses,
  And they kept their handkerchiefs in cardboard boxes.
  (l. 1–4)

GoJo; GrPl; MoShBr; OxBChV

JOHN MILTON (1608–1674)

At a Solemn Musick

1 Blest pair of Sirens, pledges of Heav'n's joy,
  Sphear-born harmonious Sisters, Voice, and Vers,
  (l. 1–2)

2 till disproportion'd sin
  Jarr'd against natures chime, and with harsh din
  Broke the fair musick that all creatures made
  To their great Lord, whose love their motion sway'd
  In perfect Diapason, whilst they stood
  In first obedience, and their state of good. (l. 19–24)

GTBS; GTBS-P; HeIP; NOBE; OBEV; OBS; PoEL-3;
UnS

Comus; a Masque Presented at Ludlow Castle

3 A hidden strength
  Which if Heav'n gave it, may be term'd her own:
  'Tis chastity, my brother, chastity:
  She that has that, is clad in compleat steel,
  And like a quiver'd Nymph with Arrows keen
  May trace huge Forests, and unharbour'd Heaths,
  Infamous Hills, and sandy perilous wildes,
  Where through the sacred rayes of Chastity,
  No savage fierce, Bandite, or mountaneer
  Will dare to soyl her Virgin purity,

4 but when lust
  By unchaste looks, loose gestures, and foul talk,
  But most by lewd and lavish act of sin,
  Lets in defilement to the inward parts,
  The soul grows clotted by contagion,
  Imbodies, and imbrutes, till she quite loose
  The divine property of her first being.

OAEL-1; OBS

5 Wherefore did Nature powre her bounties forth,
  With such a full and unwithdrawing hand,
  Covering the earth with odours, fruits, and flocks,
  Thronging the Seas with spawn innumerable,
  But all to please, and sate the curious taste?

6 List Lady be not coy, and be not cosen'd
  With that same vaunted name Virginity,
  Beauty is natures coyn, must not be hoorded,
  But must be current, and the good thereof
  Consists in mutual and partak'n bliss,
  Unsavoury in th'injoyment of it self
  If you let slip time, like a neglected rose
  It withers on the stalk with languish't head.

OAEL-1; PoEL-3

7 Listen where thou art sitting
  Under the glassy, cool, translucent wave,
  In twisted braids of lilies knitting
  The loose train of thy amber-dropping hair;
  Listen for dear honour's sake,
  Goddess of the silver lake,
  Listen and save.

OAEL-1; OBS

8 The Star that bids the Shepherd fold,
Now the top of Heav'n doth hold,
And the gilded Car of Day,
His glowing Axle doth allay
In the steep Atlantick stream, (l. 1–5)

FaBoCh; FiP; NOBE; OAEL-1; OBEV; OBS; TrGrPo

9 Sweet Echo, sweetest Nymph that liv'st unseen
Within thy airy shell
By slow Meander's margent green,
And in the violet imbroider'd vale
Where the love-lorn Nightingale
Nightly to thee her sad Song mourneth well.
Canst thou not tell me of a gently Pair
That likest thy Narcissus are?
O if thou have
Hid them in som flowry Cave,
Tell me but where,
Sweet Queen of Parly, Daughter of the Sphear,
So maist thou be translated to the skies,
And give resounding grace to all Heav'n's Harmonies.

ELP; NOBE; OAEL-1; OBEV; OBS; TrGrPo

10 To the Ocean now I fly,
And those happy climes that ly
Where day never shuts his eye,
Up in the broad fields of the sky:

11 The Graces, and the rosie-boosom'd Howres,
Thither all their bounties bring,
That there eternal Summer dwels,
And West winds, with musky wing
About the cedar'n alleys fling
Nard, and Cassia's balmy smels.

12 Celestial Cupid her fam'd son advanc't,
Holds his dear Psyche sweet intranc't
After her wandring labours long,
Till free consent the gods among
Make her his eternal Bride,
And from her fair unspotted side
Two blissful twins are to be born,
Youth and Joy; so Jove hath sworn,

13 Mortals that would follow me,
Love vertue, she alone is free,
She can teach ye how to clime
Higher than the Spheary chime;
Or if Vertue feeble were,
Heav'n it self would stoop to her.

NOBE; OAEL-1; OBEV; OBS; TrGrPo

How Soon Hath Time

14 How soon hath Time the subtle thief of youth,
Stol'n on his wing my three and twentieth year!
My hasting days fly on with full career,
By my late spring no bud or blossom shew'th.

Perhaps my semblance might deceive the truth,
That I to manhood am arriv'd so near,
And inward ripeness doth much less appear,
That some more timely-happy spirits endu'th.

Yet be it less or more, or soon or slow,
It shall be still in strictest measure ev'n,
To that same lot, however mean, or high,
Toward which Time leads me, and the will of Heav'n;
All is, if I have grace to use it so,
As ever in my great Task-Master's eye. (l. 1–14)

FF; HeIP; InPS; LiTB; NAEL-1; NAs; PoE; SeCePo; Son

Il Penseroso

15 But hail thou Goddess, sage and holy,
Hail divinest Melancholy,
Whose saintly visage is too bright
To hit the sense of human sight,
And therefore to our weaker view
O'erlaid with black, staid Wisdom's hue; (l. 11–16)

16 Come pensive Nun, devout and pure,
Sober, steadfast, and demure,
All in a robe of darkest grain,
Flowing with majestic train,
And sable stole of cypress lawn,
Over thy decent shoulders drawn.
Come, but keep thy wonted state,
With even step and musing gait,
And looks commercing with the skies,
Thy rapt soul sitting in thine eyes;
There held in holy passion still,
Forget thyself to marble, (l. 31–42)

17 Or bid the soul of Orpheus sing
Such notes as, warbled to the string,
Drew iron tears down Pluto's cheek,
And made Hell grant what love did seek; (l. 105–108)

18 But let my due feet never fail
To walk the studious cloister's pale,
And love the high embowed roof,
With antic pillars massy proof,
And storied windows richly dight,
Casting a dim, religious light. (l. 155–160)

19 Find out the peaceful hermitage,
The hairy gown and mossy cell,
Where I may sit and rightly spell
Of every star that heaven doth show,
And every herb that sips the dew;
Till old experience do attain
To something like prophetic strain.
These pleasures Melancholy give,
And I with thee will choose to live. (l. 168–176)

AWP; FiP; GTBS; GTBS-P; HAP; HoPM; JCP; LiTB;
NoP; OAEL-1; OBEV; OBS; PPP; TEP; TrGrPo

L'Allegro

20 Haste thee Nymph, and bring with thee
Jest and youthful jollity,
Quips and cranks, and wanton wiles,
Nods and becks, and wreathed smiles, (l. 25–28)

21 Come, and trip it as ye go
On the light fantastic toe,
And in thy right hand lead with thee,
The mountain nymph, sweet Liberty; (l. 33–36)

22 When the merry bells ring round,
And the jocund rebecks sound
To many a youth and many a maid,
Dancing in the chequered shade;
And young and old come forth to play
On a sunshine holiday, (l. 93–98)

23 Tells how the drudging goblin sweat,
To earn his cream-bowl duly set,
When in one night, ere glimpse of morn,
His shadowy flail hath threshed the corn
That ten day-laborers could not end:
Then lies him down the lubber fend,
And stretched out all the chimney's length,
Basks at the fire his hairy strength;
And crop-full out of doors he flings,
Ere the first cock his matin rings. (l. 105–114)

24 Lap me in soft Lydian airs,
Married to immortal verse,
Such as the meeting soul may pierce
In notes with many a winding bout
Of linked sweetness long drawn out,
With wanton heed and giddy cunning,
The melting voice through mazes running,
Untwisting all the chains that tie
The hidden soul of harmony; (l. 136–144)

AWP; FaFP; FiP; GTBS; GTBS-P; HAP; HoPM; JCP;
LiTB; NoP; OAEL-1; OBEV; OBS; PPP; SeCePo; TEP;
TrGrPo

Lycidas

25 Yet once more, O ye laurels, and once more,
Ye myrtles brown, with ivy never-sere,
I come to pluck your berries harsh and crude,
And with forc'd fingers rude
Shatter your leaves before the mellowing year.
Bitter constraint and sad occasion dear
Compels me to disturb your season due:
For Lycidas is dead, dead ere his prime

26 Alas! What boots it with uncessant care
To tend the homely slighted shepherd's trade,
And strictly meditate the thankless Muse?
Were it not better done as others use,
To sport with Amaryllis in the shade,
Hid in the tangles of Neaera's hair?

27 Fame is the spur that the clear spirit doth raise
(That last infirmity of noble mind)
To scorn delights and live laborious days;
But the fair guerdon where we hope to find,
And think to burst out into sudden blaze,
Comes the blind Fury with th'abhorred shears
And slits the thin-spun life.

28 Last came, and last did go,
The pilot of the Galilean lake.

29 Blind mouths! that scarce themselves know how to hold
A sheephook, or have learn'd ought else the least
That to the faithful herdman's art belongs!
What recks it them? What need they? They are sped.
And when they list their lean and flashy songs
Grate on their scrannel pipes of wretched straw,
The hungry sheep look up, and are not fed,

30 But that two-handed engine at the door
Stands ready to smite once, and smites no more."
Return, Alpheus, the dread voice is pass'd

31 Ay me! whilst thee the shores and sounding seas
Wash far away, where e'er thy bones are hurl'd,
Whether beyond the stormy Hebrides,
Where thou perhaps under the humming tide
Visit'st the bottom of the monstrous world,
Or whether thou, to our moist vows deni'd,
Sleep'st by the fable of Bellerus old,
Where the great vision of the guarded Mount
Looks toward Namancos and Bayona's hold.
Look homeward Angel now, and melt with ruth,
And O ye dolphins, waft the hapless youth.

32 So Lycidas sunk low, but mounted high
Through the dear might of him that walk'd the waves,
Where other groves and other streams along
With nectar pure his oozy locks he laves
And hears the unexpressive nuptial song
In the bless'd kingdoms meek of joy and love.
There entertain him all the saints above
In solemn troops and sweet societies,
That sing, and singing in their glory move,
And wipe the tears for ever from his eyes.

33 At last he rose, and twitch'd his mantle blue,
Tomorrow to fresh woods and pastures new.

AWP; ChTr; EBEV; FiP; GTBS; GTBS-P; HAP; InPS;
JCP; LiTB; NOBE; NoP; OAEL-1; OBEV; OBS; PoEL-3;
PPP; PrIm; TrGrPo; UnPo; WeW; WGRP

On His Deceased Wife

34 Came vested all in white, pure as her mind.
Her face was veiled; yet to my fancied sight
Love, sweetness, goodness, in her person shined
So clear as in no face with more delight.

But, O! as to embrace me she inclined,
I waked, she fled, and day brought back my night.
(l. 9–14)

BLPL; BoLoP; EBEV; EnLoPo; FaFP; GBL; HAP; LiTB;
NAEL-1; NOBE; NoP; OAEL-1; OBEV; OBS; PoE;
PoEL-3; SCV; Son; TEP; WeW

On Shakespeare

35 What needs my Shakespeare for his honored bones
The labor of an age in piled stones?
Or that his hallowed relics should be hid
Under a star-ypointing pyramid?
Dear son of memory, great heir of fame,
What need'st thou such weak witness of thy name?
Thou in our wonder and astonishment
Has built thyself a livelong monument.
For whilst, to the shame of slow-endeavoring art,
Thy easy numbers flow, and that each heart
Hath from the leaves of thy unvalued book
Those Delphic lines with deep impression took;
Then thou, our fancy of itself bereaving,
Dost make us marble with too much conceiving,
And so sepulchred in such pomp dost lie
That kings for such a tomb would wish to die.
(l. 1–16)

FaBoEE; InvP; MeLP; MePo; NAEL-1; NoP; PoE; PoRA;
SeCePo; TrGrPo

On the Late Massacre in Piedmont

36 Their martyred blood and ashes sow
O'er all the Italian fields where still doth sway
The triple tyrant; that from these may grow
A hundredfold, who, having learnt thy way,
Early may fly the Babylonian woe. (l. 10–14)

AWP; GTBS; GTBS-P; HAP; HeIP; JCP; LiTB; NAEL-1;
NOBE; NOCV; NoP; OAEL-1; OBS; OBWP; PoEL-3;
PPP; Son; TW; UnPo; WaaP; WeW

On the Morning of Christ's Nativity

37 But he her fears to cease
Sent down the meek-eyed Peace;
She, crowned with olive green, came softly sliding
Down through the turning sphere,
His ready harbinger,
With turtle wing the amorous clouds dividing,
And waving wide her myrtle wand,
She strikes a universal peace through sea and land.
(l. 17–24)

38 And though the shady gloom
Had given day her room,
The sun himself withheld his wonted speed,
And hid his head for shame,

As his inferior flame
The new-enlightened world no more should need;
He saw a greater Sun appear
Than his bright throne or burning axle-tree could bear.
(l. 49–56)

39 Ring out, ye crystal spheres,
Once bless our human ears
(If ye have power to touch our senses so),
And let your silver chime
Move in melodious time,
And let the bass of heaven's deep organ blow;
And with your ninefold harmony
Make up full consort to the angelic symphony.
(l. 97–104)

40 And then at last our bliss
Full and perfect is,
But now begins; for from this happy day
The old Dragon underground,
In straiter limits bound,
Not half so far casts his usurped sway,
And, wroth to see his kingdom fail,
Swinges the scaly horror of his folded tail.
(l. 137–144)

41 But see, the Virgin blest
Hath laid her Babe to rest:
Time is our tedious song should here have ending;
Heaven's youngest teemed star,
Hath fixed her polished car,
Her sleeping Lord with handmaid lamp attending;
And all about the courtly stable,
Bright-harnessed angels sit in order serviceable.
(l. 209–216)

FiP; GTBS; GTBS-P; LiTB; MeLP; NAEL-1; NAs;
NOBE; NOCV; NoP; OBEV; OBS; PoEL-3; WGRP

42 See how from far upon the eastern road
The star-led Wizards haste with odours sweet . . .

ChTr; GTBS; GTBS-P; LiTB; MeLP; NAs; NOCV; NoP;
OBS; PoEL-3; WGRP

On the University Carrier (Who Sickn'd in the Time of His Vacancy)

43 Shew'd him his room where he must lodge that night,
Pull'd off his Boots, and took away the light:
If any ask for him, it shall be sed,
Hobson has supt, and 's newly gon to bed. (l. 15–18)

EBEV; FaBoCh; FaBoEE; MePo; PrIm; SaC

On Time

44 For when as each thing bad thou hast entomb'd,
And last of all, thy greedy self consum'd,
Then long Eternity shall greet our bliss
With an individual kiss; (l. 9–12)

45 Triumphing over Death, and Chance, and thee O Time.

                         (l. 22)

BLPL; LiTB; MePo; OBEV; OBS

Paradise Lost

46 Of Mans First Disobedience, and the Fruit
   Of that Forbidden Tree, whose mortal taste
   Brought Death into the World, and all our woe,
   With loss of Eden, till one greater Man
   Restore us, and regain the blissful Seat,
   Sing Heav'nly Muse, that on the secret top
   Of Oreb, or of Sinai, didst inspire
   That Shepherd, who first taught the chosen Seed,
   In the Beginning how the Heav'ns and Earth
   Rose out of Chaos: (Bk. I, l. 1–10)

47 What in me is dark
   Illumine, what is low raise and support;
   That to the highth of this great Argument
   I may assert Eternal Providence,
   And justifie the wayes of God to men.
                   (Bk. I, l. 22–26)

48 Who first seduc'd them to that fowl revolt?
   Th' infernal Serpent; he it was, whose guile
   Stird up with Envy and Revenge, deceiv'd
   The Mother of Mankinde, what time his Pride
   Had cast him out from Heav'n, with all his Host
   Of Rebel Angels, (Bk. I, l. 33–38)

49 Him the Almighty Power
   Hurld headlong flaming from th' Ethereal Skie
   With hideous ruine and combustion down
   To bottomless perdition, there to dwell
   In Adamantine Chains and penal Fire,
   Who durst defie th' Omnipotent to Arms.
   Nine times the Space that measures Day and Night
   To mortal men, he with his horrid crew
   Lay vanquisht, rowling in the fiery Gulfe
                   (Bk. I, l. 44–52)

50 A Dungeon horrible, on all sides round
   As one great Furnace flam'd, yet from those flames
   No light, but rather darkness visible
   Serv'd only to discover sights of woe,
   Regions of sorrow, doleful shades, where peace
   And rest can never dwell, hope never comes
   That comes to all; but torture without end
                   (Bk. I, l. 61–67)

51 What though the field be lost?
   All is not lost; the unconquerable Will,
   And study of revenge, immortal hate,
   And courage never to submit or yield:
   And what is else not to be overcome?
                   (Bk. I, l. 105–109)

52 In Arms not worse, in foresight much advanc't,
   We may with more successful hope resolve
   To wage by force or guile eternal Warr
   Irreconcileable, to our grand Foe, (Bk. I, l. 119–122)

53 Thus Satan talking to his neerest Mate
   With Head up-lift above the wave, and Eyes
   That sparkling blaz'd, his other Parts besides
   Prone on the Flood, extended long and large
   Lay floating many a rood, in bulk as huge
   As whom the Fables name of monstrous size,
   Titanian, or Earth-born, that warr'd on Jove,
   Briarios or Typhon, whom the Den
   By ancient Tarsus held, or that Sea-beast
   Leviathan, (Bk. I, l. 192–201)

54 Farewel happy Fields
   Where Joy for ever dwells: Hail horrours, hail
   Infernal world, and thou profoundest Hell
   Receive thy new Possessor: One who brings
   A mind not to be chang'd by Place or Time.
   The mind is its own place, and in it self
   Can make a Heav'n of Hell, a Hell of Heav'n.
                   (Bk. I, l. 249–255)

EBEV; FaBoRV; FiP; NAEL-1; NAWM-1; NIP; NoP;
OAEL-1; PoE; PoEL-3; TOF

55 His legions, angel forms, who lay intranst
   Thick as autumnal leaves that strow the brooks
   In Vallombrosa, where th'Etrurian shades
   High overarcht imbowr. (Bk. I, l. 301–304)

FaBoPP

56 But he his wonted pride
   Soon recollecting, with high words, that bore
   Semblance of worth not substance, gently rais'd
   Thir fainting courage, and dispel'd thir fears.
                   (Bk. I, l. 527–530)

57 Thir dread commander: he above the rest
   In shape and gesture proudly eminent
   Stood like a Towr; his form had yet not lost
   All her Original brightness, nor appear'd
   Less than Arch Angel ruind, and th' excess
   Of Glory obscur'd: As when the Sun new ris'n
   Looks through the Horizontal misty Air
   Shorn of his Beams, or from behind the Moon
   In dim Eclips disastrous twilight sheds
   On half the Nations, and with fear of change
   Perplexes Monarchs. (Bk. I, l. 589–599)

OBS

58 High on a throne of royal state, which far
   Outshone the wealth of Ormus and of Ind,
   Or where the gorgeous East with richest hand
   Show'rs on her kings barbaric pearl and gold,
   Satan exalted sat, by merit raised
   To that bad eminence; and, from despair
   Thus high uplifted beyond hope, aspires
   Beyond thus high, insatiate to pursue
   Vain war with Heav'n, and by success untaught,
   His proud imaginations (Bk. II, l. 1–10)

NIP; OAEL-1

59 Towards him they bend
With awful reverence prone; and as a God
Extoll him equal to the highest in Heav'n:
Nor fail'd they to express how much they prais'd,
That for the general safety he despis'd
His own: for neither do the Spirits damn'd
Loose all thir vertue; lest bad men should boast
Thir specious deeds on earth, which glory excites,
Or close ambition varnisht o'er with zeal.
(Bk. II, l. 477−485)

60 Others apart sat on a Hill retir'd,
In thoughts more elevate, and reason'd high
Of Providence, Foreknowledge, Will, and Fate,
Fixt Fate, free will, foreknowledge absolute,
And found no end, in wandring mazes lost.
Of good and evil much they argu'd then,
Of happiness and final misery,
Passion and Apathie, and glory and shame,
Vain wisdom all, and false Philosophie:
(Bk. II, l. 557−565)

61 Thus roving on
In confus'd march forlorn, th' adventrous Bands,
With shuddring horror pale, and eyes agast
View'd first thir lamentable lot, and found
No rest: through many a dark and drearie Vale
They pass'd, and many a Region dolorous,
O'er many a Frozen, many a fierie Alpe,
Rocks, Caves, Lakes, Fens, Bogs, Dens, and shades of
death,
A Universe of death, which God by curse
Created evil, for evil only good,
Where all life dies, death lives, and Nature breeds,
Perverse, all monstrous, all prodigious things,
Abominable, inutterable, and worse
Than Fables yet have feign'd, or fear conceiv'd,
Gorgons and Hydras, and Chimeras dire.
(Bk. II, l. 614−628)

OBS

62 So he with difficulty and labour hard
Moved on, with difficulty and labour he;
But he once passed, soon after when man fell,
Strange alteration! Sin and Death amain
Following his track, such was the will of Heaven,
Paved after him a broad and beaten way
Over the dark abyss, whose boiling gulf
Tamely endured a bridge of wondrous length
From hell continued reaching th' utmost orb
Of this frail world; (Bk. II, l. 1021−1030)

SeCePo

63 Hail holy Light, of spring of Heav'n first-born,
Or of th' Eternal Coeternal beam
May I express thee unblam'd? since God is Light,
And never but in unapproached Light
Dwelt from Eternitie, dwelt then in thee,
Bright effluence of bright essence in create.

Or hear'st thou rather pure Ethereal stream,
Whose Fountain who shall tell? (Bk. III, l. 1−8)

FiP; LiTB; NOBE; OAEL-1; OBEV; OBS; SCV; TOF

64 My Vanquisher, spoild of his vanted spoile;
Death his deaths wound shall then receive, & stoop
Inglorious, of his mortall sting disarm'd.
I through the ample Air in Triumph high
Shall lead Hell Captive maugre Hell, and show
The powers of darkness bound. Thou at the sight
Pleas'd, out of Heaven shalt look down and smile,
(Bk. III, l. 251−257)

OBS

65 then from Pole to Pole
He views in bredth, and without longer pause
Down right into the Worlds first Region throws
His flight precipitant, and windes with ease
Through the pure marble Airhis oblique way
Amongst innumerable Stars, that shon
Stars distant, but nigh hand seemd other Worlds,
Or other Worlds they seemd, or happy Iles,
Like those Hesperian Gardens fam'd of old,
Fortunate Fields, and Groves and flowrie Vales,
Thrice happy Iles, but who dwelt happy there
He stayd not to enquire. (Bk. III, l. 560−571)

OBS

66 ". . . Me miserable! which way shall I fly
Infinite wrath and infinite despair?
Which way I fly is Hell; myself am Hell;
And, in the lowest deep, a lower deep
Still threat'ning to devour me opens wide,
To which the Hell I suffer seems a Heaven.
(Bk. IV, l. 73−78)

67 So farewell hope, and with hope, farewell fear,
Farewell remorse! All good to me is lost;
Evil, be thou my Good: by thee at least
Divided empire with Heaven's King I hold,
By thee, and more than half perhaps will reign;
As Man ere long, and this new World, shall know."
(Bk. IV, l. 108−113)

68 As when a prowling wolf,
Whom hunger drives to seek new haunt for prey,
Watching where shepherds pen their flocks at eve,
In hurdled cotes amid the field secure,
Leaps o'er the fence with ease into the fold;
Or as a thief, bent to unhoard the cash
Of some rich burgher, whose substantial doors,
Cross-barred and bolted fast, fear no assault,
In at the window climbs, or o'er the tiles;
So clomb this first grand Thief into God's fold:
So since into his Church lewd hirelings climb.
Thence up he flew, and on the Tree of Life,
The middle tree and highest there that grew,
Sat like a cormorant; yet not true life
Thereby regained, but say devising death

To them who lived; nor on the virtue thought
Of that life-giving plant, but only used
For prospect what, well used, had been the pledge
Of immortality. (Bk. IV, l. 183–201)

69 A happy rural seat of various view:
Groves whose rich trees wept odorous gums and balm;
Others whose fruit, burnished with golden rind,
Hung amiable — Hesperian fables true.
If true, here only — and of delicious taste.
Betwixt them lawns, or level downs, and flocks
Gracing the tender herb, were interposed,
Or palmy hillock; or the flowery lap
Of some irriguous valley spread her store,
Flowers of all hue, and without thorn the rose.
Another side, umbrageous grots and caves
Of cool recess, o'er which the mantling vine
Lays forth her purple grape, and gently creeps
Luxuriant: meanwhile murmuring waters fall
Down the slope hills dispersed, or in a lake,
That to the fringed bank with myrtle crowned
Her crystal mirror holds, unite their streams.
(Bk. IV, l. 247–263)

70 The birds their quire apply; airs, vernal airs,
Breathing the smell of field and grove, attune
The trembling leaves, while universal Pan,
Knit with the Graces and the Hours in dance,
Led on th' eternal Spring. (Bk. IV, l. 264–268)

71 the Fiend
Saw undelighted all delight, all kind
Of living creatures, new to sight and strange:
Two of far nobler shape, erect and tall,
God-like erect, with native honour clad
In naked majesty, seemed lords of all,
And worthy seemed; for in their looks divine
The image of their glorious Maker shone,
(Bk. IV, l. 285–292)

72 Whence true authority in men: though both
Not equal, as their sex not equal seemed;
For contemplation he and valour formed,
For softness she and sweet attractive grace;
He for God only, she for God in him.
(Bk. IV, l. 295–299)

73 She, as a veil down to the slender waist,
Her unadorned golden tresses wore
Dishevelled, but in wanton ringlets waved
As the vine curls her tendrils, which implied
Subjection, but required with gentle sway,
And by her yielded, by him best received,
Yielded with coy submission, modest pride,
And sweet, reluctant, amorous delay.
Nor those mysterious parts were then concealed:
Then was not guilty shame: dishonest Shame
Of Nature's works, Honour dishonourable.
(Bk. IV, l. 304–314)

74 Adam, the goodliest man of men since born
His sons; the fairest of her daughters Eve.
(Bk. IV, l. 323–324)

PoE

75 "My author and disposer, what thou biddest
Unargued I obey; so God ordains,
God is thy law, thou mine: to know no more
Is woman's happiest knowledge and her praise.
(Bk. IV, l. 635–638)

FaBV

76 With thee conversing I forget all time,
All seasons and their change, all please alike.
Sweet is the breath of morn, her rising sweet,
With charm of earliest birds; pleasant the sun
When first on this delightful land he spreads
His orient beams, on herb, tree, fruit, and flower,
Glistring with dew; fragrant the fertile earth
After soft showers; and sweet the coming on
Of grateful evening mild, then silent night
With this her solemn bird and this fair moon,
And these the gems of heav'n, her starry train:
But neither breath of morn when she ascends
With charm of earliest birds, nor rising sun
On this delightful land, (Bk. IV, l. 639–652)

ChTr; GEL; TrGrPo; WiR

77 Into thir inmost bower
Handed they went; and eas'd the putting off
These troublesom disguises which wee wear,
Strait side by side were laid, nor turnd I weene
Adam from his fair Spouse, nor Eve the Rites
Mysterious of connubial Love refus'd:
Whatever Hypocrites austerely talk
Of puritie and place and innocence,
Defaming as impure what God declares
Pure, and commands to som, leaves free to all.
Our Maker bids increase, who bids abstain
But our Destroyer, foe to God and Man?
(Bk. IV, l. 738–749)

FF; TOF

78 Hail wedded love, mysterious law, true source
Of human offspring, sole propriety,
In paradise of all things common else.
By thee adulterous lust was driven from men
Among the bestial herds to range, by thee
Founded in reason, loyal, just, and pure,
Relations dear, and all the charities
Of father, son, and brother first were known.
Far be it, that I should write thee sin or blame,
Of think thee unbefitting holiest place,
Perpetual fountain of domestic sweets,
Whose bed is undefiled and chaste pronounced,
Present, or past, as saints and patriarchs used.
Here love his golden shafts employs, here lights
His constant lamp, and waves his purple wings,
Reigns here and revels; not in the bought smile
Of harlots, loveless, joyless, unendeared,
Casual fruition, nor in court amours
Mixed dance, or wanton mask, or midnight ball,
Or serenade, which the starved lover sings
To his proud fair, best quitted with disdain.

These lulled by Nightingales embracing slept,
And on their naked limbs the flowery roof
Showered roses, which the morn repaired. Sleep on,
Blest pair; and O yet happiest if ye seek
No happier state, and know to know no more.
(Bk. IV, l. 750–775)

OBS; SeCePo

79 "Awake,
My fairest, my espoused, my latest found,
Heaven's last best gift, my ever new delight,
Awake, the morning shines, and the fresh field
Calls us: we lose the prime, to mark how spring
Our tended plants, how blows the citron grove,
What drops the myrrh and what the balmy reed,
How nature paints her colors, how the bee
Sits on the bloom extracting liquid sweet."
(Bk. V, l. 17–25)

80 But know that in the soul
Are many lesser faculties that serve
Reason as chief; among these fancy next
Her office holds. Of all external things.
Which the five watchful senses represent
She forms imaginations, airy shapes
Which reason, joining or disjoining, frames
All what we affirm or what deny, and call
Our knowledge or opinion; then retires
Into her private cell when nature rests
Oft in her absence mimic fancy wakes
To imitate her; but, misjoining shapes,
Wild work produces oft, and most in dreams,
Ill matching words and deeds long past or late.
(Bk. V, l. 100–113)

NAEL-1; OAEL-1

81 These are thy glorious works, parent of good,
Almighty, thine this universal frame,
Thus wondrous fair; thyself how wondrous then!
Unspeakable, who sittest above these heavens
To us invisible or dimly seen
In these thy lowest works, yet these declare
Thy goodness beyond thought, and power divine:
Speak ye who best can tell, ye sons of light,
Angels, for ye behold him, and with songs
And choral symphonies, day without night,
Circle his throne rejoicing, ye in heaven,
On earth join all ye creatures to extol
Him first, him last, him midst, and without end.
(Bk. V, l. 153–165)

82 Fountains and ye, that warble, as ye flow,
Melodious murmurs, warbling tune his praise.
Join voices all ye living souls, ye birds,
That singing up to heaven gate ascend,
Bear on your wings and in your notes his praise;
Ye that in waters glide, and ye that walk
The earth, and stately tread, or lowly creep;
Witness if I be silent, morn or even,
To hill, or valley, fountain, or fresh shade

Made vocal by my song, and taught his praise.
Hail universal Lord, be bounteous still
To give us only good; and if the night
Have gathered aught of evil or concealed,
Disperse it, as now light dispels the dark.
(Bk. V, l. 195–208)

TrPWD; WGRP

83 Descend from Heav'n Urania, by that name
If rightly thou art call'd, whose Voice divine
Following, above th' Olympian Hill I soare,
Above the flight of Pegasean wing.
The meaning, not the Name I call: for thou
Nor of the Muses nine, nor on the top
Of old Olympus dwell'st, but Heav'nlie borne,
Before the Hills appeerd, or Fountain flow'd,
Thou with Eternal wisdom didst converse,
Wisdom thy Sister, and with her didst play
In presence of th' Almightie Father, pleas'd
With thy Celestial Song. (Bk. VII, l. 1–12)

84 In darkness, and with dangers compast round,
And solitude; yet not alone, while thou
Visit'st my slumbers Nightly, or when Morn
Purples the East: still govern thou my Song,
Urania, and fit audience find, though few.
(Bk. VII, l. 27–31)

EBEV; FiP; NAEL-1; OAEL-1; OBS; TOF

85 And God said, Let the waters generate,
Reptile with spawn abundant, living soul:
And let fowl fly above the earth, with wings
Displayed on the open firmament of heaven.
And God created the great whales, and each
Soul living, each that crept, which plenteously
The waters generated by their kinds,
And every bird of wing after his kind;
And saw that it was good, and blessed them, saying,
Be fruitful, multiply, and in the seas
And lakes and running streams the waters fill;
And let the fowl be multiplied on the earth.
(Bk. VII, l. 387–398)

FM

86 The sixth, and of creation last arose
With evening harps and matin, when God said,
Let the earth bring forth soul living in her kind,
Cattle and creeping things, and beast of the earth,
Each in their kind. The earth obeyed, and straight
Opening her fertile womb teemed at a birth
Innumerous living creatures, perfect forms,
Limbed and full grown: out of the ground up rose
As from his lair the wild beast where he wons
In forest wild, in thicket, brake, or den;
Among the trees in pairs they rose, they walked:
The cattle in the fields and meadows green:
Those rare and solitary, these in flocks
Pasturing at once, and in broad herds upsprung.
The grassy clods now calved, now half appeared

The tawny lion, pawing to get free
His hinder parts, then springs as broke from bonds,
(Bk. VII, l. 449–465)

FM

87 If answerable style I can obtaine
Of my Celestial Patroness, who deignes
Her nightly visitation unimplor'd,
And dictates to me slumbring, or inspires
Easie my unpremeditated Verse: (Bk. IX, l. 20–24)

88 Mee of these
Nor skilld nor studious, higher Argument
Remaines, sufficient of it self to raise
That name, unless an age too late, or cold
Climat, or Years damp my intended wing
Deprest, and much they may, if all be mine,
Not Hers who brings it nightly to my Ear.
(Bk. IX, l. 41–47)

NAEL-1; NAWM-1; NoP; OBS; TOF

89 Them she upstays
Gently with myrtle band, mindless the while
Herself, though fairest unsupported flower,
From her best prop so far, and storm so nigh.
(Bk. IX, l. 430–433)

90 Her heavenly form
Angelic, but more soft and feminine,
Her graceful innocence, her every air
Of gesture or least action, overawed
His malice, and with rapine sweet bereaved
His fierceness of the fierce intent it brought.
That space of Evil One abstracted stood
From his own evil, and for the time remained
Stupidly good, of enmity disarmed,
(Bk. IX, l. 457–465)

91 But the hot hell that always in him burns,
Though in mid Heaven, soon ended his delight,
And tortures him now more, the more he sees
Of pleasure not for him ordained. Then soon
Fierce hate he recollects, and all his thoughts
Of mischief, gratulating, thus excites:
(Bk. IX, l. 467–472)

92 She fair, divinely fair, fit love for Gods,
Not terrible, though terror be in love,
And beauty, not approached by stronger hate,
Hate stronger under show of love well feigned —
The way which to her ruin now I tend."
(Bk. IX, l. 489–493)

93 "What may this mean? Language of Man pronounced
By tongue of brute, and human sense expressed!
The first at least of these I thought denied
To beasts, whom God on their creation-day
Created mute to all articulate sound;

The latter I demur, for in their looks
Much reason, and in their actions, oft appears.
(Bk. IX, l. 553–559)

94 For many are the trees of God that grow
In Paradise, and various, yet unknown
To us; in such abundance lies our choice
As leaves a greater store of fruit untouched,
Still hanging incorruptible, till men
Grow up to their provision, and more hands
Help to disburden Nature of her bearth."
(Bk. IX, l. 618–624)

95 Rather your dauntless virtue, whom the pain
Of death denounced, whatever thing Death be,
Deterred not from achieving what might lead
To happier life, knowledge of Good and Evil?
Of good, how just! Of evil-if what is evil
Be real, why not known, since easier shunned?
(Bk. IX, l. 694–699)

96 So saying, her rash hand in evil hour
Forth-reaching to the Fruit, she plucked, she eat.
Earth felt the wound, and Nature from her seat,
Sighing through all her works, gave signs of woe
That all was lost. (Bk. IX, l. 780–784)

OBS; TEP

97 How shall I behold the face
Henceforth of God or Angel, earst with joy
And rapture so oft beheld? those heav'nly shapes
Will dazle now this earthly, with thir blaze
Insufferably bright. O might I here
In solitude live savage, in some glade
Obscur'd, where highest Woods impenetrable
To Starr or Sun-light, spread thir umbrage broad,
And brown as Eevening: Cover me ye Pines,
Ye Cedars, with innumerable boughs
Hide me, where I may never see them more.
But let us now, as in bad plight, devise
What best may for the present serve to hide
The Parts of each from other, that seem most
To Shame obnoxious, and unseemliest seen,
Some Tree whose broad smooth Leaves together sowd,
And girded on our loins, my cover round
Those middle parts, that this new commer, Shame,
There sit not, and reproach us as unclean.
(Bk. IX, l. 1080–1098)

TOF

98 Be it so, for I submit; his doom is fair,
That dust I am and shall to dust return.
O welcome hour whenever! Why delays
His hand to execute what his decree
Fixed on this day? Why do I overlive?
Why am I mocked with death, and lengthened out
To deathless pain? How gladly would I meet
Mortality, my sentence, and be earth
Insensible! how glad would lay me down
As in my mother's lap! (Bk. X, l. 769–778)

99 Ah, why should all mankind
For one man's fault thus guiltless be condemned,
If guiltless? But from me what can proceed,
But all corrupt, both mind and will depraved,
Not to do only, but to will the same
With me? How can they then acquitted stand
In sight of God? Him, after all disputes,
Forced I absolve. All my evasions vain
And reasonings, though through mazes, lead me still
But to my own conviction: first and last
On me, me only, as the source and spring
Of all corruption, all the blame lights due;
So might the wrath! (Bk. X, l. 822–834)

100 O Conscience! into what abyss of fears
And horrors hast thou driven me; out of which
I find no way, from deep to deeper plunged!"
(Bk. X, l. 842–844)

101 "Forsake me not thus, Adam! witness Heaven
What love sincere and reverence in my heart
I bear thee, and unweeting have offended,
Unhappily deceived! Thy suppliant
I beg, and clasp thy knees; beereave me not,
Whereon I live, thy gentle looks, thy aid,
Thy counsel in this uttermost distress,
My only strength and stay: forlorn of thee,
Whither shall I betake me, where subsist?
(Bk. X, l. 914–922)

102 Thy hatred for this misery befallen;
On me already lost, me than thyself
More miserable. Both have sinned, but thou
Against God only; I against God and thee,
And to the place of judgment will return,
There with my cries importune Heaven, that all
The sentence, from thy head removed, may light
On me, sole cause to thee of all this woe,
Me, me only, just object of his ire."
(Bk. X, l. 928–936)

103 So spake our Father penitent; nor Eve
Felt less remorse. They, forthwith to the place
Repairing where he judged them, prostrate fell
Before him reverent, and both confessed
Humbly their faults, and pardon begged, with tears
Watering the ground, and with their sighs the air
Frequenting, sent from hearts contrite, in sign
Of sorrow unfeigned and humiliation meek.
(Bk. X, l. 1097–1104)

NAWM-1

104 God from the mount of Sinai, whose grey top
Shall tremble, he descending, will himself
In thunder lightning and loud trumpets' sound
Ordain them laws; part such as appertain
To civil justice, part religious rites
Of sacrifice, informing them, by types
And shadows, of that destined seed to bruise
The serpent, by what means he shall achieve
Mankind's deliverance. (Bk. XII, l. 227–235)

FaBoPV

105 He ended; and thus Adam last replied:
"How soon hath thy prediction, seer blest,
Measured this transient world, the race of time,
Till time stand fixed! Beyond is all abyss,
Eternity, whose end no eye can reach.
Greatly instructed I shall hence depart,
Greatly in peace of thought, and have my fill
Of knowledge, what this vessel can contain,
Beyond which was my folly to aspire.
Henceforth I learn that to obey is best,
And love with fear the only God, to walk
As in his presence, ever to observe
His providence, and on him sole depend,
(Bk. XII, l. 552–563)

106 Only add
Deeds to thy knowledge answerable; add faith;
Add virtue, patience, temperance; add love,
By name to come called charity, the soul
Of all the rest: then wilt thou not be loath
To leave this Paradise; but shalt possess
A paradise within thee, happier far.
(Bk. XII, l. 581–587)

HeIP; PoEL-3

107 'Whence thou return'st, and whither wentst, I know;
For God is also in sleep; and dreams advise,
Which he hath sent propitious, some great good
Presaging, since, with sorrow and heart's distress,
Wearied I fell asleep: but now lead on;
In me is no delay; without thee here to stay,
Is to go hence unwilling; thou to me
Art all things under Heaven, all places thou,
(Bk. XII, l. 610–617)

108 Some natural tears they dropped, but wiped them soon;
The world was all before them, where to choose
Their place of rest, and Providence their guide;
They, hand in hand, with wandering steps and slow
Through Eden took their solitary way.
(Bk. XII, l. 645–649)

NOCV

Paradise Regained

109 To whom thus Jesus temperately reply'd:
Said'st thou not that to all things I had right?
And who withholds my pow'r that right to use?
Shall I receive by gift what of my own,
When and where likes me best, I can command?
I can at will, doubt not, as soon as thou,
Command a Table in this Wilderness,
And call swift flights of Angels ministrant
Array'd in Glory on my cup to attend:
Why shouldst thou then obtrude this diligence,
In vain, where no acceptance it can find,
And with my hunger what hast thou to do?
(II, l. 378–389)

EBEV

Samson Agonistes

110 But who is this, what thing of sea or land?
Female of sex it seems,
That so bedecked, ornate, and gay,
Comes this way sailing
Like a stately ship
Of Tarsus, bound for the isles
Of Javan or Gadier
With all her bravery on, and tackle trim,
Sails filled, and streamers waving, (l. 710–718)

OAEL-1; PoEL-3; SeCePo

111 Let me obtain forgiveness of thee, Samson,
Afford me place to shew what recompence
Towards thee I intend for what I have misdone,
Misguided; only what remains past cure
Bear not too sensibly, nor still insist
To afflict thy self in vain: though sight be lost,
Life yet hath many solaces, enjoy'd
Where other senses want not their delights
At home in leisure and domestic ease, (l. 909–917)

112 Let me approach at least, and touch thy hand.
[Samson:] Not for thy life, lest fierce remembrance wake
My sudden rage to tear thee joint by joint.
At distance I forgive thee, go with that;
Bewail thy falsehood, and the pious works
It hath brought forth to make thee memorable
Among illustrious women, faithful wives:
Cherish thy hast'n'd widowhood with the gold
Of Matrimonial treason: so farewel. (l. 951–959)

EBEV; OAEL-1; PoEL-3

113 He all their ammunition
And feats of war defeats
With plain heroic magnitude of mind
And celestial vigour armed; (l. 1277–1280)

114 Between the pillars he his guide requested
(For so from such as nearer stood we heard)
As over-tir'd to let him lean a while
With both his arms on those two massie Pillars
That to the arched roof gave main support.
He unsuspitious led him; which when Samson
Felt in his arms, with head a while enclin'd,
And eyes fast fixt he stood, as one who pray'd,
Or some great matter in his mind revolv'd.
(l. 1630–1638)

115 O dearly-bought revenge, yet glorious!
Living or dying thou hast fulfill'd
The work for which thou wast foretold
To Israel, and now ly'st victorious
Among thy slain self-kill'd
Not willingly, but tangl'd in the fold
Of dire necessity (l. 1660–1666)

116 But he though blind of sight,
Despis'd and thought extinguish't quite,
With inward eyes illuminated
His fierie vertue rouz'd
From under ashes into sudden flame,
And as an ev'ning Dragon came, (l. 1687–1692)

117 but as an Eagle
His cloudless thunderbolted on thir heads.
So vertue giv'n for lost,
Deprest, and overthrown, as seem'd,
Like that self-begott'n bird
In the Arabian woods embost,
That no second knows nor third,
And lay e're while a Holocaust,
From out her ashie womb now teem'd
Revives, reflourishes, then vigorous most
When most unactive deem'd,
And though her body die, her fame survives,
A secular bird ages of lives. (l. 1695–1707)

118 All is best, though we oft doubt,
What th' unsearchable dispose
Of highest wisdom brings about,
And ever best found in the close.
Oft he seems to hide his face,
But unexpectedly returns
And to his faithful Champion hath in place
Bore witness gloriously; whence Gaza mourns
And all that band them to resist
His uncontroulable intent,
His servants he with new acquist
Of true experience from this great event
With peace and consolation hath dismist,
And calm of mind all passion spent. (l. 1745–1758)

EBEV; OAEL-1; PoEL-3

Song on May Morning

119 Hail, bounteous May, that does inspire
Mirth and youth and warm desire!
Woods and groves are of thy dressing,
Hill and dale doth boast thy blessing.
Thus we salute thee with our early song,
And welcome thee, and wish thee long. (l. 5–10)

BoNaP; CH; GN; TrGrPo

To Cyriack Skinner

120 To measure life learn thou betimes, and know
Toward solid good what leads the nearest way;
For other things mild Heaven a time ordains,

And disapproves that care, though wise in show,
That with superfluous burden loads the day,
And, when God sends a cheerful hour, refrains.
(l. 9–14)

GTBS; GTBS-P; NoP; OBEV; OBS; Son

To Mr. Lawrence

121 What neat repast shall feast us, light and choice,
Of Attick tast, with Wine, whence we may rise
To hear the Lute well toucht, or artfull voice
Warble immortal Notes and Tuskan Ayre?
He who of those delights can judge, and spare
To interpose them oft, is not unwise. (l. 9–14)

AWP; GTBS; GTBS-P; OBEV; OBS; PoE

To the Lady Margaret Ley

122 Daughter to that good Earl, once President
Of England's Council and her Treasury,
Who lived in both, unstain'd with gold or fee,
And left them both, more in himself content.

Till the sad breaking of that Parliament
Broke him, as that dishonest victory
At Chaeronea, fatal to liberty,
Kill'd with report that old man eloquent; — (l. 1–8)

GTBS; GTBS-P; OBEV; OBS

To the Lord General Cromwell

123 peace hath her victories
No less renowned than war; new foes arise,
Threatening to bind our souls with secular chains:
Help us to save free conscience from the paw
Of hireling wolves whose gospel is their maw.
(l. 10–14)

FaBoPV; NAEL-1; NoP; OBS; Son; TrGrPo

When I Consider How My Light Is Spent

124 When I consider how my light is spent,
Ere half my days, in this dark world and wide,
And that one talent which is death to hide
Lodged with me useless, though my soul more bent
To serve therewith my Maker, and present
My true account, lest he returning chide,
"Doth God exact day labor, light denied?"
I fondly ask; by Patience, to prevent
That murmur, soon replies: "God doth not need
Either man's work or his own gifts; who best
Bear his mild yoke, they serve him best. His state
Is kingly: thousands at his bidding speed
And post o'er land and ocean without rest.
They also serve who only stand and wait." (l. 1–14)

AWP; ChTr; FaBV; FiP; FPL; GN; GTBS; HAP; HeIP;
InPK; LiTB; NAEL-1; NOBE; OBEV; PoE; PoEL-3;
PoLF; PoRA; PrIm; SoSe; TrGrPo; WeW

When the Assault Was Intended to the City

125 Lift not thy spear against the Muses' bower:
The great Emathian conqueror bid spare
The house of Pindarus, when temple and tower

Went to the ground; and the repeated air
Of sad Electra's poet had the power
To save the Athenian walls from ruin bare. (l. 9–14)

GTBS; GTBS-P; NoP; OAEL-1; Son

N. SCOTT MOMADAY (b. 1934)

Angle of Geese

1 How shall we adorn
Recognition with our speech? — (l. 1–2)

2 So much symmetry!
Like the pale angle of time
And eternity.
The great shape labored and fell. (l. 17–20)

CDW; HATNAP; NOVW; QFR

The Delight Song of Tsoai-Talee

3 I am a feather on the bright sky
I am the blue horse that runs in the plain
I am the fish that rolls, shining, in the water (l. 1–3)

4 You see, I am alive, I am alive
I stand in good relation to the earth
I stand in good relation to the gods
I stand in good relation to all that is beautiful
I stand in good relation to the daughter of Tsen-tainte
You see, I am alive, I am alive (l. 19–24)

CDW; GrPl; InPK; STE

Earth and I Gave You Turquoise

5 Earth and I gave you turquoise
when you walked singing
We lived laughing in my house
and told old stories (l. 1–4)

6 I saw a crow by Red Rock
standing on one leg
It was the black of your hair
The years are heavy (l. 25–28)

CDW; HATNAP; NOVW; UnPo

COSMO MONKHOUSE (1840–1901)

There Was a Young Lady of Niger (attributed to Monkhouse)

1 There was a young lady of Niger
Who smiled as she rode on a Tiger;
They came back from the ride

With the lady inside,
And the smile on the face of the Tiger. (l. 1–5)

FaFP; FaPON; InvP; NA; NBLV; PDV

HAROLD MONRO (1879–1932)

Milk for the Cat

1 When the tea is brought at five o'clock,
And all the neat curtains are drawn with care,
The little black cat with bright green eyes
Is suddenly purring there. (l. 1–4)

2 But the cat is grown small and thin with desire,
Transformed to a creeping lust for milk. (l. 19–20)

BoTP; FaBoBe; FaFP; MoBrPo; OBMV

JOHN MONTAGUE (b. 1929)

All Legendary Obstacles

1 All legendary obstacles lay between
Us, the long imaginary plain,
The monstrous ruck of mountains (l. 1–3)

2 You had been travelling for days
With an old lady, who marked
A neat circle on the glass
With her glove, to watch us
Move into the wet darkness
Kissing, still unable to speak. (l. 19–24)

BIrV; CIP; FaBCIP; IPY; NOIV

The Wild Dog Rose

3 The only true madness is loneliness,
the monotonous voice in the skull
that never stops
because never heard. (l. 45–48)

4 And still
the dog rose shines in the hedge. (l. 81–82)

5 its crumbled yellow cup
and pale bleeding lips
fading to white
at the rim
of each bruised and heart-
shaped petal. (l. 99–104)

BIrV; CIP; IPY; PoE

ALEXANDER MONTGOMERIE
(1540?–1610?)

The Night Is Near Gone

1 Hay! now the day dawis;
The jolie Cok crawis;
Now shroudis the shawis,
Throw Natur anone.
The thissell-cok cryis
On lovers wha lyis.
Now skaillis the skyis:
The nicht is neir gone. (l. 1–8)

CH; GoTS; OBEV; OxBS

JAMES GRAHAM, MARQUESS OF
MONTROSE (1612–1650)

His Metrical Vow

1 But since Thy loud-tongu'd Blood demands Supplies,
More from BriareusHands, than Argus Eyes,
I'll tune Thy Elegies to Trumpet-sounds,
And write Thy Epitaph in Blood and Wounds! (l. 5–8)

GoTS; NOEE OBS; OxBS

Montrose to His Mistress

2 My dear and only Love, I pray
That little world of thee
Be govern'd by no other sway
Than purest monarchy;
For if confusion have a part
(Which virtuous souls abhor),
And hold a synod in thine heart,
I'll never love thee more. (l. 1–8)

3 I'll make thee glorious by my pen
And famous by my sword;
I'll serve thee in such noble ways
Was never heard before;
I'll crown and deck thee all with bays,
And love thee more and more. (l. 25–32)

GBL; JCP; NOBE; OBEV; OBS; OxBS

On Himself, upon Hearing What Was His Sentence

4 Scatter my ashes, strew them in the air:
Lord since thou know'st where all these atoms are,
I'm hopeful thou'lt recover once my dust,
And confident thou'lt raise me with the just. (l. 5–8)

ChTr; FaBoEE; OBS; OxBS; PrIm; SeCePo

PERCY MONTROSS

Oh, My Darling Clementine (*attributed to* Montross)

1 In a cavern, in a canyon,
  Excavating for a mine,
  Dwelt a miner, 'Forty-Niner,
  And his daughter Clementine. (l. 1–4)

2 Light she was and like a fairy,
  And her shoes were number nine; (l. 5–6)

3 Drove she ducklings to the water,
  Every morning just at nine; (l. 9–10)

AmFP; AnAmPo; FaBoBe; FaFP; OBAL

CLEMENT CLARKE MOORE (1779–1863)

A Visit from St. Nicholas

1 'Twas the night before Christmas, when all through the
    house
  Not a creature was stirring, not even a mouse.
  The stockings were hung by the chimney with care,
  In hopes that St. Nicholas soon would be there;
  The children were nestled all snug in their beds,
  While visions of sugarplums danced in their heads;
                                    (l. 1–6)

2 More rapid than eagles his coursers they came,
  And he whistled, and shouted, and called them by
    name:
  "Now, Dasher! now, Dancer! now, Prancer and Vixen!
  On, Comet! on, Cupid! on, Donder and Blitzen!
  To the top of the porch! to the top of the wall!
  Now dash away! dash away! dash away all!"
                                    (l. 19–24)

3 Down the chimney St. Nicholas came with a bound.
  He was dressed all in fur, from his head to his foot,
  And his clothes were all tarnished with ashes and soot;
                                    (l. 32–34)

4 He had a broad face and a little round belly,
  That shook, when he laughed, like a bowlful of jelly.
  He was chubby and plump, a right jolly old elf,
                                    (l. 43–45)

5 giving a nod, up the chimney he rose.
  He sprang to his sleigh, to his team gave a whistle,
  And away they all flew like the down of a thistle,
  But I heard him exclaim, ere he drove out of sight,
  " Happy Christmas to all, and to all a good-night."

AA; AiP; AnAmPo; BeLS; BLPA; FaBoBe; FaBV; FaFP;
FaPON; FPL; NTCP; OBAL; OBCA; OBCP; OHIP;
OnMSP; OxBChV; PChr; PWR; RHPC; WBLP

MARIANNE MOORE (1887–1972)

A Carriage from Sweden

1 At all events there is in Brooklyn
  something that makes me feel at home. (l. 4–5)

2 swirling crustacean-
  tailed equine amphibious creatures
  that garnish the axle-tree! What

  a fine thing! What unannoying
  romance! (l. 18–22)

3 The deft white-stockinged dance in thick-soled
  shoes! Denmark's sanctuaried Jews! (l. 34–35)

4 Sweden,
  what makes the people dress that way
  and those who see you wish to stay? (l. 46–48)

HAP; LiTA; LiTM; MoAB; TwCP; WeW

Critics and Connoisseurs

5 There is a great amount of poetry in unconscious
  fastidiousness. (l. 1–2)

6 I have seen this swan and
  I have seen you; I have seen ambition without
  understanding in a variety of forms. (l. 19–21)

7 What is
  there in being able
  to say that one has dominated the stream in an attitude
    of self-defense;

  in proving that one has had the experience
  of carrying a stick? (l. 31–35)

AmPP; CMoP; FaBoWP; NoAM; NOBA; OxBA

England

8 the
  criterion of suitability and convenience: (l. 3–4)

9 the East with its snails, its emotional

  shorthand and jade cockroaches, its rock crystal and its
  imperturbability,
  all of museum quality:

10 Does it follow that because there are poisonous
    toadstools
  which resemble mushrooms, both are dangerous?
                                    (l. 28–29)

LiTA; MoAB; MoAmPo

The Fish

11 Of the crow-blue mussel shells, one keeps
adjusting the ash heaps;
opening and shutting itself like

an
injured fan. (l. 3–7)

AmPP; FaBoWP; MoAB; MoAmPo; MoP; MOS; NAAL-2;
NoAM; OxBA

A Grave

12 repression, however, is not the most obvious
characteristic of the sea;
the sea is a collector, quick to return a rapacious look.
(l. 9–10)

13 the ocean, under the pulsation of lighthouses and noise
of bell buoys,
advances as usual, looking as if it were not that ocean
in which dropped things are bound to sink —
in which if they turn and twist, it is neither with
volition nor consciousness. (l. 23–26)

CMoP; FaBoWP; HAP; HeIP; LiTA; MoP; MOS; NAAL-2;
NoAM; NOBA; PoE; TAP; UnPo; WeW; WPE

I May, I Might, I Must

14 tell my why the fen
appears impassable, (l. 1–2)

FaBoWP; FF; OBAL; OxBSP

In Distrust of Merits

15 Hate-hardened heart, O heart of iron,
iron is iron till it is rust.
There never was a war that was
not inward; I must
fight till I have conquered in myself what
causes war, but I would not believe it. (l. 71–76)

16 Beauty is everlasting
and dust is for a time. (l. 79–80)

EaLo; LiTA; LiTM; MoAB; MoAmPo; NAAL-2; OBWP;
OxBA; TrGrPo; WaaP; WaP

The Mind Is an Enchanting Thing

17 is an enchanted thing
like the glaze on a
katydid-wing (l. 1–3)

18 it is a power of
strong enchantment. It
is like the dove-
neck animated by
sun; it is memory's eye;
it's conscientious inconsistency. (l. 19–24)

CMoP; HeIP; InPK; InvP; MoAB; MoAmPo; NAAL-2;
OxBA; PoE; PPP; WPOW

The Monkeys

19 The monkeys winked too much and were afraid of
snakes. The zebras, supreme in their abnormality; the
elephants with their fog-colored skin
and strictly practical appendages (l. 1–3)

CMoP; LiTA; NOBA; OxBA

Nevertheless

20 Victory won't come

to me unless I go
to it; a grape tendril
ties a knot in knots till

knotted thirty times, — (l. 21–25)

21 What is there

like fortitude! What sap
went through that little thread
to make the cherry red! (l. 30–33)

CMoP; MoAB; NAAL-2; OxBA; SoSe

The Pangolin

22 Another armored animal — scale
lapping scale with spruce-cone regularity until they
form the uninterrupted central
tail-row! (l. 1–4)

23 Sun and moon and day and night and man and beast
each with a splendor
which man in all his vileness cannot
set aside; each with an excellence! (l. 31–34)

24 this ant-and stone-swallowing uninjurable
artichoke which simpletons thought a living fable
whom the stones had nourished, whereas ants had done
so. (l. 49–52)

25 Bedizened or stark
naked, man, the self, the being we call human, writing-
master to this world, griffons a dark
"Like does not like like that is obnoxious"; (l. 78–81)

26 Unignorant,
modest and unemotional, and all emotion,
he has everlasting vigor,
power to grow,
though there are few creatures who can make one
breathe faster and make one erecter. (l. 83–88)

HAP; NoAM; NOBA; PBWP

Part of a Novel, Part of a Poem, Part of a Play

27 We do not like some things, and the hero
doesn't; deviating head-stones
and uncertainty;
going where one does not wish
to go; suffering and not
saying so; (l. 10–15)

28 He's not out
seeing a sight but the rock
crystal thing to see — the startling El Greco
brimming with inner light — that
covets nothing that it has let go. This then you may
   know
as the hero. (l. 49–54)

CMoP; NOBA; OxBA; PoA

29 Durer would have seen a reason for living
in a town like this, with eight stranded whales
to look at; (l. 1–3)

BoWoP; CMoP; FaBoMo; FaBoWP; HAP; InPS; NoAM;
NOBA; NoP; OxBA; PBWP; WeW; WPE

Peter

30 the small tuft of fronds or katydid legs above each eye,
   still numbering the units in each group;
the shadbones regularly set about the mouth, to droop
   or rise   (l. 3–4)

CMoP; NAAL-2; NoP; OxBA

Poetry

31 I, too, dislike it: there are things that are important
   beyond all this fiddle. (l. 1)

32 the immovable critic twitching his skin like a horse
   that feels a flea, (l. 13)

33 nor till the poets among us can be
literalists of
the imagination — above
insolence and triviality and can present

for inspection, 'imaginary gardens with real toads in
   them', shall we have (l. 20–24)

34 the raw material of poetry in
all its rawness and
that which is on the other hand
genuine, you are interested in poetry. (l. 25–28)

AmPP; BLPL; BoWoP; CMoP; FaBoWP; FF; HAP; HeIP;
LiTA; LiTM; MoAB; MoAmPo; MoP; NAAL-2; NIP;
NoAM; NOBA; NoP; OxBA; PoE; TAP; UnPo

Spenser's Ireland

35 a place as kind as it is green,
the greenest place I've never seen.
Every name is a tune. (l. 2–4)

36 Hindered characters
seldom have mothers
in Irish stories, but they all have grandmothers.
(l. 20–22)

37 Concurring hands divide

flax for damask
that when bleached by Irish weather
has the silvered chamois-leather
water-tightness of a
skin. (l. 34–39)

38 The Irish say your trouble is their
trouble and your
joy their joy? I wish
I could believe it;
I am troubled, I'm dissatisfied, I'm Irish. (l. 52–56)

FaBoWP; LiTA; LiTM; NoAM; NOBA; OxBA; TAP

To a Snail

39 If "compression is the first grace of style,"
you have it. (l. 1–2)

40 in the absence of feet, "a method of conclusions";
"a knowledge of principles,"
in the curious phenomenon of your occipital horn.
(l. 10–12)

CMoP; FaBoMo; FaBoWP; NAAL-2

To a Steam Roller

41 As for butterflies, I can hardly conceive
of one's attending upon you; but to question
the congruence of the complement is vain, if it exists.
(l. 11–13)

BoWoP; CMoP; FaBoMo; MoAB; MoAmPo; OxBA; VGW

What Are Years?

42 What is our innocence,
what is our guilt? All are
naked, none is safe. (l. 1–3)

43 Though he is captive,
his mighty singing
says, satisfaction is a lowly
thing, how pure a thing is joy.
This is mortality,
this is eternity. (l. 22–27)

BLPL; CMoP; EaLo; LiTA; MoAB; MoAmPo; MoP;
NoAM; NOBA; OxBA; TrGrPo

THOMAS MOORE (1779–1852)

At the Mid Hour of Night

1 At the mid hour of night, when stars are weeping, I fly
To the lone vale we loved when life was warm in thine
eye, (l. 1–2)

GTBS; GTBS-P; NOBE; OBEV; OBNC; PoEL-4

Believe Me, If All Those Endearing Young Charms

2 Believe me, if all those endearing young charms,
Which I gaze on so fondly today,
Were to change by tomorrow, and fleet in my arms,
Like fairy-gifts fading away.

3 No, the heart that has truly loved never forgets,
But as truly loves on to the close,
As the sunflower turns on her god, when he sets,
The same look which she turned when he rose.
(l. 13–16)

BLPA; ELP; EnRP; FaBoBe; FaBV; FaFP; FPL; LiTB;
NAEL-2; OBNC; PoEL-4; TEP; WBLP

Come Rest in This Bosom

4 Come rest in this bosom, my own stricken deer,
Though the herd hath fled from thee, thy love is still
here. (l. 1–2)

The Harp That Once through Tara's Halls

5 The harp that once through Tara's halls
The soul of music shed,
Now hangs as mute on Tara's walls
As if that soul were fled. (l. 1–4)

6 And hearts that once beat high for praise
Now feel that pulse no more! (l. 7–8)

ACP; AmIL; BLPL; EnRP; FaPoR; GN; NAEL-2; OBNC;
PoLF

The Meeting of the Waters

7 There is not in the wide world a valley so sweet
As that vale in whose bosom the bright waters meet;
(l. 1–2)

8 'Twas that friends, the belov'd of my bosom, were near,
Who made every dear scene of enchantment more dear,
(l. 9–10)

AnIL; NOIV; OxBoLi; PoEL-4

The Minstrel Boy

9 The Minstrel Boy to the war is gone
In the ranks of death you'll find him,
His father's sword he has girded on,
And his wild harp slung behind him. (l. 1–4)

ACP; AnIL; FaBoBe; FaFP; GN; PrIm

Oft, in the Stilly Night

10 Oft in the stilly night,
Ere slumber's chain has bound me,
Fond Memory brings the light
Of other days around me: (l. 1–4)

EnRP; FaBoBe; FaFP; GTBS; GTBS-P; LiTB; NOBE;
OBEV; OBNC; PoEL-4; Prf

Oh! Breathe Not His Name

11 Oh! breathe not his name, let it sleep in the shade,
Where cold and unhonour'd his relics are laid. (l. 1–2)

Pro Patria Mori

12 When he who adores thee has left but the name
Of his fault and his sorrows behind,
O! say wilt thou weep, when they darken the fame
Of a life that for thee was resign'd! (l. 1–4)

GTBS; GTBS-P; HoPM

Rich and Rare Were the Gems She Wore

13 Rich and rare were the gems she wore,
And a bright gold ring on her hand she bore. (l. 1–2)

'Tis the Last Rose of Summer

14 'Tis the last rose of summer
Left blooming alone;
All her lovely companions
Are faded and gone; (l. 1–4)

BLPA; BoNaP; ELP; FaBoBe; FaFP; FPL; NOIV;
OxBoLi; PoEL-4; WBLP

THOMAS OSBERT MORDAUNT
(1730–1809)

Verses Written during the War, 1756–1763
(*attributed to* Mordaunt)

1 Sound, sound the clarion, fill the fife!
Throughout the sensual world proclaim,
One crowded hour of glorious life
Is worth an age without a name. (l. 1–4)

EBEV; FaBoEE; FaPoR; NOBE; NOEC; OBEV; TrGrPo

SIR THOMAS MORE (SAINT THOMAS MORE)   (1478–1535)

A Rueful Lamentation on the Death of Queen Elizabeth

1 O Ye that put your trust and confidence
In worldly joy and frail prosperity,
That so live here as ye should never hence,
Remember death and look here upon me.

2 Was I not born of old worthy lineage?
Was not my mother queen, my father king?
Was I not a king's fere in marriage?
Had I not plenty of every pleasant thing?

3 If worship have kept me, I had not gone.
If wit might have me saved, I needed not fear.

4 Where are our castles now, where are our towers?

AAS; FaBoRV; LiTB; OBSC

ROBERT MORGAN   (b. 1944)

Mountain Bride

1 Under that wide hearth
a nest of rattlers,
they'll knot a hundred together,

had wintered and were coming awake.
The warming rock
flushed them out early. (l. 14–19)

GeTw; MAYP; MOWH; MT

WILLIAM MORRIS   (1834–1896)

The Earthly Paradise

1 Of Heaven of Hell I have no power to sing,
I cannot ease the burden of your fears,
Or make quick-coming death a little thing,
Or bring again the pleasure of past years, (l. 1–4)

2 Nor for my words shall ye forget your tears,
Or hope again for aught that I can say,
The idle singer of an empty day. (l. 5–7)

3 Dreamer of dreams,born out of my due time,
Why should I strive to set the crooked straight?
Let it suffice me that my murmuring rhyme
Beats with light wing against the ivory gate,
(l. 22–25)

AWP; EBVV; LiTB; NAEL-2; NoP; OAEL-2; OBNC;
OPOP

The Haystack in the Floods

4 Had she come all the way for this,
To part at last without a kiss?
Yea, had she borne the dirt and rain
That her own eyes might see him slain
Beside the haystack in the floods? (l. 1–5)

BeLS; EBEV; EBVV; HAP; NAEL-2; NoP; OAEL-2;
OBNC; OBNV; PoEL-5; PoRA; WeW

Inscription for an Old Bed

5 The wind's on the wold
And the night is a-cold,
And Thames runs chill
'Twixt mead and hill.
But kind and dear
Is the old house here
And my heart is warm
Midst winter's harm. (l. 1–8)

CH; FaBoRV; OBEV; PoEL-5; WiR

The Life and Death of Jason

6 I know a little garden-close
Set thick with lily and red rose,
Where I would wander if I might
From dewy dawn to dewy night,

CH; NOBE; OAEL-2; OBEV; OBNC; PoEL-5

Summer Dawn

7 Pray but one prayer for me 'twixt thy closed lips,
Think but one thought of me up in the stars. (l. 1—2)

Mes; NOBE; NOBVV; OAEL-2; OBEV; OBNC

HOWARD MOSS (b. 1922)

Elegy for My Father

1 Father, whom I murdered every night but one,
That one, when your death murdered me, (l. 1—2)

2 Two months dead, I wrestle with your name
Whose separate letters make a paltry sum
That is not you. (l. 25—27)

3 When in the sea-light every early game
Was played with love and, if death's waters came,
You'd rescue me. How I would take you from,
Now, if I could, its whirling vacuum. (l. 29—32)

CoAP; DiL; LiTM; NePoEA; VWA

Water Island

4 The senseless drowned
Have faces nobody would care to see,
But water loves those gradual erasures
Of flesh and shoreline, greenery and glass, (l. 4—7)

5 Grown onto every inch of plate, except
Where the hinges let it move, were living things,
Barnacles, mussels, water weeds — and one
Blue bit of polished glass, glued there by time:
The origins of art. (l. 16—20)

6 Wild roses, at your back porch, break their blood,
And bud to test surprises of sea air, (l. 29—30)

CoAP; NePoEA-2; NYBP; Prf

MOTHER GOOSE (*fl.* 17th—18th century)

A frog he would a-wooing go

1 A frog he would a-wooing go,
Heigh ho! says Rowley,
Whether his mother would let him or no.
With a rowley, powley, gammon and spinach,
Heigh ho! says Anthony Rowley. (l. 1—5)

OxNR

Hey, diddle, diddle

2 Hey, diddle, diddle,
The cat and the fiddle,
The cow jumped over the moon;
The little dog laughed
To see such sport,
And the dish ran away with the spoon. (l. 1—6)

FaBoBe; FaF?; HoPM; OxBoLi; OxNR

The House That Jack Built

3 This is the house that Jack built.

This is the malt
That lay in the house that Jack built. (l. 1—3)

4 This is the rat
That ate the malt
That lay in the house that Jack built. (l. 4—6)

5 This is the cat
That killed the rat (l. 7—8)

6 This is the dog
That worried the cat (l. 11—12)

7 This is the cow with the crumpled horn
That tossed the dog (l. 16—17)

8 This is the maiden all forlorn
That milked the cow with the crumpled horn
(l. 22—23)

9 That is the man all tattered and torn
That kissed the maiden all forlorn (l. 29—30)

10 This is the priest all shaven and shorn
That married the man all tattered and torn (l. 37—38)

11 This is the cock that crowed in the morn
That waked the priest all shaven and shorn (l. 46—47)

BoTP; FaBoBe; OxBoLi; OxNR

How many miles to Babylon ?

12 How many miles to Babylon?
Three score and ten.
Can I get there by candlelight?
Yes, and back again. (l. 1—4)

BoTP; FaBoCh; GBP; MoShBr; OxBoLi; OxBSP; OxNR

I had a little nut-tree, nothing would it bear

13 I had a little nut-tree, nothing would it bear
But a golden nutmeg and a silver pear; (l. 1—2)

BoTP; CH; GBP; MoShBr; OxBoLi; OxNR

I saw a ship a-sailing

14 I saw a ship a-sailing,
A-sailing on the sea, (l. 1–2)

15 The captain was a duck
With a packet on his back,
And when the ship began to move
The captain said, Quack! Quack! (l. 13–16)

FaBoBe; MoShBr; NTCP; OxNR

In marble walls as white as milk (Riddle: An Egg)

16 In marble halls as white as milk,
Lined with a skin as soft as silk,
Within a fountain crystal-clear,
A golden apple doth appear.
No doors there are to this stronghold,
Yet thieves break in and steal the gold. (l. 1–6)

ChTr; GBP; OxNR; TSS

Jack and Jill

17 Jack and Jill
Went up the hill,
To fetch a pail of water;
Jack fell down,
And broke his crown,
And Jill came tumbling after. (l. 1–6)

FaBoBe; FaFP; OxBoLi; OxNR

Little Boy Blue

18 Little Boy Blue,
Come blow your horn, (l. 1–2)

19 He's under a haycock
Fast asleep.
Will you wake him?
No, not I,
For if I do,
He's sure to cry. (l. 7–12)

BoTP; FaBoBe; FaFP; OxNR

Little Jack Horner

20 Little Jack Horner
Sat in the corner,
Eating a Christmas pie;
He put in his thumb,
And pulled out a plum,
And said, What a good boy am I! (l. 1–6)

FaBoBe; FaFP; OxNR; SoSe

The man in the wilderness

21 The man in the wilderness said to me,
How many strawberries grow in the sea?
I answered him as I thought good,
As many red herrings as grow in the wood. (l. 1–4)

BoTP; FaBoCh; FaBoCo; FaBoNo; GBP; NA; OxNR

Monday's child is fair of face

22 Monday's child is fair of face,
Tuesday's child is full of grace,
Wednesday's child is full of woe,
Thursday's child has far to go,
Friday's child is loving and giving,
Saturday's child works for its living,
And a child that's born on the Sabbath day
Is fair and wise and good and gay. (l. 1–8)

BLPA; BLPL; BoTP; FaBoBe; FaBoCh; MoShBr; NBLV;
OxNR; PYC

Peter Piper picked a peck of pickled peppers

23 Peter Piper picked a peck of pickled pepper;
A peck of pickled pepper Peter Piper picked.
If Peter Piper picked a peck of pickled pepper,
Where's the peck of pickled pepper Peter Piper picked?
(l. 1–4)

FaBoBe; FaFP; FaPON; OxNR

Pussy Cat, Pussy Cat, where have you been?

24 Pussy-cat, pussy-cat, where have you been?
I've been to London to look at the Queen.
Pussy-cat, pussy-cat, what did you there?
I frightened a little mouse under the chair. (l. 1–4)

BoTP; FaBoBe; FaFP; OxNR

Ride a cock-horse to Banbury Cross

25 Ride a cock-horse to Banbury-Cross,
To see an old woman get up on her horse.
Rings on her fingers, and bells on her toes,
And so she makes music wherever she goes. (l. 1–4)

BoTP; FaBoBe; FaFP; OxBoLi; OxNR

Solomon Grundy

26 Solomon Grundy,
Born on a Monday,
Christened on Tuesday,
Married on Wednesday,

Took ill on Thursday,
Worse on Friday,
Died on Saturday,
Buried on Sunday,
This is the end
Of Solomon Grundy.

NBLV; OxBoLi; OxNR; RHPC

There was a crooked man, and he went a crooked mile

27 There was a crooked man, and he went a crooked mile,
He found a crooked sixpence against a crooked stile:
He bought a crooked cat which caught a crooked
mouse,
And they all lived together in a little crooked house.
(l. 1–4)

BoTP; FaBoBe; FaFP; OxBoLi; OxNR; PYC

There Was a Little Girl (attributed to Mother Goose)

28 There was a little girl, she had a little curl
Right in the middle of her forehead;
And when she was good, she was very, very good,
And when she was bad, she was horrid. (l. 1–4)

BLPA; FaBoCh; FaFP; NA; OxBChV; OxNR; RHPC

There was an old woman, as I've heard tell

29 "Lawk a mercy on me,
This is none of I!

"But if this be I,
As I do hope it be,
I have a little dog at home
And he knows me; (l. 23–28)

InvP; MoShBr; OnMSP; OxNR

There was an old woman who lived in a shoe

30 There was an old woman and she lived in a shoe,
She had so many children, she didn't know what to do.
She crumm'd 'em some porridge without any bread
And she borrowed a beetle, and she knocked 'em all on
the head.
Then out went the old woman to bespeak 'em a coffin
And when she came back she found 'em all a-loffing.
(l. 1–6)

FaBoBe; FaFP; OxBoLi; OxNR

Three wise men of Gotham

31 Three wise men of Gotham
Went to sea in a bowl;

If the bowl had been stronger,
My story would have been longer. (l. 1–4)

FaBoBe; FaBoNo; FaFP; OxNR

Who killed Cock Robin?

32 Who killed Cock Robin?
I, said the sparrow,
With my bow and arrow,
I killed Cock Robin. (l. 1–4)

33 Who'll be chief mourner?
I, said the dove,
I'll mourn for my love,
I'll be chief mourner. (l. 33–36)

AmFP; OxEoLi; OxNR; PBBP

EDWIN MUIR (1887–1959)

The Animals

1 They do not live in the world,
Are not in time and space.
From birth to death hurled
No word do they have, not one
To plant a foot upon,
Were never in any place. (l. 1–6)

CMoP; CRP; EBEV; HeIP; MoBrPo; NoP

The Brothers

2 Last night I watched my brothers play,
The gentle and the reckless one,
In a field two yards away.
For half a century they were gone
Beyond the other side of care
To be among the peaceful dead. (l. 1–6)

3 I have observed in foolish awe
The dateless mid-days of the law
And seen indifferent justice done
By everyone on everyone. (l. 29–32)

GTBS-P; HeIP; Mes; NoP; PrIm

Childhood

4 Long time he lay upon the sunny hill,
To his father's house below securely bound. (l. 1–2)

CMoP; HeIP; NoP; SeCePo

The Horses

5 Barely a twelvemonth after
The seven days war that put the world to sleep,
Late in the evening the strange horses came. (l. 1–3)

6 Sometimes we think of the nations lying asleep,
Curled blindly in impenetrable sorrow,
And then the thought confounds us with its strangeness.
(l. 21–23)

CMoP; HAP; HeIP; MoBrPo; MoP; NoAM; NOBE; NoP;
OAEL-2; OxBTC; PoE; RB; TEP; WeW

Horses

7 Those lumbering horses in the steady plough,
On the bare field — I wonder why, just now,
They seemed terrible, so wild and strange,
Like magic power on the stony grange. (l. 1–4)

CMoP; FaBoCh; OAEL-2; SeCePo

One Foot in Eden

8 The world's great day is growing late,
Yet strange these fields that we have planted
So long with crops of love and hate. (l. 3–5)

9 But famished field and blackened tree
Bear flowers in Eden never known.
Blossoms of grief and charity
Bloom in these darkened fields alone. (l. 20–23)

CMoP; GTBS-P; NoAM; NOBE; OPOP

The Road

10 There is a road that turning always
Cuts off the country of Again.
Archers stand there on every side
And as it runs time's deer is slain,
And lies where it has lain. (l. 1–5)

11 The ancestral deed is thought and done,
And in a million Edens fall
A million Adams drowned in darkness,
For small is great and great is small,
And a blind seed all. (l. 31–35)

CMoP; FaFP; LiTB; LiTM; Mes

ANTHONY MUNDAY (1553–1633)

Death of Robert, Earl of Huntingdon

1 Your master Robin Hood lies dead,
Therefore sigh as you sing.

Here lie his primer and his beads,
His bent bow and his arrows keen,
His good sword and his holy cross:

CH; CTC; ElL; OBSC; WiR

Primaleon of Greece

2 Beauty sat bathing by a spring,
Where fairest shades did hide her;
The winds blew calm, the birds did sing,
The cool streams ran beside her.
My wanton thoughts enticed mine eye
To see what was forbidden:
But better memory said Fie;
So vain desire was chidden —

ElL; GTBS; GTBS-P; NOBE; OBEV; OBSC

CAROLINA OLIPHANT, BARONESS NAIRNE (1766–1845)

The Land o' the Leal

1 We'll meet and ay be fain
In the land o' the leal. (l. 23–24)

GTBS; GTBS-P; OBEV; OxBS; WBLP; WGRP

OGDEN NASH (1902–1971)

Adventures of Isabel

1 Isabel, Isabel, didn't worry,
Isabel didn't scream or scurry.
She washed her hands and she straightened her hair
up,
Then Isabel quietly ate the bear up. (l. 7–10)

2 The witch's face was cross and wrinkled,
The witch's gums with teeth were sprinkled.
(l. 13–14)

3 The giant was hairy, the giant was horrid,
He had one eye in the middle of his forehead.
(l. 23–24)

CenHV; MoAmPo; MoShBr; NTCP; OBAL; OBCA;
OnMSP; OnUR; PDV; RHPC

Celery

4 Celery, raw,
Develops the jaw, (l. 1–2)

FaBoUs; FaPON; RHPC; TDD

The Cow

5 The cow is of the bovine ilk; (l. 1)

CenHV; NBLV; NoP; RB; RHPC

I Never Even Suggested It

6 Passivity can be a provoking modus operandi;
Consider the Empire and Gandhi. (l. 13–14)

7 It is my duty, gentlemen, to inform you that women are
  dictators all, and I recommend to you this moral:
In real life it takes only one to make a quarrel.
                              (l. 17–18)

FiBHP; FPL; LiTA; PoLF

The Panther

8 Better yet, if called by a panther,
Don't anther. (l. 5–6)

FaPON; MoShBr; OBAL; OBCA

Portrait of the Artist as a Prematurely Old Man

9 It is common knowledge to every schoolboy and even
  every Bachelor of Arts,
That all sin is divided into two parts.
One kind of sin is called a sin of commission, and that
  is very important, (l. 1–3)

10 It is the sin of omission, the second kind of sin,
That lays eggs under your skin. (l. 20–21)

11 The moral is that it is probably better not to sin at all,
  but if some kind of sin you must be pursuing,
Well, remember to do it by doing rather than by not
  doing. (l. 45–46)

BLPL; FaFP; InPS; LiTA; LiTM

The Purist

12 Camped on a tropic riverside,
One day he missed his loving bride.
She had, the guide informed him later,
Been eaten by an alligator.
Professor Twist could not but smile.
"You mean," he said, "a crocodile." (l. 5–10)

FiBHP; GoJo; MoAmPo; McShBr; NBLV; OBCA

The Rhinoceros

13 Farewell, farewell, you old rhinoceros,
I'll stare at something less prepoceros. (l. 3–4)

CenHV; FiBHP; MoAmPo; OBAL; OnUR

Song of the Open Road

14 I think that I shall never see
A billboard lovely as a tree. (l. 1–2)

AnAmPo; FaBoCo; FPL; OBAL

The Tale of Custard the Dragon

15 Belinda lived in a little white house,
With a little black kitten and a little gray mouse,
And a little yellow dog and a little red wagon,
And a realio, trulio, little pet dragon. (l. 1–4)

16 The pirate gaped at Belinda's dragon,
And gulped some grog from his pocket flagon,
He fired two bullets, but they didn't hit,
And Custard gobbled him, every bit. (l. 41–44)

FaPON; OBCA; OnUR; PoRA; PYC

The Turtle

17 The turtle lives 'twixt plated decks
Which practically conceal its sex. (l. 1–2)

FaFP; FiBHP; NoP; OBAL; SoSe; TAP

Very like a Whale

18 One thing that literature would be greatly the better for
Would be a more restricted employment by authors of
  simile and metaphor. (l. 1–2)

19 What does it mean when we are told
That the Assyrian came down like a wolf on the fold?
                              (l. 5–6)

20 But that wasn't fancy enough for Lord Byron, oh dear
  me no, he had to invent a lot of figures of speech and
  then interpolate them,
With the result that whenever you mention Old
  Testament soldiers to people they say Oh yes, they're
  the ones that a lot of wolves dressed up in gold and
  purple ate them. (l. 19–20)

BLPL; HAP; InPK; InPS; PoLF; TrGrPo; WeW

THOMAS NASHE (1567–1601)

Summer's Last Will and Testament

1 Beauty is but a flower,
Which wrinkles will devour;
Brightness falls from the air;

Queens have died young and fair;
Dust hath closed Helen's eye.
I am sick, I must die.

ChTr; CH; DL; EBEV; ElL; ELP; FaBoCh; FaPoR; HAP;
HeIP; HoPM; InvP; NAEL-1; NOBE; NoP; OAEL-1;
OBEV; OBSC; PoEL-2; PoRA; PPP; PrIm; QFR; SCV;
SeCePo; TEP; TrGrPo; WeW

2 Autumn hath all the summer's fruitful treasure;
Gone is our sport, fled is poor Croydon's pleasure.
Short days, sharp days, long nights come on apace,
Ah! who shall hide us from the winter's face?
Cold doth increase, the sickness will not cease,
And here we lie, God knows, with little ease.
From winter, plague, and pestilence, good Lord, deliver
us!

ElL; OAEL-1; OBSC; QFR; TrGrPo

3 Spring, the sweet spring, is the year's pleasant king;
Then blooms each thing, then maids dance in a ring,
Cold doth not sting, the pretty birds do sing,
"Cuckoo, jug-jug, pu-we, to-witta-woo!"

BoNaP; CH; ElL; GTBS; GTBS-P; HeIP; LiTB; NAEL-1;
NOBE; NoP; OBEV; OBSC; OnUR; TrGrPo; WiR

ALICE DUNBAR MOORE NELSON
(1875–1935)

I had no thought of violets of late

1 And now — unwittingly, you've made me dream
Of violets, and my soul's forgotten gleam. (l. 13–14)

BANP; BlSi; CDC; PoBA; PoNe; Son

HOWARD NEMEROV (b. 1920)

The Goose Fish

1 The ordinary night was graced
For them by the swift tide of blood
That silently they took at flood,
And for a little time they prized
Themselves emparadised. (l. 5–9)

2 It was a wide and moony grin
Together peaceful and obscene; (l. 28–29)

CMoP; HeIP; LiTM; NePoEA; NIP; NoAM; NoP; PoE;
SM

SIR HENRY NEWBOLT (1862–1938)

Drake's Drum

1 Drake he's in his hammock till the great Armadas
come,
(Capten, art tha sleepin' there below?)
Slung atween the round shot listenin' for the drum,
An' dreamin' arl the time o' Plymouth Hoe. (l. 17–20)

FaBoCh; FaPoR; OBMV; PoRA

He Fell among Thieves

2 'Ye have robbed,' said he, 'ye have slaughtered and
made an end,
Take your ill-got plunder, and bury the dead:
What will ye more of your guest and sometime friend?'
'Blood for our blood,' they said. (l. 1–4)

3 He saw the dark wainscot and timbered roof,
The long tables, and the faces merry and keen;
The College Eight and their trainer dining aloof,
The Dons on the dais serene. (l. 29–32)

4 'O glorious Life, Who dwellest in earth and sun,
I have lived, I praise and adore Thee."
A sword swept.
Over the pass the voices one by one
Faded, and the hill slept. (l. 45–49)

EBVV; FaPoR; OBEV; OBWP; OnMSP; OxBTC

MARY EFFIE LEE NEWSOME
(1885–1979)

Morning Light

1 Through heavy menace and mystery
Of half-waking tropic dawn,
Behold a little black boy,
A naked black boy, (l. 5–8)

AmNP; CDC; PoBA; PoNe

EILÉAN NÍ CHUILLEANÁIN (b. 1942)

Swineherd

1 'I mean to retire, where
Nobody will have heard about my special skills
And conversation is mainly about the weather. (l. 2–4)

BIrV; CIP; FaBoWP; WPOW

JOHN FREDERICK NIMS (b. 1913)

Love and Death

1 And yet a kiss (like blubber)'d blur and slip, (l. 1)

HoPM; KS; SM; WeW

My clumsiest dear, whose hands shipwreck vases

2 The refugee uncertain at the door
  You make at home; deftly you steady
  The drunk clambering on his undulant floor. (l. 6–8)

3 Only
  With words and people and love you move at ease.
                                    (l. 13–14)

4 For should your hands drop white and empty
  All the toys of the world would break. (l. 23–24)

FF; HoPM; InPK; SoSe

HENRY NOEL *AND* WILLIAM STRODE

Beauty Extolled (*attributed to* Noel *and to* Strode)

1 Gaze not on swans, in whose soft breast,
  A full-hatched beauty seems to nest,
  Nor snow, which falling from the sky,
  Hovers in its virginity.

2 Swans moulting die, snow melts to tears,
  Roses do blush and hang their heads,

ChTr; ELP; OBS

ALFRED NOYES (1880–1958)

The Barrel-Organ

1 Yes; as the music changes,
  Like a prismatic glass,
  It takes the light and ranges
  Through all the moods that pass; (l. 17–20)

2 Go down to Kew in lilac-time, in lilac-time, in lilac-
    time;
  Go down to Kew in lilac-time (it isn't far from
    London!) (l. 33–34)

3 The linnet and the throstle, too, and after dark the long
    halloo
  And golden-eyed tu-whit, tu-whooof owls that ogle
    London. (l. 47–48)

4 she cannot understand
  What she wants or why she wanders to that
    undiscovered land,
  For the parties there are not at all the sort of thing she
    planned,
  In the land where the dead dreams go. (l. 84–87)

5 Once more La Traviata sighs
  Another sadder song:
  Once more Il Trovatore cries
  A tale of deeper wrong; (l. 153–156)

BLPL; FaBV; MoBrPo; PoRA

The Highwayman

6 The road was a ribbon of moonlight over the purple
    moor,
  And the highwayman came riding —
  Riding — riding —
  The highwayman came riding, up to the old inn-door.
                                    (l. 3–6)

7 Then look for me moonlight,
  Watch for me by moonlight,
  I'll come to thee by moonlight, though hell should bar
    the way.' (l. 29–31)

8 When they shot him down in the highway,
  Down like a dog in the highway,
  And he lay in his blood on the highway, with the bunch
    of lace at his throat. (l. 105–108)

BeLS; FaBV; FaFP; FaPON; FPL; OBNV; OHFP; PoLF

ANGUS O'GILLAN (*fl.* 14th century)

The Dead at Clonmacnois

1 They they laid to rest the seven Kings of Tara, (l. 9)

2 And in Clonmacnois they laid the men of Teffia, (l. 13)

AnIL; FaBoPP; OBEV; OBMV

FRANK O'HARA (1926–1966)

Autobiographia Literaria

1 And here I am, the
  center of all beauty!
  writing these poems!
  Imagine! (l. 13–16)

CAPP; NNaP; NOBA; TTTS

Ave Maria

2 Mothers of America
  let your kids go to the movies!
  get them out of the house so they won't know what
      you're up to
  it's true that fresh air is good for the body
  but what about the soul
  that grows in darkness, embossed by silvery images
                                    (l. 1–6)

3 oh mothers you will have made the little tykes
  so happy because if nobody does pick them up in the
      movies
  they won't know the difference
  and if somebody does it'll be sheer gravy (l. 22–25)

  HCAP; NAAL-2; NNaP; NoP; PoM

Chez Jane

4 "Saint-Saens!" it seems to be whispering,
  curling unerringly around the furry nuts
  of the terrible puss, who is mentally flexing.
  Ah be with me always, spirit of noisy
  contemplation in the studio, the Garden
  of Zoos, the eternally fixed afternoons! (l. 9–14)

  CoAP; NeAP; NoAM; NOBA; PoA; PoE

The Day Lady Died

5 I get a little Verlaine
  for Patsy with drawings by Bonnard although I do
  think of Hesiod, trans. Richmond Lattimore or
  Brendan Behan's new play or Le Balcon or Les Negres
  of Genet, but I don't, I stick with Verlaine
  after practically going to sleep with quandariness
                                    (l. 14–19)

6 thinking of
  leaning on the john door in the 5 SPOT
  while she whispered a song along the keyboard
  to Mal Waldron and everyone and I stopped breathing
                                    (l. 26–29)

  CAPP; HCAP; MoP; NAAL-2; NeAP; NoAM; NOBA; NoP;
  PoE; PoM; SOTW

The Eager note on my door said "Call me"

7 And he was

  there in the hall, flat on a sheet of blood that
  ran down the stairs. I did appreciate it. There are few
  hosts who so thoroughly prepare to greet a guest
  only casually invited, and that several months ago.
                                    (l. 12–16)

  CAPP; EAS; NoAM; NOBA

Ode: Salute to the French Negro Poets

8 I call
  to the spirits of other lands to make fecund my
  existence (l. 1–2)

9 trying to live in the terrible western world

  here where to love at all's to be a politician, as to love
  a poem
  is pretentious, (l. 7–9)

10 the beauty of America, neither cool jazz nor devoured
   Egyptian heroes, lies in
   lives in the darkness I inhabit in the midst of sterile
   millions (l. 34–36)

11 the only truth is face to face, the poem whose words
   become your mouth
   and dying in black and white we fight for what we
   love, not are (l. 37–39)

   GLP; NeAP; NNaP; PoM; PoNe

A Step Away from Them

12 down the sidewalk
   where laborers feed their dirty
   glistening torsos sandwiches
   and Coca-Cola, with yellow helmets
   on. They protect them from falling
   bricks, I guess. (l. 3–8)

13 And one has eaten and one walks,
   past the magazines with nudes
   and the posters for bullfight and
   the Manhattan Storage Warehouse,
   which they'll soon tear down. (l. 40–44)

14 A glass of papaya juice
   and back to work. My heart is in my
   pocket, it is Poems by Pierre Reverdy. (l. 47–49)

   HCAP; InPS; NAAL-2; VGW

To the Harbormaster

15 I am always tying up
   and then deciding to depart. (l. 3–4)

16 Yet
   I trust the sanity of my vessel; and
   if it sinks, it may well be in answer
   to the reasoning of the eternal voices,
   the waves which have kept me from reaching you.
                                    (l. 13–17)

   CoAP; CRP; MOS; NAAL-2; PoM

A True Account of Talking to the Sun at Fire Island

17 If you don't appear
at all one day they think you're lazy
or dead. (l. 42–44)

18 And don't worry about your lineage
poetic or natural. (l. 45–46)

19 And
always embrace things, people earth
sky stars, as I do, freely and with
the appropriate sense of space. (l. 64–67)

20 Go back to sleep now
Frank, and I may leave a tiny poem
in that brain of yours as my farewell.' (l. 73–75)

21 'No, go I must, they're calling
me.'
'Who are they?'
Rising he said "Some
day you'll know. They're calling to you
too.' Darkly he rose, and then I slept. (l. 77–82)

HCAP; NNaP; RB; SOTW; TTTS

Why I Am Not a Painter

22 I look
up. "You have sardines in it."
"Yes, it needed something there."
"Oh." (l. 7–10)

23 It is even in
prose, I am a real poet. My poem
is finished and I haven't mentioned
orange yet It's twelve poems, I call
it oranges. (l. 24–28)

CAPP; HCAP; MoP; NeAP; NoAM; NOBA; PoE; PoM

CHARLES OLSON (1910–1970)

The Kingfishers

1 What does not change is the will to change (l. 1)

2 Dead, hung up indoors, the kingfisher
will not indicate a favoring wind,
or avert the thunderbolt. (l. 42–44)

3 And all now is war
where so lately there was peace,
and the sweet brotherhood, the use
of tilled fields. (l. 96–99)

4 Not one death but many,
not accumulation but change, the feed-back proves, the
feed-back is the law (l. 100–102)

5 what pudor pejorocracy affronts
how awe, night-rest and neighborhood can rot
what breeds where dirtiness is law
what crawls
below (l. 175–179)

CMoP; InPS; NAAL-2; NeAP; NOBA; PoM

The Maximus Poems

6 all senses

including the mind, that worker on what is

7 what can we do
when even the public conveyances
sing?
how can we go anywhere,
even cross-town
how get out of anywhere

NoAM

8 flight
(of the bird
o kylix, o
Antony of Padua
sweep low, o bless
the roofs,

9 love is form, and cannot be without
important substance

10 But that which matters, that which insists, that which
will last,
that! o my people, where shall you find it, how, where,
where shall you listen
when all is become billboards, when, all, even silence,
is spray-gunned?

11 one loves only form,
and form only comes
into existence when
the thing is born

born of yourself,

12 love is not easy
but how shall you know,
New England, now
that pejorocracy is here,

LiTM; NoAM; NOBA; PoM

13 I have had to learn the simplest things
last. Which made for difficulties.

14 But the known?
This, I have had to be given,
a life, love, and from one man
the world.

CAPP; CMoP; NeAP; NOBA; PoE; PoM; VGW

A Newly Discovered "Homeric" Hymn

15 Hail them, and fall off. Fall off! The drink is not yours,
it is not yours! You do not come
from the same place, you do not suffer as the dead do,
they do not suffer, they need, because they have drunk
of the pot,
they need. (l. 34–38)

16 Beware the dead. And hail them. They teach you
drunkenness.
You have your own place to drink. Hail and beware
them, when they come. (l. 40–41)

MoP; NeAP; NoAM; PoM

Variations Done for Gerald Van de Wiele

17 bees
dig the plum blossoms (l. 8–9)

18 iris and lilac, birds
birds, yellow flowers
white flowers, the Diesel
does not let up dragging
the plow (l. 13–17)

19 My life

has been given its orders: the seasons
seize

the soul and the body, and make mock
of any dispersed effort. The hour of death

is the only trespass (l. 31–36)

20 by night only crazy things
like the full moon and the whippoorwill

and us, are busy. (l. 49–51)

21 The flowers are ravined
by bees, the fruit blossoms

are thrown to the ground, the wind
the rain forces everything. (l. 74–77)

22 The body

whips the soul. In its great desire
it demands the elixir

In the roar of spring,
transmutations. (l. 85–89)

23 we salute you
season of no bungling (l. 93–94)

NeAP; NoAM; NOBA; NoP

OMAR KHAYYÁM (d. 1123)

The Rubáiyát of Omar Khayyám of Naishápúr

1 Come, fill the Cup, and in the fire of Spring
Your Winter-garment of Repentance fling:
The Bird of Time has but a little way
To flutter — and the Bird is on the Wing. (l. 25–28)

2 A Book of Verses underneath the Bough,
A Jug of Wine, a Loaf of Bread — and Thou
Beside me singing in the Wilderness —
Oh, Wilderness were Paradise enow! (l. 45–48)

3 Some for the Glories of This World; and some
Sigh for the Prophet's Paradise to come;
Ah, take the Cash, and let the Credit go,
Nor heed the rumble of a distant Drum! (l. 49–52)

4 Ah, make the most of what we yet may spend,
Before we too into the Dust descend;
Dust into Dust, and under Dust to lie,
Sans Wine, sans Song, sans Singer, and — sans End!
(l. 93–96)

5 Myself when young did eagerly frequent
Doctor and Saint, and heard great argument
About it and about: but evermore
Came out by the same door where in I went.
(l. 105–108)

6 Then to the Lip of this poor earthen Urn
I leaned, the Secret of my Life to learn:
And Lip to Lip it murmured — "While you live,
Drink! — for, once dead, you never shall return."
(l. 137–140)

7 Oh Thou, who Man of baser Earth didst make,
And even with Paradise devise the Snake:
For all the Sin wherewith the Face of Man
Is blackened — Man's forgiveness give — and take!
(l. 321–324)

8 Indeed the Idols I have loved so long
Have done my credit in this World much wrong:
Have drowned my Gloryin a shallow Cup,
And sold my Reputation for a Song. (l. 369–372)

AWP; EBVV; FaBoBe; FaBoRV; FaFP; FaPON; FaPoR;
FF; HAP; HeIP; LiTB; NAEL-2; NoP; OBNC; PoEL-5;
PrIm; TrGrPo; WeW

JOHN BOYLE O'REILLY (1844–1890)

A White Rose

1 The red rose whispers of passion,
And the white rose breathes of love;
O, the red rose is a falcon,
And the white rose is a dove. (l. 1–4)

2 For the love that is purest and sweetest
Has a kiss of desire on the lips. (l. 7–8)

AA; ACP; OBEV; SoSe

CHARLES, DUC D' ORLÉANS (1391–1465)

My Ghostly Father, I me confess

1 My ghostly fadir, I me confess,
First to God and then to you
That at a window (wot ye how)
I stole a kiss of great sweetness,

ACP; BoLoP; ChTr; EnLoPo; GBL; MeEL; NOBE

ARTHUR WILLIAM EDGAR O'SHAUGHNESSY (1844–1881)

Ode

1 We are the music-makers,
And we are the dreamers of dreams,
Wandering by lone sea-breakers,
And sitting by desolate streams;
World-losers and world-forsakers,
On whom the pale moon gleams: (l. 1–6)

2 With wonderful deathless ditties
We build up the world's great cities, (l. 9–10)

3 One man with a dream, at pleasure,
Shall go forth and conquer a crown; (l. 13–14)

4 We, in the ages lying
In the buried past of the earth,
Built Nineveh with our sighing,
And Babel itself with our mirth; (l. 17–20)

5 For each age is a dream that is dying,
Or one that is coming to birth. (l. 23–24)

FaBV; FaPoR; OBEV; TrGrPo

"SEUMAS O'SULLIVAN" (pseudonym of JAMES STARKEY) (1879–1958)

A Piper

1 A piper in the streets to-day
Set up, and tuned, and started to play, (l. 1–2)

2 And men left down their work and came,
And women with petticoats coloured like flame.
And little bare feet that were blue with cold,
Went dancing back to the age of gold,
And all the world went gay, went gay,
For half an hour in the street to-day. (l. 6–11)

BoTP; CH; FaPON; MoShBr; PDV

LADY OTOMO NO SAKONOE (fl. 8th century)

Unknown Love

1 Unknown love
Is as bitter a thing
As the maiden-lily (l. 1–3)

AWP; PBWP

OVID (PUBLIUS OVIDIUS NASO) (43 B.C.–A.D. 17)

Amores

1 Then came Corinna in a long loose gown,
Her white neck hid with tresses hanging down,
Resembling fair Semiramis going to bed, (I, 5)

2 Jove send me more such afternoons as this. (I, 5)

BoLoP; EBEV; GBL; OBVE

Constant Penelope sends to thee, careless Ulysses

3 Constant Penelope sends to thee, careless Ulysses.
Write not again, but come, sweet mate, (l. 1–2)

EnLoPo; GBL; NAEL-1; OAEL-1

Metamorphoses: Philemon and Baucis

4 Here Jove with Hermes came; but in disguise
Of mortal men conceal'd their deities;
One laid aside his thunder, one his rod,

5 Now old in love, though little was their store,
Inured to want, their poverty they bore,
Nor aim'd at wealth, professing to be poor.

6 'Speak thy desire, thou only just of men;
And thou, O woman, only worthy found
To be with such a man in marriage bound.'

7 We beg one hour of death, that neither she
With widow's tears may live to bury me,
Nor weeping I, with wither'd arms, may bear
My breathless Baucis to the sepulchre.'

CTC

WILFRED OWEN (1893–1918)

A Terre

1 I tried to peg out soldierly, — no use!
One dies of war like any old disease. (l. 5–6)

2 A short life and a merry one, my buck!
We used to say we'd hate to live dead-old, —
Yet now . . . I'd willingly be puffy, bald,
And patriotic. (l. 11–14)

3 Dead men may envy living mites in cheese,
Or good germs even. Microbes have their joys,
And subdivide, and never come to death. (l. 40–42)

4 'I shall be one with nature, herb, and stone',
Shelley would tell me. Shelley wound be stunned:

The dullest Tommy hugs that fancy now.
'Pushing up daisies' is their creed, you know.
(l. 44–47)

5 Soldiers may grow a soul when turned to fronds,
But here the thing's best left at home with friends.

6 My soul's a little grief, grappling your chest,
To climb your throat on sobs; easily chased
On other sighs and wiped by fresher winds. (l. 60–64)

LiTM; MMA; OxBTC; WaP

Anthem for Doomed Youth

7 What passing-bells for these who die as cattle?
Only the monstrous anger of the guns. (l. 1–2)

8 The pallor of girl's brows shall be their pall;
Their flowers the tenderness of patient minds,
And each slow dusk a drawing-down of blinds.
(l. 12–14)

BrPo; ChTr; CMoP; EBEV; FaBoMo; FaBoRV; FaFP;
GTBS-P; HAP; HeIP; HoPM; InPK; InPS; LiTM; MoAB;
MoBrPo; MoP; NAEL-2; NoAM; NOBE; NoP; OAEL-2;
OBEV; OBWP; OxBTC; PoE; PPP; SCV; SeCePo; Son;
SoSe; TrGrPo; WaP; WeW

Apologia pro Poemate Meo

9 I, too, saw God through mud — (l. 1)

10 War brought more glory to their eyes than blood,
And gave their laughs more glee than shakes a child.
(l. 3–4)

11 I have perceived much beauty
In the hoarse oaths that kept our courage straight;
Heard music in the silentness of duty;
Found peace where shell-storms spouted reddest spate.
(l. 25–28)

12 These men are worth
Your tears: You are not worth their merriment.
(l. 35–36)

FaBoRV; LiTM; MoAB; MoBrPo; NAEL-2

Arms and the Boy

13 these blind, blunt bullet-leads
Which long to nuzzle in the hearts of lads, (l. 5–6)

14 For his teeth seem for laughing round an apple.
There lurk no claws behind his fingers supple;
And God will grow no talons at his heels,
Nor antlers through the thickness of his curls.
(l. 9–12)

BrPo; CMoP; FaFP; HAP; LiTB; LiTM; MoAB; MoBrPo;
OAEL-2; OxBSP; PoE; WaP; WeW

Disabled

15 He sat in a wheeled chair, waiting for dark,
And shivered in his ghastly suit of grey,
Legless, sewn short at elbow. (l. 1–3)

16 There was an artist silly for his face,
For it was younger than his youth, last year.
(l. 14–15)

17 To-night he noticed how the women's eyes
Passed from him to the strong men that were whole.
How cold and late it is! Why don't they come
And put him into bed? Why don't they come?
(l. 43–46)

BrPo; CMoP; FF; InPS; LiTM; MMA; MoP; NAEL-2;
NIP; NoAM; OBWVE; OxBTC; WaP

Dulce et Decorum Est

18 Men marched asleep. Many had lost their boots
But limped on, blood-shod. All went lame; all blind;
Drunk with fatigue; deaf even to the hoots
Of tired, outstripped Five-Nines that dropped behind.
(l. 5–8)

19 the white eyes writhing in his face,
His hanging face, like a devil's sick of sin;
If you could hear, at every jolt, the blood
Come gargling from the froth-corrupted lungs,
Obscene as cancer, (l. 19—23)

20 My friend, you would not tell with such high zest
To children ardent for some desperate glory,
The old Lie: Dulce et decorum est
Pro patria mori. (l. 25—28)

CMoP; DL; FaBoPV; FaBoTw; FaBV; FF; HeIP; HoPM;
InPK; InvP; LiTB; LiTM; MMA; MoAB; MoBrPo;
NAEL-2; NIP; NoAM; NoP; OAEL-2; OBWP; PoE; PPP;
PrIm; TW; UnPo; WaP

Exposure

21 We only know war lasts, rain soaks, and clouds sag
stormy. (l. 12)

22 Pale flakes with fingering stealth come feeling for our
faces —
We cringe in holes, back on forgotten dreams, and
stare, snow-dazed,
Deep into grassier ditches. (l. 21—23)

23 To-night, His frost will fasten on this mud and us,
Shriveling many hands, puckering foreheads crisp.
The burying-party, picks and shovels in their shaking
grasp,
Pause over half-known faces. All their eyes are ice,
But nothing happens. (l. 36—40)

FaBoMo; InPS; MMA; NoAM; OBWP; RB; WaP

From My Diary, July 1914

24 Bees
Shaking the heavy dews from bloom and frond.
Boys
Bursting the surface of the ebony pond. (l. 9—12)

25 A mead
Bordered about with warbling water brooks.
A maid
Laughing the love-laugh with me; proud of looks.
(l. 17—20)

FaBoMo; LiTM; MoAB; MoBrPo

Futility

26 Move him into the sun —
Gently its touch awoke him once,
At home, whispering of fields half-sown. (l. 1—3)

27 Was it for this the clay grew tall?
— O what made fatuous sunbeams toil
To break earth's sleep at all? (l. 12—14)

CMoP; FaBoMo; GTBS-P; MMA; MoAB; MoBrPo;
NAEL-2; NoAM; NoP; OBWP; RB; SeCePo; TrGrPo

Greater Love

28 Red lips are not so red.
As the stained stones kissed by the English dead.
(l. 1—2)

29 Your slender attitude
Trembles not exquisite like limbs knife-skewed,
(l. 7—8)

30 Heart, you were never hot
Nor large, nor full like hearts made great with shot;
(l. 19—20)

BrPo; CMoP; EnLoPo; FaBoMo; FaBoRV; FaFP;
GTBS-P; LiTB; LiTM; MoAB; MoBrPo; MoP; NoAM;
WaaP; WaP

Insensibility

31 Happy are men who yet before they are killed
Can let their veins run cold. (l. 1—2)

32 And some cease feeling
Even themselves or for themselves.
Dullness best solves
The tease and doubt of shelling, (l. 12—15)

33 By choice they made themselves immune
To pity and whatever moans in man
Before the last sea and the hapless stars;
Whatever mourns when many leave these shores;
Whatever shares
The eternal reciprocity of tears. (l. 54—59)

CMoP; FaBoTw; InPS; LiTB; LiTM; MMA; MoAB;
OBWP; OxBTC; WaP

Mental Cases

34 — These are men whose minds the Dead have ravished
Memory fingers in their hair of murders,
Multitudinous murders they once witnessed. (l. 10—12)

35 — Thus their hands are plucking at each other;
Picking at the rope-knouts of their scourging;
Snatching after us who smote them, brother,
Pawing us who dealt them war and madness.
(l. 25—28)

BrPo; CMoP; FaBoMo; MMA; NoAM; WaP

Miners

36 I thought of all that worked dark pits
Of war, and died
Digging the rock where Death reputes
Peace lies indeed. (l. 21–24)

37 The centuries will burn rich loads
With which we groaned,
Whose warmth shall lull their dreaming lids,
While songs are crooned:
But they will not dream of us poor lads,
Left in the ground. (l. 29–34)

BrPo; MoAB; MoBrPo; NAEL-2; NOBE; OBWVE

The Send-off

38 A few, a few, too few for drums and yells,
May creep back, silent, to village wells
Up half-known roads. (l. 18–20)

BrPo; LiTB; MoAB; MoBrPo; OBWP; OBWVE; OxBTC;
RB

The Show

39 And Death fell with me, like a deepening moan.
And He, picking a manner of worm, which half had hid
Its bruises in the earth, but crawled no further,
Showed me its feet, the feet of many men,
And the fresh-severed head of it, my head. (l. 25–29)

LiTB; LiTM; MoAB; MoBrPo; OBWVE; OxBTC; WaaP;
WaP

Strange Meeting

40 I am the enemy you killed, my friend.
I knew you in this dark; for so you frowned
Yesterday through me as you jabbed and killed.
I parried; but my hands were loath and cold.
Let us sleep now. (l. 40–44)

BrPo; CMoP; FaBoMo; FaBoRV; GTBS-P; HeIP; HoPM;
LiTB; MMA; MoAB; MoBrPo; MoP; NAEL-2; NoAM;
NOBE; NoP; OAEL-2; OBWP; PoE; RB; SCV; TrGrPo;
WaaP; WaP

ROBERT PACK (b. 1929)

The Boat

1 I asked, "What happens, father, when you die?"

He told where all the running water goes,
And dressed me gently in my little clothes. (l. 15–17)

CoAP; DiL; NePoEA-2; SM

PATRICIA K. PAGE (b. 1916)

The Stenographers

1 After the brief bivouac of Sunday,
their eyes, in the forced march of Monday to Saturday,
hoist the white flag, flutter in the snow storm of paper,
(l. 1–3)

2 In the felt of the morning the calico minded,
sufficiently starched, insert papers, hit keys,
efficient and sure as their adding machines;
yet they weep in the vault, (l. 30–33)

3 In their eyes I have seen
the pin men of madness in marathon trim
race round the track of the stadium pupil. (l. 34–36)

CaP; HeIP; LiTM; NoAM; NoP; OBCV

Stories of Snow

4 And of the swan in death these dreamers tell
of its last flight and how it falls, a plummet,
pierced by the freezing bullet
and how three feathers, loosened by the shot,
descend like snow upon it. (l. 33–37)

5 that warm metamorphosis of snow
as gentle as the sort that woodsmen know
who, lost in the white circle, fall at last
and dream their way to death. (l. 41–44)

NOBC; NoP; OBCV; PoA

DOROTHY PARKER (1893–1967)

One Perfect Rose

1 Why is it no one ever sent me yet
One perfect limousine, do you suppose?
Ah no, it's always just my luck to get
One perfect rose. (l. 9–12)

FiBHP; NBLV; NIP; NoP; OBAL

Some Beautiful Letters

2 Guns aren't lawful;
Nooses give;
Gas smells awful;
You might as well live. (l. 5–8)

AnAmPo; DL; HeIP; InPK; NAAL-2; NBLV; NoP; OBAL;
TrJP

ANDREW BARTON PATERSON
(1864–1941)

Waltzing Matilda

1 Once a jolly swagman camped by a billabong
  Under the shade of a coolibah tree; (l. 1–2)

2 Waltzing Matilda, Waltzing Matilda,
  Who'll come a-waltzing Matilda with me?
  And he sang as he watched and waited while his billy
    boiled:
  'Who'll come a-waltzing Matilda with me?' (l. 5–8)

3 And his ghost may be heard as you pass by that
    billabong,
  'You'll come a-waltzing Matilda with me!' (l. 27–28)

CBAP; ChTr; GBP; PoAu-1

COVENTRY KERSEY DIGHTON
PATMORE (1823–1896)

The Angel in the House

1 'I saw you take his kiss!' ''Tis true.'
  'O, modesty!' ''Twas strictly kept:
  'He thought me asleep; at least, I knew
  'He thought I thought he thought I slept.' (l. 1–4)

BoLoP; EnLoPo; FiBHP; NOBVV

2 The world, unfathomably fair,
  Is duller than a witling's jest.
  Love wakes men, once a lifetime each;
  They lift their heavy lids, and look;
  And, lo, what one sweet page can teach,
  They read with joy, then shut the book. (l. 3–8)

EnLoPo; GBL; GTBS-P; HAP; OBNC; OxBSP

The Unknown Eros

3 He had put, within his reach,
  A box of counters and a red-veined stone,
  A piece of glass abraded by the beach,
  And six or seven shells,
  A bottle with bluebells,
  And two French copper coins, ranged there with careful
    art, (l. 15–20)

4 And thou rememberest of what toys
  We made our joys, (l. 26–27)

ACP; BeLS; EBEV; EBVV; FaFP; NOBVV; OBEV; SoSe;
TrGrPo; TrPWD

5 With not one kiss, or a good-bye,
  And the only loveless look the look with which you
    passed:
  'Twas all unlike your great and gracious ways.
                                        (l. 30–32)

ACP; NOBE; OBEV; OBNC; SeCePo

6 Here, in this little Bay,
  Full of tumultuous life and great repose,
  Where, twice a day,
  The purposeless, glad ocean comes and goes, (l. 1–4)

7 For want of me the world's course will not fail:
  When all its work is done, the lie shall rot;
  The truth is great, and shall prevail,
  When none cares whether it prevail or not. (l. 7–10)

BoNaP; GTBS-P; HAP; NOBE; NOBVV; OBEV; OBNC;
OxBSP; TrGrPo

8 With all my will, but much against my heart,
  We two now part. (l. 1–2)

9 Go thou to East, I West.
  We will not say
  There's any hope, it is so far away. (l. 9–11)

10 Perchance we may,
   Where now this night is day,
   And even through faith of still averted feet,
   Making full circle of our banishment,
   Amazed meet; (l. 18–22)

ACP; BoLoP; EnLoPo; GTBS-P; NOBE; OBEV; OBNC;
PoEL-5; TrGrPo

RAYMOND R. PATTERSON (b. 1929)

You Are the Brave

1 You are the brave who do not break
  In the grip of the mob when the blow comes straight
  To the shattered bone; (l. 1–3)

IDB; NBP; NIP; PoBA

THOMAS LOVE PEACOCK (1785–1866)

The Misfortunes of Elphin

1 The mountain sheep are sweeter,
  But the valley sheep are fatter;
  We therefore deemed it meeter

To carry off the latter.

AWP; EnRP; FaBoCh; FaPoR; HAP; InvP; NAEL-2;
NOBE; OAEL-2; OnMSP; PrIm; WaaP; WeW; WiR

Nightmare Abbey

2 In a bowl to sea went wise men three,
   On a brilliant night of June:
   They carried a net, and their hearts were set
   On fishing up the moon.

BXAP; CH; FaBoCh; FaBoNo; OBEV; WiR

Rich and Poor; or, Saint and Sinner

3 The rich man goes out yachting,
   Where sanctity can't pursue him;
   The poor goes afloat
   In a fourpenny boat,
   Where the bishop groans to view him. (l. 36–40)

FaBoCo; NOBE; NOBL; OBSV

GEORGE PEELE (1559–1596)

The Arraignment of Paris

1 My love is fair, my love is gay,
   As fresh as bin the flowers in May
   And of my love my roundelay,
   My merry, merry, merry roundelay,
   Concludes with Cupid's curse, —
   'They that do change old love for new
   Pray gods they change for worse!'

ElL; NOBE; OBEV; OBSC

David and Bethsabe

2 Let not my beauty's fire
   Inflame unstaid desire,
   Nor pierce any bright eye
   That wandereth lightly.

ElL; GBL; NOBE; NoP; OBSC; OxBoLi; OxBSP;
PoEL-2; RB; TEP; TrGrPo

The Hunting of Cupid

3 And as my wit doth best devise,
   Love's dwelling is in ladies' eyes,
   From whence do glance love's piercing darts,
   That make such holes into our hearts;
   And all the world herein accord,
   Love is a great and mighty lord;

4 Mars and she played even and odd.

ElL; ELP; NOBE; OBSC; SeCePo

The Old Wives' Tale

5 Fair maid, white and red,
   Comb me smooth, and stroke my head;
   And every hair a sheave shall be.
   And every sheave a golden tree.

FaBoCh; NOBE; OBSC; OxBoLi

6 When as the rye reach to the chin,
   And chopcherry, chopcherry ripe within,
   Strawberries swimming in the cream,
   And school-boys playing in the stream;

ElL; ELP; EnLoPo; FaBoCh; GBL; InvP; NOBE; NoP;
OBEV; OBSC; OxBoLi; PoEL-2; SeCePo; TEP

Polyhymnia

7 His golden locks time hath to silver turned;
   O time too swift, O swiftness never ceasing!
   His youth 'gainst time and age hath ever spurned,
   But spurned in vain; youth waneth by increasing.
   Beauty, strength, youth are flowers but fading seen;
   Duty, faith, love are roots, and ever green.

ChTr; ElL; ELP; FaBoRV; HeIP; InPS; NOBE; NoP;
OBEV; OBSC; OBWP; PoEL-2; PoRA; TrGrPo

PETRARCH (FRANCESCO PETRARCA)
(1304–1374)

Secretum

1 Whyle I was abowte to chaunge myn olde lyff —
   What sorowe I suffred, dyseese, angre and stryff,
   Cracchynge myn here, my chekys all totare,
   Wrythynge my fyngres for angwysshe and care,
   Watrynge the erthe with my byttre salte teres
   That the crye of my syghes ascended to Goddys eres,
   My knees with myn handys grasped togedyre soore,
   And yitt I stode the same man I was afore
   Tyl a depe profounde remembraunce att the laste
   Hadd all my wrecchednesse afore myn eyn caste

OxBLMV

Sonnets to Laura in Death

2 My flowery and green age was passing away, and I
   feeling a chill in the fires had been wasting my heart,
   for I was drawing near the hillside above the grave.

3 Death had his grudge against me, and he got up in the
   way, like an armed robber, with a pike in his hand.

BIrV; OBMV

4 Go, grieving rimes of mine, to that hard stone
  Whereunder lies my darling, lies my dear,
  And cry to her to speak from heaven's sphere.

5 Tell her, I'm sick of living; that I'm blown
  By winds of grief from the course I ought to steer,

6 Oh, may she deign to stand at my bedside
  When I come to die; and may she call to me
  And draw me to her in the blessed place!

NAWM-1

7 Great is my envy of you, earth, in your greed
  Folding her in invisible embrace,
  Denying me the look of the sweet face
  Where I found peace from all my strife at need!

8 Great is my envy of death whose curt hard sword
  Carried her whom I called my life away;
  Me he disdains, and mocks me from her eyes!

NAWM-1

9 What a grudge I am bearing the earth that has its arms
  about her,

10 what a grudge I am bearing against Death, that is
   standing in her two eyes, and will not call me with a
   word.

MoBrPo

11 The eyes that drew from me such fervent praise,
   The arms and hands and feet and countenance
   Which made me a stranger in my own romance
   And set me apart from the well-trodden ways;

12 And I live on, but in grief and self-contempt,
   Left here without the light I loved so much,
   In a great tempest and with shrouds unkempt.

13 And tears are heard within the harp I touch.

NAWM-1

PETRONIUS ARBITER (CAIUS PETRONIUS ARBITER) (d. A.D. 66)

Doing, a Filthy Pleasure Is, and Short

1 Doing, a filthy pleasure is, and short;
  And done, we straight repent us of the sport:
  Let us not then rush blindly on unto it,
  Like lustfull beasts, that onely know to doe it:
                                    (l. 1–4)

2 Let us together closely lie, and kisse,
  There is no labour, nor no shame in this;
  This hath pleas'd, doth please, and long will please;
        never
  Can this decay, but is beginning ever. (l. 7–10)

BoLoP; ErPo; LLLT; OBVE; OxBSP

AMBROSE PHILIPS (1675–1749)

To Miss Charlotte Pulteney in Her Mother's Arms

1 Timely blossom, Infant fair,
  Fondling of a happy pair,

2 Wearied then and glad of rest,
  Like the linnet in the nest: —

3 And thou shalt in thy daughter see,
  This picture, once, resembled thee.

ELP; GTBS; GTBS-P; NOEC

KATHERINE PHILIPS ("ORINDA") (1631–1664)

To My Excellent Lucasia, on Our Friendship

1 I did not live until this time
  Crown'd my felicity,
  When I could say without a crime,
  I am not thine, but Thee.

  This carcase breath'd, and walkt, and slept,
  So that the World believ'd
  There was a soul the motions kept;
  But they were all deceiv'd. (l. 1–8)

MeLP; OBS; PeHV; WPE; WPOW

JOHN PHILLIPS (1676–1709)

The Splendid Shilling

1 Happy the Man, who void of Cares and Strife,
  In Silken, or in Leathern Purse retains
  A Splendid Shilling: He nor hears with Pain
  New Oysters cry'd, nor sighs for chearful Ale; (l. 1–4)

2 So pass my Days. But when Nocturnal Shades
  This World invelop, and th' inclement Air
  Persuades Men to repel benumming Frosts,
  With pleasant Wines, and crackling blaze of Wood;
  Me Lonely sitting, nor the glimmering Light

Of Make-weight Candle, nor the joyous Talk
Of loving Friend delights; distress'd, forlorn,
Amidst the horrors of the tedious Night,
Darkling I sigh, and feed with dismal Thoughts
My anxious Mind; or sometimes mournful Verse
Indite, and sing of Groves and Myrtle Shades,
Or desperate Lady near a purling Stream,
Or Lover pendent on a Willow-Tree: (l. 93–105)

BXAP; NOEC; OAEL-1; Par

ROBERT PINSKY (b. 1940)

The Figured Wheel

1 The figured wheel rolls through shopping malls and
      prisons,
   Over farms, small and immense, and the rotten little
      downtowns. (l. 1–2)

2 Even in the scorched and frozen world of the dead after
      the holocaust
   The wheel as it turns goes on accreting ornaments.
                                                    (l. 34–35)

3 Of the wheel as it rolls unrelentingly over

   A cow plodding through car-traffic on a street in Iasi,
   And over the haunts of Robert Pinsky's mother and
      father
   And wife and children and his sweet self (l. 44–47)

MAYP; NAmP; NoAM; NPGG; PPR

RUTH PITTER (b. 1897)

Time's Fool

1 Poor comfort all comfort: once what the mouse had
      spared
   Was enough, was delight, there where the heart was at
      home; (l. 7–8)

2 The lily in splendor, the vine in her grace,
   The fox in the forest, all had their desire,
   As then I had mine, in the place that was happy and
      poor. (l. 16–18)

MoBrPo; OxBTC; PoRA; WPE

SYLVIA PLATH (1932–1963)

The Applicant

1 First, are you our sort of a person?
   Do you wear
   A glass eye, false teeth or a crutch,
   A brace or a hook,

Rubber breasts or a rubber crotch,

Stitches to show something's missing? (l. 1–6)

2 Black and stiff, but not a bad fit.
   Will you marry it? (l. 21–22)

3 Naked as paper to start

   But in twenty-five years she'll be silver,
   In fifty, gold. (l. 30–32)

4 It works, there is nothing wrong with it.
   You have a hole, it's a poultice.
   You have an eye, it's an image.
   My boy, it's your last resort.
   Will you marry it, marry it, marry it. (l. 36–40)

MAT; NAAL-2; NaP; NMM; NOBA; TwCP

Ariel

5 God's lioness,
   How one we grow,
   Pivot of heels and knees! — (l. 3–6)

6 White
   Godiva, I unpeel —
   Dead hands, dead stringencies. (l. 19–21)

7 I
   Am the arrow,

   The dew that flies
   Suicidal, at one with the drive
   Into the red

   Eye, the cauldron of morning. (l. 26–31)

CMoP; HCAP; HeIP; LCAP; MoP; NAAL-2; NoAM;
NOBA; NoP; PBWP; PoE

The Arrival of the Bee Box

8 I would say it was the coffin of a midget
   Or a square baby
   Were there not such a din in it. (l. 3–5)

9 I have simply ordered a box of maniacs.
   They can be sent back.
   They can die, I need feed them nothing, I am the
      owner. (l. 23–25)

10 I am no source of honey
   So why should they turn on me?
   Tomorrow I will be sweet God, I will set them free.

   The box is only temporary. (l. 33–36)

FaBoMo; FaBoWP; HCAP; NaP

The Bee Meeting

11 They are the villagers —
The rector, the midwife, the sexton, the agent for bees.
In my sleeveless summery dress I have no protection,
And they are all gloved and covered, why did nobody
    tell me? (l. 1–4)

12 I am nude as a chicken neck, does nobody love me?
Yes, here is the secretary of bees with her white shop
    smock, (l. 6–7)

13 Creamy bean flowers with black eyes and leaves like
    bored hearts.
Is it blood clots the tendrils are dragging up that
    string?
No, no, it is scarlet flowers that will one day be edible.
    (l. 18–20)

14 The white hive is snug as a virgin,
Sealing off her brood cells, her honey, and quietly
    humming.

Smoke rolls and scarves in the grove.
The mind of the hive thinks this is the end of
    everything. (l. 34–37)

15 She is very clever.
She is old, old, old, she must live another year, and she
    knows it.
While in their fingerjoint cells the new virgins

Dream of a duel they will win inevitably, (l. 43–46)

16 A curtain of wax dividing them from the bride flight,
The upflight of the murderess into a heaven that loves
    her. (l. 47–48)

17 The villagers are untying their disguises, they are
    shaking hands.
Whose is that long white box in the grove, what have
    they accomplished, why am I cold? (l. 54–56)

HCAP; InPS; PPP; WPE

Black Rook in Rainy Weather

18 A certain minor light may still
Leap incandescent

Out of kitchen table or chair
As if a celestial burning took
Possession of the most obtuse objects now and then —
    (l. 14–18)

19 I only know that a rook
Ordering its black feathers can so shine
As to seize me senses, haul
My eyelids up, and grant

A brief respite from fear
Of total neutrality. (l. 27–32)

20 Miracles occur,
if you care to call those spasmodic
Tricks of radiance miracles. The wait's begun again,
The long wait for the angel,
For that rare, random descent. (l. 36–40)

LiTM; NAAL-2; NePoEA-2; NIP; SM

Blackberrying

21 Blackberries
Big as the ball of my thumb, and dumb as eyes
Ebon in the hedges, fat
With blue-red juices. These they squander on my
    fingers.
I had not asked for such a blood sisterhood; they must
    love me. (l. 4–8)

22 I come to one bush of berries so ripe it is a bush of
    flies,
Hanging their bluegreen bellies and their wing panes in
    a Chinese screen.
The honey-feast of the berries has stunned them; they
    believe in heaven. (l. 15–17)

23 a great space
Of white and pewter lights, and a din like silversmiths
Beating and beating at an intractable metal.
    (l. 25–27)

HAP; HCAP; NAAL-2; NoAM; NOBA; NYBP

The Colossus

24 Thirty years now I have labored
To dredge the silt from your throat.
I am none the wiser. (l. 8–10)

25 Nights, I squat in the cornucopia
Of your left ear, out of the wind,

Counting the red stars and those of plum-color.
The sun rises under the pillar of your tongue.
    (l. 24–26)

CAPP; FaBoWP; HCAP; LiTM; NePoEA-2; NoAM;
NOBA; NoP; TAP

Daddy

26 You do not do, you do not do
Any more, black shoe
In which I have lived like a foot
For thirty years, (l. 1–4)

27 Daddy, I have had to kill you. (l. 6)

28 I used to pray to recover you.
Ach, du. (l. 14–15)

29 the language obscene

An engine, an engine
Chuffing me off like a Jew. (l. 30–32)

30 Every woman adores a Fascist,
The boot in the face, the brute
Brute heart of a brute like you. (l. 48–50)

31 I was ten when they buried you.
At twenty I tried to die
And get back, back, back to you. (l. 57–59)

32 If I've killed one man, I've killed two —
The vampire who said he was you
And drank my blood for a year,
Seven years, if you want to know. (l. 71–74)

33 There's a stake in your fat black heart
And the villagers never liked you.
They are dancing and stamping on you.
They always knew it was you.
Daddy, daddy, you bastard, I'm through. (l. 76–80)

BoWoP; CAPP; CMoP; CoAP; HCAP; HeIP; InPK; InPS;
LiTM; MoP; NAAL-2; NaP; NIP; NMM; NoAM; NOBA;
NoP; OPOP; PoE; PrIm; TwCP; TW; UnPo

Death and Co.

34 He tells me how sweet
The babies look in their hospital
Icebox, (l. 13–15)

35 His hair long and plausive.
Bastard
Masturbating a glitter,
He wants to be loved. (l. 22–25)

36 The dead bell,
The dead bell.

Somebody's done for. (l. 29–31)

CMoP; FF; LCAP; PrIm

Edge

37 The woman is perfected.
Her dead

Body wears the smile of accomplishment, (l. 1–3)

38 Each dead child coiled, a white serpent,
One at each little

Pitcher of milk, now empty. (l. 9–11)

39 The moon has nothing to be sad about,
Staring from her hood of bone.

She is used to this sort of thing.
Her blacks crackle and drag. (l. 17–18)

FaBoWP; HCAP; NAAL-2; PoE; TAP

Elm

40 I know the bottom, she says. I know it with my great
      tap root:
It is what you fear.
I do not fear it: I have been there. (l. 1–3)

41 Love is a shadow.
How you lie and cry after it.
Listen: these are its hooves: it has gone off, like a horse.
                                    (l. 7–9)

42 The moon, also, is merciless: she would drag me
Cruelly, being barren.
Her radiance scathes me. Or perhaps I have caught her.
                                    (l. 22–24)

43 What is this, this face
So murderous in its strangle of branches? —
                        (l. 38–39)

44 Its snaky acids kiss.
It petrifies the will. These are the isolate, slow faults
That kill, that kill, that kill. (l. 40–42)

NoAM; NOBA; NoP; NYBP

Fever 103°

45 Devilish leopard!
Radiation turned it white (l. 22–23)

46 Greasing the bodies of adulterers
Like Hiroshima ash and eating in.
The sin. The sin. (l. 25–27)

47 Darling, all night
I have been flickering, off, on, off, on.
The sheets grow heavy as a lecher's kiss. (l. 28–30)

48 I am too pure for you or anyone. (l. 34)

49 I am a lantern —

My head a moon
Of Japanese paper, my gold beaten skin
Infinitely delicate and infinitely expensive. (l. 36–39)

50 I

Am a pure acetylene
Virgin
Attended by roses,

By kisses, by cherubim,
By whatever these pink things mean. (l. 45–50)

51 Not him, nor him
(My selves dissolving, old whore petticoats) –
To Paradise. (l. 52–54)

CMoP; FaBoWP; NoAM; NOBA; VGW

Lady Lazarus

52 I have done it again.
One year in every ten
I manage it – (l. 1–3)

53 Do I terrify? –

The nose, the eye pits, the full set of teeth?
The sour breath
Will vanish in a day. (l. 12–15)

54 like the cat I have nine times to die.

This is Number Three.
What a trash
To annihilate each decade. (l. 21–24)

55 Dying
Is an art, like everything else.
I do it exceptionally well.

I do it so it feels like hell.
I do it so it feels real.
I guess you could say I've a call. (l. 43–48)

56 Herr God, Herr Lucifer,
Beware.
Beware.

Out of the ash
I rise with my red hair
And I eat men like air. (l. 79–84)

CAPP; FaBoWP; HCAP; MAT; MoP; NAAL-2; NaP; NIP;
NoAM; NOBA; NoP; PrIm; TAP; VGW

The Moon and the Yew Tree

57 The trees of the mind are black. (l. 2)

58 The moon is door. It is a face in its own right,
White as a knuckle and terribly upset.
It drags the sea after it like a dark crime; it is quiet
With the O-gape of complete despair. (l. 8–11)

59 The moon is my mother. She is not sweet like Mary.
Her blue garments unloose small bats and owls.
(l. 17–18)

60 The moon sees nothing of this. She is bald and wild.
(l. 27)

CoAP; FaBoMo; FaBoWP; NaP; NYBP; PPP; VGW;
WPE; WPOW

Morning Song

61 Love set you going like a fat gold watch.
The midwife slapped your footsoles, and your bald cry
Took its place among the elements. (l. 1–3)

62 All night your moth-breath
Flickers among the flat pink roses. I wake to listen:
A far sea moves in my ear. (l. 10–12)

63 One cry, and I stumble from bed, cow-heavy and floral
In my Victorian nightgown. (l. 13–14)

64 And now you try
Your handful of notes;
The clear vowels rise like balloons. (l. 16–18)

BoWoP; HCAP; HeIP; IHMS; InPK; InPS; LCAP;
NAAL-2; NAs; NOBA; PrIm

Mushrooms

65 Overnight, very
Whitely, discreetly,
Very quietly

Our toes, our noses
Take hold on the loam,
Acquire the air. (l. 1–6)

66 Bland-mannered, asking

Little or nothing.
So many of us!
So many of us! (l. 21–24)

67 Our kind multiplies:

We shall by morning
Inherit the earth.
Our foot's in the door. (l. 30–33)

BoNaP; FaBoWP; NePoEA-2; RB; WeW; WPOW

Nick and the Candlestick

68 Even the newts are white,

Those holy Joes.
And the fish, the fish –
Christ! they are panes of ice. (l. 12–15)

69 The candle
Gulps and recovers its small altitude,

Its yellows heaten. (l. 17–19)

70 The blood blooms clean

In you, ruby.
The pain
You wake to is not yours. (l. 24–27)

71 You are the one
Solid the spaces lean on, envious.
You are the baby in the barn. (l. 37–39)

CAPP; CoAP; LCAP; PBWP

Poppies in July

72 You flicker. I cannot touch you.
I put my hands among the flames. Nothing burns.

And it exhausts me to watch you
Flickering like that, wrinkly and clear red, like the skin
of a mouth. (l. 3–6)

73 Or your liquors seep to me, in this glass capsule,
Dulling and stilling.

But colourless. Colourless. (l. 13–15)

FaBoWP; LCAP; NaP; RB

Poppies in October

74 the woman in the ambulance
Whose red heart blooms through her coat so
astoundingly — (l. 2–3)

75 O my God, what am I
That these late mouths should cry open
In a forest of frost, in a dawn of cornflowers.
(l. 10–12)

FaBoWP; HCAP; LCAP; NoAM

Sheep in Fog

76 All morning the
Morning has been blackening,

A flower left out. (l. 8–10)

77 Fields melt my heart.

They threaten
To let me through to a heaven
Starless and fatherless, a dark water. (l. 12–15)

FaBoWP; HCAP; LCAP; NaP

Winter Trees

78 Knowing neither abortions nor bitchery,
Truer than women,
They seed so effortlessly! (l. 6–8)

79 Who are these pietas?
The shadows of ringdoves chanting, but easing nothing.
(l. 14–15)

CAPP; HCAP; LCAP; NMM

Words

80 Words dry and riderless,
The indefatigable hoof-taps.
While
From the bottom of the pool, fixed stars
Govern a life. (l. 16–20)

HCAP; LCAP; NAAL-2; PoE

You're

81 Clownlike, happiest on your hands
Feet to the stars, and moon-skulled,
Gilled like a fish. (l. 1–3)

82 Mute as a turnip from the Fourth
Of July to All Fools' Day,
O high-riser, my little loaf. (l. 7–9)

83 Snug as a bud and at home
Like a sprat in a pickle jug (l. 13–14)

84 Right, like a well-done sum.
A clean slate, with your own face on. (l. 17–18)

FaBoTw; FaBoWP; NAs; RB

PLATO (*fl.* 492–347 B.C.)

The Lover to His Lady (*attributed to* Plato)

1 My girl, thou gazest much
upon the golden skies: (l. 1–2)

CTC; FaBoEE; FF; OBSC

To Stella

2 Thou wert the morning star among the living (l. 1)

3   thou art as Hesperus, giving
New splendour to the dead. (l. 3–4)

AWP; EnLoPo; FaBoEE; OBVE

STANLEY PLUMLY   (b. 1939)

Out-of-the-Body Travel

1   And then he would lift this finest
of furniture to his big left shoulder
and tuck it in and draw the bow
so carefully as to make the music

almost visible on the air. (l. 1–5)

2   The violin
sustains him. It is pain remembered. (l. 18–19)

3   I know if I wake up cold,

and go out into the clear spring night,
still dark and precise with stars,
I will feel the wind coming down hard
like his hand, in fever, on my forehead. (l. 20–24)

AmPA; DiL; GeTw; LCAP

JOSEPH MARY PLUNKETT   (1887–1916)

I See His Blood upon the Rose

1   I see His blood upon the rose,
And in the stars the glory of His eyes
His body gleams amid eternal snows,
His tears fall from the skies. (l. 1–4)

2   All pathways by His feet are worn,
His strong heart stirs the ever-beating sea;
His crown of thorns is twined with every thorn;
His cross is every tree. (l. 9–12)

PoLF; TIRV; WGRP

EDGAR ALLAN POE   (1809–1849)

Al Aaraaf

1   Science! true daughter of old Time thou art!
Who alterest all things with thy peering eyes.
Why preyest thou thus upon the poet's heart,
Vulture, whose wings are dull realities?
How should he love thee — or how deem thee wise
Who wouldst not leave him in his wandering,

2   Hast thou not dragged Diana from her car,
And driven the hamadryad from the wood
To seek a shelter in some happier star?
Hast thou not torn the naiad from her flood,
The elfin from the green grass, and from me
The summer dream beneath the tamarind tree?

AmPP; NAAL-1; NoP; OxBA; TAP; TW

Annabel Lee

3   It was many and many a year ago,
In a kingdom by the sea,
That a maiden there lived whom you may know
By the name of Annabel Lee;
And this maiden she lived with no other thought
Than to love and be loved by me. (l. 1–6)

4   She was a child and I was a child,
In this kingdom by the sea,
But we loved with a love that was more than love —
I and my Annabel Lee —
With a love that the winged seraphs of Heaven
Coveted her and me. (l. 7–12)

5   the wind came out of the cloud chilling
And killing my Annabel Lee. (l. 25–26)

6   And so all the night-tide, I lie down by the side
Of my darling, my darling, my life and my bride
In her sepulchre there by the sea —
In her tomb by the side of the sea. (l. 38–41)

AA; AiP; AmPP; AnAmPo; AWP; BeLS; BLPA; CH; DL;
FaFP; FaPON; FPL; HeIP; LiTA; NAAL-1; NOBA; NoP;
OBCA; OnMSP; OPOP; OxBA; PrIm; TAP; TrGrPo;
WBLP

The Assignation

7   Thou wast all that to me, love,
For which my soul did pine:

8   And all my days are trances,
And all my nightly dreams
Are where thy dark eye glances,
And where thy footstep gleams —
In what ethereal dances,
By what eternal streams.

AA; AmPP; AnAmPo; BLPL; BoLoP; LiTA; OBEV; OxBA;
PoLF; TAP; TrGrPo

The Bells

9   Hear the sledges with the bells —
Silver bells! (l. 1–2)

10 While the stars that oversprinkle
All the heavens, seem to twinkle
With a crystalline delight;
Keeping time, time, time,
In a sort of Runic rhyme,
To the tintinnabulation that so musically wells
From the bells, bells, bells, bells, (l. 6–12)

AA; AnAmPo; FaFP; FaPON; FaPON; FPL; GN; LiTA;
OBAL; OBCA; OHFP; PoLF; RR; TAP; WBLP

The City in the Sea

11 Lo! Death has reared himself a throne
In a strange city lying alone
Far down within the dim West,
Where the good and the bad and the worst and the best
Have gone to their eternal rest. (l. 1–5)

12 Resignedly beneath the sky
The melancholy waters lie.
So blend the turrets and shadows there
That all seem pendulous in air,
While from a proud tower in the town
Death looks gigantically down. (l. 24–29)

13 The waves have now a redder glow —
The hours are breathing faint and low —
And when, amid no earthly moans,
Down, down that town shall settle hence,
Hell, rising from a thousand thrones,
Shall do it reverence. (l. 48–53)

AA; AmPP; AnAmPo; LiTA; MAT; MOS; NAAL-1; NOBA;
NoP; OxBA; PoE; PoEL-4; SCV; TAP; TrGrPo

A Dream within a Dream

14 I stand amid the roar
Of a surf-tormented shore,
And I hold within my hand
Grains of the golden sand —
How few! yet how they creep
Through my fingers to the deep,
While I weep — while I weep! (l. 1–7)

15 Is all that we see or seem
But a dream within a dream? (l. 12–13)

AmPP; AnAmPo; BLPL; ChTr; GBL; NOBA; OxBA; TAP;
TrGrPo

Dream-Land

16 By a route obscure and lonely,
Haunted by ill angels only,
Where an eidolon, named Night,
On a black throne reigns upright,
I have reached these lands but newly

From an ultimate dim Thule —
From a wild weird clime that lieth, sublime,
Out of space — out of time. (l. 1–8)

17 There the traveler meets, aghast,
Sheeted memories of the past —
Shrouded forms that start and sigh
As they pass the wanderer by —
White-robed forms of friends long given,
In agony, to the earth — and heaven. (l. 33–38)

AmPP; AnAmPo; LiTA; NAAL-1; NOBA; OxBA; TAP

Eldorado

18 Gaily bedight,
A gallant knight,
In sunshine and in shadow,
Had journeyed long,
Singing a song,
In search of Eldorado.

19 "Over the mountains
Of the moon,
Down the valley of the shadow,
Ride, boldly ride,"
The shade replied, —
"If you seek for Eldorado!"

AmPP; AnAmPo; AWP; FaBoBe; FaBoCh; FPL; NOBA;
NoP; OxBA; RR; TAP; WiR

The Fall of the House of Usher

20 In the greenest of our valleys
By good angels tenanted,
Once a fair and stately palace —
Radiant palace — reared its head.
In the monarch Thought's dominion,
It stood there!

21 Banners yellow, glorious, golden,
On its roof did float and flow

22 But evil things, in robes of sorrow,
Assailed the monarch's high estate;

23 like a ghastly rapid river,
Through the pale door
A hideous throng rush out forever,
And laugh — but smile no more.

AA; AnAmPo; BeLS; CH; ChTr; LiTA; NOBA; OxBA;
PoEL-4; PrIm; TAP; TrGrPo; WiR; WSC

For Annie

24 When the light was extinguished,
She covered me warm,
And she prayed to the angels
To keep me from harm — (l. 79–82)

25 It glows with the light
Of the love of my Annie —
With the thought of the light
Of the eyes of my Annie. (l. 99–102)

AmPP; AnAmPo; BLPL; LiTA; NOBA; OBEV; OxBA

Israfel

26 In Heaven a spirit doth dwell
"Whose heart-strings are a lute;"
None sing so wildly well
As the angel Israfel,
And the giddy stars (so legends tell)
Ceasing their hymns, attend the spell
Of his voice, all mute. (l. 1–7)

27 Yes, Heaven is thine; but this
Is a world of sweets and sours;
Our flowers are merely — flowers,
And the shadow of thy perfect bliss
Is the sunshine of ours. (l. 40–44)

28 a bolder note than this might swell
From my lyre within the sky. (l. 50–51)

AA; AmPP; AWP; BLPL; LiTA; NAAL-1; NOBA; OxBA;
PoE; PoEL-4; TAP

Lenore

29 Ah, broken is the golden bowl! the spirit flown forever!
Let the bell toll! — a saintly soul floats on the Stygian
river;
And, Guy De Vere, hast thou no tear? — weep now or
never more!
See! on yon drear and rigid bier low lies thy love,
Lenore!

30 "Avaunt! to-night my heart is light. No dirge will I
upraise.
"But waft the angel on her flight with a pæan of old
days!
"Let no bell toll! — lest her sweet soul, amid its
hallowed mirth,
"Should catch the note, as it doth float up from the
damned Earth.
"To friends above, from fiends below, the indignant
ghost is riven —
"From Hell unto a high estate far up within the
Heaven —
"From grief and groan, to a golden throne, beside the
King of Heaven."

AA; AmPP; AnAmPo; LiTA

Ligeia

31 But see, amid the mimic rout
A crawling shape intrude! (l. 25–26)

32 The mimes become its food,
And seraphs sob at vermin fangs
In human gore imbued. (l. 30–32)

33 While the angels, all pallid and wan,
Uprising, unveiling, affirm
That the play is the tragedy "Man",
And its hero the Conqueror Worm. (l. 38–40)

AA; AnAmPo; AWP; BLPL; DL; LiTA; NOBA; OBD

The Raven

34 Once upon a midnight dreary, while I pondered, weak
and weary,
Over many a quaint and curious volume of forgotten
lore,
While I nodded, nearly napping, suddenly there came a
tapping,
As of some one gently rapping, rapping at my chamber
door. (l. 1–4)

35 Ah, distinctly I remember it was in the bleak
December,
And each separate dying ember wrought its ghost upon
the floor.
Eagerly I wished the morrow; — vainly I had sought to
borrow
From my books surcease of sorrow — sorrow for the lost
Lenore — (l. 7–10)

36 "Though thy crest be shorn and shaven, thou," I said,
"art sure no craven,
Ghastly grim and ancient raven wandering from the
Nightly shore —
Tell me what thy lordly name is on the Night's
Plutonian shore!"
Quoth the raven, "Nevermore." (l. 44–47)

37 And the raven, never flitting, still is sitting, still is
sitting
On the pallid bust of Pallas just above my chamber
door;
And his eyes have all the seeming of a demon's that is
dreaming,
And the lamp-light o'er him streaming throws his
shadow on the floor;
And my soul from out that shadow that lies floating on
the floor
Shall be lifted — nevermore! (l. 102–107)

AA; AmPP; AnAmPo; BeLS; BLPA; CH; FaBoBe;
FaBoCh; FaBV; FaFP; FPL; GN; GoJo; HeIP; LiTA;
NAAL-1; NIP; NOBA; OBCA; OBNV; OHFP; OxBA;
PoRA; PWR; TAP; WBLP

Romance

38 Romance, who loves to nod and sing,
With drowsy head and folded wing, (l. 1–2)

39 Taught me my alphabet to say,
To lisp my very earliest word. (l. 7–8)

40 Of late, eternal Condor years
So shake the very Heaven on high
With tumult as they thunder by,
I have no time for idle cares
Through gazing on the unquiet sky. (l. 11–15)

AmPP; AnAmPo; NAAL-1; NOBA; OxBA

The Sleeper

41 The lady sleeps! Oh, may her sleep,
Which is enduring, so be deep!
Heaven have her in its sacred keep! (l. 37–39)

42 Far in the forest, dim and old,
For her may some tall vault unfold — (l. 48–49)

43 Some sepulcher, remote, alone,
Against whose portal she hath thrown,
In childhood, many an idle stone —
Some tomb from out whose sounding door
She ne'er shall force an echo more,
Thrilling to think, poor child of sin!
It was the dead who groaned within. (l. 54–60)

AA; AmPP; AnAmPo; LiTA; NAAL-1; NOBA; OxBA;
PoEL-4; TAP; TrGrPo

To Helen

44 Helen, thy beauty is to me
Like those Nicean barks of yore, (l. 1–2)

45 On desperate seas long wont to roam,
The hyacinth hair, thy classic face,
Thy Naiad airs have brought me home
To the glory that was Greece,
And the grandeur that was Rome. (l. 6–10)

AA; AmPP; AnAmPo; AWP; BoLoP; CH; ChTr; FaBoBe;
FaBV; FaFP; FL; FPL; GBL; HAP; HeIP; HoPM; InPS;
InvP; LiTA; NAAL-1; NIP; NOBA; NOBE; NoP; OBEV;
OxBA; PoE; PoEL-4; PoLF; PoRA; PrIm; TAP; TrGrPo;
WeW

Ulalume

46 The skies they were ashen and sober; (l. 1)

47 It was night, in the lonesome October (l. 4)

48 In the misty mid region of Weir — (l. 7)

49 And we passed to the end of a vista,
But were stopped by the door of a tomb —
By the door of a legended tomb;

And I said — " What is written, sweet sister,
On the door of this legended tomb?"
She replied — "Ulalume — Ulalume! —
'Tis the vault of thy lost Ulalume!" (l. 75–81)

AA; AmPP; AnAmPo; AWP; BLPL; LiTA; NAAL-1;
NOBA; OxBA; TAP

ALEXANDER POPE (1688–1744)

The Dunciad

1 She comes! She comes! The sable throne behold
Of Night primaeval, and of Chaos old!

2 Physic of Metaphysic begs defence,
And Metaphysic calls for aid on Sense!
See Mystery to Mathematics fly!
In vain! they gaze, turn giddy, rave, and die.
Religion blushingveils her sacred fires,
And unawares Morality expires.
Nor public flame, nor private, dares to shine;
Nor human spark is left, nor glimpse divine!
Lo! thy dread Empire, Chaos, is restored;
Light dies before thy uncreating word:
Thy hand, great Anarch, lets the curtain fall;
And Universal Darkness buries All.

EBEV; FaBoPV; FiP; NOBE; NOEC; NoP; SCV

Elegy to the Memory of an Unfortunate Lady

3 Is it, in Heav'n, a crime to love too well?
To bear too tender or too firm a heart,
To act a lover's or a Roman's part? (l. 6–8)

4 Most souls, 'tis true, but peep out once an age,
Dull sullen pris'ners in the body's cage:
Dim lights of life, that burn a length of years,
Useless, unseen, as lamps in sepulchres; (l. 17–20)

ACP; FiP; NOBE; NOEC; OAEL-1; OBD; OBEV; TEP

Epigram Engraved on the Collar of a Dog Given to His Royal Highness

5 I am his Highness' dog at Kew;
Pray tell me, sir, whose dog are you? (l. 1–2)

ChTr; FaBoCo; FaBoEE; FM; InPK; LiTB; NOEC;
NTCP; OxBoLi; OxBSP; RHPC; SoSe; TTTS

Epistle to Dr. Arbuthnot

6 Blest with each talent, and each art to please,
And born to write, converse, and live with ease

7 Damn with faint praise, assent with civil leer,
And, without sneering, teach the rest to sneer;
Willing to wound, and yet afraid to strike,
Just hint a fault, and hesitate dislike;
Alike reserved to blame, or to commend,
A timorous foe, and a suspicious friend;
Dreading e'en fools, by flatterers besieged,
And so obliging, that he ne'er obliged;
Like Cato, give his little senate laws,
And sit attentive to his own applause:

8 Who but must laugh, if such a man there be?
Who would not weep, if Atticus were he?

AWP; InPK; InPS; NOBE; NOEC; NoP; OAEL-1;
OxBoLi; PoE; PoEL-3; SeCePo

9 Let Sporus tremble — 'What? That thing of silk,
Sporus, that mere white curd of ass's milk?
Satire or sense, alas, can Sporus feel,
Who breaks a butterfly upon a wheel?'
Yet let me flap this bug with gilded wings,
This painted child of dirt, that stinks and stings;
Whose buzz the witty and the fair annoys,
Yet wit ne'er tastes, and beauty ne'er enjoys:

10 Eternal smiles his emptiness betray,
As shallow streams run dimpling all the way.

11 His wit all see-saw, between that and this,
Now high, now low, now Master up, now Miss,
And he himself one vile antithesis.

12 Beauty that shocks you, parts that none will trust,
Wit that can creep, and pride that licks the dust.

AWP; ChTr; InPS; NOBE; NOEC; NoP; OAEL-1; OBSV;
OxBoLi; PoE; PoEL-3; SCV

13 Why did I write? what sin to me unknown
Dipp'd me in ink, my parents', or my own?
As yet a child, nor yet a fool to fame,
I lisp'd in numbers, for the numbers came.

14 The Muse but served to ease some friend, not wife,
To help me through this long disease, my life;

15 Did some more sober critic come abroad —
If wrong, I smiled; if right, I kiss'd the rod.

16 A man's true merit 'tis not hard to find;
But each man's secret standard in his mind,
That casting-weight pride adds to emptiness,
This, who can gratify, for who can guess?

ChTr; EBEV; FiP; InPS; NOEC; NoP; OAEL-1; OxBoLi;
PoE; PoEL-3; TOF

Epistle to Miss Blount, on Her Leaving the Town after the Coronation

17 She sigh'd not that They stay'd, but that She went.

18 To muse, and spill her solitary Tea,

19

Up to her godly garret after sev'n,
There starve and pray, for that's the way to heav'n.

20 Whose laughs are hearty, tho' his jests are coarse,
And loves you best of all things — but his horse.

BoLoP; EBEV; NAEL-1; NOBE; NOEC; NoP; OPOP;
PoEL-3; PPP

Essay on Criticism

21 'Tis hard to say, if greater want of skill
Appear in writing or in judging ill; (Fr. I)

22 'Tis with our judgments as our watches, none
Go just alike, yet each believes his own. (Fr. I)

23 Some have at first for wits, then poets passed,
Turned critics next, and proved plain fools at last.
(Fr. I)

24 So vast is art, so narrow human wit. (Fr. I)

25 First follow Nature, and your judgment frame
By her just standard, which is still the same;
Unerring Nature, still divinely bright,
One clear, unchanged, and universal light,
Life, force, and beauty must to all impart,
At once the source, and end, and test of art. (Fr. I)

26 For wit and judgment often are at strife,
Though meant each other's aid, like man and wife.
(Fr. I)

27 Those rules of old discovered, not devised,
Are Nature still, but Nature methodized;
Nature, like liberty, is but restrained
By the same laws which first herself ordained. (Fr. I)

28 Nature and Homer were, he found, the same. (Fr. I)

29 Learn hence for ancient rules a just esteem;
To copy Nature is to copy them. (Fr. I)

30 Thus Pegasus, a nearer way to take,
May boldly deviate from the common track.
From vulgar bounds with brave disorder part,
And snatch a grace beyond the reach of art,
Which without passing through the judgment, gains
The heart, and all its end at once attains. (Fr. I)

31 Still green with bays each ancient altar stands
Above the reach of sacrilegious hands, (Fr. I)

32 Is pride, the never-failing vice of fools. (Fr. II)

33 A little learning is a dang'rous thing;
Drink deep, or taste not the Pierian spring:
There shallow draughts intoxicate the brain,
And drinking largely sobers us again. (Fr. II)

34 Th' increasing prospect tires our wand'ring eyes.
   Hills peep o'er hills, and Alps on Alps arise!
   A perfect Judge will read each work of Wit
   With the same spirit that its author writ:
   Survey the Whole, nor seek slight faults to find
   Where nature moves, and rapture warms the mind;
                          (Fr. II)

35 what affects our hearts
   Is not the exactness of peculiar parts;
   'Tis not a lip, or eye, we beauty call,
   But the joint force and full result of all. (Fr. II)

HAP; PoEL-3

36 All comes unitedto th' admiring eyes; (Fr. II)

ChTr; FaFP; FPL; HAP; HoPM; LiTB; NOBE; PoEL-3;
PoLF; SeCePo; TrGrPo

37 True wit is Nature to advantage dressed,
   What oft was thought, but ne'er so well expressed;
   Something whose truth convinced at sight we find,
   That gives us back the image of our mind. (Fr. II)

38 Words are like leaves; and where they most abound,
   Much fruit of sense beneath is rarely found. (Fr. II)

39 Be not the first by whom the new are tried,
   Nor yet the last to lay the old aside. (Fr. II)

40 These equal syllables alone require,
   Though oft the ear the open vowels tire; (Fr. II)

41 And ten low words oft creep in one dull line: (Fr. II)

42 Where'er you find 'the cooling western breeze,'
   In the next line, it 'whispers through the trees':
   If crystal streams 'with pleasing murmurs creep':
   The reader's threaten'd (not in vain) with 'sleep.'
                          (Fr. II)

43 A needless Alexandrine ends the song,
   That, like a wounded snake, drags its slow length along.
                          (Fr. II)

44 True ease in writing comes from art, not chance,
   As those move easiest who have learn'd to dance.
   'Tis not enough no harshness gives offence,
   The sound must seem an echo to the sense: (Fr. II)

FaBoUs; HAP; NIP; PoEL-3; SeCePo

45 For fools admire, but men of sense approve: (Fr. II)

46 Some ne'er advance a judgment of their own,
   But catch the spreading notion of the town; (Fr. II)

47 Some judge of authors' names, not works, and then
   Nor praise nor blame the writings, but the men.
                          (Fr. II)

48 Some praise at morning what they blame at night,
   But always think the last opinion right. (Fr. II)

49 Be thou the first true merit to befriend;
   His praise is lost who stays till all commend. (Fr. II)

50 Our sons their fathers' failing language see,
   And such as Chaucer is shall Dryden be. (Fr. II)

51 Good nature and good sense must ever join;
   To err is human, to forgive divine. (Fr. II)

52 Learn then what morals critics ought to show,
   For 'tis but half a judge's task, to know. (Fr. III)

53 Be silent always when you doubt your sense;
   And speak, though sure, with seeming diffidence:
                          (Fr. III)

54 Fear most to tax an honorable fool,
   Whose right it is, uncensured to be dull; (Fr. III)

55 The bookful blockhead, ignorantly read,
   With loads of learned lumber in his head.
   With his own tongue still edifies his ears,
   And always listening to himself appears. (Fr. III)

56 For fools rush in where angels fear to tread. (Fr. III)

57 Though learned, well-bred; and though well-bred,
     sincere;
   Modestly bold, and humanly severe:
   Who to a friend his faults can freely show,
   And gladly praise the merit of a foe? (Fr. III)

FiP; HAP; NAEL-1; OAEL-1; PoEL-3

An Essay on Man

58 Awake, my St. John! leave all meaner things
   To low ambition, and the pride of Kings.
   Let us (since Life can little more supply
   Than just to look about us and to die)
   Expatiate free o'er all this scene of Man;
   A mighty maze! but not without a plan; (Fr. Epistle I)

59 Laugh where we must, be candid where we can;
   But vindicate the ways of God to Man. (Fr. Epistle I)

60 Say first, of God above, or Man below,
   What can we reason, but from what we know?
                       (Fr. Epistle I)

61 'Tis but a part we see, and not a whole. (Fr. Epistle I)

62 Then say not Man's imperfect, Heav'n in fault;
   Say rather, Man's as perfect as he ought:
                      (Fr. Epistle I)

63 Heav'n from all creatures, hides the book of Fate,
All but the page prescrib'd, their present state:
(Fr. Epistle I)

64 Oh blindness to the future! kindly giv'n,
That each may fill the circle mark'd by Heav'n:
(Fr. Epistle I)

65 Hope springs eternal in the human breast:
Man never Is, but always To be blest: (Fr. Epistle I)

66 In Pride, in reas'ning Pride, our error lies;
All quit their sphere, and rush into the skies.
Pride still is aiming at the blest abodes,
Men would be Angels, Angels would be Gods.
(Fr. Epistle I)

67 From pride, from pride, our very reas'ning springs;
Account for moral, as for nat'ral things:
Why charge we Heav'n in those, in these acquit?
In both, to reason right is to submit. (Fr. Epistle I)

68 But all subsists by elemental strife;
And Passions are the elements of Life. (Fr. Epistle I)

69 Why has not Man a microscopic eye?
For this plain reason, Man is not a Fly. (Fr. Epistle I)

70 Die of a rose in aromatic pain? (Fr. Epistle I)

71 The spider's touch, how exquisitely fine!
Feels at each thread, and lives along the line:
(Fr. Epistle I)

72 Vast chain of Being, which from God began,
Natures æthereal, human, angel, man,
Beast, bird, fish, insect! what no eye can see,
No glass can reach; from Infinite to thee,
From thee to Nothing! — (Fr. Epistle I)

73 From Nature's chain whatever link you strike,
Tenth or ten thousandth, breaks the chain alike.
(Fr. Epistle I)

74 All are but parts of one stupendous whole,
Whose body Nature is, and God the soul;
(Fr. Epistle I)

75 And, spite of Pride, in erring Reason's spite,
One truth is clear, Whatever is, is right. (Fr. Epistle I)

NAEL-1; NoP; PoEL-3; PrIm

76 Lo, the poor Indian! whose untutor'd mind
Sees God in clouds, or hears him in the wind;
(Fr. Epistle I)

77 To be, contents his natural desire;
He asks no Angel's wing, no Seraph's fire;
But thinks, admitted to that equal sky,
His faithful dog shall bear him company.
(Fr. Epistle I)

78 Know then thyself, presume not God to scan,
The proper study of mankind is Man.
Placed on this isthmus of a middle state,
A being darkly wise and rudely great:
With too much knowledge for the Sceptic side,
With too much weakness for the Stoic's pride,
He hangs between; in doubt to act or rest,
In doubt to deem himself a God or Beast,
In doubt his mind or body to prefer;
Born but to die, and reasoning but to err;
Alike in ignorance, his reason such
Whether he thinks too little or too much:
Chaos of thought and passion, all confused;
Still by himself abused, or disabused;
Created half to rise and half to fall;
Great lord of all things, yet a prey to all;
Sole judge of truth, in endless error hurled;
The glory, jest, and riddle of the world!
(Fr. Epistle II)

ACP; BLPL; FaFP; FiP; LiTB; NAEL-1; NOBE; NOEC;
NoP; OAEL-1; PoEL-3; PrIm; SeCePo; TrGrPo

79 some strange comfort every state attend,
And pride bestowed on all, a common friend;
(Fr. Epistle II)

80 Hope travels through, nor quits us when we die.
(Fr. Epistle II)

81 Scarfs, garters, gold, amuse his riper stage,
And beads and prayer-books are the toys of age:
Pleased with this bauble still, as that before;
'Till tired he sleeps, and life's poor play is o'er.
(Fr. Epistle II)

SeCePo

82 See! and confess, one comfort still must rise,
'Tis this, — Though man's a fool, yet God is wise.
(Fr. Epistle II)

83 For forms of government let fools contest;
Whate'er is best administered is best: (Fr. Epistle III)

84 What's fame? A fancied life in others' breath,
(Fr. Epistle IV)

85 An honest man's the noblest work of God.
(Fr. Epistle IV)

86 Know then this truth (enough for man to know)
"Virtue alone is happiness below." (Fr. Epistle IV)

NU

The First Satire of the Second Book of Horace

87 There are (I scarce can think it, but am told)
There are, to whom my satire seems too bold: (l. 1–2)

88 I love to pour out all my self, as plain
As downright Shippen or as old Montaigne:

89 Satire's my weapon, but I'm too discreet
To run amuck, and tilt at all I meet; (l. 69–70)

90 P — xed by her love, or libeled by her hate. (l. 84)

91 Yes, while I live, no rich or noble knave
Shall walk the world, in credit, to his grave.
To Virtue only and her friends, a friend,
The world beside may murmur, or commend.
(l. 119–122)

92 There St. John mingles with my friendly bowl
The feast of reason and the flow of soul; (l. 127–128)

OAEL-1; PPP

Moral Essays: Epistle to a Lady

93 Nothing so true as what you once let fall:
'Most women have no characters at all.'

94 Ladies, like variegated tulips, show,
'Tis to their changes that their charms we owe;

95 And die of nothing but a rage to live.

96 Woman and fool are two hard things to hit,
For true no-meaning puzzles more than wit.

97 In men we various ruling passions find,
In women, two almost divide the kind;
Those, only fixed, they first or last obey,
The love of pleasure, and the love of sway.

98 by man's oppression cursed,
They seek the second not to lose the first.
Men, some to bus'ness, some to pleasure take;
But ev'ry woman is at heart a rake:

99 Woman's at best a contradiction still.

NAEL-1; NOEC; OAEL-1; OxBoLi

Moral Essays: Epistle to Richard Boyle, Earl of Burlington

100 At Timon's villalet us pass a day,
Where all cry out,What sums are thrown away!'

101 Lo, what huge heaps of littleness around!

102 My Lord advances with majestic mien,
Smit with the mighty pleasure to be seen:

103 And now the chapel's silver bell you hear,
That summons you to all the pride of pray'r:

104 To rest, the cushion and soft dean invite,
Who never mentions hell to ears polite.

105 Is this a dinner? this a genial room?
No, 'tis a temple, and a hecatomb.
A solemn sacrifice, performed in state,
You drink by measure, and to minutes eat.

NOEC; OAEL-1; OBSV; PoEL-3; PPP

Nature and Nature's laws lay hid in Night

106 Nature and Nature's laws lay hid in night:
God said, Let Newton be! and all was light. (l. 1–2)

FaBoCo; FaBoEE; FiP; ImOP; InPK; WeW

Ode on Solitude

107 Happy the man whose wish and care
A few paternal acres bound,
Content to breathe his native air
In his own ground: (l. 1–4)

108 Thus let me live, unseen, unknown;
Thus unlamented let me die;
Steal from the world, and not a stone
Tell where I lie. (l. 17–20)

AWP; FaFP; FiP; FL; GTBS; GTBS-P; HeIP; InvP; NAEL-1; PoRA; Prf; TEP; TrGrPo

On a Certain Lady at Court

109 I know the thing that's most uncommon
(Envy be silent and attend!);
I know a reasonable woman,
Handsome and witty, yet a friend.

Not warped by passion, awed by rumour,
Not grave through pride, or gay through folly;
An equal mixture of good humour
And sensible soft melancholy.

'Has she no faults, then (Envy says), sir?'
Yes, she has one, I must aver:
When all the world conspires to praise her,
The woman's deaf, and does not hear. (l. 1–12)

NOBE; NOEC; OBEV; OxBSP; TrGrPo

The Rape of the Lock

110 What dire offence from am'rous causes springs,
What mighty contests rise from trivial things,
I sing — (Fr. I)

111 Now lapdogs give themselves the rousing shake,
And sleepless lovers, just at twelve, awake: (Fr. I)

112 With varying vanities, from ev'ry part,
They shift the moving toyshop of their heart; (Fr. I)

113 Th' inferior priestess, at her altar's side,
Trembling, begins the sacred rites of pride. (Fr. I)

114 Here files of pins extend their shining rows,
Puffs, powders, patches, bibles, billet-doux. (Fr. I)

HAP; NOEC; NoP; OAEL-1; OBNV; PoEL-3; TEP;
TrGrPo

115 On her white breast a sparkling cross she wore,
Which Jews might kiss, and infidels adore. (Fr. II)

116 Smooth flow the waves, the zephyrs gently play,
Belinda smiled, and all the world was gay. (Fr. II)

117 Whether the nymph shall break Diana's law,
Or some frail china jar receive a flaw,
Or stain her honour, or her new brocade, (Fr. II)

EBEV; HAP; NOBE; NOEC; NoP; OAEL-1; OBNV;
PoEL-3; TEP; TrGrPo

118 Here thou, great Anna! whom three realms obey,
Dost sometimes counsel take — and sometimes tea.
(Fr. III)

119 At every word a reputation dies. (Fr. III)

120 And wretches hang that jury-men may dine; (Fr. III)

121 The skilful Nymph reviews her force with care:
Let Spades be trumps! she said, and trumps they were.
(Fr. III)

122 The Nymph exulting fills with shouts the sky;
The walls, the woods, and long canals reply. (Fr. III)

123 But when to mischief mortals bend their will,
How soon they find fit instruments of ill! (Fr. III)

124 The Peer now spreads the glitt'ring Forfex wide,
T'inclose the Lock; now joins it, to divide. (Fr. III)

FaBoPP; FiP; HAP; NoP; OAEL-1; OBNV; OBSV;
OxBoLi; PoEL-3; TEP; TrGrPo

Sir, I admit your general rule (*attributed to* Pope)

125 Sir, I admit your gen'ral rule
That every poet is a fool:
But you yourself may serve to show it,
That every fool is not a poet. (l. 1–4)

FaBoEE; FiBHP; LiTB; NBLV

The Universal Prayer

126 Father of all in every age,
In every clime adored,
By saint, by savage, and by sage,
Jehovah, Jove, or Lord!

127 What blessings thy free bounty gives
Let me not cast away;
For God is paid when man receives,
To enjoy is to obey.

128 If I am right, thy grace impart
Still in the right to stay;
If I am wrong, O, teach my heart
To find that better way!

BLPA; FaEoBe; FPL; NoP; WGRP

When other fair ones to the shades go down

129 When other Ladies to the Shades go down,
Still Flavia, Chloris, Celia stay in Town;
Those Ghosts of Beauty ling'ring there abide,
And haunt the places where their Honour dy'd.

FaBoCo; FaEoEE; OxBSP; PoEL-3

J. R. POPE (1909–1991)

A Word of Encouragement

1 O what a tangled web we weave
When first we practice to deceive!
But when we've practised quite a while (l. 1–3)

FiBHP; FPL; NBLV; NOBL

BEATRIX POTTER (1866–1943)

The Old Woman

1 I think if she lived in
A little shoe-house —
That little old woman was
Surely a mouse! (l. 5–8)

GoJo; NTCP; PDV; RAR

EZRA POUND (1885–1972)

Alba

1 As cool as the pale wet leaves of lily-of-the-valley
(l. 1)

GBL; HAP; SOTW; WeW

Ancient Music

2 Winter is icummen in,
Lhude sing Goddamm,
Raineth drop and staineth slop,
And how the wind doth ramm! (l. 1–4)

BXAP; FaBoCo; FaBoPa; FF; HeIP; LiTM; NBLV; OBAL;
OxBA; Par; TW

Ballad of the Goodly Fere

3 Oh we drunk his "Hale" in the good red wine
When we last made company,
No capon priest was the Goodly Fere
But a man o' men was he. (l. 13–16)

4 A master of men was the Goodly Fere,
A mate of the wind and sea,
If they think they ha' slain our Goodly Fere
They are fools eternally.

I ha' seen him eat o' the honey-comb
Sin' they nailed him to the tree. (l. 49–54)

CMoP; LiTA; LiTM; MoAB; MoAmPo; MoBS; OFD;
PoRA; TrCP; TrGrPo

CANTOS (the following 3 poems)

I

5 But first Elpenor came, our friend Elpenor,
Unburied, cast on the wide earth,
Limbs that we left in the house of Circe,
Unwept, unwrapped in sepulchre, since toils urged
    other. (l. 42–45)

6 "But thou, O King, I bid remember me, unwept,
    unburied,
"Heap up mine arms, be tomb by sea-bord, and
    inscribed:
"A man of no fortune, and with a name to come.
                    (l. 54–56)

7 Lie quiet Divus. (l. 68)

8 Venerandam,
In the Cretan's phrase, with the golden crown,
    Aphrodite,
Cypri munimenta sortita est, mirthful, oricalchi, with
    golden
Girdles and breast bands, thou with dark eyelids
Bearing the golden bough of Argicida. (l. 72–76)

AmPP; CMoP; LiTA; MoAB; MoAmPo; MoP; NoAM;
NoP; OBVE; PoE; TrGrPo; VGW

XLV

9 no picture is made to endure nor to live with
but it is made to sell and sell quickly
with usura, sin against nature,

is thy bread ever more of stale rags
is thy bread dry as paper,

10 Duccio came not by usura
nor Pier della Francesca; Zuan Bellin' not by usura
nor was 'La Calunnia' painted.
Came not by usura Angelico; came not Ambrogio
    Praedis,
Came no church of cut stone signed: Adamo me fecit.

11 It hath brought palsey to bed, lyeth
between the young bride and her bridegroom
CONTRA NATURAM
They have brought whores for Eleusis
Corpses are set to banquet
at behest of usura.

CMoP; LiTM; NAAL-2; NOBA; PoE; TW

LXXXI

12 "You the one, I the few"
said John Adams
speaking of fears in the abstract
to his volatile friend Mr. Jefferson, (l. 49–52)

13 (To break the pentameter, that was the first heave)
                    (l. 53)

14 What counts is the cultural level, (l. 64)

15 Yet
Ere the season died a-cold
Borne upon a zephyr's shoulder
Irose through the aureate sky (l. 94–97)

16 Hast 'ou fashioned so airy a mood
To draw up leaf from the root?
Hast 'ou found a cloud so light
As seemed neither mist nor shade? (l. 105–108)

17 And for 180 years almost nothing. (l. 113)

18 What thou lovest well remains, (l. 131)

19 What thou lov'st well shall not be reft from thee
What thou lov'st well is thy true heritage
Whose world, or mine or theirs
or is it of none? (l. 133–136)

20 The ant's a centaur in his dragon world.
Pull down thy vanity, it is not man
Made courage, or made order, or made grace.
Pull down thy vanity, I say pull down. (l. 141–144)

21 Learn of the green world what can be thy place
In scaled invention or true artistry, (l. 145–146)

22 Thou art a beaten dog beneath the hail,
    A swollen magpie in a fitful sun,
    Half black half white
    Nor knowst'ou wing from tail
    Pull down thy vanity
    How mean thy hates (l. 152–157)

23 To have gathered from the air a live tradition
    or from a fine old eye the unconquered flame
    This is not vanity.
    Here error is all in the not done,
    all in the diffidence that faltered . . . (l. 167–171)

    FaBoMo; MoP; NAAL-2; NoAM; NOBA; VGW

Commission

24 Go, my songs, to the lonely and the unsatisfied,
    Go also to the nerve-racked, go to the enslaved-by-
        convention,
    Bear to them my contempt for their oppressors.
                                        (l. 1–3)

25 Speak against unconscious oppression,
    Speak against the tyranny of the unimaginative.
    Speak against bonds. (l. 6–8)

26 Go to the adolescent who are smothered in family —
    Oh how hideous it is
    To see three generations of one house gathered
        together!
    It is like an old tree with shoots,
    And with some branches rotted and falling. (l. 28–32)

    BoLoP; NIP; OPOP; TwCP

The Garden

27 Like a skein of loose silk blown against a wall
    She walks by the railing of a path in Kensington
        Gardens,
    And she is dying piecemeal
    of a sort of emotional anemia. (l. 1–4)

28 In her is the end of breeding.
    Her boredom is exquisite and excessive.
    She would like some one to speak to her,
    And is almost afraid that I
    will commit that indiscretion. (l. 8–12)

    AWP; HeIP; LiTA; MoAB; MoAmPo; NIP; NoP; OxBSP;
    PPP; SOTW; TwCP

Homage to Sextus Propertius

29 Out-weariers of Apollo will, as we know, continue their
        Martian generalities,
    We have kept our erasers in order.

30 Celebrities from the Trans-Caucasus will belaud Roman
        celebrities
    And expound the distentions of Empire,
    But for something to read in normal circumstances?

31 I ask a wreath which will not crush my head.
    And there is no hurry about it;
    I shall have, doubtless, a boom after my funeral,
    Seeing that long standing increases all things
    regardless of quality.

32 And in the mean time my songs will travel,
    And the devirginated young ladies will enjoy them
    when they have got over the strangeness,

33 There will be a crowd of young women doing homage
        to my palaver,

34 Yet the companions of the Muses
    will keep their collective nose in my books
    And weary with historical data, they will turn to my
        dance tune.

35 Flame burns, rain sinks into the cracks
    And they all go to rack ruin beneath the thud of the
        years,
    Stands genius a deathless adornment,
    a name not to be worn out with the years.

    CMoP; HAP; MoAB; NOBA; OBVE; OxBA

Hugh Selwyn Mauberley. (Life and Contacts)

36 For three years, out of key with his time,
    He strove to resuscitate the dead art
    Of poetry; to maintain "the sublime"
    In the old sense. (l. 1–4)

37 he had been born
    In a half savage country, out of date;
    Bent resolutely on wringing lilies from the acorn;
                                        (l. 5–8)

38 His true Penelope was Flaubert, (l. 15)

39 Unaffected by "the march of events,"
    He passed from men's memory in l'an trentiesme
    De son eage; the case presents
    No adjunct to the Muses' diadem. (l. 19–23)

40 The age demanded and image
    Of its accelerated grimace, (l. 24–25)

41 Christ follows Dionysus,
    Phallic and ambrosial
    Made way for macerations;
    Caliban casts out Ariel. (l. 41–44)

42 All things are a flowing,
Sage Heracleitus says;
But a tawdry cheapness
Shall outlast our days. (l. 45—48)

43 There died a myriad,
And of the best, among them,
For an old bitch gone in the teeth,
For a botched civilization, (l. 92—95)

AmPP; CMoP; FaBoMo; HAP; InPS; LiTA; LiTM;
MoAmPo; MoP; NAAL-2; NoAM; NOBA; NoP; OxBA;
TAP; UnPo; VGW

Hugh Selwyn Mauberley. Envoi (1919)

44 Go, dumb-born book,

45 Tell her that goes
With song upon her lips
But sings not out the song, nor knows
The maker of it, some other mouth,
May be as fair as hers,

46 When our two dusts with Waller's shall be laid,
Siftings on siftings in oblivion,
Till change hath broken down
All things save Beauty alone.

AmPP; CMoP; HAP; InPS; LiTA; LiTM; MoAB;
MoAmPo; MoP; NoAM; NOBA; NoP; OxBA; TAP; UnPo;
VGW

In a Station of the Metro

47 The apparition of these faces in the crowd; (l. 1)

AmPP; HAP; HeIP; InPK; MoAB; MoAmPo; MoP;
NAAL-2; NIP; NoAM; NOBA; NoP; OxBA; PoE; TAP;
UnPo; VGW; WeW

The Lake Isle

48 the loose fragrant cavendish
and the shag,
And the bright Virginia
loose under the bright glass cases, (l. 5—8)

49 install me in any profession
Save this damn'd profession of writing,
where one needs one's brains all the time. (l. 14—16)

FaBoCo; FaBoPa; OxBSP; PoA

Lustra

50 Artists broken against her,
Astray, lost in the villages,
Mistrusted, spoken against,

Lovers of beauty, starved,
Thwarted with systems,
Helpless against the control;

51 I have weathered the storm,
I have beaten out my exile.

AmPP; MoAB; MoAmPo; NoAM; NOBA; OxBA; PoA

A Pact

52 I make a pact with you, Walt Whitman —
I have detested you long enough. (l. 1—2)

53 It was you that broke the new wood,
Now is a time for carving.
We have one sap and one root —
Let there be commerce between us. (l. 6—9)

AmPP; AnAmPo; LiTA; MoP; NAAL-2; NoAM; NOBA;
OxBA; TAP

Portrait d'une Femme

54 Your mind and you are our Sargasso Sea,
London has swept about you this score years
And bright ships left you this or that in fee:
Ideas, old gossip, oddments of all things,
Strange spars of knowledge and dimmed wares of price.
(l. 1—5)

55 You preferred it to the usual thing:
One dull man, dulling and uxorious,
One average mind — with one thought less, each year.
(l. 8—10)

56 For all this sea-hoard of deciduous things,
Strange woods half sodden, and new brighter stuff:
In the slow float of differing light and deep,
No! there is nothing! In the whole and all,
Nothing that's quite your own.
Yet this is you. (l. 25—30)

CMoP; FF; InPS; MoAB; MoAmPo; MoP; NAAL-2;
NoAM; NOBA; NoP; PPP; TAP; TwCP

The Return

57 See, they return; ah, see the tentative
Movements, and the slow feet,
The trouble in the pace and the uncertain
Wavering! (l. 1—4)

58 See, they return, one, and by one,
With fear, as half-awakened; (l. 5—6)

59 Haie! Haie!
These were the swift to harry;
These the keen-scented;
These were the souls of blood.

Slow on the leash,
pallid the leash-men! (l. 15–20)

AmPP; CMoP; HAP; MoAB; MoAmPo; MoP; NoAM;
NOBA; OxBA; PoE; RB; VGW; WeW

Sestina: Altaforte

60 Damn it all! all this our South stinks peace.
You whoreson dog, Papiols, come! Let's to music!
(l. 9–10)

61 Hell grant soon we hear again the swords clash!
And the shrill neighs of destriers in battle rejoicing,
Spiked breast to spiked breast opposing! (l. 23–25)

62 Bah! there's no wine like the blood's crimson! (l. 28)

63 The man who fears war and squats opposing
My words for stour, hath no blood of crimson
But is fit only to rot in womanish peace (l. 35–37)

64 May God damn for ever all who cry 'Peace!' (l. 46)

CMoP; FaBoTw; LiTA; MoAB; MoAmPo; NOBA; SoSe;
SOTW

The Temperaments

65 Bastidides, on the contrary, who both talks and writes
of nothing save copulation,
Has become the father of twins,
But he accomplished this feat at some cost:
He had to be four times cuckold. (l. 6–10)

BoLoP; ErPo; NoAM; NOBA

A Virginal

66 Slight are her arms, yet they have bound me straitly
And left me cloaked as with a gauze of ther;
As with sweet leaves; as with subtle clearness.
(l. 4–6)

67 No, no! Go from me. I have still the flavour,
Soft as spring wind that's come from birchen bowers.
(l. 9–10)

68 As white their bark, so white this lady's hours. (l. 14)

CMoP; MoAB; MoAmPo; NAAL-2; NIP; NOBA; OxBA;
Son; TAP

WINTHROP MACKWORTH PRAED
(1802–1839)

Every-Day Characters

1 His talk was like a spring, which runs
With rapid change from rocks to roses:
It slipped from politics to puns,

It passed from Mahomet to Moses;
Beginning with the laws which keep
The planets in their radiant courses,
And ending with some precept deep
For dressing eels, or shoeing horses.

2 And when religious sects ran mad,
He held, in spite of all his learning,
That if a man's belief is bad,
It will not be improved by burning.

EnRP; OBEV; OBNC; PoEL-4

Goodnight to the Season!

3 Good-night to the Season! — the dances,
The fillings of hot little rooms,
The glancings of rapturous glances,
The fancyings of fancy costumes;
The pleasures which Fashion makes duties,
The praisings of fiddles and flutes,
The luxury of looking at beauties,
The tedium of talking to mutes; (l. 37–44)

4 When all who had money and leisure
Grew rural o'er ices and wines,
All pleasantly toiling for pleasure,
All hungrily pining for pines,
And making of beautiful speeches,
And marring of beautiful shows,
And feeding on delicate peaches,
And treading on delicate toes. (l. 76–83)

InvP; NOBE; NOBL; OBNC; OxBoLi; PoEL-4

EDWIN JOHN PRATT (1882–1964)

Towards the Last Spike

1 So motionless, she seemed stone dead — just seemed:
She was too old for death, too old for life,
For as if jealous of all living forms
She had lain there before bivalves began
To catacomb their shells on western mountains.

MoCV; NOBC; OBCV

FRANK TEMPLETON PRINCE (b. 1912)

Soldiers Bathing

1 All's pathos now. The body that was gross,
Rank, ravenous, disgusting in the act or in repose,
All fever, filth and sweat, its bestial strength
And bestial decay, by pain and labour grows at length
Fragile and luminous. (l. 7–11)

2 For that rage, that bitterness, those blows,
That hatred of the slain, what could it be
But indirectly or directly a commentary
On the Crucifixion? (l. 43–47)

3 And even we must know, that nobody has understood,
That some great love is over all we do,
And that is what has driven us to this fury, for so few
Can suffer all the terror of that love: (l. 57–60)

4 I feel a strange delight that fills me full,
Strange gratitude, as if evil itself were beautiful,
(l. 67–68)

GTBS-P; LiTB; LiTM; MoBrPo; NOCV; OBWP; OxBTC;
PeSA; WaP

MATTHEW PRIOR (1664–1721)

Answer to Cloe Jealous

1 Dear Chloe, how blubbered is that pretty face!
Thy cheek all on fire, and thy hair all uncurled.
Prithee, quit this caprice; and (as old Falstaff says)
Let us e'en talk a little like folks of this world.
(l. 1–4)

2 What I speak, my fair Chloe, and what I write, shows
The difference there is betwixt Nature and Art:
I court others in verse, but I love thee in prose;
And they have my whimsies, but thou hast my heart.
(l. 13–16)

AWP; ELP; NAEL-1; NOBE; NOEC; PoEL-3; SeCePo

Interred beneath this marble stone

3 Interred beneath this marble stone
Lie Saunt'ring Jack and Idle Joan. (l. 1–2)

4 Nor good, nor bad, nor fools, nor wise,
They would not learn, nor could advise:
Without love, hatred, joy or fear,
They led — a kind of — as it were:
Nor wished, nor cared, nor laughed, nor cried:
And so they lived; and so they died. (l. 57–62)

FaBoEE; NAEL-1; OAEL-1; OBD; OBSV; PoEL-3

Jinny the Just

5 But Thou that know'st Love above Intrest or lust
Strew the Myrtle and Rose on this once belov'd Dust
And shed one pious tear upon Jinny the Just

Tread soft on her Grave, and do right to her honor
Let neither rude hand no ill Tongue light upon her
Do all the smal Favors that now can be done her
(l. 13–18)

6 Less smooth than her Skin and less white than her
breast
Was this pollisht stone beneath which she lyes prest
Stop, Reader, and Sigh while thou thinkst on the rest

With a just trim of Virtue her Soul was endu'd
Not affectedly Pious nor secretly lewd,
She cut even between the Cocquet and the Prude.
(l. 62–68)

NOBE; NOEC; OBEV; PoEL-3

The Lady Who Offers Her Looking-Glass to Venus

7 Venus, take my votive glass:
Since I am not what I was,
What from this day I shall be,
Venus, let me never see. (l. 1–4)

AWP; FaBoEE; NOEC; OBEV; OxBSP

A Letter to the Honourable Lady Miss Margaret Cavendish Holles-Harley

8 At dawn of morn, and close of even,
To lift your heart and hands to Heaven.
In double beauty say your prayer:
Our Father first, then Notre Pere.
And, dearest child, along the day,
In every thing you do and say,
Obey and please my lord and lady,
So God shall love and angels aid ye. (l. 3–10)

NoAM; NOBE; NOEC; NoP; OBEV; OxBC; OxBChV;
OxBSP; SeCePo

The Merchant, to secure his treasure

9 Euphelia serves to grace my measure,
But Chloe is my real flame. (l. 3–4)

10 And Venus to the Loves around
Remarked how ill we all dissembled. (l. 15–16)

AWP; EnLoPo; GTBS; GTBS-P; NOEC; NoP; OBEV;
PoRA; TrGrPo

A Reasonable Affliction

11 A diff'rent cause, says Parson Sly,
The same effect may give:
Poor Lubin fears, that he shall die;
His wife, that he may live. (l. 5–8)

NBLV; NOEC; NoP; TrGrPo

To a Child of Quality

12 For, as our different ages move,
'Tis so ordain'd (would Fate but mend it!),
That I shall be past making love
When she begins to comprehend it. (l. 25–28)

GN; LiTB; NIP; NOBE; NOEC; OBEV; PoEL-3

To John I ow'd great obligation

13 publish it to all the nation; (l. 3)

AWP; FaBoCo; FaBoEE; FaFP; OBVE

A True Maid

14 'No, no; for my virginity,
When I lose that,' says Rose, 'I'll die':
'Behind the elms last night,' cried Dick,
'Rose, were you not extremely sick?' (l. 1–4)

ErPo; FaBoCo; FaBoEE; NAEL-1; NIP; NOEC

THOMAS PROCTOR (fl. c. 1578)

A Proper Sonnet, How Time Consumeth All Earthly Things (attributed to Proctor)

1 Down goeth the grass, soon wrought to withered hay;
Ay me alas, ay me alas, that beauty needs must yield
And princes pass, as grass doth fade away. (l. 2–4)

ChTr; ElL; FaBoRV; OBSC; TrGrPo

ALFRED WELLINGTON PURDY (b. 1919)

Wilderness Gothic

1 Someone hangs in the sky
over there from a piece of rope,
hammering and fitting God's belly-scratcher,
working his way up along the spire
until there's nothing left to nail on – (l. 3–7)

2 An age and a faith moving into transition,
the dinner cold and new-baked bread a failure,
(l. 31–32)

3 Something is about to happen. Leaves are still.
Two shores away, a man hammering in the sky.
Perhaps he will fall. (l. 35–37)

HeIP; MoCV; NOBC; NoP

FRANCIS QUARLES (1592–1644)

EMBLEMS (the following 4 poems)

I Am My Beloved's

1 Like to the Artick needle, that doth guide
The wand'ring shade by his magnetick pow'r,
And leaves his silken Gnomon to decide
The question of the controverted houre;

Now first be lov'd

2 Eternall God, O thou that onely art
The sacred Fountain of eternall light,
And blessed Loadstone of my better part;
O thou my heart's desire, my soul's delight,
Reflect upon my soul, and touch my heart,
And then my heart shall prize no good above thee;
And then my soul shall know thee; knowing, love thee;
And then my trembling thoughts shall never start
From thy commands, or swerve the least degree,
Or once presume to move, but as they move in thee.

EBEV; NOCV; OAEL-1; OBS

My Beloved Is Mine

3 Even like two little bank-dividing brooks,
That wash the pebbles with their wanton streams,
And having ranged and searched a thousand nooks,
Meet both at length in silver-breasted Thames
Where in a greater current they conjoin:
So I my Best-Beloved's am, so he is mine.

MeLP; MePo; NOBE; OBEV; OBS; TrGrPo

Why dost thou shade thy lovely face?

4 Disclose thy Sun beames; close thy wings, and stay;
See, see, how I am blind, and dead, and stray,
O thou that art my Light, my Life, my Way.

MeLP; MePo; OBS; TrPWD

SIR WALTER RALEGH (1552?–1618)

As You Came from the Holy Land (attributed to Ralegh)

1 I have loved her all my youth,
But now old, as you see;
Love likes not the falling fruit
From the withered tree.

Know that love is a careless child
And forgets promise past;
He is blind, he is deaf when he list
And in faith never fast. (l. 25–32)

2 But true love is a durable fire
In the mind ever burning;
Never sick, never old, never dead,
From itself never turning. (l. 41–44)

AAS; BoLoP; ChTr; ElL; EnLoPo; EnSB; FaBoCh; GBL;
HAP; InPS; LiTB; NOBE; NoP; OBEV; OBSC; PoEL-2;
PPP; PrIm; TrGrPo; RB

Even Such Is Time

3 Even such is time that takes in trust
Our youth, our joys, our all we have,
And pays us but with age and dust, (l. 1–3)

4 But from this earth, this grave, this dust,
My God shall raise me up, I trust. (l. 7–8)

AAS; BLPL; ChTr; CTC; ElL; FaBoEE; FaBoRV; HAP;
LiTB; NAEL-1; NOBE; OBEV; OBSC; OxBSP; PoRA;
RB; SiPS; TrGrPo; WGRP

A Farewell to False Love

5 Farewell, false love, the oracle of lies,
A mortal foe and enemy to rest;
An envious boy, from whom all cares arise,
A bastard vile, a beast with rage possessed;
A way of error, a temple full of treason,
In all effects contrary unto reason. (l. 1–6)

BoLoP; ElL; NAEL-1; OBSC; SiPS

The Lie

6 Go, Soul, the body's guest,
Upon a thankless arrant:
Fear not to touch the best;
The truth shall be thy warrant:
Go, since I needs must die,
And give the world the lie. (l. 1–6)

AAS; ChTr; CTC; EBEV; FaBoPV; HAP; InvP; LiTB;
NAEL-1; NOBE; NoP; OBSC; OPOP; PoEL-2; QFR; RB;
SCV; SiPS; TEP; TrGrPo; WGRP

The Nymph's Reply to the Shepherd

7 If all the world and love were young,
And truth in every shepherd's tongue,
These pretty pleasures might me move
To live with thee and be thy Love.

8 Thy gowns, thy shoes,thy beds of roses,
Thy cap, thy kirtle, and thy posies,
Soon break, soon wither — soon forgotten,
In folly ripe,in reason rotten.

9 But could youth last, and love still breed,
Had joys no date, nor age no need,
Then these delights my mind might move
To live with thee and be thy Love.

AAS; BoLoP; CTC; ElL; FaBoPa; FF; HAP; HeIP; HoPM;
InPK; InPS; LiTB; NAEL-1; NBLV; NIP; NOBE; NoP;
OAEL-1; OBEV; OBSC; PoE; PPP; RB; SeCePo; SiPS;
TrGrPo; WeW

The Passionate Man's Pilgrimage

10 Give me my scallop-shell of quiet,
My staff of faith to walk upon,
My scrip of joy, immortal diet,
My bottle of salvation,
My gown of glory, hope's true gage,
And thus I'll take my pilgrimage. (l. 1–6)

11 Just at the stroke when my veins start and spread,
Set on my soul an everlasting head.
Then am I ready, like a palmer fit,
To tread those blest paths which before I writ.
                                    (l. 55–58)

AAS; ChTr; ElL; LiTB; MePo; NOBE; NoP; OBSC; PoE;
PoEL-2; PoRA; RB; SeCePo; TrGrPo

The Sun May Set and Rise

12 The sun may set and rise:
But we contrariwise
Sleep after our short light
One everlasting night. (l. 1–4)

FaBoEE; FaBoRV; OBVE; SiPS

Three Things There Be That Prosper All Apace

13 And they be these: the wood, the weed, the wag.
The wood is that which makes the gallow tree;
The weed is that which strings the hangman's bag;
                                    (l. 5–7)

14 Green springs the tree, hemp grows, the wag is wild,
But when they meet, it makes the timber rot;
It frets the halter, and it chokes the child. (l. 10–12)

InPS; NAEL-1; NoP; OxBSP; PoEL-2; RB; SiPS; Son

What Is Our Life? A Play of Passion

15 What is our life? a play of passion;
Our mirth the music of division;
Our mothers' wombs the tiring-houses be
Where we are dressed for this short comedy. (l. 1–4)

16 Our graves that hide us from the searching sun
Are like drawn curtains when the play is done.
Thus march we, playing, to our latest rest,
Only, we die in earnest — that's no jest. (l. 7–10)

EBEV; FaBoEE; MePo; NAEL-1; NOBE; OBSC; OxBSP;
SiPS

SIR WALTER ALEXANDER RALEIGH
(1861–1922)

Wishes of an Elderly Man

1 And when I'm introduced to one
I wish I thought What Jolly Fun! (l. 5–6)

CenHV; FaBoCh; FaBoCo; FaBoEE; FiBHP; FPL; NBLV;
NOBL

DUDLEY RANDALL (b. 1914)

Ballad of Birmingham

1 "But, mother, I won't be alone.
Other children will go with me,
And march the streets of Birmingham
To make our country free." (l. 9–12)

BPo; HeIP; InPK; MoP; NIP; NoAM

Blackberry Sweet

2 Black girl black girl
lips as curved as cherries
full as grape bunches
sweet as blackberries (l. 1–4)

CNA; HAP; InPS; NBP; PoBA; WeW

A Different Image

3 Shatter the icons of slavery and fear.
Replace
the leer
of the minstrel's burnt-cork face
with a proud, serene
and classic bronze of Benin. (l. 7–12)

BPo; CNA; FF; TAP

Memorial Wreath

4 Fit gravefellows you are for Lincoln, Brown
And Douglass and Toussaint. . . all whose rapt eyes
Fashioned a new world in this wilderness.

American earth is richer for your bones;
Our hearts beat prouder for the blood we inherit.
(l. 15–19)

CNA; IDE; PoBA; PoNe

Roses and Revolutions

5 and men strive with each other not for power or the
accumulation of paper
but in joy create for others the house, the poem, the
game of athletic beauty.

Then washed in the brightness of the vision,
I saw how in its radiance would grow and be nourished
and suddenly
burst into terrible and splendid bloom
the blood-red flower of revolution. (l. 20–27)

BPo; CNA; PoBA; TAP

JAMES RYDER RANDALL (1839–1908)

My Maryland

1 The despot's heel is on thy shore,
Maryland
His torch is at thy temple door,
Maryland
Avenge the patriotic gore
That flecked the streets of Baltimore,
And be the battle-queen of yore,
Maryland! my Maryland!

2 She is not dead, nor deaf, nor dumb;
Huzza! she spurns the Northern scum!
She breathes! She burns! She'll come!
She'll come!
Maryland, my Maryland!

AA; AnAmPo; FaBoBe; FaFP; PAH

WILLIAM BRIGHTY RANDS
("MATTHEW BROWNE") (1823–1880)

The Wonderful World

1 Great, wide, beautiful, wonderful world, (l. 1)

2 World, you are beautifully drest. (l. 4)

3 you are so great, and I am so small,
I hardly can think of you, World, at all; (l. 13–14)

4 You are more than the Earth, though you are such a
   dot!
   You can love and think, and the Earth cannot!"
                                        (l. 19–20)

BoTP; FaPON; OHIP; OxBChV

JOHN CROWE RANSOM (1888–1874)

Antique Harvesters

1 Tawny are the leaves turned, but they still hold.
   It is the harvest; what shall this land produce?
   A meager hill of kernels, a runnel of juice.
   Declension looks from our land, it is old. (l. 1–4)

2 The horn, the hounds, the lank mares coursing by
   Under quaint archetypes of chivalry;
   And the fox, lovely ritualist, in flight
   Offering his unearthly ghost to quarry; (l. 20–23)

MoAB; MoAmPo; NoP; OxBA

Bells for John Whiteside's Daughter

3 There was such speed in her little body,
   And such lightness in her footfall,
   It is no wonder her brown study
   Astonishes us all. (l. 1–4)

4 Alas,

   For the tireless heart within the little
   Lady with rod that made them rise
   From their noon apple-dreams, and scuttle
   Goose-fashion under the skies! (l. 16–20)

CMoP; FF; HAP; HeIP; HoPM; InPK; InPS; LiTA; LiTM;
MoAB; MoAmPo; MoP; NAAL-2; NIP; NoAM; NOBA;
NoP; OxBA; PoE; PPP; PrIm; RB; SoSe; TAP; UnPo;
VGW; WeW

Blue Girls

5 For I could tell you a story which is true;
   I know a lady with a terrible tongue,
   Blear eyes fallen from blue,
   All her perfections tarnished — and yet it is not long
   Since she was lovelier than any of you. (l. 13–17)

ChTr; CMoP; GBL; LiTA; MoAB; MoAmPo; NoAM;
PrIm; RB; TAP; VGW; WeW

Captain Carpenter

6 Captain Carpenter rose up in his prime
   Put on his pistols and went riding out
   But had got wellnigh nowhere at that time
   Till he fell in with ladies in a rout. (l. 1–4)

7 But where she should have made off like a hind
   The bitch bit off his arms at the elbows. (l. 23–24)

8 I would not knock old fellows in the dust
   But there lay Captain Carpenter on his back
   His weapons were the old heart in his bust
   And a blade shook between rotten teeth alack.
                                        (l. 45–48)

9 The curse of hell upon the sleek upstart
   That got the Captain finally on his back
   And took the red red vitals of his heart
   And made the kites to whet their beaks clack clack.
                                        (l. 61–64)

FaBoMo; HoPM; LiTA; LiTM; MoAB; MoAmPo; MoP;
NoAM; NOBA; OxBA; TwCP

Dead Boy

10 A boy not beautiful, nor good, nor clever,
   A black cloud full of storms too hot for keeping,
   A sword beneath his mother's heart — yet never
   Woman bewept her babe as this is weeping. (l. 5–8)

11 But this was the old tree's late branch wrenched away,
   Grieving the sapless limbs, the shorn and shaken.
                                        (l. 19–20)

CMoP; FaBoMo; LiTA; Mes; NoAM; NoP; OBD; OxBA;
PoE; TwCP

The Equilibrists

12 Full of her long white arms and milky skin
   He had a thousand times remembered sin. (l. 1–2)

13 Predicament indeed, which thus discovers
   Honor among thieves Honor between lovers.
   O such a little word is Honor, they feel!
   But the grey word is between them cold as steel.
                                        (l. 21–24)

14 They burned with fierce love always to come near,
   But honor beat them back and kept them clear.
                                        (l. 31–32)

15 Would you ascend to Heaven and bodiless dwell?
   Or take your bodies honorless to Hell?

   In Heaven you have heard no marriage is,
   No white flesh tinder to your lecheries, (l. 39–42)

16 Great lovers lie in Hell, the stubborn ones
   Infatuate of the flesh upon the bones;
   Stuprate, they rend each other when they kiss,
   The pieces kiss again, no end to this. (l. 45–48)

17 Equilibrists lie here; stranger, tread light;
Close, but untouching in each other's sight;
Mouldered the lips and ashy the tall skull.
Let them lie perilous and beautiful. (l. 53–56)

CMoP; HAP; LiTM; MoAB; MoP; NAAL-2; NIP; NoAM;
NOBA; OxBA; PPP; TAP

Here Lies a Lady

18 Sweet ladies, long may ye bloom, and toughly I hope ye
    may thole,
But was she not lucky? In flowers and lace and
    mourning,
In love and great honor we bade God rest her soul
After six little spaces of chill, and six of burning.
                                            (l. 13–16)

AWP; CMoP; HAP; InvP; LiTM; MoAB; MoAmPo; MoP;
NAAL-2; NoAM; PoRA; RB; TAP; VGW

Janet Waking

19 It was a transmogrifying bee
Came droning down on Chucky's old bald head
And sat and put the poison. It scarcely bled,
                                            (l. 13–15)

20 Now the poor comb stood up straight
But Chucky did not. (l. 19–20)

21 And weeping fast as she had breath
Janet implored us, 'Wake her from her sleep!'
And would not be instructed in how deep
Was the forgetful kingdom of death. (l. 25–28)

CMoP; InPK; MoAB; MoAmPo; MoP; NAAL-2; NoAM;
NoP; OBD; PoE; RB; TAP

Judith of Bethulia

22 And a wandering beauty is a blade out of its scabbard.
You know how dangerous, gentlemen of threescore?
May you know it yet ten more. (l. 4–6)

23 For even within his tent she accomplished his derision;
She loosed one veil and another, standing unafraid;
And he perished. (l. 27–29)

24 And the chieftain's head, with grinning sockets, and
    varnished —
Is it hung on the sky with a hideous epitaphy?
No, the woman keeps the trophy. (l. 34–36)

FaBoMo; FYAP; LiTA; LiTM; NoAM; NOBA

Lady Lost

25 This morning, there flew up the lane
A timid lady-bird to our bird-bath
And eyed her image dolefully as death; (l. 1–3)

MoAB; MoAmPo; TrGrPo; UnPo

Painted Head

26 The body bears the head
(So hardly one they terribly are two)
Feeds and obeys and unto please what end?
Not to the glory of tyrant head but to

The being of body. Beauty is of body. (l. 25–29)

LiTA; LiTM; MoAB; MoAmPo; NoAM; NOBA; OxBA

Parting, without a Sequel

27 Away went the messenger's bicycle,
His serpent's track went up the hill forever.
And all the time she stood there hot as fever
And cold as any icicle. (l. 21–24)

MoAB; MoAmPo; OxBA; SoSe

Philomela

28 Not to these shores she came! this other Thrace,
Environ barbarous to the royal Attic;
How could her delicate dirge run democratic,
Delivered in a cloudless boundless public place
To an inordinate race? (l. 17–20)

29 Out of the darkness where Philomela sat,
Her fairy numbers issued. What then ailed me?
My ears are called capacious but they failed me,
Her classics registered a little flat!
I rose, and venomously spat. (l. 31–35)

ChTr; CMoP; FaBoPP; NAAL-2; NoAM; NOBA; OBAL;
OBSV; OxBA

Piazza Piece

30 For I must have my lovely lady soon,
I am a gentleman in a dustcoat trying. (l. 7–8)

31 —I am a lady young in beauty waiting
Until my truelove comes, and then we kiss. (l. 9–10)

AnAmPo; BoLoP; ErPo; HeIP; MoAB; MoAmPo; MoP;
NAAL-2; NoAM; NOBA; NoP; OPOP; OxBA; Son; SoSe;
TAP; TrGrPo

Prelude to an Evening

32 Do not enforce the tired wolf
Dragging his infected wound homeward
To sit tonight with the warm children
Naming the pretty kings of France. (l. 1–4)

EAS; MoAB; MoAmPo; OxBA

Survey of Literature

33   In all the good Greek of Plato
     I lack my roastbeef and potato.

     A better man was Aristotle,
     Pulling steady on the bottle. (l. 1–4)

34   God have mercy on the sinner
     Who must write with no dinner,

     No gravy and no grub,
     No pewter and no pub.

     No belly and no bowels,
     Only consonants and vowels. (l. 23–28)

FaBoCh; LiTA; NBLV; OBAL; TAP; TwCP; VGW

Vision by Sweetwater

35   Where have I seen before, against the wind,
     These bright virgins, robed and bare of bonnet,

     Flowing with music of their strange quick tongue
     And adventuring with delicate paces by the stream, —
     Myself a child, old suddenly at the scream
     From one of the white throats which it hid among?
                                    (l. 11–16)

CMoP; FaBoMo; MoAB; NOBA; OxBA; RB

SIR HERBERT READ   (1893–1968)

To a Conscript of 1940

1   But the old world was restored and we returned
     To the dreary field and workshop, and the immemorial
       feud

     Of rich and poor. Our victory was our defeat.
                              (l. 19–21)

2   To fight without hope is to fight with grace,
     The self reconstructed, the false heart repaired.'
                              (l. 32–33)

LiTB; LiTM; OBWP; WaP

THOMAS BUCHANAN READ
(1822–1872)

Sheridan's Ride

1   Up from the South at break of day,
     Bringing to Winchester fresh dismay,
     The affrighted air with a shudder bore,

Like a herald in haste, to the chieftain's door,
The terrible grumble, and rumble, and roar,
Telling the battle was on once more,
And Sheridan twenty miles away.

2   Hurrah! Hurrah for Sheridan!
     Hurrah! Hurrah for horse and man! (l. 64–65)

3   "Here is the steed that saved the day,
     By carrying Sheridan into the fight,
     From Winchester, twenty miles away!" (l. 71–73)

AnAmPo; BeLS; FaBoBe; FaBV; FaFP; GN; OHFP;
OHIP; PAH; WBLP

HENRY REED   (1914–1986)

Chard Whitlow

1   And the frigid burnings of purgatory will not be
     touched
     By any emollient. (l. 13–14)

2   And pray for me also under the draughty stair.
     As we get older we do not get any younger.

     And pray for Kharma under the holy mountain.
                              (l. 22–24)

BXAP; FaBoCo; FaBoNo; FaBoPa; FiBHP; LiTM;
MoBrPo; NBLV; NOBL; NoP; OxBTC; Par; UnPo

LESSONS OF THE WAR *(the following 2 poems)*

Judging Distances

3   And at least you know

     That maps are of time, not place, so far as the army
     Happens to be concerned — the reason being,
     Is one which need not delay us. (l. 6–9)

BoLoP; GTBS-P; HeIP; LiTB; MoAB; NIP; NOBE; NoP;
OBWP; SoSe

Naming of Parts

4   Today we have naming of parts. Yesterday,
     We had daily cleaning. And tomorrow morning,
     We shall have what to do after firing. But today,
     Today we have naming of parts. (l. 1–4)

5   We can slide it
     Rapidly backwards and forwards: we call this
     Easing the spring. And rapidly backwards and forwards

The early bees are assaulting and fumbling the flowers:
They call it easing the Spring. (l. 20–24)

FF; GoJo; HeIP; HoPM; InPS; LiTB; MoAB; MoBrPo;
NOBE; NoP; OBWP; OxBTC; PoRA; PrIm; SeCePo;
SoSe; TrGrPo; UnPo; WaP

ISHMAEL REED　(b. 1938)

Beware: Do Not Read This Poem

1 the hunger of this poem is legendary
it has taken in many victims
back off from this poem
it has drawn in yr feet
back off from this poem
it has drawn in yr legs (l. 18–22)

2 statistic: the us bureau of missing persons reports
that in 1968 over 100,000 people disappeared
leaving no solid clues
nor traceonly
a space
in the lives of their friends. (l. 40–44)

BPo; CNA; NIP; NoP; PoBA; WSC

I Am a Cowboy in the Boat of Ra

3 I am a cowboy in the boat of Ra. I bedded
down with Isis, Lady of the Boogaloo, dove
down deep in her horny, stuck up her Wells-Far-ago
in daring midday get away. (l. 10–13)

4 The price on the wanted
poster was a-going down, outlaw alias copped my
　　stance
and moody greenhorns were making me dance; while
　　my mouth's
shooting iron got its chambers jammed. (l. 20–23)

5 I am a cowboy in the boat of Ra. Lord of the lash,
the Loup Garou Kid. Half breed son of Pisces and
Aquarius. I hold the souls of men in my pot. I do
the dirty boogie with scorpions. I make the bulls
keep still and was the first swinger to grape the taste.
　　　　　　　　　　　　　　　　(l. 31–35)

NBP; NoP; PoBA; PrIm

LIZETTE WOODWORTH REESE
(1856–1935)

A Christmas Folk-Song

1 The little Jesus came to town;
With ox and sheep He laid Him down;
Peace to the byre, peace to the fold,
For that they housed Him from the cold! (l. 13–16)

FaPON; OBCA; OHIP; OnMSP; TrCP

Tears

2 I wonder at the idleness of tears. (l. 8)

3 Loose me from tears, and make me see aright
How each hath back what once he stayed to weep;
Homer his sight, David his little lad! (l. 12–14)

AA; AnAmPo; MoAmPo; WGRP

CHARLES REZNIKOFF　(1894–1976)

About an Excavation

1 a flock of bright red lanterns
has settled　(l. 2–3)

NTCP; PCP; PrIm; VGW

ADRIENNE RICH　(b. 1929)

Aunt Jennifer's Tigers

1 Aunt Jennifer's tigers prance across a screen,
Bright topaz denizens of a world of green. (l. 1–2)

2 The massive weight of Uncle's wedding band
Sits heavily upon Aunt Jennifer's hand. (l. 7–8)

CAPP; FaBoWP; HeIP; InPK; NIP; NoAM; NoP; SM

Diving into the Wreck

3 I put on
the body-armor of black rubber
the absurd flippers
the grave and awkward mask. (l. 5–7)

4 I came to explore the wreck.
The words are purposes.
The words are maps.
I came to see the damage that was done
and the treasures that prevail. (l. 51–54)

5 the thing I came for:
the wreck and not the story of the wreck
the thing itself and not the myth
the drowned face always staring
toward the sun (l. 61–65)

CAPP; HCAP; HeIP; InPK; InPS; MoP; MOS; NAAL-2;
NIP; NoAM; NOBA; NoP

Face to Face

6 How people used to meet!
starved, intense, the old
Christmas gifts saved up till spring,
and the old plain words, (l. 13–16)

7 behind dry lips
a loaded gun. (l. 19–20)

LiTM; NAAL-2; NoAM; NoP

I wake up in your bed (Twenty-one Love Poems)

8 I want to show her one poem
which is the poem of my life. But I hesitate,
and wake. (l. 7–9)

9 the pull of gravity, which is not simple
which carries the feathered grass a long way down the
upbreathing air. (l. 15–16)

GLP; NAAL-2; NoAM; UnAS

Living in Sin

10 She had thought the studio would keep itself;
no dust upon the furniture of love.
Half heresy, to wish the taps less vocal,
the panes relieved of grime. (l. 1–4)

11 By evening she was back in love again,
though not so wholly but throughout the night
she woke sometimes to feel the daylight coming
like a relentless milkman up the stairs. (l. 23–26)

FF; IHMS; NePoEA; NoP; NYBP; SoSe; TAP; UnPo

Orion

12 children are dying my death
and eating crumbs of my life. (l. 29–30)

13 Pity is not your forte.
Calmly you ache up there
pinned aloft in your crow's nest,
my speechless pirate! (l. 31–34)

MoP; NAAL-2; NIP; NoAM; NoP; WPE

Snapshots of a Daughter-in-Law

14 Your mind now, moldering like wedding-cake,
heavy with useless experience, rich
with suspicion, rumor, fantasy,
crumbling to pieces under the knife-edge
of mere fact. In the prime of your life. (l. 7–11)

15 A thinking woman sleeps with monsters. (l. 26)

16 The argument ad feminam,all the old knives
that have rusted in my back, I drive in yours,
ma semblable, ma soeur! (l. 37–39)

17 Reading while waiting
for the iron to heat,
writing, My Life had stood — a Loaded Gun —
(l. 43–45)

18 Poised, trembling and unsatisfied, before
an unlocked door, that cage of cages,
tell us, you bird, you tragical machine — (l. 59–61)

19 has Nature shown
her household books to you, daughter-in-law,
that her sons never saw? (l. 65–67)

20 Thus wrote
a woman, partly brave and partly good,
who fought with what she partly understood.
Few men about her would or could do more,
hence she was labeled harpy, shrew and whore.
(l. 72–75)

21 all that we might have been,
all that we were — fire, tears,
wit, taste, martyred ambition —
stirs like the memory of refused adultery
the drained and flagging bosom of our middle years.
(l. 80–84)

22 This luxury of the precocious child,
Time's precious chronic invalid, —
would we, darlings, resign it if we could?
Our blight has been our sinecure:
mere talent was enough for us —
glitter in fragments and rough drafts. (l. 88–93)

23 Sigh no more, ladies.
Time is male
and in his cups drinks to the fair. (l. 94–96)

24 indolence read as abnegation,
slattern thought styled intuition,
every lapse forgiven, our crime
only to cast too bold a shadow
or smash the mold straight off. (l. 99–103)

25 her fine blades making the air wince
but her cargo
no promise then:
delivered
palpable
ours. (l. 115–120)

FaBoWP; HCAP; NAAL-2; NIP; NMM; NoAM; NoP

Storm Warnings

26 The glass has been falling all the afternoon (l. 1)

27 Weather abroad
and weather in the heart alike come on
Regardless of prediction. (l. 12−14)

28 Time in the hand is not control of time,
Nor shattered fragments of an instrument
A proof against the wind; the wind will rise,
We can only close the shutters. (l. 18−21)

29 These are the things that we have learned to do
Who live in troubled regions. (l. 27−28)

AiP; GOYP; NAAL-2; NIP

EDWARD HERSEY RICHARDS (b. 1874)

A Wise Old Owl

1 A wise old owl lived in an oak;
The more he saw the less he spoke; (l. 1−2)

BLPA; FaBoBe; FaFP; OxNR; PYC

LAURA ELIZABETH RICHARDS
(1850−1943)

Antonio

1 "Oh, nonio, Antonio!
You're far too bleak and bonio!
And all that I wish,
You singular fish,
Is that you will quickly begonio." (l. 18−20)

MoShBr; OBCA; PDV; RHPC

Eletelephony

2 Once there was an elephant,
Who tried to use the telephant −
No! no! I mean an elephone
Who tried to use the telephone − (l. 1−4)

FaPON; GoJo; MoShBr; NBLV; NTCP; OBCA; OnUR;
OxBChV; PDV; PYC; RHPC

JAMES WHITCOMB RILEY (1849−1916)

Little Orphant Annie

1 Little Orphant Annie's come to our house to stay,
An' wash the cups an' saucers up, an' brush the crumbs
away, (l. 1−2)

2 A-list'nin' to the witch-tales 'at Annie tells about,
An' the Gobble-uns 'at gits you
Ef you
Don't
Watch
Out! (l. 7−12)

AA; AnAmPo; FaFP; FaPON; MoShBr; NBLV; OBAL;
OBCA; OxBChV

When She Comes Home

3 the ache here in the throat,
To know that I so ill deserve the place
Her arms make for me; (l. 10−12)

AA; AnAmPo; BLPL; FaBoBe

When the Frost Is on the Punkin

4 When the frost is on the punkin and the fodder's in the
shock,
And you hear the kyouck and gobble of the struttin'
turkey-cock. (l. 1−2)

5 a feller is a-feelin' at his best,
With the risin' sun to greet him from a night of
peaceful rest,
As he leaves the house, bare-headed, and goes out to
feed the stock,
When the frost is on the punkin and the fodder's in the
shock. (l. 5−8)

AnAmPo; BoNaP; FaBoBe; FaBV; FaFP; FPL; OBAL;
PoLF

CONRAD KENT RIVERS (1933−1968)

Four Sheets to the Wind and a One-Way Ticket to France

1 I would watch the funny people make love the way
Maupassant said,
my youth allowed me the opportunity to hear all those
strange
verbs conjugated in erotic affirmations. (l. 5−8)

2 Main Street was never the same. I read Gide and tried
to
translate Proust. Now nothing is real except French
wine.
For absurdity is reality, my loneliness unreal, my mind
tired.

And I shall die an old Parisian. (l. 22−25)

AmNP; BPo; IDB; PoBA; PoNe

ELIZABETH MADOX ROBERTS
(1880–1941)

Firefly

1 I never could have thought of it,
   To have a little bug all lit
   And made to go on wings. (l. 4–6)

   GoJo; NTCP; PDV; RAR; TSS

Strange Tree

2 And then I ran to get away,
   But when I stopped and turned to see,
   The tree was bending to the side
   And leaning out to look at me. (l. 13–15)

   BoNaP; FaPON; GrPl; WSC

EDWIN ARLINGTON ROBINSON
(1869–1935)

Bewick Finzer

1 He comes unfailing for the loan
   We give and then forget;
   He comes, and probably for years
   Will he be coming yet, —
   Familiar as an old mistake,
   And futile as regret. (l. 25–30)

   CMoP; MoAB; MoAmPo; NAAL-2; PPP

Calvary

2 Friendless and faint, with martyred steps and slow,
   Faint for the flesh, but for the spirit free, (l. 1–2)

3 Ah, when shall come love's courage to be strong!
   Tell me, O Lord — tell me, O Lord, how long
   Are we to keep Christ writhing on the cross!
                                    (l. 12–14)

   MoAmPo; OFD; Son; WGRP

Cassandra

4 Your Dollar is your only Word,
   The wrath of it your only fear.

   "You build it altars tall enough
   To make you see, but your are blind;
   You cannot leave it long enough
   To look before you or behind. (l. 3–8)

5 "Because a few complacent years
   Have made your peril of your pride,
   Think you that you are to go on
   Forever pampered and untired? (l. 17–20)

   CMoP; LiTA; LiTM; NoAM; OxBA

Charles Carville's Eyes

6 his mouth redeemed
   His insufficient eyes, forever sad:
   In them there was no life-glimpse, good or bad,
   Nor joy nor passion in them ever gleamed; (l. 3–6)

   AnAmPo; CMoP; OxBA; TAP

The Clerks

7 Poets and kings are but the clerks of Time,
   Tiering the same dull webs of discontent,
   Clipping the same sad alnage of the years. (l. 12–14)

   AA; AnAmPo; MoAB; MoAmPo; NAAL-2; PoEL-5

Cliff Klingenhagen

8 And though I know the fellow, I have spent
   Long time a-wondering when I shall be
   As happy as Cliff Klingenhagen is. (l. 12–14)

   AmPP; AnAmPo; MoAB; MoAmPo; Son

Credo

9 I cannot find my way: there is no star
   In all the shrouded heavens anywhere; (l. 1–2)

10 For through it all — above, beyond it all —
   I know the far-sent message of the years,
   I feel the coming glory of the Light. (l. 12–14)

   AmPP; CMoP; LiTM; MoAmPo; NAAL-2; OxBA; TAP;
   TrCP; WGRP

The Dark Hills

11 You fade — as if the last of days
   Were fading and all wars were done. (l. 7–8)

   AiP; FaFP; GoJo; HAP; LiTA; LiTM; MoAB; MoAmPo;
   NoAM; WeW

Eros Turannos

12 But what she meets and what she fears
   Are less than are the downward years,
   Drawn slowly to the foamless weirs
   Of age, were she to lose him. (l. 5–8)

   CMoP; GBL; HAP; HeIP; LiTA; LiTM; MoAB; MoAmPo;
   MoP; NAAL-2; NoAM; NOBA; NoP; OxBA; PoA; PoE;
   QFR; TAP

Flammonde

13 He never told us what he was,
Or what mischance, or other cause,
Had banished him from better days
To play the Prince of Castaways. (l. 17–20)

14 We cannot know how much we learn
From those who never will return,
Until a flash of unforeseen
Remembrance falls on what has been. (l. 89–92)

AmPP; CMoP; LiTA; LiTM; NoAM

For a Dead Lady

15 The forehead and the little ears
Have gone where Saturn keeps the years;
The breast where roses could not live
Has done with rising and with falling. (l. 13–16)

16 And we who delve in beauty's lore
Know all that we have known before
Of what inexorable cause
Makes Time so vicious in his reaping. (l. 21–24)

CMoP; DL; FYAP; HeIP; HoPM; InvP; LiTA; LiTM;
MoAB; MoAmPo; MoP; NoAM; NOBA; OxBA; PoEL-5;
PoRA

George Crabbe

17 Give him the darkest inch your shelf allows,
Hide him in lonely garrets, if you will, —
But his hard, human pulse is throbbing still
With the sure strength that fearless truth endows.
(l. 1–4)

BLPL; CMoP; LiTA; LiTM; MoAB; MoAmPo; NAAL-2;
NOBA; NoP; OxBA; PoEL-5; TAP

The House on the Hill

18 They are all gone away,
The house is shut and still,
There is nothing more to say. (l. 1–3)

AA; FaPON; GoJo; MoAmPo; NAAL-2; PrIm; TrGrPo

How Annandale Went Out

19 I watched him; and the sight was not so fair
As one or two that I have seen elsewhere:
An apparatus not for me to mend —
A wreck, with hell between him and the end. (l. 4–7)

20 Now view yourself as I was, on the spot —
With a slight kind of engine. Do you see?
Like this . . . You wouldn't hang me? I thought not."
(l. 12–14)

MoAB; MoAmPo; NoAM; NOBA

Karma

21 And from the fulness of his heart he fished
A dime for Jesus who had died for men. (l. 13–14)

AmPP; CMoP; HeIP; MoAB; MoAmPo; OFD; TrCP

Luke Havergal

22 But go, and if you listen she will call,
Go to the western gate, Luke Havergal —
Luke Havergal. (l. 6–8)

23 Out of a grave I come to tell you this,
Out of a grave I come to quench the kiss
That flames upon your forehead with a glow
That blinds you to the way that you must go.
(l. 17–20)

AA; AmPP; AWP; GBL; LiTA; LiTM; MoAB; MoAmPo;
NAAL-2; NoAM; NOBA; PoEL-5; QFR; UnPo

The Man against the Sky

24 Dark, marvelous, and inscrutable he moved on
Till down the fiery distance he was gone, (l. 10–11)

25 If he go on too far to find a grave,
Mostly alone he goes. (l. 21–22)

26 He may, be seeing all things for the best,
Incite futurity to do the rest. (l. 69–70)

27 He may have had for evil or for good
No argument; he may have had no care
For what without himself went anywhere (l. 77–79)

28 And at his heart there may have gnawed
Sick memories of a dead faith foiled and flawed
(l. 116–117)

29 seizing the swift logic of a woman,
Curse God and die. (l. 135–136)

30 He may have seen with his mechanic eyes
A world without a meaning, and had room,
Alone amid magnificence and doom,
To build himself an airy monument (l. 151–154)

31 He may have been a master of his fate,
And of his atoms, — ready as another
In his emergence to exonerate
His father and his mother; (l. 169–172)

32 And we, with all our wounds and all our powers,
Must each await alone at his own height
Another darkness or another light; (l. 190–192)

33 Are we no greater than the noise we make
Along one blind atomic pilgrimage
Whereon by crass chance billeted we go
Because our brains and bones and cartilage
Will have it so? (l. 216–220)

34 Where was he going, this man against the sky?
You know not, nor do I. (l. 224–225)

35 When infant Science makes a pleasant face
And waves again that hollow toy, the Race; (l. 253–254)

36 If after all that we have lived and thought,
All comes to Nought, —
If there be nothing after Now,
And we be nothing anyhow,
And we know that, — why live? (l. 304–308)

37 the cold eternal shores
That look sheer down
To the dark tideless floods of Nothingness
Where all who know may drown. (l. 311–314)

AmPP; CMoP; LiTA; OxBA

The Master

38 The face we see was never young,
Nor could it ever have been old.

For he, to whom we had applied
Our shopman's test of age and worth,
Was elemental when he died,
As he was ancient at his birth: (l. 39–44)

LiTA; LiTM; MoAB; MoAmPo; OHIP

The Mill

39 "There are no millers any more,"
Was all that she had heard him say:
And he had lingered at the door
So long that it seemed yesterday. (l. 5–8)

40 Black water, smooth above the weir
Like starry velvet in the night,
Though ruffled once, would soon appear
The same as ever to the sight. (l. 21–24)

CMoP; DL; HAP; NAAL-2; NoAM; NoP; PrIm; SoSe;
TAP; WeW

Miniver Cheevy

41 Miniver Cheevy, child of scorn
Grew lean while he assailed the seasons;
He wept that he was ever born,
And he had reasons. (l. 1–4)

42 He mourned Romance, now on the town,
And Art, a vagrant. (l. 15–16)

43 Miniver loved the Medici,
Albeit he hand never seen one;
He would have sinned incessantly
Could he have been one. (l. 17–20)

44 Miniver Cheevy, born too late,
Scratched his head and kept on thinking;
Miniver coughed, and called it fate,
And kept on drinking. (l. 29–32)

AmPP; AWP; ChTr; CMoP; FaBoCh; FaBV; FaFP; FF;
FPL; HeIP; LiTA; LiTM; MoAB; MoAmPo; MoP;
NAAL-2; NBLV; NIP; NoAM; NOBA; NoP; OBSV;
OxBA; PoEL-5; PoLF; PoRA; SCV; TAP; TrGrPo

Mr. Flood's Party

45 He set the jug down slowly at his feet
With trembling care, knowing that most things break; (l. 27–28)

46 For soon amid the silver loneliness
Of night he lifted up his voice and sang,
Secure, with only two moons listening, (l. 45–47)

47 There was not much that was ahead of him,
And there was nothing in the town below —
Where strangers would have shut the many doors
That many friends had opened long ago. (l. 53–56)

AmPP; AWP; BLPL; CMoP; FaFP; FF; HAP; HeIP;
HoPM; LiTA; LiTM; MAT; MoAB; MoAmPo; MoP;
NAAL-2; NIP; NoAM; NOBA; NoP; OxBA; PoE; PoRA;
PPP; PrIm; SoSe; TAP; TrGrPo; UnPo; WeW

New England

48 Passion is here a soilure of the wits,
We're told, and Love a cross for them to bear;
Joy shivers in the corner where she knits
And Conscience always has the rocking-chair,
Cheerful as when she tortured into fits
The first cat that was ever killed by Care. (l. 9–14)

GOA; HeIP; MoAB; MoAmPo; NAAL-2; NOBA; NoP;
OxBA; TAP

Reuben Bright

49 Because he was a butcher and thereby
Did earn an honest living (and did right),
I would not have you think that Reuben Bright
Was any more a brute than you or I; (l. 1–4)

50 He packed a lot of things that she had made
Most mournfully away in an old chest
Of hers, and put some chopped-up cedar boughs
In with them, and tore down the slaughterhouse.
(l. 11–14)

AnAmPo; MoAB; MoAmPo; NOBA; NoP; Son; TAP;
TrGrPo

Richard Cory

51 But still he fluttered pulses when he said,
"Good-morning," and he glittered when he walked.
(l. 7–8)

52 So on we worked, and waited for the light,
And went without the meat, and cursed the bread;
And Richard Cory, one calm summer night,
Went home and put a bullet through his head.
(l. 13–16)

AmPP; AnAmPo; CMoP; DL; FaFP; FF; FPL; HAP; InPK;
LiTA; LiTM; MoAB; MoAmPo; NAAL-2; NIP; NOBA;
NoP; OxBA; PoLF; PoRA; PrIm; SoSe; TAP; TrGrPo

The Sheaves

53 A thousand golden sheaves were lying there,
Shining and still, but not for long to stay—
As if a thousand girls with golden hair
Might rise from where they slept and go away.
(l. 11–14)

AWP; CMoP; FaBV; HAP; MoAB; MoAmPo; MoP;
NoAM; NOBA; OxBA; TAP

JOHN WILMOT, 2D EARL OF
ROCHESTER (1647–1680)

Absent from thee, I languish still

1 Lest, once more wandering from that heaven,
I fall on some base heart unblest,
Faithless to thee, false, unforgiven,
And lose my everlasting rest. (l. 13–16)

BoLoP; ELP; EnLoPo; GBL; MePo; NOBE; OBEV; OBS;
SeCePo; SeCV-2

The Disabled Debauchee

2 So, when my days of impotence approach,
And I'm by pox and wine's unlucky chance
Forced from the pleasing billows of debauch
On the dull shore of lazy temperance,

My pains at least some respite shall afford
While I behold the battles you maintain
When fleets of glasses sail about the board,
From whose broadsides volleys of wit shall rain.
(l. 13–20)

3 Thus, statesmanlike, I'll saucily impose,
And safe from action, valiantly advise;
Sheltered in impotence, urge you to blows,
And being good for nothing else, be wise. (l. 45–48)

BoLoP; HAP; NAEL-1; NOBL; OBSV; PoEL-3; PPP;
WeW

Impromptu on Charles II

4 God bless our good and gracious King,
Whose promise none relies on;
Who never said a foolish thing,
Nor ever did a wise one. (l. 1–4)

FaBoEE; NBLV; NOBL; OBSV

Love a woman! y'are an ass

5 Farewell, woman! I intend
Henceforth every night to sit
With my lewd, well-natured friend,
Drinking to engender wit. (l. 9–12)

GBL; NBLV; NOBL; PeHV; TEP; TW

Love and Life

6 The talk not of Inconstancy,
False Hearts, and broken Vows;
If I, by Miracle, can be
This live-long Minute true to thee,
'Tis all that Heav'n allows. (l. 11–15)

BoLoP; ELP; EnLoPo; FF; GBL; HAP; MePo; NOBE;
OBEV; OBS; PoEL-3; SeCV-2; TrGrPo

The Mistress: A Song

7 But oh, how slowly minutes roll
When absent from her eyes,
That feed my love, which is my soul:
It languishes and dies. (l. 5–8)

EBEV; MePo; NOBE; OBS

A Satire against Mankind

8 A Spirit free, to choose for my own share,
What sort of Flesh and Blood I pleas'd to wear,
I'd be a Dog, a Monkey or a Bear,

Or any thing, but that vain Animal,
Who is so proud of being rational. (l. 3–7)

9 Mountains of Whimseys, heaped in his own Brain,
Stumbling from thought to thought, falls headlong
down
Into Doubt's boundless Sea, where like to drown,
Books bear him up a while, and make him try
To swim with Bladders of Philosophy, (l. 17–21)

10 For all Men would be Cowards if they durst:
And Honesty's against all common sense —

11 Most Men are Cowards, all Men should be Knaves.
The Difference lies, as far as I can see,
Not in the thing it self, but the degree;

12 a meek humble Man of modest sense,
Who preaching peace does practice continence;
Whose pious life's a proof he does believe,
Mysterious truths, which no Man can conceive.

13 Man differs more from Man, than Man from Beast.

LiTB; NOBE; NoP; OAEL-1; OBS; OBSV; PoEL-3; SCV;
SeCV-2

A Song of a Young Lady to Her Ancient Lover

14 On thy wither'd lips and dry,
Which like barren furrows lie,
Brooding kisses I will pour,
Shall thy youthful heart restore.
(Such kind showers in autumn fall,
And a second spring recall);
Nor from thee will ever part,
Ancient Person of my Heart. (l. 7–14)

BoLoP; EBEV; ErPo; GBL; MePo; OPOP

Upon Leaving His Mistress

15 See the kind seed-receiving earth
To every grain affords a birth:
On her no showers unwelcome fall,
Her willing womb retains 'em all,
And shall my Caelia be confined?
No, live up to thy mighty mind,
And be the mistress of Mankind! (l. 15–21)

EnLoPo; GBL; NBLV; TEP; TrGrPo

Upon Nothing

16 Great Negative, how vainly would the Wise
Enquire, define, distinguish, teach, devise,
Didst thou not stand to point their dull Philosophies?

Is, or is not, the two great Ends of Fate,
And, true or false, the Subject of Debate,
That perfect, or destroy, the vast Designs of Fate,
(l. 28–33)

MePo; OBS; OBSV; PoEL-3; TrGrPo

WILLIAM ROBERT RODGERS
(1909–1969)

Neither Here nor There

1 In that land all Is and nothing's Ought;
No owners or notices, only birds; (l. 1–2)

2 No bones made, bans laid, or boons expected,
No contracts, entails, hereditaments,
Anything at all that might tie or hem. (l. 8–10)

LiTB; LiTM; MoAB; MoBrPo

The Net

3 But I, being man, can kiss
And bed-spread-eagle too;
All flesh shall come to this,
Being less than angel is,
Yet higher far in bliss
As it entwines with you. (l. 29–34)

AnIL; BoLoP; CIP; ErPo

White Christmas

4 Punctually at Christmas the soft plush
Of sentiment snows down, embosoms all
The sharp and pointed shapes of venom, (l. 1–3)

5 And the member for the constituency
Feeds the five thousand, and has plenty back.
(l. 17–18)

6 this is the night, and this the happy time
When the tinned milk of human kindness is
Upheld and holed by radio-appeal. (l. 21–23)

7 Over the stark plain
The stilted mill-chimneys once again spread
Their sackcloth and ashes a flowing mane
Of repentance for the false day that's fled. (l. 33–36)

LiTM; MoAB; MoBrPo; SeCePo

THEODORE ROETHKE   (1908–1963)

The Bat

1 For something is amiss or out of place
When mice with wings can wear a human face.
(l. 9–10)

GoJo; OBCA; PDV; PYC; RHPC; WSC

Big Wind

2 But she rode it out,
That old rose-house,
She hove into the teeth of it, (l. 21–23)

3 She sailed until the calm morning,
Carrying her full cargo of roses. (l. 32–33)

AmPP; CMoP; GoJo; InvP; NoP; VGW

CUTTINGS (the following 2 poems)

"Sticks-in-a-drowse droop over sugary loam"

4 But still the delicate slips keep coaxing up water;
The small cells bulge;

One nub of growth
Nudges a sand-crumb loose, (l. 3–6)

HCAP; LCAP; MoP; NAAL-2; NoAM; NOBA; TAP; UnPo

"This urge, wrestle, resurrection of dry sticks"

5 I can hear, underground, that sucking and sobbing,
In my veins, in my bones I feel it, —
The small waters seeping upward,
The tight grains parting at last. (l. 5–8)

CAPP; HCAP; LCAP; MoP; NAAL-2; NoAM; NOBA; TAP;
UnPo

Dinky

6 Last night you lay a-sleeping? No!
The room was thirty-five below;
The sheets and blankets turned to snow.
—He'd got in: Dirty Dinky. (l. 13–16)

OBAL; OBCA; RHPC; SM

Dolor

7 I have known the inexorable sadness of pencils.
Neat in their boxes, dolor of pad and paper-weight.
All the misery of manilla folders and mucilage,
Desolation in immaculate public places, (l. 1–4)

8 And I have seen dust from the walls of institutions,
Finer than flour, alive, more dangerous than silica,
Sift, almost invisible, through long afternoons of
tedium, (l. 9–11)

AmPP; CMoP; HCAP; HeIP; HoPM; LiTM; MoP; NoAM;
OxBSP; PoA

The Dream

9 Love is not love until love's vulnerable.
She slowed to sigh, in that long interval. (l. 17–18)

10 Like a wet log, I sang within a flame.
In that last while, eternity's confine,
I came to love, I came into my own. (l. 30–32)

LLLT; NoP; NYBP; UnPo

Elegy for Jane

11 I remember the neckcurls, limp and damp as tendrils;
And her quick look, a sidelong pickerel smile;
And how, once startled into talk, the light syllables
leaped for her. (l. 1–4)

12 If only I could nudge you from this sleep,
My maimed darling, my skittery pigeon.
Over this damp grave I speak the words of my love:
I, with no rights in this matter,
Neither father nor lover. (l. 18–22)

AmPP; CAPP; CoAP; FF; HAP; HCAP; InPK; InPS;
LiTM; MoAB; MoAmPo; NoP; PoE; TAP; TwCP; WeW

The Far Field

13 I suffered for birds, for young rabbits caught in the
mower,
My grief was not excessive.
For to come upon warblers in early May
Was to forget time and death: (l. 24–27)

14 I have come to a still, but not a deep center,
A point outside the glittering current;
My eyes stare at the bottom of a river, (l. 70–72)

15 I am renewed by death, thought of my death,
The dry scent of a dying garden in September,
The wind fanning the ash of a low fire.
What I love is near at hand,
Always, in earth and air. (l. 76–80)

16 An old man with his feet before the fire,
In robes of green, in garments of adieu. (l. 84–85)

17 All finite things reveal infinitude: (l. 93)

18 The pure serene of memory in one man, —
A ripple widening from a single stone
Winding around the waters of the world. (l. 98–100)

NAAL-2; NoAM; NoP; PrIm

FOUR FOR SIR JOHN DAVIES (the following 3 poems)

The Dance

19 Is that dance slowing in the mind of man
That made him think the universe could hum? (l. 1–2)

The Partner

20 What is desire? —
The impulse to make someone else complete?
That woman would set sodden straw on fire.
(l. 26—28)

21 The living all assemble! What's the cue? —
Do what the clumsy partner wants to do! (l. 41—42)

22 The body and the soul know how to play
In that dark world where gods have lost their way.
(l. 47—48)

The Vigil

23 All lovers live by longing, and endure:
Summon a vision and declare it pure. (l. 77—78)

24 Who rise from flesh to spirit know the fall:
The word outleaps the world, and light is all.
(l. 95—96)

MoAmPo; NoAM; NOBA

Frau Bauman, Frau Schmidt, and Frau Schwartze

25 Like witches they flew along rows
Keeping creation at ease;
With a tendril for needle
They sewed up the air with a stem; (l. 19—22)

26 I remember how they picked me up, a spindly kid,
Pinching and poking my thin ribs
Till I lay in their laps, laughing,
Weak as a whiffet; (l. 26—29)

CoAP; MoAB; MoP; NAAL-2; NoAM; NOBA; NYBP; SaC; TAP

I Knew a Woman

27 I knew a woman, lovely in her bones,
When small birds sighed, she would sigh back at them;
Ah, when she moved, she moved more ways than one;
(l. 1—3)

28 She was the sickle; I, poor I, the rake,
Coming behind her for her pretty sake
(But what prodigious mowing we did make).
(l. 12—15)

29 I swear she cast a shadow white as stone.
But who would count eternity in days?
These old bones live to learn her wanton ways:
(I measure time by how a body sways.) (l. 25—28)

AmPP; BoLoP; CAPP; ErPo; HAP; HeIP; HoPM; InPK;
LiTM; MAT; MoAmPo; MoP; NAAL-2; NIP; NoAM;
NOBA; NoP; PoE; PrIm; SM; SoSe; TAP; TrGrPo;
TwCP; UnPo

In a Dark Time

30 What's madness but nobility of soul
At odds with circumstance? (l. 7—8)

31 I know the purity of pure despair,
My shadow pinned against a sweating wall. (l. 9—10)

32 Death of the self in a long, tearless night,
All natural shapes blazing unnatural light. (l. 17—18)

33 Dark, dark my light, and darker my desire
My soul, like some heat-maddened summer fly,
Keeps buzzing at the sill. (l. 19—21)

34 The mind enters itself, and God the mind,
And one is One, free in the tearing wind. (l. 23—24)

CAPP; EaLo; HAP; HeIP; MAT; MoAmPo; MoP; NAAL-2;
NoAM; NOBA; NoP; NYBP; PoE; PPP; TAP

The Lost Son

35 The shape of a rat?
It's bigger than that.
It's less than a leg
And more than a nose,
Just under the water
It usually goes. (l. 44—49)

36 I'm cold. I'm cold all over. Rub me in father and
mother.
Fear was my father, Father Fear.
His look drained the stones. (l. 74—76)

37 It was beginning winter,
An in-between time,
The landscape still partly brown:
The bones of weeds kept swinging in the wind,
Above the blue snow. (l. 139—143)

38 A lively understandable spirit
Once entertained you.
It will come again.
Be still.
Wait. (l. 159—163)

DiL; HAP; HCAP; LiTM; VGW

The Meadow Mouse

39 A little quaker, the whole body of him trembling,
His absurd whiskers sticking out like a cartoon-mouse,
His feet like small leaves,
Little lizard-feet,
Whitish and spread wide when he tried to struggle
away, (l. 6—10)

40 Do I imagine he no longer trembles
When I come close to him?
He seems no longer to tremble. (l. 18–20)

41 I think of the nestling fallen into the deep grass,
The turtle gasping in the dusty rubble of the highway,
The paralytic stunned in the tub, and the water
rising, —
All things innocent, hapless, forsaken. (l. 27–30)

HeIP; NaP; NIP; RB

Meditation at Oyster River

42 Over the low, barnacled, elephant-colored rocks,
Come the first tide-ripples, moving, almost without
sound, toward me,
Running along the narrow furrows of the shore, the
rows of dead clam shells; (l. 1–3)

43 The self persists like a dying star,
In sleep, afraid. (l. 24–25)

44 With these I would be.
And with water: the waves coming forward, without
cessation,
The waves, altered by sand-bars, beds of kelp,
miscellaneous driftwood,
Topped by cross-winds, tugged at by sinuous
undercurrents
The tide rustling in, sliding between the ridges of stone,
The tongues of water, creeping in, quietly. (l. 30–35)

45 In this first heaven of knowing,
The flesh takes on the pure poise of the spirit,
(l. 37–38)

46 Water's my will, and my way,
And the spirit runs, intermittently,
In and out of the small waves, (l. 63–65)

47 In the first of the moon,
All's a scattering,
A shining. (l. 68–70)

CAPP; CMoP; MoAMPo; NYBP

The Minimal

48 bacterial creepers
Wriggling through wounds
Like elvers in ponds,
Their wan mouths kissing the warm sutures,
Cleaning and caressing,
Creeping and healing. (l. 6–11)

HCAP; MoP; NoAM; NOBA; RB; TSS

My Papa's Waltz

49 The whisky on your breath
Could make a small boy dizzy;
But I hung on like death;
Such waltzing was not easy. (l. 1–4)

AnAmPo; CAPP; CMoP; DiL; FF; HAP; HCAP; HeIP;
HoPM; InPK; InPS; LCAP; LiTM; MoAB; MoP; NAAL-2;
NBLV; NIP; NoAM; NOBA; NoP; PoE; PPP; PrIm; SM;
TAP; VGW; WeW

Night Crow

50 When I saw that clumsy crow
Flap from a wasted tree,
A shape in the mind rose up: (l. 1–3)

HoPM; InPK; OxBSP; VGW

Night Journey

51 Wheels shake the roadbed stone,
The pistons jerk and shove,
I stay up half the night
To see the land I love. (l. 24–27)

AmFN; GOA; NYBP; RR

Root Cellar

52 Nothing would sleep in that cellar, dank as a ditch,
Bulbs broke out of boxes hunting for chinks in the dark,
(l. 1–2)

53 Nothing would give up life;
Even the dirt kept breathing a small breath.
(l. 10–11)

AmPP; AnAmPo; BoNaP; HeIP; InPK; NoP; PPP

The Shape of the Fire

54 Time for the flat-headed man. I recognize that listener,
Him with the platitudes and rubber doughnuts,
Melting at the knees, a varicose horror.
Hello, hello. My nerves knew you, dear boy.
Have you come to unhinge my shadow? (l. 30–34)

CMoP; LCAP; LiTA; MoAB

The Sloth

55 In moving-slow he has no Peer.
You ask him something in his ear;
He thinks about it for a Year; (l. 1–4)

AnAmPo; FiBHP; OBAL; OBCA; RHPC

The Visitant

56 A tree swayed overwater.
A voice said:
Stay. Stay by the slip-ooze. Stay. (l. 2—4)

57 Slow, slow, as a fish she came,
Slow as a fish coming forward,
Swaying in a long wave;
Her skirts not touching a leaf,
Her white arms reaching towards me. (l. 10—14)

CMoP; PoE; RB; UnPo

The Waking

58 We think by feeling. What is there to know? (l. 4)

59 This shaking keeps me steady. I should know.
What falls away is always. And is near.
I wake to sleep, and take my waking slow.
I learn by going where I have to go. (l. 16—19)

AmPP; CAPP; CoAP; CRP; HAP; HCAP; HeIP; InPK;
InPS; LiTM; MoAmPo; MoP; NAAL-2; NIP; NoAM;
NOBA; NoP; OPOP; PPP; PrIm; SM; SoSe; TAP; TwCP;
WeW

Wish for a Young Wife

60 May you live out your life
Without hate, without grief
And your hair ever blaze,
In the sun, in the sun,
When I am undone,
When I am no one. (l. 6—11)

MoP; NAAL-2; NoAM; NoP; OxBSP; TAP

SAMUEL ROGERS (1763—1855)

A Wish

1 Mine be a cot beside the hill;
A bee-hive's hum shall soothe my ear;
A willowy brook, that turns a mill,
With many a fall shall linger near. (l. 1—4)

FaPoR; GTBS; GTBS-P; NOBE; OBEV

JOHN JEROME ROONEY (1866—1934)

The Men behind the Guns

1 But off with your hat and three times three for
Columbia's true-blue sons,
The men below who batter the foe — the men behind
the guns! (l. 5—6)

2 Then down, deep down, in the mighty ship, unseen by
the midday suns,
You'll find the chaps who are giving the raps — the men
behind the guns! (l. 17—18)

3 The steel decks rock with the lightning shock, and
shake with the great recoil,
And the sea grows red with the blood of the dead and
reaches for his spoil —
But not till the foe has gone below or turns his prow
and runs,
Shall the voice of peace bring sweet release to the men
behind the guns! (l. 21—24)

AA; BLPA; FaBoBe; PAH

ISAAC ROSENBERG (1890—1918)

August 1914

1 Iron are our lives
Molten right through our youth.
A burnt space through ripe fields
A fair mouth's broken tooth. (l. 9—12)

EBEV; NOBE; OBWP; OPOP; OxBTC

Break of Day in the Trenches

2 Bonds to the whims of murder,
Sprawled in the bowels of the earth,
The torn fields of France. (l. 16—18)

3 Poppies whose roots are in man's veins
Drop, and are ever dropping;
But mine in my ear is safe,
Just a little white with the dust. (l. 23—26)

BrPo; FaBoMo; GTBS-P; MMA; MoBrPo; NAEL-2; NIP;
NoAM; NOBE; NoP; OAEL-2; OBWP; PoA; SeCePo;
VWA; WaaP; WaP

Dead Man's Dump

4 Earth has waited for them,
All the time of their growth
Fretting for their decay:
Now she has them at last! (l. 14—17)

5 When the swift iron burning bee
Drained the wild honey of their youth. (l. 30—31)

6 The grass and coloured clay
More motion have than they,
Joined to the great sunk silences. (l. 66—68)

BrPo; FaBoMo; GTBS-P; LiTM; MMA; NAEL-2; NoAM;
NoP; OBWP; TrJP; VWA; WaP

Louse Hunting

7 For a shirt verminously busy
Yon soldier tore from his throat, with oaths
Godhead might shrink at, but not the lice. (l. 5–7)

EBEV; NAEL-2; NoAM; NoP; OxBTC

Returning, We Hear the Larks

8 Death could drop from the dark
As easily as song –
But song only dropped, (l. 10–12)

BrPo; FaBoMo; MMA; NAEL-2; NoAM; OAEL-2; OBWP;
VWA; WaaP

CHRISTINA GEORGINA ROSSETTI
(1830–1894)

A Birthday

1 My heart is like a singing bird
Whose nest is in a watered shoot;
My heart is like an apple-tree
Whose boughs are bent with thickset fruit;
My heart is like a rainbow shell
That paddles in a halcyon sea; (l. 1–6)

2 the birthday of my life
Is come, my love is come to me. (l. 15–16)

AWP; BLPL; CH; FaFP; InvP; LiTB; NA; NAEL-2;
NOBE; NOBVV; OAEL-2; OBEV; PoE; TrGrPo; TTTS;
WiR; WPE

The Caterpillar (Sing-Song)

3 Brown and furry
Caterpillar in a hurry,
Take your walk
To the shady leaf, or stalk, (l. 1–4)

4 Spin and die,
To live again as butterfly. (l. 7–8)

BoTP; FaPON; GoJo; OxBChV; RHPC

The City Mouse and the Garden Mouse (Sing-Song)

5 The city mouse lives in a house; –
The garden mouse lives in a bower, (l. 1–2)

6 The city mouse eats bread and cheese; –
The garden mouse eats what he can;
We will not grudge him seeds and stocks,
Poor little timid furry man. (l. 5–8)

BoTP; FaBoBe; FaPON; NTCP

Echo

7 Yet come to me in dreams that I may live
My very life again though cold in death:
Come back to me in dreams, that I may give
Pulse for pulse, breath for breath:
Speak low, lean low,
As long ago, my love, how long ago. (l. 13–18)

BoLoP; CH; EBVV; ELP; GBL; NOBE; NoP; OAEL-2;
OBNC; PoE; PoEL-5

Eve

8 As a tree my sin stands
To darken all lands;
Death is the fruit it bore. (l. 5–7)

CH; FM; GTBS-P; NIP; PoEL-5

Ferry me across the river (Sing-Song)

9 "Ferry me across the water,
Do, boatman, do."
"If you've a penny in your purse
I'll ferry you." (l. 1–4)

10 And my eyes are blue;
So ferry me across the water,
Do, boatman, do!'

"Step into my ferry-boat,
Be they black or blue, (l. 6–10)

BoTP; ChTr; GoJo; OxBChV; PDV

Goblin Market

11 Morning and evening
Maids heard the goblins cry:
'Come buy our orchard fruits,
Come buy, come buy: (l. 1–4)

12 One had a cat's face,
One whisked a tail,
One tramped at a rat's pace,
One crawled like a snail,
One like a wombat prowled obtuse and furry,
One like a ratel tumbled hurry skurry. (l. 71–76)

13 The customary cry,
'Come buy, come buy,'
With its iterated jingle
Of sugar-bated words: (l. 232–235)

14 Their fruits like honey to the throat
But poison in the blood (l. 557–558)

15 'For there is no friend like a sister
In calm or stormy weather;
To cheer one on the tedious way,
To fetch one if one goes astray,
To lift one if one totters down,
To strengthen whilst one stands.' (l. 565–570)

BoTP; EBEV; NAEL-2; NOBVV; OBNV

Hurt No Living Thing (Sing-Song)

16 Hurt no living thing:
Ladybird, nor butterfly,
Nor moth with dusty wing, (l. 1–3)

FaPON; FM; PDV; RHPC; TSS

Monna Innominata: The First Day

17 So unrecorded did it slip away,
So blind was I to see and to foresee,
So dull to mark the budding of my tree
That would not blossom yet for many a May.
If only I could recollect it, such
A day of days! I let it come and go
As traceless as a thaw of bygone snow;
It seemed to mean so little, meant so much;
If only now I could recall that touch,
First touch of hand in hand — Did one but know!
(l. 5–14)

BLPL; BoLoP; FaBoBe; GBL; Son

Old and New Year Ditties

18 Passing away, saith the World, passing away:
Chances, beauty and youth sapped day by day:
Thy life never continueth in one stay.
Is the eye waxen dim, is the dark hair changing to gray
That hath won neither laurel nor bay? (l. 1–5)

NoP; OAEL-2; OBNC; WPE

Remember

19 Remember me when I am gone away,
Gone far away into the silent land; (l. 1–2)

20 Yet if you should forget me for a while
And afterwards remember, do not grieve:
For if the darkness and corruption leave
A vestige of the thoughts that once I had,
Better by far you should forget and smile
Than that you should remember and be sad. (l. 9–14)

AWP; BoLoP; CH; EnLoPo; FaBV; FPL; NOBE; NoP;
OAEL-2; OBEV; OBNC; PoLF; PoRA; TrGrPo

Rest

21 Hush'd in and curtain'd with a blessed dearth
Of all that irk'd her from the hour of birth;
With stillness that is almost Paradise.
Darkness more clear than noonday holdeth her,
(l. 6–9)

22 Until the morning of Eternity
Her rest shall not begin nor end, but be;
And when she wakes she will not think it long.
(l. 12–14)

NOBE; OAEL-2; OBEV; OBNC; TrGrPo

Spring Quiet

23 Gone were but the Winter,
Come were but the Spring,
I would go to a covert
Where the birds sing. (l. 1–4)

BoNaP; BoTP; CH; GTBS-P; InPS; PoE; PoEL-5; WPE

The Thread of Life

24 The irresponsive silence of the land,
The irresponsive sounding of the sea,
Speak both one message of one sense to me: —
'Aloof, aloof, we stand aloof,

25 And sometimes I remember days of old
When fellowship seemed not so far to seek,
And all the world and I seemed much less cold,
And at the rainbow's foot lay surely gold,
And hope felt strong, and life itself not weak.

NOBE; OBEV; OBNC; TrGrPo

Twice

26 You took my heart in your hand
With a friendly smile,
With a critical eye you scanned,
Then set it down,
And said: It is still unripe,
Better wait awhile; (l. 9–14)

27 I smiled at the speech you spoke,
At your judgement that I heard:
But I have not often smiled
Since then, nor questioned since,
Nor cared for corn-flowers wild,
Nor sung with the singing bird. (l. 18–24)

GBL; NOBE; OBEV; OBNC; TOF; TrCP

Uphill

28 Does the road wind uphill all the way?
Yes, to the very end.
Will the day's journey take the whole long day?
From morn to night, my friend.

But is there for the night a resting-place?
A roof for when the slow, dark hours begin, (l. 1–6)

29 Shall I find comfort, travel-sore and weak?
Of labour you shall find the sum.
Will there be beds for me and all who seek?
Yea, beds for all who come. (l. 13–16)

BLPA; CH; EBVV; FaBoBe; FaBoRV; FPL; HAP; InPK;
NAEL-2; NOBE; NoP; OAEL-2; OBD; OBEV; OBNC;
PoE; PoRA; PPP; TrCP; TrGrPo; WeW; WGRP; WiR;
WPE

What Are Heavy?

30 What are heavy? Sea-sand and sorrow;
What are brief? Today and tomorrow;
What are frail? Spring blossoms and youth;
What are deep? The ocean and truth. (l. 1–4)

ChTr; FaBoEE; FaBoRV; OxBChV

What Is Pink? (Sing-Song)

31 What is pink? A rose is pink
By the fountain's brink. (l. 1–2)

32 What is green? The grass is green,
With small flowers between.
What is violet? Clouds are violet
In the summer twilight.
What is orange? Why, an orange,
Just an orange! (l. 11–16)

GoJo; OnUR; OxBChV; RHPC

When I am dead, my dearest

33 When I am dead, my dearest,
Sing no sad songs for me;
Plant thou no roses at my head,
Nor shady cypress tree:

Be the green grass above me
With showers and dewdrops wet; (l. 1–6)

34 And dreaming through the twilight
That doth not rise nor set,
Haply I may remember,
And haply may forget. (l. 13–16)

AWP; BoLoP; CH; DL; EBEV; ELP; FaFP; FF; FPL;
GBL; InPS; LiTB; NAEL-2; NOBE; NOBVV; NoP;
OAEL-2; OBD; OBEV; PoLF; PoRA; SCV; SoSe; TrGrPo;
WPE

Who has seen the wind? (Sing-Song)

35 Who has seen the wind?
Neither I nor you:
But when the leaves hang trembling,
The wind is passing through. (l. 1–4)

36 when the trees bow down their heads,
The wind is passing by. (l. 7–8)

BLPL; FaBoBe; FaPON; GoJo; NTCP; OxBChV; PDV;
RHPC

Winter: My Secret

37 Spring's an expansive time: yet I don't trust
March with its peck of dust,
Nor April with its rainbow-crowned brief showers,
Nor even May, whose flowers
One frost may wither thro' the sunless hours.
(l. 23–27)

BrRo; NAEL-2; NOBVV; TEP

DANTE GABRIEL ROSSETTI
(1828–1882)

THE HOUSE OF LIFE (the following 7 poems)

Barren Spring

1 So Spring comes merry towards me here, but earns
No answering smile from me, whose life is twin'd
With the dead boughs that winter still must bind,

EBVV; NoP; OAEL-2; OBNC; PoEL-5

Body's Beauty

2 The rose and poppy are her flowers; for where
Is he not found, O Lilith, whom shed scent
And soft-shed kisses and soft sleep shall snare?
Lo! as that youth's eyes burned at thine, so went

Thy spell through him, and left his straight neck bent
And round his heart one strangling golden hair.

OAEL-2; PoEL-5; Son; TrGrPo

Lovesight

3 O love, my love! if I no more should see
Thyself, nor on the earth the shadow of thee,
Nor image of thine eyes in any spring, —
How then should sound upon Life's darkening slope
The ground-whirl of the perished leaves of Hope,
The wind of Death's imperishable wing?

EBVV; GTBS-P; NAEL-2; OBNC; TrGrPo

Silent Noon

4 Deep in the sun-searched growths the dragonfly
Hangs like a blue thread loosened from the sky —
So this winged hour is dropped to us from above.
Oh! clasp we to our hearts, for deathless dower,
This close-companioned inarticulate hour
When twofold silence was the song of love.

HAP; NAEL-2; NoP; OBNC; PoEL-5; TrGrPo; UnAS

A Sonnet

5 A Sonnet is a moment's monument, —
Memorial from the Soul's eternity
To one dead deathless hour.

HeIP; NAEL-2; NoP; Son

A Superscription

6 Look in my face; my name is Might-have-been;
I am also called No-more, Too-late, Farewell;

EBVV; GTBS-P; NAEL-2; NoP; OAEL-2; OBNC; PoEL-5;
SeCePo

Without Her

7 What of the heart without her? Nay, poor heart,
Of thee what word remains ere speech be still?
A wayfarer by barren ways and chill,
Steep ways and weary, without her thou art,
Where the long cloud, the long wood's counterpart,
Sheds doubled darkness up the labouring hill.

GBL; OBNC; PoEL-5; Son

Sudden Light

8 I have been here before,
But when or how I cannot tell:
I know the grass beyond the door,
The sweet keen smell,
The sighing sound, the lights around the shore.
(l. 1–5)

BoLoP; CTC; ELP; FPL; NOBE; NOBVV; NoP; OAEL-2;
OBNC; OPOP; PoLF; TrGrPo

The Woodspurge

9 The wind flapped loose, the wind was still,
Shaken out dead from tree and hill:
I had walked on at the wind's will, —
I sat now, for the wind was still. (l. 1–4)

10 Among those few, out of the sun,
The woodspurge flowered, three cups in one.

From perfect grief there need not be
Wisdom or even memory:
One thing then learnt remains to me, —
The woodspurge has a cup of three. (l. 11–16)

EBEV; ELP; GTBS-P; HAP; HeIP; NOBE; NoP; OAEL-2;
OBEV; OBNC; PoEL-5; PrIm; UnPo; WeW

SAMUEL ROWLANDS (1570?–1630?)

The Melancholy Knight

1 Sir Eglamour, that worthy knight,
He took his sword and went to fight;
And as he rode both hill and dale,
Armed upon his shirt of mail,
A dragon came out of his den,
Had slain, God knows how many men! (l. 1–6)

ElL; FaBoCh; FaBoNo; InvP

MURIEL RUKEYSER (1913–1980)

Ajanta

1 a star
called Wormwood rose and flickered, shattering
bent light over the dead boiling up in the ground,
the biting yellow their corrupted lives
streaming to war, denying all our words. (l. 4–8)

2 The heavy sensual shoulders, the thighs, the blood-born
      flesh
and earth turning into color, rocks into their crystals,
water to sound, fire to form: life flickers
uncounted into the supple arms of love. (l. 35–38)

3 I am haunted by interrupted acts,
introspective as a leper, enchanted
by a repulsive clew,
a gross and fugitive movement of the limbs.
Is this the love that shook the lights to flame?
(l. 92–96)

4 "Try to live as if there were a God." (l. 119)

5 Came to Ajanta cave, the painted space of the breast,
the real world where everything is complete,
there are no shadows, the forms of incompleteness,
The great cloak blows in the light, rider and horse
arrive,
the shoulders turn and every gift is made.
(l. 120–124)

6 The naked world, and the old noise of tears,
the fear, the expiation and the love,
a world of the shadowed and alone.
The journey, and the struggles of the moon.
(l. 147–150)

LiTA; LiTM; MoAB; MoAmPo; NNaP

Boy with His Hair Cut Short

7 Twilight and bulb define
the brown room, the overstuffed plum sofa,
the boy, and the girl's thin hands above his head.
(l. 2–4)

8 He sits at the table, head down, the young clear neck
exposed,
watching the drugstore sign from the tail of his eye;
(l. 5–6)

9 Erasing the failure of weeks with level fingers,
she sleeks the fine hair, combing: "You'll look fine
tomorrow! (l. 15–16)

LiTM; MoAB; NoAM; TwCP; VGW; WPE

Effort at Speech between Two People

10 Speak to me. Take my hand. What are you now?
I will tell you all. I will conceal nothing. (l. 1–2)

11 it was my birthday, and a candle
burnt a sore spot on my finger, and I was told to be
happy, (l. 5–6)

12 What are you now? If we could touch one another,
if these our separate entities could come to grips,
clenched like a Chinese puzzle . . . yesterday
I stood in a crowded street that was live with people,
and no one spoke a word, and the morning shone.

Everyone silent, moving. . . . Take my hand. Speak to
me. (l. 31–36)

FYAP; MoAB; MoAmPo; TrGrPo; TrJP; TwCP; WeW

CHARLES SACKVILLE, 6TH EARL OF DORSET (1688–1706)

Dorinda's sparkling wit, and eyes

1 Dorinda's sparkling wit and eyes,
United, cast too fierce a light,
Which blazes high, but quickly dies,
Pains not the heart, but hurts the sight,

Love is a calmer, gentler joy:
Smooth are his looks, and soft his pace;
Her Cupid is a blackguard boy
That runs his link full in your face. (l. 1–8)

APAS; OBEV; OBS; OxBSP; SeCePo; SeCV-2

Song Written at Sea in the First Dutch War (1665), the Night before an Engagement

2 Then if we write not by each Post,
Think not we are unkind;
Nor yet conclude our Ships are lost,

3 When any mournful Tune you hear,
That dies in ev'ry Note;
As if it sigh'd with each Man's Care,
For being so remote;
Think then how often Love we've made
To you, when all those Tunes were play'd, (l. 29–34)

CoMu; EnLoPo; NOBE; OBEV; OBS; OBWP; SeCV-2

SONIA SANCHEZ (b. 1934)

Poem at Thirty

1 it is midnight
no magical bewitching
hour for me (l. 1–3)

2 no one touches
me anymore. (l. 22–23)

3 you you black man
stretching scraping
the mold from your body.
here is my hand.

i am not afraid
of the night. (l. 27–32)

BlSi; BPo; CNA; NMM; PoBA

Summer Words for a Sistuh Addict

4 the first day i shot dope
was on a sunday.
i had just come
home from church
got mad at my mother
cuz she got mad at me. u dig? (l. 1–6)

BlSi; BPo; TV; UnPo

CARL SANDBURG (1878–1967)

A. E. F.

1 There will be a rusty gun on the wall, sweetheart,
The rifle grooves curling with flakes of rust.
A spider will make a silver string nest in the darkest,
   warmest corner of it. (l. 1–3)

CMoP; MoAB; MoAmPo; WaaP

Buffalo Dusk

2 The buffaloes are gone.
And those who saw the buffaloes are gone. (l. 1–2)

GOA; OBCA; PDV; RFM; RHPC

Chicago

3 Hog Butcher for the World,
Tool Maker, Stacker of Wheat,
Player with Railroads and the Nation's Freight
   Handler;
Stormy, husky, brawling,
City of the Big Shoulders: (l. 1–5)

4 And they tell me you are brutal and my reply is: On
   the faces of women and children I have seen the
   marks of wanton hunger.
And having answered so I turn once more to those who
   sneer at this my city, and I give them back the sneer
   and say to them:
Come and show me another city with lifted head
   singing so proud to be alive and coarse and strong
   and cunning. (l. 10–12)

AiP; AmPP; AnAmPo; BLPL; CMoP; FaBV; LiTM;
MoAB; MoAmPo; MoP; NAAL-2; NoAM; NOBA; NoP;
OxBA; PoA; TAP; UnPo; VGW

Cool Tombs

5 Pocahontas' body, lovely as a poplar, sweet as a red
   haw in November (l. 3)

6 tell me if the lovers are losers ... tell me if any get
   more than the lovers ... in the dust ... in the cool
   tombs. (l. 4)

AmPP; BLPL; CMoP; HAP; HeIP; MoAB; MoAmPo; MoP;
NAAL-2; NoAM; NOBA; OPP; OxBSP; PoLF; TAP;
TrGrPo

Four Preludes on Playthings of the Wind

7 The woman named Tomorrow
sits with a hairpin in her teeth
and takes her time (l. 1–3)

8 and the girls chanted:
We are the greatest city,
and the greatest nation:
nothing like us ever was. (l. 13–16)

9 The feet of the rats
scribble on the doorsills;
the hieroglyphs of the rat footprints
chatter the pedigrees of the rats (l. 50–53)

CMoP; MoAB; MoAmPo; NOBA

Grass

10 Pile the bodies high at Austerlitz and Waterloo.
Shovel them under and let me work—
I am the grass; I cover all. (l. 1–3)

AWP; BLPL; FaBV; MoAB; MoAmPo; MoP; NAAL-2;
NoAM; NOBA; NoP; OBWP; OHFP; OxBA; PoLF;
TrGrPo; WaaP

Jazz Fantasia

11 Drum on your drums, batter on your banjos, sob on the
   long cool winding saxophones. Go to it, O jazzmen.
                                                    (l. 1)

AiP; MoAB; MoAmPo; PoNe

Limited

12 (All the coaches shall be scrap and rust and all the men
   and women laughing in the diners and sleepers shall
   pass to ashes.)
I ask a man in the smoker where he is going and he
   answers: 'Omaha.' (l. 3–4)

HAP; MoAB; MoAmPo; OxBA

Losers

13   Jack Cade, John Brown, Jesse James,
There too I could sit down and stop for a while.
I think I could tell their headstones:
"God, let me remember all good losers." (l. 16–19)

CMoP; MoAB; MoAmPo; NoAM; TrGrPo

The People, Yes

14   The people will live on.
The learning and blundering people will live on.

15   The mammoth rests between his cyclonic dramas.

16   Once having marched
Over the margins of animal necessity,
Over the grim line of sheer subsistence
Then man came
To the deeper rituals of his bones,

17   Who else speaks for the Family of Man?
They are in tune and step
with constellations of universal law.

18   Man is a long time coming.
Man will yet win.
Brother may yet line up with brother:

19   Time is a great teacher,
Who can live without hope?

MoAB; MoAmPo; NoAM; NOBA; OxBA; TrGrPo

Prayers of Steel

20   Lay me on an anvil, O God.
Beat me and hammer me into a steel spike. (l. 5–6)

CMoP; FaPON; MoAmPo; PDV; TrCP; TrPWD

Threes

21   out of great Russia came three
dusky syllables workmen took guns and went out to die
for: Bread, Peace, Land. (l. 12–14)

22   Tell me how to say three things
and I always get by — gimme a plate of ham and
eggs —
how much? — and — do you love me, kid? (l. 17–19)

AnAmPo; CMoP; OxBA; PoLF

Washington Monument by Night

23   The wind bit hard at Valley Forge one Christmas.
Soldiers tied rags on their feet.
Red footprints wrote on the snow ... (l. 12–14)

24   Tongues wrangled dark at a man.
He buttoned his overcoat and stood alone.
In a snowstorm, red hollyberries, thoughts, he stood
alone. (l. 17–19)

CMoP; FaPON; OFD; OHIP

GEORGE SANTAYANA (1863–1952)

World, Thou Choosest Not the Better Part!

1   Columbus found a world, and had no chart,
Save one that faith deciphered in the skies; (l. 5–6)

2   Our knowledge is a torch of smoky pine
That lights the pathway but one step ahead
Across a void of mystery and dread. (l. 9–11)

AnAmPo; FPL; TrGrPo; WGRP

LEW SARETT (1888–1954)

Four Little Foxes

1   Walk softly, March, forbear the bitter blow;
Her feet within a trap, her blood upon the snow,
The four little foxes saw their mother go —
Walk softly. (l. 5–8)

FaPON; PDV; RFM; RHPC

SIEGFRIED SASSOON (1886–1967)

Aftermath

1   But the past is just the same, — and War's a bloody
game. . . .
Have you forgotten yet? . . .
Look down, and swear by the slain of the War that
you'll never forget. (l. 7–9)

2   Do you remember the stretcher-cases lurching back
With dying eyes and lolling heads, those ashen-gray
Masks of the lads who once were keen and kind and
gay? (l. 19–21)

BrPo; MoBrPo; TrJP; WaP

Base Details

3   If I were fierce, and bald, and short of breath,
I'd live with scarlet Majors at the Base,
And speed glum heroes up the line to death, (l. 1–3)

4 And when the war is done and youth stone dead,
I'd toddle safely home and die — in bed. (l. 9—10)

FF; HeIP; MMA; MoBrPo; OxBSP; SoSe

Blighters

5 And there'd be no more jokes in Music-halls
To mock the riddled corpses round Bapaume. (l. 7—8)

CMoP; FaBoTw; MMA; MoP; NoAM; OxBSP

Dreamers

6 Soldiers are citizens of death's grey land,
Drawing no dividend from time's to-morrows. (l. 1—2)

7 mocked by hopeless longing to regain
Bank-holidays, and picture shows, and spats,
And going to the office in the train. (l. 12—14)

BrPo; MoBrPo; NoAM; Son

The Dug-out

8 You are too young to fall asleep for ever;
And when you sleep you remind me of the dead.
(l. 7—8)

CH; MoBrPo; OHIP; WaaP; WaP

Everyone Sang

9 O, but Everyone
Was a bird; and the song was wordless; the singing will
never be done. (l. 9—10)

BrPo; FaBV; GTBS-P; InvP; MoBrPo; NAEL-2; NoAM;
NOBE; OBEV; OBWP; OxBSP; OxBTC; TrJP; WaP

The General

10 "He's a cheery old card," grunted Harry to Jack
As they slogged up to Arras with rifle and pack.
(l. 5—6)

11 But he did for them both by his plan of attack.

BrPo; CMoP; FaBV; FiBHP; LiTM; MMA; NAEL-2;
NoAM; OBWP; OxBoLi; OxBSP; OxBTC; PoE; TW

On Passing the New Menin Gate

12 "Their name liveth for ever," the Gateway claims.
Was ever an immolation so belied
As these intolerably nameless names?

Well might the Dead who struggled in the slime
Rise and deride this sepulchre of crime. (l. 11—15)

NAEL-2; NoAM; OBMV; Son

The Rear-Guard

13 At last, with sweat of horror in his hair,
He climbed through darkness to the twilight air,
Unloading hell behind him step by step. (l. 23—25)

MoBrPo; NAEL-2; NoAM; OBWP; WaP

Repression of War Experience

14 And it's been proved that soldiers don't go mad
Unless they lose control of ugly thoughts
That drive them out to jabber among the trees.
(l. 6—8)

15 Those whispering guns — O Christ, I want to go out
And screech at them to stop — I'm going crazy;
I'm going stark, staring mad because of the guns.
(l. 36—38)

BrPo; CMoP; MMA; NIP; NoAM; PoE

They

16 And Bert's gone syphilitic: you'll not find
A chap who's served that hasn't found some change.'
And the Bishop said: 'The ways of God are strange!'
(l. 10—12)

CMoP; NAEL-2; OBSV; OBWP

DELMORE SCHWARTZ (1913—1966)

For the One Who Would Take Man's Life in His Hands

1 Tiger Christ unsheathed his sword,
Threw it down, became a lamb. (l. 1—2)

2 Troy burned for a sea-tax, also for
Possession of a charming whore. (l. 9—10)

3 Love is the tact of every good,
The only warmth, the only peace. (l. 21—22)

4 — What do all examples show?
What can any actor know?
The contradiction in every act,
The infinite task of the human heart." (l. 29—32)

LiTA; LiTM; MoAB; MoAmPo; VGW; WaP

In the Naked Bed, in Plato's Cave

5 Morning, softly
Melting the air, lifted the half-covered chair
From underseas, (l. 21–23)

6 So, so,
O son of man, the ignorant night, the travail

Of early morning, the mystery of beginning
Again and again,
while History is unforgiven. (l. 27–31)

LiTA; LiTM; MoAB; MoAmPo; NoAM; NOBA; PoA;
VGW

The Repetitive Heart

7 Each minute bursts in the burning room,
The great globe reels in the solar fire,
Spinning the trivial and unique away,
(How all things flash! How all things flare!)

8 May memory restore again and again
The smallest color of the smallest day:
Time is the school in which we learn,
Time is the fire in which we burn.

LiTA; LiTM; MoAB; MoAmPo; OxBA; PrIm

9 The heavy bear who goes with me,
A manifold honey to smear his face,
Clumsy and lumbering here and there,
The central ton of every place,
The hungry beating brutish one
In love with candy, anger, and sleep,

10 —The strutting show-off is terrified,
Dressed in his dress-suit, bulging his pants,
Trembles to think that his quivering meat
Must finally wince to nothing at all.

11 Dragging me with him in his mouthing care,
Amid the hundred million of his kind,
The scrimmage of appetite everywhere.

LiTA; LiTM; NoAM; NOBA; TAP; TrJP; TwCP; UnPo

SIR WALTER SCOTT (1771–1832)

The Bride of Lammermoor

1 Look not thou on beauty's charming;
Sit thou still when kings are arming;
Taste not when the wine-cup glistens;
Speak not when the people listens;

2 Vacant heart and hand and eye,
Easy live and quiet die.

EnRP; GoTS; NOBE; OBEV; OxBS; OxBSP

The Doom of Devorgoil

3 'Ere the King's crown shall fall, there are crowns to be
 broke;
So let each Cavalier who loves honour and me,
Come follow the bonnet of Bonny Dundee.

EnRP; FaBoCh; OxBoLi; OxBS; Par

The Dreary Change

4 With listless look along the plain
I see Tweed's silver current glide,
And coldly mark the holy fane
Of Melrose rise in ruin'd pride. (l. 9–12)

FaBoPP; NAEL-2; OAEL-2; OBNC

The Heart of Midlothian

5 'The glowworm o'er grave and stone
Shall light thee steady;
The owl from the steeple sing
Welcome, proud lady.'

CH; ChTr; EnRP; FaBoCh; FF; GoTS; GTBS; GTBS-P;
HAP; Mes; NAEL-2; NOBE; OAEL-2; OBEV; OBNC;
OxBS; PBBP; PoEL-4; SeCePo; TEP; TrGrPo; UnPo

Jock of Hazeldean

6 The priest and bridegroom wait the bride
And dame and knight are there.
They sought her baith by bower and ha
The ladie was not seen!
She's o'er the Border and awa'
Wi' Jock of Hazeldean. (l. 27–32)

BeLS; EnRP; GN; GTBS; GTBS-P; NAEL-2; OxBS; TEP

The Lady of the Lake

7 He is gone on the mountain,
He is lost to the forest,
Like a summer-dried fountain,
When our need was the sorest.

8 Like the dew on the mountain,
Like the foam on the river,
Like the bubble on the fountain,
Thou art gone, and for ever!

CH; EnRP; GTBS; GTBS-P; OHIP; TrGrPo; WiR

9 Soldier, rest! thy warfare o'er,
Sleep the sleep that knows not breaking;
Dream of battled fields no more,
Days of danger, nights of waking.

10 Huntsman, rest!thy chase is done;

AWP; GN; MoShBr; NOBE; OBNC; PoRA; TrGrPo

The Lay of the Last Minstrel

11 Breathes there the man with soul so dead,
Who never to himself hath said,
This is my own, my native land!

12 For him no Minstrel raptures swell;
High though his titles, proud his name,
Boundless his wealth as wish can claim;
Despite those titles, power, and pelf,
The wretch, concentred all in self,
Living, shall forfeit fair renown,
And, doubly dying, shall go down
To the vile dust, from whence he sprung,
Unwept, unhonour'd, and unsung.

BLPA; EnRP; FaFP; FaPoR; FPL; GN; NOBE; OBEV; OBNC; OHFP; OPP; OxBS; TrGrPo; WBLP

13 We can show you where he lies,
Fleet of foot and tall of size;
We can show the marks he made
When 'gainst the oak his antlers fray'd;
You shall see him brought to bay;
Waken, lords and ladies gay.

EnRP; GN; GTBS; GTBS-P; TrGrPo; WiR

14 But that my sire the wine will chide
If 'tis not fill'd by Rosabelle."

15 And each Saint Clair was buried there
With candle, with book, and with knell;
But the sea-caves rung, and the wild winds sung
The dirge of lovely Rosabelle.

BeLS; EnRP; GTBS; GTBS-P

The Maid of Neidpath

16 O Lovers' eyes are sharp to see,
And lovers' ears in hearing' (l. 1–2)

17 Till through her wasted hand, at night,
You saw the taper shining. (l. 11–12)

BeLS; EnRP; GTBS; GTBS-P

Marmion

18 Oh, young Lochinvar is come out of the West, —
Through all the wide Border his steed was the best,
And, save his good broadsword, he weapon had none, —
He rode all unarmed, and he rode all alone.
So faithful in love, and so dauntless in war,
There never was knight like the young Lochinvar.

19 With a smile on her lips, and a tear in her eye.

BeLS; BoTP; EnRP; FaBoBe; FaBV; FaFP; FaPON; FPL; GN; GoTS; NOBE; OBNV; OxBS; PoRA

20 Where shall the traitor rest,
He, the deceiver,
Who could win maiden's breast,
Ruin, and leave her?
In the lost battle,
Borne down by the flying,
Where mingles war's rattle
With groans of the dying;

CH; EnRP; GTBS; GTBS-P; PoEL-4

Pibroch of Donuil Dhu

21 Come away, come away,
Hark to the summons!
Come in your war-array,
Gentles and commons.

22 Come as the winds come, when
Forests are rended,
Come as the waves come, when
Navies are stranded:

EnRP; FaBoCh; FaPoR; GN; GTBS; GTBS-P; OxBS; PoEL-4

Rokeby

23 O Brignall banks are wild and fair,
And Greta woods are green,
And you may gather garlands there,
Would grace a summer queen:

EnRP; GTBS; GTBS-P; OBEV; PoRA

24 "A weary lot is thine, fair maid,
A weary lot is thine!
To pull the thorn thy brow to braid,
And press the rue for wine.

CH; EnLoPo; GTBS; GTBS-P; NOBE; OBEV; OBNC

WINFIELD TOWNLEY SCOTT
(1910–1968)

Annual Legend

1 A million butterflies rose up from South America,
All together, and flew in a gold storm toward Spain:

Eastward, the annual legend, (l. 1–3)

2 Balboa lies dead somewhere and Pizarro's helmet
Is a spider's kingdom; (l. 7–8)

CoAP; LiTA; LiTM; WaP

SIR CHARLES SEDLEY (1639–1701)

Love still has something of the sea

1 Love still has something of the Sea,
From whence his Mother rose;
No time his Slaves from Doubt can free,
Nor give their Thoughts repose: (l. 1–4)

GBL; NOBE; OBS; SeCV-2

The Mulberry Garden

2 Your Charms in harmless Childhood lay,
Like metals in the mine,
Age from no face took more away,
Than Youth conceal'd in thine.

3 Lovers, like dying men, may well
At first disorder'd be,
Since none alive can truly tell
What Fortune they must see.

OBS

Not, Celia, that I juster am

4 Not, Celia, that I juster am
Or better than the rest!
For I would change each hour, like them,
Were not my heart at rest. (l. 1–4)

AWP; GTBS; GTBS-P; NOBE; OBEV; OBS; SeCePo

ALAN SEEGER (1888–1916)

I Have a Rendezvous with Death

1 I have a rendezvous with Death
At some disputed barricade, (l. 1–2)

AiP; BLPA; DL; FaBV; FaFP; FaPoR; OHFP; WaP;
WGRP

SENECA (4 B.C.–A.D. 65)

Thyestes

1 Stond who so list upon the Slipper toppe
Of courtes estates, and lett me heare rejoyce;

2 I may dye aged after the common trace.
For hym death greep'the right hard by the croppe
That is moche knowen of other, and of him self alas,
Doth dye unknowen, dazed with dreadfull face.

AAS; NoP; OBVE; PoEL-1; SeCV-1; SiPS

IAN SERRAILLIER (b. 1912)

The Tickle Rhyme

1 "Who's that tickling my back?" said the wall. (l. 1)

2 "I'm learning
To crawl." (l. 3–4)

NTCP; OnUR; PYC; RHPC

ROBERT W. SERVICE (1874–1958)

The Cremation of Sam McGee

1 The Northern Lights have seen queer sights,
But the queerest they ever did see
Was the night on the marge of Lake Lebarge
I cremated Sam McGee. (l. 5–8)

2 Yet 'tain't being dead — it's my awful dread of the icy
grave that pains;
So I want you to swear that, foul or fair, you'll cremate
my last remains." (l. 23–24)

3 Now a promise made is a debt unpaid, and the trail
has its own stern code. (l. 33)

4 Then I made a hike, for I didn't like to hear him sizzle
so;
And the heavens scowled, and the huskies howled, and
the wind began to blow. (l. 49–51)

5 And there sat Sam, looking cold and calm, in the heart
of the furnace roar;
And he wore a smile you could see a mile, and he said:
"Please close that door. (l. 58–59)

BLPL; FaFP; NOBC; OBNV; PoLF

The Shooting of Dan McGrew

6 Back of the bar, in a solo game, sat Dangerous Dan
   McGrew;
   And watching his luck was his light-o'-love, the lady
   that's known as Lou. (l. 3–4)

7 He looked like a man with a foot in the grave and
   scarcely the strength of a louse,
   Yet he tilted a poke of dust on the bar, and he called
   for drinks for the house. (l. 7–8)

8 Then you've a hunch what the music meant . . . hunger
   and night and the stars. (l. 28)

9 For a fireside far from the cares that are, four walls
   and a roof above;
   But oh! so cramful of cosy joy, and crowned with a
   woman's love — (l. 31–32)

10 The woman that kissed him and — pinched his poke —
    was the lady that's known as Lou. (l. 58)

BeLS; FaBoBe; FaFP; FPL; PoLF; PoRA; RB

The Spell of the Yukon

11 I wanted the gold, and I sought it;
   I scrabbled and mucked like a slave,
   Was it famine or scurvy — I fought it;
   I hurled my youth into a grave. (l. 1–4)

12 No! There's the land. (Have you seen it?)
   It's the cussedest land that I know,
   From the big, dizzy mountains that screen it
   To the deep, deathlike valleys below. (l. 9–12)

13 There's a land where the mountains are nameless,
   And the rivers all run God knows where; (l. 49–50)

14 Yet it isn't the gold that I'm wanting
   So much as just finding the gold. (l. 67–68)

BLPA; BLPL; FaBoBe; FaFP

ANNE SEXTON (1928–1974)

The Abortion

1 Somebody who should have been born
  is gone.

  Yes, woman, such logic will lead
  to loss without death. Or say what you meant,
  you coward . . . this baby that I bleed. (l. 21–24)

CAPP; IHMS; MAT; NMM; SM; VGW

For My Lover, Returning to His Wife

2 She has always been there, my darling.
  She is, in fact, exquisite.
  Fireworks in the dull middle of February
  and as real as a cast-iron pot. (l. 5–8)

3 Let's face it, I have been momentary.
  A luxury. A bright red sloop in the harbor, (l. 9–10)

4 set forth three children under the moon,
  three cherubs drawn by Michelangelo,
  done this with her legs spread out
  in the terrible months in the chapel. (l. 19–22)

5 She is so naked and singular.
  She is the sum of yourself and your dream.
  Climb her like a monument, step after step.
  She is solid. (l. 43–46)

6 As for me, I am a watercolor.
  I wash off. (l. 47–48)

HCAP; IHMS; NMM; UnPo; WPE

Her Kind

7 I have gone out, a possessed witch,
  haunting the black air, braver at night;
  dreaming evil, (l. 1–3)

8 A woman like that is not a woman, quite.
  I have been her kind. (l. 6–7)

CAPP; CoAP; FF; HCAP; HeIP; LiTM; PPP; TAP; TwCP;
WPOW

Letter Written on a Ferry while Crossing Long
Island Sound

9 The sea is very old.
  The sea is the face of Mary,
  without miracles or rage
  or unusual hope,
  grown rough and wrinkled
  with incurable age. (l. 16–21)

10 I see four nuns
   who sit like a bridge club,
   their faces poked out
   from under their habits, (l. 35–38)

11 They call back to us
   from the gauzy edge of paradise,
   good news, good news. (l. 94–95)

CoAP; NAAL-2; NYBP; TwCP

Ringing the Bells

12 we are the circle of the crazy ladies
who sit in the lounge of the mental house
and smile at the smiling woman
who passes us each a bell, (l. 9–12)

13 and although we are no better for it,
they tell you to go. And you do. (l. 28–29)

FF; HCAP; PoE; TAP; VGW

The Truth the Dead Know

14 when we touch
we enter touch entirely. No one's alone.
Men kill for this, or for as much. (l. 10–12)

15 And what of the dead? They lie without shoes
in their stone boats. They are more like stone
(l. 13–14)

MoAmPo; NePoEA-2; NoAM; PBWP; TAP

Wanting to Die

16 But suicides have a special language.
Like carpenters they want to know which tools.
They never ask why build. (l. 7–9)

17 Death's a sad bone; bruised, you'd say,

and yet she waits for me, year after year, (l. 24–25)

18 leaving the page of the book carelessly open,
something unsaid, the phone off the hook
and the love, whatever it was, an infection. (l. 31–33)

IHMS; MoP; NoAM; TAP

WILLIAM SHAKESPEARE (1564–1616)

All's Well That Ends Well

1 Our remedies oft in ourselves do lie,
Which we ascribe to heaven. The fated sky
Gives us free scope, only doth backward pull
Our slow designs when we ourselves are dull. (I, i)

2 Thy blood and virtue
Contend for empire in thee, and thy goodness
Share with thy birthright! Love all, trust a few,
Do wrong to none. Be able for thine enemy
Rather in power than use, and keep thy friend
Under thy own life's key. Be checked for silence
But never taxed for speech. (I, i)

Antony and Cleopatra

3 Let Rome in Tiber melt and the wide arch
Of the ranged empire fall! Here is my space.
Kingdoms are clay; our dungy earth alike
Feeds beast as man. The nobleness of life
Is to do thus; when such a mutual pair
And such a twain can do 't, in which I bind,
On pain of punishment, the world to weet
We stand up peerless. (I, i)

4 When thou once
Was beaten from Modena, where thou slew'st
Hirtius and Pasa, consuls, at thy heel
Did famine follow, whom thou fought'st against,
Thou daintily brought up, with patience more
Than savages could suffer. Thou didst drink
The stale of horses and the gilded puddle
Which beasts would cough at. Thy palate then did
deign
The roughest berry on the rudest hedge.
Yea, like the stag, when snow the pasture sheets,
The barks of trees thou browsed. On the Alps
It is reported thou didst eat strange flesh,
Which some did die to look on. (I, iv)

5 The barge she sat in, like a burnished throne,
Burnt on the water. The poop was beaten gold;
Purple the sails, and so perfumed that
The winds were lovesick with them. The oars were
silver,
Which to the tune of flutes kept stroke, and made
The water which they beat to follow faster,
As amorous of their strokes. For her own person,
It beggared all description: she did lie
In her pavilion — cloth-of-gold of tissue —
O'erpicturing that Venus where we see
The fancy outwork nature. On each side her
Stood pretty dimpled boys, like smiling Cupids,
With divers-colored fans, whose wind did seem
To glow the delicate cheeks which they did cool,
And what they undid did. (II, ii)

6 Mine honesty and I begin to square.
The loyalty well held to fools does make
Our faith mere folly; yet he that can endure
To follow with allegiance a fall'n lord
Does conquer him that did his master conquer
And earns a place i' the story. (III, xiii)

7 His legs bestrid the ocean; his reared arm
Crested the world; his voice was propertied
As all the tuned spheres, and that to friends;
But when he meant to quail and shake the orb,
He was as rattling thunder. For his bounty,
There was no winter in 't; an autumn it was
That grew the more by reaping. His delights
Were dolphinlike; they showed his back above
The element they lived in. In his livery
Walked crowns and crownets; realms and islands were
As plates dropped from his pocket. (V, ii)

8 O sovereign mistress of true melancholy,
The poisonous damp of night dispunge upon me,
That life, a very rebel to my will,
May hang no longer on me. Throw my heart
Against the flint and hardness of my fault,
Which, being dried with grief, will break to powder
And finish all foul thoughts. O Antony,
Nobler than my revolt is infamous,
Forgive me in thine own particular,
But let the world rank me in register
A master-leaver and a fugitive. (IV, ix)

9 Sometimes we see a cloud that's dragonish,
A vapor sometimes like a bear or lion,
A towered citadel, a pendant rock,
A forked mountain, or blue promontory
With trees upon 't that nod unto the world
And mock our eyes with air. Thou hast seen these signs;
They are black vesper's pageants. (IV, xiv)

10 The quick comedians
Extemporally will stage us and present
Our Alexandrian revels; Antony
Shall be brought drunken forth, and I shall see
Some squeaking Cleopatra boy my greatness
I' the posture of a whore. (V, ii)

As You Like It

11 All the world's a stage,
And all the men and women merely players:
They have their exits and their entrances;
And one man in his time plays many parts,
His acts being seven ages. (II,vii)

12 Last scene of all,
That ends this strange eventful history,
Is second childishness and mere oblivion,
Sans teeth, sans eyes, sans taste, sans everything.
(II,vii)

FaFP; FaPoR; FiP; FF; LiTB; PoLF; RB; TrGrPo

13 Blow, blow, thou winter wind!
Thou art not so unkind
As man's ingratitude;
Thy tooth is not so keen
Because thou art not seen,
Although thy breath be rude. (II, vii)

14 Freeze, freeze, thou bitter sky,
Thou dost not bite so nigh
As benefits forgot:
Though thou the waters warp,
Thy sting is not so sharp
As friend remembered not. (II, vii)

AWP; CH; ChTr; CTC; ElL; ELP; FaFP; FiP; GBL;
GTBS; GTBS-P; HeIP; InPS; LiTB; NAEL-1; NOBE;
NoP; OAEL-1; OBEV; OBSC; PoEL-2; PrIm; TrGrPo;
WiR

15 A fool, A fool! I met a fool i' the forest,
A motley fool. A miserable world!
As I do live by food, I met a fool,
Who laid him down and basked him in the sun,
And railed on Lady Fortune in good terms,
In good set terms, and yet a motley fool. (II, vii)

16 Wedding is great Juno's crown,
O blessed bond of board and bed!
'Tis Hymen peoples every town;
High wedlock then be honored.
Honor, high honor, and renown,
To Hymen, god of every town! (V, iv)

Cymbeline

17 Hark, hark! the lark at heaven's gate sings,
And Phoebus 'gins arise,
His steeds to water at those springs
On chaliced flowers that lies;
And winking Mary-buds begin
To ope their golden eyes:
With every thing that pretty is,
My lady sweet, arise!
Arise, arise! (II, iii)

AWP; BoTP; CH; ChTr; ElL; FaBoCh; FaBV; FaFP;
FaPON; FiP; GN; HeIP; LiTB; NIP; NoP; OBEV; OBSC;
PrIm; TrGrPo

18 Fear no more the heat o' the sun
Nor the furious winter's rages;
Thou thy worldly task hast done,
Home art gone, and ta'en thy wages;
Golden lads and girls all must,
As chimney-sweepers, come to dust.

Fear no more the frown o' the great,
Thou art past the tyrant's stroke;
Care no more to clothe and eat,
To thee the reed is as the oak:
The sceptre, learning, physic, must
All follow this and come to dust.

Fear no more the lightning flash,
Nor the all-dreaded thunder-stone;
Fear not slander, censure rash;
Thou hast finished joy and moan:
All lovers young, all lovers must
Consign to thee and come to dust. (IV, ii)

AWP; CH; ChTr; CTC; EBEV; ElL; ELP; FaBoCh; FaFP;
FF; FiP; GBL; GTBS; GTBS-P; HAP; HeIP; InPS; LiTB;
Mes; NAEL-1; NOBE; NoP; OAEL-1; OBD; OBEV;
OBSC; PoE; PoEL-2; PoRA; PrIm; QFR; RB; SCV; SoSe;
TrGrPo

Hamlet

19 Some say that ever 'gainst that season comes
Wherein our Saviour's birth is celebrated,
The bird of dawning singeth all night long:

And then, they say, no spirit dare stir abroad,
The nights are wholesome, then no planets strike,
No fairy tale nor witch hath power to charm,
So hallow'd and so gracious is the time. (I, i)

ChTr; FaBoRV; GN; NAWM-1; OFD; PChr

20 A mote it is to trouble the mind's eye.
In the most high and palmy state of Rome,
A little ere the mightiest Julius fell,
The graves stood tenantless and the sheeted dead
Did squeak and gibber in the Roman streets;
As stars with trains of fire and dews of blood,
Disasters in the sun; and the moist star
Upon whose influence Neptune's empire stands
Was sick almost to doomsday with eclipse.
And even the like precurse of feared events,
As harbingers preceding still the fates
And prologue to the omen coming on,
Have heaven and earth together demonstrated
Unto our climatures and countrymen. (I, i)

NAWM-1

21 Seems, madam? Nay, it is. I know not "seems".
'Tis not alone my inky cloak, good Mother,
Nor customary suits of solemn black,
Nor windy suspiration of forced breath,
No nor the fruitful river in the eye,
Nor the dejected havior of the visage,
Together with all forms, moods, shapes of grief,
That can denote me truly. These indeed seem,
For they are actions that a man might play.
But I have that within which passes show;
These but the trappings and the suits of woe. (I, ii)

NAWM-1

22 O! that this too too solid flesh would melt,
Thaw and resolve itself into a dew;
Or that the Everlasting had not fix'd
His canon 'gainst self-slaughter! O God! O God!
How weary, stale, flat, and unprofitable
Seem to me all the uses of this world.
Fie on't! O fie! 'tis an unweeded garden,
That grows to seed; (I, ii)

NAWM-1; SCV; TrGrPo

23 The friends thou hast, and their adoption tried,
Grapple them to thy soul with hoops of steel;
But do not dull thy palm with entertainment
Of each new-hatched, unfledged comrade. Beware
Of entrance to a quarrel; but being in,
Bear't that the opposed may beware of thee. (I, iii)

24 Neither a borrower nor a lender be,
For loan oft loses both itself and friend,
And borrowing dulls the edge of husbandry.
This above all: to thine own self be true,

And it must follow, as the night the day,
Thou canst not then be false to any man. (I, iii)

FaFP; GN; LiTB; NAWM-1; OHFP; TrGrPo

25 But to my mind, though I am native here
And to the manner born, it is a custom
More honored in the breach than the observance. (I, iv)

NAWM-1

26 I am thy father's spirit,
Doomed for a certain term to walk the night,
And for the day confined to fast in fires,
Till the foul crimes done in my days of nature
Are burnt and purged away. But that I am forbid
To tell the secrets of my prison house,
I could a tale unfold whose lightest word
Would harrow up thy soul, freeze thy young blood,
Make thy two eyes like stars start from their spheres,
Thy knotted and combined locks to part,
And each particular hair to stand on end
Like quills upon the fretful porpentine.
But this eternal blazon must not be
To ears of flesh and blood. (I, v)

NAWM-1; OBD

27 But virtue, as it never will be moved,
Though lewdness court it in a shape of heaven,
So lust, though to a radiant angel linked,
Will sate itself in a celestial bed
And prey on garbage. (I, v)

NAWM-1

28 Remember thee?
Ay, thou poor ghost, whiles memory holds a seat
In this distracted globe. Remember thee?
Yea, from the table of my memory
I'll wipe away all trivial fond records,
All saws of books, all forms, all pressures past
That youth and observation copied there,
And thy commandment all alone shall live
Within the book and volume of my brain, (I, v)

NAWM-1

29 There are more things in heaven and earth, Horatio,
Than are dreamt of in your philosophy. (I, v)

NAWM-1

30 "The rugged Pyrrhus, he whose sable arms,
Black as his purpose, did the night resemble
When he lay couched in the ominous horse,
Hath now this dread and black complexion smeared
With heraldry more dismal. Head to foot
Now is he total gules, horridly tricked
With blood of fathers, mothers, daughters, sons,
Baked and impasted with the parching streets,

That lend a tyrannous and a damned light
To their lord's murder. Roasted in wrath and fire,
And thus o'ersized with coagulate gore,
With eyes like carbuncles, the hellish Pyrrhus
Old grandsire Priam seeks." (II, ii)

NAWM-1

31 What's Hecuba to him, or he to Hecuba,
That he should weep for her? What would he do
Had he the motive and the cue for passion
That I have? He would drown the stage with tears
And cleave the general ear with horrid speech,
Make mad the guilty and appall the free,
Confound the ignorant, and amaze indeed
The very faculties of eyes and ears. Yet I,
A dull and muddy-mettled rascal, peak
Like John-a-dreams, unpregnant of my cause,
And can say nothing — no, not for a king
Upon whose property and most dear life
A damned defeat was made. (II, ii)

32 The play's the thing
Wherein I'll catch the conscience of the King. (II, ii)

NAWM-1

33 O, what a noble mind is here o'erthrown!
The courtier's, soldier's, scholar's, eye, tongue, sword,
Th' expectancy and rose of the fair state,
The glass of fashion and the mold of form,
Th' observed of all observers, quite, quite down! (III, i)

NAWM-1

34 O, my offense is rank, it smells to heaven;
It hath the primal eldest curse upon 't,
A brother's murder. Pray can I not,
Though inclination be as sharp as will;
My stronger guilt defeats my strong intent,
And like a man to double business bound
I stand in pause where I shall first begin,
And both neglect. What if this cursed hand
Were thicker than itself with brother's blood,
Is there not rain enough in the sweet heavens
To wash it white as snow? (III, iii)

NAWM-1

35 What is a man,
If his chief good and market of his time
Be but to sleep and feed? A beast, no more.
Sure he that made us with such large discourse,
Looking before and after, gave us not
That capability and godlike reason
To fust in us unused. Now, whether it be
Bestial oblivion, or some craven scruple
Of thinking too precisely on th' event —
A thought which, quartered, hath but one part wisdom
And ever three parts coward — I do not know
Why yet I live to say "This thing's to do,"

Sith I have cause, and will, and strength, and means
To do 't. Examples gross as earth exhort me: (IV, iv)

NAWM-1

36 Tomorrow is Saint Valentine's day,
All in the morning betime,
And I a maid at your window,
To be your Valentine. (IV, v)

CH; EnLoPo; FaPON; LiTB; NAWM-1; NTCP; OFD

37 How should I your true love know
From another one? (IV, v)

CH; ChTr; EBEV; EnLoPo; GBL; LiTB; Mes; NAWM-1;
OBSC; PoRA; QFR; TrGrPo

38 No place, indeed, should murder sanctuarize;
Revenge should have no bounds. (IV, vii)

NAWM-1

39 To be, or not to be: that is the question:
Whether 'tis nobler in the mind to suffer
The slings and arrows of outrageous fortune,
Or to take arms against a sea of troubles,
And by opposing end them? To die: to sleep;
No more; and by a sleep to say we end
The heart-ache and the thousand natural shocks
That flesh is heir to, 'tis a consummation
Devoutly to be wished. To die, to sleep;
To sleep; perchance to dream: ay, there's the rub;
For in that sleep of death what dreams may come
When we have shuffled off this mortal coil,
Must give us pause: there's the respect
That makes calamity of so long life; (V, i.)

40 who would fardels bear,
To grunt and sweat under a weary life,
But that the dread of something after death,
The undiscovered country from whose bourn
No traveler returns, puzzles the will,
And makes us rather bear those ills we have
Than fly to others that we know not of?
Thus conscience does make cowards of us all;
And thus the native hue of resolution
Is sicklied o'er with the pale cast of thought. (V, i)

FaFP; FF; FiP; HoPM; LiTB; NAWM-1; OBD; OHFP;
TrGrPo; WBLP

41 If thou didst ever hold me in thy heart,
Absent thee from felicity awhile,
And in this harsh world draw thy breath in pain
To tell my story. (V, ii)

NAWM-1

42 This quarry cries on havoc. O proud Death,
What feast is toward in thine eternal cell,
That thou so many princes at a shot
So bloodily hast struck? (V, ii)

NAWM-1

Julius Caesar

43 Men at some time are masters of their fates,
The fault, dear Brutus, is not in our stars,
But in ourselves, that we are underlings. (I, ii)

44 But 'tis a common proof
That lowliness is young ambition's ladder,
Whereto the climber-upward turns his face;
But when he once attains the upmost round
He then unto the ladder turns his back,
Looks in the clouds, scorning the base degrees
By which he did ascend. (II, i)

45 When beggars die there are no comets seen;
The heavens themselves blaze forth the death of
prices. (II, ii)

46 That we shall die, we know; 'tis but the time,
And drawing days out, that men stand upon. (III, i)

47 How many ages hence
Shall this our lofty scene be acted over
In states unborn and accents yet unknown! (III, i)

48 The evil that men do lives after them;
The good is oft interred with their bones. (III, ii)

49 Ambition should be made of sterner stuff. (III, ii)

50 There is a tide in the affairs of men
Which, taken at the flood, leads on to fortune;
Omitted, all the voyage of their life
Is bound in shallows and in miseries.
On such a full sea are we now afloat,
And we must take the current when it serves
Or lose our ventures. (IV, iii)

King Henry IV, Pt. I

51 Yet herein will I imitate the sun,
Who doth permit the base contagious clouds
To smother up his beauty from the world,
That when he please again to be himself,
Being wanted, he may be more wondered at
By breaking through the foul and ugly mists
Of vapors that did seem to strangle him (I, ii)

52 If all the year were playing holidays,
To sport would be as tedious as to work;
But when they seldom come, they wished-for come,
And nothing pleaseth but rare accidents. (I, ii)

NAEL-1

53 Rebellion lay in his way, and he found it. (V, i)

NAEL-1

King Henry IV, Pt. II

54 O sleep, O gentle sleep,
Nature's soft nurse, how have I frighted thee,
That thou no more wilt weigh my eyelids down
And steep my senses in forgetfulness?
Why rather, sleep, liest thou in smoky cribs,
Upon uneasy pallets stretching thee,
And hushed with buzzing night-flies to thy slumber,
Than in the perfumed chambers of the great,
Under the canopies of costly state,
And lulled with sound of sweetest melody? (III, i)

King Henry V

55 Therefore doth heaven divide
The state of man in divers functions,
Setting endeavor in continual motion,
To which is fixed, as an aim or butt,
Obedience; for so work the honeybees,
Creatures that by a rule in nature teach
The act of order to a peopled kingdom. (I, ii)

56 Once more unto the breach, dear friends, once more,
Or close the wall up with our English dead!
In peace there's nothing so becomes a man
As modest stillness and humility.
But when the blast of war blows in our ears,
Then imitate the action of the tiger:
Stiffen the sinews, conjure up the blood,
Disguise fair nature with hard-favored rage.
Then lend the eye a terrible aspect:
Let it pry through the portage of the head
Like the brass cannon; let the brow o'erwhelm it
As fearfully as doth a galled rock
O'erhang and jutty his confounded base,
Swilled with the wild and wasteful ocean.
Now set the teeth and stretch the nostril wide,
Hold hard the breath, and bend up every spirit
To his full height. (III, i)

57 From camp to camp, through the foul womb of night,
The hum of either army stilly sounds,
That the fixed sentinels almost receive
The secret whispers of each other's watch.
Fire answers fire, and through their play flames
Each battle sees the other's umbered face.
Steed threatens steed, in high and boastful neighs
Piercing the night's dull ear; and from the tents
The armorers accomplishing the knights,
With busy hammers closing rivets up,
Give dreadful note of preparation. (IV, Prologue)

ChTr; EBEV; RB; WaaP

58 Upon the King! Let us our lives, our souls,
Our debts, our careful wives,
Our children, and our sins lay on the King!

We must bear all. O hard condition,
Twin-born with greatness, subject to the breath
Of every fool, whose sense no more can feel
But his own wringing! What infinite heartsease
Must kings neglect that private men enjoy!
And what have kings that privates have not too,
Save ceremony, save general ceremony?
And what art thou, thou idol ceremony?
What kind of god art thou, that suffer'st more
Of mortal griefs than do thy worshipers?
What are thy rents? What are thy comings-in?
O ceremony, show me but thy worth!
What is thy soul of adoration?
Art thou aught else but place, degree, and form,
Creating awe and fear in other men? (IV, i)

59 By Jove, I am not covetous for gold,
Nor care I who doth feed upon my cost;
It yearns me not if men my garments wear;
Such outward things dwell not in my desires.
But if it be a sin to covet honor
I am the most offending soul alive. (IV, iii)

60 This day is called the Feast of Crispian.
He that outlives this day and comes safe home
Will stand a-tiptoe when this day is nam'd
And rouse him at the name of Crispian.
He that shall live this day, and see old age,
Will yearly on the vigil feast his neighbours
And say, "Tomorrow is Saint Crispian." (IV, iii)

FaPoR

King Henry VI, Pt. III

61 O tiger's heart wrapped in a woman's hide!
How couldst thou drain the lifeblood of the child,
To bid the father wipe his eyes withal,
And yet be seen to bear a woman's face?
Women are soft, mild, pitiful, and flexible;
Thou stern, obdurate, flinty, rough, remorseless. (I, iv)

62 I can add colors to the chameleon,
Change shapes with Proteus for advantages,
And set the murderous Machiavel to school. (III, ii)

King Henry VIII (by Shakespeare *and probably* John Fletcher)

63 No man's pie is freed
From his ambitious finger. (I, i)

TrGrPo

64 Orpheus with his Lute made Trees,
And the Mountaine tops that freeze,
Bow themselves when he did sing.
To his Musicke, Plants and Flowers
Ever spring; as Sunne and Showres,
There had been a lasting Spring.

Every thing that heard him play,
Even the Billowes of the Sea,
Hung their heads, and then lay by.
In sweet Musicke is such Art,
Killing care, and griefe of heart,
Fall asleepe, or hearing dye. (III, i)

ChTr; GN; OBS; TrGrPo

65 I have touched the highest point of all my greatness,
And from that full meridian of my glory
I haste now to my setting. I shall fall
Like a bright exhalation in the evening,
And no man see me more. (III, ii)

OHFP

66 I have ventured
Like little wanton boys that swim on bladders,
This many summers in a sea of glory,
But far beyond my depth. My high-blown pride
At length broke under me and now has left me,
Weary and old with service, to the mercy
Of a rude stream that must forever hide me. (III, ii)

OHFP

67 Had I but served my God with half the zeal
I served my king, he would not in mine age
Have left me naked to mine enemies. (III, ii)

OHFP

King Lear

68 Good my lord,
You have begot me, bred me, loved me. I
Return those duties back as are right fit,
Obey you, love you, and most honor you.
Why have my sisters husbands if they say
They love you all? Haply, when I shall wed,
That lord whose hand must take my plight shall carry
Half my love with him, half my care and duty.
Sure I shall never marry like my sisters,
To love my father all. (I, i)

69 My life I never held but as a pawn
To wage against thine enemies' nor fear to lose it,
Thy safety being motive. (I, i)

70 Thou, Nature, art my goddess; to thy law
My services are bound. Wherefore should I
Stand in the plague of custom and permit
The curiosity of nations to deprive me,
For that I am some twelve or fourteen moonshines
Lag of a brother? Why bastard? Wherefore base?
When my dimensions are as well compact,
My mind as generous, and my shape as true,
As honest madam's issue? Why brand they us
With base? With baseness? Bastardy? Base, base?
Who in the lusty stealth of nature take

More composition and fierce quality
Than doth within a dull, stale, tired bed
Go to th' creating a whole tribe of fops
Got 'tween asleep and wake? (I, ii)

71 Have more than thou showest,
Speak less than thou knowest,
Lend less than thou owest,
Ride more than thou goest,
Learn more than thou trowest,
Set less than thou throwest;
Leave thy drink and thy whore,
And keep in-a-door,
And thou shalt have more
Than two tens to a score. (I, iv)

72 If she must teem,
Create her child of spleen, that it may live
And be a thwart disnatured torment to her!
Let it stamp wrinkles in her brow of youth,
With cadent tears fret channels in her cheeks,
Turn all her mother's pains and benefits
To laughter and contempt, that she may feel
How sharper than a serpent's tooth it is
To have a thankless child! (I, iv)

73 Fathers that wear rags
Do make their children blind,
But fathers that bear bags
Shall see their children kind.
Fortune, that arrant whore,
Ne'er turns the key to the poor. (II, iv)

74 O, reason not the need! Our basest beggars
Are in the poorest thing superfluous.
Allow not nature more than nature needs,
Man's life is cheap as beast's. Thou art a lady;
If only to go warm were gorgeous,
Why, nature needs not what thou gorgeous wear'st,
Which scarcely keeps thee warm. But, for true need —
You heavens, give me that patience, patience I need!
                                    (II, iv)

75 Blow, winds, and crack your cheeks! Rage, blow!
You cataracts and hurricanoes, spout
Till you have drenched our steeples, drowned the cocks!
You sulfurous and thought-executing fires,
Vaunt-couriers of oak-cleaving thunderbolts,
Singe my white head! And thou, all-shaking thunder,
Strike flat the thick rotundity o' the world!
Crack nature's molds, all germens spill at once
That makes ingrateful man! (III, ii)

76 When priests are more in word than matter;
When brewers mar their malt with water;
When nobles are their tailors' tutors,
No heretics burned but wenches' suitors,
Then shall the realm of Albion
Come to great confusion.

When every case in law is right,
No squire in debt, nor no poor knight;
When slanders do not live in tongues,

Nor cutpurses come not to throngs;
When usurers tell their gold i' the field,
And bawds and whores do churches build,
Then comes the time, who lives to see 't,
That going shall be used with feet. (III, ii)

77 To be worst,
The lowest and most dejected thing of fortune,
Stands still in esperance, lives not in fear.
The lamentable change is from the best;
The worst returns to laughter. Welcome, then,
Thou unsubstantial air that I embrace!
The wretch that thou hast blown unto the worst
Owes nothing to thy blasts. (IV, i)

78 The worst is not
So long as we can say, "This is the worst." (IV, i)

79 O you mighty gods!
This world I do renounce, and in your sights
Shake patiently my great affliction off.
If I could bear it longer, and not fall
To quarrel with your great opposeless wills,
My snuff and loathed part of nature should
Burn itself out. (IV, vi)

80 Adultery?
Thou shalt not die. Die for adultery? No.
The wren goes to 't, and the small gilded fly
Does lecher in my sight.
Let copulation thrive; for Gloucester's bastard son
Was kinder to his father than my daughters
Got 'tween the lawful sheets.
To 't, luxury, pell-mell, for I lack soldiers. (IV, vi)

81 Thou rascal beadle, hold thy bloody hand!
Why dost thou lash that whore? Strip thine own back;
Thou hotly lusts to use her in that kind
For which thou whipp'st her. The usurer hangs the
        cozener
Through tattered clothes small vices do appear;
Robes and furred gowns hide all. Plate sin with gold,
And the strong lance of justice hurtless breaks;
Arm it in rags, a pygmy's straw does pierce it.
None does offend, none, I say, none. I'll able 'em.
Take that of me, my friend, who have the power
To seal th' accuser's lips. Get thee glass eyes,
And like a scurvy politician seem
To see the things thou dost not. (IV, vi)

82 Thou must be patient. We came crying hither.
Thou know'st the first time that we smell the air
We wawl and cry. (IV, vi)

83 When we are born, we cry that we are come
To this great stage of fools. — (IV, vi)

84 Come, let's away to prison.
We two alone will sing like birds i' the cage.
When thou dost ask me blessing, I'll kneel down
And ask of thee forgiveness. So we'll live,
And pray, and sing, and tell old tales, and laugh

At gilded butterflies, and hear poor rogues
Talk of court news; and we'll talk with them too —
Who loses and who wins; who's in, who's out —
And take upon 's the mystery of things,
As if we were God's spies; and we'll wear out,
In a walled prison, packs and sects of great ones,
That ebb and flow by the moon. (V, iii)

85 Howl, howl, howl! O, you are men of stones!
Had I your tongues and eyes, I'd use them so
That heaven's vault should crack. She's gone forever.
I know when one is dead and when one lives;
She's dead as earth. (V, iii)

King Richard II

86 A heavy sentence, my most sovereign liege,
And all unlooked-for from Your Highness' mouth.
A dearer merit, not so deep a maim
As to be cast forth in the common air,
Have I deserved at Your Highness' hands.
The language I have learned these forty years,
My native English, now I must forgo;
And now my tongue's use is to me nor more
Than an unstringed viol or a harp.
Or like a cunning instrument cased up,
Or, being open, put into his hands
That knows no touch to tune the harmony.
Within my mouth you have enjailed my tongue,
Doubly portcullised with my teeth and lips,
And dull unfeeling barren ignorance
Is made my jailer to attend on me. (I, iii)

87 O, but they say the tongues of dying men
Enforce attention like deep harmony.
Where words are scarce, they are seldom spent in vain,
For they breathe truth that breathe their words in pain.
He that no more must say is listened more
Than they whom youth and ease have taught to glose.
More are men's ends marked than their lives before.
The setting sun, and music at the close,
As the last taste of sweets, is sweetest last,
Writ in remembrance more than things long past.
(II, i)

88 This royal throne of kings, this sceptered isle,
This earth of majesty, this seat of Mars,
This other Eden, demi-Paradise,
This fortress built by Nature for herself
Against infection and the hand of war,
This happy breed of men, this little world,
This precious stone set in the silver sea,
Which serves it in the office of a wall,
Or as a moat defensive to a house,
Against the envy of less happier lands;
This blessed plot, this earth, this realm, this England,
(II, i)

BoTP; TrGrPo

89 For God's sake, let us sit upon the ground
And tell sad stories of the death of kings!
How some have been deposed, some slain in war,

Some haunted by the ghosts they have deposed,
Some poisoned by their wives, some sleeping killed —
All murdered; for within the hollow crown
That rounds the mortal temples of a king
Keeps Death his court, and there the antic sits,
Scoffing his state and grinning at his pomp,
Allowing him a breath, a little scene,
To monarchize, be feared, and kill with looks,
Infusing him with self and vain conceit,
As if this flesh which walls about our life
Were brass impregnable; and humored thus,
Comes at the last and with a little pin
Bores through his castle wall, and — farewell, king!
(III, ii)

90 Go bind thou up young dangling apricots
Which, like unruly children, make their sire
Stoop with oppression of their prodigal weight.
Give some supportance to the bending twigs.
Go thou, and like an executioner
Cut off the heads of too-fast-growing sprays
That look too lofty in our commonwealth.
All must be even in our government.
You thus employed, I will go root away
The noisome weeds which without profit suck
The soil's fertility from wholesome flowers. (III, iv)

91 The shadow of your sorrow hath destroyed
The shadow of your face. (IV, i)

92 As in a theater the eyes of men,
After a well-graced actor leaves the stage,
Are idly bent on him that enters next,
Thinking his prattle to be tedious, (V, ii)

93 How sour sweet music is,
When time is broke and no proportion kept!
So is it in the music of men's lives,
And here have I the daintiness of ear
To check time broke in a disordered string;
But for the concord of my state and time
Had not an ear to hear my true time broke.
I wasted time, and now doth time waste me;
For now hath Time made me his numbering clock.
My thoughts are minutes, and with sighs they jar
Their watches on unto mine eyes, the outward watch,
Whereto my finger, like a dial's point,
Is pointing still, in cleansing them from tears.
Now sir, the sound that tells what hour it is
Are clamorous groans which strike upon my heart,
Which is the bell. (V, v)

King Richard III

94 Now is the winter of our discontent
Made glorious summer by this sun of York,
And all the clouds that loured upon our house (I, i)

95 Grim-visaged War hath smoothed his wrinkled front;
And now, instead of mounting barbed steeds
To fright the souls of fearful adversaries,

He capers nimbly in a lady's chamber
To the lascivious pleasing of a lute. (I, i)

96 I, that am rudely stamped, and want love's majesty
To strut before a wanton ambling nymph;
I, that am curtailed of this fair proportion,
Cheated of feature by dissembling Nature,
Deformed, unfinished, sent before my time
Into this breathing world scarce half made up,
And that so lamely and unfashionable
That dogs bark at me as I halt by them —
Why, I, in this weak piping time of peace,
Have no delight to pass away the time,
Unless to see my shadow in the sun
And descant on mine own deformity. (I, i)

97 O Lord, methought what pain it was to drown!
What dreadful noise of waters in my ears!
What sights of ugly death within my eyes!
Methought I saw a thousand fearful wracks;
Ten thousand men that fishes gnawed upon;
Wedges of gold, great anchors, heaps of pearl,
Inestimable stones, unvalued jewels,
All scattered in the bottom of the sea.
Some lay in dead men's skulls, and in the holes
Where eyes did once inhabit there were crept
As 'twere in scorn of eyes, reflecting gems,
That wooed the slimy bottom of the deep
And mocked the dead bones that lay scattered by.
(I, iv)

98 The great King of kings
Hath in the table of his law commanded
That thou shalt do no murder. Will you then
Spurn at his edict, and fulfill a man's?
Take heed; for he holds vengeance in his hand
To hurl upon their heads that break his law. (I, iv)

99 I am a villain. Yet I lie, I am not.
Fool, of thyself speak well. Fool, do not flatter.
My conscience hath a thousand several tongues,
And every tongue brings in a several tale,
And every tale condemns me for a villain.
Perjury, perjury, in the highest degree,
Murder, stern murder, in the direst degree,
All several sins, all used in each degree,
Throng to the bar, crying all, "Guilty! Guilty!"
I shall despair. There is no creature loves me,
And if I die no soul will pity me.
And wherefore should they, since that I myself
Find in myself no pity to myself? (V, iii)

Love's Labour's Lost

100 When daisies pied and violets blue,
And lady-smocks all silver-white,
And cuckoo-buds of yellow hue
Do paint the meadows with delight,
The cuckoo then, on every tree,
Mocks married men, for thus sings he,

Cuckoo, cuckoo! O word of fear,
Unpleasing to a married ear.

When shepherds pipe on oaten straws,
And merry larks are ploughmen's clocks,
When turtles tread, and rooks, and daws,
And maidens bleach their summer smocks, (V, ii)

BoTP; ElL; FF; FiP; HAP; HeIP; InPK; NAEL-1; NBLV;
NIP; NOBE; NoP; OAEL-1; OBEV; OBSC; PBBP;
PoEL-2; PoRA PrIm; SeCePo; TEP; TrGrPo; UnPo

101 When icicles hang by the wall,
And Dick the shepherd blows his nail
And Tom bears logs into the hall,
And milk comes frozen home in pail,
When blood is nipp'd and ways be foul,
Then nightly sings the staring owl,
To-whit!
To-who! — a merry note,
While greasy Joan doth keel the pot. (V, ii)

Macbeth

102 Fair is foul, and foul is fair.
Hover through the fog and filthy air. (I, i)

103 This supernatural soliciting
Cannot be ill, cannot be good. (I, iii)

104 The sin of my ingratitude even now
Was heavy on me. Thou art so far before
That swiftest wing of recompense is slow
To overtake thee. Would thou hadst less deserved,
That the proportion both of thanks and payment
Might have been mine! Only I have left to say,
More is thy due than more than all can pay. (I, iv)

105 And Pity, like a naked newborn babe
Striding the blast, or heaven's cherubin, horsed
Upon the sightless couriers of the air,
Shall blow the horrid deed in every eye,
That tears shall drown the wind. I have no spur
To prick the sides of my intent, but only
Vaulting ambition, which o'erleaps itself
And falls on th' other — (I, vii)

106 Methought I heard a voice cry, "Sleep no more!
Macbeth does murder sleep," the innocent sleep,
Sleep that knits up the raveled sleave of care,
The death of each day's life, sore labor's bath,
Balm of hurt minds, great nature's second course,
Chief nourisher in life's feast — (II, ii)

107 'Tis the eye of childhood
That fears a painted devil. (II, ii)

108 Will all great Neptune's ocean wash this blood
Clean from my hand? No, this my hand will rather
The multitudinous seas incarnadine,
Making the green one red. (II, ii)

109 Had I but died an hour before this chance
    I had lived a blessed time; for from this instant
    There's nothing serious in mortality.
    All is but toys. Renown and grace is dead;
    The wine of life is drawn, and the mere lees
    Is left this vault to brag of. (II, iii)

110 What man dare, I dare.
    Approach thou like the rugged Russian bear,
    The armed rhinoceros, or the Hyrcan tiger;
    Take any shape but that, and my firm nerves
    Shall never tremble. Or be alive again
    And dare me to the desert with thy sword. (III, iv)

111 Thrice the brinded cat hath mew'd.
    Thrice and once the hedge-pig whin'd.
    Harper cries: 'Tis time, 'tis time.
    Round about the cauldron go;
    In the poison'd entrails throw. (IV, i)

112 Double, double toil and trouble;
    Fire burn and cauldron bubble. (IV, i)

    ElL; InvP; OFD; RB; WSC

113 Time, thou anticipat'st my dread exploits.
    The flighty purpose never is o'ertook
    Unless the deed go with it. From this moment
    The very firstlings of my heart shall be
    The firstlings of my hand. And even now,
    To crown my thoughts with acts, be it thought and
        done: (IV, i)

114 To-morrow, and to-morrow, and to-morrow,
    Creeps in this petty pace from day to day
    To the last syllable of recorded time,
    And all our yesterdays have lighted fools
    The way to dusty death. Out, out, brief candle!
    Life's but a walking shadow, a poor player
    That struts and frets his hour upon the stage
    And then is heard no more: it is a tale
    Told by an idiot, full of sound and fury,
    Signifying nothing. (V, v)

    ChTr; DL; FaBoRV; FaFP; FF; FiP; LiTB; SoSe; TrGrPo

Measure for Measure

115 Ay, but to die, and go we know not where,
    To lie in cold obstruction and to rot,
    This sensible warm motion to become
    A kneaded clod; and the delighted spirit
    To bathe in fiery floods, or to reside
    In thrilling region of thick-ribbed ice,
    To be imprisoned in the viewless winds
    And blown with restless violence round about
    The pendent world; or to be worse than worst
    Of those that lawless and incertain thought
    Imagine howling — 'tis too horrible! (III, i)

116 He who the sword of heaven will bear
    Should be as holy as severe;
    Pattern in himself to know,
    Grace to stand, and virtue go;
    More nor less to others paying
    Than by self-offenses weighing.
    Shame to him whose cruel striking
    Kills for faults of his own liking! (III, ii)

117 Take, O take, those lips away,
    That so sweetly were forsworn;
    And those eyes, the break of day,
    Lights that do mislead the morn:
    But my kisses bring again
    Bring again:
    Seals of love but sealed in vain, (IV, i)

    AWP; EBEV; ElL; ELP; EnLoPo; FaBV; FiP; GBL; HeIP;
    InPS; LiTB; NOBE; NoP; OAEL-1; OBEV; OBSC;
    PoEL-2; TrGrPo

The Merchant of Venice

118 Signor Antonio, many a time and oft
    In the Rialto you have rated me
    About my moneys and my usances.
    Still have I borne it with a patient shrug,
    For sufferance is the badge of all our tribe.
    You call me misbeliever, cutthroat dog,
    And spit upon my Jewish gaberdine,
    And all for use of that which is mine own. (I, iii)

119 "All that glisters is not gold;
    Often have you heard that told.
    Many a man his life hath sold
    But my outside to behold.
    Gilded tombs do worms infold.
    Had you been as wise as bold,
    Young in limbs, in judgment old,
    Your answer had not been enscrolled.
    Fare you well; your suit is cold." (II, vii)

120 Tell me, where is fancy bred,
    Or in the heart, or in the head?
    How begot, how nourished? (III, ii)

121 It is engend'red in the eyes,
    With gazing fed; and fancy dies
    In the cradle where it lies.
    Let us all ring fancy's knell.
    I'll begin it — Ding, dong, bell. (III, ii)

    CH; CTC; ElL; ELP; FaPON; GTBS; GTBS-P; LiTB;
    NAEL-1; OAEL-1; OBEV; OBSC; PoEL-2; TrGrPo

122 How many cowards, whose hearts are all as false
    As stairs of sand, wear yet upon their chins
    The beards of Hercules and frowning Mars,
    Who, inward searched, have livers white as milk!
                                    (III, ii)

123 The quality of mercy is not strain'd,
It droppeth as the gentle rain from heaven
Upon the place beneath: it is twice bless'd;
It blesseth him that gives and him that takes:
'Tis mightiest in the mightiest; it becomes
The throned monarch better than his crown;
His sceptre shows the force of temporal power,
The attribute to awe and majesty,
Wherein doth sit the dread and fear of kings;
But mercy is above this sceptred sway,
It is enthroned in the hearts of kings,
It is an attribute to God himself,
And earthly power doth then show likest God's
When mercy seasons justice. (IV, i)

FaFP; LiTB; OHFP; TrGrPo; WBLP

124 Thou almost mak'st me waver in my faith
To hold opinion with Pythagoras,
That souls of animals infuse themselves
Into the trunks of men. (IV, i)

125 For do but note a wild and wanton herd
Or race of youthful and unhandled colts
Fetching mad bounds, bellowing and neighing loud,
Which is the hot condition of their blood;
If they but hear perchance a trumpet sound,
Or any air of music touch their ears,
You shall perceive them make a mutual stand,
Their savage eyes turned to a modest gaze
By the sweet power of music. (V, i)

A Midsummer Night's Dream

126 Over hill, over dale,
Thorough bush, thorough brier,
Over park, over pale,
Thorough flood, thorough fire:
I do wander everywhere,
Swifter than the moones sphere;
And I serve the fairy queen,
To dew her orbs upon the green.
The cowslips tall her pensioners be;
In their gold coats spots you see;
Those be rubies, fairy favours,
In those freckles live their savours. (II, ii)

ElL; FaPON; GN; InvP; NOBE; OBEV; OBSC; TrGrPo

127 The lunatic, the lover, and the poet
Are of imagination all compact.
One sees more devils than vast hell can hold;
That is the madman. The lover, all as frantic,
Sees Helen's beauty in a brow of Egypt.
The poet's eye, in a fine frenzy rolling,
Doth glance from heaven to earth, from earth to
    heaven;
And as imagination bodies forth
The forms of things unknown, the poet's pen
Turns them to shapes and gives to airy nothing
A local habitation and a name.

Such tricks hath strong imagination
That, if it would but apprehend some joy,
It comprehends some bringer of that joy;
Or in the night, imagining some fear,
How easy is a bush supposed a bear! (V, i)

128 Now the hungry lion roars,
And the wolf behowls the moon;
Whilst the heavy ploughman snores,
All with weary task fordone.
Now the wasted brands do glow,
Whilst the screech-owl, screeching loud,
Puts the wretch that lies in woe
In remembrance of a shroud.
Now it is the time of night,
That the graves, all gaping wide,
Every one lets forth his sprite,
In the church-way paths to glide: (V, i)

CH; ChTr; CTC; ElL; LiTB; MoShBr; OBSC; OxBoLi;
TrGrPo; WiR; WSC

129 If we shadows have offended,
Think but this, and all is mended,
That you have but slumbered here
While these visions did appear.
And this weak and idle theme,
No more yielding but a dream, (V, i)

Much Ado about Nothing

130 Sigh no more Ladies, sigh no more
Men were deceivers ever,
One foote in Sea, and one on shore,
To one thing constant never, (II, iii)

AWP; CTC; ElL; ELP; FF; FiP; LiTB; OBSC; PoEL-2;
TrGrPo

131 For there was never yet philosopher
That could endure the toothache patiently,
However they have writ the style of gods
And made a push at chance and sufferance. (V, i)

132 Pardon, goddess of the night,
Those that slew thy virgin knight,
For the which, with songs of woe,
Round about her tomb they go.
Midnight, assist our moan;
Help us to sigh and groan,
Heavily, heavily.
Graves, yawn and yield your dead,
Till death be uttered,
Heavily, heavily.
Now unto thy bones good night!
Yearly will I do this rite. (V, iii)

CTC; OESC

Othello

133 'Tis the curse of service,
Preferment goes by letter and affection,
And not by old gradation, where each second
Stood heir to th' first. (I, i)

134 O, beware, my lord, of jealousy!
     It is the green-ey'd monster which doth mock
     The meat it feeds on. That cuckold lives in bliss
     Who, certain of his fate, loves not his wronger;
     But, O, what damned minutes tells he o'er
     Who dotes, yet doubts, suspects, yet strongly loves!
     (III, iii)

135 Poor and content is rich, and rich enough,
     But riches fineless is as poor as winter
     To him that ever fears he shall be poor.
     Good God, the souls of all my tribe defend
     From jealousy! (III, iii)

136 Think'st thou I'd make a life of jealousy,
     To follow still the changes of the moon
     With fresh suspicions? No! To be once in doubt
     Is once to be resolv'd. Exchange me for a goat
     When I shall turn the business of my soul
     To such exsufflicate and blown surmises,
     Matching thy inference. 'Tis not to make me jealous
     To say my wife is fair, feeds well, loves company,
     Is free of speech, sings, plays, and dances well;
     Where virtue is, these are more virtuous.
     Nor from mine own weak merits will I draw
     The smallest fear or doubt of her revolt,
     For she had eyes, and chose me. No, Iago,
     I'll see before I doubt; when I doubt, prove;
     And on the proof, there is no more but this—
     Away at once with love or jealousy! (III, iii)

137 It is the cause, it is the cause, my soul.
     Let me not name it to you, you chaste stars!
     It is the cause. Yet I'll not shed her blood,
     Nor scar that whiter skin of hers than snow,
     And smooth as monumental alabaster.
     Yet she must die, else she'll betray more men.
     Put out the light, and then put out the light.
     If I quench thee, thou flaming minister,
     I can again thy former light restore,
     Should I repent me; but once put out thy light,
     Thou cunning'st pattern of excelling nature,
     I know not where is that Promethean heat
     That can thy light relume. When I have pluck'd the
       rose,
     I cannot give it vital growth again,
     It needs must wither. I'll smell thee on the tree.
     (V, ii)

138 Then must you speak
     Of one the lov'd not wisely but too well;
     Of one not easily jealous, but, being wrought,
     Perplex'd in the extreme; of one whose hand,
     Like the base Indian, threw a pearl away
     Richer than all his tribe; (V, ii)

Pericles

139 Time's the king of men;
     He's both their parent and he is their grave,
     And gives them what he will, not what they crave.
     (II, iii)

The Rape of Lucrece

140 'O opportunity! thy guilt is great,
     'Tis thou that execut'st the traitor's treason;
     Thou set'st the wolf where he the lamb may get;
     Whoever plots the sin, thou point'st the season;
     'Tis thou that spurn'st at right, at law, at reason;
     And in thy shady cell, where none may spy him,
     Sits Sin to seize the souls that wander by him.
     (l. 1–8)

BeLS; LiTB; NOBE; OBSC; PoEL-2

Romeo and Juliet

141 O, then, I see Queen Mab hath been with you.
     She is the fairies' midwife, and she comes
     In shape no bigger than an agate-stone
     On the fore-finger of an alderman,
     Drawn with a team of little atomies
     Athwart men's noses as they lie asleep;
     Her waggon-spokes made of long spinners' legs,
     The cover of the wings of grasshoppers,
     The traces of the smallest spider's web,
     The collars of the moonshine's watery beams,
     Her whip of cricket's bone, the lash of film,
     Her waggoner a small grey-coated gnat,
     Not half so big as a round little worm
     Prick'd from the lazy finger of a maid; (I, iv)

FaPON; FiP; LiTB; WSC

142 True, I talk of dreams,
     Which are the children of an idle brain,
     Begot of nothing but vain fantasy,
     Which is as thin of substance as the air,
     And more inconstant than the wind, who woos
     Even now the frozen bosom of the north,
     And being angered, puffs away from thence,
     Turning his side to the dew-dropping south. (I, iv)

143 It is nor hand, nor foot,
     Nor arm, nor face, nor any other part
     Belonging to a man. O, be some other name!
     What's in a name? That which we call a rose
     By any other word would smell as sweet;
     So Romeo would, were he not Romeo called,
     Retain that dear perfection which he owes
     Without that title. Romeo, doff thy name,
     And for thy name, which is no part of thee,
     Take all myself. (II, ii)

144 Bondage is hoarse and may not speak aloud,
     Else would I tear the cave where Echo lies
     And make her airy tongue more hoarse than mine
     With repetition of "My Romeo!" (II, ii)

145 I shall forget, to have thee still stand there,
     Remembering how I love thy company. (II, ii)

146 Good night, good night! Parting is such sweet sorrow
That I shall say good night till it be morrow. (II, ii)

147 The gray-eyed morn smiles on the frowning night,
Check'ring the eastern clouds with streaks of light,
And fleckled darkness like a drunkard reels
From forth day's path and Titan's fiery wheels.
(II, iii)

148 But come what sorrow can,
It cannot countervail the exchange of joy
That one short minute gives me in her sight. (II, vi)

149 These violent delights have violent ends
And in their triumph die, like fire and powder,
Which as they kiss consume. (II, vi)

150 Come, civil night,
Thou sober-suited matron all in black,
And learn me how to lose a winning match
Played for a pair of stainless maidenhoods.
Hood my unmanned blood, bating in my cheeks,
With thy black mantle till strange love grow bold,
Think true love acted simple modesty.
Come, night. Come, Romeo. Come, thou day in night;
For thou wilt lie upon the wings of night
Whiter than new snow upon a raven's back.
Come, gentle night, come, loving, black-browed night,
(III, ii)

151 Let me have
A dram of poison, such soon-speeding gear
As will disperse itself through all the veins
That the life-weary taker may fall dead,
And that the trunk may be discharged of breath
As violently as hasty powder fired
Doth hurry from the fatal cannon's womb. (V, i)

152 There is thy gold — worse poison to men's souls,
Doing more murder in this loathsome world
Than these poor compounds that thou mayst not sell.
I sell thee poison; thou hast sold me none. (V, i)

153 How oft when men are at the point of death
Have they been merry! which their keepers call
A lightning before death: O, how may I
Call this a lightning? O my love! my wife!
Death, that hath sucked the honey of thy breath,
Hath had no power yet upon thy beauty:
Thou art not conquered; beauty's ensign yet
Is crimson in thy lips and in thy cheeks,
And death's pale flag is not advanced there. (V, iii)

FaFP; TrGrPo

The Taming of the Shrew

154 And where two raging fires meet together;
They do consume the thing that feeds their fury.
Though little fire grows great with little wind,
Yet extreme gusts will blow out fire and all. (II, i)

155 Thy husband is thy lord, thy life, thy keeper,
Thy head, thy sovereign; one that cares for thee,
And for thy maintenance commits his body
To painful labor both by sea and land,
To watch the night in storms, the day in cold,
Whilst thou liest warm at home, secure and safe;
And craves no other tribute at thy hands
But love, fair looks, and true obedience —
Too little payment for so great a debt.
Such duty as the subject owes the prince,
Even such a woman oweth to her husband;
And when she is froward, peevish, sullen, sour,
And not obedient to his honest will,
What is she but a foul contending rebel
And graceless traitor to her loving lord? (V, ii)

The Tempest

156 Full fathom five thy father lies;
Of his bones are coral made;
Those are pearls that were his eyes:
Nothing of him that doth fade
But doth suffer a sea-change
Into something rich and strange.
Sea-nymphs hourly ring his knell:
Dingdong.
Hark! now I hear them, — dingdong, bell. (I, ii)

AWP; ChTr; EBEV; ElL; ELP; FaBoCh; GN; GoJo;
GTBS; GTBS-P; HAP; HeIP; HoPM; InPK; InPS; LiTB;
MOS; NAEL-1; NOBE; NoP; OAEL-1; OBEV; OBSC;
OxBSP; PoE; PoEL-2; PoRA; SeCePo; TEP; TrGrPo

157 This island's mine, by Sycorax my mother,
Which thou tak'st from me. When thou cam'st first,
Thou strok'st me and made much of me, wouldst give
me
Water with berries in 't, and teach me how
To name the bigger light, and how the less,
That burn by day and night. And then I loved thee
And showed thee all the qualities o' th' isle,
The fresh springs, brine pits, barren place and fertile.
Cursed be I that did so! All the charms
Of Sycorax, toads, beetles, bats, light on you!
For I am all the subjects that you have,
Which first was mine own king; and here you sty me
In this hard rock, whiles you do keep from me
The rest o' the' island. (I, ii)

OAEL-1

158 While you here do snoring lie,
Open-eyed conspiracy
His time doth take.
If of life you keep a care,
Shake off slumber, and beware.
Awake, Awake! (II, i)

OAEL-1

159 The master, the swabber, the boatswain and I,
The gunner and his mate,
Loved Mall, Meg, and Marian and Margery,

But none of us cared for Kate;
For she had a tongue with a tang,
Would cry to a sailor, 'Go hang!'
She loved not the savour of tar nor of pitch,
Yet a tailor might scratch her where'er she did itch:
Then to sea, boys, and let her go hang. (II, ii)

FF; MOS; NBLV; NOBL; OAEL-1; OxBSP

160 There be some sports are painful, and their labor
Delight in them sets off. Some kinds of baseness
Are nobly undergone, and most poor matters
Point to rich ends. (III, i)

OAEL-1

161 Honor, riches, marriage blessing,
Long continuance, and increasing,
Hourly joys be still upon you!
Juno sings her blessings on you. (IV, i)

OAEL-1

162 Earth's increase, foison plenty,
Barns and garners never empty,
Vines with clustering bunches growing,
Plants with goodly burden bowing;

Spring come to you at the farthest
In the very end of harvest!
Scarcity and want shall shun you;
Ceres' blessing so is on you. (IV, i)

OAEL-1

163 Our revels now are ended. These our actors,
As I foretold you, were all spirits, and
Are melted into air, into thin air.
And, like the baseless fabric of this vision,
The cloud-capped towers, the gorgeous palaces,
The solemn temples, the great globe itself—
Yea, all which it inherit—shall dissolve
And, like this insubstantial pageant faded,
Leave not a rack behind. We are such stuff
As dreams are made on, and our little life
Is rounded with a sleep. (IV, i)

FaBV; LiTB; OAEL-1; RB; TrGrPo

164 Ye elves of hills, brooks, standing lakes, and groves,
And ye that on the sands with printless foot
Do chase the ebbing Neptune, and do fly him
When he comes back; you demi-puppets that
By moonshine do the green sour ringlets make,
Whereof the ewe not bites; and you whose pastime
Is to make midnight mushrooms, (V, i)

165 But this rough magic
I here abjure, and when I have required
Some heavenly music—which even now I do—
To work mine end upon their senses that
This airy charm is for, I'll break my staff,

Bury it certain fathoms in the earth,
And deeper than did ever plummet sound
I'll drown my book. (V, i)

OAEL-1

166 Where the bee sucks, there suck I;
In a cowslip's bell I lie;
There I couch when owls do cry.
On the bat's back I do fly
After summer merrily.
Merrily, merrily shall I live now
Under the blossom that hangs on the bough. (V, i)

AWP; BoTP; CH; CTC; ElL; FaBV; GN; HeIP; NAEL-1;
NBLV; NOBE; NoP; OAEL-1; OBEV; OBSC; OxBSP;
PDV; TTTS

167 Now my charms are all o'erthrown,
And what strength I have 's mine own,
Which is most faint. (V, Epilogue)

168 As you from crimes would pardoned be,
Let your indulgence set me free. (V, Epilogue)

OAEL-1

Troilus and Cressida

169 Women are angels, wooing;
Things won are done, joy's soul lies in the doing.
That she beloved knows naught that knows not this:
Men prize the thing ungained more than it is.
That she was never yet that ever knew
Love got so sweet as when desire did sue.
Therefore this maxim out of love I teach:
Achievement is command; ungained, beseech.
Then though my heart's content firm love doth bear,
Nothing of that shall from mine eyes appear. (I, iii)

TrGrPo

170 The heavens themselves, the planets, and this center
Observe degree, priority, and place,
Insisture, course, proportion, season, form,
Office, and custom, in all line of order. (I, iii)

171 O, when degree is shaked,
Which is the ladder of all high designs,
The enterprise is sick. How could communities,
Degrees in schools, and brotherhoods in cities,
Peaceful commerce from dividable shores,
The primogeniture and due of birth,
Prerogative of age, crowns, scepters, laurels,
But by degree stand in authentic place?
Take but degree away, untune that string,
And hark what discord follows. Each thing meets
In mere oppugnancy. (I, iii)

172 And appetite, an universal wolf,
So doubly seconded with will and power,
Must make perforce an universal prey
And last eat up himself. (I, iii)

173 Time hath, my lord, a wallet at his back,
Wherein he puts alms for oblivion,
A great-sized monster of ingratitudes.
Those scraps are good deeds past, which are devoured
As fast as they are made, forgot as soon
As done. (III, iii)

LiTB

Twelfth Night

174 If music be the food of love, play on;
Give me excess of it, that surfeiting,
The appetite may sicken and so die. (I, i)

175 What is love? 'tis not hereafter;
Present mirth hath present laughter;
What's to come is still unsure:
In delay there lies no plenty;
Then come kiss me, sweet and twenty,
Youth's a stuff will not endure. (II, iii)

AWP; BoLoP; CTC; ElL; ELP; FaBV; FaFP; FiP; GBL;
GoJo; GTBS; GTBS-P; HAP; HeIP; InPS; LiTB; NAEL-1;
NBLV; NOBE; NoP; OAEL-1; OBEV; OBSC; OxBoLi;
OxBSP; PoE; PoRA; TrGrPo

176 Come away, come away, death,
And in sad cypress let me be laid.
Fly away, fly away, breath;
I am slain by a fair cruel maid.
My shroud of white, stuck all with yew,
O! prepare it.
My part of death, no one so true
Did share it. (II, iv)

CTC; ElL; ELP; FiP; GBL; GTBS; GTBS-P; NOBE; NoP;
OBEV; OBSC; PoEL-2; PoRA; TrGrPo

177 When that I was and a little tiny boy,
With hey, ho, the wind and the rain,
A foolish thing was but a toy,
For the rain it raineth every day.

But when I came to man's estate
With hey, ho, the wind and the rain,
'Gainst knaves and thieves men shut their gate,
For the rain it raineth every day.

But when I came, alas! to wive,
With hey, ho, the wind and the rain,
By swaggering could I never thrive,
For the rain it raineth every day. (V, i)

CH; EBEV; ElL; FaBoCh; FiP; HeIP; LiTB; NBLV;
NOBE; NoP; OAEL-1; OBSC; OxBoLi; PoEL-2; PoRA;
WiR

The Winter's Tale

178 We were as twinned lambs that did frisk i' the sun
And bleat the one at th' other. What we changed
Was innocence for innocence; we knew not
The doctrine of ill-doing, nor dreamed
That any did. Had we pursued that life,
And our weak spirits ne'er been higher reared
With stronger blood, we should have answered heaven
Boldly "Not guilty," the imposition cleared
Hereditary ours. (I, ii)

179 There have been,
Or I am much deceived, cuckolds ere now;
And many a man there is, even at this present,
Now while I speak this, holds his wife by th' arm,
That little thinks she has been sluiced in 's absence
And his pond fished by his next neighbor, by
Sir Smile, his neighbor. Nay, there's comfort in 't
Whiles other men have gates and those gates opened,
As mine, against their will. Should all despair
That have revolted wives, the tenth of mankind
Would hang themselves. (I, ii)

180 Jog on, jog on, the footpath way,
And merrily hent the stile-a;
A merry heart goes all the day,
Your sad tires in a mile-a. (IV, ii)

BoTP; ElL; FaBoCh; GN; OBSC; OxBSP; TrGrPo

181 When daffodils begin to peer,
With heigh! the doxy, over the dale,
Why, then comes in the sweet o' the year;
For the red blood reigns in the winter's pale. (IV, ii)

ChTr; ElL; FaBoBe; FaBoCh; FiP; NBLV; NOBE; NoP;
OAEL-1; OBSC; OxBoLi; OxBSP; PoEL-2; PrIm

182 Will you buy any tape,
Or lace for your cape,
My dainty duck, my dear-a?
Any silk, and thread,
And toys for your head,
Of the new'st and finest, finest wear-a?
Come to the pedlar;
Money's a meddler,
That doth utter all men's ware-a. (IV, iii)

OBSC

183 When you do dance, I wish you
A wave o' the sea, that you might ever do
Nothing but that — move still, still so,
And own no other function. (IV, iv)

184 It is required
You do awake your faith. (V, iii)

SONNETS (the following 49 sonnets)

II. When forty winters shall beseige thy brow

185 When forty winters shall besiege thy brow
And dig deep trenches in thy beauty's field,
Thy youth's proud livery, so gaz'd on now,

Will be a tatter'd weed of small worth held.
Then being ask'd where all thy beauty lies,
Where all the treasure of thy lusty days,
To say, within thine own deep-sunken eyes
Were an all-eating shame and thriftless praise.
How much more praise deserv'd thy beauty's use
If thou couldst answer, 'This fair child of mine
Shall sum my count and make my old excuse,'
Proving his beauty by succession thine!
This were to be new made when thou art old
And see thy blood warm when thou feel'st it cold.
                                    (l. 1–14)

BLPL; FF; LiTB; OBSC; Son; TEP

XII. *When I do count the clock that tells the time*

186   When I do count the clock that tells the time,
      And see the brave day sunk in hideous night,
      When I behold the violet past prime,
      And sable curls all silvered o'er with white:
      When lofty trees I see barren of leaves,
      Which erst from heat did canopy the herd
      And summer's green all girded up in sheaves
      Borne on the bier with white and bristly beard:
      Then of thy beauty do I question make
      That thou among the wastes of time must go,
      Since sweets and beauties do themselves forsake,
      And die as fast as they see others grow,
      And nothing 'gainst Time's scythe can make defence
      Save breed to brave him, when he takes thee hence.
                                          (l. 1–14)

AWP; ElL; FaFP; InPS; NAEL-1; NoP; OAEL-1; OBSC;
Son; TEP

XV. *When I consider everything that grows*

187   When I consider every thing that grows
      Holds in perfection but a little moment,
      That this huge stage presenteth naught but shows
      Whereon the stars in secret influence comment;
      When I perceive that men as plants increase,
      Cheered and checked even by the self-same sky,
      Vaunt in their youthful sap, at height decrease,
      And wear their brave state out of memory:
      Then the conceit of this inconstant stay
      Sets you most rich in youth before my sight.
      Where wasteful Time debateth with Decay,
      To change your day of youth to sullied night;
      And all in war with Time for love of you,
      As he takes from you, I engraft you new. (l. 1–14)

AWP; BLPL; NAEL-1; OBSC; Son; TEP; TrGrPo

XVIII. *Shall I compare thee to a summer's day*

188   Shall I compare thee to a summer's day?
      Thou art more lovely and more temperate.
      Rough winds do shake the darling buds of May,

And summer's lease hath all too short a date.
Sometime too hot the eye of heaven shines,
And often is his gold complexion dimmed;
And every fair from fair sometime declines,
By chance, or nature's changing course, untrimmed;
But thy eternal summer shall not fade
Nor lose possession of that fair thou ow'st,
Nor shall Death brag thou wand'rest in his shade
When in eternal lines to time thou grow'st.
So long as men can breathe or eyes can see,
So long lives this, and this gives life to thee. (l. 1–14)

BoLoP; CTC; ElL; EnLoPo; FaBoBe; FaBV; FaFP; FiP;
FPL; GBL; GTBS; GTBS-P; HAP; HeIP; InPK; InPS;
InvP; LiTB; MAT; NIP; NOBE; NoP; OAEL-1; OBEV;
OBSC; PoE; PoEL-2; PoLF; PoRA; PrIm; SCV; SeCePo;
Son; TEP; TrGrPo; WeW

XIX. *Devouring Time, blunt thou the lion's paws*

189   Devouring Time, blunt thou the lion's paws,
      And make the earth devour her own sweet brood;
      Pluck the keen teeth from the fierce tiger's jaws,
      And burn the long-liv'd phoenix in her blood;
      Make glad and sorry seasons as thou fleet'st,
      And do what'er thou wilt, swift-footed Time,
      To the wide world and all her fading sweets; (l. 1–7)

AWP; ChTr; EBEV; MAT; NAEL-1; OAEL-1; OBSC;
PoE; PoEL-2; TrGrPo

XXII. *My glass shall not persuade me I am old*

190   My glass shall not persuade me I am old
      So long as youth and thou are of one date,
      But when in thee time's furrows I behold,
      Then look I death my days should expiate. (l. 1–4)

OBSC; Son

XXIV. *Mine eye hath play'd the painter*

191   Mine eye hath play'd the painter, and hath steel'd
      Thy beauty's form in table of my heart: (l. 1–2)

192   For through the painter must you see his skill,
      To find where your true image pictured lies,
      Which in my bosom's shop is hanging still, (l. 5–7)

EyDe

XXVII. *Weary with toil, I haste me to my bed*

193   Weary with toil, I haste me to my bed,
      The dear repose for limbs with travel tired;
      But then begins a journey in my head
      To work my mind, when body's work's expired:
                                          (l. 1–4)

OBSC

XXIX. *When in disgrace with fortune and men's eyes*

194 When, in disgrace with fortune and men's eyes,
I all alone beweep my outcast state,
And trouble deaf heaven with my bootless cries,
And look upon myself, and curse my fate,
Wishing me like to one more rich in hope,
Featured like him, like him with friends possessed,
Desiring this man's art, and that man's scope,
With what I most enjoy contented least;
Yet in these thoughts myself almost despising,
Haply I think on thee, and then my state,
Like to the lark at break of day arising
From sullen earth, sings hymns at heaven's gate;
For thy sweet love remembered such wealth brings
That then I scorn to change my state with kings.
(l. 1–14)

AWP; CTC; EBEV; ElL; FaBoRV; FaBV; GBL; GTBS;
GTBS-P; HAP; HeIP; InPK; InPS; InvP; LiTB; NAEL-1;
NOBE NoP; OAEL-1; OBEV; OBSC; OPOP; PeHV;
PoEL-2; Son

XXX. *When to the sessions of sweet silent thought*

195 When to the sessions of sweet silent thought
I summon up remembrance of things past,
I sigh the lack of many a thing I sought,
And with old woes new wail my dear time's waste.
Then can I drown an eye, unus'd to flow.
For precious friends hid in death's dateless night
And weep afresh love's long since cancell'd woe,
And moan th' expense of many a vanish'd sight.
Then can I grieve at grievances foregone.
And heavily from woe to woe tell o'er
The sad account of fore-bemoaned moan,
Which I new pay as if not paid before.
But if the while I think on thee, dear friend,
All losses are restor'd and sorrows end. (l. 1–14)

AWP; CTC; EBEV; ElL; FaBoRV; FaBV; FaFP; FF; FPL;
GBL; GTBS; GTBS-P; HAP; InPS; LiTB; NAEL-1;
NOBE; NoP; OAEL-1; OBEV; OBSC; PoE; PoEL-2;
PoLF; PoRA; PPP; PrIm; TEP; TrGrPo

XXXII. *If thou survive my well-contented day*

196 If thou survive my well-contented day
When that churl death my bones with dust shall cover,
And shalt by fortune once more re-survey
These poor rude lines of thy deceased lover;
Compare them with the bettering of the time,
And though they be outstripped by every pen,
Reserve them for my love, not for their rhyme
Exceeded by the height of happier men.
Oh, then vouchsafe me but this loving thought —
'Had my friend's Muse grown with this growing age,
A dearer birth than this his love had brought,

To march in ranks of better equipage:
But since he died, and poets better prove,
Theirs for their style I'll read, his for his love.'
(l. 1–14)

ElL; GTBS; GTBS-P; OBSC

XXXIII. *Full many a glorious morning have I seen*

197 Full many a glorious morning have I seen
Flatter the mountain-tops with sovereign eye,
Kissing with golden face the meadows green,
Gilding pale streams with heavenly alchemy; (l. 1–4)

AWP; EBEV; ElL; FaFP; HAP; LiTB; NoP; OAEL-1;
OBSC; PoRA; PPP; SeCePo; Son; TEP; TrGrPo; WeW

XXXIV. *Why didst thou promise such a beauteous day*

198 Why didst thou promise such a beauteous day,
And make me travel forth without my cloak,
To let base clouds o'ertake me in my way,

OBSC

XXXV. *No more be grieved at that which thou hast done*

199 No more be grieved at that which thou hast done,
Roses have thorns, and silver fountains mud,
Clouds and eclipses stain both moon and sun,
And loathsome canker lives in sweetest bud.
All men make faults, and even I in this,
Authorizing thy trespass with compare,
My self corrupting salving thy amiss,
Excusing thy sins more than thy sins are: (l. 1–8)

NAEL-1; PeHV; PoE; TEP; UnPo

XL. *Take all my loves, my love, yea take them all*

200 I do forgive thy robbery, gentle thief,
Although thou steal thee all my poverty;
And yet love knows, it is a greater grief
To bear love's wrong, than hate's known injury.
(l. 9–12)

InvP; OBSC

XLI. *Those petty wrongs that liberty commits*

201 when a woman woos, what woman's son
Will sourly leave her till she have prevailed? (l. 7–8)

InvP

XLVI. *Mine eye and heart are at a mortal war*

202 Mine eye and heart are at a mortal war,
How to divide the conquest of thy sight;
Mine eye my heart thy picture's sight would bar,
My heart mine eye the freedom of that right. (l. 1–4)

203 Mine eye's due is thine outward part,
And my heart's right thine inward love of heart.
(l. 13–14)

EyDe

XLVII. *Betwixt mine eye and heart a league is took*

204 either by thy picture or my love,
Thyself away art present still with me;
For thou not farther than my thoughts canst move,
And I am still with them, and they with thee;
Or, if they sleep, thy picture in my sight
Awakes my heart to heart's and eye's delight. (l. 9–14)

EyDe

LIII. *What is your substance, whereof are you made*

205 What is your substance, whereof are you made,
That millions of strange shadows on you tend?
Since every one hath, every one, one shade,
And you, but one, can every shadow lend.
Describe Adonis, and the counterfiet
Is poorly imitated after you;
On Helen's cheek all art of beauty set,
And you in Grecian tires are painted new;
Speak of the spring and foison of the year,
The one doth shadow of your beauty show,
The other as your bounty doth appear;
And you in every blessed shape we know.
In all external grace you have some part,
But you like none, none you, for constant heart.
(l. 1–14)

CTC; EBEV; ElL; FaFP; LiTB; OAEL-1; OBEV; OBSC;
PeHV

LIV. *O, how much more doth beauty beauteous seem*

206 O, how much more doth beauty beauteous seem
By that sweet ornament which truth doth give!
The rose looks fair, but fairer we it deem
For that sweet odor which doth in it live.
The canker-blooms have full as deep a dye
As the perfumed tincture of the roses,
Hang on such thorns, and play as wantonly
When summer's breath their masked buds discloses.
But, for their virtue only is their show.

They live unwooed and unrespected fade,
Die to themselves. Sweet roses do not so;
Of their sweet deaths are sweetest odors made.
And so of you, beauteous and lovely youth,
When that shall vade, by verse distills your truth
(l. 1–14)

AWP; ElL; OBEV; OBSC; PoE

LV. *Not marble nor the gilded monuments*

207 Not marble nor the gilded monuments
Of princes shall outlive this powerful rime;
But you shall shine more bright in these contents
Than unswept stone, besmeared with sluttish time.
When wasteful war shall statues overturn,
And broils root out the work of masonry,
Nor Mars his sword nor war's quick fire shall burn
The living record of your memory. (l. 1–8)

AWP; BLPL; CTC; FaFP; FF; HeIP; LiTB; NAEL-1; NIP;
NOBE; NoP; OAEL-1; OBSC; PeHV; PoE; PoEL-2;
PoRA; Son; TEP; TrGrPo

LVII. *Being your slave, what should I do but tend*

208 Being your slave, what should I do but tend
Upon the hours and times of your desire?
I have no precious time at all to spend
Nor services to do, till you require:
Nor dare I chide the world-without-end hour
Whilst I, my sovereign, watch the clock for you,
Nor think the bitterness of absence sour
When you have bid your servant once adieu;
Nor dare I question with my jealous thought
Where you may be, or your affairs suppose,
But like a sad slave, stay and think of nought
Save, where you are, how happy you make those; —
So true a fool is love, that in your will
Though you do anything, he thinks no ill. (l. 1–14)

GTBS; GTBS-P; HAP; OBEV; PeHV; PoEL-2

LX. *Like as the waves make towards the pebbled shore*

209 Like as the waves make towards the pebbled shore,
So do our minutes hasten to their end;
Each changing place with that which goes before,
In sequent toil all forwards do contend. (l. 1–4)

210 Time doth transfix the flourish set on youth
And delves the parallels in beauty's brow,
Feeds on the rarities of nature's truth,
And nothing stands but for his scythe to mow:
And yet to times in hope my verse shall stand,
Praising thy worth, despite his cruel hand. (l. 9–14)

ChTr; EBEV; ElL; FaFP; FPL; GTBS; GTBS-P; LiTB;
NIP; NOBE; OBSC; PeHV; PoRA; Son; TEP; UnPo

LXIV. *When I have seen by Time's fell hand defaced*

211 Then I have seen by Time's fell hand defaced
The rich proud cost of outworn buried age;
When sometime lofty towers I see down-rased,
And brass eternal slave to mortal rage;
When I have seen the hungry ocean gain
Advantage on the kingdom of the shore,
And the firm soil win of the wat'ry main,
Increasing store with loss and loss with store;
When I have seen such interchange of state,
Or state itself confounded to decay,
Ruin hath taught me thus to ruminate,
That Time will come and take my love away.
This thought is as a death, which cannot choose
But weep to have that which it fears to lose. (l. 1–14)

AWP; BLPL; ElL; EnLoPo; FaFP; GTBS; GTBS-P; HAP;
HeIP; LiTB; NOBE; NoP; OAEL-1; OBSC; PoE; PoRA;
Son

LXV. *Since brass, nor stone, nor earth, nor boundless sea*

212 Since brass, nor stone, nor earth, nor boundless sea,
But sad mortality o'ersways their power,
How with this rage shall beauty hold a plea,
Whose action is no stronger than a flower?
O how shall summer's honey breath hold out
Against the wrackful siege of batt'ring days,
When rocks impregnable are not so stout,
Nor gates of steel so strong but time decays?
O fearful meditation, where alack,
Shall Time's best jewel from Time's chest lie hid?
Or what strong hand can hold his swift foot back,
Or who his spoil of beauty can forbid? (l. 1–12)

AWP; FaFP; FF; FiP; GTBS; GTBS-P; HAP; InPS; LiTB;
NAEL-1; NOBE; NoP; PoRA; Son; UnPo

LXVI. *Tired with all these, for restful death I cry*

213 Tired with all these, for restful death I cry,
As, to behold desert a beggar born,
And needy nothing trimm'd in jollity,
And purest faith unhappily forsworn,
And gilded honour shamefully misplac'd,
And maiden virtue rudely strumpeted,
And right perfection wrongfully disgrac'd,
And strength by limping sway disabled,
And art made tongue-tied by authority,
And folly, doctor-like, controlling skill,
And simple truth miscall'd simplicity,
And captive good attending captain ill:
Tir'd with all these, from these would I be gone,
Save that, to die, I leave my love alone. (l. 1–14)

AWP; CTC; EBEV; FaBoPV; FaFP; GTBS; GTBS-P;
HAP InPS; LiTB; NOBE; OAEL-1; OBSC; PoEL-2;
TrGrPo; WeW

LXXI. *No longer mourn for me when I am dead*

214 No longer mourn for me when I am dead
Than you shall hear the surly sullen bell
Give warning to the world that I am fled
From this vile world, with vilest worms to dwell:
Nay, if you read this line, remember not
The hand that writ it; for I love you so,
That I in your sweet thoughts would be forgot,
If thinking on me then should make you woe. (l. 1–8)

AWP; EBEV; ElL; FaBoRV; GBL; GTBS; GTBS-P; HAP;
LiTB; NAEL-1; NoP; OBSC; PoRA; Son; TEP; TrGrPo

LXXIII. *That time of year thou mayst in me behold*

215 That time of year thou mayst in me behold
When yellow leaves, or none, or few, do hang
Upon those boughs which shake against the cold,
Bare ruined choirs, where late the sweet birds sang.
In me thou see'st the twilight of such day
As after sunset fadeth in the west;
Which by and by black night doth take away,
Death's second self, that seals up all in rest.
In me thou see'st the glowing of such fire,
That on the ashes of his youth doth lie,
As the deathbed whereon it must expire,
Consumed with that which it was nourished by.
This thou perceiv'st, which makes thy love more strong,
To love that well which thou must leave ere long.
(l. 1–14)

AWP; BoLoP; ChTr; CTC; EBEV; ElL; EnLoPo;
FaBoRV; FaBV; FF; FiP; GBL; GTBS; GTBS-P; HAP;
HeIP; HoPM; InPK; InPS; InvP; LiTB; NAEL-1; NIP;
NOBE; NoP; OAEL-1; OBD; OBEV; OBSC; OHFP; PoE;
PoEL-2; PoRA; PPP; PrIm; QFR; Son; SoSe; TEP;
TrGrPo; UnPo; WeW

LXXXI. *Or I shall live your epitaph to make*

216 Or I shall live your epitaph to make,
Or you survive when I in earth am rotten;
From hence your memory death cannot take,
Although in me each part will be forgotten.
Your name from hence immortal life shall have,
Though I, once gone, to all the world must die:
(l. 1–6)

OBSC

LXXXVI. *Was it the proud full sail of his great verse*

217 Was it the proud full sail of his great verse,
Bound for the prize of all too precious you,
That did my ripe thoughts in my brain inherse,
Making their tomb the womb wherein they grew?

Was it his spirit, by spirits taught to write
Above a mortal pitch, that struck me dead? (l. 1–6)

218   But when your countenance filled up his line,
Then lacked I matter; that enfeebled mine. (l. 13–14)

InvP; OAEL-1; Son; TEP

LXXXVII. *Farewell! thou art too dear for my possessing*

219   Farewell! thou art too dear for my possessing,
And like enough thou know'st thy estimate:
The charter of thy worth gives thee releasing;
My bonds in thee are all determinate. (l. 1–4)

220   Thyself thou gav'st, thy own worth then not knowing,
Or me, to whom thou gav'st it, else mistaking;
So thy great gift, upon misprision growing,
Comes home again, on better judgement making.
Thus have I had thee, as a dream doth flatter,
In sleep a king, but, waking, no such matter. (l. 9–14)

EBEV; ElL; GTBS; GTBS-P; InPS; InvP; LiTB; NAEL-1;
NOBE; OAEL-1; OBEV; OBSC; PeHV; PoEL-2; QFR;
Son; TrGrPo

XC. *Then hate me when thou wilt, if ever now*

221   Then hate me when thou wilt; if ever, now;
Now, while the world is bent my deeds to cross,
Join with the spite of fortune, make me bow,
And do not drop in for an after-loss:
Ah! do not, when my heart hath 'scaped this sorrow,
Come in the rearward of a conquered woe;
Give not a windy night a rainy morrow,
To linger out a purposed overthrow.
If thou wilt leave me, do not leave me last,
When other petty griefs have done their spite,
But in the onset come; so shall I taste
At first the very worst of fortune's might. (l. 1–12)

AWP; EBEV; ElL; NOBE; OBEV; OBSC; PoEL-2

XCIV. *They that have power to hurt and will do none*

222   They that have power to hurt and will do none,
That do not do the thing they most do show,
Who, moving others, are themselves as stone,
Unmoved, cold, and to temptation slow —
They rightly do inherit heaven's graces
And husband nature's riches from expense;
They are the lords and owners of their faces,
Others but stewards of their excellence.
The summer's flower is to the summer sweet,
Though to itself it only live and die;
But if that flower with base infection meet,
The basest weed outbraves his dignity:

For sweetest things turn sourest by their deeds;
Lilies that fester smell far worse than weeds. (l. 1–14)

BLPL; ElL; GTBS; GTBS-P; InPS; LiTB; NAEL-1;
NOBE; NoP; OAEL-1; OBEV; PeHV; PoE; PoEL-2; PPP;
SCV; Son; TEP; TrGrPo

XCVII. *How like a winter hath my absence beene*

223   How like a winter hath my absence beene
From thee, the pleasure of the fleeting yeare!
What freezings have I felt, what darke daies seene!
What old December's barenesse every where! (l. 1–4)

224   Yet this aboundant issue seem'd to me,
But hope of Orphans, and un-fathered fruite,
For sommer and his pleasures waite on thee,
And thou away, the very birds are mute.
Or if they sing, tis with so dull a cheere.
That leaves looke pale, dreading the winter's neere.
(l. 9–14)

AWP; ElL; EnLoPo; EyDe; GTBS; GTBS-P; NAEL-1;
NOBE; OAEL-1; OBEV; OBSC; PoRA; Son; TEP;
TrGrPo

XCVIII. *From you have I been absent in the spring*

225   From you have I been absent in the spring,
When proud pied April, dressed in all his trim,
Hath put a spirit of youth in every thing,
That heavy Saturn laughed and leaped with him.
(l. 1–4)

226   Yet seemed it winter still, and, you away,
As with your shadow I with these did play. (l. 13–14)

AWP; ChTr; EBEV; ElL; LiTB; NAEL-1; NOBE; OBEV;
OBSC; TEP

CIV. *To me, fair friend, you never can be old*

227   To me, fair friend, you never can be old,
For as you were when first your eye I ey'd,
Such seems your beauty still. Three winters cold
Have from the forests shook three summer's pride,
Three beauteous springs to yellow autumns turn'd
In process of the seasons have I seen,
Three April perfumes in three hot Junes burn'd,
Since first I saw you fresh, which yet are green.
Ah, yet doth beauty, like a dial hand,
Steal from his figure, and no pace perceiv'd!
So your sweet hue, which methinks still doth stand,
Hath motion, and mine eye may be deceiv'd;
For fear of which, hear this, thou age unbred:
Ere you were born was beauty's summer dead.
(l. 1–14)

ElL; FPL; GBL; GTBS; GTBS-P; HeIP; OBEV; OBSC;
PeHV; Prf

CVI. *When in the chronicle of wasted time*

228 When in the chronicle of wasted time
I see descriptions of the fairest wights,
And beauty making beautiful old rhyme
In praise of ladies dead and lovely knights,
Then, in the blazon of sweet beauty's best,
Of hand, of foot, of lip, of eye, of brow,
I see their antique pen would have express'd
Even such a beauty as you master now.
So all their praises are but prophecies
Of this our time, all you prefiguring;
And, for they look'd but with divining eyes,
They had not skill enough your worth to sing;
For we which now behold these present days,
Have eyes to wonder, but lack tongues to praise.
(l. 1–14)

AWP; BLPL; CTC; ElL; EnLoPo; FaBoCh; FaBV; FiP;
GTBS; GTBS-P; LiTB; NAEL-1; NOBE; NoP; OBEV;
OBSC; PoRA; Son; TEP; TrGrPo

CVII. *Not mine own fears nor the prophetic soul*

229 Not mine own fears nor the prophetic soul
Of the wide world dreaming on things to come
Can yet the lease of my true love control,
Supposed as forfeit to a confined doom.
The mortal moon hath her eclipse endured,
And the sad augurs mock their own presage,
Incertainties now crown themselves assured,
And peace proclaims olives of endless age.
Now with the drops of this most balmy time
My love looks fresh, and death to me subscribes,
Since, spite of him, I'll live in this poor rhyme,
While he insults o'er dull and speechless tribes:
And thou in this shalt find thy monument,
When tyrants' crests and tombs of brass are spent.
(l. 1–14)

AWP; CTC; EBEV; FiP; HAP; LiTB; NAEL-1; NoP;
OAEL-1; OBSC

CIX. *O! never say that I was false of heart*

230 O! never say that I was false of heart,
Though absence seemed my flame to qualify.
As easy might I from myself depart
As from my soul, which in thy breast doth lie:
That is my home of love; if I have ranged,
Like him that travels, I return again,
Just to the time, not with the time exchanged,
So that myself bring water for my stain.
Never believe, though in my nature reigned
All frailties that besiege all kinds of blood,
That it could so preposterously be stained,
To leave for nothing all thy sum of good;
For nothing this wide universe I call,
Save thou, my rose; in it thou art my all. (l. 1–14)

ElL; GTBS; GTBS-P; NOBE; OBEV; OBSC

CXVI. *Let me not to the marriage of true minds*

231 Let me not to the marriage of true minds
Admit impediments. Love is not love
Which alters when it alteration finds,
Or bends with the remover to remove. (l. 1–4)

232 It is the star to every wand'ring bark,
Whose worth's unknown, although his height be taken.
Love's not Time's fool, though rosy lips and cheeks
Within his bending sickle's compass come;
Love alters not with his brief hours and weeks,
But bears it out even to the edge of doom. (l. 7–12)

AWP; ElL; EnLoPo; FaBV; FaFP; FPL; GBL; GTBS;
GTBS-P; HAP; HeIP; InPS; InvP; LiTB; NAEL-1; NIP;
NOBE; NoP; OAEL-1; OBEV; OBSC; PeHV; PoE; PoEL-
2; PoRA; PPP; PrIm; SCV; SeCePo; Son; SoSe; TEP;
TrGrPo; UnPo; WeW

CXXIII. *No, Time, thou shalt not boast that I do change*

233 No, Time, thou shalt not boast that I do change. (l. 1)

234 Our dates are brief, and therefore we admire
What thou dost foist upon us that is old, (l. 5–6)

235 This I do now, and this shall ever be,
I will be true, despite thy scythe and thee. (l. 13–14)

OBSC; Son; TrGrPo

CXXIX. *The expense of spirit in a waste of shame*

236 The expense of spirit in a waste of shame
Is lust in action; and, till action, lust
Is perjured, murderous, bloody, full of blame,
Savage, extreme, rude, cruel not to trust;
Enjoyed no sooner but despised straight;
Past reason hunted, and no sooner had,
Past reason hated as a swallowed bait
On purpose laid to make the taker mad;
Mad in pursuit, and in possession so;
Had, having, and in quest to have, extreme;
A bliss in proof, and proved, a very woe,
Before, a joy proposed; behind, a dream.
All this the world well knows, yet none knows well
To shun the heaven that leads men to this hell.
(l. 1–14)

AWP; EBEV; ErPo; GBL; HAP; HeIP; InPS; LiTB;
NAEL-1; NIP; NOBE; NoP; OAEL-1; OBEV; OBSC;
PoE; PoEL-2; PPP; QFR; SCV; SeCePo; Son; TEP;
TrGrPo; UnPo; WeW

CXXX. *My mistriss' eyes are nothing like the sun*

237 My mistress' eyes are nothing like the sun;
Coral is far more red than her lips' red;
If snow be white, why then her breasts are dun;

If hairs be wires, black wires grow on her head.
I have seen roses damasked, red and white,
But no such roses see I in her cheeks,
And in some perfumes there is more delight
Than in the breath that from my mistress reeks.
I love to hear her speak, yet well I know
That music hath a far more pleasing sound;
I grant I never saw a goddess go:
My mistress when she walks treads on the ground.
And yet by heaven I think my love as rare
As any she belied with false compare. (l. 1–14)

AWP; BoLoP; EBEV; FF; HAP; HoPM; InPK; InPS;
InvP; LiTB; NAEL-1; NIP; NoP; OAEL-1; PoE; PPP;
PrIm; Son; SoSe; TEP; WeW

CXXXVIII. *When my love swears that she is made of truth*

238 When my love swears that she is made of truth,
I do believe her, though I know she lies,
That she might think me some untutor'd youth,
Unlearned in the world's false subtleties.
Thus vainly thinking that she thinks me young,
Although she knows my days are past the best,
Simply I credit her false-speaking tongue:
On both sides thus is simple truth suppress'd.
But wherefore says she not she is unjust?
And wherefore say not I that I am old?
O, love's best habit is in seeming trust,
And age in love loves not to have years told:
Therefore I lie with her and she with me,
And in our faults by lies we flatter'd be. (l. 1–14)

AWP; EBEV; NAEL-1; NoP; OAEL-1; PoEL-2; PPP;
SoSe; TEP; TrGrPo

CXLI. *In faith I do not love thee with mine eyes*

239 In faith I do not love thee with mine eyes,
For they in thee a thousand errors note,
But 'tis my heart that loves what they dispise, (l. 1–3)

PoEL-2; TrGrPo

CXLIV. *Two loves I have of comfort and despair*

240 Two loves I have of comfort and despair
Which like two spirits do suggest me still;
The better angel is a man right fair,
The worser spirit a woman, colored ill.
To win me soon to hell, my female evil
Tempteth my better angel from my side,
And would corrupt my saint to be a devil,
Wooing his purity with her foul pride.
And whether that my angel be turned fiend,
Suspect I may, yet not directly tell;
But being both from me; both to each friend,
I guess one angel in another's hell.

Yet this shall I ne'er know, but live in doubt,
Till my bad angel fire my good one out. (l. 1–14)

EBEV; InvP; NAEL-1; NIP; OAEL-1; PeHV; PoEL-2; Son

CXLV. *Those lips that love's own hand did make*

241 "I hate" from hate away she threw,
And saved my life, saying "not you." (l. 13–14)

Son

CXLVII. *My love is as a fever, longing still*

242 My love is as a fever, longing still
For that which longer nurseth the disease;
Feeding on that which doth preserve the ill,
The uncertain sickly appetite to please.
My reason, the physician to my love,
Angry that his prescriptions are not kept,
Hath left me, and I desperate now approve,
Desire his death, which physic did except.
Past cure I am, now reason is past care,
And frantic-mad with evermore unrest;
My thoughts and my discourse as madmen's are,
At random from the truth vainly express'd;
For I have sworn thee fair, and thought thee bright,
Who art as black as hell, as dark as night. (l. 1–14)

EBEV; HoPM; NAEL-1; PoEL-2; TEP

CLI. *Love is too young to know what conscience is*

243 Love is too young to know what conscience is,
Yet who knows not conscience is born of love?
Then, gentle cheater, urge not my amiss,
Lest guilty of my faults, thy sweet self prove.
For, thou betraying me, I do betray
My nobler part to my gross body's treason;
My soul doth tell my body that he may
Triumph in love: flesh stays no farther reason,
But rising at thy name doth point out thee
As his triumphant prize. Proud of this pride,
He is contented thy poor drudge to be,
To stand in thy affairs, fall by thy side.
No want of conscience hold it that I call
Her "love" for whose dear love I rise and fall.
(l. 1–14)

EBEV; HeIP; PoE; PoEL-2

KARL SHAPIRO (b. 1913)

Auto Wreck

1 Its quick silver bell beating, beating
And down the dark one ruby flare
Pulsing out red light like an artery, (l. 1–3)

2 We are deranged, walking among the cops
  Who sweep glass and are large and composed.
  (l. 15–16)

3 Already old, the question Who shall die?
  Becomes unspoken Who is innocent? (l. 31–32)

4 But this invites the occult mind,
  Cancels our physics with a sneer,
  And spatters all we knew of denouement
  Across the expedient and wicked stones. (l. 35–38)

CMoP; FF; LiTM; NIP; RB; VGW

Buick

5 Flouncing your skirts, you blueness of joy, you flirt of
    politeness,
  You leap, you intelligence, essence of wheelness with
    silvery nose,
  And your platinum clocks of excitement stir like the
    hairs of a fern. (l. 8–10)

6 But with exquisite breathing you smile, with
    satisfaction of love,
  And I touch you again as you tick in the silence and
    settle in sleep. (l. 19–20)

CMoP; EoPM; MoAB; RR; TrGrPo

The Dome of Sunday

7 Sunday at noon through hyaline thin air
  Sees down the street,
  And in the camera of my eye depicts
  Row-houses and row-lives:
  Glass after glass, door after door the same, (l. 4–8)

8 I see slip to the curb the long machines
  Out of whose warm and windowed rooms pirouette
  Shellacked with silk and light
  The hard legs of our women. (l. 17–20)

9 No direct hit to smash the shatter-proof
  And lodge at last the quivering needle
  Clean in the eye of one who stands transfixed
  In fascination of her brightness. (l. 45–48)

CMoP; CoAP; LiTM; MoAB; MoAmPo; NoAM; OxBA;
WaP

Elegy for a Dead Soldier

10 We too are ashes as we watch and hear
   The psalm, the sorrow, and the simple praise
   Of one whose promised thoughts of other days
   Were such as ours, but now wholly destroyed,

The service record of his youth wiped out,
His dream dispersed by shot, must disappear.
(l. 13–18)

11 We ask for no statistics of the killed,
   For nothing political impinges on
   This single casualty, or all those gone,
   Missing or healing, sinking or dispersed,
   Hundreds of thousands counted, millions lost.
   (l. 49–53)

12 However others calculate the cost,
   To us the final aggregate is one,
   One with a name, one transferred to the blest;
   And though another stoops and takes the gun,
   We cannot add the second to the first. (l. 56–60)

HAP; LiTM; OBWP; OxBA; WaaP; WaP

The Fly

13 O hideous little bat, the size of snot,
   With polyhedral eye and shabby clothes, (l. 1–2)

14 And in a comic mood
   In mid-air take to bed a wife. (l. 7–8)

15 In the tight belly of the dead
   Burrow with hungry head
   And inlay maggots like a jewel. (l. 14–16)

16 I sweep. One gyrates like a top and falls
   And stunned, stone blind, and deaf
   Buzzes its frightful F
   And dies between three cannibals. (l. 45–48)

LiTM; MoP; NIP; NoAM; TW

The Leg

17 One day beside some flowers near his nose
   He will be thinking, When will I look at it?
   And pain, still in the middle distance, will reply,
   At what? and he will know it's gone,
   O where! and begin to tremble and cry. (l. 8–12)

18 The body, what is it, Father, but a sign
   To love the force that grows us, to give back
   What in Thy palm is senselessness and mud?
   (l. 29–31)

HAP; MoAB; MoAmPo; TrGrPo; UnPo; WeW

Nostalgia

19 My soul is now her day, my day her night,
   So I lie down, and so I rise; (l. 11–12)

20 Laughter and grief join hands. Always the heart
Clumps in the breast with heavy stride;
The face grows lined and wrinkled like a chart,
The eyes bloodshot with tears and tide.
Let the wind blow, for many a man shall die.
(l. 21–25)

CMoP; CoAP; TrJP; TwCP; WaaP

Poet

21 Oh, it is I,
Incredibly skinny, stooped, and neat as pie,
Ignorant as dirt, erotic as an ape,
Dreamy as puberty — with dirty hair! (l. 9–12)

22 To girls and wives always alive and fated;
To men and scholars always dead like Greek
And always mistranslated. (l. 38–40)

23 Sentio ergo sum: he feels his way
And words themselves stand up for him like Braille
And punch and perforate his parchment ear.
(l. 44–46)

24 He shall eat flowers,
Chew honey and spit out gall. They shall all smile
And love and pity him.

His death shall be by drowning. (l. 63–66)

25 Lastly, his tomb
Shall list and founder in the troughs of grass
And none shall speak his name. (l. 71–73)

CMoP; LiTM; MoAB; MoAmPo; NoAM

Scyros

26 The doctor punched my vein
The captain called me Cain
Upon my belly sat the sow of fear (l. 1–3)

27 The roof of England fell
Great Paris tolled her bell
And China staunched her milk and wept for bread
(l. 16–18)

HoPM; LiTA; LiTM; WaP

V-Letter

28 Give me the free and poor inheritance
Of our own kind, not furniture
Of education, or the prophet's pose,
The general cause of words, the hero's stance,
The ambitions incommensurable with flesh, (l. 45–49)

29 As groceries in a pantry gleam and smile
Because they are important weights
Bought with the metal minutes of your pay,
So do these hours stand in solid rows,
The dowry for a use in common life. (l. 56–60)

NoAM; NYBP; TrJP; WaP

PERCY BYSSHE SHELLEY (1792–1822)

Adonais

1 To that high Capital, where kingly Death
Keeps his pale court in beauty and decay,
He came. (Fr. VII)

2 As long as skies are blue, and fields are green
Evening must usher night, night urge the morrow,
Month follow month with woe, and year wake year to
sorrow (Fr. XXI)

3 But I am chained to Time, and cannot thence depart!
(Fr. XXVI)

4 Why didst thou leave the trodden paths of men
Too soon, and with weak hands though mighty heart
Dare the unpastured dragon in his den? (Fr. XXVII)

5 The Pilgrim of Eternity (Fr. XXX)

6 A pard-like Spirit beautiful and swift — (Fr. XXXII)

7 A herd-abandoned deer struck by the hunter's dart
(Fr. XXXIII)

8 He hath awakened from the dream of life —
(Fr. XXXIX)

9 He has out-soared the shadow of our night; (Fr. XL)

10 He lives, he wakes, — 'tis Death is dead, not he;
(Fr. XLI)

11 He is a portion of the loveliness
Which once he made more lovely: (Fr. XLIII)

12 The inheritors of unfulfilled renown (Fr. XLV)

13 The One remains, the many change and pass;
Heaven's light forever shines, Earth's shadows fly;
Life, like a dome of many-coloured glass,
Stains the white radiance of Eternity,
Until Death tramples it to fragments. (Fr. LII)

14 The soul of Adonais, like a star,
Beacons from the abode where the Eternal are.
(Fr. LV)

Alastor; or, The Spirit of Solitude

15 I have made my bed
In charnels and on coffins, where black death
Keeps record of the trophies won (l. 23–25)

16 she drew back a while,
Then, yielding to the irresistible joy,
With frantic gesture and short breathless cry
Folded his frame in her dissolving arms.
Now blackness veiled his dizzy eyes, and night
Involved and swallowed up the vision; sleep,
Like a dark flood suspended in its course,
Rolled back its impulse on his vacant brain.
　　　　　　　　　　　　　　　(l. 185–192)

17 At night the passion came,
Like the fierce fiend of a distempered dream,
And shook him from his rest, and led him forth
Into the darkness. — (l. 226–229)

18 At length upon the lone Chorasmian shore
He paused, a wide and melancholy waste
Of putrid marshes. (l. 274–276)

19 The slimy caverns of the populous deep. (l. 309)

20 Obedient to the light
That shone within his soul, he went, (l. 498–499)

21 But thou art fled
Like some frail exhalation; (l. 693–694)

22 But pale despair and cold tranquillity,
Nature's vast frame, the web of human things,
Birth and the grave, that are not as they were.
　　　　　　　　　　　　　　　(l. 725–727)

EnRP; OAEL-2

Charles the First

23 . . . A widow bird sat mourning for her love
Upon a wintry bough;
The frozen wind crept on above,
The freezing stream below. (l. 1–4)

BoTP; CH; ELP; FaPON; GTBS; GTBS-P; NOBE;
OBNC; OxBSP; PoEL-4

The Cloud

24 That orbed maiden with white fire laden,
Whom mortals call the Moon. (l. 45–46)

25 I am the daughter of Earth and Water,
And the nursling of the Sky;
I pass through the pores of the ocean and shores;
I change, but I cannot die. (l. 73–76)

26 I silently laugh at my own cenotaph,
And out of the caverns of rain,
Like a child from the womb, like a ghost from the
　　tomb,
I arise and unbuild it again. (l. 81–84)

BLPL; ChER; EnRP; FaPON; GN; ImOP; LiTB;
NAEL-2; NoP; OHFP; PoEL-4; PWR; TrGrPo

England in 1819

27 An old, mad, blind, despised, and dying king, (l. 1)

EnRP; FaBoPV; FF; FiP; MAT; NAEL-2; NAWM-2;
NOBE; NoP; OAEL-2; PPP; SeCePo; Son; TrGrPo; TW;
UnPo

Hymn of Pan

28 I pursued a maiden and clasped a reed.
Gods and men, we are all deluded thus! (l. 31–32)

EnRP; FaBoCh; OBEV; PoEL-4

Hymn to Intellectual Beauty

29 The awful shadow of some unseen Power
Floats though unseen among us, visiting
This various world with as inconstant wing
As summer winds that creep from flower to flower;
　　　　　　　　　　　　　　　(l. 1–4)

30 Spirit of Beauty, that dost consecrate
With thine own hues all thou dost shine upon
Of human thought or form, (l. 13–15)

31 While yet a boy I sought for ghosts, and sped
Through many a listening chamber, cave and ruin,
And starlight wood, with fearful steps pursuing
Hopes of high talk with the departed dead. (l. 49–52)

BLPL; EnRP; HAP; HeIP; NAEL-2; NoP; OAEL-2;
OBNC; PoE; TOF

The Indian Serenade

32 Oh, lift me from the grass!
I die! I faint! I fail!
Let thy love in kisses rain
On my lips and eyelids pale. (l. 17–19)

AWP; BLPL; EnRP; FaBoBe; FiP; GTBS; GTBS-P;
HoPM; LiTB; NAEL-2; OBEV; TrGrPo; TTTS

The Invitation

33 And like a prophetess of May
Strew'd flowers upon the barren way,
Making the wintry world appear
Like one on whom thou smilest, dear. (l. 17–20)

CH; GTBS; GTBS-P; NAEL-2; OBEV

A Lament: "O world! O life! O time!"

34 O world! O life! O time!
On whose last steps I climb, (l. 1–2)

ChER; ChTr; EnRP; GTBS; GTBS-P; NAEL-2; NOBE;
PoRA; TEP; TrGrPo

Lines Written among the Euganean Hills

35 Many a green isle needs must be
In the deep wide sea of Misery,
Or the mariner, worn and wan,
Never thus could voyage on (l. 1–4)

36 Underneath Day's azure eyes,
Ocean's nursling, Venice lies, —
A peopled labyrinth of walls,
Amphitrite's destined halls, (l. 55–58)

37 Sun-girt City! thou hast been
Ocean's child, and then his queen;
Now is come a darker day,
And thou soon must be his prey, (l. 76–79)

EnRP; GTBS; GTBS-P; PoEL-4

Love's Philosophy

38 Nothing in the world is single;
All things by a law divine
In one spirit meet and mingle.
Why not I with thine? (l. 5–8)

BLPA; BLPL; BoLoP; EnRP; FaBoBe; FaBV; GTBS;
GTBS-P; HoPM; TrGrPo

The Mask of Anarchy

39 I met Murder on the way —
He had a mask like Castlereagh —

40 'Rise like Lions after slumber
In unvanquishable number,
Shake your chains to earth like dew
Which in sleep had fallen on you —
Ye are many — they are few.

EnRP; Mes; OBSV; RB; SCV

Mont Blanc

41 My own, my human mind, which passively
Now renders and receives fast influencings,
Holding an unremitting interchange
With the clear universe of things around; (l. 37–40)

42 Some say that gleams of a remoter world
Visit the soul in sleep, — that death is slumber,
And that its shapes the busy thoughts outnumber
Of those who wake and live. — (l. 49–52)

EnRP; InPS; NAEL-2; NIP; NoP; OAEL-2; OBTV; TEP

Music, When Soft Voices Die

43 Music, when soft voices die,
Vibrates in the memory;
Odours, when sweet violets sicken,
Live within the sense they quicken. (l. 1–4)

AWP; CH; EnRP; FaBV; FiP; GTBS; GTBS-P; HeIP;
LiTB; NOBE; NoP; OBEV; OBNC; OxBSP; PCP;
PoEL-4; SeCePo; TrGrPo

Mutability

44 Man's yesterday may ne'er be like his morrow;
Nought may endure but mutability. (l. 15–16)

EnRP; NoP; OBNC; TEP

Ode to the West Wind

45 Oh! lift me as a wave, a leaf, a cloud!
I fall upon the thorns of life! I bleed! (l. 53–54)

46 Drive my dead thoughts over the universe
Like withered leaves to quicken a new birth!
And, by the incantation of this verse,

Scatter, as from an unextinguished hearth
Ashes and sparks, my words among mankind!
(l. 63–67)

47 If Winter comes, can Spring be far behind? (l. 70)

AWP; BoNaP; CH; EBEV; EnRP; FaBoBe; FaBV; FaFP;
FiP; FPL; GTBS; GTBS-P; HAP; HeIP; InPS; LiTB;
MOS; NAEL-2; NAWM-2; NIP; NOBE; NoP; OAEL-2;
OBEV; OBNC; OHFP; PoE; PoEL-4; PoLF; PoRA; PPP;
PrIm; TEP; TrGrPo; WeW

One word is too often profaned

48 One word is too often profaned
For me to profane it,
One feeling too falsely disdained
For thee to disdain it; (l. 1–4)

49 The desire of the moth for the star, (l. 13)

BLPL; BoLoP; ELP; EnRP; FaBV; FiP; GTBS; GTBS-P;
LiTB; NOBE; OBEV; OBNC; OPOP; PoLF; PPP; TrGrPo

Ozymandias

50 And on the pedestal these words appear:
"My name is Ozymandias, King of Kings:
Look on my works, ye Mighty, and despair!"
Nothing beside remains. Round the decay
Of that colossal wreck, boundless and bare
The lone and level sands stretch far away. (l. 9–14)

AWP; BeLS; CH; DL; EnRP; FaBoBe; FaBoCh; FaBoRV;
FaFP; FaPoR; FF; FiP; FPL; GTBS; GTBS-P; HAP; HeIP;
HoPM; InPK; InPS; NAEL-2; NIP; NOBE; NoP;
OAEL-2; OBNC; PoE; PoLF; PoRA; PrIm; RB; SCV;
Son; SoSe; TEP; TrGrPo; WeW

Prometheus Unbound

51 He will watch from dawn to gloom
The lake-reflected sun illume
The yellow bees in the ivy-bloom,
Nor heed nor see, what things they be;
But from these create he can
Forms more real than living man,
Nurslings of immortality! (Fr. I)

ChER; ELP; EnRP; FiP; GTBS; GTBS-P; OAEL-2; TOF

52 The good want power, but to weep barren tears.
The powerful goodness want: worse need for them.
The wise want love; and those who love want wisdom;
(Fr. I)

53 Child of Light! thy limbs are burning
Through the vest which seems to hide them;
As the radiant lines of morning
Through the clouds ere they divide them;
And this atmosphere divinest
Shrouds thee wheresoe'er thou shinest. (Fr. II)

CH; EnRP; FiP; GTBS; GTBS-P; NOBE; OAEL-2;
PoEL-4; PoE

54 He gave man speech, and speech created thought,
Which is the measure of the universe; (Fr. II)

55 Fate, Time, Occasion, Chance, and Change? To these
All things are subject but eternal Love. (Fr. II)

56 My soul is an enchanted Boat (Fr. II)

57 Death is the veil which those who live call life:
They sleep — and it is lifted (Fr. III)

58 To suffer woes which Hope thinks infinite;
To forgive wrongs darker than Death or Night;
To defy Power, which seems Omnipotent;
To love, and bear; to hope, till Hope creates
From its own wreck the thing it contemplates;
Neither to change nor falter nor repent;
This, like thy glory, Titan! is to be

Good, great and joyous, beautiful and free;
This is alone Life, Joy, Empire and Victory. (Fr. IV)

Question, The

59 There grew pied wind-flowers and violets,
Daisies, those pearl'd Arcturi of the earth,
The constellated flower that never sets;
Faint oxlips; tender bluebells at whose birth
The sod scarce heaved; and that tall flower that wets
Its mother's face with heaven-collected tears,
When the low wind, its playmate's voice, it hears.
(l. 9–15)

CH; EnRP; FiP; GTBS; GTBS-P; OBEV

Rarely, Rarely, Comest Thou

60 Rarely, rarely comest thou,
Spirit of Delight! (l. 1–2)

61 I love snow, and all the forms
Of the radiant frost;
I love waves, and winds and storms,
Everything almost
Which is Nature's, and may be
Untainted by man's misery. (l. 31–36)

CH; EnRP; GTBS; GTBS-P; Mes; OBNC; TEP; TrGrPo

Rough wind, that moanest loud

62 Bare woods, whose branches strain,
Deep caves and dreary main, —
Wail, for the world's wrong. (l. 6–8)

ChTr; EnRP; NAEL-2; NOBE; PoRA; SoSe; TEP;
TrGrPo; WiR

Similes for Two Political Characters of 1819

63 Two bloodless wolves whose dry throats rattle,
Two crows perched on the murrained cattle,
Two vipers tangled into one. (l. 18–20)

FaBoPV; NAEL-2; RB; TW

Song to the Men of England

64 Sow seed — but let no tyrant reap;
Find wealth — let no imposter heap;
Weave robes — let not the idle wear;
Forge arms — in your defence to bear. (l. 21–24)

65 With plough and spade, and hoe and loom,
Trace your grave, and build your tomb,
And weave your winding-sheet, till fair
England be your sepulchre. (l. 29–32)

EnRP; FiP; InPS; NAEL-2; SaC; TrGrPo

Stanzas — April 1814

66 Thy remembrance, and repentance, and deep musings
     are not free
   From the music of two voices and the light of one
     sweet smile.

   ChER; EnRP; FiP; OBEV; OBNC

Stanzas Written in Dejection, near Naples

67 I could lie down like a tired child,
   And weep away the life of care
   Which I have borne and yet must bear,
   Till death like sleep might steal on me, (l. 30–33)

   ChER; EnRP; FaBV; FiP; GTBS; GTBS-P; NAEL-2;
   NAWM-2; NoP; PoRA; TEP

Time

68 Thou shoreless flood, which in thy ebb and flow
   Claspest the limits of mortality,
   And sick of prey, yet howling on for more,
   Vomitest thy wrecks on its inhospitable shore; (l. 4–7)

   FaBoRV; FPL; MOS; Par; PoLF

To a Skylark

69 Hail to thee, blithe spirit!
   Bird thou never wert, (l. 1–2)

70 Like a poet hidden
   In the light of thought,
   Singing hymns unbidden,
   Till the world is wrought
   To sympathy with hopes and fears it heeded not:
                                        (l. 36–40)

71 We look before and after,
   And pine for what is not:
   Our sincerest laughter
   With some pain is fraught;
   Our sweetest songs are those that tell of saddest
     thought. (l. 86–90)

72 Teach me half the gladness
   That thy brain must know,
   Such harmonious madness
   From my lips would flow,
   The world should listen then, as I am listening now.
                                        (l. 101–105)

   EnRP; FaBoBe; FaBV; FaFP; FaPON; FPL; GN; GTBS;
   GTBS-P; HAP; InPS; InvP; LiTB; NAEL-2; NOBE; NoP;
   OAEL-2; OBEV; OBNC; OHFP; PBBP; PoLF; TEP;
   TrGrPo

To Jane: The Recollection

73 The whispering waves were half asleep,
   The clouds were gone to play,
   And on the bosom of the deep
   The smile of Heaven lay; (l. 13–16)

   ChER; GTBS; GTBS-P; OBNC

To Night

74 Thy sweet child Sleep, the filmy-eyed,
   Murmured like a noontide bee,
   Shall I nestle near thy side?
   Wouldst thou me? — And I replied,
   No, not thee! (l. 24–28)

   AWP; ChER; CH; EnRP; FPL; GTBS; GTBS-P; NAEL-2;
   NoP; OAEL-2; OBEV; OBNC; PoLF; PoRA; TEP;
   TrGrPo; WiR

To Wordsworth

75 In honored poverty thy voice did weave
   Songs consecrate to truth and liberty; —
   Deserting these, thou leavest me to grieve,
   Thus having been, that thou shouldst cease to be.
                                        (l. 11–14)

   EnRP; FiP; NoP; Son

The Triumph of Life

76 Mixed in one mighty torrent did appear,
   Some flying from the thing they feared, and some
   Seeking the object of another's fear; (l. 52–54)

77 the sacred few who could not tame
   Their spirits to the conquerors — (l. 127–128)

78 Yet ere I can say where — the chariot hath
   Passed over them — nor other trace I find
   But as of foam after the ocean's wrath (l. 136–138)

79 'I feared, loved, hated, suffered, did and died,
   And if the spark with which Heaven lit my spirit
   Had been with purer nutriment supplied, (l. 175–177)

80 I felt my cheek
   Alter, to see the shadow pass away,
   Whose grasp had left the giant world so weak

   That every pigmy kicked it as it lay; (l. 201–204)

81 'As the old faded.' — 'Figures ever new
   Rise on the bubble, paint them as you may;
   We have but thrown, as those before us threw,
                                        (l. 225–227)

82 'All that is mortal of great Plato there
Expiates the joy and woe his master knew not;
The star that ruled his doom was far too fair.
(l. 231–233)

83 And whether life had been before that sleep
The Heaven which I imagine, or a Hell

'Like this harsh world in which I wake to weep,
I know not. (l. 305–307)

84 'A Shape all light, which with one hand did fling
Dew on the earth, as if she were the dawn,
And the invisible rain did ever sing

'A silver music on the mossy lawn; (l. 352–355)

85 'All that was, seemed as if it had been not;
And all the gazer's mind was strewn beneath
Her feet like embers; and she, thought by thought,

'Trampled its sparks into the dust of death;
(l. 360–363)

86 'Or like small gnats and flies, as thick as mist
On evening marches, thronged about the brow
Of lawyers, statesmen, priest and theorist; —
(l. 435–437)

ChER; NAEL-2; OAEL-2; PoEL-4

The Two Spirits

87 Within my heart is the lamp of love,
And that is day! (l. 11–12)

CH; OAEL-2; Prf; WiR

The Waning Moon

88 Art thou pale for weariness
Of climbing heaven and gazing on the earth,
Wandering companionless
Among the stars that have a different birth, (l. 7–10)

ChER; CH; FaBoCh; OBEV; OxBSP; TrGrPo

When the Lamp Is Shattered

89 When the lamp is shattered,
The light in the dust lies dead;
When the cloud is scattered,
The rainbow's glory is shed;
When the lute is broken,
Sweet tones are remembered not;
When the lips have spoken,
Loved accents are soon forgot. (l. 1–8)

90 When hearts have one mingled,
Love first leaves the well-built nest;
The weak one is singled
To endure what it once possessed.
O Love! who bewailest
The frailty of all things here,
Why choose you the frailest,
For your cradle, your home, and your bier. (l. 17–24)

CH; EnRP; FF; FiP; NAEL-2; NoP; OBEV; OBNC;
PoEL-4; PPP; TEP; TrGrPo

With a Guitar, to Jane

91 and so this tree —
Oh, that such our death may be! —
Died in sleep, and felt no pain,
To live in happier form again:
From which, beneath Heaven's fairest star,
The artist wrought this loved guitar; (l. 53–58)

EnRP; GTBS; GTBS-P; OAEL-2

WILLIAM SHENSTONE (1714–1763)

Written at an Inn at Henley

1 To thee, fair Freedom! I retire
From flattery, cards, and dice, and din:
Nor art thou found in mansions higher
Than the low cot, or humble inn.

'Tis here with boundless pow'r I reign;
And ev'ry health which I begin
Converts dull port to bright champagne;
Such Freedom crowns it, at an inn. (l. 1–8)

2 Whoe'er has travelled life's dull round,
Where'er his stages may have been,
May sigh to think he still has found
The warmest welcome, at an inn. (l. 21–24)

AWP; NOBE; NOEC; OBEV

SIR EDWARD SHERBURNE (1618–1702)

And She Washed His Feet with Her Tears, and Wiped Them with the Hairs of Her Head

1 The proud Ægyptian Queen, her Roman guest,
(T'express her love in height of state, and pleasure)
With pearl dissolv'd in gold did feast, (l. 1–3)

2 And now (dear Lord!) thy lover, on the fair
And silver tables of thy feet, behold!
Pearl in her tears, and in her hair
Offers thee gold. (l. 5–8)

ACP; ChTr; MeLP; OBS; OxBSP

RICHARD BRINSLEY SHERIDAN
(1751–1816)

The School for Scandal

1 Here's to the maiden of bashful fifteen;
Here's to the widow of fifty;
Here's to the flaunting extravagant quean,
And here's to the housewife that's thrifty. (l. 1–4)

2 For let 'em be clumsy, or let 'em be slim,
Young or ancient, I care not a feather;
So fill a pint bumper quite up to the brim,
And let us e'en toast them together. (l. 16–19)

ELP; NOEC; NOIV; OxBoLi; PoRA

JAMES SHIRLEY (1596–1666)

The Contention of Ajax and Ulysses

1 The glories of our blood and state
Are shadows, not substantial things;
There is no armour against fate;
Death lays his icy hand on kings:
Sceptre and crown
Must tumble down,
And in the dust be equal made
With the poor crooked scythe and spade. (l. 1–8)

2 They stoop to fate,
And must give up their murmuring breath,
When they, pale captives, creep to death. (l. 14–16)

3 Only the actions of the just
Smell sweet and blossom in their dust. (l. 23–24)

ACP; AWP; BLPL; ChTr; FaBoRV; FaPoR; FF; GTBS;
GTBS-P; HAP; InvP; JCP; LiTB; NOBE; NoP; OAEL-1;
OBD; OBEV; OBS; PoEL-2; PoRA; PPP; TrGrPo; UnPo;
WaaP

Cupid and Death

4 Victorious men of earth, no more
Proclaim how wide your empires are;
Though you bind in every shore
And your triumphs reach as far
As night or day,
Yet you, proud monarchs, must obey
And mingle with forgotten ashes, when
Death calls ye to the crowd of common men.

GTBS; GTBS-P; OBS; TrGrPo

RICHARD SHUCKBURG *AND* EDWARD BANGS (1756–1818)

Yankee Doodle (*attributed to* Shuckburg *and to* Bangs)

1 Yankee Doodle, keep it up,

Yankee Doodle, dandy,
Mind the music and the step,
And with the girls be handy. (l. 5–8)

AmFP; AnAmPo; ChTr; FaFP; FaPON; GBP; OBAL; OPP;
OxBoLi; OxNR; PAH

SIR PHILIP SIDNEY (1554–1586)

Arcadia

1 My true love hath my heart, and I have his,
By just exchange, one for the other given.
I hold his dear, and mine he cannot miss,
There never was a better bargain driven.

2 Both equal hurt, in this change sought our bliss:
My true love hath my heart and I have his.

AWP; BoLoP; CH; ChTr; ElL; FaBoBe; GBL; GTBS;
GTBS-P; LiTB; NOBE; OBEV; OBSC; PoE; PoEL-1;
SiPS; TrGrPo

3 O sweet woods, the delight of solitariness!

4 Nor envy's snaky eye, finds harbour here,
Nor flatterers' venomous insinuations,
Nor cunning humorists' puddled opinions,
Nor courteous ruin of proffered usury,
Nor time prattled away, cradle of ignorance,
Nor causeless duty, nor comber of arrogance,
Nor trifling title of vanity dazzleth us,
Nor golden manacles stand for a paradise;

FaBoRV; LiTB; OBSC; PoEL-1; SiPS

ASTROPHEL AND STELLA (*the following 13 sonnets and songs*)

Sonnets

5 Loving in truth, and fain in verse my love to show,
That she, dear she, might take some pleasure of my
pain,
Pleasure might cause her read, reading might make her
know,
Knowledge might pity win, and pity grace obtain,
I sought fit words to paint the blackest face of woe:
(Fr. I, l. 1–5)

6 Thus, great with child to speak, and helpless in my
throes,
Biting my truant pen, beating myself for spite:
"Fool," said my Muse to me, "look in thy heart and
write!" (Fr. I, l. 12–14)

AAS; AWP; BLPL; EBEV; GBL; HAP; InPS; LiTB;
NAEL-1; NoP; OAEL-1; OBSC; PoE; SeCePo; SiPS; Son;
TEP; TrGrPo

7 It is most true, what we call Cupid's dart
An image is, which for ourselves we carve
And, fools, adore in temple of our heart,
(Fr. V, l. 5–7)

8 True, that true beauty virtue is indeed,
Whereof this beauty can be but a shade,
Which elements with mortal mixture breed.
True, that on earth we are but pilgrims made,
And should in soul up to our country move.
True, and yet true that I must Stella love.
(Fr. V, l. 9–14)

AAS; NAEL-1; OAEL-1; OBSC; SiPS; Son

9 You that do search for every purling spring
Which from the ribs of old Parnassus flows,
And every flower, not sweet perhaps, which grows
Near thereabouts into your poesy wring;
You that do dictionary's method bring
Into your rhymes, running in rattling rows;
(Fr. XV, l. 1–6)

10 these far-fet helps be such
As do bewray a want of inward touch,
and sure at length stolen goods do come to light.
But if, both for your love and skill, your name
You seek to nurse at fullest breasts of Fame,
Stella behold, and then begin to indite.
(Fr. XV, l. 9–14)

AAS; NAEL-1; OAEL-1; OBSC; SiPS; Son

11 That busy archer his sharp arrows tries?
(Fr. XXXI, l. 4)

12 Is constant love deemed there but want of wit?
(Fr. XXXI, l. 10)

13 Those lovers scorn whom that love doth possess?
Do they call virtue there ungratefulness?
(Fr. XXXI, l. 13–14)

AAS; AWP; BoLoP; BoNaP; CH; ChTr; ElL; EnLoPo;
GBL; HAP; HeIP; InPS; InvP; MAT; NAEL-1; NOBE;
NoP; OBEV; OBSC; PoE; PoEL-1; PoRA; PPP; SiPS;
Son; TEP; TrGrPo; WeW

14 Come, Sleep, O Sleep, the certain knot of peace,
The baiting-place of wit, the balm of woe,
The poor man's wealth, the prisoner's release,
The indifferent judge between the high and low;
(Fr. XXXIX, l. 1–4)

AAS; ElL; NAEL-1; NIP; NOBE; NoP; OBEV; OBSC;
PoE; PoRA; PPP; SCV; SiPS; Son; TEP; TrGrPo

15 What have I thus betrayed my libertie?
Can those blacke beames such burning markes engrave
In my free side? or am I borne a slave,
Whose necke becomes such yoke of tyranny?
(Fr. XLVII, l. 1–5)

16 Let her go: soft, but here she comes, go to,
Unkind, I love you not: O me, that eye
Doth make my heart give to my tongue the lie.
(Fr. XLVII, l. 12–14)

AAS; GBL; NAEL-1; NoP; PoEL-1; SiPS; TrGrPo

17 I on my horse, and Love on me, doth try
Our horsemanships, while by strange work I prove
A horseman to my horse, a horse to Love,
(Fr. XLIX, l. 1–3)

18 The wand is will; thou, fancy, saddle art,
Girt fast by memory; and while I spur
My horse, he spurs with sharp desire my heart;
(Fr. XLIX, l. 9–11)

19 And now hath made me to his hand so right
That in the manage myself takes delight.
(Fr. XLIX, l. 13–14)

AAS; NAEL-1; NoP; OAEL-1; PoE; SiPS

20 Who will in fairest book of Nature know
How virtue may best lodged in beauty be,
Let him but learn of love to read in thee,
Stella, those fair lines which true goodness show.
There shall he find all vices' overthrow,
Not by rude force, but sweetest sovereignty
Of reason, (Fr. LXXI, l. 1–6)

21 "But ah," Desire still cries, "give me some food."
(Fr. LXXI, l. 14)

AAS; InPS; NAEL-1; NoP; OAEL-1; PoE; SiPS

22 I never drank of Aganippe well,
Nor ever did in shade of Tempe sit,
And muses scorn with vulgar brains to dwell;
Poor layman I, for sacred rites unfit.
Some do I hear of poets' fury tell,
But, God wot, wot not what they mean by it;
And this I swear by blackest brook of hell,
I am no pickpurse of another's wit.
(Fr. LXXIV, l. 1–8)

23 My lips are sweet, inspired with Stella's kiss.
(Fr. LXXIV, l. 14)

AAS; HeIP; NAEL-1; OBSC; SiPS; Son

24 Highway, since you my chief Parnassus be,
And that my Muse, to some ears not unsweet,
Tempers her words to trampling horses' feet
More oft than to a chamber-melody,
(Fr. LXXXIV, l. 1–4)

25 Of highest wish, I wish you so much bliss,—
Hundreds of years you Stella's feet may kiss!
(Fr. LXXIV, l. 13–14)

AAS; ElL; LiTB; OBEV; OBSC; SiPS

26 Leave me, O Love, which reachest but to dust;
And thou, my mind, aspire to higher things;
Grow rich in that which never taketh rust;
Whatever fades but fading pleasure brings.
(Fr. CX, l. 1–4)

27 Then farewell, world; thy uttermost I see;
Eternal Love, maintain thy life in me.
(Frr. CX, l. 13–14)

AAS; FaBoRV; GBL; HeIP; LiTB; NIP; NOBE; PPP;
SeCePo; SiPS; Son

Songs

28 Let my whispering voice obtain
Sweet reward for sharpest pain;
(Fr. Fourth Song, l. 3–4)

29 Night hath closed all in her cloak,
Twinkling stars love-thoughts provoke,
Danger hence good care doth keep,
Jealousy itself doth sleep; (Fr. Fourth Song, l. 7–10)

AAS; ElL; GBL; HAP; InvP; NAEL-1; NoP; OBSC; SiPS

30 'Who is it that this dark night
Underneath my window plaineth?'
(Fr. Eleventh Song, l. 1–2)

31 Well, begone, begone, I say,
Lest that Argus' eyes perceive you.'
Oh, unjust Fortunes sway,
Which can make me thus to leave you,
And from louts to run away.
(Fr. Eleventh Song, l. 41–45)

AAS; ElL; NAEL-1; NOBE; OBEV; OBSC; PoE; PoEL-1;
SeCePo; SiPS; TEP

Certain Sonnets: A Farewell

32 Oft have I mused, but now at length I find,
Why those that die, men say they do depart. (l. 1–2)

33 Yea, worse than death: death parts both woe and joy:
From joy I part, still living in annoy. (l. 13–14)

ElL; GBL; NOBE; OBSC; SiPS

Love Me, O Love

34 Draw in thy beams and humble all thy might
To that sweet yoke where lasting freedoms be,
Which breaks the clouds and opens forth the light
That doth both shine and give us sight to see. (l. 5–8)

35 O take fast hold; let that light be thy guide
In this small course which birth draws out to death,
(l. 9–10)

HeIP

Ring Out Your Bells

36 Ring out your bells, let mourning shows be spread.
(l. 1)

37 All Love is dead, infected
With plague of deep disdain: (l. 3–4)

38 And Faith fair scorn doth gain.
From so ungrateful fancy,
From such a female franzy,
From them that use men thus,
Good Lord deliver us. (l. 6–10)

ElL; GBL; NoP; OBSC; SiPS; TEP; UnPo

Thou Blind Man's Mark

39 Thou blind man's mark, thou fool's self-chosen snare,
Fond Fancy's scum and dregs of scattered thought,
Band of all evils, cradle of causeless care,
Thou web of will whose end is never wrought;
Desire! desire, I have too dearly bought
With price of mangled mind thy worthless ware;
(l. 1–6)

40 In vain thou kindlest all thy smoky fire,
For virtue hath this better lesson taught,
Within myself to seek my only hire,
Desiring nought but how to kill desire. (l. 11–14)

ErPo; HeIP; LiTB; NAEL-1; NOBE; OBSC; PPP; SiPS;
Son; TrGrPo

Who Hath His Fancy Pleased

41 Let here his eyes be raised
On Nature's sweetest light; (l. 3–4)

42 She never dies, but lasteth
In life of lover's heart;
He ever dies that wasteth
In love his chiefest part. (l. 9–12)

ElL; OBSC; PoEL-1; QFR

LYDIA HUNTLEY SIGOURNEY
(1791–1865)

Indian Names

1 Ye say they all have passed away,
That noble race and brave;
That their light canoes have vanished

From off the crested wave;
That, mid the forests where they roamed,
There rings no hunters' shout;
But their name is on your waters,
Ye may not wash it out. (l. 1–8)

2 Wachusett hides its lingering voice
Within its rocky heart,
And Allegheny graves its tone
Throughout his lofty chart.
Monadnock, on his forehead hoar,
Doth seal the sacred trust,
Your mountains build their monument,
Though ye destroy their dust. (l. 33–40)

AmFN; FaPON; GOA; OBCA; PAH; PoLF

JON SILKIN (b. 1930)

Death of a Son

1 Something has ceased to come along with me.
Something like a person: something very like one.
And there was no nobility in it
Or anything like that. (l. 1–4)

2 He turned over on his side with his one year
Red as a wound
He turned over as if he could be sorry for this
And out of his eyes two great tears rolled, like stones,
and he died. (l. 40–43)

FF GTBS-P; MoP; NePoEA; OxBTC; VWA

LESLIE MARMON SILKO (b. 1948)

Toe'osh; a Laguna Coyote Story

1 How coyote got his
ratty old fur coat
bits of old fur
the sparrows stuck on him
with dabs of pitch.
That was after he lost his proud original one in a poker
game. (l. 5–10)

2 Howling and roaring
Toe'osh scattered white people
out of bars all over Wisconsin. (l. 61–63)

CDW; NoAM; STE; VoR

SHEL SILVERSTEIN (SHELLEY SILVERSTEIN) (b. 1932)

The Slithergadee

1 No you won't catch me, old Slithergadee,
You may catch all the others, but you wo ... (l. 3–4)

AmMo; NBLV; NTCP; OnUR; RHPC; WSC

CHARLES SIMIC (b. 1938)

Brooms

1 Only brooms
Know the devil
Still exists,

That the snow grows whiter
After a crow has flown over it. (l. 1–5)

2 They are sworn enemies of lyric poetry.
In prison they accompany the jailer,
Enter cells to hear confessions.
Their short-end comes down
When you least expect it. (l. 17–21)

3 And then finally there's your grandmother
Sweeping the dust of the nineteenth century
Into the twentieth, and your grandfather plucking
A straw out of the broom to pick his teeth. (l. 55–58)

AmPA; LCAP; NNaP

Butcher Shop

4 There are knives that glitter like altars
In a dark church
Where they bring the cripple and the imbecile
To be healed.

There's a woden block where bones are broken,
Scraped clean — a river dried to its bed (l. 9–14)

AmPA; InPK; LCAP; NNaP

Fork

5 This strange thing must have crept
Right out of hell.
It resembles a bird's foot
Worn around the cannibal's neck. (l. 1–4)

AmPA; HCAP; LCAP; PCP

WILLIAM GILMORE SIMMS (1806–1872)

The Swamp Fox

1 We follow where the Swamp Fox guides,
His friends and merry men are we;
And when the troop of Tarleton rides,
We burrow in the cypress tree.
The turfy hammock is our bed,
Our home is in the red deer's den,
Our roof, the tree-top overhead,
For we are wild and hunted men. (l. 1–8)

2 The Tory camp is now in sight,
And there he cowers within his den;
He hears our shouts, he dreads the fight,
He fears, and flies from Marion's men. (l. 77–80)

AA; BeLS; FaBoBe; PAH

LOUIS SIMPSON (b. 1923)

American Poetry

1 Like the shark, it contains a shoe.
It must swim for miles through the desert
Uttering cries that are almost human. (l. 4–6)

CAPP; MoP; NoAM; NOBA; TAP

Carentan O Carentan

2 The watchers in their leopard suits
Waited till it was time,
And aimed between the belt and boot
And let the barrel climb. (l. 21–24)

3 Carentan O Carentan
Before we met with you
We never yet had lost a man
Or known what death could do. (l. 53–56)

CoAP; MoBS; NOBA; OBWP; PoE; PrIm; RB

Chocolates

4 For people may not know what they think
about politics in the Balkans,
or the vexed question of men and women,

but everyone has a definite opinion
about the flavour of shredded coconut. (l. 18–22)

InPS; LCAP; Mes; OxBC

The Man Who Married Magdalene

5 The man who married Magdalene
Had not forgiven her.
God might pardon every sin . . .
Love is no pardoner. (l. 1–4)

MoP; NePoEA; NoAM; SM; TAP

My Father in the Night Commanding No

6 My father in the night commanding No
Has work to do. (l. 1–2)

CoAP; DiL; HeIP; LCAP; NePoEA-2; NoAM; NOBA;
NYBP; SM; TAP; TwCP; VGW

On the Lawn at the Villa

7 On the lawn at the villa —
That's the way to start, eh, reader?
We know where we stand — somewhere expensive —
(l. 1–4)

8 It's complicated, being an American,
Having the money and the bad conscience, both at the
same time.
Perhaps, after all, this is not the right subject for a
poem. (l. 14–16)

CoAP; GOA; LCAP; OBAL; OxBC; PPP

Squeal

9 I saw the best minds of my generation
Reading their poems to Vassar girls,
Being interviewed by Mademoiselle.
Having their publicity handled by professionals.
When can I go into an editorial office
And have my stuff published because I'm weird?
I could go on writing like this forever . . . (l. 28–34)

BXAP; FiBHP; Par; UnPo

A Story about Chicken Soup

10 In my grandmother's house there was always chicken
soup
And talk of the old country — mud and boards,
Poverty,
The snow falling down and necks of lovers. (l. 1–4)

11 The sun is shining.
The shadows of the lovers have disappeared.
They are all eyes; they have some demand on me —
They want me to be more serious than I want to be.
(l. 23–26)

LCAP; NNaP; PoE; TAP

To the Western World

12 The treasures of Cathay were never found.
In this America, this wilderness
Where the axe echoes with a lonely sound,
The generations labor to possess
And grave by grave we civilize the ground. (l. 11–15)

CAPP; CoAP; GOA; LiTM; NePoEA-2; NOBA; SM; TAP

Walt Whitman at Bear Mountain

13 "Where is the Mississippi panorama
And the girl who played the piano?
Where are you, Walt?
The Open Road goes to the used-car lot. (l. 6–9)

14 "I gave no prescriptions,
And those who have taken my moods for prophecies
Mistake the matter." (l. 20–22)

15 All that grave weight of America
Cancelled! Like Greece and Rome.
The future in ruins! (l. 35–37)

16 And the angel in the gate, the flowering plum,
Dances like Italy, imagining red. (l. 43–44)

CaPP; LiTM; NePoEA-2

DAME EDITH SITWELL (1887–1964)

FAÇADE (the following 2 poems)

Sailors Come

1 In a borealic iceberg came Victoria; she
Knew Prince Albert's tall memorial took the colours of
the floreal
And the borealic iceberg;

FaBoMo; GTBS-P; OAEL-2; SeCePo

Sir Beelzebub

2 When
Sir
Beelzebub called for his syllabub in the hotel in Hell
Where Proserpine first fell,

3 Enhances the chances to bless with a benison
Alfred Lord Tennyson crossing the barlaid
With cold vegetation from pale deputations
Of temperance workers (all signed In Memoriam)

BoWoP; FaBoMo; FaBoWP; HoPM; MoAB; MoBrPo;
OxBTC; PrIm

Jane, Jane,/ Tall as a crane

4 Jane, Jane,
Tall as a crane,
The morning light creaks down again; (l. 1–3)

5 The light would show (if it could harden)
Eternities of kitchen garden, (l. 14–15)

CMoP; MoAB; MoBrPo; MoP; NoAM; PoRA

Poems of the Atomic Bomb: Dirge for the New Sunrise

6 The ghost of the heart of manred Cain
And the more murderous brain
Of Man, still redder Nero that conceived the death

Of his mother Earth, and tore
Her womb, to know the place where he was conceived.
(l. 6–10)

7 Mother or Murderer, you have
given or taken life —
Now all is one! (l. 14–16)

8 Our hearts seemed safe in our breasts and sang to the
Light —
The marrow in the bone
We dreamed was safe ... the blood in the veins, the
sap in the tree
Were springs of Deity. (l. 20–24)

9 But I saw the little-Ant men as they ran
Carrying the world's weight of the world's filth
And the filth in the heart of Man —
Compressed till those lusts and greeds had a greater
heat
than that of the Sun. (l. 25–29)

10 The living blind and seeing Dead together lie
As if in love ... There was no more hating then,
And no more love; Gone is the heart of Man.
(l. 36–38)

CMoP; EaLo; MoAB; MoBrPo; SeCePo

Still Falls the Rain

11 Still falls the Rain —
Dark as the world of man, black as our loss —
Blind as the nineteen hundred and forty nails
Upon the Cross. (l. 1–4)

12 The last faint spark
In the self-murdered heart, the wounds of the sad
uncomprehending dark,
The wounds of the baited bear, —
The blind and weeping bear whom the keepers beat
On his helpless flesh ... the tears of the hunted hare.
(l. 22–27)

13 Then sounds the voice of One who like the heart of man
Was once a child who among beasts has lain —
'Still do I love, still shed my innocent light, my Blood,
for thee.' (l. 35–37)

BoWoP; CN; LiTM; MoAB; MoBrPo; MoP; NAEL-2;
NoAM; NOBE; OBWP; SeCePo; TEP; TrGrPo; TwCP;
WaaP

JOHN SKELTON (1460?–1529)

THE GARLANDE OF LAURELL (the following 3 poems)

To Mistress Isabel Pennell

1 My maiden Isabel,
Reflaring rosabel.
The fragrant camomel;

The ruddy rosary,
The sovereign rosemary,
The pretty strawberry;
The columbine, the nept,
The jelofer well set,
The proper violet: (l. 4–12)

AAS; CH; InPS; NAs; NOBE; OBEV; OBSC; OxBoLi;
PoEL-1; TrGrPo; TTTS

To Mistress Margaret Hussey

2 Merry Margaret,
As midsummer flower,
Gentle as falcon
Or hawk of the tower: (l. 1–4)

AAS; ACP; EBEV; EnLoPo; FaBoCh; GN; GoJo; HeIP;
HoPM; InPS; NAEL-1; NBLV; NOBE; NoP; OAEL-1;
OBEV; OBSC; OPOP; PoE; PoEL-1; PoRA; PPP; SCV;
TrGrPo

To Mistress Margery Wentworth

3 With margeran gentle,
The flower of goodlihood,
Embroidered the mantle
Is of your maidenhood. (l. 1–4)

EBEV; EnLoPo; NOBE; OAEL-1; OBEV; OBSC; TrGrPo

Mannerly Margery Mylk and Ale

4 Gup, Christian Clout, gup, Jack of the Vale!
With Mannerly Margery Milk and Ale. (l. 6–7)

AAS; FaBoNo; NAEL-1; NoP

Phyllyp Sparowe

5 Place bo!
Who is there, who? (l. 1–2)

6 For the soul of Philip Sparrow
That was late slain at Carrow,
Among the Nunnes Black. (l. 7–10)

7 And with the corner of a Creed,
The more shall be your meed. (l. 15–16)

8 The bird of Araby,
That potentially
May never die, (l. 230–232)

9 A phoenix it is
This hearse that must bless
With aromatic gums
That cost great sums,

The way of thurification
To make a fumigation,
Sweet of reflare,
And redolent of air, (l. 235–242)

10 There riseth a new creation
Of the same fashion
Without alteration, (l. 258–260)

AAS; NOBE; OAEL-1; OxBoLi; PoEL-1

Upon a Dead Man's Head

11 No man may him hide
From Death hollow-eyed, (l. 10–11)

12 With his worm-eaten maw,
And his ghastly jaw
Gasping aside,
Naked of hide,
Neither flesh nor fell. (l. 14–18)

HAP; SeCePo

KENNETH SLESSOR (1901–1971)

Five Bells

1 Time that is moved by little fidget wheels
Is not my Time, (l. 1–2)

2 Are you shouting at me, dead man, squeezing your face
In agonies of speech on speechless panes?
Cry louder, beat the windows, bawl your name!
(l. 20–22)

3 These funeral-cakes of sweet and sculptured stone.
(l. 96)

4 Where have you gone? The tide is over you,
The turn of midnight water's over you,
As Time is over you, and mystery,
And memory, the flood that does not flow. (l. 97–100)

5 And tried to hear your voice, but all I heard
Was a boat's whistle, and the scraping squeal
Of seabird's voices far away, and bells,
Five bells. Five bells coldly ringing out.
Five bells. (l. 124–128)

CBAP; PoAu-2; PoRA; SeCePo

CHRISTOPHER SMART (1722–1771)

Hymns for the Amusement of Children

1 Now's the time for mirth and play,
Saturday's an holiday;
Praise to heaven unceasing yield,
I've found a lark's nest in the field.

FaBoCh; FaBoCh; NOEC; OxBChV

Jubilate Agno

2 For I will consider my Cat Jeoffry.
  For he is the servant of the Living God, duly and daily
  serving him.
  For at the first glance of the glory of God in the East
  he worships in his way.
  For is this done by wreathing his body seven times
  round with elegant quickness.

3 For if he meets another cat he will kiss her in kindness.
  For when he takes his prey he plays with it to give it
  chance.

4 For in his morning orison she loves the sun and the sun
  loves him.

5 For he purrs in thankfulness, when God tell him he's a
  good Cat.
  For he is an instrument for the children to learn
  benevolence upon.

6 For every family had one cat at least in the bag.

7 For he is the cleanest in the use of his forepaws of any
  quadruped.
  For the dexterity of his defense is an instance of the
  love of God to him exceedingly.

8 For he is a mixture of gravity and waggery.
  For he knows that God is his Saviour.
  For there is nothing sweeter than his peace when at
  rest.

ChTr; CTC; FaBoCh; FM; HAP; HeIP; LiTB; NAEL-1;
NOEC; NoP; NU; OAEL-1; OBWVE; PoE; PoEL-3; PPP;
Prf; PrIm; RB; SCV; SeCePo; TTTS; WeW; WiR

A Song to David

9 Glorious the northern lights astream;
  Glorious the song, when God's the theme
  Glorious the thunder's roar:
  Glorious hosanna from the den;
  Glorious the catholic amen:
  Glorious the martyr's gore:

  Glorious — more glorious is the crown
  Of him that brought salvation down
  By meekness, called thy Son;
  Thou that stupendous truth believed,
  And now the matchless deed's achieved,
  Determined, Dared, and Done.

ChTr; EBEV; LaA; NAEL-1; NOBE; OAEL-1; OBWVE;
PoE PoEL-3; TrGrPo

LANGDON SMITH (1858–1908)

Evolution

1 When you were a tadpole and I was a fish
  In the Paleozoic time,
  And side by side, on the ebbing tide,

We sprawled through the ooze and slime,
Or skittered with many a caudal flip
Through the depths of the Cambrian fen,
My heart was rife with the joy of life,
For I loved you even then. (l. 1–8)

2 I was thewed like an Auroch bull,
  And tusked like the great Cave Bear;
  And you, my sweet, from head to feet,
  Were gowned in your glorious hair. (l. 49–52)

3 Our love is old, our lives are old,
  And death shall come amain:
  Should it come today, what man may say
  We shall not live again? (l. 93–96)

4 He sowed our spawn in the world's dim dawn,
  And I know that it shall not die; (l. 99–100)

5 Let us drink anew to the time when you
  Were a tadpole and I was a fish. (l. 111–112)

BeLS; BLPA; FaBoBe; FaFP

SAMUEL FRANCIS SMITH (1808–1895)

America

1 My country, 'tis of thee,
  Sweet land of liberty,
  Of thee I sing;
  Land where my fathers died,
  Land of the pilgrims' pride,
  From every mountain-side
  Let freedom ring! (l. 1–7)

2 Our fathers' God! to Thee,
  Author of liberty,
  To Thee we sing;
  Long may our land be bright
  With freedom's holy light;
  Protect us by thy might,
  Great God, our King! (l. 22–28)

AA; AiP; AnAmPo; FaBoBe; FaFP; FaPON; OPP; PoLF;
WBLP

STEVIE SMITH (1902–1971)

I Remember

1 It was my bridal night I remember,
  An old man of seventy-three
  I lay with my young bride in my arms,
  A girl with t.b. (l. 1–4)

BoLoP; BoWoP; FaBoWP; InPK; OxBC

Not Waving but Drowning

2 Oh, no no no, it was too cold always
(Still the dead one lay moaning)
I was much too far out all my life
And not waving but drowning. (l. 9–12)

FaBoWP; FF; GTBS-P; HAP; HeIP; MoP; NAEL-2;
NoAM; NOBE; NoP; OAEL-2; OxBTC; PoE; PPP; PrIm;
TEP; WeW

Our Bog is Dood

3 Our Bog is dood, our Bog is dood,
They lisped in accents mild,
But when I asked them to explain
They grew a little wild. (l. 1–4)

FaBoNo; NAEL-2; NBLV; PoE; WeW

Pretty

4 As Nature is always careless and indifferent
Who sees, who steps, means nothing and this is pretty.
(l. 27–28)

5 Cry pretty, pretty, pretty and you'll be able
Very soon not even to cry pretty
And so be delivered entirely from humanity
This is prettiest of all, it is very pretty. (l. 33–36)

NAEL-2; NoAM; NoP; TEP

The River God

6 I may be smelly and I may be old,
Rough in my pebbles, reedy in my pools,
But where my fish float by I bless their swimming
And I like the people to bathe in me, especially women.
(l. 1–4)

7 Hi yih, yippity-yap, merrily I flow,
O I may be an old foul river but I have plenty of go.
(l. 9–10)

BrRo; FaBoNo; FaBoTw; FaBoWP; PBWP

Thoughts about the Person from Porlock

8 Coleridge received the Person from Porlock
And ever after called him a curse,
Then why did he hurry to let him in?
He could have hid in the house. (l. 1–4)

9 I am hungry to be interrupted
For ever and ever amen
O Person from Porlock come quickly
And bring my thoughts to an end. (l. 34–37)

FaBoCo; NAEL-2; NoAM; NoP

WILLIAM JAY SMITH (b. 1918)

American Primitive

1 He hangs in the hall by his black cravat,
The ladies faint, and the children holler:
Only my Daddy could look like that,
And I love my Daddy like he loves his Dollar.
(l. 9–12)

DiL; FF; InPK; MoAmPo; NePoEA; OxBSP; TwCP

The Closing of the Rodeo

2 The lariat snaps; the cowboy rolls
His pack, and mounts and rides away.
Back to the land the cowboy goes. (l. 1–3)

AiP; ASP; GOA; NePoEA; SaC; SD; TwCP

Morels

3 Not ringed but rare, not gilled but polyp-like, having
sprung up overnight —

These mushrooms of the gods, resembling human
organs uprooted, rooted only on the air, (l. 12–13)

4 Tasting of the sweet damp woods and of the rain one
inch above the meadow:

It was like feasting upon air. (l. 29–31)

BoNaP; MAT; NYBP; RFM

WILLIAM DEWITT SNODGRASS
(b. 1926)

After Experience Taught Me

1 After experience taught me that all the ordinary
Surroundings of social life are futile and vain;
(l. 1–2)

2 You must call up every strength you own
And you can rip off the whole facial mask. (l. 23–24)

3 And you, whiner, who wastes your time
Dawdling over the remorseless earth,
What evil, what unspeakable crime
Have you made your life worth? (l. 27–30)

CAPP; CoAP; OBWP; PPP; TAP

April Inventory

4 The sleek, expensive girls I teach,
Younger and pinker every year,
Bloom gradually out of reach. (l. 8–10)

5 I haven't read one book about
A book or memorized one plot,
Or found a mind I did not doubt,
I learned one date. And then forgot.
And one by one the solid scholars
Get the degrees, the jobs, the dollars. (l. 25–30)

6 I taught myself to name my name,
To bark back, loosen love and crying;
To ease my woman so she came,
To ease an old man who was dying. (l. 37–40)

7 Though trees turn bare and girls turn wives,
We shall afford our costly seasons;
There is a gentleness survives
That will outspeak and has its reasons.
There is a loveliness exists,
Preserves us, not for specialists. (l. 55–60)

CAPP; CoAP; HAP; LiTM; NePoEA; NoAM; NoP; TAP;
TwCP

The Campus on the Hill

8 Up the reputable walks of old established trees
They stalk, children of the nouveaux riches; chimes
Of the tall Clock Tower drench their heads in blessing:
"I don't wanna play at your house;
I don't like you any more."
My house stands opposite, on the other hill, (l. 1–6)

9 Riot in Algeria, in Cyprus, in Alabama;
Aged in wrong, the empires are declining,
And China gathers, soundlessly, like evidence.
What shall I say to the young on such a morning? —
Mind is the one salvation? — also grammar? —
No; my little ones lean not toward revolt. (l. 20–25)

10 They wear their godhead lightly.
They look out from their hill and say,
To themselves, "We have nowhere to go but down;
The great destination is to stay." (l. 29–32)

AiP; LiTM; NIP; NoAM; TAP; TwCP

A Flat One

11 You seem to be all finished, so
We'll plug your old recalcitrant anus
And tie up your discouraged penis
In a great, snow-white bow of gauze, (l. 25–28)

12 — All this Dark Age machinery
On which we had tormented you
To life. (l. 49–51)

13 You still whispered you would not die.
Yet in the nights I heard you cry
Like a whipped child; (l. 86–88)

CAPP; LiTM; NePoEA-2; SM

Sorting out letters and piles of my old canceled checks

14 I happened to find
Your picture. That picture. I stopped there cold,
Like a man raking piles of dead leaves in his yard
Who has turned up a severed hand. (l. 3–6)

15 Before we drained out one another's force
With lies, self-denial, unspoken regret
And the sick eyes that blame; before the divorce
And the treachery. (l. 19–22)

FF; HeIP; MoAmPo; NePoEA-2; UnPo

Sweet beast, I have gone prowling

16 in darkness and in hedges
I sang my sour tone
and all my love was howling
conspicuously alone. (l. 5–8)

LLLT; MoAmPo; NYBP; SM

GARY SNYDER (b. 1930)

Above Pate Valley

1 Hands and knees
Pushing the Bear grass, thousands
Of arrowhead leavings over a
Hundred yards. (l. 16–19)

2 They came to camp. On their
Own trails I followed my own
Trail here. Picked up the cold-drill,
Pick, singlejack, and sack
Of dynamite
Ten thousand years. (l. 23–28)

CoAP; LCAP; NaP; NoP

The Bath

3 He stands in warm water
Soap all over the smooth of his thigh and stomach
"Gary don't soap my hair!"
— his eye-sting fear — (l. 8–11)

4 The sucking milk from this our body sends through
jolts of light; the son, the father,
sharing mother's joy
That brings a softness to the flower of the awesome
open curling lotus gate I cup and kiss (l. 46–50)

5 Kai's little scrotum up close to his groin,
the seed still tucked away, that moved from us to him
(l. 55–56)

6 Or me within her,
Or him emerging,
this is our body: (l. 60–62)

7 These boys who love their mother
who loves men, who passes on
her sons to other women;

The cloud across the sky. The windy pines.
the trickle gurgle in the swampy meadow

this is our body. (l. 72–77)

8 This is our body. Drawn up crosslegged by the flames
drinking icy water
hugging babies, kissing bellies,

Laughing on the Great Earth

Come out from the bath. (l. 87–91)

CAPP; DiL; NNaP; TAP

FOUR POEMS FOR ROBIN (the following 4 poems)

An Autumn Morning in Shokoku-ji

9 Bitter memory like vomit
Choked my throat. (l. 3–4)

10 In dream you appeared
(Three times in nine years)
Wild, cold, and accusing.
I woke shamed and angry:
The pointless wars of the heart. (l. 8–12)

HAP; MoP; NNaP; NoAM; NOBA; NoP; SOTW; SOTW;
VGW

December at Yase

11 Only in dream, like this dawn,
Does the grave, awed intensity
Of our young love
Return to my mind, to my flesh. (l. 17–20)

12 I feel ancient, as though I had
Lived many lives.
And may never now know
If I am a fool
Or have done what my karma demands. (l. 24–28)

MoP; NNaP; NoAM; NoAM; NOBA; NoP; SOTW

Siwashing It Out Once

13 sometimes sleeping in the open
I think backwhen I had you. (l. 15–16)

MoP; NNaP; NoAM; NOBA; NoP; SOTW

A Spring Night in Shokoku-ji

14 I remember your cool body
Naked under a summer cotton dress. (l. 9–10)

MoP; NNaP; NoAM; NOBA; NoP; SOTW; VGW

I Went into the Maverick Bar

15 My long hair was tucked up under a cap
I'd left the earring in the car. (l. 5–6)

16 I recalled when I worked in the woods
and the bars of Madras, Oregon.
That short-haired joy and roughness —
America — your stupidity.
I could almost love you again. (l. 17–21)

17 I came back to myself,
To the real work, to
"What is to be done." (l. 25–27)

CAPP; HCAP; MAT; NAAL-2; PoE

Mid-August at Sourdough Mountain Lookout

18 I cannot remember things I once read
A few friends, but they are in cities.
Drinking cold snow-water from a tin cup
Looking down for miles
Through high still air. (l. 6–10)

HAP; InPK; MAT; NaP; NoP; TAP

Milton by Firelight

19 What use Milton, a silly story
Of our lost general parents,
eaters of fruit? (l. 10–12)

20 In ten thousand years the Sierras
Will be dry and dead, home of the scorpion. (l. 22–23)

21 No paradise, no fall,
Only the weathering land
The wheeling sky,
Man, with is Satan
Scouring the chaos of the mind.
Oh Hell! (l. 25–30)

CAPP; CoAP; InPS; NAAL-2; PPP

MYTHS AND TEXTS (the following 3 poems)

Burning

22 He will not go,
But wait through fish scale, shale dust, bone
of hawk and marmot,
caught leaves in ice,
Til flung on a new net of atoms: (l. 9–13)

23 Your empty happy body
Swarming in the light (l. 16–17)

24 Bodhidharma sailing the Yangtze on a reed
Lenin in a sealed train through Germany
Hsuan Tsang, crossing the Pamirs
Joseph, Crazy Horse, living the last free
starving high-country winter of their tribes.
Surrender into freedom revolt into slavery —
(l. 17–22)

25 If, after obtaining Buddhahood, anyone in my land
gets tossed in jail on a vagrancy rap, may I
not attain highest perfect enlightenment. (l. 1–3)

26 Poetry a riprap on the slick rock of metaphysics (l. 9)

27 riding flatcars to Fresno,
Across the whole country
Steep towns, flat towns, even New York,
And oceans and Europe & libraries & galleries
And the factories they make rubbers in (l. 15–19)

28 Blotting the sun
Stinging the eyes.
The hot seeds steam underground
still alive. (l. 40–43)

29 Rain falls for centuries
Soaking the loose rocks in space
Sweet rain, the fire's out
The black snag glistens in the rain
& the last wisp of smoke floats up (l. 24–28)

30 Black pit cold and light-year
Flame tongue of the dragon
Licks the sun

The sun is but a morning star (l. 33–36)

NeAP; PoM

Hunting

31 The white gulls south of Victoria
catch tossed crumbs in midair.
When anyone hears the Catbird
he gets lonesome. (l. 9–12)

32 subtle birds
Wheel and go, leaving air in shreds
black beaks shine in gray haze.
Brushed by the hawk's wing
of vision. (l. 21–25)

33 Raven
on a roost of furs
No bird in a bird-book,
black as the sun. (l. 35–38)

34 — I think I'll go hunt bears.
"hunt bears?
Why shit Snyder,
You couldn't hit a bear in the ass
with a handful of rice!" (l. 51–55)

35 All beaded with dew
dawn grass runway
Open-eyed rabbits hang
dangle, loose feet in tall grass
From alder snares. (l. 1–5)

36 Our girls get layed by Coyote
We get along
just fine.
The Shuswap tribe. (l. 24–27)

37 Stiff springy jumps down the snowfields
Head held back, forefeet out,
Balls tight in a tough hair sack (l. 19–21)

38 How rare to be born a human being!
Wash him off with cedar-bark and milkweed
send the damned doctors home.
Baby, baby, noble baby,
Noble-hearted baby (l. 1–5)

39 Wearing a spotted fawnskin
sleeping under trees
bacchantes, drunk
On wine or truth, what you will,
Meaning: compassion. (l. 22–25)

40 beasts
Got the buddha-nature
All but
Coyote. (l. 26–29)

Logging

41 But it's hard to farm
Between the stumps:
The cows get thin, the milk tastes funny,
The kids grow up and go to college
They don't come back
the little fir-trees do (l. 20–25)

42 Again the ancient, meaningless
Abstractions of the educated mind. (l. 1–2)

43 a big picture of K. Marx with an axe,
"Where I cut off one it will never grow again."
O Karl would it were true
I'd put my saw to work for you
& the wicked social tree would fall right down.
(l. 21–25)

44 Each dawn is clear
Cold air bites the throat.
Thick frost on the pine bough
Leaps from the tree
snapped by the diesel (l. 1–5)

45 Bulldozed by Luther and Weyerhaeuser
Crosscut and chainsaw
squareheads and finns
high-lead and cat-skidding
Trees down
Creeks choked, trout killed, roads. (l. 13–18)

46 Lodgepole
coneseed waits for fire
And then thin forests of silver-grey.
in the void
a pine cone falls (l. 1–5)

47 so you and I must wait
Until the next blaze
Of the world, the universe,
Millions of worlds, burning
—oh let it lie. (l. 12–16)

48 Pa-ta Shan-jen
(A painter who watched Ming fall)
lived in a tree:
"The brush
May paint the mountains and streams
Though the territory is lost." (l. 26–31)

Piute Creek

49 All the junk that goes with being human
Drops away, hard rock wavers
Even the heavy present seems to fail
This bubble of a heart. (l. 12–15)

50 A clear, attentive mind
Has no meaning but that
Which sees is truly seen.
No one loves rock, yet we are here. (l. 19–22)

CoAP; NAAL-2; NaP; NOBA

Riprap

51 These poems, people,
lost ponies with
Dragging saddles —
and rocky sure-foot trails. (l. 11–14)

52 each rock a word
a creek-washed stone
Granite: ingrained
with torment of fire and weight (l. 19–22)

CAPP; HCAP; NAAL-2; NeAP; NoAM; NOBA; PoM

CHARLES HAMILTON SORLEY (1895–1915)

All the Hills and Vales Along

1 All the hills and vales along
Earth is bursting into song,
And the singers are the chaps

Who are going to die perhaps. (l. 1–4)

2 Earth that bore with joyful ease
Hemlock for Socrates,
Earth that blossomed and was glad
'Neath the cross that Christ had,
Shall rejoice and blossom too
When the bullet reaches you. (l. 21–26)

3 Strew your gladness on earth's bed,
So be merry, so be dead. (l. 43–44)

EBEV; FaBoCh; MMA; MoBrPo; OBWP

WILLIAM SOUTAR (1898–1943)

The Tryst

1 Sae luely, luely, cam she in
Saie luely was she gaen;
And wi' her a' my simmer days
Like they had never been. (l. 13–16)

BoLoP; EBEV; ErPo; GoTS; OxBS

ROBERT SOUTHEY (1774–1843)

The Battle of Blenheim

1 And everybody praised the Duke
Who such a fight did win. —
But what good came of it at last?
Quoth little Peterkin. —
Why that I cannot tell, said he,
But 'twas a famous victory. (l. 61–66)

BeLS; EnRP; FaBoPV; FaBV; FaPoR; FPL; GN; GTBS;
GTBS-P; OBNC; OBWP; PoLF; TrGrPo; WBLP

God's Judgment on a Wicked Bishop

2 Then when he saw it could hold no more,
Bishop Hatto, he made fast the door;
And while for mercy on Christ they call,
He set fire to the barn and burnt them all. (l. 17–20)

3 They have whetted their teeth against the stones,
And now they pick the Bishop's bones;
They gnawed the flesh from every limb,
For they were sent to do judgement on him!
(l. 73–76)

ChTr; EnRP; OBNV; OnMSP

The Inchcape Rock

4 No stir in the air, no stir in the sea,
The ship was still as she could be; (l. 1–2)

5 When the rock was hid by the surges' swell,
The mariners heard the warning bell,
And then they knew the perilous rock,
And bless'd the Abbot of Aberbrothok. (l. 13–16)

6 One dreadful sound could the Rover hear,
A sound as if, with the Inchcape Bell,
The Devil below was ringing his knell. (l. 74–76)

BeLS; ChTr; FaBoBe; GN; OBNV

The Old Man's Comforts and How He Gained Them

7 "You are old, Father William," the young man cried,
"And life must be hastening away;
You are cheerful, and love to converse upon death:
Now tell me the reason, I pray.'

"I am cheerful, young man," Father William replied;
"Let the cause thy attention engage;
In the days of my youth I remembered my God,
And He hath not forgotten my age." (l. 17–24)

HoPM; OxBChV; Par; UnPo

To a Goose

8 Departed Goose! I neither know nor care.
But this I know, that we pronounced thee fine,
Seasoned with sage and onions, and port wine.

BXAP; FM; NOBL; Son

ROBERT SOUTHWELL (1561?–1595)

The Burning Babe

1 As in hoary winter's night stood shivering in the snow,
Surprised I was with sudden heat which made my
  heart to glow;
And lifting up a fearful eye to view what fire was near,
A pretty Babe all burning bright did in the air appear;
                                                    (l. 1–4)

2 'Alas!' quoth he, 'but newly born in fiery heats I fry,
Yet none approach to warm their hearts or feel my fire
  but I.
My faultless breast the furnace is, the fuel wounding
  thorns;
Love is the fire, and sighs the smoke, the ashes shame
  and scorns;

The fuel justice layeth on, and mercy blows the coals;
The metal in this furnace wrought are men's defiled
  souls; (l. 7–12)

ACP; CH; ElL; FaBoCh; HAP; HeIP; InPS; LiTB; MePo;
NAEL-1; NAs; NOBE; NOCV; NoP; OAEL-1; OBCP;
OBEV; OBSC; PoEL-2; Prf; RB; SeCePo; TOF; TrCP;
TrGrPo

New Heaven, New War

3 Within his crib is surest ward,
This little babe will be thy guard,
If thou wilt foil thy foes with joy,
Then flit not from this heavenly boy. (l. 45–48)

MePo; NOBE; NoP; OBSC

New Prince, New Pomp

4 Behold, a silly, tender babe
In freezing winter night,
In homely manger trembling lies:
Alas, a piteous sight. (l. 1–4)

5 This stable is a Prince's court.
This crib His chair of state;
The beasts are parcel of His pomp.
The wooden dish His plate. (l. 17–20)

6 Do homage to thy King,
And highly praise His humble pomp
Which He from Heaven doth bring. (l. 26–28)

ELP; GN; NOBE; NOCV; OBSC; OHIP; TrCP

Times Go by Turns

7 The lopped tree in time may grow again,
Most naked plants renew both fruit and flower;
                                                    (l. 1–2)

8 Times go by turns, and chances change by course,
From foul to fair, from better hap to worse.

The sea of Fortune doth not ever flow,
She draws her favours to the lowest ebb;
Her tides have equal times to come and go,
Her loom doth weave the fine and Coarsest web;
                                                    (l. 5–10)

ACP; ElL; LiTB; OBSC; PoEL-2

Upon the Image of Death

9 I often look upon a face
Most ugly, grisly, bare and thin;
I often view the hollow place,
Where eyes and nose had sometimes been; (l. 7–10)

10 'Remember, man, that thou art dust!'
But yet, alas, but seldom I
Do think indeed that I must die . . . (l. 16–18)

11 Not Solomon, for all his wit,
Nor Samson, though he were so strong,
No king nor person ever yet
Could 'scape, but death laid him along: (l. 37–40)

12 Though all the East did quake to hear
Of Alexander's dreadful name,
And all the West likewise did fear
To hear of Julius Caesar's fame, (l. 43–46)

13 grant me grace, O god, that I
My life may mend, sith I must die. (l. 53–54)

CH; ElL; NOBE; OBD; OBSC

ANNE SPENCER (1882–1975)

At the Carnival

1 Guilt pins a fig-leaf; Innocence is its own adorning.
(l. 12)

2 Here the sausage and garlic booth
Sent unholy incense skyward;
There a quivering female-thing
Gestured assignations, and lied
To call it dancing; (l. 23–27)

3 I have seen the queer in queer places,
But never before a heaven-fed
Naiad of the Carnival-Tank! (l. 43–45)

BANP; BlSi; CDC; PoNe

Letter to My Sister

4 It is dangerous for a woman to defy the gods;
To taunt them with the tongue's thin tip,
Or strut in the weakness of mere humanity,
Or draw a line daring them to cross; (l. 1–4)

AmNP; BlSi; PoBA; PoNe

BERNARD SPENCER (1909–1963)

Part of Plenty

1 Whether in the bringing of the flowers or the food
She offers plenty, and is part of plenty,
And whether I see her stooping, or leaning with the
flowers,

What she does is ages old, and she is not simply,
No, but lovely in that way. (l. 17–21)

ErPo; GBL; LiTB; LiTM

STEPHEN SPENDER (b. 1909)

An Elementary School Classroom in a Slum

1 Far far from gusty waves, these children's faces.
Like rootless weeds the torn hair round their paleness.
(l. 1–2)

2 Surely Shakespeare is wicked, the map a bad example
With ships and sun and love tempting them to steal —
(l. 17–18)

3 On their slag heap, these children
Wear skins peeped through by bones and spectacles of
steel
With mended glass, like bottle bits in slag. (l. 20–22)

4 Unless, governor, teacher inspector, visitor,
This map becomes their window and these windows
That open on their lives like crouching tombs
Break, O break open, (l. 25–28)

FaBoMo; FF; LiTB; MoAB; MoBrPo; NIP; TrGrPo;
TwCP; UnPo

The Express

5 After the first powerful plain manifesto
The black statement of pistons, without more fuss
But gliding like a queen, she leaves the station.
(l. 1–3)

6 She passes the houses which humbly crowd outside,
The gasworks and at last the heavy page
Of death, printed by gravestones in the cemetery.
(l. 5–7)

7 Ah, like a comet through flame she moves entranced
Wrapt in her music no bird song, no, nor bough
Breaking with honey buds, shall ever equal. (l. 25–27)

CMoP; GoJo; HeIP; LiTM; MoAB; MoBrPo; MoP; NoAM;
TwCP

The Funeral

8 Death is another milestone on their way.
With laughter on their lips and with winds blowing
round them
They record simply
How this one excelled all others in making driving
belts. (l. 1–4)

9 They think how one life hums, revolves and toils,
One cog in a golden singing hive: (l. 13–14)

10 The decline of a culture
Mourned by scholars who dream of the ghosts of Greek
boys. (l. 19–20)

CMoP; MoAB; MoBrPo; NoAM

I Think Continually of Those Who Were Truly Great

11 I think continually of those who were truly great.
Who, from the womb, remembered the soul's history
Through corridors of light where the hours are suns,
Endless and singing. (l. 1–4)

12 The names of those who in their lives fought for life,
Who wore at their hearts the fire's centre.
Born of the sun they traveled a short while towards the
sun,
And left the vivid air signed with their honour.
(l. 22–26)

ChTr; CMoP; EaLo; HAP; HeIP; LiTB; LiTM; MoAB;
MoBrPo; NOBE; NoP; OAEL-2; OxBTC; PoRA; TrGrPo;
WaP

The Landscape near an Aerodrome

13 More beautiful and soft than any moth
With turring furred antennae feeling its huge path
Through dusk, the air liner with shut-off engines
Glides over suburbs (l. 1–4)

14 they hear the tolling bell
Reaching across the landscape of hysteria, (l. 27–28)

15 Religion stands, the Church blocking the sun. (l. 31)

LiTM; MoAB; MoBrPo; NoAM; OxBTC

Not Palaces

16 I say, stamping the words with emphasis,
Drink from here energy and only energy, (l. 8–9)

17 Eye, gazelle, delicate wanderer,
Drinker of horizon's fluid line;
Ear that suspends on a chord
The spirit drinking timelessness;
Touch, love, all senses; (l. 12–16)

18 No one
Shall hunger: Man shall spend equally.
Our goal which we compel: Man shall be man.
(l. 23–25)

19 Death to the killers, bringing light to life. (l. 32)

CMoP; FaBcMo; LiTB; LiTM; MoAB; MoBrPo; NoAM;
NoP; WaP

Ultima Ratio Regum

20 Consider his life which was valueless
In terms of employment, hotel ledgers, news files.
Consider. One bullet in ten thousand kills a man.
Ask. Was so much expenditure justified
On the death of one so young and so silly
Lying under the olive tree, O world, O death?
(l. 19–24)

CMoP; FaFP; LiTB; LiTM; OAEL-2; OBWP; SeCePo;
WaaP; WaP

What I Expected Was

21 What I had not foreseen
Was the gradual day
Weakening the will
Leaking the brightness away, (l. 9–12)

22 For I had expected always
Some brightness to hold in trust,
Some final innocence
To save from dust; (l. 25–28)

MoAB; MoBrPo; NoAM; NOBE

EDMUND SPENSER ("COLIN CLOUT")
(1552?–1599)

AMORETTI (the following 12 poems)

I. Happy ye leaves!

1 Happy ye leaves! whenas those lily hands,
Which hold my life in their dead-doing might,
Shall handle you, and hold in love's soft bands,
(l. 1–3)

2 And happy lines! on which, with starry light,
Those lamping eyes will deign sometimes to look,
(l. 5–6)

3 Leaves, lines, and rhymes, seek her to please alone,
Whom if ye please, I care for other none! (l. 13–14)

AAS; EBEV; NAEL-1; OAEL-1; PoE; Son

VIII. More than most fair

4 More than most fair, full of the living fire,
Kindled above unto the Maker near; (l. 1–2)

5 But angels come to lead frail minds to rest
In chaste desires, on heavenly beauty bound.
You frame my thoughts, and fashion me within;
You stop my tongue, and teach my heart to speak;
(l. 7–10)

6 Dark is the world, where your light shined never;
Well is he born, that may behold you ever. (l. 13–14)

AAS; NoP; PoE; Son; TEP; TrGrPo

XV. *Ye tradeful merchants*

7 Ye tradeful Merchants, that, with weary toil,
Do seek most precious things to make your gain,
And both the Indias of their treasure spoil, (l. 1–3)

8 But that which fairest is but few behold:
Her mind, adorned with virtues manifold. (l. 13–14)

AAS; HeIP; LiTB; NIP; OAEL-1; Son; TrGrPo

XXX. *My love is like to ice*

9 My Love is like to ice, and I to fire:
How comes it then that this her cold so great
Is not dissolved through my so hot desire,
But harder grows the more I her entreat? (l. 1–4)

10 Such is the power of love in gentle mind,
That it can alter all the course of kind. (l. 13–14)

AAS; ErPo; FF; FPL; LiTB; TrGrPo

XXXVII. *What guyle is this*

11 What guyle is this, that those her golden tresses,
She doth attyre under a net of gold: (l. 1–2)

12 Is it that mens frayle eyes, which gaze too bold,
She may entangle in that golden snare: (l. 5–6)

13 Fondnesse it were for any being free,
To covet fetters, though they golden bee. (l. 13–14)

AAS; NAEL-1; NoP; OBSC; Son; TrGrPo

LXIV. *Coming to kiss her lips*

14 Coming to kiss her lips, (such grace I found,)
Meseem'd, I smelt a garden of sweet flowers, (l. 1–2)

15 Such fragrant flowers do give most odorous smell;
But her sweet odour did them all excel. (l. 13–14)

AAS; EBEV; NAEL-1; OAEL-1; Son

LXVII. *Lyke as a huntsman*

16 Lyke as a huntsman after weary chace,
Seeing the game from him escapt away,
Sits downe to rest him in some shady place, (l. 1–3)

17 Strange thing me seemd to see a beast so wyld,
So goodly wonne with her owne will beguyld.
(l. 13–14)

AAS; GBL; HeIP; NAEL-1; NoP; PoE; PoEL-1; SeCePo;
Son; TrGrPo

LXVIII. *Most glorious Lord of life!*

18 Most glorious Lord of life! that, on this day,
Didst make thy triumph over death and sin;
And, having harrowed hell, didst bring away
Captivity thence captive, us to win: (l. 1–4)

19 So let us love, dear Love, like as we ought;
Love is the lesson which the Lord us taught.
(l. 13–14)

AAS; ElL; HAP; InPS; LiTB; NAEL-1; NOBE; NOCV;
NoP; OBEV; OHIP; PoE; Son; TrPWD

LXX. *Fresh Spring*

20 Fresh Spring, the herald of love's mighty king, (l. 1)

21 All sorts of flowers the which on earth do spring
In goodly colours gloriously arrayed;
Go to my love, where she is careless laid, (l. 3–4)

22 Make haste therefore, sweet love, whilst it is prime,
For none can call again the passed time. (l. 13–14)

AAS; AWP; ChTr; ElL; FF; HAP; InPS; LiTB; NoP;
OBEV; OBSC; PoE; Son

LXXV. *One day I wrote her name upon the strand*

23 One day I wrote her name upon the strand;
But came the waves, and washed it away:
Again, I wrote it with a second hand;
But came the tide, and made my pains his prey.
(l. 1–4)

24 My verse your virtues rare shall eternize,
And in the heavens write your glorious name.
Where, whenas death shall all the world subdue,
Our love shall live, and later life renew. (l. 11–14)

AAS; AWP; BLPL; BoLoP; EBEV; ElL; FiP; GBL; HAP;
HeIP; InPS; LiTB; NAEL-1; NoP; OAEL-1; PoE; SeCePo;
Son; WeW

LXXIX. *Men call you fair*

25 Men call you fair, and you do credit it,
For that yourself ye daily such do see:
But the true fair, that is the gentle wit
And virtuous mind, is much more praised of me:
(l. 1–4)

26 He only fair, and what he fair hath made;
All other fair, like flowers, untimely fade. (l. 13–14)

AAS; AWP; BLPL; FaBoBe; NAEL-1; NoP; Son

LXXXIX. *Like as the culver*

27 Like as the culver on the bared bough
Sits mourning for the absence of her mate, (l. 1–2)

28 Dark is my day whiles her fair light I miss,
And dead my life, that wants such lively bliss.
(l. 13–14)

AAS; FF; GBL; PBBP; PoE

Epithalamion

29 Ye learned sisters which have oftentimes
Beene to me ayding, others to adorne:
Whom ye thought worthy of your gracefull rymes,
That even the greatest did not greatly scorne
To heare theyr names sung in your simple layes,
(l. 1–5)

30 So Orpheus did for his owne bride,
So I unto my selfe alone will sing
The woods shall to me answer and my Eccho ring.
(l. 16–18)

AAS; BoLoP; ElL; InPS; NOBE; NoP; OAEL-1; OBEV;
OBSC; PoEL-1; TEP

The Faerie Queene

31 Eftsoones they heard a most melodious sound,
Of all that mote delight a daintie eare,

32 For all that pleasing is to living eare,
Was there consorted in one harmonee,
Birdes, voyces, instruments, windes, waters, all agree.

33 'So passeth, in the passing of a day,
Of mortall life the leafe, the bud, the flowre,

34 Gather therefore the Rose, whilest yet is prime,
For soone comes age, that will her pride deflowre:
Gather the Rose of love, whilest yet is time,
Whilest loving thou mayst loved be with equall crime.'

PoEL-1

Iambicum Trimetrum

35 Unhappie Verse, the witnesse of my unhappie state,
Make thy selfe fluttring wings of thy fast flying
Thought, (l. 1–3)

36 Whether lying reastlesse in heavy bedde, or else
Sitting so cheerelesse at the cheerfull boorde, or else
Playing alone carelesse on hir heavenlie virginals.
(l. 4–6)

37 Waking love suffereth no sleepe:
Say, that raging love dothe appall the weake stomacke:
Say, that lamenting love marreth the musicall.
(l. 10–12)

BoLoP; EBEV; ElL; OBEV; OPOP; OxBoLi; PoEL-1

Prothalamion

38 Sweet breathing Zephyrus did softly play,
A gentle spirit, that lightly did delay
Hot Titan's beams, which then did glister fair; (l. 2–4)

39 Walked forth to ease my pain
Along the shore of silver streaming Thames,
Whose rutty bank, the which his river hems,
Was painted all with variable flowers, (l. 10–13)

40 Sweet Thames, run softly, till I end my song. (l. 18)

41 The snow, which doth the top of Pindus strew,
Did never whiter shew,
Nor Jove himself, when he a swan would be
For love of Leda, whiter did appear: (l. 40–43)

42 Eftsoones the Nymphes, which now had Flowers their
fill,
Ran all in haste, to see that silver brood,
As they came floating on the Christal Flood, (l. 55–57)

43 Joy may you have and gentle hearts content
Of your loves couplement:
And let faire Venus, that is Queene of love,
With her heart-quelling Sonne upon you smile,
(l. 94–97)

44 So forth those joyous Birdes did passe along,
Adowne the Lee, that to them murmurde low,
As he would speake, but that he lackt a tong,
(l. 114–116)

45 At length they all to merry London came,
To merry London, my most kindly nurse,
That to me gave this life's first native source;
Though from another place I take my name,
An house of ancient fame. (l. 127–131)

46 Yet therein now doth lodge a noble peer,
Great England's glory and the world's wide wonder,
Whose dreadful name late through all Spain did
thunder, (l. 145–147)

47 That through thy prowess and victorious arms,
Thy country may be freed from foreign harms;
And great Elisa's glorious name may ring
Through all the world (l. 155–158)

AAS; AWP; ChTr; EBEV; ElL; FaBoPP; GTBS; GTBS-P;
HAP; LiTB; Mes; NoP; OBEV; OBSC; PPP; SeCePo

The Shepheardes Calender

48 good Hobbinoll, what garres thee greete?
What! hath some wolfe thy tender lambes ytorne?
Or is thy bagpype broke, that soundes so sweete?
Or art thou of thy loved lasse forlorne? (l. 1–4)

49 Shepheards delights he dooth them all forsweare,
Hys pleasaunt pipe, whych made us meriment,
He wylfully hath broke, and doth forbeare,
His wonted songs, wherein he all outwent. (l. 13–16)

50 Contented I: then will I singe his laye
Of fayre Elisa,queene of shepheardes all; (l. 33–34)

51 "Ye dayntye Nymphs, that in this blessed brooke
Doe bathe your brest,
Forsake you watry bowres, (l. 37–39)

52 eke you Virgins that on Parnasse dwell,
Whence floweth Helicon, the learned well,
Helpe me to blaze
Her worthy praise (l. 41–44)

53 "Of fayre Elisa be your silver song,
That blessed wight:
The flowre of virgins, may shee florish long
In princely plight. (l. 46–49)

54 No mortall blemishe may her blotte. (l. 54)

55 "I sawe Phœbus thrust out his golden hedde,
Upon her to gaze:
But when he sawe how broade her beames did spredde
It did him amaze. (l. 73–76)

56 "Lo, how finely the Graces can it foote
To the instrument:
They dauncen deffly, and singen soote,
In their meriment.
Wants not a fourth Grace, to make the daunce even?
(l. 109–113)

57 "Bring hether the pincke and purple cullambine,
With gelliflowres;
Bring coronations, and sops in wine,
Worne of paramoures;
Strowe me the ground with daffadowndillies,
(l. 136–140)

NAEL-1; OBEV; OBSC; PoEL-1

SIR JOHN COLLINGS SQUIRE ("SOLOMON EAGLE") (1884–1958)

There was an Indian, who had known no change

1 Columbus's doom-burdened caravels
Slant to the shore, and all their seamen land.
(l. 13–14)

AmFN; CH; FaPON; OFD

WILLIAM STAFFORD (1914–1941)

At the Bomb Testing Site

1 At noon in the desert a panting lizard
waited for history, its elbows tense,
watching the curve of a particular road
as if something might happen. (l. 1–4)

CAPP; CoAP; LiTM; NoAM; NoP; OBWP; RB

Traveling through the Dark

2 a doe, a recent killing;
she had stiffened already, almost cold.
I dragged her off she was large in the belly. (l. 6–8)

3 around our group I could hear the wilderness listen.
(l. 16)

CAPP; CoAP; GrPl; HAP; HeIP; InPK; LCAP; LiTM; NIP;
NoAM; NoP; SM; SoSe; WeW

THOMAS STANLEY (1625–1678)

La Belle Confidente

1 Learn by our friendship to create
An immaterial fire, (l. 5–6)

2 For when we must resign our vital breath,
Our Loves by Fate benighted,
We by this friendship shall survive in death,
Even in divorce united.
Weak Love through fortune or distrust
In time forgets to burn,
But this pursues us to the Urn,
And marries either's Dust. (l. 17–21)

JCP; MeLP; MePo; OBS

Quickness

3 Thou art a toilsome mole, or less,
A moving mist;
But life is what none can express,
A quickness which my God hath kissed. (l. 17–20)

ELP; MeLP; MePo; NOBE; NOCV; OBS; SeCePo; SeCP;
SeCV-1

FRANK LEBBY STANTON (1857–1927)

Keep a-Goin'

1 See the wild birds on the wing,
Hear the bells that sweetly ring,
When you feel like singin', sing —
Keep a-goin'! (l. 23–26)

FaFP; OHFP; PWR; WBLP

JAMES KENNETH STEPHEN
(1859–1892)

Sincere Flattery of R. B.

1 Birthdays? yes, in a general way;
For the most if not for the best of men:
You were born (I suppose) on a certain day:
So was I: or perhaps in the night: what then? (l. 1–4)

FaBoPa; NOBL; Par

To R. K.

2 Will there never come a season
Which shall rid us from the curse
Of a prose which knows no reason
And an unmelodious verse: (l. 1–4)

BXAP; CenHV; FaBoCo; FaBoEE; FaBoPa; NBLV;
NOBL; Par

Two voices are there: one is of the deep

3 Two voices are there: one is of the deep;
It learns the storm-cloud's thunderous melody, (l. 1–2)

4 And one is of an old half-witted sheep
Which bleats articulate monotony, (l. 5–6)

5 And, Wordsworth, both are thine: at certain times
Forth from the heart of thy melodious rhymes.
(l. 9–10)

6 Quite unacquainted with the ABC
Than write such hopeless rubbish as thy worst.
(l. 13–14)

BXAP; CenHV; FaBoCo; FaBoPa; FiBHP; NOBL; Par

JAMES STEPHENS (1882–1950)

Deirdre

1 The time comes when our hearts sink utterly;
When we remember Deirdre and her tale,
And that her lips are dust. (l. 4–6)

2 More than a thousand years it is since she
Was beautiful: she trod the living grass;
She saw the clouds. (l. 10–12)

AWP; CMoP; OBMV; PoRA

A Glass of Beer

3 The lanky hank of a she in the inn over there
Nearly killed me for asking the loan of a glass of beer;
May the devil grip the whey-faced slut by the hair
And beat bad manners out of her skin for a year.
(l. 1–4)

4 If I asked her master he'd give me a cask a day;
But she, with the beer at hand, not a gill would
arrange!
May she marry a ghost and bear him a kitten, and may
The High King of Glory permit her to get the mange.
(l. 9–12)

CMoP; FaBoCo; FiBHP; InPK; MoAB; MoBrPo; MoP;
NBLV; OBMV; OxBS; OxBTC; RB; SeCePo; TW

The Goat Paths

5 Crouching down where nothing stirs
In the silence of the furze,
Crouching down again to brood
In the sunny solitude. (l. 21–24)

6 I would think until I found
Something I can never find,
Something lying on the ground,
In the bottom of my mind. (l. 42–45)

AWP; CH; GoJo; LiTB; UnPo

Little Things

7 As we forgive those done to us,
— The lamb, the linnet, and the hare —

Forgive us all our trespasses,
Little creatures, everywhere! (l. 7–10)

EaLo; FaPON; GoJo; MoBrPo; PDV; PoRA; RHPC; TSS

The Main-Deep

8 The long, rolling,
Steady-pouring,
Deep-trenched
Green billow: (l. 1–4)

MoBrPo; MOS; OBMV; RR; UnPo

The Rivals

9 I was singing at the time,
Just as prettily as he! (l. 11–12)

BoTP; FaPON; InvP; OBEV; OBMV

The Shell

10 straightway like a bell
Came low and clear
The slow, sad murmur of the distant seas, (l. 4–6)

BoNaP; BoTP; CH; CMoP; MoAB; MoBrPo; MoShBr;
MOS

The Snare

11 And I cannot find the place
Where his paw is the snare!
Little One! Oh, Little One!
I am searching everywhere! (l. 13–16)

BoTP; CH; CMoP; PDV

To the Four Courts, Please

12 God help the horse, and the driver too!
And the people and beasts who have never a friend!
For the driver easily might have been you,
And the horse be me by a different end!
And nobody knows how their days will cease!
And the poor, when they're old, have little of peace!
(l. 13–18)

BIrV; MoAB; MoBrPo; UnPo

What Thomas an Buile Said in a Pub

13 I saw God! Do you doubt it?
Do you dare to doubt it?
I saw the Almighty Man! His hand
Was resting on a mountain! (l. 1–4)

CMoP; MoAB; MoBrPo; MoP; NoAM; PoRA; TrGrPo;
WGRP

The Wind

14 And said he'd kill, and kill, and kill;
And so he will! And so he will! (l. 5–6)

AnIL; BoNaP; HeIP; InPK; MoP; NoAM

WALLACE STEVENS (1879–1955)

Anecdote of the Jar

1 I placed a jar in Tennessee,
And round it was, upon a hill.
It made the slovenly wilderness
Surround that hill. (l. 1–4)

AmPP; CMoP; HCAP; HeIP; HoPM; InPK; LiTA; MoAB;
MoAmPo; MoP; NAAL-2; NAWM-2; NIP; NoAM; NOBA;
NoP; OxBA; OxBSP; PoA; PPP; PrIm; SOTW; TAP;
UnPo

Bantams in Pine-Woods

2 Chieftain Iffucan of Azcan in caftan
Of tan with henna hackles, halt!

Damned universal cock, as if the sun
Was blackamoor to bear your blazing tail. (l. 1–4)

CMoP; InPS; NoAM; NOBA; OxBA; UnPo

The Death of a Soldier

3 Life contracts and death is expected,
As in a season of autumn.
The soldier falls. (l. 1–3)

OBWP; OFD; OxBSP; QFR

Disillusionment of Ten o'Clock

4 The houses are haunted
By white night-gowns. (l. 1–2)

5 Only, here and there, an old sailor,
Drunk and asleep in his boots,
Catches tigers
In red weather. (l. 12–15)

AnAmPo; CMoP; FF; InPS; NAAL-2; NoAM; OxBA; RB;
SOTW; TTTS

Domination of Black

6 Yes: but the color of the heavy hemlocks
Came striding.
And I remembered the cry of the peacocks. (l. 8–10)

7 Out of the window,
I saw how the planets gathered
Like the leaves themselves
Turning in the wind. (l. 29–32)

AmPP; MoAB; MoAmPo; OxBA

Earthy Anecdote

8 Every time the bucks went clattering
Over Oklahoma
A firecat bristled in the way. (l. 1–3)

CMoP; GoJo; RB; RFM

The Emperor of Ice-Cream

9 Call the roller of big cigars,
The muscular one, and bid him whip
In kitchen cups concupiscent curds. (l. 1–3)

10 Let be be finale of seem.
The only emperor is the emperor of ice-cream. (l. 7–8)

11 If her horny feet protrude, they come
To show how cold she is, and dumb. (l. 13–14)

AmPP; AnAmPo; CMoP; FaBoMo; FF; HAP; HCAP;
HeIP; InPK; LiTA; MoP; NAAL-2; NAWM-2; NIP;
NoAM; NOBA; OPOP; OxBA; PoE; TAP; WeW

Esthétique du Mal

12 For the soldier of time, it breathes a summer sleep,

In which his wound is good because life was.
No part of him was ever part of death.
A woman smoothes her forehead with her hand
And the soldier of time lies calm beneath that stroke.

CMoP; LiTM; NOBA; WaaP; WaP

The Glass of Water

13 Here in the centre stands the glass. Light
Is the lion that comes down to drink. There
And in that state, the glass is a pool.
Ruddy are his eyes and ruddy are his claws
When light comes down to wet his frothy jaws
                                    (l. 6–10)

MoAB; MoAmPo; OxBA; TAP

A High-toned Old Christian Woman

14 Poetry is the supreme fiction, madame.
Take the moral law and make a nave of it
And from the nave build haunted heaven. Thus,

The conscience is converted into palms,
Like windy citherns hankering for hymns. (l. 1–5)

15 This will make widows wince. But fictive things
Wink as they will. Wink most when widows wince.
                                    (l. 21–22)

CMoP; MoP; NAAL-2; NoAM; NOBA; PPP; TAP

The House Was Quiet and the World Was Calm

16 The truth in a calm world,
In which there is no other meaning, itself

Is calm, itself is summer and night, itself
Is the reader leaning late and reading there.
                                    (l. 13–16)

AiP; HAP; NoP; VGW

The Idea of Order at Key West

17 The water never formed to mind or voice,
Like a body wholly body, fluttering
Its empty sleeves; and yet its mimic motion
Made constant cry, (l. 2–5)

18 The ever-hooded, tragic-gestured sea
Was merely a place by which she walked to sing.
                                    (l. 16–17)

19 Oh, Blessed rage for order, pale Ramon,
The maker's rage to order words of the sea,
Words of the fragrant portals, dimly-starred,
And of ourselves and of our origins,
In ghostlier demarcations, keener sounds. (l. 52–56)

CMoP; FF; HAP; HCAP; HeIP; MoAB; MoAmPo; MoP;
MOS; NAAL-2; NAWM-2; NIP; NoAM; NOBA; NoP;
OxBA; PoE; PPP; PrIm; TAP

The Irish Cliffs of Moher

20 My father's father, his father's father, his —
Shadows like winds

Go back to a parent before thought, before speech,
At the head of the past. (l. 3–6)

21 This is my father or, maybe,
It is as he was,

A likeness, one of the race of fathers: earth
And sea and air. (l. 13–16)

DiL; LCAP; NOBA; TOF; VGW

The Man with the Blue Guitar

22 I sing a hero's head, large eye
And bearded bronze, but not a man,

Although I patch him as I can
And reach through him almost to man. (l. 3–6)

23 Say that it is the serenade
Of a man that plays a blue guitar. (l. 9–10)

CMoP; LiTA; MoP; NoAM

Men Made out of Words

24 the human

Revery is a solitude in which
We compose these propositions, torn by dreams,
(l. 4–6)

25 The whole race is a poet that writes down
The eccentric propositions of its fate. (l. 9–10)

MoAB; NOBA; OxBSP; TAP; VGW

No Possum, No Sop, No Taters

26 Snow sparkles like eyesight falling to earth,

Like seeing fallen brightly away. (l. 10–11)

27 It is deep January. The sky is hard.
The stalks are firmly rooted in ice. (l. 13–14)

HCAP; OxBA; TAP; VGW

Not Ideas about the Thing but the Thing Itself

28 The sun was rising at six,
No longer a battered panache above snow.... (l. 7–8)

29 That scrawny cry — it was
A chorister whose C preceded the choir.
It was part of the colossal sun,

Surrounded by its choral rings,
Still far away. It was like
A new knowledge of reality. (l. 13–18)

HAP; HCAP; LCAP; TAP

Of Modern Poetry

30 The poem of the mind in the act of finding
What will suffice. It has not always had
To find: the scene was set; it repeated what
Was in the script.

Then the theatre was changed
To something else. Its past was a souvenir. (l. 1–6)

31 And it has to find what will suffice. It has
To construct a new stage. (l. 10–11)

32 It must
Be the finding of a satisfaction, and may
Be of a man skating, a woman dancing, a woman
Combing. The poem of the act of the mind. (l. 25–28)

InvP; MoP; NAAL-2; NoAM; OxBA; PrIm; TAP

Peter Quince at the Clavier

33 Music is feeling, then, not sound;
And thus it is that what I feel,
Here in this room, desiring you, (l. 4–6)

34 Of a green evening, clear and warm,
She bathed in her still garden, while
The red-eyed elders watching, felt

The basses of their beings throb
In witching chords, and their thin blood
Pulse pizzicati of Hosanna. (l. 10–15)

35 Soon, with a noise like tambourines,
Came her attendant Byzantines. (l. 41–42)

36 Beauty is momentary in the mind —
The fitful tracing of a portal;
But in the flesh it is immortal. (l. 51–53)

37 The body dies; the body's beauty lives.
So evenings die, in their green going,
A wave, interminably flowing. (l. 54–56)

38 Susanna's music touched the bawdy strings
Of those white elders; but, escaping,
Left only Death's ironic scraping.
Now, in its immortality, it plays
On the clear viol of her memory,
And makes a constant sacrament of praise. (l. 61–66)

AmPP; CMoP; HeIP; InPK; InPS; LiTM; MoAB;
MoAmPo; NAWM-2; NoAM; NOBA; OxBA; PoE; PPP;
TAP; TrGrPo; TwCP

Ploughing on Sunday

39 Remus, blow your horn!
I'm ploughing on Sunday,
Ploughing North America.
Blow your horn! (l. 9–12)

FaPON; GoJo; RB; SOTW; TTTS

The Poems of Our Climate

40 The imperfect is our paradise.
Note that, in this bitterness, delight,
Since the imperfect is so hot in us,
Lies in flawed words and stubborn sounds. (l. 21–24)

NoP; OxBA; TrGrPo; TwCP

A Postcard from the Volcano

41 with our bones
We left much more, left what still is
The look of things, left what we felt

At what we saw. (l. 7–10)

42 the windy sky

Cries out a literate despair. (l. 12–13)

43 A dirty house in a gutted world,
A tatter of shadows peaked to white,
Smeared with the gold of the opulent sun. (l. 22–24)

HAP; HCAP; LiTA; NoAM; WeW

The River of Rivers in Connecticut

44 There is a great river this side of Stygia, (l. 1)

45 the folk-lore
Of each of the senses; call it, again and again,
The river that flows nowhere, like a sea. (l. 16–18)

HAP; HCAP; NOBA; VGW

Sea Surface Full of Clouds

46 In that November off Tehuantepec,
The slopping of the sea grew still one night
And in the morning summer hued the deck

And made one think of rosy chocolate
And gilt umbrellas. (l. 1–5)

47 An uncertain green,
Piano-polished, held the tranced machine

Of ocean, as a prelude holds and holds. (l. 41–43)

48 A too-fluent green
Suggested malice in the dry machine

Of ocean, pondering dank stratagem.
Who then beheld the figures of the clouds
Like blooms secluded in the thick marine? (l. 59–63)

AmPP; CMoP; MoAB; MoAmPo; MOS; VGW

The Sense of the Sleight-of-Hand Man

49 It may be that the ignorant man, alone,
Has any chance to mate his life with life
That is the sensual, pearly spouse, the life
That is fluent in even the wintriest bronze. (l. 16–19)

HAP; LiTM; McAB; MoAmPo; NoAM; NOBA; PoA;
TwCP; WeW

The Snow Man

50 One must have a mind of winter
To regard the frost and the boughs
Of the pine-trees crusted with snow; (l. 1–3)

51 the listener, who listens in the snow,
And, nothing himself, beholds
Nothing that is not there and the nothing that is.
(l. 13–15)

CMoP; GoJo; HAP; HCAP; HeIP; MAT; NAAL-2; NoAM;
NoP; NU; PoE; PrIm; QFR; SoSe; WeW

Study of Two Pears

52 They are not flat surfaces
Having curved outlines.
They are round
Tapering toward the top. (l. 9–12)

53 The pears are not seen
As the observer wills. (l. 23–24)

InPS; NAAL-2; NoAM; NU; OxBA

Sunday Morning

54 Complacencies of the peignoir, and late
Coffee and oranges in a sunny chair,
And the green freedom of a cockatoo
Upon a rug mingle to dissipate
The holy hush of ancient sacrifice. (l. 1–5)

55 Why should she give her bounty to the dead?
What is divinity if it can come
Only in silent shadows and in dreams? (l. 16–18)

56 And shall the earth
Seem all of paradise that we shall know?
The sky will be much friendlier then than now,
A part of labor and a part of pain,
And next in glory to enduring love,
Not this dividing and indifferent blue. (l. 40–45)

57 She says, "But in contentment I still feel
The need of some imperishable bliss."
Death is the mother of beauty; hence from her,

Alone, shall come fulfilment to our dreams
And our desires. (l. 61–65)

58 She makes the willow shiver in the sun
For maidens who were wont to sit and gaze
Upon the grass, relinquished to their feet.
She causes boys to pile new plums and pears
On disregarded plate. The maidens taste
And stray impassioned in the littering leaves.
(l. 70–75)

59 Does ripe fruit never fall? (l. 77)

60 Death is the mother of beauty, mystical,
Within whose burning bosom we devise
Our earthly mothers waiting, sleeplessly. (l. 88–90)

61 She hears, upon that water without sound,
A voice that cries, "The tomb in Palestine
Is not the porch of spirits lingering.
It is the grave of Jesus, where he lay." (l. 106–109)

62 At evening, casual flocks of pigeons make
Ambiguous undulations as they sink,
Downward to darkness, on extended wings.
(l. 118–120)

AmPP; BLPL; CMoP; HAP; HCAP; HeIP; InPS; LiTA;
LiTM; MoAB; MoAmPo; MoP; NAAL-2; NAWM-2; NIP;
NoAM; NOBA; NoP; OxBA; PoA; PoE; QFR; TAP; WeW

Thirteen Ways of Looking at a Blackbird

63 Among twenty snowy mountains
The only moving thing
Was the eye of the blackbird. (l. 1–3)

64 A man and a woman
Are one.
A man and a woman and a blackbird (l. 9–11)

65 I do not know which to prefer,
The beauty of inflexions
Or the beauty of innuendos, (l. 13–15)

66 But I know, too,
That the blackbird is involved
In what I know. (l. 32–34)

67 It was evening all afternoon.
It was snowing
And it was going to snow.
The blackbird sat
In the cedar limbs. (l. 50–54)

BLPL; CMoP; HCAP; HeIP; InPK; InPS; LiTM; MoP;
NAAL-2; NoAM; NOBA; NoP; PoE; RB; SOTW; TAP

The World as Meditation

68 She has composed, so long, a self with which to
welcome him,
Companion to his self for her, which she imagined,
Two in a deep-founded sheltering, friend and dear
friend. (l. 7–9)

HeIP; LCAP; MoAB; NIP; PPP

ROBERT LOUIS STEVENSON
(1850–1894)

Blows the Wind Today

1 Blows the wind to-day, and the sun and the rain are
flying,
Blows the wind on the moors to-day and now,
Where about the graves of the martyrs the whaups are
crying,
My heart remembers how! (l. 1–4)

CH; EBVV; FaBoPP; NOBE; OBNC; PoSH

The Celestial Surgeon

2 Lord, thy most pointed pleasure take
And stab my spirit broad awake;
Or, Lord, if too obdurate I,
Choose thou, before that spirit die,
A piercing pain, a killing sin,
And to my dead heart run them in! (l. 9–14)

BrPo; EBVV; MoBrPo; TrGrPo; TrPWD; WGRP

A CHILD'S GARDEN OF VERSES (the following 2 poems)

The Lamplighter

3 My tea is nearly ready and the sun has left the sky;
It's time to take the window to see Leerie going by;
For every night at tea-time and before you take your
seat,
With lantern and with ladder he comes posting up the
street. (l. 1–4)

EBVV; FaFP; OxBChV; SaC

Good and Bad Children

4 Cruel children,crying babies,
All grow up as geese and gabies,
Hated, as their age increases,
By their nephews and their nieces.

EBVV; FaBoCh; FaFP; OxBChV

Christmas at Sea

5 The frost was on the village roofs as white as ocean
   foam;
   The good red fires were burning bright in every
   'longshore home;
   The windows sparkled clear, and the chimneys volleyed
   out;
   And I vow we sniffed the victuals as the vessel went
   about. (l. 17–20)

6 And they heaved a mighty breath, every soul on board
   but me,
   As they saw her nose again pointing handsome out to
   sea;
   But all that I could think of, in the darkness and the
   cold,
   Was just that I was leaving home and my folks were
   growing old. (l. 41–44)

BLPL; BrPo; CH; EBVV; FaBoBe; FaBV; Mes; MOS;
OBTV

The Cow

7 The friendly cow, all red and white,
   I love with all my heart:
   She gives me cream with all her might,
   To eat with apple tart. (l. 1–4)

BrPo; FaPON; FM; NTCP; OxBChV; PWR

From a Railway Carriage

8 Faster than fairies, faster than witches,
   Bridges and houses, hedges and ditches;
   And charging along like troops in a battle,
   All through the meadows the horses and cattle;
                                          (l. 1–4)

BoTP; FaPON; OxBChV; PDV; PYC; RHPC

Happy Thought

9 The world is so full of a number of things,
   I'm sure we should all be as happy as kings. (l. 1–2)

BoTP; FaBoBe; OxBChV; PWR; RAR; RHPC

In the Highlands

10 O to dream, O to awake and wander
   There, and with delight to take and render,
   Through the trance of silence,
   Quiet breath;
   Lo! for there, among the flowers and grasses,

Only the mightier movement sounds and passes;
Only winds and rivers,
Life and death. (l. 17–24)

BrPo; FaBoCh; FaBV; GoTS; OBEV; OxBS; PoSH

The Land of Counterpane

11 When I was sick and lay a-bed,
   I had two pillows at my head,
   And all my toys beside me lay
   To keep me happy all the day. (l. 1–4)

12 The pleasant land of counterpane. (l. 16)

BrPo; EBEV; FaBoBe; FaFP; NBLV; NTCP; OxBChV;
PWR

My Shadow

13 I have a little shadow that goes in and out with me,
   And what can be the use of him is more than I can see.
   He is very, very like me from the heels up to the head;
   And I see him jump before me, when I jump into my
   bed. (l. 1–4)

14 my lazy little shadow, like an arrant sleepy-head,
   Had stayed at home behind me and was fast asleep in
   bed. (l. 15–16)

FaBoBe; FaBV; FaPON; OnUR; OxBChV; PDV; PWR;
TEP

Romance

15 And this shall be for music when no one else is near,
   The fine song for singing, the rare song to hear!
   That only I remember, that only you admire,
   Of the broad road that stretches and the roadside fire.
                                          (l. 9–12)

BLPL; BoTP; BrPo; EBVV; FaPON; GoTS; GrPl;
MoBrPo; OBEV; OFD; TrGrPo

Songs of Travel: If This Were Faith

16 God, if this were enough,
   That I see things bare to the buff (l. 1–2)

17 With the half of a broken hope for a pillow at night
   That somehow the right is the right
   And the smooth shall bloom from the rough:
   Lord, if that were enough? (l. 33–36)

BrPo; OBNC; TrPWD; WGRP

The Swing

18 How do you like to go up in a swing,
Up in the air so blue?
Oh, I do think it the pleasantest thing
Ever a child can do! (l. 1–4)

FaBoBe; FaFP; GoJo; NTCP; PDV; TEP

Travel

19 I should like to rise and go
Where the golden apples grow; —
Where below another sky
Parrot islands anchored lie,
And, watched by cockatoos and goats,
Lonely Crusoes building boats; — (l. 1–6)

BrPo; FaBoCh; FaPON; MoShBr

Under the wide and starry sky

20 Under the wide and starry sky,
Dig the grave and let me lie. (l. 1–2)

21 This be the verse you grave for me:
Here he lies where he longed to be;
Home is the sailor, home from the sea,
And the hunter home from the hill. (l. 5–8)

BrPo; DL; EBVV; FaBV; FaPoR; FPL; GoTS; MoBrPo;
NBLV; NOBE; NOBVV; OBD; OBEV; OBNC; OHFP;
PoLF; PoRA; TrGrPo; WGRP

When I am grown to man's estate

22 And tell the other girls and boys
Not to meddle with my toys. (l. 3–4)

BrPo; CenHV; NBLV; OxBChV

Where Go the Boats?

23 Away down the river,
A hundred miles or more,
Other little children
Shall bring my boats ashore. (l. 13–16)

FaBoBe; FaBoCh; GoJo; Mes; NTCP; OxBChV; PYC

Windy Nights

24 Whenever the moon and stars are set,
Whenever the wind is high,
All night long in the dark and wet,
A man goes riding by. (l. 1–4)

25 By at the gallop he goes, and then
By he comes back at the gallop again. (l. 11–12)

BoTP; GoJo; OxBChV; PoRA; RHPC; RR

WILLIAM STEVENSON *AND* JOHN STILL (1530?–1575)

Gammer Gurton's Needle: Drinking Song
(*attributed to* Stevenson *and to* Still)

1 I love no roast but a nut-brown toast, and a crab laid
in the fire;
A little bread shall do me stead! much bread I do not
desire; (l. 13–14)

2 I am so wrapped, and throughly lapped of jolly good
ale and old! (l. 16)

3 Back and side go bare, go bare,
Both foot and hand go cold;
But belly, God send thee good ale enough;
Whether it be new or old! (l. 17–20)

ElL; HeIP; InvP; LiTB; NAEL-1; OBSC; TrGrPo; WiR

WILLIAM ALEXANDER, EARL OF STIRLING (1580?–1640)

Aurora: Sonnet

1 Oh, if thy pride did not our joys control,
What world of loving wonders shouldst thou see!
For if I saw thee once transformed in me,
Then in thy bosom I would pour my soul; (l. 5–8)

ElL; FaFP; GTBS; GTBS-P; Son

RICHARD HENRY STODDARD
(1825–1903)

Abraham Lincoln

1 Cursed be the hand that fired the shot,
The frenzied brain that hatched the plot,
Thy country's Father slain
By thee, thou worse than Cain! (l. 77–80)

2 One of the People! Born to be
Their curious epitome;
To share yet rise above
Their shifting hate and love. (l. 113–116)

3 Go, grandly borne, with such a train
As greatest kings might die to gain.
The just, the wise, the brave,
Attend thee to the grave. (l. 133–136)

AA; AnAmPo; FaBoBe; GN; OHIP; PAH

MARK STRAND (b. 1934)

Eating Poetry

1 Ink runs from the corners of my mouth.
There is no happiness like mine.
I have been eating poetry. (l. 1–3)

CAPP; GrPl; MAT; MoP; NoAM; PPP; TAP

Elegy for My Father

2 The hands were yours, the arms were yours
But you were not there. (l. 1–2)

3 Why are you going?
Because nothing means much to me anymore
Why are you going?
I don't know. I have never known. (l. 38–41)

4 You went on with your dying.
Nothing could stop you. Not your son. Not your
daughter
Who fed you and made you into a child again.
(l. 53–55)

5 It came to my house.
It sat on my shoulders.
Your shadow is yours. I told it so. I said it was yours.
I have carried it with me too long. I give it back.
(l. 142–145)

6 Nobody knows you. You are the neighbor of nothing.
(l. 179)

DiL; GeTw; HCAP; LCAP; UnPo

Keeping Things Whole

7 We all have reasons
for moving.
I move
to keep things whole. (l. 14–17)

CoAP; HCAP; HeIP; LCAP; PPP; TAP

WILLIAM STRODE (1602?–1645)

On Chloris Walking in the Snow

1 The wanton snow flew to her breast,
Like pretty birds into their nest,
But, overcome with whiteness there,

For grief it thaw'd into a tear:
Thence falling on her garments' hem,
To deck her, froze into a gem. (l. 5–10)

ELP; JCP; NOBE; OAEL-1; OBEV; OBS; OxBSP

GEORGE A. STRONG (1832–1912)

The Song of Milkanwatha

1 He killed the noble Mudjokivis.
Of the skin he made him mittens,
Made them with the fur side inside,
Made them with the skin side outside.
He, to get the warm side inside,
Put the inside skin side outside; (l. 1–6)

BXAP; FaBoCo; FaBoPa; FaFP; FaPON; FiBHP;
MoShBr; NA; Par; RHPC

SIR JOHN SUCKLING (1609–1642)

Aglaura

1 Why so pale and wan, fond lover
Prithee, why so pale?

2 Will, when speaking well can't win her,
Saying nothing do't?
Prithee, why so mute?

3 Quit, quit, for shame; this will not move,
This cannot take her.
If of herself she will not love,
Nothing can make her:
The devil take her!

AWP; BoLoP; CaPo; ELP; EnLoPo; FaBV; FaFP; FPL;
GTBS; GTBS-P; HAP; HeIP; HoPM; InPS; JCP; MePo;
NOBE; OBEV; OBS; PoE; PoEL-3; PoRA; PrIm; SeCePo;
SeCP; SeCV-1; TEP; TrGrPo; UnPo

Of thee (kind boy) I ask no red and white

4 Of thee (kind boy) I ask no red and white
to make up my delight,
no odd becoming graces,
Black eyes, or little know-not-whats, in faces;
Make me but mad enough, give me good store
Of Love, for her I Court
I ask no more,
'Tis love in love that makes the sport.

There's no such thing as that we beauty call,
it is meer cousenage all; (l. 1–10)

5 If I a fancy take
  To black and blue,
  That fancy doth it beauty make. (l. 14–16)

CaPo; MeLP; MePo; NoP; OBS; OxBoLi; SeCP; SeCV-1

Oh! for some honest lover's ghost

6 Oh for some honest lover's ghost,
  Some kind unbodied post
  Sent from the shades below!
  I strangely long to know
  Whether the nobler chaplets wear
  Those that their mistress' scorn did bear,
  Or those that were used kindly. (l. 1–7)

BoLoP; BXAP; CaPo; JCP; MeLP; MePo; NOBE; OBEV;
OBS; Par; PoEL-3; SeCP; SeCV-1

'Tis Now, Since I Sat Down Before

7 'Tis now since I sat down before
  That foolish fort, a heart,
  (Time strangely spent) a year, and more,
  And still I did my part: (l. 1–4)

CaPo; JCP; PoEL-3; SeCV-1

SIR JOHN SUCKLING *AND* OWEN FELLTHAM (c. 1602–1668)

When, dearest, I but think on thee (*attributed to* Suckling *and to* Felltham)

1 For beauties from worth arise
  Are like the grace of deities, (l. 4–5)

2 Thus while I sit and sigh the day
  With all his borrow'd lights away,
  Till night's black wings do overtake me,
  Thinking on thee, thy beauties then,
  As sudden lights do sleepy men,
  So they by their bright rays awake me. (l. 7–12)

JCP; MePo; OBEV; OBS

HENRY HOWARD, EARL OF SURREY (1517?–1547)

Brittle beauty, that nature made so frail

1 Brittle beauty that nature made so frail,
  Whereof the gift is small, and short the season,
  Flow'ring today, tomorrow apt to fail,
  Tickle treasure, abhorred of reason,

Dangerous to deal with, vain, of none avail,
Costly in keeping, passed not worth two peason,
                                        (l. 1–6)

2 Jewel of jeopardy that peril doth assail,
  False and untrue, enticed oft to treason,
  Enemy to youth (that most may I bewail!),
  Ah, bitter sweet! infecting as the poison,
  Thou farest as fruit that with the frost is taken:
  Today ready ripe, tomorrow all too shaken. (l. 9–14)

AAS; EnLoPo; HoPM; SiPS; TrGrPo

A Complaint by Night of the Lover Not Beloved

3 Alas, so all things now do hold their peace:
  Heaven and earth disturbed in no thing:
  The beasts, the air, the birds their song do cease;
  The nightes chare the stars about doth bring. (l. 1–4)

4 by and by, the cause of my disease
  Gives me a pang that inwardly doth sting,
  When that I think what grief it is again
  To live and lack the thing should rid my pain.
                                        (l. 11–14)

AAS; AWP; EBEV; ElL; NAEL-1; OAEL-1; OBSC;
OBVE; SiPS; Son; TEP

Complaint of the Absence of Her Lover Being upon the Sea

5 Help to bewail the woeful case
  And eke the heavy plight
  Of me, that wonted to rejoice
  The fortunes of my pleasant choice.
  Good ladies, help to fill my mourning voice. (l. 3–7)

AAS; EBEV; ElL; ELP; GBL; NOBE; OBEV; SiPS

Consolation

6 When raging love with extreme pain
  Most cruelly distrains my heart,
  When that my tears, as floods of rain,
  Bear witness of my woeful smart;
  When sighs have wasted so my breath
  That I lie at the point of death, (l. 1–6)

7 I call to mind the navy great
  That the Greeks brought to Troye town,
  And how the boistous winds did beat
  Their ships, and rent their sails adown;
  Till Agamemnon's daughter's blood
  Appeased the gods that them withstood. (l. 7–12)

8 Then think I thus: sith such repair,
  So long time war of valiant men,
  Was all to win a lady fair,

Shall I not learn to suffer then,
And think my life well spent to be,
Serving a worthier wight than she? (l. 19–24)

AAS; EBEV; EnLoPo; NOBE; OBSC; SiPS; TEP

I never saw you madam, lay apart

9 I never saw youe madam laye aparte
Your cornet black, in colde nor yet in heate,
Sythe first ye knew of my desire so greate,
Which other fances chac'd cleane from my harte.
(l. 1–4)

AAS; OBSC; PoEL-1; SiPS

So cruel prison how could betide, alas

10 So cruel prison how could betide, alas,
As proud Windsor, Where I in lust and joy
With a king's son my childish years did pass
In greater feast than Priam's sons of Troy?
Where each sweet place returns a taste full sour;
(l. 1–5)

11 Thus I alone, where all my freedom grew,
In prison pine with bondage and restraint;
And with remembrance of the greater grief
To banish the less, I find my chief relief. (l. 51–54)

AAS; HAP; NOBE; NoP; OBSC; SeCePo; SiPS

MAY SWENSON (b. 1919)

The Centaur

1 The summer that I was ten —
Can it be there was only one
summer that I was ten? It must

have been a long one then — (l. 1–4)

2 I was the horse and the rider,
and the leather I slapped to his rump

spanked my own behind. (l. 38–40)

3 quiet, negligent riding,
my toes standing the stirrups,
my thighs hugging his ribs. (l. 46–48)

4 Go tie back your hair, said my mother,
and Why is your mouth all green?
Rob Roy, he pulled some clover
as we crossed the field, I told her. (l. 61–64)

FaBoWP; GrPl; NMM; SO; TwCP

Question

5 Body my house
my horse my hound
what will I do
when you are fallen (l. 1–4)

HeIP; LiTM; NePoEA; PrIm; SM; VGW

JONATHAN SWIFT (1667–1745)

Baucis and Philemon; Imitated from the Eighth Book of Ovid

1 Description would but tire my Muse:
In short, they both were turned to yews. (l. 163–164)

2 He gathers all the parish there;
Points out the place of either yew,
Here Baucis, there Philemon, grew.
Till once a parson of our town,
To mend his barn, cut Baucis down;
At which, 'tis hard to be believed
How much the other tree was grieved,
Grew scrubby, died a-top, was stunted:
So the next parson stubbed and burnt it. (l. 170–178)

GN; NOEC; OAEL-1

The Day of Judgement

3 With a whirl of thought oppressed
I sink from reverie to rest.
An horrid vision seized my head,
I saw the graves give up their dead. (l. 1–4)

4 Jove, nodding, shook the Heavens, and said,
'Offending race of human kind,
By nature, reason, learning, blind;
You who through frailty stepped aside,
And you who never fell — through pride; (l. 10–14)

5 I to such blockheads set my wit!
I damn such fools! — Go, go, you're bit.' (l. 21–22)

BIrV; FaBoRV; NOBE; NOEC; OAEL-1; OBSV; PPP; TW

A Description of a City Shower

6 Careful observers may foretell the hour
(By sure prognostics) when to dread a show'r.
While rain depends, the pensive cat gives o'er
Her frolics, and pursues her tail no more. (l. 1–4)

7 Now in contiguous drops the flood comes down,
Threat'ning with deluge this devoted town.
To shops in crowds the daggled females fly,
Pretend to cheapen goods, but nothing buy. (l. 31–34)

8 Triumphant Tories, and desponding Whigs,
Forget their feuds, and join to save their wigs.
(l. 41–42)

9 Sweeping from butcher's stalls, dung, guts, and blood,
Drown'd puppies, stinking sprats, all drench'd in mud,
Dead cats, and turnip-tops, come tumbling down the
flood. (l. 61–63)

HeIP; MAT; NAEL-1; NOEC; NoP; OAEL-1; OBSV; PoE;
PPP; SeCePo; TEP; UnPo

A Description of the Morning

10 Now hardly here and there an hackney coach
Appearing, showed the ruddy morn's approach.
Now Betty from her master's bed had flown,
And softly stole to discompose her own;
The slipshod 'prentice from his master's door
Had pared the dirt, and sprinkled round the floor.
(l. 1–6)

11 Duns at his lordship's gate began to meet;
And brickdust Moll had screamed through half the
street.
The turnkey now his flock returning sees,
Duly let out a-nights to steal for fees:
The watchful bailiffs take their silent stands,
And schoolboys lag with satchels in their hands.
(l. 13–18)

EBEV; FF; HAP; HeIP; InPS; NOBE; NOEC; NoP;
OAEL-1; PPP; Prf; SoSe; TEP; WeW

On the Vowels — a Riddle

12 We are little airy creatures,
All of different voice and features:
One of us in glass is set,
One of us you'll find in jet,
T'other you may see in tin,
And the fourth a box within;
If the fifth you should pursue,
It can never fly from you. (l. 1–8)

FaBoUs; GN

Phyllis; or, The Progress of Love

13 Desponding Phyllis was endu'd
With ev'ry Talent of a Prude,
She trembled when a Man drew near;
Salute her, and she turn'd her Ear:

If o'er against her you were plac'd
She durst not look above your Waist; (l. 1–6)

14 Or on the Mat devoutly kneeling
Would lift her Eyes up to the Ceiling,
And heave her Bosom unaware
For neighb'ring Beaux to see it bare. (l. 15–18)

15 When Food and Raiment now grew scarce
Fate put a Period to the Farce;
And with exact Poetic Justice:
For John is Landlord, Phyllis Hostess;
They keep at Stains the old Blue Boar,
Are Cat and Dog, and Rogue and Whore. (l. 95–100)

OAEL-1; OBSV; PoE; PoEL-3

A Satirical Elegy on the Death of a Late Famous General

16 Come hither, all ye empty things,
Ye bubbles rais'd by breath of Kings;
Who float upon the tide of state,
Come hither, and behold your fate.
Let pride be taught by this rebuke,
How very mean a thing's a Duke;
From all his ill-got honours flung,
Turn'd to that dirt from whence he sprung. (l. 25–32)

FF; HoPM; NBLV; NoP; OBSV; PoE; PoEL-3

Stella's Birthday, March 13, 1726/27

17 This Day, whate'er the Fates decree;
Shall still be kept with Joy by me:
This Day then, let us not be told,
That you are sick, and I grown old, (l. 1–4)

18 From not the gravest of Divines,
Accept for once some serious Lines. (l. 13–14)

19 And, is not Virtue in Mankind
The Nutriment that feeds the Mind? (l. 61–62)

20 For Virtue in her daily Race,
Like Janus bears a double Face;
Looks back with Joy where she has gone,
And therefore goes with Courage on. (l. 73–76)

NAs; NoP; OAEL-1; PoE; PoEL-3

Stella's Birthday, 1718/19

21 Stella this day is thirty-four
(We shan't dispute a year or more) —
However, Stella, be not troubled,
Although thy size and years are doubled,
Since first I saw thee at sixteen,
The brightest virgin on the green,

So little is thy form declined,
Made up so largely in thy mind.
Oh, would it please the gods, to split
Thy beauty, size, and years, and wit,
No age could furnish out a pair
Of nymphs so graceful, wise, and fair, (l. 1–12)

EnLoPo; InPK; NAs; NIP; NOIV; OAEL-1

Verses on the Death of Doctor Swift

22 As with a moral view designed
To cure the vices of mankind;
His vein, ironically grave,
Exposed the fool, and lashed the knave; (l. 15–18)

23 He never courted men in station
Nor persons had in admiration;
Of no man's greatness was afraid,
Because he sought for no man's aid.

24 Fair Liberty was all his cry;
For her he stood prepared to die;
For her he boldly stood alone;
For her he oft exposed his own.

25 Had he but spared his tongue and pen
He might have rose like other men;
But power was never in his thought,
And wealth he valued not a groat;

NOBE; NOEC; OxBoLi; PoEL-3; TEP

26 For poetry, he's past his prime,
He takes an hour to find a rhyme;
His fire is out, his wit decayed,
His fancy sunk, his muse a jade.
I'd have him throw away his pen,
But there's no talking to some men.

27 'He hardly drinks a pint of wine,
And that, I doubt, is no good sign.
His stomach too begins to fail:
Last year we thought him strong and hale,
But now, he's quite another thing;
I wish he may hold out till spring.'

Then hug themselves, and reason thus;
'It is not yet so bad with us.'

EBEV; Mes; NOBE; NOBL; NOIV

ALGERNON CHARLES SWINBURNE
(1837–1909)

Atalanta in Calydon

1 Before the beginning of years
There came to the making of man
Time, with a gift of tears;
Grief, with a glass that ran;

2 His speech is a burning fire;
With his lips he travaileth;
In his heart is a blind desire,
In his eyes foreknowledge of death:
He weaves, and is clothed with derision;
Sows, and he shall not reap;
His life is a watch or a vision
Between a sleep and a sleep. (l. 39–46)

EBVV; FaFP; HeIP; LiTB; NAEL-2; NoP; OBEV; TrGrPo

3 When the hounds of spring are on winter's traces,
The mother of months in meadow or plain
Fills the shadows and windy places
With lisp of leaves and ripple of rain;

4 Come with bows bent and with emptying of quivers,
Maiden most perfect, lady of light,

AWP; CTC; EBVV; FaBoBe; FaBV; GTBS-P; HAP; HeIP;
LiTB; NAEL-2; NOBE; NoP; OAEL-2; OBEV; PoE;
PrIm; TEP; TrGrPo; WeW

Ave atque Vale

5 O sleepless heart and sombre soul unsleeping,
That were athirst for sleep and no more life
And no more love, for peace and no more strife!
(l. 34–36)

6 Hast thou found any likeness for thy vision?
O gardener of strange flowers, what bud, what bloom,
Hast thou found sown, what gather'd in the gloom?
(l. 67–70)

7 Dreams pursue death as winds a flying fire,
Our dreams pursue our dead and do not find.
(l. 94–95)

8 Sleep; and if life was bitter to thee, pardon,
If sweet, give thanks; thou hast no more to live;
And to give thanks is good, and to forgive.
(l. 167–169)

9 Content thee, howsoe'er, whose days are done;
There lies not any troublous thing before,
Nor sight nor sound to war against thee more,
For whom all winds are quiet as the sun,
All waters as the shore. (l. 182–186)

NAEL-2; NOBE; OAEL-2; OBEV; OBNC

A Forsaken Garden

10 In a coign of the cliff between lowland and highland,
At the sea-down's edge between windward and lee,
Walled round with rocks as an inland island,
The ghost of a garden fronts the sea. (l. 1–4)

EBEV; FaBoPP; GTBS-P; LiTB; NOBE; NOBVV; NoP;
OAEL-2; OBNC; TEP

The Garden of Proserpine

11 Here, where the world is quiet,
Here, where all trouble seems
Dead winds' and spent waves' riot
In doubtful dreams of dreams; (l. 1–4)

12 I am tired of tears and laughter,
And men that laugh and weep;

13 I am weary of days and hours,
Blown buds of barren flowers,
Desires and dreams and powers
And everything but sleep. (l. 10–16)

14 We are not sure of sorrow,
And joy was never sure;
To-day will die to-morrow;
Time stoops to no man's lure; (l. 73–76)

15 From too much love of living,
From hope and fear set free,
We thank with brief thanksgiving
Whatever gods may be
That no life lives for ever;
That dead men rise up never;
That even the weariest river
Winds somewhere safe to sea. (l. 81–88)

AWP; BLPA; BLPL; FaBoRV; FaBV; FaPoR; HAP; LiTB;
NAEL-2; NOBE; NOBVV; NoP; OBNC; PoE; PoEL-5;
PoRA; SCV; SeCePo; TrGrPo

The Heptalogia

16 One, who is not, we see: but one, whom we see not, is;
Surely this is not that: but that is assuredly this.

17 Doubt is faith in the main: but faith, on the whole, is
doubt;
We cannot believe by proof: but could we believe
without?

18 God whom we see not, is: and God, who is not, we see;
Fiddle, we know, is diddle: and diddle, we take it, is
dee.

BXAP; FaBoNo; NA; Par

19 From the depth of the dreamydecline of the dawn
through a notable nimbus of nebulous noonshine,

20 Life is the lust of a lamp for the light that is dark till
the dawn of the day when we die.

BXAP; FaBoCo; FaBoNo; FaBoPa; HoPM; NA; Par

Hymn to Proserpine

21 I have lived long enough, having seen one thing, that
love hath an end; (l. 1)

22 I am sick of singing; the bays burn deep and chafe: I
am fain
To rest a little from praise and grievous pleasure and
pain. (l. 9–10)

23 Thou hast conquered, O pale Galilean; the world has
grown grey from thy breath;
We have drunken of things Lethean; and fed on the
fullness of death.
Laurel is green for a season, and love is sweet for a
day;
But love grows bitter with treason, and laurel outlives
not May.
Sleep, shall we sleep after all? for the world is not
sweet in the end;
For the old faiths loosen and fall, the new years ruin
and rend. (l. 35–40)

24 And its noise as the noise in a dream; and its depth as
the roots of the sea: (l. 62)

25 I shall die as my fathers died, and sleep as they sleep;
even so.
For the glass of the years is brittle wherein we gaze for
a span;
A little soul for a little bears up this corpse which is
man.
So long I endure, no longer; and laugh not again,
neither weep.
For there is no God found stronger than death; and
death is a sleep. (l. 106–110)

EBVV; NAEL-2; OAEL-2; OBNC; PoEL-5; TEP

A Leave-taking

26 Love is a barren sea, bitter and deep;
And though she saw all heaven in flower above,
She would not love. (l. 26–28)

CH; NOBE; NOBVV; OBNC; OPOP; PoEL-5; PoLF

JOSHUA SYLVESTER (1561–1618)

Were I as base as is the lowly plain (attributed to Sylvester)

1 Were I as base as is the lowly plain,
And you, my Love, as high as heaven above,
Yet should the thoughts of me, your humble swain,
Ascend to heaven in honour of my love. (l. 1–4)

2 Were you the earth, dear Love, and I the skies,
My love should shine on you like to the Sun,
And look upon you with ten thousand eyes,
Till heaven wax'd blind, and till the world were done.

Whereso'er I am, — below, or else above you —
Whereso'er you are, my heart shall truly love you.
(l. 9–14)

ElL; GTBS; GTBS-P; OBEV; OBSC; Son

JOHN MILLINGTON SYNGE
(1871–1909)

The Curse

1 Lord, confound this surly sister,
Blight her brow with blotch and blister,
Cramp her larynx, lung and liver,
In her guts a galling give her. (l. 1–4)

ChTr; FaBoCo; FaBoEE; NOIV; TW

Queens

2 All the rare and royal names
Wormy sheepskin yet retains: (l. 2–3)

3 Bert, the big-foot, sung by Villon,
Cassandra, Ronsard found in Lyon.
Queens of Sheba, Meath, and Connaught,
Coifed with crown, or gaudy bonnet; (l. 6–9)

4 These are rotten, so you're the Queen
Of all are living, or have been. (l. 24–25)

ChTr; GBL; MoBrPo; OBMV

A Question

5 I asked if I got sick and died, would you
With my black funeral go walking too,
If you'd stand close to hear them talk or pray
While I'm let down in that steep bank of clay.

6 they alive, I dead beneath
That board — you'd rave and rend them with your
teeth.

MoBrPo; NOIV; OBMV; OxBTC

Still south I went and west and south again

7 I knew the stars, the flowers, and the birds,
The gray and wintry sides of many glens,
And did but half remember human words,
In converse with the mountains, moors, and fens.

AWP; BoNaP; ChTr; FaBoPP; MoBrPo; OBMV

TORQUATO TASSO (1544–1595)

Aminta

1 O happy, golden age!
Not for that rivers ran
With streams of milk, and honey dropped from trees;
(l. 1–3)

2 Her voluntary fruits,free without fees; (l. 6)

3 Not for no cold did freeze,
Nor any cloud beguile
Th'eternal flowering spring, (l. 7–9)

4 Then amongst flowers and springs,
Making delightful sport,
Sat lovers without conflict, without flame; (l. 27–29)

5 Honour, thou first didst close
The spring of all delight,
Denying water to the amorous thirst; (l. 40–42)

6 Thou madest loose grace unkind;
Gavest bridle to their words, art to their pace.
O Honour, it is thou
That makest that stealth, which Love doth free allow.
(l. 49–52)

AWP; OAEL-1; OBSC; OBVE; PFI; PoEL-2

ALLEN TATE (1899–1979)

Aeneas at Washington

1 I myself saw furious with blood
Neoptolemus, at his side the black Atridae,
Hecuba and the hundred daughters, Priam
Cut down, his filth drenching the holy fires. (l. 1–4)

2 The singular passion
Abides its object and consumes desire
In the circling shadow of its appetite. (l. 27–29)

FYAP; LiTA; NoAM; NOBA; OxBA

Last Days of Alice

3 Alice grown lazy, mammoth but not fat,
Declines upon her lost and twilight age;
Above in the dozing leaves the grinning cat
Quivers forever with his abstract rage: (l. 1–4)

4 O God of our flesh, return us to Your wrath,
Let us be evil could we enter in
Your grace, and falter on the stony path! (l. 34–36)

NAAL-2; NOBA; OxBA; UnPo

The Mediterranean

5 We've cracked the hemispheres with careless hand!
Now, from the Gates of Hercules we flood

Westward, westward till the barbarous brine
Whelms us to the tired world where tasseling corn,
Fat beans, grapes sweeter than muscadine
Rot on the vine: in the land were we born. (l. 31–36)

FaBoMo; GOA; HAP; LiTA; LiTM; MoAB; MoAmPo;
MOS; VGW; WeW

More Sonnets at Christmas

6 Get up and once again politely lying
Invite the ladies toward the mistletoe
With greedy eyes that stare like an old crow.
(l. 17–19)

7 Give me this day a faith not personal
As follows: The American people fully armed
With assurance policies, righteous and harmed,
Battle the world of which they're not at all.
(l. 29–32)

LiTA; LiTM; WaP

Mr. Pope

8 For Pope's tight back was rather a goat's than man's.
(l. 4)

9 And he who dribbled couplets like a snake
Coiled to a lithe precision in the sun
Is missing. (l. 9–11)

MoAB; NoAM; NOBA; TwCP; VGW

The Oath

10 Uncle Ben's brass bullet-mould
And powder horn, and Major Bogan's face
Above the fire, in the half-light, plainly said
There's naught to kill but the animated dead; (l. 2–5)

FaBoMo; LiTM; OxBA; VGW

Ode to the Confederate Dead

11 Row after row with strict impunity
The headstones yield their names to the element,
(l. 1–2)

12 Turn your eyes to the immoderate past,
Turn to the inscrutable infantry rising
Demons out of the earth — they will not last.

Stonewall, Stonewall, and the sunken fields of hemp,
Shiloh, Antietam, Malvern Hill, Bull Run. (l. 44–48)

13 What shall we say of the bones, unclean,
Whose verdurous anonymity will grow?
The ragged arms, the ragged heads and eyes
Lost in these acres of the insane green? (l. 63–66)

14 What shall we say who have knowledge
Carried to the heart? Shall we take the act
To the grave? Shall we, more hopeful, set up the grave
In the house? The ravenous grave? (l. 82–85)

15 The gentle serpent, green in the mulberry bush,
Riots with his tongue through the hush —
Sentinel of the grave who counts us all! (l. 87–89)

AiP; FaBoMo; HeIP; LiTA; LiTM; MoAB; MoAmPo;
MoP; NAAL-2; NoAM; NOBA; NoP; OBD; OBWP; OxBA;
PrIm; TAP; UnPo

The Swimmers

16 sullen fun

Savage as childhood's thin harmonious tear:
O fountain, bosom source undying-dead
Replenish me the spring of love and fear (l. 6–9)

17 Peering, I heard the hooves come down the hill.
The posse passed, twelve horse; the leader's face
Was worn as limestone on an ancient sill. (l. 25–27)

18 Alone in the public clearing
This private thing was owned by all the town,
Though never claimed by us within my hearing.
(l. 82–84)

InPS; MoAmPo; NoAM; NOBA

The Wolves

19 So this
Is man; so — what better conclusion is there —
The day will not follow night, and the heart
Of man has a little dignity, but less patience
Than a wolf's, (l. 14–18)

20 Now remember courage, go to the door,
Open it and see whether coiled on the bed
Or cringing by the wall, a savage beast
Maybe with golden hair, with deep eyes
Like a bearded spider on a sunlit floor
Will snarl — and man can never be alone. (l. 22–27)

LiTA; LiTM; NOBA; OxBA; PoA

JAMES TATE (b. 1943)

The Blue Booby

1 Rather,
they gather the blue

objects of the world
and construct from them

a nest — (l. 11–15)

2 the stars turn slowly
in the blue foil beside them
like the eyes of a mild savior. (l. 39–41)

AmPA; EAS; NoAM; NoP

The Lost Pilot

3 when I see you,
as I have seen you at least

once every year of my life,
spin across the wilds of the sky
like a tiny, African god,

I feel dead. (l. 32–37)

4 fast, perfect, and unwilling
to tell me that you are doing
well, or that it was mistake

that placed you in that world,
and me in this; or that misfortune
placed these worlds in us. (l. 43–48)

CoAP; DiL; NoAM; NoP; OBWP; TwCP; UnPo

NAHUM TATE (1652–1715)

While Shepherds Watched

1 While shepherds watched their flocks by night,
All seated on the ground,
The angel of the Lord came down,
And glory shone around. (l. 1–4)

2 The heavenly Babe you there shall find
To human view displayed,
All meanly wrapped in swaddling bands
And in a manger laid. (l. 13–16)

AmFP; GN; NOCV; OHIP; TIRV

ANN TAYLOR (1783–1824)

My Mother

1 Who fed me from her gentle breast,
And hushed me in her arms to rest,
And on my cheek sweet kisses prest?
My Mother. (l. 1–4)

BLPA; BLPL; OHIP; OxBChV

BAYARD TAYLOR (1825–1878)

The Ballad of Hiram Hover

1 Where the Moosatockmaguntic
Pours its waters in the Skuntic,
Met, along the forest side
Hiram Hover, Huldah Hyde.

She, a maiden fair and dapper,
He, a red-haired, stalwart trapper,
Hunting beaver, mink, and skunk
In the woodlands of Squeedunk. (l. 1–8)

AnAmPo; BXAP; FaBoCo; OBAL

The Song of the Camp

2 They sang of love, and not of fame;
Forgot was Britain's glory;
Each heart recalled a different name.
But all sang " Annie Laurie." (l. 17–20)

AA; AnAmPo; BeLS; GN; WBLP

EDWARD TAYLOR (1645–1729)

An Address to the Soul Occasioned by a Rain

1 One sorry fret,
An anvill Sparke, rose higher,
And in thy Temple falling, almost set
The house on fire.
Such fireballs dropping in the Temple Flame
Burns up the building: Lord, forbid the same.
                    (l. 25–30)

NAAL-1; NOBA; OxBA; PoEL-3

God's Determinations: Preface

2 Oh, what a might is this whose single frown
Doth shake the world as it would shake it down?
Which all from nothing fet, from nothing all;
Hath all on nothing set, lets nothing fall.
Gave all to nothing man indeed, whereby
Through nothing man all might Him glorify.

3 That now his brightest diamond is grown
Darker by far than any coalpit stone.

AmPP; HAP; NAAL-1; NOBA; OxBA; SCAP

God's Determinations: The Joy of Church Fellowship Rightly Attended

4 Oh! joyous hearts! enfired with holy flame!
Is speech thus tasseled with praise?
Will not your inward fire of joy contain:

That it in open flames doth blaze?
For in Christ's coach saints sweetly sing,
As they to glory ride therein.

AH; AmPP; NAAL-1; OxBA; SCAP

Huswifery

5 Make me thy Spinning Wheele of use for thee,
Thy Grace my Distaffe, and my heart thy Spoole.
Turn thou the wheele: let mine Affections bee
The flyer filling with thy yarne my soule. (l. 1–4)

6 Make me thy Loome: thy Grace the warfe therein,
My duties Woofe, and let thy word winde Quills.
The shuttle shoot. Cut off the ends my sins.
Thy Ordinances make my fulling mills,
My Life thy Web: and cloath me all my dayes
With this Gold-web of Glory to thy praise. (l. 7–12)

EaLo; FaBV; LiTA; NAAL-1; NIP; NOBA; NOBE; NoP;
OxBA; SaC; SCAP; TAP

**PREPARATORY MEDITATIONS BEFORE MY APPROACH TO
THE LORD'S SUPPER** *(the following 3 poems)*

I. What love is this of thine

7 Oh! that thy love might overflow my Heart!
To fire the same with Love: for Love I would.
But oh! my streight'ned Breast! my Lifeless Sparke!
My Fireless Flame! What Chilly Love, and Cold?
In measure small! In Manner Chilly! See!
Lord, blow the Coal: Thy Love Enflame in mee.
(l. 13–18)

AmPP; NOCV; PoEL-3; SCAP

IV. Lord, art thou at the table head above

8 Once at thy Feast, I saw thee Pearle-like stand
'Tween Heaven and Earth, where Heavens Bright glory
all
In streams fell on thee, as a floodgate and
Like Sun Beams through thee on the World to Fall.
Oh! Sugar sweet then! My Deare sweet Lord, I see
Saints Heaven-lost Happiness restor'd by thee.
(l. 25–30)

AmPP; OxBA

VIII. I Am the Living Bread

9 In this sad state, God Tender Bowells run
Out streams of Grace: And he to end all strife
The Purest Wheate in Heaven, his deare-dear Son
Grinds, and kneads up into this Bread of Life.

Which Bread of Life from Heaven down came and
stands
Disht on thy Table up by Angells Hands. (l. 19–24)

AmPP; LiTA; NAAL-1; NOBA; NoP; OxBA; PoEL-3;
SCAP; TAP

Upon a Spider Catching a Fly

10 This goes to pot, that not
Nature doth call.
Strive not above what strength hath got,
Lest in the brawle
Thou fall. (l. 26–30)

11 This Frey seems thus to us:
Hells Spider gets
His intrails spun to whip Cords thus,
And wove to nets,
And sets. (l. 31–35)

12 To tangle Adams race
In's stratagems (l. 36–37)

AmPP; NOBA; NoP; OxBA; PoEL-3; SCAP; TAP

Upon a Wasp Chilled with Cold

13 As if her velvet helmet high
Did turret rationality.
She fans her wing up to the winde
As if her Pettycoate were lin'de
With reasons fleece, and hoises saile
And humming flies in thankfull gaile (l. 21–26)

14 Here of this fustian animall,
Till I enravisht climb into
The Godhead on this ladder doe:
Where all my pipes inspir'de upraise
And Heavenly musick, furr'd with praise. (l. 40–44)

NAAL-1; NOBA; NOCV; PoEL-3

JANE TAYLOR (1783–1824)

The Star

1 Twinkle, twinkle, little star,
How I wonder what you are!
Up above the world so high,
Like a diamond in the sky. (l. 1–4)

BoTP; FaBoBe; FaFP; FaPON; NTCP; OxBChV; OxNR;
Par; PYC; RAR; RHPC

SARA TEASDALE (1884–1933)

February Twilight

1 I stood and watched the evening star
As long as it watched me. (l. 7–8)

FaPON; OBCA; PDV; RHPC

Let it be forgotten, as a flower is forgotten

2 Let it be forgotten as a flower is forgotten,
Forgotten as a fire that once was singing gold.
(l. 1–2)

3 As a flower, as a fire, as a hushed footfall
In a long forgotten snow. (l. 7–8)

AnAmPo; MoAmPo; PoA; TrGrPo

Spring Night

4 The park is filled with night and fog,
The veils are drawn about the world, (l. 1–2)

5 O beauty, are you not enough?
Why am I crying after love? (l. 23–24)

BLPL; FaBoBe; LiTA; MoAmPo

ALFRED TENNYSON, 1ST BARON TENNYSON (1809–1892)

Break, Break, Break

1 Break, break, break,
On thy cold gray stones, O Sea!
And I would that my tongue could utter
The thoughts that arise in me. (l. 1–4)

2 But O for the touch of a vanished hand,
And the sound of a voice that is still! (l. 11–12)

3 But the tender grace of a day that is dead
Will never come back to me. (l. 15–16)

AWP; BLPL; CH; DL; FaBoBe; FaBV; FaPoR; FF; FiP;
GoJo; GTBS-P; HAP; HeIP; LiTB; MOS; NAEL-2; NIP;
NOBE; NOBVV; NoP; OBNC; PoEL-5; PoRA; PrIm;
PWR; RB; TEP; TrGrPo; WBLP; WeW

The Brook; an Idyl

4 I come from haunts of coot and hern,
I make a sudden sally,
And sparkle out among the fern
To bicker down a valley. (l. 1–4)

5 And out again I curve and flow
To join the brimming river,
For men may come and men may go,
But I go on forever. (l. 43–44)

BoNaP; BoTP; FaBoBe; FaBV; FaFP; FaPON; GN; GoJo

The Charge of the Light Brigade

6 Half a league, half a league,
Half a league onward,
All in the valley of Death
Rode the six hundred.
"Forward the Light Brigade! (l. 1–5)

7 Theirs not to make reply,
Theirs not to reason why,
Theirs but to do and die. (l. 13–15)

8 Cannon to right of them,
Cannon to left of them,
Cannon in front of them
Volleyed and thundered; (l. 18–21)

BeLS; BLPA; FaBoBe; FaBV; FaFP; FaPON; FaPoR;
FPL; GN; HoPM; NAEL-2; NIP; NOBVV; OBWP; OHFP;
PrIm; TEP; WBLP

Crossing the Bar

9 Sunset and evening star,
And one clear call for me!
And may there be no moaning of the bar,
When I put out to sea,

10 Twilight and evening bell.
And after that the dark!
And may there be no sadness of farewell,
When I embark;

For though from out our bourne of Time and Place
The flood may bear me far,
I hope to see my Pilot face to face
When I have crossed the bar.

BLRP; DL; EBVV; FaBoRV; FaBV; FaFP; FaPoR; FF;
FiP; FPL; HeIP; LiTB; MOS; NAEL-2; NOBE; NOBVV;
NoP; OAEL-2; OBEV; OBNC; OHFP; PoLF; PoRA; PWR;
SoSe; TEP; TrCP; TrGrPo; WBLP; WGRP

The Daisy

11 O Love, what hours were thine and mine,
In lands of palm and southern pine;
In lands of palm, of orange-blossom,
Of olive, aloe, and maize and vine. (l. 1–4)

EnLoPo; NOBVV; OBNC; PoEL-5

The Eagle

12 He clasps the crag with crooked hands;
Close to the sun in lonely lands,
Ringed with the azure world, he stands.

The wrinkled sea beneath him crawls;
He watches from his mountain walls,
And like a thunderbolt he falls.

BoTP; CH; FaBoCh; FaPON; FF; FiP; FM; GN; GoJo;
GTBS-P; HeIP; InPK; NAEL-2; NOBVV; NoP; NTCP;
OAEL-2; OxBSP; PBBP; PDV; PrIm; RHPC; SeCePo;
TrGrPo; UnPo; WiR

Flower in the Crannied Wall

13 Flower in the crannied wall,
I pluck you out of the crannies,
I hold you here, root and all, in my hand,
Little flower — but if I could understand
What you are, root and all, and all in all,
I should know what God and man is.

BLPA; BoNaP; FaBV; FaFP; FaPON; FPL; InPK; LiTB;
NAEL-2; NIP; TEP; TrGrPo; TSS; WGRP

"Frater Ave atque Vale"

14 There beneath the Roman ruin where the purple
    flowers grow,
Came that "Ave atque Vale" of the poet's hopeless woe,
Tenderest of Roman poets nineteen hundred years ago,
                                      (l. 4–6)

ChTr; EBVV; FaBoPP; GTBS-P; HAP; InPS; NAEL-2;
NoP; OBTV; OxBSP

Idylls of the King

15 In Love, if Love be Love,if Love be ours,
Faith and unfaith can ne'er be equal powers:
Unfaith in aught is want of faith in all.

In Memoriam A. H. H.

16 Strong Son of God, immortal Love,
Whom we, that have not seen thy face,
By faith, and faith alone, embrace,
Believing where we cannot prove; (Fr. Proem, l. 1–4)

17 Our little systems have their day;
They have their day and cease to be:
They are but broken lights of thee,
And thou, O Lord, art more than they.
                          (Fr. Proem, l. 17–20)

EaLo; EBVV; HAP; LiTB; NAWM-2; OAEL-2; TrCP;
TrGrPo; TrPWD; WGRP

18 I held it truth, with him who sings
To one clear harp in diverse tones,
That men may rise on stepping-stones
Of their dead selves to higher things. (Fr. I, l. 1–4

EBVV; HeIP; LiTB; NoP; OAEL-2; OBNC

19 the clock
Beats out the little lives of men. (Fr. II, l. 7–8)

EBVV; ELP; GTBS-P; NOBE; NoP; OAEL-2; OBNC;
PoEL-5; UnPo

20 Dark house, by which once more I stand
Here in the long unlovely street,
Doors, where my heart was used to beat
                          (Fr. VII, l. 1–3)

21 The noise of life begins again,
And ghastly through the drizzling rain
On the bald street breaks the blank day.
                          (Fr. VII, l. 10–12)

EBEV; EBVV; GTBS-P; HAP; HeIP; LiTB; NOBE; NoP;
OAEL-2; OBD; OBNC; PeHV; PoEL-5; SCV; UnPo

22 Calm is the morn without a sound,
Calm as to suit a calmer grief,
And only through the faded leaf
The chestnut pattering to the ground: (Fr. XI, l. 1–4)

ChTr; EBEV; EBVV; ELP; FaBoPP; FaBoRV; FiP; HeIP;
LiTB; NOBE; NoP; OAEL-2; OBNC; PoEL-5; TrGrPo

23 To-night the winds begin to rise
And roar from yonder dropping day:
The last red leaf is whirl'd away,
The rooks are blown about the skies;

The forest crack'd, the waters curl'd,
The cattle huddled on the lea; (Fr. XV, l. 1–6)

24 And but for fancies, which aver
That all thy motions gently pass
Athwart a plane of molten glass,
I scarce could brook the strain and stir
                          (Fr. XV, l. 9–12)

EBVV; GTBS-P; LiTB; NOBE; OAEL-2; OBNC; PoEL-5

25 The Danube to the Severn gave
The darken'd heart that beat no more;
They laid him by the pleasant shore,
And in the hearing of the wave. (Fr. XIX, l. 1–4)

26 The Wye is hush'd nor moved along,
And hush'd my deepest grief of all,
When fill'd with tears that cannot fall,
I brim with sorrow drowning song. (Fr. XIX, l. 9–12)

EBVV; FaBoPP; FF; GTBS-P; NoP; OAEL-2

27 Be near me when my light is low, (Fr. L, l. 1)

28 And Time, a maniac scattering dust,
And Life, a Fury slinging flame. (Fr. L, l. 7–8)

29 Be near me when I fade away,
To point the term of human strife,
And on the low dark verge of life
The twilight of eternal day. (Fr. L, l. 13–16)

EBVV; ELP; HAP; HeIP; LiTB; NOCV; NoP; OAEL-2;
PoEL-5; SCV

30 Oh yet we trust that somehow good
Will be the final goal of ill,
To pangs of nature, sins of will,
Defects of doubt, and taints of blood; (Fr. LIV, l. 1–4)

31 So runs my dream: but what am I?
An infant crying in the night;
An infant crying for the light:
And with no language but a cry. (Fr. LIV, l. 17–20)

EaLo; EBVV; LiTB; NoP; OAEL-2; OBNC; TrGrPo;
WGRP

32 Are God and Nature then at strife,
That Nature lends such evil dreams?
So careful of the type she seems,
So careless of the single life; (Fr. LV, l. 5–8)

33 I falter where I firmly trod,
And falling with my weight of cares
Upon the great world's altar-stairs
That slope thro' darkness up to God,
(Fr. LV, l. 13–16)

34 I stretch lame hands of faith, and grope,
And gather dust and chaff, and call
To what I feel is Lord of all,
And faintly trust the larger hope. (Fr. LV, l. 17–20)

EBVV; HAP; NoP; OAEL-2; OBNC; TOF

35 "So careful of the type?" but no.
From scarped cliff and quarried stone
She cries, "A thousand types are gone;
I care for nothing, all shall go. (Fr. LVI, l. 1–4)

36 Man, her last work, who seemed so fair,
Such splendid purpose in his eyes,
Who rolled the psalm to wintry skies,
Who built him fanes of fruitless prayer,

Who trusted God was love indeed
And love Creation's final law —
Though Nature, red in tooth and claw
With ravine, shrieked against his creed —
(Fr. LVI, l. 9–16)

37 O life as futile, then, as frail!
O for thy voice to soothe and bless!
What hope of answer, or redress?
Behind the veil, behind the veil. (Fr. LVI, l. 25–28)

FF; HAP; NoF; OAEL-2; OBNC; TOF

38 I wage not any feud with Death
For changes wrought on form and face;
No lower life that earth's embrace
May breed with him can fright my faith.
(Fr. LXXXII, l. 1–4)

39 Nor blame I Death, because he bare
The use of virtue out of earth;
I know transplanted human worth
Will bloom to profit, otherwhere.

For this alone on Death I wreak
The wrath that garners in my heart:
He put our lives so far apart
We cannot hear each other speak.
(Fr. LXXXII, l. 9–16)

EBVV; LiTB; OAEL-2

40 By night we lingered on the lawn,
For underfoot the herb was dry;
And genial warmth; and o'er the sky
The silvery haze of summer drawn; (Fr. XCV, l. 1–4)

41 A hunger seized my heart; I read
Of that glad year which once had been,
In those fallen leaves which kept their green,
The noble letters of the dead. (Fr. XCV, l. 21–24)

EBVV; HAP; NoP; OAEL-2; OBNC; PoEL-5; TOF

42 Unloved, that beech will gather brown,
This maple burn itself away;

Unloved, the sun-flower, shining fair,
Ray round with flames her disk of seed,
And many a rose-carnation feed
With summer spice the humming air; (Fr. CI, l. 3–8)

43 gird the windy grove,
And flood the haunts of hern and crake;
(Fr. CI, l. 13–14)

44 And year by year the landscape grow
Familiar to the stranger's child; (Fr. CI, l. 19–20)

45 And year by year our memory fades
From all the circle of the hills. (Fr. CI, l. 23–24)

EBVV; ELP; FaBoPP; GTBS-P; OAEL-2; OBNC; PoEL-5;
SCV

46 Ring out, wild bells, to the wild sky; (Fr. CVI, l. 10)

47 Ring out the old, ring in the new,
Ring happy bells, across the snow:
The year is going, let him go;
Ring out the false,ring in the true. (Fr. CVI, l. 4–8)

48 Ring out a slowly dying cause,
And ancient forms of party strife;
Ring in the nobler modes of life,
With sweeter manners, purer laws. (Fr. CVI, l. 13–16)

49 Ring out, ring out thy mournful rhymes,
But ring the fuller minstrel in. (Fr. CVI, l. 19–20)

50 Ring out the darkness of the land,
Ring in the Christ that is to be.

BLPL; EBVV; FaFP; FaPON; FaPoR; FiP; LiTB;
OAEL-2; OFD; TrGrPo; WBLP; WiR

51 Now fades the lasts long streak of snow,
Now burgeons every maze of quick
About the flowering squares, and thick
By ashen roots the violets blow. (Fr. CXV, l. 1–4)

52 From land to land; and in my breast
Spring wakens too; and my regret
Becomes an April violet,
And buds and blossoms like the rest.
     (Fr. CXV, l. 17–20)

EBVV; FaBoRV; GTBS-P; NOBE; OAEL-2; OBNC

53 Doors, where my heart was used to beat
So quickly, not as one that weeps
I come once more; the city sleeps;
I smell the meadow in the street; (Fr. CXIX, l. 1–4)

54 Betwixt the black fronts long-withdrawn
A light-blue lane of early dawn, (Fr. CXIX, l. 6–7)

EBVV; NoP; OAEL-2; OBNC; PoEL-5; SCV

55 O earth, what changes hast thou seen!
     (Fr. CXXIII, l. 2)

56 For through my lips may breathe adieu,
I cannot think the thing farewell.
     (Fr. CXXIII, l. 11–12)

EBVV; FaBoRV; HAP; NOBE; OAEL-2; SeCePo

57 Love is and was my Lord and King,
And in his presence I attend
To hear the tidings of my friend,
Which every hour his couriers bring.
     (Fr. CXXVI, l. 1–4)

ChTr; EBVV; NOBE; NOCV; OAEL-2; OBEV; OBNC

The Kraken

58 Below the thunders of the upper deep;
Far, far beneath in the abysmal sea,
His ancient, dreamless, uninvaded sleep
The Kraken sleepeth: (l. 1–4)

AmMo; NAEL-2; NoP; OAEL-2; OBNC; PoEL-5; TOF;
WiR; WSC

The Lady of Shalott

59 And through the field the road runs by
To many-towered Camelot; (l. 4–5)

60 the silent isle imbowers
The Lady of Shalott. (l. 17–18)

61 There she weaves by night and day
A magic web with colours gay. (l. 37–38)

62 A curse is on her if she stay
To look down to Camelot. (l. 40–41)

63 The sun came dazzling through the leaves,
And flamed upon the brazen greaves
Of bold Sir Lancelot. (l. 75–77)

64 'Tirra Tirra,' by the river
Sang Sir Lancelot. (l. 107–108)

65 She left the web, she left the loom, (l. 109)

66 Out flew the web and floated wide;
The mirror cracked from side to side;
'The curse is come upon me,' cried
The Lady of Shalott. (l. 114–117)

67 Heard a carol, mournful, holy,
Chanted loudly, chanted lowly, (l. 145–146)

BeLS; BLPL; FaFP; FiP; GN; InPS; NAEL-2; NOBE;
OAEL-2; OBEV; OBNV; PoE; TEP; TOF; WiR

Locksley Hall

68 Comrades, leave me here a little, while as yet 'tis early
    morn:
Leave me here, and when you want me, sound upon the
    bugle-horn. (l. 1–2)

69 In the spring a livelier iris changes on the burnished
    dove;
In the spring a young man's fancy lightly turns to
    thoughts of love. (l. 19–20)

70 Love took up the glass of Time, and turned it in his
    glowing hands;
Every moment, lightly shaken, ran itself in golden
    sands.

Love took up the harp of Life, and smote on all the
chords with might;
Smote the chord of Self, that, trembling, passed in
music out of sight. (l. 31–34)

71 As the husband is, the wife is: thou art mated with a
clown, (l. 47)

72 Cursed be the social wants that sin against the strength
of youth!
Cursed be the social lies that warp us from the living
truth! (l. 59–60)

73 Can I think of her as dead, and love her for the love she
bore?
No—she never loved me truly: love is love for
evermore. (l. 73–74)

74 a sorrow's crown of sorrow is remembering happier
things.

Drug thy memories, lest thou learn it, lest thy heart be
put to proof,
In the dead unhappy night, and when the rain is on the
roof. (l. 76–78)

75 For I dipped into the future, far as human eye could
see,
Saw the Vision of the world, and all the wonder that
would be;

Saw the heavens fill with commerce, argosies of magic
sails,
Pilots of the purple twilight, dropping down with costly
bales;

Heard the heavens fill with shouting, and there rained
a ghastly dew
From the nations' airy navies grappling in the central
blue;

Far along the world-wide whisper of the south-wind
rushing warm,
With the standards of the peoples plunging through the
thunder-storm; (l. 119–126)

76 Till the war-drum throbbed no longer, and the battle-
flags were furled
In the Parliament of man, the Federation of the world.

There the common sense of most shall hold a fretful
realm in awe,
And the kindly earth shall slumber, lapped in universal
law. (l. 127–130)

77 Yet I doubt not through the ages one increasing
purpose runs,
And the thoughts of men are widened with the process
of the suns. (l. 137–138)

78 Knowledge comes, but wisdom lingers, (l. 143)

79 Not in vain the distance beacons. Forward let us range,
Let the great world spin for ever down the ringing
grooves of change. (l. 181–182)

BLPL; EBEV; FaBoBe; FaFP; NAEL-2; OAEL-2

The Lotus-Eaters

80 "Courage!" he said, and pointed toward the land,
"This mounting wave will roll us shoreward soon."
In the afternoon they came unto a land
In which it seemed always afternoon. (l. 1–4)

81 A land where all things always seemed the same!
And round about the keel with faces pale,
Dark faces pale against that rosy flame,
The mild-eyed melancholy Lotos-eaters came.
(l. 24–27)

82 And sweet it was to dream of Fatherland,
Of child, and wife, and slave; but evermore
Most weary seemed the sea, weary the oar,
Weary the wandering fields of barren foam. (l. 39–42)

83 "Our island home
Is far beyond the wave; we will no longer roam."
(l. 44–45)

ChTr; FiP; LiTB; NAEL-2; NoP; OAEL-2; OnMSP; PoEL-
5; TEP

84 There is sweet music here that softer falls
Than petals from blown roses on the grass,
Or night-dews on still waters between walls
Of shadowy granite, in a gleaming pass;
Music that gentlier on the spirit lies,
Than tired eyelids upon tired eyes;
Music that brings sweet sleep down from the blissful
skies. (l. 46–52)

85 Why are we weighed upon with heaviness,
And utterly consumed with sharp distress, (l. 57–58)

86 Death is the end of life; ah, why
Should life all labor be? (l. 86–87)

87 To muse and brood and live again in memory,
With those old faces of our infancy
Heaped over with a mound of grass,
Two handfuls of white dust, shut in an urn of brass!
(l. 110–113)

88 We have had enough of action, and of motion we,
Rolled to starboard, rolled to larboard, when the surge
was seething free, (l. 150–151)

89 In the hollow Lotos land to live and lie reclined
On the hills like Gods together, careless of mankind.
(l. 154–155)

90 they smile in secret, looking over wasted lands,
Blight and famine, plague and earthquake, roaring
   deeps and fiery sands,
Clanging fights, and flaming towns, and sinking ships,
   and praying hands. (l. 159–161)

91 Like a tale of little meaning though the words are
   strong;
Chanted from an ill-used race of men that cleave the
   soil,
Sow the seed, and reap the harvest with enduring toil,
Storing yearly little dues of wheat, and wine and oil;
Till they perish and they suffer — some, 'tis whispered —
   down in hell (l. 164–168)

ChTr; FaBV; FaFP; FiP; HeIP; LiTB; NAEL-2; NOBE;
NoP; OAEL-2; OBEV; OBNC; OnMSP; PoEL-5; TEP

Mariana

92 She only said, 'My life is dreary,
He cometh not,' she said;
She said, 'I am aweary, aweary,
I would that I were dead!'

AWP; CH; ChER; InPS; NAEL-2; NOBE; NoP; OAEL-2;
OBEV; OBNC; PoE; PoEL-5; TEP; TrGrPo; UnPo; WiR

Maud

93 Come into the garden, Maud,
For the black bat, night, has flown,
Come into the garden, Maud,
I am here at the gate alone;
And the woodbine spices are wafted abroad,
And the musk of the rose is blown.

94 There has fallen a splendid tear
From the passion-flower at the gate.
She is coming, my dove, my dear;
She is coming, my life, my fate;
The red rose cries, 'She is near, she is near;'
And the white rose weeps, 'She is late;'
The larkspur listens, 'I hear, I hear;'
And the lily whispers, 'I wait.'

AWP; EBVV; FaBV; FiP; NOBE; NOBVV; OAEL-2; PoE

95 I have led her home, my love, my only friend.
There is none like her, none.
And never yet so warmly ran my blood
And sweetly, on and on
Calming itself to the long-wished-for end,
Full to the banks, close on the promised good.

96 O, why should Love, like men in drinking-songs,
Spice his fair banquet with the dust of death?

ChER; EBVV; ELP; FiP; NAEL-2; NOBVV; PoEL-5

97 O that 'twere possible,
After long grief and pain,
To find the arms of my true-love
Round me once again! . . .

98 Ah God! that it were possible
For one short hour to see
The souls we loved, that they might tell us
What and where they be. . . .

BoLoP; NAEL-2; NOBE; NOBVV; OAEL-2; OBEV; PoE

99 See what a lovely shell,
Small and pure as a pearl,

100 How exquisitely minute,
A miracle of design!

101 What is it? a learned man
Could give it a clumsy name.
Let him name it who can,
The beauty would be the same.

BoNaP; GN; GoJo; PoEL-5

Morte d'Arthur

102 Were it well to obey then, if a king demand
An act unprofitable, against himself?

103 'The old order changeth, yielding place to new
And God fulfils Himself in many ways,
Lest one good custom should corrupt the world.

104 More things are wrought by prayer
Than this world dreams of. Wherefore, let thy voice
Rise like a fountain for me night and day.

DL; FaBoBe; FaBoRV; FiP; NIP; NOBVV; OAEL-2;
OBNV; PoEL-5

The Owl

105 When cats run home and light is come,
And dew is cold upon the ground,
And the far-off stream is dumb,
And the whirring sail goes round,
And the whirring sail goes round;
Alone and warming his five wits,
The white owl in the belfry sits.

BoTP; CH; FaBoCh; FaPON; GoJo; MoShBr; PBBP

The Princess

106 Ask me no more: thy fate and mine are sealed;
I strove against the stream and all in vain;
Let the great river take me to the main.

No more, dear love, for at a touch I yield;
Ask me no more.

GBL; LiTB; NAEL-2; OBNC; PoEL-5; TrGrPo

107 the children call, and I
Thy shepherd pipe, and sweet is every sound,
Sweeter thy voice, but every sound is sweet;
Myriads of rivulets hurrying through the lawn,
The moan of doves in immemorial elms,
And murmuring of innumerable bees.'

108 all her labour was but as a block
Left in the quarry;

EBVV; FF; GTBS-P; NAEL-2; NOBVV; OAEL-2; OBEV;
OBNC; TrGrPo

109 Now sleeps the crimson petal, now the white;
Nor waves the cypress in the palace walk;
Nor winks the gold fin in the porphyry font.
The firefly wakens; waken thou with me.

Now droops the milk-white peacock like a ghost,
And like a ghost she glimmers on to me.

Now lies the Earth all Danae to the stars,
And all thy heart lies open unto me.

BLPL; BoLoP; ChER; ChTr; EBEV; EBVV; ELP;
FaBoBe; FiP; GBL; GTBS-P; LLLT; NAEL-2; NIP;
NOBE; NoP; OBEV; OBNC; PoEL-5; PPP; SCV; SeCePo;
TrGrPo

110 Heavily hangs the broad sunflower
Over its grave i' the earth so chilly;
Heavily hangs the hollyhock,
Heavily hangs the tiger-lily.

GTBS-P; HeIP; InvP; OBNC

111 The splendor falls on castle walls
And snowy summits old in story;
The long light shakes across the lakes,
And the wild cataract leaps in glory.
Blow, bugle, blow, set the wild echoes flying,
Blow, bugle; answer, echoes, dying, dying, dying.

112 O, sweet and far from cliff and scar
The horns of Elfland faintly blowing!

AWP; BLPL; CH; ChTr; EBVV; ELP; FaBoCh; FaBoPP;
FaBV; FaFP; FaPON; FiP; GN; GoJo; GTBS-P; HeIP;
InPK; LiTB; NAEL-2; NOBE; NoP; OAEL-2; OBEV;
OBNC; PoEL-5; PrIm; TrGrPo; UnPo; UnS; WiR; WSC

113 Sweet and low, sweet and low,
Wind of the western sea,
Low, low, breathe and blow,
Wind of the western sea!
Over the rolling waters go,
Come from the dying moon, and blow,

Blow him again to me;
While my little one, while my pretty one, sleeps.

BLPL; BoTP; FaBoBe; FaPON; MOS; NAEL-2; OxBChV;
PoLF; TrGrPo

114 Tears, idle tears, I know not what they mean,
Tears from the depth of some divine despair
Rise in the heart, and gather to the eyes,
In looking on the happy autumn-fields,
And thinking of the days that are no more.

115 Dear as remembered kisses after death,
And sweet as those by hopeless fancy feigned
On lips that are for others; deep as love,
Deep as first love, and wild with all regret;
O Death in Life, the days that are no more.

AWP; EBVV; ELP; FaBoRV; FaFP; FaPoR; FiP; FPL;
GTBS-P; HAP; InPS; InvP; LiTB; NAEL-2; NIP; NOBE;
NoP; OAEL-2; OBNC; PoE; PoEL-5; PPP; TEP; TrGrPo;
UnPo; WeW

The Revenge

116 At Flores in the Azores Sir Richard Grenville lay,
And a pinnace like a fluttered bird, came flying from
far away:
'Spanish ships of war at sea! we have sighted fifty-
three!' (l. 1–3)

117 I should count myself the coward if I left them, my
Lord Howard.
To these Inquisition dogs and the devildoms of Spain.'
(l. 11–12)

118 'Shall we fight or shall we fly?
Good Sir Richard, tell us now,
For to fight is but to die! (l. 25–27)

119 Sir Richard cried in his English pride,
'We have fought such a fight for a day and a night
As may never be fought again!
We have won great glory, my men!
And a day less or more
At sea or ashore,
We die — does it matter when? (l. 82–88)

BeLS; EBVV; FaBoCh; FaPoR; OBWP; OnMSP; PoRA

Tithonus

120 The woods decay, the woods decay and fall,
The vapours weep their burthen to the ground,
Man comes and tills the field and lies beneath,
And after many a summer dies the swan.

121 Why should a man desire in any way
To vary from the kindly race of men,
Or pass beyond the goal of ordinance
Where all should pause, as is most meet for all?

122 'The Gods themselves cannot recall their gifts.'

     HAP; LiTB; NAEL-2; NAWM-2; NOBE; NOBVV; NoP; OAEL-2; OBNC; PoEL-5; PoE; PPP; TEP

To Virgil

123 Roman Virgil, thou that singest
     Ilion's lofty temples robed in fire, (l. 1–2)

124 All the chosen coin of fancy
     flashing out from many a golden phrase; (l. 7–8)

125 All the charm of all the Muses
     often flowering in a lonely word; (l. 11–12)

126 Thou majestic in thy sadness
     at the doubtful doom of human kind; (l. 23–24)

127 Wielder of the stateliest measure
     ever moulded by the lips of man. (l. 39–40)

     AWP; ChTr; GTBS-P; NoP; OAEL-2; PoEL-5

Ulysses

128 It little profits that an idle king,
     By this still hearth, among these barren crags,
     Matched with an aged wife, I mete and dole
     Unequal laws unto a savage race
     That hoard, and sleep, and feed, (l. 1–5)

129 I cannot rest from travel; I will drink
     Life to the lees. (l. 6–7)

130 Much have I seen and known — cities of men
     And manners, climates, councils, governments,
     Myself not least, but honored of them all —
     And drunk delight of battle with my peers,
     Far on the ringing plains of windy Troy.
     I am a part of all that I have met; (l. 13–18)

131 How dull it is to pause, to make and end,
     To rust unburnished, not to shine in use!
     As though to breathe were life! (l. 22–24)

132 And this gray spirit yearning in desire
     To follow knowledge like a sinking star,
     Beyond the utmost bound of human thought.
     (l. 30–32)

133 Death closes all; but something ere the end,
     Some work of noble note, may yet be done,
     Not unbecoming men that strove with Gods.
     (l. 49–50)

134 'Tis not too late to seek a newer world. (l. 44)

135 Though much is taken, much abides; and though
     We are not now that strength which in old days
     Moved earth and heaven, that which we are, we are —
     One equal temper of heroic hearts,
     Made weak by time and fate, but strong in will
     To strive, to seek, to find, and not to yield. (l. 52–57)

     AWP; EBEV; FaPoR; FF; FiP; FPL; HAP; HeIP; HoPM; InPK; InPS; LiTB; MOS; NAEL-2; NAWM-2; NIP; NOBE; NOBVV; NoP; OAEL-2; PoE; PoRA; PPP; PrIm; SCV; SeCePo; SoSe; TEP; TrGrPo; UnPo; WeW

WILLIAM MAKEPEACE THACKERAY
(1811–1863)

Pocahontas

1 Now they heap the funeral pyre,
     And the torch of death they light;
     Ah! 'tis hard to die by fire! (l. 9–11)

2 In the woods of Powhatan,
     Still 'tis told by Indian fires
     How a daughter of their sires
     Saved a captive Englishman. (l. 29–32)

     AmFN; FaPON; GN; OnMSP; OPP; PAH

The Sorrows of Werther

3 Werther had a love for Charlotte
     Such as words could never utter;
     Would you know how first he met her?
     She was cutting bread and butter. (l. 1–4)

     BLPA; CenHV; FaBoCo; FiBHP; FPL; NA; NBLV; NOBL; NOBVV; OBD

CELIA THAXTER ("LAIGHTON")
(1835–1894)

The Sandpiper

1 Across the lonely beach we flit,
     One little sandpiper and I;
     And fast I gather, bit by bit,
     The scattered driftwood, bleached and dry.
     The wild waves reach their hands for it,
     The wild wind raves, the tide runs high,
     As up and down the beach we flit —
     One little sandpiper and I. (l. 1–8)

     AA; FaBoBe; FaPON; GN; OBCA; OxBChV; PWR; WBLP

ERNEST LAWRENCE THAYER
(1863–1940)

Casey at the Bat

1 It looked extremely rocky for the Mudville nine that day;
The score stood two to four, with but one inning left to play. (l. 1–2)

2 There was ease in Casey's manner as he stepped into his place,
There was pride in Casey's bearing and a smile on Casey's face; (l. 21–22)

3 With a smile of Christian charity great Casey's visage shone;
He stilled the rising tumult, he made the game go on;
(l. 37–38)

4 Oh, somewhere in this favored land the sun is shining bright,
The band is playing somewhere, and somewhere hearts are light;
And somewhere men are laughing, and somewhere children shout,
But there is no joy in Mudville — Mighty Casey has struck out. (l. 49–52)

AnAmPo; BeLS; BLPA; FaBoBe; FaFP; FPL; PoRA

SAINT THERESA, OF AVILA
(1515–1582)

Lines Written in Her Breviary

1 Let nothing disturb thee,
Nothing affright thee;
All things are passing;
God never changeth; (l. 1–4)

2 Who God possesseth
In nothing is wanting;
Alone God sufficeth. (l. 7–9)

AWP; CTC; EaLo; PoEL-5; WPOW

DYLAN THOMAS (1914–1953)

After the Funeral

1 After the funeral, mule praises, brays, (l. 1)

2 Morning smack of the spade that wakes up sleep,
Shakes a desolate boy who slits his throat
In the dark of the coffin and sheds dry leaves, (l. 6–8)

3 In a room with a stuffed fox and a stale fern, (l. 11)

4 In a fiercely mourning house in a crooked year. (l. 30)

5 Her fist of a face died clenched on a round pain;
And sculptured Ann is seventy years of stone.
These cloud-sopped, marble hands, this monumental
Argument of the hewn voice, gesture and psalm,
Storm me forever over her grave (l. 34–38)

CMoP; FaBoMo; NAEL-2; NoP; OAEL-2; OBWVE

Altarwise by Owl-Light

6 Altarwise by owl-light in the half-way house
The gentleman lay graveward with his furies;
Abaddon in the hangnail cracked from Adam,
And, from his fork, a dog among the fairies,
The atlas-eater with a jaw for news,
Bit out the mandrake with to-morrow's scream.

7 I am the long world's gentleman, he said,
And share my bedwith Capricorn and Cancer.

8 Now stamp the Lord's Prayer on a grain of rice,
A Bible-leaved of all the written woods
Strip to this tree: a rocking alphabet,
Genesis in the root, the scarecrow word,
And one light's language in the book of trees.

CMoP; FaBoMo; LiTM; MoAB; Son

And Death Shall Have No Dominion

9 And death shall have no dominion.
Dead men naked they shall be one
With the man in the wind and the west moon; (l. 1–3)

10 Though they be mad and dead as nails,
Heads of the characters hammer through daisies;
Break in the sun till the sun breaks down,
And death shall have no dominion. (l. 23–26)

CMoP; EaLo; LiTM; MoAB; MoBrPo; NoAM; RB;
SeCePo

Do Not Go Gentle into That Good Night

11 Do not go gentle into that good night,
Old age should burn and rave at close of day;
Rage, rage against the dying of the light. (l. 1–3)

12 And you, my father, there on the sad height,
Curse, bless, me now with your fierce tears, I pray.
Do not go gentle into that good night.
Rage, rage against the dying of the light. (l. 16–19)

DL; FaFP; FF; HAP; HeIP; HoPM; InPK; InPS; LiTM;
MoAB; MoBrPo; MoP; NAEL-2; NIP; NoAM; NOBE;
NoP; OAEL-2; OBD; OxBTC; PoE; PrIm; RB; SCV;
SoSe; TEP; TOF; TW; TwCP; UnPo; WeW

Especially When the October Wind

13 Especially when the October wind
     With frosty fingers punishes my hair, (l. 1–2)

14 My busy heart who shudders as she talks
     Sheds the syllabic blood and drains her words.
                      (l. 7–8)

15 Behind a pot of ferns the wagging clock
     Tells me the hour's word, the neural meaning
     Flies on the shafted disc, declaims the morning
     And tells the windy weather in the cock. (l. 17–20)

16 Some let me make you of the heartless words.
     The heart is drained that, spelling in the scurry
     Of chemic blood, warned of the coming fury.
     By the sea's side hear the dark-vowelled birds.
                     (l. 29–32)

LiTB; MoAB; MoBrPo; OBWVE; OxBTC

Fern Hill

17 Now as I was young and easy under the apple boughs
     About the lilting house and happy as the grass was
         green,
     The night above the dingle starry, (l. 1–3)

18 And nightly under the simple stars
     As I rode to sleep the owls were bearing the farm away,
                     (l. 23–24)

19 it was all
     Shining, it was Adam and maiden, (l. 29–30)

20 And nothing I cared, at my sky blue trades, that time
         allows
     In all his tuneful turning so few and such morning
         songs
     Before the children green and golden
     Follow him out of grace. (l. 42–45)

21 Oh as I was young and easy in the mercy of his means,
     Time held me green and dying
     Though I sang in my chains like the sea. (l. 52–54)

CMoP; FaBoPP; FaBV; FPL; GoJo; GTBS-P; HAP; HeIP;
InPK; InPS; LiTB; LiTM; MoAB; MoBrPo; MoP;
NAEL-2; NIP; NoAM; NOBE; NoP; OAEL-2; OBWVE;
OxBTC; PoE; PoLF; PoRA; PPP; SoSe; TrGrPo; TwCP;
WeW

The Force That through the Green Fuse Drives the Flower

22 The force that through the green fuse drives the flower
     Drives my green age; that blasts the roots of trees
     Is my destroyer.

And I am dumb to tell the crooked rose
My youth is bent by the same wintry fever. (l. 1–5)

23 And I am dumb to tell the lover's tomb
     How at my sheet goes the same crooked worm.
                     (l. 21–22)

BLPL; CMoP; EBEV; FaBoMo; ImOP; InPS; LiTB;
LiTM; MoAB; MoBrPo; MoP; NAEL-2; NIP; NoAM;
NOBE; NoP; OBWVE; OxBTC; PoE; PPP; PrIm; RB;
SCV; TEP; UnPo

The Hand That Signed the Paper Felled a City

24 The hand that signed the paper felled a city;
     Five sovereign fingers taxed the breath,
     Doubled the globe of dead and halved a country;
     These five kings did a king to death. (l. 1–4)

25 The five kings count the dead but do not soften
     The crusted wound nor stroke the brow;
     A hand rules pity as a hand rules heaven;
     Hands have no tears to flow. (l. 13–16)

MoAB; MoBrPo; MoP; NoAM; NOBE; NoP; OBWP; RB;
SeCePo; TrGrPo; WaP

The Hunchback in the Park

26 All night in the unmade park
     After the railings and shrubberies
     The birds the grass the trees the lake
     And the wild boys innocent as strawberries
     Had followed the hunchback
     To his kennel in the dark. (l. 37–42)

EBEV; FaBoTw; MoAB; MoBrPo; NAEL-2; NoAM; NoP;
PrIm; TwCP

In My Craft or Sullen Art

27 In my craft or sullen art
     Exercised in the still night
     When only the moon rages
     And the lovers lie abed
     With all their griefs in their arms, (l. 1–5)

28 But for the lovers, their arms
     Round the griefs of the ages,
     Who pay no praise or wages
     Nor heed my craft or art. (l. 17–20)

BoLoP; CMoP; GTBS-P; HAP; HeIP; InvP; LiTM; MAT;
MoP; NIP; NoAM; NoP; PoE; WeW

Light Breaks Where No Sun Shines

29 Light breaks where no sun shines;
     Where no sea runs, the waters of the heart
     Push in their tides; (l. 1–3)

30 A candle in the thighs
Warms youth and seed and burns the seeds of age;
(l. 7–8)

31 When logics die,
The secret of the soil grows through the eye,
And blood jumps in the sun;
Above the waste allotments the dawn halts. (l. 27–30)

CMoP; ErPo; FaBoMo; LiTB; MoAB; MoBrPo; OxBTC;
SeCePo

Poem in October

32 It was my thirtieth year to heaven
Woke to my hearing from harbor and neighbor wood
(l. 1–2)

33 And I rose
In rainy autumn
And walked abroad in a shower of all my days.
(l. 14–16)

34 a child's
Forgotten mornings when he walked with his mother
Through the parables
Of sunlight
And the legends of the green chapels

And the twice-told fields of infancy (l. 46–51)

35 And there could I marvel my birthday
Away but the weather turned around. And the true
Joy of the long dead child sang burning
In the sun. (l. 61–64)

36 Oh may my heart's truth
Still be sung
On this high hill in a year's turning. (l. 68–70)

LiTB; NAEL-2; NAs; NoAM; PoA; PoRA; PrIm; RB;
SeCePo; SoSe

A Refusal to Mourn the Death, by Fire, of a Child in London

37 mourn

The majesty and burning of the child's death.
I shall not murder
The mankind of her going with a grave truth
Nor blaspheme down the stations of the breath
(l. 12–16)

38 Deep with the first dead lies London's daughter,
Robed in the long friends,
The grains beyond age, the dark veins of her mother,
Secret by the unmourning water

Of the riding Thames.
After the first death, there is no other. (l. 19–24)

BLPL; CMoP; EBEV; FaBoMo; FaFP; FF; GTBS-P; HeIP;
HoPM; LiTB; LiTM; MoAB; MoBrPo; MoP; NoAM;
NOBE; NoP OAEL-2; OBWVE; OxBTC; PoE; SeCePo;
TEP; TwCP; UnPo; WaaP

The Song of the Mischievous Dog

39 There are many who say that a dog has his day,
And a cat has a number of lives; (l. 1–2)

40 But my greatest delight is to take a good bite
At a calf that is plump and delicious;
And if I indulge in a bite at a bulge,
Let's hope you won't think me too vicious. (l. 13–16)

FaFP; FL; FPL; GrPl

Twenty-four Years

41 Dressed to die, the sensual strut begun,
With my red veins full of money,
In the final direction of the elementary town
I advance for as long as forever is. (l. 6–9)

CMoP; MAT; MoAB; NAs; OxBSP

Under Milk Wood

42 For Johnnie Crack and Flossie Snail
Always used to say that stout and ale
Was good for a baby in a milking pail. (l. 13–15)

FaPON; FiBHP; GoJo; PDV; RHPC

When All My Five and Country Senses See

43 When all my five and country senses see, (l. 1)

44 My one and noble heart has witnesses
In all love's countries, that will watch awake;
And when blind sleep falls on the spying senses,
The heart is sensual, though five eyes break.
(l. 11–14)

MoAB; MoBrPo; NoAM; PoA; SeCePo; Son

EDWARD THOMAS ("EDWARD EASTAWAY") (1878–1917)

Adlestrop

1 No one left and no one came
On the bare platform. What I saw
Was Adlestrop — only the name —

And willows, willow-herb, and grass, (l. 6–9)

BrPo; CH; FaBoPF; GoJo; HAP; LiTB; NAEL-2; NOBE;
OBEV; OxBTC

As the Team's Head-Brass

2 As the team's head-brass flashed out on the turn
The lovers disappeared into the wood. (l. 1–2)

3 Everything
Would have been different. For it would have been
Another world.' 'Ay, and a better, though
If we could see all all might seem good.' (l. 30–33)

GTBS-P; MMA; NAEL-2; OBWP; OxBTC; PoE; RB

Cock-Crow

4 Out of the wood of thoughts that grows by night
To be cut down by the sharp ax of light —,
Out of the night, two cocks together crow,
Cleaving the darkness with a silver blow: (l. 1–4)

GTBS-P; MoAB; MoBrPo; OxBSP; RB

Digging

5 Today I think Only with scents, — scents dead leaves
   yield, (l. 1–2)

6 It is enough
To smell, to crumble the dark earth,
While the robin sings over again
Sad songs of Autumn mirth. (l. 13–16)

BrPo; MoAB; MoBrPo; OxBTC

The Gallows

7 There was a weasel lived in the sun
With all his family,
Till a keeper shot him with his gun (l. 1–3)

8 Where he swings in the wind and rain,
In the sun and in the snow,
Without pleasure, without pain,
On the dead oak tree bough. (l. 5–8)

FM; InPS; LiTB; MoAB; MoBrPo; MoP; NoAM; UnPo

Haymaking

9 After night's thunder far away had rolled
The fiery day had a kernel sweet of cold (l. 1–2)

10 Under the heavens that know not what years be
The men, the beasts, the trees, the implements
Uttered even what they will in times far hence —
All of us gone out of the reach of change —
Immortal in a picture of an old grange. (l. 38–42)

BrPo; MoAB; MoBrPo; SeCePo

If I Should Ever by Chance

11 Whenever I am sufficiently rich:
Codham, Cockridden, and Childerditch,
Roses, Pyrgo, and Lapwater —
I shall give them all to my elder daughter. (l. 11–14)

FaBoCh; GoJo; MoAB; MoBrPo; MoShBr; OBMV;
OBWVE; OxBChV

In Memoriam (Easter, 1915)

12 The flowers left thick at nightfall in the wood
This Eastertide call into mind the men
Now far from home, (l. 1–3)

GTBS-P; NOBE; OBWP; OBWVE; OxBTC

Lights Out

13 There is not any book
Or face of dearest look
That I would not turn from now
To go into the unknown
I must enter, and leave, alone,
I know not how. (l. 19–24)

BrPo; Mes; MMA; NOBE; OBD

The New House

14 Nights of storm, days of mist, without end;
Sad days when the sun
Shone in vain: old griefs and griefs
Not yet begun. (l. 9–12)

EBEV; MoAB; MoBrPo; NOBE; OBEV; OBWVE

Out in the Dark

15 How weak and little is the light,
All the universe of sight,
Love and delight,
Before the might,
If you love it not, of night. (l. 16–20)

BrPo; CH; GTBS-P; LiTM; MoAB; MoBrPo; NOBE;
OBWVE; RB

The Owl

16 And salted was my food, and my repose,
Salted and sobered, too, by the bird's voice
Speaking for all who lay under the stars,
Soldiers and poor, unable to rejoice. (l. 13–16)

ChTr; EBEV; FaBoRV; FaBoTw; FF; GTBS-P; LiTB;
MoP; NAEL-2; NIP; NoAM; NOBE; NoP; OAEL-2;
OBWVE; PoE; RB; SoSe; UnPo

Tall Nettles

17 I like the dust on the nettles, never lost
Except to prove the sweetness of a shower. (l. 7–8)

BoTP; BrPo; ChTr; FaBoTw; MoAB; MoBrPo; OxBSP

Thaw

18 Over the land freckled with snow half-thawed
The speculating rooks at their nests cawed (l. 1–2)

EBEV; FaBoTw; FM; GTBS-P; MoAB; MoBrPo; OxBSP;
OxBTC

Will You Come?

19 If you come
Haste and come.
Owls have cried,
It grows dark
To ride.
Beloved, beautiful, come! (l. 25–30)

CH; GoJo; GrPl; RR

FRANCIS THOMPSON (1859–1907)

Daisy

1 The fairest things have fleetest end,
Their scent survives their close:
But the rose's scent is bitterness
To him that loved the rose. (l. 37–40)

2 She went her unremembering way,
She went and left in me
The pang of all the partings gone,
And partings yet to be. (l. 45–48)

3 Nothing begins, and nothing ends,
That is not paid with moan,
For we are born in other's pain,
And perish in our own. (l. 57–60)

AWP; BeLS; BrPo; FaBV; MoAB; MoBrPo; OBEV;
OBNC

Ex Ore Infantium

4 Little Jesus, wast Thou shy
Once, and just so small as I?
And what did it feel like to be
Out of Heaven, and just like me? (l. 1–4)

BoTP; FaBV; OHIP; OxBChV

The Heart

5 All's vast that vastness means. Nay, I affirm
Nature is whole in her least things exprest,
Nor know we with what scope God builds the worm.
Our towns are copied fragments from our breast;
And all man's Babylons strive but to impart
The grandeurs of his Babylonian heart.

GTBS-P; MoAB; MoBrPo; OBMV; Son

The Hound of Heaven

6 I fled Him, down the nights and down the days;
I fled Him, down the arches of the years;
I fled Him, down the labyrinthine ways
Of my own mind; and in the midst of tears
I hid from Him, and under running laughter. (l. 1–5)

7 Still with unhurrying chase,
And unperturbed pace,
Deliberate speed, majestic instancy,
Came on the following Feet,
And a Voice above their beat —
" Naught shelters thee, who wilt not shelter Me."
(l. 46–51)

8 I stand amid the dust o' the mounded years —
My mangled youth lies dead beneath the heap,
My days have crackled and gone up in smoke,
Have puffed and burst as sun-starts on a stream.
(l. 120–123)

9 All which I took from thee I did but take,
Not for thy harms,
But just that thou might'st seek it in My arms.
(l. 171–173)

10 "Ah, fondest, blindest, weakest,
I am He Whom thou seekest!
Thou dravest love from thee, who dravest Me."
(l. 180–183)

ACP; BLPL; BrPo; FaBV; FaFP; LiTB; LiTM; MoAB;
MoBrPo; NAEL-2; OBMV; PoEL-5; SeCePo; TrGrPo;
WGRP

The Kingdom of God

11 Cry; — and upon thy so sore loss
Shall shine the traffic of Jacob's ladder
Pitched betwixt Heaven and Charing Cross. (l. 18–20)

12 Cry, — clinging Heaven by the hems;
And lo, Christ walking on the water
Not of Gennesareth, but Thames! (l. 22–24)

BrPo; EaLo; FaPoR; GTBS-P; HAP; LiTB; MoAB;
MoBrPo; NOBE; NOCV; OBEV; TrCP; TrGrPo; WGRP

To a Snowflake

13 What heart could have thought you? —
Past our devisal
(O filigree petall)
Fashioned so purely, (l. 1–4)

14 From what Paradisal
Imagineless metal,
Too costly for cost?
Who hammered you, wrought you,
From argentine vapor? — (l. 6–10)

BoNaP; FaBV; ImOP; MoAB; MoBrPo; SeCePo; TrGrPo

WILL HENRY THOMPSON (1848–1918)

The High Tide at Gettysburg

1 Above the bayonets, mixed and crossed,
Men saw a gray, gigantic ghost
Receding through the battle cloud,
And heard across the tempest loud
The death cry of a nation lost! (l. 46–50)

2 They smote and fell, who set the bars
Against the progress of the stars,
And stayed the march of Motherland! (l. 58–60)

3 God lives! He forged the iron will
That clutched and held that trembling hill! (l. 66–67)

4 Fold up the banners! Smelt the guns!
Love rules, Her gentler purpose runs.
A mighty mother turns in tears
The pages of her battle years,
Lamenting all her fallen sons! (l. 71–75)

AA; AnAmPo; BeLS; BLPA; FaBoBe; PAH

JAMES THOMSON (1700–1748)

THE SEASONS (the following 4 poems)

Autumn

1 Poor is the triumph o'er the timid hare!
Scared from the corn, and now to some lone seat
Retired —

2 The savage soul of game is up at once —
The pack full-opening various, the shrill horn
Resounded from the hills, the neighing steed
Wild for the chase, and the loud hunter's shout —
O'er a weak, harmless, flying creature, all
Mixed in mad tumult and discordant joy.

Spring

3 But who can paint
Like Nature? Can imagination boast
Amid its gay creation, hues like hers?

4 If fancy then
Unequal fails beneath the pleasing task,
Ah, what shall language do?

5 The negligence of Nature wide and wild,
Where, undisguised by mimic art, she spreads
Unbounded beauty to the roving eye.

6 Hail, Source of Being! Universal Soul
Of heaven and earth! Essential Presence, hail!
To thee I bend the knee; to thee my thoughts
Continual climb, who with a master-hand
Hast the great whole into perfection touched.

7 Now 'tis nought
But restless hurry through the busy air,
Beat by unnumbered wings.

8 High from the summit of a craggy cliff,
Hung o'er the deep, such as amazing frowns
On utmost Kilda's shore, whose lonely race
Resign the setting sun to Indian worlds,
The royal eagle draws his vigorous young

Summer

9 To sunny waters some
By fatal instinct fly; where on the pool
They sportive wheel, or, sailing down the stream,
Are snatched immediate by the quick-eyed trout
Or darting salmon.

10 But chief to heedless flies the window proves
A constant death; where gloomily retired,
The villain spider lives, cunning and fierce,
Mixture abhorred! Amid a mangled heap
Of carcases in eager watch he sits,
O'erlooking all his waving snares around.

11 he dreadful darts
With rapid glide along the leaning line;
And, fixing in the wretch his cruel fangs

Winter

12 See, Winter comes, to rule the varied year,
Sullen, and sad, with all his rising train;
Vapours, and clouds, and storms. Be these my theme,
These, that exalt the soul to solemn thought,
And heavenly musing. Welcome, kindred glooms!
Congenial horrors, hail!

13 Thus Winter falls,
A heavy gloom oppressive o'er the world
Through Nature shedding influence malign,
And rouses up the seeds of dark disease.
The soul of man dies in him, loathing life,
And black with more than melancholy views.

JAMES THOMSON (1700–1748) *AND* DAVID MALLET (1705?–1765)

Alfred, A Masque: Rule Brittania

1 When Britain first, at Heaven's command,
Arose from out the azure main,
This was the charter of her land,
And guardian angels sung the strain:
Rule, Britannia! Britannia rules the waves!
Britons never shall be slaves. (l. 1–6)

FaPoR; GTBS; GTBS-P; NAEL-1; NOEC; OBWP; WBLP

JAMES THOMSON ("B.V."; "BYSSHE VANOLIS") (1834–1882)

The City of Dreadful Night

1 The City is of Night; perchance of Death,
But certainly of Night; for never there
Can come the lucid morning's fragrant breath
After the dewy dawning's cold grey air;

2 For life is but a dream whose shapes return,
Some frequently, some seldom, some by night
And some by day,

3 The street-lamps burn amidst the baleful glooms,
Amidst the soundless solitudes immense
Of ranged mansions dark and still as tombs.

4 The City is of Night, but not of Sleep;
There sweet sleep is not for the weary brain;
The pitiless hours like years and ages creep,

5 They have much wisdom yet they are not wise,
They have much goodness yet they do not well,
(The fools we know have their own Paradise,
The wicked also have their proper Hell);

6 The mighty river flowing dark and deep,
With ebb and flood from the remote sea-tides
Vague-sounding through the City's sleepless sleep,
Is named the River of the Suicides;

7 And all sad scenes and thoughts and feelings vanish
In that sweet sleep no power can ever banish,
That one best sleep which never wakes again.

EBVV; LiTB; OBNC; PoEL-5

8 Lo, thus, as prostrate, 'In the dust I write
My heart's deep languor and my soul's sad tears.'
Yet why evoke the spectres of black night
To blot the sunshine of exultant years?

GoTS; NOBE; OBNC; OxBS

HENRY DAVID THOREAU (1817–1862)

I Am a Parcel of Vain Strivings Tied

1 I am a parcel of vain strivings tied
By a chance bond together,
Dangling this way and that, their links
Were made so loose and wide,
Methinks,
For milder weather. (l. 1–6)

2 But now I see I was not plucked for naught,
And after in life's vase
Of glass set while I might survive,
But by a kind hand brought
Alive
To a strange place. (l. 31–36)

3 And by another year,
Such as God knows, with freer air,
More fruits and fairer flowers
Will bear,
While I droop here. (l. 38–42)

AmPP; AnAmPo; NOBA; NoP; OxBA; PoEL-4; TAP

Inspiration

4 If with light head erect I sing,
Though all the muses lend their force,
From my poor love of anything,
The verse is weak and shallow as its source.

But if with bended neck I grope,
Listening behind me for my wit,
With faith superior to hope,
More anxious to keep back than forward it, (l. 5–12)

5 A clear and ancient harmony
Pierces my soul through all its din,
As through its utmost melody, —
Farther behind than they — farther within.

More swift its bolt than lightning is,
Its voice than thunder is more loud,
It doth expand my privacies
To all, and leave me single in the crowd. (l. 33–40)

AA; AmPP; BLPL; FaBoBe; NOBA; OxBA

Walden

6 Light-winged Smoke, Icarian bird,
  Melting thy pinions in thy upward flight,
  Lark without song, and messenger of dawn,
  Circling above the hamlets as thy nest; (l. 1–4)

7 Go thou my incense upward from this hearth,
  And ask the gods to pardon this clear flame. (l. 9–10)

  AA; AWP; HeIP; NOBA; NoP; OxBA; TAP

A Week on the Concord and Merrimack Rivers

8 Low-anchored cloud,
  Newfoundland air,
  Fountain-head and source of rivers,
  Dew-cloth, dream drapery,
  And napkin spread by fays;

9 Bear only perfumes and the scent
  Of healing herbs to just men's fields!

  AA; AmPP; AnAmPo; AWP; ImOP; NoP; OxBA

Winter Memories

10 Within the circuit of this plodding life
   There enter moments of an azure hue,
   Untarnished fair as is the violet
   Or anemone, when the spring strews them
   By some meandering rivulet, which make
   The best philosophy untrue that aims
   But to console man for his grievances.
   I have remembered when the winter came, (l. 1–8)

11 Or seen the furrows shine but late upturned,
   And where the fieldfare followed in the rear,
   When all the fields around lay bound and hoar
   Beneath a thick integument of snow.
   So by God's cheap economy made rich
   To go upon my winter's task again. (l. 25–30)

   AmPP; AnAmPo; NOBA; OxBA

CHIDIOCK TICHBORNE   (1558–1586)

Tichborne's Elegy

1 My prime of youth is but a frost of cares,
  My feast of joy is but a dish of pain,
  My crop of corn is but a field of tares,
  And all my good is but vain hope of gain:
  The day is past, and yet I saw no sun,
  And now I live, and now my life is done. (l. 1–6)

  ACP; ChTr; DL; EBEV; ElL; FaBoRV; FF; HAP; HeIP;
  InPK; InPS; LiTB; NOBE; NoP; OAEL-1; OBD; OBSC;
  RB; SCV; TrGrPo; WeW

FRANCIS ORRERY TICKNOR
(1822–1874)

Little Giffen

1 Out of the focal and foremost fire,
  Our of the hospital walls as dire;
  Smitten of grape-shot and gangrene,
  (Eighteenth battle, and he sixteen!)
  Specter! such as you seldom see,
  Little Giffen, of Tennessee! (l. 1–6)

2 Word of gloom from the war, one day;
  Johnston pressed at the front, they say.
  Little Giffen was up and away;
  A tear — his first — as he bade good-by,
  Dimmed the glint of his steel-blue eye.
  "I'll write, if spared!" There was news of the fight;
  But none of Giffen. — He did not write.

  AA; AnAmPo; GOA; PAH

HENRY TIMROD   (1828–1867)

Charleston

1 Calm as that second summer which precedes
  The first fall of the snow,
  In the broad sunlight of heroic deeds,
  The City bides the foe. (l. 1–4)

2 Shall the Spring dawn, and she still clad in smiles,
  And with an unscathed brow,
  Rest in the strong arms of her palm-crowned isles,
  As fair and free as now?

  We know not; in the temple of the Fates
  God has inscribed her doom;
  And, all untroubled in her faith, she waits
  The triumph or the tomb. (l. 37–44)

  AA; AmPP; AnAmPo; NOBA; OxBA; PAH; TAP

Ethnogenesis

3 Hath not the morning dawned with added light?
  And shall not evening call another star
  Out of the infinite regions of the night,
  To mark this day in Heaven? At last, we are
  A nation among nations; and the world
  Shall soon behold in many a distant port
  Another flag unfurled! (l. 1–6)

4 What if, both mad and blinded in their rage,
  Our foes should fling us down their mortal gage,
  And with a hostile step profane our sod!
  We shall not shrink, my brothers, but go forth
                                   (l. 36–39)

5 To doubt the end were want of trust in God,
   Who, if he has decreed
   That we must pass a redder sea
   Than that which rang to Miriam's holy glee,
   Will surely raise at need
   A Moses with his rod! (l. 81–86)

AmPP; AnAmPo; NOBA; OxBA

Sleep sweetly in your humble graves

6 Sleep sweetly in your humble graves,
   Sleep, martyrs of a fallen cause;
   Though yet no marble column craves
   The pilgrim here to pause. (l. 1–4)

7 Stoop, angels, hither from the skies!
   There is no holier spot of ground
   Than where defeated valor lies,
   By mourning beauty crowned! (l. 17–20)

AH; AnAmPo; GOA; NOBA; OxBA; TAP

CHARLES TOMLINSON (b. 1927)

Paring the Apple

1 There are portraits and still-lifes
   And the first, because 'human'
   Does not excel the second, (l. 9–11)

2 The cool blade
   Severs between coolness, apple-rind
   Compelling a recognition. (l. 15–17)

CMoP; NePoEA-2; OxBTC; PoE

JEAN TOOMER (1894–1967)

Georgia Dusk

1 some genius of the South
   With blood-hot eyes and cane-lipped scented mouth,
   Surprised in making folk-songs from soul sounds.
   (l. 6–8)

2 Meanwhile, the men, with vestiges of pomp,
   Race memories of king and caravan,
   High-priests, an ostrich, and a juju-man,
   Go singing through the footpaths of the swamp.
   (l. 17–20)

3 O singers, resinous and soft your songs
   Above the sacred whisper of the pines,
   Give virgin lips to cornfield concubines,
   Bring dreams of Christ to dusky cane-lipped throngs.
   (l. 25–28)

AmNP; BPo; CDC; NAAL-2; NoAM; NoP; PoBA

November Cotton Flower

4 Superstition saw
   Something it had never seen before:
   Brown eyes that loved without a trace of fear,
   Beauty so sudden for that time of year. (l. 11–14)

CDC; MoP; NoAM; UnPo

Reapers

5 And there, a field rat, startled, squealing bleeds,
   His belly close to ground. I see the blade,
   Blood-stained, continue cutting weeds and shade.
   (l. 6–8)

BPo; CDC; HAP; MoP; NoAM; PoBA; PPP; WeW

Song of the Son

6 O land and soil, red soil and sweet-gum tree,
   So scant of grass, so profligate of pines, (l. 6–7)

7 one seed becomes

   An everlasting song, a singing tree,
   Caroling softly souls of slavery,
   What they were, and what they are to me,
   Caroling softly souls of slavery. (l. 19–23)

AmNP; CDC; NIP; PoBA

AUGUSTUS MONTAGUE TOPLADY
(1740–1778)

Rock of Ages

1 Rock of ages, cleft for me,
   Let me hide myself in thee!
   Let the water and the blood,
   From thy riven side which flowed,
   Be of sin the double cure;
   Cleanse me from its guilt and pow'r. (l. 1–6)

BLRP; FaFP; FaPoR; NOCV; NOEC; WGRP

AURELIAN TOWNSHEND
(c. 1583–c. 1651)

A Dialogue betwixt Time and a Pilgrime

1 Because Time cannot alter but obey Fate's laws.
   [Chorus:] Then happy those whom Fate, that is the
       stronger,

Together twists their threads, and yet draws hers the
   longer. (l. 19–21)

MePo; NOBE; OAEL-1; OBS; PoEL-2; SeCP

To the Countesse of Salisbury

2 The taking of a little prize,
  Do not a single heart dispise. (l. 4–5)

3 But neither steele nor stony breast
  Are proof against those lookes of thine,
  Nor can a Beauty lesse divine
  Of any heart be long possest,
  Where thou pretend'st an interest. (l. 11–15)

MeLP; MePo; OBS; SeCP

THOMAS TRAHERNE (1636–1674)

On Leaping over the Moon

1 Sinks to the deep abyss where Satan crawls
  Where horrid Death and Despair lies. (l. 59–60)

2 Thus did he yield me in the shady night
  A wondrous and instructive light,
  Which taught me that under our feet there is,
  As o'er our heads, a place of bliss. (l. 67–70)

LiTB; Mes; NAEL-1; SeCV-2

The Salutation

3 I that so long
  Was Nothing from Eternity,
  Did little think such Joys as Ear and Tongue
  To celebrate or see:
  Such Sounds to hear, such Hands to feel, such Feet,
  Such Eyes and Objects, on the Ground to meet.
                         (l. 13–18)

4 Such sacred Treasures are the Limbs of Boys
  In which a Soul doth dwell: (l. 21–22)

5 But that they mine should be who Nothing was,
  That Strangest is of all; yet brought to pass.
                         (l. 35–36.)

InvP; NOCV; NoP; OBS; SeCP; SeCV-2

Shadows in the Water

6 Within the regions of the air,
  Compassed about with heavens fair,
  Great tracts of land there may be found

Enriched with fields and fertile ground;
Where many numerous hosts
In those far distant coasts,
For other great and glorious ends,
Inhabit, my yet unknown friends. (l. 49–56)

HAP; LiTB; MePo; NoP; OAEL-1; OBS; PoEL-2; SeCP

The Third Century: News

7 What sacred instinct did inspire
  My soul in childhood with a hope so strong?

8 The Heavenly eye,
  Much wider than the sky,
  Wherein they all included were,
  The glorious Soul, that was the King
  Made to possess them, did appear
  A small and little thing!

MePo; NOBE; OBEV; QFR; SeCV-2

To Walk Abroad

9 And are not men than they more blind,
  Who having eyes yet never find
  The bliss in which they move:
  Like statues dead
  They up and down are carried,
  Yet neither see nor love. (l. 13–18)

EBEV; ELP; SD; TrGrPo

Wonder

10 A native health and innocence
  Within my bones did grow,
  And while my God did all his glories show,
  I felt a vigour in my sense
  That was all spirit: I within did flow
  With seas of life like wine;
  I nothing in the world did know
  But 'twas divine. (l. 17–24)

CH; HAP; LiTB; NAEL-1; NoP; PoE; SeCePo; SeCP;
SeCV-2; TOF; TrGrPo

HENRY DUFF TRAILL (1842–1900)

After Dilettante Concetti

1 'Why do you wear your hair like a man, (l. 1)

2 'But why does your figure appear so lean, (l. 8)

3 'But why is your face so yellowy white, (l. 15)

4 'But the finical fashion has had its day, (l. 43)

5 'Look in my face. My name is Used-to-was,
I am also called Played-out and Done-to-death,
And It-will-wash-no-more. (l. 50–52)

BXAP; CenHV; FaBoCo; Par

RICHARD CHENEVIX TRENCH
(1807–1886)

Lord, what a change within us one short hour

1 Lord, what a change within us one short hour
Spent in Thy presence will avail to make! (l. 1–2)

2 Why, therefore, should we do ourselves this wrong,
Or others — that we are not always strong —
That we are sometimes overborne with care —
That we should ever weak or heartless be,
Anxious or troubled — when with us is prayer,
And joy and strength and courage are with Thee?
(l. 9–14)

BLRP; TrPWD; WBLP; WGRP

JOHN TOWNSEND TROWBRIDGE
(1827–1916)

Darius Green and His Flying-Machine

1 An aspiring genius was D. Green:
The son of a farmer, age fourteen;
His body was long and lank and lean —
Just right for flying, as will be seen; (l. 15–18)

2 Dizzily down the abyss he wheels —
So fell Darius. Upon his crown,
In the midst of the barn-yard he came down,
In a wonderful whirl of tangled strings,
Broken braces and broken springs,
Broken tail and broken wings, (l. 242–247)

3 And this is the moral — Stick to your sphere,
Or if you insist, as you have a right,
On spreading your wings for a loftier flight,
The moral is — Take care how you light. (l. 263–266)

AnAmPo; BeLS; BLPL; FaBoBe; MoShBr; OBAL; OBCA;
OxBChV; PoLF

The Vagabonds

4 We are two travelers, Roger and I.
Roger's my dog. — Come here, you scamp! (l. 1–2)

5 We've learned what comfort is, I tell you!
A bed on the floor, a bit of rosin,
A fire to thaw our thumbs (poor fellow!
The paw he holds up there's been frozen),
Plenty of catgut for my fiddle
(This outdoor business is bad for strings), (l. 9–14)

AA; AnAmPo; BeLS; BLPA

FREDERICK GODDARD TUCKERMAN
(1821–1873)

And Change with hurried hand has swept these scenes

1 And Change with hurried hand has swept these scenes:
The woods have fallen, across the meadow-lot
The hunter's trail and trap-path is forgot,
And fire has drunk the swamps of evergreens;
Yet for a moment let my fancy plant
These autumn hills again: the wild dove's haunt,
The wild deer's walk: in golden umbrage shut, (l. 1–7)

HAP; NOBA; OFR; TAP

GEORGE TURBERVILLE
(c. 1540–c. 1610)

The Lover to the Thames of London, to Favour His Lady Passing Thereon

1 Thou stately stream that with the swelling tide
'Gainst London walls incessantly dost beat,
Thou Thames, I say, where barge and boat doth ride,
And snow-white swans do fish for needful meat:
(l. 1–4)

ChTr; ElL; NoP; OBSC

WALTER JAMES TURNER　(1889–1946)

Romance

1 O shining Popocatapetl, It was thy magic hour:

The houses, people, traffic seemed
Thin fading dreams by day;
Chimborazo, Cotopaxi
They had stolen my soul away! (l. 23–28)

CH; GoJo; MoBrPo; NOBE; OBMV; PoRA; TrGrPo

LOUIS UNTERMEYER (1885–1977)

Mother Goose Up-to-Date: Edgar A. Guest Considers the Good "Old Woman Who Lived in a Shoe"

1 It takes a heap o' children to make a home that's true,
And home can be a palace grand, or just a plain, old
    shoe;
But if it has a mother dear, and a good old dad or two,
Why, that's the sort of good old home for good old me
    and you. (l. 1–4)

2 And fathers are a blessing, too, they give the place a
    tone;
In fact each child should try and have some parents of
    its own. (l. 8–10)

FiBHP; MoAmPo; NIP; OBAL

Prayer for This House

3 Laughter shall drown the raucous shout;
And, though these shelt'ring walls are thin,
May they be strong to keep hate out
And hold love in. (l. 13–16)

BLPL; FaPON; PoLF; TrPWD

JOHN UPDIKE (b. 1932)

Ex-Basketball Player

1 Flick stands tall among the idiot pumps—
Five on a side, the old bubble-head style,
Their rubber elbows hanging loose and low. (l. 7–9)

2 The ball loved Flick.
I saw him rack up thirty-eight or forty
In one home game. His hands were like wild birds.
               (l. 16–18)

ASP; InPK; NYBP; SM

MARK VAN DOREN (1894–1973)

The Distant Runners

1 Ferdinand De Soto, sleeping
In the river, never heard
Four-and-twenty Spanish hooves
Fling off their iron and cut the green,
Leaving circles new and clean
While overhead the wing-tips whirred. (l. 13–18)

2 But I am here,
And they are far, and time is old.
Within my dream the grass is cold;
The legs and locked; the sky is dead. (l. 33–36)

GOA; LiTA; LiTM; MoAmPo

HENRY VAN DYKE (1852–1933)

America for Me

1 Oh, London is a man's town, there's power in the air;
And Paris is a woman's town, with flowers in her hair;
And it's sweet to dream in Venice, and it's great to
    study Rome;
But when it comes to living, there is no place like
    home. (l. 9–12)

2 I know that Europe's wonderful, yet something seems
    to lack;
The Past is too much with her, and the people looking
    back. (l. 17–18)

3 Oh, it's home again, and home again, America for me!
I want a ship that's westward bound to plow the
    rolling sea,
To the blessed Land of Room Enough beyond the ocean
    bars,
Where the air is full of sunlight and the flag is full of
    stars. (l. 21–24)

BLPA; BLPL; FaFP; OHFP; OPP; SoSe; WBLP

The Toiling of Felix

4 The legend of Felix is ended, the toiling of Felix is
    done;
The Master has paid him his wages, the goal of his
    journey is won;
He rests, but he never is idle; a thousand years pass
    like a day,
In the glad surprise of Paradise where work is sweeter
    than play. (l. 1–4)

5 This is the gospel of labour, ring it, ye bells of the kirk!
The Lord of Love came down from above, to live with
    the men who work.
This is the rose that He planted, here in the thorn-curst
    soil:
Heaven is blest with perfect rest, but the blessing of
    Earth is toil.

BLPA

HENRY VAUGHAN (1622–1695)

The Bird

1 So hills and valleys into singing break;
And though poor stones have neither speech nor tongue,
While active winds and streams both run and speak,

Yet stones are deep in admiration.
Thus praise and prayer here beneath the Sun
Make lesser mornings when the great are done.
(l. 13–18)

2 For each inclosed spirit is a star
Enlightening his own little sphere, (l. 19–20)

FM; OBEV; PoE; PoEL-2; SeCV-1

Cock-crowing

3 O thou immortal light and heat!
Whose hand so shines through all this frame,
That by the beauty of the seat,
We plainly see who made the same.
Seeing thy seed abides in me,
Dwell thou in it, and I in thee. (l. 19–24)

MePo; OAEL-1; PBBP; SeCV-1

Corruption

4 He drew the curse upon the world, and cracked
The whole frame with his fall.
This made him long for home, as loth to stay
With murmurers and foes; (l. 15–18)

5 He sighed for Eden, and would often say,
"Ah! what bright days were those!" (l. 19–20)

JCP; NAEL-1; NOCV; OAEL-1; OBS; Prf; SeCP; SeCV-1

The Dwelling-Place

6 But I am sure, thou dost now come
Oft to a narrow, homely room,
Where thou too hast but the least part,
My God, I mean my sinful heart. (l. 13–16)

MeLP; OBS; TrPWD; WGRP

Man

7 Weighing the steadfastness and state
Of some mean things which here below reside,
Where birds like watchful clocks the noiseless date
And intercourse of times divide. (l. 1–4)

8 Early, as well as late,
Rise with the sun, and set in the same bowers;
(l. 6–7)

9 The flowers without clothes live,
Yet Solomon was never dressed so fine. (l. 13–14)

10 Man is the shuttle, to whose winding quest
And passage through these looms
God ordered motion, but ordained no rest. (l. 26–28)

MeLP; MePo; NOBE; NOCV; OBEV; OBS; PoEL-2;
SeCV-1

The Morning Watch

11 O Joys! infinite sweetness! with what flowers
And shoots of glory my soul breaks and buds! (l. 1–2)

12 Prayer is
The world in tune,
A spirit-voice,
And vocal joys,
Whose echo is Heaven's bliss. (l. 18–22)

LiTB; MePo; OBS; SeCePo

The Night

13 Most blest believer he!
Who in that land of darkness and blind eyes
Thy long-expected healing wings could see,
When thou didst rise,
And what can never more be done
Did at midnight speak with the Sun! (l. 7–12)

EBEV; LiTB; MeLP; MePo; NAEL-1; NOBE; NOCV;
NoP; OAEL-1; OBEV; OBS; OBWVE; PoEL-2; SeCV-1;
TOF

Peace

14 My Soul, there is a Countrie
Far beyond the stars (l. 1–2)

15 Sweet peace sits crown'd with smiles
And one born in a Manger
Commands the Beauteous files, (l. 6–8)

16 He is thy gracious friend
And (O my Soul awake!)
Did in pure love descend
To die here for thy sake, (l. 9–12)

17 There growes the flowre of peace,
The Rose that cannot wither, (l. 14–15)

AWP; CaTr; EaLo; EBEV; ELP; FaBoCh; GN; HAP;
MePo; NOBE; NOCV; OBD; OBEV; OBS; PoE; SeCV-1;
TEP; TOF; TrCP; WeW; WGRP

Regeneration

18 A ward, and still in bonds, one day
I stole abroad;
It was high spring, and all the way

Primrosed and hung with shade;
Yet was it frost within,
And surly winds
Blasted my infant buds, and sin
Like clouds eclipsed my mind. (l. 1–8)

19 "Lord," then said I, "on me one breath,
And let me die before my death!"

JCP; MeLP; MePo; NAEL-1; NoP; OBS; PoE

Religion

20 No, no; Religion is a Spring
That from some secret, golden Mine
Derives her birth, and thence doth bring
Cordials in every drop, and Wine; (l. 29–32)

NOCV; OAEL-1; OBS; TOF

The Retreat

21 Happy those early days! when I
Shined in my angel-infancy.
Before I understood this place
Appointed for my second race,
Or taught my soul to fancy aught
But a white, celestial thought; (l. 1–6)

22 But felt through all this fleshly dress
Bright shoots of everlastingness. (l. 19–20)

AWP; BLPL; FF; GTBS; GTBS-P; HAP; HeIP; InPK;
InPS; InvP; JCP; LiTB; MeLP; MePo; NAEL-1; NIP;
NOBE; NOCV; NoP; OAEL-1; OBEV; OBS; OBWVE;
PoE; PoEL-2; PoRA; PPP; SeCePo; SeCP; SeCV-1; TOF;
TrGrPo

The Revival

23 Unfold, unfold! take in his light,
Who makes thy cares more short than night,
The joys which with his day-star rise
He deals to all but drowsy eyes;
And (what the men of this world miss)
Some drops and dews of future bliss. (l. 1–6)

ELP; NOCV; OBS; PoEL-2; TrGrPo

The Shower

24 Waters above! Eternal springs!
The dew that silvers the Dove's wings!
O welcome, welcome to the sad:
Give dry dust drink, drink that makes glad!
Many fair ev'nings, many flow'rs
Sweetened with rich and gentle showers,
Have I enjoyed, (l. 1–7)

25 But never, till this happy hour,
Was blest with such an evening-shower! (l. 9–10)

BoNaP; ChTr; MePo; OBS; SeCP

They Are All Gone into the World of Light

26 They are all gone into the world of light!
And I alone sit ling'ring here; (l. 1–2)

27 Dear, beauteous Death! the jewel of the just,
Shining nowhere, but in the dark; (l. 17–18)

28 Either disperse these mists, which blot and fill
My perspective, still, as they pass:
Or else remove me hence unto that hill
Where I shall need no glass. (l. 37–40)

BLPL; CH; ChTr; FaBoRV; HeIP; InPS; JCP; LiTB;
MeLP; MePo; NAEL-1; NOBE; NOCV; NoP; OAEL-1;
OBEV; OBS; PoEL-2; SeCePo; SeCP; SeCV-1; WGRP

The Timber

29 But thou beneath the sad and heavy line
Of death, doth waste all senseless, cold, and dark;
Where not so much as dreams of light may shine,
Nor any thought of greenness, leaf, or bark. (l. 9–12)

FaBoRV; NoP; OBEV; SeCP; SeCV-1

To Amoret

30 Then whisper by that holy spring,
Where for her sake I would have died,
Whilst those water-nymphs did bring
Flowers to cure what she had tried;
And of my faith and love did sing. (l. 11–15)

EnLoPo

The Waterfall

31 Should poor souls fear a shade or night,
Who came sure from a sea of light?
Or since those drops are all sent back
So sure to thee, that none doth lack,
Why should frail flesh doubt any more
That what God takes, He'll not restore? (l. 17–22)

FaBoPP; MeLP; MePo; NAEL-1; NOBE; NOCV; NoP;
OBS; OBWVE; PoEL-2; PrIm; SeCV-1; WiR

The World

32 I saw Eternity the other night,
Like a great ring of pure and endless light, (l. 1–2)

33 Yet some, who all this while did weep and sing,
    And sing and weep, soared up into the ring;
    But most would use no wing.
    O fools, said I, thus to prefer dark night
    Before true light! (l. 46–50)

    AWP; EBEV; FaBV; HAP; HeIP; ImOP; JCP; LiTB;
    MePo; NAEL-1; NOBE; NOCV; OAEL-1; OBEV; OBS;
    PoEL-2; PPP; SeCP; SeCV-1; TEP; TrCP; TrGrPo; WGRP

THOMAS VAUTOR (fl. c. 1590?)

Sweet Suffolk Owl (attributed to Vautor)

1   Sweet Suffolk Owl, so trimly dight
    With feathers, like a lady bright,
    Thou sing'st alone, sitting by night,
    Te whit! Te whoo! Te whit! To whit! (l. 1–4)

    CH; ChTr; EBEV; ElL; FaBoRV; PBBP

THOMAS VAUX, 2D BARON VAUX OF HARROWDEN (1510–1566)

The Aged Lover Renounceth Love

1   I loathe that I did love,
    In youth that I thought sweet; (l. 1–2)

2   My lusts they do me leave,
    My fancies all be fled,
    And tract of time begins to weave
    Grey hairs upon my head. (l. 5–8)

3   For age with stealing steps
    Hath clawed me with his crutch, (l. 9–10)

4   My hand and pen are not in plight,
    As they have been of yore. (l. 15–16)

5   The wrinkles in my brow,
    The furrows in my face,
    Say, limping age will lodge him now
    Where youth must give him place. (l. 21–24)

6   As ye of clay were cast by kind,
    So shall ye waste to dust. (l. 55–56)

    ElL; OAEL-1; PoEL-1

JONES VERY (1831–1880)

The Dead

1   I see them, — crowd on crowd they walk the earth,
    Dry leafless trees no autumn wind laid bare:
    And in their nakedness find cause for mirth,
    And all unclad would winter's rudeness dare; (l. 1–4)

2   They borrow words for thoughts they cannot feel,
    That with a seeming heart their tongue may speak;
    And in their show of life more dead they live
    Than those that to the earth with many tears they give. (l. 11–14)

    AA; AnAmPo; HAP; NOBA; OxBA; TAP

The Hand and Foot

3   The hand and foot that stir not, they shall find
    Sooner than all the rightful place to go; (l. 1–2)

4   It is the way unseen, the certain route,
    Where ever bound, yet thou art ever free;
    The path of Him, whose perfect law of love
    Bids spheres and atoms in just order move. (l. 11–14)

    OxBA; PoEL-4; QFR; TAP

Yourself

5   'Tis to yourself I speak; you cannot know
    Him whom I call in speaking such a one,
    For you beneath the earth lie buried low,
    Which he alone as living walks upon: (l. 1–4)

6   A word perhaps loud spoken you may get,
    Or hear our feet when heavily they tread;
    But he who speaks, or him who's spoken to,
    Must both remain as strangers still to you. (l. 11–14)

    AA; NOBA; OxBA; PoEL-4; Son

FRANCOIS VILLON (1431–1465)

The Ballade of Dead Ladies

1   Where's Heloise, the learned nun,
    For whose sake Abeillard, I ween,
    Lost manhood and put priesthood on? (l. 9–11)

2   But where are the snows of yester-year? (l. 16)

3   And that good Joan whom Englishmen
    At Rouen doomed and burned her there, —
    Mother of God, where are they then? . . . (l. 21–23)

    AWP; CTC; FaFP; OBVE; PoRA; PrIm; WiR

DAVID WAGONER (b. 1926)

The Shooting of John Dillinger outside the Biograph Theater, July 22, 1934

1   Did Johnny look flashy?
    Yes, his white-on-white shirt and tie were luminous.

His trousers were creased like knives to the tops of his
    shoes
And his yellow straw hat came down to his dark
    glasses. (l. 61−64)

2 he lay down with those strange women, his face in the
    alley,
One shoe off, cinders in his mouth, his eyelids heavy.
When they shouted questions at him, he talked back to
    nobody. (l. 83−86)

3 Does anyone remember?
Everyone still alive. And some dead ones. (l. 129−130)

CoAP; FYAP; RB; SM

DEREK WALCOTT (b. 1930)

A Far Cry from Africa

1 A wind is ruffling the tawny pelt
Of Africa. Kikuyu, quick as flies,
Batten upon the bloodstreams of the veldt. (l. 1−3)

2 Statistics justify and scholars seize
The salients of colonial policy.
What is that to the white child hacked in bed?
To savages, expendable as Jews? (l. 7−10)

3 Again brutish necessity wipes its hands
Upon the napkin of a dirty cause, (l. 22−23)

4 I who have cursed
The drunken officer of British rule, how choose
Between this Africa and the English tongue I love?
Betray them both, or give back what they give?
How can I face such slaughter and be cool?
How can I turn from Africa and live? (l. 28−33)

HeIP; MoP; NAEL-2; NoAM; PBCV; TTY; UnPo

MARGARET ABIGAIL WALKER (b. 1915)

Childhood

1 croppers rotting shacks
with famine, terror, flood, and plague near by;
where sentiment and hatred still held sway
and only bitter land was washed away. (l. 11−14)

IHMS; PBWP; PoBA; Son; WPOW

For Malcolm X

2 All you violated ones with gentle hearts;
You violent dreamers whose cries shout heartbreak;
                                            (l. 1−2)

3 Snow-white moslem head-dress around a dead black
    face!
Beautiful were your sand-papering words against our
    skins! (l. 9−10)

4 When and where will another come to take your holy
    place?
Old man mumbling in his dotage, or crying child,
    unborn? (l. 13−14)

BPo; CNA; PoBA; Son

For My People

5 For my people lending their strength to the years: to
    the gone years and the now years and the maybe
    years, washing ironing cooking scrubbing sewing
    mending hoeing plowing digging planting pruning
    patching dragging along never gaining never reaping
    never knowing and never understanding; (l. 2)

6 Let the martial songs be written, let the dirges
    disappear. Let a race of men now rise and take
    control! (l. 10)

AmNP; CNA; IDB; PoBA; PoNe

Lineage

7 With veins rolling roughly over quick hands
They have many clean words to say.
My grandmothers were strong.
Why am I not as they? (l. 9−12)

BlSi; CNA; NMM; PBWP; PoBA

Molly Means

8 Old Molly Means was a hag and a witch;
Chile of the devil, the dark, and sitch. (l. 1−2)

9 Imp at three and wench at 'leben
She counted her husbands to the number seben.
                                            (l. 5−6)

10 Her voice is thin and her moan is high,
And her cackling laugh or her barking cold
Bring terror to the young and old.
O Molly, Molly, Molly Means
Lean is the ghost of Molly Means. (l. 52−56)

AmNP; BlSi; NMM; PoNe

October Journey

11 Traveller take heed for journeys undertaken in the dark
    of the year.
Go in the bright blaze of Autumn's equinox. (l. 2)

12 An evil moon bleeds drops of death.
The earth burns brown.
Grass shrivels and dries to a yellowish mass.
Earth wears a dun-colored dress
like an old woman wooing the sun to be her lover,
be her sweetheart and her husband bound in one.
(l. 40–45)

13 The clock runs down
timeless and still.
The days and nights turn hours to years
and water in a gutter marks the circle of another world
hating, resentful, and afraid
stagnant, and green, and full of slimy things.
(l. 70–75)

AmNP; IDB; PoBA; PoNe

Street Demonstration

14 Hurry up, Lucille, Hurry up
We're Going to Miss Our Chance to go to Jail.

BPo; CNA

EDMUND WALLER (1606–1687)

Go, Lovely Rose

1 Go, lovely Rose —
Tell her that wastes her time and me
That now she knows.
When I resemble her to thee,
How sweet and fair she seems to be. (l. 1–5)

2 Then die that she
The common fate of all things rare
May read in thee; (l. 16–18)

AWP; BoLoP; CTC; ELP; EnLoPo; FF; GBL; GoJo;
GTBS; GTBS-P; HAP; HeIP; InPK; JCP; MePo; NAEL-1;
NIP; NOBE; NoP; OAEL-1; OBEV; OBS; OPOP; PoE;
PoEL-3; PoRA; PrIm; SeCP; SeCV-1; TEP; TrGrPo;
UnPo; WeW

Of English Verse

3 Poets that lasting Marble seek
Must carve in Latine or in Greek,
We write in Sand, our Language grows,
And like the Tide our work o'erflows. (l. 13–16)

NAEL-1; OAEL-1; OBS; PoE; SeCP

Of The Last Verses in the Book

4 The soul's dark cottage, battered and decayed,
Lets in new light through chinks that Time has made:
Stronger by weakness, wiser men become

As they draw near to their eternal home.
Leaving the old, both worlds at once they view
That stand upon the threshold of the new. (l. 7–12)

BLPL; EBEV; FaBoRV; HAP; MePo; NOBE; NOCV;
NoP; OBEV; OBS; SeCP; SeCV-1

On a Girdle

5 It was my heaven's extremest sphere,
The pale which held that lovely deer;
My joy, my grief, my hope, my love,
Did all within this circle move! (l. 5–8)

6 A narrow compass! and yet there
Dwelt all that's good, and all that's fair! (l. 9–10)

AWP; BLPL; FF; GTBS; GTBS-P; HeIP; InPK; LiTB;
NAEL-1; NoP; OBEV; OBS; PoE; PoRA; SeCePo; SeCV-
1; TrGrPo

To a Fair Lady Playing with a Snake

7 Take heed, fair Eve! you do not make
Another tempter of this snake;
A marble one so warmed would speak. (l. 16–18)

EBEV; HoPM; PoE; PoEL-3

To a Very Young Lady

8 Yet fairest blossome do not slight
That age which you may know so soon:
The rosie Morn resignes her light,
And milder glory to the Noon:
And then what wonder shall you do,
Whose dawning beauty warms us so? (l. 7–12)

MePo; OBS; SeCP; TrGrPo; WiR

WILLIAM WALSH (1663–1708)

The Despairing Lover

1 That a lover forsaken
A new love may get;
But a neck, when once broken,
Can never be set:
And, that he could die
Whenever he would;
But, that he could live
But as long as he could; (l. 18–25)

ELP; FaBoCh; NBLV; NOBL; OxBoLi

WALTHER VON DER VOGELWEIDE
(1170?–1230?)

Under the Lindens

1 Under the lindens on the heather,
There was our double resting-place. (l. 1–2)

2 Sweetly sang the nightingale. (l. 7)

CTC; ErPo; GBL; OBVE

ROBERT PENN WARREN (b. 1905)

Bearded Oaks

1 The oaks, how subtle and marine!
Bearded, and all the layered light
Above them swims; and thus the scene,
Recessed, awaits the positive night. (l. 1–4)

2 So little time we live in Time,
And we learn all so painfully,
That we may spare this hour's term
To practice for Eternity. (l. 37–40)

LiTM; MoAmPo; MoP; NAAL-2; NoAM; NOBA; PoA;
PoE; TAP; TwCP

Original Sin; a Short Story

3 Nodding, its great head rattling like a gourd,
And locks like seaweed strung on the stinking stone,
The nightmare stumbles past, (l. 1–3)

4 But it thought no bed too narrow — it stood with lips
askew
And shook its great head sadly like the abstract Jew.
(l. 24–25)

5 Later you hear it wander the dark house
Like a mother who rises at night to seek a childhood
picture;
Or it goes to the backyard and stands like an old horse
cold in the pasture. (l. 43–45)

HoPM; LiTA; LiTM; NOCV; PPP; SM; TAP

Pursuit

6 The hunchback on the corner, with gum and shoelaces,
Has his own wisdom and pleasures, (l. 1–2)

7 the pomp
Of pain swells like the Indies, or a plum (l. 13–14)

8 The doctor will take you now. He is burly and clean;
Listening, like lover or worshiper, bends at your heart.
(l. 21–22)

9 In Florida consider the flamingo,
Its color passion but its neck a question. (l. 31–32)

10 She blinks and croaks, like a toad or a Norn, in the
horrible light,
And rattles her crutch, which may put forth a small
bloom, perhaps white. (l. 49–50)

HAP; LiTA; MoAmPo; TwCP

ROSAMUND MARRIOTT WATSON
("GRAHAM R. TOMSON"; "R.
ARMYTAGE") (1863–1911)

Ave atque Vale

1 Farewell, my Youth! for now we needs must part,
For here the paths divide;
Here hand from hand must sever, heart from heart, —
Divergence deep and wide. (l. 1–4)

NOBE; OAEL-2; OBEV; OBNC

SIR WILLIAM WATSON (1858–1935)

April, April

1 April, April,
Laugh thy girlish laughter,
But, the moment after,
Weep thy golden tears! (l. 9–12)

BoTP; FaBV; GN; OBEV; TrGrPo

ALARIC ALEXANDER WATTS
(1797–1864)

An Austrian Army (attributed to Watts)

1 An Austrian army, awfully array'd,
Boldly by battery besiege Belgrade;
Cossack commanders cannonading come,
Deal devastation's dire destructive doom; (l. 1–4)

BLPA; ChTr; FaBoCo; FiBHP; NOBL

ISAAC WATTS (1674–1748)

The Day of Judgement; an Ode

1 Thoughts, like old vultures, prey upon their heart-
    strings, (l. 21)

HAP; NOBE; NOEC; NoP; OBEV; SeCePo

Our God, Our Help in Ages Past

2 Our God, our help in ages past,
    Our hope for years to come,
    Our shelter from the stormy blast,
    And our eternal home; (l. 1–4)

3 The busy tribes of flesh and blood,
    With all their lives and cares,
    Are carried downwards by thy flood,
    And lost in following years.

    Time, like an ever-rolling stream,
    Bears all its sons away;
    They fly forgotten, as a dream
    Dies at the opening day. (l. 21–28)

4 Be thou our guard while troubles last,
    And our eternal home. (l. 35–36)

NoP; OBVE; PWR; TOF

The Sluggard

5 'Tis the voice of the Sluggard; I heard him complain,
    "You have wak'd me too soon; I must slumber again."
                                        (l. 1–2)

6 Thus he wastes half his days, and his hours without
    number, (l. 6)

7 thanks to my friends for their care in my breeding,
    Who taught me betimes to love working and reading."
                                        (l. 19–20)

CH; HAP; Mes; MoShBr; NOEC; OxBChV; OxBoLi; Par;
PoEL-3

There is a land of pure delight

8 There is a land of pure delight,
    Where saints immortal reign;
    Infinite day excludes the night,
    And pleasures banish pain. (l. 1–4)

ELP; NOCV; NoP; OBD; TOF; WGRP

When I Survey the Wondrous Cross

9 When I survey the wondrous cross
    On which the Prince of Glory died,
    My richest gain I count but loss,
    And pour contempt on all my pride. (l. 1–4)

10 Were the whole realm of nature mine,
    That were a present far too small.
    Love so amazing, so divine,
    Demands my soul, my life, my all. (l. 17–20)

AmFP; FaPoR; NOCV; NOEC; WGRP

JOHN WEBSTER (c. 1580–1638)

The Devil's Law Case

1 All the flowers of the spring
    Meet to perfume our burying;
    These have but their growing prime,
    And man does flourish but his time.
    Survey our progress from our birth —
    We are set, we grow, we turn to earth (l. 1–6)

2 To leave a living name behind,
    And weave but nets to catch the wind. (l. 15–16)

CH; ElL; ELP; LiTB; NOBE; OBEV; OBS; PoEL-2;
PoRA; TrGrPo

The Duchess of Malfi

3 Your length in clay's now competent,
    A long war disturbed your mind; (l. 6–7)

4 Sin their conception, their birth weeping,
    Their life a general mist of error,
    Their death a hideous storm of terror. (l. 10–12)

CH; ElL; HAP; NAEL-1; NOBE; NoP; OBD; OBEV;
OBS; QFR; SeCePo

The White Devil

5 But keepe the wolfe far thence, that's foe to men,
    For with his nailes he'll dig them up agen. (l. 9–10)

CH; ChTr; EBEV; ElL; FaBoCh; GTBS; GTBS-P; HAP;
HeIP; LiTB; NOBE; NoP; OBEV; OBS; PoEL-2; PoRA;
PrIm; RB; SeCePo; TrGrPo

JOHN WEBSTER (c. 1580–1638) *AND*
WILLIAM ROWLEY (c. 1585?–1642?)

The Thracian Wonder (*attributed to* Webster *and*
to Rowley)

1 Art thou gone in haste?
    I'll not forsake thee!
    Runn'st thou ne'er so fast,
    I'll o'ertake thee! (l. 1–4)

2 Echo, then, shall again
Tell her I follow, (l. 13–14)

CH; ChTr; ElL; ELP; GBL; OxBoLi

JAMES WELCH (b. 1940)

Harlem, Montana; Just off the Reservation

1 We need no runners here. Booze is law
and all the Indians drink in the best tavern.
Money is free if you're poor enough. (l. 1–3)

2 Harlem, your hotel is overnamed, your children
are raggedy-assed but you go on, survive
the bad food from the two cafes and peddle
your hate for the wild who bring you money.
(l. 28–31)

CDW; HATNAP; NOVW; STE

The Man from Washington

3 He promised
that life would go on as usual,
that treaties would be signed, and everyone —
man, woman and child — would be inoculate
against a world in which we had no part,
a world of money, promise and disease. (l. 8–13)

CDW; HATNAP; NoAM; NOVW

CAROLYN WELLS (1862–1942)

How to Tell the Wild Animals

1 If he roars at you as you're dyin'
You'll know it is the Asian Lion. (l. 5–6)

2 The true Chameleon is small,
A lizard sort of thing;
He hasn't any ears at all,
And not a single wing.
If there is nothing on the tree,
'Tis the Chameleon you see. (l. 31–36)

FaFP; FaPON; FiBHP; NBLV

CHARLES WESLEY (1707–1788)

Wrestling Jacob

1 I rise superior to my pain,
When I am weak then I am strong; (l. 33–34)

2 Lame as I am, I take the prey,
Hell, earth, and sin with ease o'ercome;
I leap for joy, pursue my way,
And as a bounding hart fly home,
Through all eternity to prove,
Thy nature, and Thy name is Love. (l. 79–84)

NOBE; NOCV; NOEC; OBEV; PoEL-3; SeCePo; TOF

SAMUEL WESLEY (1691–1739)

On the Setting Up of Mr. Butler's Monument in Westminster Abbey

1 See him, when starved to death and turned to dust,
Presented with a monumental bust!
The poet's fate is here in emblem shown:
He asked for bread, and he received a stone. (l. 3–6)

InvP; NBLV; NOEC; OBD; OxBSP

ROBERT WEVER (fl. c. 1550)

Lusty Juventus

1 In a herber green, asleep where I lay,
The birds sang sweet in the mids of the day;
I dreamed fast of mirth and play.
In youth is pleasure, in youth is pleasure. (l. 1–4)

2 Of her alone to have a sight,
Which is my joy and heart's delight. (l. 10–11)

ChTr; ElL; ELP; NOBE; OBEV; OBSC

PHILLIS WHEATLEY (c. 1753–1784)

On Being Brought from Africa to America

1 'Twas mercy brought me from my Pagan land,
Taught my benighted soul to understand
That there's a God, that there's a Saviour too:
Once I redemption neither sought nor knew.
Some view our sable race with scornful eye,
"Their color is a diabolic die."

Remember, Christians, Negroes, black as Cain,
May be refin'd, and join th' angelic train. (l. 1–8)

FF; GOA; HeIP; NAAL-1; NOBA; NOEC; TAP; TTY;
WPE

JOSEPH BLANCO WHITE (1775–1841)

To Night

1 Mysterious Night! when our first parent knew
Thee from report divine, and heard thy name,
Did he not tremble for this lovely frame,
This glorious canopy of light and blue? (l. 1–4)

2 Why do we then shun death with anxious strife?
If Light can thus deceive, wherefore not Life?
(l. 13–14)

EBEV; OBEV; Son; WGRP

WALT WHITMAN (1819–1892)

As I Ebb'd with the Ocean of Life

1 As I ebb'd with the ocean of life,
As I wended the shores I know,
As I walk'd where the ripples continually wash you
Paumanok, (l. 1–3)

2 Was seiz'd by the spirit that trails in the lines
underfoot,
The rim, the sediment that stands for all the water and
all the land of the globe.

Fascinated, my eyes reverting from the south, dropt, to
follow those slender windrows,
Chaff, straw, splinters of wood, weeds, and the sea-
gluten,
Scum, scales from shining rocks, leaves of salt-lettuce,
left by the tide, (l. 8–12)

3 I too but signify at the utmost a little wash'd-up drift,
A few sands and dead leaves to gather,
Gather, and merge myself as part of the sands and
drift. (l. 22–24)

4 I perceive I have not really understood any thing, not a
single object, and that no man ever can,
Nature here in sight of the sea taking advantage of me
to dart upon me and sting me,
Because I have dared to open my mouth to sing at all.
(l. 32–34)

5 Ebb, ocean of life, (the flow will return,)
Cease not your moaning you fierce old mother,

Endlessly cry for your castaways, but fear not, deny not
me,
Rustle not up so hoarse and angry against my feet as I
touch you or gather from you.
I mean tenderly by you and all,
I gather for myself and for this phantom looking down
where we lead, and following me and mine.
(l. 51–56)

6 Just as much for us that sobbing dirge of Nature,
Just as much whence we come that blare of the cloud-
trumpets,
We, capricious, brought hither we know not whence,
spread out before you,
You up there walking or sitting,
Whoever you are, we too lie in drifts at your feet.
(l. 67–71)

AmPP; NAAL-1; NOBA; PrIm; TAP

Beat! Beat! Drums!

7 Beat! beat! drums! — blow! bugles! blow!
Through the windows — through doors — burst like a
ruthless force,
Into the solemn church, and scatter the congregation;
Into the school where the scholar is studying;
Leave not the bridegroom quiet — no happiness must he
have now with his bride;
Nor the peaceful farmer any peace, plough his field or
gathering his grain;
So fierce you whirr and pound, you drums — so shrill
you bugles blow. (l. 1–7)

8 Mind not the old man beseeching the young man;
Let not the child's voice be heard, nor the mother's
entreaties;
Make even the trestles to shake the dead, where they lie
awaiting the hearses,
So strong you thump, O terrible drums — so loud you
bugles blow. (l. 18–21)

AnAmPo; FaBV; FPL; InPK; InPS; NAAL-1; NoF;
OBWP; PoLF

Bivouac on a Mountain Side

9 I see before me now a traveling army halting,
Below a fertile valley spread, with barns and the
orchards of summer,
Behind, the terraced sides of a mountain, abrupt, in
places rising high, (l. 1–3)

10 And over all the sky — the sky! far, far out of reach,
studded, breaking out, the eternal stars.

AA; AiP; ChTr; OxBA; PoLF

By the Bivouac's Fitful Flame

11 By the bivouac's fitful flame,
A procession winding around me, solemn and sweet and
slow (l. 1–2)

12 The shrubs and trees, (as I lift my eyes they seem to be
   stealthily watching me.)
   While wind in procession thoughts, O tender and
   wondrous thoughts,
   Of life and death, of home and the past and loved, and
   of those that are far away; (l. 6—8)

NoAM; NoP; OxBA; PoE

Cavalry Crossing a Ford

13 A line in long array, where they wind betwixt green
   islands;
   They take a serpentine course — their arms flash in the
   sun — hark to the musical clank; (l. 1—2)

14 Scarlet, and blue, and snowy white,
   The guidon flags flutter gaily in the wind. (l. 6—7)

AA; AiP; AmPP; ChTr; HeIP; InPK; InPS; MoP; NAAL-1;
NoAM; NoP; OxBA; PPP; TAP; UnPo

Come Up from the Fields, Father

15 Come up from the fields father, here's a letter from our
   Pete,
   And come to the front door mother, here's a letter from
   thy dear son. (l. 1—2)

16 Open the envelope quickly,
   O this is not our son's writing, yet his name is sign'd,
   O a strange hand writes for our dear son, O stricken
   mother's soul!
   All swims before her eyes, flashes with black, she
   catches the main words only,
   Sentences broken, gunshot wound in the breast, cavalry
   skirmish, taken to hospital,
   At present low, but will soon be better. (l. 16—21)

17 While they stand at home at the door he is dead
   already,
   The only son is dead.

   But the mother needs to be better,
   She with thin form presently drest in black,
   By day her meals untouch'd, then at night fitfully
   sleeping, often waking,
   In the midnight waking, weeping, longing with one
   deep longing,
   O that she might withdraw unnoticed, silent from life
   escape and withdraw,
   To follow, to seek, to be with her dear dead son.
                                          (l. 30—37)

AnAmPo; MoAmPo; OBWP; OxBA; PPP; UnPo

Crossing Brooklyn Ferry

18 Flood-tide below me! I see you face to face!
   Clouds of the west — sun there half an hour high — I see
   you also face to face.

Crowds of men and women attired in the usual
   costumes, how curious you are to me!
On the ferry-boats the hundreds and hundreds that
   cross, returning home, are more curious to me than
   you suppose,
And you that shall cross from shore to shore years
   hence are more to me, and more in my meditations,
   than you might suppose. (l. 1—5)

19 Others will see the islands large and small;
   Fifty years hence, others will see them as they cross,
   the sun half an hour high.
   A hundred years hence, or ever so many hundred years
   hence, others will see them,
   Will enjoy the sunset, the pouring-in of the flood-tide,
   the falling-back to the sea of the ebb-tide.

   It avails not, time nor place — distance avails not,
   I am with you, you men and women of a generation, or
   ever so many generations hence,
   Just as you feel when you look on the river and sky, so
   I felt,
   Just as any of you is one of a living crowd, I was one of
   a crowd, (l. 16—23)

20 What is it then between us?
   What is the count of the scores or hundreds of years
   between us?

   Whatever it is, it avails not — distance avails not, and
   place avails not, (l. 54—56)

21 What is more subtle than this which ties me to the
   woman or man that looks in my face?
   Which fuses me into you now, and pours my meaning
   into you?

   We understand men do we not?
   What I promis'd without mentioning it, have you not
   accepted?
   What the study could not teach — what the preaching
   could not accomplish is accomplish'd, is it not?
                                          (l. 97—101)

22 You have waited, you always wait, you dumb, beautiful
   ministers,
   We receive you with free sense at last, and are insatiate
   hence-forward,
   Not you any more shall be able to foil us, or withhold
   yourselves from us,
   We use you, and do not cast you aside — we plant you
   permanently within us,
   We fathom you not — we love you — there is perfection
   in you also,
   You furnish your parts, toward eternity,
   Great or small, you furnish your parts toward the soul.
                                          (l. 127—133)

AmPP; InPS; LiTA; MoP; NAAL-1; NoAM; NOBA; NoP;
TAP

The Dalliance of the Eagles

23 Skirting the river road, (my forenoon walk, my rest,)
Skyward in air a sudden muffled sound, the dalliance
of the eagles,
The rushing amorous contact high in space together,
(l. 1–3)

24 A motionless still balance in the air, then parting,
talons loosing,
Upward again on slow-firm pinions slanting, their
separate diverse flight,
She hers, he his, pursuing. (l. 8–10)

AA; AmPP; FM; HAP; HeIP; NAAL-1; NoP; PPP; PrIm;
TAP

Dirge for Two Veterans

25 The last sunbeam
Lightly falls from the finished Sabbath,
On the pavement here, and there beyond it is looking,
Down a new-made double grave, (l. 1–4)

26 For the son is brought with the father,
(On the foremost ranks of the fierce assault they fell,
Two veterans son and father dropt together,
And the double grave awaits them). (l. 17–20)

27 The moon gives you light,
And the bugles and the drums give you music,
And my heart, O my soldiers, my veterans,
My heart gives you love. (l. 33–36)

AnAmPo; GN; MoAmPo; PoEL-5

The Dismantled Ship

28 In some unused lagoon, some nameless bay,
On sluggish, lonesome waters, anchor'd near the shore,
An old, dismasted, gray and batter'd ship, disabled,
done,
After free voyages to all the seas of earth, haul'd up at
last and hawser'd tight,
Lies rusting, mouldering. (l. 1–5)

AmPP; MOS; NoP; OxBA

Give Me the Splendid Silent Sun

29 Give me the splendid silent sun
with all his beams full-dazzling,
Give me juicy autumnal fruit ripe and red from the
orchard,
Give me a field where the unmow'd grass grows,
Give me an arbor, give me the trellis'd grape,
Give me fresh corn and wheat, give me serene-moving
animals teaching content, (l. 1–5)

30 These demanding to have them, (tired with ceaseless
excitement, and rack'd by the war-strife,)
These to procure incessantly asking, rising in cries from
my heart,
While yet incessantly asking still I adhere to my city,
Day upon day and year upon year O city, walking your
streets,
Where you hold me enchain'd a certain time refusing to
give me up, (l. 12–16)

31 (O I see what I sought to escape confronting, reversing
my cries,
I see my own soul trampling down what it ask'd for.)

Keep your splendid silent sun,
Keep your woods O Nature, and the quiet places by the
woods,
Keep your fields of clover and timothy, and your corn-
fields and orchards,
Keep the blossoming buckwheat fields where the Ninth-
month bees hum;
Give me faces and streets — give me these phantoms
incessant and endless along the trottoirs! (l. 18–24)

32 Manhattan streets with their powerful throbs, with
beating drums as now,
The endless and noisy chorus, the rustle and clank of
muskets, (even the sight of the wounded,)
Manhattan crowds, with their turbulent musical chorus!
Manhattan faces and eyes forever for me. (l. 37–40)

AA; BoNaF; FaPON; HAP; MoAmPo; NOBA

A Glimpse

33 A glimpse through an interstice caught,
Of a crowd of workmen and drivers in a barroom
around the stove late of a winter night, and I
unremarked seated in a corner,
Of a youth who loves me and whom I love, silently
approaching and seating himself near, that he may
hold me by the hand,
A long while amid the noises of coming and going, of
drinking and oath and smutty jest,
There we two, content, happy in being together,
speaking little, perhaps not a word. (l. 1–6)

AmPP; AnAmPo; OxBA; PeHV; PPP

Good-bye My Fancy!

34 Good-bye my Fancy!
Farewell dear mate, dear love!
I'm going away, I know not where,
Or to what fortune, or whether I may ever see you
again,
So Good-bye my Fancy. (l. 1–5)

35 Yet let me not be too hasty,
Long indeed have we lived, slept, filtered, become
really blended into one; (l. 11–12)

36 Maybe it is yourself now really ushering me to the true
    songs, (who knows?),
    Maybe it is you the mortal knob really undoing,
    turning — so now finally,
    Good-bye — and hail! my Fancy. (l. 16–18)

    FaFP; LiTA; NAAL-1; PrIm; TAP

I Hear America Singing

37 I hear America singing, the varied carols I hear,
    Those of mechanics, each one singing his as it should
    be blithe and strong,
    The carpenter singing his as he measures his plank or
    beam,
    The mason singing his as he makes ready for work, or
    leaves off work, (l. 1–4)

38 Each singing what belongs to him or her and to none
    else,
    The day what belongs to the day — at night the party of
    young fellows, robust, friendly,
    Singing with open mouths their strong melodious
    songs. (l. 9–11)

    AiP; AmFN; AnAmPo; AWP; FaBoBe; FaBV; FaFP;
    FaPON; FF; FPL; HAP; LiTA; MoAmPo; OPP; PDV; SaC;
    TrGrPo; WeW

I Saw in Louisiana a Live-Oak Growing

39 I saw in Louisiana a live-oak growing,
    All alone stood it and the moss hung down from the
    branches,
    Without any companion it grew there uttering joyous
    leaves of dark green,
    And its look, rude, unbending, lusty, made me think of
    myself,
    But I wonder'd how it could utter joyous leaves
    standing alone there without its friend near, for I
    knew I could not, (l. 1–5)

    AiP; AWP; InPK; InPS; LiTA; MAT; NAAL-1; NIP;
    NoAM; NOBA; NoP; OxBA; PrIm

I Sit and Look Out

40 I sit and look out upon all the sorrows of the world,
    and upon all oppression and shame, (l. 1)

    AnAmPo; NAAL-1; OxBA; TAP

Joy, Shipmate, Joy!

41 Joy, shipmate, joy!
    (Pleas'd to my soul at death I cry,)
    Our life is closed, our life begins, (l. 1–3)

    MoAmPo; MOS; OHIP; TAP

The Last Invocation

42 At the last, tenderly,
    From the walls of the powerful fortress'd house,
    From the clasp of the knitted locks, from the keep of
    the well-closed doors,
    Let me be wafted.

    Let me glide noiselessly forth;
    With the key of softness unlock the locks — with a
    whisper,
    Set ope the doors O soul. (l. 1–8)

    MoAmPo; OBD; OBEV; OxBA; OxBSP; PoEL-5; TrGrPo;
    TrPWD; WGRP

Mannahatta

43 I was asking for something specific and perfect for my
    city,
    Whereupon lo! upsprang the aboriginal name.

    Now I see what there is in a name, a word, liquid,
    sane, unruly, musical, self-sufficient,
    I see that the word of my city is that word from of old,
    Because I see that word nested in nests of water-bays,
    superb,
    Rich, hemm'd thick all around with sailships and
    steamships, an island sixteen miles long, solid-
    founded, (l. 1–6)

44 A million people — manners free and superb — open
    voices — hospitality — the most courageous and
    friendly young men,
    City of hurried and sparkling waters! city of spires and
    masts!
    City nested in bays! my city! (l. 18–20)

    AA; EyDe; GOA; MoAmPo

Memories of President Lincoln

45 O Captain! my Captain! our fearful trip is done,
    The ship has weather'd every rack, the prize we sought
    is won,
    The port is near, the bells I hear, the people all
    exulting,
    While follow eyes the steady keel, the vessel grim and
    daring;
    But O heart! heart! heart!
    O the bleeding drops of red,
    Where on the deck my Captain lies,
    Fallen cold and dead.

    AA; FaBoBe; FaBoCh; FaBV; FaFP; FaPON; FaPoR;
    FPL; GN; GOA; InPK; LiTA; MoAmPo; MOS; OBCA;
    OHFP; OHIP; PAH; PoLF; TAP; TrGrPo

46 When lilacs last in the dooryard bloomed
    And the great star early drooped in the western sky in
    the night,
    I mourned, and yet shall mourn with ever-returning
    spring.

Ever-returning spring, trinity sure to me you bring,
Lilac blooming perennial and drooping star in the west,
And thought of him I love.

47 In the swamp in secluded recesses,
A shy and hidden bird is warbling a song.

Solitary the thrush,
The hermit withdrawn to himself, avoiding the
settlements,
Sings by himself a song.

Song of the bleeding throat,
Death's outlet song of life, (for well dear brother I
know,
If thou wast not granted to sing thou would'st surely
die.)

48 O western orb sailing the heaven,
Now I know what you must have meant as a month
since I walked,
As I walked in silence the transparent shadowy night,

49 Sing on dearest brother, warble your reedy song,
Loud human song, with voice of uttermost woe.

O liquid and free and tender!
O wild and loose to my soul — O wondrous singer!
You only I hear — yet the star holds me, (but will soon
depart,)
Yet the lilac with mastering odor holds me.

50 And the voice of my spirit tallied the song of the bird.

Come lovely and soothing death,
Undulate round the world, serenely arriving, arriving,
In the day, in the night, to all, to each,
Sooner or later delicate death.

51 Over the tree-tops I float thee a song,
Over the rising and sinking waves, over the myriad
fields and the prairies wide,
Over the dense-packed cities all and the teeming
wharves and ways,
I float this carol with joy, with joy to thee, O death,

52 I cease my song for thee,
From my gaze on thee in the west, fronting the
west, communing with thee,
O comrade lustrous with silver face in the night,
Yet each to keep and all, retrievements out of the night,
The song, the wondrous chant of the grey-brown bird,
And the tallying chant, the echo aroused in my soul,
With the lustrous and drooping star with the
countenance full of woe,

53 With the holders holding my hand nearing the call of
the bird,
Comrades mine and I in the midst, and their memory
ever to keep, for the dead I loved so well,
For the sweetest, wisest soul of all my days and lands —
and this for his dear sake,

Lilac and star and bird twined with the chant of my
soul,
There in the fragrant pines and the cedars dusk and
dim.

AmPP; AWP; FPL; HAP; LiTA; MoAmPo; NAAL-1;
NOBA; NoP; OFD; OxBA; PoEL-5; PoRA; PPP; TAP;
TrGrPo

A Noiseless Patient Spider

54 A noiseless patient spider, (l. 1)

55 It launch'd forth filament, filament, filament, out of
itself,
Ever unreeling them, ever tirelessly speeding them.

And you O my soul where you stand,
Surrounded, detached, in measureless oceans of space,
Ceaselessly musing, venturing, throwing, seeking the
spheres to connect them,
Till the bridge you will need be form'd, till the ductile
anchor hold,
Till the gossamer thread you fling catch somewhere, O,
my soul.

AmPP; AnAmPo; AWP; BLPL; FF; HAP; HeIP; InPK;
InPS; LiTA; MoAmPo; NAAL-1; NIP; NOBA; NoP;
OxBA; OxBSP; PoE; SCV; SoSe; TAP; TrGrPo; WiR

On the Beach at Night

56 On the beach at night,
Stands a child with her father,
Watching the east, the autumn sky.

Up through the darkness,
While ravening clouds, the burial clouds, in black
masses spreading,
Lower sullen and fast athwart and down the sky,
(l. 1–6)

57 From the beach the child holding the hand of her
father,
Those burial clouds that lower victorious soon to
devour all,
Watching, silently weeps. (l. 11–13)

58 Then dearest child mournest thou only for Jupiter?
Considerest thou alone the burial of the stars?
(l. 23–24)

59 Something there is more immortal even than the stars,
(Many the burials, many the days and nights, passing
away,)
Something that shall endure longer even than lustrous
Jupiter.
Longer than sun or any revolving satellite,
Or the radiant sisters the Pleiades. (l. 28–32)

AmPP; AWP; ChTr; MoAmPo; NOBA; NoP; OxBA

Once I Pass'd through a Populous City

60 Once I pass'd through a populous city imprinting my
      brain for future use with its shows, architecture,
      customs, traditions,
    Yet now of all that city I remember only a woman I
      casually met there who detain'd me for love of me,
                                                    (l. 1–2)

61 I see her close beside me with silent lips sad and
      tremulous. (l. 7)

AmPP; AnAmPo; NAAL-1; OxBA

Out of the Cradle Endlessly Rocking

62 Out of the cradle endlessly rocking,
    Out of the mocking-bird's throat, the musical shuttle,
    Out of the Ninth-month midnight,
    Over the sterile sands and the fields beyond, where the
      child leaving his bed wandered alone, bareheaded,
      barefoot (l. 1–4)

63 A man, yet by these tears a little boy again,
    Throwing myself on the sand, confronting the waves,
    I, chanter of pains and joys, uniter of here and
      hereafter,
    Taking all hints to use them, but swiftly leaping beyond
      them,
    A reminiscence sing. (l. 18–22)

64 Two feathered guests from Alabama, two together,
    And their nest, and four light-green eggs spotted with
      brown,
    And every day the he-bird to and fro near at hand,
    And every day the she-bird crouched on her nest, silent,
      with bright eyes,
    And every day I, a curious boy, never too close, never
      disturbing them,
    Cautiously peering, absorbing, translating. (l. 26–31)

65 Pour down your warmth, great sun!
    While we bask, we two together.

    Two together!
    Winds blow south, or winds blow north,
    Day come white, or night come black,
    Home, or rivers and mountains from home,
    Singing all time, minding no time,
    While we two keep together. (l. 33–40)

66 O past! O happy life! O songs of joy!
    In the air, in the woods, over fields,
    Loved! loved! loved! loved! loved!
    But my mate no more, no more with me!
    We two together no more. (l. 125–129)

67 O you singers solitary, singing by yourself, projecting
      me,
    O solitary me listening, never more shall I cease
      perpetuating you

Never more shall I escape, never more the
      reverberations,
Never more the cries of unsatisfied love be absent from
      me,
Never again leave me to be the peaceful child I was
      before what there in the night,
By the sea under the yellow and sagging moon,
The messenger there aroused, the fire, the sweet hell
      within,
The unknown want, the destiny of me. (l. 150–157)

68 My own songs awakened from that hour,
    And with them the key, the word up from the waves,
    The word of the sweetest song and all songs,
    That strong and delicious word which, creeping to my
      feet,
    (Or like some old crone rocking the cradle, swathed in
      sweet garments, bending aside)
    The sea whispered me. (l. 176–181)

AA; AmPP; AWP; HAP; HeIP; MoAmPo; NAAL-1;
NAWM-2; NOBA; NoP; OxBA; PoE; PoEL-5; PrIm; TAP;
WeW

Reconciliation

69 For my enemy is dead, a man divine as myself is dead,
    I look where he lies white-faced and still in the coffin —
      I draw near,
    Bend down and touch lightly with my lips the white
      face in the coffin. (l. 4–6)

HAP; MoAmPo; NAAL-1; NoP; OBWP; OxBA; OxBSP;
TrGrPo; WaaP; WeW

The Runner

70 On a flat road runs the well-trained runner,
    He is lean and sinewy with muscular legs,
    He is thinly clothed, he leans forward as he runs,
    With lightly closed fists and arms partially raised.
                                                    (l. 1–4)

ASP; InPK; InPS; SD

A Sight in Camp in the Daybreak Gray and Dim

71 Three forms I see on stretchers lying, brought out there
      untended lying,
    Over each the blanket spread, ample brownish woolen
      blanket,
    Gray and heavy blanket, folding, covering all. (l. 4–6)

72 Then to the third — a face nor child nor old, very calm,
      as of beautiful yellow-white ivory,
    Young man I think I know you — I think this face is the
      face of the Christ himself,
    Dead and divine and brother of all, and here again he
      lies. (l. 13–15)

AA; AmPP; MoP; NAAL-1; NoAM; OFD; OxBA; PoE;
PoEL-5; TAP

Song of Myself

73 I celebrate myself, and sing myself,
And what I assume you shall assume,
For every atom belonging to me as good belongs to you.
(Fr. I, l. 1–3)

74 I lean and loafeat my ease observing a spear of summer
grass.

My tongue, every atom of my blood, form'd from this
soil, this air,
Born here of parents born here from parents the same,
and their parents the same,
I, now thirty-seven years old in perfect health begin,
Hoping to cease not till death. (Fr. I, l. 5–9)

Creeds and schools in abeyance,
Retiring back a while sufficed at whey they are, but
never forgotten,
I harbor for good or bad, I permit to speak at every
hazard,
Nature without check without original energy.
(Fr. I, l. 10–13)

75 The atmosphere is not a perfume, it has no taste of the
distillation, it is odorless,
It is for my mouth forever, I am in love with it,
I will go to the bank by the wood and become
undisguised and naked,
I am mad for it to be in contact with me.
(Fr. II, l. 17–20)

76 Stop this day and night with me and you shall possess
the origin of all poems,
You shall possess the good of the earth and sun, (there
are millions of suns left,)
You shall no longer take things at second or third hand,
nor look through the eyes of the dead, nor feed on the
spectres in books,
You shall not look through my eyes either, nor take
things from me,
You shall listen to all sides and filter them from your
self. (Fr. II, l. 33–37)

77 I believe in you my soul, the other I am must not abase
itself to you,
And you must not be abased to the other.
(Fr. V, l. 82–83)

78 I mind how once we lay such a transparent summer
morning,
How you settled your head athwart my hips and gently
turn'd over upon me,
And parted the shirt from my bosom-bone, and plunged
your tongue to my bare-stript heart,
And reach'd till you felt my beard, and reach'd till you
held my feet. (Fr. V, l. 87–90)

79 Twenty-eight young men bathe by the shore,
Twenty-eight young men and all so friendly;
(Fr. XI, l. 199–200)

80 The young men float on their backs, their white bellies
bulge to the sun, they do not ask who seizes fast to
them,
They do not know who puffs and declines with pendant
and bending arch,
They do not think whom they souse with spray.

81 Walt Whitman, a kosmos, of Manhattan the son,
Turbulent, fleshy, sensual, eating, drinking and
breeding,
No sentimentalist, no stander above men and women or
apart from them,
No more modest than immodest.
(Fr. XXIV, l. 497–500)

82 I believe in the flesh and the appetites,
Seeing, hearing, feeling, are miracles, and each part
and tag of me is a miracle.

Divine am I inside and out, and I make holy whatever I
touch or am touch'd from,
The scent of these arm-pits aroma finer than prayer,
This head more than churches, bibles, and all the
creeds. (Fr. XXIV, l. 522–526)

83 To behold the day-break!
The little light fades the immense and diaphanous
shadows,
The air tastes good to my palate.

Hefts of the moving world at innocent gambols silently
rising, freshly exuding,
Scooting obliquely high and low.
(Fr. XXIV, l. 550–554)

84 Seas of bright juice suffuse heaven.

The earth by the sky staid with, the daily close of their
junction,
The heav'd challenge from the east that moment over
my head,
The mocking taunt, See then whether you shall be
master! (Fr. XXIV, l. 556–559)

85 Is this then a touch? quivering me to a new identity,
Flames and ether making a rush for my veins,
Treacherous tip of me reaching and crowding to help
them,
My flesh and blood playing out lightning to strike what
is hardly different from myself,
On all sides prurient provokers stiffening my limbs,
(Fr. XXVIII, l. 619–623)

86 I am given up by traitors,
I talk wildly, I have lost my wits, I and nobody else am
the greatest traitor,
I went myself first to the headland, my own hands
carried me there.

You villain touch! what are you doing? my breath is
tight in its throat,
Unclench your floodgates, you are too much for me.
(Fr. XXVIII, l. 637–641)

87 I think I could turn and live with animals, they are so
   placid and self-contained,

88 They do not sweat and whine about their condition,
   They do not lie awake in the dark and weep for their
   sins,
   They do not make me sick discussing their duty to God,
   Not one is dissatisfied — not one is demented with the
   mania of owning things,
   Not one kneels to another, nor to his kind that lived
   thousands of years ago,
   Not one is respectable or industrious over the whole
   earth. (Fr. XXXII, l. 694–691)

89 Would you hear of an old-time sea-fight?
   Would you learn who won by the light of the moon and
   stars?
   List to the yarn, as my grandmother's father the sailor
   told it to me. (Fr. XXXV, l. 897–899)

90 Our frigate takes fire,
   The other asks if we demand quarter?
   If our colors are struck and the fighting done?
   Now I laugh content for I hear the voice of my little
   captain,
   We have not struck, he composedly cries, we have just
   begun our part of the fighting.
                      (Fr. XXXV, l. 912–916)

91 Serene stands the little captain,
   He is not hurried, his voice is neither high nor low,
   His eyes give more light to us than our battle-lanterns.

   Toward twelve there in the beams of the moon they
   surrender to us. (Fr. XXXV, l. 925–928)

92 Formless stacks of bodies and bodies by themselves,
   dabs of flesh upon the masts and spars,
   Cut of cordage, dangle of rigging, slight shock of the
   soothe of waves,
   Black and impassive guns, litter of powder-parcels,
   strong scent,
   A few large stars overhead, silent and mournful shining,
   Delicate sniffs of sea-breeze, smells of sedgy grass and
   fields by the shore, death-messages given in charge to
   survivors,
   The hiss of the surgeon's knife, the gnawing teeth of his
   saw,
   Wheeze, cluck, swash of falling blood, short wild
   scream, and long, dull, tapering groan,
   These so, these irretrievable.
      (Fr. XXXVI, l. 937–944)

AmPP; LiTA; MoAmPo; MOS; NOBA; OnMSP; OxBA;
RB; SOTW; UnPo

93 The spotted hawk swoops by and accuses me, he
   complains of my gab and my loitering.

   I too am not a bit tamed, I too am untranslatable,
   I sound my barbaric yawp over the roofs of the world.
                      (Fr. LII, l. 1331–1333)

94 You will hardly know who I am or what I mean,
   But I shall be good health to you nevertheless,
   And filter and fibre your blood.

   Failing to fetch me at first keep encouraged,
   Missing me one place search another,
   I stop somewhere waiting for you.
                      (Fr. LII, l. 1341–1346)

AA; AmPP; BLPL; FaBoBe; LiTA; MoAmPo; NAWM-2;
NoAM; NOBA; NoP; OxBA; PoE; SOTW

This Compost

95 Something startles me where I thought I was safest,
   I withdraw from the still woods I loved, (l. 1–2)

96 O how can it be that the ground itself does not sicken?
   How can you be alive you growths of spring?
   How can you furnish health you blood of herbs, roots,
   orchards, grain?
   Are they not continually putting distemper'd corpses
   within you?
   Is not every continent work'd over and over with sour
   dead? (l. 6–10)

97 What chemistry!
   That the winds are really not infectious,
   That this is no cheat, this transparent green-wash of the
   sea which is so amorous after me,
   That it is safe to allow it to lick my naked body all
   over with its tongues,

   That it will not endanger me with the fevers that have
   deposited themselves in it,
   That all is clean forever and forever, (l. 31–36)

98 Now I am terrified at the Earth, it is that calm and
   patient,
   It grows such sweet things out of such corruptions,
   It turns harmless and stainless on its axis, with such
   endless successions of diseas'd corpses,
   It distills such exquisite winds out of such infused fetor,
   It renews with such unwitting looks its prodigal,
   annual, sumptuous crops,
   It gives such divine materials to men, and accepts such
   leavings from them at last. (l. 42–47)

AWP; LiTA; MoAmPo; NAAL-1

To a Locomotive in Winter

99 Thee for my recitative,
   Thee in the driving storm even as now, the snow, the
   winter-day declining,
   Thee in thy panoply, thy measur'd dual throbbing and
   thy beat convulsive,
   Thy black cylindric body, golden brass and silvery steel,
                      (l. 1–4)

100 Type of the modern — emblem of motion and power —
   pulse of the continent. (l. 13)

101 By day thy warning ringing bell to sound its notes,
   By night thy silent signal lamps to swing. (l. 16–17)

102 Thy madly-whistled laughter, echoing, rumbling like an
      earthquake, rousing all,
   Law of thyself complete, thine own track firmly
      holding,
   (No sweetness debonair of tearful harp or glib piano
      thine,)
   Thy trills of shrieks by rocks and hills return'd,
   Launch'd o'er the prairies wide, across the lakes,
   To the free skies unpent and glad and strong.
                                          (l. 20–25)

   AmPP; FaBV; InPK; MoAmPo; MoP; NAAL-1; NoAM;
   NoP; PoEL-5; TAP

To the Man-of-War-Bird

103 Thou who hast slept all night upon the storm,
   Waking renew'd on thy prodigious pinions. (l. 1–2)

104 Thou born to match the gale, (thou art all wings,)
   To cope with heaven and earth and sea and hurricane,
                                             (l. 14–15)

105 That sport'st amid the lightning-flash and thunder-
      cloud,
   In them, in thy experiences, had'st thou my soul,
   What joys! what joys were thine! (l. 19–21)

   AA; AmPP; FaBoBe; FM

Vigil Strange I Kept on the Field One Night

106 Vigil strange I kept on the field one night;
   When you my son and my comrade dropt at my side
      that day,
   One look I but gave which your dear eyes return'd with
      a look I shall never forget.
   One touch of your hand to mine O boy, reach'd up as
      you lay on the ground, (l. 1–4)

107 Till at latest lingering of the night, indeed just as the
      dawn appear'd,
   My comrade I wrapt in his blanket, envelop'd well his
      form,
   Folded the blanket well, tucking it carefully over head
      and carefully under feet,
   And there and then and bathed by the rising sun, my
      son in his grave, in his rude-dug grave I deposited,
   Ending my vigil strange with that, vigil of night and
      battle-field dim,
   Vigil for boy of responding kisses, (never again on
      earth responding,)
   Vigil for comrade swiftly slain, vigil I never forget, how
      as day brighten'd,

I rose from the chill ground and folded my soldier well
   in his blanket,
And buried him where he fell. (l. 18–26)

MoAmPo; NAAL-1; NOBA; NoP; OBWP; PeHV; PoE;
TAP; WaaP

When I Heard at the Close of the Day

108 When I heard at the close of the day how my name had
      been receiv'd with plaudits in the capitol, still it was
      not a happy night for me that follow'd,
   And else when I carous'd, or when my plans were
      accomplish'd, still I was not happy,
   But the day when I rose at dawn from the bed of
      perfect health, refresh'd, singing, inhaling the ripe
      breath of autumn, (l. 1–3)

109 I heard the hissing rustle of the liquid and sands as
      directed to me whispering to congratulate me,
   For the one I love most lay sleeping by me under the
      same cover in the cool night,
   In the stillness in the autumn moonbeams his face was
      inclined toward me,
   And his arm lay lightly around my breast — and that
      night I was happy. (l. 10–13)

   AmPP; GEL; NAAL-1; NoAM; OxBA; PoE

When I Heard the Learn'd Astronomer

110 When I heard the learn'd astronomer,
   When the proofs, the figures, were ranged in columns
      before me, (l. 1–2)

111 How soon unaccountable I became tired and sick,
   Till rising and gliding out, I wander'd off by myself,
   In the mystical moist night-air, and from time to time,
   Look'd up in perfect silence at the stars. (l. 5–8)

   AmPP; AnAmPo; FF; FPL; HAP; MoAmPo; NAAL-1;
   NoP; OxBA; SoSe; TAP; TrGrPo; WeW

The World below the Brine

112 The world below the brine,
   Forests at the bottom of the sea, the branches and
      leaves, (l. 1–2)

   BoNaP; FM; MAT; NoP

The Wound-Dresser

113 An old man bending I come among new faces,
   Years looking backward resuming in answer to
      children,
   Come tell us old man, (l. 1–3)

114 What stays with you latest and deepest? of curious
      panics,
    Of hard-fought engagements or sieges tremendous what
      deepest remains? (l. 11–12)

115 Bearing the bandages, water and sponge,
    Straight and swift to my wounded I go,
    Where they lie on the ground after the battle brought
      in,
    Where their priceless blood reddens the grass the
      ground,
    Or to the rows of the hospital tent, or under the roof'd
      hospital,
    To the long rows of cots up and down each side I
      return,
    To each and all one after another I draw near, not one
      do I miss,
    An attendant follows holding a tray, he carries a refuse
      pail,
    Soon to be fill'd with clotted rags and blood, emptied,
      and fill'd again. (l. 25–33)

116 I sit by the restless all the dark night, some are so
      young,
    Some suffer so much, I recall the experience sweet and
      sad,
    (Many a soldier's loving arms about this neck have
      cross'd and rested,
    Many a soldier's kiss dwells on these bearded lips.)
                                              (l. 62–65)

AmPP; NAAL-1; NOBA; OBWP; PrIm; TAP

JOHN GREENLEAF WHITTIER
(1807–1892)

Barbara Frietchie

1 Up from the meadows rich with corn,
  Clear in the cool September morn, (l. 1–2)

2 Up rose old Barbara Frietchie then,
  Bowed with her fourscore years and ten;

  Bravest of all in Frederick town,
  She took up the flag the men hauled down; (l. 17–20)

3 She leaned far out on the window-sill,
  And shook it forth with a royal will.

  "Shoot, if you must, this old gray head,
  But spare your country's flag," she said.

  A shade of sadness, a blush of shame,
  Over the face of the leader came; (l. 33–38)

4 "Who touches a hair of yon gray head
  Dies like a dog! March on!" he said (l. 41–42)

5 Honor to her! and let a tear
  Fall, for her sake, on Stonewall's bier.

  Over Barbara Frietchie's grave,
  Flag of Freedom and Union, wave! (l. 53–56)

AiP; AnAmPo; BeLS; BoTP; CTC; FaBoBe; FaBV; FaFP;
FaPON; FaPoR; FF; FPL; GN; NOBA; OBAL; OBCA;
PAH; PoLF; TrGrPo; WBLP

The Barefoot Boy

6 Blessings on thee, little man,
  Barefoot boy, with cheek of tan! (l. 1–2)

7 For, eschewing books and tasks,
  Nature answers all he asks;
  Hand in hand with her he walks,
  Face to face with her he talks,
  Part and parcel of her joy, —
  Blessings on the barefoot boy! (l. 40–45)

8 All too soon these feet must hide
  In the prison cells of pride,
  Lose the freedom of the sod,
  Like a colt's for work be shod, (l. 91–94)

9 Ah! that thou couldst know thy joy,
  Ere it passes, barefoot boy! (l. 101–102)

AA; FaBoBe; FaPON; FPL; GN; LiTA; OBAL; OBCA;
OHFP; PoLF; WBLP

I love the old melodious lays

10 Yet here at least an earnest sense
   Of human right and weal is shown;
   A hate of tyranny intense,
   And hearty in its vehemence,
   As if my brother's pain and sorrow were my own.

   O Freedom! if to me belong
   Nor mighty Milton's gift divine,
   Nor Marvell's wit and graceful song.
   Still with a love as deep and strong
   As theirs, I lay, like them, my best gifts on thy shrine!
                                              (l. 26–35)

AA; AnAmPo; NoP; OxBA; TAP

Ichabod

11 So fallen! so lost! the light withdrawn
   Which once he wore!
   The glory from his gray hairs gone
   Forevermore! (l. 1–4)

12 All else is gone; from those great eyes
   The soul has fled:
   When faith is lost, when honor dies,

The man is dead!

Then, pay the reverence of old days
To his dead fame;
Walk backward, with averted gaze,
And hide the shame! (l. 29–36)

AA; AnAmPo; LiTA; NAAL-1; NOBA; OxBA; PAH;
PoEL-4; TAP

In School-Days

13 For near her stood the little boy
Her childish favour singled:
His cap pulled low upon a face
Where pride and shame were mingled. (l. 21–24)

14 'I'm sorry that I spelt the word:
I hate to go above you,
Because' — the brown eyes lower fell —
'Because, you see, I love you!'

Still memory to a grey-haired man
That sweet child-face is showing.
Dear girl! the grasses on her grave
Have forty years been growing. (l. 33–40)

AA; AnAmPo; BLPA; FaBoBe; FaPON; FPL; OBCA;
OxBChV

Maud Muller

15 Maud Muller on a summer's day
Raked the meadow sweet with hay. (l. 1–2)

16 Maud Muller looked and sighed: "Ah me!
That I the Judge's bride might be!

"He would dress me up in silks so fine,
And praise and toast me at his wine.

"My father should wear a broadcloth coat,
My brother should sail a painted boat. (l. 35–40)

17 The Judge looked back as he climbed the hill,
And saw Maud Muller standing still. (l. 45–46)

18 "Would she were mine, and I to-day,
Like her, a harvester of hay; (l. 51–52)

19 But he thought of his sisters, proud and cold,
And his mother, vain of her rank and gold. (l. 57–58)

20 Then she took up her burden of life again
Saying only, "It might have been."

21 God pity them both! and pity us all,
Who vainly the dreams of youth recall.

For of all sad words of tongue or pen,
The saddest are these: "It might have been!"
(l. 103–106)

AA; AnAmPo; BeLS; BLPL; FaBoBe; OHFP; PoLF; TAP;
WBLP

Skipper Ireson's Ride

22 Of all the rides since the birth of time,
Told in story or sung in rhyme, — (l. 1–2)

23 The strangest ride that ever was sped
Was Ireson's, out from Marblehead!
Old Floyd Ireson, for his hard heart,
Tarred and feathered and carried in a cart
by the women of Marblehead! (l. 7–11)

24 Small pity for him! — He sailed away
From a leaking ship in Chaleur Bay, — (l. 34–35)

25 "Here me, neighbors!" at last he cried, —
"What to me is this noisy ride? (l. 78–79)

26 Waking or sleeping, I see a wreck,
And hear a cry from a reeling deck! (l. 82–83)

27 Then the wife of the skipper lost at sea
Said, "God has touched him! why should we!"
(l. 89–90)

AA; AnAmPo; BeLS; NOBA; OBAL; OBCA; OxBA; PAH;
PoLF

Snow-bound; a Winter Idyl

28 O Time and Change! — with hair as gray
As was my sire's that winter day,
How strange it seems, with so much gone
Of life and love, to still live on!
Ah, brother! only I and thou
Are left of all that circle now, —
The dear home faces whereupon
That fitful firelight paled and shone. (l. 178–185)

29 The voices of that hearth are still;
Look where we may, the wide earth o'er,
Those lighted faces smile no more. (l. 187–189)

30 Yet, haply in some lull of life,
Some Truce of God which breaks its strife,
The worldling's eyes shall gather dew,
Dreaming in throngful city ways
Of winter joys his boyhood knew;
And dear and early friends — the few (l. 748–753)

31 These Flemish pictures of old days;
Sit with me by the homestead hearth,
And stretch the hands of memory forth
To warm them at the wood-fire's blaze! (l. 755–758)

AiP; AmPF; FaBV; GN; NAAL-1; NOBA; OxBA; TAP;
TrGrPo; WiR

Telling the Bees

32 Here is the place; right over the hill
Runs the path I took;
You can see the gap in the old wall still,
And the stepping-stones in the shallow brook. (l. 1–4)

33 Just the same as a month before, —
The house and the trees,
The barn's brown gable, the vine by the door, —
Nothing changed but the hives of bees. (l. 33–36)

34 Went drearily singing the chore-girl small,
Draping each hive with a shred of black. (l. 39–40)

35 And the song she was singing ever since
In my ear sounds on: —
"Stay at home, pretty bees, fly not hence!
Mistress Mary is dead and gone!" (l. 53–56)

AnAmPo; AWP; BLPL; NOBA; TAP

RICHARD WILBUR (b. 1921)

Advice to a Prophet

1 Nor shall you scare us with talk of the
death of the race.
How should we dream of this place without us? —
The sun mere fire, the leaves untroubled about us,
A stone look on the stone's face? (l. 9–12)

2 What should we be without
The dolphin's arc, the dove's return,

These things in which we have seen ourselves and
spoken? (l. 23–25)

3 Ask us, ask us whether with the worldless rose
Our hearts shall fail us; come demanding
Whether there shall be lofty or long standing
When the bronze annals of the oak-tree close.
(l. 33–36)

AmPP; CAPP; FYAP; MAT; MoAmPo; NYBP; OBWP;
OxBC; PoE; PPP; TwCP

After the Last Bulletins

4 Oh none too soon through the air white and dry
Will the clear announcer's voice
Beat like a dove, and you and I

From the heart's anarch and responsible town
Return by subway-mouth to life again,
Bearing the morning papers, (l. 22–27)

CoAP; MoAB; MoAmPo; NYBP; TrGrPo

A Baroque Wall-Fountain in the Villa Sciarra

5 — the main jet
Struggling aloft unti it seems at rest

In the act of rising, until
The very wish of water is reversed, (l. 31–34)

6 As near and far as grass,
Where eyes become the sunlight, and the hand
Is worthy of water: the dreamt land
Toward which all hungers leap, all pleasures pass.
(l. 56–60)

AmPP; CAPP; NAAL-2; NePoEA; NoP; NYBP; TwCP

Beasts

7 Beasts in their major freedom
Slumber in peace tonight. (l. 1–2)

AmPP; LCAP; NU; PPP; TwCP

The Beautiful Changes

8 the beautiful changes
In such kind ways,
Wishing ever to sunder
Things and things' selves for a second finding, to lose
For a moment all that it touches back to wonder.
(l. 14–18)

CMoP; CoAP; HCAP; InPS; PoE

Ceremony

9 But ceremony never did conceal,
Save to the silly eye, which all allows,
How much we are the woods we wander in. (l. 4–6)

10 What's lightly hid is deepest understood, (l. 15)

CoAP; MoP; NAAL-2; NoAM

A Christmas Hymn

11 A barn shall harbour heaven,
A stall become a shrine. (l. 7–8)

12 And every stone shall cry,
In praises of the child
By whose descent among us
The worlds are reconciled. (l. 29–32)

OBCP; OFD; PChr; TrCP

The Death of a Toad

13 The rare original heartsblood goes,
    Spends on the earthen hide, in the folds and wizenings,
        flows

    In the gutters of the banked and staring eyes. (l. 7–9)

    CMoP; LiTM; MoP; NAAL-2; NoAM; NoP; PoA

Epistemology

14 Kick at the rock, Sam Johnson, break your bones:
                                        (l. 1)

15 We milk the cow of the world, (l. 3)

    CRP; NePoEA; NoAM; NOBA; OxBSP

Exeunt

16 All cries are thin and terse;
    The field has droned the summer's final mass;
    A cricket like a dwindled hearse
    Crawls from the dry grass. (l. 5–8)

    BoNaP; HeIP; PoLF; Psk

Grasse: The Olive Trees

17 Even when seen from near, the olive shows
    A hue of far away. Perhaps for this
    The dove brought olive back, a tree which grows
    Unearthly pale, which ever dims and dries,
    And whose great thirst, exceeding all excess,
    Teaches the South it is not paradise. (l. 25–30)

    NAAL-2; NoAM; NOBA; NYBP

In the Elegy Season

18 Haze, char, and the weather of All Souls:
    A giant absence mopes upon the trees: (l. 1–2)

    InPK; MoAB; NePoEA; NYBP

Juggler

19 the earth falls
    So in our hearts from brilliance,
    Settles and is forgot. (l. 3–5)

20 If the juggler is tired now, if the broom stands
    In the dust again, if the table starts to drop
    Through the daily dark again, and though the plate
    Lies flat on the table top,

    For him we batter our hands
    Who has won for once over the world's weight.
                                        (l. 25–30)

    CMoP; LiTM; MoAB; NePoEA; NYBP; TAP

Junk

21 Haul them off! Hide them!
    The heart winces
    For junk and gimcrack,
    for jerrybuilt things
    And the men who make them
    for a little money, (l. 21–26)

22 Yet the things themselves
    in thoughtless honor
    Have kept composure, (l. 33–35)

    HAP; NoF; SaC; SM; WeW

Love Calls Us to the Things of This World

23 Outside the open window
    The morning air is all awash with angels.

    Some are in bed-sheets, some are in blouses,
    Some are in smocks: but truly there they are. (l. 5–8)

24 The soul shrinks

    From all that it is about to remember,
    From the punctual rape of every blessed day,
    And cries,
    "Oh, let there be nothing on earth but laundry,
    Nothing but rosy hands in the rising steam
    And clear dances done in the sight of heaven."
                                        (l. 17–22)

    AmPP; CAPP; CMoP; HAP; HeIP; InPS; MoAmPo;
    NePoEA; NIP; NoAM; PoE; PoRA; PPP; TAP; TrGrPo;
    UnPo; VGW

Lying

25 To claim, at a dead party, to have spotted a grackle,
    When in fact you haven't of late, can do no harm.
                                        (l. 1–2)

26 We know what boredom is: it is a dull
    Impatience or a fierce velleity,
    A champing wish, stalled by our lassitude,
    To make or do. In the strict sense, of course,
    We invent nothing, merely bearing witness
    To what each morning brings again to light:
                                        (l. 13–18)

27 And so with that most rare conception, nothing.
    What is it, after all, but something missed? (l. 33–34)

28 Or of the garden where we first mislaid
Simplicity of wish and will, forgetting
Out of what cognate splendor all things came
To take their scattering names; (l. 75–78)

29 Roland, who to Charles his King
And to the dove that hatched the dovetailed world
Was faithful unto death, and shamed the Devil.
(l. 83–85)

BLA; DiPo; HCAP; SV

Mind

30 Mind in its purest play is like some bat
That beats about in caverns all alone,
Contriving by a kind of senseless wit
Not to conclude against a wall of stone. (l. 1–4)

CMoP; HCAP; HoPM; NePoEA; OxBSP; PPP

Museum Piece

31 The good grey guardians of art
Patrol the halls on spongy shoes,
Impartially protective, though
Perhaps suspicious of Toulouse. (l. 1–4)

CMoP; FaBoMo; InPK; NIP; NoP; TAP

The Pardon

32 My dog lay dead five days without a grave (l. 1)

33 I started in to cry and call his name,

Asking forgiveness of his tongueless head.
. . . I dreamt the past was never past redeeming:
But whether this was false or honest dreaming
I beg death's pardon now. And mourn the dead.
(l. 20–24)

MoP; NePoEA; NIP; NoAM; NOBA; NoP; OBD

Piazza di Spagna, Early Morning

34 I can't forget
How she stood at the top of that long marble stair
Amazed, and then with a sleepy pirouette
Went dancing slowly down to the fountain-quieted
square; (l. 1–4)

GrPl; InPS; OxBSP; SM; VGW

Playboy

35 But what now grips his fancy is her face,

And how the cunning picture holds her still
At just that smiling instant when her soul,
Grown sweetly faint, and swept beyond control,
Consents to his inexorable will. (l. 24–28)

FF; MoP; NIP; NoAM; NOBA; NoP; WeW

Potato

36 An underground grower, blind and a common brown;
Got a misshapen look, it's nudged where it could;
Simple as soil yet crowded as earth with all. (l. 1–3)

CAPP; LiTA; MoAB; TrGrPo

Still, Citizen Sparrow

37 He shoulders nature there, the frightfully free,

The naked-headed one. Pardon him, you
Who dart in the orchard aisles, for it is he
Devours death, mocks mutability,
Has heart to make an end, keeps nature new. (l. 8–12)

38 Forgive the hero, you who would have died
Gladly with all you knew; he rode that tide
To Ararat; all men are Noah's sons. (l. 22–24)

AmPP; CMoP; HoPM; LiTM; MoAB; MoP; NoAM

Tywater

39 The violent, neat and practiced skill
Was all he loved and all he learned;
When he was hit, his body turned
To clumsy dirt before it fell.

And what to say of him, God knows.
Such violence. And such repose. (l. 13–18)

CMoP; LiTA; LiTM; MoAB

A Voice from under the Table

40 All true enough: and true as well that she
Was beautiful, and danced, and is now dead.
(l. 31–32)

41 A devil told me it was all the same
Whether to fail by spirit or by sense. (l. 39–40)

42 I am a sort of martyr, as you see,
A horizontal monument to patience.
The calves of waitresses parade about
My helpless head upon this sodden floor.
Well, I am down again, but not yet out.
O sweet frustrations, I shall be back for more.
(l. 43–48)

AmPP; HAP; NePoEA; NOBA

"A World without Objects Is a Sensible Emptiness"

43 The tall camels of the spirit
Steer for their deserts, (l. 1–2)

44 Wisely watch for the sight
Of the supernova burgeoning over the barn,
Lampshine blurred in the steam of beasts, the spirit's right
Oasis, light incarnate. (l. 25–28)

LiTM; MoAmPo; McP; NAAL-2; NoAM; NOBA; PoA

The Writer

45 Young as she is, the stuff
Of her life is a great cargo, and some of it heavy:
I wish her a lucky passage. (l. 7–9)

46 It is always a matter, my darling,
Of life or death, as I had forgotten. I wish
What I wished you before, but harder. (l. 31–33)

CAPP; HCAP; NoAM; OxBC

Year's End

47 Great mammoths overthrown
Composedly have made their long sojourns,
Like palaces of patience, in the gray
And changeless lands of ice. (l. 15–18)

48 The little dog lay curled and did not rise
But slept the deeper as the ashes rose
And found the people incomplete, (l. 19–21)

49 These sudden ends of time must give us pause.
We fray into the future, rarely wrought
Save in the tapestries of afterthought.
More time, more time. (l. 25–28)

CAPP; CoAP; HeIP; LiTM; NAAL-2; NePoEA; NYBP; SM

ELLA WHEELER WILCOX (1850–1919)

Solitude

1 Laugh, and the world laughs with you;
Weep, and you weep alone,
For the sad old earth must borrow its mirth,
But has trouble enough of its own. (l. 1–4)

2 Rejoice, and men will seek you;
Grieve, and they turn and go.
They want full measure of all your pleasure,
But they do not need your woe (l. 9–12)

3 There is room in the halls of pleasure
For a large and lordly train,
But one by one we must all file on
Through the narrow aisles of pain. (l. 21–24)

AnAmPo; FaFP; FPL; OHFP; PoLF; PWR; WBLP

The Winds of Fate

4 It's the set of the sails and not the gales,
That bids them where to go. (l. 3–4)

5 It's the set of the soul that decides the goal,
And not the storms or the strife. (l. 7–8)

AnAmPo; BLPA; FPL; WBLP

OSCAR WILDE (1854–1900)

The Ballad of Reading Gaol

1 I never saw a man who looked
With such a wistful eye
Upon that little tent of blue
Which prisoners call the sky, (l. 13–16)

2 I walked, with other souls in pain, (l. 19)

3 Yet each man kills the thing he loves,
By each let this be heard,
Some do it with a bitter look,
Some with a flattering word,
The coward does it with a kiss,
The brave man with a sword! (l. 37–42)

4 Like two doomed ships that pass in storm
We had crossed each other's way:
But we made no sign, we said no word,
We had no word to say; (l. 163–166)

5 Alas! it is a fearful thing
To feel another's guilt! (l. 265–266)

6 But neither milk-white rose nor red
May bloom in prison air;
The shard, the pebble, and the flint,
Are what they give us there:
For flowers have been known to heal
A common man's despair. (l. 487–492)

7 I know not whether Laws be right,
Or whether Laws be wrong;
All that we know who lie in gaol
Is that the wall is strong;
And that each day is like a year,
A year whose days are long. (l. 535–540)

8 The vilest deeds like poison weeds,
Bloom well in prison-air;
It is only what is good in Man
That wastes and withers there:
Pale Anguish keeps the heavy gate,
And the Warder is Despair. (l. 559–564)

9 And thus we rust Life's iron chain
Degraded and alone:
And some men curse, and some men weep,
And some men make no moan:
But God's eternal Laws are kind
And break the heart of stone: (l. 601–606)

BeLS; BrPo; MoBrPo; NoAM; NOBE; NOBVV; OBMV;
OBNC; OBNV

E Tenebris

10 Come down, O Christ, and help me! reach thy hand,
For I am drowning in a stormier sea
Than Simon on thy lake of Galilee: (l. 1–3)

11 My heart is as some famine-murdered land
Whence all good things have perished utterly,
And well I know my soul in Hell must lie
If I this night before God's throne should stand.
                                    (l. 5–8)

BrPo; MoBrPo; NAEL-2; Son; TIRV; TrPWD

The Harlot's House

12 Like strange mechanical grotesques,
Making fantastic arabesques,
The shadows raced across the blind. (l. 7–9)

EBVV; MoBrPo; NAEL-2; NoAM

Hélas!

13 To drift with every passion till my soul
Is a stringed lute on which all winds can play,
Is it for this that I have given away
Mine ancient wisdom, and austere control?
Methinks my life is a twice-written scroll
Scrawled over on some boyish holiday (l. 1–6)

14 I did but touch the honey of romance —
And must I lose a soul's inheritance? (l. 13–14)

BrPo; MoBrPo; NAEL-2; Son; TEP; TIRV

Impression du Matin

15 St. Paul's
Loomed like a bubble o'er the town. (l. 7–8)

16 one pale woman all alone,
The daylight kissing her wan hair,
Loitered beneath the gas lamps' flare,
With lips of flame and heart of stone. (l. 13–16)

BrPo; EBVV; MoBrPo; NAEL-2; NoAM

Requiescat

17 Tread lightly, she is near
Under the snow,
Speak gently, she can hear
The daisies grow. (l. 1–4)

BrPo; EBVV; FL; InvP; MoBrPo; OBNC; TrGrPo

Symphony in Yellow

18 An omnibus across the bridge
Crawls like a yellow butterfly,
And, here and there, a passer-by
Shows like a little restless midge. (l. 1–4)

EBVV; FaBoPP; MoBrPo; NoAM; NOBVV; OxBSP

EMMA HART WILLARD   (1787–1870)
Rocked in the Cradle of the Deep

1 Rocked in the cradle of the deep
I lay me down in peace to sleep;
Secure I rest upon the wave,
For Thou, O Lord! hast power to save. (l. 1–4)

2 And such the trust that still were mine,
Though stormy winds swept o'er the brine,
Or though the tempest's fiery breath
Roused me from sleep to wreck and death.
In ocean cave, still safe with Thee
The germ of immortality!
And calm and peaceful shall I sleep,
Rocked in the cradle of the deep. (l. 17–24)

AA; AnAmPo; BLPL; FaBoBe; FaFP; MOS; PWR; WBLP;
WGRP

WILLIAM CARLOS WILLIAMS
(1883–1963)
The Artist

1 Then he whirled about
bounded
into the air
and with an entrechat
perfectly achieved
completed the figure. (l. 11–15)

InPS; LCAP; NYBP; RB

As the cat

2 the cat
climbed over
the top of

the jamcloset (l. 1—4)

3 the hind
stepped down

into the pit of
the empty
flowerpot (l. 6—10)

FaPON; InPS; InvP; NoP; PDV; RR; TTTS

At the Ball Game

4 all to no end save beauty
the eternal —

So in detail they, the crowd,
are beautiful (l. 9—12)

5 It is alive, venomous
it smiles grimly
its words cut — (l. 16—18)

6 It is summer, it is the solstice
the crowd is

cheering, the crowd is laughing
in detail

permanently, seriously
without thought (l. 31—36)

CMoP; MoP; NoAM; NOBA; OxBA; PoE

Between Walls

7 the black wings
of the

hospital where
nothing

will grow (l. 1—5)

HoPM; SOTW; TAP; VGW

Burning the Christmas Greens

8 Their time past, pulled down
cracked and flung to the fire
— go up in a roar

All recognition lost, burnt clean
clean in the flame, the green
dispersed, (l. 1—6)

9 At the thick of the dark
the moment of the cold's
deepest plunge we brought branches
cut from the green trees

to fill our need, (l. 16—20)

10 Green is a solace
a promise of peace a fort
against the cold (though we

did not say so) (l. 41—44)

11 we, in
that instant, lost,

breathless to be witnesses,
as if we stood
ourselves refreshed among
the shining fauna of that fire. (l. 70—75)

LiTM; MoP NAAL-2; NoAM; NOBA

The Dance

12 Kicking and rolling about
the Fair Grounds, swinging their butts, those
shanks must be sound to bear up under such
rollicking measures, prance as they dance
in Breughel's great picture, The Kermess. (l. 8—12)

AmPP; CMoP; GoJo; GrPl; HAP; HeIP; InPK; LiTM;
MoP; NAAL-2; NIP; NoAM; NOBA; NoP; OxBA; PoE;
PrIm; SoSe TAP; WeW

Danse Russe

13 If I admire my arms, my face,
my shoulders, flanks, buttocks
against the yellow drawn shades, —

Who shall say I am not
the happy genius of my household?

CMoP; InPS; NOBA; NoP; PoE; PPP; TAP

Flowers by the Sea

14 the sea is circled and sways
peacefully upon its plantlike stem (l. 7—8)

CMoP; GoJc; MoAB; MoAmPo; NoAM; RB; TAP

The Great Figure

15 I saw the figure 5
in gold

on a red
firetruck (l. 3–6)

AiP; InPK; MoP; NoAM; QFR; TTTS

The Horse Show

16 You said, Unless there is some spark, some
spirit we keep within ourselves, life, a
continuing life's impossible — and it is all
we have. There is no other life, only the one.
(l. 8–11)

17 just like you sitting
there they come and talk to me, just the same.

They come to bother us. Why? I said I don't
know. Perhaps to find out what we are doing.
Jealous, do you think? I don't know. (l. 13–17)

18 Oh is that
all? I tho't it was something else. Oh
they jump and run too. I wish you had been
there, I was so interested to hear about it. (l. 39–42)

CMoP; NOBA; TAP; VGW

The Ivy Crown

19 We are only mortal
but being mortal
can defy our fate.
We may
by an outside chance
even win! (l. 25–30)

20 The business of love is
cruelty which,
by our wills,
we transform
to live together. (l. 38–42)

21 Sure
love is cruel
and selfish
and totally obtuse —
at least, blinded by the light,
young love is. (l. 71–76)

22 the jeweled prize
always
at our finger tips.
We will it so
and so it is
past all accident. (l. 84–89)

NAAL-2; NoAM; NoP; PrIm

Nantucket

23 Sunshine of late afternoon —
On the glass tray

a glass pitcher, the tumbler
turned down, by which

a key is lying — And the
immaculate white bed (l. 5–10)

AnAmPo; HAP; InPS; OxBA; SOTW; TAP; WeW

The Poor

24 It's the anarchy of poverty
delights me, the old
yellow wooden house indented
among the new brick tenements (l. 1–4)

MoAB; MoAmPo; NoP; PPP

Portrait of a Lady

25 Your thighs are appletrees
whose blossoms touch the sky.
Which sky? The sky
where Watteau hung a lady's
slipper. (l. 1–5)

26 Which shore?
Agh, petals maybe. How
should I know?
Which shore? Which shore?
I said petals from an appletree. (l. 18–22)

AmPP; CMoP; MoP; NAAL-2; NoAM; NOBA; OxBA

Queen-Ann's-Lace

27 the whole field is a
white desire, empty, a single stem;
a cluster, flower by flower,
a pious wish to whiteness gone over —
or nothing. (l. 17–21)

AmPP; BLPL; MoAB; MoAmPo; NAAL-2; NoAM; NOBA;
NoP; PrIm; TAP

The Red Wheelbarrow

28 so much depends
upon

a red wheel
barrow (l. 1–4)

AnAmPo; BLPL; CMoP; GrPl; HeIP; HoPM; InPK; LiTA;
LiTM; MoAB; MoAmPo; MoP; NAAL-2; NIP; NoAM;
NOBA; NoP; PoE; PrIm; SoSe; SOTW; TAP; TTTS;
UnPo; WeW

A Sort of a Song

29 Compose. (No ideas
but in things) Invent!
Saxifrage is my flower that splits
the rocks. (l. 9–12)

HoPM; NAAL-2; NoP; OxBSP; TAP

The Sparrow

30 What is more pretentiously
useless
or about which
we more pride ourselves?
It leads as often as not
to our undoing. (l. 29–34)

31 At that,
his small size,
keen eyes,
serviceable beak
and general truculence
assure his survival — (l. 62–67)

32 Practical to the end,
it is the poem
of his existence
that triumphed
finally; (l. 118–122)

33 This was I,
a sparrow.
I did my best;
farewell. (l. 136–139)

DiL; InPS; LCAP; PrIm; VGW

Spring and All

34 By the road to the contagious hospital
under the surge of the blue
mottled clouds driven from the
northwest — a cold wind. (l. 1–4)

35 Lifeless in appearance, sluggish
dazed spring approaches — (l. 14–15)

36 One by one objects are defined —
It quickens: clarity, outline of leaf

But now the stark dignity of
entrance — Still, the profound change
has come upon them: rooted, they
grip down and begin to awaken (l. 22–27)

CMoP; HAP; InPK; InPS; LiTM; MoAB; MoAmPo; MoP;
NAAL-2; NoAM; NOBA; OxBA; PoE; QFR; TAP; UnPo

These

37 These are the desolate, dark weeks
when nature in its barrenness
equals the stupidity of man. (l. 1–3)

38 (They
whine and whistle) among

the flashes of blooms of war; (l. 17–19)

39 The source of poetry that
seeing the clock stopped, says,
The clock has stopped

that ticked yesterday so well? (l. 31–34)

MoAB; MoAmPo; MoP; NOBA; NoP; OxBA

This Is Just to Say

40 Forgive me
they were delicious
so sweet
and so cold. (l. 9–12)

FF; GoJo; HoPM; InPK; InPS; NAAL-2; NIP; NoAM;
NOBA; NoP; RHPC; SOTW; TAP

To a Poor Old Woman

41 Comforted
a solace of ripe plums
seeming to fill the air
They taste good to her (l. 12–15)

AnAmPo; OBAL; SOTW; TAP; TTTS

To Elsie

42 The pure products of America
go crazy — (l. 1–2)

CMoP InPS; NAAL-2; NOBA; OxBA; PoE

To Waken an Old Lady

43 Old age is
a flight of small
cheeping birds
skimming
bare trees
above a snow glaze. (l. 1–6)

HAP; InPK; NoP; QFR; WeW

Tract

44 I begin with a design for a hearse.
For Christ's sake not black —
nor white either — and not polished!
Let it be weathered — like a farm wagon — (l. 8–11)

45 no little brass rollers
and small easy wheels on the bottom —
my townspeople what are you thinking of!
A rough plain hearse then
with gilt wheels and no top at all. (l. 28–32)

BLPL; DL; FF; LiTA; LiTM; MoAB; MoAmPo; MoP;
NoAM; NOBA; TAP; TrGrPo; TwCP; VGW

The Widow's Lament in Springtime

46 Thirty-five years
I lived with my husband.
The plumtree is white today
with masses of flowers. (l. 7–10)

CMoP; HAP; LiTM; MoP; NAAL-2; NoAM; NOBA; PoE;
TAP

The Yachts

47 they appear youthful, rare

as the light of a happy eye, live with the grace
of all that in the mind is fleckless, free and
naturally to be desired. (l. 15–18)

48 the whole sea become an entanglement of watery
     bodies
lost to the world bearing what they cannot hold.
     Broken,

beaten, desolate, reaching from the dead to be taken up
they cry out, failing, failing! their cries rising
in waves still as the skillful yachts pass over.
                          (l. 29–33)

AmPP; CMoP; HeIP; LiTA; LiTM; MoAB; MoAmPo;
MoP; MOS; NoAM; NOBA; NoP; OxBA; PoE; PPP

The Young Housewife

49 I compare her
to a fallen leaf.

The noiseless wheels of my car
rush with a crackling sound over
dried leaves as I bow and pass smiling. (l. 8–11)

HeIP; NAAL-2; NoP; TAP

ANNE FINCH, COUNTESS OF WINCHILSEA (1661–1720)

A Nocturnal Reverie

1 In such a night, when passing clouds give place,
Or thinly veil the heaven's mysterious face;
When in some river, overhung with green,
The waving moon and trembling leaves are seen;
                          (l. 7–10)

EBEV; NAEL-1; NOEC; NoP; PBWP; PoE; PoEL-3;
SeCePo; WPE

YVOR WINTERS (1900–1968)

At the San Francisco Airport

1 And you are here beside me, small,
Contained and fragile, and intent
On things that I but half recall — (l. 6–8)

2 The rain of matter upon sense
Destroys me momently. The score:
There comes what will come. (l. 16–18)

AiP; HeIP; InPK; NIP; NOBA; QFR

John Sutter

3 Metal, intrinsic value, deep and dense,
Preanimate, inimitable, still,
Real, but an evil with no human sense,
Dispersed the mind to concentrate the will. (l. 17–20)

4 What calm catastrophe will yet assuage
This final drouth of penitential tears? (l. 35–36)

MoAmPo; MoP; NoAM; NOBA; QFR

Sir Gawaine and the Green Knight

5 Reptilian green the wrinkled throat,
Green as a bough of yew the beard;
He bent his head, and so I smote; (l. 1–3)

6 By practice and conviction formed,
With ancient stubbornness ingrained,
Although her body clung and swarmed,
My own identity remained. (l. 21–24)

MoP; NoAM; PoRA; QFR; VGW

The Slow Pacific Swell

7 Far out of sight forever stands the sea,
Bounding the land with pale tranquillity. (l. 1–2)

8 And one rose in a tent of sea and gave
A darkening shudder; water fell away;
The whale stood shining, and then sank in spray. (l. 26–28)

9 The land is numb.
It stands beneath the feet, and one may come
Walking securely, till the sea extends
Its limber margin, and precision ends. (l. 33–36)

HeIP; MOS; NOBA; QFR

Time and the Garden

10 Gascoigne, Ben Jonson, Greville, Raleigh, Donne,
Poets who wrote great poems, one by one,
And spaced by many years, each line an act
Through which few labor, which no men retract.
This passion is the scholar's heritage. (l. 17–21)

11 The passion to condense from book to book
Unbroken wisdom in a single look,
Though we know well that when this fix the head,
The mind's immortal, but the man is dead. (l. 23–26)

MoAmPo; NoAM; QFR; VGW

GEORGE WITHER (1588–1667)

Fair Virtue, the Mistress of Philarete: A Lover's Resolution

1 Shall I, wasting in despair,
Die because a woman's fair?
Or make pale my cheeks with care
'Cause another's rosy are?

2 If she be not so to me,
What care I how fair she be?

AWP; BoLoP; ElL; FaBV; GTBS; GTBS-P; LiTB; NOBE; OBEV; OBS; SeCV-1; TrGrPo

I Loved a Lass

3 To maidens' vows and swearing
Henceforth no credit give,
You may give them the hearing
But never them believe.
They are as false as fair,
Unconstant, frail, untrue; (l. 64–69)

CH; ElL; FaBoPP; GBL; NOBE; OBEV; OBS

CHARLES WOLFE (1791–1823)

The Burial of Sir John Moore after Corunna

1 Not a drum was heard, not a funeral note,
As his corse to the rampart we hurried; (l. 1–2)

2 But he lay like a warrior taking his rest
With his martial cloak around him. (l. 11–12)

3 We carved not a line, and we raised not a stone,
But we left him alone with his glory. (l. 31–32)

ChTr; EnRP; FaBoPa; FaBoRV; FaFP; FaPoR; GN; GTBS; GTBS-P; NOBE; OBEV; OBWP; PoRA; PWR; WaaP; WBLP

HUMBERT WOLFE (1885–1940)

The Blackbird

1 His bill's so yellow,
his coat's so black,
that he makes a fellow
whistle back. (l. 5–8)

BoTP; FaPON; GoJo; GrPl; RHPC

SAMUEL WOODWORTH (1788–1842)

The Old Oaken Bucket

1 How dear to my heart are the scenes of my childhood,
When fond recollection presents them to view!
The orchard, the meadow, the deep tangled wildwood,
And every loved spot which my infancy knew. (l. 1–4)

2 That moss-covered bucket I hailed as a treasure,
For often at noon, when returned from the field,
I found it the source of an exquisite pleasure,
The purest and sweetest that nature can yield. (l. 9–12)

3 And now, far removed from the loved habitation,
The tear of regret will intrusively swell,
As fancy reverts to my father's plantation,
And sighs for the bucket that hung in the well. (l. 21–24)

AA; AnAmPo; BLPA; FaBoBe; FaFP; FaPON; FPL; WBLP

CONSTANCE FENIMORE WOOLSON
(1840–1894)

Kentucky Belle

1 I was at work that morning. Someone came riding like mad
Over the bridge and up the road—Farmer Rouf's little lad.

Bareback he rode; he had no hat; he hardly stopped to
   say,
" Morgan's men are coming, Frau, they're galloping on
   this way. (l. 25–28)

2 On like the wind they hurried, and Morgan rode in
   advance;
Bright were his eyes like live coals, as he gave me a
   sideways glance;
And I was just breathing freely, after my choking pain,
When the last one of the troopers suddenly drew his
   rein. (l. 53–56)

3 O, pluck was he to the backbone and clear grit through
   and through;
Boasted and bragged like a trooper; but the big words
   wouldn't do;
The boy was dying, sir, dying, as plain as plain could
   be,
Worn out by his ride with Morgan up from the
   Tennessee. (l. 65–68)

4 But, after the war was over, just think what came to
   pass —
A letter, sir; and the two were safe back in the old
   Bluegrass.

The lad had got across the border, riding Kentucky
   Belle;
And Kentuck she was thriving, and fat, and hearty, and
   well;
He cared for her, and kept her, nor touched her with
   whip or spur:
Ah! we've had many horses, but never a horse like her!
                                    (l. 111–116)

BeLS; BLPA; FaBoBe; PAH

WILLIAM WORDSWORTH   (1770–1850)

The Affliction of Margaret

1 Where art thou, my beloved Son,
Where art thou, worse to me than dead? (l. 1–2)

2 Or hast been summoned to the deep,
Thou, thou and all thy mates, to keep
An incommunicable sleep. (l. 54–56)

3 My apprehensions come in crowds;
I dread the rustling of the grass;
The very shadows of the clouds
Have power to shake me as they pass: (l. 64–67)

EnRP; GTBS; GTBS-P; PoEL-4

Character of the Happy Warrior

4 Who is the happy Warrior? Who is he
That every man in arms should wish to be?

It is the generous spirit, who, when brought
Among the tasks of real life, hath wrought
Upon the plan that pleased his boyish thought:
Whose high endeavors are an inward light
That makes the path before him always bright:
Who, with a natural instinct to discern
What knowledge can perform, is diligent to learn;
And in himself posses his own desire; (l. 1–9, 38)

5 And therefore does not stoop, nor lie in wait
For wealth, or honors, or for worldly state; (l. 41–42)

EnRP; FaBoBe; FaFP; LiTB; OHFP

Composed upon Westminster Bridge September 3, 1802

6 Earth has not anything to show more fair:
Dull would he be of soul who could pass by
A sight so touching in its majesty:
This City now doth, like a garment, wear
The beauty of the morning; silent, bare,
Ships, towers, domes, theatres, and temples lie
Open unto the fields, and to the sky; (l. 1–7)

7 Dear God! the very houses seem asleep;
And all that mighty heart is lying still! (l. 13–14)

AWP; BLPL; ChTr; EnRP; EyDe; FaBoCh; FaBoPP;
FaBoRV; FaBV; FaFP; FF; FiP; HAP; HeIP; InPK; InPS;
InvP; NAEL-2; NAWM-2; NoP; OAEL-2; OBNC; PoE;
PoEL-4; PoLF; PrIm; Son; TEP; TrGrPo; UnPo; WeW

ECCLESIASTICAL SONNETS (the following 2 sonnets)

Mutability

8 From low to high doth dissolution climb,
And sink from high to low, along a scale
Of awful notes, whose concord shall not fail; (l. 1–3)

9 could not even sustain
Some casual shout that broke the silent air,
Or the unimaginable touch of Time. (l. 12–14)

EBEV; EnRP; HeIP; InPK; LiTB; NOBE; NoP; OAEL-2;
OBEV; PoEL-4; PrIm

Tax Not the Royal Saint

10 Give all thou canst; high Heaven rejects the lore
Of nicely-calculated less or more; (l. 6–7)

EnRP; GTBS; GTBS-P; OBNC

Elegiac Stanzas

11 The light that never was, on sea or land,
The consecration, and the Poet's dream; (l. 15–16)

12 A deep distress hath humanized my Soul. (l. 36)

13 Not without hope we suffer and we mourn. (l. 60)

ChER; EnRP; FaBoPP; GTBS; GTBS-P; NAEL-2; NoP; OAEL-2; OBNC; PoE

The Excursion: The Recluse

14 On Man, on Nature, and on Human Life,
Musing is solitude, (l. 1–2)

15 the Mind of Man —
My haunt, and the main region of my song. (l. 40–41)

16 For the discerning intellect of Man,
When wedded to this goodly universe
In love and holy passion, shall find these
A simple produce of the common day.
— I, long before the blissful hour arrives,
Would chant, in lonely peace, the spousal verse
Of this great consummation — (l. 52–58)

EnRP; NoP; OAEL-2; PoE

Extempore Effusion upon the Death of James Hogg

17 The rapt One, of the godlike forehead,
The heaven-eyed creature sleeps in earth:
And Lamb, the frolic and the gentle,
Has vanished from his lonely hearth. (l. 17–20)

18 Our haughty life is crowned with darkness,
Like London with its own black wreath, (l. 29–30)

EBEV; FaBoRV; FiP; NOBE; NoP; OAEL-2; SCV

The Fountain

19 the wiser mind
Mourns less for what Age takes away,
Than what it leaves behind. (l. 34–36)

20 We wear a face of joy, because
We have been glad of yore. (l. 47–48)

EnRP; GTBS; GTBS-P; SeCePo

Great Men Have Been among Us

21 Great men have been among us; hands that penn'd
And tongues that utter'd wisdom — better none:
(l. 1–2)

22 No master spirit, no determined road;
But equally a want of books and men!

EnRP; FaBoPV; OBEV; PoEL-4; Son

The Green Linnet

23 Too blest with any one to pair;
Thyself thy own enjoyment. (l. 23–24)

EnRP; GTBS; GTBS-P; PBBP

I Wandered Lonely as a Cloud

24 I wandered lonely as a cloud
That floats on high o'er vales and hills,
When all at once I saw a crowd,
A host, of golden daffodils; (l. 1–4)

25 They flash upon that inward eye
Which is the bliss of solitude;
And then my heart with pleasure fills,
And dances with the daffodils. (l. 21–24)

BLPA; BoNaP; EnRP; FaBoBe; FaBoPP; FaBV; FaFP;
FaPON; FiP; FPL; GN; GoJo; GTBS; GTBS-P; InPK;
InPS; LiTB; NAEL-2; NOBE; NoP; OAEL-2; OBEV;
OBNC; OHFP; PoRA; PWR; SCV; TEP; TrGrPo; TTTS;
UnPo; WBLP

It Is a Beauteous Evening

26 It is a beauteous evening, calm and free,
The holy time is quiet as a Nun
Breathless with adoration; (l. 1–3)

27 Thou liest in Abraham's bosom all the year;
And worshipp'st at the Temple's inner shrine,
God being with thee when we know it not. (l. 12–14)

AWP; BLPL; ChTr; EnRP; FaBoPP; FaBoRV; FiP; HeIP;
LiTB; NAEL-2; NIP; NoP; OAEL-2; OBEV; OBTV;
PoEL-4; PoLF; PPP; SeCePo; Son; TEP; TrGrPo

It Is Not to Be Thought Of

28 We must be free or die, who speak the tongue
That Shakespeare spake; the faith and morals hold
Which Milton held. (l. 11–13)

EnRP; FaPoR; FiP; GN; NOBE; OBEV

Lines Composed a Few Miles above Tintern Abbey

29 feelings too
Of unremembered pleasure; such, perhaps,
As may have had no trivial influence

On that best portion of a good man's life;
His little, nameless, unremembered acts
Of kindness and of love. (l. 31–36)

30 that blessed mood,
In which the burthen of the mystery,
In which the heavy and the weary weight
Of all this unintelligible world
Is lightened: — (l. 38–42)

31 we are laid asleep
In body, and become a living soul:
While with an eye made quiet by the power
Of harmony, and the deep power of joy,
We see into the life of things. (l. 46–50)

32 the fretful stir
Unprofitable, and the fever of the world, (l. 53–54)

33 The sounding cataract
Haunted me like a passion: the tall rock,
The mountain, and the deep and gloomy wood,
Their colours and their forms, were then to me
An appetite: a feeling and a love,
That had no need of a remoter charm,
By thought supplied, or any interest
Unborrowed from the eye. — (l. 77–84)

34 The still, sad music of humanity, (l. 92)

35 something far more deeply interfused,
Whose dwelling is the light of setting suns, (l. 97–98)

36 in the mind of man,
A motion and a spirit, that impels
All thinking things, all objects of all thought,
And rolls through all things. (l. 100–103)

37 Knowing that Nature never did betray
The heart that loved her, (l. 123–124)

BLPL; ChER; EnRP; FaBoPP; FF; FiP; HeIP; InPS;
LiTB; NoP; OAEL-2; OBNC; PoEL-4; PPP; PrIm;
SeCePo; TEP; TrGrPo

Lines Written in Early Spring

38 And 'tis my faith that every flower
Enjoys the air it breathes. (l. 11–12)

39 Have I not reason to lament
What Man has made of Man? (l. 23–24)

EnRP; FPL; GTBS; GTBS-P; NAEL-2; OAEL-2; PoLF

London, 1802

40 Milton! thou should'st be living at this hour:
England hath need of thee: (l. 1–2)

41 And give us manners, virtue, freedom, power.
Thy soul was like a star, and dwelt apart. (l. 8–9)

42 So didst thou travel on life's common way,
In cheerful godliness; and yet thy heart
The lowliest duties on herself did lay. (l. 12–14)

AWP; EnRP; FaBoPV; FaBV; FaPoR; FF; GTBS;
GTBS-P; HAP; HeIP; InvP; LiTB; NAEL-2; NIP; NoP;
OBEV; OBNC; PoEL-4; PoRA; Son; TEP; TrGrPo

LUCY (the following 5 poems)

I. *Strange fits of passion have I known*

43 Strange fits of passion have I known:

44 What fond and wayward thoughts will slide
Into a Lover's head!
'O mercy!' to myself I cried,
'If Lucy should be dead!' (l. 25–28)

EBEV; EnRP; FiP; GBL; NOBE; OAEL-2; OBEV;
OBNC; TrGrPo

II. *She dwelt among the untrodden ways*

45 A violet by a mossy stone
Half hidden from the eye!
Fair as a star, when only one
Is shining in the sky.

46 She lived unknown, and few could know
When Lucy ceased to be;
But she is in her grave, and oh,
The difference to me! (l. 5–12)

AWP; BLPA; BoLoP; EBEV; ELP; EnLoPo; EnRP; FaBV;
FF; FiP; FPL; GBL; GTBS; GTBS-P; HAP; HeIP; LiTB;
NIP; NOBE; NoP; OAEL-2; OBEV; OBNC; OxBSP; PPP;
PrIm; PWR; TEP; TrGrPo; UnPo; WeW

III. *I traveled among unknown men*

47 I traveled among unknown men,
In lands beyond the sea;
Nor, England! did I know till then
What love I bore to thee. (l. 1–4)

AWP; EBEV; EnRP; FaBV; FiP; GBL; GTBS; GTBS-P;
NOBE; OAEL-2; OBEV; OBNC; TrGrPo

IV. *Three years she grew in sun and shower*

48 Three years she grew in sun and shower,
Then Nature said, 'A lovelier flower
On earth was never sown;
This Child I to myself will take; (l. 1–4)

EBEV; EnRP; FiP; GBL; GN; GTBS; GTBS-P; HAP;
NOBE; NoP; OAEL-2; OBEV; OBNC; PoEL-4; TrGrPo

V. *A slumber did my spirit seal*

49 She seemed a thing that could not feel
The touch of earthly years. (l. 3–4)

AWP; BLPL; EBEV; ELP; EnLoPo; EnRP; FaBoCh; FiP;
GBL; GTBS; GTBS-P; HAP; HeIP; InPK; InPS; InvP;
NOBE; NoP; OAEL-2; OBEV; OBNC; PoEL-4; PoRA;
PPP; PrIm; SCV; TEP; TrGrPo; UnPo; WeW

Lucy Gray; or, Solitude

50 No mate, no comrade Lucy knew;
She dwelt on a wide moor,
— The sweetest thing that ever grew
Beside a human door! (l. 5–8)

BeLS; CH; EnRP; FiP; NAEL-2; OAEL-2; OxBChV; TEP

Michael

51 Careless of books, yet having felt the power
Of Nature, by the gentle agency
Of natural objects, led me on to feel
For passions that were not my own, and think
(At random and imperfectly indeed)
On man, the heart of man, and human life. (l. 28–33)

52 he had been alone
Amid the heart of many thousand mists, (l. 57–58)

53 Our Luke shall leave us, Isabel; the land
Shall not go from us, and it shall be free;
He shall possess it, free as is the wind
That passes over it. (l. 244–247)

54 A work which is not here: a covenant
'Twill be between us; but, whatever fate
Befal thee, I shall love thee to the last,
And bear thy memory with me to the grave."
(l. 414–417)

55 There is a comfort in the strength of love;
'Twill make a thing endurable, which else
Would overset the brain, or break the heart:
(l. 448–450)

56 many and many a day he thither went,
And never lifted up a single stone. (l. 465–466)

EnRP; NAEL-2; OAEL-2

My Heart Leaps Up When I Behold

57 My heart leaps up when I behold
A rainbow in the sky: (l. 1–2)

58 The Child is father of the Man;
And I could wish my days to be
Bound each to each by natural piety. (l. 7–9)

BLPA; EnRP; FaBV; FaFP; FPL; GTBS; GTBS-P; InPK;
InPS; LiTB; NAEL-2; NOBE; NoP; OAEL-2; OBEV;
OBNC; OxBSP; TEP; TrGrPo

Nuns Fret Not at Their Convent's Narrow Room

59 Nuns fret not at their convent's narrow room; (l. 1)

60 In truth the prison, unto which we doom
Ourselves, no prison is:

EBEV; EnRP; NIP; NoP; OBEV; Son

Nutting

61 One of those heavenly days that cannot die; (l. 2)

62 Breathing with such suppression of the heart
As joy delights in; and, with wise restraint (l. 21–22)

63 In that sweet mood when pleasure loves to pay
Tribute to ease; and, of its joy secure,
The heart luxuriates with indifferent things,
Wasting its kindliness on stocks and stones,
And on the vacant air. (l. 38–42)

EnRP; NAEL-2; NU; OAEL-2; RB

Ode: Intimations of Immortality from Recollections of Early Childhood

64 The glory and the freshness of a dream. (l. 5)

65 The things which I have seen I now can see no more.
(l. 9)

66 The Rainbow comes and goes,
And lovely is the Rose, (l. 10–11)

67 To me alone there came a thought of grief;
A timely utterance gave that thought relief,
And I again am strong: (l. 22–24)

68 Whither is fled the visionary gleam?
Where is it now, the glory and the dream? (l. 56–57)

69 Our birth is but a sleep and a forgetting:
The Soul that rises with us, our life's Star,
Hath had elsewhere its setting,
And cometh from afar: (l. 58–61)

70 And not in utter nakedness,
But trailing clouds of glory do we come
From God, who is our home:

Heaven lies about us in our infancy!
Shades of the prison-house begin to close (l. 63–67)

71 And fade into the light of common day. (l. 76)

72 Earth fills her lap with pleasures of her own; (l. 77)

73 The homely Nurse doth all she can
To make her Foster-child, her Inmate Man,
Forget the glories he hath known,
And that imperial palace whence he came. (l. 81–84)

74 Behold the Child among his new-born blisses,
A six years' Darling of a pigmy size! (l. 85–86)

75 some little plan or chart,
Some fragment from his dream of human life,
Shaped by himself with newly-learned art; (l. 90–92)

76 As if his whole vocation
Were endless imitation. (l. 106–107)

77 Thou, whose exterior semblance doth belie
Thy Soul's immensity;
Thou best Philosopher, who yet dost keep
Thy heritage, thou Eye among the blind,
That, deaf and silent, read'st the eternal deep,
Haunted for ever by the eternal mind, — (l. 108–113)

78 Thou little Child, yet glorious in the might
Of heaven-born freedom on thy being's height,
Why with such earnest pains dost thou provoke
The years to bring the inevitable yoke, (l. 121–124)

79 O joy! that in our embers
Is something that doth live, (l. 129–130)

80 The thought of our past years in me doth breed
Perpetual benediction: not indeed
For that which is most worthy to be blest —
Delight and liberty, the simple creed
Of Childhood, whether busy or at rest,
With new-fledged hope still fluttering in his breast: —
(l. 133–138)

81 Those shadowy recollections,
Which, be they what they may,
Are yet the fountain light of all our day,
Are yet a master light of all our seeing; (l. 149–152)

82 Hence in a season of calm weather
Though inland far we be,
Our Souls have sight of that immortal sea
Which brought us hither, (l. 161–164)

83 let the young Lambs bound
As to the tabor's sound! (l. 169–170)

84 Though nothing can bring back the hour
Of splendour in the grass, of glory in the flower;
We will grieve not, rather find
Strength in what remains behind; (l. 177–180)

85 In the faith that looks through death,
In years that bring the philosophic mind. (l. 185–186)

86 The innocent brightness of a new-born Day
Is lovely yet;
The Clouds that gather round the setting sun
Do take a sober colouring from an eye
That hath kept watch o'er man's mortality;
(l. 194–197)

87 To me the meanest flower that blows can give
Thoughts that do often lie too deep for tears.
(l. 201–202)

AWP; BLPL; ChER; EnRP; FaBoRV; FaFP; FiP; GTBS;
GTBS-P; HAP; HeIP; InvP; LiTB; NAs; NOBE; NoP;
OAEL-2; OBEV; OBNC; OHFP; PoE; PoEL-4; PPP;
PrIm; TEP; TrGrPo

Ode to Duty

88 Stern Daughter of the Voice of God!
O Duty! if that name thou love,
Who art a light to guide, a rod
To check the erring, and reprove; (l. 1–4)

89 Flowers laugh before thee upon their beds
And fragrance in thy footing treads;
Thou dost preserve the stars from wrong;
And the most ancient heavens, through thee, are fresh
and strong. (l. 45–48)

AWP; EnRP; FPL; GTBS; GTBS-P; NAEL-2; NoP;
OAEL-2; OBEV; WGRP

On the Extinction of the Venetian Republic

90 Once did She hold the gorgeous East in fee;
And was the safeguard of the West: (l. 1–2)

91 And, when she took unto herself a Mate,
She must espouse the everlasting Sea. (l. 7–8)

92 Men are we, and must grieve when even the Shade
Of that which once was great, is passed away.
(l. 13–14)

EnRP; FaBoRV; GTBS; GTBS-P; NOBE; NoP; OBEV;
OBNC; TrGrPo

THE PRELUDE (the following 11 poems)

I. Childhood and School-Time

93 Fair seed-time had my soul, and I grew up
Fostered alike by beauty and by fear:

94 I heard among the solitary hills
Low breathings coming after me,

95 though mean
Our object and inglorious, yet the end
Was not ignoble.

96 Dust as we are, the immortal spirit grows
Like harmony in music; there is a dark
Inscrutable workmanship that reconciles
Discordant elements, makes them cling together
In one society.

97 my brain
Worked with a dim and undetermined sense
Of unknown modes of being; o'er my thoughts
There hung a darkness, call it solitude
Or blank desertion.

98 Wisdom and Spirit of the universe!
Thou Soul that art the eternity of thought,
That givest to forms and images a breath
And everlasting motion,

CH; EnRP; FaBoPP; GN; HAP; NOBE; NoP; NU;
OAEL-2; OBNC; PoE; PoEL-4; SCV

II. School-Time (Conclusion)

99 the soul,
Remembering how she felt, but what she felt
Remembering not, retains an obscure sense
Of possible sublimity,

III. Residence at Cambridge

100 I was the Dreamer, they the Dream; I roam'd
Delighted, through the motley spectacle;
Gowns grave or gaudy, Doctors, Students, Streets,
Lamps, Gateways, Flocks of Churches, Courts and
    Towers:

101 where the Statue stood
Of Newton, with his Prism and silent Face
The marble index of a Mind for ever
Voyaging through strange seas of Thought, alone.

EnRP; FaBoPP; HAP; ImOP; OAEL-2

IV. Summer Vacation

102 And open field,through which the pathway wound,
And homeward led my steps. Magnificent
The morning rose, in memorable pomp,
Glorious as e'er I had beheld — in front,
The sea lay laughing at a distance; near,
The solid mountains shone, bright as the clouds,
Grain-tinctured, drenched in empyrean light;

103 I made no vows, but vows
Were then made for me; bond unknown to me
Was given, that I should be, else sinning greatly,
A dedicated Spirit.

EnRP; OAEL-2; PoEL-4

V. Books

104 Knowledge and increase of enduring joy
From the great Nature that exists in works
Of mighty Poets.

EnRP; OAEL-2

105 With all its solemn imagery, its rocks,
Its woods, and that uncertain heaven, received
Into the bosom of the steady lake.

VI. Cambridge and the Alps

106 In verity, an independent world,
Created out of pure intelligence.

EnRP; FiP; ImOP; OAEL-2; PoEL-4

107 Our destiny, our being's heart and home,
Is with infinitude, and only there;
With hope it is, hope that can never die,

VII. Residence in London

108 Caught by the spectacle my mind turned round
As with the might of waters; an apt type
This label seemed of the utmost we can know,
Both of ourselves and of the universe;
And, on the shape of that unmoving man,
His steadfast face and sightless eyes, I gazed,
As if admonished from another world.

109 Oh, blank confusion! true epitome
Of what the mighty city is herself,
To thousands upon thousands of her sons,
Living amid the same perpetual whirl
Of trivial objects, melted and reduced
To one identity, by differences
That have no law, no meaning, and no end —

EnRP; HAP; OAEL-2; PoEL-4

X. Residence in France

110 The horse is taught his manage, and no star
Of wildest course but treads back his own steps;

EnRP; OAEL-2

XI. France

111 Bliss was it in that dawn to be alive,
But to be young was very Heaven!

112 Not in Utopia — subterranean Fields, —
Or some secreted Island, Heaven knows where!
But in the very world, which is the world

Of all of us, — the place where in the end
We find our happiness, or not at all!

XII. *Imagination and Taste*

113 There are in our existence spots of time,

114 I should need
Colours and words that are unknown to man,
To paint the visionary dreariness

115 Oh! mystery of man, from what a depth
Proceed thy honours. I am lost, but see
In simple childhood something of the base
On which thy greatness stands; but this I feel,
That from thyself it comes, that thou must give,
Else never canst receive. The days gone by
Return upon me almost from the dawn
Of life: the hiding-places of man's power
Open; I would approach them, but they close.

EnRP; OAEL-2; PoE; PoEL-4; TOF

116 One great Society alone on Earth,
The noble Living, and the noble Dead.

XIV. *Conclusion*

117 The power, which all
Acknowledge when thus moved, which Nature thus
To bodily sense exhibits, is the express
Resemblance of that glorious faculty
That higher minds bear with them as their own.

EnRP; OAEL-2; PoEL-4

118 Imagination, which in truth
Is but another name for absolute power
And clearest insight, amplitude of mind,
And reason, in her most exalted mood.

119 Instruct them how the mind of Man becomes
A thousand times more beautiful than the earth
On which he dwells,

Resolution and Independence

120 But how can he expect that others should
Build for him, sow for him, and at his call
Love him, who for himself will take no heed at all?

121 I thought of Chatterton, the marvellous boy,
The sleepless soul that perished in his pride;
Of him who walked in glory and in joy
Following his plough, along the mountain side:
By our own spirits are we deified:
We poets in our youth begin in gladness;
But thereof come in the end despondency and madness.

122 The oldest man he seemed that ever wore grey hairs.

123 Choice word and measured phrase, above the reach
Of ordinary men; a stately speech;
Such as grave livers do in Scotland use,

124 And mighty poets in their misery dead.

125 'How is it that you live, and what is it you do?'

The Reverie of Poor Susan

126 And a single small cottage, a nest like a dove's,
The one only dwelling on earth that she loves.
                                        (l. 11—12)

CH; EnRP; GTBS; GTBS-P; OxBoLi; WiR

The River Duddon

127 Still glides the Stream, and shall for ever glide;
The Forms remains, the Function never dies;

128 Through love, through hope, and faith's transcendent
      dower,
We feel that we are greater than we know.

EnRP; FaBoPP; FaBoRV; NOBE; OBEV; OBNC; SeCePo

Ruth; or, The Influences of Nature

129 Among the Indians he had fought;
And with him many tales he brought
Of pleasure and of fear;
Such tales as told to any Maid
By such a Youth, in the green shade,
Were perilous to hear. (l. 43—48)

130 He told of the Magnolia, spread
High as a cloud, high over head!
The Cypress and her spire;
— Of flowers that with one scarlet gleam
Cover a hundred leagues, and seem
To set the hills on fire. (l. 61—66)

ChER; EnRP; GTBS; GTBS-P; PoEL-4

Scorn not the sonnet; critic, you have frowned

131 Scorn not the sonnet; critic, you have frowned,
Mindless of its just honors; with this key
Shakespeare unlocked his heart; (l. 1—3)

132 Milton, in his hand
The thing became a trumpet;

EBEV; EnRP; HeIP; NIP; NoP; OBEV; Son; TrGrPo

She Was a Phantom of Delight

133 She was a phantom of delight
When first she gleamed upon my sight;
A lovely apparition, sent
To be a moment's ornament; (l. 1–4)

134 A creature not too bright or good
For human nature's daily food;
For transient sorrows, simple wiles,
Praise, blame, love, kisses, tears, and smiles.
(l. 17–20)

135 A perfect Woman, nobly planned,
To warn, to comfort, and command;
And yet a Spirit still, and bright
With something of angelic light. (l. 27–30)

BLPL; EnRP; FaBoBe; FaBV; FaFP; GTBS; GTBS-P;
HeIP; LiTB; NoP; OAEL-2; OBEV; OHFP; PoEL-4;
PWR; TrGrPo

Simon Lee

136 O Reader! had you in your mind
Such stores as silent thought can bring,
O gentle Reader! you would find
A tale in every thing. (l. 65–68)

137 —I've heard of hearts unkind, kind deeds
With coldness still returning;
Alas! the gratitude of men
Hath oftener left me mourning. (l. 93–96)

EnRP; GTBS; GTBS-P; NAEL-2

The Solitary Reaper

138 Behold her, single in the field,
Yon solitary Highland Lass! (l. 1–2)

139 A voice so thrilling ne'er was heard
In spring-time from the Cuckoo-bird,
Breaking the silence of the seas
Among the farthest Hebrides. (l. 13–16)

140 Will no one tell me what she sings?—
Perhaps the plaintive numbers flow
For old, unhappy, far-off things,
And battles long ago: (l. 17–20)

141 The music in my heart I bore,
Long after it was heard no more. (l. 31–32)

AWP; BLPL; CH; ChER; EnRP; FaBoCh; FaPoR; FiP;
GN; GTBS; GTBS-P; HAP; HeIP; InPS; LiTB; NAEL-2;
NOBE; NoP; OAEL-2; OBEV; OBNC; PoEL-4; PoRA;
PPP; SCV; SoSe; TEP; TrGrPo; UnPo; WeW

Surprised by Joy

142 Surprised by joy—impatient as the wind (l. 1)

143 Love, faithful love, recalled thee to my mind—
But how could I forget thee? (l. 5–6)

144 That neither present time, nor years unborn
Could to my sight that heavenly face restore.
(l. 13–14)

BLPL; BoLoP; EnRP; GTBS; GTBS-P; HAP; LiTB;
NAEL-2; NOBE; NoP; OAEL-2; OBD; OBEV; PoE; Son;
TEP

The Tables Turned

145 One impulse from a vernal wood
May teach you more of man,
Of moral evil and of good,
Than all the sages can. (l. 21–24)

146 We murder to dissect. (l. 28)

EnRP; NAEL-2; OAEL-2; TOF

Thought of a Briton on the Subjugation of Switzerland

147 Two voices are there; one is of the Sea,
One of the Mountains; each a mighty Voice:
In both from age to age Thou didst rejoice,
They were thy chosen Music, Liberty! (l. 1–4)

ChER; EnRP; GTBS; GTBS-P

To a Skylark

148 Type of the wise, who soar, but never roam—
True to the kindred points of Heaven and Home!
(l. 17–18)

EnRP; FaFP; GTBS; GTBS-P; PBBP; TrGrPo

To Sleep

149 Come, blessed barrier between day and day,
Dear mother of fresh thoughts and joyous health!
(l. 13–14)

EnRP; GTBS; GTBS-P; TrGrPo

To the Cuckoo

150 O Cuckoo! shall I call thee Bird,
Or but a wandering Voice? (l. 2–4)

151 Thrice welcome, darling of the Spring! (l. 13)

152 And thou wert still a hope, a love;
Still longed for, never seen. (l. 23–24)

BoTP; ELP; EnRP; FaFP; FiP; GTBS; GTBS-P; PoLF;
TrGrPo

To Toussaint L'Ouverture

153 Thou hast left behind
Powers that will work for thee; air, earth, and skies;
There's not a breathing of the common wind
That will forget thee; thou hast great allies;
Thy friends are exultations, agonies,
And love, and man's unconquerable mind. (l. 8–14)

EnRP; FaBoPV; InPK; NOBE; OBNC; PoNe; PoRA; PPP;
TrGrPo

The Two April Mornings

154 No fountain from its rocky cave
E'er tripped with foot so free;
She seemed as happy as a wave
That dances on the sea. (l. 49–52)

EBEV; EnRP; GTBS; GTBS-P; NAEL-2

We Are Seven

155 A simple child,
That lightly draws its breath,
And feels its life in every limb,
What should it know of death? (l. 1–4)

156 'But they are dead; those two are dead!
Their spirits are in heaven!'
'Twas throwing words away; for still
The little maid would have her will,
And said, 'Nay, we are seven!' (l. 65–69)

BLPA; BLPL; EnRP; GN; NAEL-2; OxBChV; TEP;
WBLP

When I Have Borne in Memory

157 When men change swords for ledgers, and desert
The student's bower for gold, some fears unnamed
I had, my Country — am I to be blamed? (l. 3–5)

EnRP; GTBS; GTBS-P; OBEV

Where Lies the Land to Which Yon Ship Must Go?

158 Where lies the Land to which yon Ship must go? (l. 1)

ChER; EnRP; MOS; OBNC; PoEL-4

The World Is Too Much with Us

159 The world is too much with us; late and soon,
Getting and spending, we lay waste our powers:
(l. 1–2)

160 I'd rather be
A Pagan suckled in a creed outworn;
So might I, standing on this pleasant lea,
Have glimpses that would make me less forlorn;
Have sight of Proteus rising from the sea;
Or hear old Triton blow his wreathed horn. (l. 10–14)

AWP; ChER; ChTr; EnRP; FaFP; FaPoR; FiP; FPL;
GTBS; GTBS-P; HAP; HeIP; HoPM; InPK; InPS; LiTB;
MAT; NAEL-2; NAWM-2; NOBE; NoP; OAEL-2; OBEV;
OBNC; OHFP; PoE; PoEL-4; PoLF; PoRA; PPP; PrIm;
PWR; Son; SoSe; TEP; TrGrPo; WeW; WGRP

Written in London, September 1802

161 The wealthiest man among us is the best: (l. 7)

162 The homely beauty of the good old cause
Is gone; (l. 12–13)

ChER; EnRP; FaBoPV; GTBS; GTBS-P; OBEV; TrGrPo

Written in March

163 The cattle are grazing,
Their heads never raising;
There are forty feeding like one! (l. 8–10)

164 Like an army defeated
The snow hath retreated, (l. 11–12)

BoNaP; BoTP; EnRP; FaPON; GoJo; MoShBr; NAEL-2;
NTCP; PYC; UnPo

Yarrow Unvisited

165 'Twill soothe us in our sorrow
That earth has something yet to show,
The bonny holms of Yarrow!' (l. 62–64)

EnRP; GTBS; GTBS-P; PoRA

SIR HENRY WOTTON (1568–1639)

The Character of a Happy Life

1 How happy is he born and taught
That serveth not another's will;
Whose armour is his honest thought,
And simple truth his utmost skill! (l. 1–4)

2 Lord of himself, though not of lands,
And having nothing, yet hath all. (l. 23–24)

ElL; GTBS; GTBS-P; LiTB; NOBE; OBEV; OBS;
TrGrPo; WGRP

On His Mistress, the Queen of Bohemia

3 You common people of the skies,
What are you when the moon doth rise? (l. 4–5)

4 By weaker accents, what's your praise
When Philomel her voice doth raise? (l. 9–10)

5 As if the spring were all your own,
What are you when the rose is blown? (l. 14–15)

6 So, when my mistress shall be seen
In form and beauty of her mind,
By virtue first, then choice, a queen, (l. 16–18)

BoLoP; ElL; ELP; EnLoPo; FaBoCh; GBL; GTBS;
GTBS-P; HAP; JCP; MeLP; MePo; NOBE; NoP; OBEV;
OBS; SeCP; TrGrPo

Upon the Death of Sir Albert Morton's Wife

7 He first deceas'd; She for a little tri'd
To live without him: lik'd it not, and di'd. (l. 1–2)

BoLoP; EnLoPo; FaBoEE; NoP; OBD; OBEV; OBS;
SeCP; TrGrPo; WeW

Upon the Sudden Restraint of the Earl of Somerset, Then Falling from Favor

8 Then, though darkened, you shall say,
When friends fail, and Princes frown,
Virtue is the roughest way,
But proves at night a bed of down. (l. 13–16)

ELP; JCP; MePo; NOBE; NoP; OBS; SeCP

ERNEST VINCENT WRIGHT
(1872–1939)

When Father Carves the Duck

1 And mother almost always sighs,
When father carves the duck.
Then all of us prepare to rise,
And hold our bibs before our eyes,
And be prepared for some surprise,
When father carves the duck. (l. 3–8)

BLPL; FaBV; FaFP; NTCP; PoLF

JAMES WRIGHT (1927–1980)
Autumn Begins in Martins Ferry, Ohio

1 All the proud fathers are ashamed to go home.
Their women cluck like starved pullets,
Dying for love. (l. 6–8)

CAPP; HCAP; InPK; InPS; NaP; NoAM; TSL

A Blessing

2 Her mane falls wild on her forehead,
And the light breeze moves me to caress her long ear
That is delicate as the skin over a girl's wrist.
Suddenly I realize
That if I stepped out of my body I would break
Into blossom. (l. 19–24)

CAPP; GrPl; InPK; InPS; LLLT; NAAL-2; NaP; NoAM;
NOBA; NoP; PoE; PPP; TwCP

In Response to a Rumor That the Oldest Whorehouse in Wheeling, West Virginia, Has Been Condemned

3 And nobody would commit suicide, only
To find beyond death
Bridgeport, Ohio. (l. 22–24)

CAPP; CoAP; NNaP; NoAM; TW

Lying in a Hammock at William Duffy's Farm in Pine Island, Minnesota

4 I lean back, as the evening darkens and comes on.
A chicken hawk floats over, looking for home.
I have wasted my life. (l. 11–13)

CAPP; HAP; HCAP; HoPM; NaP; NOBA; OPOP

Milkweed

5 Whatever it was I lost, whatever I wept for
Was a wild, gentle thing, the small dark eyes
Loving me in secret.
It is here. At a touch of my hand,
The air fills with delicate creatures
From the other world. (l. 7–12)

LCAP; NaP; NOBA; NU

Speak

6 To speak in a flat voice
Is all that I can do. (l. 1–2)

7 I have gone forward with
   Some, a few lonely some.
   They have fallen to death.
   I die with them. (l. 33–36)

8 Come down. Come down. Why dost
   Thou hide thy face? (l. 39–40)

HAP; SM; TAP; WeW

RICHARD WRIGHT (1808–1860)

Between the World and Me

1 Panting, begging I clutched childlike, clutched to the
   hot sides of death.
   Now I am dry bones and my face a stony skull staring
   in yellow surprise at the sun.... (l. 47–50)

AmNP; IDB; LiTM; MoP; PoBA

SIR THOMAS WYATT (1503?–1542)

And Wilt Thou Leave Me Thus?

1 And wilt thou leave me thus?
   That hath loved thee so long
   In wealth and woe among:
   And is thy heart so strong
   As for to leave me thus?
   Say nay! say nay! (l. 7–12)

AAS; ElL; EnLoPo; GTBS; GTBS-P; NAEL-1; SiPS

Blame not my lute for he must sound

2 Blame but thyself that hast misdone,
   And well deserved to have blame;
   Change thou thy way so evil begun,
   And then my lute shall sound that same:
   But if till then my fingers play
   By thy desert their wonted way,
   Blame not my lute. (l. 29–35)

AAS; EBEV; ElL; NAEL-1; OAEL-1; OBSC; PoE; QFR;
SiPS

Divers Doth Use

3 Divers doth use, as I have heard and know,
   (When that to change their ladies do begin),
   To mourn and wail and never for to lin,
   Hoping thereby to pease their painful woe. (l. 1–4)

4 But let it pass, and think it is of kind
   That often change doth please a woman's mind.
                   (l. 13–14)

AAS; NAEL-1; SiPS; Son

Farewell love and all thy laws for ever

5 Farewell, Love, and all thy laws for ever:
   Thy baited hooks shall tangle me no more;
   Senec and Plato call me from thy lore,
   To perfect wealth my wit for to endeavour. (l. 1–4)

6 Thy sharp repulse, that pricketh ay so sore,
   Hath taught me to set in trifles no store,
   And scape forth, since liberty is lever. (l. 6–8)

AAS; GBL; LiTB; NAEL-1; OAEL-1; SiPS; Son; TrGrPo

Forget Not Yet

7 Forget not yet the tried intent
   Of such a truth as I have meant;
   My great travail so gladly spent
   Forget not yet! (l. 1–4)

AAS; ElL; GTBS; GTBS-P; HAP; NAEL-1; NOBE; NoP;
OBEV; OBSC; SiPS

Help Me to Seek

8 Help me to seek, for I lost it there
   And if that ye have found it, ye that be here,
   And seek to convey it secretly,
   Handle it soft and treat it tenderly,
   Or else it will plain and then appear: (l. 1–5)

AAS; FF; InvP; SiPS

If in the World There Be More Woe

9 If in the world there be more woe
   Than I have in my heart,
   Whereso it is, it doth come fro,
   And in my breast there doth it grow, (l. 1–4)

ElL; OBSC; SiPS; TrGrPo

Is It Possible?

10 Is it possible
   That any may find
   Within one heart so diverse mind,
   To change or turn as weather and wind?
   Is it possible? (l. 11–15)

11 All is possible,
   Who so list believe;
   Trust therefore first, and after preve,
   As men wed ladies by license and leave,
   All is possible. (l. 26–30)

   ELP; GBL; NoP; OBSC; QFR; SiPS

The Lover Complaineth the Unkindness of His Love

12 My lute awake! perform the last
   Labour that thou and I shall waste,
   And end that I have now begun;
   For when this song is sung and past,
   My lute be still, for I have done. (l. 1–5)

   AAS; BoLoP; EBEV; EiL; ELP; GBL; HAP; InPS;
   NAEL-1; NOBE; NoP; OAEL-1; OBEV; OBSC; PoEL-1;
   QFR; SiPS; TrGrPo

The Lover Rejoiceth

13 Tangled was I in Love's snare.
   Oppressed with pain, torment with care;
   Of grief right sure, of joy quite bare,
   Clean in despair by cruelty. (l. 1–4)

   AAS; OBSC; SiPS; TrGrPo

The Lover Rejoiceth the Enjoying of His Love

14 My most desire my hand may reach,
   My will is alway at my hand;
   Me need not long for to beseech
   Her that hath power me to command. (l. 17–20)

15 Nothing on earth more would I have,
   Save that I have, to have it still. (l. 23–24)

   AAS; BoLoP; OBSC; SiPS

Lux my fair falcon, and your fellows all

16 Lux my fair falcon, and your fellows all,
   How well pleasant it were your liberty!
   Ye not forsake me that fair might ye befall. (l. 1–3)

   AAS; OxBSP; SiPS

Madame, withouten Many Wordes

17 Madame, withouten many wordes,
   Ons I ame sure ye will or no;
   And if ye will, then leve your bordes,
   And use your wit and shew it so. (l. 1–4)

18 Aunswer him faire with yea or nay. (l. 8)

   AAS; EiL; EnLoPo; NAEL-1; NoP; OBSC; OBVE;
   OxBSP; SeCePo; SiPS

Patience, Though I Have Not

19 I must of force, God wot,
   Forbear my most desire;
   For no ways can I find
   To sail against the wind. (l. 3–6)

20 Patience, do what they will
   To work me woe or spite, (l. 7–8)

21 To think and hold my peace,
   Since there is no redress. (l. 11–12)

   NoP; OBSC; SiPS; TrGrPo

Satires: Mine Own John Poins

22 My Poynz, I cannot frame me tune to fayne,
   To cloke the trothe for praisse withowt desart,
   Of them that lyst all vice for to retayne.
   I cannot honour them that settes their part
   With Venus and Baccus all theire lyf long;
   Nor holld my pece of them allthoo I smart. (l. 19–24)

23 I cannot speke and loke lyke a saynct,
   Use wiles for witt and make deceyt a pleasure,
   And call crafft counsell, for proffet styll to paint.
   I cannot wrest the law to fill the coffer
   With innocent blode to fede my sellff fat,
   And doo most hurt where most hellp I offer.
                                        (l. 31–36)

24 Nor I ame not where Christe is geven in pray
   For mony, poison and traison at Rome, (l. 97–98)

25 here I ame in Kent and Christendome
   Emong the muses where I rede and ryme;
                                        (l. 100–101)

   AAS; NoP; OBSC; OBSV; OBVE; PoEL-1; SiPS

They Flee from Me That Sometime Did Me Seek

26 They flee from me that sometime did me seek,
   With naked foot stalking in my chamber. (l. 1–2)

   AAS; BLPL; BoLoP; EiL; ELP; EnLoPo; FaBoPV; FF;
   HAP; HeiP; HoPM; InPK; InPS; LiTB; NAEL-1; NOBE;
   NoP; OAEL-1; OBEV; OBSC; OPOP; OxBC; PoE;
   PoEL-1; PoRA; PPP; PrIm; QFR; SCV; SiPS; TEP;
   TrGrPo; WeW

What no, perdy! ye may be sure!

27 Trouth is trayed where craft is in ure;
But though ye have had my hertes cure,
Trow ye I dote withoute ending?
What no, perdy! (l. 6–9)

AAS; MeEL; OBSC; PoEL-1

What should I say

28 What should I say,
Since faith is dead,
And truth away
From you is fled?
Should I be led
With doubleness? (l. 1–6)

29 since I see
Your double heart,
Farewell my part! (l. 12–14)

GBL; Mes; NOBE; NoP; OBEV; OBSC; PoEL-1; SiPS

Whoso List to Hunt

30 The vain travail hath wearied me so sore, (l. 3)

31 as she fleeth afore
Fainting I follow. I leave off therefore
Since in a net I seek to hold the wind. (l. 6–8)

32 And graven with diamonds in letters plain
There is written her fair neck round about:
"Noli me tangerefor Caesar's I am,
And wild for to hold though I seem tame." (l. 11–14)

AAS; BoLoP; EBEV; GBL; HAP; InvP; NAEL-1; NoP;
OAEL-1; OBVE; PoE; PoEL-1; PrIm; SiPS

With Serving Still

33 With serving still
This have I won,
For my goodwill
To be undone; (l. 1–4)

34 Disdainfulness
I have again; (l. 7–8)

ElL; InPK; OBSC; SiPS

ELINOR WYLIE (1885–1928)

The Eagle and the Mole

1 Avoid the reeking herd,
Shun the polluted flock,
Live like that stoic bird,
The eagle of the rock. (l. 1–4)

2 If you would keep your soul
From spotted sight or sound,
Live like the velvet mole;
Go burrow underground. (l. 17–20)

AWP; BoWoP; LiTA; LiTM; MoAB; MoAmPo; UnPo

Full Moon

3 The ermine muffled mouth and chin;
I could not suck the moonlight in. (l. 4–5)

4 Along the pavement my footsoles
Trod warily on living coals.

MoAB; MoAmPo; OPOP; VGW

Let No Charitable Hope

5 I was, being human, born alone;
I am, being woman, hard beset;
I live by squeezing from a stone
The little nourishment I get. (l. 5–8)

6 The years go by in single file;
But none has merited my fear,
And none has quite escaped my smile. (l. 10–12)

LiTA; LiTM; MoAB; MoAmPo; NAAL-2; OxBA; OxBSP;
TrGrPo; VGW

One Person

7 I hereby swear that to uphold your house
I would lay my bones in quick destroying lime (l. 1–2)

8 My lord, adjudge my strength, and set me where
I bear a little more than I can bear. (l. 13–14)

LiTA; LiTA; MoAB; MoAmPo; NAAL-2; OxBA; Son

Prophecy

9 I shall lie folded like a saint,
Lapped in a scented linen sheet,
On a bedstead striped with bright-blue paint,
Narrow and cold and neat. (l. 5–8)

BLPL; BoWoP; FaBoWP; PrIm; VGW

Velvet Shoes

10 We shall walk in velvet shoes:
Wherever we go
Silence will fall like dews
On white silence below.
We shall walk in the snow. (l. 16–20)

CH; FaPON; FPL; GoJo; MoAB; MoAmPo; TrGrPo

Wild Peaches

11 Peaches grow wild, and pigs can live in clover;
A barrel of salted herrings lasts a year;
The spring begins before the winter's over. (l. 23–25)

12 When strawberries go begging, and the sleek
Blue plums lie open to the blackbird's beak,
We shall live well — we shall live very well.
(l. 33–35)

13 That spring, briefer than apple-blossom's breath,
Summer, so much too beautiful to stay,
Swift autumn, like a bonfire of leaves,
And sleepy winter, like the sleep of death. (l. 52–55)

FaBoWP; LiTA; LiTM; NAAL-2; OxBA; WPE

14 Down to the Puritan marrow of my bones
There's something in this richness that I hate.
I love the look, austere, immaculate,
Of landscapes drawn in pearly monotones. (l. 1–4)

BoWoP; FPL; LiTA; LiTM; MoAB; MoAmPo; OxBA;
TrGrPo; WPE

R. J. YEATMAN (1898–1968) AND W. C. SELLAR (1898–1951)

How I Brought the Good News from Aix to Ghent (or Vice Versa)

1 For imagine my shame when they asked what I meant
And I had to confess that I'd been, gone and went
And forgotten the news I was bringing to Ghent,
(l. 18–20)

BXAP; FaBoPa; FiBHP; OnMSP

WILLIAM BUTLER YEATS (1865–1939)

Adam's Curse

1 I said: "A line will take us hours maybe;
Yet if it does not seem a moment's thought,
Our stitching and unstitching has been naught.
(l. 4–6)

2 "To be born woman is to know —
Although they do not talk of it at school —
That we must labour to be beautiful." (l. 18–20)

3 I had a thought for no one's but your ears:
That you were beautiful, and that I strove
To love you in the old high way of love;

That it had all seemed happy, and yet we'd grown
As weary-hearted as that hollow moon. (l. 34–38)

BIrV; CMoP; NAEL-2; NoAM; NoP; OAEL-2; SOTW;
TEP

Aedh Wishes for the Cloths of Heaven

4 I have spread my dreams under your feet;
Tread softly because you tread on my dreams. (l. 7–8)

MoBrPo; NoAM; OBEV

After Long Silence

5 Speech after long silence; it is right,
All other lovers being estranged or dead, (l. 1–2)

6 Bodily decrepitude is wisdom; young
We loved each other and were ignorant. (l. 7–8)

BoLoP; CMoP; EnLoPo; HeIP; HoPM; LiTM; NAEL-2;
OAEL-2; OBMV; PPP; PrIm; UnPo

Among School Children

7 — the children's eyes
In momentary wonder stare upon
A sixty-year-old smiling public man. (l. 6–8)

8 I dream of a Ledaean body, bent
Above a sinking fire, (l. 9–10)

9 For even daughters of the swan can share
Something of every paddler's heritage — (l. 20–21)

10 Hollow of cheek as though it drank the wind
And took a mess of shadows for its meat? (l. 27–28)

11 Better to smile on all that smile, and show
There is a comfortable kind of old scarecrow.
(l. 31–32)

12 Both nuns and mothers worship images,
But those the candles light are not as those
That animate a mother's reveries,
But keep a marble or a bronze repose. (l. 49–52)

13 O chestnut-tree, great-rooted blossomer,
Are you the leaf, the blossom or the bole?
O body swayed to music, O brightening glance,
How can we know the dancer from the dance?
(l. 61–64)

AnIL; BLPL; CMoP; GTBS-P; HAP; InPS; LiTB; LiTM;
MoAB; MoBrPo; MoP; NAEL-2; NAWM-2; NIP; NoAM;
NOBE; NoP; OAEL-2; OxBTC; PoE; PPP; PrIm; TrGrPo;
WeW

The Ballad of Father Gilligan

14 The old priest Peter Gilligan
Was weary night and day;
For half his flock were in their beds,
Or under green sods lay. (l. 1–4)

15 "He Who is wrapped in purple robes,
With planets in His care,
Had pity on the least of things
Asleep upon a chair." (l. 45–48)

EaLo; EBVV; MoBrPo; PoRA

Brown Penny

16 O love is the crooked thing,
There is nobody wise enough
To find out all that is in it,
For he would be thinking of love
Till the stars had run away (l. 9–13)

BoLoP; CMoP; ELP; FaBoCh; LLLT

Byzantium

17 A starlit or a moonlit dome disdains
All that man is,
All mere complexities,
The fury and the mire of human veins. (l. 5–8)

18 A mouth that has no moisture and no breath
Breathless mouths may summon;
I hail the superhuman;
I call it death-in-life and life-in-death. (l. 13–16)

19 Those images that yet
Fresh images beget,
That dolphin-torn, that gong-tormented sea. (l. 38–40)

CMoP; EBEV; FaBoMo; HAP; InPS; LiTM; MoAB;
MoBrPo; MoP; NAEL-2; NAWM-2; NIP; NoAM; NOBE;
NoP; OAEL-2; OxBTC; PoE; PPP; SeCePo; TEP

The Cap and Bells

20 'I have cap and bells,' he pondered,
'I will send them to her and die';
And when the morning whitened
He left them where she went by. (l. 21–24)

21 They set up a noise like crickets,
A chattering wise and sweet,
And her hair was a folded flower
And the quiet of love in her feet. (l. 33–36)

BrPo; ChTr; MoAB; MoBrPo; NoAM; NoP; OnMSP; RB;
WSC

The Cat and the Moon

22 Minnaloushe creeps through the grass
Alone, important and wise,
And lifts to the changing moon
His changing eyes. (l. 25–28)

CMoP; CRH; FaBoCh; GoJo; TTTS

The Choice

23 The intellect of man is forced to choose
Perfection of the life, or of the work, (l. 1–2)

24 In luck or out the toil has left its mark:
That old perplexity an empty purse,
Or the day's vanity, the night's remorse. (l. 6–8)

CMoP; NoAM; OxBSP; OxBTC

The Circus Animals' Desertion

25 I sought a theme and sought for it in vain,
I sought it daily for six weeks or so. (l. 1–2)

26 Winter and summer till old age began
My circus animals were all on show,
Those stilted boys, that burnished chariot,
Lion and woman and the Lord knows what. (l. 5–8)

27 What can I but enumerate old themes? (l. 9)

28 yet when all is said
It was the dream itself enchanted me:
Character isolated by a deed
To engross the present and dominate memory.
(l. 27–30)

29 A mound of refuse or the sweepings of a street,
Old kettles, old bottles, and a broken can,
Old iron, old bones, old rags, that raving slut
Who keeps the till. Now that my ladder's gone,
I must lie down where all the ladders start,
In the foul rag-and-bone shop of the heart. (l. 35–40)

CMoP; FaBoMo; FaBoTw; LiTB; MAT; MoP; NAEL-2;
NAWM-2; NIP; NoAM; NOBE; NOIV; NoP; OAEL-2;
OxBTC; PrIm; TEP

A Coat

30 I made my song a coat
Covered with embroideries
Out of old mythologies (l. 1–3)

31 Song, let them take it,
For there's more enterprise
In walking naked. (l. 8–10)

CMoP; LiTM; NAEL-2; NoAM; OxBSP; PoEL-5

The Cold Heaven

32 Suddenly I saw the cold and rook-delighting heaven
That seemed as though ice burned and was but the
more ice, (l. 1–2)

33 Ah! when the ghost begins to quicken,
Confusion of the death-bed over, is it sent
Out naked on the roads, as the books say, and stricken
By the injustice of the skies for punishment? (l. 9–12)

AWP; CTC; GTBS-P; HAP; NoAM; OAEL-2; OxBSP; RB;
TEP; WeW

Coole Park and Ballylee, 1931

34 What's water but the generated soul? (l. 8)

35 A spot whereon the founders lived and died
Seemed once more dear than life; ancestral trees,
Or gardens rich in memory glorified
Marriages, alliances, and families,
And every bride's ambition satisfied. (l. 33–37)

36 We were the last romantics — chose for theme
Traditional sanctity and loveliness; (l. 41–42)

37 But all is changed, that high horse riderless,
Though mounted in that saddle Homer rode
Where the swan drifts upon a darkening flood.
(l. 46–48)

CMoP; GTBS-P; NoAM; NOIV; OBMV; PPP

Crazy Jane on God

38 I had wild Jack for a lover;
Though like a road
That men pass over
My body makes no moan
But sings on:
All things remain in God. (l. 19–24)

CMoP; EBEV; MoAB; OxBTC

Crazy Jane Talks with the Bishop

39 "A woman can be proud and stiff
When on love intent;
But Love has pitched his mansion in
The place of excrement;
For nothing can be sole or whole
That has not been rent." (l. 13–18)

BoLoP; CMoP; EBEV; ErPo; InPK; MoP; NAEL-2;
NoAM; NoP; OAEL-2; PoE; PPP; TOF

Cuchulain Comforted

40 'Now must we sing and sing the best we can,
But first you must be told your character:
Convicted cowards all, by kindred slain. (l. 19–21)

41 They sang, but had not human tunes nor words,
Though all was done in common as before;

They had changed their throats and had the throats of
birds. (l. 23–25)

CMoP; LiTM; OAEL-2; TOF

A Deep-sworn Vow

42 Yet always when I look death in the face,
When I clamber to the heights of sleep,
Or when I grow excited with wine,
Suddenly I meet your face. (l. 3–6)

CMoP; OAEL-2; PCP; PoE; UnPo

A Dialogue of Self and Soul

43 I summon to the winding ancient stair;
Set all your mind upon the steep ascent, (l. 1–2)

44 Who can distinguish darkness from the soul? (l. 8)

45 Why should the imagination of a man
Long past his prime remember things that are
Emblematical of love and war? (l. 17–19)

46 A living man is blind and drinks his drop.
What matter if the ditches are impure?
What matter if I live it all once more? (l. 41–42)

47 I am content to live it all again,
And yet again, if it be life to pitch
Into the frog-spawn of a blind man's ditch. (l. 56–58)

48 When such as I cast out remorse
So great a sweetness flows into the breast
We must laugh and we must sing,
We are blest by everything,
Everything we look upon is blest. (l. 66–70)

CMoP; FaBoMo; LiTB; LiTM; MoBrPo; NAEL-2; NoAM;
PoE

The Dolls

49 A doll in the doll-maker's house
Looks at the cradle and bawls:
"That is an insult to us." (l. 1–3)

BrPo; CMoP; NoAM; PoE

Down by the Salley Gardens

50   Down by the salley gardens my love and I did meet;
She passed the salley gardens with little snow-white
  feet.
She bid me take love easy, as the leaves grow on the
  tree;
But I, being young and foolish, with her would not
  agree. (l. 1–4)

CMoP; CTC; EBVV; EnLoPo; MoAB; MoBrPo; NAEL-2;
NoAM; OBEV; PoEL-5; PrIm; SoSe

Easter 1916

51   That woman's days were spent
In ignorant good-will,
Her nights in argument
Until her voice grew shrill. (l. 17–20)

52   Hearts with one purpose alone
Through summer and winter seem
Enchanted to a stone
To trouble the living stream. (l. 41–44)

53   The rider, the birds that range
From cloud to tumbling cloud,
Minute by minute they change; (l. 46–48)

54   Too long a sacrifice
Can make a stone of the heart.
O when may it suffice? (l. 57–59)

55   our part
To murmur name upon name,
As a mother names her child
When sleep at last has come
On limbs that had run wild. (l. 60–64)

56   MacDonagh and MacBride
And Connolly and Pearse
Now and in time to be,
Wherever green is worn,
Are changed, changed utterly:
A terrible beauty is born. (l. 75–80)

BrPo; CMoP; FaBoMo; FaBoPV; FaPoR; HAP; HeIP;
InPS; LiTM; MoAB; MoP; NAEL-2; NAWM-2; NIP;
NoAM; NOBE; NOIV; NoP; OAEL-2; OBWP; OxBTC;
PoE; PPP

The Fascination of What's Difficult

57   The fascination of what's difficult
Has dried the sap out of my veins, and rent
Spontaneous joy and natural content
Out of my heart. (l. 1–4)

58   My curse on plays
That have to be set up in fifty ways,
On the day's war with every knave and dolt,
Theater business, management of men. (l. 8–11)

BIrV; BrPo; NAEL-2; PoEL-5

The Fisherman

59   All day I'd looked in the face
What I had hoped 'twould be
To write for my own race
And the reality; (l. 9–12)

60   And cried, 'Before I am old
I shall have written him one
Poem maybe as cold
And passionate as the dawn.' (l. 37–40)

CMoP; HAP; NoAM; SD

The Folly of Being Comforted

61   Because of that great nobleness of hers
The fire that stirs about her, when she stirs,
Burns but more clearly. (l. 10–11)

62   O heart! O heart! if she'd but turn her head,
You'd know the folly of being comforted. (l. 14–15)

AnIL; BrPo; GBL; HeIP; NAEL-2

For Anne Gregory

63   "Never shall a young man,
Thrown into despair
By those great honey-coloured
Ramparts at your ear,
Love you for yourself alone
And not your yellow hair." (l. 1–6)

64   "I heard an old religious man
But yesternight declare
That he had found a text to prove
That only God, my dear,
Could love you for yourself alone
And not your yellow hair." (l. 13–18)

CMoP; FaFP; LiTM; NAEL-2; SOTW

The Great Day

65   Hurrah for revolution and cannon come again!
The beggars have changed places, but the lash goes on.
          (l. 3–4)

BIrV; CMoP; FF; OxBSP

In Memory of Eva Gore-Booth and Con Markiewicz

66 I know not what the younger dreams —
    Some vague Utopia — and she seems,
    When withered old and skeleton-gaunt,
    An image of such politics. (l. 10–13)

67 Two girls in silk kimonos, both
    Beautiful, one a gazelle. (l. 19–20)

68 The innocent and the beautiful
    Have no enemy but time; (l. 24–25)

69 Should the conflagration climb,
    Run till all the sages know.
    We the great gazebo built,
    They convicted us of guilt;
    Bid me strike a match and blow. (l. 28–32)

    FaBoPV; MoAB; NoAM; OAEL-2; OBMV; OxBTC

An Irish Airman Foresees His Death

70 Those that I fight I do not hate,
    Those that I guard I do not love; (l. 3–4)

71 I balanced all, brought all to mind,
    The years to come seemed waste of breath,
    A waste of breath the years behind
    In balance with this life, this death. (l. 13–16)

    FaBoCh; FaBoMo; GoJo; GTBS-P; HeIP; HoPM; LiTM;
    MMA; MoAB; MoBrPo; MoP; NoAM; NOBE; NoP; OBD;
    OBMV; OBWP; PPP; SCV; TrGrPo; WaaP; WaP; WeW

John Kinsella's Lament for Mrs. Mary Moore

72 But nothing satisfied the fool
    But my dear Mary Moore,
    None other knows what pleasures man
    At table or in bed.
    What shall I do for pretty girls
    Now my old bawd is dead? (l. 7–12)

73 No expectation fails there,
    No pleasing habit ends,
    No man grows old, no girl grows cold,
    But friends walk by friends. (l. 29–32)

    CMoP; LiTM; MoAB; NoP; OAEL-2; RB

The Lake Isle of Innisfree

74 I will arise and go now, and go to Innisfree,
    And a small cabin build there, of clay and wattles
    made:

Nine bean-rows will I have there, a hive for the honey-
    bee,
    And live alone in the bee-loud glade. (l. 1–4)

75 I hear lake water lapping with low sounds by the shore;
    While I stand on the roadway, or on the pavements
    gray,
    I hear it in the deep heart's core.

    BrPo; CMoP; FaBoPP; FaBV; FaFP; FaPON; FaPoR;
    FPL; HeIP; InPK; InPS; LiTM; MoAB; MoBrPo; MoP;
    NAEL-2; NoAM; NOBE; NoP; OBEV; OxBTC; PoE;
    PoRA; PrIm; TEP; TrGrPo; WeW

The Lamentation of the Old Pensioner

76 I had a chair at every hearth,
    When no one turned to see,
    With 'Look at that old fellow there,
    'And who may he be? (l. 1–4)

    HAP; InPK NoAM; TW; WeW

Lapis Lazuli

77 I have heard that hysterical women say
    They are sick of the palette and fiddle-bow,
    Of poets that are always gay, (l. 1–3)

78 All perform their tragic play,
    There struts Hamlet, there is Lear,
    That's Ophelia, that Cordelia; (l. 9–11)

79 They know that Hamlet and Lear are gay;
    Gaiety transfiguring all that dread. (l. 16–17)

80 On their own feet they came, or on shipboard,
    Camelback, horseback, ass-back, mule-back,
    Old civilizations put to the sword.
    Then they and their wisdom went to rack: (l. 25–28)

81 All things fall and are built again,
    And those that build them again are gay. (l. 35–36)

82 There, on the mountain and the sky,
    On all the tragic scene they stare.
    One asks for mournful melodies;
    Accomplished fingers begin to play.
    Their eyes mid many wrinkles, their eyes,
    Their ancient, glittering eyes, are gay. (l. 51–56)

    CMoP; FaBoMo; FaBoTw; FF; HeIP; InPS; LiTB; LiTM;
    MAT; MoP; NAEL-2; NAWM-2; NoAM; NOBE; NoP;
    OAEL-2; TEP

A Last Confession

83 He fancied that I gave a soul
    Did but our bodies touch,
    And laughed upon his breast to think
    Beast gave beast as much. (l. 9–12)

    BoLoP; CMoP; ELP; ErPo; HAP; NIP; OAEL-2; WeW

Leda and the Swan

84 A sudden blow; the great wings beating still
Above the staggering girl, (l. 1–2)

85 A shudder in the loins engenders there
The broken wall, the burning roof and tower (l. 9–10)

86 Being so caught up,
So mastered by the brute blood of the air,
Did she put on his knowledge with his power
Before the indifferent beak could let her drop?
(l. 11–14)

AnIL; CMoP; EBEV; ErPo; FF; FPL; GTBS-P; HAP;
HeIP; InPK; LiTM; MoAB; MoBrPo; MoP; NAEL-2;
NAWM-2; NIP; NoAM; NOBE; NoP; OAEL-2; PBBP;
PoE; PPP; PrIm; SCV; Son; SoSe; TEP; TrGrPo; WeW

Long-legged Fly

87 That civilisation may not sink,
Its great battle lost, (l. 1–2)

88 She thinks, part woman, three parts a child,
That nobody looks; her feet
Practise a tinker shuffle
Picked up on a street. (l. 15–18)

89 Shut the door of the Pope's chapel,
Keep those children out. (l. 23–24)

90 Like a long-legged fly upon the stream
His mind moves upon silence. (l. 29–30)

CMoP; FaBoMo; FaBoTw; InPS; LiTM; MoP; NAEL-2;
NoAM; NOBE; NoP; OPOP; PoE; TEP

The Magi

91 Now as at all times I can see in the mind's eye,
In their stiff, painted clothes, the pale unsatisfied ones
Appear and disappear in the blue depth of the sky
(l. 1–3)

92 their eyes still fixed, hoping to find once more,
Being by Calvary's turbulence unsatisfied,
The uncontrollable mystery on the bestial floor.
(l. 6–8)

BrPo; CMoP; FaBoRV; HAP; InPK; NoAM; OAEL-2;
OFD; PChr; PoA; PoE; TrCP

The Man Who Dreamed of Faeryland

93 But when a man poured fish into a pile,
It seemed they raised their little silver heads,
And sang (l. 5–7)

94 That Time can never mar a lover's vows
Under that woven changeless roof of boughs:
The singing shook him out of his new ease. (l. 10–12)

95 That if a dancer stayed his hungry foot
It seemed the sun and moon were in the fruit:
(l. 23–24)

96 That God has laid His fingers on the sky,
That from those fingers glittering summer runs
Upon the dancer by the dreamless wave.
Why should those lovers that no lovers miss
Dream, until God burn Nature with a kiss?
The man has found no comfort in the grave.
(l. 43–48)

CMoP; NAEL-2; NoAM; NoP

MEDITATIONS IN TIME OF CIVIL WAR (the following 2
poems)

The Road at My Door

97 I count those feathered balls of soot
The moor-hen guides upon the stream,
To silence the envy in my thought;
And turn towards my chamber, caught
In the cold snows of a dream. (l. 11–15)

BIrV; LiTB; NOBE; PoE

The Stare's Nest by My Window

98 We are closed in, and the key is turned
On our uncertainty; (l. 6–7)

99 We had fed the heart on fantasies,
The heart's grown brutal from the fare;
More substance in our enmities
Than in our love; O honey-bees,
Come build in the empty house of the stare. (l. 16–21)

BIrV; FaBoPV; GTBS-P; InPS; LiTB; NOBE

News for the Delphic Oracle

100 From where Pan's cavern is
Intolerable music falls.
Foul goat-head, brutal arm appear,
Belly, shoulder, bum,
Flash fishlike; nymphs and satyrs
Copulate in the foam. (l. 31–36)

CMoP; FaBoMo; LiTB; LiTM; NoAM

No Second Troy

101 a mind
That nobleness made simple as a fire,
With beauty like a tightened bow, (l. 6–8)

102 Why, what could she have done, being what she is?
Was there another Troy for her to burn? (l. 11–12)

BrPo; CMoP; EnLoPo; GTBS-P; MoP; NAEL-2; NoAM;
NOBE; OAEL-2; OxBTC; PoEL-5; PPP; SeCePo; WeW

The Old Men Admiring Themselves in the Water

103 I heard the old, old men say,
"All that's beautiful drifts away
Like the waters." (l. 7–9)

CMoP; FaBoCh; GoJo; PCP

Politics

104 How can I, that girl standing there,
My attention fix
On Roman or on Russian
Or on Spanish politics? (l. 1–4)

CMoP; FF; HeIP; InPS; OxBTC; PoE; SCV

A Prayer for My Daughter

105 Once more the storm is howling, and half hid
Under this cradle-hood and coverlid
My child sleeps on. (l. 1–3)

106 May she be granted beauty and yet not
Beauty to make a stranger's eye distraught,
Or hers before a looking-glass, for such,
Being made beautiful overmuch,
Consider beauty a sufficient end,
Lose natural kindness (l. 17–22)

107 It's certain that fine women eat
A crazy salad with their meat
Whereby the Horn of Plenty is undone. (l. 30–32)

108 In courtesy I'd have her chiefly learned;
Hearts are not had as a gift but hearts are earned
By those that are not entirely beautiful; (l. 33–35)

109 And many a poor man that has roved,
Loved and thought himself beloved,
From a glad kindness cannot take his eyes. (l. 38–40)

110 O may she live like some green laurel
Rooted in one dear perpetual place. (l. 47–48)

111 to be choked with hate
May well be of all evil chances chief. (l. 52–53)

112 An intellectual hatred is the worst,
So let her think opinions are accursed. (l. 57–58)

113 Considering that, all hatred driven hence,
The soul recovers radical innocence
And learns at last that it is self-delighting,
Self-appeasing, self-affrighting,
And that its own sweet will is Heaven's will;
(l. 65–69)

114 And may her bridegroom bring her to a house
Where all's accustomed, ceremonious; (l. 73–74)

115 How but in custom and in ceremony
Are innocence and beauty born? (l. 77–78)

BLPL; CMoP; HAP; LiTB; LiTM; MoAB; MoP; NAEL-2;
NAs; NoAM; NoP; OxBTC; PoA; PoLF; PoRA; PrIm; TEP

The Resurrection: Songs from a Play

116 I saw a staring virgin stand
Where holy Dionysus died,
And tear the heart out of his side,
And lay the heart upon her hand
And bear that beating heart away; (l. 1–5)

117 The Roman Empire stood appalled:
It dropped the reins of peace and war
When that fierce virgin and her Star
Out of the fabulous darkness called. (l. 13–16)

118 Odour of blood when Christ was slain
Made all Platonic tolerance vain
And vain all Doric discipline. (l. 22–24)

119 Everything that man esteems
Endures a moment or a day. (l. 25–26)

120 Whatever flames upon the night
Man's own resinous heart has fed. (l. 31–32)

CMoP; FaBoTw; HAP; LiTB; NOBE; NoP; OAEL-2; PoE;
PPP; PrIm

The Rose of the World

121 Who dreamed that beauty passes like a dream?
For these red lips, with all their mournful pride,
Mournful that no new wonder may betide,
Troy passed away in one high funeral gleam,
And Usna's children died.

122 He made the world to be a grassy road
Before her wandering feet.

BrPo; CMoP; MoAB; MoBrPo; NAEL-2

The Rose Tree

123 'But where can we draw water,'
Said Pearse to Connolly,
'When all the wells are parched away?

O plain as plain can be
There's nothing but our own red blood
Can make a right Rose Tree.' (l. 13–18)

CMoP; ELP; FaBoPV; OBMV

Sailing to Byzantium

124 That is no country for old men. The young
In one another's arms, birds in the trees
— Those dying generations — at their song, (l. 1–3)

125 Fish, flesh, or fowl, commend all summer long
Whatever is begotten, born, and dies.
Caught in that sensual music all neglect
Monuments of unaging intellect. (l. 5–8)

126 An aged man is but a paltry thing,
A tattered coat upon a stick, (l. 9–10)

127 Nor is there singing school but studying
Monuments of its own magnificence;
And therefore I have sailed the seas and come
To the holy city of Byzantium. (l. 13–16)

128 Come from the holy fire, perne in a gyre,
And be the singing-masters of my soul. (l. 19–20)

129 Once out of nature I shall never take
My bodily form from any natural thing,
But such a form as Grecian goldsmiths make
(l. 25–27)

130 set upon a golden bough to sing
To lords and ladies of Byzantium
Of what is past, or passing, or to come. (l. 30–32)

AnIL; CMoP; FaFP; FF; FPL; GTBS-P; HAP; HeIP;
HoPM; InPK; InPS; InvP; LiTB; LiTM; MoAB; MoBrPo;
MoP; NAEL-2; NAWM-2; NIP; NoAM; NOBE; NoP;
OAEL-2; OBMV; OxBTC; PoE; PoRA; PPP; PrIm;
SeCePo; SoSe; TEP; TIRV; TOF; UnPo; WeW

The Scholars

131 young men, tossing on their beds,
Rhymed out in love's despair
To flatter beauty's ignorant ear. (l. 4–6)

132 All think what other people think;
All know the man their neighbor knows.
Lord, what would they say
Did their Catullus walk that way? (l. 9–12)

CMoP; NoP; OAEL-2; PoA

The Second Coming

133 Turning and turning in the widening gyre
The falcon cannot hear the falconer;
Things fall apart; the centre cannot hold;
Mere anarchy is loosed upon the world, (l. 1–4)

134 The ceremony of innocence is drowned;
The best lack all conviction, while the worst
Are full of passionate intensity. (l. 6–8)

135 somewhere in sands of the desert
A shape with lion body and the head of a man,
A gaze blank and pitiless as the sun,
Is moving its slow thighs, while all about it
Reel shadows of the indignant desert birds. (l. 13–17)

136 twenty centuries of stony sleep
Were vexed to nightmare by a rocking cradle,
And what rough beast, its hour come round at last,
Slouches towards Bethlehem to be born? (l. 19–22)

BIrV; BLPL; CMoP; EaLo; FaBoMo; FaBoPV; FF;
GTBS-P; HAP; HeIP; HoPM; InPK; InPS; LiTB; LiTM;
MAT; MoAB; MoBrPo; MoP; NAEL-2; NAWM-2; NIP;
NoAM; NOBE; NoP; OAEL-2; OxBTC; PoE; PPP; PrIm;
SCV; SeCePo; SoSe; TEP; UnPo; WaP; WeW

September 1913

137 For men were born to pray and save:
Romantic Ireland's dead and gone,
It's with O'Leary in the grave. (l. 6–8)

138 They have gone about the world like wind,
But little time had they to pray
For whom the hangman's rope was spun,
And what, God help us, could they save? (l. 11–14)

BrPo; CMoP; FaBoPV; GTBS-P; HAP; MoP; NAEL-2;
NoAM; PoRA

The Song of Wandering Aengus

139 I will find out where she has gone,
And kiss her lips and take her hands;
And walk among long dappled grass,
And pluck till time and times are done
The silver apples of the moon,
The golden apples of the sun. (l. 19–24)

BrPo; CH; CMoP; FaBoCh; GoJo; MAT; MoAB; MoBrPo;
PoEL-5; PoRA; SOTW; TTTS; UnAS; WSC

The Sorrow of Love

140 The quarrel of the sparrows in the eaves,
The full round moon and the star-laden sky,
And the loud song of the ever-singing leaves,
Had hid away earth's old and weary cry. (l. 1–4)

141 And now the sparrows warring in the eaves,
The curd-pale moon, the white stars in the sky,
And the loud chaunting of the unquiet leaves,
Are shaken with earth's old and weary cry. (l. 9–12)

MoAB; MoBrPo; NoAM; NOBVV; OAEL-2; PoEL-5; TEP

The Statues

142 But boys and girls, pale from the imagined love
Of solitary beds, knew what they were,
That passion could bring character enough
And pressed at midnighht in some public place
Live lips upon a plummet-measured face. (l. 4–8)

143 We Irish, born into that ancient sect
But thrown upon this filthy modern tide
And by its formless spawning fury wrecked,
Climb to our proper dark, that we may trace
The lineaments of a plummet-measured face.
(l. 28–32)

AnIL; NoAM; OAEL-2; WeW

The Stolen Child

144 Come away, O human child!
To the waters and the wild
With a faery, hand in hand,
For the world's more full of weeping than you can
understand. (l. 9–12)

145 Away with us he's going,
The solemn-eyed:
He'll hear no more the lowing
Of the calves on the warm hillside
Or the kettle on the hob
Sing peace into his breast, (l. 43–48)

CMoP; NAEL-2; NoP; WSC

To a Friend Whose Work Has Come to Nothing

146 For how can you compete,
Being honor bred, with one
Who, were it proved he lies,
Were neither shamed in his own
Nor in his neighbors' eyes? (l. 4–8)

147 Be secret and exult,
Because of all things known
That is most difficult. (l. 14–16)

AWP; InPK; LiTM; MoAB; MoBrPo; OAEL-2; OBMV;
PoA

To a Shade

148 Unquiet wanderer
Draw the Glasnevin coverlet anew
About your head till the dust stops your ear,
The time for you to taste of that salt breath
And listen at the corners has not come;
You had enough of sorrow before death — (l. 20–25)

AnIL; LiTB; NAEL-2; PoEL-5

To a Squirrel at Kyle-na-no

149 Come play with me;
Why should you run
Through the shaking tree
As though I'd a gun
To strike you dead? (l. 1–5)

FaPON; FM; PDV; RHPC

The Tower

150 this caricature,
Decrepit age that has been tied to me
As to a dog's tail? (l. 2–4)

151 It seems that I must bid the Muse to pack,
Choose Plato and Plotinus for a friend
Until imagination, ear and eye,
Can be content with argument and deal
In abstract things; or be derided by
A sort of battered kettle at the heel. (l. 11–16)

152 It is time that I wrote my will;
I choose upstanding men
That climb the streams until
The fountain leap, and at dawn
Drop their cast at the side
Of dripping stone; (l. 105–110)

153 When the swan must fix his eye
Upon a fading gleam,
Float out upon a long
Last reach of glittering stream
And there sing his last song. (l. 124–128)

154 Death and life were not
Till man made up the whole,
Made lock, stock and barrel
Out of his bitter soul, (l. 132–135)

CMoP; LiTB; LiTM; NoAM; PoE

Under Ben Bulben

155 Many times man lives and dies
Betweeen his two eternities,
That of race and that of soul,
And ancient Ireland knew it all.
Whether man die in his bed
Or the rifle knocks him dead, (l. 13–18)

156 Even the wisest man grows tense
With some sort of violence
Before he can accomplish fate,
Know his work or choose his mate.

Poet and sculptor, do the work,
Nor let the modish painter shirk (l. 33–38)

157 Irish poets, learn your trade,
   Sing whatever is well made,
   Scorn the sort now growing up
   All out of shape from toe to top, (l. 68–71)

158 Cast your mind on other days
   That we in coming days may be
   Still the indomitable Irishry. (l. 81–83)

159 Under bare Ben Bulben's head
   In Drumcliff churchyard Yeats is laid. (l. 84–85)

160 By his command these words are cut:
   Cast a cold eye
   On life, on death.
   Horseman, pass by! (l. 91–94)

   CMoP; HAP; LiTM; MoP; NAEL-2; NoAM; NoP; OxBTC

When You Are Old

161 When you are old and gray and full of sleep,
   And nodding by the fire, take down this book, (l. 1–2)

162 But one man loved the pilgrim soul in you,
   And loved the sorrows of your changing face. (l. 7–8)

   AWP; BoLoP; CMoP; CTC; EBVV; FaBV; FaFP; FPL;
   GBL; GoJo; HeIP; InvP; LiTM; MoAB; MoBrPo; MoP;
   NAEL-2; NAWM-2; NoAM; NOBVV; NoP; OBEV;
   OxBTC; PCP; PoLF; PrIm; TEP

Who Goes with Fergus?

163 Who will go drive with Fergus now,
   And pierce the deep wood's woven shade,
   And dance upon the level shore? (l. 1–3)

164 Fergus rules the brazen cars,
   And rules the shadows of the wood,
   And the white breast of the dim sea
   And all dishevelled wandering stars. (l. 9–12)

   CMoP; FaBoCh; GoJo; InPK; MoP; NAEL-2; NoAM;
   NOBE; NOBVV; PoE; PoRA

The Wild Swans at Coole

165 I saw, before I had well finished,
   All suddenly mount
   And scatter wheeling in great broken rings
   Upon their clamorous wings. (l. 9–12)

166 Unwearied still, lover by lover,
   They paddle in the cold
   Companionable streams or climb the air;
   Their hearts have not grown old; (l. 19–22)

167 But now they drift on the still water,
   Mysterious, beautiful; (l. 25–26)

   ChTr; CMoP; FaBoPP; FaBoRV; FM; HeIP; InPS; MoAB;
   MoBrPo; MoP; NAEL-2; NoAM; NoP; PBBP; PPP; SoSe;
   SOTW; TEP; UnPo

ANDREW YOUNG (1885–1971)

The Dead Crab

1 I cannot think this creature died
   By storm or fish or sea-fowl harmed
   Walking the sea so heavily armed;
   Or does it make for death to be
   Oneself a living armoury? (l. 10–14)

   FaBoTw; FM; OBD; RB

DOUGLAS YOUNG (1913–1973)

Last Lauch

1 Hit's growin, stark and heich,
   derk and straucht and sinister,
   kirkyairdie-like and dreich.
   But whaur's the Minister? (l. 5–8)

   FaBoCo; NBLV; OxBS; SeCePo

SUBJECT INDEX

The subjects assigned to the quotations in this book may (sometimes) not be the subjects of the poems from which they derive. Under each subject heading are listed the author and title of the poem quoted, with the number of the quotation.

KEY WORD INDEX

The truncated code printed after each Key Word phrase indicates the poet whose work is quoted in the Poetry Quotations section and the number of the quotation by him or her. Quotations from poems by unknown poets are indexed numerically. A possessive noun is alphabetized under the noun itself, e.g., Lord's Prayer is alphabetized under **Lord** as L's Prayer.

A

a-bed: sick and lay a., STEVENSO R 11

a-callin': 'eard the East a., KIPL 11

a-cold: night is a., MOOR 5
season died a. POUN 15

A-combing: A. his milk-white steed, UNKN 177

a-crossed: since Sophia have a. the sea.' UNKN 320

a-cutting: trade was a. of Broom, green Broom; UNKN 43

a-dabbling: rushes tall,/ Ducks are a., GRAHAME 1

a-flying: Old Time is still a. HERR 55

a-goin': Christ ain't a. HAY 4
keep a. STAN 1

a-gurgling: loves to hear the little brook a., GILB 38

a-hold: keep a. of Nurse BELL 11

a-laying: Six geese a., UNKN 279

a-leaping: Twelve lords a. UNKN 285

a-maying: All in our gowns of green so gay/ Into the Park a. UNKN 229
Life went a. COLE SAM 47
we're not a. HERR 7

a-milking: Eight maids a., UNKN 281

A-preaching: A. that drinking is sinful, GOLD 6

a-roving: we'll go no more a. BYRO 62

a-sailing: I saw a ship a., MOTH 14

a-singin': branch'll go a. DUNB 2

a-sleeping: night you lay a. ROET 6

a-smokin': seed her first a. KIPL 101

a-swimming: Seven swans a. UNKN 280

a-wondering: Long time a. ROBI 8

a-wooing: frog he would a. go, MOTH 1

Aarhus: go to A. HEAN 22

Aarons: true A. drest. HERB G 1

Abaddon: A. in the hangnail cracked from Adam, THOMA D 6

Abak: A. he sterte, CHAU 54

abandon: lithe a. of your walk, BENN G 6

abandoned: a. by each venal friend, GRAY 21

abase: a. itself to you, WHITM 77

abased: a. to the other. WHITM 77

abate: a. His ancient brutal claim. MELV 8

abated: obscene nightmare a. BOGA 7

abbey: clock or an a. horologe. CHAU 66

Abbot: bless'd the A. of Aberbrothok. SOUTHE 5

ABC: unacquainted with the A. STEPHEN 6

abed: lovers lie a. THOMA D 27
Morns a. and daylight slumber HOUS 47

abedde: somme seyden, lust a., CHAU 109

Aberdour: haf owre to A., UNKN 228

abeyance: Creeds and schools in a., WHITM 74

abhor: in extreames lov'd and a.'d. CLEV 1
virtuous souls a.), MONTROSE 2

Abide: A. with me: fast falls the eventide; LYTE 1
come to us, a. with us, BROO P 8
fellow-wight who yet a. HARD 22

Part steals, lets part a.; HARD 27
yet a. the World! DICKI 139

Abides: A. for me undesecrate:/ Dark Angel, JOHN L 6
much is taken, much a.; TENN 135
thy seed a. in me, VAUG 3

abiding: stupid and a. jelly. DE VR 1

Abishag: once the beauty A., FROS 88

abjure: this rough magic/ I here a., SHAK 165

ablution: Of pure a. KEAT 3

abnegation: indolence read as a., RICH 22

abnormality: zebras, supreme in their a.; MOOR M 19

abode: a. where the Eternal are. SHEL 14
fix your best a., BARL 1
gods pine for my a., EMER 7

abolished: hunger is a. GILB 52

abolishes: a. divorces. GILB 50

Abominable: all prodigious things,/ A., inutterable, MILT 61
wlatsom and a. CHAU 70

aboriginal: upsprang the a. name. WHITM 43

abortions: a. are hidden. MAST 5
A. will not let you forget. BROO B 17

abound: Fair face show friends when riches do a.; GOOG 1

aboundant: this a. issue SHAK 224

about: nightes car the stars a, doth bring. SURR 3

above: a. insolence and triviality MOOR M 33
a. the reach/ Of ordinary men; WORD 123
A. the rolling ball MERE G 8

a. the world so high, TAYL J 1
float up from the damnèd Earth./
"To friends a., POE 30
God a., or Man below,
POPE A 60
green grass a. ROSS C 33
hate to go a. you, WHITT 14
my arise is from a., BRAD 9
my roof the greenwood a.,
UNKN 201
share yet rise a. STOD 2
true as the stars a.; UNKN 101
Voice a. their beat— THOMP F 7
abraded: a. by the beach, PATM 3
Abraham: liest in A.'s bosom
WORD 27
abreast: we galloped a.
BROWNI R 35
abroad: flame is blown a. LONG 20
he next doth ride a., COWP 7
men/ Who went a. to die. LETT 1
'No more,/ I will a.! HERB G 17
no spirit dare stir a., SHAK 19
owl is a., the bat and the toad,
JONS 16
pilgrim, which a. hath done
DONN 44
absence: a. has gone through me
MERW 10
A., hear my protestation/ Against
thy strength HOSK 1
a. of feet, MOOR M 40
a. of her mate, SPENS 27
a. seemed my flame to qualify.
SHAK 230
a. therefore like I best. GOOG 3
been sluiced in 's a. SHAK 179
bitterness of a. sour SHAK 208
giant a. mopes WILB 18
hath my a. beene SHAK 223
hearts of truest metal/ A. doth
join, HOSK 1
month of his a. LEWI 4
re-begot/ Of a., darkness, death:
DONN 43
absent: a. from her eyes, ROCH 7
a. in the spring, SHAK 225
A. thee from felicity SHAK 41
Absolon: joly lovere A., CHAU 51
Absolute: A. across the hall
BELL 13
another name for a. power
WORD 114
foreknowledge a., MILT 60
Of the a. Heavens. BROWNI E 1
Reaching no a., GUNN 14
absorbing: peering, a., translating.
WHITM 64
abstention: a. from movement;
ELIOT T 21
Abstinence: A. sows sand BLAK 21
abstract: deal/ In a. things;
YEATS 151

sadly like the a. Jew. WARR 4
speaking of fears in the a.
POUN 12
with his a. rage: TATE A 3
abstracted: Evil One a. stood
MILT 90
Abstractions: ancient, meaningless/
A. SNYD 42
absurd: a. whiskers ROET 39
question is a. AUDE 94
absurdity: a. is reality, RIVE 2
Constantly risking a. FERL 1
abundance: in such a. lies our
choice MILT 94
pours its a. AMMO 1
abundant: generate,/ Reptile with
spawn a., MILT 85
abuse: mankind a. thee; CALV 6
abused: by himself a., or
disabused; POPE A 78
abysmal: beneath in the a. sea,
TENN 58
abyss: a. of fears/ And horrors
MILT 100
Beyond is all a., MILT 105
dark a., whose boiling gulf
MILT 62
deep a. where Satan crawls
TRAH 1
Dizzily down the a. TROW 2
fill the a.'s void FROS 137
secrets of the A. to spy: GRAY 29
accents: agèd a. and untimely
words,/ Paint shadows,
DANI S 11
caught his clear a.,
BROWNI R 45
follow with a. sweet; CAMPI 2
In states unborn and a. yet
unknown! SHAK 47
lisped in a. mild, SMIT ST 3
Loved a. are soon forgot.
SHEL 89
weaker a., WOTT 4
Accept: A. for once some serious
Lines. SWIF 13
bow and a. the end FROS 93
acceptable: a. in thy sight,
BIBL, O.T. 30
acceptance: no a. it can find,
MILT 109
accepted: a. into as much light
AMMO 2
accepts: a. such leavings
WHITM 98
accident: past all a. WILLI 22
accidents: nothing pleaseth but rare
a. SHAK 52
accompany: In prison they a. the
jailer, SIMI 2
accomplish: can a. fate, YEATS 156
preaching could not a.
WHITM 21

accomplish'd: no a.'d blackguards,
BYRO 47
plans were a.'d, WHITM 108
Accomplished: A. fingers YEATS 82
what have they a., PLATH 17
accomplishing: armorers a. the
knights, SHAK 57
accomplishment: smile of a.,
PLATH 37
Accorded: Nicholas and Alisoun/ A.
been CHAU 53
account: a. beyond the a.: AMMO 4
A. for moral, POPE A 67
sad a. of fore-bemoaned moan,
SHAK 195
accounting: a. beyond the account:
AMMO 4
accumulates: Where wealth a.
GOLD 1
accumulation: a. of paper
RANDA D 5
accursed: opinions are a.
YEATS 112
accusations: a. had begun,
AUDE 28
accuser: power/ To seal th' a.'s lips.
SHAK 81
accuses: spotted hawk swoops by
and a. WHITM 73
accusing: Wild, cold, and a.
SNYD 10
accustomed: all's a., ceremonious;
YEATS 114
acetylene: pure a. Virgin PLATH 50
ache: a. here in the throat,
RILE 3
a. of marriage; LEVE 1
deep unending/ A. of love!
JOYC 3
fingers a., my lips are dry:
LAND 11
made my heart to a.: BLAK 112
Pity is not your forte./ Calmly you
a. RICH 11
thoughts that made it a.,
COWP 3
aches: My heart a., KEAT 44
track a. GRAV 21
achieve: a. in time— GILB 28
a. Mankind's deliverance.
MILT 104
Achieved: A. that stillness
CRAN R 46
with an entrechat/ perfectly a.
WILLI 1
Achievement: A. is command;
SHAK 169
achieving: a., still pursuing,
LONG 37
Achilles: Iron-hearted man-slaying
A. AUDE 83
aching: with thine a. lust
JOHN L 6

agree: Birdes, voyces, instruments, windes, waters, all a. SPENS 32

agrees: it a. well to be amorous. CAMPI 28

ague: drowned, and I've the a. BYRO 76

ahead: angel gone a. HARP 4
What blazed a. of you? HEAN 21

Ahkond: A. of Swat? LEAR 1

Ahkoond: A. of Swat/ Is not! LANIG 1

Ai: A.! a.! GINS 22

aid: God shall love and angels a. ye. PRIO 8
meant each other's a., POPE A 26
Metaphysic calls for a. on Sense! POPE A 2
sought for no man's a. SWIF 23
thy gentle looks, thy a., MILT 101

ail: high heaven and earth a. HOUS 24

aim: a. at human hearts: JONS 28
as an a. or butt, SHAK 55
practicing their a. on stray dogs KINN 19

aimed: a. between the belt and boot SIMP 2

aiming: their a. fury BIBL, O.T. 42

aims: a. But to console man THOR 10
finger a. Always elsewhere: HOLLA 1

ain't: a. no flies on me, FIEL E 4
You a.'t ruined,' HARD 37

air: Acquire the a. PLATH 65
affrighted a. with a shudder bore, READ T 1
a.-bridged harbor LAZA 1
a., earth, and skies; WORD 153
a. is all awash with angels. WILB 23
a. is full of sunlight VAN DY 3
A. is hush'd, COLL 10
a. it breathes. WORD 38
a.-like leave no pression HERR 29
a. liner with shut-off engines SPEND 13
a. or pent in stone, EMER 10
a. tastes good to my palate. WHITM 75
a. that kills/ From yon far country blows: HOUS 34
a. white and dry WILB 4
Always, in earth and a. ROET 15
as males they disliked his a. KAVA 17
astounding crate full of a. HEAN 2
bloom in prison a.; WILD 1

bombs bursting in a., KEY 1
bosom of the A., LONG 38
breath of wild a.; MERE G 1
breathed a song into the a., LONG 2
Brightness falls from the a.; NASHE 1
broke the silent a., WORD 9
bud to test surprises of sea a., MOSS 6
bursts in the violet a. ELIOT T 148
cast forth in the common a., SHAK 86
climb the a.; YEATS 166
Cold a. bites the throat. SNYD 44
Content to breathe his native a. POPE A 107
daisies push inches of yellow a., GINS 42
dewy dawning's cold grey a.; THOMS J (1834–1882) 1
down the upbreathing a. RICH 29
dusty bondage into luminous a. MILLA 8
earth/ And sea and a. STEVENS 21
everlasting wash of a. — BROWNI R 80
fill the a. WILLI 41
fire-folk sitting in the a.! HOPKINS 23
first time that we smell the a. SHAK 82
flower in foreign a.? ARNO 40
Flyin' through the a., MAXW 1
fog and filthy a. SHAK 102
fresh a. is good OHAR 2
gathered from the a. POUN 23
God knows, with freer a., THOR 3
haunting the black a., SEXT 7
his a. of lost connections.... LOWE R 32
Horizontal misty A. Shorn of his Beams, MILT 57
horsed/ Upon the sightless couriers of the a., SHAK 105
House without a., MILLA 41
human season on this sterile a. MACL 6
humming a.; TENN 42
hyaline thin a. SHAP 7
I eat men like a. PLATH 56
I lived on a. FROS 112
in his right and honor took the a. HECH 16
Jesus choking in the a., LOWE R 22
kept head in a. GRAV 23

kiss that a. HERR 46
leaving a. in shreds SNYD 32
left the vivid a. SPEND 12
like feasting upon a. SMIT W 4
liquid gold is the a.; CLARE 1
making the a. wince/ but her cargo RICH 23
mastered by the brute blood of the a., YEATS 86
melted into a., SHAK 163
Mixing fresher a. DICKI 92
mock our eyes with a. SHAK 9
moral in the a.; GRAV 6
my hand,/ The a. fills WRIG J 5
needful to man as a., HAYD 5
Newfoundland a., THOR 8
No stir in the a., SOUTHE 4
obliging a. of retrievers, BISH 8
on earth the a. of paradise. MICH 3
on the vacant a. WORD 63
pause with his needle in the a. LEVE 9
pendulous in a., POE 12
poem of the a., LONG 39
power in the a.; VAN DY 1
pure marble A. MILT 65
Queen of a. and darkness, HOUS 12
redolent of a., SKEL 9
rooted only on the a., SMIT W 3
sawis in the a.; BOYD 1
sewed up the a. with a stem; ROET 25
shot an arrow into the a., LONG 1
sighs the a. Frequenting, MILT 98
sitting through crisp a., HECH 15
smiles and languish'd a.,/ By Love are driv'n away; BLAK 40
spiders marching through the a., LOWE R 33
still/ in the thunder a., LAWR 56
strew them in the a.: MONTROSE 4
such a conscience-stricken a.? HOUS 21
sultriness pervades the a. MELV 10
Swans in the winter a. AUDE 9
they sleep in a. JARR 2
thin of substance as the a., SHAK 141
thing in the a. LAWR 1
this thick a. DOOL 3
Thou unsubstantial a. SHAK 77
Through high still a. SNYD 18
through the busy a., THOMS J (1700–1748) 7
toothless mouth of sunny a., GINS 34

along: a. the backwater,
   GRAHAME 1
a. the spire PURD 1
come a. with me./ Something like
   a person: SILKI 1
getting to heaven at last,/ I'm
   going all a.! DICKI 131
aloof: dining a., NEWB 3
familiar, and a. CUNN J 1
we stand a., ROSS C 24
Alpe: many a Frozen, many a fierie
   A., MILT 61
alphabet: rocking a., THOMA D 8
Taught me my a. to say, POE 39
Alpine: round yon A. height;
   EMER 18
through an A. village LONG 21
Alps: A. on A. arise! POPE A 34
already: dead a., WHITM 17
twice a. on earth KINN 13
also: They a. serve MILT 124
altar: broken a., Lord, thy servant
   rears, HERB G 7
candles gutter by an empty a.,
   LOWE R 5
each ancient a. stands POPE A 31
great world's a.-stairs TENN 33
inferior priestess, at her a.'s side,
   POPE A 113
sanctify this a. to be thine.
   HERB G 8
altars: a. In a dark church SIMI 4
build it a. tall ROBI 4
Altarwise: A. by owl-light
   THOMA D 6
alter: a. all the course of kind.
   SPENS 10
A. or mend eternal fact.
   EMER 37
I felt my cheek/ A., SHEL 80
Time cannot a. but obey Fate's
   laws. TOWN 1
alteration: alters when it a. finds,
   SHAK 231
Altered: A., estranged,
   disintegrated, MILLA 2
a. fluid run, MILLA 18
alterest: a. all things POE 1
altering: Eye a. alters all; BLAK 33
alters: a. when it alteration finds,
   SHAK 231
Love a. not SHAK 232
alway: thou bewrayest murder a.!
   CHAU 70
always: a. alive and fated;
   SHAP 22
A. and last, CRAN H 25
a. embrace things, OHAR 19
a. just my luck PARK 1
a. To be blest: POPE A 65
a. tying up OHAR 15
has a. been there, SEXT 2
I a. get by — SAND 22

I had expected a. SPEND 22
If you are a. kind." HALE 2
mother almost a. sighs,
   WRIG E 1
too cold a. SMIT ST 2
you a. wait, WHITM 22
Alysoun: lyht on A. UNKN 4
amain: death shall come a.:
   SMIT L 3
Sin and Death a. MILT 62
amaine: Sound out your trumpetts,
   sound out a.! UNKN 223
Amaryllis: A., The wanton country
   maid CAMPI 6
sport with A. in the shade,
   MILT 26
amaze: Sometimes these cogitations
   still a. ELIOT T 54
amazed: many are a. and many
   doubt. LONG 20
winds and trees a. DRUM 1
amazing: a. frowns/ On utmost
   Kilda's shore,
   THOMS J (1700–1748) 8
Love so a., so divine, WATT I 10
Ambassador: A. Puser MACL 8
amber: a. waves of grain, BATE 1
a.-dropping hair; MILT 7
look mild as a.; ADAM L 2
melodious words to lutes of a.
   HERR 63
Ambiguous: A. undulations
   STEVENS 62
Ambition: A. mock their useful toil,
   GRAY 8
A. should be made of sterner
   stuff. SHAK 49
a. varnish o'er with zeal.
   MILT 59
A. was my idol, BYRO 22
a. without/ understanding
   MOOR M 6
bride's a. satisfied. YEATS 35
leave all meaner things/ To low
   a., POPE A 58
lowliness is young a.'s ladder,
   SHAK 44
martyred a. RICH 19
Vaulting a., which o'erleaps itself
   SHAK 105
ambitions: a. incommensurable with
   flesh, SHAP 28
ambitious: a. vine DRAY 18
freed/ From his a. finger.
   FLET/SHAK 2
proud, a. heaps, JONS 37
women are a. naturallie, MARL 4
amble: a. amiably here, CAME 2
ambling: a. bear BIRN 2
strut before a wanton a. nymph;
   SHAK 96
Ambrogio: A. Praedis, POUN 10
ambrosia: nectar and a., EMER 5

ambrosial: Christ follows Dionysus,/
   Phallic and a. POUN 41
ambush: land of a.,/ Purblind
   manifestoes, MACN 4
amen: ever and ever a. SMIT ST 9
Glorious the catholic a.;/ SMAR 9
amends: beauty made a.:
   JOHN L 4
America: A. for me! VAN DY 3
a. i/ love you CUMM 28
A., I've given you all GINS 1
A.! my new-found-land, DONN 15
A. stop pushing GINS 3
A. the plum blossoms GINS 3
A., this wilderness SIMP 12
beauty of A., OHAR 10
grave weight of A. Cancelled!
   SIMP 15
hear A. singing, WHITM 37
I, too, am A. HUGH L 7
I, too, sing A. HUGH L 6
Mothers of A. OHAR 2
Ploughing North A. STEVENS 39
pure products of A. go crazy —
   WILLI 42
While this A. settles JEFFE 37
American: complicated, being an
   A., SIMP 8
fallen in love with A. names,
   BENE 1
one A. Poet LIND V 4
Americayour: A. stupidity.
   SNYD 16
amiably: amble a. here, CAME 2
amid: a. no earthly moans, POE 13
A. the heart WORD 52
a. the mimic rout POE 31
lonely Earth a. the balls EMER 9
amidde: a. the ers he smoot:
   CHAU 58
amiss: salving thy a., SHAK 199
urge not my a., SHAK 243
amitie: head with foot hath private
   a., HERB G 53
ammunition: a. And feats of war
   defeats MILT 113
amnesia: pingpong & a., GINS 15
amo: "a.," I love! BROWNI R 27
Among: A. the Nunnes Black.
   SKEL 6
a. the snow BLAK 55
come a. new faces, WHITM 113
my hands a. the flames.
   PLATH 72
wealth and woe a.: WYAT 1
amore: Quia a. langueo. UNKN 206
amorous: a. after me, WHITM 97
a. as this lovely green. MARV 16
a. clouds dividing, MILT 37
a. Descant join; GRAY 32
a. of their strokes. SHAK 5
a. scul court Thy mild Dove,
   DONN 52

a. thirst; TASS 5
it agrees well to be a. CAMPI 28
rushing a. contact WHITM 23
sweet, reluctant, a. delay.
MILT 73
undo the a. world. BEHN 2
amorousnesse: a. of an harmonious
Soule, DONN 31
amphibious: equine a. creatures
MOOR M 2
Amphitrite: A.'s destined halls,
SHEL 36
Ample: A. make this bed. DICKI 3
from an a. nation— DICKI 133
am'rous: from a. causes springs,/
What mighty contests
POPE A 110
what a. I? TENN 31
amuck: To run a., POPE A 89
amuse: a. his riper stage,
POPE A 81
Anacreon: wanting thee./ Horace,
A. HERR 16
Anapaests: thĕ swĭft A. thrŏng;
COLE SAM 24
anarch: From the heart's a. WILB 4
great A., lets the curtain fall;
POPE A 2
anarchic: weeping a. Aphrodite.
AUDE 34
anarchy: a. is loosed upon the
world, YEATS 133
a. of poverty WILLI 24
anatomy: clear a. arrive,
CAMPB R 1
love's true a.: HOLLA 5
ancestral: a. deed MUIR 11
a. trees, YEATS 35
on the a. tree HERF 1
anchor: a.-watches calm, MELV 22
a. weeps/ Its red rust BOGA 12
ductile a. hold, WHITM 55
anchor'd: a. near the shore,
WHITM 28
anchored: below another sky/ Parrot
islands a. lie, STEVENSO R 19
Hushed willows a. CRAN H 52
anchorites: seek these a., ARNO 31
anchors: great a., heaps of pearl,
SHAK 97
ancient: abate/ His a. brutal claim.
MELV 8
a. at his birth: ROBI 38
a. ditty, long since mute, KEAT 5
a., dreamless, uninvaded sleep
TENN 58
A., dusky rivers. HUGH L 12
a. floor,/ Footworn and hollowed
HARD 40
a. forms of party strife; TENN 48
a., glittering eyes, YEATS 82
a. heavenly connection GINS 8

a. Ireland sweeping/ In again
KAVA 7
a., meaningless/ Abstractions
SNYD 42
A. Person of my Heart. ROCH 14
a. slogan/ Noblesse oblige.
MILE 1
a. stubbornness ingrained,
WINT 6
a., thoroughfare,/ The Roman
Road. HARD 35
a. wisdom, WILD 13
born into that a. sect YEATS 143
clear and a. harmony THOR 5
each a. altar stands POPE A 31
for a. rules a just esteem;
POPE A 29
Ghastly grim and a. raven
POE 36
holy hush of a. sacrifice.
STEVENS 54
house of a. fame. SPENS 45
I feel a., SNYD 12
left the a. love BLAK 111
limestone on an a. sill.
TATE A 17
most a. heavens, WORD 89
not a. nor modern, LOWE J 7
sodden as the bed of an a. lake,
HUGH T 3
stand'st an a. pile, JONS 35
suit of a. black, LIND V 2
That a. kiss HUGO 2
Thine a. sacrifice, KIPL 18
voice/ From the a. room, Æ 1
winding a. stair; YEATS 43
Young or a., SHERI 2
ancients: a. of these lands—
FRENE 1
birds and a. GLÜC 1
ancyents: spread out your a.!
UNKN 223
Andalusian: like a true-born A.,
BYRO 47
Andrew: for Scotland and Saint A.
UNKN 226
Andrews: Saint A. crosse, that is his
guide; UNKN 222
ane: a. to heaven BURN 32
anecdotes: a. disparaging their
wives; GILB 11
anemia: emotional a. POUN 27
anemone: as is the violet/ Or a.,
THOR 10
anemones: plant some more dew-
wet a. UNKN 255
seven a. with down-dropped
heads/ Wept tears of dew
UNKN 253
anew: both of us were born a.
CART 2
Let us drink a. SMIT L 5
world is born a., GINS 31

Angel: Abides for me undesecrate:/
Dark A., JOHN L 6
a. gone ahead HARP 4
a. in the gate, the flowering
plum, SIMP 16
a. of the Lord came down,
TATE N 1
a., robed in spotless white,
DUNB P 1
A. that presided o'er my birth
BLAK 22
a. throng, bewinged, bedight/ In
veils, POE 30
a.'s voice. GODO 1
As the a. Israfel, POE 26
asks no A.'s wing, POPE A 60
Being less than a. RODG 3
better a. is a man right fair,
SHAK 240
Dark A., JOHN L 6
drive an a. from your door.
BLAK 92
Fair-haired A. of the Evening,
BLAK 109
good wicked spirit, sweet a. devil.
DRAY 6
legions, a. forms, MILT 55
long wait for the a., PLATH 20
Look homeward A. MILT 31
Malicious A., JOHN L 6
my a. be turned fiend,
SHAK 240
Natures æthereal, human, a.,
man, POPE A 72
Shined in my a.-infancy.
VAUG 21
Tempteth my better a. SHAK 240
to a radiant a. linked, SHAK 27
turn/ Thine a. eyes BLAK 108
waft the a. POE 30
angelheaded: a. hipsters burning
GINS 8
angelic: a. as lightbulbs—
GINS 40
a. symphony. MILT 39
heavenly form/ A., MILT 90
join th' a. train. WHEA 1
something of a. light.
WORD 135
when will you be a.? GINS 2
Angelico: not by usura A.;
POUN 10
angels: Afro a., black saints
HAYD 1
a., all pallid and wan, POE 33
A. alone, LOVE 5
A. led him COWL 13
A. sing to thee their ayres divine,
COWL 11
air is all awash with a. WILB 23
A.' song, BRID R 16
A. would be Gods. POPE A 66
black-and-white a. follow DAY 11

b'lieve in God an' the a., HAY 5
Bright-harnessed a. sit in order
  serviceable. MILT 41
drink of gods and a.! Wine
  HERR 15
flie with a., fall with dust,
  HERB G 65
God shall love and a. aid ye.
  PRIO 8
greenest of our valleys/ By good a.
  tenanted, POE 20
greet as a. greet. LOVE 7
guardian a. sung the strain:
  THOMS J (1700–1748)/MALL 1
Haunted by ill a. POE 16
Host/ Of Rebel A., MILT 48
little lower than the a.,
  BIBL, O.T. 25
Liveried a. robed in green,
  LAND 7
Men would be A., POPE A 66
pass in," the a. say, EMER 33
radiant evanescence/ for a.' feet
  LEVE 10
she prayed to the a. POE 24
staring a. go through.
  HUGH T 9
Stoop, a., TIMR 7
swift flights of A. ministrant
  MILT 109
three strange a. LAWR 49
two a. white, BRID R 12
where a. fear to tread.
  POPE A 23
Women are a., wooing;
  SHAK 169
Anger: A. heaving high, HARD 9
banish our a. forever FINC 2
candy, a., and sleep, SCHW 9
dead is all the innocence of a.
  CHES 11
monstrous a. of the guns.
  OWEN 7
angle: pale a. of time/ And eternity.
  MOMA 2
Angleworm: bit an A. DICKI 12
anglican: born to the a. order,
  MACN 14
angre: dyseese, a. and stryff,
  PETRA 1
angry: a. nigardes of dispence,
  CHAU 111
dear a. Lord, HERB G 10
hoarse and a. WHITM 5
I was a. with my foe: BLAK 78
I was a. with my friend:
  BLAK 78
not an a. father.' CAMPB T 5
raise/ Your a. head GRAV 7
Their sons are often a. BLY 2
vindictive rod of a. justice
  COWP 16
woke shamed and a.: SNYD 10

anguish: a. none can draw;
  MELV 19
a. of a land BRYA 5
drinking deep of that divinest a.,
  BRON 13
Pale A. keeps the heavy gate,
  WILD 3
Which A. was the utterest —
  DICKI 153
anguished: liquid, a. eyes
  LAWR 24
anguishes: Out of their a.
  BIBL, O.T. 57
angwysshe: for a. and care,
  PETRA 1
animal: Another armored a.
  MOOR M 22
each gentle a. HALE 2
Epicurean A.!) COWL 3
information vegetable, a., and
  mineral; GILB 35
kind of a. would you get.
  CREE 10
margins of a. necessity, SAND 16
No a. will more repay BELL 6
that high, a. face DEVL 2
that vain A., ROCH 8
animall: fustian a., TAYL E 14
animals: circus a. were all on
  show, YEATS 26
cooked rotten a. GINS 14
First, a.; MERE G 15
live with a., WHITM 74
serene-moving a. WHITM 29
souls of a. SHAK 124
animate: a. a mother's reveries,
  YEATS 12
animated: a. dead; TATE A 10
dove-/ neck a. by/ sun;
  MOOR M 18
if all of a. nature/ Be but organic
  Harps COLE SAM 12
ankles: bells on their a. LIND V 12
Ann: sculptured A. THOMA D 5
Anna: A.! whom three realms obey,
  POPE A 118
Annabel: chilling/ And killing my A.
  Lee. POE 5
name of A. Lee; POE 3
annals: bronze a. of the oak-tree
  close. WILB 3
Come whispering by:/ War's a.
  will cloud HARD 30
Rome's a. wax'd but dirty.
  BYRO 34
short and simple a. of the poor.
  GRAY 8
Anne: I am A. Rutledge MAST 2
Annie: all sang " A. Laurie."
  TAYL B 2
eyes of my A. POE 25
for bonnie A. Laurie DOUG W 1

love of my A. POE 25
reivers they stole Fair A.,
  UNKN 93
Annie's: Little Orphant A. RILE 1
annihilate: a. each decade.
  PLATH 54
Annihilating: Far other worlds and
  other seas,/ A. all that's made
  MARV 18
announcement: seems/ a pure a.:
  HUGO 2
announcer: clear a.'s voice WILB 4
annoy: does it to a., CARRO 2
still living in a. SIDN 33
annoyed: without getting a. "I will
  not kiss your f.ing flag"
  CUMM 15
annual: Eastward, the a. legend,
  SCOT WI 1
prodigal, a., sumptuous crops,
  WHITM 98
annually: a. coos in Our Lady's ear
  HECH 1
anointed: each a. sense will see.
  DOWS 2
exalt the horn of his a.
  BIBL, O.T. 8
for a. dullness he was made.
  DRYD 12
look upon the face of thine a.
  BIBL, O.T. 43
anointest: a. my head with oil;
  BIBL, O.T. 31
anomaly: that singular a., GILB 27
anon: languish and a. must die;
  CAREW 9
anonymity: Whose verdurous a.
  TATE A 13
Another: A. tempter of this snake;
  WALL 7
a.'s guilt! WILD 5
Death ere thou has slain a.,
  BROWNE 3
drained out one a.'s force
  SNOD 15
Gone is a. summer's day.
  DE LA 26
lamp lights a., LOWE J 21
like love/ From a. world
  DICKEY 27
object of a.'s fear; SHEL 76
One sure, if a. fails:
  BROWNI R 78
pickpurse of a.'s wit. SIDN 22
river had a. shore, LOWE R 26
say a. is an ass — HART 4
search a., WHITM 74
To-morrow sees a. race BYRO 34
would have been/ A. world.'
  THOMA E 3
anothers: one, and one a. All.
  DONN 37

answer: a. had not been enscrolled.
  SHAK 119
  a. my questions three,/ Thy life
  and thy living   UNKN 162
  a. to children,   WHITM 113
  have their a. home.   HERB G 64
  in a. to the reasoning   OHAR 16
  silver a. rang,   BROWNI E 8
  soothe and bless!/ What hope of
  a.,   TENN 37
  woods shall to me a.   SPENS 30

answerable: thy knowledge a.;
  MILT 106

answered: her measures are, how
  well/ Each syllab'e a.,   JONS 40
  like a Host — 'Come in'/ I boldly
  a.   DICKI 162

answering: No a. smile   ROSS D 1

answers: a. to every prayer
  KAVA 13
  he a.: 'Omaha.'   SAND 12
  Kind are her a.,   CAMPI 10
  Nature a. all he asks;   WHITT 7
  secret whispers of each other's
  watch./ Fire a. fire,   SHAK 57

ant: a. and the mole sit both in a
  hole,   JONS 16
  a. on the tablecloth   FROS 30
  a.-and stone-swallowing
  MOOR M 24

antennae: burring furred a.
  SPEND 13

anther: Don't a.   NASH 8

Anticipation: eye their hopeful
  years;/ A. forward points
  BURN 18

anticipat'st: a. my dread exploits.
  SHAK 113

antics: arts, the a. of dancers,
  JEFFE 6

antient: plead the a. Rights in
  vain: MARV 21

Antietam: Shiloh, A., Malvern Hill,
  Bull Run.   TATE A 12

antique: a. pen would have
  express'd   SHAK 228
  most a. springs!   JONS 47

antithesis: himself one vile a.
  POPE A 11

antlers: 'gainst the oak his a.
  fray'd;   SCOT WA 13
  moves in a wood of desire,/ pale a.
  barely stirring   GUNN 2

Antonio: "Oh, nonio, A.!"
  RICHA L 1

Ant's: a. a centaur   POUN 20

Ants: A. are a curious race;
  FROS 31
  a. had done/ so.   MOOR M 24

anus: old recalcitrant a.   SNOD 11

anvil: Lay me on an a.,   SAND 20
  Muses' a.;   JONS 45

sounding a. shaped   LONG 50
  What the a.?   BLAK 82

anvill: a. Sparke, rose higher,
  TAYL E 1

anxiety: repose is taboo'd by a.,
  GILB 25

anxious: a. for to shine   GILB 30
  A. or troubled —   TREN 2
  a. to expatiate   DAIC 2
  a. to keep back   THOR 4

any: assuming that he's got a.
  GILB 21
  I can love a., so she be not true.
  DONN 35

anybody: "Is there a. there?"
  DE LA 11

anyone: a. lived   CUMM 4
  Does a. remember?   WAGO 3
  one day a. died   CUMM 6

Anything: A. does for me.   CARRY 1
  a. to show more fair: WORD 6
  Last year's a.?   CULL 7
  never did a. properly;   LEAR 15
  poor love of a.,   THOR 4

Anywhere: A. does for me.
  CARRY 2

apace: long nights come on a.,
  NASHE 2

apart: a. from the well-trodden
  ways;   PETRA 11
  a. from them,   WHITM 73
  joy a. from thee,   EMER 24
  our lives so far a.   TENN 39
  smithereened a.!   CRAN H 38

aparte: laye a. Your cornet black,
  SURR 9

Apathie: Passion and A.,   MILT 60

ape: a. the ways of pride.   BRYA 36
  erotic as an a.,   SHAP 21
  Tullia's a. a marmasyte
  UNKN 95

aped: a. his way?   LIND V 7

Apes: lead/ A. in Avernus.   CAMPI 4

Aphrodite: golden crown, A.,
  POUN 8
  weeping anarchic A.   AUDE 34

Apollo: A., courted for her haire,
  MARL 5
  fit only for A.   BEAU 1
  God A.'s golden mean —
  GRAV 41
  not A. can,   HERR 16
  Out-weariers of A. will,   POUN 29
  pipe that strikes A. dumb;
  LYLY 5

Apollo's: A. first,   CAREW 4

apoplexy: died of a.   DAVIS 6

Apostles: A. were so many
  fishermen?   MARV 3
  A. would have done   BYRO 20
  Twelve for the twelve A.
  UNKN 52

appall: a. the free,   SHAK 31
  a. the weake stomacke:
  SPENS 37

appalled: Roman Empire stood a.:
  YEATS 117

apparatus: a. not for me to mend —
  ROBI 19

apparel: her brave a. on)   MELV 1
  in a. that glittered   CRAN S 5

apparent: a. space between them.
  HOLLA 2

Apparently: A. they have reached
  their destination.   BISH 27
  A. with no surprise   DICKI 4

apparition: a. of these faces
  POUN 47
  lovely a.,   WORD 133

appassionato: great black piano a.
  LAWR 32

appeal: a. to heaven breaks off.
  KINN 10

appear: a. at all one day   OHAR 17
  flowers a. on the earth;
  BIBL, O.T. 72
  from mine eyes a.   SHAK 169
  greater Sun a.   MILT 38
  small vices do a.   SHAK 81
  soon a. The same   ROBI 40
  these visions did a.   SHAK 129
  they a. in/ the darkness: GUNN 9
  your bounty doth a.;   SHAK 205

appearance: a. of choice   FULL 4
  Lifeless in a.,   WILLI 35
  London's first a.   BYRO 52

appear'd: just as the dawn a.,
  WHITM 107

appeare: starres/ Watch an
  advantage to a.   HERB G 30

appeared: dream you a.   SNYD 10

appears: sun a., astonished Art
  EMER 45
  when a woman a.;   GAY 3

appel: al was for an a.,   UNKN 2

appendages: strictly practical a.
  MOOR M 19

appertain: a. To civil justice,
  MILT 104

appetite: a healthy a.:   AUDE 58
  a. was good?   BYRO 32
  circling shadow of its a.
  TATE A 2
  delight/ Nature or unrestrainèd a.
  CAREW 13
  scrimmage of a.   SCHW 11
  surfeiting,/ The a. may sicken
  SHAK 174
  uncertain sickly a.   SHAK 242

appetites: flesh and the a.,
  WHITM 74

applaud: a. His coming!
  LAWR 25

Apple: A. orchards blossom there,
  MASE 14

branch/ Of mossy a.-tree,
COLE SAM 16
cool blade/ Severs between
coolness, a.-rind/ Compelling a
recognition. TOML 2
done with a.-picking now.
FROS 3
eat with a. tart. STEVENSO R 7
golden a. doth appear. MOTH 16
laughing round an a. OWEN 14
My heart is like an a.-tree
ROSS C 1
noon a.-dreams, RANS 4
Of a.-picking: I am overtired
FROS 5
spring, briefer than a.-blossom's
breath, WYLI 13
Swing up into the a. tree.
ELIOT T 58
trees in a. orchards JACK 3
Two sticks and an a., UNKN 24
under the a. boughs
THOMA D 17
apple's: a. a rose FROS 96
apples: a. appear and disappear,
FROS 4
a. are laid in rows, DRIN 1
A. I didn't pick FROS 3
chawnk green a. FIEL E 4
few herbs and a., EMER 16
golden a. grow; —
STEVENSO R 19
golden a. of the sun. YEATS 139
Ripe a. drop MARV 17
silver a. of the moon, YEATS 139
Some bring a capon, some a rural
cake,/ Some nuts, some a.;
JONS 36
with the unpicked a., LOWE R 1
appletree: petals from an a.
WILLI 26
appletrees: thighs are a. WILLI 25
apply: birds their quire a.; airs,
vernal airs, MILT 70
Appomattox: from A. stretched to
Somme! CRAN H 13
appreciate: did a. it. OHAR 7
apprehend: a. some joy, SHAK 127
apprehensions: a. come in crowds;
WORD 3
apprentice: bound a., UNKN 172
approach: a. at least, MILT 112
days of impotence a., ROCH 2
hackney coach/ Appearing, showed
the ruddy morn's a. SWIF 10
hails thy a., O Spring!
BLAK 108
approached: a. by stronger hate,
MILT 92
approaches: sluggish/ dazed spring
a. WILLI 35
approaching: silently a. WHITM 33

appropriate: a. sense of space.
OHAR 19
judged me by their a. tool.
FROS 124
Approval: A. of what is approved
BETJ 1
approve: but men of sense a.:
POPE A 29
still the Charmer I a., CONG 1
approving: measure off another day/
For an a. God. DICKI 5
approximate: thunder of a. words.
GUNN 10
apricots: young dangling a.
SHAK 90
April: A. Comes like an idiot,
MILLA 37
A. in a face. MASE 4
A. is in my mistress' face,
UNKN 6
A. is the cruellest month,
ELIOT T 113
A.,/ Laugh thy girlish laughter,
WATS W 1
A., May, of June and July-flowers;
HERR 1
eighteenth of A., in Seventy-five;
LONG 43
flag to A.'s breeze unfurled,
EMER 11
No A. can revive thy withered
flowers, DANI S 14
Now that A.'s there,
BROWNI R 32
packs wool sheared in A., HALL 4
proud pied A., SHAK 225
regret/ Becomes an A. violet,
TENN 52
small clumsy feet of A. CUMM 20
Three A. perfumes SHAK 227
To what purpose, A., MILLA 36
Aprill: A. with his shoures soote
CHAU 3
apron: Nature was in her beryl a.,
DICKI 92
see my a. rising. UNKN 207
spread her a. to it. FROS 26
aproned: a. young and lovely
CORS 5
Aquarium: A. is gone. LOWE R 21
arabesques: fantastic a., WILD 12
Arabian: In the A. woods embost,
MILT 117
Arabs: fold their tents, like the A.,
LONG 16
kill the A., LIND V 10
Araby: bird of A., SKEL 8
Ararat: rode that tide/ To A.;
WILB 38
arbor: Give me an a., WHITM 29
arc: without/ The dolphin's a.,
WILB 2

Arch: A. Fear in a visible form,
BROWNI R 68
crawling a. of stars, KINS 2
in the belfry a. LONG 44
pendant and bending a.,
WHITM 73
wide a. Of the ranged empire
fall! SHAK 3
arched: rude bridge that a. the
flood, EMER 11
to the a. roof MILT 114
archer: busy a. his sharp arrows
tries? SIDN 11
Archers: A. stand there MUIR 10
noise of a. BIBL, O.T. 18
arches: a. of the years; THOMP F 6
Architect: Blest be the A.,
HERB G 16
mighty A., BRAD 12
architects: a. of Fate, LONG 4
architecture: frolic a. of the snow.
EMER 45
New styles of a., AUDE 69
shows, a., WHITM 60
archway: shining a. through,
HOLM 2
Arcturi: Daisies, those pearl'd A.
SHEL 59
Arcturus: strange stars near A.
MACL 5
ardent: many an a. wish,
GRAY 19
ardour: With the a. and the passion,
JONS 1
argentine: From a. vapor? —
THOMP F 14
Argicida: golden bough of A.
POUN 8
argosies: a. of magic sails,
TENN 75
argument: a. ad feminam, RICH 14
content with a. YEATS 151
He thought he saw an A.
CARRO 30
heard great a. OMAR 5
Her nights in a. YEATS 51
higher A. MILT 88
highth of this great A. MILT 47
like a tedious a. ELIOT T 76
monumental/ A. of the hewn
voice, THOMA D 5
Argus: A. Eyes, MONTROSE 1
A.' eyes perceive you.' SIDN 31
aria: Flutter, or sing an a.
BROO G 16
arid: that a. square, AUDE 87
with the a. plain behind me
ELIOT T 155
Ariel: Caliban casts out A.
POUN 41
aright: here is all a. CHES 2
arise: a. From death, you
numberless infinities DONN 5

a. Races of living things,
    BRYA 17
I will a. and go now,   YEATS 74
my a. is from above,   BRAD 9
Phoebus 'gins a.,   SHAK 17
thoughts that a. in me.   TENN 1
Arisen: A. at sunrise   DICKEY 15
arising: break of day a.   SHAK 194
Aristotelian: moderate A. city
    AUDE 14
Aristotle: better man was A.,
    RANS 33
Every Poet his own A.'   BYRO 20
arithmetic: thine a. is quite correct.
    HOUS 11
ark: a. of faith   LAWR 39
dove from Noah's a.,   BYRO 43
entered the A.   MACDI 5
two by two in the a.   LEVE 2
arks: a., the trophies,   DANI S 12
arm: brutal a. appear,   YEATS 100
clasp'd by an a.,   BYRO 45
Fly lost in sunset./ Throwing a.
    gone bad.   FITZ 2
gallant a. that strikes   DRAK 3
God/ Stretcheth out his a.,
    MARL 2
his a. lay lightly   WHITM 109
holds his wife by th' a.,
    SHAK 179
jointed wooden a.   GRAV 21
loving that old a.-chair?   COOK 1
nor hand, nor foot,/ Nor a., nor
    face,   SHAK 142
pearls upon an Ethiop's a.
    DYER J 2
reared a. Crested the world;
    SHAK 7
scent of these a.-pits   WHITM 74
stinking a.-pits,   GRAV 18
weak of will, the strong of a.,
    MAST 6
Armadas: great A. come,/ (Capten,
    art tha sleepin'   NEWB 1
armchair: used to silence and an
    a.:   HEAN 15
arme: auld moone in hir a.,
    UNKN 227
armed: a. rhinoceros,   SHAK 110
a. With assurance policies,
    TATE A 7
A. with her briars,   AYTON 1
host of a. men.   BERT 1
like an a. robber,   PETRA 3
o'er the campana knights a. and
    horses arrayed.   BERT 1
Walking the sea so heavily a.;
    YOUN A 1
Armestrong: Jonnë A. men did him
    call,   UNKN 153
armies: Boys sobbing in a.!
    GINS 16

handmaid a. back to spin,
    LOWE J 14
ignorant a. clash by night.
    ARNO 4
arming: kings are a.;   SCOT WA 1
armor: a. shone like gold.
    UNKN 60
bloody swords and a.   CAMPI 16
armored: Another a. animal —
    MOOR M 22
a. Diesel fishing tubs   LOWE R 6
armorers: a. accomplishing the
    knights,   SHAK 57
armour: a. is his honest thought,
    WOTT 1
no a. against fate;   SHIR 1
armoury: Oneself a living a.?
    YOUN A 1
arms: all their griefs in their a.,
    THOMA D 27
a. about her,   PETRA 9
a. and hands and feet and
    countenance   PETRA 11
A. and Honour,   DRYD 23
a. flash in the sun —   WHITM 13
a. hang down to laugh,
    ELIOT T 111
a. have lain/ Under my head
    MILLA 39
a. make for me;   RILE 3
a. partially raised.   WHITM 70
a. reaching towards me.
    ROET 57
a. Round the griefs of the ages,
    THOMA D 28
A. that are braceleted
    ELIOT T 85
a. were yours   STRA 2
a. you bear are brittle,   HOUS 23
bitch bit off his a.   RANS 7
dark/ of the a. Plutonic,   LAWR 5
every bone in a.   WORD 4
Felt in his a.,   MILT 114
find the a. of my true-love
    TENN 97
Forge a.   SHEL 64
hushed me in her a. to rest,
    TAYL A 1
If I admire my a.,   WILLI 13
In A. not worse,   MILT 52
in her dissolving a.   SHEL 16
in My a.   THOMP F 9
in my A. embrac'd my Lass;
    GAY 4
laid down his a.   HOOD 4
long white a.   RANS 12
love gives again into our a.
    KINN 2
muscles of his brawny a.
    LONG 48
put up your little a.   CUMM 13
ragged a., the ragged heads and
    eyes   TATE A 13

remember me, unwept, unburied,/
    "Heap up mine a.,   POUN 6
Rest in the strong a.   TIMR 2
sable a.,/ Black as his purpose,
    SHAK 30
Slight are her a.,   POUN 66
soldier's loving a.   WHITM 116
strong white a. to fold you,
    KIPL 16
supple a. of love.   RUKE 2
take a. against a sea of troubles,
    SHAK 39
To war and a. I fly.   LOVE 8
weeping I, with wither'd a.,
    OVID 7
young bride in my a.,
    SMIT ST 1
army: as the a.   REED H 3
Austrian a., awfully array'd,/
    WATT A 1
hum of either a. stilly sounds,
    SHAK 57
join the A.   GINS 6
Like an a. defeated   WORD 164
traveling a. halting,   WHITM 9
Arnold: Matthew A. and this girl
    HECH 3
aroma: a. finer than prayer,
    WHITM 74
aromatic: a. gums   SKEL 9
Burnt up with a. fire!   DARL 2
Die of a rose in a. pain?
    POPE A 70
around: a. the cannibal's neck.
    SIMI 5
lights a. the shore.   ROSS D 8
procession winding a.   WHITM 11
shudder ran a. the sky;
    EMER 50
aroused: echo a. in my soul,
    WHITM 52
messenger there a.,   WHITM 67
arraigning: Usurp the chair of wit:/
    Indicting and a.   JONS 20
arrange: not a gill would a.!
    STEPHENS 4
arrant: a. sleepy-head,
    STEVENSO R 14
Fortune, that a. whore,   SHAK 73
Arras: they slogged up to A.
    SASS 10
wavering a. of leaves, —   LANIE 3
Array: line in long a.,   WHITM 13
silks and fine a.,   BLAK 40
Array'd: A. in Glory   MILT 109
Attic robe a.,   COLL 11
Austrian army, awfully a.,
    WATT A 1
arrayed: goodly colours gloriously
    a.;   SPENS 21
Gorgeously a.,/ Boned and stayed.
    LOWE A 10

Lets his own a. choke his soul.
  HERB G 29
martyred blood and a. sow
  MILT 36
mingle with forgotten a., SHIR 4
sackcloth and a. RODG 7
Scatter my a., MONTROSE 4
sleepers shall pass to a.)
  SAND 12
under a. into sudden flame,
  MILT 116
We too are a. SHAP 10
ashie: out her a. womb MILT 117
ashore: At sea or a., TENN 119
  bring my boats a.
  STEVENSO R 23
  cast the vessel a. CARRY 11
Asia: A. is rising against me.
  GINS 4
  long moon drifts/ toward A.
  HAIN 1
Asian: home European or A.,
  HILT 2
  know it is the A. Lion. WELL 1
aside: do not cast you a.
  WHITM 22
Ask: A. me no more CAREW 1
  A. me no more. TENN 106
  a. the favour; CONG 2
  I dare not a. a kiss, HERR 46
  kneel down/ And a. of thee
  forgiveness. SHAK 84
  never a. why build. SEXT 16
  never thought to a., EMER 42
  sages a. thee why EMER 42
askance: looked a. and hated;
  LOWE J 14
asked: a. a crumb DICKI 30
  a. her master STEPHENS 4
  a. them to explain SMIT ST 3
  I have a. to be HOPKINS 10
Askelon: streets of A.;
  BIBL, O.T. 68
askew: stood with lips a. WARR 4
asking: a. too much. CANN 1
  Bland-mannered, a. PLATH 66
  incessantly a. WHITM 30
  Nearly killed me for a.
  STEPHENS 3
asks: a. no Angel's wing,
  POPE A 60
  Nature answers all he a.;
  WHITT 7
asleep: all are laid a.: BRON 14
  A. are the ranks FINC 1
  a. by thy murmuring stream,
  BURN 22
  A. on the hills. ARNO 7
  A. upon a chair." YEATS 15
  Death, rock me a., BOLE 1
  Drunk and a. in his boots,
  STEVENS 5
  fall a. for ever; SASS 8

fast a. in bed. STEVENSO R 14
fathoms down, how I'll dream fast
  a. MELV 4
Half a. as they stalk. HARD 29
'He thought me a.; PATM 1
love while half a. GRAV 24
Men marched a. OWEN 18
nations lying a., MUIR 6
pretty Baby lies/ Sung a. with
  Lullabies: HERR 13
'tween a. and wake? SHAK 70
under a haycock/ Fast a.
  MOTH 19
very houses seem a.; WORD 7
we are laid a. In body, WORD 31
Wearied I fell a.: MILT 107
asleepe: Fall a., or hearing dye.
  FLET/SHAK 1
aspect: in each a. death is pure.
  JARR 23
  lend the eye a terrible a.:
  SHAK 56
aspens: My a. dear, HOPKINS 2
aspiration: a. of my youth,
  LONG 28
  Be thou my a. CARM 1
aspire: bodies shall a. KING H 3
  folly to a. MILT 105
  mind, a. to higher things;
  SIDN 26
aspired: What I a. to be,
  BROWNI R 74
aspiring: a. genius TROW 1
ass: a.-back, mule-back, YEATS 80
  fucked in the a. GINS 11
  hit a bear in the a. SNYD 34
  man is but an a. GILB 40
  mere white curd of a.'s milk?
  POPE A 9
  nothing but sit on her a.
  GINS 12
  say another is an a. HART 4
assail: scholar's life a.,
  JOHN S (1709–1784) 18
assassin: met an a. CRAN S 5
assault: fierce a. they fell,
  WHITM 26
assaulting: early bees are a.
  REED H 5
Assemble: A. the engine again.
  UNKN 82
  living all a.! ROET 21
Assent: A., and you are sane;
  DICKI 106
  a. with civil leer, POPE A 7
asses: backs like a. load: JONS 34
  dull a. hoofe. JONS 21
  ride on white a., BIBL, O.T. 18
assignations: Gestured a.,
  SPENC A 2
assign'd: rain, from clouds to drop
  a., BIBL, O.T. 67

To wicked spirits are horrid
  shapes a., DONN 67
assigned: task by God a. me,
  BANK 1
assignments: soul has no a.,
  JARR 9
assist: Midnight, a. our moan;
  SHAK 132
assume: I a. WHITM 73
  That it a. thy body, I allow,
  DONN 1
assuming: a. that he's got any.
  GILB 21
assurance: armed/ With a. policies,
  TATE A 7
assure: a. his survival — WILLI 31
assured: a. of escape; AUDE 32
assures: beauteous form a. a piteous
  mind. DONN 67
Assyrian: A. came down BYRO 12
  A. came down NASH 19
asteroid: Supplemental a., EMER 9
astir: old couple, just a., DICKI 52
  Parties all a. DICKI 121
astonished: say a. critics,
  AUDE 100
  stopped,/ a.: AMMO 13
  sun appears, a. Art EMER 45
Astonishes: brown study/ A.
  RANS 3
Astonishment: A. takes from us
  sense of pain. CONS 1
  wonder and a. MILT 35
Astound: A. the girl next door
  CORS 1
astounding: a. crate full of air.
  HEAN 2
astray: fetch one if one goes a.,
  ROSS C 12
  moon-shine a.! MELV 3
astream: Glorious the northern
  lights a.; SMAR 9
astride: conquering limbs a.
  LAZA 1
astrologye: yfounde in myn a.,
  CHAU 54
astronomer: heard the learn'd a.,
  WHITM 110
astronomye: grounded in a.
  CHAU 8
asunder: body and soul begin to fall
  a. ELIOT T 5
ate: a. the cheeses BROWNI R 60
  chickens/ a. the vegetables
  CUMM 30
  gulped what he a.; LA FO 1
  Held his heart in his hands,/ And
  a. of it. CRAN S 3
  quietly a. the bear up. NASH 1
  rat/ That a. the malt MOTH 4
  they a. each other up! FIEL E 2
atheist: Rebel and a. too, DONN 40
Athelstan: A. King, UNKN 18

Athenian: save the A. walls
MILT 125

Athens: Jerusalem A. Alexandria
ELIOT T 148

athirst: a. for sleep SWIN 5

athletic: game of a. beauty.
RANDA D 5

athwart: a. a cedarn cover!/ A
savage place! COLE SAM 20
a. my hips WHITM 78
sullen and fast a. WHITM 56
team of little atomies/ A. men's
noses SHAK 153

Atlantic: A. and Caribbean love,
GINS 11
A. billows roar'd, COWP 1
A. wall are singing: LOWE R 3
beyond the A. roar./ Fair these
broad meads — GALT 1
bogholes might be A. seepage.
HEAN 3
picture postcards of A. City
GINS 10

Atlantick: steep A. stream, MILT 8

atlas: a.-eater with a jaw for news,
THOMA D 6

atmosphere: a. is not a perfume,
WHITM 75
this a. divinest/ Shrouds thee
SHEL 53

atom: every a. belonging to me
WHITM 73
every a. of my blood, WHITM 74

AtomI: Behold the A. preferred —
DICKI 114

atomic: blind a. pilgrimage
ROBI 33

atomies: team of little a. Athwart
men's noses SHAK 153

atoms: a. of Democritus BLAK 39
Bids spheres and a. VERY 4
flung on a new net of a.:
SNYD 22
green a. shimmer GINS 42
grey a. wet GINS 45
of his a., ROBI 31
these a. are, MONTROSE 4

attachment: a. à la Plato GILB 32

attack: lead such dire a.; MACA 4
plan of a. SASS 11

attacked: Word in the desert/ Is
most a. ELIOT T 25

attain: things for to a. MARTIA 1

attained: a. by humankind!
HARD 47
a. with ease, DANI S 18
Joys seldom yet a. HARD 47

attains: a. the upmost round
SHAK 44

attempted: Something a., something
done, LONG 49

attend: a. the spell/ Of his voice,
POE 26

A. thee to the grave. STOD 3
on my cup to a.: MILT 109
shooting stars a. thee; HERR 32

attendance: with a., CHAU 110

Attendant: A. and withdrawn.
HUGH T 5
a. follows WHITM 115
her a. Byzantines. STEVENS 35

attendants: Roman Catholic a.
LOWE R 54

Attended: A., or alone DICKI 112

attending: a. upon you;
MOOR M 41

attenes: a. in stonen showers.
CHAT 2

attention: a. like deep harmony.
SHAK 87
cause thy a. engage;/ In the days
of my youth SOUTHE 7
close the Valves of her a.
DICKI 133
give me your a., GILB 6

attentive: clear, a. mind SNYD 50

Attic: A. robe array'd, COLL 11
barbarous to the royal A.;
RANS 28
quiet of my a. KINS 2

Attica: looked down over A.;
BYRO 52

Atticus: if A. were he? POPE A 8

Attire: cheerful Fields resume their
green A.: GRAY 32

attired: a. in the usual costumes,
WHITM 18

attitude: a. of self-defense;
MOOR M 7

attitude's: a. considered quaint,'
GILB 3

Attorneys: A.-general, awful
BYRO 48

Attract: A. a Silver Churn! GILB 34

attractive: sweet a. grace; MILT 72

attribute: a. to awe and majesty,
SHAK 123
a. to God himself, SHAK 123

attune: smell of field and grove, a.
MILT 70

Auburn: mound in sweet A.
LOWE J 12
Sweet A., GOLD 1

audience: fit a. find, though few.
MILT 84

aught: a. of evil MILT 82
Unfaith in a. TENN 15

augurs: sad a. mock SHAK 229

August: yellow with A. LI PO 6

Augustine: Old Chrysostom, best A.
EMER 40

auld: a. lang syne? BURN 13
a. moone in hir arme, UNKN 227
For a. lang syne, BURN 14
Should a. acquaintance be forgot,
BURN 13

Aunswer: A. him faire with yea or
nay. WYAT 18

Aunt: A. Jennifer's hand. RICH 2

aunts: died like a. of pets or
foreigners. JARR 14
sisters, cousins, a., and niece,
GILB 5

Auroch: thewed like an A. bull,
SMIT L 2

Aurora: Sprungin is A. radius and
bricht, DUNB W 2

auroral: pendulous a. beaches, —
CRAN H 11

austere: a. control? WILD 13
look, a., immaculate, WYLI 14
love's a. and lonely offices?
HAYD 23

austerely: Hypocrites a. talk
MILT 77

Austerlitz: A. and Waterloo.
SAND 10

Austrian: A. army, awfully array'd,
WATT A 1

authentic: a.! I said LEVE 14
a.! Shadows of it LEVE 13

author: a. and disposer, MILT 75
A. of liberty, SMIT SA 2

authority: true a. in men: MILT 72
what a. in thy speech! JONS 47

Authorizing: A. thy trespass
SHAK 199

authors: employment by a.
NASH 18
judge of a.' names, not works,
POPE A 31

automaton: dragoon me into a
lethal a. MACN 16

automobiles: high-strung a.
BISH 13

autopsy: gone into a., HARP 4

autumn: a. and the falling fruit
LAWR 35
a.'s best of cheer. JACK 4
a. hills again: TUCK 1
a., like a bonfire of leaves,
WYLI 13
a. long since gone. MACL 6
A.'s power FRENE 6
A. resumes the land, HILL G 1
a. wind laid bare; VERY 1
bright blaze of A.'s equinox.
WALK 11
child with her father,/ Watching
the east, the a. sky. WHITM 56
faces like a. fruit, KLEI 2
happy a.-fields, TENN 114
in a season of a./ The soldier
falls. STEVENS 3
in the a. moonbeams WHITM 109
ripe breath of a., WHITM 108
Sad songs of A. mirth.
THOMA E 6
saw old A. HOOD 1

spring entombed in a. lies;
KING H 5
spring summer a. winter
CUMM 4
Watching the east, the a. sky
WHITM 56
yellow with a. LI PO 1
autumnal: juicy a. fruit WHITM 29
on the a. blast LONG 29
one a. face. DONN 42
Thick as a. leaves MILT 55
autumns: yellow a. SHAK 227
avail: love a. you in your hour.
MILLA 2
tyrant, shall a. GRAY 2
availeth: struggle nought a.,
CLOU 8
avails: a. not, time nor place —
WHITM 19
distance a. not, WHITM 19, 20
place a. not, WHITM 20
avalanche: Beware the awful a.!"
LONG 22
avaryce: twinne/ From a., CHAU 84
Ave: " A. atque Vale" TENN 14
Avenge: A. the patriotic gore
RANDA J 1
Roaring their readiness to a.,
HARD 15
avenged: Thou art a., my first-born,
LOWE J 22
avenger: still the enemy and the a.
BIBL, O.T. 23
aventures: a. that whilom han
bifalle. CHAU 6
avenue: a. of cypresses, LAWR 9
average: dull man, dulling and
uxorious,/ One a. mind —
POUN 55
their a. day: AUDE 75
Avernus: lead/ Apes in A. CAMPI 4
averse: To coxcombs a., GOLD 4
averted: backward, with a. gaze,
WHITT 12
faith of still a. feet, PATM 10
upstart wealth's a. eye, EMER 27
avidity: Beast ravens in its own a.?
EBER 3
avocado: a. in a glass of water —
MERR 6
avocados: Wives in the a., GINS 37
Avoid: A. the reeking herd, WYLI 1
those who a. the face ELIOT T 14
avoiding: a. the settlements,
WHITM 47
Avon: Sweet Swan of A.! JONS 46
time, where lucid A. stray'd,
GRAY 28
avow'd: first a. intent, BUNY 2
await: friend a. Felicity of doom.
DICKI 20
next year's words a. another
voice. ELIOT T 66

awaited: a. the expected guest.
ELIOT T 135
awaiting: lie a. the hearses,
WHITM 8
awaits: a. my spirit BANK 1
double grave a. them).
WHITM 26
Wind, lake, lip, everything a.
HECH 6
Awake: A., my St. John!
POPE A 58
a. your faith. SHAK 184
fairy queen Bids you a., CAMPI 3
he's always wide a. ELIOT T 94
lie a. in the dark WHITM 75
mortal sounds can sing a.,
KINN 2
My lute a.! WYAT 12
O to a. and wander
STEVENSO R 10
stab my spirit broad a.;
STEVENSO R 2
wintered and were coming a.
MORG 1
you're lying a. GILB 25
awaken: begin to a. WILLI 36
awakened: a. from the dream of
life — SHEL 8
a., lips parted, ELIOT T 96
love's a. root DONN 41
own songs a. WHITM 68
award: Time renders/ His last a.,
BYRO 34
aware: infant child is not a.
HOUS 15
awash: air is all a. with angels.
WILB 23
Away: A. at once with love or
jealousy! SHAK 136
A. delights, BEAU/FLET 1
a. down South in Dixie! EMME 2
bear that beating heart a.;
YEATS 116
bring a. Captivity thence captive,
SPENS 18
burglars stole that pair a.!
FIEL E 2
Come a., SCOT WA 21
come a., death, SHAK 176
darkness silvers a., BRID R 1
days and nights, passing a.,)
WHITM 59
Drops a., hard rock wavers
SNYD 49
Far, far a., FOST 3
flowers may fade and pass a.
MCCRE 2
fly a., breath; SHAK 176
I broke a. KAVA 13
last red leaf is whirl'd a.,
TENN 23
let's a. to prison. SHAK 84
Look a.! Dixie Land. EMME 1

maple burn itself a. TENN 42
marvel my birthday/ A.
THOMA D 35
melts a. As doth the dawn
COWL 5
moulder in dust a.! LONG 10
mounts and rides a. SMIT W 2
near me when I fade a.,
TENN 29
Passing a., saith the World,
ROSS C 18
Remember me when I am gone
a., ROSS C 19
sailed a. From a leaking ship
WHITT 24
silently steal a. LONG 16
so fair, and you a.? COWL 7
so far a. PATM 9
stars had run a. YEATS 16
take my love a. SHAK 211
take, those lips a., SHAK 117
takes a. Our playthings LONG 34
those that are far a.; WHITM 12
Thyself a. art present still
SHAK 204
time prattled a., SIDN 4
truth a. From you is fled?
WYAT 28
unrecorded did it slip a.,
ROSS C 17
what Age takes a., WORD 19
awe: admire with a. ARNO 37
attribute to a. and majesty,
SHAK 123
a. of thy imperious wit CAREW 3
a. that hushes all, BRYA 5
Creating a. and fear in other
men? SHAK 58
honor and reverend a.;
BENN H 2
Make this bed with a.; DICKI 3
observed in foolish a. MUIR 3
aweary: 'I am a., aweary, TENN 92
awed: a. by rumour, POPE A 109
a. with dreadful expectation
LUCR 2
grave, a. intensity SNYD 11
awful: Attorneys-general, a.
BYRO 48
a. brain CULL 19
a. but cheerful. BISH 10
a. calm, DODG 1
a. dread of the icy grave SERV 2
a. shadow SHEL 29
Beware the a. avalanche!"
LONG 22
compels His a. hand. CULL 19
Gas smells a.;/ You might as well
live. PARK 2
mighty mother did unveil/ Her a.
face: GRAY 28
scale/ Of a. notes, WORD 8
With a. reverence prone; MILT 59

Wild roses, at your b. porch,
  MOSS 6
Yes, and b. again. MOTH 12
backbone: cam-shaft from out of my
  b., UNKN 82
pluck was he to the b. WOOL 3
backs: b. like asses load: JONS 34
blows at our b., HENL 2
feel behind/ Their b., MASE 9
float on their b., WHITM 73
nothing on their b., or heads, or
  feet. ALBI 1
backward: b., with averted gaze,
  WHITT 12
nothing to look b. to with pride,
  FROS 25
Spelling it b., LONG 27
Years looking b. WHITM 113
backwards: film/ played b. HARP 1
Turn it b. BARA 5
backwater: along the b.,
  GRAHAME 1
bacon: b.'s not the only thing
  KINGSM 2
bacterial: b. creepers ROET 48
bad: as in b. plight, MILT 97
b. against the worse. DAY 13
beat b. manners STEPHENS 3
do not, on the other hand, be b.;
  HOUS 8
God b. us for to wexe and
  multiplye: CHAU 88
good and the b. POE 11
harbor for good or b., WHITM 74
Madame B. Luck HAY 2
map a b. example SPEND 2
money and the b. conscience,
  SIMP 8
no life-glimpse, good or b.,/ Nor
  joy nor passion ROBI 6
Nor good, nor b., nor fools, nor
  wise, PRIO 4
not yet so b. with us.' SWIF 27
outdoor business is b. for strings),
  TROW 5
sad and b. and mad
  BROWNI R 24
that b. eminence; MILT 58
thing so very b. FROS 28
when as each thing b. MILT 44
when she was b., she was horrid.
  MOTH 28
bade: Love b. me welcome:
  HERB G 48
There b. me gaze, ARNO 30
badge: sufferance is the b. of all our
  tribe. SHAK 118
badly: is my heart not b. shaken?
  KAVA 26
Baffle: B. and dissipate your soul.
  LOWE R 35
baffled: b. hand with vain
  endeavour COLL 5

bafflin: your b. odd sobriety.
  BERRYM 7
bag: in the b. SMAR 6
Lays eggs inside a paper b.
  ISHE 1
strings the hangman's b.;
  RALEG 13
tasted the b. of the bee?/ O so
  white, O so soft, O so sweet is
  she! JONS 2
Bag-pipe: like B. drone BUTL 7
baggage: blind b. CRAN H 19
Baggot: Inquire for me in B. Street
  KAVA 16
bagpype: is thy b. broke,
  SPENS 48
bags: our b. & our brushes
  BLAK 87
bailiffs: watchful b. take their silent
  stands, SWIF 11
bairn: Marie Hamilton gangs wi' b.
  UNKN 187
teachit by a b. BOYD 1
bait: thou thyself art thine own b.;
  DONN 7
baited: with a b. hook, BRET 5
wounds of the b. bear, —
  SITW 12
baith: b. by bower SCOT WA 6
baiting: b.-place of wit, SIDN 14
Baked: B. and impasted SHAK 30
b. me too brown, CARRO 1
in the brown b. features
  ELIOT T 65
baker: South Wind is a b.
  LIND V 20
balance: b. of belief and art,
  KIRK 1
b. with this life, YEATS 71
fertile lack of b. FULL 4
motionless still b. WHITM 24
Balanced: B. and just LOWE J 22
Balboa: B. lies dead somewhere
  SCOT WI 2
balck: a fleet of small b. ships,
  BISH 25
Balcon: Le B. or Les Nègres/ of
  Genet, OHAR 5
bald: B. head, GRAV 1
b. spot in the middle of my hair —
  ELIOT T 80
b. street breaks the blank day.
  TENN 21
Chucky's old b. head RANS 19
fierce, b. and b., and short of
  breath, SASS 3
Flabby, b., lobotomized,
  LOWE R 32
log at last, dry, b., and sere:
  JONS 41
on b. men's hair CUMM 7
puffy, b.,/ And patriotic. OWEN 2
She is b. and wild. PLATH 60

Baldwin: walk among us, as B. has
  said. ALBA 1
bale: whole b. of isms LOWE J 4
baleful: amidst the b. glooms,
  THOMS J (1834–1882) 3
bales: with costly b.; TENN 75
Balkans: politics in the B., SIMP 4
ball: Above the rolling b.
  MERE G 8
after partridges, or a little rubber
  b.? LAWR 14
all/ Our sweetness, up into one
  b.: MARV 35
b. is lost and the mallet slipped
  MACN 20
b. loved Flick. UPDI 2
Blackberries/ Big as the b.
  PLATH 21
bowler and the b., LANG 2
flat Earth becomes a B. BLAK 33
play at b. UNKN 35
ply the b.: MERE G 9
Roll on, thou b., GILB 47
'Throw down the b., Jew's
  daughter. UNKN 133
wanton mask, or midnight b./ Or
  serenade, MILT 78
ballad: grand old b. of Sir Patrick
  Spence, COLE SAM 6
I met with a b., CALV 1
I'll sing you a new b., DICKEN 1
Ballades: B. by the score MAST 10
ballads: b. of the plains; LAND 9
balloonman: lame b. whistles
  CUMM 12
balloons: school-children rise like
  b. LOWE R 20
vowels rise like b. PLATH 64
Balls: B. tight in a tough hair sack
  SNYD 37
feathered b. of soot YEATS 97
lonely Earth amid the b. EMER 9
Balm: B. of hurt minds, SHAK 106
b. of woe, SIDN 14
breathed primeval b. MELV 22
trees wept odorous gums and b.;
  MILT 69
balmy: b. isle of Rum-ti-Foo,
  GILB 1
b. reed, MILT 79
b. summer evening, DARC 1
drops of this most b. time
  SHAK 229
We saw Thee in Thy b. nest,
  CRAS 4
Baltimore: flecked the streets of B.,
  RANDA J 1
bamboo: came by on b. stilts,
  LI PO 3
ban: end of the Chatterley b.
  LARK 1
in every b., BLAK 74

Pangur B., my cat,
  UNKN 202, 203
Spreading ruin and scattering b.,
  BROWNI E 2
banana: tincan b. dock GINS 33
Banbury-Cross: to B., MOTH 25
band: b. is playing somewhere,
  THAY 4
B. of all evils, SIDN 39
b. of brothers joined,
  HOPKINSO 2
b. of exiles HEMA 4
b. them to resist MILT 118
dog following a brass b. BARK 4
Gently with myrtle b., MILT 89
heaven-born b.! HOPKINSO 1
one sure b. Ties the whole frame,
  HERB G 15
rest in peace, our patriot b.;
  FRENE 4
soldier in that gallant b. GILB 15
Uncle's wedding b. RICH 2
bandage: multitude saw why she
  wore the b." MAST 3
bandages: Bearing the b.,
  WHITM 115
Bandite: savage fierce, B., or
  mountaineer MILT 3
bandrols: torn b. of Napoleon's
  war. BARL 1
Bands: adventrous B., MILT 61
gown, b., and wig, CARRO 13
love's soft b., SPENS 1
Striving against my swaddling b.,
  BLAK 73
strong as iron b. LONG 48
too many b.: BRID R 7
wrapped in swaddling b.
  TATE N 2
bane: Selfish, vain,/ Eternal b.!
  BLAK 62
thy b.; FANS S 1
bang: Not with a b. but a
  whimper. ELIOT T 48
shout and b. and roar and brawl
  BELL 13
banish: b. all offense CAREW 12
b. our anger forever FINC 2
b. the thoughts of day. LONG 15
Every thing did b. moan,/ Save
  the Nightingale alone.
  BARNF 1
faithful, b. fear, EMER 47
greater grief/ To be the less,
  SURR 11
sweet sleep no power can ever b.,
  THOMS J (1834–1882) 7
banished: b. him from better days
  ROBI 13
banishment: full circle of our b.,
  PATM 10
banjos: batter on your b., SAND 11
bank: b. by the wood WHITM 75

b.-dividing brooks, QUAR 3
fringed b. with myrtle crowned
  MILT 69
let down in that steep b. of clay.
  SYNG 5
regain/ B.-holidays, SASS 7
shop was just upon the b.,
  HOLM 10
True Thomas lay on Huntlie b.;
  UNKN 245
Under a brod b. LANGL 1
banked: gutters of the b. and staring
  eyes. WILB 13
Banker: B., engaged CARRO 14
BankerFather: Burglar! B.!
  DICKI 58
banks: Full to the b., TENN 95
king/ Of b. and stones KAVA 22
Leafy-with-love b. KAVA 1
O Brignall b. SCOT WA 23
walked on the b. GINS 33
Ye b. and braes BURN 15
Banned: B. for ever MACN 14
Banner: B. by turns and bugle
  woo: ARNO 39
b. in the sky; HOLM 17
b. with the strange device,
  LONG 21
Freedom's b. streaming DRAK 4
star-spangled b. yet wave, KEY 1
wing trails like a b. JEFFE 13
banners: b. flashing through the
  trees ARNO 39
B. yellow, glorious, golden,/ On its
  roof POE 21
Confusion on thy b. wait,
  GRAY 1
Fold up the b.! THOMP W 4
Pass, b., pass, ARNO 40
trumpets sound, the b. fly,
  BURN 49
banquet: Corpses are set to b.
  POUN 11
Nature's b. share: MARV 9
Prayer the Churches b.,
  HERB G 66
Spice his fair b. TENN 96
bans: b. laid, RODG 2
Baptized: B. with fairy water;
  MACN 5
bar: Alfred Lord Tennyson crossing
  the b. SITW 3
b. and its moaning. KINGSL 4
b. in the back, KENN 1
crossed the b. TENN 10
Faces along the b. AUDE 75
harbour b. be moaning.
  KINGSL 3
hell should b. the way." NOYE 7
no moaning of the b., TENN 9

thy picture's sight would b.,
  SHAK 202
treat if met where any b. is,
  HARD 31
Barbara: B. Frietchie's grave,
  WHITT 5
Fell in love with B. Allan.
  UNKN 38
Up rose old B. Frietchie WHITT 2
barbaric: b. pearl and gold,
  MILT 58
sound my b. yawp WHITM 73
barbarous: b. brine/ Whelms us to
  the tired world TATE A 5
b. to the royal Attic; RANS 28
by the b. king ELIOT T 122
barbed: mounting b. steeds
  SHAK 95
Barbourville: care of/ The B. Jail.
  UNKN 81
barb'rous: o'er her b. Foes
  JOHN S (1709–1784) 5
Bard: B. was weather-wise,
  COLE SAM 6
b. whom there were none to
  praise, COLE H 1
fate of simple B., BURN 60
From B., to B.,
  JOHN S (1709–1784) 7
learned b. or gifted child;
  GRAV 33
lover and the b.; BROWNI R 3
manners, of the b. EMER 33
O sightless b., LONG 30
voice of the B.! BLAK 66
bards: b. of old enjoyed in you!
  BLAK 111
B. of Passion and of Mirth
  KEAT 2
b. sublime, LONG 15
black and unknown b.
  JOHN J 5
bare: autumn wind laid b.;
  VERY 1
Back and side go b., go bare,
  STEVENSO W 3
B. ruined choirs, SHAK 215
b.-stript heart, WHITM 78
B. woods, SHEL 62
boundless and b. SHEL 50
Euclid alone has looked on Beauty
  b., MILLA 7
For neighb'ring Beaux to see it b.
  SWIF 14
laid b. The root of life, KIRK 1
lies b. to heaven BROWNI R 81
of joy quite b., WYAT 13
On the b. field — MUIR 7
On the b. platform. THOMA E 1
Sae black and b., BURN 40
see things b. to the buff
  STEVENSO R 16
trees turn b. SNOD 7

ugly, grisly, b. and thin;
　SOUTHW 9
with a b. bodkin?　LAWR 37
woodlands brown and b.,
　LONG 38
woods are b. and birds are flown,
　BRYA 32
Bareback: B. he rode;　WOOL 1
bared: b. snow and thy unbraided
　gold.　CAREW 12
culver on the b. bough　SPENS 27
Barefoot: B. boy,　WHITT 6
b. dervishes,　EMER 13
bareheaded, b.,　WHITM 62
Blessings on the b. boy!　WHITT 7
go b. and be warm　GIOV 2
bareheaded: b., barefoot,
　WHITM 62
barenesse: old December's b.
　SHAK 223
bargain: better b. driven.　SIDN 1
barge: b. and boat doth ride,
　TURB 1
b. That nobody roweth　UNKN 89
barges: b. drift/ With the turning
　tide　ELIOT T 138
bark: b. back,　SNOD 6
check that speeding b.　DUNB P 8
dogs b. at me　SHAK 96
moored their b.　HEMA 4
star to every wand'ring b.,
　SHAK 232
white their b.,　POUN 68
wood was gray and the b. warping
　off it　FROS 140
barking: cackling laugh or her b.
　cold　WALK 10
barks: b. of trees thou browsèd.
　SHAK 4
Creep back into their silent B.
　COWL 7
Helen, thy beauty is to me/ Like
　those Nicéan b. of yore,
　POE 44
barley: b. grew up out of the grave.
　HEAN 18
To see me thro' the b.　BURN 46
Barleycorn: Inspiring bold John B.!
　BURN 55
barn: b. shall harbour heaven,
　WILB 11
b.'s brown gable,　WHITT 33
Before the B.-Door crowing,
　GAY 2
burgeoning over the b.,　WILB 44
"Farewell to b. and stack and
　tree,　HOUS 28
midst of the b.-yard　TROW 2
set fire to the b. and burnt them
　all.　SOUTHE 2
To mend his b.,　SWIF 2
You are the baby in the b.
　PLATH 71

Barnaby: Poe, with his raven, like
　B. Rudge,/ Three fifths of him
　genius　LOWE J 5
Barnacles: B., mussels, water
　weeds—　MOSS 5
Barns: B. and garners　SHAK 162
spread, with b.　WHITM 9
Baron: B. of Barons,　UNKN 18
like a b. bold,　UNKN 60
barrel: B.-house kings,　LIND V 8
b. of salted herrings　WYLI 11
Beat an empty b.　LIND V 8
let the b. climb.　SIMP 2
Made lock, stock and b.
　YEATS 154
old b. with many a bung.
　KENN 2
Pour from the b.,　JEFFE 9
vinegar in a b.　HALL 4
barrels: Of the spraying b.
　KAVA 27
barren: among these b. crags,
　TENN 128
b. place and fertile.　SHAK 157
b. places where men gather
　HECH 11
b. way,　SHEL 33
Blown buds of b. flowers,
　SWIN 13
dull unfeeling b. ignorance
　SHAK 86
Let me not wander in a b.
　dream,　KEAT 57
lofty trees I see b. of leaves,
　SHAK 186
Love is a b. sea,　SWIN 26
makes her b. rocks　ADDI 2
unassisted heart is b. clay,
　MICH 1
wandering fields of b. foam.
　TENN 82
wayfarer by b. ways　ROSS D 7
weep b. tears.　SHEL 52
barrenness: nature in its b.
　WILLI 37
barricade: some disputed b.,
　SEEG 1
barrier: blessèd b. between day and
　day,　WORD 149
barroom: drivers in a b.
　WHITM 33
filled Joe's b.　DARC 1
barrow: depends/ upon/ a red wheel/
　b.　WILLI 28
bars: b. of Madras, Oregon.
　SNYD 16
breaks on the sheltering b.
　JOHN G 1
cocktail smells in b.　ELIOT T 105
iron b. a cage;/ Minds innocent
　and quiet　LOVE 5
key is in the b.,　GINS 32

lets and b.　MELV 17
Put gently up the evening B.
　DICKI 81
barstools: bottoms off b.　KENN 2
barton: see the oxen kneel,/ "In the
　lonely b.　HARD 33
base: b. as is the lowly plain,
　SYLV 1
b. contagious clouds　SHAK 51
b. On which thy greatness stands;
　WORD 115
For b. designs,　MAST 4
let b. clouds o'ertake me
　SHAK 198
Like the b. Indian,　SHAK 138
O'erhang and jutty his confounded
　b.,　SHAK 56
Other than b. and fetid:
　FROS 111
scorning the b. degrees　SHAK 44
with b. infection meet,　SHAK 222
baseless: b. fabric of this vision,
　SHAK 163
baseness: Some kinds of b.
　SHAK 160
baser: Man of b. Earth didst make,
　OMAR 1
basest: b. beggars　SHAK 74
bashful: b. young potato,　GILB 32
basin: bathing in a marble b.,
　LOWE A 8
bask: b., we two together.
　WHITM 65
basked: b. him in the sun,
　SHAK 15
baskets: b. bear　JONS 36
Basks: B. at the fire　MILT 23
bass: b. of heaven's deep organ
　MILT 39
small-mouth b. breaks water,
　LOWE R 1
basses: b. of their beings
　STEVENS 34
bastard: b. vile,　RALEG 5
Daddy, daddy, you b.,
　PLATH 33
rock my b. baby.　UNKN 208
Bastidides: B., on the contrary,
　POUN 65
bastions: fierce artificer/ Curves his
　white b.　EMER 44
bat: b. is born　JARR 1
b. That beats about in caverns
　WILB 30
black b., night,　TENN 93
bloodsucking b. or the rat or the
　stoat　MACN 15
flitting of the b.　MERE G 13
hideous little b.,　SHAP 13
I couch when owls do cry./ On the
　b.'s back I do fly　SHAK 166

owl is abroad, the b. and the
toad, JONS 16
where the weak-ey'd B., COLL 10
Bateman: Lord B. was a noble
lord, UNKN 316
bath: out from the b. SNYD 8
sore labor's b., SHAK 106
bathe: delighted spirit/ To b. in fiery
floods, SHAK 115
good wif was ther of biside B.,
CHAU 10
like the people to b. in me,
SMIT ST 6
young men b. WHITM 79
bathed: b. by the rising sun,
WHITM 107
b. every veyne CHAU 3
b. in her still garden,
STEVENS 34
We have b., BEDD 1
bathing: b. in a marble basin,
LOWE A 8
Beauty sat b. MUND 2
bathroom: b. in the free world!
DURE 2
bathtubs: b. and the washbasins
MAHON 1
batons: swapping b. back and forth
DICKEY 10
Bats: grinning in their sleep./ B.!
LAWR 3
swallows gave way to b. LAWR 2
toads, beetles, b., SHAK 157
unloose small b. and owls.
PLATH 59
batsman: b. thinks he's bowled,
LANG 1
batted: b. His eyes, JOHN J 2
battell: b. on the dragon blak,
DUNB W 1
Battels: Diseases, B., Inundations.
BUTL 8
Batter: B. my heart, three-personed
God; DONN 8
b. on your banjos, SAND 11
b. the foe — ROON 1
feed oneself on b., CARRO 42
we b. our hands WILB 20
batter'd: dismasted, gray and b.
ship, WHITM 28
battered: b. bleak of brain GINS 9
b. kettle at the heel. YEATS 151
soul's dark cottage, b. and
decayed, WALL 4
battery: Boldly by b. besiege
Belgrade; WATT A 1
endless ride from B. GINS 9
battle: b. closes thick and bloody;
BURN 49
b.-flags were furled TENN 76
b.-queen of yore, RANDA J 1
b.-smoked flag, with stars
eclipsed, MELV 16

B. the world TATE A 7
b. to the strong, BIBL, O.T. 1
Ben B. was a soldier bold,
HOOD 4
drunk delight of b. with my
peers, TENN 130
(Eighteenth b., and he sixteen!)
TICK 1
great b. lost, YEATS 87
Heave in wild wreaths the b.-
shroud, DRAK 2
implements of b. CULL 14
In the lost b., SCOT WA 20
Joshua fit de b. ob Jerico,
UNKN 158
like troops in a b.,
STEVENSO R 8
Love, power, the huzza of b.
LAYT 1
pages of her b. years,
THOMP W 4
thundering line of b. GREN 4
We shall renew the b. ARNO 15
win the b. LUTH 3
battled: Dream of b. fields
SCOT WA 9
battles: b. long ago: WORD 140
battleshield: Hacked the b.,
UNKN 20
batt'ring: wrackful siege of b. days,
SHAK 212
bauble: Pleased with this b.
POPE A 81
Baucis: bear/ My breathless B.
OVID 7
Here B., there Philemon, SWIF 2
Baudelaire: if one were B. BISH 7
baul'd: gifted most that loudest b.
DRYD 19
bawd: my old b. is dead?
YEATS 72
bawds: b. and whores do churches
build, SHAK 76
bawdy: touched the b. strings
STEVENS 38
bawl: b. your name! SLES 2
bay: brought to b.; SCOT WA 13
call from the b., ARNO 9
Echo beyond the Mexique bay."
MARV 2
Here, in this little B., PATM 6
McClellan's men/ Here stood at
b.? MELV 15
neither laurel nor b.? ROSS C 18
some nameless b., WHITM 28
bayliffes: b. daughter deare,
UNKN 15
bayonets: b., mixed and crossed,
THOMP W 1
bays: b. burn deep and chafe:
SWIN 22
City nested in b.! WHITM 44

deck thee all with b.,
MONTROSE 3
green with b. POPE A 31
whiteness other b. LUCR 4
be: b. with us yet, KIPL 17
cowlèd churchman b. EMER 38
Depart, — b. off, — HOLM 1
expressions b. of inward evils.
GREV 5
if Love b. Love, TENN 15
if thou a livesman b. UNKN 166
Judge's bride might b.!
WHITT 16
Lucy ceased to b.; WORD 46
mothers' wombs the tiring-houses
b. RALEG 15
nor e'er again shall b. MACA 1
partings yet to b. THOMP F 2
To b., or not to b.: SHAK 39
we shall not b. LUCR 3
where he longed to b.;
STEVENSO R 21
beach: abraded by the b., PATM 3
Across the lonely b. THAX 1
b. at night, WHITM 56
b. hisses like fat. BISH 40
boat on the b. we flit — MILLA 4
down the b. we flit — THAX 1
left behind on the b. CARRO 16
saffron b., DAVID 3
beaches: pendulous auroral b., —
CRAN H 11
beacon: From her b.-hand LAZA 1
beacons: in vain the distance b.
TENN 79
beaded: b. bubbles winking at the
brim, KEAT 45
b. with dew SNYD 35
beadle: rascal b., hold thy bloody
hand! SHAK 81
beads: b. and prayer-books
POPE A 81
b. of surge, DAVID 3
his primer and his b., MUND 1
how many b. BEDD 12
beak: be eaten by that b. JEFFE 44
b. down my throat LA FO 2
His b. is focussed; BISH 41
his long b. LAWR 16
indifferent b. could let her drop?
YEATS 86
keen eyes/ serviceable b.
WILLI 31
Lightning showed a Yellow B.
DICKI 161
mud/ Flies from his hunching
wings and b. LOWE R 7
open to the blackbird's b.,
WYLI 12
beaker: b. full of the warm South,
KEAT 45
beaks: b. its cage. LOWE R 24

b. of cool feet   DOOL 4
b./ of fruit-trees.   DOOL 7
b. of inflexions   STEVENS 65
b. of innuendos,   STEVENS 65
b. of the Cyclades.   BYRO 51
b. of the morning;   WORD 6
b. of the night   JOHN J 4
b. of the woods,   MARV 32
b. passes like a dream?
   YEATS 121
b. purely loving   CAMPI 19
B., ripe, and calm, and fresh,
   DAVE 6
B. sat bathing   MUND 2
b. seems to nest,   NOEL H 1
b. she doth miss,   UNKN 191
b., size, and years, and wit,
   SWIF 21
B. so sudden   TOOM 4
B. stands and waits   FERL 2
B., Strength, and Discretion do
   man forsake,   UNKN 90
B. that shocks you,   POPE A 12
B. through my senses stole;
   EMER 19
b. to forego her wreath?
   ARNO 11
b. vanishes; b. passes;   DE LA 9
b., which is varying   MICH 3
B., wisdom and passion,
   MASE 5
b. with sorrow   DE LA 18
b. would be the same.
   TENN 101
b. of fruit-trees.   DOOL 7
b.'s brow,   SHAK 210
b.'s charming;   SCOT WA 1
b.'s ensign yet/ Is crimson
   SHAK 152
b.'s fire/ Inflame unstaid desire,
   PEEL 2
B.'s self she is,   UNKN 191
b.'s summer dead.   SHAK 227
blazon of sweet b.'s best,
   SHAK 228
body's b. lives.   STEVENS 37
Brittle b.   SURR 1
By mourning b. crowned!   TIMR 7
center of all b.!   OHAR 1
conceale no b. grace,   KYNA 1
dawning b. warms us so?
   WALL 8
Death is the mother of b.,
   STEVENS 57, 60
delve in b.'s lore   ROBI 16
deserv'd thy b.'s use   SHAK 185
desolate sinners/ Demented with
   b.! MACDONO 2
does not know/ Her b.,   CUNE 1
doth b. beauteous seem
   SHAK 206
earnestness/ That makes b.;
   JEFFE 6

Euclid alone has looked on B.
   bare,   MILLA 7
evil spirit, your b.,   DRAY 4
Except thy b., virtues, and thy
   friend.   FLET G EL 1
Fame to their b.,   CAREW 16
famous b. of dead women:
   MACL 11
fancy doth it b. make.   SUCK 5
flatter b.'s ignorant ear.
   YEATS 131
Fortune, honour, b., youth,
   CAMPI 29
Fostered alike by b. and by fear:
   WORD 93
game of athletic b.   RANDA D 5
Ghosts of B. ling'ring
   POPE A 129
Give b. back, b.,   HOPKINS 12
guess the b. been.
   HOPKINS 3
Helen, thy b. is to me   POE 44
Helen's b. in a brow of Egypt.
   SHAK 127
Her b. is her own.   CAMPI 6
her own increasing b.
   MACDONO 1
his spoil of b.   SHAK 212
homely b.   WORD 162
I died for B.   DICKI 37
I have perceived much b.
   OWEN 11
'I who was b.   DELA 7
in b. and decay,/ He came.
   SHEL 1
In double b.   PRIO 8
in her youthful b. died,   BRYA 9
innocence and b. born?
   YEATS 115
is there B. yet to find?
   BROO R 20
judge all b. vain;/ Wise, if too
   weak,   UNKN 74
lady young in b.   RANS 31
Life, force, and b.   POPE A 25
Lovers of b., starved,   POUN 50
Love's name, Or B.,   SHAK 228
no power yet upon thy b.:
   SHAK 152
none of b.'s daughters
   BYRO 64
of thy b. do I question make
   SHAK 186
On death and b.   LEWI 3
once the b. Abishag,   FROS 88
perfect b. of a sunflower!
   GINS 35
Proving his b.   SHAK 185
save b. the eternal —   WILLI 4
scent and b. both   AYTON 1
sense of law and b.,   CARRU 1
shadow of your b.   SHAK 205
She walks in B.,   BYRO 61

since she/ Was b.:   STEPHENS 2
smother up his b.   SHAK 51
Sorrow more beautiful than B.'s
   self.   KEAT 21
Sovran of b.!   GREE 4
Spirit of B.,   SHEL 30
Spirits of power and b.
   CAMPB R 4
spreads/ Unbounded b.
   THOMS J (1700–1748) 5
steel'd/ Thy b.'s form   SHAK 191
Such seems your b. still.
   SHAK 227
terrible b. is born.   YEATS 56
that's the b. of it.   DAY 10
thing of b. is a joy for ever:
   KEAT 4
thy b.'s field,   SHAK 185
thy brittle b. so deceives,
   FANS S 1
trodden b. like our trodden pride,
   JOHN H 3
True b. dwells on high:
   HERB G 36
true b. virtue is indeed,   SIDN 8
truth no b.?   HERB G 44
virtue may best lodged in b. be,
   SIDN 20
we b. call,   POPE A 35
where all thy b. lies,   SHAK 185
Beaux: For neighb'ring B. to see it
   bare.   SWIF 14
Beaver: B., that paced   CARRO 15
his B. Hat.   LEAR 13
Hunting b.,   TAYL B 1
wool of the b.,   JONS 2
bebby: Got no need, b.,
   BROWN S 3
lady rocks, b.,   BROWN S 2
became: b. a lamb.   SCHW 1
I b. tired and sick,   WHITM 111
soon b. like brothers   GILB 11
beckoning: jack-muh-lanterns b.
   HAYD 19
becks: Nods and b., and wreathèd
   smiles,   MILT 20
become: b. of all the gold
   BROWNI R 79
fictions only and false hair/ B. a
   verse?   HERB G 44
mimes b. its food,   POE 32
poem whose words b. your
   mouth   OHAR 11
Stronger by weakness, wiser men
   b.   WALL 4
such as she would b.   FROS 50
becomes: b. The throned monarch
   SHAK 123
map b. their window   SPEND 4
nothing so b. a man   SHAK 56
becomming: odd b. graces,   SUCK 4
bed: Ample make this b.   DICKI 3
b. and board,   DAY 1

rector, the midwife, the sexton, the agent for b. PLATH 11
secretary of b. PLATH 12
swarm of b. CHAU 71
swarm of b. in May UNKN 235
yellow b. in the ivy-bloom, SHEL 51
Beeth: B. hevy again, CHAU 118
B. ware, ye lordès of her treachery. CHAU 70
beetle: fond of b.-pie. CARRY 5
where the B. winds COLL 10
beetles: toads, b., bats, SHAK 157
befall: fair might ye b. WYAT 16
befallen: hatred for this misery b.; MILT 102
before: be as b., BROWNI R 85
b. God's throne WILD 11
b. my time SHAK 96
B. the beginning of years SWIN 1
forth I march, thou goest b.; BIBL, O.T. 64
look b. you or behind. ROBI 4
man has borne b.! LONG 25
paths which b. I writ. RALEG 11
pay as if not paid b. SHAK 195
peaceful child I was b. WHITM 67
ranged in columns b. me, WHITM 110
same as a month b., — WHITT 33
see him jump b. me, STEVENSO R 13
swims b. her eyes, WHITM 16
world was all b. them, MILT 108
befriend: first true merit to b.; POPE A 33
beg: b. a smile, HERR 46
b. death's pardon WILB 33
b. or borrow. CULL 16
b. pardon for him and for me." UNKN 164
b. the favor with a graveyard grin. DAY 8
began: before the light b., UNKN 257
universal Frame b.: DRYD 25
begat: Love closed what he b.: MERE G 13
beget: Fresh images b., YEATS 19
begets: rest that peace b. UNKN 301
Begetters: Our fond B., DRYD 1
beggar: b. may be liberal of love. UNKN 96
B.'s Rags, fluttering BLAK 6
beggared: b. all description: SHAK 5
beggars: basest b. SHAK 74
B. enjoy, GREE 1
b. have changed places, YEATS 65

lovely time of b.' luck— ADAM L 1
pays us poor b. in red. KIPL 30
When b. die SHAK 45
begging: b. at my gate. UNKN 77
b. I clutched childlike, WRIG R 1
When strawberries go b., WYLI 12
begin: b. over. FROS 13
b. to awaken WILLI 36
b. with a swelled head LOWE R 16
morning sees some task b., LONG 49
My tender age in sorrow did b.: HERB G 27
perfect health b., WHITM 74
slow, dark hours b., ROSS C 28
to change their ladies do b.), WYAT 3
waits for the world to b. MERW 9
winds b. to rise TENN 23
beginning: b. at his feet. BELL 10
b. is often the end ELIOT T 71
but is b. ever. PETRO 2
Lonely from the b. LI PO 1
mystery of b. SCHW 6
night is b. to lower, LONG 9
song, from b. to end,/ I found again LONG 3
to make an end is to make a b. ELIOT T 71
beginnings: b. of necks, KINN 18
new b., ARNO 26
begins: Nothing b., and nothing ends, THOMP F 3
our life b., WHITM 41
tract of time b. to weave/ Grey hairs upon my head. VAUX 2
begone: Well, b., b., I say, SIDN 31
begonio: quickly b." RICHA L 1
begorra: Ye haven't! Oh, b.! FRENC 2
begot: b. me, bred me, loved me. SHAK 68
B. of nothing but vain fantasy, SHAK 141
How b., how nourished? SHAK 120
Thou by old Adam wast b., BRAD 9
Vainly b., GREV 9
begotten: b. by despair/ Upon impossibility. MARV 6
begs: Physic of Metaphysic b. defence, POPE A 2
beguile: any cloud b. TASS 3
he would oft b. COWP 3
sleeps as may b. the night; MARTIA 2
what was there to b. DAY 7
beguiled: b. the world. BROO G 11

begun: b. our part of the fighting. WHITM 90
blotted what I had b.: HERB G 41
life's journey just b.? COWP 10
sensual strut b., THOMA D 41
beguyld: wonne with her owne will b. SPENS 17
Behan: Brendan B.'s new play OHAR 5
behave: How well did I b. HOUS 41
beheads: frost b. it at its play DICKI 4
beheld: joy/ And rapture so oft b.? MILT 97
behest: Corpses are set to banquet/ at b. of usura. POUN 11
Behind: B., a sealèd route, DICKI 116
cast my love b.: JONS 18
embracing from b., HOPE A 1
Farther b. THOR 5
feel b. Their backs, MASE 9
He followed—close b. DICKI 64
I, the rake,/ Coming b. her ROET 28
Leave not a rack b. SHAK 163
led his regiment from b. GILB 14
left b. her ain grey tail: BURN 56
look before you or b. ROBI 4
spanked my own b. SWEN 2
Spring be far b.? SHEL 47
they look b.,/ They hear a voice GRAY 15
true heart was left b.! HARD 7
Unloading hell b. him SASS 13
what it leaves b. WORD 19
Behold: B. the Atom—I preferred— DICKI 114
b. the Chimpanzee: HERF 1
b. the day-break! WHITM 75
b. the violet past prime, SHAK 186
b. these present days, SHAK 228
mayst in me b. SHAK 215
Mortality, b., and fear, BEAU/BASS 1
O mortal folk, you may b. and see HAWE 1
time's furrows I b., SHAK 190
your light shined never;/ Well is he born, that may b. you ever. SPENS 6
behowls: wolf b. the moon; SHAK 128
being: b. we call human, MOOR M 25
destiny, our b.'s heart WORD 101
divine property of her first b. MILT 4
independent b. in his day— BYRO 19

junk that goes with b. human
SNYD 49
little b. came: FRENE 7
out of b. AMMO 20
rare to be born a human b.!
SNYD 38
Source of B.!
THOMS J (1700–1748) 6
struggling and doing without and
b. colored HAYD 13
unknown modes of b.; WORD 97
Vast chain of B., POPE A 72
beings: basses of their b.
STEVENS 34
beleeve: b. no Paradice. KYNA 1
belfry: in the b. arch LONG 44
shouted through the b. tower,
LONG 18
white owl in the b. sits.
TENN 105
Belgrade: Boldly by battery besiege
B. WATT A 1
belie: b. Thy Soul's immensity;
WORD 77
belied: b. with false compare.
SHAK 237
immolation so b. SASS 12
belief: balance of b. and art,
KIRK 1
B. to regulate — DICKI 100
man's b. is bad, PRAE 2
superstition, like b., must die,
LARK 5
Thought can but share' B.
CLARK A 1
believe: b. in Christ and
Longfellow, CUMM 53
b. in you my soul, WHITM 77
B. not what the landmen say,
GAY 7
cannot b. by proof: SWIN 17
could we b. without? SWIN 17
do b. her, SHAK 238
he couldn't/ b. it CUMM 37
Kiss me as if you made b.
BROWNI R 37
Last of the people who b.!
ARNO 33
make the boy b. FROS 23
practice all that we b.: CHAR 1
We are led to B. a Lie BLAK 11
what I b. DRYD 18
wish/ I could b. it; MOOR M 38
believes: each b. his own.
POPE A 22
one at first b.? BROWNI R 46
Believing: B. where we cannot
prove; TENN 16
belilaced: b. cellar hole, FROS 42
Belinda: B. lived in a little white
house, NASH 15

B. smiled, POPE A 116
pirate gaped at B.'s dragon,
NASH 16
bell: b.! proclaim the hour."
LONG 18
b. tolled on thy burial day,
COWP 11
b.-cheeked Negro infantry
LOWE R 17
chapel's silver b. you hear,
POPE A 103
dead b., PLATH 36
Ding, dong, b. SHAK 121
dingdong, b. SHAK 156
great b. of Bow. UNKN 25
Great Paris tolled her b. SHAP 27
hear the tolling b. SPEND 14
In a cowslip's b. I lie; SHAK 166
Let the b. toll! — POE 29
mouth of a b. KIPL 2
noise of b. buoys, MOOR M 13
passes us each a b., SEXT 12
quick silver b. SHAP 1
straightway like a b.
STEPHENS 10
surly sullen b. SHAK 214
tingle his b. CARRO 17
Toll on, thou passing b.; BOLE 2
tolling his b. at noon, EMER 18
Twilight and evening b. TENN 10
warning ringing b. WHITM 101
Which is the b. SHAK 93
with the Inchcape B., SOUTHE 6
belladonna: enlarged by b.,
MERR 11
bellboy: winking b. knowing
CORS 4
belle: "La b. dame sans merci
KEAT 32
night of the Prairie B.? HAY 3
riding Kentucky B.; WOOL 4
bellies: b. bulge to the sun,
WHITM 73
bluegreen b. PLATH 22
hugging babies, kissing b.,
SNYD 8
Bellin': Zuan B. not by usura
POUN 10
bellowing: b. and neighing loud,
SHAK 125
bells: b., that kept the /hours
ELIOT T 150
b. break down their tower;
CRAN H 35
b.,/ Five b. SLES 5
b. I hear, WHITM 45
b. more loud and deep: LONG 12
b. of death do ring? UNKN 128
b. of Old Bailey. UNKN 25
b. of Shoreditch. UNKN 25
b. of St. Clement's. UNKN 23
b. of St. Helen's. UNKN 25
b. of St. Martin's. UNKN 23

b. of St. Peter's. UNKN 24
b. of Stepney. UNKN 25
b. of Whitechapel. UNKN 24
b. on earth did ring UNKN 9
b. on her toes, MOTH 25
b. on their ankles LIND V 12
b. or merry Lincoln/ UNKN 134
b. that sweetly ring, STANT 1
b. they sound on Bredon,
HOUS 27
church spire/ Opens its eight b.
out, MACN 22
Five b. coldly ringing out.
SLES 5
flock of b. MEYN 1
From the b., b., b., POE 10
Harmonious b. below,
HERB G 1
have cap and b.,' YEATS 20
heard the b., LONG 11
many b. down) CUMM 4
noisy b. be dumb; HOUS 27
Ring out, wild b., TENN 46
Ring out your b., SIDN 36
ring the b. of London town.
UNKN 23
sledges with the b. POE 9
smoking roofs, soft b., LONG 29
think of the Shandon b.,
MAHONY 1
thy b. of Shandon, MAHONY 2
towers/ Tolling reminiscent b.,
ELIOT T 150
belly: b., buttocks, and her waist
HERR 68
b. close to ground. TOOM 5
b., God send thee good ale
enough; STEVENSO W 3
b. of the grape, EMER 1
B., shoulder, bum, YEATS 100
broad face and a little round b.,
MOOR C 4
door of her b. LAWR 21
Dragging its slimy b.
ELIOT T 130
fits a little b, HERR 38
Frog's b. distended KIZE 1
God's b.-scratcher, PURD 1
great b. JONS 32
large in the b. STAF 2
make room for the bouncing b.,
JONS 26
No b. and no bowels, RANS 34
Rests on his b. in the mud;
ELIOT T 36
tight b. of the dead SHAP 15
Upon my b. SHAP 26
Water inflated the b. FULL 3
belong: b. to other nations,
GILB 20
Freedom! if to me b. WHITT 10
belonging: every atom b. to me
WHITM 73

When and where likes me b., MILT 109

worst and the b. POE 11

would Heaven seem b.? BROWNI R 42

bestial: Among the b. herds to range, MILT 78

be/ B. oblivion, SHAK 35

b. decay, PRIN 1

b. strength PRIN 1

creature, naked, b., CRAN S 3

on the b. floor. YEATS 92

bestials: collapse of b., idols. BROO G 14

bestowed: pride b. on all, POPE A 79

bestrid: legs b. the ocean; SHAK 7

Bet: B. is to be wedded than to brinne. CHAU 89

betake: Whither shall I b. me, MILT 101

beter: chyld in Bedlem born is b. than we alle.' UNKN 213

beth: Where b. they biforen us weren, UNKN 287

Bethink: Malvern Wood/ B. itself, MELV 16

Bethlehem: holy Child of B.! BROO P 7

O little town of B., BROO P 3

Slouches towards B. YEATS 136

betide: no new wonder may b., YEATS 121

betraies: b. poore lovers. MARL 4

Betray: B., kind husband, Thy spouse DONN 52

b. more men. SHAK 137

betraying me, I do b. SHAK 243

Eternal smiles his emptiness b., POPE A 10

finds too late that men b., GOLD 9

Nature never did b. WORD 37

thoughts that please me less and less b. me. GREV 3

betrayal: forget cruelty and past b., GRAV 43

betrayed: b. my libertie? SIDN 15

sin hath b. DONN 33

skin has b. me LORD 4

betraying: b. me, I do betray SHAK 243

keys b. HERR 7

Betsy: Sweet B. from Pike. UNKN 236

better: banished him from b. days ROBI 13

b. angel is a man right fair, SHAK 240

b. bargain driven. SIDN 1

b. gone to the gallows. UNKN 151

b. not to sin at all, NASH 11

b. swimmer BYRO 44

b. than his crown; SHAK 123

can man die b. MACA 3

doth make man b. be, JONS 41

find that b. way! POPE A 128

For b. or worse, GOGA 1

greatly the b. for NASH 18

It is still unripe,/ B. wait awhile; ROSS C 26

likely to go b. FROS 13

love thee b. after death. BROWNI E 6

march in ranks of b. equipage: SHAK 196

mother needs to be b., WHITM 17

poets b. prove, SHAK 196

sang far b. than you knew; JOHN J 7

Tempteth my b. angel SHAK 240

Theirs was the b. right — FROS 125

they are b., painted — BROWNI R 25

virtue hath this b. lesson taught, SIDN 40

warranted no b., LARK 16

we are no b. for it, SEXT 13

will soon be b. WHITM 16

bettering: b. of the time, SHAK 196

earth was b. slowly HARD 10

Betty: B. from her master's bed had flown, SWIF 10

Wee image of my bonnie B., BURN 43

betumble: showers b. the chestnut HARD 49

Between: B. a sleep and a sleep. SWIN 2

B. the stumps: SNYD 41

B. yourself and me. CARRO 4

cool blade/ Severs b. coolness, apple-rind TOML 2

dies b. three cannibals. SHAP 16

indifferent judge b. the high and low; SIDN 14

lay b. Us, MONTA 1

lives contentedly b. HORA 6

mammoth rests b. his cyclonic dramas. SAND 15

What is it then b. us? WHITM 20

betwixt: b. Heaven and Charing Cross. THOMP F 11

b. Nature and Art: PRIO 2

one night went b. CAMPI 12

bevere: Flaundryssh b. hat, CHAU 21

bewail: b. the woeful case SURR 5

B. thy falsehood, MILT 112

bewailest: Love! who b. SHEL 90

beware: b., my lord, of jealousy! SHAK 134

B. the awful avalanche!" LONG 22

B. the dead. OLSO 16

B. the Fury of a Patient Man. DRYD 1

"B. the Jabberwock, CARRO 35

B. The soft-voiced owl, HILL G 3

opposed may b. of thee. SHAK 23

beweep: b. my outcast state, SHAK 194

bewildered: nourishing in thy b. brain ARNO 18

bewinged: angel throng, b., bedight/ In veils, POE 30

bewitch: more b. me HERR 8

bewitching: magical b. hour SANC 1

your more b., HERR 35

bewrayest: thou b. murder alway!/ Murder will out, CHAU 70

beyond: accounting/ b. the account: AMMO 4

B. all dreams DE LA 7

b. death/ Bridgeport, Ohio. WRIG J 3

b. his control, BISH 38

b. the plain LANIE 5

b. the starres HERB G 68

fire b. the language of the living. ELIOT T 64

grass b. the door, ROSS D 8

sterile sands and the fields b., WHITM 62

swiftly leaping b. them, WHITM 63

Bible: B. chopped and crucified LOWE R 49

bibles: head more than churches, b., WHITM 74

Puffs, powders, patches, bibles, billet-doux. POPE A 114

bibs: b. before our eyes, WRIG E 1

milk-stiff b., MERR 10

bickering: b. brattle! BURN 62

bicycle: curate passed on a b. KAVA 8

messenger's b., RANS 27

bid: b. me take love easy, YEATS 50

b. the Muse to pack, YEATS 151

b. the soul of Orpheus sing MILT 17

they were b.; GILB 5

To b. the father wipe his eyes SHAK 61

bidding: double dead: going, and b. go. DONN 23

bide: goo where you do b.; BARNE 2

bides: City b. the foe. TIMR 1

bideth: naught now b. CRAN H 38

bids: b. afflicted worth retire to peace. JOHN S (1709–1784) 21

b. her navies, LOWE J 14
B. spheres and atoms VERY 4
fairy queen B. you awake,
  CAMPI 3
Our Maker b. increase, MILT 77
Star that b. the Shepherd fold,
  MILT 8
sting that b. BROWNI R 73
bier: b. and the shroud — KNOX 3
Borne on the b. SHAK 186
In sorrow by thy b. BRYA 5
lay down the bigly b.,
  BROWN A 1
on Stonewall's b. WHITT 5
yon drear and rigid b. POE 29
your cradle, your home, and your
  b. SHEL 90
bifalle: aventures that whilom han
  b. CHAU 6
biforen: Where beth they b. us
  weren, UNKN 287
big: Bert, the b.-foot, SYNG 3
  b., dizzy mountains SERV 12
  b. picture of K. Marx SNYD 43
  B. Rock Candy Mountains.
  UNKN 26
  Blackberries/ B. as the ball
  PLATH 21
  City of the B. Shoulders: SAND 3
  eyes b. love-crumbs, CUMM 51
  quite as b. for me, BANG 2
  roller of b. cigars, STEVENS 9
  shining B.-Sea-Water, LONG 40
  world and life's too b.
  BROWNI R 29
  you are b. for you." BANG 2
bigamy: b., sir, is a crime.'
  LEAR 20
bigger: name the b. light,
  SHAK 157
  shape no b. than an agate-stone
  SHAK 153
bigile: sely jalous housbonde to b.,
  CHAU 53
bilious: was born b. BYRO 21
Bill: Buffalo B.'s/ defunct
  CUMM 10
  fellers call me B.! FIEL E 3
  headwaiter/ puts the b., CREE 15
  His b.'s so yellow, WOLF H 1
  my butcher's b. is due; GILB 49
billabong: camped by a b. PATE 1
  pass by that b., PATE 3
billboard: b. lovely as a tree.
  NASH 14
billboards: all is become b.,
  OLSO 10
billet: Puffs, powders, patches,
  bibles, b.-doux. POPE A 114
billeted: crass chance b. ROBI 33
Billiard: B.-marker, whose skill
  CARRO 13

billion: silver-thin/ Shatters into a b.
  fragments DAVIS 5
billow: Deep-trenchèd/ Green b.:
  STEPHENS 8
billows: Atlantic b. roar'd, COWP 1
  b. of my bood have ridden,
  MILLE V 1
  b. smooth and bright —
  CARRO 37
bills: b. to be paid, AUDE 17
  cannot meet my b.? GILB 48
Billy: B. boy, B. boy? UNKN 27
  dawning of B.'s last day. MELV 3
  heart to poke poor B.
  GRAHAM H 4
  way for B. and me. HOGG 1
  while his b. boiled: PATE 2
bind: all human ties that b.
  BANK 1
  b. another to Its delight,
  BLAK 58
  B. us in time, CRAN H 50
  confidence may b., HALE 2
  dead boughs that winter still must
  b., ROSS D 1
  love which us doth b., MARV 7
  sweet Chordage cannot b.
  MARV 10
  with her eyes my heart does b.,
  MARV 13
binding: b. with briars my joys
  BLAK 65
binds: b. the brain — MELV 10
  b. to himself a joy BLAK 47
  b. of thought/ into the hues,
  AMMO 3
bine: have gone to stall and b.,
  FROS 100
Bing: Poor old Jonathan B.
  BROWN B 1
Binnorie: By the bonnie milldams o'
  B. UNKN 29
biplane: O sinewy silver b.,
  CRAN H 9
birch: Better dressed and stacking
  b., LOWE R 48
birchen: come from b. bowers.
  POUN 67
birches: b. bend to left and right
  FROS 10
  swinger of b. FROS 14
bird: Beast, b., fish, insect!
  POPE A 72
  Beats the golden b. no more.
  MILLA 19
  B. came down the Walk —
  DICKI 12
  b. deprived of wings HARD 28
  b. in a b.-book, SNYD 33
  B. is on the Wing. OMAR 1
  b. of Araby, SKEL 8
  b. of dawning singeth all night
  long: SHAK 19

B. of Time OMAR 1
b. of wing MILT 85
b. trims her to the gale,
  EMER 47
b. with the head of an ass,
  BEDD 7
b. would cease FROS 86
b., you tragical machine —
  RICH 16
b.'s voice/ Speaking for all
  THOMA E 16
chilled/ The cooked b., KINN 16
crouched an outrageous b.
  HECH 2
cuckoo is a lazy b., UNKN 73
cuckoo is a merry b., UNKN 72
every b. its language, LONG 42
Everyone/ Was a b.; SASS 9
Go, said the b., ELIOT T 18
grey-brown b., WHITM 52
Icarian b., THOR 6
let no b. call. MILLA 11
like a b., it sits and sings,
  MARV 19
like a singing b. ROSS C 1
Lilac and star and b. WHITM 53
marsh b. that children dread.
  KINS 4
one b. singing alone to his nest,
  MERE O 1
our b.-bath RANS 25
pinnace, like a fluttered b.,
  TENN 116
Poor b., he is obsessed! BISH 41
repeat,/ Cuckoo, b., HOPKINS 5
resembles a b.'s foot SIMI 5
secular b. ages of lives. MILT 117
self-begott'n b. MILT 117
shall I call thee B., WORD 150
shy and hidden b. WHITM 47
sung with the singing b.
  ROSS C 27
that stoic b., WYLI 1
thou warbling b., BURN 15
throat of one b. JEFFE 17
what the caged b. feels,
  DUNB P 9
why the caged b. sings!
  DUNB P 10
widow b. sat mourning SHEL 23
wonderful b. the frog are —
  UNKN 110
young b. in this bush!' LEAR 16
Birdes: B., voyces, instruments,
  windes, waters, all agree.
  SPENS 32
blissful b. how they sing,
  CHAU 68
birdless: Treed with iron and b.
  HUGH T 3
birds: all o' the b. o' the sea.'
  MASE 10
  be as other b. FROS 86

blackening: Morning has been b., PLATH 76

Blackens: age/ B. the heart of Adam. LOWE R 24

blackest: b. brook of hell, SIDN 22
b. face of woe: SIDN 5

blackguard: Cupid is a b. boy SACK 1

blackguards: no accomplish'd b., BYRO 47

blacklegged: white b. egret, AMMO 6

blackness: b. and a strong glare BISH 44
b. veiled his dizzy eyes, SHEL 16
bouquet of b. DAVIS 1
in the sudden b. the black pall/ Of nothing, MACL 4

blacks: b. crackle and drag. PLATH 39
b., naked women BISH 22
B. rebellious. Crew uneasy. HAYD 8

bladders: swim on b., FLET/SHAK 3
swim with B. of Philosophy, ROCH 9

blade: beauty is a b. out of its scabbard. RANS 22
b. that opens the hole LEVI 2
b. Of grass KAVA 6
broad/ B. of his glance LAWR 25
cool b. Severs between coolness, apple-rind TOML 2
Hessian blood on the b." CLARK J 3
horrible poison b. BETJ 3

blades: b. of the grave-grass quiver, FINC 1

blak: battell on the dragon b., DUNB W 1

Blake: longe nyghtes b. CHAU 121
nosethirles b. were and wyde. CHAU 17
student of B. BISH 39

blame: b. lights due; MILT 99
B. not my lute. WYAT 2
himself to b., KIPL 26
Nor blame I Death, TENN 39
Nor praise nor b. the writings, POPE A 31
poor that gets the b., UNKN 219
Praise, b., love, WORD 134
sick eyes that b.; SNOD 15
They don't b. you — GILB 60
what they b. at night, POPE A 32

blaming: losing theirs and b. it on you; KIPL 7

blanched: hedgerow/ Is b. for an hour ELIOT T 62

blanching: b., vertical eye-glare BROWNI E 1

bland: b. smile from these sages; GILB 59
B.-mannered, asking PLATH 66

blank: bald street breaks the b. day. TENN 21
b. confusion! true epitome WORD 109
gaze b. and pitiless YEATS 135
moon stands b. above; HOUS 64
Pain has an element of b. DICKI 117
solitude/ Or b. desertion. WORD 97

blanket: brownish woolen b., WHITM 71
comrade I wrapt in his b., WHITM 107
folded my soldier well in his b., WHITM 107
Folded the b. well, WHITM 107
Gray and heavy b., WHITM 71
star-eaten b. of the sky, HULM 2

blankets: b. turned to snow. ROET 6
wrapt in their b. ARNO 7

blankness: b. is the real thing strange. EMPS 11

blare: b. of the cloud-trumpets, WHITM 6

blaspheme: b. down the stations of the breath THOMA D 37

blasphemies: Blessing turned to b., UNKN 170

blast: b.-beruffled plume, HARD 18
b. of triumph o'er thy grave. BRYA 4
b. of war blows in our ears SHAK 56
on the autumnal b. LONG 29
piano's martial b. Rouse the Echoes of the Past, GILE 43
shelter from the stormy b., WATT I 2
wert thou in the cauld b., BURN 39

Blasted: winds/ B. my infant buds, VAUG 18

blasts: b. denote/ I am nearing the place, BROWNI R 68
b. the roots of trees THOMA D 22
sudden b. or slow decline JOHN S (1709–1784) 2

blaw: airts the wind can b. BURN 41

blaz'd: Eyes/ That sparkling b., MILT 53

blaze: b. Insufferably bright. MILT 97
bright b. of Autumn's equinox. WALK 11
hair ever b.,/ In the sun, ROET 60

heavens themselves b. forth SHAK 45
Helpe me to b. Her worthy praise SPENS 52
next b. Of the world, the universe, SNYD 47
warm them at the wood-fire's b.! WHITT 29

blazed: What b. ahead of you? HEAN 21

blazes: b. high, but quickly dies, SACK 1

blazing: blackamoor to bear your b. tail. STEVENS 2
natural shapes b. unnatural ROET 32

blazon: b. of sweet beauty's best, SHAK 228
this eternal b. SHAK 26

bleach: b. their summer smocks, SHAK 100

bleached: b. and dry. THAX 1
b. by Irish weather MOOR M 37

bleak: battered b. of brain GINS 9
b. and bonio! RICHA L 1
b. mountains smile. ADDI 2
b. sea-beach, LONG 52
Unhappy, eagle wings and b., JEFFE 11

Blear: B. eyes fallen from blue, RANS 5

bleat: b. the one at th' other. SHAK 178
my lungs could b. like butter'd pease; UNKN 194

bleating: Naked and b. LUCR 5

bleats: b. articulate monotony, STEPHEN 4

bled: fought and b. HOPKINSO 1
put the poison. It scarcely b., RANS 19
Scots, wha hae wi' Wallace b., BURN 47

bleed: baby that I b. SEXT 1
Crucified maun b. MACDI 4
lay mee downe and b. a-while UNKN 225

bleeding: b. drops of red, WHITM 45
b. hearts around him flowed, BEHN 1
b. to death of time GRAV 4
left our bosoms b.? CAMPB T 7
Lily and b.-heart and rose, JUST 4
pageant of his b. heart? ARNO 35
pale b. lips MONTA 5
Song of the b. throat, WHITM 47
torn and b. hearts DUNB P 12

bleeds: evil moon b. drops of death. WALK 12

field rat, startled, squealing b.,
  TOOM 5
heart that b., CULL 4
bleezing: ingle, b. finely, BURN 52
blemishe: No mortall b. may her
  blotte. SPENS 54
blend: b. the turrets and shadows
  POE 12
blended: really b. into one;
  WHITM 35
blends: flowing bends and b. of
  sight: AMMO 3
bless: at hand to b.;/ Ills have no
  weights, LYTE 2
b. the quest — CRAN H 46
b. their swimming SMIT ST 6
b. with a benison SITW 3
Curse, b., me now with your fierce
  tears, THOMA D 12
Evil will b., EMER 50
Gawd b. this world! KIPL 21
God b. my babe, and lullaby
  BRET 3
soothe and b.!/ What hope of
  answer, TENN 37
sweep low, o b. the roofs,
  OLSO 8
Though taste, though genius b.
  COLL 12
bless'd: b. kingdoms meek of joy
  and love. MILT 32
b. the Abbot of Aberbrothok.
  SOUTHE 5
it is twice b.; SHAK 123
blesse: b. this land UNKN 63
blessed: b. barrier between day and
  day, WORD 149
b. bond of board and bed!
  SHAK 16
b. is the man that trusteth
  BIBL, O.T. 44
b. Land of Room Enough
  VAN DY 3
b. Loadstone QUAR 2
B. rage for order, STEVENS 19
b. sacrifice be mine,
  HERB G 8
b. sight to see FANS C 1
b. structures, plot and rhyme —
  LOWE R 42
b. sunny day: BRET 5
b. their lucky stars GILB 42
b. them unaware: COLE SAM 36
b. to have seen — DICKI 94
came Our B. Lady, UNKN 49
curtain'd with a b. dearth
  ROSS C 21
draw me to her in the b. place!
  PETRA 6
every b. shape we know.
  SHAK 205
punctual rape of every b. day,
  WILB 24

that b. mood, WORD 30
This b. plot, this earth, SHAK 88
Blesses: B. without obliging
  DEVL 2
blesseth: b. him that gives
  SHAK 123
blessing: b. of Earth is toil.
  VAN DY 5
B. turned to blasphemies,
  UNKN 170
Ceres' b. so is on you. SHAK 162
drench their heads in b.: SNOD 8
fathers are a b., UNTE 2
Honor, riches, marriage b.,
  SHAK 161
prophetic b. — Be thou dull;
  DRYD/TATE 2
Blessings: B. on the barefoot boy!
  WHITT 7
B. on thee, WHITT 6
b. thy free bounty gives
  POPE A 127
glass of b. standing by,
  HERB G 61
Juno sings her b. SHAK 161
blest: always To be b.: POPE A 65
B. be the Architect, HERB G 16
b. by everything, YEATS 48
B. with each talent, POPE A 6
b. with perfect rest, VAN DY 5
Kings may be b., BURN 53
most worthy to be b. WORD 80
one transferred to the b.;
  SHAP 12
Too b. with any one WORD 23
Virgin b. MILT 41
blew: b. and were blown GINS 11
When breath b. back, DICKI 96
Blight: B. her brow SYNG 1
b. man was born for,
  HOPKINS 22
characters of death and b.
  FROS 37
smile in secret, looking over
  wasted lands,/ B. and famine,
  TENN 90
blights: b. with plagues the
  Marriage hearse BLAK 76
December b. my lagging May;
  COLE H 2
blind: all before is b., MASE 9
All but b. In his chambered hole
  DE LA 1
Although a poor b. boy! CIBB 1
bad licker that/ Almost made me
  b. HUGH L 11
b. and a common brown;
  WILB 36
b. and weeping bear SITW 12
B. as the nineteen hundred and
  forty nails SITW 11
b. atomic pilgrimage ROBI 33
b., blunt bullet-leads OWEN 13

b. date that has stood you up:
  JARR 10
B. fists of nothing, CRAN H 21
b. Fury with th'abhorred shears
  MILT 27
b. laboring roar, JARR 23
b. man's ditch. YEATS 47
b. man's mark, SIDN 39
B. mouths! MILT 29
b. of sight, MILT 116
b. seed all. MUIR 11
b. skyscrapers AUDE 74
B. to all of it all MAST 11
b. to Someone/ I must be.
  DE LA 2
b. us here MCCRE 3
b. wantons like the gulls MACN 2
b. was I to see ROSS C 17
brave sun/ Die b. JEFFE 43
By nature, reason, learning, b.;
  SWIF 4
cripple or b. they will ca' me,
  UNKN 113
Cupid b. did rise. LYLY 2
every man be b. DICKI 137
firelight of a long, b., dreaming
  story JARR 11
flesh had made him b.,/ Flesh had
  one pleasure GRAV 37
follows on a woman thro the fire,/
  Led by a b. BOYD 1
heart is a b. desire, SWIN 2
heaven wax'd b., SYLV 2
I am b., and dead, and stray,
  QUAR 4
land of darkness and b. eyes
  VAUG 13
living b. and seeing Dead
  SITW 10
living man is b. YEATS 46
Love is rather deafe, than b.,
  JONS 18
make their children b., SHAK 73
men than they more b., TRAH 9
Naked and b. and pale. JARR 1
not b. to Him; LANIE 1
old, mad, b., despised, and dying
  king, SHEL 27
shadows raced across the b.
  WILD 1
stunned, stone b., and deaf
  SHAP 16
thou Eye among the b.,
  WORD 77
voice a b. man dreams GARR 1
Walloping Window B.; CARRY 8
when b. sleep falls THOMA D 44
wretched, b. pit ponies HODG 1
you see, but your are b.; ROBI 4
your God is b. CHAP G 1
blinded: b. by the light, WILLI 21
b. in their rage, TIMR 4
b. man sees GRAV 21

B. they into folly run UNKN 185
b. with an eye; MARV 11
blindest: fondest, b., weakest,
THOMP F 10
Blindfolded: touch, quick, merciful/
B. me. MERR 7
blinding: ocean, multiple to a b.
oneness AMMO 11
blindly: Curled b. MUIR 6
rush b. on unto it, PETRO 1
blindness: b. to the future!
POPE A 64
joy and b. he shall know,
GREN 3
blinds: glow/ That b. ROBI 23
Blinking: B. out of silly eyes
HODG 3
blinks: b. and croaks, like a toad or
a Norn, WARR 10
bliss: All my life's b. BRON 12
b. As it RODG 3
b. in proof, SHAK 236
b. of solitude; WORD 25
B. was it WORD 111
cuckold lives in b. SHAK 134
drops and dews of future b.
VAUG 23
Eternity shall greet our b.
MILT 44
fled to b. or woe! COLE SAM 35
I wish you so much b., —
SIDN 25
In our arts we find our b.,
UNKN 203
mannès joy and all his b."
CHAU 67
mutual and partak'n b., MILT 6
my worldès b., CHAU 68
place of b. TRAH 2
promise of pneumatic b.
ELIOT T 159
shadow of thy perfect b. POE 27
some imperishable b."
STEVENS 57
such lively b. SPENS 28
To our souls' b.: KING H 3
trembling at the gate of b.;
CRAS 10
where ignorance is b. GRAY 17
blisses: Child among his new-born
b., WORD 74
blissful: before the b. hour
WORD 16
b. birdès how they sing, CHAU 68
b. cloud of summer-indolence
KEAT 41
down from the b. skies. TENN 84
blister: blotch and b., SYNG 1
blithe: b. earth die, JEFFE 43
b. Hexameters. GOGA 2
b. spirit! SHEL 69
Creation's b. and petaled word
CRAN H 51

kidlings b. and merry. GAY 1
should be b. and strong,
WHITM 37
this b. mood present, MELV 13
blithesome: meete for a b. age;
CAMPI 28
pledge of b. May, LOWE J 15
Blitzen: on, Donder and B.!
MOOR C 2
block: faked road b.? HEAN 21
labour was but as a b. TENN 108
woden b. where bones are
broken, SIMI 4
blocked: b. my eyes — DICKI 26
blockhead: bookful b., ignorantly
read, POPE A 22
blockheads: to such b. set my wit!/ I
damn such fools! — SWIF 5
blocking: Church b. the sun.
SPEND 15
blocks: b. with which we build.
LONG 5
blond: more b. than you. CUMM 18
blood: all kinds of b., SHAK 230
best of bone and b. UNKN 100
b. blooms PLATH 70
b. clots the tendrils PLATH 13
b. Come gargling OWEN 19
B. for our B.,' NEWB 2
b.-hot eyes TOOM 1
b. in the veins, SITW 8
b. jumps in the sun;
THOMA D 31
b. like water, GALT 1
b. of fathers, mothers, daughters,
sons, SHAK 30
b. of herbs, WHITM 96
b. that burns! BROWNI R 49
b. that freezes, BROWNI R 49
b. to make up the flood. JONS 17
b. we inherit. RANDA D 4
brand so drop with b., UNKN 85
break their b., MOSS 6
buried in flesh and b., JONS 25
busy tribes of flesh and b.,
WATT I 3
By b. we live, HILL G 4
clotted rags and b., WHITM 115
conjure up the b., SHAK 56
cool my b., CULL 11
creature of heroic b., HEMA 1
dense with happy b., LAWR 58
dews of b., SHAK 20
dung, guts, and b., SWIF 9
Epitaph in B. and Wounds!
MONTROSE 1
every atom of my b.,
WHITM 74
filter and fibre your b.
WHITM 74
flat on a sheet of b. OHAR 7
flavor of b., KINN 4
flesh and b. WHITM 77

flesh and b. so cheap! HOOD 13
freeze thy young b., SHAK 26
furious with b. Neoptolemus, at
his side TATE A 1
glories of our b. and state
SHIR 1
guiltie of True-loves b., MARL 4
He is merely flesh and b.
ELIOT T 36
he'll bring you b. BARL 1
her b. upon the snow, SARE 1
Hessian b. on the blade."
CLARK J 3
His b. upon the rose, PLUN 1
Hood my unmanned b.,
SHAK 149
hot condition of their b.;
SHAK 125
landless b. of Cain LOWE R 5
lay in his b. NOYE 8
Let the water and the b., TOPL 1
loud-tongu'd B. demands
Supplies, MONTROSE 1
martyred b. and ashes sow
MILT 36
massive b. moves LAWR 8
mastered by the brute b. of the
air, YEATS 86
measured b. BOGA 9
no wine like the b.'s POUN 62
nothing but our own red b.
YEATS 123
Odour of b. YEATS 118
poinsettia's red, b.-red in warm
December. MCKA 3
poison in the b. ROSS C 11
poison the whole b. stream fills.
EMPS 12
precious b. may not be shed
MCKA 1
priceless b. reddens
WHITM 115
red b. reigns in the winter's pale.
SHAK 181
red with b. will Xanthus be;
ARNO 15
Runs in b. down Palace walls
BLAK 75
scurry/ Of chemic b.,
THOMA D 16
sea contains/ the hottest b.
LAWR 57
see thy b. warm SHAK 185
Sell flesh and b. BYRO 32
shed her b., SHAK 137
shed my innocent light, my B.,
SITW 13
Sheds the syllabic b.
THOMA D 14
souls of b. POUN 59
such a b. sisterhood;
PLATH 21
swash of falling b., WHITM 92

swift tide of b. NEME 1
taints of b.; TENN 30
their b. dance ARNO 39
their loins filled with heart's b.
  DICKEY 15
their thin b. Pulse STEVENS 34
thicker than itself with brother's
  b., SHAK 34
this of thine own B. CRAS 11
token of the drops of b.
  UNKN 130
Vexing their b. MELV 10
warmly ran my b. TENN 95
wash this b. Clean from my
  hand? SHAK 108
When b. is nipp'd SHAK 101
wish thine own heart dry of b.
  KEAT 61
With stronger b., SHAK 178
Young b. KINGSL 6
bloodily: So b. hast struck?
  SHAK 42
bloodless: b. lay the untrodden
  snow, CAMPB T 3
corpse was b., LOWE R 37
no b. myth will hold. HILL G 4
Two b. wolves SHEL 63
bloodshot: eyes b. with tears
  SHAP 20
bloodstreams: b. of the veldt.
  WALC 1
bloodsucking: b. bat or the rat or
  the stoat MACN 15
bloody: battle closes thick and b.;
  BURN 49
b. leaves. FANS S 1
b. swords and armor CAMPI 16
him squealing b. Jesus HAYD 14
its b. close BRYA 6
rascal beadle, hold thy b. hand!
  SHAK 81
Wallowing in this b. sty,
  LOWE R 11
War's a b. game.... SASS 1
where's the b. horse? CAMPB R 5
bloom: bee/ Sits on the b. MILT 79
B. gradually out of reach.
  SNOD 4
b. in prison air; WILD 1
B. in these darkened fields
  MUIR 9
b. more sudden/ Than that of
  summer, ELIOT T 62
b. sae fresh and fair? BURN 15
b. to profit, TENN 39
B. well in prison-air; WILD 3
Bud and b. and go to seed;
  MILLA 18
flowers that did in Eden b.;
  FRENE 6
Full on thy b., BURN 61
heavy dews from b. OWEN 24

hung with b. along the bough,
  HOUS 38
its b. is shed; BURN 54
leaping tongue of b. FROS 119
look at things in b. Fifty springs
  are little room, HOUS 40
meadow's in the b., FOST 1
opening sweet of earliest b.,
  COLL 1
put forth a small b., WARR 10
smooth shall b. from the rough:
  STEVENSO R 17
terrible and splendid.
  RANDA D 5
Will it b. this year? ELIOT T 120
bloomed: in the dooryard b.
  WHITM 46
blooming: b. grace adorns
  DANI S 14
b. shame?' UNKN 219
every b. thing. KAVA 22
hyacinths are b. in bowls
  ELIOT T 108
Left b. alone; MOOR T 14
Lilac b. perennial WHITM 46
thy b. years. BRYA 12
bloomlets: grass-daisies' pink tiny/
  b. GINS 40
blooms: blood b. PLATH 70
b. a deathless flower, MICH 3
flashes of b. of war; WILLI 38
hawthorn b. the sweetest,
  HOGG 1
midst the gorgeous b. of May,
  BRYA 35
parting summer's lingering b.
  delayed, GOLD 1
red heart b. PLATH 74
Slowly the night b., DAVIS 1
blossom: Apple orchards b. there,
  MASE 14
b.- and the fruit-time:
  ELIOT T 57
b. bright with autumn dew,
  BRYA 31
b. in their dust. SHIR 3
b. or the bole? YEATS 13
b. that hangs on the bough.
  SHAK 166
break/ Into b. WRIG J 2
Even the night will b. as the
  rose. MASE 5
fair meek b. BRYA 9
imaginations b. KAVA 10
late spring no bud or b. shew'th.
  MILT 14
lime-tree is in b. LOWE A 7
Nip in the b. all our hopes
  MARV 32
No b. stayed away/ In gentle
  deference DICKI 42
rank tongue b. into speech.]
  BROWNI R 15

rejoice and b. SORL 2
seasonably/ leaf and b. uncurl
  LAYT 2
Stem end and b. end, FROS 4
Timely b., Infant fair, PHILI A 1
to delight in b., LEVE 24
transitory b. Of snow,
  ELIOT T 62
would not b. yet ROSS C 17
blossomed: Earth that b. SORL 2
till b. stalks KAVA 27
blossomer: chestnut-tree, great-
  rooted b., YEATS 13
blossoming: b. buckwheat fields
  WHITM 31
Hope, b. within my heart,
  BRYA 33
blossoms: America the plum b.
  GINS 3
bees/ dig the plum b. OLSO 17
B. of grief and charity MUIR 9
b. on a bough, DONN 41
b. touch the sky. WILLI 25
brooks, of b., birds and bowers,
  HERR 1
buds and b. like the rest.
  TENN 52
Fortune, honour, beauty, youth,/
  Are but b. dying;/ Wanton
  pleasures, doting love,/ Are but
  shadows flying. CAMPI 29
Spring b. and summer; ROSS C 30
whitethorn b., KAVA 7
yellow b. flourished HALL 3
blotch: b. and blister, SYNG 1
blotte: No mortall blemishe may her
  b. SPENS 54
blotted: b. what I had begun:
  HERB G 41
man will be b. out, JEFFE 43
Blotting: B. the sun SNYD 28
bloud: Saviours death did put some
  b. Into thy face; HERB G 20
blouse: Poe printed cotton b.
  KOCH 6
blouses: some are in b., WILB 23
blow: azure flowers that b.;
  GRAY 18
B., B., thou winter wind!
  SHAK 13
b.! bugles! b.! WHITM 7
B. him again to me; TENN 113
b. the gay Pantechnicon GILB 44
b. the horrid deed SHAK 105
B. the spirit-stirring harp
  GILB 43
B., winds, and crack your cheeks!
  SHAK 75
By ashen roots the violets b.
  TENN 51
Come b. your horn, MOTH 18
forbear the bitter b.; SARE 1
Hear the train b. UNKN 80

Liberty's in every b.! BURN 48
loud you bugles b. WHITM 3
low, breathe and b., TENN 113
old Triton b. his wreathèd horn.
  WORD 160
poppies b. Between the crosses,
  MCCRA 1
Remus, b. your horn!
  STEVENS 39
shrill you bugles b. WHITM 7
soon will b. us home HENL 2
strike a match and b. YEATS 69
there they b., LAWR 57
when the b. comes PATT 1
when will thou b.? UNKN 302
wild cataract leaps in glory./ B.,
  bugle, B., TENN 111
wind doth b. today, my love,"
  UNKN 292
winds b. north, WHITM 65
winds b. south, WHITM 65
winds shoreward b., ARNO 9
with a silver b.: THOMA E 4
blowes: Chill Sirocco b., BONH 1
blowing: horns of Elfland faintly
  b.! TENN 112
horns of glory b. AIKE 10
winds b. round them SPEND 8
blown: bee that now is b., BLUN 2
blew and were b. GINS 11
B. buds of barren flowers,
  SWIN 13
B. hair is sweet, ELIOT T 11
b. unto the worst SHAK 77
b. with restless violence
  SHAK 115
b. By winds of grief PETRA 5
brown hair over the mouth b.,
  ELIOT T 11
buds new b., BRAD 10
dust b. through the streets of
  Rome, MASE 8
exsufflicate and b. surmises,
  SHAK 136
flame is b. abroad LONG 20
musk of the rose is b. TENN 93
petals from b. roses TENN 84
rooks are b. about the skies;
  TENN 23
when the rose is b.? WOTT 5
blows: blast of war b. in our ears,
  SHAK 56
B. all the dust HERB G 16
b. at our backs, HENL 2
b. his nail SHAK 101
b. the citron grove, MILT 79
B. the wind to-day,
  STEVENSO R 1
cruel wind b. KUNI 1
fear/ worse than b. HAYD 24
hoarse wind b. coldly; ARNO 10
meanest flower that b. WORD 87
mercy b. the coals; SOUTHW 2

wild wind b. on the mountain-
  side. BRON 6
wind b. out, the bubble dies;
  KING H 5
wind that b. through me!
  LAWR 47
blubber: freeze it in b. KINN 3
kiss (like b.)'d NIMS 1
blubbered: b. is that pretty face!
  PRIO 1
blubs: necks of light b., BISH 22
Bludso: Jimmy B. HAY 3
blue: Above the b. snow. ROET 37
all through b. Monday? HAYD 13
at my sky b. trades,
  THOMA D 20
Blear eyes fallen from b., RANS 5
b. depth of the sky YEATS 91
b.-eyed men BONT 4
b., forked torch of this flower
  LAWR 4
b. horse that runs in the plain
  MOMA 3
b. light/ Shed by a tinted
  window. DICKEY 20
b./ objects of the world TATE J 1
b. promontory SHAK 9
b. veined unconscious girl
  GINS 39
daisies pied and violets b.,
  SHAK 100
dividing and indifferent b.
  STEVENS 56
dragonfly/ Hangs like a b. thread
  ROSS D 4
feet that were b. with cold,
  OSUL 2
grappling in the central b.;
  TENN 75
hands are b., LEAR 9
heaven's own b., BRYA 31
I wear the b.; GRAHAM R 1
Lilacs,/ False b., LOWE A 1
Little Boy B., MOTH 18
Little Boy B. Kissed them and
  FIEL E 6
Little Boy B.,/ Since he kissed
  them FIEL E 7
little tent of b. WILD 1
long as skies are b., SHEL 2
Love and tears for the B.; FINC 2
my eyes are b.; ROSS C 10
my eyes were b., LAND 12
October's bright b. weather.
  JACK 1, 2
pink and b. Of the sky LAWR 51
plays a b. guitar. STEVENS 23
prospects all look b. GILB 49
Scarlet, and b., and snowy white,
  WHITM 14
sheer b. milken dreaminess
  KINN 15
sleek/ B. plums WYLI 12

stars turn slowly/ in the b. foil
  TATE J 2
"Step into my ferry-boat,/ Be they
  black or b., ROSS C 10
Up in the air so b.?
  STEVENSO R 18
wings were b., LEAR 2
your eyes so b.?/ Out of the sky
  MACDONA 1
bluebells: bottle with b., PATM 3
Faint oxlips; tender b. SHEL 59
blueeyed: (a yearning nation's b.
  pride) CUMM 16
your b. boy CUMM 11
Bluegrass: back in the old B.
  WOOL 4
bluegreen: b. bellies PLATH 22
blueness: you b. of joy, SHAP 5
Blues: B. echoed through his head.
  HUGH L 19
blunder: frae monie a b. free us
  BURN 58
blundering: learning and b. people
  SAND 14
blunt: blind, b. bullet-leads
  OWEN 13
b. as a Celtic cross, HEAN 15
b.-faced ignorant one GUNN 1
b. it into a ninth, BROWNI R 5
b. thou the lion's paws,
  SHAK 189
blur: b. and slip, NIMS 1
b. no whisper, LAWR 48
blurred: Lampshine b. WILB 44
blush: a b. of shame, WHITT 3
b. tinged the upper sky,
  EMER 51
decked with a b. of honour,
  DANI S 9
flower is born to b. unseen,
  GRAY 10
Men saw the b. DUNB P 1
Night woke to b.; DUNB P 1
Roses do b. NOEL H 2
blushes: b. of the bride.
  BEAU/FLET 4
blushful: true, the b. Hippocrene,
  KEAT 45
blushing: Religion b. POPE A 2
Short is the glory of the b. rose,
  DANI S 6
bluster: fierce as storms that b.
  GAY 1
Blynken: Wynken and B. FIEL E 9
Boanerges: neigh like B. DICKI 56
boar: b. trampled down in ivy
  time. GRAV 35
board: bed and b., DAY 1
blessed bond of b. and bed!
  SHAK 16
headlong from on b., COWP 1
soul on b. but me,
  STEVENSO R 6

Your perfect b. JOHN H 4
your poppy b. DAVIS 2
Bog: B. is dood, SMIT ST 3
To an admiring b. DICKI 83
Bogan: Major B.'s face TATE A 10
bogholes: b. might be Atlantic
    seepage. HEAN 3
Bogs: Rocks, Caves, Lakes, Fens, B.,
    Dens, MILT 61
boiled: while his billy b.: PATE 2
boiling: b. up in the ground,
    RUKE 1
dark abyss, whose b. gulf
    MILT 62
fountains of the b. stars, JEFFE 4
In the b. squares, MAHON 5
boistous: b. winds did beat/ Their
    ships, SURR 7
bold: as wise as b., SHAK 119
Ben Battle was a soldier b.,
    HOOD 4
b. peasantry, their country's
    pride, GOLD 3
b. Sir Lancelot. TENN 63
cook and a captain b., GILB 55
like a baron b., UNKN 60
Modestly b., and humanly severe:
    POPE A 24
strange love grow b., SHAK 149
to whom my satire seems too b.:
    POPE A 87
wine-flushed, b.-eyed boys,
    MCKA 5
bolder: b. note than this POE 28
Boldly: B. by battery besiege
    Belgrade; WATT A 1
b. stood alone; SWIF 24
like a Host — 'Come in'/ I b.
    answered — DICKI 162
Ride, b. ride," POE 19
bole: blossom or the b.? YEATS 13
bolt: next bright b. may fall.
    GRAV 43
swift its b. than lightning
    THOR 5
Bolted: B. against me. COWP 15
b. on thir heads. MILT 117
Cross-barred and b. fast, MILT 68
bolts: b. of bones, MARV 11
bombardment: fury of aerial b.
    EBER 2
bombast: met'phor in the b. way,
    COWL 9
bombers: beneath a b.' moon
    BOWER 1
b. named for girls, JARR 15
bombs: b. bursting in air, KEY 1
dropping b. on Rome, LEWI 1
Bonaparte: Wellington thrashed B.,
    GILB 24
bonbon: b. mottoes GILB 12
bond: Adam lay y-bounden,/
    Bounden in a b.; UNKN 1

blessed b. of board and bed!
    SHAK 16
b. unknown to me/ Was given,
    WORD 103
tied/ By a chance b. THOR 1
bondage: b. and restraint;
    SURR 11
B. is hoarse SHAK 143
dusty b. into luminous air.
    MILLA 8
free love with b. bound.'
    BLAK 62
bondmen: Chains of b. BONT 9
bonds: b. in thee are all
    determinate. SHAK 219
Speak against b. POUN 25
springs as broke from b.,
    MILT 86
bone: best of b. and blood.
    UNKN 100
b. by infant b. CRAN H 26
b. choked a wolf LA FO 1
b. of thy b., BRAD 11
b.-crushing waterfall —
    LOWE R 47
bracelet of bright hair about the
    b., DONN 49
cheat fond death of all but b.
    DAY 2
contention was our only b.
    CREE 1
Death's a sad b.; SEXT 17
Dove-note, b. marrow, deer dung,
    KIZE 1
error bred in the b. AUDE 77
fish scale, shale dust, b. SNYD 22
get her poor dog a b.: MARTIN 1
marrow in the b. SITW 8
Mumbles a b., DE LA 25
rag and a b. and a hank of hair,
    KIPL 27
Staring from her hood of b.
    PLATH 39
straight/ To the shattered b.;
    PATT 1
through the b. LAWR 53
whip of cricket's b., SHAK 153
Zero at the B. DICKI 112
Boned: Gorgeously arrayed,/ B. and
    stayed. LOWE A 10
bones: Because our brains and b.
    ROBI 33
Bleach the b. of comrades slain,
    HOUS 43
bolts of b., MARV 11
b. Cry out in the long night
    LOWE R 38
b. didn't try/ The door; FROS 129
b., how they grind AIKE 12
b. of birth have cried,
    BEAU/BASS 4
b. of leading statesmen, BETJ 6
b. of weeds ROET 37

b. sang chirping ELIOT T 8
b. with dust shall cover,
    SHAK 196
break your b.: WILB 14
dead men lost their b.
    ELIOT T 124
deeper rituals of his b., SAND 16
dice of drowned men's b.
    CRAN H 1
Dry b. can harm no one.
    ELIOT T 151
freeze my b. around./ Selfish,
    vain,/ Eternal bane! BLAK 62
frost heaved your b. HALL 3
God said/ Shall these b. live?
    ELIOT T 6
good is oft interrèd with their b.
    SHAK 48
his b. are coral made;
    SHAK 156
his honored b. MILT 35
I knew a woman, lovely in her b.,
    ROET 27
Knight's b. are dust,
    COLE SAM 18
lightning of Lenin's b. MACDI 6
mocked the dead b. SHAK 97
No b. made, RODG 2
Now I am dry b. WRIG R 1
old b. live ROET 29
Old iron, old b., old rags,
    YEATS 29
peeped through by b. SPEND 3
pick the Bishop's b.; SOUTHE 3
pick the b. HAIN 1
Puritan marrow of my b.
    WYLI 14
Redman's b.; LOWE R 4
richer for your b.; RANDA D 4
royal b. BEAU/BASS 1
salted it down with our b.
    KIPL 31
shall these/ B. live? ELIOT T 6
stout fellows left their b. behind.
    DAY 7
stretch our b. FLET J 3
trim the year or strip its b.;
    MILLA 33
upon the b.; RANS 16
veins, in my b. I feel it, —
    ROET 5
whiteness of b. ELIOT T 7
woden block where b. are broken,
    SIMI 4
boneyard: Above the b. HECH 7
bonfire: autumn, like a b. of leaves,
    WYLI 13
Bong-Tree: where the B. grows,
    LEAR 11
bonio: bleak and b.! RICHA L 1
Bonnard: drawings by B. OHAR 5
bonnet: follow the b. of Bonny
    Dundee. SCOT WA 3

gaudy b.; SYNG 3
virgins, robed and bare of b.,
  RANS 35
Bonnets: maker of B. and Hoods —
  CARRO 12
Bonnie: B. George Campbell
  UNKN 37
By the b. milldams o' Binnorie.
  UNKN 29
for b. Annie Laurie DOUG W 1
o' b. Doon, BURN 15
there the b. lassie lives, BURN 41
Thou b. gem. BURN 59
Wee image of my b. Betty,
  BURN 43
bonny: b. holms of Yarrow!'
  WORD 165
follow the bonnet of B. Dundee.
  SCOT WA 3
he's b., UNKN 140
bony: gripped in b. vise HAYD 24
bood: billows of my b. have ridden,
  MILLE V 1
Boogaloo: I bedded/ down with Isis,
  Lady of the B., REED I 3
boogie: dirty b. with scorpions.
  REED I 5
book: Africa? A b. one thumbs
  CULL 6
body is his b. DONN 22
b. a churchyard tomb. KEAT 35
b. and volume of my brain,
  SHAK 28
B. By seraphs writ COWP 22
B. itself before me lies, EMER 40
b. of iambs and pentameters,
  LOWE J 5
B. of Verses OMAR 2
candle, with b., and with knell;
  SCOT WA 15
dumb-born b., POUN 44
fairest b. of Nature SIDN 20
from b. to book WINT 11
hides the b. of Fate, POPE A 63
I'll drown my b. SHAK 165
leaves of thy unvalued b.
  MILT 35
like a b., KIPL 20
living pages of God's b.
  LOWE J 16
man who never reads in brook or
  b.; KAVA 8
no Frigate like a B. DICKI 140
one b. about/ A b. SNOD 5
one light's language in the b. of
  trees. THOMA D 8
Open the b. BISH 34
page of the b. carelessly open,
  SEXT 18
read with joy, then shut the b.
  PATM 2
thy b. doth live JONS 43

bookful: b. blockhead, ignorantly
  read, POPE A 22
books: All saws of b., SHAK 28
B. are a load of crap. LARK 19
B. bear him up ROCH 9
B. from Boots BETJ 4
b. to you, daughter-in-law,
  RICH 17
b. will show:/ I reade, and sigh,
  and wish I were a tree;
  HERB G 5
borrow/ From my b. POE 35
Careless of b., WORD 51
collective nose in my b. POUN 34
eschewing b. and tasks, WHITT 7
far unlike his b. GREV 10
few friends, and many b.,
  COWL 8
his b. were read.' BELL 18
history b. have showed;
  GRAHAME 2
making many b. BIBL, O.T. 7
spectres in b., WHITM 76
walls of b. will deaden MACN 10
want of b. and men! WORD 22
boom: b. after my funeral,
  POUN 31
Boomlay, boomlay, boomlay,
  Boom," LIND V 9
b. of the tingling strings
  LAWR 31
boomlay: B., b., b., Boom,"
  LIND V 9
boons: b. expected,/ No contracts,
  RODG 2
boorde: at the cheerfull b.,
  SPENS 36
boot: aimed between the belt and
  b. SIMP 2
b. in the face, PLATH 30
bootes: b. clasped faire and fetisly.
  CHAU 21
booth: sausage and garlic b.
  SPENC A 2
bootless: my b. cries, SHAK 194
Boots: Books from B. BETJ 4
b. — b. — b. — KIPL 4
Drunk and asleep in his b.,
  STEVENS 5
heels of their b. FOOT 1
million b. in line, AUDE 79
bootsbootsboots: b. KIPL 4
Booze: B. and the blowens HENL 5
B. is law WELC 1
boozer: clown, the b., the fighter?
  MAST 6
bop: b.-cool/ice box cool LEE 3
Border: B., nor Breed, nor Birth,
  KIPL 3
death as a mere b. EMPS 4
sent our lads to the B.; ELLI 2
bordes: leve your b., WYAT 17

bore: affrighted air with a shudder
  b., READ T 1
b. me in the southern wild,
  BLAK 97
B. witness gloriously; MILT 118
Death is the fruit it b. ROSS C 8
Earth that b. SORL 2
hearse that b. thee COWP 11
love she b.? TENN 73
that bee/ Which b. my love away.
  HERR 30
that Byron b., ARNO 35
who b., 'mid snow and ice,
  LONG 21
borealic: In a b. iceberg came
  Victoria; SITW 1
bored: b. a hole in his head,
  KNIG 5
b. by a bee; LEAR 14
B. with the foolish things
  CAMPB R 7
leaves like b. hearts. PLATH 13
she is b. and tired, ELIOT T 136
boredom: Her b. is exquisite
  POUN 28
know what b. is: WILB 26
Bores: B. through his castle wall,
  SHAK 89
literature b. me, BERRYM 11
boring: b. meeting. AUDE 90
Life, friends, is b. BERRYM 10
born: all thy subject life was b.!
  COLL 7
bat is b. JARR 1
being human, b. alone; WYLI 5
better lord was never b.
  UNKN 79
blight man was b. for,
  HOPKINS 22
b. a woman MILLA 14
B. but to die, POPE A 78
b. but to smile and fall?
  BLAK 13
b. here from parents WHITM 74
b. hym weel, CHAU 9
b. in days ARNO 27
b. in other's pain, THOMP F 3
b. into that ancient sect
  YEATS 143
b. into the world alive, GILB 22
B. of Mortal Birth BLAK 85
B. of the sun SPEND 12
B. on a Monday,/ Christened on
  Tuesday, MOTH 26
b. out of my due time, MORR 3
b. to be and do, BROWNI R 7
b. to drill and die. CRAN S 9
b. to love freedom. JEFFE 41
b. to match the gale, WHITM 104
b. to rule the storm; HEMA 1
b. to the anglican order,
  MACN 14
both of us were b. anew. CART 2

bursting b. of May, BRID R 14
chopped-up cedar b. ROBI 50
dead b. that winter still must
  bind, ROSS D 1
Leafy the b. DAY 6
soul into the b. does glide:
  MARV 19
sturdy oak with broad-spread b.
  DYER J 1
under the apple b. THOMA D 17
woven changeless roof of b.:
  YEATS 94
bought: b. smile/ Of harlots,
  MILT 78
dearly b. SIDN 39
boughten: b. friendship FROS 90
boulders: spite of brambles and b.,
  LOWE J 4
bouncing: make room for the b.
  belly, JONS 26
Bound: B. and weary, BLAK 73
b. apprentice, UNKN 172
b. by vows and by promotion,
  GREV 10
B. each to each WORD 58
B. for the prize SHAK 217
b. in shallows and in miseries.
  SHAK 50
b. me straitly POUN 66
dropped things are b. to sink —
  MOOR M 13
few paternal acres b.,
  POPE A 107
fields around lay b. and hoar
  THOR 11
led forth and b. AUDE 81
let the young Lambs b.
  WORD 83
long-loved mistress Rhyme./
  Passion's too fierce to be in
  fetters b., DRYD 8
loosely b. FROS 102
man to double business b.
  SHAK 34
My services are b. SHAK 70
powers of darkness b. MILT 64
securely b. MUIR 4
ship that's westward b.
  VAN DY 3
slumber's chain has b. me,
  MOOR T 10
sweetheart and her husband b. in
  one. WALK 12
tyrant spell has b. me BRON 2
utmost b. of human thought.
  TENN 132
way unseen, the certain route,/
  Where ever b., VERY 4
boundaries: erected no b.,
  AMMO 5
bounded: b. into the air WILLI 1
bounding: as a b. hart fly home,
  WESL C 2

B. the land WINT 7
heart less b. at emotion ARNO 45
boundless: b. and bare SHEL 50
b. Godhead; COWL 12
b. universe/ Is Life — MCCRE 4
brass, nor stone, nor earth, nor b.
  sea, SHAK 212
Doubt's b. Sea, ROCH 9
from zone to zone,/ Guides
  through the b. sky BRYA 27
proud his name,/ B. his wealth
  SCOT WA 12
unshorn fields, b. and beautiful,
  BRYA 15
with b. pow'r I reign; SHEN 1
bounds: certain b. hold against
  chaos, DUNC 1
From vulgar b. POPE A 30
Revenge should have no b.
  SHAK 38
Soul and body have no b.:
  AUDE 55
thin Partitions do their B. divide;
  DRYD 2
bounteous: be b. still MILT 82
b. May, MILT 119
bounties: all their b. bring,
  MILT 11
Nature powre her b. forth,
  MILT 5
bounty: blessings thy free b. gives
  POPE A 127
give her b. to the dead?
  STEVENS 55
St Patrick's b., LAND 7
your b. doth appear; SHAK 205
bouquet: b. of blackness DAVIS 1
bour: twa sisters sat in a b.;
  UNKN 29
bourgeois: How beastly the b. is
  LAWR 13
bourn: from whose b. No traveler
  returns, SHAK 40
bourne: b. of Time and Place
  TENN 10
bournes: by a b. side; LANGL 1
bout: winding b. Of linkèd
  sweetness MILT 24
bovine: cow is of the b. ilk;
  NASH 5
bow: beauty like a tightened b.,
  YEATS 101
bent b. and his arrows keen,
  MUND 1
b. and accept the end FROS 93
b. and pass smiling. WILLI 49
B. down, LONG 18
B. of burning gold: BLAK 35
b. of power is bent, LOWE J 20
boy with the b. beside you
  JONS 11
great bell of B. UNKN 25
head must b., FOST 2

Made huge Plinlimmon b.
  GRAY 4
Reason's self shall b. the knee
  FRENE 2
snow-white b. of gauze, SNOD 11
thou takest thy b., LOVE 2
trees b. down their heads,
  ROSS C 36
where all the stars b. down.
  HUGH T 9
Who can 'scape his b.?
  HERB G 23
With my b. and arrow, MOTH 32
Bowe: After the scole of Stratford
  atte B., CHAU 14
Bowed: B. by the weight of
  centuries MARK 5
b. down the highest tree
  UNKN 57
b. my head and wept. MCKA 8
b. So low for long, FROS 11
B. with her fourscore years and
  ten; WHITT 2
studs are b., DUGA 1
bowels: b. of the earth, ROSE 2
No belly and no b., RANS 34
bower: baith by b. SCOT WA 6
b. at Bucklesfordbery,
  UNKN 173
garden mouse lives in a b.,
  ROSS C 5
spear against the Muses' b.:
  MILT 125
student's b. for gold, WORD 157
thir inmost b. MILT 77
bowers: b. of innocence and ease,
  GOLD 1
brooks, of blossoms, birds and b.,
  HERR 1
come from birchen b. POUN 67
set in the same b.; VAUG 8
bowing: Plants with goodly burden
  b.; SHAK 162
put the puppet b. DICKI 18
bowingwith: b. a Mighty look —
  DICKI 65
bowl: broken is the golden b.!
  POE 29
golden b. BIBL, O.T. 6
jolly nut-brown b., DEKK 3
love in a golden b.? BLAK 12
St. John mingles with my friendly
  b. POPE A 92
to sea in a b.; MOTH 31
bowled: batsman thinks he's b.,
  LANG 1
bowler: b. and the ball, LANG 2
wild b. thinks he bowls,
  LANG 1
bowls: wild bowler thinks he b.,
  LANG 1
bows: b. bent SWIN 4

box: b. is only temporary.
PLATH 10
b. of counters PATM 3
fourth a b. within; SWIF 12
ivory b. is broken, MILLA 19
one hired b. LARK 16
ordered a b. of maniacs.
PLATH 9
boxes: b., all carefully packed,
CARRO 16
b. out his man HIRS 1
Bulbs broke out of b. ROET 52
cardboard b., ELIOT T 129
handkerchiefs in cardboard b.
MILN 3
boy: Although a poor blind b.!
CIBB 1
Barefoot b., WHITT 6
Billy b., Billy b.? UNKN 27
Blessings on the barefoot b.!
WHITT 7
b. not beautiful, RANS 10
b. of responding kisses,
WHITM 107
b. was dying, WOOL 3
b., when you sing, JOHN H 1
b. with the bow beside you
JONS 11
b.'s been swinging FROS 10
b.'s will is the wind's will,
LONG 32
Chatterton, the marvellous b.,
WORD 121
Cupid is a blackguard b. SACK 1
curious b., never too close,
WHITM 64
every b. and every gal, GILB 22
if the Babe is born a B. BLAK 31
little black b., NEWS 1
little b. again, WHITM 63
Little B. BLAK 106
Little B. Blue/ Kissed them and
FIEL E 6
Little B. Blue, MOTH 18
Little B. Blue,/ Since he kissed
them FIEL E 7
little tiny b., SHAK 177
make a small b. dizzy; ROET 49
Minstrel B. to the war is gone
MOOR T 9
My b., it's your last resort.
PLATH 4
naked black b., NEWS 1
none like the B. that sold Broom,
UNKN 44
own dear b. is far away." BRIN 3
read to by a b., ELIOT T 30
Smiling the b. fell dead.
BROWNI R 38
squeaking Cleopatra b. SHAK 10
stood the little b. WHITT 13
What a good b. am I! MOTH 20
What is the b. now, BERRYM 1

your blueeyed b. CUMM 11
youthful burning b.? BLAK 18
boyes: My merrie, merrie b.,
HERR 4
boyish: All wars are b., MELV 17
plan that pleased his b. thought:
WORD 4
some b. holiday WILD 13
Boys: B. sobbing in armies!
GINS 16
b. who love their mother SNYD 7
B. In which a Soul doth dwell:
TRAH 4
eyeing the grocery b. GINS 38
Farm b. wild to couple
DICKEY 26
ghosts of Greek b. SPEND 10
little wanton b. FLET/SHAK 3
other girls and b.
STEVENSO R 22
pretty dimpled b., SHAK 5
spindling b. BROWN S 1
still whistling 'The Protestant B.'.
UNKN 198
Those stilted b., YEATS 26
two b. knife a third, AUDE 82
wild b. innocent as strawberries
THOMA D 26
wine-flushed, bold-eyed b.,
MCKA 5
brace: b. or a hook, PLATH 1
braced: b. his mind, MARK 2
bracelet: b. of bright hair about the
bone, DONN 49
B.-bestower UNKN 18
braceleted: Arms that are b.
ELIOT T 85
braces: Broken b. and broken
springs, TROW 2
bracket: b.-bold, BROD 2
braes: among thy green b.,
BURN 22
Ye banks and b. BURN 15
brag: b. and chant of Bryan,
LIND V 4
mere lees/ Is left this vault to b.
of. SHAK 109
Nor shall Death b. SHAK 188
bragged: Boasted and b. like a
trooper; WOOL 3
Brahmin: hymn the B. sings.
EMER 7
braid: brow to b., SCOT WA 24
braided: In b. dance COLL 9
brain: awful b. CULL 19
battered bleak of b. GINS 9
binds the b. MELV 10
book and volume of my b.,
SHAK 28
b. allows one half-formed thought
ELIOT T 137
b. and cerebellum, GILB 23
b. behind the dog's b., DAY 10

b. is dull, HOOD 14
B. is just the weight of God —
DICKI 15
burnt-out b. and sapless cinders.
BYRO 34
chicken b. JEFFE 11
children of an idle b., SHAK 141
connecting-rod out of my b.,
UNKN 82
Cut out part of his b., KNIG 5
dull b. perplexes and retards:
KEAT 48
eyes that petrified my b., DARC 3
felt a Funeral, in my B.,
DICKI 45
fibre from the B. does tear.
BLAK 4
frenzied b. that hatched the plot,
STOD 1
grows one in the human b.
BLAK 71
his daft old b., HODG 4
human b.-vault: JEFFE 4
imprinting my b. WHITM 60
in my b. inherse, SHAK 217
in the b. Are tunnels that re-wind
CRAN H 31
In what furnace was thy b.?
BLAK 82
leave that b. outside, GILB 23
legs waken salads in the b.
CRAN H 24
light doth seize my b. BLAK 46
made out of the carver's b.,
COLE SAM 3
murderous b. Of Man, SITW 6
Northern breast and b. HARD 20
nourishing in thy bewildered b.
ARNO 18
on his vacant b. SHEL 16
overset the b., WORD 52
pen has gleaned my teeming b.,
KEAT 68
Rises to my b. as opium DAVIS 2
school-masters puzzle their b.
GOLD 5
sequence in the b. AIKE 4
shall not his b. encumber
EMER 33
shallow draughts intoxicate the
b., POPE A 33
shepherd is the b. DAY 10
sweet sleep is not for the weary
b.; THOMS J (1834–1882) 4
Thoughts of a dry b. ELIOT T 35
tiny poem/ in that b. OHAR 20
Brains: B. wider than the Sky —
DICKI 14
brains: Because our b. and bones
ROBI 33
exercises of his b., GILB 21

fades from b. Of living men,
BROO R 7

needs one's b. all the time.
POUN 49

partake of the treat — / Eyes and
b. MELV 14

with vulgar b. SIDN 22

Brake: B. the shield-wall,
UNKN 20

In forest wild, in thicket, b., or
den; MILT 86

brakes: sudden b. and stalling/
Engine, HEAN 21

brambles: b., buttress, sky,
LARK 5

spite of b. and boulders,
LOWE J 4

branch: b. Of mossy apple-tree,
COLE SAM 16

b.-charmed by the earnest stars,
KEAT 22

b.'ll go a-singin' DUNB P 2

dove has brought an olive b.
LOWE R 61

old tree's late b. RANS 11

pine-tree's withered b.! LONG 22

branches: b. and leaves,
WHITM 112

b. ne'er remember/ Their green
felicity: KEAT 28

b. rotted and falling. POUN 26

b. strain, SHEL 62

its strangle of b.? — PLATH 43

moss hung down from the b.,
WHITM 39

branch'll: b. go a-singin' DUNE P 2

Brand: she being B. -new;
CUMM 43

slain brother's b., UNKN 84

branded: b. E on the right cheek, R
on the left, HAYD 20

brands: wasted b. do glow,
SHAK 128

brandy: Like an old b. CUNN J 1

on b. and summer gloves JOSE 1

brane: that is made of b.,
UNKN 42

brash: b. and terrible weather;
BROO G 14

brass: b. eternal slave to mortal
rage; SHAK 211

b. impregnable; SHAK 89

b., nor stone, nor earth, nor
boundless sea, SHAK 212

golden b. and silvery steel,
WHITM 99

Like the b. cannon; SHAK 56

no little b. rollers WILLI 45

Out-during marble, b., or jet,
HERR 37

shut in an urn of b.! TENN 87

tyrants' crests and tombs of b.
SHAK 229

Uncle Ben's b. bullet-mould/ And
powder horn, TATE A 10

braste: full cloudes are b. CHAT 2

brattle: bickering b.! BURN 62

brattling: his own beloved b.
GILB 17

brave: b. and partly good,
RICH 18

b. man with a sword! WILD 3

B. prick-song! LYLY 3

b. sun/ Die blind JEFFE 43

b. who do not break PATT 1

breed to b. him, SHAK 186

cheap, choice, b. and new,
UNKN 96

clothes b. enough/ To be a
courtier, JONS 24

come it b. and meek DAVID 7

gushed the life-blood of her b.
BRYA 2

heart of the b., KNOX 2

her b. apparel on) MELV 1

home of the b.? KEY 1

intelligent, the witty, the b.
MILLA 6

just, the wise, the b., STOD 3

loyal hearts, there are spirits b.,
BRID 1

more b. than me: CUMM 18

noble race and b.; SIGO 1

O b.-hearted, LIND V 14

see the b. day SHAK 186

sleep the b. COLL 3

still the valiant b., DAVE 1

story 'bout a b. engineer;
UNKN 53

Then I was clean and b.,
HOUS 41

Toll for the b. COWP 8

wear their b. state SHAK 187

with b. disorder part, POPE A 30

braved: flag has b. a thousand
years CAMPB T 10

bravely: i would die etcetera/ b.
CUMM 26

sheet turned down so b.,
UNKN 312

bravery: b. on, and tackle trim,
MILT 110

braves: Where are the b., KLEI 2

Bravest: B. of all in Frederick town,/
She took up the flag WHITT 2

b. warrior ALEX 6

brawl: shout and bang and roar and
b. The Absolute across the hall,
BELL 13

brawle: Lest in the b. Thou fall.
TAYL E 10

brawling: Stormy, husky, b.,/ City of
the Big Shoulders: SAND 3

brawny: muscles of his b. arms
LONG 48

Bray: I'll be the Vicar of B.,
UNKN 297

brays: mule praises, b.,
THOMA D 1

brazen: b. giant of Greek fame,
LAZA 1

Fergus rules the b. cars,
YEATS 164

flamed upon the b. greaves
TENN 63

breach: custom/ More honored in
the b. than the observance.
SHAK 25

Once more unto the b., SHAK 56

bread: asked for b., WESL S 1

b. dry as paper, POUN 9

b. ever more of stale rags
POUN 9

b. I broke AIKE 1

B. of Life. TAYL E 9

B., Peace, Land. SAND 21

B. to the soul, MASE 5

B. to the wise, BIBL, O.T. 1

city mouse eats b. and cheese;
ROSS C 6

cursed the b.; ROBI 52

cutting b. and butter. THAC 3

eaten b. and pulse?/ Unarmed,
faced danger EMER 22

feeds me b. of bitterness,
MCKA 2

gummery b. each day. CARRY 10

little b. shall do me stead!
STEVENSO W 1

loaf of b.," CARRO 40

more than b.; AIKE 1

new-baked b. a failure, PURD 2

one was given b. and meat
JUST 2

Pigeons settling on the bears' b.,
JARR 28

that b. should be so dear,
HOOD 13

To eat dusty b. BOGA 14

wept for b. SHAP 27

'Wi' cauk and keel I'll win your
b., UNKN 112

wrung their b. LOWE R 4

Breadand: Loaf of B. Thou
OMAR 2

breadth: b. and the sweep LANIE 4

b. was but bitterness sore,
LANIE 4

breadwinner: dole-kept b. HEAN 4

break: brave who do not b. PATT 1

b. and wave and flow, BROO R 1

B., b., b., TENN 1

b. faith with us who die
MCCRA 3

b. his law. SHAK 98

b. Into blossom. WRIG J 2

b. my staff, SHAK 165

b. of day arising SHAK 194

b. the heart: WORD 52
b. the heart of stone: WILD 4
b. their blood, MOSS 6
B. this heavy chain BLAK 62
b. to powder SHAK 8
b. your bones: WILB 14
doubted clouds would b.,
  BROWNI R 12
five eyes b. THOMA D 44
hills and valleys into singing b.;
  VAUG 1
hold or b. MARV 21
morn doth b., BRID R 1
most things b.; ROBI 45
O, b. open SPEND 4
seem not to b.; FROS 11
teeth b. off at the edges. HARJ 3
thieves b. in and steal the gold.
  MOTH 16
till b. of day AUDE 55
toys of the world would b.
  NIMS 4
Up from the South at b. of day,
  READ T 1
weary fu' o' care?/ Thou'lt b. my
  heart, BURN 15
Words strain,/ Crack and
  sometimes b., ELIOT T 24
breakdown: education marriage
  nervous b., GINS 21
breakes: golden morning b.:
  DOWL 1
breakfast: clears her b.,
  ELIOT T 134
want any b., UNKN 98
Breaking: bough/ B. with honey
  buds, SPEND 7
b. the golden lilies BROWNI E 2
b. through the foul and ugly
  mists SHAK 51
b. waves dashed high HEMA 3
If I can stop one heart from b.
  DICKI 74
sleep that knows not b.;
  SCOT WA 9
studded, b. out, WHITM 10
without b. anything. CUMM 55
breaks: bald street b. the blank
  day. TENN 21
b. a butterfly upon a wheel?'
  POPE A 9
b. his heart LIND V 3
b. its strife, WHITT 28
b. like the Atlantic Ocean on my
  head. LOWE R 29
b. my dream, BRYA 18
b. on the sheltering bars.
  JOHN G 1
b. the chain POPE A 73
b. the veldt HARD 19
day b. not, it is my heart,
  DONN 12

Light b. where no sun shines;
  THOMA D 29
morning b.; LONG 47
break'st: b. forth a god. JONS 27
Thou b. all thy girdles, JONS 27
breast: bear your body's weight
  upon my b.: MILLA 14
b. against a briar. DEKK 2
b. high amid the corn, HOOD 8
b. where roses could not live
  ROBI 15
b.'s star of hope JARR 3
Built up of odours, burneth in her
  b. HERR 34
cheer and tune my heartless b.,
  HERB G 22
copied fragments from our b.;
  THOMP F 5
cross I wear upon my b.
  LONG 14
evening's anxious b. LAWR 23
faultless b. the furnace is,
  SOUTHW 2
fear to b. the sea! LONG 7
fed me from her gentle b.,
  TAYL A 1
fluttering in his b.: — WORD 80
golden/ Girdles and b. bands,
  POUN 8
grass is soft as the b. of doves
  CORN 2
gunshot wound in the b.,
  WHITM 16
harmony that sounds within the
  b., FLET G YO 1
harp of her b.-bane, UNKN 32
heart/ Clumps in the b. SHAP 20
His b. was deep and white,
  BISH 14
in my b. there doth it grow,
  WYAT 9
in the human b.: POPE A 65
laughed upon his b. YEATS 83
less white than her b. PRIO 6
lucent, million-pleasured b., —
  KEAT 64
maiden's b., SCOT WA 20
marched b. forward,
  BROWNI R 12
Mute music soothes my b.
  BRON 10
my careful b. BOLE 1
my soul, which in thy b. doth lie:
  SHAK 230
neither steele nor stony b.
  TOWN 3
night whose sable b. CULL 3
Northern b. and brain HARD 20
nunnery!/ Of thy chaste b.
  LOVE 8
On her white b. POPE A 115
onely heart and b., HERB G 2

painted space of the b.,
  RUKE 5
perfections on the b., HERB G 1
put inside my b. BROWNI R 53
Sing peace into his b.,
  YEATS 145
sulk upon my mother's b.
  BLAK 73
throat and b. and wings vibrates
  BLAK 37
thru b. and neck, GINS 44
twining in his speckled b.,
  MARV 4
very soul within my b. MACW 1
wanton snow flew to her b.,
  STROD 1
white b. of the dim sea
  YEATS 164
breastie: panic's in thy b.!
  BURN 62
breastless: b. creatures under
  ground ELIOT T 157
breasts: b. must suckle slaves.
  BYRO 42
b. they could never suck.
  BROO G 18
derived from the rocky b. BISH 6
fullest b. of Fame, SIDN 10
hearts seemed safe in our b.
  SITW 8
Rubber b. or a rubber crotch,
  PLATH 1
snub b. and little neat posteriors,
  MANI 2
swung b. Sway LAWR 11
Their b. were horrifying. BISH 22
then her b. are dun; SHAK 237
breastsbegotten: b. sons —
  GINS 24
breath: blaspheme down the
  stations of the b. THOMA D 37
b. can make them, GOLD 3
b. for breath: ROSS C 7
b. is tight in its throat,
  WHITM 73
b. Of every fool, SHAK 58
b. of kings, BURN 20
b./ Of life be kindled,
  HERB CH 4
b. of morn, MILT 76
b. of things unseen! CARM 2
b. of wild air; MERE G 1
b.,/ Smiles, tears, of all my life! —
  BROWNI E 6
b. that from my mistress reeks.
  SHAK 237
b. to life might move
  CONS/CHET 2
Brief is the b. LARK 7
bubbles rais'd by b. of Kings;
  SWIF 16
by deep and deeper b., Æ 2
draw this weary b. DANI S 10

draw thy b. in pain SHAK 41
fancied life in others' b.,
  POPE A 84
fierce, and bald, and short of b.,
  SASS 3
fluttered and failed for b.
  ARNO 21
fly away, b.; SHAK 176
givest to forms and images a b.
  WORD 98
Gods b. in man HERB G 66
heaved a mighty b.,
  STEVENSO R 6
Hold hard the b., SHAK 56
hot wild white b. LAWR 57
lightly draws its b., WORD 155
lucid morning's fragrant b.
  THOMS J (1834–1882) 1
move upon the tree of b.;
  LOWE R 59
no moisture and no b. Breathless
  mouths may summon;
  YEATS 18
one last b. Curls JARR 4
passing of his b. JOHN L 4
perish, as the quickening b. of
  God BRYA 17
resign our vital b., STANL 2
ripe b. of autumn, WHITM 108
seemed waste of b., YEATS 71
Shadows — hold their b.
  DICKI 144
sighs have wasted so my b.
  SURR 6
small b. ROET 53
spring, briefer than appple-
  blossom's b., WYLI 13
Stealing my b. of life, MCKA 2
strength & b., BLAK 63
sucked the honey of thy b.,
  SHAK 152
summer's b. SHAK 206
summer's honey b. SHAK 212
sweet a B.! MARV 28
taste of that salt b. YEATS 148
taxed the b., THOMA D 24
tempest's fiery b. WILLA 2
thou takest away their b., they
  die, BIBL, O.T. 53
thy b. be rude. SHAK 13
trunk may be discharged of b.
  SHAK 150
twilight hour of b., DOWS 1
warm, sweet b. of May.
  MCCRE 2
Weary of b., HOOD 2
When b. blew back, DICKI 96
whisky on your b. ROET 49
windy suspiration of forced b.,
  SHAK 21
words outcarry b. MACL 6
breath'd: carcase b., and walkt, and
  slept, PHILI K 1

breathe: As though to b. were life!
  TENN 131
b. a second spring. GRAY 14
b. out the tender tale, BURN 19
b. their words in pain.
  SHAK 87
b. those thoughts MICH 2
find we b. again, KIRK 3
lips may b. adieu, TENN 56
low, b. and blow, TENN 113
make one/ b. faster MOOR M 26
men can b. SHAK 188
they b. truth SHAK 87
Valleys b., GINS 42
yearning to b. free, LAZA 2
breathed: b. a song into the air,
  LONG 2
b. joy and woe BROWNI R 48
b. primeval balm MELV 22
ever b. a word; ALEX 6
god b. from my lips. MERR 7
breathes: air it b. WORD 38
Beauty b. her last Æ 2
b. the foe DRAK 4
noon-heat b. it back HARD 22
She b.! She burns! She'll come!
  RANDA J 2
white rose b. of love; OREI 1
breathing: b. faint and low —
  POE 13
b. of the common wind
  WORD 153
consciousness by diet and b.
  AUDE 88
dirt kept b. ROET 53
I stopped b. OHAR 6
rifle all the b. spring. COLL 1
with exquisite b. SHAP 6
Without a tighter b. DICKI 112
breathings: Low b. coming after
  me, WORD 94
breathless: bear/ My b. Baucis
  OVID 7
b. to be witnesses, WILLI 11
B. with adoration; WORD 26
hanging b. on thy fate! LONG 6
no moisture and no breath/ B.
  mouths may summon;
  YEATS 18
With frantic gesture and short b.
  cry SHEL 16
bred: begot me, b. me, loved me.
  SHAK 68
Bring us in no browne b.,
  UNKN 42
error b. in the bone AUDE 77
out of hardship b., CAMPB R 4
virtue may in me be b. MICH 2
where is fancy b., SHAK 120
Bredon: bells they sound on B.,
  HOUS 27
bredth: views in b., MILT 65
Breeches: Thar sot Little B. HAY 6

breed: absolescent b. of heroes,
  DOUG K 1
Border, nor B., nor Birth, KIPL 3
b. Perpetual benediction:
  WORD 80
b. to brave him, SHAK 186
earth's embrace/ May b.
  TENN 38
England b. again/ Such a King
  Harry? DRAY 2
found the b. of men. HOPE A 1
happy b. of men, SHAK 88
love still b.,/ Had joys no date,
  RALEG 9
with mortal mixture b. SIDN 8
breeding: b. Lilacs out of the dead
  land, ELIOT T 113
drinking and b.,/ No
  sentimentalist, WHITM 73
end of b. POUN 28
words live in my throat/ b. like
  adders. LORD 1
breeds: all life dies, death lives, and
  Nature b., MILT 61
breeth: his sweete b. CHAU 3
breeze: b. through the bridge's eye.
  KAVA 15
bugle-music on the b. ARNO 39
cooling western b.,' POPE A 26
dreading every b. BRON 14
flag to April's b. unfurled,
  EMER 11
golden monthly b.! GINS 35
light b. moves me WRIG J 2
one intellectual b., COLE SAM 12
sunny summer b. FROS 101
Brendan: B. Behan's new play
  OHAR 5
brethren: twa b. in the north,
  UNKN 268
Breughel: B.'s great picture, The
  Kermess. WILLI 12
brewed: taste a liquor never b.
  DICKI 68
brewers: b. mar their malt with
  water; SHAK 76
brewing: like the b. of men;
  UNKN 201
briar: breast against a b. DEKK 2
out of Lord Lovel's a b.,
  UNKN 178
out of Lord Thomas a b.
  UNKN 179
Briareus: B. Hands, MONTROSE 1
briars: Armed with her b.,
  AYTON 1
binding with b. my joys BLAK 65
bricht: Sprungin is Aurora radius
  and b., DUNB W 2
brick: among the new b. tenements
  WILLI 24
brickdust: b. Moll had screamed
  SWIF 11

bricks: always throwing b.,
    LIND V 15
amidst the b. of Nineveh,
    BYRO 52
protect them from falling/ b.,
    OHAR 12

bridal: b. night I remember,
    SMIT ST 1
bridegrooms, brides and of their b.
    cakes; HERR 1

bride: blushes of the b.
    BEAU/FLET 4
b. and her b. POUN 11
b.'s ambition satisfied. YEATS 35
fortunate b., BOGA 5
Judge's b. might be! WHITT 16
lost b. and her groom. LAWR 5
missed his loving b. NASH 12
my life and my b. POE 6
Never turns him to the b.
    HOUS 61
priest and b. wait the b.
    SCOT WA 6
readye to be thy b. UNKN 16
resigning yet resisting b.
    HERR 14
sought me for his b.; LIND L 1
unravished b. of quietness,
    KEAT 36
young b. in my arms,
    SMIT ST 1

bridegroom: b. all night through
    HOUS 61
b. bring her to a house
    YEATS 114
b. coming out of his chamber.
    BIBL, O.T. 27
Leave not the b. quiet —
    WHITM 7
priest and b. wait the bride
    SCOT WA 6
wish'd B. of the earth.
    HERB CH 3

bridegrooms: b., brides and of their
    bridal cakes; HERR 1

brides: bridegrooms, b. and of their
    bridal cakes; HERR 1

bridge: breeze through the b.'s eye.
    KAVA 15
b. and up the road — WOOL 1
b. of wondrous length MILT 62
crowd flowed over London B.,
    ELIOT T 118
London B. is broken down,
    UNKN 175
omnibus across the b. Crawls like
    a yellow butterfly, WILD 18
quick parabola under the b.
    LAWR 1
rude b. that arched the flood,
    EMER 11

sit like a b. club, SEXT 10
Women, and Champagne and B.)
    BELL 17

Bridgeport: beyond death/ B., Ohio.
    WRIG J 3

bridges: builder of b. ELIOT T 27
faster than witches,/ B. and
    houses, STEVENSO R 8
not leap/ From steel b.,
    KNIG 2

bridled: saddled, he b., and gallant
    rode he, UNKN 37

brief: b. bivouac of Sunday,
    PAGE 1
b. hours and weeks, SHAK 232
B. is the breath LARK 7
dates are b., SHAK 234
life so b.; BRYA 10
out, b. candle! SHAK 114
rainbow-crowned b. showers,
    ROSS C 37
thank with b. thanksgiving
    SWIN 15
What are b.? ROSS C 30

briefer: garland b. than a girl's.
    HOUS 58
spring, b. than appple-blossom's
    breath, WYLI 13

brier: bud of the b., JONS 2
swinging on b. and weed,
    BRYA 19
Thorough bush, thorough b.,
    SHAK 126

brig: mate of the Nancy b.,
    GILB 55

Brigade: "Forward the Light B.!
    TENN 6

bright: actions just and b.
    COWP 22
all burning b. SOUTHW 1
All things b. and beautiful,
    ALEX 1
beautiful and b. he stood,
    HEMA 1
bedstead striped with b.-blue
    paint, WYLI 9
behold how dark and b.
    HOUS 4
best of dark and b. BYRO 61
blaze/ Insufferably b. MILT 97
bracelet of b. hair about the
    bone, DONN 49
b. as the clouds, WORD 102
b. blaze of Autumn's equinox.
    WALK 11
B. effluence of B. essence
    MILT 63
b. eye/ That wandereth lightly.
    PEEL 2
b. green eyes MONR 1
B.-harnessed angels sit in order
    serviceable. MILT 41
b. hopes yet to find me, BANK 1

b. ironical names HAYD 10
B. jewels of the mine? HEMA 5
b. lily grow/ Before rude hands
    have touch'd it? JONS 2
b. sword by his side, UNKN 154
b. torch, KEAT 54
broad stripes and b. stars, KEY 1
creature not too b. or good
    WORD 134
fall/ Like a b. exhalation
    FLET/SHAK 4
feather on the b. sky MOMA 3
feathers, like a lady b., VAUT 1
Glory is more b. DANI S 3
Heavens B. glory TAYL E 8
Hesperus entreats thy light,/
    Goddess excellently b. JONS 3
Israel's tents do shine so b.
    BLAK 39
keep that earlier, wilder image b.
    BRYA 30
light of the b. world BOUR 1
Long may our land be b.
    SMIT SA 2
Nymph more b. GAY 1
October's b. blue weather.
    JACK 1, 2
Rigid and b. HECH 2
saw a lady b., UNKN 245
Seas of b. juice WHITM 76
silent, with b. eyes, WHITM 64
so joyous and b., GILB 56
sun is shining b., THAY 4
sun shines b. FOST 1
think that Reuben B. ROBI 49
this fleshly dress/ B. shoots of
    everlastingness, VAUG 22
thought thee b., SHAK 242
Tiger, burning b. BLAK 81
to b. champagne; SHEN 1
tossed her b. hair; MANI 1
Unerring Nature, still divinely b.,
    POPE A 25
young lady named B., BULL 1

brightening: b. glance, YEATS 13

Brightens: B. up a gloomy place;
    UNKN 267

brighter: b. fares my stream, —
    EMER 49
b. light and softer airs, BRYA 8
b. sunshine FRENE 4

brightest: b. diamond TAYL E 3
b. virgin on the green,/ So little is
    thy form declined, SWIF 21

Brightness: B. falls from the air;
    NASHE 1
b. of the skies BRYA 14
b. to hold in trust, SPEND 22
fascination of her b. SHAP 9
innocent b. of a new-born Day
    WORD 86
Leaking the b. away, SPEND 21

Brignall: O B. banks SCOT WA 23

brilliance: drained of b. GINS 9

brilliant: b. night of June: PEAC 2

brillig: 'Twas b., CARRO 35

brim: beaded bubbles winking at the b., KEAT 45
b. with sorrow drowning song. TENN 26
quite up to the b., SHERI 2

brimming: b. golden, spilling cry! JOHN H 3
b. Saucer of wax, MERR 1
b. with inner light — MOOR M 28

brims: b. the poisoned well. MELV 9

brinded: Thrice the b. cat hath mew'd. SHAK 111

brine: barbarous b. Whelms us to the tired world TATE A 5
fresh springs, b. pits, SHAK 157
river-ark on the ocean b., EMER 26
world below the b., WHITM 112

bring: b. away/ Captivity thence captive, SPENS 18
b. forth soul living MILT 86
b. the inevitable yoke, WORD 78
b. white peace LIND V 3
every hour his couriers b. TENN 57
nightes car the stars about doth b. SURR 3
Reason and speech we onely b. HERB G 51
years that b. the philosophic mind. WORD 85

bringer: some b. of that joy; SHAK 127

bringing: b. light to life. SPEND 19
b. peace and mirth/ By flight of sin. HERB G 56
news I was b. to Ghent, YEATM 1

brings: b. us glad tidings UNKN 72
such wealth b. SHAK 194

bring'st: thou b. the Spring. COWL 16

brininess: b. and volubility. GRAV 3

brink: brown b. eastward, HOPKINS 8
By the fountain's b. ROSS C 31

brinne: to be wedded is no sinne:/ Bet is to be wedded than to b. CHAU 89

brisk: b. as b. can be, UNKN 45
b. Cherub something sips, CRAS 7
b. fond lackey to fetch and carry, HOUS 3

briskly: b. for so slow a thing, FROS 131
wind came b. ALDR T 2

Bristled: B. with cities, ARNO 6
firecat b. in the way. STEVENS 8

bristly: white and b. beard: SHAK 186

Bristol: ear-drop I gave to B. Molly — MELV 3
rich squire in B. doth dwell, UNKN 231

Britain: Forgot was B.'s glory; TAYL B 2

Britannia: B. needs no bulwarks, CAMPB T 11
B. rules the waves! THOMS J (1700–1748)/MALL 1
Liberty that crowns B.'s Isle, ADDI 2

brithers: Shall b. be BURN 27

British: "Come you back, you B. soldier; KIPL 9
Dirty B. coaster MASE 2
hardy B. tars GILB 42

Britons: B. never shall be slaves. THOMS J (1700–1748)/MALL 1

brittle: arms you bear are b., HOUS 23
B. beauty SURR 1
b. crazie glasse: HERB G 73
b. world so full of doubleness, HAWE 2
Night's b. song, DAVIS 5
pale and b. pencils ever JEFFE 17
Redemption, b. lady, DICKI 156

broad: beyond the Atlantic roar./ Fair these b. meads — GALT 1
b. and beaten way MILT 62
b.-backed wave! MERE G 11
b. Blade of his glance LAWR 25
b. cloud-driving moon BRID R 19
b. face and a little round belly, MOOR C 4
b. fields of the sky: MILT 10
b. herds upsprung. MILT 86
b. of bustle; GUIT 1
b. road that stretches STEVENSO R 15
b. stripes and bright stars, KEY 1
cross thy stream, b. Hellespont! BYRO 75
great glory, and not b. JONS 34
spread thir umbrage b., MILT 97
sturdy oak with b.-spread boughs. DYER J 1
Tree whose b. smooth Leaves MILT 97

broadcloth: father should wear a b. coat, WHITT 16

broade: how b. her beames did spredde SPENS 55

brocade: her new b., POPE A 117
Only whalebone and b. LOWE A 6
weight of this b., LOWE A 9

brogue: played on a man a cursed b., BURN 3

broke: bread I b. AIKE 1
b. on me the smile GARR 1
b. the silent air, WORD 9
b. up our society HART 3
check time b. in a disordered string; SHAK 93
Death b. at once the vital chain, JOHN S (1709–1784) 4
he b. into a roar; HOLM 13
hear my true time b. SHAK 93
I b. away KAVA 13
is thy bagpype b., SPENS 48
Plank in Reason, b., DICKI 47
springs as b. from bonds, MILT 86
sun and the moon b. over my head. EBER 6
When something b. DICKI 151
When time is b. SHAK 93

broken: adversaries of the Lord shall be b. to pieces; BIBL, O.T. 8
b. altar, Lord, thy servant rears, HERB G 7
B.,/ beaten, desolate, WILLI 48
B. braces and B. springs, TROW 1
b. character and constitution. GRAY 21
b. heart, JONS 13
b. heart lies here. MACA 2
b. is the golden bowl! POE 29
b. lights of thee, TENN 17
b. like a battered crown, GINS 34
b. pillar of the wing JEFFE 13
engenders there/ The b. wall, YEATS 85
Factory windows are always b. LIND V 15
fair mouth's b. tooth. ROSE 1
for a moment a b. Coriolanus ELIOT T 154
half of a b. hope STEVENSO R 17
heart was no more b. CHES 15
ivory box is b., MILLA 19
London Bridge is b. down, UNKN 175
lute is b., SHEL 89
My slumber b. LAND 10
ne'er been b. hearted. BURN 12
old egg of my desire is b., UNKN 230
Pity our b. sleep; DAY 9

blocks with which we b.
LONG 5
B. for him, sow for him,
WORD 120
b. haunted heaven. STEVENS 14
b. it altars tall ROBI 4
b. it up again? UNKN 175
b. Some tower of song LONG 28
b. your ship of death, LAWR 36
b. your tomb, SHEL 65
Found a family, b. a state,
MELV 8
honey-bees,/ Come b. YEATS 99
never ask why b. SEXT 16
ship of martial b. MELV 1
small cabin b. there, YEATS 74
builder: Eros, b. of cities,
AUDE 34
building: Burns up the b.:
TAYL E 1
Crusoes b. boats; —
STEVENSO R 19
builds: b. glorious temples,
LOWE J 9
God b. the worm. THOMP F 5
never b. a nest, UNKN 73
built: b. in such a logical way
HOLM 4
B. Nineveh with our sighing,
OSHA 4
b. their nests in my beard!"
LEAR 18
b. to envious show, JONS 35
B. up its idle door, HOLM 2
city b. upon mud; MACN 6
culture b. upon profit; MACN 6
hand that b. the firmament
BRYA 16
their lords have b., JONS 37
They b. by rivers AUDE 21
things fall and are b. YEATS 81
bulb: Twilight and b. define
RUKE 7
Bulben: Under bare Ben B.'s head
YEATS 159
Bulbs: B. broke out of boxes
ROET 52
bulge: bellies b. to the sun,
WHITM 73
indulge in a bite at a b.,
THOMA D 40
Bulges: hum/ B. to thunder
GUNN 11
bulging: b. his pants, SCHW 10
b. Eyeball of water, JEFFE 12
bulk: b. as huge/ As whom the
Fables name MILT 53
growing like a tree/ In b.,
JONS 41
bull: again the b. supreme HODG 4
b. enough to bear the part
HODG 4

chaunged to a milk-white B.,
LODG 2
See an old unhappy b., HODG 2
sunken fields of hemp,/ Shiloh,
Antietam, Malvern Hill, B.
Run. TATE A 12
thewed like an Auroch b.,
SMIT L 2
bulldog: Hanna, b. Hanna,
LIND V 6
Bulldozed: B. by Luther and
Weyerhaeuser SNYD 45
bulles: fear of blacke bears, or b.
black, CHAU 69
bullet: blind, blunt b.-leads
OWEN 13
b. reaches you. SORL 2
b. through his head. ROBI 52
like a b. can undeceive!)
MELV 20
One b. in ten thousand
SPEND 20
pierced by the freezing b. PAGE 4
Uncle Ben's brass b.-mould
TATE A 10
bullets: b. made of platinum,
BELL 9
fired two b., NASH 16
four b. hushed her. HAYD 12
bullfight: posters for b. OHAR 13
bulling: b. through wave-wrack,
MERW 7
bulls: b. keep still REED I 5
b. mellow to the touch, MACDI 3
bullshit: boatload of sensitive b.!
GINS 18
bully: b.'s thin superiority.
HECH 11
bulwark: b. never failing; LUTH 2
bulwarks: Britannia needs no b.,
CAMPB T 11
bum: Belly, shoulder, b.,
YEATS 100
bumper: fill a pint b. SHERI 2
bumpity: b. ride in a wagon of hay
DE LA 6
bumpy: b. and humpy — CARRY 3
bunch: b. of lace at his throat.
NOYE 8
b. of red berries. LEVE 20
Bunched: B. upside down, JARR 2
bunches: b. like birds' nests.
FROS 24
with clustering b. growing,
SHAK 162
bunders: Rumbletum b. roar.
CARRY 11
bundle: b. he has on his shoulders,
LOWE J 4
round it like a b. FROS 140
bundled: b. together? LOWE R 9
bundles: b. every forkful FROS 24

bung: old barrel with many a b.
KENN 2
bungling: season of no b. OLSO 23
Bunn: world we roved, Ned B.?
MELV 21
buoyancy: In b. afloat. MERE G 9
buoys: noise of bell b.,
MOOR M 13
burden: b. hard to be borne:
DE LA 18
b. of life WHITT 20
b. of my song: HERR 28
b. of the grasshopper,
ELIOT T 8
b. of the world. MARK 5
b. of your fears, MORR 1
Plants with goodly b. bowing;
SHAK 162
superfluous b. MILT 120
burdens: stranger,/ hoist your b.,
AMMO 18
burgeoning: b. over the barn,
WILB 44
burgher: many a b.'s pate
BROWNI R 64
Burglar: B.! Banker — Father!
DICKI 58
enterprising b. isn't burgling,
GILB 38
burglars: b. stole that pair away!
FIEL E 2
burgling: enterprising burglar isn't
b., GILB 38
burial: above my b.? AIKE 10
bell tolled on thy b. day,
COWP 11
b. clouds, WHITM 56
b. of the stars? WHITM 58
Give thou my sacred relics b.
HERR 24
in one red b. blent! BYRO 8
buried: beneath the earth lie b.
low, VERY 5
B. above ground. COWP 16
b. him where he fell.
WHITM 107
b. in flesh and blood,
JONS 25
b. in the dust of marching feet.
KNIG 3
b. in the /ink that /writes.
PLATO 3
b. past of the earth, OSHA 4
B. together, LOWE R 8
b. us without shroud or coffin
HEAN 18
Died on Saturday,/ B. on Sunday,
MOTH 26
Lord Thomas was b. in the
church, UNKN 179
not born, yet b., JONS 32

iron bars a c.;/ Minds innocent
    and quiet LOVE 5
Robin Redbreast in a C. BLAK 2
shut me in his golden c.
    BLAK 24
sing like birds i' the c. SHAK 84
unlocked door, that c. of c.,
    RICH 16
world goes by my c. JARR 27
caged: what the c. bird feels,
    DUNB P 9
why the c. bird sings!
    DUNB P 10
Cain: captain called me C.
    SHAP 26
landless blood of C. LOWE R 5
Negroes, black as C.,
    WHEA 1
red C. SITW 6
worse than C.! STOD 1
cajole: flatter, c., and persuade
    GILB 61
cake: Some bring a capon, some a
    rural c., JONS 36
cakes: bridegrooms, brides and of
    their bridal c.; HERR 1
calamity: makes c. of so long life;
    SHAK 39
calculate: c. the cost, SHAP 12
calf: c. that is plump and delicious;
    THOMA D 40
fetch the little c. FROS 87
held by c. and thigh. GUNN 11
Caliban: C. casts out Ariel.
    POUN 41
calico: c. minded,/ sufficiently
    starched, PAGE 2
C. Pie, LEAR 2
c. tree, LEAR 2
gingham dog and the c. cat
    FIEL E 1
call: at his c. Love him,
    WORD 120
c. crafft counsell, WYAT 23
c. for death I shall: UNKN 167
C. him not home. Æ 1
c. of the running tide MASE 12
c. to come in/ To the dark and
    lament. FROS 16
evening c. another star TIMR 3
ev'ry star by proper name to c.?
    BIBL, O.T. 66
fellers c. me Bill! FIEL E 3
for mercy on Christ they c.,
    SOUTHE 2
heeds no c. to die. HARD 26
Jonnë Armestrong men did him
    c., UNKN 153
let no bird c. MILLA 11
lied/ To c. it dancing; SPENC A 2
must c. up SNOD 2
none can c. again the passed
    time. SPENS 22

none dare c. it treason. HARI 2
one clear c. for me! TENN 9
others c. it God. CARRU 1, 2
Senec and Plato c. me WYAT 5
shall I c. thee Bird, WORD 150
That which we c. a rose
    SHAK 142
to cry and c. his name, WILB 33
vengeful god would c. to me
    HARD 24
we beauty c. POPE A 35
wild c. and a clear c. MASE 12
will not c. me with a word.
    PETRA 10
you could say I've a c. PLATH 55
called: By name to come c. charity,
    MILT 106
c. by a panther, NASH 8
c. by thy name, BLAK 95
c. for drinks for the house.
    SERV 7
c. him a curse, SMIT ST 8
c. them by name: MOOR C 2
c. through all our tribes 'The
    Good.' " LOWE J 20
He is c. Leviathan, MERW 8
Sir/ Beelzebub c. for his syllabub
    SITW 2
calling: I heard one c., 'Child!'
    HERB G 18
laughing and c. MANI 1
they're c. me.' OHAR 21
Wresting words from their true
    c.;
    JONS 9
calls: as the hostler c.; LONG 47
c. her children back, LOWE J 14
Father c. me William, FIEL E 3
Mother c. me Willie, FIEL E 3
sister c. me Will, FIEL E 3
twilight darkens, the curlew c.;
    LONG 46
Verse c. them forth; 'tis verse that
    gives LAND 5
calm: anchor-watches c., MELV 22
awful c., DODG 1
beauteous evening, c. and free,
    WORD 26
Beauty, ripe, and c., and fresh,
    DAVE 6
birds of c. LOWE J 14
C. and distressed ELIOT T 9
c. and heav'nly frame; COWP 25
c. and patient, WHITM 98
C. as that second summer
    TIMR 1
C. fell. From Heaven HARD 11
C. is the morn TENN 22
c. of mind all passion spent.
    MILT 118
c. region, where no night
    KING H 3

drifted in a sheepish c.,
    LOWE R 32
In c. or stormy weather;
    ROSS C 12
lies c. beneath that stroke.
    STEVENS 12
Sam, looking cold and c.,
    SERV 5
season of c. weather WORD 82
soundless c. descends; BRON 10
stars in their c. ARNO 8
truth in a c. world, STEVENS 16
What c. catastrophe WINT 4
winds blew c., MUND 2
calmer: Love is a c., gentler joy:
    SACK 1
suit a c. grief, TENN 22
Calmly: Pity is not your forte./ C.
    you ache RICH 11
Calunnia: 'La C.' painted. POUN 10
Calvarie: Paradise and C.,/ Christs
    Crosse, and Adams tree,
    DONN 32
Calvary: by C.'s turbulence
    unsatisfied, YEATS 92
on C. were shed. UNKN 130
Queen of C. DICKI 42
calved: grassy clods now c.,
    MILT 86
calves: c., grown muscular with
    certainties; JARR 7
c. of waitresses WILB 42
lowing/ Of the c. YEATS 145
Calvin: code corroborating C.'s
    creed MELV 12
cam: c. a knight to be their wooer,
    UNKN 29
c.-shaft from out of my backbone,
    UNKN 82
eldest c. and push'd her in.
    UNKN 30
never c. he. UNKN 37
cam': he took them as they c.
    MACDI 5
Cambria: From C.'s curse, GRAY 2
Cambrian: depths of the C. fen,
    SMIT L 1
Cambridge: C. ladies CUMM 52
C. people rarely smile,
    BROO R 18
came: c. into my own. ROET 10
c. riding like mad WOOL 1
c. to camp. SNYD 2
c. to my house. STRA 5
Down the chimney St. Nicholas
    c. MOOR C 3
his coursers they c., MOOR C 2
I c., alas! to wive, SHAK 177
in beauty and decay,/ He c.
    SHEL 1
Juliana c., MARV 27
my Master c., LANIE 1
passion c., SHEL 17

captain: c. and the crew; GILB 10
c. called me Cain SHAP 26
C. Carpenter on his back RANS 8
C. Carpenter rose RANS 6
C. finally on his back RANS 9
c. said, Quack! Quack! MOTH 15
C. they trusted so well CARRO 17
c. tickled the crew. CARRY 9
cook and a c. bold, GILB 55
crew and c. CARRY 4
crew of the c.'s gig!' " GILB 55
from the c.'s store, GILB 4
O C.! my C.! WHITM 45
on the deck my C. lies,
  WHITM 45
Serene stands the little c.,
  WHITM 91
train-band c. COWP 6
troubled the c.'s mind. CARRY 8
voice of my little c., WHITM 90
widowed ma of C. Reece, GILB 5
captaines: c. of great might;
  UNKN 61
Captains: C. and the Kings depart:
  KIPL 18
known to c. HECH 9
Capten: (C., art tha sleepin'
  NEWB 1
captivate: with her voice might c.
  my mind. MARV 13
captive: bring away/ Captivity
  thence c., SPENS 18
daughter of their sires/ Saved a c.
  Englishman. THAC 2
he is c., MOOR M 43
lead Hell C. MILT 64
captives: pale c., creep to death.
  SHIR 2
Captivity: bring away/ C. thence
  captive, SPENS 18
capture: c. The secret of self;
  AIKE 11
car: buy a goddamn big c., CREE 9
c. like the Roxy KENN 1
c. park till twenty to one
  BETJ 11
c. rattling BYRO 6
dragged Diana from her c.,
  POE 2
gilded C. of Day, MILT 8
god inside the c.: FULL 1
left the earring in the c.
  SNYD 15
nightes c. the stars about doth
  bring. SURR 3
noiseless wheels of my c.
  WILLI 49
plodding through c.-traffic
  PINS 3
Caramel: Brown sugar lassie,/ C.
  treat,/ Honey-gold baby
  HUGH L 5

caravan: innumerable c. that
  moves BRYA 24
Put up your c. HODG 11
Race memories of king and c.,
  TOOM 2
caravels: Columbus's doom-
  burdened c. SQUI 1
carbuncles: eyes like c., SHAK 30
carbuncular: young man c.,
  ELIOT T 135
carcase: c. breath'd, and walkt, and
  slept, PHILI K 1
carcases: mangled heap/ Of c.
  THOMS J (1700–1748) 10
card: "He's a cheery old c.,"
  SASS 10
cardboard: c. boxes, ELIOT T 129
handkerchiefs in c. boxes.
  MILN 3
cards: flattery, c., and dice, and
  din: SHEN 1
played at c. and dice, UNKN 207
played/ At c. for kisses, LYLY 1
wicked pack of c. ELIOT T 116
care: can read and c. for just so
  long, KIPL 20
C.-charmer Sleep, DANI S 8
c. for nothing, TENN 35
c. in my breeding, WATT I 7
C. less eyes, lips, and hands to
  miss. DONN 63
chosen out with C. MARV 5
cradle of causeless c., SIDN 39
for angwysshe and c., PETRA 1
Free from c., DOAN 1
fret of c.; GLAD 1
greatness is but c., BEAU/BASS 2
horrid c., MARV 15
in his mouthing c., SCHW 11
killed by C. ROBI 48
Killing c., and griefe
  FLET/SHAK 1
landed his crew with c.;
  CARRO 11
life of c. SHEL 67
lips of C., LONG 25
make pale my cheeks with c.
  WITH 1
mock at fate and c., EMER 31
night discharg'd of all c.
  MARTIA 2
No grief, no c., no toil.
  UNKN 147
nobody would c. to see, MOSS 4
nought but c. on ev'ry han',
  BURN 29
other side of c. MUIR 2
ought not to have to c. FROS 52
overborne with c. TREN 2
planets in His c., YEATS 15
power whose c. BRYA 26
reason is past c., SHAK 242

sigh'd with each Man's C.,
  SACK 3
Sleep that knits up the raveled
  sleeve of c., SHAK 106
streaks of c. Like wires KAVA 28
Take c. how you light. TROW 3
torment with c.; WYAT 13
uncessant c. MILT 26
weary fu' o' c.?/ Thou'lt break my
  heart, BURN 15
What c. I how fair she be?
  WITH 2
whose wish and c. POPE A 107
with trembling c. DICKI 72
woman who did not c.), KIPL 27
Worn out with life's c., CRAB 2
your crops and your c.; COLUM 2
cared: Nor wished, nor c., PRIO 4
Nought c. this body
  COLE SAM 48
careful: c. of the type TENN 32
i was/ c. of her CUMM 43
my c. breast. BOLE 1
Our debts, our c. wives, SHAK 58
ranged there with c. art,
  PATM 3
carefully: c. compare it GILB 8
Careless: C. of books, WORD 51
c. of mankind. TENN 89
c. of the single life; TENN 32
c. shoestring, HERR 8
my c. childhood stray'd,
  GRAY 13
Nature is always c. and
  indifferent SMIT ST 4
of c. mice, HAIN 1
thee, c. Ulysses. OVID 3
carelessly: page of the book c.
  open, SEXT 18
Carentan: C. O C. SIMP 3
cares: all their lives and c.,
  WATT I 3
c. for us here below. LOWE J 12
c., that infest the day, LONG 16
dark forgetting of my c.
  DANI S 8
falling with my weight of c.
  TENN 33
fireside far from the c. SERV 9
hidden should be my c.; DE VE 1
mind too strewn/ With petty c.
  CULL 19
My prime of youth is but a frost
  of c., TICH 1
no time for idle c. POE 40
nobody c. for thee.' UNKN 10
void of C. and Strife, PHILL 1
With c. and fears. BACO 1
caress: c. her long ear WRIG J 2
caressable: cold and c.;/ his eyes
  were red glass, BISH 14
caresses: engage her in c.
  ELIOT T 136

caressing: Cleaning and c.,
ROET 48
carf: c. biforn his fader at the
table. CHAU 11
cargo: full c. of roses. ROET 3
is a great c., WILB 45
making the air wince/ but her c.
RICH 23
Caribbean: Atlantic and C. love,
GINS 11
caricature: this c., YEATS 150
caring: c. much to know, GREN 3
carl: millere was a stout c.
CHAU 16
carnal: hermit's c. ecstasy.
AUDE 57
lumbering sort of c. spirit,
HECH 9
Carnival: heaven-fed/ Naiad of the
C.-Tank! SPENC A 3
carol: c. of joy or glee, DUNB P 10
float this c. with joy, WHITM 51
Heard a c., mournful, holy./
Chanted loudly, chanted lowly,
TENN 67
Caroling: C. softly TOOM 7
carols: old, familiar c. play,
LONG 11
varied as I hear, WHITM 37
carous'd: when I c., WHITM 108
carpe: c. diem, Juan, BYRO 34
Carpenter: Captain C. on his back
RANS 8
Captain C. rose RANS 6
c. singing WHITM 37
haberdasshere and a c., CHAU 5
Walrus and the C. CARRO 38
Carpenters: C., coal-passers —
CLARK J 1
Like c. SEXT 16
carpet: Persian c., HORA 10
carping: obnoxious to each c.
tongue BRAD 16
carried: c. downwards by thy flood,
WATT I 3
identified — / And c. Me away —
DICKI 109
knowledge/ C. to the heart?
TATE A 14
carriers: c. of her epidemics —
GRAV 2
carries: c. a refuse pail,
WHITM 115
c. the feathered grass RICH 29
carrion: I'll not, c. comfort,
HOPKINS 4
Old Adam, the c. crow, BEDD 4
carrot: take along a c. CARRY 6
carrots: butchered snakes and c.
HUGO 6
kept the c. clean, HUGO 6
Carrow: slain at C., SKEL 6

carry: brisk fond lackey to fetch and
c., HOUS 3
cannot c. forests EMER 36
c. Half my love SHAK 68
c. home as prizes CARRY 7
c. precept to the highest pitch:
BYRO 20
c. the gaberlunzie on. UNKN 112
c. to the Catacombs of Age,
GILB 46
It will c. and fetch, BELL 20
carrying: experience/ of c. a stick?
MOOR M 7
cars: c. nose forward like fish;
LOWE R 21
Fergus rules the brazen c.,
YEATS 164
Carthage: To C. then I came
ELIOT T 140
cartilage: c. Will have it so?
ROBI 33
cartoon: c. by Raphael BISH 43
like a c.-mouse, ROET 39
carve: c. deep your heel-marks.
JEFFE 42
c. in Latine or in Greek, WALL 3
Carved: C. with figures strange and
sweet, COLE SAM 3
We c. not a line, WOLF C 3
carver: made out of the c.'s brain,
COLE SAM 3
carves: When father c. the duck.
WRIG E 1
carving: time for c. POUN 53
case: argued each c. CARRO 6
bewail the woeful c. SURR 5
every c. in law is right, SHAK 76
help your c., UNKN 267
casement: c. ope at night, KEAT 54
on this c. shone the wintry moon,
KEAT 10
casements: Charmed magic c.,
KEAT 50
cases: thoroughbred mental c.,
LOWE R 55
Casey: ease in C.'s manner THAY 2
great C.'s visage shone; THAY 3
no joy in Mudville — Mighty C.
has struck out. THAY 4
pride in C.'s bearing THAY 2
smile on C.'s face; THAY 2
Cash: C. that goes therewith!
CHES 1
take the C., OMAR 3
unhoard the c. MILT 68
cask: give me a c. a day;
STEPHENS 4
Like a stored c., HEAN 20
Cassandra: C., Ronsard found in
Lyon. SYNG 3
Cast: C. a cold eye YEATS 160
c. a shadow white as stone.
ROET 29

c. forth in the common air,
SHAK 86
c. my love behind: JONS 18
c. out remorse YEATS 48
c. the vessel ashore CARRY 11
c. them all away
BROWNI E/GUIN 1
c. too fierce a light, SACK 1
C. up by a lonely sea, MELV 23
colours all to black are c.,
GREV 4
despite they c. on female wits:
BRAD 17
do not c. you aside — WHITM 22
Drop their c. YEATS 152
Pride/ Had c. him out from
Heav'n, MILT 48
real as a c.-iron pot. SEXT 2
sicklied o'er with the pale c. of
thought. SHAK 40
Why art thou c. down, O my
soul? BIBL, O.T. 36
ye of clay were c. by kind,
VAUX 6
Castalian: C. sisters sing, HERR 16
castaways: cry for your c.,
WHITM 5
Prince of C. ROBI 13
caste: afore myn eyn c. PETRA 1
castigated: when your c. pulse
BURN 5
Casting: C. a dim, religious light.
MILT 18
c.-weight pride POPE A 16
castle: Bores through his c. wall,
SHAK 89
lay in Lie C.! LEVE 5
splendor falls on c. walls
TENN 111
stood at his c. gate UNKN 177
Castlereagh: eunuch C.? BYRO 16
mask like C. SHEL 39
castles: Where are our c. now,
MORE 4
casual: c. flocks of pigeons
STEVENS 62
C. fruition, MILT 78
sustain/ Some c. shout WORD 9
casually: only c. invited, OHAR 7
casualty: This single c., SHAP 11
Cat: And he a c., CHAU 52
as grey as a c., FLAT 2
C. and Dog, SWIF 15
c. has a number of lives;
THOMA D 39
C. I keep, HERR 18
c. is grown small MONR 2
c. climbed over WILLI 2
c. That killed the rat MOTH 5
c.'s face, ROSS C 12
cocaine dog and a cocaine c.,
UNKN 67
consider my C. Jeoffry. SMAR 2

She was a c. POE 4
simple c., WORD 155
sweet c.-face is showing.
  WHITT 14
think it the pleasantest thing/ Ever
  a c. can do! STEVENSO R 18
thou gaes wi' c. UNKN 239
thou hast been/ Ocean's c.,
  SHEL 37
thou hast gotten a c. LAWR 60
Thou little C., WORD 78
Thursday's c. has far to go,
  MOTH 22
waters wild went o'er his c.,
  CAMPB T 6
Wednesday's c. is full of woe,
  MOTH 22
weep like a c. for the past.
  LAWR 32
white c. hacked in bed? WALC 2
Wise c., didst hastily return
  JONS 38
With crayons the c. draws a rigid
  house BISH 46
childbirth: elated after c.! BOGA 5
Childerditch: Codham, Cockridden,
  and C., THOMA E 11
childermas: I say this c. HECH 13
childfull: bodiless c. of life BEDD 6
childhood: as it was in my c.
  EBER 6
Charms in harmless C. SEDL 2
C. remembrances GIOV 3
c.'s thin harmonious tear:
  TATE A 16
eye of c. SHAK 107
In my days of c., LAMB 2
In simple c. WORD 115
liv'd my c. o'er again; COWP 12
my careless c. stray'd, GRAY 13
sacred instinct did inspire/ My
  soul in c. TRAH 7
scenes of my c., WOOD 1
seek a c. picture; WARR 5
simple creed/ Of C., WORD 80
talk about my hard c. GIOV 4
with my c.'s faith. BROWNI E 5
childish: c. favour singled:
  WHITT 13
It was a c. ignorance, HOOD 5
childishness: second c. and mere
  oblivion, SHAK 12
childlike: begging I clutched c.,
  WRIG R 1
proud though c. form. HEMA 1
children: added five c. to the
  population, AUDE 94
All yonge c. to slay. UNKN 70
answer to c., WHITM 113
be honest like c. AUDE 26
calls her c. back, LOWE J 14
came the c. running.
  BROWNI R 62

charm for c. JEFFE 6
C. afraid of the night AUDE 76
c. are dying RICH 10
c. are grown;/ Fun and frolic
  BRYA 20
c., come down! ARNO 10
c. frowned/ At something dull;
  LARK 21
c. glean in fields BONT 1
c. green and golden THOMA D 20
C., if you dare GRAV 39
c. into the river; JOHN F 1
c. laugh and play, HALE 1
c. of an idle brain, SHAK 141
c. of the nouveaux riches;
  SNOD 8
c. run naked in the field GINS 31
C. screaming GINS 16
c./ Wear skins SPEND 3
c. were killed LEVE 24
c. were nestled MOOR C 1
c. will go with me, RANDA D 1
c.'s faces./ Like rootless weeds
  SPEND 1
C.'s voices in the orchard
  ELIOT T 57
Cruel c., STEVENSO R 4
dear c., let us away; ARNO 9
fade these c. of the Spring,
  BLAK 13
gives her c. neither sense nor
  money MACN 7
go as little c. sent. DODG 2
instrument for the c. SMAR 5
Jeered at by crooked c.,
  MILLA 34
known as the C.'s Hour. LONG 9
ladies faint, and the c. holler:
  SMIT W 1
leave their c. free, EMER 12
leaves were full of c.,/ Hidden
  excitedly, ELIOT T 18
Listen, my c., LONG 43
little c. died in the streets.
  AUDE 5
make their c. blind, SHAK 73
mother for her c., BINY 1
my children's c. ELIOT T 109
noise of wheels and c. GINS 9
On the faces of women and c.
  SAND 4
Other little c. STEVENSO R 23
Our c., and our sins SHAK 58
remember the c. BROO G 17
somewhere c. shout, THAY 4
takes a heap o' c. UNTE 1
three c. under the moon, SEXT 4
Two c., all alone BINY 5
Usna's c. died. YEATS 121
voices of c. BLAK 77
warm c. RANS 32

wife and c. will be quiet
  HEAN 15
your c. are raggedy-assed
  WELC 2
Chile: C. of the devil, WALK 8
chill: cheek so pale and c.;
  DODG 1
c. in the fires PETRA 2
C. Sirocco blowes, BONH 1
crept upon/ A C. DICKI 154
huddled c. CUNN J 4
I rose from the c. ground
  WHITM 107
six little spaces of c., RANS 18
Thames runs c. MORR 5
chilled: c. The cooked bird,
  KINN 16
chilling: c. And killing my Annabel
  Lee. POE 5
chilly: c. and grown old.
  BROWNI R 79
c. winter's night; BARNE 4
earth so c.; TENN 110
Chimborazo: C., Cotopaxi TURN 1
chime: listen to the merry village
  c. GILB 38
mind may c., HERB G 22
silver c. Move in melodious time,
  MILT 39
whirr and c.: AUDE 2
Chimeras: Gorgons and Hydras, and
  C. dire. MILT 61
lament of the disconsolate c.
  ELIOT T 25
chimes: c. Of the tall Clock Tower
  SNOD 8
chiming: c. of a passing-bell.
  HERB G 31
chimney: above the c. stack
  MACL 7
As c.-sweepers, come to dust.
  SHAK 18
C.-sweepers cry BLAK 75
Down the c. St. Nicholas came
  MOOR C 3
from the monstrous c.... JARR 4
Sitting in the c. corner, CAREY 3
stockings were hung by the c.
  MOOR C 1
up the c. he rose. MOOR C 5
chimneys: c. volleyed out;
  STEVENSO R 5
your c. I sweep BLAK 86
Chimpanzee: behold the C.:
  HERF 1
chin: dimple of his c.: LYLY 2
ermine muffled mouth and c.;
  WYLI 3
little Cupid lose/ Eyes and ears
  and c. and nose, JUST 4
rye reach to the c., PEEL 6
China: C. and Africa meet, AUDE 1

C. gathers, soundlessly, like
　evidence. SNOD 9
C. staunched her milk SHAP 27
C.'s gayest art had dyed
　GRAY 18
frail c. jar POPE A 117
small-eyed C.'s BYRO 52
Survey mankind from C. to Peru;
　JOHN S (1709–1784) 15
chinaman: c.'s chance. GINS 4
Chinee: heathen C. is peculiar:
　HART 1
Chinese: C. jar still/ Moves
　perpetually ELIOT T 23
clenched like a C. puzzle . . .
　RUKE 12
chinook: like the c. salmon
　LOWE R 47
Chins: haven't any/ C. at all.
　FYLE 1
wear yet upon their c. SHAK 122
Chipmunks: C. jump, HALL 6
Chippendale: Turtle soup, C.,
　BROO G 9
chirche: Housbondes at c. dore
　CHAU 11, 87
chirp: birds do c. and sing:
　BRET 5
nestlings c. and flee, HOGG 1
chirper: Fear,/ The yellow c.,
　LOWE R 24
chirping: bones sang c. ELIOT T 8
chits: livingest c. In all the land.
　BROO G 13
chivalrie: loved c.,/ Trouthe and
　honour, CHAU 7
chivalry: archetypes of c.; RANS 2
Chloe: C. is my real flame. PRIO 9
my fair C., PRIO 2
chocolate: think of rosy c.
　STEVENS 46
choice: appearance of c. FULL 4
By virtue first, then c., a queen,
　WOTT 6
cheap, c., brave and new,
　UNKN 96
C. word and measured phrase,
　WORD 123
flowers the winter's c.? CLARE 4
fortunes of my pleasant c.
　SURR 5
in such abundance lies our c.
　MILT 94
leave to heaven the measure and
　the c., JOHN S (1709–1784) 22
"Take your c., KAVA 15
Choicer: C. than the Mermaid
　Tavern? KEAT 33
choir: c. invisible ELIOT G 1
chorister whose C preceded the c.
　STEVENS 29
Fair Ellinor in the c.; UNKN 179

He leads the C. of Day —
　BLAK 36
innumerable c. of day BRID R 14
choirs: Bare ruined c., SHAK 215
choke: Lets his own ashes c. his
　soul. HERB G 29
choked: bone c. a wolf LA FO 1
C. my throat. SNYD 9
c. with hate YEATS 111
Trees down/ Creeks c., trout
　killed, SNYD 45
chokes: c. the child. RALEG 14
choking: Jesus c. in the air,
　LOWE R 22
my c. pain, WOOL 2
choose: c. his mate./ Poet and
　sculptor, YEATS 156
c. Never to stoop. BROWNI R 57
C. One — DICKI 133
c. Plato and Plotinus for a friend.
　YEATS 151
c. the Summer Queen; CAMPI 3
c. Their place of rest, MILT 108
C. then your climate, BARL 1
c. upstanding men YEATS 152
c. you the frailest, SHEL 90
forced to c. Perfection YEATS 23
I will wear what dresses I c.!
　CREE 3
language you c. GILB 25
let them c.!' FROS 54
never c. again;/ Sweet, if you
　shrink, UNKN 74
thought that I would c. thee
　CALV 6
vexes me to c. another guide:
　BRON 6
why should poet in the twilight
　c.? KAVA 9
choosers: lovely shall be c.,
　FROS 54
choosing: man of God's own c.
　LUTH 3
Chop: C. some wood, HILL J 4
chopped: Bible c. and crucified
　LOWE R 49
c. down the house KOCH 5
poem, or c. prose, KINN 6
chopping: large around as the c.
　block; FROS 122
choral: songs/ And c. symphonies,
　MILT 81
Surrounded by its c. rings,
　STEVENS 29
Chorasmian: lone C. shore
　SHEL 18
chord: common c. again,
　BROWNI R 5
Ear that suspends on a c.
　SPEND 17
Chordage: sweet C. cannot bind.
　MARV 10
chords: c. that tenderest KEAT 5

smote on all the c. TENN 70
throb/ In witching c.,
　STEVENS 34
chore: c.-girl small, WHITT 34
chores: To do celestial c. CULL 1
chorister: c. whose C preceded the
　choir. STEVENS 29
sweet-warbling c.! HERR 53
choristers: chanting c., LAWR 9
chorus: endless and noisy c.,
　WHITM 32
sing the sweet c. BLAK 96
turbulent musical c.! WHITM 32
what a c.! LAND 14
chose: she had eyes, and c. me.
　SHAK 136
chosen: c. coin of fancy TENN 124
c. out with Care. MARV 5
c. race JOHN S (1822–1882) 1
thy c. Music, Liberty! WORD 147
Christ: believe in C. and
　Longfellow, CUMM 53
Came C. the tiger ELIOT T 31
catch C. with a greased worm,
　LOWE R 14
C. ain't a-goin' HAY 4
C. and his mother HOPKINS 24
C.-child lay on Mary's CHES 2
C.-child who comes BROO P 2
C. follows Dionysus, POUN 41
C. is born of Mary; BROO P 4
C. Jesus, it is he, LUTH 3
C. of His gentleness GRAV 13
C. save us all from a death
　LONG 53
C. that is to be. TENN 50
C. walking on the water
　THOMP F 12
C. writhing on the cross! ROBI 3
C.'s Crosse and Adam's tree,
　DONN 32
Come down, O C., WILD 10
comfort of C. BRID R 16
cross that C. had, SORL 2
dear C. enters in. BROO P 6
face of the C. himself, WHITM 72
For C.'s sake not black —
　WILLI 44
For Jesus C. his sake.' UNKN 77
For Jesus C., our Saviour, CRAI 1
for mercy on C. they call,
　SOUTHE 2
from wood and stone to C.
　JOHN J 7
half a drop! ah, my C.! —
　MARL 2
in C.'s coach saints sweetly sing,
　TAYL E 4
picture of C. crucified, DONN 66
Tiger C. unsheathed SCHW 1
when C. was slain YEATS 118
Christal'd: C. Lillie HERR 27

floating on the C. Flood,
SPENS 42

Tomb'd in a C. stone, HERR 26

Christe: C. receive thy saule.
UNKN 186

Christendome: Kent and C./ Emong
the muses where I rede and
ryme; WYAT 25

Christened: c. In white wine or red,
UNKN 13

C. on Tuesday, MOTH 26

we were c." UNKN 13

Christian: a-wastin' C. kisses
KIPL 10

Gup, C. Clout, SKEL 4

maybe it ain't like a C.) —
MASE 10

smell from ditches that were not
C. KAVA 7

smile of C. charity THAY 3

souls of C. peoples . . . CHES 1

Christians: C. have burnt BYRO 20

Christmas: But jest 'fore C.
FIEL E 4

C. Eve, and twelve of the clock.
HARD 32

C. grace KINN 16

C. is Kid Stuff . . . HORN 1

C. Log to the firing; HERR 4

Eating a C. pie; MOTH 20

Eating of a C. pie, CAREY 3

everywhere, C. tonight BROO P 1

first day of C., UNKN 274

"Happy C. to all, MOOR C 5

holly torn for C. LOWE R 23

Jes 'fore C. FIEL E 5

night before C., MOOR C 1

old/ C. gifts RICH 6

on C. Day, LONG 11

Christs: C. Crosse, and Adams tree,
DONN 32

chronic: c. invalid, — RICH 20

chronically: cathedrals c. on show,
LARK 4

chronicle: c. of wasted time
SHAK 228

chronology: not much besides c.,
BYRO 21

Chrysostom: Old C., best
Augustine. EMER 40

Chryst: campioun C. DUNB W 1

chubby: c. and plump, a right jolly
old elf, MOOR C 4

Chuck: C. it, Smith! CHES 1

chuckle: I've an irritating c.,
GILB 9

Chucky: C. did not. RANS 20

C.'s old bald head RANS 19

church: altars/ In a dark c. SIMI 4

Babies and gin and c. HUGH L 3

Beneath the c.-yard stone
BRON 4

blackning C. appalls, BLAK 75

C. blocking the sun. SPEND 15

C. can sleep and feed at once.
ELIOT T 38

C. clock at ten to three?
BROO R 20

c. of St. Geryon COLE SAM 26

c. spire/ Opens its eight bells out,
MACN 22

"Come all to c., good people, — "
HOUS 27

going to c.; DICKI 130

gone up to the c. to pray.
BLAK 55

home from c. got mad at my
mother SANC 4

I like a c.; EMER 38

In the c.-way paths to glide:
SHAK 128

Into the solemn c., WHITM 7

Lord Thomas was buried in the
c., UNKN 179

lost with the Faithful at C.
LOWE R 48

no c. of cut stone signed:
POUN 10

North C. tower LONG 44

Pardon, my Mother C., COWL 13

past life a ruined c. MACN 25

scattered at the old c. door,
KLEI 3

went to c. alone. HOUS 26

churches: bawds and whores do c.
build, SHAK 76

c. fall completely out of use
LARK 4

Flocks of C., WORD 100

head more than c., bibles,
WHITM 74

Prayer the C. banquet,
HERB G 66

churchman: cowlèd c. be.
EMER 38

churchyard: book a c. tomb.
KEAT 35

c. with a sigh, LONG 18

In Drumcliff c. YEATS 159

palsy-stricken, c. thing, KEAT 9

churl: that c. death SHAK 196

Churn: Attract a Silver C.! GILB 34

Why not a Silver C.?" GILB 33

chyld: c. in Bedlem born is beter
than we alle.' UNKN 213

cigarette: c. ends ELIOT T 129

forgotten/ C. LAWR 50

cigarettes: c. in corridors
ELIOT T 105

cigars: roller of big c., STEVENS 9

cinders: always heaving c.,
LIND V 15

burnt-out brain and sapless c.
BYRO 34

c. in his mouth, WAGO 2

Turned to c. by her eye?
JONS 12

cinnamon: Perspiring pounded c.
HERR 34

Circe: house of C., POUN 5

Circle: C. his throne rejoicing,
MILT 81

c. of the crazy ladies SEXT 12

c. of the hills. TENN 45

c. swoop, LAWR 1

fill the c. POPE A 64

full c. of our banishment,
PATM 10

lost in the white c., PAGE 5

marks the c. of another world
WALK 13

neat c. on the glass MONTA 2

of all that c. WHITT 28

Weave a c. round him
COLE SAM 22

within this c. WALL 5

circled: sea is c. and sways/
peacefully WILLI 14

circler: restless one; the c. of
circles; AIKE 11

circles: Leaving c. new and clean
VAN DO 1

restless one; the circler of c.;
AIKE 11

whirling c. of time. JEFFE 23

Circling: C. above the hamlets
THOR 6

c. shadow of its appetite.
TATE A 2

pure and c. thoughts, MARV 31

circuit: c. of his fate, GRAV 34

Success in c. lies, DICKI 136

Within the c. THOR 10

circumspect: c. and right; MEYN 4

circumstance: odds with c.?
ROET 30

circumstances: read in normal c.?
POUN 30

circus: c. animals were all on
show, YEATS 26

cisterns: empty c. and exhausted
wells ELIOT T 150

voices singing out of empty c.
ELIOT T 150

citadel: towered c., SHAK 9

citherns: windy c. hankering for
hymns. STEVENS 14

cities: Bristled with c., ARNO 6

C. and Thrones and Powers
KIPL 14

dense-packed c. WHITM 51

Eros, builder of c., AUDE 34

few friends, but they are in c.
SNYD 18

founders of these starving c.,
AUDE 19

London, thou art the flour of C.
  all DUNB W 4
Soveraign of c., DUNB W 4
Thine alabaster c. gleam BATE 3
through learned c., AUDE 20
To life, to c., and to war!
  ARNO 38
twin c. frame. LAZA 1
we burned/ The c. JARR 15
world's great c., OSHA 2
citizen: c. Of credit and renown,
  COWP 6
citizens: c. of death's grey land,
  SASS 6
citron: blows the c. grove, MILT 79
citties: opposit two c. stood,
  MARL 4
city: been long in c. pent,
  KEAT 66
c. among men, DUNC 2
C. bides the foe. TIMR 1
c. built upon mud; MACN 6
c. in the twilight LONG 29
C. is of Night;
  THOMS J (1834–1882) 1
c. mouse eats bread and cheese; —
  ROSS C 6
c. mouse lives in a house; —
  ROSS C 5
C. nested in bays! WHITM 44
c. of Boston, BOSS 1
c. of spires and masts!
  WHITM 44
c. sleeps; JOHN L 5
c. sleeps; TENN 53
c. with lifted head singing
  SAND 4
clocks in the c. AUDE 2
day in the c.-square,
  BROWNI R 84
falling on the c. brown,
  BRID R 8
famous Hanover c.;
  BROWNI R 59
felled a c.; THOMA D 24
fishbone/ in the c.'s throat.
  LOWE R 18
holy c. of Byzantium. YEATS 127
house in the c.-square;
  BROWNI R 83
I adhere to my c., WHITM 30
in the just c. HOUS 3
Kingdom is a c.; UNKN 242
moderate Aristotelian c. AUDE 14
my c.! WHITM 44
now of all that c. WHITM 60
·O my C., CRAN H 34
pass'd through a populous c.
  WHITM 60
perfect for my c., WHITM 43
shall gather dew,/ Dreaming in
  throngful c. WHITT 28
sneer at this my c., SAND 4

Stormy, husky, brawling,/ C. of the
  Big Shoulders: SAND 3
Sun-girt C.! SHEL 37
through the C.'s sleepless sleep,
  THOMS J (1834–1882) 6
Unreal c., ELIOT T 118
We are the greatest c., SAND 8
Without a c. wall, ALEX 8
word of my c. WHITM 43
year upon year O c., WHITM 30
civil: appertain/ To c. justice,
  MILT 104
assent with c. leer, POPE A 7
c. fury first grew high, BUTL 1
shaking C. War relief,
  LOWE R 17
since c. war days, MAHON 2
civilisation: c. may not sink,
  YEATS 87
civility: wild c.: HERR 8
civilization: botched c., POUN 43
c. has given us too many.
  JOHN F 1
c. is a transient sickness.
  JEFFE 27
I am tired of c. JOHN F 1
If c. goes down, JEFFE 24
civilize: c. the ground. SIMP 12
civilized: connive/ in c. outrage
  HEAN 17
They and I are c. CULL 12
they are growing c.; JEFFE 25
civilly: most c. steering, GOLD 4
clad: c. in compleat steel, MILT 3
c. in smiles, TIMR 2
too richly c.; CRAS 11
claim: abate/ His ancient brutal c.
  MELV 8
claimed: never c. by us TATE A 18
clairvoyante: Madame Sosostris,
  famous c., ELIOT T 116
clam: rows of dead c. shells;
  ROET 42
clamb: We c. the hill the gither;
  BURN 35
clamber: c. to the heights of sleep,
  YEATS 42
clambering: c. on his undulant
  floor. NIMS 2
clamor: burst into c. LAWR 32
clamorous: c. groans SHAK 93
Upon their c. wings. YEATS 165
clamp: jaws' hooked c. and fangs
  HUGH T 11
clan: learned c.; EMER 29
Clanging: C. fights, and flaming
  towns, TENN 90
clangs: then embollen c., CHAT 2
clank: hark to the musical c.;
  WHITM 13
rustle and c. of muskets,
  WHITM 32

clap: Let the floods c. their hands;
  BIBL, O.T. 47
clapped: c. His hands, JOHN J 2
claps: Those that for c. do write,
  JONS 34
clapte: c. the windowe to.
  CHAU 55
clarion: sound the c., MORD 1
Clary's Grove: horse-races of long
  ago at C., MAST 7
clasp: c. of the knitted locks,
  WHITM 42
c. thee again, BROWNI R 70
c. thy knees; MILT 101
clasp'd: c. by an arm, BYRO 45
clasped: bootes c. faire and fetisly.
  CHAU 21
c. a reed. SHEL 28
Claspest: C. the limits of mortality,
  SHEL 68
clasping: hands c. a black cross.
  IREM 1
clasps: He c. the crag TENN 12
class: only colored student in my c.
  HUGH L 15
classes: noblest work she c.,
  BURN 30
classic: c. bronze of Benin.
  RANDA D 3
hyacinth hair, thy c. face, POE 45
classics: c. registered a little flat!
  RANS 29
claw: Nature, red in tooth and c.
  TENN 36
No c. or web here: GUNN 6
odor, talon, c., KIZE 3
then a livid C. DICKI 161
whisker first and then a c.,
  GRAY 19
clawed: c. me with his crutch,
  VAUX 3
claws: c. and teeth grown perfect,
  DICKEY 18
pair of ragged c./ Scuttling
  ELIOT T 86
ruddy are his c. STEVENS 13
spreads his c., CARRO 9
There lurk no c. OWEN 14
Clay: all the lists of C.! DICKI 114
cauld in the c. ELLI 2
C. house mouldring away,
  BRAD 1
c. is vile DUNB P 13
c. was not granted LOWE J 3
for this the c. grew tall?
  OWEN 27
grass and coloured c. ROSE 6
homage to the perishable c.,
  BROWNI R 28
I'll lie as cold as c. BLAK 41
Kingdoms are c.; SHAK 3
length in c.'s now competent,
  WEBS 3

let down in that steep bank of c.
SYNG 5

lying in the wet c. KAVA 19

mock us in the c. BEAU/FLET 2

of c. and wattles made:
YEATS 74

Toiling over a lump of c.
JOHN J 3

unassisted heart is barren c.,
MICH 1

Weeping in weak & mortal c.;
BLAK 26

ye of c. were cast by kind,
VAUX 6

clean: burly and c.; WARR 8

c. forever and forever,
WHITM 97

C. forspent, LANIE 1

c. hands, and a pure heart;
BIBL, O.T. 33

c./ In you, ruby. PLATH 70

c. in the flame, WILLI 8

C. the spittoons. HUGH L 2

c. upstanding chap like you?
KINGSM 1

kept the carrots c., HUGO 6

Leaving circles new and c.
VAN DO 1

Like the c. beasts, HOPE A 1

lodge at last the quivering needle/
C. in the eye SHAP 9

Scraped c. SIMI 4

Then I was c. and brave,
HOUS 41

though I am c. forgot, HERB G 6

wash this blood/ C. from my
hand? SHAK 108

wounds are silvered c., GRAV 21

cleaner: c., greener land! KIPL 12

cleanest: c. in the use of his
forepaws SMAR 7

Cleaning: C. and caressing,
ROET 48

We had daily c. REED H 4

cleanly: c. wantonness; HERR 1

Cleanse: C. me from its guilt and
pow'r. TOPL 1

cleansing: c. them from tears.
SHAK 93

clear: Burst agonized and c.!
DICKI 135

caught his c. accents,
BROWNI R 45

c. and ancient harmony THOR 5

C. and diminished MILLA 4

c. announcer's voice WILB 4

c., attentive mind SNYD 50

c. grit through and through;
WOOL 3

c. harp in diverse tones,
TENN 18

c. the upper pasture, FROS 21

c. universe SHEL 41

c. windows of the morning;
BLAK 108

Cold dark deep and absolutely c.,
BISH 4

Darkness more c. than noonday
ROSS C 21

dawn is c. SNYD 44

doubt is slow to c., BROWNI R 4

every highway's c. BYRO 53

Free from Corruption, or intire, or
c., DRYD 18

lark so shrill and c.; LYLY 3

made my own opinions c.;
DRYD 20

one c. call for me! TENN 9

One truth is c., POPE A 58

pardon this c. flame. THOR 7

rising steam/ And c. dances
WILB 24

uncorrupt, sufficient, c., intire,
DRYD 18

wild call and a c. call MASE 12

windows sparkled c.,
STEVENSO R 5

wits were fresh and c., ARNO 27

wrinkly and c. red, PLATH 72

clearer: c. as the years go by.
LARK 15

clearing: Alone in the public c.
TATE A 18

clearly: Burns but more c.
YEATS 61

clearness: with subtle c. POUN 66

cleave: c. the general ear with
horrid speech, SHAK 31

ill-used race of men that c. the
soil, TENN 91

Cleaving: two cocks together crow,/
C. the darkness THOMA E 4

cleft: c. for me, TOPL 1

clemency: distilled a c.; HARD 11

Clementine: his daughter C.
MONTROSS 1

clenched: c. like a Chinese puzzle
... RUKE 12

c. on a round pain;
THOMA D 5

one fist c. AUDE 59

Cleopatra: squeaking C. boy
SHAK 10

cleped: c. madame Eglentyne.
CHAU 13

clergy: c. banish from the mind,
CLARK A 3

clergyman: God preaches, — a noted
c., — DICKI 131

clerk: c. ther was of Oxenford
CHAU 22

Seynt Stevene was a c.
UNKN 212

unimportant c. Writes AUDE 7

clerks: c. of Time, ROBI 7

Whippersnapper c. BROWN S 1

clever: c. at mechanics, JEFFE 5

c. servant, insufferable master.
JEFFE 39

pacified by a c. line AUDE 48

clew: enchanted/ by a repulsive c.,
RUKE 3

cliff: c. in being backed by
continent; FROS 77

coign of the c. SWIN 10

from c. and scar TENN 112

happy as C. Klingenhagen
ROBI 8

scarpéd c. and quarried stone
TENN 35

summit of a craggy c.,
THOMS J (1700–1748) 8

cliffs: c. of England crumbling
HECH 3

swift it foamed,/ Black under c. it
raced, ARNO 5

climacteric: Gored by the c. of his
want, LOWE R 46

climate: Choose then your c.,
BARL 1

whole c. of opinion. AUDE 31

climates: manners, c., councils,
governments, TENN 130

climatures: Unto our c. and
countrymen. SHAK 20

Climb: C. her like a monument,
SEXT 5

c. the air; YEATS 166

c. the look out? LI PO 5

c. the streams YEATS 152

c./ Through violence MERR 9

C. to our proper dark,
YEATS 143

c. to wealth, BRYA 36

He shall aye c. EMER 33

last steps I c., SHEL 34

let the barrel c. SIMP 2

lewd hirelings c. MILT 68

Should the conflagration c.,
YEATS 69

thoughts/ Continual c.,
THOMS J (1700–1748) 6

to high doth dissolution c.,
WORD 8

climbed: cat/ c. over WILLI 2

c. the mountain, JUST 7

c. through darkness SASS 13

he c. the hill, WHITT 17

climber: c.-upward turns his face;
SHAK 44

climbing: c. heaven SHEL 88

c. ticklishness, CHAU 1

man c. must scrape his knees,
LEVE 11

clime: c. for me. EMER 30

In every c. adored, POPE A 126

warmer c., ADDI 2

wild weird c. POE 16

climes: those happy c. MILT 10

Cling: C., swing,/ Spring, sing,
  ELIOT T 58
  C. with life to the maid;
    EMER 24
  Love must c.   MERE O 3
  Where I c.   HOLM 16
Clinging: C. close with the crush of
  the Python, HILT 4
  Cry, — c. Heaven by the hems;
    THOMP F 12
clings: c. to twig, JEFFE 17
clippers: meet/ the close c.   LEVI 4
cloak: closed all in her c.,
  SIDN 29
  great c. blows in the light,
    RUKE 5
  martial c. around him.   WOLF C 2
  my inky c., SHAK 21
  travel forth without my c.,
    SHAK 198
cloaked: left me c. POUN 66
cloakrooms: in the c., HILL G 6
cloaks: scarlet c. and surplices/ Of
  linen, LAWR 9
Clock: chimes/ Of the tall C. Tower
  SNOD 8
  Christmas Eve, and twelve of the
  c. HARD 32
  Church c. at ten to three?
    BROO R 20
  c. Beats out TENN 19
  c. or an abbey horologe.
    CHAU 66
  c. runs down WALK 13
  C. stopped — DICKI 18
  count the c. that tells the time,
    SHAK 186
  Devil in the c., AUDE 10
  Dutch c. it told me FIEL E 2
  One luminary c. FROS 2
  seeing the c. stopped, WILLI 39
  Time made me his numbering c.
    SHAK 93
  wagging c. Tells me the hour's
  word, THOMA D 15
  watch the c. for you, SHAK 208
clocks: birds like watchful c.
  VAUG 7
  c., bodies, consciousness, shoe,
    GINS 24
  c. in the city AUDE 2
  merry larks are ploughmen's c.,
    SHAK 100
  platinum c. of excitement
    SHAP 5
clod: become/ A kneaded c.;
  SHAK 115
  face turned from the c. CARRU 1
  Must dullness turn me to a c.?
    HERB G 34
clods: grassy c. now calved,
  MILT 86

king of speechless c. LOWE R 22
man harrowing c. HARD 29
cloister: walk the studious c.'s pale,
  MILT 18
cloistral: early in this c. round
  ARNO 40
Clonmacnois: in C. OGIL 2
Clootie: Hornie, Satan, Nick, or C.,
  BURN 1
close: before its c. DICKI 107
  belly c. to ground. TOOM 5
  bronze annals of the oak-tree c.
    WILB 3
  Clinging c. with the crush of the
  Python, HILT 4
  c. beside me with silent lips
    WHITM 61
  c. my ears JOHN H 1
  c. of even, PRIO 8
  c. of heavy flowers, LANG 3
  c. on the promised good.
    TENN 95
  c. the Valves of her attention —
    DICKI 133
  c. the wall up SHAK 56
  c. to his groin, SNYD 5
  c. your eyes with holy dread,
    COLE SAM 22
  c. your term here, HARD 23
  c.-companioned inarticulate hour
    ROSS D 4
  curious boy, never too c.,
    WHITM 64
  daily c. of their junction,
    WHITM 76
  evening sees its c.; LONG 49
  Folded c. under deepening snow.
    LOWE J 13
  found in the c. MILT 118
  heard at the c. of the day
    WHITM 108
  its bloody c. BRYA 6
  Lashed c. to a drifting mast.
    LONG 52
  Learn to c. softly JUST 5
  loves on to the c., MOOR T 3
  music at the c., SHAK 87
  our c. ivy twines, CAREW 12
  "Please c. that door. SERV 5
  scent survives their c.:
    THOMP F 1
  Stand c. around, LAND 13
closed: c. all in her cloak, SIDN 29
  C. his eyes in endless night.
    GRAY 30
  Love c. what he begat:
    MERE G 13
  My life c. twice DICKI 107
  on the world's c. door. CRAN H 3
  Our life is c., WHITM 41
  street door was partially c.;
    LEAR 17

'twixt thy c. lips, MORR 7
With lightly c. fists WHITM 70
closely: together c. lie, and kisse,
  PETRO 2
closer: c. walk with God, COWP 25
  In c., dearer company, GLAD 2
closets: c. of lone desire, LANIE 3
closing: Diapason c. full in Man.
  DRYD 25
  fixed forever in your c. eyes,
    JARR 11
cloth: c.-of-gold of tissue —
  SHAK 5
  Slips and pulls the table c.
    ELIOT T 111
  wrap it in a damp c. HUGO 5
clothe: c. me with dark thoughts,
  DANI S 10
  summer c. the general earth
    COLE SAM 16
clothed: c. alle in o lyveree
  CHAU 5
  c. his neck with thunder?
    BIBL, O.T. 17
  c. with derision; SWIN 2
  c. your wife, DURE 1
  God c. himself in vile man's
  flesh, DONN 54
  thinly c., WHITM 70
clothes: c. brave enough/ To be a
  courtier, JONS 24
  c. were all tarnished MOOR C 3
  flowers without c. VAUG 9
  his suit of c.? LIND V 5
  Kindles in c. a wantonness:
    HERR 8
  liquefaction of her c. HERR 61
  polyhedral eye and shabby c.,
    SHAP 13
  stiff, painted c., YEATS 91
  take off all my c. BERRYM 14
  take off your c.? GINS 2
  Through tattered c. SHAK 81
  when no c. they were worn.
    UNKN 41
clothing: saw wrong c. BETJ 7
clots: blood c. the tendrils
  PLATH 13
clotted: c. rags and blood,
  WHITM 115
  jags from the c. shoulder,
    JEFFE 13
  soul grows c. by contagion,
    MILT 4
cloud: any c. beguile TASS 3
  black c. full of storms RANS 10
  blare of the c.-trumpets,
    WHITM 6
  blissful c. of summer-indolence
    KEAT 41
  broad c.-driving moon BRID R 19
  c. across the sky. SNYD 7
  c.-capped towers, SHAK 163

c.-folds of her garments LONG 38
c. is scattered, SHEL 89
c. of sorrow, CAMPI 2
c. part screened, MERE G 8
c.-sopped, marble hands,
  THOMA D 5
c./ That seemed to twinkle.
  KOCH 1
c. that's dragonish, SHAK 9
eye in the black c. GINS 23
fast-flying c., KNOX 1
fiend hid in a c. BLAK 72
found a c.—so light POUN 16
From c. to tumbling cloud,
  YEATS 53
High as a c., WORD 130
his c.-topped head. GRAY 4
immense and lonely as a c.
  AIKE 7
lift me as a wave, a leaf, a c.!
  SHEL 45
Like a fiend in a c. BLAK 45
lonely as a c. WORD 24
Low-anchored c., THOR 8
Moloch whose fate is a c.
  GINS 17
War's annals will c. HARD 30
wind came out of the c. POE 5
clouded: c. forms of long-past
  history. BRON 5
wild the c. gleam. DIXO 1
cloudes: full c. are braste CHAT 2
cloudless: His c. thunder MILT 117
clouds: amorous c. dividing,
  MILT 37
base contagious c. SHAK 51
blue/ mottled c. WILLI 34
bright as the c., WORD 102
burial c., WHITM 56
Check'ring the eastern c.
  SHAK 146
C. and eclipses stain both moon
  and sun, SHAK 199
c. are mean, DICKI 128
C. are violet ROSS C 32
c. congeal, CHAU 46
c. ere they divide them; SHEL 53
c. of June, JACK 1
C. of the west — WHITM 18
C. shade the sun, EMER 5
C. that gather WORD 86
c. that loured upon our house
  SHAK 94
c. the c. chase; MERE G 3
c. were gone to play, SHEL 73
dark c. are massing; DUNB P 6
doubted c. would break,
  BROWNI R 12
figures of the c. STEVENS 48
God in c., POPE A 59
Grow as the c. grew. DAY 6
let base c. o'ertake me SHAK 198
Looks in the c., SHAK 44

Pack, c., away, and welcome,
  day! HEYW 1
rain, from c. to drop assign'd,
  BIBL, O.T. 67
ravening c., WHITM 56
shadows of the c. WORD 3
She saw the c. STEPHENS 2
sin/ Like c. eclipsed my mind.
  VAUG 18
skies with c. are lin'd;
  BIBL, O.T. 67
trailing c. of glory WORD 70
Vapours, and c., and storms.
  THOMS J (1700–1748) 12
whither the c. have fled?
  LOWE J 19
cloudy: c. bosom hoarded,
  LONG 39
c. foreheads of the great.
  HORA 10
Clout: Gup, Christian C., SKEL 4
clove: Flower o' the c.,
  BROWNI R 27
cloven: splinterless as a c. rock.
  FROS 122
clover: bees in the purple c.,
  COOP 1
c. and one bee, — DICKI 148
c. and timothy, WHITM 31
c.-scented grass,
  BROWNI E/GUIN 1
I'm in c. now, nor know/ Who
  made honey long ago. BLUN 3
Like a lovely white c. KENN 2
pigs can live in c.; WYLI 11
pulled some c. SWEN 4
clown: c., the boozer, the fighter?
  MAST 6
emperor and c.: KEAT 50
mated with a c., TENN 71
yon red-cloaked c., EMER 17
cloyed: heart high-sorrowful and c.,
  KEAT 39
club: c.-footed ghoul MACN 15
sit like a bridge c., SEXT 10
cluck: c. like starved pullets,
  WRIG J 1
clump: some umbrageous c., —
  HOLM 1
Clumps: heart/ C. in the breast
  SHAP 20
clumsy: alien/ As our c. traps,
  KIZE 3
body turned/ To c. dirt WILB 39
C. and lumbering SCHW 9
c. partner wants to do! ROET 21
give it a c. name. TENN 101
let 'em be c., SHERI 2
saw that c. crow ROET 50
clung: body c. and swarmed,
  WINT 6
cluster: Ripe as the melting c.,
  GAY 1

clustered: Nouns were c. in the
  street. KOCH 3
clustering: my c. fruits I tend;
  AKEN 2
with c. bunches growing,
  SHAK 162
clusters: luscious c. of the vine
  MARV 17
we such c. had, HERR 36
clutched: begging I c. childlike,
  WRIG R 1
iron will/ That c. THOMP W 3
clutching: c. the inviolable shade,
  ARNO 28
cluttered: c. eyes BARA 9
clymmynge: thunder's rattling c.
  sound CHAT 2
coach: hackney c. Appearing,
  showed the ruddy morn's
  approach. SWIF 10
in Christ's c. saints sweetly sing,
  TAYL E 4
coaches: c. shall be scrap and rust
  SAND 12
coagulate: o'ersized with c. gore,
  SHAK 30
coal: Carpenters, c.-passers —
  CLARK J 1
C.-black maidens LIND V 12
quick c. Of mortall fire:
  HERB G 29
whole world turn to c.,
  HERB G 72
coalpit: Darker by far than any c.
  stone. TAYL E 3
coals: eyes like live c., WOOL 2
footsoles/ trod warily on living c.
  WYLI 4
mercy blows the c.; SOUTHW 2
one peck of purgatorial c.,
  BYRO 43
coarse: c. and strong and cunning.
  SAND 4
jests are c., POPE A 20
thou art too c. to love.' HERR 70
coarseness: c. of our heaven repine,
  ADDI 2
Coarsest: fine and C. web;
  SOUTHW 8
coast: along that pathless c., —
  BRYA 26
c. crying out for tragedy JEFFE 1
C. of Coromandel LEAR 4
laid on Greenland's C., GAY 4
stern and rock-bound c., HEMA 3
coaster: Dirty British c. MASE 2
coat: coyote got his/ ratty old fur c.
  SILKO 1
father should wear a broadcloth
  c., WHITT 16

I made my song a c. YEATS 30
riband to stick in his c.
 BROWNI R 44
coat's: his c. so black, WOLF H 1
coats: creamy iridescent c. of mail,
 BISH 3
In their gold c. spots SHAK 126
coaxing: c. up water, ROET 4
cobweb: Fearless — the c. DICKI 32
Coca-Cola: sandwiches/ and C.,
 OHAR 12
cocaine: c. dog and a c. cat,
 UNKN 67
C. town on C. hill, UNKN 67
fought all night with a c. rat,
 UNKN 67
hear about C. Lil? UNKN 67
sniffing c.' UNKN 68
Cock: C. by Hens attended, GAY 2
c. doth craw, UNKN 307
c., hight Chanticleer. CHAU 66
c. that crowed in the morn
 MOTH 11
Damned universal c.,
 STEVENS 2
first c. his matin rings. MILT 23
hear the crowing c., LONG 8
My tale is of a c., CHAU 69
Ride a c.-horse MOTH 25
Who killed C. Robin? MOTH 32
cockatoo: green freedom of a c.
 STEVENS 54
cockatoos: watched by c. and
 goats, STEVENSO R 19
cocked: c. On sods; HEAN 10
Cockridden: Codham, C., and
 Childerditch, THOMA E 11
cockroaches: jade c., MOOR M 9
cocks: drowned the c.! SHAK 75
two c. together crow,/ Cleaving the
 darkness THOMA E 4
cocktail: c. smells in bars.
 ELIOT T 105
cocky: c. little ogre dozes off,
 AUDE 59
coconut: flavour of shredded c.
 SIMP 4
Cocquet: cut even between the C.
 and the Prude. PRIO 6
cod: home of the bean and the c.,
 BOSS 1
code: half-talk c. of mysteries
 KAVA 21
trail has its own stern c. SERV 3
Codham: C., Cockridden, and
 Childerditch, THOMA E 11
coexist: cheek-by-jowl c.;
 LOWE J 9
Coffee: late/ C. and oranges
 STEVENS 54
measured out my life with c.
 spoons; ELIOT T 82
Overturns a c.-cup, ELIOT T 111

coffer: wrest the law to fill the c.
 WYAT 23
coffin: buried us without shroud or
 c. HEAN 18
C. after C. HEAN 5
dark of the c. THOMA D 2
in the c. WHITM 69
white face in the c. WHITM 69
coffins: great guns, unawares,/
 Shook all our c. HARD 13
In charnels and on c., SHEL 15
coffles: chained you in c.,
 BROWN S 4
cofre: litel gold in c. CHAU 2
cog: c. in a golden singing hive:
 SPEND 9
c. in a machine, MACN 16
cogitations: Sometimes these c. still
 amaze ELIOT T 54
cognate: Out of what c. splendor
 WILB 28
Coifed: C. with crown, SYNG 3
coign: c. of the cliff SWIN 10
coil: c. and hissed, FROS 8
c. of rhythm and number;
 EMER 33
c. of ticking towers. . . .
 CRAN H 34
shuffled off this mortal c.,
 SHAK 39
spread his lustrous c.; HOLM 2
coiled: c., hurdling muscles of his
 thighs: LOWE R 37
c. on the bed TATE A 20
C. to a lithe precision TATE A 9
Each dead child c., PLATH 33
coin: chosen c. of fancy TENN 124
c., or counterfeit BUTL 5
Gold on a c., LARK 11
Cok: jolie C. crawis; MONTG 1
cold: "Are you c. too, poor Pleiads,
 GRAV 30
Black pit c. and light-year
 SNYD 30
boughs which shake against the
 c., SHAK 215
cackling laugh or her barking c.
 WALK 10
Cast a c. eye YEATS 160
clear/ Water, c., so cold! JARR 26
C. air bites the throat. SNYD 44
c. and caressable;/ his eyes were
 red glass, BISH 14
c. And passionate as the dawn.'
 YEATS 60
c. and rook-delighting heaven
 YEATS 32
c. as any icicle. RANS 27
c. as death: CAMPB R 8
c. charities of man CRAB 7
c. coming we had of it,
 ELIOT T 49
c. did freeze, TASS 3

C. doth increase, NASHE 2
C. doth not sting, NASHE 3
c.-drill,/ Pick, singlejack, SNYD 2
c. Earth wanderers BLAK 29
c. eternal shores ROBI 37
c. friction of expiring sense
 ELIOT T 68
c. gradations of decay,
 JOHN S (1709–1784) 4
c. hard mouth/ of the world,
 BISH 6
c. in death: ROSS C 7
c. in the pasture. WARR 5
c.-nosed gun? HEAN 21
c. snow-water from a tin cup
 SNYD 18
c. snows of a dream. YEATS 97
c. surrounds our warm bed,
 LEVE 4
c. To meet it when it woos
 HERR 35
c. tranquillity, SHEL 22
cross the damp c. lawn
 BERRYM 14
dark c. day. AUDE 36
darkness and the c.,
 STEVENSO R 6
death with c.; JONS 28
dew is c. upon the ground,
 TENN 105
dinner c. PURD 2
dinner will be c." HOUS 30
Fallen c. and dead. WHITM 45
Fare you well; your suit is c.
 SHAK 119
Fed with c. and usurous hand?
 BLAK 68
feet that were blue with c.,
 OSUL 2
fiery day had a kernel sweet of c.
 THOMA E 9
fort/ against the c. WILLI 10
grass is c.; VAN DO 2
heart a c. December. UNKN 6
his grasp is so c.! GOET 1
housed Him from the c.! REES 1
I'll lie as c. as clay. BLAK 41
I'm c. all over. ROET 36
In c. grave she was lain.
 UNKN 292
jewel c. and pure; MILLA 5
laid/ With c. vegetation SITW 3
let their veins run c. OWEN 31
lie in c. obstruction SHAK 115
moment of the c.'s/ deepest
 plunge WILLI 9
much less c., ROSS C 25
Narrow and c. and neat. WYLI 9
nose was long and c., UNKN 146
On thy c. gray stones, O Sea!
 TENN 1
paddle in the c. Companionable
 streams YEATS 166

pain, darkness and c.
  BROWNI R 69
quenched with the c. of death.
  HERB CH 4
Sam, looking c. and calm,
  SERV 5
serpents whistle at the c.
  LOWE R 60
sisters, proud and c., WHITT 19
so sweet/ and so c. WILLI 40
stroked your c., pulsing throat
  LEVE 22
thou feel'st it c. SHAK 185
Three winters c. SHAK 227
too c. always SMIT ST 2
Trembling, c., in ghastly fears —
  BLAK 43
twilight c. and gray, LONG 23
water was too c. for us.
  LOWE R 58
whitest sheets of Lillies c.
  MARV 29
Wild, c., and accusing. SNYD 10
coldly: c. die GRAV 3
c. mark the holy fane
  SCOT WA 4
Five bells c. ringing out. SLES 5
hoarse wind blows c.; ARNO 10
cole: Derk was the night as pich or
  as the c., CHAU 53
colera: your reddè c. CHAU 68
Coleridge: C. received SMIT ST 8
C. was a dope. FULL 3
Wordsworth, C., Southey;
  BYRO 21
colerik: reve was a sclendre c.
  man. CHAU 19
collapse: c. of bestials, idols.
  BROO G 14
collars: c. of the moonshine's watery
  beams, SHAK 153
collect: c. for the Community Chest
  CORS 6
collected: c. in one place
  AMMO 14
collective: c. nose in my books
  POUN 34
strength of C. Man, AUDE 74
collector: sea is a c., MOOR M 12
College: C. Eight and their trainer
  NEWB 3
c. rolls receive his name,
  JOHN S (1709–1784) 17
go to c. SNYD 41
Maud went to c. BROO G 12
said son at c. BYRO 47
two sons through c. DURE 1
collision: tingling bruises of c.,
  HECH 9
colly: Four c. birds, UNKN 277
Cologne: body-and-soul-stinking
  town of C. COLE SAM 26
city of C.; COLE SAM 5

Colonel: C.'s son has taken a horse,
  KIPL 2
colonial: salients of c. policy.
  WALC 2
colonnade: whispering sound of the
  cool c., COWP 13
color: c. is a diabolic die." WHEA 1
c. of everything MERW 2
c. of the heavy hemlocks
  STEVENS 6
c. passion but its neck a question.
  WARR 9
earth turning into c., RUKE 2
seems the c. of iris, LOWE R 57
colored: only c. student in my
  class. HUGH L 15
see the c. counties, HOUS 25
struggling and doing without and
  being c. HAYD 13
to the c. rest room; DURE 2
worser spirit a woman, c. ill.
  SHAK 240
you are c. JOHN F 1
colors: c. are struck WHITM 90
c. to the chameleon, SHAK 62
nature paints her c., MILT 79
sell the c. of your sunset
  JOHN H 2
colossal: c. wreck, SHEL 50
part of the c. sun, STEVENS 29
Colour: C. of lilac, LOWE A 1
taking him to prison for the c. of
  his hair. HOUS 21
coloured: child from the c.
  frontispiece? KLEI 2
In vials of ivory and c. glass
  ELIOT T 121
petticoats c. like flame. OSUL 2
colouring: take a sober c.
  WORD 86
Colourless: But colourless. C.
  PLATH 73
colours: c. all to black are cast,
  GREV 4
C. and words WORD 114
c. of the floreal SITW 1
glaring c. HERR 27
goodly c. gloriously arrayed;
  SPENS 21
magic web with c. gay. TENN 61
colt: Like a c.'s WHITT 8
colts: youthful and unhandled c.
  SHAK 125
Columbia: C.'s true-blue sons,
  ROON 1
Hail, C.! happy land!
  HOPKINSO 1
columbine: c., the nept, SKEL 1
Columbus: C. found a world,
  SANT 1
C.'s doom-burdened caravels
  SQUI 1

column: no marble c. craves
  TIMR 6
skunk with her c. of kittens
  LOWE R 41
columns: ranged in c. before me,
  WHITM 110
unending c. press BROO R 1
comanded: c. he virginitee?
  CHAU 90
comandement: conseiling nis no c.
  CHAU 91
comb: c. stood up straight
  RANS 20
Fair maid, white and red,/ C. me
  smooth, PEEL 5
fine-tooth c. BROO G 12
comber: c. of arrogance, SIDN 4
combine: With Thee/ Let me c.
  HERB G 27
combined: c. with gout, GILB 18
knotted and c. locks to part,
  SHAK 26
Combing: woman/ C. STEVENS 32
combs: honey/ in c., HALL 4
combustion: hideous ruine and c.
  MILT 49
come: beds for all who c.
  ROSS C 29
Brother, c.! COTTE 1
call to c. in FROS 16
c. along with me./ Something like
  a person: SILKI 1
c. among new faces, WHITM 113
c. and buy': HERR 5
c. and go ROSS C 17
C. and lick BLAK 107
C. away, SCOT WA 21
c. away, death, SHAK 176
c. buy: ROSS C 11, 13
C. down. WRIG J 8
C. down, O Christ, WILD 10
C., fill the Cup, OMAR 1
c. from, Baby dear? MACDONA 1
c. from the ends of the earth!
  KIPL 3
c. in the end despondency and
  madness. WORD 121
C. in your war-array,
  SCOT WA 21
C. into the garden, Maud,
  TENN 93
c. let us kiss and part; DRAY 15
C. live with me MARL 18
c. once more; TENN 53
C. play with me; YEATS 149
c. to bother us. WILLI 17
c. to dust. SHAK 18
c. to me in dreams ROSS C 7
C. to me, pretty peat, UNKN 204
c. to pass. BUTL 3
c. to take your holy place?
  WALK 4

c. to us, abide with us,
BROO P 8
C. were but the Spring,
ROSS C 23
c. where comfort is, CAMPI 7
curse is c. upon me,' cried/ The
Lady of Shalott. TENN 66
Day c. white, WHITM 65
harbingers are c. HERB G 34
Haste and c. THOMA E 19
How much can c. DICKI 139
how purposed art thou c.
HOUS 6
I c. to quench the kiss ROBI 23
I c. to tell you this, ROBI 23
If Death should c. UNKN 183
is past, or passing, or to c.
YEATS 130
It will c. again./ Be still./ Wait.
ROET 38
light is c., TENN 105
loves have c. and gone;
MILLA 40
men may c. and men may go.
TENN 5
my love is c. to me. ROSS C 2
never c. back to me. TENN 3
night c. black, WHITM 65
no more c. near thee.' UNKN 126
O! c. quickly, sweetest Lord,
CAMPI 17
Person from Porlock c. quickly
SMIT ST 9
redness suddenly c. LAWR 23
shall my ghost c. to thy bed,
DONN 4
She breathes! She burns! She'll
c.! RANDA J 2
Sir Francis is c.; UNKN 294
stolen goods do c. to light.
SIDN 10
they c. and talk to me, WILLI 17
whistle, and I'll c. to you,
BURN 64
Why don't they c.? OWEN 17
You c. too. FROS 87
comedians: quick c. Extemporally
will stage us SHAK 10
comedy: dressed for this short c.
RALEG 15
comely: c. soul in white BARNE 3
dost so c. grow, FRENE 5
for c. grace, UNKN 181
comen: wele is c. to weylaway,
UNKN 289
Comes: April/ C. like an idiot,
MILLA 37
c. safe home, SHAK 60
consummation c., HARD 16
evening darkens and c. on.
WRIG J 4
glad ocean c. and goes, PATM 6
hope never c. MILT 50

Joy c., grief goes, LOWE J 18
no one c.? HUGO 2
Rainbow c. and goes, WORD 66
soberly c. And stays — HAY 2
Spring c. merry towards me
ROSS D 1
There c. what will come. WINT 2
Venus c. not ev'ry Day. DRYD 24
when it c. to living, VAN DY 1
youth c. back to me. LONG 32
comest: Death! thou c. UNKN 90
rarely c. thou, SHEL 60
comet: c. through flame SPEND 7
dreadful C., BUTL 8
On, C.! on, Cupid! MOOR C 2
cometh: c. from afar: WORD 69
he c. to judge the earth;
BIBL, O.T. 47
whence c. my help. BIBL, O.T. 58
comets: no c. seen; SHAK 45
comfort: come where c. is,
CAMPI 7
c. and despair SHAK 240
c. of Christ BRID R 16
c. of her mother's tears, JONS 22
C., where true meaning is.
BRET 7
found no c. in the grave.
YEATS 96
I my sins confess,/ Sweet Spirit c.
me! HERR 19
I'll not, carrion c., HOPKINS 4
in c. lie. HULM 2
learned what c. is, TROW 5
one c. still must rise, POPE A 82
Poor c. all comfort: PITT 1
rod and thy staff they c. me.
BIBL, O.T. 31
some strange c. POPE A 79
there's c. in 't SHAK 179
tidings of c. and joy! CRAI 1
warn, to c., and command;
WORD 135
words with heavenly c. fraught,
GILM 1
comfortable: c. kind of old
scarecrow. YEATS 11
c. minds CUMM 52
c. smell BROO R 5
Progress is a c. disease:
CUMM 35
comforted: folly of being c.
YEATS 62
comforting: c., melodic sigh,
JOHN J 6
comforts: social c. drop away.
JOHN S (1709–1784) 2
comfy: a dirty dog, quite c.
BISH 12
comic: in a c. mood SHAP 14
comical: think it's c. GILB 22
coming: applaud/ His c.! LAWR 25
cold c. we had of it, ELIOT T 49

c. in the Fall, DICKI 75
c. of the King of Heaven
UNKN 314
c. on/ Of grateful evening mild,
MILT 76
c. to birth. OSHA 5
ear may hear His c., BROO P 6
glory of the c. of the Lord;
HOWE 1
going and c. back. FROS 14
I, the rake,/ C. behind her
ROET 28
Man is a long time c. SAND 18
"Morgan's men are c., WOOL 1
Moses — was c. next. HOLM 8
noises of c. and going,
WHITM 33
reflected in the c. time. LONG 27
rooms they will not be/ C. back
to. JUST 5
warned of the c. fury.
THOMA D 16
wintered and were c. awake.
MORG 1
command: Achievement is c.;
SHAK 169
at Heaven's c.,
THOMS J (1700–1748)/MALL 1
charge of the c. CREE 6
C. a Table in this Wilderness,
MILT 109
c. me to my rest, DRAY 3
c. my heart CRAS 12
Her that hath power me to c.
WYAT 14
I can c.? MILT 109
I could c. content; DE VE 1
I have cherries at c." UNKN 57
mild eyes c. LAZA 1
should c. a regiment, CAME 2
warn, to comfort, and c.;
WORD 135
commander: Thir dread c.:
MILT 57
commanders: Cossack c.
cannonading WATT A 1
commanding: c. No SIMP 6
C. words; DRYD 18
commandment: thy c. all alone shall
live SHAK 28
commandments: Fear God, and keep
his c.: BIBL, O.T. 7
no Ten C. KIPL 13
Ten for the Ten C. UNKN 52
write poetical c., BYRO 20
commands: I gave c.;
BROWNI R 57
commemorate: O c. me KAVA 23
commend: c./ A timorous foe,
POPE A 7
c. me the Yak. BELL 20
c. This way to husbands,
JONS 36

comment: stars in secret influence
c.; SHAK 187
commentary: c. On the Crucifixion?
PRIN 2
commer: this new c., Shame,
MILT 97
commerce: c. between us. POUN 53
c. or contemplation. BISH 27
conveyor of c.; ELIOT T 27
In matters of c. CANN 1
Saw the heavens fill with c.,
TENN 75
commercing: c. with the skies,
MILT 16
comming: c. of the long'd-for May.
CAREW 14
commission: sin of c., NASH 9
commodore: sat in a c.'s hat
CARRY 10
common: aged after the c. trace.
SENE 2
all was done in c. YEATS 41
blind and a c. brown; WILB 36
breathing of the c. wind
WORD 153
cast forth in the c. air, SHAK 86
c. chord again, BROWNI R 5
c. fate of all things rare WALL 2
c. friend; POPE A 79
c. man's despair. WILD 1
c. people of the skies, WOTT 3
C. Rule was made the C. Prey;
DRYD 19
Dear c. flower, LOWE J 15
deviate from the c. track.
POPE A 30
dowry for a use in c. life.
SHAP 29
forgotten crowd/ Of c. beauties,
CAREW 7
He nothing c. did, or mean,
MARV 22
Honesty's against all c. sense —
ROCH 10
It is c. knowledge NASH 9
It was a C. Night DICKI 98
life's c. way, WORD 42
light of c. day. WORD 71
people of c. sense damn metres,
LOWE J 5
raise up C.-wealths DRYD 1
simple produce of the c. day.
WORD 16
voted by c. consent)
BROWNI R 36
commonplace: life, that is c. and
solitary. JARR 19
commons: Gentles and c.
SCOT WA 21
commonwealth: too lofty in our c.
SHAK 90
commune: c. with Thee. DOAN 1

communication: c. Of the dead is
tongued ELIOT T 64
communing: c. with thee,
WHITM 52
communion: live to hold c.
BANK 2
pleasure of that c. LEVE 12
Communism: your C. 'Paranoia' into
hospitals. GINS 24
community: c. of wrongs; GILB 11
served the Greater C. AUDE 93
compact: dimensions are as well c.,
SHAK 70
imagination all c. SHAK 127
compaignye: frankeleyn was in his
c. CHAU 4
nyne and twenty in a c. CHAU 6
Withouten oother c. CHAU 11
companie: desire your c.: JONS 14
companion: c. of the dead) LINC 2
C. to his self for her,
STEVENS 68
Without any c. WHITM 39
Companionable: paddle in the cold/
C. streams YEATS 166
companionless: gazing on the earth,/
Wandering c. SHEL 88
companions: All her lovely c.
MOOR T 14
company: be in such good c.
DARC 2
bear him c. LONG 51
bear him c. POPE A 60
formost of his c., UNKN 60
I love thy c. SHAK 144
In closer, dearer c., GLAD 2
Pastime with good c. HENR 1
visionary c. of love, CRAN H 36
When c. comes, HUGH L 6
compare: belied with false c.
SHAK 237
carefully c. it GILB 8
c. her/ to a fallen leaf. WILLI 49
c. thee to a summer's day?
SHAK 188
compared: there's nothing c. with
UNKN 196
compass: c. round, FROS 102
faithful c. that still points to
thee. GAY 7
lean/ as a c.-needle. LOWE R 18
lordly great c. within, LANIE 4
narrow c.! WALL 6
rosy lips and cheeks/ Within his
bending sickle's c. SHAK 232
compasses: stiff twin c. DONN 64
compassion: Informing a correct c.,
KIRK 4
Meaning: c. SNYD 39
compast: with dangers c. round,
MILT 84
compel: Our goal which we c.:
SPEND 18

Compelling: C. a recognition.
TOML 2
compendious: Portable and c.
Oceans. CRAS 8
Compensate: C.?" he inquired
LA FO 2
compensatory: c. spark, EMER 9
competent: length in clay's now c.,
WEBS 3
Complacencies: C. of the peignoir,
STEVENS 54
complacent: few c. years ROBI 5
complain: Birds c.: GRAY 33
c. no more. LONG 25
Justice against Fate c., MARV 21
peach c. GRAV 2
complaining: great dolour c.
UNKN 206
soft c. flute DRYD 26
complains: c. of my gab and my
loitering. WHITM 73
complaint: c. of present days
BYRO 15
mourn in my c., BIBL, O.T. 37
complaints: never-ending c.,
MACN 4
compleat: clad in c. steel, MILT 3
complement: congruence of the c.
MOOR M 41
complete: everything is c., RUKE 5
Law of thyself c., WHITM 102
make someone else c.? ROET 20
complex: c., manifold involvedness
LAWR 55
whole/ Is c.; FULL 2
complexion: c.'s loss? JONS 32
dread and black c. smeared
SHAK 30
gold c. dimmed; SHAK 188
complexities: All mere c.,
YEATS 17
complicated: c., being an American,
SIMP 8
c. state of mind, GILB 30
compose: happiest when I c.
poems: LAYT 1
signs that stars c., HOLLA 2
composed: large and c. SHAP 2
composedly: he c. cries, WHITM 90
composure: Have kept c., WILB 22
compound: a familiar c. ghost
ELIOT T 65
compression: c. is the first grace
MOOR M 39
compulsions: all our c. meet,
LARK 6
compute: I c. the weary hours
KING H 2
partly may c., BURN 9
comrade: c. I wrapt in his blanket,
WHITM 107
have no c., HARD 51
my son and my c. WHITM 106

new-hatched, unfledged c.
   SHAK 23
no c. Lucy knew; WORD 50
O c. lustrous WHITM 52
Vigil for c. WHITM 107

comrades: Bleach the bones of c.
   slain, HOUS 43
C., leave me here a little,
   TENN 68
C. mine WHITM 53
Pompeius, best of all my c.,
   HORA 7

conceal: ceremony never did c.,
   WILB 9
I will c. nothing. RUKE 10
practically c. its sex. NASH 17

conceal'd: c. their deities; OVID 4
love that is c., MARL 4

conceale: c. no beauty grace,
   KYNA 1

concealed: mysterious parts were
   then c.: MILT 73

concedes: eye c. to/ Encroaching
   horizon, HEAN 1

conceit: c. of this inconstant stay
   SHAK 187
Infusing him with self and vain
   c., SHAK 89

conceive: c. you may use GILB 25
I can hardly c. MOOR M 41

conceived: C. in sin, and unto labor
   born, JONS 33
honour is a thing c. DANI S 20
place where he was c. SITW 6

conceiving: marble with too much
   c., MILT 35

concentrate: c. the will. WINT 3

concentrated: c. in purpose.
   ELIOT T 7

concentration: c. of the electric
   chair — LOWE R 32

concentred: c. all in self,
   SCOT WA 12

conception: his c. wretched,
   BACO 1
most rare c., nothing. WILB 27
Sin their c., their birth weeping,
   WEBS 4

concepts: c. linked like chainmail
   GUNN 1

concern: Does not c. the Bee,
   DICKI 119
our c. was speech, ELIOT T 67

concerned: c. with outer, FROS 116
Happens to be c. REED H 3

concertina: c.'s melancholy string!
   GILB 43

conclave: In stately c. CHES 5

conclude: c. against a wall of stone.
   WILB 30
c. our Ships are lost, SACK 2

Concludes: C. with Cupid's curse. —
   PEEL 1

conclusion: logical and/ beautiful c.
   HARJ 3
Murder will out, this my c
   CHAU 71

conclusions: c. with those
   Janizaries, BYRO 35
method of c."; MOOR M 40
reached no c., AMMO 5

concord: c. of my state and time
   SHAK 93
c. shall not fail; WORD 8
through C. Plain. EMER 48

concrete: c. void of insulin
   GINS 15

concubines: to cornfield c.,
   TOOM 3

concupiscent: c. curds. STEVENS 9

Concurring: C. hands MOOR M 37

condemn: nor the years c. BINY 3
rage, sweat, censure, and c.:
   JONS 20

condemn'd: by their Conscience, be
   c. or freed. DRYD 17

Condemned: C. to Hope's delusive
   mine, JOHN S (1709–1784) 2
guiltless be c., MILT 99

condemns: c. me for a villain.
   SHAK 99

condense: passion to c. WINT 11

condescend: c. to prose, BYRO 20

condition: hot c. of their blood;
   SHAK 125
wearisome c. of humanity!
   GREV 9

conditions: all the c. of its
   existence, BISH 30

Condor: eternal C. years POE 40

conduct: reports on his c. agree
   AUDE 93
wise c.; JEFFE 34

cone: Lodgepole/ c. SNYD 46
pine c. falls SNYD 46
sweet volcanic c.; LOWE R 51

confess: I me c., ORLE 1
I my sins c.,/ Sweet Spirit comfort
   me! HERR 19
See! and c., POPE A 82

confessed: c. Humbly their faults,
   MILT 98

confession: c. to despair,
   CLARK A 1

confessions: cells to hear c. SIMI 2

confidence: c. may bind, HALE 2
put your trust and c. MORE 1
Quire above,/ Is C.: HERB G 14

confine: eternity's c., ROET 10

confined: c. to fast in fires,
   SHAK 26
unstinted tide c.;
   JOHN S (1822–1882) 1

confines: a Canon which c.
   BELL 14

conflagration: Should the c. climb,
   YEATS 69

conflict: lovers without c., TASS 4

Confound: C. the ignorant,
   SHAK 31
c. this surly sister, SYNG 1

confounded: O'erhang and jutty his
   c. base, SHAK 56
state itself c. to decay, SHAK 211

confounds: thought c. us MUIR 6

confront: Marvelous Truth, c. us
   LEVE 16

confronting: c., reversing my cries,
   WHITM 31
c. the waves, WHITM 63

confus'd: c. march forlorn,
   MILT 61

confusion: blank c.! true epitome
   WORD 109
C. of the death-bed YEATS 33
C. on thy banners wait, GRAY 1
without discord or c. COWL 10

congeal: clouds c., CHAU 46

Congenial: C. horrors, hail!
   THOMS J (1700–1748) 12

Congo: mouth of the C. LIND V 9
Mumbo-Jumbo, god of the C.,
   LIND V 11

congratulate: whispering to c. me,
   WHITM 109

congregation: scatter the c.;
   WHITM 7

Congress: C., lobster, love, luau,
   BROO G 5
in c. meet — LEAR 3

congruence: c. of the complement
   MOOR M 41

conjo: night is c. HAYD 18

conjoin: in a greater current they
   c. QUAR 3

Conjoined: C. by love, BALD 1

conjugated: strange/ verbs c.
   RIVE 1

conjunction: c. of the mind,
   MARV 7

conjure: c. up the blood, SHAK 56

Connaught: Queens of Sheba,
   Meath, and C., SYNG 3

connecting: c.-rod out of my brain,
   UNKN 82

connections: his air/ of lost c. . . . .
   LOWE R 32

connive: c. in civilized outrage
   HEAN 17

connubial: Rites/ Mysterious of c.
   Love MILT 77

conquer: cannot c. Time. AUDE 2
c. a crown; OSHA 3
c. but to save:— CAMPB T 2
c. him that did his master c.
   SHAK 6
c. one resolved Heart. MARV 8

love is hard to catch and c.,
MERE G 4
conquered: c. in myself
MOOR M 15
c. woe; SHAK 221
Thou hast c., SWIN 23
conquering: c. limbs astride
LAZA 1
conqueror: c. at least; BYRO 34
its hero the C. Worm. POE 33
conquerors: tame/ Their spirits to
the c. SHEL 77
conquest: divide the c. SHAK 202
final c. MARV 13
Conscience: by their C., be
condemn'd or freed. DRYD 17
catch the c. of the King.
SHAK 32
C. always has ROBI 48
c. and tendre herte. CHAU 17
c. ask a curious sort of question,
BYRO 32
c. does make cowards of us all;
SHAK 40
c. hath a thousand several
tongues, SHAK 99
c. is born of love? SHAK 243
c. is converted into palms,
STEVENS 14
know what c. is, SHAK 243
money and the bad c., SIMP 8
O C.! MILT 100
quiet c. BYRO 20
spiced c., CHAU 14
such a c.-stricken air? HOUS 21
want of c. SHAK 243
conscientious: c. inconsistency.
MOOR M 18
c. object-or CUMM 14
c. still, BROWNI R 33
conscious: c. impotence of rage/ At
human folly, ELIOT T 68
c. occupation/ Of the praying
mind, ELIOT T 63
c. of the tears COWP 10
weep and sing/ Duty's c. wrong,
AUDE 10
consciousness: clocks, bodies, c.,
shoe, GINS 24
c. by diet and breathing.
AUDE 88
that span of c. CRAN H 15
volition nor c. MOOR M 13
consecrate: c. to thee. LAND 15
consecration: c., and the Poet's
dream; WORD 11
Some call it C., CARRU 2
conseile: c. a womman CHAU 91
conseiling: c. nis no comandement.
CHAU 91
consent: voted by common c.)
BROWNI R 36

whispering 'I will ne'er c.'
BYRO 20
Consented: C., and was dead —
DICKI 100
Consents: C. to his inexorable will.
WILB 35
rich results of the divine c.
EMER 4
Consequently: C. I rejoice,
ELIOT T 4
Conservative: Or else a little C.!
GILB 22
consider: c. every thing that grows
SHAK 187
c. the radiance, AMMO 1
Florida c. the flamingo, WARR 9
considered: attitude's c. quaint,'
GILB 3
Consign: lovers must/ C. to thee
SHAK 18
consolation: habitual/ Slow c.
HEAN 6
peace and c. MILT 118
console: aims/ But to c. man
THOR 10
consoles: cut stone/ c. his groping
feet. LEVE 11
consonants: c. and vowels.
RANS 34
conspicuously: c. alone. SNOD 16
conspiracy: here do snoring lie,/
Open-eyed c. SHAK 158
conspires: c. to praise her,
POPE A 109
constancy: seal joint c., DONN 47
constant: c. faith and service vow,
CAREW 2
c. love deemed SIDN 12
C. Penelope OVID 3
for a c. heart! UNKN 181
for c. heart. SHAK 205
lights/ His c. lamp, MILT 78
Love is a growing, or full c. light;
DONN 36
mimic motion/ Made c. cry,
STEVENS 17
one on shore,/ To one thing c.
never, SHAK 130
tempt with doubts thy c. mind:
GAY 7
window proves/ A c. death;
THOMS J (1700–1748) 10
Constantinople: picturesque C.
BYRO 52
constellated: c. flower that never
sets; SHEL 59
c. sounds BRID R 15
constellations: c. of universal law.
SAND 17
strange-eyed c. HARD 20
unknown c. sway — MACL 7
constituency: for the c. Feeds the
five thousand, RODG 5

constitution: broken character and
c. GRAY 21
constrained: c. to honor us though
dead! MCKA 6
constraint: Bitter c. and sad
occasion MILT 25
construct: c. a new stage.
STEVENS 31
c. from them/ a nest — TATE J 1
having to c. something
ELIOT T 4
construe: All the Latin I c.
BROWNI R 27
consum'd: thy greedy self c.,
MILT 44
consume: c. His soul to ash-heaps
HERR 34
like fire and powder,/ Which as
they kiss c. SHAK 148
consumed: c. in the fire, KEAT 57
c. with the Earth BLAK 85
utterly c. with sharp distress,
TENN 85
Consuming: C. and serene! CARM 1
Time's c. rage. DANI S 12
consummation: c. comes, HARD 16
c. Devoutly to be wished.
SHAK 39
this great c. WORD 16
contact: rushing amorous c.
WHITM 23
contagion: Burns from the strong c.
of the gown;
JOHN S (1709–1784) 17
soul grows clotted by c., MILT 4
contagious: base c. clouds
SHAK 51
most c. game:/ Hiding the
Skeleton, MERE G 9
road to the c. hospital WILLI 34
contain: Its infinite c. Its past —
DICKI 118
their lives would all c. this hour.
LARK 22
Contained: small,/ C. and fragile,
WINT 1
contains: sea c. the hottest blood
LAWR 57
contemplates: thing it c.; SHEL 58
contemplation: By c.'s help,
COWP 12
c. he and valour formed,
MILT 72
hard to say what brought them
there,/ commerce or c. BISH 27
spirit of noisy/ c. OHAR 4
contempt: c. for their oppressors.
POUN 24
c. of luxury. JEFFE 42
laughter and c., SHAK 72
pour c. on all my pride.
WATT I 9

couch: I c. when owls do cry.
  SHAK 166
couched: c. in the ominous horse,
  SHAK 30
couches: c. of the dead, BLAK 16
Couetousness: as the Welchman
  sayd,/ C. getts no gaine.
  UNKN 224
cough: gilded puddle/ Which beasts
  would c. at. SHAK 4
  smoker's c. in the hall. HEAN 15
coughed: c., and called it fate,
  ROBI 44
could: c. I rise with you, DICKI 35
  I c. command content; DE VE 1
  I c. not die with you, DICKI 34
  you c. say I've a call. PLATH 55
councils: manners, climates, c.,
  governments, TENN 130
counsel: c. in this uttermost
  distress, MILT 101
  Dost sometimes c. take —
  POPE A 118
  Scorn their c. and their pother,
  JOHN S (1709–1784) 12
  took his c. of his wife, CHAU 69
  took sweet c. together,
  BIBL, O.T. 39
  walketh not in the c. of the
  ungodly, BIBL, O.T. 21
counsell: call crafft c., WYAT 23
counsels: how mony c. sweet,
  BURN 51
  Womenes c. CHAU 69
Count: C. all your boasts JACK 2
  c. myself the coward TENN 117
  c. the clock that tells the time,
  SHAK 186
  c. the ways. BROWNI E 4
  c. them on my Hand, DICKI 77
  five kings c. the dead
  THOMA D 25
  sum my c. SHAK 185
counted: c. her husbands WALK 9
  Hundreds of thousands c.,
  SHAP 11
  Success is c. sweetest DICKI 134
  thousands c. every groan,
  ARNO 35
countenance: arms and hands and
  feet and c. PETRA 11
  c. filled up his line, SHAK 218
  c. full of woe, WHITM 52
counter: All things c., HOPKINS 19
  c.-love, original response.
  FROS 60
counterfeit: coin, or c. New words,
  BUTL 5
counterpane: pleasant land of c.
  STEVENSO R 12
counterpart: long wood's c.,
  ROSS D 7
counters: box of c. PATM 3

countervail: c. the exchange of joy
  SHAK 147
counties: see the colored c.,
  HOUS 25
Counting: C. the slow heart beats,
  GRAV 4
countless: swallow c. pills?
  GILB 48
Countrie: C. Far beyond the stars
  VAUG 14
countries: In souls as c.,
  BROWNI E 1
  witnesses/ In all love's c.,
  THOMA D 44
country: air that kills/ From yon far
  c. blows: HOUS 34
  bold peasantry, their c.'s pride,
  GOLD 3
  born/ In a half savage c.,
  POUN 37
  cheap cabin in the c., GINS 27
  c. lover and his lass; HOUS 22
  c. of Again. MUIR 10
  C. of hunchbacks! — MILLA 34
  c.'s Father slain STOD 1
  five and c. senses THOMA D 43
  Foemen at morn, but friends at
  eve —/ Fame or c. MELV 20
  halved a c.; THOMA D 24
  in soul up to our c. move.
  SIDN 8
  it is my c. LOWE A 3
  make our c. free." RANDA D 1
  merry c. lad? BRET 4
  My c., 'tis of thee, SMIT SA 1
  native c., repossessed HERR 24
  no c. for old men. YEATS 124
  raw c. girl, HARD 37
  seen a green c., useful to the
  race, BLUN 5
  sink to rest/ By all their c.'s
  wishes blest! COLL 3
  spare your c.'s flag," WHITT 3
  talk of the old c. SIMP 10
  undiscovered c. SHAK 40
  Unhappy c. JEFFE 10
  versed in c. things FROS 66
  wanton c. maid. CAMPI 6
  whole c. tremble HALL 5
countrymen: demonstrated/ Unto
  our climatures and c. SHAK 20
  For love of her, sweet c.,
  DICKI 146
counts: What c. is the cultural
  level, POUN 14
county: Emeralds big as half the c.
  LAND 7
  In the C. Tyrone, UNKN 195
couple: Farm boys wild to c.
  DICKEY 26
  loving c. lies DONN 49

  never-singling Hymen c.
  MARL 10
  old c., just astir, DICKI 52
coupled: c. to foul thraldom.
  BARBO 2
couplets: dribbled c. like a snake
  TATE A 9
courage: C.!" he said, TENN 80
  c. never to submit or yield:
  MILT 51
  fragile ship of c., LAWR 39
  goes with C. on. SWIF 20
  joy and strength and c. TREN 2
  love's c. ROBI 3
  Neither fear nor c. saves us.
  ELIOT T 33
  Now remember c., TATE A 20
  rais'd/ Thir fainting c. MILT 56
  To keep men's c. up, DAY 3
  With c. to endure! BRON 8
courageous: c. WHITM 44
  patient eyes, c. hearts! GREN 2
couriers: every hour his c. bring.
  TENN 57
  horsed/ Upon the sightless c. of
  the air, SHAK 105
course: alter all the c. of kind.
  SPENS 10
  c. I ought to steer, PETRA 5
  great nature's second c.,
  SHAK 106
  high star our c. is set, MACN 26
  Like a dark flood suspended in its
  c., SHEL 16
  must have its c., KINGSL 6
  nature's changing c., SHAK 188
  shrilling from the solar c.,
  EMER 51
  take a serpentine c. WHITM 13
  Time's c. to slower speeding,
  CAMPB T 7
  world's c. will not fail: PATM 7
coursers: his c. they came,
  MOOR C 2
courses: her wicked c., GILB 50
  planets in their radiant c.,
  PRAE 1
  steer their c. BUTL 6
court: amorous soul c. Thy mild
  Dove, DONN 52
  c. a mistris, shee denyes you;
  JONS 29
  c. others in verse, PRIO 2
  Keeps Death his c., SHAK 89
  kingly Death/ Keeps his pale c.
  SHEL 1
  Near the old c.-house LIND V 1
  poor rogues/ Talk of c. news;
  SHAK 84
  stable is a Prince's c. SOUTHW 5
  stood in a shadowy C.,
  CARRO 13

Though lewdness c. it SHAK 27
you live at c., JONS 32
courted: Apollo, c. for her haire,
　MARL 5
c. men in station SWIF 23
courteous: c. ruin of proffered
　usury, SIDN 4
c., yet harrowing Grace, DICKI 7
courtes: Slipper toppe/ Of c.
　estates, SENE 1
courtesy: In c. YEATS 108
courtier: clothes brave enough/ To
　be a c., JONS 24
c.'s, soldier's, scholar's, SHAK 33
courtly: c. dames and knights,
　CAMPI 9
c. stable,/ Bright-harnessed angels
　sit in order serviceable.
　MILT 41
Was c. once BROWNI R 33
Courts: C. and Towers: WORD 100
C. thee on Roses HORA 3
day in thy c. BIBL, O.T. 43
empties our police c., GILB 50
into his c. with praise:
　BIBL, O.T. 50
Nature c. MARV 32
cousins: sisters, c., aunts, and
　niece, GILB 5
covenant: c. 'Twill be between us;
　WORD 51
cover: art her guilt to c., GOLD 9
athwart a cedarn c.!/ A savage
　place! COLE SAM 20
bones with dust shall c.,
　SHAK 196
C. a hundred leagues, WORD 130
c. lightly, gentle earth. JONS 22
C. me ye Pines, MILT 97
I am the grass; I c. all. SAND 10
same c. in the cool night,
　WHITM 109
covered: c. up — our names —
　DICKI 38
c. with dust, FIEL E 6
C. with embroideries YEATS 30
earth is c. thick BYRO 8
limbs with dust are c. FRENE 3
once was c. with thyme, HABE 2
She c. me warm, POE 24
covering: Cowslips for her c.
　HERR 10
folding, c. all. WHITM 71
coverlet: Draw the Glasnevin c.
　YEATS 148
From the white c. CRAN H 41
coverlid: cradle-hood and c.
　YEATS 105
covers: earth that lightly c. her.
　HERR 58
easie earth that c. her. HERR 13
mimic desolation c. all. GRAY 22

covert: go to a c. ROSS C 23
murdered corpse, in c. laid,
　CHAU 48
coverts: c. from a horse; BETJ 7
covet: c. fetters, though they golden
　bee. SPENS 13
sin to c. honor SHAK 59
Thou shalt not c., CLOU 7
Coveted: C. her and me. POE 4
covetous: not c. for gold, SHAK 59
covets: c. nothing that it has let go.
　MOOR M 28
cow: c., all white and red,
　UNKN 107
c.-heavy and floral PLATH 63
c. is of the bovine ilk; NASH 5
c. of late FROS 17
c. with the crumpled horn
　MOTH 7
friendly c., all red and white,
　STEVENSO R 7
milk the c. of the world,
　WILB 15
saw a Purple C., BURG 2
wrapped him up in an old c.'s
　hide, UNKN 118
coward: count myself the c.
　TENN 117
c. does it with a kiss, WILD 3
dirty little c. UNKN 148
three parts c. SHAK 35
cowardly: face the murderous, c.
　pack, MCKA 7
cowards: conscience does make c. of
　us all; SHAK 40
Convicted c. all, YEATS 40
How many c., SHAK 122
Men are C., ROCH 11
Men would be C. ROCH 10
cowboy: c. in the boat of Ra.
　REED I 3
c. in the boat of Ra. REED I 5
c. rolls/ His pack, SMIT W 2
Roosevelt, the young dude c.,
　LIND V 7
cowering: c. foes shall shrink
　DRAK 3
cowers: c. within his den; SIMM 2
cowl: I like a c.; EMER 38
cowled: c. churchman be.
　EMER 38
cowran: Wee, sleeket, c., BURN 62
cows: c. get thin, SNYD 41
cowslip: In a c.'s bell I lie;
　SHAK 166
Cowslips: C. for her covering.
　HERR 10
c. tall her pensioners be;/ In their
　gold coats spots SHAK 126
with c. pale, AKEN 1
coxcombs: To c. averse, GOLD 4
coy: c. submission, modest pride,
　MILT 73

ful symple and c.; CHAU 13
Lady be not c., MILT 6
coyn: vaunted name Virginity,/
　Beauty is natures c., MILT 6
coyness: c., Lady, were no crime.
　MARV 33
Coyote: All but/ C. SNYD 40
c. got his/ ratty old fur coat
　SILKO 1
girls get layed by C. SNYD 36
cozener: usurer hangs the c./
　Through tattered clothes
　SHAK 81
Cozening: Spoiling senses of their
　treasure,/ C. judgment with a
　measure, JONS 9
crabs: sidelong c. had scrawled their
　crooked race; CRAB 1
crack: Blow, winds, and c. your
　cheeks! SHAK 75
can you c. a nut." EMER 36
c. in the tea-cup opens AUDE 3
C. nature's molds, SHAK 75
c. of deputies' rifles KINN 19
c. their teeth! BIBL, O.T. 42
footstool c., and the sun wink.
　DONN 28
heaven's vault should c. SHAK 85
jests that you c. GILB 59
Johnnie C. and Flossie Snail
　THOMA D 42
Words strain,/ C. and sometimes
　break, ELIOT T 24
crack'd: forest c., TENN 23
cracked: Abaddon in the hangnail c.
　from Adam, THOMA D 6
c. and flung to the fire WILLI 8
c. the hemispheres TATE A 5
mirror c. from side to side;
　TENN 66
cracker: those lovely c. mottoes!'
　GILB 12
crackers: inside the c.' — GILB 13
crackle: blacks c. and drag.
　PLATH 39
crackled: days have c. THOMP F 8
crackling: c. sound over/ dried
　leaves WILLI 49
Cracks: bough/ C. LOWE R 1
C. and reforms ELIOT T 148
cradle: c.-hood and coverlid
　YEATS 105
c. of causeless care, SIDN 39
c. of ignorance, SIDN 4
Curst from his c., BACO 1
fancy dies/ In the c. SHAK 121
in her c.-coffin lying; LAMB 3
in his linden c., LONG 41
Looks at the c. YEATS 49
old crone rocking the c.,
　WHITM 68
Out of the c. WHITM 62

Rocked in the c. of the deep
WILLA 1

vexed to nightmare by a rocking
c., YEATS 136

wise men came from far,/ Led to
thy c. by a star, GODO 1

your c., your home, and your
bier. SHEL 90

cradles: in the c., BROWNI R 60

crafft: call c. counsell, WYAT 23

craft: By its own c., EMER 3
c. or sullen art THOMA D 27
heed my c. or art. THOMA D 28

craftie: curious search, but c. sinnes
delight. GREV 6

craftsman: c.'s loom, GINS 12

crag: He clasps the c. TENN 12

Cragged: huge hill,/ C., and steep,
Truth stands, DONN 51

craggy: summit of a c. cliff,
THOMS J (1700–1748) 8

crags: among these barren c.,
TENN 128

crake: hern and c.; TENN 43

cramful: so c. of cosy joy, SERV 9

crammed: c. in a monster toy
MACN 1
c. with straw and stones. ALBI 1

Cramp: C. her larynx, SYNG 1
c. of hope MARV 12
taken with the c., HOLM 11

cramps: eyes gone gray/ from c.
HUGO 7

cranberry: c. tart." DE LA 5

Crane: Hart C., and of Shelly.
FULL 3
Jane,/ Tall as a c., SITW 4

cranks: Quips and c., and wanton
wiles, MILT 20

crannied: Flower in the c. wall,
TENN 13

crannies: pluck you out of the c.,
TENN 13

cranny: into every/ nook and c.
AMMO 1

Cranston: divinity of Lamont C.?
BARA 4

crap: Books are a load of c.
LARK 19

crass: c. chance billeted ROBI 33

crate: astounding c. full of air.
HEAN 2

craters: Like burnt-out c.
LOWE J 19

cravat: by his black c., SMIT W 1

crave: grace to those that c. it.
LODG 5
my mind forbids to c. DYER E 1
not what they c. SHAK 139
Some have too much, yet still do
c.; DYER E 2

craven: "art sure no c.,/ Ghastly
grim and ancient raven POE 36
some c. scruple SHAK 35

Craves: C. what it cannot have,
AUDE 77
no marble column c. TIMR 6

craw: cock doth c., UNKN 307

crawis: jolie Cok c.; MONTG 1

crawl: learning/ To c." SERR 2

crawled: c. like a snail, ROSS C 12

crawling: c. shape intrude! POE 31

Crawls: C. from the dry grass.
WILB 16
deep abyss where Satan c.
TRAH 1
omnibus across the bridge/ C. like
a yellow butterfly, WILD 18
wrinkled sea beneath him c.;
TENN 12

crayons: With c. the child draws a
rigid house BISH 46

crazed: c. beyond all hope,
BYRO 21

crazie: brittle c. glasse: HERB G 73

crazier: World is c. MACN 18

crazy: circle of the c. ladies
SEXT 12
c. salad with their meat
YEATS 107
only c. things OLSO 20
pure products of America/ go c.
WILLI 42

creaking: brought him to that c.
room FROS 73
c. of the tented sky, MILLA 29

creaks: morning light c. down
again; SITW 4

cream: gives me c. STEVENSO R 7
Hellespont of c. DAVIE J
junket of c. DE LA 5
Strawberries swimming in the c.,
PEEL 6

Creamy: C. bean flowers PLATH 13

creased: trousers were c. like
knives WAGO 1

Create: C. her child of spleen
SHAK 72
"I shall c.! BROO G 2
that stand c. DICKI 113

Created: C. mute to all articulate
sound; MILT 93
C. out of pure intelligence.
WORD 106
God by curse/ C. evil, MILT 61
God c. the great whales, MILT 85
speech c. thought, SHEL 54

createdst: Lord, who c. man in
wealth and store, HERB G 26

creates: Hope c. From its own
wreck SHEL 58

Creating: C. awe and fear in other
men? SHAK 58

Creation: 'alf o' C. she owns:
KIPL 31
all c. is duly respected
LOWE J 10
Amid its gay c.,
THOMS J (1700–1748) 3
c. at ease; ROET 25
C.'s blithe and petaled word
CRAN H 51
C.'s final law — TENN 36
hold C. in my foot HUGH T 2
humming-bird flashed ahead of c.
LAWR 16
of c. last arose MILT 86
riseth a new c. SKEL 10

Creations: Welcome the C. Guest,
MARV 9

Creator: C., whom sin nor nature
tied, DONN 68
C.'s Pow'r display, ADDI 3

creature: c. died/ By storm
YOUN A 1
c. God has used it for. HOLLA 4
c., naked, bestial, CRAN S 3
c. not too bright or good
WORD 134
c. of heroic blood, HEMA 1
every c. drink but I? COWL 2
heaven-eyed c. sleeps in earth:
WORD 17
living c. lie./ Mortal, guilty,
AUDE 55
no c. loves me, SHAK 99
not a c. failed, DICKI 42
Not a c. was stirring, MOOR C 1

creatures: All c. living beneath the
sun, BROWNI R 61
c. going about their business
JEFFE 7
c. great and small, ALEX 1
c. that do people harm,
BROWNI R 61
C. that hang LAWR 3
delicate c. From the other world.
WRIG J 5
equine amphibious c. MOOR M 2
fair musick that all c. made
MILT 1
Heav'n from all c. POPE A 63
human c.' lives! HOOD 12
Innumerous living c., MILT 86
join all ye c. to extol MILT 81
little airy c., SWIF 12
Little c., everywhere!
STEPHENS 7
my erring fellow c., GILB 6
there are few c. MOOR M 26
What soft, cherubic c. These
gentlewomen are! DICKI 155

credit: citizen/ Of c. and renown,
COWP 6
let the C. go, OMAR 3
you do c. it, SPENS 25

creed: code corroborating Calvin's
  c. MELV 12
  corner of a C., SKEL 7
  c. that will not let you dance?
    JOHN H 2
  neighbor's c. has lent. EMER 18
  Pagan suckled in a c. outworn;
    WORD 160
  shrieked against his c. TENN 36
  simple c. Of Childhood,
    WORD 80
creeds: all the c. WHITM 74
  C. and schools in abeyance,
    WHITM 74
creek: c.-washed stone SNYD 52
creeks: c. get fat HUGO 3
  Trees down/ C. choked, trout
    killed, SNYD 45
Creep: C. back into their silent
    Barks COWL 7
  c. from flower to flower;
    SHEL 29
  c./ Through my fingers POE 14
  crystal streams 'with pleasing
    murmurs c.': POPE A 26
  cunning wiles that c. BLAK 51
  low words oft c. in one dull line:
    POPE A 25
  pale captives, c. to death. SHIR 2
  pitiless hours like years and ages
    c., THOMS J (1834–1882) 4
  timorously c. HORA 5
  Wit that can c., POPE A 12
creeping: Cattle and c. things,
    MILT 86
  C. and healing. ROET 48
  c. in, quietly. ROET 44
  c./ In windows and doors,
    DAVIS 4
  thin with desire,/ Transformed to
    a c. MONR 2
creeps: gently c. Luxuriant:
    MILT 69
  How lazily time c. KING H 2
  Minnaloushe c. through the grass
    YEATS 22
cremate: c. my last remains."
    SERV 2
cremated: I c. Sam McGee. SERV 1
crept: c. upon/ A Chill —
    DICKI 154
  c. Right out of hell. SIMI 5
  frozen wind c. on SHEL 23
Crescendo: piped rats to its siren/
    C., MERW 4
Crescent: in the C. DICKI 126
crest: c. be shorn and shaven,
    POE 36
  c. of red and gold, CRAN S 9
crested: off the c. wave; SIGO 1
  reared arm/ C. the world;
    SHAK 7

crests: tyrants' c. and tombs of
  brass SHAK 229
Cretan: Venerandam,/ In the C.'s
  phrase, POUN 8
Crew: Blacks rebellious. C. uneasy.
    HAYD 8
  captain and the c.; GILB 10
  captain tickled the c. CARRY 9
  c. and captain CARRY 4
  c. of the captain's gig!' " GILB 55
  c. was complete: CARRO 12
  Dead Nelson and his half-dead c.,
    HARD 21
  dismayed her c. CARRY 8
  landed his c. with care;
    CARRO 11
  singles from the C., GAY 2
  under the c. haircuts LOWE R 54
  with his horrid c. MILT 49
crib: C. His chair of state;
    SOUTHW 5
cribbage: To c. pegs — GILB 41
cribs: liest thou in smoky c.,
    SHAK 54
Criccieth: Pwllheli, C.,/ Portmadoc,
  Borth, GRAV 40
cricket: c. like a dwindled hearse
    WILB 16
  fireside for the c., ALLI 3
  seat at the c. matches JARR 12
  whip of c.'s bone, SHAK 153
crickets: set up a noise like c.,
    YEATS 21
  twilight sound/ Of the c., JUST 6
cried: And still she c., ELIOT T 122
  bones of birth have c.,
    BEAU/BASS 4
  c. in his English pride,
    TENN 119
  cursed and sighed and c. and
    swore HOLLA 4
  neighbors!" at last he c., —
    WHITT 25
  nor laughed, nor c.: PRIO 4
  Out of the depths have I c.
    BIBL, O.T. 60
  Owls have c., THOMA E 19
Crier: C. on his round HOLM 15
cries: confronting, reversing my c.,
    WHITM 31
  c. and hungers HALL 1
  c. are thin and terse; WILB 16
  c. from my heart, WHITM 30
  c. of unsatisfied love WHITM 67
  C. out a literate despair.
    STEVENS 42
  c. rising/ in waves WILLI 48
  c. that are almost human.
    SIMP 1
  full of birds' c.; MASE 13
  harsh c. of wild fowl.
    MACDONO 3
  he composedly c., WHITM 90

  my bootless c., SHAK 194
  quarry c. on havoc. SHAK 42
  red rose c., 'She is near,
    TENN 94
  Il Trovatore c. NOYE 5
  so many routine c. HILL G 7
  with my c. importune Heaven,
    MILT 102
crime: bigamy, sir, is a c.'
    LEAR 20
  coyness, Lady, were no c.
    MARV 33
  cut-throat isn't occupied in c.,
    GILB 38
  deride this sepulchre of c.
    SASS 12
  exempt from scorn or c.;
    JOHN S (1709–1784) 13
  footprints of the c." KAVA 12
  I have made no c." HECH 14
  Is it, in Heav'n, a c. to love too
    well? POPE A 3
  let the punishment fit the c.
    GILB 28
  loving thou mayst loved be with
    equall c.' SPENS 34
  Napoleon of C.! ELIOT T 95
  our c. RICH 22
  What evil, what unspeakable c.
    SNOD 3
  winter called it a dreadful c.
    BLAK 52
crimes: c. done in my days of
  nature SHAK 26
  from c. would pardoned be,
    SHAK 168
  never among my c.! CARRO 21
  our impudent c. ELIOT T 33
crimson: beauty's ensign yet/ Is c.
    SHAK 152
  modest, c.-tippèd flow'r,
    BURN 59
  Now sleeps the c. petal,
    TENN 109
  thy bed/ Of c. joy: BLAK 80
cringing: c. by the wall, TATE A 20
cripple: c. and the imbecile SIMI 4
  c. or blind they will ca' me,
    UNKN 113
  That hoary c., BROWNI R 20
crisp: sitting through c. air,
    HECH 15
Crispian: Feast of C.: SHAK 60
  rouse him at the name of C.
    SHAK 60
  'To-morrow is Saint C.:'
    SHAK 60
Crispin: Upon Saint C.'s day
    DRAY 2
Crisping: C. the brook ALDR T 2
criterion: c. of suitability and
  convenience: MOOR M 8

Critic: C. spits on what is done, —
  HOOD 7
immovable c. twitching his skin
  MOOR M 32
sober c. come abroad — / If wrong,
  I smiled; POPE A 15
critical: c. eye you scanned,
  ROSS C 26
critics: say astonished c.,
  AUDE 100
Turned c. next, POPE A 23
what morals c. ought to show,
  POPE A 36
croaks: blinks and c., like a toad or
  a Norn, WARR 10
crockery: c.-ware metropolis,
  BYRO 52
crocodile: "You mean," he said, "a
  c." NASH 12
Cromwell: with mighty C.
  LIND V 7
crone: old c. rocking the cradle,
  WHITM 68
crooked: in a c. year. THOMA D 4
Jeered at by c. children,
  MILLA 34
little c. house. MOTH 27
love is the c. thing, YEATS 16
My c. winding ways, HERB G 74
same c. worm. THOMA D 23
set the c. straight? MORR 3
sidelong crabs had scrawled their
  c. race; CRAB 1
tell the c. rose THOMA D 22
was a c. man, MOTH 27
with c. hands; TENN 12
croon: mellow c., HUGH L 18
Crop: c./ A flower and a
  maidenhead. LOVE 3
C. your numbers CAREY 2
Disdains to c. a weed, DRUM 3
croppe: hym death greep'the right
  hard by the c. SENE 2
croppers: c. rotting shacks WALK 1
crops: c. of love and hate. MUIR 8
prodigal, annual, sumptuous c.,
  WHITM 98
your c. and your care; COLUM 2
cross: bear/ His c. upon my back;
  CULL 17
betwixt Heaven and Charing C.
  THOMP F 11
blunt as a Celtic c., HEAN 15
Christ writhing on the c.! ROBI 3
c. and wrinkled, NASH 2
C.-barred and bolted fast,
  MILT 68
c. from shore to shore WHITM 18
c. I wear upon my breast
  LONG 14
c. of snow upon its side.
  LONG 14
c. roads tree. HUGH L 13

c. that Christ had, SORL 2
C., the Cross/ Goes deeper
  LAWR 53
c. thy stream, broad Hellespont!
  BYRO 75
daring them to c.; SPENC A 4
even c.-town OLSO 7
going by Charing C., UNKN 12
hands clasping a black c. IREM 1
help you c., BRIN 2
His c. is every tree. PLUN 2
hundreds and hundreds that c.,
  WHITM 18
kelp, miscellaneous driftwood,/
  Topped by c.-winds, ROET 44
Like the whizz of my c.-bow!
  COLE SAM 35
Love a c. for them ROBI 48
my deeds to c., SHAK 221
sparkling c. she wore,
  POPE A 115
survey the wondrous c. WATT I 9
sword and his holy c.: MUND 1
swords about the C., CHES 3
Upon the C. SITW 11
crossbars: c. were ash, HOLM 6
Crosscut: C. and chainsaw
  SNYD 45
cross'd: about this neck have c and
  rested, WHITM 116
Crosse: Christs C., and Adams
  tree, DONN 32
Saint Andrews c., that is his
  guide; UNKN 222
crossed: bayonets, mixed and c.,
  THOMP W 1
c. each other's way: WILD 4
c. the bar. TENN 10
c. the dark defile MACL 12
crosses: poppies blow/ Between the
  c., MCCRA 1
crossing: Alfred Lord Tennyson c.
  the bar SITW 3
Hsüan Tsang, c. the Pamirs
  SNYD 24
crosslegged: c. by the flames
  SNYD 8
crotch: Rubber breasts or a rubber
  c., PLATH 1
crouch: c. to my television set,
  LOWE R 20
ghosts of the tribe/ C. JEFFE 3
crouched: c. an outrageous bird.
  HECH 2
c. on her nest, WHITM 64
perpetually c., CUMM 40
Crouching: C. down where nothing
  stirs STEPHENS 5
like c. tombs SPEND 4
crow: aloft in your c.'s nest,
  RICH 11
c.-blue mussel shells,
  MOOR M 11

c. by Red Rock MOMA 6
c. has flown over it, SIMI 1
c. Shook down FROS 46
I'd rather c. And be a rooster
  UNKN 261
Old Adam, the carrion c.,
  BEDD 4
roost/ And be a c. UNKN 261
saw that clumsy c. ROET 50
stare like an old c. TATE A 6
two cocks together c.,/ Cleaving
  the darkness THOMA E 4
crowd: After night I do c.,
  BLAK 45
c. flowed over London Bridge,
  ELIOT T 118
c. is/ cheering, WILLI 6
c. is laughing/ in detail WILLI 6
c. of ordinary decent folk
  AUDE 81
c. of workmen WHITM 33
c. of young women POUN 33
c. on c. VERY 1
drives the noisy c. CLARE 2
forgotten c. Of common beauties,
  CAREW 7
goodly c. was there. DARC 1
humbly c. outside, SPEND 6
leave me single in the c. THOR 5
madding c.'s ignoble strife,
  GRAY 11
one of a c., WHITM 19
one of a living c., WHITM 19
they, the c./ are beautiful
  WILLI 4
trampled by a hurrying c.,
  BRYA 1
crowded: c. hour of glorious life
  MORD 1
Simple as soil yet c. as earth
  WILB 36
stood in a c. street RUKE 12
theatres of c. men KEAT 25
crowding: reaching and c.
  WHITM 77
crowds: apprehensions come in c.;
  WORD 3
C. of men and women WHITM 18
I see c. of people, ELIOT T 117
Manhattan c., WHITM 32
To shops in c. SWIF 7
weary c. I roam; EMER 26
crowed: cock that c. in the morn
  MOTH 11
crowing: Before the Barn-Door c.,
  GAY 2
hear the c. cock, LONG 8
crown: better than his c.;
  SHAK 123
broke his c., MOTH 17
broken like a battered c.,
  GINS 34
Coifed with c., SYNG 3

conquer a c.; OSHA 3
c. my thoughts with acts,
　SHAK 113
c. of thorns PLUN 2
c. of thorns our Saviour wore
　UNKN 131
c. of verdure weaves, ALEX 5
c. thy Feet, MARV 5
c. thy Head. MARV 5
For this poor wreath, give Thee a
　c. of praise. HERB G 76
fountain at salute, a c. in view —
　CRAN H 45
golden c., Aphrodite, POUN 8
hairy gold c. on 'er 'ead?
　KIPL 30
heaven's jewelled c. MCCRE 1
holly bears the c. UNKN 129
more glorious is the c. SMAR 9
quiet mind is richer than a c.;
　GREE 1
radiant c. Put on, BLAK 109
reserve for me a c., BETJ 5
sorrow's c. of sorrow TENN 74
Take the neon lights and make a
　c., HUGH L 8
Upon his c., TROW 2
wager the rascals a c. GOLD 6
Wedding is great Juno's c.,
　SHAK 16
within the hollow c. SHAK 89
crown'd: time/ C. my felicity,
　PHILI K 1
With spoils of meaner beauties c.
　LOVE 4
crowned: By mourning beauty c.!
　TIMR 7
C., and again discrowned.
　JOHN L 2
c. him with glory and honor.
　BIBL, O.T. 25
c. knot of fire ELIOT T 74
c. with a woman's love —
　SERV 9
c. with darkness, WORD 18
due to be c. again. LAWR 45
fringed bank with myrtle c.
　MILT 69
head with roses c., HERR 3
With endless life are c. HERR 49
crownede: c. wythe reytes, CHAT 1
crowner: c.'s quest goes hard
　COLM 2
crownets: livery/ Walked crowns and
　c.; SHAK 7
Crowns: C. they dazzle so. KIPL 23
"Give c. and pounds and guineas
　HOUS 59
Liberty that c. Britannia's Isle,
　ADDI 2
livery/ Walked c. and crownets;
　SHAK 7

crows: dry throats rattle,/ Two c.
　perched SHEL 63
Pyes and Dawes and Rookes and
　C., BONH 1
crucible: c. of endless space,
　CRAN H 5
crucified: Bible chopped and c.
　LOWE R 49
C. maun bleed. MACDI 4
Imagine a painter c. ASHB 5
Lord was c., ALEX 8
picture of Christ c., DONN 66
Crucifixion: commentary/ On the
　C.? PRIN 2
crude: declare it's c. and mean;
　GILB 31
pluck your berries harsh and c.,
　MILT 25
cruel: c. as she's fair DANI S 9
C. children, STEVENSO R 4
c. wind blows. KUNI 1
despite his c. hand. SHAK 210
England is a c. place KINGSL 1
fertile shop of c. arts: MARV 14
fixing in the wretch his c. fangs,
　THOMS J (1700–1748) 11
love is c. and selfish WILLI 21
lovers, c. as their flame,
　MARV 16
slain by a fair c. maid.
　SHAK 176
thou c. lord, BURN 36
whose c. striking SHAK 116
cruell: deaffe and c., MARL 5
cruellest: April is the c. month,
　ELIOT T 113
cruelty: business of love is/ c.
　WILLI 20
C. has a Human Heart, BLAK 59
forget c. and past betrayal,
　GRAV 43
cruised: Ere Paul Pry c. MELV 21
crulle: lokkes c. CHAU 8
crumb: asked a c. DICKI 30
crumble: c. the dark earth,
　THOMA E 6
walls shall c. to ruin, LONG 10
when I c., DE LA 9
crumbled: c. yellow cup MONTA 5
crumbles: flesh how it c. to dust
　AIKE 12
crumbling: against our c. Troy.
　MACN 1
agape on the c. ridge MERW 4
cliffs of England c. HECH 3
c., leafy terraces. ASHB 2
c. Pageant shall devour, DRYD 27
c. to pieces RICH 12
crumbs: brush the c. away, RILE 1
catch tossed c. SNYD 31
c. of my life. RICH 10
few c. In this world COAT 1
Crumpetty: C. Tree LEAR 13

crumpled: cow with the c. horn
　MOTH 7
crunchy: crisp, c., malted, BROD 3
crush: Clinging close with the c. of
　the Python, HILT 4
c. amang the stoure BURN 59
c. these lions' jaws! BIBL, O.T. 42
crush'd: c. beneath the furrow's
　weight, BURN 61
crushed: flow'ret c. in the bud,
　LAMB 3
Truth, c. to earth, BRYA 3
Crusoes: C. building boats; —
　STEVENSO R 19
crust: watermelons gutted to the c.,
　LOWE R 6
crustacean: swirling c./ tailed
　MOOR M 2
crusted: pine-trees c. with snow;
　STEVENS 50
soften/ The c. wound
　THOMA D 25
crutch: clawed me with his c.,
　VAUX 3
rattles her c., WARR 10
cry: all c., FLET J 6
Babe maun c. MACDI 4
began to c., FOLL 1
begin to tremble and c. SHAP 17
brimming golden, spilling c.!
　JOHN H 3
Chimney-sweepers c. BLAK 75
C.; — and unto thy so sore loss
　THOMP F 11
C., — clinging Heaven by the
　hems; THOMP F 12
c., c., again. UNKN 189
c. for your castaways, WHITM 5
c. from a reeling deck! WHITT 26
c. Like a whipped child;
　SNOD 13
C. louder, beat the windows,
　SLES 2
c. of defiance, LONG 45
c. of every Man, BLAK 74
c. of the peacocks. STEVENS 6
C. pretty, pretty, SMIT ST 5
customary c., ROSS C 13
dead man's c. MACL 6
death c. of a nation lost!
　THOMP W 1
did they to Jehovah c.
　BIBL, O.T. 57
earth's old and weary c.
　YEATS 140
earth's old and weary c.
　YEATS 141
every stone shall c., WILB 12
Fair Liberty was all his c.;
　SWIF 24
falling fire and piercing c.
　BISH 2
for restful death I c., SHAK 213

Forgot the c. of gulls,
ELIOT T 142

goblins c.: ROSS C 11

hounds in c. BRET 5

I couch when owls do c.
SHAK 166

let us pass a day,/ Where all c.
out, POPE A 100

make thee c., FLET J 2

mimic motion/ Made constant c.,
STEVENS 17

no language but a c. TENN 31

overhear/ a c. of pain BISH 23

owlet's c. Came loud —
COLE SAM 13

shout and a c. BOGA 16

soul at death I c.,) WHITM 41

That scrawny c. STEVENS 29

to c. and call his name, WILB 33

undying c. of the void DICKEY 8

war c. sever, FINC 2

We wawl and c. SHAK 82

went his c. of alarm LONG 45

why do you c., JEFFE 23

With frantic gesture and short
breathless c. SHEL 16

crye: c. of my syghes PETRA 1

cryes: with their c. UNKN 59

crying: c. after love? TEAS 5

c. an unknown name in the sky
MACL 5

c. at the lock, MILLE W 1

c. babies, STEVENSO R 4

c. child, unborn? WALK 4

c. shadow in the funeral dance,
ELIOT T 25

infant c. for the light: TENN 31

infant c. in the night; TENN 31

loosen love and c.; SNOD 6

Papooses c. CRAN H 22

trailing your legs and c.!
MILLA 41

whaups are c., STEVENSO R 1

cryings: laughed their c. CUMM 5

cryis: thissell-cok c. MONTG 1

crypt: each prison c. CRAN H 6

crystal: Beside the c. fountains.
UNKN 26

c. glorious ye shine, CHAU 122

c. mirror holds, unite their
streams. MILT 69

c. of his brow, LYLY 2

c. spheres, MILT 39

c. streams 'with pleasing murmurs
creep': POPE A 26

deep into her c. body MILLA 20

fountain c.-clear, MOTH 16

gathered up the c. manna
BRID R 9

golden sands, and c. brooks,
DONN 6

river of c. light,/ Into a sea of
dew. FIEL E 8

rock c. and its/ imperturbability,
MOOR M 9

rock/ c. thing to see —
MOOR M 28

through the c. vault CHAU 46

crystalline: twinkle/ With a c.
delight; POE 10

cuccu: Sumer is icumen in,/ Lhude
sing c.! UNKN 234

cuckold: c. lives in bliss SHAK 134

four times c. POUN 65

cuckolds: c. ere now; SHAK 179

cuckoo: c.-buds of yellow hue
SHAK 100

c. is a lazy bird, UNKN 73

c. is a merry bird, UNKN 72

C., jug-jug, NASHE 3

repeat,/ C., bird, HOPKINS 5

weather the c. likes, HARD 49

cuckoos: jolly c. sing LYLY 4

cuddle: c. and hug," GRAV 30

cue: motive and the c. for passion
SHAK 31

What's the c.? — ROET 21

cuirass: Who fights in a c.,
GILB 40

cullambine: pincke and purple c.,
SPENS 57

cultural: What counts is the c.
level, POUN 14

culture: c. built upon profit;
MACN 6

decline of a c. SPEND 10

man of c. rare, GILB 30

cultured: c. hell that tests my
youth! MCKA 2

cultures: c. of nations EMPS 1

culver: c. on the barèd bough
SPENS 27

cum: we will c. to harme.'
UNKN 227

cumber: thews that lie and c.
HOUS 47

cumbered: c. with itself MERW 9

cunning: coarse and strong and c.
SAND 4

c. and fierce,
THOMS J (1700–1748) 10

c. humorists' puddled opinions,
SIDN 4

c. passages, contrived corridors
ELIOT T 32

c. picture holds her still WILB 35

c. wiles that creep BLAK 51

for c. ends; MAST 4

giddy c., MILT 24

History has many c. passages,
ELIOT T 32

like a c. instrument SHAK 86

right hand forget her c.
BIBL, O.T. 63

cunningly: little world made c.
DONN 33

cunning'st: c. pattern of excelling
nature, SHAK 137

cup: cold snow-water from a tin c.
SNYD 18

Come, fill the C., OMAR 1

crumbled yellow c. MONTA 5

c. and kiss SNYD 4

empty c., a flight of uncarpeted
stairs. MILLA 37

in a shallow C., OMAR 2

leave a kiss but in the c.,
JONS 31

my c. runneth over.
BIBL, O.T. 31

on my c. to attend: MILT 109

We'll tak a c. o' kindness yet
BURN 14

woodspurge has a c. of three.
ROSS D 10

you c. your hands/ And gulp
JARR 26

cupboard: What's in the c.?
UNKN 303

Cupid: Celestial C. MILT 12

Concludes with C.'s curse, —
PEEL 1

C. and my Campaspe LYLY 1

C. blind did rise. LYLY 2

C. is a blackguard boy SACK 1

little C. lose/ Eyes and ears and
chin and nose, JUST 4

On, Comet! on, C.! MOOR C 2

we call C.'s dart SIDN 7

cups: Catches his shrieks in c. of
gold. BLAK 31

c. drinks to the fair. RICH 21

wash the c. an' saucers RILE 1

whip/ In kitchen c. STEVENS 9

White plates and c., BROO R 3

woodspurge flowered, three c. in
one. ROSS D 10

curate: c. passed on a bicycle —
KAVA 8

curb: c. the long machines SHAP 8

use the snaffle and the c.
CAMPB R 5

curbing: weep soon on the lonely c.
HORA 2

curd: c.-pale moon, YEATS 141

mere white c. of ass's milk?
POPE A 9

curds: concupiscent c. STEVENS 9

quivering c.! CARRO 20

cure: Be of sin the double c.;
TOPL 1

c. the vices of mankind; SWIF 22

c. this place, BROWNI R 22

let your poison be your c.
MACN 25

miraculous c. at the fountain;
AUDE 84

Past c. I am, SHAK 242

Cycles: C. wheel! DICKI 97
cyclical: at c. turns JEFFE 32
cyclonic: mammoth rests between his c. dramas. SAND 15
cylinders: c. out of my kindneys, UNKN 82
cylindric: black c. body, WHITM 99
cynic: c. tyrannies of honest kings; MELV 12
cypress: burrow in the c. tree. SIMM 1
  C. and her spire; WORD 130
  c., pine,/ And useful sassafras. DRAY 18
  in sad c. let me be laid. SHAK 176
  sable stole of c. lawn, MILT 16
cypresses: avenue of c., LAWR 9
Cyprus: Riot in Algeria, in C., in Alabama; SNOD 9

D

Da: Then spoke the thunder/ D. ELIOT T 152
dabs: d. of flesh WHITM 92
  d. of pitch. SILKO 1
dad: good old d. or two, UNTE 1
Daddy: D., daddy, you bastard, PLATH 33
  I love my D. SMIT W 1
  Only my D. SMIT W 1
  thy poor worthless d.'s spirit, BURN 44
daffadowndillies: with d., SPENS 57
daffadowndilly: like the d., CONS/CHET 1
Daffodil: D. bulbs instead of balls ELIOT T 157
  withered d. JONS 4
daffodils: d. Are blowing, LOWE A 4
  dances with the d. WORD 25
  Fair d., HERR 42
  host, of golden d.; WORD 24
  meet the d., DICKI 40
  When d. begin to peer, SHAK 181
daft: his d. old brain, HODG 4
daggled: d. females fly, SWIF 7
daies: darke d. seene. SHAK 223
dailiness: d. of life. JARR 26
daily: d. close of their junction, WHITM 76
  human nature's d. food; WORD 134
  I sought it d. YEATS 25
  see thee d. weaker grow — COWP 21
  Through the d. dark WILB 20

Virtue in her d. Race, SWIF 20
We had d. cleaning. REED H 4
Which d. die: KIPL 14
Daintie: D. age,/ Cannot indure reproofe, JONS 21
  d. eare, SPENS 31
dainties: spicéd d., KEAT 13
daintiness: d. of ear SHAK 93
dainty: Many d. mistresses: HERR 65
  My d. duck, SHAK 182
daintyly: Full d. it is deight; UNKN 173
dais: Dons on the d. serene. NEWB 3
daisies: d. pied and violets blue. SHAK 100
  d. push inches of yellow air, GINS 42
  D., those pearl'd Arcturi SHEL 59
  hammer through d.; THOMA D 10
  hear/ The d. grow. WILD 17
  lie upon the d. GILB 30
  Propped with d. EBER 1
Daisieslain: in D.! DICKI 32
Daisy: mourn'st the D.'s fate, BURN 61
  "Piccadilly D." CARRY 4
Dakotas: drinking in the D. CRAN H 17
dale: doxy, over the d., SHAK 181
  Hill and d. MILT 119
  Over hill, over d., SHAK 126
dales: hills and d. UNKN 59
daliaunce: kan/ So muchel of d. and fair langage. CHAU 20
dalliance: d. of the eagles, WHITM 23
Dally: D. the doom CRAN H 37
dam': cam to the miller's d. UNKN 31
damage: d. that was done RICH 4
damask: divide/ flax for d. MOOR M 37
  placed/ 'Fore d. roses. HERR 56
damasked: d. like the chasuble HEAN 19
  roses d., red and white, SHAK 237
dame: belle d. sans merci" KEAT 5, 32
  d. and knight are there. SCOT WA 6
  d. or maid, be not afraid, UNKN 263
  D. Religion, BUTL 1
  nest of his litle d., BRYA 19
  our sulky, sullen d., BURN 50
  smild at the d. BLAK 25
dames: Ah, gentle d.! BURN 51

courtly d. and knights, CAMPI 9
elder d., thy haughty peers, BRYA 12
damming: gray stone wall d. my stream, KNIG 8
Damn: D. with faint praise, POPE A 7
  D. yo' soul; BROWN S 3
  D. your eyes BYRO 53
  God d. for ever POUN 64
  people of common sense d. metres, LOWE J 5
  to such blockheads set my wit!/ I d. such fools! — SWIF 5
damnations: Twenty-nine distinct d., BROWNI R 78
damn'd: Spirits d. MILT 59
damned: d. defeat was made. SHAK 31
  d. stood up to see. DAVID 1
  D. universal cock, STEVENS 2
  d. would make no noise, HERR 63
  float up from the d. Earth./ "To friends above, POE 30
  last pain for the d. EMPS 13
  lend a tyrannous and a d. light SHAK 30
  let poor, d. bodies bee; BURN 2
  one may be d. BYRO 71
  send the d. doctors SNYD 38
  what d. minutes SHAK 134
damns: half d. me with untruth, HERR 20
damp: cross the d. cold lawn BERRYM 14
  d. grave ROET 12
  d. my intended wing MILT 88
  neckcurls, limp and d. as tendrils; ROET 11
  poisonous d. of night SHAK 8
  sea-sands d. and brown LONG 46
  Tasting of the sweet d. woods SMIT W 4
  wrap it in a d. cloth. HUGO 5
dampned: d. wedding with the deede; CHAU 91
damselle: d. spake, and dyed. CHAT 1
Dan: sat D. D. McGrew; SERV 6
Danae: Now lies the Earth all D. to the stars. TENN 109
danc'd: drunk, and d., and sung/ Thy fill, COWL 3
dance: bent nails/ d. DUGA 2
  creed that will not let you d.? JOHN H 2
  crying shadow in the funeral d., ELIOT T 25
  d. above your green, green grave UNKN 48
  d. from the d.? YEATS 13
  d. on the surface HUGH T 10

d. exhausted eye, KINS 5
D. faces pale against that rosy
　flame, TENN 81
d. forgetting of my cares
　DANI S 8
d. hair changing to gray
　ROSS C 18
D. house, TENN 20
d. Inscrutable workmanship
　WORD 96
D. is my day SPENS 28
D. is the world, SPENS 6
D., marvelous, ROBI 24
d. my light, ROET 33
d. Night, BEAU/FLET 4
D. night is all his own,
　JOHN L 3
d. of December. HERF 3
d. of the arms Plutonic, LAWR 5
d. of the coffin THOMA D 2
d. secret love BLAK 80
D.—that—in that God? GINS 23
d. the long halloo NOYE 3
d. vapours have oppress'd
　KEAT 1
d. vault above BRID R 15
d. wainscot and timbered roof,
　NEWB 3
deep d.: AMMO 12
desolate, d. weeks WILLI 37
do in the d. CAMPI 3
Doom is d. AUDE 95
down to his d. glasses. WAGO 1
fir trees d. and high; HOOD 5
fire—devils, d. or anything,
　KIPL 4
hear the d.-vowelled birds.
　THOMA D 16
heavy night hung d. HEMA 4
I knew you in this d.; OWEN 40
in the d. and wet,
　STEVENSO R 24
in the d. of the year. WALK 11
in the d. we hide CULL 4
It grows d. To ride. THOMA E 19
it was dusk outside,/ Inside it was
　d. FROS 15
joyous leaves of d. green,
　WHITM 39
kennel in the d. THOMA D 26
know how to play/ In that d.
　world ROET 22
lie awake in the d. WHITM 75
light dispels the d. MILT 82
light that is d. SWIN 20
Like a d. flood suspended in its
　course, SHEL 16
Lord, I fashion d. gods, too,
　CULL 10
low d. verge of life TENN 29
many a d. and drearie Vale
　MILT 61

moonlight/ In the sweetgum d.
　HAYD 14
night of d. intent FROS 77
no less lovely being d., CULL 3
Of the d. past JOYC 1
Playing till too d. to see, BLUN 1
ranged mansions d.
　THOMS J (1834–1882) 3
river flowing d. and deep,
　THOMS J (1834–1882) 6
rouses up the seeds of d. disease.
　THOMS J (1700–1748) 13
Shoots across the neutral D.
　EMER 9
short d. passage DAVE 1
slow, d. hours begin, ROSS C 28
thick of the d. WILLI 9
this d. night SIDN 30
Through the daily d. WILB 20
through the spaces of the d.
　ELIOT T 103
Tired of his d. dominion,
　MERE G 8
Tongues wrangled d. SAND 24
void, d., and drear, COLE SAM 7
ways that are d. HART 1
we rose in the d. BLAK 87
where thy d. eye glances, POE 8
winter, dead and d., ALLI 4
woods are lovely, d. FROS 108
wounds of the sad
　uncomprehending d., SITW 12
darke: d. daies seene! SHAK 223
darken: d. all lands; ROSS C 8
d. the fame/ Of a life MOOR T 12
darken'd: d. heart that beat no
　more; TENN 25
darkened: Bloom in these d. fields
　MUIR 9
sky is d. AIKE 8
darkening: gave/ A d. shudder;
　WINT 8
Life's d. slope ROSS D 3
night is d. BRON 2
swan drifts upon a d. flood.
　YEATS 37
upon the d. plain MACL 12
darkens: evening d. and comes on.
　WRIG J 4
twilight d., the curlew calls;
　LONG 46
Darker: D. by far than any coalpit
　stone. TAYL E 3
D. grows the valley, MERE G 5
d. my desire ROET 33
d. than Death SHEL 58
I am the d. brother. HUGH L 6
in d. fortunes tried. BRYA 36
is come a d. day, SHEL 37
world's tide is bearing me along /
　Sterner desires and d. hopes
　BRON 11

darkest: d. inch your shelf allows,
　ROBI 17
darkey: Wherever the d. may go;
　FOST 2
darkeys: d. are gay; FOST 1
Darkling: D. I listen; KEAT 49
horrors of the tedious Night,/ D. I
　sigh, PHILL 2
Darkly: D. he rose, OHAR 21
d. wise and rudely great:
　POPE A 78
darkness: ascend from d. AIKE 8
climbed through d. SASS 13
crowned with d., WORD 18
d. and corruption leave
　ROSS C 20
d. and in hedges SNOD 16
d. and silence reign LEAR 6
d. and the cold, STEVENSO R 6
d. deepens; LYTE 1
d. I inhabit OHAR 10
D. more clear than noonday
　ROSS C 21
d. of the grave MILLA 6
d. of the land, TENN 50
d. or another light; ROBI 32
d. silvers away, BRID R 1
d. visible MILT 50
descending/ D. of fear JOYC 4
distinguish d. from the soul?
　YEATS 44
doubled d. up the labouring hill.
　ROSS D 7
dwell in d.; CHAP G 1
fleckled d. like a drunkard reels
　SHAK 146
Flowers of d., DAVIS 1
from d. into d. HAYD 19
Gods perfect D. GINS 25
into the wet d. Kissing, still
　MONTA 2
land of d. and blind eyes
　VAUG 13
leaves the world to d. and to me.
　GRAY 7
on the shores of d. there is light,
　KEAT 65
Out of the fabulous d.
　YEATS 117
Pain comes from the d. JARR 21
pain, d. and cold. BROWNI R 69
ploughman in d. plough?
　BLAK 61
powers of d. bound. MILT 64
Prince of D. stalks LOWE R 14
Queen of air and d., HOUS 12
re-begot/ Of absence, d., death:
　DONN 43
sink,/ Downward to d.,
　STEVENS 62
slope thro' d. up to God,
　TENN 33
soul/ that grows in d., OHAR 2

There hung a d., WORD 97
they appear in/ the d.: GUNN 9
through the d., WHITM 56
two cocks together crow,/ Cleaving the d. THOMA E 4
Universal D. buries All. POPE A 2
voice in the d., LONG 45
wicked shall be silent in d.; BIBL, O.T. 8
wrung from the d. JARR 21
darling: d. buds of May, SHAK 188
d. of my heart, CAREY 4
d. of the Spring! WORD 151
find thy D. in an urn. CAREW 6
maimed d., ROET 12
Nature's D. laid, GRAY 28
say Goodbye, my d., LEWI 7
side/ Of my d., POE 6
six years' D. of a pigmy size! WORD 74
twelve-year-old d. MANI 1
dart: d. in the orchard aisles, WILB 37
d. upon me and sting WHITM 4
Fate wings with every wish th' afflictive d., JOHN S (1709–1784) 16
struck by the hunter's d. SHEL 7
throw a d. at BROWNE 3
we call Cupid's d. SIDN 7
darting: quick-eyed trout/ Or d. salmon. THOMS J (1700–1748) 9
darts: both bear d., JONS 28
d. to shore/ to stab — AMMO 6
love's piercing d., PEEL 3
dash: d. away all!" MOOR C 2
dashed: breaking waves d. high HEMA 3
Dasher: "Now, D.! now, Dancer! MOOR C 2
dashin: your d. Jimmy? UNKN 150
data: weary with historical d., POUN 34
date: all too short a d. SHAK 188
blind d. that has stood you up: JARR 10
have so short a d., BRAD 10
learned one d. SNOD 5
looking out of d. LARK 14
love still breed,/ Had joys no d., RALEG 9
renewed her charter's d. DRYD 7
youth and thou are of one d., SHAK 190
dateless: d. mid-days of the law MUIR 3
death's d. night SHAK 195
dates: d. are brief, SHAK 234
d. of wars ALDR T 1
Datta: D.: what have we given? ELIOT T 152

daubing: d. The entire neighborhood DAVIS 4
daughter: bayliffes d. deare, UNKN 15
books to you, d.-in-law, RICH 17
D. d. whistle UNKN 305
d. of a fisherman, HOLM 10
d. of Earth and Water, SHEL 25
D. of the Moon, Nokomis. LONG 40
d. of their sires/ Saved a captive Englishman. THAC 2
d. of their youth: JONS 22
his d. Clementine. MONTROSS 1
in thy d. see, PHILI A 3
lies London's d., THOMA D 38
nine months' d., LOWE R 30
Science! true d. of old Time POE 1
skipper had taken his little d., LONG 51
Stern D. WORD 88
"Throw down the ball, ye Jew's d., UNKN 133
to my elder d. THOMA E 11
undaunted d. of desires! CRAS 3
daughter's: my d. brown, DURE 2
daughters: blood of fathers, mothers, d., sons, SHAK 30
d. Got 'tween the lawful sheets. SHAK 80
d. of Israel, weep over Saul, BIBL, O.T. 69
d. of the swan YEATS 9
D. of Time, EMER 13
Degenerate sons and d., MAST 9
fairest of her d. Eve. MILT 74
Hecuba and the hundred d., TATE A 1
ripe d., JONS 36
daunce: d. to an harpe smale, CHAU 87
dauncen: They d. deffly, SPENS 56
daunt: d. his spirit; BUNY 3
daunten: weird shall never d. me." UNKN 246
dauntless: d. in war, SCOT WA 18
Rather your d. virtue, MILT 95
David: D. his little lad! REES 3
daw: day doth d., UNKN 307
Dawdling: D. over the remorseless earth, SNOD 3
Dawes: Pyes and D. and Rookes and Crows, BONH 1
dawis: now the day d.; MONTG 1
dawn: At d. of morn, PRIO 8
brown fog of a winter d., ELIOT T 118
called it D. DUNB P 1
cold/ And passionate as the d.' YEATS 60
d. goes down to day./ Nothing gold can stay. FROS 71

d. grass runway SNYD 35
d. halts. THOMA D 31
d. is clear SNYD 44
d. of cornflowers. PLATH 75
d./ Of life: WORD 115
D. of our Eternal Day! CRAS 4
d. of the day when we die. SWIN 20
D.-sniffing revenant, HEAN 8
d.'s early light, KEY 1
day when I rose at d. WHITM 108
decline of the d. SWIN 19
dewdrops to greet the d., COOP 1
dewy d. to dewy night, MORR 6
endless pilgrimage,/ D. and dusk, GRAV 36
ever-returning roses of d. JEFFE 4
half-waking tropic d., NEWS 1
harbor at d.; BLY 5
if she were the d., SHEL 77
in that d. to be alive, WORD 111
just as the d. appear'd, WHITM 107
light-blue lane of early d., TENN 54
like this d., SNYD 11
lived, felt d., MCCRA 2
may d. an age, ARNO 36
melts away/ As doth the d. COWL 5
messenger of d., THOR 6
poet of the d., LONG 8
Shall the Spring d., TIMR 2
watch from d. to gloom SHEL 51
Welcome the d. BRID R 14
world's dim d., SMIT L 4
dawned: d. with added light? TIMR 3
dawning: bird of d. singeth all night long: SHAK 19
d. beauty warms us so? WALL 8
d. of Billy's last day. MELV 3
dewy d.'s cold grey air; THOMS J (1834–1882) 1
with the d. of morn, CAMPB T 9
Day: All d. long CULL 11
All d. long. JUST 2
All d. long in unrest, MACW 1
appear/ at all one d. OHAR 17
bald street breaks the blank d. TENN 21
banish the thoughts of d. LONG 15
behold the d.-break! WHITM 75
bell tolled on thy burial d., COWP 11
blessèd barrier between d. and d., WORD 149
blessèd sunny d.: BRET 5
break of d. arising SHAK 194

by d. and night I yearn,
  LOWE J 22
by guile won the d.: ELLI 2
cares, that infest the d., LONG 16
change your d. of youth
  SHAK 187
child that's born on the Sabbath
  d. MOTH 22
clear fountain of eternal d.,
  MARV 31
compare thee to a summer's d.?
  SHAK 188
curfew tolls the knell of parting
  d., GRAY 7
dark cold d. AUDE 36
Dark is my d. SPENS 28
dawn goes down to d./ Nothing
  gold can stay. FROS 71
Dawn of our Eternal D.! CRAS 4
dawn of the d. when we die.
  SWIN 20
d. and night MOOR M 23
D. and Night; BLAK 105
D. as huge DICKI 26
d. breaks not, it is my heart,
  DONN 12
d. brought back my night.
  MILT 34
d. but one; BOUR 1
D. come white, WHITM 65
d. doth daw, UNKN 307
d. in his hotness, ARNO 8
d. in the city-square,
  BROWNI R 84
d., in the night, WHITM 50
d. in thy courts BIBL, O.T. 43
d. less or more TENN 119
d. never shuts his eye, MILT 10
d. of his death AUDE 36
d./ Of mortall life SPENS 33
d. perish wherein I was born,
  BIBL, O.T. 9
d. returns, LONG 47
D. shall clasp him GREN 4
d. when I rose at dawn
  WHITM 108
D. Turned and departed
  EMER 16
d. Weakening the will SPEND 21
d.'s journey ROSS C 28
d.'s vanity, the night's remorse.
  YEATS 24
death of each d.'s life, SHAK 106
Dies at the opening d. WATT I 3
dog has his d., THOMA D 39
draughts of intellectual d.,
  CRAS 3
dropt at my side that d.,
  WHITM 106
each d. dies with sleep.
  HOPKINS 15
each d. is like a year, WILD 2

every d. came mute HECH 15
every dog his d. KINGSL 6
false d. that's fled. RODG 7
Feels shorter than the D.
  DICKI 11
fiery d. had a kernel sweet of
  cold THOMA E 9
first D.'s Night DICKI 25
floytynge al the d. CHAU 9
follow, as the night the d.,
  SHAK 24
for a d. and a night TENN 119
for me night and d. TENN 104
forever and a d., LONG 10
fountain light of all our d.,
  WORD 81
gilded Car of D., MILT 8
give me a cask a d.;
  STEPHENS 4
give the d. a scientific tone.
  CARRY 7
give you the time of d.
  MERE W 1
glory of the d. was in her face,
  JOHN J 4
glory of this perfect d. JOHN G 2
Gone is another summer's d.
  DE LA 26
grow on Irish ground!/ No more
  Saint Patrick's D. UNKN 299
happy all the d.
  STEVENSO R 11
He leads the Choir of D.
  BLAK 36
heard at the close of the d.
  WHITM 108
hippopotamus's d. Is passed in
  sleep; ELIOT T 38
idle singer of an empty d.
  MORR 2
In the cool of the d., ELIOT T 6
independent being in his d.
  BYRO 19
Infinite d. excludes the night,
  WATT I 8
innocent brightness of a new-born
  D. WORD 86
innumerable choir of d.
  BRID R 14
is come a darker d., SHEL 37
joyful world salutes the rising d.
  COWL 4
joys which with his d.-star rise
  VAUG 23
Just for one riotous d., DUNE P 4
kindest hour of d., MILLA 34
labour night and d. BUNY 4
last steps of d., BRYA 25
leav'st their losses open to the d.
  BEAU/FLET 4
left alone with our d., AUDE 91
let us pass a d.,/ Where all cry
  out, POPE A 100

light of common d. WORD 71
limits of d., LOWE R 54
little systems have their d.;
  TEN J 17
love is sweet for a d.; SWIN 23
love you all the D., GAY 5
mark this d. in Heaven? TIMR 3
Maud Muller on a summer's d.
  WHITT 15
measure off another d. For an
  approving God. DICKI 5
morn/ Of nobler d., LOWE J 14
mouth of the dying d. AUDE 36
My soul is now her d., SHAP 19
my whole d. in the quest, —
  BROWNI R 50
nearer, every D., DICKI 150
Night and d. on me she cries;
  UNKN 127
night is d., PATM 10
now the d. dawis; MONTG 1
O frabjous d.! CARRO 36
on a certain d.: STEPHEN 1
on a salty d. MILLA 12
on Christmas D., LONG 11
one d. anyone died CUMM 6
One d. beside some flowers
  SHAP 17
our master has left us for the d.
  BLY 5
outlives this d. SHAK 60
Pack, clouds, away, and welcome,
  d.! HEYW 1
paint till d. of doom,
  BEAU/BASS 6
papers are delivered every d.;
  KUNI 3
pause in the d.'s occupations,
  LONG 9
performance keeps no d.;
  CAMPI 1
pray/ Devoutly on the holy d.;/
  Skip and trip it on the green,
  CAMPI 8
promise such a beauteous d.,
  SHAK 198
punctual rape of every blesséd d.,
  WILB 24
ran a hundred years to a d.,
  HOLM 4
rare as a d. in June? LOWE J 17
remembers that famous d.
  LONG 43
sad and sorrowful d. UNKN 207
see the brave d. SHAK 186
she weaves by night and d.
  TENN 61
simple produce of the common d.
  WORD 16
since the d. she died. LONG 14
smite thee by d., BIBL, O.T. 59
Softly now the light of d.
  DOAN 1

"Some/ d. you'll know. OHAR 21
steed that saved the d.,
  READ T 3
Stella this d. is thirty-four
  SWIF 21
Stop this d. and night WHITM 76
study all d., GILB 61
survive my well-contented d.
  SHAK 196
tender grace of a d. that is dead
  TENN 3
their average d.: AUDE 75
this amazing/ d.: CUMM 19
till a D. The Owner passed —
  DICKI 109
till break of d. AUDE 55
till the Judgment d. LIND V 7
toil from d. to d.,
  JOHN S (1709–1784) 2
toils of the d.: CARRO 15
twice a d., PATM 6
twilight of eternal d. TENN 29
twilight of such d. SHAK 215
Underneath D.'s azure eyes,
  SHEL 36
Up from the South at break of d.,
  READ T 1
Upon Saint Crispin's d. DRAY 2
Ushers in a drearier d. BRON 1
Venus comes not ev'ry D.
  DRYD 24
Waiting the Judgment D.: FINC 2
weary night and d.; YEATS 14
went on Yule d. UNKN 157
what belongs to the d.
  WHITM 38
What the d. doth forbid. CAMPI 3
whole long d.? ROSS C 28
winter's morn, on a stormy d.,
  LEAR 8
world's great d. MUIR 8
year and a d., LEAR 11
Yet the d. wears, BROWNI R 50
yonder dropping d.: TENN 23
youth sapped d. by d.:
  ROSS C 18

dayes: see not half my d. that's
  due, BRAD 2

daylight: dark and the d., LONG 9
d. kissing her wan hair, WILD 16
feel the d. coming/ like a relentless
  milkman RICH 9
Noiselessly as the d. ALEX 4
Sunlit pallets never thrive;/ Morns
  abed and d. slumber HOUS 47
When d. comes, CLOU 9

dayntye: "Ye d. Nymphs,
  SPENS 51

day's: d. at the morn;
  BROWNI R 66

days: all my d. are trances, POE 8
banished him from better d.
  ROBI 13

behold these present d.,
  SHAK 228
better d. when I am gone
  BONT 7
burnt-out ends of smoky d.
  ELIOT T 97
but two d. old. BLAK 93
come perfect d.; LOWE J 17
count eternity in d.? ROET 29
crimes done in my d. of nature
  SHAK 26
d.; WHITT 29
d. and nights WALK 13
d. and nights, passing away,)
  WHITM 59
d. are in the yellow leaf;
  BYRO 57
d. are long, CARRO 33
d. are past the best, SHAK 238
D. are where we live. LARK 8
d. gone by/ Return upon me
  WORD 115
d. have crackled THOMP F 8
D. of danger, nights of waking.
  SCOT WA 9
d. of impotence approach,
  ROCH 2
d. of mist, THOMA E 14
d. of old ROSS C 25
D. of plenty BENN H 2
d. that are no more.
  TENN 114, 115
d. were a joy, HARD 3
d. yet called two CAMPI 12
dog lay dead five d. WILB 32
down the d.; THOMP F 6
embalmed the d., MCKA 4
forty nights and d. GRAV 14
heavenly d. that cannot die;
  WORD 61
how their d. will cease!
  STEPHENS 12
hypocritic D., EMER 13
in a shower of all my d.
  THOMA D 33
In my d. of childhood, LAMB 2
In the d. of my youth SOUTHE 7
last of d. Were fading ROBI 11
melancholy d. are come, BRYA 7
my d. and lands — WHITM 53
pæan of old d.! POE 30
prison of his d. AUDE 46
reverence of old d. WHITT 12
scorn delights and live laborious
  d.; MILT 27
September d. are here, JACK 4
shadowed d. are done, AUDE 10
Short d., sharp d., NASHE 2
silent d. In harmless joys are
  spent, CAMPI 13
since civil war d., MAHON 2
singing d. are done; MILLA 18
swift d. near their goal, BRON 8

Ten d. and nights, HOLM 14
thoughts of other d. SHAP 10
treasure of thy lusty d.,
  SHAK 185
Twist our narrow d.; AUDE 11
wastes half his d., WATT I 6
weary of d. and hours, SWIN 13
What are d. for? LARK 8
wi' her a' my simmer d. SOUT 1
wrackful siege of batt'ring d.,
  SHAK 212
year whose d. are long. WILD 2

dazed: d. with dreadfull face.
  SENE 2
sluggish/ d. spring approaches —
  WILLI 35

dazle: d. now this earthly, MILT 97

dazzle: Crowns they d. so. KIPL 23
d. our eyes? HILT 1
truth must d. gradually
  DICKI 137

dazzling: d. through the leaves,
  TENN 63

De Soto: Ferdinand D., sleeping/ In
  the river, VAN DO 1

De Vere: Guy D., hast thou no
  tear? — POE 29

deacon: make a d. proud. DARC 2

dead: always d. like Greek
  SHAP 22
among the peaceful d. MUIR 2
animated d.; TATE A 10
at a d. party, WILB 25
at the headstones of the d.
  HECH 5
Balboa lies d. somewhere
  SCOT WI 2
be with her dear d. son.
  WHITM 17
beauty's summer d. SHAK 227
bent light over the d. RUKE 1
between two worlds, one d.,
  ARNO 32
Beware the d. OLSO 16
breeding/ Lilacs out of the d.
  land, ELIOT T 113
bury the d.: NEWB 2
by thy scorn, O murderess, I am
  d., DONN 4
communication/ Of the d. is
  tongued ELIOT T 64
(companion of the d.) LINC 2
Consented, and was d. DICKI 100
constrained to honor us though
  d.! MCKA 6
couches of the d., BLAK 16
danced, and is now d. WILB 40
d. against the d. MACL 12
d. already, WHITM 17
D. and divine WHITM 72
d. and rotten;/ None that go
  return again. HOUS 43

d. are keeping back? FROS 128
d. bell, PLATH 36
d. black face! WALK 3
d. boughs that winter still must
  bind, ROSS D 1
D. cats, and turnip-tops, SWIF 9
D. Died. Will die. Want. CREE 10
d. faith foiled and flawed
  ROBI 28
d. fed you LOWE A 2
d. feet walked in. HARD 40
d. girl but a shadowy ghost
  MACL 10
d. had souls, FROS 128
D. hands, dead stringencies.
  PLATH 6
d. heart run them in!
  STEVENSO R 2
D., hung up indoors, OLSO 2
d. I loved so well, WHITM 53
d. is all the innocence of anger
  CHES 11
d. is the world's delight.
  GREV/DYER 2
d. land ELIOT T 44
d. man out of mind. HOUS 33
d. man's cry MACL 6
d. man's sweetheart, HOUS 37
d. man's voice MACL 10
d. men lost their bones.
  ELIOT T 124
D. men may envy OWEN 3
D. men naked THOMA D 9
d. men rise up never; SWIN 15
d. men's skulls, SHAK 97
D. Nelson and his half-d. crew,
  HARD 21
d., nor deaf, nor dumb;
  RANDA J 2
d. oak tree bough. THOMA E 8
d. one lay moaning) SMIT ST 2
d. selves to higher things.
  TENN 18
d. shall live, the living die,
  DRYD 27
d. they live VERY 2
d. thing, DONN 43
d. unhappy night, TENN 74
"D.," was all he answered.
  FROS 29
d. who groaned within. POE 43
D. who struggled in the slime
  SASS 12
d. who will not fight; GREN 1
D. winds' and spent waves' riot
  SWIN 11
d., you never shall return."
  OMAR 6
Dear d. women, BROWNI R 79
Death is d., SHEL 10
death is to the d. DODG 2
Deep with the first d.
  THOMA D 38

Deliberately stabbed him d.
  FROS 45
departed d. SHEL 31
disappeared in the d. of winter.
  AUDE 35
dispersed and d. MILLA 35
divine as myself is d.,
  WHITM 69
do not suffer as the d. do,
  OLSO 15
dog lay d. five days WILB 32
double d.: going, and bidding go.
  DONN 23
Doubled the globe of d.
  THOMA D 24
dreams pursue our d. SWIN 7
Drive my d. thoughts SHEL 46
duty, a d.-sure thing, — HAY 4
Each d. child coiled, PLATH 38
England mourns for her d.
  BINY 1
eyes of the d., WHITM 76
face of one long d. LONG 13
faith is d., WYAT 28
Fallen cold and d. WHITM 45
famous beauty of d. women:
  MACL 11
fell across the picture — d.
  DARC 4
few sands and d. leaves
  WHITM 3
five kings count the d.
  THOMA D 25
flock to gaze the strengthless d.,
  HOUS 58
frozen world of the d. PINS 2
give her bounty to the d.?
  STEVENS 55
"God is not d.; LONG 12
graves give up their d. SWIF 3
Graves, yawn and yield your d.,
  SHAK 132
Harrow the house of the d.
  AUDE 69
He who was living is now d.
  ELIOT T 143
hear the D. March play, KIPL 5
here alive, she is not d.,
  UNKN 16
house of the d.; AUDE 69
How shall the d. taste JEFFE 36
I am blind, and d., and stray,
  QUAR 4
I learnt that thou wast d.,
  COWP 10
I would that I were d.!' TENN 52
if I/ am really/ D. EVAN 2
immortal d. who live again
  ELIOT G 1
in their d.-doing might, SPENS 1
join the living with the d.
  CLARE 8

kissed by the English d.
  OWEN 28
know not you are d. in vain,
  HOUS 4
land where the d. dreams go.
  NOYE 4
lane to the land of the d. AUDE 3
laurel the graves of our d.!
  FINC 2
lazy/ or d. OHAR 17
leaves are all d. FROS 92
life became a Legend of the D.
  LONG 27
life-weary taker may fall d.,
  SHAK 150
Like statues d. TRAH 9
list of the d. CLARK J 1
living blind and seeing D.
  SITW 10
Love is d., SIDN 37
Love is d.; FORD J 1
lovers being estranged or d.,
  YEATS 5
Lycidas is d., MILT 25
mad and d. as nails,
  THOMA D 10
madman shakes a d. geranium.
  ELIOT T 103
magnificence of the d., AIKE 9
man is d.! WHITT 12
man is d. WINT 11
man that's d. HUGH L 19
mangled youth lies d.
  THOMP F 8
marriage is d., when the pleasure
  is fled: DRYD 16
master Robin Hood lies d.,
  MUND 1
mocked the d. bones SHAK 97
mourn the d. WILB 33
my enemy is d., WHITM 69
my old bawd is d.? YEATS 72
New splendour to the d. PLATO 3
noble letters of the d. TENN 41
noble Living, and the noble D.
  WORD 116
Nothing to bury but d. KING B 3
o'er the d. HERR 59
one d. deathless hour. ROSS D 5
only son is d. WHITM 17
open eyes of the d. MERW 2
our English d.! SHAK 56
parking lot of the d. DICKEY 6
pasture of d. horses,/ roots of pine
  trees HALL 3
pine-tree drops its d.; MERE G 2
poets in their misery d.
  WORD 124
praise of ladies d. SHAK 228
purposes to kill me d. HOUS 10
quiet d. and the loud celebrities
  LEWI 1
ranks of the d.: — FINC 1

reaching from the d. WILLI 48
remind me of the d. SASS 8
Renown and grace is d.;
   SHAK 109
rifle knocks him d., YEATS 155
round him o'er the d. HEMA 1
rows of d. clam shells; ROET 42
scents d. leaves yield,
   THOMA E 5
seemed stone d. PRAT 1
self-effacement of the d. LEWI 6
sheeted d./ Did squeak and gibber
   SHAK 20
shouting at me, d. man, SLES 2
Sidney is d., d. is my friend,
   GREV/DYER 2
Sierras/ Will be dry and d.,
   SNYD 20
sky is d. VAN DO 2
Smiling the boy fell d.
   BROWNI R 38
So be merry, so be d. SORL 3
soul is d. that slumbers,
   LONG 35
soul so d., SCOT WA 11
strike you d.? YEATS 149
striking me ev'n d.; HERB G 2
struck me d.? SHAK 217
tender grace of a day that is d.
   TENN 3
there are no d.! MCCRE 4
these heroic happy d. CUMM 29
they/ Were not the one d.,
   FROS 84
thy d. indifference of walls.
   MELV 2
tight belly of the d. SHAP 15
To his d. fame; WHITT 12
Treating alike its d. HUGH T 8
trestles to shake the d., WHITM 8
Two months d., MOSS 2
walk d. still. JONS 25
was alive and is d., UNKN 200
We are born with the d.:
   ELIOT T 72
what of the d.? SEXT 15
When I am d., my dearest,
   ROSS C 33
wind was still,/ Shaken out d.
   ROSS D 9
winter, d. and dark, ALLI 4
With a d. sound ELIOT T 119
with sour d.? WHITM 96
words of a d. man AUDE 38
worse to me than d.? WORD 1
youth stone d., SASS 4
deaden: walls of books will d.
   MACN 10
deadens: d. and endures. MACN 22
deadlie: knife in Sir Willie's pouch,/
   Gied him a d. wound. .
   UNKN 269

deaf: dead, nor d., nor dumb;
   RANDA J 2
d. and silent, read'st the eternal
   deep, WORD 77
D. with the drumming of an ear;
   MARV 11
dreamed as d. men hear, GARR 1
stunned, stone blind, and d.
   SHAP 16
trouble d. heaven SHAK 194
woman's d., and does not hear.
   POPE A 109
deafe: Love is rather d., than blind,
   JONS 18
deaffe: d. and cruell, MARL 5
deal: Dangerous to d. with,
   SURR 1
d. In abstract things; YEATS 151
deals: Nature d. with us, LONG 34
dealt: us who d. them war
   OWEN 35
dean: soft d. invite, POPE A 104
de-animalize: d. human mentality,
   KINN 12
dear: be with her d. dead son.
   WHITM 17
come from, Baby d.?
   MACDONA 1
d. and early friends — WHITT 28
d. angry Lord, HERB G 10
D. as remembered kisses after
   death, TENN 115
D. dead women, BROWNI R 79
d. God who loveth us,
   COLE SAM 30
d. home faces WHITT 28
D., if you change, UNKN 74
d. knows who I'll marry.
   UNKN 139
d. the schoolboy spot BYRO 22
Farewell d. mate, WHITM 34
has a mother d., UNTE 1
his offspring d. GILB 19
How d. to my heart WOOD 1
letter from thy d. son. WHITM 15
loved thee d. DANI S 13
my dove, my d.; TENN 94
new wail my d. time's waste.
   SHAK 195
own d. boy is far away." BRIN 3
Retain that d. perfection
   SHAK 142
So near or d. HERR 14
that bread should be so d.,
   HOOD 13
Three things there be in man's
   opinion d., GREV 7
too d. for my possession,
   SHAK 219
your d. eyes return'd WHITM 106
deare: Farewell d. flowers,
   HERB G 47

dearer: d. birth SHAK 196
In closer, d. company, GLAD 2
dearest: face of d. look
   THOMA E 13
him my d. guest. BRAD 11
Sing on d. brother, WHITM 49
When I am dead, my d.,
   ROSS C 33
dearly: d. bought SIDN 39
d.-bought revenge, MILT 115
d. like the west, BURN 41
heart that lo'ed me d.! BURN 31
dears: eased/ My dim d.
   BROO G 18
dearth: curtain'd with a blessèd d.
   ROSS C 21
death: Adrift dissolving, bound for
   d.; MELV 2
After the first d., THOMA D 38
age, d.'s twilight,/ Thy Soul rest,
   DONN 51
air D. moans and sings: GREN 4
All eager-lipped I kissed the
   mouth of D. BENN G 3
all/ Life d. does end HOPKINS 15
all life dies, d. lives, and Nature
   breeds, MILT 61
all slaves/ Of d., DICKEY 3
all that way for/ Birth or D.?
   ELIOT T 51
allotment of d. HUGH T 2
arise/ From d., you numberless
   infinities DONN 5
at my d. thy Sonne DONN 30
at the point of d. SHAK 152
be glad of another d. ELIOT T 52
beg d.'s pardon WILB 33
beg one hour of d., OVID 7
bells of d. do ring? UNKN 128
beyond d./ Bridgeport, Ohio.
   WRIG J 3
birth to d. hurled MUIR 1
black d./ Keeps record SHEL 15
Black Widow, d. LOWE R 36
bleeding to d. of time GRAV 4
Brother to D., DANI S 8
bugbear D. to frighten LUCR 1
build your ship of d., LAWR 36
call for d. I shall: UNKN 167
cataract of D. LONG 29
cease not till d./ Creeds and
   schools in abeyance,
   WHITM 74
chamber in the silent halls of d.,
   BRYA 24
characters of d. and blight
   FROS 37
cheat fond d. of all but bone —
   DAY 2
Christ save us all from a d.
   LONG 53
citizens of d.'s grey land, SASS 6
cold as d.: CAMPB R 8

cold in d.: ROSS C 7
come away, d., SHAK 176
Confusion of the d.-bed
    YEATS 33
Content with d. LANIE 2
contrive to agree about d.
    EMPS 3
converse upon d.: SOUTHE 7
could not stop for D. DICKI 9
darker than D. SHEL 58
day of his d. AUDE 36
Dear as remembered kisses after
    d., TENN 115
d. a hideous storm of terror.
    WEBS 4
D. and life were not YEATS 154
D. as a mere border EMPS 4
D. august and royal BINY 2
D., be not proud, DONN 17
D. broke at once the vital chain,
    JOHN S (1709–1784) 4
D. closes all; TENN 133
d., come close mine eyes;
    GIBB 1
D. cometh soon or late. MACA 3
D. could drop ROSE 8
d. could never end it: AMMO 17
d. cry of a nation lost!
    THOMP W 1
D. cut the strings CULL 16
D. ere thou has slain another,
    BROWNE 3
D. fell with me, OWEN 39
D. had his grudge PETRA 3
D. had the Mercy, GINS 22
d. had undone so many.
    ELIOT T 118
D. has reared himself a throne
    POE 11
D. his D. wound MILT 64
D. hollow-eyed, SKEL 11
d. i think is no parenthesis
    CUMM 47
d.,/ Immediate BYRO 11
d.-in-life and life-in-d. YEATS 18
D. into the World, MILT 46
d. is a sleep. SWIN 25
D. is another milestone SPEND 8
D. is dead, SHEL 10
d. is expected, STEVENS 3
d. is no evil. JEFFE 31
d. is slumber, SHEL 42
D. is the end of life; TENN 86
D. is the fruit it bore. ROSS C 8
D. is the mother of beauty,
    STEVENS 60
D. is the veil SHEL 57
d. is to the dead. DODG 2
D. laid him along: SOUTHW 11
D. lays his icy hand on kings:
    SHIR 1
D. let you out, GINS 22
D.-light of Africa! CHES 9

D. looks gigantically down.
    POE 12
d.-messages given WHITM 92
d. my days should expiate.
    SHAK 190
d. of each day's life, SHAK 106
D. of Great Men, BUTL 8
D. Of his mother Earth, SITW 6
d. of kings! SHAK 89
D. Of men; JARR 4
d. of one so young SPEND 20
d. of princes. SHAK 45
d. of the race. WILB 1
D. of the self ROET 32
d. parts both woe and joy:
    SIDN 33
D., puffing at the doore,
    HERB G 16
D., rock me asleep, BOLE 1
D., sad refuge GRAY 26
d. shall the world subdue,/ Our
    love shall live, SPENS 24
d. shall be by drowning.
    SHAP 24
d. shall come amain: SMIT L 3
d. shall have no dominion.
    THOMA D 9
D. stands above me, LAND 1
D., stay thy phantoms! GINS 25
D.! the jewel of the just,/ Shining
    nowhere, VAUG 27
D.! thou comest UNKN 90
D., thou shalt die. DONN 13
d. to me subscribes, SHAK 229
D. to the killers, SPEND 19
D. tramples it to fragments.
    SHEL 13
d. were no divorce. DONN 3
d. will drive us from the scene
    EBER 5
d. with cold; JONS 28
d.'s agony/ Besieged COWL 14
D.'s cold hand! BLAK 28
d.'s dateless night SHAK 195
D.'s dream kingdom ELIOT T 43
D.'s ironic scraping.
    STEVENS 38
d.'s other Kingdom ELIOT T 42
D.'s outlet song of life,
    WHITM 47
d.'s pale flag SHAK 152
D.'s second self, SHAK 215
D.'s self is sorry. JONS 7
d.'s waters came, MOSS 3
Devours d., WILB 37
Digging the rock where D.
    OWEN 36
disapprove of d. EMPS 3
dream their way to d. PAGE 5
Dreams pursue d. SWIN 7
Ease me with d. DONN 23
easer of all woes,/ Brother to D.,
    FLET J 4

enemy is but D. BROO R 12
enough of sorrow before d.
    YEATS 148
evil moon bleeds drops of d.
    WALK 12
eyed her image dolefully as d.;
    RANS 25
eyes foreknowledge of d.: SWIN 2
faith that looks through d.,
    WORD 85
faithful unto d., WILB 29
fallen to d. WRIG J 7
Fear d. by water. ELIOT T 117
Fear d.? — to feel the fog
    BROWNI R 68
fed on the fullness of d. SWIN 23
feud with D. TENN 38
five kings did a king to d.
    THOMA D 24
folded/ her up like d., HARJ 3
for restful d. I cry, SHAK 213
forget time and d.: ROET 13
forgetful kingdom of d.
    RANS 21
From d. to life thou mightst him
    yet recover. DRAY 13
gentle sleep the sleep of d.,
    BLAK 14
gluttonous d., will instantly
    unjoynt DONN 58
Gon to hys d.-bedde, CHAT 1
Gone to her d.! HOOD 2
gorgeous d.-bed! DARL 2
Graves, yawn and yield your
    dead,/ Till d. be uttered,
    SHAK 132
Great is my envy of d. PETRA 8
grudge I am bearing against D.,
    PETRA 10
half in love with easeful D.,
    KEAT 49
hand dipping downwards to d.
    GINS 30
Happy in d. are they MANG 1
hastes me on unto a sudden d.,
    DRAY 5
heard D. say; HARD 44
heavy page/ Of d., SPEND 6
his d., which physic did except.
    SHAK 242
hot sides of d. WRIG R 1
hour of d. draw near BRYA 33
hym d. greep'the right hard by the
    croppe SENE 2
I am dying in my own d.
    ELIOT T 110
I hung on like d.; ROET 49
If D. should come UNKN 183
in each aspect d. is pure.
    JARR 23
In the ranks of d. MOOR T 9
in their d. they were not divided:
    BIBL, O.T. 69

into the dust of d.; SHEL 78
joy to thee, O d., WHITM 51
Keeps D. his court, SHAK 89
Kind/ d. BARA 8
kingly D./ Keeps his pale court
　SHEL 1
known what d. could do. SIMP 3
knows herself in d. Æ 2
Laid out for d., HERR 53
let me die before my d.!"
　VAUG 19
lets d. descend/ Upon him
　FROS 79
life after d. JEFFE 44
Life and d. STEVENSO R 10
lighted fools/ The way to dusty d.
　SHAK 114
lightning before d.: SHAK 152
live a living d., DANI S 10
long for d., BIBL, O.T. 12
look d. in the face, YEATS 42
loss without d. SEXT 1
love thee better after d.
　BROWNI E 6
lovely and soothing d.,
　WHITM 50
messenger of d. DRAK 3
Mister D. CUMM 11
mocked with d., MILT 98
Morning after D. DICKI 16
much possessed by d.
　ELIOT T 157
My part of d., SHAK 176
no God found stronger than d.;
　SWIN 25
no thing but d. will serve thy
　turn, DRAY 14
Nor blame I D., TENN 39
Nor shall D. brag SHAK 188
'Not D., but Love.' BROWNI E 8
Not one d. but many, OLSO 4
Nothing of d. can any feel
　LAND 3
O d., come quick, CORN 3
O world, O d.? SPEND 20
Of life and d., of home
　WHITM 12
Of life or d., WILB 46
of the swan in d. PAGE 4
Often faced d. HORA 7
On d. and beauty — LEWI 3
On the look of D. DICKI 144
pain/ Of d. denounced, MILT 95
pale captives, creep to d. SHIR 2
peace instead of d. let us bring:
　CAMPB T 2
quenched with the cold of d.
　HERB CH 4
quick-coming d. MORR 1
re-begot/ Of absence, darkness, d.:
　DONN 43
Remember d. MORE 1
rendezvous with D. SEEG 1

renewed by d., ROET 15
sad and heavy line/ Of d.,
　VAUG 29
Saviours d. did put some bloud/
　Into thy face; HERB G 20
scythers, Time and D.,/ Helmed
　locusts, LOWE R 59
sentence of thy early d.
　FANS S 1
shades of d., MILT 61
sickness, d.'s herald, and
　champion; DONN 44
sights of ugly d. SHAK 97
silence deep as d.; CAMPB T 1
Sin and D. amain MILT 62
sleep of d. WYLI 13
Sooner or later delicate d.
　WHITM 50
soul at d. I cry,) WHITM 41
starved to d. and turned to dust,
　WESL S 1
stay the d.-flood rising LAWR 38
Sweet d., small son, HALL 1
sweeten and perfume my d.
　KING H 1
symbol perfected in d.
　ELIOT T 69
talent which is d. to hide
　MILT 124
teach me to see d., KING H 1
that churl d. SHAK 196
that is D. DICKI 144
that sleep of d. SHAK 39
There is no d.! MCCRE 1
they are gone to early d.,
　EBER 4
those who enter d. DODG 2
thought is as a d., SHAK 211
thought of my d., ROET 15
Time and d. shall depart DRYD 9
to start her d.-defying leap
　FERL 2
to wreck and d./ In ocean cave,
　WILLA 2
too old for d., too old for life,
　PRAT 1
torch of d. they light; THAC 1
triumph over d. and sin;
　SPENS 18
Triumphing over D., and Chance,
　MILT 45
true face of d.? DOWS 1
'Twixt life and d., CRAS 10
Universe of d., MILT 61
up the line to d., SASS 3
valley of D. TENN 6
valley of the shadow of d.,
　BIBL, O.T. 31
Vanquished in life, his d.
　JOHN L 4
vasty hall of d. ARNO 21
violent d. in thousand shapes
　CHAU 48

Voyage through d. HAYD 11
want/ Of thought is d.; BLAK 63
'What caused my d. DAVIE W 1
what d. or love is JONS 28
while he lived never thought of
　d. GREV 8
Why do we then shun d.
　WHITE 2
wind of D.'s imperishable wing?
　ROSS D 3
window proves/ A constant d.;
　THOMS J (1700–1748) 10
winter d. has never tried
　FROS 80
wish d., nor fear his might.
　MARTIA 2
with the dust of d.? TENN 96
your d. murdered me, MOSS 1
Your friends to d. HOUS 50
your memory d. cannot take,
　SHAK 216
your ship of d., LAWR 36
deathbed: d. whereon it must
　expire, SHAK 215
deathless: blooms a d. flower,
　MICH 3
d. dower, ROSS D 4
genius a d. adornment, POUN 35
lengthened out/ To d. pain?
　MILT 98
one dead d. hour. ROSS D 5
vibrations of d. music; MAST 1
With wonderful d. ditties OSHA 2
deathlike: deep, d. valleys SERV 12
death's: D. a sad bone; SEXT 17
deaths: by feigned d. to die.
　DONN 57
d. of kings, ALDR T 1
debars: fate so enviously d.,
　MARV 7
debat: youthe and elde is often at
　d. CHAU 51
debate: d., that eke discord doth
　sow, ELIZ 1
foule d. Twixt noble men
　UNKN 63
true or false, the Subject of D.,
　ROCH 16
wife wise, without d.; MARTIA 2
debated: d. empire of the world,
　LUCR 2
debateth: wasteful Time d. with
　Decay, SHAK 187
Debauchee: D. of Dew — DICKI 69
Debauchery: D. and Drinking:
　BURN 6
debt: contracted much more d. than
　knowledge. BYRO 47
No squire in d., SHAK 76
paid her last d. To Nature,
　DONN 53
promise made is a d. unpaid,
　SERV 3

Cold dark d. and absolutely clear,
  BISH 4
deaf and silent, read'st the eternal
  d., WORD 77
d. and dense, WINT 3
d. and dreamless sleep BROO P 3
d. and gloomy wood, WORD 33
D. caves SHEL 62
d., deathlike valleys SERV 12
d. distress WORD 12
d.-founded sheltering,
  STEVENS 68
d. heart's core. YEATS 75
d. January. STEVENS 27
d. like the rivers. HUGH L 12
D., majestic, GRAY 24
d. nor hill there is, UNKN 250
d. sea swell ELIOT T 142
d. tangled wildwood, WOOD 1
d. to d. plunged!" MILT 100
d. unending/ Ache of love!
  JOYC 4
d. wide sea of Misery, SHEL 35
D. with the first dead
  THOMA D 38
dig d. trenches SHAK 185
Divergence d. and wide.
  WATS R 1
drinking d. of that divinest
  anguish, BRON 13
ending with some precept d.
  PRAE 1
full as d. a dye SHAK 206
heart's d. core, DUNB P 10
heart's d. languor
  THOMS J (1834–1882) 8
heights I rolled from into the d.;
  BROWNI R 5
hides them d., ALEX 7
Hung o'er the d.,
  THOMS J (1700–1748) 8
I'th d. his wonders BIBL, O.T. 56
love as d. and strong WHITT 10
one is of the d.; STEPHEN 3
plague of d. disdain: SIDN 37
populous d. SHEL 19
renders vain their d. desire? —
  ARNO 42
river flowing dark and d.,
  THOMS J (1834–1882) 6
Rocked in the cradle of the d.
  WILLA 1
silence d. and white. LOWE J 11
silence d. as death; CAMPB T 1
sleep so d. and still; DODG 1
so be d.! POE 41
summoned to the d., WORD 2
sun-defying, in its d. ravines
  LONG 14
tempt the distant d., HORA 5
thine own d.-sunken eyes
  SHAK 185

thunders of the upper d.;
  TENN 58
thunders shook the mighty d.,
  HOLM 18
tongues dissemble d. CAMPI 9
too d. for tears. WORD 87
weeping, longing with one d.
  longing, WHITM 17
What are d.? ROSS C 30
wild, unquenched, d.-sunken,
  ARNO 18
with d. impression MILT 35
wooed the slimy bottom of the d.
  SHAK 97
Deep-trenched: D./ Green billow:
  STEPHENS 8
deepening: Folded close under d.
  snow. LOWE J 13
deepens: darkness d.; LYTE 1
deeper: Cross, the Cross/ Goes d.
  LAWR 53
  d. as the ashes rose WILB 48
  d. rituals of his bones, SAND 16
  d. than any sea-dingle.
    AUDE 95
  tale of d. wrong; NOYE 5
  to a d. roar! FROS 7
  try/ A d. plague, DONN 40
deepest: d. grief of all, TENN 26
  d. understood, WILB 10
  latest and d.? WHITM 114
  what d. remains? WHITM 114
deeply: more d. interfused,
  WORD 35
deeps: over intellectual d.
  MERE G 9
  roaring d. and fiery sands,
    TENN 90
  stars and heavenly d. JOHN L 5
  whales in the wider d., LAWR 57
deer: Dove-note, bone marrow, d.
  dung, KIZE 1
  herd-abandoned d. SHEL 7
  time's d. is slain, MUIR 10
  wild d.'s walk: TUCK 1
deere: nimble d. to take, UNKN 59
deerhide: leather/ tanned from d.,
  HALL 4
Deever: they're hangin' Danny D.,
  KIPL 5
defaced: by Time's fell hand d.
  SHAK 211
Defaming: D. as impure MILT 77
defeat: damned d. was made.
  SHAK 31
  Isn't this d. so accurate, HUGO 2
  Reverse we proved was not d.;
    MELV 16
  victory was our d. READ H 1
defeated: d. valor lies, TIMR 7
  History to the d. AUDE 91
  Like an army d. WORD 164

We have taken from the d.
  ELIOT T 69
Won his d. ends. JOHN L 4
defeats: ammunition/ And feats of
  war d. MILT 113
  stronger guilt d. my strong
  intent, SHAK 34
Defect: Chief D. of Henry King
  BELL 8
  each social d. GILB 6
Defects: sins of will,/ D. of doubt,
  TENN 30
defence: make d. SHAK 186
  Physic of Metaphysic begs d.,
  POPE A 2
defend: d. From jealousy!
  SHAK 135
defense: dexterity of his d. SMAR 7
defensive: moat d. to a house,
  SHAK 88
deference: No blossom stayed away/
  In gentle d. DICKI 42
deferred: What happens to a dream
  d.? HUGH L 9
deffly: They dauncen d., SPENS 56
defiance: cry of d., LONG 45
defile: crossed the dark d.
  MACL 12
defiled: depleted and d., MILLA 32
  men's d. souls; SOUTHW 2
defilement: d. to the inward parts,
  MILT 1
define: We only can by negatives
  d.? COWL 9
  Wise/ Enquire, d., distinguish,
  teach, devise, ROCH 16
defined: One by one objects are d.
  WILLI 36
definite: has a d. opinion SIMP 4
  with certain d. views HEAN 14
definition: d. is a doubt CRAS 10
  Is God by d. indifferent, EBER 3
Deformed: D., unfinished, SHAK 96
deformity: descant on mine own d.
  SHAK 96
deft: d. dumb-show HARD 39
  d. white-stockinged dance
  MOOR M 3
deftly: d. you steady/ The drunk
  NIMS 2
defunct: Buffalo Bill's/ d. CUMM 10
defy: d. our fate. WILLI 19
  even the monsters we d. MCKA 6
  To d. Power, SHEL 58
  woman to d. the /gods;
  SPENC A 4
Degenerate: D. sons and daughters,
  MAST 9
degraded: All Nature was d.;
  BLAK 49
  D. and alone: WILD 4
degree: but the d.; ROCH 11
  lord of high d., UNKN 316

murder in the second d.,
  UNKN 104
perjury, in the highest d.,
  SHAK 99
place, d., and form. SHAK 58
sins, all used in each d.,
  SHAK 99
Spirit gave the Doctoral D.:
  DRYD 19
stern murder, in the direst d.,
  SHAK 99
worthy men in hir d. CHAU 87
degrees: scorning the base d.
  SHAK 44
solid scholars/ Get the d.,
  SNOD 5
ten d. of more indulgent skies,
  ADDI 2
deid: lang syne d., MACDI 4
deified: By our own spirits are we
  d.: WORD 121
Deirdre: D. and her tale,
  STEPHENS 1
deities: conceal'd their d.; OVID 4
Deity: D. disowns me. COWP 15
springs of D. SITW 8
strange mirror of the D.
  COWL 10
dejected: d. havior of the visage,
  SHAK 21
lowest and most d. thing of
  fortune, SHAK 77
delay: endure d. of execution:
  COWP 14
fame did not d. DRAY 2
In d. SHAK 175
In me is no d.; MILT 107
Love loves no d.; CAMPI 14
need not d. us. REED H 3
sweet, reluctant, amorous d.
  MILT 73
To will, implies d., DONN 51
delayed: If only Centuries, d.,
  DICKI 77
parting summer's lingering blooms
  d., GOLD 1
delays: d. His hand MILT 98
delectable: All are d. ELIOT T 56
buttocks less d. JARR 12
range of d. mountains,
  LOWE R 26
deliberate: hawk's d. stoop
  HILL G 3
unperturbèd pace,/ D. speed,
  THOMP F 7
delicate: d. creatures/ From the
  other world. WRIG J 5
feeding on d. peaches,/ And
  treading on d. toes. PRAE 4
gazelle, d. wanderer, SPEND 17
glow the d. cheeks SHAK 5
O d. walker, MACN 13
seas in d. haze LUCR 4

Sooner or later d. death.
  WHITM 50
tassel-yarded/ D.-stomached
  GRAV 19
delicious: calf that is plump and
  d.; THOMA D 40
compact & d. body BERRYM 4
d. solitude. MARV 16
strong and d. word WHITM 68
they were d. WILLI 40
delight: 'All Time's d. Hath she
  DE LA 24
beds are empty of d., CAMPB R 7
bind another to Its d., BLAK 58
Birds d. BLAK 105
But my greatest d. is to take a
  good bite THOMA D 40
Caught up in a formal d.,
  KINN 9
curious search, but craftie sinnes
  d. GREV 6
dead is the world's d.
  GREV/DYER 2
D. and liberty, WORD 80
d./ Chained in night BLAK 60
d. in momentariness, GRAV 25
d./ Nature or unrestrainèd
  appetite. CAREW 13
d. of solitariness! SIDN 3
d. on a shining night, UNKN 172
d. that fills me full, PRIN 4
drunk d. of battle with my peers,
  TENN 130
ended his d., MILT 91
flocks have took d. BLAK 101
From heav'nly thoughts all true d.
  doth spring. CAMPI 27
having ease me given,/ With full
  d., HERR 51
heart's and eye's d. SHAK 204
Hunting mice is his d.,
  UNKN 202
in the manege myself takes d.
  SIDN 19
lady of my d. MEYN 3
land of pure d., WATT I 8
Love and d., THOMA E 15
made of mere d. CAMPI 25
more d. SHAK 237
My d. and thy d. BRID R 12
my joy and heart's d. WEVE 2
no d. to pass away the time,
  SHAK 96
Of all d.,' HUME 1
paint the meadows with d.,
  SHAK 100
phantom of d. WORD 133
Spirit of D.! SHEL 60
spring of all d., TASS 5
still moves d., CAMPI 19
temple of D. KEAT 43
to a more rich d. EMER 3
to d. in blossom, LEVE 24

twinkle/ With a crystalline d.;
  POE 10
valley of love and d. UNKN 260
wink-and-elbow language of d.
  KAVA 21
with d. to take and render,
  STEVENSO R 10
you did Them, They you d.,
  COWL 7
delighted: d. spirit/ To bathe in fiery
  floods, SHAK 115
Delighting: Candor here, and lustre
  there/ D.: HERR 73
delights: Away d., BEAU/FLET 1
d. my mind might move
  RALEG 9
d. thy mind may move, MARL 21
d. Were dolphinlike; SHAK 7
heaven's wonders and d.
  GREV 10
misery still d. COWP 2
scorn d. and live laborious days;
  MILT 27
Shepheards d. SPENS 49
violent d. have violent ends
  SHAK 148
winter his d.; CAMPI 18
deliver: Good Lord d. us. SIDN 38
good Lord, d. us! NASHE 2
Truthe shall d., CHAU 2
deliverance: achieve/ Mankind's d.
  MILT 104
delivered: d. entirely from
  humanity SMIT ST 5
d. palpable/ ours. RICH 23
papers are d. every day; KUNI 3
thoughts, d. to me CRAN H 41
della: Pier d. Francesca; POUN 10
Delphic: Those D. lines MILT 35
delude: hopes cannot d., CAMPI 13
deluded: we are all d. SHEL 28
deluge: Threat'ning with d. SWIF 7
delusions: shadows and d. here.
  FRENE 2
delusive: Condemned to Hope's d.
  mine, JOHN S (1709–1784) 2
delve: When we hew or d.:
  HOPKINS 3
delves: d. the parallels SHAK 210
delyvere: wonderly d., CHAU 8
demand: if a king d. TENN 102
if we d. quarter? WHITM 90
demands: what my karma d.
  SNYD 12
demarcations: ghostlier d.,
  STEVENS 19
demented: by passion once d.
  DE VR 1
desolate sinners./ D. with beauty!
  MACDONO 2
demi-Paradise: other Eden, d.,
  SHAK 88
demi-puppets: you d. SHAK 164

Democracy: class distinction,/ D.
BETJ 4
/ D. and proper /drains. BETJ 4
democratic: dirge run d., RANS 28
Democritus: atoms of D. BLAK 39
demolishing: d. the pre-
Raphaelites: KINN 5
demon: d. of pursuit FROS 110
d.'s that is dreaming, POE 37
drumming of the d. in their ears.
MACN 10
wailing for her d.-lover!
COLE SAM 20
Demons: D. out of the earth —
TATE A 12
demonstrated: d. Unto our
climatures and countrymen.
SHAK 20
Demur: D., — you're straightway
dangerous, DICKI 106
demure: Sober, steadfast, and d.,
MILT 16
Demurest: D. of the tabby kind,
GRAY 18
den: cowers within his d.; SIMM 2
d. Of savage men: BACO 2
Glorious hosanna from the d.;
SMAR 9
In forest wild, in thicket, brake, or
d.; MILT 86
in his d.? SHEL 4
denial: dishonest mood of d.,
AUDE 30
denied: fatal zone to her d.!
COLL 5
nothing was d., MARL 5
that may not be d.; MASE 12
denizens: d. can turn upon the
world KIZE 3
tigers prance across a screen,/
Bright topaz d. RICH 1
Denmark: D.'s sanctuaried Jews!
MOOR M 3
denote: blasts d. I am nearing the
place, BROWNI R 68
d. me truly. SHAK 21
Dénouement: D. to d., FEAR 1
spatters all we knew of d.
SHAP 4
denounced: pain/ Of death d.,
MILT 95
Dens: Rocks, Caves, Lakes, Fens,
Bogs, D., MILT 61
dense: deep and d., WINT 3
d. oppression, MELV 10
d. with happy blood, LAWR 58
d.-packed cities WHITM 51
deny: curse and to d. your truth;
ARNO 31
fear not, d. not me, WHITM 5
Grudge who list, but none d.!
HENR 1

walk among noise and d. the
voice ELIOT T 14
what we affirm or what d.,
MILT 80
denyes: court a mistris, shee d.
you; JONS 29
denying: d. all our words. RUKE 1
Deo: D. gratias, UNKN 3
depart: cannot thence d.! SHEL 3
Captains and the Kings d.:
KIPL 18
deciding to d. OHAR 15
d. on the winds of space AIKE 8
d. peaceful, pacified, and
thankless, LAWR 43
D., — be off, — HOLM 1
men say they do d. SIDN 32
they d., and we go with them.
ELIOT T 72
Time and death shall d. DRYD 9
departed: Day/ Turned and d.
EMER 16
d. dead. SHEL 31
D. Goose! SOUTHE 8
minds me o' d. joys,/ d. never to
return. BURN 15
nymphs are d. ELIOT T 129
of her d. lover; ELIOT T 137
departmental: how thoroughly d.
FROS 34
departure: gravel-crunching,
interminable d. MAHON 2
depend: on him sole d., MILT 105
dependin': all d. whether FRENC 3
depends: d. upon/ a red wheel/
barrow WILLI 28
depicts: camera of my eye d.
SHAP 7
depleted: d. and defiled, MILLA 32
deplore: I d. her change. CONG 1
deposed: some have been d.,
SHAK 89
depressed: by poverty d.:
JOHN S (1709–1784) 1
Deprest: D., and overthrown,
MILT 117
d. with cares, GAY 3
deprived: bird d. of wings
HARD 28
depth: d. as the roots of the sea:
SWIN 24
d. of some divine despair
TENN 114
d. of the dreamy SWIN 19
d. of the grave. KNOX 2
far beyond my d. FLET/SHAK 3
Stilled legendary d.: HUGH T 12
depths: d. of the Cambrian fen,
SMIT L 1
Out of the d. have I cried
BIBL, O.T. 60
through their rosy d., BRYA 25

deputations: pale d. Of temperance
workers SITW 3
deputies: crack of d.' rifles
KINN 19
deranged: We are d., SHAP 2
dere: Greet prees at market maketh
d. ware, CHAU 89
deride: d. this sepulchre of crime.
SASS 12
derision: accomplished his d.;
RANS 23
clothed with d.; SWIN 2
derive: d. from weakness
BROWNI R 18
derk: d. and straucht and sinister,
YOUN D 1
D. was the night as pich or as the
cole, CHAU 53
derke: d. and dredful of sight.
LANGL 2
dervishes: barefoot d., EMER 13
desart: praisse withowt d.,
WYAT 22
Descant: amorous D. join;
GRAY 32
d. on mine own deformity.
SHAK 96
descend: d. as a dove AUDE 85
D. from Heav'n Urania, MILT 83
d. the stair. AIKE 8
D. to us, we pray; BROO P 7
d. To die here for thy sake,
VAUG 16
into the Dust d.; OMAR 4
turn and d. again. HARD 42
descending: d. Darkness of fear
JOYC 4
sun d. in the west, BLAK 100
Descends: D. the snow. LONG 38
Holy Ghost d. At random KAVA 9
soundless calm d.; BRON 10
descent: d. among us WILB 12
d. from Olympus LOWE J 1
Describe: D. Adonis, SHAK 205
description: beggared all d.:
SHAK 5
D. would but tire my Muse:
SWIF 1
descriptions: d. of the fairest
wights, SHAK 228
desert: dare me to the d. with thy
sword. SHAK 110
d. sighs in the bed, AUDE 3
d. were a Paradise, BURN 40
gardens in the d. DUNC 3
Gardens of the D., BRYA 15
in wide d. HOOD 10
indignant d. birds. YEATS 135
leave our d. to its peace!"
ARNO 40
lost d.-folk GRAV 13
nightingale/ Filled all the d.
ELIOT T 122

noon in the d. STAF 1
sands of the d. YEATS 135
swim for miles through the d.
  SIMP 1
waste its sweetness on the d. air.
  GRAY 10
with my own d. places. FROS 36
Word in the d. Is most attacked
  ELIOT T 25
yields no mercy to d., LODG 5
desertion: solitude/ Or blank d.
  WORD 97
deserts: d. of the heart AUDE 46
D. of vast eternity. MARV 34
He'll make you d. BARL 1
Steer for their d., WILB 43
deserv'd: d. thy beauty's use
  SHAK 185
deserve: ill d. the place RILE 3
you somehow haven't to d."
  FROS 27
deserved: wreathed garland of d.
  praise, HERB G 74
Desiccation: D. of the world of
  sense, ELIOT T 21
design: d. for a hearse. WILLI 44
d. of darkness to appall? —
  FROS 38
miracle of d.! TENN 100
designe: houre of thy d.
  HERB G 64
designs: passions of the human
  family/ For base d., MAST 4
vast D. of Fate, ROCH 16
desire: Arrows of d.: BLAK 35
beauty's fire/ Inflame unstaid d.,
  PEEL 2
bed of our d.?" BLAK 18
closets of lone d., LANIE 3
contents his natural d.;
  POPE A 60
darker my d. ROET 33
d. for the melodious, CHES 18
D. Gratified/ Plants fruits
  BLAK 21
D. illimitable, BROO R 2
d. is full/ of endless distances.
  HASS 3
d. of the moth for the star,
  SHEL 49
D. takes charge, LARK 10
d. your companie: JONS 14
Fear contended with d. HOUS 46
Forbear my most d.; WYAT 19
heart is a blind d., SWIN 2
hours and times of your d.?
  SHAK 208
how to kill d. SIDN 40
in pleasures lappe did lye,/ I
  might refresh d., LODG 3
kiss of d. on the lips. OREI 2
lineaments of gratified d.
  BLAK 48

Mirth and youth and warm d.!/
  Woods and groves MILT 119
mixing/ Memory and d.,
  ELIOT T 113
moves in a wood of d.,/ pale
  antlers barely stirring
  GUNN 2
My d. and thy d. BRID R 13
My most d. my hand may reach,
  WYAT 14
old egg of my d. is broken,
  UNKN 230
possess his own d.: WORD 4
renders vain their deep d.? —
  ARNO 42
sanctify d.'s idolatry. GREV 7
sharp d. my heart; SIDN 18
sick with d. of the sun
  UNKN 121
'Speak thy d., OVID 6
taste of soul's d. BONT 5
thin with d.,/ Transformed to a
  creeping MONR 2
'Twixt fears of dying and d. of
  life: CRAB 3
vain d. was chidden —
  MUND 2
What is d.? — ROET 20
when d. did sue. SHAK 169
whole field is a/ white d.,
  WILLI 27
Why should a man d.
  TENN 121
will unto d.,/ As smoke we vanish
  Æ 3
yearning in d. TENN 132
Youth pined away with d.,
  BLAK 54
desired: d. above all things
  GRAV 42
I have d. to go HOPKINS 9
looked upon it and d. it.
  UNKN 256
naturally to be d. WILLI 47
of none d.' C., J 1
who d. so much — CRAN H 46
desiren: Forbede us thing, and that
  d. we; CHAU 89
desires: d. and affections meet
  MARL 5
D. and dreams and powers
  SWIN 13
In chaste d., SPENS 5
Love that so d. MERE G 6
Move then with new d., DAY 5
outward things dwell not in my
  d. SHAK 59
providently Pimps for ill d.:
  DRYD 1
Sterner d. and darker hopes
  BRON 11
undaunted daughter of d.!
  CRAS 3

Desiring: D. this man's art,
  SHAK 194
in motion, still d. change;
  DRAY 9
desk: when the eyes and back/ Turn
  upward from the d.
  ELIOT T 133
desolate: Broken,/ beaten, d.,
  WILLI 48
d., dark weeks WILLI 37
d. sinners/ Demented with
  beauty! MACDONO 2
eternal whisperings around/ D.
  shores, KEAT 59
place where I lie d. BONT 7
Shakes a d. boy THOMA D 2
sitting by d. streams; OSHA 1
Desolation: D. in ROET 7
mimic d. covers all. GRAY 22
despair: begotten by d. Upon
  impossibility. MARV 6
comfort and d. SHAK 240
common man's d. WILD 1
confession to d., CLARK A 1
Cries out a literate d.
  STEVENS 42
depth of some divine d.
  TENN 114
desolate d.; BRON 9
D., not feast on thee: HOPKINS 4
Hatred out of Envy by D.
  CUNN J 3
Heaven in Hell's d." BLAK 57
hopes greater than my d.,
  GREE 3
hurries me back to d. COWP 24
incredulous of d., BROWNI E 1
Infinite wrath and infinite d.?
  MILT 66
learn a style from a d. EMPS 17
mournful lean D. BLAK 40
mourning dove whistles of d.
  KINN 9
Negation and d., AUDE 78
pale d. SHEL 22
pale sustenance,/ D.! DICKI 36
purity of pure d., ROET 31
Rhymed out in love's d.
  YEATS 131
secret of d., LONG 39
Should all d. That have revolted
  wives, SHAK 179
Thrown into d. YEATS 63
'Tis the Seal D. DICKI 143
to cheat d., BROO R 2
Warder is D. WILD 3
despairing: Dark d. features
  CULL 10
despairs: blind hopes and blind d.,
  ARNO 16
leaden-eyed d., KEAT 47
desperate: behind his d. eyes,
  BERRYM 2

On d. seas POE 45
some d. glory, OWEN 20
Despis'd: D. and thought
    extinguish't MILT 116
Despise: D. the human span/ Of
    durance — HARD 26
ladies that d., FLET J 5
despised: d. straight; SHAK 236
old, mad, blind, d., and dying
    king, SHEL 27
despises: husband frae the wife d.!
    BURN 51
despising: myself almost d.,
    SHAK 194
despite: d. his cruel hand.
    SHAK 210
d. they cast on female wits:
    BRAD 17
d. thy scythe and thee.
    SHAK 235
Hell in Heaven's d." BLAK 58
despites: Holy deeds to d.
    UNKN 170
despondency: come in the end d.
    and madness. WORD 121
Desponding: D. Phyllis was endu'd
    SWIF 13
d. Whigs,/ Forget their feuds,
    SWIF 8
despot: d.'s heel is on thy shore,
    RANDA J 1
despots: d. ride a Russian.
    BYRO 47
destin'd: such a d. wretch as I,
    COWP 1
destination: Apparently they have
    reached their d. BISH 27
great d. is to stay." SNOD 10
destined: Amphitrite's d. halls,
    SHEL 36
d. unto judgment, JONS 33
that d. seed MILT 104
destinies: robed as d., LARK 6
destiny: d. of me. WHITM 67
d. that makes us brothers;
    MARK 1
His own funereal d.; BYRO 60
homely joys, and d. obscure;
    GRAY 8
stars mark our d. JOHN F 1
destroy: cheer of mind d. CIBB 1
Does thy life d. BLAK 80
Though ye d. their dust. SIGO 2
winged life d.; BLAK 47
destroyed: d. by madness, GINS 7
once d., can never be supplied.
    GOLD 3
destroying: quick d. lime WYLI 7
Destroys: D. me momently.
    WINT 2
destruction: d. of language.
    KOCH 4

ear be closed to its own d.?
    BLAK 17
for d. ice/ Is also great FROS 48
destructive: devastation's dire d.
    doom; WATT A 1
desyren: Wommen d. to have
    sovereyntee CHAU 111
detached: Surrounded, d.,
    WHITM 55
detail: crowd is laughing/ in d.
    WILLI 6
detain: d. her vesture's hem,
    EMER 24
detain'd: d. me for love of me,
    WHITM 60
detective: weird d. ways —
    HARD 52
deterioration: long process of d.
    JEFFE 33
determinate: bonds in thee are all
    d. SHAK 219
Determined: D., Dared, and Done.
    SMAR 9
no d. road; WORD 22
detest: do d. my life, DRUM 2
Persian garlands I d., HORA 11
detested: pact with you, Walt
    Whitman — / I have d. you
    POUN 52
devastation: d.'s dire destructive
    doom; WATT A 1
devel: Lat go, farewel, the d. go
    therwith! CHAU 88
Develops: D. the jaw, NASH 4
Nothing lets up or d. HUGH T 9
deviate: d. from the common track.
    POPE A 30
deviates: never d. into sense.
    DRYD 11
deviating: d. head-stones
    MOOR M 27
device: banner with the strange d.,
    LONG 21
devil: Chile of the d., WALK 8
corrupt my saint to be a d.,
    SHAK 240
D. below was ringing his knell.
    SOUTHE 6
d. grip the whey-faced slut
    STEPHENS 3
D. in the clock, AUDE 10
D. is still at hand DRYD 1
d./ Still exists, SIMI 1
d. take her! SUCK 3
d.'s walking parody CHES 3
dream or d. You will answer,
    CHES 1
fears a painted d. SHAK 107
good wicked spirit, sweet angel d.
    DRAY 6
like a d.'s sick of sin; OWEN 19
shamed the D. WILB 29

Subdue the d. HAWE 2
we'll face the d.! BURN 55
devildoms: d. of Spain.' TENN 117
Devilish: D. leopard! PLATH 45
devils: blackė d. will them take.
    CHAU 69
more d. than vast hell can hold;
    SHAK 127
tells news of d., GREV 5
two d., that blow BEDD 5
devirginated: d. young ladies
    POUN 32
devisal: Past our d. THOMP F 13
devise: d. the Snake! OMAR 1
Enquire, define, distinguish, teach,
    d., ROCH 16
my wit doth best d., PEEL 3
devocioun: continence eek with d.,
    CHAU 93
Devoted: D. to the memory of me:
    HERR 52
this d. town. SWIF 7
devotion: I change in vows, and in
    d. DONN 45
devour: crumbling Pageant shall d.,
    DRYD 27
make the earth d. SHAK 189
soon to d. all, WHITM 57
wrinkles will d.; NASHE 1
devour'd: d. by the same harpy.
    BYRO 34
devoured: cool jazz nor d. Egyptian
    heroes, OHAR 10
d. As fast as they are made,
    SHAK 173
D. her with their eager, passionate
    gaze; MCKA 5
Devouring: D. Time, SHAK 189
Devours: D. death, WILB 37
Us he d. ELIOT T 34
devout: d. have laid out gardens
    DUNC 3
pensive Nun, d. and pure,
    MILT 16
sorcery d. and vertical
    BROO G 11
Devoutly: consummation/ D. to be
    wished. SHAK 39
on the Mat d. kneeling SWIF 14
pray/ D. on the holy day;
    CAMPI 8
dew: beaded with d. SNYD 35
Debauchee of D. DICKI 69
D.-cloth, dream drapery, THOR 8
d. dries up, the star is shot;
    KING H 5
d.-dropping south. SHAK 141
d. her orbs upon the green.
    SHAK 126
d. is cold upon the ground,
    TENN 105
d. o' the wild white rose
    KEAT 35

d. on the mountain, SCOT WA 8
Draw up the d. DAY 6
dried the d. FROS 101
early d. woos UNKN 251
every herb that sips the d.;
    MILT 19
footprints in the d.; BROO R 6
Glistring with d.; fragrant the
    fertile earth MILT 76
hillside's d.-pearled;
    BROWNI R 66
keep her from the foggy, foggy d.
    UNKN 99
like the morning d., DANI S 5
meet the morning d., ARNO 45
Pearled wi' d. like fishes' eyes,
    CLARE 3
pearls of morning's d. HERR 43
plant some more d.-wet
    anemones UNKN 255
rained a ghastly d. TENN 75
river of crystal light,/ Into a sea of
    d. FIEL E 8
seven anemones with down-
    dropped heads/ Wept tears of d.
    UNKN 253
shall gather d., WHITT 28
shutters like the d., AIKE 6
with one hand did fling/ D. on the
    earth, SHEL 77
dewdrops: d. to greet the dawn,
    COOP 1
With showers and d. wet;
    ROSS C 33
dews: ask amid the d. of morning
    HOUS 65
d. of blood, SHAK 20
drops and d. of future bliss.
    VAUG 23
heavy d. from bloom OWEN 24
Silence will fall like d. WYLI 10
sweet May d. my wings were
    wet, BLAK 24
dewy: d. dawn to d. night,
    MORR 6
d. dawning's cold grey air;
    THOMS J (1834–1882) 1
from out the d. grass; BLAK 67
with d. locks, BLAK 108
dexterity: d. of his defense SMAR 7
diabolic: color is a d. die."
    WHEA 1
diadem: From her summer d.
    EMER 24
great Neptune's d. CAMPI 5
Without her d. DICKI 129
diademe: sought to keepe his d.;
    MARL 6
dial: beauty, like a d. hand,
    SHAK 227
D. life — / And Him — DICKI 19
my finger, like a d.'s point,
    SHAK 93

dialect: purify the d. of the tribe
    ELIOT T 67
dialectician: babbler, d. Fire,
    MACN 13
dialogue: d. with eyes CRAN H 51
diamond: brightest d. TAYL E 3
d. in the sky. TAYL J 1
star, contracted in a d., DAVE 3
diamonds: graven with d. WYAT 32
Diana: dragged D. from her car,
    POE 2
nymph shall break D.'s law,
    POPE A 117
Diapason: D. closing full in Man.
    DRYD 25
perfect D., MILT 2
diaphanous: immense and d.
    shadows, WHITM 75
dice: d. of drowned men's bones
    CRAN H 1
flattery, cards, and d., and din:
    SHEN 1
played at cards and d.,
    UNKN 207
Dickens: Duke of D. GILB 54
Dicky: D.-bird, why do you sit
    GILB 29
dictators: women are d. all,
    NASH 1
dictionary: d.'s method SIDN 9
diddle: d., we take it, is dee.
    SWIN 18
God, who is not, we see;/ Fiddle,
    we know, is d.: SWIN 18
Hey, d., d.,/ The cat and the
    fiddle, MOTH 2
die: all must d. HERB G 72
As much beauty as could d.;
    JONS 6
as she died so must we d.
    BROWNI R 14
Ay, but to d., SHAK 115
before that spirit d.,
    STEVENSO R 2
Black Poets d. as trumpets,
    KNIG 3
Born but to d., POPE A 78
born to drill and d. CRAN S 9
both parts must d. DONN 33
break faith with us who d.
    MCCRA 3
by feigned deaths to d. DONN 57
can man d. better MACA 3
coldly d. GRAV 3
color is a diabolic d." WHEA 1
come to d., BROWNI R 23
comes back to d. alone.
    CRAN H 26
dawn of the day when we d.
    SWIN 20
Dead. Died. Will d. Want.
    CREE 10

dead shall live, the living d.,
    DRYD 27
Death, thou shalt d. DONN 18
descend/ To d. here for thy sake,
    VAUG 16
d. as fast SHAK 186
d. as my fathers d., SWIN 25
d. as some have done: BONT 3
D. because a woman's fair?
    WITH 1
d. before I wake, UNKN 193
d., dear, d.; BEDD 3
d. dishevelled and soft.
    LOWE R 25
D. early and avoid the fate.
    FROS 89
d. experienced ere three days be
    spent — MELV 18
D. for adultery? SHAK 80
d. for him tomorrow." UNKN 39
d. — in bed. SASS 4
d. in earnest — RALEG 16
d. in his bed YEATS 155
d. in state. FROS 89
d. like sheep. LIND V 17
D. of a rose in aromatic pain?
    POPE A 70
d. of nothing POPE A 95
D. soon. BROO G 20
D. to themselves. SHAK 206
d. you are the same; FRENE 7
d. you must (faire Maid)
    HERR 31
Dressed to d., THOMA D 41
Easy live and quiet d.
    SCOT WA 2
Ere their story d. HARD 30
fight as we will, we d.; ARNO 17
fighting races don't d. out,
    CLARK J 4
fools that wish to d.! UNKN 128
gaze, turn giddy, rave, and d.
    POPE A 2
going to d. perhaps. SORL 1
hard to d. by fire! THAC 1
he could d. Whenever he would;
    WALS 1
heavenly days that cannot d.;
    WORD 61
heeds no call to d. HARD 26
He's come to d. KOCH 2
I am sick, I must d. NASHE 1
I could not d. with you,
    DICKI 34
I have nine times to d. PLATH 54
I shall d. an old Parisian. RIVE 2
I shall d. to-morrow; HOUS 12
I tried to d. And get back,
    PLATH 31
I want to d. JOHN G 2
i would d. etcetera/ bravely
    CUMM 26

If I should d., think only this of
me: BROO R 13

ill thoughts d. and good are
born— BROWNI E/GUIN 1

'im that doth not work must
surely d.; KIPL 19

languish and anon must d.;
CAREW 9

let me d. before my death!"
VAUG 19

let us d. to make men free;
HOWE 3

Let us do, or d.! BURN 48

let us nobly d., MCKA 6

lib and d. in Dixie! EMME 2

live and d. for thee. HERR 40

living/ Can only d. ELIOT T 22

logic of a woman,/ Curse God and
d. ROBI 29

many a man shall d. SHAP 20

men/ Who went abroad to d.
LETT 1

might d. to gain. STOD 3

millions must d., JEFFE 23

needs must d., RALEG 6

Not that they d., LIND V 17

pie in the sky when you d.
HILL J 1

privilege to d. DICKI 28

question Who shall d.? SHAP 3

quits us when we d. POPE A 80

rather had to d. in troth
UNKN 167

rose and silver lilies d.,
FLET G EL 1

seldom d. in bed, CLARK J 4

So evenings d., STEVENS 37

souls can d., LUCR 1

Spin and d., ROSS C 4

stood prepared to d.; SWIF 24

superstition, like belief, must d.,
LARK 5

Swans moulting d., NOEL H 2

that he shall d.; PRIO 11

Theirs but to do and d. TENN 7

They can d., PLATH 9

think indeed that I must d. . . . .
SOUTHW 10

those heroes dare/ To d., and
EMER 12

thou takest away their breath,
they d., BIBL, O.T. 53

thou would'st surely d.
WHITM 47

though her body d., MILT 117

time to d.; BIBL, O.T. 3

to all the world must d.:
SHAK 216

To d. and know it. LOWE R 36

to d. late, FROS 89

To d.: to sleep; SHAK 39

to fight is but to d.! TENN 118

to look about us and to d.
POPE A 58

to see God d.! DONN 28

To-day will d. to-morrow;
SWIN 14

unlamented let me d.;
POPE A 108

We d., HERR 43

We d. and rise the same,
DONN 14

We d.—does it matter when?
TENN 119

we d. in you,/ You d. in Time,
HERB CH 5

We d. with the dying:
ELIOT T 72

We must be free or d., WORD 28

When beggars d. SHAK 45

When logics d., THOMA D 31

when soft voices d., SHEL 43

Which daily d.: KIPL 14

wish to d. MILT 35

Without—the power to d.
DICKI 110

yet I love her till I d. FORD T 1

you will d. to-day. HOUS 12

you would not d. SNOD 13

zowie did he d., FEAR 2

died: As estimated, you d.
HILL G 7

as men they d. BEAU/BASS 4

creature d. By storm YOUN A 1

Dead. D. Will die. Want.
CREE 10

d. a myriad, POUN 43

d. an hour before this chance
SHAK 109

d., content. CRAN S 7

d. for men. ROBI 21

d. for Truth, DICKI 37

D. in sleep, SHEL 91

d. like aunts of pets or foreigners.
JARR 14

d. of apoplexy DAVIS 6

d. of grieving: KEAT 27

D. on Saturday, MOTH 26

d. to save us all. ALEX 8

dog it was that d. GOLD 8

dungeon, where he d. CUMM 17

elemental when he d., ROBI 38

everybody d. JARR 13

for her sake I would have d.,
VAUG 30

founders lived and d. YEATS 35

he d. old. HOUS 54

He d. to make men holy,
HOWE 3

I d. for Beauty— DICKI 37

in her youthful beauty d.,
BRYA 9

Jew who d. in exile. AUDE 25

Land where my fathers d.,
SMIT SA 1

Light has d. out JEFFE 3

lived Knott, d. Knott, UNKN 88

man that d. for me. HAY 4

Mine only d. BROWNE 1

name. d. before the man.
HOUS 57

night I d. I dreamed JARR 16

nightmare fighters./ When I d.
they washed me JARR 5

nymph d. more quick, and the
shepherd more slow. DRYD 15

one day anyone d. CUMM 6

Queens have d. young and fair;
NASHE 1

Say I d. true. BEAU/FLET 3

since the day she d. LONG 14

so they d. PRIO 4

Southwell d. on a rope. FULL 3

Terraced thousands d., HEAN 18

they d. instead CUMM 29

valiant d.; FRENE 3

when I d. DICKI 48

Where holy Dionysus d.,
YEATS 116

Why d. I not from the womb?
BIBL, O.T. 10

diem: carpe d., Juan, BYRO 34

dien: Men may d. of imaginacioun,
CHAU 50

dies: all life d., death lives, and
Nature breeds, MILT 61

belovéd above all else that d.
MILLA 3

blazes high, but quickly d.,
SACK 1

cackles, groans, and d. CLARE 2

d. among his worshippers.
BRYA 3

d. between three cannibals.
SHAP 16

d. fighting has increase. GREN 1

D. like a dog! WHITT 4

d. the swan. TENN 120

fancy d./ In the cradle SHAK 121

Function never d.; WORD 127

Light d. before thy uncreating
word: POPE A 2

light of a whole life d. BOUR 2

Love d. FORD J 1

when honor d., WHITT 12

Diesel: armored D. fishing tubs
LOWE R 6

Leaps from the tree/ snapped by
the d. SNYD 44

diet: consciousness by d. and
breathing. AUDE 88

scrip of joy, immortal d.,
RALEG 10

differ: Talents d.; EMER 36

they will d. DICKI 15

difference: all the d. FROS 95

d. to me! WORD 46

druidic d. Enhances nature
  DICKI 24
know the d. OHAR 3
different: as our d. ages move,
  PRIO 12
Made Nature d. DICKI 98
Something that's d. JARR 25
stars that have a d. birth,
  SHEL 88
differs: d. more from Man,
  ROCH 13
difficult: fascination of what's d.
  YEATS 57
difficulty: with d. and labour hard
  MILT 62
diffidence: with seeming d.:
  POPE A 37
diff'rent: d. views engage,
  JOHN S (1709–1784) 14
Diffus'd: D. unseen KEAT 20
dig: bees/ d. the plum blossoms
  OLSO 17
d. deep trenches SHAK 185
D. the grave and let me lie.
  STEVENSO R 20
d. with it. HEAN 13
fitting spot to d. Love's grave;
  MERE G 11
he'll d. it up again! ELIOT T 120
with his nailes he'll d. WEBS 5
digestion: About my d. CARRY 1
Or, if it were, if also his d.?
  BYRO 32
digging: d. on my grave HARD 6
D. the rock where Death
  OWEN 36
dight: storied windows richly d.,
  MILT 18
Sweet Suffolk Owl, so trimly d.
  VAUT 1
dignifie: your worth will d. our
  feast, JONS 14
dignified: go down d. FROS 90
dignify: d. the labor, CRAN H 46
dignity: heart/ Of man has a little
  d., TATE A 19
outbraves his d.: SHAK 222
starched d. and the quietness
  IREM 1
stark d. of/ entrance — WILLI 36
digressions: no silkworms, no d.
  MOOR M 10
Dijon: yellow/ Gloire de D. roses.
  LAWR 11
diligence: obtrude this d.,
  MILT 109
diligent: d. to learn; WORD 4
diligently: He would d. play
  GILB 44
dim: cedars dusk and d.
  WHITM 53
down within the d. West, POE 11
eye waxen d., ROSS C 18

forest, d. and old, POE 42
From an ultimate d. Thule —
  POE 16
Grow d., or cease to be!
  JOHN G 2
marbly and d. MERR 1
Nor d. nor red, COLE SAM 30
not too dirty nor too d.
  BROO G 7
tears shall d. thy sight, BRYA 30
truth do d. BALD 1
white breast of the d. sea
  YEATS 164
with a d. and undetermined sense
  WORD 97
world's d. dawn, SMIT L 4
dime: fished/ A d. for Jesus
  ROBI 21
dimensions: d. are as well compact,
  SHAK 70
dimes: d. and/ Dollars HUGH L 3
diminished: Clear and d. MILLA 4
d. thing. FROS 86
dimly: fragrant portals, d.-starred.
  STEVENS 19
invisible or d. seen MILT 81
dimmed: d. ere it had nooned
  LANIG 1
gold complexion d.; SHAK 188
dimple: d. of his chin: LYLY 2
dimpled: pretty d. boys, SHAK 5
dimpling: shallow streams run d. all
  the way. POPE A 10
dims: her parting d. the day,
  EMER 25
din: d. like silversmiths PLATH 23
flattery, cards, and dice, and d.:
  SHEN 1
shattered water made a misty d.
  FROS 76
through all its d., THOR 5
dine: gang and d. today?"
  UNKN 271
jury-men may d.; POPE A 120
dined: d. in a royal way CARRY 10
diners: laughing in the d. SAND 12
Ding: D., dong, bell. SHAK 121
dingdong: d., bell. SHAK 156
dingle: night above the d. starry,
  THOMA D 17
dining: d. aloof, NEWB 3
Dinky: Dirty D. ROET 6
dinna: d. grieve your Sarah;
  UNKN 79
dinner: d. will be cold." HOUS 30
Kings sit down to d., KIPL 23
this a d.? POPE A 105
write with no d., RANS 34
Dionysus: Christ follows D.,
  POUN 41
Where holy D. died, YEATS 116
dip: d. to the water. LAWR 1
Dipp'd: D. me in ink, POPE A 13

dipped: I d. into the future,
  TENN 75
dipping: d. for fish MASE 10
Phoebus, d. in the West,
  COTTO 1
Dirce: With D. in one boat
  convey'd, LAND 13
dire: devastation's d. destructive
  doom; WATT A 1
fold/ Of d. necessity MILT 115
Gorgons and Hydras, and
  Chimeras d. MILT 61
hospital walls as d.; TICK 1
What d. offence POPE A 110
Directed: D. as by madness
  MELV 1
direction: final d. of the elementary
  town THOMA D 41
new d. of Time. LAWR 47
direst: stern murder, in the d.
  degree, SHAK 99
Dirge: D. is whisper'd by the
  warbling LUTE. DRYD 26
d. of lovely Rosabelle.
  SCOT WA 15
d. run democratic, RANS 28
no d., except the hollow sea's,
  BYRO 51
No d. will I upraise. POE 30
sing a d. for Saint Hugh's soul,
  DEKK 1
Sing thou my d., HERR 53
sobbing d. of Nature, WHITM 6
dirges: let the d. disappear.
  WALK 6
Dirigible: O thou D., CRAN H 11
dirt: body turned/ To clumsy d.
  WILB 39
d. kept breathing ROET 53
Had pared the d., SWIF 10
Ignorant as d., SHAP 21
painted child of d., POPE A 9
poverty, hunger, and d.,
  HOOD 12
Turn'd to that d. SWIF 16
dirtiness: where d. is law OLSO 5
Dirty: D. British coaster MASE 2
D. Dinky. ROET 6
d. house in a gutted world,
  STEVENS 43
d. little coward UNKN 148
napkin of a d. cause, WALC 3
not too d. nor too dim BROO G 7
Oh, but it is d.! BISH 11
Rome's annals wax'd but d.
  BYRO 34
their d. glistening torsos
  OHAR 12
disabused: by himself abused, or
  d.; POPE A 78
disagreeable: I'm such a d. man!
  GILB 7

disappear: let the dirges d.
  WALK 6
suffered her to d. GARR 2
disappeared: d. in the dead of
  winter. AUDE 35
lovers d. into the wood.
  THOMA E 2
100,000 people d. REED I 2
disappointed: heard recede the d.
  tide! DICKI 96
sorry to have d. him. JEFFE 44
disappointing: Faithful and d.!
  LARK 13
disappointments: d. new; ARNO 26
disarm'd: mortall sting d. MILT 64
disarmed: of enmity d., MILT 90
disaster: responsible for a d.
  unverified, MILE 1
their loss is no d. BISH 31
Disasters: D. in the sun; SHAK 20
disastrous: d. twilight sheds
  MILT 57
disavows: Man d., COWP 15
disbelief: when d. has gone?
  LARK 5
disburden: d. Nature of her
  bearth." MILT 94
Disc: on a D. of Snow —
  DICKI 127
discern: natural instinct to d.
  WORD 4
discerning: d. intellect of Man,
  WORD 16
Gives genus a better d. GOLD 5
To a d. eye; DICKI 105
discharge: no d. in the war! KIPL 4
discharged: night d. of all care
  MARTIA 2
trunk may be d. of breath
  SHAK 150
discipline: vain all Doric d.
  YEATS 118
disciplines: into exquisite d.
  MERR 9
Disclose: D. thy Sun beames;
  QUAR 4
discloses: their masked buds d.
  SHAK 206
disclosing: d. what it be DICKI 94
discontent: dull webs of d., ROBI 7
sorrow d.: CAMPI 13
winter of our d. SHAK 94
discord: debate, that eke d. doth
  sow, ELIZ 1
d. of flags GRAV 22
Knows no d., CAMPI 19
without d. or confusion COWL 10
Discordant: reconciles/ D. elements,
  WORD 96
discords: old mistakes/ And d.
  KINS 3
discouraged: tie up your d. penis
  SNOD 11

Discouragement: no D., BUNY 2
discourse: d. in novel phrases
  GILB 30
fittest for d. DRYD 20
such large d., SHAK 35
thoughts and my d. as madmen's
  SHAK 242
discovers: dying Notes d. DRYD 26
Discretion: Beauty, Strength, and D.
  do man forsake, UNKN 90
passions now and then outran/
  D., BYRO 21
discrowned: Crowned, and again d.
  JOHN L 2
discuss: with myself I too much d.
  ELIOT T 5
disdain: lover's thoughts d.,
  CAMPI 21
plague of deep d.: SIDN 37
disdained: too falsely d. SHEL 48
disdaineth: Nature art d. CAMPI 6
disdainful: d. and magnificent —
  JOHN H 4
with a d. smile, GRAY 8
Disdainfulness: D. I have again;
  WYAT 34
Disdains: D. to crop a weed,
  DRUM 3
Me he d., PETRA 8
starlit or a moonlit dome d.
  YEATS 17
diseas'd: successions of d. corpses,
  WHITM 98
disease: cause of my d. SURR 4
D., and Sorrow's weeping train,
  GRAY 26
D. Not even God — can heal —
  DICKI 122
D., or sorrows strike CLOU 4
Progress is a comfortable d.:
  CUMM 35
rouses up the seeds of dark d.
  THOMS J (1700–1748) 13
shocking d.' AUDE 67
strange d. of modern life,
  ARNO 27
this long d., my life; POPE A 14
war like any old d. OWEN 1
world of money, promise and d.
  WELC 3
Diseases: D., Battels, Inundations.
  BUTL 8
disentangle: my heart is fast, and
  cannot d. UNKN 220
disgrac'd: right perfection
  wrongfully d., SHAK 213
disgrace: in d. with fortune and
  men's eyes, SHAK 194
Intellectual d. Stares AUDE 44
Disguise: D. fair nature SHAK 56
disguises: troublesom d. MILT 77
disgusting: d. in the act PRIN 1

disgustingly: d. upside down.
  LAWR 3
dish: d. of pain, TICH 1
savory d., a homely treat,
  HORA 10
wooden d. His plate. SOUTHW 5
dishes: Some shattered d. FROS 41
dishevelled: die d. and soft.
  LOWE R 25
d. wandering stars. YEATS 164
dishonest: d. mood of denial,
  AUDE 30
guilty shame: d. Shame MILT 73
low d. decade: AUDE 70
dishonored: To stain the stiff d.
  shroud. ELIOT T 112
dishoused: melt as the d. snail
  BIBL, O.T. 42
disintegrated: Altered, estranged,
  d., MILLA 2
disjoin'd: d. by Neptunes might:
  MARL 4
disk: d. of seed, TENN 42
disliked: as males they d. his air.
  KAVA 17
dismal: heraldry more d. SHAK 30
with a d. headaches, GILB 25
dismasted: d., gray and batter'd
  ship, WHITM 28
dismayed: d. her crew CARRY 8
disnatured: thwart d. torment
  SHAK 72
disobedient: His d. servant,
  AUDE 13
disorder: grasps of d., AMMO 9
sweet d. in the dress HERR 8
with brave d. part, POPE A 30
disordered: check time broke in a d.
  string; SHAK 93
disowns: Deity d. me. COWP 15
disparaging: anecdotes d. their
  wives; GILB 11
dispel'd: d. thir fears. MILT 56
dispell'd: mist is d. GAY 3
dispels: light d. the dark. MILT 82
dispence: angry nigardes of d.,
  CHAU 111
dispended: losst, d., drown'd,
  CHAT 2
disperse: d. these mists, VAUG 28
dispersed: d. and dead MILLA 35
D. the mind WINT 3
dream d. by shot, SHAP 10
sinking or d., SHAP 11
dispise: Do not a single heart d.
  TOWN 2
heart that loves what they d.,
  SHAK 239
displaced: she my mind hath so d.
  MARV 26
display: Creator's Pow'r d., ADDI 3
disponge: d. upon me, SHAK 8

dispose: unsearchable d. Of highest wisdom   MILT 118
disposed: much d. to fear,   GILB 19
spoils of war are easily d. GRAV 28
disposer: author and d.,   MILT 75
disposes: as the snake d.   LAWR 34
dispute: d. a year or more) — SWIF 21
there is none to d.;   COWP 23
disputed: some d. barricade, SEEG 1
dissatisfied: I'm d.,   MOOR M 38
Not one is d.   WHITM 75
dissect: We murder to d. WORD 146
dissemble: tongues d. deep CAMPI 9
dissembled: ill we all d.   PRIO 10
dissembling: d. Nature,   SHAK 96
dissipate: Baffle and d. your soul. LOWE R 35
dissolution: to high doth d. climb, WORD 8
dissolv'd: With pearl d. in gold SHERB 1
dissolved: my heaven d. so. DONN 65
dissolves: d. in water. AUDE 47
dissolving: Adrift d., bound for death;   MELV 2
in her d. arms.   SHEL 16
Distaffe: Thy Grace my D., TAYL E 5
Distance: D. and length,   HOSK 1
d. avails not,   WHITM 19, 20
d. throws them forth,   GUNN 11
fiery d.   ROBI 24
future in the d.,   BANK 4
ghosts then keep their d.; HARD 53
in vain the d. beacons.   TENN 79
pain, still in the middle d., SHAP 17
sea lay laughing at a d.; WORD 102
sixty seconds' worth of d. run, KIPL 8
'tis like the D.   DICKI 144
distances: desire is full/ of endless d.   HASS 3
distant: d. footsteps echo   LONG 15
d. northern sea.   ARNO 2
d. shadow of the tomb, MERE G 15
from d. Ophir   MASE 1
in many a d. port   TIMR 3
keep his d. way   GRAY 31
light of d. skies: BRYA 28
mountain in the d. West LONG 14
murmur of the d. seas, STEPHENS 10

no d. date;   BURN 61
tempt the d. deep,   HORA 5
Till, in a d. town,   DICKI 89
distemper'd: d. corpses within you? WHITM 96
distempered: fierce fiend of a d. dream,   SHEL 17
distended: Frog's belly d.   KIZE 1
distillation: taste of the d., WHITM 75
distilled: d. a clemency;   HARD 11
distills: d. such exquisite winds WHITM 98
verse d. your truth   SHAK 206
distinct: Twenty-nine d. damnations,   BROWNI R 78
distinction: d. 'twixt singing and preaching;   LOWE J 4
distinctly: d. I remember   POE 35
distinguish: d. darkness from the soul?   YEATS 44
Wise/ Enquire, define, d., teach, devise,   ROCH 16
distortions: d. of ingrown virginity. AUDE 68
distracted: In this d. globe. SHAK 28
distraught: make a stranger's eye d.,   YEATS 106
distress: counsel in this uttermost d.,   MILT 101
deep d.   WORD 12
d. that brought thee low, COWP 21
hour of my d.,   HERR 19
sorrow and heart's d.,   MILT 107
utterly consumed with sharp d., TENN 85
distressed: Calm and d.   ELIOT T 9
d. By all the needs and notions MILLA 14
distrusting: my d. self   HARP 3
disturbed: frost d. its bed? ELIOT T 120
guns d. the hour,   HARD 15
disturbing: never d. them, WHITM 64
disus'd: rust d., and shine no more. COWP 21
disused: in a d. shed   MAHON 1
ditch: blind man's d.   YEATS 47
dank as a d.,   ROET 52
ditches: d. are impure?   YEATS 46
hedges and d.;   STEVENSO R 8
smell from d. that were not Christian.   KAVA 7
ditties: d. of no tone: KEAT 38
With wonderful deathless d. OSHA 2
ditty: ancient d., long since mute. KEAT 5
dive: d. beneath the icebergs. LAWR 57

for the d. Under the river — CRAN H 33
dive-bomber: d.'s screaming orgasm   JEFFE 22
diverged: roads d. in a wood, FROS 95
Two roads d.   FROS 94
Divergence: D. deep and wide. WATS R 1
divers: d.-colored fans,   SHAK 5
in d. functions,   SHAK 55
diverse: clear harp in d. tones, TENN 18
separate d. flight,   WHITM 24
dives: blue kingfisher d. on you in fire.   LOWE R 7
d./ On Fifty-second Street AUDE 70
divide: clouds ere they d. them; SHEL 53
d. the conquest   SHAK 202
d. flax for damask   MOOR M 37
heaven d. The state of man SHAK 55
here the paths d.;   WATS R 1
intercourse of times d.,   VAUG 7
thin Partitions do their Bounds d.;   DRYD 2
divided: in their death they were not d.:   BIBL, O.T. 69
sin is d. into two parts.   NASH 9
dividend: Drawing no d.   SASS 6
dividing: d. and indifferent blue. STEVENS 56
divine: About the right d.   BYRO 32
all that is d.,   BANK 2
Angels sing to thee their ayres d., COWL 11
Dead and d.   WHITM 72
depth of some d. despair TENN 114
D. am I   WHITM 74
d. as myself is dead,   WHITM 69
d. Musæus soong)   MARL 6
d. property of her first being. MILT 4
D. Vision still was seen,   BLAK 26
drink d.;   JONS 31
effluence D.   BLAK 37
gives such d. materials WHITM 98
glimpse d.!   POPE A 2
Hand that made us is D.   ADDI 4
human form d.   BLAK 26
Love so amazing, so d., WATT I 10
Man is in part d.,   BYRO 60
mercies temporal and d.! BURN 33
mighty Milton's gift d., WHITT 10
no less d.:   BYRO 19
No voice d.   COWP 2

Poets, though d., are men:
JONS 1
power d.: MILT 81
rich results of the d. consents
EMER 4
some d. excess, COLL 12
Style; Majestick and D.,
DRYD 18
symbols d., KEAT 20
their looks d. MILT 71
things by a law d. SHEL 38
those eyes d., KEAT 64
to forgive d. POPE A 35
virtues so d.: LODG 7
you're d.! said he CUMM 24
divinely: fair, d. fair, MILT 92
reaming swats that drank d.;
BURN 52
Unerring Nature, still d. bright,
POPE A 25
diviner: Himself in some d. mood,
COLL 6
Divines: gravest of D., SWIF 18
Taylor, the Shakespeare of d.
EMER 41
divinest: drinking deep of that d.
anguish, BRON 13
Hail d. Melancholy, MILT 15
Much madness is d. sense
DICKI 105
this atmosphere d./ Shrouds thee
SHEL 53
diving: hill of dark underfoot d.,
MERW 8
divining: look'd but with d. eyes,
SHAK 228
divinity: d. of Lamont Cranston?
BARA 4
What is d. STEVENS 55
division: mirth the music of d.;
RALEG 15
"Woe weeps out her d. when she
sings." JONS 4
divorce: death were no d. DONN 3
d. And the treachery. SNOD 15
divorces: abolishes d. GILB 50
Divus: Lie quiet D. POUN 7
Dixie: away down South in D.!
EMME 2
D. Land whar I was born
EMME 1
lib and die in D.! EMME 2
Look away! D. Land. EMME 1
Way Down South in D.
HUGH L 13
Dizzily: D. down the abyss
TROW 2
dizzy: big, d. mountains SERV 12
blackness veiled his d. eyes,
SHEL 16
make a small boy d.; ROET 49
Do: D., boatman, d.!"
ROSS C 9, 10

D. diddle di do, DE LA 10
d. it by d. NASH 11
Let us d., or die! BURN 48
Theirs but to d. and die. TENN 7
dock: tincan banana d. GINS 33
doctor: d. punched my vein
SHAP 26
frequent/ D. and Saint, OMAR 5
Doctoral: Spirit gave the D.
Degree: DRYD 19
doctors: send the damned d.
SNYD 38
doctour: d. of phisik; CHAU 8
doctrine: d. of ill-doing, SHAK 178
document: d. Our bodily decay.
HALL 1
doe: d., a recent killing; STAF 2
strike me the largest d. LOVE 2
doeth: whatsoever he d. shall
prosper. BIBL, O.T. 21
doff: d. thy name, SHAK 142
dog: beaten d. beneath the hail,
POUN 22
brain behind the d.'s /brain,
DAY 10
call me misbeliever, cutthroat d.,
SHAK 118
Cat and D., SWIF 15
cocaine d. and a cocaine cat,
UNKN 67
Dies like a d.! WHITT 4
dirty d., quite comfy. BISH 12
d. among the fairies, THOMA D 6
d. and man at first were friends;
GOLD 7
d. following a brass band.
BARK 4
d. has his day, THOMA D 39
d. in the highway, NOYE 8
d. it was that died. GOLD 8
d. lay dead five days WILB 32
d. looking for a place to sleep in,
BISH 28
d. rose shines in the hedge.
MONTA 4
d. starv'd at his Master's BLAK 3
d. That worried the cat MOTH 6
d.'s fidelity!" HARD 7
every d. his day. KINGSL 6
faithful d. POPE A 60
get her poor d. a bone:
MARTIN 1
gingham d. and the calico cat
FIEL E 1
his control of d., DAY 10
his Highness' d. at Kew;
POPE A 5
I'd be a D., a Monkey or a Bear,
ROCH 8
kids, frisk with your d.,
CRAN H 47
little d. lay curled WILB 48
little toy d. FIEL E 6

little yellow d. NASH 15
mouth of the drowned d.
HUGH T 3
My d. and I are old, MASE 3
no trace of d. or cat; FIEL E 2
"O keep the D. far hence,
ELIOT T 120
tied to me/ As to a d.'s tail?
YEATS 150
Took my d. DICKI 62
walk the d. BARA 15
whose d. are you? POPE A 5
ye auld, snick-drawing d.!
BURN 3
You whoreson d., POUN 60
doggy: go on with their d. life
AUDE 63
dogs: beats the d. in noises loud.
CLARE 2
dancing d. and bears, HODG 1
d. bark at me SHAK 96
Mad d. and Englishmen COWA 1
practicing their aim on stray d.
KINN 19
Rats!/ They fought the d.,
BROWNI R 60
these Inquisition d. TENN 117
doing: joy's soul lies in the d.
SHAK 169
rather than by not d. NASH 11
struggling and d. without and
being colored HAYD 13
up and d., LONG 37
dole: d.-kept breadwinner HEAN 4
doleful: Ring out my d. knell;
BOLE 2
doll: all white, like a d. BISH 15
d. in the d.-maker's house
YEATS 49
Dollar: D. is your only Word,
ROBI 4
heterosexual d. GINS 12
like he loves his D. SMIT W 1
Dollars: dimes and/ D. HUGH L 3
jobs, the d. SNOD 5
unobtainable d.! GINS 16
dolorous: many a Region d.,
MILT 61
dolour: great d. complaining
UNKN 206
dolphin: d.-torn, that gong-
tormented sea. YEATS 19
without/ The d.'s arc, WILB 2
dolphinlike: delights/ Were d.;
SHAK 7
dolphins: plunging like d.
JEFFE 12
dolt: war with every knave and d.,
YEATS 58
domain: traverse old love's d.
HARD 12
dome: d. more vast, HOLM 3

infatuate ship went d. MELV 1

Lay me d. DUNB P 2

lie d. in dust, AIKE 10

like the d. of a thistle, MOOR C 5

lofty towers I see d.-rased,
SHAK 211

Look not thou d. but up!
BROWNI R 76

Looking d. for miles SNYD 18

moss hung d. from the branches,
WHITM 39

movin' up an' d. again, KIPL 4

must not bruise you d.
JOHN H 3

nowhere to go but d.; SNOD 10

one totters d., ROSS C 12

own soul trampling d. WHITM 31

phantom looking d. WHITM 5

Pour d. your warmth, WHITM 65

ran d. the stairs. OHAR 7

seven anemones with d.-dropped
heads UNKN 253

shoot a fellow d. HARD 31

short-end comes d. SIMI 2

sits at the table, head d.,
RUKE 8

snow falling d. and necks of
lovers. SIMP 10

soft young d. of her, MEW 4

stars go d. MCCRE 1

swan's d. JONS 2

sword,/ Threw it d., SCHW 1

terrible to come d. JUST 7

those meandering d. HARD 42

time brings d. BRAD 10

tone their rumble d. HUGH L 8

Trees d./ Creeks choked, trout
killed, SNYD 45

up and d. I sow them HOUS 33

warsled up, they warsled d.,
UNKN 269

'Way d. upon de Swanee ribber,
FOST 3

downe: goe d. to 'th sea in ships:
BIBL, O.T. 56

downed: d. with light brown hair!)
ELIOT T 85

downs: lawns, or level d., MILT 69

downstairs: I'll kick you d.!"
CARRO 7

downtowns: rotten little d. PINS 1

downtrodden: Earth's d. and
oppressed, BRYA 13

downturning: dry d. mouth.
KINS 5

Downward: sink,/ D. to darkness,
STEVENS 62

downwards: carried d. by thy
flood, WATT I 3

dowry: d. for a use in common life.
SHAP 29

doxy: d., over the dale, SHAK 181

doze: they d. over muskets
LOWE R 19

Dozens: D. of pale hands
DICKEY 21

whirligig of d. LAWR 54

dozing: Burly, d. humble-bee,
EMER 30

Draco: Wise D. comes, MELV 12

drafts: fragments and rough d.
RICH 20

drag: blacks crackle and d.
PLATH 39

look like a d. BERRYM 12

dragged: d. Diana from her car,
POE 2

d. me home alive....
LOWE R 28

d. you from homeland,
BROWN S 4

I d. her off STAF 2

Dragging: D. its slimy belly
ELIOT T 130

d. the plow OLSO 18

D. the whole sky with it
FROS 26

lost ponies with/ D. saddles —
SNYD 51

dragon: battell on the d. blak,
DUNB W 1

Dare the unpastured d. SHEL 4

d.-fly came/ And sat FARJ E 1

d.-fly on the river. BROWNI E 2

d. world. POUN 20

duskish river d. BEDD 10

ev'ning D. MILT 116

fiery red d. UNKN 243

Flame tongue of the d. SNYD 30

knight slew the d., UNKN 244

old D. underground, MILT 40

pirate gaped at Belinda's d.,
NASH 16

realio, trulio, little pet d.
NASH 15

dragonflies: d. draw flame;
HOPKINS 1

dragonfly: d. Hangs like a blue
thread ROSS D 4

dragonish: cloud that's d., SHAK 9

dragoon: d. me into a lethal
automaton MACN 16

drags: It d. the sea after it
PLATH 58

drain: d. the lifeblood of the child,
SHAK 61

drained: d. and flagging bosom
RICH 19

d. faces LOWE R 20

d. out one another's force
SNOD 15

His look d. the stones. ROET 36

drains: Democracy and proper d.
BETJ 4

d. her words. THOMA D 14

Drake: D. he's in his hammock
NEWB 1

duck do get a d.; UNKN 123

welcome home, Sir Francis D.'
UNKN 295

dram: d. of poison, SHAK 150

Drama: D.'s Laws the D.'s Patrons
give, JOHN S (1709–1784) 9

dramas: mammoth rests between
his cyclonic d. SAND 15

drank: as though it d. the wind
YEATS 10

d. of Aganippe well, SIDN 22

d. the valorous youth of a new
world. MARK 2

reaming swats that d. divinely;
BURN 52

drapery: Dew-cloth, dream d.,
THOR 8

Draping: D. each hive WHITT 34

draught: d. of heavenly pleasure
spare, BURN 19

draughte: d. of sweete win.
CHAU 87

draughts: d. of intellectual day,
CRAS 3

shallow d. intoxicate the brain,
POPE A 33

dravest: d. love from thee,
THOMP F 10

who d. Me." THOMP F 10

draw: anguish none can d.;
MELV 19

d. a line SPENC A 4

d. me to her in the blessed place!
PETRA 6

D. the Glasnevin coverlet
YEATS 148

d. the Thing as he sees It
KIPL 29

d. this weary breath. DANI S 10

D. up the dew. DAY 7

hour of death d. near BRYA 33

unicorns d. by the gilded hearse.
ELIOT T 12

where can we d. water,'
YEATS 123

drawer: open like a d. of knives.
LARK 9

Drawing: D. no dividend SASS 6

dusk a d.-down OWEN 8

Grishkin in a d.-room.
ELIOT T 160

places of d. water, BIBL, O.T. 18

time,/ And d. days out, SHAK 46

drawings: d. by Bonnard OHAR 5

drawn: d. curtains when the play is
done. RALEG 16

d. no lines: AMMO 5

landscapes d. in pearly
monotones. WYLI 14

neat curtains are d. MONR 1

voice in my d. ear melted away.
CAMPB T 9
wide world d. on things to come
SHAK 229
dreamland: quiet steeps of d.,
DE LA 17
dreamless: ancient, d., uninvaded
sleep TENN 58
dancer by the d. wave. YEATS 96
deep and d. sleep BROO P 3
dreams: all my nightly d. POE 8
back on forgotten d., OWEN 22
Beyond all d. DE LA 7
by night we are hurled/ By d.,
HERR 9
come to me in d. ROSS C 7
Desires and d. and powers
SWIN 13
doubtful d. of d.; SWIN 11
Dreamer of d., MORR 3
dreamers of d., OSHA 1
D.! adorations! GINS 18
d. come MACL 5
d. happy as her day; BROO R 14
d. of home, AUDE 96
D. pursue death SWIN 7
d. pursue our dead SWIN 7
d. truths and fables histories;
DONN 19
d. under your feet; YEATS 4
d.,/ with what frivolity LEVE 8
endless d., FORD J 1
folding up my little d. JOHN G 3
fulfilment to our d. STEVENS 57
Hold fast your d.! DRIS 1
If there were d. to sell, BEDD 9
Joys as wingëd d. fly fast,
FLET/OTHE 1
know not what the younger d.
YEATS 66
land of d. JOHN L 7
land of d., ARNO 3
land where the dead d. go.
NOYE 4
lived by honest d. DAY 13
Nature lends such evil d.?
TENN 32
object among d., you sit JARR 6
our d. used to run?' HARD 10
Plato smiling carves d., JEFFE 34
silent shadows and in d.?
STEVENS 55
such stuff/ As d. are made on,
SHAK 163
sweep past in d., LEVE 13
talk of d., SHAK 141
this world d. of. TENN 104
torn by d., STEVENS 24
tread on my d. YEATS 4
vainly the d. of youth recall.
WHITT 21
voice a blind man d. GARR 1
what d. can do/ — CUMM 9

what d. may come SHAK 39
Where d. may go, DRIS 1
dreamt: d. of in your philosophy.
SHAK 29
dreamy: depth of the d. SWIN 19
D. as puberty — SHAP 21
d. shadows rise, LINC 1
drear: void, dark, and d.,
COLE SAM 7
yon d. and rigid bier POE 29
drearie: many a dark and d. Vale
MILT 61
drearier: Ushers in a d. day
BRON 1
drearily: Went d. singing
WHITT 34
dreariness: paint the visionary d.
WORD 114
dreary: d. main, — SHEL 62
d. sorrow at the North LI PO 2
d. unnamable pain LANIE 4
For a long d. season, KEAT 1
How d. to be somebody.
DICKI 83
'My life is d., TENN 92
Once upon a midnight d., POE 34
dredful: derke and d. of sight.
LANGL 2
dredge: labored/ To d. the silt
PLATH 24
dregs: d. of scattered thought,
SIDN 39
dreich: kirkyairdie-like and d.
YOUN D 1
drench'd: all d. in mud, SWIF 9
d. their heads in blessing:
SNOD 8
drenched: d. our steeples, SHAK 75
d. there/ with purpose, GUNN 2
Grain-tinctured, d. in empyrean
light; WORD 102
drenching: d. the holy fires.
TATE A 1
dress: airs in d. an' gait BURN 58
d. me up in silks WHITT 16
d./ Of an inhuman murderess;
MARV 14
d. woven/ From green and blue
things KAVA 4
dressed in his d.-suit, SCHW 10
Peace, the human d. BLAK 88
people d. that way MOOR M 4
sweet disorder in the d. HERR 8
under a summer cotton d.
SNYD 14
wears a dun-colored d. WALK 12
dressed: Better d. and stacking
birch, LOWE R 48
d. all in fur, MOOR C 3
d. for this short comedy.
RALEG 15
d. in all his trim, SHAK 225
D. in his dress-suit, SCHW 10

d. me gently PACK 1
d. or undressed or partly.
CREE 4
D. to die, THOMA D 41
lot of wolves d. up in gold and
purple NASH 20
marks when you're d., GILD 1
Solomon was never d. so fine.
VAUG 9
to advantage d., POPE A 21
truth severe, by fairy fiction d.
GRAY 6
undressed, operated-on, d. body
JARR 18
dresses: I will wear what d. I
choose! CREE 3
dressing: For d. eels, or shoeing
horses. PRAE 1
drest: presently d. in black,
WHITM 17
you are beautifully d. RANDS 2
drew: suddenly d. his rein.
WOOL 3
trees they d. Him last: LANIE 2
woman d. her long black hair
ELIOT T 149
dribbled: d. couplets like a snake
TATE A 9
dried: boasted their scars of d.
snot; HILL G 6
d. the sap out of my veins,
YEATS 57
d. with grief, SHAK 8
river d. to its bed SIMI 4
dries: dew d. up, the star is shot;
KING H 5
Grass shrivels and d. WALK 12
drift: barges d. With the turning
tide ELIOT T 138
d. on the still water, YEATS 167
d. with every passion WILD 13
little wash'd-up d., WHITM 3
part of the sands and d.
WHITM 3
rioted in a d., BRID R 9
whirls the 'wildering d.,
BRON 14
drifted: d. in a sheepish calm,
LOWE R 32
drifting: Lashed close to a d. mast.
LONG 52
drifts: beautiful d. away
YEATS 103
lie in d. at your feet. WHITM 6
long moon d. toward Asia
HAIN 1
swan d. upon a darkening flood.
YEATS 37
driftwood: kelp, miscellaneous d.,
ROET 44
scattered d. THAX 1
drill: born to d. and die. CRAN S 9

drink: comes down to d.
　　STEVENS 13
d. a tear out of thine eye.
　　LOVE 6
D. and be whole again FROS 44
d., and leave the world unseen,
　　KEAT 46
d. at my water-trough LAWR 43
d. by measure, POPE A 105
d. divine; JONS 31
D. from here energy SPEND 16
d. it shall not thirst EMER 49
d. lemonade, UNKN 240
d. Life to the lees. TENN 129
d. like any toper. HORA 9
d. of gods and angels! Wine
　　HERR 15
d. The stale of horses SHAK 4
D. to me only with thine eyes
　　JONS 31
drinks and gapes for d. again;
　　COWL 1
every creature d. but I? COWL 2
five reasons we should d.:
　　ALDR H 1
Give dry dust d., VAUG 24
Indians d. in the best tavern.
　　WELC 1
Let us d. anew SMIT L 5
Nor any drop to d.
　　COLE SAM 33
not meat nor d. MILLA 16
rate you d. your beer. HOUS 49
shook to see him d. it up:
　　HOUS 53
taste for d., GILB 18
throats of hell to d., CHES 7
thy d. and thy whore, SHAK 71
"While you live,/ D.! — OMAR 6
drinking: A-preaching that d. is
　　sinful, GOLD 6
d. and breeding,/ No
　　sentimentalist, WHITM 73
d. and oath and smutty jest,
　　WHITM 33
d. deep of that divinest anguish,
　　BRON 13
d. icy water SNYD 8
d. in the Dakotas CRAN H 17
d. largely sobers us again.
　　POPE A 33
D. to engender wit. ROCH 5
eating and d. JONS 27
kept on d. ROBI 44
like men in d.-songs, TENN 96
quite transmugrified, they're
　　grown/ Debauchery and D.:
　　BURN 6
Socrates d. the hemlock,
　　CARRU 2
spirit d. timelessness; SPEND 17
drinks: called for d. for the house.
　　SERV 7

cups d. to the fair. RICH 21
d. and gapes for drink again;
　　COWL 1
d. his drop. YEATS 46
hardly d. a pint of wine, SWIF 27
drip: beeches d. in browns and
　　duns, HARD 50
dripping: d. in tangles green,
　　MELV 23
d. sack-wise down LAWR 21
side/ Of d. stone; YEATS 152
drips: She d. herself with water,
　　LAWR 12
When the light d. AIKE 6
drive: death will d. us from the
　　scene EBER 5
d., he sd, CREE 9
d./ Into the red/ Eye, PLATH 7
D. my dead thoughts SHEL 46
d. the brute off? LARK 20
d. with Fergus now, YEATS 163
to d., DAY 12
ugly thoughts/ That d. them
　　SASS 14
driven: adulterous lust was d.
　　MILT 78
better bargain d. SIDN 1
d. from the/ northwest —
　　WILLI 34
d. us to this fury, PRIN 3
d. wild/ by snakes HUGO 6
driver: d. easily might have been
　　you, STEPHENS 12
drivers: d. in a barroom
　　WHITM 33
drives: d. my green age;
　　THOMA D 22
d. the flower THOMA D 22
d. the noisy crowd CLARE 2
driving: D. around, I will waste
　　more time. BLY 1
d. storm even as now, WHITM 99
making d. belts. SPEND 8
drizzling: ghastly through the d.
　　rain TENN 21
droghte: d. of March CHAU 3
drone: like Bag-pipe d., BUTL 7
Snuffy old d. HOLM 5
droned: d. the summer's final
　　mass; WILB 16
droop: D. herbs and flowers;
　　JONS 4
While I d. here. THOR 3
drooped: great star early d.
　　WHITM 46
drooping: d. star in the west,
　　WHITM 46
d. weary sire, CRAB 6
lustrous and d. star WHITM 52
Tears, still d., MARV 30
drop: ages d. in it like rain.
　　EMER 49

brand so d. with blood,
　　UNKN 85
Cordials in every d., and Wine;
　　VAUG 20
Death could d. ROSE 8
drinks his d. YEATS 46
d. in for an after-loss: SHAK 221
d. like the fruits of the tree,
　　MERE G 3
d. of a hat AUDE 59
d. sleep on her eyes UNKN 254
D. their cast YEATS 152
half a d.! ah, my Christ! —
　　MARL 2
hands d. white and empty
　　NIMS 4
indifferent beak could let her d.?
　　YEATS 86
liquid d. that is heavy, LAWR 19
Nor any d. to drink.
　　COLE SAM 33
One d. would save my soul —
　　MARL 2
rain, from clouds to d. assign'd,
　　BIBL, O.T. 67
Ripe apples d. MARV 17
soul, that d., that ray MARV 31
table starts to d. WILB 20
drope: no d. ne fille CHAU 15
dropped: d. so low in my regard
　　DICKI 90
d. things are bound to sink —
　　MOOR M 13
d. upon my bosom. LOWE A 7
honey d. from trees; TASS 1
I d. down, and down —
　　DICKI 47
natural tears they d., MILT 108
plates d. from his pocket.
　　SHAK 7
droppeth: d. as the gentle rain from
　　heaven SHAK 123
dropping: dank and d. weeds
　　HORA 4
d. houses and eek smoke
　　CHAU 98
d. Victorian shoulders. LAWR 20
yonder d. day: TENN 23
drops: bleeding d. of red,
　　WHITM 45
d. and dews of future bliss.
　　VAUG 23
.D. away, hard rock wavers
　　SNYD 49
d. her ostrich tail, LOWE R 41
d. of this most balmy time
　　SHAK 229
d. of water, CARN 1
evil moon bleeds d. of death.
　　WALK 12
in contiguous d. SWIF 7
pine-tree d. its dead; MERE G 2

token of the d. of blood
    UNKN 130
What d. the myrrh MILT 79
dropt: d. at my side that day,
    WHITM 106
Two veterans son and father d.
    together, WHITM 26
you d., lost, DICKI 151
drounken: Eten and d. and maden
    hem glad; UNKN 288
drouth: d. of penitential tears?
    WINT 4
drove: d. out of sight, MOOR C 5
Verb d. up, KOCH 3
drown: all who know may d.
    ROBI 37
can I d. an eye, SHAK 195
d. the raucous shout; UNTE 3
d. the stage with tears SHAK 31
d./ The night with you in floods of
    down. HERR 35
hang or d.
    JOHN S (1709–1784) 12
I'll d. my book. SHAK 165
pain it was to d.! SHAK 97
tears shall d. the wind.
    SHAK 105
voices wake us, and we d.
    ELIOT T 91
drown'd: D. puppies, stinking
    sprats, SWIF 9
he found a d. woman. UNKN 273
in the burnt ship d. DONN 13
losst, dispended, d., CHAT 2
drowne: d. your paine, HERR 25
drowned: ceremony of innocence is
    d.; YEATS 134
dice of d. men's bones CRAN H 1
d., and I've the ague. BYRO 76
d. face always staring/ toward the
    sun RICH 5
d. my Glory OMAR 2
d. the cocks! SHAK 75
d. the sense in odours;
    ELIOT T 121
In Lethe to be d., HERR 49
in the waves was d.; HOLM 11
million Adams d. MUIR 11
mouth of the d. dog. HUGH T 3
senseless d. Have faces MOSS 4
drowning: brim with sorrow d.
    song. TENN 26
death shall be by d. SHAP 24
d. in a stormier sea WILD 10
d. their speaking BROWNI R 60
not waving but d. SMIT ST 2
drowsy: d. head and folded wing,
    POE 38
d. numbness pains/ My sense,
    KEAT 44
d. syncopated tune,/ Rocking back
    and forth HUGH L 18

d. town; BRID R 8
Where d. poppies nod
    BROWNI E/GUIN 1
drudge: contented thy poor d. to
    be, SHAK 243
drudging: d. goblin sweat, MILT 23
Drug: D. thy memories, TENN 74
drugs: married Allen don't take d.
    GINS 32
drugstore: watching the d. sign
    RUKE 8
druidic: d. difference/ Enhances
    nature DICKI 24
drum: beat the d. slowly UNKN 11
d. nor trumpet peaceful sleeps
    should move, CAMPI 16
D. on your D., SAND 11
listenin' for the d., NEWB 1
Not a d. was heard, WOLF C 1
Only the d. is confident,
    JEFFE 26
pulse, like a soft d. KING H 4
rumble of a distant D.! OMAR 3
Service, like a D. DICKI 46
Drumcliff: In D. churchyard
    YEATS 159
Drummer: throw in D. Hodge,
    HARD 19
drummers: Nine d. drumming,
    UNKN 282
drummes: Strike on your d.,
    UNKN 223
drumming: Deaf with the d. of an
    ear; MARV 11
d. of the demon in their ears.
    MACN 10
Nine drummers d., UNKN 282
drums: Beat! beat! d.! — WHITM 7
d. give you music, WHITM 27
Loud are the thunder d.
    UNKN 120
pound, you d. WHITM 7
strong you thump, O terrible d.
    WHITM 8
too few for d. and yells,
    OWEN 38
with beating d. WHITM 32
With d. and guns, UNKN 156
drunk: bacchantes, d. On wine or
    truth, SNYD 39
Could man be d. for ever
    HOUS 2
deftly you steady/ The d. NIMS 2
D. and asleep in his boots,
    STEVENS 5
d., and danc'd, and sung/ Thy fill,
    COWL 3
d. delight of battle with my
    peers, TENN 130
D. with fatigue; OWEN 18
fight, like mad or d., BUTL 1
fire has d. the swamps of
    evergreens; TUCK 1

having d. such a lot, AUDE 12
I am as d. as you are.) CHES 16
men were d. like water, JARR 3
of hemlock I had d., KEAT 44
second d., BYRO 21
drunkard: fleckled darkness like a d.
    reels SHAK 146
rolling English d. CHES 14
drunken: cursed/ The d. officer
    WALC 4
d. of things Lethean; SWIN 23
drunkenness: They teach you d.
    OLSO 16
dry: air white and d. WILB 4
bleached and d. THAX 1
bread d. as paper, POUN 9
Crawls from the d. grass.
    WILB 16
D. bones can harm no one.
    ELIOT T 151
d. downturning mouth. KINS 5
d. fields burn, LANIE 5
D. leafless trees VERY 1
d. scent of a dying garden
    ROET 15
d. the starting tear, GILB 10
d. throats rattle, SHEL 63
d. up/ like a raisin in the sun?
    HUGH L 9
fingers ache, my lips are d.:
    LAND 11
herb was d.; TENN 40
log at last, d., bald, and sere:
    JONS 41
malice in the d. machine
    STEVENS 48
Now I am d. bones WRIG R 1
old man in a d. month,
    ELIOT T 30
rondels, rondeaus,/ Seeds in a d.
    pod, MAST 11
seasons are D. and Wet;
    AUDE 60
sheds d. leaves, THOMA D 2
Sierras/ Will be d. and dead,
    SNYD 20
stalk is withered d., UNKN 293
Thoughts of a d. brain
    ELIOT T 35
wish thine own heart d. of blood
    KEAT 61
Words d. and riderless,
    PLATH 80
Dryden: as Chaucer is shall D. be.
    POPE A 34
dual: measur'd d. throbbing
    WHITM 99
Dublin: If ever you go to D. town
    KAVA 16
Duccio: D. came not by usura
    POUN 10
Duchess: my last D. painted on the
    wall, BROWNI R 54

duck: d. do get a drake;
UNKN 123
My dainty d., SHAK 182
When father carves the d.
WRIG E 1

ducklings: d. to the water,
MONTROSS 3

Ducks: D. are a-dabbling,
GRAHAME 1
young d. with white straw flats,
UNKN 258

ductile: d. anchor hold, WHITM 55

dude: d. Who lets the girl down
LARK 19
Roosevelt, the young d. cowboy,
LIND V 7

due: born out of my d. time,
MORR 3
Mine eye's d. SHAK 203
More is thy d. SHAK 104
my butcher's bill is d.; GILB 49
no more than his d.
BROWNI R 36
see not half my dayes that's d.,
BRAD 2

duel: Dream of a d. PLATH 15

dues: little d. of wheat, TENN 91

dugs: old man with wrinkled d.
ELIOT T 135

Duke: D. of Dickens — GILB 54
D. of Plaza-Toro! GILB 16
everybody praised the D.
SOUTHE 1

dull: brain is d., HOOD 14
children frowned/ At something
d.; LARK 21
Converts d. port SHEN 1
Don d., Don brutish, BELL 12
dotard lethargic and d., MELV 14
d. and hopeless CRAB 1
d. and muddy-mettled rascal,
SHAK 31
d. and slow and mild. JARR 2
d. and speechless tribes:
SHAK 229
d. brain perplexes and retards:
KEAT 48
d.-eyed night HERR 44
d. Impatience or a fierce velleity,
WILB 26
d. it is to pause, TENN 131
d. man, d. and uxorious,
POUN 55
d. shore of lazy temperance,
ROCH 2
d., stale, tired bed SHAK 70
d. thy palm with entertainment
SHAK 23
d. unfeeling barren ignorance
SHAK 86
D. would he be of soul WORD 6
emptied some d. opiate KEAT 44

Fireworks in the d. middle of
February SEXT 2
I was fishing in the d. canal
ELIOT T 130
long, d., tapering groan,
WHITM 92
low words oft creep in one d.
line: POPE A 25
Piercing the night's d. ear;
SHAK 57
point their d. Philosophies?
ROCH 16
prophetic blessing — Be thou d.;
DRYD/TATE 2
silent, d. retreat, FRENE 5
so d. a cheere. SHAK 224
travelled life's d. round, SHEN 2
uncensured to be d.; POPE A 21

duller: d. than a witling's jest.
PATM 2

dullness: filial d.: DRYD 14
for anointed d. he was made.
DRYD 12
lambent d. played around his
face. DRYD 13
Must d. turn me to a clod?
HERB G 34

dulls: borrowing d. the edge of
husbandry. SHAK 24

dully: walking d. along; AUDE 62

Dumb: dead, nor deaf, nor d.;
RANDA J 2
deft d.-show HARD 39
d. Terror shall rise MARK 8
D./ As old medallions to the
thumb, MACL 1
far-off stream is d., TENN 105
Muffled and d. EMER 13
noisy bells, be d.: HOUS 27
pipe that strikes Apollo d.;
LYLY 5
rational voice is d.: AUDE 34
you d., beautiful ministers,
WHITM 22

dun: raw rough d. was he, KIPL 2
then her breasts are d.;
SHAK 237
wears a d.-colored dress
WALK 12

Dunce: Satan, thou art but a D.,
BLAK 20

Dundee: follow the bonnet of Bonny
D. SCOT WA 3

dung: Dove-note, bone marrow, deer
d., KIZE 1
d., guts, and blood, SWIF 9
feet of d. KINS 4

Dungannon: in the town of D.,
UNKN 195

dungeon: down into the d.
LONG 10

d., where he died CUMM 17
fat d. I could rise to skin
GUNN 8

dungeons: Brightest in d., BYRO 58

dungeoun: d. thereinne LANGL 2

dungy: d. earth alike/ Feeds beast as
man. SHAK 3

duns: beeches drip in browns and
d., HARD 50
D. at his lordship's gate SWIF 11

dupe: Pity him, this d. of dream,
HODG 4

duration: frail d. of a flower.
FRENE 7

Durer: D. would have seen
MOOR M 29

dusk: cedars d. and dim.
WHITM 53
d. a drawing-down OWEN 8
endless pilgrimage,/ Dawn and d.,
GRAV 36
feeling its huge path/ Through d.,
SPEND 13
it was d. outside, FROS 15
wash the d. with silver.
BLAK 110

dusks: Beautiful glooms, soft d.
LANIE 3

dusky: Ancient, d. rivers.
HUGH L 12
d. cane-lipped throngs. TOOM 3
three/ d. syllables SAND 21

dust: As chimney-sweepers, come to
d. SHAK 18
bite the d. KLEI 3
blossom in their d. SHIR 3
Blows all the d. HERB G 16
bones with d. shall cover,
SHAK 196
broom stands/ In the d. WILB 20
buried in the d. of marching feet.
KNIG 3
come to d. SHAK 18
covered with d., FIEL E 6
D. and ashes?' BROWNI R 79
d. and chaff, TENN 34
D. as we are, WORD 96
d. blown through the streets of
Rome, MASE 8
D. did scoop itself like Hands
DICKI 160
D. hath closed Helen's eye.
NASHE 1
d., here running in the glass,
JONS 12
d. I am and shall to d. return.
MILT 98
D. in an urn MILLA 35
D. into D., OMAR 4
d. is for a time. MOOR M 16
d. Is on this skipping heart
LOWE R 6

d. o' the mounded years —
THOMP F 8

d. of snow/ From a hemlock tree.
FROS 46

d. of that little chair, FIEL E 7

d. on the nettles, THOMA E 17

d. return to the earth
BIBL, O.T. 6

d. stops your ear, YEATS 148

D. thou art, LONG 35

d. to be mingled with yours/
Forever LI PO 5

feathery, faery d.; BROO R 3

fish scale, shale d., bone
SNYD 22

flesh how it crumbles to d.
AIKE 12

flie with angels, fall with d.,
HERB G 65

follow this and come to d.
SHAK 18

Give dry d. drink, VAUG 24

Guilty of d. and sin. HERB G 48

haughty brought to d.? AIKE 9

her lips are d. STEPHENS 1

holds the d. HERB G 11

hot and sorrowful sweetness of the
d.: MILLA 20

I have seen d. ROET 8

in a handful of d. ELIOT T 115

'In the d. I write
THOMS J (1834–1882) 8

into the D. descend; OMAR 4

into the d. of death; SHEL 78

Kneeled down in the d.
JOHN J 3

lie down in d., AIKE 10

light in the d. lies dead;
SHEL 89

limbs with d. are covered
FRENE 3

lovers' hearts to d. DARL 1

March with its peck of d.,
ROSS C 37

moldering now in silent d.
BURN 31

moulder in d. away! LONG 10

no d. upon RICH 8

Of Eros and of d., AUDE 78

old fellows in the d. RANS 8

on this once belov'd D. PRIO 5

pays us but with age and d.,
RALEG 3

precious d. is layd; CAREW 8

pride that licks the d. POPE A 12

pulpits sealed with d.
BEAU/BASS 3

quaint honor turn to d.,
MARV 34

quiet D. was Gentlemen and
Ladies, DICKI 147

raiseth up the poor out of the d.,
BIBL, O.T. 8

reachest but to d.; SIDN 26

recover once my d.,
MONTROSE 4

save from d.; SPEND 22

shed one English tear/ O'er
English d. MACA 2

starved to death and turned to d.,
WESL S 1

Sweeping the d. SIMI 3

this earth, this grave, this d.,
RALEG 4

thou art d.!' SOUTHW 10

Though ye destroy their d.
SIGO 2

tilted a poke of d. SERV 7

Time, a maniac scattering d.,
TENN 28

to d. returnest, LONG 35

To the vile d., SCOT WA 12

Two handfuls of white d.,
TENN 87

under D. to lie, OMAR 4

waste to d. VAUX 6

white with the d. ROSE 3

with the d. of death? TENN 96

With years-deep d., HARD 41

dustcoat: gentleman in a d.
RANS 30

dusts: our two d. POUN 46

dusty: d. bondage into luminous
air. MILLA 8

d. rubble of the highway,
ROET 41

Fringing the d. road LOWE J 15

lighted fools/ The way to d.
death. SHAK 114

moth with d. wing, ROSS C 16

To eat d. bread. BOGA 14

Dutch: D. but be converted,
MARV 3

D. clock it told me FIEL E 2

fault of the D. CANN 1

I said it in D. CARRO 22

duteous: d. thing UNKN 313

duties: lowliest d. WORD 42

thy d. be/ To warm the world,
DONN 56

dutiful: d. weighing of ill with
good; — LANIE 3

duty: causeless d., SIDN 4

d., a dead-sure thing, — HAY 4

D., faith, love are roots, and ever
green. PEEL 7

my d., gentlemen, NASH 7

stuck by his d. UNKN 54

their d., and they did. GILB 5

their d. to God, WHITM 75

voices of D. call — LANIE 5

weep and sing/ D.'s conscious
wrong, AUDE 10

whole of man. BIBL, O.T. 7

dwalt: d. on me sae kindly;
BURN 31

dwell: Boys/ In which a Soul doth
d.: TRAH 4

cell/ Wherein to d.; HERR 39

cool waters where we used to d.,
HOPE L 3

d. in darkness; CHAP G 1

d. in Possibility — DICKI 43

d. in the house of the Lord for
ever. BIBL, O.T. 31

d. in the midst of alarms,
COWP 23

d. in the tents of wickedness.
BIBL, O.T. 43

d. with soothfastness; CHAU 1

In Heaven a spirit doth d.
POE 26

Persians do not d. upon GRAV 20

rest can never d., MILT 50

that in the heavens does d.!
BURN 32

Virgins that on Parnasse d.,
SPENS 52

where the cave men d.; CARRU 1

with vilest worms to d.:
SHAK 214

dwellers: d. In Pygmy Alley,
GRAV 19

dwellest: d. in earth and sun,
NEWB 4

dwelleth: way where light d.?
BIBL, O.T. 15

dwelling: d. is in Sule Skerrie."
UNKN 122

d. is the light of setting suns,
WORD 35

left the past year's d. HOLM 2

My heart has left its d.-place
CLARE 5

only d. on earth WORD 126

dwells: earth/ On which he d.
WORD 115

soldier's kiss d. WHITM 116

thy lord d. JONS 37

True beauty d. on high:
HERB G 36

dwelt: d. on a wide moor,
WORD 50

unapproached Light/ D. from
Eternitie, MILT 63

dwindled: cricket like a d. hearse
WILB 16

dy'd: where their Honour d.
POPE A 129

dye: Doth d. unknowen, SENE 2

Fall asleepe, or hearing d.
FLET/SHAK 1

full as deep a d. SHAK 206

if not pluckt we d., FLET J 6

dyed: China's gayest art had d.
GRAY 18

damselle spake, and d. CHAT 1

dyen: dreadë for to d.; CHAU 66

flushed them out e. MORG 1
getting up e. GILB 58
light-blue lane of e. dawn,
   TENN 54
love rose up so e. HOUS 26
sea-light every e. game MOSS 3
she is e. up and out, MILLA 33
soul e. into heaven ravished,
   DONN 53
that e.-laurelled head HOUS 58
earn: little to e., KINGSL 3
earned: e. a night's repose.
   LONG 49
hearts are e. YEATS 108
earnest: at least an e. sense
   WHITT 10
branch-charmed by the e. stars,
   KEAT 22
die in e. RALEG 16
equally/ E. elements of nature.
   JEFFE 7
Life is e.! LONG 35
So e., so graceful, LOWE J 1
with such e. pains WORD 78
earns: what everybody e., GILB 8
Earring: E., or stone, DICKI 51
left the e. in the car. SNYD 15
ears: blast of war blows in our e.,
   SHAK 56
buzzing in my e.? BROWNI R 23
charms our e. GAY 3
close my e. JOHN H 1
drumming of the demon in their
   e. MACN 10
e. and hands GRAV 21
e. like errant wings, CHES 3
Eyes and e. and chin and nose,
   JUST 4
forehead and the little e.
   ROBI 15
hasn't any e. at all, WELL 2
held my e., DICKI 73
"Jug Jug" to dirty e.
   ELIOT T 122
lend me your e.!' CARRO 18
lost in your eyes, e., nose, and
   throat — KOCH 4
lovers' e. in hearing'
   SCOT WA 16
memories plague their e. LARK 2
mentions hell to e. polite.
   POPE A 104
My e. are called capacious
   RANS 29
no one's but your e.: YEATS 3
rabbit presses back her e.,
   LAWR 24
receive those charms/ With open
   e., CAREW 2
Their sharp e., JARR 2
tongue still edifies his e.,
   POPE A 22

voices were in all men's e.
   ARNO 34
was a shout about my e., CHES 4
earth: air, e., and skies; WORD 153
All the e., DOWL 1
all the seas of e., WHITM 28
Always, in e. and air. ROET 15
American e. RANDA D 4
bells on e. did ring UNKN 9
beneath the e. lie buried low,
   VERY 5
blessing of E. is toil. VAN DY 5
blithe e. die, JEFFE 43
bought/ Long since on e.,
   HERB G 70
bowels of the e., ROSE 2
brass, nor stone, nor e., nor
   boundless sea, SHAK 212
break e.'s sleep OWEN 27
buried past of the e., OSHA 4
Bury it certain fathoms in the e.
   SHAK 165
by morning/ Inherit the e.
   PLATH 67
cold E. wanderers BLAK 29
come from the e.'s inside LORD 3
come from the ends of the e.!
   KIPL 3
consumed with the E. BLAK 85
cope with heaven and e.
   WHITM 104
cover lightly, gentle e. JONS 22
covering/ E. in forgetful snow,
   ELIOT T 113
crumble the dark e., THOMA E 6
daughter of E. and Water,
   SHEL 25
Dawdling over the remorseless e.,
   SNOD 3
dead as e. SHAK 85
death/ Of his mother E., SITW 6
Demons out of the e. TATE A 12
dungy e. alike/ Feeds beast as
   man. SHAK 3
dust return to the e. BIBL, O.T. 6
dwellest in e. and sun,/ I have
   lived, NEWB 4
e. an Eden,/ Like the heaven
   above. CARN 2
E. and I gave you turquoise
   MOMA 5
e. And sea and air. STEVENS 21
e. burns brown. WALK 12
e. by the sky staid WHITM 76
E. cannot!" RANDS 4
e. compels, MACN 24
E. does not understand her child,
   MILLA 32
e. falls/ So in our hearts WILB 19
E. felt the wound, MILT 89
E. fills her lap WORD 72
e. has something yet to show,
   WORD 165

E. has waited for them, ROSE 4
e. in our day is our curse.
   LOWE R 10
E. is bursting into song, SORL 1
E. is but a star, FLEC 3
e. is covered thick BYRO 8
e. is rigid, MACL 9
E. is the Lord's, BIBL, O.T. 32
e.-lipped fissure LAWR 44
e. of majesty, SHAK 88
E., receive AUDE 43
e. shall be forgiven CLARE 6
e. shall slumber, TENN 76
e. so chilly; TENN 110
E. that blossomed SORL 2
E. that bore SORL 2
e. that lightly covers her.
   HERR 58
e. to ugly e., GRAV 23
e. turning into color, RUKE 2
e. was bettering slowly HARD 10
e. was but one thought —
   BYRO 11
E.'s affections and longings
   MANG 1
E.'s downtrodden and oppressed,
   BRYA 13
e.'s embrace/ May breed TENN 38
e.'s hubbub and strife LOWE J 7
e.'s human shores, KEAT 3
e.'s increase, foison plenty,
   SHAK 162
e.'s old and weary cry.
   YEATS 140, 141
E.'s shadows fly; SHEL 13
easie e. that covers her. HERR 13
ever passed on e.; ALEX 3
every man upon this e. MACA 3
everything on e. FROS 102
Examples gross as e. exhort me:
   SHAK 35
eyesight falling to e.,
   STEVENS 26
Father Time and Mother E.,
   MERR 3
fell to e., LONG 1, 2
flat E. becomes a Ball. BLAK 33
float up from the damnèd
   E., POE 30
flowers appear on the e.;
   BIBL, O.T. 72
flowery e. HERR 48
fowl be multiplied on the e.
   MILT 85
fowl fly above the e., MILT 85
fresh as the young e., BRYA 15
From sullen e., SHAK 194
gazing on the e.,/ Wandering
   companionless SHEL 88
get away from e. FROS 13
given,/ In agony, to the e. POE 17
glance from heaven to e.,
   SHAK 127

Glistring with dew; fragrant the
fertile e. MILT 76
Go e.-bound wilfully! HARD 28
gods of the e. and sea BLAK 71
good of the e. and sun,
WHITM 76
good relation to the e. MOMA 4
Great is my envy of you, e., in
your greed PETRA 7
great Society alone on E.,
WORD 116
grudge I am bearing the e.
PETRA 9
Harriet Tubman, / woman of e.,
HAYD 21
heaven and e. move together,
GINS 42
heaven-eyed creature sleeps in e.:
WORD 17
Heaven tries e. LOWE J 17
Heav'ns and E. MILT 46
Hell, e., and sin WESL C 2
high heaven and e. ail HOUS 24
I in e. am rotten; SHAK 216
I laid the foundations of the e.?
BIBL, O.T. 13
judge the ends of the e.;
BIBL, O.T. 8
just touches e. LAWR 19
kind seed-receiving e. ROCH 15
laid her in e. CAREW 5
lap of E. GRAY 12
Laughing on the Great E.
SNYD 8
leaveth her eggs in the e.,
BIBL, O.T. 16
left your souls on e.! KEAT 2
lie with e. above, HOUS 22
Lifts e. to heaven, CRAS 5
lonely E. amid the balls EMER 9
lovelier flower/ On e. WORD 48
lust of e. below, CLARE 14
made of e. and sea HOUS 20
make the e. devour SHAK 189
Man marks the e. BYRO 2
Man of baser E. didst make,
OMAR 1
mirror of the acts of e. KINN 17
more than the E., RANDS 4
more things in heaven and e.,
SHAK 29
Moved e. and heaven, TENN 135
moves the nearest to the naked e.
CAMPB R 6
My E., DANI G 1
(never again on e. WHITM 107
never dream, till E. BRON 10
nothing on e. but laundry,
WILB 24
Now lies the E. all Danaë to the
stars, TENN 109
O e., what changes hast thou
seen! TENN 55

O Mary, marry e., LOWE R 10
of e. or mold celestiall, MARL 11
Oh! to e. heart GINS 44
on e. the air of paradise. MICH 3
on e.'s bed, SORL 3
only dwelling on e. WORD 126
our e. is a tomb! BROWNI R 26
Out of the e. MASE 6
over the whole e. WHITM 75
peace on e., LONG 11, 12
people e. sky stars, OHAR 19
pilgrim I on e. perplext, BRAD 1
poetry of e. KEAT 58
police the e., LOWE R 52
put on e. a little space, BLAK 98
ran sprinkling on e.'s floor
BRID R 15
round e.'s imagined corners,
DONN 5
sad old e. WILC 1
sagged ominously upon the e.
GRAV 22
scraped puffs from the e.
DICKEY 23
sense and worth, o'er a' the e.,
BURN 27
serious house on serious e.
LARK 6
shuddering from the quest./ E.
being so good, BROWNI R 42
Simple as soil yet crowded as e.
WILB 36
sleeping e. was fair. BRON 3
specious deeds on e., MILT 59
summer clothe the general e.
COLE SAM 16
sweet spontaneous/ e. CUMM 32
terrified at the E., WHITM 98
they walk the e., VERY 1
thirsty e. soaks up the rain,
COWL 1
This blessed plot, this e.,
SHAK 88
this e., this grave, this dust,
RALEG 4
till e. was but a name. CLARE 15
too good for e., JONS 8
Truth, crushed to e., BRYA 3
turns e.'s smoothness rough,
BROWNI R 73
twice already on e. KINN 13
'Twixt e. and paradise, LINC 1
Universal Soul/ Of heaven and e.!
THOMS J (1700–1748) 6
Virginia,/ E.'s only paradise.
DRAY 17
wandering/ Between e. and sky,
DAVIS 4
we grow, we turn to e., WEBS 1
Were you the e., dear Love,
SYLV 2
wide e. o'er, WHITT 29

wish'd Bridegroom of the e.
HERB CH 3
with one hand did fling/ Dew on
the e., SHEL 77
wretched We, Poets of E.!
COWL 11
Yours is the E. KIPL 8
earthen: Lip of this poor e. Urn
OMAR 6
Spends on the e. hide, WILB 13
earthly: amid no e. moans, POE 13
dazle now this e., MILT 97
e. mothers waiting, sleeplessly.
STEVENS 60
e. power doth then show
SHAK 123
e. things is but vanity: UNKN 90
e. turmoil grows, ARNO 46
honor to an e. king; UNKN 313
touch of e. years. WORD 49
earthquake: against the garage's e.
LOWE R 17
hour of the E. shock! HOLM 9
plague and e., TENN 90
rumbling like an e., WHITM 102
earth's: e.'s as cauld's the mune
MACDI 4
E.'s the right place for love:
FROS 13
ease: another's loss of e., BLAK 58
at my e. observing WHITM 74
attained with e., DANI S 18
bowers of innocence and e.,
GOLD 2
domestic e., MILT 111
dream of rural e., CRAB 6
e. an old man SNOD 6
e. in Casey's manner THAY 2
E. me with death DONN 23
e. my woman SNOD 6
give us e. ARNO 33
having e. me given, HERR 51
live with e. POPE A 6
lives at e. that freely lives!
BARBO 1
move at e. NIMS 3
Muse but served to e. some
friend, POPE A 14
pleasure loves to pay/ Tribute to
e.; WORD 63
sense of pleasant e. BROWNI E 9
toyes, to give my heart some e.:
HERR 18
True e. in writing comes from
art, POPE A 28
with e. o'ercome; WESL C 2
with joyful e. SORL 2
young enthusiast quits his e. for
fame; JOHN S (1709–1784) 17
youth and e. have taught to
glose. SHAK 87
eased: e. My dim dears BROO G 18

flowers that did in E. bloom;
FRENE 6
He sighed for E., VAUG 5
loss of E., MILT 46
other E., demi-Paradise, SHAK 88
Through E. took their solitary
way. MILT 108
When the birds of E. sang?
CULL 5
Edens: E. ere yet over-run;
MELV 22
million E. fall MUIR 11
edge: At the sea-down's e. SWIN 10
borrowing dulls the e. of
husbandry. SHAK 24
e. of doom. SHAK 232
e. of the world JOHN J 2
gauzy e. of paradise, SEXT 11
his keener Eye/ The Axes e. did
try: MARV 22
rip the e. off any ideal or dream.
MACN 2
edges: gilt rubs off the e. BISH 34
teeth break off at the e. HARJ 3
edict: Spurn at his e., SHAK 98
edifices: will proportion thee/ With
other e., JONS 37
edifies: tongue still e. his ears,
POPE A 22
editorial: into an e. office SIMP 9
educated: of the e. mind. SNYD 42
education: e. marriage nervous
breakdown, GINS 21
furniture/ Of e., SHAP 28
Edward: E., E.? UNKN 85
winding-sheet of E.'s race.
GRAY 5
'eed: never e. naught else." KIPL 11
eel: e.'s/ Oil of water body,
HUGH T 4
eels: For dressing e., or shoeing
horses. PRAE 1
Effects: E. of necessary Law!
DRYD 1
effete: English are e. COWA 2
effluence: Bright e. of bright
essence MILT 63
e. Divine. BLAK 37
our life a ruling e. ARNO 17
Effund: E. your albid hausts,
HOLM 1
egg: Killers from the e.:
HUGH T 10
new-laid/ e. LEVE 15
old e. of my desire is broken,
UNKN 230
eggs: Butter and e. CALV 2
e. under your skin. NASH 10
four light-green e. WHITM 64
Lays e. inside a paper bag.
ISHE 1

leaveth her e. in the earth,
BIBL, O.T. 16
plate of ham and e. SAND 22
Eglamour: Sir E., that worthy
knight, ROWL 1
Eglentyne: cleped madame E.
CHAU 13
egret: white blacklegged e.,
AMMO 6
Egypt: down in E. land, UNKN 115
Helen's beauty in a brow of E.
SHAK 127
old hushed E. and its sands,
HUNT 6
Egyptian: cool jazz nor devoured E.
heroes, OHAR 10
E.'s gold mist LOWE J 9
eidolon: e., named Night, POE 16
eie: essence subject to the e.,
MARL 11
eies: censur'd by our e. MARL 9
Eight: College E. and their trainer
NEWB 3
e.-limbed and e.-handed HILT 1
E. maids a-milking, UNKN 281
e. stranded whales MOOR M 29
heavy e.-wheeler UNKN 53
I was e. and very small, CULL 13
kept e. score men UNKN 153
eighteen: These e. years, LONG 14
Eighteenth: E. battle, and he
sixteen!) TICK 1
e. of April, in Seventy-five;
LONG 43
eighth: e. day of Christmas,
UNKN 281
Our noble King, King Henery the
e., UNKN 221
eighty: Young, at e. BYRO 36
Eildon: All underneath the E. Tree.
UNKN 246
down by the E. Tree. UNKN 245
either: e. grew a portion of the
other; JONS 42
Ekenhead: Leander, Mr. E., and I
did. BYRO 44
el: old sixth/ avenue/ e.; CUMM 38
El Greco: startling E. MOOR 28
elated: e. after childbirth! BOGA 5
elation: Lord of the world's e.,
CARM 2
my heart's e., CARM 1
elbow: sewn short at e. OWEN 15
elbows: knees and e. are only glued
BLAK 113
old bubble-head style,/ Their
rubber e. UPDI 1
elde: youthe and e. is often at
debat. CHAU 51
elder: e. dames, thy haughty peers,
BRYA 12
to my e. daughter. THOMA E 11

to the e. world, LOWE J 14
truth a little e. is; DONN 50
elders: red-eyed e. watching,
STEVENS 34
eldest: e. cam and push'd her in.
UNKN 30
primal e. curse upon 't, SHAK 34
Eldorado: E. in the grass
LOWE J 15
In search of E. POE 18
elect: e., the elected LOWE R 25
elected: I have e.—One DICKI 113
Electra: sad E.'s poet MILT 125
electric: concentration of the e.
chair— LOWE R 32
e. storm/ of the vibrator LEVI 4
their e. messages, KNIG 7
electricity: metrasol e.
hydrotherapy GINS 15
Moloch whose soul is e. GINS 17
shot e. Through the rest. KNIG 5
elegance: curious nervous e.
KIRK 1
e. also is force; LOWE J 6
elegant: It's so e. So intelligent
ELIOT T 125
with e. quickness. SMAR 2
Elegies: E. to Trumpet-sounds,
MONTROSE 1
e. Of birds. KINN 9
elegy: word is e. HASS 2
element: e. bearable to no mortal,
BISH 4
Pain has an e. of blank—
DICKI 117
to the e., TATE A 11
elemental: e. when he died,
ROBI 38
subsists by e. strife; POPE A 68
elementary: final direction of the e.
town THOMA D 41
elements: By time and the e.;
CRAN H 47
e. of worth MACDI 2
equally/ Earnest e. of nature.
JEFFE 7
left the rest/ to e., HUGO 4
Passions are the e. of Life.
POPE A 68
place among the e. PLATH 61
reconciles/ Discordant e.,
WORD 96
self-made from e. least visible
BISH 20
elephant: e.-colored rocks,
ROET 42
e. sneezed UNKN 7
e., the huge old beast, LAWR 6
Funnyface Or E. AUDE 60
He thought he saw an E.,
CARRO 29
hot e. hearts/ grow full LAWR 7

see the e. jump the fence.
UNKN 135

there was an e., RICHA L 2

Elephants: E. walking LINK 1
e. with their fog-colored skin
MOOR M 19

elephone: I mean an e. RICHA L 2

Eleusis: brought whores for E.
POUN 11

elevate: thoughts more e., MILT 60

elevator: e. man he knowing
CORS 4

Eleven: E. for the 'leven that went
to heaven UNKN 52
E. ladies dancing, UNKN 284

eleventh: e. day of Christmas,
UNKN 284

Elf: met a little E.-man, BANG 1
wee E. Smiled a wee smile,
HERF 2

elfin: e. from the green grass,
POE 2

Elfland: horns of E. faintly
blowing! TENN 112

Elisa: great E.'s glorious name
SPENS 47
laye/ Of fayre E., SPENS 50
"Of fayre E. be your silver song,
SPENS 53

'Ell: marched — six — weeks in E.
KIPL 4

Ellinor: Fair E. in the choir;
UNKN 179

ellum: from the "Settler's e.," —
HOLM 6

elm: single e.-tree bright ARNO 43

elmen: lofty e. swanges; CHAT 2

elms: 'Behind the e. last night,'
PRIO 14
moan of doves in immemorial e.,
TENN 107
Ye e. that wave MELV 15

Eloquence: Wit, E., and Poetry,
COWL 15

eloquent: e. tum-tum, GILB 2
that old man e.; — MILT 122

Elpenor: friend E., POUN 5

else: e. mistaking; SHAK 220

elsewhere: Hath had e. its setting,
WORD 69

eludes: e. my grasp, AMMO 9

elvers: Like e. in ponds, ROET 48

elves: e. of hills, brooks, standing
lakes, and groves, SHAK 164

Elvira: E. pulls at supper?'
GILB 12

Elysium: E. is as far DICKI 20

'em: hasty noise he spoke e.;
BUTL 5

emancipated: than less/ e. evening
CUMM 22

embalmed: e. the days, MCKA 4

embalmer: soft e. of the still
midnight, KEAT 67

embark: When I e.; TENN 10

embattled: e. farmers stood
EMER 11

ember: separate dying e. POE 35

embers: Her feet like e.; SHEL 78
in our e. Is something that doth
live, WORD 79

emblem: — e. of motion and
power — WHITM 100
e. of themselves in plum or pear.
JONS 36
here in e. shown: WESL S 1

Emblematical: E. of love and war?
YEATS 45

Emblems: All Love's E. FLET J 6

embodied: stand/ perfectly e.,
GUNN 9

embollen: then e. clangs, CHAT 2

embossed: e. by silvery images
OHAR 2

embost: In the Arabian woods e.,
MILT 117

embowed: high e. roof, MILT 18

embrac'd: my Arm's e. my Lass;
GAY 4

embrace: always e. things,
OHAR 19
earth's e. May breed TENN 33
e. me she inclined, MILT 34
none, I think, do there e.
MARV 34
odour, light, e., FLET G YO 1

embraced: By my soft nervelets
were e.; HERR 68

embracing: e. from behind,
HOPE A 1

embroideries: Covered with e.
YEATS 30

Embrouded: E. was he, CHAU 9

Emeralds: E. big as half the
county. LAND 7

Emergency: In an E. DICKI 22

emerges: body, like a worn sea-shell/
e. LAWR 42

emerging: him e., SNYD 6

Emerson: "There comes E. first,
LOWE J 8

eminence: that bad e.; MILT 58
upon yon e. our pace COWP 17

eminent: no greater, but more e.,
DONN 41
proudly e. Stood like a Tower;
MILT 57

Emmet: E.'s Inch and Eagle's Mile
BLAK 10

Emong: Kent and Christendome/ E.
the muses where I rede and
ryme; WYAT 25

emotion: heart less bounding at e.
ARNO 45
unemotional, and all e.,
MOOR M 26

emotional: e. shorthand
MOOR M 9

emparadised: Themselves e.
NEME 1

emperor: e. and clown: KEAT 50
E. of France?' KIPL 23
e. of ice-cream. STEVENS 10

emphasis: stamping the words with
e., SPEND 16

emphatic: Sophias are not so e.,
BYRO 47

empire: debated e. of the world,
LUCR 2
distentions of E., POUN 30
E. and Gandhi. NASH 6
heavily thickening to e.,
JEFFE 37
Life, Joy, E. and Victory.
SHEL 58
Neptune's e. stands SHAK 20
Roman E. stood appalled:
YEATS 117
thy dread E., POPE A 2
Westward the course of e.
BERK 1
wide arch/ Of the ranged e. fall!
SHAK 3

empires: e. are declining, SNOD 9
how wide your e. are; SHIR 4
spur away o'er e. BYRO 21

employ'd: eternal Verse e.
COWL 12

employed: single talent well e.
JOHN S (1709–1784) 3

employment: e. by authors
NASH 18
e. may afford. DAY 1
e. to the artisan. BELL 15
in his e. GILB 37
terms of e., SPEND 20

employs: golden shafts e., MILT 78

emptied: e., and fill'd again.
WHITM 115
E. of its poetry. AUDE 43
e. some dull opiate KEAT 44

empties: e. our police courts,
GILB 50

emptiness: adds to e., POPE A 16
e. of ages in his face, MARK 5
Eternal smiles his e. betray,
POPE A 10

empty: Beat an e. barrel LIND V 8
beds are e. of delight,
CAMPB R 7
candles gutter by an e. altar,
LOWE R 5
Don puffed and e., BELL 12
e. cup, a flight of uncarpeted
stairs. MILLA 37

e. doorway and a maple leaf.
MACL 2

e. grows every bed. BERRYM 9

e. happy body SNYD 23

e. house of the stare. YEATS 99

e. victual-wagons up the street
ALBI 1

e. words of a dream BRID R 6

hands drop white and e. NIMS 4

hollow e. Soul BUTL 7

Honour but an e. bubble.
DRYD 5

idle singer of an e. day. MORR 2

Life is but an e. dream! —
LONG 35

long will stand the e. plate,
HOUS 30

old perplexity an e. purse,
YEATS 24

There is the e. chapel,
ELIOT T 151

think in this e. world LAWR 30

voices singing out of e. cisterns
ELIOT T 150

With e. hand men may no hawkes
lure. CHAU 86

with their e. spaces FROS 36

emptying: e. of quivers, SWIN 4

Empyræum: E. of pure Harmony.
CRAS 6

empyrean: Grain-tinctured,
drenched in e. light;
WORD 102

enchain'd: hold me e. WHITM 30

enchant: e. your generous Mind;
DRYD 1

enchanted: as holy and e.
COLE SAM 20

dream itself e. me: YEATS 28

e./ by a repulsive clew, RUKE 3

e. me with a single kiss KOCH 4

E. to a stone YEATS 52

"I am e., CRAN S 6

is an e. thing MOOR M 17

soul is an e. Boat SHEL 56

Enchanting: E. shell! GRAY 25

Lovely e. language, HERB G 35

enchantment: power of/ strong e.
MOOR M 18

scene of e. more dear, MOOR T 8

sense/ Without e., ELIOT T 68

enchantress: Like an e. MARV 15

enclin'd: head a while e., MILT 114

enclose: things which e. me,
CUMM 48

Thou all sweetness dost e.
CAMPI 15

encomium: e., as a change. CALV 6

encroached: trade had suddenly e.
DICKI 102

Encroaching: eye concedes to/ E.
horizon, HEAN 1

encumber: e.'d with his hood, — /
Explaining Metaphysics
BYRO 14

shall not his brain e. EMER 33

end: all to no e. WILLI 4

appointed E., BROO R 10

At once the source, and e.,
POPE A 25

beginning is often the e.
ELIOT T 71

beyond the wide world's e.:
UNKN 265

bow and accept the e. FROS 93

bring my thoughts to an e.
SMIT ST 9

come in the e. despondency and
madness. WORD 121

death could never e. it:
AMMO 17

Death is the e. of life; TENN 86

e. is Life. MACN 26

e. is never wrought; SIDN 39

e. is where we start from.
ELIOT T 71

e. no eye can reach. MILT 105

e./ Of a love or a season?
FROS 93

e. of everything. PLATH 14

e. of joy and all prosperity
HAWE 1

e. of lying down together.
LEWI 7

e. of the monk, UNKN 7

e./ The heart-ache SHAK 39

e. this life of mine? MASE 7

e./ Was not ignoble. WORD 95

e. with swelled feet." LOWE R 16

envy strangely rues his e.,
GREV/DYER 2

eternall Glasse,/ Where time doth
e., GREV 8

fairest things have fleetest e.,
THOMP F 1

grave/ Should e. thy pilgrimage
HARD 44

Has heart to make an e.,
WILB 37

hell between him and the e.
ROBI 19

just or larger e., MELV 17

latter e. of joy is woe. CHAU 68

long-wished-for e., TENN 95

love hath an e.; SWIN 21

make and e., TENN 131

minutes hasten to their e.;
SHAK 209

Motive and e. GRAV 6

no law, no meaning, and no e.
WORD 109

one e., which is always present.
ELIOT T 19

passed to the e. of a vista,
POE 49

pledged event is still the same:/
Matter in e. MELV 8

Practical to the e., WILLI 32

quiet-coloured e. of evening
BROWNI R 47

sans Singer, and — sans E.!
OMAR 4

slaughtered and made an e.,
NEWB 2

song, from beginning to e.,
LONG 3

sorrows e. SHAK 195

styled by his e., JONS 42

Such e. true lovers have.
BLAK 40

This is the e., GINS 25

till I e. my song. ELIOT T 129

to make an e. is to make a
beginning. ELIOT T 71

trouble all will e., FOST 2

very e. of harvest! SHAK 162

waiting for the e.? EMPS 8

we cannot wholly e. ARNO 17

What a sublime e. JEFFE 44

work mine e. upon their senses
SHAK 165

world is not sweet in the e.;
SWIN 23

world may e. tonight?
BROWNI R 39

world's at an e., DAVE 5

wrath did e. BLAK 78

endanger: e. me with the fevers
WHITM 97

ende: every shires e. Of Engelond
CHAU 5

endeared: humble happiness e. each
scene. GOLD 1

endearing: e. young charms,
MOOR T 2

endeavor: By no e. GILB 34

e. to correct. GILB 6

Setting e. in continual motion,
SHAK 55

endeavors: high e. are an inward
light WORD 4

endeavour: baffled hand with vain
e. COLL 5

wit for to e. WYAT 5

endeavoured: e. to say CARRO 16

ended: e. her life and mine.
LAWR 17

lengthy service e., HORA 8

meal is e., ELIOT T 136

revels now are e. SHAK 163

Ending: E. my vigil strange
WHITM 107

that has e.; BROO R 12

endless: Closed his eyes in e. night.
GRAY 30

desire is full/ of e. distances.
HASS 3

e. age. SHAK 229

E. are effete COWA 2

E. cut on Greek and Latin,
BUTL 4

E. heaven. BROO R 14

E. is what you speak! CARRO 22

E. unofficial rose; BROO R 16

fine old E. Tory times;
DICKEN 1

hold on the sentimental E.
MACN 5

in fluent E., GRAV 40

kissed by the E. dead. OWEN 28

My native E., SHAK 86

my page for E. B. HUGH L 17

our E. dead! SHAK 56

rolling E. drunkard CHES 14

rolling E. road. CHES 14

shed one E. tear/ O'er E. dust.
MACA 2

Theocritus written in E.,
LOWE J 7

Englishman: daughter of their sires/
Saved a captive E. THAC 2

remains an E.! GILB 20

Englishmen: Joan whom E. At
Rouen doomed VILL 3

like most E., BYRO 47

Mad dogs and E. COWA 1

engraft: e. you new. SHAK 187

engrave: blacke beames such
burning markes e. SIDN 15

engross: e. the present and dominate
memory. YEATS 28

Enhances: druidic difference/ E.
nature DICKI 24

E. the chances SITW 3

enisled: sea of life e., ARNO 41

enjailed: e. my tongue, SHAK 86

enjoy: Beggars e., GREE 1

E. such liberty. LOVE 5

e. the sunset, WHITM 19

kings neglect that private men e.!
SHAK 58

To e. is to obey. POPE A 127

With what I most e. SHAK 194

enjoyed: still to be e., KEAT 39

enjoying: e. the freedom AMMO 9

enjoyment: capacity for innocent e.
GILB 37

Thyself thy own e. WORD 23

enjoys: beauty ne'er e.: POPE A 9

every flower/ E. WORD 38

enkindleth: nobleness e. nobleness.
LOWE J 21

enlarged: e. by belladonna,
MERR 11

Stars by the sun are not e.,
DONN 41

enlightened: e. by the vollied glare;/
Or shame survive, MELV 18

e. to perceive DICKI 118

enlightenment: highest perfect e.
SNYD 25

enmities: substance in our e.
YEATS 99

enmity: of e. disarmed, MILT 90

enormous: swooning out of an e.
willow hamper MERR 10

enough: Beauty is not e. MILLA 36

belly, God send thee good ale e.;
STEVENSO W 3

blessed Land of Room E.
VAN DY 3

e. for man to know POPE A 86

e. of action, and of motion
TENN 88

e. of sorrow before death —
YEATS 148

e. to provoke GILB 58

God, if this were e.,
STEVENSO R 16

grief e. for thee. GREE 2

if that were e.? STEVENSO R 17

if you're poor e. WELC 1

it was never e. AUDE 24

'Tis not e. POPE A 28

world e., and time, MARV 33

world is/ not with us e. LEVE 18

enquire: stayd not to e. MILT 65

Wise/ E., define, distinguish, teach,
devise, ROCH 16

enrapture: O unworn world e. me,
KAVA 2

enscrolled: answer had not been e.
SHAK 119

ensign: beauty's e. yet/ Is crimson
SHAK 152

image was my e.: GRAV 16

tear her tattered e. down!
HOLM 17

enskyment: what an e.; JEFFE 44

enslaved: e.-by-convention,
POUN 24

soul e. MARV 11

Ensnared: E. with flowers, I fall on
grass. MARV 17

entangle: e. in that golden snare:
SPENS 12

entanglement: e. of watery bodies
WILLI 48

entangles: with smoky wings, e.
them. HILL G 1

enter: dared not e., DICKI 71

e., and leave, alone, THOMA E 13

E. into his gates with
thanksgiving, BIBL, O.T. 50

e. touch entirely. SEXT 14

those who e. death DODG 2

entered: e. the Ark MACDI 5

enterprise: e. In walking naked.
YEATS 31

e. of martial kind, GILB 14

enterprising: e. burglar isn't
burgling, GILB 38

her e. movements, GILB 53

enters: child who e. life DODG 2

dear Christ e. in. BROO P 6

e. some alien cage JOHN G 1

entertain: e. him always like a
stranger, UNKN 315

entertained: Once e. you. ROET 38

entertaining: I've an e. snigger,
GILB 9

entertainment: dull thy palm with
e. SHAK 23

enthroned: e. between her subject
seas.' LOWE J 14

e. in the hearts of kings,
SHAK 123

Enthusiast: loved E. wooed,
COLL 6

young e. quits his ease for fame;
JOHN S (1709–1784) 17

enthusiasts: champions and e.
MELV 17

enticed: e. oft to treason, SURR 2

thoughts e. mine eye MUND 2

enticing: her e. parts. UNKN 141

entirely: delivered e. from
humanity SMIT ST 5

enter touch e. SEXT 14

not e. beautiful; YEATS 108

rain/ Possesses us e., LEWI 2

entomb'd: thou hast e., MILT 44

entombed: spring e. in autumn lies;
KING H 5

entrails: poison'd e. throw.
SHAK 111

rave/ Over his e., MARV 15

entrance: e. to a quarrel; SHAK 23

stark dignity of/ e. WILLI 36

entranced: she moves e. SPEND 7

entrances: their exits and their e.;
SHAK 11

entreat: harder grows the more I
her e.? SPENS 9

entreaties: mother's e.; WHITM 8

entrechat: with an e. perfectly
achieved WILLI 1

entrust: e. them to a safe GRAV 29

Entuned: E. in hir nose CHAU 14

entwined: there it e. UNKN 180

entwines: e. with you. RODG 3

enumerate: e. old themes?
YEATS 27

envelop'd: e. well his form,
WHITM 107

envelope: Open the e. quickly,
WHITM 16

envelopes: ground opens up and e.
me BARA 15

envenime: al wol e., CHAU 88

envied: mouth, dear child, is e. of
the bees. UNKN 252

envies: only the various e.,
AUDE 50

envious: built to e. show, JONS 35

enviously: fate so e. debars,
MARV 7

Envy: Dead men may e. OWEN 3
(E. be silent and attend!);
POPE A 109
e., listlessness, or sport,
BROWNI R 16
e. of less happier lands; SHAK 88
e. strangely rues his end,
GREV/DYER 2
e. the intransigence MACN 3
e.'s snaky eye, SIDN 4
Great is my e. of death PETRA 8
Great is my e. of you, earth, in
your greed PETRA 7
Hatred out of E. by Despair.
CUNN J 3
I e. no man's nightingale or
spring; HERB G 46
I e. not FULL 4
silence the e. in my thought;
YEATS 97
Toil, e., want,
JOHN S (1709–1784) 18
ephemeral: flat e. pamphlet
AUDE 90
grave/ Proves the child e.:
AUDE 54
epic: roaring, e., ragtime tune
LIND V 9
Epicurean: E. Animal!) COWL 3
epidemics: carriers of her e.
GRAV 2
epistemology: e. of loss,
BERRYM 2
Epitaph: E. in Blood and Wounds!
MONTROSE 1
For e., in foliage, HERR 53
live your e. to make, SHAK 216
epitaphy: hideous e.? RANS 24
epitome: blank confusion! true e.
WORD 109
Their curious e.; STOD 2
equal: admitted to that e. sky,
POPE A 60
Beauties e., but excel our
Strength. DRYD 29
Both e. hurt, SIDN 2
e. among human kind HARD 7
E. justice, right and law,
BENN H 2
e. syllables alone require,
POPE A 24
e. temper of heroic hearts,
TENN 135
Extoll him e. MILT 59
mine e., my guide, and mine
acquaintance. BIBL, O.T. 39
ne'er be e. powers: TENN 15
poem should be e. to: MACL 2
sex not e. seemed; MILT 72
stains its e. gleam, EMER 49
tides have e. times SOUTHW 8
equall: loving thou mayst loved be
with e. crime.' SPENS 34

equally: Man shall spend e.
SPEND 18
so e. join'd. DRYD 6
Equilibrists: E. lie here; RANS 17
equine: e. amphibious creatures
MOOR M 2
equinox: bright blaze of Autumn's
e. WALK 11
equipage: march in ranks of better
e.: SHAK 196
equity: people with e.
BIBL, O.T. 47
eradicate: plants new set to be e.,
BRAD 10
erasers: kept our e. in order.
POUN 29
erasures: gradual e. Of flesh
MOSS 4
E're: E. their story die. HARD 30
nor e. again shall be MACA 1
erect: drew the Head e. DICKI 100
God-like e., with native honour
MILT 71
house on high e., BRAD 12
keep thy Sword e.: MARV 23
souls stand up e. and strong,
BROWNI E 10
erected: fleshed, fair, e. indivisible.
BISH 20
erecter: make one e. MOOR M 26
ergo: Sentio e. sum: SHAP 23
Erith: men in the village of E.
UNKN 89
Erl-King: E. has seized me —
GOET 1
erles: two stout e. did meet,
UNKN 61
ermine: e. muffled mouth and chin;
WYLI 3
Eros: E., builder of cities, AUDE 34
Of E. and of dust, AUDE 78
erotic: e. affirmations. RIVE 1
e. as an ape, SHAP 21
err: reasoning but to e.; POPE A 78
To e. is human, POPE A 35
erratic: readings will grow e.?
LARK 10
erring: e. Reason's spite,
POPE A 58
my e. fellow creatures, GILB 6
rod/ To check the e., WORD 83
error: e. bred in the bone AUDE 77
e. is all in the not done,
POUN 23
E., wounded, writhes in pain
BRYA 3
even in E. COWL 13
in endless e. hurled; POPE A 78
our e. lies; POPE A 66
way of e., RALEG 5
errors: in thee a thousand e. note,
SHAK 239

Repent, repent, and from old e.
turn!' DRUM 7
ers: amidde the e. he smoot:
CHAU 58
kisse his e. er that he scape.
CHAU 56
kiste hir naked e., CHAU 53
out his e. he putteth prively,
CHAU 56
erst: e. from heat did canopy the
herd SHAK 186
erthe: Watrynge the e. PETRA 1
erump: excede, — evade, — e.!
HOLM 1
escalator: intent e. lifts a serenade
CRAN H 32
escape: assured of e.; AUDE 32
e. that fatal Mama — GINS 29
e. the knife. FULL 2
Never more shall I e., WHITM 67
possibilities/ of e. open: AMMO 8
secures/ E. from the weekday
time. MACN 22
silent from life e. WHITM 17
struggle to e.? KEAT 37
Summer made her light e.
DICKI 8
what I sought to e., WHITM 31
escaped: e. my smile. WYLI 6
escapt: game from him e. away,
SPENS 16
eschewing: e. books and tasks,
WHITT 7
ese: for office and for e. CHAU 96
especially: e. to women, BYRO 21
e. women. SMIT ST 6
esperance: Stands still in e.,
SHAK 77
espouse: e. the everlasting Sea.
WORD 91
espoused: my e., my latest found,
MILT 79
espy: then the heaven e.
HERB G 28
essence: Bright effluence of bright
e. MILT 63
e. of wheelness SHAP 5
e. subject to the eie, MARL 11
essential: Against the e. reality
JEFFE 7
E. Presence,
THOMS J (1700–1748) 6
more e. thing. DICKI 120
established: reputable walks of old
e. trees SNOD 8
estat: keep eek myn e.," CHAU 88
estate: Contented with thine own
e.; MARTIA 2
Hell unto a high e. POE 30
I came to man's e. SHAK 177
monarch's high e.; POE 22
estates: Slipper toppe/ Of courtes
e., SENE 1

exhalation: fall/ Like a bright e.
FLET/SHAK 4
Like some frail e.; SHEL 21
exhal'd: my verse e. thy name,
CAREW 7
exhale: Mown stalks e., LARK 7
exhausted: dark e. eye, KINS 5
empty cisterns and e. wells
ELIOT T 150
E. Worlds,
JOHN S (1709–1784) 5
exhibits: Nature thus/ To bodily
sense e., WORD 117
exhort: Examples gross as earth e.
me: SHAK 35
Exhorting: E. us to slaughter,
LEWI 1
exile: beaten out my e. POUN 51
Jew who died in e. AUDE 25
Like a king in e., LAWR 45
Versing, like an e., KINS 3
Exiled: E. Thucydides knew
AUDE 72
exiles: band of e. HEMA 4
e. from our fathers' land. GALT 1
her name/ Mother of E. LAZA 1
exist: where the two e. in twain
FROS 125
existence: all the conditions of its
e., BISH 30
excellent lovely sunflower e.!
GINS 35
e. like a Pirouot FROS 137
make fecund my e. OHAR 8
poem/ of his e. WILLI 32
exists: devil/ Still e., SIMI 1
light e. in spring DICKI 101
loveliness e., SNOD 7
vain, if it e. MOOR M 41
exits: their e. and their entrances;
SHAK 11
exonerate: emergence to e.
ROBI 31
expand: e. my privacies THOR 5
expansive: Spring's an e. time:
ROSS C 37
expatiate: anxious to e. DAIC 2
E. free POPE A 58
expect: e. as much. BROWNI R 34
neither praise e., nor censure
fear: DRYD 20
short-end comes down/ When you
least e. it. SIMI 2
wise e., the sorrowful invite,
DAVE 1
expectancy: e. and rose of the fair
state, SHAK 33
expectation: awed with dreadful e.
LUCR 2
No e. fails there, YEATS 73
expected: awaited the e. guest.
ELIOT T 135

death is e., STEVENS 3
I had e. always SPEND 22
expedient: e. and wicked stones.
SHAP 4
expendable: savages, e. as Jews?
WALC 2
expending: e. of powers AUDE 90
expenditure: much e. justified
SPEND 20
expense: At the e. of man?
GRAV 27
e. of spirit SHAK 236
moan th' e. SHAK 195
save e.." HERB G 43
expensive: sleek, e. girls I teach,
SNOD 4
somewhere e. SIMP 7
experience: By sad e. KING H 7
e./ of carrying a stick?
MOOR M 7
e. sweet and sad, WHITM 116
e. taught me SNOD 1
heavy with useless e., rich/ with
suspicion, RICH 12
Some call E. DICKI 67
experienced: die e. ere three days be
spent — MELV 18
experiences: in thy e., WHITM 105
expiate: death my days should e.
SHAK 190
something to e.;/ A pettiness.
LAWR 46
Expiates: E. the joy and woe
SHEL 82
expire: deathbed whereon it must
e., SHAK 215
expired: body's work's e.:
SHAK 193
expiring: cold friction of e. sense
ELIOT T 68
explain: asked them to e.
SMIT ST 3
e. his Explanation. BYRO 14
e. to them his prayer ASHB 4
How you e. that? — BERRYM 7
I'm glad I can't e. LARK 17
Too much e. ELIOT T 5
Explaining: encumber'd with his
hood, — / E. Metaphysics
BYRO 14
explode: does it e.? HUGH L 10
e. through my lips LORD 1
exploding: poets e. AUDE 89
exploits: anticipat'st my dread e.
SHAK 113
exploration: We shall not cease from
e. ELIOT T 73
exploring: end of all our e.
ELIOT T 73
E. hands encounter ELIOT T 136
explosion: Wives saw men of the e.
LARK 11
Exposed: E. the fool, SWIF 22

oft e. his own. SWIF 24
young clear neck e., RUKE 8
express: e. how much they prais'd,
MILT 59
life is what none can e., STANL 3
express'd: antique pen would have
e. SHAK 228
expressed: ne'er so well e.;
POPE A 21
expression: e./ expresses hiding:
AMMO 12
spoil no e. LAWR 48
expressions: e. be of inward evils.
GREV 5
exprest: her least things e.,
THOMP F 5
expropriated: Of the e. mycologist.
MAHON 2
exquisite: distills such e. winds
WHITM 98
his e. sense LOWE J 7
into e. disciplines MERR 9
She is, in fact, e. SEXT 2
source of an e. pleasure, WOOD 2
with e. breathing SHAP 6
exquisitely: how e. fine! POPE A 71
How e. minute, TENN 100
exsufflicate: e. and blown surmises,
SHAK 136
Extemporally: quick comedians/ E.
will stage us SHAK 10
extend: fingers thus e.; GILB 3
extended: face e. flat GILB 45
extensive: Let observation with e.
view, JOHN S (1709–1784) 15
extent: to any great e. HART 4
exterior: Thou, whose e. semblance
WORD 77
external: In all e. grace SHAK 205
Extinction: E. of each happy art
GRAV 23
extinguish't: Despis'd and thought
e. MILT 116
extirpate: e. the vipers, AYTOU 1
extol: join all ye creatures to e.
MILT 81
extracting: e. liquid sweet."
MILT 79
extravagant: flaunting e. quean,
SHERI 1
extreames: in e. lov'd and abhor'd.
CLEV 1
extreme: love's e./ Leander-like, —
DAVIE J 1
Perplex'd in the e.; SHAK 138
raging love with e. pain SURR 6
extremely: were you not e. sick?'
PRIO 14
extremes: e. of all extremes,
FORD J 1
Extremity: never, in E., DICKI 30
exuberant: e. voices of music,
JEFFE 6

blackness veiled his dizzy e.,
  SHEL 16
blear e., GRAV 1
Blear e. fallen from blue, RANS 5
Blinking out of silly e. HODG 3
blocked my e. DICKI 26
blood-hot e. TOOM 1
both his e. GRAV 21
bright green e. MONR 1
brown e. lower fell — WHITT 14
burn its golden e. HECH 7
cannot take his e. YEATS 109
Care less e., lips, and hands to
  miss. DONN 63
chain their e.; ARNO 39
close your e. with holy dread,
  COLE SAM 22
Closed his e. in endless night.
  GRAY 30
cluttered e. BARA 9
cold and caressable;/ his e. were
  red glass, BISH 14
curve, forsake our e. CRAN H 27
"Damn your e. BYRO 53
dazzle our e.? HILT 1
death, come close mine e.;
  GIBB 1
dialogue with e. CRAN H 51
Drink to me only with thine e.
  JONS 31
drop sleep on her e. UNKN 254
dying e. and lolling heads,
  SASS 2
Eastern e. to see, COWA 2
engend'red in the e. SHAK 121
e. agast MILT 61
e. are burning. AUDE 66
E. around him throwing, GAY 2
e., as black as sloe; UNKN 45
e., as hanged men's, turning the
  wrong way; ALBI 1
e. become the sunlight, WILB 6
e. big love-crumbs, CUMM 51
e. bloodshot with tears SHAP 20
e. can see, SHAK 188
e. did once inhabit SHAK 97
e. fast fixt MILT 114
e. flashing solemnly with hate,
  JOHN H 4
e. foreknowledge of death:
  SWIN 2
e. forever for me. WHITM 32
e. forget the tears LOWE J 19
e. give more light WHITM 91
E. glaze once — DICKI 54
e. gone gray/ from cramps
  HUGO 7
e./ In momentary wonder
  YEATS 7
e. like carbuncles, SHAK 30
e. like live coals, WOOL 2
e. like stars start from their
  spheres, SHAK 26

e. mid many wrinkles, YEATS 82
e. of a familiar compound ghost
  ELIOT T 65
e. of a mild savior. TATE J 2
e. of an eyewitness, KINN 11
e. of God not rarely look,
  COWP 22
e. of me: HERR 40
e. of men, SHAK 92
e. of my Annie. POE 25
e. of the dead, WHITM 76
e. reappear ELIOT T 47
e. that fix you ELIOT T 83
e. that petrified my brain,
  DARC 3
e. that saw not, LOWE J 13
E./ That sparkling blaz'd,
  MILT 53
e. the glow-worm lend thee
  HERR 32
e. were frosted starlight, GRAV 9
e. were made for seeing,
  EMER 42
Fascinated, my e. reverting
  WHITM 2
feral glint/ In the caught e.
  KIZE 2
five e. break. THOMA D 44
fixed forever in your closing e.,
  JARR 11
follow e. the steady keel,
  WHITM 45
from mine e. appear. SHAK 169
from those great e. WHITT 12
Get thee glass e., SHAK 81
girl with the staring e. JEFFE 8
Golden slumbers kiss your e.,
  DEKK/OTHE 1
gutters of the banked and staring
  e. WILB 13
has the secret/ e. KNIG 6
Have e. to wonder, SHAK 228
having e. yet never find TRAH 9
He gave us e. ALEX 2
he had no e. HECH 2
hid sorrow from mine e./ 11. Why
  died I not from the womb?
  BIBL, O.T. 10
His changing e. YEATS 22
his grandson's e. HARP 1
his realmless e. were closed;
  KEAT 20
horror-stricken e., KINS 4
image of thine e. ROSS D 3
in disgrace with fortune and men's
  e., SHAK 194
in her e. JOHN J 4
in his neighbors' e.? YEATS 146
In those fair e. UNKN 141
increasing prospect tires our
  wand'ring e. POPE A 34
insufficient e., forever sad:
  ROBI 6

inward e. illuminated MILT 116
July in her e. hath place,
  UNKN 6
June in her e., in her heart
  January. CAREW 15
keen e.,/ serviceable beak
  WILLI 31
lamping e. SPENS 2
land of darkness and blind e.
  VAUG 13
lift up mine e. unto the hills,
  BIBL, O.T. 58
liquid, anguished e. LAWR 24
little Cupid lose/ E. and ears and
  chin and nose, JUST 4
look'd but with divining e.,
  SHAK 223
lost in your e., ears, nose, and
  throat — KOCH 4
love thee with mine e.,
  SHAK 239
Love your e. that can see,
  JEFFE 19
lovers' e., FORD J 1
Lovers' e. are sharp SCOT WA 16
mechanic e. ROBI 30
mild e. command LAZA 1
million e., AUDE 79
mock our e. with air. SHAK 9
mocks me from her e.! PETRA 8
mustard scansions of the e.,
  CRAN H 53
my e. are blue; ROSS C 10
my e. were blue, LAND 12
My mistress' e. SHAK 237
night has a thousand e., BOUR 1
ope their golden e.: SHAK 17
open e. of the dead MERW 2
our sick e., EMER 5
out of his e. SILKI 2
Parched body, hollow e., DRUM 6
partake of the treat —/ E. and
  brains MELV 14
patient e., courageous hearts!
  GREN 2
Pearled wi' dew like fishes' e.,
  CLARE 3
pearls that were his e.:
  SHAK 156
pigs' e. followed him, BISH 36
Pressing lidless e. ELIOT T 126
ragged arms, the ragged heads
  and e. TATE A 13
rapt e. Fashioned a new world
  RANDA 4
rapt prophetic e., ARNO 12
rapt soul sitting in thine e.;
  MILT 16
Ruddy are his e. STEVENS 13
Sans teeth, sans e., sans taste,
  sans everything. SHAK 12
savage e. turned to a modest
  gaze SHAK 125

F

fadeth: after sunset f. in the west; SHAK 215

fading: all her f. sweets; SHAK 189
f. to white MONTA 5
fairy-gifts f. away. MOOR T 2
last of days/ Were f. ROBI 11
Upon a f. gleam, YEATS 153

fadom: fiftie f. deip, UNKN 228

faery: f. beam upon you, JONS 10
in f. lands forlorn. KEAT 50
'twas some f. place),
COLE SAM 43
With a f., hand in hand,
YEATS 144

faggot: f. of useless memories.
MACN 7

fail: concord shall not f.; WORD 8
f. by spirit or by sense. WILB 41
F. I alone, BROWNI R 40
friends f., and Princes frown,
WOTT 8
heavy present seems to f.
SNYD 49
it seems to f.: BROWNI R 74
Let my muse/ F. HERR 17
I die! I faint! I f.! SHEL 32
never think of love;/ Fair, if you
f., UNKN 74
Our hearts shall f. us; WILB 3
stomach too begins to f.:
SWIF 27
world's course will not f.:
PATM 7
wrong shall f., LONG 12

failed: fluttered and f. for breath.
ARNO 21
not a creature f., DICKI 42
then the Windows f. DICKI 49

failing: bulwark never f.; LUTH 2
F. to fetch me WHITM 74
sons their fathers' f. language see,
POPE A 34

failins: Without his f.; BURN 44

fails: fancy then/ Unequal f.
THOMS J (1700–1748) 4
No expectation f. there,
YEATS 73
One sure, if another f.:
BROWNI R 78

failure: f. of weeks RUKE 9
length was f., LANIE 4
new-baked bread a f., PURD 2

fain: f. for to water the plain.
LANIE 5
unafraid, I am f. to face LANIE 4
We'll meet and ay be f. NAIR 1

faint: breathing f. and low —
POE 13
Damn with f. praise, POPE A 7
F. for the flesh, ROBI 2
Friendless and f., ROBI 2
I die! I f.! I fail! SHEL 32

ladies f., and the children holler:
SMIT W 1
last f. spark SITW 12
to some f. meaning make
pretense, DRYD 11
what strength I have 's mine own,/
Which is most f. SHAK 167

fainter: spirits have a f. flow,
COWP 21

Fainting: F. I follow. WYAT 31
rais'd/ Thir f. courage MILT 56

faint's: F. the cold work COLL 12

faints: enemy f. not, CLOU 8

fair: All other f., like flowers,
untimely fade. SPENS 26
anything to show more f.:
WORD 6
At market and f., UNKN 44
beyond the Atlantic roar./ F. these
broad meads — GALT 1
bloom sae fresh and f.? BURN 15
cruel as she's f. DANI S 9
cups drinks to the f. RICH 21
curtailed of this f. proportion,
SHAK 96
Disguise f. nature SHAK 56
doom is f., MILT 98
Excellent and f. DICKI 3
expectancy and rose of the f.
state, SHAK 33
f. and fatal king: JOHN L 3
f. and free as now? TIMR 2
f. and stately palace — POE 20
f. and wise and good and gay.
MOTH 22
F. as a star, WORD 45
F. as Eve in Paradise: HERR 59
F. be thy wives, right lovesom,
white and small; DUNB W 5
f. child of mine SHAK 185
f., divinely f., MILT 92
F. face show friends when riches
do abound; GOOG 1
F. flower, FRENE 5
f. for the maistrie, CHAU 18
f. garments, such prosperi-ty?' —
HARD 36
F. is foul, SHAK 102
F. is my Love, DANI S 9
F. Liberty was all his cry;
SWIF 24
f. lines which true goodness
show. SIDN 20
f. meek blossom BRYA 9
f. might ye befall. WYAT 16
F., rich, and young: HARI 1
F. scenes shall greet thee
BRYA 29
F. seed-time had my soul,
WORD 93
F. stood the wind for France,
DRAY 1
f. there's fairer none, LODG 7

Faith f. scorn doth gain. SIDN 38
false as f.,/ Unconstant, frail,
untrue; WITH 3
far too f. SHEL 82
find/ Your person f., MILLA 14
fool he called her his lady f.
KIPL 27
forfeit f. renown, SCOT WA 12
form of a maiden f., LONG 52
forms are f., BROWNI R 1
foul is f. SHAK 102
from f. sometime declines,
SHAK 188
glister f.; SPENS 38
Heigh ho, f. Rosaline! LODG 7
I can love both f. and brown;
DONN 35
In those f. eyes UNKN 141
kan/ So muchel of daliaunce and f.
langage. CHAU 20
lies a thing so f.,/ No stone is
there BYRO 51
life would all be f. HARD 25
Lord Thomas was buried in the
church,/ F. Ellinor in the choir;
UNKN 179
love is f., my love is gay, PEEL 1
Lux my f. falcon, WYAT 16
maiden f. and dapper, TAYL B 1
manhood full and f.! BRID R 17
mistress moderately f., COWL 8
Monday's child is f. of face,
MOTH 22
More than most f., full of the
living fire, SPENS 4
my f. Chloe, PRIO 2
never think of love;/ F., if you
fail, UNKN 74
Nothing is f. or good alone.
EMER 18
nymphs so graceful, wise, and f.,
SWIF 21
pitiful as she is f., GREE 3
Queen and huntress, chaste and
f., JONS 3
Queens have died young and f.;
NASHE 1
rose looks f., SHAK 206
see her sweet and is f.: BURN 42
Seeing only what is f., EMER 31
sight was not so f. ROBI 19
slain by a f. cruel maid.
SHAK 176
sleeping earth was f. BRON 3
so f., and you away? COWL 7
soldier was passing f.; FIEL E 6
Spice his f. banquet TENN 96
swear that, foul or f., SERV 2
sworn thee f., SHAK 242
Take heed, f. Eve! WALL 7
tell her I lie in Kirk-land f.,
UNKN 270

his own house & f.; BLAK 27
lulled within, a f. with pets,
 BISH 35
passions of the human f.
 MAST 4
smothered in f. POUN 26
speaks for the F. of Man?
 SAND 17
to pray for our f. HARP 4
famine: at thy heel/ Did f. follow,
 SHAK 4
f.-murdered land WILD 11
f. or scurvy — I fought it;
 SERV 11
f., terror, flood, and plague
 WALK 1
smile in secret, looking over
 wasted lands,/ Blight and f.,
 TENN 90
famished: f. field and blackened
 tree MUIR 9
famous: f. beauty of dead women:
 MACL 11
f. by my sword; MONTROSE 3
f. high top-hat LIND V 2
f. Lincolnshire, UNKN 172
f. men of old, the Ogres —
 GRAV 18
Madame Sosostris, f.
 clairvoyante, ELIOT T 116
remembers that f. day LONG 43
fan: injured f. MOOR M 11
powdered hair and jeweled f.,
 LOWE A 5
fancied: f. life in others' breath,
 POPE A 84
sweets of f. love, CLARE 14
fancies: but for f., TENN 24
f. all be fled, VAUX 2
fancy: As f. reverts WOOD 3
chosen coin of f. TENN 124
Evacuation of the world of f.,
 ELIOT T 21
f. dies/ In the cradle SHAK 121
f. doth it beauty make. SUCK 5
f. enough for Lord Byron,
 NASH 20
f. has she for flitting; HAY 2
f. next/ Her office holds. MILT 80
f. of f. costumes; PRAE 3
f. of itself bereaving, MILT 35
F. the sunrise DICKI 52
f. then/ Unequal fails
 THOMS J (1700–1748) 4
fish of f. teem MILLE V 1
Fond F.'s scum SIDN 39
Free be she, f.-free; EMER 24
From so ungrateful f., SIDN 38
giant f., CAREW 3
Good-bye my F.!/ Farewell dear
 mate, WHITM 34
grips his f. WILB 35
His f. sunk, SWIF 26

If I a f. take SUCK 5
In the spring a young man's f.
 lightly turns TENN 69
let my f. plant TUCK 1
let the F. roam! KEAT 16
long shall timorous f. FRENE 2
mimic f. wakes MILT 80
mockingbird,/ His f. warbler;
 HAYD 12
ring f.'s knell. SHAK 121
those by hopeless f. feigned
 TENN 115
where is f. bred, SHAK 120
fancyings: f. of fancy costumes;
 PRAE 3
fane: be thy priest, and build a f.
 KEAT 53
coldly mark the holy f.
 SCOT WA 4
fanes: f. of fruitless prayer,
 TENN 36
fangs: fixing in the wretch his cruel
 f., THOMS J (1700–1748) 11
jaws' hooked clamp and f.
 HUGH T 11
fanning: wind f. the ash ROET 15
fans: divers-colored f., SHAK 5
fantasies: fed the heart on f.,
 YEATS 99
fantastic: f. arabesques, WILD 12
light f. toe, MILT 21
Love in f. triumph BEHN 1
fantasy: Begot of nothing but vain
 f., SHAK 141
far: Elysium is as f. DICKI 20
f. beyond the wave; TENN 83
F., F. away, FOST 3
f.-fet helps SIDN 10
f. from gusty waves, SPEND 1
f. out of reach, WHITM 10
f. upon the eastern road MILT 42
fireside f. from the cares SERV 9
'How f. is St Helena KIPL 23
isn't f. from London!) NOYE 2
land that's f. away UNKN 26
near and f. as grass, WILB 6
"O keep the Dog f. hence,
 ELIOT T 120
Over the Hills and f. away.
 GAY 3
sky, serene and f., LONG 23
so f. away. PATM 9
so f. to seek, ROSS C 25
Spring be f. behind? SHEL 47
those that are f. away;
 WHITM 12
unhappy, f.-off things, WORD 140
wise men came from f., GODO 1
wiser f. than I. DONN 7
Farce: Fate put a Period to the F.;
 SWIF 15
farcical: Success so huge and wholly
 f.; LARK 21

farcically: insect/ Looks f. human;
 GRAV 1
fardels: who would f. bear,
 SHAK 40
fare: f. like my peers
 BROWNI R 69
f. thee well: BYRO 54
F. you well; your suit is cold.
 SHAK 119
fared: Better men f. thus ARNO 13
fares: brighter f. my stream, —
 EMER 49
how with the soul it f. ARNO 16
Ill f. the land, GOLD 1
fareweel: then we sever!/ Ae f.,
 BURN 10
Farewell: last F. did take. BRAD 3
Lat go, f., the devel go therwith!
 CHAU 83
farewell: as my f.' OHAR 20
bade f.! GINS 19
Bid the slaves of thrift f.
 JOHN S (1709–1784) 11
did my best;/ f. WILLI 33
F. deare flowers, HERB G 47
F. green fields BLAK 101
f. journey to the Promised Land.
 UNKN 55
F., Love, and all thy laws for
 ever: WYAT 5
F., my Youth! WATS R 1
F., thou child of my right hand,
 JONS 23
F. to barn and stack and tree,
 HOUS 28
f. to the shade COWP 13
F., woman! ROCH 5
f., you old rhinoceros, NASH 13
Good-bye my Fancy!/ F. dear
 mate, WHITM 34
no f. can know. CRAN H 52
No-more, Too-late, F.; ROSS D 6
no sadness of f., TENN 10
O f. griefe, and welcome joye,
 UNKN 17
think the thing f. TENN 56
Walsingham, Oh f.! UNKN 170
waving me f.! HOPE L 3
with hope, f. fear, MILT 67
farm: every Middlesex village and
 f., LONG 44
hard to f. SNYD 41
Middlesex village and f., —
 LONG 45
owls were bearing the f. away,
 THOMA D 18
started a worm f.) CUMM 31
Uncle Sol's f. CUMM 30
weathered — like a f. wagon —
 WILLI 44
Farmer: F. Rouf's little lad.
 WOOL 1

peaceful f. any peace, WHITM 7
son of a f., age fourteen; TROW 1
farmers: embattled f. stood
   EMER 11
farming: f. of a verse AUDE 45
farms: Monroe, NY the chicken f.
   GINS 27
fart: leet flee a f. CHAU 57
Farther: F. behind THOR 5
F. in summer DICKI 23
f. within. THOR 5
not f. than my thoughts
   SHAK 204
farthest: Among the f. Hebrides.
   WORD 139
farthings: Halfpence and f.,
   UNKN 23
Fascinated: F., my eyes reverting
   WHITM 2
fascinating: I've a f. leer; GILB 9
fascination: f. of her brightness.
   SHAP 9
f. of what's difficult YEATS 57
Fascist: Every woman adores a F.,
   PLATH 30
fashion: art doth give the f.;
   JONS 45
f. me within; SPENS 5
f. out of rods, CULL 8
finical f. has had its day, TRAI 4
Gives the lover weight and f.
   JONS 1
glass of f. SHAK 33
in my f. DOWS 3
In this mediæval f., CRAN S 6
Lord, I f. dark gods, too,
   CULL 10
vegetable f. GILB 32
fashionable: f. or/ Important
   personage: AUDE 61
fashioned: f. so airy a mood
   POUN 16
F. so purely, THOMP F 13
F. so slenderly, HOOD 2
old f. tirade — LOWE R 29
rapt eyes/ F. a new world
   RANDA D 4
fast: confined to f. in fires,
   SHAK 26
devoured/ As f. as they are made,
   SHAK 173
die as f. SHAK 186
eyes f. fixt MILT 114
f. asleep in bed. STEVENSO R 14
f.-flying cloud, KNOX 1
f. I gather, bit by bit, THAX 1
f. in my fortress, LONG 10
f., perfect, and unwilling
   TATE J 4
fluttring wings of thy f. flying
   SPENS 35
Girt f. by memory; SIDN 18
Hold f. your dreams! DRIS 1

made f. the door; SOUTHE 2
my heart is f., and cannot
   disentangle. UNKN 220
Runn'st thou ne'er so f.,
   WEBS/ROWL 1
shades of night were falling f.,
   LONG 21
Sorrow and mourn and f.
   UNKN 190
soule grew so f. within, CAREW 8
sullen and f. athwart WHITM 56
who seizes f. to them, WHITM 73
fasted: I hae f. for your sake
   BROWN A 1
fasten: f. into order AMMO 9
Faster: F. than fairies,
   STEVENSO R 8
f. than light. BULL 1
f. than witches, STEVENSO R 8
make one/ breathe f. MOOR M 26
fastest: travels the f. who travels
   alone. KIPL 25
fastidiousness: poetry in
   unconscious/ f. MOOR M 5
fasting: kind/ Not well, nor full, nor
   f. DANI S 1
fat: beach hisses like f. BISH 40
creeks get f. HUGO 3
F. black bucks LIND V 8
f. little worm" UNKN 97
f. of good/ And evil, JARR 3
f. white woman whom nobody
   loves, CORN 2
like a f. gold watch. PLATH 61
mammoth but not f., TATE A 3
nas nat right f., CHAU 22
tasseling corn,/ F. beans,
   TATE A 5
fatal: fair and f. king: JOHN L 3
f. harmony; MARV 13
f. zone to her denied! COLL 5
first strange and f. interview,
   DONN 46
hurry from the f. cannon's womb.
   SHAK 150
some/ By f. instinct fly;
   THOMS J (1700–1748) 9
their sad and f. voice. FULL 4
Fate: architects of F., LONG 4
behold your f. SWIF 16
can accomplish f., YEATS 156
circuit of his f., GRAV 34
common f. of all things rare
   WALL 2
coughed, and called it f.,
   ROBI 44
curse my f., SHAK 194
defy our f. WILLI 19
Die early and avoid the f.
   FROS 89
eccentric propositions of its f.
   STEVENS 25

F. has metamorphosed them,
   HOLM 11
f. of simple Bard, BURN 60
F. put a Period to the Farce;
   SWIF 15
f. so enviously debars, MARV 7
F., Time, Occasion, Chance, and
   Change? SHEL 55
f. willfully misunderstand
   FROS 13
F. wings with every wish th'
   afflictive dart,
   JOHN S (1709–1784) 16
full lips laugh at F.! BENN G 7
full reward and glorious f.
   CAREW 17
guides nature and f. BRAD 10
hanging breathless on thy f.!
   LONG 6
heart for any f.; LONG 37
hides the book of F., POPE A 63
its f. was pathetic, UNKN 198
Justice against F. complain,
   MARV 21
labouring with a mighty f.,
   DRYD 7
limits of a vulgar f.: GRAY 31
Loves by F. benighted, STANL 2
Made weak by time and f.,
   TENN 135
master of his f., ROBI 31
mock at f. and care, EMER 31
Moloch whose f. is a cloud
   GINS 17
mourn'st the Daisy's f.,/ That f. is
   thine — BURN 61
my life, my f.; TENN 94
no armour against f.; SHIR 1
poet's f. WESL S 1
Providence, Foreknowledge, Will,
   and F., MILT 60
stoop to f., SHIR 2
storms of F.! GRAY 26
three old shrews of f. GINS 12
thy f. and mine are sealed;
   TENN 106
Time cannot alter but obey F.'s
   laws. TOWN 1
two great Ends of F., ROCH 16
vast Designs of F., ROCH 16
will in us is over-rul'd by f.
   MARL 8
(would F. but mend it!), PRIO 12
fated: always alive and f.; SHAP 22
fateful: loosed the f. lightning
   HOWE 1
fates: harbingers preceding still the
   f. SHAK 20
masters of their f., SHAK 43
Secret f. Guide our states
   CAMPI 31
temple of the F. TIMR 2

whate'er the F. decree; SWIF 17
where the F. Change horses,
  BYRO 21
father: afraid for my f. DICKEY 22
As my f. once watched me;
  BLUN 1
as my grandmother's f.
  WHITM 89
Child is f. of the Man; WORD 58
child with her f.,/ Watching the
  east, the autumn sky.
  WHITM 56
come down from my f.
  DICKEY 20
country's F. slain STOD 1
face of that f., JUST 6
fallen from my f.'s beard. KLEI 1
f. and his mother; ROBI 31
f. and mither BURN 64
F. calls me William, FIEL E 3
f. forsaken,/ Forgive your son!
  JOYC 2
f. in the night SIMP 6
F. of all! POPE A 126
f. of twins, POUN 65
f. should wear a broadcloth coat,
  WHITT 16
F., Son, and Holy Ghost,
  CULL 9
F. Time and Mother Earth,
  MERR 3
f. was Knott UNKN 88
F. who endest all, DAY 9
"F., who makes it snow?"
  LOWE J 12
F., whom I murdered MOSS 1
f.'s house below MUIR 4
Fear was my f., ROET 36
Full fathom five thy f. lies;
  SHAK 156
God for his f. BLAK 87
his f.'s f., STEVENS 20
holding the hand of her f.,
  WHITM 57
I wold thy f. were a king,
  UNKN 64
kinder to his f. SHAK 80
lean in joy upon our f.'s knee;
  BLAK 99
love my f. all. SHAK 68
mother groaned, my f. wept.
  BLAK 72
my f. and my mother JENN 2
my f. moved CUMM 25
my f.'s plantation, WOOD 3
Neither f. nor lover. ROET 12
not an angry f.' CAMPB T 5
sacked land/ of my f. BARA 7
see/ The F. and the Son,
  CHAR 1
son is brought with the f.,
  WHITM 26
Sore trembled the f.: GOET 1

spake our F. penitent; MILT 98
Struggling in my f.'s hands,
  BLAK 73
Sweet to the f. BYRO 21
Thy f.'s shame, thy mother's
  grief, BRET 1
thy f.'s spirit,/ Doomed for a
  certain term SHAK 26
To bid the f. wipe his eyes
  SHAK 61
Two veterans son and f. dropt
  together, WHITM 26
up from the fields f., WHITM 15
When f. carves the duck.
  WRIG E 1
Where are thy f. & mother?
  BLAK 55
your f.'s f., CRAN H 23
Fatherland: sweet it was to dream
  of F., TENN 82
fatherless: Starless and f.,
  PLATH 77
fatherly: f. will kiss and daut thee,
  BURN 43
fathers: As their f. watched them
  once, BLUN 1
ashes of his f. MACA 3
blood of f., mothers, daughters,
  sons, SHAK 30
die as my f. died, SWIN 25
exiles from our f.' land. GALT 1
f. are a blessing, UNTE 2
f. feel justified; BOGA 7
F. that wear rags SHAK 73
He f.-forth HOPKINS 19
Land where my f. died,
  SMIT SA 1
more f. than sons JUST 6
Our f.' God! to Thee, SMIT SA 2
proud f. are ashamed WRIG J 1
race of f.: STEVENS 21
sons their f.' failing language see,
  POPE A 34
sons your f. got, HOUS 32
things my f. learned to do.
  AIKE 6
what say the f. wise, — EMER 40
fathom: f. to this pond's black bed.
  BLUN 4
f. you not — WHITM 22
Full f. five thy father lies;
  SHAK 156
fathoms: Bury it certain f. in the
  earth, SHAK 165
down in f. many GILB 10
f. down, how I'll dream fast
  asleep. MELV 4
fatigue: Drunk with f.; OWEN 18
research on f. AUDE 88
fatigued: f. at evening, AUDE 96
fatter: Getting a little f. CARRO 42
valley sheep are f.; PEAC 1
fatuous: f. sunbeams toil OWEN 27

fatuousness: tiredness, the f.,
  CREE 11
faucets: God/ with giant f.
  HUGO 4
fauld: sheep are in the f., LIND L 1
fault: Against the flint and hardness
  of my f., SHAK 8
f. of the Dutch CANN 1
Heav'n in f.; POPE A 62
little f. of temper GILB 6
Of his f. and his sorrows
  MOOR T 12
without f. or stain BRID R 17
faultless: f. breast the furnace is,
  SOUTHW 2
try to imagine a f. love AUDE 52
faults: All men make f., SHAK 199
confessed/ Humbly their f.,
  MILT 98
f. of his own liking! SHAK 116
guilty of my f., SHAK 243
his f. can freely show, POPE A 24
in our f. SHAK 238
seek slight f. to find POPE A 34
fauna: f. of that fire. WILLI 11
Faustus: F. may repent MARL 1
velvet suit and f. hood? CORS 1
fauts: neebour's f. and folly!
  BURN 4
favor: beg the f. with a graveyard
  grin. DAY 8
favored: somewhere in this f. land
  THAY 4
favoring: indicate a f. wind,
  OLSO 2
favorite: f. scenic view, HAYD 7
favour: ask the f.; CONG 2
childish f. singled: WHITT 13
f. to men of skill; BIBL, O.T. 1
favours: rubies, fairy f., SHAK 126
fawning: flattery's f. face,
  EMER 27
fawnskin: Wearing a spotted f.
  SNYD 39
fayne: cannot frame me tune to f.,
  WYAT 22
fayre: laye/ Of f. Elisa, SPENS 50
"Of f. Elisa be your silver song,
  SPENS 53
fays: napkin spread by f.; THOR 8
feace: your vaice an' f. BARNE 2
Fear: Arch F. in a visible form,
  BROWNI R 68
Creating awe and f. in other
  men? SHAK 58
descending/ Darkness of f.
  JOYC 4
Do not f. to put thy feet/ Naked in
  the river sweet; FLET J 2
dread and f. of kings; SHAK 123
faithful, banish f., EMER 47
f. at its rising JEFFE 16

F. contended with desire.
  HOUS 46
F. death by water. ELIOT T 117
F. examples, FLET J 5
F. God, and keep his
  commandments: BIBL, O.T. 7
F. most to tax an honorable fool,
  POPE A 21
f. no foe LYTE 2
f. not, deny not me, WHITM 5
f. of blackė bears, or bullės black,
  CHAU 69
f. of change MILT 57
f. of finding something worse.
  BELL 11
f. of little men; ALLI 1
f./ Of total neutrality. PLATH 19
f. or doubt of her revolt,
  SHAK 136
F.,/ The yellow chirper,
  LOWE R 24
F., then, so wounded GARR 1
f., thirst, hunger, CUNN J 4
f. to breast the sea! LONG 7
F. was my father, ROET 36
f. what they will do HARP 2
f./ worse than blows HAYD 24
f. you not: HOUS 32
Fostered alike by beauty and by
  f.: WORD 93
From hope and f. set free,
  SWIN 15
He that is down needs f. no fall,
  BUNY 5
his eye-sting f.— SNYD 3
hive whose honey is f. and worry,
  AUDE 32
Horror and scorn and hate and f.
  and indignation— HOUS 24
hunger in the prison of my f.
  GARR 2
I will show you f. ELIOT T 115
imagining some f., SHAK 127
Infants cry of f., BLAK 74
innocence of f.; BROO G 6
Life-stifling f., COLE SAM 27
lives not in f. SHAK 77
love, hatred, joy or f., PRIO 4
love with f. the only God,
  MILT 105
Mortality, behold, and f.,
  BEAU/BASS 1
much disposed to f., GILB 19
needed not f. MORE 3
Neither f. nor courage saves us.
  ELIOT T 33
neither praise expect, nor censure
  f.: DRYD 20
Noiseless as f. in a wide
  wilderness, KEAT 12
none has merited my f., WYLI 6
not of f., LONG 45
O word of f., SHAK 100

object of another's f.; SHEL 76
Of pleasure and of f.; WORD 129
palsy shakes of f.; MARV 12
poor souls f. a shade or night,
  VAUG 31
pulse of f., LUCR 6
sat the sow of f. SHAP 26
Senses roll themselves in f.
  BLAK 33
soul that knew not f. DAVID 2
spring of love and f. TATE A 16
to feel no f., DICKEY 19
too much f.: GRAV 3
we f. nae evil; BURN 55
where angels f. to tread.
  POPE A 23
wherefore should you f., JONS 32
wish death, nor f. his might.
  MARTIA 2
With f., as half-awakened;
  POUN 58
with hope, farewell f., MILT 67
with my great tap root:/ It is what
  you f. PLATH 40
without a trace of f., TOOM 4
work me no f. LANIE 4
wrath of it your only f. ROBI 4
feare: for f. flewen over the trees;
  CHAU 71
I f. no more. DONN 30
feared: f. by all, is now a rug.
  GUIT 2
f., loved, hated, suffered,
  SHEL 79
flying from the thing they f.,
  SHEL 76
just as I f.!— LEAR 18
precurse of f. events, SHAK 20
To monarchize, be f., SHAK 89
fearful: facing f. odds MACA 3
f. eye SOUTHW 1
f. meditation, SHAK 212
f. steps SHEL 31
f. thing WILD 5
f. trip is done, WHITM 45
frame thy f. symmetry? BLAK 84
fright the souls of f. adversaries,
  SHAK 95
snatch a f. joy. GRAY 15
thousand f. wracks; SHAK 97
With a f. shriek, DARC 4
fearfully: f. as doth a gallèd rock
  SHAK 56
fearless: F.— the cobweb DICKI 32
f. truth endows. ROBI 17
fears: abyss of f. And horrors
  MILT 100
burden of your f., MORR 1
child with nameless f.; LEWI 8
dispel'd thir f. MILT 56
faith triumphant o'er our f.,
  LONG 7
f. a painted devil. SHAK 107

f., and flies from Marion's men.
  SIMM 2
f. he shall be poor. SHAK 135
f. that I may cease KEAT 68
foolish f. of what might happen.
  BROWNI E/GUIN 1
from nightly f., GRAY 2
gathering place of f.: JOHN L 7
hard words, jealousies, and f.,
  BUTL 1
hopes and f. it heeded not:
  SHEL 70
hopes and f. of all the years
  BROO P 3
Humanity with all its f., LONG 6
man who f. war POUN 63
Not mine own f. SHAK 229
play of hopes and f., POE 30
speaking of f. in the abstract
  POUN 12
Trembling, cold, in ghastly f.
  BLAK 43
'Twixt f. of dying and desire of
  life: CRAB 3
which it f. to lose. SHAK 211
With cares and f. BACO 1
feast: Chief nourisher in life's f.
  SHAK 106
Despair, not f. on thee:
  HOPKINS 4
F. of Crispian: SHAK 60
f. of reason POPE A 92
inward f., FLET G YO 1
kept a solemne f., MARL 7
neat repast shall f. us, MILT 121
shares again the joyous f.
  FRENE 1
What f. is toward SHAK 42
your worth will dignifie our f.,
  JONS 14
feasting: like f. upon air. SMIT W 4
feat: f. on which ourselves we
  prided) BYRO 44
feather: after him for a f.
  FROS 139
f. bed had every man, GILB 4
f. on the bright sky MOMA 3
I care not a f.; SHERI 2
light as f.
  JOHN S (1709–1784) 11
love was a f., CREE 14
moulted f., an eagle-feather!
  BROWNI R 53
feathered: f. balls of soot
  YEATS 97
f. with flying hours, DANI S 14
Tarred and f. WHITT 23
Two f. guests from Alabama,
  WHITM 64
feathers: f., like a lady bright,
  VAUT 1
f. of the willow DIXO 1

"Hope" is the thing with f.
    DICKI 29
— 'I wish I had f., HARD 37
unrolled his f. DICKI 13
wings and f. unto the ostrich?
    BIBL, O.T. 16
feats: ammunition/ And f. of war
    defeats MILT 113
feature: Cheated of f. SHAK 96
In f. as the worm DICKI 87
years-heired f. HARD 26
Featured: F. like him, SHAK 194
features: Dark despairing f.
    CULL 10
different voice and f.: SWIF 12
in the brown baked f.
    ELIOT T 65
February: Fireworks in the dull
    middle of F. SEXT 2
fecund: make f. my existence
    OHAR 8
fed: dead f. you LOWE A 2
f. me from her gentle breast,
    TAYL A 1
f. on the fullness of death.
    SWIN 23
f. the heart on fantasies,
    YEATS 99
F. with cold and usurous hand?
    BLAK 68
f. with judgements, COWP 16
f. your hunger like an endless
    task, CRAN H 46
freely f. on straw, BISH 35
having f. to satiety ELIOT T 6
let the world be f., CHES 12
On cheeks and roses free he f.;
    LOVE 3
With gazing f.; SHAK 121
Federation: Parliament of man, the
    F. of the world. TENN 76
fee: Go, birds of spring: let winter
    have his f.; HERB G 37
hold the gorgeous East in f.;
    WORD 90
unstain'd with gold or f.,
    MILT 122
feeble: Man's f. race GRAY 26
offspring round their f. fire,
    CRAB 6
She winks a f. eye, ELIOT T 104
with a f. grin, HUGO 7
feed: Church can sleep and f. at
    once. ELIOT T 38
f.-back is the law OLSO 4
F. him HERR 25
f. upon my cost; SHAK 59
hoard, and sleep, and f.,
    TENN 128
many a rose-carnation f.
    TENN 42
native self can nothing f.;
    MICH 1

shepherds f. their flocks
    MARL 18
sleep and f.? SHAK 35
where laborers f. OHAR 12
feeding: admiration, f. at the eye,
    COWP 17
f. on delicate peaches, PRAE 4
Feeds: dungy earth alike/ F. beast as
    man. SHAK 3
F. and obeys RANS 26
f. me bread of bitterness,
    MCKA 2
F. on the rarities SHAK 210
mock/ The meat it f. on.
    SHAK 134
Nutriment that f. the Mind?
    SWIF 19
feel: don't f. so well myself. GUIT 2
f. like singin', sing— STANT 1
f. that pulse MOOR T 6
f. the free/ Shrill wind LANG 3
his whiskers would f. like
    HECH 4
I f. ancient, SNYD 12
makes me f. at home. MOOR M 1
making men f. As small KAVA 17
may i f. said he CUMM 23
mountains, there you f. free.
    ELIOT T 114
thing that could not f. WORD 49
thoughts they cannot f., VERY 2
veins, in my bones I f. it, —
    ROET 5
We shall not f., LUCR 3
feeld: fair f. ful of folk LANGL 3
feeling: f. and a love, WORD 33
f. and looking queer. HOLM 7
f., are miracles, WHITM 74
f. is first CUMM 44
f. its huge path/ Through dusk,
    SPEND 13
formal f. comes— DICKI 1
Music is f., STEVENS 33
some cease f. OWEN 32
soothe this restless f., LONG 15
We think by f.. What is there to
    know? ROET 58
feelings: sad scenes and thoughts
    and f. vanish
    THOMS J (1834–1882) 7
use great f. MAST 4
Feels: F. at each thread, POPE A 71
horse that f. a flea, MOOR M 32
I sympathize, I know just how it
    f. FROS 22
what the caged bird f.,
    DUNB P 9
feel'st: thou f.'st it cold. SHAK 135
fees: free without f.; TASS 2
feet: absence of f., MOOR M 40
against my f. WHITM 5
arms and hands and f. and
    countenance PETRA 11

beauty of cool f. DOOL 4
Before her wandering f.
    YEATS 122
beginning at his f. BELL 10
buried in the dust of marching f.
    KNIG 3
crown thy F., MARV 5
cut stone/ consoles his groping f.
    LEVE 11
dead f. walked in. HARD 40
Do not fear to put thy f.
    FLET J 2
drawn in yr f. REED I 1
dreams under your f.; YEATS 4
end with swelled f.." LOWE R 16
faith of still averted f., PATM 10
fall at her flying f. CAMPI 2
fall down at your f. IGNA 1
f. are heavy on the floor
    AUDE 66
f. before the fire, ROET 16
f. like small leaves, ROET 39
f. of dung KINS 4
f. of the rats SAND 9
f. that were blue with cold,
    OSUL 2
f. together toes pointed
    DICKEY 12
Flashed from his matted head and
    marble f., LOWE R 37
going shall be used with f.
    SHAK 76
hear our f. VERY 6
Her f. like embers; SHEL 78
hooked head and hooked f.:
    HUGH T 1
If her horny f. protrude,
    STEVENS 11
keep the f. of his saints,
    BIBL, O.T. 8
lie in drifts at your f. WHITM 6
lightly threaded with nimble f.
    BINY 5
little black f. LIND V 12
little snow-white f. YEATS 50
loose f. in tall grass SNYD 35
lung heart f. tail GINS 14
"My f. are at Moorgate,
    ELIOT T 139
my heart/ Under my f.
    ELIOT T 139
on the following F., THOMP F 7
On winged f., EMER 10
palms before my f. CHES 4
quiet of love in her f.
    YEATS 21
rats' f. over broken glass
    ELIOT T 41
sentence, of as subtile f.,
    JONS 18
shoes were full of f. UNKN 146
small clumsy f. of April
    CUMM 20

small, poised f. LAWR 31
soles of his f. rise KUMI 1
stands beneath the f., WINT 9
strength and riches at thy f.
    BRYA 14
stuck out their little f. BISH 37
these f. must hide WHITT 8
these low f. staggered —
    DICKI 31
Thy silv'ry f. HERR 33
tied rags on their f. SAND 23
trampling horses' f. SIDN 24
with f. unstable, LIND V 8
you held my f. WHITM 78
you Stella's f. may kiss! SIDN 25
feign: Impossible to f. DICKI 54
feign'd: worse/ Than Fables yet have
    f.'d, MILT 61
feigned: by f. deaths to die.
    DONN 57
those by hopeless fancy f.
    TENN 115
under show of love well f.
    MILT 92
feit: Scots lords at his f.
    UNKN 228
felaweshipe: sorwe of Noee with his
    f.? CHAU 49
felicitous: French, f. tongue,
    MACL 8
felicity: Absent thee from f.
    SHAK 41
branches ne'er remember/ Their
    green f.: KEAT 28
friend await/ F. of doom.
    DICKI 20
time/ Crown'd my f., PHILI K 1
feline: so rank a f. smell
    ELIOT T 160
Felix: legend of F. is VAN DY 4
poor F. Randal; HOPKINS 6
fell: all f. to playing the game
    FOOT 1
brown eyes lower f. WHITT 14
buried him where he f.
    WHITM 107
by Time's f. hand defaced
    SHAK 211
Calm f.. From Heaven HARD 11
Death f. with me, OWEN 39
f. across the picture — dead.
    DARC 4
f. on his knees, UNKN 7
f. to earth, LONG 1, 2
f. upon my ear GARR 1
fierce assault they f., WHITM 26
foremost fighting, f. BYRO 7
grandfather f. on Vinegar Hill,
    CLARK J 3
great shape labored and f.
    MOMA 2
his nice new sashes,/ F. in the fire
    GRAHAM H 3

knife of penance f. KAVA 6
Neither flesh nor f. SKEL 12
never f. — Through pride; SWIF 4
Proserpine first f., SITW 2
prostrate f. Before him reverent,
    MILT 98
roof of England f. SHAP 27
They smote and f., THOMP W 2
voice f., like a falling star,
    LONG 23
felled: are all f.; HOPKINS 2
f. a city; THOMA D 24
poplars are f., COWP 13
fellers: f. call me Bill! FIEL E 3
Fellow: f.-wight who yet abide —
    HARD 22
hope some f. will lend a hand
    BRIN 3
I'll not have the f. back,"
    FROS 20
'Look at that old f. YEATS 76
makes a f. whistle back.
    WOLF H 1
my erring f. creatures, GILB 6
narrow F. in the Grass DICKI 111
never met this F. DICKI 112
one that loves his f.-men."
    HUNT 3
rear this f. up/ to lutch, BIRN 3
shoot a f. down HARD 31
whale his f.-man, HART 3
fellows: at night the party of young
    f., WHITM 38
old f. in the dust RANS 8
stout f. left their bones behind.
    DAY 7
felon: secret f. wrought, CHAU 47
When a f.'s not engaged
    GILB 37
felonious: maturing his f. little
    plans, GILB 37
felt: Earth f. the wound, MILT 89
f. a Funeral, in my Brain,
    DICKI 45
F. in his arms, MILT 114
F. less remorse. MILT 98
f. no pain, SHEL 91
f. you round my throat
    HOPE L 3
freezings have I f., SHAK 223
lived, f. dawn, MCCRA 1
Remembering how she f.,
    WORD 99
you f. my beard, WHITM 78
you tell/ What we f. only;
    BROWNI R 41
young rats with black f. hats,
    UNKN 258
female: despite they cast on f. wits:
    BRAD 17
f. heart can gold despise?
    GRAY 19

f. smells in shuttered rooms,
    ELIOT T 105
f. tunny-fish, LAWR 58
From such a f. franzy, SIDN 38
quivering f.-thing SPENC A 2
thing of sea or land?/ F. of sex
    MILT 110
females: daggled f. fly, SWIF 7
feminine: Owl-downy, soft f.
    JEFFE 16
soft and f., MILT 90
fen: depths of the Cambrian f.,
    SMIT L 1
f. appears impassable,
    MOOR M 14
fence: see the elephant jump the f.
    UNKN 135
thinne and lean without a f. or
    friend, HERB G 4
fenced: f. their gardens LOWE R 4
fences: 'Good f. make good
    neighbors.' FROS 57
fend: lies him down the lubber f.,
    MILT 23
fennel: f. that grows so green!
    UNKN 216
fens: converse with the mountains,
    moors, and f. SYNG 7
Rocks, Caves, Lakes, F., Bogs,
    Dens, MILT 61
feral: f. glint/ In the caught eyes.
    KIZE 2
Ferdinand: F. De Soto, sleeping/ In
    the river, VAN DO 1
Fere: Goodly F. POUN 3
king's f. in marriage? MORE 2
slain our Goodly F. POUN 4
Fergus: drive with F. now,
    YEATS 163
F. rules the brazen cars,
    YEATS 164
ferly: Me befel a f., LANGL 1
fern: hairs of a f. SHAP 5
sparkle out among the f. TENN 4
stale f., THOMA D 3
ferns: Behind a pot of f.
    THOMA D 15
ferny: grey flocks in f. glens
    BRON 6
ferret: f.'s smile, HILL G 3
Ferry: "F. me across the water,
    ROSS C 9
gone back and forth all night on
    the f. MILLA 26
On the f.-boats WHITM 18
"Step into my f.-boat, ROSS C 10
fertile: barren place and f.
    SHAK 157
Below a f. valley WHITM 9
f. lack of balance FULL 4
Glistring with dew; fragrant the f.
    earth MILT 76
Opening her f. womb MILT 86

fertility: suck/ The soil's f.
   SHAK 90
fervors: Pour forth thy f.
   JOHN S (1709–1784) 23
festal: feel your f. fame MELV 6
fester: Lilies that f. SHAK 222
fetch: brisk fond lackey to f. and
   carry, HOUS 3
Failing to f. me WHITM 74
f. one if one goes astray,
   ROSS C 12
It will carry and f., BELL 20
to f., DAY 12
fetid: Other than base and f.:
   FROS 111
fetisly: bootes clasped faire and f.
   CHAU 21
faire and f., CHAU 14
fetor: such infused f., WHITM 98
fetters: covet f., though they golden
   bee. SPENS 13
Fastening vowels, as with f.
   JONS 9
f. of my tongue MICH 2
Passion's too fierce to be in f.
   bound, DRYD 8
feud: f. with Death TENN 38
immemorial f. Of rich and poor.
   READ H 1
feuds: desponding Whigs,/ Forget
   their f., SWIF 8
Forget all f., MACA 2
theological f. in the taverns
   AUDE 84
fever: All f., filth and sweat,
   PRIN 1
by the same wintry f.
   THOMA D 22
f. of renown
   JOHN S (1709–1784) 17
had caught a f. COLM 1
hot as f. RANS 27
like his hand, in f., PLUM 3
My love is as a f., SHAK 242
tossed hours upon the tides of f.,
   MILLE V 1
feverish: f. fits of strife, CRAB 3
fevers: endanger me with the f.
   WHITM 97
Time and f. burn away AUDE 54
few: better for men/ To be f.
   JEFFE 21
f. friends, but they are in cities.
   SNYD 18
f. large stars overhead,
   WHITM 92
fit audience find, though f.
   MILT 84
God has a f. of us BROWNI R 4
If bees are f. DICKI 149
sacred f. SHEL 77
there are f. creatures
   MOOR M 26

There are f. hosts OHAR 7
too f. for drums and yells,
   OWEN 38
very f. to read. COLE H 1
"You the one, I the f." POUN 12
Fewness: rareness, muchness,/ F.
   GRAV 39
ffight: rise and f. againe.
   UNKN 225
Fiat: first F. that produc'd our
   Frame. DRYD 18
fibre: f. from the Brain does tear.
   BLAK 4
f. With fissures BROO G 10
filter and f. your blood.
   WHITM 74
fickle: Whatever is f., HOPKINS 19
your wills are f., MACN 25
fiction: Poetry is the supreme f.,
   STEVENS 14
truth severe, by fairy f. dressed.
   GRAY 6
fictions: f. only and false hair
   HERB G 44
fictive: f. things/ Wink as they will.
   STEVENS 15
Fiddle: cat and the f., MOTH 2
F., we know, is diddle: SWIN 18
important beyond all this f
   MOOR M 31
notes of a f., GAY 3
sick of the palette and f.-bow,
   YEATS 77
fiddled: f. whisper music
   ELIOT T 149
fiddles: in finesse of f. HULM 1
praisings of f. and flutes, PRAE 3
Fidele: fair F.'s grassy tomb
   COLL 1
fidelity: dog's f.!" HARD 7
fidget: little f. wheels SLES 1
fidgety: f. revenge. BROO G 3
Fie: better memory said F.;
   MUND 2
field: And open f., WORD 102
children run naked in the f.
   GINS 31
corner of a foreign f. BROO R 13
dreary f. and workshop,
   READ H 1
each f., each flower, each stick;
   ARNO 44
famished f. and blackened tree
   MUIR 9
f. rat, startled, squealing bleeds,
   TOOM 5
f. two yards away. MUIR 2
flying from f. and tree: BRID R 2
Give me a f. WHITM 29
Happy f. or mossy cavern,
   KEAT 33
heaping f. and highway
   LOWE J 11

in a f. a silken tent FROS 101
lark's nest in the f. SMAR 1
On the bare f MUIR 7
on the f. one night; WHITM 106
plough his f. WHITM 7
Rise odors of ploughed f. LONG 8
rushed into the f., BYRO 7
sanity of f. and mountain
   JEFFE 21
Sleep falls on forest and f.
   BRID R 19
sleep in a cold open f.,
   UNKN 312
smell of f. and grove MILT 70
thy beauty's f., SHAK 185
time the f. were mown. HOUS 29
To wood and f. LONG 39
whole f. is a/ white desire,
   WILLI 27
fieldes: midst the gladsome f.
   LODG 2
fieldfare: f. followed in the rear,
   THOR 11
fields: And favourite f. BETJ 7
Bloom in these darkened f.
   MUIR 9
blossoming buckwheat f.
   WHITM 31
broad f. of the sky: MILT 10
cheerful F. resume their green
   Attire: GRAY 32
Dream of battled f. SCOT WA 9
driving o'er the f., EMER 43
dry f. burn, LANIE 5
East and west on f. forgotten
   HOUS 43
Farewell green f. BLAK 101
f. are green SHEL 2
f. around lay bound and hoar
   THOR 11
f. beloved in vain! GRAY 13
F. melt my heart. PLATH 77
f. that we have planted
   MUIR 8
f. where glory does not stay,
   HOUS 56
In Flanders f. MCCRA 1
Keep your f. WHITM 31
myriad f. and the prairies wide,
   WHITM 51
Open unto the f., WORD 6
Out in the f. with God.
   BROWNI E/GUIN 1
range the f. LINC 2
space through ripe f. ROSE 1
sterile sands and the f. beyond,
   WHITM 62
subterranean F., — WORD 112
summer-scorched f.,
   BIBL, O.T. 67
sunken f. of hemp, TATE A 12
to just men's f.! THOR 9
torn f. of France. ROSE 2

firmly: falter where I f. trod,
    TENN 33
  f. gript the granite truth.
    MARK 2
  stalks are f. rooted in ice.
    STEVENS 27
  thine own track f. holding,
    WHITM 102
first: After the f. death,
    THOMA D 38
  Be not the f. POPE A 23
  Deep with the f. dead
    THOMA D 38
  divine property of her f. being.
    MILT 4
  each second/ Stood heir to th' f.
    SHAK 133
  feeling is f. CUMM 44
  F., animals; MERE G 15
  F. — Chill — then Stupor DICKI 2
  f. day i shot dope SANC 4
  f. day of Christmas, UNKN 274
  f. fall of the snow, TIMR 1
  f. Fiat that produc'd our Frame.
    DRYD 18
  f.-fruits of the bed; HERR 14
  f. grand Thief MILT 68
  F. he loved her, UNKN 218
  f. he wroghte, CHAU 13
  f. line he read, HOLM 12
  f. obedience, MILT 2
  f. strange and fatal interview,
    DONN 46
  F. time he kissed me,
    BROWNI E 3
  f. to the headland, WHITM 73
  four f. acts already past, BERK 1
  He taughte, but f. he folwed it
    hymselve. CHAU 14
  his f.-born's birth, BYRO 21
  how f. he met her? THAC 3
  King Charles the F. UNKN 12
  love is f. in their hearts,
    CLARK J 4
  not to lose the f. POPE A 98
  soil where f. they trod; HEMA 5
  tear — his f. TICK 2
  Thou art avenged, my f.-born,
    LOWE J 22
  Trust therefore f., WYAT 11
  we love/ F. BROWNI R 25
  When f. my lines of heavenly joys
    made mention, HERB G 40
  When God at f. made man,
    HERB G 61
  when our f. parent knew/ Thee
    WHITE 1
  whether he be f. or last.
    COLE SAM 44
firstlings: very f. of my heart
    SHAK 113
fish: Beast, bird, f., insect!
    POPE A 72

cars nose forward like f.;
    LOWE R 21
Cat's averse to f.? GRAY 19
dipping for f. MASE 10
F., flesh, or fowl, YEATS 125
F. (fly-replete, BROO R 9
f. of fancy teem MILLE V 1
f. or sea-fowl harmed YOUN A 1
f. scale, shale dust, bone
    SNYD 22
f., that is not catch'd thereby,
    DONN 7
f. that pleased my eye
    LOWE R 11
f. that rolls, MOMA 3
Gilled like a f. PLATH 81
hung five old pieces of f.-line,
    BISH 18
I was a f. SMIT L 5
I was a f. In the Paleozoic time,
    SMIT L 1
man poured f. into a pile,
    YEATS 93
moveless f. in the water gleam,
    DE LA 22
my f. float by SMIT ST 6
neither f. nor beast HUGH T 4
slow, as a f. she came, ROET 57
snow-white swans do f. for needful
    meat: TURB 1
tiny f. enjoy themselves LAWR 22
You singular f., RICHA L 1
fishbone: f. in the city's throat.
    LOWE R 18
  lick/ The f. bare. HUGH T 7
fished: f. A dime for Jesus ROBI 21
  his pond f. by his next neighbor,
    SHAK 179
fisherman: daughter of a f.,
    HOLM 10
  f. stood aghast, LONG 52
fishermen: Apostles were so many
    f.? MARV 3
Fishes: F. in the flood, UNKN 100
  f. leap and play BRET 5
  f. that are taken in an evil net,
    BIBL, O.T. 2
  men that f. gnawed upon;
    SHAK 97
  notes like little f. MACN 21
  Pearled wi' dew like f.' eyes,
    CLARE 3
  Venus among the f. LAWR 58
fishing: armored Diesel f. tubs
    LOWE R 6
  f. up the moon. PEAC 2
  f. was a rabbit's foot —
    LOWE R 12
  I sat upon the shore/ F.,
    ELIOT T 155
  I was f. in the dull canal
    ELIOT T 130
fishlike: Flash f.; YEATS 100

fissure: earth-lipped f. LAWR 44
fissures: fibre/ With f. BROO G 10
fist: f. of a face died THOMA D 5
  f. of trees, HALL 5
  one f. clenched AUDE 59
  weak mailed f. BISH 2
fists: Blind f. of nothing,
    CRAN H 21
  tender Page with horney F. was
    gual'd; DRYD 19
  they groan and shake their f.?
    HOUS 21
  With lightly closed f. WHITM 70
fit: f. audience find, though few.
    MILT 84
  f. into me ATWO 1
  f. of poverty: HORA 10
  f. only for Apollo BEAU 1
  f. words to paint SIDN 5
  Joshua f. de battle ob Jerico,
    UNKN 158
  let the punishment f. the crime —
    GILB 28
  lies at the f. o' the tree,
    UNKN 168
  like a palmer f., RALEG 11
  tumbled in a f. HOLM 13
fitful: bivouac's f. flame,
    WHITM 11
  f. firelight paled and shone.
    WHITT 28
  f. tracing of a portal;
    STEVENS 36
fitfully: at night f. sleeping,
    WHITM 17
fithele: robes riche, or f., or gay
    sautrie. CHAU 2
fits: feverish f. of strife, CRAB 3
  hand a needle better f., BRAD 16
fitted: I f. to the Latch/ My Hand,
    DICKI 72
fittest: f. for discourse DRYD 20
fitting: f. spot to dig Love's grave;
    MERE G 11
Five: bells,/ F. bells. SLES 5
  burst f. buttons off, HOLM 13
  dog lay dead f. days WILB 32
  figure 5./ in gold WILLI 15
  f. and country senses
    THOMA D 43
  F. bells coldly ringing out.
    SLES 5
  f. eyes break. THOMA D 44
  F. gold rings, UNKN 278
  f. kings count the dead
    THOMA D 25
  f. kings did a king to death.
    THOMA D 24
  F. sovereign fingers THOMA D 24
  f. watchful senses MILT 80
  for the constituency/ Feeds the f.
    thousand, RODG 5

Full fathom f. thy father lies;
SHAK 156
Housbondes at chirche dore I have
had f. CHAU 87
hung f. old pieces of fish-line,
BISH 18
in a f.-pound note. LEAR 10
in the 5. SPOT OHAR 6
tea is brought at f. MONR 1
Fives: F., and tens, LAWR 54
fix: swan must f. his eye
YEATS 153
We are in a f.! GINS 22
when this f. the head, WINT 11
fix'd: f./ His canon 'gainst self-
slaughter! SHAK 22
fixed: eternally f. afternoons!
OHAR 4
execute what his decree/ F.
MILT 98
f. forever in your closing eyes,
JARR 11
f. sentinels SHAK 57
f. stars/ Govern a life. PLATH 80
soul, the f. foot, DONN 64
time stand f.! MILT 105
fixing: f. in the wretch his cruel
fangs,
THOMS J (1700–1748) 11
fixt: eyes fast f. MILT 114
fixture: another issue/ of f., CREE 6
fizzing: f., hopeless fight. BETJ 3
Flabby: F., bald, lobotomized,
LOWE R 32
flag: Another f. unfurled! TIMR 3
battle-smoked f., with stars
eclipsed, MELV 16
death's pale f. SHAK 152
Eternity's white f. DICKI 116
f. has braved a thousand years
CAMPB T 10
f. is full of stars. VAN DY 3
f. is passing by! BENN H 1
F. of Freedom and Union,
WHITT 5
f. of the regiment, CRAN S 9
f. snaps in the glare JARR 20
f. the men hauled down;
WHITT 2
f. to April's breeze unfurled,
EMER 11
f. was still there; KEY 1
Nail to the mast her holy f.,
HOLM 18
She took up the f. WHITT 2
spare your country's f.," WHITT 3
flagon: from his pocket f.,
NASH 16
flags: discord of f. GRAV 22
guidon f. flutter WHITM 14
flail: shadowy f. hath threshed the
corn MILT 23
flak: woke to black f. JARR 5

flaked: f. off the paint, BISH 30
flakes: f. have lost their way,
HARD 42
f. were folding it gently,
LOWE J 12
f. with fingering stealth
OWEN 22
Night sank: like f. DAVID 4
rifle grooves curling with f. of
rust. SAND 1
flame: absence seemed my f. to
qualify. SHAK 230
As raging f., GAY 1
bivouac's fitful f., WHITM 11
Chloe is my real f. PRIO 9
clean in the f., WILLI 8
comet through f. SPEND 7
Dark faces pale against that rosy
f., TENN 81
dragonflies draw f.; HOPKINS 1
f./ But borrowed thence
HERB G 36
f.-flamingo infants' wear.
LOWE R 30
f. is blown abroad LONG 20
f. that lit HEMA 1
F. tongue of the dragon SNYD 30
Freedom's holy f. GRAY 27
in the f.-heart's shade. MCKA 4
inferior f. MILT 38
intolerable shirt of f. ELIOT T 70
joyous hearts! enfired with holy
f.! TAYL E 4
kindled the f. LIND V 14
Life, a Fury slinging f. TENN 28
lips of f. WILD 16
lovers, cruel as their f., MARV 16
pardon this clear f. THOR 7
petticoats coloured like f. OSUL 2
public f., nor private, POPE A 2
sang within a f. ROET 10
Show an affirming f. AUDE 78
smoke into the f. return Æ 3
sword an' the f., KIPL 31
thy fire and f. HERR 16
tongues of f. are in-folded
ELIOT T 74
unconquered f. POUN 23
under ashes into sudden f.,
MILT 116
undisturbed, unbreathing f.,
BISH 35
flamed: f. upon the brazen greaves
TENN 63
flames: crosslegged by the f.
SNYD 8
F. and ether WHITM 77
f. do work and wind when they
ascend, HERB G 42
f. upon the night/ Man's own
resinous heart YEATS 120
f. upon your forehead ROBI 23

my hands among the f.
PLATH 72
Ray round with f. TENN 42
through their play f. SHAK 57
flaming: Clanging fights, and f.
towns, TENN 90
f. forge of life LONG 50
f. from th' Ethereal Skie MILT 49
ruddy limbs and f. hair, BLAK 21
thou f. minister, SHAK 137
flamingo: Florida consider the f.,
WARR 9
Flanders: In F. fields MCCRA 1
flank: blading the wind's f.,
CRAN H 9
flanks: my shoulders, f., buttocks
WILLI 13
flannel: a fuzzed moth in a f. of
storm BIRN 4
flap: f. this bug with gilded wings,
POPE A 9
flapped: wind f. loose, ROSS D 9
flare: How all things f.!) SCHW 7
Loitered beneath the gas lamps'
f., WILD 16
one ruby f. SHAP 1
flash: arms f. in the sun —
WHITM 13
F. fishlike; YEATS 100
lightning f., SHAK 18
sparkled a f., a white flash.
KINN 13
white f. sparkled. KINN 11
Flashed: F. from his matted head
and marble feet, LOWE R 37
f. her golden smile HAYD 7
lightnings f.; JOHN J 2
team's head-brass f. THOMA E 2
flashes: f. of blooms of war;
WILLI 38
f. with black, WHITM 16
flashing: banners f. through the
trees ARNO 39
eyes f. solemnly with hate,
JOHN H 4
f. out TENN 124
flashy: Did Johnny look f.?
WAGO 1
flat: face extended f. GILB 45
f. Earth becomes a Ball.
BLAK 33
f.-headed man. ROET 54
f. on a sheet of blood OHAR 7
f. pink roses. PLATH 62
f. sleeping thing. CREE 14
On a f. road runs WHITM 70
plate/ Lies f. on the table top,
WILB 20
soul is f. MILLA 31
speak in a f. voice WRIG J 6
Steep towns, f. towns, SNYD 27
weary, stale, f., and unprofitable
SHAK 22

flatcars: riding f. to Fresno,
 SNYD 27
flaterye: winne us best with f.;
 CHAU 110
flats: fifty different sharps and f.
 BROWNI R 60
 young ducks with white straw f.,
 UNKN 258
Flattened: F. your words MILLA 13
flatter: dream doth f., SHAK 220
 f. beauty's ignorant ear.
 YEATS 131
 f., cajole, and persuade GILB 61
 F. the mountain-tops SHAK 197
flatter'd: by lies we f. be.
 SHAK 238
Flattered: F. to tears KEAT 5
flatterer: many a false f. CHAU 70
flatterers: by f. besieged, POPE A 7
 f.' venomous insinuations,
 SIDN 4
flattering: f. word, WILD 3
 idle, silly, f. words, HOWI 2
flattery: f., cards, and dice, and
 din: SHEN 1
 f.'s fawning face, EMER 27
Flaubert: Penelope was F.,
 POUN 38
Flaundryssh: F. bevere hat,
 CHAU 21
flaunting: f. extravagant quean,
 SHERI 1
flavor: f. of blood, KINN 4
flavour: f. of shredded coconut.
 SIMP 4
 I have still the f., POUN 67
flaw: receive a f., POPE A 117
flawed: dead faith foiled and f.
 ROBI 28
 f. words and stubborn sounds.
 STEVENS 40
flax: divide/ f. for damask
 MOOR M 37
flaxen: f.-haired,/ undernourished,
 HEAN 16
 rosy cheeks and f. curls,
 BROWNI R 62
flayed: you have f. us DOOL 7
flea: f. is you and I, DONN 25
 horse that feels a f., MOOR M 32
 snapped at a f. LIND V 18
fleck: every f. of russet FROS 4
flecked: f. the streets of Baltimore,
 RANDA J 1
fleckled: f. darkness like a drunkard
 reels SHAK 146
fleckless: mind is f., free WILLI 47
fled: dynasties that f. CRAN H 22
 false day that's f. RODG 7
 fancies all be f., VAUX 2
 F. gasping from the House —
 DICKI 73
 F. is that music: — KEAT 51

f. the visionary gleam? WORD 68
f. to bliss or woe! COLE SAM 35
I f. Him, down the nights
 THOMP F 6
marriage is dead, when the
 pleasure is f.: DRYD 16
soul has f.: WHITT 12
truth away/ From you is f.?
 WYAT 28
whither the clouds have f.?
 LOWE J 19
flee: chiding wives maken men to f.
 CHAU 98
 F. from the press CHAU 1
 leet f. a fart CHAU 57
 nestlings chirp and f., HOGG 1
 Swift doth young Love f.,
 MERE G 16
 They f. from me that sometime
 did me seek, WYAT 26
fleece: f. was white as snow,
 HALE 1
 skin nor hide nor f. DOOL 5
 wood's in trouble;/ His forest f.
 HOUS 44
fleet: a f. of small balck ships,
 BISH 25
 F. of foot SCOT WA 13
 so lithe and so f., LOWE J 1
fleetest: fairest things have f. end,
 THOMP F 1
fleeth: f. save Good Deeds,
 UNKN 90
fleeting: pleasure of the f. yeare!
 SHAK 223
fleets: f. of iron have fled, FINC 1
Flemish: F. pictures of old
 WHITT 29
flesh: 'All f. is grass.' UNKN 199
 All f. shall come to this, RODG 3
 ambitions incommensurable with
 f., SHAP 2
 beat/ On his helpless f....
 SITW 12
 buried in f. and blood, JONS 25
 busy tribes of f. and blood,
 WATT I 3
 change of f. BEAU/BASS 1
 dabs of f. WHITM 92
 eat strange f., SHAK 4
 Faint for the f., ROBI 2
 Fish, f., or fowl, YEATS 125
 f. and blood WHITM 77
 f. and blood so cheap! HOOD 13
 f. and the appetites, WHITM 74
 f. had made him blind,/ f. had one
 pleasure GRAV 37
 f. how it crumbles to dust
 AIKE 12
 f. is bruckle, DUNB W 3
 f. is but the glass, HERB G 11
 f. of mine/ More like a stock than
 like a vine. HERR 69

F. of thy flesh, BRAD 11
F. set one purpose GRAV 37
f. takes on the pure ROET 45
f. which walls about our life
 SHAK 89
frail f. VAUG 31
gnawed the f. SOUTHE 3
God clothed himself in vile man's
 f., DONN 54
God of our f., TATE A 4
good f. continuing/ Such
 tenderness, those afternoons
 HASS 4
gradual erasures/ Of f. MOSS 4
He is merely f. and blood.
 ELIOT T 36
in the f. it is immortal.
 STEVENS 36
Infatuate of the f. RANS 16
little curtain of f. BLAK 18
Neither f. nor fell. SKEL 12
Sell f. and blood. BYRO 32
so soon 'scaped world's and f.'s
 rage, JONS 23
study is a weariness of the f.
 BIBL, O.T. 7
such a thing as f. BROWNI R 28
terrors wherewith f. was racked.
 GRAV 37
thousand natural shocks/ That f. is
 heir to, SHAK 39
to my f. SNYD 11
too too solid f. would melt,
 SHAK 22
trapeze of your f., CRAN H 26
Triumph of f. GRAV 37
Waiting for the f. HODG 5
walls of f. grow weak, DOWS 2
Young soul put off your f.,
 BEDD 11
fleshy: in a f. tomb, COWP 16
 Turbulent, f., WHITM 73
flew: away they f. LEAR 2
 f. in a gold storm SCOT WI 1
 Holding it over him/ Gaily he f.
 HERF 2
 Out f. the web TENN 66
 out there f. a trope; BUTL 2
 That time I f., DICKI 88
 This morning, there f. RANS 25
 wanton snow f. to her breast,
 STROD 1
 witches they f. along rows
 ROET 25
flewen: for feare f. over the trees;
 CHAU 71
flexible: mild, pitiful, and f.;
 SHAK 61
flexing: my fingers f. HUGO 7
 who is mentally f. OHAR 4
Flick: ball loved F. UPDI 2
 F. stands tall UPDI 1

flicker: life, the f. of men and
  moths JEFFE 30
flickering: I have been f.,
  PLATH 47
flie: f. with angels, fall with dust,
  HERB G 65
flies: ain't no f. on me, FIEL E 4
  as f. hanging in heat, GUNN 11
  bush of f., PLATH 22
  chief to heedless f.
    THOMS J (1700–1748) 10
  fears, and f. from Marion's men.
    SIMM 2
  f. are on the plane tree,
    LOWE R 3
  f. in the night. BLAK 80
  Follow a shaddow, it still f. you;
    JONS 29
  heaven-ward f., HABI 2
  Kikuyu, quick as f., WALC 1
  like small gnats and f., SHEL 79
  mud/ F. from his hunching wings
    and beak— LOWE R 7
  sings as he f., UNKN 72
  small iridescent f. crawling on
    them. BISH 3
  swatting f., ASHB 2
flight: By f. of sin. HERB G 56
  empty cup, a f. of uncarpeted
    stairs. MILLA 37
  f. is past: and man forgot.
    KING H 5
  f. of Pegasean wing. MILT 83
  f. of small/ cheeping birds
    WILLI 43
  for a loftier f., TROW 3
  fox, lovely ritualist, in f.
    RANS 2
  His f. precipitant, MILT 65
  honest idiocy of f.) GRAV 8
  my f. HERR 51
  separate diverse f., WHITM 24
  thy upward f., THOR 6
flights: prepared for longer f.,
  MARV 19
  swift f. of Angels ministrant
  MILT 109
flighty: f. purpose never is o'ertook
  SHAK 113
fling: f. him down. MILLA 32
  f. his soul HARD 18
  F. off their iron VAN DO 1
  F. out imagination EBER 5
  f. the net, MERE G 6
  foes should f. us TIMR 4
  gossamer thread you f.
    WHITM 55
  with one hand did f. SHEL 77
flings: to Heaven he f. DUNB P 10
flint: Against the f. and hardness of
  my fault, SHAK 8
  shard, the pebble, and the f.,
    WILD 1

flinty: stern, obdurate, f., rough,
  remorseless. SHAK 61
flippers: absurd f. RICH 3
flirt: you f. of politeness, SHAP 5
flit: down the beach we f. THAX 1
  sweeter rivers pulsing f.
    EMER 48
Flits: F. across her bosom
  EMER 24
  f. by on leathern Wing, COLL 10
flitting: fancy has she for f.; HAY 2
  f. of the bat. MERE G 13
  raven, never f., POE 37
float: f. and flow POE 21
  f. from the door HEAN 5
  f. on their backs, WHITM 73
  f. that standard sheet! DRAK 4
  f. this carol with joy, WHITM 51
  f. up from the damnèd Earth.
    POE 30
  f. upon the tide of state, SWIF 16
  I f. thee a song, WHITM 51
  my fish f. by SMIT ST 6
  no sons/ to f. in the space
    KNIG 8
floating: f. home for ever left.
  COWP 1
  f. niggers swell. CRAN H 23
  f. on the Christal Flood,
    SPENS 42
  thin grey strand/ F. up LAWR 50
floats: chicken hawk f. over,
  WRIG J 4
  saintly soul f. POE 29
  wisp of smoke f. up SNYD 29
flock: f. of bells MEYN 1
  good increase/ Of f. and fold.
    HERB G 55
  half his f. were in their beds,
    YEATS 14
  led the f. away— DICKI 81
  Phillis hath a gallant f. LODG 4
  Shun the polluted f., WYLI 1
  to his sorrowful f.: BRID R 16
  turnkey now his f. returning sees,
    SWIF 11
  witless offspring f. MERW 4
Flocking: loathly birds/ F. round
  HODG 5
flocks: casual f. of pigeons
  STEVENS 62
  f. are thoughts. MEYN 3
  f. have took delight. BLAK 101
  F. of Churches, WORD 100
  grey f. in ferny glens BRON 6
  odours, fruits, and f., MILT 5
  quips and quibbles heard in f.,
    GILB 36
  shepherds feed their f. MARL 18
  shepherds pen their f. MILT 68
  shepherds watched their f. by
    night, TATE N 1

flood: blood to make up the f.
  JONS 17
  carried downwards by thy f.,
    WATT I 3
  come tumbling down the f.
    SWIF 9
  ebb and f. from the remote sea-
    tides THOMS J (1834–1882) 6
  famine, terror, f., and plague
    WALK 1
  Fishes in the f., UNKN 100
  floating on the Christal F.,
    SPENS 42
  f. comes down, SWIF 7
  f. may bear me far, TENN 10
  f./ Of mortal ills LUTH 2
  f. of remembrance, LAWR 32
  f. subsides, LAWR 42
  f. that does not flow. SLES 4
  f. the haunts TENN 43
  F.-tide below WHITM 18
  f./ Westward, westward
    TATE A 5
  Frowns o'er old Conway's foaming
    f., GRAY 3
  half so greet was nevere Noees f.
    CHAU 54
  heavenly Lethean f., DONN 34
  Like a dark f. suspended in its
    course, SHEL 16
  Over park, over pale,/ Thorough f.,
    thorough fire: SHAK 126
  perish in the f. CULL 11
  pouring-in of the f.-tide,
    WHITM 19
  rude bridge that arched the f.,
    EMER 11
  shoreless f., SHEL 68
  silently they took at f., NEME 1
  swan drifts upon a darkening f.
    YEATS 37
  taken at the f., SHAK 50
  torn the naiad from her f., POE 2
flooded: night-herons by the f. river
  JEFFE 16
floodgates: Unclench your f.,
  WHITM 73
floods: drown/ The night with you
  in f. of down. HERR 35
  F. all the soul LONG 30
  f. of rain, SURR 6
  Let the f. clap their hands;
    BIBL, O.T. 47
  poise/ Their f. LOVE 1
  tideless f. of Nothingness
    ROBI 37
  To bathe in fiery f., SHAK 115
floor: across the f. of hell; DAVID 1
  ancient f.,/ Footworn and
    hollowed HARD 40
  bearded spider on a sunlit f.
    TATE A 20
  bed on the f., TROW 5

fall at her f. feet. CAMPI 2
feathered with f. hours,
　DANI S 14
fluttring wings of thy fast f.
　SPENS 35
f. from field and tree: BRID R 2
f. from the thing they feared,
　SHEL 76
f. to the void, EMER 9
Heaven is not like f. or
　swimming, BISH 44
Just right for f., TROW 1
snow came f., BRID R 8
sun and the rain are f.,
　STEVENSO R 1
foam: 'as ships on the f. KIPL 30
Copulate in the f. YEATS 100
f. after the ocean's wrath
　SHEL 78
f./ Of perilous seas, KEAT 50
f. on the river, SCOT WA 8
gates of f., DE TA 1
pass like f., MASE 8
white as ocean f.;
　STEVENSO R 5
foamed: swift it f., ARNO 5
foaming: Frowns o'er old Conway's
　f. flood, GRAY 3
focal: f. and foremost fire, TICK 1
focused: f. beam/ folds all energy
　AMMO 19
f. energy of will. HAYD 16
focussed: His beak is f.; BISH 41
fodder: f.'s in the shock, RILE 4
foe: batter the f. ROON 1
breathes the f. DRAK 4
City bides the f. TIMR 1
commend,/ A timorous f.,
　POPE A 7
fear no f. LYTE 2
f. outstretch'd beneath the tree.
　BLAK 79
gladly praise the merit of a f.?
　POPE A 24
hell itself my only f. CLARE 14
I was angry with my f.: BLAK 78
old subtle f. so tempteth me
　DONN 60
post of the f.; BROWNI R 68
Tyrants fall in every f.! BURN 48
Foemen: F. at morn, but friends at
　eve — MELV 20
foes: cowering f. shall shrink
　DRAK 3
f. should fling us TIMR 4
foil thy f. with joy, SOUTHW 3
o'er her barb'rous F.
　JOHN S (1709–1784) 5
quick-eyed Pleasure's f.!
　FLET/SHAK 6
save/His life from f. HERB G 55
foetor: waiting for us in a f. Of
　vegetable sweat MAHON 2

fog: brown f. of a winter dawn,
　ELIOT T 118
elephants with their f.-colored
　skin MOOR M 19
Fear death? — to feel the f.
　BROWNI R 68
f. and filthy air. SHAK 102
night and f., TEAS 4
yellow f. that rubs its back.
　ELIOT T 78
foggy: keep her from the f., f. dew.
　UNKN 99
foil: f. thy foes with joy,
　SOUTHW 3
stars turn slowly/ in the blue f.
　TATE J 2
foiled: dead faith f. and flawed
　ROBI 28
foison: Earth's increase, f. plenty,
　SHAK 162
spring and f. of the year,
　SHAK 205
foist: admire/ What thou dost f.
　upon us SHAK 234
fold: f. it round me HULM 2
f. my towel KINS 6
f./ Of dire necessity MILT 115
f. their tents, like the Arabs,
　LONG 16
F. up the banners! THOMP W 4
good increase/ Of flock and f.
　HERB G 55
long will wait the f., HOUS 30
Star that bids the Shepherd f.,
　MILT 8
strong white arms to f. you,
　KIPL 16
walking to Blackberry F.
　UNKN 232
wolf on the f.? NASH 19
folded: drowsy head and f. wing,
　POE 38
F. close under deepening snow.
　LOWE J 13
f. hands, DODG 1
f./ her up like death, HARJ 3
F. his frame SHEL 16
f. like a saint, WYLI 9
f. my soldier well in his blanket,
　WHITM 107
F. the blanket well, WHITM 107
folders: misery of manilla f.
　ROET 7
folding: flakes were f. it gently,
　LOWE J 12
f., covering all. WHITM 71
f. up my little dreams JOHN G 3
folds: f. all energy AMMO 19
f. and wizenings, WILB 13
f. her wings JARR 2
foliage: For epitaph, in f.,
　HERR 53
Rise and put on your f., HERR 6

folk: crowd of ordinary decent f.
　AUDE 81
fair feeld ful of f. LANGL 3
f.-lore/ Of each of the senses;
　STEVENS 45
making f.-songs TOOM 1
O mortal f., you may behold and
　see HAWE 1
Thanne longen f. CHAU 4
folks: f. frown on that in Texas,
　DURE 2
heard f. tell HAY 3
like f. of this world. PRIO 1
my f. were growing old.
　STEVENSO R 6
old f. at home. FOST 4
old f. stay. FOST 3
poor f. as I; KINGSL 1
follow: at thy heel/ Did famine f.,
　SHAK 4
black-and-white angels f.
　DAY 11
Fainting I f. WYAT 31
First f. Nature, POPE A 25
F. a shaddow, it still flies you;
　JONS 29
f. eyes the steady keel,
　WHITM 45
F. him out of grace.
　THOMA D 20
f. knowledge like a sinking star,
　TENN 132
f. the bonnet of Bonny Dundee.
　SCOT WA 3
f. this and come to dust.
　SHAK 18
f. those slender windrows,
　WHITM 2
f. with accents sweet; CAMPI 2
F. your saint, CAMPI 2
goodness and mercy shall f. me
　BIBL, O.T. 31
make them f. HALE 2
thin ghost that I now frailly f.!
　HARD 2
those who f. MASE 9
To f., to seek, WHITM 17
We f. where the Swamp Fox
　guides, SIMM 1
years that f. victory MELV 6
Followe: F. thy faire sunne,
　CAMPI 1
followed: fieldfare f. in the rear,
　THOR 11
f. her to school HALE 1
f. him, honored him,
　BROWNI R 45
f. my own/ Trail SNYD 2
f. the hunchback THOMA D 26
He f. — close behind — DICKI 64
following: dog f. a brass band.
　BARK 4
F. his plough, WORD 121

follows

F. his track, MILT 62
lost in f. years. WATT I 3
on the f. Feet, THOMP F 7
follows: attendant f. WHITM 115
f. on a woman thro the fire,
   BOYD 1
folly: Blinded they into f. run
   UNKN 185
filled with f. and sin, MERE O 3
f. of being comforted. YEATS 62
f. to aspire. MILT 105
forts of f. fall, ARNO 14
gay through f.; POPE A 109
He knew human f. AUDE 4
impotence of rage/ At human f.,
   ELIOT T 68
In f. ripe, RALEG 8
lovely woman stoops to f.,
   GOLD 9
make/ Our faith mere f.;
   SHAK 6
neebour's fauts and f.! BURN 4
of f., noise and sin!
   BROWNI R 49
Sighs for f. said AUDE 11
'Tis f. to be wise. GRAY 17
folwed: He taughte, but first he f. it
   hymselve. CHAU 14
fond: As a f. mother, LONG 33
brisk f. lackey to fetch and carry,
   HOUS 3
f. and wayward thoughts
   WORD 44
F. Fancy's scum SIDN 39
F. Memory brings the light
   MOOR T 10
f. of beetle-pie. CARRY 5
f. recollection presents WOOD 1
Our f. Begetters, DRYD 1
wipe away all trivial f. records,
   SHAK 28
fonder: grow f., sweet Cork, of
   thee; MAHONY 2
fondest: f., blindest, weakest,
   THOMP F 10
Fondle: kids, frisk with your dog,/ F.
   your shells CRAN H 47
fondly: I aft hae kissed sae f.;
   BURN 31
food: and lays out f. in tins.
   ELIOT T 134
bad f. from the two cafes
   WELC 2
flowers or the f. SPENC B 1
F. and Raiment now grew scarce
   SWIF 15
for shelter and for f., LOWE J 20
give me some f." SIDN 21
human nature's daily f.;
   WORD 134
If music be the f. of love,
   SHAK 174
mimes become its f., POE 32

Nothing to eat but f., KING B 1
salted was my f., THOMA E 16
soft f. for worms, MAHON 3
trade the memory of this night for
   f. MILLA 17
whose f. fills you. HERR 25
fool: breath/ Of every f., SHAK 58
Busy old f., unruly sun, DONN 55
every f. is not a poet.
   POPE A 125
every poet is a f.: POPE A 125
Exposed the f., SWIF 22
Fear most to tax an honorable f.,
   POPE A 21
f. and herb, DOUG K 1
f. he called her his lady fair —
   KIPL 27
f.'s self-chosen snare, SIDN 39
I met a f. i' the forest, SHAK 15
know/ If I am a f. SNYD 12
Love's not Time's f., SHAK 232
motley f. SHAK 15
no way of knowing a f. FROS 124
nor yet a f. to fame, POPE A 13
nothing satisfied the f. YEATS 72
Poor verdant f., LOVE 1
So true a f. is love, SHAK 208
tender f.'s in tears, CONG 2
Though man's a f., POPE A 82
to be a f. CUMM 45
when we play the f., LAND 14
Woman and f. POPE A 96
You are a proper f., ELIOT T 127
foolish: being young and f.,
   YEATS 50
Bored with the f. things
   CAMPB R 7
f. fears of what might happen.
   BROWNI E/GUIN 1
f. fort, a heart,/ (Time strangely
   spent) SUCK 7
F. friends and kinsmen,
   UNKN 90
F. prater, COWL 16
f. thing was but a toy, SHAK 177
never said a f. thing, ROCH 4
observed in f. awe MUIR 3
paltry, f., painted things,
   DRAY 10
fools: all family f., GILB 57
come/ To this great stage of f.. —
   SHAK 83
Dreading e'en f., POPE A 7
f. rush in POPE A 23
f. that wish to die! UNKN 128
For f. admire, POPE A 29
Gie f. their silks, BURN 25
I damn such f.! — SWIF 5
let f. contest; POPE A 83
lighted f. The way to dusty
   death. SHAK 114
loyalty well held to f. SHAK 6
more f. than wise. GIBB 1

Nor good, nor bad, nor f., nor
   wise, PRIO 4
Poems are made by f. like me,
   KILM 2
pride, the never-failing vice of f.
   POPE A 32
proved plain f. at last.
   POPE A 23
To dandle f.: BACO 2
wall-builders than f. FROS 17
foot: at the rainbow's f. ROSS C 25
chase into the house a lucky f.
   HOUS 8
dancer stayed his hungry f.
   YEATS 95
dared not stir a f., FROS 110
'eathen idol's f.: KIPL 10
fishing was a rabbit's f.
   LOWE R 12
Fleet of f. SCOT WA 13
f. ends in hoof. GUNN 6
fountain's sliding f., MARV 19
hand and f. that stir not,
   VERY 3
hand, of f., of lip, of eye, of brow,
   SHAK 228
head with f. hath private amitie,
   HERB G 53
his f. upon the stirrup, DE LA 13
hold his swift f. back, SHAK 212
lived like a f. PLATH 26
man with a f. in the grave
   SERV 7
nor hand, nor f.,/ Nor arm, nor
   face, SHAK 142
plant a f. upon, MUIR 1
resembles a bird's f. SIMI 5
soul, the fixed f., DONN 64
with f. so free; WORD 154
with printless f. SHAK 164
foote: Men were deceivers ever,/ One
   f. in Sea, SHAK 130
footfall: as a hushed f. In a long
   forgotten snow. TEAS 3
lightness in her f., RANS 3
Footfalls: F. echo in the memory
   ELIOT T 16
footing: fragrance in thy f. treads;
   WORD 89
Footman: seen the eternal F.
   ELIOT T 87
footmarks: left his little f.,
   CLARE 10
footpath: Jog on, jog on, the f.
   way, SHAK 180
footpaths: f. for the thought of
   Italy! LONG 20
f. of the swamp. TOOM 2
footprints: f. in the dew;
   BROO R 6
f. of the crime." KAVA 12
F. on the sands of time;
   LONG 36

hieroglyphs of the rat f. SAND 9
Red f. wrote on the snow
SAND 23
foot's: Our f. in the door.
PLATH 67
footsoles: f./ Trod warily on living
coals. WYLI 4
slapped your f., PLATH 61
footstep: where thy f. gleams —
POE 8
footsteps: distant f. echo LONG 15
He plants his f. COWP 4
holy f. I may tread: MICH 2
trace thy f. CLARE 8
footstool: f. crack, and the sun
wink. DONN 28
Footworn: ancient floor,/ F. and
hollowed HARD 40
foppery: For f. he gave not any
figs, HECH 16
fops: whole tribe of f. SHAK 70
forager: Our selfless f. Jerry.
FROS 32
Forbear: F. my most desire;
WYAT 19
f. the bitter blow; SARE 1
forbeare: f.,/ His wonted songs,
SPENS 49
Forbede: F. us thing, and that
desiren we; CHAU 89
forbid: shamrock is by law f.
UNKN 299
What the day doth f. CAMPI 3
Forbidden: F. mixtures MARV 25
Fruit/ Of that F. Tree, MILT 46
On whose f. ear DICKI 135
yet f. vanity, GREV 9
forbids: my mind f. to crave.
DYER E 1
forc'd: f. fingers rude MILT 25
f., like Heav'n, against my mind,
DRYD 1
force: burst like a ruthless f.,
WHITM 7
cease your pleading f.!
UNKN 237
drained out one another's f.
SNOD 15
elegance also is f.;/ After polishing
granite LOWE J 6
f. an echo more, POE 43
f. me to a smile. COWP 3
f. More dreadful AUDE 16
f. that through the green fuse
THOMA D 22
fruit of chemic f., EMER 51
joint f. and full result of all.
POPE A 35
Life, f., and beauty POPE A 25
love the f. that grows us,
SHAP 18
muses lend their f., THOR 4

Our realm it brooks no stranger's
f., ELIZ 1
sceptre shows the f. of temporal
power, SHAK 123
skilful Nymph reviews her f.
POPE A 121
wage by f. or guile MILT 52
forced: f. march of Monday
PAGE 1
f. to choose/ Perfection YEATS 23
Virtues/ Are f. upon us
ELIOT T 33
windy suspiration of f. breath,
SHAK 21
forcing: no f. of image, AMMO 8
fordone: its strength f., BRID R 18
with weary task f. SHAK 128
fore: sad account of f.-bemoaned
moan, SHAK 195
foredoomed: Luna presence,/ f.,
HAYD 17
forefeet: Head held back, f. out,
SNYD 37
fore-finger: f. of an alderman
SHAK 153
forego: beauty to f. her wreath?
ARNO 11
foregone: grieve at grievances f.
SHAK 195
forehead: burning f., KEAT 39
flames upon your f. ROBI 23
f. and the little ears ROBI 15
middle of his f. NASH 3
Monadnock, on his f. hoar,
SIGO 2
of the godlike f., WORD 17
serpents on the f. BOGA 8
wild on her f.,
WRIG J 2
woman smoothes her f.
STEVENS 12
foreheads: cloudy f. of the great.
HORA 10
foreign: corner of a f. field
BROO R 13
flower in f. air? ARNO 40
freed from f. harms; SPENS 47
from frost or f. wind. HUGO 4
hawk-like f. faces MACN 11
loving a f. muse. BENE 3
foreigners: died like aunts of pets or
f. JARR 14
foreknowledge: eyes f. of death:
SWIN 2
f. absolute, MILT 60
Providence, F., Will, and Fate,
MILT 60
foreman: God is a f. HEAN 14
foremost: focal and f. fire, TICK 1
f. fighting, fell. BYRO 7
f. of his company, UNKN 60
foucht aye the f., ELLI 2
(On the f. ranks WHITM 26

forenoon: f. walk, my rest,
WHITM 23
forepaws: cleanest in the use of his
f. SMAR 7
foresight: f. much advanc't,
MILT 52
mind to aftersight and f.,
ELIOT T 67
forest: along the f. side TAYL B 1
fade away into the f. dim:
KEAT 46
Flowers of the F., ELLI 2
f. crack'd, TENN 23
f., dim and old, POE 42
fox in the f., PITT 2
I met a fool i' the f., SHAK 15
In f. wild, in thicket, brake, or
den; MILT 86
lost to the f., SCOT WA 7
old oak f. I KEAT 57
passionate wonder of your f.
JOHN H 2
Sleep falls on f. and field.
BRID R 19
walk in a grim f. CRAN S 5
wild as f. doe. UNKN 45
wood's in trouble;/ His f. fleece
HOUS 44
forests: cannot carry f. EMER 36
F. are rended, SCOT WA 22
F. at the bottom of the sea,
WHITM 112
f. of the night, BLAK 81, 84
f. where they roamed, SIGO 1
strength of virgin f. MARK 2
thin f. of silver-grey. SNYD 46
trace huge F., MILT 3
foretell: observers may f. the hour
SWIF 6
forethought: f. of grief. BERRY 1
rule and pale f., EMER 33
foretold: work for which thou wast
f. MILT 115
forever: advance for as long as f. is.
THOMA D 41
banish our anger f. FINC 2
clean f. and f., WHITM 97
eyes f. for me. WHITM 32
f. and a day, LONG 10
f. stands the sea, WINT 7
f. with reverted look LONG 27
grinning cat/ Quivers f. TATE A 3
Heaven's light f. shines, SHEL 13
I go on f. TENN 5
life f. old yet new, BROWNI R 43
Storm me f. THOMA D 5
Time will not be ours f.,
JONS 48
up the hill f. RANS 27
will I keep you f., LONG 10
winter's not f., CUMM 1
forevermore: shine f. MCCRE 1

forfeit: f. fair renown,　SCOT WA 12
f. to a confined doom.　SHAK 229
Forfex: glitt'ring F. wide,
　POPE A 124
forge: at the f.'s fire.　HALL 4
flaming f. of life　LONG 50
f. a name,　EMER 37
F. arms —　SHEL 64
random grim f.,　HOPKINS 6
Wit's f. and fire-blast,
　COLE SAM 25
forget: Abortions will not let you f.
　BROO G 17
eyes f. the tears　LOWE J 19
F. all feuds,　MACA 2
f. all things but one,　DE TA 2
f. and smile　ROSS C 20
f. cruelty and past betrayal,
　GRAV 43
f./ The friends　BRYA 36
F. the glories　WORD 73
F. thyself to marble,　MILT 16
f. time and death:　ROET 13
f. what flowers　GRAV 35
f. your tears,　MORR 2
give and then f.;　ROBI 1
haply may f.　ROSS C 34
I f. the rest.　BROWNI R 53
I pray that I may f. These
　matters　ELIOT T 5
If I f. thee, O Jerusalem,
　BIBL, O.T. 63
Lest we f.　KIPL 17
look I shall never f.,　WHITM 106
Make them f.　BROWNI R 28
mercy, if thou wilt f.　DONN 34
praying I may soon f.
　JOHN G 3
right hand f. her cunning.
　BIBL, O.T. 63
so I would f.　ELIOT T 7
tree/ Budding yearly must f.
　CULL 7
vigil I never f.,　WHITM 107
you'll never f.　SASS 1
forgetful: covering/ Earth in f.
　snow,　ELIOT T 113
f. kingdom of death.　RANS 21
forgetfulness: atone to f.
　ELIOT T 7
steep my senses in f.?　SHAK 54
forgets: / f. his /leg of /wood.
　GRAV 21
heart f. its sorrow　LOWE J 19
heart that has truly loved never
　f.,　MOOR T 3
one-legged man f.　GRAV 21
sun in time f. for to retire
　FLET G EL 1
forgetting: birth is but a sleep and a
　f.:　WORD 69
dark f. of my cares　DANI S 8
if f. could be willed.　MERE G 5

Forgive: father forsaken,/ F. your
　son!　JOYC 2
F. the hero,　WILB 38
f. those done to us,　STEPHENS 7
f. thy robbery, gentle thief,
　SHAK 200
F. us all our trespasses,
　STEPHENS 7
to f. divine.　POPE A 35
To f. wrongs　SHEL 58
forgiven: come back, and be f.
　MERE O 4
earth shall be f.　CLARE 6
every lapse f.,　RICH 22
Had not f. her.　SIMP 5
forgiveness: After such knowledge,
　what f.?　ELIOT T 32
Asking f. of his tongueless head.
　WILB 33
kneel down/ And ask of thee f.
　SHAK 84
Man's f. give —　OMAR 1
obtain f.　MILT 111
forgot: flight is past: and man f.
　KING H 5
f. as soon/ As done.　SHAK 173
F. the cry of gulls,　ELIOT T 142
F. was Britain's glory;
　TAYL B 2
I had f. My selfe and thee.
　JONS 13
Loved accents are soon f.
　SHEL 89
Philon the shepherd, late f.,
　UNKN 290
Settles and is f.　WILB 19
Should auld acquaintance be f.,
　BURN 13
though I am clean f.,　HERB G 6
Which ne'er f. will be;
　DOUG W 1
forgotten: am not f.,　EMME 1
as a hushed footfall/ In a long f.
　snow.　TEAS 3
back on f. dreams,　OWEN 22
child's/ F. mornings　THOMA D 34
each part will be f.　SHAK 216
flower is f.,　TEAS 2
fly f., as a dream　WATT I 3
F. as a fire　TEAS 2
f. crowd/ Of common beauties,
　CAREW 2
f., whom no poet sings,　DRAY 10
hath not f. my age."　SOUTHE 7
Have you f. yet? . . .　SASS 1
Let it be f.　TEAS 2
Li Po's name f.,　LI PO 2
mingle with f. ashes,　SHIR 4
of f. lore,　POE 34
old f. queens　BENN G 6
Sleep softly . . . eagle f. . . . under
　the stone.　LIND V 13

something we have f.?　BONT 6
soul's f. gleam.　NELS 1
forked: f. mountain,　SHAK 9
with a f. berd,　CHAU 21
forkful: bundles every f.　FROS 24
forks: pursued it with f.
　CARRO 12
forlorn: confus'd march f.,　MILT 61
I wait f.　ARNO 32
in faery lands f.　KEAT 50
maiden all f.　MOTH 8
That music, remote, f.　DE LA 18
forlorne: of thy loved lasse f.?
　SPENS 48
form: all must love the human f.,
　BLAK 89
Arch Fear in a visible f.,
　BROWNI R 68
beauteous f. assures a piteous
　mind.　DONN 67
changes wrought on f. and face;
　TENN 38
envelop'd well his f.,　WHITM 107
f. of a maiden fair,　LONG 52
f. was thine!　BLAK 26
heavenly f. Angelic,　MILT 90
human thought or f.,　SHEL 30
live in happier f.　SHEL 91
lose the glory of the f.,　ARNO 11
love is f.,　OLSO 9
Love, the human f. divine,
　BLAK 88
mold of f.,　SHAK 33
mother's f. upon my ken,
　HARD 35
one loves only f.,　OLSO 11
Only by the f., the pattern,
　ELIOT T 23
pink official f.　AUDE 7
place, degree, and f.,　SHAK 58
proud though childlike f.
　HEMA 1
repeated f.,　CREE 6
So little is thy f. declined,
　SWIF 21
take/ My bodily f.　YEATS 129
water to sound, fire to f.:
　RUKE 2
formal: Caught up in a f. delight,
　KINN 9
f. feeling comes —　DICKI 1
form'd: f. from this soil,
　WHITM 74
forme: capable of any f. at all.
　MARL 11
formed: f. of Joy and Mirth,
　BLAK 22
former: one jot of f. love retain.
　DRAY 15
she joined the f. two.　DRYD 10
thy f. light restore,　SHAK 137
formless: all our f. prayers,
　HECH 6

f. spawning fury wrecked,
YEATS 143
F. stacks of bodies WHITM 92
forms: all f., moods, shapes of
grief, SHAK 21
ancient f. of party strife;
TENN 48
cacophony of dusty f. GUNN 4
change the f. of being. BRYA 17
clouded f. of long-past history.
BRON 5
f. are fair, BROWNI R 1
f. I see on stretchers WHITM 71
f. imaginations, MILT 80
F. more real than living man,
SHEL 51
f. of government POPE A 83
f. of incompleteness, RUKE 5
f. of things unknown, SHAK 127
F. remains, WORD 127
givest to f. and images a breath
WORD 98
jealous of all living f. PRAT 1
legions, angel f., MILT 55
pass the wanderer by — / White-
robed f. POE 17
released from f., AMMO 3
Shrouded f. that start and sigh
POE 17
variety of f. MOOR M 6
formulated: in a f. phrase,
ELIOT T 83
forsak: f. the, Kyng Herowdes,
UNKN 213
forsake: Beauty, Strength, and
Discretion do man f., UNKN 90
f. his Muses dear, MARV 20
F. me not thus, MILT 101
moonéd sands f. LUCR 4
sweets and beauties do themselves
f., SHAK 186
Which if men f., UNKN 185
woman that you f. her, KIPL 15
forsaken: father f.,/ Forgive your
son! JOYC 2
harvest-fields f., LONG 38
live f. so. UNKN 167
lover f. WALS 1
old f. bough HOLM 16
Society has quite f. GILB 50
things innocent, hapless, f.
ROET 41
forsakes: f. his heavenly fires
LODG 6
Forseen: F. for so many years:
JEFFE 20
forspent: Clean f. LANIE 1
F. with love and shame, LANIE 1
forsworn: sweetly were f.;
SHAK 117
fort: foolish f., a heart, SUCK 7
f. against the cold WILLI 10
Unbreachable the f. ARNO 46

forte: Pity is not your f. RICH 11
forth: but go f. TIMR 4
distance throws them f.,
GUNN 11
f. I march, thou goest before;
BIBL, O.T. 64
F.-reaching to the Fruit, MILT 89
glide noiselessly f.; WHITM 42
gone back and f. all night on the
ferry. MILLA 26
launch'd forth filament,
WHITM 55
lets f. his sprite, SHAK 128
Verse calls them f. LAND 5
forties: f. & menopause GINS 30
fortify: f. thy name against old age;
DANI S 12
fortitude: f. of mien, CARM 2
What is there/ like f.!
MOOR M 21
fortress: fast in my f., LONG 10
f. against ideas MACN 1
f. built by Nature SHAK 88
mighty f. is our God LUTH 2
fortress'd: powerful f. house,
WHITM 42
forts: f. of folly fall, ARNO 14
fortunate: f. bride, BOGA 5
we inherit from the f.
ELIOT T 69
Fortune: adverse F.'s pow'r;
HORA 5
F. and to Fame unknown,
GRAY 12
F., honour, beauty, youth,
CAMPI 29
F., that arrant whore, SHAK 73
here by F. plac'd,
JOHN S (1709–1784) 8
in disgrace with f. and mens
eyes, SHAK 194
leads on to f.; SHAK 50
lowest and most dejected thing of
f., SHAK 77
man of no f., POUN 6
railed on Lady F. SHAK 15
sea of F. SOUTHW 8
shalt by f. SHAK 196
slings and arrows of outrageous
f., SHAK 39
spite of f., SHAK 221
to what f., WHITM 34
try the fresh f. BROWNI R 50
very worst of f.'s might.
SHAK 221
wheel of f. guide you, JONS 11
fortunes: f. must be wrought;
LONG 50
f. of my pleasant choice.
SURR 5
in darker f. tried. BRYA 36
unjust F. sway, SIDN 31

forty: Blind as the nineteen hundred
and f. nails SITW 11
f. feeding like one! WORD 163
f. years ago,/ When you were all
aglow, HARD 2
f. years been growing. WHITT 14
Men at f. JUST 5
rack up thirty-eight or f. UPDI 2
When f. winters SHAK 185
forty-four: took out her f.
UNKN 102
Forward: behind cried "F.!"
MACA 4
cars nose f. like fish; LOWE R 21
F. let us range, TENN 79
F. the Light Brigade! TENN 6
f., without cessation, ROET 44
gone f. with/ Some, WRIG J 7
marched breast f., BROWNI R 12
nothing to look f. to with hope,
FROS 25
foster: f.-child of silence KEAT 36
make her F.-child, WORD 73
Fostered: F. alike by beauty and by
fear: WORD 93
foucht: f. aye the foremost, ELLI 2
fought: famine or scurvy — I f. it;
SERV 11
f. all night with a cocaine rat,
UNKN 67
f. and bled HOPKINSO 1
f. for life, SPEND 12
f. such a fight TENN 119
f. with her, she f. with me,
CREE 1
skirmish f. near Marathon.
GRAV 20
soil they f. to save. BRYA 2
foul: breaking through the f. and
ugly mists SHAK 51
coupled to f. thraldom. BARBO 2
Fair is f., SHAK 102
F. goat-head, YEATS 100
f. is fair. SHAK 102
f. rag-and-bone shop of the heart.
YEATS 29
From camp to camp, through the
f. womb of night, SHAK 57
Hobgoblin nor f. Fiend BUNY 3
my sight is f., HOOD 14
old f. river SMIT ST 7
swear that, f. or fair, SERV 2
unchaste looks, loose gestures, and
f. talk, MILT 4
ways be f., SHAK 101
with her f. pride. SHAK 240
foule: f. debate/ Twixt noble men
UNKN 63
found: better man was f. HOLM 15
birth had never f. it AMMO 17
Columbus f. a world, SANT 1
F. a family, build a state,
MELV 8

f. a text to prove   YEATS 64

f./ A white hair   KLEI 1

f./ At Roncevaux   MACL 12

f. in the close.   MILT 118

f. no comfort in the grave.
YEATS 96

f. on his nails,   HART 2

f. the arrow,   LONG 3

f. the people incomplete,
WILB 48

he f. it.   SHAK 53

I've f. it good.   KIPL 21

just as f.:   HARD 19

'Line in nature is not f.;
EMER 50

my espoused, my latest f.,
MILT 79

my resting-place is f.,
BROWNI R 5

No name shall but your own be
f.   MARV 16

no sorrow may be f.   UNKN 147

Nothing in Nature's sober f.,
COWL 2

song, from beginning to end,/ I f.
again   LONG 3

Stretched in his last-f. home,
HOLM 2

That in a little cottage I have f.;
KEAT 30

think the parson f.,   HOLM 9

victim must be f.,   GILB 26

foundation: from the prime f.;
HOUS 24

foundations: I laid the f. of the
earth?   BIBL, O.T. 13

oxen near/ The worn f.
LOWE R 23

Founded: F. in reason,   MILT 78

founder: f. of taste   JONS 27

tomb/ Shall list and f.   SHAP 25

foundering: War was f. of
sublimities,   GRAV 23

founders: f. lived and died
YEATS 35

f. of these starving cities,
AUDE 19

fount: Slow, slow, fresh f.,   JONS 4

fountain: bubble on the f.,
SCOT WA 8

By the f.'s brink.   ROSS C 31

clear f. of eternal day,   MARV 31

down to the f.-quieted square;
WILB 34

f. at salute, a crown in view —
CRAN H 45

f. crystal-clear,   MOTH 16

f. from its rocky cave   WORD 154

F.-head and source of rivers,
THOR 8

f. light of all our day,   WORD 81

f. of domestic sweets,   MILT 78

F. sweet of heart and mind!
JOHN S (1822–1882) 1

f.'s sliding foot,   MARV 19

frog peeps out o' the f.   JONS 16

healing f. start,   AUDE 46

miraculous cure at the f.;
AUDE 84

Rise like a f.   TENN 104

sacred F. of eternall light,
QUAR 2

summer-dried f.,   SCOT WA 7

fountaines: two faithfull f.,   CRAS 8

fountains: Beside the crystal f.
UNKN 26

F. and ye, that warble,   MILT 82

f. of the boiling stars,   JEFFE 4

silver f. mud,   SHAK 199

four: F.-and-twenty Spanish
hooves   VAN DO 1

f. bullets hushed her.   HAYD 12

f.-clawed Mole.   DE LA 1

F. colly birds,   UNKN 277

f. first acts already past,   BERK 1

f.-footed in berries.   BIRN 2

f.-honed-down ivory toes   LEVI 1

f. light-green eggs   WHITM 64

f. little foxes saw their mother
go —   SARE 1

"Last night there was f. Maries,
UNKN 188

sick f.-story hulk,   BROO G 10

valet, too, to every f.   GILB 4

fourpenny: f. boat,   PEAC 3

fours: Threes and f. and twelves,
LAWR 54

fourscore: Bowed with her f. years
and ten;   WHITT 2

fourteen: f. teats into the fourteen
mouths   KINN 15

son of a farmer, age f.;   TROW 1

twelve or f. moonshines   SHAK 70

Fourth: didn't get back till the F. of
July.   UNKN 135

f. day of Christmas,   UNKN 277

foweles: smale f. maken melodye,
CHAU 4

fowl: Fish, flesh, or f.,   YEATS 125

f. be multiplied on the earth.
MILT 85

f. fly above the earth,   MILT 85

harsh cries of wild f.
MACDONO 3

lord of the f. and the brute.
COWP 23

Fowls: F. in the frith,   UNKN 100

fox: berd as any sowe or f. was
reed,   CHAU 17

f. in the forest,   PITT 2

f., lovely ritualist, in flight
RANS 2

f.'s nose touches twig,
HUGH T 13

room with a stuffed f.
THOMA D 3

sharp hot stink of f.   HUGH T 14

We follow where the Swamp F.
guides,   SIMM 1

foxes: four little f. saw their mother
go —   SARE 1

little f., that spoil the vines:
BIBL, O.T. 73

three little f.   MILN 3

fraction: perhaps/ f. of flower
CUMM 55

Fragile: F. and luminous.   PRIN 1

f. ship of courage,   LAWR 39

shakes this f. frame at eve
HARD 27

small,/ Contained and f.,   WINT 1

fragment: f. from his dream of
human life,   WORD 75

fragments: copied f. from our
breast;   THOMP F 5

Death tramples it to f.   SHEL 13

f. and rough drafts.   RICH 20

f. / Of quiet shadows   DAVIS 5

not control of time,/ Nor shattered
f.   RICH 26

silver-thin/ Shatters into a billion
f.   DAVIS 5

These f. I have shored
ELIOT T 156

With f. strewed the sea; —
HEMA 2

fragrance: f. in thy footing treads;
WORD 89

f. Of your flowers,   JOHN H 2

fragrant: f. camomel;   SKEL 1

f. flowers   KING H 1

f. portals, dimly-starred,
STEVENS 19

Glistring with dew; f. the fertile
earth   MILT 76

in the f. pines   WHITM 53

lucid morning's f. breath
THOMS J (1834–1882) 1

frail: aged thrush, f., gaunt,
HARD 18

Cut grass lies f.:   LARK 7

f. china jar   POPE A 117

f. duration of a flower.   FRENE 7

f. flesh   VAUG 31

joy and f. prosperity,   MORE 1

lead f. minds to rest   SPENS 5

lift f. heads   MAHON 3

Like some f. exhalation;   SHEL 21

this f. world;   MILT 62

Unconstant, f., untrue;   WITH 3

What are f.?   ROSS C 30

your most f. gesture   CUMM 48

frailest: choose you the f.,   SHEL 90

frailly: thin ghost that I now f.
follow!   HARD 2

frailties: in my nature reigned/ All
   f. SHAK 230
man f. hath, HERB G 24
frailty: f. of all things here,
   SHEL 90
through f. stepped aside, SWIF 4
frame: calm and heav'nly f.;
   COWP 25
cannot f. me tune to fayne,
   WYAT 22
first Fiat that produc'd our F.
   DRYD 18
Folded his f. SHEL 16
f. my thoughts, SPENS 5
f. so robust, LOWE J 1
f. thy fearful symmetry?
   BLAK 81, 84
Graunt me to f. UNKN 169
my curious f.: MARV 5
Nature's vast f., SHEL 22
one sure band/ Ties the whole f.,
   HERB G 15
shakes this fragile f. at eve
   HARD 27
spangled Heav'ns, a Shining F.,
   ADDI 3
stirs this mortal f., COLE SAM 23
tremble for this lovely f.,
   WHITE 1
twin cities f. LAZA 1
universal F. began: DRYD 25
frames: question that he f.
   FROS 86
France: Emperor of F.?' KIPL 23
Fair stood the wind for F.,
   DRAY 1
imported from F., GILB 59
pretty kings of F. RANS 32
torn fields of F. ROSE 2
Francesca: Pier della F.: POUN 10
Francis: Sir F. is come; UNKN 294
welcome home, Sir F. Drake.'
   UNKN 295
francs: costs three f. BYRO 43
Frank: back to sleep now/ F.,
   OHAR 20
outlaws F. and Jesse James.
   UNKN 149
they are f. and free. UNKN 209
frankeleyn: f. was in his
   compaignye. CHAU 4
Frankie: F. and Johnny were
   lovers, UNKN 101
frantic: f.-mad with evermore
   unrest; SHAK 242
lover, all as f., SHAK 127
With f. gesture and short
   breathless cry SHEL 16
With f. pain. BLAK 46
franzy: From such a female f.,
   SIDN 38
fraternitee: greet f. CHAU 5
fraud: He loathed to f. GRAV 38

fraught: sincerest laughter/ With
   some pain is f.; SHEL 71
words with heavenly comfort f.,
   GILM 1
fray: f. into the future, WILB 49
fray'd: 'gainst the oak his antlers
   f.; SCOT WA 13
freckled: land f. with snow half-
   thawed THOMA E 18
freckles: In those f. live their
   savours. SHAK 126
Fred: 'tis only F., UNKN 200
Frederick: Bravest of all in F.
   town, WHITT 2
fredom: f. and curteisie. CHAU 7
free: After f. voyages WHITM 28
appall the f., SHAK 31
bathroom in the f. world!
   DURE 2
beauteous evening, calm and f.
   WORD 26
dark, salt, clear, moving, utterly
   f., BISH 6
deliver his raw materials f.
   AUDE 58
Expatiate f. POPE A 58
fair and f. as now? TIMR 2
feel the f. Shrill wind LANG 3
for the spirit f., ROBI 2
f. and poor inheritance SHAP 28
f. as is the wind WORD 53
F. be she, fancy-free; EMER 24
F. from care, DOAN 1
F. from Corruption, or intire, or
   clear, DRYD 18
f. from this restraint, CONG 2
f. in the tearing wind.
   ROET 34
f. land of the grave. HOUS 3
f. man how to praise. AUDE 46
f./ myth from reality BIRN 3
f. sense at last, WHITM 22
F. speech nipped in the bud.
   MACN 6
F. to mortgage or to sell,
   JOHN S (1709–1784) 11
f.-will, an' that sort of thing —
   HAY 5
f. without fees; TASS 2
from labor f., DOAN 1
Greece might still be f.; BYRO 41
Grief makes us f. LAWR 18
he from white cloud f., BLAK 99
husbandes hardy, wise, and f.,
   CHAU 67
icily f. above the stones, BISH 5
I'm f. of you, CREE 3
invisible and f.: AUDE 53
land of the f., KEY 1
leave their children f., EMER 12
let us die to make men f.;
   HOWE 3

Let your indulgence set me f.
   SHAK 168
liquid and f. and tender!
   WHITM 49
Love vertue, she alone is f.,
   MILT 13
lowly paths of service f.; GLAD 1
made of the mettle so f.,
   UNKN 154
make our country f.."
   RANDA D 1
manners f. and superb —
   WHITM 44
mind is fleckless, f. WILLI 47
Money is f. WELC 1
mountains, there you feel f.
   ELIOT T 114
My lines and life are f.,
   HERB G 17
pen that set a people f. MARK 3
Spirit f., ROCH 8
stealth, which Love doth f. allow.
   TASS 6
tawny lion, pawing to get f.
   MILT 86
they are frank and f. UNKN 209
they pipe us f., BROWNI R 65
thou art ever f.; VERY 4
thou at length art f., HOLM 3
to be f./ Is often to be lonely;
   AUDE 33
unspent and f.,
   JOHN S (1822–1882) 1
Was he f.? AUDE 94
We must be f. or die, WORD 28
We'll sport and be f. JORD 1
with foot so f.; WORD 154
yearning to breathe f., LAZA 2
freed: by their Conscience, be
   condemn'd or f. DRYD 17
f. from foreign harms;
   SPENS 47
f./ From his ambitious finger.
   FLET/SHAK 2
f. his soul the nearest way.
   JOHN S (1709–1784) 4
freedom: almost convinced of his f.,
   AUDE 39
Beasts in their major f. WILB 7
born to love f. JEFFE 41
enjoying the f. AMMO 9
Flag of F. and Union, WHITT 5
F. all solace to man gives:
   BARBO 1
f. at thy gates BRYA 13
F., from her mountain DRAK 1
F.! if to me belong WHITT 10
f. in my love LOVE 5
f. is excluded, AUDE 32
f. more to prize BARBO 2
f. of that right. SHAK 202
f. of the sod, WHITT 8
f. staying thee! CRAN H 28

F. to worship God. HEMA 5
F.'s banner streaming DRAK 4
F.'s holy flame. GRAY 27
f.'s holy light; SMIT SA 2
F.'s soil beneath our feet,
   DRAK 4
glorious in the might/ Of heaven-
   born f. WORD 78
green f. of a cockatoo
   STEVENS 54
in F.'s cause, HOPKINSO 1
Let f. ring! SMIT SA 1
Lost is our f. CAMPI 11
love of f. JEFFE 40, 42
luxuries and f. also. JEFFE 41
manners, virtue, f., power.
   WORD 41
Surrender into f. SNYD 24
this f., this liberty, HAYD 5
To thee, fair F.! SHEN 1
When a man hath no f. BYRO 72
freely: as I do, f. OHAR 19
his faults can f. show, POPE A 24
lives at ease that f. lives!
   BARBO 1
freer: God knows, with f. air,
   THOR 3
freeways: f. fifty lanes wide
   FERL 4
freeze: cold did f., TASS 3
f. it in blubber KINN 3
f. my bones around. BLAK 62
f. my/ humanity, MACN 16
f./ Their tongues BRID R 9
f., thou bitter sky, SHAK 14
f. thy young blood, SHAK 26
Mountaine tops that f.,
   FLET/SHAK 1
freezes: blood that f.,
   BROWNI R 49
freezing: As F. persons, DICKI 2
Between melting and f.
   ELIOT T 61
f. aloft in a snorter, MASE 10
f. stream below. SHEL 23
night is f. fast, HOUS 19
freezings: f. have I felt, SHAK 223
freight: hopping the slow f.
   CRAN H 21
Nation's F. Handler; SAND 3
French: except F. wine. RIVE 2
F., felicitous tongue, MACL 8
F., or Turk, or Proosian,
   GILB 20
not-too-French F. bean! GILB 32
Three F. hens, UNKN 276
frendes: verray f. see. CHAU 110
Frenssh: F. she spak CHAU 14
frenzied: f. brain that hatched the
   plot, STOD 1
frenzy: f. insufficient reason
   MILLA 15

frequent: f. in tapers, — that's wax.
   HART 2
Frequenting: sighs the air/ F.,
   MILT 98
frere: f. ther was, CHAU 20
shave as neigh as any f.
   CHAU 118
fresh: Beauty, ripe, and calm, and
   f., DAVE 6
bloom sae f. and fair? BURN 15
cheeks were wont more f. C., J 1
f. air is good OHAR 2
f. and green, HERR 50
f. as a queen; UNKN 210
f. as bin the flowers PEEL 1
f. as the young earth, BRYA 15
F. garlands weave, AKEN 2
F. images beget, YEATS 19
f.-severed head of it, OWEN 39
f. springs, brine pits, SHAK 157
f. the level pasture lay, INGE 1
Give me f. corn WHITM 29
meadows f. and gay, MARV 27
mother of f. thoughts WORD 149
My love looks f., SHAK 229
pooh-pooh whatever's f. and new,
   GILB 31
springtime, f. and green, HERR 6
Tomorrow to f. woods and
   pastures new. MILT 33
try the f. fortune —
   BROWNI R 50
With f. suspicions? SHAK 136
wits were f. and clear, ARNO 27
freshe: f. flowers how they spring;
   CHAU 68
fresher: f. wind sweeps by,
   BRYA 18
freshly: rising, f. exuding,
   WHITM 75
freshness: glory and the f. of a
   dream. WORD 64
Fresno: riding flatcars to F.,
   SNYD 27
fressh: as f. as in the monthe of
   May. CHAU 9
fresshe: meede/ Al ful of f. floures,
   CHAU 9
fret: cadent tears f. channels in her
   cheeks, SHAK 72
f. of care; GLAD 1
Nuns f. not WORD 59
fretful: hold a f. realm TENN 76
quills upon the f. porpentine.
   SHAK 26
frets: f. the halter, RALEG 14
poor player/ That struts and f.
   SHAK 114
Fretting: time of their growth/ F. for
   their decay: ROSE 4
friction: cold f. of expiring sense
   ELIOT T 68

friend: abandoned by each venal f.,
   GRAY 21
be a f. to man. FOSS 2
Choose Plato and Plotinus for a f.
   YEATS 151
common f.; POPE A 79
copy of his f. JONS 42
Except thy beauty, virtues, and
   thy f. FLET G EL 1
f. await/ Felicity of doom.
   DICKI 20
f. remembered not. SHAK 14
f. unseen, unborn, unknown,
   FLEC 9
guest and sometime f.?' NEWB 2
have never a f.! STEPHENS 12
heart of a f. LONG 3
I was angry with my f.: BLAK 78
literati keep/ An imaginary f.
   AUDE 6
loan oft loses both itself and f.,
   SHAK 24
lone man's f. HARD 51
Modestly bold, and humanly
   severe:/ Who to a f. POPE A 24
Muse but served to ease some f.,
   POPE A 14
My f.'s cold made-up face,
   JARR 18
my love, my only f. TENN 95
my worthy f., LONG 50
no f. like a sister ROSS C 12
Nobility more nobly to repay?/ O,
   be my f., EMER 23
perfect patriot and a noble f.,
   JONS 39
Sidney is dead, dead is my f.,
   GREV/DYER 2
suspicious f.;/ Dreading e'en fools,
   POPE A 7
that's f. to men, ELIOT T 120
thinne and lean without a fence or
   f., HERB G 4
Thou art not my f., EMER 26
tidings of my f., TENN 57
volatile f. Mr. Jefferson, POUN 12
without its f. near, WHITM 39
worst f. BROO R 12
Friendless: F. and faint, ROBI 2
friendlier: sky will be much f.
   STEVENS 56
friendliness: brimfull of the f.
   KEAT 30
friendly: By a f., helping hand,
   UNKN 145
f. they guide him MELV 14
f. young men, WHITM 44
gossiping of f. spheres,
   MILLA 29
robust, f., WHITM 38
St. John mingles with my f. bowl
   POPE A 92

friends: dear and early f.
  WHITT 28
dog and man at first were f.;
  GOLD 7
Fair face show f. when riches do
  abound; GOOG 1
few f., and many books, COWL 8
few f., but they are in cities.
  SNYD 18
float up from the damnèd Earth./
  "To f. above, POE 30
Foemen at morn, but f. at eve —/
  Fame or country MELV 20
Foolish f. and kinsmen, UNKN 90
For precious f. SHAK 195
forget/ The f. BRYA 36
f. are exultations, agonies,
  WORD 153
f. fail, and Princes frown,/ Virtue
  is the roughest way, WOTT 8
f. forsake me like a memory lost;
  CLARE 7
f. had opened ROBI 47
f., the belov'd of my bosom, were
  near, MOOR T 8
f. thou hast, SHAK 23
f. walk by friends. YEATS 73
golden f. I had, HOUS 62
Health, love, f., scope HARD 47
heart is warm with the f. I make,
  MILLA 38
In spite of all their f. LEAR 8
laughter, learnt of f.; BROO R 14
man makes f. CHAP A 2
one by one our f. have gone
  CAMPB T 7
Robed in the long f.,
  THOMA D 38
seated with his f., FRENE 1
space/ in the lives of their f.
  REED I 2
To Virtue only and her f.,
  POPE A 91
with f. possessed, SHAK 194
yet unknown f. TRAH 6
Your f. to death HOUS 50
friendship: Be my enemy for f.'s
  sake. BLAK 112
boughten f. FROS 90
Pretty 'tis to rhyme HOUS 50
Frietchie: Barbara F.'s grave,
  WHITT 5
Up rose old Barbara F. WHITT 2
frigate: f. takes fire, WHITM 90
no F. like a Book DICKI 140
fright: f. my faith. TENN 38
f. the souls of fearful adversaries,
  SHAK 95
frighten: bugbear Death to f.
  LUCR 1
frightful: Buzzes its f. F SHAP 16
frigid: f. Caution crept,
  JOHN S (1709–1784) 7

frigidly: f. stretched, IREM 1
fringed: f. bank with myrtle
  crowned MILT 69
f. with light LONG 24
fringes: vases and f. BROO G 1
Fringing: F. the dusty road
  LOWE J 15
frisk: f. i' the sun SHAK 178
frith: Fowls in the f., UNKN 100
fritters: Pancakes and f., UNKN 24
frivolity: dreams,/ with what f.
  LEVE 8
gay without f. ARNO 36
fro: To and f. MACW 1
frocks: Holding their tattered f.,
  BINY 5
frog: f. he would a-wooing go,
  MOTH 1
f. peeps out o' the fountain.
  JONS 16
F.'s belly distended KIZE 1
How public — like a f. DICKI 83
Into the f.-spawn YEATS 47
keep a f. BELL 6
kind and tender to the F.,
  BELL 5
wonderful bird the f. are —
  UNKN 110
frogs: gross-bellied f. HEAN 10
frolic: f. architecture of the snow.
  EMER 45
Fun and f. BRYA 20
Outdid the meat, outdid the f.
  wine. HERR 36
frolics: pensive cat gives o'er/ Her
  f., SWIF 6
fronds: tuft of f. or katydid legs
  MOOR M 30
front: Cannon in f. of them
  TENN 8
Johnston pressed at the f.,
  TICK 2
smoothed his wrinkled f.;
  SHAK 95
to the f. door mother, WHITM 15
fronting: west, f. the west,
  WHITM 52
frontispiece: child from the coloured
  f.? KLEI 2
fronts: black f. long-withdrawn
  TENN 54
f. the sea. SWIN 10
frost: from f. or foreign wind.
  HUGO 4
f., almost in separate stars
  FROS 72
f. beheads it at its play DICKI 4
f. disturbed its bed? ELICT T 120
f. heaved your bones HALL 3
f. is on the punkin RILE 4
f. on the pine bough SNYD 44
f. stings sweetly CAMPB R 8
f. was glitt'ring BARNE 4

f. was on the village roofs
  STEVENSO R 5
F. was spectre-gray HARD 17
f. within, VAUG 18
fruit that with the f. is taken:
  SURR 2
furred/ With a light f., HECH 2
like f. upon a Glass — DICKI 154
My prime of youth is but a f. of
  cares, TICH 1
radiant f.; SHEL 61
secret ministry of f.
  COLE SAM 17
Warm amidst eternal F., GAY 4
frosted: eyes were f. starlight,
  GRAV 9
frosts: cursing of the f. and snowes;
  BONH 1
frosty: Early on one f. mornin',
  EMME 1
f. fingers punishes my hair,
  THOMA D 13
f. sagas, CRAN H 8
This f. night?" GRAV 30
frothy: wet his f. jaws
  STEVENS 13
frown: folks f. on that in Texas,
  DURE 2
friends fail, and Princes f.,
  WOTT 8
Sigh then, or f., GRAV 6
single f. Doth shake the world
  TAYL E 2
frown'd: f. not on his humble birth,
  GRAY 12
frowned: children f. At something
  dull; LARK 21
frowning: beards of Hercules and f.
  Mars, SHAK 122
gray-eyed morn smiles on the f.
  night, SHAK 146
frowns: amazing f. On utmost
  Kilda's shore,
  THOMS J (1700–1748) 8
F. o'er old Conway's foaming
  flood, GRAY 3
froze: Heaven f. above, CHAU 46
frozen: f. bosom of the north,
  SHAK 141
f. in each eye. AUDE 44
f. Pleiads shine: ADDI 2
f. wind crept on SHEL 23
f. world of the dead PINS 2
many a F., many a fierie Alpe,
  MILT 61
milk comes f. home in pail,/ When
  blood is nipp'd SHAK 101
Utterly f. DANT 1
frugal: How f. is the Chariot
  DICKI 141
on such f. pastures fed
  CAMPB R 4

fruit: among sweet- and f.-boxes.
  KINS 1
As a globed f., MACL 1
autumn and the falling f.
  LAWR 35
beauty/ of f.-trees. DOOL 7
bitter tastelessness of shadow f.
  ELIOT T 68
blossom- and the f.-time:
  ELIOT T 57
borne many another f.: CAME 3
boughs are bent with thickset f.;
  ROSS C 1
Death is the f. it bore. ROSS C 8
dying for a jungle f. BONT 8
eaters of f.? SNYD 19
faces like autumn f., KLEI 2
feed on bitter f. BONT 1
Forth-reaching to the F., MILT 89
f. and flower; SOUTHW 7
F. cannot drop DOOL 3
f. of chemic force, EMER 51
f. of sense beneath POPE A 22
F./ Of that Forbidden Tree,
  MILT 46
f. that with the frost is taken:
  SURR 2
f.-tree's mossy root, MARV 19
greater store of f. untouched,
  MILT 94
juicy autumnal f. WHITM 29
Last season's f. is eaten
  ELIOT T 66
no sin love's f. to steal; JONS 49
preferred fallen f. LOWE R 31
ripe f. never fall? STEVENS 59
sun and moon were in the f.:
  YEATS 95
tasted f., FROS 18
they also hide big f. DAY 6
With f. are bending down.
  JACK 3
fruite: un-fathered f., SHAK 224
fruited: Above the f. plain! BATE 1
fruitful: Be f., multiply, MILT 85
f. ground, MARTIA 1
f. river in the eye, SHAK 21
rich and f. land, BLAK 68
summer's f. treasure; NASHE 2
fruitfulness: Season of mists and
  mellow f., KEAT 62
fruition: Casual f., MILT 78
fruitless: fanes of f. prayer,
  TENN 36
f. sleep DARL 3
fruits: all pleasant f. do flow.
  CAMPI 23
drop like the f. of the tree,
  MERE G 3
flowers and f. of Love BYRO 57
f. and fairer flowers THOR 3
f. in vale and mountain,
  UNKN 290

f. like honey to the throat
  ROSS C 11
F. of the Two seasons. BLAK 8
Her voluntary f., TASS 2
my clustering f. I tend; AKEN 2
No f., HOOD 6
odours, f., and flocks, MILT 5
our orchard f., ROSS C 11
Plants f. BLAK 21
summer and ripe f. DOOL 9
frustrations: O sweet f., WILB 42
fry: how to cook and to f.;
  HILL J 4
in fiery heats I f., SOUTHW 2
fucked: f. in the ass GINS 11
fudge: two fifths sheer f.,
  LOWE J 5
fuel: f. wounding thorns;
  SOUTHW 2
Gathering f. in vacant lots.
  ELIOT T 102
fugitive: gross and f. movement
  RUKE 3
master-leaver and a f. SHAK 8
Ful: F. worthy was he CHAU 7
meede/ Al f. of fresshe floures,
  CHAU 9
fulfilment: f. to our dreams
  STEVENS 57
fulfils: God f. Himself TENN 103
full: beams f.-dazzling,
  WHITM 29
both their hearts so f. of glee.
  UNKN 320
brittle world so f. of doubleness,
  HAWE 2
countenance f. of woe,
  WHITM 52
face was f. of woe; UNKN 141
F. fathom five thy father lies;
  SHAK 156
f. measure of all your pleasure,
  WILC 2
f. meridian of my glory
  FLET/SHAK 4
f. moon OLSO 20
f. of thy riches. BIBL, O.T. 51
F. of tumultuous life PATM 6
f. reward and glorious fate
  CAREW 17
f.-sized a man LOWE J 3
F. to the banks, TENN 95
manhood f. and fair!
  BRID R 17
More than most fair, f. of the
  living fire, SPENS 4
Not well, nor f., nor fasting.
  DANI S 1
On such a f. sea SHAK 50
proud f. sail SHAK 217
so f. of a number of things,
  STEVENSO R 9
taste f. sour; SURR 10

temple f. of treason, RALEG 5
thought came like a f.-blown
  rose, KEAT 8
To his f. height. SHAK 56
too f. of sleep LONG 34
Tuesday's child is f. of grace,
  MOTH 22
Wednesday's child is f. of woe,
  MOTH 22
world's more f. of weeping
  YEATS 144
fuller: ring the f. minstrel in.
  TENN 49
fullest: f. breasts of Fame, SIDN 10
fullfed: f. beast shall kick
  ELIOT T 66
fullness: fed on the f. of death.
  SWIN 23
f. of the past, ARNO 12
fully: f. and perfectly man.
  LOWE J 3
fumbling: f. the flowers: REED H 5
fume: f. of space foams CRAN H 4
fumes: f. a little with pallor
  LAWR 41
fumigation: make a f.,/ Sweet of
  reflare, SKEL 9
Fun: F. and frolic BRYA 20
I wish I thought What Jolly F.!
  RALEI 1
sullen f. TATE A 16
Function: F. never dies; WORD 127
own no other f. SHAK 183
functions: in divers f., SHAK 55
fundamental: f. project of
  technology; KINN 12
funeral: After the f., THOMA D 1
At a f. mass, HEAN 19
boom after my f., POUN 31
crying shadow in the f. dance,
  ELIOT T 25
felt a F., in my Brain, DICKI 45
f.-cakes of sweet and sculptured
  stone. SLES 3
grandest f. ALEX 3
have a/ Big F. EVAN 1
heap the f. pyre, THAC 1
in one high f. gleam, YEATS 121
not a f. note, WOLF C 1
secret like a happy f.; LARK 21
With my black f. SYNG 5
funereal: His own f. destiny;
  BYRO 60
funny: As f. as I can. HOLM 14
as long as you're f.! GILB 60
F. bugs, of handy sizes, CARRY 7
f. people make love RIVE 1
milk tastes f., SNYD 41
peas taste f., UNKN 137
Funnyface: F. Or Elephant
  AUDE 60
fur: bits of old f. SILKO 1

coyote got his/ ratty old f. coat
　SILKO 1
dressed all in f.,　MOOR C 3
f. side inside,　STRON 1
grey f. is pulsing in its grip.
　HECH 7
furies: lay graveward with his f.;
　THOMA D 6
furious: f. papa　AUDE 85
　f. winter's rages;　SHAK 18
　f. with blood　TATE A 1
furled: battle-flags were f.
　TENN 76
furnace: faultless breast the f. is,
　SOUTHW 2
　heart of the f. roar;　SERV 5
　In what f. was thy brain?
　BLAK 82
furnish: f. health　WHITM 96
　f. out a pair　SWIF 21
Furnish'd: F. and burnish'd by
　Aldershot sun,　BETJ 9
Furnished: F. with tile,　EMER 44
　live in f. souls　CUMM 52
　thousand f. rooms.　ELIOT T 98
　With glory richly f.,　BRAD 12
furniture: f. Of education,
　SHAP 28
　f. of love.　RICH 8
　this finest/ of f.　PLUM 1
furred: burring f. antennae
　SPEND 13
　f. With a light frost,　HECH 2
　Robes and f. gowns hide all.
　SHAK 81
furriners: what them f. do),
　GILB 42
furrow: crush'd beneath the f.'s
　weight,　BURN 61
　f. on the glow,　DICKI 24
furrows: f. in my face,　VAUX 5
　f. of the shore,　ROET 42
　f. shine but late upturned,
　THOR 11
　time's f. I behold,　SHAK 190
furry: f. nuts/ of the terrible puss,
　OHAR 4
　Poor little timid f. man.
　ROSS C 6
　wombat prowled obtuse and f.,
　ROSS C 12
furs: Raven/ on a roost of f.
　SNYD 33
Fury: Beware the F. of a Patient
　Man.　DRYD 1
　blind F. with th'abhorred shears
　MILT 27
　civil f. first grew high,　BUTL 1
　driven us to this f.,　PRIN 3
　formless spawning f. wrecked,
　YEATS 143
　full of sound and f.,　SHAK 114

f. of aerial bombardment
　EBER 2
Life, a F. slinging flame.
　TENN 28
poets' f.　SIDN 22
their aiming f.　BIBL, O.T 42
warned of the coming f.
　THOMA D 16
furze: silence of the f.,
　STEPHENS 5
fuse: force that through the green f.
　THOMA D 22
fused: f. to the inside of a helmet;
　KINN 11
fuses: f. me into you now,
　WHITM 21
fust: f. in us unused.　SHAK 35
fustian: f. animall,　TAYL E 14
futile: f. and vain;　SNOD 1
　f. as regret.　ROBI 1
　"It is f.," I said,　CRAN S 2
　life as f.,　TENN 37
future: blindness to the f.!
　POPE A 64
　fray into the f.,　WILB 49
　f. in ruins!　SIMP 15
　f. in the distance,　BANK 4
　f. is a serious matter—　BYRO 33
　f. is ever a misted landscape,
　JEFFE 32
　f. veils its face,　MELV 19
　Heaven and the f.'s sakes.
　FROS 126
　hopes of f. years,　LONG 6
　I dipped into the f.,　TENN 75
　no f. but itself—　DICKI 118
　numbers it for f. reference,
　FROS 24
　perhaps present in time f.,
　ELIOT T 15
　see the shaky f.　LOWE R 55
　time f. contained in time past.
　ELIOT T 15
　Time past and time f.
　ELIOT T 19
　what they imperfectly control/ To
　dare a f.　GUNN 12
　Who Present, Past and F., sees;
　BLAK 66
futurity: f. to do the rest.　ROBI 26
fyngres: Ne wette hir f.　CHAU 15
　Wrythynge my f.　PETRA 1
fyr: f.-reed cherubynnes face,
　CHAU 3
fyve: Housbondes at chirche dore
　she hadde f./　CHAU 11

G

gab: complains of my g. and my
　loitering.　WHITM 73

Gabble: geese/ G. and hiss,
　MILLA 8
gaberdine: spit upon my Jewish g.,
　SHAK 118
gaberlunzie: carry the g. on.
　UNKN 112
　wearifu' g. man.'　UNKN 111
gabies: grow up as geese and g.,
　STEVENSO R 4
gable: barn's brown g.,　WHITT 33
Gadier: isles/ Of Javan or G.
　MILT 110
gage: down their mortal g.,　TIMR 4
　glory, hope's true g.,　RALEG 10
gaily: g. as the sparkling Thames;
　ARNO 27
gain: Faith fair scorn doth g.
　SIDN 38
　hope of g.　GILB 10
　hungry ocean g. Advantage
　SHAK 211
　might die to g.　STOD 3
　richest g. I count but loss,
　WATT I 9
　to g. some private ends,　GOLD 7
　vain hope of g.:　TICH 1
gain'd: what we g. in Skill we lost
　in Strength.　DRYD 29
gaine: Couetousness getts no g.
　UNKN 224
gaining: never g. never reaping
　WALK 5
'Gainst: G. knaves and thieves
　SHAK 177
gait: airs in dress an' g.　BURN 58
　that precarious G.　DICKI 67
　your pompous g.,　JOHN H 4
gal: every boy and every g.,
　GILB 22
gala: 'tis a g. night　POE 30
Galatians: great text in G.,
　BROWNI R 78
gale: bird trims her to the g.,
　EMER 47
　born to match the g.,
　WHITM 104
　g., it plies the saplings　HOUS 45
　lightning and the g.!　HOLM 18
　Warping the g.,　CRAN H 9
gales: not the g.,　WILC 4
Galilaean: he strayes/ Among the G.
　mountains,　CRAS 8
Galilean: O pale G.;　SWIN 23
　pilot of the G. lake.　MILT 28
Galilee: God kissed in G.,　CHES 11
　Simon on thy lake of G.:
　WILD 10
gall: Chew honey and spit out g.
　SHAP 24
gallant: bends the g. mast;
　CUNN A 1
　g. arm that strikes　DRAK 3

g. knight,/ In sunshine and in
　shadow, POE 18
Phillis hath a g. flock LODG 4
saddled, he bridled, and g. rode
　he, UNKN 37
soldier in that g. band GILB 15
gallantly: so g. streaming? KEY 1
gallard: g. eare of terroure CHAT 2
galled: fearfully as doth a g. rock
　SHAK 56
galleons: minstrel g. of Carib fire,
　CRAN H 50
galleries: libraries & g. SNYD 27
galling: g. give her. SYNG 1
gallop: back at the g. again.
　STEVENSO R 25
g. for what must be joy, LARK 3
g. he goes, STEVENSO R 25
still eternal g.: BURN 5
galloped: we g. abreast.
　BROWNI R 35
we g. all three; BROWNI R 35
galloping: g. on this way. WOOL 1
gallow: makes the g. tree;
　RALEG 13
gallows: better gone to the g.
　UNKN 151
head of a g.-tree. KIPL 2
when the g. is high UNKN 192
galvanic: quick, g. tread — GILB 3
galvanizing: g. my genes. KNIG 7
gamble: g. for your little garments.
　HORN 2
game: all fell to playing the g.
　FOOT 1
g. from him escapt away,
　SPENS 16
Hating you shall be a g.
　BENN G 1
"High-low Jack and the g.."
　UNKN 103
in a poker g. SILKO 1
inventor of the g. EMER 20
made the g. go on; THAY 3
most contagious g. MERE G 9
play a g. of chess, ELIOT T 126
sea-light every early g. MOSS 3
War's a bloody g. SASS 1
games: any sinful g.; HART 3
Gandhi: Empire and G. NASH 6
gane: till seven years were g. and
　past, UNKN 249
Word's g. to the kitchen,
　UNKN 187
Gang: G. aft agley, BURN 63
g. to the high heavens, UNKN 49
g. to your men again? UNKN 49
will ye g. wi me? UNKN 49
gangly: our g. starting center
　HIRS 1
gangrene: grape-shot and g.,
　TICK 1

gangs: Marie Hamilton g. wi' bairn
　UNKN 187
gaol: lie in g. WILD 2
gap: g. in the old wall still,
　WHITT 32
gaped: pirate g. at Belinda's
　dragon, NASH 16
gapes: drinks and g. for drink
　again; COWL 1
gaping: graves, all g. wide,
　SHAK 128
garage: against the g.'s earthquake.
　LOWE R 17
garb: Robed in the sable g. of woe,
　GRAY 3
garbage: empty cans and g.
　MAST 5
holding a g. can lid. KOCH 7
prey on g. SHAK 27
swills the g. pail. LOWE R 41
yesterday's g. ripening
　BROO G 16
Garcia Lorca: G., what were you
　doing GINS 37
garden: bathed in her still g.,
　STEVENS 34
Come into the g., Maud,
　TENN 93
down the g.-paths, LOWE A 4
dry scent of a dying g. ROET 15
Eternities of kitchen g., SITW 5
g. for us HERB G 33
g. in her face, CAMPI 23
g. is a lovesome thing,
　BROWN T 1
g. mouse eats what he can;
　ROSS C 6
g. mouse lives in a bower,
　ROSS C 5
g. walks we go." GRAV 12
ghost of a g. SWIN 10
go to the g. CREE 8
Him that walketh in the g.
　BLAK 14
I went to the G. of Love,
　BLAK 64
in my pleached g., EMER 15
know a little g.-close MORR 6
Meseem'd, I smelt a g. of sweet
　flowers, SPENS 14
My g. is run wild! HABE 2
nearer God's heart in a g.
　GURN 1
none of the g. noticed BETJ 3
small house and large g. COWL 8
strangers in the g. LAWR 56
studio, the G. of Zoos, OHAR 4
sunlight on the g. Hardens
　MACN 23
unweeded g.,/ That grows to seed;
　SHAK 22
gardener: g. of strange flowers,
　SWIN 6

gardens: devout have laid out g.
　DUNC 3
Down by the salley g. YEATS 50
fenced their g. LOWE R 4
g. in the desert. DUNC 3
G. of the Desert, BRYA 15
g. rich in memory glorified
　YEATS 35
gates of no g., MERW 8
Hesperian G. fam'd of old,
　MILT 65
'imaginary g. MOOR M 33
Leaving the g. tidy, LARK 18
path in Kensington G., POUN 27
gargling: blood/ Come g. OWEN 19
garland: g. briefer than a girl's.
　HOUS 58
g. on my hearse, BEAU/FLET 3
wreathed g. of deserved praise,
　HERB G 74
garlands: Fresh g. weave, AKEN 2
gather g. there, SCOT WA 23
Persian g. I detest, HORA 11
garlic: sausage and g. booth
　SPENC A 2
garment: g. too good/ For thee
　CRAS 11
know the G. from the Man.
　BLAK 20
life as in a strange g. MERW 6
like a g., wear WORD 6
garments: cloud-folds of her g.
　LONG 38
fair g., such prosperi-ty?' —
　HARD 36
gamble for your little g. HORN 2
g. of adieu. ROET 16
if men my g. wear; SHAK 59
smoky smell of our g. UNKN 121
swathed in sweet g., WHITM 68
trailing g. of the Night LONG 24
garners: Barns and g. SHAK 162
g. in my heart: TENN 39
garnish: g. the axle-tree!
　MOOR M 2
garnished: wrists and knees g. with
　impetigo. HILL G 6
garres: Hobbinoll, what g. thee
　greete? SPENC 48
garret: godly g. after sev'n,
　POPE A 19
garrets: Hide him in lonely g.,
　ROBI 17
gars: it g. me greet, BURN 51
garters: Scarfs, g., gold, POPE A 81
Garyulies: Jobillies,/ and the G.,
　FOOT 1
gas: G. smells awful;/ You might as
　well live. PARK 2
Loitered beneath the g. lamps'
　flare, WILD 16
pale dull pallor of an old g. light
　HUGH L 18

saved them from the g. HECH 13
smell it turning to g.; BISH 7
Gascon: G.'s shrewd wit LOWE J 9
gasping: Fled g. from the House —
  DICKI 73
turtle g. ROET 41
Gat-toothed: G. was I, CHAU 90
gate: angel in the g., the flowering
  plum, SIMP 16
as the g.-bolts undrew,
  BROWNI R 35
begging at my g. UNKN 77
By the North G., LI PO 1
Duns at his lordship's g. SWIF 11
Go to the western g., ROBI 22
God at every g. DICKI 116
Heaven's G. Opes to the rich
  BROWNI R 64
here at the g. alone; TENN 93
leant upon a coppice g. HARD 17
light wing against the ivory g.,
  MORR 3
men shut their g., SHAK 177
open curling lotus g. SNYD 4
Pale Anguish keeps the heavy g.,
  WILD 3
passion-flower at the g. TENN 94
played about the front g.,
  LI PO 3
sings hymns at heaven's g.;
  SHAK 194
stood at his castle g. UNKN 177
Those flowers, that g., LARK 14
trembling at the g. of bliss;
  CRAS 10
unlock the g. Of heaven ALEX 9
up to heaven g. ascend, MILT 82
wall than an open g., FROS 17
We pass the g. DOWS 5
gates: Enter into his g. with
  thanksgiving, BIBL, O.T. 50
freedom at thy g. BRYA 13
g. of foam, DE TA 1
g. of no gardens, MERW 8
g. of steel so strong SHAK 212
g. of this Chapel were shut,
  BLAK 64
iron g. of life. MARV 35
Lift up your heads, O ye g.;
  BIBL, O.T. 34
other men have g. SHAK 179
sea-washed, sunset g. LAZA 1
Gath: Tell it not in G.,
  BIBL, O.T. 68
gather: barren places where men g.
  HECH 11
beech will g. brown, TENN 42
Clouds that g. WORD 86
fast I g., bit by bit, THAX 1
G., and merge myself WHITM 3
g. garlands there, SCOT WA 23
g. Paradise — DICKI 44

G. the flowers, but spare the
  buds; MARV 32
G. therefore the Rose, SPENS 34
G. ye rosebuds HERR 55
merchant g. wealth,
  BEAU/BASS 6
shall g. dew, WHITT 28
gather'd: what g. in the gloom?
  SWIN 6
gathered: g. up the crystal manna
  BRID R 9
how the planets g. STEVENS 7
they g. once LEVE 24
gathering: brows like g. storm,
  BURN 50
g. as we stray, MASE 9
g. his grain; WHITM 7
g. many a shell, MAST 8
g. place of fears: JOHN L 7
g. the orange leather HIRS 1
g. together of spirit. DUNC 2
gathers: China g., soundlessly, like
  evidence. SNOD 9
g. all the parish there; SWIF 2
gaudy: g. bonnet; SYNG 3
Gowns grave or g., WORD 100
gaunt: aged thrush, frail, g.,
  HARD 18
his mother g. and lean HODG 3
skeletons/ Of their g. horses;
  ALBI 1
gauze: g. of æther; POUN 66
snow-white bow of g., SNOD 11
gauzy: g. edge of paradise,
  SEXT 11
gav'st: Thyself thou g., SHAK 220
gave: Danube to the Severn g.
  TENN 25
Earth and I g. you turquoise
  MOMA 5
g. their laughs more glee
  OWEN 10
He g. us eyes ALEX 2
I g. commands; BROWNI R 57
I that g. thee thy renowne:
  CAREW 7
midwife g. o'er. UNKN 75
One look I but g. WHITM 106
she g. him milk; BIBL, O.T. 19
we g. ourselves outright FROS 50
Gawd: G. bless this world! KIPL 21
gay: All in our gowns of green so g.
  UNKN 229
all the world was g. POPE A 116
all the world went g., OSUL 2
Amid its g. creation,
  THOMS J (1700–1748) 3
as g. And transient, BYRO 34
bedecked, ornate, and g.,
  MILT 110
blow the g. Pantechnicon
  GILB 44
darkeys are g.; FOST 1

fair and wise and good and g.
  MOTH 22
g., delighted porpoise LAWR 58
g. through folly; POPE A 109
g. without frivolity. ARNO 36
"God the G. is not the Wise."
  KAVA 14
I'm a g. deceiver.' COLM 1
lady was g., UNKN 244
love is fair, my love is g., PEEL 1
meadows fresh and g., MARV 27
once were keen and kind and g.?
  SASS 2
poets that are always g.,
  YEATS 77
robes riche, or fithele, or g.
  sautrie. CHAU 2
gayest: g. laddie of all BRIN 2
Good luck is the g. HAY 1
gaz'd: so g. on now, SHAK 185
Gaza: G. mourns MILT 118
gaze: backward, with averted g.,
  WHITT 12
Devoured her with their eager,
  passionate g.; MCKA 5
face to face they g., BINY 5
From my g. on thee WHITM 52
g. blank and pitiless YEATS 135
g., turn giddy, rave, and die.
  POPE A 2
savage eyes turned to a modest g.
  SHAK 125
sit and g. Upon the grass,
  STEVENS 58
sit for men to g. upon. MARL 5
spindrift g. toward paradise.
  CRAN H 50
There bade me g., ARNO 30
turn my g. ASHB 3
gazebo: great g. built, YEATS 69
Gazed: G. on the lake below.
  GRAY 18
gazelle: g., delicate wanderer,
  SPEND 17
one a g. YEATS 67
gazer: all the g.'s mind SHEL 78
gazes: g. on the ground, MARK 5
gazest: thou g. much/ upon the
  golden skies: PLATO 1
gazing: g. on the earth, SHEL 88
g. on the unquiet sky. POE 40
With g. fed; SHAK 121
gear: for grace and g. may shine,
  BURN 33
soon-speeding g. SHAK 150
geese: clanging chains/ of g.
  CAMPB R 2
g. Gabble and hiss, MILLA 8
grow up as g. and gabies,
  STEVENSO R 4
More g. than swans GIBB 1

Six g. a-laying, UNKN 279
Something told the wild g.
  FIEL R 2
Gehenna: Down to G. KIPL 25
gelliflowres: With g.; SPENS 57
gem: g. of purest ray serene,
  GRAY 10
Thou bonnie g. BURN 59
Gemara: G. of your gentleness,
  KUNI 4
gemme: Hero this inestimable g.
  MARL 6
gems: g. of heav'n, her starry train:
  MILT 76
gen: Their Cause was g.'ral,
  JOHN S (1709–1784) 6
general: Birthdays? yes, in a g.
  STEPHEN 1
for the g. safety MILT 59
g. truculence WILLI 31
lost g. parents, SNYD 19
save g. ceremony? SHAK 58
generate: g./ Reptile with spawn
  abundant, MILT 85
generated: g. by their kinds,
  MILT 85
What's water but the g. soul?
  YEATS 34
generation: best minds of my g.
  SIMP 9
best minds of my g. GINS 7
old age shall this g. waste,
  KEAT 40
parent of his g., AUDE 94
robes of red g. BARK 1
women of a g., WHITM 19
generations: dying g. YEATS 124
g. labor to possess SIMP 12
g. of thy peers ARNO 23
his truth endureth to all g.
  BIBL, O.T. 50
many g. hence, WHITM 19
three g. of one house POUN 26
generous: enchant your g. Mind;
  DRYD 1
g. wine with age grows strong,
  COWL 5
Glory pursue, and g. Shame,
  GRAY 27
My mind as g. SHAK 70
genes: falling leaves stir my g.,
  KNIG 8
galvanizing my g. KNIG 7
Genesis: G. in the root,
  THOMA D 8
Genet: Le Balcon or Les Nègres/ of
  G., OHAR 5
Geneva: G.'s farthest skill DICKI 18
genial: g. warmth; TENN 40
his g. way CARRO 11
this a g. room? POPE A 105
genius: aspiring g. TROW 1
g. of the South TOOM 1

g. so shrinking and rare
  LOWE J 1
happy g. of my household?
  WILLI 13
specter of g.! GINS 17
Though taste, though g. bless
  COLL 12
Three fifths of him g. LOWE J 5
what is g.?) AIKE 2
Gennesareth: Not of G., but
  Thames! THOMP F 12
gent: decent for a scientific g.
  HART 4
gentian: Reach me a g., LAWR 4
gentil: g. maunciple CHAU 18
g. pardoner/ Of Rouncivale,
  CHAU 42
Gentile: might of the G., BYRO 13
gentle: Ah, g. dames! BURN 51
Born of the g. South, KEAT 1
droppeth as the g. rain from
  heaven SHAK 123
each g. animal HALE 2
fed me from her g. breast,
  TAYL A 1
flow'rs/ Sweetened with rich and
  g. showers, VAUG 24
forgive thy robbery, g. thief,
  SHAK 200
g. agency/ Of natural objects,
  WORD 51
g. and the reckless one, MUIR 2
G. as falcon SKEL 2
g. cheater, SHAK 243
g.-hearted Charles, COLE SAM 42
g. hearts content SPENS 43
G. love deeds, DONN 41
g. rising, HERB G 14
g. serpent, TATE A 15
g. Shakespeare, JONS 45
g. sleep the sleep of death,
  BLAK 14
g. wit/ And virtuous mind,
  SPENS 25
go g. into that good night,
  THOMA D 11
In g. deference DICKI 42
margeran g., SKEL 3
O g. sleep, SHAK 54
rose, the g. rose, UNKN 216
sleep! it is a g. thing,
  COLE SAM 29
So g. and so beautiful, BRYA 11
thy g. looks, thy aid, MILT 101
violated ones with g. hearts;
  WALK 2
wild, g. thing, WRIG J 5
gentleman: g. born, UNKN 41
g. in a dustcoat RANS 30
long world's g., THOMA D 7
gentlemen: dangerous, g. of
  threescore? RANS 22
g. in stays, BYRO 47

God rest you merry, g., CRAI 1
my duty, g., NASH 7
quiet Dust was G. and Ladies,
  DICKI 147
some pious g. HAY 4
gentleness: Christ of His g.
  GRAV 13
Gemara of your g., KUNI 4
g. survives SNOD 7
gentler: g. purpose runs.
  THOMP W 4
Love is a calmer, g. joy: SACK 1
Still g. sister Woman; BURN 7
Gentles: G. and commons.
  SCOT WA 21
gentlewomen: What soft, cherubic
  creatures/ These g. are!
  DICKI 155
gentlier: g. on the spirit lies,
  TENN 84
gently: dressed me g. PACK 1
flakes were folding it g.,
  LOWE J 12
g. creeps/ Luxuriant: MILT 69
G. its touch awoke him
  OWEN 26
g. scan your brother Man,
  BURN 7
g. turn'd over upon me,
  WHITM 78
G. with myrtle band, MILT 89
some one g. rapping, POE 34
Speak g., WILD 17
Time and Nature g. spare
  EMER 12
way/ Of speaking g.,—
  BROWNI E 9
gentrye: prys of his g. CHAU 112
genuine: I'm a g. philanthropist—
  GILB 6
genus: Gives g. a better discerning.
  GOLD 5
geometry: Euclid's g. AUDE 14
George: Bonnie G. Campbell
  UNKN 37
G. the Third. KOCH 7
G. the Third BENT 1
Georges: G. ended. LAND 2
Georgia: stranger from G. DAVIS 6
Georgius Secundus: G. was then
  alive,— HOLM 5
geranium: madman shakes a dead
  g. ELIOT T 103
geraniums: pot of pink g. MACN 9
germ: g. of immortality! WILLA 2
German: "Being G. my hero is
  Hitler," KINN 5
from the G. hive. HOLM 5
germens: all g. spill at once
  SHAK 75
germs: get up all the g. GILB 30
gesture: g. and psalm, THOMA D 5
g. or least action, MILT 90

gladly: wife most g.!' LEAR 5
gladness: half the g. SHEL 72
  lark is so brimful of g. and love,
    COLE SAM 1
  poets in our youth begin in g.;
    WORD 121
  Serve the Lord with g.:
    BIBL, O.T. 48
  sheer morning g. FROS 119
  Strew your g. SORL 3
gladsome: midst the g. fieldes
    LODG 2
glance: brightening g., YEATS 13
  broad/ Blade of his g. LAWR 25
  first g. of the glory of God
    SMAR 2
  for ay, the sparkling g. BURN 31
  g. from heaven to earth,
    SHAK 127
  g. in their tread, LEVE 10
  g. Of passing troops ARNO 38
  kind g. from my love. UNKN 201
  Many a kiss, both odd and even;/
  Many a HERR 7
  woman's g. instinctive thrown:
    MELV 6
glances: glancings of rapturous g.,
    PRAE 3
  meteor g. glow, DRAK 3
  where thy dark eye g., POE 8
glancings: g. of rapturous glances,
    PRAE 3
glare: blackness and a strong g.
    BISH 44
  enlightened by the vollied g.;
    MELV 18
  flag snaps in the g. JARR 20
  rocket's red g., KEY 1
glares: image g. AMMO 19
glaring: g. colours HERR 27
Glass: As cautiously as G.
    DICKI 73
  avocado in a g. of water —
    MERR 6
  Blue bit of polished g., MOSS 5
  boldly shines your shuttered door
  of g. MCKA 10
  bright g. cases, POUN 48
  cops/ Who sweep g. SHAP 2
  dome of many-colored g.,
    SHEL 13
  dust, here running in the g.,
    JONS 12
  flesh is but the g., HERB G 11
  Get thee g. eyes, SHAK 81
  g. eye, false teeth PLATH 1
  g. has been falling RICH 24
  g. is a pool. STEVENS 13
  g. of blessings standing by,
    HERB G 61
  g. of fashion SHAK 33
  g. of papaya juice OHAR 14

  g. shall not persuade me
    SHAK 190
  Grief, with a g. that ran; SWIN 1
  his eyes were red g., BISH 14
  I shall need no g. VAUG 28
  in g. is set, SWIF 12
  In vials of ivory and coloured g.
    ELIOT T 121
  life's vase/ Of g. THOR 2
  Like a prismatic g., NOYE 1
  like frost upon a G. DICKI 154
  loan of a g. of beer;
    STEPHENS 3
  looks a moment in the g.,
    ELIOT T 137
  man that looks on g. HERB G 28
  mended g., like bottle bits
    SPEND 3
  message from thy g., DANI S 15
  neat circle on the g. MONTA 2
  No g. can reach; POPE A 72
  On the g. tray WILLI 23
  piece of g. PATM 3
  plane of molten g., TENN 24
  rats' feet over broken g.
    ELIOT T 41
  riotous g. houses built on rock,
    LOWE R 5
  sea smooths g. HALL 2
  shoreline, greenery and g.
    MOSS 4
  took up the g. of Time, TENN 70
  Venus, take my votive g.: PRIO 7
glasse: brittle crazie g.:
    HERB G 73
  eternall G.,/ Where time doth
  end, GREV 8
glasses: down to his dark g.
    WAGO 1
glassy: g., cool, translucent wave,
    MILT 7
glaze: above a snow g. WILLI 43
  Eyes g. once — DICKI 54
  g. on a/ katydid-wing
    MOOR M 17
gleam: fled the visionary g.?
    WORD 68
  groceries in a pantry g. SHAP 29
  in one high funeral g.,
    YEATS 121
  reflects in joy its scanty g.
    LOWE J 16
  soul's forgotten g. NELS 1
  stains its equal g., EMER 49
  Upon a fading g., YEATS 153
  wild the clouded g. DIXC 1
  with one scarlet g. WORD 130
gleamed: g. upon my sight;
    WORD 133
gleaming: g. lights, — LONG 29
  g. of a random light, DUNB P 7
  thing of g. strands LEVE 10
  twilight's last g., KEY 1

gleams: g. of a remoter world
    SHEL 42
  pale moon g.: OSHA 1
  where thy footstep g. POE 8
glean: children g. in fields BONT 1
gleaned: pen has g. my teeming
  brain, KEAT 68
glee: both their hearts so full of g.
    UNKN 320
  carol of joy or g., DUNB P 10
  gave their laughs more g.
    OWEN 10
  gete gold with here g. LANGL 4
  private and corporal g., HECH 10
  rang to Miriam's holy g., TIMR 5
  Social-life and G. BURN 6
glen: Down the rushy g., ALLI 1
  good ale in the g., UNKN 201
glens: grey flocks in ferny g.
    BRON 6
  wintry sides of many g., SYNG 7
glib: tearful harp or g. piano
    WHITM 102
glide: flowers that g. HERB G 33
  g./ Into the grave. HERR 41
  g. noiselessly forth; WHITM 42
  In the church-way paths to g.:
    SHAK 128
  rapid g. along the leaning line;
    THOMS J (1700–1748) 11
  soul into the boughs does g.:
    MARV 19
  sunny beams did g.! BLAK 23
  Tweed's silver current g.,
    SCOT WA 4
glides: g. in modest Innocence
  away; JOHN S (1709–1784) 13
  G. over suburbs SPEND 13
  preacher g. to the vestry-door,
    HARD 38
  shark/ G. white MELV 7
  Still g. the Stream, WORD 127
gliding: g. like a queen, SPEND 5
  rising and g. out, WHITM 111
glimmering: speak silence with thy
  g. eyes, BLAK 110
glimpse: g. divine! POPE A 2
  g. through an interstice
    WHITM 33
glint: feral g. In the caught eyes.
    KIZE 2
  g. of his steel-blue eye. TICK 2
glisten: see it g.; LOWE J 17
  shoulders/ G. as silver, LAWR 12
  stars to g. on you, JONS 10
glistening: g. eye to the poison of a
  smile? BLAK 17
  their dirty/ g. torsos OHAR 12
glistens: black snag g. SNYD 29
  wine-cup g.; SCOT WA 1
glister: g. fair; SPENS 38
glisters: All that g. SHAK 119
  Nor all, that g., gold. GRAY 20

Glistring: G. with dew; fragrant the fertile earth MILT 76

glitter: knives that g. SIMI 4

Masturbating a g., PLATH 35

glittered: g. when he walked. ROBI 51

in apparel that g. CRAN S 5

stars g. on the snow KINN 17

glittering: ancient, g. eyes, YEATS 82

g. current; ROET 14

g. stars JEFFE 21

g. summer runs YEATS 96

his g. heaps, BYRO 21

holds him with his g. eye — COLE SAM 29

how that g. taketh me! HERR 62

of g. stream YEATS 153

glitt'ring: frost was g. BARNE 4

g. Forfex wide, POPE A 124

gloaming: snow had begun in the g., LOWE J 11

globe: all the land of the g. WHITM 2

Doubled the g. of dead THOMA D 24

great g. itself — SHAK 163

great g. reels SCHW 7

In this distracted g. SHAK 28

wears the turning g. HOUS 20

globed: As a g. fruit, MACL 1

Gloire: yellow/ G. de Dijon roses. LAWR 11

gloom: g. from the war, TICK 2

g. oppressive o'er the world, THOMS J (1700–1748) 13

go with him in the g., HARD 33

street/ Into its g. retires, BINY 4

Upon the growing g. HARD 18

watch from dawn to g. SHEL 51

what gather'd in the g.? SWIN 6

whispers pierce the g.: ARNO 30

gloomily: where g. retired, THOMS J (1700–1748) 10

glooms: amidst the baleful g., THOMS J (1834–1882) 3

Beautiful g., soft dusks LANIE 3

Welcome, kindred g.! THOMS J (1700–1748) 12

gloomy: Brightens up a g. place; UNKN 267

deep and g. wood, WORD 33

glories: Forget the g. WORD 73

g. of our blood and state SHIR 1

G. of This World; OMAR 3

Immortal g. in my mind ADDI 1

triumphs and their g. BROWNI R 49

glorified: gardens rich in memory g. YEATS 35

glorify: all might Him g. TAYL E 2

glorious: Banners yellow, g., golden, POE 21

builds g. temples, LOWE J 9

crowded hour of g. life MORD 1

crystal g. ye shine, CHAU 122

full reward and g. fate CAREW 17

g. by my pen MONTROSE 3

g. canopy of light WHITE 1

g. faculty WORD 117

G. hosanna from the den;/ G. the catholic amen;/ G. the martyr's gore: SMAR 9

g. in the might WORD 78

g. land in the sky; HILL J 1

g. Lord of life! SPENS 18

g. Sun uprist: COLE SAM 30

G. the northern lights astream; SMAR 9

G. the song, SMAR 9

G. the thunder's roar: SMAR 9

gowned in your g. hair. SMIT L 2

great Elisa's g. name SPENS 47

heaven was g. BRON 3

image of their g. Maker MILT 71

Made g. summer SHAK 94

many a g. morning SHAK 197

more g. is the crown SMAR 9

'O g. Life, NEWB 4

other great and g. ends, TRAH 6

passion in a lover's g., BYRO 18

Tam was g., BURN 53

thy g. works, MILT 81

upon thy g. canvas BRYA 28

utter forth a g. Voice, ADDI 4

gloriously: Bore witness g.; MILT 118

goodly colours g. arrayed; SPENS 21

glory: a' the g. shall be thine! BURN 33

all vain g., DUNB W 3

alone with his g. WOLF C 3

Array'd in G. MILT 109

crowned him with g. and honor. BIBL, O.T. 25

days of our g.; BYRO 66

drowned my G. OMAR 2

excess/ Of G. obscur'd: MILT 57

fields where g. does not stay, HOUS 56

first glance of the g. of God SMAR 2

Forgot was Britain's g.; TAYL B 2

full meridian of my g. FLET/SHAK 4

g. and shame, MILT 60

g. and the dream? WORD 68

g. and the freshness of a dream. WORD 64

g. excites, MILT 59

g. from his gray hairs WHITT 11

G.! G.! Hallelujah! HOWE 2

g., hope's true gage, RALEG 10

g. in His bosom HOWE 3

g. in the flower; WORD 84

G. is more bright DANI S 3

g., jest, and riddle of the world! POPE A 78

g. of the coming of the Lord; HOWE 1

g. of the day was in her face, JOHN J 4

g. of the Light. ROBI 10

g. of the winning MERE G 4

g. of this perfect day JOHN G 2

g. of tyrant head RANS 26

G. pursue, and generous Shame, GRAY 27

g. that was Greece, POE 45

Great England's g. SPENS 46

great g., and not broad. JONS 34

Heavens Bright g. TAYL E 8

heavens declare the g. of God; BIBL, O.T. 26

her brown body/ Has no g. CUNE 1

High King of G. STEPHENS 4

horns of g. blowing AIKE 10

infirm g. of the positive hour ELIOT T 3

inherit the throne of g.: BIBL, O.T. 8

leaves a white/ Unbroken g., BROO R 11

like thy g., Titan! SHEL 58

lose the g. of the form, ARNO 11

Lust of g. pricked their hearts up, BROWNI R 48

next in g. to enduring love, STEVENS 56

paths of g. lead but to the grave. GRAY 9

praise, pomp, g., joy BOLT 1

Prince of G. died, WATT I 9

rainbow's g. is shed; SHEL 89

sea of g. FLET/SHAK 3

Short is the g. of the blushing rose, DANI S 6

some desperate g., OWEN 20

stars of g. there; DRAK 1

stars the g. of His eyes PLUN 1

thronging years in g. rise. BRYA 14

thy flow'r, thy g., pass, DANI S 15

trailing clouds of g. WORD 70

walked in g. WORD 121

War brought more g. OWEN 10

what is in g. above them, DICKEY 19

wild cataract leaps in g. TENN 111

With g. richly furnished, BRAD 12

won great g., TENN 119

goest: forth I march, thou g.
  before; BIBL, O.T. 64
Ride more than thou g.,
  SHAK 71
goggles: smiling under their g.
  DICKEY 10
going: double dead: g., and bidding
  go. DONN 23
g. and coming back. FROS 14
g. shall be used with feet.
  SHAK 76
g. to die perhaps. SORL 1
g. to snow. STEVENS 67
I'm g. all along! DICKI 131
I'm G. home; EMER 26
murder/ The mankind of her g.
  THOMA D 37
noises of coming and going,
  WHITM 33
old and g. KINGSL 2
preserve thy g. out BIBL, O.T. 59
Why are you g.? STRA 3
gold: armor shone like g. UNKN 60
barbaric pearl and g., MILT 58
bared snow and thy unbraided g.
  CAREW 12
become of all the g.
  BROWNI R 79
Bow of burning g.: BLAK 35
bringing home/ black g., HAYD 9
cage the minute/ Within its nets of
  g., MACN 23
Catches his shrieks in cups of g.
  BLAK 31
chains red and g. CUMM 13
dancing back to the age of g.,
  OSUL 2
Egyptian's g. mist LOWE J 9
female heart can g. despise?
  GRAY 19
figure 5/ in g. WILLI 15
Five g. rings, UNKN 278
flew in a g. storm SCOT WI 1
gete g. with here glee LANGL 4
G. as on a coin, LARK 11
g. complexion dimmed;
  SHAK 188
g. enough around her middle/ To
  buy Northumberland
  UNKN 319
g. in phisik is a cordial; CHAU 9
g. Of Matrimonial treason:
  MILT 112
g. of the opulent sun.
  STEVENS 43
green tigering the g. HUGH T 10
hairy g. crown on 'er 'ead?
  KIPL 30
hearts of g. BELL 13
her rank and g. WHITT 19
if g. ruste, what shal iren do?
  CHAU 13
In their g. coats spots SHAK 126

is not g.; SHAK 119
just finding the g. SERV 14
like a fat g. watch. PLATH 61
liquid g. is the air; CLARE 1
litel g. in cofre. CHAU 2
lot of wolves dressed up in g. and
  purple NASH 20
Much have I traveled in the
  realms of g., KEAT 55
my g. beaten skin PLATH 49
Nature's first green is g.,
  FROS 70
Nor all, that glisters, g. GRAY 20
not covetous for g., SHAK 59
Nothing g. can stay. FROS 71
Of two g. Ingots MARL 9
Offers thee g. SHERB 2
once was singing g. TEAS 2
Plate sin with g., SHAK 81
poop was beaten g.; SHAK 5
priests in g. and black, LAWR 9
roof of g.; JONS 35
Scarfs, garters, g., POPE A 81
straight was a path of g.
  BROWNI R 58
student's bower for g.,
  WORD 157
There is thy g. SHAK 151
thieves break in and steal the g.
  MOTH 16
unstain'd with g. or fee,
  MILT 122
usurers tell their g. SHAK 76
wanted the g., SERV 11
Wedges of g., SHAK 97
with harmless g., LOWE J 15
With pearl dissolv'd in g.
  SHERB 1
Yet it isn't the g. SERV 14
golden: Banners yellow, glorious,
  g., POE 21
Beats the g. bird no more.
  MILLA 19
beside the g. door!" LAZA 2
breaking the g. lilies
  BROWNI E 2
brimming g., spilling cry!
  JOHN H 3
broken is the g. bowl! POE 29
burn its g. eyes. HECH 7
burnished with g. rind, MILT 69
children green and g.
  THOMA D 20
cog in a g. singing hive:
  SPEND 9
corn by her g. hair, DAVIE W 3
covet fetters, though they g. bee.
  SPENS 13
entangle in that g. snare:
  SPENS 12
girls with g. hair ROBI 53
G. Age HERR 2
g. apple doth appear. MOTH 16

g. apples grow; —
  STEVENSO R 19
g. apples of the sun. YEATS 139
g. bough of Argicida. POUN 8
g. bowl BIBL, O.T. 6
g. brass and silvery steel,
  WHITM 99
g. crown, Aphrodite, POUN 8
g.-eyed tu-whit, tu-whoo NOYE 3
g. friends I had, HOUS 62
g./ Girdles and breast bands,
  POUN 8
G. lads and girls SHAK 18
g. lamps in a green night,
  MARV 1
g. light of morn, HOOD 8
g. manacles stand for a paradise;
  SIDN 4
g. monthly breeze! GINS 35
g. morning breakes: DOWL 1
g. nutmeg and a silver pear;
  MOTH 13
g. pomp HERR 48
g. sands, and crystal brooks,
  DONN 6
g. shafts employs, MILT 78
G. slumbers kiss your eyes,
  DEKK/OTHE 1
g. umbrage shut, TUCK 1
Grains of the g. sand — POE 14
happy, g. age! TASS 1
His g. locks PEEL 7
holds fast the g. mean, HORA 6
host, of g. daffodils; WORD 24
Kissing with g. face the meadows
  green, SHAK 197
Lock'd me up with a g. Key.
  BLAK 19
many a g. phrase; TENN 124
miles of g. moss, AUDE 8
Music's g. tongue KEAT 5
one strangling g. hair. ROSS D 2
ope their g. eyes: SHAK 17
Phœbus thrust out his g. hedde,
  SPENS 55
ran itself in g. sands. TENN 70
redd'ning Phoebus lifts his g.
  Fire: GRAY 32
rich and g. coloured raine,
  LODG 1
set upon a g. bough YEATS 130
shut me in his g. cage. BLAK 24
snip the intellectual g. threads
  GINS 12
stretches out my g. wing,
  BLAK 24
thousand g. sheaves ROBI 53
to a g. throne, POE 30
unadornèd g. tresses MILT 73
upon the g. skies: PLATO 1
Weep thy g. tears! WATS W 1
Goldengrove: G. unleaving?
  HOPKINS 21

goldenrod: g. is yellow,   JACK 3
goldsmiths: form as Grecian g.
    make   YEATS 129
gondolier: highly respectable g.,
    GILB 17
    highly respectable g.   GILB 19
gone: All else is g.,   WHITT 12
    all g. away,   ROBI 18
    all her robes are g.   UNKN 191
    All is g.;   DANI S 15
    Aquarium is g.   LOWE R 21
    Art thou g. in haste?
        WEBS/ROWL 1
    better days when I am g.
        BONT 7
    better g. to the gallows.
        UNKN 151
    body is g. completely   LAWR 40
    buffaloes are g.   SAND 2
    g. in the wind.   MANG 1
    g. into the world of light!
        VAUG 26
    G. is another summer's day.
        DE LA 26
    G. is our sport,   NASHE 2
    G. is the heart of Man.   SITW 10
    g. off, like a horse.   PLATH 41
    g. on the mountain,   SCOT WA 7
    g. on the wind's wings.   BYRO 37
    g. out, a possessed witch,   SEXT 7
    g. out of the reach of change —
        THOMA E 10
    g. up in smoke,   THOMP F 8
    g. up to the church to pray.
        BLAK 55
    G. were but the Winter,
        ROSS C 23
    g. years and the now years and
        the maybe years,   WALK 5
    Guest, that would be g.   DICKI 7
    half a century they were g.
        MUIR 2
    Half of my life is g.,   LONG 28
    I miss it! is it g.?   ARNO 43
    I'd been, g. and went   YEATM 1
    know it's g.,   SHAP 17
    loves have come and g.;
        MILLA 40
    old man g.   JOYC 2
    pang of all the partings g.,
        THOMP F 2
    Remember me when I am g.
        away,   ROSS C 19
    shine when all of these are g.
        BRAD 8
    sweet cheat g.   DE LA 8
    "thousand types are g.;   TENN 35
    up and be g.   HARD 23
    when disbelief has g.?   LARK 5
    When love is g.   BOUR 2
    your world of Beautie 's g.
        HERR 45

gong-tormented: dolphin-torn, that
    g. sea.   YEATS 19
good: air tastes g. to my palate.
        WHITM 75
    all might seem g..'   THOMA E 3
    all the g. I can —   GILB 7
    all thy sum of g.;   SHAK 230
    appetite was g.?   BYRO 32
    be in such g. company   DARC 2
    be, on the one hand, g.,   HOUS 8
    being g. for nothing else, be wise.
        ROCH 3
    bid the world G.-night.   HERR 21
    brave and partly g.,   RICH 13
    bubbles with wit and g. humour!
        GILB 56
    But my greatest delight is to take
        a g. bite   THOMA D 40
    called through all our tribes 'The
        G..' "   LOWE J 20
    causeless g. or ill decree.   GREV 1
    chief g. and market of his time
        SHAK 35
    close on the promised g.
        TENN 95
    creature not too bright or g.
        WORD 134
    doing us some g.,   AUDE 24
    dutiful weighing of ill with g.; —
        LANIE 3
    fair and wise and g. and gay.
        MOTH 22
    fat of g. And evil,   JARR 3
    find a g. wife too,   CREE 13
    fleeth save G. Deeds,   UNKN 90
    for evil or for g.   ROBI 27
    fresh air is g.   OHAR 2
    garment too g. For thee   CRAS 11
    gave me a g. character,   CARRO 3
    g. ale in the glen,   UNKN 201
    g. and the bad   POE 11
    g. as I kin be!   FIEL E 4
    g. as yer kin be!   FIEL E 5
    G.-bye — and hail!   WHITM 36
    G.-bye my Fancy!   WHITM 34
    G.-bye, proud world!   EMER 26
    g.-bye to the bar   KINGSL 4
    G.-night to the Season! —
        PRAE 3
    g. for a baby in a milking pail.
        THOMA D 42
    g. for the body   OHAR 2
    G. how far —   GRAY 31
    g. is oft interrèd with their bones.
        SHAK 48
    G. Lord deliver us.   SIDN 38
    G. luck is the gayest   HAY 1
    g. news, g. news.   SEXT 11
    G. night, ladies,   ELIOT T 128
    G.-night to the Season!   PRAE 3
    g. of evil born,   EMER 51
    g. of the earth and sun,
        WHITM 76

    g. old cause   WORD 162
    g. old me and you.   UNTE 1
    g. red fires were burning
        STEVENSO R 5
    g. relation to the earth   MOMA 4
    g. relation to the gods   MOMA 4
    g. that I can do.   BANK 1,4
    g. things have perished utterly,
        WILD 11
    g. want power,   SHEL 52
    g. wicked spirit, sweet angel
        devil.   DRAY 6
    g. wif was ther of biside Bathe,
        CHAU 10
    g. will to men.   LONG 11, 12
    graveyard of g. and evil,   MERR 5
    greenest of our valleys/ By g.
        angels tenanted,   POE 20
    harbor for g. or bad,   WHITM 74
    He is g. i' the main,
        BROWNI R 7
    he isn't quite as g.   FROS 28
    heart shall prize no g. above
        thee;   QUAR 2
    I shall be g. health   WHITM 74
    Ill and g., old,   HERB CH 5
    ill thoughts die and g. are born —
        BROWNI E/GUIN 1
    in g. satire,   BYRO 35
    in g. sooth,   HARD 10
    in gravity and g. faith.   MAHON 3
    I've found it g.   KIPL 21
    jolly g. ale and old!
        STEVENSO W 2
    Kentucky home, g.-night!   FOST 2
    kissed and bade my love g.-bye.
        CLARE 12
    knowledge of G. and Evil?
        MILT 95
    let no man hope least g.,
        JONS 25
    Man is naturally g.,   MELV 12
    meek lover of the g.!   EMER 7
    much less g. than ill,   HOUS 52
    my sent be g.,   HERB G 47
    never been happy or g.   AUDE 76
    no g. sign.   SWIF 27
    no life-glimpse, g. or bad,   ROBI 6
    no other g. enough   ALEX 9
    Nor g., nor bad, nor fools, nor
        wise,   PRIO 4
    Nothing is fair or g. alone.
        EMER 18
    of g. humour   POPE A 109
    Of moral evil and of g.,
        WORD 145
    one g. custom   TENN 103
    Or a g. lay: AUDE 48
    our g. will sever.   JONS 48
    parent of g.,   MILT 81
    Pastime with g. company
        HENR 1
    peasant's last G.-night,   LONG 22

lovely in thy youthful g.:
BRYA 12
madest loose g. unkind; TASS 6
No place of g. ELIOT T 14
nobler g. than now. BRYA 14
pity g. obtain, SIDN 5
Remit as yet no g., DICKI 24
Renown and g. is dead;
SHAK 109
simplicity a g.; JONS 5
single g. HERR 26
snatch a g. POPE A 30
Stealing g. from all EMER 25
stonden in his lady g. CHAU 9
sweet attractive g.; MILT 72
tender g. of a day that is dead
TENN 3
thy g. impart POPE A 128
Thy G. my Distaffe, TAYL E 5
Thy mither's person, g., an'
merit, BURN 44
Tuesday's child is full of g.,
MOTH 22
Wants not a fourth G., SPENS 56
window, through thy g.
HERB G 73
with g. and mekeness, HAWE 2
with proper g. KIRK 4
with what g. I can, KINS 6
words of g. GRAV 13
yield with a g. to reason,
FROS 93
graced: g. with birds that sing,
BROWNE 1
ordinary night was g. NEME 1
graceful: g. innocence, MILT 90
Marvell's wit and g. song.
WHITT 10
nymphs so g., wise, and fair,
SWIF 21
So earnest, so g., LOWE J 1
gracefull: worthy of your g. rymes,
SPENS 29
Graces: G. naked danced DRUM 1
inherit heaven's g. SHAK 222
odd becomming g., SUCK 4
Gracing: G. the tender herb,
MILT 69
gracious: So hallow'd and so g. is
the time. SHAK 19
your great and g. ways. PATM 5
graciousness: Dwell on her g.,
GRAV 35
grackle: spotted a g., WILB 25
gradation: not by old g., SHAK 133
gradations: cold g. of decay,
JOHN S (1709–1784) 4
gradual: g. erasures/ Of flesh
MOSS 4
g. ruin spreading like a stain;
AUDE 97
in g. vision through my tears,
BROWNI E 7

gradually: Bloom g. out of reach.
SNOD 4
truth must dazzle g. DICKI 137
grafts: He g. upon the Wild the
Tame: MARV 25
grain: amber waves of g., BATE 1
burning the unburied g.
LOWE R 5
cheweth g. and licoris, CHAU 51
gathering his g.; WHITM 7
G.-tinctured, drenched in
empyrean light; WORD 102
Lord's Prayer on a g. of rice,
THOMA D 8
roots, orchards, g.? WHITM 96
sparrows pecking the llamas' g.
JARR 28
Take of this g., HERB G 57
grains: g. beyond age,
THOMA D 38
g. of sand, CARN 1
G. of the golden sand — POE 14
millions of g. are black, white,
tan, and gray, BISH 42
mixed with quartz g., rose and
amethyst. BISH 42
grammar: also g.? — SNOD 9
g., and nonsense, and learning;
GOLD 5
grand: first g. Thief MILT 68
G. go the Years — DICKI 126
g. old ballad of Sir Patrick
Spence, COLE SAM 6
g. old masters, LONG 15
palace g., or just a plain, old
shoe; UNTE 1
grandest: g. funeral ALEX 3
grandeur: g. that was Rome.
POE 45
g., with his wise grimace,
EMER 27
Nor G. hear GRAY 8
old Scotia's g. springs, BURN 20
grandeurs: g. of his Babylonian
heart. THOMP F 5
grandfather: g. fell on Vinegar Hill,
CLARK J 3
g. plucking/ A straw SIMI 3
grandfathers: graves of my g. call
me, KNIG 7
grandly: Go, g. borne, STOD 3
grandmama: sewing a new/
button FREE 1
grandmamma: match the g./ Staid
sleeping there. DICKI 51
grandmother: as my g.'s father
WHITM 89
g. sings BISH 47
her g.'s voice, HARJ 2
In my g.'s house SIMP 10
play g.'s-steps DAY 11
there's your g. SIMI 3

grandmothers: all have g.
MOOR M 36
My g. were strong. WALK 7
grandson: his g.'s eyes. HARP 1
grange: magic power on the stony
g. MUIR 5
of an old g. THOMA E 10
granite: After polishing g.
LOWE J 6
firmly gript the g. truth. MARK 2
g. among its flowers, JARR 18
G.: ingrained SNYD 52
g./ quarries on the islands.
LOWE R 56
walls/ Of shadowy g., TENN 84
grant: God g. you find KINGSL 8
g. me grace, SOUTHW 13
Hell g. what love did seek;
MILT 17
Grantchester: would I were!/ In G.,
BROO R 17
granted: be g. beauty YEATS 106
clay was not g. LOWE J 3
g. to sing WHITM 47
little is not g.." COAT 1
Your suit is g., HERB G 71
granting: g. my request,
HERB G 22
g. we have sinned, DRYD 17
grants: Government g., MACN 9
grape: belly of the g., EMER 1
full as g. bunches RANDA D 2
g.-shot and gangrene, TICK 1
g. tendril/ ties a knot
MOOR M 20
mantling vine/ Lays forth her
purple g., MILT 69
swinger to g. the taste. REED I 5
trellis'd g., WHITM 29
grapes: "Bunches of g.," DE LA 5
g. sweeter than muscadine
TATE A 5
g. the morn salute EMER 2
vines have tender g.
BIBL, O.T. 73
where the g. of wrath are stored;
HOWE 1
Grapple: G. them to thy soul
SHAK 23
grappled: g. at the net LOWE R 37
grappling: g. in the central blue;
TENN 75
grasp: eludes my g., AMMO 9
g. had left the giant world so
weak SHEL 80
guardian g. BRID R 10
his g. is so cold! GOET 1
What dread g. BLAK 82
grasps: g. of disorder, AMMO 9
Grass: 'All flesh is g.' UNKN 199
as grows the g.; EMER 39
blade/ Of g. KAVA 6
carries the feathered g. RICH 29

through the g.? GINS 2
too far to find a g., ROBI 25
Trace your g., SHEL 65
Tread soft on her G., PRIO 5
verse you g. for me:
  STEVENSO R 21
vortex of our g. CRAN H 50
web of human things,/ Birth and
  the g., SHEL 22
with me to the g.." WORD 51
without a g. WILB 32
yew to deck my g.: BLAK 40
graved: g. in the white stone
  BRAD 8
gravefellows: Fit g. RANDA D 4
gravel: g.-crunching, interminable
  departure MAHON 2
stepped out onto the g. MERR 4
graven: g. with diamonds WYAT 32
No g. images CLOU 5
grave's: g. a fine and private place,
  MARV 34
g. the second Marriage-bed.
  CRAS 1
graves: all are in their g.; BRYA 8
Allegheny g. its tone SIGO 2
filled with g., BLAK 65
g., all gaping wide, SHAK 128
g. by glow-worm night. BEDD 8
g. give up their dead. SWIF 3
g. of my grandfathers call me,
  KNIG 7
g. of the martyrs STEVENSO R 1
g. stood tenantless SHAK 20
G., yawn and yield your dead,/ Till
  death be uttered, SHAK 132
in your humble g., TIMR 6
laurel the g. of our dead! FINC 2
They have no g. as yet. CHES 5
gravest: g. of Divines, SWIF 18
gravestones: g. in the cemetery.
  SPEND 6
graveward: lay g. with his furies;
  THOMA D 6
graveyard: beg the favor with a g.
  grin. DAY 8
g. marble sculpture FROS 39
g. of good and evil, MERR 5
g. shelves on the town.
  LOWE R 39
Monaghan g.; KAVA 19
old Quaker g. LOWE R 38
graveyards: slant stones of g.
  LOWE A 2
gravity: breaks the law of g.
  ELIOT T 93
g., which is not simple RICH 29
in g. and good faith. MAHON 3
mixture of g. and waggery.
  SMAR 8
gravy: it'll be sheer g. OHAR 3
No g. and no grub, RANS 34

Gray: auld Robin G. he is kind
  LIND L 2
dark hair changing to g.
  ROSS C 18
dismasted, g. and batter'd ship,
  WHITM 28
Dominie in G. DICKI 81
eyes gone g. from cramps
  HUGO 7
glory from his g. hairs WHITT 11
g./ And changeless lands of ice.
  WILB 47
G. and heavy blanket, WHITM 71
g.-eyed morn smiles on the
  frowning night, SHAK 146
g., gigantic ghost THOMP W 1
hair as g. As was my sire's
  WHITT 28
little g. mouse, NASH 15
old and g. and full of sleep,
  YEATS 161
old and ragged and g. BRIN 1
on the pavements g., YEATS 75
On thy cold g. stones, O Sea!
  TENN 1
scorn the home-spun g. CAMPI 9
Tears and love for the G. FINC 2
this g. spirit TENN 132
this old g. head, WHITT 3
twilight cold and g., LONG 23
wood was g. and the bark warping
  off it FROS 140
yon g. head WHITT 4
grazing: cattle are g., WORD 163
grease: g.-/ impregnated
  wickerwork; BISH 12
slides by on g. LOWE R 21
greased: catch Christ with a g.
  worm, LOWE R 14
greasy: g. Joan doth keel the pot.
  SHAK 101
great: all g. Neptune's ocean
  SHAK 108
Be g., JEFFE 42
chestnut-tree, g.-rooted
  blossomer, YEATS 13
cloudy foreheads of the g.
  HORA 10
creatures g. and small, ALEX 1
Death of G. Men, BUTL 8
did g. wrong, and maintained
  little right. UNKN 159
far above the G. GRAY 31
from those g. eyes WHITT 12
g. as any honest man's. GILB 37
g. as God had made them
  KAVA 17
g. bell of Bow. UNKN 25
g. belly. JONS 32
g. destination is to stay."
  SNOD 10
g. dolour complaining UNKN 206
g. events were decided, KAVA 4

g. globe reels SCHW 7
g. glory, and not broad. JONS 34
G. God, our King! SMIT SA 2
g. guns, unawares, HARD 13
g. head rattling like a gourd,
  WARR 3
g. is God Almighty, ALEX 2
G. is my envy of death PETRA 8
G. is my envy of you, earth, in
  your greed PETRA 7
g. is small, MUIR 11
G. is the art, EMER 33
g. man humbled, AIKE 9
G. men have been among us;
  WORD 21
g. Nature WORD 104
G. Negative, ROCH 16
g. Neptune's diadem. CAMPI 5
G. or small, WHITM 22
g. Original proclaim: ADDI 3
g. Panjandrum himself, FOOT 1
g. river this side of Stygia,
  STEVENS 44
g. shape labored and fell.
  MOMA 2
g. shout upon the hills, MARK 4
G. Sir John,
  JOHN S (1709–1784) 10
g.-sized monster of ingratitudes.
  SHAK 173
g. star early drooped WHITM 46
g. to study Rome; VAN DY 1
g. traditions of the Past LONG 27
g.-uncle painted a big picture.
  BISH 24
g. whole THOMS J (1700–1748) 6
g. with child to speak, SIDN 6
G. Wits DRYD 2
hearts made g. with shot;
  OWEN 30
In a g. tempest PETRA 12
Laughing on the G. Earth
  SNYD 8
Lives of g. men LONG 36
long-yarded and g.-bellied
  GRAV 18
lordly g. compass within,
  LANIE 4
Love is a g. and mighty lord;
  PEEL 3
name g. in story — BYRO 66
other g. and glorious ends,
  TRAH 6
out of g. Russia SAND 21
palace too g., BROO P 2
perfumed chambers of the g.,
  SHAK 54
quaint g. figure that men love,
  LIND V 2
Shake patiently my g. affliction
  off. SHAK 79
small is g. MUIR 11

So g. a sweetness flows
  YEATS 48
so g. a wrong, UNKN 190
so g., and I am so small,
  RANDS 3
So thy g. gift, SHAK 220
That cost g. sums, SKEL 9
things both g. and small;
  COLE SAM 30
This G. God, JOHN J 3
those who were truly g.
  SPEND 11
truth is g., PATM 7
which once was g., WORD 92
world's g. cities, OSHA 2
world's g. day MUIR 8
world's g. hands. HUNT 7
your g. and gracious ways.
  PATM 5
greater: g. grief/ To banish the less,
  SURR 11
g. heat/ than that of the Sun.
  SITW 9
g. heaven in an heaven less.
  MARV 31
g. Sun appear MILT 38
g. than we know. WORD 128
g. torment/ Of love satisfied
  ELIOT T 10
it is a g. grief SHAK 200
no g., but more eminent,
  DONN 41
served the G. Community.
  AUDE 93
wonder at a g. wonder, DONN 68
greatest: As g. kings STOD 3
But my g. delight is to take a
  good bite THOMA D 40
g. Herald of Heaven's King,
  DRUM 5
g. nation: SAND 8
g. traitor, WHITM 73
We are the g. city, SAND 8
greatly: else sinning g., WORD 103
G. instructed MILT 105
g. the better for NASH 18
greatness: base/ On which thy g.
  stands; WORD 115
g. is but care, BEAU/BASS 2
g. is no trust'. BEAU/BASS 3
highest point of all my g.,
  FLET/SHAK 4
Of no man's g. was afraid,
  SWIF 23
think/ Of the g., GRAV 39
Twin-born with g., SHAK 58
greaves: flamed upon the brazen g.
  TENN 63
Grecian: form as G. goldsmiths
  make YEATS 129
you in G. tires SHAK 205
gree: bear the g., BURN 27
Greece: glories of G. BYRO 72

glory that was G., POE 45
G. might still be free; BYRO 41
isles of G.! BYRO 40
Like G. and Rome. SIMP 15
greed: Great is my envy of you,
  earth, in your g. PETRA 7
greeds: lusts and g. SITW 9
greedy: thy g. self consum'd,
  MILT 44
With g. eyes TATE A 6
Greek: always dead like G.
  SHAP 22
brazen giant of G. fame, LAZA 1
carve in Latine or in G., WALL 3
English cut on G. and Latin,
  BUTL 4
ghosts of G. boys. SPEND 10
G. name for Swine's Snout?
  BROWNI R 77
G. of Plato RANS 33
hive the G. honey. JEFFE 34
Greeks: G. brought to Troye town,
  SURR 7
green: acres of the insane g.?
  TATE A 13
All in g. CUMM 3
All in our gowns of g. so gay
  UNKN 229
all the trees are g.; KINGSL 5
among thy g. braes, BURN 22
amorous as this lovely g.
  MARV 16
Bossom'd in yon g. EMER 28
bright g. eyes MONR 1
brightest virgin on the g.,
  SWIF 21
chawnk g. apples FIEL E 4
children g. and golden
  THOMA D 20
cut the g., VAN DO 1
dance above your green, g. grave
  UNKN 48
Deep-trenchèd/ G. billow:
  STEPHENS 8
dew her orbs upon the g.
  SHAK 126
dripping in tangles g., MELV 23
Drives my g. age; THOMA D 22
Duty, faith, love are roots, and
  ever g. PEEL 7
elfin from the g. grass, POE 2
England's g. & pleasant Land.
  BLAK 35
Farewell g. fields BLAK 101
fennel that grows so g.!
  UNKN 216
fields are g. SHEL 2
flowery and g. age PETRA 2
force that through the g. fuse
  THOMA D 22
fresh and g., HERR 50
golden lamps in a g. night,
  MARV 1

grass is g., ROSS C 32
g. atoms shimmer GINS 42
g./ Before my threshold, AKEN 1
g.-ey'd monster SHAK 134
g. for a season, SWIN 23
g. freedom of a cockatoo
  STEVENS 54
g. grass above ROSS C 33
g. grass glows upwards,
  LAWR 56
G. grow the rashes, BURN 28
G. grow the rushes-O UNKN 51
g. ice! LOVE 1
g. in the mulberry bush,
  TATE A 15
G. is a solace WILLI 10
g. is El Aghir . CAME 3
g.-rob'd senators of mighty
  woods, KEAT 22
G. Snake, when I hung you
  LEVE 22
g. sour ringlets make, SHAK 164
G. springs the tree, RALEG 14
g. thought in a green shade,
  MARV 18
g. tigering the gold. HUGH T 10
g. waters of the canal KAVA 1
g. with bays POPE A 31
Greta woods are g., SCOT WA 23
happy as the grass was g.,
  THOMA D 17
heads are g., LEAR 9
joyous leaves of dark g.,
  WHITM 39
kind as it is g., MOOR M 35
Kissing with golden face the
  meadows g., SHAK 197
laid him on the g. UNKN 40
Learn of the g. world POUN 21
legends of the g. chapels
  THOMA D 34
live like some g. laurel
  YEATS 110
loitered o'er the g., GOLD 1
maketh me to lie down in g.
  pastures: BIBL, O.T. 31
Making the g. one red. SHAK 108
Many a g. isle SHEL 35
mouth all g.? SWEN 4
Nature's first g. is gold, FROS 70
On the Echoing G.." BLAK 90
On the g. BLUN 1
patient lies/ Within a tent of g.,
  KIRK 2
pray/ Devoutly on the holy day;/
  Skip and trip it on the g.,
  CAMPI 8
precipices show untrodden g.;
  KEAT 65
Reptilian g. the wrinkled throat,
  WINT 5
robes of g., ROET 16

seen a g. country, useful to the
  race, and mines, BLUN 5
singing to the g. valleys. MAST 8
slow Meander's margent g.,
  MILT 9
springtime, fresh and g., HERR 6
summer's g. all girded up in
  sheaves SHAK 186
Time held me g. and dying
  THOMA D 21
to the g. valley, UNKN 11
tomb among g. shades
  UNKN 253
too-fluent g. STEVENS 48
transparent g.-wash of the sea
  WHITM 97
uncertain g.,/ Piano-polished,
  STEVENS 47
under the g. sods lay. YEATS 14
valley warm and g., HODG 3
wearin' o' the G.! UNKN 299
Wherever g. is worn, YEATS 56
wind betwixt g. islands;
  WHITM 13
woods are getting g., CARRO 32
world of g. RICH 1
greener: cleaner, g. land! KIPL 12
greenery: shoreline, g. and glass,
  MOSS 4
greenest: g. of our valleys POE 20
g. place MOOR M 35
greenhorns: moody g. REED I 4
Greenland: laid on G.'s Coast,
  GAY 4
greenness: g. of the grass MARV 27
Greensnakes: G. slither. HALL 6
Greenwich: pavement of G. Village.
  GINS 20
greenwood: my roof the g. above,
  UNKN 201
Greeny: G. at the heart of summer.
  KAVA 23
greep'the: hym death g. right hard
  by the croppe SENE 2
greet: dewdrops to g. the dawn,
  COOP 1
Fair scenes shall g. thee BRYA 29
g. as angels greet. LOVE 7
G. prees at market maketh dere
  ware, CHAU 89
How should I g. thee? BYRO 74
it gars me g., BURN 51
message g. him UNKN 183
prepare to g. a guest OHAR 7
risin' sun to g. him RILE 5
too g. chepe is holden at litel
  pris. CHAU 89
greete: Hobbinoll, what garres thee
  g.? SPENS 48
gregarious: g. people, JEFFE 5
loud g. town MILLA 32
Grenville: Sir Richard G. lay,
  TENN 116

Greta: G. woods are green,
  SCOT WA 23
gretteste: Hire g. ooth CHAU 13
grew: as the spiral g., HOLM 2
for this the clay g. tall?
  OWEN 27
g. a red rose UNKN 178
g. the more by reaping. SHAK 7
sweetest thing that ever g.
  WORD 50
They g. a little wild. SMIT ST 3
Three years she g. WORD 48
wine which never g. EMER 1
womb wherein they g.?
  SHAK 217
grey: as g. as a cat, FLAT 2
ever wore g. hairs. WORD 122
good g. guardians of art WILB 31
g.-brown bird, WHITM 52
g. flocks in ferny glens BRON 6
G. hairs upon my head. VAUX 2
g. monsters BARA 12
g. rigid uniform GUNN 1
g. word is RANS 13
memory to a g.-haired man
  WHITT 14
old g. Widow-maker? KIPL 15
small g.-coated gnat, SHAK 153
world has grown g. SWIN 23
grief: After long g. and pain,
  TENN 97
all forms, moods, shapes of g.,
  SHAK 21
As imperceptibly as G. DICKI 6
Blossoms of g. and charity
  MUIR 9
blown/ By winds of g. PETRA 5
canker, and the g. BYRO 57
cannot tell our g., HERB CH 2
deepest g. of all, TENN 26
dried with g., SHAK 8
Each to his g., BROO G 3
Eden sank to g., FROS 71
Fall g. in showers; JONS 4
feels nor joy nor g.,
  BROWNI R 18
forethought/ of g. BERRY 1
"From g. and groan, POE 30
greater g. To banish the less,
  SURR 11
g. ageän awoke. BARNE 3
g. an' pain, BURN 63
g. enough for thee. GREE 2
g. for pleasure take. UNKN 185
G. is but a wound to woe;
  FLET/OTHE 1
G. makes us free LAWR 18
G., with a glass that ran; SWIN 1
g. without a pant, COLE SAM 7
history of g. MACL 2
hopeless g. is passionless;
  BROWNI E 1

in g. and self-contempt,
  PETRA 12
it is a greater g. SHAK 200
joy and g. JOYC 1
Joy comes, g. goes, LOWE J 18
Laughter and g. join hands.
  SHAP 20
My g. was not excessive.
  ROET 13
My joy, my g., my hope, my love,
  WALL 5
My soul's a little g., OWEN 6
No g., no care, no toil.
  UNKN 147
Of g. right sure, WYAT 13
perfect g. ROSS D 10
quickened so with g. GRAV 15
sense of g. and pain LUCR 3
Silence augmenteth g., writing
  increaseth rage, GREV/DYER 1
suit a calmer g. TENN 22
thought of g.; WORD 67
Thy father's shame, thy mother's
  g., BRET 1
Without hate, without g.
  ROET 60
griefe: O farewell g., and welcome
  joye, UNKN 17
griefs: all their g. in their arms,
  THOMA D 27
arms/ Round the g. of the ages,
  THOMA D 28
g. that bow, ARNO 29
my g. enfold: BLAK 44
old g. and g. Not yet begun.
  THOMA E 14
other petty g. SHAK 221
suffer'st more/ Of mortal g.
  SHAK 58
grievances: for his g. THOR 10
grieve at g. foregone. SHAK 195
grieve: dinna g. your Sarah;
  UNKN 79
g. at grievances foregone.
  SHAK 195
g. they lived not in these times
  DRAY 8
race of them who g. ARNO 33
Rejoice, and men will seek you;/
  G., and they turn WILC 2
thou leavest me to g., SHEL 75
Time, to make me g., HARD 27
We will g. not, WORD 84
women g. to think they must be
  old. DANI S 7
grieved: No more be g. SHAK 199
other tree was g., SWIF 2
grieves: prayer to the soul that g.,
  LANIE 3
single heart that g. GRAV 32
grieving: died of g.: KEAT 27
g. rimes of mine, PETRA 4

G. the sapless limbs, RANS 11
Margaret, are you g.
  HOPKINS 21
grievous: g. pleasure and pain.
  SWIN 22
grim: Ghastly g. and ancient raven
  POE 36
g. grinning King, DRUM 3
g. line of sheer subsistence
  SAND 16
G.-visaged War SHAK 95
Portly and g., — EMER 20
vessel g. and daring; WHITM 45
walk in a g. forest. CRAN S 5
grimace: accelerated g., POUN 40
grandeur, with his wise g.,
  EMER 27
grimaces: senseless g. CARRO 16
grime: panes relieved of g. RICH 8
grimly: smiles g. its words cut —
  WILLI 5
grimy: g. slur on the Republic's
  faith MELV 12
grin: all upon the g. HOLM 12
beg the favor with a graveyard g.
  DAY 8
changeless g. CUMM 22
cheerfully he seems to g.,
  CARRO 9
lipless g./ Daffodil bulbs instead
  of balls ELIOT T 157
malevolent aged g. HUGH T 10
wide and moony g. NEME 2
with a feeble g., HUGO 7
grind: bones, how they g. AIKE 12
Grinder: Tell me, G., if thou
  grindest CALV 4
grindest: who serenely g. CALV 3
grinning: grim g. King, DRUM 3
g. at his pomp, SHAK 89
g. cat/ Quivers forever TATE A 3
g. in their sleep./ Bats! LAWR 3
grins: g. and lies, DUNB P 11
grip: devil g. the whey-faced slut
  STEPHENS 3
grey fur is pulsing in its g.
  HECH 7
g. of the mob PATT 1
g. that swung the ax in Illinois
  MARK 3
rooted, they/ g. down WILLI 36
gripped: g. in bony vise HAYD 24
grips: g. his fancy WILB 35
gript: firmly g. the granite truth.
  MARK 2
Grishkin: G. in a drawing-room.
  ELIOT T 160
grisly: ugly, g., bare and thin;
  SOUTHW 9
grit: clear g. through and through;
  WOOL 3
grizzly: To stop a g. bear, AUST 1
groan: crazy pierstakes g.; JOYC 3

"From grief and g., POE 30
long, dull, tapering g., WHITM 92
men sit and hear each other g.;
  KEAT 47
they g. and shake their fists?
  HOUS 21
thousands counted every g.,
  ARNO 35
groaned: dead who g. within.
  POE 43
mother g., my father wept.
  BLAK 72
groaning: bends the g. trees.
  BRON 14
TV g. KINN 19
groans: bishop g. to view him.
  PEAC 3
cackles, g., and dies. CLARE 2
clamorous g. SHAK 93
g. of the dying; SCOT WA 20
groat: wealth he valued not a g.;
  SWIF 25
Grocer: From the G.'s Shoppy-
  Shop, CAREY 1
groceries: boy putting g. in my car
  JARR 17
g. in a pantry gleam SHAP 29
grocery: eyeing the g. boys.
  GINS 38
grog: gulped some g. NASH 16
groin: close to his g., SNYD 5
Gromboolian: great G. plain,
  LEAR 6
grooved: stars have g. our eyes
  CRAN H 12
grooves: rifle g. curling with flakes
  of rust. SAND 1
ringing g. of change. TENN 79
grope: g. back upward, HARD 42
with bended neck I g., THOR 4
Gropes: G. for worms DE LA 1
groping: cut stone/ consoles his g.
  feet. LEVE 11
gross: body that was g., PRIN 1
Examples g. as earth exhort me:
  SHAK 35
g. and fugitive movement
  RUKE 3
g.-bellied frogs HEAN 10
g. body's treason; SHAK 243
Grossly: G. overestimated our
  powers. AUDE 12
grote: Ye, for a g.! CHAU 85
grotesques: strange mechanical g.,
  WILD 12
grots: umbrageous g. and caves
  MILT 69
ground: as you lay on the g.,
  WHITM 106

belly close to g. TOOM 5
boiling up in the g., RUKE 1
breastless creatures under g.
  ELIOT T 157
Buried above g. COWP 16
Burning hot is the g., CLARE 1
call it holy g., HEMA 5
chestnut pattering to the g.:
  TENN 22
civilize the g. SIMP 12
dew is cold upon the g.,
  TENN 105
fruitful g., MARTIA 1
gazes on the g., MARK 5
grass the g., WHITM 115
g. itself does not sicken?
  WHITM 96
g. of his making, KINN 2
g. opens up and envelopes me
  BARA 15
g. that late did mourn,
  HERB CH 3
g. Was as hard KEAT 60
grow in other g.? ARNO 40
grow on Irish g.! UNKN 299
heard it hit the g., DICKI 90
I rose from the chill g.
  WHITM 107
In his own g.: POPE A 107
lying on the g., STEPHENS 6
no holier spot of g. TIMR 7
passion that left the g.
  BROWNI R 3
sit upon the g. SHAK 89
squatting upon the g., CRAN S 3
stained this heirloomed g.,
  KLEI 1
sweet music makes the g. to
  move, GRIF 1
Swelling of the G. DICKI 10
tears/ Watering the g., MILT 98
they lie on the g. WHITM 115
to the mill and g.! HOLM 9
treads on the g. SHAK 237
vapours weep their burthen to the
  g., TENN 120
whispering to the g. FROS 62
grounded: g. in astronomye.
  CHAU 8
grounds: g. of a burnt-out hotel,
  MAHON 1
group: around our g. STAF 3
grove: blows the citron g., MILT 79
gird the windy g., TENN 43
horse-races of long ago at Clary's
  G., MAST 7
smell of field and g., attune
  MILT 70
groves: elves of hills, brooks,
  standing lakes, and g.,
  SHAK 164
G. and flowrie Vales, MILT 65
happy g., BLAK 101

Mirth and youth and warm
   desire!/ Woods and g.   MILT 119
grow: dost so comely g.,   FRENE 5
Green g. the rashes,   BURN 28
G. as the clouds grew.   DAY 6
G. dim, or cease to be!
   JOHN G 2
g. excited with wine,   YEATS 42
g. fonder, sweet Cork, of thee;
   MAHONY 2
g. in other ground?   ARNO 40
g. in the woods   UNKN 129
g. no talons at his heels,
   OWEN 14
g. on Irish ground!   UNKN 299
g. proud   HERR 46
g. sea-green at last   GRAV 3
g. up as geese and gabies,
   STEVENSO R 4
hear/ The daisies g.   WILD 17
in my breast there doth it g.,
   WYAT 9
kids g. up   SNYD 41
leaves g. on the tree;   YEATS 50
loppèd tree in time may g. again,
   SOUTHW 7
Love's mysteries in souls do g.,
   DONN 22
never g. again."   SNYD 43
nothing/ will g.   WILLI 7
Peaches g. wild,   WYLI 11
power to g.,   MOOR M 26
see thee daily weaker g.
   COWP 21
Soldiers may g. a soul   OWEN 5
sorrow did twist and g.
   HERB G 3
sugar-canes g.   FOST 2
taught still peace to g.   ELIZ 1
they see others g.,   SHAK 186
They shall g. not old,   BINY 3
we g., we turn to earth,   WEBS 1
What is it to g. old?   ARNO 11
why he didn't g.   BANG 1
wires g. on her head.   SHAK 237
year by year the landscape g.
   TENN 44
growe: Virginitee, thanne wherof
   sholde it g.?   CHAU 92
grower: underground g.,   WILB 36
growing: forty years been g.
   WHITT 14
g. late,   MUIR 8
g. like a tree/ In bulk,   JONS 41
in Louisiana a live-oak g.,
   WHITM 39
Love is a g., or full constant
   light;   DONN 36
misprision g.,/ Comes home
   again,   SHAK 220
Muse grown with this g. age,
   SHAK 196

my folks were g. old.
   STEVENSO R 6
they are g. civilized;   JEFFE 25
Upon the g. gloom.   HARD 18
with clustering bunches g.,
   SHAK 162
growling: listen to it g.   BISH 28
grown: Alice g. lazy,   TATE A 3
cat is g. small   MONR 2
chilly and g. old.   BROWNI R 79
G. beyond nature now,   MAHON 3
g. man's work,"   CLARK J 2
g. rough and wrinkled/ with
   incurable age.   SEXT 9
Love by the spring is g.;
   DONN 41
Muse g. with this growing age,
   SHAK 196
My soul has g.   HUGH L 12
quite transmugrified, they're g.
   BURN 6
spirit is g.   LANIE 4
world has g. grey   SWIN 23
grown-up: waiting room/ was full of
   g. people,   BISH 21
grows: as g. the grass;   EMER 39
consider every thing that g.
   SHAK 187
Darker g. the valley,   MERE G 5
earthly turmoil g.,   ARNO 46
empty g. every bed.   BERRYM 9
g. by night   THOMA E 4
g. one in the human brain.
   BLAK 71
g. such sweet things   WHITM 98
g. through the eye,   THOMA D 31
harder g. the more I her entreat?
   SPENS 9
love g. bitter with treason,
   SWIN 23
love the force that g. us,
   SHAP 18
man g. old, lies down,   BRAD 5
soul/ that g. in darkness,   OHAR 2
unmow'd grass g.,   WHITM 29
unweeded garden,/ That g. to
   seed;   SHAK 22
where the Bong-Tree g.,   LEAR 11
growth: nub of g.   ROET 4
time of their g.   ROSE 4
growths: g. of spring?   WHITM 96
sun-searched g.   ROSS D 4
grub: No gravy and no g.,
   RANS 34
grubber: Walt Whitman, childless,
   lonely old g.,   GINS 38
grudge: Death had his g.   PETRA 3
g. I am bearing against Death,
   PETRA 10
g. I am bearing the earth
   PETRA 9
g. the poor old man   FROS 21

G. who list, but none deny!
   HENR 1
no g. nor strife;   MARTIA 1
grumble: g., and rumble, and roar,
   READ T 1
Grundy: Solomon G.,   MOTH 26
grunt: To g. and sweat   SHAK 40
grunts: g. in my throat   LEVE 21
Guadalajara: dream of G.   ASHB 3
gual'd: tender Page with horney
   Fists was g.;   DRYD 19
guarantee: g. they shall be bodies.
   KINN 18
guard: babe will be thy g.,
   SOUTHW 3
Be thou our g.   WATT I 4
Changing g.   LAWR 2
I g. I do not love;   YEATS 70
tips the g.'s cutlass   MELV 3
guardian: g. angels sung the strain:
   THOMS J (1700–1748)/MALL 1
g. grasp   BRID R 10
g. or the mother
   JOHN S (1709–1784) 12
guardians: good grey g. of art
   WILB 31
wise g. of the poor;   BLAK 92
guards: Beauty g. thy looks:
   CAMPI 15
g. them from the steep.   MEYN 3
guardsman: many a g. knows,
   GILB 39
guardsmen: g. fed to the tigers.
   LI PO 2
gude: g. wife ay to be,   LIND L 2
no for ony g. or ill   BURN 32
gudeman: g. lies sound by me.
   LIND L 1
Guess: G. now who holds thee?' —
   BROWNI E 8
g. the beauty been.   HOPKINS 3
guessed: Placable if His mind and
   ways were g.,   BROWNI R 17
guessing: better only g.'   CLOU 2
guest: awaited the expected g.
   ELIOT T 135
g. and sometime friend?'
   NEWB 2
g. in quiet,   LAWR 43
G., that would be gone —
   DICKI 7
her Roman g.,   SHERB 1
him my dearest g.   BRAD 11
honoured g./ William Yeats is
   laid   AUDE 43
prepare to greet a g.   OHAR 7
Rapid — footless G.   DICKI 162
Soul, the body's g.,   RALEG 6
Welcome the Creations G.,
   MARV 9
guests: be a while our g.:
   BROWNE 2

Two feathered g. from Alabama, WHITM 64

guid: hame cam his g. horse, UNKN 37

ye wha are sae g. yoursel, BURN 4

guide: be thy g. UNKN 90

friendly they g. him MELV 14

g. informed him later, NASH 12

he his g. requested MILT 114

light to g., WORD 88

mine equal, my g., and mine acquaintance. BIBL, O.T. 39

Namby-Pamby is your g., CAREY 2

Providence their g.; MILT 108

Saint Andrews crosse, that is his g.; UNKN 222

Secret fates/ G. our states CAMPI 31

vexes me to choose another g.: BRON 6

wheel of fortune g. you, JONS 11

Guides: g. nature and fate. BRAD 10

G. through the boundless sky BRYA 27

moor-hen g. upon the stream, YEATS 97

We follow where the Swamp Fox g., SIMM 1

Guiding: G. my infant steps, HARD 35

guidon: g. flags flutter WHITM 14

guile: by g. won the day: ELLI 2

packed with g.; BROO R 18

shadows neither love nor g., BRID R 4

wage by force or g. MILT 52

guileless: g. old scapegoat; GRAV 14

guilt: all seemed g., remorse or woe, COLE SAM 27

another's g.! WILD 5

art can wash her g. away? GOLD 9

art her g. to cover, GOLD 9

Cleanse me from its g. and pow'r. TOPL 1

convicted us of g.; YEATS 69

G. pins a fig-leaf; SPENC A 1

stronger g. defeats my strong intent, SHAK 34

thy g. is great, SHAK 140

what is our g.? MOOR M 42

guiltie: g. of True-loves blood, MARL 4

guiltless: g. be condemned, MILT 99

weary g. ghost BOLE 1

Guilty: crying all, "G.! G.!" SHAK 99

G. of dust and sin. HERB G 48

g. of my faults, SHAK 243

g. shame: dishonest Shame MILT 73

Make mad the g. SHAK 31

minority always g. MACN 6

"Not g.," SHAK 178

guinea: rank is but the g. stamp — BURN 24

guineas: "Give crowns and pounds and g. HOUS 59

guise: In their own g., EMER 20

guitar: artist wrought this loved g.; SHEL 91

plays a blue g. STEVENS 23

guitars: g. and bridgework, BROO G 21

gules: Now is he total g., SHAK 30

gulf: dark abyss, whose boiling g. MILT 62

Gulfe: rowling in the fiery G. MILT 49

Gulliby: On the G. Isles CARRY 11

gullies: brown/ hills and red g. of mississippi KNIG 7

gulls: blind wantons like the g. MACN 2

Forgot the cry of g., ELIOT T 142

return like a g. LOWE R 58

white g. south of Victoria SNYD 31

gulp: you cup your hands/ And g. JARR 26

gulped: g. some grog NASH 16

g. what he ate; LA FO 1

gulphs: whelm'd in deeper g. COWP 2

Gulps: candle/ G. PLATH 69

gum: with g. and shoelaces, WARR 6

Gumee: shores of Gitche G., LONG 40

gummery: g. bread each day. CARRY 10

gums: aromatic g. SKEL 9

trees wept odorous g. and balm; MILT 69

witch's g. NASH 2

Gun: As though I'd a g. YEATS 149

birds without a g.? EMER 22

cold-nosed g.? HEAN 21

have no g. LAWR 28

keeper shot him with his g. THOMA E 7

Loaded G. DICKI 109

loaded g. RICH 7, 15

rusty g. on the wall, SAND 1

stoops and takes the g., SHAP 12

gunner: g. and his mate, SHAK 159

gunners: Officers, seamen, g., marines, CLARK J 1

gunnery: g. practice out at sea HARD 14

gunpowder: till the g. ran out FOOT 1

guns: because of the g. SASS 15

Black and impassive g., WHITM 92

great g., unawares,/ Shook all our coffins HARD 13

G. aren't lawful; PARK 2

g. disturbed the hour, HARD 15

g. drawn/ they came running LEE 1

Knocked silly with g. and mines, BLUN 5

men behind the g.! ROON 1

monstrous anger of the g. OWEN 7

Smelt the g.! THOMP W 4

Those whispering g. SASS 15

With drums and g., UNKN 156

gunshot: g. wound in the breast, WHITM 16

Gup: G., Christian Clout, SKEL 4

g., Jack of the Vale! SKEL 4

gurgle: trickle g. in the swampy meadow SNYD 7

gush: g., flush, green AUDE 23

gushed: g. the life-blood of her brave — BRYA 2

spring of love g. from my heart, COLE SAM 36

gusty: far from g. waves, SPEND 1

guts: dung, g., and blood, SWIF 9

lung and liver,/ In her g. SYNG 1

modified in the g. of the living. AUDE 38

gutted: dirty house in a g. world, STEVENS 43

gutter: candles g. by an empty altar, LOWE R 5

rain makes running pools in the g. HUGH L 1

water in a g. WALK 13

gutters: g. of the banked and staring eyes. WILB 13

guttural: g. sorrow of the refugees. MACN 11

Guy: G. De Vere, hast thou no tear? — POE 29

guyle: What g. is this, SPENS 11

guys: wise g. tell me HORN 1

Gynglen: G. in a whistlynge wynd CHAU 19

gypsies: g. in the wood, UNKN 125

seeking like g. LORD 1

gyrates: g. like a top SHAP 16

gyre: perne in a g., YEATS 128

turning in the widening g. YEATS 133

H

H: H.[olland] took the pious resolution GRAY 21

h. a century they were gone
  MUIR 2
H.-a-crown is stopped out of your
  wages! GILB 59
H. a league onward, TENN 6
h. damns me with untruth,
  HERR 20
h.-gods go,/ The gods arrive.
  EMER 25
H. hidden from the eye!
  WORD 45
h. his flock were in their beds,
  YEATS 14
h. in love with easeful Death,
  KEAT 49
h. of a broken hope
  STEVENSO R 17
H. of my life is gone, LONG 28
h.-opened flowers, UNKN 251
h. perhaps will reign; MILT 67
h.-talk code of mysteries
  KAVA 21
h. that's got my keys."
  GRAHAM H 2
h. the gladness SHEL 72
H. the world's hopes, HECH 1
h. to rise and h. to fall;
  POPE A 78
h.-waking tropic dawn, NEWS 1
h.-way house THOMA D 6
h.-way up the hill, LONG 29
h.-words whispered low:
  GRAV 24
H. Year's Night GAY 4
help to h.-a-crown.' HARD 31
in h. a minute — GILB 9
land freckled with snow h.-
  thawed THOMA E 18
lifted the h.-covered chair
  SCHW 5
old h.-witted sheep STEPHEN 4
Pause over h.-known faces.
  OWEN 23
scarce h. made up, SHAK 96
see not h. my dayes that's due,
  BRAD 2
servant's cut in h.; GRAHAM H 1
sun h. an hour high. WHITM 19
sun there h. an hour high —
  WHITM 18
things that I but h. recall —
  WINT 1
With fear, as h.-awakened;
  POUN 58
Halfpence: H. and farthings,
  UNKN 23
hall: Absolute across the h.,
  BELL 13
bears logs into the h., SHAK 101
hangs in the h. SMIT W 1
in the h., OHAR 7
smoker's cough in the h.
  HEAN 15

valleys of H. LANIE 5
vasty h. of death. ARNO 21
Hallelujah: Glory! Glory! H.!
  HOWE 2
halloo: dark the long h. NOYE 3
hallow'd: So h. and so gracious is
  the time. SHAK 19
hallowed: amid its h. mirth,
  POE 30
h. relics should be hid MILT 35
halls: Amphitrite's destined h.,
  SHEL 36
chamber in the silent h. of death,
  BRYA 24
harp that once through Tara's h.
  MOOR T 5
hurry through the eternal h.,
  EMER 9
In social h. MELV 6
marble h. as white as milk,
  MOTH 16
Patrol the h. on spongy shoes,
  WILB 31
room in the h. of pleasure
  WILC 3
through her marble h.! LONG 24
Halt: H. by the headstone HOUS 1
halter: frets the h., RALEG 14
halting: traveling army h.,
  WHITM 9
halts: dawn h. THOMA D 31
halved: h. a country; THOMA D 24
ham: plate of h. and eggs —
  SAND 22
hamadryad: h. from the wood
  POE 2
hame: kye at h., LIND L 1
Noah was at h. wi' them a',
  MACDI 5
Hamelin: alas for H.!
  BROWNI R 64
H. Town's in Brunswick,
  BROWNI R 59
Hamilton: Marie H. gangs wi'
  bairn UNKN 187
Hamlet: H. and Lear are gay;
  YEATS 79
I am not Prince H., ELIOT T 89
There struts H., YEATS 78
hamlets: Circling above the h.
  THOR 6
hammer: Beat me and h. me
  SAND 20
h. through daisies; THOMA D 10
hand to the workmen's h.;
  BIBL, O.T. 19
What the h.? BLAK 82
with the h. she smote Sis'e-ra,
  BIBL, O.T. 19
hammered: h. you, wrought you,
  THOMP F 14
hammering: man h. in the sky.
  PURD 3

hammers: busy h. closing rivets up,
  SHAK 57
h., muffled h., HODG 8
Silent h. of decay. HODG 8
hammock: Drake he's in his h.
  NEWB 1
turfy h. is our bed, SIMM 1
hamper: swooning out of an
  enormous willow h. MERR 10
hand: Against infection and the h. of
  war, SHAK 88
at h. to bless;/ Ills have no
  weights, LYTE 2
Aunt Jennifer's h. RICH 2
beauty, like a dial h., SHAK 227
beer at h., STEPHENS 4
By a friendly, helping h.,
  UNKN 145
by a kind h. brought/ Alive/ To a
  strange place. THOR 2
by his h. alone BRAD 10
by Time's fell h. defaced
  SHAK 211
Change with hurried h. TUCK 1
compels His awful h. CULL 19
count them on my H., DICKI 77
Cursed be the h. STOD 1
cut my h. off — FROS 83
Death lays his icy h. on kings:
  SHIR 1
Death's cold h.! BLAK 28
delays/ His h. MILT 98
despite his cruel h. SHAK 210
Devil is still at h. DRYD 1
Farewell, thou child of my right
  h., JONS 23
Fed with cold and usurous h.?
  BLAK 68
fingers of this h. BROWNI E 3
full and unwithdrawing h.,
  MILT 5
God's h. that leadeth me. GILM 1
h. a needle better fits, BRAD 16
h. and foot that stir not, VERY 3
h. and pen are not in plight,
  VAUX 4
h.-clasp's a little stronger,
  CHAP A 1
h. dipping downwards to death —
  GINS 30
h. from hand must sever,
  WATS R 1
h. in h., LEAR 12
h. in h., MILT 108
h. in h. ROSS C 17
h. in hand we'll go; BURN 35
h./ Is worthy of water: WILB 6
h. no yet contented MERW 9
h. of the king KNOX 2
h. rules heaven; THOMA D 25
h. rules pity THOMA D 25
h. stiff — heaviness GINS 30

Nothing but rosy h. WILB 24
over quick h. WALK 7
Pale h. I love HOPE L 1
Pale h., pink-tipped, HOPE L 3
raising their innocent h. BLAK 91
reach of sacrilegious h.,
  POPE A 31
schoolboys lag with satchels in
  their h. SWIF 11
sinking ships, and praying h.
  TENN 90
spreading wide my narrow H.
  DICKI 44
stand on his h., DICKEY 24
stretch the h. of memory
  WHITT 29
strong h., GREN 4
Struggling in my father's h.,
  BLAK 73
take her h.; YEATS 139
thin h. above his head. RUKE 7
through ruder h., AYTON 1
washed her h. NASH 1
washed the pity from her h.
  KIZE 3
we batter our h. WILB 20
weak h. though mighty heart
  SHEL 4
wild waves reach their h.
  THAX 1
with crooked h.; TENN 12
Without men's h. were rung,
  UNKN 3
world's great h. HUNT 7
you cup your h. And gulp
  JARR 26
handsome: h. pigtail wore;
  CHAM 1
h., winsome Johnny. UNKN 140
pointing h. out to sea;
  STEVENSO R 6
handy: camel comes h. CARRY 2
Funny bugs, of h. sizes, CARRY 7
with the girls be h. SHUC 1
hang: arms h. down to laugh,
  ELIOT T 111
come to h. you, lad: KINGSM 2
Creatures that h. LAWR 3
H. a lantern aloft LONG 44
h. and brush their bosoms?
  BROWNI R 79
h. or drown
  JOHN S (1709–1784) 12
h. your hat on a pension.
  MACN 9
icicles h. by the wall, SHAK 101
leaves h. trembling, ROSS C 35
let her go h. SHAK 159
to h. trophies on, LOWE J 8
Would h. themselves. SHAK 179
wretches h. POPE A 120
You wouldn't h. me? ROBI 20

hangars: larval-silver h.
  CRAN H 10
hange'd: say we were h.,
  UNKN 155
Hanged: I do not find/ The H. Man.
  ELIOT T 117
longed to see him h. BELL 1
Hangie: Hear me, auld H., BURN 2
hangin': they're h. Danny Deever,
  KIPL 5
hanging: as flies h. in heat,
  GUNN 11
cured by h. from a string.
  KINGSM 2
h. breathless on thy fate! LONG 6
h. from the 13th floor/ window.
  HARJ 1
h. like an oasis LOWE R 32
h. loose and low. UPDI 1
Still h. incorruptible, MILT 94
windows h. low, DICKI 50
young ones h. at her teats;
  CLARE 11
hangings: through the red h.
  KINS 1
hangman: h.'s rope was spun,
  YEATS 138
strings the h.'s bag; RALEG 13
hangnail: Abaddon in the h. cracked
  from Adam, THOMA D 6
hangs: blossom that h. on the
  bough. SHAK 166
dragonfly/ H. like a blue thread
  ROSS D 4 lily. TENN 110
h. in the hall SMIT W 1
Heavily h. the broad sunflower
  TENN 110
Heavily h. the hollyhock,/ Heavily
  h. the tiger-
jury h. o'er/ The rose marie.
  UNKN 286
Someone h. in the sky PURD 1
usurer h. the cozener. SHAK 81
hank: lanky h. of a she
  STEPHENS 3
rag and a bone and a h. of hair,
  KIPL 27
hankering: windy citherns h. for
  hymns. STEVENS 14
hankie: like a h. LEVI 2
Hanna: H., bulldog H., LIND V 6
Low-browed H., LIND V 6
Mark H.'s McKinley, LIND V 5
Hanover: famous H. city;
  BROWNI R 59
hansom: helped to a h. BETJ 2
hapless: h. Nymph with wonder
  saw: GRAY 19
things innocent, h., forsaken.
  ROET 41
Haply: H. I may remember,
  ROSS C 34
H. I think on thee, SHAK 194

h., in some lull of life, WHITT 28
h. may forget. ROSS C 34
happen: foolish fears of what might
  h. BROWNI E/GUIN 1
Something is about to h. PURD 3
something might h. STAF 1
happening: way of h., AUDE 42
happens: world is everything that h.
  to/ Be true. HOLLA 3
happier: envy of less h. lands;
  SHAK 88
find a h. land, FRENE 4
H., hopeless fair, COLL 5
height of h. men. SHAK 196
live in h. form SHEL 91
remembering h. things. TENN 74
shelter in some h. star? POE 2
happiest: h. on your hands
  PLATH 81
h. when I compose poems:
  LAYT 1
h. with hyphens, BROD 2
woman's h. knowledge MILT 75
happiness: find our h., or not at
  all! WORD 112
first song of his h., KINN 8
h. and final misery, MILT 60
humble h. endeared each scene.
  GOLD 1
imbecile illusions of h. FERL 4
love, h., riches — " KAVA 13
on the verge/ Of h., BROO G 21
roof with inward h., CAREW 19
Saints Heaven-lost H. TAYL E 8
"Virtue alone is h. below."
  POPE A 86
Withdraws into its h.; MARV 18
happinesse: straw'd with flow'rs and
  h.; HERB G 3
happy: Ah h. hills! GRAY 13
all were as h. as we; BLAK 70
any h. flower, DICKI 4
as h. as a wave WORD 154
cheers the h. Hen; GAY 2
dense with h. blood, LAWR 58
empty h. body SNYD 23
Everything is h. now, LOWE J 18
Extinction of each h. art
  GRAV 23
Hail, Columbia! h. land!
  HOPKINSO 1
h. all the day. STEVENSO R 11
h. as Cliff Klingenhagen ROBI 8
h. as kings. STEVENSO R 9
h. as the grass was green,
  THOMA D 17
h. breed of men, SHAK 88
" H. Christmas to all, MOOR C 5
H. enough to chat and play
  MEW 3
H. field or mossy cavern,
  KEAT 33

h. genius of my household?
   WILLI 13
h., golden age! TASS 1
h. groves, BLAK 101
h. harbour of the saints,
   UNKN 147
h. highways where I went
   HOUS 35
h. Iles, MILT 65
h. in being together, WHITM 33
H. in death are they MANG 1
h. life be these, MARTIA 1
H. the man POPE A 107
I was quite h. GIOV 4
I was told to be h., RUKE 11
made the little tykes/ so h.
   OHAR 3
More h. love! KEAT 39
never been h. or good. AUDE 76
not a h. night WHITM 108
O past! O h. life! WHITM 66
place that was h. PITT 2
rare/ as the light of a h. eye,
   WILLI 47
secret like a h. funeral; LARK 21
that night I was h. WHITM 109
these heroic h. dead CUMM 29
Thrice h. Iles, MILT 65
Who is the h. Warrior? WORD 4
harbingers: h. are come.
   HERB G 34
h. preceding still the fates
   SHAK 20
harbor: air-bridged h. LAZA 1
bright red sloop in the h.,
   SEXT 3
h. and neighbor wood
   THOMA D 32
h. at dawn; BLY 5
h. for good or bad, WHITM 74
h. him/ At his age FROS 20
h., silver-paced CRAN H 28
Mud for the mole-tide h.,
   LOWE R 6
northerly h. of Labrador,
   BISH 24
this thy h., CRAN H 34
harbour: barn shall h. heaven,
   WILB 11
happy h. of the saints,
   UNKN 147
h. bar be moaning. KINGSL 3
hard: being woman, h. beset;
   WYLI 5
Drops away, h. rock wavers
   SNYD 49
early love unfortunate and h.,
   MILLA 5
for his h. heart, WHITT 23
ground/ Was as h. KEAT 60
h. as a floor, LEVE 9
h.-favored rage. SHAK 56
h.-fought engagements

H. is his lot,
   JOHN S (1709–1784) 8
h. legs of our women. SHAP 8
H. Rock wasn't a mean nigger
   KNIG 5
h. to die by fire! THAC 1
h. to farm SNYD 41
h. to say what brought them
   there, BISH 27
h. to tame, GAY 1
h. words, jealousies, and fears,
   BUTL 1
h. words ready to show why,
   BUTL 2 WHITM 114
hym death greep'the right h. by
   the croppe SENE 2
love her as h. as you can.
   CREE 13
love is h. to catch and conquer,
   MERE G 4
Phillis hath so h. a heart —
   LODG 4
sky is h. STEVENS 27
Sorrow is h. to bear,
   BROWNI R 4
straight, h. pathway plod —
   CARRU 2
sty me/ In this h. rock,
   SHAK 157
two h. things to hit, POPE A 96
with difficulty and labour h.
   MILT 62
world's so h., KINGSL 2
harden: (if it could h.) SITW 5
Hardens: sunlight on the garden/
   H. MACN 23
harder: h. grows the more I her
   entreat? SPENS 9
hardinesse: Mars yaf me my sturdy
   h. CHAU 92
hardly: h. different from myself,
   WHITM 77
I can h. conceive MOOR M 41
Johnny, I h. knew ye! UNKN 156
hardned: Lust the Master of a h.
   Face, COWL 4
hardness: Against the flint and h. of
   my fault, SHAK 8
all this h., LEWI 6
without h. will be sage, ARNO 36
hardship: out of h. bred,
   CAMPB R 4
hardy: h. British tars GILB 42
husbandes h., wise, and free,
   CHAU 67
hare: h. go stealing by: BRET 5
lamb, the linnet, and the h.
   STEPHENS 7
outcry of the hunted H. BLAK 4
tears of the hunted h. SITW 12
hares: little hunted h. HODG 1
Hark: H., H.! the lark SHAK 17

h. to the musical clank;
   WHITM 13
H. to the summons! SCOT WA 21
Harlem: H., your hotel is
   overnamed, WELC 2
hill above H. HUGH L 15
take the H. night HUGH L 8
Harlot: Every H. was a Virgin
   once, BLAK 20
harlots: bought smile/ Of h.,
   MILT 78
youthful H. curse BLAK 76
harm: can do no h. WILB 25
creatures that do people h.,
   BROWNI R 61
do us h. LAWR 49
Dry bones can h. no one.
   ELIOT T 151
Midst winter's h. MORR 5
need not fear h. BLAK 87
No h. on thy body! GINS 43
To keep me from h. POE 24
harme: we will cum to h..'
   UNKN 227
harmed: fish or sea-fowl h.
   YOUN A 1
righteous and h., TATE A 7
harmless: more h. vanity? LAMB 4
silent days/ In h. joys are spent,
   CAMPI 13
turns h. and stainless WHITM 98
with h. gold, LOWE J 15
Harmonies: grace to all Heav'ns H.
   MILT 9
harmonious: amorousnesse of an h.
   Soule, DONN 31
childhood's thin h. tear:
   TATE A 16
H. bells below, HERB G 1
h. Sisters, Voice, and Vers,
   MILT 1
Helicon's h. springs GRAY 23
make h. mix of voice and string
   BIBL, O.T. 67
Such h. madness SHEL 72
harmony: attention like deep h.
   SHAK 87
by the power/ Of h., WORD 31
clear and ancient h. THOR 5
Empyræum of pure H. CRAS 6
fatal h.; MARV 13
h. in music; WORD 96
h. that sounds within the breast,
   FLET G YO 1
heavenly H. DRYD 25
hidden soul of h.; MILT 24
ninefold h. MILT 39
touch to tune the h. SHAK 86
harms: freed from foreign h.;
   SPENS 47
Not for thy h.. THOMP F 9
harness: hear the h. jingle
   HOUS 36

harnessed: h. to the moon:
  CAMPB R 2
harp: Blow the spirit-stirring h.
  GILB 43
clear h. in diverse tones,
  TENN 18
h. of her breast-bane, UNKN 32
h. that once through Tara's halls
  MOOR T 5
Love took up the h. of Life,
  TENN 70
strung his h. UNKN 32
tearful h. or glib piano
  WHITM 102
unstringèd viol or a h. SHAK 86
wild h. slung behind MOOR T 9
with the h., BIBL, O.T. 46
within the h. I touch. PETRA 13
harpe: daunce to an h. smale,
  CHAU 87
harpoon: h. were sparring for the
  kill. LOWE R 53
harps: Be but organic H.
  COLE SAM 12
evening h. and matin, MILT 86
harpy: devour'd by the same h.
  BYRO 34
h., shrew and whore. RICH 18
Harrow: H. the house of the dead;
  AUDE 69
h. up thy soul, SHAK 26
harrowed: having h. hell,
  SPENS 18
harrowing: courteous, yet h. Grace,
  DICKI 7
man h. clods HARD 29
Harry: Such a King H.? DRAY 2
swift to h.; POUN 59
harsh: h. cries of wild fowl.
  MACDONO 3
h. world in which I wake to
  weep, SHEL 76
pluck your berries h. and crude,
  MILT 25
harshness: no h. gives offence,
  POPE A 28
hart: as a bounding h. fly home,
  WESL C 2
H. Crane, and of Shelly. FULL 3
h. panteth after the water brooks,
  BIBL, O.T. 35
like a roe or a young h.:
  BIBL, O.T. 71
harvest: h. evening now KAVA 20
h.-fields forsaken, LONG 38
It is the h.; RANS 1
reap the h. with enduring toil,
  TENN 91
very end of h.! SHAK 162
harvester: faithful h.! BARL 1
h. of hay; WHITT 18
has: a dog h. his day,
  THOMA D 39

haste: Art thou gone in h.?
  WEBS/ROWL 1
convulsed in undignified h.,
  LAWR 44
H. and come. THOMA E 19
h. away so soon: HERR 42
h. me to my bed, SHAK 193
h. now to my setting.
  FLET/SHAK 4
h. with odours sweet . . . MILT 42
Like a herald in h., READ T 1
hasten: minutes h. to their end;
  SHAK 209
hastening: h. ill a prey, GOLD 1
h. ills a prey, GOLD 3
life must be h. away; SOUTHE 7
hastens: traveler h. toward the
  town, LONG 46
hastes: h. me on unto a sudden
  death, DRAY 5
hast'n'd: Cherish thy h. widowhood
  MILT 112
hasty: h. noise he spoke 'em;
  BUTL 5
not be too h., WHITM 35
violently as h. powder fired
  SHAK 150
hat: drop of a h. AUDE 59
Flaundryssh bevere h., CHAU 21
hang your h. on a pension.
  MACN 9
his Beaver H. LEAR 13
his yellow straw h. WAGO 1
off with your h. ROON 1
only as big as his h. BISH 29
sat in a commodore's h.
  CARRY 10
wear purple/ With a red h.
  JOSE 1
hatch: head withdraws into its h.
  JARR 23
hatch'd: h. a Cherubin. CAREW 8
hatched: dove that h. the dovetailed
  world WILB 29
frenzied brain that h. the plot,
  STOD 1
hatchet: smitten with a h.'s jaw;
  HOUS 10
hate: Admire and h. BRYA 12
approached by stronger h.,
  MILT 92
choked with h. YEATS 111
crops of love and h. MUIR 8
eyes flashing solemnly with h.,
  JOHN H 4
Falsehood is worse than h.;
  DONN 40
Fierce h. he recollects, MILT 91
from h. away she threw,
  SHAK 241
H.-hardened heart, MOOR M 15
h. me when thou wilt; SHAK 221
h. of tyranny intense, WHITT 10

h. to go above you, WHITT 14
h. you died to quench HOUS 4
h.'s known injury. SHAK 200
hoard hath h. CHAU 1
Horror and scorn and h. and fear
  and indignation— HOUS 24
I fight I do not h., YEATS 70
"I h. my verses, JEFFE 17
I know enough of h. FROS 48
keep h. out UNTE 3
libeled by her h. POPE A 90
"Lord, I do not h., COTTE 1
love and h. mee too, DONN 48
muse my life-long h., MCKA 9
my h.'s profiting!" HARD 24
peddle/ your h. WELC 2
People's violent Love and H.;
  CLEV 1
potent poison of your h.
  MCKA 11
power to love, or h., MARL 8
shifting h. and love. STOD 2
study of revenge, immortal h.,
  MILT 51
time to h.; BIBL, O.T. 5
Without h., without grief
  ROET 60
world see the utmost of thy h.;
  DRAY 14
hated: feared, loved, h., suffered,
  SHEL 79
H., as their age increases,
  STEVENSO R 4
I am h. COTTE 1
looked askance and h.;
  LOWE J 14
hateful: Povert is h. good,
  CHAU 109
hates: How mean thy h. POUN 22
Hating: H. you shall be a game
  BENN G 1
no more h. then, SITW 10
hatless: young man lands h.
  BETJ 8
hatred: all h. driven hence,
  YEATS 113
H. and vengeance, COWP 14
h. for this misery befallen;
  MILT 102
h. of the slain, PRIN 2
H. out of Envy by Despair.
  CUNN J 3
h.'s hidden ulcer MARV 12
intellectual h. is the worst,
  YEATS 112
love, h., joy or fear, PRIO 4
sentiment and h. WALK 1
understand/ My h. BENN G 2
Hats: H. off! BENN H 1
inside men's Sunday h.,
  BROWNI R 60
men are selling h. ASHB 2

young rats with black felt h.,
UNKN 258
haud: h. thy peace!" the lady said,
UNKN 248
h. your tongue, UNKN 79
haughty: elder dames, thy h. peers,
BRYA 12
h. brought to dust? AIKE 9
h. intellectual look KAVA 8
h. old copper-bound albatross
MASE 10
h. scorn which mock'd the smart,
ARNO 35
whose h. brow, GRAY 3
Haul: H. them off! WILB 21
h. My eyelids up, PLATH 19
haul'd: h. up at last WHITM 28
hauled: flag the men h. down;
WHITT 2
haunche: buttok to the h.-boon.
CHAU 56
haunt: h. the places POPE A 129
h. the rich man's door, HORA 6
new h. for prey, MILT 68
wild dove's h., TUCK 1
haunted: build h. heaven.
STEVENS 14
ghost has h. AUDE 92
H. by ill angels POE 16
h. by interrupted acts, RUKE 3
h. by the ghosts SHAK 89
H. for ever WORD 77
H. me like a passion: WORD 33
houses are h. STEVENS 4
Lost in a h. wood, AUDE 76
we h. here together, HARD 1
haunting: h. my memory LONG 32
h. the black air, SEXT 7
H. untrodden paths DANI S 10
haunts: flood the h. TENN 43
h. of coot and hern, TENN 4
h. of Robert Pinsky's PINS 3
hausts: Effund your albid h.,
HOLM 1
haven: Rowing home to h. MASE 1
havens: green swell is in the h.
HOPKINS 10
Havergal: Luke H. ROBI 22
havior: dejected h. of the visage,
SHAK 21
havoc: quarry cries on h. SHAK 42
haw: sweet as a red h. SAND 5
hawk: chicken h. floats over,
WRIG J 4
from Kill Devils Hill at Kitty H.
CRAN H 9
h. and marmot, SNYD 22
h.-like foreign faces MACN 11
h. of the tower: SKEL 2
h.'s deliberate stoop HILL G 3
h.'s wing/ of vision. SNYD 32
killed my h. so good, UNKN 86

spotted h. swoops by and accuses
WHITM 73
hawkes: With empty hand men may
no h. lure. CHAU 86
hawser'd: h. tight, WHITM 28
hawthorn: Beneath the h. lying,
HOUS 14
h. blooms the sweetest, HOGG 1
Hawthorne: "There is H.,
LOWE J 1
hay: bumpity ride in a wagon of h.
DE LA 6
dance the h., BRET 6
harvester of h.; WHITT 18
h. is dried-up grass KOCH 2
left the h. to make. FROS 63
live on h., HILL J 1
new-mown h.,
BROWNI E/GUIN 1
sweet with h. WHITT 15
wrought to withered h.; PROC 1
haycock: under a h. Fast asleep.
MOTH 19
haying: told him so last h.,
FROS 20
hazard: speak at every h.,
WHITM 74
haze: seas in delicate h. LUCR 4
silvery h. of summer drawn;
TENN 40
hazel: water with a h. prong —
FROS 23
Hazeldean: Wi' Jock of H.
SCOT WA 6
hazy: night was thick and h
CARRY 4
head: anointest my h. with oil;
BIBL, O.T. 31
arms have lain/ Under my h.
MILLA 39
Asking forgiveness of his
tongueless h. WILB 33
Bald h., GRAV 1
begin with a swelled h.
LOWE R 16
body bears the h. RANS 26
bored a hole in his h., KNIG 5
bowed my h. and wept. MCKA 8
breaks like the Atlantic Ocean on
my h. LOWE R 29
bullet through his h. ROBI 52
Burrow with hungry h. SHAP 15
Camden, most reverend h.,
JONS 47
chieftain's h., RANS 24
Chucky's old bald h. RANS 19
city with lifted h. singing
SAND 4
crown thy H. MARV 5
dark hole of the h. HUGH T 14
deviating h.-stones MOOR M 27
drew the H. erect — DICKI 100

drowsy h. and folded wing,
POE 38
everlasting h. RALEG 11
Flashed from his matted h. and
marble feet, LOWE R 37
fresh-severed h. of it, OWEN 39
glory of tyrant h. RANS 26
great h. rattling like a gourd,
WARR 3
hath not where to lay his h.;
LOWE J 20
h. a while enclin'd, MILT 114
h. falls AMMO 19
h. falls forward, AUDE 96
H. held back, forefeet out,
SNYD 37
h. more than churches, bibles,
WHITM 74
h. must bow, FOST 2
h. of a gallows-tree. KIPL 2
h. of a man, YEATS 135
h. of the past. STEVENS 20
H. up-lift above the wave,
MILT 53
h. with foot hath private amitie,
HERB G 53
h. with roses crowned, HERR 3
h. withdraws into its hatch
JARR 23
heels up to the h.;
STEVENSO R 13
hid his h. for shame, MILT 38
high over h.! WORD 130
hings his h., BURN 23
his cloud-topped h. GRAY 4
his peat-brown h., HEAN 22
Holinesse on the h., HERB G 1
hooked h. and hooked feet:
HUGH T 1
horrid vision seized my h.,
SWIF 3
horse by the h. FROS 45
huge of h. GUIT 1
I sing a hero's h., STEVENS 22
I turned my h. DAVIE W 3
If you can keep your h. KIPL 7
in the h.? SHAK 120
journey in my h. SHAK 193
kept h. in air. GRAV 23
Knock at a star with my exalted
h. HERR 3
My h. a moon PLATH 49
my heart or h. CULL 12
my onely h., HERB G 2
Nod is a little h., FIEL E 9
nowhere yet to rest my h.,
ARNO 32
parade about/ My helpless h.
WILB 42
portage of the h. SHAK 56
pound his h. upon the sidewalk.
IGNA 1
put down his h. in love. BOGA 3

raise/ Your angry h. GRAV 7
reared its h. POE 20
rests his h. GRAY 12
sairer, sairer akes my h.;
  UNKN 65
scar on her h., GINS 30
settled your h. WHITM 78
showers his h. and eyes,
  HARD 43
Singe my white h.! SHAK 75
smitten his h. from his faire
  boddë. UNKN 153
Snow-white moslem h.-dress
  WALK 3
something quiet o'er His h.,
  BROWNI R 18
stick in your h., GILB 3
stroke my h.; PEEL 5
sun and the moon broke over my
  h. EBER 6
sunrays obliterated on its hairy
  h. GINS 34
team's h.-brass flashed
  THOMA E 2
that early-laurelled h. HOUS 58
that moment over my h.,
  WHITM 76
thin hands above his h. RUKE 7
this old gray h., WHITT 3
thumped him on the h.
  CARRO 41
toys for your h., SHAK 182
turn her h., YEATS 62
two pillows at my h.,
  STEVENSO R 11
upon the shapely h., DARC 4
weave/ Grey hairs upon my h.
  VAUX 2
when this fix the h., WINT 11
which will not crush my h.
  POUN 31
wires grow on her h. SHAK 237
with languish't h. MILT 6
with light h. erect I sing,
  THOR 4
With monstrous h. CHES 3
yon gray h. WHITT 4
headaches: with a dismal h.,
  GILB 25
Headings: Gods of the Copybook
  H., KIPL 6
headland: beyond stormy h.
  JEFFE 12
first to the h., WHITM 73
headlands: round h. shone.
  ARNO 5
headlong: h. from on board,
  COWP 1
heads: bolted on thir h. MILT 117
Cut off the h. SHAK 90
danced in their h.; MOOR C 1
drench their h. in blessing:
  SNOD 8

dying eyes and lolling h., SASS 2
h. are green, LEAR 9
h. hooded HEAN 21
h. of strong old age JEFFE 35
H. of the characters
  THOMA D 10
lift frail h. MAHON 3
Lift up your h., O ye gates;
  BIBL, O.T. 34
manners are tearing off h.
  HUGH T 2
ragged arms, the ragged h. and
  eyes TATE A 13
seven anemones with down-
  dropped h. UNKN 253
shake their h. LARK 2
surmised the Horses H. DICKI 11
their little silver h., YEATS 93
To hurl upon their h. SHAK 98
trees bow down their h.,
  ROSS C 36
young, h. trailed KINN 18
headstone: Halt by the h. HOUS 1
little h. stood; LOWE J 12
On her h. UNKN 68
headstones: at the h. of the dead
  HECH 5
could tell their h.: SAND 13
h. yield their names TATE A 11
headwaiter: h. puts the bill,
  CREE 15
heal: Disease/ Not even God — can
  h. DICKI 122
flowers have been known to h.
  WILD 1
will it never h.? ARNO 18
healed: h. with snow. LOWE J 19
To be h. SIMI 4
healing: Creeping and h. ROET 48
h. fountain start, AUDE 46
Missing or h., SHAP 11
scent/ Of h. herbs THOR 9
health: bed of perfect h.,
  WHITM 108
flush/ Of h. and toilets, HECH 10
furnish h. WHITM 96
h. and plenty GOLD 1
H., love, friends, scope HARD 47
I shall be good h. WHITM 74
joyous h.! WORD 149
native h. and innocence TRAH 10
perfect h. begin, WHITM 74
Say that h. and wealth have
  missed HUNT 5
state of h. is poor; HOUS 11
healthful: for a h. mind,
  JOHN S (1709–1784) 23
healthy: h. appetite: AUDE 58
heap: chaise in a h. or mound,
  HOLM 9
h. the funeral pyre, THAC 1
imposter h.; SHEL 64

mangled h. Of carcases
  THOMS J (1700–1748) 10
On their slag h., SPEND 3
takes a h. o' children UNTE 1
heaped: all he had h. together;
  DRAY 16
H. over with a mound of grass,
  TENN 87
heaping: h. field and highway
  LOWE J 11
heaps: adjusting the ash h.;
  MOOR M 11
great anchors, h. of pearl,
  SHAK 97
his glittering h., BYRO 21
proud, ambitious h., JONS 37
what huge h. of littleness around!
  POPE A 101
hear: bells I h., WHITM 45
But spiritual Eve-droppers can h.
  BUTL 7
cells to h. confessions. SIMI 2
Do you h., Eadwacer? UNKN 83
dreamed as deaf men h., GARR 1
ear may h. His coming,
  BROO P 6
h. America singing, WHITM 37
h. but do not read, LOWE R 49
h. each other speak. TENN 39
h. her charm the air: BURN 42
h. her speak, SHAK 237
h. him sizzle so; SERV 4
h. his cannons roar? UNKN 217
h. it by and by. BROWNI R 3
h. life murmur, LOWE J 17
h. like ocean LANG 3
H. me, auld Hangie, BURN 2
h. my true time broke. SHAK 93
h. of a thing like that?
  LIND V 21
h. our feet VERY 6
h. the chanting BENN G 4
h. the crowing cock, LONG 8
h./ The daisies grow. WILD 17
h. the Dead March play, KIPL 5
h. the surgeon hum. KIRK 3
h. the tolling bell SPEND 14
H. the train blow. UNKN 80
h. the wilderness listen. STAF 3
h. them talk or pray SYNG 5
h. thy true Love's tale: DEKK 2
h. Thy Word BETJ 6
h. tom-toms just as plain.
  JOHN H 1
h. us squeel! BURN 2
I can h., underground, ROET 5
interested to h. about it.
  WILLI 18
larkspur listens, 'I h., TENN 94
men sit and h. each other groan;
  KEAT 47
mind that can/ H. the music,
  JEFFE 19

h. is in my/ pocket, OHAR 14

h. is sensual, THOMA D 44

h. is slow to learn MILLA 24

h. is true, UNKN 96

h. is turning ebber, FOST 3

h. is warm/ Midst winter's harm.
MORR 5

h. is warm with the friends I
make, MILLA 38

h. keeps its tough old persistency
still; LOWE J 6

h. leaps up WORD 57

h. less bounding at emotion
ARNO 45

h. luxuriates WORD 63

h. monastic aisles EMER 38

h. no longer stirred, HOUS 1

h. of a friend. LONG 3

h. of a woman JOHN G 1

h. of iron, MOOR M 15

h. of man FROS 93

h. of man, and human life.
WORD 51

h./ Of man has a little dignity,
TATE A 19

h. of revel and solace!' CHAU 68

h. of stone. WILD 16

h. of the brave, KNOX 2

h. of the furnace roar; SERV 5

h. of trust? EMER 22

h. profoundly stirred; ARNO 12

h.-quelling Sonne SPENS 43

h. recoiled at war: CUMM 14

h. regularly/ Thunders. —
KIRK 3

h. remembers how!
STEVENSO R 1

h. shall prize no good above thee;
QUAR 2

h. so glad BRET 4

h. stirs the ever-beating sea;
PLUN 2

h. that bleeds, CULL 4

h. that has truly loved never
forgets, MOOR T 3

h. that lo'ed me dearly! BURN 31

h. that loved her, WORD 37

h. that loves what they dispise,
SHAK 239

h. to poke poor Billy.
GRAHAM H 4

h. was no more broken CHES 15

h. was used to beat TENN 20, 53

h. winces WILB 21

h. without her? ROSS D 7

H., you were never hot OWEN 30

h.'s and eye's delight. SHAK 204

h.'s changes, AUDE 92

h.'s deep core, DUNB P 10

h.'s deep languor
THOMS J (1834–1882) 8

h.'s grown brutal YEATS 99

heaven-entreated h. CRAS 10

Held his h. in his hands,
CRAN S 3

he'll have her h. HOLLA 5

Her black h. . . . KINS 1

hold me in thy h., SHAK 41

hollow as a h. HAYD 2

Hope, blossoming within my h.,
BRYA 33

How dear to my h. WOOD 1

humble and a contrite h. KIPL 18

hunger seized my h.; TENN 41

I came home to your h.
BROWNI R 10

I have your face by h., BOGA 11

I have your h. by heart, BOGA 13

I see/ Your double h., WYAT 29

I told her all my h., BLAK 43

I was false of h., SHAK 230

If I can stop one h. from
breaking DICKI 74

If the h. of a man GAY 3

I'll chain my h. UNKN 171

in his tameless h. HODG 4

In life of lover's h.; SIDN 42

in the h., SHAK 120

infinite task of the human h.."
SCHW 4

is my h. not badly shaken?
KAVA 26

it is my h.." CRAN S 4

June in her eyes, in her h.
January. CAREW 15

keep my h. inviolate MCKA 11

knowledge/ Carried to the h.?
TATE A 14

lay the h. upon her hand
YEATS 116

'Leave the h. BRON 7

lift your h. and hands to Heaven.
PRIO 8

like adamant draw mine iron h.
DONN 60

like the h. of man SITW 13

lines that speak the passionate h.,
KAVA 18

"look in thy h. and write!"
SIDN 6

love might overflow my H.!
TAYL E 7

love with all my h.:
STEVENSO R 7

lung h. feet tail GINS 14

made my h. to ache: BLAK 112

make a stone of the h. YEATS 54

Man's own resinous h.
YEATS 120

may my h.'s truth THOMA D 36

meditation of my h.,
BIBL, O.T. 30

Mercy has a human h., BLAK 88

merry h. goes all the day,
SHAK 180

mighty h. is lying still! WORD 7

mony a h. thou hast made sair
BURN 36

more woe/ Than I have in my h.,
WYAT 9

moving toyshop of their h.;
POPE A 112

much against my h., PATM 8

music in my h. I bore,
WORD 141

My busy h. THOMA D 14

My h. aches, KEAT 44

My h. gives you love. WHITM 27

My h. grows tense LOWE R 53

My h. has left its dwelling-place
CLARE 5

my h. in your hand ROSS C 26

my h. is fast, and cannot
disentangle. UNKN 220

my h. is light. POE 30

My h. is like a rainbow shell
ROSS C 1

My h. is like an apple-tree
ROSS C 1

my h. is like nothing CARRO 20

My h. is torn JOYC 1

my h., O my soldiers, WHITM 27

my h. or head CULL 12

my h./ Under my feet.
ELIOT T 139

my h. with pleasure fills,
WORD 25

my h.'s content SHAK 169

my h.'s elation, CARM 1

my h.'s right SHAK 203

my hinny and my h.? UNKN 126

my joy and h.'s delight. WEVE 2

my life, my love, my h.,
HERR 40

My own h. let me HOPKINS 14

my sinful h. VAUG 6

My true love hath my h.
SIDN 1, 2

naked thinking h. DONN 11

Nature's h. and mine; BANK 2

nearer God's h. in a garden
GURN 1

O h.! h.! h.! WHITM 45

O sleepless h. SWIN 5

O tiger's h. SHAK 61

Oh! to earth h. GINS 44

old h. in his bust RANS 8

On my legs my h. my liver
ELIOT T 6

one and noble h. THOMA D 44

onely h. and breast, HERB G 2

pageant of his bleeding h.?
ARNO 35

Pains not the h., SACK 1

perish all at the h..' UNKN 36

Phillis hath so hard a h. LODG 4

pointless wars of the h. SNYD 10

prey upon their h.-strings,
WATT I 1

Prepare your h. BLAK 28
score of h. BRID 2
see those two h., MERR 5
So will our h. decay; UNKN 293
somewhere h. are light; THAY 4
their h. united, MARL 5
there's kindly h. DARC 2
tired half-healed h.; BOGA 4
torn and bleeding h. DUNB P 12
violated ones with gentle h.;
    WALK 2
wins more h. UNKN 141
heartsblood: rare original h. goes,
    WILB 13
heartsease: What infinite h.
    SHAK 58
hearty: h. in its vehemence,
    WHITT 10
Whose laughs are h., POPE A 20
heat: as flies hanging in h.,
    GUNN 11
erst from h. did canopy the herd
    SHAK 186
greater h. than that of the Sun.
    SITW 9
h. o' the sun SHAK 18
immortal light and h.! VAUG 3
Love wounds with h., JONS 28
quite impervious to h. COWA 2
shade him from the h. BLAK 99
that Promethean h. SHAK 137
wind, rend open the h., DOOL 3
heath: Across the h. HARD 34
heathen: Around a h. fire
    BENN G 4
h. Chinee is peculiar: HART 1
h. gods CULL 8
h., Turk, or Jew. BLAK 89
heather: how the h. looks DICKI 60
picked up on the h.
    BROWNI R 53
Under the lindens on the h.,
    WALT 1
Heaths: unharbour'd H., MILT 3
heats: in fiery h. I fry, SOUTHW 2
heave: h. her Bosom unaware
    SWIF 14
H. in wild wreaths the battle-
shroud, DRAK 2
heaved: h. a mighty breath,
    STEVENSO R 6
sod scarce h.; SHEL 59
Heaven: all things under H.,
    MILT 107
alone with h., MERE G 7
ane to h. BURN 32
appeal to h. breaks off. KINN 10
ascend to H. RANS 15
at H.'s command,
    THOMS J (1700–1748)/MALL 1
barn shall harbour h., WILB 11
bass of h.'s deep organ MILT 39
beside the King of H.." POE 30

betwixt H. and Charing Cross.
    THOMP F 11
build haunted h. STEVENS 14
Calm fell. From H. HARD 11
candidate of H. DRYD 31
climbing h. SHEL 88
clinging H. by the hems;
    THOMP F 12
coarseness of our h. repine,
    ADDI 2
cold and rook-delighting h.
    YEATS 32
coming of the King of H.
    UNKN 314
cope with h. and earth
    WHITM 104
done in the sight of h.." WILB 24
doors of H. and of Hell,
    HOPE L 2
droppeth as the gentle rain from
h. SHAK 123
Eleven for the 'leven that went to
h. UNKN 52
English h. BROO R 14
ever-moving spheres of h.,
    MARL 1
every purpose under the h.:
    BIBL, O.T. 3
far up within the H. POE 30
first h. of knowing, ROET 45
For H. HERR 51
further off from H. HOOD 5
getting to h. at last, DICKI 131
glance from h. to earth,
    SHAK 127
God's in His H. BROWNI R 66
greater h. in an h. less. MARV 31
greatest Herald of H.'s King,
    DRUM 5
hand rules h.; THOMA D 25
h. a perfect round. BROWNI R 2
h. also I will be. CREE 8
h. and earth move together,
    GINS 42
H. and she are beyond this ride.
    BROWNI R 42
H. and the future's sakes.
    FROS 126
h. be in these lips, MARL 3
h.-born band! HOPKINSO 1
h. did prepare CAREW 1
h. divide/ The state of man
    SHAK 55
h.-entreated heart CRAS 10
h.-eyed creature sleeps in earth:
    WORD 17
h.-fed/ Naiad of the Carnival-
Tank! SPENC A 3
H. froze above, CHAU 46
H. in a Rage. BLAK 2
H. in a Wild Flower, BLAK 1
H. in Hell's despair." BLAK 57

H. is not like flying or swimming,
    BISH 44
H. is thine; POE 27
H. rejects the lore WORD 10
H. that smiles BANK 1
H. tries earth LOWE J 17
H. turned is to hell, UNKN 170
H. vows to keep him. JONS 8
h.-ward flies, HABI 2
h. was glorious BRON 3
h. wax'd blind, SYLV 2
H. which I imagine, SHEL 76
h.'s cherubin, SHAK 105
h.'s fairest star, SHEL 91
H.'s Gate/ Opes to the rich
    BROWNI R 64
h.'s immortal store, DRAY 11
h.'s jewelled crown MCCRE 1
H.'s last best gift, MILT 79
h.'s light forever shines,
    SHEL 13
h.'s own blue, BRYA 31
H.'s vault, MARV 2
h.'s vault should crack. SHAK 85
h.'s wonders and delights —
    GREV 10
Hell I suffer seems a H. MILT 66
Hell in H.'s despite." BLAK 58
high as h. above, SYLV 1
high h. and earth ail HOUS 24
holds you like a h., LARK 15
Hope! our earlier H.! COWL 5
In H. a spirit doth dwell POE 26
In h. you'll learn to sing, CRAS 9
In the unscarred h. LOWE J 19
Indolence is h.'s ally MELV 9
inherit h.'s graces SHAK 222
journey is shorter to h.
    UNKN 192
leave to h. the measure and the
choice, JOHN S (1709–1784) 22
lies bare to h. BROWNI R 81
lift your heart and hands to H.
    PRIO 8
Lifts earth to h., CRAS 5
lightened up my h., BRON 12
Like the h. above. CARN 2
Lord's mother from h. UNKN 215
love of h. above, CLARE 14
make up a h. of our misery.
    BLAK 56
mark this day in H.? TIMR 3
might/ Of h.-born freedom
    WORD 78
mild H. a time ordains,
    MILT 120
more things in h. and earth,
    SHAK 29
Moved earth and h., TENN 135
my h. dissolvèd so. DONN 65
Of H. of Hell MORR 1
open face of h., — KEAT 66
open firmament of h. MILT 85

Out of H., THOMP F 4
own sweet will is H.'s will;
  YEATS 113
Parting is all we know of h.,
  DICKI 108
Praise to h. SMAR 1
Purest Wheate in H., TAYL E 9
river, and the h., EMER 43
rose was H. to smell, HODG 9
Saints H.-lost Happiness
  TAYL E 8
saw all h. in flower SWIN 26
shake the very H. POE 40
Shut thee from h. HOLM 3
sings hymns at h.'s gate;
  SHAK 194
smells to h.; SHAK 34
smile of H. lay; SHEL 73
soul early into h. ravished,
  DONN 53
spark from h.! ARNO 25
spark with which H. lit my spirit
  SHEL 79
speak from h.'s sphere. PETRA 4
sphæares/ Of Musicks h.; CRAS 6
spirits are in h.!' WORD 156
suffuse h. WHITM 76
sword of h. will bear SHAK 116
that uncertain h. WORD 105
then the h. espy. HERB G 28
thirtieth year to h. THOMA D 32
to be young was very H.!
  WORD 111
to H. he flings — DUNB P 10
To shun the h. SHAK 236
too hot the eye of h. shines,
  SHAK 188
Toward h. still, FROS 3
trouble deaf h. SHAK 194
turn thy back on h. EMER 7
Universal Soul/ Of h. and earth!
  THOMS J (1700–1748) 6
unlock the gate/ Of h. ALEX 9
up to h. gate ascend, MILT 82
veil the h.'s mysterious face;
  WINC 1
visited in H. DICKI 61
wandering from that h., ROCH 1
western orb sailing the h.,
  WHITM 48
wingèd seraphs of H. POE 4
with h.-collected tears, SHEL 59
with my cries importune H.,
  MILT 102
world were h., GREE 3
would H. seem best?
  BROWNI R 42
ye souls in h. KEAT 2
your humble swain,/ Ascend to h.
  SYLV 1
heavenlie: on hir h. virginals.
  SPENS 36

heavenly: ancient h. connection
  GINS 8
beams of h. light, COWP 22
draught of h. pleasure spare,
  BURN 19
forsakes his h. fires LODG 6
h. alchemy; SHAK 197
h. Babe TATE N 2
h. days that cannot die;
  WORD 61
H. eye,/ Much wider than the sky,
  TRAH 8
h. form/ Angelic, MILT 90
h. Harmony DRYD 25
h. Lethean flood, DONN 34
H. musick, TAYL E 14
h. things DONN 53
Some h. music — SHAK 165
stars and h. deeps JOHN L 5
that h. face restore. WORD 144
When first my lines of h. joys
  made mention, HERB G 40
words with h. comfort fraught,
  GILM 1
heavens: by h. he must be poor."
  KAVA 26
Does to Rags the H. tear.
  BLAK 6
gang to the high h., UNKN 49
H. Bright glory TAYL E 8
h. declare the glory of God;
  BIBL, O.T. 26
h. fill with shouting, TENN 75
h. reward thee manifold
  BRAD 14
h. scowled, and the huskies
  howled, SERV 4
h. that know not what years be
  THOMA E 10
h., the work of thy fingers,
  BIBL, O.T. 24
h. themselves blaze forth
  SHAK 45
most ancient h., WORD 89
not rain enough in the sweet h.
  SHAK 34
Of the absolute H. BROWNI E 1
Pluck the stars out of the h.
  JOHN F 1
Saw the h. fill with commerce
  TENN 75
seven h. came roaring down
  CHES 7
shook the H., SWIF 4
shrouded h. anywhere; ROBI 9
stars that oversprinkle/ All the h.
  POE 10
that in the h. does dwell!
  BURN 32
Heavily: h. from woe to woe
  SHAK 195
H. hangs the broad sunflower
  TENN 110

H. hangs the hollyhock,/ H. hangs
  the tiger-lily. TENN 110
h. they tread; VERY 6
h. thickening to empire,
  JEFFE 37
Walking the sea so h. armed;
  YOUN A 1
were h. insured. GILB 10
heaviness: sleep of mortal h.;
  HAWE 2
weighed upon with h., TENN 85
heaving: always h. cinders,
  LIND V 15
Reply by h. rocks HART 4
heav'n: charge we H. POPE A 67
Descend from H. Urania,
  MILT 83
gems of h., her starry train:
  MILT 76
H. from all creatures POPE A 63
H. in fault; POPE A 62
H. of Hell, a Hell of H.'n.
  MILT 54
highest in H.: MILT 59
Is it, in H., a crime to love too
  well? POPE A 3
Light, ofspring of H. MILT 63
mark'd by H.: POPE A 64
Pride/ Had cast him out from H.,
  MILT 48
pursue/ Vain war with H.,
  MILT 58
that's the way to h. POPE A 19
will of H.; MILT 14
heav'nly: calm and h. frame;
  COWP 25
From h. thoughts all true delight
  doth spring. CAMPI 27
h. shapes MILT 97
heav'ns: grace to all H. Harmonies.
  MILT 9
H. and Earth MILT 46
spangled H., a Shining Frame,
  ADDI 3
heavy: close of h. flowers, LANG 3
color of the h. hemlocks
  STEVENS 6
feet are h. on the floor AUDE 66
Gray and h. blanket, WHITM 71
h. and the weary weight
  WORD 30
h. as a lecher's kiss. PLATH 47
h. bear who goes with me,
  SCHW 9
h. dews from bloom OWEN 24
h. eight-wheeler UNKN 53
h. menace and mystery NEWS 1
h. night hung dark HEMA 4
h. page/ Of death, SPEND 6
h. ploughman snores, SHAK 128
h. present seems to fail SNYD 49
h. Saturn laughed and leaped
  SHAK 225

more devils than vast h. can
  hold; SHAK 127
my soul in H. must lie WILD 11
myself am H.; MILT 66
Of Heaven of H. MORR 1
out o' h. BURN 43
place prepared in h., UNKN 78
profoundest H. MILT 54
sell/ myself in h., CREE 8
sweet h. within, WHITM 67
ten to h., BURN 32
throats of h. to drink, CHES 7
To H. with the Pope, MACN 4
Unloading h. behind him
  SASS 13
wicked also have their proper
  H.); THOMS J (1834–1882) 5
win me soon to h., SHAK 240
You shall know H. HORN 2
helle: lien in h. UNKN 289
Hellespont: cross thy stream, broad
  H.! BYRO 75
H. of cream DAVIE J 1
pass'd the H., BYRO 44
hellp: doo most hurt where most h.
  I offer. WYAT 23
hells: green h. of the sea CHES 10
H. Spider gets/ His intrails spun
  TAYL E 11
helm: h. she doth unbind,
  LOWE J 14
Helmed: Time and Death,/ H.
  locusts, LOWE R 59
helmet: fused to the inside of a h.;
  KINN 14
off that h. goes. GILB 39
Pizarro's h. Is a spider's
  kingdom; SCOT WI 2
velvet h. TAYL E 13
helmets: with yellow h. on.
  OHAR 12
help: By contemplation's h.,
  COWP 12
cannot h. or pardon. AUDE 91
God h. the horse, STEPHENS 12
God, our h. in ages past,
  WATT I 2
h., a love, a you, a wife. DUGA 3
h. me bear GLAD 1
H. me to seek, WYAT 8
h. to half-a-crown.' HARD 31
h. you cross, BRIN 2
h. your case, UNKN 267
love without the h. of any thing
  BLAK 22
no h. to me now LOWE R 42
nor h. for pain; ARNO 3
Since there's no h., DRAY 15
whence cometh my h.
  BIBL, O.T. 58
Helpe: H. me to blaze/ Her worthy
  praise SPENS 52

helped: all have h. to save her!
  LOWE J 14
helping: By a friendly, h. hand,
  UNKN 145
helpless: h. in my throes, SIDN 6
H., naked, piping loud, BLAK 72
parade about/ My h. head
  WILB 42
rolled h. in the sea, LEWI 5
helps: far-fet h. SIDN 10
hem: detain her vesture's h.,
  EMER 24
Eten and drounken and maden h.
  glad; UNKN 288
putte h. to plow, LANGL 3
hemispheres: cracked the h.
  TATE A 5
jars two h. HARD 16
hemlock: dust of snow/ From a h.
  tree. FROS 46
H. for Socrates, SORL 2
of h. I had drunk, KEAT 44
Socrates drinking the h.,
  CARRU 2
hemlocks: color of the heavy h.
  STEVENS 6
hemm'd: Rich, h. thick all around
  WHITM 14
hemp: sunken fields of h.,
  TATE A 12
hems: clinging Heaven by the h.;
  THOMP F 12
Hen: cheers the happy H.; GAY 2
have they not h.-peck'd BYRO 20
owls and a h., LEAR 18
hence: Fifty years h., WHITM 19
hundred years h., WHITM 19
insatiate h.-forward, WHITM 22
many generations h., WHITM 19
so many hundred years h.,
  WHITM 19
takes thee h. SHAK 186
what he thinks of it a year h.!
  BYRO 52
Henery: Our noble King, King H.
  the eighth, UNKN 221
henna: tan with h. hackles,
  STEVENS 2
Henry: H. Wadsworth, Alfred,
  GILB 14
John H. was a little fellow,
  UNKN 152
Hens: Cock by H. attended, GAY 2
Three French h., UNKN 276
hent: merrily h. the stile-a;
  SHAK 180
her: Molded to h. Æ 2
Heracleitus: Sage H. says;
  POUN 42
Herald: greatest H. of Heaven's
  King, DRUM 5
Like a h. in haste, READ T 1

sickness, death's h., and
  champion; DONN 44
Spring, the h. of love's mighty
  king, SPENS 20
heraldry: h. more dismal. SHAK 30
herb: every h. that sips the dew;
  MILT 19
fool and h., DOUG K 1
Gracing the tender h., MILT 69
h. was dry; TENN 40
herbage: sown their slopes/ With
  h., BRYA 16
herbs: blood of h., WHITM 96
Droop h. and flowers; JONS 4
few h. and apples, EMER 16
scent/ Of healing h. THOR 9
Hercules: beards of H. and frowning
  Mars, SHAK 122
herd: Avoid the reeking h., WYLI 1
erst from heat did canopy the h.
  SHAK 186
h.-abandoned deer SHEL 7
Leader of the h. HODG 4
lowing h. wind slowly o'er the
  lea, GRAY 7
wild and wanton h. SHAK 125
herds: Among the bestial h. to
  range, MILT 78
broad h. upsprung. MILT 86
vast/ H. of reindeer AUDE 8
Herdsman: H. and roper of stars,
  AIKE 11
here: h. alive, she is not dead,
  UNKN 16
h. am I. HOUS 63
Hoere paradis hy nomen h.,
  UNKN 289
into the h. MACDONA 1
persist h. and there MACDI 2
uniter of h. and h., WHITM 63
You there, I h., DICKI 36
hereafter: Here and h., touch a
  Paradise. MELV 22
'tis not h.; SHAK 175
Hereditary: H. ours. SHAK 178
heresy: Half h., RICH 8
heretic: burned at the stake as h.,
  UNKN 198
heretics: burning/ Witches and h.
  MAHON 5
No h. burned SHAK 76
heritage: every paddler's h.
  YEATS 9
h. thou'st signalled CRAN H 15
Our h. the sea. CUNN A 2
passion is the scholar's h.,
  WINT 10
thy true h. Whose world,
  POUN 19
yet dost keep/ Thy h., WORD 77
Hermes: Jove with H. came;
  OVID 4

hermit: h. withdrawn to himself,
  WHITM 47
  h.'s carnal ecstasy. AUDE 57
hermit-thrush: h. sings
  ELIOT T 147
hermitage: peaceful h., MILT 19
  take/ That for an h.; LOVE 5
hern: haunts of coot and h.,
  TENN 4
  h. and crake; TENN 43
hero: "Being German my h. is
  Hitler," KINN 5
  Forgive the h., WILB 38
  H. this inestimable gemme.
  MARL 6
  I sing a h.'s head, STEVENS 22
  its h. the Conqueror Worm.
  POE 33
  know/ as the h. MOOR M 28
  with no h.-courageous/ Tomb —
  KAVA 24
Herod: H. shrieking vengeance
  LOWE R 22
  world out-Herods H.; LOWE R 22
heroes: cool jazz nor devoured
  Egyptian h., OHAR 10
  Hail, ye h.! HOPKINSO 1
  h. are no more! FRENE 3
  h. of old, BROWNI R 69
  h. seek release MILLA 8
  speed glum h. SASS 3
  those h. dare/ To die EMER 12
  world has held great H.,
  GRAHAME 2
heroic: creature of h. blood,
  HEMA 1
  equal temper of h. hearts,
  TENN 135
  h. magnitude of mind MILT 113
  in old h. traces, BRON 5
  sunlight of h. deeds, TIMR 1
  these h. happy dead CUMM 29
Herowdes: forsak the, Kyng H.,
  UNKN 213
Herrick: H.'s left alone, HERR 66
  tomb of Robin H. HERR 53
herrings: As many red h. MOTH 21
  barrel of salted h. WYLI 11
Herse: sad sighs honour my absent
  H.; BRAD 3
herself: knows h. in death. Æ 2
herte: beautè fro your h. chaced
  CHAU 120
  conscience and tendre h.
  CHAU 17
herys: werte, and theron stood a toft
  of h. CHAU 17
Hesiod: think of H., OHAR 5
hesitate: They h. We h. LAWR 28
  They h. We hesitate. LAWR 28
Hesperian: H. fables true. MILT 69
  H. Gardens fam'd of old,
  MILT 65

Hesperus: H. entreats thy light,
  JONS 3
  H. thy twinkling ray CLARE 6
  was the schooner H., LONG 51
  wreck of the H., LONG 53
Hessian: H. blood on the blade."
  CLARK J 3
heterosexual: h. dollar GINS 12
hevy: Beeth h. again, CHAU 118
hew: When we h. or delve:
  HOPKINS 3
hewe: reed of h. CHAU 11
Hewed: H. the lindenwood,
  UNKN 20
hewn: monumental/ Argument of the
  h. voice, THOMA D 5
  On a white stone were h.
  HARD 41
Hexameters: blithe/ H. GOGA 2
Hey: H., diddle, diddle, MOTH 2
Hiawatha: Nursed the little H.,
  LONG 41
Hibernia: Albion's joy, H.'s pride.
  CAREY 2
hid: hallowed relics should be h.
  MILT 35
  H. half as well GILB 15
  h. his head for shame, MILT 38
  h. in the house. SMIT ST 8
  h. sorrow from mine eyes./ 11.
  Why died I not from the
  womb? BIBL, O.T. 10
  Nature's laws lay h. in night:
  POPE A 106
  Night will have all h. CAMPI 3
  What's lightly h. WILB 10
hidden: abortions are h. MAST 5
  Half h. from the eye! WORD 45
  h. and lost KNOX 2
  H. by a minstrel-smile.
  BENN G 5
  H. excitedly, ELIOT T 18
  H. from the buzzing fly, CLARE 3
  H. in the cap MELV 19
  h./ In the light of thought,
  h. should be my cares; DE VE 1
  h. soul of harmony; MILT 24
  h. strength MILT 3 SHEL 70
  shy and h. bird WHITM 47
hide: fairest shades did h. her;
  MUND 2
  forever h. me. FLET/SHAK 3
  h. her shame from every eye,
  GOLD 9
  H. him in lonely garrets,
  ROBI 17
  h. his face, MILT 118
  h. is tough. GUNN 6
  h. the pieces, BERRYM 13
  h. the shame! WHITT 12
  H. them! WILB 21
  h. us from each other's sight.
  KING H 3

  h. us from the searching sun
  RALEG 16
  in the dark we h. CULL 4
  Let me h. myself in thee! TOPL 1
  Naked of h., SKEL 12
  No man may him h. SKEL 11
  power their love to h., MARL 4
  rose I h., UNKN 256
  serve to h. MILT 97
  skin nor h. nor fleece DOOL 5
  Spends on the earthen h.,
  WILB 13
  talent which is death to h.
  MILT 124
  these feet must h. WHITT 8
  vest which seems to h. them;
  SHEL 53
  Why dost/ Thou h. thy face?
  WRIG J 8
  wrapped him up in an old cow's
  h., UNKN 118
  wrapped in a woman's h.!
  SHAK 61
hideous: death a h. storm of terror.
  WEBS 4
  h. little bat, SHAP 13
  h. ruine and combustion MILT 49
  h. throng rush out forever,
  POE 23
  h. was the noise, CHAU 72
  how h. it is POUN 26
  sunk in h. night, SHAK 186
  uncouth h. thing, HERB G 19
hides: h. the book of Fate,
  POPE A 63
  h. them deep, ALEX 7
  whited air/ H. hills and woods,
  EMER 43
hidest: h. thy face, BIBL, O.T. 53
hiding: expression/ expresses h.:
  AMMO 12
  h.-places of man's power
  WORD 115
  H. the Skeleton, MERE G 9
hierarchy: Olympus' faded h.!
  KEAT 52
hieroglyphs: h. of the rat footprints
  SAND 9
high: above the world so h.,
  TAYL J 1
  Anger heaving h., HARD 9
  dove, from the rafters h.,
  UNKN 109
  famous h. top-hat LIND V 2
  fir trees dark and h.; HOOD 5
  gang to the h. heavens, UNKN 49
  heart h.-sorrowful and cloyed,
  KEAT 39
  Hell unto a h. estate POE 30
  h. and boastful neighs SHAK 57
  h. and palmy state of Rome,
  SHAK 20
  H. as a cloud, WORD 130

h. as heaven above, SYLV 1
h.-blown pride FLET/SHAK 3
h. embowèd roof, MILT 18
h. endeavors are an inward light WORD 4
h. esthetic line GILB 30
h. horse riderless, YEATS 37
h. in space together, WHITM 23
H. King of Glory STEPHENS 4
h.-lead and cat-skidding SNYD 45
H.-low Jack and the game." UNKN 103
h. over all/ Uplifted, LONG 30
h. over head! WORD 130
h. star our course is set, MACN 26
h.-strung automobiles. BISH 13
h. than the soul is h. MILLA 30
H. though his titles, SCOT WA 12
H. wedlock then be honorèd. SHAK 16
h., white star of Truth, ARNO 30
Hold the h. way CHAU 2
Hopes of h. talk SHEL 31
house on h. erect, BRAD 12
in one h. funeral gleam, YEATS 121
in Triumph h. MILT 64
indifferent judge between the h. and low; SIDN 14
jumped so h. UNKN 135
Long has it waved on h., HOLM 17
lord of h. degree, UNKN 316
moan is h., WALK 10
monarch's h. estate; POE 22
O h.-riser, my little loaf. PLATH 82
paths of h. morality, BRON 5
Pile the bodies h. SAND 10
reason'd h. MILT 60
rich and h., KINGSL 1
Scooting obliquely h. and low. WHITM 75
slam in thine h. places. BIBL, O.T. 69
starving h.-country winter SNYD 24
sun half an hour h. WHITM 19
sun there half an hour h. WHITM 18
that h., animal face DEVL 2
that h. Capital, SHEL 1
Through h. still air. SNYD 18
tide runs h., THAX 1
to h. doth dissolution climb, WORD 8
True beauty dwells on h.: HERB G 36
voice is neither h. nor low, WHITM 91

when the gallows is h. UNKN 192
wind is h., STEVENSO R 24
Highbury: H. bore me. ELIOT T 139
higher: anvill Sparke, rose h., TAYL E 1
dead selves to h. things. TENN 18
h. Argument MILT 88
h. minds bear WORD 117
h. than the soul is high. MILLA 30
mind, aspire to h. things; SIDN 26
unread vision in the h. dream ELIOT T 12
weak spirits ne'er been h. reared SHAK 178
highest: bowed down the h. tree UNKN 57
carry precept to the h. pitch: BYRO 20
h. in Heav'n: MILT 59
h. point of all my greatness, FLET/SHAK 4
h. Woods impenetrable/ To Starr or Sun-light, MILT 97
Of h. wish, SIDN 25
perjury, in the h. degree, SHAK 99
unsearchable dispose/ Of h. wisdom MILT 118
highland: between lowland and h., SWIN 10
Yon solitary H. Lass! WORD 133
Highlands: Ye H. and ye Lawlands. UNKN 40
highly: h. respectable gondolier, GILB 17, 19
Highness: his H.' dog at Kew; POPE A 5
hight: cock, h. Chanticleer. CHAU 66
H.-hearted buccaneers, LOWE J 15
highth: h. of this great Argument MILT 47
highway: dog in the h., NOYE 8
down in the h., NOYE 8
dusty rubble of the h., ROET 41
every h.'s clear — BYRO 53
heaping field and h. LOWE J 11
on the h., NOYE 8
highwayman: h. came riding — NOYE 6
highways: happy h. where I went HOUS 35
hill: Cocaine town on Cocaine h., UNKN 67
cot beside the h.; ROGE 1
deep nor h. there is, UNKN 250

doubled darkness up the labouring h. ROSS D 7
from Kill Devils H. at Kitty Hawk CRAN H 9
grandfather fell on Vinegar H., CLARK J 3
grave below the h., MERE O 2
green h. far away, ALEX 8
half-way up the h., LONG 29
he climbed the h., WHITT 17
held that trembling h.! THOMP W 3
h. above Harlem HUGH L 15
H. and dale MILT 119
h. of dark underfoot diving, MERW 8
h. slept. NEWB 4
huge h.,/ Cragged, and steep, Truth stands, DONN 51
hunter home from the h. STEVENSO R 21
idle h. of summer, HOUS 42
lay upon the sunny h., MUIR 4
look out from their h. SNOD 10
melting snow upon some craggy h., JONS 4
Olympian H. MILT 83
on the slant h. a putrid lamb, EBER 1
On this high h. THOMA D 36
outside the H., BROWNI R 63
Over h., over dale, SHAK 126
right over the h. WHITT 32
sleep upon his h. again? LIND V 3
sleeping on the h. MAST 6
Shiloh, Antietam, Malvern H., Bull Run. TATE A 12
'Twixt mead and h. MORR 5
up the h. forever. RANS 27
We clamb the h. the gither; BURN 35
Went up the h., MOTH 17
hillock: palmy h.; or the flowery lap MILT 69
hills: Ah happy h.! GRAY 13
Asleep on the h. ARNO 7
autumn h. again: TUCK 1
brown/ h. and red gullies of mississippi KNIG 7
by rocks and h. return'd, WHITM 102
circle of the h. TENN 45
elves of h., brooks, standing lakes, and groves, SHAK 164
great shout upon the h., MARK 4
heard among the solitary h. WORD 94
Hides h. and woods, EMER 43
h. and dales UNKN 59
h. and vales SORL 1
h. and valleys into singing break; VAUG 1

h. and waters o'er, HEMA 4
h. be joyful BIBL, O.T. 47
h. of Habersham, LANIE 5
H. peep o'er hills, POPE A 34
Infamous H., MILT 3
lift up mine eyes unto the h.,
  BIBL, O.T. 58
My black h. KAVA 25
o'er vales and h., WORD 24
Over the H. and far away. GAY 5
rive the h. EMER 10
set the h. on fire. WORD 130
Shouting to the wooded h.,
  MAST 8
sunset over the box house h.
  GINS 33
"Up in the h. to roll and play."
  MILN 2
"Who owns them hungry h.
  KAVA 26
wind/ undulating on mossy h.
  GINS 41
hillside: h. above the grave.
  PETRA 2
on the warm h. YEATS 145
hillside's: h. dew-pearled;
  BROWNI R 66
hilt: swear by the h. of my spear,
  UNKN 126
himself: As parts of h.—just a little
  projected; LOWE J 10
each in the cell of h. AUDE 39
falls by h. Falls by h. KIPL 26
falls by h. Falls by himself
  KIPL 26
from eternity doth teach/ H. in
  all, COLE SAM 15
God fulfils H. TENN 103
hermit withdrawn to h.,
  WHITM 47
H. in some diviner mood, COLL 6
h. to blame, KIPL 26
h. to knowe. CHAU 110
Lord of h., though not of lands,
  WOTT 2
Man's pity for h., BYRO 47
hind: h. stepped down WILLI 3
hinder: His h. parts, MILT 86
Hindered: H. characters
  MOOR M 36
hinds: Soft maids and village h.
  COLL 1
hinges: h. let it move, MOSS 5
hings: h. his head, BURN 23
hinny: my h. and my heart?
  UNKN 126
hint: give no h. that night
  HARD 23
hip: new h. moon, GINS 35
Hippocrene: true, the blushful H.,
  KEAT 45
hippopotamus: broad-backed h.
  ELIOT T 36

h. is strong GUIT 1
h.'s day/ Is passed in sleep;
  ELIOT T 38
shoot the H. BELL 9
hippopotomuscle: big with h.
  GUIT 1
hips: athwart my h. WHITM 78
hipsters: angelheaded h. burning
  GINS 8
Hiram: H. Hover, Huldah Hyde.
  TAYL B 1
hire: heeld h. narwe in cage,
  CHAU 50
hired: one h. box LARK 16
hireling: Of h. wolves whose gospel
  is their maw. MILT 123
hirelings: lewd h. climb. MILT 68
Hiroshima: H. ash and eating in.
  PLATH 46
hiss: geese/ Gabble and h.,
  MILLA 8
h. of the surgeon's knife,
  WHITM 92
hissed: coil and h., FROS 8
hissing: heard the h. WHITM 109
h. hair, BOGA 8
H. to leeward like a ton of spray,
  MILLA 12
historical: few with h. names.
  GUNN 9
I quote the fights h., GILB 35
our knowledge is h., BISH 6
weary with h. data, POUN 34
histories: dreams truths and fables
  h.; DONN 19
history: clouded forms of long-past
  h. BRON 5
h. books have showed;
  GRAHAME 2
h. change its tune, BYRO 21
H. has many cunning passages,
  ELIOT T 32
H. is unforgiven. SCHW 6
H. of grief MACL 2
H. to the defeated AUDE 91
panting lizard/ waited for h.,
  STAF 1
remembered the soul's h.
  SPEND 11
rocking loom of h., HAYD 10
this strange eventful h., SHAK 12
history's: all h. a winter sport
  CUMM 1
hit: body h. a body, MAXW 1
heard it h. the ground, DICKI 90
h. a bear in the ass SNYD 34
h. a more excellent plan
  LOWE J 3
h. a World, at every plunge,
  DICKI 47
not to h. the mark FRANC 1
When he was h., WILB 39

hither: immortal sea/ Which brought
  us h., WORD 82
Hitler: "Being German my hero is
  H.," KINN 5
hits: h. the streets LOWE R 45
hive: cog in a golden singing h.:
  SPEND 9
Draping each h. WHITT 34
from the German h. HOLM 5
h. for the honey-bee, YEATS 74
h. the Greek honey. JEFFE 34
h. whose honey is fear and worry,
  AUDE 32
mind of the h. PLATH 14
hives: changed but the h. of bees.
  WHITT 33
hoar: fields around lay bound and
  h. THOR 11
Monadnock, on his forehead h.,
  SIGO 2
hoard: h., and sleep, and feed,
  TENN 128
h. hath hate CHAU 1
hoarded: cloudy bosom h.,
  LONG 39
Bondage is h. SHAK 143
hoarse: h. and angry WHITM 5
h. oaths that kept OWEN 11
make her airy tongue more h.
  SHAK 143
till you're h., LOWE J 6
hoary: h. winter's night
  SOUTHW 1
h. woods are grand: GALT 1
That h. cripple, BROWNI R 20
hob: kettle on the h. YEATS 145
Hobbinoll: H., what garres thee
  greete? SPENS 48
Hobgoblin: H. nor foul Fiend
  BUNY 3
Hobson: H. has supt, MILT 43
hock: h. and soda-water! BYRO 33
May-poles, h.-carts, wassails,
  wakes, HERR 1
Hodge: throw in Drummer H.,
  HARD 19
hoe: h. and loom, SHEL 65
leans/ Upon his h. MARK 5
o' Plymouth H. NEWB 1
with a h. HUGO 6
Hoere: H. paradis hy nomen here,
  UNKN 289
Hog: H. Butcher for the World,
  SAND 3
to buy a fine h.;/ Home again,
  home again, UNKN 262
hoist: stranger,/ h. your burdens,
  AMMO 18
hold: all things now do h. their
  peace: SURR 3
beauty h. a plea, SHAK 212
brightness to h. in trust,
  SPEND 22

For it's h., dearie, home —
   HENL 3
from distant Ophir/ Rowing h. to
   haven MASE 1
God, who is our h.: WORD 70
have their answer h. HERB G 64
hearth-fire and the h.-acre,
   KIPL 15
h. again, and h. again, VAN DY 3
H. comes the rover, ALLI 5
h. European or Asian, HILT 2
h. from the sea, STEVENSO R 21
h. in leisure MILT 111
H. is the place where, FROS 27
H. is the sailor, STEVENSO R 21
h. of the bean and the cod,
   BOSS 1
h. of the brave? KEY 1
h. of the scorpion. SNYD 20
h. shall never come." UNKN 270
h. we brought you shoulder-high.
   HOUS 55
house t' make it h., GUES 1
hunter h. from the hill.
   STEVENSO R 21
I came h. to your heart.
   BROWNI R 10
I come h. no more. HOUS 28
I have led her h., TENN 95
I was leaving h. STEVENSO R 6
I Years had been from H.
   DICKI 71
I'm Going h.; EMER 26
Kentucky h., good-night! FOST 2
kindred points of Heaven and H.!
   WORD 148
make a h. that's true, UNTE 1
makes me feel at h. MOOR M 1
march for h., GRAV 28
misprision growing,/ Comes h.
   again, SHAK 220
much nearer h. FROS 36
my h. of love; SHAK 230
Naiad airs have brought me h.
   POE 45
no place like h. VAN DY 1
Of life and death, of h.
   WHITM 12
old folks at h. FOST 4
old Kentucky h.; FOST 1
one was sent h., JUST 2
only the wind's h. ELIOT T 151
our eternal h.; WATT I 2
our hugest h.; CUMM 57
"Our island h. TENN 83
Pleasure never is at h.: KEAT 16
returning h., WHITM 18
Sadie stayed at h. BROO G 12
saviors come not h. tonight:
   HOUS 31
scorn the h.-spun gray CAMPI 9
Snug as a bud and at h.
   PLATH 83

soon will blow us h. HENL 2
"Stay at h., pretty bees,
   WHITT 35
staying at h., DICKI 130
Stretched in his last-found h.,
   HOLM 2
to buy a fine hog;/ H. again, home
   again, UNKN 262
to make his mind up to go h.
   BISH 38
toddle safely h. SASS 4
typist h. at teatime, ELIOT T 134
we have no h., MASE 8
weep t' make it h., GUES 3
welcome h., Sir Francis Drake.'
   UNKN 295
where the heart was at h.;
   PITT 1
with him at h. DICKI 85
your cradle, your h., and your
   bier. SHEL 90
homeland: dragged you from h.,
   BROWN S 4
homeless: h., tempest-tost to me.
   LAZA 2
homelier: made it h. than it was.
   BISH 30
homely: h. beauty WORD 162
   h. joys, and destiny obscure;
   GRAY 8
   h. manger SOUTHW 4
   h. Nurse doth all she can
   WORD 73
   h. slighted shepherd's trade,
   MILT 26
narrow, h. room, VAUG 6
savory dish, a h. treat, HORA 10
Homer: H. his sight, REES 3
   H.'s ghost came KAVA 5
   Nature and H. were, he found, the
   same. POPE A 28
   saddle H. rode YEATS 37
home's: h. the best place
   BROWN B 1
homestead: by the h. hearth,
   WHITT 29
Homeward: evening hour that
   strives/ H., ELIOT T 134
   h. led my steps. WORD 102
   infected wound h. RANS 32
   Look h. Angel MILT 31
   plowman h. plods his weary way,
   GRAY 7
homicidal: hackneyed speech, its h.
   eye — LOWE R 28
homicide: love that kisses with a h.
   BARK 1
homward: h. he shal tellen othere
   two, CHAU 6
honest: armour is his h. thought,
   WOTT 1
   be h. if ever so poor, UNKN 233
   be h. like children. AUDE 26

cynic tyrannies of h. kings;
   MELV 12
earn an h. living ROBI 49
false or h. dreaming WILB 33
great as any h. man's. GILB 37
h. idiocy of flight) GRAV 8
H. labour bears a lovely face;
   DEKK/OTHE 2
h. lover's ghost, SUCK 6
h. man, though e'er sae poor,
   BURN 26
h. man's the noblest work of
   God!" BURN 20
h. man's the noblest work of God.
   POPE A 85
h. wealth's BROO S 1
Is there for h. poverty BURN 23
lived by h. dreams DAY 13
poor, but she was h., UNKN 218
honesty: h. and I begin to square.
   SHAK 6
honesty's: H. against all common
   sense — ROCH 10
Honey: bough/ Breaking with h.
   buds, SPEND 7
Chew h. and spit out gall.
   SHAP 24
eat my peas with h., UNKN 136
eat o' the h.-comb POUN 4
fruits like h. to the throat
   ROSS C 11
hive for the h.-bee, YEATS 74
hive the Greek h. JEFFE 34
hive whose h. is fear and worry,
   AUDE 32
h., and plenty of money,
   LEAR 10
h.-bees,/ Come build YEATS 99
h.-coloured/ Ramparts YEATS 63
h. dropped from trees; TASS 1
h.-feast of the berries PLATH 22
H.-gold baby/ Sweet enough to
   eat. HUGH L 5
H.-heavy on my hand, BLUN 2
h. of peace in old poems.
   JEFFE 43
h. of romance — WILD 14
H. of roses, HERB G 35
h. still for tea? BROO R 20
h. to smear his face, SCHW 9
I am no source of h. PLATH 10
I'm in clover now, nor know/ Who
   made h. long ago. BLUN 3
on h.-dew hath fed,
   COLE SAM 22
pedigree of H. DICKI 119
poets h. their truth JEFFE 9
sucked the h. of thy breath,
   SHAK 152
summer's h. breath SHAK 212
wild h. of their youth. ROSE 5
honeybees: so work the h.,
   SHAK 55

with more successful h. resolve
   MILT 52
With new-fledged h. WORD 80
Work without H. COLE SAM 46
Hoped: H. to improve a little
   AUDE 24
What I had h. YEATS 59
hopeful: eye their h. years;
   BURN 18
hopefulness: Liberal h. EMPS 4
hopeless: dull and h. CRAB 1
Happier, h. fair, COLL 5
h. grief is passionless;
   BROWNI E 1
mocked by h. longing SASS 7
poet's h. woe, TENN 14
those by h. fancy feigned
   TENN 115
Woes of h. Lovers, DRYD 26
write such h. rubbish
   STEPHEN 6
hopes: blind h. and blind despairs,
   ARNO 16
bright h. yet to find me, BANK 1
clever h. expire AUDE 70
Half the world's h., HECH 1
h. and fears it heeded not:
   SHEL 70
h. and fears of all the years
   BROO P 3
h. cannot delude, CAMPI 13
h. dance best CUMM 7
h. greater than my despair,
   GREE 3
h. of future years, LONG 6
H. of high talk SHEL 31
h. to win her; CONG 2
H. which obscure, BRON 11
Love wing'd my H. UNKN 184
Nip in the blossom all our h.
   MARV 32
our h., our prayers, our tears,
   LONG 7
play of h. and fears, POE 30
Sterner desires and darker h.
   BRON 11
hopped: Some h.: HEAN 10
hopping: h. the slow freight
   CRAN H 21
hoppy-hop: away did h. CAREY 1
hopscotch: he played h. CARRY 9
Horace: wanting thee./ H.,
   Anacreon HERR 16
horizon: eye concedes to/
   Encroaching h., HEAN 1
Faded to last h. notes. DODS 1
h.'s fluid line; SPEND 17
I saw a man pursuing the h.;
   CRAN S 1
horizons: h., launched above/
   Mortality — CRAN H 45

Horizontal: H. misty Air MILT 57
h. monument to patience.
   WILB 42
horn: bullet-mould/ And powder h.,
   TATE A 10
Come blow your h., MOTH 18
cow with the crumpled h.
   MOTH 7
exalt the h. of his anointed.
   BIBL, O.T. 8
H. of Plenty is undone.
   YEATS 107
h., the hounds, RANS 2
old Triton blow his wreathèd h.
   WORD 160
Remus, blow your h.!
   STEVENS 39
sheep, with curly h., UNKN 108
small but sullen H., COLL 10
your occipital h. MOOR M 40
Hornell: Xenia, Burnt Cabins, H.
   KINN 7
Horner: Little Jack H. MOTH 20
sings of Jacky H., CAREY 3
horney: tender Page with h. Fists
   was gual'd; DRYD 19
Hornie: H., Satan, Nick, or Clootie,
   BURN 1
horns: h. of Elfland faintly
   blowing! TENN 112
h. of glory blowing AIKE 10
sound of h. and motors,
   ELIOT T 131
horny: deep in her h., REED I 3
If her h. feet protrude,
   STEVENS 11
horologe: clock or an abbey h.
   CHAU 66
horrible: Dungeon h., MILT 50
ravener of h. meat. MELV 14
reign in this h. place. COWP 23
'tis too h.! SHAK 115
horrid: blow the h. deed SHAK 105
cleave the general ear with h.
   speech, SHAK 31
giant was h., NASH 3
h. care, MARV 15
h. vision seized my head, SWIF 3
To wicked spirits are h. shapes
   assign'd, DONN 67
when she was bad, she was h.
   MOTH 28
with his h. crew MILT 49
horrifying: Their breasts were h.
   BISH 22
Horror: H. and scorn and hate and
   fear and indignation —
   HOUS 24
h.-stricken eyes, KINS 4
scaly h. of his folded tail.
   MILT 40
shook with h. at thy fall. BRYA 5
shuddring h. pale, MILT 61

sweat of h. in his hair, SASS 13
Unrolled its h. in my face —
   DICKI 26
varicose h. ROET 54
horrors: abyss of fears/ And h.
   MILT 100
Congenial h., hail!
   THOMS J (1700–1748) 12
h. of the tedious Night, PHILL 2
hors: Wel koude he sitte on h.
   CHAU 10
horse: all things — but his h.
   POPE A 20
black man upon a black h.;
   UNKN 12
blue h. that runs in the plain
   MOMA 3
Colonel's son has taken a h.,
   KIPL 2
couchèd in the ominous h.,
   SHAK 30
Could back a h., BYRO 47
coverts from a h.; BETJ 7
God help the h., STEPHENS 12
gone off, like a h. PLATH 41
great Napoleon/ Stops his h.,
   EMER 18
hame cam his guid h., UNKN 37
Hast thou given the h. strength?
   BIBL, O.T. 17
high h. riderless, YEATS 37
h. and the rider, SWEN 2
h. by the head FROS 45
h. is taught his manage,
   WORD 110
h.-races of long ago at Clary's
   Grove, MAST 7
h. that feels a flea, MOOR M 32
h. to Love, SIDN 17
Hurrah for h. and man!
   READ T 2
Joseph, Crazy H., SNYD 24
Kicking H. fills up. HUGO 3
my h. my hound SWEN 5
never a h. like her! WOOL 4
old h. that stumbles and nods
   HARD 29
posse passed, twelve h.;
   TATE A 17
scorneth the h. and his rider.
   BIBL, O.T. 17
stands like an old h. WARR 5
terrible h. began BOGA 2
torturer's h. Scratches AUDE 63
where's the bloody h.?
   CAMPB R 5
horseback: Camelback, h.,
   YEATS 80
horsed: h. Upon the sightless
   couriers of the air, SHAK 105
Horseman: H., pass by! YEATS 160
horsemanships: try/ Our h.,
   SIDN 17

felt the lapse of h.! ARNO 22
Hold back thy h., BEAU/FLET 4
h. and times of your desire?
  SHAK 208
h. are numbered, EMER 45
h. are suns, SPEND 11
h. of travail LIND V 3
h. stand in solid rows, SHAP 29
h. were thine and mine,
  TENN 11
I compute the weary h.
  KING H 2
in twenty-four h. you'll ride it
  about." UNKN 163
line will take us h. YEATS 1
music of the languid h., LANG 3
needful h. of Rest? DRYD 2
pitiless h. like years and ages
  creep, THOMS J (1834–1882) 4
slow, dark h. begin, ROSS C 28
social h., swift-winged, BURN 18
spoken three h., CARRO 14
sweetest h. that e'er I spend,
  BURN 28
thine oblivious h.! DOWS 4
turn h. to years WALK 13
wait, through wintry h.,
  MCCRE 2
weary of days and h., SWIN 13
wither thro' the sunless h.
  ROSS C 37
hous: governance of h. and land,
  CHAU 87
housbond: over hir h. as hir love,
  CHAU 111
housbonde: sely jalous h. to bigile,
  CHAU 53
Housbondes: H. at chirche dore I
  have had five CHAU 87
  H. at chirche dore she hadde
  fyve, CHAU 11
  H. mekė, yonge, CHAU 111
house: At the top of the h. DRIN 1
before a H. DICKI 10
Belinda lived in a little white h.,
  NASH 15
Body my h. SWEN 5
bridegroom bring her to a h.
  YEATS 114
bring down the h. AUDE 49
Bustle in a H. DICKI 16
called for drinks for the h.
  SERV 7
came to my h. STRA 5
chase into the h. a lucky foot.
  HOUS 8
child draws another inscrutable
  h. BISH 47
chopped down the h. KOCH 5
city mouse lives in a h.; —
  ROSS C 5
Clay h. mouldring away, BRAD 1

clouds that loured upon our h.
  SHAK 94
come to our h. to stay, RILE 1
Dark h., TENN 20
dirty h. in a gutted world,
  STEVENS 43
doll in the doll-maker's h.
  YEATS 49
doorkeeper in the h. of my God,
  BIBL, O.T. 43
dwell in the h. of the Lord for
  ever. BIBL, O.T. 31
empty h. of the stare. YEATS 99
fairer H. than Prose — DICKI 43
father's h. below MUIR 4
fiercely mourning h. THOMA D 4
Fled gasping from the H.
  DICKI 73
half-way h. THOMA D 6
Harrow the h. of the dead;
  AUDE 69
haunted h. BRID R 11
hid in the h. SMIT ST 8
his moss-greened h. DE LA 25
his own h. & family; BLAK 27
h. and the trees, WHITT 33
h. by the side of the road FOSS 2
h. in the city-square;
  BROWNI R 83
h. is in the village FROS 107
h. is shut and still, ROBI 18
h. of ancient fame. SPENS 45
h. of make believe, FROS 41
H. of Peers, GILB 24
h. of the /dead; AUDE 69
h. on high erect, BRAD 12
h. rent to pay. HUGH L 3
H. sought for All, GINS 25
h. stands opposite, SNOD 8
h. t' make it home, GUES 1
h. that is no more FROS 42
h., the poem, RANDA D 5
H. without air, MILLA 41
In my grandmother's h. SIMP 10
little crooked h. MOTH 27
lived laughing in my h. MOMA 5
lounge of the mental h. SEXT 12
malt/ That lay in the h. MOTH 3
master of this h., UNKN 116
moat defensive to a h., SHAK 88
my poore h., and I JONS 14
old h. here MORR 5
one man — can't keep a h.,
  FROS 75
opera h. sparkled MERR 11
out of the h. OHAR 2
powerful fortress'd h., WHITM 42
Range the wide h. BROWNI R 50
retinue from the magician's h.
  AUDE 53
secrets of my prison h., SHAK 26
serious h. on serious earth
  LARK 6

set/ The h. on fire. TAYL E 1
shakes my h., LOWE R 6
Silent is the h.: BRON 14
small h. and large garden
  COWL 8
sound within the h. HOUS 10
sunset over the box h. hills
  GINS 33
Tenants of the h., ELIOT T 35
Tending the h., MERR 2
three generations of one h.
  POUN 26
uphold your h. WYLI 7
wander the dark h. WARR 5
wanna play at your h.; SNOD 8
With crayons the child draws a
  rigid h. BISH 46
yellow wooden h. indented
  WILLI 24
household: happy genius of my h.?
  WILLI 13
h. of Impulse AUDE 34
Nature shown/ her h. RICH 17
housemaid: as the prying h.
  EMPS 14
houses: dropping h. and eek smoke
  CHAU 98
faster than witches,/ Bridges and
  h., STEVENSO R 8
h. are haunted STEVENS 4
know some lonely h. DICKI 50
passes the h. SPEND 6
riotous glass h. built on rock,
  LOWE R 5
very h. seem asleep; WORD 7
housewife: h. that's thrifty.
  SHERI 1
Indolent H. DICKI 32
Hover: Hiram H., Huldah Hyde.
  TAYL B 1
Hovered: H. thy spirit COWP 10
Hovers: H. in its virginity.
  NOEL H 1
How: H. is it that you live,
  WORD 125
h. much? — SAND 22
H. shall we adorn MOMA 1
h. their days will cease!
  STEPHENS 12
h. to kill desire. SIDN 40
know not h.; LOWE J 18
tell me h. to woo! GRAHAM R 1
Howard: shot Mister H.,
  UNKN 148
Howl: H., H., H.! SHAK 85
wild cayotes will h. o'er me,
  UNKN 50
howlds: ould engin' h. together —'
  FRENC 1
howled: heavens scowled, and the
  huskies h., SERV 4
Howling: H. and roaring SILKO 2
h. on for more, SHEL 68

In the h. storm, BLAK 80
love was h. SNOD 16
quick and h., COWP 16
storm is h., YEATS 105
With h. woe, BLAK 45
Howres: rosie-boosom'd H.,
  MILT 11
Hsüan Tsang: H., crossing the
  Pamirs SNYD 24
Hubbard: Says Mr. H. UNKN 303
hubbub: Earth's h. and strife
  LOWE J 7
H. increases more they call
  KEAT 25
hubs: h. of logs HOLM 6
huddled: and h. chill. CUNN J 4
cattle h. on the lea; TENN 23
h. you spoon-fashion BROWN S 4
Your h. masses LAZA 2
hue: black, staid Wisdom's h.;
  MILT 15
h. of far away. WILB 17
moments of an azure h.,
  THOR 10
native h. of resolution SHAK 40
your sweet h., SHAK 227
hued: summer h. the deck
  STEVENS 46
hues: binds/ of thought/ into the h.,
  AMMO 3
fallen skies and evil h. CHES 10
h. like hers?
  THOMS J (1700–1748) 3
thine own h. SHEL 30
hug: cuddle and h.," GRAV 30
grizzly bear whose potent h.
  GUIT 2
huge: bulk as h. As whom the
  Fables name MILT 53
Day as h. DICKI 26
feeling its h. path SPEND 13
h. hill,/ Cragged, and steep,
  DONN 51
h. of head GUIT 1
h. stage presenteth naught but
  shows SHAK 187
Success so h. and wholly farcical;
  LARK 21
trace h. Forests, MILT 3
what h. heaps of littleness
  around! POPE A 101
hugest: our h. home; CUMM 57
hugging: h. babies, kissing bellies,
  SNYD 8
thighs h. his ribs. SWEN 3
Hugh: sing a dirge for Saint H.'s
  soul, DEKK 1
Huldah: Hiram Hover, H. Hyde.
  TAYL B 1
hulk: her shattered h. HOLM 18
sick four-story h., BROO G 10
hull: together, h. to h., LOWE R 39
hum: bee-hive's h. ROGE 1

Buz, quoth the blue fly,/ H., quoth
  the bee, JONS 19
hear the surgeon h. KIRK 3
h./ Bulges to thunder GUNN 11
h. of either army stilly sounds,
  SHAK 57
h. of multitudes BLAK 91
Ninth-month bees h.; WHITM 31
universe could h.? ROET 19
human: all h. ties that bind
  BANK 1
all must love the h. form,
  BLAK 89
bears the H. soul. DICKI 141
being h., born alone; WYLI 5
being we call h., MOOR M 25
cries that are almost h. SIMP 1
de-animalize h. mentality,
  KINN 12
doubtful doom of h. kind;
  TENN 126
earth's h. shores, KEAT 3
equal among h. kind HARD 7
every h. face, AUDE 44
every h. heart, LOWE J 16
evil with no h. sense, WINT 3
half remember h. words, SYNG 7
hard, h. pulse ROBI 17
He knew h. folly AUDE 4
heart of man, and h. life.
  WORD 51
how well they understood/ Its h.
  position; AUDE 62
h. brain-vault: JEFFE 4
h. child! YEATS 144
h. creatures' lives! HOOD 12
h. flower MARV 31
h. form divine BLAK 26
h. kind/ Cannot bear very much
  reality./ Time past and time
  future ELIOT T 19
h. nature's daily food; WORD 134
h. power cannot remove.
  ELIOT T 70
h./ Revery is a solitude
  STEVENS 24
h. right and weal WHITT 10
h. season on this sterile air
  MACL 6
h. seraphim, the sailors, GINS 11
h. thought or form, SHEL 30
h. title, putting pig within.
  GUNN 8
h. tunes nor words, YEATS 41
idol of the h. race, BRID R 3
In curve and voice and eye/
  Despise the h. span/ Of
  durance — HARD 26
In h. gore imbued. POE 32
in the h. breast: POPE A 65
infinite task of the h. heart."
  SCHW 4

insect/ Looks farcically h.;
  GRAV 1
junk that goes with being h.
  SNYD 49
just some h. sleep. FROS 6
Loud h. song, WHITM 49
Love the h. form divine,
  BLAK 88
Mercy has a h. heart, BLAK 88
Natures æthereal, h., angel, man,
  POPE A 72
Nor h. spark is left, POPE A 2
' Offending race of h. kind,
  SWIF 4
older than h. cries, HAYD 17
passions of the h. family MAST 4
Peace, the h. dress. BLAK 88
Pity, a h. face; BLAK 88
potent quack, long versed in h.
  ills, CRAB 8
rare to be born a h. being!
  SNYD 38
read h. and exact. GRAV 6
resembling h. organs SMIT W 3
smells of the h. body, KINN 19
so narrow h. wit. POPE A 24
stars where no h. race FROS 36
sweetest thing that ever grew/
  Beside a h. door! WORD 50
term of h. strife, TENN 29
tinned milk of h. kindness
  RODG 6
To err is h., POPE A 35
To soothe and satisfy the h. ear.
  COWP 20
To step aside is h.: BURN 7
transplanted h. worth TENN 39
true source/ Of h. offspring,
  MILT 78
turbid ebb and flow/ Of h.
  misery; ARNO 2
tyrant of the h. heart, BRID R 3
Undimmed by h. tears! BATE 3
utmost bound of h. thought.
  TENN 132
wear a h. face. ROET 1
web of h. things,/ Birth and the
  grave, SHEL 22
when the h. engine waits
  ELIOT T 133
Wiser far than h. seer, EMER 31
humanised: h. my Soul. WORD 12
humanity: delivered entirely from
  h. SMIT ST 5
freeze my/ h., MACN 16
His life was of h. the sphere.
  JONS 39
H. with all its fears, LONG 6
still, sad music of h., WORD 34
'suffering h.' FERL 3
weakness of mere h., SPENC A 4
wearisome condition of h.!
  GREV 9

humankind: / /attained by h.!
  HARD 47
humanly: Modestly bold, and h.
  severe: POPE A 24
humans: spare a million or two of
  h. LAWR 30
humble: Burly, dozing h.-bee,
  EMER 30
  frown'd not on his h. birth,
  GRAY 12
  h. and a contrite heart. KIPL 18
  h. happiness endeared each scene.
  GOLD 1
  h. Man of modest sense,
  ROCH 12
  h. roof/ Is weather-proof;
  HERR 39
  h. way to save his self-respect.
  FROS 21
  in your h. graves, TIMR 6
  praise His h. pomp SOUTHW 6
  thy h. stalk. BRYA 35
  your h. swain, SYLV 1
humbled: great man h., AIKE 9
humbling: no h. of reality AMMO 8
Humbly: confessed/ H. their faults,
  MILT 98
  h. crowd outside, SPEND 6
humiliation: Pride and h. LONG 26
  sorrow unfeigned and h. meek.
  MILT 98
Humilitie: checker'd all along,/ H.:
  HERB G 13
humility: modest stillness and h.
  SHAK 56
humming: h. air; TENN 42
humming-bird: h. flashed ahead of
  creation. LAWR 16
humorist: h., I infer! LA FO 2
humorists: cunning h.' puddled
  opinions, SIDN 4
humour: bubbles with wit and good
  h.! GILB 56
  for his h.'s sake, COWP 3
  h. of melancholy CHAU 69
  increase that loving h. more.
  CAMPI 4
  of good h. POPE A 109
hump: doesn't h. a sump," KOCH 1
humpty-dumpty: h. clods.
  CRAN H 21
humpy: bumpy and h. CARRY 3
hums: one life h., SPEND 9
hunch: h. what the music meant
  SERV 8
hunchback: followed the h.
  THOMA D 26
  h. on the corner, WARR 6
hunchbacks: Country of h.! —
  MILLA 34
hunched: boy's h. body KINN 8
hunching: mud/ Flies from his h.
  wings and beak — LOWE R 7

hundred: At a h. mysteries;
  HODG 3
  Blind as the nineteen h. and forty
  nails SITW 11
  Cover a h. leagues, WORD 130
  Hecuba and the h. daughters,
  TATE A 1
  h. different lives; ARNO 24
  h. miles or more,
  STEVENSO R 23
  h. years hence, WHITM 19
  knot a h. together, MORG 1
  nothing a h. years hence. JORD 1
  ran a h. years to a day, HOLM 4
  Rode the six h. TENN 6
  so many h. years hence,
  WHITM 19
hundreds: h. and h. that cross,
  WHITM 18
  H. of thousands counted,
  SHAP 11
Hundredth: H. Psalm, CALV 3
  morn of its h. year HOLM 7
hung: bucket that h. in the well.
  WOOD 3
  Green Snake, when I h. you
  LEVE 22
  heavy night h. dark HEMA 4
  h. my black young lover
  HUGH L 13
  H. o'er the deep,
  THOMS J (1700–1748) 8
  h. with bloom along the bough,
  HOUS 38
  h. with stars!), HOLLA 3
  I h. on like death; ROET 49
  moss h. down from the branches,
  WHITM 39
  our boat/ H. poised ARNO 5
  stockings were h. by the chimney
  MOOR C 1
  There h. a darkness, WORD 97
  Watteau h. a lady's/ slipper.
  WILLI 25
hunger: Babe can never h. there,
  BLAK 69
  fear, thirst, h., CUNN J 4
  fed your h. like an endless task,
  CRAN H 46
  h. and night and the stars.
  SERV 8
  h. fer 'em somehow, GUES 1
  h. in the prison of my fear.
  GARR 2
  h. is abolished — GILB 52
  h. of this poem REED I 1
  h. seized my heart; TENN 41
  H. shall make thy modest zone
  DAY 2
  h. was a more immediate sorrow;
  AUDE 22
  marks of wanton h. SAND 4
  No one/ Shall h.: SPEND 18

poverty, h., and dirt, HOOD 12
  with my h. MILT 109
hungering: Thirsting and h.,
  GRAV 13
hungers: all h. leap, WILB 6
  cries and h. HALL 1
hungrily: h. pining for pines,
  PRAE 4
hungry: Burrow with h. head
  SHAP 15
  dancer stayed his h. foot
  YEATS 95
  h. beating brutish one SCHW 9
  h. for the old, familiar ways,
  MCKA 8
  h. lion roars, SHAK 128
  h. ocean gain/ Advantage
  SHAK 211
  h. on the tracks, CRAN H 16
  h. to be interrupted SMIT ST 9
  h. weed grows. BROO G 19
  listeners' h. hearts JOHN J 7
  "Who owns them h. hills
  KAVA 26
hunt: go h. bears. SNYD 34
hunted: little h. hares. HODG 1
  none h., alien, HAYD 6
  Past reason h., SHAK 236
  tears of the h. hare. SITW 12
  we are wild and h. men. SIMM 1
hunter: h. home from the hill.
  STEVENSO R 21
  h. strangled by the boars;
  CHAU 48
  h.'s trail and trap-path TUCK 1
  Miss J, H. Dunn, BETJ 9
  struck by the h.'s dart SHEL 7
hunters: rings no h.' shout; SIGO 1
Hunting: H. beaver, TAYL B 1
  h. for chinks ROET 52
  H. mice is his delight,/ H. words I
  sit UNKN 202
Huntlie: True Thomas lay on H.
  bank; UNKN 245
huntress: Queen and h., chaste and
  fair, JONS 3
hunts: h. for flowers. UNKN 250
huntsman: h. after weary chace,
  SPENS 16
  H., rest! SCOT WA 10
hurdled: h. cotes MILT 68
hurdling: coiled, h. muscles of his
  thighs: LOWE R 37
hurl: To h. upon their heads
  SHAK 98
hurled: birth to death h. MUIR 1
  both hurler and the h., GUNN 13
  by night we are h. By dreams,
  HERR 9
  h. my youth into a grave.
  SERV 11
  in endless error h.; POPE A 78

hurler: both h. and the hurled,
GUNN 13
Hurrah: H. for horse and man!
READ T 2
H. for revolution   YEATS 65
H.! H. for Sheridan!   READ T 2
hurricane: sea and h.,   WHITM 104
hurricanoes: cataracts and h.,
SHAK 75
hurried: Change with h. hand
TUCK 1
h. and sparkling waters!
WHITM 44
like the wind they h.,   WOOL 2
hurries: h. me back to despair.
COWP 24
hurry: Caterpillar in a h.,
ROSS C 3
h. from the fatal cannon's womb.
SHAK 150
h. through the eternal halls,
EMER 9
h. to let him in?   SMIT ST 8
H. up please its time
ELIOT T 128
nought/ But restless h.
THOMS J (1700–1748) 7
ratel tumbled h. skurry.
ROSS C 12
sick h.,   ARNO 27
hurrying: trampled by a h. crowd,
BRYA 1
hurt: Balm of h. minds,   SHAK 106
Both equal h.,   SIDN 2
doo most h. where most hellp I
offer.   WYAT 23
h. is not enough: FROS 114
H. no living thing: ROSS C 16
I am h.   UNKN 225
Mad Ireland h. you   AUDE 40
power to h.   SHAK 222
They h. me.   LI PO 6
hurts: h. the sight,   SACK 1
husband: As the h. is, the wife is:
TENN 71
Betray, kind h., Thy spouse
DONN 52
fact of her h.   BERRYM 5
h. frae the wife despises!
BURN 51
h. nature's riches   SHAK 222
in a h.   BYRO 18
lived with my h.   WILLI 46
My hoppped up h.   LOWE R 45
sweetheart and her h. bound in
one.   WALK 12
husbanded: silence h. our strength —
MELV 16
husbandes: h. hardy, wise, and
free,   CHAU 67
husbandry: borrowing dulls the edge
of h.   SHAK 24
husbands: Aisles full of h.!   GINS 37

commend/ This way to h.,
JONS 36
counted her h.   WALK 9
God's supply of tolerable h.
GRAV 27
Why have my sisters h.   SHAK 68
hush: /call out H.!"   KEAT 25
holy h. of ancient sacrifice.
STEVENS 54
h. of peace —   BRON 10
h. of spacious prairies   MARK 2
Old Man who said, H.!   LEAR 16
hush'd: Air is h.,   COLL 10
hushed: all is h. at Shiloh.
MELV 20
as a h. footfall   TEAS 3
four bullets h. her.   HAYD 12
h. me in her arms to rest,
TAYL A 1
H. willows anchored   CRAN H 52
h. with buzzing night-flies
SHAK 54
old h. Egypt and its sands.
HUNT 6
hushes: awe that h. all,   BRYA 5
land h. to rest: BRID R 13
Hushing: H. the latest traffic
BRID R 8
huskies: heavens scowled, and the h.
howled,   SERV 4
husking: h. of the corn,
BROWNI E/GUIN 1
husky: Stormy, h., brawling,/ City of
the Big Shoulders: SAND 3
huts: wearied of our h.   UNKN 121
huzza: Love, power, the h. of battle
LAYT 1
hyacinth: h. hair, thy classic face,
POE 45
h. I wished me   DRUM 1
hyacinths: h. are blooming in
bowls   ELIOT T 108
Hyads: so are the H.:   GRAV 30
hyaline: h. thin air   SHAP 7
Hyde: Hiram Hover, Huldah H.
TAYL B 1
Hydras: Gorgons and H., and
Chimera's dire.   MILT 61
hydrogen: sexless h.!   GINS 17
hydrotherapy: metrasol electricity
h.   GINS 15
hym: born h. weel,   CHAU 9
h. death greep'the right hard by
the croppe   SENE 2
Hymen: H. peoples every town;
SHAK 16
never-singling H. couple
MARL 10
hymn: h. the Brahmin sings.
EMER 7
hymns: Ceasing their h.,   PCE 25
Singing h. unbidden,   SHEL 70

sings h. at heaven's gate;
SHAK 194
windy citherns hankering for h.
STEVENS 14
hymselve: He taughte, but first he
folwed it h.   CHAU 14
hyphens: happiest with h.,   BROD 2
hypocrisy: love is taught h. from
youth.   BYRO 21
Hypocrite: H. women, how seldom
LEVE 7
Hypocrites: H. austerely talk
MILT 77
hypocritic: h. Days,   EMER 13
hypocritical: Be h., be cautious,
BYRO 35
Hyrcan: H. tiger;   SHAK 110
hysteria: landscape of h.,
SPEND 14
hysterical: h. women say   YEATS 77
starving h. naked,   GINS 7

I

iambs: book of i. and pentameters,
LOWE J 5
Ianthe: find I.'s name agen.
LAND 6
Iasi: street in I.,   PINS 3
Icarian: I. bird,   THOR 6
ice: All their eyes are i.,   OWEN 23
as though i. burned   YEATS 32
caught leaves in i.,   SNYD 22
for destruction i. Is also great
FROS 48
gray/ And changeless lands of i.
WILB 47
green i.!   LOVE 1
i. will burn.'   EMER 50
matter-of-fact about the i.-storm
FROS 12
My Love is like to i., and I to
fire: SPENS 9
panes of i.   PLATH 68
silence/ Of the unbroken i.
JARR 20
Some say in i.   FROS 47
stalks are firmly rooted in i.
STEVENS 27
thick-ribbèd i.,   SHAK 115
through their veins in i. and fire
HOUS 46
who bore, 'mid snow and i.,
LONG 21
ice-cream: emperor of i.
STEVENS 10
iceberg: Against a stolid i. steer,
MELV 1
In a borealic i. came Victoria;
SITW 1
icebergs: dive beneath the i.
LAWR 57
I. behoove the soul   BISH 20

Icebox: in their hospital/ I.,
  PLATH 34
ices: rural o'er i. and wines,
  PRAE 4
icicle: cold as any i. RANS 27
icicles: i. hang by the wall,
  SHAK 101
  in silent i., COLE SAM 17
icily: i. free above the stones,
  BISH 5
icons: Shatter the i. of slavery
  RANDA D 3
icy: awful dread of the i. grave
  SERV 2
  Death lays his i. hand on kings:
  SHIR 1
  drinking i. water SNYD 8
idea: held in i., a little handful.
  EBER 5
ideal: rip the edge off any i. or
  dream. MACN 2
ideas: fortress against i. MACN 1
  I., old gossip, POUN 54
  (No i. but in things) WILLI 29
identified: i. / And carried Me
  away — DICKI 109
identity: melted and reduced/ To
  one i., WORD 109
  My own i. remained. WINT 6
  to a new i., WHITM 77
idiocy: honest i. of flight) GRAV 8
idioms: well-meant i. CRAN H 42
idiot: among the i. pumps —
  UPDI 1
  April/ Comes like an i., MILLA 37
  tale/ Told by an i., SHAK 114
idle: Built up its i. door, HOLM 2
  children of an i. brain, SHAK 141
  I make an i. boast; CULL 9
  i. as a painted ship
  COLE SAM 32
  i., silly, flattering words, HOWI 2
  i. singer of an empty day.
  MORR 2
  i. wear; SHEL 64
  Lie Saunt'ring Jack and I. Joan.
  PRIO 3
  little profits that an i. king,
  TENN 128
  many an i. stone — POE 43
  never is i.; VAN DY 4
  no time for i. cares POE 40
  only i. chatter GILB 30
  Tears, i. tears, TENN 114
  weak and i. theme, SHAK 129
idleness: i. of tears. REES 2
idly: Who fluctuate i. ARNO 24
idol: Ambition was my i., BYRO 22
  'eathen i.'s foot: KIPL 10
  i. of the human race, BRID R 3
idolatry: sanctify desire's i.
  GREV 7

idoll: i. which you terme Virginitie,
  MARL 11
idols: collapse of bestials, i.
  BROO G 14
  I. I have loved so long OMAR 2
if: Decking the sense as i. it were to
  sell. HERB G 40
  I. you can keep your head KIPL 7
  Thy word is all, i. we could spell.
  HERB G 32
Iffucan: I. of Azcan in caftan
  STEVENS 2
ignoble: end/ Was not i. WORD 95
  madding crowd's i. strife,
  GRAY 11
  starved i. nature; BROWNI R 21
ignorance: cradle of i., SIDN 4
  dull unfeeling barren i. SHAK 86
  i. toboggans into know CUMM 1
  It was a childish i., HOOD 5
  my simple i., EMER 42
  trudges up to i. CUMM 1
  where i. is bliss GRAY 17
  worthless as i.: JARR 21
ignorant: blunt-faced i. one
  GUNN 1
  clenched i. against the sky!
  BISH 2
  Confound the i., SHAK 31
  flatter beauty's i. ear. YEATS 131
  i. armies clash by night. ARNO 4
  I. as dirt, SHAP 21
  i. for current took 'em; BUTL 5
  i. goodwill, YEATS 51
  i. night, the travail SCHW 6
  loved each other and were i.
  YEATS 6
  Luxury, then is a way of/ being
  i., BARA 14
  Youth must its i. impulse lend —
  MELV 17
ignorantly: bookful blockhead, i.
  read, POPE A 22
Ike: with her lover I., UNKN 236
Iles: happy I., MILT 65
  Thrice happy I., MILT 65
Iliad: made the I. from such
  KAVA 5
Ilion: I.'s lofty temples TENN 123
Ilium: topless towers of I.?
  MARL 3
ilk: cow is of the bovine i.;
  NASH 5
ill: as little i.,/ For I will dare
  none." JONS 25
  causeless good or i. decree.
  GREV 1
  doctrine of i.-doing, SHAK 178
  dutiful weighing of i. with good; —
  LANIE 3
  final goal of i., TENN 30
  find fit instruments of i.!
  POPE A 123

  hastening i. a prey, GOLD 1
  Haunted by i. angels POE 16
  he thinks no i. SHAK 208
  his i.-got honours flung, SWIF 16
  I. and good, old, HERB CH 5
  i. brought up, BYRO 21
  i. deserve the place RILE 3
  I. fares the land, GOLD 1
  i.-got plunder, NEWB 2
  I. matching words MILT 80
  i.-tempered and queer, LEAR 7
  i. thoughts die and good are
  born — BROWNI E/GUIN 1
  i.-used race of men that cleave the
  soil, TENN 91
  i. we all dissembled. PRIO 10
  in judging i.; POPE A 21
  much less good than i., HOUS 52
  no for ony gude or i. BURN 32
  reckon i. who leave me out;
  EMER 7
  that which doth preserve the i.,
  SHAK 242
  think no i., CAMPI 8
  worser spirit a woman, colored i.
  SHAK 240
Illinois: grip that swung the ax in
  I. MARK 3
Ills: bear those i. we have
  SHAK 40
  flood/ Of mortal i. LUTH 2
  hastening i. a prey, GOLD 3
  I. have no weights, LYTE 2
  O'er a' the i. o' life victorious!
  BURN 53
  potent quack, long versed in
  human i., CRAB 8
  suffer toothache's i.? GILB 48
  There mark what i.
  JOHN S (1709–1784) 18
  what i. await! GRAY 26
illuminated: inward eyes i.
  MILT 116
illuminations: i.! religions!
  GINS 18
illusion: that was i., MERR 7
illusions: imbecile i. of happiness
  FERL 4
illustrious: Among i. women,
  MILT 112
image: age demanded and i.
  POUN 40
  enemy and i. of ourselves,
  MACN 13
  eyed her i. dolefully as death;
  RANS 25
  find where your true i. pictured
  lies, SHAK 192
  i. glares AMMO 19
  i. of our mind. POPE A 21
  i. of such politics. YEATS 66
  i. of their glorious Maker
  MILT 71

i. of thine eyes ROSS D 3
i. was my ensign: GRAV 16
i. Warped in the weather,
   GRAV 17
Isn't it god's own i.? LAWR 14
keep that earlier, wilder i. bright.
   BRYA 30
living i. of our own bright land,
   BRYA 28
no forcing of i., AMMO 8
shaped it in His own i.;
   JOHN J 3
thine I. be/ White as I can,
   MARV 30
verse is the true i. of my mind,
   DRAY 9
Wee i. of my bonnie Betty,
   BURN 43
imaged: i. word, CRAN H 52
images: embossed by silvery i.
   OHAR 2
Fresh i. beget, YEATS 19
givest to forms and i. a breath
   WORD 98
i. of pastoral CUNN J 4
i. of self-confusednesses GREV 5
No graven i. CLOU 5
imaginacioun: Men may dien of i.,
   CHAU 56
imaginary: i. gardens MOOR M 33
literati keep/ An i. friend.
   AUDE 6
long i. plain, MONTA 1
imagination: as i. bodies forth
   SHAK 127
Can i. boast,
   THOMS J (1700–1748) 3
Fling out i. EBER 5
i. all compact. SHAK 127
i. of a man YEATS 45
literalists of/ the i. MOOR M 33
shaping spirit of I. COLE SAM 10
Such tricks hath strong i.
   SHAK 127
imaginations: forms i., MILT 80
His proud i. MILT 58
i. blossom. KAVA 10
imagine: Heaven which I i.,
   SHEL 76
i. he no longer trembles ROET 40
i. my shame YEATM 1
i. thee exempt from age
   ARNO 23
try to i. a faultless love AUDE 52
writing these poems!/ I.! OHAR 1
imagined: i. love/ Of solitary beds,
   YEATS 142
make/ something i., LOWE R 42
round earth's i. corners, DONN 5
Imagineless: Paradisal/ I. metal.
   THOMP F 14

imagining: Dances like Italy, i. red.
   SIMP 16
i. some fear, SHAK 127
imbecile: cripple and the i. SIMI 4
Imbitt'ring: I. all his state.
   HORA 6
Imbodies: I., and imbrutes, MILT 4
imbracements: i. sweet, MARL 5
imbroider: violet i.'d vale MILT 9
imbrutes: Imbodies, and i., MILT 4
imbued: In human gore i. POE 32
imitate: i. the action of the tiger:
   SHAK 56
i. the sun, SHAK 51
imitated: counterfiet/ Is poorly i.
   SHAK 205
imitation: Were endless i.
   WORD 76
immaculate: i. white bed WILLI 23
look, austere, i., WYLI 14
Immanuel: Our Lord, I. BROO P 8
immaterial: i. fire, STANL 1
immature: dangle of an i. paw,
   LAWR 20
immediate: hunger was a more i.
   sorrow; AUDE 22
immelodious: i. winds DRUM 4
immemorial: moan of doves in i.
   elms, TENN 107
immense: held/ Pike too i. to stir,
   HUGH T 12
i. and diaphanous shadows,
   WHITM 75
i. and lonely as a cloud. AIKE 7
immensity: belie/ Thy Soul's i.;
   WORD 77
immoderate: to the i. past,
   TATE A 12
immodest: modest than i.
   WHITM 73
immolation: i. so belied SASS 12
immoral: art thou i., HILT 3
immortal: heaven's i. store,
   DRAY 11
i. dead who live again
   ELIOT G 1
I. glories in my mind ADDI 1
i. hand or eye BLAK 81
I. in a picture THOMA E 10
i. light and heat! VAUG 3
i. sea/ Which brought us hither,
   WORD 82
i. Shakespear rose;
   JOHN S (1709–1784) 5
i. spirit grows WORD 96
i. with a kiss. — MARL 3
I. youth to mortal maids.
   LAND 5
in the flesh it is i. STEVENS 36
life i. from my verse. HERR 54
Married to i. verse, MILT 24
mind's i., WINT 11
more i. WHITM 59

pains the i. spirit must endure,
   ARNO 29
possessest an i. lot, ARNO 23
saints i. reign; WATT I 8
scrip of joy, i. diet, RALEG 10
Strong Son of God, i. Love,
   TENN 16
study of revenge, i. hate,
   MILT 51
subject for i. verse — DAY 13
survive in my i. song. DRAY 8
Warble i. Notes MILT 121
immortality: germ of i.! WILLA 2
instrument/ Of i., HALL 1
Nurslings of i.! SHEL 51
pledge/ Of i. MILT 68
immovable: i. critic twitching his
   skin MOOR M 32
immune: i. To catechism CULL 19
made themselves i. OWEN 33
Imp: I. at three and wench at
   'leben WALK 9
impairs: All weakness that i.,
   ARNO 29
impart: thy grace i. POPE A 128
Impartially: I. protective, WILB 31
impassable: fen/ appears i.,
   MOOR M 14
impassioned: i. in the littering
   leaves. STEVENS 58
impassive: Black and i. guns,
   WHITM 92
impasted: Baked and i. SHAK 30
Impatience: dull/ I. or a fierce
   velleity, WILB 26
fierce i. ends; BRON 10
impatient: i. as the wind
   WORD 142
Wait, with i. readiness, COWP 14
impediments: Admit i. SHAK 231
impelled: i. by stirrings HAYD 15
impels: i. All thinking things,
   WORD 36
impenetrable: highest Woods i.
   MILT 97
in i. sorrow, MUIR 6
imperceptibly: As i. as Grief
   DICKI 6
imperfect: i. is our paradise.
   STEVENS 40
i. is so hot in us, STEVENS 40
say not Man's i., POPE A 62
imperfection: No i. GINS 42
imperfectly: (At random and i.
   WORD 51
what they i. control GUNN 12
imperial: i. multiplicator BARK 2
i. palace whence he came.
   WORD 73
imperious: awe of thy i. wit
   CAREW 3

sacred i. CRAS 7
stars in secret i. comment;
    SHAK 187
infold: Gilded tombs do worms i.
    SHAK 119
in-folded: tongues of flame are i.
    ELIOT T 74
information: i. vegetable, animal,
    and mineral; GILB 35
least i. BARA 14
informed: guide i. him later,
    NASH 12
Informing: I. a correct compassion,
    KIRK 4
infused: such i. fetor, WHITM 98
Infusing: I. him with self and vain
    conceit, SHAK 89
infusion: that sticky i., KINN 4
ingender: i. windmills on a bitch.
    UNKN 194
ingenious: most i. paradox!
    GILB 36
ingle: i., bleezing finely, BURN 52
inglorious: mean/ Our object and i.,
    WORD 95
stoop/ I., MILT 64
Ingots: Of two gold I. MARL 9
ingrained: ancient stubbornness i.,
    WINT 6
Granite: i. SNYD 52
ingratitude: man's i. SHAK 13
sin of my i. SHAK 104
ingratitudes: great-sized monster of
    i. SHAK 173
ingrown: distortions of i. virginity.
    AUDE 68
inhabit: darkness I i. OHAR 10
eyes did once i. SHAK 97
inhaling: refresh'd, singing, i.
    WHITM 108
inherit: all which it i. SHAK 163
blood we i. RANDA D 4
by morning/ I. the earth.
    PLATH 67
i. heaven's graces SHAK 222
i. the throne of glory:
    BIBL, O.T. 8
Shall Life i. BUNY 3
we i. from the fortunate
    ELIOT T 69
inheritance: free and poor i.
    SHAP 28
lose a soul's i.? WILD 14
inheritances: were i. Delicate riders
    of the storm. CRAN H 41
inheritors: i. of unfulfilled renown
    SHEL 12
inherse: in my brain i., SHAK 217
inhospitable: i. shore; SHEL 68
inhuman: dress/ Of an i.
    murderess; MARV 14
inimitable: Preanimate, i., still,
    WINT 3

injoyment: Unsavoury in the i.
    MILT 6
injure: Tom will i. nothing.
    UNKN 263
injured: i. fan. MOOR M 11
its i. stone, HILL G 2
injury: done me no i., BLAK 56
hate's known i. SHAK 200
injustice: i. of the skies YEATS 33
ink: buried in the i. that writes.
    PLATO 3
Dipp'd me in i., POPE A 13
I. runs STRA 1
Soul lies buried in the i. that
    writes. CLARE 9
inky: my i. cloak, SHAK 21
inland: flow of the i. river, FINC 1
i. woods were pushed by winds,
    MILLA 12
Walled round with rocks as an i.
    island, SWIN 10
inlay: i. maggots like a jewel.
    SHAP 15
inmost: thir i. bower MILT 77
inn: chamber in the i. UNKN 314
Do you remember an I.?
    BELL 19
up to the old i.-door. NOYE 6
warmest welcome, at an i.
    SHEN 2
inner: brimming with i. light —
    MOOR M 28
i., weather. FROS 116
Temple's i. shrine, WORD 27
walking with an i. peace, ASHB 1
inning: one i. left to play. THAY 1
Innings: I. and afternoons. FITZ 2
Innisfree: go to I., YEATS 74
innocence: bowers of i. and ease,
    GOLD 1
ceremony of i. is drowned;
    YEATS 134
dead is all the i. of anger
    CHES 11
glides in modest I. away;
    JOHN S (1709–1784) 13
graceful i., MILT 90
i. and beauty born? YEATS 115
i. for i.; SHAK 178
I. is its own adorning.
    SPENC A 1
i. itself has many a wile,
    BYRO 21
i. of fear; BROO G 6
native health and i. TRAH 10
Never such i. again. LARK 18
no penance, much less i.
    DONN 16
puritie and place and i., MILT 77
Queens of Love and I.,
    CAREW 12
safety of her i.; JONS 22
Some final i. SPEND 22

soul recovers radical i.
    YEATS 113
What is our i., MOOR M 42
innocent: Art thou i., HILT 3
capacity for i. enjoyment
    GILB 37
i. and the beautiful YEATS 68
i. as now thou art. CORB 1
i. behind on a tree. AUDE 63
i. brightness of a new-born Day
    WORD 86
i. of passion, uncorrupt, MCKA 4
iron bars a cage;/ Minds i. and
    quiet LOVE 5
raising their i. hands. BLAK 91
shed my i. light, my Blood,
    SITW 13
things i., hapless, forsaken.
    ROET 41
Who is i.? SHAP 3
wild boys i. as strawberries
    THOMA D 26
innuendos: beauty of i.,
    STEVENS 65
innumerable: Amongst i. Stars,
    MILT 65
i. caravan that moves BRYA 24
i. choir of day BRID R 14
murmuring of i. bees.' TENN 107
spawn i., MILT 5
Innumerous: I. living creatures,
    MILT 86
inoculate: i. against a world
    WELC 3
Inoperancy: I. of the world of
    spirit; ELIOT T 21
inopportune: i. joke GILB 58
Inquire: I. for me in Baggot Street
    KAVA 16
inquired: "Compensate?" he i.
    LA FO 2
Inquisition: these I. dogs
    TENN 117
insane: acres of the i. green?
    TATE A 13
insatiate: i. hence-forward,
    WHITM 22
i. to pursue/ Vain war with
    Heav'n, MILT 58
inscribed: God has i. her doom;
    TIMR 2
inscrutable: child draws another i.
    house. BISH 47
dark/ I. workmanship WORD 96
i. he moved on ROBI 24
I. His ways are, CULL 19
i. infantry rising TATE A 12
insect: Beast, bird, fish, i.!
    POPE A 72
i. Looks farcically human;
    GRAV 1
insensible: stones and trees, i. of
    time, BRAD 4

insert: i. her into water like a
   needle   DICKEY 12
inside: all wormy i.,   LAWR 15
   burns the thing/ i. it.   BARA 2
   Candor and secrecy i.   GUNN 5
   come from the earth's i.   LORD 3
   fur side i.,   STRON 1
   fused to the i. of a helmet;
     KINN 11
   i. skin side outside;   STRON 1
   i. someone/ who hates me.
     BARA 1
   i. the crackers' —   GILB 13
   it was dusk outside,/ I. it was
     dark.   FROS 15
   My outside Woman, and your i.
     Man.   COWL 6
   rather tough worm in your little
     i.?"   GILB 29
   warm side i.,   STRON 1
insidious: Shuddering i. shock
   MACN 1
insights: his shuddering i.,   BISH 38
insinuations: flatterers' venomous
   i.,   SIDN 4
insolence: above/ i. and triviality
   MOOR M 33
insolent: i. old lechers   HORA 2
inspection: present/ for i.,
   MOOR M 33
inspector: i., visitor,   SPEND 4
inspiration: little throat labours
   with i.,   BLAK 37
   rapture of an i.   HOPKINS 26
inspire: i. the whole;   COLL 12
   sacred instinct did i.   TRAH 7
inspired: i. with Stella's kiss.
   SIDN 23
Inspiring: I. bold John Barleycorn!
   BURN 55
instance: i. of the love of God
   SMAR 7
instancy: majestic i.,   THOMP F 7
instant: At a wavering i.   LAWR 2
   smiling i. when her soul,
     WILB 35
instantly: gluttonous death, will i.
   unjoynt   DONN 58
instead: they died i.   CUMM 29
instinct: natural i. to discern
   WORD 4
   sacred i. did inspire   TRAH 7
   some/ By fatal i. fly;
     THOMS J (1700–1748) 9
instinctive: woman's glance i.
   thrown: MELV 6
institution: 'tis His i.   DICKI 122
institutions: walls of i.,   ROET 8
Instruct: I. Your son,   KUNI 4
instructed: Greatly i.   MILT 105
instructional: write the i. manual
   ASHB 1

instructive: wondrous and i. light,
   TRAH 2
instrument: i. for the children
   SMAR 5
   life subdued to its i.;   HUGH T 11
   like a cunning i.   SHAK 86
instruments: Birdes, voyces, i.,
   windes, waters, all agree.
     SPENS 32
   find fit i. of ill!   POPE A 123
   Keen i.,   CRAN H 18
insubstantial: this i. pageant faded,
   SHAK 163
insufferable: clever servant, i.
   master.   JEFFE 39
Insufferably: blaze/ I. bright.
   MILT 97
insulin: concrete void of i.   GINS 15
insult: "That is an i. to us."
   YEATS 49
insults: i. the victim whom he kills
   CRAB 8
insured: were heavily i.   GILB 10
intact: There lies i.   HARD 48
integument: thick i. of snow.
   THOR 11
intellect: discerning i. of Man,
   WORD 16
   i. of man   YEATS 23
   Monuments of unaging i.
     YEATS 125
   weakness of i.,   GILB 29
intellectual: draughts of i. day,
   CRAS 3
   haughty i. look   KAVA 8
   I. disgrace/ Stares   AUDE 44
   i. hatred is the worst,   YEATS 112
   lords of ladies i.,   BYRO 20
   one i. breeze,   COLE SAM 12
   our i. chickens   GILB 54
   over i. deeps   MERE G 9
   snip the i. golden threads
     GINS 12
   what an i. war   BYRO 35
intelligence: Created out of pure i.
   WORD 106
Intelligences: I. at a leap;
   MERE G 15
   i., they the sphere.   DONN 21
intelligent: i., the witty, the brave.
   MILLA 6
   It's so elegant/ So i.   ELIOT T 125
intended: damp my i. wing
   MILT 88
intense: hate of tyranny i.,
   WHITT 10
   so lovely and i.,   MASE 9
   starved, i.,   RICH 6
intensity: full of passionate i.
   YEATS 134
   grave, awed i.   SNYD 11
intent: filled with the i.   BISH 31
   first avow'd i.,   BUNY 2

His uncontroulable i.,   MILT 118
on love i.;   YEATS 39
stronger guilt defeats my strong
   i.,   SHAK 34
To prick the sides of my i.,
   SHAK 105
tried i. Of such a truth   WYAT 7
truth that's told with bad i.
   BLAK 5
with knowledge or i.,   DODG 2
intention: Curling with metaphors a
   plain i.,   HERB G 40
intents: all i. a corpse   CUMM 15
inter: wood-nymphs my cold corpse
   i.,   HERR 53
interchange: i. of state,   SHAK 211
   unremitting i.   SHEL 41
intercourse: i. of times divide,
   VAUG 7
   Sexual i. began   LARK 1
interest: God! but the i.!   DUNB P 5
   i. Unborrowed from the eye. —
     WORD 33
   wreaths of Fame and I.   MARV 4
interested: i. in poetry.
   MOOR M 34
   i. to hear about it.   WILLI 18
interests: i. of a black man
   CRAN H 3
interfered: he never i.   AUDE 94
interfused: more deeply i.,
   WORD 35
interminable: gravel-crunching, i.
   departure   MAHON 2
interminably: wave, i. flowing.
   STEVENS 37
interpolate: then i. them,   NASH 20
interposed: i. a Fly —   DICKI 49
interr'd: i. her Infant-birth,
   HERB CH 3
interred: good is oft i. with their
   bones.   SHAK 48
   have so often been i.   BETJ 6
   I. beneath this marble stone
     PRIO 3
interrupted: hungry to be i.
   SMIT ST 9
   i. by a knife,   BYRO 53
interstice: glimpse through an i.
   WHITM 33
interview: first strange and fatal i.,
   DONN 46
interviewed: i. by *Mademoiselle*.
   SIMP 9
intestines: shake out the i.   LEVI 2
intimate: Both i. and
   unidentifiable.   ELIOT T 65
   i. as love,   CAMPB R 8
   tribal, i. revenge.   HEAN 17
intire: Free from Corruption, or i.,
   or clear,   DRYD 18
   uncorrupt, sufficient, clear, i.,
   DRYD 18

intolerably: i. nameless names?
   SASS 12

intoxicate: shallow draughts i. the brain, POPE A 33

intoxicated: writers stagger i. BROD 2

intrails: Hells Spider gets/ His i. spun TAYL E 11

intranc't: Psyche sweet i. MILT 12

intransigence: envy the i. MACN 3

Intrest: above I. or lust PRIO 5

intrinsic: Metal, i. value, WINT 3

introspective: i. as a leper, RUKE 3

intrude: crawling shape i.! POE 31

intuition: thought styled i., RICH 22

Inundations: Diseases, Battels, I. BUTL 8

inutterable: all prodigious things,/ Abominable, i., MILT 61

invalid: chronic i., — RICH 20

invelop: This World i., PHILL 2

invent: Beats all the Lies you can i. BLAK 5
  i. a lot of figures of speech
  NASH 20
  To remember or i. FROS 51

invention: "Faith" is a fine i. DICKI 21
  quaint words and trim i.;
  HERB G 40
  scaled i. or true artistry,
  POUN 21

inventive: i. Europe, AUDE 87

inventor: i. of the game EMER 20

inviolable: clutching the i. shade, ARNO 28
  with i. voice ELIOT T 122

inviolate: keep my heart i. MCKA 11

invisible: i. and free: AUDE 53
  i. or dimly seen MILT 81
  i. rain did ever sing SHEL 77
  live with an i. limp, BLY 2
  throne/ Of the I.! BYRO 4

Invite: I. the ladies toward the mistletoe TATE A 6
  wise expect, the sorrowful i.,
  DAVE 1

invited: only casually i., OHAR 7

invites: i. the occult mind, SHAP 4

inviting: wooden beams were so i. KOCH 5

involv'd: i. the sky, COWP 1

involved: blackbird is i. STEVENS 66
  night/ I. and swallowed up the vision; SHEL 16

involvedness: complex, manifold i. LAWR 55

inward: defilement to the i. parts, MILT 4
  expressions be of i. evils. GREV 5

---

high endeavors are an i. light
  WORD 4

i. eyes illuminated MILT 116

i. Light, a way as good, BUTL 8

roof with i. happiness, CAREW 19

thine i. love of heart. SHAK 203

want of i. touch, SIDN 10

war that was/ not i.; MOOR M 15

Io: Why should I mention I.? HOUS 9

ioy: plentye, i., and peace, UNKN 63

ire: just object of his i.." MILT 102

Ireland: ancient I. knew it all. YEATS 155
  ancient I. sweeping/ In again
  KAVA 7
  Mad I. hurt you AUDE 40

Ireland's: Romantic I. dead YEATS 137

iren: if gold ruste, what shal i. do? CHAU 13
  redy with his i. hoot, CHAU 64

Ireson: Old Floyd I., WHITT 23

Ireson's: I., out from Marblehead! WHITT 23

iridescent: small i. flies crawling on them. BISH 3

iris: In the spring a livelier i. TENN 69
  seems the color/ of i., LOWE R 57

Irish: bleached by I. weather MOOR M 37
  candles of the I. poor; MACN 14
  grow on I. ground! UNKN 299
  I'm I. MOOR M 38
  I. say your trouble is their/ trouble MOOR M 38
  Let the I. vessel lie AUDE 43
  mangy as the I. Seas, UNKN 194
  seldom have mothers/ in I.
  stories, MOOR M 36

Irishry: indomitable I. YEATS 158

irk'd: all that i. her ROSS C 21

iron: fleets of i. have fled, FINC 1
  Fling off their i. VAN DO 1
  heart of i., MOOR M 15
  I. are our lives ROSE 1
  i. bars a cage;/ Minds innocent and quiet LOVE 5
  i. door of the north KUNI 1
  i. gates of life. MARV 35
  I.-hearted man-slaying Achilles
  AUDE 83
  i. is i. till it is rust. MOOR M 15
  i. tears down Pluto's cheek,
  MILT 17
  i. to heat,/ writing, RICH 15
  i. will/ That clutched
  THOMP W 3
  lasts like i. HOLM 6

---

like adamant draw mine i. heart. DONN 60

mouth's/ shooting i. REED I 4

Old i., old bones, old rags, YEATS 29

rust Life's i. chain WILD 4

strong as i. bands. LONG 48

swift i. burning bee ROSE 5

Treed with i. and birdless. HUGH T 3

ironic: Death's i. scraping. STEVENS 38

ironical: bright i. names HAYD 10

Irreconcileable: Warr/ I., MILT 52

Irregular: I. verbs to learn, AUDE 17

irresistible: yielding to the i. joy, SHEL 16

irresponsive: i. silence of the land, ROSS C 24
  i. sounding of the sea, ROSS C 24

irretrievable: These so, these i. WHITM 92

irriguous: some i. valley MILT 69

irritating: I've an i. chuckle, GILB 9

Isabel: I., didn't worry,/ I. didn't scream NASH 1
  Luke shall leave us, I.; WORD 53

Isar: By the I., in the twilight LAWR 33
  men mowing down by the I.; LAWR 59

Iser: dark as winter was the flow/ Of I., CAMPB T 3

Isis: I bedded/ down with I., Lady of the Boogaloo, REED I 3

island: i. sixteen miles long, WHITM 43
  "Our i. home TENN 83
  some secreted I., WORD 112
  This i.'s mine, SHAK 157
  Walled round with rocks as an inland i., SWIN 10
  whiter I., HERR 73

islands: dream of i. AUDE 23
  granite/ quarries on the i. LOWE R 56
  i. large and small; WHITM 19
  Parrot i. anchored lie, STEVENSO R 19
  realms and i. SHAK 7
  wind betwixt green i.; WHITM 13

isle: all the qualities o' th' i., SHAK 157
  balmy i. of Rum-ti-Foo, GILB 1
  legendary i. Where sirens sang DAY 7
  Many a green i. SHEL 35
  Nearing again the legendary i. DAY 7
  our western i., BLAK 108

J

royal throne of kings, this
　sceptered i., SHAK 88
isles: her palm-crowned i., TIMR 2
　i. of Greece! BYRO 40
　i. Of Javan or Gadier MILT 110
　On the Gulliby I. CARRY 11
Islington: That lived in I.
　UNKN 15
isms: whole bale of i. LOWE J 4
isolate: i., slow faults/ That kill,
　PLATH 44
isolated: Character i. by a deed
　YEATS 28
Israel: daughters of I., weep over
　Saul, BIBL, O.T. 69
　I.'s tents do shine so bright.
　BLAK 39
　Let I. hope in the Lord,
　BIBL, O.T. 61
　redeem I. BIBL, O.T. 61
Israfel: As the angel I., POE 26
issue: this aboundant i. SHAK 224
isthmus: i. of a middle state,
　POPE A 78
Itali-an: perhaps I.! GILB 20
Italy: Dances like I., imagining red.
　SIMP 16
　footpaths for the thought of I.!
　LONG 20
itch: lungs hath caught the i.,
　UNKN 194
　where'er she did i.: SHAK 159
iterated: i. jingle ROSS C 13
Ithaca: lands to him were I.:
　GRAV 38
itself: abase i. to you, WHITM 77
　filament, out of i., WHITM 55
　life i. not weak. ROSS C 25
　maple burn i. away; TENN 42
　Vaulting ambition, which o'erleaps
　i. SHAK 105
ivory: beautiful yellow-white i.,
　WHITM 72
　black i., black seed. HAYD 9
　four-honed-down i. toes LEVI 1
　In vials of i. and coloured glass
　ELIOT T 121
　i. box is broken, MILLA 19
　light wing against the i. gate,
　MORR 3
　o'er thy naked polished i.
　CAREW 12
　ornaments of i., BONT 8
ivy: boar trampled down in i. time.
　GRAV 35
　heart's i., Patience HOPKINS 16
　holly and the i. UNKN 129
　our close i. twines, CAREW 12
　yellow bees in the i.-bloom,
　SHEL 51

jabber: j. among the trees.
　SASS 14
Jabberwock: "Beware the J.,
　CARRO 35
jabs: j. her wedge-head
　LOWE R 41
Jack: gup, J. of the Vale! SKEL 4
　"High-low J. and the game.'
　UNKN 103
　J. and Jill MOTH 17
　J., eating rotten cheese, FRANK 1
　j.-muh-lanterns beckoning
　HAYD 19
　Lie Saunt'ring J. and Idle Joan.
　PRIO 3
　Little J. Horner MOTH 20
　Naughty Paughty J.-a-Dandy,
　CAREY 1
　wild J. for a lover; YEATS 38
Jacke: J. Straw and his meinie
　CHAU 81
jacket: one was put in a j., JUST 2
Jacky: sings of J. Horner, CAREY 3
Jacob: traffic of J.'s ladder
　THOMP F 11
jade: his muse a j. SWIF 26
　j. cockroaches, MOOR M 9
jags: j. from the clotted shoulder,
　JEFFE 13
jaguar: sleek Brazilian j.
　ELIOT T 160
Jail: care of/ The Barbourville J.
　UNKN 81
　go to J. WALK 14
　patron, and the j.
　JOHN S (1709–1784) 18
　tossed in j. on a vagrancy rap,
　SNYD 25
jailer: In prison they accompany the
　j., SIMI 2
　made my j. SHAK 86
jails: sealed in doorless j. HECH 12
jalous: sely j. housbonde to bigile,
　CHAU 53
jam: j. and judicious advice —
　CARRO 19
jamcloset: top of/ the j. WILLI 2
James: Jack Cade, John Brown,
　Jesse J., SAND 13
　outlaws Frank and Jesse J.
　UNKN 149
Jamie: Young J. lo'ed me weel,
　LIND L 1
jan: Jelly flower j.; UNKN 286
Jane: J.,/ Tall as a crane, SITW 4
　Queen J. was in labor UNKN 75
Janet: J. implored us, 'Wake her
　from her sleep!' RANS 21
Janizaries: conclusions with those
　J., BYRO 35

Jankin: Knew I jolly J. UNKN 157
January: deep J. STEVENS 27
　June in her eyes, in her heart J.
　CAREW 15
Janus: Like J. bears a double Face;
　SWIF 20
Japanese: / /moon / Of J. /paper,
　PLATH 49
jar: Chinese j. still/ Moves
　perpetually ELIOT T 23
　folks in the front that I j.
　EUWE 1
　frail china j. POPE A 117
　j. in Tennessee, STEVENS 1
　with sighs they j. Their watches
　SHAK 93
jars: j. two hemispheres. HARD 16
jassamine: with the j. sweet,
　LIND V 12
Javan: isles/ Of J. or Gadier
　MILT 110
javelin: pressing wind shoots j.-like
　MERE G 11
jaw: atlas-eater with a j. for news,
　THOMA D 6
　Develops the j., NASH 4
　loosened and let down this brutal
　j.? MARK 6
　smitten with a hatchet's j.;
　HOUS 10
　towel my shaven j. KINS 5
　wolves black j., JONS 21
　zebra stripes along his j.
　ELIOT T 111
jaws: crush these lions' j.!
　BIBL, O.T. 42
　fierce tiger's j., SHAK 189
　in what j. you were to suppurate:
　LARK 17
　j.' hooked clamp and fangs
　HUGH T 11
　wet his frothy j. STEVENS 13
jazz: cool j. nor devoured Egyptian
　heroes, OHAR 10
　J. June. BROO G 20
jazzmen: Go to it, O j. SAND 11
Jealous: J., do you think? WILLI 17
　j. of all living forms PRAT 1
　not easily j., SHAK 138
　question with my j. thought
　SHAK 208
　thou' Art J., Lord, DONN 31
jealousies: Doubled sighs and j.
　GRAV 32
　hard words, j., and fears, BUTL 1
jealousy: Away at once with love or
　j.! SHAK 136
　beware, my lord, of j.! SHAK 134
　defend/ From j.! SHAK 135
　J. a Human Face; BLAK 59
　J. itself doth sleep; SIDN 29
　life of j., SHAK 136

Jeered: J. at by crooked children, MILLA 34

jeers: cheers and the j. BELL 19

Jefferson: volatile friend Mr. J., POUN 12

Jehovah: did they to J. cry BIBL, O.T. 57

  J., Jove, or Lord! POPE A 126

  that men would J. prayse BIBL, O.T. 55

Jelly: J. flower jan; UNKN 286

  stupid and abiding j. DE VR 1

  this little J. HERR 38

jellyfish: j. and a saurian, CARRU 1

jelofer: j. well set, SKEL 1

Jenny: J. kissed me. HUNT 5

Jeoffry: consider my Cat J. SMAR 2

jeopardy: Jewel of j. SURR 2

Jerico: Joshua fit de battle ob J., UNKN 158

jerk: pistons j. and shove, ROET 51

jerrybuilt: for j. things WILB 21

Jerusalem: If I forget thee, O J., BIBL, O.T. 63

  J. Athens Alexandria ELIOT T 148

  was J. builded here, BLAK 34

Jesse: laid poor J. in his grave. UNKN 148

  outlaws Frank and J. James. UNKN 149

jest: drinking and oath and smutty j., WHITM 33

  duller than a witling's j. PATM 2

  eye, love's firmament;/ Many a j. HERR 7

  glory, j., and riddle of the world! POPE A 78

  J. and youthful jollity, MILT 20

  Life is a j.; GAY 6

  lost his labor, I my j.; BYRO 76

  that's no j. RALEG 16

jests: j. are coarse, POPE A 20

  j. that you crack GILB 59

  like j. of kindness HAYD 10

Jesus: Christ J., it is he, LUTH 3

  dove of J. LOWE R 61

  face/ Would put out J.', DICKI 35

  fished/ A dime for J. ROBI 21

  For J. Christ his sake.' UNKN 77

  For J. Christ, our Saviour, CRAI 1

  grave of J., STEVENS 61

  him squealing bloody J. HAYD 14

  J. came to town; REES 1

  J. choking in the air, LOWE R 22

  J., look with pitying eye. DOAN 2

  J. of the twice-turned cheek CULL 9

  J. on the rood; CARRU 2

  J. our brother, UNKN 106

J. temperately reply'd: MILT 109

  Little J., wast Thou shy THOMP F 4

  who will sing J. down HAYD 13

Jet: living walls of J. DONN 25

  Out-during marble, brass, or j., HERR 37

  you'll find in j., SWIF 12

Jew: doen him to the J.'s castell, UNKN 132

  heathen, Turk, or J. BLAK 89

  J. who died in exile. AUDE 25

  sadly like the abstract J. WARR 4

  Through the J.'s window UNKN 132

  Throw down the ball, ye J.'s daughter. UNKN 133

jewel: Death! the j. of the just, VAUG 27

  inlay maggots like a j. SHAP 15

  j. cold and pure; MILLA 5

  J. of jeopardy SURR 2

  take my word for j. LORD 3

  Time's best j. SHAK 212

jeweled: j. prize/ always/ at our finger tips. WILLI 22

  powdered hair and j. fan, LOWE A 5

jewelled: heaven's j. crown MCCRE 1

jewelry: deal in fake j. AUDE 49

jewels: Bright j. of the mine? HEMA 5

  Inestimable stones, unvalued j., SHAK 97

  J. being lost are found MARL 7

  J. more rich than Ormus MARV 1

Jewish: spit upon my J. gaberdine, SHAK 118

Jews: Denmark's sanctuaried J.! MOOR M 3

  savages, expendable as J.? WALC 2

  Which J. might kiss, POPE A 115

Jill: Jack and J. MOTH 17

  make sure of his J.! GILB 62

Jim: run my chance with J., HAY 4

Jimmy: J. Bludso HAY 3

  your dashin J.? UNKN 150

jingle: hear the harness j. HOUS 36

  iterated j. ROSS C 13

jingles: Learn your j. CAREY 2

Jinny: upon J. the Just PRIO 5

Joan: J. whom Englishmen VILL 3

  Lie Saunt'ring Jack and Idle J. PRIO 3

job: difficultest j. a man DAVID 7

  down to the j. GINS 6

Jobillies: J./ and the Garyulies, FOOT 1

jobs: j., the dollars. SNOD 5

Jock: Wi' J. of Hazeldean. SCOT WA 6

jocund: j. rebecks MILT 22

Joe: filled J.'s barroom DARC 1

Jog: J. on, J. on, the footpath way, SHAK 180

John: Great Sir J., JOHN S (1709–1784) 10

  J. Anderson my jo, BURN 35

  J. Henry was a little fellow, UNKN 152

  leaning on the j. door OHAR 6

  notable prince that was called King J.; UNKN 159

  peak/ Like J.-a-dreams, SHAK 31

  St. J. mingles with my friendly bowl POPE A 92

Johnnie: J. Crack and Flossie Snail THOMA D 42

Johnny: Did J. look flashy? WAGO 1

  Frankie and J. were lovers, UNKN 101

  handsome, winsome J. UNKN 140

  J., I hardly knew ye! UNKN 156

Johnson: Kick at the rock, Sam J., WILB 14

Johnston: J. pressed at the front, TICK 2

join: Gone to j. the shadows, LIND V 5

  hearts of truest metal/ Absence doth j., HOSK 1

  j. all ye creatures to extol MILT 81

  j. th' angelic train. WHEA 1

  j. the Army GINS 6

  j. the shadows LIND V 7

  J. voices all ye living souls, MILT 82

  Laughter and grief j. hands. SHAP 20

  must ever j.; POPE A 35

  summons comes to j. BRYA 24

join'd: so equally j. DRYD 6

joined: band of brothers j., HOPKINSO 2

  she j. the former two. DRYD 10

  their murmurs j., COLL 9

joins: One j. the movement GUNN 13

joint: j. force and full result of all. POPE A 35

  seal j. constancy, DONN 47

  tear thee j. by j. MILT 112

joists: j./ are shaky by nature, DUGA 1

joke: form of practical j.? GINS 3

  inopportune j. GILB 58

jokes: no more j. in Music-halls SASS 5

  understand my j.? LOWE R 15

jollity: Jest and youthful j.,
  MILT 20
jolly: chubby and plump, a right j.
  old elf, MOOR C 4
  I wish I thought What J. Fun!
  RALEI 1
  j. cuckoos sing LYLY 4
  j. good ale and old!
  STEVENSO W 2
  Knew I j. Jankin UNKN 157
jolts: j. of light; SNYD 4
joly: j. lovere Absolon, CHAU 51
  Stibourne and strong and j. as a
  pie: CHAU 87
jolynesse: somme seyde, j.;
  CHAU 109
Jonnë: faire Westmerland,/ J.
  Armestrong men did him call,
  UNKN 153
Jonson: Here lies J. HERR 60
Joris: and J. and he;
  BROWNI R 35
Joseph: J. and his mother ABRA 2
  J., Crazy Horse, SNYD 24
Joshua: J. fit de battle ob Jerico,
  UNKN 158
jostled: Too j. were Our Souls to
  speak DICKI 99
jot: one j. of former love retain.
  DRAY 15
journey: day's j. ROSS C 28
  farewell j. to the Promised Land.
  UNKN 55
  goal of his j. VAN DY 4
  j. had advanced; DICKI 115
  j. in my head SHAK 193
  j. is shorter to heaven.
  UNKN 192
  life's j. just begun? COWP 10
  like a mole I j. DAVID 6
  long j. towards oblivion.
  LAWR 35
  Methinks it is no j. UNKN 265
  worst time of the year/ For a j.,
  ELIOT T 49
journeys: for j. undertaken
  WALK 11
Jove: Jehovah, J., or Lord!
  POPE A 126
  J., nodding, SWIF 4
  J. with Hermes came; OVID 4
  J.'s nectar JONS 31
jowled: seeps from heavily j.
  MACN 11
joy: Albion's j., Hibernia's pride.
  CAREY 2
  apprehend some j., SHAK 127
  be kept with J. SWIF 17
  binds to himself a j. BLAK 47
  bless'd kingdoms meek of j. and
  love. MILT 32
  breathed j. and woe
  BROWNI R 48

carol of j. or glee, DUNB F 10
countervail the exchange of j.
  SHAK 147
days were a j., HARD 3
death parts both woe and j.:
  SIDN 33
end of j. and all prosperity
  HAWE 1
Expiates the j. and woe SHEL 82
feels nor j. nor grief,
  BROWNI R 18
float this carol with j.,
  WHITM 51
foil thy foes with j., SOUTHW 3
For promis'd j.! BURN 63
formed of J. and Mirth, BLAK 22
From j. I part, SIDN 33
Full of j.; BLAK 106
full of j. and of solace CHAU 67
gallop for what must be j.,
  LARK 3
I leap for j., pursue my way,
  WESL C 2
increase of enduring j.
  WORD 104
its own strange j., DICKEY 25
j. and blindness he shall know,
  GREN 3
j. and frail prosperity, MORE 1
j. and grief JOYC 1
j. and natural content/ Out
  YEATS 57
j. and peace, BROWNI R 80
j./ And rapture so oft beheld?
  MILT 97
j. and strength and courage
  TREN 2
j. apart from thee, EMER 24
J. comes, grief goes, LOWE J 18
j. create for others RANDA D 5
J. is my name. BLAK 93
J. may you have SPENS 43
j., nor love, nor light, ARNO 3
j. of the working, KIPL 29
j. proposed; SHAK 236
J., shipmate, J.! WHITM 41
J. shivers in the corner ROBI 48
j., to solely seek BROWNI R 72
j. to thee, O death, WHITM 51
j. was never sure; SWIN 14
J.'s cheerful madness MARV 12
j.'s soul lies in the doing.
  SHAK 169
kisses the j. as it flies BLAK 47
know you, terrible j. LEVE 17
latter end of j. is woe. CHAU 68
lean in j. upon our father's knee;
  BLAK 99
Life, J., Empire and Victory.
  SHEL 58
Light, j., and leisure; HERB G 39
like lambs we j., BLAK 99
Looks back with J. SWIF 20

Love and j. UNKN 117
love, hatred, j. or fear, PRIO 4
Love is a calmer, gentler j.:
  SACK 1
mannes j. and all his bliss."
  CHAU 76
my j. and heart's delight.
  WEVE 2
My j., my grief, my hope, my
  love, WALL 5
never want j. BLAK 87
no j. but lacks salt FROS 113
no j. in Mudville — Mighty Casey
  has struck out. THAY 4
Nor j. nor passion ROBI 6
not a j. the world can give
  BYRO 65
O songs of j.! WHITM 66
of j. quite bare, WYAT 13
Part and parcel of her j., —
  WHITT 7
power of j., WORD 31
praise, pomp, glory, j. BOLT 1
pure a thing is j. MOOR M 43
read with j., then shut the book.
  PATM 2
Reap in j. the fruit BLAK 30
redolent of j. and youth,
  GRAY 14
reflects in j. its scanty gleam
  LOWE J 16
rife with the j. of life, SMIT L 1
sadness of j. KINN 8
screamed with j., GINS 11
scrip of j., immortal diet,
  RALEG 10
sharing mother's j. SNYD 4
short-haired j. and roughness —
  SNYD 16
shouted for j.? BIBL, O.T. 14
snatch a fearful j. GRAY 15
so cramful of cosy j., SERV 9
some bringer of that j.;
  SHAK 127
some j. from with'ring life
  JOHN S (1709–1784) 14
some j. not to be known LEVE 2
Surprised by j. WORD 142
Sweet j. befall thee! BLAK 93
thing of beauty is a j. for ever:
  KEAT 4
thou couldst know thy j.,
  WHITT 9
tidings of comfort and j.! CRAI 1
'tis little j. HOOD 5
too much j. GRAV 3
twins are to be born,/ Youth and
  J.; MILT 12
voice of one that jumps for j.
  HOUS 10
wager in their j. GILB 42
We wear a face of j., WORD 20
Wi' j. unfeigned BURN 18

you blueness of j., SHAP 5
your/ j. their j.? MOOR M 38
joye: O farewell griefe, and welcome
  j., UNKN 17
joyful: hills be j. BIBL, O.T. 47
in my j. school-days, LAMB 2
j. noise unto the Lord,
  BIBL, O.T. 48
j. world salutes the rising day.
  COWL 4
sound of cornet make a j. noise
  before the Lord, BIBL, O.T. 46
joyless: loveless, j., unendeared,
  MILT 78
joyous: All j. and unthinking,
  BURN 6
j. health! WORD 149
j. hearts! enfired with holy flame!
  TAYL E 4
j. leaves of dark green,
  WHITM 39
shares again the j. feast.
  FRENE 1
so j. and bright, GILB 56
utter j. leaves WHITM 39
joy's: j. the voice CUMM 8
joys: All our j. Are but toys,
  CAMPI 30
attend love's j. in vain. CAMPI 21
binding with briars my j.
  BLAK 65
Celia, let us reap our j.
  CAREW 10
chanter of pains and j.,
  WHITM 63
homely j., and destiny obscure;
  GRAY 8
increasing,/ Hourly j. SHAK 161
J. as wingèd dreams fly fast,
  FLET/OTHE 1
J. seldom yet attained HARD 47
j. which with his day-star rise
  VAUG 23
love still breed,/ Had j. no date,
  RALEG 9
Microbes have their j., OWEN 3
minds me o' departed j.,
  BURN 15
pale dispensers of my J.
  HOPE L 2
pride did not our j. control,
  STIR 1
renew'd the j. COWP 12
Secret j. and secret smiles,
  BLAK 50
silent days/ In harmless j. are
  spent, CAMPI 13
such were the j. BLAK 90
summer hath his j. CAMPI 18
ways/ Of winter is. WHITT 28
We made our j., PATM 4
what j. were thine! WHITM 105

When first my lines of heavenly j.
  made mention, HERB G 40
Juan: carpe diem, J., BYRO 34
juba: Night is j., HAYD 18
Judas: J. to a tittle, BROWNI R 25
judge: half a j.'s task, POPE A 36
he cometh to j. the earth;
  BIBL, O.T. 47
indifferent j. between the high and
  low; SIDN 14
j. all beauty vain; UNKN 74
J. looked back WHITT 17
j. of authors' names, not works,
  POPE A 31
J. tenderly of me! DICKI 146
j. the ends of the earth;
  BIBL, O.T. 8
j. womans thoughts by tears,
  DONN 61
J.'s bride might be! WHITT 16
perfect J. will read each work of
  Wit POPE A 34
preacher, j., and poet, JEFFR 1
Sole j. of truth, POPE A 78
to j. the world, MARK 8
judged: j. me by their appropriate
  tool. FROS 124
they j. without skill GOLD 4
judgement: better j. making.
  SHAK 220
j. that I heard: ROSS C 27
sent to do j. on him! SOUTHE 3
judgements: fed with j., COWP 16
judging: in j. ill; POPE A 21
judgment: advance a j. of their
  own, POPE A 30
Cozening j. with a measure,
  JONS 9
destined unto j., JONS 33
in j. old, SHAK 119
Last J.'s fire BROWNI R 22
Mark tardy j. CRAN H 3
place of j. MILT 102
thought it was the J.-day
  HARD 13
till the J. day. LIND V 7
wait till j. break DICKI 3
Waiting the J. Day: FINC 2
wit and j. POPE A 26
without passing through the j.,
  POPE A 30
judgments: j. warp us BYRO 48
with our j. as our watches,
  POPE A 22
judicious: jam and j. advice —
  CARRO 19
jug: "Cuckoo, j.-j., NASHE 3
He set the j. down ROBI 45
J. j. j. j. j. j. ELIOT T 132
"J. J." to dirty ears. ELIOT T 122
J. of Wine, OMAR 2
j. without a handle, — LEAR 4
juggement: oure owene j. CHAU 91

juggler: j. is tired WILB 20
juice: glass of papaya j. OHAR 14
runnel of j. RANS 1
Seas of bright j. WHITM 76
juicy: j. autumnal fruit WHITM 29
juju-man: ostrich, and a j.,
  TOOM 2
Julia: in silks my J. goes, HERR 61
Juliana: J. came, MARV 27
Julius: mightiest J. fell, SHAK 20
July: April, May, of June and J.-
  flowers; HERR 1
didn't get back till the Fourth of
  J. UNKN 135
J. in her eyes hath place,
  UNKN 6
Jumblies: lands where the J. live;
  LEAR 9
jump: j. and run WILLI 18
j. into my bed. STEVENSO R 13
ragged papooses j., KLEI 3
see him j. before me,
  STEVENSO R 13
jumped: j. off the roof! GINS 19
j. so high UNKN 135
j. without a chute DICKEY 10
Jumpers: Holy Rollers and J.
  HILL J 3
jumping: j. and falling back,
  LOWE R 47
jumps: blood j. in the sun;
  THOMA D 31
Stiff springy j. SNYD 37
voice of one that j. for joy.
  HOUS 10
junction: daily close of their j.,
  WHITM 76
June: April, May, of J. and Jùly-
  flowers; HERR 1
clouds of J., JACK 1
flowers of J. JACK 1
flowers of J., JACK 2
Jazz J. BROO G 20
J. in her eyes, in her heart
  January. CAREW 15
livelong J. DICKI 83
newly sprung in J.; BURN 45
rare as a day in J.? LOWE J 17
Junes: three hot J. SHAK 227
jungle: dying for a j. fruit. BONT 8
J. star or J. track, CULL 5
jungleberry: can of j. tea. CARRY 6
juniper: /sat under a j.-tree
  ELIOT T 6
junk: For j. and gimcrack,
  WILB 21
j. that goes with being human
  SNYD 49
junket: j. of cream DE LA 5
Juno: J. sings her blessings
  SHAK 161
Wedding is great J.'s crown,
  SHAK 16

Richmond and K. Undid me.
ELIOT T 139

key: k. is in my pocket, AIKE 8
k. is in the bars, GINS 32
k. is in the window, GINS 32
k. is lying — WILLI 23
k. is turned/ On our uncertainty;
YEATS 98
k. of softness WHITM 42
K. of the Kingdom: UNKN 242
listening at the k.-hole GILB 45
Lock'd me up with a golden K.
BLAK 19
out of k. with his time, POUN 36
someone else slips/ The k.
JARR 12
turns the k. to the poor.
SHAK 73
with them the k., WHITM 68
keyboard: along the k. OHAR 6
keyes: I have the k.: HERB G 60
keyhole: thousand mushrooms
crowd to a k. MAHON 1
keys: Give me the k. BROWNI R 5
half that's got my k.."
GRAHAM H 2
k. betraying HERR 7
Kharma: pray for K. REED H 2
kick: fullfed beast shall k.
ELIOT T 66
I'll k. you downstairs!" CARRO 7
K. at the rock, Sam Johnson,
WILB 14
kicked: every pigmy k. it SHEL 80
k. by boys and men, CLARE 2
Kicking: K. and rolling about
WILLI 12
K. his mother AUDE 58
K. Horse fills up. HUGO 3
kid: Christmas/ is K. Stuff . . .
HORN 1
do you love me, k.? SAND 22
Loup Garou K. REED I 5
spindly k., ROET 26
kidlings: k. blithe and merry.
GAY 1
kidneys: cylinders out of my k.,
UNKN 82
kids: k., frisk with your dog,
CRAN H 47
k. go to the movies! OHAR 2
k. grow up SNYD 41
Kikuyu: K., quick as flies, WALC 1
Kilda: On utmost K.'s shore,
THOMS J (1700–1748) 8
kill: Can k. a tiger. LOWE R 34
except the penalties, k. a man
JEFFE 15
Forever bent upon the k.'
HILL G 3
from K. Devils Hill at Kitty
Hawk CRAN H 9

harpoon were sparring for the k.
LOWE R 53
how to k. desire. SIDN 40
I have had to k. you. PLATH 27
I'll K. you if you Quote it.
BURG 1
k. the Arabs, LIND V 10
k. the white men, LIND V 10
k. with looks, SHAK 89
Men k. for this, SEXT 14
naught to k. TATE A 10
Otherwise k. me. MACN 17
power to k., DICKI 110
said he'd k., and k.,
STEPHENS 14
shoot to k. MACN 3
Thou shalt not k.; CLOU 6
kill'd: k. the cats, BROWNI R 60
killed: cat/ That k. the rat MOTH 5
children were k. LEVE 24
I am the enemy you k.,
OWEN 40
If I've k. one man, PLATH 32
k. by Care. ROBI 48
k. my hawk so good, UNKN 86
k. the noble Mudjokivis.
STRON 1
Nearly k. me for asking
STEPHENS 3
no statistics of the k., SHAP 11
people we had k. JARR 15
Trees down/ Creeks choked, trout
k., SNYD 45
Who k. Cock Robin? MOTH 32
killer: lover and k. are mingled
DOUG K 2
killers: Death to the k., SPEND 19
K. from the egg: HUGH T 10
killeth: Christian k. Christian
CHES 11
Lord k., and maketh alive;
BIBL, O.T. 8
killing: chilling/ And k. my Annabel
Lee. POE 5
doe, a recent k.; STAF 2
excellence of k. CRAN S 9
K. and quickning, HERB G 31
k. sin, STEVENSO R 2
killings: fightings and k. GINS 28
kills: air that k. From yon far
country blows: HOUS 34
k. the thing he loves, WILD 3
rehearse perfect k. HUGH T 1
true, because her truth k. mee.
DONN 61
waste remains and k. EMPS 12
kimono: threw back her k.,
UNKN 102
kimonos: Two girls in silk k.,
YEATS 67
kin: good as yer k. be! FIEL E 5
kind: alter all the course of k.
SPENS 10

auld Robin Gray he is k.
LIND L 2
beautiful, the tender, the k.;
MILLA 6
by a k. hand brought/ Alive
THOR 2
comfortable k. of old scarecrow.
YEATS 11
Demurest of the tabby k.,
GRAY 18
Do not weep, maiden, for war is
k. CRAN S 8
doubtful doom of human k.;
TENN 126
enterprise of martial k., GILB 14
equal among human k. HARD 7
Godlike crime was to be k.,
BYRO 59
hearts are k. and true; BANK 1
hundred million of his k.,
SCHW 11
I have been her k. SEXT 8
If you are always k.." HALE 2
In spite of all their k. MACDI 2
In such k. ways, WILB 8
jolly deed of k.: HOPE A 1
k. and tender to the Frog,
BELL 5
K. are her answers, CAMPI 10
k. as it is green, MOOR M 35
K./ death. BARA 8
k./ Not well, nor full, nor fasting.
k. of animal would you get.
CREE 10
k. of ghost. DONN 11
k. of senseless wit WILB 30
k. seed-receiving earth ROCH 15
DANI S 1
man thinning out his k.
LOWE R 50
my sad self hereafter k.,
HOPKINS 14
Nature, strong and k., EMER 21
Natures trick to propagate her K.
DRYD 1
of a transcendental k. GILB 30
'Offending race of human k.,
SWIF 4
once were keen and k. and gay?
SASS 2
they're exceedingly k. GILB 60
ye of clay were cast by k.,
VAUX 6
your gift will be paid in k.,
BRID 3
kinde: k. of tune, HERB G 67
kindenes: loving k. lasts
BIBL, O.T. 54
kinder: k. to his father SHAK 80
kindest: k. hour of day, MILLA 34
kindled: as soon as k., cooled?
ARNO 42

breath/ Of life be k., HERB CH 4
k. the flame — LIND V 14
Kindles: K. in clothes a
wantonness: HERR 8
kindlest: k. all thy smoky fire,
SIDN 40
kindliness: cool k. of sheets,
BROO R 4
Wasting its k. WORD 63
kindly: dwalt on me sae k.;
BURN 31
for other's weelfare k. spiers:
BURN 18
k. stopped for me — DICKI 9
my most k. nurse, SPENS 45
there's k. hearts DARC 2
vary from the k. race TENN 121
kindness: deeds of k., CARN 2
From a glad k. YEATS 109
kiss her in k. SMAR 3
last k. HERR 53
like jests of k. HAYD 10
little, nameless, unremembered
acts/ Of k. and of love.
WORD 29
Lose natural k. YEATS 106
shoot reformed k., GREV 3
tinned milk of human k. RODG 6
We'll tak a cup o' k. yet
BURN 14
kindred: by k. slain. YEATS 40
k. points of Heaven and Home!
WORD 148
Welcome, k. glooms!
THOMS J (1700–1748) 12
kinds: generated by their k.,
MILT 85
other k. are sham. GILB 6
Some k. of baseness SHAK 160
King: beside the K. of Heaven."
POE 30
by the barbarous k. ELIOT T 122
catch the conscience of the K.
SHAK 32
coming of the K. of Heaven
UNKN 314
Corn K. beckoning JARR 11
fair and fatal k.: JOHN L 3
five k. did a k. to death.
THOMA D 24
God save our k., UNKN 63
Great God, our K.! SMIT SA 2
greatest Herald of Heaven's K.,
DRUM 5
grim grinning K., DRUM 3
hand of the k. KNOX 2
High K. of Glory STEPHENS 4
homage to thy K., SOUTHW 6
honor to an earthly k.;
UNKN 313
I wold thy father were a k.,
UNKN 64
if a k. demand TENN 102

In sleep a k., SHAK 220
k. o' men, BURN 26
K. o' Scots, and a' his power
UNKN 309
k./ Of banks and stones KAVA 22
k. of speechless clods LOWE R 22
k.'s fere in marriage? MORE 2
life is the mirror of k. and slave —
BRID 5
Like a k. in exile, LAWR 45
little profits that an idle k.,
TENN 128
Long live the k., COWP 7
my Lord and K., TENN 57
notable prince that was called K.
John; UNKN 159
old, mad, blind, despised, and
dying k., SHEL 27
Ozymandias, K. of Kings:
SHEL 50
palace of a k., GUES 2
play at queen and k. GRAV 12
praise God & his Priest & K.,
BLAK 56
praises sing to God the K.,
BROO P 5
pray for our k. and queen.
UNKN 216
prosper long our noble k.,
UNKN 58
Race memories of k. and caravan,
TOOM 2
resurrection of the K.,"
LOWE R 3
'Ruin seize thee, ruthless k.!
GRAY 1
short note to the K.:
BROWN B 1
Spring, the herald of love's mighty
k., SPENS 20
Such a K. Harry? DRAY 2
tall K. Saul, LIND V 7
Time's the k. of men; SHAK 139
whatsoever k. shall reign,
UNKN 297
Whilst thus I sing, I am a k,
CIBB 1
Who plainly say, My God, My K.
HERB G 46
kingdom: death's dream k.
ELIOT T 43
death's other K. ELIOT T 42
faced the k. of the mad —
LOWE R 28
forgetful k. of death. RANS 21
Key of the K.: UNKN 242
k. by the sea, POE 3
K. is a city; UNKN 242
k. of the shore, SHAK 211
k., or a cottage, or a grave.
DE VE 2
mile of k., KAVA 22

My mind to me a k. is;
DYER E 1
peopled k. SHAK 55
Pizarro's helmet/ Is a spider's k.;
SCOT WI 2
pure vegetable k., GINS 14
kingdoms: bless'd k. meek of joy
and love. MILT 32
K. are clay; SHAK 3
We returned to our places, these
K., ELIOT T 52
with k. and with kings —
MARK 8
kingfisher: blue k. dives on you in
fire. LOWE R 7
kingfishers: k. catch fire,
HOPKINS 1
kingly: k. Death/ Keeps his pale
court SHEL 1
kings: As greatest k. STOD 3
Barrel-house k., LIND V 8
breath of k., BURN 20
bubbles rais'd by breath of K.;
SWIF 16
Captains and the K. depart:
KIPL 18
cynic tyrannies of honest k.;
MELV 12
Death lays his icy hand on k.: .
SHIR 1
death of k.! SHAK 89
deaths of k., ALDR T 1
dread and fear of k.; SHAK 123
enthroned in the hearts of k.,
SHAK 123
five k. count the dead
THOMA D 25
five k. did a king to death.
THOMA D 24
happy as k. STEVENSO R 9
k. are arming; SCOT WA 1
k. for such a tomb MILT 35
K. may be blest, BURN 53
k. must murder still, LIND V 3
k. neglect that private men enjoy!
SHAK 58
K. sit down to dinner, KIPL 23
know the k. of England, GILB 35
Of cabbages — and k. CARRO 39
pale k., and princes too, KEAT 32
Poets and k. ROBI 1
pretty k. of France. RANS 32
pride of K. POPE A 58
queens, patriots, k., BYRO 37
royal throne of k., this sceptered
isle, SHAK 88
ruine K. DRYD 1
saddest of all k. JOHN L 2
scythe that mows down k.
BEAU/BASS 5
seven K. of Tara, OGIL 1
with kingdoms and with k.
MARK 8

kinsmen: Foolish friends and k.,
   UNKN 90
Kirk-land: tell her I lie in K. fair,
   UNKN 270
kirkyairdie: k.-like and dreich.
   YOUN D 1
kirtle: Thy cap, thy k., and thy
   posies, RALEG 8
kiss: Ae fond k., BURN 10
being man, can k. RODG 3
burning k. CAMPB R 8
come k. me, SHAK 175
come let us k. and part;
   DRAY 15
coward does it with a k., WILD 3
cup and k. SNYD 4
each point he nameth with a k.
   BROWNE 2
enchanted me with a single k.
   KOCH 4
Every Night would k. and play,
   GAY 5
fatherly will k. and daut thee,
   BURN 43
God burn Nature with a k.?
   YEATS 96
Golden slumbers k. your eyes,
   DEKK/OTHE 1
heavy as a lecher's k. PLATH 47
I come to quench the k. ROBI 23
I dare not ask a k., HERR 46
'I saw you take his k.!' PATM 1
"I will not k. your f.ing flag"
if I k. thy com'ly mouth
   UNKN 66
immortal with a k..— MARL 3
In this last k. I here surrender
   thee KING H 6
inspired with Stella's k. SIDN 23
Its snaky acids k. PLATH 44
k. again, no end to this. RANS 16
k. her in kindness. SMAR 3
k. her lips YEATS 139
k. (like blubber)'d NIMS 1
K. me as if you made believe
   BROWNI R 37
k. of desire on the lips. OREI 2
k. of great sweetness, ORLE 1
k. of the sun for pardon, GURN 1
k. of virgins HERR 14
k. off that falling tear, GAY 7
k. that air HERR 46
k. this paper BRAD 3
last good k. you had HUGO 1
learn to k., BRET 7
leave a k. but in the cup,
   JONS 31
Many a k., both odd and even;
   HERR 7
mother's k. sweeter this ALLI 5
moth's k. first! BROWNI R 37
my k. was given to her sister,
   LOWE J 13

never wholly k. you; CUMM 44
noone stooped to k. his face)
   CUMM 6
part at last without a k.?
   MORR 4
rend each other when they k.,
   RANS 16
rough male k. BROO R 4
soldier's k. dwells WHITM 116
Syrinx' lips I k. LYLY 6
That ancient k. HUGO 2
then we k. RANS 31
these that k. and pass? HOUS 22
unclosed in a last long k.
   LAWR 17
Which as they k. consume.
   SHAK 148
Which Jews might k.,
   POPE A 115
With an individual k.; MILT 44
With not one k., PATM 5
   CUMM 15
you Stella's feet may k.! SIDN 25
kiss'd: he but only k. BROWNI E 3
kisse: k. his ers er that he scape.
   CHAU 56
k. the relikes everychon,
   CHAU 85
together closely lie, and k.,
   PETRO 2
kissed: All eager-lipped I k. the
   mouth of Death. BENN G 3
First time he k. me,
   BROWNI E 3
God k. in Galilee, CHES 11
I aft hae k. sae fondly; BURN 31
Jenny k. me. HUNT 5
k. and bade my love good-bye.
   CLARE 12
k. by the English dead. OWEN 28
k. each other's cheek GILB 42
k. her if the rain HARD 46
k. the sleeping Night. DUNB P 1
K. them and put them there
   FIEL E 6, 7
lips my lips have k., MILLA 39
quickness which my God hath k.
   STANL 3
That lately k. thee. HERR 46
woman that k. him SERV 10
kisses: a-wastin' Christian k.
   KIPL 10
boy of responding k., WHITM 107
Dear as remembered k. after
   death, TENN 115
k., tears, and smiles. WORD 134
k. the joy as it flies BLAK 47
love in k. rain SHEL 32
love that k. with a homicide
   BARK 1
my k. bring again SHAK 117
on my cheek sweet k. prest?
   TAYL A 1

played/ At cards for k., LYLY 1
soft-shed k. ROSS D 2
Sweet are the k., MARL 5
Your k. close my eyes LEWI 8
kissing: daylight k. her wan hair,
   WILD 16
hugging babies, k. bellies,
   SNYD 8
into the wet darkness/ K., still
   MONTA 2
k. had to stop? BROWNI R 79
K. with golden face the meadows
   green, SHAK 197
mouths k. the warm sutures,
   ROET 48
kiste: k. hir naked ers, CHAU 53
kitchen: dancing in the k. CLIF 1
do tiny dances on the k. floor.
   BLY 5
eat in the k. HUGH L 6
Eternities of k. garden, SITW 5
k. table exists AUDE 14
swept to the k. KIZE 3
whip/ In k. cups STEVENS 9
Word's gane to the k., UNKN 187
kitchens: steam in hotel k.,
   HUGH L 2
kites: k. to whet their beaks
   RANS 9
kitten: bear him a k.,
   STEPHENS 4
little black k. NASH 15
kittens: naughty k.! FOLL/COOK 1
skunk with her column of k.
   LOWE R 41
Three little k. FOLL/COOK 1
Kitty: from Kill Devils Hill at K.
   Hawk CRAN H 9
Klingenhagen: happy as Cliff K.
   ROBI 8
knack: had the k. KAVA 17
must study the k. GILB 62
knacks: Fine k. for ladies,
   UNKN 96
knave: lashed the k.; SWIF 22
rich or noble k. POPE A 91
war with every k. and dolt,
   YEATS 58
knaves: 'Gainst k. and thieves
   SHAK 177
k. their wine— BURN 25
Men should be K. ROCH 11
kneaded: become/ A k. clod;
   SHAK 115
Knee: Bury my heart at Wounded
   K. BENE 4
I bend the k.;
   THOMS J (1700–1748) 6
K. skirts trimmed LIND V 12
lean in joy upon our father's k.;
   BLAK 99
obedience to the k.; CLARK A 2

Reason's self shall bow the k.
FRENE 2
shoulder, bosom, lip, and k.
HOLLA 5
sit upon a serpent's k.' UNKN 78
smile upon my k.; GREE 2
struck at my k. FROS 8
kneel: k. down/ And ask of thee
forgiveness. SHAK 84
see the oxen k., HARD 33
Who will k. them gently down
UNKN 310
Kneeled: K. down in the dust
JOHN J 3
kneeling: on the Mat devoutly k.
SWIF 14
kneels: k. to another, WHITM 75
knees: all on their k.," HARD 32
By Richmond I raised my k.
ELIOT T 139
clasp thy k.; MILT 101
fell on his k., UNKN 7
Hands and k. SNYD 1
k. and elbows are only glued
BLAK 113
man climbing/ must scrape his k.,
LEVE 11
Pivot of heels and k.! — PLATH 5
plunging up to the k.; BRID R 9
round her mighty k. LOWE J 14
rubber doughnuts,/ Melting at the
k., ROET 54
Sweeney spreads his k.
ELIOT T 111
Tries to sit on Sweeney's k.
ELIOT T 111
wrists and k. garnished with
impetigo. HILL G 6
knell: candle, with book, and with
k.; SCOT WA 15
curfew tolls the k. of parting day,
GRAY 7
Devil below was ringing his k.
SOUTHE 6
I end my Evening k. FLET J 1
like a rising k.! BYRO 5
ring fancy's k. SHAK 121
Ring out my doleful k.;
BOLE/BOLE 2
something rich and strange./ Sea-
nymphs hourly ring his k.:
SHAK 156
knew: face that I/ no longer k.
HAYD 24
gods shook, they k. not why.
EMER 51
I k. a woman, lovely in her
bones, ROET 27
I k. you in this dark; OWEN 40
Johnny, I hardly k. ye!
UNKN 156
k. not where; LONG 1
k. not where; LONG 2

spatters all we k. of dénouement
SHAP 4
which my infancy k., WOOD 1
knife: blind/ swipe of the pruner
and his k. LOWE R 50
escape the k. FULL 2
hiss of the surgeon's k.,
WHITM 92
interrupted by a k., BYRO 53
keeps them on the k. UNKN 137
k.-edge/ of mere fact. RICH 12
k. in Sir Willie's pouch,
UNKN 269
k. of penance fell KAVA 6
k. or a needle, GILB 33
limbs k.-skewed, OWEN 29
two boys k. a third, AUDE 82
knight: cam a k. to be their wooer,
UNKN 29
dame and k. are there.
SCOT WA 6
gallant k.,/ In sunshine and in
shadow, POE 18
k. of ghosts and shadows
UNKN 265
k. slew the dragon, UNKN 244
K.'s bones are dust,
COLE SAM 18
no poor k.; SHAK 76
noble k. was her ransom soon,
UNKN 93
Sir Eglamour, that worthy k.,
ROWL 1
slew thy virgin k., SHAK 132
valor hath slain her k.,
GREV/DYER 2
knights: armorers accomplishing the
k., SHAK 57
courtly dames and k., CAMPI 9
lovely k., SHAK 228
o'er the campana k. armed and
horses arrayed. BERT 1
sing of k. and paladins
DANI S 11
knit: k. with his doom. Æ 1
stuff of life to k. me HOUS 63
Unwind a love k. up KING H 6
knits: Sleep that k. up the raveled
sleave of care, SHAK 106
knitted: clasp of the k. locks,
WHITM 42
knives: all the old k. RICH 14
k. that glitter SIMI 1
open like a drawer of k. LARK 9
trousers were creased like k.
WAGO 1
knob: mortal k. really undoing,
WHITM 36
Knock: K. at a star with my exalted
head. HERR 3
k. at the door, LONG 45
waiting for a k. upon the door.
ELIOT T 126

Knocked: K. silly with guns and
mines, BLUN 5
knocking: Some one came k.
DE LA 23
knot: certain k. of peace, SIDN 14
crowned k. of fire ELIOT T 74
grape tendril/ ties a k.
MOOR M 20
k. a hundred together, MORG 1
k. of little purposeful nature!
EBER 8
k.'s untied that made us one,
BRAD 2
true love's k. UNKN 180
knots: k. till/ knotted thirty times, —
MOOR M 20
ugly K. inside. BELL 8
Knott: father was K. UNKN 88
lies John K.: UNKN 88
lived K., died K., UNKN 88
knotted: knots till/ k. thirty times, —
MOOR M 20
k. and combined locks to part,
SHAK 26
know: all who k. may drown.
ROBI 37
all ye need to k. KEAT 40
at least you k. REED H 3
Because I k. it's true — DICKI 53
caring much to k., GREN 3
Did one but k.! ROSS C 17
does not k. Her beauty, CUNE 1
Don't let him k. CARRO 4
enough for man to k. POPE A 86
from what we k.? POPE A 60
greater than we k. WORD 128
He did not k. I saw — DICKI 12
heavens that k. not what years be
THOMA E 10
how he set — I k. not — DICKI 80
how I came to k..) FIEL E 2
I k. about the row HART 3
I k. everybody's income GILB 8
I sympathize. I k. just how it
feels FROS 22
I think I k. FROS 107
k./ About tom-toms? JOHN H 1
k./ as the hero. MOOR M 28
K. his work YEATS 156
k. how to play ROET 22
k./ If I am a fool SNYD 12
k. it as it is k. AMMO 17
k. it's gone, SHAP 17
k. much about gods; ELIOT T 26
k. not how; LOWE J 18
k. not what the younger dreams —
YEATS 66
k. not where, WHITM 34
k. not why! UNKN 182
k. not you are dead in vain,
HOUS 4
k. some lonely houses DICKI 50
k. the difference OHAR 3

labouring: cheered the l. swain,
GOLD 2
doubled darkness up the l. hill.
ROSS D 7
l. with a mighty fate, DRYD 7
Labrador: northerly harbor of L.,
BISH 24
labyrinth: peopled l. of walls,
SHEL 36
labyrinthine: down the l. ways
THOMP F 6
lace: bunch of l. at his throat.
NOYE 8
flowers and l. and mourning.
RANS 18
l. for your cape, SHAK 182
lacerate: l./ Simply by being over;
LARK 14
lack: l. tongues to praise.
SHAK 228
our l. of faith, AUDE 30
sigh the l. SHAK 195
something seems to l.; VAN DY 2
lacked: If I l. any thing.
HERB G 48
l. I matter; SHAK 218
lackey: brisk fond l. to fetch and
carry, HOUS 3
lackt: he l. a tong, SPENS 44
lacquers: supper-table l.; GILB 13
lactiferous: l. maids! HOLM 1
lad: come to hang you, l.:
KINGSM 2
Farmer Rouf's little l. WOOL 1
l. that loved you HOUS 1
many a lightfoot l. HOUS 62
merry country l.? BRET 4
Yes, l., I lie easy, HOUS 37
ladder: lowliness is young
ambition's l., SHAK 44
traffic of Jacob's l. THOMP F 11
With lantern and with l.
STEVENSO R 3
ladder's: l. sticking through a tree
FROS 3
my l. gone, YEATS 29
ladders: where all the l. start,
YEATS 29
laddie: gayest l. of all BRIN 2
lie with an east-shore l.,
UNKN 209
laden: white fire l., SHEL 24
ladies: Cambridge l. CUMM 52
circle of the crazy l. SEXT 12
devirginated young l. POUN 32
Eleven l. dancing, UNKN 284
Fine knacks for l., UNKN 96
Good night, l., ELIOT T 128
Invite the l. toward the mistletoe
TATE A 6
l. faint, and the children holler:
SMIT W 1
l. in a rout. RANS 6

L., like variegated tulips,
POPE A 94
l. of honour UNKN 231
l. that despise, FLET J 5
l. that do sleep! CAMPI 3
lords and l. of Byzantium
YEATS 130
lords of l. intellectual, BYRO 20
praise of l. dead SHAK 228
quiet Dust was Gentlemen and
L., DICKI 147
Sigh no more L., SHAK 130
Sigh no more, l./ Time is male
RICH 21
sweet l., good night,
ELIOT T 128
Sweet l., long may ye RANS 18
these l./ That must be wooed and
prayed; CAMPI 6
to change their l. do begin),
WYAT 3
wed l. by license and leave,
WYAT 11
"Yessum" to the l., FIEL E 5
ladles: soup from the cook's own l..
BROWNI R 60
lads: ashen-gray/ Masks of the l.
SASS 2
Golden l. and girls SHAK 18
L. and Girls; DICKI 147
lie as l. would choose; HOUS 37
sent our l. to the Border; ELLI 2
Lady: annually coos in Our L.'s ear
HECH 1
ask'd a lithe l. BLAK 25
came Our Blessed L., UNKN 49
capers nimbly in a l.'s chamber
SHAK 95
feathers, like a l. bright, VAUT 1
fool he called her his l. fair—
KIPL 27
he's made her his l. UNKN 233
I bedded/ down with Isis, L. of the
Boogaloo, REED I 3
L. be not coy, MILT 6
L. has always moved CREE 7
l. novelist— GILB 27
l. of light, SWIN 4
l. of my delight— MEYN 3
L. of Shalott. TENN 60
L. of silences ELIOT T 9
l. of the West Country? DE LA 9
l. rocks, bebby, BROWN S 2
l. sleeps! POE 41
l. that's known as Lou. SERV 6
l. was gay, UNKN 244
l. wept sorely, UNKN 243
l. with a terrible tongue, RANS 5
l. young in beauty RANS 31
little/ L. with rod RANS 4
must have my lovely l. RANS 30
Oh most lovely l., CREE 4
old l., who marked MONTA 2

Redemption, brittle l., DICKI 156
saw a l. bright, UNKN 245
saw my l. weep, UNKN 141
Sin is where our L. sat,
UNKN 170
stonden in his l. grace. CHAU 9
this youthful l., DANT 1
Venus, love's l., was born of the
sea; JORD 1
Watteau hung a l.'s/ slipper.
WILLI 25
white this l.'s hours. POUN 68
young l. named Bright, BULL 1
young l. of Niger MONK 1
lady-bird: timid l. RANS 25
Ladybird: L., nor butterfly,
ROSS C 16
lady-smocks: l. all silver-white,
SHAK 100
lag: schoolboys l. with satchels in
their hands. SWIF 11
lagging: December blights my l.
May; COLE H 2
l. far behind you, DAIC 1
lagoon: In some unused l.,
WHITM 28
lags: diff'rent views engage,/
Superfluous l.
JOHN S (1709–1784) 14
Superfluous l. the veteran on the
stage, JOHN S (1709–1784) 21
laid: autumn wind l. bare; VERY 1
death l. him along: SOUTHW 11
God has l. His fingers YEATS 96
I l. the foundations of the earth?
BIBL, O.T. 13
in a manger l. TATE N 2
in sad cypress let me be l.
SHAK 176
In this little urn is l. HERR 64
l. bare/ The root of life, KIRK 1
l. him on the green. UNKN 40
l. on Greenland's Coast, GAY 4
L. out for death, HERR 53
l./ With cold vegetation SITW 3
Nature's Darling l., GRAY 28
laily: made me the l. worm
UNKN 168
lain: child who among beasts has l.
SITW 13
In cold grave she was l.
UNKN 292
l./ In an adjoining Room—
DICKI 37
lies where it has l. MUIR 10
lake: bosom of the steady l.
WORD 105
Gazed on the l. below. GRAY 18
Goddess of the silver l., MILT 7
l. water lapping YEATS 75
l.-reflected sun SHEL 51
marge of L. Lebarge SERV 1
pilot of the Galilean l. MILT 28

sedge has wither'd from the l.,
KEAT 31
Simon on thy l. of Galilee:
WILD 10
sodden as the bed of an ancient
l., HUGH T 3
swimmin' in the l..— FIEL E 4
Wind, l., lip, everything awaits
HECH 6
lakes: elves of hills, brooks, standing
l., and groves, SHAK 164
light shakes across the l.,
TENN 111
Rocks, Caves, L., Fens, Bogs,
Dens, MILT 61
lamb: became a l. SCHW 1
he calls himself a L., BLAK 95
L. of God, CULL 9
L. of the shepherds, LOWE R 23
l., the linnet, and the hare—
STEPHENS 7
l. was sure to go; HALE 1
leads me to the L.! COWP 25
lion and the l., MACDI 5
Little L., who made thee?
BLAK 94
Mary had a little l., HALE 1
on the slant hill a putrid l.,
EBER 1
"Pipe a song about a L.";
BLAK 104
see a l. at school. HALE 1
set'st the wolf where he the l. may
get; SHAK 140
shut up the l. at night. HAY 6
thou a l., BLAK 95
lambent: l. dullness played around
his face. DRYD 13
lambes: tender l. ytorne?
SPENS 48
Lambs: let the young L. bound
WORD 83
like l. we joy, BLAK 99
multitudes of l., BLAK 91
We were as twinned l. SHAK 178
Lame: L. as I am, WESL C 2
l. hands of faith, TENN 34
l. now— wrinkles— GINS 30
lamely: so l. and unfashionable
SHAK 96
lament: l. of the disconsolate
chimera. ELIOT T 25
reason to l. WORD 39
To the dark and l. FROS 16
lamentable: l. change is from the
best; SHAK 77
thir l. lot, MILT 61
lamenting: he was left l.
CAMPB T 6
L. all her fallen sons!
THOMP W 4
l. love marreth the musicall.
SPENS 37

lamp: l.-flame at the table
FROS 19
l. is shattered, SHEL 89
l.-light o'er him streaming
POE 37
l. lights another, LOWE J 21
l. of love, SHEL 87
Life is the lust of a l. SWIN 20
lift my l. LAZA 2
lights/ His constant l., MILT 78
smell of the l., HERR 17
lamping: l. eyes SPENS 2
lamps: golden l. in a green night,
MARV 1
Loitered beneath the gas l.' flare,
WILD 16
silent signal l. to swing.
WHITM 101
unseen, as l. in sepulchres;
POPE A 4
Lampshine: L. blurred WILB 44
lan: man upo the l., UNKN 122
lance: flashing l.! ARNO 38
strong l. of justice SHAK 81
that fallen l. FROS 103
Lancelot: bold Sir L. TENN 63
Sang Sir L. TENN 64
lancewood: l. to make the thills;
HOLM 6
land: all the l. of the globe.
WHITM 2
Autumn resumes the l., HILL G 1
Back to the l. SMIT W 2
before we were the l.'s. FROS 49
bitter l. was washed away.
WALK 1
blesse this l. UNKN 63
blessed L. of Room Enough
VAN DY 3
Bounding the l. WINT 7
Bread, Peace, L. SAND 21
breeding/ Lilacs out of the dead
l., ELIOT T 113
cactus l. ELIOT T 44
charter of her l.,
THOMS J (1700–1748)/MALL 1
citizens of death's grey l., SASS 6
cleaner, greener l.! KIPL 12
cussedest l. that I know,
SERV 12
darkness of the l., TENN 50
dead l. ELIOT T 44
Dixie L. whar I was born
EMME 1
down in Egypt l., UNKN 115
England's green & pleasant L.
BLAK 35
famine-murdered l. WILD 11
farewell journey to the Promised
L. UNKN 55
find a happier l., FRENE 4
fine l., the west l., MASE 14
free l. of the grave. HOUS 3

glorious l. in the sky; HILL J 1
gone/ About some l., HERB G 70
governance of hous and l.,
CHAU 87
Hail, Columbia! happy l.!
HOPKINSO 1
Ill fares the l., GOLD 3
In that l. all Is RODG 1
In the green tempestuous l.
BLUN 2
In the hollow Lotos l. TENN 89
in the l. were we born. TATE A 5
irresponsive silence of the l.,
ROSS C 24
Is no man's l., DAY 5
l. and soil, TOOM 6
l. freckled with snow half-thawed
THOMA E 18
l. hushes to rest: BRID R 18
l. in the yard, JARR 24
l. is bright! CLOU 9
l. is numb. WINT 9
l. is scattered with light,
BRID R 2
l. is wrapt in sleep. BRID R 19
l. may vary more; FROS 67
l. o' the leal. NAIR 1
l. ob cotton, EMME 1
l. of Abraham Lincoln CUMM 39
l. of ambush, MACN 4
l. of darkness and blind eyes
VAUG 13
l. of dreams JOHN L 7
l. of lost content HOUS 35
L. of Men & Women BLAK 29
l. of pure delight, WATT I 8
l. of scholars and saints: MACN 4
l. of spices; HERB G 68
l. of the free, KEY 1
L. of the pilgrims' pride,
SMIT SA 1
l. that's far away UNKN 26
l. was our FROS 49
L. where my fathers died,
SMIT SA 1
l. where the dead dreams go.
NOYE 4
lane to the l. of the dead.
AUDE 3
living image of our own bright l.,
BRYA 28
livingest chits/ In all the l.
BROO G 13
Long may our l. be bright
SMIT SA 2
Look away! Dixie L. EMME 1
my native l.! SCOT WA 11
my own native l., COWP 24
One, if by l., LONG 44
our l., it is old. RANS 1
pleasant l. of counterpane.
STEVENSO R 12
pointed toward the l., TENN 80

prime o' our l., ELLI 2
publishes to every L. ADDI 3
rich and fruitful l., BLAK 68
sacked l. of my father. BARA 7
seas and l. be 'twixt us both,
LOVE 7
secret nook in a pleasant l.,
EMER 28
see the l. I love. ROET 51
silent l.; ROSS C 19
sing the Lord's song in a strange
l.? BIBL, O.T. 63
somewhere in this favored l.
THAY 4
strong l.'s swift increase;
BENN H 2
Sweet l. of liberty, SMIT SA 1
their seamen l. SQUI 1
thing of sea or l.? MILT 110
thro' a L. of Men BLAK 29
universal peace through sea and
l. MILT 37
Utopia's quite another l.;
GILB 53
voice of the turtle is heard in our
l.; BIBL, O.T. 72
weathering l. SNYD 21
Where lies the L. WORD 158
landless: l. blood of Cain
LOWE R 5
landmark: l. is a kopje-crest
HARD 19
landmen: 'Believe not what the l.
say, GAY 7
lands: ancients of these l. FRENE 1
darken all l.; ROSS C 8
envy of less happier l.; SHAK 88
gray/ And changeless l. of ice.
WILB 47
in lonely l., TENN 12
l. beyond the sea; WORD 47
l. of palm and southern pine;
TENN 11
l. where the Jumblies live;
LEAR 9
Lord of himself, though not of l.,
WOTT 2
my days and l. WHITM 53
set my l. in order? ELIOT T 155
smile in secret, looking over
wasted l., TENN 90
spirits of other l. OHAR 8
landscape: future is ever a misted
l., JEFFE 32
L. listens — DICKI 144
l. of hysteria, SPEND 14
l. still partly brown: ROET 37
limestone l. AUDE 52
year by year the l. grow
TENN 44
landscapes: l. drawn in pearly
monotones. WYLI 14

lane: l. to the land of the dead.
AUDE 3
light-blue l. of early dawn,
TENN 54
lanes: poets loiter'd in green l.,
LAND 9
lang: For auld l. syne,
BURN 13, 14
l. syne deid, MACDI 4
langage: So muchel of daliaunce
and fair l. CHAU 20
language: cool web of l. GRAV 3
destruction of l. KOCH 4
eternal l., which thy God/ Utters,
COLE SAM 15
every bird its l., LONG 42
fire beyond the l. of the living.
ELIOT T 64
l., and the truth, JONS 1
L. has not the power to speak
CLARE 9
l. I have learned SHAK 86
l. obscene PLATH 29
L. of Man pronounced MILT 93
l. to her, was as sweet, JONS 18
l. you choose GILB 25
last year's l. ELIOT T 66
Learned his great l.,
BROWNI R 45
Lovely enchanting l., HERB G 35
my l. is plain — HART 1
New splendour to the dead./ L.
has not the power to speak
PLATO 3
no l. but a cry. TENN 31
one light's l. in the book of trees.
THOMA D 8
sons their fathers' failing l. see,
POPE A 34
speaks/ A various l.: BRYA 22
suicides have a special l.
SEXT 16
tell in simple l. HART 3
their own l. LONG 20
those lips had l.! COWP 9
what shall l. do?
THOMS J (1700–1748) 4
wink-and-elbow l. of delight.
KAVA 21
langueo: Quia amore l. UNKN 206
languid: excite your l. spleen,
GILB 32
music of the l. hours, LANG 3
tone of l. Nature. COWP 19
languish: l. and anon must die;
CAREW 9
Relieve my l. DANI S 8
languishing: Numbers l. MARV 20
languish't: with l. head. MILT 6
languor: heart's deep l.
THOMS J (1834–1882) 8
Indian Psyche's l. MELV 22
lank: bronzed, l. man! LIND V 2

lanky: l. hank of a she
STEPHENS 3
lantern: Hang a l. aloft LONG 44
Thou ! ast no l. JONS 35
With l. and with ladder
STEVENSO R 3
lanterns: flock of bright red l.
REZN 1
l. of stone? LEVE 23
lap: Earth fills her l. WORD 72
in my mother's l.! MILT 98
In thy green l. GRAY 28
l. of Earth GRAY 12
light poured softly in her l.
FROS 26
see it l. the Miles — DICKI 55
lapdogs: l. give themselves the
rousing shake, POPE A 111
Lapland: verse of a L. song
LONG 32
lappe: in pleasures l. did lye,
LODG 3
lapped: l. in universal law.
TENN 76
lapping: lake water l. YEATS 75
scale/ l. scale MOOR M 22
laps: lay in their l., laughing,
ROET 26
lapse: felt the l. of hours! ARNO 22
lapsed: Summer l. away —
DICKI 6
Lapwater: Roses, Pyrgo, and L.
THOMA E 11
large: few l. stars overhead,
WHITM 92
islands l. and small; WHITM 19
l. and composed. SHAP 2
l. and lordly train, WILC 3
l. and sinewy hands; LONG 48
l. in the belly. STAF 2
small house and l. garden
COWL 8
such l. discourse, SHAK 35
larger: just or l. end, MELV 17
L. than in life LARK 11
new and l. life MCCRE 3
trust the l. hope. TENN 34
largest: strike me the l. doe.
LOVE 2
lariat: l. snaps; SMIT W 2
lark: Hark, hark! the l. SHAK 17
have a l. instead. HOOD 14
l. is so brimful of gladness and
love, COLE SAM 1
l. sitting upon his earthy bed,
BLAK 36
l. so shrill and clear; LYLY 3
L. without song, THOR 6
l.'s nest in the field. SMAR 1
Like to the l. SHAK 194
note/ Of l. and linnet, LONG 8
lark's: l. on the wing;
BROWNI R 66

laughed: heavy Saturn l. and
    leaped SHAK 225
    l. their cryings CUMM 5
    l. upon his breast YEATS 83
    nor l., nor cried: PRIO 4
laughing: crowd is l./ in detail/
    WILLI 6
    l. and calling MANI 1
    l. in the diners SAND 12
    l. is heard on the hill, BLAK 77
    L. on the Great Earth SNYD 8
    l. queen HUNT 7
    l. round an apple./ There lurk no
    claws OWEN 14
    L. the love-laugh OWEN 25
    lay in their laps, l./ Weak as a
    whiffet; ROET 26
    lived l. in my house MOMA 5
    sea lay l. at a distance;
    WORD 102
    somewhere men are l., THAY 4
laughs: gave their l. more glee
    OWEN 10
    l. not and sees not! AIKE 12
    Whose l. are hearty, POPE A 20
    world l. with you; WILC 1
laughter: containing l. ELIOT T 18
    holy l. in the river! GINS 19
    l. and contempt, SHAK 72
    L. and grief join hands. SHAP 20
    l., learnt of friends; BROO R 14
    l. on their lips SPEND 8
    l., pain, and love. MERR 8
    madly-whistled l., WHITM 102
    Our sincerest l. SHEL 71
    Present mirth hath present l.;
    SHAK 175
    respectable senators burst with l.,
    AUDE 5
    seismic with l., BARK 3
    shouting and l. BROWNI R 62
    tired of tears and l. SWIN 12
    under running l. THOMP F 6
    weeping and the l., DOWS 5
    worst returns to l. SHAK 77
launch: l. the small ship, LAWR 39
    l.'d forth filament, WHITM 55
    L.'d o'er the prairies wide,
    WHITM 102
    life departs, l. out, LAWR 39
launched: l. a thousand ships,
    MARL 3
laundry: nothing on earth but l.,
    WILB 24
laurel: beneath my l. tree. HORA 8
    early though the l. grows
    HOUS 56
    l. also bears a thorn. LAND 10
    l. outlives not May. SWIN 23
    l. the graves of our dead! FINC 2
    live like some green l.
    YEATS 110
    neither l. nor bay? ROSS C 18

laurels: once more, O ye l.,
    MILT 25
    rests in its l. HILL G 2
Laurie: all sang " Annie L.."
    TAYL B 2
    for bonnie Annie L. DOUG W 1
lavish: lewd and l. act of sin,
    MILT 4
law: Booze is l. WELC 1
    both Rule and L. alone:
    DRYD 17
    break his l. SHAK 98
    by L. requir'd; DRYD 17
    constellations of universal l.
    SAND 17
    Creation's final l. TENN 36
    dateless mid-days of the l.
    MUIR 3
    Effects of necessary L.! DRYD 1
    Equal justice, right and l.,
    BENN H 2
    every case in l. is right, SHAK 76
    feed-back is the l. OLSO 4
    give the universe your l.,
    ARNO 37
    God is thy l., thou mine:
    MILT 75
    Hail wedded love, mysterious l.,
    MILT 78
    his l. a curse, BLAK 27
    "I took to the l., CARRO 6
    lapped in universal l. TENN 76
    L. makes long spokes EMPS 9
    l. of the Lord is perfect,
    BIBL, O.T. 28
    L. of thyself complete,
    WHITM 102
    no l., no meaning, and no end—
    WORD 109
    nymph shall break Diana's l.,
    POPE A 117
    perfect l. of love VERY 4
    sense of l. and beauty, CARRU 1
    shamrock is by l. forbid
    UNKN 299
    spurn'st at right, at l., at reason;
    SHAK 140
    table of his l. SHAK 98
    things by a l. divine SHEL 38
    this is l., UNKN 297
    where dirtiness is l. OLSO 5
    wrest the l. to fill the coffer
    WYAT 23
lawe: sergeant of the l., war and
    wys, CHAU 3
lawful: All things are l. there
    CAREW 13
    Got 'tween the l. sheets.
    SHAK 80
    l. prize; GRAY 20
Lawk: " L. a mercy MOTH 29
Lawlands: Ye Highlands and ye L.
    UNKN 40

lawless: those that l. and incertain
    thought SHAK 115
lawn: butterflies on the l., COOP 1
    cross the damp cold l.
    BERRYM 14
    l. at the villa— SIMP 7
    lingered on the l., TENN 40
    loveliest of the l. GOLD 2
    mossy l.; SHEL 77
    sable stole of cypress l., MILT 16
lawns: l., or level downs, MILT 69
Lawrel: L. wear, DRYD 30
laws: art in obedience to l.,
    BROWNI R 1
    By the same l. POPE A 27
    dole/ Unequal l. TENN 128
    Drama's L. the Drama's Patrons
    give, JOHN S (1709–1784) 9
    Farewell, Love, and all thy l. for
    ever: WYAT 5
    God's eternal L. WILD 4
    L. be right, WILD 2
    L. be wrong; WILD 2
    l. of God, HOUS 16
    l. of God, and man and metre.
    JEFFR 1
    l. of man, HOUS 16
    l. of propriety, CARRO 11
    Like Cato, give his little senate l.,
    POPE A 7
    Love likes no l. but his own!
    GREV 1
    Nature's l. lay hid in night:
    POPE A 106
    Ordain them l.; MILT 104
    sweeter manners, purer l.
    TENN 48
    Time cannot alter but obey Fate's
    l. TOWN 1
lawyers: Of l., statesmen, priest and
    theorist; — SHEL 79
lax: Too tense, or too l. BOGA 15
lay: alone of all His treasure/ Rest
    in the bottom l. HERB G 62
    as you l. on the ground,
    WHITM 106
    fields around l. bound and hoar
    THOR 11
    hath not where to l. his head;
    LOWE J 20
    he l. like a warrior WOLF C 2
    I'd l. me doune and dee.
    DOUG W 1
    l. between/ Us, MONTA 1
    l. by that young man UNKN 304
    l. down with those strange
    women, WAGO 2
    l. in his bed till 'twas noon,
    UNKN 43
    l. in his blood NOYE 8
    l. in Lie Castle! LEVE 5
    l. in their laps, laughing,
    ROET 26

L. me down   DUNB P 2
l. me down to sleep,   UNKN 193
L. me on an anvil,   SAND 20
l. mee downe and bleed a-while
   UNKN 225
l. out their money   BYRO 43
l. rich in shade   MELV 21
l. upon the sunny hill,   MUIR 4
love most l. sleeping by me
   WHITM 109
malt/ That l. in the house
   MOTH 3
mind how once we l.   WHITM 78
my soul l. out of sight,
   HERB G 21
Or a good l.:   AUDE 48
sea l. laughing at a distance;
   WORD 102
sick and l. a-bed,
   STEVENSO R 11
simple and heartfelt l.,   LONG 15
smile of Heaven l.;   SHEL 73
toys beside me l.
   STEVENSO R 11
True Thomas l. on Huntlie bank;
   UNKN 245
we l. waste our powers:
   WORD 159
We like sepulchral statues l.;
   DONN 20
layd: precious dust is l.;   CAREW 8
laye: l. aparte/ Your cornet black,
   SURR 9
l./ Of fayre Elisa,   SPENS 50
layed: girls get l. by Coyote
   SNYD 36
layered: l. light/ Above them
   swims;   WARR 1
layes: names sung in your simple
   l.,   SPENS 29
layest: l. thy finger   LONG 25
lays: sucks in thy sacred l.
   CAREW 18
lazily: How l. time creeps
   KING H 2
lazy: Alice grown l.,   TATE A 3
cuckoo is a l. bird,   UNKN 73
l. finger of a maid;   SHAK 153
l. little shadow,   STEVENSO R 14
l./ or dead.   OHAR 17
lea: cattle huddled on the l.;
   TENN 23
lowing herd wind slowly o'er the
   l.,   GRAY 7
standing on this pleasant l.,
   WORD 160
lead: for the Moon to l.,   BEAU 1
ghost thee l.   CHAU 2
Hour of L.   DICKI 2
l./ Apes in Avernus.   CAMPI 4
l. frail minds to rest   SPENS 5
l. Hell Captive   MILT 64
l. me still   MILT 99

l. my steps aright.   BRYA 27
l. nor steel shall reach him,
   GREN 3
l. such dire attack;   MACA 4
l. the world the way to rest.
   COTTO 1
leade: l. them unto life and rest.
   HERB G 1
leaden: l.-eyed despairs,   KEAT 47
leader: face of the l.   WHITT 3
L. of the herd   HODG 4
leaders: vote just as their l. tell 'em
   to.   GILB 23
leadeth: God's hand that l. me.
   GILM 1
He l. me   GILM 1
l. me beside the still waters.
   BIBL, O.T. 31
l. me in the paths of
   righteousness   BIBL, O.T. 31
leading: l. me on   HARD 1
nature would be l.:   BRON 6
leads: from walls and l.,   HARD 22
l. as often as not/ to our undoing.
   WILLI 30
L. by the hand   LONG 33
l. me from my love.   HOUS 64
l. me to the Lamb!   COWP 25
l. men to this hell.   SHAK 236
such a life, as one l.
   BROWNI R 83
Time l. me,   MILT 14
leaf: compare her/ to a fallen l.
   WILLI 49
draw up l. from the root?
   POUN 16
empty doorway and a maple l.
   MACL 1
flower and the l.,   AIKE 5
last l. upon the tree   HOLM 16
last red l. is whirl'd away,
   TENN 23
l. subsides to l.   FROS 71
let fall/ No burning l.;   MILLA 11
lift me as a wave, a l., a cloud!
   SHEL 45
seasonably/ l. and blossom uncurl
   LAYT 2
shady l., or stalk,   ROSS C 3
shape of a l. lay once   MACL 11
skirts not touching a l.,   ROET 57
(this life one l.)   CUMM 9
through the faded l.   TENN 22
turned a l.   KLEI 1
leafe: l., the bud, the flowre,
   SPENS 33
leafless: Dry l. trees   VERY 1
Leafy: L. the boughs —   DAY 6
L.-with-love banks   KAVA 1
league: Half a l. onward,   TENN 6
leagues: Cover a hundred l.,
   WORD 130

Leaking: L. the brightness away,
   SPEND 21
sailed away/ From a l. ship
   WHITT 24
leal: land o' the l.   NAIR 1
lean: figure appear so l.,   TRAI 2
his mother gaunt and l.   HODG 3
l. and loafe   WHITM 74
l. and sinewy   WHITM 70
l./ as a compass-needle.
   LOWE R 18
l. in joy upon our father's knee;
   BLAK 99
L. is the ghost of Molly Means.
   WALK 10
l. not toward revolt.   SNOD 9
let him l. a while   MILT 114
Speak low, l. low,   ROSS C 7
thinne and l. without a fence or
   friend,   HERB G 4
Leander: L., beautifull and yoong,
   MARL 6
L., Mr. Ekenhead, and I did.
   BYRO 44
L., who was nightly wont
   BYRO 75
love's extreme,/ L.-like, —
   DAVIE J 1
leaned: l. far out on the window-
   sill,   WHITT 3
Leaning: L. against the — Sun —
   DICKI 70
l. on the john door   OHAR 6
l. with the flowers,   SPENC B 1
rapid glide along the l. line;
   THOMS J (1700–1748) 11
reader l. late   STEVENS 16
leans: l./ Upon his hoe   MARK 5
to Sin our byast Nature l.,
   DRYD 1
leant: l. upon a coppice gate
   HARD 17
leap: all hungers l.,   WILB 6
Beasts did l.,   BARNF 1
fishes l. and play   BRET 5
I l. for joy, pursue my way,
   WESL C 2
Intelligences at a l.;   MERE G 15
L. incandescent   PLATH 18
l. into a dance,   BEAU 1
L., plashless   DICKI 13
l. to head off a straggler   DAY 11
never l. up that way again,
   LAWR 29
not l. From steel bridges,   KNIG 2
to start her death-defying l.
   FERL 2
leaping: swiftly l. beyond them,
   WHITM 63
leaps: heart l. up   WORD 57
L. from the tree/ snapped by the
   diesel   SNYD 44
l. in the sky: BRID R 1

wild cataract l. in glory./ Blow,
  bugle, blow,   TENN 111
Lear: Hamlet and L. are gay;
  YEATS 79
pleasant to know Mr. L.!'   LEAR 7
there is L.,   YEATS 78
learn: As I l. from you,/ I guess you
  l. from me —   HUGH L 17
diligent to l.;   WORD 4
heart is slow to l.   MILLA 24
how much we l.   ROBI 14
I l. by going where I have to go.
  ROET 59
I l. to bear   LONG 25
In heaven you'll l. to sing,
  CRAS 9
Irregular verbs to l.,   AUDE 17
l. all so painfully,   WARR 2
l. her wanton ways:/ (I measure
  time   ROET 29
L. more than thou trowest,
  SHAK 71
l. the simplest things   OLSO 13
l. to bear the beams of love,
  BLAK 98
L. to close softly   JUST 5
l. to kiss,   BRET 7
L. to labor and to wait.   LONG 37
l. who won   WHITM 89
L. your jingles   CAREY 2
l. your trade,   YEATS 157
Stand in a row and l.   MERW 4
To measure life l. thou   MILT 120
would not l.,   PRIO 4
learned: all he l.;   WILB 39
have her chiefly l.;   YEATS 108
Héloïse, the l. nun,   VILL 1
In spite of all the l.   FRENE 1
language I have l.   SHAK 86
l. bard or gifted child;   GRAV 33
l. clan;   EMER 29
L. his great language,
  BROWNI R 45
l. one date.   SNOD 5
l., well-bred;   POPE A 24
l. what comfort is,   TROW 5
loads of l. lumber   POPE A 22
things my fathers l. to do.
  AIKE 6
things that we have l.   RICH 27
through l. cities,   AUDE 20
Ye l. sisters   SPENS 29
learn'd: heard the l. astronomer,
  WHITM 110
l. to dance.   POPE A 28
learnin: l.' 'ere in London   KIPL 11
learning: By nature, reason, l.,
  blind;   SWIF 4
grammar, and nonsense, and l.;
  GOLD 5
l. and blundering people
  SAND 14

little l. is a dangerous thing.
  POPE A 33
l. to be mad,   GINS 21
l./ To crawl."   SERR 2
love of l.,   MACN 10
sceptre, l., physic,   SHAK 18
wayes of l.;   HERB G 59
When L.'s Triumph
  JOHN S (1709–1784) 5
learns: l. the storm-cloud's
  thunderous melody,
  STEPHEN 3
learnt: I l. that thou wast dead,
  COWP 10
lease: l. of my true love   SHAK 229
new small-rented l.,   HERB G 69
squalid l. of sin   BRID R 11
summer's l.   SHAK 188
leash: Slow on the l.,/ pallid the l.-
  men!   POUN 59
least: at l. an earnest sense
  WHITT 10
conqueror at l.;   BYRO 34
contented l.;   SHAK 194
had thee l. in mind!   UNKN 90
her l. things exprest,   THOMP F 5
made me so much admired/ Is l.
  regarded,   C., J 1
pity on the l. of things   YEATS 15
When you l. expect it.   SIMI 2
leathalle: to yer l. tyde.   CHAT 1
leather: gathering the orange l.
  HIRS 1
l. I slapped to his rump   SWEN 2
l./ tanned from deerhide,   HALL 4
so much Zyklon and l.,   HILL G 7
leathern: flits by on l. Wing,
  COLL 10
leav: l.'st their losses open to the
  day.   BEAU/FLET 4
leave: cannot l. her mother."
  UNKN 28
Comrades, l. me here a little,
  TENN 68
darkness and corruption l.
  ROSS C 20
drink, and l. the world unseen,
  KEAT 46
enter, and l., alone,   THOMA E 13
give me l. to love,   CAREW 16
I l. this light;   HERR 51
l. a kiss but in the cup,   JONS 31
l. all meaner things/ To low
  ambition,   POPE A 58
l. Mankind without a way:
  DRYD 18
L. me, O Love,   SIDN 26
l. me single in the crowd.
  THOR 5
l. no wake,   LOWE J 19
l. our desert to its peace!"
  ARNO 40
l. that brain outside,   GILB 23

L. the chaff,   EMER 31
l. the loathèd stage,   JONS 20
l. the trodden paths of men
  SHEL 4
l. their children free,   EMER 12
l. to your own mother dear,
  UNKN 87
loath/ To l. this Paradise;
  MILT 106
lusts they do me l.,   VAUX 2
make me thus to l. you,   SIDN 31
reckon ill who l. me out;
  EMER 7
sourly l. her   SHAK 201
they had to l. us — a symbol:
  ELIOT T 69
thou must l. ere long.   SHAK 215
wed ladies by license and l.,
  WYAT 11
wilt thou l. me thus?   WYAT 1
worst that love could do?/ Love
  may make me l. loving,
  DONN 40
leaves: Amongst the l. so green.
  UNKN 210
attune/ The trembling l.,   MILT 70
autumn, like a bonfire of l.,
  WYLI 13
bloody l.   FANS S 1
branches and l.,   WHITM 112
caught l. in ice,   SNYD 22
chaunting of the unquiet l.,
  YEATS 141
crackling sound over/ dried l.
  WILLI 49
dazzling through the l.,   TENN 63
falling l. stir my genes,   KNIG 8
feet like small l.,/ Little lizard-
  feet,   ROET 39
few sands and dead l.   WHITM 3
green l. were afalling,   UNKN 38
impassioned in the littering l.
  STEVENS 58
joyous l. of dark green,
  WHITM 39
l. a lonesome place against the
  sky.   MARK 4
l. and moss-work   HERR 53
l. are all dead   FROS 92
l. are brown,   CARRO 34
l. come down in hosts;   ALLI 2
L. got up   FROS 8
l. grow on the tree;   YEATS 50
l. hang trembling,   ROSS C 35
l. like bored hearts.   PLATH 13
L., lines, and rhymes, seek her to
  please   SPENS 3
l. looke pale,   SHAK 224
l. may fall,   MCCRE 2
l. never a doorway   LOWE J 9
l. of salt-lettuce,   WHITM 2
L. of the summer,   BARNE 1
l. of thy unvalued book   MILT 35

l. off work, WHITM 37
l. the well-built nest; SHEL 90
l. untroubled about us, WILB 1
l. were full of children,/ Hidden
    excitedly, ELIOT T 18
lisp of l. SWIN 3
lofty trees I see barren of l.,
    SHAK 186
no l., no birds — November!
    HOOD 6
on Severn snow the l. HOUS 44
perished l. of Hope, ROSS D 3
raking piles of dead l. SNOD 14
scents dead l. yield, THOMA E 5
she l. the station. SPEND 5
sheds dry l., THOMA D 2
song of the ever-singing l.,
    YEATS 140
Tawny are the l. turned, RANS 1
Thick as autumnal l. MILT 55
Tree whose broad smooth L.
    MILT 97
utter joyous l. WHITM 39
wavering arras of l., — LANIE 3
waving moon and trembling l.
    WINC 1
what it l. behind. WORD 19
when l. depart, CAMPB R 1
with sweet l.; POUN 66
withered l. SHEL 46
Words are like l.; POPE A 22
leaving: child l. his bed WHITM 62
I must be l. AUDE 65
I was l. home STEVENSO R 6
L. circles new and clean
    VAN DO 1
l. thee, my bonnie Mary.
    BURN 49
leavings: accepts such l. WHITM 98
thousands/ Of arrowhead l.
    SNYD 1
leaze: Upon the l. HARD 25
Lebanon: to cedared L. KEAT 13
Lebarge: marge of Lake L. SERV 1
'leben: Imp at three and wench at
    l. WALK 9
lecher: heavy as a l.'s kiss.
    PLATH 47
l. in my sight. SHAK 80
lecherous: l. as a sparwe, CHAU 3
lechers: insolent old l. HORA 2
Led: I have l. her home, TENN 95
L. by a blind BOYD 1
l. his regiment from behind
    GILB 14
l. the flock away — DICKI 81
l. With doubleness? WYAT 28
unsuspitious l. him; MILT 114
Leda: L.'s goose a swan. UNKN 95
love of L., SPENS 41
Ledaean: dream of a L. body,
    YEATS 8

ledge: wave, wide from this l.
    CRAN H 1
ledgers: change swords for l.,
    WORD 157
hotel l., news files. SPEND 20
Lee: Adowne the L., SPENS 44
between windward and l.,
    SWIN 10
chilling/ And killing my Annabel
    L. POE 5
name of Annabel L.; POE 3
leech: l., or newt, or toad FLET J 2
leer: assent with civil l., POPE A 7
I've a fascinating l.; GILB 9
Replace/ the l. RANDA D 3
Leerie: see L. going by;
    STEVENSO R 3
lees: drink/ Life to the l. TENN 129
mere l. Is left this vault
    SHAK 109
leet: l. no morsel from hir lippes
    falle, CHAU 15
leeward: Hissing to l. like a ton of
    spray, MILLA 12
left: Cannon to l. of them, TENN 8
enough/ L. overs AUDE 12
floating home for ever l. COWP 1
He l. the name,
    JOHN S (1709–1784) 19
l. a void; JOHN S (1709–1784) 3
l. behind her ain grey tail:
    BURN 56
l. by the tide, WHITM 2
l. in loneliness behind. BARNE 5
L. in the quarry; TENN 108
l. it on its stalk? EMER 22
l. the ancient love BLAK 111
l. the past year's dwelling
    HOLM 2
l. thee naked, Lord, CRAS 11
l. what still is STEVENS 41
l. your souls on earth! KEAT 2
lit what's l. of my life. MERR 1
millions of suns l.,) WHITM 76
nail my l. palm DUGA 3
She l. the web, she left the loom,
    TENN 65
then he l. her, UNKN 218
They have l. unstained HEMA 5
What of soul was l.,
    BROWNI R 79
leg: forgets his l. of wood.
    GRAV 21
less than a l. ROET 35
standing on one l. MOMA 6
Swing out my long lean l.
    ALLE 1
legend: Eastward, the annual l.,
    SCOT WI 1
l. of Felix is VAN DY 4
L. of Love DRYD 6
life became a L. of the Dead.
    LONG 27

legendary: All l. obstacles
    MONTA 1
l. isle/ Where sirens sang DAY 7
Stilled l. depth: HUGH T 12
legended: door of a l. tomb;
    POE 49
legends: l. of the green chapels
    THOMA D 34
l. of their own: DICKEY 26
legions: l., angel forms, MILT 55
legs: cannon-ball took off his l.,
    HOOD 4
curl your l. up under you;
    JARR 6
drawn in yr l. REED I 1
hard l. of our women. SHAP 8
l. and locked; VAN DO 2
l. bestrid the ocean; SHAK 7
l. of the race run/ forwards,
    HARP 1
l. waken salads in the brain
    CRAN H 24
long, small l. and thighs
    HERR 68
long spinners' l., SHAK 153
On my l. my heart my liver
    ELIOT T 6
trailing your l. and crying!
    MILLA 41
tuft of fronds or katydid l.
    MOOR M 30
turn one's l. GILB 41
with her l. spread out SEXT 4
with muscular l., WHITM 70
leisure: all who had money and l.
    PRAE 4
home in l. MILT 111
life in shifts of work and l.
    HEAN 14
Light, joy, and l.; HERB G 39
then an awful l. was DICKI 100
lemonade: drink l., UNKN 240
lemons: Oranges and l., UNKN 23
lend: hope some fellow will l. a
    hand BRIN 3
its ignorant impulse l. MELV 17
l. a tyrannous and a damnèd
    light SHAK 30
L. less than thou owest, SHAK 71
l. the eye a terrible aspect:
    SHAK 56
muses l. their force, THOR 4
truest heart that lover e'er did l.
    KING H 6
lender: Neither a borrower nor a l.
    SHAK 24
lending: l. their strength WALK 5
lends: Nature l. such evil dreams?
    TENN 32
length: bridge of wondrous l.
    MILT 62
Distance and l., HOSK 1

l. in clay's now competent,
   WEBS 3
l. was failure, LANIE 4
now at l. I find, SIDN 32
touching along the l. of our
   bodies, KINN 1
lengthe: of evene l., CHAU 8
lengthen'd: l., sage advices,
   BURN 51
lengthened: l. out/ To deathless
   pain? MILT 98
length'n: Thought must l.
   DANI S 4
lengthy: l. service ended, HORA 8
Lenin: L. in a sealed train
   SNYD 24
lightning of L.'s bones. MACDI 6
Lenore: low lies thy love, L.!
   POE 29
sorrow for the lost L. POE 35
Lenox: Down on L. Avenue
   HUGH L 18
lent: neighbor's creed has l.
   EMER 18
Seven years thou wert l.
   JONS 23
lentil: likes l. soup.' GINS 28
leopard: Devilish l.! PLATH 45
watchers in their l. suits SIMP 2
leopards: three white l. sat
   ELIOT T 6
leper: introspective as a l., RUKE 3
less: day l. or more TENN 119
envy of l. happier lands;
   SHAK 88
greater grief/ To banish the l.,
   SURR 11
greater heaven in an heaven l.
   MARV 31
Lend l. than thou owest,
   SHAK 71
l. is more, BROWNI R 9
l. patience/ Than a wolf's,
   TATE A 19
l. subject than Eternitie;
   COWL 12
l. than a leg ROET 35
L. then a span: BACO 1
much l. cold, ROSS C 25
nicely-calculated l. or more;
   WORD 10
Set l. than thou throwest;
   SHAK 71
something l. prepoceros.
   NASH 13
Speak l. than thou knowest,
   SHAK 71
thoughts that please me l. and l.
   betray me. GREV 3
lesser: many l. faculties MILT 80
lesson: l. thou hast taught!
   LONG 50
Like a poetry l. AUDE 27

Love is the l. SPENS 19
take a l. from this tale HOWI 2
virtue hath this better l. taught,
   SIDN 40
lest: l. fierce remembrance
   MILT 112
L. we forget — KIPL 17
let: come l. us kiss and part
   DRAY 15
creed that will not l. you dance?
   JOHN H 2
Go, birds of spring: l. winter have
   his fee; HERB G 37
hurry to l. him in? SMIT ST 8
l. down in that steep bank of
   clay. SYNG 5
L. him be rich and weary,
   HERB G 63
l. it go by. BOGA 16
l. it pass, WYAT 4
l. me die before my death!"
   VAUG 19
l. me walk with thee GLAD 1
l. my people go. UNKN 115
l. that light be thy guide
   SIDN 35
l. the punishment fit the crime —
   GILB 28
l. their veins run cold. OWEN 31
though I am clean forgot, L me
   not love thee, if I love thee not.
   HERB G 6
Will you never l. us go? KIPL 22
lethal: dragoon me into a l.
   automaton MACN 16
lethargic: dotard l. and dull,
   MELV 14
Lethe: go not to L., KEAT 42
In L. to be drowned, HERR 49
L.-wards had sunk: KEAT 44
Lethean: drunken of things L.;
   SWIN 23
heavenly L. flood, DONN 34
lets: l. and bars MELV 17
l. forth his sprite, SHAK 123
L. his own ashes choke his soul.
   HERB G 29
letter: l. from his wife. CARRO 29
l. from our Pete, WHITM 15
l. from thy dear son. WHITM 15
my l. to the world, DICKI 145
Preferment goes by l. and
   affection, SHAK 133
Write me a l., UNKN 81
write your l., DONN 27
letters: his long marvelous l.
   AUDE 101
Jointing syllables, drowning l,
   JONS 9
l. make a paltry sum MOSS 2
long,/ neat-scripted l. KINN 5
noble l. of the dead. TENN 41
letting: — then the l. go — DICKI 2

leve: l. your bordes, WYAT 17
lordinges, by youre l., that am nat
   I. CHAU 94
level: all's one l. plain UNKN 250
dance upon the l. shore?
   YEATS 163
fresh the l. pasture lay, INGE 1
lawns, or l. downs, MILT 69
lone and l. sands SHEL 50
Nothing is plumb, l. or square:
   DUGA 1
Taking the final l. CRAN H 33
What counts is the cultural l.,
   POUN 14
leveling: l. of the marshes
   CRAN H 43
lever: liberty is l. WYAT 6
Leviathan: He is called L.,
   MERW 8
there is that l., BIBL, O.T. 52
levynne: l. and the thunder poures,
   CHAT 2
lewd: affectedly Pious nor secretly
   l., PRIO 6
l. and lavish act of sin, MILT 4
l. hirelings climb. MILT 68
lewdness: Though l. court it
   SHAK 27
leyd: l. in presse. CHAU 8
Lhude: L. sing Goddamm, POUN 2
liable: l. to melt as snow.
   CRAN H 40
Liar: They only answered 'Little
   L.'! BELL 16
lib: l. and die in Dixie! EMME 2
libeled: l. by her hate. POPE A 90
liberal: beggar may be l. of love.
   UNKN 96
either a litle L., GILB 22
liberating: proved/ In l. strife,
   BATE 2
walk l., AMMO 3
libertie: betrayed my l.? SIDN 15
Who ever gives, takes l.:
   DONN 31
liberty: Author of l., SMIT SA 2
chained bay waters L.
   CRAN H 27
Delight and l., WORD 80
Enjoy such l. LOVE 5
Fair L. was all his cry; SWIF 24
give me l.' BRON 7
l. is lever. WYAT 6
L. that crowns Britannia's Isle,
   ADDI 2
mocks my loss of l. BLAK 24
mountain nymph, sweet L.;
   MILT 21
Nature, like l., is but restrained
   POPE A 27
People's l.!
   JOHN S (1822–1882) 1

l.'s headlong train; — ARNO 45

l.'s journey just begun? COWP 10

l.'s poor play is o'er. POPE A 81

L.'s struggle BROWNI R 75

L.'s troubled bubble broken'? —
DE LA 24

l.'s unresting sea! HOLM 3

l.'s vase/ Of glass THOR 2

light of a whole l. dies BOUR 2

lit what's left of my l. MERR 1

live out your l. ROET 60

lived his own, private l., FEAR 1

lords of l. EMER 20

Love, maintain thy l. in me.
SIDN 27

Love took up the harp of L.,
TENN 70

low dark verge of l. TENN 29

made your l. worth? SNOD 3

makes calamity of so long l.;
SHAK 39

man should labour all/ 'Is l.
KIPL 19

Man's l. is cheap as beast's.
SHAK 74

mate his l. with l. STEVENS 49

measured out my l. with coffee
spoons; ELIOT T 82

mercy more than l.! BATE 2

my l. and my bride POE 6

My l. closed twice DICKI 107

My L. had stood — DICKI 109

My L. had stood — RICH 15

'My l. is dreary, TENN 92

My l. may mend, SOUTHW 13

my l., my fate; TENN 94

my l., my love, my heart,
HERR 40

My L. thy Web: TAYL E 6

my Light, my L., my Way.
QUAR 4

My lines and l. are free,
HERB G 17

My pulse of l., LAWR 26

My very l. ROSS C 7

new and larger l. MCCRE 3

no l.-glimpse, good or bad,/ Nor
joy nor passion ROBI 6

no l. lives for ever; SWIN 15

No sound is dissonant which tells
of L. COLE SAM 42

no such pleasure in l.!
BROWNI R 84

nobleness of l. SHAK 3

nobler modes of l., TENN 48

noise of l. TENN 21

Nothing would give up l.;
ROET 53

now I live, and now my l. is
done. TICH 1

'O glorious L., NEWB 4

O l. unlike to ours! ARNO 24

O past! O happy l.! WHITM 66

O world! O l.! O time! SHEL 34

Of l. and death, of home
WHITM 12

Of l. or death, WILB 46

of this plodding l. THOR 10

On l.'s rough ocean luckless
starr'd: BURN 60

on the Tree of L., MILT 68

one l. hums, SPEND 9

one L. within us and abroad,
COLE SAM 11

one of the lords/ Of l. LAWR 46

Onward through l. he goes;
LONG 49

ordinary/ Surroundings of social
l. SNOD 1

our l. a ruling effluence ARNO 17

our l. begins, WHITM 41

Our l. is closed, WHITM 41

our l.'s Star, WORD 69

our little l. SHAK 163

passeth from l. KNOX 1

Passions are the elements of L.
POPE A 68

past l. a ruined church —
MACN 25

pay glad l.'s arrears
BROWNI R 69

poem of my l. RICH 28

Poor vaunt of l. BROWNI R 72

prime of your l. RICH 12

Pure was thy l.; BRYA 6

put forth all our l., ARNO 16

red l. might stream again,
KEAT 61

rife with the joy of l., SMIT L 1

rust L.'s iron chain WILD 4

Sadie scraped l. BROO G 12

saved my l., saying "not you."
SHAK 241

scholar's l. assail,
JOHN S (1709–1784) 18

sea of l. enisled, ARNO 41

seas of l. like wine; TRAH 10

Secret of my L. to learn:
OMAR 6

sense/ Of L., MASE 9

Shall L. inherit. BUNY 3

Shall l. succeed BROWNI R 74

sheets and towels of a l.
MERR 10

shilling l. AUDE 98

short l. and a merry one,
OWEN 2

short l., eternal liberty. BRON 9

show of l. VERY 2

signifies the l. o' man, BURN 29

silent from l. escape WHITM 17

simple l. that Nature yields;
CRAB 5

Sleep; and if l. was bitter
SWIN 8

slits the thin-spun l. MILT 27

some joy from with'ring l.
JOHN S (1709–1784) 14

soul of man dies in him, loathing
l., THOMS J (1700–1748) 13

spectacles to my l. GREV 3

Squat on my l.? LARK 20

Stealing my breath of l., MCKA 2

stuff/ Of her l. WILB 45

stuff of l. to knit me HOUS 63

such a l., as one leads
BROWNI R 83

such is l. LEAR 3

sucked the l. BARA 3

sun's l.-giving power,
CONS/CHET 2

sweetness did not save/ His l. from
foes. HERB G 55

tasks of real l., WORD 4

There is no l. in them.
ELIOT T 7

These make the lines of l.,
JONS 40

(this l. one leaf) CUMM 9

this long disease, my l.;
POPE A 14

thorns of l.! SHEL 45

those who live call l.: SHEL 57

Thou gav'st me l., but mortal;
HERR 54

thought is l. BLAK 63

threatened its l. CARRO 12

To l., to cities, and to war!
ARNO 38

To measure l. learn thou
MILT 120

too far out all my l. SMIT ST 2

too old for death, too old for l.,
PRAT 1

tormented you/ To l. SNOD 12

travelled l.'s dull round,/ Where'er
his stages SHEN 2

twinned the sweet babe o' its l.,
UNKN 71

'Twixt fears of dying and desire of
l.: CRAB 3

'Twixt l. and death, CRAS 10

unknown unwanted l. JARR 22

upon the road of l. KAVA 12

Vanquished in l., his death
JOHN L 4

voyage of their l. SHAK 50

waste of l., MERE O 1

watched me all your l., DURE 1

what good in l. since?
BROWNI R 26

What is this l. DAVIE W 2

what is this l.? GINS 21

What l. is best? BACO 2

What wondrous l. MARV 17

wine of l. is drawn, SHAK 109

winged l. destroy; BLAK 47

With endless l. are crowned.
HERR 49

womanly l. WHITM 72
Word I was in my l. alone,
  FROS 9
Worn with l.'s care, CRAB 2
your l. broke down. HUGO 1
your money or your l.!" —
  BYRO 53
life's: L. a piece in bloom HENL 4
L. but a walking shadow,
  SHAK 114
l. none so long. KIPL 19
l. not a paragraph CUMM 46
world and l. too big
  BROWNI R 29
lifeblood: drain the l. of the child,
  SHAK 61
Lifeless: L., but beautiful,
  LONG 23
L. in appearance, WILLI 35
lifeward: Lug us back l.
  CRAN H 26
liffes: l. and saftyes all! UNKN 58
lift: lids that will not l. DODG 1
l. frail heads MAHON 3
l. me as a wave, a leaf, a cloud!
  SHEL 45
l. me from the grass!/ I die! I
  faint! I fail! SHEL 32
l. my lamp LAZA 2
l. their heavy lids, PATM 2
l. up mine eyes unto the hills,
  BIBL, O.T. 58
L. up your heads, O ye gates;
  BIBL, O.T. 34
To l., DAY 12
Would l. her Eyes SWIF 14
lifted: attains his l. mark —
  MELV 7
city with l. head singing SAND 4
l. the half-covered chair SCHW 5
l. up a single stone. WORD 53
Shall be l. nevermore! POE 37
sleep — and it is l. SHEL 57
Lifts: L. earth to heaven, CRAS 5
l. to the changing moon
  YEATS 22
light: accepted into as much l.
  AMMO 2
Add l. to some small Star.
  DAVE 6
all was l. POPE A 106
as a signal l., — LONG 44
beams of heavenly l., COWP 22
before the l. began, UNKN 257
bent l. over the dead RUKE 1
Between the l. — and me —
  DICKI 49
Black pit cold and l.-year
  SNYD 30
blasted with excess of l.,
  GRAY 30
blinded by the l., WILLI 21

blue l. Shed by a tinted window.
  DICKEY 20
borrowed l. KING H 5
brighter l. and softer airs,
  BRYA 8
brimming with inner l.
  MOOR M 28
bringing l. to life. SPEND 19
brings again to l.: WILB 26
cast too fierce a l., SACK 1
Casting a dim, religious l.
  MILT 18
certain Slant of l., DICKI 142
cheerful beams send forth their l.
  CAREW 20
Child of L.! SHEL 53
comes in the l.; CLOU 9
corridors of l. SPEND 11
danced by the l. of the moon,
  LEAR 12
dark my l., ROET 33
darkness or another l.; ROBI 32
dawned with added l.? TIMR 3
dawn's early l., KEY 1
drear l. of Zoo, GINS 9
drenched in empyrean l.
  WORD 102
dwelling is the l. of setting suns,
  WORD 35
eternal l. DAVE 1
Everlasting L.; BROO P 3
eyes give more l. WHITM 91
faster than l. BULL 1
Fond Memory brings the l.
  MOOR T 10
"Forward the L. Brigade!
  TENN 6
found a cloud so l. POUN 16
fountain l. of all our day,
  WORD 81
four l.-green eggs WHITM 64
freedom's holy l.; SMIT SA 2
fringed with l. LONG 24
from th' eternal L. DAVIE S 1
furred/ With a l. frost, HECH 2
gigantic men of l. whispering
  HARJ 2
gleaming of a random l.,
  DUNB P 7
glorious canopy of l. WHITE 1
glory of the L. ROBI 10
glows with the l. POE 25
gone into the world of l.!
  VAUG 26
Grain-tinctured, drenched in
  empyrean l.; WORD 102
great cloak blows in the l.,
  RUKE 5
hair was like a l. CHES 2
Heaven's l. forever shines,
  SHEL 13
Hesperus entreats thy l., JONS 3

hidden/ In the l. of thought,
  SHEL 70
high endeavors are an inward l.
  WORD 4
I leave this l.; HERR 51
If L. can thus deceive, WHITE 2
I'm so l., it don't seem right
  DURE 2
immortal l. and heat! VAUG 3
in her tranquil l. BRID R 19
In the pink l. the small red sun
  goes rolling, BISH 26
infant crying for the l.: TENN 31
inward L., a way as good,
  BUTL 8
jolts of l.; SNYD 4
joy, nor love, nor l., ARNO 3
lady of l., SWIN 4
land is scattered with l.,
  BRID R 2
layered l. Above them swims;
  WARR 1
lend a tyrannous and a damnèd l.
  SHAK 30
let that l. be thy guide SIDN 35
l. and a shadow on every man
  MELV 7
l. as feather
  JOHN S (1709–1784) 11
l.-blue lane of early dawn,
  TENN 54
L. breaks where no sun shines;
  THOMA D 29
l. canoes have vanished SIGO 1
L. dies before thy uncreating
  word: POPE A 2
l. dispels the dark. MILT 82
l. doth seize my brain BLAK 46
l. exists in spring DICKI 101
l. fantastic toe, MILT 21
l. for thighs KINS 4
l. he was to no one FROS 74
l. I loved so much, PETRA 12
l. in the dust lies dead; SHEL 89
l. incarnate. WILB 44
l. is come, TENN 105
L./ Is the lion STEVENS 13
L., joy, and leisure; HERB G 39
l. of a whole life dies BOUR 2
l. of common day. WORD 71
l. of distant skies: BRYA 28
l. of hidden fire MARL 4
l. of one sweet smile. SHEL 66
l. of the bright world BOUR 1
l. of the moon and stars?
  WHITM 89
L., ofspring of Heav'n MILT 63
l. passes DOOL 1
l. poured softly in her lap.
  FROS 26
l. pushes through; LAWR 1
l. shakes across the lakes,
  TENN 111

L. she was MONTROSS 2
l./ that comes and goes, like
  hearts. BISH 1
l. that is dark SWIN 20
l. that never was, WORD 11
l. thee steady; SCOT WA 5
l. to guide, WORD 88
l. wing against the ivory gate,
  MORR 3
L.-winged Smoke, THOR 6
l. withdrawn WHITT 11
l. would show SITW 5
little l. fades WHITM 75
long l. on the sea — MACL 13
Love is a growing, or full constant
  l.; DONN 36
luck was his l.-o'-love, SERV 6
master l. of all our seeing;
  WORD 81
moon gives you l., WHITM 27
morning l. creaks down again;
  SITW 4
my heart is l. POE 30
my l. is low, TENN 27
my l. is spent, MILT 124
my L., my Life, my Way.
  QUAR 4
my lives l. And saviour,
  CHAU 117
name the bigger l., SHAK 157
Nature's sweetest l.; SIDN 41
Newton's particles of l. BLAK 39
No l. propitious shone; COWP 2
Obedient to the l. SHEL 20
odour, l., embrace, FLET G YO 1
on the shores of darkness there is
  l., KEAT 65
one l.'s language in the book of
  trees. THOMA D 8
opens forth the l. SIDN 34
pale dull pallor of an old gas l.
  HUGH L 18
pause in the l. AIKE 7
placed thee with the sons of l.,
  BRYA 6
prefer dark night/ Before true l.!
  VAUG 33
private buffoon is a l.-hearted
  loon, GILB 56
Pulsing out red l. SHAP 1
put out the l. SHAK 137
Rage, rage against the dying of
  the l. THOMA D 11
rare/ as the l. of a happy eye,
  WILLI 47
ring of pure and endless l.,
  VAUG 32
river of crystal l., FIEL E 8
rocks breaking with l., BISH 35
rosie Morn resignes her l.,
  WALL 8
sacred Fountain of eternall l.,
  QUAR 2

sang to the L. SITW 8
sea of l.? VAUG 31
seizure on the l., HERR 44
Shape all l., SHEL 77
sharp ax of l., THOMA E 4
she made all of l., CAMPI 1
shed my innocent l., my Blood,
  SITW 13
shores of l.? LUCR 5
Softly now the l. of day DOAN 1
something of angelic l.
  WORD 135
somewhere hearts are l.; THAY 4
stolen goods do come to l.
  SIDN 10
Swarming in the l. SNYD 23
Take care how you l. TROW 3
takes the l. and ranges NOYE 1
thought of the l. POE 25
thy former l. restore, SHAK 137
took away the l.: MILT 43
torch of death they l.; THAC 1
unapproached L./ Dwelt from
  Eternitie, MILT 63
waited for the l., ROBI 52
way where l. dwelleth?
  BIBL, O.T. 15
weak and little is the l.,
  THOMA E 15
When l. if over, UNKN 257
When the l. drips AIKE 6
will never be l.; FOST 2
with l. head erect I sing, THOR 4
with starry l., SPENS 2
with streaks of l., SHAK 146
wonder came to l., GOLD 8
wondrous and instructive l.,
  TRAH 2
your l. shined never; SPENS 6
lightbulbs: angelic as l. GINS 40
lighted: l. at the sex again. CART 1
l. faces smile no more. WHITT 29
l. fools/ The way to dusty death.
  SHAK 114
lightened: l. up my heaven,
  BRON 12
unintelligible world/ Is l.: —
  WORD 30
lightfoot: many a l. lad. HOUS 62
lighthouses: pulsation of l.
  MOOR M 13
lightly: bright eye/ That wandereth
  l. PEEL 2
cover l., gentle earth. JONS 22
his arm lay l. WHITM 109
In the spring a young man's fancy
  l. turns TENN 69
l. draws its breath, WORD 155
l. threaded with nimble feet
  BINY 5
l. with my lips WHITM 69
slight things do l. please.
  HERR 18

Tread l., WILD 17
wear their godhead l. SNOD 10
What's l. hid WILB 10
With l. closed fists WHITM 70
ye tread/ L., HERR 59
lightness: l. in her footfall, RANS 3
lightning: flame/ Is the imprisoned
  l., LAZA 1
In thunder l. MILT 104
l. and the gale! HOLM 18
l. before death: SHAK 152
l. flash, SHAK 18
l. of Lenin's bones. MACDI 6
L. showed a Yellow Beak
  DICKI 161
looked like l. or a scribble.
  FROS 131
loosed the fateful l. HOWE 1
playing out l. WHITM 77
smiles are l., DANI S 9
sport'st amid the l.-flash and
  thunder-cloud, WHITM 105
steel decks rock with the l. shock,
  ROON 3
swift its bolt than l. THOR 5
Writhed like l., LAWR 44
lightnings: l. flashed; JOHN J 2
lights: blame l. due; MILT 99
broken l. of thee, TENN 17
courteous l. MARV 26
false l. on the shore, LONG 7
gleaming l., — LONG 29
Glorious the northern l. astream;
  SMAR 9
in the body's cage:/ Dim l. of life,
  POPE A 4
lamp l. another, LOWE J 21
l. around the shore. ROSS D 8
l./ Her stove, ELIOT T 134
l./ His constant lamp, MILT 78
L. that do mislead the morn:
  SHAK 117
l. the pathway SANT 2
love that shook the l. RUKE 3
Northern L. have seen queer
  sights, SERV 1
Take the neon l. and make a
  crown, HUGH L 8
white and pewter l., PLATH 23
lightsome: in l. files they fare,
  MELV 18
like: absence therefore l. I best.
  GOOG 3
dearly l. the west, BURN 41
I l. a church; EMER 38
I l. a cowl; EMER 38
I l. a look of Agony, DICKI 53
I l. it CRAN S 4
i l. my body CUMM 50
i l. the thrill CUMM 51
L. and unlike, EMER 20
L. as the waves SHAK 209
l. task we are at; UNKN 202

l. the heart of man SITW 13
l. the morning dew, DANI S 5
l. this dawn, SNYD 11
l. to rise and go
  STEVENSO R 19
L. to the lark SHAK 194
l. you any more." SNOD 8
My Love is l. to ice, and I to fire:
  SPENS 9
mysteries/ Are l. the Sun,
  DONN 51
not l. some things, MOOR M 27
Something l. a person: SILKI 1
something very l. one. SILKI 1
very, very l. me STEVENSO R 13
liked: ' 'E l. it all!' KIPL 21
she l. them best, CARRO 4
likeness: l. for thy vision? SWIN 6
smashed into a l. KOCH 7
likerous: so propre and sweete and
  l., CHAU 52
likerousnesse: my lust, my l.,
  CHAU 92
likes: Love l. no laws but his own!
  GREV 1
weather the cuckoo l., HARD 49
When and where l. me best
  MILT 109
Likewise: master of this house,/ L.
  the mistress UNKN 116
liking: faults of his own l.!
  SHAK 116
Tuned to my l., MILLA 12
Lil: hear about Cocaine L.?
  UNKN 67
lilac: Colour of l., LOWE A 1
Kew in l.-time, NOYE 2
L. and brown hair; ELIOT T 11
L. and star and bird WHITM 53
L. blooming perennial WHITM 46
l. is in bloom, BROO R 15
l. with mastering odor
  WHITM 49
Lilacs: breeding/ L. out of the dead
  land, ELIOT T 113
L.,/ False blue, LOWE A 1
When l. last WHITM 46
lilies: breaking the golden l.
  BROWNI E 2
L. that fester SHAK 222
rose and silver l. die,
  FLET G EL 1
roses and white l. grow;
  CAMPI 23
wringing l. from the acorn;
  POUN 37
Lillie: Christal'd L. HERR 27
Lillies: L. without, Roses within.
  MARV 29
whitest sheets of L. cold.
  MARV 29
lilting: l. at our yowe-milking,
  ELLI 1

lily: bright l. grow JONS 2
know a little garden-close/ Set
  thick with l. MORR 6
L. and bleeding-heart and rose,
  JUST 4
l. in splendor, PITT 2
l. of a day/ Is fairer far in May
  JONS 41
l. of the valleys. BIBL, O.T. 70
l. whispers, 'I wait.' TENN 94
No l. has such lustre, GAY 1
pale wet leaves of l.-of-the-valley
  POUN 1
limb: life in every l., WORD 155
limbs: blackbird sat/ In the cedar l.
  STEVENS 67
brown habergeon of his l.
  BEDD 10
conquering l. astride LAZA 1
Grieving the sapless l., RANS 11
l. are burning SHEL 53
l. knife-skewed, OWEN 29
l. that had run wild. YEATS 55
L. that we left POUN 5
l. with dust are covered
  FRENE 3
repose for l. with travel tired;
  SHAK 193
ruddy l. and flaming hair,
  BLAK 21
stiffening my l., WHITM 77
Young in l., SHAK 119
lime: l. and copper smell KAVA 27
l.-tree is in blossom LOWE A 7
quick destroying l. WYLI 7
limestone: l. landscape. AUDE 52
l. on an ancient sill. TATE A 17
Limited: so/ whizzed the L.
  CRAN H 16
limits: Claspest the l. of mortality,
  SHEL 68
l. of a vulgar fate: GRAY 31
l. of day, LOWE R 54
nature's l. thrown, FRENE 4
limousine: All we want is a l.
  MACN 8
One perfect l., PARK 1
limp: hides his l., BLY 3
live with an invisible l., BLY 2
neckcurls, l. and damp as
  tendrils; ROET 11
surroundings l. BLY 3
limping: l. age will lodge him now
  VAUX 5
l. as before, BROWNI R 63
lin'd: skies with clouds are l.;
  BIBL, O.T. 67
Lincoln: bells of merry L.
  UNKN 134
Beloved in life of Abraham L.,
  MAST 2
land of Abraham L. CUMM 39
L., Brown RANDA D 4

Robert of L. is telling his name:
  BRYA 19
Lincolnshire: famous L.,
  UNKN 172
linden: in his l. cradle, LONG 41
lindens: Under the l. on the
  heather, WALT 1
lindenwood: Hewed the l.,
  UNKN 20
line: countenance filled up his l.,
  SHAK 218
draw a l. SPENC A 4
each l. an act WINT 10
first l. he read, HOLM 12
God in every L.: DRYD 18
grim l. of sheer subsistence
  SAND 16
high esthetic l. GILB 30
horizon's fluid l.; SPEND 17
it faltered at the l. AUDE 27
l. in array, WHITM 13
L. in nature is not found;
  EMER 50
l. up with brother: SAND 18
l. will take us hours YEATS 1
l./ You must not cross
  CRAN H 47
lives along the l.: POPE A 71
low words oft creep in one dull
  l.: POPE A 25
meet to walk the l. FROS 56
million boots in l., AUDE 79
pacified by a clever l. AUDE 48
rapid glide along the leaning l.;
  THOMS J (1700–1748) 11
scarce change a l. LOWE J 7
up the l. to death, SASS 3
We carved not a l., WOLF C 3
lineage: born of old worthy l.?
  MORE 2
don't worry about your l.
  OHAR 18
Poets of the proud old l. FLEC 1
lineaments: l. of a plummet-
  measured face. YEATS 143
l. of gratified desire. BLAK 48
lined: face grows l. and wrinkled
  SHAP 20
Photographically l. GILB 46
linen: in a scented l. sheet, WYLI 9
l. you're wearing out HOOD 12
scarlet cloaks and surplices/ Of l.,
  LAWR 9
liner: air l. with shut-off engines
  SPEND 13
Lines: Accept for once some serious
  L. SWIF 18
drawn no l.: AMMO 5
fair l. which true goodness show.
  SIDN 20
in eternal l. SHAK 188
Leaves, l., and rhymes, seek her to
  please SPENS 3

lisp: l. my very earliest word,
  POE 39
  l. of leaves   SWIN 3
lisped: l. in accents mild,
  SMIT ST 3
list: Doth as yow l.,   CHAU 111
  Grudge who l., but none deny!
  HENR 1
  I've got a little l.   GILB 26
  l. of the dead.   CLARK J 1
  L. to the yarn,   WHITM 89
  l./ To Nature's teachings,
  BRYA 23
  Names on a l.,   EBER 4
  tomb/ Shall l. and founder
  SHAP 25
listen: Darkling I l.;   KEAT 49
  hear the wilderness l.   STAF 3
  L. and save.   MILT 7
  l. at the corners   YEATS 148
  L., my children,   LONG 43
  l. she will call,   ROBI 22
  l. to all sides   WHITM 76
  l. to popular rumour;   GILB 56
  l. to the merry village chime.
  GILB 38
  world should l. then,   SHEL 72
listened: l. wondering.   GRAV 13
  we l. to Red Lantern   BARA 6
listeners: l.' hungry hearts
  JOHN J 7
listenin': l. for the drum,   NEWB 1
listening: l. at the key-hole
  GILB 45
  L. behind me for my wit,
  THOR 4
  l. chamber,   SHEL 31
  L., like lover or worshiper,
  WARR 8
  l./ To silence,   HOOD 1
  only two moons l.,   ROBI 46
  solitary me l.,   WHITM 67
listens: Landscape l.   DICKI 144
  l. in the snow,   STEVENS 51
  l. like a three years' child:
  COLE SAM 29
  people l.;   SCOT WA 1
listless: l. look along the plain
  SCOT WA 4
  nerveless, l., dead,   KEAT 20
Listlessly: L., till slumber comes.
  CULL 6
listlessness: envy, l., or sport,
  BROWNI R 16
lit: flame that l.   HEMA 1
  little bug all l.   ROBE 1
litany: write a holy l.   GINS 5
litel: l. gold in cofre.   CHAU 2
  too greet chepe is holden at l.
  pris.   CHAU 89
literalists: l. of/ the imagination —
  MOOR M 33

literate: Cries out a l. despair.
  STEVENS 42
literati: l. keep/ An imaginary
  friend.   AUDE 6
literature: l. bores me,
  BERRYM 11
  One thing that l.   NASH 18
lithe: ask'd a l. lady   BLAK 25
  Build with l. love.   BROO G 15
  Coiled to a l. precision   TATE A 9
  l. abandon of your walk,
  BENN G 6
  so l. and so fleet,   LOWE J 1
litter: l. of powder-parcels,
  WHITM 92
littering: impassioned in the l.
  leaves.   STEVENS 58
Litters: filmy trash/ L.   JARR 4
little: called the latter " L. Prig";
  EMER 35
  either a l. Liberal,   GILB 22
  Farmer Rouf's l. lad.   WOOL 1
  fear of l. men;   ALLI 1
  fits a l. belly,   HERR 38
  go as l. children sent.   DODG 2
  have l. of peace!   STEPHENS 12
  Here, in this l. Bay,   PATM 6
  I have a l. shadow
  STEVENSO R 13
  left his l. footmarks,   CLARE 10
  l.-Ant men as they ran   SITW S
  l. being came: FRENE 7
  l. black cat   MONR 1
  l. black feet,   LIND V 12
  l. black thing   BLAK 55
  l. boy again,   WHITM 63
  L. Boy Blue/ Kissed them
  FIEL E 6, 7
  L. Boy Blue,   MOTH 18
  l. bread shall do me stead!
  STEVENSO W 1
  l. by l. and was by was   CUMM 6
  l. child to bed,   LONG 33
  l. fidget wheels   SLES 1
  l. fir-trees do   SNYD 41
  l. foxes, that spoil the vines:
  BIBL, O.T. 73
  L. Giffen, of Tennessee!   TICK 1
  l. girl, she had a l. curl   MOTH 28
  l. he can do?   FROS 20
  l. is not granted."   COAT 1
  L. Jack Horner   MOTH 20
  L. Jesus, wast Thou shy
  THOMP F 4
  l. learning is a dangerous thing;
  POPE 33
  l. lives of men.   TENN 19
  l. lizard-feet   ROET 39
  l. man,   WHITT 6
  L. Orphant Annie's   RILE 1
  l. profits that an idle king,
  TENN 128
  l. restless midge.   WILD 18

  l. Saviour;   HERR 47
  l. scrotum   SNYD 5
  l. soul   SWIN 25
  l. still she strove, and much
  repented,   BYRO 20
  l. systems have their day;
  TENN 17
  l. time they prized   NEME 1
  l. tiny boy,   SHAK 177
  l. to earn,   KINGSL 3
  l. tom-tit   GILB 29
  l. toy dog   FIEL E 6
  L. Trotty Wagtail,   CLARE 10
  l. troubles pass   LAND 4
  l. was their store,   OVID 5
  l. world made cunningly
  DONN 33
  Love me l., love me long,
  HERR 28
  loves to hear the l. brook a-
  gurgling,   GILB 38
  made the l. tykes/ so happy
  OHAR 3
  Mary had a l. lamb,   HALE 1
  Nursed the l. Hiawatha,
  LONG 41
  O high-riser, my l. loaf.
  PLATH 82
  offering too l.   CANN 1
  one l. room an everywhere.
  DONN 29
  One l. sandpiper and I;   THAX 1
  Or else a l. Conservative!
  GILB 22
  Other l. children
  STEVENSO R 23
  our l. life   SHAK 163
  rotten l. downtowns.   PINS 1
  round l. worm   SHAK 153
  Serene stands the l. captain,
  WHITM 91
  speaking l., perhaps not a word.
  WHITM 33
  stood the l. boy   WHITT 13
  team of l. atomies/ Athwart men's
  noses   SHAK 153
  Thar sot L. Breeches   HAY 6
  That in a l. cottage I have found;
  KEAT 30
  this l. Jelly.   HERR 38
  This l. Pipkin   HERR 38
  this l. world,   SHAK 88
  Three l. kittens   FOLL 1
  voice of my l. captain,
  WHITM 90
  weak and l. is the light,
  THOMA E 15
littleness: what huge heaps of l.
  around!   POPE A 101
live: Almanacked, their names l.;
  LARK 3
  Black Poets should l.   KNIG 2

breast where roses could not l.
  ROBI 15
but a rage to l. POPE A 95
by which men long l. well
  EMPS 15
Come, l. with me DAY 1
Come l. with me MARL 18
content to l. it all again,
  YEATS 47
Days are where we l. LARK 8
dead shall l., the living die,
  DRYD 27
dead they l. VERY 2
death shall all the world subdue,/
  Our love shall l., SPENS 24
Easy l. and quiet die.
  SCOT WA 2
Gas smells awful;/ You might as
  well l. PARK 2
ghosts can l. Between two fires.
  DAY 5
Give me simplicity, that I may l.,
  HERB G 76
God said/ Shall these bones l.?
  ELIOT T 6
He spak to hem that wolde l.
  parfitly — CHAU 94
How is it that you l., WORD 125
I cannot l. with you. DICKI 33
I shall not l. in vain: DICKI 74
I than He — may longer l.
  DICKI 110
if I should l. to be HOLM 16
immortal dead who l. again
  ELIOT G 1
in Louisiana a l.-oak growing,
  WHITM 39
In solitude l. savage, MILT 97
lands where the Jumblies l.;
  LEAR 9
let me l., unseen, unknown;
  POPE A 108
l. a living death, DANI S 10
l. again as butterfly. ROSS C 4
l. again in memory, TENN 87
l. and die for thee. HERR 40
l. and lie reclined TENN 89
l. as if there were a God."
  RUKE 4
l. beyond the reach HORA 5
l. forsaken so. UNKN 167
l. in a name, LIND V 14
l. in furnished souls CUMM 52
l. in happier form SHEL 91
l. in mankind LIND V 14
l. in the terrible western world
  OHAR 9
l. in this poor rhyme, SHAK 229
l. like some green laurel
  YEATS 110
L. like the velvet mole; WYLI 2
L. lips YEATS 142

l.-long Minute true to thee,
  ROCH 6
l. on hay, HILL J 1
l. on toasted lizards, CARRY 5
l. out your life ROET 60
l. to bury me, OVID 7
l. with animals, WHITM 74
l. with ease POPE A 6
l. with scarlet Majors SASS 3
l. with the grace WILLI 47
l. with the men who work.
  VAN DY 5
l. with thee and be thy Love.
  RALEG 7, 9
l. within the spirit's fire; Æ 3
l. without hope? SAND 19
l. your epitaph to make,
  SHAK 216
Long l. the king, COWP 7
Love in all my parts shall l.
  COWL 6
lovers l. by longing, ROET 23
loving l., and merry still;
  CAMPI 8
Made him our pattern to l.
  BROWNI R 45
mortal millions l. alone.
  ARNO 41
must please to l.
  JOHN S (1709–1784) 9
not l. in the world, MUIR 1
now I l., and now my life is
  done. TICH 1
old bones l. ROET 29
one bare hour to l., MARL 1
people will l. on. SAND 14
pigs can l. in clover; WYLI 11
scorn delights and l. laborious
  days; MILT 27
see this day, and l. old age,
  SHAK 60
shall these/ Bones l.? ELIOT T 6
So little time we l. in Time,
  WARR 2
something that doth l., WORD 79
Stand and l., LOWE R 61
tell me how you l.!' CARRO 41
they pine, I l. DYER E 2
those who l. call life: SHEL 57
thy book doth l. JONS 43
To perish, or to l.? DICKI 153
to still l. on! WHITT 28
tri'd/ To l. without him: WOTT 7
wake and l.. — SHEL 42
way to l., by dying. DRYD 9
we shall l. very well. WYLI 12
We shall not l. again? SMIT L 3
we that l. to please,
  JOHN S (1709–1784) 9
"While you l.,/ Drink! — OMAR 6
why l.? ROBI 36
will I l. long enough LORD 5

words l. in my throat/ breeding
  like adders. LORD 1
you l. at court, JONS 32
you say/ You l., GRAV 39
lived: anyone l. in a pretty how
  town CUMM 4
At ninety-six I had l. enough,
  MAST 8
Belinda l. in a little white house,
  NASH 15
dwellest in earth and sun,/ I have
  l., NEWB 4
founders l. and died YEATS 35
grieve they l. not in these times
  DRAY 8
l. and thought, ROBI 36
l. by honest dreams DAY 13
l. by the river-side, HOLM 10
l., felt dawn, MCCRA 2
l. in a tree: SNYD 48
l. in an oak; RICHA E 1
l. in important places, times
  KAVA 4
l. Knott, died Knott, UNKN 88
l. laughing in my house MOMA 5
l. long enough, SWIN 21
L. many lives. SNYD 12
l. thousands of years ago,
  WHITM 75
l. with my husband. WILLI 46
Long indeed have we l.,
  WHITM 35
old woman and she l. in a shoe,
  MOTH 30
She l. unknown, WORD 46
so they l.; PRIO 4
sweetly l.; yet sweetness did not
  save/ His life from foes.
  HERB G 55
weasel l. in the sun THOMA E 7
When I was a bachelor, I l. by
  myself UNKN 99
while he l. never thought of
  death. GREV 8
livelier: In the spring a l. iris
  TENN 69
lively: l. understandable spirit
  ROET 38
such l. bliss. SPENS 28
liver: lung and l.,/ In her guts
  SYNG 1
On my legs my heart my l.
  ELIOT T 6
Liveried: L. angels robed in green,
  LAND 7
livers: grave l. do in Scotland use,
  WORD 123
l. I stick with needles quick;
  JONS 17
l. white as milk! SHAK 122
livery: l./ Walked crowns and
  crownets; SHAK 7
youth's proud l., SHAK 185

lives: all life dies, death l., and
  Nature breeds, MILT 61
all their l. and cares, WATT I 3
body's beauty l. STEVENS 37
cat has a number of l.;
  THOMA D 39
cuckold l. in bliss SHAK 134
Every thing that l. BLAK 15
evil that men do l. after them;
  SHAK 48
hundred different l.; ARNO 24
in their l. SPEND 12
Iron are our l. ROSE 1
lead their l. in love like me,
  CAMPI 16
lies in/ l. OHAR 10
little l. of men. TENN 19
Lived many l. SNYD 12
l. along the line: POPE A 71
l. at ease that freely l.! BARBO 1
l. contentedly between HORA 6
l. not in fear. SHAK 77
L. of great men LONG 36
make our l. sublime, LONG 36
music of men's l., SHAK 93
my l. light/ And saviour,
  CHAU 117
no life l. for ever; SWIN 15
our l., our souls, SHAK 58
our l. so far apart TENN 39
saved each other's l. GILB 11
secular bird ages of l. MILT 117
Securer l. the silly swain.
  CAMPI 9
space/ in the l. of their friends.
  REED I 2
spirit that l. alone. KAVA 18
their l. would all contain this
  hour. LARK 22
there the bonnie lassie l.,
  BURN 41
true pleasure/ L. in measure,
  UNKN 185
turtle l. NASH 17
villain spider l.,
  THOMS J (1700–1748) 10
whole l. were a preparation.
  JENN 1
windows/ That open on their l.
  SPEND 4
yellow their corrupted l. streaming
  to war, RUKE 1
livesman: if thou a l. be.
  UNKN 166
liveth: name l. for ever," SASS 12
livid: then a l. Claw. DICKI 161
Livie: piece of Virgil, Tacitus,/ L.,
  JONS 15
livin': It takes a heap o' l. GUES 1
living: answer my questions three,/
  Thy life and thy l. UNKN 162
become a l. soul: WORD 31
bring forth soul l. MILT 86

dead shall live, the l. die,
  DRYD 27
dost thou in this l. tomb?
  ARNO 30
earn an honest l. ROBI 49
every l. thing in/ siege: AMMO 6
fire beyond the language of the l
  ELIOT T 64
Forms more real than l. man,
  SHEL 51
He who was l. is now dead
  ELIOT T 143
his l. name. LOWE R 44
Hurt no l. thing: ROSS C 16
Innumerous l. creatures, MILT 86
jealous of all l. forms PRAT 1
join the l. with the dead
  CLARE 8
life is to the l., DODG 2
live a l. death, DANI S 10
l. all assemble! ROET 21
l. are now dying ELIOT T 143
l. at this hour: WORD 40
l. blind and seeing Dead SITW 10
l./ Can only die. ELIOT T 22
l. creature lie,/ Mortal, guilty,
  AUDE 55
l. gave you roome, HABI 3
l. image of our own bright land,
  BRYA 28
l. in the tombs. LINC 2
l. is a pain. DRYD 28
l. man is blind YEATS 46
l. name behind, WEBS 2
l. pages of God's book.
  LOWE J 16
l. record of your memory.
  SHAK 207
l. walks upon: VERY 5
l. walls of Jet. DONN 25
love of l., SWIN 15
modified in the guts of the l.
  AUDE 38
More than most fair, full of the l.
  fire, SPENS 4
morning star among the l.
  PLATO 2
noble L., and the noble Dead.
  WORD 116
one of a l. crowd, WHITM 19
pleasing is to l. eare, SPENS 32
Queen/ Of all are l., SYNG 4
reason for l. MOOR M 29
Saturday's child works for its l.,
  MOTH 22
servant of the L. God, SMAR 2
simpletons thought a l. fable
  MOOR M 24
still l. in annoy. SIDN 33
Tell her, I'm sick of l.; PETRA 5
Tiresome heart, forever l. and
  dying, MILLA 41
trod the l. grass; STEPHENS 2

warp us from the l. truth!
  TENN 72
"Were she only l. still, MERE O 2
when it comes to l., VAN DY 1
livingest: l. chits/ In all the land.
  BROO G 13
lizard: feet like small leaves,/ Little
  l.-feet, ROET 39
l. sort of thing; WELL 2
panting l. waited for history,
  STAF 1
lizards: Like l. on rocks. KNIG 1
live on toasted l., CARRY 5
llamas: sparrows pecking the l.'
  grain, JARR 28
Lo: L., the poor Indian! POPE A 59
load: Books are a l. of crap.
  LARK 19
its l. Of pine-scents, ALDR T 2
sags/ like a heavy l. HUGH L 10
tote the weary l., — FOST 2
Loaded: L. Gun — DICKI 109
loads: l. of learned lumber
  POPE A 22
Loadstone: blessed L. QUAR 2
loaf: l. of bread," CARRO 40
L. of Bread — and Thou OMAR 2
O high-riser, my little l.
  PLATH 82
loafe: lean and l. WHITM 74
loan: l. of a glass of beer;
  STEPHENS 3
l. oft loses both itself and friend,
  SHAK 24
Poor was the l. DUNB P 5
loath: l./ To leave this Paradise;
  MILT 106
summer l. to go BOGA 10
loathe: l. that I did love, VAUX 1
loathed: He l. to fraud, GRAV 38
leave the l. stage, JONS 20
snuff and l. part of nature
  SHAK 79
loathing: soul of man dies in him, l.
  life, THOMS J (1700–1748) 13
loathly: l. birds/ Flocking round
  HODG 5
loathsome: l. canker lives in
  sweetest bud. SHAK 199
more murder in this l. world
  SHAK 151
lobbies: smoke in hotel l.,
  HUGH L 2
lobotomized: Flabby, bald, l.,
  LOWE R 32
lobotomy: l. — ruin, GINS 30
lobster: Congress, l., love, luau,
  BROO G 5
voice of the L.; CARRO 1
lobsterpot: shattered l.,
  ELIOT T 29
lobsters: l. and oysters to cure
  melancholy; JORD 1

local: l. habitation and a name.
SHAK 127
made the Iliad from such/ A l.
row. KAVA 5
Lochinvar: young L. SCOT WA 18
lock: crying at the l., MILLE W 1
l. of her safety-deposit box
JARR 12
l. your door. MILLA 41
Made l., stock and barrel
YEATS 154
T'inclose the L.; POPE A 124
Lock'd: L. me up with a golden
Key. BLAK 19
locked: legs and l.; VAN DO 2
locker: horseplay of the l. room,
HECH 8
locks: clasp of the knitted l.,
WHITM 42
His golden l. PEEL 7
l. like seaweed WARR 3
l. picked; HERR 7
l. with ointments shine, HERR 72
three l. o' her yellow hair,
UNKN 32
unlock the l. WHITM 42
with dewy l., BLAK 108
locomotive: shade of a Southern
Pacific l. GINS 33
locomotives: where the l. sing
LIND V 16
locusts: Helmed l., LOWE R 59
lodge: limping age will l. him now
VAUX 5
l. at last the quivering needle
SHAP 9
l. him in the manger. UNKN 315
lodged: virtue may best l. in beauty
be, SIDN 20
Lodgepole: L./ cone SNYD 46
loftier: for a l. flight, TROW 3
loftiness: first in l. of thought
DRYD 10
lofty: l. elmen swanges; CHAT 2
l. or long standing WILB 3
l. towers I see down-rased,
SHAK 211
l. trees I see barren of leaves,
SHAK 186
l. vase's side, GRAY 18
our l. scene be acted over
SHAK 47
Throughout his l. chart. SIGO 2
too l. in our commonwealth.
SHAK 90
with l. parapet. LONG 28
Log: Christmas L. to the firing;
HERR 4
Like a wet l., ROET 10
l. at last, dry, bald, and sere:
JONS 41
logic: l. of a woman, ROBI 29

l. of our times, DAY 13
superb in love and l., HAYD 6
logical: built in such a l. way
HOLM 4
l. and/ beautiful conclusion.
HARJ 3
logics: When l. die, THOMA D 31
logs: bears l. into the hall,
SHAK 101
hubs of l. HOLM 6
loins: girded on our l., MILT 97
shudder in the l. YEATS 85
their l. filled with heart's blood
DICKEY 15
Women/ from whose l. I sprang
CULL 5
loiter'd: poets l. in green lanes,
LAND 9
Loitered: L. beneath the gas lamps'
flare, WILD 16
l. o'er the green, GOLD 1
loitering: complains of my gab and
my l. WHITM 73
lumbering lubbard l. slow,
MELV 2
loke: speke and l. lyke a saynct,
WYAT 23
lokkes: l. crulle CHAU 8
lolling: dying eyes and l. heads,
SASS 2
London: crowd flowed over L.
Bridge, ELIOT T 118
isn't far from L.!) NOYE 2
learnin' 'ere in L. KIPL 11
lies L.'s daughter, THOMA D 38
L. Bridge is broken down,
UNKN 175
L. has swept about you POUN 54
L. is a man's town, VAN DY 1
L. spread out in the sun,
LARK 22
L., thou art the flour of Cities all
DUNB W 4
L. with its own black wreath,
WORD 18
L.'s first appearance— BYRO 52
merry L. SPENS 45
owls that ogle L. NOYE 3
ring the bells of L. town.
UNKN 23
Vienna L. ELIOT T 148
lone: bury me not on the l. prairie,
UNKN 50
closets of l. desire, LANIE 3
l. and level sands SHEL 50
l. Chorasmian shore SHEL 18
l. man's friend— HARD 51
Wandering by l. sea-breakers,
OSHA 1
lonelier: Life is grown sweeter and
l., JEFFE 31
loneliness: each to/ his l.
BROO G 3

left in l. behind. BARNE 5
l./ given away in poems, KINN 7
l. unreal, RIVE 2
lonely as it is, that l. FROS 35
silver l. ROBI 46
true madness is l., MONTA 3
vision which echoes l. CREE 5
lonelinesses: 4 a.m. HARJ 3
lonely: Across the l. beach THAX 1
axe echoes with a l. sound,
SIMP 12
Cast up by a l. sea, MELV 23
dark and l. wood. DAVIE W 3
flowering in a l. word; TENN 125
Hide him in l. garrets, ROBI 17
How l. all the years DE TA 2
"I'm l. JOHN J 1
immense and l. as a cloud.
AIKE 7
in l. lands, TENN 12
in l. peace, the spousal verse
WORD 16
"In the l. barton HARD 33
l. and the unsatisfied, POUN 24
l. as a cloud WORD 24
l. as it is, that loneliness
FROS 35
l. Earth amid the balls EMER 9
l. ere it will be less— FROS 35
L. from the beginning LI PO 1
l. old man with a white beard.
GINS 27
l. scene shall thee restore;
COLL 2
l. sea and the sky, MASE 11
love's austere and l. offices?
HAYD 23
on the l. shore, BYRO 1
route obscure and l., POE 16
to be free/ Is often to be l.;
AUDE 33
vanished from his l. hearth.
WORD 17
Walt Whitman, childless, l. old
grubber, GINS 38
weep soon on the l. curbing
HORA 2
lonesome: all so l. WHITM 72
hears the Catbird/ he gets l.
SNYD 31
leaves a l. place against the sky.
MARK 4
l. latter years; POE 30
night, in the l. October POE 47
sluggish, l. waters, WHITM 28
long: advance for as l. as forever is.
THOMA D 41
After l. rain HUGH T 3
All day l. in unrest, MACW 1
all this l. pretense! HERB G 43
alone again l. since, LEVE 12
as a hushed footfall/ In a l.
forgotten snow. TEAS 3

sit and l. out   WHITM 40

stone l. on the stone's face?
WILB 1

They cannot l. out far./ They
cannot l. in deep.   FROS 68

to l. about us and to die
POPE A 58

Unbroken wisdom in a single l.,
WINT 11

When will I l. at it?   SHAP 17

you may l. for snow!)   KIPL 23

look'd: l. but with divining eyes,
SHAK 228

looke: leaves l. pale,   SHAK 224

looked: Judge l. back   WHITT 17

l. askance and hated;   LOWE J 14

l. down over Attica;   BYRO 52

l. holwe,   CHAU 22

l. upon it and desired it.
UNKN 256

Maud Muller l.   WHITT 16

whate'er/ She l. on,
BROWNI R 55

looking: feeling and l. queer.
HOLM 7

L. down for miles   SNYD 18

l. for something,   BISH 41

l. out of a window   ASHB 1

l. out of date.   LARK 14

luxury of l. at beauties,   PRAE 3

people l. back.   VAN DY 2

phantom l. down   WHITM 5

Years l. backward   WHITM 113

looking-glass: before a l.,
YEATS 106

looks: Beauty guards thy l.:
CAMPI 15

Death l. gigantically down.
POE 12

her l. went everywhere.
BROWNI R 55

in their l. Much reason,   MILT 93

kill with l.,   SHAK 89

l. a moment in the glass,
ELIOT T 137

L. at me from the wall,   LONG 13

l. grave enough/ To seem a
statesman.   JONS 24

L. in the clouds,   SHAK 44

man that l. in my face?
WHITM 21

man that l. on glass   HERB G 28

My love l. fresh,   SHAK 229

stood amid the stooks,/ Praising
God with sweetest l.: —
HOOD 9

their l. divine   MILT 71

thy gentle l., thy aid,   MILT 101

unchaste l., loose gestures, and
foul talk,   MILT 4

loom: craftsman's l.,   GINS 12

hoe and l.,   SHEL 65

rocking l. of history,   HAYD 10

She left the web, she left the l.,
TENN 65

Tyrian l.,   HORA 10

Loome: Make me thy L.:   TAYL E 6

Loomed: St. Paul's / L.   WILD 15

loon: private buffoon is a light-
hearted l.,   GILB 56

loose: cabin of l. imaginings,
HECH 6

give thy soul a l.,   HORA 10

hanging l. and low.   UPDI 1

L. all thir vertue;   MILT 59

L. as the wind,   HERB G 17

l. feet in tall grass   SNYD 35

l. rocks in space   SNYD 29

made so l. and wide,   THOR 1

madest l. grace unkind;   TASS 6

man who should l. me
LOWE A 11

pavement slabs burn l.   MCKA 10

unchaste looks, l. gestures, and
foul talk,   MILT 4

wild and l. to my soul —
WHITM 49

wind flapped l.,   ROSS D 9

loosed: anarchy is l. upon the
world,   YEATS 133

l. the fateful lightning   HOWE 1

loosely: settling and l. lying,
BRID R 8

loosen: l. love and crying;   SNOD 6

old faiths l. and fall,   SWIN 23

loosened: l. and let down this brutal
jaw?   MARK 6

L. from the minor's tether;
JOHN S (1709–1784) 11

l. from the sky —   ROSS D 4

loosing: parting, talons l.,
WHITM 24

lopped: l. tree in time may grow
again,   SOUTHW 7

Lorca: Garcia L., what were you
doing   GINS 37

Lord: adversaries of the L. shall be
broken to pieces;   BIBL, O.T. 8

Alfred L. Tennyson crossing the
bar   SITW 3

angel of the L. came down,
TATE N 1

before the L., new-born?
UNKN 310

better l. was never born
UNKN 79

broken altar, L., thy servant
rears,   HERB G 7

dear angry L.,   HERB G 10

dwell in the house of the L. for
ever.   BIBL, O.T. 31

earth is the L.'s,   BIBL, O.T. 32

fancy enough for L. Byron,
NASH 20

Give yee thanks unto the L.,
BIBL, O.T. 54

glance of the L.!   BYRO 13

glorious L. of life!   SPENS 18

glory of the coming of the L.;
HOWE 1

good L., deliver us!   NASHE 2

Good L. deliver us.   SIDN 38

Great l. of all things,   POPE A 78

Hail universal L.,   MILT 82

I replied, 'My L..'   HERB G 18

Jehovah, Jove, or L.!   POPE A 126

joyful noise unto the L.,
BIBL, O.T. 48

knows not the hand of the L.
DUNC 4

law of the L. is perfect,
BIBL, O.T. 28

Let Israel hope in the L.,
BIBL, O.T. 61

L. among Earls,   UNKN 18

L. Bateman was a noble L.,
UNKN 316

L. Chamberlain with his white
staff,   UNKN 295

l. endures/ much care   UNKN 308

L. God is a sun and shield:
BIBL, O.T. 43

L. God made them all.   ALEX 1

L. God of Hosts,   KIPL 17

L.! hast power to save.   WILLA 1

L., how manifold are thy works!
BIBL, O.T. 51

L., if too obdurate I,
STEVENSO R 2

L. in the Void?   GINS 23

L. is my shepherd;   BIBL, O.T. 31

L. is thy keeper;   BIBL, O.T. 59

L. killeth, and maketh alive;
BIBL, O.T. 8

L. maketh poor, and maketh rich:
BIBL, O.T. 8

L. of all,   TENN 34

l. of high degree,   UNKN 316

L. of himself, though not of
lands,   WOTT 2

l. of the fowl and the brute.
COWP 23

L. of the lash,   REED I 5

L. of the world's elation,   CARM 2

L., remember me and mine
BURN 33

L. Sabaoth is his name,   LUTH 3

L. shall preserve thee from all
evil;   BIBL, O.T. 59

L. was crucified,   ALEX 8

L., who createdst man in wealth
and store,   HERB G 26

L. with me abide: LYTE 1

L.'s Prayer on a grain of rice,
THOMA D 8

Love is a great and mighty l.;
PEEL 3

married My L. you.   LI PO 4

suburbs, where they will be l.
  CRAN H 42
territory is l.." SNYD 48
vault of thy l. Ulalume!" POE 49
vertue giv'n for l., MILT 117
what we gain'd in Skill we l. in
  Strength. DRYD 29
Whatever it was I l., WRIG J 5
wife of the skipper l. at sea
  WHITT 27
Wold I had l. my hand;
  UNKN 62
you dropt, l., DICKI 151
lot: Hard is his l.,
  JOHN S (1709–1784) 8
having drunk such a l., AUDE 12
Open Road goes to the used-car l.
  SIMP 13
parking l. of the dead. DICKEY 6
thir lamentable l., MILT 61
weary l. is thine, SCOT WA 24
weighs a l., GILB 39
Lotos: In the hollow L. land
  TENN 89
mild-eyed melancholy L.-eaters
  TENN 81
lotus: fades the l. of the water?
  BLAK 13
like L. buds that float HOPE L 3
open curling l. gate SNYD 4
Lou: lady that's known as L.
  SERV 6
loud: beats the dogs in noises l.
  CLARE 2
bells more l. and deep: LONG 12
cannon-mouthings l. DRAK 2
heard across the tempest l.
  THOMP W 1
Helpless, naked, piping l.,
  BLAK 72
L. are the thunder drums
  UNKN 120
l. gregarious town MILLA 32
L. human song, WHITM 49
l. trumpets' sound MILT 104
l. you bugles blow. WHITM 8
quiet dead and the l. celebrities
  LEWI 1
voice than thunder is more l.,
  THOR 5
word perhaps l. spoken VERY 6
louder: Cry l., beat the windows,
  SLES 2
loudest: gifted most that l. baul'd:
  DRYD 19
loudly: Chanted l., chanted lowly,
  TENN 67
Louisiana: in L. a live-oak growing,
  WHITM 39
lounge: l. of the mental house
  SEXT 12
Loup Garou: L. Kid. REED I 5

loured: clouds that l. upon our
  house SHAK 94
louse: scarcely the strength of a l.,
  SERV 7
louts: from l. to run away.
  SIDN 31
lov'd: in extreames l. and abhor'd.
  CLEV 1
love was l. out in us both;
  DRYD 16
l. not at first sight? MARL 9
l. not wisely but too well;
  SHAK 138
man were l. by wife, BRAD 13
Who ever l., MARL 9
love: add l., MILT 106
Adieu L., adieu L., untrue L.,
  UNKN 291
after making l., quiet, KINN 1
age in l. SHAK 238
all but ministers of L.,
  COLE SAM 23
All L.'s Emblems FLET J 6
all must l. the human form,
  BLAK 89
all the world and l. were young,
  RALEG 7
almost l. you again. SNYD 16
america i/ l. you CUMM 28
"amo," I l.! BROWNI R 27
at his call/ L. him, WORD 120
Atlantic and Caribbean l.,
  GINS 11
attend l.'s joys in vain. CAMPI 21
Away at once with l. or jealousy!
  SHAK 136
back in l. again, RICH 9
be for nought/ Except for l.'s sake
  only. BROWNI E 9
be my L., MARL 18
be my l., DAY 1
bear l.'s wrong, SHAK 200
beauty is no beauty without l.
  CAMPI 26
beggar may be liberal of l.
  UNKN 96
bid me take l. easy, YEATS 50
Black l. is Black wealth GIOV 4
bless'd kingdoms meek of joy and
  l. MILT 32
boys who l. their mother SNYD 7
bright torch of l.; BLAK 109
Build with lithe l BROO G 15
burned with fierce l. RANS 14
business of l. is/ cruelty WILLI 20
but eternal L. SHEL 55
By L. are driv'n away; BLAK 40
came to l., ROET 10
camp of l. CAMPI 16
carry/ Half my l. SHAK 68
cast my l. behind: JONS 18
change old l. for new PEEL 1

composing/ L.-letters again,
  HEAN 20
Congress, lobster, l., luau,
  BROO G 5
Conjoined by l., BALD 1
conscience is born of l,?
  SHAK 243
constant l. deemed SIDN 12
cries of unsatisfied l. WHITM 67
crops of l. and hate. MUIR 8
crowned with a woman's l.
  SERV 9
crying after l.? TEAS 5
dark and sultry/ l. BARA 8
dark secret l. BLAK 80
deep unending/ Ache of l.!
  JOYC 4
detain'd me for l. of me,
  WHITM 60
do you l. me, kid? SAND 22
dost l., yet strike; HERB G 10
dravest l. from thee,
  THOMP F 10
Duty, faith, l. are roots, and ever
  green. PEEL 7
Dying for l. WRIG J 1
early l. unfortunate and hard,
  MILLA 5
Earth's the right place for l.:
  FROS 13
Emblematical of l. and war?
  YEATS 45
end / Of a l. or a /season?
  FROS 93
eye, l.'s firmament; HERR 7
eyes big l.-crumbs, CUMM 51
Fair is my L., DANI S 9
faithful in l., SCOT WA 18
faithful l., recalled thee to my
  mind— WORD 143
Farewell, L., and all thy laws for
  ever: WYAT 5
feeling and a l., WORD 33
Fierce war and faithful l.,
  GRAY 6
fight for what we l., OHAR 11
firm l. doth bear, SHAK 169
fitting spot to dig L.'s grave;
  MERE G 11
For l. of her, sweet countrymen,
  DICKI 146
for l. of you, SHAK 187
for your l. song HUGH L 8
Forspent with l. and shame,
  LANIE 1
Fortune, honour, beauty, youth,/
  Are but blossoms dying;/
  Wanton pleasures, doting l.,/ Are
  but shadows flying. CAMPI 29
free l. with bondage bound.'
  BLAK 62
freedom in my l. LOVE 5
furniture of l. RICH 8

Gentle l. deeds, DONN 41
Give it Endymion's l., DAVE 4
give me leave to l., CAREW 16
god of l. was born. DONN 39
God shall l. and angels aid ye.
 PRIO 8
God was l. indeed TENN 36
great l. is over all we do, PRIN 3
greater torment/ Of l. satisfied
 ELIOT T 10
Hail wedded l., mysterious law,
 MILT 78
half in l. with easeful Death,
 KEAT 49
Health, l., friends, scope
 HARD 47
hear thy true L.'s tale: DEKK 2
Hell grant what l. did seek;
 MILT 17
high way of l.; YEATS 3
his l. had brought, SHAK 196
hold l. in. UNTE 3
honour of my l. SYLV 1
horse to L., SIDN 17
How do I l. thee? BROWNI E 4
how often L. we've made SACK 3
I am in l. with it, WHITM 75
I can l. any, so she be not true.
 DONN 35
I can l. both fair and brown;
 DONN 35
I could not l. thee, LOVE 9
I guard I do not l.; YEATS 70
I hae parted frae my L.,
 BURN 34
I have the keyes:/ Yet I l. thee.
 HERB G 60
I hid my l. when young
 CLARE 12
"I l. her for her smile —
 BROWNI E 9
I l. my Daddy SMIT W 1
I l. not man the less, BYRO 1
I l. thy company. SHAK 144
"I l. you"? GRAV 9
I shall be past making l. PRIO 12
I sowed the seeds of l., HABE 1
I watched for l.-cars. LOWE R 39
I went to the Garden of L.,
 BLAK 64
I write of youth, of l., HERR 1
if L. be Love, TENN 15
if L. be ours, TENN 15
If music be the food of l.,
 SHAK 174
If this be l., DANI S 10
If thou must l. me, BROWNI E 9
I'll l. you AUDE 1
I'm tired of L.: BELL 3
imagined l. Of solitary beds,
 YEATS 142
In l. and holy passion, WORD 16
in l. lets so persever, BRAD 14

in verse my l. to show, SIDN 5
In whom l. wrought new
 alchemy. DONN 43
indomitable l. Kept me in chains.
 KUNI 2
instance of the l. of God SMAR 7
intimate as l., CAMPB R 8
Is it, in Heav'n, a crime to l. too
 well? POPE A 3
Is l.'s bed always snow? CLARE 4
It takes life to l. Life. MAST 9
joy, nor l., nor light, ARNO 3
kind glance from my l.
 UNKN 201
lamenting l. marreth the
 musicall. SPENS 37
lamp of l., SHEL 87
lark is so brimful of gladness and
 l., COLE SAM 1
Laughing the l.-laugh OWEN 25
laughter, pain, and l. MERR 8
lead their lives in l. like me,
 CAMPI 16
leads me from my l. HOUS 64
learn to bear the beams of l.,
 BLAK 98
lease of my true l. SHAK 229
Leave me, O L., SIDN 26
left the ancient l. BLAK 111
Legend of L. DRYD 6
Let me not l. thee, if I l. thee not.
 HERB G 6
let the warm L. in! KEAT 54
Let's contend no more, L.,
 BROWNI R 85
lies under L. DUNC 4
like l. From another world
 DICKEY 27
Like shadows in l.'s frenzied
 stifled throes? CLARE 7
liquor, l., or fights, HOUS 2
little, nameless, unremembered
 acts/ Of kindness and of l.
 WORD 29
live with me, and be my l.,
 DONN 6
live with thee and be thy L.
 RALEG 7, 9
loathe that I did l., VAUX 1
long ago, my l., ROSS C 7
loosen l. and crying; SNOD 6
l./ A burnt match CRAN E 31
L. a cross for them ROBI 48
l. a poem/ is pretentious, OHAR 9
l. a prophet of the soul;
 EMER 38
l. a wall, FROS 55, 58
l. all beauteous things, BRID R 5
L. alters not SHAK 232
l. and be l. POE 3
l., and bear; to hope, SHEL 58
L./ And Charitie, HERB G 15
L. and delight, THOMA E 15

l. and hate mee too, DONN 48
L. and joy UNKN 117
l. and need are one, FROS 126
l. and pity him. SHAP 24
l. and skill, SIDN 10
l., and then be wise? BYRO 20
l. and think, RANDS 4
l. as deep and strong WHITT 10
l. as odd as wearing shoes —
 CORS 8
l. at all's to be a politician,
 OHAR 9
L. at the lips was touch
 FROS 112
l. avail you in your hour.
 MILLA 2
L. bade me welcome: HERB G 48
l. but her for ever; BURN 16
L. but themselves DRYD 1
L. by the spring is grown;
 DONN 41
L. closed what he begat:
 MERE G 13
L. dies. FORD J 1
l. for Charlotte THAC 3
l. for evermore. TENN 73
l. gives again into our arms.
 KINN 2
L. got so sweet SHAK 169
l. grows bitter with treason,
 SWIN 23
l., happiness, riches — " KAVA 13
L. has pitched his mansion
 YEATS 39
l. hath an end; SWIN 21
l., hatred, joy or fear, PRIO 4
l. her as hard as you can.
 CREE 13
l I seemed to lose BROWNI E 6
L., if you love me, CREE 11
l. in a golden bowl? BLAK 12
L. in all my parts shall live.
 COWL 6
L. in fantastic triumph BEHN 1
l. in kisses rain SHEL 32
L. is a barren sea, SWIN 26
L. is a calmer, gentler joy:
 SACK 1
l. is a careless child RALEG 1
L. is a great and mighty lord;
 PEEL 3
L. is a growing, or full constant
 light; DONN 36
L. is a naked shadow HUGH L 14
L. is a shadow. PLATH 41
L. is a torment of the mind,
 DANI S 1
L. is an evil word. BARA 5
L. is best. BROWNI R 49
l is cruel/ and selfish WILLI 21
L. is dead; FORD J 1
L. is dead, SIDN 37
l. is fair, my love is gay, PEEL 1

l. is first in their hearts,
CLARK J 4
l. is form, OLSO 9
l. is hard to catch and conquer,
MERE G 4
l. is near at hand, ROET 15
L. is no pardoner. SIMP 5
L. is not ful of pittie MARL 5
L. is not L. ROET 9
l. is old, SMIT L 3
L. is rather deafe, than blind,
JONS 18
l. is sweet for a day; SWIN 23
l. is taught hypocrisy from youth.
BYRO 21
l. is the crooked thing, YEATS 16
L. is the fire, SOUTHW 2
L. is the lesson SPENS 19
L. is the perfect sum HUME 1
l. is the sky CUMM 9
L. is the tact SCHW 3
L. is the unfamiliar Name
ELIOT T 70
L. is too young SHAK 243
l., let us be true ARNO 3
L.-light of Spain — CHES 9
l. like black, our black —
BROO G 15
l. like lion-eyes. BROO G 15
l. like morningrise. BROO G 15
L. likes no laws but his own!
GREV 1
L. L. no delay; CAMPI 14
l.-lorn Nightingale MILT 9
L. made the bed; CRAS 2
L., maintain thy life in me.
SIDN 27
L. me little, love me long,
HERR 28
l. might overflow my Heart!
TAYL E 7
l. most lay sleeping by me
WHITM 109
L. must cling MERE O 3
L. must not be, but take a body
too, DONN 1
l. my father all. SHAK 68
l. no roast but a nut-brown toast,
STEVENSO W 1
L. of God JOHN S (1822–1882) 1
l. of heaven above, CLARE 14
l. of learning, MACN 10
l. of Leda, SPENS 41
l. of living, SWIN 15
l. of my Annie — POE 25
l. of Nature, BRYA 22
l. of pleasure, POPE A 97
L. of youth, forgive, BRON 11
l. one which did scorn. DONN 39
L. pine at them KEAT 47
L., power, the huzza of battle
LAYT 1
l. rose up so early HOUS 26

"L. seeketh not Itself BLAK 57
"L. seeketh only Self BLAK 58
l. shall be; UNKN 257
l. shall hourly sing, BROWNE 2
l. she bore? TENN 73
l. sincere MILT 101
L. sits in the beds of spices,
GRIF 1
L. so amazing, so divine,
WATT I 10
l. still breed, RALEG 9
L. still has something of the Sea,
SEDL 1
L., sweetness, goodness, MILT 34
l. tempting them to steal —
SPEND 2
L. that had robbed us
MERE G 14
l. that is conceal'd, MARL 4
l. that is purest and sweetest
OREI 2
l. that kisses with a homicide
BARK 1
l. that shook the lights RUKE 3
L. that so desires MERE G 6
l. the force that grows us,
SHAP 18
L., the human form divine,
BLAK 88
L. the wild swan. JEFFE 19
L. thee in prose; PRIO 2
l. thee more and more.
MONTROSE 3
l. thee to the last, WORD 51
l. thee with mine eyes, SHAK 239
l. their profession. GILB 57
L. took up the harp of Life,
TENN 70
L. vertue, she alone is free,
MILT 13
L. wakes men, PATM 2
l. was a feather, CREE 14
l. was howling SNOD 16
l. was lov'd out in us both;
DRYD 16
L., we are in God's hand.
BROWNI R 7
l., whatever it was, an infection.
SEXT 18
l. which us doth bind, MARV 7
l. while half asleep GRAV 24
l. whilst that thou mayst be l.
again. DANI S 14
L.! who bewailest SHEL 90
L. will find out the way!
UNKN 183
L. will have his Hour at last:
DRYD 24
L. wing'd my Hopes UNKN 184
l. with fear the only God,
MILT 105
l. without the help of any thing
BLAK 22

l. working and reading."
WATT I 7
L. wounds with heat, JONS 28
l. yet was love. CRAB 2
l. you all the Day, GAY 5
L. you for yourself alone
YEATS 63, 64
l.'s awakened root DONN 41
l.'s best habit SHAK 238
l.'s courage ROBI 3
l.'s extreme,/ Leander-like, —
DAVIE J 1
l.'s impetuous rage, DONN 47
l.'s long since cancell'd woe,
SHAK 195
l.'s manners in bed CREE 12
L.'s martyr, DONN 26
L.'s mysteries in souls do grow,
DONN 22
l.'s piercing darts, PEEL 3
l.'s soft bands, SPENS 1
l.'s true anatomy: HOLLA 5
low lies thy l., Lenore! POE 29
make yourself content, my l.,
UNKN 293
makes thy l. more strong,
SHAK 215
many times do I l. again.
BEDD 12
Mercy, L., and Pity dwell
BLAK 89
Mie l. ys dedde, CHAT 1
mie true l. waytes. CHAT 1
mighty L. has done; FLET J 5
Moloch whose l. GINS 17
More happy l.! KEAT 39
Much ado there was, God wot,/ He
would l. BRET/OTHE 2
music shrill/ Give my fair L. good
morrow! HEYW 2
My dear and only L.,
MONTROSE 2
My heart gives you l. WHITM 27
my home of l.; SHAK 230
My joy, my grief, my hope, my l.,
WALL 5
my life, my l., my heart,
HERR 40
my l. as rare SHAK 237
My L. in me BALD 1
My l. is as a fever, SHAK 242
my l. is come to me. ROSS C 2
My L. is like to ice, and I to fire:
SPENS 9
My l. lies underground LAWR 17
My l. looks fresh, SHAK 229
my l., my only friend. TENN 95
my l. my roundelay, PEEL 1
My right might be l. FROS 125
My true l. hath my heart
SIDN 1, 2
my unrespected l.; GRIF 1

Nae living man I'll l. again,
UNKN 171
neither see nor l. TRAH 9
Never seek to tell thy l. BLAK 42
never think of l.;/ Fair, if you fail,
UNKN 74
new l. may get; WALS 1
next in glory to enduring l.,
STEVENS 56
no more l.; SITW 10
no sin l.'s fruit to steal; JONS 49
'Not Death, but L..' BROWNI E 8
Not universal l. AUDE 77
Now old in l., OVID 5
Of l. and pleasure speakes.
DOWL 1
Of l. unsatisfied ELIOT T 10
of my faith and l. did sing.
VAUG 30
on l. intent; YEATS 39
one jot of former l. retain.
DRAY 15
our l. hath no decay; DONN 2
Our l. shall live, SPENS 24
over hir housbond as hir l.,
CHAU 111
Pale hands I l. HOPE L 1
people and l. NIMS 3
People's violent L. and Hate;
CLEV 1
perfect law of l. VERY 4
performs its l., KIRK 4
pestilence of l. MARV 12
physician to my l., SHAK 242
played with l. MOSS 3
poor l. of anything, THOR 4
power of l. SPENS 10
power their l. to hide, MARL 4
power to l., or hate, MARL 8
Praise, blame, l., WORD 134
presence adds to the rhyme of l.
HARD 48
Prince of L. beheld BLAK 23
profane L., DONN 45
pull up your pants,/ L. never lets
you go. AMIS 1
put down his head in l. BOGA 3
putting L. away DICKI 17
P—xed by her l., POPE A 90
Queens of L. and Innocence,
CAREW 12
quick-eyed L., HERB G 48
quiet of l. in her feet. YEATS 21
raging l. with extreme pain
SURR 6
refuse l. safe FROS 54
Reserve them for my l.,
SHAK 196
Rhymed out in l.'s despair
YEATS 131
Rise up, my l., BIBL, O.T. 72
Rites/ Mysterious of connubial L.
MILT 77

Rose of l., SPENS 34
Seals of l. SHAK 117
see the land I l. ROET 51
seed of l. was sick. LEWI 4
seeking lost l. GRAV 15
sell your l. for peace, MILLA 17
send a l.-letter, UNKN 46
shadows neither l. nor guile,
BRID R 4
She would not l. SWIN 26
shifting hate and l. STOD 2
silken ties of l. and thought
FROS 102
sin when l.'s rites are not done.
CAREW 13
smile on your l., GINS 31
So true a fool is l., SHAK 208
sporting with l. and the sea
LAWR 58
sports of l.;/ Time will not be ours
forever, JONS 48
spring of l. and fear TATE A 16
spring of l. gushed from my
heart, COLE SAM 36
Spring, the herald of l.'s mighty
king, SPENS 20
stars l.-thoughts provoke,
SIDN 29
stealth, which L. doth free allow.
TASS 6
'Still do I l., SITW 13
strange l. grow bold, SHAK 149
strength of l.; WORD 52
Strong Son of God, immortal L.,
TENN 16
sublunary l.' l., DONN 63
sunlight in the window./ L.,/ your
mother' GINS 32
superb in l. and logic, HAYD 6
supple arms of l. RUKE 2
sweet l. remembered SHAK 194
sweet minor zest/ Of l., KEAT 64
Sweetest l., I do not go DONN 57
sweets of fancied l., CLARE 14
Take away l., BROWNI R 26
take my l. away. SHAK 211
Tangled was I in L.'s snare.
WYAT 13
Tears and l. for the Gray. FINC 2
terror be in l., MILT 92
terror of that l.: PRIN 3
that bee/ Which bore my l. away.
HERR 30
There is a privacy I l. in this
snowy night. BLY 1
These are thy wonders, Lord of l.,
HERB G 33
They sang of l., TAYL B 2
thine inward l. of heart.
SHAK 203
Those l. scorn whom that l. doth
possess? SIDN 13
those who l. me, BANK 1

those who l. want wisdom;
SHEL 52
thou art too coarse to l..'
HERR 70
Thou that know'st L. PRIO 5
thought of him I l. WHITM 46
thoughts of l. TENN 69
through dooms of l. CUMM 25
Through l., through hope,
WORD 128
Thy L. Enflame in mee.
TAYL E 7
thy l. to every one AYTON 2
thy l.'s loss HARD 24
Thy name is L. WESL C 2
thy picture or my l., SHAK 204
Till l. and fame to nothingness do
sink. KEAT 69
time to l., BIBL, O.T. 5
'Tis l. in l. that makes the sport.
SUCK 4
To l. or not to love?
BROWNI R 81
to l. so, be so l., BROWNI R 11
To see her is to l. her, BURN 16
to see her, was to l. her;
BURN 11
Touch, l., all senses; SPEND 17
traverse old l.'s domain HARD 12
trew L. shall never twain
UNKN 66
Triumph in l.: SHAK 243
true l. acted simple modesty.
SHAK 149
True l. doth pass away! BLAK 41
True L. doth stay, UNKN 183
true l. is a durable fire RALEG 2
true l. sent to me UNKN 274
true l.'s knot UNKN 180
true that I must Stella l. SIDN 8
try to imagine a faultless l.
AUDE 52
twofold silence was the song of l.
ROSS D 4
under show of l. well feigned —
MILT 92
Unknown l. OTOM 1
unstinted, L. did sip, LOVE 3
until l.'s vulnerable. ROET 9
Unwind a l. knit up KING H 6
valley of l. and delight.
UNKN 260
vanity, sets l. a task like that."
HUNT 4
Venus, l.'s lady, was born of the
sea; JORD 1
Venus, that is Queene of l.,
SPENS 43
Waking l. suffereth no sleepe:
SPENS 37
want l.'s majesty SHAK 96
wasted for you, l.! MACW 1

wasteth/ In l. his chiefest part.
  SIDN 42
we l./ First BROWNI R 25
we l. our luxuries. JEFFE 5
we l. you — WHITM 22
went my l. riding CUMM 3
Were you the earth, dear L.,
  SYLV 2
what death or l. is JONS 28
What is l.? SHAK 175
What l. I bore to thee. WORD 47
what l. indites: CLARE 9
When l. is gone. BOUR 2
When my l. swears SHAK 238
while you l. me, JOHN G 2
whisper of L.'s name, GRAV 7
white rose breathes of l.; OREI 1
wind doth blow today, my l.,"
  UNKN 292
wise want l.; SHEL 52
witnesses/ In all l.'s countries,
  THOMA D 44
words of l., CARN 2
words of my l.: ROET 12
worst that l. could do? DONN 40
wound of l. goes home! LAWR 23
yet I l. her till I die. FORD T 1
you see, I l. you!' WHITT 14
your true l. know SHAK 37
loveboys: lost their l. GINS 12
Loved: all he l. WILB 39
artist wrought this l. guitar;
  SHEL 91
be l. by none. AYTON 2
begot me, bred me, l. me.
  SHAK 68
But to be l. alone. AUDE 77
dead I l. so well, WHITM 53
decayed and l. ones lost LINC 1
did not know we l. you. HARP 5
every l. spot WOOD 1
feared, l., hated, suffered,
  SHEL 79
First he l. her, UNKN 218
for a l. one
  must wait UNKN 308
heart that l. her, WORD 37
him that l. the rose. THOMP F 1
Idols I have l. so long OMAR 2
lad that l. you HOUS 1
light I l. so much, PETRA 12
L. accents are soon forgot.
  SHEL 89
L. and thought himself beloved,
  YEATS 109
L. and were L., MCCRA 2
l. chivalrie,/ Trouthe and honour,
  CHAU 7
l. each other and were ignorant.
  YEATS 6
l. Enthusiast wooed, COLL 6
L.! L.! WHITM 66
l. more than his lif. CHAU 49

l. the pilgrim soul in you,
  YEATS 162
l. the races; BYRO 47
L. the wood rose, EMER 22
l. thee dear. DANI S 13
never l. me truly: TENN 73
no more he l. me, UNKN 46
Of one that l.? JONS 12
past and l., WHITM 12
removed from the l. habitation,
  WOOD 3
say, "He l.." BROO R 8
secret sleep/ Of him he l. ALEX 7
souls we l., TENN 98
still woods I l., WHITM 95
We that had l. him so,
  BROWNI R 45
You l. when all was young.
  KINGSL 8
lovede: l. venerie, CHAU 18
Lovel: out of Lord L.'s a briar,
  UNKN 178
loveless: l., joyless, unendeared,
  MILT 78
only l. look PATM 5
lovelier: l. flower/ On earth
  WORD 48
l. than any of you. RANS 5
loveliest: latest-born and l. vision
  far KEAT 52
l. village GOLD 1
loveliness: long, perfect l. of sow.
  KINN 15
l. exists, SNOD 7
l. increases; KEAT 4
portion of the l. SHEL 11
Traditional sanctity and l.;
  YEATS 36
lovely: billboard l. as a tree.
  NASH 14
dirge of l. Rosabelle.
  SCOT WA 15
excellent l. sunflower existence!
  GINS 35
flower of l. youth BRID R 3
fox, l. ritualist, in flight RANS 2
he made more l.: SHEL 11
Honest labour bears a l. face;
  DEKK/OTHE 1
I knew a woman, l. in her bones,
  ROET 27
keep that l. body. GLÜC 2
lie/ Unvariably l. there, LARK 15
Like a l. white clover KENN 2
l. and soothing death, WHITM 50
l. apparition, WORD 133
l., gifted girls/ Married impossible
  men? GRAV 26
l. in that way. SPENC B 1
l. in thy youthful grace! BRYA 12
l. is the Rose, WORD 66
l. knights, SHAK 228
l. shall be choosers, FROS 54

l. woman stoops to folly, GOLD 9
more l. and more temperate.
  SHAK 188
must have my l. lady RANS 30
no less l. being dark, CULL 3
Oh most l. lady, CREE 4
one so l. BRYA 10
Pocahontas' body, l. as a poplar,
  SAND 5
poem l. as a tree. KILM 1
See what a l. shell, TENN 99
shoot long and l. HOPKINS 20
so l. and intense, MASE 9
these l. tokens JACK 4
those l. cracker mottoes!'
  GILB 12
tremble for this l. frame,
  WHITE 1
What l. things DE LA 20
Wonderful l. there she sat,
  DE LA 19
woods are l., dark FROS 108
loven: wommen l. best richesse,
  CHAU 109
lover: act a l.'s or a Roman's part?
  POPE A 3
country l. and his lass; HOUS 22
give repentance to her l., GOLD 9
Gives the l. weight and fashion.
  JONS 1
honest l.'s ghost, SUCK 6
hung my black young l.
  HUGH L 13
In life of l.'s heart; SIDN 42
Listening, like l. or worshiper,
  WARR 8
l., all as frantic, SHAK 127
l. and his lass HOUS 14
l. and killer are mingled
  DOUG K 2
l. and the bard; BROWNI R 3
l. forsaken WALS 1
l.'s thoughts disdain, CAMPI 21
lunatic, the l., and the poet
  SHAK 127
magnetic,/ Peripatetic/ L.
  GILB 34
mar a l.'s vows YEATS 94
meek l. of the good! EMER 7
Neither father nor l. ROET 12
of her departed l.; ELIOT T 137
restless l.'s ghost; MARV 15
secret l. is saying KAVA 11
sipped l.'s wine." HARD 48
some old l.'s ghost DONN 39
Tears like a l. wept. GRAV 14
tell the l.'s tomb THOMA D 23
thy deceasèd l.; SHAK 196
truest heart that l. e'er did lend.
  KING H 6
Why so pale and wan, fond l.
  SUCK 1

wild Jack for a l.; YEATS 38
wooing the sun to be her l.,
   WALK 12
lover's: passion in a l. glorious,
   BYRO 18
lovere: joly l. Absolon, CHAU 51
lovers: ashes of l. find no rest.
   JONS 12
betraies poore l. MARL 4
Frankie and Johnny were l.,
   UNKN 101
Great l. lie in Hell, RANS 16
Honor between l. RANS 13
l. being estranged or dead,
   YEATS 5
l., cruel as their flame, MARV 16
l. disappeared into the wood.
   THOMA E 2
l.' ears in hearing' SCOT WA 16
L.' eyes are sharp SCOT WA 16
L.' eyes,/ Locked in endless
   dreams FORD J 1
l.' hearts to dust DARL 1
l. lie abed THOMA D 27
L., like dying men, SEDL 3
l. live by longing, ROET 23
l. looking to be wed; HOUS 22
L. lying two and two HOUS 61
l. must/ Consign to thee SHAK 18
L. of beauty, starved, POUN 50
l. that no lovers miss YEATS 96
L., the conclusion GRAV 32
l. without conflict, TASS 4
On l. wha lyis. MONTG 1
shades where buried l. lie.
   DAVE 2
shadows of the l. SIMP 11
sleepless l., just at twelve, awake:
   POPE A 111
snow falling down and necks of l.
   SIMP 10
sublunary l.' love, DONN 63
Such end true l. have. BLAK 40
tell me if the l. are losers
   SAND 6
Those l. scorn whom that love
   doth possess? SIDN 13
Woes of hopeless L., DRYD 26
loves: Cavalier who l. honour and
   me, SCOT WA 3
fat white woman whom nobody
   l., CORN 2
For all true l. to admire.
   UNKN 180
heart that l. what they dispise,
   SHAK 239
kills the thing he l., WILD 3
like he l. his Dollar. SMIT W 1
L. by Fate benighted, STANL 2
l. fire HERB CH 4
l. have come and gone; MILLA 40
l. not his wronger; SHAK 134
L. riddles DONN 37

l. to hear the little brook a-
   gurgling, GILB 38
l. you best POPE A 20
no creature l. me, SHAK 99
No one l. rock, SNYD 50
one l. only form, OLSO 11
one that l. his fellow-men."
   HUNT 2
pleasure l. to pay/ Tribute to
   ease; WORD 63
Romance, who l. to nod and sing,
   POE 38
Somebody l. us all. BISH 13
sun l. him. SMAR 4
suspects, yet strongly l.!
   SHAK 134
Towards L. holy land, CAMPI 28
warm their little L. GRAY 33
water l. MOSS 4
who l. men, SNYD 7
youth who l. me WHITM 33
lovesick: perfumèd that/ The winds
   were l. SHAK 5
lovesom: Fair be thy wives, right l.,
   white and small; DUNB W 5
lovest: What thou l. well remains,
   POUN 18
loveth: l. best of all the year
   JACK 2
who l. best COLE SAM 30
loving: beauty purely l. CAMPI 19
increase that l. humour more.
   CAMPI 4
l. a foreign muse. BENE 3
l., black-browed night, SHAK 149
l. couple lies DONN 49
L. in truth, SIDN 5
l. live, and merry still; CAMPI 8
L. me in secret. WRIG J 5
Love may make me leave l.
   DONN 40
l., rapid, merciless — LOWE R 29
l. thou mayst loved be with equall
   crime.' SPENS 34
missed his l. bride. NASH 12
soldier's l. arms WHITM 116
those two l. ones! HOLM 11
vouchsafe me but this l. thought —
   SHAK 196
Whase only faut is l. thee?
   BURN 38
world of l. wonders STIR 1
youthful, l., modest pair
   BURN 19
lovyere: yong squier,/ A l. and a
   lusty bacheler, CHAU 8
low: At present l., WHITM 16
beneath the earth lie buried l.,
   VERY 5
breathing faint and l. POE 13
cap pulled l. upon a face
   WHITT 13
chariot "swing l."? JOHN J 6

dropped so l. in my regard
   DICKI 90
hanging loose and l. UPDI 1
indifferent judge between the high
   and l.; SIDN 14
leave all meaner things/ To l.
   ambition, POPE A 58
L.-anchored cloud, THOR 8
l., breathe and blow, TENN 113
L. breathings coming after me,
   WORD 94
L.-browed Hanna, LIND V 6
l. dark verge of life TENN 29
l.-vaulted past! HOLM 3
l. words oft creep in one dull
   line: POPE A 25
my light is l., TENN 27
prairie flowers lie l.: —
   LIND V 16
Scooting obliquely high and l.
   WHITM 75
sky is l., DICKI 128
Speak l., lean low, ROSS C 7
sunk him in the l. l. UNKN 118
sweep l., o bless/ the roofs,
   OLSO 8
Sweet and l., TENN 113
Valley so l., UNKN 80
voice is neither high nor l.,
   WHITM 91
Lowell: "There is L., LOWE J 4
lower: brown eyes l. fell —
   WHITT 14
little l. than the angels,
   BIBL, O.T. 25
l. victorious WHITM 57
night is beginning to l., LONG 9
lowest: l. and most dejected thing of
   fortune, SHAK 77
to the l. ebb; SOUTHW 8
lowing: l. herd wind slowly o'er the
   lea, GRAY 7
l. Of the calves YEATS 145
lowland: between l. and highland,
   SWIN 10
sunk him in the L. sea,
   UNKN 118
lowlands: In the l. HARD 51
sunk him in the L. low.
   UNKN 118
lowliest: l. duties WORD 42
us l. sometime sweep,
   CRAN H 29
lowliness: l. is young ambition's
   ladder, SHAK 44
lowly: base as is the l. plain,
   SYLV 1
bereft, and meek, and l.,
   HARD 10
Chanted loudly, chanted l.,
   TENN 67
l. paths of service free; GLAD 1

play the fife l.,　UNKN 11
satisfaction is a l. thing,
　MOOR M 43
Loy: by Seint L.　CHAU 13
loyal: l. hearts, there are spirits
　brave,　BRID 1
l., just, and pure,　MILT 78
loyalty: l. well held to fools
　SHAK 6
luau: Congress, lobster, love, l.,
　BROO G 5
lubbard: lumbering l. loitering
　slow,　MELV 2
lubber: lies him down the l. fend,
　MILT 23
Lubin: Poor L. fears,　PRIO 11
lucent: l., million-pleasured
　breast, —　KEAT 64
lucid: l. morning's fragrant breath
　THOMS J (1834–1882) 1
time, where l. Avon stray'd,
　GRAY 28
Lucifer: Herr God, Herr L.,
　PLATH 56
Prince L. uprose,　MERE G 8
luck: always just my l.　PARK 1
Good l. is the gayest　HAY 1
In l. or out　YEATS 24
l. was his light-o'-love,　SERV 6
Madame Bad L.　HAY 2
luckless: On life's rough ocean l.
　starr'd:　BURN 60
lucky: blessed their l. stars
　GILB 42
chase into the house a l. foot.
　HOUS 8
l. older wife,　BOGA 5
shore was l. in being backed by
　cliff,　FROS 77
wish her a l. passage.　WILB 45
Lucretius: L. Sings　JEFFE 34
Lucy: L. ceased to be;　WORD 46
no comrade L. knew;　WORD 50
luely: l., cam she in　SOUT 1
Luke: L. Havergal —　ROBI 22
L. shall leave us, Isabel;
　WORD 53
lull: haply, in some l. of life,
　WHITT 28
l. their dreaming lids,　OWEN 37
Lullabies: Sung asleep with L.:
　HERR 13
lullaby: sing a l.:　DEKK/OTHE 1
Sing l. and be thou still;　BRET 3
Sing l., as women do,　GASC 1
sit by thee and wail my fill:/ God
　bless my babe, and l.　BRET 3
lull'd: l. by the rills,　ARNO 7
lulled: l. with sound of sweetest
　melody?　SHAK 54
l. within, a family with pets,
　BISH 35

lumber: loads of learned l.
　POPE A 22
lumbering: Clumsy and l.　SCHW 9
l. lubbard loitering slow,　MELV 2
l. sort of carnal spirit,　HECH 9
Those l. horses　MUIR 7
lumberjacks: woods and l.,
　FROS 124
luminous: dusty bondage into l.
　air.　MILLA 8
Fragile and l.　PRIN 1
shirt and tie were l.　WAGO 1
lump: snow l. thrice his own slight
　size　HARD 43
Toiling over a l. of clay
　JOHN J 3
lumpy: camel's all l.　CARRY 3
lunatic: l., the lover, and the poet
　SHAK 127
lung: l. and liver,　SYNG 1
l. heart feet tail　GINS 14
lungs: froth-corrupted l.,　OWEN 19
l. hath caught the itch,
　UNKN 194
l. of bronze,　BELL 13
my l. could bleat like butter'd
　pease;　UNKN 194
lure: Time stoops to no man's l.;
　SWIN 14
With empty hand men may no
　hawkes l.　CHAU 86
luscious: l. clusters of the vine
　MARV 17
world is mud-/ l.　CUMM 12
lust: above Intrest or l.　PRIO 5
adulterous l. was driven　MILT 78
burlesque of our l.　CRAN H 26
into ashes all my l.:　MARV 34
Life is the l. of a lamp　SWIN 20
l. for milk.　MONR 2
l. in action;　SHAK 236
l./ Is perjured, murderous,
　SHAK 236
l. of earth below,　CLARE 14
L. of glory pricked their hearts
　up,　BROWNI R 48
L. the Master of a hardned Face,
　COWL 4
my l., my likerousnesse,　CHAU 92
oftener seen, the more I l.,
　GOOG 2
semi-/ l. of intentional
　indifference.　CREE 11
somme seyden, l. abedde,
　CHAU 109
Uncorseted, her friendly l.
　ELIOT T 159
with thine aching l.　JOHN L 6
luster: l. of the eye?　ARNO 11
Such was their l.,　HERB G 40
lustfull: l. beasts,　PETRO 1

lustre: Candor here, and l. there
　HERR 73
No lily has such l.,　GAY 1
lustrous: Beauty cannot keep her
　l.-eyes,　KEAT 47
l. and drooping star　WHITM 52
l. Jupiter,　WHITM 59
O comrade l.　WHITM 52
spread his l. coil;　HOLM 2
lusts: in toys, in l., or wine,
　COWL 15
l. and greeds　SITW 9
l. they do me leave,　VAUX 2
lusty: lovyere and a l. bacheler,
　CHAU 8
l. stealth of nature　SHAK 70
rude, unbending, l.,　WHITM 39
treasure of thy l. days,　SHAK 185
was a l. oon,　CHAU 90
lutch: rear this fellow up/ to l.,
　BIRN 3
lute: Blame not my l.　WYAT 2
Dirge is whisper'd by the warbling
　L.　DRYD 26
lascivious pleasing of a l.
　SHAK 95
l. is broken,　SHEL 89
l., nor gittern can　LYLY 5
My l. awake!　WYAT 12
My l., be as thou wert　DRUM 4
My l. be still, for I have done.
　WYAT 12
Orpheus with his L.
　FLET/SHAK 1
stringed l. on which all winds can
　play,　WILD 13
tune her l.　GRIF 1
"Whose heart-strings are a l.;"
　POE 26
lutes: l. were strewn　HARD 41
melodious words to l. of amber.
　HERR 63
Luther: Bulldozed by L. and
　Weyerhaeuser　SNYD 45
Luve: L.'s like a red, red rose,
　BURN 45
Lux: L. my fair falcon,　WYAT 16
Luxuriant: gently creeps/ L.:
　MILT 69
luxuriates: heart l.　WORD 63
luxuries: l. and freedom also.
　JEFFE 41
we love our l.　JEFFE 5
Luxurious: L. Man,　MARV 24
luxuriously: spend the time l.
　DANI S 19
luxury: contempt of l.　JEFFE 42
l. of looking at beauties,　PRAE 3
l. of the precocious　RICH 20
L., then is a way of/ being
　ignorant,　BARA 14
Wild Nights should be/ Our l.!
　DICKI 157

maggots: inlay m. like a jewel.
  SHAP 15
over the surfacing/ like m.
  DUGA 2
magic: argosies of m. sails,
  TENN 75
Charmed m. casements, KEAT 50
m.-lanterned on the smoke of
  hell; EMPS 15
m. power on the stony grange.
  MUIR 7
m. web with colours gay.
  TENN 61
Mighty m. is a mother, CREE 6
Modred, whose m. song GRAY 4
of m. and might, COAT 2
this rough m. I here abjure,
  SHAK 165
magical: m. bewitching/ hour
  SANC 1
magician: retinue from the m.'s
  house AUDE 53
magnet: Can a m. ever GILB 34
magnetic: m.,/ Peripatetic/ Lover
  GILB 34
magnetick: m. pow'r, QUAR 1
magnificence: Alone amid m.
  ROBI 30
m. of the dead, AIKE 9
magnificent: disdainful and m.
  JOHN H 4
M. in piles of ruin ADDI 1
M. The morning rose, WORD 102
mild and m. eye, BROWNI R 45
Magnified: M. one thousand times,
  GRAV 1
magnitude: heroic m. of mind
  MILT 113
Magnolia: told of the M.,
  WORD 130
magpie: swollen m. in a fitful sun,
  POUN 22
Mahomet: from M. to Moses;
  PRAE 1
maid: Amaryllis,/ The wanton
  country m. CAMPI 6
Cling with life to the m.;
  EMER 24
com'st a decent m., COLL 11
dame or m., be not afraid,
  UNKN 263
die you must (faire M.) HERR 31
Fair m., white and red, PEEL 5
lazy finger of a m.; SHAK 153
m. again I'll never be. UNKN 298
m. and her wight HARD 30
m. at your window, SHAK 36
once my m. HERR 64
slain by a fair cruel m.
  SHAK 176
steals the heart of m. HOUS 14
Wondering m.; HODG 6
woo a fair m., GILB 61

maiden: Adam and m.,
  THOMA D 19
form of a m. fair, LONG 52
I pursued a m. SHEL 28
m. all forlorn MOTH 8
m. fair and dapper, TAYL B 1
M. most perfect, SWIN 4
m. of bashful fifteen; SHERI 1
m. posies, HERR 56
m.'s breast, SCOT WA 20
many a rose-lipt m. HOUS 62
neater, sweeter m. KIPL 12
orbed m. SHEL 24
To a m. true UNKN 84
maidenhead: crop/ A flower and a
  m. LOVE 3
losse of m., DONN 24
maidenhood: mantle/ Is of your m.
  SKEL 3
maidenhoods: pair of stainless m.
  SHAK 149
maidens: Coal-black m. LIND V 12
dismal yew;/ M., willow branches
  BEAU/FLET 3
m. taste/ And stray STEVENS 58
m.' vows and swearing WITH 3
maids: Eight m. a-milking,
  UNKN 281
gives Immortal youth to mortal
  m. LAND 5
lactiferous m.! HOLM 1
m. dance in a ring, NASHE 3
M. have spent their houres.
  HERR 50
Soft m. and village hinds COLL 1
mail: creamy iridescent coats of
  m., BISH 3
m. from Tunis, probably,
  DICKI 124
mailed: weak m. fist BISH 2
mailins: Than stockit m. BURN 44
maimed: m. darling, ROET 12
spent and m. KINGSL 8
main: catches the m. words only,
  WHITM 16
Doubt is faith in the m.:
  SWIN 17
dreary m., — SHEL 62
from out the azure m.,
  THOMS J (1700–1748)/MALL 1
gave m. support. MILT 114
great river take me to the m.
  TENN 106
He is good i' the m.,
  BROWNI R 17
lordly m. LANIE 5
m. region of my song. WORD 15
M. Street was never the same.
  RIVE 2
sailor frae the m., BURN 34
wat'ry m., SHAK 211
with m. and with might,
  UNKN 159

Maine: as populous as M. today,
  MERE W 1
M. lobster town — LOWE R 56
mainly: conversation is m. NÍ CH 1
maintain: Good liquor, I stoutly
  m., GOLD 5
Love, m. thy life in me. SIDN 27
m. "the sublime" POUN 36
maintained: did great wrong, and
  m. little right. UNKN 159
Maisry: Lady M. is gone home,
  UNKN 134
maistrie: fair for the m., CHAU 18
maize: m. and vine. TENN 11
majestic: Deep, m., GRAY 24
Flowing with m. train, MILT 16
in m. cadence LONG 30
m. in thy sadness TENN 126
m. instancy, THOMP F 7
My Lord advances with m. mien,
  POPE A 102
Majestick: Style; M. and Divine,
  DRYD 18
majesties: purple mountain m.
  BATE 1
majesty: attribute to awe and m.,
  SHAK 123
earth of m., SHAK 88
m. and riches of the mind,
  CHAP G 1
mourn/ The m. and burning
  THOMA D 37
next in m., DRYD 10
touching in its m.: WORD 6
want love's m. SHAK 96
major: Beasts in their m. freedom
  WILB 7
C M. of this life: BROWNI R 5
M. Bogan's face TATE A 10
Major-Gineral: of a modern M.,
  GILB 35
Majors: live with scarlet M.
  SASS 3
make: factories they m. rubbers in
  SNYD 27
heart is warm with the friends I
  m., MILLA 38
I'll m. me a world." JOHN J 1
live your epitaph to m.,
  SHAK 216
Love may m. me leave loving,
  DONN 40
m. a nave STEVENS 14
m. a quarrel. NASH 7
m. and end, TENN 131
m. him run. MARV 35
m. me sick WHITM 75
m. me thus to leave you,
  SIDN 31
M. me thy Loome: TAYL E 6
M. me thy Spinning Wheele
  TAYL E 5
m. of me a saint, CONG 2

m. one/ breathe faster
MOOR M 26

m. one erecter. MOOR M 26

M. one place ev'rywhere.
HERB G 65

m. our lives sublime, LONG 36

m. sure of his Jill! GILB 62

m. that, which was nothing, all;
DONN 65

m. the earth devour SHAK 189

m. the taker mad; SHAK 236

m. them follow HALE 2

M. them forget BROWNI R 28

m. yourself content, my love,
UNKN 293

m. something imagined,
LOWE R 42

men who m. them WILB 21

Some let me m. you of the
heartless words. THOMA D 16

spider will m. a silver string nest
SAND 1

Theirs not to m. reply, TENN 7

To m. a prairie DICKI 148

To m. a third DRYD 10

to m. an end is to m. a
beginning. ELIOT T 71

maken: smale foweles m. melodye,
CHAU 4

Maker: image of their glorious M.
MILT 71

Our M. bids increase, MILT 77

thy m. is not by; BLAK 103

thy m. is not near. BLAK 103

makers: old toilers, soil m.:
HALL 3

makes: m. ready for work,
WHITM 37

m. the gallow tree; RALEG 13

m. the timber rot; RALEG 14

sweet music m. the ground to
move, GRIF 1

'Tis love in love that m. the
sport. SUCK 4

maketh: Greet prees at market m.
dere ware, CHAU 89

Lord killeth, and m. alive;
BIBL, O.T. 8

m. me to lie down in green
pastures: BIBL, O.T. 31

making: after m. love, quiet,
KINN 1

ground of his m., KINN 2

I shall be past m. love PRIO 12

m. driving belts. SPEND 8

m. folk-songs TOOM 1

m. of man SWIN 1

M. their tomb SHAK 217

m. wise the simple. BIBL, O.T. 28

poet of God's m.; DRYD/TATE 2

Mal: to M. Waldron OHAR 6

Malcolm: M.'s words BARA 11

Maldive: sot of the M. sea,
MELV 13

male: m. of the species —
LAWR 13

rough m. kiss BROO R 4

Time is m. RICH 21

males: as m. they disliked his air
KAVA 17

malevolent: m. aged grin.
HUGH T 10

malice: gesture or least action,
overawed/ His m., MILT 90

m. in the dry machine
STEVENS 48

Malicious: M. Angel, JOHN L 5

with m. eye BROWNI R 20

malign: Nature shedding influence
m., THOMS J (1700–1748) 13

mallet: ball is lost and the m.
slipped MACN 20

malls: shopping m. and prisons,
PINS 1

malorum: Radix m. est cupiditas.
CHAU 83

malt: brewers mar their m. with
water; SHAK 76

m. does more than Milton can
HOUS 51

m. That lay in the house
MOTH 3

rat! That ate the m. MOTH 4

Malvern: M. Wood/ Bethink itself,
MELV 16

on M. Hill MELV 15

Shiloh, Antietam, M. Hill, Bull
Run. TATE A 12

Malverne: upon M. hilles LANGL 1

Mama: escape that fatal M.
GINS 29

mammoth: m. but not fat,
TATE A 3

m. rests between his cyclonic
dramas. SAND 15

mammoths: Great m. overthrown
WILB 47

mammy: m. bending over her
baby, JOHN J 3

man: aims/ But to console m.
THOR 10

all m.'s Babylons THOMP F 5

almost to m. STEVENS 22

any scientific m. HART 3

At the expense of m.? GRAV 27

be a friend to m. FOSS 2

being m., can kiss RODG 3

beseeching the young m.;
WHITM 8

better m. was found HOLM 15

Beware the Fury of a Patient M
DRYD 1

blind m.'s ditch. YEATS 47

blind m.'s mark, SIDN 39

blinded m. sees GRAV 21

bluidy m. I trow thou be;
BURN 36

boxes out his m. HIRS 1

brave m. with a sword! WILD 3

bronzed, lank m.! LIND V 2

buy the soul of any m. DARC 4

by m.'s oppression cursed,
POPE A 98

can m. die better MACA 3

canst not then be false to any m.
SHAK 24

Child is father of the M.;
WORD 58

Child's Toys and the Old M.'s
Reasons BLAK 8

cold charities of m. CRAB 7

corpse which is m. SWIN 25

Could m. be drunk for ever
HOUS 2

cry of every M., BLAK 74

Dark as the world of m.,
SITW 11

dead m. out of mind. HOUS 33

dead m.'s cry MACL 6

dead m.'s voice MACL 10

Diapason closing full in M.
DRYD 25

differs more from M., ROCH 13

difficultest job a m. DAVID 7

discerning intellect of M.,
WORD 16

dog and m. at first were friends;
GOLD 7

doth make m. better be, JONS 41

dull m., dulling and uxorious,
POUN 55

ease an old m. SNOD 6

ere m. had sinned — BRYA 15

eternal thing in m., HARD 26

eternal truth m.'s fighting soul
EBER 3

every m. be blind. DICKI 137

every m. in arms WORD 4

every m. upon this earth MACA 3

Everything that m. esteems
YEATS 119

Face of M. Is blackened —
OMAR 1

feather bed had every m., GILB 4

Feeds beast as m. SHAK 3

filth in the heart of M. SITW 9

flat-headed m. ROET 54

flight is past: and m. forgot.
KING H 5

flower had marred a m.,
FROS 111

four seasons in the mind of m.:
KEAT 19

free m. how to praise. AUDE 46

Freedom all solace to m. gives:
BARBO 1

from one m. the world. OLSO 14

full-sized a m. LOWE J 3

fully and perfectly m. LOWE J 3
ghost of the heart of m. SITW 6
God above, or M. below,
  POPE A 60
Gods breath in m. HERB G 66
Gone is the heart of M. SITW 10
great as any honest m.'s. GILB 37
grown m.'s work," CLARK J 2
grudge the poor old m. FROS 21
Happy the m. POPE A 107
Hardly a m. is now alive
  LONG 43
heart of m. FROS 93
heart of m., and human life.
  WORD 51
heart/ Of m. has a little dignity,
  TATE A 19
heaven divide/ The state of m.
  SHAK 55
hiding-places of m.'s power
  WORD 115
Hurrah for horse and m.!
  READ T 2
I came to m.'s estate SHAK 177
I do not find/ The Hanged M.
  ELIOT T 117
I envy no m.'s nightingale or
  spring; HERB G 46
I have killed a naked m.
  UNKN 174
I love not m. the less, BYRO 1
I saw a m. pursuing the horizon;
  CRAN S 1
I Tiresias, old m. ELIOT T 135
If I've killed one m., PLATH 32
If the heart of a m. GAY 3
I'm such a disagreeable m.!
  GILB 7
imagination of a m. YEATS 45
in m.'s veins ROSE 3
In the spring a young m.'s fancy
  lightly turns TENN 69
intellect of m. YEATS 23
Iron-hearted m.-slaying Achilles
  AUDE 83
Is no m.'s land, DAY 5
Just like his old m. HEAN 11
justify God's ways to m.
  HOUS 51
kept watch o'er m.'s mortality;
  WORD 86
know the Garment from the M.
  BLAK 20
know what God and m. is.
  TENN 13
knowing each m., CREE 13
Language of M. pronounced
  MILT 93
laws of God, and m. and metre.
  JEFFR 1
laws of m., HOUS 16
let God and m. decree HOUS 16

light and a shadow on every m.
  MELV 7
like a tired M. DICKI 162
like m. and wife. POPE A 26
like the heart of m. SITW 13
little m., WHITT 6
living m. is blind YEATS 46
London is a m.'s town,
  VAN DY 1
lone m.'s friend — HARD 51
lonely old m. with a white beard.
  GINS 27
Lord, who createdst m. in wealth
  and store, HERB G 26
lost a m. SIMP 3
love of m., JEFFE 39
Luxurious M., MARV 24
making of m. SWIN 1
m. against the sky? ROBI 34
m. all tattered and torn MOTH 9
m. and a woman/ Are one.
  STEVENS 64
m. and beast MOOR M 23
m. can never be alone.
  TATE A 20
m. can raise a thirst; KIPL 13
m. climbing/ must scrape his
  knees, LEVE 11
M. comes and tills the field
  TENN 120
M. disavows, COWP 15
m. does flourish but his time.
  WEBS 1
M., dreame no more GREV 6
M. from Beast. ROCH 13
m. goes riding by.
  STEVENSO R 24
m. grows old, lies down, BRAD 5
m. harrowing clods HARD 29
m. has borne before! LONG 25
m. has married a wife, BLAK 113
M. hath no part BRYA 16
M., her last work, TENN 36
m. his own quietus make
  LAWR 37
m. in all his vileness
  MOOR M 23
m. in marriage bound.' OVID 6
m. in the bush with God
  EMER 29
m. in the smoker SAND 12
M. is a long time coming.
  SAND 18
M. is all symmetrie, HERB G 52
m. is but an ass GILB 40
m. is dead! WHITT 12
m. is dead. WINT 11
M. is ev'ry thing,/ And more:
  HERB G 50
M. is in part divine, BYRO 60
M. is naturally good, MELV 12
M. is no starre, HERB G 29
M. is not a Fly. POPE A 69

M. is the shuttle, VAUG 10
m. makes friends CHAP A 2
m. marks the earth BYRO 2
m. o' men was he. POUN 3
M. of baser Earth didst make,
  OMAR 1
m. of culture rare, GILB 30
m. of God's own choosing.
  LUTH 3
m. of no fortune, POUN 6
m. poured fish into a pile,
  YEATS 93
m. recover'd of the bite, GOLD 8
M. shall be M. SPEND 18
M. shall spend equally.
  SPEND 18
m. should labour all/ 'Is life
  KIPL 19
m. skating, STEVENS 32
m. that died for me. HAY 4
m. that looks in my face?
  WHITM 21
m., that thou art mindful of him?
  BIBL, O.T. 24
m. that's dead. HUGH L 19
m. the rudder, EMER 47
m., the self, MOOR M 25
m. their neighbor knows.
  YEATS 132
m. thinning out his kind
  LOWE R 50
m. to double business bound
  SHAK 34
m. were lov'd by wife, BRAD 13
m. who fears war POUN 63
m. who married Magdalene
  SIMP 5
m. who never reads in brook or
  book; KAVA 8
m. who should loose me
  LOWE A 11
m. who used to notice HARD 4
m. will be blotted out, JEFFE 43
M. will yet win. SAND 18
m. with a foot in the grave
  SERV 7
M., with is Satan SNYD 21
m., yet by these tears WHITM 63
M.'s feeble race GRAY 26
M.'s forgiveness give — OMAR 1
M.'s own resinous heart
  YEATS 120
M.'s pity for himself, BYRO 47
m.'s unconquerable mind.
  WORD 153
M.'s yesterday SHEL 44
many a m. shall die. SHAP 20
memory to a grey-haired m.
  WHITT 14
Mind not the old m. WHITM 8
Mind of M. WORD 15, 36
mother m. in his doubt! LEVE 7

moulded by the lips of m.
  TENN 127
murderous brain/ Of M., SITW 6
My outside Woman, and your
  inside M. COWL 6
mystery of m., WORD 115
name died before the m.
  HOUS 57
Natures æthereal, human, angel,
  m., POPE A 72
never m. was true;
  BRET/OTHE 2
no m. ever can, WHITM 4
No m. grows old, YEATS 73
No m. may him hide SKEL 11
no M. moved Me— DICKI 63
nothing so becomes a m.
  SHAK 56
of m.'s infirmity! DOAN 2
Of no m.'s greatness was afraid,
  SWIF 23
offence/ Of m. DRYD 17
old m. bending WHITM 113
old m. gone. JOYC 2
old m. in a dry month,
  ELIOT T 30
Old M. in a tree, LEAR 14
old m. of seventy-three
  SMIT ST 1
old m. of Thermopylae, LEAR 15
old m. with a beard, LEAR 18
old m. with his feet before the
  fire ROET 16
old m. with wrinkled dugs
  ELIOT T 135
oldest m. he seemed WORD 122
ole m. died— BROWN S 2
On water the M.-Fisher walks.
  LOWE R 14
one m.—can't keep a house,
  FROS 75
One m. with a dream, OSHA 3
one m.'s fault MILT 99
one/ With the m. in the wind and
  the west moon; THOMA D 9
one-armed m. GRAV 21
one-legged m. forgets GRAV 21
Parliament of m., the Federation
  of the world. TENN 76
play is the tragedy M.", POE 33
played on a m. a cursed brogue,
  BURN 3
Poor little timid furry m.
  ROSS C 6
poor m.'s wealth, SIDN 14
prentice han' she try'd on m.,
  BURN 30
pride of m. EMER 29
proper study of Mankind is M.
  POPE A 78
rather a goat's than m.'s.
  TATE A 8

reve was a sclendre colerik m.
  CHAU 19
reverend good old man.,
  HERB G 54
right m. on our side, LUTH 3
sadder and a wiser m.,
  COLE SAM 31
same m. I was afore PETRA 1
saw the Almighty M.!
  STEPHENS 13
scene of M.; POPE A 58
shape of that unmoving m.,
  WORD 108
shouting at me, dead m., SLES 2
sigh'd with each M.'s Care,
  SACK 3
signifies the life o' m., BURN 29
smiling public m. YEATS 7
smith, a mighty m. LONG 48
So, so,/ O son of m., SCHW 6
Sober as m. can get, BERRYM 7
solempne m. CHAU 20
sought for no m.'s aid. SWIF 23
soul of m. dies in him, loathing
  life, THOMS J (1700–1748) 13
speaks for the Family of M.?
  SAND 17
Spring-time of m. MASE 4
strong m. must go:
  BROWNI R 68
stupidity of m. WILLI 37
Summer of m. its sunlight
  MASE 4
teach you more of m., WORD 145
tell us old m., WHITM 113
that m.'s scope, SHAK 94
this aged m. and poor; KEAT 5
Three things there be in m.'s
  opinion dear, GREV 7
Time stoops to no m.'s lure;
  SWIN 14
Time, you old gipsy m.,
  HODG 11
trembled when a M. drew near;
  SWIF 13
Unhappy is the m. for evermair
  BOYD 1
Untainted by m.'s misery.
  SHEL 61
vindicate the ways of God to M.
  POPE A 59
voice a blind m. dreams GARR 1
Was m. made stupid EBER 3
watched that wretched m.,
  HOLM 14
wealthiest m. among us is the
  best: WORD 161
wear your hair like a m., TRAI 1
wearifu' gaberlunzie m..'
  UNKN 111
What is a m., SHAK 35
what is good in M. WILD 3

what m. does not know of God
  EBER 9
What M. has made of Man?
  WORD 39
what pleasures m. YEATS 72
When God at first made m.,
  HERB G 61
When I was m. alive? HOUS 36
when m. receives, POPE A 127
White m. tells me— BROWN S 3
whole duty of m. BIBL, O.T. 7
whole shadow of M. BISH 29
Why should a m. desire
  TENN 121
wisest m. grows tense YEATS 156
words of a dead m. AUDE 38
world in which a m. was born?'
  BYRO 36
you black m. SANC 3
you'll be a M., my son! KIPL 8
young m. carbuncular,
  ELIOT T 135
Young m. I think I know you—
  WHITM 72
young m. of Montrose BENN A 1
man's: honest m. the noblest work
  of God!" BURN 20
honest m. the noblest work of
  God. POPE A 85
m. the gowd for a' that!
  BURN 24
m. a m. for a' that! BURN 25
say not M. imperfect, POPE A 62
Though m. a fool, POPE A 82
manacled: m. in hands: MARV 11
manacles: golden m. stand for a
  paradise; SIDN 4
mind-forg'd m. BLAK 74
manage: horse is taught his m.,
  WORD 110
We are easy to m., JEFFE 5
management: Theater business, m.
  of men. YEATS 58
Mandalay: come you back to M.!"
  KIPL 9
mandatory: slaughter's m. every
  spring HUGO 3
mandibles: hairy black m., GRAV 1
mandrake: m. with to-morrow's
  scream. THOMA D 6
mane: flowing m. Of repentance
  RODG 7
m. falls wild WRIG J 2
twa corbies making a m.;
  UNKN 271
wind's long m. Screamed redskin
  CRAN H 22
manege: in the m. myself takes
  delight. SIDN 19
maner: alle m. of men, LANGL 3
mange: permit her to get the m.
  STEPHENS 4

manger: Away in a m., LUTH 1
holy m. LOWE R 23
homely m. SOUTHW 4
in a m. laid. TATE N 2
lodge him in the m. UNKN 315
one born in a M. VAUG 15

mangled: m. heap/ Of carcases
THOMS J (1700–1748) 10
m. youth lies dead THOMP F 8
price of m. mind SIDN 39

mangy: m. as the Irish Seas,
UNKN 194

Manhattan: M. crowds, WHITM 32
M. faces WHITM 32
M. Storage Warehouse, OHAR 13
M. streets WHITM 32
M. the son, WHITM 73

manhood: Lost m. and put
priesthood on? VILL 1
m. full and fair! BRID R 17
m. of the poor, LOWE J 14

mania: m. of owning things,
WHITM 75

maniac: Time, a m. scattering dust,
TENN 28

maniacs: ordered a box of m.
PLATH 9

Manifestations: M. of that beauteous
life KEAT 20

manifesto: powerful plain m.
SPEND 4

manifestoes: land of ambush,/
Purblind m., MACN 4

manifold: complex, m. involvedness
LAWR 55
heavens reward thee m. BRAD 14
Lord, how m. are thy works!
BIBL, O.T. 51
mind, adorned with virtues m.
SPENS 8

manilla: misery of m. folders
ROET 7

Mankind: achieve/ M.'s deliverance.
MILT 104
alone of all m. BARNE 5
careless of m. TENN 89
cure the vices of m.; SWIF 22
live in m. LIND V 14
m. abuse thee; CALV 6
M. made plausible, MILLA 21
mistress of M.! ROCH 15
murder/ The m. of her going
THOMA D 37
proper study of m. is Man.
POPE A 78
Survey m. from China to Peru;
JOHN S (1709–1784) 15
tenth of m. SHAK 179
Virtue in M. SWIF 19
words among m.! SHEL 46

mankinde: m. brought to
wrecchednesse, CHAU 86

Mother of M., MILT 48
womman was the los of al m.
CHAU 86

manly: m. man, CHAU 18
open thou thy m. mouth,
UNKN 166

manna: gathered up the crystal m.
BRID R 9

manner: All m. of thing shall be
well ELIOT T 74
ease in Casey's m. THAY 2
picking a m. of worm, OWEN 39
to the m. born, SHAK 25

Mannerly: M. Margery Milk and
Ale. SKEL 4

manners: beat bad m.
STEPHENS 3
love's m. in bed CREE 12
m. are tearing off heads —
HUGH T 2
m., climates, councils,
governments, TENN 130
m. free and superb — WHITM 44
m., of the bard. EMER 33
m., virtue, freedom, power.
WORD 41
sweeter m., purer laws. TENN 48

mannes: m. joy and all his bliss."
CHAU 67

Mans: M. First Disobedience,
MILT 46

mansion: Love has pitched his m.
YEATS 39

mansions: found in m. higher
SHEN 1
more stately m., HOLM 3
ranged m. dark
THOMS J (1834–1882) 3

Mantel: Not the M.'s — DICKI 18

Mantels: candelabra,/ M.,
BROO G 9

mantle: m. Is of your maidenhood.
SKEL 3

mantling: m. vine/ Lays forth her
purple grape, MILT 69

manual: m. on schedule ASHB 1
write the instructional m.
ASHB 1

manufacture: m. both machine and
soul, GUNN 12

manunkind: busy monster, m.,
CUMM 35

many: Change of m.-colour'd Life he
drew, JOHN S (1709–1784) 5
civilization has given us too m.
JOHN F 1
dome of m.-colored glass,
SHEL 13
m. a fall shall linger near.
ROGE 1
m. a May. ROSS C 17
m. a rose-carnation feed
TENN 42

m. generations hence, WHITM 19
m. thousand mists, WORD 52
m. to keep, KINGSL 3
m.-towered Camelot; TENN 59
m. wanton babes have I, GASC 2
Not one death but m., OLSO 4
so m. hundred years hence,
WHITM 19
So m. of us! PLATH 66
withouten m. wordes, WYAT 17

map: m. a bad example SPEND 2
m. becomes their window
SPEND 4

mapemounde: cercled is the m.:
CHAU 122

maple: empty doorway and a m.
leaf. MACL 2
m. burn itself away; TENN 42

maps: "Here are the m."; JARR 16
m. are of time, not place,
REED H 3
words are m. RICH 4

mar: m. a lover's vows YEATS 94

Marathon: From M. to Waterloo,
GILB 35
m. trim PAGE 3
skirmish fought near M. GRAV 20

marble: bathing in a m. basin,
LOWE A 8
brest hath m. beene HABI 3
Chess on a m. table AIKE 2
Chichesters knelt in m. MACN 14
cloud-sopped, m. hands,
THOMA D 5
Flashed from his matted head and
m. feet, LOWE R 37
Forget thyself to m., MILT 16
Interred beneath this m. stone
PRIO 3
m. for a tombe, HABI 3
m. halls as white as milk,
MOTH 16
m. index of a Mind WORD 101
m. or a bronze repose. YEATS 12
m. with too much conceiving,
MILT 35
no m. column craves TIMR 6
Not m. SHAK 207
Out-during m., brass, or jet,
HERR 37
power/ To melt that m. yce,
CAREW 14
pure m. Air MILT 65
Rung from their m. caves
DRUM 7
stood at the top of that long m.
stair WILB 34
through her m. halls! LONG 24

Marblehead: Ireson's, out from M.!
WHITT 23
women of M.! WHITT 23

marbly: m. and dim — MERR 1

march: confus'd m. forlorn,
 MILT 61
droghte of M. CHAU 3
forced m. of Monday PAGE 1
forth I m., thou goest before;
 BIBL, O.T. 64
hear the Dead M. play, KIPL 5
m. for home, GRAV 28
m. in ranks of better equipage:
 SHAK 196
M. indefatigably MARV 23
m. of Motherland! THOMP W 2
m. the streets of Birmingham
 RANDA D 1
M. with its peck of dust,
 ROSS C 37
Walk softly, M., SARE 1
marchant: m. was ther CHAU 21
marched: m. breast forward,
 BROWNI R 12
m. — six — weeks in 'Ell KIPL 4
Men m. asleep. OWEN 18
marches: thick as mist/ On evening
 m., SHEL 79
marching: buried in the dust of m.
 feet. KNIG 3
His truth is m. on. HOWE 2
spiders m. through the air,
 LOWE R 33
mare: black m. CUNN J 3
mares: lank m. coursing by
 RANS 2
Margaret: Merry M.,' As midsummer
 flower, SKEL 2
marge: m. of Lake Lebarge SERV 1
margent: slow Meander's m. green,
 MILT 9
margeran: m. gentle, SKEL 3
Margery: Mannerly M. Milk and
 Ale. SKEL 4
margins: m. of animal necessity,
 SAND 16
mariage: in fruit of m. CHAU 95
speke of wo that is in m.:
 CHAU 86
marie: M. Hamilton gangs wi'
 bairn UNKN 187
Maries: "Last night there was four
 M., UNKN 188
marimba: turning to m. music.
 BISH 7
marine: mystical monster m.?
 HILT 2
oaks, how subtle and m.!
 WARR 1
secluded in the thick m.?
 STEVENS 48
mariner: m., worn and wan,
 SHEL 35
Mariners: M. of England
 CAMPB T 10
m. were skinned, DAY 7

marines: Officers, seamen, gunners,
 m., CLARK J 1
Marion: fears, and flies from M.'s
 men. SIMM 2
mark: attains his lifted m. MELV 7
blind man's m., SIDN 39
M. Hanna's McKinley, LIND V 5
m. this day in Heaven? TIMR 3
M. you the floore? HERB G 12
Melancholy m.'d him for her
 own. GRAY 12
No m. of her late time HARD 45
not to hit the m. FRANC 1
nought to do but m. and tell
 BURN 4
There m. what ills
 JOHN S (1709–1784) 18
toil has left its m.: YEATS 24
Marke: Beautie be the M. of praise,
 JONS 30
marked: More are men's ends m.
 SHAK 87
old lady, who m. MONTA 2
markes: blacke beames such
 burning m. engrave SIDN 15
market: At m. and fair, UNKN 44
chaired you through the m.-place;
 HOUS 55
chief good and m. of his time
 SHAK 35
from m. or plough, MACDONO 1
Gods of the M.-Place. KIPL 6
Greet prees at m. maketh dere
 ware, CHAU 89
to m.-place and people HOUS 5
to m., to buy a fat pig;
 UNKN 262
marks: m. he made SCOT WA 13
m. of wanton hunger. SAND 4
m. the circle of another world
 WALK 13
m. when you're dressed, GILD 1
marmasyte: Tullia's ape a m.
 UNKN 95
marmot: hawk and m., SNYD 22
marred: flower had m. a man,
 FROS 111
marreth: lamenting love m. the
 musicall. SPENS 37
marriage: ache of m.; LEVE 1
blights with plagues the M.
 hearse BLAK 76
education m. nervous breakdown,
 GINS 21
grave's the second M.-bed.
 CRAS 1
Honor, riches, m. blessing,
 SHAK 161
king's fere in m.? MORE 2
man in m. bound.' OVID 6
m. is dead, when the pleasure is
 fled: DRYD 16

m. of true minds SHAK 231
m. on the rocks. MERR 3
Marriages: M., alliances, and
 families, YEATS 35
thousands of m. LARK 18
married: He was m. AUDE 94
longs to get m. UNKN 304
man has m. a wife, BLAK 113
man who m. Magdalene SIMP 5
m. Allen don't take drugs —
 GINS 32
m., charming, chaste, and twenty-
 three. BYRO 20
M. impossible men? GRAV 26
m. their everyones CUMM 5
m. three wives at one time.
 LEAR 19
M. to immortal verse, MILT 24
Mocks m. men, SHAK 100
mostly m. people; CLOU 3
Should I get m.? CORS 1
60 years old and not m., CORS 9
Unpleasing to a m. ear.
 SHAK 100
wherever corpses m. LOWE R 9
marries: m. its own mother,
 JARR 8
marring: m. of beautiful shows,
 PRAE 4
marrow: Dove-note, bone m., deer
 dung, KIZE 1
m.-bone might seize! UNKN 230
m. in the bone SITW 8
Puritan m. of my bones WYLI 14
Right into the m. LAWR 53
marry: dear knows who I'll m.
 UNKN 139
m. a ghost STEPHENS 4
m. you young KENN 2
not the bodies m., but the minds,
 DONN 38
Will you m. it? PLATH 2, 4
Mars: beards of Hercules and
 frowning M., SHAK 122
dome of mighty M. the red,
 CHAU 45
M. yaf me my sturdy hardinesse.
 CHAU 92
seat of M., SHAK 88
marsh: in this simmering m..'
 LAWR 34
m. bird that children dread.
 KINS 4
marshes: leveling of the m.
 CRAN H 43
of the m. of Glynn LANIE 4
putrid m. SHEL 18
martial: enterprise of m. kind,
 GILB 14
Let the m. songs be written,
 WALK 6
m. cloak around him. WOLF C 2
piano's m. blast GILB 43

Set the M. Mind on Fire,
DRYD 23
ship of m. build MELV 1
Martian: M. generalities, POUN 29
Martinmas: about the M. time,
UNKN 38
martyr: Glorious the m.'s gore:
SMAR 9
Love's m., DONN 26
sort of m., WILB 42
martyrdom: dreadful m. AUDE 63
martyred: m. ambition — RICH 19
m. blood and ashes sow MILT 36
m. steps and slow, ROBI 2
martyrs: graves of the m.
STEVENSO R 1
m. of a fallen cause; TIMR 6
marvel: m. at this /curious thing;
CULL 19
m. my birthday/ Away
THOMA D 35
Yet do I m. CULL 19
Marvell: M.'s wit and graceful
song. WHITT 10
marvellous: Chatterton, the m. boy,
WORD 121
marvelous: Dark, m., ROBI 24
Marx: big picture of K. M.
SNYD 43
Mary: all thy deeds, my faithful M.,
shine; COWP 22
Christ-child lay on M.'s CHES 2
Christ is born of M.; BROO P 4
every where that M. went
HALE 1
leaving thee, my bonnie M.
BURN 49
M., at thy window be, BURN 37
M. had a little lamb, HALE 1
M. sat musing FROS 19
Mistress M. is dead WHITT 35
my dear M. Moore, YEATS 72
O M., marry earth, LOWE R 10
rise on M.'s day LOWE R 9
sea is the face of M., SEXT 9
winking M.-buds SHAK 17
marybones: with the m. CHAU 6
Maryland: M.! my M.! RANDA J 1
Marys: Three Hail M. KAVA 11
Masery: my sister M. UNKN 168
mask: grave and awkward m.
RICH 3
m. like Castlereagh — SHEL 39
rip off the whole facial m.
SNOD 2
wanton m., or midnight ball,
MILT 78
wear the m. DUNB P 11, 13
masked: everywhere beside me, m.,
MERR 8
their m. buds discloses.
SHAK 206

Masks: ashen-gray/ M. of the lads
SASS 2
mason: m. singing WHITM 37
masonry: north wind's m.
EMER 44
work of m., SHAK 207
mass: At a funeral m., HEAN 19
bubble in the molten m.,
JEFFE 37
droned the summer's final m.;
WILB 16
every m. that's said. BYRO 43
his purple m. DRAY 18
Its unobtrusive m. DICKI 23
m. hardens, JEFFE 37
several weeks before a m.
BYRO 43
masses: black m. spreading,
WHITM 56
m. of flowers. WILLI 46
poor,/ Your huddled m. LAZA 2
massie: those two m. Pillars
MILT 114
massing: dark clouds are m.;
DUNB P 6
massive: m. blood/ moves LAWR 8
m. buttocks slipping LEVI 1
m. deeds and great, LONG 4
mast: bends the gallant m.;
CUNN A 1
Lashed close to a drifting m.
LONG 52
m. burst open with a rose,
FLEC 5
Nail to the m. her holy flag,
HOLM 18
master: art of losing isn't hard to
m.; BISH 31
asked her m. STEPHENS 4
beauty as you m. now. SHAK 228
Betty from her m.'s bed had
flown, SWIF 10
clever servant, insufferable m.
JEFFE 39
conquer him that did his m.
conquer SHAK 6
dog starv'd at his M.'s BLAK 3
her m. hale, BURN 56
lose its evoked m. shape
DICKEY 11
Lust the M. of a hardned Face,
COWL 4
m. is surly, GILB 58
m.-leaver and a fugitive. SHAK 8
m. light of all our seeing;
WORD 81
M. of all; BROO P 2
m. of his fate, ROBI 31
m. of this house, UNKN 116
m., the swabber, the boatswain
SHAK 159
my M. came, LANIE 1
my M. went, LANIE 1

No m. spirit, WORD 22
our m. has left us for the day.
BLY 5
prairie-lawyer, m. of us all.
LIND V 2
slipshod 'prentice from his m.'s
door SWIF 10
steed bit his m.; UNKN 199
sure the Eternal M. found
JOHN S (1709–1784) 3
whether you shall be m.!
WHITM 76
with a m.-hand
THOMS J (1700–1748) 6
writing-/ m. to this world,
MOOR M 25
mastered: he is m. now, DICKI 39
m. by the brute blood of the air,
YEATS 86
mastering: lilac with m. odor
WHITM 49
masters: grand old m., LONG 15
m. of their fates, SHAK 43
Old M.: how well they
understood AUDE 62
masts: city of spires and m.!
WHITM 44
m. and spars, WHITM 92
M. in the offing DAVID 3
Masturbating: M. a glitter,
PLATH 35
Mat: on the M. devoutly kneeling
SWIF 14
match: born to m. the gale,
WHITM 104
careful with that m.! BISH 11
lose a winning m. SHAK 149
love/ A burnt m. CRAN H 31
m.-girl strikes it rich. HECH 12
m. in wealth LOWE J 15
m. the grandmamma, DICKI 51
strike a m. and blow. YEATS 69
Matched: M. with an aged wife,
TENN 128
matches: seat at the cricket m.
JARR 12
matching: Ill m. words MILT 80
M. thy inference. SHAK 136
matchless: m. deed's achieved,
SMAR 9
matchsticks: spars like burned m.
BISH 25
mate: absence of her m., SPENS 27
boatswain's m. was very sedate,
CARRY 9
born for sorrow's m., BENN G 7
choose his m./ Poet and sculptor,
YEATS 156
England I've a m., LEAR 5
Farewell dear m., WHITM 34
great beasts m. in secret LAWR 7
gunner and his m., SHAK 159
he wants you for his m. DAIC 2

vain travail hath wearied m.
　WYAT 30
way for Billy and m.　HOGG 1
What is Africa to m.:　CULL 5
who dravest M.."　THOMP F 10
why did nobody tell m.?
　PLATH 11
Wi my dear son and m.?"
　UNKN 49
wilt thou leave m. thus?　WYAT 1
worse to m. than dead?　WORD 1
You from m.　GRAV 31
your death murdered m.,
　MOSS 1
your liquors seep to m.,
　PLATH 73
mead: flowery m.　LONG 8
'Twixt m. and hill.　MORR 5
meadow: in m. or plain　SWIN 3
m. in the street;　TENN 53
m. where the bees hum:　LEVE 3
orchard, the m.,　WOOD 1
ragged m. of my soul.　CUMM 20
rain one inch above the m.:
　SMIT W 4
Raked the m.　WHITT 15
stranger's feet may find the m.
　HOUS 65
to return to a m.　DUNC 1
trickle gurgle in the swampy m.
　SNYD 7
meadow's: m. in the bloom,
　FOST 1
meadows: Kissing with golden face
　the m. green,　SHAK 197
m. brown and sear.　BRYA 7
m. fresh and gay,　MARV 27
paint the m. with delight,
　SHAK 100
through the m.　STEVENSO R 8
Up from the m.　WHITT 1
Woodlands, m.,　MAST 11
meads: Fair these broad m.
　GALT 1
sweet-springing m.　BRID R 14
meal: maketh her murderous m.!
　HILT 4
m. is ended,　ELIOT T 136
meals: at m. some odd thoughts
　BYRO 32
her m. untouch'd,　WHITM 17
mean: clouds are m.,　DICKI 128
declare it's crude and m.;
　GILB 31
God Apollo's golden m.　GRAV 41
Hard Rock wasn't a m. nigger
　KNIG 5
He nothing common did, or m.,
　MARV 22
holds fast the golden m.,　HORA 6
How m. thy hates　POUN 22
m. tenderly by you　WHITM 5

m. Our object and inglorious,
　WORD 95
poem should not m.　MACL 3
What does it m.　NASH 19
Meander: slow M.'s margent green,
　MILT 9
meandering: Five miles m. with a
　mazy motion　COLE SAM 21
some m. rivulet,　THOR 10
those m. down　HARD 42
meaner: Exempts no m. mortal
　things.　BEAU/BASS 5
leave all m. things　POPE A 58
With spoils of m. beauties
　crown'd　LOVE 4
meanest: m. flower that blows
　WORD 87
meaning: Comfort, where true m.
　is.　BRET 7
M.: compassion.　SNYD 39
m. doesn't matter　GILB 30
m.'s press and screw.
　COLE SAM 25
neural m. Flies　THOMA D 15
no law, no m., and no end—
　WORD 109
pours my m. into you?
　WHITM 21
tale of little m.　TENN 91
to some faint m. make pretense,
　DRYD 11
world without a m.,　ROBI 30
meaningless: ancient, m.
　Abstractions　SNYD 42
its m. voice,　HUGH T 8
meaninglessness: eager m.
　BOGA 15
means: All's vast that vastness m.
　THOMP F 5
cause, and will, and strength, and
　m.　SHAK 35
Lean is the ghost of Molly M.
　WALK 10
m. of a secret charm,
　BROWNI R 61
mercy of his m.,　THOMA D 21
Molly M. was a hag and a witch;
　WALK 8
meant: hunch what the music
　m. . . .　SERV 8
m. each other's aid,　POPE A 26
not what I m. at all.　ELIOT T 88
say what you m.,　SEXT 1
what you must have m.
　WHITM 48
measur'd: m. dual throbbing
　WHITM 99
measure: Cozening judgment with a
　m.,　JONS 9
drink by m.,　POPE A 105
full m. of all your pleasure,
　WILC 2
grace my m.,　PRIO 9

In weight in m., number, sound,
　JONS 39
leave to heaven the m. and the
　choice,　JOHN S (1709–1784) 22
m. in phenomena:　JEFFE 4
m. of the universe;　SHEL 54
m. of the year;　KEAT 19
m. off another day　DICKI 5
our last m. of wine,
　BROWNI R 36
To m. life learn thou　MILT 120
true pleasure/ Lives in m.,
　UNKN 185
Wielder of the stateliest m.
　TENN 127
measured: Choice word and m.
　phrase,　WORD 123
m. blood　BOGA 9
m. by the Lord and found
　wanting.　DUNC 2
m. out my life with coffee
　spoons;　ELIOT T 82
M. this transient world,
　MILT 105
measureless: caverns m. to man
　COLE SAM 19
m. oceans of space,　WHITM 55
measures: her m. are, how well/
　Each syllab'e answered,
　JONS 40
m. all our time;　HERB G 11
m. his plank or beam,　WHITM 37
m. our own nature,　LARK 16
short m.　JONS 41
such/ rollicking m.,　WILLI 12
meat: arsenic in his m.　HOUS 53
buzzards/ Tearing the m.
　JARR 28
crazy salad with their m.
　YEATS 107
mess of shadows for its m.?
　YEATS 10
mock/ The m. it feeds on.
　SHAK 134
not m. nor drink　MILLA 16
one was given bread and m.
　JUST 2
Outdid the m., outdid the frolic
　wine.　HERR 36
ravener of horrible m.　MELV 14
snow-white swans do fish for
　needful m.:　TURB 1
Some hae m. and canna eat,
　BURN 17
taste my m.:　HERB G 49
we hae m. and we can eat,
　BURN 17
went without the m.,　ROBI 52
Meath: M. of the pastures,
　COLUM 1
Queens of Sheba, M., and
　Connaught,　SYNG 3
meats: fresh m.,　JONS 27

poking among the m. in the
refrigerator GINS 38
mechanic: m. eyes ROBI 30
mechanical: strange m. grotesques,
WILD 12
mechanics: clever at m., JEFFE 5
Newton's m. AUDE 14
Those of m., WHITM 37
medallions: As a globed fruit,/
Dumb/ As old m. to the thumb,
MACL 1
meddle: m. with my toys.
STEVENSO R 22
meddler: Come to the pedlar;/
Money's a m., SHAK 182
mediæval: In this m. fashion,
CRAN S 6
Medici: Miniver loved the M.,
ROBI 43
medicinal: flower and m. weed —
MAST 8
meditate: m. day and night.
BIBL, O.T. 21
m. the thankless Muse? MILT 26
meditation: fearful m., SHAK 212
m. of my heart, BIBL, O.T. 30
meditations: more in my m.,
WHITM 18
meditative: Then you arrived, m.,
HAYD 3
medium: m.-sized pink
strawberries JARR 7
meed: more shall be your m.
SKEL 7
meede: m. Al ful of fresshe floures,
CHAU 9
meek: bereft, and m., and lowly,
HARD 10
come it brave and m. DAVID 7
fair m. blossom BRYA 9
Holy & m. she cries — BLAK 25
m.-eyed Peace; MILT 37
m. lover of the good! EMER 7
m. members of the Resurrection —
DICKI 125
m. souls will receive BROO P 6
sorrow unfeigned and humiliation
m. MILT 98
strength is so tender, his wildness
so m., LOWE J 2
meeker: morns are m. than they
were, DICKI 103
meekness: By m., called thy Son;
SMAR 9
meet: all our compulsions m.,
LARK 6
bodies m. HERR 49
body m. a body MAXW 1
brothers and sisters m., BURN 18
cannot m. my bills? GILB 48
China and Africa m., AUDE 1
cold/ To m. it when it woos
HERR 35

contraries m. in one: DONN 45
honor will honor m.; BRID 3
I shall m., HERR 33
I will come out to m. you
LI PO 7
m. a holy God! BLAK 28
m. and mingle. SHEL 38
M. at this grave, DONN 49
m. my face no more, HARD 5
m./ the close clippers, LEVI 4
m. the daffodils, DICKI 40
m. the morning dew, ARNO 45
m. Mortality, my sentence,
MILT 98
m. the close clippers LEVI 4
most m. for all? TENN 121
never the twain shall m., KIPL 1
Never to m. again. BURN 34
others they would never m.
LARK 22
part to m. again. GAY 7
rushes thee to m.; EMER 10
sod what thousands m.! —
MELV 16
We'll m. and ay be fain NAIR 1
With m. tranquility, HARD 28
meete: m. for a blithesome age;
CAMPI 28
meeter: deemed it m. PEAC 1
with M. safe, BUTL 6
meeting: boring m. AUDE 90
raise the m. soul! COLL 12
meets: traveler m., aghast, POE 17
Meg: M. she was a Gipsy KEAT 34
meinie: Jacké Straw and his m.
CHAU 72
meke: Housbondes m., yonge,
CHAU 111
mekeness: with grace and m.,
HAWE 2
melancholy: black with more than
m. views.
THOMS J (1700–1748) 13
charm can soothe her m.,
GOLD 9
concertina's m. string! GILB 43
cordial in this m. vale, BURN 19
Hail divinest M., MILT 15
humour of m. CHAU 69
lobsters and oysters to cure m.;
JORD 1
lovely m. FLET J 3
m. days are come, BRYA 7
M. mark'd him for her own.
GRAY 12
m. waters lie. POE 12
mild-eyed m. Lotos-eaters
TENN 81
Moping m. mad: HOUS 50
sensible soft m. POPE A 109
sovereign mistress of true m.,
SHAK 8

sweet, sad years, the m. years,
BROWNI E 7
Veil'd M. has her sovran shrine,
KEAT 43
wide and m. waste SHEL 18
mellow: bulls m. to the touch,
MACDI 3
m. croon, HUGH L 18
Season of mists and m.
fruitfulness, KEAT 62
melodic: comforting, m. sigh,
JOHN J 6
melodie: My Luve's like the m.
BURN 45
melodies: asks for mournful m.;
YEATS 82
Heard m. are sweet, KEAT 38
melodious: desire for the m.,
CHES 18
M. birds sing madrigals.
MARL 18
M. murmurs, MILT 82
m. words to lutes of amber.
HERR 63
most m. sound, SPENS 31
silver chime/ Move in m. time,
MILT 39
strong m. songs. WHITM 38
thy m. rhymes. STEPHEN 5
with its m. seas. LONG 30
melody: learns the storm-cloud's
thunderous m., STEPHEN 3
lulled with sound of sweetest m.?
SHAK 54
through its utmost m., —
THOR 5
melodye: smale foweles maken m.,
CHAU 4
Melrose: M. rise in ruin'd pride.
SCOT WA 4
melt: Fields m. my heart.
PLATH 77
Let Rome in Tiber m. SHAK 3
liable to m. as snow. CRAN H 40
m. as the dishoused snail
BIBL, O.T. 42
power/ To m. that marble yce,
CAREW 14
too too solid flesh would m.,
SHAK 22
melted: m. into air, SHAK 163
perpetual whirl/ Of trivial objects,
m. and reduced WORD 109
she m. in all her prime, BLAK 52
voice in my dreaming ear m.
away. CAMPB T 9
melting: Between m. and freezing
ELIOT T 61
M. at the knees, ROET 54
m. snow upon some craggy hill,
JONS 4
M. thy pinions THOR 6
m. voice MILT 24

Morning, softly/ M. SCHW 5
Ripe as the m. cluster, GAY 1
melts: even snow/ m.; CUMM 1
m. away/ As doth the dawn
    COWL 5
m. for ever; BURN 54
m. with unperceived decay,
    JOHN S (1709–1784) 13
members: meek m. of the
    Resurrection — DICKI 125
m. of a world that never was,
    MACN 5
memorable: in m. pomp,
    WORD 102
make thee m. MILT 112
m. Scene: MARV 22
Memorial: M. from the Soul's
    eternity ROSS D 5
Prince Albert's tall m. SITW 1
Memoriall: M. Of any men
    HERR 22
Memoriam: signed In M. SITW 3
memories: Drug thy m., TENN 74
faggot of useless m. MACN 7
gnawed/ Sick m. ROBI 28
m. plague their ears LARK 2
night of m. and of sighs LAND 15
Race m. of king and caravan,
    TOOM 2
Sheeted m. of the past — POE 17
memorized: m. one plot, SNOD 5
memory: And stretch the hands of
    m. WHITT 29
bear thy m. WORD 51
better m. said Fie; MUND 2
Bitter m. like vomit SNYD 9
clear viol of her m.,
    STEVENS 38
Devoted to the m. of me:
    HERR 52
engross the present and dominate
    m. YEATS 28
Fond M. brings the light
    MOOR T 10
Footfalls echo in the m.
    ELIOT T 16
friends forsake me like a m. lost;
    CLARE 7
gardens rich in m. glorified
    YEATS 35
Girt fast by m.; SIDN 18
habit of m. propels KINN 2
haunting my m. LONG 32
left her m. in each place;
    CLARE 12
live again in m., TENN 87
living record of your m.
    SHAK 207
May m. restore SCHW 8
M. fingers in their hair OWEN 34
m. of refused adultery RICH 19
m.! thou midway world LINC 1

m. to a grey-haired man
    WHITT 14
M. will lay its hands BENN G 2
m.'s eye; MOOR M 18
m.'s rapturous pain; BRON 13
Midnight shakes the m.
    ELIOT T 103
mixing/ M. and desire,
    ELIOT T 113
moon has lost her m.
    ELIOT T 104
mystery,/ And m., SLES 4
our m. fades TENN 45
out of m.: SHAK 187
passed from men's m. POUN 39
Remorse — is M. — awake
    DICKI 121
room for m. CRAN H 39
serene of m. ROET 18
sins' black m. DONN 34
son of m., great heir of fame,
    MILT 35
stem/ Of m. KAVA 10
table of my m. SHAK 28
their m. ever to keep, WHITM 53
those of m. CRAN H 39
trade the m. of this night for
    food. MILLA 17
when soft voices die,/ Vibrates in
    the m.; SHEL 43
whiles m. holds a seat SHAK 28
your m. death cannot take,
    SHAK 216
men: above the reach/ Of ordinary
    m.; WORD 123
All m. make faults, SHAK 199
all the m. and women merely
    players: SHAK 11
alle maner of m., LANGL 3
as m. strive for Right;
    BROWNI E 5
as m. they died'. BEAU/BASS 4
barren places where m. gather
    HECH 11
betray more m. SHAK 137
better for m. To be few JEFFE 21
Better m. fared thus ARNO 13
blue-eyed m. BONT 4
but m. of sense approve:
    POPE A 29
by which m. long live well
    EMPS 15
catch m. with show,
    BROWNI R 28
city among m., DUNC 2
courted m. in station SWIF 23
Creating awe and fear in other
    m.? SHAK 58
Crowds of m. and women
    WHITM 18
dead m. lost their bones.
    ELIOT T 124
Dead m. may envy OWEN 3

dead m. rise up never; SWIN 15
dead m.'s skulls, SHAK 97
Death of Great M., BUTL 8
den/ Of savage m.: BACO 2
died for m. ROBI 21
dreamed as deaf m. hear,
    GARR 1
evil that m. do lives after them;
    SHAK 48
eyes of m., SHAK 92
famous m. of old, the Ogres —
    GRAV 18
favour to m. of skill;
    BIBL, O.T. 1
fear of little m.; ALLI 1
fears, and flies from Marion's m.
    SIMM 2
Few m. about her would
    RICH 18
finds too late that m. betray,
    GOLD 9
foe to m. WEBS 5
for the best of m.:/ You were
    born STEPHEN 1
foule debate/ Twixt noble m.
    UNKN 63
found the breed of m. HOPE A 1
friendly young m., WHITM 44
gang to your m. again? UNKN 49
gigantic m. of light whispering
    HARJ 2
good will to m." LONG 12
gratitude of m. WORD 137
Great m. have been among us;
    WORD 21
happy breed of m., SHAK 88
heard the old, old m. say,
    YEATS 103
here the race of m. go by.
    FOSS 3
host of armed m. BERT 1
I eat m. like air. PLATH 56
if m. my garments wear;
    SHAK 59
ill-used race of m. that cleave the
    soil, TENN 91
in disgrace with fortune and m.'s
    eyes, SHAK 194
Jonnë Armestrong m. did him
    call, UNKN 153
justifie the wayes of God to m.
    MILT 47
kept eight score m. UNKN 153
kill the white m., LIND V 10
Land of M. & Women BLAK 29
leads m. to this hell. SHAK 236
leave the trodden paths of m.
    SHEL 4
Let a race of m. now rise
    WALK 6
life, the flicker of m. and moths
    JEFFE 30

like m. in drinking-songs,
  TENN 96
like the brewing of m.;
  UNKN 201
little-Ant m. as they ran   SITW 9
little lives of m.   TENN 19
little sardine m.   MACN 1
Lives of great m.   LONG 36
Love wakes m.,   PATM 2
lovely, gifted girls./ Married
  impossible m.?   GRAV 26
Lovers, like dying m.,   SEDL 3
making m. feel/ As small
  KAVA 17
master of m.   POUN 4
M. are Cowards,   ROCH 11
m. are worth/ Your tears:
  OWEN 12
M. at forty   JUST 5
m. at weakest, they are strongest,
  JONS 29
m. behind the guns!   ROON 1
m. can breathe   SHAK 188
m. decay: GOLD 1
m.-folk keep away.   MEW 3
m. in women do require?
  BLAK 48
M. kill for this,   SEXT 14
m. make no moan: WILD 4
m. may come and men may go,
  TENN 5
M. may dien of imaginacioun,
  CHAU 50
m. may rise on stepping-stones
  TENN 18
m. must work,   KINGSL 3
m./ Now far from home,
  THOMA E 12
m. of wealthie Sestos,   MARL 7
m. of worth.   DANI S 19
M. saw the blush   DUNB P 1
m. say they do depart.   SIDN 32
M. should be Knaves.   ROCH 11
m. smoot it with a yerde smerte —
  CHAU 17
m. strive with each other
  RANDA D 5
m. than they more blind,   TRAH 9
m. that laugh and weep;
  SWIN 12
M. were deceivers ever,/ One foote
  in Sea,   SHAK 130
m. were drunk like water.
  JARR 3
m. who make them   WILB 21
m./ Who went abroad to die.
  LETT 1
M. would be Angels,   POPE A 66
M. would be Cowards   ROCH 10
m. you've been,   HOUS 32
m.'s defiled souls;   SOUTHW 2
Mens sana in m.'s sauna,
  HECH 10

"Morgan's m. are coming,
  WOOL 1
multitude of m.   BROWNI R 48
music of m.'s lives,   SHAK 93
need of a world of m.
  BROWNI R 58
no country for old m.   YEATS 124
no talking to some m.   SWIF 26
Not unbecoming m.   TENN 133
o' Mice an' M.,   BURN 63
Old m. weeping in the parks!
  GINS 16
Old m. who never cheated,
  BETJ 8
on bald m.'s hair   CUMM 7
other m. may use deceit;
  LAND 12
peace to m. on earth.   BROO P 5
perceive that m.   SHAK 187
pin m. of madness   PAGE 3
Poets, though divine, are m.:
  JONS 1
rich m.'s tables   EMER 22
riches to m. of understanding,
  BIBL, O.T. 1
sit for m. to gaze upon.   MARL 5
So long time war of valiant m.,
  SURR 8
sober m.   GRAV 41
some m. curse,   WILD 4
some m. weep,   WILD 4
souls of m. in my pot.   REED I 5
stander above m.   WHITM 73
Stil'd but the shaddowes of us
  m.?   JONS 29
Strong bronzed m., or regal black
  CULL 5
strong m. git stronger . . .
  BROWN S 5
strong m. keep a-comin'
  BROWN S 5
strong m. stand face to face,
  KIPL 3
sweet societie of m.   MARL 10
sweetly sang of m. in pow'r,
  DICKEN 2
team of little atomies/ Athwart
  m.'s noses   SHAK 153
that m. would Jehovah prayse
  BIBL, O.T. 55
that's friend to m.,   ELIOT T 120
Theater business, management of
  m.   YEATS 58
they strove, those worn-out m.,
  HARD 21
thro' a Land of M.   BLAK 29
Time's the king of m.;   SHAK 139
to just m.'s fields!   THOR 9
To keep m.'s courage up,   DAY 3
to sea went wise m. three,
  PEAC 3
tongues of dying m.   SHAK 87
tranced dancing of m.   BIRN 3

traveled among unknown m.,
  WORD 47
true authority in m.:   MILT 72
trunks of m.   SHAK 124
understand m. do we not?
  WHITM 21
vexed question of m.   SIMP 4
virtuous m. pass mildly away,
  DONN 62
voices were in all m.'s ears
  ARNO 34
want of books and m.!   WORD 22
Warning of thinges that m. after
  seen.   CHAU 72
wealth accumulates, and m.
  decay: GOLD 3
What m. or gods   KEAT 37
what m. Unborn shall read
  LAND 6
where the cave m. dwell;
  CARRU 1
which no m. retract.   WINT 10
who loves m.,   SNYD 7
wise m. came from far,/ Led to
  thy cradle by a star,   GODO 1
Wives saw m. of the explosion
  LARK 11
women do in m. require?
  BLAK 48
worthy m. in hir degree.
  CHAU 87
"Yessur" to the m.,   FIEL E 5
you are m. of stones!   SHAK 85
young m. and girls pray for:
  KAVA 13
young m. bathe   WHITM 79
young m. think it is,   HOUS 13

menace: heavy m. and mystery
  NEWS 1

mend: Alter or m. eternal fact.
  EMER 37
apparatus not for me to m.
  ROBI 19
m. my rhyme.   HERB G 22
My life may m.,   SOUTHW 13
strive to m.   GRAY 21
To m. his barn,   SWIF 2
(would Fate but m. it!),   PRIO 12

mended: all is m.,   SHAK 129
m. glass, like bottle bits
  SPEND 3

mendicants: m. in public places;
  CRAN H 14

mending: m. the socks.   MERR 2

Mendip: deep as a M. mine,
  CHES 7

menopause: forties & m.   GINS 30

mental: back home from the m.
  hospital —   GINS 26
lounge of the m. house   SEXT 12

thoroughbred m. cases,
LOWE R 55
will not cease from M. Fight,
BLAK 35
mentality: de-animalize human m.,
KINN 12
mentally: who is m. flexing.
OHAR 4
mention: lines of heavenly joys
made m., HERB G 40
Why should I m. Io? HOUS 9
mentioned: m. orange yet OHAR 23
mentioning: promis'd without m.
it, WHITM 21
mentions: m. hell to ears polite.
POPE A 104
merchant: m. gather wealth,
BEAU/BASS 6
Merchants: tradeful M., SPENS 7
merci: belle dame sans m.":
KEAT 5
mercies: m. temporal and divine!
BURN 33
merciful: touch, quick, m.
Blindfolded me. MERR 7
merciless: loving, rapid, m.
LOWE R 29
m. miles of the plain, — LANIE 4
moon, also, is m.: PLATH 42
mercury: m. sank AUDE 36
mercy: at the m. of the Rabble
DRYD 19
Death had the M., GINS 22
first stop M. HAYD 22
for m. on Christ they call,
SOUTHE 2
goodness and m. shall follow me
BIBL, O.T. 31
"Lawk a m. MOTH 29
m. blows the coals; SOUTHW 2
m. brought me from my Pagan
land, WHEA 1
m., if thou wilt forget. DONN 34
m. is above this sceptred sway,
SHAK 123
M., Love, and Pity dwell
BLAK 89
m. more than life! BATE 2
m. no more could be, BLAK 70
m./ Of a rude stream
FLET/SHAK 3
m. of his means, THOMA D 21
m. on the sinner RANS 34
most tender m. CRAB 8
pray to God to have m. upon us
ELIOT T 5
quality of m. is not strain'd,
SHAK 123
Those at His m., —
BROWNI R 19
When m. seasons justice.
SHAK 123
yields no m. to desert, LODG 5

mere: All m. complexities,
YEATS 17
made of m. delight CAMPI 25
merge: Gather, and m. myself
WHITM 3
meridian: full m. of my glory
FLET/SHAK 4
merit: first true m. to befriend;
POPE A 33
gladly praise the m. of a foe?
POPE A 24
man's true m. POPE A 16
Thy mither's person, grace, an'
m., BURN 44
merited: none has m. my fear,
WYLI 6
merits: mine own weak m.
SHAK 136
Mermaid: Choicer than the M.
Tavern? KEAT 33
m. sings, HABI 1
Mer-maids: Muses are not M.,
CLEV 2
mermaids: I have heard the m.
singing, ELIOT T 90
oyster-shop for m. HOLM 11
Quadroon m., HAYD 1
merrie: My merrie, m. boyes,
HERR 4
merrier: m. than the merry organ
CHAU 66
merrily: m. hent the stile-a;
SHAK 180
m. I flow, SMIT ST 7
things went on right m. CREE 1
merry: By his m. tone —
UNKN 157
cuckoo is a m. bird, UNKN 72
faces m. and keen; NEWB 3
kidlings blithe and m. GAY 1
listen to the m. village chime.
GILB 38
loving live, and m. still; CAMPI 8
merrier than the m. organ
CHAU 66
m. country lad? BRET 4
m. heart goes all the day,
SHAK 180
m. larks are ploughmen's clocks,
SHAK 100
m. London SPENS 45
M. Margaret, flower, SKEL 2
m. month of May, BARNF 1
m. month of May, BRET/OTHE 1
one of the m. troop, BRIN 2
short life and a m. one, OWEN 2
So be m., so be dead. SORL 3
Spring comes m. towards me
ROSS D 1
we were m., COLE M 1
merry-go-round: no go the m.,
MACN 8
merthes: m. to make, LANGL 4

merye: swyede so m. LANGL 1
wantowne and a m., CHAU 20
Meseem'd: M., I smelt a garden of
sweet flowers, SPENS 14
mess: m. of shadows for its meat?
YEATS 10
message: m. from thy glass,
DANI S 15
m. greet him UNKN 183
m. of the years, ROBI 10
Speak both one m. ROSS C 24
messages: their electric/ m.,
KNIG 7
messenger: m. of dawn, THOR 6
m. of death. DRAK 3
m. there aroused, WHITM 67
m.'s bicycle, RANS 27
met: finde both Adams m. in me;
DONN 32
hadst ever m. my soul. MEYN 2
how first he m. her? THAC 3
I m. a woman — DARC 3
m. a little Elf-man, BANG 1
m. an assassin CRAN S 5
m. in thee tonight. BROO P 3
m. me in an evil hour; BURN 59
m. with virgins seven, UNKN 215
part of all that I have m.;
TENN 130
they m., or parting place
HERR 29
treat if m. where any bar is,
HARD 31
We m. the Solid Town —
DICKI 65
metal: hearts of truest m. HOSK 1
M., intrinsic value, WINT 3
m. minutes of your pay, SHAP 29
Paradisal/ Imagineless m.,
THOMP F 14
uses of a new m. ASHB 1
metamorphosed: Fate has m. them,
HOLM 11
m. to a vine, HERR 67
metamorphosis: warm m. of snow
PAGE 5
metaphor: simile and m. NASH 18
metaphors: Curling with m. a plain
intention, HERB G 40
Metaphysic: M. calls for aid on
Sense! POPE A 2
Physic of M. begs defence,
POPE A 2
Metaphysics: encumber'd with his
hood, — / Explaining M.
BYRO 14
slick rock of m. SNYD 26
meteor: m. glances glow, DRAK 3
m. of the war. MELV 19
swift-fleeting m., KNOX 1
Methinks: M./ For milder weather.
THOR 1

method: dictionary's m. SIDN 9
  m. of conclusions'; MCOR M 40
methodical: In m. way, GILB 61
Methodist: M. preachers come
  down GOLD 6
met'phor: m. in the bombast way,
  COWL 9
metrasol: m. electricity
  hydrotherapy GINS 15
metre: laws of God, and man and
  m. JEFFR 1
metres: people of common sense
  damn m., LOWE J 5
  speaking of m.; LOWE J 8
metropolis: crockery-ware m.,
  BYRO 52
mettle: made of the m. so free,
  UNKN 154
mew'd: Thrice the brinded cat hath
  m. SHAK 111
mewing: little cats m. and
  scratching HARJ 2
Mexique: Echo beyond the M. bay."
  MARV 2
miasmal: Wrapt in the old m. mist.
  ELIOT T 39
mice: from rats or from m.,
  BROWNI R 65
  Hunting m. is his delight,
  UNKN 202
  m. Are rather nice. FYLE 1
  m. with wings ROET 1
  o' M. an' Men, BURN 63
Michael: Still ye might now, M.,
  FRENC 1
Michelangelo: cherubs drawn by
  M., SEXT 4
  Talking of M. ELIOT T 77
Microbes: M. have their joys,
  OWEN 3
Microscopes: M. are prudent
  DICKI 22
microscopic: m. eye? POPE A 69
mid: dateless m.-days of the law
  MUIR 3
  m.-air take to bed a wife.
  SHAP 14
midday: out in the m. sun.
  COWA 1
  unseen by the m. suns, ROON 2
middle: Fireworks in the dull m. of
  February SEXT 2
  gold enough around her m.
  UNKN 319
  isthmus of a m. state, POPE A 78
  m. of his forehead. NASH 3
  m. of the woods LEAR 4
  only kind of m. wife CULL 16
  pain, still in the m. distance,
  SHAP 17
  Those m. parts, MILT 97
Middlesex: M. village and farm, —
  LONG 44, 45

midge: little restless m. WILD 18
midnight: at m. speak with the
  Sun! VAUG 13
  In the m. waking, WHITM 17
  into the m. BROWNI R 35
  make m. mushrooms, SHAK 164
  M., assist our moan; SHAK 132
  m. never come! MARL 1
  m. ride of Paul Revere, LONG 43
  m. roll/ Of black artillery;
  MELV 12
  M. shakes the memory
  ELIOT T 103
  m. sky a sunset glow. FROS 64
  Ninth-month m., WHITM 62
  Once upon a m. dreary, POE 34
  Plodder through m. rain, HEAN 8
  soft embalmer of the still m.,
  KEAT 67
  thro' m. streets BLAK 76
  troubled m. and the noon's
  repose. ELIOT T 54
  turn of m. water's SLES 4
  wanton mask, or m. ball,/ Or
  serenade, MILT 78
  woes at m. rise. LYLY 3
midshipmite: bos'sun tight, and a
  m., GILB 55
midst: dwell in the m. of alarms,
  COWP 23
  m. of spoils EMER 5
  m. of tears THOMP F 6
  m. of the barn-yard TROW 2
  M. winter's harm. MORR 5
Midsummer: I awoke in the M.
  HOPKINS 13
  Merry Margaret,/ As m. flower,
  SKEL 2
midway: memory! thou m. world
  LINC 1
midwife: fairies' m., SHAK 153
  m. gave o'er. UNKN 75
  rector, the m., the sexton, the
  agent for bees. PLATH 11
Midwinter: M. spring is its own
  season ELIOT T 60
mien: fortitude of m., CARM 2
  My Lord advances with majestic
  m.,/ Smit with the mighty
  pleasure POPE A 102
  thy m. is stately, CALV 5
might: all that we m. have been,
  RICH 19
  captaines of great m.; UNKN 61
  disjoin'd by Neptunes m.:
  MARL 4
  driver easily m. have been you,
  STEPHENS 12
  fair m. ye befall. WYAT 16
  Gas smells awful;/ You m. as well
  live. PARK 2
  glorious in the m. Of heaven-born
  freedom WORD 78

in their dead-doing m., SPENS 1
  "It m. have been." WHITT 20, 21
  Judge's bride m. be! WHITT 16
  m. have been!" WHITT 20, 21
  m. of the Gentile, BYRO 13
  m. withdraw unnoticed,
  WHITM 17
  of magic and m., COAT 2
  Protect us by thy m., SMIT SA 2
  set while I m. survive, THOR 2
  Still ye m. now, Michael,
  FRENC 1
  very worst of fortune's m.
  SHAK 221
  whose heedless m., LUCR 5
  wish death, nor fear his m.
  MARTIA 2
  with main and with m.,
  UNKN 159
  with the m. of waters;
  WORD 108
Might-have-been: my name is M.;
  ROSS D 6
mightier: m. movement sounds and
  passes; STEVENSO R 10
mightiest: m. Julius fell, SHAK 20
  'Tis m. in the m.; SHAK 123
Mighty: bowing — with a M. look —
  DICKI 65
  dome of m. Mars the red,
  CHAU 45
  green-rob'd senators of m. woods,
  KEAT 22
  heaved a m. breath,
  STEVENSO R 6
  his m. singing MOOR M 43
  how are the m. fallen!
  BIBL, O.T. 68. 69
  labouring with a m. fate,
  DRYD 7
  Love is a great and m. lord;
  PEEL 3
  Make the m. ocean CARN 1
  M. and dreadful, DONN 17
  m. Architect, BRAD 12
  m. fortress is our God LUTH 2
  m. heart is lying still! WORD 7
  m. maze! POPE A 58
  m. Milton's gift divine,
  WHITT 10
  m. mother did unveil/ Her awful
  face: GRAY 28
  m. mother turns in tears
  THOMP W 4
  m. thought HUNT 6
  m. undulations of thy song,
  LONG 30
  m. woman with a torch, LAZA 1
  mother of a m. race, BRYA 12
  no joy in Mudville — M. Casey has
  struck out. THAY 4
  one m. torrent SHEL 76
  round her m. knees LOWE J 14

Smit with the m. pleasure
POPE A 102

smith, a m. man LONG 48

Spring, the herald of love's m.
king, SPENS 20

springs,/ What m. contests
POPE A 110

sweeps along to the m. sea;
MANG 2

thunders shook the m. deep,
HOLM 18

weak hands though m. heart
SHEL 4

with m. Cromwell LIND V 7

works/ Of m. Poets. WORD 104

you m. gods!/ This world I do
renounce, SHAK 79

mild: coming on/ Of grateful
evening m., MILT 76

dull and slow and m. JARR 2

eyes of a m. savior. TATE J 2

lisped in accents m., SMIT ST 3

look m. as amber; ADAM L 2

m. and magnificent eye,
BROWNI R 45

m. engineer: AUDE 85

m.-eyed melancholy Lotos-eaters
TENN 81

m. eyes command LAZA 1

m., pitiful, and flexible; SHAK 61

m. pods of his eye-lids, HEAN 22

milder: Methinks,/ For m. weather.
THOR 1

mildly: virtuous men pass m.
away, DONN 62

Mile: Emmet's Inch and Eagle's M.
BLAK 10

long the m.; DUNB P 13

m. after m., GRAV 36

m. of kingdom, KAVA 22

My pilgrimages last m.;
DONN 58

smile you could see a m.,
SERV 5

tires in a m.-a. SHAK 180

went a crooked m., MOTH 27

miles: hundred m. or more,
STEVENSO R 23

island sixteen m. long,
WHITM 43

Looking down for m. SNYD 18

merciless m. of the plain, —
LANIE 4

m. around the wonder grew
HOUS 41

m. to Babylon? MOTH 12

m. to go before I sleep,
FROS 108

see it lap the M. DICKI 55

Sheridan twenty m. away.
READ T 1

swim for m. through the desert
SIMP 1

tramping his thirty m. LAWR 14

milestone: Death is another m.
SPEND 8

milk: A-combing his m.-white
steed, UNKN 177

chaunged to a m.-white Bull,
LODG 2

China staunched her m. SHAP 27

drunk the m. of Paradise.
COLE SAM 22

livers white as m.! SHAK 122

lust for m. MONR 2

Mannerly Margery M. and Ale.
SKEL 4

marble halls as white as m.,
MOTH 16

mere white curd of ass's m.?
POPE A 9

M. all the way. CRAS 9

m. and sweetnesses; HERB G 3

m. comes frozen home in pail,/
When blood is nipp'd
SHAK 101

m.-stiff bibs, MERR 10

m. tastes funny, SNYD 41

m. the cow of the world,
WILB 15

m.-white mistress, DAVIE J 1

neither m.-white rose nor red
WILD 1

on his m.-white steede, UNKN 60

Pitcher of m., now empty.
PLATH 38

she gave him m.; BIBL, O.T. 19

sucking m. from this our body
SNYD 4

sweetest m., and sugar, MARV 28

tinned m. of human kindness
RODG 6

milken: sheer blue m. dreaminess
KINN 15

milking: good for a baby in a m.
pail. THOMA D 42

milkmaid: in love with a charming
m. UNKN 231

milkman: feel the daylight coming/
like a relentless m. RICH 9

milkweed: cedar-bark and m.
SNYD 38

milky: eye-balls were seared with a
m. mucus; MAST 3

mill: to the m. and ground!
HOLM 9

turns a m., ROGE 1

milldams: By the bonnie m. o'
Binnorie. UNKN 29

miller: cam to the m.'s dam.
UNKN 31

millere: m. was a stout carl
CHAU 16

millers: no m. any more," ROBI 39

million: hundred m. of his kind,
SCHW 11

lucent, m.-pleasured breast, —
KEAT 64

m. Adams drowned MUIR 11

m. boots in line, AUDE 79

m. butterflies rose up SCOT WI 1

m. Edens fall MUIR 11

m. eyes, AUDE 79

m. people — WHITM 44

One year/ They sent a m. JARR 3

spare a m. or two of humans
LAWR 30

your m. Trotskyites? GINS 2

millions: 'as m. at 'ome, KIPL 30

midst of sterile m. OHAR 10

m. lost. SHAP 11

m. must die, JEFFE 23

m. of grains are black, white, tan,
and gray, BISH 42

m. of strange shadows SHAK 205

m. of suns left,) WHITM 76

M. of worlds, burning SNYD 47

mortal m. live alone. ARNO 41

mills: m. are to turn, LANIE 5

these dark Satanic M.? BLAK 34

Milton: malt does more than M.
can HOUS 51

mighty M.'s gift divine,
WHITT 10

What use M., SNYD 19

Milton's: M. the prince of poets —
BYRO 19

Miltown: Tamed by M.,
LOWE R 27

mimes: m. become its food, POE 32

mimic: amid the m. rout POE 31

m. desolation covers all.
GRAY 22

m. fancy wakes MILT 80

m. in slow structures, EMER 45

m. motion/ Made constant cry,
STEVENS 17

undisguised by m. art,
THOMS J (1700–1748) 5

mimsy: All m. were the borogoves,
CARRO 35

mind: all the gazer's m. SHEL 78

allus on yer m. GUES 1

beauteous form assures a piteous
m. DONN 67

bottom of my m.; DICKI 90

bottom of my m. STEPHENS 6

braced his m., MARK 2

brought all to m., YEATS 71

by the eternal m., — WORD 77

calm of m. all passion spent.
MILT 118

change doth please a woman's m.
WYAT 4

clear, attentive m. SNYD 50

clergy banish from the m.,
CLARK A 3

iron bars a cage;/ M. innocent and
     quiet   LOVE 5
lead frail m. to rest   SPENS 5
marriage of true m.   SHAK 231
m. made better   ELIOT G 1
m. me o' departed joys,/ Departed
     never to return.   BURN 15
not the bodies marry, but the m.,
     DONN 38
tenderness of patient m.,
     OWEN 8
mine: Bright jewels of the m.?
     HEMA 5
certainly it is m.   LOWE A 3
Comrades m.   WHITM 53
Condemned to Hope's delusive
     m.,   JOHN S (1709–1784) 2
end this life of m.?   MASE 7
Excavating for a m.,
     MONTROSS 1
falls in well with m.,
     BROWNI E 9
God is thy law, thou m.:
     MILT 75
grieving rimes of m.,   PETRA 4
in a greater current they conjoin:/
     So I my Best-Beloved's am, so
     he is m.   QUAR 3
Lord, remember me and m.
     BURN 33
M. only died.   BROWNE 1
Nature's heart and m.;   BANK 2
none of m.,   UNKN 77
that enfeebled m.   SHAK 218
they m. should be who Nothing
     was,   TRAH 5
This island's m.,   SHAK 157
thy tears mixed with m. do
     overflow   DONN 65
trust that still were m.,   WILLA 2
"Would she were m.,   WHITT 18
would she were m.   LODG 6
(you are M. said she)   CUMM 24
yours from m.,   GRAV 31
miner: m., 'Forty-Niner,
     MONTROSS 1
mineral: information vegetable,
     animal, and m.;   GILB 35
mines: Knocked silly with guns and
     m.,   BLUN 5
Ming: watched M. fall)   SNYD 48
mingle: meet and m.   SHEL 38
m. with forgotten ashes,   SHIR 4
mingled: dust to be m. with yours
     LI PO 5
hearts have one m.,   SHEL 90
pride and shame were m.
     WHITT 13
mingles: St. John m. with my
     friendly bowl   POPE A 92
Where m. war's rattle
     SCOT WA 20

minister: thou flaming m.,
     SHAK 137
whaur's the M.?   YOUN D 1
ministers: Are all but m. of Love,
     COLE SAM 23
you dumb, beautiful m.,
     WHITM 22
ministrant: swift flights of Angels
     m.   MILT 109
ministry: performs its secret m.,
     COLE SAM 13
secret m. of frost   COLE SAM 17
Miniver: M. loved the Medici,
     ROBI 43
mink: m., and skunk   TAYL B 1
Minnaloushe: M. creeps through the
     grass   YEATS 22
minnow: snapped at a m.
     LIND V 18
minor: Loosened from the m.'s
     tether;   JOHN S (1709–1784) 11
m. nation celebrates   DICKI 23
sink to a m., —   BROWNI R 5
that sweet m. zest   KEAT 64
minority: m. always guilty.
     MACN 6
minors: music is in m.   BROO G 4
minstrel: Hidden by a m.-smile.
     BENN G 5
M. Boy to the war is gone
     MOOR T 9
m. galleons of Carib fire,
     CRAN H 50
m.'s burnt-cork face   RANDA D 3
no M. raptures swell;
     SCOT WA 12
ring the fuller m. in.   TENN 49
minstrelsy: Pan sounds up his m.;
     LYLY 6
minute: cage the m. Within its nets
     of gold,   MACN 23
Each m. bursts   SCHW 7
fill the unforgiving m.   KIPL 8
How exquisitely m.,   TENN 100
in half a m.   GILB 9
lasted a m. more.   HARD 46
live-long M. true to thee,   ROCH 6
M. after M.,   HUGH T 9
one short m. gives me in her
     sight.   SHAK 147
minutes: how slowly m. roll
     ROCH 7
metal m. of your pay,   SHAP 29
m. hasten to their end;/ Each
     changing place   SHAK 209
m. wing'd their way   BURN 53
My thoughts are m.,   SHAK 93
ten m. to see me go past.
     KENN 1
to m. eat.   POPE A 105
what damned m.   SHAK 134
miracle: m. of design!   TENN 100
m. swayed/ stiffly   HAYD 15

tag of me is a m./ Divine am I
     WHITM 74
miracles: feeling, are m.,
     WHITM 74
without m. or rage   SEXT 9
miraculous: m. cure at the
     fountain;   AUDE 84
mirage: Sister of the m. and echo.
     GRAV 42
mire: m. of human veins.
     YEATS 17
Miriam: rang to M.'s holy glee,
     TIMR 5
mirror: crystal m. holds, unite their
     streams.   MILT 69
life is the m. of king and slave—
     BRID 5
m. cracked from side to side;
     TENN 66
m. of the acts of earth.   KINN 17
strange m. of the Deity.
     COWL 10
mirth: amid its hallowed m.,
     POE 30
Babel itself with our m.;   OSHA 4
Bards of Passion and of M.
     KEAT 2
borrow its m.,   WILC 1
bringing peace and m. By flight of
     sin.   HERB G 56
find cause for m.,   VERY 1
formed of Joy and M.,   BLAK 22
m. and mourning.   CAMPI 31
M. and youth and warm desire!/
     Woods and groves   MILT 119
M. can do   UNKN 141
m./ Of thieves and murderers:
     HERB G 71
m. the music of division;
     RALEG 15
Sad songs of Autumn m.
     THOMA E 6
song of the birds for m., —
     GURN 1
time for m.,   HERR 48
time for m. and play,   SMAR 1
Present m. hath present laughter;
     SHAK 175
misbeliever: call me m., cutthroat
     dog,   SHAK 118
miscall'd: simple truth m.
     simplicity,   SHAK 213
mischief: when to m.   POPE A 123
mischiefs: purge the m. that
     DANI S 22
misdone: thyself that hast m.,
     WYAT 2
what I have m.,/ Misguided;
     MILT 111
miser: Sweet to the m.   BYRO 21

miseries: afford my m. a shelter;
   COWP 15
bound in shallows and in m.
   SHAK 50
Misery: Babes reduced to m.,
   BLAK 68
deep wide sea of M., SHEL 35
happiness and final m., MILT 60
hatred for this m. befallen;
   MILT 102
him that is in m., BIBL, O.T. 12
make up a heaven of our m.
   BLAK 56
m. of manilla folders ROET 7
m. still delights COWP 2
poets in their m. dead.
   WORD 124
shake off m.: HARD 11
turbid ebb and flow/ Of human
   m.; ARNO 2
Untainted by man's m. SHEL 61
misfortune: m. placed these worlds
   TATE J 4
misguided: poor m. souls, LANG 1
what I have misdone,/ M.;
   MILT 111
mislaid: m. Simplicity of wish and
   will, WILB 28
mislead: Lights that do m. the
   morn: SHAK 117
mislikes: what He m. or slights,
   BROWNI R 16
misprision: m. growing,/ Comes
   home again, SHAK 220
miss: beauty she doth m.,
   UNKN 191
Care less eyes, lips, and hands to
   m. DONN 63
I m. it! is it gone? ARNO 43
lovers that no lovers m.
   YEATS 96
M. Our Chance WALK 14
never m. them. LAWR 30
not one do I m., WHITM 115
whatever M. T. eats DE LA 14
missed: m. his loving bride.
   NASH 12
something m.? WILB 27
who never would be m. GILB 26
missiles: guided m., DAY 11
Missing: M. me one place
   WHITM 74
M. or healing, SHAP 11
show something's m.? PLATH 1
missionary: m. endeavour,
   GRAV 26
mississippi: brown/ hills and red
   gullies of m. KNIG 7
"Where is the M. panorama
   SIMP 13
mist: days of m., THOMA E 14
Egyptian's gold m. LOWE J 9
m. in my face, BROWNI R 68

m. is dispell'd GAY 3
neither m. nor shade? POUN 16
thick as m. On evening marches.
   SHEL 79
Wrapt in the old miasmal m.
   ELIOT T 39
mistake: Familiar as an old m.,
   ROBI 1
M. the matter." SIMP 14
mistaken: yet so m.!
   BROWNI R 11
mistakes: old m. And discords
   KINS 3
mistaking: else m.; SHAK 220
misted: future is ever a m.
   landscape, JEFFE 32
mister: We got to say m.
   BROWN S 1
mistletoe: Invite the ladies toward
   the m. TATE A 6
mistranslated: always m. SHAP 22
mistress: April is in my m.' face,
   UNKN 6
breath that from my m. reeks.
   SHAK 237
In ev'ry port a m. find. GAY 7
long-loved m. Rhyme. DRYD 8
master of this house,/ Likewise the
   m. UNKN 116
milk-white m., DAVIE J 1
m. moderately fair, COWL 8
m. of Mankind! ROCH 15
m. shall be seen WOTT 6
My m.' eyes SHAK 237
On ev'ry m., DICKEN 1
sovereign m. of true melancholy,
   SHAK 8
these trees their m.' name:
   MARV 16
mistresses: Many dainty m.:
   HERR 65
mistris: court a m., shee denyes
   you; JONS 29
mists: Beyond the m. MOORE 3
breaking through the foul and
   ugly m. SHAK 51
disperse these m., VAUG 28
many thousand m., WORD 52
m., make room for me."
   LONG 17
Season of m. and mellow
   fruitfulness, KEAT 62
misty: Horizontal m. Air/ Shorn of
   his Beams, MILT 57
in the m. morn HOOD 1
m. mid region of Weir— POE 48
m. parks and motors, LARK 14
shattered water made a m. din.
   FROS 76
miter: m. hath worn; KNOX 2
mither: father and m. BURN 64
Thy m.'s person, grace, an' merit,
   BURN 44

mittens: lost their m.,
   FOLL/COOK 1
skin he made him m., STRON 1
mix: make harmonious m. of voice
   and string BIBL, O.T. 67
mixed: bayonets, m. and crossed,
   THOMP W 1
thy tears m. with mine do
   overflow DONN 65
Mixing: M. fresher air. DICKI 92
m. Memory and desire,
   ELIOT T 113
mixture: m. of gravity and
   waggery. SMAR 8
with mortal m. breed. SIDN 8
mixtures: Forbidden m. MARV 25
moan: body makes no m.
   YEATS 38
Every thing did banish m.,
   BARNF 1
men make no m.: WILD 4
Midnight, assist our m.;
   SHAK 132
m. is high, WALK 10
m. of doves in immemorial elms,
   TENN 107
m. th' expense SHAK 195
paid with m., THOMP F 3
Pray her regard my m.; LODG 5
sad account of fore-bemoaned m.,
   SHAK 195
moaning: bar and its m. KINGSL 4
Cease not your m. WHITM 5
dead one lay m.) SMIT ST 2
harbour bar be m. KINGSL 3
no m. of the bar, TENN 9
their m. is a prayer HAYD 8
moans: air Death m. and sings:
   GREN 4
amid no earthly m., POE 13
moat: m. defensive to a house,
   SHAK 88
mob: grip of the m. PATT 1
mock: Ambition m. their useful
   toil, GRAY 8
m. at fate and care, EMER 31
m. our eyes with air. SHAK 9
m./ The meat it feeds on.
   SHAK 134
m. the riddled corpses SASS 5
m. us in the clay. BEAU/FLET 2
sad augurs m. SHAK 229
thirty/ M. tyrants, BYRO 34
mock'd: haughty scorn which m. the
   smart, ARNO 35
mocked: m. by hopeless longing
   SASS 7
m. the dead bones SHAK 97
m. with death, MILT 98
mockery: m. of hell BYRO 69
mocking: m. taunt, WHITM 76
mocking-bird: m.'s throat,
   WHITM 62

mockingbird: m.,/ His fancy
warbler; HAYD 12

mocks: admires and m.
BROWNI R 16
M. married men, SHAK 100
m. me from her eyes! PETRA 8
m. mutability, WILB 37

Modena: beaten from M., SHAK 4

moderate: m. Aristotelian city
AUDE 14
nothing so m. JEFFE 39

moderately: mistress m. fair,
COWL 8

modern: filthy m. tide YEATS 143
in the m. sense AUDE 93
not ancient nor m., LOWE J 7
of a m. Major-Gineral, GILB 35
songs of m. speech LANG 3
strange disease of m. life,
ARNO 27

modes: nobler m. of life, TENN 48
unknown m. of being; WORD 97

modest: coy submission, m. pride,
MILT 73
glides in m. Innocence away;
JOHN S (1709–1784) 13
humble Man of m. sense,
ROCH 12
Hunger shall make thy m. zone
DAY 2
m., crimson-tippèd flow'r,
BURN 59
m. stillness and humility.
SHAK 56
m. than immodest. WHITM 73
savage eyes turned to a m. gaze
SHAK 125
two too m.; HERR 35
Unignorant,/ m. MOOR M 26
youthful, loving, m. pair
BURN 19

Modestly: M. bold, and humanly
severe: POPE A 24

modesty: 'O, m.!' PATM 1
true love acted simple m.
SHAK 149

modified: m. in the guts of the
living. AUDE 38

modish: m. painter shirk
YEATS 156

Modred: M., whose magic song
GRAY 4

modus: m. operandi; NASH 6

moist: m. star SHAK 20
mystical m. night-air,
WHITM 111

moisture: no m. and no breath
YEATS 18

mold: m. of form, SHAK 33
of earth or m. celestiall,
MARL 11

scraping/ the m. from your body.
SANC 3
smash the m. straight off.
RICH 22

Molded: M. to her Æ 2

moldering: m. now in silent dust
BURN 31

molds: Crack nature's m., SHAK 75

mole: ant and the m. sit both in a
hole, JONS 16
four-clawed M. DE LA 1
like a m. I journey DAVID 6
Live like the velvet m.; WYLI 2
m., and toad, BROWNI R 61
Mud for the m.-tide harbor,
LOWE R 6
wilt thou go ask the M.?
BLAK 12

Moll: brickdust M. had screamed
SWIF 11

Molly: ear-drop I gave to Bristol
M. MELV 3
Lean is the ghost of M. Means.
WALK 10
M. Means was a hag and a witch;
WALK 9

Moloch: M.! Solitude! Filth!
GINS 16
M. whose fate is a cloud GINS 17
M. whose love GINS 17
M. whose name is the Mind!
GINS 17
M. whose poverty GINS 17
M. whose soul is electricity
GINS 17

molten: bubble in the m. mass,
JEFFE 37
plane of m. glass, TENN 24

moly: deep in grass, the m.:
GUNN 7

moment: but a little m., SHAK 187
daring of a m.'s surrender
ELIOT T 153
Endures a m. or a day.
YEATS 119
for a m. a broken Coriolanus
ELIOT T 154
looks a m. in the glass,
ELIOT T 137
m. of the cold's/ deepest plunge
WILLI 9
seem a m.'s thought, YEATS 1
seize my/ Soul in a m. COWP 14
Sonnet is a m.'s monument, —
ROSS D 5
that m. over my head,
WHITM 76
To be a m.'s ornament;
WORD 133

momentariness: delight in m.,
GRAV 25

momentary: Beauty is m.
STEVENS 36

eyes/ In m. wonder YEATS 7
I have been m. SEXT 3

momently: Destroys me m. WINT 2

moments: sacred m. when we
played, MCKA 4

momma: m.'s in the bedroom
LORD 5

Monadnock: M., on his forehead
hoar, SIGO 2

Monaghan: M. graveyard; KAVA 19

monarch: becomes/ The throned m.
SHAK 123
m. of all I survey; COWP 23
m. Thought's dominion, POE 20
m.'s high estate; POE 22

monarchize: To m., be feared,
SHAK 89

monarchy: purest m.;
MONTROSE 2
universal m. of wit; CAREW 4

monastic: heart m. aisles EMER 38

Monday: all through blue M.?
HAYD 13
Born on a M., MOTH 26
forced march of M. PAGE 1
M.'s child is fair of face,
MOTH 22

money: all who had m. and leisure
PRAE 4
for a little m., WILB 21
Give m. me, GOOG 1
gives her children neither sense
nor m. MACN 7
lay out their m. BYRO 43
m. and the bad conscience,
SIMP 8
m. enough and to spare,
BROWNI R 83
M. gives me pleasure BELL 4
M. is free WELC 1
no m. for butter. JOSE 1
no one shall work for m.,
KIPL 29
plenty of m., BROWNI R 83
red veins full of m.,
THOMA D 41
spent the public m. DICKEN 1
where our m. talks LOWE R 2
wild who bring you m. WELC 2
world of m., promise and disease.
WELC 3
your m. or your life!" —
BYRO 53

Money's: Come to the pedlar;/ M. a
meddler, SHAK 182

moneys: my m. and my usances.
SHAK 118

monie: frae m. a blunder free us
BURN 58
gowd and white m. UNKN 93

monk: end of the m., UNKN 7
m. ther was, CHAU 18

Monkey: I'd be a Dog, a M. or a Bear, ROCH 8

monkeys: m. winked too much MOOR M 19

monotone: underground, the m. of motion CRAN H 30

monotones: landscapes drawn in pearly m. WYLI 14

monotonous: m. sublime. LOWE R 52

m. voice in the skull MONTA 3

monotony: bleats articulate m., STEPHEN 4

Monroe: M., NY the chicken farms GINS 27

monster: busy m., manunkind, CUMM 35

crammed in a m. toy MACN 1

great-sized m. of ingratitudes. SHAK 173

green-ey'd m. SHAK 134

mystical m. marine? HILT 2

monsters: even the m. we defy MCKA 6

grey m. BARA 12

sleeps with m. RICH 13

monstrous: bottom of the m. world, MILT 31

from the m. chimney.... JARR 4

m. anger of the guns. OWEN 7

m. ruck of mountains MONTA 1

Perverse, all m., MILT 61

this m. violence, JEFFE 20

With m. head CHES 3

Montaigne: as old M.: POPE A 88

month: April is the cruellest m., ELIOT T 113

merry m. of May BARNF 1

merry m. of May, BRET/OTHE 1

M. follow M. with woe, SHEL 2

m. of his absence LEWI 4

m. since I walked, WHITM 48

m.'s warning. GILB 58

old man in a dry m., ELIOT T 30

same as a m. before, — WHITT 33

There was no m. but May. HERB G 3

monthe: as fressh as in the m. of May. CHAU 9

monthly: golden m. breeze! GINS 35

months: mother of m. SWIN 3

nine m.' daughter, LOWE R 30

several m. ago. OHAR 7

terrible m. in the chapel. SEXT 4

wind the m. in balls — DICKI 76

Montrose: a young man of M. BENN A 1

monument: airy m. ROBI 30

Climb her like a m., SEXT 5

find thy m., SHAK 229

horizontal m. to patience. WILB 42

livelong m. MILT 35

m. without a tomb, JONS 43

Sonnet is a moment's m. — ROSS D 5

wanted no m. LOWE R 19

Your mountains build their m. SIGO 2

monumental: m. Argument of the hewn voice, THOMA D 5

Presented with a m. bust! WESL S 1

smooth as m. alabaster. SHAK 137

monuments: gilded m. Of princes SHAK 207

M. of unaging intellect. YEATS 125

studying/ M. YEATS 127

mony: how m. counsels sweet, BURN 51

m. a canty day, BURN 35

mood: dishonest m. of denial, AUDE 30

fashioned so airy a m. POUN 16

Himself in some diviner m., COLL 6

in a comic m. SHAP 14

that blessed m., WORD 30

this blithe m. present, MELV 18

your silly m.? GINS 5

moods: all forms, m., shapes of grief, SHAK 21

m. that pass; NOYE 1

taken my m. for prophecies SIMP 14

moon: beneath a bombers' m. BOWER 1

broad cloud-driving m. BRID R 19

changes of the m. SHAK 136

Clouds and eclipses stain both m. and sun, SHAK 199

Come from the dying m., TENN 113

curd-pale m., YEATS 141

danced by the light of the m., LEAR 12

Daughter of the M., Nokomis. LONG 40

ebb and flow by the m SHAK 84

evil m. bleeds drops of death. WALK 12

first of the m., ROET 47

fishing up the m. PEAC 2

for the M. to lead, BEAU 1

full m. OLSO 20

full round m. YEATS 140

harnessed to the m.: CAMPB R 2

lifts to the changing m. YEATS 22

light of the m. and stars? WHITM 89

long m. drifts/ toward Asia HAIN 1

m., also, is merciless: PLATH 42

m. and stars are set, STEVENSO R 24

m. by night. BIBL, O.T. 59

m. gives you light, WHITM 27

m. has lost her memory. ELIOT T 104

m. I watch goes down, LEVE 12

m. is a sow LEVE 21

m. is door. PLATH 58

m. is my mother. PLATH 59

m.-marbly boards. MERR 10

m. Of Japanese paper, PLATH 49

m.-quake. GRAV 17

m. sees me; UNKN 142

m.-shine astray! MELV 3

m. stands blank above; HOUS 64

m. tenderly shone, GRAV 16

m./ Walks the night DE LA 21

m. was falling FROS 26

mortal m. hath her eclipse endured, SHAK 229

mortals call the M., SHEL 24

Mountains of the M. LIND V 9

My head a m. PLATH 49

new hip m., GINS 35

Of the m., POE 19

on this casement shone the wintry m., KEAT 10

one/ With the man in the wind and the west m.; THOMA D 9

only the m. rages THOMA D 27

pale m. gleams: OSHA 1

see the m., UNKN 142

shining to the quiet M. COLE SAM 17

Shut out that stealing m., HARD 41

silver apples of the m., YEATS 139

struggles of the m. RUKE 6

Sun and m. MOOR M 23

sun and m. were in the fruit: YEATS 95

sun and the m. broke over my head. EBER 6

three children under the m., SEXT 4

Thy m.-kissed roses seem: DOWS 4

tide is full, the m. lies fair ARNO 1

waving m. and trembling leaves WINC 1

weary-hearted as that hollow m. YEATS 3

when the m. WOTT 3

White in the m. HOUS 64

from eve and m. HOUS 63
From m. to night GILB 56
golden m. breakes: DOWL 1
I caught this m. HOPKINS 27
in his m. orisons SMAR 4
In the m. glad I see BLAK 79
Lief should I rouse at m. HOUS 2
like the m. dew, DANI S 5
lucid m.'s fragrant breath
  THOMS J (1834–1882) 1
Magnificent/ The m. rose,
  WORD 102
many a glorious m. SHAK 197
meet the m. dew, ARNO 45
M. after Death DICKI 16
M. and evening ROSS C 11
m. and with night. EMER 8
m. breaks; LONG 47
M. has been blackening,
  PLATH 76
m. just at nine; MONTROSS 3
m. light creaks down again;
  SITW 4
m. of Eternity ROSS C 22
m. sees some task begin,
  LONG 49
M. smack of the spade
  THOMA D 2
M., softly/ Melting SCHW 5
m. star among the living
  PLATO 2
m. stars sang together,
  BIBL, O.T. 14
M.'s at seven; BROWNI R 66
on such a m.? — SNOD 9
praise at m. POPE A 32
radiant lines of m. SHEL 53
shadow at m. striding behind you
  ELIOT T 115
sheer m. gladness FROS 119
Sleep well and see no m.
  HOUS 4
star of m. and of liberty!
  LONG 19
such m. songs THOMA D 20
sun is but a m. star SNYD 30
Sun keeps rising every m.
  DURE 1
This m., there flew RANS 25
transparent summer m.,
  WHITM 78
Untouched by M. DICKI 125
virgins of youth and m. BLAK 60
walk of the m.: HOPKINS 13
when the m. whitened YEATS 20
mornings: child's/ Forgotten m.
  THOMA D 34
M. purple bed, COWL 4
smiling M. shine, GRAY 32
sober m. HERR 71
morns: M. abed and daylight
  slumber HOUS 47

m. are meeker than they were,
  DICKI 103
morrow: be like his m.; SHEL 44
Give my fair Love good m.!
  HEYW 2
good m. to our waking souls,
  DONN 29
night urge the m., SHEL 2
say good night till it be m.
  SHAK 145
windy night a rainy m.,
  SHAK 221
wished the m.; POE 35
morsel: leet no m. from hir lippes
  falle, CHAU 15
mortal: Above a m. pitch,
  SHAK 217
'All that is m. of great Plato
  SHEL 82
Better than m. flowers, DOWS 4
Born of M. Birth BLAK 85
brass eternal slave to m. rage;
  SHAK 211
down their m. gage, TIMR 4
element bearable to no m.,
  BISH 4
Exempts no meaner m. things.
  BEAU/BASS 5
eye and heart are at a m. war,
  SHAK 202
flood/ Of m. ills LUTH 2
gives/ Immortal youth to m.
  maids. LAND 5
life of m. men? ARNO 22
m. knob really undoing,
  WHITM 36
m. millions live alone. ARNO 41
m. moon hath her eclipse
  endured, SHAK 229
m. Muse thy praise rehearse,
  DRYD 31
m. sounds can sing awake,
  KINN 2
m. splendor: JEFFE 38
My thoughts hold m. strife;
  DRUM 2
no m. Ear BUTL 7
O m. folk, you may behold and
  see HAWE 1
rounds the m. temples of a king
  SHAK 89
shuffled off this m. coil, SHAK 39
sleep of m. heaviness; HAWE 2
spirit of m. be proud? KNOX 1
stirs this m. frame, COLE SAM 23
suffer'st more/ Of m. griefs
  SHAK 58
Thou Echo, thou art m.,
  HERB G 38
Thou gav'st me life, but m.;
  HERR 54
Time the fatal wrack of m.
  things, BRAD 7

We are only m. WILLI 19
with m. mixture breed. SIDN 8
mortality: Claspest the limits of m.,
  SHEL 68
horizons, launched above/ M.
  ascending emerald-bright,
  CRAN H 45
kept watch o'er man's m.;
  WORD 86
meet/ M., my sentence, MILT 98
M., behold, and fear,
  BEAU/BASS 1
nothing serious in m. SHAK 109
sad m. SHAK 212
This is m., MOOR M 43
mortall: day,/ Of m. life SPENS 33
m. sting disarm'd. MILT 64
No m. blemishe may her blotte.
  SPENS 54
quick coal/ Of m. fire:
  HERB G 29
mortally: myriad flowers m. yearn,
  LANIE 5
mortals: m. bend their will,
  POPE A 123
m. call the Moon, SHEL 24
mortgage: Free to m. or to sell,
  JOHN S (1709–1784) 11
Moses: from Mahomet to M.;
  PRAE 1
Go down, M. UNKN 115
M. with his rod! TIMR 5
what the — M. — was coming
  next. HOLM 8
moslem: Snow-white m. head-dress
  WALK 3
mosquito: snapped at a m.
  LIND V 18
moss: his m.-greened house
  DE LA 25
in m. and rushes, LONG 41
leaves and m.-work HERR 53
miles of golden m., AUDE 8
M. had reached our lips —
  DICKI 38
m. hung down from the branches,
  WHITM 39
m.-covered bucket WOOD 2
mosses: m. that glow MERE G 1
mossy: branch/ Of m. apple-tree,
  COLE SAM 16
fruit-tree's m. root, MARV 19
Happy field or m. cavern,
  KEAT 33
m. lawn: SHEL 77
violet by a m. stone WORD 45
wind/ undulating on m. hills
  GINS 41
most: doo m. hurt where m. hellp I
  offer. WYAT 23
Forbear my m. desire; WYAT 19
make the m. OMAR 4

More than m. fair, full of the
living fire, SPENS 4
m. melodious sound, SPENS 31
m. offending soul alive. SHAK 59
My m. desire my hand may
reach, WYAT 14
they please Him m.
BROWNI R 19
mote: m. it is SHAK 20
shadowe m. by seene, INGE 1
moth: desire of the m. for the star,
SHEL 49
fuzzed m. in a flannel of storm
BIRN 4
m. with dusty wing, ROSS C 16
than any m. SPEND 13
your m.-breath PLATH 62
mother: animate a m.'s reveries,
YEATS 12
As a fond m., LONG 33
boys who love their m. SNYD 7
by Sycorax my m., SHAK 157
cannot leave her m." UNKN 28
Christ and his m. HOPKINS 24
comfort of her m.'s tears,
JONS 22
dark veins of her m.,
THOMA D 38
Death is the m. of beauty,
STEVENS 60
death/ Of his m. Earth, SITW 6
doors of my m.'s womb,
BIBL, O.T. 10
father and his m.; ROBI 31
Father Time and M. Earth,
MERR 3
fierce old m., WHITM 5
four little foxes saw their m. go—
SARE 1
girl who was like my m. CORS 8
got mad at my m. SANC 4
guardian or the m.
JOHN S (1709–1784) 12
has a m. dear, UNTE 1
his m. gaunt and lean HODG 3
his m., vain WHITT 19
holy m., GINS 31
I'm your m.' GINS 26
in my m.'s lap! MILT 98
kept the newspapers from M.,
MILE 1
Kicking his m. AUDE 58
leave to your own m. dear,
UNKN 87
lie on M.'s bed; LOWE R 27
Lord's m. from heaven.
UNKN 215
Love,/ your m. GINS 32
mad'st thy m.'s womb thine urn.
JONS 38
marries its own m., JARR 8
Mighty magic is a m., CREE 6

mighty m. did unveil/ Her awful
face: GRAY 28
mighty m. turns in tears
THOMP W 4
moon is my m. PLATH 59
m. almost always sighs,
WRIG E 1
M. calls me Willie, FIEL E 3
m. for her children, BINY 1
m. groaned, my father wept./ Into
the dangerous world BLAK 72
m., I won't be alone. RANDA D 1
M., let me go! GRAV 9
m. makes a pocket of her tail
JARR 1
m. man in his doubt! LEVE 7
M., M.; UNKN 86
m. needs to be better, WHITM 17
m. of a mighty race, BRYA 12
m. of fresh thoughts WORD 149
M. of Mankinde, MILT 48
m. of months SWIN 3
M. or Murderer, SITW 7
m. said that I never should
UNKN 125
m. thinks us long away;
HOUS 29
m. who smiles as she sings.
LAWR 31
m.'s entreaties; WHITM 8
m.'s form upon my ken,
HARD 35
m.'s kiss — sweeter this ALLI 5
m.'s pains and benefits SHAK 72
my father and my m. JENN 2
My m. Nature BARK 2
O great Wetness, O M., GINS 43
only one m. COOP 1
Pardon, my M. Church, COWL 13
Perhaps my m. murdered me.'
DAVIE W 1
sharing m.'s joy SNYD 4
some imperishable bliss."/ Death is
the m. of beauty; STEVENS 57
somebody's m., BRIN 3
stricken m.'s soul! WHITM 16
such a lady/ Goddès m. be.
UNKN 143
sword beneath his m.'s heart —
RANS 10
tall flower that wets/ Its m.'s face
SHEL 59
Thy father's shame, thy m.'s
grief, BRET 1
to the front door m., WHITM 15
Where are thy father & m.?
BLAK 55
Motherland: march of M.!
THOMP W 2
mothers: blood of fathers, m.,
daughters, sons, SHAK 30
earthly m. waiting, sleeplessly.
STEVENS 60

M. of America OHAR 2
m. relieved. BOGA 7
m.' wombs the tiring-houses be
RALEG 15
nuns and m. worship images,
YEATS 12
seldom have m. in Irish stories,
MOOR M 36
moths: life, the flicker of men and
m. JEFFE 30
mothy: m. curfew-tide, HARD 22
motion: airy maze/ Of m. BINY 5
At worst, one is in m.; GUNN 14
emblem of m. and power —
WHITM 100
enough of action, and of m.
TENN 88
everlasting m., WORD 98
Five miles meandering with a
mazy m. COLE SAM 21
God ordered m., but ordained no
rest. VAUG 10
in m., still desiring change;
DRAY 9
mimic m. Made constant cry,
STEVENS 17
More m. have than they, ROSE 6
m. and a spirit, WORD 36
one extended m., GINS 41
overtone of m. CRAN H 30
Setting endeavor in continual m.,
SHAK 55
sluiced by m., — CRAN H 5
Some m. ever unspent
CRAN H 28
This sensible warm m. SHAK 115
underground, the monotone/ of
m. CRAN H 30
motionless: m. still balance
WHITM 24
Motive: M. and end GRAV 6
m. and the cue for passion
SHAK 31
m. sabotage their motives.
MACN 3
Thy safety being m. SHAK 69
motley: m. fool. SHAK 15
through the m. spectacle;
WORD 100
motorcyclists: saintly m., GINS 11
motors: misty parks and m.,
LARK 14
sound of horns and m.,
ELIOT T 131
Taut m. surge, CRAN H 10
mottled: blue/ m. clouds WILLI 34
mottles: snake, with m. rare,
DICKI 87
mottoes: bonbon m. GILB 12
those lovely cracker m.!' GILB 12
write the pretty m. GILB 13

brown hair over the m. blown,
ELIOT T 11
cane-lipped scented m., TOOM 1
cinders in his m., WAGO 2
cold hard m. of the world,
BISH 6
corners of my m. STRA 1
could not ope/ His m., BUTL 2
dared to open my m. WHITM 4
dry downturning m. KINS 5
ermine muffled m. and chin;
WYLI 3
fair m.'s broken tooth. ROSE 1
for my m. forever, WHITM 75
his m. redeemed ROBI 6
I speak/ With my m. thus,
CULL 9
m. all green? SWEN 4
m., dear child, is envied of the
bees. UNKN 252
m. of a bell KIPL 2
m. of the Congo LIND V 9
m. of the drowned dog.
HUGH T 3
m. of the dying day. AUDE 36
m.'s/ shooting iron REED I 4
muzzle as a m., HAYD 2
my m. with wind I fill, LYLY 6
on a murderer's m.; HAYD 10
Only the soldered m. DICKI 31
open thou thy manly m.,
UNKN 166
Out of the m. of babes and
sucklings BIBL, O.T. 23
poem whose words become your
m. OHAR 11
purple-stainèd m.; KEAT 45
scorn/ Plays o'er her m.,
LOWE J 14
shadbones regularly set about the
m., MOOR M 30
shuddering m.-wracked GINS 9
smile,/ And m. DUNB P 12
toothless m. of sunny air,
GINS 34
trumpet's m. is pealed BRYA 4
words of my m., BIBL, O.T. 30
mouthing: in his m. care, SCHW 11
mouths: Blind m.! MILT 29
fourteen teats into the fourteen
m. KINN 15
hell keeps her everhungry m.
COWP 15
m. kissing the warm sutures,
ROET 48
no moisture and no breath/
Breathless m. may summon;
YEATS 18
Singing with open m. WHITM 38
skulls' m. which will not tire
MACN 22
mouthy: third so quaint and m.:
BYRO 21

move: delights my mind might m.
RALEG 9
delights thy mind may m.,
MARL 21
hinges let it m., MOSS 5
I suffer and m., BERRYM 3
in just order m. VERY 4
in soul up to our country m.
SIDN 8
m. at ease. NIMS 3
m. upon the tree of breath;
LOWE R 59
no show/ To m., DONN 64
pleasures may thee m., MARL 20
pretty pleasures might me m.
RALEG 7
sweet music makes the ground to
m., GRIF 1
Words m., music m. ELIOT T 22
moved: Lady has always m.
CREE 7
M. earth and heaven, TENN 135
m. from us to him SNYD 5
m. more ways than one;
ROET 27
my father m. CUMM 25
no Man m. Me — DICKI 63
Nouns were struck, m., changed.
KOCH 3
suffer the righteous to be m.
BIBL, O.T. 40
Then m. my Fingers off DICKI 73
Time that is m. SLES 1
virtue, as it never will be m.,
SHAK 27
when she m., ROET 27
moveless: m. fish in the water
gleam, DE LA 22
movement: abstention from m.;
ELIOT T 21
gross and fugitive m. RUKE 3
Lest m. should provoke
FROS 110
mightier m. sounds and passes;
STEVENSO R 10
no music or m. MACN 22
One joins the m. GUNN 13
Two eyes serve a m., HUGH T 13
movements: her enterprising m.,
GILB 53
m. of packers; AUDE 88
see the tentative/ M., POUN 57
movering: on a sabre track m.
HAYD 22
Moves: Chinese jar still/ M.
perpetually ELIOT T 23
innumerable caravan that m.
BRYA 24
light breeze m. me WRIG J 2
m. in a wood of desire, GUNN 2
only prayer/ That m. my lips
BRON 7

she m. entranced SPEND 7
still m. delight, CAMPI 19
Where nature m., POPE A 34
movies: kids go to the m.! OHAR 2
pick them up in the m. OHAR 3
movin': m. up an' down again,
KIPL 4
moving: Hefts of the m. world
WHITM 75
m. into transition, PURD 2
m.-slow he has no Peer. ROET 55
m. toyshop of their heart;
POPE A 112
m. waters at their priestlike task
KEAT 3
only m. thing STEVENS 63
reasons/ for m. STRA 7
mow: for his scythe to m.:
SHAK 210
M. with their scythes LUCR 4
mowed: m. it in the dew FROS 117
mower: rabbits caught in the m.,/
ROET 13
mowing: men m. down by the Isar;
LAWR 59
prodigious m. ROET 28
Mown: M. stalks exhale, LARK 7
time the field were m. HOUS 29
mows: scythe that m. down kings
BEAU/BASS 5
much: asking too m. CANN 1
how m.? — SAND 22
How m. can come DICKI 139
light I loved so m., PETRA 12
M. ado there was, God wot,
BRET/OTHE 2
m. against my heart, PATM 8
m. can go, DICKI 139
m. disposed to fear, GILB 19
m. is taken, m. abides;
TENN 135
m. less cold, ROSS C 25
Past is too m. with her,
VAN DY 2
Some have too m., yet still do
crave; DYER E 2
world is too m. with us;
WORD 159
muchel: So m. of daliaunce and fair
langage. CHAU 20
muchness: rareness, m.,/ Fewness
GRAV 39
mucked: scrabbled and m. like a
slave, SERV 11
mucus: eye-balls were seared with a
milky m.; MAST 3
mud: all drench'd in m., SWIF 9
city built upon m.; MACN 6
I, too, saw God through m.
OWEN 3
m. and boards,/ Poverty, SIMP 10
m./ Flies from his hunching wings
and beak — LOWE R 7

m. for mouse, LOWE R 6

M. for the mole-tide harbor,
  LOWE R 6

M. unto mud! — BROO R 10

Out of the m. FROS 121

Rests on his belly in the m.;
  ELIOT T 36

senselessness and m.? SHAP 18

silver fountains m., SHAK 199

waddled in the m., CLARE 10

muddy: dull and m.-mettled rascal,
  SHAK 31

Mudjokivis: killed the noble M.
  STRON 1

Mudville: no joy in M. THAY 4

rocky for the M. nine THAY 1

muffins: They roused him with m.
  CARRO 19

muffled: ermine m. mouth and
  chin; WYLI 3

M. and dumb EMER 13

sudden m. sound, WHITM 23

mulatto: likely young m. HAYD 20

mulberry: green in the m. bush,
  TATE A 15

mule: ass-back, m.-back, YEATS 80

m. praises, brays, THOMA D 1

muleteers: young m. BELL 19

Muller: Maud M. looked WHITT 16

Maud M. on a summer's day
  WHITT 15

saw Maud M. standing still.
  WHITT 17

multiple: ocean, m. to a blinding/
  oneness AMMO 11

multiplicator: imperial m. BARK 2

multiplied: fowl be m. on the
  earth. MILT 85

multiply: Be fruitful, m., MILT 85

bison m. so fast HUGO 3

multiplye: God bad us for to wexe
  and m.: CHAU 88

multitude: m. of men
  BROWNI R 48

m. saw why she wore the
  bandage." MAST 3

multitudes: hum of m. BLAK 91

m. of lambs, BLAK 91

multitudinous: m. seas incarnadine,
  SHAK 108

Mumbles: M. a bone, DE LA 25

mumbling: Old man m. in his
  dotage, WALK 4

Mumbo-Jumbo: M., god of the
  Congo, LIND V 11

mune: earth's as cauld's the m.
  MACDI 4

murder: brother's m. SHAK 34

charge me with m. CARRO 21

I met M. SHEL 39

kings must m. still, LIND V 3

Macbeth does m. sleep,"
  SHAK 106

more m. in this loathsome world
  SHAK 151

m. in the second degree,
  UNKN 104

m./ The mankind of her going
  THOMA D 37

M. will out, this my conclusión.
  CHAU 71

ripened plot to m. CHAU 47

should m. sanctuarize; SHAK 38

stern m., in the direst degree,
  SHAK 99

tell. O! tell, how thou didst m.
  me. CAMPI 32

thou bewrayest m. alway! m. will
  out, CHAU 70

thou shalt do no m. SHAK 98

We m. to dissect. WORD 146

whims of m., ROSE 2

murdered: Father, whom I m.
  MOSS 1

m. corpse, in covert laid,
  CHAU 48

Perhaps my mother m. me.'
  DAVIE W 1

your death m. me, MOSS 1

murderer: first m. HOPE A 2

Mother or M., SITW 7

on a m.'s mouth; HAYD 10

murderers: mirth/ Of thieves and
  m.: HERB G 71

murderess: by thy scorn, O m., I am
  dead, DONN 4

dress/ Of an inhuman m.;
  MARV 14

upflight of the m. PLATH 16

murderous: face the m., cowardly
  pack, MCKA 7

lust/ Is perjured, m., SHAK 236

maketh her m. meal! HILT 4

m. brain/ Of Man, SITW 6

m. Machiavel to school. SHAK 62

murd'ring: Wi' m. pattle! BURN 62

murmur: hear life m., LOWE J 17

m. more like the sigh FROS 65

m. name upon name, YEATS 55

m. of the distant seas,
  STEPHENS 10

m. Of underground streams,
  AUDE 52

murmured: Lip to Lip it m
  OMAR 6

M. like a noontide bee, SHEL 74

murmuring: asleep by thy m.
  stream, BURN 22

m. of innumerable bees.'
  TENN 107

m. seal DARL 3

m. waters fall MILT 69

my m. rhyme MORR 3

murmurs: crystal streams 'with
  pleasing m. creep': POPE A 26

Melodious m., MILT 82

their m. joined, COLL 9

murrained: m. cattle, SHEL 63

Murray: slain the Earl of M.,
  UNKN 40

Musæus: divine M. soong MARL 6

muscadine: grapes sweeter than m.
  TATE A 5

muscle: Big trout m. HUGH T 6

m. or turf, HECH 11

muscles: coiled, hurdling m. of his
  thighs: LOWE R 37

m. of his brawny arms LONG 48

quaking m. in the act of birth,
  HOPE A 2

muscular: calves, grown m. with
  certainties; JARR 7

with m. legs, WHITM 70

Muse: bid the M. to pack,
  YEATS 151

Description would but tire my
  M.: SWIF 1

his m. a jade. SWIF 26

Let my m. Fail HERR 17

loving a foreign m. BENE 3

meditate the thankless M.?
  MILT 26

mortal M. thy praise rehearse,
  DRYD 31

m. and brood? MELV 16

m. and brood TENN 87

M. but served to ease some
  friend, POPE A 14

M. grown with this growing age,
  SHAK 196

M. herself/ All Time fulfils,
  GOGA 2

m. my life-long hate, MCKA 9

m. through their sideburns . . .
  LOWE R 19

Sweet fire of the sire of m.,
  HOPKINS 26

To m., and spill her solitary Tea,
  POPE A 18

unwashed M. CAREW 18

Muses: charm of all the M.
  TENN 125

companions of the M. POUN 34

forsake his M. dear, MARV 20

Kent and Christendome/ Emong
  the m. where I rede and ryme;
  WYAT 25

M.' anvil; JONS 45

M. are not Mer-maids, CLEV 2

M.' diadem, POUN 39

m. lend their force, THOR 4

M. never knew their pains.
  CRAB 4

spear against the M.' bower:
  MILT 125

museum: all of m. quality:
  MOOR M 9

mushroom: like an old m.,
   LAWR 15
mushrooms: make midnight m.,
   SHAK 164
m. of the gods, SMIT W 3
thousand m. crowd to a keyhole.
   MAHON 1
which resemble m., MOOR M 10
music: after/ The wonderful m.
   BROWNI R 62
as the m. changes, NOYE 1
beautiful m., do not cease!
   MILLA 21
body swayed to m., YEATS 13
Caught in that sensual m.
   YEATS 125
drums give you m., WHITM 27
exuberant voices of m., JEFFE 6
fiddled whisper m. ELIOT T 149
fierce impatience ends;/ Mute m.
   soothes my breast — BRON 10
Fled is that m.: — KEAT 51
Flowing with m. RANS 35
harmony in m.; WORD 96
have you wine and m. still,
   FLEC 8
Hear your lame m., DODS 2
How sour sweet m. is, SHAK 93
hunch what the m. meant . . .
   SERV 8
If m. be the food of love,
   SHAK 174
Intolerable m. falls. YEATS 100
like m. on the waters BYRO 64
makes m. wherever she goes.
   MOTH 25
Mind the m. and the step,
   SHUC 1
mirth the m. of division;
   RALEG 15
more than m., AIKE 1
m. almost visible PLUM 1
m. and sweet poetry BARNF 2
m. at the close, SHAK 87
m. hath a far more pleasing
   sound; SHAK 237
M. I heard with you AIKE 1
m. in my heart I bore,
   WORD 141
m. in the spheres, HERB G 9
M. is feeling, STEVENS 33
m. is in minors. BROO G 4
m. must always play, AUDE 75
M. my rampart, MILLA 22
m. of men's lives, SHAK 93
m. of the languid hours, LANG 3
m. of the rain; EMER 48
m. of two voices SHEL 66
m. sent up to God BROWNI R 3
m. shrill/ Give my fair Love good
   morrow! HEYW 2
m. stopp'd, and I stood still,
   BROWNI R 63

m. when no one else is near,
   STEVENSO R 15
m./ Which can be made AUDE 51
m., yearning like a God in pain,
   KEAT 7
M.'s golden tongue KEAT 5
night shall be filled with m.,
   LONG 16
no more jokes in M.-halls SASS 5
no m. or movement MACN 22
passed in m. out of sight.
   TENN 70
rich stream of M. winds GRAY 24
silver m. SHEL 77
Some heavenly m. SHAK 165
soul of m. shed, MOOR T 5
sound of m. echoing BONT 9
still, sad m. of humanity,
   WORD 34
sweet m. here that softer falls
   TENN 84
sweet m. makes the ground to
   move, GRIF 1
sweet power of m. SHAK 125
That m., remote, forlorn.
   DE LA 18
Thrush m. — hark! FROS 15
thy chosen M., Liberty!
   WORD 147
tired eyelids upon tired eyes;/ M.
   that brings sweet sleep
   TENN 84
turning to marimba m. BISH 7
vibrations of deathless m.;
   MAST 1
We are the m.-makers, OSHA 1
words are m. in my ear,
   EMER 41
Words move, m. moves
   ELIOT T 22
Wrapt in her m. SPEND 7
musical: hark to the m. clank;
   WHITM 13
m., self-sufficient, WHITM 43
m. shuttle, WHITM 62
stuff keeps him m.: MERW 3
turbulent m. chorus! WHITM 32
musicall: lamenting love marreth
   the m. SPENS 37
musically: tintinnabulation that so
   m. wells POE 10
musicians: we m. know.
   BROWNI R 4
musick: fair m. that all creatures
   made MILT 2
Heavenly m., TAYL E 14
In m.'s ravish't soule CRAS 6
M. shall untune the Sky.
   DRYD 27
My onely m., HERB G 2
Musicke: M., Plants and Flowers
   FLET/SHAK 1

sweet M. is such Art,
   FLET/SHAK 1
Musicks: sphæares/ Of M. heaven;
   CRAS 6
musing: Ceaselessly m., WHITM 55
Mary sat m. FROS 19
M. is solitude, WORD 14
musk: m. of the rose is blown.
   TENN 93
musket: m. moulds in his hands.
   FIEL E 6
Musketaquit: summer voice, M.,
   EMER 48
muskets: rustle and clank of m.,
   WHITM 32
they doze over m. LOWE R 19
musky: West winds, with m. wing
   MILT 11
mussel: crow-blue m. shells,
   MOOR M 11
mussels: Barnacles, m., water
   weeds — MOSS 5
must: I m. fight MOOR M 15
Love m. not be, but take a body
   too, DONN 1
M. all be veiled, HERB G 45
m. call up SNOD 2
M. dullness turn me to a clod?
   HERB G 34
M. observe GILB 57
m. pass like smoke Æ 3
"Shoot, if you m., WHITT 3
we needs m. part, WATS R 1
mustard: m. scansions of the eyes,
   CRAN H 53
musty: m. reek that lingers
   BROO R 5
Musus: divine M. soong) MARL 6
mutability: mocks m., WILB 37
Nought may endure but m.
   SHEL 44
mutation: Nature, m., strife?
   FULL 2
mute: all m. POE 26
ancient ditty, long since m.,
   KEAT 5
Created m. to all articulate
   sound; MILT 93
every day came m. HECH 15
fierce impatience ends;/ M. music
   soothes my breast — BRON 10
M. as a turnip PLATH 82
Now it's m. BLAK 105
poem should be palpable and m.
   MACL 1
Prithee, why so m.? SUCK 2
very birds are m. SHAK 224
we stand m., ARNO 34
mutes: tedium of talking to m.;
   PRAE 3
Mutton: To the Shoulder o' M.
   LEWI 3

mutual: make a m. stand,
  SHAK 125
m. and partak'n bliss, MILT 6
muzzle: m. as a mouth, HAYD 2
my: Blame not m. lute. WYAT 2
cause of m. disease SURR 4
day breaks not, it is m. heart,
  DONN 12
I replied, M. Lord.' HERB G 18
m. beloved Son, WORD 1
m. city! WHITM 44
M. crooked winding ways,
  HERB G 74
M. faith shall wax, DANI S 16
M. garden is run wild! HABE 2
m. heart is fast, and cannot
  disentangle. UNKN 220
m. joy and heart's delight.
  WEVE 2
M. most desire my hand may
  reach, WYAT 14
m. roof the greenwood above,
  UNKN 201
M. tender age in sorrow did
  begin: HERB G 27
M. thoughts hold mortal strife;
  DRUM 2
M. very life ROSS C 7
now I live, and now m. life is
  done. TICH 1
O m. God, what am I PLATH 75
old egg of m. desire is broken,
  UNKN 230
see m. apron rising. UNKN 207
Who plainly say, M. God, M.
  King. HERB G 46
mycologist: Of the expropriated m.
  MAHON 2
myriad: m. fields and the prairies
  wide, WHITM 51
m. flowers mortally yearn,
  LANIE 5
with m. subtleties. DUNB P 12
Myriads: M. of rivulets TENN 107
myrrh: camphor, m., and roses,
  GRIF 1
What drops the m. MILT 79
myrtle: fringed bank with m.
  crowned MILT 69
Gently with m. band, MILT 89
M. more becoming thee,
  HORA 11
Plainer m. pleases me HORA 11
Strew the M. and Rose PRIO 5
myself: back to m., SNYD 17
Child I to m. will take; WORD 48
conquered in m. MOOR M 15
count m. the coward TENN 117
deem m. a slave. BYRO 41
I celebrate m., WHITM 73
I m. am hell; LOWE R 40
I taught m. SNOD 6

I wander'd off by m.,
  WHITM 111
in the manege m. takes delight.
  SIDN 19
look upon m., SHAK 194
made me think of m., WHITM 39
m. am Hell; MILT 66
no pity to m.? SHAK 99
sing m., WHITM 73
Throwing m. on the sand,
  WHITM 63
When I was a bachelor, I lived by
  m. UNKN 99
with m. I too much discuss
  ELIOT T 5
yielded m. EMER 19
Mysteries: Almighty's M. to read
  HABI 2
At a hundred m.; HODG 3
God hath his m. of grace,
  ALEX 7
had an eye for such m."?
  HARD 5
half-talk code of m. KAVA 21
Love's m. in souls do grow,
  DONN 22
m. that dwell CRAS 6
m. Are like the Sun, DONN 51
Mysterious: believe,/ M. truths,
  ROCH 12
God moves in a m. way, COWP 4
Hail wedded love, m. law,
  MILT 78
m. as the silence LEVE 9
m. night. BARA 9
m. parts were then concealed:
  MILT 73
proud m. cat. LIND V 21
Rites/ M. of connubial Love
  MILT 77
To that m. realm, BRYA 24
veil the heaven's m. face
  WINC 1
mystery: burthen of the m ,
  WORD 30
heavy menace and m. NEWS 1
lay bare/ The m. to me, HODG 9
m.,/ And memory, SLES 4
m. of beginning SCHW 6
m. of man, WORD 115
m. of things, SHAK 84
M. to Mathematics fly! POPE A 2
uncontrollable m. YEATS 92
void of m. and dread. SANT 2
warm with the m. of lather.
  JUST 6
mystic: m. volume of the world
  LONG 27
mystical: m. moist night-air,
  WHITM 111
m. monster marine? HILT 2
myth: curveship lend a m. to God.
  CRAN H 29

free/ m. from reality BIRN 3
no bloodless m. will hold.
  HILL G 4
not the m. RICH 5
tall as a m., BIRN 1
mythologies: Out of old m.
  YEATS 30

N

Nagoya: Snow is falling on N.
  MAHON 4
Naiad: heaven-fed/ N. of the
  Carnival-Tank! SPENC A 3
N. airs have brought me home
  POE 45
torn the n. from her flood, POE 2
nail: blows his n. SHAK 101
hand to n. the right, DUGA 3
hand to the n., BIBL, O.T. 19
n. my left palm DUGA 3
N. to the mast her holy flag,
  HOLM 18
n. you up twixt thieves HORN 2
nailed: n. him to the tree. POUN 4
with their n. prows UNKN 21
nailes: with his n. he'll dig
  WEBS 5
nails: bent n./ dance DUGA 2
Blind as the nineteen hundred and
  forty n. SITW 11
found on his n., HART 2
gold n. in temples LOWE J 8
mad and dead as n.,
  THOMA D 10
n. him down upon a rock
  BLAK 31
naked: All are/ n., MOOR M 42
Bedizened or stark/ n.,
  MOOR M 25
blacks, n. women BISH 22
children run n. in the field
  GINS 31
cool body/ N. SNYD 14
creature, n., bestial, CRAN S 3
Dead men n. THOMA D 9
Do not fear to put thy feet/ N. in
  the river sweet; FLET J 2
enterprise/ In walking n.
  YEATS 31
gnarled and n. tree. HUGH L 14
Graces n. danced DRUM 1
Helpless, n., piping loud,
  BLAK 72
I have killed a n. man.
  UNKN 174
kiste hir n. ers, CHAU 53
left thee n., Lord, CRAS 11
lick my n. body WHITM 97
Love is a n. shadow HUGH L 14
moves the nearest to the n. earth
  CAMPB R 6

N. and bleating   LUCR 5
N. and blind and pale.   JARR 1
N. as paper to start   PLATH 3
n. black boy,   NEWS 1
n.-headed one.   WILB 37
N. I came,   CUNN J 2
N. of hide,   SKEL 12
n. on the roads,   YEATS 33
n. thinking heart   DONN 11
n. to mine enemies.
    FLET/SHAK 5
n. world,   RUKE 6
no penance, much less innocence./
    To teach thee, I am n. first;
    DONN 16
o'er thy n. polished ivory
    CAREW 12
Pity, like a n. newborn babe
    SHAK 105
so n. and singular.   SEXT 5
starving hysterical n.,   GINS 7
undisguised and n.,   WHITM 75
wailing winds and n. woods
    BRYA 7
nakedness: in their n.   VERY 1
not in utter n.,   WORD 70
nakednesse: n. must reach:
    HERR 27
Namby-Pamby: N. is your guide,
    CAREY 2
name: age without a n.   MORD 1
Alexander's dreadful n.,
    SOUTHW 12
another n. for absolute power
    WORD 118
bawl your n.!   SLES 2
Ben Adhem's n. led all the rest!
    HUNT 3
Bitter woe for thy n.   UNKN 169
bulk as huge/ As whom the Fables
    n.   MILT 53
By n. to come called charity,
    MILT 106
called by thy n.,   BLAK 95
called them by n.:   MOOR C 2
college rolls receive his n.,
    JOHN S (1709–1784) 17
crying an unknown n. in the sky
    MACL 5
Dame Poverty gave me my n.,
    CULL 15
doff thy n.,   SHAK 142
ev'ry star by proper n. to call?
    BIBL, O.T. 66
fall we n. the fall.   FROS 85
forge a n.,   EMER 37
fortify thy n. against old age;
    DANI S 12
give it a clumsy n.   TENN 101
He left the n.,
    JOHN S (1709–1784) 19
her n./ Mother of Exiles.   LAZA 1
his living n.   LOWE R 44

I have no n.   BLAK 93
Joy is my n.   BLAK 93
left but the n.   MOOR T 12
Let him n. it   TENN 101
live in a n.,   LIND V 14
living n. behind,   WEBS 2
local habitation and a n.
    SHAK 127
Lord Sabaoth is his n.,   LUTH 3
Love is the unfamiliar N.
    ELIOT T 70
Moloch whose n. is the Mind!
    GINS 17
murmur n. upon name,
    YEATS 55
my n. is Might-have-been;
    ROSS D 6
my n. is Truthful James;   HART 3
my n. shall mount upon
    Eternitie.   DRAY 12
my verse exhal'd thy n.,
    CAREW 7
n. great in story —   BYRO 66
n. had been receiv'd with
    plaudits   WHITM 108
n. his tools.   BUTL 3
n. is a tune.   MOOR M 35
n. is sign'd,   WHITM 16
n. is Used-to-was,   TRAI 5
n. liveth for ever,"   SASS 12
n. my n.,   SNOD 6
n. of Annabel Lee;   POE 3
n. the bigger light,   SHAK 157
n. to come.   POUN 6
n. to go down to fame
    GRAHAME 2
Nature all the N.,   CRAS 13
nine-hundred-years-old n.
    BROWNI R 56
No n. shall but your own be
    found.   MARV 16
none shall speak his n.   SHAP 25
Omnipresent without n.; —
    EMER 20
out of our n.   BROWN S 1
proud his n.,   SCOT WA 12
Reason is my middle n.   MILE 2
Robert of Lincoln is telling his n.
    BRYA 19
terrible n. of rectitude,   HECH 11
their n. is on your waters,
    SIGO 1
these trees their mistress' n.:
    MARV 16
Thy n. is Love.   WESL C 2
till earth was but a n.   CLARE 15
to cry and call his n.,   WILB 33
To tell your n.   DICKI 83
upsprang the aboriginal n.
    WHITM 43
weak witness of thy n.?   MILT 35
What n., what skill, what faith
    JONS 47

what thy lordly n. is   POE 36
What's in a n.?   SHAK 142
whisper of Love's n.,   GRAV 7
whose n. I knew,   LEVE 5
wrestle with your n.   MOSS 2
wrote her n. upon the strand;
    SPENS 23
"you'll find my n.   CLARK J 2
named: also n. Pompilius),
    BYRO 21
woman n. Tomorrow   SAND 7
nameless: child with n. fears;
    LEWI 8
intolerably n. names?   SASS 12
little, n., unremembered acts/ Of
    kindness and of love.   WORD 29
mountains are n.,   SERV 13
n. piece of Babyhood,   LAMB 3
some n. bay,   WHITM 28
names: Almanacked, their n. live;
    LARK 3
bright ironical n.   HAYD 10
change their n.   BYRO 18
covered up — our n.   DICKI 38
fallen in love with American n.,
    BENE 1
few with historical/ n.   GUNN 9
habitations long their n. retain,
    BRAD 6
headstones yield their n.
    TATE A 1
intolerably nameless n.?   SASS 12
judge of authors' n., not works,
    POPE A 31
n. and all their secrets,   LONG 42
N. on a list,   EBER 4
n. sung in your simple layes,
    SPENS 29
rare and royal n./ Wormy
    sheepskin   SYNG 2
slipped their n.,   LARK 3
their scattering n.;   WILB 28
nameth: each point he n. with a
    kiss.   BROWNE 2
naming: Today we have n. of parts.
    REED H 4
Nancy: mate of the N. brig,
    GILB 55
nane: Excelled by n.!   BURN 33
napkin: n. of a dirty cause,
    WALC 3
n. spread by fays;   THOR 8
Napoleon: great N./ Stops his
    horse,   EMER 18
N. of Crime!   ELIOT T 95
torn bandrols of N.'s war.
    BARL 1
napping: nodded, nearly n.,   POE 34
nard: n. in the fire?   JONS 2
narrow: convent's n. room;
    WORD 59
n. aisles of pain.   WILC 3
N. and cold and neat.   WYLI 9

n. compass! WALL 6
n. Fellow in the Grass DICKI 111
n. grave just six by three,
UNKN 50
n., homely room, VAUG 6
no bed too n. WARR 4
saft and n.! UNKN 39
so n. human wit. POPE A 24
spreading wide my n. Hands
DICKI 44
Twist our n. days; AUDE 11
virtues walked their n. round,
JOHN S (1709–1784) 3
narrowing: n. its boiling Wheel
DICKI 150
Narsissus: N. so she were a spring
LODG 3
narwe: heeld hire n. in cage,
CHAU 50
nas: n. nat right fat, CHAU 22
nation: death cry of a n. lost!
THOMP W 1
from an ample n. DICKI 133
greatest n.: SAND 8
minor n. celebrates DICKI 23
n. among n.; TIMR 3
N.'s Freight Handler; SAND 3
publish it to all the n.; PRIO 13
what our N. stands for, BETJ 4
(yearning n.'s blueeyed pride)
CUMM 16
nations: belong to other n.,
GILB 20
cultures of n. EMPS 1
curiosity of n. SHAK 70
n. lying asleep, MUIR 6
n.' airy navies TENN 75
surcease of n. . . . . CRAN H 12
Through all the n., LONG 20
native: Content to breathe his n.
air POPE A 107
Fast by their n. shore. COWP 8
God-like erect, with n. honour
MILT 71
guard our n. seas! CAMPB T 10
I am n. here SHAK 25
life's first n. source; SPENS 45
My n. English, SHAK 86
my n. land! SCOT WA 11
my n. soil! BURN 21
my own n. land, COWP 24
n. country, repossessed HERR 24
n. health and innocence TRAH 10
n. hue of resolution SHAK 40
n. self can nothing feed; MICH 1
natives: what the n. shun. COWA 3
nat'ral: as for n. things: POPE A 67
natural: by n. piety. WORD 58
contents his n. desire; POPE A 60
everything/ which is n. CUMM 19
gentle agency/ Of n. objects,
WORD 51

joy and n. content/ Out
YEATS 57
Lose n. kindness YEATS 106
n. for work. HEAN 4
n. instinct to discern WORD 4
n. shapes blazing unnatural
ROET 32
n. tears they dropped, MILT 108
poetic or n. OHAR 18
reach its n. term; EMER 5
sweet n. eye GINS 35
theory of n. origins JEFFE 34
thousand n. shocks SHAK 39
naturally: Man is n. good,
MELV 12
n. to be desired. WILLI 47
Nature: all life dies, death lives, and
N. breeds, MILT 61
All N. was degraded; BLAK 49
Auld N. swears, BURN 30
Beauty, and N. CAREW 12
betwixt N. and Art: PRIO 2
By n., reason, learning, blind;
SWIF 4
Crack n.'s molds, SHAK 75
Creator, whom sin nor n. tied,
DONN 68
crimes done in my days of n.
SHAK 26
cunning'st pattern of excelling n.,
SHAK 137
darken n. FROS 106
delight/ N. or unrestrained
appetite. CAREW 13
disburden N. of her bearth."
MILT 94
Disguise fair n. SHAK 56
dissembling N., SHAK 96
doth n. seem, LOWE J 15
druidic difference/ Enhances n.
DICKI 24
Each gift of n.,
JOHN S (1709–1784) 16
equally/ Earnest elements of n.
JEFFE 7
Fair N.'s eye, rise, MARL 1
fairest book of N. SIDN 20
faults to find/ Where n. moves,
POPE A 34
First follow N., POPE A 25
fortress built by N. SHAK 88
From N.'s chain POPE A 73
God and N. TENN 32
God burn N. with a kiss?
YEATS 96
Good n. and good sense
POPE A 51
great N. WORD 104
great n.'s second course,
SHAK 106
Grown beyond n. now, MAHON 3
guides n. and fate. BRAD 10

He obeys the orders of n.
EBER 8
human n.'s daily food;
WORD 134
husband n.'s riches SHAK 222
if all of animated n.
COLE SAM 12
in my n. reigned SHAK 230
in our life alone does N. live:
COLE SAM 9
is N.'s Roman, MELV 12
joists/ are shaky by n., DUGA 1
Keep your woods O N.,
WHITM 31
keeps n. new. WILB 37
knot of little purposeful n.!
EBER 8
lies/ within something of another
n., LEVE 19
'Line in n. is not found;
EMER 50
list/ To N.'s teachings, BRYA 23
love of N., BRYA 22
lusty stealth of n. SHAK 70
Made N. different DICKI 98
man rebounds whole æons back in
n. MELV 11
measures our own n., LARK 16
My mother N. BARK 2
N. all the Name, CRAS 13
N. always does contrive GILB 22
N. and Homer were, he found, the
same. POPE A 28
N. answers all he asks; WHITT 7
N. art disdaineth; CAMPI 6
N., art my goddess; SHAK 70
N. courts MARV 32
N. deals with us, LONG 34
n. gave me any my birth,
COLE SAM 10
n., heartless, witless nature,
HOUS 65
N. here in sight WHITM 4
n. in its barrenness WILLI 37
N. inanimate employs sweet
sounds, COWP 20
N. is always careless and
indifferent SMIT ST 4
N. is whole THOMP F 5
N. lends such evil dreams?
TENN 32
N., like liberty, is but restrained
POPE A 27
N., like us, is sometimes caught
DICKI 129
N. made her what she is,
BURN 16
N. made thy own, EMER 10
N., mutation, strife? FULL 2
N. ne'er deserts the wise and
pure; COLE SAM 41
N. never did betray WORD 37
n., not art, ASHB 4

n. paints her colors, MILT 79

N. powre her bounties forth,
MILT 5

N., red in tooth and claw
TENN 36

N. shedding influence malign,
THOMS J (1700–1748) 13

N. shown/ her household
RICH 17

n. so sweet, LOWE J 1

N., strong and kind, EMER 21

N. thus/ To bodily sense exhibits,
WORD 117

N. wants an Art MARV 8

N. was in her beryl apron,
DICKI 92

N. was shaping him, LOWE J 3

N. without check WHITM 74

n. would be leading: BRON 6

N.'s banquet share: MARV 9

n.'s changing course, SHAK 188

N.'s Darling laid, GRAY 28

N.'s first green is gold, FROS 70

N.'s heart and mine; BANK 2

N.'s laws lay hid in night:
POPE A 106

n.'s limits thrown, FRENE 4

n.'s pride JONS 4

N.'s soft nurse, SHAK 54

N.'s sweetest light; SIDN 41

n.'s truth, SHAK 210

N.'s vast frame, SHEL 22

negligence of N.
THOMS J (1700–1748) 5

out of n. YEATS 129

paid her last debt/ To N.,
DONN 53

paint/ Like N.?
THOMS J (1700–1748) 3

pangs of n., TENN 30

poet's matter N. be, JONS 45

power/ Of N., WORD 51

priketh hem n. CHAU 4

simple life that N. yields;
CRAB 5

simple news that N. told,
DICKI 145

snuff and loathèd part of n.
SHAK 79

sobbing dirge of N., WHITM 6

starved ignoble n.;
BROWNI R 21

that n. can yield. WOOD 2

Till pitying N. signs the last
release,
JOHN S (1709–1784) 21

Time and N. gently spare
EMER 12

To copy N. POPE A 29

to Sin our byast N. leans,
DRYD 1

tone of languid N. COWP 19

True wit is N. POPE A 21

Unerring N., still divinely bright,
POPE A 25

usura, sin against n., POUN 9

whole realm of n. mine,
WATT I 10

Whose body N. is, POPE A 74

worth my strife:/ N. I loved,
LAND 8

Nature's: Nothing in N. sober
found, COWL 2

Natures: Beauty is n. coyn, MILT 6

N. æthereal, human, angel, man,
POPE A 72

N. plain Indictment DRYD 17

n. sad decree BRAD 11

N. trick to propagate her Kind.
DRYD 1

Naught: huge stage presenteth n.
but shows SHAK 187

knows n. that knows not this:
SHAK 169

"N. shelters thee, THOMP F 7

n. to kill TATE A 10

never 'eed n. else." KIPL 11

plucked for n., THOR 2

naughty: n. kittens! FOLL/COOK 1

N. Paughty Jack-a-Dandy,
CAREY 1

nave: make a n. STEVENS 14

navies: bids her n., LOWE J 14

nations' airy n. TENN 75

N. are stranded: SCOT WA 22

nay: Aunswer him faire with yea or
n. WYAT 18

N., I have done, DRAY 15

N., we are seven!' WORD 156

Say n.! say n.! WYAT 1

near: anchor'd n. the shore,
WHITM 28

Be n. me TENN 27

music when no one else is n.,
STEVENSO R 15

n. and far as grass, WILB 6

n. me when I fade away,
TENN 29

no more come n. thee.'
UNKN 126

pitch that is n. madness EBER 6

port is n., WHITM 45

red rose cries, 'She is n.,
TENN 94

So n. or dear HERR 14

without its friend n., WHITM 39

nearer: n. by not keeping still.
GUNN 14

n., every Day, DICKI 150

n. God's heart in a garden
GURN 1

Space is n. LOWE R 20

"We are n. to Spring HERF 3

nearest: n. prose; DRYD 20

very n. room, DICKI 20

nearing: I am n. the place,
BROWNI R 68

N. again the legendary isle
DAY 7

nearsighted: n. and psychopathic
GINS 6

neat: long,/ n.-scripted letters
KINN 5

Narrow and cold and n. WYLI 9

n. circle on the glass MONTA 2

n. curtains are drawn MONR 1

n. prints into the snow
HUGH T 13

One of the n. ones CAME 2

skinny, stooped, and n. as pie,
SHAP 21

snub breasts and little n.
posteriors, MANI 2

violent, n. and practiced skill
WILB 39

Where all is plain, where all is
n., HORA 10

neater: n., sweeter maiden KIPL 12

nebulous: notable nimbus of n.
noonshine, SWIN 19

necessary: n. things, DRYD 1

necessity: brutish n. wipes its
hands WALC 3

fold/ Of dire n. MILT 115

margins of animal n., SAND 16

neck: about this n. have cross'd and
rested, WHITM 116

around the cannibal's n. SIMI 5

back of her n. HECH 4

clothed his n. with thunder?
BIBL, O.T. 17

color passion but its n. a
question. WARR 9

dove-/ n. animated by/ sun;
MOOR M 18

his straight n. bent ROSS D 2

I am nude as a chicken n.,
PLATH 12

My white n.; BLAK 107

n. rubbed the windowsill HALL 2

take godhead by the n. AIKE 4

thru breast and n., GINS 44

white n. hid with tresses OVID 1

with bended n. I grope, THOR 4

wring its n.! . . .' AIKE 3

young clear n. exposed, RUKE 8

neckcurls: n., limp and damp as
tendrils; ROET 11

necks: beginnings of n., KINN 18

n. of light blubs, BISH 22

n. pulsed like sails. HEAN 10

n./ wound round and round with
wire BISH 22

ruffs about their n., MACN 14

snow falling down and n. of
lovers. SIMP 10

nectar: draws n. in a sieve,
COLE SAM 46

Jove's n. JONS 31
n. and ambrosia, EMER 5
nectarine: n. and curious peach
MARV 17
Ned: world we roved, N. Bunn?
MELV 21
neebour: n.'s fauts and folly!
BURN 4
need: age no n., RALEG 9
all we n. of hell. DICKI 108
all ye n. to know. KEAT 40
do not n. your woe WILC 2
England hath n. of thee:
WORD 40
everyday's/ Most quiet n.,
BROWNI E 5
I shall n. no glass. VAUG 28
love and n. are one, FROS 126
n. no runners WELC 1
n. of a world of men
BROWNI R 58
n.'st not make new Songs,
COWL 11
no n. of a remoter charm,
WORD 33
reason not the n.! SHAK 74
round of their n., DICKEY 28
theirs was n. FROS 125
to fill our n., WILLI 9
what n. you a heart? DONN 10
what we chiefly n.: CARRO 40
needed: it n. something OHAR 22
n. not fear. MORE 3
needful: n. to man as air, HAYD 5
snow-white swans do fish for n.
meat: TURB 1
needfull: things which our n. Faith
require. DRYD 18
needle: Artick n., QUAR 1
hand a n. better fits, BRAD 16
insert her into water like a n.
DICKEY 12
knife or a n., GILB 33
lodge at last the quivering n.
SHAP 9
n.'s eye takes a camel
BROWNI R 64
pause with his n. in the air.
LEVE 9
Plying her n. and thread —
HOOD 11
tendril for n. ROET 25
thread through a n. MERW 10
needles: livers I stick with n. quick;
JONS 17
n., once a shining store, COWP 21
needs: distressed/ By all the n. and
notions MILLA 14
He that is down n. fear no fall,
BUNY 5
mother n. to be better,
WHITM 17
n. must die, RALEG 6

n. must wither. SHAK 137
we n. must part, WATS R 1
What n. my Shakespeare
MILT 35
wrong that n. resistance, BANK 4
neere: dreading the winter's n.
SHAK 224
Negation: N. and despair, AUDE 78
Negative: Great N., ROCH 16
negatives: We only can by n.
define? COWL 9
neglect: kings n. that private men
enjoy! SHAK 58
sweet n. JONS 5
neglected: like a n. rose MILT 6
Ye do lie,/ Poor girls, n.
HERR 56
negligence: n. of Nature
THOMS J (1700–1748) 5
negligent: quiet, n. riding, SWEN 3
negotiate: souls n. DONN 20
Negres: Le Balcon or Les N. of
Genet, OHAR 5
Negro: bell-cheeked N. infantry
LOWE R 17
Negroes: N., black as Cain,
WHEA 1
neigh: n. like Boanerges —
DICKI 56
shave as n. as any frere.
CHAU 118
Stamp and n., LONG 47
neighbor: harbor and n. wood
THOMA D 32
his pond fished by his next n.,
SHAK 179
I let my n. know FROS 56
man their n. knows. YEATS 132
n. of nothing. STRA 6
n.'s creed has lent. EMER 18
neighborhood: daubing/ The entire
n. DAVIS 4
neighboring: To something n.,
DICKI 85
neighbors: 'Good fences make good
n.' FROS 57
in his n.' eyes? YEATS 146
n.!" at last he cried, — WHITT 25
neighb'ring: For n. Beaux to see it
bare. SWIF 14
neighing: bellowing and n. loud,
SHAK 125
neighs: high and boastful n.
SHAK 57
Neither: N. flesh nor fell. SKEL 12
N. I nor you: ROSS C 35
n. laurel nor bay? ROSS C 18
n. milk-white rose nor red
WILD 1
Nelson: Dead N. and his half-dead
crew, HARD 21
Neoptolemus: N., at his side
TATE A 1

nephews: n. and their nieces.
STEVENSO R 4
nept: columbine, the n., SKEL 1
Neptune: all great N.'s ocean
SHAK 108
ebbing N., SHAK 164
great N.'s diadem. CAMPI 5
N.'s empire stands SHAK 20
Neptunes: disjoin'd by N. might:
MARL 4
Nero: still redder N. SITW 6
nerveless: n., listless, dead,
KEAT 20
nervelets: By my soft n. were
embraced; HERR 68
nerves: chains/ Of n., and arteries,
and veins; MARV 11
my firm n. Shall never tremble.
SHAK 110
My n. knew you, ROET 54
nervous: curious n. elegance
KIRK 1
education marriage n.
breakdown, GINS 21
nest: aloft in your crow's n.,
RICH 11
as thy n.; THOR 6
beauty seems to n., NOEL H 1
construct from them/ a n.
TATE J 1
crouched on her n., WHITM 64
lark's n. in the field. SMAR 1
leaves the well-built n.; SHEL 90
n. is in a watered shoot;
ROSS C 1
n. like a dove's, WORD 126
n. of his litle dame, BRYA 19
n. of rattlers, MORG 1
never builds a n., UNKN 73
one bird singing alone to his n.,
MERE O 1
spider will make a silver string n.
SAND 1
Wake from thy n., robin
redbreast! HEYW 2
We saw Thee in Thy balmy n.,
CRAS 4
nested: City n. in bays! WHITM 44
see that word n. WHITM 43
nestle: n. near thy side? SHEL 74
nestled: children were n.
MOOR C 1
nestling: n. fallen ROET 41
nestlings: n. chirp and flee,
HOGG 1
nests: at their n. cawed
THOMA E 18
built their n. in my beard!"
LEAR 18
bunches like birds' n. FROS 24
n. of water-bays, WHITM 43
net: carried a n., PEAC 2

caught me in his silken n.,
BLAK 24

fishes that are taken in an evil n.,
BIBL, O.T. 2

fling the n., MERE G 6

flung on a new n. of atoms:
SNYD 22

grappled at the n. LOWE R 37

in a n. I seek to hold the wind.
WYAT 31

nets: weave but n. to catch the
wind. WEBS 2

Within its n. of gold, MACN 23

nettles: dust on the n.,
THOMA E 17

neural: n. meaning/ Flies
THOMA D 15

neutral: Shoots across the n. Dark.
EMER 9

neutrality: fear/ Of total n.
PLATH 19

never: choose/ N. to stoop.
BROWNI R 57

Departed n. to return. BURN 15

face we see was n. young,
ROBI 38

it was n. enough AUDE 24

look I shall n. forget, WHITM 106

man can n. be alone. TATE A 20

mother said that I n. should
UNKN 125

n. a horse like her! WOOL 4

N. a ploughman. BELL 7

n. a question CARRY 1

(n. again on earth WHITM 107

n. ask why build. SEXT 16

n. come back to me. TENN 3

n. deviates into sense. DRYD 11

n.-ending complaints, MACN 4

n. heard. MONTA 3

n. in any place. MUIR 1

n., in Extremity, DICKI 30

n. man was true; BRET/OTHE 2

N. more shall I escape,
WHITM 67

n.-singling Hymen couple
MARL 10

n. stops MONTA 3

n. to have occurred. BENT 1

N. to meet again. BURN 34

n. wholly kiss you; CUMM 44

n. yet philosopher SHAK 131

pride, the n.-failing vice of fools.
POPE A 32

shall n. see KILM 1

Something I can n. find,
STEPHENS 6

that which n. taketh rust;
SIDN 26

To one thing constant n.,
SHAK 130

Treason doth n. prosper; HARI 2

vigil I n. forget, WHITM 107

weird shall n. daunten me."
UNKN 246

while he lived n. thought of
death. GREV 8

who n. would be missed —
GILB 26

Will you n. let us go? KIPL 22

words could n. utter; THAC 3

"You can n." CRAN S 2

you n. can be old, SHAK 227

you'll n. forget. SASS 1

Nevermore: Quoth the raven, "N."
POE 36

Shall be lifted — n.! POE 37

nevers: said their n. CUMM 5

new: America! my n.-found-land,
DONN 15

among the n. brick tenements
WILLI 24

by whom the n. are tried,
POPE A 23

change old love for n. PEEL 1

cheap, choice, brave and n.,
UNKN 96

Child among his n.-born blisses,
WORD 74

come among n. faces,
WHITM 113

construct a n. stage.
STEVENS 31

disappointments n.; ARNO 26

each n. temple, HOLM 3

engraft you n. SHAK 187

Ever charming, ever n.,
DYER J 2

'Figures ever n. SHEL 81

flung on a n. net of atoms:
SNYD 22

innocent brightness of a n.-born
Day WORD 86

keeps nature n. WILB 37

life forever old yet n.,
BROWNI R 43

little toy dog was n., FIEL E 6

Move then with n. desires, DAY 5

need'st not make n. Songs,
COWL 11

n. and larger life MCCRE 3

n. beginnings, ARNO 26

n.-born Infants tear BLAK 76

n.-found seas, HERB G 60

n.-hatched, unfledged comrade.
SHAK 23

n. knowledge of reality.
STEVENS 29

n. lies on the old, JEFFE 9

n. love may get; WALS 1

n.-made double grave, WHITM 25

n. made when thou art old
SHAK 185

n.-mown hay,
BROWNI E/GUIN 1

n. pleasures prove DONN 6

n. proselytes, LONG 20

N. splendour to the dead./
Language has not the power to
speak PLATO 3

n. to sight and strange: MILT 71

n. wail my dear time's waste.
SHAK 195

no n. wonder may betide,
YEATS 121

pile n. plums and pears
STEVENS 58

pooh-pooh whatever's fresh and
n., GILB 31

ring in the n., TENN 47

riseth a n. creation SKEL 10

rôle/ In the N. Order AUDE 58

saw the n. moone, UNKN 227

So various, so beautiful, so n.,
ARNO 3

strange it seems and n.!
BROWNI R 52

this n. commer, Shame, MILT 97

tiger springs in the n. year.
ELIOT T 34

Tomorrow to fresh woods and
pastures n. MILT 33

under me you so quite n.
CUMM 51

uses of a n. metal. ASHB 1

what's n. HERB CH 5

Whiter than n. snow SHAK 149

wild N. England shore. HEMA 4

With n.-fledged hope WORD 80

yielding place to n. TENN 103

newborn: Pity, like a naked n. babe
SHAK 105

newer: seek a n. world. TENN 134

Newfoundland: N. air, THOR 8

newly: n. gon to bed. MILT 43

n. sprung in June; BURN 45

n.-learned art; WORD 75

news: are ye sure the n. is true?
MICKLE 1

atlas-eater with a jaw for n.,
THOMA D 6

brought good n. from Ghent.
BROWNI R 36

forgotten the n. YEATM 1

good n., good n. SEXT 11

hotel ledgers, n. files. SPEND 20

n. I was bringing to
Ghent YEATM 1

n. of the fight; TICK 2

poor rogues/ Talk of court n.;
SHAK 84

simple n. that Nature told,
DICKI 145

tells n. of devils, GREV 5

'What n., what news, my proud
young porter, UNKN 318

newspapers: kept the n. from
Mother, MILE 1

newt: leech, or n., or toad
FLET J 2
n., and viper; BROWNI R 61
Newton: Let N. be! POPE A 106
N.'s mechanics AUDE 14
N.'s particles of light BLAK 39
Statue stood/ Of N., WORD 101
newts: Even the n. are white,
PLATH 68
next: n. blaze/ Of the world
SNYD 47
nice: his n. new sashes,
GRAHAM H 3
mice/ Are rather n. FYLE 1
Nicean: Like those N. barks of
yore, POE 44
nicely: n.-calculated less or more;
WORD 10
nicetee: suffre him do his n.
CHAU 86
Nicholas: Down the chimney St. N.
came MOOR C 3
N. and Alisoun/ Accorded been
CHAU 53
N. was risen for to pisse,
CHAU 56
St. N. soon would be there;
MOOR C 1
nicht-gown: doon stairs in his n.
MILLE W 1
n. is neir gone. MONTG 1
Nick: Hornie, Satan, N., or Clootie,
BURN 1
niece: sisters, cousins, aunts, and
n., GILB 5
nieces: nephews and their n.
STEVENSO R 4
nigardes: angry n. of dispence,
CHAU 111
Niger: young lady of N. MONK 1
Nigger: called me, N." CULL 13
Hard Rock wasn't a mean n.
KNIG 5
some unknown n. BARA 3
niggers: floating n. swell.
CRAN H 23
lost with his n." LOWE R 19
nigh: drawing n. and nigher,
BROWNI E 10
storm so n. MILT 89
night: acquainted with the n.
FROS 1
After n. I do crowd, BLAK 45
all n. through, CULL 11
all n. without a stir, KEAT 22
at latest lingering of the n.,
WHITM 107
at n. fitfully sleeping, WHITM 17
at n. the party of young fellows,
WHITM 38
At the mid hour of n., MOOR T 1
awaits the positive n. WARR 1
azure robe of n., DRAK 1

be there before the n.? FRENC 1
beach at n., WHITM 56
beauty of the n. JOHN J 4
'Behind the elms last n.,'
PRIO 14
black as hell, as dark as n.
SHAK 242
black bat, n., TENN 93
black n. doth take away,
SHAK 215
bones/ Cry out in the long n.
LOWE R 38
bridal n. I remember, SMIT ST 1
bridegroom all n. through
HOUS 61
by day and n. I yearn,
LOWE J 22
by n. we are hurled/ By dreams,
HERR 9
calm region, where no n.
KING H 3
calm summer n., ROBI 52
Casement ope at n. KEAT 54
Children afraid of the n.
AUDE 76
chilly winter's n.; BARNE 4
City is of N.;
THOMS J (1834–1882) 1
Closed his eyes in endless n.
GRAY 30
comes every n. to me, BRON 9
Dark n. is all his own, JOHN L 3
day and n. MOOR M 23
Day and N.; BLAK 105
day brought back my n. MILT 34
day, in the n., WHITM 50
day's vanity, the n.'s remorse.
YEATS 24
dead unhappy n., TENN 74
death's dateless n. SHAK 195
delight/ Chained in n. BLAK 60
delight on a shining n.,
UNKN 172
Derk was the n. as pich or as the
cole, CHAU 53
dewy dawn to dewy n., MORR 6
dreadful n. shall break. BLAK 51
drown/ The n. with you in floods
of down. HERR 35
dull-eyed n. HERR 44
each returns unto his love at n.
DRAY 3
earned a n.'s repose. LONG 49
eidolon, named N., POE 16
Even the n. will blossom as the
rose. MASE 5
Evening must usher n., SHEL 2
every n. but one, MOSS 1
Every N. would kiss and play,
GAY 5
Exercised in the still n.
THOMA D 27
families shopping at n.! GINS 37

father in the n. SIMP 6
first Day's N. DICKI 25
flames upon the n. YEATS 120
flies in the n. BLAK 80
follow, as the n. the day,
SHAK 24
for a day and a n. TENN 119
for me n. and day. TENN 104
forests of the n., BLAK 81, 84
From camp to camp, through the
foul womb of n., SHAK 57
From morn to n., ROSS C 28
From morning to n. GILB 56
give no hint that n. HARD 23
go gentle into that good n.,
THOMA D 11
golden lamps in a green n.,
MARV 1
gone back and forth all n. on the
ferry. MILLA 26
graves by glow-worm n. BEDD 8
gray-eyed morn smiles on the
frowning n., SHAK 146
grows by n. THOMA E 4
Half Year's N. GAY 4
heavy n. hung dark HEMA 4
hoary winter's n. SOUTHW 1
horrors of the tedious N.,
PHILL 2
hunger and n. and the stars.
SERV 8
hushed with buzzing n.-flies
SHAK 54
i am not afraid/ of the n. SANC 3
I saw Eternity the other n.,
VAUG 32
ignorant armies clash by n.
ARNO 4
ignorant n., the travail SCHW 6
in the stilly n., MOOR T 10
infant crying in the n.; TENN 31
Infinite day excludes the n.,
WATT I 8
infinite regions of the n., TIMR 3
into the pregnant n., DUNB P 6
kissed the sleeping N. DUNB P 1
labour n. and day BUNY 4
last N. that She lived DICKI 98
"Last n. there was four Maries,
UNKN 188
last the n.; MILLA 10
lie upon the wings of n.
SHAK 149
long, tearless n., ROET 32
loving, black-browed n.,
SHAK 149
machinery of n., GINS 8
mad wind's n.-work, EMER 45
middle of the n. CARRO 37
moon by n. BIBL, O.T. 59
moon/ Walks the n. DE LA 21
moonshine n., GAY 1
morning and with n. EMER 8

mysterious n. BARA 9
Mysterious N.! WHITE 1
mystical moist n.-air,
  WHITM 111
Nature's laws lay hid in n.:
  POPE A 106
n. above the dingle starry,
  THOMA D 17
N. and day on me she cries;
  UNKN 127
n. and fog, TEAS 4
n. as welcome ARNO 46
n. before Christmas, MOOR C 1
n. come black, WHITM 65
n. comes on; FROS 115
N. comes to the room DAVIS 3
N. coming tenderly HUGH L 4
n.-dews on still waters TENN 84
n. dischargèd of all care
  MARTIA 2
n. has a thousand eyes, BOUR 1
n.-herons by the flooded river
  JEFFE 16
n. I died I dreamed JARR 16
n. in her silence, ARNO 8
n., in the lonesome October
  POE 47
n./ Involved and swallowed up the
  vision; SHEL 16
n. is a-cold, MORR 5
N. is a curious child, DAVIS 4
n. is beginning to lower, LONG 9
n. is conjo. HAYD 18
n. is darkening BRON 2
n. is day, PATM 10
n. is done, ALEX 4
n. is freezing fast, HOUS 19
N. is juba, HAYD 18
n. is withdrawn BRID R 14
N. is worn, BLAK 67
n. of dark intent FROS 77
n. of memories and of sighs
  LAND 15
n. of peaceful rest, RILE 5
n. of the Prairie Belle? HAY 3
N. sank: like flakes DAVID 4
n. shall be filled with music,
  LONG 16
N. shall fold him GREN 4
n. upon the storm, WHITM 103
n. urge the morrow, SHEL 2
N. was ordained DRAY 3
n. was thick and hazy CARRY 4
n. whose sable breast CULL 3
N. will have all hid. CAMPI 3
n. will slip away FARJ E 2
n. you lay a-sleeping? ROET 6
n.'s black wings SUCK/FELL 2
N.'s brittle song, DAVIS 5
n.'s thunder far away had rolled
  THOMA E 9
not a happy n. WHITM 108
not-to-call n., HOPKINS 13

O holy N.! LONG 25
Obscurest n. COWP 1
Of N. primaeval, POPE A 1
on our roof at n. HUGH L 1
on the field one n.; WHITM 106
on the N.'s Plutonian shore!"
  POE 36
on the previous n. BULL 2
One everlasting n. RALEG 12
one n. went betwixt. CAMPI 12
only a n., an age. FROS 77
ordinary n. was graced NEME 1
out-soared the shadow of our n.;
  SHEL 9
paid to n. KING H 5
Pardon, goddess of the n.,
  SHAK 132
Piercing the n.'s dull ear;
  SHAK 57
pillow at n. STEVENSO R 17
poisonous damp of n. SHAK 8
poor souls fear a shade or n.,
  VAUG 31
prefer dark n. VAUG 33
proof through the n. KEY 1
quarry-slave at n., BRYA 24
retrievements out of the n.,
  WHITM 52
same cover in the cool n.,
  WHITM 109
say good n. till it be morrow.
  SHAK 145
scribbled all n. GINS 13
sence one n. last spring. HAY 5
shades of n. were falling fast,
  LONG 21
shadow of the n. comes on
  MACL 13
she weaves by n. and day
  TENN 61
sheltered for the n. MCKA 1
shepherds watched their flocks by
  n., TATE N 1
shut up the lamb at n. HAY 6
silent n. MILT 76
silver face in the n. WHITM 52
sing'st alone, sitting by n.,
  VAUT 1
sleepless watches of the n.,
  LONG 13
sleeps as may beguile the n.;
  MARTIA 2
Slowly the n. blooms, DAVIS 1
son of the sable N., DANI S 8, 17
sower/ Sow by n., BLAK 61
spectres of black n.
  THOMS J (1834–1882) 8
Spirits of the shady N.; MARV 23
starry velvet in the n., ROBI 40
stay up half the n. ROET 51
Stop this day and n. WHITM 76
stove late of a winter n.,
  WHITM 33

stranger came one n. LOWE J 20
Such n. in England MACA 1
summer and n., STEVENS 16
sunk in hideous n., SHAK 186
Sympathizing N. COWL 4
take the Harlem n. HUGH L 8
tender is the n., KEAT 48
that n. at Trafalgár! HARD 21
that n. I was happy. WHITM 109
There is a privacy I love in this
  snowy n./ Driving around, I will
  waste more time. BLY 1
this dark n. SIDN 30
This frosty n.?" GRAV 30
through the n. CAMPB R 4
through the n. LONG 45
throughout the n. she woke
  RICH 9
time of n., SHAK 128
'tis a gala n. POE 30
To let the warm Love in!
  KEAT 54
to sullied n.; SHAK 187
trailing garments of the N.
  LONG 24
transparent shadowy n.,
  WHITM 48
trembling n.-winds whistle
  ALLI 3
turns the woe of N., EMER 3
vigil of n. WHITM 107
voice I hear this passing n.
  KEAT 50
weary n. and day; YEATS 14
western sky in the n., WHITM 46
what they blame at n.,
  POPE A 32
when n.'s decay BRON 1
white n.-gowns. STEVENS 4
wind changes at n. MACL 5
windy n. a rainy morrow,
  SHAK 221
with n. will go; BLAK 45
nighte: This ae n., UNKN 185
nightes: n. car the stars about doth
  bring. SURR 3
nightfall: flowers left thick at n.
  THOMA E 12
Only at n., ELIOT T 154
nightgown: In my Victorian n.
  PLATH 63
Nightingale: I envy no man's n. or
  spring; HERB G 46
love-lorn N. MILT 9
n./ Filled all the desert
  ELIOT T 122
pretty n., DEKK 2
Save the N. alone. BARNF 1
Sweetly sang the n. WALT 2
tongues of n. GRAV 16
nightingales: n. are singing
  ELIOT T 112
nightly: all my n. dreams POE 8

nobody: barge/ That n. roweth
　　UNKN 89
fat white woman whom n. loves,
　　CORN 2
I'm n., who are you? DICKI 82
n. cares for thee.' UNKN 10
n. has understood, PRIN 3
N. knows de trouble I see"?
　　JOHN J 6
N. sings anymore. BARA 16
N. will have heard NÍ CH 1
n. would care to see, MOSS 4
n. would commit suicide,
　　WRIG J 3
take no shit/ From n.," KNIG 4
talked back to n. WAGO 2
why did n. tell me? PLATH 11
nocturnal: From a n. root, EMER 2
N. Shades PHILL 2
Nod: N. is a little head, FIEL E 9
Old N., the shepherd, DE LA 16
Romance, who loves to n. and
　　sing, POE 38
Where drowsy poppies n.
　　BROWNI E/GUIN 1
nodded: n., nearly napping, POE 34
nodding: Jove, n., SWIF 4
n. by the fire, YEATS 161
Nods: N. and becks, and wreathed
　　smiles, MILT 20
old horse that stumbles and n.
　　HARD 29
Noee: sorwe of N. with his
　　felaweshipe? CHAU 49
Noees: half so greet was nevere N.
　　flood. CHAU 54
noise: damned would make no n.,
　　HERR 63
dreadful n. of waters SHAK 97
hasty n. he spoke 'em; BUTL 5
heard a ragged n. HERB G 71
heard a strange n. UNKN 198
hideous was the n., CHAU 72
joyful n. unto the Lord,
　　BIBL, O.T. 48
made a great n., UNKN 197
no greater than the n. ROBI 33
n. as the n. in a dream; SWIN 24
n. like tambourines,
　　STEVENS 35
n. of archers BIBL, O.T. 18
n. of bell buoys, MOOR M 13
n. of life TENN 21
n. of the mourning LANIG 1
n. of wheels and children GINS 9
of folly, n. and sin!
　　BROWNI R 49
old n. of tears, RUKE 6
set up a n. like crickets,
　　YEATS 21
sound of cornet make a joyful n.
　　before the Lord, BIBL, O.T. 46

walk among n. and deny the
　　voice ELIOT T 14
wheels made no n., KENN 1
Noiseless: N. as fear in a wide
　　wilderness, KEAT 12
n. patient spider, WHITM 54
n. wheels of my car WILLI 49
noiselessly: glide n. forth;
　　WHITM 42
N. as the daylight ALEX 4
N. as the spring-time ALEX 5
noises: beats the dogs in n. loud.
　　CLARE 2
n. of coming and going,
　　WHITM 33
noisome: root away/ The n. weeds
　　SHAK 90
noisy: drives the n. crowd
　　CLARE 2
endless and n. chorus, WHITM 32
spirit of n./ contemplation
　　OHAR 4
to me is this n. ride? WHITT 25
Nokomis: wigwam of N.,/ Daughter
　　of the Moon, N. LONG 40
wrinkled old N. LONG 41
Noli: N. me tangere WYAT 32
nomad: n. raillery, CRAN H 20
nomen: Hoere paradis hy n. here,
　　UNKN 289
none: gluttony second to n.
　　LA FO 1
Grudge who list, but n. deny!
　　HENR 1
n. can call again the passed time.
　　SPENS 22
N. can re-enter there — EMER 37
n. dare call it treason. HARI 2
N. goes his way alone: MARK 1
n. has merited my fear, WYLI 6
n. hunted, alien, HAYD 6
n. like the Boy that sold Broom,
　　UNKN 44
n. of mine, UNKN 77
n. shall speak his name. SHAP 25
n. too soon WILB 4
of n. desired.' C., J 1
nones: cook they hadde with hem
　　for the n. CHAU 6
Nonne: N., a prioresse, CHAU 13
nonplus: nothing can n.: BARK 2
nonsense: grammar, and n., and
　　learning; GOLD 5
nonsensical: n. bachelor twinkle
　　LOWE R 54
nook: into every/ n. and cranny
　　AMMO 1
secret n. in a pleasant land,
　　EMER 28
silvers this n.; MELV 3
Noon: Butterflies, off Banks of N.
　　DICKI 13

lay in his bed till 'twas n.,
　　UNKN 43
n. apple-dreams, RANS 4
n.-day fire, — LANIE 3
n.-heat breathes it back HARD 22
n. in the desert STAF 1
Rangoon the heat of n. COWA 3
tolling his bell at n., EMER 18
troubled midnight and the n.'s
　　repose. ELIOT T 54
untouched by N. DICKI 125
noonday: Darkness more clear than
　　n. ROSS C 21
noone: n. stooped to kiss his face)
　　CUMM 6
nooned: dimmed ere it had n.;
　　LANIG 1
noonshine: notable nimbus of
　　nebulous n., SWIN 19
noontide: Murmured like a n. bee,
　　SHEL 74
throbbings of n. HARD 27
Norf: N. is up, HOLLO 1
normal: n. and selfish BOGA 6
read in n. circumstances?
　　POUN 30
Norman: reef of N.'s Woe!
　　LONG 53
Norn: blinks and croaks, like a toad
　　or a N., WARR 10
Norsemen: Parted the N.,
　　UNKN 21
North: By the N. Gate, LI PO 1
Eternally they look n. KAVA 25
frozen bosom of the n.,
　　SHAK 141
I stare/ At the N. Pole. . .
　　JARR 20
iron door of the n. KUNI 1
Moon's the N. Wind's cooky,
　　LIND V 19
N. Church tower LONG 44
n. wind's masonry. EMER 44
Ploughing N. America.
　　STEVENS 39
twa brethren in the n.,
　　UNKN 268
winds blow n., WHITM 65
northern: distant n. sea. ARNO 2
Glorious the n. lights astream;
　　SMAR 9
N. breast and brain HARD 20
N. Lights have seen queer sights,
　　SERV 1
spurns the N. scum! RANDA J 2
This n. sky; DE LA 15
Northumberland: gold enough
　　around her middle/ To buy N.
　　UNKN 319
northwest: driven from the/ n.
　　WILLI 34
nose: cars n. forward like fish;
　　LOWE R 21

man who used to n. HARD 4
What did I n.? GINS 46
notices: No owners or n., RODG 1
notify: n. subscriber. HAYD 20
notion: catch the spreading n.
POPE A 30
have no n. why. HOUS 9
notions: dispark/ Those sparkling
n., HERB G 34
distressed/ By all the needs and
n. MILLA 14
Nought: lea'e us n. BURN 63
n. but care on ev'ry han',
BURN 29
n./ But restless hurry
THOMS J (1700–1748) 7
N. may endure but mutability.
SHEL 44
n. to do but mark and tell
BURN 4
n. to find, BRID R 4
n. worth to me. GREV 2
stay and think of n. SHAK 208
Nouns: N. were clustered in the
street. KOCH 3
N. were struck, moved, changed.
KOCH 3
nourished: How begot, how n.?
SHAK 120
n. and suddenly/ burst
RANDA D 5
stones had n., MOOR M 24
nourisher: Chief n. in life's feast —
SHAK 106
nourishing: n. in thy bewildered
brain ARNO 18
nouveaux riches: children of the n.
SNOD 8
novel: discourse in n. phrases
GILB 30
novelist: lady n. — GILB 27
novelty: whose n. survives
COWP 18
November: no leaves, no birds —
N.! HOOD 6
N. off Tehuantepec, STEVENS 46
now: all things n. do hold their
peace: SURR 3
driving storm even as n.,
WHITM 99
Everything is happy n.,
LOWE J 18
gone years and the n. years and
the maybe years, WALK 5
He said, N. GILD 1
limping age will lodge him n.
VAUX 5
My soul is n. her day, SHAP 19
nothing after N., ROBI 36
n. I know it. GAY 6
n. I live, and n. my life is done.
TICH 1

Nowhere: N. to fall but off,
KING B 2
n. to go but down; SNOD 10
n. yet to rest my head, ARNO 32
n. Zen New Jersey GINS 10
river that flows n., STEVENS 45
noxious: Each thing impure or n.
AKEN 2
nude: I am n. as a chicken neck,
PLATH 12
nudes: magazines with n. OHAR 13
Nudge: N. of the impossible,
AUDE 59
n. you from this sleep, ROET 12
numb: I was n. and sick LEWI 4
land is n. WINT 9
My Mind was going n. DICKI 46
n. the elastic powers. ARNO 22
numbed: these n. wrists HARP 2
number: cat has a n. of lives;
THOMA D 39
coil of rhythm and n.; EMER 33
In unvanquishable n., SHEL 40
In weight in measure, n., sound,
JONS 39
n. sorrow HERR 66
One is no n., MARL 10
so full of a n. of things,
STEVENSO R 9
to the n. seben. WALK 9
numbered: hours are n., EMER 45
numbering: Time made me his n.
clock. SHAK 93
numberless: arise/ From death, you
n. infinities DONN 5
numbers: Crop your n. CAREY 2
easy n. flow, MILT 35
for the n. came. POPE A 13
mournful n., LONG 35
n. it for future reference,
FROS 24
N. languishing. MARV 20
n. sweet HERR 49
plaintive n. flow WORD 140
soft Silence fall in n. FLET J 1
numbness: drowsy n. pains/ My
sense, KEAT 44
numinous: body is as n. as words,
HASS 4
nun: Héloise, the learned n.,
VILL 1
pensive N., devout and pure,
MILT 16
quiet as a N. WORD 26
nunnery: n./ Of thy chaste breast
LOVE 8
Nunnes: Among the N. Black.
SKEL 6
nuns: n. and mothers worship
images, YEATS 12
N. fret not WORD 59
see four n. SEXT 10

Nurse: homely N. doth all she can
WORD 73
keep a-hold of N. BELL 11
my most kindly n., SPENS 45
Nature's soft n., SHAK 54
Nursed: N. the little Hiawatha,
LONG 41
nurses: n. and rumours; AUDE 37
Nursing: N. her wrath to keep it
warm. BURN 50
n. the unconquerable hope,
ARNO 28
nursling: n. of the Sky; SHEL 25
Ocean's n., Venice lies, —
SHEL 36
Nurslings: N. of immortality!
SHEL 51
nut: can you crack a n." EMER 36
jolly n.-brown bowl, DEKK 1
love no roast but a n.-brown
toast, STEVENSO W 1
n.-tree, nothing would it bear
MOTH 13
nutmeg: golden n. and a silver
pear; MOTH 13
Nutriment: N. that feeds the Mind?
SWIF 19
with purer n. supplied, SHEL 79
nuts: furry n./ of the terrible puss,
OHAR 4
n. are getting brown; DICKI 103
Some n., some apples; JONS 36
table with cherries and n.
BLAK 96
NY: Monroe, N. the chicken farms
GINS 27
nyghtes: slepen al the n. with open
eye — CHAU 4
nyghtes: longe n. blake. CHAU 121
nymph: chaste, unboastful n.,
COLL 11
hapless N. with wonder saw:
GRAY 19
mountain n., sweet Liberty;
MILT 21
n. died more quick, and the
shepherd more slow. DRYD 15
N. exulting fills with shouts the
sky; POPE A 122
N. more bright GAY 1
n. shall break Diana's law,
POPE A 117
quiver'd N. with Arrows keen
MILT 3
skilful N. reviews her force
POPE A 121
strut before a wanton ambling n.;
SHAK 96
Sweet Echo, sweetest N. MILT 9
nymphs: n. and satyrs YEATS 100
n. are departed. ELIOT T 129
n. so graceful, wise, and fair,
SWIF 21

ocean: all great Neptune's o.
  SHAK 108
  breaks like the Atlantic O. on my
    head. LOWE R 29
  capital ship for an o. trip,
    CARRY 8
  cold o. JEFFE 21
  crossing the o., CARRO 17
  deep and dark blue O., BYRO 2
  Ebb, o. of life, WHITM 5
  ebb'd with the o. of life,
    WHITM 1
  foam after the o.'s wrath
    SHEL 78
  glad o. comes and goes, PATM 6
  hear like o. LANG 3
  hungry o. gain/ Advantage
    SHAK 211
  legs bestrid the o.; SHAK 7
  Make the mighty o. CARN 1
  mind, that o. MARV 18
  not that o. MOOR M 13
  Oars divide the O., DICKI 13
  o. and truth. ROSS C 30
  O. might turn Helicon CLEV 2
  o., multiple to a blinding/
    oneness AMMO 11
  O.'s nursling, Venice lies, —
    SHEL 36
  On life's rough o. luckless starr'd:
    BURN 60
  over Catholics the o. rolls,
    BYRO 43
  pores of the o. and shores;
    SHEL 25
  river-ark on the o. brine,
    EMER 26
  river/ Nor o. spawns MILLE V 1
  same o. round us raves, ARNO 34
  thou hast been/ O.'s child,
    SHEL 37
  to wreck and death./ In o. cave,
    WILLA 2
  tranced machine/ Of o.,
    STEVENS 47
  Upon a painted o. COLE SAM 32
  white as o. foam;
    STEVENSO R 5
  wild and wasteful o. SHAK 56
oceans: measureless o. of space,
  WHITM 55
  o. and Europe SNYD 27
  Portable and compendious O.
    CRAS 8
Octaves: O. of radiation; AUDE 88
October: Especially when the O.
  wind THOMA D 13
  night, in the lonesome O. POE 47
  O.'s bright blue weather.
    JACK 1, 2
Octosyllabic: Rhymed O. Curse
  BELL 14

odd: love as o. as wearing shoes —
  CORS 8
  Many a kiss, both o. and even;
    HERR 7
  o. becomming graces, SUCK 4
  played even and o. PEEL 4
oddments: o. of all things,
  POUN 54
odds: facing fearful o. MACA 3
  long shot at long o., CUNN J 3
  o. with circumstance? ROET 30
odes: wrote each other little o.
  GILB 11
odor: Blendeth its o. with the
  violet — KEAT 6
  lilac with mastering o.
    WHITM 49
  o., talon, claw, KIZE 3
  steeped in the o. of ponds,
    KUNI 2
  that sweet o. which doth in it
    live. SHAK 206
odorless: it is o., WHITM 75
odorous: give most o. smell;
  SPENS 15
  trees wept o. gums and balm;
    MILT 69
odors: Rise o. of ploughed field
  LONG 8
  sweetest o. SHAK 206
odour: her sweet o. did them all
  excel. SPENS 15
  o., light, embrace, FLET G YO 1
  O. of blood YEATS 118
odours: bedew'd with liquid o.
  HORA 3
  Built up of o., burneth in her
    breast. HERR 34
  drowned the sense in o.;
    ELIOT T 121
  haste with o. sweet . . . MILT 42
  o., fruits, and flocks, MILT 5
Odysseus: O. saw the sirens;
  MANI 2
Odyssey: surge and thunder of the
  O. LANG 3
o'er: lay the sod o. me, UNKN 11
  midwife gave o. UNKN 75
O'erhang: O. and jutty his
  confounded base, SHAK 56
o'erleaps: Vaulting ambition, which
  o. itself SHAK 105
O'erpicturing: O. that Venus
  SHAK 5
o'ersized: o. with coagulate gore,
  SHAK 30
o'ertake: let base clouds o. me
  SHAK 198
  o.' thee! WEBS/ROWL 1
o'erthrown: noble mind is here o.
  SHAK 33
  Now my charms are all o.
    SHAK 167

o'ertook: flighty purpose never is o.
  SHAK 113
o'erwhelm: brow o. it SHAK 56
off: Depart, — be o., — HOLM 1
  I wander'd o. by myself,
    WHITM 111
  Nowhere to fall but o., KING B 2
  o. that helmet goes. GILB 39
  take o. all my clothes
    BERRYM 14
  to be like that, well o., LAWR 14
offence: no harshness gives o.,
  POPE A 28
  o./ Of man DRYD 17
  What dire o. POPE A 110
offended: shadows have o.,
  SHAK 129
  unweeting have o., MILT 101
offenders: Of society o. GILB 26
Offending: most o. soul alive.
  SHAK 59
  'O. race of human kind, SWIF 4
offense: banish all o. CAREW 12
  like to give o. FROS 58
  my o. is rank, SHAK 34
offer: doe most hurt where most
  hellp I o. WYAT 23
  o. gifts after his will, EMER 14
offering: o. no promise ELIOT T 68
  o. too little CANN 1
offers: She o. plenty, SPENC B 1
office: fancy next/ Her o. holds.
  MILT 80
  for o. and for ese/ Of engendrure,
    CHAU 96
  going to the o. SASS 7
  into an editorial o. SIMP 9
  o. of a wall, SHAK 88
officer: cursed/ The drunken o.
  WALC 4
Officers: O., seamen, gunners,
  marines, CLARK J 1
offices: All o. were done/ By him,
  JONS 39
  love's austere and lonely o.?
    HAYD 23
official: pink o. form. AUDE 7
offing: Masts in the o. DAVID 3
offspring: his o. dear GILB 19
  o. round their feeble fire, CRAB 6
  Time's noblest o. BERK 1
  true source/ Of human o.,
    MILT 78
  witless o. flock MERW 4
ofspring: Light, o. of Heav'n
  MILT 63
often: how o. Love we've made
  SACK 3
  I have not o. smiled ROSS C 27
  leads as o. as not/ to our
    undoing. WILLI 30
  too o. profaned SHEL 48

youthe and elde is o. at debat.
CHAU 51

oftener: o. seen, the more I lust,
GOOG 2

ogle: owls that o. London. NOYE 3

ogre: cocky little o. dozes off,
AUDE 59

Ogres: famous men of old, the O.
GRAV 18

O'Hara: Cathleen O. (he names her)
KAVA 11

Ohio: beyond death/ Bridgeport, O.
WRIG J 3

oil: anointest my head with o.;
BIBL, O.T. 31

eel's/ O. of water body,
HUGH T 4

endless o. and stone! GINS 17

o.-soaked, o.-permeated BISH 11

river sweats/ O. and tar
ELIOT T 138

wine and o.; TENN 91

words were softer than o.,
BIBL, O.T. 40

oiled: slipping/ like o. parts LEVI 1

oinement: o. unto my wounde,
CHAU 123

ointment: o. from the shells,
HORA 9

ointments: locks with o. shine,
HERR 72

Olaf: i sing of O. glad and big
CUMM 14

old: all the world is o., KINGSL 7

bards of o. enjoyed in you!
BLAK 111

'Before I am o. YEATS 60

bits of o. fur SILKO 1

catch me, o. Slithergadee, SILV 1

change o. love for new PEEL 1

Child's Toys and the O. Man's
Reasons BLAK 8

chilly and grown o.
BROWNI R 79

coyote got his/ ratty o. fur coat
SILKO 1

days of o. ROSS C 25

Do they know they're o., JENN 2

ease an o. man SNOD 6

elephant, the huge o. beast,
LAWR 6

ever have been o. ROBI 38

face nor child nor o., WHITM 72

Familiar as an o. mistake,
ROBI 1

farewell, you o. rhinoceros,
NASH 13

fierce o. mother, WHITM 5

Flemish pictures of o. WHITT 29

forest, dim and o., POE 42

fortify thy name against o. age;
DANI S 12

from a fine o. eye POUN 23

gap in the o. wall still,
WHITT 32

given to a Woman O., BLAK 31

good o. cause WORD 162

grand o. ballad of Sir Patrick
Spence, COLE SAM 6

Grow o. along with me!
BROWNI R 71

grudge the poor o. man FROS 21

guileless o. scapegoat; GRAV 14

haughty o. copper-bound
albatross MASE 10

he died o. HOUS 54

heard the o., old men say,
YEATS 103

"He's a cheery o. card," SASS 10

heroes of o., BROWNI R 69

"How o. is she, UNKN 28

hungry for the o., familiar ways,
MCKA 8

I grow o. . . . I grow o. . . .
ELIOT T 90

I shall die an o. Parisian. RIVE 2

I Tiresias, o. man ELIOTT 135

in judgment o., SHAK 119

in o. heroic traces, BRON 5

jolly good ale and o.!
STEVENSO W 2

last to lay the o. aside.
POPE A 23

Lest I should be o.-fashioned,
DICKI 104

life forever o. yet new,
BROWNI R 43

Like an o. brandy CUNN J 1

lonely o. man with a white
beard. GINS 27

longing for de o. plantation,
FOST 4

'Look at that o. fellow YEATS 76

love is o., SMIT L 3

loving that o. arm-chair? COOK 1

make my o. excuse,' SHAK 135

Mind not the o. man WHITM 8

My dog and I are o., MASE 2

my folks were growing o.
STEVENSO R 6

my o. opinion keep; FRENE 1

new lies on the o., JEFFE 9

new made when thou art o.
SHAK 185

Now o. in love, OVID 5

Now that I'm o., JARR 17

now thirty-seven years o.
WHITM 74

of Chaos o.! POPE A 1

o. age shall this generation waste,
KEAT 40

o. and going — KINGSL 2

o. and ragged and gray BRIN 1

o. and gray and full of sleep,
YEATS 161

o. barrel with many a bung.
KENN 2

o. bitch gone in the teeth,
POUN 43

o. crone rocking the cradle,
WHITM 68

o. egg of my desire is broken,
UNKN 230

o. faiths loosen and fall, SWIN 23

o., familiar carols play, LONG 11

o. familiar faces. LAMB 2

o. fashioned tirade —
LOWE R 29

O. Floyd Ireson, WHITT 23

o. folks at home. FOST 4

o. folks stay. FOST 3

o. forsaken bough HOLM 16

o. foul river SMIT ST 7

o. griefs and griefs/ Not yet
begun. THOMA E 14

o. half-witted sheep STEPHEN 4

o. lady, who marked MONTA 2

o. lost road KIPL 28

o., mad, blind, despised, and dying
king, SHEL 27

o. man bending WHITM 113

o. man gone. JOYC 2

o. man in a dry month,
ELIOT T 30

O. Man in a tree, LEAR 14

o. man of seventy-three
SMIT ST 1

o. man of Thermopylae, LEAR 15

o. man with a beard, LEAR 18

o. man with his feet ROET 16

o. man with wrinkled dugs
ELIOT T 135

O. men weeping in the parks!
GINS 16

o. mouse bolted CLARE 11

o. noise of tears, RUKE 6

o. order changeth, TENN 103

o. party of Lyme LEAR 19

o. plain words, RICH 6

o. recalcitrant anus SNOD 11

o. subtle foe so tempteth me
DONN 60

O. Testament soldiers NASH 20

O. times dar EMME 1

o. tree's late branch RANS 11

o. whore petticoats) — PLATH 51

o. world was restored READ H 1

o.-time sea-fight? WHITM 89

our land, it is o. RANS 1

Out of o. mythologies YEATS 30

pleasing habit ends,/ No man
grows o., YEATS 73

poor, when they're o.,
STEPHENS 12

remember/ Like the o. AUDE 26

Repent, repent, and from o. errors
turn!' DRUM 7

reverence of o. days WHITT 12

O., who is not, SWIN 16
o./ With the man in the wind and
   the west moon; THOMA D 9
O. year in every ten PLATH 52
Pray but o. prayer MORR 7
really blended into o.; WHITM 35
restless o.; the circler of circles;
   AIKE 11
rival for o. hour JACK 1
seen o. thing, SWIN 21
sounds the voice of O. SITW 13
takes only o. NASH 7
Too blest with any o. WORD 23
two souls therefore, which are o.,
   DONN 63
vision of the great O. GINS 46
we two being o. DONN 14
weeping, longing with o. deep
   longing, WHITM 17
When I was o.-and-twenty
   HOUS 59
"Where I cut off o. SNYD 43
wonderful o.-hoss shay, HOLM 4
woodspurge flowered, three cups
   in o. ROSS D 10
"You the o., I the few" POUN 12
onely: my o. head, HERB G 2
My o. musick, HERB G 2
o. heart and breast, HERB G 2
Reason and speech we o. bring.
   HERB G 51
oneness: ocean, multiple to a
   blinding/ o. AMMO 11
ones: decayed and loved o. lost
   LINC 1
pale unsatisfied o. YEATS 91
violated o. with gentle hearts;
   WALK 2
Oneself: O. a living armoury?
   YOUN A 1
onion: o. fumes BROO G 16
onions: Seasoned with sage and o.,
   and port wine. SOUTHE 8
only: fictions o. and false hair
   HERB G 44
my love, my o. friend. TENN 95
o. crazy things OLSO 20
O. my Daddy SMIT W 1
o., o., thing that I ever did wrong
   UNKN 99
o. son is dead. WHITM 17
o. warmth, the only peace.
   SCHW 3
Virginia,/ Earth's o. paradise.
   DRAY 17
onset: for the o. with Eternity,
   DICKI 96
onward: Half a league o., TENN 6
O. through life he goes; LONG 49
ooth: Hire gretteste o. CHAU 13
oother: Withouten o. compaignye
   CHAU 11

ooze: through the o. and slime,
   SMIT L 1
oozy: o. weeds about me twist.
   MELV 5
ope: casement o. at night, KEAT 54
could not o. His mouth, BUTL 2
o. the doors O soul. WHITM 42
o. their golden eyes: SHAK 17
open: (After o. weather KIPL 23
All these stand o., HERB G 60
And all thy heart lies o. unto me.
   TENN 109
And o. field, WORD 102
dared to o. my mouth WHITM 4
ear the o. vowels tire; POPE A 24
Go forth under the o. sky,
   BRYA 23
leav'st thy losses o. to the day.
   BEAU/FLET 4
o. always petal by petal
   CUMM 49
o. curling lotus gate SNYD 4
O.-eyed conspiracy SHAK 158
O.-eyed rabbits SNYD 35
o. eyes of the dead MERW 2
o. face of heaven, — KEAT 66
o. firmament of heaven. MILT 35
o. like a drawer of knives.
   LARK 9
O. Road goes to the used-car lot.
   SIMP 13
o. soul and o. door, LOWE J 14
O. the envelope quickly,
   WHITM 16
o. thou thy manly mouth,
   UNKN 166
O. unto the fields, WORD 6
o. voices — hospitality —
   WHITM 44
page of the book carelessly o.,
   SEXT 18
receive those charms/ With o.
   ears, CAREW 2
Singing with o. mouths
   WHITM 38
sleeping in the o. SNYD 13
slepen al the nyght with o. eye —
   CHAU 4
windows/ That o. on their lives
   SPEND 4
opened: door we never o.
   ELIOT T 16
friends had o. ROBI 47
opening: Dies at the o. day.
   WATT I 3
eating or o. a window AUDE 62
o. and shutting itself
   MOOR M 11
O. her fertile womb MILT 86
o. sweet of earliest bloom,
   COLL 1
opens: ground o. up and envelopes
   me BARA 15

opera: o. house sparkled MERR 11
operandi: modus o.; NASH 6
operated: undressed, o.-on, dressed
   body JARR 18
operation: o., teaching school,
   GINS 21
Ophelia: That's O., that Cordelia;
   YEATS 78
Ophir: from distant O. MASE 1
opiate: emptied some dull o.
   KEAT 44
opinion: Flouted o. HECH 16
has a definite o. SIMP 4
hold o. with Pythagoras,
   SHAK 124
my old o. keep; FRENE 1
Three things there be in man's o.
   dear, GREV 7
whole climate of o. AUDE 31
opinions: cunning humorists'
   puddled o., SIDN 4
held the proper o. AUDE 94
made my own o. clear; DRYD 20
o. are accursed. YEATS 112
opium: Rises to my brain as o.
   DAVIS 2
opportunity: 'O o.! SHAK 140
o. to hear all RIVE 1
oppose: remorse did not o.
   temptation; BYRO 20
opposed: o. may beware of thee.
   SHAK 23
opposeless: quarrel with your great
   o. wills, SHAK 79
opposit: o. two citties stood,
   MARL 4
opposite: house stands o., SNOD 8
on the o. shore LONG 44
opposition: o. of the stars. MARV 7
oppress: temptations me o.,
   HERR 19
oppressed: Earth's downtrodden and
   o., BRYA 13
O. with pain, WYAT 13
oppression: by man's o. cursed,
   POPE A 98
dense o., MELV 10
o. and shame, WHITM 40
o. of their prodigal weight.
   SHAK 90
unconscious o., POUN 25
oppressive: gloom o. o'er the world,
   THOMS J (1700–1748) 13
oppressor: voice of the o.
   BIBL, O.T. 11
oppressors: contempt for their o.
   POUN 24
opulent: gold of the o. sun.
   STEVENS 43
oracle: o. of lies, RALEG 5
orange: Just an o.! ROSS C 32
mentioned/ o. yet OHAR 23

of o.-blossom, TENN 11
ould O. flute. UNKN 196
Orangemen: O. no more UNKN 217
oranges: I call/ it o. OHAR 23
late/ Coffee and o. STEVENS 54
O. and lemons, UNKN 23
orators: Statesmen, chiefs, o.,
BYRO 37
orb: quail and shake the o.,
SHAK 7
reaching th' utmost o. MILT 62
western o. sailing the heaven,
WHITM 48
orbed: o. maiden SHEL 24
orbs: dew her o. upon the green.
SHAK 126
orchard: Children's voices in the o.
ELIOT T 57
dart in the o. aisles, WILB 37
from the o., WHITM 29
o., the meadow, WOOD 1
our o. fruits, ROSS C 11
that o. sprite,/ Eve, HODG 7
orchards: Apple o. blossom there,
MASE 14
corn-fields and o., WHITM 31
o. of summer, WHITM 9
roots, o., grain? WHITM 96
trees in apple o. JACK 3
Ordain: O. them laws; MILT 104
ordained: God ordered motion, but
o. no rest. VAUG 15
Night was o. DRAY 3
order: Blessed rage for o.,
STEVENS 19
Bright-harnessed angels sit in o.
serviceable. MILT 41
fasten into o. AMMO 9
in just o. move. VERY 4
in o. categorical; GILB 35
kept our erasers in o. POUN 29
old o. changeth, TENN 103
O. their populations forth,
KUNI 1
o. words of the sea, STEVENS 19
o. of words, ELIOT T 63
rôle/ In the New O. AUDE 58
set my lands in o.? ELIOT T 155
teach/ The act of o. SHAK 55
ordered: cannon o. well; MELV 16
God o. motion, but ordained no
rest. VAUG 10
o. a box of maniacs. PLATH 9
orders: He obeys the o. of nature
EBER 8
ordinance: pass beyond the goal of
o. TENN 121
ordinary: above the reach/ Of o.
men; WORD 123
crowd of o. decent folk AUDE 81
o. night was graced NEME 1
o./ Surroundings of social life
SNOD 1

Oregon: bars of Madras, O.
SNYD 16
organ: bass of heaven's deep o.
MILT 39
merrier than the merry o.
CHAU 66
organdy: her o. skirt JUST 3
organic: Be but o. Harps
COLE SAM 12
organs: resembling human o.
SMIT W 3
orgasm: dive-bomber's screaming
o. JEFFE 22
orient: spreads/ His o. beams,
MILT 76
origin: o. of all poems, WHITM 76
o. of it all. BARK 2
Original: great O. proclaim:
ADDI 3
lost his proud o. one SILKO 1
rare o. heartsblood goes,
WILB 13
origins: o. of art. MOSS 5
theory of natural o. JEFFE 34
orisons: in his morning o. SMAR 4
Ormus: Jewels more rich than O.
MARV 1
Outshone the wealth of O. and of
Ind, MILT 58
ornament: Art and o. the shame.
CRAS 13
for smell or o., HERB G 47
that sweet o. SHAK 206
To be a moment's o.; WORD 133
ornaments: goes on accreting o.
PINS 2
o. of ivory, BONT 8
o. of rhyme. LONG 4
rosy o. in thee. CAMPI 25
ornate: bedecked, o., and gay,
MILT 110
Orphans: hope of O., SHAK 224
Orphant: Little O. Annie's RILE 1
Orpheus: bid the soul of O. sing
MILT 17
O. with his Lute FLET/SHAK 1
orthodox: have an o. smack,
GILB 59
ospreys: o./ would fall like
valkyries BIRN 5
ostrich: drops her o. tail,
LOWE R 41
o., and a juju-man, TOOM 2
pinions, o.-like, COLE SAM 43
wings and feathers unto the o.?
BIBL, O.T. 16
other: abased to the o. WHITM 77
All o. fair, like flowers, untimely
fade. SPENS 26
crossed each o.'s way: WILD 4
delicate creatures/ From the o.
world. WRIG J 5

do not, on the o. hand, be bad;
HOUS 8
either grew a portion of the o.;
JONS 42
Far o. worlds and other seas,
MARV 18
only look the o. way. HOUS 17
o. Eden, demi-Paradise, SHAK 88
o. side of care MUIR 2
Parts of each from o., MILT 97
rise upon some o. shore,
MCCRE 1
they ate each o. up! FIEL E 2
thoughts of o. days SHAP 10
othere: homward he shal tellen o.
two, CHAU 6
others: catch all the o., SILV 1
o. they would never meet
LARK 22
o. will see them WHITM 19
see oursels as o. see us! BURN 58
they see o. grow, SHAK 186
this one excelled all o. SPEND 8
otherwhere: "Go, go, go seek some
o.! ELIZ 2
otter: bitch o. in a field HUGH T 7
ought: o. not to have to care
FROS 52
ould: o. engin' howlds together —'
FRENC 3
our: All in o. gowns of green so gay
UNKN 229
begun o. part of the fighting.
WHITM 90
came O. Blessed Lady, UNKN 49
O. foot's in the door. PLATH 67
O. love shall live, SPENS 24
o. sick eyes, EMER 5
smoky smell of o. garments.
UNKN 121
sucking milk from this o. body
SNYD 4
wearied of o. huts UNKN 121
what is o. guilt? MOOR M 42
What is o. innocence,
MOOR M 42
ours: if Love be o., TENN 15
ourselves: do o. this wrong,
TREN 2
enemy and image of o., MACN 13
feat on which o. we prided)
BYRO 44
o. we find in the sea CUMM 21
spirit we keep within o.,
WILLI 16
things in which we have seen o.
WILB 2
unto which we doom/ O.,
WORD 60
out: Bloom gradually o. of reach.
SNOD 4
climb the look o.? LI PO 5
clock/ Beats o. TENN 19

drained o. one another's force
SNOD 15

far o. of reach, WHITM 10

gone o. of the reach of change —
THOMA E 10

His fire is o., SWIF 26

in and o. with me,
STEVENSO R 13

joy and natural content/ O.
YEATS 57

keep hate o. UNTE 3

Murder will o., CHAU 70

my soul lay o. of sight,/ Untuned,
unstrung; HERB G 21

no, I was o. for stars; FROS 16

o., brief candle! SHAK 114

O.-during marble, brass, or jet,
HERR 37

o. of being AMMO 20

o. of great Russia SAND 21

O. of Heaven, THOMP F 4

O. of old mythologies YEATS 30

o. of such corruptions,
WHITM 98

O. of the depths have I cried
BIBL, O.T. 60

O. of the everywhere
MACDONA 1

o. of the house OHAR 2

O. of the woods LANIE 2

o.-soared the shadow of our
night; SHEL 9

o. there flew a trope; BUTL 2

reckon ill who leave me o.;
EMER 7

rising and gliding o., WHITM 111

sublime,/ O. of space — out of
time. POE 16

Sweet rain, the fire's o. SNYD 29

They o.-talked thee, ARNO 13

walling in or walling o., FROS 58

wear us o. GINS 24

world o.-Herods Herod;
LOWE R 22

your eyes so blue?/ O. of the sky
MACDONA 1

outbraves: o. his dignity:
SHAK 222

outcast: beweep my o. state,
SHAK 194

outcry: o. of the hunted Hare
BLAK 4

Outdid: O. the meat, o. the frolic
wine. HERR 36

outdoor: o. business is bad for
strings), TROW 5

outdoors: who could sing o.,
LIND V 4

outer: concerned with o., FROS 116

outgrown: Leaving thine o. shell
HOLM 3

outlast: o. our days. POUN 42

outlaws: o. Frank and Jesse James.
UNKN 149

we, o. on God's property EBER 5

outleaps: word o. the world,
ROET 24

outlet: Death's o. song of Life,
WHITM 47

outlines: Having curved o.
STEVENS 52

outlive: o. this powerful rime;
SHAK 207

outlived: Remembered, if o.,
DICKI 2

outlives: laurel o. not May
SWIN 23

o. this day SHAK 60

outnumber: busy thoughts o.
SHEL 42

outrage: connive/ in civilized o.
HEAN 17

outrageous: crouched an o. bird.
HECH 2

suffer/ The slings and arrows of o.
fortune, SHAK 39

outran: passions now and then o./
Discretion, BYRO 21

Runners whom renown o.
HOUS 57

Outshone: O. the wealth of Ormus
and of Ind, MILT 58

outside: humbly crowd o.,
SPEND 6

inside skin side o.; STRON 1

it was dusk o., FROS 15

leave that brain o., GILB 23

My o. Woman, and your inside
Man. COWL 6

O. the door! LAWR 52

o. the Hill, BROWNI R 63

point o. the ROET 14

skin side o. STRON 1

outsleep: Woe and want thou canst
o.; EMER 32

outspeak: will o. and has its
reasons. SNOD 7

outspread: for sails o.,
COLE SAM 43

outstretch: foe o.'d beneath the
tree. BLAK 79

outstretched: o. beneath my vine,
HORA 11

outstripped: o. by every pen,
SHAK 196

outward: any o. part: UNKN 181

o. things dwell not in my desires.
SHAK 59

thin and o. rind, EMER 5

outwears: soul o. the breast,
BYRO 63

sword o. its sheath, BYRO 63

outworn: o. buried age; SHAK 211

Pagan suckled in a creed o.;
WORD 160

ovens: Ghosts from the o.,
HECH 15

over: after the war was o.,
WOOL 4

continent work'd o. WHITM 96

Edens ere yet o.-run; MELV 22

gently turn'd o. upon me,
WHITM 78

Holding it o. him HERF 2

I have seen it o. and over,
BISH 5

lacerate/ Simply by being o.;
LARK 14

my cup runneth o. BIBL, O.T. 31

o. all the sky — WHITM 10

o. the purple moor, NOYE 6

party is o. MERR 4

rain is o. and gone;
BIBL, O.T. 72

same the whole world o.;
UNKN 219

Soap all o. SNYD 3

sooner it's o., KINGSL 4

spring begins before the winter's
o. WYLI 11

storm is o., BRID R 18

sword swept./ O. the pass
NEWB 4

wake us/ Time and time o.
LARK 8

will in us is o.-rul'd by fate.
MARL 8

Overall: O. is beyond me: AMMO 4

overawed: gesture or least action, o.
MILT 90

overborne: o. with care — TREN 2

overbyde: grace t'o. hem CHAU 11

overcast: our sky was o., COWP 21

overcoat: buttoned his o. SAND 24

o. for ever, HOUS 20

Overcome: Fiend/ Let go, then, O.
DICKI 152

o. with whiteness STROD 1

vertue o. by vice, KYNA 1

overestimated: Grossly o. our
powers. AUDE 12

overflow: love might o. my Heart!
TAYL E 7

mighty o. HERR 35

thy tears mixed with mine do o.
DONN 65

Overflowing: That very knowing,/
O., GILB 16

overhead: few large stars o.,
WHITM 92

God is o.; DODG 2

overhear: o. a cry of pain BISH 23

overnamed: Harlem, your hotel is
o., WELC 2

overnight: having sprung up o.
SMIT W 3

O., very/ Whitely, PLATH 65

overrun: o. with rue? HABE 2

overs: enough/ Left o. AUDE 12
overset: o. the brain, WORD 52
oversprinkle: stars that o. All the
    heavens, POE 10
overswear: unswear, and o. them
    DONN 47
overtake: slow/ To o. thee.
    SHAK 104
overthrow: vices' o., SIDN 20
overthrown: Deprest, and o.,
    MILT 117
    Great mammoths o. WILB 47
overtired: Of apple-picking: I am o.
    FROS 5
overtone: o. of motion CRAN H 30
overture: not an o., BROO G 2
overturn: wasteful war shall statues
    o., SHAK 207
overwater: tree swayed o. ROET 56
Ovid: Burn O. with the rest.
    CLARK A 3
owe: their charms we o.;
    POPE A 94
owed: beauties that those ashes o.
    HERB CH 1
owene: oure o. juggement.
    CHAU 91
owest: Lend less than thou o.,
    SHAK 71
owl: Altarwise by o.-light
    THOMA D 6
    'Beware/ The soft-voiced o.,
    HILL G 3
    nightly sings the staring o.,
    SHAK 101
    O. and the Pussy-cat LEAR 10
    O.-downy, soft feminine
    JEFFE 16
    o. from the steeple SCOT WA 5
    o. is abroad, the bat and the
    toad, JONS 16
    Sweet Suffolk O., so trimly dight
    VAUT 1
    take away thine O., HOOD 14
    white o. in the belfry sits.
    TENN 105
    wise old o. RICHA E 1
owlet: o.'s cry/ Came loud—
    COLE SAM 13
owls: I couch when o. do cry.
    SHAK 166
    o. and a hen, LEAR 18
    O. have cried, THOMA E 19
    o. in the beardusky woods
    BIRN 6
    o. that ogle London. NOYE 3
    o. trilled GRAV 16
    o. were bearing the farm away,
    THOMA D 18
    unloose small bats and o.
    PLATH 59
own: came into my o. ROET 10
    despis'd/ His o.: MILT 59

every strength you o. SNOD 2
followed my o. Trail SNYD 2
Gods make their o. importance.
    KAVA 5
Her beauty is her o. CAMPI 6
his o. house & family; BLAK 27
In their o. guise, EMER 20
Innocence is its o. adorning.
    SPENC A 1
legends of their o.: DICKEY 26
Lets his o. ashes choke his soul.
    HERB G 29
Love likes no laws but his o.!
    GREV 1
my o. conviction: MILT 99
my o. hearthstone, EMER 28
my o. mind; THOMP F 6
Nature made thy o., EMER 10
No name shall but your o. be
    found. MARV 16
oft exposed his o. SWIF 24
On their/ O. trails SNYD 2
o. no other function. SHAK 183
perish in our o. THOMP F 3
pleasures of her o.; WORD 72
receive by gift what of my o.,
    MILT 109
See the victim's face become their
    o. MACN 3
some parents of its o. UNTE 2
thine o. hues SHEL 30
owne: wonne with her o. will
    beguyld. SPENS 17
owned: o. by all the town,
    TATE A 18
Owner: —till a Day/ The O.
    passed— DICKI 109
owners: lords and o. of their faces,
    SHAK 222
    No o. or notices, RODG 1
owning: mania of o. things,
    WHITM 75
owns: 'alf o' Creation she o.:
    KIPL 31
    "Who o. them hungry hills
    KAVA 26
own'st: thou o. that praise,
    COWP 22
owre: haf o. to Aberdour,
    UNKN 228
ox: With o. and sheep REES 1
oxen: o. near/ The worn
    foundations LOWE R 23
    see the o. kneel, HARD 33
Oxenford: clerk ther was of O.
    CHAU 22
Oxford: grey spires of O. LETT 1
oxlips: Faint o.; tender bluebells
    SHEL 59
oxygen: in an o. tent GINS 39
    lack of o. HUGO 7
    seeking o., HARP 4
    terrible o. BISH 16

oyster: o.-shop for mermaids
    HOLM 11
oysterman: tall young o. HOLM 10
oysters: lobsters and o. to cure
    melancholy; JORD 1
Ozymandias: O., King of Kings:
    SHEL 50

P

pace: no p. perceiv'd! SHAK 227
    p. the hollow rooms, LINC 2
    soft his p.; SACK 1
    this petty p. SHAK 114
    tramped at a rat's p., ROSS C 12
    trouble in the p. POUN 57
    unperturbèd p.,/ Deliberate speed,
    THOMP F 7
    upon yon eminence our p.
    COWP 17
paces: delicate p. by the stream, —
    RANS 35
Pacific: shade of a Southern P.
    locomotive GINS 33
    stared at the P. KEAT 56
    Swell with p. violence. DAY 6
pacified: depart peaceful, p., and
    thankless, LAWR 43
    p. by a clever line AUDE 48
pacing: p. up and down, LIND V 1
pack: bid the Muse to p.,
    YEATS 151
    cowboy rolls/ His p., SMIT W 2
    face the murderous, cowardly p.,
    MCKA 7
    wicked p. of cards. ELIOT T 116
packed: boxes, all carefully p.,
    CARRO 16
    p. a lot of things ROBI 50
    p. like squares of wheat:
    LARK 22
packers: movements of p.;
    AUDE 88
packs: p. and sects of great ones,
    SHAK 84
    twenty-four p., — HART 2
pact: p. with you, Walt Whitman —/
    POUN 52
paction: p. tween them twa,
    UNKN 114
pad: dolor of p. and paper-weight,
    ROET 7
paddle: p. in the cold/
    Companionable streams
    YEATS 166
paddler: every p.'s heritage —
    YEATS 9
paddles: p. in a halcyon sea;
    ROSS C 1

paddling: Splashing and p. with hoofs of a goat, BROWNI E 2

pæan: p. of old days! POE 30

Pagan: mercy brought me from my P. land, WHEA 1

P. suckled in a creed outworn; WORD 160

page: All but the p. prescrib'd, POPE A 63

heavy p./ Of death, SPEND 6

my p. for English B. HUGH L 17

p. is printed. HUGH T 14

p. of the book carelessly open, SEXT 18

what one sweet p. can teach, PATM 2

Pageant: crumbling P. shall devour, DRYD 27

p. of his bleeding heart? ARNO 35

this insubstantial p. faded, SHAK 163

pageants: black vesper's p. SHAK 9

pages: living p. of God's book. LOWE J 16

p. of her battle years, THOMP W 4

thick black p.! LARK 12

Pagoda: old Moulmein P., KIPL 9

paid: bills to be p., AUDE 17

God is p. POPE A 127

p. her last debt/ To Nature, DONN 53

p. to night. KING H 5

p. with moan, THOMP F 3

pay as if not p. before. SHAK 195

your gift will be p. in kind, BRID 3

pail: carries a refuse p., WHITM 115

good for a baby in a milking p. THOMA D 42

milk comes frozen home in p., SHAK 101

pain: After great p., DICKI 1

After long grief and p., TENN 97

all pleasures are but p., BEAU/BASS 2

Astonishment takes from us sense of p. CONS 1

born in other's p., THOMP F 3

breathe their words in p. SHAK 87

brother's p. and sorrow WHITT 10

clenched on a round p.; THOMA D 5

Die of a rose in aromatic p.? POPE A 70

dish of p., TICH 1

draw thy breath in p. SHAK 41

dreary unnamable p. LANIE 4

Error, wounded, writhes in p., BRYA 3

Excuse from P. DICKI 27

felt no p., SHEL 91

grief an' p., BURN 63

grievous pleasure and p. SWIN 22

habit-forming p., AUDE 73

Is it the p. affrights? JONS 32

It is p. remembered. PLUM 2

it is the p., endures. EMPS 5

laughter, p., and love. MERR 8

lengthened out/ To deathless p.? MILT 98

living is a p. DRYD 28

memory's rapturous p.; BRON 13

music, yearning like a God in p., KEAT 7

my choking p., WOOL 2

narrow aisles of p. WILC 3

New periods of p. DICKI 118

no fiery throbbing p., JOHN S (1709–1784) 4

nor help for p.; ARNO 3

old-world p. ARNO 18

On p. of punishment, SHAK 3

Oppressed with p., WYAT 13

overhear/ a cry of p. BISH 23

p. and labour grows PRIN 1

P. comes from the darkness JARR 21

p., darkness and cold. BROWNI R 69

P. godfathered me. CULL 15

P. has an element of blank — DICKI 117

p. is worse to the strong, JEFFE 14

p. it was to drown! SHAK 97

p./ Of death denounced, MILT 95

p./ Of finite hearts that yearn BROWNI R 82

p., still in the middle distance, SHAP 17

p./ You wake to is not yours. PLATH 70

part of p., STEVENS 56

piercing p., STEVENSO R 2

pleasures banish p. WATT I 8

pomp/ Of p. swells WARR 7

racks of P., GRAY 26

raging love with extreme p SURR 6

riches left, not got with p.; MARTIA 1

rise superior to my p., WESL C 1

sense of grief and p. LUCR 3

sincerest laughter/ With some p. is fraught; SHEL 71

souls in p., WILD 2

Sweet reward for sharpest p. SIDN 28

take some pleasure of my p., SIDN 5

With frantic p. BLAK 46

Without pleasure, without p., THOMA E 8

paine: drowne your p., HERR 25

wearie out my p., LODG 3

paines: age and p. brought to decay, BRAD 1

painful: pease their p. woe. WYAT 3

some sports are p., SHAK 160

painfully: learn all so p., WARR 2

P. to the stake, HECH 14

pains: chanter of p. and joys, WHITM 63

drowsy numbness pains My sense, KEAT 44

made my p. his prey. SPENS 23

mother's p. and benefits SHAK 72

Muses never knew their p. CRAB 4

not worth His p.; BROWNI R 16

P. not the heart, SACK 1

p./ the bruising; BROO G 14

p. the immortal spirit must endure, ARNO 29

with such earnest p. WORD 78

Paint: agèd accents and untimely words,/ P. shadows, DANI S 11

bedstead striped with bright-blue p., WYLI 9

brush/ May p. the mountains and streams SNYD 48

fit words to p. SIDN 5

flaked off the p., BISH 30

p./ Like Nature? THOMS J (1700–1748) 3

p. the meadows with delight, SHAK 100

p. the souls of men — BROWNI R 28

p. the visionary dreariness WORD 114

p. them as you may; SHEL 81

p. till day of doom, BEAU/BASS 6

With purple p. DAVIS 4

painted: brother should sail a p. boat. WHITT 16

fears a p. devil. SHAK 107

idle as a p. ship COLE SAM 32

'La Calunnia' p. POUN 10

my last Duchess p. on the wall, BROWNI R 54

p. all with variable flowers, SPENS 39

p. chief, and pointed spear, FRENE 2

p. child of dirt, POPE A 9

p. space of the breast, RUKE 5

paltry, foolish, p. things DRAY 7

see them p., BROWNI R 25
stiff, p. clothes, YEATS 91
they are better, p. BROWNI R 25
thou art p. MARV 14
Upon a p. ocean. COLE SAM 32
painter: eye hath play'd the p.,
   SHAK 191
Imagine a p. crucified ASHB 5
modish p. shirk YEATS 156
p. saw what was, GUNN 5
through the p. SHAK 192
wily p., GUNN 4
paints: nature p. her colors,
   MILT 79
pair: burglars stole that p. away!
   FIEL E 2
furnish out a p. SWIF 21
p. of stainless maidenhoods.
   SHAK 149
precious p. of poets, AIKE 2
union of this ever-diverse p.!
   MERE G 13
youthful, loving, modest p.
   BURN 19
pairs: Yesterdays in p., —
   DICKI 26
palace: fair and stately p. POE 20
hollow oak our p. is, CUNN A 2
imperial p. whence he came.
   WORD 73
no go the picture p., MACN 9
p. grand, or just a plain, old
   shoe; UNTE 1
p. of a king, GUES 2
p. too great, BROO P 2
Runs in blood down P. walls
   BLAK 75
palaces: p. of patience, WILB 47
ploughs down p., CAMPB R 6
Paladin: Easygoing/ P., GILB 16
paladins: sing of knights and p.
   DANI S 11
palate: air tastes good to my p.
   WHITM 75
palaver: p. is finished. ELIOT T 56
pale: cheek so p. and chill;
   DODG 1
Dark faces p. against that rosy
   flame, TENN 81
death's p. flag SHAK 152
Gilding p. streams SHAK 197
kingly Death/ Keeps his p. court
   SHEL 1
leaves looke p., SHAK 224
make p. my cheeks with care
   WITH 1
Naked and blind and p. JARR 1
O p. Galilean; SWIN 23
Over park, over p., SHAK 126
p. and brittle pencils ever
   JEFFE 17
p. angle of time/ And eternity.
   MOMA 2

P. Anguish keeps the heavy gate,
   WILD 3
p. antlers barely stirring GUNN 2
p. bleeding lips MONTA 5
p. captives, creep to death.
   SHIR 2
p. curves of your ribs, HALL 3
p. deputations/ Of temperance
   workers SITW 3
p. despair SHEL 22
p. dispensers of my Joys
   HOPE L 2
p. dull pallor of an old gas light
   HUGH L 18
p. for weariness of climbing
   heaven SHEL 88
P. hands, pink-tipped, HOPE L 3
p. kings, and princes too,
   KEAT 32
p. moon gleams: OSHA 1
p. now, those rosy lips, BURN 31
p. parting-line in hair HARD 34
p. skull protruding under ashen
   skin GINS 39
P. warriors, KEAT 32
p. woman all alone, WILD 16
red blood reigns in the winter's
   p. SHAK 181
rule and p. forethought,
   EMER 33
shuddring horror p., MILT 61
sicklied o'er with the p. cast of
   thought. SHAK 40
three p. beautiful pilgrims:
   AIKE 5
three p. figures AUDE 81
Through the p. door POE 23
Turn p. and starve. EMER 5
walk the studious cloister's p.,
   MILT 18
Why so p. and wan, fond lover
   SUCK 1
with cowslips p., AKEN 1
with p. tranquillity. WINT 7
world grew p.,
   JOHN S (1709–1784) 19
youth grows p., and specter-thin,
   KEAT 47
paled: fitful firelight p. and shone.
   WHITT 28
paleness: torn hair round their p.
   SPEND 1
Paleozoic: I was a fish/ In the P.
   time, SMIT L 1
palest: p. rose she flung EMER 24
Palestine: in sunny P., MASE 1
tomb in P. STEVENS 61
palette: sick of the p. and fiddle-
   bow, YEATS 77
paling: piece-bright p.
   HOPKINS 24
pall: black p./ Of nothing, MACL 4
Pallas: pallid bust of P. POE 37

pallets: Sunlit p. never thrive
   HOUS 47
Upon uneasy p. SHAK 54
pallid: angels, all p. and wan,
   POE 33
p. bust of Pallas POE 37
p. there as chalk, CRAN H 13
Slow on the leash,/ p. the leash-
   men! POUN 59
pallor: fumes a little with p.
   LAWR 41
pale dull p. of an old gas light
   HUGH L 18
p. of girl's brows OWEN 8
palm: dull thy p. with
   entertainment SHAK 23
her p.-crowned isles, TIMR 2
hold him in the p. of your hand,
   UNKN 152
Infinity in the p. of your hand
   BLAK 1
lands of p. and southern pine;
   TENN 11
lashed his open p. FROS 109
nail my left p. DUGA 3
strife with the p.; ARNO 8
What in Thy p. SHAP 18
wind is in the p.-trees, KIPL 9
palmer: like a p. fit, RALEG 11
palms: brushed past the p. BETJ 2
conscience is converted into p.,
   STEVENS 14
p. before my feet. CHES 4
palmy: high and p. state of Rome,
   SHAK 20
p. hillock; or the flowery lap
   MILT 69
palpable: poem should be p. and
   mute MACL 1
palsied: its p. hearts, ARNO 27
palsy: p. plagues my pulses
   UNKN 264
p. shakes of fear; MARV 12
p.-stricken, churchyard thing,
   KEAT 9
Where p. shakes KEAT 47
paltry: letters make a p. sum
   MOSS 2
p., foolish, painted things
   DRAY 7
Pamirs: Hsüan Tsang, crossing the
   P. SNYD 24
pampered: Forever p. and untired?
   ROBI 5
pamphlet: flat ephemeral p.
   AUDE 90
Pan: From that dear reed P.'s pipe
   LYLY 5
great god P., BROWNI E 2
p. of old days! POE 30
p. out on the prophets HAY 5
P. sounds up his minstrelsy;
   LYLY 6

P.'s Syrinx was a girl LYLY 5
panache: battered p. above
    snow.... STEVENS 28
Pancakes: P. and fritters, UNKN 24
panebreaking: p. heartmadness:
    HARP 3
panels: p. of white-wood, HOLM 6
panes: agonies of speech on
    speechless p.? SLES 2
    p. relieved of grime. RICH 8
pang: cause of my disease/ Gives me
    a p. SURR 4
    p. of all the partings gone,
    THOMP F 2
pangs: p. of nature, TENN 30
Pangur Bán: P. my cat,
    UNKN 202, 203
panic: falling fire and piercing cry/
    and p., BISH 2
    in a state of controlled p.,
    BISH 39
panic's: p. in thy breastie!
    BURN 62
panics: of curious p., WHITM 114
Panjandrum: great P. himself,
    FOOT 1
panoply: Thee in thy p., WHITM 99
panorama: "Where is the Mississippi
    p. SIMP 13
pans: Kettles and p., UNKN 24
pansies: pensive p. dark; MELV 7
pant: grief without a p.,
    COLE SAM 7
Pantechnicon: blow the gay P.
    GILB 44
panteth: hart p. after the water
    brooks, BIBL, O.T. 35
panther: called by a p., NASH 8
panting: p. lizard/ waited for
    history, STAF 1
    groceries in a p. gleam
    SHAP 29
pants: bulging his p., SCHW 10
    pull up your p., AMIS 1
papa: furious p. AUDE 85
papaya: glass of p. juice OHAR 14
paper: accumulation of p.
    RANDA D 5
    bread dry as p., POUN 9
    dolor of pad and p.-weight,
    ROET 7
    hand that signed the p.
    THOMA D 24
    kiss this p. BRAD 3
    moon/ Of Japanese p., PLATH 49
    Naked as p. to start PLATH 3
    took the p., HOLM 12
    snow storm of p., PAGE 1
papers: Bearing the morning p.,
    WILB 4
    p. are delivered every day;
    KUNI 3
    sandwich p., ELIOT T 129

Papiols: P., come! POUN 60
Papooses: P. crying CRAN H 22
    ragged p. jump, KLEI 3
parables: p. Of sunlight
    THOMA D 34
parabola: quick p. under the bridge
    LAWR 1
parade: p. about/ My helpless head
    WILB 42
Paradice: beleeve no P. KYNA 1
paradis: Hoere p. hy nomen here,
    UNKN 289
Paradisal: P. Imagineless metal,
    THOMP F 14
Paradise: desert were a P.,
    BURN 40
    drunk the milk of P.
    COLE SAM 22
    Fair as Eve in P.: HERR 59
    gather P. DICKI 44
    gauzy edge of p., SEXT 11
    glad surprise of P. VAN DY 4
    golden manacles stand for a p.;
    SIDN 4
    have their own P.,
    THOMS J (1834–1882) 5
    Here and hereafter, touch a P.
    MELV 22
    imperfect is our p. STEVENS 40
    loath/ To leave this P.; MILT 106
    mount to p. EMER 34
    No p., no fall, SNYD 21
    on earth the air of p. MICH 3
    P. and Calvarie,/ Christs Crosse,
    and Adams tree, DONN 32
    p. within thee, MILT 106
    Prophet's P. to come; OMAR 3
    Seem all of p. STEVENS 56
    sole propriety,/ In p. MILT 78
    South it is not p. WILB 17
    spindrift gaze toward p.
    CRAN H 50
    stillness that is almost P.
    ROSS C 21
    'Twixt earth and p., LINC 1
    Virginia,/ Earth's only p.
    DRAY 17
    Wilderness were P. OMAR 2
    Ye cam to P. incog, BURN 3
paradox: most ingenious p.!
    GILB 36
paragraph: life's not a p. CUMM 46
parallels: delves the p. SHAK 210
paralytic: p. stunned in the tub.
    ROET 41
Paranoia: P. into hospitals.
    GINS 24
parapet: with lofty p. LONG 28
paraphrase: soul in p., HERB G 66
parcel: beasts are p. of His pomp,
    SOUTHW 5
    p. of vain strivings THOR 1

Part and p. of her joy, —
    WHITT 7
parch: rain when the summers p.
    MASE 5
Parched: P. body, hollow eyes,
    DRUM 6
    wells are p. away? YEATS 123
parching: p. streets, SHAK 30
    p. tongue. KEAT 39
parchment: punch and perforate his
    p. ear. SHAP 23
pard: p.-like Spirit SHEL 6
pardon: beg death's p. WILB 33
    beg p. for him and for me."
    UNKN 164
    brought him a p. UNKN 165
    cannot help or p. AUDE 91
    God might p. every sin . . .
    SIMP 5
    kiss of the sun for p., GURN 1
    P. free truth, JONS 47
    P., goddess of the night,
    SHAK 132
    P., my Mother Church, COWL 13
    p. this clear flame. THOR 7
pardoned: from crimes would p. be,/
    Let your indulgence set me
    free. SHAK 168
pardoner: gentil p. Of Rouncivale,
    CHAU 4
    Love is no p. SIMP 5
pared: Had p. the dirt, SWIF 10
    p. them/ like toenails, LEVE 8
parent: both their p. and he is their
    grave, SHAK 139
    p. before thought, STEVENS 20
    p. of good, MILT 81
    p. of his generation, AUDE 94
    P. of sweet and solemn-breathing
    airs, GRAY 25
    when our first p. knew/ Thee
    WHITE 1
parenthesis: death i think is no p.
    CUMM 47
    P.-proud, BROD 2
parents: born here from p.
    WHITM 74
    Here lies each her p.' ruth,
    JONS 22
    lost general p., SNYD 19
    p. that first gave her birth,
    CAREW 5
    some p. of its own. UNTE 2
parfitly: He spak to hem that wolde
    live p. CHAU 94
Paris: Great P. tolled her bell
    SHAP 27
    P. is a woman's town, VAN DY 1
parish: gathers all the p. there;
    SWIF 2
Parisian: I shall die an old P.
    RIVE 2

Long p. his prime YEATS 45
low-vaulted p.! HOLM 3
O p.! O happy life! WHITM 66
Of the dark p. JOYC 1
p. all accident. WILLI 22
p. and loved, WHITM 12
p. and present all as one
  CLARE 8
P. cure I am, SHAK 242
p. his prime, SWIF 26
p. is just the same, — SASS 1
P. is too much with her,
  VAN DY 2
P. our devisal THOMP F 13
P. reason hunted, SHAK 236
p. the tyrant's stroke; SHAK 18
p. was a souvenir. STEVENS 30
reason is p. care, SHAK 242
Rouse the Echoes of the P.,
  GILB 43
Sheeted memories of the p.
  POE 17
sleep p., we wake eternally,
  DONN 18
sweep p. in dreams, LEVE 13
ten minutes to see me go p.
  KENN 1
Their time p., WILLI 8
things long p. SHAK 87
thought of our p. years WORD 80
till seven years were gane and p.,
  UNKN 249
time future contained in time p.
  ELIOT T 15
Time p. and time future
  ELIOT T 19
Time present and time p.
  ELIOT T 15
to the immoderate p., TATE A 12
trembling ages p., Æ 2
weep like a child for the p.
  LAWR 32
Who Present, P. and Future, sees;
  BLAK 66
winter is p., BIBL, O.T. 72
World is p. its Infant Age:
  DRYD 23
wrecked p. purpose. HOPKINS 16
Pastime: P. with good company
  HENR 1
pastoral: images of p. CUNN J 4
tender, virgin-like p. Evangeline.
  LOWE J 7
pasture: bare upland p. FROS 91
clear the upper p., FROS 21
cold in the p. WARR 5
fresh the level p. lay, INGE 1
his people, and the sheep of his
  p. BIBL, O.T. 49
p. of dead horses, HALL 3
when snow the p. sheets, SHAK 4
pastures: maketh me to lie down in
  green p.: BIBL, O.T. 31

Meath of the p., COLUM 1
on such frugal p. fed CAMPB R 4
Tomorrow to fresh woods and p.
  new. MILT 33
pat: "Stand p. LIND V 6
Pata Shan-jen: P. (A Painter
  SNYD 48
patches: Puffs, powders, p., bibles,
  billet-doux. POPE A 114
pate: many a burgher's p.
  BROWNI R 64
patented: p. terror, HILL G 7
paternal: few p. acres bound,
  POPE A 107
path: falter on the stony p.!
  TATE A 4
feeling its huge p. SPEND 13
Our p. emerges for a while,
  DOWS 6
p. of Him, VERY 4
p. thru it — GINS 22
Runs the p. I took; WHITT 32
straight was a p. of gold
  BROWNI R 58
pathetic: its fate was p.,
  UNKN 198
P. from the grass, DICKI 23
pathless: along that p. coast, —
  BRYA 26
in the p. woods, BYRO 1
p. realms of Space GILB 47
pathos: All's p. now. PRIN 1
paths: Haunting untrodden p.
  DANI S 10
here the p. divide; WATS R 1
In the church-way p. to glide:
  SHAK 128
leave the trodden p. of men
  SHEL 4
lowly p. of service free; GLAD 1
p. of glory lead but to the grave.
  GRAY 9
p. of high morality, BRON 5
p. through flowers. HARD 3
p. which before I writ. RALEG 11
pathway: lights the p. SANT 2
straight, hard p. plod —
  CARRU 2
through which the p. wound,
  WORD 102
winding p. BISH 46
patience: Add virtue, p.,
  temperance; MILT 106
firm and strong,/ Is P.:
  HERB G 12
give me that p., SHAK 74
heart's ivy, P. HOPKINS 16
horizontal monument to p.
  WILB 42
less p. Than a wolf's, TATE A 19
palaces of p., WILB 47
p. more/ Than savages could
  suffer. SHAK 4

surly p. of the serf CAMPB R 6
Teach me thy p.; GLAD 2
With a little p. ELIOT T 143
Patient: Beware the Fury of a P.
  Man. DRYD 1
calm and p., WHITM 98
I borne it with a p. shrug,
  SHAK 118
noiseless p. spider, WHITM 54
p. etherized ELIOT T 75
p. eyes, courageous hearts!
  GREN 2
p. lies/ Within a tent of green,
  KIRK 2
tenderness of p. minds, OWEN 8
patiently: endure the toothache p.,
  SHAK 131
Shake p. my great affliction off.
  SHAK 79
Patrick: grand old ballad of Sir P.
  Spence, COLE SAM 6
lies guid Sir P. Spence,
  UNKN 228
No more Saint P.'s Day
  UNKN 299
St. P.'s bounty, LAND 7
patriot: perfect p. and a noble
  friend, JONS 39
rest in peace, our p. band;
  FRENE 4
patriotic: Avenge the p. gore
  RANDA J 1
puffy, bald,/ And p. OWEN 2
patriots: queens, p., kings,/ And
  dandies, BYRO 37
Patrol: P. the halls on spongy
  shoes, WILB 31
patron: p., and the jail.
  JOHN S (1709–1784) 18
Patroness: Celestial P., MILT 87
Patrons: Drama's Laws the Drama's
  P. give, JOHN S (1709–1784) 9
Patsy: Verlaine/ for P. OHAR 5
pattering: chestnut p. to the
  ground: TENN 22
pattern: am the very p. GILB 35
cunning'st p. of excelling nature,
  SHAK 137
I too am a rare/ P. LOWE A 5
Made him our p. to live
  BROWNI R 45
Only by the form, the p.,
  ELIOT T 23
p. called a war. LOWE A 11
patterns: What are p. for?
  LOWE A 11
pattle: Wi' murd'ring p.! BURN 62
Paughty: Naughty P. Jack-a-Dandy,
  CAREY 1
Paul: Ere P. Pry cruised MELV 21
midnight ride of P. Revere,
  LONG 43
Paumanok: wash you P., WHITM 1

pealed: trumpet's mouth is p.
   BRYA 4

pear: emblem of themselves in plum
   or p. JONS 36
   golden nutmeg and a silver p.;
   MOTH 13
   O, white p., DOOL 9
   partridge in a p. tree UNKN 274
   P.-tree spreads COLE SAR 1

pearl: barbaric p. and gold,
   MILT 58
   great anchors, heaps of p.,
   SHAK 97
   P. in her tears, SHERB 2
   sickness of the p.; CHES 10
   Small and pure as a p., TENN 99
   swelling p., DAVE 4
   Tankards scooped in P.! —
   DICKI 68
   threw a p. away SHAK 138
   With p. dissolv'd in gold
   SHERB 1

pearl'd: Daisies, those p. Arcturi
   SHEL 59

Pearle: I saw thee P.-like stand
   TAYL E 8

pearls: p. in their hair, LIND V 12
   p. of morning's dew HERR 43
   p. that were his eyes: SHAK 156
   p. upon an Ethiop's arm.
   DYER J 2
   yards of p., HAYD 7

pearly: landscapes drawn in p.
   monotones. WYLI 14
   sensual, p. spouse, STEVENS 49

pears: pile new plums and p.
   STEVENS 58
   Prickly p., CARRY 5

peas: eat my p. with honey,
   UNKN 136
   p. taste funny, UNKN 137

peasant: bold p., their country's
   pride, GOLD 3

peasant's: boast their p. pipes
   CRAB 4
   p. last Good-night, LONG 22

pease: my lungs could bleat like
   butter'd p.; UNKN 194
   p. their painful woe. WYAT 3

peat: his p.-brown head, HEAN 22
   squelch and slap/ Of soggy p.,
   HEAN 12

pebble: shard, the p., and the flint,
   WILD 1

pebbled: towards the p. shore,
   SHAK 209

pebbles: Rough in my p.,
   SMIT ST 6
   with impulsive p. HORA 1

pece: holld my p. of them
   WYAT 22

peck: March with its p. of dust,
   ROSS C 37

one p. of purgatorial coals,
   BYRO 43
   p. of pickled pepper; MOTH 23

pecking: sparrows p. the llamas'
   grain, JARR 28

peculiar: exactness of p. parts;
   POPE A 35
   heathen Chinee is p.: HART 1

peddle: p. your hate WELC 2

pedigree: p. of Honey DICKI 119

pedigrees: chatter the p. of the rats
   SAND 9

pedlar: Come to the p. SHAK 182

peek: p. at the back BROO G 19

peep: Hills p. o'er hills, POPE A 34
   p. out once an age, POPE A 4
   saw him p. within; HOLM 12

peeped: p. through by bones
   SPEND 3

peeps: frog p. out o' the fountain.
   JONS 16

peepshow: ticket for the p. MACN 8

Peer: moving-slow he has no P.
   ROET 55
   P. now spreads POPE A 124
   When daffodils begin to p.,
   SHAK 181

peering: p., absorbing, translating.
   WHITM 64
   P., I heard the hooves TATE A 17
   P. through reverent fingers
   KIPL 6
   with thy p. eyes. POE 1

peerless: We stand up p. SHAK 3

peers: drunk delight of battle with
   my p., TENN 130
   elder dames, thy haughty p.,
   BRYA 12
   fare like my p. BROWNI R 69
   generations of thy p. ARNO 23
   House of P., GILB 24
   twelve p. as witness GRAV 34

Pegasean: flight of P. wing.
   MILT 83

Pegasus: P., a nearer way to take,
   POPE A 30

pegs: To cribbage p. GILB 41

peignoir: Complacencies of the p.,
   STEVENS 54

pejorocracy: p. is here, OLSO 12
   what pudor p. OLSO 5

pelf: titles, power, and p.,
   SCOT WA 12
   with P. and Trade. MELV 21

pelt: p. over the back of a chair.
   HUGH T 7
   tawny p. Of Africa. WALC 1

pen: antique p. would have
   express'd SHAK 228
   Biting my truant p., SIDN 6
   glorious by my p. MONTROSE 3
   hand and p. are not in plight,
   VAUX 4

of tongue or p., WHITT 21
outstripped by every p.
   SHAK 196
   p. has gleaned my teeming brain,
   KEAT 68
   p. that set a people free. MARK 3
   poet's p. SHAK 127
   shepherds p. their flocks MILT 68
   spared his tongue and p.
   SWIF 25
   squat p. rests. HEAN 13
   to p., DAY 12
   With such acts fill a p., DRAY 2

penal: Adamantine Chains and p.
   Fire, MILT 49

penalties: except the p., kill a man
   JEFFE 15

penance: knife of p. fell KAVA 6
   no p., much less innocence./ To
   teach thee, I am naked first;
   DONN 16

pencil: limned with a p. DANI S 17

pencils: pale and brittle p. ever
   JEFFE 17
   sadness of p., ROET 7

pendant: p. and bending arch,
   WHITM 73
   p. rock, SHAK 9

pendent: round about/ The p.
   world; SHAK 115

pendulous: p. auroral beaches, —
   CRAN H 11
   p. in air, POE 12

Penelope: Constant P. OVID 3
   P. was Flaubert, POUN 38

penis: tie up your discouraged p.
   SNOD 11

penitence: rid the world of p.:
   JOHN L 6

penitent: spake our Father p.;
   MILT 98

penitential: drouth of p. tears?
   WINT 4

penn'd: hands that p. WORD 21

penned: sweetness ready p.,
   HERB G 43

pennies: tourist's/ brown p. KLEI 3

Pennon: P., and plume, ARNO 38
   shakes our p. free, HENL 2

penny: p. in your purse ROSS C 9
   to one p. what I am worth.
   UNKN 160

pennycandystore: p. beyond the El
   FERL 5

pennyfather: some rich p.,
   DRAY 16

Penrhyndeudraeth: Tremadoc, P.,
   GRAV 40

pension: hang your hat on a p.
   MACN 9
   spend my p. JOSE 1

pensioners: cowslips tall her p. be;
   SHAK 126

pensive: p. cat gives o'er/ Her
   frolics, SWIF 6
p. Nun, devout and pure,
   MILT 16
p. pansies dark; MELV 7
p. Selima reclined, GRAY 18
p. smiles; EMER 38
with p. tread, LINC 2
pent: air or p. in stone, EMER 10
been long in city p., KEAT 66
pentameter: break the p., POUN 13
pentameters: book of iambs and p.,
   LOWE J 5
Penury: Labour, and P., GRAY 26
people: alien p. clutching their
   gods. ELIOT T 52
bring him home to his p.
   FROS 33
common p. of the skies, WOTT 3
creatures that do p. harm,
   BROWNI R 61
Did the p. of Vietnam LEVE 23
For my p. WALK 5
found the p. incomplete, WILB 48
full of grown-up p., BISH 21
funny p. make love RIVE 1
gregarious p., JEFFE 5
his p., and the sheep of his
   pasture. BIBL, O.T. 49
I see crowds of p., ELIOT T 117
Last of the p. who believe!
   ARNO 33
learning and blundering p.
   SAND 14
let my p. go. UNKN 115
like the p. to bathe in me,
   SMIT ST 6
million p. WHITM 44
mostly married p.; CLOU 3
my sad p.'s soul BENN G 5
100,000 p. disappeared REED I 2
One of the P.! STOD 2
pen that set a p. free. MARK 3
p. all exulting, WHITM 45
p. and beasts STEPHENS 12
p. and love NIMS 3
p. dress that way MOOR M 4
p. earth/ sky stars, OHAR 19
p. like me! BROWN B 1
p. listens; SCOT WA 1
p. looking back. VAN DY 2
p. make/ You feel so tired
   FIEL R 1
p. of common sense damn
   metres, LOWE J 5
p. used to meet! RICH 6
p. we had killed JARR 15
p. will live on. SAND 14
p. with equity. BIBL, O.T. 47
P.'s liberty!
   JOHN S (1822–1882) 1
P.'s violent Love and Hate;
   CLEV 1

These poems, p., SNYD 51
three kinds of p.: ABRA 1
to market-place and p. HOUS 5
Toe'osh scattered white p.
   SILKO 2
we were her p. FROS 49
what other p. think; YEATS 132
peopled: p. kingdom. SHAK 55
p. labyrinth of walls, SHEL 36
peoples: Hymen p. every town;
   SHAK 16
standards of the p. TENN 75
pepper: peck of pickled p.;
   MOTH 23
perced: p. to the roote, CHAU 3
perceiv'd: no pace p.! SHAK 227
perceive: Argus' eyes p. you.'
   SIDN 31
enlightened to p. DICKI 118
p. the world's a dream.
   BROWNI R 14
perceived: I have p. much beauty
   OWEN 11
perchance: did to nothing, p.
   BROWNI R 18
hear p. a trumpet sound,
   SHAK 125
To sleep; p. to dream: SHAK 39
perched: Two crows p. SHEL 63
perches: p. in the soul — DICKI 29
perdition: To bottomless p.,
   MILT 49
perdy: What no, p.! WYAT 27
perennial: Lilac blooming p.
   WHITM 46
perfeccioun: Virginitee is greet p.,
   CHAU 93
perfect: bed of p. health,
   WHITM 108
blest with p. rest, VAN DY 5
come p. days; LOWE J 17
fast, p., and unwilling TATE J 4
glory of this p. day JOHN G 2
heaven a p. round. BROWNI R 2
highest p. enlightenment.
   SNYD 25
law of the Lord is p.,
   BIBL, O.T. 28
long, p. loveliness of sow.
   KINN 15
'Love is the p. sum HUME 1
Maiden most p., SWIN 4
Man's as p. as he ought:
   POPE A 62
One p. limousine, PARK 1
One p. rose. PARK 1
p. beauty of a sunflower!
   GINS 35
p. Diapason, MILT 2
p. for my city, WHITM 43
p. grief ROSS D 10
p. health begin, WHITM 74

p. Judge will read each work of
   Wit POPE A 34
p. law of love VERY 4
P. little body, BRID R 17
p. silence at the stars.
   WHITM 111
p. Woman, nobly planned,
   WORD 135
to the p. whole. EMER 19
Work out a p. will. JOHN L 5
Your p. body JOHN H 4
perfected: symbol p. in death.
   ELIOT T 69
woman is p. PLATH 37
Perfection: forced to choose/ P.
   YEATS 23
her p. is my wound. KING H 7
Holds in p. SHAK 187
into p. THOMS J (1700–1748) 6
p. in you WHITM 22
Retain that dear p. SHAK 142
right p. wrongfully disgrac'd,
   SHAK 213
white p. AUDE 9
perfections: All her p. tarnished —
   RANS 5
all p. keep. UNKN 141
p. on the breast, HERB G 1
perfectly: entrechat/ p. achieved
   WILLI 1
fully and p. man. LOWE J 3
perfidy: when she felt this p.,
   DAVID 1
perforate: punch and p. his
   parchment ear. SHAP 23
perform: His wonders to p.;
   COWP 4
p. their tragic play, YEATS 78
performance: p. keeps no day;
   CAMPI 10
performed: promised that is not p.
   GRAV 5
solemn sacrifice, performed in state,
   POPE A 105
performs: p. its love, KIRK 4
p. its secret ministry,
   COLE SAM 13
perfume: atmosphere is not a p.,
   WHITM 75
downed with light brown hair!)/ Is
   it p. from a dress ELIOT T 85
p. our burying; WEBS 1
rich p., HERR 34
sweeten and p. my death.
   KING H 1
perfumed: p. chambers of the
   great, SHAK 54
p. that/ The winds were lovesick
   SHAK 5
p. tincture of the roses,
   SHAK 206
perfumes: Bear only p. THOR 9
in some p. SHAK 237

strange synthetic p., ELIOT T 121
Three April p. SHAK 227
perhaps: like a p. hand CUMM 54
p. Itali-an! GILB 20
peril: p. of your pride, ROBI 5
perilous: foam/ Of p. seas, KEAT 50
p. and beautiful. RANS 17
p. rock, SOUTHE 5
p. to hear. WORD 129
sandy p. wildes, MILT 3
through the p. fight, KEY 1
period: At any other p. DICKI 101
Fate put a P. to the Farce;
SWIF 15
periods: New p. of pain. DICKI 118
Peripatetic: magnetic,/ P. Lover
GILB 34
perish: day p. wherein I was born,
BIBL, O.T. 9
let all thine enemies p.,
BIBL, O.T. 20
p. all at the heart.' UNKN 36
p., as the quickening breath of
God BRYA 17
p. in our own. THOMP F 3
p. in the flood. CULL 11
p. with the flowers. BRYA 11
shall p. unconsoled. LANG 1
they p. and they suffer —
TENN 91
To p., or to live? DICKI 153
way of the ungodly shall p.
BIBL, O.T. 22
perishable: homage to the p. clay,
BROWNI R 28
perish'd: We p., each alone:
COWP 2
perished: good things have p.
utterly, WILD 11
Just because it p.? MILLA 23
p. in his pride; WORD 121
p. in the cause of Right. BRYA 6
p. in the simple prayer
CLARK A 2
p. leaves of Hope, ROSS D 3
perishing: shine, p. republic.
JEFFE 38
perjured: lust/ Is p., murderous,
SHAK 236
perjury: p., in the highest degree,
SHAK 99
permanent: Stands p. BRAD 12
tomorrow is our p. address
CUMM 2
permanently: p., seriously WILLI 6
plant you p. within us,
WHITM 22
permission: place of first p.,
DUNC 1
permit: p. her to get the mange.
STEPHENS 4
perne: p. in a gyre, YEATS 128

Perpetual: breed/ P. benediction:
WORD 80
P. in P. change, MASE 6
p. whirl/ Of trivial objects,
WORD 109
Rooted in one dear p. place.
YEATS 110
round at the same height/ in p.
sunset, BISH 26
perpetually: Chinese jar still/ Moves
p. ELIOT T 23
p. crouched, CUMM 40
Stealthily and p. BRID R 8
perpetuating: cease p. you,
WHITM 67
perpetuitee: loving kindenes lasts/
To p. BIBL, O.T. 54
Perplex'd: P. in the extreme;
SHAK 138
perplexed: fifthly, and stopped p.
HOLM 8
perplexes: dull brain p. and
retards: KEAT 48
P. Monarchs. MILT 57
perplexity: old p. an empty purse,
YEATS 24
perplext: pilgrim I on earth p.,
BRAD 1
Persephone: fairy queen P. Bids you
awake, CAMPI 3
P. herself is but a voice LAWR 5
Persian: P. carpet, HORA 10
P. garlands I detest, HORA 11
Persians: P. do not dwell upon
GRAV 20
persist: p. here and there MACDI 2
persistency: heart keeps its tough
old p. still; LOWE J 6
persists: self p. like a dying star,
ROET 43
Person: Ancient P. of my Heart.
ROCH 14
find/ Your p. fair, MILLA 14
no more a p. AUDE 31
P. from Porlock SMIT ST 8, 9
p. in the Spanish cape
ELIOT T 111
Something like a p.: SILKI 1
Thy mither's p., grace, an' merit,
BURN 44
personage: fashionable or/ Important
p.: AUDE 61
personal: faith not p. TATE A 7
in his p. hair; HECH 16
said as p. to himself. FROS 139
persons: p. had in admiration;
SWIF 23
random p. whom you do not
know — GRAV 5
Remembered, if outlived,/ As
Freezing p., DICKI 2
persoun: poure p. of a toun,
CHAU 12

Perspiring: P. pounded cinnamon.
HERR 34
persuade: flatter, cajole, and p.
GILB 61
glass shall not p. me SHAK 190
old men p. them. JEFFE 25
persuasion: Wi' sma' p. BURN 46
Peru: old man from P. UNKN 241
Survey mankind from China to
P.; JOHN S (1709–1784) 15
pervades: sultriness p. the air
MELV 10
Perverse: P., all monstrous,
MILT 61
p. sexe, DONN 61
pervert: To p. truth, MAST 4
pestilence: p. of love MARV 12
verray p. CHAU 111
winter, plague, and p., NASHE 2
pet: get a p. CREE 10
little p. dragon. NASH 15
petal: bruised and heart-/ shaped p.
MONTA 5
Now sleeps the crimson p.,
TENN 109
open always p. by p. CUMM 49
petaled: Creation's blithe and p.
word CRAN H 51
petall: (O filigree p.) THOMP F 13
petals: p. begin to fall, KINN 10
p. from an appletree. WILLI 26
p. from blown roses TENN 84
pursed/ Its p. up; BROWNI R 37
shook listlessly/ Two p. ALDR T 2
stint of p., DOOL 10
Pete: letter from our P., WHITM 15
Peter: Saint P. sat BYRO 67
petrified: eyes that p. my brain,
DARC 3
Petrushka: P.'s valentine pivots on
its pin." CRAN H 54
pets: died like aunts of p. or
foreigners. JARR 14
petticoat: tempestuous p.: HERR 8
petticoats: old whore p.) —
PLATH 51
p. coloured like flame. OSUL 2
pettiness: something to expiate;/ A
p. LAWR 46
petty: mind too strewn/ With p.
cares CULL 19
other p. griefs SHAK 221
this p. pace SHAK 114
pews: p. and steeples CHES 1
pewter: No p. and no pub.,
RANS 34
white and p. lights, PLATH 23
Phallic: Christ follows Dionysus,/ P.
and ambrosial POUN 41
phantom: p. looking down
WHITM 5
p. of delight WORD 133

phantoms: Death, stay thy p.!
  GINS 25
p. incessant WHITM 31
tracked by p. HARD 52
where p. may keep warm.
  EMPS 16
Pharaoh: Tell ole P., UNKN 115
phenomena: measure in p.:
  JEFFE 4
phenomenon: in the curious p.
  MOOR M 40
philanthropist: I'm a genuine p.
  GILB 6
Philemon: Here Baucis, there P.,
  SWIF 2
Phillis: P. hath a gallant flock
  LODG 4
P. hath so hard a heart —
  LODG 4
Philomel: change of P.,
  ELIOT T 122
P. her voice doth raise? WOTT 4
Philomela: darkness where P. sat,
  RANS 29
Philon: P. the shepherd, late
  forgot, UNKN 290
philosopher: never yet p.
  SHAK 131
Thou best P., WORD 77
Yellow-breeched p.! EMER 31
philosophers: fingers of/ prurient p.
  CUMM 33
philosophic: years that bring the p.
  mind. WORD 85
Philosophie: false P.: MILT 60
Philosophies: point their dull P.?
  ROCH 16
philosophre: was a p., CHAU 2
philosophy: dreamt of in your p.
  SHAK 29
Make Lame P. to smile. BLAK 10
make/ The best p. untrue
  THOR 10
search of deep P., COWL 15
swim with Bladders of P.,
  ROCH 9
phisik: gold in p. is a cordial;
  CHAU 9
p. and of a surgerye, CHAU 8
Phlebas: P. the Phoenician,
  ELIOT T 142
phlegmatical: Shark, p. one,
  MELV 13
phoebes: believe the p. wept.
  FROS 66
Phoebus: P., dipping in the West,
  COTTO 1
P. fir'd my vocal rage; BLAK 24
P. 'gins arise, SHAK 17
P. thrust out his golden hedde,
  SPENS 55
redd'ning P. lifts his golden Fire:
  GRAY 32

Phoenician: Phlebas the P.,
  ELIOT T 142
Phoenix: burn the long-liv'd p.
  SHAK 189
consuméd in the fire,/ Give me
  new P. wings KEAT 57
p.-nest, HERR 34
p. riddle DONN 14
phone: p. off the hook SEXT 18
phonographs: p. of hades
  CRAN H 31
phosphorus: through the p. sea.
  MELV 7
Photographically: P. lined GILB 46
photography: p.! as no art is,
  LARK 13
phrase: Choice word and measured
  p., WORD 123
many a golden p.; TENN 124
phrases: discourse in novel p.
  GILB 30
Phyllis: Desponding P. was endu'd
  SWIF 13
physic: his death, which p. did
  except. SHAK 242
P. of Metaphysic begs defence,
  POPE A 2
sceptre, learning, p., SHAK 18
physician: p. to my love,
  SHAK 242
physics: invites the occult mind,/
  Cancels our p. SHAP 4
piano: child sitting under the p ,
  LAWR 31
girl who played the p.? SIMP 13
great black p. appassionato.
  LAWR 32
p.'s martial blast/ Rouse the
  Echoes of the Past, GILB 43
tearful harp or glib p.
  WHITM 102
uncertain green,/ P.-polished,
  STEVENS 47
Picasso: P.'s or the Pope's HECH 1
Piccadilly Daisy: P. carried down
  the crew CARRY 4
pich: Derk was the night as p. or as
  the cole, CHAU 53
Pick: p. his teeth. SIMI 3
P., singlejack, SNYD 2
p. the Bishop's bones; SOUTHE 3
p. the bones HAIN 1
p. them up in the movies
  OHAR 3
picked: locks p.; HERR 7
P. up on a street. YEATS 88
p. up on the heather
  BROWNI R 53
sowdger boys have p. him up
  UNKN 150
pickerel: sidelong p. smile;
  ROET 11

picking: p. a manner of worm,
  OWEN 39
pickled: peck of p. pepper;
  MOTH 23
pickles: toasted pigs and p. and
  figs CARRY 10
pickpurse: p. of another's wit.
  SIDN 22
Picninnies: there were present/ the
  P., FOOT 1
picture: big p. of K. Marx
  SNYD 43
Breughel's great p., The Kermess.
  WILLI 12
cunning p. holds her still
  WILB 35
fell across the p. dead. DARC 4
find/ Your p. SNOD 14
great-uncle painted a big p.
  BISH 24
Immortal in a p. THOMA E 10
Me in my vow'd/ P. HORA 4
no go the p. palace, MACN 9
no p. is made to endure POUN 9
P. and Poesy, CRAS 13
p. her there. HARD 45
p. of Christ crucified, DONN 66
p. of Edgar Allan Poe. KOCH 6
p., once, resembled thee.
  PHILI A 3
p. postcards of Atlantic City
  GINS 10
p. shows, and spats, SASS 7
seek a childhood p.; WARR 5
take this p. DANI S 17
thy p. in my sight SHAK 204
thy p. or my love, SHAK 204
thy p.'s sight would bar,
  SHAK 202
Pictured: P. trophies to their grave,
  LAMB 4
pictures: Flemish p. of old
  WHITT 29
p. full, of wax and of wool,
  JONS 17
picturesque: p. Constantinople
  BYRO 52
Pie: Calico P., LEAR 2
Eating a Christmas p.; MOTH 20
Eating of a Christmas p.,
  CAREY 3
have no p. FOLL 1
No man's p., FLET/SHAK 2
pass yer plate for p. again;
  FIEL E 5
p. in the sky when you die.
  HILL J 1
skinny, stooped, and neat as p.,
  SHAP 21
Stibourne and strong and joly as a
  p.: CHAU 87
piece: his best p. of poetry;
  JONS 23

nameless p. of Babyhood,
  LAMB 3
p. of glass PATM 3
true p. of Wit COWL 10
Pied: call me the P. Piper."
  BROWNI R 61
daisies p. and violets blue,
  SHAK 100
p. wind-flowers and violets,
  SHEL 59
proud p. April, SHAK 225
Pier: P. della Francesca; POUN 10
pierce: p. my right side open
  UNKN 76
p. the deep wood's woven shade,
  YEATS 163
pygmy's straw does p. it.
  SHAK 81
whispers p. the gloom: ARNO 30
pierced: p. by the freezing bullet
  PAGE 4
p. the slow vegetable veins
  LAWR 16
Pierces: P. my soul THOR 5
piercing: love's p. darts, PEEL 3
p. pain, STEVENSO R 2
P. the night's dull ear; SHAK 57
Uriel spoke with p. eye,
  EMER 50
Pierian: taste not the P. spring.
  POPE A 33
Pierpont: with old P. Morgan.
  LIND V 6
Pierre: Poems by P. Reverdy.
  OHAR 14
pierstakes: crazy p. groan; JOYC 3
pietas: Who are these p.?
  PLATH 79
piety: accept my p. JONS 47
by natural p. WORD 58
so much P. as His. COWL 13
pig: defending a p. CARRO 13
human title, putting p. within.
  GUNN 8
p. himself becomes FULL 1
p. was supposed to have
  CARRO 14
to market, to buy a fat p.;
  UNKN 262
pigeon: skittery p. ROET 12
pigeons: casual flocks of p.
  STEVENS 62
P. settling on the bears' bread,
  JARR 28
pigmy: Between her legs a p. face
  HOPE A 2
every p. kicked it SHEL 80
six years' Darling of a p. size!
  WORD 74
pigs: p. can live in clover; WYLI 11
p.' eyes followed him, BISH 36

toasted p. and pickles and figs
  CARRY 10
whether p. have wings."
  CARRO 39
pigtail: handsome p. wore;
  CHAM 1
Pike: held/ P. too immense to stir,
  HUGH T 12
perfect/ P. in all parts,
  HUGH T 10
p. in his hand. PETRA 3
Sweet Betsy from P. UNKN 236
pike's: rusty p. in the cabin still,
  CLARK J 3
pile: man poured fish into a p.,
  YEATS 93
p. new plums and pears
  STEVENS 58
P. the bodies high SAND 10
stand'st an ancient p., JONS 35
piles: Magnificent in p. of ruin
  ADDI 1
raking p. of dead leaves
  SNOD 14
pilgrim: loved the p. soul in you,
  YEATS 162
p. here to pause. TIMR 6
p. I on earth perplext, BRAD 1
P. of Eternity SHEL 5
p., which abroad hath done
  DONN 44
To be a P. BUNY 2
weary p. to thy roof; CAREW 21
pilgrimage: blind atomic p.
  ROBI 33
endless p.,/ Dawn and dusk,
  GRAV 36
go on p.; BUNY 6
goe on a P. CAMPI 28
grave/ Should end thy p.
  HARD 44
thus I'll take my p. RALEG 10
pilgrimages: goon on p., CHAU 4
My p. last mile; DONN 58
pilgrims: Land of the p.' pride,
  SMIT SA 1
p.' and so forth CUMM 28
three pale beautiful p.: AIKE 5
we are but p. made, SIDN 8
piling: p. up the ricks KAVA 20
pillar: Fame's p. HERR 37
p. of your tongue. PLATH 25
pillars: Between the p.; MILT 114
row/ Of polished p., JONS 35
those two massie P. MILT 114
pillow: p. at night
  STEVENSO R 17
spread her brown hair on his p.,
  MACDONO 3
pillows: two p. at my head,
  STEVENSO R 11

pills: It's them p. I took,
  ELIOT T 127
swallow countless p.? GILB 48
pilot: p. of the Galilean lake.
  MILT 28
see my P. face to face TENN 10
pilot-fish: sleek little p., azure and
  slim, MELV 13
Pilots: P. of the purple twilight,
  TENN 75
pimp: to become a p. AUDE 49
Pimps: providently P. for ill
  desires: DRYD 1
pin: Petrushka's valentine pivots on
  its p." CRAN H 54
pinch: wants that p. the poor,
  HORA 6
pinched: p. his poke — SERV 10
p., indigenous faces LOWE R 55
pincke: p. and purple cullambine,
  SPENS 57
Pindus: top of P. SPENS 41
pine: cypress, p.,/ And useful
  sassafras. DRAY 18
frost on the p. bough SNYD 44
gods for my abode, EMER 7
In prison p. SURR 11
in the p. trees ELIOT T 147
its load/ Of p.-scents, ALDR T 2
knowledge is a torch of smoky p.
  SANT 2
lands of palm and southern p.;
  TENN 11
Love p. at them KEAT 47
my soul did p.: POE 7
pasture of dead horses,/ roots of p.
  trees HALL 3
p. cone falls SNYD 46
p. for what is not: SHEL 71
p. in vain the sacred Seven;
  EMER 7
p.-tree drops its dead; MERE G 2
p.-tree's withered branch!
  LONG 22
p.-trees crusted with snow;
  STEVENS 50
they p., I live. DYER E 2
pined: Youth p. away with desire,
  BLAK 54
Pines: Cover me ye P., MILT 97
hungrily pining for p., PRAE 4
in the fragrant p. WHITM 53
profligate of p., TOOM 6
sacred whisper of the p., TOOM 3
windy p. SNYD 7
pingpong: p. & amnesia, GINS 15
pining: hungrily p. for pines,
  PRAE 4
pinions: Melting thy p. THOR 6
p., ostrich-like, COLE SAM 43
slow-firm p. slanting, WHITM 24
thy prodigious p., WHITM 103
pink: In the p. light, BISH 26

p. and blue/ Of the sky LAWR 51
p. official form. AUDE 7
p. paint BROO G 6
pot of p. geraniums. MACN 9
rose is p. ROSS C 31
What is p.? ROSS C 31
pinker: Younger and p. every year,
   SNOD 4
Pinkham: Lydia E. P., CUMM 39
pinnace: p., like a fluttered bird,
   TENN 116
pins: files of p. POPE A 114
Guilt pins a fig-leaf; SPENC A 1
Pinsky: haunts of Robert P.'s
   PINS 3
pint: fill a p. bumper SHERI 2
hardly drinks a p. of wine,
   SWIF 27
pints: weep his p. AUDE 99
pioneer: p. souls FOSS 1
Pious: affectedly P. nor secretly
   lewd, PRIO 6
H[olland] took the p. resolution
   GRAY 21
P. Selinda goes to prayers,
   CONG 2
p. wish to whiteness WILLI 27
Sae p. and sae holy, BURN 4
shed one p. tear PRIO 5
some p. gentlemen HAY 4
pipe: for p. and dancers BELL 7
p. a tune to dance to, HOUS 50
p. that merry old strain,
   BRYA 21
p. that strikes Apollo dumb;
   LYLY 5
shepherds p. on oaten straws,
   SHAK 100
they p. us free, BROWNI R 65
turned into a reed;/ From that
   dear reed Pan's p. LYLY 5
piped: p. rats to its siren/
   Crescendo, MERW 4
Piper: call me the Pied P."
   BROWNI R 61
p. in the streets OSUL 1
pipers: especially p.;
   BROWNI R 65
Ten p. piping, UNKN 283
pipes: boast their peasants' p.,
   CRAB 4
What p. and timbrels? KEAT 37
ye soft p., play on; KEAT 38
piping: Ten pipers p., UNKN 283
weak p. time of peace, SHAK 96
Pipkin: This little P. HERR 38
pique: when a p. began, GOLD 7
pirate: p. gaped at Belinda's
   dragon, NASH 16
speechless p.! RICH 11
pirates: p. of the universe, EMER 5

pirouette: p./ Shellacked with silk
   SHAP 8
with a sleepy p. WILB 34
Pisces: Half breed son of P.
   REED I 5
pisse: Nicholas was risen for to p.,
   CHAU 56
pistil: p. after the petals go.
   FROS 64
pistols: Put on his p. RANS 6
pistons: black statement of p.,
   SPEND 5
p. jerk and shove, ROET 51
pit: Black p. cold and light-year
   SNYD 30
Does the Eagle know what is in
   the p. BLAK 12
p. of/ the empty/ flowerpot
   WILLI 3
wretched, blind p. ponies
   HODG 1
pitch: Above a mortal p.,
   SHAK 217
carry precept to the highest p :
   BYRO 20
dabs of p. SILKO 1
p. that is near madness EBER 6
roller, p., and stumps, and all
   LANG 2
savour of tar nor of p.,
   SHAK 159
pitched: Love has p. his mansion
   YEATS 39
Pitcher: P. of milk, now empty.
   PLATH 38
pouring from his p. clear
   MELV 9
pitchfork: use my wit as a p.
   LARK 20
piteous: beauteous form assures a p.
   mind. DONN 67
p. pretense of sleep! MEW 2
pith: my beautee and my p.
   CHAU 88
pitied: I p. him CAME 1
pitiful: mild, p., and flexible;
   SHAK 61
p. as she is fair, GREE 3
pitiless: gaze blank and p.
   YEATS 135
p. hours like years and ages
   creep, THOMS J (1834–1882) 4
pits: fresh springs, brine p.,
   SHAK 157
worked dark p./ Of war,
   OWEN 36
pittie: Love is not ful of p. MARL 5
pity: cherish p., BLAK 92
God p. me now MACDONO 2
God p. them both! WHITT 21
hand rules p. THOMA D 25
Knowledge might p. win, SIDN 5
love and p. him. SHAP 24

Man's p. for himself, BYRO 47
Mercy, Love, and P. dwell
   BLAK 89
no p. to myself? SHAK 99
no soul will p. me. SHAK 99
peace may wake and p. me.
   CAMPI 22
P., a human face; BLAK 88
p. grace obtain, SIDN 5
P. is not your forte./ Calmly you
   ache RICH 11
P., like a naked newborn babe
   SHAK 105
p. on a poor Parley-voo, GILB 42
p. on the least of things
   YEATS 15
P. our broken sleep; DAY 9
P. the planet, LOWE R 51
P. would be no more, BLAK 70
seas of p. AUDE 44
Small p. for him! — WHITT 24
sorrow and p. BRID 4
Spirit of P. whispered, 'Why?'
   HARD 11
washed the p. from her hands.
   KIZE 3
yield some p., woo her; LODG 5
pitying: Jesus, look with p. eye.
   DOAN 2
Till p. Nature signs the last
   release,
   JOHN S (1709–1784) 21
Pivot: P. of heels and knees! —
   PLATH 5
pivoting: p. searchlights probe to
   shock LOWE R 5
pivots: Petrushka's valentine p. on
   its pin." CRAN H 54
Pizarro: P.'s helmet! — Is a spider's
   kingdom; SCOT WI 2
pizzicati: p. of Hosanna.
   STEVENS 34
Placable: P. if His mind and ways
   were guessed, BROWNI R 17
place: Age finds p. MELV 17
athwart a cedarn cover!/ A savage
   p.! COLE SAM 20
avails not, time nor p.
   WHITM 19
barren p. and fertile. SHAK 157
blasts denote/ I am nearing the
   p., BROWNI R 68
bourne of Time and P. TENN 10
Brightens up a gloomy p.;
   UNKN 267
by a kind hand brought/ Alive/ To
   a strange p. THOR 2
cannot find the p. STEPHENS 11
central ton of every p., SCHW 9
choose/ Their p. of rest, MILT 108
collected in one p. AMMO 14
come to take your holy p.?
   WALK 4

cure this p., BROWNI R 22
draw me to her in the blessed p.!
  PETRA 6
dream of this p. WILB 1
Each changing p. SHAK 209
each sweet p. SURR 10
England is a cruel p. KINGSL 1
England is a pleasant p.
  KINGSL 1
every time and p.,
  JOHN S (1822–1882) 1
gathering p. of fears: JOHN L 7
give the p. a tone; UNTE 2
grave's a fine and private p.,
  MARV 34
greenest p. MOOR M 35
Here is the p.; WHITT 32
ill deserve the p. RILE 3
July in her eyes hath p., UNKN 6
know the p. for the first time.
  ELIOT T 73
leaves a lonesome p. against the
  sky. MARK 4
Long in one p., HAY 1
Make one p. ev'rywhere.
  HERB G 65
maps are of time, not p.,
  REED H 3
mind is its own p., MILT 54
Missing me one p. WHITM 74
never in any p. MUIR 1
no p. like home. VAN DY 1
not in that strange p. MCKA 5
p. among the elements.
  PLATH 61
p. avails not, WHITM 20
P. bo! SKEL 5
p., degree, and form, SHAK 58
p. i' the story. SHAK 6
p. of bliss. TRAH 2
p. of judgment MILT 102
p. prepared in hell, UNKN 78
p. that was happy PITT 2
p. to shew what recompence
  MILT 111
Points out the p. of either yew,
  SWIF 2
puritie and p. and innocence,
  MILT 77
reign in this horrible p. COWP 23
rightful p. to go; VERY 3
Rooted in one dear perpetual p.
  YEATS 110
seeks to p. it there CULL 17
"Stand pat"?/ Gone to his p.
  LIND V 6
'twas some faery p.),
  COLE SAM 43
unbefitting holiest p., MILT 78
yielding p. to new TENN 103
placed: p./ 'Fore damask roses.
  HERR 56

places: barren p. where men gather
  HECH 11
beggars have changed p.,
  YEATS 65
haunt the p. POPE A 129
immaculate public p., ROET 7
lived in important p., times
  KAVA 4
p. of drawing water,
  BIBL, O.T. 18
queer in queer p., SPENC A 3
shadows and windy p. SWIN 3
slam in thine high p.
  BIBL, O.T. 69
placid: p. and self-contained,
  WHITM 74
plague: famine, terror, flood, and p.
  WALK 1
gods still p. you! BYRO 76
memories p. their ears LARK 2
p. and earthquake, TENN 90
p. of custom SHAK 70
p. of deep disdain: SIDN 37
try/ A deeper p., DONN 40
winter, p., and pestilence,
  NASHE 2
plagues: blights with p. the
  Marriage hearse BLAK 76
palsy plagues my pulses UNKN 264
plaidie: p. to the angry airt,
  BURN 39
plain: Above the fruited p.! BATE 1
all's one level p. UNKN 250
base as is the lowly p., SYLV 1
beyond the p. LANIE 5
blue horse that runs in the p.
  MOMA 3
Curling with metaphors a p.
  intention, HERB G 40
fain for to water the p. LANIE 5
great Gromboolian p., LEAR 6
hear tom-toms just as p.
  JOHN H 1
horses of the windy p.
  CAMPB R 3
I'm a p. man, BYRO 20
in meadow or p. SWIN 3
listless look along the p.
  SCOT WA 4
long imaginary p., MONTA 1
merciless miles of the p., —
  LANIE 4
my language is p. HART 1
Natures p. Indictment DRYD 17
of the p., GOLD 1
palace grand, or just a p., old
  shoe; UNTE 1
p. as p. can be; UNKN 104
p. worn shawl LIND V 2
powerful p. manifesto SPEND 5
proved p. fools at last.
  POPE A 23
rough p. hearse WILLI 45

see it shining p., HOUS 35
see Shelley p., BROWNI R 52
stints Thy smiling p. GOLD 2
this p. reason, POPE A 69
through Concord P. EMER 48
upon the darkening p. MACL 12
Where all is p., where all is neat,
  HORA 10
with the arid p. behind me
  ELIOT T 155
Plainer: P. myrtle pleases me
  HORA 11
plaineth: Underneath my window
  p.?' SIDN 30
plainly: Who p. say, My God, My
  King. HERB G 46
plains: ballads of the p.; LAND 9
ringing p. of windy Troy.
  TENN 130
us burning p., ARNO 6
plaintive: p. numbers flow
  WORD 140
plaints: Bitter p. to rue thy wrong,
  UNKN 169
plan: hit a more excellent p.
  LOWE J 3
indication of the p. LAWR 55
little p. or chart, WORD 75
not a proper p. HART 3
not without a p.; POPE A 58
p. of attack. SASS 11
p. that pleased his boyish
  thought: WORD 4
plane: p. of molten glass, TENN 24
planes: After the p. unloaded,
  LOWE R 8
planet: half the p.: JEFFE 12
her in her cooling p. EMPS 18
new p. swims into his ken;
  KEAT 56
Pity the p., LOWE R 51
planets: how the p. gathered
  STEVENS 7
no p. strike, SHAK 19
p. in His care, YEATS 15
p. in their radiant courses,
  PRAE 1
plangency: p./ older than human/
  cries, HAYD 17
plank: measures his p. or beam,
  WHITM 37
P. in Reason, broke, DICKI 47
propped by a p. splint
  LOWE R 17
stepped from P. to P. DICKI 66
planned: perfect Woman, nobly p.,
  WORD 135
sort of thing she p., NOYE 4
plans: maturing his felonious little
  p., GILB 37
p. were accomplish'd,
  WHITM 108

pleached: in my p. garden,
    EMER 15
Plead: P., Sleep, my cause,
    CAMPI 22
p. the antient Rights in vain:
    MARV 21
so what I p. is just. HOPKINS 25
pleading: cease your p. force!
    UNKN 237
pleasant: all p. fruits do flow.
    CAMPI 23
by the p. shore, TENN 25
England is a p. place KINGSL 1
England's green & p. Land.
    BLAK 35
fortunes of my p. choice. SURR 5
How p. it is CLOU 1
p. land of counterpane.
    STEVENSO R 12
p. to know Mr. Lear!' LEAR 7
secret nook in a p. land,
    EMER 28
standing on this p. lea,
    WORD 160
sweet and p. soil, UNKN 147
think him p. enough. LEAR 7
Thou prov'st the p. she, LOVE 4
pleasantest: think it the p. thing
    STEVENSO R 18
pleasantly: p. toiling for pleasure,
    PRAE 4
please: all to p., MILT 5
change doth p. a woman's mind.
    WYAT 4
each art to p., POPE A 6
every sport could p., GOLD 1
Leaves, lines, and rhymes, seek
    her to p. SPENS 3
must p. to live.
    JOHN S (1709–1784) 9
P. close that door. SERV 5
slight things do lightly p.
    HERR 18
they p. Him most BROWNI R 19
thoughts that p. me less and less
    betray me. GREV 3
we that live to p.,
    JOHN S (1709–1784) 9
pleased: fish that p. my eye
    LOWE R 11
plan that p. his boyish thought:
    WORD 4
P. with this bauble POPE A 81
pleases: as it p. best thysel,
    BURN 32
pleaseth: it p. me when I see
    BERT 1
nothing p. but rare accidents.
    SHAK 52
pleasing: beneath the p. task,
    THOMS J (1700–1748) 4
crystal streams 'with p. murmurs
    creep': POPE A 26

lascivious p. of a lute. SHAK 95
music hath a far more p. sound;
    SHAK 237
my p. eye or face, UNKN 181
p. habit ends,/ No man grows
    old, YEATS 73
p. shade! GRAY 13
pleasure: Cells for the passionate p.
    LANIE 3
did Kubla Khan/ A stately p.-dome
    decree: COLE SAM 19
draught of heavenly p. spare,
    BURN 19
dying is a p., DRYD 28
filthy p. is, PETRO 1
flesh had made him blind,/ Flesh
    had one p. GRAV 37
full measure of all your p.,
    WILC 2
grave with a perfect p. BINY 5
grief for p. take. UNKN 185
grievous p. and pain. SWIN 22
Heart asks P. DICKI 27
In youth is p., WEVE 1
less to your p. than surprise,
    BROWNI R 34
love of p., POPE A 97
marriage is dead, when the p. is
    fled: DRYD 16
Money gives me p. BELL 4
most pointed p. take
    STEVENSO R 2
my heart with p. fills, WORD 25
no such p. in life! BROWNI R 84
Of love and p. speakes. DOWL 1
Of p. and of fear; WORD 129
Of unremembered p.; WORD 29
pleasantly toiling for p., PRAE 4
p. is like raine, HERR 25
p. loves to pay/ Tribute to ease;
    WORD 63
P. never is at home: KEAT 16
p. of past years, MORR 1
p. of that communion LEVE 12
p. of the fleeting yeare!
    SHAK 223
Pomp and p.,
    JOHN S (1709–1784) 10
quick-eyed P.'s foes!
    FLET/SHAK 6
rich that gets the p. UNKN 219
room in the halls of p. WILC 3
shrines of Sorrow, and of P.;
    BYRO 22
sma' p. it can gie, BURN 2
Smit with the mighty p.
    POPE A 102
some to p. take; POPE A 98
source of an exquisite p.,
    WOOD 2
take some p. of my pain, SIDN 5
true p./ Lives in measure,
    UNKN 185

when Youth and P. meet BYRO 6
Without p., without pain,
    THOMA E 8
pleasures: all p. are but pain,
    BEAU/BASS 2
all p. pass. WILB 6
all the p. prove MARL 18
all the p. prove DAY 1
he soothed his soul to p. DRYD 5
his own wisdom and p., WARR 6
in p. lappe did lye, LODG 3
new p. prove DONN 6
p. are but toys, CAMPI 18
p. are like poppies spread,
    BURN 54
p. are like yesterday. DONN 59
P. are not, if they last; DANI S 3
p. banish pain. WATT I 8
p. may thee move, MARL 20
p. of her own; WORD 72
P. only shadows be, DANI S 2
p. which Fashion makes duties,
    PRAE 3
pretty might me move
    RALEG 7
sommer and his p. waite on thee,
    SHAK 224
taste the p. of the poor. HORA 10
tear our p. with rough strife
    MARV 35
Wanton p., doting love, CAMPI 29
what p. man YEATS 72
pledge: p. of blithesome May,
    LOWE J 15
p./ Of immortality. MILT 68
pledged: p. event is still the same:
    MELV 8
Pleiades: Plato and the swing of P.?
    MARK 7
radiant sisters the P. WHITM 59
Pleiads: "Are you cold too, poor P.,
    GRAV 30
frozen P. shine: ADDI 2
plenteous: p. redemption.
    BIBL, O.T. 61
plenty: Days of p. BENN H 2
Earth's increase, foison p.,
    SHAK 162
have p. of go. SMIT ST 7
health and p. GOLD 1
honey, and p. of money, LEAR 10
Horn of P. is undone. YEATS 107
Of peace and p., DAY 1
part of p., SPENC B 1
p. of every pleasant thing?
    MORE 2
p. of money, BROWNI R 83
pride and p.,
    JOHN S (1709–1784) 10
She offers p., SPENC B 1
there lies no p.; SHAK 175
plentye: p., ioy, and peace,
    UNKN 63

plies: p. the saplings, HOUS 44, 45
plight: as in bad p., MILT 97
  hand and pen are not in p.,
    VAUX 4
Plinlimmon: Made huge P. bow
  GRAY 4
plod: p. behind the plough;
  CRAB 4
  straight, hard pathway p.
    CARRU 2
Plodder: P. through midnight rain,
  HEAN 8
plodding: of this p. life THOR 10
  p. through car-traffic PINS 3
ploddingly: p./ watching
  CRAN H 16
plop: slap and p. HEAN 10
plot: blessed structures, p. and
  rhyme — LOWE R 42
  frenzied brain that hatched the
    p., STOD 1
  memorized one p., SNOD 5
  Passions spin the p.: MERE G 12
  ripened p. to murder CHAU 47
  This blessed p., this earth,
    SHAK 88
Plotinus: Choose Plato and P. for a
  friend YEATS 151
  P.-Montaigne, LOWE J 9
Plots: P., true or false, DRYD 1
  Whoever p. the sin, SHAK 140
plough: Following his p.,
  WORD 121
  from market or p., MACDONO 1
  in the steady p., MUIR 7
  plod behind the p.; CRAB 4
  p. his field WHITM 7
  With p. and spade, SHEL 65
ploughed: Rise odors of p. field
  LONG 8
Ploughing: P. North America.
  STEVENS 39
  p. on Sunday, STEVENS 39
ploughman: heavy p. snores,
  SHAK 128
  Never a p. BELL 7
  p. in darkness plough? BLAK 61
ploughmen: merry larks are p.'s
  clocks, SHAK 100
ploughs: yok'd us unto p.,
  UNKN 296
ploughshare: Stern Ruin's p.
  BURN 61
plow: dragging/ the p. OLSO 18
  p. the rolling sea, VAN DY 3
  putte hem to p., LANGL 3
plowed: pointed as it p. the dust.
  FROS 103
plowman: p. homeward plods his
  weary way, GRAY 7
  p., was his brother, CHAU 15
Pluck: P. the keen teeth SHAK 189

P. the stars out of the heavens.
  JOHN F 1
p. was he to the backbone
  WOOL 3
p. you out of the crannies,
  TENN 13
p. your berries harsh and crude,
  MILT 25
pluck'd: p. the rose, SHAK 137
plucked: p. and strained AYTON 1
  p. for naught, THOR 2
  she p., she eat. MILT 89
  willing to be p. and worn,
  GREE 4
pluckest: O Lord Thou p./ burning
  ELIOT T 141
plucking: grandfather p./ A straw
  SIMI 3
pluckt: if not p. we dye, FLET J 6
plum: America the p. blossoms
  GINS 3
  angel in the gate, the flowering
  p., SIMP 16
  bees/ dig the p. blossoms
  OLSO 17
  emblem of themselves in p. or
  pear. JONS 36
  overstuffed p. sofa, RUKE 7
  pulled out a p., MOTH 20
plumb: Nothing is p., level or
  square! DUGA 1
plume: blast-beruffled p., HARD 18
  Pennon, and p., ARNO 38
plummet: p.-measured face.
  YEATS 142, 143
  p. sound SHAK 165
plump: calf that is p. and
  delicious; THOMA D 40
  chubby and p., a right jolly old
  elf, MOOR C 4
  proud,/ P. bed bear up, HERR 35
plumper: berry's cheek is p.,
  DICKI 103
plums: pile new p. and pears
  STEVENS 58
  sleek/ Blue ripe. WYLI 12
  solace of ripe p. WILLI 41
plumtree: p. is white today
  WILLI 46
plunder: ill-got p., NEWB 2
plunderwhere: There's p.?
  DICKI 51
plunge: hit a World, at every p.,
  DICKI 47
  moment of the cold's/ deepest p.
  WILLI 9
plunged: deep to deeper p.!"
  MILT 100
  p. your tongue WHITM 78
plunging: p. like dolphins
  JEFFE 12

p. through the thunder-storm;
  TENN 75
p. up to the knees; BRID R 9
plural: Incorrigibly p. MACN 18
plush: soft p./ Of sentiment
  RODG 4
Pluto: iron tears down P.'s cheek,
  MILT 17
Plutonian: on the Night's P. shore!"
  POE 36
Plutonic: dark/ of the arms P.,
  LAWR 5
ply: in peace our tasks we p.,
  UNKN 203
  p. the ball: MERE G 9
  thresh, and p.; HARD 50
Plying: P. her needle and thread —
  HOOD 11
Plymouth: P. Hoe. NEWB 1
pneumatic: promise of p. bliss.
  ELIOT T 159
Pocahontas: P.' body, lovely as a
  poplar, SAND 5
pocket: from his p. flagon,
  NASH 16
  heart is in my/ p., OHAR 14
  key is in my p., AIKE 8
  mother makes a p. of her tail
  JARR 1
  plates dropped from his p.
  SHAK 7
pod: Seeds in a dry p., MAST 11
pods: mild p. of his eye-lids,
  HEAN 22
Poe: picture of Edgar Allan P.
  KOCH 6
  P. printed cotton blouse. KOCH 6
  P., with his raven, like Barnaby
  Rudge, LOWE J 5
poem: house, the p., RANDA D 5
  hunger of this p. REED I 1
  love a p., OHAR 9
  Mark Van Doren,/ a p. of
  remembrance, HAYD 4
  p. includes them like a pool
  LAYT 1
  p./ is finished OHAR 23
  p. lovely as a tree. KILM 1
  p./ of his existence WILLI 32
  p. of my life. RICH 28
  p. of the act of the mind.
  STEVENS 32
  p. of the air, LONG 39
  p. of the mind STEVENS 30
  p., or chopped prose, KINN 6
  p. should be equal to: MACL 2
  p. should be palpable and mute
  MACL 1
  p. should not mean MACL 3
  p. whose words become your
  mouth OHAR 11
  read to me some p., LONG 15
  right subject for a p. SIMP 8

show her one p. RICH 28
taken in many victims/ back off
  from this p. REED I 1
tiny p. in that brain OHAR 20
written him one/ P. YEATS 60
poems: happiest when I compose
  p.: LAYT 1
honey of peace in old p.
  JEFFE 43
loneliness/ given away in p.,
  KINN 7
origin of all p., WHITM 76
P. are made by fools like me,
  KILM 2
P. by Pierre Reverdy. OHAR 14
Poets who wrote great p.,
  WINT 10
Reading their p. to Vassar girls,
  SIMP 9
These p., people, SNYD 51
writing these p.!/ Imagine!
  OHAR 1
Poesy: Picture and P., CRAS 13
viewless wings of P., KEAT 48
poet: Beneath this sod/ A p. lies,
  COLE SAM 40
choose his mate./ P. and sculptor,
  YEATS 156
consecration, and the P.'s dream;
  WORD 11
deck its P.'s sylvan Grave!
  COLL 4
every fool is not a p. POPE A 125
Every P. his own Aristotle.'
  BYRO 20
every p. is a fool: POPE A 125
forgotten, whom no p. sings,
  DRAY 10
I am a real p. OHAR 23
I was a p., I was young. FLEC 9
lunatic, the lover, and the p.
  SHAK 127
most gifted p. ALEX 6
one American P. LIND V 4
p. is a man speaking to men":
  BERRYM 15
p. like an acrobat FERL 1
p. lost to potato-fields, KAVA 27
p. of God's making;
  DRYD/TATE 2
p. of the dawn, LONG 8
p.'s eye, SHAK 127
p.'s fate WESL S 1
p.'s hopeless woe, TENN 14
p.'s matter Nature be, JONS 45
p.'s pen SHAK 127
preacher, judge, and p., JEFFR 1
sad Electra's p. MILT 125
smash of p." LOWE R 15
speckled shell/ the p. fondles
  LEVE 15
To make a p. black, CULL 19
upon the p.'s heart, POE 1

whole race is a p. STEVENS 25
why should p. in the twilight
  choose? KAVA 9
With haggard eyes the P. stood;
  GRAY 3
poetic: p. or natural. OHAR 18
with exact P. Justice: SWIF 15
poetical: write p. commandments,
  BYRO 20
poetry: dead art/ Of p.; POUN 36
eating p. STRA 1
Emptied of its p. AUDE 43
enemies of lyric p. SIMI 2
his best piece of p.; JONS 23
interested in p. MOOR M 34
Like a p. lesson AUDE 27
music and sweet p. BARNF 2
P. a riprap SNYD 26
p., by which I lived? KINN 4
p. in unconscious/ fastidiousness.
  MOOR M 5
P. is the supreme fiction,
  STEVENS 14
p. makes nothing happen:
  AUDE 41
p. of earth KEAT 58
raw material of p. MOOR M 34
source of p. WILLI 39
Wit, Eloquence, and P., COWL 15
poet's: good p. made, as well as
  born. JONS 45
poets: All ye p. of the age,
  CAREY 2
Black P. die as trumpets, KNIG 3
Black P. should live — KNIG 2
Milton's the prince of p.
  BYRO 19
p. among us MOOR M 33
P. and kings ROBI 7
p. better prove, SHAK 196
P. could not praise too much./
  Virgins come, HERR 59
p. exploding AUDE 89
p. honey their truth JEFFE 9
p. in our youth begin in gladness;
  WORD 121
p. in their misery dead.
  WORD 124
p. loiter'd in green lanes, LAND 9
P. of the proud old lineage
  FLEC 1
p. that are always gay, YEATS 77
P., though divine, are men:
  JONS 1
P. who wrote great poems,
  WINT 10
p.' fury SIDN 22
precious pair of p., AIKE 2
puling P. whine,/ Fame to their
  beauty, CAREW 16
sculptors and the p. were half
  sad, AUDE 53

Souls of P. dead and gone,
  KEAT 33
Tenderest of Roman p. TENN 14
then p. passed, POPE A 23
works/ Of mighty P. WORD 104
wretched We, P. of Earth!
  COWL 11
poinsettia's: p. red, blood-red in
  warm December. MCKA 3
point: at the p. of death SHAK 152
come to the p. GINS 3
each he nameth with a kiss.
  BROWNE 2
highest p. of all my greatness,
  FLET/SHAK 4
my finger, like a dial's p.,
  SHAK 93
Never to get the p. HOLLA 1
P. for them CRAN S 9
p., the still p., ELIOT T 20
p. their dull Philosophies?
  ROCH 16
To p. a moral,
  JOHN S (1709–1784) 19
point'st: p. the season; SHAK 140
pointed: feet together
  toes p. DICKEY 12
His p. skin cap. HEAN 22
most p. pleasure take
  STEVENSO R 2
painted chief, and p. spear,
  FRENE 2
p. toward the land, TENN 80
p. as it plowed the dust.
  FROS 103
pointing: p. handsome out to sea;
  STEVENSO R 6
p. At any stars. HOLLA 1
pointless: its p. sound MERW 2
p. wars of the heart. SNYD 10
points: faithful compass that still p.
  to thee. GAY 7
her hair/ Spread out in fiery p.
  ELIOT T 123
kindred p. of Heaven and Home!
  WORD 148
P. out the place of either yew,
  SWIF 2
Weaker in most p., stronger in a
  few, BROWNI R 16
poise: p. of the spirit, ROET 45
p./ Their floods LOVE 1
pride its p. DAY 4
poised: our boat/ Hung p. ARNO 5
small, p. feet LAWR 31
poison: dram of p., SHAK 150
glistening eye to the p. of a
  smile? BLAK 17
I sell thee p.; SHAK 151
let your p. be your cure.
  MACN 25
p. and traison at Rome,
  WYAT 24

p. in the blood ROSS C 11
p. the whole blood stream fills.
  EMPS 12
potent p. of your hate. MCKA 11
pumps yet the p. draught
  EMPS 7
put the p. It scarcely bled,
  RANS 19
vilest deeds like p. weeds,
  WILD 3
worse p. to men's souls,
  SHAK 151
poison'd: p. entrails throw.
  SHAK 111
poisoned: brims the p. well.
  MELV 9
p. by their wives, SHAK 89
poisonous: p. damp of night
  SHAK 8
p. toadstools MOOR M 10
poke: heart to p. poor Billy.
  GRAHAM H 4
pinched his p. SERV 10
tilted a p. of dust SERV 7
poked: faces p. out SEXT 10
he p. out/ His tongue, CULL 13
poker: in a p. game SILKO 1
poking: p. among the meats in the
  refrigerator GINS 38
p. my thin ribs ROET 26
pole: Beloved from p. to pole!
  COLE SAM 29
between p. and tropic.
  ELIOT T 60
from P. to P. MILT 65
I stare/ At the North P. . .
  JARR 20
police: empties our p. courts,
  GILB 50
p. the earth, LOWE R 52
policies: armed/ With assurance p.,
  TATE A 7
policy: salients of colonial p.
  WALC 2
polish: p. all the silver, GILB 13
polished: Blue bit of p. glass,
  MOSS 5
o'er thy naked p. ivory
  CAREW 12
row/ Of p. pillars, JONS 35
polishing: After p. granite
  LOWE J 6
polite: mentions hell to ears p.
  POPE A 104
politely: once again p. lying
  TATE A 6
politeness: you flirt of p., SHAP 5
politic: No thief so p., EMER 37
political: nothing p. impinges
  SHAP 11
religion-/ Vendors and p. men,
  JEFFE 9

politician: like a scurvy p.
  SHAK 81
love at all's to be a p., OHAR 9
p. is an arse CUMM 41
P.'s corpse was laid away.
  BELL 1
politics: from p. to puns, PRAE 1
image of such p. YEATS 66
Or on Spanish p.? YEATS 104
p. in the Balkans, SIMP 4
pollinates: p. the fingertips.
  BISH 34
polluted: Shun the p. flock, WYLI 1
Polly-wog: 'Slimy skin', or P.,
  BELL 5
polyhedral: p. eye and shabby
  clothes, SHAP 13
polyp: gilled but p.-like, SMIT W 3
Pomegranates: Breathes vineyards
  and p.: HERR 34
P. pink," DE LA 5
pomp: beasts are parcel of His p.,
  SOUTHW 5
golden p. HERR 48
in memorable p., WORD 102
P. and pleasure,
  JOHN S (1709–1784) 10
p. and train, CAMPI 9
p. of holy sacrifice GREV 10
p./ Of pain swells WARR 7
praise His humble p. SOUTHW 6
praise, p., glory, joy BOLT 1
sepulchred in such p. MILT 35
vestiges of p., TOOM 2
watched the p., EMER 15
Pompeius: P., best of all my
  comrades, HORA 7
Pompilius: also named P.),
  BYRO 21
pompous: your p. gait, JOHN H 4
pomps: p. of that time, LIND V 5
pond: every print of a hoof a p.
  FROS 123
fathom to this p.'s black bed.
  BLUN 4
his p. fished by his next
  neighbor, SHAK 179
surface of the ebony p. OWEN 24
ponder: I p. where'er I wander,
  MAHONY 2
pondered: I p., weak and weary,
  POE 34
pondering: p. dank stratagem.
  STEVENS 48
ponds: Like elvers in p., ROET 48
steeped in the odor of p., KUNI 2
ponies: lost p. with/ Dragging
  saddles — SNYD 51
wretched, blind pit p. HODG 1
Pooh-pooh: P. smiles, CARRY 11
p. whatever's fresh and new,
  GILB 31
pool: glass is a p. STEVENS 13

on the p./ They sportive wheel,
  THOMS J (1700–1748) 9
poem includes them like a p.
  LAYT 1
p. among the rock ELIOT T 146
water in a stagnant p.! BONT 8
pools: rain makes running p. in the
  gutter. HUGH L 1
rain makes still p. on the
  sidewalk. HUGH L 1
reedy in my p., SMIT ST 6
poop: p. was beaten gold; SHAK 5
poor: Although a p. blind boy!
  CIBB 1
"Are you cold too, p. Pleiads,
  GRAV 30
be honest if ever so p.,
  UNKN 233
beautiful p. BROO G 7
by heavens he must be p."
  KAVA 26
candles of the Irish p.; MACN 14
fears he shall be p. SHAK 135
fineless is as p. as winter
  SHAK 135
For this p. wreath, give Thee a
  crown of praise. HERB G 76
free and p. inheritance SHAP 28
get her p. dog a bone: MARTIN 1
grudge the p. old man FROS 21
heart to poke p. Billy.
  GRAHAM H 4
honest man, though e'er sae p.,
  BURN 26
I am p. once more! DICKI 58
if you're p. enough. WELC 1
immemorial feud/ Of rich and p.
  READ H 1
let p., damnèd bodies bee;
  BURN 2
life's p. play is o'er. POPE A 81
live in this p. rhyme, SHAK 229
Lo, the p. Indian! POPE A 59
Lord maketh p., and maketh rich:
  BIBL, O.T. 8
make somebody p.; BLAK 70
manhood of the p., LOWE J 14
most p. matters/ Point to rich
  ends. SHAK 160
no p. knight; SHAK 76
pity on a p. Parley-voo, GILB 42
P. and content is rich, SHAK 135
P. bird, he is obsessed! BISH 41
p. black cherubs rise at seven
  CULL 1
p., but she was honest,
  UNKN 218
P. comfort all comfort: PITT 1
p. folks as I; KINGSL 1
p. goes afloat PEAC 3
P. little timid furry man.
  ROSS C 6
p. love of anything, THOR 4

lack my roastbeef and p.
RANS 33

poet lost to p.-fields, KAVA 27

Rub a half p. on your wart
HUGO 5

smell of p. mould, HEAN 12

potatoes: fight with fried p.
BROO G 16

potent: grizzly bear whose p. hug
GUIT 2

p. poison of your hate. MCKA 11

p. quack, long versed in human
ills, CRAB 8

pother: woes of willful waste,/ Scorn
their counsel and their p.,
JOHN S (1709–1784) 12

pouch: knife in Sir Willie's p.,
UNKN 269

Pound: Heft them — P. for P.
DICKI 15

p. his head upon the sidewalk.
IGNA 1

p., you drums — WHITM 7

pounded: p. on the table, LIND V 8

pounds: "Give crowns and p. and
guineas HOUS 59

Pour: in thy bosom I would p. my
soul; STIR 1

p. contempt on all my pride.
WATT I 9

P. down your warmth,
WHITM 65

P. from the barrel, JEFFE 9

p. out all my self, POPE A 88

Thy silv'ry feet/ My soul I'll p.
HERR 33

poure: p. persoun of a toun,
CHAU 12

poured: Life of Ages, richly p.,
JOHN S (1822–1882) 1

man p. fish into a pile,
YEATS 93

p. down his throat
BROWNI R 36

pouring: p. from his pitcher clear
MELV 9

p.-in of the flood-tide, WHITM 19

P. redemption for me, KAVA 1

pours: p. its abundance AMMO 1

p. my meaning into you?
WHITM 21

Povert: P. a spectacle is, CHAU 110

P. is hateful good, CHAU 109

poverty: anarchy of p. WILLI 24

by p. depressed:
JOHN S (1709–1784) 1

Dame P. gave me my name,
CULL 15

fit of p.: HORA 10

honest p., BROO S 1

honored p. SHEL 75

Is there for honest p. BURN 23

Moloch whose p. GINS 17

mud and boards,/ P., SIMP 10

p., hunger, and dirt, HOOD 12

p. is obsolete GILB 52

p. the mind appall. BLAK 69

steal thee all my p.; SHAK 200

powder: brass bullet-mould/ And p.
horn, TATE A 10

break to p. SHAK 8

like fire and p., SHAK 148

litter of p.-parcels, WHITM 92

violently as hasty p. fired
SHAK 150

powdered: p. hair and jeweled fan,
LOWE A 5

powders: Puffs, p., patches, bibles,
billet-doux. POPE A 114

Those p. CAREW 1

power: another name for absolute
p. WORD 118

Autumn's p. FRENE 6

bow of p. is bent, LOWE J 20

by the p./ Of harmony, WORD 31

earthly p. doth then show
SHAK 123

emblem of motion and p.
WHITM 100

good want p., SHEL 52

Her that hath p. me to command.
WYAT 14

hiding-places of man's p.
WORD 115

his knowledge with his p.
YEATS 86

human p. cannot remove.
ELIOT T 70

King o' Scots, and a' his p.
UNKN 309

Language has not the p. to speak
CLARE 9

Lord! hast p. to save. WILLA 1

Love, p., the huzza of battle
LAYT 1

magic p. on the stony grange.
MUIR 7

manners, virtue, freedom, p.
WORD 41

no p. to sing, MORR 1

no p. yet upon thy beauty:
SHAK 152

not for p. RANDA D 5

p. divine: MILT 81

p. in the air; VAN DY 1

p. of joy, WORD 31

p. of love SPENS 10

p. Of Nature, WORD 51

p. of/ strong enchantment.
MOOR M 18

p. their love to hide, MARL 4

p. to charm, SHAK 19

p. to grow, MOOR M 26

p. to hurt SHAK 222

p. to kill, DICKI 110

p. to love, or hate, MARL 8

p. To melt that marble yce,
CAREW 14

p. To seal th' accuser's lips.
SHAK 81

p. to shake me WORD 3

p. to sing of thee MICH 2

p. was never in his thought,
SWIF 25

p. whose care BRYA 26

ringed with p. DICKI 87

sceptre shows the force of
temporal p., SHAK 123

self-same P. EMER 42

some unseen P. SHEL 29

Spirits of p. and beauty
CAMPB R 4

sun's life-giving p.,
CONS/CHET 2

sweet p. of music. SHAK 125

sweet sleep no p. can ever
banish,
THOMS J (1834–1882) 7

this that had the p.,' FROS 109

titles, p., and pelf, SCOT WA 12

To defy P., SHEL 58

Without — the p. to die —
DICKI 110

powerful: outlive this p. rime;
SHAK 207

p. fortress'd house, WHITM 42

p. goodness want: SHEL 52

p. plain manifesto SPEND 5

their p. throbs, WHITM 32

powerless: p. to be born, ARNO 32

Powers: Cities and Thrones and P.
KIPL 14

Desires and dreams and P.
SWIN 13

expending of P. AUDE 90

Grossly overestimated our p.
AUDE 12

ne'er be equal p.: TENN 15

numb the elastic P. ARNO 22

p. of darkness bound. MILT 64

P. that will work for thee;
WORD 153

pride of life, your tireless p.,/ We
laud them, ARNO 37

vanquished p. were glad
AUDE 53

we lay waste our p.: WORD 159

wounds and all our p., ROBI 32

Powhatan: woods of P., THAC 2

pow'r: adverse Fortune's p.;
HORA 5

Cleanse me from its guilt and p.
TOPL 1

Creator's P. display, ADDI 3

magnetick p., QUAR 1

sweetly sang of men in p.,
DICKEN 2

wad some P. the giftie gie us
BURN 58

with boundless p. I reign;
SHEN 1

withholds my p. that right to
use? MILT 109

powre: Nature p. her bounties
forth, MILT 5

practical: form of p. joke? GINS 3

P. to the end, WILLI 32

strictly p. appendages
MOOR M 19

practically: p. conceal its sex.
NASH 17

practice: gunnery p. out at sea
HARD 14

p. all that we believe: CHAR 1

p. and conviction WINT 6

p. continence; ROCH 12

p. for Eternity. WARR 2

p. to deceive! POPE J 1

practiced: violent, neat and p. skill
WILB 39

practicing: p. their aim on stray
dogs KINN 19

Practise: P. a tinker shuffle
YEATS 88

Praedis: Ambrogio P., POUN 10

prairie: bury me not on the lone p.,
UNKN 50

night of the P. Belle? HAY 3

p. flowers lie low: — LIND V 16

p.-lawyer, master of us all.
LIND V 2

To make a p. DICKI 148

prairies: hush of spacious p.
MARK 2

Launch'd o'er the p. wide,
WHITM 102

myriad fields and the p. wide,
WHITM 51

Vaulting the sea, the p. dreaming
sod, CRAN H 29

prais'd: express how much they p.,
MILT 59

praise: all-eating shame and
thriftless p. SHAK 185

bard whom there were none to
p., COLE H 1

Beautie be the Marke of p.,
JONS 30

conspires to p. her, POPE A 109

constant sacrament of p.
STEVENS 38

Damn with faint p., POPE A 7

For this poor wreath, give Thee a
crown of p. HERB G 76

free man how to p. AUDE 46

gladly p. the merit of a foe?
POPE A 24

hearts that once beat high for p.
MOOR T 6

Helpe me to blaze/ Her worthy p.
SPENS 52

How much more p. SHAK 185

in your notes his p.; MILT 82

into his courts with p.:
BIBL, O.T. 50

lack tongues to p. SHAK 228

mortal Muse thy p. rehearse,
DRYD 31

neither p. expect, nor censure
fear: DRYD 20

Nor p. nor blame the writings,
POPE A 31

pay no p. or wages THOMA D 28

Poets could not p. too much.
HERR 59

p. and adore Thee." NEWB 4

p. at morning POPE A 32

P., blame, love, WORD 134

p. God & his Priest & King,
BLAK 56

p. His humble pomp SOUTHW 6

P. is deeper than the lips:
BROWNI R 31

p. of ladies dead SHAK 228

p., pomp, glory, joy BOLT 1

p. to give. JONS 43

P. to heaven SMAR 1

psalm, the sorrow, and the simple
p. SHAP 10

rest a little from p. SWIN 22

sing thee a song in thy p.;
BURN 22

taught his p. MILT 82

thou own'st that p., COWP 22

turn from P. BROWNI E 5

wreathed garland of deserved p.,
HERB G 74

praised: p. in every kind of art,
HOLLA 5

praises: mule p., brays,
THOMA D 1

p. are but prophecies SHAK 228

p. of the child WILB 12

p. sing to God the King,
BROO P 5

sound thy p. everlastingly
MICH 2

Praising: P. God with sweetest
looks: — HOOD 9

P. thy worth, SHAK 210

praisings: p. of fiddles and flutes,
PRAE 3

praisse: p. withowt desart,
WYAT 22

prance: p. as they dance WILLI 12

Prancer: now, P. and Vixen!
MOOR C 2

prater: Foolish p., COWL 16

prattle: Thinking his p. to be
tedious, SHAK 92

prattled: time p. away, SIDN 4

pray: born to p. and save:
YEATS 137

Descend to us, we p.; BROO P 7

gone up to the church to p.
BLAK 55

hear them talk or p. SYNG 5

I p. that I may forget ELIOT T 5

I used to p. PLATH 28

I'll p. wi' woone said vaice
BARNE 2

P. but one P. MORR 7

p. for Kharma REED H 2

p. for me REED H 2

p. for our king and queen.
UNKN 216

P. her regard my moan; LODG 5

p. that come it may, — BURN 27

p. the Lord my soul to take.
UNKN 193

p. to God to have mercy upon us
ELIOT T 5

spirit give by which I p.; MICH 1

There starve and p., POPE A 19

to p. for our family — HARP 4

young men and girls p. for:
KAVA 13

prayed: Know I have p. thee,
HERR 23

ladies,/ That must be wooed and
p.; CAMPI 6

she p. to the angels POE 24

prayer: answers to every p.
KAVA 13

aroma finer than p., WHITM 74

beads and p.-books POPE A 81

explain to them his p. ASHB 4

fanes of fruitless p., TENN 36

Give ear to my p., O God;
BIBL, O.T. 37

Lord's P. on a grain of rice,
THOMA D 8

only p./ That moves my lips
BRON 7

perished in the simple p.
CLARK A 2

p. is more/ Than an order of
words, ELIOT T 63

P. is/ The world in tune,
VAUG 12

p. that he sends DUNB P 10

P. the Churches banquet,
HERB G 66

p. to the soul that grieves,
LANIE 3

reverie, of shade, of p., ARNO 40

say your p.: PRIO 8

their moaning is a p. HAYD 8

with us is p., TREN 2

wrought by p. TENN 104

prayers: all our formless p.,
HECH 6

hopes, our p., our tears, LONG 7

in spite of her p., AUDE 18

No p. or incense rose HECH 15

Pious Selinda goes to p., CONG 2

p. to broken stone. ELIOT T 45

p. thy soul. BIBL, O.T. 59
that which doth p. the ill,
SHAK 242
preserved: long p. virginity:
MARV 34
Preserves: P. us, SNOD 7
presided: Angel that p. o'er my
birth BLAK 22
president: our p., being of which
CUMM 17
press: Flee from the p. CHAU 1
meaning's p. and screw.
COLE SAM 25
p. of the storm, BROWNI R 68
p. the rue for wine. SCOT WA 24
p. was seldom known to
DICKEN 2
presse: leyd in p. CHAU 8
pressed: Johnston p. at the front,
TICK 2
P. to the wall, MCKA 7
Pressing: P. lidless eyes
ELIOT T 126
p. wind shoots javelin-like
MERE G 11
pression: air-like leave no p.
HERR 29
prest: on my cheek sweet kisses p.?
TAYL A 1
presume: p. not God to scan,
POPE A 78
presumptuous: p. sins;
BIBL, O.T. 29
pretense: piteous p. of sleep!
MEW 2
to some faint meaning make p.,
DRYD 11
pretentious: love a poem/ is p.,
OHAR 9
pretentiously: more p./ useless
WILLI 30
prettiest: p. little parlor HOWI 1
This is p. of all, SMIT ST 5
prettily: as p. as he! STEPHENS 9
pretty: Cry p., SMIT ST 5
for her p. sake ROET 28
in a p. how town CUMM 4
none like p. Sally; CAREY 4
p. dimpled boys, SHAK 5
p. pleasures might me move
RALEG 7
p. strawberry; SKEL 1
p. toys with thee to lie —
LAMB 4
this is p. SMIT ST 4
while my p. one, sleeps.
TENN 113
write the p. mottoes GILB 13
prevail: right p., LONG 12
whether it p. or not. PATM 7
prevailed: till she have p.?
SHAK 201
previous: on the p. night. BULL 2

Prey: Common Rule was made the
common P.; DRYD 19
greedy vulture's p. MARV 15
hastening ills a p., GOLD 3
made my pains his p. SPENS 23
new haunt for p., MILT 68
p. on garbage. SHAK 27
p. to all; POPE A 78
sick of p., SHEL 68
soon must be his p., SHEL 37
take the p., WESL C 2
takes his p. SMAR 3
preyest: p. thou thus POE 1
Priam: P. Cut down, TATE A 1
price: dimmed wares of p.
POUN 54
p. of mangled mind SIDN 39
p. on the wanted/ poster
REED I 4
p. that bears proportion
DRYD 17
priceless: p. blood reddens
WHITM 115
prick: no spur/ To p. the sides of my
intent, SHAK 105
woes at midnight rise./ Brave p.-
song! LYLY 3
you little p., CREE 3
pricked: Lust of glory p. their hearts
up, BROWNI R 48
prickles: in the holly p. UNKN 131
Prickly: P. pears, CARRY 5
pride: acned shame, punk's p.,
HECH 11
Albion's joy, Hibernia's p.
CAREY 2
all the summer's p., BLAK 23
all their mournful p., YEATS 121
ape the ways of p. BRYA 36
bold peasantry, their country's p.,
GOLD 3
casting-weight p. POPE A 16
coy submission, modest p.,
MILT 73
cried in his English p.,
TENN 119
from p., our very reas'ning
springs; POPE A 67
grave through p., POPE A 109
high-blown p. FLET/SHAK 3
In P., in reas'ning P., POPE A 66
Land of the pilgrims' p.,
SMIT SA 1
Let p. be taught SWIF 16
lovely summer's p., BARNE 1
Melrose rise in ruin'd p.
SCOT WA 4
nature's p. JONS 4
never fell — through p.; SWIF 4
nothing to look backward to with
p., FROS 25
Of that white p., HERR 35
peril of your p., ROBI 5

perished in his p.; WORD 121
pour contempt on all my p.
WATT I 9
P. and humiliation LONG 26
p. and impudence JONS 20
p. and plenty,
JOHN S (1709–1784) 10
p. and shame were mingled.
WHITT 13
p. bestowed on all, POPE A 79
p. did not our joys control,
STIR 1
P./ Had cast him out from
Heav'n, MILT 48
p. in Casey's bearing THAY 2
p. its poise. DAY 4
p. of Kings. POPE A 58
p. of life, your tireless powers,
ARNO 37
p. of man EMER 29
p. of pray'r: POPE A 103
p. that licks the dust. POPE A 12
p., the never-failing vice of fools.
POPE A 32
prison cells of p., WHITT 8
Quench my p. CULL 11
shown their p. HERR 41
soldier's p./ Touched to the quick,
BROWNI R 38
spite of P., POPE A 58
three summer's p., SHAK 227
too much weakness for the Stoic's
p., POPE A 78
Trembling, begins the sacred rites
of p. POPE A 113
trodden beauty like our trodden
p., JOHN H 3
we more p. ourselves? WILLI 30
with her foul p. SHAK 240
wonted p. MILT 56
worth any man's p. MACDI 1
yearning nation's blueeyed p.
CUMM 16
prided: feat on which ourselves we
p.) BYRO 44
priest: be thy p., and build a fane,
KEAT 53
brow of the p. KNOX 2
No capon p. POUN 3
Of lawyers, statesmen, p. and
theorist; — SHEL 79
old p. Peter Gilligan YEATS 14
praise God & his P. & King,
BLAK 56
p. all shaven and shorn MOTH 10
p. and bridegroom wait the bride
SCOT WA 6
true God's p. CAREW 4
priestess: inferior p., at her altar's
side, POPE A 113
priesthood: Lost manhood and put
p. on? VILL 1

pumps: among the idiot p.　UPDI 1
p. yet the poison draught
　EMPS 7
punch: p. and perforate his
　parchment ear.　SHAP 23
punched: doctor p. my vein
　SHAP 26
punctual: p. as a Star　DICKI 56
p. rape of every blessèd day,
　WILB 24
Punctually: P. at Christmas
　RODG 4
punish: so p. sin,　HERB G 27
punishes: frosty fingers p. my hair,
　THOMA D 13
punishment: let the p. fit the
　crime —　GILB 28
On pain of p.,　SHAK 3
punk: acned shame, p.'s pride,
　HECH 11
punkin: frost is on the p.　RILE 4
puns: from politics to p.,　PRAE 1
pup: truth about the cat and p.
　FIEL E 2
puppet: put the p. bowing —
　DICKI 18
puppies: Drown'd p., stinking
　sprats,　SWIF 9
Puppy: (I said to the P.　MILN 2
Purblind: land of ambush,/ P.
　manifestoes,　MACN 4
purchase: If a man might p. a wife
　FLAT 1
pure: clean hands, and a p. heart;
　BIBL, O.T. 33
Created out of p. intelligence.
　WORD 106
declare it p.　ROET 23
faith's p. shrine!　HEMA 5
flesh takes on the p.　ROET 45
I am too p. for you　PLATH 48
in each aspect death is p.
　JARR 23
jewel cold and p.;　MILLA 5
land of p. delight,　WATT I 8
Nature ne'er deserts the wise and
　p.;　COLE SAM 41
Of p. ablution　KEAT 3
pensive Nun, devout and p.,
　MILT 16
p. a thing is joy.　MOOR M 43
p. acetylene/ Virgin　PLATH 50
p. and circling thoughts,
　MARV 31
p. marble Air　MILT 65
p. products of America/ go crazy —
　WILLI 42
P. was thy life;　BRYA 6
purity of p. despair,　ROET 31
realm of p. Art,　LOWE J 7
ring of p. and endless light,
　VAUG 32

rose/ In them p. and eternal is.
　CAMPI 15
seems/ a p. announcement:
　HUGO 2
silence p. and smooth,
　LOWE J 19
Small and p. as a pearl,
　TENN 99
souls that are p. and true;
　BRID 1
white, p. as her mind.　MILT 34
purely: beauty p. loving　CAMPI 19
Fashioned so p.,　THOMP F 13
purer: sweeter manners, p. laws.
　TENN 48
with p. nutriment supplied,
　SHEL 79
purest: gem of p. ray serene,
　GRAY 10
love that is p. and sweetest
　OREI 2
Mind in its p. play　WILB 30
p. and sweetest　WOOD 2
p. kind of wit,　KIRK 1
P. Wheate in Heaven,　TAYL E 9
purgatorial: one peck of p. coals,
　BYRO 43
Purgatory: been in P.?"
　LOWE R 16
frigid burnings of p.　REED H 1
purge: p. the mischiefs that
　DANI S 22
purged: burnt and p. away.
　SHAK 26
p. its faith,　ARNO 30
purify: p. the dialect of the tribe
　ELIOT T 67
Puritan: P. marrow of my bones
　WYLI 14
puritie: p. and place and
　innocence,　MILT 77
purity: p. of pure despair,　ROET 31
soyl her Virgin p.,　MILT 3
Wooing his p.　SHAK 240
purling: search for every p. spring
　SIDN 9
purple: bees in the p. clover,
　COOP 1
deep twilight's p. charm.
　BYRO 45
his p. mass　DRAY 18
in their p. hearts.　DOOL 9
lot of wolves dressed up in gold
　and p.　NASH 20
mantling vine/ Lays forth her p.
　grape,　MILT 69
Mornings p. bed,　COWL 4
over the p. moor,　NOYE 6
Pilots of the p. twilight,
　TENN 75
pincke and p. cullambine,
　SPENS 57
Primrose, and p. lychnis,　AKEN 1

p. dark must bruise　JUST 4
p. flowers grow,　TENN 14
p. mountain majesties　BATE 1
p.-stainèd mouth;　KEAT 45
P. the sails,　SHAK 5
p. wardrobe in thy side.　CRAS 11
saw a P. Cow,　BURG 2
waves his p. wings,　MILT 78
wear p. With a red hat　JOSE 1
With p. paint.　DAVIS 4
wrapped in p. robes,　YEATS 15
purpler: rotting and turning p.,
　LOWE R 57
Purples: Morn/ P. the East:
　MILT 84
purpose: Black as his p.,　SHAK 30
concentrated in p.　ELIOT T 7
drenched there/ with p.,　GUNN 2
every p. under the heaven:
　BIBL, O.T. 3
Flesh set one p.　GRAV 37
flighty p. never is o'ertook
　SHAK 113
gentler p. runs.　THOMP W 4
Hearts with one p.　YEATS 52
one increasing p. runs,　TENN 77
ride it for a p.,　MAST 4
splendid p. in his eyes,　TENN 36
To what p., April,　MILLA 36
wrecked past p.　HOPKINS 16
purposed: how p. art thou come
　HOUS 6
purposeful: knot of little p. nature!
　EBER 8
purposes: p. to kill me dead
　HOUS 10
p. will ripen fast,　COWP 5
purring: suddenly p. there.
　MONR 1
purrs: p. in thankfulness,　SMAR 5
purs: Ye p.,　CHAU 117
purse: old perplexity an empty p.,
　YEATS 24
penny in your p.　ROSS C 9
pursed: p./ Its petals up;
　BROWNI R 37
pursue: Dreams p. death　SWIN 7
dreams p. our dead　SWIN 7
fifth you should p.,　SWIF 12
Glory p., and generous Shame,
　GRAY 27
I leap for joy, p. my way,
　WESL C 2
insatiate to p. Vain war with
　Heav'n,　MILT 58
p./ Thy solitary way!　BRYA 25
sanctity can't p. him;　PEAC 3
pursued: I p. a maiden　SHEL 28
pursues: decay p. decay,
　JOHN S (1709–1784) 14
p. her tail no more.　SWIF 6
p. us to the Urn,　STANL 2
pursueth: tempter me p.　HERR 20

pursuing: achieving, still p., LONG 37

I saw a man p. the horizon; CRAN S 1

She hers, he his, p. WHITM 24

sin you must be p., NASH 11

pursuit: demon of p. FROS 110

What mad p.? KEAT 37

Puser: Ambassador P. MACL 8

push'd: eldest cam and p. her in. UNKN 30

p. at chance and sufferance. SHAK 131

P. in their tides; THOMA D 29

pushed: inland woods were p. by winds, MILLA 12

pushes: light p. through; LAWR 1

pushing: America stop p. GINS 3

P. the Bear grass, SNYD 1

puss: furry nuts/ of the terrible p., OHAR 4

Pussy: Owl and the P.-cat LEAR 10

P.-cat, p.-cat, MOTH 24

put: Lost manhood and p. priesthood on? VILL 1

one was p. in a jacket, JUST 2

p. on earth a little space, BLAK 98

p. them there. FIEL E 6

p. them there. FIEL E 7

p. up your little arms CUMM 13

Saviours death did p. some bloud/ Into thy face; HERB G 20

putrid: on the slant hill a p. lamb, EBER 1

p. marshes. SHEL 18

putte: at the windowe out she p. hir hole, CHAU 53

putteth: out his ers he p. prively, CHAU 56

putting: p. Love away DICKI 17

puzzle: clenched like a Chinese p. RUKE 12

school-masters p. their brain. GOLD 5

puzzles: no-meaning p. more than wit. POPE A 96

puzzling: p./ Our sense of HOLLA 2

Pwllheli: P., Criccieth,/ Portmadoc, Borth, GRAV 40

P — xed: P. by her love, POPE A 90

Pyes: P. and Dawes and Rookes and Crows, BONH 1

pygmies: steal the p., LIND V 10

Pygmy: dwellers/ In P. Alley, GRAV 19

p.'s straw does pierce it. SHAK 81

pyramid: star-ypointing p.? MILT 35

pyre: heap the funeral p., THAC 1

Pyrgo: Roses, P., and Lapwater — THOMA E 11

Pythagoras: hold opinion with P., SHAK 124

Python: Clinging close with the crush of the P., HILT 4

Q

Quack: captain said, Q.! Q.! MOTH 15

potent q., long versed in human ills, CRAB 8

Quadroon: Q. mermaids, HAYD 1

quail: q. and shake the orb, SHAK 7

quaint: attitude's considered q ,' GILB 3

q. and curious volume POE 34

q. and curious war is! HARD 31

q. great figure that men love, LIND V 2

q. honor turn to dust, MARV 34

q. words and trim invention; HERB G 40

third so q. and mouthy: BYRO 21

quake: East did q. SOUTHW 12

we were woken by the q. EMPS 2

quaker: A little q., ROET 39

old Q. graveyard LOWE R 38

quaking: q. muscles in the act of birth, HOPE A 2

qualify: absence seemed my flame to q. SHAK 230

qualities: all the q. o' th' isle, SHAK 157

quality: all of museum q.: MOOR M 9

q. of loss DICKI 102

q. of mercy is not strain'd, SHAK 123

q. of Western man. JEFFE 40

regardless of q. POUN 31

quandariness: sleep with q. OHAR 5

Quangle Wangle: Q. sat, LEAR 13

quarrel: entrance to a q.; SHAK 23

Had a q., EMER 35

make a q. NASH 7

q. of the sparrows YEATS 140

q. with your great opposeless wills, SHAK 79

quarrels: little q. and strife, MERE O 1

quarried: scarped cliff and q. stone TENN 35

quarries: granite/ q. on the islands. LOWE R 56

quarry: Left in the q.; TENN 108

of an unseen q. EMER 44

q. cries on havoc. SHAK 42

q.-slave at night, BRYA 24

quarter: if we demand q.? WHITM 90

poorer q., ASHB 2

rich q., ASHB 2

quarters: Sprinkle the q. on the morning town. HOUS 5

quartz: mixed with q. grains, rose and amethyst. BISH 42

quean: flaunting extravagant q., SHERI 1

queen: By virtue first, then choice, a q., WOTT 6

choose the Summer Q.; CAMPI 8

every lass a q.; KINGSL 5

fairy q. Bids you awake, CAMPI 3

fresh as a q.; UNKN 210

gliding like a q., SPEND 5

God will save the Q. HOUS 32

grace a summer q.: SCOT WA 23

I serve the fairy q., SHAK 126

laughing q. HUNT 7

play at q. and king GRAV 12

pray for our king and q. UNKN 216

Q. all flowers among, HERR 31

Q. and huntress, chaste and fair, JONS 3

Q. Jane was in labor UNKN 75

Q.-Moon is on her throne, KEAT 48

Q. of air and darkness, HOUS 12

Q./ Of all are living, SYNG 4

Q. of Calvary. DICKI 42

then his q.; SHEL 37

queene: q. of shepheardes all; SPENS 50

Venus, that is Q. of love, SPENS 43

queens: old forgotten q. BENN G 6

Q. have died young and fair; NASHE 1

Q. of Love and Innocence, CAREW 12

Q. of Sheba, Meath, and Connaught, SYNG 3

q., patriots, kings,/ And dandies, BYRO 37

Q. stand up to dance. KIPL 23

queer: feeling and looking q. HOLM 7

ill-tempered and q., LEAR 7

Northern Lights have seen q. sights, SERV 1

q. in q. places, SPENC A 3

q. little squirm, UNKN 97

q. shoulder to the wheel. GINS 6

you look so q., UNKN 156

quench: hate you died to q. HOUS 4

I come to q. the kiss ROBI 23

Q. my pride CULL 11

quenched: q. with the cold of death. HERB CH 4

quercine: curr to q. shades! HOLM 1

quest: bless the q.   CRAN H 46
  crowner's q. goes hard   COLM 2
  my whole day in the q., —
    BROWNI R 50
  shuddering from the q.
    BROWNI R 42

question: color passion but its neck
    a q.   WARR 9
  never a q.   CARRY 1
  of thy beauty do I q. make
    SHAK 186
  q. is absurd.   AUDE 94
  Q. me again.   HEAN 8
  q. that he frames   FROS 86
  q. Who shall die?   SHAP 3
  q. with my jealous thought
    SHAK 208
  see every side of every q.;
    MAST 4
  that is the q.:   SHAK 39
  vexed q. of men   SIMP 4

Questioner: Q., who sits so sly,
    BLAK 9

questions: answer my q. three,
    UNKN 162

Quia: Q. amore langueo.
    UNKN 206

quibbles: quips and q. heard in
  flocks,   GILB 36

quick: every maze of q.   TENN 51
  Kikuyu, q. as flies,   WALC 1
  less q. to spring   ARNO 45
  nymph died more q., and the
    shepherd more slow.   DRYD 15
  O death, come q.,   CORN 3
  over q. hands   WALK 7
  q. and howling,   COWP 16
  q. coal/ Of mortall fire:
    HERB G 29
  q. comedians/ Extemporally will
    stage us   SHAK 10
  q.-coming death   MORR 1
  q. destroying lime   WYLI 7
  q.-eyed Love,   HERB G 48
  q.-eyed trout/ Or darting salmon.
    THOMS J (1700–1748) 9
  q., galvanic tread —   GILB 3
  q. silver bell   SHAP 1
  soldier's pride/ Touched to the q.,
    BROWNI R 38
  war's q. fire   SHAK 207

quicken: ghost begins to q.,
    YEATS 33
  q. a new birth!   SHEL 46
  within the sense they q.   SHEL 43

quickened: q. so with grief.
    GRAV 15

quickening: perish, as the q. breath
  of God   BRYA 17

quickly: O! come q., sweetest Lord,
    CAMPI 17

Open the envelope q.,   WHITM 16
Person from Porlock come q.
  SMIT ST 9

quickness: q. which my God hath
  kissed.   STANL 3
  with elegant q.   SMAR 2

quickning: Killing and q.,
    HERB G 31

quiet: after making love, q.,
    KINN 1
Easy live and q. die.   SCOT WA 2
everyday's/ Most q. need,
    BROWNI E 5
guest in q.,   LAWR 43
Leave not the bridegroom q.
    WHITM 7
Minds innocent and q.   LOVE 5
q. and chaste   LOWE J 7
q. as a Nun   WORD 26
q., as under the sea.   MERE G 2
q.-coloured end of evening
    BROWNI R 47
q. dead and the loud celebrities
    LEWI 1
q. mind;   MARTIA 1
q. mind is richer than a crown;
    GREE 1
q., negligent riding,   SWEN 3
q. of love in her feet.   YEATS 21
q. of my attic.   KINS 2
q. she reposes;   ARNO 20
scallop-shell of q.,   RALEG 10
something q. o'er His head,
    BROWNI R 18
to q. rest,   BOLE 1
where the world is q.,   SWIN 11
wife and children will be q.
    HEAN 15
winds are q. as the sun,   SWIN 9

quietly: q. ate the bear up.   NASH 1
q. stalks and spears/ the shallows,
    AMMO 6

quietness: q. of the womb
    JEFFE 30
starched dignity and the q.
    IREM 1
unravished bride of q.,   KEAT 36

quietus: man his own q. make
    LAWR 37

quills: q. upon the fretful
  porpentine.   SHAK 26

quince: Flower o' the q.,
    BROWNI R 26

Quinquireme: Q. of Nineveh
    MASE 1

quintessence: q. even from
  nothingness,   DONN 43

Quips: Q. and cranks, and wanton
  wiles,   MILT 20
  q. and quibbles heard in flocks,
    GILB 36

quire: birds their q. apply; airs,
  vernal airs,   MILT 70

Q. above,/ Is Confidence:
    HERB G 14
Q. of Birds   COWL 4

Quit: Q., Q., for shame;   SUCK 3
  q. their sphere,   POPE A 66
  q. this caprice;   PRIO 1

quits: q. us when we die.
    POPE A 80
  young enthusiast q. his ease for
    fame;   JOHN S (1709–1784) 17

quiver: blades of the grave-grass q.,
    FINC 1

quiver'd: q. Nymph with Arrows
  keen   MILT 3

quivered: Valley q.   GINS 41

quivering: lodge at last the q.
  needle   SHAP 9
  q. curds!   CARRO 20
  q. female-thing   SPENC A 2
  q. me   WHITM 77

quivers: emptying of q.,   SWIN 4
  grinning cat/ Q. forever   TATE A 3
  soul's sap q.   ELIOT T 61

quoniam: beste q. mighte be.
    CHAU 91

quotations: fond of q.:   CARRO 18

quote: I q. the fights historical,
    GILB 35
  I'll Kill you if you Q. it.   BURG 1

Quoth: Q. the raven, "Nevermore."
    POE 36

R

Ra: cowboy in the boat of R.
    REED I 3, 5

rabbit: fishing was a r.'s foot —
    LOWE R 12
  r. presses back her ears,
    LAWR 24

rabbits: Open-eyed r.   SNYD 35
  r. caught in the mower,   ROET 13

Rabble: at the mercy of the R.
    DRYD 19

raccoon: as the black r.   CULL 14

race: Ants are a curious r.;
    FROS 31
  brown as my r. is brown,
    JOHN H 3
  death of the r.   WILB 1
  exulting thunder of your r.;
    ARNO 37
  here the r. of men go by.   FOSS 3
  hollow toy, the R.;   ROBI 35
  idol of the human r.,   BRID R 3
  ill-used r. of men that cleave the
    soil,   TENN 91
  inordiante r.?   RANS 28
  legs of the r. run/ forwards,
    HARP 1
  Let a r. of men now rise   WALK 6

love in kisses r. SHEL 32
music of the r.; EMER 48
Nor slumber nor a roof against
    the r.; MILLA 16
not r. enough in the sweet
    heavens SHAK 34
Plodder through midnight r.,
    HEAN 8
R. falls for centuries SNYD 29
r., from clouds to drop assign'd,
    BIBL, O.T. 67
r. is on the roof. TENN 74
r. is over and gone;
    BIBL, O.T. 72
r. it r. every day. SHAK 177
r. it r. on the just BOWEN 1
r. makes running pools in the
    gutter. HUGH L 1
r. makes still pools on the
    sidewalk. HUGH L 1
r.-mist curtains wave GINS 45
r. of matter upon sense WINT 2
r. one inch above the meadow:
    SMIT W 4
r. plays a little sleep-song
    HUGH L 1
r./ Possesses us entirely, LEWI 2
r. reminds. GRAV 21
r. when the summers parch.
    MASE 5
ripple of r.; SWIN 3
small r. down can rain.
    UNKN 302
spout,/ Where the r. water of my
    eyes CLEV 2
Still falls the R. SITW 11
stirring/ Dull roots with spring r.
    ELIOT T 113
streets/ Burst suddenly in r. . . .
    CRAN H 32
suddenly, and all at once, the r.!
    MACL 9
summer's r.; HERR 43
sun and the r. are flying,
    STEVENSO R 1
Sweet r., the fire's out SNYD 29
swings in the wind and r.,
    THOMA E 8
thirsty earth soaks up the r.,
    COWL 1
waiting for r. ELIOT T 30
war lasts, r. soaks, OWEN 21
wind and the r., SHAK 177
rainbow: at the r.'s foot ROSS C 25
dark r. bliss in the sea. LAWR 58
everything/ was r., BISH 19
My heart is like a r. shell
    ROSS C 1
R. comes and goes, WORD 66
r.-crowned brief showers,
    ROSS C 37
r. in the sky: WORD 57
r.'s glory is shed; SHEL 89

raine: pleasure is like r., HERR 25
rich and golden coloured r.,
    LODG 1
rained: r. a ghastly dew TENN 75
Raineth: R. drop POUN 2
rains: r. that come in time
    KAVA 12
rainy: windy night a r. morrow,
    SHAK 221
rais'd: r./ Thir fainting courage
    MILT 56
raise: My God shall r. me up,
    RALEG 4
Philomel her voice doth r.?
    WOTT 4
r. for good the supplicating voice,
    JOHN S (1709–1784) 22
r. me with the just.
    MONTROSE 4
r. the meeting soul! COLL 12
r. up Common-wealths DRYD 1
r./ Your angry head GRAV 7
shaft we r. to them EMER 12
structure that we r., LONG 5
your vertue now I r. JONS 30
raised: arms partially r. WHITM 70
By Richmond I r. my knees
    ELIOT T 139
we r. not a stone, WOLF C 3
Raises: R. the spirits, GAY 3
raiseth: r. up the poor out of the
    dust, BIBL, O.T. 8
raisin: dry up/ like a r. in the sun?
    HUGH L 9
rake: ev'ry woman is at heart a r.:
    POPE A 98
I, the r.,/ Coming behind her
    ROET 28
Raked: R. the meadow WHITT 15
raking: r. piles of dead leaves
    SNOD 14
Rallying: R. round our Liberty;
    HOPKINSO 2
ram: caverns of r., SHEL 26
rampart: his corse to the r.
    WOLF C 1
Music my r., MILLA 22
r. to the mind. MASE 9
Ramparts: honey-coloured/ R.
    YEATS 63
r. we watched KEY 1
ran: And r. on. CRAN S 2
Grief, with a glass that r.;
    SWIN 1
r. a hundred years to a day,
    HOLM 4
r. down the stairs. OHAR 7
r. itself in golden sands.
    TENN 70
r. sprinkling on earth's floor
    BRID R 15
r. to get away, ROBE 2

shudder r. around the sky;
    EMER 50
slipped his hand and r. away!
    BELL 10
warmly r. my blood TENN 95
Randal: poor Felix R.; HOPKINS 6
random: (At r. and imperfectly
    WORD 51
At r. from the truth SHAK 242
gleaming of a r. light, DUNB P 7
Holy Ghost descends/ At r.
    KAVA 9
r. persons whom you do not
    know — GRAV 5
r. scatter of shot. KIZE 3
rang: r. to Miriam's holy glee,
    TIMR 5
range: Among the bestial herds to
    r., MILT 78
birds that r. YEATS 53
Forward let us r., TENN 79
r. of delectable mountains,
    LOWE R 26
r. the fields LINC 2
R. the wide house BROWNI R 50
to rest or r. MASE 6
ranged: if I have r., SHAK 230
r. in columns before me,
    WHITM 110
r. mansions dark
    THOMS J (1834–1882) 3
r. there with careful art, PATM 3
wide arch/ Of the r. empire fall!
    SHAK 3
ranges: takes the light and r.
    NOYE 1
Rangoon: R. the heat of noon
    COWA 3
rank: her r. and gold. WHITT 19
my offense is r., SHAK 34
r. is but the guinea stamp —
    BURN 24
r. me in register SHAK 8
r. tongue blossom into speech.]
    BROWNI R 15
so r. a feline smell ELIOT T 160
ranked: she r./ My gift
    BROWNI R 56
ranks: In the r. of death MOOR T 9
march in r. of better equipage:
    SHAK 196
(On the foremost r. WHITM 26
r. of the dead: — FINC 1
ransom: noble knight was her r.
    soon, UNKN 93
rap: tossed in jail on a vagrancy r.,
    SNYD 25
rapacious: return a r. look.
    MOOR M 12
rape: punctual r. of every blessed
    day, WILB 24
raped: girls are r., AUDE 82

Raphaels: talked of their R.,
    Corregios and stuff, GOLD 4
rapid: ghastly r. river, POE 23
    loving, r., merciless —
    LOWE R 29
    More r. than eagles MOOR C 2
    on the r.'s top, ARNO 5
    r. falcons in a snare, MERE G 13
    R. — footless Guest — DICKI 162
    r. glide along the leaning line;
    THOMS J (1700–1748) 11
rapidly: Iser, rolling r. CAMPB T 3
    We can slide it/ R. REED H 5
rapine: with r. sweet MILT 90
rapping: some one gently r.,
    POE 34
raps: chaps who are giving the r.
    ROON 2
rapt: r. prophetic eyes, ARNO 12
    r. soul sitting in thine eyes;
    MILT 16
rapture: joy/ And r. so oft beheld?
    MILT 97
    r. of an inspiration. HOPKINS 26
    r. warms the mind; POPE A 34
raptures: no Minstrel r. swell;
    SCOT WA 12
rapturous: glancings of r. glances,
    PRAE 3
    memory's r. pain; BRON 13
rare: common fate of all things r.
    WALL 2
    genius so shrinking and r.
    LOWE J 1
    I too am a r. Pattern. LOWE A 5
    man of culture r., GILB 30
    most r. conception, nothing.
    WILB 27
    my love as r. SHAK 237
    My verse your virtues r. shall
    eternize, SPENS 24
    Not ringed but r., SMIT W 3
    nothing pleaseth but r. accidents.
    SHAK 52
    r. and royal names SYNG 2
    r. and solitary, MILT 86
    r. as a day in June? LOWE J 17
    r. as the light of a happy eye,
    WILLI 47
    r. original heartsblood goes,
    WILB 13
    r. to be born a human being!
    SNYD 38
    rule all dominions that are r.;
    KAVA 13
    too r., grow now my visits
    ARNO 44
rarely: r. comest thou, SHEL 60
rareness: r., muchness,/ Fewness
    GRAV 39
rarities: Feeds on the r. SHAK 210
rascal: dull and muddy-mettled r.,
    SHAK 31

r. beadle, hold thy bloody hand!
    SHAK 81
rascals: wager the r. a crown
    GOLD 6
rash: r. hand in evil hour MILT 89
    slander, censure r.; SHAK 18
rashes: Green grow the r.,
    BURN 28
Rashly: R. importunate, HOOD 2
rat: bloodsucking bat or the r. or
    the stoat MACN 15
    cat/ That killed the r. MOTH 5
    field r., startled, squealing bleeds,
    TOOM 5
    fought all night with a cocaine r.,
    UNKN 67
    hieroglyphs of the r. footprints
    SAND 9
    r. crept softly through the
    vegetation ELIOT T 130
    r./ That ate the malt MOTH 4
    shape of a r.? ROET 35
    tramped at a r.'s pace,
    ROSS C 12
rate: r. you drink your beer.
    HOUS 49
    such a r.; BYRO 18
    You skate at such a r. DAIC 1
ratel: r. tumbled hurry skurry.
    ROSS C 12
rather: r. see than be one. BURG 3
    r. than by not doing. NASH 11
    r. tough worm in your little
    inside?" GILB 29
rational: proud of being r. ROCH 8
    r. voice is dumb: AUDE 34
rationality: turret r. TAYL E 13
rats: chatter the pedigrees of the r.
    SAND 9
    feet of the r. SAND 9
    from r. or from mice,
    BROWNI R 65
    I think we are in r.' alley
    ELIOT T 124
    piped r. to its siren/ Crescendo,
    MERW 4
    R.!/ They fought the dogs,
    BROWNI R 60
    young r. with black felt hats,
    UNKN 258
rattle: dry throats r.,/ Two crows
    perched SHEL 63
    Where mingles war's r.
    SCOT WA 20
rattlers: nest of r., MORG 1
rattles: r. her crutch, WARR 10
rattling: as r. thunder. SHAK 7
    car r. BYRO 6
    dry r. of a shutter, FROS 132
    great head r. like a gourd,
    WARR 3

running in r. rows; SIDN 9
thunder's r. clymmynge sound
    CHAT 2
ratty: coyote got his/ r. old fur coat
    SILKO 1
raucous: drown the r. shout;
    UNTE 3
raunson: r. unto me; CHAU 86
ravage: making apt for r. MELV 10
    To r. and redeem the world:
    HILL G 4
rave: gaze, turn giddy, r., and die.
    POPE A 2
    if I should brood or r., CHES 12
    Old age should burn and r.
    THOMA D 11
    r./ Over his entrails, MARV 15
    you'd r. and rend them SYNG 6
raveled: Sleep that knits up the r.
    sleave of care, SHAK 106
raven: Ghastly grim and ancient r.
    POE 36
    No R.'s wing can stretch BARL 1
    on the Night's Plutonian shore!"/
    Quoth the r., "Nevermore."
    POE 36
    Poe, with his r., like Barnaby
    Rudge, LOWE J 5
    r., never flitting, POE 37
    R./ on a roost of furs SNYD 33
    upon a r.'s back. SHAK 149
ravener: r. of horrible meat.
    MELV 14
ravening: r. clouds, WHITM 56
ravenous: r. grave? TATE A 14
ravens: Beast r. in its own avidity?
    EBER 3
raves: same ocean round us r.,
    ARNO 34
    wild wind r., THAX 1
ravined: flowers are r./ by bees,
    OLSO 21
ravines: sun-defying, in its deep r.
    LONG 14
raving: that r. slut YEATS 29
ravish: chaste, except you r. me.
    DONN 9
    In musick's r.'t soule CRAS 6
    notes, to r. all DANI G 1
ravished: soul early into heaven r.,
    DONN 53
raw: Celery, r., NASH 4
    deliver his r. materials free;
    AUDE 58
    r. country girl, HARD 37
    r. material of poetry MOOR M 34
    r. rough dun was he, KIPL 2
rawness: in/ all its r. MOOR M 34
ray: gem of purest r. serene,
    GRAY 10
    Hesperus thy twinkling r. Beams
    CLARE 6

I snatched the sun's eternal r.
CLARE 15
R. round with flames TENN 42
soul, that drop, that r. MARV 31
rayes: sacred r. of Chastity, MILT 3
rays: splendor without r., JEFFE 28
vain produced, all r. return;
EMER 50
razor: holds a locked r.
LOWE R 55
reach: above the r. Of ordinary
men; WORD 123
beyond the r. of art, POPE A 30
Bloom gradually out of r.
SNOD 4
end no eye can r. MILT 105
far out of r., WHITM 10
gone out of the r. of change —
THOMA E 10
live beyond the r. HORA 5
long/ Last r. YEATS 153
My most desire my hand may r.,
WYAT 14
r. its natural term; EMER 5
r. of sacrilegious hands,
POPE A 31
r. thy hand, WILD 10
rye r. to the chin, PEEL 6
wild waves r. their hands
THAX 1
within his r., PATM 3
reached: r. the sky, UNKN 135
reaches: bullet r. you. SORL 2
reachest: r. but to dust; SIDN 26
r. me too late! JOHN L 6
reaching: arms r. towards me.
ROET 57
kept me from r. you. OHAR 16
r. and crowding WHITM 77
r. from the dead WILLI 48
R. no absolute, GUNN 14
r. th' utmost orb MILT 62
read: Almighty's Mysteries to r.
HABI 2
can r. and care for just so long,
KIPL 20
first line he r., HOLM 12
hear but do not r., LOWE R 49
I r. Gide RIVE 2
r. human and exact. GRAV 6
r. in normal circumstances?
POUN 30
r. to by a boy, ELIOT T 30
r. to me some poem, LONG 15
r. with joy, then shut the book.
PATM 2
remember things I once r.
SNYD 18
rigid Cato r. these lines of mine.
HERR 72
very few to r. COLE H 1
Who rides may r. KIPL 24
wits to r. JONS 43

read'st: deaf and silent, r. the
eternal deep, WORD 77
reade: I r., and sigh, and wish I
were a tree; HERB G 5
reader: r. leaning late
STEVENS 16
way to start, eh, r.? SIMP 7
reader's: r. threaten'd (not in vain)
with 'sleep.' POPE A 26
Readeth: R. Ecclesiasticus
CHAU 70
readiness: Roaring their r. to
avenge, HARD 15
Wait, with impatient r., COWP 14
reading: love working and r."
WATT I 7
r. in these treatises KLEI 1
r. might make her know, SIDN 5
R. while waiting RICH 15
readings: r. will grow erratic?
LARK 10
reads: man who never r. in brook or
book; KAVA 8
ready: makes r. for work,
WHITM 37
not r. for others to go, AMMO 15
sweetness r. penned, HERB G 43
tea is nearly r. STEVENSO R 3
Today r. ripe, SURR 2
readye: r. to be thy bride.
UNKN 16
real: Forms more r. than living
man, SHEL 51
I am a r. poet. OHAR 23
if what is evil/ Be r., MILT 95
Life is r.! LONG 35
Now nothing is r. RIVE 2
r. as a cast-iron pot. SEXT 2
r. toads in them', MOOR M 33
tasks of r. life, WORD 4
To the r. work, SNYD 17
realio: r., trulio, little pet dragon.
NASH 15
realities: Vulture, whose wings are
dull r.? POE 1
reality: absurdity is r., RIVE 2
Against the essential r. JEFFE 7
free/ myth from r. BIRN 3
human kind/ Cannot bear very
much r. ELIOT T 19
my own race/ And the r.;
YEATS 59
new knowledge of r.
STEVENS 29
no humbling of r. AMMO 8
unsheathed from r. JEFFE 16
realized: In the least way r.
CULL 12
really: r. blended into one;
WHITM 35
realm: hold a fretful r. TENN 76
Our r. it brooks no stranger's
force, ELIZ 1

r. of pure Art, LOWE J 7
r., this England, SHAK 88
To that mysterious r., BRYA 24
whole r. of nature mine,
WATT I 10
realmless: his r. eyes were closed;
KEAT 20
realms: Anna! whom three r. obey,
POPE A 118
Much have I traveled in the r. of
gold, KEAT 55
pathless r. of Space GILB 47
r. and islands SHAK 7
seeken acts of sundry r. CHAU 65
reaming: r. swats that drank
divinely; BURN 52
reap: always plant while others r.
CULL 2
Celia, let us r. our joys
CAREW 10
he shall not r.; SWIN 2
r. the harvest with enduring toil,
TENN 91
tyrant r.; SHEL 64
reaping: grew the more by r.
SHAK 7
in his r. ROBI 16
never gaining never r. WALK 5
reappear: eyes r. ELIOT T 47
reappraisal: no agonizing r.
LOWE R 32
rear: fieldfare followed in the r.,
THOR 11
promised the Royal babe to r.
GILB 17
rear'd: First r. the Stage,
JOHN S (1709–1784) 5
reared: Death has r. himself a
throne POE 11
r. arm/ Crested the world;
SHAK 7
r. its head. POE 20
weak spirits ne'er been higher r.
SHAK 178
rears: broken altar, Lord, thy
servant r., HERB G 7
reas'ning: from pride, our very r.
springs; POPE A 67
In Pride, in r. Pride, POPE A 66
reason: By nature, r., learning,
blind; SWIF 4
capability and godlike r.
SHAK 35
contrary unto r. RALEG 5
erring R.'s spite, POPE A 58
feast of r. POPE A 92
Founded in r., MILT 78
frenzy insufficient r. MILLA 15
in r. rotten. RALEG 8
in their looks/ Much r., MILT 93
Passion and r. self-division cause.
GREV 9
Past r. hunted, SHAK 236

region: calm r., where no night
  KING H 3
main r. of my song. WORD 15
many a R. dolorous, MILT 61
misty mid r. of Weir — POE 48
reside/ In thrilling r. SHAK 115
some untrodden r. of my mind,
  KEAT 53
Worlds first R. MILT 65
regions: in troubled r. RICH 27
infinite r. of the night, TIMR 3
R. of sorrow, MILT 50
Within the r. of the air, TRAH 6
register: rank me in r. SHAK 8
regret: futile as r. ROBI 1
lies, self-denial, unspoken r.
  SNOD 15
r./ Becomes an April violet,
  TENN 52
tear of r. WOOD 3
wild with all r.; TENN 115
regularity: spruce-cone r.
  MOOR M 22
regularly: heart r./ Thunders. —
  KIRK 3
regulate: Belief to r. DICKI 100
rehearse: mortal Muse thy praise
  r., DRYD 31
r. perfect kills HUGH T 1
r. The holy incantation of a
  verse; HERR 71
reign: darkness and silence r.
  LEAR 6
half perhaps will r.; MILT 67
r./ His stars eternally. HARD 20
r. in this horrible place.
  COWP 23
their R. was long;
  JOHN S (1709–1784) 6
whatsoever king shall r.,
  UNKN 297
with boundless pow'r I r.;
  SHEN 1
reigned: in my nature r. SHAK 230
reigns: On a black throne r.
  POE 16
red blood r. in the winter's pale.
  SHAK 181
R. here and revels; MILT 78
rose r., HERR 72
vast silence r. JOHN L 1
rein: r. of a wimpling wing
  HOPKINS 27
suddenly drew his r. WOOL 2
reindeer: vast/ Herds of r. AUDE 8
reins: r. of peace and war
  YEATS 117
reivers: r. they stole Fair Annie,
  UNKN 93
rejects: Heaven r. the lore
  WORD 10
rejoice: Consequently I r.,
  ELIOT T 4

from age to age Thou didst r.,
  WORD 147
No time to r. ELIOT T 14
Reason's Ear they all r., ADDI 4
r. and blossom SORL 2
R., and men will seek you;
  WILC 2
shepherds too r., GODO 1
something/ Upon which to r.
  ELIOT T 4
unable to r. THOMA E 16
rejoicing: Circle his throne r.,
  MILT 81
Toiling, — r., — sorrowing,
  LONG 49
relation: good r. to the earth
  MOMA 4
good r. to the gods MOMA 4
stand in good r. MOMA 4
release: heroes seek r. MILLA 8
prisoner's r., SIDN 14
signs the last r.,
  JOHN S (1709–1784) 14
sorrow finds a swift r. in song
  DAY 4
Till pitying Nature signs the last
  r., JOHN S (1709–1784) 21
voice of peace bring sweet r.
  ROON 3
released: Indian, when from life r.,
  FRENE 1
r. from forms, AMMO 3
releasing: gives thee r.; SHAK 219
relent: make him once r., BUNY 2
Would rouse God to r.; EBER 2
relics: Give thou my sacred r.
  burial. HERR 24
hallowed r. should be hid
  MILT 35
relief: Or hope r. HERB CH 2
shaking Civil War r., LOWE R 17
timely utterance gave that thought
  r., WORD 67
Relieve: R. my languish DANI S 18
relieved: mothers r. BOGA 7
relieves: r. the stark,/ White stars,
  CULL 3
Religion: Dame R., BUTL 1
For all r.'s sake, HERR 23
R. after this!/ Came next MARV 3
R. blushing POPE A 2
R. is a Spring VAUG 20
R. stands, SPEND 15
r.-/ Vendors and political men
  JEFFE 9
religions: illuminations! r.!
  GINS 18
religious: Casting a dim, r. light.
  MILT 18
heard an old r. man YEATS 64
r. rites/ Of sacrifice, MILT 104
r. sects ran mad, PRAE 2

relikes: kisse the r. everychon,
  CHAU 85
reluctant: Half willing, half r.
  LONG 33
sweet, r., amorous delay.
  MILT 73
remain: oblivion to the final day r.
  BRAD 6
r. as strangers VERY 6
things r. in God. YEATS 38
vows shall ever true r.; GAY 7
remained: My own identity r.
  WINT 6
remains: cremate my last r."
  SERV 2
Forms r., WORD 127
Nothing r. BROO R 8
r. an Englishman! GILB 20
Strength in what r. behind;
  WORD 84
what deepest r.? WHITM 114
What thou lovest well r.,
  POUN 18
remember: bridal night I r.,
  SMIT ST 1
distinctly I r. POE 35
Do you r. an Inn? BELL 19
Does anyone r.? WAGO 3
half r. human words, SYNG 7
Haply I may r., ROSS C 34
I could never r. CRAN H 43
I r. only a woman WHITM 60
Lord, r. me and mine BURN 33
Now r. courage, TATE A 20
r. all good losers." SAND 13
r. and be sad. ROSS C 20
r. God? AIKE 7
r. me, unwept, unburied, POUN 6
R. me when I am gone away,
  ROSS C 19
r. the stretcher-cases SASS 2
r. things I once read SNYD 18
R. us — ELIOT T 42
r./ Like the old AUDE 26
To r. or invent FROS 51
will not the tale r.?) BYRO 75
remembered: Dear as r. kisses after
  death, TENN 115
friend r. not. SHAK 14
It is pain r. PLUM 2
R., if outlived, DICKI 2
R. on waking. BRID R 6
r. sin. RANS 12
r. the soul's history SPEND 11
sweet love r. SHAK 194
Sweet tones are r. not; SHEL 89
rememberest: thou r. of what toys
  PATM 4
remembering: r. happier things.
  TENN 74
R. how she felt, WORD 99
R. not, WORD 99

R. the stable AUDE 15
R. the Strait of Belle Isle
BISH 24
remembers: heart r. how!
STEVENSO R 1
r. that famous day LONG 43
Remembrance: flash of unforeseen/
R. falls ROBI 14
flood of r., LAWR 32
In r. of a shroud. SHAK 128
lest fierce r. MILT 112
Mark Van Doren,/ a poem of r.,
HAYD 4
r., and repentance, SHEL 66
r. of things past, SHAK 195
summon up r. SHAK 195
Writ in r. SHAK 87
remembrances: Childhood r.
GIOV 3
remembraunce: depe profounde r.
PETRA 1
remind: r. me of the dead. SASS 8
reminds: rain r. GRAV 21
reminiscence: r. sing. WHITM 63
Remit: R. as yet no grace,
DICKI 24
remorse: all seemed guilt, r. or
woe, COLE SAM 27
cast out r. YEATS 48
day's vanity, the night's r.
YEATS 24
Felt less r. MILT 98
r. did not oppose temptation;
BYRO 20
R. is cureless — DICKI 122
R. — is Memory — awake —
DICKI 121
remorseless: Dawdling over the r.
earth, SNOD 3
stern, obdurate, flinty, rough, r.
SHAK 61
remote: ebb and flood from the r.
sea-tides
THOMS J (1834–1882) 6
sepulcher, r., alone, POE 43
That music, r., forlorn. DE LA 18
remoter: gleams of a r. world
SHEL 42
no need of a r. charm, WORD 33
remove: 'Hence, r., HERR 70
human power cannot r.
ELIOT T 70
removed: r. from the loved
habitation, WOOD 3
remover: bends with the r.
SHAK 231
removes: Catching the sense at two
r.? HERB G 45
Remus: R., blow your horn!
STEVENS 39
rend: new years ruin and r.
SWIN 23

r. each other when they kiss,
RANS 16
r. not my heart MARL 2
you'd rave and r. them SYNG 6
rended: Forests are r., SCOT WA 22
render: with delight to take and r.,
STEVENSO R 10
rendered: r. into soap. JARR 3
renders: r. and receives SHEL 41
r. vain their deep desire? —
ARNO 42
Time r. His last award, BYRO 34
rendezvous: r. with Death SEEG 1
renew: We shall r. the battle
ARNO 15
renewable: Not young, and not r.,
KINS 6
renewal: race r., CREE 6
renew'd: r. the joys COWP 12
Waking r. WHITM 103
renewed: r. by death, ROET 15
r. her charter's date DRYD 7
renounce: This world I do r.,
SHAK 79
renown: citizen/ Of credit and r.,
COWP 6
fever of r.
JOHN S (1709–1784) 17
forfeit fair r., SCOT WA 12
inheritors of unfulfilled r.
SHEL 12
R. and grace is dead; SHAK 109
Runners whom r. outran
HOUS 57
renowne: I that gave thee thy r.:
CAREW 7
renowned: No less r. than war;
MILT 123
rent: house r. to pay. HUGH L 3
That has not been r." YEATS 39
rents: What are thy r.? SHAK 58
Reorganized: R. upon the floor
ELIOT T 111
repair: machines to keep in r.,
AUDE 17
repaired: false heart r.' READ H 2
Repairing: forthwith to the place/
R. MILT 98
repast: neat r. shall feast us,
MILT 121
repay: Nobility more nobly to r.?
EMER 23
Repeat: R. that, HOPKINS 5
R. thy song, LONG 20
words r. LONG 11
repeate: no verses to r.: JONS 15
repeated: word too much r.
AMMO 20
repent: change nor falter nor r.;
SHEL 58
Faustus may r. MARL 1

R., R., and from old errors turn!'
DRUM 7
r. us of the sport: PETRO 1
repentance: flowing mane/ Of r.
RODG 7
give r. to her lover, GOLD 9
remembrance, and r., SHEL 66
Winter-garment of R. OMAR 1
repented: little still she strove, and
much r., BYRO 20
repine: coarseness of our heaven r.,
ADDI 2
repining: r. restlessness:
HERB G 63
Replace: R./ the leer RANDA D 3
replied: Adam last r.: MILT 105
I r., 'My Lord.' HERB G 18
shade r., — POE 19
voice r., far up the height,
LONG 22
reply: having no r. CARRO 41
know how to R. BLAK 9
long canals r. POPE A 122
R. by heaving rocks HART 4
Theirs not to make r., TENN 7
reply'd: Jesus temperately r.:
MILT 109
report: r. how we were slaine.'
UNKN 155
reports: r. on his conduct agree
AUDE 93
repose: charm of thy r., ARNO 46
earned a night's r. LONG 49
marble or a bronze r. YEATS 12
passed to a sweet r. MAST 8
r./ And peace, HERB G 58
r. for limbs with travel tired;
SHAK 193
r. is taboo'd by anxiety, GILB 25
R. is yours — your deed is known,
MELV 6
r.,/ Salted and sobered,
THOMA E 16
smile unsearchable r. CRAN H 51
Such violence. And such r.
WILB 39
troubled midnight and the noon's
r. ELIOT T 54
reposes: quiet she r.; ARNO 20
repossessed: native country, r.
HERR 24
reproach: r. us as unclean.
MILT 97
reproached: enemy that r.
BIBL, O.T. 39
reproofe: Daintie age,/ Cannot
indure r., JONS 21
Reptile: generate,/ R. with spawn
abundant, MILT 85
Reptilian: R. green the wrinkled
throat, WINT 5

Republic: grimy slur on the R.'s
faith MELV 12
shine, perishing r. JEFFE 38
repulse: Thy sharp r., WYAT 6
repulsive: enchanted/ by a r. clew,
RUKE 3
reputable: r. walks of old
established trees SNOD 8
reputation: At every word a r. dies.
POPE A 119
sold my R. for a Song. OMAR 2
request: granting my r.,
HERB G 22
requested: he his guide r.
MILT 114
requiem: supremest r. sing;
HERR 59
requir'd: by Law r.; DRYD 17
require: equal syllables alone r.,
POPE A 24
men in women do r.? BLAK 48
things which our needfull Faith r.
DRYD 18
women do in men r.? BLAK 48
requited: she willingly r. MARL 5
res': las' long r. DUNB P 3
rescue: You'd r. me. MOSS 3
research: r. on fatigue AUDE 88
resemble: which r. mushrooms,
MOOR M 10
resembled: picture, once, r. thee.
PHILI A 3
resembles: r. a bird's foot SIMI 5
r. all the old thinking. HASS 1
Resembling: R. fair Semiramis
OVID 1
r. human organs SMIT W 3
resentment: looked with cold r.
HOLLA 4
Reserve: r. for me a crown,
BETJ 5
R. them for my love, SHAK 196
reside: r. at Table Mountain,
HART 3
r./ In thrilling region SHAK 115
Residence: entered then/ My R.
DICKI 162
resign: r. our vital breath,
STANL 2
R. the setting sun
THOMS J (1700–1748) 8
resign'd: so much r. — ARNO 31
resigned: I am not r. MILLA 6
will r.; JOHN S (1709–1784) 23
Resignedly: R. beneath the sky
POE 12
resignes: rosie Morn r. her light,
WALL 8
resigning: r. yet resisting bride.
HERR 14
resinous: Man's own r. heart
YEATS 120
r. and soft your songs TOOM 3

resist: band them to r. MILT 118
resistance: wrong that needs r.,
BANK 4
resisted: know not what's r.
BURN 9
resisting: resigning yet r. bride.
HERR 14
resolution: H[olland] took the pious
r. GRAY 21
native hue of r. SHAK 40
resolve: with more successful hope
r. MILT 52
resons: r. he spak ful solempnely,
CHAU 21
resort: My boy, it's your last r.
PLATH 4
respectable: highly r. gondolier,
GILB 17, 19
Not one is r. WHITM 75
r. senators burst with laughter,
AUDE 5
respected: all creation is duly r.;
LOWE J 10
responding: boy of r. kisses,
WHITM 107
responsibility: nightmare begins r.
HARP 3
responsible: r. for a disaster
unverified, MILE 1
rest: ashes of lovers find no r.
JONS 12
best thing of our life, our r.,
DANI S 21
blest with perfect r., VAN DY 5
buds and blossoms like the r.
TENN 52
choose/ Their place of r.,
MILT 108
command me to my r., DRAY 3
convicts r. KNIG 1
enemy to r.; RALEG 5
forenoon walk, my r., WHITM 23
futurity to do the r. ROBI 26
God ordered motion, but ordained
no r. VAUG 10
gone to their eternal r. POE 11
how I long to be at r. BRAD 1
Huntsman, r.! SCOT WA 10
hushed me in her arms to r.,
TAYL A 1
I cannot r. from travel;
TENN 129
I r. upon the wave, WILLA 1
in doubt to act or r., POPE A 78
land hushes to r.: BRID R 18
lead frail minds to r. SPENS 5
lead the world the way to r.
COTTO 1
leade them unto life and r.
HERB G 1
lose my everlasting r. ROCH 1
may thy soul have r." UNKN 47
My r. a stone; ADAMS S 1

needful hours of R.? DRYD 2
night of peaceful r., RILE 5
nothing sweeter than his peace
when at r. SMAR 8
nowhere yet to r. my head,
ARNO 32
r. a little from praise SWIN 22
r. can never dwell, MILT 50
r. in peace, our patriot band;
FRENE 4
R. in soft peace, JONS 23
r./ In the act of rising, WILB 5
R. in the bottom lay. HERB G 62
r. in the grave. KNOX 1
R. in the strong arms TIMR 2
R., r., and r. again." DE LA 17
r. that peace begets. UNKN 301
r.! thy warfare o'er, SCOT WA 9
retir'st to endless R. COWL 3
seals up all in r. SHAK 215
shook him from his r., SHEL 17
shot electricity/ Through the r.
KNIG 5
singing to the r. UNKN 73
sink from reverie to r. SWIF 3
sink to r./ By all their country's
wishes blest! COLL 3
thy heart is laid to r. BRON 4
Thy Soul r., DONN 51
to quiet r., BOLE 1
to r. or range MASE 6
To r., the cushion POPE A 104
to r. Uncoffined — HARD 19
to the colored r. room; DURE 2
Until I r. by thee. DE TA 2
warld to r. are gane, LIND L 1
Wearied then and glad of r.,
PHILI A 2
weary be at r. BIBL, O.T. 11
Were not my heart at r. SEDL 4
rested: about this neck have cross'd
and r., WHITM 116
restful: for r. death I cry,
SHAK 213
resting: His hand/ Was r. on a
mountain! STEPHENS 13
my r.-place is found,
BROWNI R 5
their r.-place, LOWE R 23
your r.-place." HARD 8
restless: blown with r. violence
SHAK 115
little r. midge. WILD 18
nought/ But r. hurry
THOMS J (1700–1748) 7
r. one; the circler of circles;
AIKE 11
sit by the r. WHITM 116
soothe this r. feeling, LONG 15
vale of r. mind UNKN 205
restlessness: repining r.
HERB G 63
restor'd: All losses are r. SHAK 195

restore: lonely scene shall thee r.; COLL 2

May memory r. SCHW 8

pot/ That can r. that. JONS 32

that heavenly face r. WORD 144

thy former light r., SHAK 137

restored: Chaos, is r.; POPE A 2

old world was r. READ H 1

restoreth: r. my soul: BIBL, O.T. 31

restraine: sleepe hir sence with slomber doth r. LODG 2

restrained: Nature, like liberty, is but r. POPE A 27

restraint: bondage and r.; SURR 11

free from this r., CONG 2

wise r. WORD 62

rests: r. his head GRAY 12

r. in its laurels HILL G 2

R. on his belly in the mud; ELIOT T 36

r. your face — UNKN 267

result: joint force and full r. of all. POPE A 35

results: rich r. of the divine consents EMER 4

resume: cheerful Fields r. their green Attire: GRAY 32

resurrect: r. the dead ALBA 1

Resurrection: meek members of the R. DICKI 125

r. of the King," LOWE R 3

re-survey: once more r. SHAK 196

resuscitate: He strove to r. POUN 36

retain: habitations long their names r., BRAD 6

one jot of former love r. DRAY 15

R. that dear perfection SHAK 142

retains: r. an obscure sense WORD 99

retards: dull brain perplexes and r.: KEAT 48

retinue: r. from the magician's house AUDE 53

retire: bids afflicted worth r. to peace. JOHN S (1709–1784) 21

'I mean to r., NÍ CH 1

sun in time forgets for to r. FLET G EL 1

retired: where gloomily r., THOMS J (1700–1748) 10

retires: r./ Into her private cell MILT 80

street/ Into its gloom r., BINY 4

retir'st: r. to endless Rest. COWL 3

retract: age of prudence can never r. ELIOT T 153

which no men r. WINT 10

Retreat: R. was out of hope, — DICKI 116

shrine of r. LOWE J 7

silent, dull r., FRENE 5

retreated: snow hath r., WORD 164

retrievements: r. out of the night, WHITM 52

retrievers: obliging air of r., BISH 8

return: days gone by/ R. upon me WORD 115

dead, you never shall r." OMAR 6

Departed never to r. BURN 15

Do evil in r. AUDE 71

dove's r., WILB 2

dust I am and shall to dust r. MILT 98

dust r. to the earth BIBL, O.T. 6

flow will r.,) WHITM 5

None that go r. again. HOUS 43

not/ to r. my stare. BISH 17

r. a rapacious look. MOOR M 12

R. by subway-mouth WILB 4

R. to my mind, SNYD 11

r. us to Your wrath, TATE A 4

See, they r.; POUN 57

spirit shall r. unto God BIBL, O.T. 6

they r., and bring us with them. ELIOT T 72

they r., one, and by one, POUN 58

those who never will r., ROBI 14

to r. to a meadow DUNC 1

vain produced, all rays r.; EMER 50

whose shapes r., THOMS J (1834–1882) 2

Wise child, didst hastily r. JONS 38

return'd: But sorrow r. CAMPB T 9

your dear eyes r. WHITM 106

returnest: to dust r., LONG 35

returning: r. home, WHITM 18

returns: day r., LONG 47

each r. unto his love at night. DRAY 3

from whose bourn/ No traveler r. SHAK 40

income-tax r.; GILB 8

nevermore/ R. the traveler LONG 47

unexpectedly r. MILT 118

worst r. to laughter. SHAK 77

Reuben: think that R. Bright ROBI 49

reve: r. was a sclendre colerik man. CHAU 19

reveal: sweet theft to r., JONS 49

revealed: whispered and r. LONG 39

revel: heart of r. and soláce!' CHAU 68

revelry: sound of r. by night, BYRO 5

revels: present/ Our Alexandrian r.; SHAK 10

Reigns here and r.; MILT 78

r. now are ended. SHAK 163

revenant: Dawn-sniffing r., HEAN 8

revenge: artist will have had his r. JUST 1

dearly-bought r., MILT 115

fidgety r. BROO G 3

I'll ne'er pursue R.; CONG 1

r. for being made to wait, JUST 1

R. should have no bounds. SHAK 38

study of r., immortal hate, MILT 51

Sweet is r. BYRO 21

tribal, intimate r. HEAN 17

Reverdy: Poems by Pierre R. OHAR 14

Revere: midnight ride of Paul R., LONG 43

reverence: r. in my heart MILT 101

r. of old days WHITT 12

Shall do it r. POE 13

With awful r. prone; MILT 59

reverend: Ah, r. sir, BROWNI R 23

Camden, most r. head, JONS 47

honor and r. awe; BENN H 2

r. good old man, HERB G 54

reverent: Peering through r. fingers KIPL 6

prostrate fell/ Before him r., MILT 98

reverie: r., of shade, of prayer, ARNO 40

sink from r. to rest. SWIF 3

reveries: animate a mother's r., YEATS 12

Reverse: R. we proved was not defeat; MELV 16

reversed: wish of water is r., WILB 5

reversing: confronting, r. my cries, WHITM 31

reverted: forever with r. look LONG 27

reverting: Fascinated, my eyes r. WHITM 2

reverts: As fancy r. WOOD 3

Revery: human/ R. is a solitude STEVENS 24

r. alone will do DICKI 149

revile: saints r. her, GRAV 41

reviv'd: Good Old Cause, r., DRYD 1

Revive: aethereal rumours/ R. ELIOT T 154

No April can r. thy withered flowers, DANI S 14

Revives: R., reflourishes, MILT 117

revolt: fear or doubt of her r., SHAK 136

lean not toward r. SNOD 9

Nobler than my r. is infamous,
SHAK 8

r. into slavery— SNYD 24

revolted: Should all despair/ That
have r. wives, SHAK 179

revolution: blood-red flower of r.
RANDA D 5

Hurrah for r. YEATS 65

revolv'd: great matter in his mind
r. MILT 114

revolve: r. it all slowly—
HUGH T 2

revolves: r. and toils, SPEND 9

revolving: r. satellite, WHITM 59

With a r. Wheel— DICKI 123

reward: full r. and glorious fate
CAREW 17

heavens r. thee manifold
BRAD 14

Sweet r. for sharpest pain;
SIDN 28

re-wind: tunnels that r. CRAN H 31

reytes: crownede wythe r., CHAT 1

rhetoric: must take r., AIKE 3

with it, r. AIKE 4

rhetorician: r.'s rules/ Teach
nothing BUTL 3

Rhime: R. the Rudder is of Verses,
BUTL 6

Rhine: wash the river R.?
COLE SAM 5

rhinoceros: armed r., SHAK 110

farewell, you old r., NASH 13

rhyme: beauty making beautiful old
r. SHAK 228

blessed structures, plot and r.
LOWE R 42

For his r. EMER 33

In a sort of Runic r., POE 10

live in this poor r., SHAK 229

long-loved mistress R., DRYD 8

mend my r. HERB G 22

my murmuring r. MORR 3

not for their r. SHAK 196

ornaments of r. LONG 4

presence adds to the r. of love
HARD 48

Pretty friendship 'tis to r.
HOUS 50

r. for roman FLEM 1

R., the rack of finest wits,
JONS 9

story or sung in r.,— WHITT 22

tied together with r., LOWE J 4

to find a r.; SWIF 26

Rhymed: R. Octosyllabic Curse
BELL 14

R. out in love's despair
YEATS 131

rhymes: Leaves, lines, and r., seek
her to please SPENS 3

thy melodious r. STEPHEN 5

thy mournful r., TENN 49

rhythm: change felt in the r.
JEFFE 32

coil of r. and number; EMER 33

smile/ As you find a r. HEAN 7

Sprung r. sprang, BROD 1

Rialto: In the R. SHAK 118

rib: Adam found his r. was gone
HOLLA 4

His r. is gone; HOLLA 5

take a wolf's r. KINN 3

Ribald: R. romeos HORA 1

riband: r. to stick in his coat—
BROWNI R 44

ribber: 'Way down upon de Swanee
r., FOST 3

Ribbon: R. at a time— DICKI 79

road was a r. of moonlight
NOYE 6

ribs: pale curves of your r., HALL 3

poking my thin r. ROET 26

r. and all the skeletons; ALBI 1

r. of old Parnassus flows, SIDN 9

thighs hugging his r. SWEN 3

rice: handful of r.!" SNYD 34

Lord's Prayer on a grain of r.,
THOMA D 8

stabs/ the r. of the world,
KINN 19

rich: At r. men's tables EMER 22

dare be r. for a' that. BROO S 1

Fair, r., and young: HARI 1

haunt the r. man's door, HORA 6

Heaven's Gate/ Opes to the r.
BROWNI R 64

immemorial feud/ Of r. and poor.
READ H 1

Jewels more r. than Ormus
MARV 1

lay r. in shade MELV 21

Let him be r. and weary,
HERB G 63

Lord maketh poor, and maketh
r.: BIBL, O.T. 8

match-girl strikes it r. HECH 12

most poor matters/ Point to r.
ends. SHAK 160

one more r. in hope, SHAK 194

Poor and content is r., SHAK 135

r. and fruitful land, BLAK 68

r. and golden coloured raine,
LODG 1

r. and high, KINGSL 1

r.-haired youth of morn, COLL 7

R., hemm'd thick all around
WHITM 43

R. in the simple worship of a
day. KEAT 18

r. or noble knave POPE A 91

r. proud cost SHAK 211

r. quarter, ASHB 2

r. results of the divine consents
EMER 4

r. that gets the pleasure.
UNKN 219

r. with corn, WHITT 1

r. words, every one, LOWE J 8

Sets you most r. in youth
SHAK 187

Sombre and r., the skies;
JOHN L 1

some r. pennyfather, DRAY 16

something r. and
strange. SHAK 156

to a more r. delight. EMER 3

When I grow r., UNKN 25

Whenever I am sufficiently r.:
THOMA E 11

Richard: R. Cory, ROBI 52

riche: robes r., or fithele, or gay
sautrie. CHAU 2

richer: quiet mind is r. than a
crown; GREE 1

R. than all his tribe; SHAK 138

riches: children of the nouveaux r.;
SNOD 8

Fair face show friends when r. do
abound; GOOG 1

full of thy r. BIBL, O.T. 51

Honor, r., marriage blessing,
SHAK 161

husband nature's r. SHAK 222

love, happiness, r." KAVA 13

majesty and r. of the mind,
CHAP G 1

r. left, not got with pain;
MARTIA 1

r. to men of understanding,
BIBL, O.T. 1

strength and r. at thy feet.
BRYA 14

world's r., HERB G 61

richesse: wommen loven best r.,
CHAU 109

richest: r. gain I count but loss,
WATT I 9

richly: Life of Ages, r. poured,
JOHN S (1822–1882) 1

storied windows r. dight,
MILT 18

too r. clad: CRAS 11

With glory r. furnished, BRAD 12

Richmond: By R. I raised my knees
ELIOT T 139

R. and Kew/ Undid me.
ELIOT T 139

richness: something in this r.
WYLI 14

ricks: piling up the r. KAVA 20

rickshaw: no go the r. MACN 8

rid: r. us from the curse
STEPHEN 2

ridden: billows of my bood have r.,
MILLE V 1

riddle: glory, jest, and r. of the
world! POPE A 78
phœnix r. DONN 14
riddled: mock the r. corpses
SASS 5
riddles: Loves r. DONN 37
ride: barge and boat doth r.,
TURB 1
despots r. a Russian. BYRO 47
easy Morning's R. DICKI 124
endless r. from Battery GINS 9
For you alone I r. the ring,
GRAHAM R 1
he next doth r. abroad, COWP 7
Heaven and she are beyond this
r. BROWNI R 42
in twenty-four hours you'll r. it
about." UNKN 163
It grows dark/ To r. THOMA E 19
may not on you r., CHAU 67
midnight r. of Paul Revere,
LONG 43
R. a cock-horse MOTH 25
r. and spread the alarm LONG 44
R., boldly R.," POE 19
r. it for a purpose, MAST 4
R. more than thou goest,
SHAK 71
r. on its back, BELL 20
r. on white asses, BIBL, O.T. 18
r. the whole world about;
UNKN 161
r. with Morgan WOOL 3
strangest r. that ever was
WHITT 23
to me is this noisy r.? WHITT 25
rider: horse and the r., SWEN 2
scorneth the horse and his r.
BIBL, O.T. 17
riderless: high horse r., YEATS 37
Words dry and r., PLATH 80
riders: Delicate r. of the storm.
CRAN H 41
rides: Alone he r., alone, JOHN L 3
mounts and r. away. SMIT W 2
Occasionally r. DICKI 111
Of all the r. WHITT 22
r. upon the storm. COWP 4
Who r. may read. KIPL 24
ridest: Lo, Lord, Thou r.!
CRAN H 38
ridge: agape on the crumbling r.
MERW 4
ridiculous: sleep makes r.
EMER 32
riding: came r. like mad WOOL 1
highwayman came r. NOYE 6
man goes r. by. STEVENSO R 24
quiet, negligent r., SWEN 3
r. flatcars to Fresno, SNYD 27
r. Kentucky Belle; WOOL 4
r. the rods, CRAN H 21

went my love r. CUMM 3
went r. out RANS 6
rife: r. with the joy of life,
SMIT L 1
rifle: r. all the breathing spring.
COLL 1
r. grooves curling with flakes of
rust. SAND 1
r. knocks him dead, YEATS 155
rifles: crack of deputies' r.
KINN 19
rifts: sulphurous r. of passion and
woe LOWE J 19
rigging: dangle of r., WHITM 92
right: About the r. divine BYRO 32
All's r. with the world!
BROWNI R 66
as men strive for R.;
BROWNI E 5
Cannon to r. of them, TENN 8
circumspect and r.; MEYN 4
crept/ R. out of hell. SIMI 5
did great wrong, and maintained
little r. UNKN 159
do r. to her honor PRIO 5
Equal justice, r. and law,
BENN H 2
every case in law is r., SHAK 76
Fair be thy wives, r. lovesom,
white and small; DUNB W 5
Farewell, thou child of my r.
hand, JONS 23
freedom of that r. SHAK 202
hand to nail the r., DUGA 3
human r. and weal WHITT 10
hym death greep'the r. hard by
the croppe SENE 2
If I am r., POPE A 128
if r., I kiss'd the rod. POPE A 15
I'm so light, it don't seem r.
DURE 2
in his r. and honor took the air.
HECH 16
Just r. for flying, TROW 1
Laws be r., WILD 2
made me to his hand so r.
SIDN 19
my heart's r. SHAK 203
My mind's not r. LOWE R 39
My r. might be love FROS 125
nas nat r. fat, CHAU 22
never r. themselves: FROS 11
Of grief r. sure, WYAT 13
perished in the cause of R.
BRYA 6
planted unco r., BURN 52
R. as a Ribstone Pippin!" BELL 2
r. is the r. STEVENSO R 17
R., like a well-done sum.
PLATH 84
r. man on our side, LUTH 3
r. of way to Tripoli DICKI 120
r. over the hill WHITT 32

r. perfection wrongfully disgrac'd,
SHAK 213
r. prevail, LONG 12
r. to stay; POPE A 128
shade upon thy r. hand.
BIBL, O.T. 59
spurn'st at r., at law, at reason;
SHAK 140
Theirs was the better r.
FROS 125
things would come r. again
LARK 17
think of the r. thing to say
FROS 22
though r. were worsted, wrong
would triumph, BROWNI R 12
to all things I had r.? MILT 109
to reason r. is to submit.
POPE A 67
Whatever is, is r. POPE A 58
what's wrong and what's r.;
HILL J 2
withholds my pow'r that r. to
use? MILT 109
righteous: r. and harmed,
TATE A 7
suffer the r. to be moved.
BIBL, O.T. 40
righteousness: leadeth me in the
paths of r. BIBL, O.T. 31
r. from the God of his salvation.
BIBL, O.T. 33
rightful: r. place to go; VERY 3
rights: no r. in this matter,
ROET 12
plead the antient R. in vain:
MARV 21
Your r. reach down EMPS 10
rigid: earth is r., MACL 9
grey r. uniform GUNN 1
R. and bright HECH 2
r. Cato read these lines of mine.
HERR 72
yon drear and r. bier POE 29
rigorous: r. teachers seized my
youth, ARNO 30
rills: lull'd by the r., ARNO 7
thousand r. their mazy progress
GRAY 23
rim: at the r. MONTA 5
hook shot kisses the r. HIRS 1
over the mountain's r.:
BROWNI R 58
r., the sediment WHITM 2
Rimbaud: R. and Verlaine, AIKE 2
rime: outlive this powerful r.;
SHAK 207
rimes: grieving r. of mine,
PETRA 4
rin: r. an' chase thee, BURN 62

rind: burnished with golden r.,
  MILT 69
toss it yonder, like a R.,
  DICKI 78
ring: before the final r. CRAN H 25
bells of death do r.? UNKN 128
bells on earth did r. UNKN 9
bells that sweetly r. STANT 1
For you alone I ride the r.,
  GRAHAM R 1
Let freedom r.! SMIT SA 1
maids dance in a r., NASHE 3
my Eccho r. SPENS 30
r. fancy's knell. SHAK 121
r. in the new, TENN 47
r. in the true. TENN 47
r. of pure and endless light,
  VAUG 32
r. of skull-/ bone KINN 11
R. out my doleful knell; BOLE 2
R. out the false, TENN 47
R. out the old, TENN 47
R. out, wild bells, TENN 46
R. out your bells, SIDN 36
r. the bells of London town.
  UNKN 23
r. the fuller minstrel in. TENN 49
Sea-nymphs hourly r. his knell:
  SHAK 156
walking round in a r.
  ELIOT T 117
ringdoves: shadows of r. PLATH 79
ringed: Not r. but rare, SMIT W 3
r. with power. DICKI 87
R. with the azure world, he
  stands. TENN 12
ringing: Devil below was r. his
  knell. SOUTHE 6
Five bells coldly r. out. SLES 5
r. grooves of change. TENN 79
r. plains of windy Troy.
  TENN 130
warning r. bell WHITM 101
ringlets: green sour r. make,
  SHAK 164
wanton r. waved MILT 73
rings: first cock his matin r.
  MILT 23
Five gold r., UNKN 278
r. no hunters' shout; SIGO 1
r. on every finger, UNKN 319
R. on her fingers, MOTH 25
scatter wheeling in great broken
  r. YEATS 165
Surrounded by its choral r.,
  STEVENS 29
white r. of tumult, CRAN H 27
riot: Dead winds' and spent waves'
  r. SWIN 11
R. in Algeria, in Cyprus, in
  Alabama; SNOD 9
rioted: r. in a drift, BRID R 9

riotous: Just for one r. day,
  DUNB P 4
r. glass houses built on rock,
  LOWE R 5
Riots: R. with his tongue
  TATE A 15
rip: r. the edge off any ideal or
  dream. MACN 2
ripe: Beauty, r., and calm, and
  fresh, DAVE 6
'Cherry-r., r., r.', HERR 5
corn-top's r., FOST 1
In folly r., RALEG 8
my r. thoughts SHAK 217
r. and red WHITM 29
R. as the melting cluster, GAY 1
r. breath of autumn, WHITM 108
r. daughters, JONS 36
r. fruit never fall? STEVENS 59
Today ready r., SURR 2
ripen: purposes will r. fast,
  COWP 5
ripened: r. plot to murder
  CHAU 47
riper: amuse his r. stage,
  POPE A 81
ripple: r. of rain; SWIN 3
r. widening ROET 18
ripples: r. down a sunny river;
  LAND 4
walk'd where the r. WHITM 1
riprap: Poetry a r. SNYD 26
rise: all of us prepare to r.,
  WRIG E 1
could I r. with you, DICKI 35
dead men r. up never; SWIN 15
doth not r. nor set, ROSS C 34
dreamy shadows r., LINC 1
dumb Terror shall r. MARK 8
exultant labor of his r.; HALL 5
Fair Nature's eye, r., MARL 1
half to r. and half to fall;
  POPE A 78
Let a race of men now r.
  WALK 6
like to r. and go
  STEVENSO R 19
men may r. on stepping-stones
  TENN 18
one comfort still must r.,
  POPE A 82
poor black cherubs r. at seven
  CULL 1
r. and fall LONG 30
r. and fall. SHAK 243
r. and ffight againe. UNKN 225
R. and put on your foliage,
  HERR 6
r. from out thy hearse, HERR 54
r. from trivial things,
  POPE A 110
r. from where they slept ROBI 53
R. like a fountain TENN 104

R. like Lions after slumber
  SHEL 40
R. odors of ploughed field
  LONG 8
r. on Mary's day LOWE R 9
R. on the bubble, SHEL 81
R. up, my love, BIBL, O.T. 72
r. upon some other shore,
  MCCRE 1
school-children r. like balloons.
  LOWE R 20
shall r. again; BRYA 3
share yet r. above STOD 2
soles of his feet r. KUMI 1
starry r. and starry fall. GRAV 34
struggle and r. brooding
  DICKEY 14
sun may set and r.: RALEG 12
thronging years in glory r.
  BRYA 14
trees unnumbered r., DYER J 1
vowels r. like balloons. PLATH 64
We die and r. the same,
  DONN 14
we fall to r., BROWNI R 12
winds begin to r. TENN 23
risen: Nicholas was r. for to pisse,
  CHAU 56
rises: Runs falls r. stumbles
  HAYD 19
Slow r. worth,
  JOHN S (1709–1784) 1
tide r., the tide falls, LONG 46
riseth: r. a new creation SKEL 10
risin': r. sun to greet him RILE 5
rising: bathed by the r. sun,
  WHITM 107
cries r. in waves WILLI 48
done with r. ROBI 15
gentle r., HERB G 14
Hell, r. from a thousand thrones,
  POE 13
inscrutable infantry r. TATE A 12
joyful world salutes the r. day.
  COWL 4
like a r. knell! BYRO 5
never seen the sun r., KAVA 25
Proteus r. from the sea;
  WORD 160
rest/ In the act of r., WILB 5
r. and gliding out, WHITM 111
r. and sinking waves, WHITM 51
r., freshly exuding, WHITM 75
r. from the toilet seat. LEVE 14
r. steam/ And clear dances
  WILB 24
see my apron r. UNKN 207
shadow at evening r. to meet
  you; ELIOT T 115
stilled the r. tumult, THAY 3
Sun keeps r. every morning.
  DURE 1
two sons at r. day, HOUS 29

water r., — ROET 41
with all his r. train;
  THOMS J (1700–1748) 12
risk: r. is full: AMMO 6
rissin: lyk a lyone r. up agane,
  DUNB W 2
rite: Yearly will I do this r.
  SHAK 132
rites: for sacred r. unfit. SIDN 22
religious r. Of sacrifice, MILT 104
R. Mysterious of connubial Love
  MILT 77
sin when love's r. are not done.
  CAREW 13
Trembling, begins the sacred r. of
  pride. POPE A 113
rituals: deeper r. of his bones,
  SAND 16
rival: r. for one hour JACK 1
r. of the rose! EMER 42
rive: r. the hills EMER 10
thoughts to r. the heart HOUS 24
riven: From thy r. side which
  flowed, TOPL 1
indignant ghost is r. POE 30
river: at the bottom of a r.,
  ROET 14
by Spoon R. MAST 8
children into the r.; JOHN F 1
down the r., STEVENSO R 23
dragon-fly on the r. BROWNI E 2
even the weariest r. sea.
  SWIN 15
Ferdinand De Soto, sleeping/ In
  the r., VAN DO 1
flow of the inland r., FINC 1
foam on the r., SCOT WA 8
for the dive/ Under the r.
  CRAN H 33
fruitful r. in the eye, SHAK 21
ghastly rapid r., POE 23
great r. take me to the main.
  TENN 106
great r. this side of Stygia,
  STEVENS 44
holy laughter in the r.! GINS 19
lived by the r.-side, HOLM 10
look on the r. and sky,
  WHITM 19
my song, like the rushing r.,
  MANG 2
night-herons by the flooded r.
  JEFFE 16
O Sleepless as the r. CRAN H 29
old foul r. SMIT ST 7
on the Stygian r.; POE 29
put thy feet/ Naked in the r.
  sweet; FLET J 2
reeds by the r.? BROWNI E 2
ripples down a sunny r.; LAND 4
r., and the heaven, EMER 43
r.-ark on the ocean brine,
  EMER 26

r. bears no empty bottles,
  ELIOT T 129
r. dried to its bed SIMI 4
r. flowing dark and deep,
  THOMS J (1834–1882) 6
r. had another shore, LOWE R 26
r./ Is a strong brown god —
  ELIOT T 26
r. jumps over the mountain
  AUDE 1
r./ Nor ocean spawns MILLE V 1
r. of crystal light,/ Into a sea of
  dew. FIEL E 8
R. of the Suicides;
  THOMS J (1834–1882) 6
R., spreading, flows —
  CRAN H 23
r. sweats/ Oil and tar
  ELIOT T 138
r. that flows nowhere,
  STEVENS 45
R. that is East — CRAN H 34
Skirting the r. road, WHITM 23
snow falls in the r., BURN 54
'Tirra Tirra,' by the r. TENN 64
to the r.! into the street! GINS 19
tree by a r. GILB 29
rivered: subways, r. under streets
  CRAN H 30
rivers: Ancient, dusky r.
  HUGH L 12
By the r. of Babylon,
  BIBL, O.T. 62
deep like the r. HUGH L 12
Fountain-head and source of r.,
  THOR 8
Only winds and r.,
  STEVENSO R 10
r. all run God knows where;
  SERV 13
streams and r. MAST 11
sweeter r. pulsing flit EMER 48
They built by r. AUDE 21
tree planted by the r.
  BIBL, O.T. 21
winding r. be red: FINC 2
riverside: Camped on a tropic r.,
  NASH 12
rivets: busy hammers closing r. up,
  SHAK 57
rivulet: some meandering r.,
  THOR 10
this r.'s sands, BRYA 1
rivulets: Myriads of r. TENN 107
road: Ah, little r., JOHN H 3
ancient, thoroughfare,/ The Roman
  R. HARD 35
bridge and up the r. WOOL 1
broad r. that stretches
  STEVENSO R 15
curve of a particular r. STAF 1
faked r. block? HEAN 21
far upon the eastern r. MILT 42

Fringing the dusty r. LOWE J 15
get on down the r. AMMO 18
house by the side of the r.
  FOSS 2
named/ The Open R. CRAN H 15
no determined r.; WORD 22
no r. through the woods. KIPL 28
off the r. DICKI 50
old lost r. KIPL 28
On a flat r. runs WHITM 70
Open R. goes to the used-car lot.
  SIMP 13
r. of evening, DE LA 16
r. runs near the stream, ARNO 38
r./ That men pass over YEATS 38
r. that turning MUIR 10
r. to the contagious hospital
  WILLI 34
r. was a ribbon of moonlight
  NOYE 6
r. wind uphill all the way?
  ROSS C 28
rolling English r. CHES 14
Roman R. runs straight HARD 34
shine upon the r. COWP 25
Skirting the river r., WHITM 23
threw away the R. DICKI 160
tiger on the r. JEFFE 9
totter on the r.: — FOST 2
upon the r. of life KAVA 12
we have no r. EMPS 1
world to be a grassy r.
  YEATS 122
roadbed: Wheels shake the r.
  ROET 51
roads: cross r. tree. HUGH L 13
naked on the r., YEATS 33
r. diverged in a wood, FROS 95
Two r. diverged FROS 94
roadside: r. fire. STEVENSO R 15
roadway: stand on the r.,
  YEATS 75
roam: let the Fancy r.!: KEAT 16
Sadly I r., FOST 4
soar, but never r. WORD 148
sometimes have t' r. GUES 1
we will no longer r." TENN 83
weary crowds I r.; EMER 26
world young lads no more shall
  r. MELV 21
roamed: forests where they r.,
  SIGO 1
roar: beyond the Atlantic r. —
  GALT 1
blind laboring r., JARR 23
Glorious the thunder's r.:
  SMAR 9
grumble, and rumble, and r.,
  READ T 1
he broke into a r.; HOLM 13
hear his cannons r.? UNKN 217
heart of the furnace r.; SERV 5
r. of spring, OLSO 22

rock and tempest's r., LONG 7
Rumbletum bunders r.
   CARRY 11
shout and bang and r. and brawl
   BELL 13
stand amid the r. POE 14
to a deeper r.? FROS 7
roar'd: Atlantic billows r., COWP 1
roared: r. by and left/ three men,
   CRAN H 16
roaring: Howling and r. SILKO 2
r. alongside he takes for granted,
   BISH 39
r. deeps and fiery sands,
   TENN 90
r., epic, ragtime tune LIND V 9
R. their readiness to avenge,
   HARD 15
roars: hungry lion r. SHAK 128
r. at you as you're dyin' WELL 1
roast: love no r. but a nut-brown
   toast, STEVENSO W 1
roastbeef: lack my r. and potato.
   RANS 33
Roasted: R. in wrath and fire,
   SHAK 30
robbed: Love that had r. us
   MERE G 14
r. the Danville train. UNKN 149
'Ye have r.,' NEWB 2
robber: like an armed r., PETRA 3
robber'd: r. like the look of, —
   DICKI 50
robbery: forgive thy r., gentle thief,
   SHAK 200
robe: Attic r. array'd, COLL 11
azure r. of night, DRAK 1
robed: angel, r. in spotless white,
   DUNB P 1
Liveried angels r. in green,
   LAND 7
r. as destinies, LARK 6
r. in fire, TENN 123
R. in the long friends,
   THOMA D 38
R. in the sable garb of woe,
   GRAY 3
Robert: haunts of R. Pinsky's
   PINS 3
R. of Lincoln is telling his name:
   BRYA 19
robes: all her r. are gone.
   UNKN 191
all her r. are on; UNKN 191
evil things, in r. of sorrow,
   POE 22
R. and furred gowns hide all.
   SHAK 81
R. loosely flowing, JONS 5
r. of green, ROET 16
r. of red generation BARK 1
r. riche, or fithele, or gay sautrie.
   CHAU 2

Weave r. SHEL 64
wrapped in purple r., YEATS 15
Robin: auld R. Gray he is kind
   LIND L 2
dreaded that first r. DICKI 39
master R. Hood lies dead,
   MUND 1
R. Redbreast in a Cage BLAK 2
r.-redbreast tunes his note;
   LYLY 4
r. sings over again THOMA E 6
Wake from thy nest, r. redbreast!
   HEYW 2
Where can poor R. go? ALLI 4
Who killed Cock R. MOTH 32
robins: As did r. LOWE J 12
robust: frame so r., LOWE J 1
r., friendly, WHITM 38
rock: based upon a r. ELIOT T 37
Big R. Candy Mountains.
   UNKN 26
crow by Red R. MOMA 6
Death, r. me asleep, BOLE 1
Drops away, hard r. wavers
   SNYD 49
each r. a word SNYD 52
eagle of the r. WYLI 1
fearfully as doth a gallèd r.
   SHAK 56
Hard R. wasn't a mean nigger
   KNIG 5
Kick at the r., Sam Johnson,
   WILB 14
nails him down upon a r.
   BLAK 31
No one loves r., SNYD 50
no water but only r.
   ELIOT T 144
On a r., GRAY 3
pendant r., SHAK 9
perilous r., SOUTHE 5
pool among the r. ELIOT T 146
riotous glass houses built on r.,
   LOWE R 5
r. and tempest's roar, LONG 7
r. crystal and its/
   imperturbability, MOOR M 9
r./ crystal thing to see —
   MOOR M 28
r. my bastard baby. UNKN 208
R. of ages, TOPL 1
sat on a slab of r. LOWE R 57
shadow under this red r.,
   ELIOT T 115
slept like a r. HUGH L 19
slick r. of metaphysics SNYD 26
sound of water over a r.
   ELIOT T 147
splinterless as a cloven r.
   FROS 122
steel decks r. with the lightning
   shock, ROON 3

stern and r.-bound coast,
   HEMA 3
sty me/ In this hard r., SHAK 157
tall r., WORD 33
usual gray r. LOWE R 57
warming r. MORG 1
Wind begun to r. the Grass
   DICKI 159
Rocked: R. in the cradle of the
   deep WILLA 1
rocket: r.'s red glare, KEY 1
Rocking: conscience always has the
   r.-chair, ROBI 48
endlessly r., WHITM 62
old crone r. the cradle,
   WHITM 68
r. alphabet, THOMA D 8
r. and rolling GINS 13
R. back and forth HUGH L 18
r. loom of history, HAYD 10
vexed to nightmare by a r.
   cradle, YEATS 136
rocks: by r. and hills return'd,
   WHITM 102
elephant-colored r., ROET 42
from r. to roses: PRAE 1
Like lizards on r. KNIG 1
loose r. in space SNYD 29
makes her barren r. ADDI 2
marriage on the r. MERR 3
Reply by heaving r. HART 4
r. breaking with light, BISH 35
R., Caves, Lakes, Fens, Bogs,
   Dens, MILT 61
r. impregnable are not so stout,
   SHAK 212
scales from shining r., WHITM 2
sit upon the r., MARL 18
splits/ the r. WILLI 29
stumbled through the r. FROS 61
Walled round with r. as an inland
   island, SWIN 10
rocky: forced on r. shores,
   CHAU 48
fountain from its r. cave
   WORD 154
r. for the Mudville nine THAY 1
r. sure-foot trails. SNYD 51
Within its r. heart, SIGO 2
rod: if right, I kiss'd the r.
   POPE A 15
little/ Lady with r. RANS 4
Moses with his r.! TIMR 5
r. and thy staff they comfort me.
   BIBL, O.T. 31
r./ To check the erring, WORD 88
Throw away thy r.: HERB G 24
vindictive r. of angry justice
   COWP 16
wisdom be put in a silver r.,
   BLAK 12
rode: Bareback he r.; WOOL 1
Morgan r. in advance; WOOL 2

r. out on a day. UNKN 37
r. that tide/ To Ararat; WILB 38
R. the six hundred. TENN 6
saddle Homer r. YEATS 37
saddled, he bridled, and gallant r.
  he, UNKN 37
rods: fashion out of r., CULL 8
riding the r., CRAN H 21
roe: like a r. or a young hart:
  BIBL, O.T. 71
Roger: two travelers, R. and I.
  TROW 4
Rogue: R. and Whore. SWIF 15
rogues: poor r. Talk of court news;
  SHAK 84
showed the r. they lied: GOLD 8
role: he perfected his r. DICKEY 23
roll: how slowly minutes r.
  ROCH 7
midnight r. Of black artillery;
  MELV 12
r. all our strength, MARV 35
R. on, thou ball, GILB 47
r. to the track, KENN 1
r. us shoreward soon." TENN 80
Senses r. themselves in fear
  BLAK 33
swift seasons r.! HOLM 3
"Up in the hills to r. and play."
  MILN 2
rolled: heights I r. from into the
  deep; BROWNI R 5
night's thunder far away had r.
  THOMA E 9
r. the psalm TENN 36
R. to starboard, TENN 88
tears r., like stones, SILKI 2
thunders r.; JOHN J 2
where the tide has r. you.
  KIPL 16
roller: r. of big cigars, STEVENS 9
r., pitch, and stumps, and all.
  LANG 2
Rollers: Holy R. and Jumpers
  HILL J 3
no little brass r. WILLI 45
rollicking: such/ r. measures,
  WILLI 12
rolling: Above the r. ball
  MERE G 8
Iser, r. rapidly. CAMPB T 3
Kicking and r. about WILLI 12
long, r.,/ Steady-pouring,
  STEPHENS 8
Over the r. waters go, TENN 113
plow the r. sea, VAN DY 3
rocking and r. GINS 13
r. English drunkard CHES 14
r. English road. CHES 14
small red sun goes r., BISH 26
veins r. roughly WALK 7
rolls: college r. receive his name,
  JOHN S (1709–1784) 17

cowboy r. His pack, SMIT W 2
figured wheel r. PINS 1
fish that r., MOMA 3
over Catholics the ocean r.,
  BYRO 43
r. through all things. WORD 36
Smoke r. and scarves PLATH 14
wheel as it r. PINS 3
Roman: act a lover's or a R.'s
  part? POPE A 3
ancient, thoroughfare,/ The R.
  Road. HARD 35
belaud R. celebrities POUN 30
beneath the R. ruin TENN 14
her R. guest, SHERB 1
Nature's R., MELV 12
On R. or on Russian YEATS 104
rhyme for r. FLEM 1
R. and his trouble HOUS 45
R. came to Rye CHES 14
R. Catholic attendants.
  LOWE R 54
R. Empire stood appalled:
  YEATS 117
R. Road runs straight HARD 34
R. Virgil, TENN 123
romance: honey of r. WILD 14
mourned R., ROBI 42
R., who loves to nod and sing,
  POE 38
stranger in my own r. PETRA 11
unannoying/ r.! MOOR M 2
romantic: deep r. chasm
  COLE SAM 20
I will be a r. CREE 8
R. Ireland's dead YEATS 137
romantics: were the last r.
  YEATS 36
Rome: dropping bombs on R.,
  LEWI 1
dust blown through the streets of
  R., MASE 8
grandeur that was R. POE 45
great to study R.; VAN DY 1
high and palmy state of R.,
  SHAK 20
Let R. in Tiber melt SHAK 3
Like Greece and R. SIMP 15
poison and traison at R.,
  WYAT 24
R.'s annals wax'd but dirty.
  BYRO 34
R.'s exalted beauties ADDI 1
R.'s ghost since her/ decease.
  BROWNI R 80
Strangers of R., LONG 20
romeos: Ribald r. HORA 1
Roncevaux: found/ At R. MACL 12
rondeaus: rondels, r./ Seeds in a dry
  pod, MAST 11
rondels: r., rondeaus,/ Seeds in a dry
  pod, MAST 11

Ronsard: Cassandra, R. found in
  Lyon. SYNG 3
rood: Jesus on the r.; CARRU 2
roof: Banners yellow, glorious,
  golden,/ On its r. POE 21
burning r. and tower YEATS 85
dark wainscot and timbered r.,
  NEWB 3
flowery r. Showered roses
  MILT 78
high embowed r., MILT 18
humble r. Is weather-proof;
  HERR 39
jumped off the r.! GINS 19
my r. the greenwood above,
  UNKN 201
Nor slumber nor a r. against the
  rain; MILLA 16
on our r. at night — HUGH L 1
rain is on the r. TENN 74
r. of England fell SHAP 27
r. of gold; JONS 35
r. was o' the beaten gold
  UNKN 300
r. with inward happiness,
  CAREW 19
to the arched r. MILT 114
weary pilgrim to thy r.;
  CAREW 21
with projected r. EMER 44
woven changeless r. of boughs:
  YEATS 94
roof'd: under the r. hospital,
  WHITM 115
roofs: frost was on the village r.
  STEVENSO R 5
r. of the world. WHITM 73
smoking r., soft bells, LONG 29
sweep r., o bless/ the r.,
  OLSO 8
rook: cold and r.-delighting heaven
  YEATS 32
Rookes: Pyes and Dawes and R. and
  Crows, BONH 1
rooks: r. are blown about the skies;
  TENN 23
speculating r. THOMA E 18
room: blessed Land of R. Enough
  VAN DY 3
brought him to that creaking r.
  FROS 73
brown r., RUKE 7
convent's narrow r.; WORD 59
down to the back r. KINS 1
Fifty springs are little r.,
  HOUS 40
horseplay of the locker r.,
  HECH 8
In every grave make r., DAVE 5
in that r. DICKI 20
in the burning r., SCHW 7
In winter, in my r., DICKI 84
lain/ In an adjoining R. DICKI 37

rosebuds

r.'s scent is bitterness
   THOMP F 1
Roves back the r.   DE LA 3
shape in the mind r.   ROET 50
Short is the glory of the blushing
   r.,   DANI S 6
sick of a r.   BROO G 19
smiling R.   HERR 26
Strew the Myrtle and R.   PRIO 5
tell the crooked r.   THOMA D 22
That which we call a r.
   SHAK 142
thou, my r.; in it thou art my all.
   SHAK 230
thought came like a full-blown r.,
   KEAT 8
to bear the red r. company.
   UNKN 14
twilight dim with r.,   DE LA 16
Up r. old Barbara Frietchie
   WHITT 2
up the chimney he r.   MOOR C 5
when the r. is blown?   WOTT 5
white r. breathes of love;   OREI 1
white r. is a dove.   OREI 1
white r. weeps, 'She is late;'
   TENN 94
with the worldless r.   WILB 3
withers quicker than the r.
   HOUS 56
withers/ The r.,   BOLT 1
without thorn the r.   MILT 69
You, of course, are a r.   FROS 97

rosebuds: Gather ye r.   HERR 55
rosemary: sovereign r.,   SKEL 1
roses: breast where r. could not
   live   ROBI 15
camphor, myrrh, and r.,   GRIF 1
Courts thee on R.   HORA 3
days of wine and r.:   DOWS 6
ever-returning r. of dawn.
   JEFFE 4
flat pink r.   PLATH 62
flowery roof/ Showered r.
   MILT 78
from rocks to r.:   PRAE 1
full cargo of r.   ROET 3
head with r. crowned,   HERR 3
Honey of r.,   HERB G 35
In thee all flowers and r. spring,
   BROWNE 1
Like wet and falling r.,   LAWR 12
Lillies without, R. within.
   MARV 29
make thee beds of r.   MARL 19
no such r.   SHAK 237
On cheeks and r. free he fed;
   LOVE 3
perfumèd tincture of the r.,/ Hang
   on such thorns,   SHAK 206
petals from blown r.   TENN 84
placed/ 'Fore damask r.   HERR 56
Plant thou no r.   ROSS C 33

r. and white lilies grow;
   CAMPI 23
r. damasked, red and white,
   SHAK 237
R. do blush   NOEL H 2
r./ Had the look of flowers
   ELIOT T 17
R. have thorns,   SHAK 199
R., Pyrgo, and Lapwater —
   THOMA E 11
R. thus its self to fill: MARV 29
snows and the r. of yesterday
   MAST 10
Strew on her r.,   ARNO 20
thy beds of r.,   RALEG 8
Thy moon-kissed r. seem:
   DOWS 4
Wild r., at your back porch,
   MOSS 6
yellow/ Gloire de Dijon r.
   LAWR 11

rosie: r. Morn resignes her light,
   WALL 8
r.-boosom'd Howres,   MILT 11
rosin: bit of r.,   TROW 5
rosy: Dark faces pale against that r.
   flame,   TENN 81
Nothing but r. hands   WILB 24
pale now, those r. lips,   BURN 31
r. cheeks and flaxen curls,
   BROWNI R 62
r. lips and cheeks   SHAK 232
r. ornaments in thee.   CAMPI 25
think of r. chocolate
   STEVENS 46
through their r. depths,   BRYA 25
rot: lie shall r.;   PATM 7
makes the timber r.;   RALEG 14
rotted: branches r. and falling.
   POUN 26
rotten: between r. teeth alack.
   RANS 8
cooked r. animals   GINS 14
dead and r.;   HOUS 43
I in earth am r.;   SHAK 216
in reason r.   RALEG 8
Jack, eating r. cheese,   FRANK 1
r. little downtowns.   PINS 1
These are r.,   SYNG 4
rotting: croppers r. shacks   WALK 1
r. and turning purpler,
   LOWE R 57
r./ Grave shall ne'er get out.
   BLAK 7
rotundity: thick r. o' the world!
   SHAK 75
Rouen: Joan whom Englishmen/ At
   R. doomed   VILL 3
Rouf: Farmer R.'s little lad.
   WOOL 1
rough: grown r. and wrinkled
   SEXT 9
it's r. and untended   BROO G 19

raw r. dun was he,   KIPL 2
R. in my pebbles,   SMIT ST 6
r. plain hearse   WILLI 45
R. winds do shake   SHAK 188
smooth shall bloom from the r.:
   STEVENSO R 17
stern, obdurate, flinty, r.,
   remorseless.   SHAK 61
tear our pleasures with r. strife
   MARV 35
this r. magic/ I here abjure,
   SHAK 165
turns earth's smoothness r.,
   BROWNI R 73
what r. beast,   YEATS 136
rougher: beneath a r. sea,   COWP 2
r. than His handiwork,
   BROWNI R 17
roughest: r. berry on the rudest
   hedge.   SHAK 4
Virtue is the r. way,   WOTT 8
Roughly: R. rushing on the sky!
   DYER J 2
Speak r.   CARRO 2
veins rolling r.   WALK 7
roughness: short-haired joy and r.
   SNYD 16
Round: arms/ R. the griefs of the
   ages,   THOMA D 28
attains the upmost r.   SHAK 44
broad face and a little r. belly,
   MOOR C 4
clenched on a r. pain;
   THOMA D 5
compass r.,   FROS 102
Crier on his r.   HOLM 15
early in this cloistral r.   ARNO 40
fired the shot heard r. the world.
   EMER 11
fold it r. me   HULM 2
heaven a perfect r.   BROWNI R 2
hollow r. of my skull.   ELIOT T 6
hour come r. at last,   YEATS 136
Ray r. with flames   TENN 42
R. about her tomb   SHAK 132
R. about the cauldron go;
   SHAK 111
r. at the same height/ in perpetual
   sunset,   BISH 26
r. earth's imagined corners,
   DONN 5
r. headlands shone.   ARNO 5
r. him o'er the dead.   HEMA 1
r. it like a bundle.   FROS 140
r. little worm   SHAK 153
R. me once again! . . .   TENN 97
r. of their need,   DICKEY 28
r. the setting sun   WORD 86
r. the tent of God   BLAK 99
r.-tower of my heart.   LONG 10
Slung atween the r. shot
   NEWB 1

torn hair r. their paleness.
SPEND 1
travelled life's dull r.,/ Where'er
his stages SHEN 2
Undulate r. the world,
WHITM 50
Unit and universe are r.;
EMER 50
virtues walked their narrow r.,
JOHN S (1709–1784) 3
whirring sail goes r., TENN 105
with the little r. button at top;
FOOT 1
rounded: r. with a sleep. SHAK 163
roundelay: my love my r., PEEL 1
shepherd's r. BRET 6
rounders: Come all you r.
UNKN 53
roundness: r. and withdrawal
AMMO 12
rounds: walking their r., BLAK 65
rouse: Lief should I r. at morning
HOUS 2
r. him at the name of Crispian.
SHAK 60
R. the Echoes of the Past,
GILB 43
Would r. God to relent; EBER 2
Roused: R. me from sleep WILLA 2
rouses: r. up the seeds of dark
disease.
THOMS J (1700–1748) 13
rousing: lapdogs give themselves the
r. shake, POPE A 111
Rousseau: mock on, Voltaire, R.!
BLAK 38
rout: amid the mimic r. POE 31
route: Behind, a sealed r.,
DICKI 116
no r. shut, AMMO 8
r. obscure and lonely, POE 16
R. of Evanescence DICKI 123
way unseen, the certain r.,
VERY 4
routes: from the taken r. GUNN 12
routine: so many r. cries. HILL G 7
rouz'd: fierie vertue r. MILT 116
roved: world we r., Ned Bunn?
MELV 21
Rover: dreadful sound could the R.
hear, SOUTHE 6
Home comes the r., ALLI 5
Roves: R. back the rose. DE LA 3
roving: License my r. hands,
DONN 15
to the r. eye.
THOMS J (1700–1748) 5
too old for r. MASE 3
row: I know about the r. HART 3
made the Iliad from such/ A local
r. KAVA 5
R. after R. TATE A 11
r./ Of polished pillars, JONS 35

r. on r., MCCRA 1
Stand in a r. and learn. MERW 4
rowed: r. him softer home —
DICKI 13
roweth: barge/ That nobody r.
UNKN 89
Rowing: R. home to haven MASE 1
rowling: r. in the fiery Gulfe
MILT 49
rows: apples are laid in r., DRIN 1
extend their shining r.,
POPE A 114
hours stand in solid r., SHAP 29
long r. of cots WHITM 115
r. of cans BISH 13
r. of disgusting old rags LAWR 3
r. of the hospital tent,
WHITM 115
r. that once, and somewhere else,
were young . . . MACL 8
running in rattling r.; SIDN 9
Roxy: car like the R. KENN 1
royal: dined in a r. way CARRY 10
promised the R. babe to rear
GILB 17
rare and r. names SYNG 2
r. bones BEAU/BASS 1
r. eagle draws his vigorous
young, THOMS J (1700–1748) 8
r. throne of kings, this sceptered
isle, SHAK 88
Satan with a r. trick EMER 37
shook it forth with a r. will.
WHITT 3
throne of r. state, MILT 58
which the R. stripling. GILB 19
Rub: R. a half potato on your wart
HUGO 5
there's the r.; SHAK 39
rubbed: neck r. the windowsill
HALL 2
rubber: after partridges, or a little r.
ball? LAWR 14
body-armor of black r. RICH 3
R. breasts or a rubber crotch,
PLATH 1
r. doughnuts,/ Melting at the
knees, ROET 54
Their r. elbows UPDI 1
rubbers: factories they make r. in
SNYD 27
rubbish: write such hopeless r.
STEPHEN 6
rubble: dusty r. of the highway,
ROET 41
Under the r., LOWE R 9
Rubie: R., which you weare,
HERR 45
rubies: r., fairy favours, SHAK 126
ruby: clean/ In you, r. PLATH 70
one r. flare SHAP 1
r. been youre cheekes rounde.
CHAU 122

ruck: monstrous r. of mountains
MONTA 1
rudder: man the r., EMER 47
Rhime the R. is of Verses,
BUTL 6
ruddier: r. than the cherry, GAY 1
ruddy: showed the r. morn's
approach. SWIF 10
r. are his claws STEVENS 13
R. are his eyes STEVENS 13
r. limbs and flaming hair,
BLAK 21
r. rosary, SKEL 1
rude: Before r. hands have touch'd
it? JONS 2
forc'd fingers r. MILT 25
in his r.-dug grave WHITM 107
mercy/ Of a r. stream
FLET/SHAK 3
poor r. lines SHAK 196
r. bridge that arched the flood,
EMER 11
r. hand no ill Tongue light
PRIO 5
r., unbending, lusty, WHITM 39
thy breath be r. SHAK 13
rudely: darkly wise and r. great:
POPE A 78
that am r. stamped, SHAK 96
rudeness: unclad would winter's r.
dare; VERY 1
ruder: through r. hands, AYTON 1
Rudesheimer: Mr. Mum's R.
COLE SAM 26
rudest: roughest berry on the r.
hedge. SHAK 4
Rudge: Poe, with his raven, like
Barnaby R., LOWE J 5
rue: Bitter plaints to r. thy wrong,
UNKN 169
lumbering lubbard loitering slow,/
Impingers r. thee MELV 2
overrun with r.? HABE 2
planting r.?" HARD 6
press the r. for wine.
SCOT WA 24
With r. my heart HOUS 62
rues: envy strangely r. his end,
GREV/DYER 2
ruffled: r. once, ROBI 40
ruffles: r. the woods HILL G 1
ruffling: we have borne/ The r.
wind, COWP 17
ruffs: r. about their necks,
MACN 14
rug: feared by all, is now a r.
GUIT 2
rugged: r. Russian bear, SHAK 110
unpolished, r. verse DRYD 20
ruin: all go to rack r. POUN 35
beneath the Roman r. TENN 14
courteous r. of proffered usury,
SIDN 4

gradual r. spreading like a stain;
AUDE 97

Magnificent in piles of r. ADDI 1

new years r. and rend. SWIN 23

Predicts the r. of the State.
BLAK 3

r. a fine tenor voice AUDE 49

R. hath taught SHAK 211

R. seize thee, ruthless king!
GRAY 1

Spreading r. and scattering ban,
BROWNI E 2

Stern R.'s ploughshare BURN 61

to her r. now I tend." MILT 92

walls shall crumble to r.,
LONG 10

ruin'd: Melrose rise in r. pride.
SCOT WA 4

ruine: hideous r. and combustion
MILT 49

r. Kings. DRYD 1

ruined: Bare r. choirs, SHAK 215

his life is r. IGNA 1

past life a r. church— MACN 25

You ain't r.,' HARD 37

you know I'd been r.?' HARD 36

ruins: future in r.! SIMP 15

rule: born to r. the storm; HEMA 1

both R. and Law alone: DRYD 17

charge of r. nor governance;
MARTIA 1

Charles here r. HERR 2

Common R. was made the
common Prey; DRYD 19

possibility of r. AMMO 7

r. all dominions that are rare;
KAVA 13

r. and pale forethought,
EMER 33

they that r. in England CHES 5

Winter comes, to r. the varied
year, THOMS J (1700–1748) 12

written R. and never known,
DRYD 17

ruled: God their severance r.!
ARNO 42

star that r. his doom SHEL 82

rulelessness: sum of r.: AMMO 7

rules: for ancient r. a just esteem;
POPE A 29

hand r. heaven; THOMA D 25

hand r. pity THOMA D 25

one or two r., GILB 57

rhetorician's r. Teach nothing
BUTL 3

r. the shadows of the wood,
YEATS 164

Those r. of old discovered,
POPE A 27

what r. he did it by; BUTL 2

ruling: our life a r. effluence
ARNO 17

various r. passions find,
POPE A 97

Rum: R. Tum Tugger is a Curious
Cat— ELIOT T 106

scalps served up in r. GILB 2

Rum-ti-Foo: balmy isle of R.,
GILB 1

rumble: grumble, and r., and roar,
READ T 1

r. of a distant Drum! OMAR 3

tone their r. down. HUGH L 8

Rumbletum: R. bunders roar.
CARRY 11

rumbling: r. like an earthquake,
WHITM 102

ruminate: thus to r., SHAK 211

rumour: awed by r., POPE A 109

listen to popular r.; GILB 56

rumours: aethereal r. Revive
ELIOT T 154

nurses and r.; AUDE 37

rump: leather I slapped to his r.
SWEN 2

run: beyond the r.-way BETJ 8

Blinded they into folly r.
UNKN 185

dead heart r. them in!
STEVENSO R 2

jump and r. WILLI 18

legs of the race r. forwards,
HARP 1

make him r. MARV 35

My garden is r. wild! HABE 2

our dreams used to r.?' HARD 10

rivers all r. God knows where;
SERV 13

r. its course AUDE 63

r. my chance with Jim, HAY 4

Saints—to windows r. DICKI 70

sixty seconds' worth of distance
r., KIPL 8

stars had r. away YEATS 16

Shiloh, Antietam, Malvern Hill,
Bull R. TATE A 12

Sweet Thames, r. softly,
ELIOT T 129

To r. amuck, POPE A 89

Rung: R. from their marble caves
DRUM 7

sea-caves r., SCOT WA 15

Runic: In a sort of R. rhyme,
POE 10

runnable: stag, a r. stag. DAVID 5

runner: well-trained r., WHITM 70

runners: need no r. WELC 1

R. whom renown outran
HOUS 57

runneth: my cup r. over.
BIBL, O.T. 31

running: all the r. water goes,
PACK 1

call of the r. tide MASE 12

came the children r.
BROWNI R 62

dust, here r. in the glass,
JONS 12

guns drawn they came r. LEE 1

r. in rattling rows; SIDN 9

sounded as if the streets were r.,
DICKI 91

under r. laughter. THOMP F 6

Under the r. tap MACN 20

runn'st: r. thou ne'er so fast,
WEBS/ROWL 1

runs: blue horse that r. in the plain
MOMA 3

gentler purpose r. THOMP W 4

Ink r. STRA 1

On a flat road r. WHITM 70

one increasing purpose r.,
TENN 77

road r. near the stream,
ARNO 38

R. falls rises stumbles HAYD 19

r. his link SACK 1

R. the path I took; WHITT 32

So r. my dream: TENN 31

spirit r., intermittently, ROET 46

Thames r. chill MORR 5

tide r. high, THAX 1

turns his prow and r., ROON 3

Where no sea r., THOMA D 29

runway: dawn grass r. SNYD 35

rural: dream of r. ease, CRAB 6

r. o'er ices and wines, PRAE 4

r. seat of various view: MILT 69

Some bring a capon, some a r.
cake, JONS 36

rurall: r. privacie: HERR 18

rush: fools r. in POPE A 23

hideous throng r. out forever,
POE 23

r. blindly on unto it, PETRO 1

r. for my veins, WHITM 77

r. into the skies. POPE A 66

what/ Soared: the fierce r.:
JEFFE 16

rushed: r. into the field, BYRO 7

rushes: Green grow the r.-O
UNKN 51

in moss and r., LONG 41

r. tall,/ Ducks are a-dabbling,
GRAHAME 1

r. thee to meet; EMER 10

rushing: my song, like the r. river,
MANG 2

Roughly r. on the sky! DYER J 2

r. amorous contact WHITM 23

rushy: Down the r. glen, ALLI 1

russet: every fleck of r. FROS 4

Russia: out of great R. SAND 21

Russian: despots ride a R.
BYRO 47

On Roman or on R. YEATS 104
rugged R. bear, SHAK 110
rust: anchor weeps/ Its red r.
    BOGA 12
coaches shall be scrap and r.
    SAND 12
iron is iron till it is r.
    MOOR M 15
rifle grooves curling with flakes of
    r. SAND 1
r. disus'd, and shine no more,
    COWP 21
r./ Life's iron chain WILD 4
r. unburnished, not to shine in
    use! TENN 131
that which never taketh r.:
    SIDN 34
Then we shall r. in shade,
    ARNO 16
toy soldier is red with r.,
    FIEL E 6
ruste: if gold r., what shal iren do?
    CHAU 13
rusted: r. in my back, RICH 14
rusting: Lies r., mouldering.
    WHITM 28
rustle: r. and clank of muskets,
    WHITM 32
r. of the liquid and sands
    WHITM 109
rustling: dread the r. of the grass;
    WORD 3
white and r. sail CUNN A 1
rusts: r. with its grass. KENN 2
rusty: r. gun on the wall, SAND 1
r. pike's in the cabin still,
    CLARK J 3
r. Pump pumps JARR 26
ruth: not in r., ARNO 31
sad heart of R., KEAT 50
ruthless: burst like a r. force,
    WHITM 7
'Ruin seize thee, r. king!' GRAY 1
Rutledge: I am Anne R. MAST 2
rye: put their Scotch or r. down
    COWA 3
Roman came to R. CHES 14
r. reach to the chin, PEEL 6
ryme: Emong the muses where I
    rede and r.; WYAT 25
rymes: worthy of your gracefull r.,
    SPENS 29

S

Sabaoth: Lord S. is his name,
    LUTH 3
Sabbath: child that's born on the S.
    day MOTH 22
finished S., WHITM 25
S. of Witches. AUDE 84
Some keep the S. DICKI 130

sable: night whose s. breast
    CULL 3
Robed in the s. garb of woe,
    GRAY 3
s. arms,/ Black as his purpose,
    SHAK 30
s. curls all silvered o'er with
    white: SHAK 186
s. stole of cypress lawn, MILT 16
s. throne behold POPE A 1
saw her s. skirts LONG 24
son of the s. Night, DANI S 8
Underneath this s. hearse
    BROWNE 3
view our s. race with scornful
    eye, WHEA 1
Winter snows upon thy s. hairs.
    DANI S 16
sabotage: motive s. their motives.
    MACN 3
sabre: on a s. track movering
    HAYD 22
sack: Balls tight in a tough hair s.
    SNYD 37
dripping s.-wise down LAWR 21
s. Of dynamite SNYD 2
sackcloth: s. and ashes RODG 7
sacked: s. land/ of my father.
    BARA 7
sacrament: constant s. of praise.
    STEVENS 38
Upon a s. DICKI 102
Sacred: Convent of the S. Heart,
    ELIOT T 112
dance s. AMMO 16
for s. rites unfit. SIDN 22
in its s. keep! POE 41
lips to touch the s. fire?
    JOHN J 5
pine in vain the s. Seven;
    EMER 7
s. few SHEL 77
s. Fountain of eternall light,
    QUAR 2
s. influence CRAS 7
s. instinct did inspire TRAH 7
s. moments when we played,
    MCKA 4
s. rayes of Chastity, MILT 3
s. whisper of the pines, TOOM 3
seal the s. trust, SIGO 2
sucks in thy s. lays. CAREW 18
Trembling, begins the s. rites of
    pride. POPE A 113
veils her s. fires, POPE A 2
sacredly: deem/ More s. LOWE J 16
sacrifice: blessed s. be mine,
    HERB G 8
holy hush of ancient s.
    STEVENS 54
pomp of holy s. GREV 10
religious rites/ Of s., MILT 104

solemn s., performed in state,
    POPE A 105
Thine ancient s., KIPL 18
Too long a s. YEATS 54
sacrilegious: reach of s. hands,
    POPE A 31
sad: Death, s. refuge GRAY 26
Death's a s. bone; SEXT 17
experience sweet and s.,
    WHITM 116
in s. cypress let me be laid.
    SHAK 176
insufficient eyes, forever s.:
    ROBI 6
like a s. slave, SHAK 208
my s. people's soul BENN G 5
of all s. words WHITT 21
remember and be s. ROSS C 20
s. account of fore-bemoaned
    moan, SHAK 195
s. alnage of the years. ROBI 7
s. and bad and mad
    BROWNI R 24
s. and heavy line/ Of death,
    VAUG 29
s. and solemn shows,
    FLET/SHAK 6
s. and sorrowful day UNKN 207
s. and tremulous. WHITM 61
s. augurs mock SHAK 229
s. effect of sadder grones;
    HERB G 19
s. heart of Ruth, KEAT 50
s. mortality SHAK 212
s. old earth WILC 1
s. scenes and thoughts and feelings
    vanish THOMS J (1834–1882) 7
S. songs of Autumn mirth.
    THOMA E 6
sculptors and the poets were half
    s., AUDE 53
Sing no s. songs ROSS C 33
soul's s. tears.'
    THOMS J (1834–1882) 8
still, s. music of humanity,
    WORD 34
Sullen, s.,
    THOMS J (1700–1748) 12
sweet, s. years, the melancholy
    years, . . . BROWNI E 7
tell s. stories SHAK 89
their s. and fatal voice. FULL 4
there on the s. height,
    THOMA D 12
sadder: Another s. song: NOYE 5
s. and a wiser man,
    COLE SAM 31
saddest: s. are these: WHITT 21
s. of all kings JOHN L 2
s. of the year— BRYA 7
tell of s. thought. SHEL 71
saddle: s. Homer rode YEATS 37

saddled: He s., he bridled, and gallant rode he,   UNKN 37

saddles: lost ponies with/ Dragging s.   SNYD 51

Sadly: S. I roam,   FOST 4

  s. like the abstract Jew.   WARR 4

sadness: majestic in thy s.   TENN 126

  no s. of farewell,   TENN 10

  s. longer last?/ Grief is but a wound to woe;   FLET/OTHE 1

  s. of joy.   KINN 8

  shade of s.,   WHITT 3

sae: s. the Lord be thankit.   BURN 17

safe: comes s. home,   SHAK 60

  dreamed was s. . . .   SITW 8

  entrust them to a s.   GRAV 29

  hearts seemed s. in our breasts   SITW 8

  none is s.   MOOR M 42

  s. from action, valiantly advise;   ROCH 3

  still s. with Thee   WILLA 2

  Winds somewhere s. to sea.   SWIN 15

  with Meeter s.,   BUTL 6

safeguard: s. of the West: WORD 90

safely: toddle s. home   SASS 4

safest: where I thought I was s.,   WHITM 95

safety: for the general s.   MILT 59

  lock of her s.-deposit box   JARR 12

  Peace and s.   HOPKINSO 2

  S. with virtue of the sun.   GUNN 1

  Thy s. being motive.   SHAK 69

saffron: s. beach,   DAVID 3

saft: s. and narrow!   UNKN 39

saftyes: liffes and s. all!   UNKN 58

sagas: frosty s.,   CRAN H 8

Sage: By saint, by savage, and by s.,   POPE A 126

  eye of the s.,   KNOX 2

  lengthen'd, s. advices,   BURN 51

  S. Heraclitus says;   POUN 42

  Seasoned with s. and onions, and port wine.   SOUTHE 8

  There lived a s.   CHAM 1

  without hardness will be s.,   ARNO 36

sages: all the s. can.   WORD 145

  bland smile from these s.;   GILB 59

  s. ask thee why   EMER 42

  s. have seen   COWP 23

  till all the s. know.   YEATS 69

Sagged: S. and reeled   LIND V 8

  s. ominously upon the earth   GRAV 22

sagging: yellow and s. moon,   WHITM 67

sags: s. like a heavy load.   HUGH L 10

said: God s. Shall these bones live?   ELIOT T 6

  no more to be s.   UNKN 200

  s. no word,   WILD 4

  s. their nevers   CUMM 5

  vampire who s. he was you   PLATH 32

sail: brother should s. a painted boat.   WHITT 16

  every threadbare s.,   HOLM 18

  proud full s.   SHAK 217

  reef the s.,   EMER 47

  s. against the wind.   WYAT 19

  s. on, O Ship of State!   LONG 6

  S. on, O Union,   LONG 6

  swan s.   MERE G 14

  take in s.: —   EMER 46

  weather-beaten s.   CAMPI 17

  whirring s. goes round,   TENN 105

  white and rustling s.   CUNN A 1

sailed: He s. east, he s. west,   UNKN 317

  s. away/ From a leaking ship   WHITT 24

  s. calmly on.   AUDE 64

  s. into proud Turkey,   UNKN 317

  S. off in a wooden shoe —   FIEL E 8

  s. the seas   YEATS 127

  s. the wintry sea;   LONG 51

  They s. away,   LEAR 11

  wooden shoe that s. the skies   FIEL E 9

sailing: Bodhidharma s. the Yangtze   SNYD 24

  s. down the stream,   THOMS J (1700–1748) 9

  three ships come s. by,   UNKN 8

  western orb s. the heaven,   WHITM 48

sailor: brings the s. home from sea,   ELIOT T 134

  Home is the s.,   STEVENSO R 21

  s. frae the main,   BURN 34

  s. told it to me.   WHITM 89

  some shipwrecked s.,   LUCR 5

sailors: human seraphim, the s.,   GINS 11

sails: argosies of magic s.,   TENN 75

  for s. outspread,   COLE SAM 43

  necks pulsed like s.   HEAN 10

  Purple the s.,   SHAK 5

  S. filled, and streamers waving,   MILT 110

  set of the s.   WILC 4

sailships: s. and steamships,   WHITM 43

saint: By s., by savage, and by sage,   POPE A 126

  corrupt my s. to be a devil,   SHAK 240

  folded like a s.,   WYLI 9

  Follow your s.,   CAMPI 2

  for Scotland and S. Andrew   UNKN 226

  frequent/ Doctor and S.,   OMAR 5

  he was a s.,   AUDE 93

  make of me a s.,   CONG 2

  No more S. Patrick's Day   UNKN 299

  Sweet s., 'tis true you worthy be,   GREV 2

  Tomorrow is S. Valentine's day,   SHAK 36

  Upon S. Crispin's day   DRAY 2

  weren't no s.   HAY 4

Saint-Saens: "S.!" it seems to be whispering,   OHAR 4

Sainte: prente of S. Venus seel.   CHAU 90

saintly: s. motorcyclists,   GINS 11

  s. soul floats   POE 29

  s. visage   MILT 15

saints: Afro angels, black s.   HAYD 1

  happy harbour of the s.,   UNKN 147

  in Christ's coach s. sweetly sing,   TAYL E 4

  keep the feet of his s.,   BIBL, O.T. 8

  land of scholars and s.:   MACN 4

  my lost s., —   BROWNI E 6

  S. Heaven-lost Happiness   TAYL E 8

  s. immortal reign;   WATT I 8

  s. revile her,   GRAV 41

  s. through the wood,   LANIE 3

  S. — to windows run —   DICKI 70

  s. with their beau-peers   FLET G YO 2

  soul is with the s.,   COLE SAM 18

sair: mony a heart thou hast made s.   BURN 36

saith: Passing away, s. the World,   ROSS C 18

  soothfastness unto you s.   CHAU 70

sake: descend/ To die here for thy s.,   VAUG 16

  For Christ's s. not black —   WILLI 44

  for her pretty s.   ROET 28

  For her own fair s.   UNKN 123

  for her s. I would have died,   VAUG 30

  for his humour's s.,   COWP 3

  For Jesus Christ his s.'   UNKN 77

  For old religion's s.,   HERR 23

  tear/ Fall, for her s.,   WHITT 5

salad: crazy s. with their meat
   YEATS 107
salads: legs waken s. in the brain
   CRAN H 24
sale: Nothing for s. HODG 10
salients: s. of colonial policy.
   WALC 2
salley: Down by the s. gardens
   YEATS 50
sally: make a sudden s., TENN 4
   none like pretty S.; CAREY 4
salmon: like the chinook/ s.
   LOWE R 47
   quick-eyed trout/ Or darting s.
   THOMS J (1700–1748) 9
   s. sing in the street. AUDE 1
saloon: From the gilded s. KNOX 3
salt: leaves of s.-lettuce, WHITM 2
   no joy but lacks s. FROS 113
   s.-caked smoke stack MASE 2
   taste of that s. breath YEATS 148
   unplumbed, s., estranging sea.
   ARNO 42
   with s. tears BRAD 3
salte: my byttre s. teres PETRA 1
salted: barrel of s. herrings
   WYLI 11
   kegs of s. sprats, BROWNI R 60
   repose,/ S. and sobered,
   THOMA E 16
   s. it down with our bones.
   KIPL 31
   s. was my food, THOMA E 16
salty: on a s. day MILLA 12
salute: grapes the morn s. EMER 2
   s. us on the turns. KUMI 1
salutes: joyful world s. the rising
   day. COWL 4
   s. me as he goes, DICKI 42
salvation: bottle of s., RALEG 10
   Mind is the one s.? — SNOD 9
   righteousness from the God of his
   s. BIBL, O.T. 33
   S. must its Doom receive
   DRYD 18
salver: s. of infinity, CRAN H 5
salving: s. thy amiss, SHAK 199
Sam: I cremated S. McGee.
   SERV 1
Samarcand: From silken S.
   KEAT 13
same: beauty would be the s.
   TENN 101
   devour'd by the s. harpy.
   BYRO 34
   die you are the s.; FRENE 7
   door after door the s., SHAP 7
   I've never been the s.
   ELIOT T 127
   lost the s., HERB G 26
   Nature and Homer were, he found,
   the s. POPE A 28
   past is just the s., — SASS 1

pledged event is still the s
   MELV 8
s. as a month before, —
   WHITT 33
s. cover in the cool night,
   WHITM 109
s. look which she turned
   MOOR T 3
s. the whole world over;
   UNKN 219
set in the s. bowers; VAUG 8
things always seemed the s.!
   TENN 81
We die and rise the s., DONN 14
Samson: S. I my thousands slay.'
   FRANK 1
   S., though he were so strong,
   SOUTHW 11
sanctify: s. desire's idolatry.
   GREV 7
   s. this altar to be thine.
   HERB G 8
sanctity: s. can't pursue him;
   PEAC 3
   Traditional s. and loveliness;
   YEATS 36
sanctuaried: Denmark's s. Jews!
   MOOR M 3
sanctuarize: should murder s.;
   SHAK 38
sand: Abstinence sows s. BLAK 21
   edge of the s., LEAR 12
   false/ As stairs of s., SHAK 122
   grains of s., CARN 1
   Grains of the golden s. POE 14
   my s. is sinking, HARD 12
   s. her chamber door. DE TA 1
   s.-crumb loose, ROET 4
   sink as water in the s.;
   BIBL, O.T. 42
   Such quantities of s.: CARRO 38
   they as the s., LONG 26
   Throwing myself on the s.,
   WHITM 63
   tills the s. BOYD 1
   waves, altered by s.-bars,
   ROET 44
   We write in S., WALL 3
   wind blows full of s., LI PC 1
   World in a Grain of S. BLAK 1
   your s.-papering words WALK 3
sandal: bright and battering s.!
   HOPKINS 6
   massive s. set on stone. MILLA 9
sandpile: sternly allotted s.
   CUMM 40
sandpiper: One little s. and I;
   THAX 1
sands: few s. and dead leaves
   WHITM 3
   Footprints on the s. of time
   LONG 36

golden s., and crystal brooks,
   DONN 6
mooned s. forsake LUCR 4
old hu hed Egypt and its s.,
   HUNT 6
part of the s. and drift. WHITM 3
ran itself in golden s. TENN 70
roaring deeps and fiery s.
   TENN 90
rustle of the liquid and s.
   WHITM 109
s. of the desert YEATS 135
s. upon the Red Sea shore,
   BLAK 39
sterile s. and the fields beyond,
   WHITM 62
this rivulet's s., BRYA 1
sandwich: s. papers, ELIOT T 129
sandwiches: s. and Coca-Cola,
   OHAR 12
sandy: s. perilous wildes, MILT 3
   Wherever it's s. CARRY 2
sane: Assent, and you are s.;
   DICKI 106
   word, liquid, s., WHITM 43
sang: all s. " Annie Laurie."
   TAYL B 2
   bones chirping ELIOT T 8
   legendary isle Where sirens s.
   DAY 7
   morning stars s. together,
   BIBL, O.T. 14
   s. burning/ In the sun.
   THOMA D 35
   s. far better than you knew;
   JOHN J 7
   s. his didn't CUMM 4
   s. in my chains like the sea.
   THOMA D 21
   s. my sour tone SNOD 16
   s. to the Light — SITW 8
   s. within a flame. ROET 10
   summer s. in me MILLA 40
   sweetly s. of men in pow'r,
   DICKEN 2
   Sweetly s. the nightingale.
   WALT 2
   They s. of love, TAYL B 2
   When the birds of Eden s.?
   CULL 5
   You s. a race JOHN J 7
sanguine: s. alamandines BEDD 10
   Unreasoning, s., visionary —
   HARD 47
sanity: s. of field and mountain
   JEFFE 21
   trust the s. of my vessel;
   OHAR 16
sank: mercury s. AUDE 36
   Sometimes she s., sometimes she
   swam. UNKN 31
sans: s. Singer, and — s. End!
   OMAR 4

S. teeth, S. eyes, S. taste, S. everything. SHAK 12

S. Wine, S. Song, OMAR 4

sap: dried the s. out of my veins, YEATS 57

one s. and one root — POUN 53

s. in the tree SITW 8

s. in/ the trees, AMMO 16

s. went through MOOR M 21

Vaunt in their youthful s., SHAK 187

sapless: burnt-out brain and s. cinders. BYRO 34

saplings: gale, it plies the s. HOUS 45

plies the s. double, HOUS 44

sapped: youth s. day by day: ROSS C 18

sapphire: wind flaking s., CRAN H 44

Sappho: S. loved and sung, BYRO 40

Sarah: dinna grieve your S.; UNKN 79

sardine: little s. men MACN 1

sardines: s. in it." OHAR 22

Sargasso: S. Sea, POUN 54

sashes: his nice new s. GRAHAM H 3

sat: blackbird s. In the cedar limbs. STEVENS 67

I s. me down; DICKI 89

I s. upon the shore/ Fishing, ELIOT T 155

s. in a commodore's hat CARRY 10

s. on a slab of rock. LOWE R 57

s. on my shoulders. STRA 5

s. the sow of fear SHAP 26

twa sisters s. in a bour; UNKN 29

Satan: deep abyss where S. crawls TRAH 1

Hornie, S., Nick, or Clootie, BURN 1

Man, with is S. SNYD 21

S. sweet-talked her, HAYD 12

S., thou art but a Dunce, BLAK 20

S. with a royal trick EMER 37

satanic: s. thistle GINS 40

these dark S. Mills? BLAK 34

satchels: schoolboys lag with s. in their hands. SWIF 11

sate: s. itself in a celestial bed SHAK 27

s. the curious taste? MILT 5

sated: s. with variety. LOVE 4

satellite: revolving s., WHITM 59

satiety: having fed to s. ELIOT T 6

satire: in good s., BYRO 35

S. or sense, alas, POPE A 9

to whom my s. seems too bold: POPE A 87

Satire's: S. my weapon, POPE A 89

satisfaction: finding of a s., STEVENS 32

s. is a lowly/ thing, MOOR M 43

smile, with s. SHAP 6

satisfied: bride's ambition s. YEATS 35

greater torment/ Of love s. ELIOT T 10

nothing s. the fool YEATS 72

Saturday: Died on S.,/ Buried on Sunday, MOTH 26

S.'s child works for its living, MOTH 22

Saturday's: S. an holiday; SMAR 1

Saturn: heavy S. laughed and leaped SHAK 225

where S. keeps the years; ROBI 15

satyrs: nymphs and s. YEATS 100

sauce: only s. they knew. GILB 2

Saucer: brimming/ S. of wax, MERR 1

saucers: wash the cups an' s. RILE 1

saugh: she s. a mous CHAU 16

Saul: daughters of Israel, weep over S., BIBL, O.T. 69

tall King S., LIND V 7

saule: Christe receive thy s. UNKN 186

sauna: Mens sana in men's s., HECH 10

Saunt'ring: Lie S. Jack and Idle Joan. PRIO 3

shunn'd by s. an' sinner, BURN 57

saurian: jellyfish and a s., CARRU 1

sausage: s. and garlic booth SPENC A 2

sautrie: robes riche, or fithele, or gay s. CHAU 2

savage: athwart a cedarn cover!/ A s. place! COLE SAM 20

born/ In a half s. country, POUN 37

By saint, by s., and by sage, POPE A 126

chafing s., MCKA 10

den/ Of s. men: BACO 2

In solitude live s., MILT 97

s. eyes turned to a modest gaze SHAK 125

s. fierce, Bandite, or mountaneer MILT 3

s. servility/ slides by on grease. LOWE R 21

unto a s. race TENN 128

savagely: then would be s. still. ELIOT T 123

savages: patience more/ Than s. could suffer. SHAK 4

s., expendable as Jews? WALC 2

save: all have helped to s. her! LOWE J 14

born to pray and s.: YEATS 137

Christ s. us all from a death LONG 53

conquer but to s.: — CAMPB T 2

God s. our king, UNKN 63

God will s. her, HOUS 32

Listen and s. MILT 7

Lord! hast power to s. WILLA 1

s. expense." HERB G 43

s. from dust; SPEND 22

s. my baby." UNKN 76

s. the Athenian walls MILT 125

S. the Nightingale alone. BARNF 1

soil they fought to s. BRYA 2

streams in the firmament!/ One drop would s. my soul — MARL 2

sweetness did not s. His life from foes. HERB G 55

Themselves they could not s. HOUS 31

saved: 'Be proud! for she is s., LOWE J 14

Just lost, when I was s.! DICKI 95

lie to say that these/ S., MACDI 1

S. a captive Englishman. THAC 2

s. each other's lives. GILB 11

s. my life, saying "not you." SHAK 241

s. them from the gas. HECH 13

wit might have me s., MORE 3

saves: dream of a dove that s., HECH 1

savior: eyes of a mild s. TATE J 2

saviors: s. come not home tonight: HOUS 31

Saviour: crown of thorns our S. wore UNKN 131

For Jesus Christ, our S., CRAI 1

little S.; HERR 47

my lives light/ And s., CHAU 117

Saviours: S. death did put some bloud/ Into thy face; HERB G 20

savory: s. dish, a homely treat, HORA 10

savour: s. of tar nor of pitch, SHAK 159

Sweet are the thoughts that s. of content, GREE 1

savours: In those freckles live their s. SHAK 126

saw: eyes that s. not, LOWE J 13

gnawing teeth of his s., WHITM 92

He did not know I s. DICKI 12

I never s. a Moor — DICKI 59

I s. a ship a-sailing, MOTH 14

I s. God! STEPHENS 13

I s. thee Pearle-like stand
TAYL E 8

I s. them pass EMER 20

'I s. you take his kiss!' PATM 1

I, too, s. God through mud —
OWEN 9

more he s. RICHA E 1

put my s. to work SNYD 43

s. a lady bright, UNKN 245

s. all heaven in flower SWIN 26

s. him peep within; HOLM 12

s. sunset glow, MCCRA 2

s. that it was good, MILT 85

s. the new moone, UNKN 227

She s. the clouds. STEPHENS 2

solemn fillet s. the scorn.
EMER 16

We s. Thee in Thy balmy nest,
CRAS 4

What I s. Was Adlestrop —
THOMA E 1

sawis: s. in the air; BOYD 1

saws: All s. of books, SHAK 28

Saxifrage: S. is my flower
WILLI 29

saxophones: sob on the long cool
winding s. SAND 11

say: heard the old, old men s.
YEATS 103

I s. this childermas HECH 13

Irish s. your trouble is their
trouble MOOR M 38

know not yet what you will s.
HOUS 7

no word to s.; WILD 4

nothing more to s. ROBI 18

pass in," the angels s., EMER 33

s. good night till it be morrow.
SHAK 145

S. nay! S. nay! WYAT 1

s. not I that I am old? SHAK 238

S. so. UNKN 145

s. what you meant, SEXT 1

Who plainly s., My God, My
King. HERB G 46

savd: as the Welchman s.
UNKN 224

saying: suffering and not/ s. so;
MOOR M 27

saynct: speke and loke lyke a s.
WYAT 23

scabbard: beauty is a blade out of
its s. RANS 22

scaffold: mounted to the s.
UNKN 105

scale: fish s., shale dust, bone
SNYD 22

s. lapping s. MOOR M 22

s. lapping scale MOOR M 22

s. Of awful notes, WORD 8

scales: s. from shining rocks,
WHITM 2

scallop: s.-shell of quiet, RALEG 10

scalps: s. served up in rum —
GILB 2

scaly: s. horror of his folded tail.
MILT 40

scan: gently s. your brother Man,
BURN 7

presume not God to s.,
POPE A 78

scanned: critical eye you s.,
ROSS C 26

scansions: mustard s. of the eyes,
CRAN H 53

scanty: reflects in joy its s. gleam
LOWE J 16

scape: kisse his ers er that he s.
CHAU 56

Who can s. his bow? HERB G 23

'scaped: so soon s. world's and
flesh's rage, JONS 23

when my heart hath s. this
sorrow, SHAK 221

scapegoat: guileless old s.;
GRAV 14

scar: from cliff and s. TENN 112 s.
on her head, GINS 30

s. that whiter skin SHAK 137

scarce: Food and Raiment now grew
s. SWIF 15

s. half made up, SHAK 96

s. the sense of dying: LAMB 3

s. Adjusted in the Tomb
DICKI 37

sod s. heaved; SHEL 59

struggled s. DICKI 100

Where words are s., SHAK 87

scarcely: s. six converts he's got
LOWE J 9

s. the strength of a louse,
SERV 7

Scarcity: very end of harvest!/ S.
and want SHAK 162

scare: s. myself FROS 36

s. us with talk WILB 1

They cannot s. me FROS 36

will not s. LOWE R 41

scarecrow: comfortable kind of old
s. YEATS 14

s. word, THOMA D 8

Scarfs: S., garters, gold, POPE A 81

scarlet: Copper sun or s. sea,
CULL 5

His sins were s., BELL 18

live with s. Majors SASS 3

S., and blue, and snowy white,
WHITM 14

s. cloaks and surplices/ Of linen,
LAWR 9

s. red about your eyen, CHAU 66

with one s. gleam WORD 130

scarped: s. cliff and quarried stone
TENN 35

scars: boasted their s. of dried
snot; HILL G 6

s. to prove it: KNIG 4

scarves: Smoke rolls and s.
PLATH 14

scathe: somde, deef, and that was
s. CHAU 10

scathes: Her radiance s. me.
PLATH 42

scatter: random s. of shot. KIZE 3

S. my ashes, MONTROSE 4

s. the congregation; WHITM 7

s. wheeling in great broken rings
YEATS 165

scattered: cloud is s., SHEL 89

dregs of s. thought, SIDN 39

land is s. with light, BRID R 2

s. at the old church door, KLEI 3

s. driftwood, THAX 1

s. in the bottom of the sea.
SHAK 97

to your s. bodies go, DONN 5

Toe'osh s. white people SILKO 2

scattering: All's a s./ A shining.
ROET 47

Spreading ruin and s. ban,
BROWNI E 2

their s. names; WILB 28

Time, a maniac s. dust, TENN 28

scaud: skelp an' s. poor dogs
BURN 2

scene: death will drive us from the
s. EBER 5

humble happiness endeared each
s. GOLD 1

leave him out of the s. forever.
JUST 1

lonely s. shall thee restore;
COLL 2

memorable S.: MARV 22

my playes last s., DONN 58

our lofty s. be acted over
SHAK 47

s. cut in cameo MILLA 4

s. of enchantment more dear,
MOOR T 8

s. of Man; POPE A 58

still unsated, dwelt upon the s.
COWP 17

tragic s. they stare. YEATS 82

scenes: all the changing s.
LONG 14

Fair s. shall greet thee BRYA 29

sad s. and thoughts and feelings
vanish THOMS J (1834–1882) 7

S. must be beautiful, COWP 18

s. of my childhood, WOOD 1

swept these s.: TUCK 1

scenic: favorite s. view, HAYD 7

scent: dry s. of a dying garden
ROET 15

rose's s. is bitterness   THOMP F 1
s. and beauty both   AYTON 1
s./ Of healing herbs   THOR 9
s. of these arm-pits   WHITM 74
s. of wild flowers in the wood.
   CREE 5
s. survives their close:
   THOMP F 1
scented: cane-lipped s. mouth,
   TOOM 1
in a s. linen sheet,   WYLI 9
scents: Only with s., —
   THOMA E 5
s. dead leaves yield,   THOMA E 5
scepter: s. hath borne;   KNOX 2
sceptered: royal throne of kings, this
   s. isle,   SHAK 88
Sceptic: too much knowledge for the
   S. side,   POPE A 78
sceptre: s., learning, physic,
   SHAK 18
s. shows the force of temporal
   power,   SHAK 123
sceptred: mercy is above this s.
   sway,   SHAK 123
schedule: manual on s.   ASHB 1
scheme: s. of the weal and woe:
   BROWNI R 4
schemes: best laid s.   BURN 63
scholar: courtier's, soldier's, s.'s,
   SHAK 33
passion is the s.'s heritage,
   WINT 10
s. is studying;   WHITM 7
s.'s life assail,
   JOHN S (1709–1784) 18
scholars: land of s. and saints:
   MACN 4
Mourned by s.   SPEND 10
solid s. Get the degrees,   SNOD 5
Statistics justify and s. seize
   WALC 2
school: followed her to s.   HALE 1
in my joyful s.-days,   LAMB 2
is there singing s.   YEATS 127
murderous Machiavel to s.
   SHAK 62
operation, teaching s.,   GINS 21
s.-boys playing in the stream;
   PEEL 6
s.-children rise like balloons.
   LOWE R 20
s.-masters puzzle their brain.
   GOLD 5
see a lamb at s.   HALE 1
talk of it at s.   YEATS 2
Time is the s.   SCHW 8
schoolboy: dear the s. spot
   BYRO 22
to every s.   NASH 9
schoolboys: s. lag with satchels in
   their hands.   SWIF 11

schools: Creeds and s. in abeyance,
   WHITM 74
sophist s.,   EMER 29
superficial s.   BACO 2
schoolyard: In the s.,   HILL G 6
schooner: was the s. Hesperus,
   LONG 51
Science: infant S.   ROBI 35
naughty thumb/ of s.   CUMM 34
S.! true daughter of old Time
   POE 1
scientific: any s. man   HART 3
decent for a s. gent   HART 4
give the day a s. tone.   CARRY 7
Scipio: worthy S.,   CHAU 72
sclendre: reve was a s. colerik man.
   CHAU 19
Scoffing: S. his state   SHAK 89
scold: want the heart to s.
   BROWNI R 79
scole: After the s. of Stratford atte
   Bowe,   CHAU 14
scoop: Dust did s. itself like Hands
   DICKI 160
Scooting: S. obliquely high and
   low.   WHITM 75
scope: Health, love, friends, s.
   HARD 47
that man's s.,   SHAK 194
without term or s.,   ARNO 24
score: Ballades by the s.   MAST 10
kept eight s. men   UNKN 153
s. of hearts   BRID 2
take from seventy springs a s.,
   HOUS 39
Three s. and ten.   MOTH 12
scores: wipers/ S. out
   BROWNI R 65
scorn: both full of shame and s.,/
   JONS 33
by thy s., O murderess, I am
   dead,   DONN 4
dangers thou canst make us s.!
   BURN 55
exempt from s. or crime;
   JOHN S (1709–1784) 13
Faith fair s. doth gain.   SIDN 38
haughty s. which mock'd the
   smart,   ARNO 35
Horror and s. and hate and fear
   and indignation —   HOUS 24
love one which did s.   DONN 39
Miniver Cheevy, child of s.
   ROBI 41
s. delights and live laborious
   days;   MILT 27
S. not the sonnet;   WORD 131
s. of eyes,   SHAK 97
s./ Plays o'er her mouth,
   LOWE J 14
s. the home-spun gray   CAMPI 9
s. them all,   ELIZ 2
s. to change my state   SHAK 194

solemn fillet saw the s.   EMER 16
Those lovers s. whom that love
   doth possess?   SIDN 13
Uriel's voice of cherub s.,
   EMER 51
scorn'd: s. my tears,   DANI S 16
scorneth: s. the horse and his rider.
   BIBL, O.T. 17
scornful: seat of the s.
   BIBL, O.T. 21
view our sable race with s. eye,
   WHEA 1
scorning: s. the base degrees
   SHAK 44
scorns: She s. a pasture   FROS 18
scorpion: home of the s.   SNYD 20
scorpions: dirty boogie with s.
   REED I 5
Scotch: put their S. or rye down
   COWA 3
Scotia: old S.'s grandeur springs,
   BURN 20
Scotland: away to S.   KEAT 60
grave livers do in S. use,
   WORD 123
Scots: King o' S., and a' his power
   UNKN 309
S. lords at his feit.   UNKN 228
S., wha hae wi' Wallace bled,
   BURN 47
Scottland: for S. and Saint Andrew
   UNKN 226
scourged: never to be s.   MELV 12
scourging: rope-knouts of their s.;
   OWEN 35
Scouring: S. the chaos of the mind.
   SNYD 21
scowled: heavens s., and the huskies
   howled,   SERV 4
scrabbled: s. and mucked like a
   slave,   SERV 11
scrap: coaches shall be s. and rust
   SAND 12
scrape: man climbing/ must s. his
   knees,   LEVE 11
Scraped: S. clean —   SIMI 4
scraping: Death's ironic s.
   STEVENS 38
s. squeal/ Of seabird's voices
   SLES 5
s. the mold from your body.
   SANC 3
scraps: casual bits and s.   GRAV 5
scratch: come here and s."
   UNKN 98
tailor might s.   SHAK 159
scratching: little cats mewing and
   s.   HARJ 2
scrawny: That s. cry —
   STEVENS 29
scream: bending to a s.,
   CRAN H 33

Isabel, didn't worry,/ Isabel didn't
s. NASH 1
mandrake with to-morrow's s.
THOMA D 6
short wild s., WHITM 92
screamed: s. with joy, GINS 11
wind's long mane./ S. redskin
CRAN H 22
screaming: Children s. GINS 16
dive-bomber's s. orgasm
JEFFE 22
screams: that thing/ s. BARA 2
screech: s. at them to stop —
SASS 15
screech-owl: s., screech loud,
SHAK 128
screen: tigers prance across a s.
RICH 1
screened: cloud part s., MERE G 8
screw: Go s. yourself, CREE 2
meaning's press and s.
COLE SAM 25
scribble: looked like lightning or a
s. FROS 131
s. on the doorsills; SAND 9
scribbled: s. all night GINS 13
scrimmage: s. of appetite SCHW 11
tom-tom s. CRAN H 25
scrip: s. of joy, immortal diet,
RALEG 10
scroll: life is a twice-written s.
WILD 13
scrotum: little s. SNYD 5
scroungy: handful of mine all s.
CORS 3
scrub: because I s. it. AUDE 14
scruple: some craven s. SHAK 35
scrutiny: Long knowledge and the
s. of years — COWP 18
scullery: to the s., KINS 1
sculptor: choose his mate./ Poet and
s., YEATS 156
sculptors: s. and the poets were half
sad, AUDE 53
sculpture: graveyard marble s.
FROS 39
sculptured: funeral-cakes of sweet
and s. stone. SLES 3
s. Ann THOMA D 5
scum: Fond Fancy's s. SIDN 39
sea-gluten,/ S., WHITM 2
spurns the Northern s.!
RANDA J 2
scurry: s. Of chemic blood,
THOMA D 16
scurvy: like a s. politician
SHAK 81
scurvyI: famine or s. fought it;
SERV 11
scuttle: s. Goose-fashion RANS 4
Scuttling: pair of ragged claws/ S.
ELIOT T 86
scythe: cuts with his s. GOGA 2

despite thy s. and thee.
SHAK 235
for his s. to mow: SHAK 210
long s. whispering FROS 62
nothing 'gainst Time's s.
SHAK 186
poor crooked s. and spade.
SHIR 1
s. that mows down kings
BEAU/BASS 5
s. whispered FROS 63
swish of the s.-strokes, LAWR 59
scythes: Mow with their s. LUCR 4
shaking s. at cannon. HEAN 18
sea: age had brought me to the s.
CRAN H 43
Ah, the S.! DICKI 158
At s. or ashore, TENN 119
At the s.-down's edge SWIN 10
beneath a rougher s., COWP 2
beneath in the abysmal s.,
TENN 58
Billowes of the S. FLET/SHAK 1
black s.-brute MERW 7
bleak s.-beach, LONG 52
body, like a worn s.-shell
LAWR 42
bottom of the s. is cruel.
CRAN H 48
brass, nor stone, nor earth, nor
boundless s., SHAK 212
brings the sailor home from s.,
ELIOT T 134
bud to test surprises of s. air,
MOSS 6
burst/ Into that silent s.
COLE SAM 31
Cast up by a lonely s., MELV 23
center all round to the s.
COWP 23
Copper sun or scarlet s., CULL 5
dances on the s. WORD 154
dark rainbow bliss in the s.
LAWR 58
deep s. swell ELIOT T 142
deep wide s. of Misery, SHEL 35
deeper than any s.-dingle.
AUDE 95
depth as the roots of the s.:
SWIN 24
distant northern s. ARNO 2
dolphin-torn, that gong-tormented
s. YEATS 19
Doubt's boundless S., ROCH 9
drowning in a stormier s.
WILD 10
earth/ And s. and air.
STEVENS 21
ebb and flood from the remote s.-
tides THOMS J (1834–1882) 6
espouse the everlasting S.
WORD 91

ever-hooded, tragic-gestured s.
STEVENS 18
falling-back to the s. WHITM 19
fear to breast the s.! LONG 7
fish or s.-fowl harmed YOUN A 1
Forests at the bottom of the s.,
WHITM 112
forever stands the s., WINT 7
From the grey s.-folk CHES 15
fronts the s. SWIN 10
gods of the earth and s. BLAK 71
goe downe to 'th s. in ships:
BIBL, O.T. 56
green hells of the s. CHES 10
gunnery practice out at s.
HARD 14
heart stirs the ever-beating s.;
PLUN 2
home from the s.,
STEVENSO R 21
How many strawberries grow in
the s.? MOTH 21
immortal s. Which brought us
hither, WORD 82
in the s. being burnt, DONN 13
Into a s. of dew. FIEL E 8
irresponsive sounding of the s.,
ROSS C 24
It drags the s. after it PLATH 58
kingdom by the s., POE 3
lands beyond the s.; WORD 47
last s. and the hapless stars;
OWEN 33
life's unresting s.! HOLM 3
lonely s. and the sky, MASE 11
long light on the s. MACL 13
lookin' eastward to the s., KIPL 9
Love is a barren s., SWIN 26
Love still has something of the
S., SEDL 1
machrel of the s. UNKN 168
made of earth and s. HOUS 20
mate of the wind and s., POUN 4
no dirge, except the hollow s.'s,
BYRO 51
no stir in the s., SOUTHE 4
obvious characteristic of the s.;
MOOR M 12
old-time s.-fight? WHITM 89
On such a full s. SHAK 50
On thy cold gray stones, O S.!
TENN 1
One foote in S., SHAK 130
one is of the S., WORD 147
one rose in a tent of s. WINT 8
order words of the s.,
STEVENS 19
Our heritage the s. CUNN A 2
ourselves we find in the s.
CUMM 21
paddles in a halcyon s.;
ROSS C 1
pass a redder s. TIMR 5

mangy as the Irish S., UNKN 194
multitudinous s. incarnadine,
  SHAK 108
murmur of the distant s.,
  STEPHENS 10
new-found s., HERB G 60
On desperate s. POE 45
sailed the s. YEATS 127
s. and land be 'twixt us both,
  LOVE 7
s. in delicate haze LUCR 4
s. of life like wine; TRAH 10
s. of pity AUDE 44
spat out the seven s.; JOHN J 2
strange s. of Thought, WORD 101
Thronging the S. MILT 5
wealthy of s., HEMA 5
with its melodious s. LONG 30
season: end/ Of a love or a s.?
  FROS 93
For a long dreary s., KEAT 1
Good-night to the S.! — PRAE 3
green for a s., SWIN 23
human s. on this sterile air
  MACL 6
in a s. of autumn. STEVENS 3
In s., JONS 40
Last s.'s fruit is eaten
  ELIOT T 66
Midwinter spring is its own s.
  ELIOT T 60
never come a s. STEPHEN 2
point'st the s.; SHAK 140
s. died a-cold POUN 15
s. of calm weather WORD 82
S. of mists and mellow
  fruitfulness, KEAT 62
s. of no bungling OLSO 23
s. of the year. UNKN 172
stubborn s. ELIOT T 108
To every thing there is a s.,
  BIBL, O.T. 3
seasonably: s. leaf and blossom
  uncurl LAYT 2
seasoned: Like s. timber,
  HERB G 72
S. with sage and onions, and port
  wine. SOUTHE 8
seasons: afford our costly s.;
  SNOD 7
All s. and their change, MILT 76
four s. in the mind of man:
  KEAT 19
Fruits of the Two s. BLAK 8
s. are Dry and Wet; AUDE 60
s., changeless LONG 14
s. seize/ the soul OLSO 19
s. shall be sweet COLE SAM 16
swift s. roll! HOLM 3
When mercy s. justice. SHAK 123
seat: canal-bank s. for the passer-
  by. KAVA 24
rising from the toilet s. LEVE 14

rural s. of various view: MILT 69
s. at the cricket matches
  JARR 12
s. of Mars, SHAK 88
s. of the scornful. BIBL, O.T. 21
whiles memory holds a s.
  SHAK 28
You walked about my s., LI PO 3
seated: s. by the sea; LONG 31
s. with his friends, FRENE 1
seaward: salt tides s. flow; ARNO 9
seaweed: locks like s. WARR 3
seben: to the number s. WALK 9
secluded: s. and shy. BINY 4
s. in the thick marine?
  STEVENS 48
swamp in s. recesses, WHITM 47
second: breathe a s. spring.
  GRAY 14
Calm as that s. summer TIMR 1
cannot add the s. SHAP 12
Death's s. self, SHAK 215
each s. Stood heir to th' first.
  SHAK 133
for a s. finding, WILB 8
gluttony s. to none LA FO 1
grave's the s. Marriage-bed.
  CRAS 1
great nature's s. course,
  SHAK 106
murder in the s. degree,
  UNKN 104
s. childishness and mere oblivion,
  SHAK 12
s. day of Christmas, UNKN 275
s. drunk, BYRO 21
s. kind of sin, NASH 10
s. or third hand, WHITM 76
s. self/ To be His mate:
  BROWNI R 16
seek the s. POPE A 98
seconds: sixty s.' worth of distance
  run, KIPL 8
secrecy: Candor and s. inside
  GUNN 5
secret: Be s. and exult, YEATS 147
capture/ The s. of self; AIKE 11
dark s. love BLAK 80
great beasts mate in s. LAWR 7
great s. is no s. GINS 45
has the s. eyes KNIG 6
I own to me's a s. BARBA 1
Loving me in s. WRIG J 5
means of a s. charm,
  BROWNI R 61
one still, s. spot DRIS 1
performs its s. ministry,
  COLE SAM 1
save thy s. soul GRAY 2
S. by the unmourning water
  THOMA D 38
s. chambers of my heart MCKA 9

S. fates/ Guide our states
  CAMPI 31
s. felon wrought, CHAU 47
S. joys and secret smiles,
  BLAK 50
s. kept from all CARRO 4
s. like a happy funeral; LARK 21
s. lover is saying KAVA 11
s. ministry of frost COLE SAM 17
s. nook in a pleasant land,
  EMER 28
s. of despair, LONG 39
S. of my Life to learn: OMAR 6
s. of the soil THOMA D 31
s. sleep/ Of him he loved ALEX 7
s. standard in his mind,
  POPE A 16
s. whispers of each other's watch./
  Fire answers fire, SHAK 57
smile in s., looking over wasted
  lands TENN 90
stars in s. influence comment;
  SHAK 187
sucks his thumb/ in s. LORD 4
Tell me thy s.; GLAD 1
wondrous s. show, LOWE J 16
secretary: s. of bees PLATH 12
secreted: some s. Island,
  WORD 112
secretly: affectedly Pious nor s.
  lewd, PRIO 6
convey it s., WYAT 8
how swift how s. MACL 13
secrets: names and all their s.,
  LONG 42
s. of my prison house, SHAK 26
s. of the Abyss to spy: GRAY 29
sect: born into that ancient s.
  YEATS 143
sects: packs and s. of great ones,
  SHAK 84
religious s. ran mad, PRAE 2
secular: s. bird ages of lives.
  MILT 117
Secundus: Georgius S. was then
  alive, — HOLM 5
Secured: S. him by a string
  DICKI 85
securely: come/ Walking s., WINT 9
s. bound. MUIR 4
Securer: S. lives the silly swain.
  CAMPI 9
secures: s. Escape from the weekday
  time. MACN 22
sedate: boatswain's mate was very
  s., CARRY 9
sedge: s. has wither'd from the
  lake, KEAT 31
sedgy: smells of s. grass WHITM 92
sediment: rim, the s. WHITM 2
seduce: World s.: MARV 24
see: always what you s. BYRO 35
blind was I to s. ROSS C 17

damned stood up to s. DAVID 1
Did he smile his work to s.?
  BLAK 83
eye has danced to s. HOLM 17
eyes can s., SHAK 188
face you could not s., LEAR 13
forms I s. on stretchers
  WHITM 71
God, who is not, we s.; SWIN 18
I could not s. to see — DICKI 49
I s. the Past LONG 29
I s. Your double heart, WYAT 29
it pleaseth me when I s. BERT 1
Love your eyes that can s.,
  JEFFE 19
make me s. aright REES 3
neither s. nor love. TRAH 9
nobody would care to s., MOSS 4
now can s. no more. WORD 65
O mortal folk, you may behold
  and s. HAWE 1
O! say can you s. KEY 1
O taste and s. LEVE 18
others will s. them WHITM 19
rather s. than be one. BURG 3
rock/ crystal thing to s.
  MOOR M 28
S.! and confess, POPE A 82
s. before I doubt; SHAK 136
s. every side of every question;
  MAST 4
s. her in the dewy flowers,
  BURN 42
s. her sweet and fair: BURN 42
s. him jump before me,
  STEVENSO R 13
s. it glisten; LOWE J 17
s. it lap the Miles — DICKI 55
s. my apron rising. UNKN 207
s. not half my dayes that's due,
  BRAD 2
s. oursels as others see us!
  BURN 58
s. that word nested WHITM 43
s. the brave day SHAK 186
s. the falling star, HABI 1
s./ The Father and the Son,
  CHAR 1
s. the moon, UNKN 142
s. the stars, LANG 3
s. things bare to the buff
  STEVENSO R 16
s. this day, and live old age,
  SHAK 60
s. those two hearts, MERR 5
s. upon that tree, FIEL E 5
S. what a lovely shell, TENN 99
s. you face to face! WHITM 18
s. you in a year, DICKI 76
shall never s. KILM 1
sleeping, I s. a wreck, WHITT 26
smile you could s. a mile,
  SERV 5

things unseen do s.,
  FLET G YO 2
to s. God die! DONN 28
To s. her is to love her, BURN 16
to s. her, was to love her;
  BURN 11
whom we s. not, is; SWIN 16
world; thy uttermost I s.;
  SIDN 27
you s., but your are blind;
  ROBI 4
you s., I love you!' WHITT 14
seed: black ivory, black s. HAYD 9
blind s. all. MUIR 11
Bud and bloom and go to s.;
  MILLA 18
disk of s., TENN 42
Fair s.-time had my soul,
  WORD 93
kind s.-receiving earth ROCH 15
one s. becomes/ An everlasting
  song, TOOM 7
same/ cycle of s.-time DOOL 6
s. of love was sick. LEWI 4
s. still tucked away, SNYD 5
s. waits for fire SNYD 46
Sow s. SHEL 64
that destined s. MILT 104
thy s. abides in me, VAUG 3
unweeded garden,/ That grows to
  s.; SHAK 22
Warms youth and s.
  THOMA D 30
seeds: burns the s. of age;
  THOMA D 30
hot s. steam SNYD 28
I sowed the s. of love, HABE 1
rouses up the s. of dark disease.
  THOMS J (1700–1748) 13
s. fallen out of its face, GINS 34
S. in a dry pod, MAST 11
tend our agonizing s. CULL 4
seeing: eyes were made for s.,
  EMER 42
master light of all our s.;
  WORD 81
Or Charon, s., may forget
  LAND 13
s. a sight MOOR M 28
S., hearing, WHITM 74
S. only what is fair, EMER 31
seek: beds for me and all who s.?
  ROSS C 29
each sound sets out to s. JARR 8
"Go, go, go s. some otherwhere!
  ELIZ 2
Hell grant what love did s.;
  MILT 17
Help me to s., WYAT 8
in a net I s. to hold the wind.
  WYAT 31

Leaves, lines, and rhymes, s. her
  to please SPENS 3
Rejoice, and men will s. you;
  WILC 2
s. a childhood picture; WARR 5
s. a newer world. TENN 134
s. and adore them; BRID R 5
s. slight faults to find/ Where
  nature moves, POPE A 34
s. the empty world BRON 13
s. the second POPE A 98
s. these anchorites, ARNO 31
so far to s., ROSS C 25
They flee from me that sometime
  did me s., WYAT 26
To follow, to s., WHITM 17
To strive, to s., TENN 135
seeken: s. acts of sundry realms
  CHAU 65
seekest: He Whom thou s.!
  THOMP F 10
seeking: s. lost love. GRAV 15
s. oxygen, HARP 4
s. the spheres WHITM 55
seeks: s. to place it there CULL 17
seel: prente of Sainte Venus s.
  CHAU 90
seem: all might s. good.'
  THOMA E 3
Not what you s., BYRO 35
s. a moment's thought, YEATS 1
s. to be all finished, SNOD 11
things are not what they s.
  LONG 35
seemed: it s. yesterday. ROBI 39
s. waste of breath, YEATS 71
sex not equal s.; MILT 72
things always s. the same!
  TENN 81
seeming: in s. trust, SHAK 238
with a s. heart VERY 2
seems: heavy present s. to fail
  SNYD 49
it s. to fail: BROWNI R 74
"Saint-Saëns!" it s. to be
  whispering, OHAR 4
seen: blessed to have s. DICKI 94
Durer would have s. MOOR M 29
I have s. it over and over,
  BISH 5
I have s. you; MOOR M 6
Much have I s. and known —
  TENN 130
none have s. us, BEDD 1
Northern Lights have s. queer
  sights, SERV 1
O earth, what changes hast thou
  s.! TENN 55
oftener s., the more I lust,
  GOOG 2
sages have s. COWP 23
s. no more. HARD 38
s. one thing, SWIN 21

s. this swan MOOR M 6
things in which we have s.
  ourselves WILB 2
things which I have s. WORD 65
unseemliest s., MILT 97
Warning of thinges that men after
  s. CHAU 72
Which sees is truly s. SNYD 50
Who has s. the wind? ROSS C 35
seep: your liquors s. to me,
  PLATH 73
seepage: bogholes might be Atlantic
  s. HEAN 3
seeps: s. from heavily jowled
  MACN 11
seer: Wiser far than human s.,
  EMER 31
sees: blinded man s. GRAV 21
evening s. its close; LONG 49
morning s. some task begin,
  LONG 49
s. through stone KNIG 6
Which s. is truly seen. SNYD 50
Who s. God's face, DONN 28
see-saw: His wit all s., POPE A 11
seeth: nobody s. or heareth,
  UNKN 89
seething: surge was s. free,
  TENN 88
Seint: by S. Loy. CHAU 13
seismic: s. with laughter, BARK 3
seiz'd: s. by the spirit WHITM 2
seize: marrow-bone might s.!
  UNKN 230
'Ruin s. thee, ruthless king!
  GRAY 1
seasons/ s. the soul OLSO 19
s. my/ Soul in a moment.
  COWP 14
s. the flow'r, BURN 54
s. the souls that wander by him.
  SHAK 140
Statistics justify and scholars s.
  WALC 2
seized: Erl-King has s. me —
  GOET 1
hunger s. my heart; TENN 41
rigorous teachers s. my youth,
  ARNO 30
seizes: who s. fast to them,
  WHITM 73
seizure: s. on the light, HERR 44
seldom: Joys s. yet attained
  HARD 47
s. have mothers/ in Irish stories,
  MOOR M 36
s. spent in vain, SHAK 37
selects: Soul s. her own Society —
  DICKI 132
self: afflict thy s. in vain:
  MILT 111
alike my work and s.
  BROWNI R 7

attitude of s.-defense; MOOR M 7
Beauty's s. she is, UNKN 191
by s.-offenses weighing.
  SHAK 116
capture/ The secret of s.; AIKE 11
Companion to his s. for her,
  STEVENS 68
concentred all in s., SCOT WA 12
Death's second s, SHAK 215
fight with grace,/ The s.
  reconstructed, READ H 2
filter them from your s.
  WHITM 76
fix'd/ His canon 'gainst s.-
  slaughter! SHAK 22
fool's s.-chosen snare, SIDN 39
humble way to save his s.-
  respect. FROS 21
images of s.-confusednesses
  GREV 5
in grief and s.-contempt,
  PETRA 12
Infusing him with s. and vain
  conceit, SHAK 89
know the s. AMMO 17
lies, s.-denial, unspoken regret
  SNOD 15
Light-lashed, s.-righteous,
  BISH 36
ly'st victorious/ Among thy slain
  s.-kill'd MILT 115
man, the s., MOOR M 25
more than s. BATE 2
musical, s.-sufficient, WHITM 43
my distrusting s. HARP 3
my sad s. hereafter kind,
  HOPKINS 14
My s. corrupting SHAK 199
native s. can nothing feed;
  MICH 1
Passion and reason s.-division
  cause. GREV 9
placid and s.-contained,
  WHITM 74
pour out all my s., POPE A 88
Reason's s. shall bow the knee
  FRENE 2
second s. To be His mate:
  BROWNI R 16
s.-begott'n bird MILT 117
s.-consumer of my woes,
  CLARE 7
s.-delighting,/ s.-appeasing, s.-
  affrighting, YEATS 113
s.-made from elements least
  visible BISH 20
s.-murdered heart, SITW 12
s. persists like a dying star,
  ROET 43
s.-sacrifice may be ruled out,
  GRAV 26
s.-same sky, SHAK 187
s.-same song KEAT 50

s.-same weapon, FRANK 2
s. under the eye lies, HUGH T 5
thy greedy s. consum'd, MILT 44
thy sweet s. prove. SHAK 243
to thine own s. be true, SHAK 24
selfe: I had forgot/ My s. and thee.
  JONS 13
I unto my s. alone will sing,
  SPENS 30
Selfish: love is cruel/ and s.
  WILLI 21
normal and s. BOGA 6
S., vain,/ Eternal bane! BLAK 62
Selima: pensive S. reclined,
  GRAY 18
Selinda: Pious S. goes to prayers,
  CONG 2
sell: couldn't s. 'em, HOLM 6
Decking the sense as if it were to
  s. HERB G 40
Free to mortgage or to s.,
  JOHN S (1709–1784) 11
I s. thee poison; SHAK 151
I will s. myself in hell, CREE 8
made to s. and s. quickly
  POUN 9
S. flesh and blood. BYRO 32
s. the colors of your sunset
  JOHN H 2
s. your love for peace, MILLA 17
selle: al is for to s.; CHAU 86
s. Al that he hadde CHAU 94
selling: men are s. hats ASHB 2
selves: dead s. to higher things.
  TENN 88
Things and things' s. WILB 8
sely: s. jalous housbonde to bigile,
  CHAU 53
Semblance: S. of worth not
  substance, MILT 56
Thou, whose exterior s. WORD 77
semeliest: s. in sight, DUNB W 4
semi-tones: Sliding by s.
  BROWNI R 5
Semiramis: Resembling fair S.
  OVID 1
senate: Like Cato, give his little s.
  laws, POPE A 7
senators: green-rob'd s. of mighty
  woods, KEAT 22
respectable s. burst with
  laughter, AUDE 5
send: belly, God s. thee good ale
  enough; STEVENSO W 3
s. me more such afternoons
  OVID 2
sending: lines/ I kept s. back
  KINN 6
sends: prayer that he s. DUNB P 10
Senec: S. and Plato call me
  WYAT 5
sense: appropriate s. of space.
  OHAR 19

Astonishment takes from us s. of
   pain. CONS 1
at least an earnest s. WHITT 10
bodily s. exhibits, WORD 117
but men of s. approve:
   POPE A 29
Catching the s. at two removes?
   HERB G 45
cold friction of expiring s.
   ELIOT T 68
Decking the s. as if it were to
   sell. HERB G 40
Desiccation of the world of s.,
   ELIOT T 21
drowned the s. in odours;
   ELIOT T 121
drowsy numbness pains/ My s.,
   KEAT 44
each anointed s. will see.
   DOWS 2
fail by spirit or by s. WILB 41
free s. at last, WHITM 22
fruit of s. beneath POPE A 22
gives her children neither s. nor
   money MACN 7
Good nature and good s.
   POPE A 35
his exquisite s. LOWE J 7
Honesty's against all common s.
   ROCH 10
humble Man of modest s.,
   ROCH 12
in the modern s. AUDE 93
Lips that sealed up the s. DAY 8
Metaphysic calls for aid on S.!
   POPE A 2
Much madness is divinest s.
   DICKI 105
Much s. the starkest madness.
   DICKI 105
never deviates into s. DRYD 11
one s. to me: — ROSS C 24
people of common s. damn
   metres, LOWE J 5
puzzling/ Our s. of HOLLA 2
rain of matter upon s. WINT 2
retains an obscure s. WORD 99
Satire or s., alas, POPE A 9
scarce the s. of dying: LAMB 3
s. and worth, o'er a' the earth,
   BURN 27
s. from gnawing time DAY 8
s./ Of Life, MASE 9
s. of the passing LANIE 3
s./ Without /enchantment,
   ELIOT T 68
sound must seem an echo to the
   s.: POPE A 28
vigour in my s. TRAH 10
weave myself into the s.
   HERB G 42
when you doubt your s.;
   POPE A 37

with a dim and undetermined s.
   WORD 97
within the s. they quicken.
   SHEL 43
senseless: kind of s. wit WILB 30
s. drowned/ Have faces MOSS 4
s. grimaces CARRO 16
senselessness: s. and mud?
   SHAP 18
senses: all s. OLSO 6
Beauty through my s. stole;
   EMER 19
five and country s. THOMA D 43
five watchful s. MILT 80
folk-lore/ Of each of the s.;
   STEVENS 45
on the spying s., THOMA D 44
S. fit the winds, GINS 45
S. roll themselves in fear
   BLAK 33
Spoiling s. of their treasure,/
   JONS 9
steep my s. in forgetfulness?
   SHAK 54
Touch, love, all s.; SPEND 17
work mine end upon their s.
   SHAK 165
sensible: s. soft melancholy.
   POPE A 109
This s. warm motion SHAK 115
sensibly: Bear not too s., MILT 111
sensitive: boatload of s. bullshit!
   GINS 18
sensual: Caught in that s. music
   YEATS 125
heart is s., THOMA D 44
heavy s. shoulders, RUKE 2
s., eating, WHITM 73
s., pearly spouse, STEVENS 49
s. strut begun, THOMA D 41
s. world proclaim, MORD 1
sent: go as little children s.
   DODG 2
my s. be good, HERB G 47
one was s. home, JUST 2
true love s. to me UNKN 274
sentence: adjective is lost in the s.,
   KOCH 4
heavy s., SHAK 86
meet/ Mortality, my s., MILT 98
s., of as subtile feet, JONS 18
s. of thy early death FANS S 1
'tis me, not the s. they'll suspend.
   MELV 3
sentience: tribal s. in the cactus,
   HAYD 16
sentiment: Full of s., JEFFE 5
s. and hatred WALK 1
soft plush/ Of s. RODG 4
sentimental: hold on the s. English
   MACN 5
s. passion GILB 32

sentimentalist: drinking and
   breeding,/ No s., WHITM 73
Sentinel: S. of the grave
   TATE A 15
s. stars set their watch in the
   sky; CAMPB T 8
sentinels: fixed s. SHAK 57
Sentio: S. ergo sum: SHAP 23
separate: each, in his s. star,
   KIPL 29
s. diverse flight, WHITM 24
s. dying ember POE 35
separated: s. souls,/ All time and
   space controls: LOVE 7
separates: thread/ s. itself LAWR 41
separating: s. inside/ from outside:
   AMMO 5
separation: through s. MAST 2
September: bosom is S., UNKN 6
cool S. morn, WHITT 1
S. days are here, JACK 4
we were in S.," HERF 3
sepulcher: glorious s. HABI 3
s., remote, alone, POE 43
sepulchral: We like s. statues lay;
   DONN 20
sepulchre: deride this s. of crime.
   SASS 12
England be your s. SHEL 65
s. there by the sea — POE 6
Shall be a soldier's s. CAMPB T 4
unwrapped in s., POUN 5
sepulchred: s. in such pomp
   MILT 35
sepulchres: unseen, as lamps in s.;
   POPE A 4
sequence: s. in the brain — AIKE 4
sequent: In s. toil SHAK 209
Seraph: no S.'s fire; POPE A 60
s.-wings of Ecstasy GRAY 29
seraphim: human s., the sailors,
   GINS 11
seraphs: Book/ By s. writ COWP 22
s. sob at vermin fangs POE 32
winged s. of Heaven POE 4
sere: log at last, dry, bald, and s.:
   JONS 41
serenade: intent escalator lifts a s.
   CRAN H 32
s. Of a man STEVENS 23
wanton mask, or midnight ball,/
   Or s., MILT 78
serene: Consuming and s.! CARM 1
Dons on the daïs s. NEWB 3
gem of purest ray s., GRAY 10
s.-moving animals WHITM 29
s. of memory ROET 18
S. stands the little captain,
   WHITM 91
sky, s. and far, LONG 23
serenely: s. arriving, arriving,
   WHITM 50
who s. grindest CALV 3

Severn: Danube to the S. gave
   TENN 25
  on S. snow the leaves. HOUS 44
  out to S. strode, CHES 14
Severs: S. between coolness,
   TOML 2
sev'n: godly garret after s.
   POPE A 19
sewage: s. flows from the village,
   MAST 5
sewed: s. up the air with a stem;
   ROET 25
sewers: Nymphs that reign o'er s.
  and sinks, COLE SAM 5
sewn: s. short at elbow. OWEN 15
sex: from s. to soul, from soul to
  thought; CART 1
  lighted at the s. again. CART 1
  practically conceal its s.
   NASH 17
  s. not equal seemed; MILT 72
  S. stops AMIS 1
  thing of sea or land?/ Female of
  s. MILT 110
sexe: perverse s., DONN 61
sexless: s. hydrogen! GINS 17
sexton: rector, the midwife, the s.,
  the agent for bees. PLATH 11
Sexual: S. intercourse began
  LARK 1
Seynt: S. Stevene was a clerk
  UNKN 212
shabby: polyhedral eye and s.
  clothes, SHAP 13
  tamed and s. tigers HODG 1
shacks: croppers rotting s. WALK 1
shadbones: s. regularly set about the
  mouth, MOOR M 30
shadder: sun an' s., GUES 1
shaddow: Follow a s., it still flies
  you; JONS 29
shaddowes: Stil'd but the s. of us
  men? JONS 29
shade: beauty can be but a s.,
  SIDN 8
  Clouds s. the sun, EMER 5
  clutching the inviolable s.,
   ARNO 28
  cutting weeds and s. TOOM 5
  Dancing in the chequered s.;
   MILT 22
  farewell to the s. COWP 13
  green thought in a green s.,
   MARV 18
  in the flame-heart's s. MCKA 4
  lay rich in s. MELV 21
  neither mist nor s.? POUN 16
  No s., HOOD 6
  painted birds laugh in the s.,
   BLAK 96
  pierce the deep wood's woven s.,
   YEATS 163
  pleasing s.! GRAY 13

poor souls fear a s. or night,
  VAUG 31
reverie, of s., of prayer, ARNO 40
s. him from the heat BLAK 99
s. of a coolibah tree; PATE 1
s. of a Southern Pacific
  locomotive GINS 33
s. of sadness, WHITT 3
s. of Tempe SIDN 22
S./ Of that WORD 92
s. replied, — POE 19
s. upon thy right hand.
  BIBL, O.T. 59
she a s. LAND 13
Sitting in a pleasant s., BARNF 1
snow that lies within the s.;
  DANT 1
sport with Amaryllis in the s.,
  MILT 26
Sweet is the s. BARNE 1
Then we shall rust in s.,
  ARNO 16
wand'rest in his s. SHAK 188
shades: cool and silent s. of sleep.
  HERR 52
  curr to quercine s.! HOLM 1
  Etrurian s. MILT 55
  fairest s. did hide her; MUND 2
  in matted s., MELV 10
  Nocturnal S. PHILL 2
  post/ Sent from the s. below!
   SUCK 6
  raising dingy s. ELIOT T 98
  s. of death, MILT 61
  s. of night were falling fast,
   LONG 21
  S. of the prison-house WORD 70
  s. where buried lovers lie.
   DAVE 2
  to the S. go down, POPE A 129
  tomb among green s. UNKN 253
  yellow drawn s., — WILLI 13
shadow: awful s. SHEL 29
  bitter tastelessness of s. fruit
   ELIOT T 68
  cast a s. white as stone. ROET 29
  cast too bold a s. RICH 22
  circling s. of its appetite.
   TATE A 2
  come to unhinge my s.? ROET 54
  crying s. in the funeral dance,
   ELIOT T 25
  distant s. of the tomb,
   MERE G 15
  I have a little s.
   STEVENSO R 13
  In sunshine and in s., POE 18
  Its skeleton s. MERE G 11
  lazy little s., STEVENSO R 14
  Life's but a walking s.,
   SHAK 114
  light and a s. on every man
   MELV 7

Love is a naked s. HUGH L 14
Love is a s. PLATH 41
out-soared the s. of our night;
  SHEL 9
see my s. in the sun SHAK 96
see the s. pass away, SHEL 80
s. and the steeple; CLOU 3
s. at evening rising to meet you;
  ELIOT T 115
s. at morning striding behind you
  ELIOT T 115
s. of the night comes on
  MACL 13
s. of thee, ROSS D 3
s. of thy perfect bliss POE 27
s. of your beauty SHAK 205
s. of your face. SHAK 91
s. of your sorrow SHAK 91
s. on the floor; POE 37
s. only the sea keeps. CRAN H 2
S., or she, or both, UNKN 138
s. pinned ROET 31
s. seeks s., DOOL 2
s. under this red rock,
  ELIOT T 115
shining s.,/ Peace-bringer,
  JEFFE 28
soul from out that s. POE 37
thy s., follow thee. EMER 10
vague s. of surmise EMER 24
valley of the s., POE 19
valley of the s. of death,
  BIBL, O.T. 31
whole s. of Man BISH 29
with your s. SHAK 226
shadowe: s. mote by seene, INGE 1
  unhappy s., CAMPI 1
shadowed: s. days are done,
  AUDE 10
  world of the s. RUKE 6
shadowless: Stand s. like Silence,
  HOOD 1
shadows: about it/ Reel s.
  YEATS 135
  authentic! S. of it LEVE 13
  blend the turrets and s. POE 12
  brushing by me in the s., KINS 1
  dreamy s. rise, LINC 1
  Earth's s. fly; SHEL 13
  fragments /Of quiet s. DAVIS 5
  Gone to join the s., LIND V 5
  immense and diaphanous s.,
   WHITM 75
  join the s. LIND V 7
  knight of ghosts and s.
   UNKN 265
  Like s. in love's frenzied stifled
  throes? CLARE 7
  mess of s. for its meat?
   YEATS 10
  millions of strange s. SHAK 205
  Paint s., DANI S 11
  Pleasures only s. be, DANI S 2

rules the s. of the wood,
YEATS 164
s. and delusions here. FRENE 2
s. and windy places SWIN 3
s. have offended, SHAK 129
S. — hold their breath —
DICKI 144
S. like winds STEVENS 20
s. neither love nor guile,
BRID R 4
s. of ringdoves PLATH 79
s. of the clouds WORD 3
s. of the lovers SIMP 11
s. raced across the blind.
WILD 12
silent s. and in dreams?
STEVENS 55
tatter of s. STEVENS 43
truth do dim/ All s. dark BALD 1
types/ And s., MILT 104
Wanton pleasures, doting love,/
Are but s. flying. CAMPI 29

shadowy: dead girl but a s. ghost
MACL 10
s. flail hath threshed the corn
MILT 23
sit/ in the s. spruce HAIN 1
Those s. recollections, WORD 81
transparent s. night, WHITM 48
walls/ Of s. granite, TENN 84

shad'wy: s. tribes of Mind, COLL 9

shady: in thy s. cell, SHAK 140
s. leaf, or stalk, ROSS C 3

shaft: s. we raise to them
EMER 12
Shiver the s. BIBL, O.T. 42

shafts: golden s. employs, MILT 78

shag: common cormorant or s.
ISHE 1

shaggy: donkey, s. and brown
UNKN 106

shake: boughs which s. against the
cold, SHAK 215
lapdogs give themselves the
rousing s., POPE A 111
power to s. me WORD 3
quail and s. the orb, SHAK 7
Rough winds do s. SHAK 188
s. down into a world GRAV 5
s. off misery: HARD 11
S. off slumber, SHAK 158
S. patiently my great affliction
off. SHAK 79
s. the very Heaven POE 40
s. their heads. LARK 2
s. with the great recoil, ROON 3
S. your chains SHEL 40
single frown/ Doth s. the world
TAYL E 2
then the bigger s. EMPS 2
they groan and s. their fists?
HOUS 21

trestles to s. the dead, WHITM 8
world is bound to s. BISH 39

shaken: From the s. tower MEYN 1
is my heart not badly s.?
KAVA 26
S. out dead ROSS D 9
tomorrow all too s. SURR 2

shakes: light s. across the lakes,
TENN 111
madman s. a dead geranium.
ELIOT T 103
palsy s. of fear; MARV 12
S. a desolate boy THOMA D 2
s. my house, LOWE R 6
s. this fragile frame at eve
HARD 27
Where palsy s. KEAT 47

Shakespear: immortal S. rose;
JOHN S (1709–1784) 5

Shakespeare: gentle S., JONS 45
S. is wicked, SPEND 2
S. unlocked his heart; WORD 131
Taylor, the S. of divines.
EMER 41
tongue/ That S. spake; WORD 28
What needs my S. MILT 35

Shakespeherian: that S. Rag —
ELIOT T 125

shaking: s. Civil War relief,
LOWE R 17
s. keeps me steady. ROET 59
s. scythes at cannon. HEAN 18
Through the s. tree YEATS 149

shaky: joists/ are s. by nature,
DUGA 1
see the s. future LOWE R 55

shale: fish scale, s. dust, bone
SNYD 22

shall: all s. go. TENN 35
How s. we adorn MOMA 1
Our love s. live, SPENS 24
question Who s. die? SHAP 3
S. brithers be BURN 27
think that I s. NASH 14
wrong s. fail, LONG 12

shallow: along the s. brook,
BRET 5
in a s. Cup, OMAR 2
s. draughts intoxicate the brain,
POPE A 33
s. streams run dimpling all the
way. POPE A 10
stepping-stones in the s. brock.
WHITT 32
weak and s. as its source.
THOR 4

shallows: bound in s. and in
miseries. SHAK 50
quietly stalks and spears/ the s.,
AMMO 6

Shalott: Lady of S. TENN 60

sham: other kinds are s. GILB 6

shame: acned s., punk's pride,
HECH 11
all-eating s. and thriftless praise
SHAK 185
Art and ornament the s. CRAS 13
ashes s. and scorns; SOUTHW 2
blooming s.?' UNKN 219
blush of s., WHITT 3
do s. and vileinye; CHAU 112
dread of s. BROWNI R 48
Forspent with love and s.,
LANIE 1
glory and s., MILT 60
Glory pursue, and generous S.,
GRAY 27
guilty s.: dishonest s. MILT 73
Have you no s. GRAV 7
hid his head for s., MILT 38
hide her s. from every eye,
GOLD 9
hide the s.! WHITT 12
imagine my s. YEATM 1
most/ To S. obnoxious, MILT 97
oppression and s., WHITM 40
Or s. survive, MELV 18
pride and s. were mingled.
WHITT 13
Quit, quit, for s.; SUCK 3
s. of slow-endeavoring art,
MILT 35
S. would woo Him last, LANIE 2
soul-stifling s. COLE SAM 27
state, both full of s. and scorn,
JONS 33
this new commer, S., MILT 97
Thy father's s., thy mother's grief,
BRET 1
waste of s. SHAK 236
with sicknesses and s.
HERB G 27

shamed: s. in his own YEATS 146
S. in their souls. UNKN 22
s. the Devil. WILB 29
woke s. and angry: SNYD 10

shamrock: s. is by law forbid
UNKN 299

Shan-jen: Pa-ta S./ (A painter
SNYD 4

Shan Van Vocht: Says the S.
UNKN 217

Shandon: think of the S. bells,
MAHONY 1
thy bells of S., MAHONY 2

shanks: s. must be sound to bear
up WILLI 12

shape: All out of s. YEATS 157
crawling s. intrude! POE 31
every blessed s. we know.
SHAK 205
fall into a s. BROWNI R 7
great s. labored and fell.
MOMA 2

lose its evoked master s.
DICKEY 11

my ain proper s.,   UNKN 5

S. all light,   SHEL 77

s. as true,   SHAK 70

s. in the mind rose   ROET 50

s. no bigger than an agate-stone
SHAK 153

s. of a leaf lay once   MACL 11

s. of a rat?   ROET 35

s. of that unmoving man,
WORD 108

s. of the tree,   AIKE 5

s. with lion body   YEATS 135

Take s. in silence.   DAY 6

to this s. all must be brought.
BEAU/BASS 6

shaped: bruised and heart-/ s.
petal.   MONTA 5

S. by himself   WORD 75

s. it in His own image;   JOHN J 3

sounding anvil s.   LONG 50

those who s. him   MARK 8

shapely: upon the s. head,   DARC 4

shapes: all forms, moods, s. of
grief,   SHAK 21

Change s. with Proteus   SHAK 62

eventual s.   HECH 6

heav'nly s.   MILT 97

natural s. blazing unnatural
ROET 32

pointed s. of venom,   RODG 4

s. of what might be.   HOLLA 3

thicketed with s. of terror
HAYD 19

To wicked spirits are horrid s.
assign'd,   DONN 67

Turns them to s.   SHAK 127

violent death in thousand s.
CHAU 48

whose s. return,
THOMS J (1834–1882) 2

shaping: Nature was s. him,
LOWE J 3

s. spirit of Imagination.
COLE SAM 10

shard: s., the pebble, and the flint,
WILD 1

share: Nature's banquet s.:
MARV 9

s. my bed   THOMA D 7

s. those wings   JEFFE 44

s. yet rise above   STOD 2

shares: my s. go down.   BETJ 5

s. again the joyous feast.
FRENE 1

sharing: s. mother's joy   SNYD 4

shark: Like the s.,   SIMP 1

s./ Glides white   MELV 7

S., phlegmatical one,   MELV 13

Sharon: Rose of S.   HERR 47

rose of S.,   BIBL, O.T. 70

sharp: busy archer his s. arrows
tries?   SIDN 11

inclination be as s. as will;
SHAK 34

Lovers' eyes are s.   SCOT WA 16

s. ax of light —,   THOMA E 4

s. desire my heart;   SIDN 18

s. hot stink of fox   HUGH T 14

Short days, s. days,   NASHE 2

their quick s. faces   JARR 2

Their s. ears,   JARR 2

their s. teeth,   JARR 2

Thy s. repulse,   WYAT 6

Thy sting is not so s.   SHAK 14

utterly consumed with s. distress,
TENN 85

whittle/ it s. at both ends
KINN 3

sharper: s. than a serpent's tooth
SHAK 72

sharpest: Sweet reward for s. pain;
SIDN 28

sharps: fifty different s. and flats.
BROWNI R 60

Shatter: S. the icons of slavery
RANDA D 3

smash the s.-proof   SHAP 9

shattered: her s. hulk   HOLM 18

lamp is s.,   SHEL 89

postmarks again/ of s. towns —
KINN 7

s. water made a misty din.
FROS 76

straight/ To the s. bone;   PATT 1

Shatters: silver-thin/ S. into a
billion fragments   DAVIS 5

shave: berd was s.   CHAU 19

s. as neigh as any frere.
CHAU 118

shaved: silent as a man being s.
ALBI 2

shaven: crest be shorn and s.,
POE 36

priest all s. and shorn   MOTH 10

towel my s. jaw   KINS 5

shawis: shroudis the s.,   MONTG 1

shawl: plain worn s.   LIND V 2

shay: wonderful one-hoss s.,
HOLM 4

she: lanky hank of a s.
STEPHENS 3

sheared: packs wool s. in April,
HALL 4

shears: blind Fury with th'abhorred
s.   MILT 27

sheave: every hair a s. shall be,
PEEL 5

every s. a golden tree.   PEEL 5

sheaves: summer's green all girded
up in s.   SHAK 186

thousand golden s.   ROBI 53

Sheba: Queens of S., Meath, and
Connaught,   SYNG 3

shed: alone and never s. a tear."
KUNI 3

in a disused s.   MAHON 1

on Calvary were s.   UNKN 130

precious blood may not be s.
MCKA 6

rainbow's glory is s.;   SHEL 89

s. her blood,   SHAK 137

s. my innocent light, my Blood,
SITW 3

s. them at their side.   ARNO 32

tear be duly s.;   COLL 2

to s., to pen   DAY 12

shedding: Nature s. influence
malign,
THOMS J (1700–1748) 13

sheds: disastrous twilight s.
MILT 57

s. dry leaves,   THOMA D 2

S. the syllabic blood
THOMA D 14

sheep: die like s.   LIND V 17

have a s.   UNKN 305

his people, and the s. of his
pasture.   BIBL, O.T. 49

Jesus came to town;/ With ox and
s.   REES 1

mountain s. are sweeter,   PEAC 1

old half-witted s.   STEPHEN 4

See stylish s.   MACDI 3

s. are in the fauld,   LIND L 1

s. speckle the mountainside,
GINS 42

s., with curly horn,   UNKN 108

shepherdess of s.   MEYN 3

valley s. are fatter;   PEAC 1

When snow like s. lay   HILL G 5

sheepish: drifted in a s. calm,
LOWE R 32

sheepskin: rare and royal names/
Wormy s.   SYNG 2

sheer: grim line of s. subsistence
SAND 16

it'll be s. gravy   OHAR 3

s. blue milken dreaminess
KINN 15

sheet: flat on a s. of blood   OHAR 7

float that standard s.!   DRAK 4

in a scented linen s.,   WYLI 9

s. turned down so bravely,
UNKN 312

snow shall be their winding s.,
CAMPB T 4

wet s. and a flowing sea,
CUNN A 1

sheeted: s. dead/ Did squeak and
gibber   SHAK 20

S. memories of the past —
POE 17

sheets: cool kindliness of s.,
BROO R 4

daughters/ Got 'tween the lawful
s.   SHAK 80

s. and towels of a life MERR 10
when snow the pasture s.,
SHAK 4
whitest s. of Lillies cold.
MARV 29
shelf: Caesar's bust is on the s.,
GUIT 2
darkest inch your s. allows,
ROBI 17
shell: Enchanting s.! GRAY 25
gathering many a s., MAST 8
Leaving thine outgrown s.
HOLM 3
My heart is like a rainbow s.
ROSS C 1
See what a lovely s., TENN 99
speckled s. the poet fondles
LEVE 15
where s.-storms spouted
OWEN 11
Shellacked: pirouette/ S. with silk
SHAP 8
Shelley: see S. plain,
BROWNI R 52
S. wound be stunned: OWEN 4
shelling: tease and doubt of s.,
OWEN 32
shells: catacomb their s. PRAT 1
crow-blue mussel s., MOOR M 11
ointment from the s., HORA 9
rows of dead clam s.; ROET 42
six or seven s., PATM 3
Shelly: Hart Crane, and of S.
FULL 3
shelter: afford my miseries a s.;
COWP 15
for s. and for food, LOWE J 20
s. from the stormy blast,
WATT I 2
s. in some happier star? POE 2
wilt not s. Me." THOMP F 7
sheltered: s. for the night. MCKA 1
sheltering: breaks on the s. bars.
JOHN G 1
deep-founded s., STEVENS 68
shelters: "Naught s. thee,
THOMP F 7
shelt'ring: s. walls are thin,
UNTE 3
shelves: graveyard s. on the
town.... LOWE R 39
shelving: my s. walls/ With
honeysuckle AKEN 1
shepheardes: queene of s. all;
SPENS 50
Shepheards: S. delights SPENS 49
shepherd: Dick the s. SHAK 101
homely slighted s.'s trade,
MILT 26
I'm his poor s., UNKN 164
Lord is my s.; BIBL, O.T. 31
nymph died more quick, and the
s. more slow. DRYD 15

Old Nod, the s., DE LA 16
Philon the s., late forgot,
UNKN 290
s. is the brain DAY 10
s. swains shall dance and sing
MARL 21
s.'s roundelay. BRET 6
Star that bids the S. fold, MILT 8
truth in every s.'s tongue,
RALEG 7
weather the s. shuns, HARD 50
shepherdess: s. of sheep. MEYN 3
shepherding: s. the unruly, DAY 12
shepherds: Lamb of the s.,
LOWE R 23
moonlight the s., ARNO 7
s. feed their flocks MARL 18
s. pen their flocks MILT 68
s. pipe on oaten straws,
SHAK 100
s. too rejoice, GODO 1
s. watched their flocks by night,
TATE N 1
Sheridan: Hurrah! Hurrah for S.!
READ T 2
S. into the fight, READ T 3
S. twenty miles away. READ T 1
shew'th: late spring no bud or
blossom s. MILT 14
place to s. what recompence
MILT 111
use your wit and s. it so.
WYAT 17
shield: Brake the s.-wall, UNKN 20
her shining s., BRID R 19
Lord God is a sun and s.:
BIBL, O.T. 43
shifted: s. his trumpet, GOLD 4
They s. a little, BISH 17
shifting: s. hate and love. STOD 2
shifts: life in s. of work and leisure.
HEAN 14
shilling: s. life AUDE 98
Splendid S.: PHILL 1
shillings: owe me ten s., UNKN 25
Shiloh: all is hushed at S.
MELV 20
S., Antietam, Malvern Hill, Bull
Run. TATE A 12
shine: all thy deeds, my faithful
Mary, s.; COWP 22
anxious for to s. GILB 30
baby gonna s. BROWN S 5
black beaks s. SNYD 32
crystal glorious ye s., CHAU 122
dares to s.; POPE A 2
for grace and gear may s.,
BURN 33
frozen Pleiads s.: ADDI 2
furrows s. but late upturned,
THOR 11
How late they start to s.!
GUNN 9

Israel's tents do s. so bright.
BLAK 39
locks with ointments s., HERR 72
no s., HOOD 6
rust disus'd, and s. no more,
COWP 21
rust unburnished, not to s. in
use! TENN 131
Shall s. DONN 30
s. forevermore. MCCRE 1
S. here to us, DONN 56
s. in strife, ARNO 16
s., perishing republic. JEFFE 38
s. upon the road COWP 25
s. when all of these are gone.
BRAD 8
singing, as they s., ADDI 4
smiling Mornings s., GRAY 32
Shined: S. in my angel-infancy.
VAUG 21
your light s. never; SPENS 6
shines: boldly s. your shuttered door
of glass. MCKA 10
dog rose s. in the hedge.
MONTA 4
great shining s. LEVE 21
Heaven's light forever s.,
SHEL 13
Light breaks where no sun s.;
THOMA D 29
sun s. bright FOST 1
too hot the eye of heaven s.,
SHAK 188
shinest: wheresoe'er thou s.
SHEL 53
shingle: whines the s., JOYC 3
shining: All's a scattering,/ A s.
ROET 47
dark and dark — a s. space
GRAV 25
Death! the jewel of the just,/ S.
nowhere, VAUG 27
delight on a s. night, UNKN 172
extend their s. rows, POPE A 114
great s. shines JEFFE 28
her s. shield, BRID R 19
matrix of all s. JEFFE 28
needles, once a s. store, COWP 21
one/ Is s. in the sky. WORD 45
saw the taper s. SCOT WA 17
scales from s. rocks, WHITM 2
see it s. plain, HOUS 35
s. archway through, HOLM 2
s. Big-Sea-Water, LONG 40
s., in the water MOMA 3
s. Popocatapetl, TURN 1
s. to the quiet Moon.
COLE SAM 17
silent and mournful s.,
WHITM 92
spangled Heav'ns, a S. Frame,
ADDI 3
sun is s. SIMP 11

sun is s. bright, THAY 4
whale stood s., WINT 8

shinning: summoning, a s.
HAYD 21

ship: all I ask is a tall s. MASE 11
build your s. of death, LAWR 36
capital s. for an ocean trip,
CARRY 8
dismasted, gray and batter'd s.,
WHITM 28
expensive delicate s. AUDE 64
fragile s. of courage, LAWR 39
I saw a s. a-sailing, MOTH 14
idle as a painted s.
COLE SAM 32
in the burnt s. drown'd.
DONN 13
infatuate s. went down. MELV 1
launch the small s., LAWR 39
sail on, O S. of State! LONG 6
sailed away/ From a leaking s.
WHITT 24
s. from some near star JARR 24
s. has weather'd every rack,
WHITM 45
s. I seek is passing, DUNB P 7
S. me somewheres east of Suez,
KIPL 13
s. of martial build MELV 1
s. that's westward bound
VAN DY 3
stately s. Of Tarsus, MILT 110
your s. of death, LAWR 36

shipman: s. was ther, CHAU 7

shipmate: Joy, s., joy! WHITM 41

Shippen: As downright S.
POPE A 88

ships: 'as s. on the foam —
KIPL 30
boistous winds did beat/ Their s.,
SURR 7
bright s. left you POUN 54
conclude our S. are lost, SACK 2
dark s. move, HAYD 10
fleet of small balck s., BISH 25
goe downe to 'th sea in s.:
BIBL, O.T. 56
launched a thousand s., MARL 3
new s. ELIOT T 96
old s. sail like swans asleep
FLEC 4
s. and sun SPEND 2
S. burnt in fight, CHAU 48
sinking s., and praying hands.
TENN 90
Spanish s. of war at sea!
TENN 116
three s. come sailing by, UNKN 8
two doomed s. WILD 4

shipwho: so old a s. knows, FLEC 5

shipwrecked: some s. sailor,
LUCR 5

shires: every s. ende/ Of Engelond
CHAU 5

shirk: modish painter s.
YEATS 156

shirt: intolerable s. of flame
ELIOT T 70
parted the s. WHITM 78
s. and tie were luminous.
WAGO 1
s. verminously busy ROSE 7
Shroud as well as a S. HOOD 12

shirts: no s. to wear; GILB 49

shit: take no s. From nobody,"
KNIG 4
Why s. Snyder, SNYD 34

shiver: s., and then a thrill,
HOLM 9
S. the shaft BIBL, O.T. 42
willow s. in the sun STEVENS 58

shivering: s. birds beneath the
eaves MCKA 1
s. from our dream. MERE G 16
s.-sweet to the touch? CORN 2
stood s. in the snow, SOUTHW 1

shivers: Joy s. in the corner
ROBI 48

shock: fodder's in the s., RILE 4
hour of the Earthquake s.!
HOLM 9
pivoting searchlights probe to s.
LOWE R 5
Shuddering insidious s. MACN 1
slight s. of the soothe of waves,
WHITM 92
steel decks rock with the lightning
s., ROON 3

shocking: s. disease.' AUDE 67

shocks: Beauty that s. you,
POPE A 12
repeated s., again, ARNO 22
thousand natural s. SHAK 39

shod: for work be s., WHITT 8

shoe: black s. PLATH 26
clocks, bodies, consciousness, s.,
GINS 24
contains a s. SIMP 1
each eye attending its s.,
CRAN H 32
eating his s.; UNKN 241
little s.-house — POTT 1
old woman and she lived in a s.,
MOTH 30
palace grand, or just a plain, old
s.; UNTE 1
Sailed off in a wooden s.
FIEL E 8
Went past my simple S.
DICKI 63
wooden s. that sailed the skies
FIEL E 9

shoeing: For dressing eels, or s.
horses. PRAE 1

shoelaces: with gum and s.,
WARR 6

shoes: love as odd as wearing s.
CORS 8
Patrol the halls on spongy s.,
WILB 31
s. were full of feet. UNKN 146
so vegetarian,/ he wore rope s.
LOWE R 31
They lie without s. SEXT 15
thick-soled/ s.! MOOR M 3
Thy gowns, thy s., RALEG 8
to the tops of his s. WAGO 1
walk in velvet s.: WYLI 10
with your s. off JARR 6

shoestring: careless s., HERR 8

shog: gied the infant warld a s.,
BURN 3

shone: armor s. like gold.
UNKN 60
fitful firelight paled and s.
WHITT 28
No light propitious s.; COWP 2
round headlands s. ARNO 5
solid mountains s., WORD 102
sun/ S. in vain: THOMA E 14

Shook: crow/ S. down FROS 46
gods s., they knew not why.
EMER 51
love that s. the lights RUKE 3
S. all our coffins HARD 13
s. him from his rest, SHEL 17
s. it forth with a royal will.
WHITT 3
s. listlessly/ Two petals ALDR T 2
s. the Heavens, SWIF 4
s. to see him drink it up:
HOUS 53
s. with horror at thy fall. BRYA 5
singing s. him YEATS 94
thunders s. the mighty deep,
HOLM 18

shoon: in her silver s.; DE LA 21

shoot: nest is in a watered s.;
ROSS C 1
s. a fellow down HARD 31
S., if you must, WHITT 3
s. reformed kindness, GREV 3
s. to kill MACN 3

shooting: mouth's/ s. iron
REED I 4
s. stars attend thee; HERR 32

shoots: Bright s. of everlastingness.
VAUG 22
old tree with s., POUN 26
pressing wind s. javelin-like
MERE G 11
S. across the neutral Dark.
EMER 9

shop: fertile s. of cruel arts:
MARV 14
foul rag-and-bone s. of the heart.
YEATS 29

in my bosom's s. SHAK 192
s. was just upon the bank,
   HOLM 10
shopman: s.'s test of age ROBI 38
shopping: families s. at night!
   GINS 37
s. malls and prisons, PINS 1
Shoppy-Shop: From the Grocer's S.
   CAREY 1
shops: To s. in crowds SWIF 7
shore: Along the treach'rous s.
   HORA 5
along the unharmful s.
   LOWE J 14
amazing frowns/ On utmost
   Kilda's s.,
   THOMS J (1700–1748) 8
anchor'd near the s., WHITM 28
by the pleasant s., TENN 25
by the s., WHITM 79
control/ Stops with the s.;
   BYRO 1
cross from s. to s. WHITM 18
dance upon the level s.?
   YEATS 163
darts to s. to stab— AMMO 6
despot's heel is on thy s.,
   RANDA J 1
doing something to the s.
   FROS 76
dull s. of lazy temperance,
   ROCH 2
Europe to the Aetolian s.
   ARNO 35
false lights on the s., LONG 7
Fast by their native s. COWP 8
furrows of the s., ROET 42
I sat upon the s. Fishing,
   ELIOT T 155
inhospitable s.; SHEL 68
kingdom of the s., SHAK 211
lights around the s. ROSS D 8
lone Chorasmian s. SHEL 18
low sounds by the s.; YEATS 75
more willing bent to s.,
   CAMPI 17
of your teeming s. LAZA 2
on the lonely s., BYRO 1
on the Night's Plutonian s.!"
   POE 36
on the opposite s. LONG 44
one on s./ To one thing constant
   never, SHAK 130
rise upon some other s.,
   MCCRE 1
river had another s., LOWE R 26
s. was lucky in being backed by
   cliff, FROS 77
Slant to the s., SQUI 1
surf-tormented s. POE 14
that unknown and silent s.,
   LAMB 1
to no earthly s. CRAN H 50

towards the pebbled s.,
   SHAK 209
waters as the s. SWIN 9
Which s.? WILLI 26
wild New England s. HEMA 4
your presence was s. HAYD 3
shored: These fragments I have s.
   ELIOT T 156
Shoreditch: bells of S. UNKN 25
shoreless: s. flood, SHEL 68
s. watery wild, ARNO 41
shoreline: s., greenery and glass,
   MOSS 4
shores: cold eternal s. ROBI 37
earth's human s., KEAT 3
eternal whisperings around/
   Desolate s., KEAT 59
forced on rocky s., CHAU 48
life upon these s. HAYD 11
on the s. of darkness there is
   light, KEAT 65
pores of the ocean and s.;
   SHEL 25
s. of Gitche Gumee, LONG 40
s. of light? LUCR 5
wended the s. I know, WHITM 1
shoreward: roll us s. soon."
   TENN 80
winds s. blow, ARNO 9
shorn: crest be s. and shaven,
   POE 36
Horizontal misty Air/ S. of his
   Beams, MILT 57
short: all too s. a date. SHAK 138
dressed for this s. comedy.
   RALEG 15
fierce, and bald, and s. of breath,
   SASS 3
For one s. hour TENN 98
have so s. a date, BRAD 10
one s. minute gives me in her
   sight. SHAK 147
sewn s. at elbow. OWEN 15
s. and simple annals of the poor.
   GRAY 8
s. dark passage DAVE 1
S. days, sharp days, NASHE 2
s.-end comes down/ When you
   least expect it. SIMI 2
s.-haired joy and roughness—
   SNYD 16
S. is the glory of the blushing
   rose, DANI S 6
s. life and a merry one, OWEN 2
s. measures JONS 41
s. shrill Shriek COLL 10
s. stakes of men. EMPS 9
s. wild scream, WHITM 92
tempers are s. GILB 58
time is s. AUDE 91

With frantic gesture and s.
   breathless cry SHEL 16
work until my heart is s.,
   HUGO 7
shortcomings: bear my s. HARD 28
shorten: s. tedious nights.
   CAMPI 18
shorter: Feels s. than the Day
   DICKI 11
journey is s. to heaven.
   UNKN 192
shorthand: emotional/ s.
   MOOR M 9
shot: dew cries up, the star is s.;
   KING H 5
dream dispersed by s., SHAP 10
fired the s., STOD 1
fired the s. heard round the
   world. EMER 11
first day i s. dope SANC 4
hearts made great with s.;
   OWEN 30
hook s. kisses the rim HIRS 1
keeper s. him with his gun
   THOMA E 7
last bear, s. CRAN H 17
random scatter of s. KIZE 3
s. an arrow into the air, LONG 1
s. electricity/ Through the rest.
   KNIG 5
s. Mister Howard, UNKN 148
Slung atween the round s.
   NEWB 1
so many princes at a s. SHAK 42
When they s. him NOYE 8
should: brother s. sail a painted
   boat. WHITT 16
mother said that I never s.
   UNKN 125
s. be blithe and strong,
   WHITM 37
s. be her grave; HOLM 18
Somebody who s. have been
   SEXT 1
shoulder: Belly, s., bum,
   YEATS 100
Borne upon a zephyr's s.
   POUN 15
hand upon my s., CORN 1
home we brought you s.-high.
   HOUS 55
jags from the clotted s.,
   JEFFE 13
queer s. to the wheel. GINS 6
s., bosom, lip, and knee HOLLA 5
To the S. o' Mutton LEWI 3
shoulders: bundle he has on his s.,
   LOWE J 4
dropping Victorian s. LAWR 20
face,/ my s., flanks, buttocks
   WILLI 13
heavy sensual s., RUKE 2
sat on my s. STRA 5

s. Glisten as silver, LAWR 12
Stormy, husky, brawling,/ City of
  the Big S.: SAND 3
shoures: Aprill with his s. soote
  CHAU 3
shout: drown the raucous s.;
  UNTE 3
great s. upon the hills, MARK 4
rings no hunters' s.; SIGO 1
s. and a cry. BOGA 16
s. and bang and roar and brawl
  BELL 13
somewhere children s., THAY 4
sustain/ Some casual s. WORD 9
was a s. about my ears, CHES 4
shouted: every time She s. 'Fire!'
  BELL 16
s. for joy? BIBL, O.T. 14
s. through the belfry tower,
  LONG 18
shouting: heavens fill with s.,
  TENN 75
s. and laughter. BROWNI R 62
s. at me, dead man, SLES 2
S. to the wooded hills, MAST 8
tumult and the s. dies; KIPL 18
shouts: hears our s., SIMM 2
Nymph exulting fills with s. the
  sky; POPE A 122
s. o' war are heard BURN 49
shove: pistons jerk and s., ROET 51
Shovel: S. them under SAND 10
show: books will s. HERB G 5
built to envious s., JONS 35
catch men with s.,
  BROWNI R 28
cathedrals chronically on s.,
  LARK 4
circus animals were all on s.,
  YEATS 26
earth has something yet to s.,
  WORD 165
Fair face s. friends when riches do
  abound; GOOG 1
fair lines which true goodness s.
  SIDN 20
for their virtue only is their s.
  SHAK 206
gathered s. lets down FROS 78
hard words ready to s. why,
  BUTL 2
having no more to s. LARK 16
his faults can freely s.,
  POPE A 24
in verse my love to s., SIDN 5
light would s. SITW 5
no s. To move, DONN 64
s. of life VERY 2
s. something's missing? PLATH 1
that within which passes s.;
  SHAK 21
under s. of love well feigned —
  MILT 92

What do all examples s.?
  SCHW 4
what morals critics ought to s.,
  POPE A 36
wondrous secret s., LOWE J 16
shower: in a s. of all my days.
  THOMA D 33
in sun and s., WORD 48
prove the sweetness of a s.
  THOMA E 17
stars in one great s. DAVID 4
steam of the tiled s. stalls,
  HECH 8
Showered: flowery roof/ S. roses
  MILT 78
showers: attenes in stonen s.
  CHAT 2
Fall grief in s.; JONS 4
flow'rs/ Sweetened with rich and
  gentle s., VAUG 24
rainbow-crowned brief s.,
  ROSS C 37
s. betumble the chestnut
  HARD 49
s. his head and eyes, HARD 43
sighs dissolved into s. KING H 2
With s. and dewdrops wet;
  ROSS C 33
showest: Have more than thou s.,
  SHAK 71
showing: sweet child-face is s.
  WHITT 14
shown: here in emblem s.:
  WESL S 1
s. their pride HERR 41
streaming beard is s. MELV 19
show-off: strutting s. SCHW 10
show'r: when to dread a s. SWIF 6
Showres: as Sunne and S.,
  FLET/SHAK 1
shows: huge stage presenteth naught
  but s. SHAK 187
marring of beautiful s., PRAE 4
mourning s. be spread. SIDN 36
picture s., and spats, SASS 7
sad and solemn s., FLET/SHAK 6
s., architecture, WHITM 60
s. its berries red UNKN 130
shred: s. of black. WHITT 34
shredded: flavour of s. coconut.
  SIMP 4
sugared and s. BROD 3
shrew: harpy, s. and whore.
  RICH 18
one eyed s. GINS 12
shrewd: Gascon's s. wit LOWE J 9
shrews: three old s. of fate
  GINS 12
Shriek: short shrill S. COLL 10
With a fearful s., DARC 4
shrieked: s. against his creed —
  TENN 36

shrieking: Herod s. vengeance
  LOWE R 22
s. and squeaking BROWNI R 60
shrieks: Catches his s. in cups of
  gold. BLAK 31
trills of s. WHITM 102
shrill: eccho s. did make. UNKN 59
feel the free/ S. wind LANG 3
lark so s. and clear; LYLY 3
music s. Give my fair Love good
  morrow! HEYW 2
short s. Shriek COLL 10
s. you bugles blow. WHITM 7
Until her voice grew s. YEATS 51
shrilling: s. from the solar course,
  EMER 51
shrine: best gifts on thy s.!
  WHITT 10
faith's pure s.! HEMA 5
s. of retreat LOWE J 7
stall become a s. WILB 11
Temple's inner s., WORD 27
Veil'd Melancholy has her sovran
  s., KEAT 43
shrines: s. of Sorrow, and of
  Pleasure; BYRO 22
shrink: cowering foes shall s.
  DRAK 3
Sweet, if you s., UNKN 74
We shall not s., TIMR 4
shrinking: genius so s. and rare
  LOWE J 1
shrinks: soul s. WILB 24
shrivel: thoughts begin to s. up
  FIEL R 1
shrivels: Grass s. and dries
  WALK 12
shroud: bier and the s. KNOX 3
buried us without s. or coffin
  HEAN 18
In remembrance of a s.
  SHAK 128
S. as well as a Shirt. HOOD 12
s. of white, SHAK 176
To stain the stiff dishonored s.
  ELIOT T 112
shrouded: pale Virgin s. in snow,
  BLAK 54
S. forms that start and sigh
  POE 17
s. heavens anywhere; ROBI 9
shroudis: s. the shawis, MONTG 1
shrouds: with s. unkempt.
  PETRA 12
shrubberies: railings and s.
  THOMA D 26
shrubs: s. and trees, WHITM 12
shrug: I borne it with a patient s.,
  SHAK 118
shudder: affrighted air with a s.
  bore, READ T 1
gave/ A darkening s.; WINT 8

s. in the loins YEATS 85
s. ran around the sky; EMER 50
shuddering: his s. child; GOET 1
his s. insights, BISH 38
s. from the quest. BROWNI R 42
S. insidious shock MACN 1
s. mouth-wracked GINS 9
spurting and s KINN 15
shuddring: s. horror pale, MILT 61
shuffle: Practise a tinker s.
YEATS 88
shuffled: s. off this mortal coil,
SHAK 39
Shun: S. the polluted flock,
WYLI 1
To s. the heaven SHAK 236
Why do we then s. death
WHITE 2
shunn'd: s. by saunt an' sinner,
BURN 57
shunned: since easier s.? MILT 95
shuns: weather the shepherd s.,
HARD 50
Shuswap: S. tribe SNYD 36
shut: air liner with s.-off engines
SPEND 13
Behind s. the postern,
BROWNI R 35
Eternity s. in a span, CRAS 5
gates of this Chapel were s.,
BLAK 64
golden umbrage s., TUCK 1
house is s. and still, ROBI 18
men s. their gate, SHAK 177
no route s., AMMO 8
read with joy, then s. the book.
PATM 2
s. in an urn of brass! TENN 87
S. not so soon; HERR 44
S. out that stealing moon,
HARD 41
S. thee from heaven HOLM 3
s. up the lamb at night. HAY 6
strangers would have s. the many
doors ROBI 47
shuts: s. the Door — DICKI 132
shutter: dry rattling of a s.,
FROS 132
shuttered: female smells in s.
rooms, ELIOT T 105
shutters: only close the s. RICH 26
s. like the dew, AIKE 6
shutting: opening and s. itself
MOOR M 11
s. out and shutting in, AMMO 5
shuttle: Man is the s., VAUG 10
musical s., WHITM 62
shy: Little Jesus, wast Thou s.
THOMP F 4
secluded and s. BINY 4
s. and hidden bird WHITM 47
Ye s. recluses, ARNO 39

Sick: gnawed/ S. memories
ROBI 28
I am s., I must die. NASHE 1
I am so s., so s., so s.: CORN 3
I became tired and s.,
WHITM 111
I was numb and s. LEWI 4
like a devil's s. of sin; OWEN 19
make me s. WHITM 75
our s. eyes, EMER 5
seed of love was s. LEWI 4
s. almost to doomsday with
eclipse. SHAK 20
s. and lay a-bed,
STEVENSO R 11
s. eyes that blame; SNOD 15
s. of prey, SHEL 68
s. of singing; SWIN 22
s. of the palette and fiddle-bow,
YEATS 77
s. with desire of the sun
UNKN 121
stunted trees look s., EMER 5
Tell her, I'm s. of living;
PETRA 5
true, s.-hearted slave, HOUS 3
were you not extremely s.?'
PRIO 14
you are s., and I grown old,
SWIF 17
sicken: ground itself does not s.?
WHITM 96
surfeiting,/ The appetite may s
SHAK 174
sweet violets s., SHEL 43
sickle: rosy lips and cheeks/ Within
his bending s.'s compass
SHAK 232
She was the s.; ROET 28
Time his s. brings/ In vain,
CAREW 11
sicklied: s. o'er with the pale cast of
thought. SHAK 40
sickly: uncertain s. appetite
SHAK 242
sickness: civilization is a transient
s. JEFFE 27
s., death's herald, and champion;
DONN 44
s. will not cease, NASHE 2
Splashed with a splended s.,
CHES 10
sicknesses: with s. and shame
HERB G 27
side: along the forest s. TAYL B 1
Back and s. go bare, go bare,
STEVENSO W 3
be on every s., MAST 4
bright sword by his s.,
UNKN 154
dropt at my s. that day,
WHITM 106
faded by my s., BRYA 9

fall by thy s. SHAK 243
From thy riven s. which flowed,
TOPL 1
fur s. inside, STRON 1
go by thy s. UNKN 90
inside skin s. outside; STRON 1
nestle near thy s.? SHEL 74
on the other s. DICKI 96
other s. of care MUIR 2
pierce my right s. open UNKN 76
purple wardrobe in thy s.
CRAS 11
right man on our s., LUTH 3
see every s. of every question;
MAST 4
shed them at their s. ARNO 32
s./ Of dripping stone; YEATS 152
s./ Of my darling, POE 6
skin s. outside. STRON 1
too much knowledge for the
Sceptic s., POPE A 78
turned over on his s. SILKI 2
warm s. inside, STRON 1
world stands out on either s.
MILLA 30
your softe s., CHAU 67
sideburns: muse through their
s. . . . LOWE R 19
sidelong: s. crabs had scrawled their
crooked race; CRAB 1
sides: hot s. of death. WRIG R 1
listen to all s. WHITM 76
On both s. SHAK 238
prick the s. of my intent,
SHAK 105
terraced s. of a mountain,
WHITM 9
wintry s. of many glens, SYNG 7
world from both s., DICKEY 28
sidestep: We will s., CRAN H 37
sidewalk: down the s. OHAR 12
pound his head upon the s.
IGNA 1
rain makes still pools on the s.
HUGH L 1
Sidney: S. is dead, dead is my
friend, GREV/DYER 2
siege: every living thing in/ s.:
AMMO 6
wrackful s. of batt'ring days,
SHAK 212
sieges: s. tremendous WHITM 114
Sierras: S. Will be dry and dead,
SNYD 20
sieve: draws nectar in a s.,
COLE SAM 46
went to sea in a S. LEAR 8, 9
sigh: churchyard with a s.,
LONG 18
comforting, melodic s., JOHN J 6
hapless Soldiers s. BLAK 75
horrors of the tedious Night,/
Darkling I s., PHILL 2

used to s. and an armchair:
HEAN 15
vast s. reigns. JOHN L 1
white s. below. WYLI 10
With s. and tears. BYRO 74
silences: great sunk s. ROSE 6
Lady of s. ELIOT T 9
silent: Be s. always POPE A 37
beheld the s. toil HOLM 2
below your s. tree, BARNE 1
best are s. now. ARNO 33
birds are s. in their nest,
BLAK 100
broke the s. air, WORD 9
burst/ Into that s. sea.
COLE SAM 31
center of the s. Word.
ELIOT T 13
chamber in the s. halls of death,
BRYA 24
close beside me with s. lips
WHITM 61
cool and s. shades of sleep.
HERR 52
Creep back into their s. Barks
COWL 7
deaf and s., read'st the eternal
deep, WORD 77
Envy be s. and attend!);
POPE A 109
floors of s. seas. ELIOT T 86
his Prism and s. Face WORD 101
in s. icicles, COLE SAM 17
moldering now in s. dust
BURN 31
sat in s. musing — BRON 3
sessions of sweet s. thought
SHAK 195
s. and mournful shining,
WHITM 92
S., and soft, and slow LONG 38
s. as a man being shaved. ALBI 2
s. days/ In harmless joys are
spent, CAMPI 13
s., dull retreat, FRENE 5
s. from life escape WHITM 17
S. hammers of decay. HODG 8
S. is the house: BRON 14
s. land; ROSS C 19
s. night MILT 76
s. shadows and in dreams?
STEVENS 55
s. signal lamps to swing.
WHITM 101
s. syllables recorded; LONG 39
s. thought can bring, WORD 136
s., with bright eyes, WHITM 64
slow s. walk HARD 29
splendid s. sun WHITM 29, 31
that unknown and s. shore,
LAMB 1
watchful bailiffs take their s.
stands, SWIF 11

wicked shall be s. in darkness;
BIBL, O.T. 8
silently: s. laugh at my own
cenotaph, SHEL 26
s. steal away. LONG 16
s. they took at flood, NEME 1
Watching, s. weeps. WHITM 57
silica: dangerous than s., ROET 8
silk: Any s., and thread, SHAK 182
pirouette/ Shellacked with s.
SHAP 8
s. blown against a wall POUN 27
S. handkerchiefs, ELIOT T 129
skin as soft as s., MOTH 16
That thing of s., POPE A 9
silken: caught me in his s. net,
BLAK 24
From s. Samarcand KEAT 13
in a field a s. tent FROS 101
s. lines, and silver hooks.
DONN 6
s. ties of love and thought
FROS 102
With a s. thread of my own hand's
weaving; KEAT 27
silkie: s. in the sea, UNKN 122
silks: dress me up in s. WHITT 16
Gie fools their s., BURN 25
in s. my Julia goes, HERR 61
s. and fine array, BLAK 40
sill: buzzing at the s. ROET 33
limestone on an ancient s.
TATE A 17
silly: artist s. for his face,
OWEN 16
idle, s., flattering words, HOWI 2
Save to the s. eye, WILB 9
Securer lives the s. swain.
CAMPI 9
s. story SNYD 19
s., tender babe SOUTHW 4
your s. mood? GINS 5
silt: labored/ To dredge the s.
PLATH 24
Silver: Attract a S. Churn! GILB 34
chapel's s. bell you hear
POPE A 103
for a handful of s. BROWNI R 44
Goddess of the s. lake, MILT 7
golden nutmeg and a s. pear;
MOTH 16
harbor, s.-paced CRAN H 28
in her s. shoon; DE LA 21
lady-smocks all s.-white,
SHAK 100
oars were s., SHAK 5
"Of fayre Elisa be your s. song,
SPENS 53
polish all the s., GILB 13
precious stone set in the s. sea,
SHAK 88
quick s. bell SHAP 1

rose and s. lilies die,
FLET G EL 1
Seated in thy s. chair, JONS 3
see that s. brood, SPENS 42
shoulders/ Glisten as s., LAWR 12
silken lines, and s. hooks.
DONN 6
s. answer rang, BROWNI E 8
s. apples of the moon,
YEATS 139
S. bells! POE 9
s. chime/ Move in melodious
time, MILT 39
s. cord BIBL, O.T. 6
s. face in the night. WHITM 52
s. fountains mud, SHAK 199
s. loneliness ROBI 46
s. music SHEL 77
s., snarling trumpets' KEAT 6
s. streaming Thames, SPENS 39
s.-thin/ Shatters into a billion
fragments DAVIS 5
s. wings, MARV 19
sketched a s. Zion, LIND V 4
spider will make a s. string nest
SAND 1
stroke his s. hair, BLAK 99
their little s. heads, YEATS 93
thin forests of s.-grey. SNYD 46
to s. turned; PEEL 7
Too s. for a seam — DICKI 13
Tweed's s. current glide,
SCOT WA 4
wash the dusk with s. BLAK 110
Why not a S. Churn?" GILB 33
with a s. blow: THOMA E 4
silvered: sable curls all s. o'er with
white: SHAK 186
s. chamois-leather MOOR M 37
silvers: darkness s. away, BRID R 1
s. this nook; MELV 3
silversmiths: din like s. PLATH 23
silvery: embossed by s. images
OHAR 2
golden brass and s. steel,
WHITM 99
s. haze of summer drawn;
TENN 40
So smooth, so sweet, so s., is thy
voice HERR 63
with s. nose, SHAP 5
silv'ry: Thy s. feet/ My soul I'll
pour HERR 33
simile: s. and metaphor. NASH 18
simmer: wi' her a' my s. days
SOUT 1
simmering: in this s. marsh.'
LAWR 34
Simon: S. on thy lake of Galilee:
WILD 10
simple: gift to be s. UNKN 260
gravity, which is not s. RICH 29
In s. childhood WORD 115

making wise the s. BIBL, O.T. 28
mind/ That nobleness made s.
  YEATS 101
my s. ignorance, EMER 42
names sung in your s. layes,
  SPENS 29
Rich in the s. worship of a day.
  KEAT 18
short and s. annals of the poor.
  GRAY 8
s. and heartfelt lay, LONG 15
s. as a fire, YEATS 101
S. as soil yet crowded as earth
  WILB 36
s. child, WORD 155
s. creed/ Of Childhood, WORD 80
s. I according to my skill.
  BRAD 15
s. life that Nature yields; CRAB 5
s. produce of the common day.
  WORD 16
s. truth his utmost skill! WOTT 1
s. truth miscall'd simplicity,
  SHAK 213
s. truth suppress'd. SHAK 238
tell in s. language HART 3
though I am s., FULL 2
transient sorrows, s. wiles,
  WORD 134
true love acted s. modesty.
  SHAK 149
under the s. stars THOMA D 18
simplest: learn the s. things
  OLSO 13
simpletons: s. thought a living
  fable MOOR M 24
simplicity: Give me s., that I may
  live, HERB G 76
mislaid/ S. of wish and will,
  WILB 28
simple truth miscall'd s.,
  SHAK 213
s. a grace;/ Robes loosely flowing,
  JONS 5
simply: They record s. SPEND 8
sin: As a tree my s. stands
  ROSS C 8
Be of s. the double cure; TOPL 1
better not to s. at all, NASH 11
bringing peace and mirth/ By
  flight of s. HERB G 56
Conceived in s., and unto labor
  born, JONS 33
Creator, whom s. nor nature tied,
  DONN 68
disproportion'd s. MILT 2
filled with folly and s.,
  MERE O 3
God might pardon every s. . . .
  SIMP 5
Guilty of dust and s. HERB G 48
Hell, earth, and s. WESL C 2
killing s., STEVENSO R 2

lewd and lavish act of s., MILT 4
like a devil's sick of s.; OWEN 19
no s. love's fruit to steal;
  JONS 49
of folly, noise and s.!
  BROWNI R 49
Plate s. with gold, SHAK 81
poor child of s.! POE 43
price of s.; ALEX 9
remembered s. RANS 12
second kind of s., NASH 10
S. and Death amain MILT 62
s. hath betrayed DONN 33
s. is divided into two parts.
  NASH 9
S. is where our Lady sat,
  UNKN 170
s./ Like clouds eclipsed my mind.
  VAUG 18
s. of commission, NASH 9
s. of my ingratitude SHAK 104
s. of omission, NASH 10
s. s. BROO G 20
S. their conception, their birth
  weeping, WEBS 4
s. to covet honor SHAK 59
s. when love's rites are not done.
  CAREW 13
s. you must be pursuing,
  NASH 11
so punish s., HERB G 27
social wants that s. TENN 72
squalid lease of s. BRID R 11
this world of s., BROO P 6
to S. our byast Nature leans,
  DRYD 1
triumph over death and s.;
  SPENS 18
usura, s. against nature, POUN 9
We wallow in our s.; UNKN 314
what s. to me unknown
  POPE A 13
Whoever plots the s., SHAK 140
Sinai: from the mount of S.,
  MILT 104
since: month s. I walked,
  WHITM 48
s. she/ Was beautiful:
  STEPHENS 2
s. Sophia have a-crossed the sea.'
  UNKN 320
s. the birth of time, WHITT 22
s. the day she died. LONG 14
S. there's no help, DRAY 15
sincere: declare with a mind s.
  GILB 19
evermore s.; HERR 73
love s. MILT 101
sincerest: Our s. laughter SHEL 71
sinews: Stiffen the s., SHAK 56
sinewy: large and s. hands;
  LONG 48
lean and s. WHITM 70

sinful: any s. games; HART 3
A-preaching that drinking is s.,
  GOLD 6
my s. heart. VAUG 6
vileyns s. dedès make a cherl.
  CHAU 113
sing: Angels s. to thee their ayres
  divine, COWL 11
bid him s.! CULL 19
birds do chirp and s.: BRET 5
blissful birdès how they s.,
  CHAU 68
boy, when you s., JOHN H 1
Castalian sisters s., HERR 16
feel like singin', s. STANT 1
fine to dance and s. UNKN 128
Flutter, or s. an aria BROO G 16
graced with birds that s.,
  BROWNE 1
granted to s. WHITM 47
he did whistle and she did s.,
  UNKN 9
I s. a hero's head, STEVENS 22
I strive to s., GRAHAM R 1
I, too, s. America. HUGH L 6
I unto my selfe alone will s.,
  SPENS 30
I'll s. you a new ballad,
  DICKEN 1
in Christ's coach saints sweetly
  s., TAYL E 4
In heaven you'll learn to s.,
  CRAS 9
invisible rain did ever s.
  SHEL 77
jolly cuckoos s. LYLY 4
love shall hourly s., BROWNE 2
mortal sounds can s. awake,
  KINN 2
no birds s. KEAT 31
no power to s., MORR 1
Now we s., BLY 5
of my faith and love did s.
  VAUG 30
Of thee I s.; SMIT SA 1
power to s. of thee MICH 2
praises s. to God the King,
  BROO P 5
pretty birds do s., NASHE 3
public conveyances/ s.? OLSO 7
reminiscence s. WHITM 63
Romance, who loves to nod and
  s., POE 38
salmon s. in the street. AUDE 1
she walked to s. STEVENS 18
shepherd swains shall dance and
  s. MARL 21
sigh as you s. MUND 1
s. a dirge for Saint Hugh's soul,
  DEKK 1
s. a lullaby: DEKK/OTHE 1
s. as you tackle the thing
  GUES 5

skate: You s. at such a rate DAIC 1
skating: leave behind your s. mate.
  DAIC 1
  man s., STEVENS 32
  s. in a urinal — CRAN H 31
skeleton: H. the S., MERE G 9
  Its s. shadow MERE G 11
  withered old and s.-gaunt,
  YEATS 66
skeletons: ribs and all the s.
  ALBI 1
skelp: s. an' scaud poor dogs
  BURN 2
sketch: s. a face DARC 4
sketched: s. a silver Zion,
  LIND V 4
Skie: flaming from th' Ethereal S.
  MILT 49
skies: air, earth, and s.; WORD 153
  beautiful for spacious s., BATE 1
  brightness of the s. BRYA 14
  commercing with the s., MILT 16
  down from the blissful s.
  TENN 84
  felt I like some watcher of the s.
  KEAT 56
  I the s., SYLV 2
  injustice of the s. YEATS 33
  light of distant s.: BRYA 28
  long as s. are blue, SHEL 2
  meet the raging of the s.,
  CAMPB T 5
  rooks are blown about the s.;
  TENN 23
  rush into the s. POPE A 66
  s. they were ashen and sober;
  POE 46
  s. with clouds are lin'd;
  BIBL, O.T. 67
  Sombre and rich, the s.;
  JOHN L 1
  suns and s. JACK 1
  tears fall from the s. PLUN 1
  ten degrees of more indulgent s.,
  ADDI 2
  thou gazest much/ upon the
  golden s.: PLATO 1
  translated to the s., MILT 9
  vast wings across the canceled s.,
  MACL 4
  volumes of the s. HABI 2
  wooden shoe that sailed the s.
  FIEL E 9
skilful: s. Nymph reviews her force
  POPE A 121
skill: Billiard-marker, whose s.
  CARRO 13
  favour to men of s.; BIBL, O.T. 1
  Geneva's farthest s. DICKI 18
  if greater want of s. POPE A 21
  love and s., SIDN 10
  not s. enough SHAK 228
  see his s., SHAK 192

set with S. MARV 5
simple I according to my s.
  BRAD 15
simple truth his utmost s.!
  WOTT 1
they judged without s. GOLD 4
violent, neat and practiced s.
  WILB 39
What name, what s., what faith
  JONS 47
what we gain'd in S. we lost in
  Strength. DRYD 29
with s. And nothing else;
  AUDE 100
skillful: s. yachts pass over.
  WILLI 48
skills: my special s. NÍ CH 1
skim: over them the swallows s.,
  MELV 20
skimming: small/ cheeping birds/ s.
  bare trees WILLI 43
skin: Because my s. is black."
  CULL 17
  eggs under your s. NASH 10
  elephants with their fog-colored
  s. MOOR M 19
  fat dungeon I could rise to s.
  GUNN 8
  His pointed s. cap. HEAN 22
  hollow/ under a smooth s.
  LAWR 15
  immovable critic twitching his s.
  MOOR M 32
  inside s. side outside; STRON 1
  Less smooth than her S. PRIO 6
  milky s. RANS 12
  my gold beaten s. PLATH 49
  out of her s. for a year.
  STEPHENS 3
  pale skull protruding under ashen
  s. GINS 39
  scar that whiter s. SHAK 137
  s. as soft as silk, MOTH 16
  s. has betrayed me LORD 4
  s. he made him mittens,
  STRON 1
  s. nor hide nor fleece DOOL 5
  s. over a girl's wrist. WRIG J 2
  s. side outside. STRON 1
  'Slimy s.', or 'Polly-wog' BELL 5
  spot on your s. AUDE 67
  water-tightness of a/ s.
  MOOR M 37
skinful: preach best with a s.
  GOLD 6
skinned: mariners were s., DAY 7
  peach-s. girlie HUGH L 5
skinny: s., stooped, and neat as pie,
  SHAP 21
skins: children/ Wear s. SPEND 3
Skip: S. and trip it on the green,
  CAMPI 8

skipper: s. had taken his little
  daughter, LONG 51
  wife of the s. lost at sea
  WHITT 27
skipping: dust/ Is on this s. heart
  LOWE R 6
  Tripping and s., BROWNI R 62
skirmish: cavalry s., WHITM 16
  s. fought near Marathon.
  GRAV 20
skirt: her organdy s. JUST 3
Skirting: S. the river road,
  WHITM 23
skirts: Flouncing your s., SHAP 5
  Knee s. trimmed LIND V 12
  saw her sable s. LONG 24
  s. not touching a leaf, ROET 57
skittery: s. pigeon. ROET 12
skull: ashy the tall s. RANS 17
  Brushing their chalky s.
  FROS 132
  hollow round of my s. ELIOT T 6
  monotonous voice in the s.
  MONTA 3
  my face a stony s. WRIG R 1
  pale s. protruding under ashen
  skin GINS 39
  ring of s.-/ bone KINN 11
  s., how it yawns AIKE 12
  splits my s., HOUS 10
skulls: dead men's s., SHAK 97
  s.' mouths which will not tire
  MACN 22
  terrorizes the contents of s.
  KINN 12
skunk: look for s. tracks FROS 53
  mink, and s. TAYL B 1
  s. with her column of kittens
  LOWE R 41
  skunk's tail/ Paraded the s.
  HEAN 19
skunks: s. ate the chickens
  CUMM 30
Skuntic: waters in the S.,
  TAYL B 1
skurry: ratel tumbled hurry s.
  ROSS C 12
sky: admitted to that equal s.,
  POPE A 60
  against the boding s., BOWER 1
  at my s. blue trades,
  THOMA D 20
  banner in the s.; HOLM 17
  below another s.
  STEVENSO R 19
  blossoms touch the s. WILLI 25
  blue depth of the s. YEATS 91
  blue Ethereal S., ADDI 3
  blue true dream of s.; CUMM 19
  blush tinged the upper s.,
  EMER 51
  boy falling out of the s.,
  AUDE 64

sleepers: s. shall pass to ashes.)
  SAND 12
sleepeth: Kraken s.: TENN 58
sleepin': (Capten, art tha s.
  NEWB 1
sleeping: at night fitfully s.,
  WHITM 17
child is s.: JOYC 2
Ferdinand De Soto, s. In the
  river, VAN DO 1
flat/ s. thing. CREE 14
kissed the s. Night. DUNB P 1
love most lay s. by me
  WHITM 109
s. earth was fair. BRON 3
s., I see a wreck, WHITT 26
s. in the open SNYD 13
s. on the hill. MAST 6
s. under trees SNYD 39
s. when she died. HOOD 3
slomerede into a s., LANGL 1
Staid s. there. DICKI 51
Sleepless: O S. as the river
  CRAN H 29
O s. heart SWIN 5
s. lovers, just at twelve, awake:
  POPE A 111
s. soul WORD 121
s. watches of the night, LONG 13
through the City's s. sleep,
  THOMS J (1834–1882) 6
with s. eye, HOLM 14
sleeplessly: earthly mothers waiting,
  s. STEVENS 60
sleeps: child s. on. YEATS 105
city s.; JOHN L 5
city s.; TENN 53
heaven-eyed creature s. in earth:
  WORD 17
lady s.! POE 41
Now s. the crimson petal,
  TENN 109
s. as may beguile the night;
  MARTIA 2
s. with monsters. RICH 13
s. without a sound KIRK 2
tired he s., POPE A 81
while my pretty one, s.
  TENN 113
sleepy: s. winter, WYLI 13
warm an' s. an' white; HAY 6
with a s. pirouette WILB 34
sleepy-head: arrant s.,
  STEVENSO R 14
sleeves: fluttering/ Its empty s.;
  STEVENS 17
s., which were long, HART 2
sleigh: sprang to his s., MOOR C 5
slender: follow those s. windrows,
  WHITM 2
veil down to the s. waist,
  MILT 73
slenderly: Fashioned so s., HOOD 2

slept: carcase breath'd, and walkt,
  and s., PHILI K 1
hill s. NEWB 4
rise from where they s. ROBI 53
s. like a rock HUGH L 19
s. their dream CUMM 5
then I s. OHAR 21
Thou who hast s. WHITM 103
while Passion s.
  JOHN S (1709–1784) 7
slew: knight s. the dragon,
  UNKN 244
on a tree they s. Him — LANIE 2
s. thy virgin knight, SHAK 132
S. with the sword-edge UNKN 19
slice: s. a big sun HEAN 1
slick: s. rock of metaphysics
  SNYD 26
slide: We can s. it/ Rapidly
  REED H 5
slides: savage servility/ s. by on
  grease. LOWE R 21
Sliding: S. by semi-tones
  BROWNI R 5
slight: seek s. faults to find/ Where
  nature moves, POPE A 34
should so s. me, JONS 18
S. are her arms, POUN 66
s. shock of the soothe of waves,
  WHITM 92
s. things do lightly please.
  HERR 18
S. was the thing DUNB P 5
slighted: homely s. shepherd's
  trade, MILT 26
slights: what He mislikes or s.,
  BROWNI R 16
slim: her/ S. finger tips, HODG 7
let 'em be s., SHERI 2
sleek little pilot-fish, azure and s.,
  MELV 13
straight and s., HOLM 10
slime: Dead who struggled in the s.
  SASS 12
s. in hotel spittoons: HUGH L 2
through the ooze and s.,
  SMIT L 1
wetter water, slimier s.!
  BROO R 10
slimy: Dragging its s. belly
  ELIOT T 130
full of s. things. WALK 13
s. caverns SHEL 1
'S. skin', or 'Polly-wog', BELL 5
s. slug that sprawls MELV 2
s. things did crawl COLE SAM 34
Upon the s. sea. COLE SAM 34
wooed the s. bottom of the deep
  SHAK 97
slinging: Life, a Fury s. flame.
  TENN 28
slings: suffer/ The s. and arrows of
  outrageous fortune, SHAK 39

slip: blur and s., NIMS 1
s. thy troth UNKN 167
unrecorded did it s. away,
  ROSS C 17
years s. from me LONG 28
slipped: ball is lost and the mallet
  s. MACN 20
s. his hand and ran away!
  BELL 10
s. their names, LARK 3
s. through the straw UNKN 240
Slipper: S. toppe/ Of courtes
  estates, SENE 1
Watteau hung a lady's/ s.
  WILLI 25
slippers: Warm s. and hot-water
  can, GILB 4
slipping: massive buttocks s. like
  oiled parts LEVI 1
Slips: S. and pulls the table cloth
  ELIOT T 111
slipshod: s. 'prentice from his
  master's door SWIF 10
Slithergadee: catch me, old S.,
  SILV 1
slits: s. the thin-spun life. MILT 27
sloe: eyes as black as s.; UNKN 45
slogan: ancient s. Noblesse oblige.
  MILE 1
slogged: they s. up to Arras
  SASS 10
slomber: sleepe hir sence with s.
  doth restraine. LODG 2
sloop: bright red s. in the harbor,
  SEXT 3
slope: Life's darkening s. ROSS D 3
s. thro' darkness up to God,
  TENN 33
slopes: sown their s. With herbage,
  BRYA 16
slopping: s. of the sea
  STEVENS 46
Slouches: S. towards Bethlehem
  YEATS 136
Slouching: S. in the undergrowth
  HODG 2
slovenly: made the s. wilderness
  STEVENS 1
slow: doubt is s. to clear,
  BROWNI R 4
dull and s. and mild. JARR 2
martyred steps and s., ROBI 2
mimic in s. structures, EMER 45
moving its s. thighs, YEATS 135
nymph died more quick, and the
  shepherd more s. DRYD 15
pierced the s. vegetable veins
  LAWR 16
shame of s.-endeavoring art,
  MILT 35
Silent, and soft, and s. LONG 38
s., as a fish she came, ROET 57
s., dark hours begin, ROSS C 28

s.-firm pinions slanting,
 WHITM 24
s. silent walk HARD 29
S., s., fresh fount, JONS 4
s./ To overtake thee. SHAK 104
S. tramp the Centuries, DICKI 97
solemn and sweet and s.
 WHITM 11
sun climbs s., how slowly!
 CLOU 9
take my waking s. ROET 59
wandering steps and s. MILT 108
slowed: She s. to sigh, ROET 9
slowly: beat the drum s. UNKN 11
earth was bettering s. HARD 10
how s. minutes roll ROCH 7
revolve it all s. HUGH T 2
s. dying cause, TENN 48
stars turn s. TATE J 2
slug: slimy s. that sprawls MELV 2
Sluggard: voice of the S.;
 WATT I 5
sluggish: s., lonesome waters,
 WHITM 28
s. dazed spring approaches —
 WILLI 35
sluiced: been s. in 's absence
 SHAK 179
s. by motion, — CRAN H 5
slumber: death is s., SHEL 42
earth shall s., TENN 76
Listlessly, till s. comes. CULL 6
Morns abed and daylight s.
 HOUS 47
must s. again." WATT I 5
My s. broken LAND 10
Nor s. nor a roof against the
 rain; MILLA 16
'Rise like Lions after s. SHEL 40
Shake off s., SHAK 158
S. in peace WILB 7
s.'s chain has bound me,
 MOOR T 10
tormented s. JOHN L 7
slumbered: you have but s. here
 SHAK 129
slumberous: 'Rises from the s.
 mass. BLAK 67
slumbers: Golden s. kiss your eyes,
 DEKK/OTHE 1
s. in a brute. FROS 110
soul is dead that s., LONG 35
Sweetest S. FLET J 1
slummeries: s. in England. GILB 51
Slung: S. atween the round shot
 NEWB 1
slur: grimy s. on the Republic's
 faith MELV 12
slut: devil grip the whey-faced s.
 STEPHENS 3
that raving s. YEATS 29
sluttish: unswept stone, besmeared
 with s. time. SHAK 207

sly: Questioner, who sits so s.,
 BLAK 9
says Parson S., PRIO 11
sma': Wi' s. persuasion BURN 46
smack: have an orthodox s.,
 GILB 59
Morning s. of the spade
 THOMA D 2
smale: s. foweles maken melodye,
 CHAU 4
s. houndes hadde she CHAU 17
small: Arthur was very s. BISH 15
cat is grown s. MONR 2
chore-girl s., WHITT 34
cottage too s. BROO P 2
creatures great and s., ALEX 1
flight of s. cheeping birds
 WILLI 43
great is s., MUIR 11
Great or s., WHITM 22
I was eight and very s., CULL 13
islands large and s.; WHITM 19
just so s. as I? THOMP F 4
like s. gnats and flies, SHEL 79
making men feel/ As s. KAVA 17
new s.-rented lease, HERB G 69
not up to s. deceit, HART 3
right lovesom, white and s.;
 DUNB W 5
S. and pure as a pearl, TENN 99
s. birds they do sing. HABE 1
s. but sullen Horn, COLL 10
s./ Contained and fragile,
 WINT 1
s. easy wheels on the bottom —
 WILLI 45
s.-eyed China's BYRO 52
s. gilded fly SHAK 80
s. grey-coated gnat, SHAK 153
s. house and large garden
 COWL 8
s. is great MUIR 11
S. pity for him! — WHITT 24
s., poised feet LAWR 31
s. proportions JONS 41
s. rain down can rain. UNKN 302
S. was the debt DUNB P 5
so great, and I am so s.
 RANDS 3
Sweet and s.; BLAK 106
tatter'd weed of s. worth
 SHAK 185
things both great and s.;
 COLE SAM 30
true Chameleon is s., WELL 2
Whereof the gift is s., SURR 1
why he was so s. BANG 1
smallest: traces of the s. spider's
 web, SHAK 153
smart: allthoo I s. WYAT 22
girls that are so s. CAREY 4

haughty scorn which mock'd the
 s., ARNO 35
witness of my woeful s.; SURR 6
smash: s. of poet." LOWE R 15
s. the shatter-proof SHAP 9
smashed: s. into a likeness KOCH 7
smear: honey to s. his face,
 SCHW 9
smeared: dread and black
 complexion s. SHAK 30
Smell: actions of the just/ S. sweet
 SHIR 3
brand of soap has the same s.
 MACN 19
comfortable s. BROO R 5
does not s. AUDE 51
first time that we s. the air
 SHAK 82
for s. or ornament, HERB G 47
give most odorous s.; SPENS 15
lime and copper s. KAVA 27
rose was Heaven to s., HODG 9
s. as sweet; SHAK 142
s. far worse than weeds.
 SHAK 222
s. from ditches that were not
 Christian. KAVA 7
s. it turning to gas; BISH 7
s. of field and grove, MILT 70
s. of potato mould, HEAN 12
s. of the lamp, HERR 17
s. thee on the tree. SHAK 137
smoky s. of our garments.
 UNKN 121
sweet keen s., ROSS D 8
smellen: To s. sweete, CHAU 51
smelling: s. of vegetation,
 ELIOT T 50
smells: cocktail s. in bars.
 ELIOT T 105
female s. in shuttered rooms,
 ELIOT T 105
S. of chestnuts in the streets,
 ELIOT T 105
s. of sedgy grass WHITM 92
s. of the human body, KINN 19
s. to heaven; SHAK 34
sweet she s.! AYTON 1
smelly: s. and I may be old,
 SMIT ST 6
smelt: Meseem'd, I s. a garden of
 sweet flowers, SPENS 14
S. the guns! THOMP W 4
smerte: men smoot it with a yerde
 s. CHAU 17
smild: s. at the dame — BLAK 25
smile: all things s.; CAREW 14
beg a s., HERR 46
bland s. from these sages;
 GILB 59
bleak mountains s. ADDI 2
born but to s. and fall? BLAK 13
bought s. Of harlots, MILT 78

broke on me the s. GARR 1
Did he s. his work to see?
BLAK 83
dost thou s.? BRET 2
early s. has stayed my walk;
BRYA 35
escaped my s. WYLI 6
ferret's s., HILL G 3
flashed her golden s. HAYD 7
force me to a s. COWP 3
forget and s. ROSS C 20
glistening eye to the poison of a
s.? BLAK 17
"I love her for her s.
BROWNI E 9
laugh — but s. no more. POE 23
light of one sweet s. SHEL 66
lighted faces s. no more.
WHITT 29
look down and s., MILT 64
Make Lame Philosophy to s.
BLAK 10
No answering s. ROSS D 1
Professor Twist could not but s.
NASH 12
sidelong pickerel s.; ROET 11
s./ And mouth DUNB P 12
s., as I do now, HOLM 16
s./ As you find a rhythm HEAN 7
s. at the smiling woman SEXT 12
s. dwells a little longer,
CHAP A 1
s. in secret, looking over wasted
lands, TENN 90
s. of accomplishment, PLATH 37
s. of Christian charity THAY 3
s. of Heaven lay; SHEL 73
s. on all that s., YEATS 11
s. on Casey's face; THAY 2
s. on her lips, SCOT WA 19
s. on the face of the Tiger.
MONK 1
s. on your love, GINS 31
s. unsearchable repose —
CRAN H 51
s. up at us — eternally. KAVA 20
s. upon my knee; GREE 2
s. upon our evening bed!
BLAK 109
s., with satisfaction SHAP 6
s. you could see a mile, SERV 5
soft unchristened s., BRID R 4
Thrust close your s. LEVE 17
wee Elf/ smiled a wee s., HERF 2
with a disdainful s., GRAY 8
smiled: I have not often s.
ROSS C 27
so I s., CULL 13
wee Elf/ S. a wee smile, HERF 2
smiles: all s. stopped together.
BROWNI R 57
clad in s., TIMR 2

Eternal s. his emptiness betray,
POPE A 10
flower that s. today, HERR 55
gray-eyed morn s. on the frowning
night, SHAK 146
Heaven that s. BANK 1
kisses, tears, and s. WORD 134
mother who s. as she sings.
LAWR 31
Nods and becks, and wreathed s.,
MILT 20
pensive s.; EMER 38
Pooh-pooh s., CARRY 11
Secret joys and secret s.,
BLAK 50
She s. into corners. ELIOT T 104
s. and languish'd air, BLAK 40
s. are lightning, DANI S 9
s. grimly/ its words cut —
WILLI 5
S., tears, of all my life! —
BROWNI E 6
They charmed it with s.
CARRO 12
smilest: on whom thou s., dear.
SHEL 33
smiling: bow and pass s. WILLI 49
dwell on her s., GRAV 35
Go, s. souls, CRAS 9
smile at the s. woman SEXT 12
s. instant when her soul,
WILB 35
s. Mornings shine, GRAY 32
s. public man. YEATS 7
s. Rose HERR 26
s. spring its earliest visit paid,
GOLD 1
S. the boy fell dead.
BROWNI R 38
s. under their goggles DICKEY 10
took he the wound, s., CRAN S 7
Try s.; UNKN 266
smirk: final s. CRAN H 37
Smit: S. with the mighty pleasure
POPE A 102
smite: s. once, and smites no
more." MILT 30
s. thee by day, BIBL, O.T. 59
smith: s., a mighty man LONG 48
stock o coal-black s. UNKN 272
smithy: village s. stands; LONG 48
smitten: s. his head from his faire
boddë. UNKN 154
s. with a hatchet's jaw; HOUS 10
smock: her white shop s.,
PLATH 12
smocks: bleach their summer s.,
SHAK 100
Some are in s.: WILB 23
smoke: As s. we vanish Æ 3
Ascends in s. and fire HOUS 4
dropping houses and eek s.
CHAU 98

gone up in s., THOMP F 8
Light-winged S., THOR 6
must pass like s. Æ 3
salt-caked s. stack MASE 2
sighs the s., SOUTHW 2
s. in hotel lobbies, HUGH L 2
S. rolls and scarves PLATH 14
s. unto the flame return Æ 3
wisp of s. floats up SNYD 29
smokeless: slow s. burning of
decay. FROS 141
smoker: man in the s. SAND 12
s.'s cough in the hall. HEAN 15
smoking: s. roofs, soft bells,
LONG 29
smoky: Into the s. spring
CRAN H 42
kindlest all thy s. fire, SIDN 40
knowledge is a torch of s. pine
SANT 2
liest thou in s. cribs, SHAK 54
s. smell of our garments.
UNKN 121
with s. wings, entangles them.
HILL G 1
smoot: amidde the ers he s.:
CHAU 58
men s. it with a yerde smerte —
CHAU 17
smooth: hollow/ under a s. skin
LAWR 15
Less s. than her Skin PRIO 6
say that he's s. LOWE J 6
silence pure and s., LOWE J 19
s. and even, MERE O 4
s., and strong, GRAY 24
s. as monumental alabaster.
SHAK 137
S. flow the waves, POPE A 116
s. of his thigh and stomach
SNYD 3
s. shall bloom from the rough:
STEVENSO R 17
So s., so sweet, so silvery, is thy
voice HERR 63
Supple and s. HODG 7
Tree whose broad s. Leaves
MILT 97
smoothed: s. his wrinkled front;
SHAK 95
s. these verdant swells, BRYA 16
smoother: s. than butter,
BIBL, O.T. 40
smoothes: woman s. her forehead
STEVENS 12
smoothing: s. the wood HALL 2
smoothness: turns earth's s. rough,
BROWNI R 73
smooths: She s. the hair of the
grass. ELIOT T 104
smote: s. on all the chords
TENN 70
They s. and fell, THOMP W 2

with the hammer she s. Sis'e-ra,
  BIBL, O.T. 19
smother: s. up his beauty SHAK 51
smothered: s. in family —
  POUN 26
smuggle: s. some few years
  GRAY 21
smutch'd: Before the soil hath s. it?
  JONS 2
smutty: drinking and oath and s.
  jest, WHITM 33
smylyng: hir s. CHAU 13
snaffle: use the s. and the curb
  CAMPB R 5
snag: black s. glistens SNYD 29
snail: crawled like a s., ROSS C 12
  Johnnie Crack and Flossie S.
  THOMA D 42
  melt as the dishoused s.
  BIBL, O.T. 42
snail's: s. on the thorn:
  BROWNI R 66
snails: East with its s., MOOR M 9
snake: Another tempter of this s.;
  WALL 7
  as the s. disposes LAWR 34
  devise the S.: OMAR 1
  dribbled couplets like a s.
  TATE A 9
  Green S., when I hung you
  LEVE 22
  like a wounded s., POPE A 27
  s.-hips with a hiss, BROO G 21
  s., with mottles rare, DICKI 87
snakes: afraid of s. MOOR M 19
  butchered s. and carrots HUGO 6
  driven wild/ by s. HUGO 6
snaky: envy's s. eye, SIDN 4
  Its s. acids kiss. PLATH 44
snapped: s. at a flea. LIND V 18
  s. at a minnow. LIND V 18
  s. at a mosquito. LIND V 18
  s. at me. LIND V 18
  s. by the diesel SNYD 44
snaps: lariat s.; SMIT W 2
snare: birds that are caught in the
  s.; BIBL, O.T. 2
  entangle in that golden s.:
  SPENS 12
  fool's self-chosen s., SIDN 39
  I am caught in a s.! LAWR 26
  paw is the s.! STEPHENS 11
  rapid falcons in a s., MERE G 13
  soft sleep shall s.? ROSS D 2
  Tangled was I in Love's s.
  WYAT 13
  world's a s., BEAU/BASS 2
snared: sons of men s. in an evil
  time, BIBL, O.T. 2
snares: From alder s. SNYD 35
  O'erlooking all his waving s.
  THOMS J (1700–1748) 10

Snark: place for a S.!" CARRO 11
  S. found the verdict, CARRO 15
snarling: silver, s. trumpets'
  KEAT 6
snatch: s. a fearful joy. GRAY 15
snatch'd: s. away BYRO 56
snatched: Are s. immediate
  THOMS J (1700–1748) 9
  I s. the sun's eternal ray
  CLARE 15
sneer: I give them back the s.
  SAND 4
  I've a celebrated s., GILB 9
  s. at this my city, SAND 4
  teach the rest to s.; POPE A 7
sneered: Sinister Spirit s.:
  HARD 11
  s. and slanged, BELL 1
sneezed: elephant s. UNKN 7
sneezes: beat him when he s.:
  CARRO 2
snick: ye auld, s.-drawing dog!
  BURN 3
sniffed: s. the victuals
  STEVENSO R 5
sniffing: s. cocaine.' UNKN 68
sniffs: s. of sea-breeze, WHITM 92
snigger: I've an entertaining s.,
  GILB 9
snip: s. the intellectual golden
  threads GINS 12
snored: s. BISH 37
snores: heavy ploughman s.,
  SHAK 128
snoring: here do s. lie, SHAK 158
snorter: freezing aloft in a s.,
  MASE 10
snot: boasted their scars of dried
  s.; HILL G 6
  size of s., SHAP 13
Snout: Greek name for Swine's S.?
  BROWNI R 77
snouts: above moving s., BISH 36
snow: above a s. glaze. WILLI 43
  Above the blue s. ROET 37
  among the s. BLAK 55
  Arrives the s., EMER 43
  as a hushed footfall/ In a long
  forgotten s. TEAS 3
  asked the soft s. with me to play;
  BLAK 52
  bared s. and thy unbraided gold.
  CAREW 12
  battered panache above s. . . . .
  STEVENS 28
  Betwixt the tufts of s.
  COLE SAM 16
  blankets turned to s. ROET 6
  bloodless lay the untrodden s.,
  CAMPB T 3
  cold s.-water from a tin cup
  SNYD 18

covering/ Earth in forgetful s.,
  ELIOT T 113
  cross of s. upon its side.
  LONG 14
  Descends the s. LONG 38
  dust of s. From a hemlock tree.
  FROS 46
  even s. melts; CUMM 1
  fall of the s. Before the soil hath
  smutch'd it? JONS 2
  "Father, who makes it s.?"
  LOWE J 12
  first fall of the s., TIMR 1
  fleece was white as s., HALE 1
  Folded close under deepening s.
  LOWE J 13
  frolic architecture of the s.
  EMER 45
  going to s. STEVENS 67
  healed with s. LOWE J 19
  heart fire and s. GRAV 9
  her blood upon the s., SARE 1
  I, this incessant s., DE LA 15
  If s. be white, SHAK 237
  In the sun and in the s.,
  THOMA E 8
  Is love's bed always s.? CLARE 4
  land freckled with s. half-thawed
  THOMA E 18
  last year's s. to me, CULL 7
  lasts long streak of s., TENN 51
  liable to melt as s. CRAN H 40
  lie upon the wings of night
  SHAK 149
  listens in the s., STEVENS 51
  little s.-white feet. YEATS 50
  melting s. upon some craggy hill,
  JONS 4
  neat prints into the s.
  HUGH T 13
  o'er the s.-wreaths deep,
  BRON 14
  on a Disc of S. DICKI 127
  on Severn s. the leaves. HOUS 44
  One thinks of s., JUST 7
  pale Virgin shrouded in s.,
  BLAK 54
  pine-trees crusted with s.;
  STEVENS 50
  recollect the S. DICKI 2
  s. came flying, BRID R 8
  s. falling down and necks of
  lovers. SIMP 10
  s. falls in the river, BURN 54
  s. grows whiter SIMI 1
  s. had begun in the gloaming,
  LOWE J 11
  s. has possessed the mountains.
  UNKN 119
  s. hath retreated, WORD 164
  S. is falling on Nagoya
  MAHON 4

s. lump thrice his own slight size
HARD 43

s. melts to tears, NOEL H 2

s. shall be their winding sheet,
CAMPB T 4

s. storm of paper, PAGE 1

s. that lies within the shade;
DANT 1

s.-white bow of gauze, SNOD 11

S.-white moslem head-dress
WALK 3

s.-white swans do fish for needful
meat: TURB 1

Something whispered — S."
FIEL R 2

stars glittered on the s. KINN 17

stood shivering in the s.,
SOUTHW 1

temperate valley,/ Wet, below the
s. line, ELIOT T 50

thick integument of s. THOR 11

traceless as a thaw of bygone s.;
ROSS C 17

Under the s., WILD 17

walk in the s. WYLI 10

wanton s. flew to her breast,
STROD 1

warm metamorphosis of s.
PAGE 5

wash it white as s.? SHAK 34

When s. like sheep lay HILL G 5

when s. the pasture sheets,
SHAK 4

when winter s. DANI 17

who bore, 'mid s. and ice,
LONG 21

wreaths of s. BRON 1

you may look for s.!) KIPL 23

snowballing: hands with s.;
BRID R 9

snowes: cursing of the frosts and s.;
BONH 1

snowfields: down the s. SNYD 37

Snowing: Goes-tiddely-pom/ On/ S.
MILN 1

snowman: we saw a s. KOCH 7

snows: body gleams amid eternal
s., PLUN 1

cold s. of a dream. YEATS 97

s. and the roses of yesterday
MAST 10

s. melted, GRAV 16

where are the s. of yester-year?
VILL 2

Winter s. upon thy sable hairs.
DANI S 16

snowy: privacy I love in this s.
night. BLY 1

Scarlet, and blue, and s. white,
WHITM 14

s. summits old in story;
TENN 111

twenty s. mountains
STEVENS 63

snub: s. breasts and little neat
posteriors, MANI 2

snuff: only took s. GOLD 4

s. and loathed part of nature
SHAK 79

Snuffy: S. old drone HOLM 5

snug: all s. in their beds,
MOOR C 1

S. as a bud and at home
PLATH 83

s. as a virgin, PLATH 14

soaks: thirsty earth s. up the rain,
COWL 1

Soap: Bar of Mottled S. CARRO 30

brand of s. has the same smell
MACN 19

don't s. my hair!" SNYD 3

rendered into s. JARR 3

S. all over SNYD 3

soar: s., but never roam —
WORD 148

Soared: what/ S.: the fierce rush:
JEFFE 16

sob: seraphs s. at vermin fangs
POE 32

s. on the long cool winding
saxophones. SAND 11

sobbing: Boys s. in armies!
GINS 16

s. dirge of Nature, WHITM 6

sucking and s., ROET 5

sober: Nothing in Nature's s.
found, COWL 2

pensive Nun, devout and pure,/ S.,
steadfast, and demure, MILT 16

skies they were ashen and s.;
POE 46

S. as man can get, BERRYM 7

s. critic come abroad —
POPE A 15

s. men GRAV 41

s. mornings HERR 71

s.-suited matron SHAK 149

s. wishes never learn'd to stray;
GRAY 11

take a s. colouring WORD 86

sobered: repose,/ Salted and s.,
THOMA E 16

soberly: s. comes/ And stays —
HAY 2

sobers: drinking largely s. us again.
POPE A 33

sobriety: your bafflin odd s.
BERRYM 7

social: each s. defect GILB 6

In s. halls MELV 6

ordinary/ Surroundings of s. life
SNOD 1

s. comforts drop away.
JOHN S (1709–1784) 2

s. hours, swift-winged, BURN 18

S.-life and Glee BURN 6

s. wants that sin TENN 72

wicked s. tree SNYD 43

societie: sweet s. of men. MARL 10

societies: solemn troops and sweet
s., MILT 32

society: broke up our s. HART 3

great S. alone on Earth,
WORD 116

Of s. offenders GILB 26

S. has quite forsaken GILB 50

Soul selects her own S.
DICKI 132

thrill in S.), CARRO 11

sockets: grinning s., RANS 24

Stared from the s. ELIOT T 157

socks: mending the s. MERR 2

sockses: didn't wear s., MILN 3

Socrates: Hemlock for S., SORL 2

S. drinking the hemlock,
CARRU 2

sod: Beneath this s. COLE SAM 40

freedom of the s., WHITT 8

lay the s. o'er me, UNKN 11

profane our s.! TIMR 4

s. scarce heaved; SHEL 59

s. what thousands meet! —
MELV 16

that was in the s. DICKI 57

Vaulting the sea, the prairies
dreaming s., CRAN H 39

sodden: s. as the bed of an ancient
lake, HUGH T 3

s. towards sundown, ELIOT T 60

upon this s. floor. WILB 42

sodenly: slee me s., CHAU 119

Sodom: world like Great S.
DUNC 4

sods: cocked/ On s.; HEAN 10

heaped-up s. upon the fire,
COLUM 3

under green s. lay. YEATS 14

sofa: overstuffed plum s., RUKE 7

soft: asked the s. snow with me to
play; BLAK 52

Beautiful glooms, s. dusks
LANIE 3

Bedded s. LONG 41

'Beware/ The s.-voiced owl,
HILL G 3

die dishevelled and s.
LOWE R 25

Handle it s. WYAT 8

loose girdle of s. rain.
CRAN H 39

love's s. bands, SPENS 1

More beautiful and s. SPEND 13

Nature's s. nurse, SHAK 54

O so white, O so s., O so sweet is
she! JONS 2

Owl-downy, s. feminine JEFFE 16
pulse, like a s. drum KING H 4
resinous and s. your songs
TOOM 3
sensible s. melancholy.
POPE A 109
Silent, and s., and slow LONG 38
smoking roofs, s. bells, LONG 29
s. and feminine, MILT 90
s. and fundamental hour
BROO G 11
s. complaining FLUTE DRYD 26
s. embalmer of the still midnight,
KEAT 67
s. food for worms, MAHON 3
s. his pace; SACK 1
s. like thee, CAMPI 22
s. mouse body, KIZE 2
s. sleep shall snare? ROSS D 2
s. unchristened smile, BRID R 4
s.-shed kisses ROSS D 2
Stole with s. step HOLM 2
they are brown and s.,
CRAN H 40
this s. turf, BRYA 1
thy tones are s.; CALV 5
when s. voices die, SHEL 43
Women are s., SHAK 61
softe: somer, with thy sonne s.,
CHAU 121
your s. side, CHAU 67
soften: s./ The crusted wound
THOMA D 25
softer: brighter light and s. airs,
BRYA 8
rowed him s. home — DICKI 13
sweet music here that s. falls
TENN 84
words were s. than oil,
BIBL, O.T. 40
softly: Caroling s. TOOM 7
rat crept s. through the
vegetation ELIOT T 130
silence surged s. backward,
DE LA 13
Sleep s.... eagle forgotten ...
under the stone. LIND V 13
s. her warm ear LOWE J 17
S. now the light of day DOAN 1
Sweet Thames, run s.,
ELIOT T 129
Sweet Thames, run s., SPENS 40
Walk s., March, SARE 1
softness: For s. she MILT 72
key of s. WHITM 42
s. of a woman LOWE A 8
s. to the flower SNYD 4
soger: s. frae the wars returns,
BURN 34
soggy: squelch and slap/ Of s. peat,
HEAN 12
soil: Before the s. hath smutch'd it?
JONS 2

firm s. win SHAK 211
form'd from this s., WHITM 74
Freedom's s. beneath our feet,
DRAK 4
ill-used race of men that cleave
the s., TENN 91
land and s., TOOM 6
my native s.! BURN 21
old toilers, s. makers: HALL 3
red s. and sweet-gum tree,
TOOM 6
secret of the s. THOMA D 21
Simple as s. yet crowded as earth
WILB 36
s. they fought to save. BRYA 2
s. where first they trod; HEMA 5
suck/ The s.'s fertility SHAK 90
sweet and pleasant s., UNKN 147
thorn-curst s.: VAN DY 5
To sting or s. benevolence,
KIZE 3
wealth of its s. CAME 3
soiled: Trampled or s., MERR 10
soilure: s. of the wits, ROBI 48
sojourns: made their long s.,
WILB 47
solace: Freedom all s. to man
gives: BARBO 1
full of joy and of s. CHAU 67
Green is a s. WILLI 10
heart of revel and s.!' CHAU 68
s. of ripe plums WILLI 41
solaces: Life yet hath many s.,
MILT 111
solar: in the s. fire, SCHW 7
shrilling from the s. course,
EMER 51
sold: his life hath s. SHAK 119
none like the Boy that s. Broom,
UNKN 44
s. my Reputation for a Song.
OMAR 2
soldered: be s. down DICKI 94
Only the s. mouth DICKI 31
soldier: Ben Battle was a s. bold,
HOOD 4
"Come you back, you British s.;
KIPL 9
courtier's, s.'s, scholar's,
SHAK 33
curses of the s. KINN 19
folded my s. well in his blanket,
WHITM 107
s. falls. STEVENS 3
Shall be a s.'s sepulchre.
CAMPB T 4
s. in that gallant band GILB 15
s. of time, STEVENS 12
s. tore from his throat, ROSE 7
s. was passing fair; FIEL E 6
s.'s is the trade: HOUS 14
s.'s kiss dwells WHITM 116
s.'s loving arms WHITM 116

s.'s pride/ Touched to the quick,
BROWNI R 38
s.'s rage CHAU 48
ten-year s. tells: KIPL 11
toy s. is red with rust, FIEL E 6
Soldiers: hapless S. sigh BLAK 75
my heart, O my s., WHITM 27
Old Testament s. NASH 20
S. and poor, THOMA E 16
s. don't go mad SASS 14
S. may grow a soul OWEN 5
those s. fare, ARNO 38
sole: nothing can be s. or whole
YEATS 39
on him s. depend, MILT 105
s. cause to thee of all this woe,
MILT 102
s. propriety,/ In paradise MILT 78
s. unbusy thing, COLE SAM 45
solemn: exalt the soul to s.
thought,
THOMS J (1700–1748) 12
Into the s. church, WHITM 7
Parent of sweet and s.-breathing
airs, GRAY 25
sad and s. shows, FLET/SHAK 6
s. and sweet and slow WHITM 11
s. fillet saw the scorn. EMER 16
s. sacrifice, performed in state,
POPE A 105
s. temples, SHAK 163
s. troops and sweet societies,
MILT 32
strange and s. thing. JOHN L 3
solemnly: eyes flashing s. with
hate, JOHN H 4
solempne: s. man. CHAU 20
solempnely: resons he spak ful s.,
CHAU 21
soles: s. of his feet rise KUMI 1
soliciting: This supernatural s.
SHAK 103
solid: hours stand in s. rows,
SHAP 29
She is s. SEXT 5
s. mountains shone, WORD 102
s. scholars/ Get the degrees,
SNOD 5
too too s. flesh would melt,
SHAK 22
solitariness: delight of s.! SIDN 3
solitary: heard among the s. hills
WORD 94
imagined love/ Of s. beds,
YEATS 142
life, that is commonplace and s.
JARR 19
pursue/ Thy s. way! BRYA 25
rare and s., MILT 86
singers s., WHITM 67
s. me listening, WHITM 67
S. the thrush, WHITM 47

Through Eden took their s. way.
MILT 108
To muse, and spill her s. Tea,
POPE A 18
Yon s. Highland Lass! WORD 138
solitude: bliss of s.; WORD 25
delicious s. MARV 16
human/ Revery is a s.
STEVENS 24
In s. live savage, MILT 97
In the sunny s. STEPHENS 5
Moloch! S.! Filth! GINS 16
Musing is s., WORD 14
only their s. kept. KINN 7
s. in the mountains ELIOT T 145
s./ Or blank desertion. WORD 97
s.! waving! GINS 19
S.! where are the charms
COWP 23
star-crowned s. DOWS 4
white s. of peace DODG 1
solitudes: Platonic England, house of
s., HILL G 2
soundless s. immense
THOMS J (1834–1882) 3
solitudinous: s. sea DE LA 19
Solomon: S., for all his wit,
SOUTHW 11
S. Grundy, MOTH 26
S. was never dressed so fine.
VAUG 9
solstice: summer, it is the s.
WILLI 6
Solution: S. sweet: KEAT 6
Sombre: S. and rich, the skies;
JOHN L 1
s. soul unsleeping, SWIN 5
somebody: How dreary to be s.
DICKI 83
make s. poor; BLAK 70
S. loves us all. BISH 13
S. who should have been SEXT 1
s.'s mother, BRIN 3
Somebody's: S. done for. PLATH 36
somedeal: s. stape in age, CHAU 65
Somehow: walking/ S. from the sun
LARK 11
somer: s., with thy sonne softe,
CHAU 121
something: brisk Cherub's. sips,
CRAS 7
earth has s. yet to show,
WORD 165
having to construct s. ELIOT T 4
in our embers/ Is s. that doth
live, WORD 79
Love still has s. of the Sea,
SEDL 1
make/ s. imagined, LOWE R 42
S. attempted, S. done, LONG 49
S. has ceased SILKI 1
S. I can never find, STEPHENS 6
s. in this richness WYLI 14

S. is about to happen. PURD 3
s. less prepoceros. NASH 13
S. like a person: SILKI 1
s. of angelic light. WORD 135
S. startles me WHITM 95
s. understood. HERB G 68
s./ Upon which to rejoice
ELIOT T 4
s. very like one. SILKI 1
Superstition saw/ S. TOOM 4
something's: show s. missing?
PLATH 1
sometime: from fair s. declines,
SHAK 188
They flee from me that s. did me
seek, WYAT 26
Sometimes: S. she sank, S. she
swam, UNKN 31
somewhere: Balboa lies dead s.
SCOT WI 2
s. expensive— SIMP 7
s. in this favored land THAY 4
Somme: from Appomattox stretched
to S.! CRAN H 13
sommer: s. and his pleasures waite
on thee, SHAK 224
somonour: s. was ther CHAU 3
son: be with her dear dead s.
WHITM 17
By meekness, called thy S.;
SMAR 9
father forsaken,/ Forgive your s.!
JOYC 2
Father, S., and Holy Ghost,
CULL 9
gang to the high heavens,/ Wi my
dear s. and me?" UNKN 49
Half breed s. of Pisces REED I 5
Instruct/ Your s., KUNI 4
letter from thy dear s. WHITM 15
Manhattan the s., WHITM 73
my beloved S., WORD 1
my s. and my comrade
WHITM 106
my s. in his grave, WHITM 107
not our s.'s writing, WHITM 16
o'er thy sorrowing s., COWP 10
only s. is dead. WHITM 17
said s. at college BYRO 47
see/ The Father and the S.,
CHAR 1
So, so,/ O s. of man, SCHW 6
s. is brought with the father,
WHITM 26
s. of memory, great heir of fame,
MILT 35
s. of the sable night, DANI S 8
s.'s body was thrown LOWE R 19
Strong S. of God, immortal Love,
TENN 16
Sweet death, small s., HALL 1
Two veterans s. and father dropt
together, WHITM 26

virtuous s., JONS 39
you'll be a Man, my s.! KIPL 8
song: Angels' s., BRID R 16
Another sadder s.: NOYE 5
As easily as s. ROSE 8
at their s., YEATS 124
beautiful with s.; LONG 8
becomes/ An everlasting s.,
TOOM 7
breathed a s. into the air,
LONG 2
brim with sorrow drowning s.
TENN 26
build/ Some tower of s. LONG 28
bullet stopped his s. LEWI 3
burden of my s.: HERR 28
Celestial S. MILT 83
Death's outlet s. of life,
WHITM 47
Earth is bursting into s., SORL 1
fine s. for singing,
STEVENSO R 15
first s. of his happiness, KINN 8
for your love s. HUGH L 8
Glorious the s., SMAR 9
I cease my s. WHITM 52
I float thee a s., WHITM 51
I made my s. a coat YEATS 30
Lark without s., THOR 6
Loud human s., WHITM 49
Made vocal by my s., MILT 82
main region of my s. WORD 15
Marvell's wit and graceful s.
WHITT 10
Modred, whose magic s. GRAY 4
my s., like the rushing river,
MANG 2
needless Alexandrine ends the s.,
POPE A 27
new s., BIBL, O.T. 45
Night's brittle s., DAVIS 5
"Of fayre Elisa be your silver s.,
SPENS 53
"Pipe a s. about a Lamb";
BLAK 104
Repeat thy s., LONG 20
Sans Wine, sans S., OMAR 4
self-same s. KEAT 50
sing his last s. YEATS 153
sing the Lord's s. in a strange
land? BIBL, O.T. 63
sing thee a s. in thy praise;
BURN 22
Singing a s., POE 18
Sings by himself a s. WHITM 47
sold my Reputation for a S.
OMAR 2
s., from beginning to end,/ I found
again LONG 3
s. is consider'd CALV 2
S., let them take it, YEATS 31
s. of the bird. WHITM 50

s. of the birds for mirth, —
GURN 1
S. of the bleeding throat,
WHITM 47
s. of the ever-singing leaves,
YEATS 140
s. only dropped, ROSE 8
s. she was singing WHITT 35
s., the wondrous chant
WHITM 52
s. upon her lips POUN 45
s. was wordless; SASS 9
s. woke/ His heart KINN 8
sorrow finds a swift release in s.
DAY 4
survive in my immortal s.
DRAY 8
sweetest s. and all s., WHITM 68
tedious s. MILT 41
till I end my s. ELIOT T 129
twofold silence was the s. of love.
ROSS D 4
warble your reedy s., WHITM 49
warbling a s. WHITM 47
whispered a s. OHAR 6
songs: forbeare,/ His wonted s.,
SPENS 49
Let the martial s. be written,
WALK 6
my s. will travel, POUN 32
need'st not make new S.,
COWL 11
O s. of joy! WHITM 66
own s. awakened WHITM 68
pine for what is not:/ Our
sincerest laughter/ With some
pain is fraught;/ Our sweetest s.
SHEL 71
resinous and soft your s. TOOM 3
Sad s. of Autumn mirth.
THOMA E 6
Sing no sad s. ROSS C 33
s. of modern speech LANG 3
s. of spring? KEAT 63
s./ And choral symphonies,
MILT 81
strong melodious s. WHITM 38
such morning s. THOMA D 20
ushering me to the true s.,
WHITM 36
voice did weave/ S. SHEL 75
with s. of woe, SHAK 132
Sonne: at my death thy S.
DONN 30
heart-quelling S. SPENS 43
somer, with thy s. softe,
CHAU 121
yonge s. CHAU 4
sonnet: Scorn not the s.;
WORD 131
S. is a moment's monument, —
ROSS D 5

sons: all men are Noah's s.
WILB 38
blood of fathers, mothers,
daughters, s., SHAK 30
breasts — begotten s. GINS 24
Columbia's true-blue s., ROON 1
Degenerate s. and daughters,
MAST 9
her s. never saw? RICH 17
Lamenting all her fallen s.!
THOMP W 4
more fathers than s. JUST 6
My brother's s. BONT 1
no s. to float in the space
KNIG 8
placed thee with the s. of light,
BRYA 6
s. of men snared in an evil time,
BIBL, O.T. 2
S. of the world, ARNO 36
s. their fathers' failing language
see, POPE A 34
s. to other women; SNYD 7
s. your fathers got, HOUS 32
Their s. are often angry. BLY 2
thousands of her s., WORD 109
three stout and stalwart s.,
UNKN 306
two s. at rising day, HOUS 29
two s. through college. DURE 1
soon: Death cometh s. or late.
MACA 3
haste away so s.: HERR 42
late and s., WORD 159
none too s. WILB 4
Shut not so s.; HERR 44
s.-speeding gear SHAK 150
s. to devour all, WHITM 57
too s. made glad, BROWNI R 55
will s. be better. WHITM 15
Sooner: shall find/ S. than all
VERY 3
s. it's over, KINGSL 4
S. or later delicate death.
WHITM 50
s. to sleep; KINGSL 4
soore: s. wepte she CHAU 17
soot: ashes and s.; MOOR C 3
feathered balls of s. YEATS 97
in s. I sleep. BLAK 86
upon his eyes in a black s.
HECH 15
soote: Aprill with his shoures s.
CHAU 3
singen s., SPENS 56
sooth: in good s., HARD 10
soothe: charm can s. her
melancholy, GOLD 9
slight shock of the s. of waves,
WHITM 92
s. and bless!/ What hope of
answer, TENN 37
s. my ear; ROGE 1

s. my sperrit bes' DUNB P 3
s. this restless feeling, LONG 15
s. us in our sorrow WORD 165
they seem to s., GRAY 14
soothed: he s. his soul to pleasures.
DRYD 5
soothes: Mute music s. my breast —
BRON 10
soothfastness: dwell with s.;
CHAU 1
s. unto you saith. CHAU 70
soothing: lovely and s. death,
WHITM 50
Sophia: since S. have a-crossed the
sea.' UNKN 320
Sophias: S. are not so emphatic,
BYRO 47
sophist: s. schools, EMER 29
sophistry: no s. in my body:
HUGH T 2
Sophocles: S. long ago ARNO 2
sorcery: s. devout and vertical
BROO G 11
sore: breadth was but bitterness s.,
LANIE 4
burnt a s. spot RUKE 11
Cry; — and upon thy so s. loss
THOMP F 11
sorely: lady wept s., UNKN 243
sorowe: What s. I suffred, PETRA 1
sorrow: beauty with s. DE LA 18
born for s.'s mate, BENN G 7
brim with s. drowning song.
TENN 26
brother's pain and s. WHITT 10
But s. return'd CAMPB T 9
cloud of s., CAMPI 2
Disease, and S.'s weeping train,
GRAY 5
dreary s. at the North LI PO 2
enough of s. before death —
YEATS 148
evil things, in robes of s., POE 22
feel my s.'s share? BLAK 102
guttural s. of the refugees.
MACN 11
handed me to S., CULL 16
heart forgets its s. LOWE J 19
hid s. from mine eyes./ 11. Why
died I not from the womb?
BIBL, O.T. 10
hunger was a more immediate s.;
AUDE 22
in impenetrable s., MUIR 6
In s. by thy bier BRYA 5
Like s. or a tune. FARJ E 2
My tender age in s. did begin:
HERB G 27
Naught but vast s. DE LA 8
no s. may be found UNKN 147
not sure of s., SWIN 14
number s. HERR 66

Parting is such sweet s.
  SHAK 145

psalm, the s., and the simple
  praise SHAP 10

Regions of s., MILT 50

Sea-sand and s.; ROSS C 30

shadow of your s. SHAK 91

shrines of S., and of Pleasure;
  BYRO 22

Sings s. up BINY 2

soothe us in our s. WORD 165

s. and heart's distress, MILT 107

S. and mourn and fast.
  UNKN 190

s. and pity BRID 4

s. did twist and grow, HERB G 3

s. discontent: CAMPI 13

s. finds a swift release in song
  DAY 4

s. for the lost Lenore — POE 35

s. I walk with UNKN 100

S. is hard to bear, BROWNI R 4

S. more beautiful than Beauty's
  self. KEAT 21

S. proud UNKN 141

s. unfeigned and humiliation
  meek. MILT 98

s.'s crown of s. TENN 74

s.'s other madness MARV 12

surcease of s. POE 35

thy s. is my ecstasy, HARD 24

to think is to be full of s.
  KEAT 47

when my heart hath 'scaped this
  s., SHAK 221

year wake year to s. SHEL 2

sorrowful: hot and s. sweetness of
  the dust: MILLA 20

sad and s. day UNKN 207

to his s. flock: BRID R 16

wise expect, the s. invite, DAVE 1

sorrowing: o'er thy s. son,
  COWP 10

Toiling, — rejoicing, — s.,
  LONG 49

sorrows: Disease, or s. strike
  CLOU 4

Of his fault and his s.
  MOOR T 12

s. end. SHAK 195

s. of the world, WHITM 40

s. of your changing face.
  YEATS 162

transient s., simple wiles,
  WORD 134

sorry: Death's self is s. JONS 7

he could be s. SILKI 2

I'm S., now, I Wrote it, BURG 1

s. to have disappointed him.
  JEFFE 44

sort: free-will, an' that s. of thing —
  HAY 5

sorts: s. of flowers SPENS 21

sorwe: s. of Noee with his
  felaweshipe? CHAU 49

sory: gooth forth a s. pas. CHAU 55

Sosostris: Madame S., famous
  clairvoyante, ELIOT T 116

sot: s. of the Maldive sea, MELV 13

Souf: An' S. is down, HOLLO 1

sought: I s. a theme YEATS 25

many a thing I s., SHAK 195

not s. in vain, COWP 12

prize we s. is won, WHITM 45

s. for as a good. HERB G 20

s. for no man's aid. SWIF 23

s. me for his bride; LIND L 1

s. they thus afar? HEMA 5

what I s. to escape, WHITM 31

Soul: age, death's twilight,/ Thy S.
  rest, DONN 51

amorous s. court Thy mild Dove,
  DONN 52

Baffle and dissipate your s.
  LOWE R 35

Be still, my s., be still; HOUS 23

bears the Human s. DICKI 141

become a living s.: WORD 31

belie/ Thy S.'s immensity;
  WORD 77

believe in you my s., WHITM 77

bid the s. of Orpheus sing
  MILT 17

bitter in s.; BIBL, O.T. 12

body and s. begin to fall asunder.
  ELIOT T 68

body and the s. ROET 22

body/ whips the s. OLSO 22

Boys/ In which a S. doth dwell:
  TRAH 4

Bread to the s., MASE 5

bring forth s. living MILT 86

business of my s. SHAK 136

buy the s. of any man. DARC 4

cause, my s. SHAK 137

chainless s./ With courage to
  endure! BRON 8

chant of my s., WHITM 53

comely s. in white BARNE 3

consume/ His s. to ash-heaps
  HERR 34

Demands my s., my life,
  WATT I 10

distinguish darkness from the s.?
  YEATS 44

dost/ My s. JOHN L 6

Dull would he be of s. WORD 6

echo aroused in my s.,
  WHITM 52

eternal truth man's fighting s.
  EBER 3

every s., it passed me by,
  COLE SAM 35

exalt the s. to solemn thought,
  THOMS J (1700–1748) 12

Fair seed-time had my s.,
  WORD 93

fling his s. HARD 18

Floods all the s. LONG 30

flow of s.; POPE A 92

For anything but the s., KAVA 18

freed his s. the nearest way.
  JOHN S (1709–1784) 4

from sex to s., from s. to thought;
  CART 1

from s. sounds. TOOM 1

from thought to s., CART 1

give me my s. again. MARL 3

give thy s. a loose, HORA 10

God rest her s. RANS 18

God the s.; POPE A 74

Grapple them to thy s. SHAK 23

hadst ever met my s. MEYN 2

had'st thou my s., WHITM 105

harrow up thy s., SHAK 26

has a wiry s. FULL 2

has her s. to keep. MEYN 4

he soothed his s. to pleasures.
  DRYD 5

her S. was endu'd PRIO 6

her sweet s., POE 30

hidden s. of harmony; MILT 24

higher than the s. is high.
  MILLA 30

hollow empty S. BUTL 7

how with the s. it fares.
  ARNO 16

humanised my S. WORD 12

Icebergs behoove the s. BISH 20

in s. up to our country move.
  SIDN 8

in thy bosom I would pour my s.;
  STIR 1

joy's s. lies in the doing.
  SHAK 169

keep your s. WYLI 2

Let us be unashamed of s.,
  BROWNI R 81

Lets his own ashes choke his s.
  HERB G 29

lips suck forth my s.; MARL 3

little s. SWIN 25

lose a s.'s inheritance? WILD 14

love a prophet of the s.;
  EMER 38

loved the pilgrim s. in you,
  YEATS 162

madness but nobility of s.
  ROET 30

madness of a dying s. MAST 3

manufacture both machine and
  s., GUNN 12

may thy s. have rest." UNKN 47

Memorial from the S.'s eternity
  ROSS D 5

Moloch whose s. is electricity
  GINS 17

most offending s. alive. SHAK 59

south: away down S. in Dixie!
  EMME 2
beaker full of the warm S.,
  KEAT 45
bereaving points/ S. GLÜC 1
Born of the gentle S., KEAT 1
dew-dropping s. SHAK 141
from the s., WHITM 2
genius of the S. TOOM 1
he runs to the s., BISH 39
my step is to the s. JARR 20
S. it is not paradise. WILB 17
S. stinks peace. POUN 60
S. Wind is a baker. LIND V 20
Up from the S. at break of day,
  READ T 1
Way Down S. in Dixie
  HUGH L 13
whisper of the s.-wind TENN 75
white gulls s. of Victoria
  SNYD 31
Winds blow s., WHITM 65
southern: bore me in the s. wild,
  BLAK 97
shade of a S. Pacific locomotive
  GINS 33
Southey: Wordsworth, Coleridge,
  S.; BYRO 21
Southwell: S. died on a rope.
  FULL 3
Southwerk: S. at the Tabard
  CHAU 6
souvenir: gift, a s. for you. HAYD 4
past was a s. STEVENS 30
Soveraign: S. of cities, DUNB W 4
sovereign: Five s. fingers
  THOMA D 24
s. mistress of true melancholy,
  SHAK 8
S. of the willing soul, GRAY 25
s. rosemary, SKEL 1
with s. eye, SHAK 197
sovereignty: sweetest s. Of reason,
  SIDN 20
wine may bear no s.; MARTIA 2
sovereyntee: Wommen desyren to
  have s. CHAU 111
sov'raign: s. thing and proud;
  MARV 25
sov'reign: hold the s. throne?
  BIBL, O.T. 41
Sovran: S. of beauty! GREE 4
Veil'd Melancholy has her s.
  shrine, KEAT 43
sow: Build for him, s. for him,
  WORD 120
debate, that eke discord doth s.,
  ELIZ 1
long, perfect loveliness of s.
  KINN 15
moon is a s. LEVE 21
sat the s. of fear SHAP 26
S. seed — SHEL 64

s. that always ate her young —
  BISH 36
sower/ s. by night. BLAK 61
up and down I s. them HOUS 33
sowdger: s. boys have picked him
  up UNKN 150
sowe: berd as any s. or fox was
  reed, CHAU 17
sowed: I s. the seeds of love,
  HABE 1
s. our spawn SMIT L 4
sower: s./ Sow by night, BLAK 61
sown: s. their slopes/ With herbage,
  BRYA 16
soyl: s. her Virgin purity, MILT 3
space: All time and s. controls:
  LOVE 7
apparent s. between them.
  HOLLA 2
appropriate sense of s. OHAR 19
crucible of endless s., CRAN H 5
dark and dark — a shining s.
  GRAV 25
depart on the winds of s. AIKE 8
47 black faces across the s.
  KNIG 8
fume of s. foams CRAN H 4
God stepped out on s., JOHN J 1
Here is my s. SHAK 3
high in s. together, WHITM 23
loose rocks in s. SNYD 29
measureless oceans of s.,
  WHITM 55
no sons/ to float in the s. KNIG 8
not in time and s. MUIR 15
painted s. of the breast, RUKE 5
pathless realms of S. GILB 47
put on earth a little s., BLAK 98
s. between, is but an hour,
  FRENE 7
s. in the lives of their friends.
  REED I 2
S. is nearer. LOWE R 20
s. through ripe fields ROSE 1
S. with gaunt grey eyes FLEC 7
throughout eternal s.: KEAT 20
triumph over time and s.!
  ARNO 37
vast sweet visage of s. LANIE 4
spaced: s. by many years, WINT 10
spaceout: Out of s. of time. POE 16
spaces: through the s. of the dark
  ELIOT T 103
with their empty s. FROS 36
spacious: beautiful for s. skies,
  BATE 1
hush of s. prairies MARK 2
S. Firmament ADDI 3
stately s. room, HORA 10
spade: Bring me an axe and s.,
  BLAK 41
brood, as though it were a s.
  CHAU 17

handle a s. HEAN 11
I've no s. to follow men HEAN 12
Morning smack of the s.
  THOMA D 2
poor crooked scythe and s.
  SHIR 1
With plough and s., SHEL 65
Spades: Let S. be trumps!
  POPE A 121
Spain: devildoms of S.' TENN 117
Love-light of S. CHES 9
war in S. has ended GINS 39
yes, I am S.' AUDE 86
spak: Frenssh she s. CHAU 14
He s. to hem that wolde live
  parfitly — CHAU 94
resons he s. ful solempnely,
  CHAU 21
spake: damselle s., and dyed.
  CHAT 1
he s. tenderly BRID R 16
s. our Father penitent; MILT 98
tongue/ That Shakespeare s.;
  WORD 28
span: Contract into a s.
  HERB G 61
Despise the human s. HARD 26
Eternity shut in a s., CRAS 5
Less then a s.: BACO 1
that s. of consciousness
  CRAN H 15
spangled: s. Heav'ns, a Shining
  Frame, ADDI 3
with stars was s. BRID R 15
spangles: s. that sleep CUMM 13
Spanish: Four-and-twenty S.
  hooves VAN DO 1
Or on S. politics? YEATS 104
person in the S. cape
  ELIOT T 111
S. ships of war at sea! TENN 116
spanked: s. my own behind.
  SWEN 2
spare: Gather the flowers, but s. the
  buds; MARV 32
money enough and to s.,
  BROWNI R 83
s. a million or two of humans
  LAWR 30
s. me, Lucifer! — MARL 2
s. this hour's term WARR 2
s. your country's flag," WHITT 3
Time and Nature gently s.
  EMER 12
spared: s. his tongue and pen
  SWIF 25
what the mouse had s. PITT 1
spark: compensatory s., EMER 9
ethereal s. MELV 7
happy s. HERR 64
last faint s. SITW 12
Nor human s. is left, POPE A 2
s. from heaven! ARNO 25

s. with which Heaven lit my
   spirit SHEL 79
Unless there is some s., WILLI 16
Sparke: anvill S., rose higher,
   TAYL E 1
sparkle: s. out among the fern
   TENN 4
sparkled: s. a flash, a white flash.
   KINN 13
white flash s. KINN 11
sparkling: dispark/ Those s.
   notions, HERB G 34
Dorinda's s. wit SACK 1
for ay, the s. glance BURN 31
gaily as the s. Thames; ARNO 27
hurried and s. waters! WHITM 44
s. cross she wore, POPE A 115
s. surface-eyes MERE G 9
sparks: Ashes and s., SHEL 46
thought by thought,/ 'Trampled its
   s. SHEL 78
sparring: harpoon were s. for the
   kill. LOWE R 53
sparrow: I,/ a s. WILLI 33
I, said the s., MOTH 32
quick hear the song s.,
   ELIOT T 55
s. enters the tree, HARD 43
s. flutters. LAWR 51
sparrows: quarrel of the s.
   YEATS 140
s. pecking the llamas' grain,
   JARR 28
s. stuck on him SILKO 1
s. warring in the eaves,
   YEATS 141
spars: masts and s., WHITM 92
s. like burned matchsticks.
   BISH 25
Strange s. of knowledge POUN 54
sparwe: lecherous as a s., CHAU 3
spat: rose, and venomously s.
   RANS 29
s. out the seven seas; JOHN J 2
spats: picture shows, and s.,
   SASS 7
spatters: s. all we knew of
   dénouement SHAP 4
spawn: generate,/ Reptile with s.
   abundant, MILT 85
gorged with s. LOWE R 1
sowed our s. SMIT L 4
s. innumerable, MILT 5
spawning: formless s. fury wrecked,
   YEATS 143
spawns: river/ Nor ocean s.
   MILLE V 1
speak: English is what you s.!
   CARRO 22
great with child to s., SIDN 6
hear each other s. TENN 39
hear her s., SHAK 237
I s. With my mouth thus, CULL 9

Language has not the power to s.
   PLATO 3
lines that s. the passionate heart,
   KAVA 18
none shall s. his name. SHAP 25
S. against bonds. POUN 25
s. at every hazard, WHITM 74
S. both one message ROSS C 24
s. from heaven's sphere. PETRA 4
S. gently, WILD 17
s. in a flat voice WRIG J 6
S. less than thou knowest,
   SHAK 71
S. low, lean low, ROSS C 7
s. my heart out MERE G 7
s. silence with thy glimmering
   eyes, BLAK 110
s., though sure, POPE A 37
S. thy desire, OVID 6
s. to it of itself LOWE A 3
S. to me. RUKE 10
S. to me. RUKE 12
teach my heart to s.; SPENS 5
tongue may s.; VERY 2
Too jostled were Our Souls to s.
   DICKI 99
unable to s. MONTA 2
speake: he would s., SPENS 44
speakes: Of love and pleasure s.
   DOWL 1
speaking: against your s. mouth.
   MILLA 13
bird's voice/ S. for all
   THOMA E 16
drowning their s. BROWNI R 60
s. little, perhaps not a word.
   WHITM 33
s. of fears in the abstract
   POUN 12
s. of metres; LOWE J 8
way/ Of s. gently, —
   BROWNI E 9
speaks: every whisper that s.
   BOGA 16
nothing/ s. in its own tongue,
   LEVE 6
s./ A various language: BRYA 22
s. for the Family of Man?
   SAND 17
spear: painted chief, and pointed s.,
   FRENE 2
s. against the Muses' bower:
   MILT 125
s. of summer grass. WHITM 74
swear by the hilt of my s.,
   UNKN 126
spears: glittering s. are rankèd
   BURN 49
quietly stalks and s., AMMO 6
special: my s. skills NÍ CH 1
suicides have a s. language.
   SEXT 16
specialists: not for s. SNOD 7

species: male of the s. LAWR 13
specious: s. deeds on earth,
   MILT 59
speckled: s. shell/ the poet fondles
   LEVE 15
square & s. stone, HERB G 12
spectacle: Caught by the s.
   WORD 108
Povert a s. is, CHAU 110
through the motley s., WORD 100
spectacles: s. of steel SPEND 3
s. to my life GREV 3
specter: s. of genius! GINS 17
youth grows pale, and s.-thin,
   KEAT 47
spectral: s. wrong, EMER 20
spectre: Frost was s.-gray HARD 17
spectres: s. in books, WHITM 76
s. of black night
   THOMS J (1834–1882) 8
speculating: s. rooks THOMA E 18
speech: agonies of s. on s. panes?
   SLES 2
cleave the general ear with horrid
   s., SHAK 31
Free s., free passes, BETJ 4
Free s. nipped in the bud,
   MACN 6
gave man s., SHEL 54
hackneyed s., its homicidal eye —
   LOWE R 28
invent a lot of figures of s.
   NASH 20
our concern was s., ELIOT T 67
rank tongue blossom into s.]
   BROWNI R 15
Reason and s. we onely bring.
   HERB G 51
Recognition with our s.? —
   MOMA 1
songs of modern s. LANG 3
S. after long silence; YEATS 5
s. be still? ROSS D 7
s. created thought, SHEL 54
s. for that unspoken, ELIOT T 96
s. in stars, HERB G 9
s. is a burning fire; SWIN 2
s. you spoke, ROSS C 27
stones have neither s. nor tongue,
   VAUG 1
what authority in thy s.!
   JONS 47
Words, after s., ELIOT T 22
speeches: making of beautiful s.,
   PRAE 4
speechless: dull and s. tribes:
   SHAK 229
hold my s. tongue. HOUS 7
king of s. clods LOWE R 22
Speechlesse: lie/ S. still, CLEV 1
speed: S. echoed the wall
   BROWNI R 35
s. glum heroes SASS 3

s. in her little body, RANS 3
s. those years; ARNO 36
unperturbèd pace,/ Deliberate s.,
   THOMP F 7
With the vegetative s. DEVL 1
Your splendid s. DAIC 1
speeding: check that s. bark
   DUNB P 8
s. change of water, EMER 51
Swift s. Time, DANI S 14
Time's course to slower s.,
   CAMPB T 7
tirelessly s. them. WHITM 55
speke: s. and bere him wrong
   CHAU 97
s. and loke lyke a saynct,
   WYAT 23
s. of wo that is in mariage:
   CHAU 86
spell: attend the s. Of his voice,
   POE 26
cannot weave a s. KAVA 27
lies beneath your s.? HOPE L 1
Thy s. through him, ROSS D 2
Thy word is all, if we could s.
   HERB G 32
tyrant s. has bound me BRON 2
within this tideless s.?
   CRAN H 23
Spelling: S. it backward, LONG 27
Spence: grand old ballad of Sir
   Patrick S., COLE SAM 6
lies guid Sir Patrick S.
   UNKN 228
spend: Man shall s. equally.
   SPEND 18
s. my pension JOSE 1
s. the time luxuriously
   DANI S 19
sweetest hours that e'er I s.,
   BURN 28
spending: Getting and s.,
   WORD 159
Spends: S. on the earthen hide,
   WILB 13
s. your dream. CRAN H 23
spent: calm of mind all passion s.
   MILT 118
foolish fort, a heart,/ (Time
   strangely s.) SUCK 7
seldom s. in vain, SHAK 87
short hour/ S. in Thy presence
   TREN 1
silent days/ In harmless joys are
   s., CAMPI 13
s. and maimed KINGSL 8
sperrit: soothe my s. bes'
   DUNB P 3
sphæares: s./ Of Musicks heaven;
   CRAS 6
sphere: highest s. LOVE 7
His life was of humanity the s.
   JONS 39

intelligences, they the s.
   DONN 21
quit their s., POPE A 66
speak from heaven's s. PETRA 4
Stick to your s., TROW 3
Swifter than the moones s.;
   SHAK 126
that serener s. MCCRE 3
turning s., MILT 37
spheres: As all the tunèd s.,
   SHAK 7
Bids s. and atoms VERY 4
crystal s., MILT 39
ever-moving s. of heaven,
   MARL 1
eyes like stars start from their s.,
   SHAK 26
gossiping of friendly s., MILLA 29
into immortal s. BINY 2
music in the s., HERB G 9
seeking the s. WHITM 55
Spice: S. his fair banquet TENN 96
s. of danger CLARK J 2
summer s. TENN 42
spiced: s. conscience, CHAU 14
s. dainties, KEAT 13
spices: land of s.; HERB G 68
Love sits in the beds of s.,
   GRIF 1
woodbine s. are wafted abroad,
   TENN 93
spider: bearded s. on a sunlit floor
   TATE A 20
dimpled s., fat and white,
   FROS 37
Hells S. gets/ His intrails spun
   TAYL E 11
hourglass-blazoned s.,
   LOWE R 34
noiseless patient s., WHITM 54
Pizarro's helmet/ Is a s.'s
   kingdom; SCOT WI 2
said the s. to the fly; HOWI 1
S. and the Fly. HOWI 2
s. will make a silver string nest
   SAND 1
s.'s touch, POPE A 71
traces of the smallest s.'s web,
   SHAK 153
villain s. lives,
   THOMS J (1700–1748) 10
spiders: s. marching through the
   air, LOWE R 33
spiderweb: dried wire s., GINS 34
spiers: for other's welfare kindly
   s.: BURN 18
spies: As if we were God's s.;
   SHAK 84
spike: into a steel s. SAND 20
spikes: corolla of bleary s. GINS 34
spill: all germens s. at once
   SHAK 75
let them not s. me. MACN 17

To muse, and s. her solitary Tea,
   POPE A 18
spilling: brimming golden, s. cry!
   JOHN H 3
spin: handmaid armies back to s.,
   LOWE J 14
Passions s. the plot: MERE G 12
s. across the wilds of the sky
   TATE J 3
S. and die, ROSS C 4
spindling: s. boys BROWN S 1
spindly: s. kid, ROET 26
spine: strong, straight s. MILLA 34
Spinner: S. of the Years HARD 16
spinners: long s.' legs, SHAK 153
Spinning: Make me thy S. Wheele
   TAYL E 5
S. the trivial and unique SCHW 7
spiral: as the s. grew, HOLM 2
spire: along the s. PURD 1
church s. Opens its eight bells
   out, MACN 22
Cypress and her s.; WORD 130
spires: city of s. and masts!
   WHITM 44
grey s. of Oxford LETT 1
spirit: awaits my s. BANK 1
before that s. die,
   STEVENSO R 2
bend up every s. SHAK 56
blithe s.! SHEL 69
Blow the s.-stirring harp GILB 43
cabined, ample s., ARNO 21
camels of the s. WILB 43
daunt his s.; BUNY 3
dedicated S. WORD 103
delighted s. To bathe in fiery
   floods, SHAK 115
each inclosed s. is a star VAUG 2
evil s., your beauty, DRAY 4
expense of s. SHAK 236
fail by s. or by sense. WILB 41
for the s. free, ROBI 2
gathering together of s. DUNC 2
gentlier on the s. lies, TENN 84
good wicked s., sweet angel devil.
   DRAY 6
Hovered thy s. COWP 10
immortal s. grows WORD 96
In Heaven a s. doth dwell
   POE 26
Inoperancy of the world of s.;
   ELIOT T 21
live within the s.'s fire; Æ 3
lively understandable s. ROET 38
lumbering sort of carnal s.,
   HECH 9
motion and a s., WORD 36
No master s., WORD 22
no s. dare stir abroad, SHAK 19
pains the immortal s. must
   endure, ARNO 29
pard-like S. SHEL 6

poise of the s., ROET 45
seiz'd by the s. WHITM 2
shaping s. of Imagination.
   COLE SAM 10
shot the s. on FROS 105
Sinister S. sneered: HARD 11
spark with which Heaven lit my
   s. SHEL 79
s. drinking timelessness;
   SPEND 17
s. flown forever! POE 29
S. free, ROCH 8
S. gave the Doctoral Degree:
   DRYD 19
s. give by which I pray; MICH 1
s. is grown LANIE 4
S. of Beauty, SHEL 30
S. of Delight! SHEL 60
S. of her I love, CLARE 13
s. of mortal be proud? KNOX 1
s. of noisy/ contemplation
   OHAR 4
S. of Pity whispered, 'Why?'
   HARD 11
S. of things unseen, CARM 1
s. of youth in every thing,
   SHAK 225
s. runs, intermittently, ROET 46
s. shall return unto God
   BIBL, O.T. 6
s. that lives alone. KAVA 18
S., that made EMER 12
s. we keep within ourselves,
   WILLI 16
s.'s right/ Oasis, WILB 44
stab my s. broad awake;
   STEVENSO R 2
Sweet S. comfort me! HERR 19
this gray s. TENN 132
thy father's s.,/ Doomed for a
   certain term SHAK 26
thy poor worthless daddy's s.,
   BURN 44
voice of my s. tallied WHITM 50
Wisdom and S. of the universe!
   WORD 98
worser s. a woman, colored ill.
   SHAK 240
spirits: By our own s. are we
   deified: WORD 121
by s. taught to write SHAK 217
greenly s. of trees CUMM 19
loyal hearts, there are s. brave,
   BRID 1
porch of s. lingering.
   STEVENS 61
Raises the s., GAY 3
s. are in heaven!' WORD 156
S. damn'd MILT 59
s. have a fainter flow, COWP 21
s. of other lands OHAR 8
S. of power and beauty
   CAMPB R 4

S. of the shady Night; MARV 23
Summoning s. FROS 127
tame/ Their s. to the conquerors —
   SHEL 77
To wicked s. are horrid shapes
   assign'd, DONN 67
trap that catches noblest s.,
   JEFFE 39
weak s. ne'er been higher reared
   SHAK 178
were all s., SHAK 163
Where he gets his s. MERW 3
spiritual: But s. Eve-droppers can
   hear. BUTL 7
spit: Chew honey and s. out gall.
   SHAP 24
s. out all the butt-ends
   ELIOT T 84
s. upon my Jewish gaberdine,
   SHAK 118
spite: beating myself for s.: SIDN 6
erring Reason's s., POPE A 58
in s. of all temptations, GILB 20
In s. of all the learned FRENE 1
In s. of all their friends LEAR 8
In s. of all their kind MACDI 2
in s. of her prayers, AUDE 18
s. of fortune, SHAK 221
work me woe or s., WYAT 20
spitting: object to your s.),
   CHES 17
With s. tongue, KIZE 3
spittoons: Clean the s. HUGH L 2
slime in hotel s.: HUGH L 2
Splashed: S. with a splended
   sickness, CHES 10
Splashing: S. and paddling with
   hoofs of a goat, BROWNI E 2
spleen: Create her child of s.,
   SHAK 72
excite your languid s., GILB 32
splendid: s. purpose in his eyes,
   TENN 36
S. Shilling: PHILL 1
s. silent sun WHITM 29, 31
terrible and s. bloom RANDA D 5
Your s. speed DAIC 1
splendor: each with a s.
   MOOR M 23
lily in s., PITT 2
mortal s.: JEFFE 38
Out of what cognate s. WILB 28
s. falls on castle walls TENN 111
s. without rays, JEFFE 28
splendour: New s. to the dead.
   PLATO 3
s. in the grass, WORD 84
splint: propped by a plank s.
   LOWE R 17
splinters: Chaff, straw, s. WHITM 2
split: ends of/ s. hair. LEVE 8
his waistband s.; HOLM 13

splits: s. my skull, HOUS 10
s. the rocks. WILLI 29
spoil: both the Indias of their
   treasure s., SPENS 7
his s. of beauty SHAK 212
if spring should s. CUMM 1
little foxes, that s. the vines:
   BIBL, O.T. 73
s. no expression. LAWR 48
thinks to s. the room,
   HERB G 16
spoil'd: s. of his vanted spoile;
   MILT 64
s. the women's chats,
   BROWNI R 60
spoile: spoil'd of his vanted s.;
   MILT 64
Spoiling: S. senses of their treasure,
   JONS 9
spoils: midst of s. EMER 5
on both their S. dost tread,
   MARV 5
s. of war? — HEMA 5
s. of war are easily disposed
   GRAV 28
With s. of meaner beauties
   crown'd LOVE 4
spoilt: Everything is s. by use:
   KEAT 17
spoke: hasty noise he s. 'em;
   BUTL 5
I never s. with God DICKI 61
less he s.; RICHA E 1
no one s. a word, RUKE 12
speech you s., ROSS C 27
Then s. the thunder/ Da
   ELIOT T 152
Uriel s. with piercing eye,
   EMER 5
spoken: lips have s., SHEL 89
not s. of the soul. LONG 35
word perhaps loud s. VERY 6
spokes: Law makes long s. EMPS 9
sponge: frowsy s. boats BISH 8
water and s., WHITM 115
spongy: Patrol the halls on s. shoes,
   WILB 31
Spontaneous: rent/ S. YEATS 57
sweet s. earth CUMM 32
Spoon: by S. River MAST 8
eating with or without a s.
   CREE 4
huddled you s.-fashion
   BROWN S 4
Tankard, or s., DICKI 51
spoonbowl: s.-metal is thin
   BENE 2
spoons: measured out my life with
   coffee s.; ELIOT T 82
sport: All goodly s. HENR 2
envy, listlessness, or s.,
   BROWNI R 16
every s. could please, GOLD 1

S. comes slowly up this way.
COLE SAM 2
s. entombed in autumn lies;
KING H 5
S. is in the world CUMM 45
s. of all delight, TASS 5
s. of love and fear TATE A 16
s. of love gushed from my heart,
COLE SAM 36
s./ Our tended plants, MILT 79
s. strews them THOR 10
s. summer autumn winter
CUMM 4
S., the herald of love's mighty
king, SPENS 20
S. the purple violet. HERR 64
S., the sweet spring, NASHE 3
S.-time of man MASE 4
S. wakens too; TENN 52
stirring/ Dull roots with s. rain.
ELIOT T 113
talk was like a s., PRAE 1
taste not the Pierian s.:
POPE A 33
They call it easing the S.
REED H 5
thou bring'st the S. COWL 16
"We are nearer to S. HERF 3
we call this/ Easing the s.
REED H 5
welcome in the s.! LYLY 4
wild s. Spurts LAWR 24
with ever-returning s. WHITM 46
year's at the s., BROWNI R 66
Spring's: S. an expansive time:
ROSS C 37
Springs: At Eutaw S. FRENE 3
Broken braces and broken s.,
TROW 2
Eternal s.! VAUG 24
Fifty s. are little room, HOUS 40
fresh s., brine pits, SHAK 157
from am'rous causes s.,
POPE A 110
from pride, our very reas'ning s.;
POPE A 67
Green s. the tree, RALEG 14
Helicon's harmonious s. GRAY 23
most antique s.! JONS 47
old Scotia's grandeur s.,
BURN 20
s. as broke from bonds, MILT 86
s. of Deity. SITW 8
take from seventy s. a score,
HOUS 39
Three beauteous s. SHAK 227
tiger s. in the new year.
ELIOT T 34
Weep on, ye s., FRENE 3
springtime: s., fresh and green,
HERR 6
springy: Stiff s. jumps SNYD 37

Sprinkle: S. the quarters on the
morning town. HOUS 5
sprinkled: s. round the floor.
SWIF 10
teeth were s. NASH 2
sprinkling: ran s. on earth's floor
BRID R 15
sprite: lets forth his s., SHAK 128
that orchard s.,/ Eve, HODG 7
sprout: "Has it begun to s.?
ELIOT T 120
spruce: sit/ in the shadowy s.
HAIN 1
s.-cone regularity MOOR M 22
sprung: having s. up overnight —
SMIT W 3
newly s. in June; BURN 45
S. from the West, MARK 2
S. rhythm sprang, BROD 1
Sprungin: S. is Aurora radius and
bricht, DUNB W 2
spud: bury rag and s. HUGO 5
spun: hangman's rope was s.,
YEATS 138
Hells Spider gets/ His intrails s.
TAYL E 11
spur: Fame is the s. MILT 27
no s. To prick the sides of my
intent, SHAK 105
s. away o'er empires BYRO 21
touched her with whip or s.:
WOOL 4
Spurn: S. at his edict, SHAK 98
spurns: the Northern scum!
RANDA J 2
spurn'st: s. at right, at law, at
reason; SHAK 140
spurting: s. and shuddering
KINN 15
Spurts: wild spring/ S. LAWR 24
sput: s. of cattleprod, KINN 19
spy: secrets of the Abyss to s.:
GRAY 29
spying: on the s. senses,
THOMA D 44
spyre: Shakes the hie s., CHAT 2
squad: your awkward s. CAME 2
squalid: s. lease of sin BRID R 11
Squalor: S.! This sick four-story
hulk BROO G 10
square: corner of the s., DARC 1
down to the fountain-quieted s.;
WILB 34
honesty and I begin to s. SHAK 6
Nothing is plumb, level or s.:
DUGA 1
Or a s. baby PLATH 8
Regiment's in 'ollow s. KIPL 5
s. & speckled stone, HERB G 12
s.-rigged, sails furled, motionless,
BISH 25
that arid s., AUDE 87
squareheads: s. and finns SNYD 45

squares: flowering s., TENN 51
In the boiling s., MAHON 5
packed like s. of wheat: LARK 22
s. of his mind were empty,
AUDE 37
Squat: toad work/ S. on my life?
LARK 20
squatting: s. upon the ground,
CRAN S 3
squeak: sheeted dead/ Did s. and
gibber SHAK 20
squeaking: shrieking and s.
BROWNI R 60
s. Cleopatra boy SHAK 10
squeaks: s. of radio static,
CRAN H 4
squeal: i'll s. said she CUMM 23
scraping s. Of seabird's voices
SLES 5
squealing: field rat, startled, s.
bleeds, TOOM 5
him s. bloody Jesus HAYD 14
Squeedunk: woodlands of S.
TAYL B 1
squeel: hear us s.! BURN 2
squeezed: s. out by the mind,
LOWE J 5
squeezing: s. from a stone WYLI 5
s. your face SLES 2
squelch: s. and slap/ Of soggy peat,
HEAN 12
squier: yong s.,/ A lovyere and a
lusty bacheler, CHAU 8
squire: No s. in debt, SHAK 76
no S. Westerns as of old;
BYRO 47
rich s. in Bristol doth dwell,
UNKN 231
squirm: queer little s., UNKN 97
squirrel: mountain and the s.
EMER 35
stab: darts to shore/ to s. AMMO 6
s. my spirit broad awake;
STEVENSO R 2
stabbed: Deliberately s. him dead.
FROS 45
s. me through CAME 1
stable: courtly s., MILT 41
its own s. door — DICKI 56
Remembering the s. AUDE 15
s. is a Prince's court. SOUTHW 5
stabs: s. me to the heart HOUS 11
s. the rice of the world, KINN 19
stack: above the chimney s.
MACL 7
"Farewell to barn and s. and tree,
HOUS 28
salt-caked smoke s. MASE 2
Stacker: Tool Maker, S. of Wheat,
SAND 3
stacking: Better dressed and s.
birch, LOWE R 48

stacks: Formless s. of bodies
  WHITM 92
stadium: no go the s., MACN 9
staff: break my s., SHAK 165
  Lord Chamberlain with his white
  s., UNKN 295
  s. of faith to walk upon,
  RALEG 10
  thy rod and thy s. they comfort
  me. BIBL, O.T. 31
stag: here the patient s.
  ELIOT T 59
  stag, a runnable s. DAVID 5
  s. of warrant, DAVID 5
stage: All the world's a s.,
  SHAK 11
  All ye witlings of the s., CAREY 2
  amuse his riper s., POPE A 81
  came out on the s. HAYD 7
  come/ To this great s. of fools. —
  SHAK 83
  construct a new s. STEVENS 31
  drown the s. with tears SHAK 31
  First rear'd the S.,
  JOHN S (1709–1784) 5
  hour upon the s. SHAK 114
  huge s. presenteth naught but
  shows SHAK 187
  leave the loathèd s., JONS 20
  quick comedians/ Extemporally
  will s. us SHAK 10
  S. but echoes
  JOHN S (1709–1784) 9
  s.-fairy wings, GRAV 1
  stumble, s. by s. GRAV 36
  Superfluous lags the veteran on
  the s., JOHN S (1709–1784) 21
  that strumpet the S., JONS 21
  vet'ran on the s.,
  JOHN S (1709–1784) 14
  well-graced actor leaves the s.,
  SHAK 92
stages: travelled life's dull round,/
  Where'er his s. SHEN 2
staggered: s., — and terrible-eyed,
  BETJ 2
  these low feet s. DICKI 31
staggering: Above the s. girl,
  YEATS 84
stagnant: water in a s. pool!
  BONT 3
staid: earth by the sky s.
  WHITM 76
  S. sleeping there. DICKI 51
stain: bring water for my s.
  SHAK 230
  Clouds and eclipses s. both moon
  and sun, SHAK 199
  gradual ruin spreading like a s.;
  AUDE 97
  s. her honour, POPE A 117

To s. the stiff dishonored shroud.
  ELIOT T 112
  without fault or s. BRID R 17
stained: s. this heirloomed ground,
  KLEI 1
staineth: s. slop, POUN 2
stainless: pair of s. maidenhoods.
  SHAK 149
  turns harmless and s. WHITM 98
stains: all unseemly s. KEAT 1
  s. its equal gleam, EMER 49
  s. on my underwear CORS 9
stair: descend the s. AIKE 8
  ran down the s. MANI 1
  ruffian on the s. HENL 4
  stood at the top of that long
  marble s. WILB 34
  under the draughty s. REED H 2
  up a winding s., HOWI 1
  winding ancient s.; YEATS 43
stairs: doon s. in his nicht-gown,
  MILLE W 1
  empty cup, a flight of uncarpeted
  s. MILLA 37
  false!/ As s. of sand, SHAK 122
  ran down the s. OHAR 7
  up the s. RICH 9
stairway: s. of surprise." EMER 34
stairways: under the s.! GINS 16
stake: burned at the s. as heretic,
  UNKN 198
  Painfully to the s., HECH 14
stakes: short s. of men. EMPS 9
  work is play for mortal s.,
  FROS 126
stale: drink/ The s. of horses
  SHAK 4
  dull, s., tired bed SHAK 70
  he's s., he's been there LAWR 15
  s. fern, THOMA D 3
  weary, s., flat, and unprofitable
  SHAK 22
stalk: Half asleep as they s.
  HARD 29
  left it on its s.? EMER 22
  shady leaf, or s., ROSS C 3
  s. is withered dry, UNKN 293
  thy humble s. BRYA 3
  withers on the s. MILT 6
stalking: s. in my chamber.
  WYAT 26
stalks: Mown s. exhale, LARK 7
  Prince of Darkness s. LOWE R 14
  quietly s. and spears/ the
  shallows, AMMO 6
  s. are firmly rooted in ice.
  STEVENS 27
  till blossomed s. KAVA 27
stall: have gone to s. and bine,
  FROS 100
  s. become a shrine. WILB 11
stalled: s. by our lassitude,
  WILB 26

stalling: sudden brakes and s.
  Engine, HEAN 21
stalls: he s. above me LOWE R 46
  steam of the tiled shower s.,
  HECH 8
  steeds in their s. LONG 47
  Sweeping from butcher's s.,
  SWIF 9
stalwart: red-haired, s. trapper,
  TAYL B 1
  three stout and s. sons,
  UNKN 306
stamp: rank is but the guinea s.
  BURN 24
  S. and neigh, LONG 47
stamped: that am rudely s.,
  SHAK 96
stamping: s. the words with
  emphasis, SPEND 16
stance: alias copped my s.
  REED I 4
stanch: sturdy and s. he stands;
  FIEL E 6
stand: All these s. open,
  HERB G 60
  Archers s. there MUIR 10
  golden manacles s. for a
  paradise; SIDN 4
  Grace to s., and virtue go;
  SHAK 116
  hours s. in solid rows, SHAP 29
  I saw thee Pearle-like s.
  TAYL E 8
  I s. on top LOWE R 41
  know where we s. SIMP 7
  Let us s. here and admit EMPS 1
  little child I s., HERR 11
  long will s. the empty plate,
  HOUS 30
  make a mutual s., SHAK 125
  men s. upon. SHAK 46
  no time to s. and stare.
  DAVIE W 2
  nor sit nor s. but go!
  BROWNI R 73
  Nowhere to s. but on. KING B 2
  Queens s. up to dance. KIPL 23
  soul where you s., WHITM 55
  souls s. up erect and strong,
  BROWNI E 10
  s. amid the roar POE 14
  s. and wait." MILT 124
  s. at my bedside PETRA 6
  S. close around, LAND 13
  S. erect BONT 2
  S. in a row and learn. MERW 4
  s. in good relation MOMA 4
  s./ In sight of God? MILT 99
  s. in thy affairs, SHAK 243
  S. in Time's eye, KIPL 14
  s. on a star unstable, AIKE 7
  s. on alien ground, BROWNI R 5
  s. on his hands, DICKEY 24

s. on the roadway, YEATS 75
S. pat"?/ Gone to his place
   LIND V 6
s. perfectly embodied, GUNN 9
staring virgin s. YEATS 116
strong men s. face to face,
   KIPL 3
time s. fixed! MILT 105
verse shall s., SHAK 210
we cannot make our sun/ S. still,
   MARV 35
we s. aloof, ROSS C 24
we s. mute, ARNO 34
We s. up peerless. SHAK 3
Will s. a tip-toe SHAK 60
words themselves s. up SHAP 23
standard: By her just s., POPE A 25
float that s. sheet! DRAK 4
secret s. in his mind, POPE A 16
s. wave, BRYA 4
Unfurled her s. DRAK 1
standards: (Her s. set, MELV 1
s. of the peoples TENN 75
stander: s. above men WHITM 73
standing: appeared the s. hail.
   CHAU 46
elves of hills, brooks, s. lakes, and
   groves, SHAK 164
glass of blessings s. by,
   HERB G 61
lofty or long s. WILB 3
long s. increases all things
   POUN 31
saw Maud Muller s. still.
   WHITT 17
s. in her two eyes, PETRA 10
s. on one leg MOMA 6
s. on this pleasant lea,
   WORD 160
that girl s. there, YEATS 104
toes s. the stirrups, SWEN 3
stands: As a tree my sin s.
   ROSS C 8
base/ On which thy greatness s.;
   WORD 115
broom s. In the dust WILB 20
bud/ s. for all things, KINN 14
Flick s. tall UPDI 1
forever s. the sea, WINT 7
huge hill,/ Cragged, and steep,
   Truth s., DONN 51
nothing s. SHAK 210
one who s. transfixed SHAP 9
Religion s., SPEND 15
Ringed with the azure world, he
   s. TENN 12
Serene s. the little captain,
   WHITM 91
s. beneath the feet, WINT 9
s. for all the water WHITM 2
s. in warm water SNYD 3
s. like an old horse WARR 5

strengthen whilst one s.'
   ROSS C 12
sturdy and stanch he s.; FIEL E 6
village smithy s.; LONG 48
watchful bailiffs take their silent
   s., SWIF 11
With glory richly furnished,/ S.
   permanent BRAD 12
stand'st: s. an ancient pile,
   JONS 35
stane: youngest stood upon a s.,
   UNKN 30
Stanislow: upon the S. HART 3
stanzas: morning were s. of
   gibberish, GINS 13
stape: some deal s. in age,
   CHAU 65
Star: Add light to some small S.
   DAVE 6
breast's s. of hope JARR 3
desire of the moth for the s.,
   SHEL 49
dew dries up, the s. is shot;
   KING H 5
drooping s. in the west,
   WHITM 46
each, in his separate s., KIPL 29
each inclosed spirit is a s.
   VAUG 2
Earth is but a s., FLEC 3
evening call another s. TIMR 3
evening s. does shine; BLAK 100
ev'ry s. by proper name to call?
   BIBL, O.T. 66
eye of a yellow s.: — BEDD 12
Fair as a s., WORD 45
fierce virgin and her S.
   YEATS 117
follow knowledge like a sinking
   s., TENN 132
great s. early drooped WHITM 46
Heaven's fairest s., SHEL 91
high s. our course is set,
   MACN 26
high, white s. of Truth, ARNO 30
I stood and watched the evening
   s. TEAS 1
Jungle s. or jungle track, CULL 5
Knock at a s. with my exalted
   head. HERR 3
Led to thy cradle by a s.,
   GODO 1
lightened up my heaven,/ No other
   s. BRON 12
Lilac and s. and bird WHITM 53
lustrous and drooping s.
   WHITM 52
moist s. SHAK 20
morning s. among the living
   PLATO 2
one s. over the tower. MERE O 1
our life's S., WORD 69
punctual as a S. DICKI 56

runaway young s. or two,
   BYRO 68
see the falling s., HABI 1
self persists like a dying s.,
   ROET 43
shelter in some happier s.? POE 2
ship from some near s. JARR 24
soul was like a s., WORD 41
stand on a s. unstable, AIKE 7
s./ called Wormwood RUKE 1
"S. Chamber" BYRO 48
S.-climbed, wind-combed,
   MERW 9
s., contracted in a diamond,
   DAVE 3
s.-crowned solitude DOWS 4
s.-eaten blanket of the sky,
   HULM 2
s. holds me, WHITM 49
s.-laden sky, YEATS 140
s.-led Wizards MILT 42
s. of morning and of liberty!
   LONG 19
s.-spangled banner yet wave,
   KEY 1
S. that bids the Shepherd fold,
   MILT 8
s. that ruled his doom SHEL 82
s. to every wand'ring bark,
   SHAK 232
s. to steer her by, MASE 11
s.-ypointing pyramid? MILT 35
sun is but a morning s. SNYD 30
Sunset and evening s., TENN 9
there is no s. ROBI 9
Twinkle, twinkle, little s.,
   TAYL J 1
voice fell, like a falling s.,
   LONG 23
starboard: Rolled to s., TENN 88
with the s. watch, CARRY 9
starched: calico minded,/ sufficiently
   s., PAGE 2
s. dignity and the quietness
   IREM 1
stare: empty house of the s.
   YEATS 99
I s. At the North Pole. . . JARR 20
no time to stand and s.
   DAVIE W 2
not/ to return my s. BISH 17
sit and s. BETJ 8
s. like an old crow. TATE A 6
tragic scene they s. YEATS 82
stared: s. aghast to watch him eat;
   HOUS 53
s. at the Pacific — KEAT 56
staring: drowned face always s.
   RICH 5
gutters of the banked and s. eyes.
   WILB 13
nightly sings the s. owl,
   SHAK 101

s. angels go through. HUGH T 9

S. from her hood of bone.
   PLATH 39

s. in yellow surprise WRIG R 1

stark, s. mad SASS 15

stark: Bedizened or s. naked,
   MOOR M 25

growin, s. and heich, YOUN D 1

relieves the s.,/ White stars,
   CULL 3

s. dignity of/ entrance —
   WILLI 36

s., staring mad SASS 15

starkest: Much sense the s.
   madness. DICKI 105

Starless: S. and fatherless,
   PLATH 77

window is s. still; HUGH T 14

starlight: eyes were frosted s.,
   GRAV 9

s. wood, SHEL 31

starlit: s. or a moonlit dome
   disdains YEATS 17

s. Stonehenge. HARD 15

Starr: To S. or Sun-light, MILT 97

starr'd: On life's rough ocean
   luckless s.: BURN 60

starre: Man is no s., HERB G 29

starres: beyond the s. HERB G 68

s. Watch an advantage to
   appeare. HERB G 30

starry: gems of heav'n, her s. train:
   MILT 76

night above the dingle s.,
   THOMA D 17

s. dynamo GINS 8

s. rise and s. fall. GRAV 34

s. velvet in the night, ROBI 40

wide and s. sky,
   STEVENSO R 20

with s. light, SPENS 2

Stars: all the S. to follow. BEAU 1

battle-smoked flag, with s.
   eclipsed, MELV 16

Between s. FROS 36

blessed their lucky s. GILB 42

branch-charmed by the earnest s.,
   KEAT 22

broad stripes and bright s.,
   KEY 1

burial of the s.? WHITM 58

Countrie/ Far beyond the s.
   VAUG 14

crawling arch of s., KINS 2

dark and precise with s., PLUM 3

dishevelled wandering s.
   YEATS 164

dreamed of the s., JOHN G 1

eternal s. WHITM 10

even than the s., WHITM 59

evening s. were twinkling
   BARNE 4

eyes like s. start from their
   spheres, SHAK 26

few large s. overhead, WHITM 92

fixed s. Govern a life. PLATH 80

flag is full of s. VAN DY 3

fountains of the boiling s.,
   JEFFE 4

frost, almost in separate s.,
   FROS 72

giddy s. POE 26

glittering s. JEFFE 21

handfulla s. Swing out my long
   lean leg ALLE 1

Herdsman and roper of s.,
   AIKE 11

his oblique way/ Amongst
   innumerable S., MILT 65

hung with s.!), HOLLA 3

hunger and night and the s.
   SERV 8

last sea and the hapless s.;
   OWEN 33

light of the moon and s.?
   WHITM 89

Look at the s.! HOPKINS 23

moon and s. are set,
   STEVENSO R 24

morning s. sang together,
   BIBL, O.T. 14

nightes car the s. about doth
   bring. SURR 3

no, I was out for s.: FROS 16

no s. to-night CRAN H 39

not in our s., SHAK 43

Now lies the Earth all Danaë to
   the s., TENN 109

On coontless s. MACDI 4

opposition to the s. MARV 7

people earth/ sky s., OHAR 19

perfect silence at the s.
   WHITM 111

Pluck the s. out of the heavens.
   JOHN F 1

preserve the s. WORD 89

progress of the s., THOMP W 2

reign/ His s. eternally. HARD 20

relieves the stark,/ White s.,
   CULL 3

see the s., LANG 3

sentinel s. set their watch in the
   sky; CAMPB T 8

shooting s. attend thee; HERR 32

souls like s., FOSS 1

speech in s., HERB G 9

s. and heavenly deeps JOHN L 5

s. at night seem to suggest
   HOLLA 3

S. by the sun are not enlarged,
   DONN 41

s. glittered on the snow KINN 17

s. go down MCCRE 1

s. had run away YEATS 16

s. have grooved our eyes
   CRAN H 12

s. in one great shower DAVID 4

s. in secret influence comment;
   SHAK 187

s. in their calm ARNO 8

s. love-thoughts provoke,
   SIDN 29

s. mark our destiny. JOHN F 1

s. of glory there; DRAK 1

S. prick the eyes CRAN H 7

S. scribble on our eyes
   CRAN H 8

s. stand close ADAM L 2

s. that have a different birth,
   SHEL 88

s. that oversprinkle/ All the
   heavens, POE 10

s., the flowers, and the birds,
   SYNG 7

s. the glory of His eyes PLUN 1

s. to glisten on you, JONS 10

s. turn slowly/ in the blue foil
   TATE J 2

s. were settling ADAM L 2

s. where no human race FROS 36

s. with trains of fire SHAK 20

strange as the s. near Arcturus MACL 5

true as the s. above; UNKN 101

under the simple s. THOMA D 18

up in the s. MORR 7

valley of dying s. ELIOT T 46

very huge s., man, in the sky,
   CREE 16

when s. are weeping, MOOR T 1

where all the s. bow down.
   HUGH T 9

white s. in the sky, YEATS 141

with s. was spangled BRID R 15

yanks immortal s. awry?
   CUMM 56

you chaste s.! SHAK 137

start: end is where we s. from.
   ELIOT T 71

eyes like stars s. from their
   spheres, SHAK 26

healing fountain s., AUDE 46

Naked as paper to s. PLATH 3

Shrouded forms that s. and sigh
   POE 17

veins s. and spread, RALEG 11

way to s., eh, reader? SIMP 7

started: I s. Early — DICKI 62

s. a worm farm) CUMM 31

to arrive where we s. ELIOT T 73

startin': so long in s., FRENC 1

starting: dry the s. tear, GILB 10

our gangly s. center HIRS 1

startled: field rat, s., squealing
   bleeds, TOOM 5

s. into talk, ROET 11

startles: Something s. me
   WHITM 95

startling: s. El Greco   MOOR M 28
starv'd: dog s. at his Master's
    BLAK 3
starve: There s. and pray,
    POPE A 19
    Turn pale and s.   EMER 5
starved: cluck like s. pullets,
    WRIG J 1
    Lovers of beauty, s.,   POUN 50
    s. ignoble nature;   BROWNI R 21
    s., intense,   RICH 6
    s. to death and turned to dust,
    WESL S 1
starving: founders of these s. cities,
    AUDE 19
    s. high-country winter   SNYD 24
    s. hysterical naked,   GINS 7
starward: s. eye/ Saw chariot "swing
    low"?   JOHN J 6
state: beweep my outcast s.,
    SHAK 194
    canopies of costly s.,   SHAK 54
    complicated s. of mind,   GILB 30
    concord of my s. and time
    SHAK 93
    crib His chair of s.;   SOUTHW 5
    die in s.   FROS 89
    expectancy and rose of the fair s.,
    SHAK 33
    float upon the tide of s.,   SWIF 16
    for worldly s.;   WORD 5
    Found a family, build a s.,
    MELV 8
    glories of our blood and s.
    SHIR 1
    heaven divide/ The s. of man
    SHAK 55
    high and palmy s. of Rome,
    SHAK 20
    Imbitt'ring all his s.   HORA 6
    interchange of s.,   SHAK 211
    isthmus of a middle s.,
    POPE A 78
    Predicts the ruin of the S.
    BLAK 3
    sail on, O Ship of S.!   LONG 6
    Scoffing his s.   SHAK 89
    scorn to change my s.   SHAK 194
    solemn sacrifice, performed in s.,
    POPE A 105
    s., both full of shame and scorn,
    JONS 33
    s. but the facts;   HART 2
    s. itself confounded to decay,
    SHAK 211
    s. of health is poor;   HOUS 11
    wear their brave s.   SHAK 187
stateliest: Wielder of the s. measure
    TENN 127
stately: fair and s. palace —
    POE 20
    In time the strong and s. turrets
    fall,   FLET G EL 1

more s. mansions,   HOLM 3
    s. ship/ Of Tarsus,   MILT 110
    s. spacious room,   HORA 10
    s. stream   TURB 1
    thy mien is s.,   CALV 5
statement: black s. of pistons,
    SPEND 5
states: In s. unborn and accents yet
    unknown! SHAK 47
    Secret fates/ Guide our s.
    CAMPI 31
    s. of the next age   JEFFE 42
statesman: looks grave enough/ To
    seem a s.   JONS 24
statesmen: bones of leading s.,
    BETJ 6
    Of lawyers, s., priest and
    theorist; —   SHEL 79
    S., chiefs, orators,   BYRO 37
static: squeaks of radio s.,
    CRAN H 4
station: courted men in s.   SWIF 23
    in a single s.,   BYRO 20
    It has a railway s.,   CAME 3
    she leaves the s.   SPEND 5
    this little filling s.,   BISH 11
stations: blaspheme down the s. of
    the breath   THOMA D 37
statistics: no s. of the killed,
    SHAP 11
    S. justify and scholars seize
    WALC 2
    unless s. lie   CUMM 18
Statue: S. stood/ Of Newton,
    WORD 101
statues: Like s. dead   TRAH 9
    wasteful war shall s. overturn,
    SHAK 207
    We like sepulchral s. lay;
    DONN 20
stature: taller s., Sirs, than you.
    GRAV 18
staunched: China s. her milk
    SHAP 27
stay: conceit of this inconstant s.
    SHAK 187
    great destination is to s."
    SNOD 10
    It passes, and we s.:   DICKI 102
    old folks s.   FOST 3
    right to s.;/ If I am wrong,
    POPE A 128
    she will not s.:   HAY 1
    strength and s.:   MILT 101
    True Love doth s.,   UNKN 183
    wish to s.?   MOOR M 4
stay'd: sigh'd not that They s.,
    POPE A 17
    s. not to enquire.   MILT 65
staye: s., thou goodlye youthe,
    UNKN 16
stayed: dancer s. his hungry foot
    YEATS 95

early smile has s. my walk;
    BRYA 35
    Gorgeously arrayed,/ Boned and
    s. LOWE A 10
stayeth: Thy swifting heart/ Naught
    s.,   CRAN H 38
staying: s. at home,   DICKI 130
stays: gentlemen in s.,   BYRO 47
    soberly comes/ And s.   HAY 2
stead: little bread shall do me s.!
    STEVENSO W 1
steadfast: Sober, s., and demure,
    MILT 16
steadfastness: s. and state   VAUG 7
steady: deftly you s. The drunk
    NIMS 2
    follow eyes the s. keel,
    WHITM 45
    in the s. plough,   MUIR 7
    light thee s.;   SCOT WA 5
    long, rolling,/ S.-pouring,
    STEPHENS 8
    shaking keeps me s.   ROET 59
steal: love tempting them to s.
    SPEND 2
    no sin love's fruit to s.;   JONS 49
    silently s. away.   LONG 16
    sleep might s.   SHEL 67
    S. from his figure,   SHAK 227
    S. from the world,   POPE A 108
    S. in by window,   EMER 37
    s. me a peach   BLAK 25
    s. the pygmies,   LIND V 10
    s. thee all my poverty;   SHAK 200
    thieves break in and s. the gold.
    MOTH 16
    While the Ages s.   DICKI 97
stealing: age with s. steps   VAUX 3
    hare go s. by: BRET 5
    Shut out that s. moon,   HARD 41
    slowly winds the S. Wave!
    COLL 4
    S. grace from all   EMER 25
    S. my breath of life,   MCKA 2
steals: Part s., lets part abide;
    HARD 27
    s. the just's umbrella.   BOWEN 1
stealth: flakes with fingering s.
    OWEN 22
    lusty s. of nature   SHAK 70
    s., which Love doth free allow.
    TASS 6
    usurer exact by s.,   BEAU/BASS 6
Stealthily: S. and perpetually
    BRID R 8
    s. watching me.)   WHITM 12
steam: hot seeds s.   SNYD 28
    rising s. And clear dances
    WILB 24
    s. in hotel kitchens,   HUGH L 2
    s. of beasts,   WILB 44
    s. of the tiled shower stalls,
    HECH 8

steamships: sailships and s.,
  WHITM 43
steed: A-combing his milk-white s.,
  UNKN 177
  s. bit his master; UNKN 199
  s. that saved the day, READ T 3
  S. threatens S., SHAK 57
steede: on his milk-white s.,
  UNKN 60
steeds: His s. to water SHAK 17
  mounting barbèd s. SHAK 95
  s. in their stalls LONG 47
steel: bodies hooped in s.,
  HILL G 3
  burn a hole through two-foot s.
  GRAV 29
  clad in compleat s., MILT 3
  cold as s. RANS 13
  gates of s. so strong SHAK 212
  glint of his s.-blue eye. TICK 2
  golden brass and silvery s.,
  WHITM 99
  hoops of s.; SHAK 23
  into a s. spike. SAND 20
  lead nor s. shall reach him,
  GREN 3
  not leap/ From s. bridges,
  KNIG 2
  spectacles of s. SPEND 3
  s. decks rock with the lightning
  shock, ROON 3
  s.-driving man. UNKN 152
  s.-guitar trio, KENN 1
steel'd: s./ Thy beauty's form
  SHAK 191
steele: neither s. nor stony breast
  TOWN 3
steep: Cragged, and s., DONN 51
  guards them from the s. MEYN 3
  let down in that s. bank of clay.
  SYNG 5
  mind upon the s. ascent,
  YEATS 43
  s. my senses in forgetfulness?
  SHAK 54
  S. towns, flat towns, SNYD 27
  towers along the s.; CAMPB T 11
steeped: s. in the odor of ponds,
  KUNI 2
steeple: owl from the s.
  SCOT WA 5
  shadow and the s.; CLOU 3
  s. towered INGE 1
steeples: drenched our s., SHAK 75
  pews and s. CHES 1
  still the s. hum. HOUS 27
steeps: quiet s. of dreamland,
  DE LA 17
steer: Against a stolid iceberg s.,
  MELV 1
  course I ought to s., PETRA 5
  star to s. her by, MASE 11

S. for their deserts, WILB 43
  s. their courses. BUTL 6
steering: most civilly s., GOLD 4
Stella: inspired with S.'s kiss.
  SIDN 23
  S. this day is thirty-four SWIF 21
  true that I must S. love. SIDN 8
  you S.'s feet may kiss! SIDN 25
stem: sewed up the air with a s.;
  ROET 25
  S. end and blossom end, FROS 4
  s. Of memory KAVA 10
  upon its plantlike s. WILLI 14
stems: clustered s. LOWE A 2
stench: s.; the urine, cabbage,
  BROO G 8
step: every s., a stile; GRAV 36
  in tune and s. SAND 17
  Mind the music and the s.,
  SHUC 1
  my s. is to the south. JARR 20
  "S. into my ferry-boat,
  ROSS C 10
  Stole with soft s. HOLM 2
  To s. aside is human: BURN 7
  with a hostile s. TIMR 4
Stepney: bells of S. UNKN 25
stepped: God s. out on space,
  JOHN J 1
  hind/ s. down WILLI 3
  s. from Plank to Plank DICKI 66
  s. out of my body WRIG J 2
  s. out onto the gravel. MERR 4
stepping: men may rise on s.-stones
  TENN 18
  s.-stones in the shallow brock.
  WHITT 32
steps: age with stealing s. VAUX 3
  fearful s. SHEL 31
  Guiding my infant s., HARD 35
  homeward led me s. WORD 102
  last s. I climb, SHEL 34
  last s. of day, BRYA 25
  lead my s. aright. BRYA 27
  wandering s. and slow MILT 108
  who s., means nothing
  SMIT 4
sterile: dry s. thunder without rain
  ELIOT T 145
  human season on this s. air
  MACL 6
  midst of s. millions OHAR 10
  s. sands and the fields beyond,
  WHITM 62
stern: s. and rock-bound coast,
  HEMA 3
  S. Daughter WORD 88
  s. God of Sea. HORA 4
  s. murder, in the direst degree,
  SHAK 99
  s., obdurate, flinty, rough,
  remorseless. SHAK 61
  trail has its own s. code. SERV 3

sterner: Ambition should be made of
  s. stuff. SHAK 49
sterte: Abak he s., CHAU 54
Stevene: Seynt S. was a clerk
  UNKN 212
stewards: s. of their excellence.
  SHAK 222
stewed: Get s.: LARK 19
Stibourne: S. and strong and joly as
  a pie: CHAU 87
stick: each field, each flower, each
  s.; ARNO 44
  experience/ of carrying a s.?
  MOOR M 7
  I'm the one can make it s.
  CREE 3
  riband to s. in his coat —
  BROWNI R 44
  s. in your head, GILB 3
  S. to your sphere, TROW 3
  S. you your toes — GILB 3
  tattered coat upon a s.,
  YEATS 126
stickit: s. him like a swine.
  UNKN 133
sticks: Two s. and an apple,
  UNKN 24
sticky: that s. infusion, KINN 4
stiff: Black and s., PLATH 2
  s. as stones. BYRO 47
  s., painted clothes, YEATS 91
  S. springy jumps SNYD 37
  s. twin compasses DONN 64
  woman can be proud and s.
  YEATS 39
Stiffen: S. the sinews, SHAK 56
stiffened: she had s. already,
  STAF 2
  s. our wills LEVI 4
  Underneath my s. gown
  LOWE A 8
stiffening: s. my limbs, WHITM 77
stiffly: miracle swayed/ s. HAYD 15
Stil'd: S. but the shaddowes of us
  men? JONS 29
stile: every step, a s.; GRAV 36
  merrily hent the s.-a; SHAK 180
  sixpence against a crooked s.:
  MOTH 27
still: Be s., my soul, be still;
  HOUS 23
  By this s. hearth, TENN 128
  Child, how s. you lie.
  LOWE R 23
  cunning picture holds her s.
  WILB 35
  in the s. hour grew, CLARE 13
  is s. unsure: SHAK 175
  keep quite s. and wait. LARK 17
  leadeth me beside the s. waters.
  BIBL, O.T. 31
  left what s. is STEVENS 41
  lie/ Speechlesse s., CLEV 1

lies white-faced and s. WHITM 69

love me s., UNKN 182

mighty heart is lying s.! WORD 7

My lute be s., for I have done.
  WYAT 12

nearer by not keeping s.
  GUNN 14

night-dews on s. waters TENN 84

one s., secret spot DRIS 1

portraits and s.-lifes TOML 1

saw Maud Muller standing s.
  WHITT 17

Sing lullaby and be thou s.;
  BRET 3

sleep so deep and s.; DODG 1

soft embalmer of the s. midnight,
  KEAT 67

Some have too much, yet s. do
  crave; DYER E 2

sound of a voice that is s.!
  TENN 2

speech be s.? ROSS D 7

Stands s. in esperance, SHAK 77

s. as she could be; SOUTHE 4

s. as tombs.
  THOMS J (1834–1882) 3

S. do I love, SITW 13

S. falls the Rain — SITW 11

s./ in the thunder air, LAWR 56

s. is sitting, still is sitting POE 37

s. the enemy and the avenger.
  BIBL, O.T. 23

streets stood s. DICKI 91

Such seems your beauty s.
  SHAK 227

then would be savagely s.
  ELIOT T 123

Thou art s. my God. HERB G 34

Through high s. air. SNYD 18

to s. live on! WHITT 28

we cannot make our sun/ Stand
  s., MARV 35

"Were she only living s.,
  MERE O 2

wind was s.,/ Shaken out dead
  ROSS D 9

window is starless s.; HUGH T 14

stilled: s. his soul. MARK 2

S. legendary depth: HUGH T 12

s. the rising tumult, THAY 3

stillness: Achieved that s.
  CRAN H 46

modest s. and humility. SHAK 56

s. that is almost Paradise.
  ROSS C 21

stills: voice that s. LUCR 6

stilly: hum of either army s.
  sounds, SHAK 57

in the s. night, MOOR T 10

stilted: Those s. boys, YEATS 26

stilts: came by on bamboo s.,
  LI PO 3

sting: Cold doth not s., NASHE 3

dart upon me and s. WHITM 4

mortall s. disarm'd. MILT 64

s. that bids BROWNI R 73

Thy s. is not so sharp SHAK 14

To s. or soil benevolence, KIZE 3

Stinging: S. the eyes. SNYD 28

stink: sharp hot s. of fox
  HUGH T 14

stinking: Drown'd puppies, s.
  sprats, SWIF 9

s. arm-pits, GRAV 18

strung on the s. stone, WARR 3

stints: s. thy smiling plain. GOLD 2

stir: all night without a s.,
  KEAT 22

brook the strain and s. TENN 24

fretful s. Unprofitable, WORD 32

hand and foot that s. not,
  VERY 3

held/ Pike too immense to s.,
  HUGH T 12

no spirit dare s. abroad,
  SHAK 19

No s. in the air, SOUTHE 4

no s. in the sea, SOUTHE 4

stirred: heart no longer s., HOUS 1

heart profoundly s.; ARNO 12

we have not s., BROWNI R 67

stirring: Not a creature was s.,
  MOOR C 1

pale antlers barely s. GUNN 2

s. Dull roots with spring rain.
  ELIOT T 113

stirrings: impelled/ by s. HAYD 15

stirrup: his foot upon the s.,
  DE LA 13

I sprang to the s., BROWNI R 35

stirrups: toes standing the s.,
  SWEN 3

stirs: Crouching down where
  nothing s. STEPHENS 5

s. this mortal frame,
  COLE SAM 23

stitching: Our s. and unstitching
  YEATS 1

stoat: bloodsucking bat or the rat or
  the s. MACN 15

stock: Made lock, s. and barrel
  YEATS 154

More like a s. than like a vine.
  HERR 69

No Plant now knew the S.
  MARV 25

stocking: draws a s. up;
  ELIOT T 111

stockinged: neat lipsticked s.
  DICKEY 9

stockings: didn't wear s., MILN 3

s. were hung by the chimney
  MOOR C 1

stockit: Than s. mailins. BURN 44

stocks: in a world of s., —
  CRAN H 6

on s. and stones, WORD 63

s. and stones LOWE R 4

stoic: that s. bird, WYLI 1

too much weakness for the S.'s
  pride, POPE A 78

stole: Beauty through my senses s.;
  EMER 19

burglars s. that pair away!
  FIEL E 2

reivers they s. Fair Annie,
  UNKN 93

sable s. of cypress lawn, MILT 16

S. a Piece of Sugar Candy
  CAREY 1

s. out unbeknown HOUS 26

S. with soft step HOLM 2

stolen: s. goods do come to light.
  SIDN 10

s. my soul away! TURN 1

stolid: Against a s. iceberg steer,
  MELV 1

stol'n: say it's s., or else it was by
  chance. BRAD 17

stomach: smooth of his thigh and
  s. SNYD 3

s. too begins to fail: SWIF 27

stomacke: appall the weake s.:
  SPENS 37

stone: air or pent in s., EMER 10

ant-and s.-swallowing
  MOOR M 24

are themselves as s., SHAK 222

Ask his story, not this s.
  HERR 60

brass, nor s., nor earth, nor
  boundless sea, SHAK 212

break the heart of s.: WILD 4

cast a shadow white as s.
  ROET 29

conclude against a wall of s.
  WILB 30

creek-washed s. SNYD 52

cut s. consoles his groping feet.
  LEVE 11

Darker by far than any coalpit s.
  TAYL E 3

Earring, or s., DICKI 51

Enchanted to a s. YEATS 52

endless oil and s.! GINS 17

every s. shall cry, WILB 12

from wood and s. to Christ.
  JOHN J 7

funeral-cakes of sweet and
  sculptured s. SLES 3

graved in the white s. BRAD 8

gray s. wall damming my stream,
  KNIG 8

heart of s. WILD 16

in their s. boats. SEXT 15

Interred beneath this marble s.
  PRIO 3

its injured s., HILL G 2

lanterns of s.? LEVE 23

needles, once a shining s.,
COWP 21
set in trifles no s., WYAT 6
stored: Like a s. cask, HEAN 20
where the grapes of wrath are s.;
HOWE 1
storied: s. windows richly dight,
MILT 18
stories: in Irish s., MOOR M 36
S. of sweet visions, CLARE 13
tell sad s. SHAK 89
told old s. MOMA 5
storm: birds in a s.: GRAV 30
born to rule the s.; HEMA 1
brows like gathering s.,/ Nursing
her wrath to keep it warm.
BURN 50
creature died/ By s. YOUN A 1
death a hideous s. of terror.
WEBS 4
Delicate riders of the s.
CRAN H 41
driving s. even as now,
WHITM 99
electric s. of the vibrator LEVI 4
ev'ry s. and winde. HERB G 4
flew in a gold s. SCOT WI 1
fuzzed moth in a flannel of s.
BIRN 4
In the howling s., BLAK 80
learns the s.-cloud's thunderous
melody, STEPHEN 3
night upon the s., WHITM 103
Nights of s., THOMA E 14
pass in s. WILD 4
press of the s., BROWNI R 68
rides upon the s. COWP 4
s. is howling, YEATS 105
s. is over, BRID R 18
S. me forever THOMA D 5
s. of time, EMER 47
s. of war was gone, HOPKINSO 1
s. roaming the sky uneasily
BISH 28
s. so nigh. MILT 89
weathered the s., POUN 51
stormier: drowning in a s. sea
WILD 10
storms: black cloud full of s.
RANS 10
fierce as s. that bluster. GAY 1
god of s., HOLM 18
love waves, and winds and s.,
SHEL 61
s. of Fate! GRAY 26
s. or the strife. WILC 5
Vapours, and clouds, and s.
THOMS J (1700–1748) 12
Where no s. come, HOPKINS 10
stormy: beyond s. headland
JEFFE 12
In calm or s. weather;
ROSS C 12

shelter from the s. blast,
WATT I 2
s. Hebrides, MILT 31
S., husky, brawling, SAND 3
winter's morn, on a s. day,
LEAR 8
story: Ask his s., not this stone.
HERR 60
Ere their s. die. HARD 30
firelight of a long,/ blind,/
dreaming s. JARR 11
I could tell you a s. RANS 5
one s. and one s. only GRAV 33
place i' the s. SHAK 6
same old s. MERR 3
silly s. SNYD 19
snowy summits old in s.;
TENN 111
s./ Lingers upon your lips;
JARR 11
s. of the wreck RICH 5
s. or sung in rhyme, —
WHITT 22
stoure: crush amang the s.
BURN 59
stout: millere was a s. carl
CHAU 16
rocks impregnable are not so s.,
SHAK 212
say that s. and ale THOMA D 42
s. fellows left their bones behind.
DAY 7
three s. and stalwart sons,
UNKN 306
two s. erles did meet, UNKN 61
stoutly: Good liquor, I s. maintain,
GOLD 5
stove: lights/ Her s., ELIOT T 134
marvellous s. BISH 47
s. late of a winter night,
WHITM 33
straggle: s. of a long thin ear,
LAWR 20
straggler: leap to head off a s.
DAY 11
straight: despised s.; SHAK 236
hair was still cut s. LI PO 3
his s. neck bent ROSS D 2
life is s., HERB G 75
Poplar grows up s. COLE SAR 1
Roman Road runs s. HARD 34
set the crooked s.? MORR 3
s. and slim, HOLM 10
s., hard pathway plod —
CARRU 2
s. was a path of gold
BROWNI R 58
s. To the shattered bone; PATT 1
strong, s. spine MILLA 34
straightened: s. her hair up,
NASH 1

straightway: Demur, — you're s.
dangerous, DICKI 106
s. like a bell STEPHENS 10
straiked: s. me three times o'er her
knee; UNKN 5
strain: branches s., SHEL 62
brook the s. and stir TENN 24
guardian angels sung the s.:
THOMS J (1700–1748)/MALL 1
pipe that merry old s., BRYA 21
roots of the grass s., MACL 9
something like prophetic s.
MILT 19
s. of toil, GLAD 1
Words s.,/ Crack and sometimes
break, ELIOT T 24
strain'd: quality of mercy is not s.,
SHAK 123
strained: plucked and s. AYTON 1
strains: distant s. of triumph
DICKI 135
Fall like sweet s., EMER 38
Strait: Remembering the S. of Belle
Isle BISH 24
straitly: bound me s. POUN 66
straits: Upon the s.; — ARNO 1
strand: bear to Europe's s.
BRYA 28
thin grey s. Floating up LAWR 50
wrote her name upon the s.;
SPENS 23
stranded: eight s. whales
MOOR M 9
Navies are s.: SCOT WA 22
strands: thing of gleaming s.
LEVE 10
strange: banner with the s. device,
LONG 21
brought/ Alive/ To a s. place.
THOR 2
Carved with figures s. and sweet,
COLE SAM 3
eat s. flesh, SHAK 4
Ending my vigil s. WHITM 107
first s. and fatal interview,
DONN 46
gardener of s. flowers, SWIN 6
heard a s. noise — UNKN 198
lay down with those s. women,
WAGO 2
life as in a s. garment MERW 6
millions of s. shadows SHAK 205
new to sight and s.: MILT 71
not in that s. place. MCKA 5
preferring the s. to the tame:
KIZE 1
sing the Lord's song in a s. land?
BIBL, O.T. 63
some s. comfort POPE A 79
something rich and s./ Sea-nymphs
hourly ring his knell:
SHAK 156
s. and solemn thing. JOHN L 3

s. disease of modern life,
ARNO 27

s.-eyed constellations HARD 20

s. hand writes WHITM 16

s. horses came. MUIR 5

s. it seems and new!
BROWNI R 52

s. love grow bold, SHAK 149

s. mechanical grotesques,
WILD 12

s. mirror of the Deity. COWL 10

s. seas of Thought, WORD 101

s. stars near Arcturus MACL 5

s. synthetic perfumes,
ELIOT T 121

terrible, so wild and s., MUIR 7

think me s. or older, CORN 1

this s. eventful history, SHAK 12

This s. thing SIMI 5

unknown passing through the s.
MASE 6

Vigil s. I kept WHITM 106

ways of God are s.!' SASS 16

strangely: (Time s. spent) SUCK 7

strangeness: got over the s.,
POUN 32

with its s. MUIR 6

stranger: entertain him always
like a s., UNKN 315

Familiar to the s.'s child;
TENN 44

I, a s. and afraid HOUS 18

make a s.'s eye distraught,
YEATS 106

Our realm it brooks no s.'s force,
ELIZ 1

s. came one night LOWE J 20

s. from Georgia DAVIS 6

s.,/ hoist your burdens, AMMO 18

s. in my own romance PETRA 11

s., tread light; RANS 17

s.'s feet may find the meadow
HOUS 65

strangers: all s. to one another
LAWR 56

remain as s. VERY 6

s. in the garden. LAWR 56

S. of Rome, LONG 20

s. would have shut the many
doors ROBI 47

two s. came FROS 121

strangest: s. ride that ever was
WHITT 23

strangle: its s. of branches? —
PLATH 43

s. it, AIKE 4

vapors that did seem to s. him
SHAK 51

strangled: hunter s. by the boars;
CHAU 48

strangling: one s. golden hair.
ROSS D 2

stratagem: pondering dank s.
STEVENS 48

stratagems: tangle Adams race/ In's
s. TAYL E 12

strategy: his small s. CAME 1

Stratford: After the scole of S. atte
Bowe, CHAU 14

straucht: derk and s. and sinister,
YOUN D 1

straw: Chaff, s., splinters WHITM 2

crammed with s. and stones.
ALBI 1

flowers to s. thy way;
HERB G 25

freely fed on s., BISH 35

grandfather plucking/ A s. SIMI 3

his yellow s. hat WAGO 1

Jacke S. and his meinie CHAU 72

pygmy's s. does pierce it.
SHAK 81

slipped through the s. UNKN 240

sodden s. on fire. ROET 20

young ducks with white s. flats,
UNKN 258

strawberries: How many s. grow in
the sea? MOTH 21

medium-sized pink s. JARR 7

S. swimming in the cream,
PEEL 6

When s. go begging, WYLI 12

wild boys innocent as s.
THOMA D 26

strawberry: pretty s.; SKEL 1

straw'd: s. with flow'rs and
happinesse; HERB G 3

straws: shepherds pipe on oaten s.,
SHAK 100

stray: gathering as we s., MASE 9

I am blind, and dead, and s.,
QUAR 4

maidens taste/ And s.
STEVENS 58

practicing their aim on s. dogs
KINN 19

sober wishes never learn'd to s.;
GRAY 11

time, where lucid Avon s.'d,
GRAY 28

strayes: he s. Among the Galilaean
mountains, CRAS 8

streak: lasts long s. of snow,
TENN 51

streaks: s. of care/ Like wires
KAVA 28

with s. of light, SHAK 146

stream: asleep by thy murmuring
s., BURN 22

black s., FROS 135

brighter fares my s., — EMER 49

cross thy s., broad Hellespont!
BYRO 75

delicate paces by the s., —
RANS 35

dominated the s. MOOR M 7

far-off s. is dumb, TENN 105

freezing s. below. SHEL 23

gray stone wall damming my s.,
KNIG 8

mercy/ Of a rude s.
FLET/SHAK 3

moor-hen guides upon the s.,
YEATS 97

of glittering s. YEATS 153

poison the whole blood s. fills.
EMPS 12

red life might s. again, KEAT 61

rich s. of Music winds GRAY 24

road runs near the s., ARNO 38

sailing down the s.,
THOMS J (1700–1748) 9

school-boys playing in the s.;
PEEL 6

stately s. TURB 1

steep Atlantick s., MILT 8

Still glides the S., WORD 127

strove against the s. TENN 106

sun-starts on a s. THOMP F 8

Time, like an ever-rolling s.,
WATT I 3

upon the s. YEATS 90

streamers: Sails filled, and s.
waving, MILT 110

streaming: lamp-light o'er him s.
POE 37

silver s. Thames, SPENS 39

so gallantly s.? KEY 1

s. beard is shown MELV 19

streams: climb the s. YEATS 152

cool s. ran beside her. MUND 2

crystal mirror holds, unite their
s. MILT 69

crystal s. 'with pleasing murmurs
creep': POPE A 26

Gilding pale s. SHAK 197

murmur/ Of underground s.,
AUDE 52

paddle in the cold/ Companionable
s. YEATS 166

paint the mountains and s.
SNYD 48

shallow s. run dimpling all the
way. POPE A 10

sitting by desolate s.; OSHA 1

Sleepy with the flow of s.,
HOUS 42

s. and rivers — MAST 11

s. in the firmament! MARL 2

street: bald s. breaks the blank
day. TENN 21

down into the s. ASHB 1

down the decent s.; MCKA 10

in/ Stupidity S. HODG 10

Inquire for me in Baggot S.
KAVA 16

long unlovely s., TENN 20

Main S. was never the same.
RIVE 2
meadow in the s.; TENN 53
Nouns were clustered in the s.
KOCH 3
Picked up on a s. YEATS 88
posting up the s. STEVENSO R 3
salmon sing in the s. AUDE 1
stood in a crowded s. RUKE 12
s.,/ Breathes vineyards and
pomegranates: HERR 34
s. door was partially closed;
LEAR 17
s. in Iasi, PINS 3
s. Into its gloom retires, BINY 4
s.-lamps burn
THOMS J (1834–1882) 3
sweepings of a s., YEATS 29
to the river! into the s.! GINS 19
streets: dust blown through the s. of
Rome, MASE 8
flecked the s. of Baltimore,
RANDA J 1
Give me faces and s. WHITM 31
hits the s. LOWE R 45
Manhattan s. WHITM 32
march the s. of Birmingham
RANDA D 1
parching s., SHAK 30
piper in the s. OSUL 1
Smells of chestnuts in the s.,
ELIOT T 105
sounded as if the s. were running,
DICKI 91
s./ Burst suddenly in rain.
CRAN H 32
s. of Askelon; BIBL, O.T. 68
s. stood still. DICKI 91
thro' midnight s. BLAK 76
walking your s., WHITM 30
strength: Beauties equal, but excel
our S. DRYD 29
Beauty, S., and Discretion do man
forsake, UNKN 90
bestial s. PRIN 1
cause, and will, and s., and
means SHAK 35
every s. you own SNOD 2
Hast thou given the horse s.?
BIBL, O.T. 17
hidden s. MILT 3
his hairy s.; MILT 23
I long for weight and s.
FROS 114
inadulterate s. HERR 17
its s. fordone, BRID R 18
joy and s. and courage TREN 2
lending their s. WALK 5
Lord, my s., and my redeemer.
BIBL, O.T. 30
My lord, adjudge my s., WYLI 8
Nor youth, nor s., nor wisdom
BRAD 6

promise of s. BRID R 17
protestation/ Against thy s.
HOSK 1
roll all our s., MARV 35
scarcely the s. of a louse, SERV 7
see the s. LOWE J 1
silence husbanded our s.
MELV 16
s. & breath, BLAK 63
s. and riches at thy feet.
BRYA 14
s. and stay: MILT 101
S. in what remains behind;
WORD 84
s. is so tender, his wildness so
meek, LOWE J 2
s. of Collective Man, AUDE 74
s. of love; WORD 52
s. of virgin forests MARK 2
s. of youth! TENN 72
sure s. ROBI 17
tower of s.; LANIG 1
what s. I have 's mine own,
SHAK 167
what we gain'd in Skill we lost in
S. DRYD 29
strengthen: s. whilst one stands.'
ROSS C 12
strengthless: flock to gaze the s.
dead, HOUS 58
stretch: aged eagle s. its wings?)
ELIOT T 2
s. our bones FLET J 3
s. the nostril wide, SHAK 56
stretch'd: s. in vain to reach the
prize. GRAY 19
stretched: frigidly s., IREM 1
S. in his last-found home,
HOLM 2
s. the sky, — MILLA 30
stretcher: remember the s.-cases
SASS 2
stretchers: forms I see on s.
WHITM 71
stretches: broad road that s.
STEVENSO R 15
s. out my golden wing, BLAK 24
Stretcheth: God/ S. out his arm,
MARL 2
Strew: S. on her roses, ARNO 20
s. them in the air: MONTROSE 4
S. your gladness SORL 3
strew'd: S. flowers SHEL 33
s. with flow'rs HERB CH 3
strewed: With fragments s. the
sea; — HEMA 2
strewing: babbling and s. flowers.
MILLA 37
strewings: Give her s., HERR 58
s. be HERR 52
strewn: mind too s. With petty
cares CULL 19
s. beneath SHEL 78

strews: spring s. them THOR 10
stricken: s. mother's soul!
WHITM 16
strict: s. impunity TATE A 11
stride: with heavy s.; SHAP 20
striding: shadow at morning s.
behind you ELIOT T 115
strife: ancient forms of party s.;
TENN 48
breaks its s., WHITT 28
Earth's hubbub and s. LOWE J 7
feverish fits of s., CRAB 3
for peace and no more s.!
SWIN 5
little quarrels and s., MERE O 1
madding crowd's ignoble s.,
GRAY 11
My thoughts hold mortal s.;
DRUM 2
Nature, mutation, s.? FULL 2
no grudge nor s.; MARTIA 1
often are at s., POPE A 26
peace from all my s. PETRA 7
proved/ In liberating s., BATE 2
shine in s., ARNO 16
storms or the s. WILC 5
s. with the palm; ARNO 8
subsists by elemental s.;
POPE A 68
tear our pleasures with rough s.
MARV 35
term of human s., TENN 29
void of Cares and S., PHILL 1
worth my s. LAND 8
strike: dost love, yet s.;
HERB G 10
madness if I s. me dead,
CHES 12
no planets s., SHAK 19
s. a match and blow. YEATS 69
s. me the largest doe. LOVE 2
s. mine eyes, but not my heart.
JONS 5
S. on your drummes, UNKN 223
s. upon my heart, SHAK 93
s. you dead? YEATS 149
yet afraid to s., POPE A 7
strikes: deep sound s. BYRO 5
gallant arm that s. DRAK 3
pipe that s. Apollo dumb;
LYLY 5
three hot s. ALLE 1
striking: s. me ev'n dead;
HERB G 2
whose cruel s. SHAK 116
string: check time broke in a
disordered s.; SHAK 93
chewing little bits of S. BELL 8
concertina's melancholy s.!
GILB 43
cured by hanging from a s.
KINGSM 2
lead it about with a s. BELL 20

make harmonious mix of voice
and s. BIBL, O.T. 67
Secured him by a s. DICKI 85
spider will make a silver s. nest
SAND 1
warbled to the s., MILT 17
stringed: s. lute on which all winds
can play, WILD 13
stringencies: I unpeel —! Dead
hands, dead s. PLATH 6
strings: boom of the tingling s.
LAWR 31
Death cut the s. CULL 16
languid s. do scarcely BLAK 111
on those s. ELIOT T 149
outdoor business is bad for s.),
TROW 5
s. the hangman's bag; RALEG 13
touched the bawdy s.
STEVENS 38
whirl of tangled s., TROW 2
strip: s. and cool our fire LOVE 6
S. to this tree: THOMA D 8
trim the year or s. its bones;
MILLA 33
striped: bedstead s. with bright-blue
paint, WYLI 9
stripes: broad s. and bright stars,
KEY 1
cut his s. away, KIPL 5
zebra s. along his jaw
ELIOT T 111
stripling: Royal s. GILB 19
strive: all men s. and who
succeeds? BROWNI R 40
as men s. for Right;
BROWNI E 5
I s. to sing, GRAHAM R 1
men s. with each other
RANDA D 5
s. to mend GRAY 21
To s., to seek, TENN 135
striving: Everything is upward s.;
LOWE J 18
S. against my swaddling bands,
BLAK 73
s. Parnassus to climb LOWE J 4
strivings: parcel of vain s. THOR 1
strok'st: Thou s. me SHAK 157
stroke: another s.! HOUS 11
lies calm beneath that s.
STEVENS 12
on the final s. of nine.
ELIOT T 119
past the tyrant's s.; SHAK 18
s. my head; PEEL 5
s. the brow; THOMA D 25
to the tune of flutes kept s.,
SHAK 5
stroked: s. your cold, pulsing
throat LEVE 22
strokes: amorous of their s.
SHAK 5

strong: battle to the s.,
BIBL, O.T. 1
both s. and tall. BRAD 10
coarse and s. and cunning.
SAND 4
faith sweet and s., GLAD 2
firm and s.,/ Is Patience:
HERB G 12
gates of steel so s. SHAK 212
generous wine with age grows s.,
COWL 5
heads of s. old age JEFFE 35
hope felt s., ROSS C 25
I again am s.: WORD 67
I am weak then I am s.;
WESL C 1
In time the s. and stately turrets
fall, FLET G EL 1
Life is too s. for you — MAST 9
love as deep and s. WHITT 10
makes thy love more s.,
SHAK 215
Men are s. or weak. MARV 21
My grandmothers were s.
WALK 7
Nature, s. and kind, EMER 21
ninth wave superb and s.,
LONG 30
pain is worse to the s., JEFFE 14
power of/ s. enchantment.
MOOR M 18
Rest in the s. arms TIMR 2
Samson, though he were so s.,
SOUTHW 11
should be blithe and s.,
WHITM 37
smooth, and s., GRAY 24
souls stand up erect and s.,
BROWNI E 10
Stibourne and s. and joly as a
pie: CHAU 87
s. and delicious word WHITM 63
s. and good, UNKN 106
s. and hale, SWIF 27
s. as iron bands. LONG 48
S. be thy wallis DUNB W 5
S. bronzed men, or regal black
CULL 5
s. guilt defeats my s. intent,
SHAK 34
s. in a weak heart. HERB G 16
s. in will TENN 135
s. lance of justice SHAK 81
s. man must go: BROWNI R 68
s. melodious songs. WHITM 38
s. men git s. . . . BROWN S 5
s. men keep a-comin'
BROWN S 5
s. men stand face to face, KIPL 3
S. Son of God, immortal Love,
TENN 16
s., straight spine MILLA 34

s. white arms to fold you,
KIPL 16
s. you thump, O terrible drums —
WHITM 8
Such tricks hath s. imagination
SHAK 127
their Supports were s.,
JOHN S (1709–1784) 6
unpent and glad and s.
WHITM 102
wall is s.; WILD 2
weak of will, the s. of arm,
MAST 6
wears the s. sea BERRYM 9
words are s.; TENN 91
stronger: approached by s. hate,
MILT 92
hand-clasp's a little s., CHAP A 1
no God found s. than death;
SWIN 25
no s. than a flower? SHAK 212
S. by weakness, wiser men
become WALL 4
s. guilt defeats my strong intent,
SHAK 34
s. than lions. BIBL, O.T. 69
Weaker in most points, s. in a
few, BROWNI R 16
With s. blood, SHAK 178
strongest: men at weakest, they are
s., JONS 29
strongly: suspects, yet s. loves!
SHAK 134
strove: little still she s., and much
repented, BYRO 20
s. against the stream TENN 106
s. with Gods. TENN 133
they s., those worn-out men,
HARD 21
struck: colors are s. WHITM 90
no joy in Mudville — Mighty
Casey has s. out. THAY 4
Nouns were s., moved, changed.
KOCH 3
So bloodily hast s.? SHAK 42
s. by the hunter's dart SHEL 7
s. me dead? SHAK 217
S. them tame; BROWNI R 48
structure: s. that we raise, LONG 5
structures: blessèd s., plot and
rhyme — LOWE R 42
mimic in slow s., EMER 45
struggle: confused alarms of s.
ARNO 4
Life's s. BROWNI R 75
s. and rise brooding DICKEY 14
s. nought availeth, CLOU 8
s. to escape? KEAT 37
today the s. AUDE 84
writhing s. to wrench free,
HAYD 24

s., whereof are you made,
SHAK 205
thin of s. as the air, SHAK 141
substantial: s. doors, MILT 68
subterranean: s. Fields, —
WORD 112
subtile: sentence, of as s. feet,
JONS 18
such s. violence! JOHN L 6
subtle: know not well the s. ways
EMER 6
oaks, how s. and marine!
WARR 1
old s. foe so tempteth me
DONN 60
s. birds/ Wheel and go, SNYD 32
with s. clearness. POUN 66
subtleties: with myriad s.
DUNB P 12
world's false s./ Thus vainly
thinking SHAK 238
suburb: new s. stretched BETJ 8
suburbs: Glides over s. SPEND 13
s., where they will be lost.
CRAN H 42
subway: Return by s.-mouth
WILB 4
subways: chained themselves to s.
GINS 9
s., rivered under streets
CRAN H 30
succeed: first you don't s.
UNKN 189
Shall life s. BROWNI R 74
those who ne'er s. DICKI 134
succeeds: all men strive and who
s.? BROWNI R 40
door s. door; BROWNI R 50
Success: S. in circuit lies,
DICKI 136
S. is counted sweetest DICKI 134
S. so huge and wholly farcical;
LARK 21
successful: from her s. search,
BYRO 43
with more s. hope resolve
MILT 52
succession: by s. thine! SHAK 185
S. swift, EMER 20
successions: s. of diseas'd corpses,
WHITM 98
such: Even s. is time RALEG 3
s. a dot! RANDS 4
s. a rate; BYRO 18
s. a thing as flesh. BROWNI R 28
s. is life — LEAR 3
s. lively bliss. SPENS 28
S. night in England MACA 1
S. was their luster, HERB G 40
tried intent/ Of s. a truth
WYAT 7
suck: breasts they could never s.
BROO G 18

lips s. forth my soul; MARL 3
s. the moonlight in. WYLI 3
s./ The soil's fertility SHAK 90
sucked: s. the honey of thy breath,
SHAK 152
s. the life BARA 3
sucking: s. and sobbing, ROET 5
s. milk from this our body
SNYD 4
suckled: Pagan s. in a creed
outworn; WORD 160
sucklings: Out of the mouth of
babes and s. BIBL, O.T. 23
sucks: s. in thy sacred lays.
CAREW 18
Where the bee s., SHAK 166
sudden: Beauty so s. TOOM 4
bloom more s. ELIOT T 62
hastes me on unto a s. death,
DRAY 5
in the s. blackness MACL 4
make a s. sally, TENN 4
s. came the sea, BROWNI R 58
s. ends of time WILB 49
s. muffled sound, WHITM 23
under ashes into s. flame,
MILT 116
wake/ My s. rage MILT 112
suddenly: redness s. come
LAWR 23
s., and all at once, the rain!
MACL 9
s. drew his rein. WOOL 2
s. purring there. MONR 1
sue: when desire did s. SHAK 169
Suez: Ship me somewheres east of
S., KIPL 13
suffer: do not s. as the dead do,
OLSO 15
God s. little men BONT 5
Hell I s. seems a Heaven.
MILT 66
I s. and move, BERRYM 3
more/ Than savages could s.
SHAK 4
Some s. so much, WHITM 116
s. a sea-change SHAK 156
s. the righteous to be moved.
BIBL, O.T. 40
s./ The slings and arrows of
outrageous fortune, SHAK 39
s. toothache's ills? GILB 48
they perish and they s. TENN 91
we s. and we mourn. WORD 13
weak enough to s. woe. DONN 54
sufferance: push at chance and s.
SHAK 131
s. is the badge of all our tribe.
SHAK 118
suffered: feared, loved, hated, s.,
SHEL 79
I s. for birds, ROET 13
s. her to disappear GARR 2

suffereth: Waking love s. no sleepe:
SPENS 37
suffering: Infinitely s. thing.
ELIOT T 101
s. and not/ saying so;
MOOR M 27
s. is exact, LARK 10
"Thou s. thing, HARD 24
suffice: And would s. FROS 48
sufficed: s. at whey they are,
WHITM 74
sufficeth: Alone God s. THER 2
sufficient: uncorrupt, s., clear,
intire, DRYD 18
sufficiently: calico minded,/ s.
starched, PAGE 2
Whenever I am s. rich:
THOMA E 11
Suffolk: Sweet S. Owl, so trimly
dight VAUT 1
suffre: s. him do his nicetee.
CHAU 86
suffred: What sorowe I s., PETRA 1
suffuse: s. heaven. WHITM 76
sugar: Brown s. lassie, HUGH L 5
s.-bated words: ROSS C 13
s.-canes grow. FOST 2
sweetest milk, and s., MARV 28
sugared: s. and shredded. BROD 3
sugarplums: visions of s.
MOOR C 1
suggest: stars at night seem to s.
HOLLA 3
suicidal: dew that flies/ suicidal
PLATH 7
suicide: nobody would commit s.,
WRIG J 3
Suicides: River of the S.;
THOMS J (1834–1882) 6
s. have a special language.
SEXT 16
suit: Fare you well; your s. is cold.
SHAK 119
his s. of clothes? LIND V 5
make a s. unto him, HERB G 69
serviceable s. of black
BROWNI R 33
s. a calmer grief, TENN 22
s. of ancient black, LIND V 2
velvet s. and faustus hood?
CORS 1
whatever title s. thee! BURN 1
Your s. is granted, HERB G 71
suitability: criterion of s. and
convenience: MOOR M 8
suite: mathematic/ Passion of a cello
s. KINS 2
suits: trappings and the s. of woe.
SHAK 21
watchers in their leopard s.
SIMP 2
weather s. you not, UNKN 266

Sule: dwelling is in S. Skerrie."
  UNKN 122
sulfurous: s. and thought-executing
  fires, SHAK 75
sulk: s. upon my mother's breast.
  BLAK 73
sulky: our s., sullen dame,
  BURN 50
sullen: craft or s. art THOMA D 27
  Dull s. pris'ners POPE A 4
  From s. earth, SHAK 194
  our sulky, s. dame, BURN 50
  small but s. Horn, COLL 10
  s. and fast athwart WHITM 56
  s. fun TATE A 16
  S., sad, THOMS J (1700–1748) 12
  surly s. bell SHAK 214
sullied: to s. night; SHAK 187
sulphurous: s. rifts of passion and
  woe LOWE J 19
sultan: adore a s.? BYRO 16
sultriness: s. pervades the air
  MELV 10
sultry: dark and s. love. BARA 8
sum: all thy s. of good; SHAK 230
  labour you shall find the s.
  ROSS C 29
  letters make a paltry s. MOSS 2
  'Love is the perfect s. HUME 1
  Right, like a well-done s.
  PLATH 84
  Sentio ergo s.: SHAP 23
  s. my count SHAK 185
  s. of rulelessness: AMMO 7
  s. of these events AMMO 4
  s. of yourself SEXT 5
Sumer: S. is icumen in, UNKN 234
summer: after many a s.
  TENN 120
  all the s.'s pride, BLAK 23
  balmy s. evening, DARC 1
  be s. woods — FROS 106
  beauty's s. dead. SHAK 227
  bleach their s. smocks, SHAK 100
  blissful cloud of s.-indolence
  KEAT 41
  bloom more sudden/ Than that of
  s., ELIOT T 62
  brush the S. by DICKI 75
  Calm as that second s. TIMR 1
  calm s. night, ROBI 52
  choose the S. Queen; CAMPI 8
  compare thee to a s.'s day?
  SHAK 188
  droned the s.'s final mass;
  WILB 16
  eternal S. dwels, MILT 11
  Far from the sun and s.-gale
  GRAY 28
  Farther in s. DICKI 23
  From her s. diadem. EMER 24
  from me/ The s. dream POE 2
  glittering s. runs YEATS 96

Gone is another s.'s day.
  DE LA 26
grace a s. queen: SCOT WA 23
Greeny at the heart of s.
  KAVA 1
heat-maddened s. fly, ROET 33
I always like s. best GIOV 1
idle hill of s.,/ Sleepy with the
  flow of streams, HOUS 42
in the s. too; UNKN 99
In the s. twilight. ROSS C 32
last rose of s. MOOR T 14
Leaves of the s., BARNE 1
lovely s.'s pride, BARNE 1
Made glorious s. SHAK 94
Maud Muller on a s.'s day
  WHITT 15
on brandy and s. gloves JOSE 1
orchards of s., WHITM 9
parting s.'s lingering blooms
  delayed, GOLD 1
prouder s.-blooms LOWE J 15
silvery haze of s. drawn;
  TENN 40
spear of s. grass. WHITM 74
spring s. autumn winter CUMM 4
s. and night, STEVENS 16
s. and ripe fruits DOOL 9
s. clothe the general earth
  COLE SAM 16
s.-dried fountain, SCOT WA 7
s. hath his joys CAMPI 18
s. hued the deck STEVENS 46
s., it is the solstice WILLI 6
S. lapsed away — DICKI 6
s. loath to go BOGA 10
S. made her light escape DICKI 8
S. of man its sunlight MASE 4
s. sang in me MILLA 40
s.-scorched fields, BIBL, O.T. 67
s. spice TENN 42
s. that I was ten — SWEN 1
s. voice, Musketaquit, EMER 48
S. wanes; BRYA 20
s. winds SHEL 29
s.'s best of weather JACK 4
s.'s breath SHAK 206
s.'s fruitful treasure; NASHE 2
s.'s green all girded up in sheaves
  SHAK 186
s.'s honey breath SHAK 212
s.'s lease SHAK 188
s.'s rain; HERR 43
sunny s. breeze FROS 101
testimony of s. nights.
  ELIOT T 129
three s.'s pride, SHAK 227
thy eternal s. SHAK 188
to the s. sweet, SHAK 222
transparent s. morning,
  WHITM 78
under a s. cotton dress. SNYD 14
Winter and s. YEATS 26

summers: rain when the s. parch.
  MASE 5
summit: s. of a craggy cliff,
  THOMS J (1700–1748) 8
summits: snowy s. old in story;
  TENN 111
summon: Breathless mouths may
  s.; YEATS 18
  s. all to sleep? DRAY 3
  s. up remembrance SHAK 195
summon'd: I s. am to a tourney
  UNKN 265
summoned: s. to the deep,
  WORD 2
summoning: s., a shinning
  HAYD 21
summons: Hark to the s.!
  SCOT WA 21
  s. comes to join BRYA 24
sump: doesn't hump a s.," KOCH 1
sumptuous: prodigal, annual, s.
  crops, WHITM 98
sums: That cost great s., SKEL 9
  What s. are thrown away!'
  POPE A 100
sun: All creatures living beneath the
  s., BROWNI R 61
  arms flash in the s. WHITM 13
  at midnight speak with the S.!
  VAUG 13
  basked him in the s., SHAK 15
  bathed by the rising s.,
  WHITM 107
  bellies bulge to the s., WHITM 73
  black as the s. SNYD 33
  blood jumps in the s.;
  THOMA D 31
  Blotting the s. SNYD 28
  Born of the s. SPEND 12
  brave s. Die blind JEFFE 43
  Busy old fool, unruly s.,
  DONN 55
  Church blocking the s. SPEND 15
  Close bosom-friend of the
  maturing s.; KEAT 62
  Close to the s. TENN 12
  Clouds and eclipses stain both
  moon and s., SHAK 199
  Clouds shade the s., EMER 5
  Copper s. or scarlet sea, CULL 5
  Disasters in the s.; SHAK 20
  dove-/ neck animated by/ s.;
  MOOR M 18
  dwellest in earth and s., NEWB 4
  Eclipse of S., BUTL 8
  eternity's s. rise. BLAK 47
  face downward in the s. MACL 13
  Far from the s. and summer-gale
  GRAY 28
  find her/ A-sunning in the s.!
  MILLA 25
  footstool crack, and the s. wink.
  DONN 28

tendrils did s.; HERR 68
Use and s., EMER 20
Surprised: S. by joy — WORD 142
s. half the time: AMMO 10
surprises: bud to test s. of sea air,
MOSS 6
surrender: daring of a moment's s.
ELIOT T 153
In this last kiss I here s. thee
KING H 6
S. into freedom SNYD 24
they s. to us. WHITM 91
Surrounded: S. by its choral rings,
STEVENS 29
S., detached, WHITM 55
Surroundings: ordinary/ S. of social
life SNOD 1
s. limp. BLY 3
surrounds: cold/ s. our warm bed,
LEVE 4
survey: monarch of all I s.;
COWP 23
S. mankind from China to Peru;
JOHN S (1709–1784) 15
S. our progress WEBS 1
Surveyed: S. my chamber floor,
DICKI 87
survival: assure his s. WILLI 31
survive: set while I might s.,
THOR 2
shame s., MELV 18
s. in my immortal song. DRAY 8
s. my well-contented day
SHAK 196
survives: gentleness s. SNOD 7
her fame s., MILT 117
scent s. their close: THOMP F 1
suspects: s., yet strongly loves!
SHAK 134
suspend: 'tis me, not the sentence
they'll s. MELV 3
suspended: Like a dark flood s. in
its course, SHEL 16
S. in time, ELIOT T 60
suspends: Ear that s. on a chord
SPEND 17
suspicion: rich/ with s., RICH 12
suspicions: With fresh s.?
SHAK 136
suspicious: s. friend;/ Dreading e'en
fools, POPE A 7
s. of Toulouse. WILB 31
suspiration: windy s. of forced
breath, SHAK 21
sustain: he shall s. thee:
BIBL, O.T. 40
s. Some casual shout WORD 9
sustains: violin/ s. him. PLUM 2
sustenance: pale s.,/ Despair!
DICKI 36
sutures: mouths kissing the warm
s., ROET 48

swabber: master, the s., the
boatswain SHAK 159
swaddling: Striving against my s.
bands, BLAK 73
wrapped in s. bands TATE N 2
swaggering: By s. SHAK 177
swagman: Once a jolly s. PATE 1
swain: cheered the labouring s.,
GOLD 1
Securer lives the silly s. CAMPI 9
your humble s., SYLV 1
swains: shepherd s. shall dance and
sing MARL 21
swallow: s. countless pills?
GILB 48
s. leaves her nest, BEDD 2
swallowed: night/ Involved and s. up
the vision; SHEL 16
swallows: over them the s. skim,
MELV 20
s. gave way to bats LAWR 2
swam: Sometimes she sank,
sometimes s. UNKN 31
swamp: footpaths of the s. TOOM 2
s. in secluded recesses,
WHITM 47
warm the frozen s. FROS 141
We follow where the S. Fox
guides, SIMM 1
swamps: fire has drunk the s. of
evergreens; TUCK 1
swampy: trickle gurgle in the s.
meadow SNYD 7
swan: brustle like a s., HERR 35
daughters of the s. YEATS 9
dies the s. TENN 120
every goose a s., KINGSL 5
Leda's goose a s., UNKN 95
Love the wild s. JEFFE 19
of the s. in death PAGE 4
seen this s. MOOR M 6
s. drifts upon a darkening flood.
YEATS 37
s. must fix his eye YEATS 153
s. sail MERE G 14
S. spread her wings, KINN 17
s.'s down JONS 2
Sweet S. of Avon! JONS 46
when he a s. would be SPENS 41
wild s. of a world JEFFE 18
Swanee: 'Way down upon de S.
ribber, FOST 3
swanges: lofty elmen s.; CHAT 2
swans: Gaze not on s., NOEL H 1
More geese than s. GIBB 1
old ships sail like s. asleep
FLEC 4
Seven s. a-swimming. UNKN 280
snow-white s. do fish for needful
meat: TURB 1
S. in the winter air AUDE 9
S. moulting die, NOEL H 2

Wild s., come over the town,
MILLA 41
swapping: s. batons back and forth
DICKEY 10
swarm: s. of bees CHAU 71
s. of bees in May UNKN 235
swarmed: body clung and s.,
WINT 6
Swarming: S. in the light SNYD 23
swarthy: not too s.? BROO G 7
swash: s. of falling blood,
WHITM 92
Swat: Ahkond of S.? LEAR 1
Ahkoond of S. Is not! LANIG 1
swathed: s. in sweet garments,
WHITM 68
swats: reaming s. that drank
divinely; BURN 52
swatting: s. flies ASHB 2
sway: love of s. POPE A 97
mercy is above this sceptred s.,
SHAK 123
swung breasts/ S. LAWR 11
time has no s., LOWE J 7
uncertain who should s.: LUCR 2
unjust Fortunes s., SIDN 31
unknown constellations s.
MACL 7
swayed: body s. to music,
YEATS 13
miracle s. stiffly HAYD 15
sways: how a body s.) ROET 29
sea is circled and s. peacefully
WILLI 14
swear: s. by the hilt of my spear,
UNKN 126
s. by the slain of the War SASS 1
s. that, foul or fair, SERV 2
swearing: maidens' vows and s.
WITH 3
swears: Auld Nature s., BURN 30
When my love s. SHAK 238
sweat: All fever, filth and s.,
PRIN 1
foetor/ Of vegetable s. MAHON 2
rage, censure, and condemn:
JONS 20
s. and whine WHITM 75
s. of horror in his hair, SASS 13
To grunt and s. SHAK 40
sweated: stood and s. hot and cold,
HOUS 46
sweats: river s. Oil and tar
ELIOT T 138
Sweden: from India to S.
MILLE V 1
S./ what makes MOOR M 4
Sweeney: S. spreads his knees
ELIOT T 111
Tries to sit on S.'s knees
ELIOT T 111
sweep: breadth and the s. LANIE 4
cops/ Who s. glass SHAP 2

s. low, o bless/ the roofs, OLSO 8
s. past in dreams, LEVE 13
us lowliest sometime s.,
  CRAN H 29
your chimneys I s. BLAK 86
sweeping: ancient Ireland s. In
  again KAVA 7
fine s. gown, HARD 37
S. from butcher's stalls, SWIF 9
S. the dust SIMI 3
S. up the Heart DICKI 17
sweepings: s. of a street, YEATS 29
sweeps: fresher wind s. by,
  BRYA 18
s. along to the mighty sea;
  MANG 2
sweet: actions of the just/ Smell s.
  SHIR 3
among s.- and fruit-boxes.
  KINS 1
blazon of s. beauty's best,
  SHAK 228
Blown hair is s., ELIOT T 11
Carved with figures strange and
  s., COLE SAM 3
chattering wise and s., YEATS 21
each s. place SURR 10
every sound is s.; TENN 107
experience s. and sad,
  WHITM 116
extracting liquid s." MILT 79
faith s. and strong, GLAD 2
Fall like s. strains, EMER 38
fiery day had a kernel s. of cold
  THOMA E 9
follow with accents s.; CAMPI 2
Fountain s. of heart and mind!
  JOHN S (1822–1882) 1
funeral-cakes of s. and sculptured
  stone. SLES 3
good wicked spirit, s. angel devil.
  DRAY 6
grows such s. things WHITM 98
haste with odours s. . . . MILT 42
Heard melodies are s., KEAT 38
her s. odour did them all excel.
  SPENS 15
her s. soul, POE 30
how it was s.! BROWNI R 24
how many counsels s., BURN 51
How sour s. music is, SHAK 93
imbracements s., MARL 5
in your s. thoughts SHAK 214
language to her, was as s.,
  JONS 18
late the s. birds sang. SHAK 215
light of one s. smile. SHEL 66
Love got so s. SHAK 169
love is s. for a day; SWIN 23
make a fumigation,/ S. of reflare,
  SKEL 9
Meseem'd, I smelt a garden of s.
  flowers, SPENS 14

music and s. poetry BARNF 2
Music that brings s. sleep
  TENN 84
My lips are s., SIDN 23
my William, s. and true."
  UNKN 33
Nature inanimate employs s.
  sounds, COWP 20
nature so s., LOWE J 1
never choose again;/ S., if you
  shrink, UNKN 74
not in the wide world a valley so
  s. MOOR T 7
not rain enough in the s. heavens
  SHAK 34
O so s. is she! JONS 2
O s. frustrations, WILB 42
opening s. of earliest bloom,
  COLL 1
own s. will is Heaven's will;
  YEATS 113
Parent of s. and solemn-breathing
  airs, GRAY 25
Parting is such s. sorrow
  SHAK 145
Satan s.-talked her, HAYD 12
seasons shall be s. COLE SAM 16
see her s. and fair: BURN 42
Seeing only what is fair,/ Sipping
  only what is s., EMER 31
sessions of s. silent thought
  SHAK 195
smell as s.; SHAK 142
So smooth, so s., so silvery, is thy
  voice HERR 63
so s. a face CLARE 5
so s. and so cold. WILLI 40
solemn and s. and slow
  WHITM 11
solemn troops and s. societies,
  MILT 32
Solution s.: KEAT 6
Spring, the s. spring, NASHE 3
Stories of s. visions, CLARE 13
swathed in s. garments,
  WHITM 68
s. a Breath! MARV 28
S. and low, TENN 113
s. and pleasant soil, UNKN 147
s. and small; BLAK 106
s. and twenty, SHAK 175
s. and virtuous soul, HERB G 72
S. are the kisses, MARL 5
S. are the thoughts that savour of
  content, GREE 1
s. as a red haw SAND 5
s. as blackberries RANDA D 2
s. attractive grace; MILT 72
S. Auburn, GOLD 1
S. Betsy from Pike. UNKN 236
s. cement, HERB G 15
s. cheat gone. DE LA 8

s. child Sleep, the filmy-eyed,/
  SHEL 74
s. child-face is showing.
  WHITT 14
s.-cupid-lipped GRAV 19
s. disorder in the dress/ Kindles in
  clothes a wantonness: HERR 8
s. dove died; KEAT 27
S. Echo, sweetest Nymph MILT 9
S. enough to eat. HUGH L 5
s. fire sweeps across me,
  LAWR 27
s., give thanks; SWIN 8
s. hell within, WHITM 67
s. is every sound, TENN 107
S. is revenge BYRO 21
S. is the shade BARNE 1
s. it was to dream of Fatherland,
  TENN 82
s. keen smell, ROSS D 8
s. ladies, good night,
  ELIOT T 128
S. land of liberty, SMIT SA 1
S., let me go! UNKN 237
s. love remembered SHAK 194
s. music here that softer falls
  TENN 84
s. music makes the ground to
  move, GRIF 1
s. neglect JONS 5
s. o' the year; SHAK 181
s. power of music. SHAK 125
S. rain, the fire's out SNYD 29
s., reluctant, amorous delay.
  MILT 73
S. reward for sharpest pain;
  SIDN 28
s., sad years, the melancholy
  years, . . . BROWNI E 7
S. saint, 'tis true you worthy be,
  GREV 2
s. she smells! AYTON 1
s. sleep is not for the weary
  brain; THOMS J (1834–1882) 4
s. sleep no power can ever
  banish,
  THOMS J (1834–1882) 7
s. smiling village GOLD 2
s.-springing meads BRID R 14
S. Suffolk Owl, so trimly dight
  VAUT 1
s. theft to reveal, JONS 49
s. to dream in Venice, VAN DY 1
S. to the father BYRO 21
S. to the miser BYRO 21
s. tones are remembered not;
  SHEL 89
s. violets sicken, SHEL 43
s. volcanic cone; LOWE R 51
s. will be the flow'r. COWP 5
s. with hay. WHITT 15
swore my lips were s. LAND 12

Tasting of the s. damp woods
SMIT W 4
that s. minor zest KEAT 64
that s. odor which doth in it live.
SHAK 206
that s. ornament SHAK 206
thy s. self prove. SHAK 243
To that s. yoke SIDN 34
to the summer s., SHAK 222
Tomorrow I will be s. God,
PLATH 10
took s. counsel together,
BIBL, O.T. 39
vast s. visage of space. LANIE 4
voice of peace bring s. release
ROON 3
wild and s. LONG 11
with rapine s. MILT 90
with s. leaves; POUN 66
with the jassamine s., LIND V 12
world is not s. in the end;
SWIN 23
your s. hue, SHAK 227
sweete: his s. breeth CHAU 3
so propre and s. and likerous,
CHAU 52
To smellen s., CHAU 51
sweeten: s. and perfume my death.
KING H 1
Sweetened: flow'rs.' S. with rich and
gentle showers, VAUG 24
sweeter: grapes s. than muscadine
TATE A 5
mother's kiss — s. this ALLI 5
mountain sheep are s., PEAC 1
neater, s. maiden KIPL 12
nothing s. than his peace when at
rest. SMAR 8
s. manners, purer laws. TENN 48
s. rivers pulsing flit EMER 48
s. than the berry, GAY 1
those unheard/ Are s.; KEAT 38
work is s. than play. VAN DY 4
sweetest: hawthorn blooms the s.,
HOGG 1
loathsome canker lives in s. bud.
SHAK 199
love that is purest and s. OREI 2
lulled with sound of s. melody?
SHAK 54
Nature's s. light; SIDN 41
Our s. songs SHEL 71
Praising God with s. looks: —
HOOD 9
purest and s. WOOD 2
Success is counted s. DICKI 134
s. hours that e'er I spend,
BURN 28
S. love, I do not go DONN 57
s. milk, and sugar, MARV 28
s. odors SHAK 206
S. Slumbers FLET J 1
s. song and all songs, WHITM 68

s. sovereignty/ Of reason,
SIDN 20
s. thing that ever grew WORD 50
s. things turn sourest SHAK 222
s., wisest soul WHITM 53
sweetnes to his s. lips, CRAS 7
sweet-gum: red soil and s. tree,
TOOM 6
sweetgum: In the s. dark. HAYD 14
sweetheart: dead man's s.,
HOUS 37
s. and her husband bound in one
WALK 12
sweetly: bells that s. ring, STANT 1
frost stings s. CAMPB R 8
Sleep s. TIMR 6
s. lived; HERB G 55
s. played in tune. BURN 45
S. sang the nightingale. WALT 2
s. were forsworn; SHAK 117
sweetnes: s. to his sweetest lips,
CRAS 7
sweetness: all/ Our s., up into one
ball: MARV 35
hot and sorrowful s. of the dust:
MILLA 20
infinite s.! VAUG 11
kiss of great s., ORLE 1
Love, s., goodness, MILT 34
prove the s. of a shower.
THOMA E 17
So great a s. flows YEATS 48
s. did not save HERB G 55
s. ready penned, HERB G 43
Thou all s. dost enclose
CAMPI 15
waste its s. on the desert air.
GRAY 10
winding bout/ Of linkèd s.
MILT 24
sweetnesses: milk and s.;
HERB G 3
sweets: all her fading s.; SHAK 189
brought'st thy s. HERB G 25
fountain of domestic s., MILT 78
last taste of s., SHAK 87
s. and beauties do themselves
forsake, SHAK 186
s. of fancied love, CLARE 14
thousand s. HERR 14
world of s. and sours; FOE 27
Year's best S. shall duteous rise
COLL 4
swell: beechen buds begin to s.,
BRYA 34
deep sea s. ELIOT T 142
green s. is in the havens
HOPKINS 10
hid by the surges' s., SOUTHE 5
no Minstrel raptures s.;
SCOT WA 12
s. From my lyre POE 23
S. with pacific violence. DAY 6

swelled: begin with a s. head
LOWE R 16
end with s. feet." LOWE R 16
Swelling: S. of the Ground —
DICKI 10
s. pearl, DAVE 4
S. to maculate giraffe.
ELIOT T 111
with the s. tide TURB 1
swells: smoothed these verdant s.,
BRYA 16
swept: has her floor s. MILLA 25
s. beyond control, WILB 35
s. these scenes: TUCK 1
s. to the kitchen. KIZE 3
sword s./ Over the pass NEWB 4
winds s. o'er the brine, WILLA 2
Swere: S. and lie as a woman
CHAU 97
sweven: bothe s. and dream.'
CHAU 67
swich: s. licour CHAU 3
swift: His terrible s. sword;
HOWE 1
hold his s. foot back, SHAK 212
how s. how secretly MACL 13
race is not to the s., BIBL, O.T. 1
Succession s., EMER 20
s. anapaests throng;
COLE SAM 24
s. days near their goal, BRON 8
S. doth young Love flee,
MERE G 16
s.-fleeting meteor, KNOX 1
s. flights of Angels ministrant
MILT 109
s.-footed Time, SHAK 189
s. iron burning bee ROSE 5
s. its bolt than lightning THOR 5
s. seasons roll! HOLM 3
S. speeding Time, DANI S 14
s. tide of blood NEME 1
s. to harry; POUN 59
time too s., PEEL 7
swifter: s. than eagles,
BIBL, O.T. 69
S. than the moonès sphere;
SHAK 126
swiftest: s. wing of recompense
SHAK 104
swiftly: hounds ran s. UNKN 59
s. leaping beyond them,
WHITM 63
swiftness: never ceasing! PEEL 7
swills: s. the garbage pail.
LOWE R 41
swim: as they s. DICKI 13
s. for miles through the desert
SIMP 1
s. on bladders, FLET/SHAK 3
s. the sea, EMER 10
s. with Bladders of Philosophy,
ROCH 9

swimmer: better s. BYRO 44
swimmin': s. in the lake. —
  FIEL E 4
swimming: bless their s.
  SMIT ST 6
  Heaven is not like flying or s.,
  BISH 44
  Strawberries s. in the cream,
  PEEL 6
swims: layered light/ Above them
  s.; WARR 1
  new planet s. into his ken;
  KEAT 56
  s. before her eyes, WHITM 16
Swine: Greek name for S.'s Snout?
  BROWNI R 77
swing: Cling, s.,/ Spring, sing,
  ELIOT T 58
  go up in a s., STEVENSO R 18
  Plato and the s. of Pleiades?
  MARK 7
  silent signal lamps to s.
  WHITM 101
  Saw chariot "s. low"? JOHN J 6
  s. I know not where. CRAN H 35
  S. out my long lean leg ALLE 1
  S. up into the apple tree.
  ELIOT T 58
swinger: s. of birches. FROS 14
  s. to grape the taste. REED I 5
swinging: boy's been s. FROS 10
  s. above the stones, BISH 5
  s. on brier and weed, BRYA 19
  s. their butts, WILLI 12
  s. waves pealed on DAVID 3
swings: and the door s.,
  ELIOT T 151
  s. from the ceiling — DICKI 32
  s. in the wind and rain,
  THOMA E 8
  tide s. you away LEVE 12
swipe: blind/ s. of the pruner
  LOWE R 50
swirling: s. crustacean-/ tailed
  MOOR M 2
swish: s. of the scythe-strokes,
  LAWR 59
switchblades: s. of that air HAYD 1
swivel: their s. chairs BONT 4
swoon: their ordinary s., AUDE 56
  very like to s. LOWE A 9
swooning: s. out of an enormous
  willow hamper MERR 10
swoop: circle s., LAWR 1
swoops: spotted hawk s. by and
  accuses WHITM 73
sword: ah! the uplifted s. LAWR 25
  brave man with a s.! WILD 3
  bright s. by his side, UNKN 154
  dare me to the desert with thy s.
  SHAK 110
  ever buckled s.; ALEX 6
  eye, tongue, s., SHAK 33

famous by my s.; MONTROSE 3
father's s. he has girded on,
  MOOR T 9
good s. rust: — COLE SAM 18
His terrible swift s.; HOWE 1
keep thy S. erect: MARV 23
my S. sleep in my hand,
  BLAK 35
put to the s. YEATS 80
Slew with the s.-edge UNKN 19
s. an' the flame, KIPL 31
s. and his holy cross: MUND 1
s. beneath his mother's heart —
  RANS 10
s. of heaven will bear SHAK 116
S. of Justice draw? DRYD 1
s. outwears its sheath, BYRO 63
s. shall wield, BRYA 4
s. swept./ Over the pass NEWB 4
s./ Threw it down, SCHW 1
swords: bloody s. and armor
  CAMPI 16
  change s. for ledgers, WORD 157
  s. about the Cross, CHES 8
  s. clash! POUN 61
  were they drawn s. BIBL, O.T. 40
swore: cursed and sighed and cried
  and s. HOLLA 4
  S. to be true UNKN 101
  vows you s. me AUDE 65
sworn: s. deceitfully. BIBL, O.T. 33
  s. thee fair, SHAK 242
swound: waked not from her s.,
  HOLM 11
swung: grip that s. the ax in
  Illinois MARK 3
  s. breasts/ Sway LAWR 11
swyede: s. so merye. LANGL 1
Sycorax: by S. my mother,
  SHAK 157
  charms/ Of S., SHAK 157
syghes: crye of my s. PETRA 1
syllab'e: Each s. answered,
  JONS 40
syllabic: Sheds the s. blood
  THOMA D 14
syllable: last s. of recorded time,
  SHAK 114
  S. from Sound — DICKI 15
  s. Light as a flower HODG 6
syllables: equal s. alone require,
  POPE A 24
  Jointing s., drowning letters,
  JONS 9
  light s. leaped ROET 11
  silent s. recorded; LONG 39
  three/ dusky s. SAND 21
syllabub: Sir/ Beelzebub called for
  his s. SITW 2
symbol: they had to leave us — a s.:
  ELIOT T 69
  s. perfected in death. ELIOT T 69
symbols: s. divine, KEAT 20

symmetrie: Man is all s.,
  HERB G 52
symmetry: frame thy fearful s.?
  BLAK 81, 84
  horned s. GINS 40
  So much s.! MOMA 2
sympathize: I s., I know just how it
  feels FROS 22
Sympathizing: S. Night COWL 4
sympathy: s. he longed for, BLY 4
  world is wrought/ To s. SHEL 70
symphonies: songs/ And choral s.,
  MILT 81
symphony: angelic s. MILT 39
symple: ful s. and coy; CHAU 13
syncopated: drowsy s. tune,
  HUGH L 18
syne: auld lang s.? BURN 13, 14
  lang s. deid, MACDI 4
synod: a s. in thine heart,
  MONTROSE 2
syntax: s. of things CUMM 44
synthetic: strange s. perfumes,
  ELIOT T 121
syphilitic: Bert's gone s.: SASS 16
Syrinx: Pan's S. was a girl LYLY 5
  S.' lips I kiss. LYLY 6
systems: little s. have their day;
  TENN 17
  Thwarted with s., POUN 50

T

t.b.: girl with t. SMIT ST 1
TV: T. groaning KINN 19
Ta: T.t., Goonight, Goonight.
  ELIOTT 128
Tabard: Southwerk at the T.
  CHAU 6
tabby: Demurest of the t. kind,
  GRAY 18
tabernacle: t. for the sun.
  BIBL, O.T. 27
table: carf biforn his fader at the t.
  CHAU 11
  Chess on a marble t. AIKE 2
  Command a T. in this
  Wilderness, MILT 109
  kitchen t. exists AUDE 14
  lamp-flame at the t. FROS 19
  on the t. sat; FIEL E 1
  plate/ Lies flat on the t. top,
  WILB 20
  pounded on the t., LIND V 8
  preparest a t. before me
  BIBL, O.T. 31
  reside at T. Mountain, HART 3
  sits at the t., head down,
  RUKE 8
  Slips and pulls the t. cloth
  ELIOT T 111

build it altars t. ROBI 4
Flick stands t. UPDI 1
loose feet in t. grass SNYD 35
Prince Albert's t. memorial
   SITW 1
some t. vault unfold — POE 42
t. as a myth, BIRN 1
t. King Saul, LIND V 7
t. of size; SCOT WA 13
taller: t. stature, Sirs, than you.
   GRAV 18
tallest: not the t. there, BLUN 4
tallied: voice of my spirit t.
   WHITM 50
tallying: t. chant, WHITM 52
talon: odor, t., claw, KIZE 3
t. as a finger, HAYD 2
talons: grow no t. at his heels,
   OWEN 14
hairy t. BETJ 3
parting, t. loosing, WHITM 24
Tam: T. was glorious, BURN 53
tamarind: beneath the t. tree?
   POE 2
tambourines: noise like t.,
   STEVENS 35
tame: grafts upon the Wild the T.:
   MARV 25
hard to t., GAY 1
preferring the strange to the t.:
   KIZE 1
Struck them t.; BROWNI R 48
't./ Their spirits to the
   conquerors — SHEL 77
tamed: not a bit t., WHITM 73
t. and shabby tigers HODG 1
T. by Miltown, LOWE R 27
tameless: in his t. heart. HODG 4
tan: t. with henna hackles,
   STEVENS 2
tang: tongue with a t., SHAK 159
tangere: "Noli me t. WYAT 32
tangible: Wishing a t. good
   EBER 5
tangle: t. Adams race TAYL E 12
tangled: deep t. wildwood,
   WOOD 1
of t. things and texts CHES 11
T. was I in Love's snare.
   WYAT 13
Two vipers t. SHEL 63
whirl of t. strings, TROW 2
tangles: dripping in t. green,
   MELV 23
Tankard: T., or spoon, DICKI 51
Tankards: T. scooped in Pearl! —
   DICKI 68
tanned: leather/ t. from deerhide,
   HALL 4
tansy-throne: toppling t. BLUN 2
tantrums: t. thrash to a whale's
   rage. LOWE R 13
tap: Under the running t. MACN 20

with my great t. root: PLATH 40
tape: buy any t., SHAK 182
taper: saw the t. shining.
   SCOT WA 17
which were t., HART 2
tapering: long, dull, t. groan,
   WHITM 92
T. toward the top. STEVENS 52
tapers: frequent in t., HART 2
We're t. too, DONN 14
tapestries: t. of afterthought.
   WILB 49
tapestry: t. for a Pope: BISH 43
tapped: He t. — 'twas flurriedly —
   DICKI 163
tapping: there came a t., POE 34
taps: t. on the upstairs window
   LEVE 20
wish the t. less vocal, RICH 8
tapycer: webbe, a dyere, and a t.,
   CHAU 5
tar: river sweats/ Oil and t.
   ELIOT T 138
savour of t. nor of pitch,
   SHAK 159
t.-black face HEAN 16
Tara: harp that once through T.'s
   halls MOOR T 5
seven Kings of T., OGIL 1
Tarleton: troop of T. rides, SIMM 1
tarn: cyclops' eye/ Of a t. HEAN 1
tarnished: All her perfections t.
   RANS 5
clothes were all t. MOOR C 3
Tarred: T. and feathered WHITT 23
tarry: Next time, to t., DICKI 97
tars: hardy British t. GILB 42
tarsel: t.'s eyes were made; COLL 8
Tarsus: stately ship/ Of T.,
   MILT 110
tart: eat with apple t.
   STEVENSO R 7
task: beneath the pleasing t.,
   THOMS J (1834–1822) 4
fed your hunger like an endless
   t., CRAN H 46
half a judge's t., POPE A 36
infinite t. of the human heart."
   SCHW 4
morning sees some t. begin,
   LONG 49
moving waters at their priestlike
   t. KEAT 3
t. by God assigned me, BANK 1
thy worldly t. hast done,
   SHAK 18
upon my winter's t. THOR 11
with weary t. fordone. SHAK 128
Task-Master: great T.'s eye.
   MILT 14
tasks: eschewing books and t.,
   WHITT 7

in peace our t. we ply,
   UNKN 203
t. of real life, WORD 4
tassel: t.-yarded/ Delicate-
   stomached GRAV 19
tasseling: t. corn, TATE A 5
taste: bud may have a bitter t.,
   COWP 5
fire, tears,/ wit, t., RICH 19
founder of t. JONS 27
last t. of sweets, SHAK 87
maidens t. And stray
   STEVENS 58
matter of t.; AUDE 60
O t. and see LEVE 18
peas t. funny, UNKN 137
Sans teeth, sans eyes, sans t., sans
   everything. SHAK 12
sate the curious t.? MILT 5
swinger to grape the t. REED I 5
t. a liquor never brewed —
   DICKI 68
t. for drink, GILB 18
t. full sour; SURR 10
t. good to her WILLI 41
t. my meat: HERB G 49
t. not the Pierian spring:
   POPE A 33
t. of that salt breath YEATS 148
t. of the distillation, WHITM 75
t. the pleasures of the poor.
   HORA 10
terrible t. for tippling, GILB 19
Though t., though genius bless
   COLL 12
watch the wild Vicissitudes of T.;
   JOHN S (1709–1784) 8
tasted: t. the bag of the bee?
   JONS 2
tastelessness: bitter t. of shadow
   fruit ELIOT T 68
tastes: air t. good to my palate.
   WHITM 75
milk t. funny, SNYD 41
wit ne'er t., POPE A 9
Tasting: T. of the sweet damp
   woods SMIT W 4
tatter: t. of shadows STEVENS 43
tatter'd: t. weed of small worth
   SHAK 185
tattered: Holding their t. frocks,
   BINY 5
man all t. and torn MOTH 9
t. coat upon a stick, YEATS 126
tear her t. ensign down!
   HOLM 17
Through t. clothes SHAK 81
tatters: rend it to t. DOOL 3
taught: by spirits t. to write
   SHAK 217
experience t. me SNOD 1
I t. myself SNOD 6
lesson thou hast t.! LONG 50

love is t. hypocrisy from youth.
BYRO 21
Ruin hath t. SHAK 211
t. his praise. MILT 82
t. me how to fly UNKN 184
T. me my alphabet to say,
POE 39
T. my benighted soul WHEA 1
t. still peace to grow. ELIZ 1
virtue hath this better lesson t.,
SIDN 40
youth and ease have t. to glose.
SHAK 87
taughte: afterward he t. CHAU 13
He t., but first he folwed it
hymselve. CHAU 14
taunt: mocking t., WHITM 76
Tavern: Choicer than the Mermaid
T.? KEAT 33
Indians drink in the best t.
WELC 1
taverns: theological feuds in the t.
AUDE 84
tawdry: t. cheapness POUN 42
Tawny: T. are the leaves turned,
RANS 1
t. lion, pawing to get free
MILT 86
t. pelt/ Of Africa. WALC 1
t. tigers feel MELV 10
tax: Fear most to t. an honorable
fool, POPE A 21
taxed: t. the breath, THOMA D 24
taxi: Like a t. throbbing waiting,
ELIOT T 133
Taylor: T., the Shakespeare of
divines. EMER 41
tea: After t. and homemade cookies
CORS 2
can of jungleberry t. CARRY 6
crack in the t.-cup opens AUDE 3
every night at t.-time
STEVENSO R 3
honey still for t.? BROO R 20
I won't come to t.; BROWN B 1
sometimes t. POPE A 118
strenous singles we played after
t., BETJ 9
t. is brought at five MONR 1
t. is nearly ready
STEVENSO R 3
To muse, and spill her solitary
T., POPE A 18
teach: None may t. it —
DICKI 143
rhetorician's rules/ T. nothing
BUTL 3
sleek, expensive girls I t.,
SNOD 4
study could not t. WHITM 21
T. me thy patience; GLAD 2
t. me to be thine! EMER 23
t. me to see death, KING H 1

t. my heart POPE A 128
t. my heart to speak; SPENS 5
t./ The act of order SHAK 55
t. the Child to Doubt BLAK 7
t. the rest to sneer; POPE A 7
t. you more of man, WORD 145
They t. you drunkenness.
OLSO 16
To t. thee, I am naked first;
DONN 16
truths I t., HORA 5
what one sweet page can t.,
PATM 2
Wise/ Enquire, define, distinguish,
t., devise, ROCH 16
teacher: governor, t. SPEND 4
Time is a great t., SAND 19
teachers: rigorous t. seized my
youth, ARNO 30
Teaches: T. thy way BRYA 26
teaching: operation, t. school,
GINS 21
t. content, WHITM 29
teachings: list/ To Nature's t.,
BRYA 23
teachit: t. by a bairn. BOYD 1
team: t. of little atomies SHAK 153
t.'s head-brass flashed
THOMA E 2
to his t. gave a whistle,
MOOR C 5
Teams: T. in grey deploy FITZ 1
tear: alone and never shed a t."
KUNI 3
Can I see a falling t., BLAK 102
childhood's thin harmonious t.:
TATE A 16
Does to Rags the Heavens t.
BLAK 6
drink a t. out of thine eye.
LOVE 6
dry the starting t., GILB 10
fallen a splendid t. TENN 94
Guy De Vere, hast thou no t.? —
POE 29
kiss off that falling t., GAY 7
new-born Infants t. BLAK 76
shed one English t. O'er English
dust. MACA 2
shed one pious t. PRIO 5
t. be duly shed; COLL 2
t./ Fall, for her sake, WHITT 5
t. her tattered ensign down!
HOLM 17
t. in her eye. SCOT WA 19
t. of regret WOOD 3
t. our pleasures with rough strife
MARV 35
t. the cave where Echo lies
SHAK 143
t. the heart out YEATS 116
t. thee joint by joint. MILT 112
thou canst weep a t. BLAK 103

tearful: t. harp or glib piano
WHITM 102
your t. tide; FRENE 3
tearhis: t. first — TICK 2
Tearing: buzzards/ T. the meat
JARR 28
manners are t. off heads —
HUGH T 2
tearless: long, t. night, ROET 32
tears: allow our t.! ARNO 36
breath,/ Smiles, t., of all my
life! — BROWNI E 6
cadent t. fret channels in her
cheeks, SHAK 72
cemented with t.: HERB G 7
cleansing them from t. SHAK 93
comfort of her mother's t.,
JONS 22
conscious of the t. COWP 10
Curse, bless, me now with your
fierce t., THOMA D 12
drouth of penitential t.? WINT 4
drown the stage with t. SHAK 31
drowned in t., POE 30
eternal reciprocity of t. OWEN 33
eyes bloodshot with t. SHAP 20
eyes forget the t. LOWE J 19
fire, t.,/ wit, taste, RICH 19
Flattered to t. KEAT 5
forget your t., MORR 2
Hands have no t. to flow.
THOMA D 25
hopes, our prayers, our t.,
LONG 7
idleness of t. REES 2
in bitter t. did sow. BLAK 30
in gradual vision through my t.,
BROWNI E 7
In silence and t., BYRO 73
iron t. down Pluto's cheek,
MILT 17
judge womans thoughts by t.,
DONN 61
keep time with my salt t.;
JONS 4
kisses, t., and smiles. WORD 134
lie down with t. DAY 9
Loose me from t., REES 3
man with buttons like t. BISH 46
man, yet by these t. WHITM 63
many t. they give. VERY 2
men are worth/ Your t.:
OWEN 12
midst of t. THOMP F 6
mighty mother turns in t.
THOMP W 4
natural t. they dropped,
MILT 108
Nothing to weep but t.,/ Nothing
to bury but dead. KING B 3
old noise of t., RUKE 6
Pearl in her t., SHERB 2
scorn'd my t., DANI S 16

snow melts to t., NOEL H 2
soul's sad t.'
   THOMS J (1834–1882) 8
stood in t. KEAT 50
Tears and love for the Gray.
   FINC 2
t. are heard PETRA 13
t. are in my eyes. MASE 13
t. fall from the skies. PLUN 1
t. for all souls in trouble,
   MANG 3
T., idle tears, TENN 114
T. in mine eyes DANI S 10
T. like a lover wept. GRAV 14
t. no bitterness; LYTE 2
t. of the hunted hare. SITW 12
t. rolled, like stones, SILKI 2
t. shall dim thy sight, BRYA 30
t. shall drown the wind.
   SHAK 105
T., still drooping, MARV 30
t. that cannot fall, TENN 26
t./ Watering the ground, MILT 98
tender fool's in t., CONG 2
Their faith, my t., ARNO 32
thy t. mixed with mine do
   overflow DONN 65
Time to plant t., says the
   almanac. BISH 47
Time, with a gift of t.; SWIN 1
tired of t. and laughter, SWIN 12
too deep for t. WORD 87
Undimmed by human t.! BATE 3
vehemence of useless t.
   JOHN L 7
water'd with their t. ARNO 34
weep barren t. SHEL 52
Weep thy golden t.! WATS W 1
Wept t. of dew UNKN 253
with salt t. BRAD 3
With silence and t. BYRO 74
world as a vale of t.?'
   BROWNI R 23
tease: t. and doubt of shelling,
   OWEN 32
teases: he knows it t. CARRO 2
teatime: typist home at t.,
   ELIOT T 134
teats: fourteen t. into the fourteen
   mouths KINN 15
young ones hanging at her t.;
   CLARE 11
technique: t. of unsettlement
   AUDE 29
technology: fundamental project of
   t.; KINN 12
tedious: shorten t. nights.
   CAMPI 18
t. song MILT 41
t. way, ROSS C 12
Thinking his prattle to be t.,
   SHAK 92

To sport would be as t. as to
   work; SHAK 52
tedium: long afternoons of t.,
   ROET 8
t. of talking to mutes; PRAE 3
teem: fish of fancy t. MILLE V 1
teeming: of your t. shore. LAZA 2
pen has gleaned my t. brain,
   KEAT 68
t. wharves and ways, WHITM 51
teeth: between rotten t. alack.
   RANS 8
claws and t. grown perfect,
   DICKEY 18
crack their t.! BIBL, O.T. 42
glass eye, false t. PLATH 1
gnawing t. of his saw, WHITM 92
hairpin in her t. SAND 7
hove into the t. of, ROET 2
I cut my t. CULL 14
old bitch gone in the t., POUN 43
pick his t. SIMI 3
Pluck the keen t. SHAK 189
Sans t., sans eyes, sans taste, sans
   everything. SHAK 12
saying Christmas t.! CORS 5
set the t. SHAK 56
t. break off at the edges. HARJ 3
t. were sprinkled. NASH 2
their sharp t., JARR 2
thumbs and toes and t. JARR 1
whetted their t. SOUTHE 3
with my t. and lips, SHAK 86
with your t. SYNG 6
Teffia: men of T., OGIL 2
Tehuantepec: November off T.,
   STEVENS 46
telephant: tried to use the t.
   RICHA L 2
telephone: use the t. RICHA L 2
television: crouch to my t. set,
   LOWE R 20
tell: could t. their headstones:
   SAND 13
heard folks t. HAY 3
I am young and cannot t.
   JONS 28
I come to t. you this, ROBI 23
nought to do but mark and t.
   BURN 4
soul doth t. my body SHAK 243
T. all the truth DICKI 136
T. it not in Gath, BIBL, O.T. 68
t. me if the lovers are losers
   SAND 6
T. me no more how fair
   KING H 7
T. me not, LONG 35
T. me thy secret; GLAD 1
t., O! tell, how thou didst murder
   me. CAMPI 32
t. the crooked rose THOMA D 22
t. us old man, WHITM 113

t. you to go. And you do.
   SEXT 13
To t. your name DICKI 83
vote just as their leaders t. 'em
   to. GILB 23
why did nobody t. me?
   PLATH 11
you t. What we felt only;
   BROWNI R 41
telle: t. tales tweye/ To Caunterbury-
   ward, CHAU 6
tellen: homward he shal t. othere
   two, CHAU 6
telling: worth your t., GRAV 33
tells: count the clock that t. the
   time, SHAK 186
sound that t. what hour it is
   SHAK 93
t. us no lies. UNKN 72
Winter t. a heavy tale; BONH 1
Tempe: shade of T. SIDN 22
temper: equal t. of heroic hearts,
   TENN 135
god whose t.-tantrums AUDE 48
little fault of t. GILB 6
Temperament: T. without a tongue,
   EMER 20
temperance: add faith;/ Add virtue,
   patience, t.; MILT 106
dull shore of lazy t., ROCH 2
pale deputations/ Of t. workers
   SITW 3
temperate: more lovely and more t.
   SHAK 188
t. valley,/ Wet, below the snow
   line, ELIOT T 50
temperately: Jesus t. reply'd:
   MILT 109
tempers: t. are short GILB 58
tempest: heard across the t. loud
   THOMP W 1
homeless, t.-tost to me. LAZA 2
In a great t. PETRA 12
rock and t.'s roar, LONG 7
t.'s fiery breath WILLA 2
tempests: course with t.
   CAMPB R 4
Let winds and t. beat: BLAK 41
tempestuous: t. petticoat: HERR 8
toppling tansy-throne/ In the green
   t. land— BLUN 2
temple: each new t., HOLM 3
t., and a hecatomb. POPE A 105
t.-bells they say: KIPL 9
t. full of treason, RALEG 5
t. of Delight KEAT 43
t. of our heart, SIDN 7
t. of the Fates TIMR 2
T.'s inner shrine, WORD 27
torch is at thy t. door,
   RANDA J 1
temples: builds glorious t.,
   LOWE J 9

gold nails in t. LOWE J 8
rounds the mortal t. of a king
 SHAK 89
solemn t., SHAK 163
t. of his gods, MACA 3
thou that singest/ Ilion's lofty t.
 TENN 123
temporal: mercies t. and divine!
 BURN 33
sceptre shows the force of t.
 power, SHAK 123
temporary: box is only t.
 PLATH 10
temp'rate: virtues of a t. prime
 JOHN S (1709–1784) 13
tempt: t. the distant deep, HORA 5
t. with doubts thy constant mind:
 GAY 7
temptation: remorse did not oppose
 t.; BYRO 20
temptations: in spite of all t.,
 GILB 20
t. me oppress, HERR 19
tempter: Another t. of this snake;
 WALL 7
Cease T. MARV 10
t. me pursueth HERR 20
tempteth: old subtle foe so t. me
 DONN 60
T. my better angel SHAK 240
tempting: love t. them to steal —
 SPEND 2
tempts: t. your wand'ring eyes
 GRAY 20
ten: Bowed with her fourscore years
 and t.; WHITT 2
no T. Commandments KIPL 13
One bullet in t. thousand
 SPEND 20
One year in every t. PLATH 52
owe me t. shillings, UNKN 25
summer that I was t. SWEN 1
T. days and nights, HOLM 14
T. for the T. Commandments
 UNKN 52
t. minutes to see me go past.
 KENN 1
T. pipers piping, UNKN 283
T. thousand years SNYD 2, 20
t. to hell, BURN 32
t.-times-fingering weed KIPL 16
t.-year soldier tells: KIPL 11
tenant: t. long to a rich Lord,
 HERB G 69
t. of the room, HENL 4
tenanted: By good angels t.,
 POE 20
tenantless: graves stood t.
 SHAK 20
Tenants: T. of the house,
 ELIOT T 35
tend: my clustering fruits I t.;
 AKEN 2

t. our agonizing seeds. CULL 4
to her ruin now I t." MILT 92
what should I do but t.
 SHAK 208
tended: Our t. plants, MILT 79
tender: beautiful, the t., the kind;
 MILLA 6
Faint oxlips; t. bluebells
 SHEL 59
Gracing the t. herb, MILT 69
liquid and free and t.! WHITM 49
most t. mercy CRAB 8
My t. age in sorrow did begin:
 HERB G 27
strength is so t., his wildness so
 meek, LOWE J 2
t. and wondrous thoughts.
 WHITM 12
t. grace of a day that is dead
 TENN 3
t.-headed flower. FROS 109
t. is the night, KEAT 48
t. lambes ytorne? SPENS 43
t., virgin-like pastoral Evangeline.
 LOWE J 7
vines have t. grapes.
 BIBL, O.T. 73
tenderest: chords that t. KEAT 5
T. of Roman poets TENN 14
tenderly: At the last, t., WHITM 42
he spake t. BRID R 16
Judge t. of me! DICKI 146
mean t. by you WHITM 5
Night coming t. HUGH L 4
treat it t., WYAT 8
tenderness: good flesh continuing/
 Such t., those afternoons
 HASS 4
t. of patient minds, OWEN 8
Tending: T. the house, MERR 2
tendre: conscience and t. herte.
 CHAU 17
tendril: grape t. ties a knot
 MOOR M 3
t. for needle ROET 25
tendrils: blood clots the t.
 PLATH 13
neckcurls, limp and damp as t.;
 ROET 11
t. did surprise; HERR 68
vine curls her t., MILT 73
tenements: among the new brick t.
 WILLI 24
Tennessee: jar in T., STEVENS 1
Little Giffen, of T.! TICK 1
up from the T. WOOL 3
tennis: strongly adorable t.-girl's
 hand! BETJ 10
Tennyson: Alfred Lord T. crossing
 the bar SITW 3
tenor: ruin a fine t. voice AUDE 49
tens: Fives, and t., LAWR 54

tense: My heart grows t.
 LOWE R 53
Too t., or too lax. BOGA 15
wisest man grows t. YEATS 156
tent: in a field a silken t.
 FROS 101
in an oxygen t. GINS 39
little t. of blue WILD 1
one rose in a t. of sea WINT 8
round the t. of God BLAK 99
rows of the hospital t.,
 WHITM 115
t. is mine," LOWE J 20
Within a t. of green, KIRK 2
within his t. RANS 23
tentative: see the t. Movements,
 POUN 57
tented: creaking of the t. sky,
 MILLA 29
tenth: t. day of Christmas,
 UNKN 283
t. of mankind SHAK 179
tentless: wi' t. heed; BURN 46
tents: dwell in the t. of wickedness.
 BIBL, O.T. 43
fold their t., like the Arabs,
 LONG 16
Israel's t. do shine so bright.
 BLAK 39
t. of the mountains. UNKN 120
terbacky: chaw of t., HAY 6
teres: my byttre salte t. PETRA 1
tereu: "Jug, jug, jug, jug, t.,"
 LYLY 3
term: close your t. here, HARD 23
Doomed for a certain t. SHAK 26
reach its natural t.; EMER 5
spare this hour's t. WARR 2
t. of human strife, TENN 29
to its Stygian t. . . . . LOWE R 14
without t. or scope, ARNO 24
terme: of al thy lif; CHAU 88
Terminate: T. torment ELIOT T 10
terms: t. of employment,
 SPEND 20
transcendental t., GILB 30
terraced: t. sides of a mountain,
 WHITM 9
T. thousands died, HEAN 18
terraces: crumbling, leafy t.
 ASHB 2
terrible: furry nuts/ of the t. puss,
 OHAR 4
grateful that a thing/ So t. — had
 been endured — DICKI 25
His t. swift sword; HOWE 1
how t. it must be CORS 2
know you, t. joy. LEVE 17
lend the eye a t. aspect:
 SHAK 56
live in the t. western world
 OHAR 9
staggered — and, t.-eyed, BETJ 2

strong you thump, O t. drums —
  WHITM 8
t. and splendid bloom
  RANDA D 5
t. beast, BOGA 3
t. beauty is born. YEATS 56
t. horse began BOGA 2
t. name of rectitude, HECH 11
t., so wild and strange, MUIR 7
t. taste for tippling, GILB 19
t. to come down JUST 7
t. water BERRYM 14
terribly: t. are two) RANS 26
terrified: t. at the Earth,
  WHITM 98
terrify: Do I t.? — PLATH 53
territory: t. is lost." SNYD 48
terror: death a hideous storm of t.
  WEBS 4
dumb T. shall rise MARK 8
famine, t., flood, and plague
  WALK 1
no arranged t.: AMMO 8
patented/ t., HILL G 7
t. be in love, MILT 92
t. of his oncoming; LAWR 24
t. of that love: PRIN 3
t. pervades AMMO 8
t. to the young and old.
  WALK 10
thicketed with shapes of t.
  HAYD 19
terrorizes: t. the contents of skulls
  KINN 12
terrors: Dare its deadly t. clasp?
  BLAK 82
t. wherewith flesh was racked.
  GRAV 37
terroure: gallard eare of t. CHAT 2
terse: cries are thin and t.;
  WILB 16
test: bud to t. surprises of sea air,
  MOSS 6
t. of art. POPE A 25
Testament: Old T. soldiers
  NASH 20
testimony: t. of summer nights.
  ELIOT T 129
t. of the Lord BIBL, O.T. 28
tether: Loosened from the minor's
  t. JOHN S (1709–1784) 11
Texas: folks frown on that in T.,
  DURE 2
text: found a t. to prove YEATS 64
great t. in Galatians,
  BROWNI R 78
his Sunday's t., — HOLM 8
texts: of tangled things and t.
  CHES 11
Thackeray: Earl of T. GILB 54
Thames: gaily as the sparkling T.;
  ARNO 27

Not of Gennesareth, but T.!
  THOMP F 12
Ouer the riuer of T. past hee.
  UNKN 221
silver streaming T., SPENS 39
Sweet T., run softly,
  ELIOT T 129
Sweet T., run softly, SPENS 40
T. runs chill MORR 5
thank: i t. You God CUMM 19
t. with brief t. SWIN 15
thankfulness: purrs in t., SMAR 5
thankit: sae the Lord be t.
  BURN 17
thankless: depart peaceful, pacified,
  and t., LAWR 43
have a t. child! SHAK 72
thanks: Give yee t. unto the Lord,
  BIBL, O.T. 54
proportion both of t. and
  payment SHAK 104
sweet, give t.; SWIN 8
t. to thee, LONG 50
to give t. is good, SWIN 8
thanksgiving: Enter into his gates
  with t., BIBL, O.T. 50
With proud t., BINY 1
thaw: fire to t. our thumbs
  TROW 5
traceless as a t. of bygone snow;
  ROSS C 17
theater: As in a t. SHAK 92
Sit in a t., POE 30
T. business, management of men.
  YEATS 58
theatre: t. was changed
  STEVENS 30
theatres: t. of crowded men
  KEAT 25
thee: broken lights of t., TENN 17
commune with T. DOAN 1
dravest love from t.,
  THOMP F 10
faithful compass that still points
  to t. GAY 7
For this poor wreath, give T. a
  crown of praise. HERB G 76
Hobbinoll, what garres t. greete?
  SPENS 48
I am not thine, but T. PHILI K 1
I had forgot/ My selfe and t.
  JONS 13
I have been faithful to t.,
  DOWS 3
In t. all flowers and roses spring,
  BROWNE 1
joy to t., O death, WHITM 51
moor — Tonight — / In T.!
  DICKI 158
"Naught shelters t., THOMP F 7
nobody cares for t.' UNKN 10
praise and adore T." NEWB 4
rosy ornaments in t. CAMPI 25

shadow of t., ROSS D 3
sun took step of t., CRAN H 28
T. for my recitative, WHITM 99
T. in thy panoply, WHITM 99
t. O Time. MILT 45
though I am clean forgot, Let me
  not love t., if I love t. not.
  HERB G 6
thy shadow, follow t. EMER 10
Until I rest by t. DE TA 2
We saw T. in Thy balmy nest,
  CRAS 4
With T. Let me combine
  HERB G 27
Yet I love t. HERB G 60
theft: sweet t. to reveal, JONS 49
Theirs: T. but to do and die.
  TENN 7
T. not to make reply, TENN 7
T. not to reason why, TENN 7
theme: I sought a t. YEATS 25
liquid t. CRAN H 23
weak and idle t., SHAK 129
when God's the t. SMAR 9
themes: enumerate old t.?
  YEATS 27
Heft t. — Pound for Pound —
  DICKI 15
themselves: are t. as stone,
  SHAK 222
bodies by t., WHITM 92
Gods t. cannot recall their gifts.'
  TENN 122
Love but t. DRYD 1
saviors come not home tonight:/ T.
  they could not save. HOUS 31
'Tis for T. they look, DRYD 18
then: Echo, t., shall again
  WEBS/ROWL 2
t. the heaven espy. HERB G 28
thence: bring away/ Captivity t.
  captive, SPENS 18
flame/ But borrowed t.
  HERB G 36
Theocritus: T. written in English,
  LOWE J 7
theological: t. feuds in the taverns
  AUDE 84
theology: post-obits of t. BYRO 21
theorist: lawyers, statesmen, priest
  and t.; — SHEL 79
theory: t. of natural origins
  JEFFE 34
therapy: psychotherapy occupational
  t. GINS 15
therefore: Trust t. first, WYAT 11
therein: virtue lies t., HERB G 56
thereinne: dungeoun t. LANGL 2
Thermopylae: old man of T.,
  LEAR 15
theron: werte, and t. stood a toft of
  herys CHAU 17

these: grieve they lived not in t.
　times DRAY 8
lie to say that t. Saved, MACDI 1
T. are thy wonders, Lord of love,
　HERB G 33
Who are t. pietàs? PLATH 79
thewed: t. like an Auroch bull,
　SMIT L 2
thews: t. that lie and cumber
　HOUS 47
thick: flowers left t. at nightfall
　THOMA E 12
know a little garden-close/ Set t.
　with lily MORR 6
night was t. and hazy CARRY 4
Rich, hemm'd t. all around
　WHITM 43
secluded in the t. marine?
　STEVENS 48
T. as autumnal leaves MILT 55
t. as mist/ On evening marches,
　SHEL 79
t. black pages! LARK 12
t. integument of snow. THOR 11
t. of the dark WILLI 9
t.-ribbed ice, SHAK 115
t. rotundity o' the world!
　SHAK 75
t.-soled/ shoes! MOOR M 3
thickening: heavily t. to empire,
　JEFFE 37
thicker: t. than itself with brother's
　blood, SHAK 34
thicket: In forest wild, in t., brake,
　or den; MILT 86
thicketed: t. with shapes of terror
　HAYD 19
thickset: boughs are bent with t.
　fruit; ROSS C 1
Thief: first grand T. MILT 68
forgive thy robbery, gentle t.,
　SHAK 200
I askèd a t. BLAK 25
like a T. DICKI 73
No t. so politic, EMER 37
Time the subtle t. of youth,
　MILT 14
wanders god-like or like t.
　GRAV 15
wink'd at the t. BLAK 25
thieves: 'Gainst knaves and t.
　SHAK 177
Honor among t. RANS 13
honour among t. GRAV 32
mirth/ Of t. and murderers:
　HERB G 71
nail you up twixt t. HORN 2
slaves, we t. EMER 5
t. break in and steal the gold.
　MOTH 16
thigh: heel drawn up to t.
　AUDE 59
held by calf and t. GUNN 11

smooth of his t. and stomach
　SNYD 3
t. and tongue, LEVE 1
thighs: candle in the t.
　THOMA D 30
coiled, hurdling muscles of his t.:
　LOWE R 37
light for t. KINS 4
long, small legs and t. HERR 63
Long spindly t. GRAV 1
moving its slow t., YEATS 135
t. are appletrees WILLI 25
t. hugging his ribs. SWEN 3
thills: lancewood to make the t.;
　HOLM 6
thin: bully's t. superiority.
　HECH 11
childhood's t. harmonious tear:
　TATE A 16
cows get t., SNYD 41
cries are t. and terse; WILB 16
hyaline t. air SHAP 7
shelt'ring walls are t., UNTE 3
spoonbowl-metal is t. BENE 2
their t. blood STEVENS 34
t. and outward rind, EMER 5
t. forests of silver-grey. SNYD 46
t. ghost that I now frailly follow!
　HARD 2
t. of substance as the air,
　SHAK 141
t. with desire, MONR 2
tongue's t. tip, SPENC A 4
ugly, grisly, bare and t.;
　SOUTHW 9
voice is t. WALK 10
thine: by succession t.! SHAK 185
form was t.! BLAK 26
Heaven is t.; POE 27
I am not t., but Thee. PHILI K 1
image of t. eyes ROSS D 3
sanctify this altar to be t.
　HERB G 8
teach me to be t.! EMER 23
T. ancient sacrifice, KIPL 18
T. eternal throne, DOAN 2
weary lot is t., SCOT WA 24
youth's eyes burned at t.,
　ROSS D 2
thing: All manner of t. shall be
　well ELIOT T 74
best t. of our life, our rest,
　DANI S 21
burns the t. inside it. BARA 2
dead t., DONN 43
draw the T. as he sees It KIPL 29
duteous t. UNKN 313
duty, a dead-sure t.,— HAY 4
Every t. did banish moan,
　BARNF 1
fearful t. WILD 5
Forbede us t., and that desiren
　we; CHAU 89

honour is a t. conceived
　DANI S 20
Hurt no living t.: ROSS C 16
is a dang'rous t.; POPE A 33
kills the t. he loves, WILD 3
little black t. BLAK 55
Man is ev'ry t., HERB G 50
many a t. I sought, SHAK 195
many a wonder t. CHAU 65
never said a foolish t., ROCH 4
no t. but death will serve thy
　turn, DRAY 14
only moving t. STEVENS 63
only, only, t. that I ever did
　wrong UNKN 99
palsy-stricken, churchyard t.,
　KEAT 9
plays's the t. SHAK 32
seen one t., SWIN 21
She's a young t., UNKN 28
sing as you tackle the t. GUES 5
sleep! it is a gentle t.,
　COLE SAM 29
Slight was the t. DUNB P 5
sole unbusy t., COLE SAM 45
sort of t. she planned, NOYE 4
tale in every t. WORD 136
That t. of silk, POPE A 9
that t. screams. BARA 2
t. in the air. LAWR 1
t. of beauty is a joy for ever:
　KEAT 4
think it the pleasantest t. Ever a
　child can do! STEVENSO R 18
This strange t. SIMI 5
"Thou suffering t., HARD 24
To every t. there is a season,
　BIBL, O.T. 3
uncouth hideous t., HERB G 19
understood any t., WHITM 44
What/ a fine t.! MOOR M 2
thinges: Warning of t. that shall
　after fall. CHAU 72, 73
things: all prodigious t., MILT 61
All t. are a flowing,/ Sage
　Heracleitus says; POUN 42
All t. are lawful there CAREW 13
All t. are passing; THER 1
all t.— but his horse. POPE A 20
all t. for the best, ROBI 26
all t. now do hold their peace:
　SURR 3
all t. smile; CAREW 14
all t. under Heaven, MILT 107
alterest all t. POE 1
always embrace t., OHAR 19
as for nat'ral t.: POPE A 67
as t. have been CLOU 8
dead selves to higher t. TENN 18
dropped t. are bound to sink —
　MOOR M 13
fairest t. have fleetest end,
　THOMP F 1

forget all t. but one, DE TA 2
full of slimy t. WALK 13
God of T. as They are! KIPL 29
good t. have perished utterly,
  WILD 11
grows such sweet t. WHITM 98
heavenly t. DONN 53
her least t. exprest, THOMP F 5
How all t. flare!) SCHW 7
impels/ All thinking t., WORD 36
indifferent t., WORD 63
keep t. whole. STRA 7
learn the simplest t. OLSO 13
leave all meaner t. POPE A 58
love all beauteous t., BRID R 5
mania of owning t., WHITM 75
mind, aspire to higher t.;
  SIDN 26
more t. in heaven and earth,
  SHAK 29
(No ideas/ but in t.) WILLI 29
not like some t., MOOR M 27
oddments of all t., POUN 54
only crazy t. OLSO 20
paltry, foolish, painted t. DRAY 7
remember t. I once read
  SNYD 18
rolls through all t. WORD 36
sea-hoard of deciduous t.,
  POUN 56
see t. bare to the buff
  STEVENSO R 16
slimy t. did crawl COLE SAM 34
Spirit of t. unseen, CARM 1
sweetest t. turn sourest
  SHAK 222
syntax of t. CUMM 44
T. and t.' selves WILB 8
t. are not what they seem.
  LONG 35
t. fall and are built YEATS 81
T. fall apart; YEATS 133
t. for to attain MARTIA 1
t. in which we have seen
  ourselves WILB 2
t. my fathers learned to do.
  AIKE 6
t. that I but half recall—
  WINT 1
t. themselves WILB 22
t. which enclose me, CUMM 48
t. which I have seen WORD 65
t. would come right again
  LARK 17
Three t. there be in man's opinion
  dear, GREV 7
Time the fatal wrack of mortal t.,
  BRAD 7
to all t. I had right? MILT 109
two hard t. to hit, POPE A 96
unhappy, far-off t., WORD 140
web of human t., SHEL 22
What lovely t. DE LA 20

wide world dreaming on t. to
  come SHAK 229
think: can't t. why! GILB 7
Haply I t. on thee, SHAK 194
I t. back SNYD 13
I t. I know. FROS 107
I t. we are in rats' alley
  ELIOT T 124
know what they t. SIMP 4
love and t., RANDS 4
made me t. of myself, WHITM 39
never t. of love; UNKN 74
red slayer t. he slays, EMER 6
slain t. he is slain, EMER 6
stay and t. of nought SHAK 208
they did not stop to t. CUMM 29
t. continually SPEND 11
t. him pleasant enough. LEAR 7
t. it's comical GILB 22
t. me strange or older, CORN 1
t. no ill, CAMPI 8
t. of me! JARR 25
t. of the beautiful town LONG 31
t./ Of the greatness, GRAV 39
t. of the right thing to say
  FROS 22
t. on thee, dear friend, SHAK 195
t. that I shall NASH 14
t. the parson found, HOLM 9
t. the thing farewell. TENN 56
To t. and hold my peace,
  WYAT 21
to t. is to be full of sorrow
  KEAT 47
to t. of you, GINS 20
truly what I do t." UNKN 161
We t. by feeling. ROET 58
what other people t.; YEATS 132
women grieve to t. they must be
  old. DANI S 7
thinking: impels/ All t. things,
  WORD 36
naked t. heart DONN 11
new t. is about loss. HASS 1
resembles all the old t. HASS 1
T. his prattle to be tedious,
  SHAK 92
t. woman RICH 13
Thus vainly t. SHAK 238
thinks: he t. no ill. SHAK 208
One t. of snow, JUST 7
t. about it for a Year; ROET 55
t. me young, SHAK 238
t. too little or too much:
  POPE A 78
what he t. of it a year hence!
  BYRO 52
thinly: t. clothed, WHITM 70
thinne: t. and lean without a fence
  or friend, HERB G 4
Third: George the T. KOCH 7
George the T. BENT 1
make a t. DRYD 10

second or t. hand, WHITM 76
t. day of Christmas, UNKN 276
t. so quaint and mouthy:
  BYRO 21
thirst: amorous t.; TASS 5
drink it shall not t. EMER 49
fear, t., hunger, CUNN J 4
great t., exceeding all excess,
  WILB 17
man can raise a t.; KIPL 13
Thirsting: T. and hungering,
  GRAV 4
thirsty: t. earth soaks up the rain,
  COWL 1
13th: hanging from the 1. floor/
  window. HARJ 1
thirtieth: t. year to heaven
  THOMA D 32
thirty: knotted t. times, —
  MOOR M 20
t. bob a week, DAVID 7
tramping his t. miles LAWR 14
Thirty-eight: rack up t. or forty
  UPDI 2
thirty-seven: now t. years old
  WHITM 74
thissell-cok: t. cryis MONTG 1
thistle: like the down of a t.,
  MOOR C 5
satanic t. GINS 40
Wind and T. BELL 7
Thomas: Lord T. was buried in the
  church, UNKN 179
True T. lay on Huntlie bank;
  UNKN 245
thonder-dent: hadde been a t.
  CHAU 63
thorn: laurel also bears a t.
  LAND 10
pull the t. SCOT WA 24
snail's on the t.: BROWNI R 66
t.-curst soil: VAN DY 5
wantons thro' the flowering t.:
  BURN 15
without t. the rose. MILT 69
thorns: crown of t. PLUN 2
crown of t. our Saviour wore
  UNKN 131
fuel wounding t.; SOUTHW 2
Hang on such t., SHAK 206
Roses have t., SHAK 199
t. of life! SHEL 45
thoroughbred: t. mental cases,
  LOWE R 55
thoroughfare: ancient, t.,/ The
  Roman Road. HARD 35
thou: God is thy law, t. mine:
  MILT 75
Little Jesus, wast T. shy
  THOMP F 4
Lo, Lord, T. ridest! CRAN H 38
t./ Art jealous, Lord, DONN 31

T. by old Adam wast begot,
  BRAD 9
T. hast conquered, SWIN 23
T. little Child, WORD 78
t. Prince of Walsingham,
  UNKN 169
t. thyself art thine own bait;
  DONN 7
Where art t., WORD 1
Why dost/ T. hide thy face?
  WRIG J 8
wilt t. leave me thus? WYAT 1
thought: armour is his honest t.,
  WOTT 1
binds/ of t. into the hues,
  AMMO 3
brain allows one half-formed t.
  ELIOT T 137
burning deed and t.! LONG 50
Chaos of t. and passion,
  POPE A 78
dregs of scattered t., SIDN 39
eternity of t., WORD 98
exalt the soul to solemn t.,
  THOMS J (1700–1748) 12
first in loftiness of t. DRYD 10
footpaths for the t. of Italy!
  LONG 20
from sex to soul, from soul to t.;
  CART 1
from t. to soul, CART 1
goodness beyond t., MILT 81
green t. in a green shade,
  MARV 18
'He t. me asleep; PATM 1
hidden/ In the light of t.,
  SHEL 70
human t. or form, SHEL 30
I wish I t. What Jolly Fun!
  RALEI 1
lived and t., ROBI 36
mighty t. HUNT 6
monarch T.'s dominion, POE 20
my stubborn t.: HERB G 9
no other t. POE 3
no t. apparent but burns JEFFE 4
objects of all t., WORD 36
oft was t., POPE A 21
parent before t., STEVENS 20
plan that pleased his boyish t.:
  WORD 4
power was never in his t.,
  SWIF 25
question with my jealous t.
  SHAK 208
same old t.: MAST 10
seem a moment's t., YEATS 1
sessions of sweet silent t.
  SHAK 195
sicklied o'er with the pale cast of
  t. SHAK 40
silence the envy in my t.
  YEATS 97

silent t. can bring, WORD 136
silken ties of love and t.
  FROS 102
simpletons t. a living fable
  MOOR M 24
speech created t., SHEL 54
strange seas of T., WORD 101
Stumbling from t. to thought,
  ROCH 9
sulfurous and t.-executing fires,
  SHAK 75
tell of saddest t. SHEL 71
those that lawless and incertain
  t. SHAK 115
t. and done, MUIR 11
t. by thought,/ 'Trampled its
  sparks SHEL 78
t. came like a full-blown rose
  KEAT 8
T. can but share/ Belief—
  CLARK A 1
t. confounds us MUIR 6
t. has changed to dream, Æ 3
t. is as a death, SHAK 211
t. is life BLAK 63
T. must length'n DANI S 4
t. of grief; WORD 67
t. of him I love. WHITM 46
t. of my death, ROET 15
t. of our past years WORD 80
t. of the light POE 25
t. styled intuition, RICH 22
t. that I would choose thee
  CALV 6
t. thee bright, SHAK 242
timely utterance gave that t.
  relief, WORD 67
tremble into t., COLE SAM 12
trick of t. BROWNI E 9
utmost bound of human t.
  TENN 132
vouchsafe me but this loving t.
  SHAK 196
want/ Of t. is death; BLAK 63
where I t. I was safest,
  WHITM 95
while he lived never t. of death.
  GREV 8
whirl of t. oppressed SWIF 3
white, celestial t.; VAUG 21
without t. WILLI 6
thoughtless: in t. honor WILB 22
thoughts: at meals some odd t.
  BYRO 32
banish the t. of day. LONG 15
breathe those t. MICH 2
bring my t. to an end.
  SMIT ST 9
busy t. outnumber SHEL 42
clothe me with dark t.,
  DANI S 10
crown my t. with acts, SHAK 113
Drive my dead t. SHEL 46

flocks are t. MEYN 3
fond and wayward t. WORD 44
frame my t., SPENS 5
From heav'nly t. all true delight
  doth spring. CAMPI 27
holding men's t. MACDONO 1
ill t. die and good are born—
  BROWNI E/GUIN 1
in your sweet t. SHAK 214
judge womans t. by tears,
  DONN 61
lover's t. disdain, CAMPI 21
mother of fresh t. WORD 149
my ripe t. SHAK 217
my t. and me. MARV 27
My t. are minutes, SHAK 93
My t. hold mortal strife; DRUM 2
not farther than my t. SHAK 204
o'er my t. WORD 97
pure and circling t., MARV 31
red hollyberries, t., SAND 24
sad scenes and t. and feelings
  vanish THOMS J (1834–1882) 7
Sweet are the t. that savour of
  content, GREE 1
tender and wondrous t.,
  WHITM 12
t. and my discourse as madmen's
  SHAK 242
t. begin to shrivel up FIEL R 1
t./ Continual climb,
  THOMS J (1700–1748) 6
t., delivered to me CRAN H 41
t. enticed mine eye MUND 2
T., like old vultures, WATT I 1
t. more elevate, MILT 60
T. of a dry brain ELIOT T 35
t. of love. TENN 69
t. of other days SHAP 10
t. of youth LONG 32
t. that arise in me. TENN 1
T. that do often lie WORD 87
t. that made it ache, COWP 3
t. that please me less and less
  betray me. GREV 3
t. they cannot feel, VERY 2
t. to rive the heart HOUS 24
t./ Were roots MARK 2
ugly t. That drive them SASS 14
vestige of the t. ROSS C 20
What t. I have of you GINS 36
wind in procession t., WHITM 12
wood of t. THOMA E 4
thousand: conscience hath a t.
  several tongues, SHAK 99
flag has braved a t. years
  CAMPB T 10
Hell, rising from a t. thrones,
  POE 13
in the a t. errors note,
  SHAK 239
launched a t. ships, MARL 3
many t. mists, WORD 52

More than a t. years
STEPHENS 2

night has a t. eyes, BOUR 1

One bullet in ten t. SPEND 20

stones have stood for a t. years,
JEFFE 43

Ten t. times UNKN 17

ten t. years SNYD 2, 20

t. corpses lie. CRAN S 9

t. fearful wracks; SHAK 97

t. natural shocks/ That flesh is heir
to, SHAK 39

t. rills their mazy progress
GRAY 23

t. sweets HERR 14 "t. types are
gone; TENN 35

t. years pass VAN DY 4

thousands: Hundreds of t. counted,
SHAP 11

lived t. of years ago, WHITM 75

Samson I my t. slay.' FRANK 1

sod what t. meet! — MELV 16

Terraced t. died, HEAN 18

t. counted every groan, ARNO 35

t./ Of arrowhead leavings
SNYD 1

t. of her sons, WORD 109

T. of little boys BLAK 91

t. of marriages LARK 18

thraldom: coupled to foul t.
BARBO 2

thrash: tantrums t. to a whale's
rage. LOWE R 13

thrashed: Wellington t. Bonaparte,
GILB 24

thread: Any silk, and t., SHAK 182

dragonfly/ Hangs like a blue t.
ROSS D 4

Feels at each t., POPE A 71

gossamer t. you fling WHITM 55

Nor a t. of her hair, HARD 45

t. through a needle. MERW 10

t. separates itself LAWR 41

With a silken t. of my own hand's
weaving; KEAT 27

threadbare: every t. sail, HOLM 18

t. art of my eye LOWE R 43

threaded: lightly t. with nimble
feet BINY 5

threading: t. a dream, HUNT 6

threads: invisible t. above the Site,
BISH 33

snip the intellectual golden t.
GINS 12

threaten'd: reader's t. (not in vain)
with 'sleep.' POPE A 26

threatening: t. Tunes and low —
DICKI 159

threatens: Steed t. steed, SHAK 57

Threat'ning: T. with deluge SWIF 7

three: answer my questions t.,
UNKN 162

Batter my heart, t.-personed God;
DONN 8

Imp at t. and wench at 'leben
WALK 9

listens like a t. years' child:
COLE SAM 29

married t. wives at one time.
LEAR 19

narrow grave just six by t.,
UNKN 50

part woman, t. parts a child,
YEATS 88

spoken t. hours, CARRO 14

straiked me t. times o'er her
knee; UNKN 5

they gave him t. cheers,
CARRO 18

T. April perfumes SHAK 227

t./ dusky syllables SAND 21

T. French hens, UNKN 276

t. generations of one house
POUN 26

t. gipsies a-come to my door,
UNKN 311

T. Hail Marys KAVA 11

t. hot Junes SHAK 227

t. kinds of people: ABRA 1

t. locks o' her yellow hair,
UNKN 32

t. pale beautiful pilgrims: AIKE 5

t. pale figures AUDE 81

t. parts coward — SHAK 35

t. posts driven upright AUDE 81

T. score and ten. MOTH 12

t. ships come sailing by, UNKN 8

t. stout and stalwart sons,
UNKN 306

t. strange angels. LAWR 49

t. summer's pride,/ t. beauteous
springs SHAK 227

T. things there be in man's
opinion dear, GREV 7

t. times t. ROON 1

t. white leopards sat ELIOT T 6

T. winters cold SHAK 227

T. years she grew WORD 48

we galloped all t.; BROWNI R 35

woodspurge flowered, t. cups in
one. ROSS D 10

Threes: T. and fours and twelves,
LAWR 54

threescore: Now, of my t. years and
ten, HOUS 39

thresh: t., and ply; HARD 50

threshed: shadowy flail hath t. the
corn MILT 23

threshold: green/ Before my t.,
AKEN 1

t. of the new. WALL 4

threw: as those before us t.,
SHEL 81

from hate away she t., SHAK 241

t. a pearl away SHAK 138

T. it down, SCHW 1

thrice: snow lump t. his own slight
size HARD 43

T. happy Iles, MILT 65

T. the brinded cat hath mew'd.
SHAK 111

T. welcome, WORD 151

thrift: Bid the slaves of t. farewell.
JOHN S (1709–1784) 11

without t., without good,
UNKN 43

thriftless: all-eating shame and t.
praise SHAK 185

thrifty: housewife that's t. SHERI 1

thrill: i like the t. CUMM 51

shiver, and then a t., HOLM 9

thrilling: reside/ In t. region
SHAK 115

voice so t. WORD 139

thrive: could I never t., SHAK 177

Let copulation t.; SHAK 80

Sunlit pallets never t.; HOUS 47

thrives: nothing t. EMER 5

thriving: Kentuck she was t.,
WOOL 4

throat: ache here in the t., RILE 3

beak down my t. LA FO 2

body taking by the t. DICKEY 8

breath is tight in its t.,
WHITM 73

bunch of lace at his t. NOYE 8

Choked my t. SNYD 9

Cold air bites the t. SNYD 44

Cut your own t. LOWE R 1

felt you round my t. HOPE L 3

fishbone/ in the city's t.
LOWE R 18

fruits like honey to the t.
ROSS C 11

grunts in my t. LEVE 21

little t. labours with inspiration,
BLAK 37

lost in your eyes, ears, nose, and
t. KOCH 4

mocking-bird's t., WHITM 62

poured down his t.
BROWNI R 36

Reptilian green the wrinkled t.,
WINT 5

sinks into my t. her tiger's tooth,/
Stealing my breath of life,
MCKA 2

soldier tore from his t., ROSE 7

Song of the bleeding t.,
WHITM 47

stroked your cold, pulsing t.
LEVE 22

t. and breast and wings vibrates
BLAK 37

t. of one bird JEFFE 17

words live in my t. LORD 1

throats: changed their t. YEATS 41

dry t. rattle, SHEL 63

t. of birds. YEATS 41
t. of hell to drink, CHES 7
t. which it hid among? RANS 35
throb: t. In witching chords,
　STEVENS 34
throbbed: war-drum t. no longer,
　TENN 76
throbbing: huge, doomed t. FULL 2
Like a taxi t. waiting,
　ELIOT T 133
measur'd dual t. WHITM 59
no fiery t. pain,
　JOHN S (1709–1784) 4
throbbings: t. of noontide.
　HARD 27
throbs: their powerful t.,
　WHITM 32
throes: helpless in my t., SIDN 6
throne: Beat upward to God's t.
　BROWNI E 1
before God's t. WILD 11
Circle his t. rejoicing, MILT 81
Death has reared himself a t.
　POE 11
dower his burning t., MARL 5
hold the sov'reign t.?
　BIBL, O.T. 41
inherit the t. of glory:
　BIBL, O.T. 8
like a burnished t., SHAK 5
On a black t. reigns POE 16
Queen-Moon is on her t.,
　KEAT 48
royal t. of kings, this sceptered
　isle, SHAK 88
sable t. behold POPE A 1
Thine eternal t., DOAN 2
t. of royal state, MILT 58
t./ Of the Invisible! BYRO 4
T. of Wit; DRYD 30
to a golden t., POE 30
up to the T., KIPL 25
throned: becomes/ The t. monarch
　SHAK 123
Thrones: Cities and T. and Powers
　KIPL 14
Hell, rising from a thousand t.,
　POE 13
t., and towers. CAMPB R 6
throng: angel t., bewinged, bedight/
　In veils, POE 30
hideous t. rush out forever,
　POE 23
T. to the bar, SHAK 99
thronged: t. about the brow
　SHEL 79
throngful: shall gather dew,/
　Dreaming in t. city WHITT 28
Thronging: odours, fruits, and
　flocks,/ T. the Seas MILT 5
t. years in glory rise. BRYA 14

throngs: cutpurses come not to t.;
　SHAK 76
dusky cane-lipped t. TOOM 3
throstle: linnet and the t., NOYE 3
throttle: t. in his hand, UNKN 55
through: clear grit t. and t.;
　WOOL 3
dreaming t. the twilight
　ROSS C 34
Flyin' t. the air, MAXW 1
ghastly t. the drizzling rain
　TENN 21
light pushes t.; LAWR 1
no road t. the woods. KIPL 28
pass'd t. a populous city
　WHITM 60
sap/ went t. MOOR M 21
serve me seven years,/ T. weal or
　woe UNKN 247
swim for miles t. the desert
　SIMP 1
T. all his veins
　JOHN S (1709–1784) 17
t. all its din, THOR 5
t. an Alpine village LONG 21
t. doors— WHITM 7
t. the darkness, WHITM 56
t. the faded leaf TENN 22
T. the pale door POE 23
t. the town, MILLE W 1
T. the windows— WHITM 7
t. the world LONG 26
Thy spell t. him, ROSS D 2
wind is passing t. ROSS C 35
window, t. thy grace. HERB G 73
throughout: t. the war, GILB 24
throw: poison'd entrails t.
　SHAK 111
t. a dart at BROWNE 3
T. away thy rod: HERB G 24
T. away thy wrath. HERB G 24
T. down the ball, ye Jew's
　daughter, UNKN 133
t. in Drummer Hodge, HARD 19
T. my heart SHAK 8
whirl three times and t. HUGO 5
throwest: Set less than thou t.;
　SHAK 71
throwing: always t. bricks,
　LIND V 15
Eyes around him t., GAY 2
T. myself on the sand, WHITM 63
venturing, t., WHITM 55
thrown: echoing straits between us
　t., ARNO 41
nature's limits t., FRENE 4
son's body was t. LOWE R 19
t. away her electric toothbrush,
　JARR 12
T. into despair YEATS 63
We have but t., SHEL 81
What sums are t. away!'
　POPE A 100

woman's glance instinctive t.:
　MELV 6
throws: distance t. them forth,
　GUNN 11
t. His flight precipitant, MILT 65
thrush: aged t., frail, gaunt,
　HARD 18
Solitary the t., WHITM 47
thrust: Phœbus t. out his golden
　hedde, SPENS 55
T. close your smile LEVE 17
thrusts: victor's tireless/ t.,
　BARA 11
Thucydides: Exiled T. knew
　AUDE 72
Thule: From an ultimate dim T.
　POE 16
thumb: Dumb/ As old medallions to
　the t., MACL 1
naughty t. of science CUMM 34
put in his t., MOTH 20
Putting in his t., CAREY 3
sucks his t. in secret LORD 4
that inevitable t. CRAN H 37
thumbs: Africa? A book one t.
　CULL 6
fire to thaw our t. TROW 5
t. and toes and teeth. JARR 1
thump: strong you t., O terrible
　drums— WHITM 8
thunder: all-dreaded t.-stone;
　SHAK 18
all-shaking t., SHAK 75
as rattling t. SHAK 7
came a burst of t. HEMA 2
clothed his neck with t.?
　BIBL, O.T. 17
dry sterile t. without rain
　ELIOT T 145
exulting t. of your race; ARNO 37
fly/ From t.'s violence. CAMPI 13
Glorious the t.'s roar: SMAR 9
His cloudless t. MILT 117
hum/ Bulges to t. GUNN 11
In t. lightning MILT 104
laid aside his t., OVID 4
levynne and the t. poures,
　CHAT 2
Loud are the t. drums UNKN 120
night's t. far away had rolled
　THOMA E 9
plunging through the t.-storm;
　TENN 75
sport'st amid the lightning-flash
　and t.-cloud, WHITM 105
still/ in the t. air, LAWR 56
surge and t. of the Odyssey.
　LANG 3
Then spoke the t. Da
　ELIOT T 152
t. of approximate words.
　GUNN 10

t.'s rattling clymmynge sound
CHAT 2
tumult as they t. by, POE 40
voice than t. is more loud,
THOR 5
We heard the miniature t.
FROS 98
thunderbolt: like a t. he falls.
TENN 12
thunderbolts: oak-cleaving t.,
SHAK 75
thundered: Volleyed and t.;
TENN 8
thundering: t. from the heights.
LONG 29
thunderous: learns the storm-cloud's
t. melody, STEPHEN 3
Thunders: heart regularly/ T. —
KIRK 3
hold their t. in, LOWE J 14
t. of the upper deep; TENN 58
t. rolled; JOHN J 2
t. shook the mighty deep,
HOLM 18
thurification: way of t. SKEL 9
Thursday: T.'s child has far to go,
MOTH 22
thus: t. to ruminate, SHAK 211
wilt thou leave me t.? WYAT 1
thwart: t. disnatured torment
SHAK 72
thy: Bitter plaints to rue t. wrong,
UNKN 169
Farewell, Love, and all t. laws for
ever: WYAT 5
message from t. glass, DANI S 15
Not for t. harms, THOMP F 9
These are t. wonders, Lord of
love, HERB G 33
T. spell through him, ROSS D 2
T. word is all, if we could spell.
HERB G 32
thyme: once was covered with t.,
HABE 2
thysel: as it pleases best t.,
BURN 32
thyself: Know then t., POPE A 78
thou t. art thine own bait;
DONN 7
T. away art present still
SHAK 204
t. that hast misdone, WYAT 2
T. thou gav'st, SHAK 220
T. thy own enjoyment. WORD 23
Tiber: Let Rome in T. melt
SHAK 3
tick: said in every t.: CORN 3
t. in the silence SHAP 6
ticked: t. yesterday so well?
WILLI 39
ticket: t. for the peepshow.
MACN 8
ticking: t. of Eternity. MILLA 29

Tickle: T. treasure, SURR 1
tickled: captain t. the crew.
CARRY 9
tickling: "Who's that t. my back?"
SERR 1
ticklishness: climbing t., CHAU 1
tide: barges drift/ With the turning
t. ELIOT T 138
boat was on the t.; HOLM 10
call of the running t. MASE 12
filthy modern t. YEATS 143
first t.-ripples, ROET 42
float upon the t. of state,
SWIF 16
heard recede the disappointed t.!
DICKI 96
left by the t., WHITM 2
rode that t. To Ararat; WILB 38
swift t. of blood NEME 1
t. in the affairs of men SHAK 50
t. is full, the moon lies fair
ARNO 1
t. is over you, SLES 4
t. rises, the t. falls, LONG 46
t. runs high, THAX 1
t. rustling in, ROET 44
t. swings you away LEVE 12
till the T. DICKI 63
top of the t. CARRO 11
unstinted t. confined;
JOHN S (1822–1882) 1
what no t. Shall ever wash away,
LAND 6
when will that t. draw JEFFE 29
where the t. has rolled you.
KIPL 16
with the swelling t. TURB 1
world's t. is bearing me along;
BRON 11
your tearful t.; FRENE 3
tideless: t. floods of Nothingness
ROBI 37
within this t. spell? CRAN H 23
tides: Push in their t.;
THOMA D 29
salt t. seaward flow; ARNO 9
t. have equal times SOUTHW 8
tossed hours upon the t. of fever,
MILLE V 1
with moons and t. HERB G 53
tidings: brings us glad t. UNKN 72
t. of my friend, TENN 57
tidy: Leaving the gardens t.,
LARK 18
tie: shirt and t. were luminous.
WAGO 1
t. back your hair, SWEN 4
tied: Creator, whom sin nor nature
t., DONN 68
t./ By a chance bond THOR 1
t. rags on their feet. SAND 23
t. to me/ As to a dog's tail?
YEATS 150

t. together with rhyme,
LOWE J 4
tiers: t. of eyes, MERR 11
ties: grape tendril/ t. a knot
MOOR M 20
one sure band/ T. the whole
frame, HERB G 15
silken t. of love and thought
FROS 102
t. me to the woman WHITM 21
tiger: Came Christ the t.
ELIOT T 31
Can kill a t. LOWE R 34
fierce t.'s jaws, SHAK 189
Hyrcan t.; SHAK 110
imitate the action of the t.:
SHAK 56
O t.'s heart SHAK 61
rode on a t.; MONK 1
sinks into my throat her t.'s
tooth, MCKA 2
smile on the face of the T.
MONK 1
T., burning bright BLAK 81
T. Christ unsheathed SCHW 1
t. on the road. JEFFE 9
t. springs in the new year.
ELIOT T 34
tiger-lily: Heavily hangs the t.
TENN 110
tigering: green t. the gold.
HUGH T 10
tigers: Catches t. In red weather.
STEVENS 5
guardsmen fed to the t. LI PO 2
tamed and shabby t. HODG 1
tawny t. feel MELV 10
t. prance across a screen, RICH 1
tight: Balls t. in a tough hair sack
SNYD 37
bos'sun t., and a midshipmite,
GILB 55
breath is t. in its throat,
WHITM 73
hawser'd t., WHITM 28
Pope's t. back TATE A 8
t. belly of the dead SHAP 15
Wolf's-bane, t.-rooted, KEAT 42
tile: Furnished with t., EMER 44
tiled: steam of the t. shower stalls,
HECH 8
tiles: On the t. of Kyōto. MAHON 4
tillage: half a t. GOLD 2
tills: Man comes and t. the field
TENN 120
t. the sand BOYD 1
tilt: t. at all I meet; POPE A 89
t. their aggregate beast MACN 1
tilted: t. a poke of dust SERV 7
tilting: Who on a t. deck sings
DAY 3
timber: Last of its t., — HOLM 6

Like seasoned t., HERB G 72
makes the t. rot; RALEG 14
timbered: dark wainscot and t.
   roof, NEWB 3
timbrels: What pipes and t.?
   KEAT 37
Timbuctoo: seen T., BYRO 52
time: achieve in t. GILB 28
all in war with T. SHAK 137
All t. is unredeemable.
   ELIOT T 15
'All T.'s delight/ Hath she
   DE LA 24
avails not, t. nor place —
   WHITM 19
Back in a t. made simple
   FROS 39
before my t. SHAK 96
before their t. HOUS 50
bettering of the t., SHAK 196
Bind us in t., CRAN H 50
Bird of T. OMAR 1
bleeding to death of t. GRAV 4
boar trampled down in ivy t.
   GRAV 35
born out of my due t., MORR 3
bourne of T. and Place TENN 10
But at my back from t. to t.
   ELIOT T 131
By t. and the elements;
   CRAN H 47
By t.'s fell hand defaced.
   SHAK 211
cannot conquer T. AUDE 2
chained to T., SHEL 3
check t. broke in a disordered
   string; SHAK 93
chief good and market of his t.
   SHAK 35
chronicle of wasted t. SHAK 228
clerks of T., ROBI 7
count the clock that tells the t.,
   SHAK 186
Daughters of T., EMER 13
Devouring T., SHAK 189
dreamin' arl the t. NEWB 1
Driving around, I will waste more
   t. BLY 1
drops of this most balmy t.
   SHAK 229
dust is for a t. MOOR M 16
eternall Glasse,/ Where t. doth
   end, GREV 8
Even such is t. RALEG 3
every t. and place,
   JOHN S (1822–1882) 1
Fate, T., Occasion, Chance, and
   Change? SHEL 55
Father T. and Mother Earth,
   MERR 3
Footprints on the sands of t.;
   LONG 36
for that t. of year. TOOM 4

forget t. and death: ROET 13
from t. to t.,/ Look'd up
   WHITM 111
from t.'s to-morrows. SASS 6
give you the t. of day.
   MERE W 1
glued there by t.: MOSS 5
hear my true t. broke. SHAK 93
How lazily t. creeps KING H 2
human kind/ Cannot bear very
   much reality./ T. past and T.
   future ELIOT T 19
Hurry up please its t.
   ELIOT T 128
I measure t. ROET 29
I was a fish/ In the Paleozoic t.
   SMIT L 1
I wasted t., SHAK 93
If all t. is eternally present
   ELIOT T 15
In t. the strong and stately turrets
   fall, FLET G EL 1
it wastes its t. JARR 9
It will not be in our t. JEFFE 24
keep t. with my salt tears;
   JONS 4
Keeping t., time, time, POE 10
knoweth not his t.: BIBL, O.T. 2
last syllable of recorded t.,
   SHAK 114
last t. I saw you GINS 39
little t. they prized NEME 1
Long t. a-wondering ROBI 8
lopped tree in t. may grow again,
   SOUTHW 7
loss of t. and loss of sport
   JONS 3
Love's not T.'s fool, SHAK 232
Made weak by t. and fate,
   TENN 135
maps are of t., not place,
   REED H 3
married three wives at one t.
   LEAR 19
measures all our t.; HERB G 11
mild Heaven a t. ordains,
   MILT 120
minding no t., WHITM 65
Muse herself/ All T. fulfils,
   GOGA 2
new direction of T. LAWR 47
new wail my dear t.'s waste.
   SHAK 195
no delight to pass away the t.,
   SHAK 96
no enemy but t.; YEATS 68
No mark of her late t. HARD 45
no precious t. at all SHAK 208
no t. for idle cares POE 40
no t. to stand and stare.
   DAVIE W 2
none can call again the passed t.
   SPENS 22

not control of t., RICH 26
not in t. and space. MUIR 1
not my T., SLES 1
not of an age, but for all t.!
   JONS 44
nothing 'gainst T.'s scythe
   SHAK 186
O T. and Change! — WHITT 28
O world! O life! O t.! SHEL 34
Old T. is still a-flying; HERR 55
out of key with his t., POUN 36
pale angle of t. And eternity.
   MOMA 2
perhaps present in t. future,
   ELIOT T 15
pomps of that t., LIND V 5
pruning-knife of T. HOLM 15
race of t., MILT 105
rains that come in t. KAVA 12
Redeem/ The t. ELIOT T 12
reflected in the coming t.
   LONG 27
Science! true daughter of old T.
   POE 1
scythers, T. and Death,
   LOWE R 59
sea of t. ARNO 34
secures/ Escape from the weekday
   t. MACN 22
sense from gnawing t. DAY 8
separated souls,/ All t. and space
   controls: LOVE 7
Sigh no more, ladies./ T. is male
   RICH 21
silver chime/ Move in melodious
   t., MILT 39
since the birth of t., WHITT 22
sing the T.'s uncertaintie,
   DANI G 1 Singing all t.,
   WHITM 65
Singing all t. WHITM 65
singing at the t., STEPHENS 9
So hallow'd and so gracious is the
   t. SHAK 19
So little t. we live in t., WARR 2
So long t. war of valiant men,
   SURR 8
soldier of t., STEVENS 12
sons of men snared in an evil t.,
   BIBL, O.T. 2
spend the t. luxuriously
   DANI S 19
spots of t., WORD 113
Spring's an expansive t.:
   ROSS C 37
Stand in T.'s eye, KIPL 14
stones and trees, insensible of t.,
   BRAD 4
storm of t., EMER 47
sublime,/ Out of space — out of t.
   POE 16
sun in t. forgets for to retire
   FLET G EL 1

Sun-flower! weary of t., BLAK 53
surprised half the t.: AMMO 10
Suspended in t., ELIOT T 60
Swift speeding T., DANI S 14
swift-footed T., SHAK 189
takes her t. SAND 7
That t. of year SHAK 215
thee O T. MILT 45
Their t. past, WILLI 8
this our t., SHAK 228
till t. and times are done
　YEATS 139
T., a maniac scattering dust,
　TENN 28
t. allows/ In all his tuneful
　turning THOMA D 20
t. and chance happeneth to them
　all. BIBL, O.T. 1
T. and death shall depart
　DRYD 9
t.,/ And drawing days out,
　SHAK 46
T. and fevers burn away
　AUDE 54
T. and Nature gently spare
　EMER 12
t. brings down BRAD 10
T. cannot alter but obey Fate's
　laws. TOWN 1
t. comes, not only you and I,
　FLEC 2
t./ Crown'd my felicity,
　PHILI K 1
t. decays? SHAK 212
T. deceive you, AUDE 2
T. doth settle. HOSK 1
T. doth transfix SHAK 210
t. enough to mourn BRON 4
t. enough to sleep. HOUS 48
t. flew by, BURN 46
t. for carving. POUN 53
t. for mirth, HERR 48
t. for mirth and play, SMAR 1
T. for you and T. for me,
　ELIOT T 79
t. for you to wake; MEW 1
t. future contained in t. past.
　ELIOT T 15
t. has come," CARRO 39
T. has estranged you MILLA 5
t. has no sway, LOWE J 7
T. held me green and dying
　THOMA D 21
T. his sickle brings/ In vain,
　CAREW 11
T. in Eternity. HERB CH 5
T. in the hand RICH 26
T. in the heart AIKE 4
T. is a great teacher, SAND 19
t. is a tree CUMM 9
t. is inches AUDE 92
t. is now propitious, ELIOT T 136
t. is old. VAN DO 2

T. is over you, SLES 4
t. is short AUDE 91
T. is the fire SCHW 8
T. is the school SCHW 8
T. is with materials filled;
　LONG 5
T. leads me, MILT 14
T., like an ever-rolling stream,
　WATT I 3
T. made me his numbering clock.
　SHAK 93
t. may cease MARL 1
t. of night, SHAK 128
t. of peace. BIBL, O.T. 5
t. of their growth/ Fretting for
　their decay: ROSE 4
t. of war, BIBL, O.T. 5
t. prattled away, SIDN 4
T. present and T. past
　ELIOT T 15
T. renders/ His last award,
　BYRO 34
t. shall put them both to bed,
　HOUS 22
T. so vicious ROBI 16
t. stand fixed! MILT 105
T. stoops to no man's lure;
　SWIN 14
(T. strangely spent) SUCK 7
t. that cut'st down all! HERR 22
T. that is moved SLES 1
T. the fatal wrack of mortal
　things, BRAD 7
t. the field were mown. HOUS 29
T. the subtle thief of youth,
　MILT 14
t. to be born, BIBL, O.T. 3
t. to be old, EMER 46
t. to dance; BIBL, O.T. 4
t. to die; BIBL, O.T. 3
t. to hate; BIBL, O.T. 5
t. to laugh; BIBL, O.T. 4
t. to love, BIBL, O.T. 5
T., to make me grieve, HARD 27
t. to mourn, BIBL, O.T. 4
t. to plant, BIBL, O.T. 3
t. to weep, BIBL, O.T. 4
t. too swift, PEEL 7
T. was. HAYD 14
T./ Wheeling and whispering
　FLEC 7
t. when it's later CREE 15
t., where lucid Avon stray'd,
　GRAY 28
T. will come SHAK 211
T. will not be ours forever,
　JONS 48
T., with a gift of tears; SWIN 1
T. writes no wrinkles BYRO 3
T., you old gipsy man, HODG 11
T.'s best jewel SHAK 212
T.'s consuming rage. DANI S 12

T.'s course to slower speeding,
　CAMPB T 7
t.'s deer is slain, MUIR 10
t.'s furrows I behold, SHAK 190
T.'s noblest offspring BERK 1
T.'s precious chronic invalid
　RICH 22
T.'s the king of men; SHAK 139
T.'s winged chariot MARV 34
took up the glass of T., TENN 70
tract of t. begins to weave
　VAUX 2
triumph over t. and space!
　ARNO 37
unimaginable touch of T.
　WORD 9
unswept stone, besmeared with
　sluttish t. SHAK 207
wake us/ T. and time over.
　LARK 8
walls of T.; LONG 4
wasteful T. debateth with Decay,
　SHAK 187
wastes of t. SHAK 186
weak piping t. of peace, SHAK 96
When t. is broke SHAK 93
whiner, who wastes your t.
　SNOD 3
whirling circles of t. JEFFE 23
wings of T. EMER 8
wooed her in the winter t.,
　UNKN 99
world enough, and t., MARV 33
world of t. beyond me;
　ELIOT T 96
worst t. of the year/ For a
　journey, ELIOT T 49
You die in T., HERB CH 5
timelessness: spirit drinking t.;
　SPEND 17
Timely: T. blossom, Infant fair,
　PHILI A 1
t. utterance gave that thought
　relief, WORD 67
Time's: T. the king of men;
　SHAK 139
Times: grieve they lived not in these
　t. DRAY 8
hours and t. of your desire?
　SHAK 208
How many t. DICKI 31
I have nine t. to die. PLATH 54
knots till/ knotted thirty t., —
　MOOR M 20
lived in important places, t.
　KAVA 4
Old t. dar EMME 1
tides have equal t. SOUTHW 8
T. go by turns, SOUTHW 8
t. his jump HIRS 1
wreathing his body seven t.
　round SMAR 2

toil: Ambition mock their useful t.,
GRAY 8
blessing of Earth is t. VAN DY 5
Double, double t. and trouble;
SHAK 112
fatuous sunbeams t. OWEN 27
In sequent t. SHAK 209
No grief, no care, no t.
UNKN 147
reap the harvest with enduring t.,
TENN 91
strain of t., GLAD 1
T., envy, want,
JOHN S (1709–1784) 18
t. from day to day,
JOHN S (1709–1784) 2
t. has left its mark: YEATS 24
Weary with t., SHAK 193
toilers: old t., soil makers: HALL 3
toilet: rising from the t. seat.
LEVE 14
toilets: flush/ Of health and t.,
HECH 10
toiling: pleasantly t. for pleasure,
PRAE 4
T. over a lump of clay JOHN J 3
T., — rejoicing, — sorrowing,
LONG 49
toils: revolves and t., SPEND 9
t. of the day: CARRO 15
token: t. of the drops of blood
UNKN 130
tokens: these lovely t. JACK 4
told: Dutch clock it t. me FIEL E 2
have years t.: SHAK 238
I t. her all my heart, BLAK 43
I was t. to be happy, RUKE 11
sailor t. it to me. WHITM 89
simple news that Nature t.,
DICKI 145
tale/ T. by an idiot, SHAK 114
t. by Indian fires THAC 2
t. my Soul to sing — DICKI 25
t. of the good All-father
LOWE J 12
t. old stories MOMA 5
t. us what he was, ROBI 13
tole: To be t. BROWN S 3
tolerance: all Platonic t. vain
YEATS 118
toll: Let the bell t.! — POE 29
T. for the brave — COWP 8
T. on, thou passing bell; BOLE 2
tolled: bell t. on thy burial day,
COWP 11
Great Paris t. her bell SHAP 27
tolling: hear the t. bell SPEND 14
t. his bell at noon, EMER 18
towers/ T. reminiscent bells,
ELIOT T 150
Tom: T. will injure nothing.
UNKN 263

tomatoes: babies in the t.! —
GINS 37
tomb: book a churchyard t.
KEAT 35
build your t., SHEL 65
distant shadow of the t.,
MERE G 15
door of a legended t.; POE 49
dost thou in this living t.?
ARNO 30
fair Fidele's grassy t. COLL 1
ghost from the t., SHEL 26
here's the t. JONS 32
in a fleshy t., COWP 16
into the quiet t., BEDD 11
kings for such a t. MILT 35
Making their t. SHAK 217
monument without a t., JONS 43
no ponderous t.; BYRO 56
our earth is a t.! BROWNI R 26
scarce/ Adjusted in the T.
DICKI 37
tell the lover's t. THOMA D 23
t. among green shades
UNKN 253
t. by the side of the sea. POE 6
t. from out whose sounding door
POE 43
t. in Palestine STEVENS 61
t. of Robin Herrick HERR 53
t. Shall list and founder SHAP 25
t.-stones where flowers should be;
BLAK 65
waits/ The triumph or the t.
TIMR 2
with no hero-courageous/ T.
KAVA 24
with songs of woe,/ Round about
her t. SHAK 132
womb/ So to the t.; BACO 1
tomb'd: T. in a Christal stone,
HERR 26
tombe: marble for a t., HABI 3
tombless: t. as their flesh;
BYRO 11
tombs: Gilded t. do worms infold.
SHAK 119
in the cool t. SAND 6
like crouching t. SPEND 4
living in the t. LINC 2
still as t.
THOMS J (1834–1882) 3
tyrants' crests and t. of brass
SHAK 229
Tom-lin: young T. is there.
UNKN 238
tom-tit: little t. GILB 29
tomorra: comin' down t. FRENC 2
to-morrow: I shall die t.; HOUS 12
mandrake with t.'s scream.
THOMA D 6
to-day will die t.; SWIN 14
T., and T., and T., SHAK 114

T. comes December. HOUS 19
'T. is Saint Crispian:' SHAK 60
T. sees another race BYRO 34
tomorrow: change by t., MOOR T 2
die for him t." UNKN 39
flower that smiles today,/ T. will
be dying. HERR 55
nothing to wear t. LORD 5
Today and t.; ROSS C 30
t. all too shaken. SURR 2
T. I will be sweet God, PLATH 10
t. is our permanent address
CUMM 2
T. is Saint Valentine's day,
SHAK 36
T. to fresh woods and pastures
new. MILT 33
woman named T. SAND 7
to-morrows: from time's t. SASS 6
tom-tom: t. scrimmage CRAN H 25
tom-toms: hear t. just as plain.
JOHN H 1
know/ About t.? JOHN H 1
ton: central t. of every place,
SCHW 9
tone: Allegheny graves its t.
SIGO 2
By his merry t. UNKN 157
ditties of no t.: KEAT 38
give the day a scientific t.
CARRY 7
give the place a t.; UNTE 2
sang my sour t. SNOD 16
t. of languid Nature. COWP 19
t. their rumble down. HUGH L 8
tones: clear harp in diverse t.,
TENN 18
Sweet t. are remembered not;
SHEL 89
thy t. are soft; CALV 5
tong: he lackt a t., SPENS 44
tonge: his t. and his hand CHAU 87
tongue: cheek or t. be dumb;
HERR 48
enjailed my t., SHAK 86
every t. brings in a several tale,
SHAK 99
eye, t., sword, SHAK 33
false-speaking t.: SHAK 238
fetters of my t. MICH 2
Flame t. of the dragon SNYD 30
French, felicitous t., MACL 8
give to my t. the lie. SIDN 16
haud your t., UNKN 79
he poked out/ His t., CULL 13
hold my speechless t. HOUS 7
lady with a terrible t., RANS 5
leaping t. of bloom FROS 119
make her airy t. more hoarse
SHAK 143
Music's golden t. KEAT 5
my t. could utter TENN 1

nothing/ speaks in its own t.,
LEVE 6
obnoxious to each carping t.
BRAD 16
of t. or pen, WHITT 21
over my t. LORD 1
parching t. KEAT 39
pillar of your t. PLATH 25
plunged your t. WHITM 78
rank t. blossom into speech.]
BROWNI R 15
Riots with his t. TATE A 15
rude hand no ill T. light PRIO 5
so curst a t., HARI 1
spared his t. and pen SWIF 25
stones have neither speech nor t.,
VAUG 1
strange quick t. RANS 35
Temperament without a t.,
EMER 20
thigh and t., LEVE 1
t. could no longer CARRO 16
t. may speak; VERY 2
t. of brute, MILT 93
t. still edifies his ears, POPE A 22
t./ That Shakespeare spake;
WORD 28
t. with a tang, SHAK 159
t.'s thin tip, SPENC A 4
truth in every shepherd's t.,
RALEG 7
Twining to a t. of fire,
BRID R 13
With spitting t., KIZE 3
You stop my t., SPENS 5
tongued: communication/ Of the
dead is t. ELIOT T 64
tongueless: Asking forgiveness of his
t. head. WILB 33
tongues: conscience hath a thousand
several t., SHAK 99
freeze/ Their t. BRID R 9
gift of t. DICKEY 1
lack t. to praise. SHAK 228
slanders do not live in t.,
SHAK 76
t. dissemble deep CAMPI 9
t. of dying men SHAK 87
t. of flame are in-folded
ELIOT T 74
t. of water, ROET 44
t. that utter'd WORD 21
T. wrangled dark SAND 24
with its t., WHITM 97
to-night: no stars t. CRAN H 39
tonight: infected wound homeward/
To sit t. RANS 32
met in thee t. BROO P 3
moor — T. In Thee! DICKI 158
rain/ Is full of ghosts t.,
MILLA 39
T. remains, LEWI 7
world may end t.? BROWNI R 39

too: No-more, T.-late, Farewell;
ROSS D 6
of t.-fast-growing sprays
SHAK 90
t.-fluent green STEVENS 48
t. t. solid flesh SHAK 22
world is t. much with us;
WORD 159
took: All which I t. THOMP F 9
he t. them as they cam'.
MACDI 5
Runs the path I t.; WHITT 32
She t. up the flag WHITT 2
Through Eden t. their solitary
way. MILT 108
t. away the light: MILT 43
t. he the wound, smiling,
CRAN S 7
t. his counsel of his wife,
CHAU 69
t. up the glass of Time, TENN 70
tool: aghast of every t., CHAU 67
judged me by their appropriate t.
FROS 124
No workman's t. HERB G 7
T. Maker, Stacker of Wheat,
SAND 3
tools: name his t. BUTL 3
want to know which t. SEXT 16
tooth: fair mouth's broken t.
ROSE 1
Nature, red in t. and claw
TENN 36
sharper than a serpent's t.
SHAK 72
sinks into my throat her tiger's t.,
MCKA 2
Thy t. is not so keen SHAK 13
toothache: endure the t. patiently,
SHAK 131
suffer t.'s ills? GILB 43
toothbrush: thrown away her
electric t., JARR 12
toothless: t. mouth of sunny air,
GINS 34
top: At the t. of the house DRIN 1
famous high t.-hat LIND V 2
from toe to t., YEATS 157
gilt wheels and no t. at all.
WILLI 45
gyrates like a t. SHAP 16
I sit in the t. of the wood,
HUGH T 1
I stand on t. LOWE R 41
on the rapid's t., ARNO 5
plate/ Lies flat on the table t.,
WILB 20
stood at the t. of that long marble
stair WILB 34
Tapering toward the t.
STEVENS 52
t. of Pindus SPENS 41
t. of/ the jamcloset WILLI 2

t. of the porch! MOOR C 2
t. of the tide CARRO 11
t. of the wall! MOOR C 2
topaz: Bright t. denizens RICH 1
toper: drink like any t. HORA 9
topless: t. towers of Ilium? MARL 3
toppe: Slipper t. Of courtes estates,
SENE 1
Toppled: T. in two. HERF 2
tops: to the t. of his shoes WAGO 1
torch: blue, forked t. of this flower
LAWR 4
bright t., KEAT 54
bright t. of love; BLAK 109
give me a t.! LAWR 4
knowledge is a t. of smoky pine
SANT 2
mighty woman with a t., LAZA 1
t. is at thy temple door,
RANDA J 1
t. of death they light; THAC 1
tore: t./ Her womb, SITW 6
Tories: Triumphant T., SWIF 8
torment: Condemned by Jove to
endless t. DRAY 10
greater t. Of love satisfied
ELIOT T 10
Love is a t. of the mind,
DANI S 1
Terminate t. ELIOT T 10
thwart disnatured t. SHAK 72
t. of fire and weight SNYD 52
t. with care; WYAT 13
tormented: t. mind tormenting
HOPKINS 14
t. slumber JOHN L 7
t. you/ To life. SNOD 12
torn: holly t. for Christmas.
LOWE R 23
man all tattered and t. MOTH 9
my doublet t., LAND 10
My heart is t. JOYC 1
t. and bleeding hearts
DUNB P 12
T. and most whole ELIOT T 9
t. bandrols of Napoleon's war.
BARL 1
t. by dreams, STEVENS 24
t. hair round their paleness.
SPEND 1
t. the naiad from her flood,
POE 2
torrent: one mighty t. SHEL 76
torsos: their dirty/ glistening t.
OHAR 12
tortillas: borscht & t. GINS 14
tortoise: slate/ Of the baby t.
LAWR 55
torture: t. of their sight. JOHN G 3
woe, which t. us, EMER 32
torturer: t.'s horse/ Scratches
AUDE 63

Torturing: upon the T. Tree
   CHES 13
Tory: fine old English T. times;
   DICKEN 1
   T. camp is now in sight, SIMM 2
toss: t. it yonder, like a Rind,
   DICKI 78
tossed: catch t. crumbs SNYD 31
   t. her bright hair; MANI 1
   t. hours upon the tides of fever,
   MILLE V 1
   t. in jail on a vagrancy rap,
   SNYD 25
tossing: t. on their beds,
   YEATS 131
total: fear/ Of t. neutrality.
   PLATH 19
   Now is he t. gules, SHAK 30
totally: t. obtuse — WILLI 21
tote: t. the weary load, — FOST 2
totter: maun t. down, BURN 35
   t. on the road: — FOST 2
totters: one t. down, ROSS C 12
touch: allowed to t. UNKN 256
   at a t. I yield; TENN 106
   Bend down and t. WHITM 69
   blossoms t. the sky. WILLI 25
   bulls mellow to the t., MACDI 3
   enter t. entirely. SEXT 14
   familiar t. of the long-married,
   KINN 1
   Gently its t. awoke him
   OWEN 26
   Here and hereafter, t. a Paradise.
   MELV 22
   Is this then a t.? WHITM 77
   lips to t. the sacred fire?
   JOHN J 5
   One t. of your hand WHITM 106
   recall that t., ROSS C 17
   spider's t., POPE A 71
   t. a hundred flowers MILLA 1
   T., love, all senses; SPEND 17
   t. of a vanished hand, TENN 2
   t. of earthly years. WORD 49
   t. thy hand. MILT 112
   t. to tune the harmony. SHAK 86
   t. you again SHAP 6
   unimaginable t. of Time.
   WORD 9
   want of inward t., SIDN 10
   within the harp I t. PETRA 13
   You villain t.! WHITM 73
touch'd: Before rude hands have t.
   it? JONS 2
touched: "God has t. him!
   WHITT 27
   No lip has t. it HARD 48
   t. her with whip or spur:
   WOOL 4
   t. the bawdy strings
   STEVENS 38
touches: just t. earth. LAWR 19

no one t. me anymore. SANC 2
   t. back to wonder. WILB 8
   "Who t. a hair WHITT 4
touching: t. along the length of our
   bodies, KINN 1
   t. in its majesty: WORD 6
tough: Balls tight in a t. hair sack
   SNYD 37
   heart keeps its t. old persistency
   still; LOWE J 6
   hide is t. GUNN 6
   rather t. worm in your little
   inside?" GILB 29
Toulouse: suspicious of T. WILB 31
toun: poure persoun of a t.,
   CHAU 12
tourist: t.'s/ brown pennies KLEI 3
tournament: We in the t. BETJ 9
tourney: I summon'd am to a t.
   UNKN 265
Toussaint: Douglass and T.
   RANDA D 4
towards: Spring comes merry t. me
   ROSS D 1
   t. the pebbled shore, SHAK 209
   t. the sun, SPEND 12
towel: fold my t. KINS 6
   t. my shaven jaw KINS 5
towels: sheets and t. of a life
   MERR 10
tower: bells break down their t.;
   CRAN H 35
   build/ Some t. of song LONG 28
   burning roof and t. YEATS 85
   chimes/ Of the tall Clock T.
   SNOD 8
   From the shaken t. MEYN 1
   hawk of the t.: SKEL 2
   in the T. before his execution
   HECH 14
   North Church t. LONG 44
   one star over the t. MERE O 1
   proud t. in the town POE 12
   shouted through the belfry t.,
   LONG 18
   t. of strength; LANIG 1
towered: steeple t. INGE 1
   t. citadel, SHAK 9
towers: cloud-capped t., SHAK 163
   coil of ticking t. . . . CRAN H 34
   Courts and T.: WORD 100
   Falling t. ELIOT T 148
   lofty t. I see down-rased,
   SHAK 211
   thrones, and t. CAMPB R 6
   topless t. of Ilium? MARL 3
   t. along the steep; CAMPB T 11
   t./ Tolling reminiscent bells,
   ELIOT T 150
   where are our t.? MORE 4
town: Bind t. to t. CRAN H 18
   body-and-soul-stinking t. of
   Cologne. COLE SAM 26

bubble o'er the t. WILD 15
Cocaine t. on Cocaine hill,
   UNKN 67
could strut about T.!' —
   HARD 37
drowsy t.; BRID R 8
final direction of the elementary
   t. THOMA D 41
graveyard shelves on the t. . . . .
   LOWE R 39
Hymen peoples every t.;
   SHAK 16
If ever you go to Dublin t.
   KAVA 16
in a pretty how t. CUMM 4
in the t. of Dungannon,
   UNKN 195
Jesus came to t.; REES 1
lock your door./ Wild swans, come
   over the t., MILLA 41
London is a man's t., VAN DY 1
loud gregarious t. MILLA 32
Maine lobster t. LOWE R 56
nothing in the t. below —
   ROBI 47
O little t. of Bethlehem,
   BROO P 3
owned by all the t., TATE A 18
Paris is a woman's t., VAN DY 1
parson of our t., SWIF 2
proud tower in the t. POE 12
Sprinkle the quarters on the
   morning t. HOUS 5
that t. shall settle POE 13
think of the beautiful t. LONG 31
this devoted t. SWIF 7
through the t., MILLE W 1
Till, in a distant t., DICKI 89
to the next t. CREE 7
t. like this, MOOR M 29
traveler hastens toward the t.,
   LONG 46
We met the Solid T. DICKI 65
towns: Clanging fights, and flaming
   t., TENN 90
postmarks again/ of shattered t.
   KINN 7
Steep t., flat t., SNYD 27
T. on from mine — DICKI 89
Towr: proudly eminent/ Stood like a
   T.; MILT 57
   t. on a toft LANGL 2
toy: crammed in a monster t.
   MACN 1
   foolish thing was but a t.,
   SHAK 177
   hollow t., the Race; ROBI 35
   little t. dog FIEL E 6
   t. soldier is red with rust,
   FIEL E 6
toyes: t., to give my heart some
   ease: HERR 18
toys: All is but t. SHAK 109

All our joys/ Are but t., CAMPI 30
bucketful of radiant t. AMMO 12
Child's T. and the Old Man's
  Reasons BLAK 8
in t., in lusts, or wine, COWL 15
meddle with my t.
  STEVENSO R 22
pleasures are but t., CAMPI 18
pretty t. with thee to lie —
  LAMB 4
thou rememberest of what t.
  PATM 4
t. beside me lay
  STEVENSO R 11
t. for your head, SHAK 182
t. of age: POPE A 81
t. of the world would break.
  NIMS 4
toyshop: moving t. of their heart;
  POPE A 112
trace: aged after the common t.
  SENE 2
no t. of dog or cat; FIEL E 2
nor other t. SHEL 78
t. huge Forests, MILT 3
t. thy footsteps CLARE 8
T. your grave, SHEL 65
without a t. of fear, TOOM 4
traceless: t. as a thaw of bygone
  snow; ROSS C 17
traces: in old heroic t., BRON 5
on winter's t., SWIN 3
t. of the smallest spider's web,
  SHAK 153
tracing: fitful t. of a portal;
  STEVENS 36
track: deviate from the common t.
  POPE A 30
Following his t., MILT 62
Jungle star or jungle t., CULL 5
on a sabre t. movering HAYD 22
roll to the t., KENN 1
serpent's t. RANS 27
thine own t. firmly holding,
  WHITM 102
tracked: t. by phantoms HARD 52
tracks: hungry on the t.,
  CRAN H 16
tract: t. of time begins to weave
  VAUX 2
trade: homely slighted shepherd's
  t., MILT 26
learn your t., YEATS 157
'prentice himself to the t.;
  GILB 61
soldier's is the t.: HOUS 14
t. had suddenly encroached
  DICKI 102
t. of a timoneer GILB 17
t. the memory of this night for
  food. MILLA 17
t. was a-cutting of Broom, green
  Broom; UNKN 43

with Pelf and T. MELV 21
worked at the weaver's t.;
  UNKN 99
tradeful: t. Merchants, SPENS 7
trades: at my sky blue t.,
  THOMA D 20
tradition: live t. POUN 23
Traditional: T. sanctity and
  loveliness; YEATS 36
traditions: customs, t., WHITM 60
great t. of the Past LONG 27
Trafalgar: that night at T.!
  HARD 21
traffic: canyoned t.... CRAN H 6
Hushing the latest t. BRID R 8
t. of Jacob's ladder THOMP F 11
tragedy: play is the t. "Man",
  POE 33
tragic: ever-hooded, t.-gestured sea
  STEVENS 18
In t. life, God wot, MERE G 12
perform their t. play, YEATS 78
t. scene they stare. YEATS 82
Trail: followed my own/ T. SNYD 2
hunter's t. and trap-path TUCK 1
t. has its own stern code. SERV 3
t. in the sky MERW 1
trailed: young, heads/ t. KINN 18
trailing: t. clouds of glory
  WORD 70
t. garments of the Night
  LONG 24
t. your legs and crying!
  MILLA 41
trails: On their/ Own t. SNYD 2
rocky sure-foot t. SNYD 51
t. in the lines underfoot,
  WHITM 2
wing t. like a banner JEFFE 13
train: Disease, and Sorrow's
  weeping t., GRAY 26
Flowing with majestic t.,
  MILT 16
gems of heav'n, her starry t.:
  MILT 76
Hear the t. blow. UNKN 80
isn't a t. I wouldn't take,
  MILLA 38
join th' angelic t. WHEA 1
large and lordly t., WILC 3
Lenin in a sealed t. SNYD 24
pomp and t., CAMPI 9
t.-band captain COWP 6
t. rounds, CRAN H 33
with all his rising t.;
  THOMS J (1700–1748) 12
with such a t. STOD 3
trainer: College Eight and their t.
  NEWB 3
trains: stars with t. of fire
  SHAK 20
traison: poison and t. at Rome,
  WYAT 24

traitor: greatest t., WHITM 73
t.'s treason; SHAK 140
treason labouring in the t.'s
  thought, CHAU 47
Where shall the t. rest,
  SCOT WA 20
traitors: given up by t., WHITM 73
tram: not even a 'bus I'm a t.''
  HARE 1
tramp: Slow t. the Centuries,
  DICKI 97
tramped: t. at a rat's pace,
  ROSS C 12
tramping: t. his thirty miles
  LAWR 14
trampled: boar t. down in ivy time.
  GRAV 35
rag to be ever/ T. or soiled,
  MERR 10
T. and beaten LONG 26
t. by a hurrying crowd, BRYA 1
T. its sparks SHEL 78
tramples: Death t. it to fragments.
  SHEL 13
trampling: own soul t. down
  WHITM 31
t. horses' feet SIDN 24
t. out the vintage HOWE 1
trance: heavy t., BEAU 1
t. of silence, STEVENSO R 10
tranced: t. dancing of men. BIRN 3
t. machine/ Of ocean,
  STEVENS 47
trances: all my days are t., POE 8
t. of the blast, COLE SAM 17
tranquil: in her t. light BRID R 19
tranquility: With meet t., HARD 28
tranquillity: cold t., SHEL 22
with pale t. WINT 7
transcendent: faith's t. dower,
  WORD 128
transcendental: of a t. kind.
  GILB 30
one grand t. vowel. JARR 8
t. terms, GILB 30
transcends: How far the unknown
  t. LONG 34
transferred: one t. to the blest;
  SHAP 12
transfigures: that t. you and me;
  HOWE 3
transfiguring: t. all that dread.
  YEATS 79
transfix: Time doth t. SHAK 210
transfixed: one who stands t.
  SHAP 9
transform: by our wills,/ we t.
  WILLI 20
Transformed: thin with desire,/ T. to
  a creeping MONR 2
transient: as gay/ And t., BYRO 34
civilization is a t. sickness.
  JEFFE 27

Measured this t. world, MILT 105
t. sorrows, simple wiles,
WORD 134
transition: moving into t., PURD 2
transitory: t. blossom/ Of snow,
ELIOT T 62
translate: tried to/ t. Proust.
RIVE 2
translated: t. to the skies, MILT 9
translating: peering, absorbing, t.
WHITM 64
translucency: over-all/ black t.
BISH 11
translucent: glassy, cool, t. wave,
MILT 7
transmugrified: quite t., they're
grown BURN 6
transom: gotten in through the t.
LEVI 3
transparent: t. green-wash of the
sea WHITM 97
t. shadowy night, WHITM 48
t. summer morning, WHITM 78
transplanted: t. human worth
TENN 39
transprose: to write verse with him
is to t.; DRYD/TATE 1
trap: hunter's trail and t.-path
TUCK 1
t. that catches noblest spirits,
JEFFE 39
trapeze: t. of your flesh,
CRAN H 26
trappe: Kaught in a t., CHAU 16
trapper: red-haired, stalwart t.,
TAYL B 1
trappings: t. and the suits of woe.
SHAK 21
traps: alien/ As our clumsy t.,
KIZE 3
T. for the traveller— BYRO 53
trash: filmy t. Litters JARR 4
wares be t., UNKN 96
travail: hours of t. LIND V 3
ignorant night, the t. SCHW 6
vain t. hath wearied me
WYAT 30
travaileth: lips he t.; SWIN 2
travel: didst thou t. WORD 42
I cannot rest from t.; TENN 129
I could not t. both FROS 94
my songs will t., POUN 32
repose for limbs with t. tired;
SHAK 193
t. forth without my cloak,
SHAK 198
t.-sore and weak? ROSS C 29
traveled: I took the one less t.
FROS 95
Much have I t. in the realms of
gold, KEAT 55
t. among unknown men,
WORD 47

traveler: nevermore/ Returns the t.
LONG 47
No t. returns, SHAK 40
t. hastens toward the town,
LONG 46
t., long I stood FROS 94
t. meets, aghast, POE 17
travelers: two t., Roger and I.
TROW 4
traveling: t. army halting,
WHITM 9
travelled: t. life's dull round,
SHEN 2
traveller: Traps for the t. BYRO 53
T. take heed WALK 11
travels: Hope t. through,
POPE A 80
our t.:/ serious, engravable.
BISH 32
t. the fastest who t. alone.
KIPL 25
traverse: t. old love's domain
HARD 12
Traviata: La T. sighs NOYE 5
tray: On the glass t. WILLI 23
trayed: Trouth is t. WYAT 27
treacherous: hope is t. MICH 3
T. tip WHITM 77
treachery: Beeth ware, ye lordes of
her t. CHAU 70
divorce/ And the t. SNOD 15
treach'rous: Along the t. shore.
HORA 5
tread: glance in their t., LEVE 10
heavily they t.; VERY 6
holy footsteps I may t.: MICH 2
on both their Spoils dost t.,
MARV 5
quick, galvanic t. GILB 3
T. lightly, WILD 17
t. on my dreams. YEATS 4
T. soft on her Grave, PRIO 5
way that I must t. alone,
BRYA 27
When turtles t., SHAK 100
where angels fear to t.
POPE A 23
with pensive t., LINC 2
ye t. Lightly, HERR 59
treading: t. on delicate toes.
PRAE 4
t. on my tail. CARRO 10
treads: fragrance in thy footing t.;
WORD 89
t. back his own steps; WORD 110
t. on the ground. SHAK 237
treason: enticèd oft to t., SURR 2
gold/ Of Matrimonial t.:
MILT 112
gross body's t.; SHAK 243
hath done T., DONN 44
less than a t. FROS 93

love grows bitter with t.,
SWIN 23
none dare call it t. HARI 2
temple full of t., RALEG 5
traitor's t.; SHAK 140
T. doth never prosper; HARI 2
t. labouring in the traitor's
thought, CHAU 47
treasure: alone of all His t.
HERB G 62
both the Indias of their t. spoil,
SPENS 7
hailed as a t., WOOD 2
Spoiling senses of their t.,
JONS 9
summer's fruitful t.; NASHE 2
Tickle t., SURR 1
t. of thy lusty days, SHAK 185
treasures: t. of Cathay were never
found. SIMP 12
t. that prevail. RICH 4
treat: Brown sugar lassie,/ Caramel
t., HUGH L 5
partake of the t. MELV 14
savory dish, a homely t.,
HORA 10
t. if met where any bar is,
HARD 31
t. it tenderly, WYAT 8
treaties: t. would be signed,
WELC 3
Treating: T. alike its dead
HUGH T 8
treatises: reading in these t.
KLEI 1
tree: acorn's not yet/ Fallen from the
t. UNKN 56
All underneath the Eildon T.
UNKN 246
As a t. my sin stands ROSS C 8
below your silent t., BARNE 1
beneath my laurel t. HORA 8
beneath the tamarind t.? POE 2
billboard lovely as a t. NASH 14
bowed down the highest t.
UNKN 57
budding of my t. ROSS C 17
busy about the t. of life . . .
LOWE R 50
calico t., LEAR 2
child become a willow t.,
FANS C 1
Christs Crosse, and Adams t.,
DONN 32
cross roads t. HUGH L 13
Crumpetty T. LEAR 13
dead oak t. bough. THOMA E 8
down by the Eildon T.
UNKN 245
drop like the fruits of the t.,
MERE G 3
dust of snow/ From a hemlock t.
FROS 46

every sheave a golden t. PEEL 5
famished field and blackened t.
    MUIR 9
"Farewell to barn and stack and
    t., HOUS 28
flies are on the plane t.,
    LOWE R 3
flying from field and t.:
    BRID R 2
from a wasted t., ROET 50
Fruit/ Of that Forbidden T.,
    MILT 46
gnarled and naked t. HUGH L 14
Green springs the t., RALEG 14
growing like a t. In bulk,
    JONS 41
His cross is every t. PLUN 2
I reade, and sigh, and wish I were
    a t.; HERB G 5
innocent behind on a t. AUDE 63
ladder's sticking through a t.
    FROS 3
last leaf upon the t. HOLM 16
Leaps from the t. SNYD 44
leaves grow on the t.; YEATS 50
lies at the fit o' the t. UNKN 168
lived in a t.: SNYD 48
loppèd t. in time may grow
    again, SOUTHW 7
Lying under the olive t.,
    SPEND 20
makes the gallow t., RALEG 13
move up into the t. of breath;
    LOWE R 59
nailed him to the t. POUN 4
nothing on the t., WELL 2
Old Man in a t., LEAR 14
old t. with shoots. POUN 26
old t.'s late branch RANS 11
on a t. they slew Him —
    LANIE 2
on the ancestral t. HERF 1
on the T. of Life, MILT 68
only God can make a t. KILM 2
other t. was grieved, SWIF 2
Over the t.-tops WHITM 51
partridge in a pear t. UNKN 274
peach from the t. BLAK 25
poem lovely as a t. KILM 1
red soil and sweet-gum t.,
    TOOM 6
right Rose T.' YEATS 123
sap in the t. SITW 8
see upon that t., FIEL E 5
shape of the t., AIKE 5
smell thee on the t. SHAK 137
sparrow enters the t., HARD 43
Strip to this t.: THOMA D 8
Swing up into the apple t.
    ELIOT T 58
that wild-rose t. ALDR T 2
Through the shaking t.
    YEATS 149

time is a t. CUMM 9
toddle about the t. UNKN 5
t. and truth. HOLM 7
T. at my window, FROS 115
t./ Budding yearly must forget
    CULL 7
t. by a river GILB 29
t. planted by the rivers
    BIBL, O.T. 21
t. swayed overwater. ROET 56
t. was bending ROBE 2
T. whose broad smooth Leaves
    MILT 97
under the wyllowe t. CHAT 1
upon the Torturing T. CHES 13
wicked social t. SNYD 43
window t., FROS 115
trees: all the t. are green;
    KINGSL 5
ancestral t., YEATS 35
banners flashing through the t.
    ARNO 39
barks of t. thou browsed. SHAK 4
bends the groaning t. BRON 14
blasts the roots of t.
    THOMA D 22
Dry leafless t. VERY 1
fir t. dark and high; HOOD 5
fist of t., HALL 5
for fearė flewen over the t.;
    CHAU 71
greenly spirits of t. CUMM 19
honey dropped from t.; TASS 1
house and the t., WHITT 33
in the pine t. ELIOT T 147
jabber among the t. SASS 14
lofty t. I see barren of leaves,
    SHAK 186
man came out of the t. FROS 45
one light's language in the book of
    t. THOMA D 8
roots of pine t. HALL 3
sap in/ the t., AMMC 16
shrubs and t., WHITM 12
sleeping under t. SNYD 39
small/ cheeping birds/ skimming/
    bare t. WILLI 43
stones and t., insensible of time,
    BRAD 4
straighter darker t. FROS 10
stunted t. look sick, EMER 5
these t. their mistress' name:
    MARV 16
t. are brown; KINGSL 7
t. are Indian princes, ALLI 2
t. bow down their heads,
    ROSS C 36
T. down/ Creeks choked, trout
    killed, SNYD 45
t. in apple orchards JACK 3
t. of God MILT 94
t. of the mind are black.
    PLATH 57

t. that have it FROS 106
t. they drew Him last: LANIE 2
t. turn bare SNOD 7
t. unnumbered rise, DYER J 1
t. wept odorous gums and balm;
    MILT 69
'whispers through the t.':
    POPE A 26
winds and t. amazed DRUM 1
Winds through the olive t.
    UNKN 176
trellis'd: t. grape, WHITM 29
trellised: t. sky, DAVIS 1
Tremadoc: T., Penrhyndeudraeth,
    GRAV 40
tremble: begin to t. and cry.
    SHAP 17
Let Sporus t. POPE A 9
my firm nerves/ Shall never t.
    SHAK 110
t. for this lovely frame, WHITE 1
t. into thought, COLE SAM 12
whole country t. HALL 5
trembled: Sore t. the father;
    GOET 1
t. when a Man drew near;
    SWIF 13
trembles: imagine he no longer t.
    ROET 40
trembling: held that t. hill!
    THOMP W 3
leaves hang t., ROSS C 35
smell of field and grove, attune/
    The t. leaves, MILT 70
t. ages past, Æ 2
t. and unsatisfied, RICH 16
t. at the gate of bliss; CRAS 10
T., begins the sacred rites of
    pride. POPE A 113
T., cold, in ghastly fears —
    BLAK 43
t. night-winds whistle ALLI 3
waving moon and t. leaves
    WINC 1
With t. care, ROBI 45
tremendous: sieges t. WHITM 114
tremulous: sad and t. WHITM 61
trenches: dig deep t. SHAK 185
trespass: Authorizing thy t.
    SHAK 199
t. there and go, HOUS 65
trespasses: Forgive us all our t.,
    STEPHENS 7
tresses: unadornèd golden t.
    MILT 73
white neck hid with t. OVID 1
trestles: t. to shake the dead,
    WHITM 8
trewe: lik a turtle t. is my
    mooringe: CHAU 52
trial: proof maketh t. UNKN 204

trousers: bottoms of my t. rolled.
ELIOT T 90

t. were creased like knives
WAGO 1

trout: Creeks choked, t. killed,
SNYD 45

quick-eyed t.
THOMS J (1700–1748) 9

Trouth: T. is trayed WYAT 27

Trouthe: chivalrie,/ T. and honour,
CHAU 7

Trovatore: Il T. cries NOYE 5

trowest: Learn more than thou t.,
SHAK 71

Troy: against our crumbling T.
MACN 1

another T. for her to burn?
YEATS 102

ringing plains of windy T.
TENN 130

T. burned for a sea-tax, SCHW 2

T. passed away YEATS 121

Troye: Greeks brought to T. town,
SURR 7

truant: Biting my t. pen, SIDN 6

Truce: Some T. of God WHITT 28

truculence: general t. WILLI 31

true: all t. delight doth spring.
CAMPI 27

are ye sure the news is t.?
MICK 1

Because I know it's t. DICKI 53

blank confusion! t. epitome
WORD 109

Columbia's t.-blue sons, ROON 1

Comfort, where t. meaning is.
BRET 7

fair lines which t. goodness show.
SIDN 20

find the arms of my t.-love
TENN 97

find where your t. image pictured
lies, SHAK 192

first t. merit to befriend;
POPE A 33

Gie'd me her promise t.;
DOUG W 1

glory, hope's t. gage, RALEG 10

guiltie of T.-loves blood, MARL 4

hear my t. time broke. SHAK 93

heart is t., UNKN 96

hearts are kind and t.; BANK 1

I can love any, so she be not t.
DONN 35

I will be t., SHAK 235

Karl would it were t. SNYD 43

lease of my t. love SHAK 229

like a t.-born Andalusian,
BYRO 47

live-long Minute t. to thee,
ROCH 6

love, let us be t. ARNO 3

make a home that's t., UNTE 1

man's t. merit POPE A 16

marriage of t. minds SHAK 231

mie t. love waytes. CHAT 1

My t. love hath my heart
SIDN 1, 2

my William, sweet and t."
UNKN 33

never man was t.; BRET/OTHE 2

Nothing so t. POPE A 93

Plots, t. or false, DRYD 1

prefer dark night/ Before t. light!
VAUG 33

ring in the t. TENN 47

Say I died t. BEAU/FLET 3

shape as t., SHAK 70

So t. a fool is love, SHAK 208

souls that are pure and t.;
BRID 1

Such end t. lovers have. BLAK 40

Sweet saint, 'tis t. you worthy be,
GREV 2

Swore to be t. UNKN 101

Though she were t., DONN 27

'tis t., 'tis true. HOUS 60

To a maiden t. UNKN 84

to thine own self be t., SHAK 24

t. as the stars above; UNKN 101

t. authority in men: MILT 72

T. beauty dwells on high:
HERB G 36

t. beauty virtue is indeed, SIDN 8

t. because her truth kills mee.
DONN 61

T. Church can never fail/ For it is
based upon a rock. ELIOT T 37

t. fair, SPENS 25

t. God's priest. CAREW 4

t. heart was left behind. HARD 7

t. love acted simple modesty.
SHAK 149

t. love sent to me UNKN 274

t. love's knot/ For all t. loves to
admire. UNKN 180

t. madness is loneliness.
MONTA 3

t. or false, the Subject of Debate,
ROCH 16

t. pleasure/ Lives in measure,
UNKN 185

t. source/ Of human offspring.
MILT 78

t. that I must Stella love. SIDN 8

T. Thomas lay on Huntlie bank;
UNKN 245

t. Valour see, BUNY 1

T. wit is Nature POPE A 21

ushering me to the t. songs,
WHITM 36

vows shall ever t. remain; GAY 7

your t. love know SHAK 37

truelove: Until my t. comes.
RANS 31

Truer: T. than women, PLATH 78

truest: t. heart that lover e'er did
lend. KING H 6

trulio: realio, t., little pet dragon.
NASH 15

truly: denote me t. SHAK 21

never loved me t.: TENN 73

those who were t. great.
SPEND 11

t. what I do think." UNKN 161

Which sees is t. seen. SNYD 50

trumpet: drum nor t. peaceful sleeps
should move, CAMPI 16

Elegies to T.-sounds,
MONTROSE 1

hear perchance a t. sound,
SHAK 125

shifted his t., GOLD 4

thing became a t.; WORD 132

T. shall be heard on high,
DRYD 27

t.'s mouth is pealed BRYA 4

trumpets: Black Poets die as t.,
KNIG 3

loud t.' sound MILT 104

silver, snarling t.' KEAT 6

t. of the sky, EMER 43

t. sound, the banners fly,
BURN 49

With t. BIBL, O.T. 46

trumpetts: Sound out your t.,
UNKN 223

trumps: Let Spades be t.!
POPE A 121

trundle-bed: wee one's t. FIEL E 9

trunk: t. may be discharged of
breath SHAK 150

trunks: t. of men. SHAK 124

trust: brightness to hold in t.,
SPEND 22

come the t. and cheer? MELV 17

greatness is no t.'. BEAU/BASS 3

heart of t.? EMER 22

in seeming t., SHAK 238

parts that none will t.,
POPE A 12

put your t. and confidence
MORE 1

seal the sacred t., SIGO 2

t. itself with truth, BYRO 21

t. that still were mine, WILLA 2

t. that triumphs over wrong,
GLAD 2

t. the larger hope. TENN 34

t. the sanity of my vessel;
OHAR 16

T. therefore first, WYAT 11

want of t. in God, TIMR 5

trusteth: blessed is the man that t.
BIBL, O.T. 44

truth: At random from the t.
SHAK 242

Beauty is t., truth beauty, —
KEAT 40

curse and to deny your t.;
  ARNO 31
died for T., DICKI 37
does t. sound bitter
  BROWNI R 46
drunk/ On wine or t., SNYD 39
eternal t. man's fighting soul
  EBER 3
fearless t. endows. ROBI 17
firmly gript the granite t.
  MARK 2
Give t., BRID 3
her t. kills mee. DONN 61
high, white star of T., ARNO 30
his t. endureth to all generations.
  BIBL, O.T. 50
His t. is marching on. HOWE 2
if t. were told, HOUS 46
In t. the prison, WORD 60
Know then this t. POPE A 86
Loving in t., SIDN 5
Marvelous T., confront us
  LEVE 16
may my heart's t. THOMA D 36
men hate the t.; JEFFE 9
nature's t., SHAK 210
ocean and t. ROSS C 30
One t. is clear, POPE A 58
Pardon free t., JONS 47
poets honey their t. JEFFE 9
she is made of t., SHAK 238
simple t. his utmost skill!
  WOTT 1
simple t. miscall'd simplicity,
  SHAK 213
simple t. suppress'd. SHAK 238
Sole judge of t., POPE A 78
Tell all the t. DICKI 136
that stupendous t. believed,
  SMAR 9
they breathe t. SHAK 87
they worship T.; BROO R 19
'tis t. you say, HOUS 12
To pervert t., MAST 4
tree and t. HOLM 7
tried intent/ Of such a t. WYAT 7
trust itself with t., BYRO 21
t. a little elder is; DONN 50
t. about the cat and pup
  FIEL E 2
t. and falsehood be DONN 50
t. and liberty; — SHEL 75
t. away/ From you is fled?
  WYAT 28
T., crushed to earth, BRYA 3
t. do dim/ All shadows dark
  BALD 1
t. in a calm world, STEVENS 16
t. in every shepherd's tongue,
  RALEG 7
T., in sunny vest arrayed, COLL 8
t. is face to face, OHAR 11
t. is great, PATM 7

t. must dazzle gradually
  DICKI 137
t. no beauty? HERB G 44
t. severe, by fairy fiction dressed.
  GRAY 6
t. shall be thy warrant: RALEG 6
T. stands, DONN 51
t. that's told with bad intent
  BLAK 5
t. wailing there like a red babe.
  EBER 7
verse distills your t. SHAK 206
warp us from the living t.!
  TENN 72
when T. broke in FROS 12
wherever the t. may be —
  FROS 67
which t. doth give! SHAK 206
Truthe: T. shall deliver, CHAU 2
truths: believe,/ Mysterious t.,
  ROCH 12
dreams t. and fables histories;
  DONN 19
eternal t. receive, CHAR 1
t. I teach, HORA 5
try: Decidedly can t. us, BURN 8
each child should t. UNTE 2
T. smiling; UNKN 266
t. to sleep. BROWNI R 5
t. A deeper plague, DONN 40
trying: without half t. CHAP A 2
tryout: bad variant nor a t.
  HUGH T 9
trysted: t. hour! BURN 37
Tsen-tainte: daughter of T.
  MOMA 4
tub: paralytic stunned in the t.,
  ROET 41
tube: t.-kept/ prison HARP 2
tubs: armored Diesel fishing t.
  LOWE R 6
tucked: long hair was t. up
  SNYD 15
seed still t. away, SNYD 5
Tuesday: Christened on T.,
  MOTH 26
T.'s child is full of grace,
  MOTH 22
tuft: t. of fronds or katydid legs
  MOOR M 30
tufts: Betwixt the t. of snow
  COLE SAM 16
Tugged: T. till the toadstool
  HERF 2
Tugger: Rum Tum T. is a Curious
  Cat — ELIOT T 106
tulips: Here t. bloom BROO R 16
Ladies, like variegated t.,
  POPE A 94
Tullia: T.'s ape a marmasyte
  UNKN 95

tumbled: ratel t. hurry skurry.
  ROSS C 12
t. in a fit. HOLM 13
tumbler: t. turned down, WILLI 23
tumblin': walls come t. down.
  UNKN 158
tumbling: come t. down the flood.
  SWIF 9
tum: eloquent t.-t. GILB 2
tumult: stilled the rising t.,
  THAY 3
t. and the shouting dies; KIPL 18
t. as they thunder by, POE 40
tumultuous: Full of t. life PATM 6
tune: always out of t. CALV 4
cannot frame me t. to fayne,
  WYAT 22
cheer and t. my heartless breast,
  HERB G 22
drowsy syncopated t.,
  HUGH L 18
history change its t., BYRO 21
if it be in t., LOWE J 17
in t. and step SAND 17
kinde of t., HERB G 67
Like sorrow or a t. FARJ E 2
mournful T. you hear, SACK 3
name is a t. MOOR M 35
roaring, epic, ragtime t.
  LIND V 9
sweetly played in t. BURN 45
to the t. of flutes kept stroke,
  SHAK 5
touch to t. the harmony.
  SHAK 86
t. her lute GRIF 1
turn to my dance t. POUN 34
world in t., VAUG 12
tuned: As all the t. spheres,
  SHAK 7
t., and started to play, OSUL 1
T. to my liking, MILLA 12
tunefu': hear her in the t. birds,
  BURN 42
tuneful: time allows/ In all his t.
  turning THOMA D 20
Tunes: all those T. were play'd,
  SACK 3
human t. nor words, YEATS 41
robin-redbreast t. his note;
  LYLY 4
threatening T. and low —
  DICKI 159
Tunis: mail from T., probably,
  DICKI 124
tunnels: t. that re-wind themselves,
  CRAN H 31
tunny: female t.-fish, LAWR 58
Tupper: Mister T., GILB 12
turbid: t. ebb and flow ARNO 2
turbulence: by Calvary's t.
  unsatisfied, YEATS 92

Turbulent: T., fleshy, WHITM 73
t. musical chorus! WHITM 32
turd: feeds on dried goose t.
CREE 2
turf: every t., CAMPB T 4
muscle or t., HECH 11
this soft t., BRYA 1
turfy: t. hammock is our bed,
SIMM 1
Turk: French, or T., or Proosian,
GILB 20
heathen, T., or Jew. BLAK 89
turkey: gobble of the struttin' t.-
cock, RILE 4
sailed into proud T., UNKN 317
turmoil: earthly t. grows, ARNO 46
turn: change or t. as weather and
wind? WYAT 10
denizens can t. upon the world
KIZE 3
gaze, t. giddy, rave, and die.
POPE A 2
girls t. wives, SNOD 7
Grieve, and they t. WILC 2
I do not hope to t. again
ELIOT T 1
mills are to t., LANIE 5
Must dullness t. me to a clod?
HERB G 34
no thing but death will serve thy
t., DRAY 14
pass, and t. again. EMER 6
Repent, repent, and from old
errors t.!' DRUM 7
stars t. slowly TATE J 2
swift mind beholds at every t.
MILLA 24
trees t. bare SNOD 7
t. and descend again. HARD 42
t. and twist, MOOR M 13
t. Arthur O'Bower. UNKN 309
t. from Africa WALC 4
t. from Praise. BROWNI E 5
t. her head, YEATS 62
t. hours to years WALK 13
T. it backwards/ BARA 5
t. my gaze ASHB 3
t. of midnight water's SLES 4
t. one's legs GILB 41
T. pale and starve. EMER 5
t./ Thine angel eyes BLAK 108
t. thy back on heaven. EMER 7
t. towards my chamber,
YEATS 97
T. your eyes TATE A 12
we grow, we t. to earth, WEBS 1
turn'd: gently t. over upon me,
WHITM 78
turned: Blessing t. to blasphemies,
UNKN 170
Day/ T. and departed EMER 16
face t. from the clod — CARRU 1
Heaven t. is to hell, UNKN 170

key is t. YEATS 98
no one t. to see, YEATS 76
to silver t.; PEEL 7
tumbler/ t. down, WILLI 23
t. a leaf KLEI 1
t. aside AMMO 13
t. over on his side SILKI 2
T. to cinders by her eye?
JONS 12
t. up a severed hand. SNOD 14
who never t. his back
BROWNI R 12
turning: corn is t. brown, JACK 3
eyes, as hanged men's, t. the
wrong way; ALBI 1
heart is t. ebber, FOST 3
in a year's t. THOMA D 36
In all his tuneful t. THOMA D 20
road that t. MUIR 10
rotting and t. purpler,
LOWE R 57
t. in the widening gyre
YEATS 133
T. in the wind. STEVENS 7
wears the t. globe. HOUS 20
With the t. tide ELIOT T 138
turnip: Dead cats, and t.-tops,
SWIF 9
Mute as a t. PLATH 82
turnkey: t. now his flock returning
sees, SWIF 11
turns: at cyclical t. JEFFE 32
Banner by t. and bugle woo:
ARNO 39
climber-upward t. his face;
SHAK 44
mighty mother t. in tears
THOMP W 4
Never t. him to the bride.
HOUS 61
on the burnished dove/ In the
spring a young man's fancy
lightly t. TENN 69
salute us on the t. KUMI 1
Times go by t., SOUTHW 8
t. a mill, ROGE 1
t. earth's smoothness rough,
BROWNI R 73
t. harmless and stainless
WHITM 98
t. his prow and runs, ROON 3
t. the key to the poor. SHAK 73
t. the woe of Night. EMER 3
T. them to shapes SHAK 127
turquoise: Earth and I gave you t.
MOMA 5
turret: out of the t. with a hose.
JARR 5
t. rationality. TAYL E 13
turrets: blend the t. and shadows
POE 12
In time the strong and stately t.
fall, FLET G EL 1

turtle: lik a t. trewe is my
moorninge: CHAU 52
t. gasping ROET 41
t. lives NASH 17
T. soup, Chippendale, BROO G 9
Two t. doves, UNKN 275
voice of the t. is heard in our
land; BIBL, O.T. 72
turtles: When t. tread, SHAK 100
tusked: t. like the great Cave Bear;
SMIT L 2
tutors: nobles are their tailors' t.,
SHAK 76
tu-whit: golden-eyed t., t.-whoo
NOYE 3
twa: t. brethren in the north,
UNKN 268
t. corbies making a mane;
UNKN 271
t. sisters sat in a bour; UNKN 29
twain: never the t. shall meet,
KIPL 1
where the two exist in t.
FROS 125
Tweed: T.'s silver current glide,
SCOT WA 4
'tween: 't. asleep and wake?
SHAK 70
twelfth: t. day of Christmas,
UNKN 285
twelve: Christmas Eve, and t. of the
clock. HARD 32
posse passed, t. horse; TATE A 17
T. for the t. Apostles UNKN 52
T. lords a-leaping. UNKN 285
t. or fourteen moonshines
SHAK 70
t.-winded sky, HOUS 63
twelvemonth: Barely a t. MUIR 5
twelves: Threes and fours and t.,
LAWR 54
twentieth: nineteenth century/ Into
the t., SIMI 3
t. year is well-nigh past;
COWP 21
twenty: Long-expected one and t.
JOHN S (1709–1784) 10
nyne and t. in a compaignye
CHAU 6
Sheridan t. miles away.
READ T 1
sweet and t., SHAK 175
t. snowy mountains STEVENS 63
T. years hence LAND 16
twenty-four: t. packs, — HART 2
twenty-nine: T. distinct
damnations, BROWNI R 78
twenty-three: married, charming,
chaste, and t. BYRO 20
twenty-two: still alive at t.
KINGSM 1
tweye: telle tales t. To Caunterbury-
ward, CHAU 6

twice: Jesus of the t.-turned cheek
　CULL 9
life is a t.-written scroll　WILD 13
lost as much but t.,　DICKI 57
My life closed t.　DICKI 107
t. a day,　PATM 6
t. already on earth　KINN 13
t.-told fields of infancy
　THOMA D 34
t. unhappier is he,　BOYD 1
twig: clings to t.,　JEFFE 17
twigs: supportance to the bending
　t.　SHAK 90
twilight: across the t. wave
　MERE G 14
age, death's t.,　DONN 51
By the Isar, in the t.　LAWR 33
city in the t.　LONG 29
deep t.'s purple charm.　BYRO 45
disastrous t. sheds　MILT 57
dreaming through the t.
　ROSS C 34
full Surrey t.!　BETJ 10
In the summer t.　ROSS C 32
lost and t. age;　TATE A 3
Making a new t.　MERW 1
Pilots of the purple t.,　TENN 75
T. and bulb define　RUKE 7
T. and evening bell.　TENN 10
t. cold and gray,　LONG 23
t. darkens, the curlew calls;
　LONG 46
t. dim with rose,　DE LA 16
t. hour of breath,　DOWS 5
t. of eternal day.　TENN 29
t. of such day　SHAK 215
t.-piece.　BROWNI R 7
t. sound/ Of the crickets,　JUST 6
t.'s last gleaming,　KEY 1
why should poet in the t. choose?
　KAVA 9
'twill: t. do you good,　HILL J 4
twin: stiff t. compasses　DONN 64
t. cities frame.　LAZA 1
T.-born with greatness,　SHAK 58
twines: our close ivy t.,　CAREW 12
twining: t. in his speckled breast,
　MARV 4
T. to a tongue of fire,　BRID R 13
twinkle: cloud/ That seemed to t.
　KOCH 1
nonsensical bachelor t.
　LOWE R 54
T., twinkle, little star,　TAYL J 1
t. With a crystalline delight;
　POE 10
twinkling: evening stars were t.
　BARNE 4
Hesperus thy t. ray　CLARE 6
twinne: t. From avaryce,　CHAU 84
twinned: We were as t. lambs
　SHAK 178
twins: father of t.,　POUN 65

Near t.,　DONN 50
Sisters we are, yea, t. we be,
　BRAD 9
t. are to be born,　MILT 12
twirled: t. her fingers madly
　LEAR 5
twist: oozy weeds about me t.
　MELV 5
Professor T. could not but smile.
　NASH 12
sorrow did t. and grow,
　HERB G 3
turn and t.,　MOOR M 13
T. our narrow days;　AUDE 11
Twit: T. t. t.　ELIOT T 132
twitching: immovable critic t. his
　skin　MOOR M 32
twixt: seas and land be t. us both,
　LOVE 7
T. life and death,　CRAS 10
T. mead and hill.　MORR 5
t. plated decks　NASH 17
two: bask, we t. together.
　WHITM 65
Catching the sense at t. removes?
　HERB G 45
days yet called t.　CAMPI 12
field t. yards away.　MUIR 2
fired t. bullets,　NASH 16
homward he shal tellen othere t.,
　CHAU 6
I am t.-and-twenty,　HOUS 60
If ever t. were one,　BRAD 13
jars t. hemispheres.　HARD 16
Lovers lying t. and t.　HOUS 61
one or t. rules,　GILB 57
she joined the former t.　DRYD 10
sin is divided into t. parts.
　NASH 9
terribly are t.)　RANS 26
T. crows perched　SHEL 63
t. births:　CART 2
T. bloodless wolves　SHEL 63
t. by two in the ark　LEVE 2
t. doomed ships　WILD 4
T. feathered guests from
　Alabama,　WHITM 64
t.-handed engine　MILT 30
t., if by sea;　LONG 44
t. little eyes,　FIEL E 9
t. souls therefore,　DONN 63
t. souls unite,　CART 2
T. sticks and an apple,　UNKN 24
t. together no more!　WHITM 66
t. travelers, Roger and I.
　TROW 4
T. turtle doves,　UNKN 275
T. veterans son and father dropt
　together,　WHITM 26
T. vipers tangled　SHEL 63
T. voices are there:　STEPHEN 3
we t. being one　DONN 14

we t., content,　WHITM 33
We t. now part.　PATM 8
twofold: t. silence was the song of
　love.　ROSS D 4
tyde: to yer leathalle t.　CHAT 1
tying: always t. up　OHAR 15
tykes: made the little t. so happy
　OHAR 3
type: careful of the t.　TENN 32, 35
types: thousand t. are gone;
　TENN 35
t. And shadows,　MILT 104
typist: t. home at teatime,
　ELIOT T 134
tyrannies: cynic t. of honest kings;
　MELV 12
tyrannous: lend a t. and a damnèd
　light　SHAK 30
t. wind,　BRID R 18
tyranny: hate of t. intense,
　WHITT 10
tool that T. could want,　BYRO 17
t. of the unimaginative,　POUN 25
yoke of t.?　SIDN 15
tyrant: glory of t. head　RANS 26
past the t.'s stroke;　SHAK 18
triple t.;　MILT 36
t. of the human heart,　BRID R 3
t. reap;　SHEL 64
t., shall avail　GRAY 2
t. spell has bound me　BRON 2
tyrants: let my t. know,　BRON 9
thirty/ Mock t.,　BYRO 34
t.' crests and tombs of brass
　SHAK 229
T. fall in every foe!　BURN 48
Tyrian: T. loom,　HORA 10
Tyrone: In the County T.,
　UNKN 195

U

Ugliness: U.! Ashcans　GINS 16
ugly: breaking through the foul and
　u. mists　SHAK 51
earth to u. earth,　GRAV 23
sights of u. death　SHAK 97
u., creepin, blastit wonner,
　BURN 57
u., grisly, bare and thin;
　SOUTHW 9
u. thoughts　SASS 14
u. Yahoo tricks.　LIND V 15
Ulalume: vault of thy lost U.!"
　POE 49
ulcer: hatred's hidden u.　MARV 12
ultimate: seemed in u. peace
　HECH 2
u. dim Thule —　POE 16
ultrablack: super-cool/ u.　LEE 2

unplumbed: u., salt, estranging sea.
ARNO 42

unpolished: u., rugged verse
DRYD 20

unpregnant: u. of my cause,
SHAK 31

unpremeditated: u. Verse: MILT 87

unprofitable: act u., TENN 102
weary, stale, flat, and u.
SHAK 22

unquenched: wild, u., deep-sunken,
ARNO 18

unquiet: gazing on the u. sky.
POE 40
sole u. thing. COLE SAM 14
U. wanderer YEATS 148

unravished: u. bride of quietness,
KEAT 36

unread: u. vision in the higher
dream ELIOT T 12

unreal: loneliness u., RIVE 2
U. city, ELIOT T 118

Unreasoning: U., sanguine,
visionary— HARD 47

unrecorded: u. did it slip away,
ROSS C 17

unredeemable: All time is u.
ELIOT T 15

unreeling: Ever u. them,
WHITM 55

unremarked: u. seated in a corner,
WHITM 33

unremembered: little, nameless, u.
acts WORD 29
Of u. pleasure; WORD 29

unremembering: went her u. way,
THOMP F 2

unremitting: u. interchange
SHEL 41

unreproved: u., if undesired.
ELIOT T 136

unrespected: live unwooed and u.
fade, SHAK 206
my u. love; GRIF 1

unrest: All day long in u., MACW 1
frantic-mad with evermore u.;
SHAK 242

unresting: life's u. sea! HOLM 3

unrestrained: delight/ Nature or u.
appetite. CAREW 13

unripe: It is still u., ROSS C 26

unrolled: u. his feathers DICKI 13
U. its horror in my face—
DICKI 26

unruly: Busy old fool, u. sun,
DONN 55
shepherding the u., DAY 12

unsated: still u., dwelt upon the
scene. COWP 17

unsatisfied: by Calvary's turbulence
u., YEATS 92
cries of u. love WHITM 67
lonely and the u., POUN 24

Of love u. ELIOT T 10
pale u. ones YEATS 91
trembling and u., RICH 16

Unsavoury: U. in th'injoyment
MILT 6

unscarred: In the u. heaven
LOWE J 19

unscathed: with an u. brow,
TIMR 2

unsearchable: smile u. repose—
CRAN H 51
u. dispose/ Of highest wisdom
MILT 118

unseemliest: u. seen, MILT 97

unseemly: all u. stains KEAT 1

unseen: breath of things u.!
CARM 2
"Diffus'd u. KEAT 20
let me live, u., unknown;
POPE A 108
of an u. quarry EMER 44
some u. Power SHEL 29
Spirit of things u., CARM 1
things u. do see, FLET G YO 2
u., as lamps in sepulchres;
POPE A 4
u. by the midday suns, ROON 2
way u., the certain route,
VERY 4

unsettle: don't let that u. you:
GILB 49

unsettlement: technique of u.
AUDE 29

unshaken: u. as the continent.
LONG 26

unsheathed: Tiger Christ u.
SCHW 1
u. from reality. JEFFE 16

unshorn: u. fields, boundless and
beautiful, BRYA 15

unsleeping: sombre soul u.,
SWIN 5

Unspeakable: how wondrous then!/
U., MILT 81
What evil, what u. crime
SNOD 3

unspent: u. and free,
JOHN S (1822–1882) 1

unspoken: lies, self-denial, u. regret
SNOD 15
speech for that u., ELIOT T 96

unstable: stand on a star u.,
AIKE 7
with feet u., LIND V 8

unstaid: beauty's fire/ Inflame u.
desire, PEEL 2

unstain'd: u. with gold or fee,
MILT 122

unstained: They have left u.
HEMA 5

unstilled: u. world still whirled
ELIOT T 13

unstinted: u., Love did sip, LOVE 3

u. tide confined;
JOHN S (1822–1882) 1

unstitching: Our stitching and u.
YEATS 1

unstringed: u. viol or a harp.
SHAK 86

unstrung: my soul lay out of sight,/
Untuned, u.; HERB G 21

unsubstantial: Thou u. air
SHAK 77

unsung: Unwept, unhonour'd, and
u. SCOT WA 12

unsupported: fairest u. flower,
MILT 89

unsure: is still u.: SHAK 175

unsurp: u. the canvas? ASHB 4

unsuspitious: u. led him; MILT 114

unswear: u., and overswear them
DONN 47

unswept: u. stone, besmeared with
sluttish time. SHAK 207

Untainted: U. by man's misery.
SHEL 61

Untarnished: U. fair THOR 10

untended: it's rough and u.
BROO G 19
u. lying, WHITM 71

unthinking: All joyous and u.,
BURN 6

untidy: some u. spot AUDE 63
u. activity continues, BISH 10

untied: knot's u. that made us one,
BRAD 2

untimely: aged accents and u.
words, DANI S 11
All other fair, like flowers, u.
fade. SPENS 26

untired: Forever pampered and u.?
ROBI 5

untouch'd: her meals u. WHITM 17

untouched: greater store of fruit u.,
MILT 94
U. by Morning DICKI 125
u. by Noon— DICKI 125

untranslatable: I too am u.,
WHITM 73

untrodden: bloodless lay the u.
snow, CAMPB T 3
Haunting u. paths DANI S 10
precipices show u. green;
KEAT 65
some u. region of my mind,
KEAT 53

untroubled: leaves u. about us,
WILB 1
u. in her faith, TIMR 2

untrue: Adieu Love, adieu Love, u.
Love, UNKN 291
false as fair,/ Unconstant, frail,
u.; WITH 3
make/ The best philosophy u.
THOR 10

untruth: half damns me with u.,
HERR 20

untune: MUSICK shall u. the Sky.
DRYD 27

Untuned: my soul lay out of sight,/
U., unstrung; HERB G 21

untutor'd: think me some u. youth,
SHAK 238

whose u. mind POPE A 59

Untwisting: U. all the chains
MILT 24

unus'd: u. to flow. SHAK 195

unused: fust in us u. SHAK 35

In some u. lagoon, WHITM 28

unvalued: Inestimable stones, u.
jewels, SHAK 97

leaves of thy u. book MILT 35

unvanquishable: In u. number,
SHEL 40

Unvariably: lie/ U. lovely there,
LARK 15

unveil: mighty mother did u. Her
awful face: GRAY 28

unveiling: Uprising, u., affirm
POE 33

unverified: responsible for a disaster
u., MILE 1

unwanted: feeling u.! BOGA 5

unknown u. life. JARR 22

unwashed: u. Muse CAREW 18

unwearied: u. Sun, ADDI 3

unweeded: u. garden,/ That grows to
seed; SHAK 22

unweeting: u. have offended,
MILT 101

unwept: remember me, u.,
unburied, POUN 6

U., unhonour'd, and unsung.
SCOT WA 12

unwilling: fast, perfect, and u.
TATE J 4

Unwind: U. a love knit up
KING H 6

unwithdrawing: full and u. hand,
MILT 5

unwithered: find u. on its curls
HOUS 58

unwooed: live u. and unrespected
fade, SHAK 206

unworn: O u. world enrapture me,
KAVA 2

unworthy: u. and unknown
MAST 1

up: bringeth down to the grave, and
bringeth u. BIBL, O.T. 8

doubled darkness u. the labouring
hill. ROSS D 7

dress me u. in silks WHITT 16

go u. in a swing,
STEVENSO R 18

gone u. in smoke, THOMP F 8

kids grow u. SNYD 41

Look not thou down but u.!
BROWNI R 76

movin' u. an' down again,
KIPL 4

must call u. SNOD 2

pick them u. in the movies
OHAR 3

took u. the flag WHITT 2

u. and be gone HARD 23

u. and doing, LONG 37

u. and down I sow them
HOUS 33

u. from the fields father,
WHITM 15

u. in the stars. MORR 7

u. the line to death, SASS 3

u. to the Throne, KIPL 25

warsled u., they warsled down,
UNKN 269

windes are u.; CHAT 2

wisp of smoke floats u. SNYD 29

upflight: u. of the murderess
PLATH 16

uphill: road wind u. all the way?
ROSS C 28

uphold: u. your house WYLI 7

uplifted: ah! the u. sword
LAWR 25

high over all/ U., LONG 20

upmost: attains the u. round
SHAK 44

upper: blush tinged the u. sky,
EMER 51

upraise: No dirge will I u. POE 30

upright: beast that walks u.,
JEFFE 2

three posts driven u. AUDE 81

Uprising: U., unveiling, affirm
POE 33

uprose: Prince Lucifer u.,
MERE G 8

upside: disgustingly u. down.
LAWR 3

upsprang: u. the aboriginal name.
WHITM 43

upsprung: broad herds u. MILT 86

upstanding: choose u. men
YEATS 152

clean u. chap like you?
KINGSM 1

upstart: u. wealth's averted eye,
EMER 27

upturned: furrows shine but late u.,
THOR 11

upward: Beat u. to God's throne
BROWNI E 1

Everything is u. striving;
LOWE J 18

grope back u., HARD 42

I'm u. boun'. HOLLO 1

thy u. flight, THOR 6

Turn u. from the desk
ELIOT T 133

waters seeping u., ROET 5

upwards: green grass glows u.,
LAWR 56

Urania: Descend from Heav'n U.,
MILT 83

urge: night u. the morrow, SHEL 2

u. not my amiss, SHAK 243

urged: u. by your propinquity
MILLA 14

Uricon: ashes under U. HOUS 45

Uriel: U. spoke with piercing eye,
EMER 50

U.'s voice of cherub scorn,
EMER 51

urinal: skating in a u. CRAN H 31

urine: the u., cabbage, BROO G 8

urn: Dust in an u. MILLA 35

find thy Darling in an u.
CAREW 6

In this little u. is laid HERR 64

Lip of this poor earthen U.
OMAR 6

mad'st thy mother's womb thine
u. JONS 38

pursues us to the U., STANL 2

shut in an u. of brass! TENN 87

white hand holds an u. DARL 1

Us: between Me and U. AUDE 60

imperfect is so hot in u.,
STEVENS 40

insult to u." YEATS 49

lay between/ U., MONTA 1

Made all we see; and u.,
BROWNI R 16

nothing like u. ever was. SAND 8

So many of u.! PLATH 66

u. who dealt them war OWEN 35

will not dream of u. OWEN 37

With her glove, to watch u.
MONTA 2

world is too much with u.;
WORD 159

usances: my moneys and my u.
SHAK 118

use: chiefly u. my charm
BROWNI R 61

churches fall completely out of u.
LARK 4

cleanest in the u. of his forepaws
SMAR 7

conceive you may u. GILB 25

dowry for a u. in common life.
SHAP 29

Everything is spoilt by u.:
KEAT 17

passion put to u. BROWNI E 5

posterity has no u. KAVA 18

rust unburnished, not to shine in
u.! TENN 131

U. and surprise, EMER 20

u. my wit as a pitchfork
LARK 20

u. of him STEVENSO R 13

u. of virtue TENN 39
U. wiles for witt WYAT 23
u. your wit and shew it so.
  WYAT 17
want to u. again DICKI 17
We u. you, WHITM 22
withholds my pow'r that right to
  u.? MILT 109
used: heart was u. to beat
  TENN 53
I u. to pray PLATH 28
name is U.-to-was, TRAI 5
u. me ungenteelly. COLM 2
used-car: Open Road goes to the u.
  lot. SIMP 13
useful: Ambition mock their u. toil,
  GRAY 8
useless: faggot of u. memories.
  MACN 7
heavy with u. experience,
  RICH 12
more pretentiously/ u. WILLI 30
vehemence of u. tears. JOHN L 7
uses: u. of a new metal. ASHB 1
useternally: smile up at u.
  KAVA 20
usher: Evening must u. night,
  SHEL 2
wife at U.'s Well, UNKN 306
ushering: u. me to the true songs,
  WHITM 36
Ushers: U. in a drearier day.
  BRON 1
Usna: U.'s children died.
  YEATS 121
usquabae: Wi' u., BURN 55
usual: attired in the u. costumes,
  WHITM 18
usura: at behest of u. POUN 11
Duccio came not by u. POUN 10
u., sin against nature, POUN 9
Zuan Bellin' not by u. POUN 10
usurer: u. exact by stealth,
  BEAU/BASS 6
u. hangs the cozener. SHAK 81
usurers: u. tell their gold SHAK 76
Usurp: U. the chair of wit:
  JONS 20
usurpers: Lay the proud u. low!
  BURN 48
usury: courteous ruin of proffered
  u., SIDN 4
utmost: reaching th' u. orb
  MILT 62
through its u. melody, — THOR 5
u. bound of human thought.
  TENN 132
world see the u. of thy hate;
  DRAY 14
Utopia: Not in U., — WORD 112
Some vague U. YEATS 66
Utopia's: U. quite another land;
  GILB 53

utter: my tongue could u. TENN 1
not in u. nakedness, WORD 70
u. forth a glorious Voice, ADDI 4
u. joyous leaves WHITM 39
u. what is just, BIBL, O.T. 41
words could never u.; THAC 3
utter'd: tongues that u. WORD 21
utterance: timely u. gave that
  thought relief, WORD 67
uttered: Till death be u., SHAK 132
utterest: Which Anguish was the u.
  DICKI 153
utterly: changed, changed u.:
  YEATS 56
good things have perished u.,
  WILD 11
hearts sink u.; STEPHENS 1
u. consumed with sharp distress,
  TENN 85
U. frozen DANT 1
uttermost: counsel in this u.
  distress, MILT 101
voice of u. woe. WHITM 49
world; thy u. I see; SIDN 27
uxorious: dull man, dulling and u.,
  POUN 55
pronounced u. BYRO 18

V

vacancy: In chaos of v. shone;
  DE LA 8
vacant: on his v. brain. SHEL 16
on the v. air. WORD 63
V. heart SCOT WA 2
vacuum: its whirling v. MOSS 3
vagrancy: tossed in jail on a v. rap,
  SNYD 25
vagrant: Art, a v. ROBI 42
vague: Some v. Utopia —
  YEATS 66
v. shadow of surmise EMER 24
vaguely: v. realizing westward,
  FROS 50
vaice: your v. an' feace BARNE 2
vain: afflict thy self in v.:
  MILT 111
all Platonic tolerance v.
  YEATS 118
all v. glory, DUNB W 3
attend love's joys in v. CAMPI 21
Begot of nothing but v. fantasy,
  SHAK 141
distant and v. affirmation
  MACL 10
evasions v. And reasonings,
  MILT 99
fields beloved in v.! GRAY 13
futile and v.; SNOD 1
his mother, v. WHITT 19
I shall not live in v.: DICKI 74

in v. the distance beacons.
  TENN 79
Infusing him with self and v.
  conceit, SHAK 89
insatiate to pursue/ V. war with
  Heav'n, MILT 58
judge all beauty v.; UNKN 74
not sought in v., COWP 12
parcel of v. strivings THOR 1
pine in v. the sacred Seven;
  EMER 7
renders v. their deep desire? —
  ARNO 42
sealed in v., SHAK 117
Seem yet in v. LIND V 3
seldom spent in v., SHAK 87
Selfish, v./ Eternal bane!
  BLAK 62
sun/ Shone in v.: THOMA E 14
that v. Animal, ROCH 8
Time his sickle brings/ In v.,
  CAREW 11
'Tis all in v.! BLAK 38
tricks that are v., HART 1
v. all Doric discipline.
  YEATS 118
v. desire was chidden — MUND 2
v. his wings. CAREW 11
v. hope of gain: TICH 1
v., if it exists. MOOR M 41
v. produced, all rays return;
  EMER 50
v. travail hath wearied me
  WYAT 30
V. wisdom all, MILT 60
Vainly: V. begot, GREV 9
v. the dreams of youth recall.
  WHITT 21
v. thinking SHAK 238
Vale: " Ave atque V." TENN 14
fruits in v. and mountain,
  UNKN 290
gup, Jack of the V.! SKEL 4
lone v. we loved MOOR T 1
many a dark and drearie V.
  MILT 61
v. of restless mind UNKN 205
violet imbroider'd v. MILT 9
world as a v. of tears?'
  BROWNI R 23
valentine: Petrushka's v. pivots on
  its pin." CRAN H 54
Tomorrow is Saint V.'s day,
  SHAK 36
Vales: Groves and flowrie V.,
  MILT 65
hills and v. SORL 1
o'er v. and hills, WORD 24
valet: v., too, to every four. GILB 4
valiant: So long time war of v.
  men, SURR 8
still the v. brave, DAVE 1
v. died; FRENE 3

valiantly: safe from action, v. advise; ROCH 3

valkyries: ospreys/ would fall like v. BIRN 5

valley: Below a fertile v. WHITM 9
bicker down a v. TENN 4
Darker grows the v., MERE G 5
Down in the v., UNKN 80
gloomy v.; FLET J 3
not in the wide world a v. so sweet MOOR T 7
some irriguous v. MILT 69
temperate v., ELIOT T 50
to the green v., UNKN 11
v. of Death TENN 6
v. of dying stars ELIOT T 46
v. of love and delight. UNKN 260
v. of the shadow, POE 19
v. of the shadow of death, BIBL, O.T. 31
V. quivered GINS 41
v. sheep are fatter; PEAC 1
V. so low, UNKN 80
v. warm and green, HODG 3
wind bit hard at V. Forge SAND 23

valleys: deep, deathlike v. SERV 12
greenest of our v. POE 20
hills and v. into singing break; VAUG 1
lick the V. up — DICKI 55
lily of the v. BIBL, O.T. 70
singing to the green v. MAST 8
V. breathe, GINS 42
v. of Hall LANIE 5

valor: defeated v. lies, TIMR 7
peace your v. won. HOPKINSO 1
v. hath slain her knight, GREV/DYER 2

valorous: drank the v. youth of a new world. MARK 2

valour: contemplation he and v. formed, MILT 72
true V. see, BUNY 1

value: all we v. HOLM 7
Metal, intrinsic v., WINT 3

valued: wealth he v. not a groat; SWIF 25

valueless: in a v. world, GUNN 13
life which was v. SPEND 20

Valves: close the V. of her attention — DICKI 133

vampire: v. who said he was you PLATH 32

Van Doren: Mark V.,/ a poem of remembrance, HAYD 4

Van Vocht: Says the Shan V. UNKN 217

vanish: sad scenes and thoughts and feelings v. THOMS J (1834–1882) 7
v. in oblivions host, CLARE 7
v. with a wink of tails, MACN 21

will unto desire,/ As smoke we v. Æ 3

vanish'd: many a v. sight. SHAK 195

vanished: light canoes have v. SIGO 1
touch of a v. hand, TENN 2
v. from his lonely hearth. WORD 17

vanishes: beauty v.; beauty passes; DE LA 9

vanities: Vanity of v., BIBL, O.T. 6
With varying v., POPE A 112

vanity: day's v., the night's remorse. YEATS 24
earthly things is but v.: UNKN 90
more harmless v.? LAMB 4
Pull down thy v., POUN 22
soul unto v., BIBL, O.T. 33
This is not v. POUN 23
trifling title of v. SIDN 4
V. of vanities, BIBL, O.T. 6
V., saith the preacher, BROWNI R 13
v., sets love a task like that." HUNT 4
yet forbidden v., GREV 9

Vanquished: V. in life, his death JOHN L 4
v. powers were glad AUDE 53
victors and the v. HARD 21

vanted: spoild of his v. spoile; MILT 64

vapor: From argentine v.? — THOMP F 14
v. sometimes like a bear or lion, SHAK 9

vapors: v. that did seem to strangle him SHAK 51

vapours: dark v. have oppress'd KEAT 1
V., and clouds, and storms. THOMS J (1700–1748) 12
v. weep their burthen to the ground, TENN 120

variable: painted all with v. flowers, SPENS 39

variant: bad v. nor a tryout. HUGH T 9

varicose: v. horror. ROET 54

varied: v. carols I hear, WHITM 37
Winter comes, to rule the v. year, THOMS J (1700–1748) 12

variegated: Ladies, like v. tulips, POPE A 94

variety: sated with v. LOVE 4
v. of forms. MOOR M 6

various: only the v. envies, AUDE 50
rural seat of v. view: MILT 69
So v., so beautiful, so new, ARNO 3

speaks/ A v. language: BRYA 22
v. ruling passions find, POPE A 97

varnisht: ambition v. o'er with zeal. MILT 59

vary: v. from the kindly race TENN 121

varying: beauty, which is v. MICH 3
With v. vanities, POPE A 112

vase: life's v. Of glass THOR 2
lofty v.'s side, GRAY 18

vases: v. and fringes. BROO G 1

Vassar: Reading their poems to V. girls, SIMP 9

vast: All's v. that v. means. THOMP F 5
dome more v., HOLM 3
more devils than v. hell can hold; SHAK 127
Nature's v. frame, SHEL 22
Naught but v. sorrow DE LA 8
v. sweet visage of space. LANIE 4
v. wings across the canceled skies. MACL 4

vasty: v. hall of death. ARNO 21

vault: dark v. above BRID R 15
Heaven's v., MARV 2
heaven's v. should crack. SHAK 85
mere lees/ Is left this v. to brag of. SHAK 109
some tall v. unfold — POE 42
through the crystal v. CHAU 46
v. of thy lost Ulalume!" POE 49

vaulter: Green little v. in the sunny grass, HUNT 8

Vaulting: V. ambition, which o'erleaps itself SHAK 105
V. the sea, the prairies dreaming sod, CRAN H 29

Vaunt: V. in their youthful sap, SHAK 187
V.-couriers SHAK 75

vaunted: v. name Virginity, MILT 6

veal: knuckle of v., UNKN 303

vegetable: information v., animal, and mineral; GILB 35
pierced the slow v. veins LAWR 16
pure v. kingdom, GINS 14
v. fashion GILB 32
waiting for us in a foetor/ Of v. sweat MAHON 2

vegetables: chickens/ ate the v. CUMM 30
v. tremble, GINS 42

vegetarian: so v.,/ he wore rope shoes LOWE R 31

vegetation: laid/ With cold v. SITW 3
smelling of v., ELIOT T 50

rat crept softly through the v.
ELIOT T 130

vegetative: With the v. speed
DEVL 1

vehemence: hearty in its v.,
WHITT 10

v. of useless tears. JOHN L 7

veil: Behind the v., TENN 37

Death is the v. SHEL 57

v. down to the slender waist,
MILT 73

v. the heaven's mysterious face;
WINC 1

Veil'd: V. Melancholy has her
sovran shrine, KEAT 43

veiled: blackness v. his dizzy eyes,
SHEL 16

Must all be v., HERB G 45

veils: angel throng, bewinged,
bedight/ In v., POE 30

future v. its face, MELV 19

v. are drawn TEAS 4

v. her sacred fires, POPE A 2

vein: doctor punched my v.
SHAP 26

veined: blue v. unconscious girl
GINS 39

veins: blood in the v., SITW 8

chains/ Of nerves, and arteries,
and v.; MARV 11

dark v. of her mother,
THOMA D 38

dried the sap out of my v.,
YEATS 57

in man's v. ROSE 3

let their v. run cold. OWEN 31

mire of human v. YEATS 17

pierced the slow vegetable v.
LAWR 16

ragings must his v. convulse,
BURN 5

red v. full of money,
THOMA D 41

rush for my v., WHITM 77

Through all his v.
JOHN S (1709–1784) 17

through their v. in ice and fire
HOUS 46

v., in my bones I feel it, —
ROET 5

v. rolling roughly WALK 7

v. start and spread, RALEG 11

veldt: bloodstreams of the v.
WALC 1

breaks the v. HARD 19

velleity: dull/ Impatience or a fierce
v., WILB 26

velvet: Live like the v. mole;
WYLI 2

starry v. in the night, ROBI 40

v. helmet TAYL E 13

walk in v. shoes: WYLI 10

venal: abandoned by each v. friend,
GRAY 21

Venerandam: V.,/ In the Cretan's
phrase, POUN 8

venerie: lovede v., CHAU 18

vengeance: Hatred and v.,
COWP 14

Herod shrieking v. LOWE R 22

holds v. in his hand SHAK 98

vengeful: v. god would call to me
HARD 24

Venice: Eternal V. sinking
BOWER 2

Ocean's nursling, V. lies, —
SHEL 36

sweet to dream in V., VAN DY 1

venom: pointed shapes of v.,
RODG 4

venomous: flatterers' v.
insinuations, SIDN 4

is alive, v. WILLI 5

ventures: lose our v. SHAK 50

venturing: v., throwing, WHITM 55

Venus: O'erpicturing that V.
SHAK 5

prente of Sainte V. seel. CHAU 90

timid, bending V., BEDD 1

V. among the fishes LAWR 58

V. comes not ev'ry Day.
DRYD 24

V., love's lady, was born of the
sea; JORD 1

V. me yaf CHAU 92

V., take my votive glass: PRIO 7

V., that is Queene of love,
SPENS 43

V. with her ecstasy." KAVA 15

Verb: V. drove up, KOCH 3

verbs: Irregular v. to learn,
AUDE 17

strange/ v. conjugated RIVE 1

verdant: Poor v. fool, LOVE 1

smoothed these v. swells,
BRYA 16

verdict: Snark found the v.,
CARRO 15

verdure: crown of v. weaves,
ALEX 5

verdurous: Whose v. anonymity
TATE A 13

verge: low dark v. of life TENN 29

Verlaine: Rimbaud and V., AIKE 2

stick with V. OHAR 5

V. for Patsy OHAR 5

verminously: shirt v. busy ROSE 7

vernal: birds their quire apply; airs,
v. airs, MILT 70

impulse from a v. wood
WORD 145

Vers: harmonious Sisters, Voice, and
V., MILT 1

verse: court others in v., PRIO 2

eternal V. employ'd COWL 12

farming of a v. AUDE 45

fictions only and false hair/
Become a v.? HERB G 44

in lonely peace, the spousal v.
WORD 16

in v. my love to show, SIDN 5

incantation of this v., SHEL 46

Let the v. the subject fit,
CAREY 2

life immortal from my v.
HERR 54

Married to immortal v., MILT 24

mournful V. Indite, PHILL 2

my v. exhal'd thy name,
CAREW 7

My v. your virtues rare shall
eternize, SPENS 24

Propping v. for fear of falling
JONS 9

prose is grand v., LOWE J 8

rehearse/ The holy incantation of a
v.; HERR 71

subject for immortal v. DAY 13

subject of all v.: BROWNE 3

to write v. with him is to
transprose; DRYD/TATE 1

Unhappie V., SPENS 35

unmelodious v.: STEPHEN 2

unpolished, rugged v. DRYD 20

unpremeditated V.: MILT 87

V. calls them forth; 'tis V. that
gives LAND 5

v. distills your truth SHAK 206

v. is the true image of my mind,
DRAY 9

v. of a Lapland song LONG 32

v. of thine HERR 36

v. shall make, HERR 23

v. shall stand, SHAK 210

v. you grave for me:
STEVENSO R 21

Were it not for V.: GOGA 1

versed: v. in country things
FROS 66

Verses: Book of V. OMAR 2

"I hate my v., JEFFE 17

no v. to repeate: JONS 15

Rhime the Rudder is of V.,
BUTL 6

Versing: V., like an exile, KINS 3

vertical: blanching, v. eye-glare
BROWNI E 1

sorcery devout and v.
BROO G 11

vertu: v. engendred is the flour;
CHAU 3

vertue: fierie v. rouz'd MILT 116

Loose all thir v.; MILT 59

Love v., she alone is free,
MILT 13

v. giv'n for lost, MILT 117

v. overcome by vice, KYNA 1

your v. now I raise. JONS 30

very: black/ is/ to be/ v.-hot. LEE 4
It's v. hot, GILB 39
something v. like one. SILKI 1
That v. knowing,/ Overflowing,
GILB 16
vesper: black v.'s pageants.
SHAK 9
vessel: cast the v. ashore
CARRY 11
Let the Irish v. lie AUDE 43
trust the sanity of my v.;
OHAR 16
v. grim and daring; WHITM 45
vest: Truth, in sunny v. arrayed,
COLL 8
v. which seems to hide them;
SHEL 53
vestige: v. of the thoughts
ROSS C 20
v. of this flower. FRENE 6
vestiges: v. of pomp, TOOM 2
vestry: preacher glides to the v.-
door, HARD 38
re-enact at the v.-glass HARD 39
vesture: detain her v.'s hem,
EMER 24
veteran: Superfluous lags the v. on
the stage.
JOHN S (1709-1784) 21
veterans: my v., WHITM 27
Two v. son and father dropt
together, WHITM 26
vet'ran: v. on the stage,
JOHN S (1709-1784) 14
vexed: v. question of men SIMP 4
v. to nightmare by a rocking
cradle, YEATS 136
vexes: v. me to choose another
guide: BRON 6
Vexing: V. their blood MELV 10
veyne: bathed every v. CHAU 3
vials: In v. of ivory and coloured
glass ELIOT T 121
vibrates: throat and breast and
wings v. BLAK 37
when soft voices die,/ V. in the
memory, SHEL 43
vibration: brave v. HERR 62
vibrations: v. of deathless music;
MAST 1
vibrator: electric storm/ of the v.
LEVI 4
Vicar: I'll be the V. of Bray,
UNKN 297
vice: pride, the never-failing v. of
fools. POPE A 32
vertue overcome by v., KYNA 1
vices: cure the v. of mankind;
SWIF 22
small v. do appear; SHAK 81
Unnatural v. ELIOT T 33
v.' overthrow, SIDN 20

vicinity: well-nightingaled v.?
HOUS 6
vicious: think me too v.
THOMA D 40
Time so v. ROBI 16
Vicissitudes: watch the wild V. of
Taste; JOHN S (1709-1784) 8
victim: insults the v. whom he
kills; CRAB 3
See the v.'s face become their
own MACN 3
v. must be found, GILB 26
v. treads unfalteringly GRAV 34
victims: litte v. play; GRAY 16
taken in many v. REED I 1
victor: v.'s tireless/ thrusts,
BARA 11
Victoria: In a borealic iceberg came
V.; SITW 1
white gulls south of V. SNYD 31
Victorian: dropping V. shoulders.
LAWR 20
victories: peace hath her v.
MILT 123
victorious: lower v. WHITM 57
ly'st v. Among thy slain self-kill'd
MILT 115
O'er a' the ills o' life v.!
BURN 53
voice in that v. brow. ARNO 29
victors: Let the v., ARNO 14
v. and the vanquished HARD 21
Victory: Life, Joy, Empire and V.
SHEL 58
'twas a famous v. SOUTHE 1
v. was our defeat. READ H 1
V. won't come MOOR M 20
years that follow v. MELV 6
victual-wagons: empty v. up the
street ALBI 1
victuals: eat your v. fast enough;
HOUS 49
sniffed the v. STEVENSO R 5
Vienna: V. London ELIOT T 148
Vietnam: Did the people of V.
LEVE 23
view: favorite scenic v., HAYD 7
Let observation with extensive v.,
JOHN S (1709-1784) 15
rural seat of various v.: MILT 69
v. yourself as I was, ROBI 20
with a moral v. designed
SWIF 22
viewless: imprisoned in the v.
winds SHAK 115
v. wings of Poesy, KEAT 48
views: black with more than
melancholy v.
THOMS J (1700-1748) 13
diff'rent v. engage,/ Superfluous
lags JOHN S (1709-1784) 14
v. in bredth, MILT 65
with certain definite v. HEAN 14

vigil: Ending my v. strange
WHITM 107
V. for comrade WHITM 107
v. I never forget, WHITM 107
v. of night WHITM 107
V. strange I kept WHITM 106
vigor: has everlasting v.,
MOOR M 26
vigorous: royal eagle draws his v.
young, THOMS J (1700-1748) 8
vigour: celestial v. armed;
MILT 113
v. in my sense TRAH 10
Vile: always reckoned/ V., LAND 2
bastard v., RALEG 5
clay is v. DUNB P 13
God clothed himself in v. man's
flesh, DONN 54
himself one v. antithesis.
POPE A 11
To the v. dust, SCOT WA 12
vileinye: do shame and v.;
CHAU 112
vileness: man in all his v.
MOOR M 23
vilest: v. deeds like poison weeds,
WILD 3
with v. worms to dwell:
SHAK 214
vileyns: v. sinful dedes make a
cherl. CHAU 113
villa: At Timon's v. POPE A 100
lawn at the v. SIMP 7
village: every Middlesex v. and
farm, LONG 44
frost was on the v. roofs
STEVENSO R 5
house is in the v. FROS 107
listen to the merry v. chime.
GILB 38
loveliest v. GOLD 1
men in the v. of Erith UNKN 89
Middlesex v. and farm, —
LONG 45
pavement of Greenwich V.
GINS 20
sewage flows from the v.,
MAST 5
Soft maids and v. hinds COLL 1
Sweet smiling v. GOLD 2
through an Alpine v. LONG 21
v. smithy stands; LONG 48
villages: ghosts of the v. MERW 1
v. vanished, BLUN 5
villain: condemns me for a v.
SHAK 99
I am a v. SHAK 99
v. spider lives,
THOMS J (1700-1748) 10
You v. touch! WHITM 73
villanelles: Triolets, v., MAST 11
vindicate: v. the ways of God to
Man. POPE A 59

v. so divine: LODG 7
v. walked their narrow round,
  JOHN S (1709–1784) 3
virtuoso: v. of the heart, KINS 3
virtuous: gentle wit/ And v. mind,
  SPENS 25
sweet and v. soul, HERB G 72
these are more v. SHAK 136
v. men pass mildly away,
  DONN 62
v. son. JONS 39
visage: dejected havior of the v.,
  SHAK 21
great Casey's v. shone; THAY 3
saintly v. MILT 15
vast sweet v. of space. LANIE 4
vise: gripped in bony v. HAYD 24
visible: Arch Fear in a v. form,
  BROWNI R 68
darkness v. MILT 50
music/ almost v. PLUM 1
self-made from elements least v.
  BISH 20
V. is V., GINS 45
vision: baseless fabric of this v.,
  SHAK 163
brightness of the v., RANDA D 5
Divine V. still was seen, BLAK 26
finality of v., AMMO 9
hawk's wing/ of v. SNYD 32
horrid v. seized my head, SWIF 3
in gradual v. through my tears,
  BROWNI E 7
latest-born and loveliest v. far
  KEAT 52
life is a watch or a v. SWIN 2
likeness for thy v.? SWIN 6
night/ Involved and swallowed up
  the v.; SHEL 16
Saw the V. of the world,
  TENN 75
Summon a v. ROET 23
thy v. is reclaimed! CRAN H 15
unread v. in the higher dream
  ELIOT T 12
v. of the great One GINS 46
v. of them put together
  FROS 130
v., or a waking dream? KEAT 51
visionary: fled the v. gleam?
  WORD 68
paint the v. dreariness
  WORD 114
Unreasoning, sanguine, v.
  HARD 47
v. company of love, CRAN H 36
visioning: v. a world HAYD 6
visions: Stories of sweet v.,
  CLARE 13
these v. did appear. SHAK 129
v. of sugarplums MOOR C 1
visit: make our v. ELIOT T 77

smiling spring its earliest v. paid,
  GOLD 1
V. the soul in sleep, — SHEL 42
visitation: nightly v. MILT 87
visited: v. in Heaven — DICKI 61
v. the Sea — DICKI 62
visitor: inspector, v., SPEND 4
visits: too rare, grow now my v.
  ARNO 44
vista: down the v. of years,
  LAWR 31
passed to the end of a v., POE 49
vital: Death broke at once the v.
  chain, JOHN S (1709–1784) 4
resign our v. breath, STANL 2
vitals: passion rends my v. as I
  pass, MCKA 10
red v. of his heart RANS 9
vivid: left the v. air SPEND 12
Violent, v., EBER 6
Vixen: now, Prancer and V.!
  MOOR C 2
vocal: Made v. by my song,
  MILT 82
wish the taps less v., RICH 8
vocation: his whole v. WORD 76
Vocht: Says the Shan Van V.
  UNKN 217
voice: angel's v. GODO 1
attend the spell/ Of his v.
  POE 26
back the publick V.
  JOHN S (1709–1784) 9
bird's v. Speaking for all
  THOMA E 16
but a wandering V.? WORD 150
child's v. be heard, WHITM 8
clear announcer's v. WILB 4
daylong v. of Eve FROS 69
dead man's v. MACL 10
different v. and features: SWIF 12
harmonious Sisters, V., and Vers,
  MILT 1
her grandmother's v., HARJ 2
In curve and v. and eye HARD 26
joy's the v. CUMM 8
lifted up his v. and sang,
  ROBI 46
low wind, its playmate's v.,
  SHEL 59
madness chooses out my v.
  BOGA 1
make harmonious mix of v. and
  string BIBL, O.T. 67
melting v. MILT 24
monotonous v. in the skull
  MONTA 3
monumental Argument of the
  hewn v., THOMA D 5
next year's words await another
  v. ELIOT T 66
No v. divine COWP 2
Obey the v. at eve EMER 47

Persephone herself is but a v.
  LAWR 5
Philomel her v. doth raise?
  WOTT 4
raise for good the supplicating v.,
  JOHN S (1709–1784) 22
rational v. is dumb: AUDE 34
ruin a fine tenor v. AUDE 49
sing of it with my own v.
  LOWE A 3
So smooth, so sweet, so silvery, is
  thy v. HERR 63
sound of a v. that is still!
  TENN 2
sound of the v. praying.
  ELIOT T 63
sounds the v. of One SITW 13
speak in a flat v. WRIG J 6
summer v., Musketaquit,
  EMER 48
their sad and fatal v. FULL 4
They hear a v. GRAY 15
tried to hear your v., SLES 5
Until her v. grew shrill.
  YEATS 51
Uriel's v. of cherub scorn,
  EMER 51
utter forth a glorious V., ADDI 4
v. a blind man dreams GARR 1
V. above their beat —
  THOMP F 7
v. did weave/ Songs SHEL 75
v. fell, like a falling star,
  LONG 23
v./ From the ancient room, Æ 1
v. I hear this passing night
  KEAT 50
v. in my dreaming ear melted
  away. CAMPB T 9
v. in that victorious brow.
  ARNO 29
v. in the darkness, LONG 45
v. is neither high nor low,
  WHITM 91
v. is thin WALK 10
V. of God! WORD 88
v. of my little captain,
  WHITM 90
v. of my spirit tallied WHITM 50
v. of one that jumps for joy.
  HOUS 10
v. of peace bring sweet release
  ROON 3
v. of the Bard! BLAK 66
v. of the Lobster; CARRO 1
v. of the Sluggard; WATT I 5
v. of the turtle is heard in our
  land; BIBL, O.T. 72
v. of uttermost woe. WHITM 49
v. replied, far up the height,
  LONG 22
v. said: ROET 56
v. so thrilling WORD 139

voices

v. still so hollow HARD 2
v. than thunder is more loud,
　THOR 5
v. that stills LUCR 6
v. was propertied/ As all the tunèd
　spheres, SHAK 7
v. without a face AUDE 80
Wachusett hides its lingering v.
　SIGO 2
walk among noise and deny the
　v. ELIOT T 14
whispering v. SIDN 28
with her v. might captivate my
　mind. MARV 13
with inviolable v. ELIOT T 122

voices: By words, by v., a lost
　way— MACL 7
Children's v. in the orchard
　ELIOT T 57
dried v., ELIOT T 41
exuberant v. of music, JEFFE 6
Join v. all ye living souls,
　MILT 82
music of two v. SHEL 66
open v. hospitality— WHITM 44
reasoning of the eternal v.,
　OHAR 16
red faces and virile v., MACDI 3
scraping squeal/ Of seabird's v.
　SLES 5
sea has many v., ELIOT T 29
Two v. are there: STEPHEN 3
v. of children BLAK 77
v. of Duty call— LANIE 5
v. of that hearth WHITT 29
v. one by one/ Faded, NEWB 4
v. singing out of empty cisterns
　ELIOT T 150
v. were in all men's ears
　ARNO 34
web/ Of fabulous grass and eternal
　v. KAVA 2
when soft v. die, SHEL 43

void: concrete v. of insulin
　GINS 15
flying to the v., EMER 9
in the v. SNYD 46
left a v.; JOHN S (1709–1784) 3
Lord in the V.? GINS 23
undying cry of the v. DICKEY 8
v., dark, and drear, COLE SAM 7
v. of Cares and Strife, PHILL 1
v. of mystery and dread. SANT 2

volatile: v. friend Mr. Jefferson,
　POUN 12

volcanic: sweet v. cone;
　LOWE R 51

vole: might I v. HOLM 1

volition: v. nor consciousness.
　MOOR M 13

Volleyed: chimneys v. out;
　STEVENSO R 5
V. and thundered; TENN 8

vollied: enlightened by the v. glare;
　MELV 18

Voltaire: mock on, V., Rousseau!
　BLAK 38

volte: v. face of decimals, LAWR 54

volubility: brininess and v. GRAV 3

volume: book and v. of my brain,
　SHAK 28
mystic v. of the world LONG 27
quaint and curious v. POE 34

volumes: v. of the skies. HABI 2
written such v. LEAR 7

voluntary: Her v. fruits, TASS 2

vomit: Bitter memory like v.
　SNYD 9

Vomitest: howling on for more,/ V.
　thy wrecks SHEL 68

vortex: v. of our grave CRAN H 50

vote: mayor comes to get my v.
　CORS 6
v. just as their leaders tell 'em to.
　GILB 23

voted: v. by common consent)
　BROWNI R 36

votive: Venus, take my v. glass:
　PRIO 7

vouchsafe: v. me but this loving
　thought— SHAK 196

vow: as false as a well-kept v.
　BETJ 1
constant faith and service v.,
　CAREW 2

vow'd: Me in my v./ Picture
　HORA 4

vowel: one grand transcendental v.
　JARR 8

vowels: consonants and v.
　RANS 34
ear the open v. tire; POPE A 24
Fastening v., as with fetters
　JONS 9
v. rise like balloons. PLATH 64

vows: bound by v. and by
　promotion, GREV 10
cancel all our v., DRAY 15
Heaven v. to keep him. JONS 8
I change in v., and in devotion.
　DONN 45
made no v., WORD 103
maidens' v. and swearing
　WITH 3
mar a lover's v. YEATS 94
v. shall ever true remain; GAY 7
v. you swore me AUDE 65

voyage: v. of their life SHAK 50
V. through death HAYD 11

voyages: After free v. WHITM 28

Voyaging: for ever/ V. WORD 101

voyces: Birdes, v., instruments,
　windes, waters, all agree.
　SPENS 32

vulgar: From v. bounds POPE A 30

limits of a v. fate: GRAY 31
with v. brains SIDN 22

vulgarity: mould of its v.,
　JEFFE 37

vulnerable: until love's v. ROET 9

vulture: greedy v.'s prey. MARV 15
V., whose wings are dull
　realities? POE 1

vultures: Thoughts, like old v.,
　WATT I 1

W

Wachusett: W. hides its lingering
　voice SIGO 2

waddled: w. in the mud, CLARE 10
w. in the water-pudge, CLARE 10

waders: In w. and peaked cap
　HEAN 4

Wadsworth: Henry W., Alfred,
　GILB 12

wae: w. to thee, BURN 36

waft: w. the angel POE 30

wafted: Let me be w. WHITM 42
woodbine spices are w. abroad,
　TENN 93

wag: wood, the weed, the w.
　RALEG 13

wage: w. against thine enemies'
　SHAK 69
w. by force or guile MILT 52

wager: w. in their joy GILB 42
w. the rascals a crown GOLD 6

wages: Half-a-crown is stopped out
　of your w.! GILB 59
paid him his w., VAN DY 4
pay no praise or w. THOMA D 28
ta'en thy w.; SHAK 18

waggery: mixture of gravity and w.
　SMAR 8

wagging: w. clock THOMA D 15

waggon: Her w.-spokes SHAK 153

wagon: little red w., NASH 15
weathered—like a farm w.
　WILLI 44

Wagtail: Little Trotty W.,
　CLARE 10

wail: new w. my dear time's waste.
　SHAK 195
sit by thee and w. my fill:
　BRET 3
so sings, yet so does w.? LYLY 3

wailing: truth w. there like a red
　babe. EBER 7
w. winds and naked woods
　BRYA 7

wails: w. In the trees HECH 5

wainscot: dark w. and timbered
　roof, NEWB 3

waist: belly, buttocks, and her w.
  HERR 68
great weight below the w.,
  LAWR 20
look above your W.; SWIF 13
veil down to the slender w.,
  MILT 73
waistband: his w. split; HOLM 13
wait: Be still./ W. ROET 38
Better w. awhile; ROSS C 26
for a loved one
  must w. UNKN 308
I w. forlorn. ARNO 32
keep quite still and w. LARK 17
Learn to labor and to w.
  LONG 37
long w. for the angel, PLATH 20
long will w. the fold, HOUS 30
revenge for being made to w.,
  JUST 1
rick will w., HOUS 30
stand and w." MILT 124
W., Kate! DAIC 1
w., through wintry hours,
  MCCRE 2
w. till judgment break DICKI 3
W., with impatient readiness,
  COWP 14
Who w. like thee, ARNO 24
you always w., WHITM 22
waite: sommer and his pleasures w.
  on thee, SHAK 224
waited: Earth has w. for them,
  ROSE 4
panting lizard/ w. for history,
  STAF 1
w. for the light, ROBI 52
You have w., WHITM 22
waiter: former Macon w. DAVIS 6
waitest: w. late and com'st alone,
  BRYA 32
waiting: earthly mothers w.,
  sleeplessly. STEVENS 60
Like a taxi throbbing w.,
  ELIOT T 133
Reading while w. RICH 15
w. for a knock upon the door.
  ELIOT T 126
w. for a sigh. AUDE 79
w. for rain. ELIOT T 30
w. for the end? EMPS 8
W. for Warren. FROS 19
w. for you. WHITM 74
w. room/ was full of grown-up
  people, BISH 21
W. the Judgment Day: — FINC 2
w. the long years FIEL E 7
waitresses: calves of w. WILB 42
waits: seed w. for fire SNYD 46
w. for the world to begin.
  MERW 9

w./ The triumph or the tomb.
  TIMR 2
yet she w. for me, SEXT 17
wake: cannot w. itself. AMMO 19
die before I w., UNKN 193
harsh world in which I w. to
  weep, SHEL 76
I hesitate,/ and w. RICH 28
I w. to sleep, ROET 59
Janet implored us, W. her from
  her sleep!' RANS 21
leave no w., LOWE J 19
pain/ You w. to is not yours.
  PLATH 70
peace may w. and pity me.
  CAMPI 22
sleep past, we w. eternally,
  DONN 18
Sleep to w. BROWNI R 12
(sleep w. hope and then)
  CUMM 5
time for you to w.; MEW 1
'tween asleep and w.? SHAK 70
w. and live. — SHEL 42
W. from thy nest, robin
  redbreast! HEYW 2
w. or sleep? KEAT 51
w. us/ Time and time over.
  LARK 8
We w. and whisper awhile,
  DE LA 4
year w. year to sorrow. SHEL 2
waked: w. not from her swound,
  HOLM 11
wakeful: these w. eyes LAND 15
W. they lie. GRAV 4
waken: w. but to weep. DAY 9
wakens: Spring w. too; TENN 52
wakes: Love w. men, PATM 2
May-poles, hock-carts, wassails,
  w., HERR 1
mimic fancy w. MILT 80
sleep which never w. again.
  THOMS J (1834–1882) 7
w. up sleep, THOMA D 2
waking: Days of danger, nights of
  w. SCOT WA 9
good morrow to our w. souls,
  DONN 29
In the midnight w., WHITM 17
Remembered on w. BRID R 6
take my w. slow. ROET 59
vision, or a w. dream? KEAT 51
W. love suffereth no sleepe:
  SPENS 37
W. renew'd WHITM 103
wept with w. eyes: MERE G 10
Waldron: to Mal W. OHAR 6
walk: Bird came down the W.
  DICKI 12
Catullus w. that way? YEATS 132
closer w. with God, COWP 25

early smile has stayed my w.;
  BRYA 35
forenoon w., my rest, WHITM 23
friends w. by friends. YEATS 73
let me w. with thee GLAD 1
lithe abandon of your w.,
  BENN G 6
meet to w. the line FROS 56
new w. is a new walk. AMMO 9
slow silent w. HARD 29
sorrow I w. with UNKN 100
staff of faith to w. upon,
  RALEG 10
they w. the earth, VERY 1
w. among long dappled grass,
  YEATS 139
w. among us, as Baldwin has
  said. ALBA 1
w. dead still. JONS 25
W. in a gingerly manner
  BROO G 6
w. in th' old ways MEW 5
w. in the snow. WYLI 10
w. in velvet shoes: WYLI 10
w. into my parlor? HOWI 1
w. liberating, AMMO 3
w. like this,' GILB 3
W. softly, March, SARE 1
w. the dog. BARA 15
w. the studious cloister's pale,
  MILT 18
W. wide o' the Widow KIPL 31
wild deer's w.: TUCK 1
walk'd: w. where the ripples
  WHITM 1
walked: Adjective w. by, KOCH 3
dead feet w. in. HARD 40
glittered when he w. ROBI 51
I w. in silence WHITM 48
livery/ W. crowns and crownets;
  SHAK 7
month since I w., WHITM 48
she w. to sing. STEVENS 18
she w. unaware MACDONO 1
w. in glory WORD 121
W. in the wilderness; GRAV 13
W. on the banks GINS 33
W. with them LONG 26
when you w. singing MOMA 5
walker: O delicate w., MACN 13
walketh: Him that w. in the garden
  BLAK 14
w. not in the counsel of the
  ungodly, BIBL, O.T. 21
walking: Christ w. on the water
  THOMP F 12
come/ W. securely, WINT 9
enterprise/ In w. naked.
  YEATS 31
Life's but a w. shadow,
  SHAK 114
w. dully along; AUDE 62
w. or sitting, WHITM 6

w. round in a ring./ Thank you.
ELIOT T 117
w./ Somehow from the sun
LARK 11
W. the sea so heavily armed;
YOUN A 1
w. their rounds, BLAK 65
w. to Blackberry Fold.
UNKN 232
w. with an inner peace, ASHB 1
w. your streets, WHITM 30
walks: Dreaming of evening w.
AUDE 20
in hand with her he w.; WHITT 7
living w. upon: VERY 5
moon/ W. the night DE LA 21
mourning figure w., LIND V 1
On water the Man-Fisher w.
LOWE R 14
one has eaten and one w.,
OHAR 13
reputable w. of old established
trees SNOD 8
w./ In parks or alleys,
BROO G 21
when she w. SHAK 237
walkt: carcase breath'd, and w., and
slept, PHILI K 1
wall: against a sweating w.
ROET 31
body by the w.! ARNO 14
Bores through his castle w.,
SHAK 89
close the w. up SHAK 56
conclude against a w. of stone.
WILB 30
cringing by the w., TATE A 20
engenders there/ The broken w.,
YEATS 85
Flower in the crannied w.,
TENN 13
gap in the old w. still, WHITT 32
gray stone w. damming my
stream, KNIG 8
Helen will come upon the w.
ARNO 15
icicles hang by the w., SHAK 101
Looks at me from the w.,
LONG 13
love a w., FROS 55, 58
office of a w., SHAK 88
Pressed to the w., MCKA 7
rusty gun on the w., SAND 1
silk blown against a w. POUN 27
small in the w. CREE 5
"Speed!" echoed the w.
BROWNI R 35
top of the w.! MOOR C 2
w. between us as we go FROS 56
w. between us once again.
FROS 56
w.-builders than fools. FROS 17
w. is strong; WILD 2

w. than an open gate, FROS 17
Without a city w., ALEX 8
Wallace: Scots, wha hae wi' W.
bled, BURN 47
Walled: W. round with rocks as an
inland island, SWIN 10
wallet: w. at his back, SHAK 173
walling: w. in or w. out, FROS 58
wallis: Strong be thy w.
DUNB W 5
wallop: Gies now and then a w.,
BURN 5
walloped: w. with a cat GILB 45
Walloping: W. Window Blind;
CARRY 8
wallow: We w. in our sin;
UNKN 314
Wallowing: W. in this bloody sty,
LOWE R 11
walls: flesh which w. about our life
SHAK 89
From the celestial w.! LONG 24
from w. and leads, HARD 22
hospital w. as dire; TICK 1
living w. of Jet. DONN 25
my shelving w. With honeysuckle
AKEN 1
save the Athenian w. MILT 125
shelt'ring w. are thin, UNTE 3
Stone w. do not a prison make,
LOVE 5
thy dead indifference of w.
MELV 2
w. come tumblin' down.
UNKN 158
w. of books will deaden
MACN 10
w. of flesh grow weak, DOWS 2
w. of institutions,/ Finer than
flour, ROET 8
w./ Of shadowy granite, TENN 84
w. of Time; LONG 4
w. shall crumble to ruin,
LONG 10
w., the woods, POPE A 122
watches from his mountain w.,
TENN 12
Walrus: W. and the Carpenter
CARRO 38
walruses: wily w. LEAR 3
Walsingham: thou Prince of W.,
UNKN 169
W., Oh farewell! UNKN 170
Walt: pact with you, W.
Whitman — POUN 52
tonight, W. Whitman, GINS 36
W. Whitman, a kosmos,
WHITM 73
W. Whitman, childless, lonely old
grubber, GINS 38
Where are you, W.? SIMP 13
Waltzing: W. Matilda, PATE 2
w. was not easy. ROET 49

wan: angels, all pallid and w.,
POE 33
daylight kissing her w. hair,
WILD 16
mariner, worn and w., SHEL 35
Why so pale and w., fond lover
SUCK 1
wand: w. is will; SIDN 18
with a witching w., FROS 123
wander: I ponder where'er I w.,
MAHONY 2
Let me not w. in a barren dream,
KEAT 57
lingers when we w. hence,
MASE 9
O to awake and w.
STEVENSO R 10
seize the souls that w. by him.
SHAK 140
w. everywhere, SHAK 126
w. the dark house WARR 5
Where I would w. MORR 6
woods we w. in. WILB 9
wander'd: I w. off by myself,
WHITM 111
wandered: w. alone, WHITM 62
wanderer: gazelle, delicate w.,
SPEND 17
pass the w. by — / White-robed
forms POE 17
Unquiet w. YEATS 148
young w. dream on: Æ 1
wanderers: cold Earth w. BLAK 29
wandereth: bright eye/ That w.
lightly. PEEL 2
wandering: Before her w. feet.
YEATS 122
but a w. Voice? WORD 150
dishevelled w. stars. YEATS 164
gazing on the earth,/ W.
companionless SHEL 88
w. and singing, LAWR 33
w./ Between earth and sky,
DAVIS 4
W. by lone sea-breakers, OSHA 1
w. fields of barren foam.
TENN 82
w. from that heaven, ROCH 1
w. steps and slow MILT 108
wanders: w. god-like or like thief
GRAV 15
What she wants or why she w.
NOYE 4
wand'rest: w. in his shade
SHAK 188
wand'ring: increasing prospect tires
our w. eyes. POPE A 34
star to every w. bark, SHAK 232
tempts your w. eyes GRAY 20
wandring: in w. mazes lost.
MILT 60
waneth: youth w. by increasing.
PEEL 7

Greet prees at market maketh dere
w., CHAU 89
worthless w.; SIDN 39
Warehouse: Manhattan Storage W.,
OHAR 13
wares: dimmed w. of price.
POUN 54
w. be trash, UNKN 96
warfare: rest! thy w. o'er,
SCOT WA 9
warily: footsoles/ trod w. on living
coals. WYLI 4
warld: gied the infant w. a shog,
BURN 3
w. to rest are gane, LIND L 1
warm: beaker full of the w. South,
KEAT 45
cold/ surrounds our w. bed,
LEVE 4
go barefoot/ and be w. GIOV 2
heart is w./ Midst winter's harm.
MORR 5
heart is w. with the friends I
make, MILLA 38
If only to go w. were gorgeous,
SHAK 74
keeps us w.: GRAV 30
let the w. Love in! KEAT 54
life was w. in thine eye,
MOOR T 1
mouths kissing the w. sutures,
ROET 48
Nursing her wrath to keep it w.
BURN 50
on the w. hillside YEATS 145
see thy blood w. SHAK 185
She covered me w., POE 24
softly her w. ear LOWE J 17
stands in w. water SNYD 3
This sensible w. motion
SHAK 115
thy duties be/ To w. the world,
DONN 56
Twas w. — at first — like Us —
DICKI 154
valley w. and green, HODG 3
W. amidst eternal Frost, GAY 4
w. an' sleepy an' white; HAY 6
w. and windowed rooms SHAP 8
w. metamorphosis of snow
PAGE 5
w. side inside, STRON 1
W. slippers and hot-water can,
GILB 4
w. the frozen swamp FROS 141
w. their little Loves GRAY 33
w. them at the wood-fire's blaze!
WHITT 29
w. wind, the west wind,
MASE 13
w. with the mystery of lather.
JUST 6
Winter kept us w., ELIOT T 113

warmer: w. clime, ADDI 2
warming: Alone and w. his five
wits, TENN 105
w. rock MORG 1
warmly: w. ran my blood TENN 95
warms: dawning beauty w. us so?
WALL 8
rapture w. the mind; POPE A 34
W. youth and seed THOMA D 30
warmth: Pour down your w.,
WHITM 65
genial w.; TENN 40
only w., the only peace. SCHW 3
warn: w., to comfort, and
command; WORD 135
warned: w. of the coming fury.
THOMA D 16
warning: heard the w. bell,
SOUTHE 5
month's w. GILB 58
W. of thingès that men after
seen. CHAU 72
W. of thingès that shall after fall.
CHAU 73
w. ringing bell WHITM 101
warp: judgments w. us BYRO 48
w. us from the living truth!
TENN 72
waters w., SHAK 14
Weave the w. GRAY 5
warped: w. by passion, POPE A 109
Warr: W. Irreconcileable, MILT 52
warrant: stag of w., DAVID 5
truth shall be thy w.: RALEG 6
warranted: w. no better, LARK 16
Warren: Waiting for W. FROS 19
warring: sparrows w. in the eaves,
YEATS 141
warrior: bravest w. ALEX 6
he lay like a w. WOLF C 2
Who is the happy W.? WORD 4
warriors: Pale w., KEAT 32
wars: All w. are boyish, MELV 17
dates of w. ALDR T 1
daunting w., HOPKINS 17
pointless w. of the heart.
SNYD 10
soger frae the w. returns,
BURN 34
w. were done. ROBI 11
whirling between two w., KUNI 4
warsled: w. up, they w. down,
UNKN 269
wart: Rub a half potato on your w.
HUGO 5
warty: w. giant and witch
HECH 12
wash: art can w. her guilt away?
GOLD 9
everlasting w. of air —
BROWNI R 80
I w. off. SEXT 6
w. it white as snow? SHAK 34

w. the cups an' saucers RILE 1
w. the dusk with silver.
BLAK 110
w. this blood/ Clean from my
hand? SHAK 108
w. you Paumanok, WHITM 1
what no tide/ Shall ever w. away,
LAND 6
washbasins: bathtubs and the w.
MAHON 1
wash'd-up: little w. drift, WHITM 3
washed: bitter land was w. away.
WALK 1
handkerchief w. clean by
weeping — GINS 25
w. her hands NASH 1
w. the pity from her hands.
KIZE 3
When I died they w. me JARR 5
wassail: your w. too, UNKN 117
wassails: May-poles, hock-carts, w.,
wakes, HERR 1
wast: w. all that POE 7
waste: Above the w. allotments
THOMA D 31
Driving around, I will w. more
time. BLY 1
new wail my dear time's w.
SHAK 195
old age shall this generation w.,
KEAT 40
seemed w. of breath, YEATS 71
w. its sweetness on the desert air.
GRAY 10
w. of life, MERE O 1
w. of shame SHAK 236
w. remains and kills. EMPS 12
w. to dust. VAUX 6
we lay w. our powers:
WORD 159
were I in the wildest w.,
BURN 40
wide and melancholy w.
SHEL 18
woes of willful w.,
JOHN S (1709–1784) 12
wasted: charm is w. EMER 42
chronicle of w. time SHAK 228
from a w. tree, ROET 50
her w. hand, SCOT WA 17
I have w. my life. WRIG J 4
I w. time, SHAK 93
sighs have w. so my breath
SURR 6
smile in secret, looking over w.
lands, TENN 90
w. brands do glow, SHAK 128
w. for you, love! MACW 1
wasteful: w. Time debateth with
Decay, SHAK 187
w. war shall statues overturn,
SHAK 207
wild and w. ocean. SHAK 56

wastes: it w. its time. JARR 9
w. and withers WILD 3
w. half his days, WATT I 6
w. of time SHAK 186
whiner, who w. your time
  SNOD 3

wasteth: w. In love his chiefest
  part. SIDN 42

Wasting: W. its kindliness
  WORD 63
w. my heart, PETRA 2

watch: I linger to w. her; LAWR 10
in eager w. he sits,
  THOMS J (1700–1748) 10
kept w. o'er man's mortality;
  WORD 86
life is a w. or a vision SWIN 2
like a fat gold w. PLATH 61
moon I w. goes down, LEVE 12
My w. is wound, AIKE 8
secret whispers of each other's w.
  SHAK 57
sentinel stars set their w. in the
  sky; CAMPB T 8
starres/ W. an advantage to
  appeare. HERB G 30
To any w. they keep? FROS 68
w. from dawn to gloom SHEL 51
w. his woods fill up with snow.
  FROS 107
w., some ancient brooch
  DICKI 51
w. the clock for you, SHAK 208
w. the waves. ARNO 34
w. the wild Vicissitudes of Taste;
  JOHN S (1709–1784) 8
With her glove, to w. us
  MONTA 2
with the starboard w., CARRY 9

watched: I stood and w. the evening
  star TEAS 1
I w. for love-cars. LOWE R 39
long as it w. me. TEAS 1
paper, and I w., HOLM 12
ramparts we w. KEY 1
shepherds w. their flocks by
  night, TATE N 1
w. by cockatoos and goats,
  STEVENSO R 19
w. me all your life, DURE 1
w. Ming fall) SNYD 48
w. my brothers play, MUIR 2
w. that wretched man, HOLM 14
w. the pomp, EMER 15

watcher: felt I like some w. of the
  skies KEAT 56

watchers: w. in their leopard suits
  SIMP 2

watches: sleepless w. of the night,
  LONG 13
w. from his mountain walls,
  TENN 12

with our judgments as our w.,
  POPE A 22
with sighs they jar/ Their w.
  SHAK 93

watchful: birds like w. clocks
  VAUG 7
five w. senses MILT 80
w. bailiffs take their silent
  stands, SWIF 11

Watching: red-eyed elders w.,
  STEVENS 34
stealthily w. me.) WHITM 12
W., silently weeps. WHITM 57
W. the east, the autumn sky.
  WHITM 56
w. the drugstore sign RUKE 8

water: all the running w. goes
  PACK 1
avocado in a glass of w. MERR 6
Baptized with fairy w.; MACN 5
Barnacles, mussels, w. weeds —
  MOSS 5
Black w., smooth ROBI 40
blood like w., GALT 1
brewers mar their malt with w.;
  SHAK 76
bring w. for my stain. SHAK 230
Burnt on the w. SHAK 5
But there is no w. ELIOT T 147
Canal w. preferably, KAVA 23
Christ walking on the w.
  THOMP F 12
clear/ W., cold, so cold JARR 26
coaxing up w.; ROET 4
daughter of Earth and W.,
  SHEL 25
dip to the w. LAWR 1
drift on the still w., YEATS 167
drink at my w.-trough LAWR 43
drinking icy w. SNYD 8
drops of w., CARN 1
ducklings to the w.,
  MONTROSS 3
eel's/ Oil of w. body, HUGH T 4
fades the lotus of the w.?
  BLAK 13
fain for to w. the plain. LANIE 5
fair spring w.,/ With UNKN 13
Fear death by w. ELIOT T 117
"Ferry me across the w.,
  ROSS C 9
hand/ Is worthy of w.: WILB 6
hart panteth after the w. brooks,
  BIBL, O.T. 35
have plenty of w. CAME 3
hill of w.: JEFFE 12
His steeds to w. SHAK 17
in w. we were from FROS 136
insert her into w. like a needle
  DICKEY 12
Just Add Hot W. And Serve —
  CUMM 39
lake w. lapping YEATS 75

Let the w. and the blood, TOPL 1
men were drunk like w., JARR 3
nests of w.-bays, WHITM 43
no w. but only rock ELIOT T 144
On w. the Man-Fisher walks.
  LOWE R 14
places of drawing w.,
  BIBL, O.T. 18
Pushing the crumpled w.
  FROS 61
rain w. of my eyes CLEV 2
Secret by the unmourning w.
  THOMA D 38
shattered w. made a misty din.
  FROS 76
She drips herself with w.,
  LAWR 12
shining, in the w. MOMA 3
sink as w. in the sand;
  BIBL, O.T. 42
sound of w. only ELIOT T 146
sound of w. over a rock
  ELIOT T 147
speeding change of w., EMER 51
stands for all the w. WHITM 2
stands in warm w. SNYD 3
terrible w. BERRYM 14
under the w. ROET 35
waddled in the w.-pudge,
  CLARE 10
warbling w. brooks. OWEN 25
w. and sponge, WHITM 115
w. in a gutter WALK 13
w. in a stagnant pool! BONT 8
W. inflated the belly FULL 3
w. loves MOSS 4
w. rising, — ROET 41
w., rising high, FLET J 2
w.-tightness of a/ skin.
  MOOR M 37
w. to sound, fire to form:
  RUKE 2
w. was too cold for us.
  LOWE R 58
W., w., everywhere,
  COLE SAM 33
w. with a hazel prong —
  FROS 23
W. with berries in 't, SHAK 157
w. without sound, STEVENS 61
wetter w., slimier slime!
  BROO R 10
where can we draw w.,'
  YEATS 123
white w. rode FROS 135
wish of w. is reversed, WILB 5

water'd: w. with their tears
  ARNO 34

watercolor: I am a w. SEXT 6

watered: nest is in a w. shoot;
  ROSS C 1

waterfall: bone-crushing w.
  LOWE R 47

cannot find my w.: ROBI 9
crossed each other's w.: WILD 4
eyes, as hanged men's, turning the
     wrong w.; ALBI 1
find that better w.! POPE A 128
firecat bristled in the w.
     STEVENS 8
flowers to straw thy w.;
     HERB G 25
freed his soul the nearest w.
     JOHN S (1709–1784) 4
galloping on this w. WOOL 1
hell should bar the w." NOYE 7
high w. of love; YEATS 3
his genial w. CARRO 11
his oblique w. MILT 65
Hold the high w. CHAU 2
I leap for joy, pursue my w.,
     WESL C 2
In methodical w., GILB 61
Jog on, jog on, the footpath w.,
     SHAK 180
leave Mankind without a w.:
     DRYD 18
life's common w., WORD 42
Love will find out the w.!
     UNKN 183
lovely in that w. SPENC B 1
Milk all the w. CRAS 9
my Light, my Life, my W.
     QUAR 4
Pegasus, a nearer w. to take,
     POPE A 30
plowman homeward plods his
     weary w., GRAY 7
pursue/ Thy solitary w.! BRYA 25
Rebellion lay in his w., SHAK 53
right of w. to Tripoli DICKI 120
road wind uphill all the w.?
     ROSS C 28
shallow streams run dimpling all
     the w. POPE A 10
slow and cautious w. DICKI 66
Teaches thy w. BRYA 26
tedious w., ROSS C 12
that's the w. to heav'n.
     POPE A 19
This is the one w., ELIOT T 21
Thou art the W. MEYN 2
Through Eden took their solitary
     w. MILT 108
Virtue is the roughest w.,
     WOTT 8
Water's my will, and my w.,
     ROET 46
W. down upon de Swanee ribber,
     FOST 3
w. for Billy and me. HOGG 1
w. for the rising sun. BONT 3
w. of error, RALEG 5
w. of sinners, BIBL, O.T. 21
w./ Of speaking gently, —
     BROWNI E 9

w. of the ungodly shall perish.
     BIBL, O.T. 22
w. that I must tread alone,
     BRYA 27
w. the world ends ELIOT T 48
w. to dusty death. SHAK 114
w. to live, by dying. DRYD 9
w. unseen, the certain route,/
     Where ever bound, VERY 4
w. where light dwelleth?
     BIBL, O.T. 15
went her unremembering w.,
     THOMP F 2
wayes: justifie the w. of God to
     men. MILT 47
w. of learning; HERB G 59
wayfarer: w. by barren ways
     ROSS D 7
ways: apart from the well-trodden
     w.; PETRA 11
count the w. BROWNI E 4
down the labyrinthine w.
     THOMP F 6
hungry for the old, familiar w.,
     MCKA 8
In such kind w., WILB 8
know not well the subtle w.
     EMER 6
knows/ The w. of women
     KAVA 11
My crooked winding w.,
     HERB G 74
peace in all thy w., CORB 1
Placable if His mind and w. were
     guessed, BROWNI R 17
set up in fifty w., YEATS 58
teeming wharves and w.,
     WHITM 51
vindicate the w. of God to Man.
     POPE A 59
walk in th' old w. MEW 5
wayfarer by barren w. ROSS D 7
w. be foul, SHAK 101
w. of God are strange! SASS 16
w./ Of winter joys WHITT 28
w. that are dark HART 1
your great and gracious w.
     PATM 5
waytes: mie true love w. CHAT 1
wayward: fond and w. thoughts
     WORD 44
weak: grasp had left the giant world
     so w. SHEL 80
I am w. then I am strong;
     WESL C 1
I pondered, w. and weary,
     POE 34
life itself not w. ROSS C 25
Made w. by time and fate,
     TENN 135
Men are strong or w. MARV 21
mine own w. merits SHAK 136
strong in a w. heart. HERB G 16

travel-sore and w.? ROSS C 29
w. and idle theme, SHAK 129
w. and little is the light,
     THOMA E 15
w. and shallow as its source.
     THOR 4
W. as a whiffet; ROET 26
w. enough to suffer woe.
     DONN 54
w. hands though mighty heart
     SHEL 4
W. I am grown, HERR 24
w. of will, the strong of arm,
     MAST 6
w. one is singled SHEL 90
w. or heartless be, TREN 2
w. piping time of peace,
     SHAK 96
w. spirits ne'er been higher
     reared SHAK 178
where the w.-ey'd Bat, COLL 10
Wise, if too w., UNKN 74
weake: appall the w. stomacke:
     SPENS 37
Weakening: day/ W. the will
     SPEND 21
weaker: see thee daily w. grow —
     COWP 7
W. in most points, stronger in a
     few, BROWNI R 16
weakest: fondest, blindest, w.,
     THOMP F 10
men at w., they are strongest,
     JONS 29
weakness: All w. that impairs,
     ARNO 29
derive from w. BROWNI R 18
Stronger by w., wiser men
     become WALL 4
too much w. for the Stoic's pride,
     POPE A 78
w. of intellect, GILB 29
w. of mere humanity, SPENC A 4
weal: human right and w.
     WHITT 10
scheme of the w. and woe:
     BROWNI R 4
serve me seven years,/ Through w.
     or woe UNKN 247
wealth: Black love is Black w.
     GIOV 4
Boundless his w. SCOT WA 12
climb to w., BRYA 36
Find w. SHEL 64
For w., or honors, WORD 5
Lord, who createdst man in w.
     and store, HERB G 26
match in w. LOWE J 15
merchant gather w.,
     BEAU/BASS 6
Outshone the w. of Ormus and of
     Ind, MILT 58
poor man's w., SIDN 14

Say that health and w. have
  missed   HUNT 5
such w. brings   SHAK 194
upstart w.'s averted eye,
  EMER 27
w. accumulates, and men decay:
  GOLD 3
w. and honor!   FROS 54
w. and woe among: WYAT 1
w. he valued not a groat;
  SWIF 25
w. of its soil   CAME 3
Where w. accumulates   GOLD 1
with W. and Honour blest,
  DRYD 2
wealth's: honest w. a better thing
  BROO S 1
wealthiest: w. man among us is the
  best: WORD 161
wealthy: business of the w. man
  BELL 15
w. of seas,   HEMA 5
w. wife was she;   UNKN 306
weaned: w. to knowledge of the
  Will   MACN 12
weans: w. in their bed,   MILLE W 1
weapon: Satire's my w.,   POPE A 89
self-same w.,   FRANK 2
weaponlike: a lip — / grim, wet, and
  w.,   BISH 18
Wear: children/ W. skins   SPEND 3
cross I w. upon my breast
  LONG 14
father should w. a broadcloth
  coat,   WHITT 16
Fathers that w. rags   SHAK 73
flame-flamingo infants' w.
  LOWE R 30
I w. the blue;   GRAHAM R 1
I will w. what dresses I choose!
  CREE 3
idle w.;   SHEL 64
if men my garments w.;
  SHAK 59
Lawrel w.,   DRYD 30
no shirts to w.;   GILB 49
nobler chaplets w.   SUCK 6
w. another face,   EMER 21
w. purple/ With a red hat   JOSE 1
w. the mask   DUNB P 11
w. the mask!   DUNB P 13
w. their brave state   SHAK 187
w. their godhead lightly.
  SNOD 10
w. us out —   GINS 24
w. yet upon their chins
  SHAK 122
w. your hair like a man,   TRAI 1
weare: Rubie, which you w.,
  HERR 45
wearie: w. out my paine,   LODG 3
wearied: vain travail hath w. me
  WYAT 30

W. I fell asleep: MILT 107
w. of our huts   UNKN 121
W. then and glad of rest,
  PHILI A 2
weariest: even the w. river
  SWIN 15
wearifu': w. gaberlunzie man.
  UNKN 111
wearin': w. o' the Green!
  UNKN 299
weariness: Lay your w.   HORA 8
pale for w.   SHEL 88
study is a w. of the flesh.
  BIBL, O.T. 7
Wearing: W. a spotted fawnskin
  SNYD 39
wearisome: w. condition of
  humanity!   GREV 9
wears: w. a dun-colored dress
  WALK 12
w. the strong sea   BERRYM 9
Yet the day w.,   BROWNI R 50
weary: Age shall not w. them,
  BINY 3
Bound and w.,   BLAK 73
draw this w. breath.   DANI S 10
drooping w. sire,   CRAB 6
earth's old and w. cry.
  YEATS 140, 141
heavy and the w. weight
  WORD 30
huntsman after w. chace,
  SPENS 16
I pondered, weak and w.,   POE 34
Let him be rich and w.,
  HERB G 63
My w. soul   GRAY 14
my w. spright now longs to fly
  CAMPI 17
plowman homeward plods his w.
  way,   GRAY 7
sweet sleep is not for the w.
  brain;   THOMS J (1834–1882) 4
tote the w. load, —   FOST 2
W. and old with service,
  FLET/SHAK 3
w. and worn!' —   CAMPB T 9
w. be at rest.   BIBL, O.T. 11
w. crowds I roam;   EMER 26
w. fu' o' care?   BURN 15
w. guiltless ghost   BOLE 1
w.-hearted as that hollow moon.
  YEATS 3
w. lot is thine,   SCOT WA 24
w. night and day;   YEATS 14
W. of breath,   HOOD 2
w. of days and hours,   SWIN 13
w. pilgrim to thy roof;
  CAREW 21
w. seemed the sea,   TENN 82
w., stale, flat, and unprofitable
  SHAK 22
w. were the world,   CHES 2

w. with historical data,   POUN 34
W. with toil,   SHAK 193
With fingers w. and worn,
  HOOD 11
with w. task fordone.   SHAK 128
weasel: w. lived in the sun
  THOMA E 7
weather: about the w.   NÍ CH 1
(After open w.   KIPL 23
Bard was w.-wise,   COLE SAM 6
bleached by Irish w.   MOOR M 37
brash and terrible w.;/ the pains;/
  the bruising;   BROO G 14
Catches tigers/ In red w.
  STEVENS 5
change or turn as w. and wind?/ Is
  it possible?   WYAT 10
for wind or w.   COLE SAM 48
humble roof/ Is w.-proof;
  HERR 39
image/ Warped in the w.,
  GRAV 17
In any wind or w.   HOUS 14
In calm or stormy w.;
  ROSS C 12
inner, w.   FROS 116
Methinks,/ For milder w.   THOR 1
October's bright blue w.
  JACK 1, 2
season of calm w.   WORD 82
summer's best of w.   JACK 4
w.-beaten sail   CAMPI 17
w. in the heart   RICH 25
w. of All Souls: WILB 18
w. suits you not,   UNKN 266
w. the cuckoo likes,   HARD 49
w. the shepherd shuns,   HARD 50
weather'd: ship has w. every rack,
  WHITM 45
weathered: w. — like a farm
  wagon —   WILLI 44
w. the storm,   POUN 51
weathering: w. land   SNYD 21
weave: cannot w. a spell.   KAVA 27
Fresh garlands w.,   AKEN 2
O what a tangled web we w.
  POPE J 1
voice did w. Songs   SHEL 75
W. a circle round him
  COLE SAM 22
w. but nets to catch the wind.
  WEBS 2
w. Grey hairs upon my head.
  VAUX 2
w. myself into the sense.
  HERB G 42
W. robes —   SHEL 64
w. the sunlight in your hair —
  ELIOT T 53
w. the woof,   GRAY 5
w. your winding-sheet,   SHEL 65
weaver: worked at the w.'s trade;
  UNKN 99

weaves: crown of verdure w.,
ALEX 5
she w. by night and day
TENN 61
weaving: With a silken thread of my
own hand's w.; KEAT 27
web: cool w. of language GRAV 3
fine and Coarsest w.; SOUTHW 8
magic w. with colours gay.
TENN 2
My Life thy W.: TAYL E 6
No claw or w. here: GUNN 6
O what a tangled w. we weave
POPE J 1
Out flew the w. TENN 66
She left the w., she left the loom,
TENN 65
traces of the smallest spider's w.,
SHAK 153
w./ Of fabulous grass and eternal
voices KAVA 2
w. of human things, SHEL 22
w. of will SIDN 39
webbe: w., a dyere, and a tapycer,
CHAU 5
webs: dull w. of discontent, ROBI 7
wed: lovers looking to be w.;
HOUS 22
then we'll w., CAREY 5
w. ladies by license and leave,
WYAT 11
We're w. to one eternity
CLARE 8
wedde: to be widwe and w.
CHAU 109
wedded: Hail wed. love, mysterious
law, MILT 78
to be w. is no sinne:/ Bet is to be
w. than to brinne. CHAU 89
W. to him, not through union,
MAST 2
w. to this goodly universe
WORD 16
wedding: dampned w. with the
deede; CHAU 91
How happy a thing were a w.,
FLAT 1
Uncle's w. band RICH 2
W. is great Juno's crown,
SHAK 16
wedding-cake: moldering like w.,
RICH 12
wedge: jabs her w.-head
LOWE R 41
Wedges: W. of gold, SHAK 97
wedlock: High w. then be honorèd.
SHAK 16
Wednesday: W.'s child is full of
woe, MOTH 22
wee: At my w., small door;
DE LA 23
w. one's trundle-bed. FIEL E 9

W., sleeket, cowran, BURN 62
W. Willie Winkie MILLE W 1
weed: Disdains to crop a w.,
DRUM 3
flower and medicinal w. MAST 3
hungry w. grows. BROO G 19
swinging on brier and w.,
BRYA 19
tatter'd w. of small worth
SHAK 185
ten-times-fingering w. KIPL 16
wood, the w., the wag.
RALEG 13
weeds: Barnacles, mussels, water
w. MOSS 5
bones of w. ROET 37
children's faces./ Like rootless w.
SPEND 1
cutting w. and shade. TOOM 5
dank and dropping w. HORA 4
Long live the w. HOPKINS 11
oozy w. about me twist. MELV 5
root away/ The noisome w.
SHAK 90
smell far worse than w.
SHAK 222
vilest deeds like poison w..
WILD 3
wood, w., WHITM 2
weedy: Grass, w. pavement,
LARK 5
weekday: secures/ Escape from the
w. time. MACN 22
weeks: brief hours and w.,
SHAK 232
desolate, dark w. WILLI 37
failure of w. RUKE 9
several w. before a mass
BYRO 43
weel: born hym w., CHAU 9
gooth faire and w.' CHAU 55
Young Jamie lo'ed me w.,
LIND L 1
welfare: for other's w. kindly
spiers: BURN 18
weep: cannot choose.' But w.
SHAK 211
daughters of Israel, w. over Saul,
BIBL, O.T. 69
Do not w., maiden, for war is
kind CRAN S 8
harsh world in which I wake to
w., SHEL 76
he stayed to w.' REES 3
laugh not again, neither w.
SWIN 25
men that laugh and w.; SWIN 12
Nothing to w. but tears,
KING B 3
saw my lady w., UNKN 141
some men w., WILD 4
thou canst w. a tear BLAK 103
time to w., BIBL, O.T. 4

vapours w. their burthen to the
ground, TENN 120
waken but to w. DAY 9
w. afresh SHAK 195
w. and sing/ Duty's conscious
wrong, AUDE 10
w. barren tears. SHEL 52
w. because another wept.
AUDE 82
w. for her? SHAK 31
w. for their sins, WHITM 75
w. his pints AUDE 99
w. like a child for the past.
LAWR 32
W. not, my wanton, GREE 2
w. now or never more! POE 29
W. on, ye springs, FRENE 3
w. soon on the lonely curbing
HORA 2
w. t' make it home, GUES 3
w. though I be Stone: MARV 30
W. thy golden tears! WATS W 1
W. with me, JONS 7
while I w.! POE 14
Who would not w., POPE A 8
wilt thou w., MOOR T 12
women must w., KINGSL 3
you w. alone, WILC 1
weeping: blind and w. bear
SITW 12
Disease, and Sorrow's w. train,
GRAY 26
handkerchief washed clean by w.
GINS 25
Old men w. in the parks!
GINS 16
Sin their conception, their birth
w., WEBS 4
this is w. RANS 10
w. anarchic Aphrodite. AUDE 34
w. and the laughter, DOWS 5
w. fast RANS 21
w. I, with wither'd arms, OVID 7
W. in weak & mortal clay;
BLAK 26
w., longing with one deep
longing, WHITM 17
when stars are w., MOOR T 1
world's more full of w.
YEATS 144
weeps: one that w. TENN 53
Watching, silently w. WHITM 57
white rose w., 'She is late;'
TENN 94
"Woe w. out her division JONS 4
weet: world to w. SHAK 3
weigh: w. my eyelids down
SHAK 54
weighed: infinite with infinite be
w. DRYD 17
w. upon with heaviness,
TENN 85

weighing: by self-offenses w.
SHAK 116
dutiful w. of ill with good; —
LANIE 3
weighs: w. a lot, GILB 39
weight: Bowed by the w. of
centuries MARK 5
Brain is just the w. of God —
DICKI 15
crush'd beneath the furrow's w.,
BURN 61
falling with my w. of cares
TENN 33
Gives the lover w. and fashion.
JONS 1
grave w. of America/ Cancelled!
SIMP 15
great w. below the waist,
LAWR 20
heavy and the weary w.
WORD 30
his w. wilts HARP 1
I long for w. and strength
FROS 114
In w. in measure, number, sound,
JONS 39
oppression of their prodigal w.
SHAK 90
over the world's w. WILB 20
torment of fire and w. SNYD 52
w. of this brocade, LOWE A 9
world's w. of the world's filth
SITW 9
weights: are important w. SHAP 29
at hand to bless;/ Ills have no w.,
LYTE 2
Weir: misty mid region of W.
POE 48
weird: because I'm w.? SIMP 9
w. detective ways — HARD 52
(W. John Brown), MELV 19
w. shall never daunten me."
UNKN 246
wild w. clime POE 16
weirs: foamless w. Of age, ROBI 12
Wel: W. koude he sitte on hors
CHAU 10
Welchman: as the W. sayd,/
Couetousness getts no gaine.
UNKN 224
welcome: Glows world-wide w.;
LAZA 1
Love bade me w.: HERB G 48
O farewell griefe, and w. joye,
UNKN 17
Pack, clouds, away, and w., day!
HEYW 1
rest may reason and w.;
BROWNI R 4
sing/ W., proud lady.'
SCOT WA 5
Thrice w., WORD 151
warmest w., at an inn. SHEN 2

w. each rebuff BROWNI R 73
w. home, Sir Francis Drake.'
UNKN 295
w. in the spring! LYLY 4
W., kindred glooms!
THOMS J (1700–1748) 12
W. the Creations Guest, MARV 9
W. the dawn. BRID R 14
W. to your gory bed, BURN 47
wele: w. is comen to weylaway,
UNKN 289
well: All manner of thing shall be
w. ELIOT T 74
almost w. BOGA 4
And all shall be w. ELIOT T 74
apart from the w.-trodden ways;
PETRA 11
Bloom w. in prison-air; WILD 3
brims the poisoned w. MELV 9
bucket that hung in the w.
WOOD 3
did it very w.: GILB 24
drank of Aganippe w., SIDN 22
envelop'd w. his form,
WHITM 107
folded my soldier w. in his
blanket, WHITM 107
Folded the blanket w.,
WHITM 107
jelofer w. set, SKEL 1
learned, w.-bred; POPE A 24
leaves the w.-built nest; SHEL 90
lov'd not wisely but too w.;
SHAK 138
might w. be underground,
GILB 26
much goodness yet they do not
w., THOMS J (1834–1882) 5
Not w., nor full, nor fasting.
DANI S 1
Right, like a w.-done sum.
PLATH 84
survive my w.-contented day
SHAK 196
to be like that, w. off, LAWR 14
To be w. changed for war.
DANI S 22
twentieth year is w.-nigh past;
COWP 21
w.-closed doors, WHITM 42
w.-graced actor leaves the stage,
SHAK 92
W. is he born, that may behold
you ever. SPENS 6
w.-nightingaled vicinity? HOUS 6
w.-trained runner, WHITM 70
w. to obey TENN 102
w. wrapped in their winding-
sheet! DRAY 7
wife at Usher's W., UNKN 306
youthe, and a w.-loved youthe,
UNKN 15
welladay: Alack and w.! HERR 30

Wellington: W. thrashed Bonaparte,
GILB 24
wells: empty cisterns and/exhausted
w. ELIOT T 150
tintinnabulation that so musically
w. POE 10
w. are parched away?
YEATS 123
Wells-Far-ago: up her W. REED I 3
Welsh: in good W. GRAV 40
wench: Imp at three and w. at
'leben WALK 9
wended: w. the shores I know,
WHITM 1
Wenlock: On W. Edge HOUS 44
went: but that She w. POPE A 17
every where that Mary w.
HALE 1
I'd been, gone and w. YEATM 1
my Master w., LANIE 1
sap/ w. through MOOR M 21
w. on with your dying. STRA 4
W. past my simple Shoe —
DICKI 63
w. to sea in a Sieve, LEAR 8, 9
wept: bowed my head and w.
MCKA 8
he w. with joy to hear. BLAK 104
mother groaned, my father w.
BLAK 72
Tears like a lover w. GRAV 14
trees w. odorous gums and balm;
MILT 69
weep because another w.
AUDE 82
w. a last adieu! COWP 11
w. for bread SHAP 27
W. tears of dew UNKN 253
w. that he was ever born,
ROBI 41
w. with waking eyes: MERE G 10
wepte: soore w. she CHAU 17
weren: Where beth they biforen us
w., UNKN 287
wert: My lute, be as thou w.
DRUM 4
werte: w., and theron stood a toft of
herys CHAU 17
west: after sunset fadeth in the w.;
SHAK 215
Clouds of the w. WHITM 18
dearly like the w., BURN 41
down within the dim W., POE 11
drooping star in the w.,
WHITM 46
East and w. on fields forgotten
HOUS 43
fallen back in the w. BRID R 18
fine land, the w. land, MASE 14
Go thou to East, I W. PATM 9
He sailed east, he sailed w.,
UNKN 317
Let thy W. Wind sleep BLAK 110

w. my hand is set, my seal shall
  be. DONN 15
w. one does not wish/ to go;
  MOOR M 27
W. the birds sing. ROSS C 23
Whereso'er: W. I am, — SYLV 2
  W. you are, SYLV 2
Wherever: W. the darkey may go;
  FOST 2
wherof: Virginitee, thanne w. sholde
  it growe? CHAU 92
whetted: w. their teeth SOUTHE 3
whey: devil grip the w.-faced slut
  STEPHENS 3
which: Who, or why, or w., or
  what, LEAR 1
whiffet: Weak as a w.; ROET 26
Whigs: desponding W.,/ Forget their
  feuds, SWIF 8
whimper: Not with a bang but a
  w. ELIOT T 48
whims: w. of murder, ROSE 2
Whimseys: Mountains of W.,
  ROCH 9
whimsies: they have my w., PRIO 2
whin'd: once the hedge-pig w.
  SHAK 111
whine: puling Poets w., CAREW 16
  sweat and w. WHITM 75
  w. and whistle) WILLI 38
whiner: w., who wastes your time
  SNOD 3
whines: w. the shingle, JOYC 3
  Wind w. JOYC 3
whip: touched her with w. or spur:
  WOOL 4
  w./ In kitchen cups STEVENS 9
  w. of cricket's bone, SHAK 153
whipped: cry/ Like a w. child;
  SNOD 13
Whippersnapper: W. clerks
  BROWN S 1
whippoorwill: full moon and the w.
  OLSO 20
whips: body/ w. the soul. OLSO 22
whipscarred: w., HAYD 21
whirl: perpetual w. Of trivial
  objects, WORD 109
  w. of tangled strings, TROW 2
  w. of thought oppressed SWIF 3
  w. three times and throw.
  HUGO 5
  W. up, sea — DOOL 8
whirl'd: last red leaf is w. away,
  TENN 23
whirled: unstilled world still w.
  ELIOT T 13
  w. light from the day BARA 7
whirligig: w. of dozens LAWR 54
whirling: its w. vacuum. MOSS 3
  w. between two wars, KUNI 4
  w. circles of time. JEFFE 23

whirls: w. the 'wildering drift,
  BRON 14
whirr: fierce you w. WHITM 7
  w. and chime: AUDE 2
whirred: wing-tips w. VAN DO 1
whirring: w. sail goes round,
  TENN 105
whisked: w. a tail, ROSS C 12
whisker: w. first and then a claw,
  GRAY 19
whiskers: absurd w. ROET 39
  his w. would feel like HECH 4
whiskey: to run/ Corn w.
  DICKEY 5
whisky: w. on your breath
  ROET 49
whisper: blur no w., LAWR 48
  every w. that speaks BOGA 16
  fiddled w. music ELIOT T 149
  sacred w. of the pines, TOOM 3
  We wake and w. awhile, DE LA 4
  w. of Love's name, GRAV 7
  w. of the south-wind TENN 75
  with a w., WHITM 42
whisper'd: Dirge is w. by the
  warbling LUTE. DRYD 26
whispered: half-words w. low:
  GRAV 24
  scythe w. FROS 63
  sea w. me. WHITM 68
  Something w. "Snow." FIEL R 2
  Spirit of Pity w., 'Why?'
  HARD 11
  w. a song OHAR 6
  w. and revealed LONG 39
  w. to the fields LONG 18
  You still w. SNOD 13
whispering: Come w. by: HARD 30
  gigantic men of light w. HARJ 2
  long scythe w. to the ground.
  FROS 62
  "Saint-Saëns!" it seems to be w.,
  OHAR 4
  Those w. guns — SASS 15
  w. 'I will ne'er consent' BYRO 20
  w. low LAND 1
  w. sound of the cool colonnade,
  COWP 13
  w. to congratulate me,
  WHITM 109
  W. to me,/ Stories of sweet
  visions, CLARE 13
  w. to my mind. KAVA 5
  w. voice SIDN 28
  w. waves SHEL 73
whisperings: eternal w. around/
  Desolate shores, KEAT 59
whispers: lily w., 'I wait.' TENN 94
  red rose w. of passion, OREI 1
  secret w. of each other's watch.
  SHAK 57
  w. in the ear; BROWNI R 4
  w. pierce the gloom: ARNO 30

whistle: all I heard/ Was a boat's
  w., SLES 5
  Daughter daughter w. UNKN 305
  he did w. and she did sing,
  UNKN 9
  heare my w. blowe. UNKN 226
  makes a fellow/ w. back.
  WOLF H 1
  serpents w. at the cold.
  LOWE R 60
  to his team gave a w., MOOR C 5
  trembling night-winds w. ALLI 3
  whine and w.) WILLI 38
  w., and I'll come to you,
  BURN 64
whistles: lame balloonman/ w.
  CUMM 12
  mourning dove w. of despair.
  KINN 9
  Under a world of w., CRAN H 19
whistling: still w. 'The Protestant
  Boys'. UNKN 198
whistlynge: Gynglen in a w. wynd
  CHAU 19
whit: Te w.! Te whoo! VAUT 1
white: air w. and dry WILB 4
  all w., like a doll BISH 15
  angel, robed in spotless w.,
  DUNB P 1
  before the w. man. ABRA 2
  Belinda lived in a little w. house,
  NASH 15
  black and w., EMER 8
  bring w. peace LIND V 3
  cast a shadow w. as stone.
  ROET 29
  christened/ In w. wine or red,
  UNKN 13
  cow, all w. and red, UNKN 107
  Curves his w. bastions EMER 44
  Day come w., WHITM 65
  deft w.-stockinged dance
  MOOR M 3
  dying in black and w. OHAR 11
  Even the newts are w., PLATH 68
  face so yellowy w., TRAI 3
  fading to w. MONTA 5
  Fair be thy wives, right lovesom,
  w. and small; DUNB W 5
  Fair maid, w. and red, PEEL 5
  fat w. woman whom nobody
  loves, CORN 2
  fleece was w. as snow, HALE 1
  found/ A w. hair KLEI 1
  friendly cow, all red and w.,
  STEVENSO R 7
  gowd and w. monie. UNKN 93
  graved in the w. stone BRAD 8
  hair has become very w.;
  CARRO 5
  hands drop w. and empty
  NIMS 4
  he from w. cloud free, BLAK 99

Rogue and W. SWIF 15
thy drink and thy w., SHAK 71

whores: bawds and w. do churches
      build, SHAK 76
brought w. for Eleusis POUN 11

whoreson: You w. dog, POUN 60

why: can't think w.! GILB 7
know not w.! UNKN 182
never ask w. build. SEXT 16
shall we &/ w. not, CREE 9
Spirit of Pity whispered, W.?'
      HARD 11
Theirs not to reason w., TENN 7
Who, or w., or which, or what,
      LEAR 1
W. are you going? STRA 3
w. did nobody tell me?
      PLATH 11
W. don't they come? OWEN 17
W. dost/ Thou hide thy face?
      WRIG J 8

wicked: expedient and w. stones.
      SHAP 4
good w. spirit, sweet angel devil.
      DRAY 6
her w. courses, GILB 50
no God,' the w. saith, CLOU 2
see a w. peace DANI S 22
Shakespeare is w., SPEND 2
To w. spirits are horrid shapes
      assign'd, DONN 67
w. also have their proper Hell);
      THOMS J (1834–1882) 5
w. cease from troubling;
      BIBL, O.T. 11
w. pack of cards. ELIOT T 116
w. shall be silent in darkness;
      BIBL, O.T. 8
w. social tree SNYD 43

wickedness: dwell in the tents of
      w. BIBL, O.T. 43

wickerwork: grease-/ impregnated
      w.; BISH 12

wicks: w. are lighted ADAM L 2

wide: deep w. sea of Misery,
      SHEL 35
Divergence deep and w.
      WATS R 1
dwelt on a w. moor, WORD 50
glitt'ring Forfex w., POPE A 124
graves, all gaping w., SHAK 128
how w. your empires are; SHIR 4
in w. desert HOOD 10
made so loose and w., THOR 1
myriad fields and the prairies w.,
      WHITM 51
Noiseless as fear in a w.
      wilderness, KEAT 12
not in the w. world a valley so
      sweet MOOR T 7
Range the w. house
      BROWNI R 50

spreading w. my narrow Hands
      DICKI 44
stretch the nostril w., SHAK 56
Under that w. hearth MORG 1
Walk w. o' the Widow KIPL 31
w. and melancholy waste
      SHEL 18
w. and moony grin NEME 2
w. and starry sky,
      STEVENSO R 20
w. and wild,
      THOMS J (1700–1748) 5
w. arch/ Of the ranged empire
      fall! SHAK 3
w., beautiful, wonderful world,
      RANDS 1
w. earth o'er, WHITT 29
w. ope I burst. BROWNI R 37
w. than the heart is w.;
      MILLA 30
w. world dreaming on things to
      come SHAK 229
w. world over. COOP 1

widening: ripple w. ROET 18

wider: Brain — is w. than the Sky —
      DICKI 14
w. than the heart is wide;
      MILLA 30

Widow: old grey W.-maker?
      KIPL 15
Walk wide o' the W. KIPL 31
w. bird sat mourning SHEL 23
w. of fifty; SHERI 1

widowed: w. ma of Captain Reece,
      GILB 5

widowhood: Cherish thy hast'n'd
      w. MILT 112

widows: when w. wince.
      STEVENS 15

widwe: to be w. and wedde.
      CHAU 109

wield: sword shall w., BRYA 4

Wielder: W. of the stateliest
      measure TENN 127

wif: good w. was ther of biside
      Bathe, CHAU 10

wife: As the husband is, the w. is:
      TENN 71
broaching the word 'w.' HEAN 20
child, and w., and slave;
      TENN 82
clothed your w., DURE 1
dance with Chance's w. KAVA 12
fat Reichian w. screeching
      CORS 7
find a good w. too, CREE 13
gude w. ay to be, LIND L 2
help, a love, a you, a w. DUGA 3
holds his w. by th' arm,
      SHAK 179
husband frae the w. despises!
      BURN 51

If a man might purchase a w.
      FLAT 1
letter from his w. CARRO 29
like man and w. POPE A 26
lucky older w., BOGA 5
man has married a w., BLAK 113
man were lov'd by w., BRAD 13
Matched with an agèd w.,
      TENN 128
mid-air take to bed a w.
      SHAP 14
only kind of middle w. CULL 16
rank robber's w., UNKN 14
To say my w. is fair, SHAK 136
took his counsel of his w.,
      CHAU 69
wealthy w. was she; UNKN 306
w. and children will be quiet
      HEAN 15
w. and I lived all alone, CREE 1
w. at Usher's Well, UNKN 306
w. most gladly!' LEAR 5
w. of the skipper lost at sea
      WHITT 27
w. wise, without debate;
      MARTIA 2

wig: gown, bands, and w.,
      CARRO 13

wight: maid and her w. HARD 30

wigs: in a world of w., HECH 16
join to save their w. SWIF 8

wigwam: w. of Nokomis, LONG 40

wikkednesse: for hir w. CHAU 86

wild: breath of w. air; MERE G 1
caught me in the W., BLAK 19
corn-flowers w., ROSS C 27
dew o' the w. white rose
      KEAT 35
driven w. by snakes HUGO 6
Farm boys w. to couple
      DICKEY 26
grew more fierce and w.
      HERB G 18
hands were like w. birds. UPDI 2
harsh cries of w. fowl.
      MACDONO 3
He grafts upon the W. the Tame:
      MARV 25
Heave in w. wreaths the battle-
      shroud, DRAK 2
Heaven in a W. Flower, BLAK 1
In forest w., in thicket, brake, or
      den; MILT 86
limbs that had run w. YEATS 55
mane falls w. WRIG J 2
My garden is run w.! HABE 2
nobly w., not mad; HERR 36
peace of w. things BERRY 1
Peaches grow w., WYLI 11
Ring out, w. bells, TENN 46
scent of w. flowers in the wood.
      CREE 5
sea-blue eyes were w. GRAV 35

She is bald and w. PLATH 60
shoreless watery w., ARNO 41
short w. scream, WHITM 92
terrible, so w. and strange,
  MUIR 7
that w.-rose tree. ALDR T 2
They grew a little w. SMIT ST 3
Through what w. centuries
  DE LA 3
waters and the w. YEATS 144
waters w. went o'er his child,
  CAMPB T 6
we are w. and hunted men.
  SIMM 1
What w. ecstasy? KEAT 37
wide and w.,
  THOMS J (1700–1748) 5
w. and fair, SCOT WA 23
w. and loose to my soul —
  WHITM 49
w. and sweet LONG 11
w. and wanton herd SHAK 125
w. and wasteful ocean. SHAK 56
w. as forest doe. UNKN 45
W. as wind,
  JOHN S (1709–1784) 11
w. birds on the wing, STANT 1
w. boys innocent as strawberries
  THOMA D 26
w. call and a clear call MASE 12
w. cataract leaps in glory.
  TENN 111
w. civility: HERR 8
W., cold, and accusing. SNYD 10
w. deer's walk: TUCK 1
w. dove's haunt, TUCK 1
w. eyes! GINS 19
w. for to hold WYAT 32
w., gentle thing, WRIG J 5
w. harp slung behind MOOR T 9
w. honey of their youth. ROSE 5
w. Jack for a lover; YEATS 38
w. New England shore. HEMA 4
W. Nights should be/ Our luxury!
  DICKI 157
W. roses, at your back porch,
  MOSS 6
W. swans, come over the town,
  MILLA 41
w., unquenched, deep-sunken,
  ARNO 18
w. waves reach their hands
  THAX 1
w. weird clime POE 16
w. who bring you money.
  WELC 2
w. wind blows on the mountain-
  side. BRON 6
w. wind raves, THAX 1
w. winds sung SCOT WA 15
w. with all regret; TENN 115
wilde: so w. and wood, CHAU 54

wilder: keep that earlier, w. image
  bright. BRYA 30
wildering: whirls the w. drift,
  BRON 14
wilderness: America, this w.
  SIMP 12
Command a Table in this W.,
  MILT 109
hear the w. listen. STAF 3
in the w. alone. BRYA 18
in this w. RANDA D 4
made the slovenly w.
  STEVENS 1
Noiseless as fear in a wide w.,
  KEAT 12
redemption from W., GINS 25
singing in the W. OMAR 2
Walked in the w.; GRAV 13
W. were Paradise OMAR 2
Women have no w. BOGA 14
wildes: sandy perilous w., MILT 3
wildly: I talk w., WHITM 75
sing so w. well POE 26
wildness: let them be left, w.
  HOPKINS 11
strength is so tender, his w. so
  meek, LOWE J 2
wilds: spin across the w. of the sky
  TATE J 3
wildwood: deep tangled w.,
  WOOD 1
W. privacies, LANIE 3
wile: innocence itself has many a
  w., BYRO 21
wiles: cunning w. that creep
  BLAK 51
pretty infant w. BLAK 50
Quips and cranks, and wanton
  w., MILT 20
transient sorrows, simple w.,
  WORD 134
Use w. for witt WYAT 23
wilfully: Go earth-bound w.!
  HARD 28
will: alone against my w.,
  BROWNI R 63
boy's w. is the wind's w.,
  LONG 32
cause, and w., and strength, and
  means SHAK 35
concentrate the w. WINT 3
Consents to his inexorable w.
  WILB 35
day/ Weakening the w.
  SPEND 21
focused/ energy of w. HAYD 16
good w. to men. LONG 11, 12
inclination be as sharp as w.;
  SHAK 34
iron w. That clutched
  THOMP W 3
keep that w. and can; HOUS 16
mind and w. depraved, MILT 99

mortals bend their w.,
  POPE A 123
offer gifts after his w., EMER 14
own sweet w. is Heaven's w.;
  YEATS 113
Providence, Foreknowledge, W.,
  and Fate, MILT 60
rebel to my w., SHAK 8
shook it forth with a royal w.
  WHITT 3
Simplicity of wish and w.,
  WILB 28
sins of w., TENN 30
sister calls me W., FIEL E 3
strong in w. TENN 135
to the w. must yield. GUNN 12
to w. and act is one; CAREW 13
To w., implies delay, DONN 51
unconquerable W., MILT 51
wand is w.; SIDN 18
Water's my w., and my way,
  ROET 46
weak of w., the strong of arm,
  MAST 6
weaned to knowledge of the W.
  MACN 12
web of w. SIDN 39
w. in us is over-rul'd by fate.
  MARL 8
w. is alway at my hand;
  WYAT 14
w. of Heav'n; MILT 14
w. resigned;
  JOHN S (1709–1784) 23
w. unto desire, Æ 3
wind's w., — ROSS D 9
Wink as they w. STEVENS 15
wonne with her owne w. beguyld.
  SPENS 17
Work out a perfect w. JOHN L 5
wrote my w.; YEATS 152
wille: heer at your w.' CHAU 111
willed: if forgetting could be w.
  MERE G 5
willers: w. in de grass, DUNB P 2
willful: woes of w. waste,
  JOHN S (1709–1784) 12
William: Father calls me W.,
  FIEL E 3
my W., sweet and true."
  UNKN 33
"You are old, Father W.,"
  SOUTHE 7
Willie: knife in Sir W.'s pouch,
  UNKN 269
Mother calls me W., FIEL E 3
Wee W. Winkie MILLE W 1
willing: Half w., half reluctant
  LONG 33
more w. bent to shore, CAMPI 17
Sovereign of the w. soul,
  GRAY 25

Their Slaves were w.,
  JOHN S (1709–1784) 6
w. to be plucked and worn,
  GREE 4
W. to wound, POPE A 7
willow: child become a w. tree,/ His
  brother trees among. FANS C 1
feathers of the w. DIXO 1
Maidens, w. branches
  BEAU/FLET 3
swooning out of an enormous w.
  hamper MERR 10
w. shiver in the sun
  STEVENS 58
W., titwillow, titwillow!" GILB 29
willow-herb: w., w., and grass,
  THOMA E 1
willows: Hushed w. anchored
  CRAN H 52
w., willow-herb, and grass,
  THOMA E 1
willowy: w. brook, ROGE 1
wills: by our w., WILLI 20
not seen/ As the observer w.
  STEVENS 53
quarrel with your great opposeless
  w., SHAK 79
stiffened our w. LEVI 4
your w. are fickle, MACN 25
wilt: w. thou leave me thus?
  WYAT 1
w. thou weep, MOOR T 12
wilts: his weight w. HARP 1
wily: w. walruses LEAR 3
win: Beauty is easy enough to w.;
  MERE O 3
draughte of sweete w. CHAU 87
hopes to w. her; CONG 2
Knowledge might pity w.,
  SIDN 5
Man will yet w. SAND 18
such a fight did w. — SOUTHE 1
we are to w. GILD 1
'Wi' cauk and keel I'll w. your
  bread, UNKN 112
w. me soon to hell, SHAK 240
w. the battle. LUTH 3
wince: when widows w.
  STEVENS 15
w. to nothing at all. SCHW 10
winces: heart w. WILB 21
wind: about the world like w.,
  YEATS 138
against the w., RANS 35
airts the w. can blaw, BURN 41
as though it drank the w.
  YEATS 10
autumn w. laid bare; VERY 1
Blow, blow, thou winter w.!
  SHAK 13
Blows the w. to-day,
  STEVENSO R 1

boy's will is the w.'s will,
  LONG 32
breathing of the common w.
  WORD 153
change or turn as weather and
  w.?/ Is it possible? WYAT 10
cruel w. blows. KUNI 1
endless w. Whips HECH 5
Especially when the October w.
  THOMA D 13
Fair stood the w. for France,
  DRAY 1
feel the free/ Shrill w. LANG 3
flames do work and w. when they
  ascend, HERB G 42
for w. or weather COLE SAM 48
free as is the w. WORD 53
free in the tearing w. ROET 34
fresher w. sweeps by, BRYA 18
from frost or foreign w. HUGO 4
frozen w. crept on SHEL 23
gone in the w. MANG 1
gone on the w.'s wings. BYRO 37
heard this w. before FROS 7
hears him in the w.; POPE A 59
hoarse w. blows coldly; ARNO 10
impatient as the w. WORD 142
in a net I seek to hold the w.
  WYAT 31
In any w. or weather HOUS 14
in every w., GRAY 15
indicate a favoring w., OLSO 2
Is that the w. dying? BEDD 5
Let thy West W. sleep BLAK 110
like the w. they hurried, WOOL 2
Loose as the w., HERB G 17
low w., its playmate's voice,
  SHEL 59
mad w.'s night-work, EMER 45
mate of the w. and sea, POUN 4
Moon's the North W.'s cooky,
  LIND V 19
more inconstant than the w.,
  SHAK 141
my mouth with w. I fill, LYLY 6
night w. sighs; JOHN L 1
north w.'s masonry. EMER 44
one/ With the man in the w. and
  the west moon; THOMA D 9
only the w.'s home. ELIOT T 151
pied w.-flowers and violets,
  SHEL 59
pressing w. shoots javelin-like
  MERE G 11
proof against the w.; RICH 26
road w. uphill all the way?
  ROSS C 28
sail against the w. WYAT 19
saw the w., DAVIE W 3
Soft as spring w. POUN 67
soft w. waved my hair; BRON 3
South W. is a baker. LIND V 20

Star-climbed, w.-combed,
  MERW 9
swings in the w. and rain,
  THOMA E 8
tears shall drown the w.
  SHAK 105
there's a w. a-blowing, HENL 2
Turning in the w. STEVENS 7
'twas but the w., BYRO 6
tyrannous w., BRID R 18
warm w., the west w., MASE 13
we have borne/ The ruffling w.,
  COWP 17
weave but nets to catch the w.
  WEBS 2
Who has seen the w.?/ Neither I
  nor you: ROSS C 35
Wild as w.,
  JOHN S (1709–1784) 11
wild w. blows on the mountain-
  side. BRON 6
wild w. raves, THAX 1
w. and the rain, SHAK 177
W. and Thistle BELL 7
W. begun to rock the Grass
  DICKI 159
w. betwixt green islands;
  WHITM 13
w. bit hard at Valley Forge
  SAND 23
w. blows full of sand, LI PO 1
w. blows out, the bubble dies;
  KING H 5
w. came briskly ALDR T 2
w. came out of the cloud POE 5
w. came up out of the sea,
  LONG 17
w. changes at night MACL 5
w. doth blow today, my love,"
  UNKN 292
w. doth ramm! POUN 2
w. fanning the ash ROET 15
w. flaking sapphire, CRAN H 44
w. flapped loose, ROSS D 9
w. from the sea, BISH 30
w. goin' over my hand. MEW 6
w. in procession thoughts,
  WHITM 12
w. is high, STEVENSO R 24
w. is in the palm-trees, KIPL 9
w. is passing by. ROSS C 36
w. is passing through. ROSS C 35
W., lake, lip, everything awaits
  HECH 6
W. like a Bugle — DICKI 138
w. of Death's imperishable wing?
  ROSS D 3
W. of the western sea, TENN 113
w. of their endurance, MILLA 13
w., rend open the heat, DOOL 3
w. that blows through me!
  LAWR 47

no w. like the blood's POUN 62
our last measure of w.,
  BROWNI R 36
outdid the frolic w. HERR 36
press the rue for w. SCOT WA 24
Sans W., sans Song, OMAR 4
seas of life like w.; TRAH 10
Seasoned with sage and onions,
  and port w. SOUTHE 8
sipped lover's w." HARD 48
Slops the bad w. BROO G 21
toast me at his w. WHITT 16
w. and oil; TENN 91
w.-barrel room, LIND V 8
w.-cup glistens; SCOT WA 1
w.-flushed, bold-eyed boys,
  MCKA 5
w. may bear no sovereignty;
  MARTIA 2
w. of life is drawn, SHAK 109
w. redeems the sight, CRAN H 53
w. which never grew EMER 1
w. will chide SCOT WA 14
wines: rural o'er ices and w.,
  PRAE 4
wing: asks no Angel's w.,
  POPE A 60
Bird is on the W. OMAR 1
bird of w. MILT 85
broken pillar of the w. JEFFE 13
damp my intended w. MILT 88
drowsy head and folded w.,
  POE 38
ever on the w., JOHN L 6
flight of Pegasean w. MILT 83
flits by on leathern W., COLL 10
hawk's w. of vision. SNYD 32
inconstant w. SHEL 29
lark's on the w.; BROWNI R 66
light w. against the ivory gate,
  MORR 3
minutes w.'d their way BURN 53
moth with dusty w., ROSS C 16
No Raven's w. can stretch
  BARL 1
not a single w. WELL 2
rein of a wimpling w.
  HOPKINS 27
stretches out my golden w.,
  BLAK 24
swiftest w. of recompense
  SHAK 104
West winds, with musky w.
  MILT 11
wild birds on the w., STANT 1
wind of Death's imperishable w.?
  ROSS D 3
winds of the buck and w.
  DICKEY 4
w.-tips whirred. VAN DO 1
w. to the centre, BROWNI R 50
w. trails like a banner JEFFE 13

wing'd: Love w. my Hopes
  UNKN 184
winged: Joys as w. dreams fly fast,
  FLET/OTHE 1
On w. feet, EMER 10
Time's w. chariot MARV 34
w. hour ROSS D 4
w. seraphs of Heaven POE 4
wings: aged eagle stretch its w.?)
  ELIOT T 2
Beat by unnumbered w.
  THOMS J (1700–1748) 7
bird deprived of w. HARD 28
black w. of the/ hospital WILLI 7
chirrup up his w. to dry
  CLARE 10
ears like errant w., CHES 3
flap this bug with gilded w.,
  POPE A 9
Flies from his hunching w. and
  beak — LOWE R 7
fluttring w. of thy fast flying
  SPENS 35
folds her w. JARR 2
Give me new Phoenix w.
  KEAT 57
gone on the wind's w. BYRO 37
goodly w. unto the peacocks?
  BIBL, O.T. 16
great w. beating YEATS 84
I am the w.; EMER 7
lie upon the w. of night
  SHAK 149
mice with w. ROET 1
night's black w. SUCK/FELL 2
Oh that I had w. like a dove!
  BIBL, O.T. 38
presence beats its w. in wrath.
  HECH 7
seagull's w. shall dip and pivot
  CRAN H 27
silver w., MARV 19
soft w. GREN 4
soule her w. doth spread HABI 2
spreading your w. TROW 3
stage-fairy w., GRAV 1
Swan spread her w., KINN 17
sweet May dews my w. were wet,
  BLAK 24
(thou art all w.,) WHITM 104
throat and breast and w. vibrates
  BLAK 37
to go on w. ROBE 1
to share those w. JEFFE 44
Unhappy, eagle w. and bleak,
  JEFFE 11
Upon their clamorous w.
  YEATS 165
vain his w. CAREW 11
vast w. across the canceled skies,
  MELO 1
vast w. across the canceled skies,
  MACL 4

viewless w. of Poesy, KEAT 48
Vulture, whose w. are dull
  realities? POE 1
waves his purple w., MILT 78
what w. you have JEFFE 10
whether pigs have w." CARRO 39
w. and feathers unto the ostrich?
  BIBL, O.T. 16
w. break into fire BROWNI E 10
W. brush past him. LEVE 11
w. of grasshoppers, SHAK 153
w. of Time EMER 8
w. were blue, LEAR 2
with smoky w., entangles them.
  HILL G 1
young beneath her w.
  MERE G 14
Wink: fictive things/ W. as they
  will. STEVENS 15
footstool crack, and the sun w.
  DONN 28
this great w. of eternity,
  CRAN H 49
vanish with a w. of tails,
  MACN 21
w.-and-elbow language of delight.
  KAVA 21
wink'd: w. at the thief BLAK 25
winked: monkeys w. too much
  MOOR M 19
Winkie: Wee Willie W. MILLE W 1
winking: beaded bubbles w. at the
  brim, KEAT 45
w. Mary-buds SHAK 17
winks: one eyed shrew that w.
  GINS 12
She w. a feeble eye, ELIOT T 104
winne: w. us best with flaterye;
  CHAU 110
W. whoso may, CHAU 86
winning: glory of the w.
  MERE G 4
lose a w. match SHAK 149
wins: w. more hearts UNKN 141
winsome: handsome, w. Johnny.
  UNKN 140
winter: all history's a w. sport
  CUMM 1
Blow, blow, thou w. wind!
  SHAK 13
brown fog of a w. dawn,
  ELIOT T 118
chilly w.'s night; BARNE 4
dark as w. was the flow/ Of Iser,
  CAMPB T 3
dead boughs that w. still must
  bind, ROSS D 1
disappeared in the dead of w.
  AUDE 35
dreading the w.'s neere.
  SHAK 224
fineless is as poor as w.
  SHAK 135

flowers the w.'s choice? CLARE 4
furious w.'s rages; SHAK 18
Go, birds of spring: let w. have his
    fee; HERB G 37
Gone were but the W.,
    ROSS C 23
heart is warm/ Midst w.'s harm.
    MORR 5
hoary w.'s night SOUTHW 1
How like a w. SHAK 223
In w., in my room DICKI 84
It was beginning w., ROET 37
lay in 'gainst w. rain, LOVE 1
mind of w. STEVENS 50
no w. in 't; SHAK 7
on w.'s traces, SWIN 3
red blood reigns in the w.'s pale.
    SHAK 181
seemed it w. still, SHAK 226
sleepy w., WYLI 13
spring summer autumn w.
    CUMM 4
starving high-country w.
    SNYD 24
stove late of a w. night,
    WHITM 33
Swans in the w. air AUDE 9
Thus W. falls,
    THOMS J (1700–1748) 13
unclad would w.'s rudeness dare;
    VERY 1
upon my w.'s task THOR 11
ways/ Of w. joys WHITT 28
W. and summer YEATS 26
w. called it a dreadful crime.
    BLAK 52
W. comes, to rule the varied
    year, THOMS J (1700–1748) 12
w.-day declining. WHITM 99
w., dead and dark, ALLI 4
w. death has never tried
    FROS 80
w. evening settles down
    ELIOT T 97
W.-garment of Repentance
    OMAR 1
w. his delights; CAMPI 18
W. is icummen in, POUN 2
w. is past, BIBL, O.T. 72
W. kept us warm, ELIOT T 113
w. of our discontent SHAK 94
w., plague, and pestilence,
    NASHE 2
W. snows upon thy sable hairs.
    DANI S 16
W. tells a heavy tale; BONH 1
w.'s morn, on a stormy day,
    LEAR 8
wooed her in the w. time,
    UNKN 99
wintered: w. and were coming
    awake. MORG 1

winter's: spring begins before the w.
    over. WYLI 11
w. not forever, CUMM 1
winters: Three w. cold SHAK 227
When forty w. SHAK 185
wintriest: even the w. bronze.
    STEVENS 49
wintry: by the same w. fever.
    THOMA D 22
long w. nights; — LEAR 6
on this casement shone the w.
    moon, KEAT 10
sailed the w. sea; LONG 51
Upon a w. bough; SHEL 23
wait, through w. hours, MCCRE 2
w. sides of many glens, SYNG 7
w. world appear SHEL 33
wipe: To bid the father w. his eyes
    SHAK 61
w. away all trivial fond records,
    SHAK 28
wipers: w. Of scores out
    BROWNI R 65
wipes: brutish necessity w. its
    hands WALC 3
wire: dried w. spiderweb, GINS 34
necks/ wound round and round
    with w. BISH 22
wires: hairs be w., SHAK 237
streaks of care/ Like w. KAVA 28
w. grow on her head. SHAK 237
Wisconsin: all over W. SILKO 2
wisdom: ancient w., WILD 13
Beauty, w. and passion, MASE 5
black, staid W.'s hue; MILT 15
Bodily decrepitude is w.;
    YEATS 6
child's undoubting w. LOWE J 16
hath but one part w. SHAK 35
his own w. and pleasures,
    WARR 6
I thy w. may adore, BIBL, O.T. 65
Knowledge comes, but w. lingers,
    TENN 78
much w. yet they are not wise,
    THOMS J (1834–1882) 5
Nor youth, nor strength, nor w.
    BRAD 6
Of Highest W. MILT 118
those who love want w.;
    SHEL 52
Thou with Eternal w. didst
    converse, MILT 83
Unbroken w. in a single look,
    WINT 11
unsearchable dispose/ Of highest
    w. MILT 118
Vain w. all, MILT 60
we call it w. JARR 21
W. and Spirit of the universe!
    WORD 98
w. be put in a silver rod,
    BLAK 12

w. thy sister MILT 83
w. went to rack: YEATS 80
wise: Alone, important and w.,
    YEATS 22
as w. as bold, SHAK 119
being good for nothing else, be
    w. ROCH 3
bread to the w., BIBL, O.T. 1
chattering w. and sweet,
    YEATS 21
darkly w. and rudely great:
    POPE A 78
fair and w. and good and gay.
    MOTH 7
God is w. POPE A 82
"God the Gay is not the W."
    KAVA 14
grandeur, with his w. grimace,
    EMER 27
heard a w. man say, HOUS 59
husbandes hardy, w., and free,
    CHAU 67
just, the w., the brave, STOD 3
love, and then be w.? BYRO 20
making w. the simple.
    BIBL, O.T. 28
more fools than w. GIBB 1
much wisdom yet they are not
    w., THOMS J (1834–1882) 5
Nature ne'er deserts the w. and
    pure; COLE SAM 41
Nor ever did a w. one. ROCH 4
Nor good, nor bad, nor fools, nor
    w., PRIO 4
nymphs so graceful, w., and fair,
    SWIF 21
O w. man, LIND V 14
'Tis folly to be w. GRAY 17
to sea went w. men three,
    PEAC 2
Type of the w., WORD 148
we were very very w.,
    COLE M 1
what say the fathers w., —
    EMER 40
wife w., without debate;
    MARTIA 2
w. and wonderful, ALEX 1
W. Draco comes, MELV 12
W./ Enquire, define, distinguish,
    teach, devise, ROCH 16
w. expect, the sorrowful invite,
    DAVE 1
w. guys/ tell me HORN 1
W., if too weak, UNKN 74
w. men came from far, GODO 1
w. old owl RICHA E 1
w. restraint WORD 62
w. want love; SHEL 52
wisely: lov'd not w. but too well;
    SHAK 138
wiser: sadder and a w. man,
    COLE SAM 31

Every w. adores a Fascist,
  PLATH 30
ev'ry w. is at heart a rake:
  POPE A 98
Farewell, w.! ROCH 5
fat white w. whom nobody loves,
  CORN 2
follows on a w. thro the fire,
  BOYD 1
given to a W. Old, BLAK 31
Harriet Tubman, / w. of earth,
  HAYD 21
heart of a w. JOHN G 1
I knew a w., lovely in her bones,
  ROET 27
I met a w. DARC 3
I remember only a w. WHITM 60
judge w.'s thoughts by tears,
  DONN 61
know a reasonable w.,
  POPE A 109
Lion and w. YEATS 26
logic of a w., ROBI 29
lovely w. stoops to folly, GOLD 9
man and a w. Are one.
  STEVENS 64
mighty w. with a torch, LAZA 1
My outside W., and your inside
  Man. COWL 6
obliged to call him w. FLEM 1
old w. and she lived in a shoe,
  MOTH 30
over-value w. GRAV 27
pale w. all alone, WILD 16
Paris is a w.'s town, VAN DY 1
part w., three parts a child,
  YEATS 88
perfect W., nobly planned,
  WORD 135
She is the w. HARJ 1
smile at the smiling w. SEXT 12
softness of a w. LOWE A 8
Swere and lie as a w. CHAU 97
tell a w.'s age GILB 9
That w. out of Botticelli —
  DE VR 1
thinking w. RICH 13
Thus wrote/ a w., RICH 18
ties me to the w. WHITM 21
"To be born w. is to know —
  YEATS 2
what correct young w.
  DICKEY 13
when a w. appears; GAY 3
when a w. woos, SHAK 201
When I am an old w. JOSE 1
wisest w. in Europe,
  ELIOT T 116
W. and fool POPE A 96
w. can be proud and stiff
  YEATS 39
w. chaste and fair. HABI 1
w./ Combing. STEVENS 32

w. dancing, STEVENS 32
w. drew her long black hair
  ELIOT T 149
w. is perfected. PLATH 37
w. is singing to me; LAWR 31
w. keeps the trophy. RANS 24
w. like that SEXT 8
w. named Tomorrow SAND 7
w., only worthy found OVID 6
w. smoothes her forehead
  STEVENS 12
w. that kissed him SERV 10
w. that you forsake her, KIPL 15
w. to defy the gods; SPENC A 4
w. who did not care), KIPL 27
w. would set ROET 20
w.'s glance instinctive thrown:
  MELV 6
w.'s happiest knowledge MILT 75
worser spirit a w., colored ill.
  SHAK 240
wrapped in a w.'s hide! SHAK 61
young w.-smell DAVIS 2
womanish: my wish/ Is w.:
  JARR 17
w. peace POUN 63
womanly: w. life WHITM 72
woman's: W. at best a contradiction
  still. POPE A 99
w. deaf, and does not hear.
  POPE A 109
womb: child from the w., SHEL 26
doors of my mother's w.,
  BIBL, O.T. 10
from the w., SPEND 11
hurry from the fatal cannon's w.
  SHAK 150
in her wicked w. BEDD 6
mad'st thy mother's w. thine urn.
  JONS 38
Opening her fertile w. MILT 86
out her ashie w. MILT 117
out of the w. GINS 12
quietness of the w. JEFFE 30
through the foul w. of night,
  SHAK 57
tore/ Her w., SITW 6
Why died I not from the w.?
  BIBL, O.T. 10
w./ So to the tomb; BACO 1
w. wherein they grew? SHAK 217
wombat: w. prowled obtuse and
  furry, ROSS C 12
wombs: mothers' w. the tiring-
  houses be RALEG 15
women: all the men and w. merely
  players: SHAK 11
Among illustrious w., MILT 112
Back home the black w. BARA 17
blacks, naked w. BISH 22
crowd of young w. POUN 33
Crowds of men and w.
  WHITM 18

Dear dead w., BROWNI R 79
especially to w., BYRO 21
especially w. SMIT ST 6
famous beauty of dead w.:
  MACL 11
hard legs of our w. SHAP 8
Hope not for mind in w.;
  DONN 38
Hypocrite w., how seldom
  LEVE 7
hysterical w. say YEATS 77
Land of Men & W. BLAK 29
lay down with those strange w.,
  WAGO 2
men in w. do require? BLAK 48
'Most w. have no characters
  POPE A 93
On the faces of w. and children
  SAND 4
Sing lullaby, as w. do, GASC 1
sons to other w.; SNYD 7
spoil'd the w.'s chats,
  BROWNI R 60
Truer than w., PLATH 78
ways of w. KAVA 11
When we submit to w. CAMPI 11
W., and Champagne and Bridge)
  BELL 17
w. and Sunday HUGH L 3
w. are ambitious naturallie,
  MARL 4
W. are angels, wooing; SHAK 169
w. are dictators all, NASH 7
W. are soft, SHAK 61
w. do in men require? BLAK 48
W. from whose loins CULL 5
w. grieve to think they must be
  old. DANI S 7
W. have no wilderness BOGA 14
w. must weep, KINGSL 3
w. of a generation, WHITM 19
w. of Marblehead! WHITT 23
worlds revolve like ancient w.
  ELIOT T 102
Womenes: W. counsels CHAU 69
womman: conseile a w. CHAU 91
w. was the los of al mankinde.
  CHAU 86
Wommen: W. desyren to have
  sovereyntee CHAU 111
w. loven best richesse, CHAU 109
won: by guile w. the day: ELLI 2
learn who w. WHITM 89
nothing to be w. or lost.
  GRAV 38
peace your valor w.
  HOPKINSO 1
prize that was w. UNKN 84
prize we sought is w., WHITM 45
w. great glory, TENN 119
W. his defeated ends. JOHN L 4
wonder: eyes/ In momentary w.
  YEATS 7

hapless Nymph with w. saw:
GRAY 19
Have eyes to w., SHAK 228
How I w. what you are!
TAYL J 1
Let it not your w. move JONS 1
many a w. thing. CHAU 65
miles around the w. grew
HOUS 41
no new w. may betide,
YEATS 121
passionate w. of your forest
JOHN H 2
touches back to w. WILB 8
w. and astonishment MILT 35
w. at a greater w., DONN 68
w. came to light, GOLD 8
w. that bubbles LAWR 48
w. the world can bear
BERRYM 8
world's wide w., SPENS 46
wondered: be more w. at SHAK 51
Wonderer: way for the W.,
GINS 25
wonderful: after/ The w. music
BROWNI R 62
know that Europe's w.,
VAN DY 2
wide, beautiful, w. world,
RANDS 1
wise and w., ALEX 1
With w. deathless ditties OSHA 2
w. bird the frog are —
UNKN 110
W. lovely there she sat, DE LA 19
w. one-hoss shay, HOLM 4
wondering: listened w. GRAV 13
W. maid; HODG 6
wonderly: w. delyvere, CHAU 8
wonderment: Full of baby w.,
HODG 3
wonders: heaven's w. and delights —
GREV 10
His w. to perform; COWP 4
I'th deep his w. BIBL, O.T. 56
These are thy w., Lord of love,
HERB G 33
world of loving w. STIR 1
wondrous: bridge of w. length
MILT 62
hear thy w. word, LONG 20
how w. then! MILT 81
O w. singer! WHITM 49
song, the w. chant WHITM 52
survey the w. cross WATT I 9
tender and w. thoughts,
WHITM 12
What w. life MARV 17
w. and instructive light, TRAH 2
w. secret show, LOWE J 16
wonne: w. with her owne will
beguyld. SPENS 17

wonner: ugly, creepin, blastit w.,
BURN 57
wont: cheeks were w. more fresh
C., J 1
Leander, who was nightly w.
BYRO 75
wonted: forbeare,/ His w. songs,
SPENS 49
w. pride MILT 56
woo: Banner by turns and bugle
w.: ARNO 39
Shame would w. Him last,
LANIE 2
tell me how to w.! GRAHAM R 1
w. a fair maid, GILB 61
yield some pity, w. her; LODG 5
wood: babes in the w. LOWE J 12
bank by the w. WHITM 75
broke the new w., POUN 53
burnt like w. JARR 3
Chop some w., HILL J 4
dark and lonely w. DAVIE W 3
deep and gloomy w., WORD 33
forgets his leg of w. GRAV 21
from w. and stone to Christ.
JOHN J 7
gypsies in the w., UNKN 125
hamadryad from the w. POE 2
harbor and neighbor w.
THOMA D 32
I sit in the top of the w.,
HUGH T 1
impulse from a vernal w.
WORD 145
long w.'s counterpart, ROSS D 7
Lost in a haunted w., AUDE 76
Loved the w. rose, EMER 22
lovers disappeared into the w.
THOMA E 2
Malvern W. Bethink itself,
MELV 16
moves in a w. of desire, GUNN 2
pierce the deep w.'s woven shade,
YEATS 163
roads diverged in a w., FROS 95
rules the shadows of the w.,
YEATS 164
saints through the w., LANIE 3
scent of wild flowers in the w.
CREE 5
smoothing the w. HALL 2
sound beside the w. FROS 62
starlight w., SHEL 31
three long mountains and a w.;
MILLA 27
To w. and field. LONG 39
warm them at the w.-fire's blaze!
WHITT 29
w.-nymphs my cold corpse inter,
HERR 53
w. of thoughts THOMA E 4
w., the weed, the wag.
RALEG 13

w. was gray and the bark warping
off it FROS 140
w., weeds, WHITM 2
woodbine: w. spices are wafted
abroad, TENN 93
woodchuck: w. could say FROS 6
wooded: Shouting to the w. hills,
MAST 8
wooden: jointed w. arm. GRAV 21
Sailed off in a w. shoe —
FIEL E 8
w. beams were so inviting.
KOCH 5
w. shoe that sailed the skies
FIEL E 9
yellow w. house indented
WILLI 24
woodlands: w. brown and bare,
LONG 38
W., meadows, MAST 11
w. of Squeedunk. TAYL B 1
wood's: w. in trouble; HOUS 44
woods: Bare w., SHEL 62
be summer w. FROS 106
beauty of the w., MARV 32
green-rob'd senators of mighty
w., KEAT 22
Greta w. are green, SCOT WA 23
grow in the w. UNKN 129
highest W. impenetrable MILT 97
hoary w. are grand: GALT 1
In the Arabian w. embost,
MILT 117
in the pathless w., BYRO 1
inland w. were pushed by winds,
MILLA 12
Into the w. LANIE 1
Keep your w. O Nature,
WHITM 31
middle of the w. LEAR 4
no road through the w. KIPL 28
Out of the w. LANIE 2
owls in the beardusky w. BIRN 6
ruffles the w. HILL G 1
still w. I loved, WHITM 95
Strange w. POUN 56
Tasting of the sweet damp w.
SMIT W 4
through the w. UNKN 59
Tomorrow to fresh w. and
pastures new. MILT 33
wailing winds and naked w.
BRYA 7
walls, the w., POPE A 122
watch his w. fill up with snow.
FROS 107
whited air/ Hides hills and w.,
EMER 43
Whose w. these are FROS 107
W. and groves MILT 119
w. and lumberjacks, FROS 124
w. are bare and birds are flown,
BRYA 32

w. are getting green,　CARRO 32
w. are lovely, dark　FROS 108
w. decay and fall,　TENN 120
w. have fallen,　TUCK 1
w. of Powhatan,　THAC 2
w. shall to me answer　SPENS 30
w. we wander in.　WILB 9
worked in the w.　SNYD 16

woodspurge: w. flowered, three cups
　in one.　ROSS D 10
w. has a cup of three.
　ROSS D 10

wooed: ladies,/ That must be w.
　CAMPI 6
loved Enthusiast w.,　COLL 6
w. her in the winter time,
　UNKN 99
w. the slimy bottom of the deep
　SHAK 97

wooer: cam a knight to be their w.,
　UNKN 29

woof: weave the w.,　GRAY 5

wooing: Women are angels, w.;
　SHAK 169
W. his purity　SHAK 240
w. the sun to be her lover,
　WALK 12

wool: packs w. sheared in April,
　HALL 4
pictures full, of wax and of w.,
　JONS 17
w. of the beaver,　JONS 2

woolen: brownish w. blanket,
　WHITM 71

woolgathering: Controlled w. is my
　work too.　DAY 12

woos: early dew w.　UNKN 251
meet it when it w.　HERR 35
when a woman w.,　SHAK 201

Word: Against the W.　ELIOT T 13
At every w. a reputation dies.
　POPE A 119
center of the silent W.
　ELIOT T 13
Choice w. and measured phrase,
　WORD 123
Creation's blithe and petaled w.
　CRAN H 51
Dollar is your only W.,　ROBI 4
each rock a w.　SNYD 52
ever breathed a w.;　ALEX 6
faith in your w. and deed.
　BRID 2
flattering w.,　WILD 3
flowering in a lonely w.;
　TENN 125
grey w. is　RANS 13
he lied in every w.,
　BROWNI R 20
hear thy wondrous w.,　LONG 20
hear Thy W.　BETJ 6
imaged w.,　CRAN H 52

in deed and not in w. alone.
　HOUS 10
in the Prophet's w.
　JOHN S (1822–1882) 1
Light dies before thy uncreating
　w.:　POPE A 2
lisp my very earliest w.,　POE 39
little w. is Honor,　RANS 13
Love is an evil w.　BARA 5
no one spoke a w.,　RUKE 12
No w. do they have,　MUIR 1
no w. to say;　WILD 4
O w. of fear,　SHAK 100
one that kept his w.　HOUS 1
preach thy eternall w.?
　HERB G 73
priests are more in w. than
　matter;　SHAK 76
said no w.,　WILD 4
scarecrow w.,　THOMA D 8
see that w. nested　WHITM 43
speaking little, perhaps not a w.
　WHITM 33
strong and delicious w.
　WHITM 68
take my w. for jewel　LORD 3
Thy w. is all, if we could spell.
　HERB G 32
wagging clock/ Tells me the hour's
　w.,　THOMA D 15
will not call me with a w.
　PETRA 10
w. from of old,　WHITM 43
W. I was in my life alone,
　FROS 9
W. in the desert　ELIOT T 25
w. is elegy　HASS 2
w., liquid, sane,　WHITM 43
w. of my city　WHITM 43
w. outleaps the world,　ROET 24
w. perhaps loud spoken　VERY 6
w. that shall echo for evermore!
　LONG 45
w. too much repeated　AMMO 20
w. up from the waves,
　WHITM 68

wordes: withouten many w.,
　WYAT 17

wordless: song was w.;　SASS 9

Word's: W. gane to the kitchen,
　UNKN 187

words: agéd accents and untimely
　w.,　DANI S 11
Beauty and beauteous w.
　HERB G 36
body is as numinous/ as w.,
　HASS 4
breathe their w. in pain.
　SHAK 87
By w., by voices, a lost way —
　MACL 7
catches the main w. only,
　WHITM 16

coin, or counterfeit/ New w.,
　BUTL 5
Colours and w.　WORD 114
Commanding w.;　DRYD 18
denying all our w.　RUKE 1
drains her w.　THOMA D 14
dream w. most)　MACL 10
empty w. of a dream　BRID R 6
fit w. to paint　SIDN 5
Flattened your w.　MILLA 13
flawed w. and stubborn sounds.
　STEVENS 40
general cause of w.,　SHAP 28
Glowed into w.,　ELIOT T 123
half remember human w.,
　SYNG 7
hard w., jealousies, and fears,
　BUTL 1
hard w. ready to show why,
　BUTL 2
Hearing your w.,　MILLA 12
human tunes nor w.,　YEATS 41
Hunting w. I sit all night
　UNKN 202
idle, silly, flattering w.,　HOWI 2
Ill matching w.　MILT 80
in all but w.　FROS 86
in w. and deeds?　BROWNI R 40
last year's w. belong　ELIOT T 66
low w. oft creep in one dull line:
　POPE A 25
Malcolm's w.　BARA 11
melodious w. to lutes of amber.
　HERR 63
next year's w. await another
　voice.　ELIOT T 66
of all sad w.　WHITT 21
old plain w.,　RICH 6
Only/ With w.　NIMS 3
order w. of the sea,　STEVENS 19
poem whose w. become your
　mouth　OHAR 11
prayer is more/ Than an order of
　w.,　ELIOT T 63
quaint w. and trim invention;
　HERB G 40
rich w., every one,　LOWE J 8
Some let me make you of the
　heartless w.　THOMA D 16
Some w. bedevil me.　LORD 2
stamping the w. with emphasis,
　SPEND 16
sugar-bated w.:　ROSS C 13
They borrow w.　VERY 2
thunder of approximate w.
　GUNN 10
very last w. he ever said
　UNKN 103
Where w. are scarce,　SHAK 87
W., after speech,　ELIOT T 22
w. among mankind!　SHEL 46
W. are like leaves;　POPE A 22
w. are maps.　RICH 4

truth in a calm w.,
STEVENS 16
Under a w. of whistles,
CRAN H 19
undo the amorous w. BEHN 2
Undulate round the w.,
WHITM 50
unintelligible w. Is lightened: —
WORD 30
unstilled w. still whirled
ELIOT T 13
visioning a w. HAYD 6
waits for the w. to begin.
MERW 9
warm the w., DONN 56
way the w. ends ELIOT T 48
weary were the w., CHES 2
'What is the w., DE LA 15
'Where is the w.?' BYRO 36
where the w. is quiet, SWIN 11
whole w. turn to coal,
HERB G 72
whose w. shall whiten, FLEC 2
wide w. dreaming on things to
come SHAK 229
wide w. over. COOP 1
wild swan of a w. JEFFE 18
wintry w. appear SHEL 33
word outleaps the w., ROET 24
workings of the w.: AMMO 10
w. and life's too big
BROWNI R 29
w. as a vale of tears?'
BROWNI R 23
w. below the brine, WHITM 112
w. doth pass UNKN 94
w. dream otherwise, DUNB P 13
w. enough, and time, MARV 33
w. from both sides, DICKEY 28
w. goes by my cage JARR 27
w. grew pale,
JOHN S (1709–1784) 19
w. has grown grey SWIN 23
w. has held great Heroes,
GRAHAME 2
w. has not changed; JEFFE 26
w. has still/ Much good,
HOUS 52
w. I never made. HOUS 18
W. in a Grain of Sand BLAK 1
w. in which a man was born?'
BYRO 36
w. is born anew, GINS 31
w. is bound to shake. BISH 39
w. is charged HOPKINS 7
W. is crazier MACN 18
w. is everything that happens to/
Be true. HOLLA 3
w. is mud-/ luscious CUMM 12
w. is not sweet in the end:
SWIN 23
w. is/ not with us enough
LEVE 18

W. is past its Infant Age:
DRYD 23
w. is too much with us;
WORD 159
w. is wrought/ To sympathy
SHEL 70
w. laughs with you; WILC 1
w. like Great Sodom DUNC 4
W.-losers and W.-forsakers,
OSHA 1
w. may end tonight?
BROWNI R 39
w. of born- CUMM 36
w. of green. RICH 1
w. of its triumph. AUDE 18
w. of loving wonders STIR 1
w. of made CUMM 36
w. of money, promise and
disease. WELC 3
w. of sweets and sours; POE 27
w. of the shadowed RUKE 6
w. out-Herods Herod;
LOWE R 22
W. seduce: MARV 24
w. see the utmost of thy hate;
DRAY 14
w. should listen then, SHEL 72
w. stands out on either side
MILLA 30
w.; thy uttermost I see; SIDN 27
w. to be a grassy road
YEATS 122
w. to weet SHAK 3
w. too beautiful this year;
MILLA 11
w., unfathomably fair, PATM 2
w. was all before them.
MILT 108
w. we roved, Ned Bunn?
MELV 21
w. were heaven, GREE 3
w. will end in fire, FROS 47
w. without a meaning, ROBI 30
w. young lads no more shall
roam. MELV 21
w./ Is all his own, EMER 45
w.'s course will not fail: PATM 7
w.'s dim dawn, SMIT L 4
w.'s false subtleties. SHAK 238
w.'s great cities, OSHA 2
w.'s great day MUIR 8
w.'s great eye, DAVE 2
w.'s great hands. HUNT 7
w.'s more full of weeping
YEATS 144
w.'s riches, HERB G 61
w.'s tide is bearing me along;/
Sterner desires and darker
hopes BRON 11
w.'s weight of the w.'s filth
SITW 9
w.'s wide wonder, SPENS 46
w.'s wrong. SHEL 62

would have been/ Another w.'
THOMA E 3
writing-/ master to this w.,
MOOR M 25
yet abide the W.! DICKI 139
you mighty gods!/ This w. I do
renounce, SHAK 79
your w. of Beautie 's gone.
HERR 45
worldes: my w. bliss, CHAU 68
worldless: with the w. rose WILB 3
worldling: w.'s eyes WHITT 28
worldly: all his w. goods: LEAR 4
for w. state; WORD 5
thy w. task hast done, SHAK 18
world's: All the w. a stage,
SHAK 11
perceive the w. a dream.
BROWNI R 14
w. a bubble, BACO 1
w. a snare, BEAU/BASS 2
w. at an end, DAVE 5
w. so hard, KINGSL 2
worlds: between two w., one dead,
ARNO 32
Exhausted W.,
JOHN S (1709–1784) 5
Far other w. and other seas,
MARV 18
Millions of w., burning SNYD 47
misfortune/ placed these w.
TATE J 4
to Indian w.,
THOMS J (1700–1748) 8
whole w. outwear, FLET G YO 2
w. are reconciled. WILB 12
W. first Region MILT 65
w. revolve like ancient women
ELIOT T 102
worm: came upon a w., DICKI 84
catch Christ with a greased w.,
LOWE R 14
channerin w. doth chide;
UNKN 307
fat little w." UNKN 97
God builds the w. THOMP F 5
In feature as the w. DICKI 87
invisible w. BLAK 80
its hero the Conqueror W.
POE 33
little thing, a little w.,
LOWE R 34
made me the laily w. UNKN 168
picking a manner of w.,
OWEN 39
rather tough w. in your little
inside?" GILB 29
round little w. SHAK 153
same crooked w. THOMA D 23
started a w. farm) CUMM 31
w.-eaten maw, SKEL 12
worms: Gilded tombs do w. infold.
SHAK 119

damn'd profession of w.,
  POUN 49
iron to heat,/ w., RICH 15
no line of her w. have I,
  HARD 45
not our son's w., WHITM 16
True ease in w. comes from art,
  POPE A 28
w. like this forever . . . SIMP 9
w./ master to this world,
  MOOR M 25
w. these poems!/ Imagine!
  OHAR 1
writings: Nor praise nor blame the
  w., POPE A 31
written: Let the martial songs be
  w., WALK 6
Theocritus w. in English,
  LOWE J 7
What is w., sweet sister,
  POE 49
w. on her face — MAST 3
w. Rule and never known,
  DRYD 17
w. such volumes LEAR 7
wroghte: first he w., CHAU 13
wrong: Aged in w., SNOD 9
bear love's w., SHAK 200
Bitter plaints to rue thy w.,
  UNKN 169
did great w., and maintained little
  right. UNKN 159
do ourselves this w., TREN 2
done her w. UNKN 101
eyes, as hanged men's, turning the
  w. way; ALBI 1
If I am w., POPE A 128
If w., I smiled; POPE A 15
Laws be w.; WILD 2
my Love! ye do me w.
  UNKN 124
ne'er did w. to thine BURN 36
only, only, thing that I ever did
  w. UNKN 99
so great a w., UNKN 190
spectral w., EMER 20
speke and bere him w. CHAU 97
tale of deeper w.; NOYE 5
there is nothing w. PLATH 4
they were never w., AUDE 62
trust that triumphs over w.,
  GLAD 2
weep and sing/ Duty's conscious
  w., AUDE 10
what's w. and what's right;
  HILL J 2
Where did it all go w.?
  BERRY M 6
world's w. SHEL 62
w. shall fail, LONG 12
w. side of every door,
  ELIOT T 107
w. that needs resistance, BANK 4

wronger: loves not his w.;
  SHAK 134
wrongfully: right perfection w.
  disgrac'd, SHAK 213
wrongs: community of w.; GILB 11
To forgive w. SHEL 58
Wrote: I'm Sorry, now, I W. it,
  BURG 1
never w. to me — DICKI 145
Poets who w. great poems,
  WINT 10
Red footprints w. on the snow
  SAND 23
Thus w. a woman, RICH 18
w. each other little odes GILB 11
w. her name upon the strand;
  SPENS 23
w. my will; YEATS 152
w. The Canterbury Tales LONG 8
wrought: artist w. this loved
  guitar; SHEL 91
changes w. on form and face;
  TENN 38
end is never w.; SIDN 39
fortunes must be w.; LONG 50
hammered you, w. you,
  THOMP F 14
In whom love w. new alchemy.
  DONN 43
what was done and w. JONS 40
world is w. To sympathy
  SHEL 70
w. by prayer TENN 104
w. to withered hay; PROC 1
wrung: w. from the darkness —
  JARR 21
w. their bread LOWE R 4
Wrythynge: W. my fyngres
  PETRA 1
wyde: nosethirles blake were and
  w. CHAU 17
wyld: beast so w., SPENS 17
wyllowe: under the w. tree.
  CHAT 1
wymmen: From alle w. UNKN 4
wynd: Gynglen in a whistlynge w.
  CHAU 19
Wynken: W. and Blynken FIEL E 9
wys: sergeant of the lawe, war and
  w., CHAU 3
wytches: Waterre w., CHAT 1

X

Xenia: X., Burnt Cabins, Hornell —
  KINN 7

Y

y-bounden: Adam lay y./ Bounden in
  a bond; UNKN 1

yachting: goes out y., PEAC 3
yachts: skillful y. pass over.
  WILLI 48
yaf: Mars y. me my sturdy
  hardinesse. CHAU 92
Venus me y. CHAU 92
Yahoo: ugly Y. tricks. LIND V 15
Yak: commend me the Y. BELL 20
Yangtze: Bodhidharma sailing the
  Y. SNYD 24
Yankee: Y. Doodle, dandy, SHUC 1
Y. Doodle, keep it up, SHUC 1
yanks: y. immortal stars awry?
  CUMM 56
yard: front y. all my life.
  BROO G 19
hadn't gone a y. BELL 10
land in the y., JARR 24
y. Was as long, KEAT 60
yards: field two y. away. MUIR 2
y. of pearls, HAYD 7
yarn: List to the y., WHITM 89
Yarrow: bonny holms of Y.!'
  WORD 165
him I lost on Y. UNKN 79
yawl: gig and y., CLARK J 1
yawn: Graves, y. and yield your
  dead, SHAK 132
yawns: skull, how it y. AIKE 12
yawp: sound my barbaric y.
  WHITM 73
yce: power/ To melt that marble y.,
  CAREW 14
yea: Aunswer him faire with y. or
  nay. WYAT 18
year: beats out the y.'s delay.
  BOGA 9
dispute a y. or more)— SWIF 21
each day is like a y., WILD 2
each y. we see/ Breeds ARNO 26
for that time of y. TOOM 4
glad y. which once had been,
  TENN 41
Half Y.'s Night GAY 4
in a crooked y. THOMA D 4
in a y.'s turning. THOMA D 36
in the dark of the y. WALK 11
juvescence of the y. ELIOT T 31
Last y.'s anything? CULL 7
last y.'s language ELIOT T 66
last y.'s snow to me, CULL 7
last y.'s words belong
  ELIOT T 66
lasts a y.; WYLI 11
left the past y.'s dwelling
  HOLM 2
Ling'ring y. at last is flown,
  JOHN S (1709–1784) 10
loveth best of all the y. JACK 2
many a y. ago, POE 3
measure of the y.; KEAT 19
morn of its hundredth y.
  HOLM 7

Z

youthful: in her y. beauty died,
   BRYA 9

lovely in thy y. grace! BRYA 12

this y. lady, DANT 1

Vaunt in their y. sap,
   SHAK 187

y. and unhandled colts
   SHAK 125

y. burning boy? BLAK 18

y. Harlots curse BLAK 76

y., loving, modest pair
   BURN 19

Youth's: Y. a stuff will not endure.
   SHAK 175

yowe: lilting at our y.-milking,
   ELLI 1

ytorne: tender lambes y.?
   SPENS 48

Yule: went on Y. day
   UNKN 157

zeal: ambition varnisht o'er with z.
   MILT 59

served my God with half the z.
   FLET/SHAK 5

zebra: z. stripes along his jaw
   ELIOT T 111

zebras: z., supreme in their
   abnormality; MOOR M 19

Zen: nowhere Z. New Jersey
   GINS 10

zephyr: Borne upon a z.'s shoulder
   POUN 15

zephyrs: z. gently play,
   POPE A 116

Zephyrus: Sweet breathing Z.
   SPENS 38

Zero: Z. at the Bone — DICKI 112

zest: that sweet minor z. KEAT 64

Zion: sketched a silver Z.,
   LIND V 4

Zoetrope: On the Z. GILB 44

zombies: lobby z. they knowing
   CORS 4

zone: fatal z. to her denied!
   COLL 5

from z. to z. BRYA 27

Hunger shall make thy modest z.
   DAY 2

Zoo: drear light of Z., GINS 9

Zoos: studio, the Garden/ of Z.,
   OHAR 4

zowie: z. did he die, FEAR 2

Zuan: Z. Bellin' not by usura
   POUN 10

Zyklon: so much Z. and leather,
   HILL G 7